WORLD
CRICKETERS

WORLD
CRICKETERS
A Biographical Dictionary

CHRISTOPHER MARTIN-JENKINS

Oxford   New York

OXFORD UNIVERSITY PRESS

1996

Oxford University Press, Walton Street, Oxford OX2 6DP

Oxford New York

Athens Auckland Bangkok Bombay
Calcutta Cape Town Dar es Salaam Delhi
Florence Hong Kong Istanbul Karachi
Kuala Lumpur Madras Madrid Melbourne
Mexico City Nairobi Paris Singapore
Taipei Tokyo Toronto
and associated companies in
Berlin Ibadan

Oxford is a trade mark of Oxford University Press

Published in the United States
by Oxford University Press Inc., New York

British Library Cataloguing in Publication Data
Data available

Library of Congress Cataloging in Publication Data
Martin-Jenkins, Christopher.
World cricketers:
a biographical dictionary
Christopher Martin-Jenkins.
1. Cricket players—Biography—Dictionaries.
I. Title.
GV915, A1M32   1996   796.358'092'2—dc20 95–47276[B]
ISBN 0–19–210005–X

1 3 5 7 9 10 8 6 4 2

Typeset by Interactive Sciences, Gloucester
Printed in Great Britain
on acid-free paper by
The Bath Press
Bath, Avon

CONTENTS

PREFACE · vi

BIBLIOGRAPHY AND ACKNOWLEDGEMENTS · ix

AUSTRALIA · 1

ENGLAND · 151

INDIA · 411

NEW ZEALAND · 489

PAKISTAN · 549

SOUTH AFRICA · 607

SRI LANKA · 683

WEST INDIES · 705

ZIMBABWE · 793

REST OF THE WORLD

ARGENTINA · 809   BERMUDA · 809   CANADA · 811

DENMARK · 812   FIJI · 813   HOLLAND · 815

IRELAND · 816   SCOTLAND · 817   USA · 818

PREFACE

The intention behind *World Cricketers* was to produce a readable reference book containing short cricketing biographies of every notable player or influential personality from the game's earliest days as a rural pastime to its present status as a high-profile international sport. It has been the latter for at least a century and the emphasis, naturally, is on those who have played the game at Test level.

Since 1992 the proliferation of Test cricket has continued with a ninth nation, Zimbabwe, being accorded Test status and the return of South Africa in the same year. The cricketers are listed alphabetically under the Test nations for whom, or in which, they played their cricket, and additional entries appear under a Rest of the World section. All Test cricketers are included and my earlier work, *The Complete Who's Who of Test Cricketers*, last published by Queen Anne Press in 1987, is the basis for many of the entries in this volume, suitably amended and updated. I am grateful to the company's chairman, Adrian Stephenson, for his ready agreement over this.

In addition to Test players other persons included fall within the following categories: those who have toured for their country but not won a Test cap; one-day international players; and those who have made a particular impact on cricket without gaining any kind of international recognition as a player. This includes one or two minor cricketers who became famous for a particular feat—for example F. C. Cobden, who finished the University match with a hat-trick, or Ted Alletson who, one afternoon at Hove, produced an inspired and astounding innings for Nottinghamshire, a shining gem in an otherwise banal career; those whose primary significance to cricket has been other than as a player, for example John Arlott, Sir Neville Cardus, Thomas Lord, Lord Sheffield, and the Maharajah of Baroda; those with strong cricket connections who have achieved fame in other fields, for example J. M. Barrie, Robert Menzies, and Edmund Blunden.

First-class records are given for all who have played 'first-class' cricket, according to the generally accepted figures agreed by the Association of Cricket Statisticians. I have followed this estimable body, and the Editor of *Wisden*, in ignoring the edict of the International Cricket Council which attempted unsuccessfully to refuse first-class status to certain obviously 'first-class' matches played in South Africa during their years of political isolation. The designation of first-class matches was, in any case, in the hands of the press until 1947 when national Cricket Boards started to define that status themselves. All current cricket scholars depend heavily on the statistical work of Arthur Haygarth and F. S. Ashley-Cooper.

I am indebted, like all those for whom statistics are always illuminating, but often a chore, to that body of discerning moles who, on behalf of the Association of Cricket Statisticians, investigate ancient matches and keep punctilious record of contemporary ones, apparently undaunted by their growing volume. My grateful thanks are due both to leading and lesser lights in this field.

The format of the biographies is self-evident: the years and places of birth and, where applicable, death are given with full Christian or first names. Teams for which an entrant played, or has played, are given at the head of the entry. If a player has played Test cricket this is instantly identified by the inclusion of his country amongst the first-class teams listed. Test records are given at the foot of all relevant entries, except in the case of those who have played a single Test, in which case the details are in the text. Test career figures are complete to May 1995. All other figures, including first-class and one-day international statistics, are complete to September 1994. The inevitable gap between the compilation and publication of a book of this scale is regrettable, but unavoidable. In the case of some eighteenth-century players score-cards did not always give bowling analyses. In these cases wickets taken by bowlers are indicated by a plus sign (+) between the wickets figure and the average.

A list of reference books consulted in the compilation of this book is given under the bibliography on page ix. I am also, however, especially indebted to the late Jim Coldham for his original invaluable assistance on research into the *Who's Who of Test Cricketers*; to Philip Bailey, Peter Wynne-Thomas, and Philip Thorn for their seminal *Who's Who of Cricketers*, which lists all who have played first-class cricket in England to 1992; and to my team of contributors. They are, with categories for which they supplied information for entries, as follows.

Qamar Ahmed	Non-Test-playing Pakistanis and Pakistan players since 1987
Harsha Bhogle	Non-Test-playing Indians and Indian players since 1987
R. T. Brittenden	Non-Test-playing New Zealanders and New Zealand players since 1987
Tony Cozier	Non-Test-playing West Indians
Gerald Howat	Non-Test-playing British cricketers to 1987; The Rest of the World
Brian Murgatroyd	England Test cricketers since 1987
Michael Owen-Smith	Non-Test-playing South Africans and South African players since 1992
Ken Piesse	Non-Test-playing Australians and Australian players since 1987
Carol Salmon	Women cricketers
Stephen Thorpe	West Indian players since 1987
Mahinda Wijesinghe	Non-Test-playing Sri Lankans and Sri Lankan players since 1987
Mark Williams	Zimbabwe section

My warm thanks to all the above for their time and trouble, especially to Dr Howat, who could not have been more punctilious and to whose thoroughness and erudition most of the credit for the Rest of the World section is due. Thanks also to Robert Brooke, for reading all proofs; and to Polly Barnes, for help with much of the repetitive work of checking and revision, and for kindly assisting with the rapid reproduction of much of the New Zealand section, which I left in a hotel room early in the 1995 season and which a well-meaning maid tidily deposited in the nearest dustbin! It is commonplace for an author and editor to pay tribute to his or her spouse, but in my case my thanks to my wife Judy are heartfelt, for her patience, her frequent help with obscure queries when I was working on the book far from home, and her sympathy with my occasional Basil Fawltyish tantrums—notably during the New Zealand crisis.

My great hope is that this will prove to be both a reliable and an enjoyable reference book, standing apart because of its international breadth and the depth of its scope. Any mistakes and omissions are my own responsibility. I realize that, whilst the categories for those who have played Test and international cricket are clear cut, there was room, in an ideal world, for considerable expansion under the other criteria. If personalities who deserved an entry are missing, I can only apologize and ask readers to accept that there had to be limits to this as in any publishing project. Although educated at the 'other place', I deem it an honour to have compiled a book for Oxford University Press: the thoroughness of their approach to all aspects of the book's production has been an education in itself.

CHRISTOPHER MARTIN-JENKINS

Bucks Green, West Sussex, 1995

BIBLIOGRAPHY AND ACKNOWLEDGEMENTS

The following books and periodicals have been especially valuable:

The Cricketer
The Cricketer International
Wisden Anthology 1864–1900
Wisden Anthology 1900–1940
Wisden Anthology 1940–1963
Wisden Anthology 1963–1982
Wisden Cricketers Almanack (various years)
Bailey, Philip, Philip Thorne, and Peter Wynne-Thomas *(eds)*, *Who's Who of Cricketers* (Newnes Books, 1984)
Frindall, William H. (ed.), *The Wisden Book of Test Cricket 1876–77 to 1994* (Headline, 1995)
Lemmon, David (ed.), *Benson and Hedges Cricket Year* (various years)
Pollard, Jack, *Australian Cricket: The Game and the Players* (Hodder and Stoughton, 1982; Angus and Robertson, rev. edn 1988)
Swanton, E. W. and John Woodcock (eds), *Barclays World of Cricket: The Game from A–Z* (Collins, 1980; Willow Books, rev. edn 1986)

The following have also been consulted:

GENERAL
Athletic News Cricket Annual (various years)
Booklets of the Association of Cricket Statisticians
Cricket
Cricket News
The Journal of the Cricket Society
Playfair Cricket Annual (various years)
Wisden Cricket Monthly
Altham, H. S. and E. W. Swanton, *A History of Cricket* (Allen & Unwin, fifth edn 1962)
Birley, Derek, *The Willow Wand: Some Cricket Myths Explored* (Simon & Schuster, 1989)
Bowen, R., *Cricket: A History of its Growth and Development* (Eyre & Spottiswoode, 1970)
Brooke, R. W., *The Collins Who's Who of English First Class Cricket 1946–84* (Collins, 1985)

Cardus, Neville, *Cricket All the Year* (Collins, 1952)
Frindall, William H. (ed.), *The Wisden Book of Cricket Records* (Queen Anne Press, 1981)
Frith, David, *The Fast Men: A 200-Year Cavalcade of Speed Bowlers* (George Allen & Unwin, 1982)
Frith, David, *The Slow Men* (George Allen & Unwin, 1985)
Martineau, G. D., *The Valiant Stumper: A History of Wicket Keeping* (Stanley Paul, 1957)
Reese, Daniel, *Was it all Cricket?* (Allen & Unwin, 1948)
Robertson-Glasgow, R. C., *Cricket Prints: Some Batsmen and Bowlers, 1920–1940* (Laurie, 1943)
Robertson-Glasgow, R. C., *More Cricket Prints: Some Batsmen and Bowlers, 1920–1945* (Laurie, 1948)
Robinson, Ray, *The Wildest Tests* (Pelham Books, 1972)
Thomas, A. A., *Test Form at a Glance* (W. H. Allen, 1953)
Thomson, A. A., *Cricket: The Great Captains* (Stanley Paul, 1965)

AUSTRALIA
Allan's Australian Cricket Annual (various years)
Association of Cricket Statistician booklets
Australian Cricket
Victorian Cricket Association annual reports
Western Australian Cricket Association yearbooks
World of Cricket
Test Match Grounds of the World (Willow Books, 1990)
Alley, W. E. (Bill), *My Incredible Innings* (Pelham Books, 1969)
Barnes, Sid, *It Isn't Cricket* (Collins, 1953)
Border, Allan, *An Autobiography* (Methuen, 1986)
Bradman, Don, *Farewell to Cricket* (Pavilion Books, 1988)

Bibliography and Acknowledgements

Brayshaw, Ian, *Cricket West* (Transgraphics Pty Ltd, 1979)

Butler, Keith (ed.), *Howzat: Sixteen Australian Cricketers Talk to Keith Butler* (William Collins, 1979)

Cardus, Neville, *Australian Summer: The Test Matches 1936/37* (Cape, 1937)

Cashman, Richard, *Ave A Go, Yer Mug! Australian Cricket Crowds from Larrikin to Occer* (Collins, 1984)

Coleman, Robert, *Seasons in the Sun: The Story of the Victorian Cricket Association* (Hargreen Publishing Company, 1993)

Dawson, Graham (ed.), *Test Cricket Lists* (Five Mile Press, 1992)

Derriman, Richard, *True To The Blue: A History of the New South Wales Cricket Association* (Richart Smart Publishing, 1985)

Edmundson, David, *See the Conquering Hero: The Story of the Lancashire League, 1892–1992* (Mike McLeod Litho, 1992)

Fingleton, Jack, *Batting From Memory* (Collins, 1949)

Fingleton, Jack, *Brightly Fades the Don* (Collins, 1981)

Frith, David, *Archie Jackson: The Keats of Cricket* (Pavilion Books, 1987)

Hutcheon, E. H. and T. J. Bale, *A History of Australian Cricket* (1946)

Jack, David, *Mr Cricket: The Autobiography of Fergie* (Nicholas Kaye, 1957)

Moyes, A. G., *Australian Cricket: A History* (Angus & Robertson, 1959)

Mullins, Pat and Philip Derriman, *Bat & Pad: Writings on Australian Cricket 1804–1984* (Oxford University Press, 1984)

Mulvaney, John and Rex Harcourt, *Cricket Walkabout: The Australian Aborigines in England* (Macmillan, 1988)

Page, Michael, *Bradman: The Illustrated Biography* (Macmillan, 1983)

Piesse, Ken, *Cricket Year* (various years)

Piesse, Ken, *Prahran Cricket Club's Centenary History* (Prahran C.C., 1977)

Robinson, Ray, *From The Boundary* (Collins, 1950)

Robinson, Ray, *On Top Down Under: Australia's Cricket Captains* (Cassell, 1975)

Seith, Don, *The Prime Minister's XI* (self-published, 1989)

Tasker, Norman, *McGilvray. The Game Is Not The Same* (ABC, 1985)

Tatz, Colin, *Aborigines in Sport* (The Australian Society for Sports History, 1982)

Torrens, Warwick, *Queensland Cricket and Cricketers 1862–1981* (self-published, 1982)

Webster, Ray, *First Class Cricket in Australia, Vol. 1: 1850–51 to 1941–42* (self-published, 1991)

Whitington, R. S., *Keith Miller: The Golden Nugget* (Rigby, 1981)

Whitington, R. S., *The Quiet Australian: The Lindsay Hasset Story* (William Heinemann, 1970)

ENGLAND

Allen, David Rayvern (ed.), *A Word from Arlott* (Pelham Books, 1983)

Ames, Leslie, *Close of Play* (Stanley Paul, 1953)

Arlott, John, *Alletson's Innings* (Epworth, 1957)

Arlott, John (ed.), *Cricket: The Great Bowlers* (Pelham Books, 1968)

Arlott, John (ed.), *Cricket: The Great All Rounders* (Pelham Books, 1969)

Arlott, John, *Fred: Portrait of a Fast Bowler* (Eyre & Spottiswoode, 1971)

Arlott, John (ed.), *Cricket: The Great Captains* (Pelham Books, 1971)

Arrowsmith, R. L., *A History of County Cricket: Kent* (Barker, 1971)

Ashley-Cooper, F. S., *Cricket Highways and Byways* (Allen & Unwin, 1927)

Bailey, T. E., *The Greatest of My Time* (Eyre & Spottiswoode, 1968)

Barker, Ralph, *Innings of a Lifetime* (Collins, 1982)

Batchelor, Denzil, *A Gallery of Great Players: W. G. Grace to the Present Day*

Benaud, Richie, *Willow Patterns* (Hodder & Stoughton, 1969)

Berry, Scyld, *A Cricket Odyssey: England on Tour 1987–1988* (Pavilion Books, 1988)

Bettesworth, W. A., *Chats on the Cricket Field* (Merritt & Hatcher, 1910)

Bird, H. D. ('Dickie'), *Not Out* (A. Barker, 1978)

Blunden, Edmund, *Cricket Country* (Collins, 1944)

Brodribb, Gerald, *Hit for Six* (Heinemann, 1960)

Brodribb, Gerald, *Felix on the Bat* (Eyre & Spottiswoode, 1962)

Bowes, Bill, *Express Deliveries* (Stanley Paul, 1949)

Boycott, Geoffrey, *The Autobiography*

Brearley, Mike, *Phoenix from the Ashes: The Story of the England Australia Series 1981* (Hodder & Stoughton, 1981)

Carew, Dudley, *To The Wicket* (To the Wicket, 1947)

Carr, A. W., *Cricket with the Lid Off* (Hutchinson, 1935)

Chesterton, George and Hubert Doggart, *Oxford and Cambridge Cricket* (Willow Books, 1989)

Close, Brian, *I Don't Bruise Easily: The Autobiography* (Macdonald and Jane's, 1978)

Coldham, J. D., *Lord Harris* (George Allen & Unwin, 1983)

Cowdrey, Colin, *The Incomparable Game* (Hodder & Stoughton, 1970)

Cricket Writers' Club, *Cricket Heroes* (Phoenix House, 1959)

Denness, Mike, *I Declare* (Barker, 1977)

Doggart, Hubert (ed.), *The Heart of Cricket: A Memoir of H. S. Altham* (Hutchinson, 1967)

D'Oliveira, Basil, *Time to Declare: An Autobiography* (Dent, 1980)

Edrich, John, *Runs in the Family* (Stanley Paul, 1969)

Farnes, Kenneth, *Tours and Tests* (Lutterworth Press, 1940)

Fender, P. E. H., *Kissing the Rod: The Story of the Tests of 1934* (Chapman & Hall, 1934)

Frindall, William H., *England Test Cricketers: The Complete Record from 1877* (Willow Books, 1989)

Fry, C. B., *Life Worth Living* (Eyre and Spottiswoode, 1939)

Gatting, Mike, *Leading from the Front: The Autobiography of Mike Gatting* (Queen Anne Press, 1988)

Gower, David, *A Right Ambition* (Collins, 1986)

Grace, W. G., *W. G.: Cricketing Reminiscences and Personal Recollections* (Hambledon Press, 1980)

Graveney, Tom, *Cricket Through the Covers* (Muller, 1958)

Grayson, Edward, *Corinthians and Cricketers* (Naldrett Press, 1955)

Haygarth, A., *Lillywhite's Scores & Biographies, Vols 1–4* (1862)

Haygarth, A., *MCC Scores & Biographies, Vols 5–15* (Longman, various years)

Hendren, Patsy, *Big Cricket* (Hodder & Stoughton, 1934)

Heyhoe-Flint, Rachael, *Fair Play and the Story of Women's Cricket*

Hill, Alan, *The Family Fortune: A Saga of Sussex Cricket* (Scan Books, 1978)

Hill, Alan, *Hedley Verity: A Portrait of a Cricketer* (Kingswood Press, 1986)

Hobbs, J. B., *My Cricket Memories* (Heinemann, 1924)

Howat, Gerald, *Learie Constantine* (Allen & Unwin, 1975)

Howat, Gerald, *Len Hutton* (Heinemann Kingswood, 1988)

Jessop, G. L., *A Cricketer's Log* (Hodder and Stoughton, 1922)

Johnston, Brian and Roy Webber, *Armchair Cricket* (BBC, 1956; fourth edn 1975)

Kay, John, *A History of County Cricket: Lancashire* (Barker, 1972)

Kilburn, J. M., *A History of Yorkshire Cricket* (Stanley Paul, 1970)

Laker, Jim, *A Spell from Laker on Cricket and Cricketers Past and Present* (Hamlyn, 1979)

Le Quesne, A. L., *The Bodyline Controversy* (Secker & Warburg, 1983)

Lemmon, David, *'Tich' Freeman and the Decline of the Leg-Break Bowler* (George Allen & Unwin, 1982)

Lucas, E. V. (ed.), *The Hambledon Men* (Frowde, 1907; rev. edn Phoenix House, 1954)

Marshall, Michael, *Gentlemen and Players: Conversations with Cricketers* (Grafton Books, 1987)

Mason, Ronald, *Walter Hammond: A Biography* (Hollis & Carter, 1962)

Melford, Michael, *Botham Rekindles the Ashes* (Daily Telegraph, 1981)

Mitchell, Alan, *84 All Out: The Story of Sir Arthur Sims* (Kt. Locke, 1962)

Morrah, Patrick, *Alfred Mynn and the Cricketers of His Time* (Eyre & Spottiswoode, 1963)

Mulvaney, J. and R. Harcourt, *Cricket Walkabout: The Australian Aboriginal Cricketers on Tour 1867–8* (Melbourne UP and Cambridge UP, 1967)

Murphy, Patrick, *'Tiger' Smith of Warwickshire and England: The Autobiography of E. J. Smith* (Lutterworth Press, 1981)

Parkin, Cecil Henry, *Parkin on Cricket* (Hodder & Stoughton, 1923)

Parkin, Cecil Henry, *Parkin Again* (Hodder & Stoughton, 1925)

Parkin, Cecil Henry, *Cricket Triumphs and Troubles* (Nicholls, 1936)

Paynter, Eddie, *Cricket All the Way* (Richardson, 1962)

Peebles, Ian, *Batter's Castle: A Ramble Round the Realm of Cricket* (Souvenir Press, 1958)

Peebles, Ian, *'Patsy' Hendren: The Cricketer and His Times* (Macmillan, 1969)

Peebles, Ian, *Spinner's Yarn* (Collins, 1977)

Phelps, Gilbert (ed.), *Arlott and Trueman on Cricket* (BBC, 1977)

Pollock, William, *The Cream of Cricket* (Methuen, 1934)

Pollock, William, *Talking About Cricket* (Gollancz, 1941)

Pullin, A. W., *Talks with Old Yorkshire Cricketers* (Yorkshire Post, 1898)

Pullin, A. W., *Talks with Old English Cricketers* (Blackwood, 1900)

Robertson-Glasgow, R. C., *46 Not Out* (Constable, 1985)

Ross, Alan, *Australia 55: A Journal of the MCC Tour* (Michael Joseph, 1955)

Ross, Alan, *Ranji: Prince of Cricketers* (Collins, 1983)

Root, Fred, *A Cricket Pro's Lot* (Edward Arnold, 1937)

Sewell, E. H. D., *Who's Won the Toss?* (Stanley Paul, 1944)

Sheppard, David, *Parson's Pitch* (Hodder & Stoughton, 1964)

Sissons, Ric, *The Players: The Social History of the Professional Cricketer* (Pluto Press, 1988)

Snow, John, *Cricket Rebel: An Autobiography* (Hamlyn, 1976)

Bibliography and Acknowledgements

Sproat, Iain (ed.), *The Cricketers Who's Who* (various years)

Statham, Brian, *A Spell at the Top* (1969)

Steele, David, *Come in Number 3* (Pelham Books, 1977)

Stevenson, Mike, *A History of County Cricket: Yorkshire* (Barker, 1972)

Streeton, Richard, *P. G. H. Fender: A Biography* (Faber & Faber, 1981)

Sutcliffe, Herbert, *For England and Yorkshire* (Edward Arnold, 1935)

Swanton, E. W., *Denis Compton: A Cricket Sketch* (1948)

Swanton, E. W., *As I said at the Time: A Lifetime of Cricket* (Willow Books, 1983)

Swanton, E. W., *Gubby Allen: Man of Cricket* (Hutchinson/Stanley Paul, 1985)

Tate, Maurice, *My Cricketing Reminiscences* (Stanley Paul, 1934)

Thomson, A. A., *Cricketers of My Times* (Stanley Paul, 1967)

Walker, Peter, *Cricket Conversations* (Pelham Books, 1978)

Warner, Sir Pelham, *Long Innings: The Autobiography* (Harrap, 1951)

Wellings, E. M., *A History of County Cricket: Middlesex* (Barker, 1972)

Willis, Bob, *Diary of a Cricket Season* (Pelham Books, 1979)

Wooller, Wilfred, *A History of County Cricket: Glamorgan* (Barker, 1971)

Wynne-Thomas, Peter, *England on Tour* (Hamlyn, 1982)

OTHER COUNTRIES

The Cricketer, Pakistan

Indian Cricket Annual (various years)

Abbas, Zaheer, *Zed* (World's Work, 1983)

Ahmed, Qamar, *Pakistan Book of Cricket* (various years)

Bailey, Trevor, *Sir Gary: A Biography* (Collins, 1976)

Carman, A. H., Francis Payne, and Ian Smith (eds), *The Shell Cricket Almanack of New Zealand* (various years)

Cozier, Tony (ed.), *West Indies Cricket Annual* (various years)

Duffus, Louis George, *South African Cricket, 1927–1947* (1948)

Hadlee, Richard, *Rhythm and Swing: An Autobiography* (Souvenir Press, 1990)

Heesom, Denys (ed.), *The Protea Cricket Annual of South Africa* (various years)

James, C. L. R., *Beyond a Boundary* (Hutchinson, 1963)

Khan, Imran, *All Round View* (Chatto & Windus, 1988)

McConnell, Lynn, *The Shell New Zealand Cricket Encyclopaedia*

Manley, Michael, *A History of West Indies Cricket*

Reese, T. W., *New Zealand Cricket 1841–1933* (vol. 1, 1927; vol. 2, 1936)

Romanos, Joseph, *A Century of New Zealand Cricketers*

Turner, Glenn, *My Way* (Hodder & Stoughton, 1975)

The following individuals, in addition to those mentioned in the Preface, have kindly helped with various queries.

General Philip Bailey, Peter Bryne, Geoffrey Saulez, Peter Wynne-Thomas; *Argentina* David Parsons; *Australia* Ric Finlay, Roger Page, Jack Pollard, Ray Webster; *Bermuda* Alma Hunt; *Canada* Kevin Boller; *Denmark* Peter Hargreaves, Sorren Nissen; *Fiji* P. A. Snow; *Holland* H. Bordewisk; *India, statistical* Mohandas Menon; *Ireland* Derek Scott; *Scotland* Neil J. Leitch, Sandy Robertson; *West Indies* Mervyn Wong; *Zimbabwe* Don Arnott, Peter Chingoka, J. K. Clarke, Graeme Hick, John Hick, David Houghton, Alwyn Pichanick; *secretarial* Carolyn Carroll, James Pyemont.

Australia

A'BECKETT, Edward Lambert

(b. 1907, East St Kilda, Melbourne; d. 1989, Melbourne) *Victoria and Australia*

One of four members of a prominent legal family to play for Victoria, Ted A'Beckett was a fast-medium bowler and resolute, attractive batsman, some 6 ft. 3 in. tall. He retired after only five seasons of first-class cricket, partly as a result of a Rules football injury but mainly to concentrate on his career as a barrister. On his Test début, against England at Melbourne, 1928/9, he opened the bowling and his first wicket was that of Jack Hobbs. He toured England with Woodfull's team in 1930, catching Hobbs low to the ground in the third Test, a scooping, somersaulting effort at short-leg which led to some controversy. He also appeared against South Africa in 1931/2.

First-class career (1927–31): 1,636 runs (29.21) including 2 centuries, and 105 wickets (29.16)
Test matches (4): 143 runs (20.42), 3 wickets (105.66), and 4 catches

ALDERMAN, Terence Michael

(b. 1956, Subiaco, Perth) *Western Australia, Kent, Gloucestershire, and Australia*

A tall and good-looking right-arm fast-medium bowler with fine control of swing and cut who enjoyed two wonderful tours of England in 1981 and 1989, the only surprise about Terry Alderman was that recognition did not come sooner. As early as 1974/5 he had taken 5 for 65 in the first innings of his first Sheffield Shield match and he had given another impressive performance

against the MCC touring team in the same season, but such was the competition from bowlers of similar type it was not until 1977/8 that he established himself in the West Australian side in the Sheffield Shield. In that season he took 28 wickets, in the following one 26, and in 1979/80 42, the third-biggest haul in first-class cricket that season. In England in 1981 he was an immediate success, moving the ball both ways through the air and off the pitch and doing so at a pace liable to make batting a nightmare on pitches such as that at Trent Bridge, where Alderman's figures of 9 for 130 in his first Test were instrumental in a narrow Australian victory. Later he met his match—as did his partner Lillee—in Ian Botham and Australia lost a close series despite his 42 wickets (21.26) in the six Tests. No Australian has taken more wickets in a Test series in England. A modest fellow with a fierce personal pride, he was no batsman but a very accomplished slip fieldsman. His career was badly set back in the first Test of the 1982/3 series against England when he damaged his right shoulder as he tried to rugby tackle a spectator invading the ground. He missed the rest of the season. He found it difficult to reproduce his magnificent form of 1981, but seemed to have recovered his fitness, playing a full county season for Kent in 1984 when he took 76 wickets. He produced his best Test figures, 6 for 128, against the West Indies at Perth in 1984/5 and took 44 first-class wickets in the season. Originally selected for the 1985 tour of England, he pulled out in order to join the unofficial Australian tour to South Africa and was badly missed in England. He returned to Kent for the 1986 season, taking 98 wickets (19.20) through bowling, as he put it, down the 'corridor of uncertainty'. In 1988 he had a single season for Gloucestershire, another successful one with 75 Championship wickets (22.81). On the 1989 tour he was again outstanding for his accuracy and skilful variations, crucially reducing Graham Gooch to impotence. 70 wickets on tour cost only 15 runs each and in six Tests he took 41 wickets (17.36) of which 13 were opening batsmen. He coached Western Australia in 1992/3. Personable off the field, he was a stern competitor on it.

First-class career (1974–92): 1,276 runs (8.34), 936 wickets (23.47), and 189 catches

Test matches (41): 203 runs (6.54), 170 wickets (27.15), and 27 catches

ALEXANDER, George

(b. 1851, Fitzroy, Melbourne; d. 1930, Richmond, Melbourne) *Victoria and Australia*

A hard-hitting right-handed batsman, a useful fast-medium change-bowler and a smart field, George Alexander was player/manager of the Australian teams in 1880 and 1884 and manager of Hon. Ivo Bligh's team in Australia in 1882/3. He played in the first-ever Test in England, at The Oval in 1880, when his steadfast innings of 33 contributed to Australia's avoidance of an innings defeat. For Victoria against New South Wales in 1879/80 he made 75, the highest score on either side and took 5 for 64.

First-class career (1875–84): 466 runs (15.53) and 33 wickets (18.39)

Test matches (2): 52 runs (13.00), 2 wickets (46.50), and 2 catches

ALEXANDER, Harry Houston

(b. 1905, Ascot Vale, Victoria; d. 1993, Melbourne) *Victoria and Australia*

A powerful right-arm fast bowler, Harry 'Bull' Alexander toured India in 1935/6 with Jack Ryder's Australians. His sole Test was against England in the fifth match at Sydney in 1932/3, as something of a reply to Harold Larwood. He scored 17 not out, and took 1 for 154. He could be intimidatingly fast.

First-class career (1928–35): 228 runs (6.16) and 95 wickets (33.91)

ALLAN, Francis Erskine

(b. 1849, Allansford, Victoria; d. 1917, Melbourne) *Victoria and Australia*

Known as 'The Bowler of the Century', he was the first of the great Australian bowlers. Left-arm medium-pace with abundant spin and a remarkable 'curl' (or swerve), he was immediately famous in intercolonial matches. Not fully fit when coming to England with the first Australian team in 1878—though in the whole length of the tour he took no fewer than 217 wickets for 1,832 runs—his sole Test was at Melbourne in 1878/9, when he scored 5 and took 4 for 80. He had been picked for the first Test in 1877, but preferred to go to an Agricultural show. He was a skilful all-round sportsman, renowned also for shooting and angling.

First-class career (1867–82): 371 runs (10.91) and 123 wickets (13.31)

ALLAN, Peter John

(b. 1935, Brisbane) *Queensland and Australia*

A tall, strongly built, right-arm fast bowler, Peter Allan took 10 for 61 in an innings for Queensland against Victoria at Melbourne in 1965/6—the only occasion this feat has been accomplished on the Melbourne ground. By the time of his retirement he was Queensland's highest wicket-taker. He toured the West Indies in 1964/5, bowling only 65 overs on the tour, and played his sole Test against England at Brisbane in 1965/6, not batting and taking 2 for 83.

First-class career (1959–69): 689 runs (10.59) and 206 wickets (26.10)

ALLEN, Reginald Charles

(b. Sydney, 1858; d. 1952, Sydney) *New South Wales and Australia*

An uncle of 'Gubby' Allen, himself an Australian by birth, Reginald Allen was a competent batsman whose sole Test was against Shaw and Shrewsbury's team in 1886/7, the second match at Sydney; he scored 14 and 30 and held 2 catches.

First-class career (1878–87): 382 runs (12.32)

ALLEY, William Edward

(b. 1919, Sydney) *New South Wales and Somerset*

See England section.

ANDREWS, Thomas James Edwin

(b. 1890, Newton, New South Wales; d. 1970, Croydon, Sydney) *New South Wales and Australia*

A thickset, right-handed stylist with powerful wrists and a straight bat, Tommy Andrews was not a good starter, but once settled in could play attractively and entertainingly with a wide range of strokes. He was also a high-ranking fielder both close to the wicket and further away, with a deadly arm. He toured England in 1921 and 1926 and South Africa in 1921/2, in the former year hitting 92 and 94 in the Tests at Headingley and The Oval respectively. He made 1,212 runs (32.75) on the 1921 tour and, though he achieved little in the 1926 Tests, he hit a magnificent 164 against Middlesex at Lord's in about three hours, and reached an aggregate of 1,234 runs (38.56). He scored 224 for his state against Arthur Gilligan's MCC team in 1924/5 at Sydney, adding 270 for the second wicket with Herbie Collins. In the Sheffield Shield he scored 3,072 runs (42.08) with a highest score of 247 not out against Victoria in 1919/20. A lively, cheerful character, he was a stonemason by trade and his family owned funeral parlours.

First-class career (1912–30): 8,095 runs (39.49) including 14 centuries, and 95 wickets (32.10)
Test matches (16): 592 runs (26.90), 1–116, and 12 catches

ANGEL, Jo

(b. 1968, Subiaco, Western Australia) *Western Australia and Australia*

An extrovert, strapping, 6 ft. 6 in. right-arm fast bowler, Jo Angel gained a reputation for being a home-town specialist in his opening seasons of first-class cricket. Two-thirds of his wickets were taken at the bouncy WACA Ground where he could be unpleasantly hostile. Making his Test début in the final Test of the 1992/3 summer in Perth, he bowled briskly enough to strike Desmond Haynes in the face with the ninth ball of the West Indian first innings, having previously had him dropped (at fine leg) from his fifth. Failing to bowl a fuller length, however, he was pounded by Richie Richardson and took 1 for 72 from 19 nervous overs. New South Wales's Glenn McGrath was preferred for much of the 1993/4 summer, but Angel, with four 5-wicket hauls, showed he was a bowler for the future. Only one other, Shane Warne, took more wickets than Angel's 47 at 21.78. It was an exceptional effort considering he had had his finger broken, by the

New Zealander Murphy Su'a, in Perth in the opening game of the summer; and his arm fractured, by a ball from Paul Reiffel, in November. Angel's reward was his maiden Australia tour—to Pakistan and Sri Lanka in August/September, 1994. A left-hand number nine batsman, he can occasionally hit strongly and in early 1994 made successive fifties, including a career-best 84 not out against the eventual Sheffield Shield champions, New South Wales, in Sydney.

First-class career (1991–): 369 runs (16.77), 110 wickets (26.57), and 6 catches
Test matches (4): 35 runs (5.83), 10 wickets (46.30), and 1 catch

ANNETTS, Denise Audrey (later Anderson)

(b. 1964, Sydney) *New South Wales and Australia*

Australia's outstanding bat in the past decade, Denise Annetts ended her career (probably) in the most controversial of circumstances. One of the casualties of Australia's unsuccessful attempt to retain the World Cup in England in 1993, she was omitted from the party to tour New Zealand in January 1994. The 29-year-old pharmacist, who married Ross Anderson in June 1991, responded by alleging she had been discriminated against because she was heterosexual. She took her case to Australia's Anti-Discrimination Board, who told her they could not consider her cause because although it is illegal under Australian law to discriminate against homosexuals, it is not illegal to discriminate against heterosexuals. Belinda Clark, who replaced Lyn Larsen as Australian captain after the World Cup, in which the hot favourites did not even reach the final, said Annetts was left out on merit. Ann Mitchell, president of the Australian Women's Cricket Council, said Annetts had been dropped because of a decline in her batting, fielding, and fitness levels. By her exemplary standards Annetts had a poor World Cup, scoring just 79 runs in five innings at an average of 19.75. She went into the tournament as Australia's top scorer in one-day cricket. Wielding a bat that often appeared to come up to her chin, the right-hander, who is just 5 ft. $\frac{3}{4}$ in. tall, was particularly prolific on the 1987 tour to England. Her innings of 193 against England in the second Test at Collingham, Yorkshire, in August is the highest in women's Test cricket. During this magnificent display of batting, Annetts and Lindsay Reeler (110 not out) broke the third-wicket partnership record by putting on 309. Annetts also holds the all-Tests fourth-wicket record of 222, scored with Lyn

Larsen (86) against England in Sydney in February 1992.

Test matches (10): 819 runs (81.90) including 2 centuries

One-day internationals (43): 1,126 runs (41.70) including 1 century

ARCHER, Kenneth Allan

(b. 1928, Yeerongpilly, Queensland) *Queensland and Australia*

The elder brother of Ron Archer, Ken had grace of style and some good strokes including a liking for the deflection. He opened the batting for his state from 1946 to 1957 and was also an excellent fielder, once offered a contract to play baseball in the USA. He toured South Africa in 1949/50 and, although he did not make the Test side, scored 826 runs in 24 innings. In a short Test career he played against England in 1950/1 and West Indies in 1951/2. He scored 1,116 runs (93.00) for Accrington in the Lancashire League in 1954. He became a radio and television executive.

First-class career (1946–57): 3,774 runs (29.95) including 3 centuries, and 13 wickets (53.69)

Test matches (5): 234 runs (26.00)

ARCHER, Ronald Graham

(b. 1933, Brisbane) *Queensland and Australia*

A vigorous all-rounder, Ron Archer relied on a strong right arm and a keen eye to attack. Of fine physique, he used his height and reach to punch the ball hard in front of the wicket. As a fast-medium stock bowler he bowled at the stumps and was often successful with the new ball. He toured England twice, in 1953 and 1956, also the West Indies and Pakistan, and represented his country at home against England and South Africa. At The Oval in 1953 he struck hard, top-scoring with 49. In the 1956 series, he captured 18 wickets (25.05), including a remarkable spell in the third Test at Headingley when, on the first morning, he dismissed Colin Cowdrey, Alan Oakman, and Peter Richardson in nine overs for 3 runs; he took no more wickets in the innings but his 50 overs yielded only 68 runs. In the West Indies he made 364 runs (60.66) in the Tests, including 128 in the fifth Test in Kingston, when his was one of five centuries in the innings! In the Sheffield Shield he made 1,766 runs (29.43) and took 115 wickets (24.08). Back and knee injuries forced his retirement at the early age of 25, in the 1958/9 season. Like his brother Ken, he became a television executive.

First-class career (1951–8): 3,768 runs (31.93) including 4 centuries, and 255 wickets (23.36)

Test matches (19): 713 runs (24.58) including 1 century, 48 wickets (27.45), and 20 catches

ARMSTRONG, Warwick Windridge

(b. 1879, Kyneton, Victoria; d. 1947, Sydney) *Victoria and Australia*

Tall and slim when he first appeared for his country against England during the 1901/2 tour, Warwick Armstrong weighed 22 stone at the end of his playing days 20 years later. 'The Big Ship' was a highly successful captain, leading Australia to eight successive wins against England in 1920/1 and 1921. His manner was haughty, even bossy, but a kind heart lay beneath. Not a graceful or cultured right-handed batsman, he was none the less completely assured, certain in defence, confident in attack, and terribly difficult to shift even when he seemed to be floundering against spin. As a bowler he took an exceptionally long run for one of his slow pace, but he had uncanny gifts of length and control. On helpful pitches he would turn his leg-break quickly and he could keep going for hours. Touring England in 1902, 1905, 1909, and 1921, he was outstanding all round, altogether making 5,974 runs (40.36), taking 443 wickets (16.45) and holding 150 catches. He put up 428 with Monty Noble against Sussex at Hove in 1902 for the sixth wicket, an Australian record; and his 'double' record in 1905 was 2,002 runs (48.82), including his highest score, 303 not out against Somerset at Bath, and 130 wickets (17.60). He headed Australia's batting averages in 1907/8 with 410 runs (45.55) and 1911/12 with 324 runs (32.40); and he hit three of his four Test centuries against England in 1920/1 when he made 464 runs (77.33). His highest in Tests was 159 not out against South Africa at Johannesburg in 1902/3, and he reached 410 runs (51.25) against South Africa in 1910/11. His best series as a bowler was 1909, when he took 16 wickets, including 5 for 27 in the first innings of the first Test at Edgbaston, which Australia lost, and 6 for 35 in the second innings of the second Test at Lord's, which Australia won. He was independently minded, strong-willed and caustic; when a draw was certain in the last Test at The Oval in 1921, 'The Big Ship' rested his regular bowlers and retired to the deep field, where he started reading a newspaper. Asked what he was reading, he replied that he was trying to find out who his opponents were. A whisky merchant and journalist, he died a wealthy man. In the Sheffield

Shield he made 4,997 runs (50.47) and took 177 wickets (24.68).

First-class career (1898–1921): 16,158 runs (46.83) including 45 centuries, 832 wickets (19.71), and 273 catches

Test matches (50): 2,863 runs (38.68) including 6 centuries, 87 wickets (33.59), and 44 catches

BADCOCK, Clayvel Lindsay

(b. 1914, Exton, Tasmania; d. 1982, Exton)
Tasmania, South Australia, and Australia

'Jack' Badcock played for Tasmania at 15, the second-youngest Australian to play first-class cricket, but his career was linked mostly with his adopted state, South Australia. A sturdy and accomplished right-hander, he hit a century in each innings against Victoria in 1940, scored 325 in another game against Victoria (1936), 271 not out against New South Wales and 236 against Queensland. He could drive magnificently on either side of the wicket, and his square-cut was so hard and clean that cover-point had little chance of getting a hand to it. In the Sheffield Shield he hit 2,473 runs (58.88) from 30 matches. Against England in 1936/7 he opened without success in the first Test at Brisbane, but in the fifth at Melbourne made 118 at number five, adding 161 with Ross Gregory. In England in 1938 he was often devastating against the counties, overall making 1,604 runs (45.82), but he failed completely in the Tests, with scores of 9, 5, 0, and 0 (at Lord's), 4, 5 not out, 0, and 9. Recurring lumbago brought his career to a close.

First-class career (1929–41): 7,371 runs (51.54) including 26 centuries

Test matches (7): 160 runs (14.54) including 1 century, and 3 catches

BANNERMAN, Alexander Chalmers

(b. 1854, Sydney; d. 1924, Sydney) *New South Wales and Australia*

Alec Bannerman, younger brother of Charles, was a member of the Australian eleven which defeated MCC at Lord's in 1878. He played in the first Test in England in 1880 and in the classic match at The Oval in 1882 which gave birth to the Ashes. The catch by which he disposed of W.G. in the second innings was the turning-point of the latter epic struggle. He paid three other visits to England, 1884, 1888, and 1893, and, short and dour, became the most famous (or infamous) of Australian stonewallers: his patience was inexhaustible. He took seven and a half hours to make 91 in the Test at Sydney in 1892, when his side won the rubber, scoring from only five of 204 balls bowled to him by William Attewell. Though such a slow run-getter, he made many large scores and was invaluable as a partner for bigger hitters. In the field, he was superb at mid-off—fast, safe and untiring. In England he scored 4,881 runs (19.44), including two centuries, and for New South Wales against Victoria 1,209 runs (29.29). In five Sheffield Shield matches he made 197 runs.

First-class career (1876–93): 7,816 runs (22.14) including 5 centuries, 22 wickets (29.81), and 154 catches

Test matches (28): 1,108 runs (23.08), 4 wickets (40.75), and 21 catches

BANNERMAN, Charles

(b. 1851, Woolwich, Kent; d. 1930, Sydney) *New South Wales and Australia*

Immortal as the man who made the first century in Test cricket, Charles Bannerman was a fine, upstanding and polished batsman. A native of Kent, he was master of most strokes and, unlike his brother, delighted in playing them. He was also a first-rate, versatile field. In the first-ever Test at Melbourne in 1877 his chanceless 165 (before retiring hurt) in $4\frac{3}{4}$ hours, came off a reputable professional attack and none of his colleagues reached 20 in the innings. Never before had an Australian made a century off an English team. In the bowlers' summer of 1878 he scored 770 runs (34.06), including 133 at Leicester. In the whole tour, including New Zealand and Canada, he reached 2,630 runs (23.90). Ill-health prevented his visiting England again, but at various times he coached in Australia and New Zealand and served as an umpire in 12 Tests. Most of his money was spent on beer and gambling.

First-class career (1870–87): 1,687 runs (21.62) including 1 century

Test matches (3): 239 runs (59.75) including 1 century

BARDSLEY, Warren

(b. 1882, Nevertine, Warren, New South Wales; d. 1954, Sydney) *New South Wales and Australia*

A stylish left-handed opening batsman, accomplished on all wickets, Warren Bardsley played with an exemplary straight bat, had an upright stance, quick and shrewd footwork and employed a wide variety of strokes. He drove easily off the front foot, was ready to go back on his stumps to force the ball from his pads by means of powerful wrists and forearms, and was a fine outfield. At a bumper he would toss his head backwards with a contemptuous sniff of the nose. Sober, patient, and assiduous, he was also tough: he batted without a glove on his top hand. He toured England in 1909, 1912, 1921, and 1926, on his first tour heading the batting with 2,072 runs (46.04), including 136 and 130 in the fifth Test at The Oval, putting up a record 180 for the first wicket of the second innings with Sid Gregory, and becoming the first player to hit two centuries in a Test. In two other tours he exceeded 2,000 runs—reaching 2,365 runs (51.41), including eight centuries in 1912—and in the Test at Lord's in 1926 he carried his bat through the first innings for 193 not out in $6\frac{1}{2}$ hours on a turning wicket against a superb attack. He headed the batting averages against England in 1921 (46.83), and against South Africa and England in the Triangular Tournament of 1912 he was the most prolific batsman on the three sides, with 392 runs (65.33), including 164 against South Africa at Lord's, adding 242 with Charles Kelleway for the third wicket after an early collapse. In 1910/11 he made 573 runs (63.66) against the visiting South Africans. Although considered to be better in England than at home—he made 7,866 runs (49.78) in England—he still represented his country at home in each series from 1910 until 1925.

First-class career (1903–26): 17,025 runs (49.92) including 53 centuries, and 113 catches

Test matches (41): 2,469 runs (40.47) including 6 centuries, and 12 catches

BARNES, Alan Roberts

(b. 1916, Mosman, Sydney; d. 1989, Sydney)

One of the best known and respected post-war Australian cricket officials, Alan Barnes served New South Wales and Australian cricket for more than 40 years. A first-grader at Mosman in the late 1930s, he originally worked in a bank before successfully applying for the newly created NSWCA position of assistant-secretary. Becoming Association secretary in 1950, he served for 26 years, including the state's halcyon years of nine consecutive Sheffield Shield victories between 1953/4 and 1961/2. Between 1950 and 1958, he acted as joint secretary of the International Cricket Conference. From 1958 to 1973 he was secretary. In 1960 he was also secretary of the Australian Board of Control for International

Cricket, succeeding Victorian Jack Ledward, and he held that position until his retirement in 1980. In 1976 he was awarded an OBE for his services to cricket.

BARNES, Sidney George

(b. 1916, Charters Towers, Queensland; d. 1973, Sydney) *New South Wales and Australia*

A colourful, bizarre personality, from the outset Sid Barnes was renowned for his glorious right-handed off-side strokes. On board ship coming to England with the 1938 team, he fractured a wrist—an accident which developed his on-side play amazingly. After the Second World War he became sounder and tougher and, getting on to his back foot more and more, was dogged and defiant, a particularly hard man to dislodge. He set himself to accumulate runs in large quantities. Generally an opening batsman, he shared a world-record partnership for the fifth wicket of 405 with Don Bradman in the second Test at Sydney against England in 1946/7, each man making 234. He averaged 73.83 for the series. In England in 1948 he finished second in the averages with 82.25, hitting 141 at Lord's. It was at Lord's too that he was criticized for fielding so close in at point or short-leg five yards from the bat and, at Old Trafford, the beefy Dick Pollard hit him in the ribs from a full-blooded stroke. Barnes had to spend the next ten days in hospital. Following that tour, he dropped out of cricket for two years and began writing controversial pieces for the newspapers. His great days were behind him. His eccentricities increased, and he eventually took his own life. He could, however, be a man of real wit. In a match during the 1948 tour, after a strong appeal had been turned down by Alec Skelding, the umpire, a dog ran on to the field. Sid captured it and carried it to the umpire with the caustic comment: 'Now all you want is a white stick!' In the Sheffield Shield he scored 2,655 runs (48.27) and took 29 wickets (28.65).

First-class career (1936–52): 8,333 runs (54.11) including 26 centuries, and 57 wickets (32.21)

Test matches (13): 1,072 runs (63.05) including 3 centuries, 4 wickets (54.50), and 14 catches

BARNETT, Benjamin Arthur

(b. 1908, Melbourne; d. 1979, Newcastle, New South Wales) *Victoria, Buckinghamshire, and Australia*

Ben Barnett was a cricketer of great charm. Although a model wicket-keeper and steady left-handed batsman, he was overshadowed by Bert

Oldfield for several years. He toured England in 1934 and South Africa in 1935/6, without playing in any of the Tests, but his chance came on his second visit to England in 1938, when he played in all four Tests, hitting 57 at Headingley—a low-scoring match—and effecting five dismissals; and he came fourth in the Test batting averages with 27.85. Subsequently, he settled in England, playing for and captaining Buckinghamshire. Noted for his tact, he acted as Australia's ICC representative in London before returning to Australia where he died in 1979.

First-class career (1929–61): 5,531 runs (27.51) including 4 centuries, 357 dismissals (215 c., 142 st.)

Test matches (4): 195 runs (27.85) and 5 dismissals (3 c., 2 st.)

BARRETT, Dr John Edward

(b. 1866, South Melbourne; d. 1916, Peak Hill, West Australia) *Victoria and Australia*

A patient left-handed batsman and useful medium-paced change-bowler with a high action, Jack Barrett was 18 when, on his début for his state against South Australia at Melbourne, he took 5 for 31 and 6 for 49 in the two innings. He came to England with the 1890 side and in the Test at Lord's carried his bat (67 not out) through the innings of 176 against Lohmann, Peel, Attewell, Barnes, Ulyett, and W. G. Grace. A busy medical practitioner, he had a relatively short first-class career.

First-class career (1884–92): 2,039 runs (25.81) and 21 wickets (16.00)

Test matches (2): 80 runs (26.66) and 1 catch

BARTON, Rt. Hon. Sir Edmund, PC, GCMG

(b. 1849, Glebe, Sydney; d. 1920, Medlow Bath, New South Wales)

The first Prime Minister of Australia and the only Prime Minister to have umpired in first-class cricket, Sir Edmund played for Sydney University against Melbourne University, as well as officiating at intercolonial fixtures. He stood in the infamous match at Sydney in 1879 when Billy Murdoch's run-out prompted a riot.

BEAN, Ernest Edward

(b. 1866, North Melbourne; d. 1939, Hampton, Victoria) *Victoria*

Prominent in the formation of the Australian Board of Control, Ernie Bean formed a formidable back-room partnership with Prahran's 'Harry' Rush, having enjoyed some playing success at club and state level. Bean's record of service included 33 years as a delegate to the Victorian Cricket Association, 20 as chairman of the executive, 20 as VCA delegate to the Australian Board of Control, 22 as a Victorian selector, 11 as an Australian selector and 17 years as honorary secretary of North Melbourne. At the time of his death, he was patron of the VCA.

First-class career (1887–1905): 282 runs (31.33) including 1 century, 8 wickets (39.75), and 3 catches

BEARD, Graeme Robert

(b. 1950, Sydney) *New South Wales and Australia*

A versatile all-round cricketer who bowled either medium pace or slow off-spin and batted usefully in the middle-order, Graeme Beard made only slow progress after his first appearance for New South Wales in 1975/6, starting with a pair against the West Indies. But in 1979/80 he scored 230 runs (38.33) and took 23 wickets (22.17) in the Sheffield Shield, and was chosen to tour Pakistan at the end of the season, playing in all three Tests on the short tour. He gained only one expensive wicket, but at Lahore in the third Test scored 39 and 49. He was a surprising choice for Australia's 1981 tour of England but was given little chance to shine and he announced his retirement in 1982 to concentrate on his job as an Industrial Officer in the Australian Workers' Union.

First-class career (1975–83): 1,441 runs (23.62) and 125 wickets (28.19)

Test matches (3): 114 runs (22.80) and 1–109

BECKER, Gordon Charles

(b. 1936, Katanning, Western Australia) *Western Australia*

A polished wicket-keeper and right-hand number seven batsman, Becker toured with the 1966/7 Australian team to South Africa, without playing a Test. His best season was 1965/6 when he made 30 dismissals, including 6 catches in an innings against Victoria in Melbourne and 9 victims for the match (8 catches and 1 stumping). The highest of his three first-class centuries was 195 against India in Perth in his penultimate season. He later became a West Australian selector.

First-class career (1963–8): 2,227 runs (27.49) including 3 centuries, and 140 dismissals (118 c., 22 st.)

BENAUD, John

(b. 1944, Auburn, New South Wales) *New South Wales and Australia*

A tall, punishing, right-handed batsman, John Benaud's aggressive leadership of his state during 1969/70 won him considerable respect until a two-match suspension marred his season following his insistence on wearing ripple-heeled boots against the directions of the State Association. Like his elder brother, Richie, he revealed a flair for captaincy, and again led his state with success in 1972/3, when he made his Test début. In his second Test, against Pakistan at Melbourne, he hit 142—93 of them before lunch—after learning that the selectors had left him out of the third Test. He toured the West Indies in 1973 with less success. He made a powerful 134 for his state against Victoria in 1969/70 which all but won the match when the cause looked hopeless for New South Wales. For Australia against Rest of the World at Adelaide, 1971/2, he hit 99. Like his brother he is a prominent journalist and a shrewd judge of a cricketer. Until resigning in 1993, he was a selector in a period of notable Australian success with what Peter Roebuck described as a 'typically Australian fondness for fast bowlers, "leggies" and fleet-footed batsmen, players who take the game forward'.

First-class career (1966–73): 2,888 runs (36.55) including 4 centuries

Test matches (3): 223 runs (44.60) including 1 century, and 2–12

BENAUD, Richard

(b. 1930, Penrith, New South Wales) *New South Wales and Australia*

One of the great Test captains, Richie Benaud has remained a household name through his work as a cricket journalist and broadcaster. His father, Lou, was an Australian first-grade player, who once took 20 wickets in a match, and Richie himself first played for his state at 18 and for Australia in Tests against the West Indies in 1951/2, aged 21. He became a notable all-rounder, a tough competitor, and an enterprising, adroit leader who captained his country in four successive and triumphant series—against England twice, and West Indies and Pakistan once each. He lost only four of his 27 Tests as captain. His efforts lifted the game in Australia out of the doldrums. As a lithe and forcing right-handed batsman he was always worth watching. His drives, powerfully hit with a full follow-through,

were often lofted. At Scarborough in 1953, against T. N. Pearce's XI, he hit 11 sixes and 9 fours while making 135. As a leg-spinner he touched the heights. An advocate of regular practice, he drove himself to the top. From a rhythmical, high, sideways-on action, he was more accurate and had greater variety than most of his kind. He bowled the leg-break, the googly, the top-spinner, and his speciality, the 'flipper': in effect an off-spinning top-spinner. With clever changes of pace and a teasing flight, he was a more fearsome prospect on the hard wickets in Australia and overseas than he was in England. A magnificent close fielder, able to leap with cat-like agility, he brought off some spectacular catches, notably one left-handed in the gully in 1956, to dismiss Cowdrey off a full-blooded drive at Lord's. He came to England in 1953 and 1956, and appeared in the home series against England in 1954/5 and in the West Indies in 1955, but it was not until the tour of South Africa in 1957/8 that he established himself as an all-rounder of the highest class, with 817 runs, including four centuries, and 106 wickets, a record number in that country. Against India and Pakistan in 1959/60 he took 47 wickets (20.19) in the eight Tests. With 31 wickets (18.83) against England in 1958/9—his first series as captain—he was largely instrumental in Australia's winning back the Ashes. His co-operation with Frank Worrell in the exciting series against the West Indies in 1960/1 captured the imagination of the whole cricket world. On his last tour England looked set to win the Test at Old Trafford in 1961, when they needed little more than a hundred runs to win with nine wickets in hand. Benaud took the ball and (despite pain in his shoulder) bowled round the wicket into the rough, first dismissing the rampant Ted Dexter, and then Brian Close, Peter May, and Raman Subba Row in the space of five overs. From 150 for 1, England were all out for 201, Benaud taking 6 for 70, saving the Ashes for Australia. When his shoulder trouble hastened his retirement, he had taken a record number of wickets for Australia, and also for his state (322 from 86 matches). He was awarded the OBE for his services to Australian cricket. A journalist, he has written several cricket books, mainly about tours, but his continuing fame is mainly the result of his distinctive, fair, frank, and authoritative television commentaries, always as generous as possible to contemporary players. As a public relations officer he was the key adviser to those who set up Kerry Packer's World Series Cricket.

First-class career (1948–68): 11,719 runs (36.50) including 23 centuries, 945 wickets (24.73), and 254 catches
Test matches (63): 2,201 runs (24.45) including 3 centuries, 248 wickets (27.03), and 65 catches

BENNETT, Murray John

(b. 1956, Brisbane) *New South Wales and Australia*

Murray Bennett, a slow left-arm bowler and useful lower-order right-hand batsman, won a place in the Australian side by virtue of his performances for New South Wales in 1984/5. Exploiting the helpful Sydney wickets, he captured 28 wickets (16.53) for his state in that season including 6 for 32, a career best, in the defeat of the West Indies. He made his Test début in the Melbourne game in the same season against West Indies and in the final Test at Sydney, he gave vital support to his spinning partner, Bob Holland, in setting up the famous Australian victory. Previously he had enjoyed a very successful début season in 1982/3 when he took 38 wickets, including nine in the match against the English tourists. He toured Zimbabwe in 1982/3 with the Young Australians and was a member of the tour party to England in 1985. He played in the final Test at The Oval, taking 1 for 111. He played his cricket in light-reflective glasses, an idiosyncrasy at the time but one which several cricketers eventually followed to reduce glare to the eyes.
First-class career (1982–8): 1,437 runs (23.95) and 157 wickets (30.92)
Test matches (3): 71 runs (23.66), 6 wickets (54.16), and 5 catches.

BEVAN, Michael Gwyl

(b. 1970, Belconnen, Canberra) *South Australia, New South Wales, Yorkshire, and Australia*

One of the few international-class cricketers born and bred in the Australian Capital Territory, Michael Bevan joined Don Bradman and his fellow left-hander David Hookes as the only batsmen to score four Sheffield Shield centuries in a row, late in the 1990/1 season. By amassing five centuries in 42 days in New South Wales's five final matches of the season, Bevan's streak was a record by an Australian, bar Bradman, who scored six centuries in six matches (and consecutive innings) in 1938/9. Selection as the Australian 12th man for the Prime Minister's XI against the West Indies at Manuka Oval in 1988/9 was his first big break. The following season he joined the Australian Cricket Academy in Adelaide and

started in Sheffield Shield ranks with South Australia. Ironically, Bevan had been regarded as an emerging bowling all-rounder in Canberra cricket before a back injury restricted his new ball duties. Now he bowls occasional left-arm wrist spin à la Gary Sobers. His brilliant form in the 1993/4 season enabled him to win an eleventh-hour touring place to Sharjah and on Australia's 1994 winter tour of Pakistan and Sri Lanka. By scoring 1,240 runs, average 82.66, with five centuries, Bevan also went within 14 runs of Victorian Graham Yallop's competition record, established in 1982/3. Included was a career-best 203 not out against Western Australia and 113 in the championship final against Tasmania, both at the Sydney Cricket Ground. In Pakistan he made an immediate impact as a Test cricketer and, returning home, played against England in preparation for becoming Yorkshire's first Australian mercenary in 1995.
First-class career (1989–): 4,041 runs (53.88) including 15 centuries, 9 wickets (84.66), and 28 catches
Test matches (6): 324 (32.40), 1 wicket (67.00), and 5 catches.

BISHOP, Glenn Andrew

(b. 1960, Adelaide) *South Australia*

A strongly built right-hand opener who represented the Australian one-day team twice in 1986/7 (scoring 7 and 6), Bishop was a consistent player at Sheffield Shield level for almost all of his eleven first-class seasons. In 1985/6 he toured Zimbabwe with a Young Australian team and on return made 965 runs at an average of almost 50 including a double-century against New Zealand. The highest of his thirteen first-class centuries also came that year: 224 not out for South Australia against Tasmania in Adelaide. In 1991/2, during a short South Australian tour of South-East Asia, he hit thirty-one sixes in an innings on his way to 246 in just 2 hours in a fifty-over score of 528 for 8, against All Malaysia at Kuala Lumpur.
First-class career (1982–92): 6,206 runs (37.38) including 13 centuries and 67 catches

BLACKHAM, John McCarthy

(b. 1854, Melbourne; d. 1932, Melbourne) *Victoria and Australia*

Jack Blackham was an outstanding wicket-keeper who generally stood up to fast bowling without a long-stop—although he invariably went back when 'The Demon' Spofforth was bowling his fastest. He was neat, quick, and accurate, a stumper who would gather the ball and whip off the bails in a flash. He was a very useful right-handed batsman, but (like most of the early Australians) had no pretentions to style. Coming to England with each of the first eight teams, he captained that of 1893. He kept in the first Test at Melbourne in 1876/7 when Spofforth refused to take part 'because his own wicket-keeper. W. L. Murdoch, did not play'. By 1878, however, Jack Blackham was established and his most notable achievement on this historic tour was to stump six and catch four of an Eighteen of Stockport on a rough, bumpy pitch. A bank clerk, Jack grew a beard (suitably black) as a young man of 23 and kept it all through his life.

First-class career (1874–94): 6,395 runs (16.78) including 1 century, and 454 dismissals (274 c., 180 st.)

Test matches (35): 800 runs (15.68) and 61 dismissals (37 c., 24 st.)

BLACKIE, Donald Dearness

(b. 1882, Bendigo; d. 1955, Melbourne) *Victoria and Australia*

At 46 the oldest player to represent Australia for the first time, against England in 1928/9, Don 'Rock' Blackie headed the bowling averages in this, his only series. Tall and spare and somewhat bow-legged, he was a vintage right-arm off-spin bowler, starting his run near mid-off (where he could joke with the fieldsman), curving his way to the stumps, and often making the ball curl in the breeze. For his state he took 158 wickets (23.59), but his opportunities came too late, partly because of the war and four years working in the country until 1922. Joining St Kilda instead of his old club, Prahran (formerly Hawksburn) he began a legendary spin-bowling partnership with 'Dainty' Ironmonger for both St Kilda and Victoria.

First-class career (1924–33): 548 runs (12.17) and 213 wickets (23.88)

Test matches (3): 24 runs (8.00), 14 wickets (31.71), and 2 catches

BLEWETT, Gregory Scott

(b. 1971, Adelaide) *South Australia and Australia*

The son of a South Australian stalwart, Bob, Greg Blewett forced his way into the Test team against England in 1994/5 after some outstanding innings for Australia's 'A' side. A lean, tall, and dashing right-handed batsman, right-arm medium-paced bowler, and brilliant fielder, he scored a cool and attractive 102 not out in his first Test innings at Adelaide, 115 in his second match at Perth, and subsequently toured the West Indies.

First-class career (1993–   ) 1,036 runs (57.55) including 5 centuries, 5 wickets (51.80), and 1 catch.

Test matches (6): 381 runs (42.33) including 2 centuries, and 8 catches

BONNOR, George John

(b. 1855, Bathurst, New South Wales; d. 1912, East Orange, New South Wales) *Victoria, New South Wales, and Australia*

Six feet six inches tall, around 16 stone in weight, and known as either 'The Australian Giant' or 'The Australian Hercules', George Bonnor was a hitter of extraordinary power. Finely proportioned, and sporting a bushy beard, he was no mere slogger, indeed was able to play quite an orthodox game at times, much to the disgust of some colleagues who argued that his business was to hit hard and often. He toured England in 1880, 1882, 1884, 1886, and 1888. During the first Test in England at The Oval in 1880 he hit a ball to such a tremendous height that the batsman had turned for the third run when Fred Grace caught it. Bonnor, like all hitters, was as inconsistent as he could be explosive, but at Sydney in 1884/5 he slammed 128 after Australia had lost seven wickets for 134, his hundred coming in even time, the fastest Test hundred scored to that date. He was credited with a hit of 147 yards at Mitcham in 1880 and with throws of 120 and 131 yards.

First-class career (1880–90): 4,820 runs (21.23) including 5 centuries, 12 wickets (39.16), 128 catches, and 1 stumping

Test matches (17): 512 runs (17.06) including 1 century, 2 wickets (42.00), and 16 catches

BOON, David Clarence

(b. 1960, Launceston, Tasmania) *Tasmania and Australia*

David Boon looks like a bulldog and plays like one. Recognized in Tasmania as an exceptional schoolboy talent, he was coached by Lancashire's Jack Simmons, who retained a fatherly interest in his progress. With a very correct technique and quick, decisive foot movement, he soon learned to play the ball late and became especially adept against spin bowling. All the attacking shots are at his command, the most characteristic being an upright clip through mid-wicket, a fierce square-cut, and a drive played with the whole squat body moving through the ball. He toured England in 1985 and by the end of the next Australian season had established himself in the national side. He made his first-class début in 1978/9 at the age of 17 and the following year scored over 400 runs in seven matches, including 78 against the West Indian tourists, to reveal his quality as a young batsman. His opportunities to impress were limited as Tasmania were not made full members of the Sheffield Shield until 1982/3. Then, playing a full season of 12 matches, he scored 682 runs (40.11) including two centuries. He toured Zimbabwe with the Young Australians in May 1983 and impressed greatly by scoring hundreds in both first-class matches against the full Zimbabwe side. With a career-best 227 against Victoria in the 1983/4 season, he was unlucky to miss the tour of West Indies, but two centuries in successive games in the following season brought his Test début at the age of 23 when he batted bravely against the West Indian pace, making 51. He toured England in 1985 and although he was not successful in the Tests, 61 in the fourth Test being his only good score, he scored 832 runs on the overall tour, average 55.46. His record included three centuries, the best a magnificent 206 not out against Northamptonshire. In 1985/6 following a fine 81 against New Zealand in the second Test, he gained in confidence and made two hundreds against India when he was promoted to open the batting. In Australia's defeat by New Zealand at Auckland later in 1985/6, he carried his bat throughout Australia's second innings of 103, making 58 not out, but as vice-captain against England in 1986 a Test century at Adelaide was surrounded by so many low scores that he was dropped. Not, however, for long. He established a successful opening partnership with Geoff Marsh which was the bedrock of Australia's successes under Allan Border following the winning of the World Cup in 1987. In 1987/8 his patience and skill were evident in a match-saving 184 not out against England at Sydney in a Test held to mark Australia's bicentenary. Intensely loyal to family, friends, and country, the occasion meant much to Boon. Test hundreds began to be expected from him in every series now: against West Indies he scored 149 at Sydney in 1988/9 and 109 not out at Kingston in 1990/1; against New Zealand 200 in Perth in 1989/90; against India in 1991/2 centuries in Sydney, Adelaide, and Perth to add to the three scored earlier in his career; and against England a flawless 121 at

Adelaide in 1990/1 and in England in 1993, now established as the dependable first wicket down, successive Test hundreds at Lord's (164 not out), Trent Bridge, and Headingley and six more against the counties. On the tour he scored 1,437 runs (75.63). Always a dependable catcher, he became a specialist short-leg, brave and reliable.

First-class career (1978–): 16,773 runs (47.11) including 52 centuries, 6 wickets (60.66), and 196 catches

Test matches (101): 7,111 runs (44.16) including 20 centuries, and 85 catches

BOOTH, Brian Charles

(b. 1933, Bathurst, New South Wales) *New South Wales and Australia*

A very slim right-handed batsman with a great gift of timing, Brian Booth was an elegant stroke-player who looked taller than his 5 ft. $11\frac{1}{2}$ in. His unruffled, effortless style owed much to unhesitating footwork right to the pitch of spin-bowling. Besides a full range of graceful on-side shots, his cover-drives and square-drives were placed to advantage and he cut well. He was a useful change-bowler and versatile field. After playing hockey for Australia in the 1956 Olympic Games in Melbourne, he visited New Zealand with the Australian 'A' side in 1959/60, opening the tour with 105 against Auckland. A permanent member of Australia's middle order between 1961 and 1965, he toured England twice (in 1964 as vice-captain), India, Pakistan, and the West Indies and played in series at home against England, South Africa, and Pakistan. He was in this period probably Australia's most consistent scorer, reaching 1,000 runs after 11 Tests. He made 112 at Brisbane and 103 at Melbourne in 1962/3 against England; and 169 at Brisbane and 102 not out at Sydney in 1963/4 against South Africa, the former on his début against that country. Moreover, he frequently made his runs when they were most needed. He substituted as Bob Simpson's captain in two Tests against England in 1965/6 and set a notable example by standing outside England's dressing-room door and shaking each member of the opposition by the hand after Australia had been beaten by an innings. He was promptly dropped and never chosen for Australia again, although he continued for several years successfully for his state and was vice-captain of the Australian 'A' tour to New Zealand in 1967. A cricketer respected and liked by opponents and team-mates, he became a teacher, Anglican lay-reader, and the first chairman of the

Youth Advisory Committee, set up to deal with teenage vandalism and unemployment.

First-class career (1954–68): 11,265 runs (45.42) including 26 centuries, 16 wickets (59.75), and 119 catches
Test matches (29): 1,773 runs (42.21) including 5 centuries, 3 wickets (48.66), and 17 catches

BORDER, Allan Robert

(b. 1955, Cremorne, Sydney) *New South Wales, Queensland, Gloucestershire, Essex, and Australia*

The most durable cricketer of his generation, Allan Border's teak-hard toughness will become the stuff of legend. Whenever his career had any sort of setback, which was rare, he had his revenge, sooner or later. In the end he outscored all other Test batsmen, and despite a depressingly unsuccessful start as Test captain he eventually presided over a period of more or less remorseless success against all Australia's opponents except the West Indies. Along the way he knocked off the runs and the records like a machine made of cast iron. The working parts of his batting technique were so simple that little could go wrong, and his concentration and determination were apparently without limit. When one Australian talked to another about 'A.B.', no elaboration was required. He was worshipped for his mental and physical tenacity and revered for his achievement. He played in more Tests, more one-day internationals, and scored more Test runs than any other man. He learned the game at an early age on the Mosman Oval in Sydney, his home being situated opposite the ground. A stocky left-hand batsman, specialist slip fielder, and steady, slow left-arm orthodox spin bowler, Allan Border advanced quickly after a season for Gloucestershire 2nd XI (one match for the county) in 1977 and a second in the Lancashire League in 1978. Showing himself in the Sheffield Shield to be a cool, decisive, and impressive stroke-player with a good technique, quick to pull or cut the short ball but also a confident driver, he soon made his way into a struggling Australian team in 1978/9, his first Test and also England's first and only defeat in the series. In his second Test at Sydney, Border scored 45 not out and 60 not out, batting with remarkable authority against the England spinners on a turning pitch on the last day. He made his maiden Test century against Pakistan later in the year and scored 521 runs in six Tests in India at the start of the 1979/80 season, including 162 at Madras to establish himself as Australia's number three. He retained his place in the side

after the return of the Packer players and although he struggled against the West Indies, he made a gritty 115 against England and finished off his long season in great style in Pakistan by scoring 150 not out and 153 in the Lahore Test. Having moved to Queensland, his form was modest during the 1980/1 season until he made 124 in the last Test against India at Melbourne. He was easily the leading batsman on either side in the 1981 series in England with 533 runs (59.22) in the Tests, including a remarkable second innings of 123 not out at Old Trafford when he batted throughout with a broken finger. The Ashes were lost but he helped his country regain them in 1982/3 by making three fifties in his last three innings, after a disappointing start to the series. He showed enormous courage in facing the West Indian fast bowlers, especially in the first phase of his packed international career. He comfortably topped the Australian batting averages in the short 1981/2 series in Australia, scoring 336 runs (67.20), then performed heroically in the Caribbean in the early months of 1984. He made 521 runs (74.73) in the five Tests, carrying the fight almost single-handedly against the barrage of pace. He was often at his very best in the most difficult circumstances and his richest vein of form was produced as captain of an initially very weak Australian team. After taking over from a tearful Kim Hughes during the home series against West Indies in 1984/5 he made 597 runs (66.33) in the 1985 series in England, including a match-winning 196 at Lord's and 146 not out to save the Old Trafford Test. He hit eight first-class hundreds on the tour, including four in his first four matches, displaying a glorious range of strokes. Then, as Australia's fortunes went from bad to worse in 1985/6 he batted with undiminished class, hitting 152 not out against New Zealand and 163 against India, compiling 577 runs in the six home Tests. He continued his outstanding run on the tour to New Zealand by hitting two centuries in the second Test at Christchurch, passing 6,000 Test runs in the process. He played for Essex in 1986 and 1988, scoring over 1,000 runs in both seasons. By now the tide had turned for his country. Unexpectedly, Australia won the World Cup in India in 1987, well led by a captain who had learned from his mistakes—mainly ones of inflexible tactics and poor communication with struggling team-mates. The discipline and strategy instilled by the team manager, Bobby Simpson, enabled Border to deal with matters on the field and his own hardness and single-mindedness began to rub off on his players, who played a ruthlessly tough brand of cricket, occasionally declining into foul-mouthed abuse of opponents. In 1989 in England Border's team regained the Ashes, winning the series by four matches to nil and four years later he returned to pull off at least an equal triumph against his friend and rival Graham Gooch, winning four of the first five Tests before England won at The Oval under Mike Atherton. At Headingley he scored 200 not out and shared an unbroken partnership of 332 for the fifth wicket with Steve Waugh. It was Border's 26th Test hundred. On 26th February 1993 he had surpassed Sunil Gavaskar's record Test aggregate of 10,122 runs, from more matches but with an almost identical average. After a record 93 Tests (32 won, 22 lost, 38 drawn) he was relieved of the Test captaincy, against his will, after home and away series against South Africa in 1993/4. His last ambition, to help Queensland win the Sheffield Shield for the first time, was duly achieved the following season.

First-class career (1976–): 25,551 runs (51.30) including 68 centuries, 102 wickets (39.06), and 345 catches

Test matches (156): 11,174 runs (50.56) including 27 centuries, 39 wickets (39.10), and 156 catches

BOYLE, Henry Frederick

(b. 1847, Sydney; d. 1907, Bendigo) *Victoria and Australia*

More than anyone else, the full-bearded 'Harry' Boyle made the fame of the first Australian touring team of 1878. As a right-handed overarm bowler, he relied much on intelligence and accuracy; he could peg away at medium pace for an hour without bowling a bad ball, and was satisfied if he could make the ball do just enough to beat the bat. A tall man, his very high delivery made the ball rise quickly off the pitch. Spofforth, Allan, and he dismissed MCC at Lord's in 1878 twice in one day, Boyle's record being 3 for 14 and 5 for 3 (when MCC made 19). He toured England again in 1880, 1882, 1884, 1888, and 1890 (in the last tour he was player/manager). He appeared at home against England in 1878/9, and through the early 1880s. In England he appeared in the first two Tests, when he was at his peak. At The Oval in 1882 it was Harry Boyle who took the last wicket to give Australia her victory by seven runs. In first-class matches in England he secured 311 wickets (13.48), 125 coming in 1882. He was one of the most daring of fieldsmen at short mid-on.

First-class career (1871–90): 1,711 runs (10.24) including 1 century, 370 wickets (15.38), and 126 catches

Test matches (12): 153 runs (12.75), 32 wickets (20.03), and 10 catches

BRADMAN, Sir Donald George

(b. 1908, Cootamundra, New South Wales) *New South Wales, South Australia, and Australia*

The son of a farmer and carpenter, the young Don Bradman revealed precocious skill in games and athletics in the country town of Bowral and through the logical organization of Australian sport eventually made his way to the Sydney Cricket Ground for trials, to grade cricket in Sydney, into the New South Wales eleven, and into the Australian side he was to dominate for some 20 years. The mental approach of the man—the resolve, the patience, the concentration, the discipline, the shrewd assessment of any cricketing situation, and the terrier-like desire to worry the bowlers to death—was as remarkable as his natural genius. Although quite small (5 ft. 7 in.), he was physically unexceptional, and scientific tests on his eyesight suggested nothing abnormal. Yet the impression he gave was that he saw the ball earlier in flight than most mortals, and with a clear, unerring judgement, always had the right stroke at his immediate command. He became the greatest run-getter the game has ever known: in 21 years of first-class cricket he was to average a century once in every three innings played. If his actual run-scoring was mechanical, the method employed to get the runs had as much variety as any great player and the pace of his innings was almost always appropriate to the position of the match. His declared aim, indeed, was to dictate the terms of any cricketing situation in which he found himself. The little man was invariably the master and how the bowlers must have loathed him, despaired against him, but grudgingly admired him! His footwork was swift and sure, the timing of his driving, hooking, and cutting perfect. Though he six times scored more than 300, only on twelve occasions did he bat for 6 hours or more. His fielding in the deep or the covers was brilliant. He scored 118 on his début for New South Wales against South Australia at Adelaide, in 1927/8; the following season he appeared for Australia for the first time, at Brisbane in the first Test, but was relegated to 12th man for the second match. He returned for the third at Melbourne, when he made 79 and 112, invaluably for a side in transition, and was never again left out. He toured England in 1930, 1934, 1938, and 1948; the first year he made 2,960 runs (98.66), including ten centuries; the second, 2,020 runs (84.16), including seven centuries; the third, as captain, 2,429 runs (115.66), including 13 centuries; and the final tour, 2,428 runs (89.92), including 11 centuries. In the 1930 series he set a record of 974 runs (139.14), including 334 at Headingley, 254 at Lord's and 232 at The Oval. Against the West Indies and South Africa at home he was also virtually unbowlable. Against the latter, in 1931/2, he made 806 runs (201.50), including four centuries. When MCC were in Australia in 1932/3, bodyline bowling was devised to halt 'the Don's' progress; it was half successful as he averaged a mere 56.57 in four Tests! In 1934, with Bill Ponsford, he amassed 451 for the second wicket against England at The Oval and 388 for the fourth wicket at Headingley. In the series he scored 758 runs (94.75). Away from Tests he struck the then highest score ever in first-class cricket, 452 not out for New South Wales against Queensland at Sydney in 1929/30, and the previous season compiled the record aggregate in Australia of 1,690 runs (93.88), including seven centuries in 13 matches, the highest being 340 not out against Victoria at Sydney. Becoming Australia's captain against England in 1936/7, he was as astute, as tough and as mercilessly efficient as he was as a batsman, and his own batting performances lost nothing to the extra responsibility. Leading his country in five series between 1936 and 1948 he did not lose one, and, indeed, won four decisively. In 1936/7, after a quiet start, he finished with 810 runs (90.00), including 270 at Melbourne, when he added 346 for the sixth wicket with Jack Fingleton, another record, and 212 at Adelaide. He was injured while bowling his leg-breaks during England's marathon innings of 903 runs for 7 at The Oval in 1938, but he averaged 108.50 in the series. He became unfit through fibrositis and there was some doubt about his return to post-war cricket, but he continued to lead Australia. In the first Test against England at Brisbane in 1946/7 he made 187, adding 276 with Lindsay Hassett for the third wicket, and 234 in the second at Sydney, adding 405 for the fifth wicket with Sid Barnes, a record-breaking stand. He made 680 runs (97.14) in the five Tests. In 1947/8 he totalled 715 runs (178.75) against the first Indian side in Australia, including 132 and 127 not out in one match at Melbourne. On his final visit to England he led an unbeaten Australian side. He made 138 in the first Test at Trent Bridge and 173 not out at

Headingley in the fourth match. But in his last Test of all at The Oval, cricket proved its power to humble even the immortal: 'the Don' was bowled by Eric Hollies for 0, second ball. He had scored over 200 in an innings on thirty-seven occasions. In sixty-two Sheffield Shield matches for New South Wales from 1927 to 1934 and for South Australia after 1935 (he captained his second state until 1948) he made 8,896 runs (109.82). On retirement in Adelaide he became the first Australian cricketer to be knighted and at different times chairman of the Board of Control and chairman of the selectors. A public figure of immense significance—he was a businessman and writer of considerable expertise—he remained a devoted family man. In 1981 he was made a Companion of the Order of Australia (AC), his country's highest honour. He continued, while frequently going round the golf course at Royal Adelaide in fewer strokes than his age, to take a close interest in cricketing trends and techniques, answering his huge post-bag with care and courtesy and fighting a fierce but sadly vain campaign to restore the back-foot no-ball law. There can be no other candidate for the title of the greatest of all batsmen.

First-class career (1927–49): 28,067 runs (95.14) including 117 centuries, 36 wickets (37.97), 131 catches, and 1 stumping
Test matches (52): 6,996 runs (99.94) including 29 centuries, 2 wickets (36.00), and 32 catches

BRAYSHAW, Ian James

(b. 1942 South Perth) *Western Australia*

One of only three players—along with Tim Wall and Peter Allan—to take all 10 wickets in a Sheffield Shield innings, Ian Brayshaw's all-round gifts played a part in Western Australia's first six Shields in an 11-year period from 1967/8 to 1977/8. For much of the time he was vice-captain to John Inverarity. His 10 for 44 against Victoria in 1967/8 came at the WACA Ground where his right-arm medium pace seamers were invariably at their deadliest when he was bowling into the strong breeze known as 'The Fremantle Doctor'. A prominent sports writer, he wrote or edited almost a dozen cricket books, including Dennis Lillee's autobiography, *Back to the Mark*. His son, Jamie, also played first-class cricket, both for Western Australia and South Australia, amongst his achievements being a century for his adopted state against the 1994/5 England touring team.

First-class career (1960–77): 4,325 runs (31.80) including 3 centuries, 178 wickets (25.08), and 108 catches

BRIGHT, Raymond James

(b. 1954, Melbourne) *Victoria and Australia*

Ray Bright, one of the best orthodox left-arm spinners to have been produced by Australia since the Second World War, was by international standards no more than a moderate performer. Forced largely by the modern Australian emphasis on fast bowlers to become economical first and a wicket-taker second, he developed into a very steady, tight bowler, his orthodox spinner away from the right-hander being cleverly mixed with a dangerous in-swinging 'arm ball'. However, the surfeit of one-day cricket which he played during the two seasons of World Series Cricket caused his trajectory to get flatter and he lacked the curve and dip of the great slow left-handers. He was a determined and capable right-handed batsman, and an excellent gully fielder. Some useful performances for Victoria in Sheffield Shield cricket led to his selection for two tours of New Zealand, where he performed well, especially in 1976/7 when he took 25 wickets at 14.64 on the short tour to finish top of the bowling averages. With 39 wickets at 20.35 he was again top of the averages in England in 1977 when he played in three Tests. He was only on the fringes of the Australian team after the treaty between World Series Cricket and the Australian Cricket Board, playing in one match against the West Indies and one against England in 1979/80, taking only one wicket in each game. Against Pakistan on the short tour at the end of that season, however, he put in an outstanding Test performance at Karachi where Australia were defeated on a turning pitch. He took 7 for 87 in the first innings and the three Pakistan wickets to fall in the second for 24, finishing the series with 15 wickets (23.60). He was chosen for the Centenary Test at Lord's where he bowled tidily without taking a wicket and, having been ignored for the home Tests in 1980/1, he was selected as the main spinner in England in the 1981 Ashes series. Playing in all but one of the six Tests, he took 12 wickets (32.50) and in all first-class matches on the tour took 40 wickets (26.40). Dropped from the Australian side after an unsuccessful tour of Pakistan in 1982/3, he became captain of his state and was recalled in 1985/6 against New Zealand and India, serving as vice-captain for the tour of New Zealand. In India in 1986/7 he took 5 for 74 in the tied Test at Madras

in sapping, humid heat. He broke Bill Lawry's record of 110 appearances for Victoria, playing in 114 matches before retiring.

First-class career (1972–88): 4,130 runs (21.07) including 2 centuries, 471 wickets (32.08), and 107 catches

Test matches (25): 445 runs (14.35), 53 wickets (41.13), and 13 catches

BROMLEY, Ernest Harvey

(b. 1912, Fremantle; d. 1967, Melbourne) *Western Australia, Victoria, and Australia*

An attractive left-handed batsman whose game was built on attack, Ernest Bromley could hit with terrific power, but his defence was suspect; he was also a superb field, fleet of foot and a sure catch. Known as 'slogger', he had a prodigiously strong, flat throw. He toured England in 1934, but made only 312 runs in 20 innings. It was his fielding that won him a place in the Test at Lord's after representing Australia once previously in the 1932/3 series. In six years with Victoria he averaged 35.71 for the state, hitting three centuries. He appeared in the Bombay Quadrangular Tournament in December 1936.

First-class career (1929–38): 2,055 runs (28.54) including 3 centuries, and 39 wickets (42.33)

Test matches (2): 38 runs (9.50), 0–19, and 2 catches

BROWN, William Alfred

(b. 1912, Toowoomba, Queensland) *New South Wales, Queensland, and Australia*

A right-handed opening batsman of undoubted charm but rather slow in unfolding his array of strokes, Bill Brown was unruffled and assured at the wicket and a prolific scorer in Tests. An excellent field, he trained regularly with professional sprinters. Although he made a duck on his début for his adopted state, New South Wales, he made 154 in his seventh match and 205 in his thirteenth against Queensland and Victoria respectively; against Queensland he shared in a stand of 294 with Don Bradman. He was chosen in preference to Jack Fingleton for the 1934 tour of England, and among his five centuries was 105 in the Test at Lord's, when he opened for his country for the first time. In South Africa, 1935/6, he averaged 59.57 in the Tests, and, returning to England in 1938, enjoyed his best season. Coming second to Bradman in the overall tour averages with 1,854 runs (57.93), including his career-highest, 265 not out against Derbyshire at Chesterfield, he was second also in the Tests, making 512 runs (73.14). At Trent Bridge he made a stolid 133, and at Lord's carried his bat through the first innings of 422, amassing 206 in $6\frac{1}{4}$ hours. Returning to his native Queensland in 1936/7 as player-coach, he scored 1,057 runs in 11 innings in 1938/9; and he captained Australia successfully in the first post-war Test, against New Zealand at Wellington. For Australia against India in 1947/8, he was run out controversially by Mankad, when backing up too far; and in the fifth Test at Melbourne he was run out again—for 99. He later served as a Test selector. Charming and modest, he retained an eager interest in cricket into old age.

First-class career (1932–49): 13,838 runs (51.44) including 39 centuries, 6 wickets (18.33), and 110 catches

Test matches (22): 1,592 runs (46.82) including 4 centuries, and 14 catches

BRUCE, William

(b. 1864, Melbourne; d. 1925, Melbourne) *Victoria and Australia*

The first left-handed batsman sent to England with an Australian team—in 1886 and again in 1893—William Bruce was free and attractive in style, a brilliant hitter either as an opener or in the middle order, but he lacked a sound defence. More successful on his second trip, he made 60 and 37 against Surrey at The Oval, when Tom Richardson was at his best; and he headed the averages in the Tests with 39.75. To a huge record total of 843 against Oxford and Cambridge Past and Present at Portsmouth, he contributed his career-highest, 191, adding 232 in two hours twenty minutes with Hugh Trumble. In very good form against Lord Sheffield's side, 1891/2, he averaged 37.66 in the Tests; and in the third Test at Adelaide in 1894/5 he made his highest against England, a charming 80. His left-arm, medium-paced bowling brought him 69 wickets for his state, but it was infrequently used in Tests. A well-known solicitor who fell on hard times, he was found drowned near Melbourne in 1925.

First-class career (1882–1903): 5,732 runs (23.98) including 4 centuries, 143 wickets (29.68), and 101 catches

Test matches (14): 702 runs (29.25), 12 wickets (36.66), and 12 catches

BRYANT, Francis Joseph

(b. 1907, Perth; d. 1984, Perth) *Western Australia*

The youngest of three cricketing brothers, who all represented Western Australia, on one occasion in the same match, Frank Bryant was one of those most responsible for Perth's receiving Test status in 1970/1. A popular and influential cricket administrator, he managed three Australian teams to New Zealand, including the senior team tour in 1973/4. Like his brother, Dick, he was awarded an OAM and also earned life membership of the Western Australian Cricket Association

First-class career (1926–36): 1,571 runs (27.56) including 3 centuries and 12 catches

BURGE, Peter John Parnell

(b. 1932, Brisbane) *Queensland and Australia*

A tall, rugged, burly right-handed batsman who loved a fight. Peter Burge was one of the most dangerous batsmen of the 1960s. A powerful driver and natural attacker, he was an exceptionally good hooker for a tall man, and many fast bowlers had cause to regret bowling short at him. On his début for his state, against South Australia in 1952/3, he hit 54 and 46, when runs were badly needed each time. The next year he made 103 off a powerful New South Wales attack. He represented Australia for the first time at Sydney in the fifth Test against England in 1954/5 when, at his first touch of the ball, he caught Len Hutton at leg-slip off Ray Lindwall. He toured the West Indies in 1955, with his father managing the side, but did little other than make 177 against British Guiana, and then fared moderately in England in 1956. Dropped first ball, he went on to score 210 against Victoria in 1956/7, but continued to be erratic for Australia, despite touring New Zealand, South Africa, India, and Pakistan. It was after 1960/1 that he emerged as a dominant figure. From two Tests he headed the averages against the West Indies with 53.75. On the England tour of 1961 he appeared in all five Tests for the first time. At The Oval, in the last Test, he struck hard for 181. Against England in 1962/3 he came back superbly with 103 and 52 not out in the fifth match at Sydney and headed the averages with 61.25. He made his career-highest score of 283 against New South Wales at Brisbane in 1963/4 and, after a foot operation, came to England again in 1964 when he finished second to Bobby Simpson in the Test averages. He hit a magnificent 160 at Headingley, turning the match with a daring assault on the second new ball. Burge always considered he batted better against England than anyone else. His last Test century was in the second Test at Melbourne in 1965/6 when he hit 120, another decisive knock, after Australia had followed-on. He made 7,627 runs (56.08) for his state alone. He remained a prominent and popular figure in Queensland cricket. He lost weight after becoming, the locals said, the 'fastest growing sport in Queensland', and was one of the first of the ICC referees who officiated in Test matches, enforcing the new code of conduct vigorously. In 1994 he twice disciplined the England captian, Mike Atherton.

First-class career (1952–67): 14,640 runs (47.53) including 38 centuries, and 170 dismissals (166 c., 4 st.)

Test matches (42): 2,290 runs (38.16) including 4 centuries, and 23 catches

BURKE, James Wallace

(b. 1930, Sydney; d. 1979, Manly, Sydney) *New South Wales and Australia*

Dark-haired, lantern-jawed, and with his baggy cap tugged down over one eye, Jim Burke was an obdurate opening batsman who exuded a healthy dislike of English cricketers on the field. He established a fruitful opening partnership for Australia with Colin McDonald. Enthusiastic but ultra-cautious and stodgy at times, he toured New Zealand with the Australian 'A' team in 1949/50 and, as runs continued to come, made his début against England at Adelaide in 1950/1, scoring 101 not out in the second innings. He toured England (in 1956), South Africa, India, and Pakistan—scoring 161 at Bombay in 1956/7 and 189 at Cape Town in 1958/9. On his sole tour of England he topped the Test averages with 30.11, in 'Laker's year'. In the Test at Brisbane in 1958/9 Burke followed an incredibly slow innings by Trevor Bailey with an even slower one—28 not out in 250 minutes. As an occasional off-break bowler, his action was described by Ian Peebles as looking like a policeman applying his truncheon 'to a particularly short offender's head'. At the height of the 'throwing' controversy in 1958/9, when Peter May was scoring a brilliant century at Sydney, a voice bellowed from the Hill: 'Put Burke on—he can throw straight!' In 58 Sheffield Shield matches he made 3,399 runs (44.14), including his highest, 220 against South Australia at Adelaide in 1956/7. Although he had domestic and financial worries, and was facing a major hip

operation which threatened to prevent him from playing golf, a sport he loved, it was a great shock to his friends when he bought a gun one morning in Sydney early in 1979 and shot himself with it that afternoon.

First-class career (1948–58): 7,563 runs (45.01) including 21 centuries, 101 wickets (29.11), and 58 catches

Test matches (24): 1,280 runs (34.59) including 3 centuries, 8 wickets (28.75), and 18 catches

BURN, Edwin James Kenneth

(b. 1862, Richmond, Tasmania; d. 1956, Hobart) *Tasmania, Wellington, and Australia*

Ken Burn, 'The Scotsman', was a sound, painstaking batsman who made many runs for Richmond, East Hobart, Wellington, and Tasmania: in all cricket he hit 41 centuries, two above 350. He reached three figures in six successive innings in 1895/6 and three years later scored 1,200 runs at an average of 133 in club cricket. He was chosen as second-string wicket-keeper for the 1890 Australian tour of England, and it was only when they were in the Red Sea that his colleagues learnt that he had never put on the gloves in his life. During the tour he made only 355 runs (10.14), but appeared in two Tests. He captained Tasmania for 20 years. At time of death he was the oldest surviving Test cricketer.

First-class career (1883–1909): 1,750 runs (21.60) including 2 centuries, and 14 wickets (22.85)

Test matches (2): 41 runs (10.25)

BURTON, Frederick John

(b. 1865, Collingwood, Victoria; d. 1929, Wanganui, New Zealand) *New South Wales, Victoria, and Australia*

A wicket-keeper, Frederick Burton played in two Tests against England, both at Sydney, in 1886/7 and 1887/8, though Jack Blackham kept during the second match. He toured New Zealand with a New South Wales team in 1895 and settled there. He became a renowned umpire and three of his four sons played provincial cricket.

First-class career (1885–95): 376 runs (13.42) and 32 dismissals (25 c., 7 st.)

Test matches (2): 4 runs (2.00) and 2 dismissals (1 c., 1 st.)

BUSHBY, Charles Harold

(b. 1887, Carrick, Tasmania; d. 1975, Launceston)

A tall fast bowler from Launceston who represented the North of Tasmania against the South several times during the First World War, Harold Bushby's dynamic contribution to Tasmanian cricket is unequalled. A Tasmanian delegate to the Australian Board of Control from 1919 to 1969, Bushby was Board chairman in 1919 and again in 1925/6, before managing the 1934 Australian team to England. A foundation member of the Liberal Party in Tasmania, he was made an OBE in 1958 and an honorary life member of MCC in 1971.

CALDWELL, Tim Charles John

(b. 1913, Clayfield, Queensland; d. 1994, Orange, New South Wales) *New South Wales*

One of the Australian Cricket Board administrators most responsible for negotiating a settlement with Kerry Packer's breakaway World Series Cricket movement during the turbulent 1970s, Caldwell had 14 years on the ACB including four as chairman from 1972 to 1975, when he succeeded Sir Donald Bradman. He was also chairman of the New South Wales Cricket Association executive and a long-serving delegate, initially representing the Northern District club, from 1955 to 1956. A banker by profession, Caldwell was appointed an OBE in 1976 for his services to cricket. He had previously been awarded a BEM for services rendered while a member of the AIF in the Middle East in 1943. He was also a cricketer of note, representing New South Wales with his right-arm orthodox spin in three matches in the mid-1930s. As a continuing tribute, international youth teams visiting Australia contest the Tim Caldwell Cup.

First-class career (1935–6): 48 runs (9.60), 3 wickets (54.00), and 5 catches

CALLAWAY, Sydney Thomas

(b. 1868, Sydney; d. 1923, Christchurch) *New South Wales, Queensland, Canterbury, and Australia*

A splendid batsman when in form and a medium-fast bowler with a good length, Sydney Callaway represented Australia against Lord Sheffield's 1891/2 team and A. E. Stoddart's of 1894/5. In the third Test at Adelaide in 1894/5, he took 5 for 37 (England being dismissed for 124) and added 81 with Albert Trott for the last wicket. He visited New Zealand twice with teams from New South Wales, each time heading the bowling averages. Later he settled there, playing for Canterbury as well as for New Zealand against English and Australian teams. He took 167 wickets in New Zealand from 1896 to 1907. He died in New Zealand after two years of ill health.

First-class career (1888–1906): 1,747 runs (16.79) and 321 wickets (17.00)

Test matches (3): 87 runs (17.40) and 6 wickets (23.66)

CALLEN, Ian Wayne

(b. 1955, Yarck, Victoria) *Victoria, Boland, and Australia*

Ian Callen made an impressive start in the Sheffield Shield in 1976/7, taking 25 wickets in three matches. His Test career was soon blighted after a promising start against India in 1977/8. He took 6 wickets (31.83), scored 22 and 4, both times not out, and held 1 catch in his first Test at Adelaide, when Australia's inexperienced side won a high-scoring game, but on the arduous tour of the Caribbean which followed, he could take only 11 wickets at 50 each and did not get another Test cap. Tall and wiry, with a fine action and an ability to swing the ball away from the bat, he was hardly able to give a fair reflection of his potential. A back injury reduced his chances of playing further Tests but he came back into the reckoning by doing well for Victoria in 1981/2 when he took 31 wickets at 25.45 runs each in six matches (besides averaging more than 20 with the bat). He toured Pakistan in 1982/3, but did not get a chance in the Tests. A live-wire who enjoyed his cricket greatly, he played for Rams-bottom in the Lancashire League in 1981 but his suspect back obliged him to reject a preferred contract from Somerset.

First-class career (1976–86): 578 runs (12.30) and 197 wickets (27.47)

CAMPBELL, Gregory Dale

(b. 1964, Launceston, Tasmania) *Tasmania and Australia*

A surprise choice for Australia's 1989 tour of England after just twelve first-class matches, this right-arm medium pace bowler and right-hand number eleven batsman had an equally swift demise, playing just twenty more games back in Australia before injury enforced his retirement. Originally from Clarence, and one of three Tasmanians (along with David Boon and umpire Steve Randell) to figure in the state's first-ever Test match against Sri Lanka in December 1989, Campbell's selection for England ahead of more experienced bowlers like Michael Whitney was prompted by his 36-wicket season in 1988/9, which included 1 for 64 and 5 for 69 against the ultimate champions, Western Australia, at the WACA Ground. Earlier in the season, he made his highest first-class score, 41, against Queensland in Brisbane, where he shared a 10th wicket stand of 116 with the wicket-keeper, Richard Soule. Campbell played the opening Test of the 1989 Ashes tour at Headingley after Carl Rackemann withdrew with injury. On return to Australia he had another consistent season and played three Tests, doing best in the third Test against Pakistan in Adelaide when he took 3 for 79 and 1 for 83. Knee and wrist injuries shortened his 1990/1 and 1991/2 seasons. He broke a bone in his left wrist trying to field a hot return drive from Dirk Wellham and on return, 10 weeks later, broke down with a back injury and did not represent Tasmania again. Shifting to Queensland, he was unable to regain a place at Sheffield Shield level. In twelve one-day internationals, Campbell claimed 18 wickets, with a best performance of 3 for 17 against New Zealand at Christchurch.

First-class career (1986–91): 347 runs (8.46), 120 wickets (33.47), and 10 catches
Test matches (4): 10 runs (2.50), 13 wickets (38.69), and 1 catch

CARKEEK, William

(b. 1878, Walhalla, Victoria; d. 1937, Melbourne) *Victoria and Australia*

William Carkeek toured England in 1909 as second-string wicket-keeper, but was first choice in 1912, the year of the Triangular Tournament. Short and sturdily built, he was sound rather than brilliant and not in the tradition of the great Australian 'keepers. Nicknamed 'Barlow' because of his stonewalling propensities, his left-handed batting remained moderate and he averaged only 13.28 for his state. He was chosen for the tour of South Africa in 1914/15 which was abandoned because of the First World War.

First-class career (1903–14): 1,388 runs (12.17) and 160 dismissals (114 c., 46 st.)
Test matches (6): 16 runs (5.33) and 6 dismissals (6 c.)

CARLSON, Philip Henry

(b. 1951, Kedron, Queensland) *Queensland and Australia*

Phil Carlson made an outstanding start to his Sheffield Shield career, scoring a century for Queensland at the age of 18, but he was unfortunate in starting his Test career against such a strong England bowling attack as that of the 1978/9 team. Tall, strong, and Scandinavian in appearance, with a military bearing, he was a gifted batsman who loved to drive straight and hard, a good fielder (who held a superb slip catch in his first Test) and a useful, medium-pace, swing bowler. His selection against England followed a succession of high scores in Sheffield Shield cricket—in 1977/8 he scored 591 runs at 45.46 and in 1978/9 he made 448 runs (40.33) as well as taking 28 wickets at 11.00 each—but he proved vulnerable against fast bowling in Test cricket.

First-class career (1969–81): 4,167 runs (28.34) including 5 centuries, and 124 wickets (24.06)
Test matches (2): 23 runs (5.75), 2 wickets (49.50), and 2 catches

CARMODY, Douglas Keith

(b. 1919, Mosman, New South Wales; d. 1977, Concord, New South Wales) *New South Wales and Western Australia*

The originator of the 'Umbrella' or 'Carmody' field, a semi-circle of close catchers set between wicket-keeper and point, Sydney-born Keith Carmody led Western Australia to its first ever Sheffield Shield when it first competed on a restricted basis in 1947/8. A right-hand batsman and occasional wicket-keeper, his career-best score of 198 against South Australia came on his début with his adopted state. He was also a prominent Services XI cricketer, competing in the 'Victory Tests' in 1945. His former team-mate Keith Miller regarded Carmody's cricketing strategies as highly as those of the celebrated Don Bradman.

First-class career (1939–55): 3,496 runs (28.89) including 2 centuries, 3 wickets (62.33), and 42 dismissals (39 c., 3 st.)

CARTER, Hanson

(b. 1878, Halifax, Yorkshire; d. 1948, Sydney) *New South Wales and Australia*

Born in Halifax, 'Sammy' or 'Sep' Carter was only 5 ft. 5 in. tall and slightly built, and he did not stand as close to the stumps as most other noted wicket-keepers have done, but he took the ball comfortably, even when Albert Cotter, Jack Gregory, and Ted McDonald bowled their fastest, and very few byes swelled England's totals. He walked with tiny, quick, dapper strides between the wickets. He toured England in 1902, 1909, and 1921, and in the Test at Headingley in 1921 found himself the only Yorkshire-born player in the match! Generally of small account as a batsman, he could be dangerous and prolific in his own way. His chief delight was a stroke by which he lifted the ball over his left shoulder just as a labourer shovels the dirt out of a drain he is digging. An authority on the Laws of Cricket, it was Sep Carter who pointed out at Old Trafford in 1921 that England's captain had erred in closing his innings, a revelation which sent the Australians back on the field, where the Australian captain Warwick Armstrong unwittingly committed a breach of the Laws by bowling two successive overs. An undertaker by profession, Sammy sometimes came to matches in a hearse. At the age of 54, in 1932, he went on Arthur Mailey's lengthy private tour of Canada, the USA, and New Zealand.

First-class career (1897–1924): 2,897 runs (20.11) including 2 centuries, and 271 dismissals (182 c., 89 st.)

Test matches (28): 873 runs (22.97) and 65 dismissals (44 c., 21 st.)

CHAPPELL, Gregory Stephen

(b. 1948, Unley, Adelaide) *South Australia, Queensland, Somerset, and Australia*

The Chappell family provided something of an Australian answer to the Grace family. The three grandsons of the Test captain Victor Richardson —Ian, Greg, and Trevor Chappell—all played Test cricket, and the elder two were amongst their country's finest batsmen as well as providing the only instance of brothers captaining Australia. Greg, who took over from Ian in 1976/7 as captain of Australia (his brother, elder by five years, had carefully groomed him for the job), was the more brilliant. A tall, naturally graceful right-hander, his batting was cool and composed, without being casual: he had mastered even the best bowlers in the worst batting conditions. At the crease he appeared instantly and permanently at ease, rarely betraying excitement or emotion. He was quick to judge whether he should defend with a bat perfectly straight, or attack with an array of strokes which ranged from a crisp and fearless hook, through majestic drives on either side of the wicket, to delicate cuts and deflections. Starting in the Sheffield Shield with his native South Australia, he later toughened his attitude and broadened his experience by playing for Somerset. In the Championship of 1968 he made 1,108 runs and took 26 wickets, in addition to making one spectacular century in a televised John Player Sunday League

game—typical of his flair for the big occasion. He had already shown such flair when only 18 in a Sheffield Shield match against his later adopted state, Queensland, scoring a century when still in his first season, and at 22 he revealed it again in his first Test at Perth in 1970 when, coming in at 107 for 5 in a reply to an England total of 397, he made 108. The high Test average which he later built up would have been even higher had Australia's unofficial series against the Rest of the World in 1971/2 been taken into account: Chappell made 115 not out at Sydney, 197 not out at Melbourne, and 85 at Adelaide. In England in the closely fought Ashes series of 1972 he made two beautiful centuries at Lord's and The Oval. Against New Zealand at Wellington in 1973/4 he scored 247 not out and 133 in a match at which another fraternal record was established when Ian too scored two centuries. Brilliant performances rolled off his bat in the ensuing years. Against England, 1974/5, he scored 608 runs (55.27) and caught brilliantly at second slip. Tired and unwell, he was much less successful in England the following summer, but in his first match as captain of Australia in 1975/6 he scored 123 and 109 against the powerful West Indies at Brisbane. He went on to lead Australia to a 5–1 victory in the series, scoring 702 runs at an average of 117. Chappell's experience as a captain had begun with his move to Queensland in 1973/4. He was a less successful motivator of men than his brother Ian, but it is perhaps unfair to lay much of the blame for Australia's failures in England in 1977 at the door of their captain, who scored most runs for his team (371 at 41.22), including a memorable century against the tide of English success at Old Trafford, and who by then had decided, after much agonizing, to join most of his fellows in Kerry Packer's World Series Cricket. In addition to his genius as a batsman, Greg Chappell was a more than useful medium-pace swing bowler, always capable of turning in an inspirational spell, and one of the most brilliant slip fielders of modern times. He held seven catches at second slip in the Perth Test against England in 1974/5, setting a world record (subsequently equalled by India's Yajurvindra Singh). Chappell's 14 catches in that series is the second highest in a Test series by a non-wicket-keeper. After the disbandment of World Series Cricket, Greg Chappell, who had hitherto announced his retirement from Test cricket, returned to the fray as captain of Australia in 16 more Tests from 1979 to 1981 before deciding against touring England in 1981. There were times when his health was in doubt during this intense period but his cricket throughout was superb.

Against the West Indies he made 124 at Perth and against England 98 not out at Sydney and 114 at Melbourne. In the many one-day internationals he was still Australia's key batsman although in the field his captaincy sometimes lacked resource. He took the Australian team to Pakistan where the short series was lost despite the captain's 235 in the second Test at Faisalabad. Chappell's third Test double century came less than a year later against India at Sydney where his 204 out of 406 was decisive. For the 1980/1 season he led Australia, at last, to success in a one-day tournament, the triangular series with India and Pakistan, but in the third match of the best of five finals he created an international furore by ordering his brother Trevor to bowl an underarm grubber with New Zealand requiring six runs off the last ball of the match to tie the game. It was an uncharitable piece of captaincy, described by the New Zealand Prime Minister as cowardly, and it was certainly unworthy of a cricketer normally very tough but gracious in triumph or failure. In 1981/2 he had a run of unaccustomed failures, but kept his place as captain on the short tour of New Zealand at the end of the season, scoring 176 at Christchurch, his 20th Test century. In 1982/3 he at last achieved his ambition to captain Australia to victory in an Ashes series, hitting centuries at Perth and Adelaide, significantly the two games which Australia won. His Test career ended in record-breaking style against Pakistan in 1983/4. Having made 150 not out in the second Test, he came to the final Test at Sydney needing 69 to overtake Sir Donald Bradman's Australian record total of 6,996 Test runs. He made 182 to end his Test career with a classic century, just as he had begun it 13 years before. Taking three catches on his last appearance he also established a world record of 122 Test catches, passing Colin Cowdrey's total. Awarded an MBE, he was for a time a national selector, a successful businessman, and occasional TV commentator.

First-class career (1966–84): 24,535 runs (52.20) including 74 centuries, 291 wickets (29.95), and 376 catches
Test matches (87): 7,110 runs (53.86) including 24 centuries, 47 wickets (40.70), and 122 catches

CHAPPELL, Ian Michael

(b. 1943, Unley, Adelaide) *South Australia and Australia*

Ian Chappell will be remembered for many reasons: as one of Australia's best post-war batsmen, as one of her greatest captains of any era, and as a fiercely determined man who led a players' revolt against the cricket administrators of Australia. A grandson of the Test captain, Victor Richardson, and educated, like his brothers, at Prince Alfred College in Adelaide, Ian was as 'Aussie' as a gum tree, tough but straight. He played for South Australia at the age of 18 and for his country at 21. He became quickly established as a stern competitor, a right-handed batsman both gritty and attractive, a brilliant slip fielder and useful leg-spin bowler. Unlike that of his younger brother Greg, Ian Chappell's apprenticeship in Test cricket was tough. After making 348 runs against England in 1968, when he established himself in the Australian team, he scored 138 and 99 in successive Tests in India in 1969/70, but was then brought to earth as Australia were humiliated under Bill Lawry's captaincy in South Africa, losing 4–0. Chappell (whom Lawry had called at the start of the tour 'the best batsman in the world') had a top score of only 34. But from the moment that he replaced Lawry as captain, for the final Test of the 1970/1 series against England, Ian Chappell made a lasting reputation. He lost that match to the wily Illingworth, but a new spirit and new players—notably Dennis Lillee—were to transform Australian fortunes in the next few years. Although Australia failed to regain the Ashes in 1972, the match in which they squared the series at The Oval, with the Chappell brothers both making centuries and sharing a stand of 201, marked the turning point. It was Chappell's good fortune to have at his command one of Australia's greatest-ever fast bowlers, Dennis Lillee, and when he was joined by Jeff Thomson in 1974/5, there was never any doubt that he would restore the Ashes to Australian hands. He used his major assets shrewdly, never relaxing the relentless pressure on the unfortunate English batsmen and setting a fine example in the other departments of the game—batting with his characteristic concentration and dedication to the cause of victory, as well as fielding brilliantly at first slip where he was always outstanding. The following season in England he retained the Ashes, making 192 at The Oval in his final Test as captain. Under his brother's subsequent captaincy he continued to score freely. With Greg he shares a record unlikely to be equalled—both scored centuries in each innings of the first Test against New Zealand at Wellington in 1973/4, Ian making 145 and 121 (yet the match was drawn). Much of Ian Chappell's temperament and character was infused into the men under him, and his players were sometimes

21

accused of excess arrogance and bluntness. It was this very matter-of-fact approach of his, refusing to pay lip service to the niceties of the establishment, which not only resulted in his various brushes with the authorities of cricket, but also contributed to the formation of World Series Cricket in 1977. Having played a leading role, both as player and adviser, in World Series Cricket, he returned to Test cricket when WSC was disbanded, but the controversies continued to follow him. He was suspended for abusing an umpire in a Sheffield Shield match and also carried out two petulant public protests when playing for South Australia against England. He nevertheless played three more Tests in 1979/80, failing in both innings against the West Indies at Adelaide but making 152 (50.66) in four innings against England when his experience, application and determination proved invaluable. It appeared, however, that his enthusiasm for the game had turned sour and his retirement at the end of the season came as no surprise despite the fact that his final year had brought him 890 runs (40.25) and that he had led South Australia into second place in the Sheffield Shield. Thus this stormy character departed the playing scene, knowing that he was loved by few but that he had achieved much and feeling, rightly or wrongly, that he had sinned less than he had been sinned against. He became a competent and successful journalist and TV commentator.

First-class career (1961–79): 19,680 runs (48.35) including 59 centuries, 176 wickets (37.57), 312 catches, and 1 stumping

Test matches (75): 5,345 runs (42.42) including 14 centuries, 20 wickets (65.80), and 105 catches

CHAPPELL, Trevor Martin

(b. 1952, Glenelg, Adelaide) *South Australia, Western Australia, New South Wales, and Australia*

The youngest of the Chappell brothers, Trevor, like Ian and Greg, set his heart on playing for Australia and eventually achieved his ambition in England in 1981, after a long struggle to establish himself in Sheffield Shield cricket. Small, tough, curly-haired, and determined, a nuggety right-handed batsman, useful medium-paced bowler, and fine cover fielder, he eventually proved himself a valuable member of the New South Wales side, scoring 550 runs with two centuries in 1980/1 and thus earning a place on the tour of England. He played in the first three Tests, sharing not only the pleasure of victory at Trent Bridge, where his staunch 20 not out in the second innings helped to stop a sudden slide of Australian wickets, but also the humiliation of unexpected defeat at Headingley. After this match, however, he was dropped and took a back seat on the tour. Not called on at home the following season, he maintained steady form with 533 Sheffield Shield runs. Though he shared with his brothers the distinction of the only instance of three (or more) brothers playing for Australia, he was never quite the batsman Greg or Ian was.

First-class career (1972–85): 4,049 runs (29.55) including 5 centuries, and 59 wickets (24.77)

Test matches (3): 79 runs (15.80) and 2 catches

CHARLTON, Dr Percie Chator

(b. 1867, Sydney; d. 1954, Sydney) *New South Wales and Australia*

Showing promise as batsman and fast-medium bowler—for Eighteen of Sydney Juniors he took seven wickets against Shaw and Shrewsbury's team in 1887/8—Percie Charlton toured England with the 1890 team when he took 42 wickets (19.04) but averaged only 14.30 with the bat. Due to ill-health he soon retired from first-class cricket and became a medical practitioner, but remained an active club cricketer, notably for the Australian I Zingari, whose President he was from 1928 to 1947. Thereupon he became the club's Patron, 'touching nothing he did not adorn'. He was also a long-serving cricket administrator in New South Wales, although he spent six years as a doctor in England.

First-class career (1888–97): 648 runs (12.46) and 97 wickets (19.96)

Test matches (2): 29 runs (7.25) and 3 wickets (8.00)

CHEGWYN, John William

(b. 1909, Botany, New South Wales; d. 1992, Sydney) *New South Wales*

A right-hand batsman who made almost 12,000 club runs for Randwick and represented his state five times, Jack Chegwyn's major contribution came in promoting the game in New South Wales country areas, as well as during his 25-year term as a state selector, a period in which the state won the Sheffield Shield nine times. For almost 40 years from 1939 into the late 1970s, Chegwyn paraded well-known Australian Test stars with promising youngsters in series of representative games in the New South Wales bush. Along the way, he unearthed many Australian players, including Doug Walters and Steve

Rixon. He represented Randwick at the NSW Cricket Association for more than 30 years and was appointed a life member of the Association in 1956. In 1977 he was awarded an MBE for his services to cricket.

First-class career (1940–1): 375 runs (46.87) including 1 century and 3 catches

CHIPPERFIELD, Arthur Gordon

(b. 1905, Sydney; d. 1987, Sydney) *New South Wales and Australia*

Of average height, thickset, and rather slow in his movements, 'Chipper' was a solid batsman, busy and competent, essentially a front-foot player. He was also a slow spin bowler who collected useful wickets (although he often toiled more than he spun) and a quite brilliant slip field. A surprise choice for the 1934 tour—even at the age of 29 and already bald—he had played only three times for his state, though he had hit a century for Northern Districts of New South Wales against the 1932/3 MCC team. He soon justified his selection by making 99 on his Test début at Trent Bridge. He played in all five Tests. He averaged 37.58 on this tour, and 38.56 in the 1936/7 series against England. When Gubby Allen and Bill Voce bundled Australia out for 58 at Brisbane in the first Test, he alone stood his ground with 26 not out. On the 1938 tour his activities were greatly curtailed by appendicitis. His one Test century was 109 in the first Test at Durban in 1935/6.

First-class career (1933–9): 4,295 runs (38.34) including 9 centuries, 65 wickets (39.72), and 91 catches

Test matches (14): 552 runs (32.47) including 1 century, 5 wickets (87.40), and 15 catches

CLARK, Wayne Maxwell

(b. 1953, Perth) *Western Australia and Australia*

A strongly built, fast-medium right-arm swing bowler with an action very reminiscent of Graham McKenzie's, Wayne Clark was a pivotal member of the young Australian side formed under Bobby Simpson's captaincy in the wake of the defections to Kerry Packer. But after taking 43 wickets in nine successive Tests, suspicions about the legality of his action when he delivered his bouncer (certainly a mean and dangerous one) and a general loss of form at the start of the 1978/9 season, led to his replacement by Rodney Hogg as Australia's opening bowler. A back injury had caused his omission from the final Test of the 1978 tour of the West Indies, but with 15 wickets

in four Tests and 31 on an arduous tour at an average of 23 each, Clark performed manfully. His last Test was the first against Pakistan in March 1979.

First-class career (1974–84): 717 runs (12.57) and 210 wickets (29.37)

Test matches (10): 98 runs (5.76), 44 wickets (28.75), and 6 catches

COLLEY, David John

(b. 1947, Sydney) *New South Wales and Australia*

A right-arm fast-medium bowler with a long run-up and a more than useful late-order batsman, David Colley was a surprise choice for the 1972 tour of England. He appeared in three Tests, often bowling better than his figures reflected, and he hit a daring 54 at Trent Bridge. He played another remarkable hitter's innings in 1974/5 when, in a losing cause, he hit MCC for 90 off 67 balls while only 19 runs came at the other end.

First-class career (1969–77): 2,374 runs (23.74) including 1 century, and 236 wickets (31.60)

Test matches (3): 84 runs (21.00), 6 wickets (52.00), and 1 catch

COLLINS, Herbert Leslie

(b. 1889, Sydney; d. 1959, Sydney) *New South Wales and Australia*

Herbie or 'Horseshoe' Collins—a bookmaker by profession—was a right-handed batsman with unlimited patience and concentration, of practically impregnable defence, almost strokeless, seemingly without power, and yet highly effective and a regular choice in Tests from 1920 until 1926. As a slow left-arm bowler, he often broke irritating partnerships. Opening with Warren Bardsley, he made 70 and 104 in his first Test at Sydney in 1920/1, and 162 in his third at Adelaide; in that series he totalled 557 runs in nine completed innings. In South Africa, 1921/2, he hit 203 in the Test at Johannesburg. His last major successes against England were in the first Test at Sydney in 1924/5 when he scored 114 and 60. A shrewd captain who understood his men, Herbie Collins led the AIF team in England in 1919, doing the double himself, and then guided Australia to a 4–1 victory in the 1924/5 series. When he led the team that lost the Ashes in 1926 he was handicapped by neuritis. In Sheffield Shield matches he scored 2,040 runs (41.63). At 51, he married a girl of 24, the union lasting 11 years, but gambling dragged him down in the end.

23

CONINGHAM

First-class career (1909–26): 9,924 runs (40.01) including 32 centuries, 181 wickets (21.38), and 115 catches
Test matches (19): 1,352 runs (45.06) including 4 centuries, 4 wickets (63.00), and 13 catches

CONINGHAM, Arthur

(b. 1863, South Melbourne; d. 1939, Sydney) *Queensland, New South Wales, and Australia*

A left-handed batsman and fast bowler, Arthur Coningham ranked high in Australia as an all-rounder and came to England with the 1893 team but was surprisingly given little to do. His career-highest score was 151 for Queensland against New South Wales at Sydney in 1895/6; and his sole Test was the second at Melbourne in 1894/5, when he scored 10 and 3 and took 2 for 76. Volatile and over-confident, he was no-balled when bowling to England's captain, A. E. Stoddart, and, in annoyance, deliberately threw the next ball at the batsman. A champion athlete, he was also adept at billiards, rowing, shooting, and Rugby football and he earned a medal saving a boy's life in the Thames in 1893. But this was dull fare compared with the conspiracy sensation of 1900: 'Conny', revolver at his hip, conducted his own scandalous and unsuccessful divorce case with an eminent priest as the alleged 'other man'. In eleven Sheffield Shield matches he made 203 runs and took 41 wickets. He died in a mental home, but his son, Sir Arthur Coningham, became an RAF Air Marshal.

First-class career (1892–8): 896 runs (15.71) including 1 century, and 112 wickets (23.24)

CONNOLLY, Alan Norman

(b. 1939, Skipton, Victoria) *Victoria, Middlesex, and Australia*

A tall and powerfully built, right-arm, fast-medium bowler, Alan Connolly's swerve, cut, and clever changes of pace set the batsmen of several nations some insoluble problems. Genial and persevering, he toured England twice in 1964 and 1968, suffering a back injury on the former tour, but in the latter headed the Test averages with 23 wickets (25.69). He toured India twice and South Africa once. During his last tour, one of several as partner for 'Garth' Mackenzie, he took 20 wickets (26.10) in the four Tests against the victorious South Africans in 1969/70, heading the averages. Seven Tests against England brought him 25 wickets, but his finest feat was 6 for 47 in the first innings of the fourth Test at Port Elizabeth—in

the last Test played by South Africa for 22 years—before Australia were overwhelmed by 323 runs. Connolly signed for Middlesex for three years, taking 74 wickets (23.24) in 1969, but 1970 was less successful, partly because of back trouble, and he returned home. No one had taken more wickets for Victoria than his 330 at 27.04 in 83 matches.

First-class career (1959–70): 1,073 runs (8.79) and 676 wickets (26.58)
Test matches (29): 260 runs (10.40), 102 wickets (29.22), and 17 catches

COOPER, Bransby Beauchamp

(b. 1844, Dacca, India; d. 1914, Geelong, Victoria) *Middlesex, Kent, Victoria, and Australia*

Bransby Cooper was an outstanding right-handed batsman at Rugby School—attractive, hard-hitting, patient, and defensive when necessary. In 1869 he opened with W.G. at The Oval for Gentlemen against Players, putting on 105, and three weeks later—going in against a total of 475—they put on 283 in 3 hours 40 minutes for Gentlemen of the South against Players of the South. Soon afterwards he left England for the USA and then spent the rest of his life in Australia. He hit 83 for Eighteen of Victoria against W.G.'s England team in 1873/4, and he represented Australia in the first-ever Test at Melbourne in 1876/7, scoring 15 and 3 and holding 2 catches. He was also a useful wicket-keeper.

First-class career (1863–77): 1,600 runs (20.51) including 1 century and 61 dismissals (41 c., 20 st.)

COOPER, William Henry

(b. 1849, Maidstone, Kent; d. 1939, Malvern, Melbourne) *Victoria and Australia*

Born in Kent, William Cooper was, at the time of death, the oldest Australian Test player. Starting serious cricket late, at 27, he became an effective right-arm, slow, leg-break bowler, capable of prodigious turn, and in his initial Test at Melbourne, in the 1882 New Year's match, took 9 for 200 (in 98.2 overs). He toured England with the 1884 team but could not grip the ball properly because of a finger injured on the voyage over. He was successively captain of his state, a state selector and vice-president of the Victoria Cricket Association. Paul Sheahan, who also played for Victoria and Australia, is his great-grandson.

First-class career (1878–86): 247 runs (10.29) and 71 wickets (24.49)
Test matches (2): 13 runs (6.50), 9 wickets (25.11), and 1 catch

CORLING, Grahame Edward

(b. 1941, Newcastle, New South Wales) *New South Wales and Australia*

On the small side for an opening right-arm fast-medium bowler, Grahame Corling had admirable stamina and, after one season of first-class cricket, toured England in 1964 as the youngest member of the team, appearing in all the Tests. Thereafter, his first-class career fell away though he remained a keen and cheerful grade cricketer. In 40 Sheffield Shield matches he took 111 wickets (33.45).

First-class career (1963–8): 484 runs (10.52), 173 wickets (32.05), and 11 catches
Test matches (5): 5 runs (1.66) and 12 wickets (37.25)

COSIER, Gary John

(b. 1953, Richmond, Victoria) *Victoria, South Australia, Queensland, and Australia*

Red-haired, burly, and merry, like a reincarnation of the youthful Henry VIII, Gary Cosier was a cricketer of character who never quite established himself in the Australian side, either before or after the Packer Revolution. An outstanding teenage cricketer in Victoria, he moved to South Australia for whom he scored two hundreds against the 1975/6 West Indians. Rewarded with a place in the third Test at Melbourne, he scored 109, but though he played some fine innings afterwards, including 168 against Pakistan in 1976/7, technical deficiencies, and a desire to play his shots even when it was indiscreet to do so, led to a disappointing inconsistency. He batted with virtually no backlift, but very powerful arms made him a good hooker and square-cutter and in limited-overs cricket he could be a dynamic exponent of the lofted drive: a whirlwind knock helped Australia defeat England in a one-day international at his favourite Melbourne in 1978/9. A cheerful, happy-go-lucky character, he was also a good close fielder and a very useful slow-medium bowler who could swing the ball alarmingly in humid conditions. A property company in Queensland insured his future with the 'Sunshine State' by offering him a long-term contract said to be worth some £30,000 a year, but his career faded.

First-class career (1971–81): 5,005 runs (32.92) including 7 centuries, and 75 wickets (30.68)
Test matches (18): 897 runs (28.93) including 2 centuries, 5 wickets (68.20), and 14 catches

COTTAM, John Thomas

(b. 1867, Sydney; d. 1897, Coolgardie, W. Australia) *New South Wales*

A right-handed batsman and popular character, John Cottam represented Australia once against England at Sydney, 1886/7, scoring 1 and 3 and holding 1 catch. He did not appear in any Sheffield Shield matches, despite a polished style and strong physique. He died of typhoid, aged only 29.

First-class career (1886–90): 273 runs (22.75)

COTTER, Albert

(b. 1883, Sydney; d. 1917, Palestine) *New South Wales and Australia*

Once he gained command over his length and shortened his run, 'Tibby' Cotter, whose style was similar to that, later, of Jeff Thomson, could be a fearsome fast bowler. From 1904 until 1912 he was the spearhead of his country's attack. Like Larwood, Lindwall, and other very fast bowlers he was not tall, but had immense strength in his chest and shoulders. In the fifth Test at Melbourne in 1903/4, after England had regained the Ashes, he took 8 for 65, earning Australia a convincing win. He toured England in 1905 and 1909; in 1905 he took 124 wickets (including 12 for 34 at Worcester when his pace was terrific), and in 1909 he had a large hand in the winning of the Headingley Test, taking 5 for 38 in the second innings. Two years later he took four wickets in four balls for Glebe versus Sydney. Tibby was killed in action by a sniper at Beersheba while serving in the Australian Light Horse. He had had a premonition of his death.

First-class career (1901–13): 2,484 runs (16.89) and 442 wickets (24.27)
Test matches (21): 457 runs (13.05), 89 wickets (28.64), and 8 catches

COULTHARD, George

(b. 1856, Boroondarra, Victoria; d. 1883, Melbourne) *Victoria and Australia*

On the staff of the Melbourne club, George Coulthard accompanied Lord Harris's 1878/9 team in Australia as umpire, and adjudicated in the sole Test at Melbourne to general satisfaction. Then, during the match between the tourists and New South Wales at Sydney, all hell broke loose. Rivalry between Victoria and New South Wales was bitter and when George gave W. L. Murdoch out on an appeal for run out, the crowd grew angry and invaded the playing area. George appearing to be in danger, Lord Harris moved to help him but was struck by a 'larrikin' wielding a stick. The trouble subsided, and the match continued. George became the first umpire who *later* played in a Test, for Australia at Sydney in 1881/2, when he made 6 not out at number eleven and did not bowl. He died of consumption a year later.

First-class career (1880–1): 92 runs (11.50) and 5 wickets (25.00)

COWPER, Robert Maskew

(b. 1940, Melbourne) *Victoria, Western Australia, and Australia*

Known as 'Wallaby' because, like his father, he played Rugby Union in an Australian Rules stronghold, Bob Cowper was a well-built, left-handed batsman who scored readily with skilful leg-side deflections, square-cuts, hooks, and drives. Though not spectacular, he was remarkably consistent either as an opener or in the middle order. A useful off-spin bowler, he was a little quicker than most bowlers of this type and was rarely collared; and he was also a first-rate slip field. He toured England in 1964 and 1968, and South Africa, the West Indies, India, and Pakistan once each. On his first tour in 1964 he scored 1,287 runs (51.48) but did not establish himself as a Test player until his visit to the West Indies in 1965 when he headed the Test aggregates with 417, including two centuries, creating a fine impression against the fast bowlers. He was recalled for the fifth Test against England at Melbourne in 1965/6 and scored 307, the highest innings in a Test in Australia and the fourth longest in history, lasting in all 12 hours and seven minutes. Less successful against South Africa in 1966/7, he was back to his best when India toured Australia in 1967/8, scoring most runs in the four Tests, 485 (69.28), including two centuries, and taking 13 wickets (18.38). He also played as a professional in the Lancashire League. In Sheffield Shield matches, he scored 4,067 runs (53.51) and took 59 wickets (40.83). He was a very keen and studious cricketer, with an extensive knowledge of the game. He acted as adviser to Kerry Packer during his first negotiations with the Australian Cricket Board, became a respected figure in Melbourne business circles and a fine player of real tennis, and settled in Monte Carlo, a prosperous, hearty and well-travelled man with a cigar almost always in hand.

He represented Australia at the ICC and became one of the early ICC referees.

First-class career (1959–69): 10,595 runs (53.78) including 26 centuries, 183 wickets (31.19), and 152 catches

Test matches (27): 2,061 runs (46.84) including 5 centuries, 36 wickets (31.63), and 21 catches

CRAFTER, Anthony Ronald

(b. 1940, Mt Barker, South Australia)

Australia's most experienced Test umpire, Tony Crafter officiated in 33 Tests and 85 one-day internationals from 1978 to 1992 before becoming the Australian Cricket Board's national umpiring officer. A prominent club batsman who was in the South Australian Sheffield Shield squad for three seasons and played for the Leicestershire 2nd XI, Crafter made more than 3,000 first-grade runs in a 13-year career with Port Adelaide before switching to umpiring. In only his second Test match, in Perth in 1979, he was involved in controversy when the Pakistan tailender Sikander Bakht was given run-out after backing-up too far at the non-striker's end. Later in the fiery game, Australia's Andrew Hilditch was given out handled the ball. On Pakistan's next tour of Australia, in 1981/2, Crafter was sandwiched between an angry Javed Miandad and Dennis Lillee after the volatile pair had clashed in mid-pitch at the WACA Ground. Crafter had to restrain Miandad, who brandished his bat threateningly at the Australian. He was also officiating in Perth in 1983, when hundreds of fans, locked out of the Australia–West Indies international, broke down a section of the fence. The estimated attendance that day was more than 33,000. Whenever emotions were high, Tony Crafter was a calm, smiling, pacifying figure: his judgements were cool, and usually right.

CRAIG, Ian David

(b. 1935, Yass, New South Wales) *New South Wales and Australia*

At 16 years 5 months, Ian Craig became the youngest player to appear in interstate cricket, against South Australia at Sydney, when he made a sedate 91. The following season, 1952/3, an innings of 213 not out for his state against the South Africans gained him a place in the fifth Test at Melbourne, when he scored 53 and 47, starting the match, at 17 years, 239 days, as Australia's youngest player in Test cricket. Touring England in 1953, however, he averaged only 16.50, and on returning home he resumed his studies as a chemist, not coming back to first-class cricket for three years. But his skill was never in doubt: his cover-driving could be a model of perfection and his on-side play crisp and certain, with feet in the right place all the time. Though small and apparently quite slight, he had deceptive strength and timing and once hit Ian Johnson for four sixes in five balls in Lindsay Hassett's benefit match. But he had weaknesses, especially against the good-length ball just outside the off-stump, and he lacked the ruthlessness of Don Bradman, with whom in his youth he was compared. On his second visit to England in 1956 he made only 55 runs (being dismissed by Jim Laker three times out of four); he was still the youngest member of the Australian party. On the way home he did well against India and Pakistan and he captained the Australians in South Africa in 1957/8 with much success: the newly confident team won three Tests out of five and lost none. Beyond a 52 in the third Test at Durban, which saved his side in the first innings, he did little in the Tests, but averaged 36.93 for the whole tour. A serious and pleasant man by nature, Ian was being groomed for leadership against England on his return to Australia, but he contracted hepatitis the following season and was rarely in the running for a Test place subsequently. He continued to captain his state, however, and against Queensland at Sydney in 1960/1 Neil Harvey and he added 323 for the second wicket.

First-class career (1951–61): 7,328 runs (37.96) including 15 centuries
Test matches (11): 358 runs (19.88) and 2 catches

CRAWFORD, William Patrick Anthony

(b. 1933, Dubbo, New South Wales) *New South Wales and Australia*

A tall, gangling right-arm fast bowler, Pat Crawford burst on the scene in 1954/5, heading the Sheffield Shield averages with 25 wickets (12.96). He was regarded as the logical successor to Ray Lindwall in Australia's ranks and was an improving batsman. He toured England, India, and Pakistan in 1956 and captured some inexpensive wickets against India, but throughout was subject to muscular injuries, and soon dropped out of first-class cricket. He had some experience of the Lancashire League.

First-class career (1954–7): 424 runs (19.27) and 110 wickets (21.02)
Test matches (4): 53 runs (17.66), 7 wickets (15.28), and 1 catch

DANSIE, Hampton Neil

(b. 1928, Nuriootpa, South Australia) *South Australia*

Scorer of more runs (6,692) at Sheffield Shield level than any other player without making an Australian twelve, the right-handed Neil Dansie played a record 107 matches with South Australia. He was also a prominent administrator and had 20 years as a selector for South Australia, including several as chairman. In 1991 he was awarded an OAM for his services to cricket.

First-class career (1949–66): 7,543 runs (34.44) including 18 centuries, 90 wickets (33.31), and 48 catches

DARLING, Hon. Joseph

(b. 1870, Adelaide; d. 1946, Hobart) *South Australia and Australia*

Of medium height, thickset, powerful of frame and personality, his brown moustache and tanned face making him look older than he was, Joe Darling was a batsman who never seemed out of form. Frequently opening the innings, he was one of the great left-handers, who could either defend with stubborn steadiness or pull a game round by determined forcing tactics; and he was a fine mid-off. His greatest impact, however, was as a leader. He toured England in 1896, 1899, 1902, and 1905, as the inspiring captain of the last three teams. On these tours he led two Ashes-winning sides—1899 and 1902—and made, altogether, 6,302 runs (33.70) and held 92 catches. At home he led the winning side of 1901/2. In 1905, however, England were triumphant, the captain F. S. Jackson winning all five tosses in the Tests. When the two skippers met again at the Scarborough Festival at the end of the tour, Joe, with a towel round his waist, waited in the dressing-room and received 'Jacker' with the remark: 'I'm not going to risk the toss this time except by wrestling'—but the spin of the coin again favoured 'Jacker'. In the 1897/8 series Joe made 101 in the first Test at Sydney, 178 in the second at Adelaide and 160 in the fifth at Sydney, heading the batting with 537 runs (67.12). His highest in first-class cricket was 210 for his state against Queensland at Brisbane in 1898/9. Farming and politics occupied his time outside cricket once he had sold his sports store in Adelaide in 1908. Settling in Tasmania, he became a member of the Legislative Assembly in 1921, helping to form the Country Party a year later and being awarded the CBE for public services in 1938. His father had been a member of the Legislative Assembly of

South Australia and had inaugurated the Adelaide Oval, one of the most beautiful Test grounds.

First-class career (1893–1907): 10,635 runs (34.52) including 19 centuries, and 148 catches
Test matches (34): 1,657 runs (28.56) including 3 centuries, and 27 catches

DARLING, Leonard Stuart

(b. 1909, Melbourne; d. 1992, Adelaide) *Victoria and Australia*

A left-handed batsman born to attack but lacking solidity, and occasional right-arm fast-medium bowler, Len Darling had no outstanding successes for Australia; he is best remembered for his superb catches on the leg-side which disposed of Walter Hammond and Maurice Leyland on the 'sticky' wicket at Melbourne in 1936/7. He appeared occasionally for his country against England in 1932/3 and 1934—when he made over 1,000 runs on the tour—and again in 1936/7. He also played in all five Tests against South Africa in 1935/6. His highest Test score was 85 at Sydney in the last match of 1932/3. For his state he made 3,451 runs (47.93). He played baseball for both Victoria and South Australia.

First-class career (1926–36): 5,780 runs (42.50) including 16 centuries, and 32 wickets (46.93)
Test matches (12): 474 runs (27.88), 0–65, and 8 catches

DARLING, Warrick Maxwell

(b. 1957, Waikerie, South Australia) *South Australia and Australia*

Given his chance in Test cricket earlier than might have been the case if so many senior players had not played World Series Cricket for two years, 'Rick' Darling had a stern baptism against the varied skills of India (1977/8 and 1979), West Indies (1978) and England (1978/9), but his ability to shine in the highest company was clear, for all his inconsistency. Bursting with youthful keenness, this fair-haired, right-handed opening bat and brilliant cover fielder from the Murray River country, a great-nephew of Joe Darling, scored 65 and 56 in his first Test against India, and made two hundreds on his first tour, to the West Indies—although he failed in the Tests. He often threatened to disrupt the supremacy of England's bowlers in 1978/9 with his brilliant and audacious hooking and cutting. His 221 runs in the series (27.62) included a highest score of 91 at Sydney. But his flair was never exploited to the full because of accompanying rashness. He nearly

died after being hit on the heart by a ball from Bob Willis in the fifth Test at his home ground, Adelaide. The gum he was chewing lodged in the back of his throat but he was revived by England's John Emburey who administered the 'pre-cordial thump' to get him breathing again. His performances in five more Tests in India were modest; he batted sometimes as an opener and sometimes in the middle order and although he made 59 in the third Test at Kanpur, an innings of great resolution, he made only one other fifty on the tour, illness and injury more than once obstructing this unlucky cricketer. He had to retire hurt in the last innings of the tour, having been hit on the head again, this time by a ball from Kapil Dev. He came back to form with a vengeance in 1981/2, hitting 1,011 runs (72.21) with three centuries, but he was overlooked for Test matches. He remained an attractive middle-order batsman for South Australia, and he hit a century against the 1985/6 Indians in his final season.

First-class career (1975–86): 5,554 runs (35.83) including 9 centuries, and 30 catches
Test matches (14): 697 runs (26.80) and 5 catches

DAVIDSON, Alan Keith

(b. 1929, Lisarow, Gosford, New South Wales) *New South Wales and Australia*

For many years president of the New South Wales Cricket Association, Alan Davidson was a left-handed all-rounder of the highest class. Turning from left-arm 'chinamen' to fast bowling to make full use of his height and barrel-chested power, he ran a lively 15 yards, culminating in a strong wheeling action. He moved the new ball very late in the air, and off the pitch in either direction. As a left-handed batsman, he had tremendous power in his attacking strokes; and in the field he moved sharply, equally brilliant in the deep or close to the wicket. Establishing himself for the Australian 2nd XI in New Zealand in 1949/50, he took 10 for 29 off 81 balls and made 157 not out in the match against Wairarapa at Masterton. He toured England in 1953, 1956, and 1961, India and Pakistan twice, and South Africa once; and at home he had three series against England and one against the West Indies. He never knew a poor series. Richie Benaud wrote of him: 'I have never played with or against a more penetrative bowler. . . . For the five years after 1957/8, whenever the side was in trouble the captain, Craig, Harvey or myself, always looked for Davidson and seldom did he fail' (*Willow Patterns*, 1969). In 1958/9 against England he scored 180 runs and took 24 wickets (20.00). In 1960/1, far and away the best bowler on either side, he took 33 wickets (18.54), besides scoring 212 runs against the West Indies. In the first Test tie at Brisbane, he became the first player to score 100 runs and take ten wickets in a Test (44 and 80—his own Test highest—and 5 for 135 and 6 for 87). His most productive bowling in a Test innings was 7 for 93 against India at Kanpur in 1959/60. In 25 Tests against England alone he made 750 runs, took 84 wickets and held 23 catches. A modest family man, but an amusing raconteur, he was successively bank clerk, manager, and director of the Rothmans National Sports Foundation. He was awarded an OBE for services to sport. His autobiography, *Fifteen Faces*, published in 1963, was well received.

First-class career (1949–63): 6,804 runs (32.86) including 9 centuries, 672 wickets (20.90), and 168 catches

Test matches (44): 1,328 runs (24.59), 186 wickets (20.53), and 42 catches

DAVIES, Geoffrey Robert

(b. 1946, Sydney) *New South Wales*

A leanly built all-rounder who toured New Zealand twice with Australian second teams (1966/7 and 1969/70) and was 12th man in the opening Test of the 1968/9 series against the West Indies, Geoff Davies played his last game with New South Wales aged only 25. Included amongst his most satisfying moments are the highest of his five first-class centuries (127 for New South Wales against Victoria in Melbourne in 1968/9) and a career-best analysis of 6 for 43 (and 112) against Queensland at Sydney in 1967/8.

First-class career: (1965–71): 3,903 runs (36.13) including 5 centuries, 107 wickets (32.18), and 70 catches

DAVIS, Ian Charles

(b. 1953, Sydney) *New South Wales, Queensland, and Australia*

Something of an enigma, Ian Davis was a slightly built, fair-haired, neat, right-handed opening (or middle-order) batsman, who first played Test cricket for Australia at the age of 20. He faded for a time, spending one season with Queensland before returning to his native Sydney, but seemed to be re-establishing himself in the Australian team before joining the Kerry Packer troupe. He was given an extended trial in the Australian side, performing only modestly in six Test matches at

home and abroad against New Zealand in 1973/4. A good innings of 91 against the 1974/5 MCC team did not regain him his Test place but after a maiden Test century against Pakistan at Adelaide (105) he was back in favour by the time of the 1977 Centenary Test, scoring a solid 68 in the second innings at Melbourne. In three Tests in England in 1977, he could make only 107 runs (17.83) and in 13 matches on the tour averaged a modest 30. He held his own, however, in the highly competitive World Series Cricket events. An outstanding fielder, his batting had a pleasant touch at its best, with neat cutting and glancing and some sweet driving.

First-class career (1973–82): 4,609 runs (33.40) including 7 centuries

Test matches (15): 692 runs (26.61) including 1 century, and 9 catches

DAVIS, Simon Peter

(b. 1959, Brighton, Melbourne) *Victoria, Durham, and Australia)*

Simon Davis, a fair-haired, right-arm, fast-medium in-swing bowler of notable accuracy who played his only Test in New Zealand in 1986, first caught the eye in England when he played for Durham in 1982 and 1983, taking 55 wickets in two seasons in Minor Counties cricket. He also turned in two outstanding performances in one-day cricket, taking 4 for 11 for the Minor Counties against Leicestershire, and 7 for 32 for Durham against Lancashire. He made his début for Victoria the following year and some hostile performances for his state in the 1985/6 season won him a place in the Australian one-day side, for whom he took 18 wickets against New Zealand and India. In New Zealand, he played in only the first Test, taking no wickets for 70 and scoring 0. Thereafter the selectors viewed him only as a limited-overs specialist, but he five times took five wickets in a first-class innings and his wickets comfortably exceeded his runs: he was a genuine number eleven.

First-class career (1983–8): 98 runs (5.15) and 124 wickets (35.04)

De COURCY, James Harry

(b. 1927, Newcastle, New South Wales) *New South Wales and Australia)*

Although possessing a capacity to charm and the ability to play all the strokes, Jim de Courcy never took the high place his ability indicated. An attacking right-handed batsman, he frequently

29

DELL

obtained a good start without reaching big figures. He toured England in 1953, scoring 1,214 runs (41.86), including 204 against Combined Services at Kingston, but disappointed in the Tests, the only series in which he represented his country. Fifty matches for his state realized 2,362 runs.

First-class career (1947–57): 3,778 runs (37.04) including 6 centuries
Test matches (3): 81 runs (16.20) and 3 catches

DELL, Anthony Ross

(b. 1947, Lymington, England) *Queensland and Australia*

A heavily built, left-arm fast-medium bowler, born in Hampshire of English parents, Tony Dell joined Dennis Lillee in the attack for the final Test of 1970/1 against England, and made another Test appearance against New Zealand in 1973/4. But he was unable to secure a Test match place in the face of such competition as Jeff Thomson, Max Walker, Gary Gilmour, Lillee himself, and his own Queensland opening partner Geoff Dymock.

First-class career (1970–4): 169 runs (5.63) and 137 wickets (26.70)
Test matches (2): 6 runs (—) and 6 wickets (26.66)

DODEMAIDE, Anthony Ian Christopher

(b. 1963, Williamstown, Victoria) *Victoria, Sussex, and Australia*

Tony Dodemaide's great moment of fame came in the 1987/8 Christmas Test against Jeff Crowe's New Zealanders in his home town of Melbourne when he was called at the eleventh hour as a replacement for his close friend and Footscray team-mate Merv Hughes. A right-arm fast-medium bowler and right-hand number seven batsman, Dodemaide made the most effective contribution by an Australian all-rounder in his first Test for years, scoring 50 and 3, and taking 1 for 48 and a career-best 6 for 58, including the prize wicket of New Zealand's in-form Martin Crowe, caught at slip from a leg-cutter after making an imperious 79. One week later in his maiden one-day international against Sri Lanka in Perth, he became the first débutant to take five wickets, his late-swinging medium-pace deliveries being virtually unplayable. While he was unable to maintain his momentum and soon dropped back into Sheffield Shield ranks, he continued to be one of Victoria's most stalwart performers and

when needed, filled in admirably at one-day level for Australia, as shown by his record of 36 wickets in 24 matches. The highlight of his Shield career came in the championship final in 1990/1 when he took 3 for 69 and 5 for 25 to help Victoria to its first title in more than a decade. He had played little cricket that summer, having returned from an arduous season with Sussex with a stress fracture of the foot. He had three seasons of county cricket, the most notable being 1990 when he completed the double of 1,000 runs and 50 wickets. One of the few Test cricketers of recent times to have a tertiary degree to his name (in Applied Science, majoring in physics), Dodemaide now works full-time in cricket as marketing manager for the Melbourne Cricket Club.

First-class career (1983–): 5,662 runs (29.18) including 5 centuries, 486 wickets (32.26), and 85 catches
Test matches (10): 202 runs (22.44), 34 wickets (28.02), and 6 catches

DONNAN, Henry

(b. 1864, Liverpool, New South Wales; d. 1956, Sydney) *New South Wales and Australia*

Harry Donnan's patience as a right-handed batsman was monumental. He was extremely difficult to dislodge and his style was not unattractive: watching the ball right on to his bat, he could cut and drive admirably. He hit centuries against all the other states, in 32 Sheffield Shield matches alone making 1,784 runs. He first made his mark as a round-arm bowler, outstanding at Sydney Grammar School, but his indifferent fielding was against him. Touring England in 1896, he made 1,009 runs but was disappointing in the Tests. He first represented Australia against Lord Sheffield's team in 1891/2. He was brother-in-law of Syd Gregory and his wife was herself an outstanding cricketer.

First-class career (1887–1900): 4,262 runs (29.19) including 6 centuries, and 29 wickets (41.06)
Test matches (5): 75 runs (8.33), 0–22, and 1 catch

DOOLAND, Bruce

(b. 1923, Cowandilla, Adelaide; d. 1980, Adelaide) *South Australia, Nottinghamshire, and Australia*

A tall, right-arm, leg-break and googly bowler, Bruce Dooland performed the first post-war hat-trick, for his state against Victoria at Melbourne in 1945/6, and was tried in Tests against England in 1946/7 and India in 1947/8. At this stage of his

30

career, however, he lacked the subtleties of flight and the ability to beat the best batsmen off the pitch. He later became a great, rather than just good, leg-spinner but it was as a batsman that his most effective Test performances occurred: in 1946/7 at Adelaide he batted doggedly, helping to restore his country's morale in the first innings. Not selected for the team to tour England in 1948, he came to England on his own account and played in league cricket until Nottingham-shire specially registered him in 1953—and he was such a success that he just failed to achieve the double in his first season. Five times he captured 100 wickets in a season, twice achieving the double, the second time in his last county season, 1957, when he made 1,604 runs (28.64) and took 141 wickets (23.21). Throughout he was a great success for his adopted county—he had 16 for 83 against Essex at Trent Bridge in 1954 and took 8 for 20 in an innings against Worcestershire on the same ground in 1956. It was a heavy blow when he decided to return to his native South Australia. He represented Australia also at base-ball.

First-class career (1945–57): 7,141 runs (24.37) including 4 centuries, 1,016 wickets (21.98), and 186 catches
Test matches (3): 76 runs (19.00), 9 wickets (46.55), and 3 catches

DRENNAN, John

(b. 1932, Adelaide) *South Australia*

An economical right-arm fast-medium bowler and right-hand number nine batsman, Drennan toured New Zealand with the Australian second team in 1956/7, and a year later won senior representative honours to South Africa, without playing a Test. He twice took six wickets in an innings, including 6 for 69 against Victoria in Melbourne in 1956/7, his late movement result-ing in five catches to wicket-keeper Barry Jar-man.

First-class career (1953–8): 569 runs (11.85), 136 wickets (25.66), and 12 catches

DUFF, Reginald Alexander

(b. 1878, Sydney; d. 1911, Sydney) *New South Wales and Australia*

Of sturdy medium height and cheerful disposi-tion, Reggie Duff was a very punishing right-handed batsman who watched the ball closely and drove powerfully. On his Test début, against England in the second Test at Melbourne in

1901/2, he hit 104, sharing in a last-wicket partnership of 120 with Warwick Armstrong—a strange last-wicket pair!—and averaged 44.42 for the series. Coming to England as opening partner for Victor Trumper in both 1902 and 1905, he was very successful, exceeding 1,300 runs each time. In his last Test innings, at The Oval in 1905, he made 146—the highest of the series on both sides—and headed the averages with 41. 'He was never the same man after his second visit', said *Wisden*, 'quickly losing his form'—in fact he fell on hard times. At the turn of the century he was one of the half-dozen best batsmen in Aus-tralia—26 Sheffield Shield matches brought him, 2,149 runs (49.97), including his highest, 271, against South Australia at Sydney in 1903/4. At Sydney for his state against South Australia in 1902/3 he and Trumper put up 298 together for the first wicket; and against Victoria their stand was worth 367. Back in 1900/1 he contributed a modest 119 to his state's record 918 against South Australia at Sydney. C. B. Fry wrote of him, 'Reggie Duff had a face like a good-looking brown trout and was full of Australian sun-shine.'

First-class career (1898–1907): 6,589 runs (35.04) including 10 centuries, and 14 wickets (34.14)
Test matches (22): 1,317 runs (35.59) including 2 centuries, 4 wickets (21.25), and 14 catches

DUNCAN, John Ross Frederick

(b. 1944, Brisbane) *Queensland, Victoria, and Australia*

An accurate fast-medium right-arm bowler with considerable powers of swing, Ross Duncan played in the fifth Test against England at Mel-bourne in 1970/1, scoring 3 and taking no wickets for 30. He had earned his place with match figures of 13 for 125 against Victoria at Melbourne and that season he took 34 wickets for Queensland. He moved to Victoria in 1971/2, but played for only one more season.

First-class career (1964–72): 649 runs (8.42) and 218 wickets (31.19)

DYMOCK, Geoffrey

(b. 1945, Maryborough, Queensland) *Queensland and Australia*

A thoroughly genuine medium-fast left-arm opening bowler, sturdily built and with an eco-nomical action of some 12 paces, Geoff Dymock was the pivot of Queensland's attack for many years and the state's highest-ever wicket-taker.

31

His role in Test cricket was that of a stock bowler but he could swing the ball both ways and always earned respect. His first Test cricket was against New Zealand, at home and away in 1973/4. He took seven wickets in his first Test match at Adelaide and appeared in two Tests in New Zealand before losing his place to Gary Gilmour, whose bowling was of similar style but whose batting was superior. However, after taking 35 wickets at 24.66 in nine Shield matches in 1976/7, Dymock was rather surprisingly preferred to Gilmour for the 1977 tour of England where he took only 15 wickets in ten matches at an average of 31.20. Restored to a side weakened by World Series Cricket defections in 1978/9, he did a much more effective and useful job for Australia than his seven wickets in three Tests at 38.42 suggest. A cheerful, sunny-tempered character, he bowled without histrionics and enjoyed cricket whatever the results. By far the most memorable year in a worthy career came in 1979/80 when he followed a successful tour of India with some fine performances on home soil. In India 24 of his 32 wickets came in the five Tests in which he played. At Kanpur, in great heat, he took 12 wickets in the match for 166 from 63 overs and four balls. His success against England in Australia was less expected. Consistent performances earned him a place ahead of some of the former World Series Cricket stars and he produced a decisive spell with the new ball in the second innings of the Perth Test to finish with 6 for 34. Helped by Lillee's fire at the other end, he took 17 wickets (15.29) against England and 11 (26.27) in the two Tests in which he played against the West Indies, having been omitted in his native Brisbane. At the end of this busy season he toured Pakistan, taking only one wicket for 128 on the unresponsive pitches on which the three Tests were played. His service was rewarded with another visit to England for the Centenary Test but he was unsuccessful and his Test days were over. Nevertheless, he had much to tell his own children and those he taught in Queensland as his profession. In 1981/2 he made a characteristically determined maiden hundred, soon after helped Queensland win the one-day McDonalds Cup for the second time in succession, and retired on a high note. In 1985 he returned to England as assistant-manager of the touring party.

First-class career (1971–82): 1,518 runs (14.45) including 1 century, and 425 wickets (26.91)
Test matches (21): 236 runs (9.44), 78 wickets (27.13), and 1 catch

DYSON, John

(b. 1954, Sydney) *New South Wales and Australia*

John Dyson made a modest start to his Sheffield Shield career in 1976/7, but two centuries by this patient and resolute right-hand opening batsman the following season earned him a place in the Australian team against India and he began well with 53 in his first Test innings at Perth. Inconsistent but determined, he took some astounding catches in the deep and was every inch a team man. He failed later against the Indian spinners and although he batted well for New South Wales against the England touring team of 1978/9 making a solid 67 out of a total of 165, he was struggling to hold his place in the state side by the end of the season. The selectors, however, had not forgotten him and he toured England in 1980, although making only 66 in six innings and missing selection for the Centenary Test. It was an injury to Bruce Laird which enabled him to earn the place as opening partner to Graeme Wood in all six home Tests of 1980/1. The big score eluded him, against both New Zealand and India, but his 'stickability' persuaded the selectors to give him another tour of England in 1981. He made his mark with an excellent hundred in the Leeds Test and also by some spectacular fielding. He made a fine undefeated 127 against the West Indies, his highest Test score, in 1981/2 and he played several valuable innings in the Ashes series the following year. Determined and consistent batting in the Sheffield Shield over the next two seasons won him a recall against the West Indies in 1984/5, but he could make only 77 runs in six innings. He joined the unofficial tour to South Africa in 1985/6 and carried his bat in the third international with a score of 18 not out, as the Australians were bowled out for 61. In the second unofficial Test at Newlands the following year, he scored 198. His highest score was 241 in Adelaide in 1984.

First-class career (1975–89): 9,935 runs (40.22) including 19 centuries, and 2 wickets (33.00)
Test matches (30): 1,359 runs (26.64) including 2 centuries, and 10 catches

DWYER, Edmund Alfred

(b. 1893, Mosman, New South Wales; d. 1975, Mosman) *New South Wales*

A prominent Sydney-born administrator, who managed the Australian team to South Africa in 1949/50, 'Chappie' Dwyer was an Australian selector from 1930 to 1952 and a New South

Wales selector from 1930 to 1954. A Mosman delegate to the NSW Cricket Association for 20 years, Dwyer also served as Association vice-president from 1947 to 1967 and was an astute junior coach. When he was replaced by Queensland's Bill Brown as a national selector, New South Wales lacked a representative on the panel for the first time in the history of the Australian Board of Control.

First-class career (1918–28): 65 runs (16.25)

EADY, Charles John

(b. 1870, Hobart; d. 1945, Hobart) *Tasmania and Australia*

Over 6 ft. tall and weighing 15 stone, Charles Eady was best known for scoring 566 out of 911, made in less than eight hours for his club, Break O'Day, against Wellington at Hobart in 1902. He made five other double centuries in club cricket, including two in succession, against Derwent and Wellington, in 1898/9. For Tasmania against Victoria at Hobart, 1894/5, he hit 116 and 112 not out and against the same state at Melbourne in the same year he took 8 for 35. During his sole visit to England in 1896—a rare experience for a Tasmanian—he was handicapped by ill-health, his powerful batting and pacey bowling bringing only 290 runs and 16 wickets from 16 matches (including one Test). He represented his country once at home in 1901/2. He was active in almost every other sport practised in Tasmania and secretary of the Tasmanian Jockey Club from 1917 to 1927. Sometime president of the Australian Board of Control, he was also a member of the Tasmanian Legislative Council.

First-class career (1889–1907): 1,490 runs (22.92) including 3 centuries, and 136 wickets (23.13)
Test matches (2): 20 runs (6.66), 7 wickets (16.00), and 2 catches

EASTWOOD, Kenneth Humphrey

(b. 1935, Chatswood, New South Wales) *Victoria and Australia*

A solid left-handed opening batsman, strong on the leg-side, Ken Eastwood was a shock choice at the age of 36 for the seventh Test against England at Sydney in 1970/1, in place of his own state captain, Bill Lawry, who had the experience of 67 Tests but was two years younger; in an intermittent first-class career this was the first and only time he appeared for a team other than Victoria. He scored 5 and 0 and took 1 for 21 with slow left-arm spin. 1970/1 was easily his best

season: he scored two double hundreds, against New South Wales at Sydney and South Australia at Adelaide, and also made 177 against New South Wales in Melbourne. He was a stalwart of the Footscray Club.

First-class career (1959–71): 2,722 runs (41.87) including 9 centuries, and 6 wickets (63.83)

EBELING, Hans Irvine

(b. 1905, Avoca, Victoria; d. 1980, Melbourne) *Victoria and Australia*

A right-arm fast-medium bowler who swung the ball both ways after a quick arm action, Hans Ebeling was also an occasionally useful batsman, but an ordinary field. He had an irregular career with his state for 14 years because of business commitments, but captained them with success. He made two tours, with his state side to New Zealand in 1924/5 and with Australia to England in 1934. In England he took 62 wickets (20.80) and appeared in his sole Test, the fifth at the Oval, scoring 2 and 41 and taking 3 for 89. Associated with Melbourne CC since his youth, he was the originator of the outstandingly well organized Melbourne Centenary Test Match celebrations in March 1977.

First-class career (1923–37): 1,005 runs (14.15) and 217 wickets (26.58)

EDWARDS, John Dunlop

(b. 1862, Melbourne; d. 1911, Hawksburn, Victoria) *Victoria and Australia*

Jack Edwards was a steady middle-order batsman, useful leg-spinner, and good fieldsman, outstanding in school cricket for Wesley College. Shortly before leaving Australia with the 1888 team to England he hit 254 and 104, both undefeated, for Sandhurst in club cricket, but did not enjoy the wet English summer and the slow pitches, averaging 12 for the whole tour and achieving very little in the three Tests.

First-class career (1880–9): 961 runs (13.72) and 7 wickets (27.71)
Test matches (3): 48 runs (9.60) and 1 catch

EDWARDS, Ross

(b. 1942, Perth) *Western Australia, New South Wales, and Australia*

Fair-haired, strongly built, and a genial pipe-smoker, Ross Edwards was a sound and steady middle-order right-handed batsman and a superb cover fielder, swift as a hawk to swoop on the ball; at the outset of his career he was also a very competent wicket-keeper. His father, E. K. Edwards, also kept wicket for Western Australia. His batting improved with age and, after scoring four centuries for his state in 1971/2, he toured England with the 1972 side as a batsman. Opening the innings in an emergency, he hit a chanceless 170 not out at Trent Bridge in the third Test, displaying a fine array of off-side strokes, mainly off the back foot. He toured the West Indies in 1972/3, acting as reserve wicket-keeper, and was recalled to the Test side against England for 1974/5, hitting 115 in the second Test in Perth, the first West Australian to make a home Test century. Back in England he made 80 not out against Pakistan and 58 against the West Indies in the 1975 Prudential World Cup Final—the latter score being Australia's highest, but insufficient to ward off defeat—and averaged 50.60 in the Tests which followed. At Lord's he stemmed a first innings collapse with a bold 99 (out lbw). He became a Packer-contracted player in 1977, although his main employment is as an accountant. In 1979 he moved to New South Wales.

First-class career (1964–79): 7,345 runs (39.27) including 14 centuries, 111 catches, and 11 stumpings

Test matches (20): 1,171 runs (40.37) including 2 centuries, 0–20, and 7 catches

EDWARDS, Walter John

(b. 1950, Perth) *Western Australia and Australia*

Playing for the same state as Ross Edwards, but not related to him, Wally Edwards was an attractive left-hand opening batsman, who proved disappointing in Test company. In his three Tests against England in 1974/5 he twice helped Ian Redpath to put on more than 60 at the start of an innings, but his own top score was only 30. That season, however, in all first-class matches, he made 731 runs (30.46).

First-class career (1973–8): 1,381 runs (30.68) including 2 centuries

Test matches (3): 68 runs (11.33)

EGAR, Colin James

(b. 1928, Malvern, Adelaide)

A prominent umpire and forthright administrator who managed three Australian teams to Pakistan in 1982, 1988, and 1994 as well as the team to the West Indies in 1984, 'Col' Egar has had a lifetime in sport. (Always known as 'Col', one newspaper

once referred to him as 'Colonel' Egar.) He umpired top-level cricket and Australian football in 1956, his duties as a football field umpire keeping him fit for the summer game. Egar officiated in 67 Sheffield Shield matches from 1956 to 1970 and 29 Tests from 1960 to 1969—including 22 in a row—the most controversial being the opening Test of the 1963/4 Springbok summer in Brisbane when he no-balled Australian fast bowler Ian Meckiff for throwing. Meckiff never played again. Afterwards Egar channelled his energies into administration, in 1971 joining the South Australian Cricket Association's ground and finance committee and in 1981, becoming a delegate to the Australian Cricket Board. He was appointed vice-president of the SACA in 1987, managed two Australian teams overseas, and served a term as chairman of the Australian Cricket Board (1989–92).

ELLIS, John Leslie

(b. 1890, Malvern, Victoria; d. 1974, Glen Iris, Victoria) *Victoria*

A genial, fun-loving character renowned for his behind-the-stumps banter, 'Jack' Ellis is one of only three Victorian wicket-keepers to figure in 200 or more dismissals. He was a member of the Victorian team which made the world record score of 1,107 against New South Wales in Melbourne in 1926/7. On pulling New South Wales's Tommy Andrews through mid-wicket to register Victoria's 1,000, Ellis, a right-hander, said, 'Come on, there's three in it. Three to me and 1,000 up. Long live Victoria.' He toured England in 1926 as Bert Oldfield's deputy, went to New Zealand with the 1924/5 Victorians and toured India in 1935/6 with Frank Tarrant's team.

First-class career (1918–36): 2,351 runs (21.18) including 2 centuries, and 293 dismissals (187 c., 107 st.)

EMERY, Philip Allen

(b. 1964, St Ives, New South Wales) *New South Wales and Australia*

For some years a stalwart wicket-keeper and left-handed batsman for New South Wales, Phil Emery was a popular replacement for Ian Healy when Australia's normally indestructible regular 'keeper broke a thumb before the third Test in Lahore at the end of Australia's tour of Pakistan in 1994/5. A left-hander, Emery scored 8 not out in his only innings and in this, his only Test, took

4 catches and a stumping in the second innings to add to a catch in the first.

First-class career (1987–): 1,747 runs (24.95) and 234 dismissals (218 c., 17 st.)

EMERY, Sidney Hand

(b. 1885, Macdonald Town, Sydney; d. 1967, Petersham, Sydney) *New South Wales and Australia*

A right-arm googly bowler of lively medium-pace, Sid Emery could make the ball fizz from the pitch, but his length was uncertain. If he could have gained consistent control, he would have been a real match-winner. He toured England in 1912, taking 66 wickets, including 12 for 110 against Northamptonshire at the county ground, but enjoyed little success against either England or South Africa in the Triangular Tournament. In 15 Sheffield Shield matches he scored 371 runs (16.13) and took 60 wickets (24.65) including 12 for 113 against Victoria in 1909/10. 'On his day', wrote Johnny Moyes, 'Sid Emery was the most devastating bowler of the bosey ever seen.'

First-class career (1908–13): 1,192 runs (18.33) and 183 wickets (23.79)

Test matches (4): 6 runs (3.00), 5 wickets (49.80), and 2 catches

EVANS, Edwin

(b. 1849, Emu Plains, New South Wales; d. 1921, Walgett, NSW) *New South Wales and Australia*

In his prime a very accurate right-arm spin bowler with a high action, who could pitch on a sixpence, Edwin Evans was in his thirty-eighth year when he toured England for the first and only time in 1886, and, past his best, he held no terrors for English batsmen during a summer of hard wickets. He also appeared for Australia in 1881/2, 1882/3, and 1884/5. At home his career for his state was brilliant, and with 'The Demon' Spofforth he often did great things in the 1870s. He was also a useful tail-end batsman and, off the field, a fearless horseman of whom the poet Banjo Paterson wrote: 'he astounded us by taking his rifle [on horseback] and killing a kangaroo that was going past at full speed—a feat only attempted by very good professional kangaroo-shooters.'

First-class career (1874–87): 1,006 runs (12.26) and 201 wickets (16.69)

Test matches (6): 82 runs (10.25), 7 wickets (47.42), and 5 catches

EVATT, Dr Herbert Vere, QC

(b. 1894, Maitland, New South Wales; d. 1965, Canberra)

One of those most responsible for international cricket's restart so soon after the Second World War, Dr Evatt was one of Australia's most prominent wartime politicians, who later—as part of his busy public life—served as vice-president of the New South Wales Cricket Association and was a trustee of the Sydney Cricket Ground. He directly encouraged the formation of the Services XI after a wartime trip to London with Australia's Labour Prime Minister, John Curtin. The pair met Sir Pelham Warner at Lord's, and soon afterwards an Australian army team under the captaincy of Lindsay Hassett assembled for the series of matches known as the 'Victory Tests'. Educated at Fort St. High School and the University of Sydney, Dr Evatt first entered Parliament in 1925, before becoming Justice of the High Court in 1930. Returning to politics in 1940 in the Sydney seat of Barton, he became Australia's Attorney-General in 1941, Minister for External Affairs in the Curtin Cabinet, and, in 1946, Deputy Prime Minister. His doctorate was in law.

EVERETT, Samuel Charles

(b. 1901, Sydney; d. 1970, Sydney) *New South Wales*

A right-arm fast-medium bowler and big-hitting right-hand lower-order batsman, strongly built Sam Everett toured New Zealand with New South Wales in 1923/4 and England with the 1926 Australians without outstanding results. In his penultimate game, he took a career-best 6 for 23 against Queensland in Sydney in 1929/30, but the feat was totally overshadowed by Don Bradman's world record 452 not out. Everett's highest first-class score was 77 in just over an hour (12 fours and 2 sixes) for the Australian XI against Tasmania at the TCA Ground, Hobart, in 1926. He shared a 10th wicket stand of 147 in just 62 minutes with Charles Macartney, who made 163 not out.

First-class career (1921–9): 617 runs (14.69), 134 wickets (27.11), and 26 catches

FAIRFAX, Alan George

(b. 1906, Summer Hill, Sydney; d. 1955, Kensington, London) *New South Wales and Australia*

Tall and dark-haired, Alan Fairfax was a sound right-handed stroke-player who used his long reach extremely well. He was also a lively fast-medium bowler. Coming into Australia's rebuilt Test side for the fifth match of 1928/9 at Melbourne, he scored 65, sharing in a fifth-wicket record stand of 183 with young Don Bradman. On his tour of England in 1930, when he generally shared the new ball with Tim Wall, he averaged 50 with the bat in four Tests, besides taking 12 wickets; and in Australia's first-ever series against the West Indies in 1930/1, he averaged 48.75 with the bat in the five Tests and took seven wickets. Lost to Australian cricket thereafter, he returned to England in 1932 as a professional in the Lancashire League and played for Gentlemen against Players in 1934. He later organized an indoor cricket school in London and after the war became a newspaper columnist. A serious injury during war service for the RAF led to his early death from a heart attack. In 17 Sheffield Shield matches he scored 805 runs (29.81) and took 60 wickets (24.73).

First-class career (1928–34): 1,910 runs (28.93) including 1 century, and 134 wickets (27.87)
Test matches (10): 410 runs (51.25), 21 wickets (30.71), and 15 catches

FAVELL, Leslie Ernest

(b. 1929, Sydney; d. 1987, Adelaide) *South Australia and Australia*

A stocky, hard-hitting right-handed opening batsman, Les Favell tended to attack merrily from the start, believing that the new ball could be hit just as hard and as often as the old one. He was justly renowned for his courage, spirit, and impeccable sportsmanship. In particular he was a daring hooker. Against Trinidad in 1955 he hit the first four balls of the Australian innings for 22—three sixes and a four. He made 80 and 40 for his state against MCC in 1954/5 but he never did himself full justice against England, often getting himself out by chasing the ball wide of the off stump. He appeared occasionally against England and the West Indies at home, and toured the West Indies, India and Pakistan, and New Zealand in 1957 and 1967 (as captain). His sole century in Tests was 101 in the fourth Test at Madras (1959/60) when Australia beat India by an innings. He captained his state, for whom he made 8,983 runs (38.38) in 130 Sheffield Shield matches, a record 95 times. He twice made two hundreds in a match for South Australia. Later closely involved in the administration of South Australian cricket, he was also a shrewd and interesting commentator on cricket for ABC Radio in Adelaide. His career aggregate is the highest by an Australian who never toured England. His son also played for South Australia.

First-class career (1951–70): 12,379 runs (36.63) including 27 centuries, and 110 catches
Test matches (19): 757 runs (27.03) including 1 century, and 9 catches

FERGUSON, William H.

(b. 1880, Sydney; d. 1957, Bath, England)

A scorer and baggageman for touring teams for almost 50 years, Bill Ferguson worked in England with the 1905 Australian team, the first of his 41 tours and 204 Test matches. 'Fergie' was the first to keep charts showing the scoring strokes of each batsman. In 1957 he was awarded the BEM for his services to cricket.

FERRIS, John James

(b. 1867, Sydney; d. 1900, Durban, South Africa) *New South Wales, South Australia, Gloucestershire, Australia, and England*

A left-arm medium-fast swing bowler of immaculate length who could vary his pace admirably, 'J.J.' Ferris was a member of the Australian teams to England in 1888 and 1890 when he formed a phenomenally successful partnership with C. T. B. Turner, 'The Terror'. On the two tours he captured 435 wickets (13.19) in all matches. In 1888 they bowled unchanged against Middlesex at Lord's and an England XI at Stoke. On his Test début at Sydney in 1886/7 he and Turner were unchanged in the first innings, bundling out England for 45, J.J. having a match record of 9 for 103, and in the second match, also at Sydney, he took 9 for 140. In his last Test for Australia, at The Oval in 1890, he took 9 for 74 in all. He then settled in England and had three disappointing seasons for Gloucestershire. He toured South Africa with W. W. Read's side in 1891/2, representing England for the only time and taking 13 for 91 in the sole Test at Cape Town. Altogether, he took 235 wickets on this tour. He died, while serving with the British Forces during the Boer War, of enteric fever.

First-class career (1886–97): 4,264 runs (15.67) including 1 century, and 812 wickets (17.54)
Test matches (Australia—8): 98 runs (8.16), 48 wickets (14.25), and 4 catches. (England—1): 16 runs (16.00) and 13 wickets (7.00)

FINGLETON, John Henry Webb

(b. 1908, Sydney; d. 1981, Sydney) *New South Wales and Australia*

A right-hand opening batsman, often associated with Bill Brown at either Sheffield Shield or international level, Jack Fingleton had a strong defence and great courage. He became at least as famous as a cricket writer and broadcaster. Solid rather than fluent, he hit hard and could score quickly. He was always immaculately turned out. Like many of his colleagues his effectiveness was reduced by Harold Larwood and Bill Voce in the 1932/3 Bodyline series and, although he hit 83 in the second Test at Melbourne, he made 'a pair' in the third, was dropped and later omitted from the 1934 tour of England. In South Africa, however, in 1935/6 he was highly successful, making 478 runs (79.66) in the Tests. This included three successive centuries in the third, fourth and fifth matches—112 at Cape Town (putting on 233 with Bill Brown), 108 at Johannesburg and 118 at Durban. The runs continued, with 100 in the first Test against England at Brisbane in 1936/7. Then, in the third Test at Melbourne, he made 136, adding a record 346 for the sixth wicket with Don Bradman. Visiting England at last in 1938, his defence was often invaluable although he did not score highly in the Tests; on the tour he made 1,141 runs (38.03). A wise and kindly man with a mischievous sense of humour and an obstinate streak, 'Fingo' was a professional journalist of the highest calibre, also employed by the Government in Canberra. He wrote ten cricket books in an informed, literary, and scholarly way, including *Cricket Crisis*, *Brightly Fades the Don*, *The Ashes Crown the Year*, and *The Immortal Victor Trumper*. In 37 Sheffield Shield matches Fingleton scored 2,263 runs (39.70). He was awarded an OBE for services to cricket and cricket literature.

First-class career (1928–39): 6,816 runs (44.54) including 22 centuries
Test matches (18): 1,189 runs (42.46) including 5 centuries, and 13 catches

FLEETWOOD-SMITH, Leslie O'Brien

(b. 1910, Stawell, Victoria; d. 1971, Melbourne) *Victoria and Australia*

'Chuck' Fleetwood-Smith was a left-arm back-of-the-hand spin bowler who changed his style after breaking his arm as a schoolboy; he had prodigious powers of spin and made the ball twist and turn on the hardest pitches at near medium pace. After a few short steps he would deliver his natural off-break to a right-hander; the leg-break was his 'wrong 'un' and he was not easy to bat against, though Walter Hammond disagreed, thrashing his bowling in Australia in 1932/3 and at Lord's in 1938. In the late thirties the Australian strategy revolved round 'Chuck' and Bill O'Reilly. He toured England in 1934, taking 106 wickets (19.20), yet not gaining a Test place. In 1938, however, he was an integral part of Australia's attack, taking 14 wickets (though at high cost) in the four Tests. He also toured South Africa in 1935/6. At home in 1936/7 he took 19 wickets in Tests against England. Lacking the killer instinct, much of his talent was wasted in Tests, but he had some amazing performances for his state, twice dismissing nine batsmen in an innings, and taking 295 wickets (24.38). He died in poverty.

First-class career (1931–9): 617 runs (7.34) and 597 wickets (22.64)
Test matches (10): 54 runs (9.00) and 42 wickets (37.38)

FLEMING, Damien William

(b. 1970, Bentley, Western Australia) *Victoria and Australia*

Winning selection on his first major Australian tour, to Sri Lanka and Pakistan late in 1994, Damien Fleming took a hat-trick in his first Test match (1994/5) after previously replacing the injured Craig McDermott at the tail-end of Australia's 1993/4 South African tour. A right-arm medium-pace swing bowler and right-hand number nine batsman, Fleming took 6 for 37 on his state début as a teenager against Western Australia at the Junction Oval, St Kilda, in 1989/90. He had previously played several games at one-day level for Victoria as an 18-year-old, in 1988/9. Prior to his encouraging and spirited start in Tests, he had played five one-day internationals, taking 7 wickets at 26 including a best performance of 4 for 39 against New Zealand in Sharjah during the Australasian Cup tournament in 1994.

First-class career (1989–): 411 runs (14.67), 146 wickets (28.95), and 21 catches
Test matches (4): 40 runs (10.00), 17 wickets (25.58), and 2 catches

FRANCIS, Bruce Collin

(b. 1948, Sydney) *New South Wales, Essex, and Australia*

A genial and intelligent man, a graduate of Sydney University, and a strapping right-handed opening batsman who loved to attack, Bruce Francis was a popular cricketer with both players and spectators. If he got going at the start of an innings, there was no likelihood of dull cricket, for he was a handsome striker of the ball, especially to the on-side, and with his burly strength the lofted straight drive was often brought into use against even the fastest bowlers. Coming to England in 1970 to play in the Lancashire League for Accrington, he had two successful seasons for Essex in 1971 and 1973, scoring 1,578 runs (38.48) with four centuries, plus another in the Sunday League, in his first year, and 1,384 (38.44) in his last. In between he toured England with the Australian side, but at Test level one or two inadequacies in his defensive technique were uncovered, notably by John Snow. He had first represented Australia (unofficially) in two matches against the Rest of the World in 1971/2 scoring 34 runs in three innings before breaking a thumb. His highest score was 210 not out against the Combined Oxford and Cambridge side in 1972. Seldom suffering physical injury, he sometimes had to leave the field because of bad migraines. He was prominent in setting up both World Series Cricket and the 'rebel' Australian tour to South Africa.

First-class career (1968–74): 6,183 runs (33.97) including 13 centuries
Test matches (3): 52 runs (10.40) and 1 catch

FREEMAN, Eric Walter

(b. 1944, Adelaide) *South Australia and Australia*

A husky and combative cricketer, Eric Freeman had a meteoric rise in first-class cricket, even though he was originally more involved in Australian football. A right-arm fast-medium bowler, hard-hitting batsman, and excellent field, he took 7 for 52 for his state against Queensland in 1966/7; he toured New Zealand with an 'A' team; and when a visiting New Zealand side played South Australia in 1967/8 at Adelaide, he hit 50 and 39 (at number ten) and took 3 for 50 and 8 for 47, his state winning by 24 runs. Between 1967 and 1970 he toured England, South Africa, and India and represented his country at home against India and the West Indies. He took some useful wickets, but was not the penetrative opening bowler Australia was looking for and he was dropped after his drubbing at the hands of the South Africans in the 1969/70 series. His hitting brought two fifties in Tests; but he soon dropped out of Sheffield Shield cricket. His subsequent job, in banking, took him to country areas where he was immensely popular and he became both a coach and a broadcaster in Adelaide.

First-class career (1964–74): 2,244 runs (19.17) including 1 century, and 241 wickets (27.76)
Test matches (11): 345 runs (19.16), 34 wickets (33.17), and 5 catches

FREER, Frederick William

(b. 1915, Melbourne) *Victoria and Australia*

A hard-working right-arm fast-medium bowler and very useful lower-order batsman, Fred Freer replaced Ray Lindwall, who was unfit for the second Test at Sydney against England in 1946/7, scoring 28 not out and taking 3 for 74. He was not selected again when Lindwall recovered but toured India with the Commonwealth team of 1949/50. His three first-class centuries were hit on this tour, the highest being 132 against India at Bombay. He coached in both India and South Africa and played for Rishton in the Lancashire League.

First-class career (1945–9): 1,284 runs (32.10) including 3 centuries, and 104 wickets (27.75)

GANNON, John Brian

(b. 1947, Perth) *Western Australia and Australia*

A fast-medium left-arm bowler and athletic fielder, 'Sam' Gannon effectively had two first-class careers, the second bringing him Test honours in the wake of the defections to Kerry Packer. First playing for Western Australia against Victoria in 1966/7, he took 6 for 107 in that season against South Australia at Adelaide, but although a useful member of the Western Australia side for several more seasons with his often hostile new-ball bowling, he was overshadowed in a strong team by Lillee, Massie, and Brayshaw (one of the best Australian bowlers never to be capped). Gannon did not play for Western Australia between 1973/4 and 1976/7 but the following year he bowled himself into the Australian side for the second Test against India, after taking four second-innings wickets against them for Western Australia. In his first Test on his home ground at Perth he took 3 for 84 and 4 for 77, but he was dropped after failing to take a wicket in the fourth Test, which India won easily.

First-class career (1966–79): 141 runs (6.40) and 117 wickets (30.79)
Test matches (3): 3 runs (3.00), 11 wickets (32.82), and 3 catches

GARRETT, Thomas William

(b. 1848, Wollongong, New South Wales; d. 1943, Warrawee, Sydney) *New South Wales and Australia*

At the time of his death the oldest living Australian Test cricketer, Tom Garrett played in the first two matches against England in 1876/7. He toured England with the first team in 1878, again in 1882 (playing in the historic Ashes match) and 1886. A good right-arm medium-fast bowler, a fine fielder (he was an expert sprinter) and a hard-hitting, but undependable, batsman, he improved as he got older. Having an easy action, he used his height (about 6 ft.) well, came fast off the pitch, could move the ball either way and send down a telling yorker. On hard grounds many considered he was more effective than Spofforth or Boyle. On the 1882 and 1886 tours he took more than 100 wickets each time—in the former year, *four* matches against Yorkshire bringing him 27 wickets at 9 runs each. He represented Australia in seven series at home, having his best return in 1881/2, when he headed the bowling with 18 wickets (20.38), including 9 for 163 in the third match at Sydney.

First-class career (1876–97): 3,673 runs (16.18) including 2 centuries, and 446 wickets (18.72)

Test matches (19): 339 runs (12.55), 36 wickets (26.94), and 7 catches

GASCOIGNE, Stephen Harold

(b. 1878, Redfern, Sydney; d. 1942, Lidcombe, Sydney)

Popularly known as 'Yabba', the legendary Australian cricket barracker, Gascoigne's boisterous and witty comments from the Hill kept Sydney crowds amused for more than 30 years. On one occasion, when Trevor Bailey had been beaten by several balls in succession, Yabba cried, 'Send him out a piano and see if he can play that!' When an umpire put up his hand to alert the sightscreen operator of a bowler changing from over to round the wicket, Yabba yelled, 'It's no use umpire; you'll have to wait till playtime like the rest of us!' His celebrity status was assured when he was the subject of a Cinesound newsreel. When the great Englishman Jack Hobbs played his final game in Sydney, the members of the Hill chipped in to buy him a parting gift, an ornate boomerang. When Hobbs walked around to receive it, he asked for Yabba and shook his hand.

GAUNT, Ronald Arthur

(b. 1934, York, Western Australia) *Western Australia, Victoria, and Australia*

A right-arm fast-medium bowler, Ron Gaunt was a sturdily built and determined cricketer, but he bowled countless no-balls during his short career and came under the eye of the umpires for dragging. He toured New Zealand twice on 'A' tours, South Africa in 1957/8, and England in 1961, taking 40 wickets on that tour at 21.87, and 3 for 53 in the drawn Oval Test. He played at home against South Africa in 1963/4. He was a moderate left-handed batsman.

First-class career (1955–63): 616 runs (10.44) and 266 wickets (26.85)

Test matches (3): 6 runs (3.00), 7 wickets (44.28), and 1 catch

GEHRS, Donald Raeburn Algernon

(b. 1880, Port Victor, South Australia; d. 1953, Adelaide) *South Australia and Australia*

Tallish, thickset, and athletic, Algy Gehrs was an attractive right-handed batsman who could hook superbly against any type of bowler; he had many strokes and much audacity, although he was rather disappointing at representative level. He appeared once against England at home in 1903/4, and once on tour in 1905, when he averaged 21.77. Against South Africa in 1910/11 he had some glory, hitting 67 and 58 in Tests at Sydney and Melbourne respectively. In 34 Sheffield Shield matches he made 2,168 runs (35.54) and in all matches for his state he hit 3,387 runs, including 13 centuries. Against Western Australia at Fremantle in 1906 he scored two centuries in the match, one of them in only 50 minutes, which remained the fastest in Australia for 76 years until David Hookes bettered it.

First-class career (1902–21): 4,377 runs (33.67) including 13 centuries

Test matches (6): 221 runs (20.09), 0–4, and 6 catches

GIFFEN, George

(b. 1859, Adelaide; d. 1927, Adelaide) *South Australia and Australia*

Known as 'the W. G. Grace of Australia', George Giffen was a highly gifted all-rounder who performed the match double of a century and 10 wickets no fewer than nine times. A determined, attacking right-handed batsman, he stooped a little but possessed a variety of strokes, including some exceptionally powerful drives; he was also a slow-medium bowler of great accuracy who delivered very effectively a high-tossed slow ball, which resulted in many caught and bowled victims. Overshadowed on his first tour in 1882, when he played in the Ashes match at The Oval, he came to England again in 1884, 1886, 1893, and 1896 when he was usually the dominant figure, though he did not always reproduce his Australian form. Minor tours included visits to the United States, Canada, and New Zealand. He headed both batting and bowling in 1886, with 1,424 runs and 154 wickets. He hit four double-centuries for South Australia, the highest being 271 against Victoria at Adelaide in 1891/2. His highest score in England was 180 against Gloucestershire at Bristol, where he also captured 7 for 11. Although England won, his best series was 1894/5, when he scored most runs and took most wickets—475 runs (52.77) and 34 wickets (24.11). He led Australia in four Tests in all. His finest feat was in the first Test at Sydney, when he scored 161 and 41 and took eight wickets (in 118 overs)—yet was on the losing side! Like W.G., he retained his fitness for many years: in his forty-fourth year, he made 81 and 97 not out and took 15 for 185 against Victoria at Adelaide. In 38 Sheffield Shield matches he scored 2,318 runs (36.21) and took 192 wickets (29.55). He was the first Australian to make over 10,000 runs and take over 1,000 wickets in first-class cricket. On retirement from the Civil Service (Post Office branch) he delighted in coaching schoolboys. One of the main stands at the Adelaide Oval bears his name.

First-class career (1877–1903): 11,758 runs (29.54) including 18 centuries, 1,022 wickets (21.31), and 195 catches
Test matches (31): 1,238 runs (23.35) including 1 century, 103 wickets (27.09), and 24 catches

GIFFEN, Walter Frank

(b. 1861, Adelaide; d. 1949, Adelaide) *South Australia and Australia*

Walter Giffen was a sound defensive batsman and a good outfield. He was perhaps fortunate in being chosen to tour England in 1893, although he had been a prolific scorer in Adelaide club cricket. At home he appeared for Australia three times against England in 1886/7 and 1891/2 (with little success). He averaged 13.77 in England but did not play in a Test; it was said that his famous elder brother, George, had insisted on his coming. In 1886 Walter lost the top of two of his

fingers at the Brompton Gasworks, Adelaide, in an accident involving a pair of cog-wheels. In 13 Sheffield Shield matches his batting average came to 11.77.

First-class career (1882–1902): 1,178 runs (15.92)
Test matches (3): 11 runs (1.83) and 1 catch

GILBERT, David Robert

(b. 1960, Sydney) *New South Wales, Tasmania, Gloucestershire, Lincolnshire, and Australia*

David Gilbert gained a place on the tour of England in 1985 when three players withdrew to join the rebel tour of South Africa. A dark, wiry right-arm fast bowler with a fluent action and the ability to move the ball off the seam, he made his state début in 1983/4 following the retirement of Len Pascoe and took 25 wickets in eight matches including a best performance of 5 for 56. In 1984/5 he shared the new ball with Imran Khan and took 30 important wickets for the side which won the Sheffield Shield. Batting at number 11 he hit the winning boundary to bring his state victory by one wicket in the final, having told his much more renowned batting partner, 'I've waited all season to win this Shield; don't stuff it up now.' Originally awarded an Esso Scholarship in England for 1985, he instead got the chance to play in the touring side. He bowled well in the few matches he played and made his Test début in the last game at The Oval, taking 1 for 96. Back in Australia, circumstances forced him to be his country's leading strike bowler and he did well to take 12 wickets in the five Tests he played against New Zealand and India, before going on the return tour to these two countries at either end of 1986. A witty character, he was a popular member of the Gloucestershire side in 1991 and also played a season for Lincolnshire in 1984, taking 40 wickets at only 14 runs each and also scoring a century.

First-class career (1983–92): 1,374 runs (14.31), including 1 century, 354 wickets (32.39), and 34 catches
Test matches (9): 57 runs (7.12) and 16 wickets (52.68)

GILBERT, Eddie

(b. 1908, Woodford, Queensland; d. 1978, Wacol, Queensland) *Queensland*

The best-known Aboriginal cricketer to play first-class cricket, Gilbert's career was restricted to twenty-three games by a shoulder injury. A slight man of just 5 ft. 8 in. and 9 stone, Gilbert could generate express pace off just five paces, with or without boots. In December 1931 he dismissed Don Bradman for a duck, Bradman later claiming it to be the fastest bowling he had ever encountered. A right-arm fast bowler and left-hand batsman, Gilbert lacked stamina and was effective in only short bursts. So quick was his arm action that critics found it difficult to assess claims that he threw the ball. However, he was no-balled for throwing eleven times in three overs by Andy Barlow in Melbourne in 1931/2. He was also no-balled in his final season, in 1935/6, under the experimental intimidation laws that were introduced as an aftermath to the 'bodyline' trauma of 1932/3. Originally from Barambah, in country Queensland, Gilbert lived in a tent in the Queensland Cricket Association secretary's backyard when representing his state in home matches. His finest match was against the touring West Indies in 1930/1, his first season, when he took 5 for 65 and 2 for 26. He also lifted West Indian fast bowler Learie Constantine for a big six over fine leg.

First-class career (1930–5): 224 runs (7.22), 87 wickets (28.97), and 4 catches

GILMOUR, Gary John

(b. 1951, Waratah, New South Wales) *New South Wales and Australia*

A highly talented and natural cricketer, Gary Gilmour was a left-handed all-rounder—a fast-medium over-the-wicket bowler, hard-hitting batsman, and athletic fielder. Fair haired, burly, and a genial character, he was bred in the wine-growing area of the Hunter Valley of New South Wales and came to Sydney to develop his cricket skills, at once making his mark in the New South Wales side with 122 against South Australia in his first match, 1971/2. His Test career started against New Zealand at Melbourne in 1973/4 when he made 52 and took 4 for 75 in each first innings. An injury led to the temporary loss of his place to Geoff Dymock, a similar bowler, but, after New Zealand had beaten Australia for the first time at Christchurch in March 1974, Gilmour returned for the third Test at Auckland and with sharp late swing undermined New Zealand's batting with a 12-over spell in the first innings which brought him five wickets and led to swift Australian revenge. The emergence of Jeff Thomson in 1974/5 and further rivalry from Dennis Lillee and Max Walker meant that, of ten Tests against England in 1974/5, Gilmour played only one, although he bowled Australia into the final of the 1975 Prudential World Cup with a devas-

tating spell of swing bowling on a humid, cloudy day at Headingley. He lacked only the pace of several contemporary Australian fast bowlers. He was a surprise omission from Australia's 1977 side to England, after which he played two seasons of World Series Cricket with success but again was not selected for the Australian team in 1979/80. He returned to the Newcastle competition where his career had started.

First-class career (1971–9): 3,126 runs (30.64) including 5 centuries, and 233 wickets (31.52)

Test matches (15): 483 runs (23.00) including 1 century, 54 wickets (26.03), and 8 catches

GLEESON, John William

(b. 1938, Kyogle, New South Wales) *New South Wales, Eastern Province, and Australia*

Short and sinewy, with the weather-beaten face of a jockey, John Gleeson was a right-arm spin bowler who propelled the ball off a bent middle finger in the manner of Jack Iverson. A countryman who twice toured with the Emus, a team of bush cricketers, before joining the Balmain Club in Sydney at the age of 27 in 1965, he perfected his unusual style by bowling at a Eucalyptus tree in Tamworth, where he worked as a telephone engineer. He produced a greater spin variety than Iverson, making more use of the leg-break, though perhaps his staple ball was the off-break. Although he was tidy, there were enough loose balls for experienced players, even those who could not 'read' him, to feed on. Making his first-class début at the age of 28 and taking 23 wickets (18.22) in his first season, he played first for Australia against India in 1967/8. He toured England in 1968 and 1972, as well as India and South Africa. He did well generally in England in 1968 and was one of the few successes in South Africa in 1969/70, taking 59 wickets (19.49), including 19 wickets in four Tests. However, against England in 1970/1 he took 14 very expensive wickets; and in England again in 1972 he was disappointing, claiming only three wickets from three Tests. In 1974/5 he played with success for Eastern Province in the South African Currie Cup. An amusing and gregarious character, he was awarded an unofficial 30th Test Cap for the rained-off Melbourne Test of 1970/1 so that he would qualify for the ACB's superannuation Fund.

First-class career (1966–74): 1,095 runs (11.06) and 430 wickets (24.95)

Test matches (29): 395 runs (10.39), 93 wickets (36.20), and 17 catches

GRAF, Shaun Francis

(b. 1957, Mornington, Victoria) *Victoria, Hampshire, and Western Australia*

An athletic bowling all-rounder with a wristy action and consistent away-swing, Shaun Graf played eleven one-day internationals for Australia from 1980 to 1982 and was twice 12th man at Test level in 1980/1. Acting as a substitute fieldsman in the first Test at Sydney, he caught India's Kapil Dev from a towering skied drive. He represented Victoria for four years and Hampshire for one, before crossing to Western Australia and playing a key role in the state's 1983/4 Sheffield Shield victory. A right-arm fast-medium bowler and left-hand number seven batsman, Graf's best bowling figures were 5 for 95 for Victoria against Western Australia in Perth in 1982/3 and his highest first-class score 100 not out for Victoria against Western Australia in Melbourne in 1980/1. He later became a Victorian selector.

First-class career (1979–84): 1,559 runs (25.14) including 1 century, 124 wickets (33.91), and 30 catches

GRAHAM, Henry

(b. 1870, Melbourne; d. 1911, Dunedin) *Victoria, South Island, Otago, and Australia*

Although 'Harry' Graham did not play with a perfectly straight bat, he was a splendid right-handed hitter with plenty of dash and vigour. In England in 1893 he hit 219 at Derby and 107 in his first Test, at Lord's: in this Test he came in with the score faltering at 75 for 5 and immediately flayed the bowling. 'The little dasher' headed the batting for the tour with 1,435 runs (28.7), and at Sydney in 1894/5 his 105 was equally valuable against England. Dominating the hostile fast bowling of Tom Richardson, Graham inspired Australia to an innings victory. On his second tour of England in 1896 he was often unwell and his form declined. Although he recovered some of his lost skill on his return home, his career was left half-fulfilled. He went to live in New Zealand, where he died young. *Wisden* commented: 'Had he ordered his life more carefully, he might have had a much longer and more successful career.'

First-class career (1892–1906): 5,054 runs (26.32) including 7 centuries
Test matches (6): 301 runs (30.10) including 2 centuries, and 3 catches

GREEN, Douglas Carling

(b. 1902, Hobart; d. 1990, Lindisfarne, Hobart) *Tasmania*

An outstanding Tasmanian sportsman, particularly noted for his playing and cricket administrative abilities, Doug 'Dyna' Green was a reliable top-order right-hand batsman who captained Tasmania in five of his twenty-five first-class matches. At the time of his death, he was vice-patron to the Tasmanian Cricket Association.

First-class career (1924–36): 1,265 runs (30.11) including 2 centuries, and 11 catches

GREGORY, David William

(b. 1845, Fairy Meadow, New South Wales; d. 1919, Sydney) *New South Wales and Australia*

With a full, flowing beard and Ned Kelly looks, Dave Gregory appeared much older than his years. He captained Australia in the first three Tests (two in 1876/7 and one in 1878/9)—winning the first and third comprehensively—and was in charge again on the first tour of England in 1878, when MCC were overwhelmed at Lord's in a day. Except as a tactful leader among rugged types, he did not earn much distinction on English cricket grounds—it was a wet summer, the slow, treacherous wickets were too much for him and his batting average was only 11. As a batsman, he had no grace or style to commend him—a common failing amongst his contemporaries—but he could defend stubbornly and did not lack grit. In intercolonial matches against Victoria he scored 445 runs (17.80) on wickets which did not approach their later perfection. For some years he was honorary secretary of the NSW Cricket Association. His brothers, Ned, Walter, Charles, and Arthur also played for New South Wales, as did his nephews, Sydney, Charles, and Jack. Several nieces were keen lady cricketers.

First-class career (1866–82): 889 runs (14.57) and 29 wickets (19.24)
Test matches (3): 60 runs (20.00) and 0–9

GREGORY, Edward James

(b. 1839, Sydney; d. 1899, Sydney) *New South Wales and Australia*

A useful right-handed forcing batsman and for 30 years curator of the Sydney Cricket Ground, Ned Gregory played for Australia in the first-ever Test at Melbourne in 1877, under the captaincy of brother Dave, scoring 0 and 11 and holding 1 catch. He was the first man to make a duck in Test cricket. He was father of the future captain, Syd, and the eldest of five brothers to play for New South Wales. Moreover, one of his daughters married a Test cricketer, Harry Donnan. Ned himself laid out, levelled and looked after the SCG and died in his cottage between the 'number one' and 'number two' Ovals. He was the first to build a giant scoreboard, giving far more details than English boards, in letters and numbers 2 ft. high.

First-class career (1862–77): 470 runs (17.40)

GREGORY, Jack Morrison

(b. 1895, Sydney; d. 1973, Bega, New South Wales)
New South Wales and Australia

In the words of Ian Peebles, he was 'towering, tanned and powerfully lithe'; according to R. C. Robertson-Glasgow he was 'tall, strong and raw-boned, like one of his native kangaroos'. As the descriptions suggest, Jack Gregory was a spectacular as well as great all-rounder. He was a left-handed batsman, who, with great confidence and without a pair of batting gloves, could hit with tremendous power, using his long reach to attack, often with low, skimming drives. He could cover the length of the pitch with a few long strides. Primarily, however, a right-arm fast bowler, he took a 20 yard run, starting with a shuffle, then moving his 14-stone weight forward like an avalanche to finish with a huge bound as he let go of the ball. His exceptional, fearsome speed came from sheer strength, and, although he bowled a good out-swinger with the new ball and often ripped the ball back off the seam, it was speed itself rather than any subtle movement or variety which got him wickets. He simply frightened many a batsman into submission. He was also a quite superb slip fielder with marvellous anticipation and long reach. He first came to public notice with the Australian Imperial Forces Team in 1919, scoring 942 runs and taking 131 wickets. In partnership with Ted McDonald in Australia 1920/1, England 1921, and South Africa 1921/2, he was magnificent; in the first Test series he took 23 wickets (24.17) and scored 442 runs (73.66), including 100 (at number nine) and 7 for 69 in the first innings of the second Test at Melbourne; in the second 'Gregory and McDonald' were the scourge of England, Jack securing 19 wickets in the Tests; and in the third series, on matting, he took 15 wickets (18.93) in the three matches and hit 119 in 70 minutes at Johannesburg, which still remains the fastest Test century. In England in 1921 he achieved the double with 1,135 runs (36.61) and 116 wickets (16.58). Subsequently, he was not quite the same power. It is true he took 22 wickets in 1924/5 but they were gained expensively. On the 1926 England tour he broke down physically; and he had to leave the field during the first Test at Brisbane in 1928/9, after sending down 41 overs, with a recurrence of his knee injury. With tears in his eyes he told team-mates 'I'm done for.' He never represented his country again. For a time Jack Gregory had been the personification of young dynamic physical power and gusto for life. In 11 Sheffield Shield matches he made 476 runs (31.73) and took 38 wickets (28.89). He was the son of Charles Gregory and cousin of Syd Gregory. His wife, a former 'Miss Australia', died in 1963 and his last 10 years were spent living alone on the remote New South Wales Coast.

First-class career (1918–28): 5,661 runs (36.52) including 13 centuries, 504 wickets (20.99), and 195 catches

Test matches (24): 1,146 runs (36.96) including 2 centuries, 85 wickets (31.15), and 37 catches

GREGORY, Ross Gerald

(b. 1916, Melbourne; d. 1942, Assam) *Victoria and Australia*

One of the youngest ever to play in Test cricket, Ross Gregory was chosen for his state while still a schoolboy. He made 128 for Victoria against MCC in 1936/7 and in the last two Tests of the series made 23, 50 and 80. He was passed over, however, for the 1938 England tour. In his last season he averaged 44.72 for his state yet had a top score of only 77. A very quick-footed right-hander, he could produce brilliant front-of-the-wicket forcing strokes, pull confidently, send down a useful slow leg-break and field cleanly. As Sgt Observer Gregory (RAAF) he died while on active service in Assam. He was not related to the New South Wales Gregory family.

First-class career (1933–8): 1,874 runs (38.24) including 1 century, and 50 wickets (35.34)

Test matches (2): 153 runs (51.00), 0–14, and 1 catch

GREGORY, Sydney Edward

(b. 1870, Sydney; d. 1929, Sydney) *New South Wales and Australia*

Born on the site of the present Sydney Cricket Ground and son of Ned Gregory, Syd Gregory, of the curling moustache and text-book style, visited

England with the teams of 1890, 1893, 1896, 1899, 1902, 1905, 1909, and 1912. What the Graces and the Walkers were to English cricket, the Gregories were to Australian, and Syd was the second most distinguished. For many years his 58 Tests constituted an Australian record. Little more than 5 ft. tall, his quick footwork compensated for lack of inches. Right-handed, possessing a keen eye and strong wrists, and particularly strong on the off-side, he was also brilliant at cover-point, quick and deadly accurate with his returns. He helped maintain the supremacy of New South Wales in the Sheffield Shield—hitting eight centuries—and his earliest great achievement in Tests was 201 in the first Test played at Sydney in 1894/5, when he added 154 with Jack Blackham for the ninth wicket—yet the match was lost! In the first Test at Lord's in 1896, after Australia had been routed for 53 in the first innings and were 62 for 3 in the second, Syd made 103, putting on 221 for the fourth wicket with Harry Trott in just over two and a half hours—again in a losing cause. At The Oval in 1899 he scored a brave 117. He also toured South Africa in 1902/3 but did not prosper on matting. He returned to Test cricket in 1912, captaining a weakened side in the Triangular Tournament in England. In 53 Sheffield Shield matches he scored 3,659 runs (44.08).

First-class career (1889–1912): 15,190 runs (28.55) including 25 centuries, and 174 catches
Test matches (58): 2,282 runs (24.53) including 4 centuries, 0–33, and 25 catches

GRIEVES, Kenneth John

(b.1925, Sydney; d. 1992, Rawtenstall, England)
New South Wales and Lancashire

One of a select group to represent New South Wales at soccer, baseball, and cricket, Ken Grieves made his base in England after ten matches in two seasons with New South Wales immediately after the war. A right-hand batsman known for his free strokeplay and a brilliant field, he also bowled effective leg-breaks and googlies early in his career. After filling in for Keith Miller in Lancashire league ranks at Rawtenstall in 1947, Grieves had an impressive career with Lancashire, making 1,000 runs in a season on thirteen occasions and captaining his adopted county as a professional in 1963 and 1964. In one match, in 1951, he took eight catches at slip, including six in the second innings. Grieves also played first division English football with Bolton Wanderers. His career aggregate of almost 23,000 runs has been surpassed by only three other Australian-

born players: Don Bradman, Greg Chappell, and Allan Border.

First-class career (1945–64): 22,454 runs (33.66) including 29 centuries, 242 wickets (29.78), 610 catches, and 4 stumpings

GRIMMETT, Clarence Victor

(b. 1891, Caversham, Dunedin; d. 1980, Adelaide)
Wellington, Victoria, South Australia, and Australia

Small, stringy, prematurely bald, and wizened in the face, Clarrie Grimmett was a New Zealander by birth. With his short, jerky approach and almost round-arm action, 'the Gnome' or 'Scarlet' (after the Pimpernel whose enemies sought him here and there without much result) was a slow leg-break bowler, exceptionally accurate, with an obvious googly but a wicked dipping top-spinner. A signwriter by trade, he moved at the start of the First World War to Australia, settling first in Sydney, then in Melbourne and finally in Adelaide. He would practise for hours in his backyard during the war years, having laid out a turf pitch in his home in South Melbourne. He trained his black and white fox terrier, Joe, to collect and return the balls he bowled into an empty net. Prolific in Australia, he was nevertheless more consistent in England where the softer pitches were more responsive to his 'infinite variations'. On his belated Test début at the age of 34 in the final Test at Sydney in 1924/5, he took 5 for 45 and 6 for 37, routing England, and after this sensational start he toured England in 1926 in harness with his flightier leg-spin partner, Arthur Mailey. They took 27 of the 39 wickets that fell to bowlers in the Tests and they both took over 100 wickets on the tour. Clarrie was the pivot of Australia's attack against England in 1928/9, capturing 23 wickets in 398.2 overs from the five Tests; 29 wickets from 349.4 overs in 1930; and 28 wickets in 1934, bowling in tandem with Bill O'Reilly. Against other countries he was often even more deadly. He took 33 wickets against the West Indies in 1930/1, the first series in Australia; 33 against South Africa in 1931/2; and in South Africa, 1935/6, 44 wickets—at 14.59 each! This tour of South Africa witnessed his swan-song, as he was not selected for Australia against England in either 1936/7 or 1938. Sometimes a useful tail-end batsman, his all-round record in 79 Sheffield Shield matches was 1,989 runs (19.50) and 513 wickets (25.29).

First-class career (1911–40): 4,720 runs (17.67), 1,424 wickets (22.28), and 139 catches
Test matches (37): 557 runs (13.92), 216 wickets (24.21), and 17 catches

GROUBE, Thomas Underwood

(b. 1857, Taranaki, New Zealand; d. 1927, Melbourne) *Victoria and Australia*

Tom Groube was a steady right-handed batsman and good field at cover-point or long-on. He toured England in 1880, playing in the first-ever Test in England at The Oval, scoring 11 and 0. His highest score in first-class cricket was a mere 61 against Yorkshire at Huddersfield. He did not represent Australia again but ran up some fantastic averages for East Melbourne, for example 155.33 in 1879/80.

First-class career (1878–81): 179 runs (8.52)

GROUT, Arthur Theodore Wallace

(b. 1927, Mackay, Queensland; d. 1968, Brisbane) *Queensland and Australia*

A universally popular cricketer, Wally Grout was a very agile wicket-keeper who modelled himself on Don Tallon. He missed very few chances and his diving catches down the leg-side will be long remembered. He was also a good enough right-hand batsman to open for his state. He represented Australia in four home series between 1958 and 1964; in England in 1961 and 1964, and in South Africa, the West Indies, and India and Pakistan. On two occasions he claimed eight victims in a Test and his six (all caught) in an innings against South Africa at Johannesburg in 1957/8 was then a Test record; also in this match his stand of 69 for the eighth wicket with Richie Benaud sustained an important Australian recovery. On five other occasions he disposed of five men in an innings. Against the West Indies in 1960/1 he had 23 dismissals and a further 23 came his way in the series in England in 1964. For 25 years he held the world record of eight catches in an innings, for Queensland against Western Australia at Brisbane, 1959/60. He showed true sportsmanship when refusing to take off the bails during a Test against England after Fred Titmus had become stranded, having collided with Neil Hawke during a run. Grout died after a heart attack, having kept news of an earlier attack away from his team-mates.

First-class career (1946–65): 5,168 runs (22.56) including 4 centuries, and 587 dismissals (473 c., 114 st.)
Test matches (51): 890 runs (15.08) and 187 dismissals (163 c., 24 st.)

GUEST, Colin Ernest James

(b. 1937, Melbourne) *Victoria, Western Australia, and Australia*

Colin Guest was one of the army of right-arm fast bowlers competing for a place in Australia's team in succession to Lindwall and Miller. In his sole Test against England in the third Test at Sydney in 1962/3, he scored 11 and took 0 for 59 (18 overs, no maidens). Most of his Sheffield Shield cricket was played for Victoria; once he took ten wickets in a match and five times five or more wickets in an innings. Moving to Western Australia in 1964, he also represented that state at baseball and coached their under-18 cricket team. Although 74 was his top score, he regularly batted usefully.

First-class career (1958–66): 922 runs (19.20) and 115 wickets (27.13)

HAMENCE, Ronald Arthur

(b. 1915, Adelaide) *South Australia and Australia*

A shortish, compact figure, Ron Hamence possessed strong back-foot strokes and liked to attack. Although he had the big match temperament, he was rarely impressive against genuine pace. He was a good outfield. A long-serving, dependable state player, often as opening batsman, he made an assured and important 30 not out on his début in the fifth Test at Sydney in 1946/7 when Doug Wright was making short work of his partners, and the following season he twice scored 25 against India. On coming to England in 1948 he became a familiar figure with the drinks tray and was unable to force his way into the strong Test side. His good cheer survived the disappointment of being a reserve and missing a century by one against Somerset at Taunton. His excellent tenor voice enlivened many an evening on tour. For his state he hit centuries against MCC touring sides in 1946/7 and 1950/1. He also hit 130 and 103 not out against Victoria at Melbourne and 132 and 101 against New South Wales at Adelaide in 1940/1 and 1946/7 respectively, the first South Australian player to have achieved this.

First-class career (1935–50): 5,285 runs (37.75) including 11 centuries
Test matches (3): 81 runs (27.00) and 1 catch

HAMMOND, Jeffrey Roy

(b. 1950, Adelaide) *South Australia and Australia*

An enthusiastic right-arm, fast-medium bowler with a good action, Jeff Hammond took 34

HARRY

wickets (20.26) in his second season for his state in 1970/1, and looked a fine prospect for Australia in the search for fast bowlers. He was unlucky not to play in the series against the Rest of the World in 1971/2 but toured England in 1972, the youngest member of the side. He took 6 for 15 by sheer speed in the first innings of the match against the Minor Counties at Stoke, but did not appear in the Tests. He was handicapped by an earlier back strain. In the West Indies in 1972/3 he was selected for all five Tests, and showed much promise. On his return home, however, he broke a foot and then a further back injury forced him to retire temporarily.

First-class career (1969–80): 922 runs (16.46) and 184 wickets (28.88)

Test matches (5): 28 runs (9.33), 15 wickets (32.53), and 2 catches

HARRY, John

(b. 1857, Ballarat, Victoria; d. 1919, Melbourne) *Victoria and Australia*

John Harry was an above-average all-rounder: a very good right-handed batsman, useful off-break change-bowler, good wicket-keeper, and brilliant mid-off. Several times he was nearly chosen as reserve wicket-keeper to tour England, and in 1896 was actually selected, only to be discarded at the last moment ostensibly owing to a knee injury. He sued the Australian Cricket Council for damages as a result, accepting an out-of-court settlement of £180. Thereupon he came to England on his own account and joined the ground staff at Lord's but was only moderately successful. For Victoria he made many good scores and at Adelaide against South Australia in 1891/2 he bowled both left- and right-handed. In his sole Test at Adelaide in the third match of 1894/5, he scored 2 and 6 and held a catch. In club cricket, for either East Melbourne or Bendigo, he made over 11,000 runs and took 250 wickets. He was also a skittles player and an interstate baseballer.

First-class career (1883–97): 1,466 runs (25.71) including 2 centuries, 26 wickets (23.76) and 21 dismissals (18 c., 3 st.)

HARTIGAN, Roger Joseph

(b. 1879, Sydney; d. 1958, Brisbane) *New South Wales, Queensland, and Australia*

A bright and attractive right-handed batsman and a brilliant slip, Roger Hartigan, in a short career, was Queensland's star batsman long before Sheffield Shield status was attained. He played in two Tests against England in 1907/8 scoring 116 in

sweltering heat in the second innings of his first at Adelaide, having gone in at number eight when runs were badly needed. He toured England in 1909 but rarely found his form and did not play in a Test. An able administrator, he served on the Australian Board of Control for 35 years as a Queensland representative. He represented New South Wales at baseball and Queensland at lacrosse.

First-class career (1903–20): 1,901 runs (25.01) including 2 centuries

Test matches (2): 170 runs (42.50) including 1 century, 0–7, and 1 catch

HARTKOPF, Dr Albert Ernst Victor

(b. 1889, Melbourne; d. 1968, Melbourne) *Victoria and Australia*

One of the most powerful of right-handed hitters and a talented slow leg-break bowler, Albert Hartkopf was a superb athlete and was selected for the second Test at Melbourne in 1924/5 to strengthen the bowling. He took 1 for 134 (Bert Strudwick's wicket) but hit 80 out of a total of 600. Australia won by 81 runs but he did not appear in another Test. He toured New Zealand with his state in 1924/5. He was a good player, but not sufficiently outstanding for the period in which he lived. He was a GP.

First-class career (1911–28): 1,758 runs (34.47) including 2 centuries, and 121 wickets (30.79)

HARVEY, Mervyn Roye

(b. 1918, Broken Hill, New South Wales) *Victoria and Australia*

Usually an opening batsman, Mervyn Harvey was a delightfully free right-handed stroke-maker, at his happiest when the ball was coming through to him from the faster bowlers. His career was seriously interrupted by the Second World War, and in his sole Test, the fourth at Adelaide against England in 1946/7, he scored 12 and 31, putting on 116 for the first wicket with Arthur Morris. He was the eldest of four cricketing brothers who all played for Victoria, the others being 'Mick' (who became a first-class umpire), Ray, and Neil.

First-class career (1940–8): 1,147 runs (38.23) including 3 centuries

HARVEY, Robert Neil

(b. 1928, Melbourne) *Victoria, New South Wales, and Australia*

Between 1948 and 1963 Neil Harvey played in more Tests than any other Australian, scored more runs in Tests than all but Don Bradman, and was preceded only by Bradman in Australian Test centuries and averages. The sight of his trim figure coming through the gate—short, stocky, and with his neat, dark hair always capless—invariably spelt danger to opponents. One of the greatest of all left-handers, he was continually looking for runs, a clinical destroyer of the bad ball. A strong driver and cutter, it was said that when he hooked, the sound of the ball hitting the fence was like an explosion from Bikini. His footwork was brilliant, but if he was vulnerable anywhere it was outside the off-stump. Against spin he often danced down the pitch to balls an ordinary batsman would have played defensively. In the field, swooping on the ball and flicking it back to the 'keeper accurately with a minimum of effort, he was superb, usually in the covers, but sometimes on the boundary or in the slips. He burst into cricket brilliantly with a century in his first club match, another in his first game for Victoria, one in his second Test, against India in 1947, and 112 on his first appearance against England, at Headingley, in 1948, when he was the youngest member of the touring side. He made four tours of England, scoring 1,129 runs (53.76) and 2,040 runs (65.80) in 1948 and 1953 respectively. In South Africa in 1949/50 he hit eight centuries, four in the Tests and averaged 76.30 on the tour. When the South Africans visited Australia in 1952/3 he made 834 runs in the Tests, again hitting four centuries, including his Test highest, 205 at Melbourne, and beating Bradman's record of 1931/2. To crown all this, he married a South African girl. In 37 Tests against England between 1948 and 1961, he made 2,416 runs (38.34), including six centuries, the highest being 167 at Melbourne in 1958/9. A specially memorable innings was 92 not out (out of 184) at Sydney in 1954/5 when Tyson and Statham were carrying all before them. On the uncertain pitches against the dominant Jim Laker in 1956 he hit 69 (out of 140) at Headingley, resisting with superb footwork and concentration for four and a half hours. He toured the West Indies, India, and Pakistan—making 204 at Kingston and several other centuries. His highest score in first-class cricket was 231 not out for New South Wales against South Australia at Sydney in 1962/3; in all he made seven scores in excess of 200. In 75 Sheffield Shield matches he made 5,853 runs (50,46). In one such match he made 52 in forty-eight minutes before being caught. 'Why did you get out?' asked a selector, 'You could have made 300 today.' Neil's reported reply was, 'Who on earth ever wants to make 300?' He captained Australia in one Test in 1961, as substitute for Richie Benaud at Lord's, where Australia won en route to retaining the Ashes. Latterly he has been a Test selector and was awarded an MBE for services to cricket.

First-class career (1946–63): 21,699 runs (50.93) including 67 centuries, 30 wickets (36.86), and 228 catches

Test matches (79): 6,149 runs (48.42) including 21 centuries, 3 wickets (40.00), and 64 catches

HASSETT, Arthur Lindsay

(b. 1913, Geelong, Victoria; d. 1993, Bateman's Bay, New South Wales) *Victoria and Australia*

One of the smallest men ever to represent Australia, Lindsay Hassett was a glorious right-handed attacking batsman by nature who often became dour and watchful at the wicket in his country's service. Not only could he hook and cut the short ball and drive the half-volleys but he would also force the good-length ball 'on the up'. His footwork was superbly quick. Poker-faced, he was both a wit and a practical joker, at home as much with 'larrikins' as with princes and prime ministers, possessing a charm and personality all his own. The game was never for him a matter of life and death and he watched it from the ABC commentary box with dispassionate fairness for many years. His voice may have been somewhat monotonous as a summarizer, but there was a constant twinkle in his eye and his comments were often wry and wise, erring on the generous side. Having captained Geelong College at cricket, football, and tennis, he was picked for Victoria soon after leaving school but dropped after one game and not recalled for three years. He toured England in 1938, 1948, and 1953, when he succeeded Bradman as captain. He found English pitches much to his liking, on his initial tour making 1,589 runs (54.79), on his second 1,563 runs (74.42), when vice-captain, and 1,236 runs (44.14) on his final visit. Like all his contemporaries, he was overshadowed by Bradman, but when he retired only Bradman among Australians had made more runs. In his first post-war Test, at Wellington, he hit 128 in six and a half hours, adding 276 for the third wicket with Bradman. Against India in 1947/8 he came second to Bradman with an average of 110.66, which included his Test highest score of 198 not out at Adelaide. At Trent Bridge in 1948 he made 138 and, when he took over the captaincy in South Africa in 1949/50, he scored two centuries and averaged 67.00. He never had a poor series and led both Victoria and Australia with cunning and quiet authority. No side under his command would overstep the limits of fair play or acceptable behaviour. He cut his teeth as an international captain when chosen to lead the Australian Services team to Britain for the 'Victory Tests'. Off the field he enjoyed himself hugely, on this and subsequent tours. He liked a good prank, once tethering a goat to Bradman's bed, and on another occasion climbing into bed with Mr and Mrs E. W. Swanton—uninvited. When he scored 163 at Adelaide against South Africa in 1952/3 he put on 275 for the second wicket with Colin McDonald, and in his last series in 1953, against England, he headed the batting with 365 runs (36.50), becoming an opening batsman to help steady the side. He made eight scores above 200, the highest being 232 for Victoria against MCC at Melbourne in 1950/1. In 58 Sheffield Shield matches he made 5,535 runs (63.62). Happily married, he retired to the New South Wales coast where fishing was his great hobby. He was awarded an MBE for services to cricket and Jack Pollard wrote truly of him: 'in the art of making friends for Australian cricket, there has never been anybody like him.' Richie Benaud wrote: 'there are others who have made more runs and taken more wickets but very few have ever got more out of a lifetime.'

First-class career (1932–53): 16,890 runs (58.24) including 59 centuries, 18 wickets (39.05), and 170 catches

Test matches (43): 3,073 runs (46.56) including 10 centuries, 0–78 and 30 catches

HAWKE, Neil James Napier

(b. 1939, Adelaide) *Western Australia, South Australia, Tasmania, and Australia*

A renowned Australian Rules footballer, Neil Hawke was a dark, powerfully built right-arm fast-medium bowler who cut the ball off the pitch and bowled a good late in-swinger from an economical, open-chested action. He was also a useful late-order batsman. His début was against England, 1962/3, in the final match of the series; and he replaced Ian Meckiff against South Africa in 1963/4, after the latter was no-balled for 'throwing' in the first Test. He took 14 wickets (33.78) in the series. In 1967/8 he took 48 wickets in Australia, including 7 for 46 for his state against the Indians and 8 for 62 against New South Wales. He toured England in 1964 and 1968, and twelve Tests against England brought him 37

wickets, his best piece of bowling being 7 for 105 when England reached 488 in the third Test at Sydney in 1965/6. His finest hour was, however, in the West Indies in 1965, when, for a losing side, he was the best bowler with 24 wickets (21.83) in the Tests—besides earning a batting average of 28.60. Although Australia lost heavily at Georgetown, he took 10 for 115 in the match. He had success with Nelson in the Lancashire League and settled in Lancashire for some years. He made a courageous recovery from a very severe illness.

First-class career (1959–71): 3,383 runs (23.99) and 458 wickets (26.39)

Test matches (27): 365 runs (16.59), 91 wickets (29.41), and 9 catches

HAWKE, Robert James Lee

(b. 1929, Bordertown, South Australia)

Like Sir Robert Menzies before him, Bob Hawke was a cricket-loving Australian Prime Minister who had grown up with the game. A wicket-keeping batsman, he played frequently and at good standard in first-grade in Perth, Melbourne, and Canberra—and for the Oxford University Authentics—before concentrating on his political career. In Canberra his most satisfying innings was one of 78 for the Australian Capital Territory against a Newcastle combined district team in the mid-1950s. Just days after he became Prime Minister in early 1983, Hawke discussed with Phil Ridings, chairman of the Australian Cricket Board, his desire to reintroduce the Prime Minister's XI fixture, first played 32 years previously. Hawke wanted the matches to be played in earnest and to include the reigning Australian captain and as many genuine Test aspirants as possible. In 1984, when the fixture was revived, the young Tasmanian David Boon, who had been overlooked for international selection, scored 134 against the West Indies and later that year played the first of more than 100 Tests. The following summer, the Victorian Simon O'Donnell shone for the Prime Minister's XI and later made the Australian touring team to England. New South Wales's Steve Waugh was named for his first Test a week after he had played for the Prime Minister's XI in late 1985. Hawke played in several games in 1988 and 1989 against the Aboriginal Cricket Association. Batting at number six he made only 0 and 2, but his enthusiastic involvement made for several memorable days. He continued to represent the politicians in social games against teams such as the Melbourne

Crusaders and when caught on the boundary by cricket writer Ken Piesse at the Melbourne Cricket Ground one day, quipped as he was walking off, 'that's the first time in 25 years I've been caught out by a journalist!' In 1979 Hawke was named a Companion of the Order of Australia.

HAYDEN, Matthew Lawrence

(b. 1971, Kingaroy, Queensland) *Queensland and Australia*

The first Australian to score 1,000 first-class runs in each of his first three summers, the 6 ft. 4 in. left-hander Matthew Hayden is an aggressive opening batsman who intimidates bowlers with his front-foot power. His feat of scoring seven centuries in Queensland's opening six matches in 1993/4 won him Australian one-day selection and a place on the tour of South Africa, where he made his Test début. He had toured England with the 1993 Australians, uniquely scoring 1,000 first-class runs without playing a Test. He took two outstanding catches at Lord's, one in the deep and another at short-leg. The son of a Kingaroy peanut farmer, Hayden and his older brother, Gary, fashioned a home-made turf pitch, planting couch grass and lovingly rolling and mowing it before each session. They erected netting and even used shoe polish to help preserve their leather balls. The bounce was often irregular and a good defence and nimble feet were essential. Hayden tended to be too aggressive in his late-teen years and was overlooked for the Queensland under-19 team. Developing a rigid defence and drawing comparisons with Australia's 'unbowlable' between-the-wars opening batsman, Bill Woodfull, it was two seasons, 21 matches, and 39 innings before he was bowled at top level, by New South Wales's Wayne Holdsworth at Brisbane 1993. Among Hayden's laurels were a century on début for Queensland in Brisbane in 1991/2 and his 161 not out and 35 not out in his second season against South Australia, in Adelaide.

First-class career (1991–): 4,714 runs (61.22) including 15 centuries, 1 wicket (67.00), and 44 catches
Test matches (1): 20 runs (10.00) and 1 catch

HAZLITT, Gervys Rignold

(b. 1888, Sydney; d. 1915, Parramatta, New South Wales) *Victoria, New South Wales, and Australia*

Although Gerry Hazlitt was a very useful bats-man, it was his bowling which gained him his reputation. He bowled right-arm off-breaks at swerving medium pace, though there were some doubts at times about his action. He first appeared for Victoria at 17. He played in Tests against England in 1907/8 and 1911/12, and came to England for the Triangular Tournament in 1912, taking 19 wickets (20.94) in the Tests, including 7 for 25 in the second innings against England at The Oval, at one time ensnaring 5 for 1 in 17 balls. Despite having to have an eye operation, he took 101 wickets (18.96) on the tour. In Sheffield Shield matches he made 390 runs (16.25) and took 60 wickets (31.98). He was a master at the King's School, Parramatta, where he died of a heart attack at the age of 27.

First-class career (1905–13): 876 runs (12.69) and 188 wickets (26.09)
Test matches (9): 89 runs (11.12), 23 wickets (27.08), and 4 catches

HEALY, Ian Andrew

(b. 1964, Spring Hill, Queensland) *Queensland and Australia*

Rock-hard, durable, and consistent in the best traditions of the finest wicket-keepers, Ian Healy was initially a surprise selection at Test level, being named for the Test tour of Pakistan in 1988 after just six first-class matches over two seasons as substitute for the injured Queensland stumper Peter Anderson. Benefiting from the retirement of the ex-international, Ray Phillips, Healy leap-frogged all his opposition, including Greg Dyer, who had kept wicket for Australia the previous summer. Although he initially struggled on the low, turning pitches of Pakistan, he won the admiration of his team-mates and opponents alike with his passion for the game and his enthusiasm to improve. His hard work ethics include a dawn routine on match days of working out with inners and a golf ball, generally in the basement car-park of the team's hotel. It took time for him to win Australia-wide acceptance, especially with sections of Perth cricket fans, who regarded Tim Zoehrer as at least his equal and in December 1992 openly booed Healy during a World Series Cup match. He responded superbly, and in 1993 in England, dismissed 26 batsmen (21 catches and 5 stumpings), just two dismissals short of Rod Marsh's series record of 28—also against England in 1982/3—winning praise for his clean catching and sureness standing up to the spinners. His batting has also advanced and in the opening Test in England in 1993, he scored his maiden Test century at Manchester, a sparkling knock from just 133 balls. He also scored 80 at Edgbaston and 83 not out at The Oval. Brisbane-born, Healy learnt the rudiments of the game in his teen years playing on canvas-covered concrete wickets at Biloela, south-west of Rockhampton in country Queensland. Only the sixth wicket-keeper to amass 200 dismissals, Healy had by 1994 surpassed the figures of all compatriots except Rodney Marsh. His dismissals per match average of almost 3.5 is comparable with the all-time best 'keepers. Coming into Australia's packed 1994/5 home-and-away Test schedule, he had played 62 Tests in a row, a record of durability surpassed by only two Australians, Allan Border and Ian Chappell. He had also figured in 109 one-day internationals, maintaining a free-flowing strike-rate of almost a run a ball. Queensland captain since 1992/3, Healy was named Australia's deputy-captain (to Mark Taylor) for the tour of Pakistan and Sri Lanka in late 1994.

First-class career (1986–): 4,632 runs (31.29) including 2 centuries, and 430 dismissals (394 c., 36 st.)

Test matches (73): 2,558 runs (26.92) including 2 centuries, and 248 dismissals (231 c., 17 st.)

HENDRY, Hunter Scott Thomas Laurie

(b. 1895, Sydney; d. 1988, Sydney) *New South Wales, Victoria, and Australia*

Tall and slim, 'Stork' Hendry was a right-handed batsman who cut and drove effortlessly, a fast-medium change-bowler, and a fine slip field. He toured England in 1921 and 1926, disappointing in the Tests on the former tour and being kept out of them by illness on the latter. He hit 112 in the second Test at Sydney in 1928/9 and opened the bowling in two of the matches, but he had lost his place by the end of the series. Although he rarely revealed his true ability for his country, he made 325 not out for Victoria against the New Zealanders at Melbourne in 1925; and in 52 Sheffield Shield matches (33 for Victoria) he made 3,393 runs (43.50) and took 101 wickets (29.53). He toured South Africa in 1921/2 and India in 1935/6.

First-class career (1918–35): 6,799 runs (37.56) including 14 centuries, 229 wickets (29.02), and 151 catches

Test matches (11): 335 runs (20.93) including 1 century, 16 wickets (40.00), and 10 catches

HIBBERT, Paul Anthony

(b. 1952, Melbourne) *Victoria and Australia*

A dark, quite tall, and very patient left-handed opening batsman, Paul Hibbert played for Victorian Colts for four years and was selected for Australia against India for the first Test of 1977/8 after making 100 not out against the touring team for Victoria. Curiously, this was an innings without any boundaries. Less adept against spin than speed, he was dropped after only one Test, in which he scored 13 and 2, and held 1 catch. A useful change-bowler, he took 4 for 28 against South Australia at Melbourne in 1977/8 with his left-arm medium pace. He scored over 800 runs in 1983/4, nearly 700 runs in 1985/6 and a further 725 in his last season, proving himself to be a durable player.

First-class career (1974–87): 4,790 runs (38.63) including 8 centuries, 15 wickets (19.00), and 38 catches

HIGGS, James Donald

(b. 1950, Kyabram, Victoria) *Victoria and Australia*

Probably the best Australian leg-spinner between Richie Benaud and Shane Warne and a cheery, straightforward character, Jim Higgs has long since lived down his first main claim to fame, that of being bowled by the only ball he faced on the 15-match tour of England in 1975. Red-faced on the coolest days, he was a dedicated cricketer who worked hard to turn himself into a respectable batsman (in 1978/9 he was promoted to number ten) and into a serviceable fielder, although his wickets eventually outnumbered his runs. With a good, high, comfortable action, he gave the ball a strong flip and had a useful googly. These qualities allied to exceptionally good control made him an economical as well as an effective Test bowler, anything but a luxury in an attack. His selection for the 1975 tour owed much to a return of 8 for 66 against the powerful West Australian side the previous season (11 for 118 in the match), but not until the cream of Australian cricketers had left to join World Series Cricket did he make his belated Test début. In four Tests in the West Indies in 1978 he took 15 wickets (25.60) and on the tour 42 wickets at 22.21, including 12 for 163 in the match against the Leeward Islands. Against England in 1978/9 he demanded respect in all the five games he played, finishing the series with 19 wickets (24.63) though the pitches were seldom quick enough to suit his spin, which could be extremely sharp. Touring India in 1979, Higgs took 29 wickets on the tour (32.86) but his 14 wickets in the six Tests cost 50 runs apiece. He played one Test each against the West Indies and England in 1979/80, taking 3 for 122 against the former at Melbourne but suffering the misery against England at Sydney of bowling only one over in the entire game. The feeling was growing that he might be one of the last of a dying breed but he bowled Victoria to success in the Sheffield Shield in 1979/80 and played in the first four Tests of 1980/1 (three against New Zealand and one against India) taking four wickets in an innings on three occasions. Then he was dropped and left out of the tour to England in 1981. He retired from first-class cricket at the end of the 1982/3 season at the age of 32, but became part of the shrewd and closely-knit selection team which chose the Australian sides who did so well under Allan Border's captaincy from the mid-1980s.

First-class career (1970–82): 384 runs (5.41) and 399 wickets (29.67)

Test matches (22): 111 runs (5.55), 66 wickets (31.16), and 3 catches

HILDITCH, Andrew Mark Jefferson

(b. 1956, Adelaide) *New South Wales, South Australia, and Australia*

A confident and determined young solicitor and graduate of Sydney University, Andrew Hilditch was an unflappable, right-handed, opening batsman with a thoroughly sound, front-foot technique and limitless concentration. He was a good slip catcher. He was made captain of New South Wales at the age of 21. Lean, sallow-complexioned, and combative in the true Australian tradition, he was appointed state captain after he had played only two first-class matches; only Ian Craig was younger when first leading New South Wales. After several failures at the start of 1978/9 season NSW were said to be captained by Andrew 'Who?' But after scoring a determined 93 against the England touring team he batted consistently enough to earn a place as opening batsman for the sixth Test against England and for two games against Pakistan (1978/9), in the second of which he was appointed deputy to Australia's new captain, Kim Hughes. He

remained vice-captain during the Prudential World Cup in 1979 when he was a conspicuous success. In the second Test against Pakistan at Perth in 1979 he was the victim of an appalling mockery of the spirit of cricket. Picking up the ball after it had been fielded, he handed it to the bowler Safraz Nawaz, who appealed successfully for 'handling the ball'. Australia went on to win the match. He fell swiftly from grace, despite a not unsuccessful tour of India later in 1979. He opened the batting in all six Tests, passing 50 three times and making 313 runs (26.08). But the return of the World Series Cricket players, and of Rick McCosker in particular, caused him to lose the captaincy of New South Wales and his place as well for a time. He was married during the 1979/80 season to the daughter of R. B. (Bobby) Simpson. Making no progress in Sydney, however, he moved to South Australia and scored 79 against the 1982/3 England touring team. Following two fine seasons for his new state he made a triumphant return to Test cricket against the West Indies at Melbourne in 1984—he scored a determined 70 in the first innings following it with 113, his maiden Test hundred. Vice-captain on the tour to England in 1985, he started in great style with 119 and 80 in the first Test at Headingley and made 424 runs (38.54) in the series, but the hook shot often brought his downfall in the later matches. In the first Test of the next Australian season two cheap dismissals at the hands of Richard Hadlee, again the result of ill-judged hooks, led to his being dropped. That a qualified solicitor should have got himself out in the same way so often confirmed that it is one thing to have a brain, another to have a 'cricket brain'!

First-class career (1976–91): 9,984 runs (37.96) including 20 centuries, and 101 catches

Test matches (18): 1,073 runs (31.55) including 2 centuries, and 13 catches

HILEY, Sir Thomas

(b. 1905, Highgate Hill, Queensland; d. 1990, Cooroy, Queensland)

A right-hand batsman and wicket-keeper, Sir Thomas played senior club cricket in Brisbane before becoming president of the Queensland Cricket Association for the first of three years in 1965. He was also vice-president (1968–83) and a Queensland Cricket Association trustee between 1971 and 1981. He also served as a member of Queensland Parliament, rising at one time to deputy premier and treasurer.

HILL, Clement

(b. 1877, Adelaide; d. 1945, Melbourne) *South Australia and Australia*

Shortish, square, and sturdy, Clem Hill was one of the greatest of left-handed batsmen. He had an ugly wide stance, with the hands held low on the bat handle, but saw the ball early and positioned himself easily for a wide variety of strokes. Strong on the leg side, and quick into position to hook or pull, he could also drive anywhere and was an explosive cutter. With his bottom-handed grip he was merciless on anything short. Although normally an attacking player, he was also a natural fighter, who saved many a lost cause. The son of H. J. Hill, who scored the first century at Adelaide Oval, Clem at 16 hit 360 in an inter-College match—the highest innings hit in Australia at that time—and visited England with the 1896, 1899, 1902, and 1905 sides. He headed the Test averages with 60.20 in 1899, his 135 at Lord's being important in helping to win the only match decided that year. A fine fielder, especially in the deep, he made a legendary catch at Old Trafford in 1902: running from long-on to square-leg, he held a skier hit by Dick Lilley, and soon afterwards Australia won by three runs. Hill's highest score in Tests was 191 against South Africa at Sydney in 1910/11, but perhaps the best innings was his 188 against England at Melbourne in 1897/8, when he was 21. Coming together at 58 for 6, he and Hugh Trumble added 165, a stand which won the match. At Adelaide in 1907/8 he and Roger Hartigan put on 243 for the eighth wicket. When Australia retained the Ashes in 1901/2, Hill was the heaviest run-getter with 521 runs (52.10), which included 99, 98, and 97 in successive innings! He captained Australia in 1910/11 and 1911/12. During the latter series, he was involved in a 'punch-up' with another Test selector, Percy McAlister, which was a prelude to the great 'Board of Control versus Players' row. He did not tour England therefore in 1912. In 68 Sheffield Shield matches he made 6,274 runs (52.28), a record until beaten by Don Bradman. His career-highest score was 365 not out for South Australia against New South Wales at Adelaide in 1900/1. He hit three other double centuries but, in contrast, was out in the nineties no fewer than five times in Tests against England.

First-class career (1892–1923): 17,213 runs (43.57) including 45 centuries

Test matches (49): 3,412 runs (39.21) including 7 centuries, and 33 catches

HILL, John Charles

(b. 1923, Melbourne; d. 1974, Melbourne) *Victoria and Australia*

Jack Hill was an inelegant right-arm leg-break bowler who turned the ball little but made the top-spinner bounce especially awkwardly at a brisk pace. He toured England in 1953 and the West Indies in 1955, but did not represent his country at home. In the West Indies he headed the bowling in all matches with 18 wickets (21.11), and was also successful in England with 63 wickets (20.98). Seven of his eight Test wickets were recognized batsmen. He was a great Rules footballer until he twice fractured his skull.

First-class career (1945–55): 867 runs (16.05) and 218 wickets (23.11)

Test matches (3): 21 runs (7.00), 8 wickets (34.12), and 2 catches

HILL, Leslie Roy

(b. 1884, Adelaide; d. 1952, Adelaide) *South Australia*

One of six Hill brothers to play first-class cricket, including the legendary left-hander Clem Hill, Les Hill was an all-rounder good enough to score a century against New South Wales (Sydney, 1910/11) and also capture valuable wickets. A right-hand batsman and right-arm medium-pacer, Hill was once 12th man for Australia, for the Adelaide Test against England in 1907/8.

First-class career (1905–10): 583 runs (18.21) including 1 century, 28 wickets (47.14), and 8 catches

HIRD, Sydney Francis

(b. 1910, Balmain, New South Wales; d. 1980, Bloemfontein, South Africa) *New South Wales, Lancashire, Eastern Province, and Border*

An outstanding all-rounder who shifted to England to play professional cricket after failing to find work during the Great Depression, Syd Hird was Australia's 12th man for the opening Test of the 'bodyline' series, but soon afterwards left Australia never to return. He earned his place in the twelve after scoring a century for New South Wales against the visiting South Africans in only his third first-class match the previous year, as well as taking 6 for 135 with his wrist spinners in the lead-up games to the 1932/3 series. A right-hand batsman renowned for his attractive hitting and right-arm leg-break and googly bowler, Hird switched to off-spinners while playing in England,

and in five years with Ramsbottom amassed almost 400 wickets and made more than 4,000 runs. After the Second World War, he played and coached in South Africa, figuring in his last match, for Border, in his forty-second year.

First-class career (1931–50): 1,453 runs (33.02) including 5 centuries, 59 wickets (28.54), and 8 catches

HOARE, Desmond Edward

(b. 1934, Perth) *Western Australia and Australia*

Des Hoare was a tall, strong right-arm fast bowler who was unlucky to represent Australia in only one Test, at Adelaide against the West Indies in 1960/1. In a particularly exciting game his match analysis was 29–0–156–2 but his first wicket, that of Conrad Hunte in his second over, was memorable. He scored 35 and 0 and held 2 catches.

First-class career (1955–66): 1,276 runs (18.49) including 1 century, and 225 wickets (26.91)

HODGES, John Robart

(b. 1855, London; d. unknown) *Victoria and Australia*

John Hodges was a left-arm fast-medium bowler renowned for his straightness and pronounced break, but was too inclined to bowl short. An erratic batsman, he was not remarkable in the field. Much of his best cricket was played for Richmond (Victoria) and he appeared for Australia in the first two Tests of 1876/7. It is unlikely that he was the 'J. Hodges' who also umpired a Test in 1884/5.

First-class career (1876–7): 75 runs (12.50) and 12 wickets (16.50)

Test matches (2): 10 runs (3.33) and 6 wickets (14.00)

HOGAN, Thomas George

(b. 1956, Merredin, Western Australia) *Western Australia and Australia*

Tom Hogan, a tidy slow left-arm bowler and lower-order right-hand batsman, made his Test début in Australia's game in Sri Lanka in April 1983 and was his side's leading spin bowler on the 1983/4 tour of the West Indies. He made his début for his state in the 1981/2 season and immediately developed a fine spinning partnership with the Test off-spinner Bruce Yardley. He took 20 wickets in his first season and bowled beautifully throughout the following year, taking

35 wickets (26.82) with match figures of 9 for 162 against New South Wales and 8 for 101 against Queensland. His performances won him a place on the short end-of-season tour to Sri Lanka. He took 1 for 50 and 5 for 66 in the inaugural Test match between the two countries at Kandy, sharing 13 wickets with Yardley to bring Australia victory. He only played one match in the home series with Pakistan in 1983/4 but played in all five Tests in the Caribbean, where 4 for 56 at Georgetown were his best figures. Despite his modest return of eight wickets (60.37), he bowled a number of long and accurate spells on largely unresponsive wickets. He joined the rebel Australian tour to South Africa in 1985/6, having missed selection for the tour of England in 1985, and thereby effectively burnt his boats.

First-class career (1981–   ): 1,092 runs (17.06) and 157 wickets (35.34)

Test matches (7): 205 runs (18.63), 15 wickets (47.06), and 2 catches

HOGG, Rodney Malcolm

(b. 1951, Melbourne) *Victoria, South Australia, and Australia*

After a long struggle to establish himself in first-class cricket, Rodney Hogg burst into Test matches like one of his own express deliveries. Blue-eyed, with fair curly hair, six foot but strongly built around the shoulders and rump, he aimed to bowl fast and straight in short, electric spells, putting all his energy into most deliveries, except when bowling off a shorter run. Even then he was decidedly sharp. The approach from little more than 20 yards was a fine example of smoothly gathered momentum, the body leaning forward and gathering speed into the final leap and long stretch of the delivery stride. Only a certain stiffness of movement and a lack of stamina, sometimes due to a mild asthmatic condition, prevented his taking even more than his 41 wickets at a remarkable average of 12.85 against England in 1978/9. Yet before this dramatic performance Hogg had played first-class cricket in only two seasons. Time and time again, with hostile three- or four-over bursts, he undermined the confidence of the England batting, reducing the menace of the hitherto consistently successful Geoff Boycott (whom he often defeated by sheer speed) and generally saving Australia from a much heavier defeat. A serious, determined character, sometimes petulant, he had a number of jobs while struggling, first in his native Victoria and then in South Australia, to make his mark in the game. He toured England for the Prudential World Cup in 1979, and India later that year. Hogg was a grave disappointment on the Indian tour, bowling an excessive number of no-balls and taking only 11 wickets in the Tests at 53.72. He played in only one home Test in 1979/80 but won his place back the following Australian season, bowling effectively as the back-up fast bowler to Lillee and Pascoe against New Zealand and winning selection for a tour of England in 1981. Sadly, however, a serious back injury restricted him to two Test appearances. Yet he was back near his best against England in 1982/3, taking 11 important wickets in his three Tests. He took his 100th Test wicket against Pakistan in 1983 and then in two series against the West Indies collected 20 rather expensive wickets. He had lost the devastating turn of speed he had shown in 1978/9 and was not selected to tour England in 1985, although he had two successful tours of South Africa with the unofficial Australian side in 1985/6 and the following season.

First-class career (1975–87): 1,185 runs (10.48) and 378 wickets (24.36)

Test matches (38): 439 runs (9.75), 123 wickets (28.47), and 7 catches

HOHNS, Trevor Victor

(b. 1954, Nundah, Queensland) *Queensland and Australia*

A late-developing right-arm leg spinner and left-hand middle-order batsman who was 34 on his Test début in 1988/9, Trevor 'Cracka' Hohns made sterling contributions as his team's front-line spinner in the 1989 Ashes series. They were not as spectacular as Shane Warne's efforts four years later, but were equally important in Australia's runaway series victory. Playing five of the six Test matches, Hohns bowled superbly, the flipper which trapped David Gower lbw at Manchester in the third Test being a reward for his hours of toil and practice. An over later, he bowled Ian Botham for a duck and, charging down the wicket in jubilation, almost skittled close-in fieldsman Dean Jones. It was the most memorable afternoon of his career. He finished with Test-best figures of 3 for 59 from 27 overs. His emergence as an international player was buoyed by his experiences with Kim Hughes's rebel tours to South Africa in 1985/6 and 1986/7. Chosen as one of two specialist spinners (along with Western Australia's Tom Hogan), Hohns

played four of the unofficial tests, his nine wicket haul (6 for 98 and 3 for 27) against the South Africans at Kingsmead in January 1987 being his most successful stint in representative cricket. Previously, he had played mainly as a batting all-rounder with Queensland without looking likely to advance. It took him 146 innings to make his maiden first-class century, a fighting second innings ton against Western Australia in Perth in 1984/5. Four matches later, in the Shield final against New South Wales at the Sydney Cricket Ground, he made another one. So respected was he that he was enticed out of retirement, aged 37, in 1990/1 to captain Queensland. He had several outstanding spells, notably 5 for 18 from 19 overs against New South Wales at the Gabba and 6 for 102 from 55 overs in the return match in Sydney. He refused an offer to continue in Shield ranks in 1991/2.

First-class career (1972–89): 5,210 runs (27.13) including 2 centuries, 288 wickets (37.15), and 86 catches

Test matches (7): 136 runs (22.66), 17 wickets (34.11), and 3 catches

HOLE, Graeme Blake

(b. 1931, Sydney; d. 1990, Adelaide) *New South Wales, South Australia, and Australia*

A tall, right-handed middle-order batsman, Graeme Hole had an awkward knock-kneed stance and was too fond of the sweep for his own good, but he could be a powerful right-handed driver, attractive and punishing. A brilliant slip field, he twice caught four men in Tests against South Africa, at Adelaide and Sydney in 1952/3. His other series were against the West Indies and England. His sole overseas tour to England was in 1953, when, despite many opportunities, he never really established himself. He top-scored with 63 in the second innings of his first Test, against the West Indies at Melbourne in 1951/2 but, although he opened his England tour with 112 at Worcester, his ten Test innings brought only 273 runs, with 66 at Old Trafford as his best effort. He made his career-highest score of 226 against Queensland at Adelaide in 1953/4, and the following season made his last Test appearances, scoring 85 runs in three matches. A prolific run-getter for his states, in 44 Sheffield Shield matches he made 3,060 runs (42.50), besides taking 34 wickets (50.35) with off-breaks.

First-class career (1949–57): 5,647 runs (36.66) including 11 centuries, and 61 wickets (44.04)

Test matches (18): 789 runs (25.45), 3 wickets (42.00), and 21 catches

HOLLAND, Robert George

(b. 1946, Sydney) *New South Wales and Australia*

Bob Holland's first-class career began late, in the 1978/9 season, when he played his first game for his state at the age of 32. Six years later he made his Test début against the West Indies as a leg-spin bowler. A friendly and courteous man, he much enjoyed the fruits which fell in the autumn of his career. In his first match he found the transition from grade to first-class cricket a hard one, taking only 1 for 113 in 19 overs, but he soon turned in several match-winning performances for his state. He did not often use the googly but his rolling leg-breaks were dangerous on helpful wickets and his control and accuracy were extremely tight for a wrist-spinner. In the 1984/5 season his bowling helped New South Wales win the Sheffield Shield, as he ruthlessly exploited the helpful Sydney wicket. He took 4 for 81 and 3 for 38 to help bring his state a historic victory against Clive Lloyd's seemingly invincible West Indians. This achievement gained him immediate promotion to the Test side, and although unsuccessful in his first two Tests, back at Sydney in the final match he took 6 for 54 and 4 for 90 to bamboozle the West Indies again and end their long unbeaten Test record. With 59 wickets he was the leading Australian wicket-taker and so was a certainty for the 1985 tour of England. In the second Test at Lord's he took 5 for 68 in the second innings to bowl England out and set up an Australian victory. On slow, unresponsive pitches he could take only one more wicket in three Tests as the English batsmen played him with greater ease. Back once more on his favourite Sydney wicket, he took 8 for 33 for his state against New Zealand and his ten wickets in the Test against them on the same ground again brought his country victory. His Test record epitomizes the misfortunes of the leg-spinner—on three responsive pitches he took 25 wickets and each time Australia won, but in his eight other Tests he gained only nine more wickets.

First-class career (1978–87): 706 runs (9.67) and 316 wickets (31.19)

Test matches (11): 35 runs (3.18), 34 wickets (39.76), and 5 catches

HOOKES, David William

(b. 1955, Adelaide) *South Australia and Australia*

David Hookes made an indelible impression by hitting five centuries in six innings during three successive Sheffield Shield matches for South Australia at the age of 21 in 1976/7, and then hitting five successive fours off Tony Greig during an innings of 56 in the Centenary Test in Melbourne (Hookes's first). A fair-haired left-hander, he had a wonderful gift of timing, plus self-confidence and courage. Sir Donald Bradman said of his Test début, 'I thought Frank Woolley had been born again.' Hookes owed his selection to his inspired run of scores against Victoria, Queensland, and New South Wales. The innings, all played at Adelaide Oval, were 163, 9, 185, 101, 135, and 156. He had already made a mark in minor cricket in England, hitting six sixes in one six-ball over when playing club cricket for Dulwich, but his phenomenal start was followed by anti-climax in England in 1977 when, sometimes let down by impetuosity and a rather fiery temperament, be scored only 283 runs in nine innings, hitting only one hundred on the tour. However, despite breaking his jaw when trying to hook a bumper from Andy Roberts, he played some outstanding innings during two seasons of World Series Cricket, having unsuccessfully tried to obtain a release from his contract. The seasons which followed the disbandment of World Series Cricket suggested that it would have been better for him in the long run had he stayed with the 'Establishment'. Turned into a star, even an idol, by the marketing men now so powerful in Australian cricket, he lost the ability to apply himself for long periods at the crease and was ditched after only one Test in 1979/80, despite scoring 43 and 37 against the West Indies at Brisbane. Poor form in the many limited-overs internationals seemed to hasten his downfall and although he toured Pakistan at the end of the 1979/80 season he made a pair in the only Test in which he played. 'Hooksey' remained in the cold in 1980/1 but in 1981/2 he returned to the international arena and proved a very successful captain of South Australia, who won the Sheffield Shield. Hookes himself scored 703 runs (43.93). He was in magnificent form the following year. He had a fine Test series against England, scoring 344 runs (49.14), and he hit a total of 1,424 runs in the Australian season. This included a century in each innings (137 and 107) against Victoria at Adelaide, the second one reached in forty-three minutes, off 34 balls—the fastest hundred ever made by an Australian and the fastest 'authentic' century—with the opposition bowlers really trying—on record anywhere. He made his maiden Test hundred, 143 not out, against Sri Lanka, ending the season in style. Discarded from the side after touring the West Indies in 1983/4 he went to England in 1985 as a commentator for Australian television, but he was temporarily recalled for the 1985/6 series against New Zealand and India. In the same season, he made 243 as captain of South Australia against New South Wales, and eclipsed even this effort a year later when dominating Tasmania at Adelaide with a dazzling 306 not out. With Wayne Phillips he added 462 for the fourth wicket, undefeated, then the highest partnership by an Australian pair.

First-class career (1975–92): 12,671 runs (43.99) including 32 centuries, 41 wickets (58.02), and 167 catches

Test matches (23): 1,306 runs (34.36) including 1 century, 1–41, and 12 catches

HOPKINS, Albert John Young

(b. 1874, Young, New South Wales; d. 1931, Sydney) *New South Wales and Australia*

A right-arm slow-medium bowler with a pronounced swerve and break from the off, a forceful batsman and a brilliant field, Bert Hopkins toured England with the 1902, 1905, and 1909 teams—passing 1,000 runs on the first tour and taking 34 wickets (18.61) in 1902. He also went to South Africa in 1902/3, and at home played in two series against England, without really establishing himself. In the second Test at Lord's in 1902 he opened the bowling (to everyone's surprise bar his captain's) and immediately disposed of C. B. Fry and K. S. Ranjitsinhji. He did not get another wicket in the series. His highest score in England was 154 against Northamptonshire at Northampton in 1905. Usually opening the batting for his state, he made his career-highest score of 218 against South Australia at Adelaide in 1908/9, adding 283 for the second wicket with M. A. Noble in two hours and fifty minutes. In 35 Sheffield Shield matches he made 1,594 runs (30.65) and took 96 wickets (22.57).

First-class career (1896–1914): 5,563 runs (25.40) including 8 centuries, and 271 wickets (24.40)
Test matches (20): 509 runs (16.42), 26 wickets (26.76), and 11 catches

HORAN, Thomas Patrick

(b. 1854, Midleton, County Cork, Ireland; d. 1916, Melbourne) *Victoria and Australia*

A native of Ireland, Tom Horan was taken to Australia as a child and led them twice in Test matches. For more than a decade he was the 'crack' batsman for his state. He was not a stylist, but his defence was strong and he excelled against fast bowling. He was also a round-arm, medium-pace change-bowler. He played in the first-ever Test at Melbourne in 1876/7 and was a member of the 1878 and 1882 teams to England, playing in the historic Ashes match at The Oval. He was second to the captain, W. L. Murdoch, in 1882 with 1,197 runs (25.00) on the tour, including his career-highest score of 141 not out against Gloucestershire at Clifton and 112 against the United Eleven at Chichester. In the first Test at Melbourne in 1881/2 he made 124, adding 124 for the fifth wicket with George Giffen—the first century stand in Australia. A good judge of the game and a first-rate journalist, he wrote on cricket for many years under the pseudonym 'Felix' in the *Australasian*. For his state alone, in 42 matches, he made 2,101 runs (30.01).

First-class career (1874–91): 4,027 runs (23.27) including 8 centuries, and 35 wickets (23.68)
Test matches (15): 471 runs (18.84) including 1 century, 11 wickets (13.00), and 6 catches

HORDERN, Dr Herbert Vivian

(b. 1884, Sydney; d. 1938, Sydney) *New South Wales, Philadelphia, and Australia*

A googly bowler of exceptional merit and a useful batsman, 'Ranji' Hordern (so-called because of his dark complexion) was prevented by the claims of his medical career from visiting England with an Australian side, but in the Tests of 1911/12 he was sensational, taking 32 wickets (24.37), besides making 173 runs (21.62), for a losing team. The previous season he had captured 14 wickets in two Tests against South Africa. In the first Test against England at Sydney in 1911/12, opening the bowling in both innings, he took 12 for 135, Australia winning her only match of the series. In the last match, also at Sydney, he had 10 for 161. In England, on tour with Pennsylvania University in 1907, he was extraordinarily successful, capturing 110 wickets (9.68) and making 391 runs (21.72) in matches not deemed to be first-class. He also toured Jamaica with Philadelphia in 1908/9.

First-class career (1905–13): 721 runs (16.38) and 217 wickets (16.79)
Test matches (7): 254 runs (23.09), 46 wickets (23.36), and 6 catches

HORNIBROOK, Percival Mitchell

(b. 1899, Obi Obi, Queensland; d. 1976, Brisbane) *Queensland and Australia*

A tall, left-arm bowler, loose-armed and with an easy action, Percy Hornibrook often opened the attack with medium-paced swingers and then, after a few overs, slowed down to spin and flight the ball. He suffered more than most through the inability of slip fielders to hold catches off his bowling; moreover, he was selected for Australia in Tests far too late in his career. He took 81 wickets at under ten runs apiece on an Australian tour of New Zealand in 1921, but was not selected for visits to England in 1921 and 1926, and did not make his Test début until the fifth Test of 1928/9. Touring England in 1930 he took 96 wickets (18.77) but accomplished nothing in the Tests until the last at The Oval, when he took 7 for 92 in the second innings on a turning wicket, England losing the match and Ashes after making 405 in the first innings. After 1931 he played only once more for Queensland, taking 4 for 43 in 1934 against South Australia.

First-class career (1919–33): 754 runs (10.77) and 279 wickets (23.83)

Test matches (6): 60 runs (10.00), 17 wickets (39.05), and 7 catches

HOWELL, William Peter

(b. 1869, Penrith, New South Wales; d. 1940, Sydney) *New South Wales and Australia*

Heavily built and genial, Bill Howell spun the ball at medium pace from a strong right hand with cunning variations of pace. His command of length was excellent and his off-break could be deadly. A left-handed batsman who hit hard, high, and often, 'Farmer Bill' was a great entertainer. On his Test début at Adelaide in 1897/8 he bowled Archie MacLaren, who had been in great form, very cheaply (taking 4 for 70 in 54 overs). On his first match in England in 1899 he created a sensation by dismissing Surrey in the first innings—capturing all 10 for 28 in 23.2 overs —and taking 5 for 29 in the second. He toured England, again successfully, in 1902 and 1905. In the 1903/4 series he took 14 wickets (21.14), including 4 for 43 in 34.5 overs when England made 315 in the second Test at Melbourne. On matting he took 14 wickets (12.42) from two matches against South Africa, 1902/3, opening the bowling at Cape Town and taking 4 for 18 and 5 for 81. In 36 Sheffield Shield matches he scored 1,029 runs (22.86) and took 159 wickets (23.55).

First-class career (1894–1905): 2,227 runs (14.84) including 1 century, 519 wickets (21.49), and 126 catches

Test matches (18): 158 runs (7.52), 49 wickets (28.71), and 12 catches

HUBBLE, James Merrick

(b. 1942, Beaconsfield, Western Australia) *Western Australia*

A left-arm fast bowler and left-hand number ten batsman, Jim Hubble won a place on Australia's 1966/7 tour of South Africa, having played just five Sheffield Shield games, with unexceptional results. He did not play in a Test and after being selected for Western Australia's opening game the following season, was dropped. He was never again a regular at first-class level. His career-best analysis of 7 for 49 against Queensland in Perth came at the tail-end of his career, in 1972/3.

First-class career (1964–74): 279 runs (16.41), 69 wickets (28.71), and 10 catches

HUGHES, Kimberley John

(b. 1954, Margaret River, Western Australia) *Western Australia, Natal, and Australia*

Considerable natural ability took a long time to mature in Kim Hughes, a modest if impetuous man who became captain of his country at the age of 25 in his eleventh Test. A fine all-round fielder and gifted right-hand batsman with a complete array of attractive strokes, he made 119 and 60 in his first Shield match for Western Australia in 1975/6 against New South Wales, but was a long time on the fringe of the Australian Test side (several times being 12th man) before finally establishing himself against England in 1978/9. Until the moment of his breakthrough he had travelled with official Australian teams to New Zealand and England (both in 1977) and the West Indies in 1978, yet for various reasons, including an appendix operation, had played in only three Tests, which had brought him a mere 65 runs in five innings. Then, in an hour of great Australian need, he scored 129 in the second innings of the first Test at Brisbane, his stand of 170 with Graham Yallop saving Australia from a much heavier defeat after a humiliating first innings failure. By batting for only 4 minutes less than 8 hours he showed that he had concentration as well as natural and technical ability. A full-blooded stroke-maker when he committed himself to attack, his defence was also solid. Taking over the captaincy from Yallop when the latter was injured at the end of the 1978/9 season, Hughes led Australia to a convincing seven-wicket victory over Pakistan and captained the Prudential World Cup side in 1979 and the touring team to India later that year. He returned from India with his reputation enhanced. His inexperienced team lost the Test series 2–0 but the captain made 858 runs (53.62) on the tour and led by example in the Tests, hitting 594 runs (59.40) including 100 at Madras and 92 not out and 64 at Calcutta. At home in 1979/80 he played some sparkling innings against England and the West Indies in both Test and limited-overs cricket, scoring 130 not out in a bold innings against the West Indies fast-bowling battery in the Brisbane Test and a beautiful 99 against England at Perth in conditions favouring swing bowling. He was even more impressive during the Centenary Test at Lord's in 1980 when his brilliant footwork and flamboyant, inventive stroke-play in innings of 117 and 84 proved the most memorable features of the match. At home in 1980/1 his form was relatively modest until, on a perfect wicket at Adelaide, he became the third Australian after Bradman and Greg Chappell to score a double century against India, making 213 out of 528. When Chappell decided not to tour England for the 1981 Ashes series, Hughes was appointed captain in his place. The tour began well for him, with a thrilling victory in a low-scoring Test at Trent Bridge, but turned sour with Australia's defeat at Headingley after England had followed on. Hughes had little luck personally in a series eventually won 3–1 by England, scoring 300 runs at an average of 25. His 89 in the first innings of the Leeds Test was his top score of the whole tour. He was displaced as captain by Greg Chappell for the home series against West Indies and Pakistan, in which he scored further Test hundreds against each country; but then, in Chappell's absence, he captained Australia again on a disastrous short tour of Pakistan in the early part of the 1982/3 season. All three Tests were lost and not a fixture won. Chappell returned as captain for the series against England and Hughes batted superbly, making 469 runs (67.00) in the Tests with a magnificent series-clinching 137 at Sydney when his footwork against the spinners was at its sparkling best. He had another fine series with the bat against Pakistan in 1983/4, scoring 375 runs (62.50), when he took over the captaincy once more. But he had a disastrous tour of the West Indies later in the season: Australia lost 3–0. He managed a top score of just 33 in the Tests and angered people in Trinidad by his deliberately negative tactics against the Island team. After losing the first two matches in the 1984/5 home series against the mighty West Indians, and having a miserable time with the bat, Hughes tearfully submitted to official pressure and resigned the captaincy. He could score only

two runs in his next four Test innings and was dropped from the side. Not selected for the 1985 England tour he instead led the unofficial Australian sides to South Africa in 1985/6 and 1986/7. Banned as a result from playing in Australia, he successfully argued a 'restraint of trade' case against the W. A. Cricket Association, but there was a legacy of bitterness and he finished his first-class career with two seasons as captain of Natal (1989–91). As Australia's captain in a traumatic period, his team won four out of 28 Tests, losing 13.

First-class career (1975–91): 12,711 runs (36.52) including 26 centuries, and 155 catches
Test matches (70): 4,415 runs (37.41) including 9 centuries, 0–28, and 50 catches

HUGHES, Mervyn Gregory

(b. 1961, Euroa, Victoria) *Victoria, Essex, and Australia*

A tall, dark, hirsute fast bowler of mighty strength who looked like a throw-back to the early days of Test cricket but had a shrewd awareness of the commercial possibilities of his fierce public image, Merv Hughes was famous for his bushy moustache and barrel chest, but also forced respect for his prowess as a cricketer. Indeed, a canny brain lurked beneath the impression of brute force and ignorance. He employed subtle changes of pace, skilful, if sometimes overdone and deplorable use of invective to prey upon batsmen's doubts, and sheer courage to keep going with hostility in unpromising circumstances. A proud son of Footscray, a working-class district of Melbourne, he was twice disciplined for overstepping the limits of fair play by Test-match referees. In Brisbane in 1992/3 he lost 10 per cent of his match fee for dissent and abusing the umpire ('Merv spends more than that on a round of drinks' said a team-mate) and having been severely reprimanded for a further offence later in the same series he was again fined by the match referee, and subsequently given an additional $A2,000 fine by the Australian Board for abusing a batsman in the Johannesburg Test of 1993/4. Such disgrace did not prevent his becoming a popular hero, a fact which had less to do with his moustache and outlandish appearance than the fact of his becoming only the seventh Australian to take 200 Test wickets. He achieved the feat at Headingley as Australia were regaining the Ashes in 1993 but there was evidence towards the end of his most successful series—he took 31 wickets in the six Tests—that this was likely to be the high point of a determined career. Knee surgery followed and he lost his Test place to younger men but he drove himself to get fit again. Hughes had immediately looked an exciting prospect when taking 18 wickets in his first season for Victoria in 1981/2. He struggled for fitness and consistency for some seasons thereafter despite a successful season for Essex 2nd XI in 1983 (60 wickets at 18 each and six in his only first-class match against the touring New Zealanders) but had gained the confidence of the then Victorian coach Frank Tyson and in 1985/6 won his first Test cap against India. His start was inauspicious—1 for 123 and a duck but he gradually worked his way into a regular place in the Australian team, suiting Allan Border's policy of playing whole-hearted, committed players. Against the West Indies at Perth in 1988/9 he took 13 for 217 in the match and 8 for 87 in the second innings. By taking two wickets with his last two balls in the first innings and another with his first in the second he also officially claimed Australia's first Test hat-trick for more than 30 years. In England in 1989 he was picked as fourth seamer behind Alderman, Lawson, and Rackemann but played in all six Tests and against the West Indies at home in 1992/3 took 20 wickets at 21. It was the prelude to his finest hour. Losing the support of Craig McDermott, the other senior fast bowler, early in the 1993 tour of England, he carried the new ball attack and paved the way for Shane Warne to be the chief instrument of attack in four crushing victories. As a limited but watchful batsman he also contributed valuable runs and at Lord's his running-out of Michael Atherton with a throw from the Grand Stand boundary turned the game. In England, as in Australia, he had achieved cult status although behind the scenes he had become a married man who chose to spend the night quietly in his hotel on the night that the Ashes had been regained.

First-class career (1981–93): 2,569 runs (17.47), 580 wickets (28.92), and 53 catches

Test matches (53): 1,032 runs (16.64), 212 wickets (28.38), and 23 catches

HUNT, William Alfred

(b. 1908, Sydney; d. 1983, Sydney) *New South Wales and Australia*

A left-arm medium-pace bowler, Bill Hunt spent several years with Rishton in the Lancashire League, believing, as something of a rebel, that he had no chance of selection for Australia while Bill Woodfull was captain. Before leaving Australia, he represented his country in the fourth Test against South Africa at Adelaide in 1931/2, scoring 0, taking 0 for 39 and holding 1 catch. A genial raconteur, he furnished incidental material for several cricketing biographies and helped set up a cricket museum at the Sydney Cricket Ground. In 11 Sheffield Shield matches he scored 192 runs (14.76) and took 48 wickets (20.60). He is said to have taken no fewer than 11 hat-tricks in his career, including five in one year: three for Rishton and two in social matches for his home club, Balmain.

First-class career (1929–31): 301 runs (14.33) and 62 wickets (23.00)

HURST, Alan George

(b. 1950, Melbourne) *Victoria and Australia*

A tall, dark, and strapping right-arm fast bowler, Alan Hurst was considered to be almost as fast as Dennis Lillee when he made his first tour to England in 1975, taking 21 wickets at 31 each as reserve for Lillee, Thomson, and Walker without playing in a Test. A series of injuries delayed his arrival as a regular Test cricketer but in 1978/9 he finally established himself with a vengeance, taking 40 wickets in eight Tests, 25 in six matches against England, including 5 for 28 in England's first innings in the fourth Test at Sydney, and 15 in two games against Pakistan, including 9 for 155 at Perth. A modest man, he had hitherto seemed to have everything needed to make himself a success at the top level except luck, sustained fitness and the killer instinct. But with his strength and a model action—cheeks puffing during a short, rhythmical approach and then a rapid but fluent sideways-on delivery—it was no surprise that he should have proved his true worth after modest success in two isolated Test appearances, against New Zealand in 1973/4 and India in 1977/8. Against England and Pakistan, however, he bowled genuinely fast, swung the ball both ways, and only occasionally lost control. Merely an adequate fielder by modern high standards, he was a genuine number eleven batsman: he suffered no fewer than three Test pairs in the one 1978/9 season! His best performance for Victoria was 8 for 84 in Queensland in 1977/8. He toured India in 1979/80 but a serious back injury forced him to return home after playing in only the first two Tests. A loyalist, he refused to join World Series Cricket.

HURWOOD

First-class career (1972–81): 504 runs (8.68) and 280 wickets (26.28)
Test matches (12): 102 runs (6.00), 43 wickets (27.91), and 3 catches

HURWOOD, Alexander

(b. 1902, Brisbane; d. 1982, Coffs Harbour, New South Wales) *Queensland and Australia*

A tall, right-arm medium-pace bowler with a short run and exceptional control, Alec Hurwood toured England with the 1930 team, but was not called upon in the Tests. He represented his country only in the first and second Tests, at Adelaide and Sydney, against West Indies, 1930/1, when he met with encouraging success against the leading batsmen. He took 4 for 22 when West Indies fell for 90 in the second innings at Sydney, but was then dropped. He was an outstanding slip catcher.

First-class career (1925–31): 575 runs (11.27) and 113 wickets (27.62)
Test matches (2): 5 runs (2.50), 11 wickets (15.45), and 2 catches

HUTCHEON, John Silvester, QC

(b. 1882, Warwick, Queensland; d. 1957, Albion Heights, Queensland) *Queensland*

Few administrators have been as influential or as autocratic as 'Jack' Hutcheon, a right-hand batsman who played eleven state matches from 1905 to 1910 and later served as president of the Queensland Cricket Association (1926–57). With ex-Test-man 'Roger' Hartigan, Hutcheon was most responsible for Queensland's entry into the Sheffield Shield in competition in 1926/7. Known for his flamboyant debating skills, he represented Queensland on the Australian Board of Control for almost 40 years, but was not widely popular in his home state, often being referred to as 'The Tsar'. His brother, Ernie, an Australian Olympian, also played state cricket and was co-author of *A History of Queensland Cricket*, one of Australian cricket's rarest post-war reference books.

First-class career (1905–10): 599 runs (24.95) and 14 catches

INVERARITY, Robert John

(b. 1944, Perth) *Western Australia, South Australia, and Australia*

A born leader, John Inverarity achieved greater fame for Western Australia than he did for his country, leading his state to the Sheffield Shield title in four of his five seasons as captain. He would undoubtedly have been an effective captain of Australia, and deserved to be so in 1978/9 when he alone, perhaps, could have matched Brearley's leadership of England. A calm, thoughtful, and astute captain, Inverarity knew how to react under pressure and how best to put pressure on opposing sides. He was himself a talented all-rounder, a neat and very patient right-hand batsman with no frills (once dubbed 'Infor-everity') and also a good fielder and useful slow left-arm spin bowler. He is the son of a former West Australian stalwart, Mervyn Inverarity. John first attracted national attention with an innings of 177 against South Australia in 1965/6. He toured England in 1968 and 1972 and New Zealand in 1969/70. He scored a determined 56 against England at The Oval in 1968, being last out, lbw to Underwood, who had routed Australia on a wet wicket. When Underwood again destroyed Australia at Leeds in 1972, 'Invers' took 3 for 26 with his own left-arm spin. He became deputy headmaster of a school in Adelaide, marking his final season with Western Australia in 1978/9 with 187 against New South Wales at Sydney and 124 not out against Tasmania at Devonport. However, he continued to be an exceptionally valuable cricketer for South Australia and it was his slow left-arm spin which had much to do with the Shield victory of his adopted state in 1981/2, taking 30 wickets (21.30) and scoring 348 runs (38.66) in nine games. In 1983/4 he overtook Sir Donald Bradman's record number of Sheffield Shield runs and having scored over 350 runs and taken 43 wickets in the 1984/5 season he announced his retirement from first-class cricket at the age of 41. A headmastership soon followed.

First-class career (1962–85): 11,777 runs (35.90) including 26 centuries, 221 wickets (30.67), and 251 catches
Test matches (6): 174 runs (17.40), 4 wickets (23.25), and 4 catches

IREDALE, Francis Adams

(b. 1867, Sydney; d. 1926, Sydney) *New South Wales and Australia*

Tall, lean, cool, collected, and a resourceful right-handed batsman, Frank Iredale combined sound defence with good hitting power: he was a particularly graceful off-side player. In the outfield he was a quick mover with a safe pair of hands. On his Test début, at Sydney in 1894/5, he scored 81 and he finished the series with 337 runs

(37.44). Touring England in 1896 and 1899, he passed 1,000 runs on both visits and had a blaze of success during the first tour, in quick succession scoring 94 not out, 114, 106, 171, 108 (in the Test at Old Trafford), 73, and 62. He headed the Test batting averages in 1896 with 38.00 and in the 1897/8 series averaged 43.20. In 38 Sheffield Shield matches he made 2,466 runs (38.53). He became secretary of the New South Wales Cricket Association.

First-class career (1888–1901): 6,795 runs (33.63) including 12 centuries, and 111 catches
Test matches (14): 807 runs (36.68) including 2 centuries, 0–3, and 16 catches

IRONMONGER, Herbert

(b. 1882, Pine Mountain, Ipswich, Queensland; d. 1971, Melbourne) *Queensland, Victoria, and Australia*

Heavily-built, slow-moving, and awkward, 'Dainty' Ironmonger was a left-arm medium-pace bowler relying on spin which broke sharply from the leg on all pitches, most of which had surfaces like glass. He had lost the top joint of his forefinger in a saw-mill and the stump enabled him to twist the ball; his leg-break looked sometimes as if it were a Chinaman. He never went to England—there was some doubt about the legality of his action—and he was, at 46 years 237 days, the second (and still the fourth) oldest cricketer to make his Test début, at Brisbane in the first Test against England in 1928/9, when he delivered 94.3 overs (4 for 164). At Melbourne in the fifth Test against South Africa in 1931/2 he was unplayable on a soft pitch, taking 5 for 6 and 6 for 18, the visitors collapsing for 36 and 45. In that series he was supreme with 31 wickets (9.67); and the previous season against the West Indies he took 22 wickets (14.68) in four Tests, including 7 for 23 in 20 overs (11 for 79 in the match), the West Indies falling for 99 on the first day. Although he often wreaked havoc with the ball, he was no asset in the field, and as a batsman, as A. G. Moyes wrote, 'He went to the wickets mostly as a gesture to convention.' It was said (first) of Bert Ironmonger that his wife once rang him at the Melbourne ground and, on being told that he had just gone in to bat, replied, 'Oh, that's alright. I'll hold on!' In 44 Sheffield Shield matches 'Dainty' took 215 wickets (24.74). He toured New Zealand in 1920/1 with an Australian side and India with Frank Tarrant's in 1935/6. In 1932/3 he became the only Australian to play Test cricket when past the age of 50.

First-class career (1909–35): 476 runs (5.95) and 464 wickets (21.50)
Test matches (14): 42 runs (2.62), 74 wickets (17.97), and 3 catches

IRVINE, John Taylor

(b. 1944, Subiaco, Western Australia) *Western Australia*

A member of Western Australia's 1967/8 Sheffield Shield winning team, 'Jock' Irvine was initially a dour right-hand batsman, who blossomed and won a place on Bill Lawry's 1970 Australian tour to Ceylon, India, and South Africa, before retiring only one season later. His highest first-class score was 182 against South Australia in Perth in 1968/9.

First-class career (1964–70): 1,946 runs (31.90) including 3 centuries, one wicket (120.00), and 37 catches

IVERSON, John Brian

(b. 1915, Melbourne; d. 1973, Melbourne) *Victoria and Australia*

Six feet two inches tall and weighing 15 stone, 'Big Jack' Iverson was Australia's Bosanquet, creating something of a sensation during his brief first-class career. At first he bowled fastish, but while on Army Service in New Guinea during the Second World War he developed a peculiar method of spinning the ball, which he gripped in his right hand between his thumb and bent middle finger, using the bent finger as a spring to discharge 'the missile'. Batsmen with experience of Iverson came to know that if the thumb pointed straight, it was a top-spinner and if the thumb pointed to the leg-side the ball would turn from the off, a peculiar 'wrong 'un' bowled with the wrist over the ball instead of underneath it. He could bowl his wide variety of deliveries—off-breaks, leg-breaks, and googlies—without any change of action. He attracted great attention when he took 46 wickets (16.12) for Victoria in 1949/50, and 75 wickets (7.00) for Bill Brown's Australian side in New Zealand later that season. Inevitably dubbed the 'mystery bowler' when he was selected against England in 1950/1, he took 6 for 27 in England's second innings (a mere 123) at Sydney in the third match, but in the fourth match at Adelaide he suffered an ankle injury when treading on a ball and played in only one game in each of the next two years. Thereupon he gave up the game altogether in Australia. He toured India, however, with the Commonwealth team of 1953/4.

First-class career (1949–53): 277 runs (14.57) and
157 wickets (19.22)
Test matches (5): 3 runs (0.75), 21 wickets
(15.23), and 2 catches

JACKSON, Archibald Alexander

(b. 1909, Rutherglen, Lanarkshire, Scotland;
d. 1933, Brisbane) *New South Wales and Australia*

Had Archie Jackson lived longer, some authorities
believed he would have gone further than Don
Bradman. Unlikely as that is, he remains a
romantic hero, a genius who died tragically
young of tuberculosis. Settling in Balmain with
his impecunious parents from Scotland, he used
to play in the street with another future Test
cricketer, Bill Hunt. He played for Balmain under
Arthur Mailey and for Victoria under Alan Kippax, whose graceful style he echoed. With his bat
held high on the handle and his cap brim
drooping like a guardsman's, his leg glances were
casually elegant, subtle wrists steering the ball
square and late. His footwork was light and as he
cover-drove his body would incline like a ballet
dancer's. In short he was an artist with a rare gift
for timing and placing. As an outfield he was
superb. At 17 he made his début for his state, and
his first season, 1926/7, brought him 464 runs
(58.00). The following year, promoted to opening
batsman, he made 131 and 122—the latter century coming in two hours—against South Australia at Sydney. He toured New Zealand with an
Australian side in 1927/8, averaging 49.50. Australian cricket was in a transitional state and
young, classy batsmen were being eagerly
accepted. Only 19 on his Test début in the fourth
match against England at Adelaide in 1928/9, he
opened with Bill Woodfull and hit a brilliant 164.
His career-highest score of 182 in the Test Trial
for Ryder's XI against Woodfull's XI ensured his
selection for the 1930 England tour. Possibly the
sickness which carried him off less than three
years later was already affecting him, but he was
rarely at his best in England, though he reached
his 1,000 at The Oval in the final Test, when he
made 73, helping Bradman to add 243 for the
fourth wicket, then a record. He appeared against
the West Indies on the first Australian tour of
1930/1, but he was by now regularly fighting
poor health. While in hospital on his death-bed,
he became engaged to Phyllis Thomas, a dancer,
on her 21st birthday. He died on the day that
England regained the Ashes, 16 February, and in
the same city, Brisbane. Jackson had moved there
the previous year to be near his girl-friend and in

the vain hope that a warmer climate would cure
him. In twenty-three Sheffield Shield matches he
had made 1,858 runs (54.64).

First-class career (1926–30): 4,383 runs (45.65)
including 11 centuries
Test matches (8): 474 runs (47.40) including 1
century, and 7 catches

JARMAN, Barrington Noel

(b. 1936, Adelaide) *South Australia and Australia*

For years in the shadow of Wally Grout, Barry
Jarman emerged as his country's number one
wicket-keeper, a good right-handed batsman and
vice-captain on the England tour of 1968. A
cheerful character, he toured England three times,
India and Pakistan and New Zealand twice each,
and the West Indies and South Africa once each.
Except for his first Test against India at Kanpur in
1959/60 he was understudy for 27 Tests in six
series. Bulkily built—5 ft. $7\frac{1}{2}$ in. and $13\frac{1}{2}$ stone—he
was, nevertheless, agile. In his first match against
England (Grout being out because of a broken jaw)
at Melbourne in 1962/3, he made a fantastic one-
handed, diving, leg-side catch from Geoff Pullar off
'Garth' McKenzie. During the Test at Lord's in
1968 a ball from McKenzie broke his right
forefinger in three places, but he came in to bat
most gamely—only for a fast ball from David
Brown to strike the damaged finger. The following
month he led Australia for the first time in the
absence of Bill Lawry (injured) at Headingley. He
had ten New South Wales victims at Adelaide in
1962/3; and 1963/4 saw him dismiss 45 batsmen in
11 first-class matches. A hard-hitting batsman who
could have held his place in some sides as such, he
struck 26 off one over from David Allen against T.
N. Pearce's side at Scarborough in 1961. His best
score in Tests was 78 against India at Calcutta in
1964/5. His career-highest score was 196 against
New South Wales at Adelaide in 1965/6.

First-class career (1955–69): 5,615 runs (22.73)
including 5 centuries, and 560 dismissals (431 c.,
129 st.)
Test matches (19): 400 runs (14.81) and 54
dismissals (50 c., 4 st.)

JARVIS, Arthur Harwood

(b. 1860, Adelaide; d. 1933, Adelaide) *South
Australia and Australia*

The exceptional ability of Jack Blackham as
wicket-keeper limited 'Affie' Jarvis's opportunities
in representative cricket, but he toured England

as second-string in 1880, 1886, 1888, and 1893, and had a long career for his state from 1877 until 1901. In the third Test at Sydney in 1884/5 he caught five and stumped one, helping Australia to win by six runs. A dogged batsman not often among the runs, he hit 98 not out for his state against New South Wales in 1894/5, and 82—topscore for a losing side—for Australia against England in the second Test at Melbourne in 1884/5.

First-class career (1877–1901): 3,161 runs (15.57) and 198 dismissals (115 c., 82 st.)

Test matches (11): 303 runs (16.83) and 18 dismissals (9 c., 9 st.)

JENNER, Terence James

(b. 1944, Perth) *South Australia, Western Australia, Cambridgeshire, and Australia*

Ashley Mallett's 'spin-twin', Terry Jenner was a right-arm leg-break bowler with a good googly who toured New Zealand in 1969/70 and the West Indies in 1972/3. He played in Tests against England in 1970/1 and 1974/5, and when he was not selected for any tours of England came over and joined a minor county. Sometimes he bowled impressively in Tests: in the fifth match against West Indies at Port of Spain in 1972/3 he took 5 for 90 in conditions favouring the bat. A useful late-order batsman, his aggressive 74 in the fifth Test at Adelaide in 1974/5 enabled Australia to recover (after losing five wickets for 84) and win. After a fall from grace, he came back into the limelight in the early 1990s as leg-spinning adviser at the Cricket Academy in Adelaide to the brilliantly talented Shane Warne.

First-class career (1963–77): 3,580 runs (22.23) and 389 wickets (32.18)

Test matches (9): 208 runs (23.11), 24 wickets (31.20), and 5 catches

JENNINGS, Claude Barrows

(b. 1884, Melbourne; d. 1950, Adelaide) *South Australia, Queensland, and Australia*

A neat right-handed opening batsman, sound, and able to adapt his game to the circumstances but lacking real power in his strokes, Claude Jennings visited England in 1912 for the Triangular Tournament, opening the batting in all six Tests. He was fortunate to make the team as a substitute, six famous players, in dispute with the Board of Control, refusing to make the trip. In a wet summer he reached his 1,000 runs. In 16 Sheffield Shield matches for South Australia he

made only 617 runs (20.56). Sometime South Australian correspondent of the British Department of Overseas Trade and secretary of the Adelaide Chamber of Commerce, he was appointed a delegate to the Australian Cricket Board of Control in 1938.

First-class career (1902–12): 2,453 runs (25.55) including 1 century

Test matches (6): 107 runs (17.83) and 5 catches

JOHNS, Alfred Edward

(b. 1868, Hawthorn, Victoria; d. 1934, Melbourne) *Victoria*

Alf Jones twice toured England (in 1896 and 1899) as Australia's deputy wicket-keeper without playing a Test. He took over from Jack Blackham as Victoria's wicket-keeper but soft hands prevented him from fulfilling his considerable gifts. A left-hand lower-order batsman, he once shared in a 136-run tenth-wicket stand with Jim O'Halloran for Victoria against South Australia in Melbourne in 1896/7, an Australian first-class record. Johns was captain of Melbourne University's 1st XI while studying for a law degree and in 1922 he was appointed a trustee of the Melbourne Cricket Ground.

First-class career (1894–9): 429 runs (11.28) and 84 dismissals (58 c., 26 st.)

JOHNSON, Ian William

(b. 1918, Melbourne) *Victoria and Australia*

A very slow off-spinner with a teasing flight, Ian Johnson was one of the few high-class, right-arm, off-spin bowlers to emerge from Australia. He would use a wind skilfully, making the ball float away as a change from the off-break. His action was unusual with a rather staccato swing of the bowling arm, but he was not quick enough to use wet wickets effectively and was no answer to Laker in 1956. As a right-handed batsman, he had a sound defence and, able to hit very hard when necessary, was very useful in the middle order. He was a brilliant slip field. Making his first-class début at 17 and succeeding Lindsay Hassett as Australian captain in 1954/5, he did not always enjoy his team's confidence—there were those who believed that Keith Miller, not Johnson, should have got the job. But he was a cheerful captain, generous in defeat in 1956. He also toured England in 1948 and, over eight years, South Africa, the West Indies, New Zealand, and India and Pakistan. The first time he bowled against England, in the second Test at Sydney in

1946/7, he was virtually unplayable, taking 6 for 42 in 30.1 overs. In the third Test at Georgetown in 1955 he took 7 for 44 in the second innings. In South Africa in 1949/50 he was the leading bowler with 79 wickets (16.82), including 18 in the Tests. In the third Test at Durban, when Australia were 236 behind on the first innings, Johnson took 5 for 34, and South Africa were bundled out for 99. Amazingly, Australia won handsomely by five wickets. His highest score in Tests was 77 against England in the third Test at Sydney in 1950/1, and his career-highest, 132 not out against Queensland at Melbourne in 1948/9. His best bowling was 7 for 42 at Leicester in 1948. He was for 25 years, from 1957, secretary of Melbourne Cricket Club and was awarded first an MBE then an OBE (1956 and 1977) for his services to the game. His father-in-law was Dr R. L. Park, who played once for Australia, and his own father was a prominent cricket administrator who had played one match for Victoria.

First-class career (1935–56): 4,905 runs (22.92) including 2 centuries, 619 wickets (23.30), and 138 catches

Test matches (45): 1,000 runs (18.51), 109 wickets (29.19), and 30 catches

JOHNSON, Keith Ormong Edley

(b. 1895; d. 1972, Sydney)

Manager of the 1945 Australian Services team and Don Bradman's 1948 side to England, Johnson was a stalwart of Sydney's Mosman club and served on the Australian Cricket Board of Control for 17 years. Made a life member of the New South Wales Cricket Association in 1943 and awarded an MBE for his services to cricket in 1964, Johnson was Association vice-president (1965–8) and in 1972 honoured with life membership of MCC.

JOHNSON, Leonard Joseph

(b. 1919, Ipswich, Queensland; d. 1977, Ipswich) *Queensland and Australia*

One of the many right-arm fast bowlers who came and went while Ray Lindwall and Keith Miller remained in harness, Len Johnson was also a useful hitter in the lower order. He played in the fifth Test against India at Melbourne in 1947/8, scoring 23 not out, taking 3 for 66 and 3 for 8 and catching Lala Amarnath; this was his sole Test. His tally of 171 wickets (24.42) from 42 Sheffield Shield matches was a record for his state.

First-class career (1946–52): 1,139 runs (16.75) and 218 wickets (23.17)

JOHNSTON, William Arras

(b. 1922, Beeac, Victoria) *Victoria and Australia*

A sporting and good-humoured cricketer but a tough competitor, Bill Johnston was a tall, strongly built, left-arm fast-medium bowler. With a bucking and plunging run-up of ten paces, he bowled a good length, would cut and swing the ball late either way and make the ball lift disconcertingly. His batting afforded rich entertainment. He played with limbs seemingly independent of each other, aiming his bat at the ball with arms and legs flying and, on contact, prancing down the pitch in bounding good spirits. Occasionally he would connect with a really big hit. In England in 1953 he enjoyed the singular triumph of averaging 102 on the tour: in 17 innings his top score was 28 but he was out only once. He was an extremely good catcher and had a strong throw which reflected earlier baseball training. He toured England in 1948—taking 102 wickets (16.42)—and in 1953. He also toured South Africa and the West Indies. At home he was a regular (when free of injury) in five series from 1947 until 1955. On his first tour of England he was the invaluable link between Ray Lindwall and Keith Miller in the Tests, taking 27 wickets (23.33), including 9 for 183 in 84 overs in the first Test at Trent Bridge. He took 102 wickets on the tour at 16.42 from 850 overs, a huge workload by any standards. In South Africa in 1949/50, despite an early injury in a car accident, he topped the bowling in all first-class matches with 56 wickets (13.75) and took 23 Test wickets (17.04), his best haul being 6 for 44 at Johannesburg in the first Test. In two successive seasons in Australia from 1950 to 1953 he took 22 wickets (19.18) and 23 wickets (22.08). At that time he had taken 100 Test wickets faster than any other bowler in history—four years and a few days. In 38 Sheffield Shield matches he took 148 wickets (28.41), with a best innings analysis of 8 for 52 against Queensland at Melbourne in 1952/3.

First-class career (1945–54): 1,129 runs (12.68) and 554 wickets (23.35)

Test matches (40): 273 runs (11.37), 160 wickets (23.91), and 16 catches

JONES, Dean Mervyn

(b. 1961, Coburg, Victoria) *Victoria, Durham, and Australia*

Tough, assertive, and self-confident to the point of bumptiousness, Dean Jones was a tall, attractive, and commanding right-handed batsman and a superb fielder in the deep. Too cocky for some tastes in his youth, he matured to become captain of Victoria and his whole-hearted commitment enlivened many an international match. Such was his skill, it is surprising, and indicative of Australia's batting strength, that his Test career petered out in the early 1990s when he was still being picked for one-day internationals. His forceful driving, fierce hooking, and wondrously quick running between the wickets were particularly effective, certainly, in limited-overs cricket. 'Deano', as the MCG fans called him, made his first appearance against the 1982/3 England touring team and in his fifth match for Victoria scored 199 against Western Australia. In the following season 762 runs earned him a place on a tough tour of the Caribbean when 48 in the second Test was his best performance. Second in the first-class averages in 1984/5 with 681 runs at 68.10, and despite a brilliant innings in the MCG's first floodlit match, against England, he was overlooked for the 1985 tour of England but two seasons later he memorably established his right to a place in the Test team. In the stifling and enervating heat of Madras he scored 210 despite such dehydration that he regularly retched beside the crease and had to go to hospital to be fed intravenously while a famous match proceeded towards a tie. Back home against England he scored 184 in the fifth Test in Sydney which marked the start of a sustained revival for Australia. He was a central figure at first wicket down in the successful World Cup campaign in India and Pakistan in 1987. Even now he was not an automatic Test selection, prone as he was to impetuosity, but at Adelaide against the 1988/9 West Indians he made his highest Test score, 216, before being run out, and in England in 1989 he topped the tour averages with 1,510 runs at 88, including 248 against Warwickshire and Test hundreds at Edgbaston and the Oval. Returning to England to play for Durham in 1992, he scored 1,179 runs at 73 and did much to ease the county's entry to the county championship by advising and encouraging younger players. At home his consistency in Sheffield Shield cricket was a constant challenge to the Test selectors: he scored 1,248 runs at 96 in 1991/2, yet was overlooked for the 1993 tour to England; and four hundreds in fourteen innings in 1993/4. Recalled once again for the one-day matches against the touring South Africans that season he thought about retiring when once again left out of a tour—the return visit to South Africa. The captaincy of Victoria kept him involved, however,

and it was not untypical of this natural iconoclast that he should have been the first man to lead out a first-class team clad in short trousers.

First-class career (1981–): 13,586 runs (51.65) including 39 centuries, 17 wickets (62.35), and 138 catches
Test matches (52): 3,631 runs (46.55) including 11 centuries, 1 wicket (64.00), and 34 catches

JONES, Ernest

(b. 1869, Auburn, South Australia; d. 1943, Adelaide) *South Australia, West Australia, and Australia*

Barrel-chested Ernie Jones or 'Jonah' was the best Australian right-arm fast bowler of his day. Originally a miner, he was below medium height but very powerfully built and, after a fairly short run, would put all his bodily strength behind the delivery, the intense force of which often made the ball rise very unpleasantly, especially if pitched short. No-balled twice in Australia for throwing, once in the opening match of the 1897/8 tour between South Australia and A. E. Stoddart's team at Adelaide and later in a Test, he subsequently concentrated more on length and control, to very good effect. From 1894 until 1902 he represented his country regularly. In his tours of England, 1896, 1899, and 1902, he took 121, 135, and 66 wickets respectively at an average of 19 runs a wicket. In the first match of the first tour, against Lord Sheffield's XI at Sheffield Park, he allegedly bowled a ball through Dr W. G. Grace's beard, and to W. G.'s querulous, 'What do you think you're at, Jonah?' made the classic reply, 'Sorry, Doctor, she slipped.' He was especially effective against Yorkshire, taking 6 for 74 at Sheffield and 7 for 36 at Headingley. An England XI at Crystal Palace lost the last four wickets to him for no runs, Jonah finishing with 8 for 39. Not until the 1897/8 and 1899 series did he fulfil his promise in Tests, taking 22 wickets (25.13) and 26 wickets (25.26) respectively, the chief wicket-taker each time. For South Australia at Adelaide against A. E. Stoddart's 1897/8 side he captured 14 for 237, a record for the ground. In 38 Sheffield Shield matches he took 209 wickets (26.35). Of little account as a batsman, he was a fine mid-off. Stories abound about Jonah, who called a spade a spade in a genial way. He was introduced to the Prince of Wales, later Edward VII, who asked him whether he had attended St Peter's College, Adelaide, to which he replied, 'Yes, I take the dust-cart there regularly!'

JONES

First-class career (1892–1907): 2,390 runs (13.13) and 641 wickets (22.83)
Test matches (19): 126 runs (5.04), 64 wickets (29.01), and 21 catches

JONES, Samuel Percy

(b. 1861, Sydney; d. 1951, Auckland, New Zealand) *New South Wales, Queensland, Auckland, and Australia*

The last survivor of both sides in the Ashes match at The Oval in 1882, Sammy Jones was a determined and watchful right-handed batsman, a fast scorer when in the mood, a pleasing stroke-maker confident on difficult pitches, a versatile field and useful change-bowler. Before he was 20 he had hit a century; and he toured England in 1882, 1886, 1888 (when he became dangerously ill with smallpox), and 1890. At his very best in 1886, he finished second in the averages, making 1,497 runs (24.96), including 151 against the Gentlemen at The Oval and, in the first Test at Old Trafford, 87, which remained his Test highest. Settling in Queensland, he toured New Zealand with the state's team in 1896/7, and lived in New Zealand for his last 47 years, playing for Auckland from 1904 until 1908. During the 1882 Oval Test he was batting with W. L. Murdoch who played a ball to leg and ran. Sammy Jones completed the first run and, thinking the ball was dead, went out of his ground to pat the wicket. W.G. whipped the bail off and the umpire, Robert Thoms, gave him out. Sammy was furious, but did not retain ill-will for the Doctor, whose ethics on this occasion hardly bear scrutiny.

First-class career (1880–1908): 5,189 runs (21.09) including 5 centuries, and 55 wickets (33.52)
Test matches (12): 428 runs (21.40), 6 wickets (18.66), and 12 catches

JORDON, Raymond Clarence

(b. 1937, Melbourne) *Victoria*

A talkative, bubbly figure, with a mischievous twinkle in his eye, Ray 'Slug' Jordon won international honours with Bill Lawry's touring team to Ceylon, India, and South Africa in 1969/70 mainly through his habit of standing up to the medium-pace bowling of his team-mate Alan Connolly. But he could not dislodge New South Wales's Brian Taber as the number one wicket-keeper. Jordon took 6 catches in an innings for Victoria against Queensland in Melbourne in 1968/9 and 10 wickets in a game (9 catches and 1 stumping) against South Australia in Melbourne in 1970/1. A capable right-hand batsman, his highest score was 134 against South Australia in Adelaide in 1963/4. He later became a Victorian selector and a voluble radio commentator who eschewed a chair and stood behind the microphone.

First-class career (1959–70): 2,414 runs (25.95) including 1 century, and 283 dismissals (238 c., 45 st.)

JOSLIN, Leslie Ronald

(b. 1947, Melbourne) *Victoria and Australia*

Bursting into first-class cricket, Les Joslin was an aggressive left-handed batsman of brilliant potential, not alas fulfilled. Scoring 565 runs (51.36) in Australia in 1967/8, he made a Test appearance against India in the fourth match, scoring 7 and 2. He toured England in 1968, but was disappointing, averaging only 21.60 with the bat and not being selected for the Tests. He dropped out of first-class cricket after the 1969/70 season.

First-class career (1966–9): 1,816 runs (29.77) including 2 centuries

JULIAN, Brendon Paul

(b. 1970, Hamilton, New Zealand) *Western Australia and Australia*

A left-arm fast-medium swing bowler, prone to overstepping, Brendon Julian's ability to move the ball back into right-handers ensured his selection on Australia's 1993 Ashes tour. The 6 ft. 5 in. bowling all-rounder of Polynesian descent had earned his place with 43 wickets at 31.20 during the preceding Australian season, including 5 for 72 and 1 for 46 against the touring West Indians. Winning man-of-the-match honours on his one-day international début at Lord's, he played only two Tests, a match saving half-century at Trent Bridge being his major contribution. Julian moved to the West Australian north-west mining town of Port Hedland with his family when he was 5, and back to his native New Zealand between the ages of 10 and 15, before finishing his schooling in Perth. A sometimes punishing right-hand number eight batsman—he once made 80 not out off 65 balls in a non-first-class match for a West Australian representative side against a touring team from Lancashire—his highest score prior to the 1994/5 season was 87 for Western Australia against Tasmania at Bellerive in 1992/3. He toured West Indies in 1994/5.

First-class career (1989–): 1,137 runs (21.05),
129 wickets (33.95), and 25 catches
Test matches (6): 128 runs (16.00), 14 wickets
(37.64), and 3 catches

KELLEWAY, Charles

(b. 1886, Lismore, New South Wales; d. 1944,
Sydney) *New South Wales and Australia*

A very sound right-handed batsman, Charles
Kelleway possessed unlimited patience—he was
named 'Rock of Gibraltar'—and was invaluable
opening the innings or facing a crisis. He also
bowled fast-medium with a swerve that troubled
the best batsmen. Coming to England in 1912
with an Australian team weakened by internal
politics, he scored 360 runs in the six Tests,
including 114 against South Africa at Old Trafford
and 102 at Lord's; his only superior was Warren
Bardsley. He captained the Australian Imperial
Forces in 1919, but at the outset of the tour—and
after scoring 505 runs in nine innings—he left the
side and, indeed, never came to England again as
a player. In the 1920/1 series he made 330 runs
(47.14) and took 15 wickets (21.00), heading the
bowling averages in a powerful side. At Adelaide,
after England had gained a lead of 93, he was
missed before scoring but stayed nearly 7 hours
for 147, showing solid defence in an uphill
struggle. He finished his Test career in 1928/9,
falling ill during the first match at Brisbane which
England were to win by 675 runs. For his state
against South Australia at Sydney in 1920/1, he
made his career-highest score of 168, and added
397 for the fifth wicket with Bardsley—a world-
record for nearly 30 years. Awkward but indomitable, and deaf to the opinion of others, Charles
Kelleway was one of the toughest cricketers
produced by Australia. He sometimes brought his
defensive tactics to the verge of inhumanity.
Bardsley said of him that he 'only got out so that
he could go away, have a good long bite on it, and
tell you a month later "Thought that one the
other day would break from the off".' In 39
Sheffield Shield matches he made 2,304 runs
(40.42) and took 126 wickets (27.73).
First-class career (1907–28): 6,389 runs (35.10)
including 15 centuries, 339 wickets (26.32), and
103 catches
Test matches (26): 1,422 runs (37.42) including 3
centuries, 52 wickets (32.36), and 24 catches

KELLY, James Joseph

(b. 1867, Port Melbourne; d. 1938, Sydney) *New
South Wales and Australia*

An outstanding wicket-keeper, James Kelly left
Victoria—where Jack Blackham held sway—and
joined New South Wales two years before touring England for the first time in 1896. He made
other tours in 1899, 1902, and 1905. He was
particularly adept at taking very fast bowlers like
Ernest Jones and Albert Cotter. A useful batsman,
he was able to defend or attack as the game
demanded. In the Old Trafford Test of 1896, he
and Hugh Trumble batted an hour for the last 25
runs, bringing victory by three wickets after a
terrific struggle against the fast bowling of Tom
Richardson. He hit 105 against Warwickshire at
Edgbaston in 1899, and 74 out of 112 in an hour
against Gloucestershire at Bristol in 1905. He
gave up first-class cricket after his last tour largely
because of a damaged finger and a blow over the
heart by a ball from Walter Brearley at Old
Trafford.
First-class career (1894–1906): 4,108 runs (19.94)
including 3 centuries, and 355 dismissals (243 c.,
112 st.)
Test matches (36): 664 runs (17.02) and 63
dismissals (43 c., 20 st.)

KELLY, Thomas Joseph Dart

(b. 1844, County Waterford, Ireland; d. 1893,
Melbourne) *Victoria and Australia*

Playing in the second and third Tests at Melbourne in 1876/7 and 1878/9, Thomas Kelly was
a good right-handed batsman and outstanding at
point. As a child he moved with his parents to
Bristol and learned his cricket there before
migrating to Australia at the age of 19. He
startled Australians by wearing a blazer, the first
to set the trend in his adopted country.
First-class career (1863–82): 543 runs (20.11)
Test matches (2): 64 runs (21.33) and 1 catch

KENDALL, Thomas Kingston

(b. 1851, Bedford, England; d. 1924, Hobart)
Victoria, Tasmania, and Australia

Tom Kendall played purely as a left-arm slow
bowler in the first Test at Melbourne in 1876/7
and, next to Charles Bannerman, had the biggest
share in beating England, capturing 8 for 109.
Taking two walking strides to the wicket, he
bowled orthodox left-arm spin with considerable
flight and command of length and, for variety, a

ball which went with his arm. He was a surprising omission from the 1878 side. Although a poor batsman and slow in the field, he was a safe catcher. Living latterly at Hobart, he toured New Zealand with a Tasmanian side in 1883/4.

First-class career (1876–88): 141 runs (12.81) and 40 wickets (16.65)

Test matches (2): 39 runs (13.00), 14 wickets (15.35), and 2 catches

KENT, Martin Francis

(b. 1953, Mossman, Queensland) *Queensland and Australia*

Cricket fate was never very kind to Martin Kent, a tall man, who batted right-handed with aggressive intent and a handsome, upright style. He scored freely for Queensland after his début for them in 1974/5 and was one of the few men signed up to play World Series Cricket for Kerry Packer without having established himself in Test cricket. In his first Shield match, against New South Wales, he hit 140. He added to his experience by touring West Indies on an unofficial World Series tour, and made his first Test appearance in England in 1981, making 171 runs in three Tests and hitting fifties at Old Trafford, batting number five, and as a makeshift opener in the final Test at The Oval. A very good slip fielder, he lost his place the following Australian season only because of a serious back injury caused by a disc protruding into the spinal cord. He was obliged to retire prematurely from the game.

First-class career (1974–82): 3,567 runs (36.03) including 7 centuries

Test matches (3): 171 runs (28.50) and 6 catches

KERR, Robert Byers

(b. 1961, Aspley, Queensland) *Queensland and Australia*

An elegant and stylish right-handed batsman, Robbie Kerr made his first-class début in the 1981/2 season and immediately revealed his talent as an opening batsman. He scored 613 runs (47.15) in his first season, making 103 not out against South Australia and 158 and 101 against Western Australia. Over the next two seasons he gave further evidence of his potential, scoring over 800 runs in both the 1982/3 and 1983/4 seasons. Against Victoria at St Kilda in 1982/3 he and Kepler Wessels put on 388 for Queensland's first wicket, a record opening stand for the Sheffield Shield. Following a highest score of 201

not out against Tasmania, he was brought into the Australian one-day side in 1985, making 87 not out against England at Melbourne. He was unlucky not to be selected for the 1985 tour of England, but after touring Zimbabwe with Young Australia, he made his Test début in the 1985/6 series against New Zealand. He managed only 31 runs in two matches but the following season became captain of Queensland and continued to play for them until 1989/90 without quite fulfilling his early billing as another Greg Chappell.

First-class career (1981–9); 5,709 runs (37.31) including 16 centuries, 1 wicket (16.00), and 90 catches

Test matches (2): 31 runs (7.75) and 1 catch

KIPPAX, Alan Falconer

(b. 1897, Sydney; d. 1972, Sydney) *New South Wales and Australia*

Tallish, rather slim, with his shirt-sleeves rolled just like Victor Trumper's, Alan Kippax was a charming, cultured, right-handed batsman, orthodox in his stroke-play but never dull or boring. He was very quick-footed and could get to the pitch of the ball when facing the spinner or walk inside the line of flight when the short one came along. Ray Robinson wrote of the 'silken quality' of his batting. 'His leg-glancing, forward or back, had a kind of moonbeam beauty . . . when he late cut he made a lissom bow over the ball and stroked it away with his bat face downwards . . .' Not always well treated by Test Selection Committees, he remained a brilliant and prolific batsman, and captained his state for several years. He made his Test début against England in 1924/5 but was a surprise omission from the 1926 team to England, although he toured in 1930 and 1934, making 329 runs (54.83) in the Tests of the former year, and averaging more than 50 in all first-class matches on each tour. He scored 100 in the third Test against England at Melbourne in 1928/9, adding 161 with Jack Ryder after three wickets had fallen cheaply. Against the first West Indian tourists of 1930/1 he made 146 at Adelaide, top-scoring in the first Test between the two countries; and the following season he was quite effective against South Africa. In 61 Sheffield Shield matches he made 6,096 runs (70.06), his career-highest being 315 not out against Queensland in 1927/8. He made 260 not out against Victoria at Melbourne the following year, adding 307 for the last wicket with J. E. H. Hooker, which remains a world record. Altogether, he passed 200 seven times and twice scored a century in each innings. In retirement he ran a successful sports goods business and took celebrity teams to country areas to develop the game.

First-class career (1918–35): 12,762 runs (57.22) including 43 centuries, and 21 wickets (52.33)

Test matches (22): 1,192 runs (36.12) including 2 centuries, 0–19, and 13 catches

KLINE, Lindsay Francis

(b. 1934, Melbourne) *Victoria and Australia*

A left-arm off-break and googly bowler and dogged tail-end batsman, Lindsay Kline took 37 wickets (24.89) for his state in his second season in 1956/7, which led to tours to New Zealand (with an 'A' team) and South Africa in 1957/8. In his second Test, at Cape Town, he performed one of the rare hat-tricks. He headed the Test bowling averages in that series with 15 wickets (16.33). Again heading the averages against India and Pakistan in 1959/60, he collected 16 wickets (14.45) from four Tests, including 7 for 75 in the Pakistan second innings at Lahore on an easy turf pitch, clinching victory for Australia. He appeared twice against England, in 1958/9, without success, and went on the 1961 tour of England but was not selected for the Tests. In the fourth Test at Adelaide against the West Indies in the unforgettable series of 1960/1, Kline batted 100 minutes for 15 not out in a last-wicket stand of 66 with Ken Mackay which denied victory to the visitors. The whole nation listened to the commentary of the final stages.

First-class career (1955–61): 559 runs (8.60) and 276 wickets (27.39)

Test matches (13): 58 runs (8.28), 34 wickets (22.82), and 9 catches

LAIRD, Bruce Malcolm

(b. 1950, Perth) *Western Australia and Australia*

A small, gritty, fair-haired, right-hand opening batsman, Bruce Laird was unlucky to make his Test début as late as he did and to make it, moreover, against one of the fiercest fast-bowling attacks in history—the West Indians Holding, Roberts, Croft, and Garner. He had played his first match for Western Australia in 1972/3 and toured England in 1975, batting consistently without earning a cap. He scored four first-class hundreds, the highest, 171 against Queensland in 1976/7, before signing for World Series Cricket, where he gained valuable experience against

high-class fast bowling which stood him in good stead when WSC was disbanded in 1979/80. In that season Laird assured himself of Test selection with a fighting 117 in his state's first Sheffield Shield game against New South Wales, and his first innings for Australia was outstanding: 92 at Brisbane, scored during five hours of determined batting which deserved at least eight more runs. His 75 in the second innings helped Australia to draw the game and throughout the season he continued to display pluck and concentration which, allied to a compact and correct technique, made him Australia's most successful batsman with 340 runs (56.66) against the West Indies. Against England he was less successful until he made 74 and 25 in the Melbourne Test, and on the short tour of Pakistan in 1979/80 he disappointed on the slow pitches apart from scoring 63 in the third Test in Lahore. He did not get going, either, in the Centenary Test at Lord's and further appearances at Test level were prevented by a serious rupture to an Achilles' tendon which kept him out of the 1980/1 season and the 1981 England tour. He reclaimed a regular place against Pakistan and West Indies at home in 1981/2 and toured Pakistan in 1982/3. He was consistent, but a major innings eluded him. He announced his retirement from first-class cricket at the end of the 1983/4 season, having helped Western Australia to win the Sheffield Shield, scoring 63 and 54 not out in the Final, his last match.

First-class career (1972–83): 6,085 runs (35.37) including 8 centuries

Test matches (21): 1,341 runs (35.28), 0–12, and 16 catches

LANGER, Justin Lee

(b. 1970, Perth) *Western Australia and Australia*

No player, not even in the days of bodyline, has ever endured such a fiery initiation into Test cricket as the West Australian left-hander Justin Langer. In making 20 and 54 in six heroic hours against the intimidating West Indians in Adelaide in January 1993, Langer was struck a dozen times but refused to back away, or to forfeit his wicket. In one of post-war cricket's tensest finishes, Australia, needing 186 runs to win, were bowled out for 184, the narrowest defeat in Test history. Batting at number three, Langer saw Australia from 5 for 1 to 144 for 9, showing a street-fighting approach and rare flair for one playing his first Test. He had made an eleventh-hour entry into the match after his team-mate Damien Martyn had injured his eye on the eve of the match in a freak fielding accident. A nephew of Robbie Langer, the former West Australian and Australian World Series Cricket batsman, Langer toured New Zealand and was unfortunate not to go to England in 1993 and South Africa in 1994, the selectors preferring the prolific scoring of Queensland's Matthew Hayden. Amassing almost 1,200 runs during the 1993/4 Australian season, including a career-best 233 against Tasmania in Perth, he forced his way into the 1994 winter tours of Pakistan and Sri Lanka and, with his close friend Martyn, seemed likely to be an Australian regular throughout the 1990s. Another Test player to spend time at the Australian Cricket Academy, Langer's insatiable desire for success saw him bat in the nets for 6 hours one day in Adelaide. Even then he wanted to go back for more! He toured the West Indies in 1994/5.

First-class career (1991–   ): 2,696 runs (50.86) including 6 centuries, and 26 catches

Test matches (6): 241 runs (26.77) and 2 catches

LANGLEY, Gilbert Roche Andrews

(b. 1919, Adelaide) *South Australia and Australia*

At one time Speaker of the South Australian parliament, Gil Langley was for several years Australia's number one wicket-keeper. Genial and burly, he was also a stolid right-handed batsman, extremely sound though hardly a stylist, his most useful scoring strokes being past square-leg and point. His first tour was to South Africa in 1949/50, followed by trips to England in 1953 and 1956, and to the West Indies, India and Pakistan. His Test experience was packed into the years between 1951 and 1956, and, in achieving 21 dismissals in the series at home against the West Indies in 1951/2, he equalled the then world record in a rubber. Nine Tests against England brought him 37 victims (35 caught). At Lord's in 1956 he had nine in the match, a record, and 19 in the three matches in which he kept that year. His career-highest score was 150 not out for his state against New Zealand at Adelaide in 1953/4.

First-class career (1945–57): 3,236 runs (25.68) including 4 centuries, and 369 dismissals (293 c., 76 st.)

Test matches (26): 374 runs (14.96) and 98 dismissals (83 c., 15 st.)

LAUGHLIN, Trevor John

(b. 1951, Nyah West, Victoria) *Victoria and Australia*

An aggressive all-rounder, a hard-hitting left-hand batsman, steady medium-pace right-arm bowler and fine close fielder, Trevor Laughlin had a good tour of the West Indies for Bobby Simpson's reconstituted Australian team early in 1978. But his subsequent form was disappointing. He was dropped from the team after Australia had lost the first Test to England in 1978/9 (when Laughlin brought off one brilliant catch in the gully) and thereafter only shone for his country in limited-overs cricket. He was a useful member of Australia's Prudential World Cup side in England in 1979. In two Tests against the West Indies he made 24 priceless runs in a crisis to help his side win the third Test narrowly, and then took 5 for 101 in the first innings of the fifth Test, sharing the new ball with Jeff Thomson. Laughlin played cricket in the Scottish and Lancashire Leagues in 1976 and 1977 to broaden his experience. In seven matches for Victoria, 1977/8, he scored 497 runs (49.70) and took 20 wickets (29.10).

First-class career (1974–80): 2,770 runs (32.58) including 1 century, and 99 wickets (31.92)

Test matches (3): 87 runs (17.40), 6 wickets (43.66), and 3 catches

LAVER, Frank Jonas

(b. 1869, Castlemaine, Victoria; d. 1919, Melbourne) *Victoria and Australia*

A tall, powerful man, Frank Laver's right-handed batting was so ungainly that, even when he did well, little was thought of him. As a medium-pace bowler, however, he had an excellent command of length and a deceptive flight. On his first England tour in 1899 he made 859 runs and, having ten not-outs, averaged 30, but, except in the Test at Lord's when he quickly disposed of Tom Hayward, Johnny Tyldesley, and Gilbert Jessop (Australia ultimately winning), he had little chance to shine as a bowler. Returning to England in 1905 and, as player/manager, in 1909, he enjoyed greater success in the former year, virtually winning the first Test at Trent Bridge by taking 7 for 64 in the first innings. In all first-class matches on the tour he captured 115 wickets (18.19). In 1909 he headed the averages for both Tests with 17 wickets (13.50), and for all matches with 68 wickets (14.69) from 17 games. In the first innings of the Old Trafford Test, flattered by some inept batting, he took 8 for 31. Although he hit 143 against Somerset at Taunton in 1899, he was generally a more effective batsman at home, hitting five centuries there. In 59 Sheffield Shield matches he made 2,750 runs (28.65) and took 108 wickets (36.99). He was also player/manager on two tours of New Zealand. It was partly because the Board of Control refused to appoint him as manager in 1912 that six important players declined to make the trip to England. A photographer and writer, he wrote a well-illustrated book of his first two tours of England, *An Australian Cricketer on Tour*.

First-class career (1891–1913): 5,430 runs (25.02) including 6 centuries, 404 wickets (24.72), and 148 catches
Test matches (15): 196 runs (11.52), 37 wickets (26.05), and 8 catches

LAWRY, William Morris

(b. 1937, Melbourne) *Victoria and Australia*

Six feet two inches tall, lean, with a sharp jaw, prominent nose, and ready smile, Bill Lawry bore the nickname 'The Phantom' because of his youthful addiction to a comic strip character of that name. A left-handed opening batsman with a short back-lift which did not prevent him from driving well and scoring greedily on the on-side, his major quality was his quite exceptional concentration. A very fine player of fast bowling, he hooked with authority. He was also a fast out-fielder with a good arm, but opposing bowlers will recall only his broad, straight bat and his endless patience. Bill Lawry came to England comparatively unknown in 1961 and had a triumphant summer: all first-class matches brought him 2,019 runs (61.18), including nine centuries, and in the Tests he made 420 runs (52.50). This was his first Test series. In his first match at Edgbaston he made 57 and in his second, at Lord's, a memorable 130 out of 238 in 6 hours 10 minutes against the hostile fast bowling of Brian Statham and Fred Trueman on a fiery wicket. Largely due to him Australia won. At Old Trafford his 74 and 102 were also fighting match-winning innings. On return home he became captain of his state and led Australia from 1968 to 1971 against England (twice), West Indies, India, and South Africa. He was in charge of a relatively weak side who were heavily mauled by South Africa in 1970 and lost the Ashes in 1970/1 when Lawry lost the captaincy to Ian Chappell for the final Test. He toured England three times and, in 29 Tests against England alone, made 2,233 runs (48.54). At home in 1965/6 he three times stood

between England and the decisive advantage that presages victory, scoring more runs than anyone else in the series: 592 (84.57). In the first Test at Brisbane he made 166, adding 187 with Doug Walters after four wickets had fallen very cheaply; and in the fourth, at Adelaide, he put on 244 for the first wicket with his captain Bobby Simpson (by themselves they passed England's 241). In his day the hardest Australian batsman to dismiss, Lawry averaged 55.11 in the series against South Africa in 1963/4, his 157 in the second Test at Melbourne being an especially good innings. His highest Test score was 210 against West Indies in the fourth Test at Bridge-town in 1964/5 when he put on 382 with Bobby Simpson for the first wicket; they were the first opening pair in Test history to score double centuries in the same innings. He averaged 52.57 for the Tests and 65.92 for the tour. His career-highest score was 266 for Victoria against New South Wales at Sydney in 1960/1. Highly effective he was, as all these figures prove, but he was often a rather colourless cricketer to watch. Originally a plumber, he devoted more time to his hobby of racing pigeons after retiring from cricket and became a popular, if sometimes hysterical, commentator on cricket on Channel 9 Television.

First-class career (1955–71) 18,734 (50.90) including 50 centuries, and 121 catches
Test matches (67): 5,234 runs (47.15) including 13 centuries, 0–6, and 30 catches

LAWSON, Geoffrey Francis

(b. 1957, Wagga Wagga, New South Wales) *New South Wales, Lancashire, and Australia*

A tall, slim, raw-boned fast bowler and hard-hitting lower-order batsman, Geoff Lawson interrupted his degree course in optometry at the University of New South Wales to tour India (as a replacement) and Pakistan at each end of the 1979/80 season. He had come to prominence with some lively performances in the previous season and was to prove one of the most durable players of his generation, finishing his career in 1991/2 with more wickets for New South Wales than any other bowler. He dismissed Geoff Boy-cott in the match between New South Wales and England at Sydney in 1979/80 and also unleashed a series of bouncers at him in the second innings, earning a reprimand from the umpire. In that season he took 34 wickets (20.97) and five times took four or more wickets in an innings. He had little opportunity in Pakistan but won his first cap against New Zealand at Brisbane in 1980/1. Despite taking 1 for 39 and 2 for 26 in a comfortable Australian win he was considered to have sacrificed accuracy for hostility and lost his place immediately, but he was picked to tour England in 1981 as a replacement for the injured Len Pascoe. He had already had experience in England, having taken 94 wickets for Heywood in the Central Lancashire League in 1979, and he played in one first-class match for Lancashire against Cambridge University. This experience stood him in good stead on the 1981 tour until a back injury ruled him out of the remainder of the tour after three Tests. Perhaps he overstrained himself at Lord's where, in the first England innings, he took 7 for 81, figures only surpassed in a Lord's Test for Australia by Bob Massie. He was fast, persistent, and hostile. He played only one Test at home in 1981/2 when his back had mended, but on a disastrous Australian tour of Pakistan in 1982/3 he was the outstanding bowler, taking nine wickets in the three Tests at 33.44 each. His hostile fast bowling was the overriding reason for Australia's regaining of the Ashes later in the year. He took 34 wickets (20.20) in the five Tests, collecting five wickets in an innings four times, and taking over from Dennis Lillee the mantle of Australia's most dangerous fast bowler. He added another 24 wickets in the 1983/4 series against Pakistan to his growing haul of Test victims and, having endured a long, arduous tour of the Caribbean, he bowled with sustained aggression to take 8 for 112, his best Test figures, against the West Indies at Adelaide in 1984/5. Despite never being fully fit he took 22 wickets (37.72) in the 1985 Test series against England, but the following winter he suffered a serious back injury and played in only two Tests. A brief reappearance against England in 1986/7 was disappointing, yet in 1987/8, varying his pace cleverly, he took 42 Sheffield Shield wickets at 18 and he returned to England in 1989 to play a full part, with 29 wickets at 27 each, in the regaining of the Ashes.

First-class career (1977–91): 2,683 runs (14.82), 666 wickets (24.87), and 75 catches
Test matches (46): 894 runs (15.96), 180 wickets (30.56), and 10 catches

LEE, Philip Keith

(b. 1904, Gladstone, South Australia; d. 1980, Adelaide) *South Australia and Australia*

A batsman who liked to attack and an off-spin bowler with good control and shrewd knowledge

of flight, Phil Lee was particularly successful for his state against the first West Indian tourists in 1930/1. His Tests, however, were limited to one each against South Africa in 1931/2 and England in 1932/3. His 5 for 23 against Victoria at Melbourne in the latter year was the best of his six 5-wicket analyses. In 40 Sheffield Shield matches he scored 1,069 runs (15.72) and took 115 wickets (30.33). He was also a gifted football and baseball player.

First-class career (1925–35): 1,669 runs (18.54) including 2 centuries, and 152 wickets (30.16)
Test matches (2): 57 runs (19.00), 5 wickets (42.40), and 1 catch

LEHMANN, Darren Scott

(b. 1970, Gawler, South Australia) *South Australia and Victoria*

An aggressive left-hander, Darren Lehmann became one of the youngest Australian first-class players when first appearing for South Australia against Victoria at the age of 17, in December 1987. His promise was confirmed with a series of exciting performances and he was Australia's 12th man in the third and final Test against Pakistan in 1989/90. He had made four centuries in six innings for South Australia, including 228 against New Zealand, to win selection, but coming into the 1994/5 Australian season had still not broken into the actual XI, either at Test or one-day level. After three seasons with Victoria, he returned to his native South Australia.

First-class career (1987–): 4,916 runs (46.81) including 15 centuries, 8 wickets (65.75), and 37 catches

LILLEE, Dennis Keith

(b. 1949, Perth) *Western Australia and Australia*

A superb fast bowler, Dennis Lillee retired as the leading wicket-taker in Tests. A glorious action was at the heart of his success. In addition, Lillee had a fine physique, courage, exceptional stamina, and a belligerence which sometimes amounted almost to hatred. Some fast bowlers go about their business with a silent menace —Andy Roberts, Brian Statham, Jeff Thomson, Lindwall—some with histrionics and occasional invective, although with the likes of a Fred Trueman the ostentatious fire and brimstone is part bluff, part acting for the gallery. Lillee, too, was a great showman, but one who too often appeared to show a vicious streak. Quick to boil, however, he was also quick to smile again.

Starting with Western Australia in 1969/70, he took 32 Shield wickets in eight matches, then 18 wickets at 16 each on the tour of New Zealand which followed. As Australia rebuilt with the loss of the Ashes imminent in 1970/1 he bowled with hostility, but without his later control, in his first two Test matches, the last two of that series, starting with 5 for 84 on his début at Adelaide. In 1971 he broadened his experience playing for Haslingden in the Lancashire League, and in 1971/2 showed his growing maturity by taking 23 wickets in four matches against the Rest of the World in Australia, including a devastating 8 for 29 in 7.1 overs downwind on the fast Perth pitch. He was now approaching the first of his peaks, a controlled fast bowler with a long run leading to a magnificent final leap and a full-blooded, no-holds-barred delivery. Dark, moustached, with an eagle's eyes and an eagle's beak for a nose, he provided a splendid spectacle for watchers, a fearsome one for batsmen. Moreover he varied the direction of his swing and his speed intelligently. He took 31 wickets in the five Tests in 1972. At The Oval he took 10 for 81 in an Australian victory which ushered in a new era of success. However, he broke down in the West Indies with stress fractures in the back and, after spending six weeks in plaster, had a long, determined fight back to fitness before joining forces with Jeff Thomson in 1974/5 to demoralize England with one of the most destructive fast-bowling partnerships in history. Making ferocious use of the bouncer, he took 25 wickets (23.84) and 21 wickets (21.90) in the Tests in England in 1975. He also won the Centenary Test for Australia at Melbourne in 1977, with 6 for 26 and 5 for 139. A useful tail-end batsman who played very straight, he scored a fine 73 not out to rescue Australia at Lord's in 1975. After the disbandment of World Series Cricket, in which he played a prominent part, Lillee returned to the Test arena and to new triumphs. Superbly fit, he seemed to have lost very little pace, and his control of swing and cut, allied to his bristling aggression at all times, discomforted batsmen of all nationalities (but especially English ones), as he passed Richie Benaud in 1980/1 to become the highest wicket-taker in Australian Test history. His chief successes in 1979/80 were against England. He took 23 wickets (16.86) in the three Tests but spoilt this fine bowling with a public display of arrogant ill-humour at Perth when the umpires ordered him to change the aluminium bat he was using for a wooden one. The match was held up for 10 minutes, and the episode ended with Lillee

throwing the bat 20 yards. Against the West Indies he was less successful (12 wickets at 30.41) and on the short tour of Pakistan his three Test wickets cost 101 runs apiece. But in England for the Centenary Test his 4 for 43 helped to bowl England out cheaply in the first innings and in the 1980/1 season he was consistently successful with 16 wickets in three Tests against New Zealand and 21 wickets in three more against India. He passed Benaud's 248 wickets in the third Test against India at Melbourne in his 48th match for Australia. The next landmark, Lance Gibbs's all-time Test record of 309 wickets, was reached with remarkable rapidity. Despite suffering a bout of viral pneumonia at the start of the 1981 tour of England, he took 39 wickets (22.30) in the six Tests and in the first Test against West Indies in Melbourne in 1981/2—his 58th Test for Australia—he dismissed his 310th victim, Larry Gomes. A tour to New Zealand at the end of another crowded season enabled him to take his haul to 328. Sadly he marred these admirable performances by again losing his temper in the middle of a Perth Test, aiming a public kick at the Pakistan captain Javed Miandad. Further controversy surrounded his admission that he and Rodney Marsh had placed a bet on Australia to lose the 1981 Headingley Test. A serious knee injury allowed him to play in only the first Test against England in 1982/3, but in his final Test series against Pakistan in 1983/4 he took a further 20 wickets to stretch his record haul to 355, 167 of them against England. He captured five wickets in a Test innings 23 times, ten wickets in a match seven times. He led his state to victory in the Sheffield Shield Final in his last first-class match, then retired, a relatively wealthy man, to what he hoped would be a quieter life. He had always courted controversy, but he was unquestionably one of the greatest bowlers in Test history and much of his time in retirement was spent in helping aspiring fast bowlers, not least in India, where he ran an annual clinic in Madras, sponsored by an industrial company.

First-class career (1969–88): 2,377 runs (13.90) and 882 wickets (23.46)

Test matches (70): 905 runs (13.71), 355 wickets (23.92), and 23 catches

LINDWALL, Raymond Russell

(b. 1921, Sydney) *New South Wales, Queensland, and Australia*

In his youth Ray Lindwall and his friends bowled vigorously at paraffin-tins in the street down which Bill O'Reilly made his way home, hoping to catch the great man's eye; and he also watched Harold Larwood bowling in the 1932/3 series. Five feet ten inches, with broad chest and shoulders, he rose to rank with the great fast bowlers and, for a decade after the Second World War, his partnership with Keith Miller became legendary. His low-slung run to the wicket had a slow start, then an arm-pumping acceleration which brought him smoothly to his delivery and follow-through. He had genuine pace, a great variety of swing and speed, good control, and the 'killer' spirit, though he bowled the bouncer relatively rarely—a surprise weapon, which was often lethal. His 'stock' delivery was the late out-swinger. He was also a distinctly useful batsman, who could hit the ball effectively through the covers and who played some invaluable innings. In Tests his return of wickets was the best by any Australian fast bowler this century. He toured England in 1948, 1953, and 1956, also South Africa, the West Indies, and New Zealand; and from 1946 until 1958 he was a first choice at home. In 29 Tests against England alone he took 114 wickets (22.44), besides scoring 795 runs (22.08). On the 1948 England tour crowds who had been starved of a really great fast bowler gave him a tumultuous reception and in the Tests he captured 27 wickets (19.62), including one of the most remarkable spells of bowling in the whole series between the two countries, 6 for 20 at The Oval in the fifth match, England falling for 52. When England were fighting back in the third Test at Melbourne in 1946/7, Lindwall hit 100, adding 154 with Don Tallon for the eighth wicket in 88 minutes. Having taken 86 wickets at 15.68 on the 1948 tour of England, he fared equally well, with 85 at 16.40, in 1953. Against India in 1947/8 he took more wickets than anyone else on either side, 18 (16.88) including 7 for 38 in the second innings of the fourth match at Adelaide. His 7 for 43 in the second innings at Madras won Australia's first Test in India, 1956/7. Against West Indies in Australia in 1951/2 he took 21 wickets (23.04) and made 211 runs in the five matches. In the West Indies his 20 Test wickets were expensive, but in the fourth match at Bridgetown he slammed the wilting bowlers for 118. Most of his cricket was played at the highest level, on the best wickets and against strong opposition. His skill, unaccompanied by histrionics, was something for the connoisseur to savour. He reached his first hundred Test wickets after 26 matches and his second hundred after 52 matches. He led Australia once against India in

1956/7 and Queensland from 1955 until 1960. He was awarded the MBE for his services to Australian cricket, and partnered his wife in a flourishing florist business in Brisbane.

First-class career (1941–61): 5,042 runs (21.82) including 5 centuries, 794 wickets (21.35), and 123 catches

Test matches (61): 1,502 runs (21.15) including 2 centuries, 228 wickets (23.03), and 26 catches

LIVINGSTON, Leonard

(b. 1920, Marrickville, Sydney) *New South Wales and Northamptonshire*

One of the first paid players to be admitted to membership of MCC when the club opened its ranks to professionals in 1961, 'Jock' Livingston, a stocky left-hander and occasional wicket-keeper, had eight years with Northamptonshire from 1950 to 1957 before a knee injury forced his premature retirement. He scored four double-centuries and averaged more than 45 in county cricket. He also captained a Commonwealth team to India in 1949/50, a tour which did much for the game's popularity. He had five wartime games with New South Wales, including a century against Queensland at Sydney in 1946/7, before moving to England.

First-class career (1941–64): 15,260 runs (45.01) including 34 centuries, 4 wickets (12.50), 149 catches, and 23 stumpings

LOVE, Hampden Stanley Bray

(b. 1895, Sydney; d. 1969, Sydney) *Victoria, New South Wales, and Australia*

'Hammy' Love was a very sound wicket-keeper and a dependable right-handed batsman who dealt largely in deflections. Replacing Bert Oldfield, who had been disabled in the previous Test, he played once for Australia, against England in the fourth match at Brisbane in 1932/3, scoring 5 and 3 and holding 3 catches. A popular cricketer, he toured India in 1935/6.

First-class career (1919–35): 2,906 runs (35.01) including 7 centuries, and 102 dismissals (73 c., 29 st.)

LOXTON, Samuel John Everett

(b. 1921, Melbourne) *Victoria and Australia*

Looking like a boxer, with a chin jutting out belligerently not unlike Humphrey Bogart's, Sam Loxton played some glorious swashbuckling innings. His reply when told the fast bowlers would bounce the ball at his head was characteristic: 'If they do I'll hit them over the fence.' A right-hander, he also bowled as fast as he could —fast-medium—for long periods; he could move the ball in the air and was a useful accessory to a powerful Australian attack. In the field he was a fast mover and an accurate thrower. He toured England in 1948 and South Africa in 1949/50, and managed the team to India and Pakistan in 1959/60 (playing one match). At home he played against India and England. In England in 1948 he made 973 runs (57.23), including three forceful centuries; and he appeared in three Tests primarily as a batsman. In the fourth at Leeds he struck five sixes in his first-innings score of 93 which occupied only two and a quarter hours, when runs were badly needed. In his first Test against South Africa, at Johannesburg in 1949/50, he hit 101 in two and a half hours, again when runs were needed. He toured India with the Commonwealth team in 1953/4. Sam Loxton entered national politics, becoming a member of the Australian Parliament as a Liberal-Country member. He served as a member of the Test Selection Committee from 1972–81. In 66 Sheffield Shield matches he made 3,157 runs (36.28) and took 130 wickets (23.90).

First-class career (1946–59): 6,249 runs (36.97) including 13 centuries, 232 wickets (25.73), and 83 catches

Test matches (12): 554 runs (36.93) including 1 century, 8 wickets (43.62), and 7 catches

LYONS, John James

(b. 1863, Gawler, South Australia; d. 1927, Adelaide) *South Australia and Australia*

'J.J.' Lyons was a very hard-hitting right-handed opener, a quick-footed driver, especially on a hard, true wicket. But when the ball was turning, he was generally an easy victim for a spin bowler. He toured England in 1888, 1890, and 1893, and was at his best during his last tour. He made 1,377 runs (28.10) and at Lord's in May he played the most brilliant innings of his career. The touring team needed 181 against a powerful MCC XI, and got them without losing a wicket, J.J. scoring 149 in 90 minutes, his century coming in an hour. He had a penchant for Lord's: during the Test of 1890 he hit 55 out of 66 in 45 minutes on the first morning and, later, took 5 for 30 with his medium pace; against MCC he struck 99 out of 117 in 75 minutes; and in 1893, in two games against MCC, he scored 149 out of 181 in 90 minutes and 83 out of 117 in 100 minutes

respectively. At home he appeared in Tests between 1886 and 1898, heading the averages in 1891/2 with 287 runs (47.83) in the three matches, including a quick 134 in the second innings at Sydney. Australia, 162 behind and batting again, were indebted to J.J. and A. C. Bannerman for putting on 174 for the second wicket—and the match was ultimately won; J.J. reached his hundred out of 129 and batted for about three hours altogether. In 29 Sheffield Shield matches he made 1,826 runs (33.20).

First-class career (1884–1900): 6,753 runs (25.57) including 11 centuries, and 107 wickets (30.14)

Test matches (14): 731 runs (27.07) including 1 century, 6 wickets (24.83), and 3 catches

McALISTER, Peter Alexander

(b. 1869, Melbourne; d. 1938, Melbourne) *Victoria and Australia*

Peter McAlister toured England in 1909 as vice-captain and opening batsman. A veteran, he had appeared six times against England in 1903/4 and 1907/8, and on tour scored 751 runs though he achieved little in the Tests. A tall, spare, right-handed batsman, he played in 40 Sheffield Shield matches and made 2,398 runs (32.40). Active for many years in cricket administration, he sided with the Board of Control in the 1911/12 controversy and was involved in a fist-fight in the Selection Committee room, the provoked Australian captain, Clem Hill, punching him on the nose. His career-highest was 224 for Victoria against New Zealand at Melbourne in 1898/9.

First-class career (1898–1910): 4,552 runs (32.74) including 9 centuries

Test matches (8): 252 runs (16.80) and 10 catches

MACARTNEY, Charles George

(b. 1886, West Maitland, New South Wales; d. 1958, Sydney) *New South Wales, Otago, and Australia*

A little man but a great batsman, Charles Macartney, known as the 'Governor General', developed an artistry which charmed spectators and drove bowlers to distraction. A right-handed batsman, he was a brilliant improviser, though his risks were calculated and even Bradman did not dominate bowlers more ruthlessly than Macartney in his prime. He was short, square-shouldered, with forearms formidably strong, chin aggressive and eyes perpetually alive. He would dart down the pitch to drive, or go right back to hook or cut. By nature confident and a little cocky, he was always looking for runs and never resisted a challenge. 'I can't bear watching luscious half-volleys being nudged gently back to bowlers!' he would exclaim when he became a spectator. At the outset he was played more for his left-arm slow bowling than his batting. On his first tour of England in 1909, he took 64 wickets (17.85) and scored only 503 runs in 37 innings. Taking a long run for one of his pace, he had excellent control and could produce an unexpected faster one. He was an excellent fielder, with few equals at mid-off. Besides 1909, he toured England in 1912, 1921, and 1926 and South Africa in 1921/2; and between 1907 and 1921 played in four series at home, three times against England and once against South Africa. He won the third Test at Headingley in 1909 by taking 11 for 85; but against the 1910/11 South Africans he first blazed as a batsman. He hit a century in each innings for New South Wales against the tourists, and in the fifth Test at Sydney, opening the batting for the first time, scored 137 and 56. At Lord's in the first Test of 1912 he struck hard for 99. A year later he hit 2,390 runs and captured 180 wickets in an unofficial Australian visit to America; and after the First World War, usually at first wicket down, he rarely failed at the highest level. Against England in 1920/1 he headed the averages with 86.66 from two Tests, including 170 in the fifth match at Sydney. In England in 1921 he averaged 42.85 in the five Tests and in all first-class matches made 2,317 runs (59.41), including eight centuries, the highest being a punishing 345 in one day (less than four hours) against Nottinghamshire at Trent Bridge, the third of four centuries in successive innings. In reaching 115 in the third Test at Headingley, he hit a century before lunch on the first day. That winter in South Africa he averaged 73 in the Tests. Back in England for the last time in 1926 he headed the batting with 473 runs (94.60) in the Tests, including 133 not out, 151 and 109 in successive innings. Missed by the England captain before he had scored in the third match at Headingley, he added 235 with Bill Woodfull for the second wicket—again scoring his century before lunch on the first day (going on to 151). He played for Otago in 1909/10, for New South Wales from 1905 to 1926, and then, with continued success, for the Gordon Club in Sydney for several more seasons, going on tour to India and Ceylon in 1935/6.

First-class career (1905–35): 15,019 runs (45.78) including 49 centuries, 419 wickets (20.96), and 102 catches

Test matches (35): 2,131 runs (41.78) including 7 centuries, 45 wickets (27.55), and 17 catches

McCABE, Stanley Joseph

(b. 1910, Grenfell, New South Wales; d. 1968, Sydney) *New South Wales and Australia*

A right-hander of the highest class, Stan McCabe's batting had a daring and cavalier gaiety about it; his great innings lived on in the imagination. He was short, stockily built, strong, and extremely agile. His stance and strokes were perfectly balanced and he specialized in the drive, late-cut, and hook. An all-rounder, he was an accurate fastish-medium bowler, who occasionally produced a googly, and he opened the bowling in a Test on several occasions. He fielded magnificently anywhere until suffering, late in his career, from sore feet. By then, he had been the cause of many sore feet amongst his opponents! First representing his state at the age of 18, he toured England in 1930 (as the 'baby' of the side), 1934 and 1938, and South Africa in 1935/6; and he appeared at home in four series between 1930 and 1937. On the first tour he averaged 35 in the Tests and took eight inexpensive wickets. His first-class matches in 1934 brought him 2,078 runs (69.26), including eight centuries, only 12 runs less than Bradman, the headline-stealer. In his short Test career he continued to shine. In the 'bodyline' series he was second to Bradman, averaging 42.77, in the 1934 series third to Bill Ponsford and Bradman when he made 483 runs (60.37). In 1936/7 he was second to Bradman with 491 runs (54.55) and in the 1938 series, his last, he averaged 45.25. Usually batting at number four, Stan McCabe played three innings which will never be forgotten, such was their heroic stature. In the first Test at Sydney, 1932/3, he defied the fearsome Larwood with 187 not out. In South Africa, 1935/6, in the second Test at Johannesburg he scored 189 not out. And in the first Test at Trent Bridge in 1938 he scored 232 (out of 300) in less than four hours in the face of a huge England total. This was the famous occasion when Bradman begged his team not to miss a ball for, he said, they would never again see batting to equal it. On Stan's return to the pavilion Bradman said to him, 'If I could play an innings like that, I'd be a proud man, Stan!' He had the phenomenal average of 438 in the Sheffield Shield matches of 1931/2. He hit 229 not out against Queensland at Brisbane. In 37 Sheffield Shield matches he made 3,031 runs (55.10) and took 49 wickets (23.81). He did not return to first-class cricket after the Second World War, becoming a successful seller of sporting equipment until dying tragically in a fall from a cliff near his home in Sydney.

First-class career (1928–41): 11,951 runs (49.39) including 29 centuries, 159 wickets (33.72), and 139 catches

Test matches (39): 2,748 runs (48.21) including 6 centuries, 36 wickets (42.86), and 41 catches

McCOOL, Colin Leslie

(b. 1915, Sydney; d. 1986, Woy Woy, New South Wales) *New South Wales, Queensland, Somerset, and Australia*

Short but powerful, Colin McCool was a right-handed stroke-playing batsman, at his best when playing his natural attacking game, a gifted leg-break bowler with something of a round-arm delivery but a shrewd control, and a safe catcher at slip. He was handicapped by the tendency of the skin to rub off his spinning finger. He took the last New Zealand wicket at Wellington with his second ball in Tests to give Australia the victory in the first post-war Test of 1946; and against England in 1946/7 he scored 272 runs (54.40) and took 18 wickets (27.27) in the five matches, his 104 not out in the third match at Melbourne saving Australia from collapse, and his 5 for 44 in England's second innings of 186 in the fifth match at Sydney bringing the victory. He appeared against India in the first series between the two countries; toured England in 1948, doing well all round but not appearing in a Test; and toured South Africa in 1949/50. He came to England as a professional in the East Lancashire League and qualified for Somerset in 1956, when a new, highly successful, career began. In five seasons he exceeded 1,000 runs four times, his 1,967 runs (37.82) in 1956 being the best, and his best bowling feat was 8 for 74 against Nottinghamshire at Trent Bridge in 1958. His career-highest score was 172 for Queensland against South Australia at Adelaide in 1945/6. A regular watcher at Sydney in retirement, he never indulged in unjust criticism of the modern player.

First-class career (1939–60): 12,421 runs (32.85) including 18 centuries, 602 wickets (27.48), and 264 dismissals (262 c., 2 st.)

Test matches (14): 459 runs (35.30) including 1 century, 36 wickets (26.61), and 14 catches

McCORMICK, Ernest Leslie

(b. 1906, Melbourne; d. 1991, Tweed Heads, New South Wales) *Victoria and Australia*

Tall and slim, Ernie McCormick measured out a run of 31 paces. He had real, venomous pace when creaking joints or lumbago left him free to bowl at his top speed, and he brought the ball very awkwardly into the batsman but never mastered away-swing. His approach was unusual in that he carried the ball as he ran without swinging his arms. He toured South Africa in 1935/6, taking 15 wickets (27.86) in the Tests; and in his first Test against England, at Brisbane in 1936/7, he was menacing and hostile in the opening overs—sending back Stan Worthington with the first ball of the match and soon afterwards Walter Hammond for a duck. Then lumbago took charge and never again, except briefly at Lord's in 1938, was he able to bowl with such fire. He was no-balled (for overstepping) 35 times during his first match in England, at Worcester in 1938. An inveterate joker, he told a sympathizer at lunch that day at Worcester, 'It's all right. The umpire is hoarse; he can't call any more!' The English turf did not suit him and it was said in 1938 that he was faster through the air than off the pitch. He batted left-handed and moderately.

First-class career (1929–38): 582 runs (8.68) and 241 wickets (27.74)

Test matches (12): 54 runs (6.00), 36 wickets (29.97), and 8 catches

McCOSKER, Richard Bede

(b. 1946, Inverell, New South Wales) *New South Wales and Australia*

A tall, dark, broad-shouldered opening batsman from the diamond-mining area of Inverell in northern New South Wales, Rick McCosker came to Sydney to take a job in a bank and advance his cricket career. He was a player with a solid defence, considerable powers of concentration and unerring ability to hit away any ball straying towards the leg-side. After a long struggle to get into the state side, he made four centuries in four successive Shield matches and two fifties against MCC, to earn a Test cap at the age of 28 in the fourth game at Sydney in 1974/5 when Australia regained the Ashes. Opening the batting (having gone in first wicket down for New South Wales) he made a solid 80 in his first Test innings and 202 runs (40.40) in five innings overall. Thereafter he was a regular member of the Australian side until he left to join World Series Cricket. Perhaps troubled by the unsettling nature of the controversy, and by memories of breaking his jaw when missing a hook at Bob Willis during the Centenary Test (coming back with his jaw wired up he made some courageous runs late in Australia's second innings which helped to decide the game), he was disappointing in England in 1977, apart from a fine innings of 107 at Trent Bridge. But in 1975 he had topped the Test averages with 414 runs in four matches (82.80) and he hit four centuries on the tour, scoring 1,078 runs at 59.88. A quiet and modest character, clean-shaven and short-haired, he stood out in an Australian side which tended to be hirsute and extrovert. After two years with World Series Cricket Rick McCosker returned to captain New South Wales and play in three more Tests in 1979/80, two against England and one against the West Indies. He retired from first-class cricket in 1984, having scored 723 runs in his final season, as ever, a difficult man to dislodge, seldom pretty but highly effective.

First-class career (1973–83): 8,983 runs (44.03) including 27 centuries, and 144 catches
Test matches (25): 1,622 runs (39.56) including 4 centuries, and 21 catches

McCURDY, Rodney John

(b. 1959, Melbourne) *Derbyshire, Victoria, Tasmania, South Australia, Eastern Province, Natal, and Border*

A true cricketing journeyman, the barrel-chested, Victorian-born, right-arm fast bowler Rod McCurdy was an often stormy figure whose appearances with the Australian rebel teams to South Africa from 1985 to 1987 cancelled his chance of playing Test cricket. Starting at one-day level in 1984/5, he took 12 wickets at 31.25 in eleven matches. With South Australia, his third cricketing state, he took 38 wickets in nine games in 1984/5, including 7 for 55 against New South Wales in the opening match in Adelaide. He suffered from acute no-ball problems for much of his career, but at his top was very sharp and a tough competitor. A hard-hitting right-hand lower-order batsman, always on the lookout for quick runs, his contributions were invariably entertaining. In his two international seasons in South Africa, he took 20 wickets in five unofficial Test matches, including 6 for 67 at Wanderers on Christmas Eve, 1986. He settled in South Africa after the tours and took 5 wickets in Eastern Province's historic Castle Currie Cup victory in

1988/9. Later he also represented Natal and Border.

First-class career (1979–94): 725 runs (10.21), 305 wickets (29.85), and 25 catches

McDERMOTT, Craig John

(b. 1965, Ipswich, Queensland) *Queensland and Australia*

Craig McDermott, a stern, fit, red-haired, right-arm fast bowler and hard-hitting, right-handed lower-order batsman, had an incredible start to his Test career. By the end of his very successful England tour (1985), at the age of 20, he had already taken 40 wickets in eight Test matches. A six-footer with broad shoulders and powerful physique, he could bowl with exceptional pace and hostility, charging in like a bull from a long run-up, and soon learned both accuracy and change-of-pace. He toured England with the Australian under-19 side in 1983, already with quite a reputation from junior cricket in Australia. He suffered a serious muscle injury in the first representative game and took no further part in the tour but recovered quickly and worked hard on his fitness under the direction of Dennis Lillee. He made his first-class début in the 1983/4 season, forming a new-ball partnership with Jeff Thomson. In the 1984/5 season, having taken 25 wickets (20.24) in six state matches, he was thrust into the Test side at the age of 19—a veteran of only 14 first-class matches. He took 10 wickets in two Tests, troubling the West Indian batsmen with his fiery pace even on the slow Sydney wicket. Following that fine start in Test cricket, he toured England in 1985 and proved the fastest and most destructive Australian bowler. He achieved 30 wickets including 6 for 70 at Lord's and 8 for 141 at Old Trafford, though he had some problems—with his run-up at Trent Bridge and the England batsmen at Edgbaston. In the 1985/6 Australian season his inexperience caught up with him and he took only six wickets in four Tests against New Zealand and India. He was omitted from the final Test against India, and on the end-of-season tour of New Zealand took only three wickets in two Tests. More disappointment followed when on a tour of India early in 1986/7 he failed to take a wicket in two Tests. He played only one Test against England in the subsequent Ashes series, but was an immediate success when recalled to the Test team in 1990/1 for the last two Tests against England, taking 5 for 97 at Adelaide and 8 for 97 at Perth (11 for 157 in the match). He played a major part in the following series against the West Indies and then devastated the Indians in 1991/2, with 31 wickets at 12.83 in five Tests, 21 in the one-day internationals and 60 in all first-class games. Having agreed to play for Yorkshire in 1992, he had to withdraw to have an operation and early on Australia's 1993 tour of England he again found himself in hospital for a serious intestinal operation on the eve of the second Test at Lord's. It was just another setback to be overcome by this fiery Queenslander and with 32 wickets at 21 he was again the leading fast bowler in the 1994/5 Ashes series.

First-class career (1983–): 2,629 runs (16.74), 596 wickets (27.82), and 41 catches

Test matches (58): 897 runs (12.45), 270 wickets (28.50), and 15 catches

McDONALD, Colin Campbell

(b. 1928, Melbourne) *Victoria and Australia*

A fighter, but a true 'sport', Colin McDonald was a most able right-handed opening batsman. Despite a short backlift he was strong off the back foot, and a shrewd judge of when to play a shot to the swinging ball. He was a regular choice for his country from 1951 until 1961. He toured England in 1953, 1956, and 1961, South Africa, the West Indies, India, and Pakistan; and he appeared in five series at home, two against England. He had a poor first tour of England, but averaged 34.34 and 48.05 respectively in all first-class matches on his second and third tours. Indeed he developed into a scourge of England. His opening stand of 137 with Jim Burke in the 1956 Lord's Test set Australia on the way to victory and he alone threatened to prevent Jim Laker from performing his miracle at Old Trafford, when he scored 32 out of 84 and 89 out of 205. He was ahead of everyone else with 519 runs (64.87) in 1958/9, including 170 in the fourth Test at Adelaide, his Test-highest. He had another highly successful series against South Africa in 1952/3, when he made 437 runs (48.55), including 154, again in the fourth Test at Adelaide. His final home series, against West Indies in 1960/61, saw him bearing the brunt of Wesley Hall's speed with great courage. His 91 in the fifth match was valuable in deciding the rubber for Australia. He captained his state from 1958 until 1963 and in 49 Sheffield Shield matches made 3,237 runs (45.59), including his career-highest of 229 against South Australia at Adelaide in 1953/4. In 15 Tests against England alone he made 1,043 runs (38.62). After retiring he worked for some time in north Queensland, before taking a senior job with the Australian Lawn Tennis Association.

First-class career (1947–62): 11,375 runs (40.48) including 24 centuries

Test matches (47): 3,107 runs (39.32) including 5 centuries, 0–3, and 14 catches

McDONALD, Edgar Arthur

(b. 1891, Tasmania; d. 1937, Lancashire) *Tasmania, Victoria, Lancashire, and Australia*

A natural athlete, tall, strongly but not heavily built, 'Ted' McDonald ran some 16 yards easily to the crease, and with his rhythmical action, accurate length, exceptional pace, and ability to move the ball either way was one of a dominating pair of fast bowlers, the other being Jack Gregory, who proved altogether too good for England in 1921. After taking 8 for 42 for Victoria against New South Wales at Sydney in 1918/19, in conditions favourable to the bat, McDonald took only six very expensive wickets in the 1920/1 series; but, in the following summer, 'Gregory and McDonald' were the bane of practically all England's batsmen. In the first Test at Trent Bridge he had a match record of 8 for 74, and at Lord's and Headingley his early break-throughs led to decisive victories. He took 27 wickets (24.74) in the series, and in South Africa in 1921/2 collected ten wickets from three Tests. But, in accepting a professional post with Nelson in Lancashire, he deserted Australian cricket and qualified for Lancashire, spearheading the attack with great aplomb when the county was Champion in 1926, 1927, 1928, and 1930. In eight seasons (1924–31) he collected 1,040 wickets for Lancashire, also representing Players against Gentlemen. He took 205 wickets (18.67) in 1925, and 190 wickets (19.75) in 1928. Usually of small account as a batsman, he made a century in a hundred minutes against Middlesex at Old Trafford in 1926. A calm, detached cricketer of few words, he would often merely go through the motions of bowling fast against modest opposition but when a class player such as Hobbs or Bradman was at the other end he would suddenly produce a spell of bowling as fast as anything seen before or since. He was killed in the aftermath of a car accident: having accidentally crashed his car, he staggered into the road waving for traffic to stop and was run down by another car.

First-class career (1909–35): 2,663 runs (10.44) including 1 century, 1,395 wickets (20.76), and 98 catches

Test matches (11): 116 runs (16.57), 43 wickets (33.27), and 3 catches

McDONNELL, Percy Stanislaus

(b. 1858, Kennington, London; d. 1896, Brisbane)
Victoria, New South Wales, Queensland, and Australia

The only captain of Australia who was also a Greek scholar, 'Percy Greatheart' McDonnell was an attacking right-handed batsman with a strong defence. With a keen eye and remarkable footwork he was regarded as an even better batsman on bad wickets than on good. Contemporary critics considered that his sterling performances on wickets ruined by rain had never been equalled. He toured England in 1880, 1882, 1884, and finally as captain in 1888. Between 1881 and 1887 he represented his country fairly regularly at home when his medical studies allowed. When he was captain—1886/7, 1887/8, and 1888—England's cricket was in the ascendent, but McDonnell's fearless hitting frequently turned the tide; his greatest achievement being an innings of 82 with which he won the game against North of England at Old Trafford in 1888. His 147 in a low-scoring game against England in the third Test at Sydney in 1881/2 earned a six-wicket victory. In successive Tests in 1884 he hit 103 at The Oval and 124 and 83 at Adelaide in the first Test of the next series. His Test averages were quite prodigious for those years. He made 302 runs (50.33) in 1881/2, 230 runs (57.50) in 1884/5, and in England in 1884 he averaged 39.75. His career-highest score was 239 for New South Wales against Victoria at Melbourne in 1886/7.

First-class career (1877–95): 6,474 runs (23.54) including 7 centuries, and 98 catches
Test matches (19): 955 runs (28.93) including 3 centuries, 0–53, and 6 catches

McELHONE, William Percy

(b. 1870, Sydney; d. 1932, Sydney)

One of the founders of the Australian Board of Control in 1905, its first secretary and a strong-minded cricketing personality, Billy McElhone was Board chairman in 1911/12 when the famous revolt by six star players occurred. A solicitor by profession and a fearless communicator, he was also president of the New South Wales Cricket Association for 12 years from 1921 to 1931, having first served as a club delegate in 1893. Educated at St Aloysius College, McElhone was given key administrative responsibilities earlier than most after playing a leading role in the Association, successfully winning its right to the Sydney Cricket Ground in 1904 after a dispute with the SCG Trust. He was Lord Mayor of Sydney in 1922.

McGILVRAY, Alan David

(b. 1909, Paddington, Sydney) *New South Wales*

Australia's best-known cricket commentator, Alan McGilvray had 50 distinguished years with the Australian Broadcasting Commission, covering over 100 Test matches in Australia and overseas. Educated at Sydney Grammar, he was a left-hand batsman and right-arm fast-medium bowler who captained New South Wales before being forced to choose between cricket and his commentaries because officials objected to his broadcasting on matches in which he was involved. His love of good sportsmanship and the ethics of the game were always prominent in his commentaries, many Australians first developing a love of the game through McGilvray's incisive and vivid imagery. In 1974 he was awarded an MBE and in 1980, an AM. In 1985 he received the Advance Australia award for his outstanding contributions to sports broadcasting. Earlier that year, when 74-year-old McGilvray made his farewell Test match broadcast from the Sydney Cricket Ground, Prime Minister Bob Hawke made a moving speech of appreciation. McGilvray remained close to cricket via the publication of three books, including his best-selling, *The Game Is Not The Same.*

First-class career (1933–6): 684 runs (24.42), 20 wickets (56.75), and 20 catches

McGRATH, Glenn Donald

(b. 1970, Dubbo, New South Wales) *New South Wales and Australia*

A 6 ft. 5 in. fast bowler, Glenn McGrath first played for Australia after just seven matches with New South Wales. The son of a Narromine sheep and wheat farmer, McGrath was originally spotted by the legendary Doug Walters while playing for Dubbo against Parkes in a western New South Wales representative match. He had preferred tennis and basketball before being invited to Sydney to play at grade level. The first Test player to be chosen while still at the Australian Cricket Academy, McGrath, a right-arm fast bowler and right-hand number eleven batsman, benefited from expert tuition from Dennis Lillee, straightening his line and developing a potent out-swinger. His fairy-tale début with New South Wales, where he took 25 wickets in the final six matches of the 1992/3 season, included 4 for 64 and 3 for 28 against Queensland in the Shield play-off. The highlight of his first international season, which included his participation at both

Test and one-day international level, was his dismissal of the South Africans Hansie Cronje (bowled) and Jonty Rhodes (lbw) on the opening day of the second Test in Cape Town in 1994. He took 3 for 65 and 1 for 26 as Australia squared the series after an opening loss in Johannesburg. He won a place on the 1994 tour of Pakistan and Sri Lanka and in early 1995 took 17 wickets in 4 Tests in the West Indies.

First-class career (1992–): 38 runs (4.22), 62 wickets (26.38), and 2 catches

Test matches (13): 22 runs (2.00) and 42 wickets (31.59)

McILWRAITH, John

(b. 1857, Melbourne; d. 1938, Melbourne) *Victoria and Australia*

A hard-hitting right-handed batsman, John McIlwraith toured England in 1886 when he averaged only 15 and in his sole Test, the third at The Oval, scored 2 and 7 and held 1 catch. He had made 133 on his début in first-class cricket, for Victoria against New South Wales at Melbourne in 1885/6.

First-class career (1884–9): 1,468 runs (24.06) including 2 centuries

McINTYRE, Peter Edward

(b. 1966, Gisborne, Victoria) *Victoria, South Australia, and Australia*

A dark-haired, stocky, cheerful leg-spin and googly bowler, Peter McIntyre had the misfortune to be a contemporary of Shane Warne, the most talented wrist-spinner for 30 years. His path to a place in the Victorian side was blocked by Warne, although they played together on an Australian Under 25 tour of Zimbabwe with more-or-less equal success and Warne was still in the side when McIntyre, after several successful seasons at Adelaide, made his Test début on his adopted home ground against England in 1994/5. He took 2 for 87 in this his sole Test to date but was out for nought in both innings to England's matchwinner, Devon Malcolm.

First-class career (1988–): 151 runs (7.19), 81 wickets (48.35), and 14 catches

MACKAY, James Rainey Munro

(b. 1880, Kentucky, New South Wales; d. 1953, Walcha, New South Wales) *New South Wales and Transvaal*

One of the finest colonial batsmen of the Golden Age—cruelly robbed of his opportunity of play-

ing Test cricket—'Sunny Jim' Mackay was hailed as a successor to the great Victor Trumper before suffering a near fatal car accident which badly affected his sight. The legendary Clem Hill said Mackay 'was undoubtedly the best player that Australia produced who never reached a Test match. He was a batsman after the Trumper type and it is just possible that if he had gone home with the Australian Eleven and toured England he might have proved in time as marvellous as the illustrious Victor.' Born in country New South Wales of Scottish stock, the 6 ft. 2 in. Mackay was a powerful right-hand batsman who created a dazzling set of country records before thrilling Sydney grade crowds with his superlative batting. Uncoached, but with a superb eye, in his final country season before shifting from Uralla to Sydney, Mackay batted five times and scored 104 not out, 128 not out, 108 not out, 200 not out, and 65 not out! In 1905/6, having narrowly missed a place in Australia's touring team to England, Mackay amassed 902 runs at an average of 112.75 in eight completed innings, including 203 for New South Wales against Queensland, the highest of his six first-class centuries and 136 against the 1905 Australian XI. Migrating to South Africa, he represented Transvaal in 1906/7 before his accident, when he was struck from behind by a motor cycle travelling at about 40 m.p.h. For several days he was unconscious and near death in a hospital in Johannesburg. His eyesight was badly impaired. He returned to Australia and played only occasionally, but remained an enthusiastic coach of Juniors, retaining his renowned sunny temperament. His catchphrase to young batsmen was: 'If you leave your crease to meet the ball, make sure you hit it hard.'

First-class career (1902–6): 1,556 runs (50.19) including 6 centuries, and 5 catches

MACKAY, Kenneth Donald

(b. 1925, Brisbane; d. 1982, Point Loouart, Stradbroke) *Queensland and Australia*

A left-hander of infinite patience and solid skill despite an ungainly style, 'Slasher' Mackay was for a decade the most difficult batsman in Australia to dismiss. He was at his best and most frustrating when Australia were in trouble. He was also a useful right-arm medium-pace bowler with a strange, almost furtive approach to the wicket. He was one of the earliest and most vigorous of gum-chewers. While at school, he had shown outstanding promise, in one match scoring 364 not out and taking 10 wickets. His career-highest score, 223 for his state against Victoria at Brisbane in 1953/4, took him 9 hours and 45 minutes; and his next innings was an almost equally patient 198 against Western Australia on the same ground. He toured England in 1956 and 1961 and South Africa, India and Pakistan; and at home played in the series against England in 1958/9 and 1962/3, and against the West Indies in 1960/1. He took 6 for 42 against Pakistan at Dacca in 1959/60 and, although he never scored a Test century, made 13 Test fifties. He was very good at the 'bits and pieces'. On the first visit in 1956 he could make little of Jim Laker—but fought well and headed the averages for the whole tour, 52.52 for 1,103 runs. Resisting valiantly in the Test at Lord's which Australia won, he took 264 minutes over his 35, and he saved Australia with another long innings against the West Indies at Adelaide in 1961. In 100 Sheffield Shield matches he made 6,341 runs (45.29) and took 122 wickets (37.54). He was awarded an MBE for services to cricket.

First-class career (1946–63): 10,823 runs (43.64) including 23 centuries, and 251 wickets (33.31)
Test matches (37): 1,507 runs (33.48), 50 wickets (34.42), and 16 catches

McKENZIE, Colin

(b. 1880, Trawool, Victoria; d. 1930, Avenel, Victoria) *Victoria*

Colin McKenzie was Australia's 12th man at Melbourne after just five first-class matches for Victoria in his first season, the Australian selectors naming local players as 12th man for each of the final three Tests. A right-hand opening or number three batsman, he had a first-class double century to his credit, scoring 211 for Victoria against Western Australia in Perth in 1909/10. His partnership of 358 in 227 minutes with H. H. L. Kortlang was, at the time, a record for any wicket outside England. In 1913/14 he toured New Zealand with Sir Arthur Sims's Australian side.

First-class career (1907–13): 1,385 runs (31.47) including 2 centuries, 27 wickets (30.55), and 18 catches

McKENZIE, Graham Douglas

(b. 1941, Perth) *Western Australia, Transvaal, Leicestershire, and Australia*

Truly a 'gentle giant', Graham or 'Garth' McKenzie was a Rolls-Royce amongst modern fast bowlers—smooth and classy. He was a modest but often useful right-hand batsman and a safe and athletic fielder in the deep. About 6 ft. tall and of superb physique—he was nicknamed after the sizeable comic strip character—he had an economical run-up that seemed all muscular ease and a classic final stretch in his sideways-on delivery. He swung the ball late, away from the right-hander and he was often at his best on good wickets where he was able to combine genuine fast bowling with a deceptive change of pace. He 'hit the deck' hard and the lift off the pitch was often too much for the best batsmen. Geoff Boycott had his forearm broken by his bowling, and the West Indian Jackie Hendriks had to be taken to hospital for brain surgery after being struck by one of his deliveries. But they were accidents; he was a gentleman on and off the field who never abused his strength and speed. He toured England in 1961, 1964, and 1968, South Africa twice, India twice, and the West Indies and Pakistan once each. Between 1962 and 1971 he appeared in seven series at home, including three against England. He also toured India, South Africa, and Rhodesia with the International Cavaliers. At 23 he became the youngest Australian bowler ever to take 100 wickets in Tests and in the shortest time—three years 165 days. He was also the youngest to reach 150 wickets (against South Africa in 1966/7) and, at 27, the youngest to take 200 wickets (against the West Indies in 1968/9). His number of wickets in Tests was only two short of the record held by Richie Benaud and these he would surely have obtained if he had not been dropped for the last two Tests against India in 1967/8. He had taken 10 for 151 in the third Test at Melbourne and was then rested because Australia's selectors wanted to give others a chance. McKenzie had many memorable performances. He took 7 for 153 out of an England total of 611 at Old Trafford in 1964. In Australia's victory at Lord's in 1961 he took five wickets in each innings and was at the crease when the last two wickets put on 149, himself making 34 vital runs. It was not his only important innings: in the same series at Old Trafford he put on 98 for the last wicket with Alan Davidson to turn the match; and in the third Test at Sydney against South Africa in 1963/4 he made 76. From 1969 until 1975 he was registered for Leicestershire and in his last season his adopted county won the Championship for the first time. Altogether, he took 465 wickets and scored 1,830 runs for Leicestershire in first-class cricket. In 1979/80 he played for Transvaal in limited-overs matches, having married a South African and settled in Johannesburg.

First-class career (1959–75): 5,662 runs (15.64), 1,219 wickets (26.96), and 201 catches

Test matches (60): 945 runs (12.27), 246 wickets (29.78), and 34 catches

McKIBBIN, Thomas Robert

(b. 1870, Bathurst, New South Wales; d. 1939, Bathurst) *New South Wales and Australia*

A man of frank, happy character and the possessor of a flowing moustache, Tom McKibbin toured England in 1896, and his delivery raised such criticism that it was written 'there can be little doubt that he continually threw when putting on his off-break'; but he played for Australia from 1894 until 1898 and does not appear to have been actually called by the umpire for 'throwing'. Of medium height but powerfully built, he could be legitimately deadly with his right-handed slow to medium bowling when he kept a length. In England he took 101 wickets (14.27), including 11 wickets in the two Tests he played. Against Lancashire at Aigburth, bowling unchanged with Hugh Trumble, he took 13 for 38, Lancashire falling for 28 in the second innings, when his analysis was 7 for 11, including a hat-trick. (Frank Sugg did not attempt to play one that came back a prodigious amount on to the stumps, which he thought was a palpable throw.) In 18 Sheffield Shield matches his tally was 136 wickets (21.02) including 9 for 68 against Queensland in 1894/5.

First-class career (1894–8): 682 runs (10.02) and 320 wickets (19.67)

Test matches (5): 88 runs (14.66), 17 wickets (29.17), and 4 catches

MACKINNON, Donald

(b. 1859, Marida Yallock, Boorcan, Victoria; d. 1932, Melbourne)

President of the Victorian Cricket Association (1906–32), Mackinnon helped steer the Association to financial prosperity after a period of disharmony at the turn of the century. The son of a wealthy western districts pastoralist, a barrister by profession, and educated at Geelong Grammar, Mackinnon was president of Hawksburn–Prahran for 33 years until his death. He had played cricket at Oxford, being described by Victorian cricket historian Robert Coleman as a useful round-arm bowler without ever making the University's 1st XI. Mackinnon had a distin-

guished civil career, being a member of the Victorian Cabinet for 20 years, including five as a minister. He was also the Director-General of Recruiting for Australia in the United States and the Australian Commissioner to the USA.

McLACHLAN, Ian Murray

(b. 1936, Adelaide) *Cambridge University and South Australia*

A tall, fair-headed farmer from South Australia, Ian McLachlan might well have played for Australia had his business, pastoral, and political interests not taken precedence at the stage when he was on the verge of Test selection. He became the leader of Australia's Country party, often a civilizing force in the rough and tumble of Australian politics. The Adelaide-born right-hander was Australia's 12th man in the fourth Ashes Test of 1962/3—a reward for a series of scores which the previous summer had included three centuries in as many games. In a 4-year period for South Australia from 1960/3, he made eight centuries, including a career-best 188 not out against Queensland in Adelaide in 1960/1. At Cambridge University, he won cricket blues in 1957 and 1958. He also toured the West Indies with E. W. Swanton's XI in 1960/1. His brother, Angus, a tall leg-spinner, also represented Cambridge.

First-class career (1956–63): 3,743 runs (31.72) including 9 centuries, 6 wickets (63.66), and 41 catches

McLAREN, John William

(b. 1886, Brisbane; d. 1921, Brisbane) *Queensland and Australia*

A fast bowler, John McLaren toured England with the weakened Australian team of 1912, as replacement for Albert Cotter, but took only 27 wickets and did not appear in any of the Tests. His sole Test appearance was in the fifth match at Sydney against England in 1911/12: he was 0 not out in both innings and took 1 for 70. He died young of diabetes.

First-class career (1906–14): 564 runs (12.53) and 107 wickets (26.74)

MACLEAN, John Alexander

(b. 1946, Brisbane) *Queensland and Australia*

A product of the University of Queensland and a civil engineer, John Maclean was unfortunate to be selected for Australia when he was past his best, and as a wicket-keeper/batsman it was touch-and-go whether he or Rodney Marsh would be chosen in 1970/1. Throughout the 1970s Maclean gave Queensland staunch service, captaining them with enterprise and by fine example in 1972/3 and between 1977 and 1979. Very solidly built, he was a limited but determined right-hand batsman, a particularly good cutter, and a surprisingly agile wicket-keeper. First playing for Queensland in 1968/9 he toured New Zealand with the Australians in 1969/70, playing in three representative games not recognized as Tests. But his Tests were played against a confident and all-conquering England side in 1978/9 and, though he brought off some very good catches, his batting proved vulnerable against the off-spinners.

First-class career (1968–79): 3,888 runs (24.45) including 2 centuries, and 385 dismissals (354 c., 31 st.)

Test matches (4): 79 runs (11.28) and 18 dismissals (18 c.)

MACLEAY, Kenneth Hervey

(b. 1959, Bradford-on-Avon, Wiltshire) *Western Australia and Somerset*

An underrated 6 ft. 4 in. all-rounder, renowned for his contributions on home soil at the WACA ground, English-born Ken Macleay was one of Western Australia's foremost players in the 1980s and played 16 one-day internationals. While he never seriously vied for Test selection, the tall, spindly right-arm swing bowler took 15 wickets at 41.73 and made 139 runs at 12.63 from 1982/3 to 1986/7. His representative highlight came against India during the 1983 World Cup tournament when he took 6 for 39 at Trent Bridge. A right-hand number six or seven batsman, the highest of Macleay's three state centuries was a whirlwind 114 not out against New South Wales in Perth in 1986/7. He dominated a record ninth wicket stand of 168 with Tim Zoehrer, who made 91. His finest first-class bowling for Western Australia was 6 for 93, also against New South Wales, in Perth the previous season. Macleay played exactly 100 first-class matches for Western Australia before finishing his career at county level with Somerset.

First-class career (1981–92): 3,750 runs (26.97) including 3 centuries, 300 wickets (30.26), and 79 catches

McLEOD, Charles Edward

(b. 1869, Port Melbourne; d. 1918, Melbourne) *Victoria and Australia*

A right-handed batsman of the ultra-careful school, strong in defence but undistinguished in style, Charlie McLeod was also a steady, persistent medium-paced bowler. He played for his country with fair regularity from 1894 until 1905. He toured England with the 1899 and 1905 teams, making 545 runs and taking 81 wickets in the former year and 722 runs and 91 wickets in the latter. In the fifth Test at The Oval in 1899 his 31 not out and 77 did much to save the match. Promoted to opening batsman, he put on 116 with Jack Worrell for the first wicket, when Australia had to follow on 224 behind. In the 1897/8 series, when he opened several times, he came second in the batting with 352 runs (58.66), making 112 in 245 minutes in the second Test at Melbourne, very slow by contemporary but not modern standards. In 33 Sheffield Shield matches he made 1,281 runs (23.72) and took 109 wickets (25.08). He was the younger brother of R. W. McLeod.

First-class career (1893–1905): 3,321 runs (21.28) including 2 centuries, and 335 wickets (24.25)

Test matches (17): 573 runs (23.87) including 1 century, 33 wickets (40.15), and 9 catches

McLEOD, Robert William

(b. 1868, Port Melbourne; d. 1907, Melbourne) *Victoria and Australia*

A steady left-handed batsman and right-arm medium-paced bowler who hurried the ball from the pitch, Bob McLeod toured England with the 1893 side but generally did not enhance his reputation, although at Lord's against MCC he took 5 for 29 in the second innings, the premier club saving the game narrowly. On the tour he averaged 17 with the bat and took 47 wickets. One of his experiences is said to be unique: batting for Melbourne against North Melbourne in the competition final, he was run out in each innings without having a ball bowled to him. His Test cricket was confined to the 1891/2 and 1893 series. In his first Test at Melbourne he took 5 for 55 in the first innings, but achieved little subsequently. He had real ability but, according to some contemporary writers, lacked enthusiasm.

First-class career (1889–99): 1,701 runs (22.38) including 1 century, and 141 wickets (22.73)

Test matches (6): 146 runs (13.27), 12 wickets (31.83), and 3 catches

McMAHON, Norman

(b. 1922, Helidon, Queensland; d. 1991, Springhill, Queensland)

One of the longest-serving Queensland cricket administrators, 'Norm' McMahon was chairman of the Queensland Cricket Association and a forthright delegate to the Australian Cricket Board from 1967 to 1987. He was treasurer on Australia's 1977 tour of England and foundation treasurer of the Queensland Cricketers' Club in 1959.

McSHANE, Patrick George

(b. 1857, Melbourne; d. 1903, Melbourne) *Victoria and Australia*

A contemporary described McShane as 'a very fine left-hand bowler, with great command over the ball, a splendid batsman who had made some fine scores; and a good field'. He achieved some good performances in interstate matches but never came to England; his short Test career was spread over the 1884/5, 1886/7, and 1887/8 series. Indeed, he umpired the fourth Test in 1884/5 and played in the fifth. While curator (groundsman) to St Kilda CC in Melbourne, he became mentally afflicted and had to receive treatment at an asylum, where he died at the age of 46.

First-class career (1880–92): 1,117 runs (18.31) and 72 wickets (25.37)

Test matches (3): 26 runs (5.20), 1–48, and 2 catches

MADDOCKS, Leonard Victor

(b. 1926, Melbourne) *Victoria, Tasmania, and Australia*

Eventually influential on the Australian Cricket Board, Len Maddocks was a very competent wicket-keeper, the best second-string for Australia of his time, and a very useful right-handed batsman. Always a cheerful cricketer, he had the size and appearance of a racehorse jockey. In his first Test innings against England, in the third Test at Melbourne in 1954/5, he top-scored with 47 against Brian Statham and Frank Tyson, enabling his country to take an unexpected first innings lead, and in the next Test at Adelaide he again top-scored with 69, by robust methods and good running adding 92 in 95 minutes with his captain Ian Johnson for the ninth wicket. He toured England (in 1956), the West Indies and India without gaining a regular Test place. He

toured South Africa with the International Cavaliers. He had the thankless task of managing the team to England in 1977, when he discovered early in the tour that most of his team had secretly signed contracts with Kerry Packer. It was thereafter an unhappy and unsuccessful tour but Maddocks kept smiling and did his best to maintain a united front. Both his brother (R.I.) and his son (I.L.) also played cricket for Victoria.

First-class career (1946–67): 4,106 runs (32.84) including 6 centuries, and 277 dismissals (209 c., 68 st.)

Test matches (7): 177 runs (17.70) and 19 dismissals (18 c., 1 st.)

MAGUIRE, John Norman

(b. 1956, Murwillumbah, New South Wales) *Queensland, Leicestershire, Eastern Province, and Australia*

John Maguire, a tall, fit right-arm fast-medium bowler, played three Tests for Australia during the 1983/4 season. Although he took 46 wickets in the following season his selection to tour England in 1985 was withdrawn and decided to join the rebel tour to South Africa. He made his début for his state in the 1977/8 season but only gained a regular place in 1981/2. The next season brought him 28 first-class wickets and a place in the one-day side. He toured Sri Lanka in April 1983 but did not play in the Test. He played in one Test against Pakistan, taking 3 for 111 at Melbourne. On the tour to the West Indies he was his country's leading wicket-taker with 26 wickets, average 24.80. He took seven wickets in the two Tests in which he played; 4 for 57 was his best performance. He played two seasons for Eastern Province (1989–91) and for Leicestershire in 1991, taking 77 wickets at 31.64.

First-class career (1977–91): 1,162 runs (10.96) and 463 wickets (27.78)

Test matches (3): 28 runs (7.00), 10 wickets (32.30), and 2 catches.

MAILEY, Arthur Alfred

(b. 1886, Sydney; d. 1967, Sydney) *New South Wales and Australia*

Although of slight physique, Arthur Mailey was a man of many talents and one of the great right-arm leg-break and googly bowlers. He sometimes paid the penalty for poor length, but he had abnormally strong fingers which enabled him to impart tremendous spin. He gave the ball a generous amount of air, cheerfully prepared to 'buy' his wickets. He toured England in 1921 and 1926, and South Africa in 1921/2. At home he played against England in the 1920/1 and 1924/5 series. In his first series of 1920/1 he took 36 wickets (26.27) which remained the largest-ever for an Australian until exceeded by Rodney Hogg in 1978/9. In the fourth match at Melbourne he captured 9 for 121 in the second innings (13 for 236 in the match). In 1924/5 he again had a large, though expensive, haul of 24 wickets (41.62). In England he took 134 first-class wickets (19.36) and 126 wickets (19.34) respectively on his two tours. Outside the Tests his most noteworthy achievement was 10 for 66 in the Gloucestershire second innings at Cheltenham in 1921 which inspired the title of his autobiography *Ten for 66 and All That*, written 37 years later. He also took 9 for 86 in an innings against Lancashire at Aigburth in 1926. Starting his working life as a labourer, Arthur was a wit, philosopher, very clever cartoonist, painter (in oils), and journalist. He frequently revisited England and South Africa and was one of the best-loved of cricketers. In 37 Sheffield Shield matches he took 180 wickets (32.56).

First-class career (1912–30): 1,529 runs (12.33), 779 wickets (24.09), and 157 catches

Test matches (21): 222 runs (11.10), 99 wickets (33.91), and 14 catches

MALLETT, Ashley Alexander

(b. 1945, Sydney) *South Australia and Australia*

Known as 'Rowdy' because he usually kept his thoughts to himself—although he is now a successful journalist—Ashley Mallett was the best Australian off-spinner of his generation, judged by his success on different types of pitches in different countries—although on three tours of England his tallies were modest. Tall and sinewy, with thin rather strained-looking features, he was a limited right-hand batsman, often difficult to remove, and a fine close fielder, who held 95 catches in first-class cricket including some unbelievable ones in the gully against England in 1974/5. He toured England in 1968, 1972, and 1975 and India and South Africa in 1969/70, taking 28 wickets in five Tests in India. He bowled with a rather flat trajectory but with excellent control of line and length; he deployed a sharp off-break whenever conditions permitted, often with an awkward bounce, and he had a useful away-drifter. It took him a surprisingly long time to establish himself in the Australian Test side, partly because, when he did play, Bill

Lawry was reluctant to use him in long spells. After a season in the Scottish Western Union in 1967, during which he took 111 wickets for Ayr, he took 32 wickets in eight games in his first season for South Australia in 1967/8, having moved from Western Australia where his boyhood was spent. He played only one Test in 1968, the last at The Oval. But, after an analysis of 13 for 122 against Western Australia in a Shield game at Adelaide in 1971/2, as well as a score of 92 against Western Australia in the season before, he was recalled to the Test side and became virtually a fixture in the successful Ian Chappell side, taking ten wickets against England in 1972, 17 (19.94) in 1974/5 and nine (42.88) in 1975. At Adelaide in 1972/3 he took 8 for 59 against Pakistan. His best Test match analysis came during his highly successful tour of India when he took 10 for 144 at Madras. Although not one of those who joined World Series Cricket, Mallett left the first-class game after the 1976/7 season to work as a journalist in South Australia. But he returned in 1979/80 and took 48 wickets (23.75) for his state, winning back the spinning place in the national team for the last two Tests against the West Indies and England. Against the former he bowled with his old control, taking four significant wickets on a delightful batting pitch at Adelaide, and although he opted out of the subsequent tour of Pakistan he earned a farewell tour of England in 1980 for the Centenary Test in which he played and took a wicket in each innings. It seemed out of character for him, but in 1981 he was banned for life by the Queensland Cricketers' Club for telling blue jokes within the hearing of ladies. He has written biographies of the great Australian players Victor Trumper and Clarrie Grimmett and as both a Journalist and Cricket broadcaster has always been keen to pass on advice to aspiring spin bowlers. Tim May especially benefited from his accumulated wisdom, not least in bowling an attacking line outside the right-hander's off stump.

First-class career (1967–81): 2,326 runs (13.60), 693 wickets (26.27) and 105 catches

Test matches (38): 430 runs (11.62), 132 wickets (29.85) and 30 catches

MALONE, Michael Francis

(b. 1950, Perth) *Western Australia, Lancashire, and Australia*

Though he made a very good living from joining World Series Cricket from 1977 to 1979, 'Mick' Malone did himself a grave disservice by missing two years of Test cricket just as he was breaking through. A dark and strapping, right-arm, medium-fast swing bowler with the strength and will to bowl all day, he emerged in 1975/6 when he took 31 Sheffield Shield wickets at 20.58. Next season he took 40 Sheffield Shield wickets (16.13) for Western Australia and 49 wickets in the season, and he was unlucky not to gain selection for more than one Test in England in 1977, for he often bowled better than Max Walker. In this, his sole Test, he took 5 for 63 in England's first innings at The Oval in a fine demonstration of his stamina, strength and ability to swing the ball late away from the bat. In the match he took six wickets (12.83) and scored 46 runs (46.00). His action was high and classical, and he could hit the ball effectively. After two years of relative obscurity with WSC, he joined Lancashire at the end of 1979, but his success was limited and he left after two seasons. He had one further taste of international cricket in Pakistan in 1979/80, taking 1 for 123 in only two matches on unhelpful pitches. He was also a successful professional in Australian Rules football at full-back.

First-class career (1974–81): 914 runs (16.03) and 260 wickets (24.77)

MANN, Anthony Longford

(b. 1945, Perth) *Western Australia and Australia*

A fair-haired all-rounder, slow right-arm leg-break bowler, vigorous left-hand bat, and fine fielder, Tony Mann hit an electrifying hundred in his second Test match at Perth against India in 1977/8. Coming in as night-watchman at number three, he hit 105 and helped win a thrilling game by two wickets. But his leg-breaks were ineffective against Indian batsmen used to slow bowling of greater subtlety and he had lost his place by the end of the series. He was a key man in several Western Australian triumphs in the Sheffield Shield.

First-class career (1963–83): 2,544 runs (24.22) including 2 centuries, and 200 wickets (34.54)
Test matches (4): 189 runs (23.62) including 1 century, 4 wickets (79.00), and 2 catches

MARR, Alfred Percy

(b. 1862, Sydney; d. 1940, Sydney) *New South Wales and Australia*

A useful batsman and right-arm, medium-pace bowler, Alfred Marr was one of the 'might have beens': chosen three times to come to England, he was never able to do so. When New South

Wales were defeated unexpectedly by Queensland in 1884, he took 8 for 28 unavailingly in the second innings. In his sole Test, the second at Melbourne in 1884/5, he scored 0 and 5 and took 0 for 14. He remained so fit that at 67 he hit 101 in a Sydney grade competition match.

First-class career (1882–90): 304 runs (11.26) and 14 wickets (32.42)

MARSH, Geoffrey Robert

(b. 1958, Armadale, Western Australia) *Western Australia and Australia*

A farmer's boy from the tiny West Australian outpost of Wandering, Geoff 'Swampy' Marsh, no relation of the wicket-keeper, Rod, was the best type of Australian cricketer, brave, determined, fit, and loyal, never giving an opponent an inch but never stooping to anything dishonourable or tacky. An opening batsman whose staple shots were the square-cut and leg-glance, he was sturdily built and had great powers of concentration. He became vice-captain to Allan Border in the successful era which began for Australia when they won the World Cup in India and Pakistan in 1987/8. Following a successful tour of England in 1977 with the under 19 side, Marsh took time to establish himself, despite making 58 on his début for Western Australia in 1977/8. Hundreds against both Victoria and Queensland in 1985/6 led to his first Test chances against India and in the third Test he contributed 92 to an opening stand of 217 with David Boon, the first of his two regular opening partners. Later that season he made a maiden Test hundred in Auckland and in 1986/7, on his way to 1,200 runs in the Australian season, scored 56 and 110, top score in both innings, as Australia were beaten by England at Brisbane. He had also scored 101 against India in Bombay in his country's previous Test. Technical flaws were exposed by the high-class West Indies bowlers but in England in 1989 he formed another productive opening partnership with Mark Taylor and these two batted unbeaten through the whole of the first day at Trent Bridge for 301, the first pair to do so in England. Their eventual stand of 329 was the highest in Anglo-Australian Tests, Marsh's share being 138. In 1989/90 he made his highest score, 355 not out for Western against South Australia. Such was his commitment that when he was dropped from the Test side to make way for Michael Slater, Allan Border threatened to resign. The faithful Swampy had played alongside Border in 117 one-day internationals.

MARSH

First-class career (1977–93): 11,760 runs (39.46) including 33 centuries, 1 wicket (9.00), and 133 catches
Test matches (50): 2,854 runs (33.18) including 4 centuries, and 38 catches

MARSH, John

(b. 1874, Yugilbar, Clarence River, New South Wales; d. 1916, Orange, New South Wales) *New South Wales*

A right-arm fast bowler noted for his speed and late swing, 'Jack' Marsh played only six times for New South Wales at the turn of the century before becoming a victim of the anti-throwing movement which was then at its peak. According to several of his opponents, Marsh at his best was a bowler of international standard. However, as a full-blood Aboriginal, he was denied normal selection opportunities. The prominent journalist J. C. Davis said Marsh had a unique ability to make the ball do peculiar things in the air. Writing in the *Sydney Referee* he said; 'Jack Marsh would have been one of the world's greatest bowlers if he had been a white man . . . His bowling would have established a fresh standard of hard-wicket excellence and created a new type, differing altogether from anything we have ever known.' In clean-bowling the great Victor Trumper in a trial match at the Sydney Cricket Ground, Marsh's critics claimed that he was a thrower and he was subsequently no-balled regularly, forcing him out of big cricket. In one of his finest performances, however, for a Bathurst XV against the 1903/4 Englishmen, he took 5 for 55, the tourists pronouncing his action perfectly legal and naming him the best bowler they had faced all summer. Despite a six-month Australia-wide circus where he exhibited the art of fast bowling, suggestions that he should be included on the 1905 tour of England were only fleeting. He faded from the public eye and was not heard of again until his tragic death, in a street brawl in Orange in 1916. An inquiry found he had been kicked to death.

First-class career (1900–2): 40 runs (5.00), 34 wickets (21.47), and 2 catches

MARSH, Rodney William

(b. 1947, Armadale, Western Australia) *Western Australia and Australia*

Australia's most durable wicket-keeper became a folk hero, personifying the aggressive spirit of his country's cricket in the hectic and unsettled era which led to, embraced, and succeeded the Packer Revolution of 1977–9. He revealed his quality in his first match for Western Australia, scoring 106 against the West Indies. Burly and tending in his youth to be distinctly podgy, he survived a baptism of fire in his first Test series of 1970/1 to become one of Australia's finest wicket-keeper/batsmen. In that first series the Australian public dubbed him 'Irongloves' because of the amount of times he dropped the ball, but the germs of a great cricketer were evident even then in his agility, aggressive attitude, and rugged strength as a left-hand batsman. He became a regular and vital member of Ian Chappell's successful Australian side, throwing his formidable weight in all directions to take the thunderbolts of Lillee and Thomson, and then coming in at number seven, chewing gum as if he meant to grind it into oblivion, shirt half-open to reveal a hairy chest, to bludgeon often weary bowlers with calculated hitting. An immensely forceful driver, often hitting straight back over the bowler's head, and a ruthless square-cutter of anything short, he could also defend if necessary. Of his three Test hundreds perhaps his best was 110 not out in the Centenary Test in Melbourne. He toured England in 1972, dismissing 45 batsmen and scoring 664 runs (242 in the Tests), also in 1975 (28 dismissals, 464 runs), 1977 (30 dismissals, 477 runs) and 1981 (28 dismissals, 368 runs). It was partly the huge discrepancy between Marsh's earnings as a Test cricketer and those of his brother Graham, a wealthy and successful professional golfer, which persuaded Mr Packer and his associates that cricketers would willingly respond to generous financial offers. Marsh duly joined World Series Cricket then returned to Test cricket, where this indestructible bear of a man continued to be an integral part of the national team. Certainly he remained the outstanding wicket-keeper in Australia although his batting seemed to have lost its assurance and it was not until the eighth match after his return that he scored a fifty. This was in the high-scoring second Test against Pakistan at Faisalabad, when Marsh also bowled ten overs in a match in which only ten wickets fell to the bowlers. Against India at Sydney in 1980/1 he took five catches in the first innings, a record for an Australian wicket-keeper against India. Earlier in the season on his home pitch at Perth he helped to rescue Australia against New Zealand with a fighting 91. Having captained Western Australia for a season, he was replaced by Kim Hughes and became vice-captain to Hughes for the 1981 tour of England. During the momentous Headingley Test of that summer he overtook Alan Knott as the most successful wicket-keeper in Test history. Appropriately enough his 264th victim, Ian Botham, was caught behind off Dennis Lillee, who had accounted for 74 of Marsh's catches. This was the Test in which Marsh and Lillee took bets on an England victory at 500 to one. Australia lost the Test but their two senior players, hard though they tried for their side, won the money. Marsh continued indestructibly through more Test series against Pakistan, West Indies, and New Zealand in 1981/2 and against Pakistan and England in 1982/3, his wicket-keeping still as athletic and effective as ever. Indeed, he took an astonishing 28 catches in the 1982/3 Ashes series, the most-ever dismissals in a Test series. Another 21 catches the following year against Pakistan brought his final total to 355 Test dismissals, a record which should stand for a long time. He took 141 catches and seven stumpings against England. Marsh, along with Lillee and Greg Chappell, made his final appearance in first-class cricket in the 1983/4 Sheffield Shield Final; the three great Australians had also played their last Tests together. After working as a broadcaster—one whose bluntness created headlines (not least when he dubbed most English bowlers 'pie-throwers') he became the director of Australia's Cricket Academy in Adelaide. He was awarded an MBE for services to Australian Cricket.

First-class career (1968–84): 11,067 runs (31.17) including 12 centuries, and 869 dismissals (804 c., 65 st.)

Test matches (96): 3,633 runs (26.51) including 3 centuries, 0–54 and 355 dismissals (343 c., 12 st.)

MARSHAL, Alan

(b. 1883, Warwick, Queensland; d. 1915, Malta) *Queensland and Surrey*

A spectacular 'Golden Age' hitter who also fielded brilliantly and bowled a variety of medium pace and spin, Marshal was best known in England, where he played 98 games with Surrey from 1907 to 1910 after a 4,350-run season with London County, under the captaincy of W. G. Grace, in 1906. During this remarkable year he made fourteen hundreds, including 300 not out against Croydon and 245 against Egypt, both at Crystal Palace. Born in Warwick in the Darling Downs and educated at Brisbane Grammar, the 6 ft. 3 in. Marshal had eleven matches with Queensland, three in 1903/4 and 1904/5 and

eight on his return from England from 1910/11 to 1913/14. Seven of his eight first-class centuries were for Surrey, including two consecutive innings at Worcester. His highest Australian score of 110 in the second innings for an Australian XI against the 1910/11 South Africans came after he had earlier been bowled for a duck by the renowned Springbok googly specialist Bert Vogler. His second fifty took just 31 minutes. During his AIF wartime service, he served at Gallipoli, and died of enteric fever in 1915 at Imtarfa military hospital, Malta, aged 32.

First-class career (1903–13): 5,177 runs (27.98), 119 wickets (22.84), and 114 catches

MARTIN, John Wesley

(b. 1931, Wingham, New South Wales; d. 1992, Burnell Creek, New South Wales) *South Australia, New South Wales, and Australia*

Short, enthusiastic and jaunty, Johnny Martin was an unorthodox left-arm off-break and googly bowler inclined to be somewhat erratic, an aggressive left-handed batsman, and good fielder. His family gathered once a year to form a Burnell Creek XI and he was popular wherever he played. A prolific wicket-taker in Australia, he took 45 wickets (23.64) for his state in Sheffield Shield matches in 1959/60, which was the largest number taken in the competition for ten years. Making his Test début against the West Indies in 1960/1, he scored 55, helping 'Slasher' Mackay add 97 for the ninth wicket in seventy-two minutes; and he also took three wickets in four balls—those of Rohan Kanhai, Gary Sobers, and Frank Worrell—these being his first three wickets in Test cricket. Not selected to tour England in 1961, he instead came over as professional for Colne in the Lancashire League, taking 70 wickets (12.04) and scoring 706 runs (35.30). When he toured England in 1964 he did not make the Test side and, although he represented his country against South Africa and India and Pakistan in the early sixties, he never repeated his initial Test successes. He returned to England to play more league cricket for Wallsend, who organized a testimonial for him after the first of two heart attacks in 1971. He joined only three other bowlers who had taken 200 wickets for New South Wales; and he travelled 470 miles each week-end from his home in the bush to play in Sydney district cricket. In 77 Sheffield Shield matches he made 2,701 runs (27.84) and took 273 wickets (31.92).

First-class career (1956–67): 3,970 runs (23.77) including 1 century, 445 wickets (31.17), and 114 catches

Test matches (8): 214 runs (17.83), 17 wickets (48.94), and 5 catches

MARTYN, Damien Richard

(b. 1971, Darwin, Northern Territory) *Western Australia, Leicestershire, and Australia*

A flashy, authoritative right-hand batsman who first appeared for Western Australia aged 19, and for Australia at 21, Damien Martyn remained one of Australian cricket's finest young talents. His opportunities at international level were limited, however, until the retirement from Test cricket of two middle-order rivals, Dean Jones and Allan Border, at the conclusion of the 1993/4 South African tour. A former Australian youth team captain, Martyn had broken many teenage run records with his appetite for big scores and in 1992/3, when first named for Australia, he underlined his talent with four hundreds in five Sheffield Shield innings, including two centuries against Queensland in Brisbane. His 67 not out in trying circumstances against the West Indies in Melbourne was innovative and at times daring. Several times he used his feet and 'charged' at Curtly Ambrose, trying to upset the impeccable line of the West Indian express. While he failed to play a Test during Australia's 1993 Ashes tour, he still amassed more than 800 runs at an average of 69 and on return to Australia, averaged 50 at first-class level—including his highest first-class score, 197 against New South Wales in Perth—and was included for the Tests against South Africa in Melbourne and Sydney. Few are speedier between the wickets, or possess his all-round ability in the field. Not only is he a fine cover field, he can fill in as a more-than-capable reserve wicket-keeper.

First-class career (1990–): 3,947 runs (52.62) including 12 centuries, 9 wickets (47.22), 34 catches, and 2 stumpings

Test matches (7): 317 runs (28.81) and 1 catch

MASSIE, Hugh Hamon

(b. 1854, Belfast (now Point Fairy), Victoria; d. 1938, Point Piper, New South Wales) *New South Wales and Australia*

Nearly 6 ft. tall, Hugh Massie was a magnificent right-handed forcing batsman, moving forward to the pitch of the ball whenever possible. Making his Test début modestly in 1881/2, he was the last man chosen for the 1882 England tour. In the first match, however, at Oxford he opened the batting and thrashed the University's bowling for 206 in three hours—his only century in first-class cricket—scoring his second hundred while his partners were scratching only 12 runs. Later he won undying fame in the Ashes match at The Oval when he flayed the bowling in the second innings on a slowish pitch. Australia had made but 63 and England 101, when Massie struck 55 out of 66 for the first wicket in about forty-five minutes. This fine piece of attacking cricket won the match for Australia by seven runs. He scored 1,403 runs (24.64) on the tour. At home he appeared in the 1882/3 and 1884/5 series, but his duties as a banker prevented his touring again. He was selected to captain Australia in the third Test at Sydney in 1884/5, after two leaders had failed, but he did no better. In 1895 he played some more first-class cricket in England for MCC and Gentlemen of England.

First-class career (1877–95): 2,485 runs (23.00) including 1 century

Test matches (9): 249 runs (15.56) and 5 catches

MASSIE, Robert Arnold Lockyer

(b. 1947, Perth) *Western Australia and Australia*

Immortal for one amazing performance, Bob Massie was a right-arm medium-fast bowler, who could swing and cut the ball either way. He came like a comet into Test cricket as opening partner for Dennis Lillee. For a while it was believed that Ray Lindwall and Keith Miller would be replaced at last by an established match-winning pair but Massie faded almost as quickly as he had shone. Coming to England in 1972 after taking 6 for 27 in 11 overs for Australia against the Rest of the World at Sydney, he made an astounding Test début at Lord's, taking 8 for 84 and 8 for 53, swinging the ball about in humid conditions as if he had string attached to it. Bowling round the wicket, he mesmerized the English batsmen with the late swerve of the ball, and only Jim Laker and Sydney Barnes have taken more wickets in a Test. It was the performance of his life. He took only seven wickets in the remaining three Tests and eight wickets in two Tests at home the following season against Pakistan. Although he toured the West Indies in 1973 he could not swing the ball in the thin atmosphere, took only 18 wickets in six games, and his Test career was over. He lost his place in his state side in 1973/4. For some reason he could never recapture the magical power of swing. He unwisely tried to compensate by pushing the ball through faster and this made him easier to play. It was rumoured that he used lip-salve to keep the shine on the ball and that Sir Donald Bradman ordered the practice to stop, but Sir Donald has publicly denied the truth of the story. Two years before Massie achieved fame, he had been rejected by Northamptonshire after being offered a trial when playing in the Scottish League. An asthma sufferer, he often commentated on Test cricket for ABC radio, never blowing his own trumpet.

First-class career (1965–75): 385 runs (9.62) and 179 wickets (24.83)

Test matches (6): 78 runs (11.14), 31 wickets (20.87) and 1 catch

MATTHEWS, Christina (née White)

(b. 1959, Melbourne) *Victoria and Australia*

Australia's most capped player, Christina Matthews also has the best wicket-keeping record in women's cricket. It was in the 1990/1 home series against India that Matthews improved on the previous world-best of 37 career dismissals. In three Tests, she claimed the most dismissals in a series—19 (seventeen catches, two stumpings) —including a Test-best 9 (eight catches and a stumping) in the second Test in Adelaide. England's Lisa Nye set the best record in one innings with six catches and two stumpings in the third Test against New Zealand in 1992. In her début series in India in 1984, Matthews, a right-handed bat, was involved in setting an Australian ninth wicket record of 67 with Lyn Fulston in the fourth Test in Bombay. This determined side of her character was also illustrated in 1988 when she moved to New South Wales. Unable to displace the then state wicket-keeper, Cathy Smith, Matthews, also eligible to play for Australian Capital Territory, did just that in order to maintain her place in the Australian side. Later, as the National Development Officer of the Australian Women's Cricket Council, she was at the forefront of the fight to get women's sport better recognition in the media. Her constant encouragement of team-mates and ready good humour makes Matthews an important member of all the sides she played in since making her state début for Victoria in 1983/4. Now playing for New South Wales, Matthews's interstate record stood at 60 catches and 31 stumpings at the end of the 1993/4 season. She was a member of the Australian side that won the World Cup in 1988.

Test matches (19): 177 runs (11.06) and 53 dismissals (43 c., 10 st.)

One-day internationals (44): 139 runs (9.93) and 44 dismissals (31 c., 13 st.)

MATTHEWS, Gregory Richard John

(b. 1959, Newcastle, New South Wales) *New South Wales and Australia*

This often entertaining, eccentric, enigmatic, and hyperactive cricketer developed from a useful 'bits and pieces' player, right-arm off-spinner, brilliant fielder and correct, left-hand bat, into one of Australia's leading and most consistent all-rounders. As an off-spinner he was always accurate but his trajectory was flat: his greatest bowling contributions at international level came in one-day cricket. Despite an unorthodox life-style off the field (he was badly hurt in a brawl late in his career) he always played with intense pride and commitment, delighting crowds, but not opponents, with constant chattering and shameless exhibitionism. He made his début for his state in the 1982/3 season, scoring 343 runs (49.00) and taking 11 wickets. Impressive all-round performances the following season gained him a Test place and he made 75 against Pakistan at Melbourne, sharing a seventh-wicket partnership of 185 with Graham Yallop. He also took four wickets in the match. He went on tour to the West Indies, playing in the Kingston Test, and made one appearance in the series against West Indies in Australia. That season, 1984/5, he scored 674 runs including a maiden hundred and took 23 wickets in his state's Sheffield Shield triumph. He toured England in 1985 and with his punk hairstyle and restless mannerisms made quite an impression, despite playing in only one Test at Old Trafford. In the 1985/6 season he excelled both for his state and Australia, scoring a maiden Test hundred, 115 against New Zealand at Brisbane, having come in at 67 for 5 to share a partnership of 197 with Allan Border. He scored another Test century against India and in the six home Tests, batting at number seven, scored 438 runs at an average of 43.80, before going on to New Zealand where he hit his third Test hundred and also returned 4 for 61, his best Test figures. At Madras in 1986/7 he secured the second tie in Test history by claiming Maninder Singh lbw off the second-to-last ball of a pulsating match, Matthews finishing with 10 wickets in the match. It was again as a batsman that he shone against England in 1990/1; he made a painstaking 128 in the third Test in Sydney and 353 runs in the series at an average of 70. By contrast his seven wickets cost 60 runs each. Returning to the colours in Sri Lanka in 1992/3 his 10 wickets were less expensive (38.10) and his 329 runs in three Tests helped Australia to their first win in a series on the Indian subcontinent for 23 years. He played in two further Tests against the West Indies in the 1992/3 home season, once again revealing staunch qualities at his beloved Sydney, making 79 at number eight. Dropped soon after, he continued to be an all-round force for New South Wales.

First-class career (1982–): 7,570 runs (39.42) including 12 hundreds, 432 wickets (31.50), and 129 catches

Test matches (33): 1,849 runs (41.08) including 4 hundreds, 61 wickets (48.22), and 17 catches

MATTHEWS, Thomas James

(b. 1884, Williamstown, Melbourne, Victoria; d. 1943, Melbourne) *Victoria and Australia*

Pint-sized, his skin tanned by continual exposure to the sun, 'as tough as a piece of jarrah', Jimmy Matthews was an honest-to-goodness, right-arm, leg-break bowler, who was accurate, persistent, and kept the ball well up to the bat, and a right-handed batsman difficult to shift, tough, and without frills. He made his Test début in 1911/12, making 53 in the third match at Adelaide, and toured England in 1912, the year of the Triangular Tournament, earning his place in history by achieving a hat-trick in each South African innings at Old Trafford: a unique feat in Test cricket. He took 85 wickets (19.37) on the tour. In a short career he played in 19 Sheffield Shield matches, making 915 runs (29.51) and taking 38 wickets (38.72). After the First World War he became curator of the Williamstown ground, the home of Victoria cricket.

First-class career (1906–14): 2,149 runs (24.98) and 177 wickets (25.46)

Test matches (8): 153 runs (17.00), 16 wickets (26.18), and 7 catches

MAY, Timothy Brian Alexander

(b. 1962, Adelaide) *South Australia and Australia*

A product of Prince Alfred College—one of Australian cricket's most famous nurseries and responsible for the early development of the three Chappell brothers—Tim May kick-started his career in 1992/3 after it had seemed destined for a premature and unsatisfactory end. Injury-prone for much of his first eight major seasons, May, a right-arm orthodox spinner with a classic upright action, made such a sudden and pronounced improvement that he formed a front-line attack with the leg-spinner Shane Warne in Australia's 4–1 Ashes demolition of England in 1993. Rejuvenated by a more attacking attitude and his development of drift and extra spin, May regained a place at Sheffield Shield level and forced his way back into the national XI, both at Test and one-day international level. His 2 for 41 and a stunning 5 for 9 (from 6.5 overs) against the West Indies in his home town Adelaide in January 1993 heralded his return to the Test arena and reminded of the attacking approach of his mentor, Ashley Mallett. He also made a courageous 42 not out in the classic finish which saw Australia beaten by just one run. So effective did May become, used in tandem with Warne, that the Australian selectors reverted to pre-war Test selection strategies and started regularly to include two spinners in each XI. May took 21 wickets in five Tests and Warne 34 in six in England in 1993. It was commonplace to see them both operating before lunch on the opening day of Tests, a refreshing sight after years of fast bowling domination. In the fifth Test at Birmingham, May produced figures of 5 for 89 from almost 50 overs, despite lingering doubts about an injured hamstring. He gave the ball air, spun it hard, and successfully employed subtle tricks of the trade, bringing into play his side-spinner and an undercutter. He also showed a marked improvement in his fielding, which had been a weakness in his early international appearances. One of his most prized wickets came in his first Test in England, at Lord's, when he had Graeme Hick caught at slip from his 'arm' ball, delivered from round the wicket. He also played all three Texaco Cup one-dayers, highlighting his new status in the side. Following a season for Horsham in the Sussex league, he had previously toured England in 1989, without playing a Test. Knee, hamstring, and recurring injuries to his spinning fingers frustrated his attempts to regain favour and he was even dropped from South Australia's team for the final Shield match of the 1991/2 season, having taken just 17 wickets at more than 70 apiece.

First-class career (1984–): 1,550 runs (15.81) including 1 century, 368 wickets (35.32), and 38 catches

Test matches (24): 225 runs (14.06), 75 wickets (34.74), and 6 catches

MAYNE, Edgar Richard

(b. 1882, Jamestown, S. Australia; d. 1961, Carrum, Victoria) *South Australia, Victoria, and Australia*

A tall and fluent right-handed stroke-maker excelling with the cut and drive, Edgar Mayne needed a fast wicket to display his powers to the full. An opening batsman, he lived for cricket, never shirking his responsibility. He toured England in 1912 and 1921 and South Africa in 1921/2, but only played in four Tests altogether with moderate success. Such was Australia's batting strength in 1921 that, although he averaged 32.64 for the tour, he could not make the Test eleven. He captained both South Australia and Victoria, exceeding 2,300 runs for each state. Making 209, his career-highest, he put on 456 for the first wicket with Bill Ponsford for Victoria against Queensland at Melbourne in 1923/4, which remains the record stand for any Australian wicket in Australia.

First-class career (1906–25): 7,624 runs (32.72) including 14 centuries, and 13 wickets (33.84)
Test matches (4): 64 runs (21.33), 0–1, and 2 catches

MAYNE, Laurence Charles

(b. 1942, Westonia, Western Australia) *Western Australia and Australia*

All through the 1960s the Australian opening attack remained unsettled, and briefly Laurie Mayne was tried as opening partner for Graham McKenzie. A right-arm fast-medium bowler, he toured the West Indies in 1965, and South Africa and India in 1969/70, but he was then eclipsed by Dennis Lillee.

First-class career (1961–70): 667 runs (12.83) and 203 wickets (30.12)
Test matches (6): 76 runs (9.50), 19 wickets (33.05), and 3 catches

MECKIFF, Ian

(b. 1935, Melbourne) *Victoria and Australia*

A controversial left-arm fast bowler with a strong physique, whose casual approach to the crease belied the speed of his delivery, Ian Meckiff toured South Africa in 1957/8, and India and Pakistan in 1959/60 and at home played against England in 1958/9, West Indies in 1960/1, and South Africa in 1963/4. He never toured England—torn tendons in an ankle followed by loss of form caused him to be left out of the 1961 side. It was also believed that his action might not have been passed by English umpires. Certainly there was something unusual about his action and some players and journalists were convinced that he sometimes threw rather than bowled the ball. He took 17 wickets (17.17) in four Tests against England in 1958/9, taking 9 for 107 in the second Test at Melbourne when the suspicions were aired very loudly. This was a disastrous tour for MCC, and Meckiff was not the only bowler accused of an unfair action. Eventually, against South Africa at Brisbane in 1963/4, he was called by umpire Colin Egar for throwing his second, third, fifth, and ninth balls, and he was taken off at the end of this his first over, never to play first-class cricket again.

First-class career (1956–63): 778 runs (11.27) and 269 wickets (23.35)
Test matches (18): 154 runs (11.84), 45 wickets (31.62), and 9 catches

MENZIES, Rt. Hon. Sir Robert Gordon, AK, CH, LLM, QC, FRS, FRCS

(b. 1894, Jeparit, Victoria; d. 1978, Melbourne)

Prime Minister of Australia from 1939 to 1941 and again from 1949 to 1966 Sir Robert was one of cricket's greatest friends. As a cricket lover and keen follower of the game throughout his life, he instituted and hosted the Prime Minister's XI cricket matches in Canberra from 1951/2. It was fitting that his last public appearance was at the Centenary Test in Melbourne in 1977 where he was presented with his Knight of the Order of Australia award by Her Majesty, Queen Elizabeth II. At the time of his death, Sir Robert, 83, was patron of the Victorian Cricket Association—a post he had held for 35 years—and vice-president of the Australian Capital Territory Cricket Association. He had played only occasionally, mainly at primary school at Grenville College in Ballarat, and said he made the 1st XI only because the school's entire enrolment was 35. Despite his lack of ability, the young Menzies developed a deep understanding of the game, revelling in its subtleties and having an unbounded admiration for those who played it well. He had an uncanny ability to be in England around the time of the Lord's Test match. He would be pictured with the teams and delight in the cricket chat. He loved the company of cricketers almost as much as he enjoyed watching them perform. His games were light-hearted affairs, played in a relatively carefree fashion. They have become more serious. In 1962/3 he persuaded Sir Donald Bradman, then aged 54, to play one last game. In

1965/6 he named the 19-year-old Victorian Paul Sheahan in his side. Sheahan, a virtual unknown, made 79 and within two years was playing for Australia. In his first book, *Afternoon Light*, Sir Robert said, 'Cricket, in short, is illustrative of the character of players and onlookers alike. It involves a quiet humour and expresses both patience and endurance.' In *'Measure of the Years'*, he referred to cricket as 'the most delightfully illogical game on earth'. The Victorian Cricket Association honours his memory each four years by playing the Sir Robert Menzies Memorial match between its State XI and the visiting England team. Between 1965, when he was appointed Lord Warden of the Cinque Ports, and 1971, when his health failed, he spent much time in England and was president of Kent CCC in 1968.

MEULEMAN, Kenneth Douglas

(b. 1923, Melbourne) *Victoria, Western Australia, and Australia*

A sound right-handed opening batsman, very unlucky to miss regular international honours, Meuleman toured New Zealand—the first post-Second World War tour—where he played his sole Test, at Wellington in 1946, being bowled for 0 and holding 1 catch. He visited New Zealand again in 1949/50, and India with the Commonwealth team in 1953/4. For Western Australia against the South Africans at Perth in 1952/3 he scored 103, assisting in adding 170 for the third wicket, a record for the state. Later he captained Western Australia. His highest score was 234 not out against South Australia at Perth in 1956/7 and he made 206 for Victoria against Tasmania at Melbourne in 1947/8. He was a prolific scorer in Sheffield Shield games, 70 matches bringing him 4,916 runs (48.19).

First-class career (1945–60): 7,855 runs (47.60) including 22 centuries, and 19 wickets (50.31)

MIDDLETON, Roy Foster

(b. 1889, Adelaide; d. 1975, Adelaide) *South Australia*

A right-hand batsman from East Torrens who played five state games in the final seasons before big cricket was suspended because of the First World War, Middleton served at South Australian Cricket Association committee level for more than 40 years. He was also the SACA's delegate to the Australian Board of Control from 1928 to 1965, including a stint as chairman (1952–5).

First-class career (1912–14): 151 runs (16.77) and 1 catch

MIDWINTER, William Evans

(b. 1851, St Briavels, Gloucestershire; d. 1890, Melbourne) *Gloucestershire, Victoria, Australia, and England*

Born in Gloucestershire, Billy Midwinter is the only cricketer to have played both for and against Australia. He emigrated and became professional at Melbourne. Also an extremely good billiards player, he was known as 'the Bendigo Infant'. A steady right-handed batsman who could hit hard, he was a medium-paced bowler who spun the ball quite considerably and a first-rate outfielder. He appeared in the first-ever Test for Australia at Melbourne, taking 5 for 78 in England's first innings. He commuted between Victoria and Gloucestershire for some years, playing for the county from 1877 until 1882 and for Players against Gentlemen. A member of the first Australian side of 1878, he was virtually kidnapped by W. G. Grace after arriving at Lord's to represent the tourists against Middlesex; the great cricketer took him by cab to The Oval to play for his native county against Surrey, and Billy did not play for the Australians again on the tour! He toured Australia with Alfred Shaw's team in 1881/2, opening the bowling for England with Edmund Peate in two Tests; but he represented Australia again in 1882/3 and 1886/7 and toured England again (without being kidnapped) in 1884. For several years he was a professional on the Lord's ground staff. His ending was tragic: his wife and two children died, he became insane and was confined to an asylum where he died.

First-class career (1874–86): 4,534 runs (19.13) including 3 centuries, 419 wickets (17.41), and 122 catches

Test matches (Australia—8): 174 runs (13.38), 14 wickets (23.78), and 5 catches. (England—4): 95 runs (13.57), 10 wickets (27.20), and 5 catches

MILLER, Keith Ross

(b. 1919, Melbourne) *Victoria, New South Wales, Nottinghamshire, and Australia*

One of the greatest natural all-round cricketers in history, and certainly one of the most popular, Keith Miller was a wartime pilot in Britain, capable of crash-landing at 11 a.m. and joining in a game of cricket at noon. Red-faced and generous, he loves life and still lives it to the full. Matured by playing for the Australian Services side in 1945, he was brilliant in the Victory Tests and scored an unforgettable 185 in 165 minutes at Lord's for a Dominions eleven. He was a right-handed batsman in the grand manner, an especially powerful driver, who could also be a delicate late-cutter, but his success often depended on his mood: he was a somewhat wayward genius. As a natural bowler, his action was a model of co-ordination, classically high. With his height—above 6 ft.—and athlete's physique, he bowled an occasional ball faster than Ray Lindwall, his regular destructive opening partner in international matches. His speed (and the length of his run-up) depended on his state of health, which often had something to do with how he had spent the previous evening. He was at once an aggressive but also a magnificently casual cricketer, a crowd-pleaser whose long black hair would drop over his eyes as he bowled and be sent back into place with a flick of the head. He played in the first Test after the Second World War, against New Zealand at Wellington in 1945/6, and from then until 1956 was an integral part of Australia's side. He toured England in 1948, 1953, and 1956; and South Africa, the West Indies, and Pakistan; and at home appeared in six series, including three against England. In 29 Tests alone against England, he made 1,511 runs (33.57) and took 87 wickets (22.40). In his first Test against the 'ancient enemy' at Brisbane in 1946/7 he scored 79 and took 7 for 60 in the first innings, which remained his best piece of bowling for his country. His first Test hundred was 141 not out in the fourth match at Adelaide, adding a bright 150 for the fifth wicket with Ian Johnson. He finished second in the batting averages to Don Bradman with 384 runs (76.80) and second to Ray Lindwall in the bowling with 16 wickets (20.87). Often unfit to bowl in England in 1948, he had a decisive hand in the victory in the first Test at Trent Bridge, taking seven wickets. In the third match at Sydney in 1950/1 he captured 4 for 37, breaking the back of the early batting, and then slammed 145 not out. He headed the batting in the series with 350 runs (43.75), besides taking 17 wickets (17.70). In the second Test at Lord's in 1953 his 109 was invaluable. In the West Indies in 1955 he came second in the averages with 439 runs (73.16), which included three hundreds, his 147 in the first Test at Kingston, when he added 224 for the third wicket with Neil Harvey, remaining his highest for Australia. He never made runs for the sake of it (when the Australians scored more than 700 in a day against Essex in 1948, Keith was

bored and allowed himself to be dismissed for a duck) but he was always in the game at some point or another as a potential match-winner. Seven times he exceeded 200 in an innings, the highest being 281 not out against Leicestershire at Leicester in 1956. In 52 Sheffield Shield matches he made 3,803 runs (56.76) and took 109 wickets (25.86). He appeared for MCC and Nottinghamshire in 1959, in his sole match for the county making 62 and 102 not out against Cambridge University at Trent Bridge. In collaboration with R. S. Whitington, he wrote several books and became a journalist and commentator. He was awarded the MBE for his services to the game and remains a generous and popular character.

First-class career (1937–59): 14,183 runs (48.90) including 41 centuries, 497 wickets (22.30), and 136 catches

Test matches (55): 2,958 runs (36.97) including 7 centuries, 170 wickets (22.97), and 38 catches

MINNETT, Dr Roy Baldwin

(b. 1888, Sydney; d. 1955, Sydney) *New South Wales and Australia*

One of three brothers who played for the state, Minnett was essentially a right-handed forward player with a fine, free swing of the bat, and a fast-medium bowler with a longish run, his arms revolving like a windmill as he ran in to deliver the ball. He toured England in 1912 but without much success, scoring 722 runs in forty-one innings and taking 40 expensive wickets. He was unfortunate not to have made a hundred in his first Test, against England at Sydney in 1911/12. He often told the story of how Sydney Barnes —'that wily old fox'—enticed him into flashing at one outside the off-stump with his score at 90. In ten Sheffield Shield matches he made 621 runs (44.35), including his career-highest, 216 not out against Victoria at Sydney in 1911/12, and took 26 wickets (19.69).

First-class career (1906–14): 2,142 runs (28.94) including 2 centuries, and 86 wickets (25.02)

Test matches (9): 391 runs (26.06) and 11 wickets (26.36)

MISSON, Francis Michael

(b. 1938, Sydney) *New South Wales and Australia*

A blond, very determined, right-arm fast-medium bowler, useful batsman, and good field, Frank Misson was one of the many fastish bowlers tried fleetingly for Australia in the 1960s. He toured

New Zealand in 1959/60 and, on his Test début in the second match against West Indies at Melbourne in 1960/1, dismissed C. C. Hunte with his second ball. In England in 1961 his chief virtues were stamina and accuracy, and at Lord's he scored 25 not out in a vital last wicket stand of 49.

First-class career (1958–63): 1,052 runs (17.53) 177 wickets (31.13), and 58 catches
Test matches (5): 38 runs (19.00), 16 wickets (38.50), and 6 catches

MOODY, Thomas Masson

(b. 1965, Adelaide) *Western Australia, Warwickshire, Worcestershire, and Australia*

Scorer of the second fastest century in first-class cricket, in terms of time, Tom Moody's second innings 103 not out for Warwickshire against Glamorgan at Swansea in 1990 came in just 26 minutes and included 11 fours and seven sixes. However, the milestone was achieved against so-called 'declaration bowling'—two of Glamorgan's non-bowlers sending down a succession of donkey-drops—and is not considered as important as another Australian, David Hookes's century in 43 minutes (and 34 balls) almost a decade earlier. Moody made seven centuries in 15 first-class innings in an auspicious maiden season of county ranks. The following English season, this time representing Worcestershire, he was the first player to 1,000 Sunday League runs and amassed his highest first-class score, 210, against Warwickshire at Worcester, as well as hitting twin centuries against Nottinghamshire. In 1992, he scored a century before lunch, at Oxford. In 1994 he hit an amazing 180 not out against Surrey in the semi-final of the NatWest Trophy and won the man of the match award in the final as well, scoring 88 not out and returning figures of 12–4–17–1 against Warwickshire at Lord's. Holder of the Australian record for the most runs (30) from a six-ball over (against New South Wales's Adrian Tucker at Sydney in 1990/1), the 6 ft. 7 in. Moody is a right-handed batsman and handy right-arm, in-swing bowler. While he had played just eight Tests—including a century in his second Test appearance, in 1989/90 against Sri Lanka in Brisbane—he had played 34 one-day internationals to the start of the 1994/5 Australian season, including all 18 in 1991/2, when his most notable effort was 87 not out, having been controversially elevated to the number three position in place of Dean Jones, Australia's one-day match-winner. Noted for his thunderous front foot driving and athletic outfielding, Moody once knocked a ball into the top deck of the Lillee–Marsh Stand at the WACA Ground. During another one-day international, he hit another on to the roof of the members' stand at the Gabba in Brisbane. Few have been able to throw the ball as powerfully or over as great a distance. In Scotland, during a break in the 1989 tour of England, Moody created a new world record by throwing the haggis more than 230 ft. When one or two locals grumbled at an outsider beating everyone else, Tom assured them he had Scottish ancestry and reminded them that he had broken the record while wearing a kilt!

First-class career (1985–): 12,128 runs (45.59) including 37 centuries, and 117 wickets (32.97)
Test matches (8): 456 runs (32.57), 2 wickets (73.50), and 9 catches

MORONEY, John

(b. 1917, Sydney) *New South Wales and Australia*

Powerfully built and a fine right-handed opening batsman who tended to carry caution to extremes, Jack Moroney had a curious career in Test cricket. He toured South Africa in 1949/50, scoring 1,487 runs in 31 innings, including six centuries, and 352 runs in the Tests. In the fourth Test at Johannesburg he made 118 and 101 not out, the first time an Australian had achieved the feat against South Africa. However, in the first Test against England at Brisbane in 1950/1, he failed to score in either innings (dismissed by Trevor Bailey each time) and was promptly dropped from the side. Although he continued to be a prolific if laborious run-getter for his state, he appeared in only one further Test, against West Indies in 1951/2, and was again dropped, this time for good. His career-highest score was 217 for A. R. Morris's XI against A. L. Hassett's XI (Test Trial) at Sydney in 1948/9.

First-class career (1945–51): 4,023 runs (52.25) including 12 centuries
Test matches (7): 383 runs (34.81) including 2 centuries

MORRIS, Arthur Robert

(b. 1922, Sydney) *New South Wales and Australia*

A charming and relaxed person, for whom cricket was never a matter of life and death, Arthur Morris scored 148 and 111 on his first-class début for his state against Queensland at Sydney in 1940/1, the first player in any country to score two centuries on his début. He was only 18. After

War service he became Australia's regular opening batsman for a decade. Of medium height and compact build he was an elegant left-hander, at his most brilliant when facing spin, when he would sometimes move yards down the pitch to break up a length. A certain fallibility against the swinging ball around the leg-stump caused some loss of confidence and Alec Bedser exploited the weakness, dismissing him 18 times in Tests. None the less, he scored six hundreds in his first ten Tests against England; and in 24 Tests against England between 1946 and 1955 he made 2,080 runs (50.73), including seven centuries. He toured England in 1948 and 1953, South Africa and the West Indies; and at home had three series against England and one each against India, West Indies, and South Africa. Only Don Bradman scored more runs in the 1946/7 series; Morris made 503 runs (71.85). He scored 155 in the third Test at Melbourne, and 122 and 124 not out in the fourth at Adelaide. He made another century off the 1947/8 Indians and in England in 1948 he had a sequence of 105 and 62 in the second Test at Lord's; 51 and 54 not out in the third at Old Trafford; 6 and a match-winning 182 at Headingley, where Australia scored 404 to win in the fourth innings, and 196 in the fifth at The Oval. In this series he made 696 runs (87.00), far more than anyone else. In South Africa at Port Elizabeth and Johannesburg in 1949/50 he scored further Test centuries. In 1950/1 Alec Bedser dismissed him four times for scores of 25 or less. The fourth dismissal occurred on Morris's 29th birthday and that evening Bedser presented him with a book entitled *Better Cricket* by Lindsay Hassett and Ian Johnson, saying, 'I hope this will help you.' Morris promptly made his highest Test score—206—in the fourth Test at Adelaide! He held his place until his retirement in 1955, and his last major Test innings was 153 in the first Test against England at Brisbane in 1954/5 when he added 202 for the third wicket with Neil Harvey, before Frank Tyson and Brian Statham began to dominate the series. Captain of New South Wales at 25, he led Australia when the regular captain was unable to play through injury, once against West Indies in 1951/2 and once against England in 1954/5. In 37 Sheffield Shield matches he made 3,517 runs (63.94). In all, he made four double-centuries, his career-highest being 290 against Gloucestershire at Bristol in 1948. He was awarded an MBE for services to cricket, became a successful businessman, and was a member and vice-chairman of the Sydney Cricket Ground Trust.

First-class career (1940–63): 12,614 runs (53.67) including 46 centuries, 12 wickets (49.33), and 73 catches
Test matches (46): 3,533 runs (46.48) including 12 centuries, 2 wickets (25.00), and 15 catches

MORRIS, Samuel

(b. 1855, Hobart; d. 1931, Melbourne) *Victoria and Australia*

Born at Hobart of West Indian parents attracted by the gold rush, the lissom and good-humoured Sam Morris remains the only black man to have represented Australia in Tests. In the 1880s the country's cricket was rent by disputes and at times well-known players refused to play for their country, but when Sam Morris appeared in his sole Test, the second at Melbourne in 1884/5, opening the batting and scoring 4 and 10 not out and taking 2 for 73, he was genuinely considered to be 'among the best 22 in Australia'. His right-handed batting was 'first-class, of a taking, wristy kind, scientific, strong on the off'; his medium-paced bowling was generally very accurate; and he fielded with characteristic West Indian zest; at a pinch, too, he could also keep wicket. He played for Victoria for 11 years irregularly and became curator of the St Kilda ground until afflicted by blindness. He learned the game at Daylesford, and the Cricket Association there play annually for 'The Sam Morris Cup'.

First-class career (1881–92): 623 runs (18.32) and 31 wickets (26.09)

MORRISBY, Ronald Orlando George

(b. 1915 Hobart) *Tasmania*

A right-hand specialist batsman from Sandford, Hobart, Morrisby may well have played for Australia had he been born a mainlander. At 20, he was chosen on Frank Tarrant's 1935/6 tour of Ceylon and India, playing with notable cricketers, including 49-year-old Charlie Macartney. Tasmania played only a restricted programme of first-class matches, not winning a place in Sheffield Shield cricket until the late 1970s, yet Morrisby figured in 37 games, 21 as captain, starting as a 16-year-old. He continued to play senior grade cricket in Hobart until he was 47, in all representing three clubs, South Hobart, Clarence, and Kingborough.

First-class career (1931–51): 2,596 runs (32.45) including 3 centuries, and 16 catches

MOSES, Henry

(b. 1858, Windsor, New South Wales; d. 1938, Sydney) *New South Wales and Australia*

The first of a long line of famous left-handed batsmen produced by Australia, 'Harry' Moses had great defensive powers, monumental patience, and exquisite skill in on-side play, notably the leg-glance, but business prevented him from visiting England with an Australian side. He appeared occasionally in Tests during the 1886/7, 1887/8, 1891/2, and 1894/5 series, but he was disappointing. For his State against Victoria at Sydney he hit 297 not out in 1887/8, one of the highest scores ever registered in the country. In the same season he made 58 and 109 against Arthur Shrewsbury's England team. A batsman of special gifts, he was placed next to W. L. Murdoch in ability among the batsmen of his day. He was chairman of the Sydney Cricket Ground Trust for many years.

First-class career (1881–94): 2,898 runs (35.77) including 4 centuries and 1 wicket (52.00)

Test matches (6): 198 runs (19.80) and 1 catch

MOSS, Jeffrey Kenneth

(b. 1947, Melbourne) *Victoria and Australia*

A hard-hitting and uncomplicated left-handed batsman, who stood up straight and kept the blade straight too, Jeff Moss scored 748 runs at 68.00 in 1978/9 when his consistency had much to do with Victoria's winning of the Sheffield Shield. Although overlooked by the selectors while the England bowlers were causing havoc, he was called in for the final Test of the season in March 1979, making 22 and 38 not out against Pakistan in his sole Test, when Australia won by seven wickets at Perth. A fine fielder, Moss toured England for the 1979 Prudential World Cup but was not picked to tour India later that year. In 1981/2 he scored 200 against Western Australia, sharing a record third-wicket stand of 390 with Julien Wiener.

First-class career (1976–82): 3,416 runs (43.79) including 9 centuries

MOULE, William Henry

(b. 1858, Melbourne; d. 1939, Melbourne) *Victoria and Australia*

A member of the 1880 team, Moule was a good right-handed batsman and medium-pace change-bowler. In his sole Test—the first in England, at The Oval—he scored 6 and 34, took 3 for 23 (in a total of 420) and held 1 catch. As the number eleven batsman, he assisted his captain W. L. Murdoch in a last wicket stand of 88 after Australia had followed-on, which saved an innings defeat and made England bat again. A lawyer, he later became a judge.

First-class career (1878–85): 137 runs (11.41) and 5 wickets (21.20)

MOYES, Alban George

(b. 1893, Gladstone, South Australia; d. 1963, Chatswood, New South Wales) *South Australia and Victoria*

One of Australian's most prominent post-war cricket broadcasters, whose excited voice lives on in the archives of the ABC, 'Johnny' Moyes was the author of nine cricket books, including the first definitive history of Australian cricket. He had been a player of uncommon promise, denied his only Australian selection when the scheduled 1913/14 Australian tour of South Africa was cancelled because of the First World War. A school colleague of the future Test player 'Nip' Pellew at St Peter's College in Adelaide, Moyes first represented South Australia while studying at Adelaide University. In his first match, against Western Australia in Adelaide in 1912/13, he made 104 and 38 and was one of thirteen Australians named for only the second ever tour to South Africa. After distinguished wartime service in England and France, and several services matches at Lord's and The Oval, he joined Victoria for two matches in 1919/20 before shifting to Sydney with his newspaper work: there he played only at grade level. In one of his first matches for Gordon at Chatswood Oval in 1921/2, he made 218 in 83 minutes with 7 sixes and 36 fours. Moyes was part of the 1926/7 New South Wales selection panel which named Sir Donald Bradman for his first state matches. His services to sport earned him an MBE.

First-class career (1912–20): 883 runs (29.43) including 1 century, 5 wickets (53.60), and 16 catches

MULLAGH, Johnny

(b. 1841, Mullagh Station, near Harrow, Victoria; d. 1891, Pine Hills Station, Victoria) *Victoria*

The outstanding batsman on the 1868 Aboriginal tour of England, Mullagh (or Unaarrimin, his tribal name) was an intelligent and highly skilled cricketer, particularly sensitive to racial taunts. A right-hand batsman, he scored 1,679 runs, average 22.51 with a highest score of 129, the only century scored by the 14-man touring party during its historic 47-match programme. It was the highpoint of his brush with 'civilization'. Appointed a professional by the Melbourne Cricket Club for a 20-week period in 1869/70, he played only six club games before returning to Harrow in western Victoria. His only intercolonial appearance for Victoria was in 1878/9 against an England XI captained by Lord Harris: he made 4 and 36. So impressive was he in top scoring in Victoria's second innings that a £50 collection was made from the 9,000 spectators in attendance. Unhappy about legislation which restricted most Aboriginals to missionary controlled reserves, Mullagh lived his final years alone in a rabitter's shack. He played cricket until 6 months before his death, aged 50, in 1891. The Edenhope Sports Ground is named in his honour.

First-class career (1878): 40 runs (20.00) and 1 catch

MULLINS, Patrick

(b. 1923, Townsville, Queensland)

Australian cricket's premier private collector of cricket books, magazines, and memorabilia, the Brisbane-based Mullins acquired more than 8,000 cricket books before his collection was purchased by Melbourne Cricket Club in 1990. His library was described by the prominent cricket writer Phil Derriman as 'one of the treasures of the cricket world'. Mullins, a solicitor, wrote several unpublished books, including a paper updating and adding hundreds of items to the *Bibliography of Cricket*, first published in 1977. With Derriman, he co-edited a fascinating Australian cricket anthology, *Bat & Pad*, in 1984.

MURDOCH, William Lloyd

(b. 1854, Sandhurst, Victoria; d. 1911, Melbourne)
New South Wales, Sussex, Australia, and England

Of fine physique, Billy Murdoch, a great friend of W. G. Grace, was the first Australian to rank with England's best batsmen. Although a wicket-keeper—he became as deputy-keeper with the first 1878 side—he was usually played for his batting. Right-handed, he had a good style, plenty of strokes, good eyes and superb footwork, especially on difficult wickets. He made his Test début in the second match at Melbourne in 1876/7, and captained the 1880 Australians in the first Test in England, at The Oval, going in first wicket down

in the second innings and carrying his bat for 153 (exceeding W.G.'s century by one run). Altogether, he led his country in five further campaigns: 1881/2, 1882, 1882/3, 1884, and 1890. In the low-scoring classic Ashes match at The Oval in 1882, his 13 and 29 were invaluable; and in 1884 he became the first batsman to register a double-century in Tests—211 in the third match at The Oval, when he batted eight hours. Old photographs show his contented round face and Charlie Chan moustache. Genial and full of bonhomie, he was genuinely and unaffectedly amusing: the dressing-room was always relaxed while he was there. His 321 for New South Wales against Victoria at Sydney in 1881/2 remained the highest in first-class cricket in Australia for 20 years. Settling in Sussex, he captained the county from 1893 until 1899, hitting 226 against Cambridge University at Hove in 1895. He toured South Africa with W. W. Read's team in 1891/2, keeping wicket for England against South Africa at Cape Town in the sole Test match; thus, he represented both Australia and England. Finally, he appeared for W.G.'s London County Eleven for six seasons until 1904. He died, however, in Australia, suffering a heart attack during a Test between Australia and South Africa.

First-class career (1875–1904): 16,953 runs (26.86) including 19 centuries, 10 wickets (43.00) and 243 dismissals (219 c., 24 st.)
Test matches (Australia—18): 896 runs (32.00) including 2 centuries, and 14 dismissals (13 c., 1 st.). (England—1): 12 runs (12.00) and 1 dismissal (1 st.)

MUSGROVE, Henry Alfred

(b. 1858, Surbiton, Surrey; d. Sydney, 1931)
Victoria and Australia

Harry Musgrove was the tactful, courteous and popular manager of the 1896 Australian team. Though never a distinguished player, he played for Australia as a late replacement in the second Test at Melbourne in 1884/5, when many prominent players refused to take part because they disagreed with the financial terms offered. He scored 4 and 9.

First-class career (1881–96): 99 runs (8.25)

NAGEL, Lisle Ernest

(b. 1905, Bendigo, Victoria; d. 1971, Mornington, Victoria) *Victoria and Australia*

Very tall (6 ft. 6 in.) Lisle Nagel was a right-arm fast-medium swing bowler, who took 8 for

32—with an elastic bandage around his elbow after a mishap with a crank handle—for an Australian XI against MCC (all out 60) at Melbourne in 1932/3. He appeared in the first Test at Sydney, scoring 0 and 21 not out and taking 2 for 110. That was his sole Test. He toured India with Frank Tarrant's side in 1935/6, and established a Melbourne Pennant record in 1939/40 by taking 86 wickets (13.45). His twin brother, Vernon, also played for Victoria. His career was ended by a persistent neck injury.

First-class career (1927–38): 407 runs (12.33) and 67 wickets (28.35)

NASH, Laurence John

(b. 1910, Melbourne; d. 1986, Heidelburg, Victoria) *Tasmania, Victoria, and Australia*

A right-arm fast bowler and hard-hitting batsman, Laurie Nash took 7 for 50 for Tasmania against the South Africans at Hobart in 1931/2 and was selected for the fifth Test at Melbourne, taking 4 for 18 in South Africa's first innings débâcle of 36. He had appeared only once for Victoria—taking 4 for 37 against the visiting MCC—before being chosen for his second (and last) Test, the fifth against England at Melbourne in 1936/7, and he took 4 for 70 in the first innings. He never appeared in a Sheffield Shield match. A magnificent athlete, he was one of the most accomplished footballers under the Australian Rules.

First-class career (1929–36): 953 runs (28.02) including 1 century, and 69 wickets (28.33)
Test matches (2): 30 runs (15.00), 10 wickets (12.60), and 6 catches

NEWLAND, Philip Mesmer

(b. 1875, Adelaide; d. 1916, Westbury, Tasmania) *South Australia*

This slimly built, highly skilled South Australian had his career shortened when he broke his jaw while playing cricket on board the ship taking the 1905 Australians to England. He appeared in only a third of the touring programme and on his return to Australia retired to concentrate on his legal practice. A right-hand lower-order batsman, his highest first-class score was 77.

First-class career (1899–1905): 599 runs (18.15), 30 catches, and 18 stumpings

NIELSEN, Timothy John

(b. 1968, London) *South Australia*

Tim Nielsen created a South Australian wicketkeeping record at the end of his first season in 1990/1 by taking 11 catches for the match against Western Australia in Perth.

First-class career (1990–): 1,701 runs (28.83) including 1 century, 1 wicket (49.00), and 132 dismissals (118 c., 14 st.)

NITSCHKE, Holmesdale Carl

(b. 1905, Adelaide; d. 1982, Adelaide) *South Australia and Australia*

Never happier than when driving a fast bowler back over his head into the pavilion, 'Jack' or 'Slinger' Nitschke, as the opening batsman of his state, went to the wickets breathing fire and slaughter. He was known as the 'Don Quixote' of the bat. For his state he averaged 39.85 in Sheffield Shield matches, though he was often on the beaten side; but he appeared only in two Tests, both against South Africa in 1931/2. A left-hander, he hit five of his nine hundreds against New South Wales, including 130 not out, out of a South Australian total of 246 at Sydney in 1933/4. He became a noted race-horse breeder.

First-class career (1929–35): 3,320 runs (42.03) including 9 centuries
Test matches (2): 53 runs (26.50) and 3 catches

NOBLE, Montague Alfred

(b. 1873, Sydney; d. 1940, Sydney) *New South Wales and Australia*

Regarded by many as the greatest all-rounder produced by Australia, Monty Noble, also known as 'Alf' or 'Mary Ann' was over 6 ft., powerfully built and with sharp, clean-shaven features; he was a right-handed batsman of rare style and execution. Beautifully positioned and relaxed, he was able to hit very hard or play with heartbreaking patience, using his height and reach fully in driving, forcing the ball off his legs, pulling and cutting, either square or late. As a bowler, he was an off-spinner with a fairly long run-up, good control, and the ability to swerve the ball: he varied his pace considerably from slow to medium-fast. He was also a good fielder, usually at point, and an astute captain who drilled his side like a Cromwell—though off the field he was quite a genial companion. Noble toured England in 1899, 1902, 1905, and, as captain, in 1909. At home he appeared in 1897/8, 1901/2, and, as captain, in 1903/4 and 1907/8. He toured South Africa in 1902/3. He was very successful all round on each England tour: 1,608 runs and 82 wickets (1899); 1,357 runs and 93 wickets (1902); 2,053 runs and 55 wickets (1905); and 1,060 runs and 25 wickets (1909). In his whole career he made seven double-centuries. His highest score was 284 against Sussex at Hove in 1902, when he added 428 for the sixth wicket with Warwick Armstrong, which remains Australia's record for this wicket; and he hit 267 against Sussex again in 1905. He headed the Test bowling averages in 1897/8, with 19 wickets (20.26). On his début in the second Test at Melbourne he took 6 for 49 on a difficult wicket in the second innings, winning the match for his country. Perhaps his greatest achievement was in taking 7 for 17 and 6 for 60 in the second Test at Melbourne against a strong England batting side in 1901/2. In the third Test at Sheffield in 1902 he took 11 for 103. He made his sole Test century, 133 (out of a total of 285) in the first Test at Sydney in 1903/4, and on several occasions held the batting together in that series. Five of his double-centuries came in Sheffield Shield matches, in 51 of which he made 4,896 runs (68.00) and took 158 wickets (22.65). He was in turn banker, dentist, manufacturer's agent, writer, and broadcaster, and his books *Gilligan's Men*, *The Game's the Thing*, *Those Ashes* and *The Fight for the Ashes 1928–29* are classics on the game. A stand at the Sydney Cricket Ground is named after him.

First-class career (1893–1919): 13,975 runs (40.74) including 37 centuries, 624 wickets (23.14), and 190 catches

Test matches (42): 1,997 runs (30.25) including 1 century, 121 wickets (25.00), and 26 catches

NOBLET, Geffery*

(b. 1916, Adelaide) *South Australia and Australia*

Six feet three inches and very thin, Geff Noblet's endurance was remarkable. Bowling a lively right-arm medium pace, he started his long run with a peculiar hop, as in a barn-dance, and finished with a 7 ft. stride, delivering the ball with a flick which some purists thought was a throw; he could move the ball either way and his control was excellent. He toured South Africa in 1949/50 and also represented his country at home against the West Indies in 1951/2 and South Africa in 1952/3. Thirty-five Sheffield Shield matches brought him 190 wickets (17.87), but Ray Lindwall, Keith Miller, and Bill Johnston kept him out of the Australian side against England. He became president of the South Australian Cricket Association. *Christened Geffery, a mistaken entry in the register, he has always signed himself in this way.

First-class career (1946–56): 975 runs (13.92) and 282 wickets (19.26)

Test matches (3): 22 runs (7.33), 7 wickets (26.14), and 1 catch

NOTHLING, Dr Otto Ernest

(b. 1900, Teutoburg (now Witta) Queensland; d. 1965, Brisbane) *Queensland, New South Wales, and Australia*

Otto Nothling could bowl right-arm medium pace and swing a heavy bat effectively; he appeared in one Test, the second at Sydney against England in 1928/9, scoring 8 and 44 and taking 0 for 72. A notable Rugby full-back, he represented Australia against New Zealand; and for many years he was president of the Queensland Cricket Association.

First-class career (1922–9): 882 runs (24.50) including 1 century, and 36 wickets (41.06)

O'BRIEN, Leo Patrick Joseph

(b. 1907, Melbourne) *Victoria and Australia*

A small, neat, left-handed opening batsman, Leo O'Brien had a good defence and tons of courage, but a disappointing Test record. He appeared against England in 1932/3 and 1936/7, and South Africa in 1935/6, his only overseas tour. In the final match of the 'bodyline' series at Sydney, after Vic Richardson, Bill Woodfull, and Don Bradman had gone rather cheaply on the opening morning, he hit 61, adding 99 with Stan McCabe for the fourth wicket off Larwood, Voce, and company, but he was unable to consolidate his place.

First-class career (1929–37): 3,303 runs (36.70) including 7 centuries, and 3 wickets (42.33)

Test matches (5): 211 runs (26.37) and 3 catches

O'CONNOR, John Denis Alphonsus

(b. 1875, Sydney; d. 1941, Sydney) *New South Wales, South Australia, and Australia*

Right-arm, fastish medium in pace, with immaculate length, good control, able to make the ball lift and swing towards leg, Jack O'Connor played against England in 1907/8—having a match record of 8 for 150 on his début in the third Test at Adelaide. He toured England in 1909, taking 77 wickets (16.01) in all first-class matches. His best performance was 7 for 36 for South Australia against Victoria at Melbourne in 1908/9, enabling his state to snatch an unexpected victory. In 17 Sheffield Shield matches his left-handed batting was of little account, but he took 80 wickets (29.13).

First-class career (1904–9): 695 runs (11.77) and 224 wickets (23.45)

Test matches (4): 86 runs (12.28), 13 wickets (26.15), and 3 catches

O'DONNELL, Simon Patrick

(b. 1963, Deniliquin, New South Wales) *Victoria and Australia*

Simon O'Donnell was a fine, natural stroke-player and a brisk right-arm seam bowler who promised to be the all-rounder that Australia had lacked since the retirement of Keith Miller but was eventually eclipsed by Steve Waugh. Tall, dark, and powerful, he was offered professional terms as a Rules footballer. He made a sensational début for Victoria in the last match of the 1983/4 season when he scored a brilliant 130 and took 4 for 118. The following season he made another sparkling hundred as he scored almost 400 runs and took 11 wickets. He was chosen to tour England in 1985 after playing only seven first-class matches. He quickly confirmed his reputation by making a memorable undefeated century against MCC at Lord's, marked by impressive straight-driving, and was rewarded with a Test début at Headingley—only his eleventh first-class match. He made a disappointing start, with 0 in his first innings, but took 3 for 37 in England's second innings, obtaining considerable movement off the wicket with his medium pace. He played several useful innings during the series, reaching 40 three times and compiling 186 runs (26.28) but his bowling appeared to lack penetration in the later matches. He lost his Test place in 1985/6 but went back to England in 1986 as a professional in the Birmingham League, and continued to play for Australia in one-day internationals, playing a prominent all-round role in the 1987 World Cup in India and Pakistan; his one for 35 in 10 overs in a high-scoring final against England was crucial to Australia's victory. Soon afterwards he discovered that a lump on his ribs was cancerous. Chemotherapy cured him and in 1988/9 he returned to cricket after a season away, as fit as ever and still a very effective one-day all-rounder. In a tournament in Sharjah in 1989/90 he hit 50 off only 18 balls against Sri Lanka, a one-day record. He became captain of Victoria but was criticized as being 'unimaginative' and retired after a very public rift with Victoria's manager Bill Lawry, who was often absent on duty as a television commentator. It

was an unfortunate end to O'Donnell's spirited career.

First-class career (1983–92): 4,603 runs (44.37) including 2 centuries, and 41 wickets (40.85)

Test matches (6): 206 runs (29.42), 6 wickets (84.00), and 4 catches

OGILVIE, Alan David

(b. 1951, Southport, Queensland) *Queensland and Australia*

A tall, bearded schoolmaster, red-haired, and a right-hand batsman, David Ogilvie earned a place in Australia's fledging side against India (at home) and the West Indies (away) in 1977/8, but was disappointing despite a pleasing upright technique. He simply could not go wrong in the Sheffield Shield, however. In the 1977/8 season he scored 1,060 runs (66.25) with six centuries which only Bradman and Ponsford have exceeded in the Shield. He played straight and hit hard but a blow on the head from a ball by Bob Willis at Brisbane in 1978/9 did nothing to help his confidence. A late replacement on the tour of the Caribbean, he scored 296 runs (26.91).

First-class career (1974–9): 3,006 runs (34.15) including 8 centuries

Test matches (5): 178 runs (17.80) and 5 catches

O'KEEFFE, Francis Aloysius

(b. 1896, Waverley, New South Wales; d. 1924, Hampstead, London) *New South Wales and Victoria*

The Sydney-born right-hand batsman seemed set for international honours when he made 177 and 144 in Frank Iredale's benefit match in 1921. By averaging 31 in five matches with New South Wales and 96 in three with Victoria, he showed himself to be an outstanding prospect. He also bowled handy slow right-arm spinners and was an exceptional field. However, after accepting a professional contract with Church in the Lancashire League, he died from peritonitis, aged 27, just months before completing residential qualification to play at county level with Lancashire.

First-class career (1919–21): 926 runs (71.23) including 3 centuries, 12 wickets (19.16), and 5 catches

O'KEEFFE, Kerry James

(b. 1949, Sydney) *New South Wales, Somerset, and Australia*

A tall, fair-haired all-rounder, a right-arm leg-break bowler and right-hand batsman, Kerry O'Keeffe never quite fulfilled his early potential, and in an era dominated by fast bowlers he was often the man left out of an Australian twelve. He was a brisk leg-spinner, with a good high action who bowled as many top-spinners and off-breaks as he did leg-spinners. As a batsman he possessed exceptional determination and a sound technique and he could field well anywhere, especially in the slip or gully. He had wide English experience, although he made only one official tour of England, in 1977, when he averaged 50 with the bat in all matches and took 36 tour wickets (28.75) but his Test bowling, three wickets at 101.66, was very disappointing. In 1971 he took 77 wickets for Somerset (but only 19 in 1972) and in 1975 scored over 1,000 runs and took 68 wickets for the League club, East Lancashire. In Tests generally he was often chipping in with good all-round efforts at important times, but he only once took five wickets in an innings.

First-class career (1968–79): 4,169 runs (26.05), 476 wickets (28.11), and 112 catches

Test matches (24): 644 runs (25.76), 53 wickets (38.07), and 15 catches

OLDFIELD, William Albert Stanley

(b. 1894, Sydney; d. 1976, Sydney) *New South Wales and Australia*

Very small, but wiry as a weasel, Bert Oldfield was an artistic wicket-keeper who did his job with quiet efficiency, stumping batsmen with the speed and stealth of a cat and then appealing with a polite conviction. His right-handed batting was also neat and business-like. He had a good defence and could force the pace when necessary. After front-line service near Ypres, he came to notice as a member of the Australian Imperial Forces team in 1919. He toured England in 1921, 1926, 1930, and 1934 and South Africa in 1921/2 and 1935/6. Establishing himself in Tests in 1924/5 against England, he showed amazing skill in the fourth Test at Melbourne, stumping Hobbs, Woolley, Chapman, and Whysall and catching Gilligan, all in the same innings. In the fifth Test at Sydney he caught Hobbs for 0 in the first innings and stumped him for 13 in the second. He played in seven home series between 1920 and 1937, five against England. On his five tours of England he caught 155 batsmen and stumped 111. He was the unwitting cause of much Australian fury when, batting at Adelaide in the third Test of the 'bodyline' series, he was hit on the head as he ducked into a ball from Larwood and had to be carried off the field. On recovering consciousness he said, 'It was my own

fault,' and he and Larwood became great friends. He was awarded the MBE.

First-class career (1919–37): 6,135 runs (23.77) including 6 centuries, and 661 dismissals (400 c., 261 st.)

Test matches (54): 1,427 runs (22.65) and 130 dismissals (78 c., 52 st.)

O'NEILL, Norman Clifford

(b. 1937, Sydney) *New South Wales and Australia*

Heralded as 'the new Don Bradman', Norman O'Neill had a brilliant but also rather mercurial career. Without doubt he was a superb right-handed stroke-maker. Strongly built, and much taller than the Don, he was a back-foot player of the highest class, a powerful driver, very quick on his feet to the spinners, and was practically never tied down. But he was a nervous starter who had none of Bradman's air of invincibility. His character was warm-hearted and generous; but he could be quick to ire. A useful leg-spin bowler, he was also a brilliant cover field with a superb throw. He averaged 43.61 at the age of 18 in his first season of first-class cricket. He toured New Zealand with the 'A' team in his second season, averaging 72.66, and in his next season, 1957/8, made 1,005 runs (83.75)—only the third player to have totalled 1,000 runs in the Sheffield Shield in a season. He played his first Test against England in 1958/9 when he batted with admirable consistency to average 56.40. He toured England in 1961 and 1964, India twice, the West Indies and Pakistan. On his first England tour he was highly successful with 1,981 runs (60.03), including seven centuries, but on his second less so, although he averaged 45.63. His first Test century was 181 in the tied Test against the West Indies at Brisbane in 1960/1. His first century against England was in his tenth Test against them, 117 in the final match at The Oval in 1961. His superb footwork and powerful driving provided the best batting of that series. Soon after he lost form and confidence, but he redeemed himself with a memorable 143 against MCC at Sydney and 100 in the fourth Test at Adelaide in 1962/3, adding 194 for the fourth wicket with Neil Harvey after a poor Australian start. He was even more successful against other countries, scoring 163 at Bombay and 113 at Calcutta against India in 1959/60 and 134 against Pakistan at Lahore on the same tour. The tour also saw his career-highest score of 284 against the Indian President's XI at Ahmedabad. By the mid 1960s, however, the glory had departed from his batting; and at the close of his last series against the West Indies in the Caribbean controversial articles appeared under his name bitterly condemning the bowling action of Charlie Griffith. His handsome stroke-play was still in evidence in Sheffield Shield matches, however, and he was the chief run-getter in 1966/7, heading the table with 741 runs (74.10). But late in the season after a poor tour with an Australian 'A' team of New Zealand, he announced his retirement from big cricket because of recurring knee trouble. In 61 Sheffield Shield matches he made 4,749 runs (50.52). His son, Mark, was also a gifted all-round cricketer who played successfully for both Western Australia and New South Wales in the 1980s, scoring three Shield hundreds in succession in 1985/6. Father Norman was by then well established in his career as a tobacco company representative and ABC Radio Cricket summarizer.

First-class career (1955–68): 13,859 runs (50.95) including 45 centuries, 99 wickets, (41.01), and 104 catches

Test matches (42): 2,779 runs (45.55) including 6 centuries, 17 wickets (39.23), and 21 catches

O'REILLY, William Joseph

(b. 1905, White Cliffs, New South Wales; d. 1992, Sydney) *New South Wales and Australia*

In Sir Donald Bradman's view the greatest bowler of his time, Bill O'Reilly played his cricket with the fierce zeal of a fire-and-brimstone missionary. Known as 'Tiger', he had a meteoric rise to fame. He played for his State in two matches in 1927/8, without any pronounced success, and nothing more was heard of him in first-class cricket until 1931/2, when the South Africans were touring Australia. In five Sheffield Shield matches he took 25 wickets and he was selected for the fourth and fifth Tests—in the fifth at Melbourne helping to demolish South Africa's second innings for 45 (taking 3 for 19). From then until the outbreak of the Second World War he was an integral part of his country's fearsome spin attack, especially in company with Clarrie Grimmett. Over 6 ft. tall, he bowled right-arm. His run-up and action formed an ungraceful whirl of arms and legs but the result was deadly. His stock delivery was a leg-break rolled out of the hand with no great turn, but he spun his googly sharply and almost every ball he bowled had abnormal bounce. His pace was such that few batsmen could move out to the pitch of the ball, and both his accuracy and his hostility were unremitting; he had more the temperament of a fiery fast bowler than of a patient spinner. As a left-handed batsman he had no style but he could hit tremendously hard. In the 'bodyline' tour of 1932/3 he consolidated his place as the outstanding Australian bowler, with 27 wickets (26.81) taking 10 for 129 in his country's sole victory, in the second Test at Melbourne. Against England in 1934 and South Africa in 1935/6, Grimmett and O'Reilly were a host in themselves—in the former series they collected 53 wickets (O'Reilly 28) and in the latter 71 wickets (O'Reilly 27). At Trent Bridge in 1934 O'Reilly took 11 for 129 and at Old Trafford took three wickets in four balls (Walters, Wyatt, and Hammond). Although England reached 627 for 9, 'Tiger's' analysis was 7 for 189 in 59 overs. Against South Africa in 1935/6 he was consistently successful with 95 wickets (13.56). Both England tours brought him 100 wickets and first place in the averages. At Leeds in 1938, in a low-scoring match, his 10 for 122 was decisive. He appeared in the first post-war Test, against New Zealand at Wellington in 1945/6, taking 5 for 14 and 3 for 19, then retired. Originally a schoolmaster, he turned to journalism and produced two tour books, besides much characteristically well-informed, intelligent, honest, and forthright newspaper comment. A kind heart lay beneath his fiery exterior

First-class career (1927–45): 1,655 runs (13.13) and 774 wickets (16.60)

Test matches (27): 410 runs (12.81), 144 wickets (22.59), and 7 catches

OXENHAM, Ronald Keven

(b. 1891, Brisbane; d. 1939, Brisbane) *Queensland and Australia*

Perhaps the best all-rounder produced by his State, Ron Oxenham made his name comparatively late. Not a stylist, he was a much better right-handed batsman than he looked and was a right-arm slow-medium bowler who flighted the ball well and had a jerky action, 'like a toy which functions when the strings are pulled'. His best delivery was a slower ball which floated from off to leg. He was a smart slip. In his late thirties and early forties he appeared in Tests against England in 1928/9, West Indies in 1930/1, and South Africa in 1931/2. His best feat in Tests was to take 4 for 39 in 30 overs as one of the opening bowlers in the third Test against West Indies at Brisbane in 1930/1. He toured India with the Maharajah of Patiala's Australian team in 1935/6, managed by Frank Tarrant, taking 101 wickets at 8 runs each. In 46 Sheffield Shield matches he made 2,314 runs

(30.85) and took 167 wickets (22.14). Suffering serious injury in a car accident in 1937, he never fully recovered.

First-class career (1911–36): 3,693 runs (25.64) including 4 centuries, and 369 wickets (18.67)

Test matches (7): 151 runs (15.10), 14 wickets (37.28), and 4 catches

OXLADE, R. Aubrey

(b. 1887, Sydney; d. 1955, Sydney)

Chairman of the Australian Cricket Board for four separate stints (1927–30, 1933–6, 1946–8, and 1951–2), Oxlade joined the Manly club in 1905, was elected to its committee in 1906, and was a delegate to the New South Wales Cricket Association for 50 years until his death. He also served on the NSW Cricket Association executive committee from 1913 to 1955, was chairman of the Sydney Cricket Ground trust, and founding vice-president on the formation of the NSW Cricketers' Club in 1940. Like so many other cricket administrators of the day, Oxlade was a lawyer by profession. His enthusiasm for the game often saw him drive to Adelaide for a Test match, even if there were no Board meetings scheduled. He was awarded a CBE for his services to cricket.

PAGE, Roger

(b. 1936, London)

A leading collector and historian, who became the first in Australia to make his full-time livelihood as a dealer in new and second-hand cricket books, Roger Page is well known to a legion of cricket lovers in Australia and overseas who receive his catalogue. Author, in 1957, of *A History of Tasmanian Cricket*, he was also one of the founding Australian members of the Association of Cricket Statisticians, being responsible for co-ordinating a series of valuable booklets, outlining the birth and death details and personal performances of State cricketers. He moved to Tasmania as a teenager and worked as a schoolteacher before basing himself in Melbourne from 1971 and establishing his cricket book business. In 1991 he was elected vice-president of the Melbourne branch of the Australian Cricket Society.

PALMER, George Eugene

(b. 1859, Mulwala, Corowa, New South Wales; d. 1910, Baddaginnie, Victoria) *Victoria, Tasmania, and Australia*

At 19, playing for Victoria against Lord Harris's team at Melbourne in 1878/9, George or 'Joey'

Palmer took 9 for 94 in the match, greatly impressing his opponents. A right-arm medium-paced spin bowler, with the necessary command of length and direction, he was considered Australia's best bowler in the early 1880s on batsmen's pitches—'and when the wicket was sticky, he was a nasty one to face'. He toured England in 1880—playing in the first Test in England at The Oval, taking three of the five wickets to fall in England's second innings—and again in 1882, 1884, and 1886. At home he played in the 1881/2, 1882/3, and 1884/5 series. On his last England tour he almost achieved the double with 972 runs and 106 wickets, his batting having developed greatly; this was the first Australian double in England. In the second Test at Sydney in 1881/2 his match analysis, 11 for 165 in 124 overs, enabled his country to win convincingly, and in the next match at Sydney he took 9 for 90 in 85.2 overs. The four Tests brought him 24 wickets (21.75). Again the chief bowler in 1882/3, he took 21 wickets (18.90). His highest score against England, 48, was made defiantly at Lord's in 1886. On his four trips to England he captured 397 wickets (16.90).

First-class career (1878–96): 2,728 runs (16.14) including 1 century, 594 wickets (17.71), and 107 catches

Test matches (17): 296 runs (14.09), 78 wickets (21.51), and 13 catches

PARISH, Robert James

(b. 1916, Armadale, Victoria)

When Bob Parish and his close friend Ray Steele simultaneously retired from the Victorian Cricket Association in 1992, they drew stumps on the longest running and most successful administrative partnership in Australian cricket. Together they carried the banners of Victorian and Australian cricket through times of revolution, trauma, and triumph, outlasting virtually all their contemporaries. As the Victorian cricket historian Robert Coleman said, none of the legendary partnerships of Australian cricket folklore—not Woodfull and Ponsford, Lindwall and Miller, Simpson and Lawry, nor Lillee and Marsh—did more for the game. At a Victorian cricket dinner in their honour in late 1992, Sir Donald Bradman paid tribute to both men, saying how each had given 'unsurpassed service to the game of cricket at both State and international level'. Both were club standard medium-paced bowlers who had an enormous love of cricket. Educated at Melbourne Grammar, Parish played against Bill Woodfull in his maiden match, an experience he likened to bowling against a barn door. After a 130-game playing career with Prahran, including a 4-year stint as captain, Parish served as the club's delegate to the Victorian Cricket Association for more than 40 years, including 30 years as the VCA's executive chairman. His cricketing travels took him around the world but he never forgot his roots, enjoying running Prahran's scoreboard or dressing up as Santa Claus at the club's annual Christmas party. He had two separate stints as chairman of the Australian Cricket Board, from 1966 to 1969 and again from 1975 to 1980, as well as managing two Australian teams, in 1965 to the West Indies and 1968 to England. In 1975 he was awarded the OBE for services to cricket and in 1981, a CMG.

PARK, Dr Roy Lindsay

(b. 1892, Ballarat; d. 1947, Melbourne) *Victoria and Australia*

Small in stature, Roy Park was a right-hand batsman of sound defence, who went on his way relentlessly. He would have played more Test cricket but for the war and his medical commitments. He made 586 runs (83.71) for his state in 1919/20 and the following season made his sole Test appearance, against England at Melbourne in the second match, when in Australia's only innings he was bowled first ball, and never received another chance. His wife is reputed to have bent down to pick up her knitting and thus to have missed her husband's entire Test career! His career-highest score was 228 against South Australia at Melbourne in 1919/20.

First-class career (1912–24): 2,514 runs (39.28) including 9 centuries, and 3 wickets (46.33)

PASCOE, Leonard Stephen (formerly Durtanovich, Len)

(b. 1950, Bridgetown North, Western Australia) *New South Wales and Australia*

The son of Yugoslavian immigrants to Australia, Len Pascoe was a very determined right-arm fast bowler with little subtlety but plenty of strength and hostility. No scholar, he once observed that 'a tiger never changes his spots'. He was just challenging for a regular Test place at the outbreak of the Packer Revolution, which he joined. After a successful season for New South Wales in 1976/7 he toured England, taking 41 wickets on the tour at 21.78. England's players were surprised and relieved when he was left out of the Australian team at Old Trafford after a promising Test début at Lord's, where he took five wickets in the match. Later in the series he took 4 for 80 on a good pitch at Trent Bridge. He was an enthusiastic fielder, but a genuine tail-end batsman. Hostile fast bowlers thrived during the two years of World Series Cricket and Len Pascoe emerged from his time in the 'circus' a more confident and determined competitor. Looking an even more dangerous bowler then Lillee in the many one-day internationals of 1979/80 and the following season, he was not an automatic selection for the Test team but took ten wickets (24.10) in two home Tests against England and then bowled outstandingly well in England's first innings in the Centenary Test, taking 5 for 59, four of his wickets being lbws. By now he had learned the virtues of bowling straight, fast, and to a good length. He took 12 wickets in three Tests against New Zealand in 1980/1 and 16 in the three Tests against India. But a knee injury was increasingly troubling him and he decided to miss the tour to England in 1981 in order to have an operation. His last Test was the third against West Indies at Adelaide in 1981/2, when he took four wickets.

First-class career (1974–84): 502 runs (8.96) and 309 wickets (25.60)

Test matches (14): 106 runs (10.60), 64 wickets (26.06), and 2 catches.

PELLEW, Clarence Everard

(b. 1893, Port Pirie, South Australia; d. 1981, Adelaide) *South Australia and Australia*

Of average height, with strong shoulders and broad chest, 'Nip' Pellew could drive hard and straight, had a fine stroke past point—a mixture of cover-drive and cut—and was always looking for runs. He was nephew of the Shield player J. H. Pellew, also known as 'Nip'. He was a most accomplished field, sprinting round the boundary at even-time rate. 'Nip' toured England with the Australian Imperial Forces team in 1919, making 1,260 runs and returned home to hit 271 for his state against Victoria at Adelaide. In the 1920/1 series against England he made 319 runs (53.16) from four Tests, including 116 in the second at Melbourne and 104 in the third at Adelaide. He disappointed in the 1921 England tour, not even reaching 1,000 runs and appeared in only one more Test, against South Africa the following winter. In 18 Sheffield Shield matches he made 1,343 runs (39.50).

First-class career (1913–29): 4,536 runs (33.60) including 9 centuries, and 12 wickets (70.75)
Test matches (10): 484 runs (37.23) including 2 centuries, 0–34, and 4 catches

PEPPER, Cecil George

(b. 1916, Forbes, New South Wales; d. 1993 Littleborough, Lancashire, England) *New South Wales*

One of the finest post-Second World War cricketers to be denied Test status, 'Cec' Pepper was victim of his own impetuosity in an era when a loud mouth was not tolerated. A spur-of-the-moment comment to umpire Jack Scott after an lbw appeal against Don Bradman had been rejected in one of Bradman's come-back matches in Adelaide in 1946 soured his Australian career. Pepper arranged for an apology to be sent to the Australian Cricket Board of Control, but it was never received. Pepper refused to apologize a second time and returned to England where he had been so successful representing the Australian Services team in 1945. Born at Forbes in country New South Wales, Pepper was a naturally gifted right-hand batsman and right-arm wrist spinner, who is regarded as one of the first to develop the 'flipper'. While his appearances for New South Wales were limited to sixteen matches, he was an exciting player on his day. In one game against Queensland at the Gabba in his second season in 1939/40, he made 81 in an hour, all but seven runs coming in boundary hits. Along with Keith Miller he was the outstanding personality in Lindsay Hassett's 1945 Australian Services team and one of the most valuable, making 195 runs and taking 14 wickets in five 'Victory' Tests. In the opening international at Lord's, he inspired a famous victory by taking four wickets and making 40 and 54 not out, the winning runs coming with just one ball to spare, after 34 were required in 12 minutes. His feats in English league cricket are legend. With Burnley in 1949, he became the first Australian to achieve the double, making 1,070 runs and taking 113 wickets. Later he served for 15 years on England's first-class umpires' panel, prized for his down-to-earth wit.

First-class career (1938–57): 1,927 runs (29.64) including 1 century, 171 wickets (29.35), and 41 catches

PHILLIPS, James

(b. 1860, Pleasant Creek (now Stawell), Victoria; d. 1930, Burnaby, Vancouver, Canada) *Victoria, Middlesex, and Canterbury*

Best known for no-balling leading fast bowlers including the Australian Ernie Jones and the Lancastrian Arthur Mold, 'Dimboola Jim' Phillips was a much-travelled figure who appeared in first-class matches in Australia, England, and New Zealand. Before qualifying as a first-class umpire in England in 1900, his no-balling of Jones during A. E. Stoddart's 1897/8 MCC tour caused a furore. No player had ever been called in a Test match before. He stood in 29 Tests—13 in Australia, 11 in England, and five in South Africa, establishing a reputation for integrity and moral courage. His nickname came from the western districts Victorian town in which he spent his early life before appearing for Victoria in 1885/6. In his maiden match against New South Wales in 1890/1, he took 10 for 44, including a first innings analysis of 41.5–28–20–7. He conceded runs from just 15 of his 251 deliveries. A right-arm medium-pace bowler and right-hand lower-order batsman, Phillips played in 124 first-class matches, the majority with Middlesex in nine professional seasons from 1890–8.

First-class career (1885–98): 1,826 runs (12.59) including 1 century, 355 wickets (20.00), and 50 catches

PHILLIPS, Raymond Berry

(b. 1954, Sydney) *New South Wales and Queensland*

A right-hand lower-order batsman and wicket-keeper who played in dark sunglasses and was one of the first to discard the bulkier wicket-keeping pads for today's lightweight version, Ray Phillips enjoyed marked success after shifting states. He had three games with New South Wales as a substitute for Steve Rixon in 1978/9, before gaining a permanent place in Queensland's side and playing 68 games in a row from 1979/80 to 1985/6. He also toured England with the 1985 Australians as the reserve wicket-keeper for his namesake, Wayne Bentley Phillips.

First-class career (1978–85): 2,925 runs (28.96) including 1 century, and 286 dismissals (271 c., 15 st.)

PHILLIPS, Wayne Bentley

(b. 1958, Adelaide) *South Australia and Australia*

Wayne Phillips was an outstanding left-handed stroke-playing batsman who, having first come into the Test side as an opening batsman, became Australia's wicket-keeper for a time after the retirement of Rodney Marsh. Fair-haired, his batting had a rare sense of touch and timing but his wicket-keeping was not of true Test class. He first came into the state side in 1977/8 playing three matches in the middle order. His next appearance was the last match of the 1980/1 season when he revealed his rich potential with scores of 111 and 91. A magnificent 1981/2 season in which he scored 857 runs (47.61) including a monumental 260 against Queensland, won him a place on the tour to Pakistan, but he did not play in the Tests. A fit and dedicated cricketer, he eventually won a Test place in the home series against Pakistan in 1983/4 and had a wonderful début, scoring 159 at Perth in his first innings in Test cricket. He made 362 runs (60.33) in the five Tests. On the subsequent tour of West Indies, Phillips was given the job of Test wicket-keeper, although he was not keeping wicket for his state. He took 10 catches and scored 258 runs (25.80) in the Tests, now batting down the order, including a bold and attractive 120 on a fast wicket at Bridgetown. His 1984/5 season was ruined by injury and he played in only two Tests against the West Indies, but in England in 1985 he showed himself again to be a highly capable and attractive number six, scoring 350 runs in the Test series and 899 runs (47.31) on the whole tour. His scintillating square-cutting was a particular feature of his batting, but it was such a stroke, hit hard against the boot of Allan Lamb and bouncing up into the hands of David Gower, which cost him his wicket—and Australia the match—in the crucial fifth Test at Edgbaston. In the 1985/6 Australian season the burden of keeping wicket and being pushed up the order to open the batting proved heavy. Although he made 63 against New Zealand at Sydney, he had a wretched series against India, making only 67 runs (13.40) and struggling to keep wicket to the Australian spinners. He was dropped as wicket-keeper for the subsequent tour of New Zealand, but played in all three Tests as a specialist batsman. He shared in a partnership of 462, undefeated, for South Australia's fourth wicket against Tasmania at Adelaide in 1986/7, then the highest ever partnership in Australia.

First-class career (1977–90): 6,907 runs (37.74) including 13 centuries, and 161 dismissals (154 c., 7 st.)
Test matches (27): 1,485 runs (32.28) including 2 centuries, and 52 catches

PHILLIPS, Wayne Norman

(b. 1962, Geelong, Victoria) *Victoria and Australia*

Following in famous footsteps—Hassett, Shea-han, and Redpath also hail from Geelong—Wayne Phillips had one Test with Australia, aged 29, before returning to Sheffield Shield ranks. A right-handed batsman and a confident worker of the ball, particularly noted for his crisp on-side play, Phillips was 26 before playing first-class cricket. Making 111 on his début against the 1988/9 West Indians, he immediately stamped himself a fine and courageous player of fast bowling. Replacing Geoff Marsh in the XI for the fifth and final Test of the 1991/2 season, Phillips made 8 and 14 against the touring Indians and was subsequently overlooked for the winter tour of Sri Lanka. His 91 not out, including the winning runs, in the low-scoring 1990/1 Sheffield Shield final against New South Wales in Melbourne was an invaluable effort. Compact and prematurely balding, best-suited to four- and five-day cricket, Phillips led Victoria briefly at the conclusion of the 1993/4 season. Known for his calculated approach to batting, his career-best score of 205 against New South Wales at Sydney in 1992/3 took almost 10 hours.

First-class career (1988–   ): 3,859 runs (38.59) including 9 centuries, 1 wicket (124.00), and 24 catches

PHILPOTT, Peter Ian

(b. 1934, Sydney) *New South Wales and Australia*

A right-arm leg-break bowler, brilliant slip fielder, and very useful batsman, Peter Philpott toured the West Indies in 1965 and, in his first Test series, took 18 wickets (34.94). In his first Test against England in 1965/6, at Brisbane, he took 5 for 90 in the first innings. He was a member of Denis Compton's side to the Transvaal in 1959 and played in the Lancashire League, but he never toured England and retired in his prime. He was captain of New South Wales for the 1964/5 season. He became a noted coach, for a time guided Sri Lanka's national team, and was an articulate upholder of the difficult art of leg-spin wherever he travelled. Amongst his assignments was one as coach to Rossall School where he guided, amongst others, Ian Botham's son Liam. He also taught English and History at a number of schools.

First-class career (1954–66): 2,886 runs (31.36) including 4 centuries, and 245 wickets (30.31)

Test matches (8): 93 runs (10.33), 26 wickets (38.46), and 5 catches

POIDEVIN, Dr Leslie Oswald Sheridan

(b. 1876, Merrila, New South Wales; d. 1931, Sydney) *New South Wales, London County, and Lancashire*

The first Australian to reach 100 centuries at all levels of cricket (in 1918/19), Les Poidevin was a gifted all-round sportsman, good enough to represent Australia in Davis Cup tennis and to be 12th man for an Ashes Test (1901/2). An accomplished batsman and later a noted cricket writer and administrator, Poidevin reserved much of his best cricket for English soil. Only 13 of his 149 first-class matches over a 15-year span were for New South Wales. In 1900/1 he made 140 in New South Wales's then world record score of 918 in a Sheffield Shield match against South Australia. The following season he made 151 not out against Archie MacLaren's MCC tourists, but played only occasionally back in Australia while he concentrated on graduating in medicine at Edinburgh University. After captaining the Sydney grade club Waverley to three consecutive premierships after the First World War, he joined the club president, Mr F. P. Gray, in presenting an annual Shield for competition amongst teenagers from Sydney grade clubs. Most of New South Wales's élite metropolitan-born players are former Poidevin–Gray schoolboys.

First-class career (1895–1908): 7,022 runs (32.96) including 14 centuries, 46 wickets (41.89), and 163 catches

POLLARD, Jack Ernest

(b. 1926, Sydney)

An acclaimed sporting historian and writer, whose *magnum opus, Australian Cricket, The Game and the Players* won the English Cricket Society's Literary Award in 1983, Pollard has been writing about cricket since the late 1940s when he first worked in England, covering major events such as Wimbledon, Don Bradman's 1948 Australian tour, and rugby league Tests. Educated at Sydney Technical High, he played first grade cricket with Paddington, once striking the great Bill O'Reilly for six at Trumper Park. 'Tiger couldn't get the

ball back in his hands quick enough,' said Pollard. After working as a journalist and running his own publishing company until 1981, Pollard concentrated on his books, which included a five-volume *History of Australian Cricket*. In 1992 he was awarded an OA for his services to sporting history.

PONSFORD, William Harold

(b. 1900, Melbourne; d. 1991, Kyneton, Victoria) *Victoria and Australia*

Though he was humbled by Larwood in 1928/9 and again in 1932/3, there were times during his career when Bill Ponsford scored runs with the relentless efficiency of a machine. The prolific 'Ponny' was an opening right-handed batsman regularly associated first with Bill Woodfull, with whom he shared 20 partnerships of 100 or more, including one of 375 for Victoria—Ponsford scored 352—against New South Wales at Melbourne in 1926/7, then with the even more remorseless Don Bradman. Sturdy of frame, Ponsford's movements looked heavy, but in fact his footwork was quick. Bat and pad were always close together and even in defence he was perfectly positioned to push the ball for ones and twos. He was master particularly of spin bowling, sidling down the pitch and playing strokes into gaps all round the wicket, though he was especially good around the leg-stump. He toured England in 1926, 1930, and 1934, and appeared in five series at home between 1924 and 1933, three against England. On his three England tours he made 4,110 runs (55.54). On his Test début, the first match at Sydney in 1924/5, he made 110 and 128 in the second match at Melbourne. He failed, relatively, in the 1926, 1928/9 and 1932/3 series, Harold Larwood being the main bogey-man; but he was a tower of strength against England in 1930 with 330 runs (55.00); against the West Indies in 1930/1 with 467 runs (77.83), including 183 in the second Test at Sydney; and in his final series in England in 1934 when, with Bradman, he dwarfed everyone else. Ponsford headed the averages with 569 runs (94.83), although the Don made more runs. At Headingley he scored 181, adding 388 in $5\frac{1}{2}$ hours with Bradman for the fourth wicket after a batting collapse. Then, in what was to be his final Test, at The Oval, he scored 266, adding 451 with Bradman for the second wicket in only $5\frac{1}{4}$ hours, which remains an Australian record. Against MCC at Lord's in 1934 Ponsford added 389 for the third wicket with Stan McCabe, another record stand, his own share being 281 not out, the record for an Australian at Lord's. He retired from first-class cricket at the end of the 1934 tour. He made 13 scores exceeding 200, nine for his state. He scored 429 against Tasmania at Melbourne in 1922/3, then the world's highest score in a first-class match; and exceeded it with 437 against Queensland on the same ground in 1927/8. Also against Queensland at Melbourne, 1923/4, he put on 456 for the first wicket with Edgar Mayne, which remains the Australian record for the first wicket. In 43 Sheffield Shield matches his remarkable record was 5,413 runs (83.27). He was awarded an MBE and lived to be the oldest surviving Australian Test Cricketer.

First-class career (1920–34): 13,819 runs (65.18) including 47 centuries

Test matches (29): 2,122 runs (48.22) including 7 centuries, and 21 catches

POPE, Roland James

(b. 1864, Sydney; d. 1952, Sydney) *New South Wales, Scotland, and Australia*

Roland Pope, or 'The Doc', travelled through England with the 1886, 1890, and 1902 touring teams from Australia with an array of luggage and medicines. He was an honoured and welcome visitor though only a player as the last resort! After hitting 170 for Melbourne I Zingari against Richmond in 1884/5, he represented New South Wales in three matches and Australia, depleted by disagreements over pay, called on him to play in the second Test at Melbourne in the same season, when he scored 0 and 3. Wilst at Edinburgh University, he played some cricket for Scotland. He was a correct batsman, enthusiastic lob bowler, and a keen fielder in the deep.

First-class career (1884–1902): 318 runs (12.23)

PORTER, Graeme David

(b. 1955, Middle Swan, Western Australia) *Western Australia*

A member of Australia's inexperienced 1979 World Cup squad and Kim Hughes's 1979 touring team to India, Graeme Porter, a right-arm medium pacer and right-hand middle-order batsman, was a consistent Sheffield Shield all-rounder, who played one come-back match with Western Australia in 1985/6—three years after his previous appearance. Representing Australia in two one-day internationals, for 3 runs at 3 and 3 wickets at 11, Porter was fast-tracked into the national team because of the drain of quality

players who signed to play World Series Cricket from 1977 to 1979.

First-class career (1977–85): 666 runs (21.48), 52 wickets (32.26), and 20 catches

POTTER, Jack

(b. 1938, Melbourne, Victoria) *Victoria*

Widely regarded as one of Australian cricket's finest post-war batsmen never to play Test cricket, Potter toured with the Australian second team to New Zealand in 1960 and with the senior squad to England in 1964. He was Australia's 12th man three times, once in Melbourne against the 1963/4 South Africans, when he ran out Eddie Barlow as a substitute fieldsman, and twice in England in 1964. Had he not suffered a fractured skull late in the tour in Holland in 1964, he could well have made his Test début on the subcontinent, with Australia committed to three Tests against India and one against Pakistan on the way home from England. A right-hand middle-order batsman and occasional right-arm leg-spinner, Potter amassed more than 5,000 runs in 81 games for Victoria, a feature being his 221 against a New South Wales attack of Test standard in the 1965/6 Christmas match at the MCG. Potter later captained Victoria with success and in 1988 was named the inaugural coach at the AIS Australian Cricket Academy in Adelaide. Here he guided several future Test cricketers with understated wisdom.

First-class career (1956–67): 6,142 runs (41.22) including 14 centuries, 31 wickets (41.51), and 85 catches

QUICK, Ian William

(b. 1933, Geelong, Victoria) *Victoria*

A tall, left-arm orthodox spinner and right-hand late-order batsman, Ian 'Cure 'em' Quick claimed 32 wickets in his first Sheffield Shield season with Victoria in 1956/7, immediately being noted for his stamina; but he dropped quickly out of first-class cricket for business reasons after touring with the 1961 Australians to England. He was Australia's 12th man in the famous Old Trafford Test and took 50 wickets for the tour, but had no realistic chance of breaking into the XI ahead of Richie Benaud. He also toured New Zealand with an Australian second team in 1960, topping the aggregates with 28 wickets, including 7 for 20 and 5 for 78 in the opening three-day match against Auckland.

First-class career (1956–61): 816 runs (14.06), 195 wickets (30.36), and 32 catches

RACKEMANN, Carl Gray

(b. 1960, Brisbane) *Queensland, Surrey, and Australia*

Playing in only his second first-class match for his state, Carl Rackemann, a tall, blond, right-hand fast bowler, with a very powerful upper body but relatively weak legs, took 5 for 25 against the England tourists at Brisbane in 1979/80. At his best he bowled with the pace and fire of a marauding Viking, but a series of serious injuries, and his decision to join the rebel Australian tour of South Africa in 1985/6, limited his Test career. Injury restricted him to two games in the 1981/2 season but he burst back in 1982/3, taking 11 wickets in his first match and heading the bowling averages with 35 wickets (15.80). With 25 wickets in four games, he made his début in the Brisbane Test against England, taking 2 for 61 in the first innings. He broke down in the second innings and played only one more first-class match that season. Next year he was in devastating form in the first two Tests against Pakistan, taking 11 wickets at Perth and five at Brisbane, all at an average of 11.06, but injury again interrupted his season. He toured the West Indies, playing in only one Test, when he took 5 for 161 in a marathon display in Antigua. Injury, however, limited his tour appearances to three games. In 1984/5, his first full Australian season, he totalled 42 wickets but was selected for only one Test against the West Indies. Yet in the Sheffield Shield final he bowled himself to exhaustion, taking 6 for 54 from 30.2 overs in the second innings. Overlooked for the tour of England in 1985 he decided to secure his financial future by joining the rebel tour of South Africa. There he showed what the Australian Test side was missing by taking 28 wickets in the three international matches, including a career-best of 8 for 84 in the third game at Johannesburg. Back in favour for the tour of England in 1989 he was restricted to eight matches by injury, taking 32 wickets at 23. His fitful Test career resumed in 1989/90 and the following season against England it was his stout batting—mainly, in fact, his stout front pad—which defied the spinners in the Sydney Test for 32 overs. With 38 wickets at 28 for Queensland in 1993/4 he was still bowling with fire and resolution and he went as a replacement on Australia's 1994/5 tour of West Indies, prior to playing the 1995 season for Surrey.

First-class career (1979–   ): 646 runs (7.42), 450 wickets (26.25), and 30 catches.
Test matches (12): 53 runs (5.30), 39 wickets (29.15), and 2 catches

RANSFORD, Vernon Seymour

(b. 1885, Melbourne; d. 1958, Melbourne) *Victoria and Australia*

A very attractive left-handed batsman, strong on the leg-side and with a brilliant cover-drive, Vernon Ransford had a rather crouching stance, but moved rapidly into position, and was never afraid of lifting the ball into the open spaces. He was one of the best outfielders of his day. Unlucky, he once had an arm broken during a game and on another occasion deflected a full-toss on to his nose, with unpleasant results. After the First World War he was handicapped by ill-health and could not recapture his form of earlier days. He did not play in Test cricket again, although he toured New Zealand in 1921, 1925, and 1927. He appeared against England at home in 1907/8 and 1911/12, and South Africa in 1910/11. He toured England in 1909 but missed the 1912 tour owing to the dispute with the Australian Board. He paid five visits to New Zealand. In England he made 1,736 runs (43.40), including six centuries, one of 190 against MCC at Lord's in 1909 being his highest-ever score. He led the Test averages with 353 runs (58.83). On a difficult wicket in the Lord's Test he hit 143 not out. In 49 Sheffield Shield matches, spread over 22 years, he made 3,061 runs (39.24). Against New South Wales at Sydney in 1908/9 he hit 182 and 110, the first Victorian to make a century in each innings of a first-class match. From 1938 to 1957 he was Melbourne CC secretary.

First-class career (1903–27): 8,268 runs (42.40) including 25 centuries, and 29 wickets (30.62)
Test matches (20): 1,211 runs (37.84) including 1 century, 1–28, and 10 catches.

REDPATH, Ian Ritchie

(b. 1941, Geelong, Victoria) *Victoria and Australia*

For more than a decade Ian Redpath was one of the hardest Test batsmen in the world to dig out and an outstanding ambassador for his country, a charming, modest, and amusing man, though his batting was often pedestrian. Very lean, sallow skinned, with a prominent Adam's apple and bandy-legged walk, 'Redders' was a right-hander with immense powers of concentration who accumulated his runs doggedly, mainly off the back foot, though he could also drive vigorously. He played straight and got behind the ball, often looking discomforted by bouncers, but usually managing to duck back out of reach and never flinching when the next ball came down. He was also a brilliant fielder close to the wicket, especially at short-leg. He succeeded Colin McDonald as Victoria's opening batsman in 1962 and with Bill Lawry provided a highly productive opening partnership for many years, although until the initial retirement of Bobby Simpson he had to struggle to establish himself lower down the order for Australia. He toured England in 1964 and 1968, scoring 1,075 runs (32.57) in 1964 and 1,474 runs (43.35) in 1968, by which time he was a much more positive player. He was still a thorn in English flesh in 1974/5 when he played with all his old solidity to score 472 runs (42.90). In the fourth Test of this series, at Sydney, he shared a record second-wicket partnership of 220 for Australia against England and, during the course of this innings of 105, his fifth century in Test cricket, he reached 4,000 runs in his 58th match for Australia. Against the West Indies fast bowlers the following season he was again consistency itself, scoring 575 runs (52.27) and hitting Test centuries at Melbourne (twice) and Adelaide as well as a fourth century against the touring side for Victoria. His highest Test innings was 171 against England at Perth in 1970/1, when he added 219 with Greg Chappell for Australia's sixth wicket. In this series he scored 497 runs (49.70) against John Snow at his peak. Despite these efforts at home he was left out of the Australian team touring England in 1972. Instead 'Redders' spent the summer teaching cricket at Charterhouse School in Surrey and, in his spare time, engaging in his hobby of fishing. Redpath played in some of the early World Series Cricket matches before injuring himself severely as he leapt in the air to celebrate taking a rare wicket! Awarded an MBE, he returned to his business as a Melbourne antique dealer, and was active in politics.

First-class career (1961–75): 14,993 runs (41.99) including 32 centuries, 13 wickets (35.84), and 211 catches

Test matches (66): 4,737 runs (43.45) including 8 centuries, 0–41, and 83 catches

REEDMAN, John Cole

(b. 1865, Adelaide; d. 1924, Adelaide) *South Australia and Australia*

A postman, John Reedman's batting lacked polish, but never faith or courage. Known as 'Dinny' he was difficult to shift because he was prepared to take all the knocks rather than lose his wicket.

His medium-pace change-bowling broke partnerships. He was held in high regard in his state during a very long career. His sole Test was the first at Sydney in 1894/5, when he scored 17 and 4, took 1 for 24 and held 1 catch.

First-class career (1887–1909): 3,338 runs (23.34) including 2 centuries, and 118 wickets (32.09)

REID, Bruce Anthony

(b. 1963, Perth) *Western Australia and Australia*

A cousin of the New Zealand Test player J. F. Reid, Bruce Reid was a left-arm fast bowler, 6 ft. 8 in. tall, with a mean bouncer and all the attributes of a dangerous Test bowler except an inswinger. For one of such gangling build, he had exceptional rhythm and had his willowy frame stood the strain his would have been a devastating career. But he was in demand for one-day matches too and after helping Australia to win the World Cup in India in 1987 he was obliged to rest his painful back. In 1989 a metal pin was inserted to correct stress fractures. He made his first-class début for his state in the 1984/5 season, taking over the mantle of Dennis Lillee. In five matches he took 17 wickets, including a best of 4 for 88. He toured Zimbabwe with the Young Australians and back in Australia bowled well for Western Australia, taking a career-best 6 for 54 against Tasmania. He was a surprise choice for the first Test against India at the age of 22, following injuries to other candidates and in the absence of the South African rebels. Despite his inexperience, he was Australia's most successful bowler in the series, taking 11 wickets (29.54) with a best return of 4 for 100 at Melbourne. He constantly troubled the batsmen with his accuracy, awkward bounce, and movement away from the bat, and on a successful tour to New Zealand at the end of the 1985/6 season, he took nine Test wickets at 32.66, including 4 for 90 at Christchurch. Against England in 1986/7 he played with steady success throughout the series, taking 7 of his 20 wickets at Perth, but his back operation ruled him out of the following season and his recovery was slow. Remodelling his action to reduce the strain on his body, he returned with dramatic success against England in 1990/1, taking 27 wickets at 16 each, including 6 for 97 and 7 for 51 in the second Test at Melbourne. It was the high point of a career full of vicissitudes, staunchly borne by an unassuming family man.

First-class career (1984–): 489 runs (8.57) and 306 wickets (26.92)
Test matches (27): 93 runs (4.65), 113 wickets (24.63), and 5 catches

REIFFEL, Paul Ronald

(b. 1966, Box Hill, Victoria) *Victoria and Australia*

Until the 1993 Headingley Test, Paul Reiffel was just making up the numbers among Australia's Ashes tourists. He had been 'smashed' in the first two one-day internationals and omitted from the first three Tests. But because of injuries the Australian selectors had little choice but to include the 6 ft. 4 in. Victorian in their XI for the fourth Test. He responded by taking 5 for 65 and 3 for 87 and, continuing his form, took 6 for 71 at Edgbaston, finishing the series with 19 wickets. While Shane Warne cornered most of the headlines for his 'ball of the century' in dismissing Mike Gatting, Reiffel had his own magic moment at Edgbaston in the fifth Test when he bowled Nasser Hussain with a leg cutter which pitched middle stump and hit the off bail. Right-arm fast-medium and a proficient right-hand tail-end batsman, Reiffel's will to succeed and his accuracy are his major attributes. His best wicket-taking ball, an off-cutter which jags back at pace, resulted in many of his wickets in England. Less successful on his own Australian pitches, he remained one of his country's best limited-overs players, taking 48 wickets in 40 one-day games to the start of the 1994/5 Australian season. An example of his all-round value came against the South Africans in Sydney in 1993/4 when he took 4 for 13, made 29 not out and figured in a run-out. In the West Indies in 1995 he took 15 wickets at 17 runs each in the four Tests.
First-class career (1987–): 1,237 runs (21.32), 235 wickets (30.12), and 37 catches
Test matches (16): 303 runs (21.44) and 31 wickets

RENNEBERG, David Alexander

(b. 1942, Sydney) *New South Wales and Australia*

A tall, dark, and enthusiastic right-arm fast bowler, David Renneberg improved steadily during the early to mid 1960s. At first erratic, especially while using the new ball, he developed excellent control. In the second innings of his first Test, against India at Adelaide in 1967/8, he took 5 for 39. As Graham McKenzie's opening partner in the Tests in South Africa in 1966/7, he took only 11 expensive wickets, but in Australia, the following season, he had 47 wickets (19.20). He took 41 wickets in England in 1968.

First-class career (1964–70): 466 runs (7.06) and 291 wickets (29.30)
Test matches (8): 22 runs (3.66), 23 wickets (36.08), and 2 catches

RICHARDS, David Lyle

(b. 1946, Melbourne)

A useful club cricketer, David Richards was the able, personable, and articulate secretary of the Australian Cricket Board from 1980–93 and became the first full-time secretary of the Cricket Council in 1993.

RICHARDSON, Arthur John

(b. 1888, Sevenhill, Clare, South Australia, d. 1973, Adelaide) *South Australia, Western Australia, and Australia*

A tall, dark, rather lean, bespectacled figure, slow in his movements like a man accustomed to following the plough, Arthur Richardson was a right-handed opening batsman who played mainly in front of the wicket, being a powerful driver, and a medium-pace off-break bowler. He used a heavy bat with a piece of cow-hide fastened around it. He appeared against England at home in 1924/5, and on tour in 1926. In the second innings of his Test début, at Sydney in 1924/5, he went in first and made 98 before giving a return catch to Tich Freeman. In the Test at Headingley in 1926 he made 100; and throughout the series bowled economically if not very penetratively, generally pitching on middle or middle-and-leg to four short-legs. He made 111 for his state against MCC at Adelaide in 1920/1. In 1922/3, in two matches for his state against Archie MacLaren's MCC side, he scored 150 in the first and 280 in the second, reaching his first hundred before lunch on the first day. This remains the highest for a state side against MCC. In 32 Sheffield Shield matches he made 2,355 runs (39.25) and took 74 wickets (39.04). He became a professional in the Lancashire League, coached in Australia, New Zealand, and the West Indies, and even umpired Tests in the Caribbean.
First-class career (1918–33): 5,238 runs (41.57) including 13 centuries, and 209 wickets (31.36)
Test matches (9): 403 runs (31.00) including 1 century, 12 wickets (43.41), and 1 catch

RICHARDSON, Victor York

(b. 1894, Adelaide; d. 1969, Adelaide) *South Australia and Australia*

Full of life and vigour, Vic Richardson—grandfather of the Chappell brothers—was a courageous and forcing right-handed batsman, being despite his awkward stance an excellent driver on both sides of the wicket and a fine hooker. His speed, agility, and safe hands made him a remarkable fielder in any position. A cheerful, enterprising, and unorthodox leader, he captained his state for many years, was vice-captain of the 1930 Australians to England, and captain of Australia in South Africa in 1935/6. At home he represented his country in the 1924/5, 1928/9, and 1932/3 series, just failing to win a permanent place at Test level. He toured America in 1932. He hit 138 in his second Test, at Melbourne in 1924/5, and 83 in the fourth Test at Brisbane, putting on 138 for the first wicket with Bill Woodfull. In 17 years for his state he usually opened the batting, making 7,698 attractive runs (42.53), including 21 centuries. In making his career-highest score of 231 against MCC at Adelaide in 1928/9, he caused tremendous excitement by hooking Larwood into the Pavilion. He was also an outstanding athlete, representing Australia at baseball and his state at baseball, golf, and tennis. He was also good at lacrosse, basketball, and swimming. He became a journalist and highly regarded radio commentator with the ABC, especially in partnership with Arthur Gilligan, whence the catchphrase, 'What do you think, Arthur?'

First-class career (1918–37): 10,727 runs (37.63) including 27 centuries, and 217 dismissals (213 c., 4 st.)
Test matches (19): 706 runs (23.53) including 1 century, and 24 catches

RIDINGS, Philip Lovett

(b. 1917, Unley, South Australia) *South Australia*

A proficient right-hand batsman who toured New Zealand with Bill Brown's 1950 Australian team, Phil Ridings amassed more than 5,000 first-class runs before serving Australian cricket ably as a national selector and administrator, being appointed Australian Cricket Board chairman in 1980/1. He was one of those most responsible for starting the highly successful financial group, Custom Credit, in Australia.

First-class career (1937–56): 5,653 runs (36.23) including 9 centuries, 61 wickets (46.95), and 55 catches

RIGG, Keith Edward

(b. 1906, Melbourne; d. 1985, Melbourne) *Victoria and Australia*

A tall right-hander with a fluent style, Keith Rigg

had both strokes and courage but lacked opportunities at the highest level. He hit 126 for his state against the West Indians at Melbourne in 1930/1 and appeared in the fifth Test at Sydney but achieved little. The following season against South Africa, in the second Test at Sydney, he added 111 quickly for the third wicket with Don Bradman. In that series he made 253 runs (50.60). Subsequently, he appeared against England in three matches during 1936/7, but did not tour. He hit a century against MCC's 'goodwill' side in 1935/6.

First-class career (1926–38): 5,544 runs (42.00) including 14 centuries
Test matches (8): 401 runs (33.41) including 1 century, and 5 catches

RIMINGTON, Stanley Garnet

(b. 1892, Kew, Melbourne; d. 1991, Kew) *Victoria*

Stan Rimington was Australia's longest-lived first-class cricketer, dying just two months short of his 100th birthday, in November 1991.

First-class career (1921): 91 runs (91.00)

RING, Douglas Thomas

(b. 1918, Hobart) *Victoria and Australia*

A happy philosopher, a tall right-arm leg-break bowler who did not mind being hit, and a fearless and unorthodox hitter, Doug Ring toured England in 1948 and 1953, appearing in one Test on each visit—although he took altogether 60 and 68 wickets, respectively. He played at home against India in 1947/8, West Indies in 1951/2 and South Africa in 1952/3. In Tests his main successes were at Brisbane in 1951/2 when he broke through to take 6 for 80, and again in the first Test at Brisbane in 1952/3 when he took 6 for 72. Against West Indies, with scores of 65, 67, and 32 not out, his swashbuckling batting was invaluable.

First-class career (1938–53): 3,418 runs (23.25) including 1 century, 451 wickets (28.48), and 93 catches
Test matches (13): 426 runs (22.42), 35 wickets (37.28), and 5 catches

RITCHIE, Gregory Michael

(b. 1960, Stanthorpe, Queensland) *Queensland, Buckinghamshire, and Australia*

Greg Ritchie toured Pakistan in 1982/3 as a replacement for Australia's senior batsman, Greg Chappell, and filled his shoes admirably on what was otherwise a disastrous tour for Australia. At Faisalabad, where Pakistan won by an innings, he scored 106 not out in only his fourth Test innings, hitting three sixes and nine fours. A tubby, tallish, confident and aggressive right-handed batsman with fair, curly hair, Ritchie made his first appearance for Queensland in 1980/1 and that season scored 140 not out against Victoria. In 1981 he gained further experience with Buckinghamshire, scoring 433 runs from eight innings (54.12), and in 1982 he played for the Middlesex 2nd XI. His trip to Pakistan was thoroughly earned by a series of commanding innings in the 1981/2 Sheffield Shield. In all first-class cricket that season he hit 833 runs (59.50) with three centuries. Although Chappell took his place in the series against England, his retirement enabled Ritchie to get back into the Test team on the tour of the Caribbean in 1983/4 and he made two impressive fifties in a difficult series. He played only in the final Test of the home series against the West Indies the following season, scoring 37. But on the 1985 tour of England he looked an accomplished player, resolute in defence, confident in attack, and fitter and quicker in the field. He scored 422 runs (42.20) in the Test series, including 146 at Trent Bridge and 94 at Lord's, adding 216 for the fifth wicket with Border, and made 1,097 runs (54.85) on the tour with four centuries. He completed his 1,000 runs in Test cricket against New Zealand and made his third Test century, 128 against India in 1985/6.

First-class career (1980–92): 10,170 runs (44.21) including 24 centuries, and 5 wickets (49.40)
Test matches (23): 1,374 runs (35.23) including 3 centuries, 0–10, and 14 catches

RIXON, Stephen John

(b. 1954, Alluay, New South Wales) *New South Wales and Australia*

A neat and lively wicket-keeper and useful right-hand batsman, Steve Rixon played ten Tests in succession under the captaincy of Bobby Simpson in the reconstituted Australian side which played series against India at home and West Indies away in 1977/8. He was dropped, however, for the series against England in 1978/9 and a broken arm, suffered while batting at Perth, made this an unhappy season for a keen and personable cricketer. Rixon made the position of New South Wales wicket-keeper his own in 1974/5 when, after making a mere 50 runs in his first 11 innings in first-class cricket, he scored 115 against Queensland at Sydney, starting his innings as a night-watchman. In the West Indies he made his major batting contribution in the fourth Test, scoring 54 and 39 not out, and although his 'keeping was inconsistent his subsequent rejection was harsh. Although he toured England as reserve to Rodney Marsh in 1981, he was not recalled to Test cricket until 1984, seven years later, to face the West Indies. He took seven catches in the Adelaide Test. Fine 'keeping in his three Tests won him a place on the 1985 tour to England, but he chose instead to go to South Africa, and was replaced. He had an incredible series behind the stumps for the 'rebel' Australians in 1985/6, taking 19 catches in the three 'Test' matches, including ten at Johannesburg. He became captain of New South Wales.

First-class career (1974–87): 4,303 runs (23.13) including 6 centuries, and 460 dismissals (394 c., 66 st.)
Test matches (13): 394 runs (18.76) and 47 dismissals (42 c., 5 st.)

ROBERTSON, Gavin Ron

(b. 1966, St Leonards, New South Wales) *New South Wales and Tasmania*

A 6 ft. 3 in. right-arm off-spinner, Gavin Robertson was chosen on Australia's winter tours of Pakistan and Sri Lanka in 1994 after an impressive 30-wicket season haul with New South Wales. After playing only one of New South Wales's opening three games of the 1993/4 season, Robertson took full advantage of Greg Matthews's fall from grace to become one of the champion state's main bowlers. Ironically, he had spent two seasons in Tasmania early in his career in a bid to secure a regular first-class place. A handy right-hand batsman, his highest score leading into the 1994/5 Australian season was 99, for Tasmania against New South Wales in Hobart, in 1991.

First-class career (1987–): 1,014 runs (28.16), 63 wickets (44.14), and 17 catches

ROBERTSON, William Roderick

(b. 1861, Deniliquin, New South Wales; d. 1938, Melbourne) *Victoria and Australia*

In a rather fleeting career 'Digger' Robertson, a useful right-handed batsman and leg-break bowler, took eight wickets in the tied match between his state and Alfred Shaw's team in 1884/5. He filled a place in the second Test at Melbourne, after several outstanding players had defected owing to disagreements over pay and conditions. He scored 0 and 2 and took 0 for 24.

First-class career (1884–7): 109 runs (13.62) and 15 wickets (31.06)

ROBINSON, Rayford Harold

(b. 1914, Stockton, New South Wales; d. 1965, Stockton) *New South Wales, South Australia, Otago, and Australia*

Slim and slightly built, Ray Robinson was a right-handed batsman of tremendous natural ability and charm. He had made handsome centuries against South Australia and Queensland when he represented his country against England at Brisbane in the first Test of 1936/7, scoring 2 and 3 (being 'c. Hammond b. Voce' each time) and catching Hammond in the first innings before the great man had scored. This was his sole Test, although in 23 Sheffield Shield matches he made 1,539 runs (38.47). He played for South Australia in 1940 and after the Second World War he played in New Zealand.

First-class career (1934–48): 2,441 runs (31.70) including 4 centuries, and 44 wickets (37.59)

ROBINSON, Raymond John

(b. 1905, Brighton, Victoria; d. 1982, Sydney)

Australia's most internationally acclaimed cricket writer, whose book *On Top Down Under* contained thoroughly researched biographies of Australia's cricket captains and won the English Cricket Society's Literary Award, Ray Robinson's cricket stories appeared in newspapers and magazines around the world for more than 50 years. His enthusiasm for cricket was boundless and he remained a keen contributor to magazines until his death, although his eyesight had virtually gone. Few sportswriters had the unanimous trust of the players like 'Robbie', who wrote in his own style, racily rather than elegantly, injecting all kinds of personal colour into his sentences. Thus: 'Sunshine gleamed on Miller's hair and his circling bat as his front-of-the-wicket shots explored the outskirts of the 208 yard-long outfield.' (*From the Boundary*, 1950.) He received a $A10,000 Government grant via the Australian Council for the Arts to research *On Top Down Under* and his *Between Wickets*, published in 1946, the first of his five books, remains one of the finest examples of Australian sportswriting.

ROBINSON, Richard Daryl

(b. 1946, Melbourne) *Victoria and Australia*

Tall for a wicket-keeper but also very capable and an attacking right-handed batsman, 'Richie' Robinson earned three Test caps in England in 1977 as a batsman. (Rodney Marsh kept wicket.) A popular and enterprising captain of Victoria, he had finished top of the Sheffield Shield batting averages in the previous Australian season and he was successful too against the English counties, scoring 715 runs (37.63). He also claimed more victims (34) on the tour than Marsh achieved from three more matches. But in the Tests the England fast bowlers exposed some technical frailties and, apart from a buccaneering 70 in a one-day international at The Oval, he was disappointing. He also toured England as Marsh's deputy in 1975, scoring 223 runs at 37.16 in seven matches.

First-class career (1971–82): 4,776 runs (39.80) including 7 centuries, 0–6, and 329 dismissals (289 c., 40 st.)

Test matches (3): 100 runs (16.66) and 4 catches

RORKE, Gordon Frederick

(b. 1938, Sydney) *New South Wales and Australia*

A giant right-arm fast bowler, handsome, blond-haired and nicknamed 'Lothair', Gordon Rorke played with some success against England in 1958/9 and toured India and Pakistan in 1959/60. He was one of several controversial bowlers in international cricket at that time. Dragging his rear foot several feet over the bowling crease, he bowled the ball from such a height and at such a pace that even the tallest batsmen had difficulty in doing more than prodding off the chest. Unhappily, he fell victim to hepatitis, which curtailed his career. In 25 Sheffield Shield matches he took 58 wickets (31.01). His action did more than anyone's to bring about the introduction of the front-foot no-ball law.

First-class career (1957–63): 248 runs (10.77) and 88 wickets (24.60)

Test matches (4): 9 runs (4.50), 10 wickets (20.30), and 1 catch

RUSH, Henry Reynolds

(b. 1858; d. 1928, Malvern, Victoria)

'Harry' Rush served Hawksburn, Prahran, Victorian, and Australian cricket for almost 50 years, being chairman of the Australian Board of Control from 1920 to 1922. Educated at Wesley

College and a grain-broker by profession, Rush captained Hawksburn for 16 seasons and worked diligently off the field, too, representing Hawksburn–Prahran on the Victorian Cricket Association for 23 years. As treasurer of the VCA from 1905 to 1927, he was one of those most responsible for the Association being able to afford its long-time city headquarters on the corner of Flinders and Exhibition Streets. He also acted as Association chairman when Donald Mackinnon was overseas. During the First World War he took an active part in recruiting for the 'Sportsmen's Thousand' in which he represented cricket interests. In helping to rehabilitate dozens of returning soldiers, he received honorary membership of the Returned Soldiers' League. Rush also served as a Victorian cricket selector. To perpetuate his memory, the VCA instituted the H. R. Rush Trophy for Country Week competition for 12 seasons, beginning 1928/9. His brother, Eddie, three years his junior, holds the Hawksburn–Prahran club individual batting record of 293 not out, scored against Carlton in 1897–8. Eddie played three matches for Victoria.

RUTHERFORD, John Walter

(b. 1929, Bruce Rock, Western Australia) *Western Australia and Australia*

A careful, defensive right-handed opening batsman, Jack Rutherford toured England, Pakistan, and India in 1956, but appeared in only one Test, the second against India at Bombay, in which he made 30 and took 1 for 15. He was the first Western Australian to be selected for an important overseas tour and the first to be capped for Australia. In 33 Sheffield Shield matches he made 2,200 runs (37.92), including a career-highest 167. He bowled occasional leg-breaks.

First-class career (1952–61): 3,367 runs (31.76) including 6 centuries, and 29 wickets (45.27)

RYDER, John

(b. 1889; d. 1977) *Victoria and Australia*

A tall, slim, attacking right-handed batsman, Jack Ryder was largely a front-of-the-wicket player with a powerful drive. As a fast-medium changebowler, he would get lift and movement away from the bat. He was also a good fielder. He toured England in 1921 and 1926 and South Africa in 1921/2. At home he appeared in the 1920/1, 1924/5, and 1928/9 series against England, the last as captain. He visited India as

skipper of Frank Tarrant's side in 1935/6; and led his state for many years. Before the First World War he was outstanding as a bowler: in his first season for his state in 1912/13, he captured 30 wickets (15.40), including 13 for 155 against South Australia, but after the War his main forte was batting. His career-highest score of 295 against New South Wales at Melbourne in 1926/7 included six sixes, his second hundred coming in 74 minutes—the total innings of the team was the record 1,107 runs! He did not represent Australia in any of the 1921 Tests, although he made 825 runs (35.86) and took 24 wickets on the tour. Against South Africa he hit 334 runs (111.33) in the three Tests of 1921/2, including 142 in the third at Cape Town. In the third Test at Adelaide in 1924/5, coming in at 119 for 6, he made 201 not out in $6\frac{1}{2}$ hours—slow for him, but very responsible in the circumstances—and 88 in the second innings, Australia just managing to defeat England by 11 runs. As captain for 1928/9, he made more runs than anyone else, 492 runs (54.66), which included 112 in the third Test at Melbourne, when he added 161 with Alan Kippax after three wickets had gone for 57. By now one of the Test selectors, there was much surprise and resentment that he was not selected for the team to England in 1930. The first of three teetotallers to captain Australia in the 11 years before the Second World War, he was well liked as a straightforward, unpretentious, slow-spoken man. A great helper of young players, he was a selector again from 1946 until 1970, working closely with Sir Donald Bradman. Known as 'the King' in his native Collingwood, he proudly led the parade of old Australian Test players at the Centenary Test Match celebrations in March 1977, dying only a few days later.

First-class career (1912–35): 10,501 runs (44.29) including 24 centuries, 238 wickets (29.68), and 133 catches
Test matches (20): 1,394 runs (51.62) including 3 centuries, 17 wickets (43.70), and 17 catches

SAGGERS, Ronald Arthur

(b. 1917, Sydney; d. 1987, Sydney) *New South Wales and Australia*

An accomplished second-string wicket-keeper to Don Tallon in England in 1948, Ron Saggers became the regular 'keeper during the tour of South Africa in 1949/50. His style was quiet and neat and reminiscent of Bert Oldfield. He was an attractive batsman, good enough early in his career for a place in his state XI on his batting alone. He captained his state for some years. He dismissed seven (all caught) in an innings for New South Wales against a Combined XI at Brisbane in 1940/1 and six (four caught, two stumped) in an innings against Queensland at Sydney in 1946/7.

First-class career (1939–50): 1,888 runs (23.89) including 1 century, and 221 dismissals (146 c., 75 st.)

Test matches (6): 30 runs (10.00) and 24 dismissals (16 c., 8 st.)

SAUNDERS, John Victor

(b. 1876, Melbourne; d. 1927, Melbourne) *Victoria, Wellington, and Australia*

Tall and spare, like the pen-pictures of Daniel Boone, Jack Saunders had a large moustache and a corkscrew run to the wicket. Starting from around mid-on, he came round the wicket, brought his left arm over close to his ear and spun the ball viciously at near medium pace. He was a holy terror on sticky wickets. A mainstay of the 1902 side to England, taking 123 wickets (16.95) in the wet summer, he was the man who bowled out Fred Tate at Old Trafford, thus ensuring the famous three-run victory. On his Test début against England in the fourth match at Sydney in 1901/2, he took 9 for 162 in the match, bowling unchanged with Noble in the second innings. He took seven wickets at Old Trafford and six at The Oval in 1902—having 18 wickets (26.27) in the series—and in South Africa in 1902/3 he took 15 wickets at 11.73 in two Tests, including 7 for 34 in the second innings at Johannesburg. Against the losing England 1907/8 side he took 9 for 104 in the fourth Test at Melbourne and 8 for 196 in the fifth at Sydney, which was his farewell appearance. In this last series he took more wickets than anyone else on either side and at lower cost, 31 wickets (23.09). In 37 Sheffield Shield matches he took 196 wickets (26.16), four times taking ten or more wickets in a match. Jack Saunders settled in New Zealand, playing in representative matches for Wellington and New Zealand from 1910 to 1914, and helped Clarrie Grimmett enter Australian cricket.

First-class career (1899–1914): 586 runs (4.76), 553 wickets (21.81), and 71 catches

Test matches (14): 39 runs (2.29), 79 wickets (22.74), and 5 catches

SCOTT, Dr Henry James Herbert

(b. 1858, Melbourne; d. 1910, Scone, New South Wales) *Victoria and Australia*

'Tup' Scott was a right-handed batsman and—like many of his colleagues—never a stylist, but his defence was assured, and he could hit when he liked. In a career that lasted less than ten years he represented Australia in the 1884/5 series, and toured England in 1884 and as captain in 1886. He gained golden opinions from those who played with him but there is little doubt that the cares of captaincy weighed heavily on him. His more prolific tour was 1886, when he made 1,278 runs in 58 completed innings; but his peak as a Test batsman was 1884 when he averaged 73.33 in the three matches. At Lord's, when England won by an innings, he top-scored each time with 75 and 31 not out; and at The Oval he made 102, adding 207 in a run-feast for the third wicket with Billy Murdoch. During the 1886 tour the players argued among themselves and sometimes blood-stained carriages bore witness to blows having been struck. 'Tup' remained in England to pursue his medical studies, played no more big cricket and became a pioneer country doctor.

First-class career (1877–86): 2,863 runs (22.72) including 4 centuries, and 18 wickets (27.44)

Test matches (8): 359 runs (27.61) including 1 century, 0–26, and 8 catches

SCOTT, John Drake

(b. 1888, Sydney; d. 1964, Adelaide) *New South Wales and South Australia*

A right-arm fast bowler with two states, Jack Scott was also a noted umpire, standing in 10 Tests from 1936 to 1947. He was renowned for disciplining fast bowlers for the over-use of bouncers.

First-class career (1908–28): 1,113 runs (14.64) including 1 century, 227 wickets (28.31), and 35 catches

SEDDON, Cecil Dudley

(b. 1902, Sydney; d. 1978, Dulwich Hill, Sydney) *New South Wales*

'Snowy' Seddon was a right-hand batsman with a peculiar two-eyed (open) stance who represented New South Wales alongside a young Don Bradman and also played Rugby League for his state. He devoted almost 60 years to the Petersham club, was on the New South Wales executive from 1955/6 to 1968, a state selector from 1947/8 to 1966/7 and a national selector from 1954/5 to 1966/7, choosing 82 Test teams.

First-class career (1926–8): 361 runs (36.10) including 1 century

SELLERS, Reginald Hugh Durning

(b. 1940, Bulsar, India) *South Australia and Australia*

A tall leg-spin bowler, Rex Sellers took 48 wickets for his state in 1963/4, which earned him a place in the team to England in 1964, but he damaged his bowling hand in one of the preliminary games on the tour and did not appear in the Tests. He toured India in 1964/5 and made his sole Test appearance in the third match, at Calcutta, scoring 0, taking 0 for 17 and holding 1 catch.

First-class career (1959–67): 1,089 runs (18.15) and 121 wickets (38.45)

SERJEANT, Craig Stanton

(b. 1951, Perth) *Western Australia and Australia*

A tall and strongly built right-hand batsman, Craig Serjeant was a powerful hitter of the ball, especially to the on-side, and such was his consistency after breaking into the strong Western Australian side in 1977/8 that he was making his first Test appearance at Lord's after only 18 first-class innings. He had scored 730 runs at an average of 66 in his first ten innings for Western Australia, including an impressive century against MCC on their way via Perth to play in the Centenary Test at Melbourne. At Lord's in his first Test innings he played a determined innings of 81 marked by powerful leg-side hitting, but England's bowlers got the measure of him thereafter and it was only in his tenth Test, when he hit 124 against West Indies at Georgetown in 1978, that he appeared to have established himself in the Australian team. However his form was topsy-turvy the following season and he was not picked to play against England. A modest, friendly man, he is a pharmacist by trade.

First-class career (1976–83): 4,030 runs (35.04) including 9 centuries, and 90 catches

Test matches (12): 522 runs (23.72) including 1 century, and 13 catches

SHEAHAN, Andrew Paul

(b. 1946, Werribee, Victoria) *Victoria and Australia*

Although in the early part of his career Paul Sheahan was regarded as the most exciting bats-

man to emerge in Australian cricket since Norman O'Neill, he did not quite live up to that early reputation. Tall, good-looking, charming, and erudite, he was, nevertheless, a classy and stylish right-handed batsman and brilliant cover-point. In his second season with Victoria, 1966/7, he came second in the overall Sheffield Shield averages with 66, making his career-highest score of 202 against South Australia at Melbourne. He was sparkling, and, making his Test début against India in 1967/8 at Adelaide, he hit 81 and 35. Between 1967 and 1971 he appeared in 25 consecutive Tests: in England, South Africa, and India, and at home against India, West Indies, and England. He was then dropped, until making his second tour to England in 1972 and appearing against Pakistan and New Zealand in 1972/3 and 1973/4. With a highest score of 51 he averaged 36.71 against the West Indies in 1968/9, not able to build a long innings. In India in 1969 he made his first Test century, 114 in the second match at Kanpur. The previous year he had disappointed on his first tour of England, failing to reach 1,000 runs, and in the Tests excelling only with 88 in the first Test at Old Trafford when his fourth-wicket stand with Bill Lawry took Australia from danger at 174 for 4 to the safety of 326 for 5. On his second England visit in 1972 he performed quite well, making 788 runs (41.47) and in one of the two Tests he played, the last at The Oval, his 44 not out saw Australia safely home. His 127 in the second Test against Pakistan in 1972/3 helped to lay foundations for victory. His Test career ended quietly against New Zealand in 1973/4. For his state alone he made 3,988 runs (59.52) in 47 matches. He became Principal at Geelong College.

First-class career (1965–73): 7,987 runs (46.16) including 19 centuries, 1 wicket (66.00), and 89 catches

Test matches (31): 1,594 runs (33.91) including 2 centuries, and 17 catches

SHEPHERD, Barry Kenneth

(b. 1938, Donnybrook, W. Australia) *Western Australia and Australia*

A burly, hard-hitting, and very consistent left-handed batsman, Barrie Shepherd narrowly missed the 1964 tour of England. He toured the West Indies in 1964/5 and at home, between 1962 and 1965, played a sprinkling of Tests, against England, South Africa, and Pakistan. On his début against England, in the third Test at Sydney in 1962/3, he made 71 not out, holding the

SIDDONS

middle-order batting together. In his first Test against South Africa, the second at Melbourne in 1963/4, he struck hard for 96, but in the fourth Test at Adelaide his 70 and 78 could not prevent South Africa winning handsomely. In four Tests of that series he averaged 38.28. Against Pakistan at Melbourne in 1964/5 he made 55 and 43 not out. Such was Australia's batting power that he had fewer chances than he deserved. He captained Western Australia 39 times, and all his centuries, three of them doubles, were for the state.

First-class career (1955–66): 6,834 runs (41.16) including 13 centuries, and 4 wickets (85.75)
Test matches (9): 502 runs (41.83), 0–9, and 2 catches

SIDDONS, James Darren

(b. 1964, Robinvale, Victoria) *Victoria and South Australia*

Few non-Test players have a more formidable record at state level than the dashing right-hand batsman and brilliant fieldsman who left Victoria in mid-career to captain South Australia. In 1993/4, he became only the tenth player to score more than 7,000 runs in Sheffield Shield cricket. His highest first-class score, 245 for Victoria against New South Wales at the Junction Oval, St Kilda in 1990/1, included 203 runs in a day, against an attack involving Lawson, Whitney, Holdsworth, and Steve Waugh. Later that season, he scored 124 not out against New South Wales in a low-scoring Sheffield Shield final, a disciplined display on a difficult pitch which took almost 5 hours. It was to be his last innings for his home state, during which he passed 5,000 first-class runs. By taking three catches for the match, at slip, he equalled the record (23) for most catches by a non-wicket-keeper in a Sheffield Shield season. His batting average of 80-plus in matches in Adelaide, including two double-centuries, and lack of regular work opportunities was central to his decision to move. He made 650 runs in his first year in Adelaide and 1,190 in his second, but still could not win an international place ahead of younger players of lesser achievement. He underlined the point with innings of 121, and 31 out of 102, for South Australia against the 1994/5 England team. His solitary Australian appearance came at Lahore in the final one-day game of the controversial 1988 tour of Pakistan. He made 32. Siddons is one of the few 1990s Australian first-class cricketers also to have played senior Australian Rules football.

First-class career (1984–   ): 7,637 runs (48.03) including 23 centuries, 2 wickets (173.50), and 120 catches

SIEVERS, Morris William

(b. 1912, Wonthaggi, Victoria; d. 1968, Melbourne) *Victoria and Australia*

Six feet four inches, Morris Sievers was a right-arm fast-medium bowler with the invaluable lift which great height gives to a bowler, and a useful batsman. He appeared in three Tests as an opening bowler against England in 1936/7, in the third of which (his last) he was virtually unplayable on a Melbourne 'glue-pot' pitch, when the ball rose from a good length almost vertically. He took 5 for 21 in the first innings and headed the Test bowling averages. He toured South Africa in 1935/6 without, however, appearing in the Tests.

First-class career (1933–45): 2,075 runs (29.64) and 116 wickets (33.36)
Test matches (3): 67 runs (13.40), 9 wickets (17.88), and 4 catches

SIMPSON, Robert Baddeley

(b. 1936, Sydney) *New South Wales, Western Australia, and Australia*

One of Australia's finest all-round cricketers, Bobby Simpson owed his success to a rigorous dedication to cricket allied to great natural ability. A sturdily built right-hand batsman at home against all bowlers except at times the very fastest, he was also a good leg-spin and googly bowler and one of the finest slip fielders of all time. His ability was evident very early. He made his initial first-class appearance for New South Wales in 1952/3 against Victoria when still a month short of his 17th birthday. To further his career, he played Lancashire League cricket in England in 1959 and moved to Western Australia between 1956/7 and 1960/1. Brilliant footwork and lightning reflexes took him into the right position to play any stroke but, like all prolific batsmen, he had the self-discipline not to play shots involving too great a risk until he was thoroughly established at the crease. New South Wales were reminded of what they had (temporarily) lost in 1959/60 when, playing for Western Australia against them, he scored 236 not out and then took three wickets in five balls while taking 5 for 45. His highest score, 359 for New South Wales against Queensland in 1963/4, is the highest score in Australia since the Second World War. Simpson has toured all the other Test-playing countries: England (twice), New Zealand (twice), South Africa (twice), the West Indies (twice), and India and Pakistan. He captained Australia in twenty-nine Tests between 1963/4 and 1967/8, and again in a further ten in 1977/8 after accepting the invitation of the Australian Board to come back to lead the young side which had to be rebuilt after the defections to World Series Cricket. At Old Trafford in 1964 he hit 311 against England, the second highest by an Australian in Test cricket—a typically painstaking effort designed to make sure of the Ashes. He hit 23 fours and a six in this innings which stretched into the third morning of the match and which was, strangely enough, his first hundred in thirty Tests, although as opening partner to Bill Lawry he had already been a consistent run-scorer. With Lawry in 1965 he scored 382 for the first wicket against the West Indies at Bridgetown, the highest opening partnership in Australia's history, Simpson making 201. Like all their partnerships together this one was notable for a perfect understanding in their running between the wickets. Simpson always believed in taking as many short singles as possible. As a captain he was firm, decisive, always in control, but sometimes lacking imagination. His 110 catches in Test cricket was a (then) record for Australia; practically nothing escaped him at first slip. His leg-spinners were good enough to bring him 5 for 57 against India at Sydney in 1967/8, his last season in his 'first' career. Always superbly fit, Simpson conducted the game sportingly but toughly, and he was always quite immaculately turned out, with his dark hair swept back neatly above square, tough, and determined features. Director of a successful public relations business, he became manager of the Australian side in 1985/6. He set high standards, insisting on commitment, fitness, and character in his players. He was not always popular with all of them and he and Allan Border did not always see eye-to-eye, but theirs was a highly successful partnership, characterized by victories in the 1987 World Cup in India and the successful campaigns in England in 1989 and 1993. He also coached and managed Leicestershire in 1991 and 1992.

First-class career (1952–77): 21,029 runs (56.22) including 60 centuries, 349 wickets (38.07), and 383 catches

Test matches (62): 4,869 runs (46.81) including 10 centuries, 71 wickets (42.26), and 110 catches

SINCOCK, David John

(b. 1942, Adelaide) *South Australia and Australia*

A red-haired left-arm googly bowler, David Sincock was able to spin the ball on any wicket but, like many of his type, tended to lack control and direction. He toured the West Indies in 1965 and played at home against Pakistan in 1964/5, and England in 1965/6 with expensive results. His début in first-class cricket, however, had been notable: he took 6 for 52 in the first innings of the strong New South Wales side at Adelaide in 1960/1. A dentist, he had been outstanding as a scholar and baseball player at school in Adelaide. His father, Harold, and brother, Peter, also played for South Australia.

First-class career (1960–6): 838 runs (17.45) and 159 wickets (36.87)

Test matches (3): 80 runs (26.66), 8 wickets (51.25), and 2 catches

SLATER, Keith Nichol

(b. 1935, Perth) *Western Australia and Australia*

A big, strong, extrovert all-rounder, usually a slow off-spinner, sometimes a medium-pacer with the new ball, Keith Slater's action did not meet with general satisfaction, but later his sound batting enabled him to open the innings for his state. In taking 4 for 8 in one spell for Western Australia against MCC at Perth in 1958/9, he became the first of Australia's alleged 'chuckers' of the period. In his last season, 1964/5, he was called for throwing at Sydney, while playing against New South Wales, but this was only the second time he had been called. In his sole Test, the third at Sydney against England that season, he made 1 not out and took 2 for 101. He toured New Zealand in 1959/60 and was also a noted Australian Rules footballer.

First-class career (1955–65): 2,198 runs (21.13) including 1 century, and 140 wickets (42.15)

SLATER, Michael Jonathon

(b. 1970, Wagga Wagga, New South Wales) *New South Wales and Australia*

A cycling accident threatened to end Michael Slater's international career even before it started in 1990. As one of the first pupils at the newly established Australian Cricket Academy in Adelaide, the teenager was bike-riding for extra fitness with Michael Bevan when struck by a car, resulting in hip and back injuries. It took him

SLEEP

more than a year to recover fully. His flourishing progress afterwards involved selection for Australia, a century in his first Lord's Test and additional tours to Sharjah, South Africa, Pakistan, Sri Lanka, and West Indies, all in two years. A right-hand opening batsman noted for his orthodoxy, dash, and flair—his maiden Test century came from 175 balls—Slater took just 14 matches to pass 1,000 Test runs, averaging almost 50. Developing a fine understanding with his left-handed partner, Mark Taylor, who also hails from Wagga Wagga, the pair averaged 80 each time they batted in England in 1993, including an initial stand of 128 in the first Test at Old Trafford and 260 in the second at Lord's. Slater had begun the preceding Australian season with the New South Wales 2nd XI, but forced his way into the Ashes party with three centuries and more than 1,000 runs in only 10 matches with the senior New South Wales XI. Modest and friendly, Slater is the son of a cricket-playing Lancastrian who emigrated. He regarded his coach at Wagga, Warren Smith, as a second father. Smith's simple drills included asking Slater to use his feet to hit a stationary ball into the nets as straight as he could, before repeating the exercise, this time with a moving ball. Making his one-day international début in Australia in 1993/4, Slater scored 73 from just 69 balls, including a six over the MCC's extra cover boundary against Hansie Cronje. It was a surprise when he was omitted from the one-day side soon afterwards, but against England in 1994/5 he was superb, cutting the first ball of the series for four on his way to 176, and going on to score 623 runs in the five Tests.

First-class career (1991–): 3,742 runs (50.56) including 10 centuries, and 22 catches
Test matches (15): 1,157 runs (48.20) and 3 catches

SLEEP, Peter Raymond

(b. 1957, Penola, South Australia) *South Australia and Australia*

A cheerful, sturdy right-arm leg spinner with a good high action and an attacking middle-order batsman, Peter Sleep, known as 'Sounda', belied his name because he was a thoroughly lively cricketer. Establishing himself in the South Australia side in 1977/8, he scored 105 not out against Queensland and took 4 for 41 against New South Wales. Performances like these the following season took him into the national side for the first Test against Pakistan at Melbourne in March 1979. He scored 10 and 0, took 1 for 16 in the first innings and 1 for 62 in only eight overs

in the second, and was promptly dropped, but he gained further Test experience in India in 1979. His tour to India was disappointing, although in the fourth Test his determined 64 in the second innings helped to save the game for Australia. He was less successful in the other Test in which he played, the sixth, and he did not take a wicket in either game. Selection for the Test team eluded him in the following two seasons but he continued to be a considerable force for South Australia with batting becoming increasingly the strongest of his all-round qualities. Unfortunately for him the leg-spinner was becoming unfashionable, even in the country which has produced more outstanding exponents of the art than any other. He played against Pakistan in 1982/3 before returning, with more success, against England in 1986/7. His 5 for 82 in the second innings at Sydney won an exciting last Test and proved to be the start of a period of domination by Australia. He had an effective series with the bat against New Zealand in 1987/8, with scores of 39, 62, 90, and 20, and followed this with 41 in the 'one-off' Bicentenary Test against England. He toured Pakistan in 1988/9 but missed the 1989 tour of England and played his last two Tests at home to Sri Lanka and India in 1989/90. At Hobart against Sri Lanka his match figures of 5 for 175 in 69 overs represented a great contribution to his team's victory, since it followed a fighting 3-hour innings of 47 not out, the highest score in Australia's first innings. Popular and effective as a Lancashire League cricketer, Peter Sleep often played in Rest of the World teams in England and at the Scarborough Festival and in 1995 Lancashire appointed him as 2nd XI captain because of his experience and know-how.

First-class career (1976–93): 8,122 runs (34.56) including 15 centuries, 363 wickets (39.36), 104 catches, and 1 stumping
Test matches (14): 483 runs (24.15), 31 wickets (45.06), and 4 catches

SLIGHT, James

(b. 1855, Ashby, Geelong, Victoria; d. 1930, Melbourne) *Victoria and Australia*

Jim Slight was a right-handed batsman with a sound defence and a free style, and a good field at point or long-on. Impaired health, which necessitated an operation, handicapped him while in England with the 1880 team. In the first-ever Test in England at The Oval he scored 11 but did not represent Australia again.

First-class career (1874–87): 415 runs (12.57), 3 wickets (12.33), and 4 catches

SMITH, David Bertram Miller

(b. 1884, Melbourne; d. 1963, Melbourne) *Victoria and Australia*

A fast-scoring right-handed batsman, being a splendid cutter and driver, Dave Smith toured New Zealand in 1909/10 and England in 1912 as a replacement for one of the six major players who had refused to tour. He was a big disappointment, 'living it up' and making only 292 runs (13.27), although he did hit a century off Surrey at The Oval, adding 176 for the sixth wicket in less than two hours with Claude Jennings. Even then an error of judgement on his part threw away his partner's wicket—and Surrey won. He played in two Tests on this tour and also toured America in 1912.

First-class career (1908–12): 1,764 runs (23.83) including 3 centuries, 1 wicket (22.00), and 16 catches

Test matches (2): 30 runs (15.00)

SMITH, Horace Clitheroe

(b. 1892, Sandy Bay, Tasmania; d. 1977, Hobart) *Tasmania*

'Clyde' Smith became known as Tasmania's 'Mr Cricket' while serving on the Tasmanian Cricket Association's Committee of Management for more than 50 years, including 35 as its chairman. During the First World War it was largely his energy which saved the TCA from bankruptcy. A right-hand batsman good enough to captain Tasmania during his six state appearances, his administrative qualities were recognized very early in his career and at 27, he was appointed a Tasmanian delegate to the Australian Board of Control. He managed the Australian team to New Zealand in 1960 and the members' pavilion at the old TCA ground on the Domain is named in his honour.

First-class career (1913–27): 146 runs (13.27) and 1 wicket (106.00)

SMITH, Stephen Barry

(b. 1961, Sydney) *New South Wales, Transvaal, and Australia*

Steve Smith, the cousin of Norman O'Neill, was a gifted right-handed opening batsman, with a penchant for the square-cut, who was on the fringe of the Australian Test side, playing three Tests in the West Indies in 1983/4, before he joined the Australian rebel tour of South Africa. A positive, fit cricketer and fine fielder, he made his first-class début for New South Wales in 1981/2 scoring 245 runs (40.83). The following season he added to his reputation, making his maiden century against Queensland and a brilliant marathon 263 against Victoria, whilst still only 21. He made his one-day international début in the World Series Cup against New Zealand and England, scoring a fine century against New Zealand. He toured Sri Lanka in April 1983 but did not play in the Test match. After more one-day appearances, his Test chance came on the 1983/4 tour of the West Indies. He started the tour brilliantly, scoring two centuries in his first game, but in his three Test matches, against fierce bowling, scored only 41 runs. He had a disappointing season in 1984/5 but showed his talent again when he scored a superb 116 against South Africa in the third international at Johannesburg. He stayed to play several seasons for Transvaal after an unsuccessful attempt to re-establish himself in New South Wales.

First-class career (1981–91): 5,248 runs (35.94) including 12 centuries, 1 wicket (77.00), and 66 catches

Test matches (3): 41 runs (8.20) and 1 catch

SMITH, Sydney jun.

(b. 1880, Sydney; d. 1972, Sydney)

Syd Smith's contribution to Australian cricket at state and national level is legendary. A fluent speaker and great diplomat, he had a 76-year involvement with cricket administration, including a record 61 years with the New South Wales Cricket Association. At 10, he became secretary of a boys' cricket club at Annandale, starting an unbroken attachment with the game until his retirement as president of the NSWCA in 1966, aged 86. On his retirement, the Association held a dinner in his honour, attended by the State Governor, Sir Roden Cutler. Secretary and treasurer of the Australian Board of Control in its formative years from 1911 to 1926, he managed the 1921 and 1926 Australian teams to England and also served as a Sydney Cricket Ground trustee from 1940 to 1950. He was president of the NSWCA (1935–66). He referred to himself as Syd Smith junior, as his father, also Syd, was a Member of Parliament in Sydney. Smith wrote two cricket books, *With the 15th Australian XI* in 1922 and *History of the Tests* in 1946. He remained a keen club cricketer into his mid-40s and was awarded a CBE for his services to cricket.

SPOFFORTH, Frederick Robert

(b. 1853, Sydney; d. 1926, Long Ditton, Surrey, England) *New South Wales, Victoria, Derbyshire, and Australia*

'The Demon' Spofforth was the greatest figure in early Australian Test cricket, the man who finally humbled W. G. Grace. In May 1878 at Lord's he captured 6 for 4 and 5 for 16, MCC being routed in one day. He studied the methods of all the famous bowlers he had seen and put to useful effect all their lessons, but he was still an original, mixing speed, cut, and swerve with devilish accuracy. His basic pace was fast-medium. He was tall—over 6 ft.—and lean, could run 100 yards in less than 11 seconds and, unlike most of his contemporaries, studied the strengths and weaknesses of his opposing batsmen. He refused to play in the first-ever Test at Melbourne in 1876/7 as W. L. Murdoch had not been selected to keep wicket but he appeared in the second. At Melbourne in 1878/9 he was the main instrument of victory in taking 13 for 110. After his dramatic start in 1878 he toured England again in 1880 (injury prevented him appearing in the first Test at The Oval), 1882, 1884, and 1886. At The Oval in 1882—the first Ashes match—he bowled Australia to victory with his 14 for 90. In the 1886 series he was still the most effective bowler with 14 wickets (18.57). In Australia he took 18 wickets (22.66) in the 1882/3 series, including 7 for 44 in the second innings of the third match at Sydney (11 for 117 in the match), which still could not bring victory; and he was still the best bowler in the 1884/5 series with 19 wickets (16.10). In all eleven-a-side matches in England he took 123 wickets (11.37) in 1878, 188 wickets (12.12) in 1882 and 216 wickets (12.23) in 1884. Only injuries prevented similar records in 1880 and 1886. Settling in England, 'The Demon' became a director of the Star Tea Company and played for Derbyshire with success from 1889 until 1891, taking 15 for 81 against Yorkshire at Derby in the former year. It is said that in 1881 he rode 400 miles to play in a minor match in Australia and then took all 20 wickets—clean-bowled!

First-class career (1874–97): 1,928 runs (9.88), 853 wickets (14.95), and 83 catches

Test matches (18): 217 runs (9.43), 94 wickets (18.41), and 11 catches

STACKPOLE, Keith Raymond

(b. 1940, Melbourne) *Victoria and Australia*

Squarely built and red-faced, Keith Stackpole was a lusty right-handed opening batsman who almost always attacked, and often hooked and cut so hard at the new ball that his occasional edges were just too hot for fielders to hold. He was an entertainer who, in full flow, would bat with tremendous confidence, often leaving the crease to drive straight or over mid-on. As he matured, he extended his range with many more front-foot strokes. He was a useful leg-break bowler in his early days and a fine close fieldsman. His sole tour of England in 1972 was as vice-captain. From 1966 until 1973 other tours were to South Africa (twice), India, the West Indies and New Zealand. At home he appeared in two series against England, 1965/6 and 1970/1, and against West Indies, Pakistan, and New Zealand. He had a long haul to the top after making his first-class début for his state against Tasmania in 1959/60. On his Test début against England in 1965/6 he batted down the order. His first Test century was 134 against South Africa in the Cape Town match in 1966/7. He lost his place against the Indian tourists and was not selected for England in 1968, but he regained his place against the West Indies in 1968/9 and became established as an opening batsman. From then until the end of the 1970/1 England series, in which he headed the Australian averages with 627 runs (52.25) including his career-highest score of 207 in the first match at Brisbane, he played in 20 consecutive Tests. In England in 1972 he made more runs than anyone on either side and headed the averages again with 485 runs (53.88), including a fine 114 at Trent Bridge, when runs were badly needed against John Snow at his best. In all first-class matches on the tour he scored 1,309 runs (43.63). His last Test century was 122 in the first match against New Zealand at Melbourne in 1973/4, and in his final Test, against New Zealand at Auckland the same season, he was dismissed without scoring in either innings. He became a forthright TV commentator and was awarded an MBE.

First-class career (1959–73): 10,100 runs (39.29) including 22 centuries, 148 wickets (39.28), and 166 catches

Test matches (43): 2,807 runs (37.42) including 7 centuries, 15 wickets (66.73), and 47 catches

STEELE, Raymond Charles

(b. 1917, Yarraville, Victoria; d. 1993, Melbourne)

A much-loved cricketing ambassador who was president of the Victorian Cricket Association for 20 years, Ray Steele also managed three Australian teams to England, in 1961 (as assistant-manager), 1964, and 1972. With Bob Parish he formed a formidable administrative combination which was responsible for taking on and ultimately negotiating a peace settlement with Kerry Packer's World Series Cricket movement in 1979. A solicitor by profession and a talented all-round sportsman, who played in an Australian Rules premiership with the Richmond club, Steele was a cheerful extrovert, equally at ease in the hearty companionship of sportsmen, making a speech, or controlling cricket meetings. Educated at Scotch College and Melbourne University, he was a fast-medium bowler and capable lower-order batsman, who captained University and Hawthorn-East Melbourne during a 74-match senior career. He served on cricket committees for more than 45 years, was Hawthorn-East Melbourne's delegate to the Victorian Cricket Association from 1953 to 1973, and a VCA executive committee member from 1956 to 1992, including 20 years as treasurer. He was also treasurer (1969–85) of the Australian Cricket Board. In 1977 he was appointed an OBE for his services to cricket.

STEVENS, Gavin Byron

(b. 1932, Adelaide) *South Australia and Australia*

Hepatitis, contracted on tour to India and Pakistan, brought a sad and abrupt end to the promising career of Gavin Stevens, a broad-shouldered right-handed opening batsman. He had earned selection for the tour, in 1959/60, by heavy scoring for his state, scoring 666 runs and 951 runs in 1957/8 and 1958/9 respectively, including his top-score, 259 not out against New South Wales at Sydney in 1958/9. He also made three Shield hundreds in succession, two in the match against New South Wales in Sydney in January, 1958.

First-class career (1954–60); 3,061 runs (38.26) including 7 centuries
Test matches (4): 112 runs (16.00) and 2 catches

TABER, Hedley Brian

(b. 1940, Wagga Wagga, New South Wales) *New South Wales and Australia*

A small, dark, neat, unobtrusive 'keeper, Brian Taber held some fine catches standing back and supported the slow bowlers very well. Brought up in the country district of Wollongong, he made a round trip of 120 miles every Saturday from the age of 16 to play for the Gordon Club in Sydney. In his first season for his state in 1964/5 he made 31 dismissals, including eight victims

against South Australia at Sydney, and 35 the following season. He toured England in 1968 as second-string to Barry Jarman, but visited South Africa (twice) and India as the first-string. His sole home Test was against the West Indies in 1968/9. His entry into Test cricket was most striking. At Johannesburg in 1966/7 he held seven catches and made one stumping, the most victims by an Australian 'keeper against South Africa. In 1968/9 he equalled the world record for 12 victims in a match (nine caught, three stumped) against South Australia. He became a senior coach.

First-class career (1964–74): 2,648 runs (18.01) including 1 century, and 395 dismissals (345 c., 50 st.)
Test matches (16): 353 runs (16.04) and 60 dismissals (56 c., 4 st.)

TALLON, Donald

(b. 1916, Bundaberg, Queensland; d. 1984, Bundaberg) *Queensland and Australia*

A strident appealer, Don Tallon was also a quick and brilliant wicket-keeper. He equalled a long-standing world record by capturing 12 wickets in a match (nine caught, three stumped) for his state against New South Wales at Sydney in 1938/9. He was a stylish middle-order batsman with a pleasing array of strokes, making his name as a powerful driver; he hit centuries against all the other Sheffield Shield states. Against England at Melbourne in 1946/7 he hit 92 and added 154 with Ray Lindwall for the eighth wicket in 87 minutes. He had 20 victims in this series. He toured New Zealand in 1946, and England in 1948 and 1953 and, at home, played against India in 1947/8 and England in 1950/1. Hard of hearing, he once misunderstood Lindsay Hassett's message, sent from the dressing-room, to 'have a go' at appealing against bad light. Tallon immediately began attacking the bowling instead.

First-class career (1933–53): 6,034 runs (29.14) including 9 centuries, and 433 dismissals (303 c., 131 st.)
Test matches (21): 394 runs (17.13) and 58 dismissals (50 c., 8 st.)

TARRANT, Francis Alfred

(b. 1880, Fitzroy, Melbourne; d. 1951, Upper Hawthorn, Melbourne) *Victoria, Middlesex, Europeans, and Patiala*

Arguably the finest all-rounder never to appear in Test cricket, Frank Tarrant was denied international status by the restrictive qualification rules then in force. Brought up in Melbourne and a state player at 18, he played most of his cricket in England, becoming one of the premier and most versatile cricketers in county ranks in the decade immediately before the First World War. After the war he played two seasons for the Europeans in India and for Patiala from 1926 to 1934. A right-hand batsman, slow-medium left-hand bowler and reliable slip fielder, Tarrant was good enough to be chosen for either his batting or bowling. In his golden years from 1907 to 1914, he made 13,375 runs (average 37) and took 1,136 wickets (17). Of his three double hundreds for Middlesex, his 250 not out against Essex at Leyton in 1914 was the means of one of the county's greatest victories. He played 17 times for the Players v. the Gentlemen. The first player to score a Sheffield Shield and a county championship double century, Tarrant's personal feats were extraordinary. In a first-class game in India in 1918, he took 10 wickets in an innings and made 182 not out, for Maharajah of Cooch Behar's XI against Lord Willington's XI at Poona. In another match, he took 16 wickets and made a century. His career extended almost 40 years. Only four others had longer playing spans: C. K. Nayudu, W. G. Grace, Lord Harris, and A. W. Nourse. Between the wars, Tarrant was a dealer in high-priced racehorses to India and Australia and an umpire of note, standing in India's first two home Tests in 1933/4. In 1935/6, as manager of an unofficial Australian team to India, he played in three games. The following 'Indian summer', aged 56, he scored 78 and 18 and took four wickets in his final first-class match. He remains the oldest Australian-born player to play first-class cricket.

First-class career (1898–1936): 17,952 runs (36.41) including 33 centuries, 1,512 wickets (17.49), and 303 catches

TAYLOR, John Morris

(b. 1895, Sydney; d. 1971, Sydney) *New South Wales and Australia*

A schoolboy phenomenon, Johnny Taylor was a smallish man and a polished right-handed batsman, happiest when chasing runs and giving full rein to his varied array of strokes. His on-side play was excellent and he would stand back and, with certainty and power, force away anything short of a length. A brilliant fielder at cover, he was a spectacular runner and thrower. He was a member of the Australian Imperial Forces side in 1919, scoring 1,187 runs (31.23), and toured England again with the 1921 and 1926 teams, besides South Africa in 1921/2. It was in the 1924/5 home series against England that he rose to stardom, scoring 541 runs (54.10) and, in the second innings of the first Test at Sydney, saving his side with 108, when he added 127 for the last wicket with Arthur Mailey, a record for these contests. Taylor batted with the handicap of a boil on the back of the knee, just where the strap of the pad was rubbing. In the fourth Test at Melbourne, when England won handsomely, he top-scored each time with 86 and 68. On his last tour of England he was in poor health and achieved little. In 21 Sheffield Shield matches he made 1,299 runs (39.36).

First-class career (1913–26): 6,274 runs (33.37) including 11 centuries, 1 wicket (53.00), and 68 catches

Test matches (20): 997 runs (35.60) including 1 century, 1–45, and 11 catches

TAYLOR, Peter Laurence

(b. 1956, North Sydney) *New South Wales, Queensland, and Australia*

So unexpected was the foxy-haired Peter Taylor's selection in Australia's team for the fifth Ashes Test in 1986/7 that even Sydney scribes—renowned for their love of promoting their own —dubbed him 'Peter Who' and asked if the wrong Taylor (Peter instead of Mark) had accidentally been included. With only one specialist opener in the 12 (Geoff Marsh), it seemed possible that the 30-year-old Taylor's selection had come via an error in transmission. After all, he had played just four Sheffield Shield games for New South Wales, including only one of NSW's first seven matches that season. The tall right-arm off-spinner went from being an unknown to a national hero inside five days, taking an astonishing 6–78 and 2–76 to be 'man of the match'. A left-handed batsman, he also scored a fighting 42 in Australia's second innings as England suffered their only Test defeat of the summer. Taylor admitted he hardly knew his team-mates coming into the game. His chief concern was not to 'make an idiot' of himself and bowl badly. Spurred by the 'Peter Who' headlines, he had Allan Lamb caught behind in his third over and dismissed Ian Botham in both innings, including first ball in the second, to a wonderful running catch by Dirk Wellham, which helped change the fortunes of the Test. Test selector Greg Chappell said later that Taylor's promising display in the previous season's Sheffield Shield final against

Queensland in Sydney had alerted the panel to his qualities. A finger spinner was needed on the dusty SCG wicket and Taylor, despite his inexperience, was considered mature enough not to be overawed. Four of Taylor's nine Australian Tests were in Sydney, but there were to be no repeats of his fairy-tale beginning. A plucky, lower-middle order left-hander, his batting was considered just as valuable an asset and he actually opened for Australia (in the second innings against Pakistan at Karachi in 1988, having top scored with 54 not out in the first) and batted at number four (again in the second innings, against New Zealand at Wellington in 1990, when he top-scored with 87). He was never able to command a regular Test place and left Sydney for Brisbane late in his career to advance his chances, having been omitted from New South Wales's XI for the 1989/90 Shield final. But he became expert at the one-day game and in his final season, 1991/2, played 17 of Australia's 18 one-day internationals, for a career total of 83, prompting the team coach, Bob Simpson, to call him the best one-day spin bowler in the world. In 1994 he was appointed a Test selector at the age of only 38.

First-class career (1985–91): 1919 runs (30.95) including 1 century, 129 wickets (37.36), and 45 catches

Test matches (13): 431 runs (26.93), 27 wickets (39.55), and 10 catches

THOMAS, Grahame

(b. 1938, Sydney) *New South Wales and Australia*

Dark, thickset, and a beautiful stroke-player, Grahame Thomas toured New Zealand in 1959/60, West Indies in 1965, and South Africa in 1966/7. Such was his country's batting strength, however, that he could never establish himself as a Test player. He represented Australia at home against England and on a tour of the West Indies, when his overall average was 40.91 in first-class matches. His highest Test score was 61 at Port of Spain in the second Test. In 59 Sheffield Shield matches he made 3,992 runs (46.41), including his career-highest, 229 against Victoria at Melbourne, a display of brilliance sustained in 100-degree heat just before Christmas. 136 of his runs came in boundaries. With Neil Marks he added 332 for the sixth wicket against South Australia at Sydney in 1958/9, a Shield record. Of part-American Indian extraction, he was often homesick on tours and his retirement followed immediately after an unhappy tour to South Africa.

First-class career (1957–66): 5,726 runs (40.32) including 17 centuries

Test matches (8): 325 runs (29.54) and 3 catches

THOMPSON, Raelee Helen

(b. 1945, Shepparton, Victoria) *Victoria and Australia*

At the time Jeff Thomson was terrorizing many a batsman with his whiplash bowling the female 'Thommo', as she was dubbed by the press, was playing a significant part in the Australian domination of women's cricket during the late 1970s and 1980s. A right-arm medium-fast bowler with a more orthodox action than her namesake, Thompson took 57 wickets in 16 Tests to rank second on the all-time Australian list to Betty Wilson (68 in 11 Tests). Making her Test début in 1972 when Anne Gordon broke her arm, Thompson also captained her country in four Tests and three one-day internationals in the 1984/5 series against England when her equally feared opening bowling partner and international captain, Sharon Tredrea, was injured. Never one to let an opportunity slip by, Thompson took Australia from 1–0 down in the series to a 2–1 victory, their first win over England in 36 years. She was also the outstanding bowler in the series, taking 18 wickets at an average of 15.72 and claiming 5 for 33 in the final and series-winning Test in Bendigo. Thompson also played in three World Cups, 1973, 1978, and 1982, the latter two on the winning side. A policewoman specializing in fingerprinting, Thompson retired from international cricket at the age of 39. She represented her state between 1970 and 1987, and was also an Australian selector for 10 years. For her long and meritorious service to women's cricket she was made a life member of the Australian Women's Cricket Council in 1994.

Test matches (16): 162 runs (11.57) and 57 wickets (15.25)

One-day internationals (23): 207 runs (25.9) and 24 wickets (18.7)

THOMS, George Ronald

(b. 1927, Melbourne) *Victoria and Australia*

A right-handed opening batsman, George Thoms's sole Test was the fifth against West Indies at Sydney in 1951/2, when he scored 16 and 28. In the same season, as Colin McDonald's, opening partner for Victoria, he scored 150 against Western Australia and 120 against Queensland.

THOMSON

First-class career (1946–53): 1,137 runs (35.53) including 3 centuries, and 1 wicket (14.00)

THOMSON, Alan Lloyd

(b. 1945, Reservoir, Victoria) *Victoria and Australia*

Alan or 'Froggy' Thomson bowled with enthusiasm and a curious wrong-foot action which gave him some extra bounce. He was heralded as the new fast-bowling terror when MCC toured Australia in 1970/1—especially when he took 9 for 181 for Victoria against the touring team at Melbourne in an early match—but he was not genuinely fast and his performances in the Tests were very disappointing.

First-class career (1968–74): 260 runs (8.12) and 184 wickets (26.72)

Test matches (4): 22 runs (22.00) and 12 wickets (54.50)

THOMSON, Jeffrey Robert

(b. 1950, Sydney) *New South Wales, Queensland, Middlesex, and Australia*

A happy-go-lucky character with a rebellious streak, Jeff Thomson made one unsuccessful Test appearance against Pakistan in 1972/3 when it was subsequently discovered he played with a broken bone in his foot. Then, after showing his ability in his first season for Queensland in 1974/5, the selectors gambled with him for the first Test of that season and the result was one of the most awesome performances of fast bowling in cricket history. On a Gabba pitch unprepared because of tropical thunderstorms, Thomson got the ball to lift off a length after delivering it at a speed somewhere between 90 and 100 mph. Immensely strong and a former surf rider from the Sydney suburb of Bankstown, he bowled with a slinging action involving a powerful twist of the body in delivery. With the ball brought from behind his back at the last moment, he had the approach of a javelin thrower once his target was sighted. The action, however, demanded much of his body, and he never consistently achieved the ferocious pace which brought him 33 wickets (17.93) in his first five Tests against England. The bane of Thomson's life since this magnificent display of bowling, in which he earned success by sheer speed and exceptional bounce, was a suspect right shoulder, which first caused him trouble while playing tennis at Adelaide during the fifth Test in 1974/5. When Thomson missed the last Test and his partner Lillee was injured at the start of the sixth Test in Melbourne, England

who had been demoralized by the fire of these two, won the final game by an innings! Of all the great fast-bowling partnerships, perhaps none has been as crucial to their team's success as this one. The slow wickets in England in 1975 reduced Thomson's effectiveness: he took 16 Test wickets (28.56) in the four Tests. But the following winter he and Lillee outbowled an almost equally fearsome West Indian fast-bowling combination, Thomson taking 29 wickets (28.65). However, on the first day of the first Test against Pakistan at Adelaide (his unlucky ground) in 1976/7, Thomson crashed into his team-mate Alan Turner as they went for a high catch and tore his right shoulder muscle so severely that he missed the remainder of the series, and the Centenary Test. During this match Thomson signed for World Series Cricket, only to withdraw from his contract when he realized that it contravened another. He played against England in 1977, taking 23 wickets in the series (25.34) (easily the leading Australian bowler), against India in 1977/8 (22 wickets at 23.45), and West Indies in 1978 (20 wickets at 28.85). However, getting into financial trouble, he accepted a second offer to join World Series Cricket, missed the 1978/9 series with England, and played for WSC in the West Indies when the Australian Board released him early from his contract. A capable fielder, he was a right-handed batsman who occasionally hit effectively. The prospect of Jeff Thomson resuming his partnership with Dennis Lillee was eagerly awaited after the disbandment of World Series Cricket in 1979/80. He played in the first two Tests of the season, against the West Indies in Brisbane and England in Perth, but although he took seven wickets the extraordinary pace and lift of five seasons before had gone, never, it seemed, to return. He toured England in 1980, playing in several of the warm-up games but not the Centenary Test itself, and despite some good performances at home in 1980/1 he was overlooked for the national team and omitted from the 1981 touring team to England when two younger fast bowlers were preferred. Instead Thomson signed a contract for Middlesex. He went home early, however, after an appendix operation, and in 1981/2 got back into the national side, bowling heroically against the West Indies at Adelaide after Lillee had been injured. He could take only three wickets in a three-match series in Pakistan, but their old enemy from 1974/5 had one more nasty surprise in store for England's batsmen. Brought into the side for the 1982/3 Ashes confrontation only because of injuries to Alderman and Lillee, he proceeded to bowl with great hostility to take 22 wickets (18.68) in four Tests and topped the Australian bowling averages. He almost saved his side with the bat at Melbourne, making 21 of a last-wicket stand of 70 with Allan Border before he was caught at slip to allow England to win by 3 runs. Chagrined, he went to the England dressing-room to warn them in colourful language that he would get his revenge in the next Test: he duly took 5 for 50 in the first innings at Sydney, a performance which virtually guaranteed Australia the Ashes. His Test career again seemed to be over, but the desertions to South Africa gave him the chance of another England tour in 1985. He took the three wickets he needed for 200 Test wickets and 100 against England before retiring from first-class cricket at the end of the 1985/6 season. He became Queensland's coach.

First-class career (1972–86): 2,065 runs (13.58) and 675 wickets (26.46)
Test matches (51): 679 runs (12.81), 200 wickets (28.00), and 20 catches

THOMSON, Nathaniel Frampton Davis

(b. 1839, Sydney; d. 1896, Sydney) *New South Wales and Australia*

Nat Thomson was a considerable figure in early Australian cricket, playing 21 times for his state against Victoria between 1858 and 1879, achieving a batting average of 13.41 and 20 wickets. He was also a good reserve wicket-keeper. Against a Queensland XXII in 1864 he returned analyses of 7 for 9 and 7 for 25. He played against all the England sides which visited Australia up to and including Lord Harris's in 1878/9—five in all—and, in eleven-a-side matches against them, averaged 18.80 with the bat. He appeared in the first two Tests of 1876/7 as an opening batsman, but was unable to make the first tour of England in 1878. He was the first player to be dismissed in Tests—'b. A. Hill 1'.

First-class career (1857–79): 705 runs (14.10), 23 wickets (22.26), and 30 dismissals (23 c., 7 st.)
Test matches (2): 67 runs (16.75), 1–31, and 3 catches

THURLOW, Hugh Motley

(b. 1903, Townsville, Queensland; d. 1975, Brisbane) *Queensland and Australia*

A fast bowler, 'Pud' Thurlow attracted notice by taking 6 for 60 for his state against Victoria at Melbourne in 1929/30, in the course of which he broke the finger of Australia's future captain, Bill Woodfull, putting him out of action for the rest of the season. Then in 1931/2 Alan Kippax of New South Wales attempted to hook him too early and had to have his eyebrow treated in hospital. That season 'Pud' played in his sole Test, the fourth against South Africa at Adelaide, failing to score and conceding 86 runs without taking a wicket.

First-class career (1928–34): 202 runs (5.31) and 80 wickets (42.88)

TOBIN, Bertram Joseph

(b. 1910, North Adelaide; d. 1969, Adelaide) *South Australia*

A prominent Sheffield Shield all-rounder of the early 1930s, Bert Tobin was once 12th man for Australia, for the fourth 'bodyline' Test in 1932/3. A right-arm medium pacer who often opened the bowling and a right-hand middle-order batsman, his best bowling figures were 4 for 31 and highest score, 61.

First-class career (1930–4): 722 runs (16.04), 51 wickets (39.03), and 17 catches

TOOHEY, Peter Michael

(b. 1954, Blayney, New South Wales) *New South Wales and Australia*

A small, right-handed middle-order batsman, Peter Toohey had an impressive start in Test cricket in 1977/8 but failed most disappointingly against the strong England bowling attack the following season. At his best he was a fine stroke-player who drove extremely hard, and bore a strong resemblance in style to Doug Walters, whose role he took on in the New South Wales side. He was also a quick runner with a fine throw from the deep field. After scoring 1,149 runs at an average of 54.00 in Grade cricket in Sydney in 1973/4, the sixth-highest seasonal aggregate ever recorded in that competition, Toohey soon showed his ability in first-class cricket the following season and played in all the Tests against India (home) and West Indies (away) in 1977/8, scoring 705 runs at 47.00 in his first eight Tests with a highest score of 122 against the West Indies at Sabina Park where he also made 97 in the second innings. He scored 954 first-class runs in the Australian season of 1977/8 and a further 566 at 51.46 in the West Indies, but the English fast bowlers uncovered, and mercilessly exploited, a weakness outside his off-stump and in five Tests in 1978/9 he totalled only 149 runs

(16.55), including a fine innings of 81 not out in the first innings of the second Test at Perth. In 1979/80 he hit three hundreds in the Sheffield Shield and finished the season in eighth place in the national averages with 697 runs from 19 innings. The four knocks which he had in Test cricket, however, brought down the average considerably, for he was out of luck in his one game each against the West Indies and England. Despite his eclipse at international level he continued to be a valuable batsman for New South Wales for several years.

First-class career (1974–84): 5,735 runs (37.98) including 12 centuries
Test matches (15): 893 runs (31.89) including 1 century, 0–4, and 9 catches

TOSHACK, Ernest Raymond Herbert

(b. 1914, Cobar, New South Wales) *New South Wales and Australia*

Tall, dark-haired, and with a look of world-weariness, Ernie Toshack bowled a lively left-arm medium pace and, when he concentrated on the leg-stump, his main value lay in nagging accuracy of a kind which would have made him highly suitable for limited-overs cricket. In a high-scoring era he conceded approximately two and a half runs an over. He toured New Zealand in 1945/6 and England in 1948. At home he appeared against England in 1946/7 and India in 1947/8. With Lindwall, Miller, Johnston, and Toshack to contend with, England's batsmen had little respite in 1948. Toshack himself took 50 wickets (21.12) on his England tour, including 11 in Tests (in which, incidentally, he made 51 of the 78 runs he hit on the tour and had some inspired and comical last-wicket stands with Bill Johnston). In his first Test, against New Zealand at Wellington in 1945/6, Toshack delivered 29 overs and took 6 for 18. On his début against England, at Brisbane in 1946/7, his match record was 9 for 99; in the series he had 17 wickets (25.70). The following season, against India, he had his last major triumph: 5 for 2 (in two overs and three balls) and 6 for 29 (11 for 31 in the match) at Brisbane. A troublesome knee curtailed his career.

First-class career (1945–9): 185 runs (5.78), 195 wickets (20.37), and 10 catches
Test matches (12): 73 runs (14.60), 47 wickets (21.04), and 4 catches

TRAVERS, Joseph Patrick Francis

(b. 1871, Adelaide, d. 1942, Adelaide) *South Australia and Australia*

A shrewd, slow left-arm bowler of the Wilfred Rhodes school, Joe Travers took 9 for 30 in the first innings of Victoria at Melbourne in 1900/1 and captured 28 wickets in Sheffield Shield matches that season. He appeared in the fifth Test at Melbourne against England in 1901/2, scoring 9 and 1, taking 1 for 14 and holding one catch; this was his sole Test. In 28 Sheffield Shield matches he took 91 wickets (31.82).

First-class career (1895–1906): 760 runs (16.52) and 116 wickets (31.39)

TREDREA, Sharon Ann

(b. 1954, Reservoir, Victoria) *Victoria and Australia*

At the age of 22, Sharon Tredrea was billed as the fastest bowler in women's cricket when she toured England in 1976. While not officially logged, Tredrea's pace more than matched that recorded by a later Australian, Debbie Wilson, of 75 m.p.h. in 1984. On the occasion of the 1976 tour to England, Tredrea failed to make the most of the hard and fast wickets of a long, hot summer but it was a rare setback in a highly successful career that almost did not get off the ground because of a back injury. By 1979/80 Tredrea was forced to give up bowling because of a recurrence of her back trouble, and other injuries were to rob her of the chance of playing more Test cricket. Tredrea's right-handed batting was always a useful adjunct and good enough to see her selected in that role as of right. She became the first female to score a half-century at Lord's during the historic first women's match at headquarters—a one-day international—played on the 1976 tour. She will be best remembered, however, for her opening bowling partnership with Raelee Thompson. Tredrea's right-arm deliveries were characterized by a leap that took her halfway up stump height as she entered into her delivery stride. She was the only player to appear in the first four World Cup tournaments: 1973 in England, 1978 in India, 1982 in New Zealand as captain, and 1988 in Australia. Australia, beaten finalists in 1973, followed with a hat-trick of wins. Her record 28 World Cup appearances—460 runs makes her Australia's top scorer in this competition—was only surpassed by Debbie Hockley (New Zealand) during the 1993 tournament. Tredrea captained Australia in four Tests and played for Victoria for the majority of seasons between 1973 and 1990/1. Her sister, Janette, played in all three Tests of the 1976 tour to England as a 19-year-old top-order bat.

Test matches (10): 346 runs (31.45) and 30 wickets (26.13)

One-day internationals: 528 runs (27.8) and 32 wickets (16.3)

TRIBE, George Edward

(b. 1920, Melbourne) *Victoria, Northamptonshire, and Australia*

A genuine all-rounder, but best remembered as a back-of-the-hand left-arm spinner, George Tribe achieved great feats for Northamptonshire from 1951 until 1959, achieving the double seven times for his adopted county. He could bowl either slow left-arm orthodox or chinamen, spinning the ball quickly and often, and not giving the ball as much air as most bowlers. He was also a sound left-handed defender and front-of-the-wicket hitter liable to change the course of a game, and a brilliant fielder, especially at short-leg. He played in three Tests against England in 1946/7 after a season in which his 33 wickets had been largely instrumental in his state winning the Sheffield Shield, but there was a plethora of talent in Australia and he did not receive adequate recognition. Thus, he became a professional in the Central Lancashire League in 1947, capturing 426 wickets in three seasons. The rest is mainly the story of great, all-round work for Northamptonshire. Three times in his career he took 9 wickets in an innings (twice for Northamptonshire). He toured India with Commonwealth teams in 1949/50 and 1950/1.

First-class career (1945–59): 10,177 runs (27.35) including 7 centuries, 1,378 wickets (20.55), and 242 catches

Test matches (3): 35 runs (17.50) and 2 wickets (165.00)

TRIMBLE, Glenn Samuel

(b. 1963, Brisbane) *Queensland*

One of a number of solid Sheffield Shield performers who were prematurely elevated to Australian level in the mid-1980s with the exodus of the rebel players to South Africa, Glenn Trimble had two one-day games for Australia in 1985/6. He delivered a wayward bowling spell in his first game against New Zealand in Perth when his four overs cost 32. A right-hand middle-order batsman and right-arm medium-pacer, Trimble's career-best score was 138 not out for Queensland

against Tasmania at Launceston in 1987/8. His best bowling figures were 5 for 50, also against Tasmania, in Brisbane in 1985/6. His father, Sam, was a Queensland stalwart.

First-class career (1982–9): 2,881 runs (33.11) including 4 centuries, 30 wickets (29.33), and 55 catches

TRIMBLE, Samuel Christy

(b. 1934, Lismore, New South Wales) *Queensland*

No Australian has made more first-class runs without winning Test selection than the popular right-hand opener from New South Wales. In 144 first-class matches, Trimble made 26 centuries and amassed more than 10,000 runs, including a career highest of 252 for his adopted state, Queensland, against New South Wales in Sydney in 1963/4. In all first-class games that season, he made 1,006 runs at an average of 83.80, including five centuries, two of which came in the same match against Victoria, in Brisbane. He also scored 213 as captain of an Australian 2nd XI against New Zealand at Wellington in 1969/70. The closest he came to Test selection was 12th man in the fifth Test against the West Indies on Bobby Simpson's 1965 tour. He was advised to cross back to New South Wales on his return and open the state's batting with Simpson, but having already left for lack of opportunity in his early 20s, he preferred to remain in Brisbane and, playing at Shield level into his 42nd year, broke Les Favell's record for most runs in the Sheffield Shield. Initially a drab, colourless player, he became a fine strokemaker and a magnificent ambassador for Queensland cricket. He attributed his longevity in the game to his dairy-farming father, Christy, who played in the Lismore area for 60 years. Sam's son, Glenn, also played first-class cricket with success.

First-class career (1959–75): 10,282 runs (41.80) including 26 centuries, three wickets (59.00), and 86 catches

TROTT, Albert Edwin

(b. 1873, Melbourne; d. 1914, Harlesden, Middlesex) *Victoria, Middlesex, Australia, and England*

Tall, strong, moustached, and confident, 'Alberto' Trott burst into Test cricket in 1894/5 against A. E. Stoddart's England side. On his début in the third match at Adelaide he scored 38 not out and 72 not out and took 8 for 43 in the second innings, and in the next match at Sydney his contribution was 85 not out. Both times Australia won handsomely (yet lost the Ashes)—and in all matches against the English teams on the tour he made 331 runs in nine innings and took 19 wickets. 'Alberto' was omitted, however, from the 1896 team to England captained by his elder brother, Harry. Thereupon, the most promising young Australian of his generation came to England on his own account, joined Lord's ground staff and qualified for Middlesex and from 1899 until 1904 enjoyed great all-round success. He scored 1,175 runs and took 239 wickets in 1899, and scored 1,337 runs and took 211 wickets in 1900. Though his arm was low, he could bowl just about anything from fast to slow and spun the ball vigorously. Six of his eight centuries were scored at Lord's and some tremendous hits were recorded there. For MCC against Sussex in May 1899 he drove Fred Tate so hard that the ball hit the left-hand emblem of the MCC coat of arms crowning the highest pinnacle on the top of the towers of the pavilion and, two months later, for MCC against the Australians, came his unique hit: he struck a ball from Monty Noble over the top of the pavilion. The wine went to his head: he was always trying to repeat these performances, and he eventually became a mere slogger. He took all ten wickets in an innings for Middlesex against Somerset at Taunton in 1900 and on ten occasions took 13 or more wickets in a match. After 1904 he fell away, becoming heavy and muscle-bound, but in 1907, in his benefit match for Middlesex against Somerset at Lord's, he took four wickets in five balls, then finished the game early by doing the hat-trick a second time in the same innings. Thus he deprived himself of more gate money! His wry comment was that he was bowling himself 'into the workhouse'. From 1911 to 1913 he was a first-class umpire, but his health steadily worsened and he finally shot himself through the head at his lodgings at Willesden Green. Touring South Africa with Lord Hawke's team in 1898/9, he appeared in two Tests for England, very successfully.

First-class career (1893–1911): 10,696 runs (19.48) including 8 centuries, 1,674 wickets (21.09), and 452 catches

Test matches (Australia—3): 205 runs (102.50), 9 wickets (21.33), and 4 catches. (England—2): 23 runs (5.75) and 17 wickets (11.64)

TROTT, George Henry Stephens

(b. 1866), Melbourne; d. 1917, Melbourne) *Victoria and Australia*

'Harry' Trott, a genial fellow, was an elegant and forcing right-handed batsman who could also play the barn-door game if necessary, indeed was at his best in a difficult situation. An effective leg-spin change-bowler, he was also a fine fielder at point. He toured England in 1888, 1890, 1893, and 1896; and at home played against England in 1891/2, 1894/5, and 1897/8. He captained Australia in 1896 and 1897/8, winning the rubber in the latter series by four games to one. Despite little early education he was a born leader. In the Test at Lord's in 1896 he was at his best. Australia were dismissed for 53 in the first innings and, 239 runs behind, lost three quick wickets in the second, but then Trott scored 143 and, with Syd Gregory, added 221 in just over $2\frac{1}{2}$ hours. He averaged 34.33 in this series. Away from cricket he was a postman, but his later life was marred by mental breakdowns.

First-class career (1885–1907): 8,804 runs (23.54) including 9 centuries, 386 wickets (25.12), and 183 catches

Test matches (24): 921 runs (21.92) including 1 century, 29 wickets (35.13), and 21 catches

TRUMBLE, Hugh

(b. 1867, Melbourne; d. 1938, Melbourne) *Victoria and Australia*

Tall and slim, with long bones, prominent nose and ears, Hugh Trumble made the most of his height by bringing the ball over at the full extent of his right arm. A medium-paced off-spin bowler of the highest class, he kept an impeccable length, flighted the ball skilfully, turned it a little on the hard pitches and a great deal on the poor ones. Highly intelligent, he would buy the wicket of the best players if necessary. He was a more than useful right-handed batsman at times, with abundant concentration, and also a fine slip fielder. He toured England in 1890, 1893, 1896, 1899, and 1902. After a quiet first tour he took 108 wickets (16.61), 148 (15.81), 142 (18.43), and 137 (14.02) respectively, and scored 1,183 runs (27.51) in 1899, thus achieving the double that year. At home he represented his country in 1894/5, 1897/8, 1901/2, and 1903/4. He took 12 for 89 in The Oval Test in 1896; 10 for 128 at Old Trafford in 1902, when Australia won by three runs; and 12 for 173 at The Oval the same year, when England triumphed by one wicket. In the 1901/2 series he took 28 wickets (20.03), in 1902 26 wickets (14.26), and in 1903/4 24 wickets (16.58). Twice he performed the hat-trick, each time at Melbourne, and in his final match in first-class cricket he captured 7 for 28 at Melbourne in 1903/4, Australia beating England by 218 runs. He also toured South Africa in 1902/3 and North America twice. He captained Australia in two Tests. From 1911 until 1938 he was secretary of Melbourne CC and, with his tall figure, broad-brimmed hat, and kindly nature, he was a popular and respected official. He was younger brother of J. W. Trumble.

First-class career (1887–1903): 5,395 runs (19.47) including 3 centuries, 929 wickets (18.44), and 328 catches

Test matches (32): 851 runs (19.78), 141 wickets (21.78), and 45 catches

TRUMBLE, John William

(b. 1863, Melbourne; d. 1944, Melbourne) *Victoria and Australia*

John Trumble was a useful all-rounder. Tall, and bowling with a high delivery, he was noted for his accurate length. He toured England in 1886, but showed only moderate form, and at home represented his country in 1884/5. On his Test début, in the second match at Melbourne in 1884/5, he made 59. His work as a solicitor curtailed his career in big cricket.

First-class career (1883–93): 1,761 runs (18.93), 109 wickets (24.10), and 33 catches

Test matches (7): 243 runs (20.25), 10 wickets (22.20), and 3 catches

TRUMPER, Victor Thomas

(b. 1877, Sydney; d. 1915, Sydney) *New South Wales and Australia*

A genius, and the greatest Australian batsman before Bradman, Victor Trumper had the ability to make big scores in 'impossible' conditions. 'He moved into his strokes', wrote H. S. Altham, 'with effortless and perfectly balanced ease. There was no limit to their range, or flaw in their fluency or timing.' Those who saw him bat have never forgotten the extreme suppleness which gave peculiar grace to everything he did and the marvellous union of his hand and eye. Unlike Bradman, it was the style and grace of Trumper, rather than the figures he produced, which marked the man's greatness as a cricketer. Yet the figures themselves were impressive enough. His first three-figure score was 292 not out for his

state against Tasmania at Sydney in 1898/9. The following English season he hit 135 not out at Lord's in his second Test and, against Sussex at Hove, contributed a chanceless 300 not out in 6 hours 20 minutes. On this tour Trumper made 1,556 runs (34.57) and he remained an integral part of the Australian team until 1912. He came to England again in 1902, 1905, and 1909; and, at home, he appeared in the 1901/2, 1903/4, 1907/8, and 1911/12 series against England and the 1910/11 against South Africa. He established himself as the finest Australian batsman in the wet summer of 1902, making 2,570 runs (48.49)—956 runs more than his nearest rival in the team—including 11 centuries, the greatest of which was 104 on a sticky wicket at Old Trafford, when England were beaten by a mere three runs. At Sydney, in the first Test of the 1903/4 series, Trumper scored 185 not out, and in the second, on a pig of a pitch at Melbourne, he hit a superlative 74 out of a total of 122. In this series he headed the averages of both sides with 574 runs (63.77). He dominated the 1910/11 series against South Africa with 661 runs (94.42), including 214 not out in the third match at Adelaide, his Test highest. By 1914 he had scored 3,627 runs (48.36) in 46 Sheffield Shield matches, but he had never been robust and he was struck down by Bright's disease at the age of 37. When this modest, unspoilt, kindly, and popular cricketer died, it was announced on newspaper placards even though it was during the First World War.

First-class career (1894–1913): 16,939 runs (44.57) including 42 centuries, 64 wickets (31.37), and 171 catches

Test matches (48): 3,163 runs (39.04) including 8 centuries, 8 wickets (39.62), and 31 catches

TURNER, Alan

(b. 1950, Sydney) *New South Wales and Australia*

A sturdy, pigeon-chested, dark-haired left-hand opening batsman, Alan Turner was a determined player with a good temperament who did not quite have the sound technique needed for consistent success at the highest level. A steady player for several seasons in the Sheffield Shield he was picked to tour England in 1975 and hit 158 against Kent at Canterbury, earning himself a Test place. He had toured New Zealand in 1969/70 and he did so again during 1976/7 by which time he was a regular contender for a Test place. His sole Test hundred was 136 against the West Indies at Adelaide in 1975/6. He was an especially rugged square-cutter and on his day he

133

could be a highly effective attacker of anything but the most accurate bowling, as he showed in making a century before lunch against Sri Lanka during the 1975 Prudential World Cup. He became an executive of the Benson and Hedges Company who sponsored international cricket in Australia for many years.

First-class career (1968–77): 5,744 runs (30.88) including 7 centuries, 1 wicket (10.00), and 80 catches

Test matches (14): 768 runs (29.54) including 1 century, and 15 catches

TURNER, Charles Thomas Biass

(b. 1862, Bathurst, New South Wales; d. 1944, Sydney) *New South Wales and Australia*

Shortish and thickset, Charlie Turner bowled fast-medium with a chest-on action. At 19 he took 17 for 69, including all ten in the first innings, for a Bathurst XXII against Alfred Shaw's England team in 1881/2. Against Arthur Shrewsbury's team in 1886/7, playing for New South Wales XI, he took 13 for 54. Then, on his Test début at Sydney in the same season, he dismissed 6 for 15, England falling for 45, which remains their lowest against Australia. Thus was born the legend of 'Turner the Terror'. Touring England in 1888, 1890, and 1893, he found the wickets, especially after rain, just to his liking. He was coupled with J. J. Ferris on the first two tours as one of the great bowling partnerships in history. In 1888 they took 534 wickets between them (Turner 314), and in 1890, 430 (Turner 215) in all matches. Yet they were invariably on the losing side. Two of the three Tests in 1888 England won by an innings margin—yet Turner took 21 wickets (12.42) in the series, including 10 for 63 at Lord's in the only game won (and against an England XI at Hastings he captured 17 for 50). At Sydney in 1887/8 he had 12 for 87. In the second and fourth Tests of 1894/5 he took eight wickets each time and was then dropped from the side! He pleaded pressure of business when receiving his delayed invitation to tour in 1896, and thus passed out of Test cricket. He was the first man to take 100 wickets in an Australian first-class season—106 wickets (13.59) in 1887/8—and his 283 wickets (11.68) in first-class matches in 1888 remains the record for a touring bowler.

First-class career (1882–1909): 3,856 runs (15.54) including 2 centuries, 993 wickets (14.25), and 85 catches

Test matches (17): 323 runs (11.53), 101 wickets (16.53), and 8 catches

VEIVERS, Thomas Robert

(b. 1937, Beenleigh, Queensland) *Queensland and Australia*

A cheerful Queenslander, Tom Veivers came to England in 1964 as the first genuine right-arm off-break bowler selected by Australia for some years. He also visited South Africa, India, and Pakistan; and at home played against South Africa, Pakistan, and England between 1963 and 1966. His vigorous but also responsible left-handed batting helped his country considerably on several occasions. In his third Test against South Africa in 1963/4 his defiant batting at Sydney on the last day of the series in a smallish innings prevented Australia coming to England a beaten side. At Lord's in 1964 he top-scored with 54 out of 176; and at The Oval he struck 67 not out. In his next two Tests, against India, he hit further half-centuries; and in the first Test against South Africa at the New Wanderers ground in Johannesburg in 1966/7 he held the middle-order together with 55. His top score in Tests was 88 against Pakistan at Melbourne in 1964/5. He proved his stamina at Old Trafford in 1964 when he bowled 95.1 overs to take 3 for 155. He was generally a tidy and economical off-spinner but one who lacked penetration at the highest level. In 49 Sheffield Shield matches he made 2,726 runs (37.86) and took 86 wickets (37.97). Dark and thickset, Tom Veivers emerged originally from Queensland country cricket.

First-class career (1958–68): 5,100 runs (36.96) including 4 centuries, 191 wickets (38.71), and 52 catches

Test matches (21): 813 runs (31.26), 33 wickets (41.66), and 7 catches

VELETTA, Michael Robert John

(b. 1963, Subiaco, Western Australia) *Western Australia and Australia*

A busy right-hand opening batsman renowned for his consistency at Sheffield Shield level, the 5 ft. 9 in. Veletta is best known for his marathon double-century in the 1986/7 Shield final against Victoria at the WACA Ground. He batted for almost seven sessions and 766 minutes in making a career-best 262 to ensure Western Australia the title. It was the longest innings by an Australian—beating Bobby Simpson's Old Trafford marathon by 4 minutes—and the fourth longest innings in first-class cricket. Veletta forged a formidable presence with fellow international Geoff Marsh, their starts with WA including 431,

374, and 310 during a golden run in consecutive seasons in the late 1980s. Veletta's sparkling fielding, expert slip catching, and ability to keep wicket when needed made him an invaluable asset at state and, on occasions, at national level. He toured with Australian teams to England in 1989 and the West Indies in 1991 as a reserve wicket-keeper to Ian Healy. Outstandingly durable and consistent—he did not miss a West Australian match in his first eight seasons of first-class cricket—Veletta failed to make a lasting impression at international level. However, he played a leading role in Australia's unexpected 1987 World Cup victory on the subcontinent and scored 134 not out and 83 when opening the innings for the 1989 Australians against Glamorgan at Neath. Known for his intensity and tunnel-visioned concentration while batting, Veletta worked as hard at his skills as any Australian cricketer in the late 1980s and early 1990s. On being adjudged run out in a Shield game in Perth in 1991/2, a furious Veletta marched from the field straight into the team gymnasium and without removing his helmet or pads, mounted an exercise bike and pedalled furiously for 10 minutes. His 37 against the West Indies in Brisbane in 1988/9 was top score on an awkward opening day for batsmen. Equally important was his second innings 39 in Melbourne a season earlier, in the tensely fought 1987/8 Christmas Test with New Zealand. Veletta batted in the Australian middle order for much of his international career, before finally being elevated to his favourite opening spot, against Pakistan in Sydney in 1990. He made 9 runs and was not selected again. In twenty one-day internationals he made 484 runs at the excellent average of 32.26, including a highest score of 68 not out against Sri Lanka in a day–night international at Sydney in 1988.

First-class career (1983–   ): 8,309 runs (40.14) including 20 centuries, 180 catches, and 3 stumpings
Test matches (8): 207 runs (18.82) and 12 catches

WADDY, The Revd Ernest Frederick

(b. 1880, Morpeth, New South Wales; d. 1958, Evesham, Worcestershire) *New South Wales and Warwickshire*

A leading member of one of Sydney's most outstanding early sporting families, E. F. 'Mick' Waddy was once 12th man for Australia, for the fifth and final Ashes Test of 1907/8, after he made 107 not out and 54 for New South Wales against MCC earlier in the summer. His two brothers, E. L. 'Gar' and P. S. (Percival) also played first-class cricket, as did his nephew, B. B. (Bernard) Waddy. A right-hand top-order batsman, renowned for his 'free and attractive style', the highest of Ernest Waddy's four first-class centuries was 129 not out on his Sheffield Shield début for New South Wales against South Australia in Adelaide in 1904/5. He shared a record 221-run ninth-wicket stand with Bill Howell, who also made a century. Waddy captained his state once in 1910/11 and after the First World War had four seasons with Warwickshire (1919–22). His highest score in all grades was 309 for Sydney University against Melbourne University in 1904.

First-class career (1902–20): 2,326 runs (28.36) including 4 centuries, and 43 catches

WAITE, Mervyn George

(b. 1911, Adelaide; d. 1985, Georgetown, South Australia) *South Australia and Australia*

An honest type of batsman and medium-paced bowler without any special trimmings—'good at the bits 'n pieces'—Mervyn Waite toured England in 1938, scoring 684 runs and taking 56 wickets. He opened the bowling with Stan McCabe in the fifth Test at The Oval, when England made 903 for 7 declared. In 48 Sheffield Shield matches he made 2,167 runs (31.86) and took 76 wickets (36.81). His sole Test wicket was Denis Compton's—bowled for 1.

First-class career (1930–46): 3,888 runs (27.77) including 1 century, 192 wickets (31.62), and 66 catches
Test matches (2): 11 runs (3.66), 1–190, and 1 catch

WALKER, Alan Keith

(b. 1925, Sydney) *New South Wales and Nottinghamshire*

One of an élite band of post-war Australians to win representative honours at two sports, Alan Walker toured South Africa with the 1949/50 Australian cricketers and Britain, France, and the United States with the 1947/8 Australian Wallabies Rugby League team. A left-arm fast bowler and right-hand lower-order batsman, he took a hat-trick at Sheffield Shield level (against Queensland, 1948/9) and four wickets in four balls, while playing for Nottinghamshire against Leicestershire in 1955. In almost any other era he would have played at Test level, but he could not

135

overcome the competition from Ray Lindwall, Keith Miller and Bill Johnston. He had three seasons of Lancashire League cricket with Rawtenstall in the early 1950s and represented Nottinghamshire from 1954 to 1958, before being forced out of cricket after suffering a shoulder injury playing rugby.

First-class career (1948–58): 1,603 runs (17.42), 221 wickets (27.47), and 37 catches

WALKER, Charles William

(b. 1909, Brompton, South Australia; d. 1942, Soltau, Germany) *South Australia*

Deputy wicket-keeper on two Australian tours to England, in 1930 and 1938, Charlie 'Chilla' Walker had an impressive record in Sheffield Shield ranks with South Australia, where he formed a formidable partnership with Clarrie Grimmett. In 78 games, he figured in 252 dismissals, including 36 in the 1939/40 season, a state record which stood for more than two decades. In the game against New South Wales in Sydney, he took nine dismissals in the match, including six in an innings (two catches and four stumpings), a career-best performance. Injuries affected his chances of Test selection ahead of Victoria's Ben Barnett on the 1938 tour, when the job was considered open after the shock non-selection of New South Wales's Bert Oldfield. He died in 1942, killed in action in an RAAF air battle over Soltau.

First-class career (1928–41): 1,754 runs (14.99), and 320 dismissals (171 c., 149 st.)

WALKER, Maxwell Henry Norman

(b. 1948, Hobart) *Victoria and Australia*

A jovial Tasmanian, Max Walker moved to the mainland to further his cricket and Rules football careers and broke through as Victoria's main strike bowler in 1972/3, the year which also saw his emergence as a Test-class bowler. Six foot four, pigeon-chested, and thoroughly revelling in the hard work of bowling, he bowled right arm 'off the wrong foot' at fast-medium pace, usually swinging the ball into the bat with an open-chested delivery but also getting the ball to cut sharply away from the batsman in the manner of Alec Bedser. Known to his colleagues as 'Tangles' because of his action, he was also a willing and determined batsman who played some highly effective and important innings against England in 1974/5. As a fielder he was relatively ponderous by modern Test standards but his hands were

safe, as befitted a noted jumper and catcher on the football field. After two home Tests against Pakistan, in the second of which he took 6 for 15 in the second innings to bowl Australia to victory at Sydney, Walker went on to surpass Lillee and Massie in the Caribbean, taking 26 wickets (20.73) in the series and 41 (20.48) on the tour—outstanding figures on pitches which gave him little help. He was tirelessly hostile and enthusiastic. At home against England in 1974/5 he played third fiddle to Lillee and Thomson, but was none the less vital to the success of Australia, for he ensured that the England batsmen should be allowed no respite. In the six Tests he took 23 wickets (29.73) including 8 for 143 in England's first innings of 529 when, minus Lillee and Thomson, Walker had the stage to himself. In England he was less successful, taking 14 wickets (34.71) in 1975 and again 14 wickets (39.35) in 1977. He became a witty and eloquent radio and TV cricket commentator.

First-class career (1968–81): 2,014 runs (15.49), 499 wickets (26.47), and 49 catches

Test matches (34): 586 runs (19.53), 138 wickets (27.47), and 12 catches

WALL, Thomas Welbourne

(b. 1904, Adelaide; d. 1981, Adelaide) *South Australia and Australia*

One of the two outstanding Australian fast bowlers of the 1930s, 'Tim' Wall had a long, flowing approach and a vigorous kicking action like a frisky colt as he reached the crease, but his length and direction tended to be faulty. His right arm was high and he often had nasty lift and movement. He toured England in 1930 and 1934, and played at home against England in 1928/9 and 1932/3, West Indies in 1930/1, and South Africa in 1931/2. In his first Test against England, the fifth at Melbourne in 1928/9, his stamina was magnificent; he bowled 75 overs in the match, taking 8 for 189, Australia winning after five successive Test defeats. He took 13 wickets (20.23) in three Tests against South Africa in 1931/2, and in the 'bodyline' series of 1932/3 he headed Australia's averages with 16 wickets (25.56) from four Tests. On his two English tours his overall figures were unimpressive; spin bowlers tended to dictate policy. He took 56 wickets (29.25) and 42 wickets (30.71) respectively. For his state in 1932/3 he devastated New South Wales at Sydney, capturing all 10 for 36 in an innings where Bradman made the top score of 56.

First-class career (1924–36): 1,071 runs (10.50), 330 wickets (29.93), and 54 catches
Test matches (18): 121 runs (6.36), 56 wickets (35.89), and 11 catches

WALSH, John Edward

(b. 1912, Sydney; d. 1980, Wallsend, New South Wales) *New South Wales and Leicestershire*

A masterly left-arm wrist-spinner who played almost 300 first-class games, including just two for his native state, New South Wales in 1939/40, 'Jack' Walsh rates as one of the finest Australian players never to play Test cricket. His development of a well-concealed chinaman made him a dangerous player against even the surest-footed batsmen. He went to Leicestershire via Sir Julien Calvin's XI in 1936, representing the county from 1937 to 1956 and taking 100 wickets in a season seven times. His biggest hauls were 16 wickets against Oxford University in 1953 and 14 against Sussex in 1948. He was 39 when he achieved the double of 1,000 runs and 100 wickets. He was a lower-order left-hander who hit hard. In 1965 he became the first full-time coach appointed by the Newcastle Cricket Association and he also coached in Tasmania and Scotland.

First-class career (1939–56): 7,247 runs (17.76) including 2 centuries, 1,190 wickets (24.56), and 209 catches

WALTERS, Francis Henry

(b. 1860, Melbourne; d. 1922, at sea, off Bombay, India) *Victoria, New South Wales, and Australia*

Although Frank Walters had height and reach and always seemed to be on the verge of something exceptional, over-caution prevented him from achieving anything of note on the slow wickets during the 1890 England tour, other than a valuable 53 not out against Surrey at The Oval. In his sole Test at Melbourne against Arthur Shrewsbury's 1885/6 England side he scored 7 and 5 and held two catches. In interstate games, however, he could cut loose and reveal a superb array of strokes.

First-class career (1880–95): 1,755 runs (20.17) including 4 centuries, 1 wicket (81.00), and 31 catches

WALTERS, Kevin Douglas

(b. 1945, Dungog, New South Wales) *New South Wales and Australia*

Only on English and South African pitches was Doug Walters anything less than a superb bats-man and an inspiring all-round cricketer. On hard pitches his incisive footwork, crisp cutting, bold hooking, and devastating driving made him a scourge of bowlers, a match-winner who scored runs so quickly that many a game was transformed by his brilliance. He was also a useful medium-pace swing bowler with a knack of coming on to take important wickets, and a dazzling fielder in the covers who could catch with the best close to the wicket. For once, a 'new Bradman' did not disappoint when he reached Australian first-class cricket and he was popular with crowds and players wherever he went. In his first two Test matches, played against England in 1965/6, he scored 155, 22, and 115. A star was born and he finished the series with 410 runs at 68.33. However, National Service prevented him from going to South Africa the following season, and, although he was released to play on the England tour of 1968, there are many who claim that his technique was looser on his return. In a miserably wet summer he scored 933 runs (31.10), 343 in the five Tests at 38.11. He fared less well on his subsequent visits to England, scoring only 54 in seven Test innings in 1972, 125 in five innings in 1975, although in 1977 on his fourth visit he improved to make 223 runs in five Tests at 24.77, including a dashing 88 at Old Trafford, though these were nothing like the scores that a batsman of his talents should have been capable of producing. Like the South Africans a year earlier, England's bowlers, led by John Snow, had worked out his weaknesses in 1970/1, when it was realized that he would soon perish in the gully area if a fast attack was directed exclusively at his off-stump. Walters did not have the discipline to reform his technique. He was essentially a light-hearted soul, happy with a beer in one hand and a cigarette in the other. Yet, even against the confident English bowlers, he made 373 runs (37.30) in 1970/1, including 112 at Brisbane, and 383 (42.53) in 1974/5, including a superb 103 in a fraction over 2 hours at Perth. If Walters blew hot and cold against England, he was more consistently brilliant against other countries. In 1968/9 against the West Indies at home he made 699 runs in four Tests including 242 and 103 at Sydney. In West Indies in 1973 he hit 497 runs in five Tests at 71.00, including a century between lunch and tea at Port of Spain. In 1976/7 he hit his second Test double century, 250 against New Zealand at Christchurch. He joined Kerry Packer's World Series Cricket, but did not meet with much success in cricket dominated by fast bowlers. When Doug Walters reappeared for Australia in one or two limited-overs internationals in 1979/80 after a relatively unsuccessful sojourn with World Series Cricket, it looked rather like a case of a job for one of the boys for old time's sake. But the following season he returned to Test cricket and thoroughly justified his selection, hitting a fluent 107 in the third Test against New Zealand at Melbourne and batting steadily at number six in the order against India. The selectors must have thought long and hard before deciding against offering him a fifth major tour of England in 1981. On hearing the news, he decided to retire, but the award of an MBE was amongst his consolations.

First-class career (1962–80): 16,180 runs (43.84) including 45 centuries, 190 wickets (35.69), and 149 catches

Test matches (74): 5,357 runs (48.26) including 15 centuries, 49 wickets (29.08), and 43 catches

WARD, Francis Anthony

(b. 1909, Sydney; d. 1974, Sydney) *South Australia and Australia*

An honest toiler, full of courage but lacking inspiration, Frank Ward was a right-arm leg-break bowler contemporary with such masters as Clarrie Grimmett and Bill O'Reilly, and a dogged tailender. On his Test début, against England in the first match at Brisbane in 1936/7, he captured 6 for 102 in the second innings (bowling 82 overs in the match). He toured England in 1938 as a controversial replacement for Grimmett and, although he took 92 wickets (19.27) in first-class matches, he appeared in only one Test.

First-class career (1935–40): 871 runs (13.83), 320 wickets (24.68), and 42 catches

Test matches (4): 36 runs (6.00), 11 wickets (52.18), and 1 catch

WARNE, Shane Keith

(b. 1969, Ferntree Gully, Victoria) *Victoria and Australia*

Rare accuracy and an ability to spin the ball quite prodigiously made Shane 'Hollywood' Warne one of the greatest of all bowlers. He was the dominant figure in Australia's 4–1 defeat of England in the 1993 Ashes series. With 34 wickets in six Tests, including the so-called 'ball of the century', an inswinging leg-break which pitched outside the leg-stump and spun past the outside edge of an astounded Mike Gatting to hit his off-stump in the first Test at Old Trafford, Warne proved that wrist spin still commands a place of importance in world cricket. The broad-shouldered, flashy Victorian, with blond-tipped hair and a liking for custom-made jewellery, demoralized a series of leading English players, bowling an orthodox line from over the wicket, or pitching wide of the leg stump and spinning back viciously when operating from round the wicket. Brash but personable, he was soon making big money from his success. In amassing 72 wickets for the 1993 calendar year, the most by an Australian bar Dennis Lillee (who took 85 in 1981), Warne became his captain Allan Border's match-winning bowler. With the off-spinner Tim May also in the XI, Australia often attacked with specialist spin from both ends, a rare occurrence in international cricket after years of domination by fast bowlers. In addition to his stock leg-break, which often turned 2 ft., Warne used an 'under-spun' flipper—the flatter, skidding delivery delivered at increased pace—plus a top spinner and a googly. His career had taken off in his home town, Melbourne, in the 1992/3 Christmas Test when he claimed 1 for 76 and 7 for 52 to spin Australia to a rare win against the West Indies. Before his last-day heroics, he had taken just five wickets in five Tests and admitted to doubts about being able to compete at the highest level. But he bowled superbly and in one spell took 4 for 4 from 6.2 overs. Only five years previously, as a roly-poly teenager, he had been playing as an all-rounder with St Kilda's 4th XI. The former international Shaun Graf quickly promoted him to the firsts and he first played for Victoria as a 21 year old. A stint at the Australian Cricket Academy in Adelaide, practising under the former Test leg-spinner Terry Jenner, furthered his education. Working hard at his fitness, which had been questioned after he took 1 for 150 in his first Test against India at Sydney in early 1992, Warne lost a stone and a half before the winter tour of Sri Lanka. At Colombo in the opening Test, Sri Lanka looked certain of an historic win at 147 for 6, needing only 34 more runs to win. Bowling in tandem with Greg Matthews, Warne took 3 for 11 including 3 for 0 from his final eleven deliveries. Warne averaged more than four wickets a game in his first twenty-six Test matches, proving to be Australia's most successful wrist-spinner since Bill O'Reilly and Clarrie Grimmett between the wars. Possessing exceptionally strong wrists and shoulders, Warne's knack of making the ball grip and spin sharply away from the right-handers has few parallels. The Academy's head coach, Rodney Marsh, said it was not what he saw that first impressed him about Warne; it was what he heard. 'The ball really hummed out of his hand, such was the "rip" he gave it.' With 36 wickets in six Australian Tests against New Zealand and South Africa in 1993/4, Warne maintained his new status, with Pakistan's Waqar Younis, as world cricket's greatest match-winning bowler. He took 3 for 63 and 6 for 31 against New Zealand in Hobart before, for the first time in a Test, taking ten or more wickets (7 for 56 and 5 for 72) in a game, against the touring South Africans in Sydney. For the first time, he also commanded a regular place in Australia's World Series Cup team and was a clear winner of the International Cricketer of the Year award. Again heading the averages in three return Tests in South Africa, Warne's 15-wicket series haul was overshadowed by an uncharacteristic but inexcusable loss of temper on the field at Johannesburg. He was fined for abusing the South African batsman, Andrew Hudson. Against England in 1994/5 he took 27 wickets at 20.33, including a hat-tirck at Melbourne. A good fielder and capable right-hand batsman, Warne has an impressively correct technique and a highest Test score of 74 not out (v. New Zealand, Brisbane, 1993).

First-class career (1990–): 964 runs (17.21), 243 wickets (25.28), and 29 catches
Test matches (38): 597 runs (13.26), 176 wickets (24.08), and 25 catches

WATKINS, John Russell

(b. 1943, Newcastle, New South Wales) *New South Wales and Australia*

A right-arm leg-break bowler, John Watkins played against Pakistan in the third Test at Sydney in 1972/3 after only five first-class games in which he had taken a mere 11 wickets (37.18); his fame had been achieved for Newcastle. In this, his sole Test, he scored 3 not out and 36, sharing in a record ninth-wicket stand of 83 with Bob Massie, held one catch and took 0 for 21. He toured the West Indies in 1973, taking ten wickets in four matches but he was too erratic to be risked in Tests.

First-class career (1971–2): 71 runs (10.14) and 20 wickets (36.30)

WATSON, Graeme Donald

(b. 1945, Melbourne) *Victoria, Western Australia, New South Wales, and Australia*

An attractive right-handed batsman who sometimes opened, and a vigorous medium-fast bowler, Graeme Watson was the keenest of cricketers. Hit on the bridge of the nose by a ball from Tony Greig while batting for Australia against the Rest of the World at Melbourne in 1971/2, he was in an intensive-care ward for days and received 14 blood transfusions (40 pints of blood). He ignored the advice of surgeons never to play again and toured England in 1972, scoring 915 runs (36.60) and taking 25 wickets. Against Hampshire at Southampton he hit 176 (including five sixes), putting on 301 for the first wicket with Keith Stackpole in less than four hours. He did little in the Tests, but on his first tour, to South Africa in 1966/7, he had hit 50 on his début at Cape Town.

First-class career (1964–76): 4,674 runs (32.68) including 7 centuries, 186 wickets (25.31), and 73 catches
Test matches (5): 97 runs (10.77), 6 wickets (42.33), and 1 catch

WATSON, William James

(b. 1931, Sydney) *New South Wales and Australia*

A sound right-handed opening batsman, Bill Watson hit his maiden century in only his second first-class match—155 in $6\frac{1}{4}$ hours against MCC at Sydney in 1954/5. He played in the fifth Test at Sydney that season but achieved little, and a few months later toured the West Indies. He had a string of good scores against the Islands but disappointed in the Tests and was not tried again. In twenty-seven Sheffield Shield matches he made 1,233 runs (30.82).

First-class career (1953–61): 1,958 runs (32.09) including 6 centuries
Test matches (4): 106 runs (17.66), 0–5, and 2 catches

WAUGH, Mark Edward

(b. 1965, Canterbury, New South Wales) *New South Wales, Essex, and Australia*

Few modern-day players consistently delight more than Mark Waugh, an aristocratic, fast-scoring strokemaker with a novel twist of etching matchstick men on his thigh pad each time he scores a century. Until his auspicious Test début, when he made a classical 138 against England in Adelaide in 1990/1, his performances had not matched those of his twin, Steve, who had been a Test player for 5 years when Mark temporarily displaced him. In an innings he described later as the best he had ever played, the right-handed Waugh started with precision and supreme confidence, despite Australia's precarious position, 104 for four. Before he faced a ball, Waugh's close friend Robin Smith, fielding for England, said, 'Now's the time to release the handbrake, champ.' Powering a straight drive to the second delivery he faced past the bowler Phil DeFreitas, Waugh was immediately into his stride. Phil Tufnell went for 5 fours in 11 deliveries, as Waugh reached his first 50 from just 73 balls. The second 50 was even quicker, coming at almost a run a ball. Only bad light stopped him from scoring a century in the final session. It was the finest display by an Ashes newcomer since Greg Chappell's majestic first century in Perth two decades earlier. Waugh had previously played one-day cricket with Australia and dominated at Shield level with New South Wales and in county ranks with Essex before being belatedly called into the Australian side. No one had built a more auspicious first-class record coming into their first Test than Waugh, whose 100-match apprenticeship had produced 7,501 runs at an average of 55, including 13 centuries for New South Wales and 12 for Essex. He topped the Australian averages in the West Indies in 1991, scoring a Test-best 139 not out in the fifth and final Test at St John's. His ability to improvise against even the fastest bowler made him a most difficult batsman to restrict. He also averaged 60-plus on tour in England in 1993. Surviving some rocky periods, notably in Sri Lanka in 1992, when he made two pairs in a row, Waugh played 36 Tests of a possible 38 once he had established himself. His Test average of more than 40 and his one-day international average of almost 35 underline his importance to the Australian middle-order. His feats for New South Wales have also been consistently outstanding, almost 5,000 runs coming at an average approaching 60. Waugh's 229 not out against Western Australia in Perth on the eve of Christmas, 1990, remains his highest first-class score. As Don Bradman had done at Nottingham in 1938 when Stan McCabe was playing his most legendary innings, New South Wales's captain Geoff Lawson called his team-mates from the back of the dressing room into the viewing area to witness the skill of Waugh and his twin, Steve, who shared a world record stand of 464 (unbeaten) for the fifth wicket. Neither gave a chance—and against a full-strength Western Australian attack which included five international bowlers Bruce Reid, Terry Alderman, Chris Matthews, Ken Macleay, and Tom Moody. During the memorable stand, Lawson sent a message to the pair that they still had plenty of time to bat and should not become reckless. Waugh responded by hitting the next ball from Macleay into the Prindiville Stand. 'It was the first ball that either of them had hit into the air!' said Lawson. In becoming one of only ten Australians to score more than 3,000 runs for the calendar year, Waugh virtually demanded a place in the Test side. His first Australian matches had been in 1989/90 at World Series Cup level. His first one-day century (108 v. New Zealand at Hamilton, 1993), came while opening the innings; his highest one-day score (113, v. England, Birmingham, 1993) was from number three, but number four is his regular and favourite position. Stronger through the legside than his brother, Mark Waugh has a Macartney-like arrogance towards bowling. Six foot, and perfectly balanced at the crease, he cuts a relaxed but imposing figure. Anything pitched on middle and leg is fruit for the sightboard. He also has a devastating cut shot. An easier mixer than his brother Steve, like him he is also an above-average right-arm medium-pacer, with a deceptively fast bouncer which has caught even the best batsmen unawares. His close-in fielding has been consistently brilliant, several slip catches during the 1993/4 summer being as good as any taken in recent memory. He played for Essex 1988–90, 1992, and again in 1995.

First-class career (1985–): 14,346 runs (56.70) including 48 centuries, 130 wickets (38.23), and 221 catches

Test matches (48): 3,072 runs (42.08) including 8 centuries, 34 wickets (34.77), and 62 catches

WAUGH, Steven Rodger

(b. 1965, Sydney) *New South Wales, Somerset, and Australia*

Lean, pale-faced, cool, and laconic, Steve Waugh was a taciturn destroyer of anything but the highest class of bowling and a resourceful medium-paced bowler who was seldom mastered in any type of cricket. One of the most competitive and naturally gifted of Allan Border's strong Australian side between 1987 and 1994, his perfect right-handed batting technique enabled him to top the Test averages, with 126 and 83, on his tours to England in both 1989 and 1993 and he hit seven first-class centuries on the two trips. In the first and second Tests, at Headingley and Lord's, in 1989 his scores were 177 not out and 152 not out, both examples of classical batting and uncompromising concentration. In the intervening his place, temporarily and poignantly, to his twin brother, Mark, but was soon back alongside him. The first twins to play together in first-class cricket in Australia, they shared an undefeated fifth-wicket partnership of 464 for New South Wales against Western Australia at Perth in 1990/1, a record for any wicket. The sons of a Sydney newsagent they learned their cricket at the Bankstown club and their two younger brothers, Dean and Daniel, were both also outstanding players. Steve's batting, bowling, and fielding had a natural, low-slung balance. He fielded well anywhere, not least the slips early in a career which began for New South Wales in 1984/5 when his 71 in the Shield final against Queensland bore the unmistakable stamp of class. Tours to Zimbabwe and New Zealand followed and in 1986/7 he played his first Test against India. His first marks against England were made a season later when he took 5 for 69 at Perth. Three scores in the seventies gave him a series average of 44. In the World Cup in India in 1987 he was outstanding, fielding like a demon in the deep, scoring 167 rapidly acquired runs at an average of 55 and picking up 11 wickets. He bowled with characteristic shrewdness in the crucial closing stages of the final against England in Calcutta, seldom bowling a ball of the same pace twice. His batting method, with head over the ball, body sideways-on and feet moving purposefully forward or back, was polished during two seasons in England in 1987 and 1988. As understudy to Martin Crowe in the first year he played in only four games but made centuries in two of them. In 1988 he hit 1,314 runs at 64. Although a man of few words off the field, especially when there were 'Pom' opponents about, he was accused of being a 'sledger', a master of gratuitous insults, on it. Thought by some English fast bowlers not to relish their fare, he was nevertheless chosen as first wicket down against the West Indies' four-pronged fast attack in the home series of 1992/3, scoring 100 at Sydney. His most effective role, however, was as a number six batsman who frequently stabilized the listing ship and as a change-bowler always capable of getting a good player out. In South Africa in 1993/4 his 10 Test wickets cost him only 13 runs each and with 86 and 5 for 28 in the second innings at Cape Town he was Australia's match-winner. So he was again in the West Indies in 1994/5, when he averaged 107 and scored 200 in the final Test at Kingston.

First-class career (1984–   ): 11,002 runs (48.25) including 32 centuries, 210 wickets (31.82), and 155 catches
Test matches (76): 4,440 runs (47.23) including 8 centuries, 72 wickets (36.61), and 3 catches

WEBB, Sydney G., QC

(b. 1900, Sydney; d. 1976)

One of New South Wales's best-known and admired cricket administrators, Sid Webb played as a slow left-arm spin bowler for Sydney University and became the club's delegate to the New South Wales Cricket Association for more than 40 years. He was made an Association life member in 1944 and was its executive chairman for almost a decade. NSW's delegate on the Australian Cricket Board of Control for 16 years, he managed the 1961 Australian tour to England and in 1972 was awarded an OBE.

WEBSTER, Harold Wynne

(b. 1889, Sydney; d. 1949, Randwick, New South Wales) *South Australia*

Harold 'Darkie' Webster was named as Australia's deputy wicket-keeper to England and North America in 1912 following the decision of six players, including the number one 'keeper Hanson Carter, to withdraw from the selected team after a dispute with the Australian Cricket Board of Control. Webster did not play any further first-class cricket on his return.

First-class career (1910–12): 346 runs (14.41) and 35 dismissals (31 c., 4 st.)

WELLHAM, Dirk MacDonald

(b. 1959, Sydney) *New South Wales, Tasmania, Queensland, and Australia*

A small, bespectacled, fair-haired man of neat movement and quiet, studious mien, Dirk Wellham was the surprise choice on the 1981 Australian tour of England. Captain of both New South Wales and Tasmania, whom he also coached, he completed his first-class career for Queensland, making 873 runs at 58 in his first season in Brisbane in 1992/3. He justified his selection by scoring a hundred in his first Test, the sixth at The Oval, when his scores were 24 and 103. A qualified schoolmaster, and graduate of Sydney University, he impressed when scoring 95 against the 1979/80 England touring team for Combined Universities, though the first-class status of the game was later denied. The following season he forced his way into the New South Wales side and scored 408 runs in eight innings, including 100 on his début against Victoria and 128 not out against Tasmania. A compact, orthodox right-hander with the ability to concentrate and build an innings, and a complete variety of shots, he did consistently well during the 1981 tour of England, despite limited opportunities. Playing his first Test at The Oval, he seized his chance with both hands, although after his captain had delayed the declaration in order to give him his chance of glory a sudden attack of nerves made him play like a novice as his hundred came close. Dropped off a 'sitter', he recovered his poise and reached his goal. He scored 1,205 runs (66.94) for New South Wales in 1982/3 and in 1984/5, scoring 829 runs (41.45), and 1985/6 he captained his side to victory in the Sheffield Shield. After changing his mind about making an unofficial tour of South Africa, he won a place on the tour to England in 1985, and again he was given his chance in The Oval Test, but this time he could make only 13 and 5. Between 1981 and 1986/7 he appeared in five different Test series, yet played in more than one Test of each series only once, a victim of unfair selectional whims.

First-class career (1980–94): 8,662 runs (42.25) including 16 centuries, 1 wicket (25.00), and 68 catches

Test matches (6): 257 runs (23.36) including 1 century, and 5 catches

WESSELS, Kepler Christoffel

(b. 1957) See South Africa.

WHATMORE, Davenell Frederick

(b. 1954, Colombo, Ceylon) *Victoria and Australia*

A compact and strong right-handed batsman, born in Ceylon, 'Dav' Whatmore was a cricketer of wide experience when he appeared in both Tests against Pakistan, at Melbourne and Perth, in March 1979. As a club cricketer in England in 1975 and 1977, he represented Middlesex 2nd XI and toured South Africa with D. H. Robins's XI in 1975/6. The same year he appeared for Victoria for the first time and by 1977/8 was captaining the side with imagination in the absence of Graham Yallop on Test duty. He again led the side in several matches in 1978/9, when Victoria won the Shield. He could bowl medium pace, and was briefly used in this role during the 1979 Prudential Cup in England. Later that year he

toured India. For much of the Indian tour his form was modest—411 runs at 24.17 from 17 innings—but he played in all but one of the Test matches and was at his best in the fourth game at Delhi when his 77 and 54 helped save the match after a huge Indian first innings total. After this tour he faded from Test cricket, but he remained a stalwart for Victoria, not least as a reliable first slip, and he passed Warwick Armstrong's record of catches for the state.

First-class career (1975–89): 6,116 runs (33.97) including 10 centuries, 4 wickets (27.25), and 147 catches

Test matches (7): 293 runs (22.53), 0–11, and 13 catches

WHITE, Edward Clive Stewart

(b. 1913, Mosman, New South Wales) *New South Wales*

An accurate left-arm medium-pace bowler and right-hand batsman, Ted White toured England in 1938 without playing a Test. At his best on wet wickets, he took a career-best 8 for 31 against South Australia at Sydney in 1935/6. His father, A. B. S. White also represented New South Wales.

First-class career (1934–8): 1,316 runs (22.30) including 1 century, 115 wickets (26.71), and 37 catches

WHITINGTON, Richard Smallpiece

(b. 1912, Unley Park, South Australia; d. 1984, Sydney) *South Australia*

A former lawyer who opened the batting for South Australia and appeared in the 'Victory' Tests of 1945, Dick Whitington wrote more than twenty-five books, the majority on cricket, including eight in conjunction with the celebrated Australian all-rounder Keith Miller. He worked as a cricket writer in all the major cricket nations. He was married four times.

First-class career (1932–45): 2,782 runs (32.34) including 4 centuries, 1 wicket (91.00), and 32 catches

WHITNEY, Michael Roy

(b. 1959, Sydney) *New South Wales, Gloucestershire, and Australia*

A very solidly built, fast left-arm bowler and right-handed tail-ender, Mike Whitney had the sort of call-up for Test cricket that all young cricketers dream about. After just six first-class matches, four for New South Wales and two for Gloucestershire, he was playing as a professional for Fleetwood (Lancashire) in the Northern League when a series of injuries to fast bowlers picked for the official Australian touring team caused him to be selected as an almost complete unknown for the vital Ashes Test at Old Trafford. In a dramatic match his was no fairy-tale success story, but he took four worthily earned wickets for 124 in the match, bowling with some speed and hostility for one of such scant experience. This sudden opportunity at the highest level had clearly come too early, but although Whitney was brought back to earth with a bump on his return to Australia (nine wickets in six matches at 51.00 apiece in the 1981/2 Sheffield Shield season) he came back into consideration for international cricket again. With a crop of dark, curly hair and a powerful pair of shoulders, Whitney was always whole-hearted, often fiery and never prepared to give in. He returned to international cricket in 1986/7 and between then and 1992 played in ten more Tests and several one-day internationals, touring the West Indies in 1990/1. His 5 for 39 for New South Wales at Newcastle led to one of the few reverses for the 1986/7 England touring team but in Tests the performances which stood out above the rest were a remarkable analysis of 7 for 27 (11 for 95 in the match) against India at Perth in 1991/2, and another 7-wicket haul, for 89, against the West Indies at Adelaide in 1988/9. He took 46 wickets in his 38 one-day internationals.

First-class career (1980–94): 415 runs (5.60), 412 wickets (26.75), and 50 catches
Test matches (12): 68 runs (6.18), 39 wickets (33.97), and 2 catches

WHITTY, William James

(b. 1886, Sydney; d. 1974, Tantanoola, South Australia) *New South Wales, South Australia, and Australia*

Six feet and with good shoulders, Bill Whitty was a left-arm fast-medium bowler with a high and graceful action, who swung the new ball prodigiously (like George Hirst). With the ball no longer new, he would bowl slow left-arm orthodox. He toured England in 1909 and 1912 and, at home, played against South Africa in 1910/11 and England in 1911/12. On his first tour he took 77 wickets, but was chosen for only one Test. Against South Africa he was almost unplayable, taking 37 wickets (17.08): 8 wickets in the first

Test, 6 for 17 off 16 overs in the second innings of the second at Melbourne (routing the tourists for 80 when they needed only 161 to win) and 8 wickets in the third. In all five matches he opened the bowling with 'Tibby' Cotter. In the Triangular Tournament of 1912 he was again dominant, with 25 wickets (19.80), including 5 for 55 in the first innings against South Africa at Old Trafford. In all first-class matches in 1912 he took 109 wickets (18.08). He had a ready tongue. Once, refused an appeal for caught behind, he bowled a rather wide ball well clear of the batsman and appealed again. The umpire rebuked him, but Bill came back with an acid, 'Just thought you might make two mistakes in one day.' In 37 Sheffield Shield matches he took 154 wickets (32.64).

First-class career (1907–25): 1,465 runs (11.53), 491 wickets (23.39), and 35 catches
Test matches (14): 161 runs (13.41), 65 wickets (21.12), and 4 catches

WIENER, Julien Mark

(b. 1955, Melbourne) *Victoria and Australia*

The fair-haired, well-built son of Austrian immigrants to Melbourne, Julien Wiener dedicated himself to the idea of opening the batting for Australia at an early age. A season of cricket for Kent 2nd XI had an ironic twist when Graham Dilley, the young Kent and England fast bowler with whom he had stayed, ran him out in his first Test innings. A solid right-handed opener with a good range of strokes and no fear of playing them, Wiener made a century in his first Shield game for Victoria in 1977/8, scoring 31 and 106 against Queensland. In his first two seasons he hit four centuries. In addition, his occasional slow off-spin brought him two wickets for 31 for Victoria against England in 1978/9. It was no great surprise therefore when he overcame strong opposition from bigger names to win his first Test cap against England the following season. After his first innings run-out at Perth he made an impressive 58 in the second but this was his highest score in four Tests against the West Indies and England that season, although he top-scored with 40 against the fierce West Indies fast bowling in the first innings of the Melbourne Test. In Pakistan at the end of that season he played in two more Tests (March 1980), scoring 93 at Lahore. An outstanding 1981/2 season (847 runs at 52.93) included an innings of 221 not out against Western Australia at Melbourne: with Jeff Moss he added 390.

WILSON

First-class career (1977–85): 3,609 runs (30.32) including 7 centuries, and 17 wickets (68.47)
Test matches (6): 281 runs (25.54), 0–41, and 4 catches

WILSON, Elizabeth Rebecca

(b. 1921, Melbourne) *Victoria and Australia*

Betty Wilson is ranked by many observers as the finest woman cricketer of any era. Although she only played in eleven Test matches, she scored 862 runs at an average well exceeding 50 and took 68 wickets at a shade under 12 runs each. On three ocasions she took 5 wickets in an innings and scored a century, the first in Test history to do so. Wilson also took the first and so far only hat-trick in Test cricket amid figures of 7 for 7 against England at St Kilda in Melbourne in 1958. This performance was but part of her achievement in this match. After top scoring in the first innings she scored a century in Australia's second innings and finished with match bowling figures of 11 for 16. She thus became the first Test cricketer to complete such a match double. She was an attacking and fluent right-hander who normally batted in the middle order. A right-arm off-spin bowler, she delivered the ball with a classic action, rocking back in her delivery stride to take full advantage of her height. The daughter of a boot-maker, she learnt her cricket playing in her Collingwood street. She was recruited by the local side when they were impressed with the strength of her returns from the boundary. At the time she was just 10 years old and a spectator. The Second World War prevented her playing international cricket until 1948. She was meticulous in her preparation, practised every day, and was a confident, outgoing personality. Wilson retired after the 1957/8 series against England and in the 1980s was honoured by becoming the first woman cricketer admitted to the Australian Sporting Hall of Fame. Her citation reads: 'The greatest Australian woman cricketer and undisputed best player of her time.'

Test matches (11): 862 runs (57.47) including 3 centuries, and 68 wickets (11.81)

WILSON, John William

(b. 1921, Melbourne; d. 1985, Melbourne) *South Australia, Victoria, and Australia*

A stocky left-arm orthodox spinner of relatively brisk pace, Jack Wilson took 40 wickets (24.32) for South Australia in 1953/4 and toured England and India in 1956. His sole Test came towards the end of that long tour when he took 1 for 64 and did not bat in the second Test against India at Bombay. In first-class matches in England his figures were respectable: he took 43 wickets (23.06) and at Bristol had match figures of 12 for 61 against Gloucestershire.

First-class career (1949–58): 287 runs (5.74) 230 wickets (30.51), and 17 catches

WOOD, Graeme Malcolm

(b. 1956, Perth) *Western Australia and Australia*

A neat, very fit, left-handed opening batsman with an impetuous streak but a brave, determined approach, Graeme Wood made his first-class début against MCC in 1976/7, scoring 37 and 1. A year later, as a result of the defections to World Series Cricket, he was being tried as a Test cricketer. His start was auspicious: in his first six Tests, one at Adelaide against India followed by all five against the West Indies in the Caribbean, he scored 521 runs at 43.42, hitting 126 in the Georgetown Test and sharing a stand of 251 for the fourth wicket with Craig Serjeant. However, though Wood's sound technique, wide variety of strokes and rather taciturn determination were clearly in evidence against England in 1978/9, he spoilt a respectable record of 344 runs (28.66) by dreadful misjudgements when running between the wickets. Constantly taking risks with the speed of the England fielders, he was involved in all but one of the run-outs which accounted for the dismissal of at least one of the opening batsmen in every Test of the series. They nicknamed Wood the 'Kamikaze Kid', and he lost his Test place for the series against Pakistan and for the Prudential World Cup. But he returned against India later in 1979. In India he was a grave disappointment, not getting to 50 in four Test innings and scoring only 138 runs (13.80) on the whole tour, and for a time he lost his place in the Western Australia side. A promising career was in danger of being blighted but Wood showed the character to fight back and make the most of his ability. His chance came again when he was picked to tour England for the Centenary Test of 1980. He was a marginal selection and success was crucial. Shortly before the end of the first day he completed a determined and painstaking hundred. Significantly it was a spinner who eventually dismissed him for 112, for he was more at ease against fast bowling. He followed this effort with another century—111 in Australia's next Test, against New Zealand at Brisbane, but the balance was restored with a pair in his next Test! Indeed in three of the four innings he played in the last two Tests against New Zealand he was caught behind the wicket cheaply off Richard Hadlee. He came back with his fifth Test hundred—125 against India in the second Test at Adelaide, thus booking his passage to England in 1981. He had a relatively disappointing tour, scoring 310 Test runs (28.18) but had a good home series against Pakistan in 1981/2, scoring 100 at Melbourne. He made his seventh Test hundred against New Zealand in Auckland in March 1982. He played in all three Tests on the tour to Pakistan in 1982/3, but was dropped after the first Test against England. He was called out to the West Indies in 1983/4, and made 68 and 20 in his only Test, before breaking a finger. Australia's regular opener once more in the home series against the West Indies the following year, he toured England in 1985 and, having struggled in the early Tests, he made a courageous highest Test score of 172 at Trent Bridge. A dramatic surge of form in 1987/8—he scored 1,057 runs at 70.00—earned him a final run in Test cricket. He toured Pakistan with moderate success in 1988/9, but made a ninth Test hundred, 111, against the West Indies on his home ground—and 42 in the second innings against an attack led by Marshall, Patterson, Walsh, and Ambrose. Still exceptionally fit, he passed R. J. Inverarity's record of 7,607 runs for Western Australia in 1990/1, when he also made a hundred against the touring England team. He captained his state for several seasons, but was deposed controversially.

First-class career (1976–92): 13,353 runs (39.97) including 35 centuries, 6 wickets (26.00), and 155 catches

Test matches (59): 3,374 runs (31.83) including 9 centuries, and 41 catches

WOODCOCK, Ashley John

(b. 1947, Adelaide) *South Australia and Australia*

A sound and stylish right-handed batsman for his state for a decade, Ashley Woodcock represented his country against Rest of the World in 1971/2 and toured New Zealand in 1973/4. Earlier in 1973 he appeared in his sole Test, against New Zealand, in the third match at Adelaide, scoring 27 and holding 1 catch.

First-class career (1967–79): 4,550 runs (30.95) including 5 centuries

WOODFULL, William Maldon

(b. 1897, Maldon, Victoria; d. 1965, Tweed Heads South, New South Wales) *Victoria and Australia*

Bill Woodfull would hardly have appreciated the modern emphasis on limited-overs cricket. Variously known as 'The Rock', 'The Unbowlable' and 'The Worm-Killer', his backlift was a staccato bending of the wrists. But he had an imperturbable temperament, very strong defence and great patience; he built on firm foundations, learning to swing the bat harder and to place the ball firmly to one side or the other of the field with a variety of pushes and deflections. As right-handed opening partner of 'the other Bill', the heavy scoring W. H. Ponsford, for both state and country, he was never far behind as he gathered runs patiently and consistently. This stolid schoolmaster and clergyman's son toured England in 1926, 1930, and 1934, the last two occasions as captain, and played at home against England in 1928/9 and, as captain, in 1932/3. He also toured South Africa in 1931/2 (captain). He led Australia in 25 of his 35 Tests, winning back the Ashes in 1930 and 1934, and winning the series against West Indies and South Africa. A man of great moral and physical courage, he was a firm and understanding captain. He was at the heart of the bodyline controversy, both as captain and, in the more physical sense, being hit about the chest several times. He strongly denounced this form of attack as being contrary to the true spirit of cricket. At Adelaide, when Plum Warner, the MCC manager, went to the Australian dressing-room to enquire how he was, the solid Woodfull replied: 'There's two teams out there, and only one of them's playing cricket.' In England in 1926 he headed the batting overall with 1,672 runs (57.65), including eight centuries, scoring 201 against Essex at Leyton in his initial first-class match on English soil. At Headingley in the third Test he made 141, adding 235 for the second wicket with Charlie Macartney; in the series his record was 306 runs (51.00). Thereafter he never had a poor series with the bat: 1928/9, 491 runs (54.55); 1930, 345 runs (57.50); 1930/1, 195 runs (32.50); 1931/2, 421 runs (70.16) (including his Test highest, 161, in the third match at Melbourne); 1932/3, 305 runs (33.88); and 1934, 228 runs (28.50). Woodfull shared in nine three-figure stands in Tests, three with Ponsford in the 1930 series. His most prolific opening partnership was 375 with Ponsford for Victoria against New South Wales at Melbourne in 1926/7. Of seven double-centuries his highest was 284 for an Australian XI against a New Zealand XI at Auckland in 1927/8. He received the OBE for services to education.

First-class career (1921–34): 13,388 (64.99) including 49 centuries, 1 wicket (24.00), and 78 catches

Test matches (35): 2,300 runs (46.00) including 7 centuries, and 7 catches

WOODS, Samuel Moses James

(b. 1867, Sydney; d. 1931, Taunton) *Cambridge University, Somerset, Australia, and England*

A native of Glenfield, New South Wales, Sammy Woods was a player of grand physique, cheery disposition, and unflinching courage: in both senses he was 'a sport'. Academic requirements were more charitable at Cambridge University in his day and he was able to appear four times against Oxford, being three times on the winning side. He captured 36 wickets in these games. He was an accurate and genuinely fast right-arm bowler with subtlety as well as speed, also bowling a skilful slower ball. He was a fighting and vigorous batsman and fine fielder. While an undergraduate, he was selected to play for the 1888 Australian team in the Tests but was disappointing. He settled in Taunton—in time developing the 'Zummerzet' brogue—playing for the county for 21 years, from 1894 until 1906 as a popular, determined captain, and serving for a time as secretary. Four times he exceeded 1,000 runs in a season and twice took over 100 wickets in the relatively short programmes of those years. For Somerset against Sussex at Hove in 1895 he hammered 215—his career-highest—out of 282 in two hours and a half! A regular for Gentlemen against Players, he bowled unchanged in both innings with F. S. Jackson at Lord's in 1894. He toured South Africa in 1895/6 with Lord Hawke's team and represented England in the three Tests there, thus appearing for both Australia and England at cricket. He also toured America and West Indies, and played 13 times for England at Rugby football.

First-class career (1886–1910): 15,345 runs (23.43) including 19 centuries, 1,040 wickets (20.82), and 279 catches

Test matches (Australia—3): 32 runs (5.33), 5 wickets (24.20), and 1 catch. (England—3): 122 runs (30.50), 5 wickets (25.80), and 4 catches

WOOLLEY, Roger Douglas

(b. 1954, Hobart) *Tasmania and Australia*

Roger Woolley developed into a very useful wicket-keeper and an impressive right-hand middle-order batsman after his début for Tasmania in 1977/8. In the 1982/3 season he captained the state and showed outstanding all-round ability, scoring 551 runs (42.38) and taking 40 catches and two stumpings. This form won him a place in the Australia v. Sri Lanka Test match when Rodney Marsh was not available; he was not required to bat but took five catches behind the stumps. He toured the West Indies in 1983/4, playing in only one Test, but Woolley remained a heavy scorer in first-class cricket, making 717 runs (51.21) in 1984/5.

First-class career (1977–88): 4,781 runs (40.17) including 7 centuries, and 160 dismissals (144 c. 16 st.)

Test matches (2): 21 runs (10.50) and 7 catches

WORRALL, John

(b. 1861, Maryborough, Victoria; d. 1937, Melbourne) *Victoria and Australia*

Short and thickset, Jack Worrall was a right-handed hitter, full of courage and ready to fight his way out of any trouble. Touring England twice in 1888 and 1899, he did not strike form on the earlier visit but, in 1899, he generally opened the batting with his captain, Joe Darling, scoring 1,202 runs (35.35) in first-class matches. In the Tests, with a highest score of 76 (out of 172) on a wet pitch at Headingley, he averaged 45.42. At home he played in the series of 1884/5, 1887/8, 1894/5, and 1897/8. In the fifth Test at Sydney in 1897/8, although Australia were 96 behind on the first innings, Jack Worrall hit 62 not out in the second, adding 193 with Darling for the third wicket in a Homeric struggle which Australia managed to win. His 417 not out for Carlton against Melbourne University in 1896 was the then highest in Australian club cricket. Also a distinguished Australian Rules footballer, he became a well-known sports writer, and is credited with the invention of the term 'bodyline' to describe England tactics in 1932/3.

First-class career (1883–1901): 4,660 runs (20.99) including 7 centuries, 105 wickets (23.10), and 101 catches

Test matches (11): 478 runs (25.15), 1–127, and 13 catches

WRIGHT, Kevin John

(b. 1953, Fremantle, Western Australia) *Western Australia, South Australia, and Australia*

A red-headed wicket-keeper and left-handed catcher, although he batted capably right-handed,

Kevin Wright came from the same Western Australian club as Rodney Marsh. Trim, fit, neat, agile, and with great determination, he received his first Test opportunities sooner than he would have done but for Marsh's involvement with World Series Cricket. Wright took over from John Maclean as Australia's wicket-keeper for the last two Tests against England in 1978/9 and for two games against Pakistan, taking seven catches in both these last two games. He toured England for the Prudential World Cup in 1979 and India later that year. In India he batted usefully, scoring a fighting and attractive 55 not out in the fourth Test at Delhi, and he claimed three stumpings as well as ten catches in the six Tests. But when he got home the broad figure of Rodney Marsh barred his way, for Western Australia as well as for the national team. The consolation was that the international games were so many, Wright was able to play in the majority of Shield matches, and an innings of 88 not out against Queensland in the last match of 1979/80 took him to 321 runs for the season at an average of 35.66. Time was on his side but it must have been a big disappointment to this personable young man, who became State Manager of an insurance firm, when Steve Rixon was preferred to him as Marsh's deputy in England in 1981. In 1981/2 he moved to South Australia, but he retired when Wayne Phillips displaced him as wicket-keeper.

First-class career (1974–84): 2,551 runs (27.14) including 2 centuries, and 293 dismissals (267 c., 26 st.)

Test matches (10): 219 runs (16.84) and 35 dismissals (31 c., 4 st.)

YALLOP, Graham Neil

(b. 1952, Melbourne) *Victoria and Australia*

Not unlike Mike Denness in 1974/5, Graham Yallop had the misfortune to be a losing Test captain four years later in an era of intense and at times cruel publicity. A determined, vigorous, and orthodox left-hander, who hit the ball very hard, he toured Ceylon with the Australian schoolboys in 1971/2 and a year later was proving his ability by scoring 55 in his first Shield innings for Victoria. To widen his experience, he played for Walsall in the Birmingham League in 1973 and 1975 and also represented Glamorgan 2nd XI in 1977, having married a Welsh girl. The following Australian season he became only the tenth Victorian batsman to score two centuries in a match, hitting 105 and

114 not out against New South Wales at Sydney. His Test career began promisingly in 1975/6 against the West Indies. Dropped the following season, he returned for the final Test against India at Adelaide and scored 121. He followed by batting consistently in the West Indies, with 317 runs in the Tests at 45.29 and 660 runs (55.00) on the tour, including a brilliant 118 against Guyana before having his jaw broken by a ball from Colin Croft. When Bobby Simpson announced his second retirement after the tour, Yallop succeeded him for the 1978/9 Ashes series. His leadership was unimaginative, but he was captaining an inferior side. His own batting stood the stern test of the England bowlers well and he made a defiant century in the first Test at Brisbane and a brilliant 121 in the last. He scored more runs in the series (391) than any other batsman on his side. In India, under the captaincy of Kim Hughes, Yallop scored consistently throughout, making 729 runs at an average of 48.60 and reserving his highest score of 167 for the fifth Test. Yet when he returned home he found himself out of favour and out of form and he played in only one of the limited-overs internationals in 1979/80 and in none of the Tests. His consolation was to lead Victoria to the Sheffield Shield for the second year running. When others were not available he answered the call to go to Pakistan—a lesser man might not have done so—and at Faisalabad scored 172, his fifth century in twenty-three Tests. He played in the Centenary Test at Lord's but never hit form on the short tour and played in none of the 1980/1 Tests. However, he was selected for the 1981 Ashes series, when, in a mixed tour, his personal highlight was a brilliant 114 at Old Trafford. Hit by injury in 1981/2, he played only one Test, and he did not play in the Test series against England the following year. But in first-class cricket he hit 1,418 runs (67.52), beating Bill Ponsford's 55-year-old record of 1,217 Sheffield Shield runs. He played in the Test in Sri Lanka, scoring 98, and he had an outstanding series against Pakistan in 1983/4, when he hit 554 runs (92.33) including 268 in the Melbourne Test. He also scored 578 runs for Victoria in just three games, but injury prevented him from touring the Caribbean. He played just one more Test—against the West Indies in 1984/5, scoring 2 and 1—and went to South Africa with the 'rebel' Australians in 1985/6.

First-class career (1972–85): 11,615 runs (45.90) including 30 centuries, 14 wickets (62.57), 120 catches, and 1 stumping
Test matches (39): 2,756 runs (41.13) including 8 centuries, 1–116, and 23 catches

YARDLEY, Bruce

(b. 1947, Midland, Western Australia) *Western Australia and Australia*

A lively, amusing, enthusiastic, and highly strung character, Bruce Yardley was a slim and swarthy, right-handed all-rounder who hit very hard in an unorthodox way and bowled off-spinners at a brisk pace with considerable bounce and spin. Given greater control he could have been a world-beater. As it was, no regular Test spinner of his time took more wickets per Test than he did. His apprenticeship was a long one, before the advent of World Series Cricket gave him the chance to break into Test cricket. He played one game for Western Australia in 1966/7 as a new-ball bowler while still a teenager but did not establish a place in his strong state side until 1974/5 by which time he had learned to bowl off-breaks with a grip more like a leg-spinner, the ball gripped between his 'middle' and 'ring' fingers. After a promising start to his Test career against India at Adelaide (22, 26, and 4 for 134 in the second innings) Yardley was a central figure in the Australian team in the West Indies, taking 15 Test wickets and making an aggressive 74 against the West Indies fast bowlers at Bridgetown. A senior West Indian umpire was unhappy about the legality of his bowling action. Against England in 1978/9 he was mercurial, never sure of a place and never quite sustaining his efforts with bat or ball, although in defeat in the final Test at Sydney he hit the spinners effectively in a defiant innings of 61 not out. Touring India in 1979/80, Yardley was disappointing, although eight of his 17 wickets came in the two Tests in which he played—at Bangalore and Calcutta. In the latter Test, the fifth, he hit a spirited 61 not out in the first innings, all the more meritorious for the fact that he had missed the fourth Test because of a broken toe suffered when being lbw to Kapil Dev in the third. Having played in only three Shield matches for Western Australia after the return of the Packer cricketers in 1979/80, he burst back the following season and earned two more Test caps, both against India, at Adelaide and Melbourne. He bowled a great deal in both matches, taking 2 for 90 from 44.4 overs in India's first innings at Adelaide, but though the two games

brought him seven more Test wickets in all, he did not quite do enough to persuade the selectors to send him to England. His career took on a new lease of life, however, at home in 1981/2 when he was voted cricketer of the year. In three Tests against Pakistan he took 18 wickets at 22 each and against the powerful West Indies a further 20 wickets in three more Tests, also at 22 each. He continued to play with customary zest in New Zealand towards the end of a tiring season, bowling 56 overs in the first innings of the Auckland Test (4 for 142) and taking 13 wickets in the three Tests. Following a disappointing series in Pakistan he took 22 important wickets in the 1982/3 Ashes series and fielded brilliantly, mainly in the gully. He retired from first-class cricket at the end of the season after taking seven wickets in Australia's first-ever Test in Sri Lanka.

First-class career (1966–83): 2,656 runs (20.82) and 334 wickets (27.91)
Test matches (33): 978 runs (19.56), 126 wickets (31.63), and 31 catches

ZESERS, Andris Karlis

(b. 1967, Medindie, South Australia) *South Australia*

A member of Australia's 1987 victorious World Cup squad—he took one wicket in his only two international appearances—Andrew Zesers struggled to overcome persistent shoulder problems and retired from first-class ranks, aged 23. A tall, superbly-built, right-arm slow-medium bowler and capable right-hand lower-order batsman, Zesers, of Latvian parentage, was the first Australian to take 100 first-class wickets before his 21st birthday. He had started at 17, exceptionally young. Zesers scored 85 and took 5 for 51 and 1 for 25 against Victoria in Adelaide in his fifth match. The following season, also against Victoria, he took 11 wickets in two matches and scored 44 runs in two completed innings.

First-class career (1984–9): 763 runs (16.59), 142 wickets (30.44), and 14 catches

ZOEHRER, Timothy Joseph

(b. 1961, Armadale, Western Australia) *Western Australia and Australia*

Tim Zoehrer, Western Australia's talented, live-wire wicket-keeper, made his Test début on Australia's end-of-season tour to New Zealand in February 1986. He first played for his state in 1980/1, but for several seasons he had to content himself with being Rodney Marsh's deputy. Red-haired, perky, and extrovert, he always impressed behind the stumps when Marsh was on Test duty and made a century against New South Wales in 1982/3. He finally became the state's regular 'keeper after Marsh's retirement, and consistent performances over the next two seasons won him a place in the Test team in New Zealand in 1985/6 as the Australian selectors opted once more for a specialist wicket-keeper. With his clean handling and solid batting he had the chance to establish himself as Marsh's permanent successor for state and country, and he had the additional skill of bowling leg-breaks and googlies well enough to defeat good batsmen when condi-

tions suited him. But he lost his Test place after the 1986/7 season, in which he toured India (making 52 not out at Delhi) and played in four of the five Tests against England. For Western Australia he remained a valuable asset and he toured England both in 1989 and 1993 as deputy wicket-keeper to Ian Healy. By now he had learned to curb a fiery temperament which sometimes got him into trouble in his salad days.

First-class career (1980–): 5,348 runs (29.54) including 7 centuries, 38 wickets (46.52), 423 catches, and 38 stumpings
Test matches (10): 246 runs (20.50) and 19 dismissals (18 c., 1 st.)

England

ABEL, Robert

(b. 1857, Rotherhithe, Surrey; d. 1936, Stockwell, London) *Surrey and England*

Bobby Abel held a world record for 50 years: at The Oval in 1899, he put on 448 for Surrey's fourth wicket against Yorkshire, the English record until 1982. With his faded, chocolate-coloured Surrey cap, waddling walk, upright stance, resourceful, patient, and often punishing batting, 'The Guv-'nor' was a great favourite, especially at The Oval. A diminutive opening batsman (5 ft. 4 in.), he was reputedly afraid of fast bowling, yet he mastered all types of attack—and in 1901 scored 3,309 runs (55.15) after passing 2,000 for six consecutive seasons. Two years before he had carried his bat for his highest score, 357 against Somerset at The Oval. In 1897, with William Brockwell, he put on 379 for the first wicket, for Surrey against Hampshire, also at The Oval, which was a record at that time. On the third of three visits to Australia, in 1891/2, he made 388 runs (38.80) in first-class matches, including 132 in the Test at Sydney, when he carried his bat. He toured South Africa with the first English team in 1888/9, and was, in figures if not in fact, head and shoulders above the other batsmen. He made 1,075 runs (48.19) in all matches, including 120 in the second Test at Cape Town, which was the first hundred in matches between the two countries. He was also a jack-in-the-box at slip and a useful slow bowler. Two sons played for Surrey, one going on to Glamorgan.

First-class career (1881–1904): 33,124 runs (35.46) including 74 centuries, 263 wickets (24.01), and 585 catches

Test matches (13): 744 runs (37.20) including 2 centuries, and 13 catches

ABSOLOM, Charles Alfred

(b. 1846, Blackheath, Kent; d. 1889, Port of Spain, Trinidad) *Cambridge University, Kent, Essex, and England*

Known as 'the Cambridge navvy', Charlie Absolom was a large, bearded all-rounder who trained on hay-making and beer and could bowl a good medium pace, hit in lively fashion, and field actively. He was a member of Lord Harris's team to Australia in 1878/9 and rescued England with 52 at Melbourne in his only Test. On forsaking first-class cricket soon afterwards, he travelled extensively, spending much time with Red Indians in America, and became a purser, dying in agony at Port of Spain, when a crane discharged a cargo of sugar on him. (Strangely, he was one of the few cricketers who had never worn a cap or hat.) In 57 matches for Kent he made 1,644 runs (16.60) and took 89 wickets (25.22). Also a useful footballer and athlete, he represented Cambridge in the long jump and shot-put.

First-class career (1866–79): 2,515 runs (15.05), 281 wickets (19.11), and 127 catches

AGNEW, Jonathan Philip

(b. 1960, Macclesfield, Cheshire) *Leicestershire and England*

A 6 ft. 4 in. right-arm fast bowler of slim, wiry build, and cheerful demeanour, Jon Agnew left county cricket before receiving a benefit to take his chance as a broadcaster and journalist. He quickly made a second name for himself as a natural and articulate communicator with a ready humour and a contagious propensity for giggling. On and off the field the game for him has never lost its fun or enjoyment. His best season for Leicestershire came in 1987 when he decided to abandon all-out pace for the art of swing and variation: his 101 wickets were the product of bowling of high skill, and in the course of a memorable season he also made 90 against Yorkshire at Scarborough, dispatching half-volleys with elegant relish. He made his first appearances for his county, whose former batsmen Les Barry and Maurice Hallam had coached him at Uppingham, soon after a last school season in which his 37 wickets cost only 8 runs each, including 8 for 16 in the victory over Oundle. He took a wicket with his fourth ball in county cricket. It was not, however, until 1984 that the hostile pace released from his high, easy action bore extensive fruit. That season he took 84 first-class wickets and won his first two Test caps against the West Indies and Sri Lanka. Punished, like the other England bowlers, by the Sri Lankans at Lord's, he was nevertheless called out as a replacement on England's tour of India the following winter, taking seven wickets in his only first-class match and playing in the later one-day internationals. In 1985, after taking 9 for 70 against Kent, he won back his Test place for the Old Trafford match against Australia but did not take a wicket and was displaced by his friend and county partner, Les Taylor. He went on the England B tour of Sri Lanka the following winter, but when there was no further international recognition despite his successful 1987 season, he began regular winter employment for BBC Radio Leicester as a sports producer. He also wrote an observant book about the life of a professional cricketer, *Eight Days a Week* (1988). The life of a journalist both attracted and suited him: after covering England's 1990/1 tour of Australia for the *Today* newspaper he was appointed BBC cricket correspondent in 1991. A year later he again appeared for Leicestershire, in the semi-final of the NatWest, when two regular bowlers were injured. He took 1 for 31 in 12 steady overs to help his team to get to Lord's.

First-class career (1978–90): 2,118 runs (11.57) and 666 wickets (29.25)
Test matches (3): 10 runs (10.00) and 4 wickets (93.25)

AIRD, Ronald

(b. 1902, London; d. 1986, Yapton, Sussex)
Cambridge University and Hampshire

Ronnie Aird's three years in the Eton XI included a century which brought victory against Winchester (1921) in the match in which J. L. Guise made 278 for the losers. Gentle, courteous, and able, Aird was a stylish right-handed batsman whose best performance was 159 for Hampshire against Leicestershire at Lord's in 1928. Although he played for his county throughout the interwar years his appearances were limited, especially after 1926 when he became assistant secretary of MCC. From then on he served the club in various capacities for the remaining 60 years of his life. As secretary (1952–62), in succession to Colonel Rait Kerr, his hallmark was friendliness in a period of calm in the cricket world. He was just the right person to go to the dockside and present MCC membership to the returning Len Hutton, MCC's successful professional captain in the 1954/5 series against Australia. But there was a quality of steel as well, to which an MC in the Second World War testified and which was demonstrated when, as president (1968), he chaired the MCC Special General Meeting over relations with South Africa. In retrospect, his presidency marked a turning-point in the nature of that office. It had been primarily one demanding the social courtesies: henceforth the president of MCC was its titular representative in the public and political issues which confronted the game.

First-class career (1920–38): 4,482 runs (21.97) including 4 centuries, 7 wickets (59.00), and 52 catches

ALCOCK, Charles William

(b. 1842, Sunderland, County Durham; d. 1907, Brighton, Sussex)

Scores and Biographies described Charles Alcock as a 'steady bat, fair change fast bowler and an excellent long stop'. He was a club cricketer, when time permitted, even captaining a side of Englishmen in 1865 to play as 'France' against a similar 'German' XI at Hamburg in 'grand cricket week'. But it is as an administrator in two sports for which he should be best remembered. At the age of 30, he became secretary of Surrey CCC when the fortunes of the county were in decline. 'The resuscitation of the club might safely be left in his hands,' declared the chairman on his appointment, in the presence of the outgoing secretary! Events proved him right, Alcock remaining secretary for the rest of his life and Surrey enjoying a run of success comparable to that of the 1950s. It was Alcock who brought the 1880 Australians to The Oval to take part in the first Test match in England. The visitors had come unexpectedly and unwelcomed after some bitterness during England's visit to Australia the year before. Not even a match at Lord's was on their itinerary. Alcock's tact and determination secured the fixture which England won by five wickets, W. G. Grace and W. L. Murdoch each making over 150 for their respective sides. Two years later, Alcock founded the weekly periodical, *Cricket*, editing it until his death as he did *James Lillywhite's Cricketers' Annual*. His *Surrey Cricket* (with Lord Alverstone) was the first major history of a county club. Meanwhile, his winters were occupied as first secretary of the Football Association (1867–96). The memory of house-matches at Harrow prompted him to launch a knock-out competition for clubs and he himself led Wanderers to the first FA Cup Final at the Oval in 1872. Three years later, he himself captained England against Scotland on the same ground and refereed the FA Cup Final. To his credit must go the recognition that the future of both games lay in the growth of professionalism and in the body of public support which the new era of transport, communication, and literacy made possible. He was also associated with developments in other sports, staging the first home rugby match between England and Scotland in 1872 at The Oval and leasing the ground for hockey. He was a man with a keen business acumen, with influential friends such as Grace, a perceptive writer, and possessing the late-Victorian virtues of hard work and high endeavour.

ALDERMAN, Albert Edward

(b. 1907, Allenton, Derbyshire; d. 1990, Frimley Park, Surrey) *Derbyshire*

One of the unsung heroes of the county circuit, Alderman was a dependable right-handed opening batsman for Derbyshire, reaching 1,000 runs on six occasions and helping them to their only championship title in 1936. A year later he made his highest score of 175 against Leicestershire at Chesterfield and a century against the New Zealanders. In an era when outstanding fielding was less common, Alderman was a superb deepfield, two of his 202 catches—at the Oval in 1936 and Trent Bridge in 1938—leaving indelible memories on those who saw them. He was a pro-

fessional footballer for Derby County and, in his later years, a first-class umpire and coach at Repton School.

First-class career (1928–48): 12,376 runs (25.94) including 12 centuries, 4 wickets (42.75), and 204 dismissals (202 c., 2 st.)

ALLEN, David Arthur

(b. 1935, Bristol) *Gloucestershire and England*

With a comfortable amble to the crease of no more than four or five paces, David Allen could bowl accurately for long spells, turning his off-spinner substantially. His best batting came against the fastest bowling or when his side badly needed runs, and he was a very good outfield. He did the double in 1961 and twice scored 1,000 runs. Dark-haired, slim, of medium height, he always looked a neat, well-prepared cricketer. He was Jim Laker's successor as the prime England off-spinner and bowled several long containing spells on his first tour of the West Indies in 1959/60. He toured all the leading cricket countries within the next ten years, although several top-class off-spinners including Titmus, Illingworth, and Mortimore challenged him for a place. He and Titmus bowled England to big victories on turning pitches at Durban in 1964/5, when Allen took 5 for 41, and at Sydney the following year.

First-class career (1953–72): 9,291 runs (18.80) including 1 century, 1,209 wickets (23.64), and 252 catches
Test matches (39): 918 runs (25.50), 122 wickets (30.97), and 10 catches

ALLEN, Sir George Oswald Browning

(b. 1902, Sydney, Australia; d. 1989, London) *Cambridge University, Middlesex, and England*

A brave, forthright, and very determined character, 'Gubby' Allen was for many years the *eminence grise* of English cricket. In his retirement his home, later bought by MCC as the secretary's residence, stood within a six-hit of Lord's Cricket Ground and his spiritual home was the Lord's Pavilion. A stubborn supporter of the traditional virtues of cricket, he made enemies who resented his 'backroom meddling' in England's cricket politics, but his undoubtedly strong influence was invariably for the good of the game. 'Gubby' had a wider experience than any predecessor in the practicalities of cricket in England, as player, captain, selector, and administrator, although he was born in Sydney and had an uncle, R. C. Allen, who played for Australia. Attacking like 'flaming fire', his right-arm fast bowling with a classical sideways-on action often touched greatness; in full measure he possessed rhythm and the ability to make the ball hurry from the pitch. His batting was strong, courageous, and correct, and his outstanding close-in fielding completed his status as a genuine all-rounder. In 1929, arriving late for the Middlesex match against Lancashire at Lord's after a morning's work in the City, he took all ten wickets for 40. He was an amateur, with no time to play cricket full-time, whose career reached its zenith in his thirties when he toured Australia in 1932/3, taking 21 wickets in that series without resorting to bodyline, of which he disapproved. He led England to victory over India in 1936, taking 20 wickets (16.50) himself in the three Tests. Back in Australia in 1936/7, his exertions as captain were herculean, but after England had won the first two Tests, Australia recovered and retained the Ashes. First appointed a selector in 1955, he became a tough and inventive chairman of selectors, putting his faith in class rather than averages. He served as president of MCC in 1963/4 and as treasurer from 1964 until 1976. He was awarded a CBE in 1962, and was knighted for his services to cricket in 1986. He was president of Middlesex, 1977–9, and of the Association of Cricket Umpires.

First-class career (1921–54): 9,232 runs (28.67) including 11 centuries, 785 wickets (22.31), and 131 catches

Test matches (25): 750 runs (24.19) including 1 century, 81 wickets (29.37), and 20 catches

ALLETSON, Edward Boaler

(b. 1884, Welbeck, Nottinghamshire; d. 1963, Worksop, Nottinghamshire) *Nottinghamshire*

Ted Alletson was famous for a single innings. On Saturday 20 May 1911, playing for Nottinghamshire against Sussex at Hove, after a morning bathe in the sea to ease an injury, he hit 189 in 90 minutes, the last 142 runs coming in just 40 minutes. Played against strong opposition, it was the most remarkable piece of sustained hitting in the history of first-class cricket. Alletson was the son of a wheelwright on the Duke of Portland's estate and stood over 6 ft., with an arm-span of 6 ft. 6 in. Though he was a useful all-rounder, it was his batting feats that drew attention. These included hitting a ball from Schofield Haigh of Yorkshire onto the roof of the Bramall Lane pavilion and straight-driving Walter Brearley of Lancaster so hard that the ball uprooted the middle stump at the bowler's end and lifted it ten

yards even as the ball itself sped towards the boundary. His 189 against Sussex in 1911 was his only first-class hundred. Going in at number nine in the second innings when his team, at 185 for 7, were only 9 runs ahead, he scored 47 runs in 50 minutes before lunch. Play resumed at 2.15 before a small crowd who expected Sussex to wrap the game up quickly. At 260 for 9, Nottinghamshire were only 84 ahead. They were all out by 2.55, but by that time Alletson had hit a further 142 out of 152. In 7 overs he scored 115, including 34 in one over off Killick. In the end Sussex, 34 adrift with two wickets left, came close to defeat. The Duke of Portland presented Alletson with a gold watch to mark his achievement. Bob Relf of Sussex, looking back on the day, wrote in a letter to John Arlott in 1957: 'My chief memory is that shower of cricket-balls going over the boundary and the crowd mad with delight. Of course, it cost us a match we were winning, but I don't think anybody minded about that—it was such an experience to watch it.' Alletson joined the ground staff at Lord's in 1914 and during the First World War served with the Royal Garrison Artillery. After the war he settled in Worksop, working in the Manton colliery until arthritis of the hips forced his retirement.

First-class career (1906–14): 3,217 runs (18.59), 33 wickets (19.02), and 74 catches

ALLEY, William Edward

(b. 1919, Sydney, Australia) *New South Wales and Somerset*

Cricket around Bill Alley was fun. At the age of 38, when many a first-class player is thinking of hanging up his boots, he joined Somerset in 1957—getting his county cap after three weeks and 365 runs. In 1961 he scored over 3,000 runs, including 221 not out against Warwickshire at Nuneaton and ten other centuries. He took 396 runs off the Surrey attack in four innings without being dismissed and averaged 93.75 against his fellow-Australians. 265 runs and 8 for 227 on the Petersham ground in Sydney just before World War II with his aggressive left-handed batting and right-arm medium pace brought him to the attention of the New South Wales selectors but he did not play for the state till after the war. In 1948 he embarked upon a 9-year spell in the Lancashire League, playing for Colne and Blackpool, before being specially registered with Somerset. He scored 1,000 runs on ten occasions and went on four tours with Commonwealth and Cavalier sides. In his final year with the county, when in his fiftieth year, he 'played several inimitable knocks' including 110 and 64 against Kent in the Weston Festival. A further 15 years (1969–84) as a first-class umpire in which he stood in ten Test matches completed a quarter of a century on the English county circuit in which both his talents and his personality had made him a welcome figure. In his Australian days he won all his twenty-eight fights as a professional welter-weight boxer before a cricket injury to his jaw forced his retirement when his sights were set on the world welter-weight title.

First-class career (1945–68): 19,612 runs (31.88) including 31 centuries, 768 wickets (22.68), and 293 catches

ALLOM, Maurice James Carrick

(b. 1906, Northwood, Middlesex; d. 1995, Bletchingley, Surrey) *Cambridge University, Surrey, and England*

Maurice Allom was a huge but genial fast-medium right-arm bowler. He was a Cambridge blue and toured Australasia, 1929/30, securing 68 wickets (18.35) and, in the first-ever Test between England and New Zealand at Christchurch, he took four wickets in five balls, including the hat-trick. In 1930/1 he toured South Africa. With Maurice Turnbull he wrote light-hearted accounts of these two tours in *The Book of the Two Maurices* and *The Two Maurices Again* respectively, but business curtailed his career. As an under-graduate, he played the saxophone in a jazz band. President of MCC in 1969/70, he was also president of Surrey CCC from 1971 until 1979. His son Anthony, a 6 ft. 9 in. bowler, also represented Surrey in one match in 1960.

First-class career (1926–38): 1,953 runs (12.84) and 605 wickets (23.62)
Test matches (5): 14 runs (14.00) and 14 wickets (18.92)

ALLOTT, Paul John Walter

(b. 1956, Altrincham, Cheshire) *Cheshire, Lancashire, and England*

Six-foot-four, strongly built, and fair-haired, Paul Allott showed promise at Altrincham Grammar School, played for Cheshire in 1976 and for Lancashire from 1978 whilst studying at Durham University. A useful right-hand bat with a correct technique, he blossomed suddenly as a right-arm fast-medium bowler in 1981 when, with Michael Holding as an occasional new-ball partner, he bowled with stamina and determination to take

85 first-class wickets at 23.09. Not genuinely quick, his high action and strength enable him to move the ball, and he revealed a sound tempera-ment too when playing a useful all-round part in his first Test at Old Trafford, when England retained the Ashes. He took four wickets for 88 and scored 52 not out—an inspired innings—and 14. He had a disappointing tour to India and Sri Lanka in 1981/2 and injury restricted him to only two Tests in 1982. But he made a fine return to Test cricket against the West Indies at Headingley in 1984 when he took 6 for 61, his best Test figures, and he was England's best bowler in the series, taking 14 wickets (20.14) in his three matches. A back injury on the 1984/5 tour to India prevented him from playing in any of the Tests. He played in the first four matches against Australia in 1985, but did not often get the new ball and he could take only five expensive wickets. Intelligent and gregarious, he could be volubly combative on the field. Although a consistently dangerous and accurate bowler in county cricket the conclusion seemed to be that he neither moved the ball enough, nor was quite fast enough, to be a successful bowler on good Test pitches.

First-class career (1978–91): 3,360 runs (16.96) and 652 wickets (25.55)
Test matches (13): 213 runs (14.20), 26 wickets (41.69), and 4 catches

ALSTON, Arthur Reginald

(b. 1901, Farringdon, Berkshire; d. 1994, Ewhurst, Surrey)

Rex Alston was a talented all-round sportsman at Cambridge, where he ran the 100 yards against Oxford as number two to the Olympic gold medalist Harold Abrahams. He played rugby for Bedford and captained the county in the minor counties' cricket competition. He joined the BBC in 1942, after a career in schoolmastering and became an able sports commentator on tennis, athletics, rugby, and cricket, with a pleasant, precise microphone presence. He covered most of the Test matches in England and several MCC tours in the 20 years after the war, as well as several Olympic Games. In 1984, through an error, he joined the select few to have seen his own obituary in *The Times*. Possessed of rare courtesy and charm, he reported cricket into his eighties for the *Daily Telegraph* and *Sunday Tele-graph*. Until the last few years of a contented life he washed every morning in a cold bath.

ALTHAM, Harry Surtees

(b. 1888, Camberley, Surrey; d. 1965, Fulwood,
Yorkshire) *Oxford University, Surrey, and Hampshire*

Harry Altham, a charismatic cricket enthusiast
and a scholar with the common touch, had four
years in the very powerful Repton XIs of 1905–8,
making his Surrey début a month after leaving
school against Leicestershire at The Oval. After
the First World War, in which he won a DSO and
an MC and survived four years as an infantry
officer on the Western Front, he threw in his lot
with Hampshire. A chanceless century against
Kent at Canterbury in 1921 won both praise and
gratitude from Frank Woolley, whose benefit it
was, in that it prolonged the match into a third
day. He was a right-handed batsman in the
classical style with a high back-lift, but cricket saw
little of him once he had embarked on his life's
work at Winchester where he coached generations of boys with skill, kindliness, and enthusiasm, ran a house and taught classics. He was an
expert on the history of Winchester Cathedral
and a willing guide to visitors. His coaching
abilities were offered to a wider field when
he became the first chairman of MCC Young
Cricketers' Association—the forerunner of the
National Association of Young Cricketers—and
later president of the English Schools' Cricket
Association. He was the principal author of
MCC's *Coaching Book* (1952) and to him must go
much credit (as also to Sir George Allen) for the
development of national coaching policies and
the fulfilment of his aim 'to get enough boys
playing this game and playing it right'. His *History
of Cricket* (1926), still the standard work on the
game, appeared originally in articles in *The Cricketer*. In 1938 E. W. Swanton contributed the
second volume. Altham served on the MCC
Committee (1941–65) as treasurer (1951–65) and,
in his year as president (1959–60), had to chair an
ICC meeting handling the throwing issue—
brought to a head in the second Test between
England and South Africa at Lord's. A few years
earlier he had served as chairman of the selectors
who picked the MCC side, under Hutton, which
won the Ashes in 1954/5. Hampshire, for whom
his schoolmastering limited his appearances to
August, enjoyed his services as a committee
member for 40 years and as president for 19.
Cricketers throughout England appreciated the
historical depth, shrewd analysis and good
humour of his speeches and talks. Of Altham,
R. W. V. Robins declared, 'We have the Grace
Gates, the Harris Gardens and the Warner Stand

but in my humble opinion Harry very quietly did
more for cricket than any of them.'

First-class career (1908–31): 1,537 runs (19.70)
including 1 century, and 26 catches

AMES, Leslie Ethelbert George

(b. 1905, Elham, Kent; d. 1990, Canterbury, Kent)
Kent and England

A cheerful, bubbling character, Les Ames spent
most of his life in professional cricket. He was
a fine, strongly built, all-round wicket-keeper,
equally at home taking Tich Freeman, Harold
Larwood, or Bill Voce, and responded admirably
to the demands of the big occasion. He was first
choice 'keeper for England from 1931 until 1938.
The strength of the England sides in that period
owes much to the fact that he was also an
orthodox, free-scoring batsman who showed the
full face of the bat and was good enough to play
for England as a batsman alone. No other wicket-
keeper has scored 100 first-class hundreds. In
1934, particularly, his batting was invaluable
against Australia, especially when he and Maurice
Leyland were the sixth-wicket rescuers at Lord's,
adding 129: Ames scored 120. He shared the
record fifth- and eighth-wicket partnerships
against New Zealand and the fourth against
South Africa. His highest in Tests was 149 against
the West Indies at Kingston, 1929/30, in which
series he made 417 runs (59.57). Against the West
Indies at The Oval in 1933, he had eight dismissals. In 1928 and 1929 he had 122 and 128
dismissals respectively in first-class games, besides
making 1,919 and 1,795 runs. In 1932 his record
was 2,482 runs and 100 dismissals, 64 of them
stumpings. His partnership with the leg-spinner
Tich Freeman was legendary. For many years he
was hampered by fibrositis. He was an England
selector from 1950 until 1956 and again in 1958,
and the secretary/manager of Kent during the
successful years of the 1970s. He was awarded the
CBE for his services to cricket, managed three
MCC tours abroad and was president of Kent in
1975. He played soccer for Gillingham.

First-class career (1926–51): 37,248 runs (43.51)
including 102 centuries, and 1,113 dismissals
(703 c., 418 st.)
Test matches (47): 2,434 runs (40.56) including 8
centuries, and 97 dismissals (74 c., 23 st.)

AMISS, Dennis Leslie

(b. 1943, Birmingham) *Warwickshire and England*

Until his decision to secure his family's future by
accepting 'an offer I could not refuse' from Kerry

Packer's World Series Cricket (despite a record declared benefit of £34,947 from Warwickshire), the image of Dennis Amiss was one of a loyal and dedicated professional cricketer. But temporary bitterness resulting from this decision was quickly forgotten and he continued to serve Warwickshire with honour, despite premature rejection by the national selectors. Such was his natural ability that he became associated with Warwickshire at the age of only 15. At 17 he played his first County Championship match and at 23 his first Test for England against the West Indies, who were to come to respect him as a formidable opponent. His batting reflected his character: calm, determined, disciplined, cautious. An affable family man with his heart very much set in his Birmingham home, his career has had more peaks and troughs than most, but only Boycott among English batsmen in the 1970s equalled his ability patiently to accumulate runs. It took Amiss a long time to establish a regular place in the England team, which he did towards the end of the 1972/3 tour of India and Pakistan, after reaching his first Test century in his 13th Test at Lahore. In his first twelve games for England he averaged only 18; in his next twenty he made over 2,000 runs with eight centuries at an average of 71.33. In 1974 alone he scored 1,379 runs, including his most famous innings, 262 not out at Sabina Park, a marathon of concentration and endurance which saved England from defeat in a truly heroic way. He followed this run of high scores with a series of depressing failures against Australia, frequently falling to Dennis Lillee. But after being hit on the head by a ball from Michael Holding in 1976, he returned to Test cricket with another double-century at The Oval. Squarely built, his special hallmarks as a batsman were a glorious cover-drive and the flick off the legs executed with wrists of steel. Before suffering a back injury he could bowl useful medium-pace left-arm seamers, and he was a reliable if not very athletic fielder. He started his career as a middle-order batsman but achieved a new consistency from the moment that he began regularly to open the Warwickshire innings. He scored over 1,000 runs in every English season between 1965 and 1987 (23 seasons in succession) and made 1,120 runs (74.66) on the tour to the West Indies in 1973/4. He reached 1,500 runs 16 times and passed 2,000 on three occasions—in 1976, 1978, and 1984, his most prolific season, when he hit 2,239 runs (55.97). Unlucky not to be restored to the England side in the post-Packer years, he joined the unofficial tour of South Africa in March 1982, when he showed his undiminished class by heading the English batting averages. In 1985 he became the 13th player to compile 40,000 runs in first-class cricket. Five centuries in 1985 left him needing only four more to complete his 100 hundreds, and he reached the landmark—the 21st cricketer to do so—only the following summer, against Lancashire at Edgbaston. In 1992 he became chairman of the Warwickshire Cricket Committee and an England selector. Two years later he was appointed as Warwickshire's chief executive and one of his earliest decisions, to sign Brian Lara as the county's overseas player, was the catalyst for a season of unprecedented success in 1994: Warwickshire won three of the four county titles and only lost the other, the NatWest, in the final.

First-class career (1960–87): 43,423 runs (42.86) including 102 centuries, 18 wickets (39.88), and 418 catches

Test matches (50): 3,612 runs (46.30) including 11 centuries, and 24 catches

ANDERSON, John Corbet

(b. 1827, London; d. 1906, London)

John Corbet Anderson was a typical Victorian in the range of his interests and skills. He was a portrait painter in oils, an antiquarian, a genealogist, a historian, and a lithographic artist. His lithographs of some forty cricketers, produced in the era immediately before photography had established itself, coincided with the growth of cricket in popular acceptance. They are important both for their artistic ability and as representations of the players of the 1850s such as Parr, Mynn, Wisden, Clarke, Pilch, and the Lillywhites. It was Fred Lillywhite who appreciated the commercial value of printing and distributing Anderson's work while Arthur Haygarth—Lilleywhite's publisher of *Scores and Biographies*—testified to the likenesses of the pictures to the men whom he knew and played with.

ANDREW, Keith Vincent

(b. 1929, Oldham, Lancashire) *Northamptonshire and England*

Keith Andrew, in the face of much competition, played only twice for England, once on the tour to Australia, 1954/5. He was a neat, skilful, unobtrusive and very successful wicket-keeper in county cricket—once holding seven catches in an innings—and a stubborn late-order batsman. He captained Northamptonshire with distinction for five years (1962–6), one of the most successful periods in the county's history. Successively a committee man with Northamptonshire and Lancashire, he became the National Cricket Association's director of coaching, a popular and respected figure. His son, Neale, used artistic hands to equally good effect in a different field, becoming a distinguished sculptor.

First-class career (1952–66): 4,230 runs (13.38) and 903 dismissals (723 c., 181 st.)

Test matches (2): 29 runs (9.66) and 1 dismissal (1 c.)

ANDREWS, William Harry Russell

(b. 1908, Swindon, Wiltshire; d. 1989, Weston-super-Mare, Somerset) Somerset

Bill Andrews, an attacking right-handed batsman and a right-arm fast-medium bowler of in-swingers, had a colourful—if interrupted—career with Somerset as a player (1930–47) and coach. On four occasions the Committee dispensed with his services and, by temperament, he was very much a players' man. His best years were just before the Second World War when he did the 'double' twice—in 1937 and 1938. He took eight Surrey wickets for 12 at The Oval in 1937 (including a hat-trick) and in the following year bowled Don Bradman at Taunton. The great man had already made a double-century but it gave Andrews a title for his autobiography, *The Hand that bowled Bradman* (1973). His loyalty to the West Country went deep and he was popular as a coach both on village greens and in three public schools. In a career not lending itself to precise analysis, he set the record right by making exactly 5,000 runs in first-class cricket.

First-class career (1930–47): 5,000 runs (15.77), 768 wickets (23.48), and 96 catches

APPLEYARD, Robert

(b. 1924, Bradford, Yorkshire) Yorkshire and England

Tall, with an ideal physique, smooth action, and quiet, thoughtful manner, Bob Appleyard was a right-arm, medium-paced off-spin bowler, whose unusual pace combined with his high action enabled him to achieve extra bounce. Like a right-handed Derek Underwood, he was at his most devastating on a wet or damp wicket. His length was superb, and one of his greatest gifts was being able to make the ball dip. He was also an occasionally useful tail-end batsman and a safe

catcher. He was dogged by ill-health for much of his career, but despite an attack of pleurisy took 200 wickets (14.14) and headed the averages in his first full season of first-class cricket in 1951, at the relatively advanced age of 27. Unable to play in 1953, he again took his wickets at only 14, 154 of them, the following year. In Australia and New Zealand, 1954/5, he was at his best, heading the averages in the Tests against Australia with 11 wickets (20.36) and in the two Tests against New Zealand with 9 wickets (8.88), including 4 for 7 in the second innings at Auckland; but his continual struggle against sickness caused his retirement in 1958. Strongly committed to the cause of Yorkshire cricket, he devoted much time in retirement to the development of bowling talent at the Cricket Academy in Bradford. He was also a keen, competitive, and skilful golfer.

First-class career (1950–8): 776 runs (8.52) and 708 wickets (15.48)

Test matches (9): 51 runs (17.00), 31 wickets (17.87), and 4 catches

ARCHER, Alfred German

(b. 1871, Richmond, Surrey; d. 1935, Seaford, Sussex) Shropshire, Worcestershire, and England

A wicket-keeper of occasional county experience, Alfred Archer toured South Africa with Lord Hawke's team, 1898/9, and in his sole Test at Cape Town, his first match in first-class cricket, batted at number ten, scoring 7 and 24 not out, not keeping wicket and not bowling. At school he had not made the Haileybury XI.

First-class career (1899–1903): 231 runs (11.00) and 12 dismissals (10 c., 2 st.)

ARLOTT, Leslie Thomas John

(b. 1914, Basingstoke, Hampshire; d. 1991, Alderney, Channel Islands)

To condense John Arlott's achievements is no easier than selecting a bottle from his fine cellarage of 4,000. He was a man of taste, in wine as in literature; in food as in conversation, although he could be earthy too. The early years as a police detective in Southampton gave no clue to the fame which would be his from 1946 onwards as a broadcaster and writer on cricket. His first broadcast, a scripted talk in 1944, began, 'It's unfashionable to be fond of cricket nowadays . . .'. He joined the BBC as a poetry producer and from his initial commentary on the Indian tour of 1946 until he slipped quietly from the commentary box at Lord's in 1980—with the plaudits of players and spectators ringing in his ears—he never looked back. He had commentated on every single home Test in those 35 seasons. While others might better satisfy the pedant in offering technical judgements, Arlott's precious gift was to convey a vivid picture of events, by the richness and tone of his voice, which never lost its Hampshire accent, although it grew deeper and more deliberate with time, and by his persuasive and compelling choice of word or phrase. There was 'Mann's inhumanity to Mann' in 1948/9 (when 'Tufty' Mann of South Africa was hit for 6 by George Mann of England); or Asif Masood's run-up, likened to 'Groucho Marx stalking a waitress'; or the crowd at Old Trafford in the rain huddled by a 'portly' iron railing. Arlott, the moralist, had strong views on events in South Africa and a practical expression of this was to bring Basil D'Oliviera, the 'Cape Coloured' cricketer, to the Central Lancashire League. The social reformer concerned himself with players' rights and became president of the Cricketers' Association in 1968, his proudest honour. The politician stood twice for Parliament as a liberal. Away from the microphone—and in addition to his radio work he also commentated on BBC television on Sunday afternoon county matches—Arlott wrote or contributed to 93 books or booklets, mainly on cricket but also including *English Cheeses of the South and West* (1958) and *Crime and Punishment* (1961). He reported cricket and soccer for a number of newspapers, finishing with 12 years as cricket correspondent of *The Guardian* from 1968. In 1980 he retired, moving from his home at Alresford in Hampshire, a former public house, to the Channel Island of Alderney, where the pace of life slowed and his health began a slow decline. Personal tragedies—he lost a son in a car accident and the second of his three wives died young—led him to combine a certain hedonism with a brooding sadness. He was awarded an OBE for his services to cricket. His gravestone in Alderney quotes his own poem to Andrew Young:

'So clear you see these timely things
That, like a bird, the vision sings.'

ARMITAGE, Thomas

(b. 1848, Walkley, Sheffield, Yorkshire; d. 1922, Pullman, Chicago, USA) *Yorkshire and England*

Tom Armitage was a useful right-handed batsman and a round-arm, medium-pace or slow-lob bowler. He played in the first two Tests of all, both at Melbourne, 1877. Robust, tall, and bulky,

he prompted one of Tom Emmett's classic 'cracks': he likened the slender Louis Hall and Armitage to 'Law and Gospel', and when his fellow cricketer, the Revd E. S. Carter, asked him for an explanation, he replied, 'Shadow and Substance'. In 51 matches for Yorkshire between 1872 and 1879 he made 1,053 runs (13.85) and took 106 wickets (15.05).

First-class career (1872–9): 1,122 runs (13.35) and 119 wickets (14.27)

Test matches (2): 33 runs (11.00) and 0–15

ARNOLD, Edward George

(b. 1876, Exmouth, Devon; d. 1942, Worcester) *Devon, Worcestershire, and England*

A long, loose-limbed all-rounder, Ted Arnold was a right-handed batsman, strong in defence, and a powerful stroke-player all round the wicket; a right-arm bowler above medium pace, who would vary his speed intelligently; and a safe field. Starting with Devon at 16, he joined Worcestershire two years later and helped to raise his adopted county to first-class rank in 1899. In four consecutive seasons he achieved the 'double' of 1,000 runs and 100 wickets, and in 1903/4 was an integral part of P. F. Warner's team in Australia that regained the Ashes. Only Rhodes enjoyed greater success than Arnold, who secured 18 wickets (26.38) in the series.

First-class career (1899–1913): 15,853 runs (29.91) including 24 centuries, 1,069 wickets (23.16), and 187 catches

Test matches (10): 160 runs (13.33), 31 wickets (25.41), and 8 catches

ARNOLD, Geoffrey Graham

(b. 1944, Earlsfield, Surrey) *Surrey, Sussex, Orange Free State, and England*

Geoff Arnold—' 'Orse' to his fellow players—was a master of the art of swing and cut, and for most of the period in which he played for England, 1967 to 1975, was as dangerous a new-ball bowler as any in the country. Strongly built, yet prone to injury, his effectiveness was reduced more drastically than most by clear blue skies and lifeless pitches. In these conditions, lacking extreme pace and despite exceptional accuracy, he could look ordinary and on three major overseas tours—to India, Pakistan, and Sri Lanka, 1972/3, West Indies, 1973/4, and Australia, 1974/5—achieved little success apart from one outstanding return of 6 for 45 at Delhi, where the ball often swings a great deal. In overcast conditions or on a green pitch his late out-swing and prodigious cut off the seam in either direction undermined the best batsmen: Boycott, for example, seldom survived long against him in these conditions. Against Australia at Old Trafford in 1972 he had three slip catches dropped off him in successive balls. His reaction was remarkably phlegmatic although on another occasion he was disciplined for abusing an umpire. A straightforward character and a friendly family man, he seldom gave the public the impression that cricket is anything other than a stern job of work and as Surrey coach he was a stern taskmaster. He was an outstanding all-round games player and had the batting ability to develop into a genuine all-rounder but seldom got enough batting opportunity at The Oval. Despite making 59 in only his second Test, against Pakistan in 1967, he became no more than an occasionally useful tail-ender. 'Orse made his début for Surrey in 1963, was capped four years later and collected a £15,000 benefit in 1976. He played in the South African Currie Cup for the Orange Free State in 1976/7 and moved to Sussex in 1978. The pitches at Hove often proved more helpful to his skilful fast-medium bowling than the bland Oval pitches of the 1970s and he enjoyed a successful extension to his career, helping considerably towards a sustained improvement in Sussex's fortunes and to victory in the 1978 Gillette Cup Final. His best figures were his 8 for 41 (13 for 128 in the match) for Surrey against Gloucestershire at The Oval in 1967 when he took 109 wickets (18.22). He did the hat-trick for Surrey against Leicestershire at Leicester in 1974 and returned to The Oval as coach in 1983, only to be summarily dismissed from the post after the 1992 season, an apparent victim of Surrey's impatience for success. In 1992 Keith Fletcher, the new England manager, asked him to become a specialist adviser to England's leading bowlers.

First-class career (1963–82): 3,952 runs (13.67), 1,130 wickets (21.91), and 122 catches
Test matches (34): 421 runs (12.02), 115 wickets (28.29), and 9 catches

ARNOLD, John

(b. 1907, Cowley, Oxford; d. 1984, Southampton)
Oxfordshire, Hampshire, and England

John Arnold was Hampshire's outstanding opening batsman during the second decade of the inter-war period. He was a fine attacker, employing some brilliant strokes, and was undisturbed by fast bowling. He was also a quick mover in the field, especially at cover, as befitted an Association

Footballer with Southampton and Fulham who was capped for England against Scotland in 1932/3, at outside left. He also appeared once for England at cricket, scoring 0 and 34 in the first Test against New Zealand in England, at Lord's in 1931. In 1934 he scored 2,261 runs, including 109 not out against the Australians. His highest score was 227 against Glamorgan at Cardiff in 1932. He scored 1,000 runs in a season 14 times. On retirement he became a first-class umpire and stood in first-class cricket from 1961 to 1972.

First-class career (1929–50): 21,831 runs (32.82) including 37 centuries, 17 wickets (69.52), and 184 catches

ASHLEY-COOPER, Frederick Samuel

(b. 1877, London; d. 1932, Milford, Surrey)

Wisden in 1933 prefaced its normal list of obituaries with special ones of Lord Harris and of Ashley-Cooper. In their separate ways both deserved such singular attention: one a Colossus of cricket and the other its Herodotus. And, as the joint authors of *Lord's and the MCC* (1920) it was not unfitting. Unable to play or, indeed, pursue a profession because of poor health and weak eyesight, Ashley-Cooper devoted his life to the archives and statistics of cricket. There were years spent in the British Museum researching pre-Victorian newspapers. He published over a hundred books and pamphlets besides writing some 40,000 biographical and obituary notices, mostly for *Wisden*. After Arthur Haygarth's death in 1925, he compiled volume xv of his *Scores and Biographies* from Haygarth's notes and updated all the biographical entries in the preceding volumes. The hallmark of his scholarship was meticulous accuracy and clarity of expression. He collected books and pictures in an age when bargains were still possible: an unknown picture of Alfred Mynn became his for a shilling or two. Just before his death Sir Julien Cahn purchased his collection. Many of Ashley-Cooper's own books, notably *Cricket and Cricketers* (1907) and *Highways and Byways* (1927) have themselves become collectors' pieces.

ASHTON, Sir Hubert

(b. 1898, Calcutta, India; d. 1979, South Weald, Essex) *Cambridge University, Essex, Burma, and Europeans*

Seventy-five runs by Hubert Ashton, a stylish right-handed batsman, paved the way for an England XI, raised by the veteran A. C. Mac-

Laren, to beat the hitherto undefeated Australians of 1921 by 28 runs at Eastbourne. MacLaren's 'scratch' XI—also including Hubert's brothers, Claude and Gilbert, who played with him in the same Cambridge side—were 71 runs behind with six second-innings wickets left when Hubert and the South African G. A. Faulkner put on 154. Ashton had announced himself a year earlier with 236 not out for the University against the Free Foresters at Fenner's and in 1922 he would probably have become the first man to score a century in successive University matches at Lord's had he himself not declared the Cambridge innings closed when he was 90 not out. He had been an outstanding schoolboy captain at Winchester before winning an MC in the First World War and averaging 64.51 in his three years in the Cambridge XI. A career in the oil industry limited his future appearances. When the Europeans in the Far East played MCC at Calcutta in 1926 he, J. L. Guise, the Winchester hero of five years earlier, R. J. O. Meyer, and F. A. Tarrant were all in the side. Subsequently, he played off and on for Essex until the outbreak of war in 1939, becoming the county's chairman (1946–51) and president (1949–70). Besides being a Bristol Rovers footballer, he had a distinguished career in public life, as a Church Commissioner and Member of Parliament for Chelmsford (1950–64). He was president of MCC (1960). His brother Gilbert was president of Worcestershire, 1967–9. Claude, the youngest of the four brothers who played first-class cricket, won cricket, hockey, and soccer blues and played soccer for England.

First-class career (1920–39): 4,025 runs (38.70) including 8 centuries, and 72 catches

ASTILL, William Ewart

(b. 1888, Ratby, Leicestershire; d. 1948, Stoneygate, Leicester) *Leicestershire and England*

One of the best cricketers never to play a Test against Australia and one of the hardiest perennials of them all, Ewart Astill was a mainstay of the county side season after season and, indeed, with George Geary he virtually carried the side upon his shoulders between the two World Wars. He was an orthodox right-handed batsman without mannerism or oddity. As an off-spin bowler he had an enviable ease with a lolloping run and tireless wheel of the arm and could spin acutely even on true surfaces. He was also first-rate in the slips or gully. From 1921 until 1930 he achieved the double each season except 1927. In 1935 he was the first Leicestershire professional to be

appointed county captain. He played in nine Tests, all abroad, not making his first appearance until he was 39, in South Africa in 1927/8. He also toured the West Indies twice (1925/6, 1929/30), and India (1926/7) in addition to making three private (non-MCC) tours. An excellent pianist, vocalist, banjoist and billiard player, he was, especially on tour, an amusing singer of songs to his own ukulele accompaniment.

First-class career (1906–39): 22,731 runs (22.55) including 15 centuries, 2,431 wickets (23.76), and 464 catches

Test matches (9): 190 runs (12.66), 25 wickets (34.24), and 7 catches

ATHERTON, Michael Andrew

(b. 1968, Manchester) *Cambridge University, Lancashire, and England*

Mike Atherton seemed destined to captain England long before he was appointed to the job in critical circumstances, two-thirds of the way through an Ashes series in 1993, at the age of only 25. Independent, yet not a loner; articulate, yet not pompous; assiduous, but far from humourless, he approached his challenge with a matter-of-fact honesty and after England had lost his first Test in charge, the fifth game of the series at Edgbaston, they defeated Australia at The Oval, the country's first win for eleven matches. By this stage of what promised to be a long and durable Test career, he had established himself as a worthy, if unspectacular, opening batsman, capable of improving on a batting average of 35 from 29 matches. His first cricket tutor was his father Alan, a Bolton headmaster who played cricket for Woodhouses, a village team near Oldham. He was at Manchester Grammar School for seven years, captaining the first team for his last three before going up to Cambridge to read history. In his first year at Fenner's, in 1987, he made 73 not out from a total of 135 in his first match. Graham Gooch was one of the opposing Essex team. Four matches later Atherton scored 109 not out in a total of 185 against Derbyshire and at the end of that season his first appearances for Lancashire's 1st XI confirmed his ability. Leadership potential as well as a sound batting technique was obvious: he captained the university for two seasons and under him the Combined Universities qualified for the Benson and Hedges Cup Quarter Finals for the only time in 1989. Going down from Cambridge with a 2:1 history degree to become a full-time professional, he made his first Test appearance at Trent Bridge against Australia later that season at the age of 21 and a year later secured his international future with Test hundreds against both New Zealand and India and 735 Test runs at 66 in that batsman's summer *par excellence*. A loss of form in the first part of the 1990/1 tour of Australia and the back operation which kept him away from the limelight after an unhappy home series against the West Indies in 1991 gave him the chance to assess his career. He spent his time doing homely things: reading good books, seeing his girl-friend, watching Manchester United, and supping modest amounts of real ale. His come-back to the England team was swift but initially unsuccessful. Not chosen for a single one-day international and for only the final Test in India in 1992/3, he scored 80 and 99 in the Lord's Test against Australia the following summer, run out after he had slipped in the second innings. Innings of 55 and 63 as England suffered another heavy defeat at Leeds helped to persuade the selectors that he should succeed Gooch, who had resigned as captain the moment the Ashes were lost. 'It's amazing how quickly things change in this game,' Atherton said, 'never take success for granted and never get overwhelmed by failure.' With Gooch he had enjoyed one of the most successful opening partnerships in Test history: of their 16 opening stands of 50 or more in 34 innings, seven had gone past 100 and three past 200 (204 and 225 against India in 1990 and 203 against Australia at Adelaide in 1990/1). Taking a young side to the West Indies in the early months of 1994, he enjoyed something of a triumph as a batsman, scoring hundreds at Georgetown and St John's and 510 runs in the five Tests at an average of 56. England lost the series 1–3 and were bowled out for 46 in Trinidad, so it was hardly plain sailing, but at Bridgetown they became only the second side ever to win a Test in Barbados. Back home, Atherton quickly added another Test hundred at Trent Bridge as England defeated New Zealand but at Lord's against South Africa in July his world fell upon him. Not only did England lose by the humiliating margin of 356 runs, but Atherton was spotted by television cameras rubbing earth from his pocket onto the ball. His explanation, that he was trying to keep it dry in the exceptionally sticky heat, was not at first given in proper detail to the match referee, Peter Burge, and Atherton was fined £2,000 by England's chairman of selectors; £1,000 'for using dirt' (though this was not strictly against the Laws) and £1,000 'for giving incomplete information to the match referee'. Atherton weathered the subsequent media storm, resisted pressure to resign—the umpires had not, after all,

reported any malpractice—and having made a gritty 99 in the drawn Leeds Test, he led England to a victory at The Oval to level the series. Two months later he took the side to Australia, a wiser man.

First-class career (1987–): 11,644 runs (44.44) including 34 centuries, and 107 wickets (43.77)
Test matches (45): 3,324 runs (40.04) including 7 centuries, 1 wicket (282.00), and 34 catches

ATHEY, Charles William Jeffrey

(b. 1957, Middlesbrough) *Yorkshire, Gloucestershire, Sussex, and England*

A neat, 5 ft. 9 in., fair-haired, right-handed batsman of wiry build, occasional medium-paced bowler, and brilliant outfielder, Bill Athey made an impressive start for Yorkshire in 1976, soon hitting form with 131 against Sussex. Four years later, he scored 1,000 runs for the first time during a consistent season for Yorkshire but made a disappointing start to his Test career, having been talked of as the next in line to Sutcliffe, Hutton, and Boycott. After playing with great flair in a one-day international against Australia, he was selected for the 1980 Centenary Test but failed in trying circumstances. Not originally selected to tour the West Indies under Ian Botham early in 1981, he was called from a coaching job in Australia to join a team stricken by various tribulations. In four Test innings against ferocious fast bowling, he managed only seven runs but his speed in the field won frequent applause. Growing increasingly unhappy at Yorkshire, he joined Gloucestershire at the beginning of the 1984 season and he immediately redis-covered his best form. He scored 1,812 runs (37.75) including a century against his old county, and two more successful seasons in 1985 and 1986 brought him back to the notice of the Test selectors. He made a career-best 184 on the England B tour to Sri Lanka, and returned to the England side against India and New Zealand in 1986, scoring an accomplished 142 not out in a limited-overs international against New Zealand at Old Trafford but, apart from a neat 55, also against New Zealand, at Trent Bridge, having no luck in the Tests. Despite a batting average of 15, the selectors showed faith in his technique by picking him for the 1986/7 tour of Australia. This was the high point of his somewhat restless career. Opening the batting with Chris Broad, he put on 223 in the second Test at Perth, adding 96 himself to an important 76 on the first day of the series at Brisbane. Throughout this tour, he also contributed well to England's many one-day successes, both with the bat and in the field. In the Lord's Test the following season he scored 123 at number three against Pakistan but despite further tours of Pakistan and New Zealand in 1987/8, he did not reach 50 in 15 further innings for England and was obliged to become again merely one of the steadiest and most orthodox of county batsmen. Moving to Sussex in 1993, having captained Gloucestershire in 1989 and received a benefit in 1990, he had a very consistent season, scoring 1,600 runs (64.00), the eleventh time he had scored 1,000 runs. He scored four first-class hundreds in succession in 1987 and was, more than most, a man who made the most of his periods of good form.

First-class career (1976–): 22,741 runs (35.81) and 48 wickets (54.52)

Test matches (23): 919 runs (22.97) including 1 century, and 13 catches

ATTEWELL, William

(b. 1861, Keyworth, Nottinghamshire; d. 1927, Long Eaton, Derbyshire) *Nottinghamshire and England*

William Attewell, a calm and cheerful right-arm, medium-paced bowler of exceptional accuracy, could bowl for long spells without tiring. Against Kent at Trent Bridge in 1887 his analysis was 52.2–42–19–4. He was also a useful late-order batsman and a good field at cover-point. He played first for his county during the 'Nottingham Schism' of 1881 when many leading players went on strike; immediately he strengthened the attack and for 16 years was an integral part of the side. He took 100 wickets in a season ten times, and visited Australia three times, taking 55 wickets (10.72) in first-class matches on his second visit in 1887/8. He became an umpire on retirement (1902–7). His brother, Thomas, and cousin, Walter, both played briefly for Notts.

First-class career (1881–99): 8,083 runs (14.03) including 1 century, 1,951 wickets (15.32) and 364 catches

Test matches (10): 150 runs (16.66), 28 wickets (22.35), and 9 catches

BADER, Sir Douglas Robert Steuart

(b. 1910, London; d. 1982, London) *RAF*

After captaining St Edward's, Oxford, Douglas Bader played for the Royal Air Force. In 'a brilliant display' of right-handed batting he made 65 against the Army at The Oval in July 1931 in his only appearance in first-class cricket. Five months later he lost both his legs in an air crash when, as a rugby football trialist, he was on the verge of getting an England cap. Returning to the RAF soon after the outbreak of war in 1939, he won the DSO and DFC (each with bars) as a fighter pilot and later became managing director of Shell Aircraft Limited. His triumph over adversity—he played golf off a handicap of four—was an inspiration to others similarly afflicted.

First-class career (1931): 66 runs (33.00)

BAILEY, Jack Arthur

(b. 1930, London) *Oxford University and Essex*

Jack Bailey's début for Essex in 1953 brought his right-arm fast-medium bowling a spectacular return of 7 for 53 against Nottinghamshire at Southend and he ended the season top of the national bowling averages. A year later, on the same ground, he took 5 for 9 against Somerset. His namesake, Trevor, whose biographer Jack would become, was almost equally successful in the match. Going up to Oxford a little late, his captaincy of the University created an atmosphere 'of determination and enthusiasm'. Although he had made runs at Christ's Hospital as a right-handed batsman, he had little success at higher level. He was assistant secretary of MCC (1968–74) but his secretaryship (1974–87) was marred by increasingly strained relations between the club and the TCCB in which opinions were divided among members upon the future role of the premier club in the world and its proper relationship with the TCCB, which had organized the first-class game in the United Kingdom since 1968. Bailey's ability as an administrator was unquestioned and his loyalty to the club was unswerving but intransigent. His premature resignation, in MCC's bicentenary year, came after pressure from other senior figures at Lord's and led to cosier relations with the Board at the cost of some MCC independence. In the (then) dual role of ICC secretary, Bailey had won the confidence of the member-countries and handled matters well in the difficult 'Packer' years when there had also been bitter divisions. An affable character by nature and a fluent writer, he had written on Rugby Union for the *Sunday Telegraph* before his jobs at Lord's and after 1987 returned to the press-box to write cricket for *The Times*. He was a friendly and professional colleague.

First-class career (1953–68): 641 runs (5.82), 347 wickets (21.62), and 67 catches

BAILEY, Robert John

(b. 1963, Biddulph, Staffordshire) *Staffordshire, Northamptonshire, and England*

Tall and, despite a short backlift, often an imposing, hard-hitting right-handed batsman, eager to drive fast bowlers over the top off the front foot, Rob Bailey was unlucky that the first tour for which he was selected by England, to India in 1988/9, was cancelled for political reasons. He went instead to the West Indies in 1989/90 and although not out of his depth he struggled against some of the best and fiercest fast bowlers in the world. He was, indeed, very unlucky for England, being given out caught behind without touching the ball at a crucial stage of the Barbados Test and never playing for England again despite a sturdy 42 against a barrage of hostile bowling at Antigua, where England were overwhelmed. Going in at his customary number three position in 1988 he had made 43 in his first Test innings, also against West Indies, at The Oval in 1988, only to be dropped for the following match against Sri Lanka. A sound fielder and occasionally useful off-spin bowler, he gave Northamptonshire loyal, steadfast, and consistent service, equally effective in one-day and two-innings cricket. On the dry and grassless pitches of 1990 he enjoyed himself hugely, scoring 1,987 runs (64.09) and with an average of 51 in his benefit season, 1993, he pressed in vain for a Test recall.

First-class career (1982–): 16,221 runs (42.35) including 34 centuries, and 84 wickets (42.15)
Test matches (4): 119 runs (14.87)

BAILEY, Trevor Edward

(b. 1923, Westcliff-on-Sea, Essex) *Cambridge University, Essex, and England*

A born iconoclast, and a cricketer of immense character and intelligence, Trevor Bailey, like his predecessor J. W. H. T. Douglas, enjoyed a reputation as a tough competitor but, unlike Douglas, he never captained England, except in a BBC computer Test match. Prolific during his wartime schooldays at Dulwich, Bailey was an outstanding right-arm fast-medium bowler, brilliant fielder, and generally dour batsman, whose stolid defence based around an impassable forward defensive stroke played with the top hand behind the handle dug England out of many a hole. It earned him the sobriquet 'Barnacle' although he could attack effectively when the occasion demanded. He did, however, score first-class cricket's slowest-ever 50, in 357 minutes at Brisbane in 1958/9, one of fourteen matches in which he opened the batting for his country. He positively relished a crisis, although this was one of his own making. Throughout the 1950s he was the pivot of the national team, becoming a right-hand man to both Len Hutton and Peter May. He went on four major MCC tours, generally sharing the new ball with Alec Bedser as England emerged from post-war struggle to domination in the mid-1950s with the help of younger fast bowlers. Twice in 1953 England owed their survival mainly to Bailey. At Leeds he bowled leg-theory to slow down an Australian gallop to victory and at Lord's he batted $4\frac{1}{4}$ hours for 71 on the final day in a famous stand with Willie Watson. England went on to win the Ashes. In Jamaica the following winter he produced one of the great bowling spells of Test history, taking 7 for 34 in 16 overs of incisive swing bowling on a hot day and beautiful pitch against a star-studded West Indian batting team. For Essex he was even more the lynch-pin, acting as club secretary from 1955 to 1967, the days when the scoreboard had to be driven from ground to ground on a lorry, and as captain from 1961 to 1966. He did the double eight times. With his lovely high action, he was always a better bowler to watch than he was batsman. He also won a Soccer blue and an FA Amateur Cup medal with Walthamstow Avenue. He wrote on cricket in books and newspapers on his retirement and became a long-serving and popular member of Test Match Special commentaries on BBC Radio. His astringent summaries, always perceptive of the strengths and weaknesses of players, were delivered in a jaunty style with evident self-satisfaction and enjoyment. Somewhat vague, he intended to take his wife to the coast on the Sunday of his first Test at Leeds in 1949, having taken 6 for 118 in the first innings against New Zealand, but was surprised to find no sea in the inland spa resort of Harrogate. In 1993, conducting English supporters around India, he arrived at Bombay airport with a party of thirty—but no tickets. His beloved wife had thrown them away. The Bailey charm prevailed, as his determination had in many a cricketing crisis.

First-class career (1945–67): 28,641 runs (33.42) including 28 centuries, 2,082 wickets (23.13), and 427 catches
Test matches (61): 2,290 runs (29.74) including 1 century, 132 wickets (29.21), and 32 catches

BAIRSTOW, David Leslie

(b. 1951, Bradford, Yorkshire) Yorkshire, Griqualand West, and England

Red-haired, a chunkily built but very acrobatic wicket-keeper in the Godfrey Evans mould, and a determined and hard-hitting right-handed batsman who could also bowl medium pace, David Bairstow was a wholehearted extrovert and enthusiast. After making his county début in 1970 while still a Bradford schoolboy, he got his first chance at international level when he was called to Australia in 1978/9 to replace the injured Roger Tolchard. Physically as hard as nails, but emotional and full of *joie de vivre*, 'Bluey' Bairstow won his first Test cap against India at The Oval in 1979, making 9 and 59 and taking 3 catches, doing quite enough to ensure a place as Bob Taylor's deputy wicket-keeper in Australia in 1979/80. Bairstow did not play in any of the three Tests on this tour but was a valuable member of the England side in the one-day internationals, making many useful contributions with his pugnacious batting. He again showed his value with the bat when making top score of 40 against the fierce West Indies attack in the fifth Test at Headingley in 1980 and played in the Centenary Test against Australia at Lord's, but after an untidy performance behind the stumps at Bridgetown on the tour of West Indies which followed, he was not considered again for the Test team, although he played in more one-day internationals. He was Yorkshire captain between 1984 and 1986 and as the internal strife at the club gradually subsided he led his side enthusiastically from the front with his swashbuckling batting. He scored 1,000 runs in a season three times and he took 11 catches against Derbyshire at Scarborough in 1982, equalling the world record for most catches in a match. He played some professional soccer for Bradford City. His son, Andrew, was an outstanding opening batsman for Yorkshire and English school teams in 1993, but it was for Derbyshire that he first appeared in the first-class game, in 1995, as a part-time wicket-keeper.

First-class career (1970–90): 13,961 runs (26.44) including 10 centuries, 9 wickets (34.22), and 1,099 dismissals (961 c., 138 st.)
Test matches (4): 125 runs (20.83) and 13 dismissals (12 c., 1 st.)

BAKEWELL, Alfred Harry

(b. 1908, Walsall, Staffordshire, d. 1983, Westbourne, Dorset) Northamptonshire and England

A great batsman and fielder was locked up inside 'Fred' Bakewell but, in some ways, he was his own worst enemy. His right-handed batsmanship had authority and, although his stance was ugly —wide, straggling, rather crouched and very open—he had no fear of bowlers. In a small innings of 30 he would reveal every stroke in the book. Essentially a stroke-maker, not a compiler of runs, his footwork was nimble and he was an especially strong and daring off-driver. A specialist short-leg, he was almost worth playing for his fielding alone. As a change-bowler he met with some success. On his county début he held 5 catches against Essex at Kettering, 1928, and in the return at Leyton held 8 catches. In successive matches in 1933 he made the then record score by a Northamptonshire batsman—246 against Nottinghamshire at Northampton and 257 against Glamorgan at Swansea. In that season he also hit the then highest aggregate, 1,952 runs, and over 2,000 in all matches including 107 in the Test against the West Indies at The Oval. Throughout his career he was consistently effective against touring sides and, although he never appeared in a Test against Australia, he represented England with success against other countries and toured India, 1933/4, in MCC's first Test-playing tour of the subcontinent. His last match of all was at Chesterfield against Derbyshire, the champions of 1936, when Northamptonshire were bottom of the Table. He hit a chanceless 241 not out, and the champion county very nearly lost. On the way home he was involved in a car accident, and was never able to play first-class cricket again.

First-class career (1928–36): 14,570 runs (33.96) including 31 centuries, 22 wickets (57.77), and 225 catches
Test matches (6): 409 runs (45.44) including 1 century, 0–8, and 3 catches

BAKEWELL, Enid (née Turton)

(b. 1940, Newstead, Nottingham) East Midlands and England

Enid Bakewell burst on to the Test match arena with a century on her début in 1968 and her enthusiasm, energy, and appetite for the game remained undiminished. She was the first English player, male or female, to score a century and take 10 wickets in a Test. It was against the

West Indies at Edgbaston in 1979, strangely the last of her twelve Test appearances. Ian Botham repeated the feat at Bombay, during England's 1979/80 tour of India. A slight right-hand opening bat and left-arm orthodox spinner, Bakewell returned from her début tour of Australia and New Zealand having scored 1,031 runs and taken 118 wickets in 20 matches. She scored her maiden Test century (113) on her début against Australia in Adelaide and registered successive centuries of 124 (in Wellington) and 114 (in Christchurch) against New Zealand. Bakewell returned to England as the outstanding all-rounder in women's cricket, was accorded a civic reception by Nottingham County Council and became the first woman cricketer to be specially featured in Wisden. Bakewell was described in the press as England's 'prop and stay' after scoring 118 in their World Cup final win over Australia at Edgbaston in 1973 and her opening stand of 246 with Lynne Thomas against the International XI during the 1982 World Cup in New Zealand remains an all-wicket competition record. Bakewell, who had three children, continued to play representative cricket for East Midlands well past her 50th birthday. Always alert and nimble in the field, Bakewell spends countless hours coaching and encouraging youngsters and played a large part in the development of four of England's 1993 World Cup winners, captain Karen Smithies, all-rounder Jo Chamberlain, wicket-keeper Jane Smit, and opening bat Wendy Watson, who all play for the East Midlands. Herself one of the selectors of that World Cup squad, Bakewell became England under-21 coach.

Test matches (12): 1,078 runs (59.88) including 4 centuries, and 50 wickets (16.62)
One-day internationals (23): 500 runs (35.71) including 2 centuries, and 25 wickets (21.12)

BALDERSTONE, John Christopher

(b. 1940, Huddersfield, Yorkshire) *Yorkshire, Leicestershire, and England*

Had the financial reward of cricket been greater, Chris Balderstone would probably have given less of the prime years of his athletic life to football, which he played professionally for Huddersfield, Carlisle, Doncaster, and Queen of the South, and as a result might have won more than his two Test caps. He was unlucky to be picked for England against one of the most fearsome fast-bowling attacks in Test history—the 1976 West Indians. He was a brave, sound, dependable, right-hand bat with the ability to concentrate for

long periods, and a key member of the strong Leicestershire side of the 1970s in both three-day and one-day cricket. He was also an excellent fielder whose one catch in Test cricket was a brilliant diving effort following an unexpected lapse. A flighty, left-arm spinner, who could be relied on to take wickets on a turning pitch, he was shrewdly used by Ray Illingworth, whom he followed to Leicester from his native Yorkshire in 1971. Chris Balderstone was a model professional, dedicated and untemperamental and as the elder statesman of the Leicestershire side he remained a useful performer. In 1985, at the age of 44, he collected a Benson and Hedges Cup winner's medal as well as scoring over 1,200 first-class runs. On 15 September 1975 he had played Championship cricket until 6.30, then kicked off for Doncaster Rovers at 7.30 the same evening. He became a first-class umpire in 1988.

First-class career (1961–86): 19,034 runs (34.11) including 32 centuries, 310 wickets (26.32), and 210 catches
Test matches (2): 39 runs (9.75), 1 wicket (80.00), and 1 catch

BANNISTER, John David

(b. 1930, Wolverhampton, Staffordshire)
Warwickshire

A man of many parts, with a quick, retentive mind, Jack Bannister took 100 wickets on four occasions during his nineteen seasons for Warwickshire. Against Yorkshire at Leeds in 1954 his right-arm fast-medium bowling secured him 8 for 54. In the following year, against the same opponents at Sheffield, he took 9 for 35 including a hat-trick. Against the Combined Services in 1959 he took 10 for 41 in their first innings only to be dropped for the next match. Just before he retired (1968) he became the first treasurer and subsequently the second chairman and a long-serving secretary of the Cricketers' Association. He played an instrumental part in establishing a basic pay structure for county players. Later he combined a career as a bookmaker with able and thorough reporting on cricket as correspondent of the *Birmingham Post*. He was also a television and radio commentator, as well known in South Africa, where he worked regularly, as in England.

First-class career (1950–68): 3,140 runs (9.42), 1,198 wickets (21.91), and 168 catches

BARBER, Robert William

(b. 1935, Withington, Lancashire) *Cheshire, Cambridge University, Lancashire, Warwickshire, and England*

Bob Barber was one of the few England opening batsmen to spend a tour of Australia almost exclusively on the attack, but he retired early owing to the claims of business. He was a left-handed batsman with a superb array of strokes, a talented right-arm leg-break bowler, and an excellent field in the leg-trap. At his school, Ruthin, he achieved the double and also played for Lancashire. He won blues at Cambridge for cricket and the javelin, endured a stormy passage as captain of Lancashire, and reached his best form for Warwickshire. Utterly fearless against fast bowling, he changed quite suddenly from a cautious batsman into one who would attack from the start. He was an early hero of Gillette Cup cricket, winning four man-of-the-match awards and at one time making more runs in the competition than anyone else. For his new county, Warwickshire, he hit a brilliant hundred against the West Indies side who had humbled England in 1963, and the following year made a hundred before lunch on the first day against Australia. He had a Test average of 72.50 in South Africa in 1964/5, and in the Test at Sydney in 1965/6 hit a memorable 185, which remained his highest; on the latter tour he scored 1,001 runs (50.05). His best bowling was 7 for 35 for Lancashire against Derbyshire at Chesterfield in 1960. It was typical of his adventurous and independent spirit that he should have taken part, in 1980, in an arduous mountaineering expedition in the Himalayas. He also made a small fortune from a business making and selling hygienic blue colourants for lavatory cisterns.

First-class career (1954–69): 17,631 runs (29.43) including 17 centuries, 549 wickets (29.46), and 210 catches

Test matches (28): 1,495 runs (35.59) including 1 century, 42 wickets (43.00), and 21 catches

BARBER, Wilfred

(b. 1901, Cleckheaton, Yorkshire; d. 1968, Bradford, Yorkshire) *Yorkshire and England*

Wilf Barber, or 'Tiddley-push', was a text-book right-handed batsman. His speciality was to the off and, with his solid defence, he exercised a restraint typical of Yorkshire's opening batsmen. He was a first-rate outfield. During his years with the county Yorkshire were champions on eight occasions. His best year was 1935 when he exceeded 2,000 runs, hitting his highest score, 255, off Surrey at Bramall Lane, and playing for England twice against South Africa. That winter he was senior professional with MCC's 'goodwill' side to Australasia. On retirement he became a coach and groundsman to a school in Harrogate.

First-class career (1926–47): 16,402 runs (34.38) including 29 centuries, and 16 wickets (26.18)

Test matches (2): 83 runs (20.75), 1–0, and 1 catch

BARLOW, Graham Derek

(b. 1950, Folkestone, Kent) *Middlesex and England*

Graham Barlow had an influence on England's Test cricket stronger than his modest figures would suggest. The brilliance and aggressiveness of his fielding at cover and mid-wicket, in tandem with Derek Randall, saved countless runs and helped to usher in a period when much of England's success was due to the high standard of the fielding, giving extra confidence to the bowlers. An open, cheerful and amusing character, Barlow's cricket always had an engaging vitality, and at his best his rugged left-handed batting was punishing and authoritative. His rapid improvement in 1976 when he scored 1,478 runs at an average of just under 50, and usually at a brisk pace, had much to do with Middlesex's first outright Championship win since 1947. On the tour to India, Sri Lanka, and Australia the following winter he scored hundreds in his first two innings in India and finished top of the tour averages with 51, but unusual nervousness and a relatively loose defence proved fatal in his three Test appearances, the last of them against Australia at Lord's in June 1977. He was an important member of the Middlesex side which won the Championship five times between 1976 and 1985, taking up the role of opening batsman following Mike Brearley's retirement. Throwing off a persistent hip injury with the aid of a faith-healer, he scored 1,343 runs (47.96) and hit six centuries in 1985, but a further serious back injury caused his retirement in 1986 when his ebullient presence in the Middlesex team was sorely missed.

First-class career (1969–86): 12,387 runs (35.90) including 26 centuries, 3 wickets (22.66), and 136 catches

Test matches (3): 17 runs (4.25)

BARLOW, Richard Gorton

(b. 1851, Barrow Bridge, Lancashire; d. 1919, Blackpool, Lancashire) *Lancashire and England*

Cricket was the absorbing interest of Dick Barlow's life. He kept himself in first-rate condition and was always capable of doing his best; no day was too long for him. He was first among right-handed batsmen of the extremely steady or stonewalling school, using forward play excessively in defence. He was also a left-arm, medium-pace bowler, possessing implicit faith in accuracy of length, and he was a sure fieldsman. He and his captain, A. N. Hornby, were well-contrasted opening batsmen of some 'box-office' appeal, whose partnership was immortalized in Francis Thompson's poem 'At Lord's' ('O my Hornby and my Barlow long ago'). Barlow paid three visits to Australia and did not miss a single match. In Tests he was always doing something useful; his steadiness with the bat at Old Trafford in 1886 pulled England through on a crumbling wicket, and he took 7 for 44 in the second innings. At Trent Bridge in 1884, for North of England against the Australians, he had the game of his life, scoring 10 and 101 on a spiteful pitch and taking 10 for 48 in the match. On retirement he became a much-respected Test match umpire. A quiet, neighbourly man, his home was a complete cricket museum. His marriage, like that of many a wandering cricketer, was not a success.

First-class career (1871–91): 11,217 runs (20.61) including 4 centuries, 950 wickets (14.52), and 268 catches

Test matches (17): 591 runs (22.73), 34 wickets (22.55), and 14 catches

BARNES, Sydney Francis

(b. 1873, Smethwick, Staffordshire; d. 1967, Chadsmoor, Staffordshire) *Warwickshire, Staffordshire, Lancashire, and England*

A large proportion both of those who watched and of those who played against Sydney Barnes, especially on big occasions, have no hesitation in naming this dark, brooding, gaunt, eventually cadaverous-faced man as the best bowler ever. In all Test match series in which he played and was free from illness or injury, his bowling was strong and subtle enough to settle matters in England's favour. Tall, with a back as straight as a shield, he was a right-arm, medium-fast bowler who made devastating use of the seam and shine of a new ball, and combined swing and cut so subtly with spin that few batsmen could distinguish one from

the other. He made a name in the days when one new ball had to suffice for the whole innings. He had a splendid upright action after a shortish, springy approach, and his phenomenal successes stemmed from a powerful frame, immense stamina, and large hands as strong as steel. An aloof man of independent outlook, he seemed more at home in League cricket. After several appearances for Warwickshire with moderate success, he served as a professional in the Lancashire League, and at the Old Trafford nets impressed A. C. Maclaren who invited him to tour Australia with his team, 1901/2. After a successful tour and despite some injury, he had two full seasons with Lancashire. Then, when relations fell short of cordiality, he returned to League cricket, devoting much time on home territory in Staffordshire Leagues, and returned at intervals to England's Test and touring teams straight from the League. In Australia, 1911/12, he took 34 wickets (22.88) including an opening spell of 5 for 6 in 11 overs in the second Test at Melbourne, at the age of 38. In the 1912 Triangular Tournament against Australia and South Africa, he took 39 wickets (10.35); and in South Africa, 1913/14, in four of the five Tests, took 49 wickets (10.93) at the age of 40. Until his sixties he continued to achieve distinction in local League cricket and also appeared in the occasional first-class match for a variety of teams, including Wales. In 133 first-class matches he took five or more wickets in an innings on 68 occasions. For Staffordshire in the Minor Counties Championship he took 76 wickets (8.21) at the age of 55. According to his biography his overall haul in all cricket was 6,229 wickets (8.33). He captured all 10 wickets in an innings seven times.

First-class career (1894–1930): 1,573 runs (12.78) and 719 wickets (17.09)

Test matches (27): 242 runs (8.06), 189 wickets (16.43), and 12 catches

BARNES, William

(b. 1852, Sutton-in-Ashfield, Nottinghamshire; d. 1899, Mansfield Woodhouse, Nottinghamshire) *Nottinghamshire and England*

A right-handed batsman, Billy Barnes was a strong off-side player who liked to keep things moving. He was also a medium-pace bowler, one of the best change-bowlers in England, besides being a fine close field. Over six feet tall, he had a long reach but an unbecoming style. He could be a brilliant batsman—in 1880 he became the first Nottinghamshire player to reach 1,000 runs in a season—but he was not as patient as Arthur Shrewsbury or William Gunn. He played in the first Test against Australia in England in 1880, and in the second in 1882, when England lost by 7 runs in the match that gave rise to the Ashes. Three times he visited Australia and until 1890 was nearly always a first choice for England. His 104 at Adelaide in 1884/5 was a great innings on a tricky pitch. In the second (following) Test his 6 for 31 in Australia's second innings won the game for England. But in the following game he refused to bowl and on his third visit to Australia a fight with one of the opposition players led to a damaged hand and several matches missed. He found the discipline of county cricket irksome and was warned not to arrive at matches the worse for liquor. On one occasion he staggered out to the wicket and made a saving hundred for his county, and afterwards, on being reprimanded by the committee, said, 'How many of you gentlemen could make a hundred, drunk *or* sober?' On retiring from the game he became, perhaps appropriately, landlord of an inn.

First-class career (1875–94): 15,425 runs (23.19) including 21 centuries, 902 wickets (17.11), 342 catches, and 3 stumpings

Test matches (21): 725 runs (23.38) including 1 century, 51 wickets (15.54), and 19 catches

BARNETT, Charles John

(b. 1910, Cheltenham, Gloucestershire; d. 1993, Stroud, Gloucestershire) *Gloucestershire and England*

Charlie Barnett first appeared for his county at 16 in 1927, coming to the fore in 1933 with 2,280 runs (40.71). An aquiline-nosed, right-handed batsman of vigour and imagination, who opened the innings from 1932 onwards, he was specially adept at driving and square-cutting. Barnett shared in many brilliant and prolific partnerships with Walter Hammond. He was prepared to cut the ball in the first over of a Test; a little more caution, perhaps, would have stood him in better stead with the selectors. He hit 11 sixes in his 194 against Somerset at Bath, 1934. He visited Australia, 1936/7, and his century at Adelaide was a nobly aggressive innings. When he hit 126 against Australia at Trent Bridge, 1938, he reached his century off the first ball after lunch on the first day. He scored over 2,000 runs in four seasons, 1,000 in twelve, and hit four double-centuries, the highest being 259 for MCC against Queensland. He was a fast-medium change-bowler of no mean ability and a very reliable outfielder. His father,

C. S., and uncle, E. P., both played for Gloucestershire.

First-class career (1927–53): 25,389 runs (32.71) including 48 centuries, 394 wickets (30.98), and 319 catches

Test matches (20): 1,098 runs (35.41) including 2 centuries, 0–93, and 14 catches

BARNETT, Kim John

(b. 1960, Stoke-on-Trent, Staffordshire) *Staffordshire, Derbyshire, Boland, and England*

In 1983 Kim Barnett became Derbyshire's youngest-ever captain at the age of 22, and was tipped in some quarters to get the job for England as well, but he brought a halt to his Test career in 1989 when he decided to join the unofficial tour of South Africa after being dropped during the Ashes series that summer. An unorthodox batsman with a pronounced shuffle across the crease as the bowler delivered, as well as an underrated leg-spinner, the affable Barnett's decision may have been influenced by his struggles against the high-class seam bowling of Allan Border's side. But he remained a consistent performer at county level with a reputation as a fine player of quick bowling. He was a skilful improviser in limited-overs matches, and amassed over 20,000 runs in the first-class game. Barnett first showed talent as a leg-spinner, but gradually his batting became more important. From the age of 15 he played for Northamptonshire and Warwickshire's second teams and also Staffordshire, as well as touring with an English Schools side and Young England. Eventually he joined Derbyshire, making his début in 1979. Barnett spent two winters playing in South Africa, and was capped in 1982 before being given the county captaincy the following season in the wake of brief tenures by David Steele, Barry Wood, and Geoff Miller, quickly establishing a reputation as a good leader. In 1985 Barnett was appointed vice-captain of the England B tour of Sri Lanka but was forced home early by a tropical illness which cost him 28 lbs in weight and his fitness for much of the following season. Barnett led Derbyshire to the Benson and Hedges Cup Final in 1988 where they lost to Hampshire, but the same season, in which he made 1,623 runs and finished seventh in the national averages, saw his Test début against Sri Lanka at Lord's. He scored 66 and nought. In a one-day international which followed, Barnett made 84 to steer England to victory and secure a place on the winter tour of India. The tour was cancelled, and although he was not originally picked for the first Test against Australia the following summer, he was called up as a replacement for the injured Mike Gatting. A fluent Test-best 80 and 34 could not save England from defeat, and he lost his place after scores of 14, 3, and 10 in the next two matches, the latter innings hampered by a hamstring strain. The 'rebel' tour of South Africa was abandoned half-way through following political pressure, but not before Barnett had shown his ability with 136 in a one-day 'international' under floodlights at the Wanderers, Johannesburg. In 1990 he led Derbyshire to the Sunday League title for the first time and in 1993 to victory in the Benson and Hedges Cup Final. In 1994 he finished top of the first-class bowling averages, albeit with only 13 wickets, taking his career total past 150.

First-class career (1979–): 20,565 runs (39.02) and 152 wickets (36.67)

Test matches (4): 207 runs (29.57)

BARRATT, Fred

(b. 1894, Annesley, Nottinghamshire; d. 1947, Standard Hill, Nottinghamshire) *Nottinghamshire and England*

Fred Barratt was a burly coal-miner turned right-arm fast bowler. After taking more than a hundred wickets in his initial season of first-class cricket, 1914, he was slow in finding his form again after the war, but he did so and, developing also as a powerful and effective hitter, achieved the double in 1928. Touring Australasia with MCC, 1929/30, he played in the first-ever Test matches against New Zealand; the previous season he appeared once against South Africa. Against Sussex at Trent Bridge in 1924, he sent a bail 38 yards in bowling a batsman out. Renowned for hitting sixes, he twice struck three in succession. At soccer he represented Aston Villa and Sheffield Wednesday as a full-back.

First-class career (1914–32): 6,445 runs (15.53) including 2 centuries, 1,224 wickets (22.72), and 174 catches

Test matches (5): 28 runs (9.33), 5 wickets (47.00), and 2 catches

BARRIE, Sir James Matthew, Bt.

(b. 1860, Kirriemuir, Scotland; d. 1937, London)

Somewhere along the line between Kirriemuir and Kensington Gardens J. M. Barrie discovered cricket. He admired great cricketers with a passion amounting almost to envy. 'Your cricket success has been an honour to all of us,' he wrote to 'Plum' Warner and, to his friend Neville Cardus, '(Macartney) can do all that he wants to do.' The two men, Barrie and Cardus, both from humble origins, had formed a friendship in which the journalist would want to know all about Peter Pan and the dramatist all about cricket. Barrie, the cricketer, founded his own club, the Allahakbarries (a corruption of the Moorish 'God help us') in 1893 and recruited writers and artists to play for him. In 1899 he published privately a book describing the 'Test Matches' they played at Broadway in Worcestershire. Later the Allahakbarries became rather ambitious and attracted county players. Success proved their undoing, and the spirit of the founder was lost: 'The next man in was Barrie (captain). On returning he received an ovation.' The real world responded to Barrie's make-believe one. Just as *Peter Pan*, from 1904 onwards, appealed to everyone so did Barrie's personality to the cricket world. He made the welcoming speech to the 1926 Australians and *The Times* published a long letter from him when they came in 1930.

BARRINGTON, Kenneth Frank

(b. 1930, Reading, Berkshire; d. 1981, Barbados, West Indies) *Berkshire, Surrey, and England*

One of the true cricketing heroes, Ken Barrington devoted much of his life to the cause of English cricket. The son of a regular soldier, he batted for England as if the country's future depended on his success—and, in cricketing terms, it often did. A little under medium height, he was stockily built with features of considerable strength, notably a nose and a chin which might have been hewn from granite. He possessed a full array of powerful strokes, but used them only when he was sure it was safe to do so. He had to fight his way into both the Surrey and the England sides and seldom, if ever, returned to the pavilion as a result of an ill-judged shot, although he delighted often in reaching three figures with a six. Australia's wicket-keeper Wally Grout said that he always seemed to walk to the wicket with a Union Jack trailing behind. He was a useful but under-used leg-break and googly bowler and on the 1964/5 tour took 7 for 40 for MCC against Griqualand West at Kimberley. He revelled in bowling as a coach when testing the England team in the nets. He was also a thoroughly dependable fielder. He first played for England in 1955, the year he won his Surrey cap, making 0, 34 (top score), and 18 against South Africa. At this stage he was a flowing stroke-player, but he disciplined himself and by the time that he returned to England colours (and no one ever wore them with greater pride) in 1959, he was one of the hardest men in the world to dig out. A regular tourist, he made 1,329 runs (69.94) in India and Pakistan, 1961/2; 1,763 runs (80.13) in Australia and New Zealand, 1962/3; and 1,128 runs (86.76) in South Africa, 1964/5. In England he exceeded 1,000 runs in a season twelve times and three times scored over 2,000. His highest score was 256 in 11 hours 25 minutes against Australia at Old Trafford in 1964—his first Test century in England after nine abroad and England's highest at Old Trafford—and in his next match, against Nottinghamshire at The Oval, he scored 207. A cheerful, witty man and skilful mimic, he was also thoughtful, sensitive, and conscientious. He suffered a mild heart attack whilst competing in a double-wicket tournament in Australia in 1968, and retired from first-class cricket as a result. In later years he was an able Test selector and a popular manager of England touring teams. It was as assistant manager and coach of the England team in the West Indies in 1981 that he died suddenly in Barbados. It was a grievous blow to English cricket and he was mourned throughout the cricket world. Surrey's Indoor sports centre, opened by the Queen in 1991, was named after him.

First-class career (1953–68): 31,714 runs (45.63) including 76 centuries, 273 wickets (32.61), and 511 catches

Test matches (82): 6,806 runs (58.67) including 20 centuries, 29 wickets (44.82), and 58 catches

BARTON, Victor Alexander

(b. 1867, Hound, Hampshire; d. 1906, Belle Vue, Southampton) *Kent, Hampshire, and England*

Victor Barton was bought out of the army, where he was a bombardier in the Royal Artillery, to play county cricket. An attractive right-handed batsman, few men drove more powerfully to the on. He was also a useful change-bowler. He hit 205 for Hampshire against Sussex at Hove in 1900, but poor health made his retirement imperative two years later. In 1891/2 he toured South Africa with W. W. Read's side, scoring 23 in his sole Test innings at Cape Town.

First-class career (1889–1902): 6,411 runs (24.01) including 6 centuries, and 141 wickets (28.62)

BATES, William

(b. 1855, Lascelles Hall, Yorkshire; d. 1900, Lepton, Yorkshire) *Yorkshire and England*

Billy Bates's brilliant career was closed when he received a blow in the eye at net practice on the Melbourne ground in 1887; his sight was permanently injured. Then at the height of his powers, he was a brilliant, cavalier, right-handed batsman and a first-rate slow, round-arm bowler, commanding both a high degree of spin and an immaculate length. It was only his uncertain catching that prevented him from being chosen to play against Australia in his own country. He toured Australia five times and America once. He was the first Englishman to perform the hat-trick against Australia. This was in the second Test, at Melbourne, in 1882/3, for Hon. Ivo Bligh's side, when he took 14 for 102, England winning after two recent defeats. Sartorially elegant, he was a fine vocalist and his rendering of 'The Bonny Yorkshire Lass' fascinated the King of the Sandwich Islands so much that he asked him to sing it time and again on the voyage to Australia. His son was W. E. Bates (Yorkshire and Glamorgan) and his grandson, Ted, was manager of Southampton FC.

First-class career (1877–87): 10,249 runs (21.57) including 10 centuries, 874 wickets (17.13), and 238 catches

Test matches (15): 656 runs (27.33), 50 wickets (16.42), and 9 catches

BEAN, George

(b. 1864, Sutton-in-Ashfield, Nottinghamshire; d. 1923, Mansfield, Nottinghamshire) *Nottinghamshire, Sussex, and England*

George Bean was a fast-scoring right-handed batsman, especially on dry wickets, and was well-suited to the Hove ground, where, due to short boundaries and a fast outfield, he obtained numberless fours. He was a useful medium-pace bowler and above average at cover-point. In 1891/2 he went to Australia with Lord Sheffield's side, playing in the three Tests. Except for one other season the remainder of his career was an anti-climax. At the time of his death, he was the senior member of MCC's ground staff.

First-class career (1885–98): 8,634 runs (20.70) including 9 centuries, 260 wickets (27.25), and 154 catches

Test matches (3): 92 runs (18.40) and 4 catches

BEAUCLERK, The Revd Lord Frederick

(b. 1773, England; d. 1850, London) *MCC, Hampshire, and Kent*

After a slow start, Beauclerk became, in the early 1800s 'the most accomplished and graceful performer' of his day. A strong off-side right-handed batsman, he played mainly at Lord's between 1791 and 1825. Of his eight centuries there, Haygarth observed that five 'were off inferior bowling' but two were in 1805 for Hampshire (as a given man) against England and for England against Surrey. He had some success as a slow under-arm bowler in the early years and could 'set his field to foil' a batsman, but a later generation got the measure of him. He was a clergyman in the eighteenth-century *laissez-faire* tradition. Cricket and Lord's claimed his interest for 60 years. To a reputation for selfishness as a player must be added one of dishonesty, especially where wagers were involved, and he made 600 guineas a season regularly. 'My Lord, he comes next, and will make you all stare, / With his little tricks, a long way from fair.' He was president of MCC in 1826 and for the rest of his life an autocratic figure at Lord's even in the view of that later autocrat, Lord Harris. His death in 1850, in a period of religious revival espousing the moral virtues of cricket, was pointedly ignored by *The Times*.

First-class career (1801–25): 4,555 runs (27.27) including 4 centuries, 25 wickets (average not known), and 82 dismissals (81 c., 1 st.)

BECKETT, Samuel Barclay

(b. 1906, Dublin, Ireland; d. 1989, Paris, France) *Dublin University*

The author of *Waiting for Godot* and Nobel prizewinner for Literature (1969) was a left-handed all-rounder who played twice in first-class cricket, opening both the batting and bowling for his university against Northamptonshire at Northampton in 1926.

First-class career (1925–6): 35 runs (8.75) and 2 catches

BEDSER, Alec Victor

(b. 1918, Reading, Berkshire) *Surrey and England*

Giant of frame, and a strong pillar of Surrey and England cricket after the Second World War, Alec Bedser was born within minutes of his identical twin brother, Eric, who was a talented county all-rounder. He began his illustrious Test career with 11 wickets from each of his first two Tests against India in 1946. Until 1954 he seemed to be carrying the burden of England's fortunes in the field on his broad shoulders, and willingly, too, for he loved bowling. He was a leading player in Surrey's run of Championship victories from 1952 to 1958. He took 100 wickets in a season eleven times. In a long career he left the field of play only once, during a Test match in a heatwave at Adelaide. He went to the edge of the boundary to vomit, then returned to carry on bowling. Bedser was a truly great medium-fast bowler, likened by many to Maurice Tate. He had a model action: a relatively short approach, late turn of a powerful body, high arm, and full follow-through. His stock ball was the in-swinger, often with his huge right hand cutting across the seam at the moment of release. The leg-cutter was his most feared delivery: on helpful pitches it became effectively a fast leg-break. Sir Donald Bradman considers him, in some conditions, the most difficult bowler he batted against. In 1950/1 he took 30 wickets (16.06) in the Ashes series and followed this up with 39 wickets (17.48) in 1953, including 14 for 99 at Trent Bridge. His batting was wooden but straight, and often useful, especially in the role of nightwatchman, as when he made 79 against Australia at Headingley in 1948. His catching was eminently safe. Intensely loyal, patriotic, and committed, and with trenchant conservative views, he served England as a selector for a record 23-year period, starting as a member of the committee in 1962 and being chairman from 1969 until 1981, during which time England played seven Ashes series against Australia and lost only two of them. He was a popular assistant manager to the Duke of Norfolk during the MCC tour of Australia in 1962/3 and manager of the 1974/5 and 1979/80 teams in Australia. The ethics of hard work and clean living have never had a sterner champion, and they have served him well, both in his cricket career and as a successful businessman. He remains inseparable from his identical twin and only their friends can distinguish between them. He was awarded an OBE in 1964 and a CBE in 1982 for his services to cricket and was president of Surrey in 1987, an honour which meant more to him than most. He served on both the Surrey and MCC committees.

First-class career (1939–60): 5,735 runs (14.51) including 1 century, 1,924 wickets (20.41), and 289 catches
Test matches (51): 714 runs (12.75), 236 wickets (24.89), and 26 catches

BELDHAM, William

(b. 1766, Farnham, Surrey; d. 1862, Tilford, Surrey)
Surrey, Hampshire, and Kent

The last survivor of the old Hambledon club and the only one to be photographed, 'Silver Billy' learnt his cricket from Harry Hall, the gingerbread baker in Farnham. Pupil far eclipsed teacher and John Nyren, in his *The Cricketers of my Time*, called him 'the finest bat of his own, or perhaps of any age'. His right-handed batting was 'a peculiar exhibition of elegance with vigour' distinguished by his ability to cut the ball 'at the point of the bat'. Nyren described him as a 'change bowler' of moderate pace. Playing as a professional in the last years of eighteenth-century Hambledon, Beldham hedged his bets by accepting offers to play for the infant Marylebone club. Ninety-four at Lord's for Hambledon in 1789 was eclipsed by 144 for MCC at Lord's three years later. In the loose arrangements of those days, he would appear for both Surrey and Hampshire, his final appearance being for the Players against the Gentlemen at Lord's in 1821—the match arranged to mark the coronation of George IV. In old age he was visited by the historian John Mitford and in extreme old age (92) by Arthur Haygarth, then compiling his *Scores and Biographies*. Both recorded their reminiscences of him. He is said to have fathered 39 children.

First-class career (1801–21): 2,374 runs (19.30), 48 wickets (average not known), and 153 dismissals (111 c., 42 st.)

BENCRAFT, Dr Sir Henry William Russell

(b. 1858, Southampton; d. 1943, Compton, Winchester, Hampshire) *Hampshire*

After captaining St Edward's, Oxford, Bencraft studied medicine at St George's Hospital, London where he made six centuries on six consecutive days, for once out, with a highest score of 243. He was an attacking right-handed batsman, many of his best innings being played for Hampshire while the county was still second-class. His 195 against Warwickshire at Edgbaston in 1889 was the highest score in any county match that year. He was prominent in the discussions in the early 1890s on what should constitute a first-class county. Appropriately enough he was captain when Hampshire won their opening match at first-class level against Derbyshire at Southampton in 1895 making a fifty himself. He had first played for the county in 1876, held office as secretary, treasurer and captain and in 1936 became president. He was a prominent physician in Southampton and was almost equally involved, as player and administrator, in both codes of football in the city and county.

First-class career (1895–6): 932 runs (15.53), 5 wickets (39.40), and 31 catches

BENJAMIN, Joseph Emmanuel

(b. 1961, Christchurch, St Kitts, West Indies)
Staffordshire, Warwickshire, Surrey, and England

Joey Benjamin broke into the England side just as most seamers are thinking about hanging up their bowling boots, but so well did he take his chance, collecting four wickets on his début against South Africa, that he was chosen for his first overseas tour at the age of 33. A broad-shouldered, tallish, bustling fast-medium bowler capable of swinging the ball, the personable Benjamin emigrated to Britain with his parents at 16, but did not start playing county cricket until he was 27. Prior to that, he had played club cricket in the Birmingham League and also for Staffordshire in the Minor Counties Championship, while working as, amongst other things, a landscape gardener and the manager of a bookstore. In 1987 Benjamin played against Warwickshire in the NatWest Trophy, and although he took only 1 for 65 in his twelve overs, he impressed county officials sufficiently to be offered a contract for the following summer. He spent four years at Edgbaston, but found his opportunities limited. In 1990, however, he took 43 wickets, including 5 for 72 against Surrey, and when Warwickshire released him in 1991, he was quickly offered a new contract at The Oval. In 1992 he took 45 wickets, and the following season 64, including a career-best 6 for 19 against Nottinghamshire. Continuing this progress in 1994, he was the first English-qualified seamer to 50 wickets. Called up for the second Test with South Africa at Headingley, he was named 12th man, but played in the final match of the series at The Oval and took 4 for 42 in South Africa's first innings as England went on to win by eight wickets. His reward was selection for the winter tour of Australia ahead of Angus Fraser but he was given no opportunity. His sole Test produced 4 wickets (20.00) and 0 runs; no catches.

First-class career (1988–): 617 runs (10.46) and 253 wickets (28.62)

BENSON, Richard Mark

(b. 1958, Shoreham-by-Sea, Sussex) *Kent and England*

Mark Benson's chance to play for England came with quite unexpected suddenness in 1986 and went almost as quickly, though he was by no means a failure. A solidly built left-handed opening batsman of a little under medium height he had been renowned for some seasons as being a good player of quick bowling, playing straight and, rather in the manner of John Edrich, knowing when to leave the ball outside his off-stump. A product of Sutton Valence School, he scored consistently once he had established his place in the Kent side in 1981, reaching 1,000 runs in eleven seasons between 1981 and 1992, although he was restricted by persistent injuries, notably to his knees. A determined drive to get down his weight in the winter of 1985/6 led to a solid start to the 1986 season and when Wayne Larkins, who had been selected for the third Test against India at Edgbaston, withdrew with a broken thumb, Benson was called up just as he was about to start a Championship match. Rushing up the motorway to join the England team on the eve of the match, he was batting almost before he had had a chance to draw breath. Very soon England were 0 for 2 but, in company with David Gower, Benson capably stopped the rot before being bowled by the left-arm spin of Maninder Singh for 21. He was out in similar fashion in the second innings for a solid 30 and it seems the selectors decided that he was too weak against spin to be given further opportunities for after one limited-overs international against New Zealand, in which he made 24, he was summarily discarded. Consolation came through his appointment to the captaincy of a strong Kent side in 1991. A year later Kent finished second in the Championship and reached the final of the Benson and Hedges Cup.

First-class career (1980–): 17,685 runs (40.56) and 5 wickets (98.60)

BENTLEY, Henry

(b. 1782, London; d. 1857, Hereford) *Middlesex, Kent, and Hampshire*

Although playing as an all-rounder for 30 years and first appearing at Lord's for MCC against London in 1798, Henry Bentley was principally an umpire. In 1823 he published the scores of all the matches played by MCC 'and all other principal matches' from 1786 to 1822. The volume (with two supplements for 1823 and 1824–5) assumed importance as a source-book after the records at Lord's, which Bentley had used, were burnt in the Pavilion fire (1825).

First-class career (1801–22): 1,176 runs (10.69), 26 wickets (average not known), and 18 dismissals (17 c., 1 st.)

BERRY, Robert

(b. 1926, West Gorton, Manchester) *Lancashire, Worcestershire, Derbyshire, and England*

An orthodox, left-arm, spin bowler from the Lancashire and Cheshire League, Bob Berry harnessed length to flight and spin, and was a much better bowler than his figures suggested. Tired of fighting for a regular place alongside other spinners in the Lancashire team, he migrated to other counties. He was a deep field with a good arm. Picked for two Tests against the West Indies in 1950, he toured Australia and New Zealand with Freddie Brown's side, 1950/1, but was not selected for any of the Tests. All three of his counties awarded him a cap.

First-class career (1948–62): 1,463 runs (7.58) and 703 wickets (24.73)

Test matches (2): 6 runs (3.00), 9 wickets (25.33), and 2 catches

BICKNELL, Martin Paul

(b. 1969, Guildford, Surrey) *Surrey and England*

A succession of injuries prevented Martin Bicknell from fulfilling the potential which catapulted him into the Surrey first team as a promising fast-medium swing bowler at the age of 17. Tall, wiry, and combative, with a good action after a long run-up, Bicknell, along with his elder brother Darren, a left-handed batsman, was a product of the thriving Guildford club and the Nescafé scheme, set up by Surrey to help develop young talent. He took 22 wickets in his first seven Championship outings and produced figures of 1 for 25 in a tense NatWest Trophy semi-final which Surrey narrowly lost. Young England recognition followed, but he broke down with a side strain during a 'Test' at Headingley. Successive Young England tours to Sri Lanka and Australia preceded selection for the A tour of Zimbabwe and Kenya, reward for his 65 wickets in 1989. A successful trip included figures of 4 for 74 in the second 'Test' in Bulawayo. Then in 1990, a summer dominated by batsmen, Bicknell took 67 wickets at 27 each to earn a place on the winter tour to Australia. England's best bowler for the first month of the trip, his confidence suffered when he was singled out for some savage treatment by Dean Jones in the one-day internationals. An injury to Angus Fraser gave him the apparent chance of a Test appearance later on the tour, but he himself broke down with a side strain. Injury struck again in 1991, but Bicknell was still included on the winter A tour to the Caribbean only to dislocate his shoulder and miss the trip. Bouncing back with 71 wickets in 1992, he was overlooked when the winter touring parties were selected, but in 1993 was 12th man for the third Test at Trent Bridge, and at last won a Test cap at Headingley. Hard though he tried on a true pitch he took just 1 for 155 in 50 overs, removing Mark Taylor with his seventeenth ball, as Australia made 653 for four declared to win by an innings. Chosen for the next Test as one of only two specialist seamers, he took 3 for 108 in the match as England again lost, but he was forced to pull out of the final Test at The Oval through knee ligament trouble; his replacement, Fraser, took eight wickets and was named man of the match. Bicknell was chosen for the A tour to South Africa that winter but further knee trouble forced him home, and his 1994 season was disrupted by a stress fracture of the ankle and a dislocated shoulder.

First-class career (1986–): 2,128 runs (17.73) and 479 wickets (26.35)

Test matches (2): 26 runs (6.50) and 4 wickets (65.75)

BINKS, James Graham

(b. 1935, Hull) *Lincolnshire, Yorkshire, and England*

Jimmy Binks was a polished, unassuming professional playing in 412 consecutive Championship matches for Yorkshire between 1955 and 1969. Possibly even better standing up to the wicket than he was standing back, he was a highly skilled but often underrated wicket-keeper, the Bob Taylor of his day. He dismissed 107 batsmen in 1960 (96 c., 11 st.), his total of catches setting a new record for a season. Against India, 1963/4, in his only Tests, he opened the batting three times in four innings with J. B. Bolus. He was normally a useful lower-order batsman with his county, and his highest score was 95 against Middlesex, at Lord's. He flew out to India and Pakistan in 1961/2, as a replacement wicket-keeper for John Murray.

First-class career (1955–75): 6,910 runs (14.73) and 1,071 dismissals (895 c., 176 st.)

Test matches (2): 91 runs (22.75) and 8 catches

BIRD, Harold Denis

(b. 1933, Barnsley, Yorkshire) *Yorkshire and Leicestershire*

One of the best of all umpires and a rum, amusing character, 'Dickie' Bird began as an opening right-handed batsman for Yorkshire and Leicestershire. 181 not out for Yorkshire against Glamorgan at Bradford in 1959—he was left out of the next match—was, none the less, his highest score and *Wisden* coupled him with Brian Bolus—a future England player and selector—as a colt making 'good progress'. But a nervous nature restricted his progress despite over a thousand runs for Leicestershire in 1960. After a few years as a coach and as a club professional in Devon, he embarked on his umpiring career in 1970, at the age of 37. In 25 years he has become the best-known umpire in first-class cricket, winning the Yorkshire Personality of the Year Award in 1977, and standing in over sixty Test Matches, a world record. He has not allowed a certain flamboyance to get out of hand and has won the highest respect from players and public. Like a cat on a hot tin roof off the field, and anxious to please everyone, he is calmness personified when it comes to weighing up the merits of an appeal and his 'not out' verdicts (he always gives batsmen the benefit of the doubt) are delivered in a stentorian Barnsley accent. A bachelor, he has often said that he is too much married to cricket to make anyone else happy, but he has been much-loved by cricketers and cricket crowds the world over.

First-class career (1956–64): 3,314 runs (20.71) including 2 centuries, and 28 catches

BIRD, Morice Carlos

(b. 1888, Liverpool; d. Broadstone, Dorset, 1933) *Lancashire, Surrey, and England*

Scoring two separate centuries as Harrow's captain in the Eton and Harrow match, 1907, Morice Bird played seven matches for Lancashire in that season. He later captained Surrey (1910–13) and toured South Africa with MCC in 1909/10 and 1913/14. At Bloemfontein in his second tour he scored 200 against Orange Free State. In his rather meteoric career he was a fine, forcing, right-handed batsman, strong on the off, both in driving and cutting, and a good medium-pace bowler. He later coached at Harrow and at The Oval in 1924–5.

BIRKENSHAW

First-class career (1907–21): 6,920 runs (23.76) and 149 wickets (25.68)
Test matches (10): 280 runs (18.66), 8 wickets (15.00), and 5 catches

BIRKENSHAW, Jack

(b. 1940, Rothwell, Yorkshire) *Yorkshire, Leicestershire, Worcestershire, and England*

Jack Birkenshaw was a great team man and tourist. Fair-haired and small, he presented a neat appearance, whether as left-handed batsman with a fine cover-drive or when sidling up to the wicket to bowl his right-arm 'tweakers'. He was a safe slip field, but his main strength lay in bowling; an orthodox, right-arm slow off-break bowler, he had a light-footed, springy approach and a high action, combining accuracy with subtle variations of flight and spin. He played for Yorkshire between 1958 and 1960 without winning a cap but his move to Leicestershire in 1961 paid mutual dividends. His county captain, Ray Illingworth, unwittingly restricted his chances, first for Yorkshire and later for England. 'Birky's' handful of Tests were all played abroad, against the West Indies, India, and Pakistan, and he never once let England down. He was a dry humorist off the field and a determined fighter on it. He was released by Leicestershire after the 1980 season and joined Worcestershire for one year before becoming a first-class umpire. He was appointed to the Test panel for the 1986 season, but in 1989 reverted to coaching. He was manager of Somerset from 1989 to 1991 and returned to Leicester in the same role in 1992. He also coached Orange Free State in South Africa.

First-class career (1958–81): 12,780 runs (23.57) including 4 centuries, 1,073 wickets (27.28), and 318 catches
Test matches (5): 148 runs (21.14), 13 wickets (36.07), and 3 catches

BLAKEY, Richard John

(b. 1967, Huddersfield, Yorkshire) *Yorkshire and England*

Chosen as understudy to Alec Stewart on the 1992/3 tour of India and Sri Lanka after playing in one limited-overs international the previous summer, the wicket-keeper-batsman Richard Blakey endured a traumatic Test baptism. Making his début in Madras as Stewart took over the captaincy when Gooch fell ill, and retaining his place despite Gooch's return for the final match of the series in Bombay, this modest and loyal cricketer kept wicket tidily, but after making only seven runs in four innings, found himself forgotten at international level. Although he did some 'keeping at club, youth, and second-team levels, he began his career as a specialist batsman, touring the West Indies with Young England in 1984/5. In 1986 he made 1,168 runs in twelve matches for the 2nd XI, including the then-record score of 273 not out against Northamptonshire, and the following season he was named Young Player of the Year by the Cricket Writers Club after scoring 1,361 runs, including an unbeaten 204 against Gloucestershire. Keeping in over half the Championship matches in 1989 and topping 1,000 runs, Blakey was picked for the A tour of Zimbabwe and Kenya and made his highest first-class score, 221 in the second 'Test' in Bulawayo. In 1990 he took over behind the stumps for Yorkshire on a regular basis, and again toured with England A in the winter, this time to Pakistan and Sri Lanka, before, in 1992, he was called up by England for three one-day internationals against Pakistan. Playing in the second, at Lord's, he made 25 and took a catch and a stumping, and was chosen ahead of Jack Russell for the tour which followed. Sadly, his confidence was shattered by the Indian spinners, but he let no byes at Madras in a total of 560 for 6 declared.

First-class career (1985–): 9,407 runs (33.60) and 1 wicket (68.00)
Test matches (2): 7 runs (1.75)

BLIGH, Hon. Ivo Francis Walter (8th Lord Darnley)

(b. 1859, Westminster, London; d. 1927, Shorne, Kent) *Cambridge University, Kent, and England*

A tall man, Bligh was a right-handed batsman with a fine drive and, until handicapped by illness, a first-rate outfield or point. He batted well at Eton and Cambridge, where he won blues from 1878 to 1881, captained the University in his last year, and was a member of the side that defeated the Australians in 1878. He also played rackets and real tennis for Cambridge. For Kent he hit a brilliant century against Surrey at The Oval in 1880 but his health allowed him to play for his county only from 1877 until 1883. He captained the team to Australia, 1882/3, which retrieved 'the ashes of English cricket' thus avenging the historic defeat at The Oval in 1882 when according to a notice in *The Sporting Times*, English cricket 'died' and its body was cremated. The exact origins of the Ashes have been disputed by historians but Bligh met his future wife, Florence

Morphy, during the tour and on his death she presented the famous urn to MCC. Bligh had succeeded to the title of Lord Darnley in 1900. A genial and kind-hearted man, he retained his intense interest in the game, serving as president of MCC (in 1900) and of Kent in 1892.

First-class career (1877–83): 2,733 runs (20.70) including 2 centuries
Test matches (4): 62 runs (10.33) and 7 catches

BLOFELD, Henry Calthorpe

(b. 1939, Hoveton, Norfolk) *Cambridge University and Norfolk*

Keeping wicket for Norfolk at the age of 16 and scoring a hundred for the Schools against Combined Services at Lord's, 'Blowers' was a brilliant prospect at Eton. He went on to get a blue at Cambridge and in 1959 was second in the University averages as a right-handed opening batsman, scoring another century at Lord's against MCC. His promising schoolboy career had been set back when a bus knocked him off his bicycle outside Agar's Plough, however, and his fame was to come instead from a mellifluous voice and honeyed tongue. He established himself as a front-line journalist and broadcaster, achieving the feat in 1977 of reporting upon all six Test-playing countries within seven weeks. His *The Packer Affair* was a responsible study of a controversy which threatened to be more damaging than even the bodyline crisis of the 1930s, but it was as a Commentator on BBC Radio, and, less convincingly, on Sky television, that he made his firmest mark. He developed his own florid style, bringing buses and pigeons to the scene whenever they were visible and sometimes when they were not. Somewhat absent-minded, he greeted anyone he could not immediately identify as 'my dear old thing' which became a deliberate catchphrase. He took to wearing bow-ties and developed his eccentricity energetically, especially in Australia and New Zealand where his image was that of an old-fashioned English gentleman. At the height of his considerable popularity in Australia in the 1970s a group of students created an imaginary stand at the Sydney Cricket Ground which they proclaimed with a large banner, marked 'The Henry Blofly Stand'.

First-class career (1958–60): 758 runs (24.45) including 1 century, and 11 catches

BLUNDEN, Edmund Charles

(b. 1896, London; d. 1974, Long Melford, Suffolk)

The scholarship and sensitivity of Edmund Blunden as essayist, poet, and literary journalist made him well suited to be 'a frail but intrepid wicketkeeper' in Sir John Squire's Invalids, the team of literary sporting men founded after the First World War. That war, in which Blunden won a Military Cross in Flanders, affected him very deeply as did the Second, during which he wrote *Cricket Country* (1944) as a tribute to Hedley Verity and all the cricketers who fell. It was a book with cricket 'as its central core'; an appeal to a peaceful past and the expectation of a hopeful future, full of literary allusions, watchful memories, and haunting images. Cricket also finds nostalgic and sentimental echoes in much of his other prose and verse.

BLYTHE, Colin

(b. 1879, Deptford, Kent; d. 1917, Passchendaele, Belgium) *Kent and England*

'Charlie' Blythe was one of the greatest slow left-arm bowlers. In accuracy and flight he was masterly and in style he was rhythmic and graceful: a few dancing steps, a long last stride, left arm flung behind the back, right thrown high forward to balance it, long sensitive fingers wrapped round the ball and every inch of his height in use. He bowled to a full length, so could be driven on good wickets, but he made the fullest use of any turn in the pitch, possessed deceptive flight, and a faster ball which swung in with the arm. In his second county season, 1900, he took over 100 wickets in county matches alone, and he hardly ever looked back, enjoying his best season in 1909 with 215 wickets (14.54). At Northampton in 1907 he obtained 17 wickets in a day (10 for 30 and 7 for 18) and he enjoyed many other extraordinary feats. Fourteen times he exceeded a hundred wickets in a season. Artistic, highly strung and subject to epileptic fits, he found Tests emotionally trying, but he toured Australia and South Africa twice each and, at home, had a big share in England's win over Australia at Edgbaston in 1909. Two years before he had captured 26 South African wickets in the three Tests. He was killed in action in Belgium and a monument to him stands at Canterbury.

First-class career (1899–1914): 4,443 runs (9.87), 2,503 wickets (16.81), and 206 catches
Test matches (19): 183 runs (9.63), 100 wickets (18.63), and 6 catches

BOARD, John Henry

(b. 1867, Clifton, Bristol; d. 1924, at sea)
Gloucestershire, Hawkes Bay, and England

A fearless and untiring wicket-keeper, Jack Board was a contemporary of Dick Lilley, Bill Storer, and Joe Humphries and, therefore, his appearances in representative cricket were few. A long-term county 'keeper, he also developed his batting so well that, late in his career, he exceeded 1,000 runs in a season six times. He toured Australia, 1897/8, as understudy to Storer but did not reach the Test side. He had better fortune on two tours of South Africa, but died of a heart attack while on his way from a coaching assignment there. He had umpired in first-class cricket from 1921.

First-class career (1891–1914): 15,674 runs (19.37) including 9 centuries, and 1,206 dismissals (852 c., 354 st.)
Test matches (6): 108 runs (10.80) and 11 dismissals (8 c., 3 st.)

BOLUS, John Brian

(b. 1934, Whitkirk, Leeds) *Yorkshire, Nottinghamshire, Derbyshire, and England*

An opening batsman of canny technique and great resource, Brian Bolus became the third player after Bob Berry and Roy Swetman to be capped by three different first-class counties. He was also the first to captain different counties (Nottinghamshire and Derbyshire in 1972 and 1973) in successive seasons. His distinguishing features were sleek, carefully combed dark hair which turned prematurely grey and a bulbous pair of pads which he sometimes seemed to use in defence as often as his bat. Indeed, before the law governing leg-byes acquired without playing a stroke was changed, he could sometimes be seen apparently kicking the ball to the boundary! But he was also a skilful and powerful stroke-player, good off his legs, and possessing a strong square-cut and a low-slung cover-drive. He showed great courage during his brief period as a Test player, notably in 1963 against the extreme speed of Griffith and Hall, whom he on-drove for four from the first ball he received in Test cricket. In the Oval Test he drove Hall back over his head to the pavilion, a stroke which revealed character as well as talent. He toured India in 1963/4, playing with great consistency in all five Tests. He was an occasional left-arm, medium-pace bowler. In retirement he became well known for witty, whimsical, self-deprecating speeches at cricket

dinners and in 1994 joined Ray Illingworth's England selection committee.

First-class career (1956–75): 25,598 runs (34.03) including 39 centuries, 24 wickets (36.91), and 201 catches
Test matches (7): 496 runs (41.33), 0–16, and 2 catches

BOOTH, Major William

(b. 1886, Pudsey, Yorkshire; d. 1916, La Cigny, France) *Yorkshire and England*

Booth was tall, good-looking, and popular, and a fine, punishing, right-handed batsman and fast-medium bowler. He possessed a free, natural action, making the ball come quickly off the pitch: occasionally, his off-break was formidable, but his main strength lay in his swerve and pace. Winning a regular Yorkshire place in 1910 he made 1,239 runs in 1911, including 210 at Worcester. Making 1,228 runs (27.28) and taking 181 wickets (18.46) in 1913, he toured South Africa with MCC that winter, making his Test début. A native of Pudsey (hallowed in Yorkshire cricket annals), Second-Lieutenant Booth (West Yorkshire Regiment) was a player of the richest promise, still improving when war broke; but he fell on the Somme in July 1916.

First-class career (1908–14): 4,753 runs (23.29) including 2 centuries, and 603 wickets (19.82)
Test matches (2): 46 runs (23.00) and 7 wickets (18.57)

BOSANQUET, Bernard James Tindal

(b. 1877, Bulls Cross, Enfield, Middlesex; d. 1936, Ewhurst, Surrey) *Oxford University, Middlesex, and England*

Over 6 ft. in height, Bosanquet was a fine, upstanding, right-handed batsman, who put power into his drives and other forcing strokes with apparently little effort. At first a fast-medium bowler, he was a capable all-rounder successively at Eton, Oxford—where he won a blue—and Middlesex. But his main fame is due to being remembered as the inventor of the 'googly'. Certainly he was the first cricketer to make the googly, or 'Bosie' as Australians refer to it, a practical proposition at the highest levels. The googly is an off-break, delivered with a leg-break action from the back of the hand. Bringing the ball over from a great height, Bosanquet mystified the best batsman with its flight and uncertain break. He developed the ball playing billiard fives or 'twisty grab' and experimenting with bouncing a tennis ball on a table so that his opponent seated at the other end could not catch it. 'It was not unfair; only immoral,' he said of his 'Bosie'. Trying out his new style at Lord's for Middlesex against Leicestershire in 1900, he had Sammy Coe stumped at 98. In Australia, 1903/4—his only Test-playing tour out of six tours he made—he won the deciding Test for the rubber at Sydney, taking 6 for 51; and at Trent Bridge against Australia in 1905, he captured 8 for 107: England won convincingly. Remaining a very talented all-rounder, he took 11 for 138 and scored 103 and 100 not out against Sussex at Lord's in the same year. In 1908 he headed the national averages with 1,081 runs (54.05) and scored 214 in 195 minutes for the Rest of England v. Champion County (Yorkshire) at the Oval. His son was Reginald Bosanquet, the former ITV newsreader.

First-class career (1898–1919): 11,696 runs (33.42) including 21 centuries, 629 wickets (23.81), and 191 catches
Test matches (7): 147 runs (13.36), 25 wickets (24.16), and 9 catches

BOTHAM, Ian Terence

(b. 1955, Heswall, Cheshire) *Somerset, Worcestershire, Durham, and England*

The first man to complete a Test double of over 5,000 runs and 300 wickets, Ian Botham gained, too, an undisputed place amongst the supreme all-round cricketers of the game's history when in 1981 England won three Tests against Australia largely by dint of his herculean performances with bat and ball. Not since W. G. Grace had England produced such a colossus. Accompanied throughout his career by television scrutiny and tabloid hype, he had a superabundance of the qualities needed for success in cricket: immense natural ability, physical strength, determination, confidence, courage, luck, and an instinctive common sense. Though he failed in an almost impossible task when asked to captain England against the West Indies before his carefree, sometimes wild spirit was ready for such heavy responsibility, he quickly bounced back and continued to live life his own way, leading a number of long and strenuous walks in aid of charity, making a small fortune from advertising endorsements, driving fast cars, learning to fly his own aeroplanes, going fishing, or playing Fourth Division football for Scunthorpe United—in his youth he had been offered professional terms by Crystal Palace. Yet none of this interfered with a stream

of match-winning performances on the cricket field or with his determination to see as much as possible of his loyal wife, Kathy, and three children. Six feet one inch, and powerfully built, he was a brilliant, natural, orthodox attacking batsman and a superb fielder, notably in the slips; he bowled with consistent hostility in his prime at fast-medium pace and could swing the ball exceptionally in helpful conditions throughout his career. He scored three centuries in his first seven Tests and reached the double of 100 Test wickets and 1,000 runs in his 21st Test—the least number of Tests in which any all-rounder has reached this goal. Born in Cheshire of parents hailing from the East Yorkshire/North Lincolnshire area, Botham moved to Somerset before he was 3. He joined the MCC ground staff at Lord's and first played for Somerset in the John Player League in 1973 at the age of 17. The following year he played Somerset into the semi-finals of the Benson and Hedges Cup with an innings of brilliance and courage after being hit on the mouth by a ball from the West Indies fast bowler Andy Roberts. Three years later, at 21, he was making his Test début at Trent Bridge, taking five wickets against Australia on his first day at the top level. Those Australians who had seen Botham struggle to find any form in grade cricket while on a Whitbread scholarship in Melbourne the previous winter were surprised by his success but, by the time that England toured Australia, under Mike Brearley in 1978/9, Botham was already the pivotal player in the successful England side. With 23 wickets, some superb slip catches and two outstanding attacking innings, which rescued a struggling team at Sydney and Adelaide in successive Tests, he fully justified his reputation. Known to his team-mates as 'Guy the Gorilla', his toughness was already legendary. The following winter he scored a commanding 119 not out in a losing cause in the Melbourne Test and took 19 wickets in three Tests before moving to India to dominate the Jubilee Test in Bombay, scoring 114 when England were in trouble and taking 13 wickets for 106 in the match. In 1980 he was appointed England captain at the age of 24 in succession to Mike Brearley and during the season became the first England player to pass 1,500 runs and 150 wickets in Tests. But the burden of captaining England in successive series at home and away against the powerful West Indies proved too great. His phenomenal performances became ordinary, his whole demeanour lost its sparkle and aggression and off the field he was troubled by a charge of assault against a man who had provoked him in a night club: he was declared not guilty at a time when his year of misfortune had already been dramatically reversed. He continued to lead England for the first two Tests against Australia in 1981 but the first was lost and the second, in which he made a pair, was a dull draw. He resigned the captaincy which the selectors had already decided to take from him. At the same time he gave the opinion that Brearley should take over the reins again and under the latter's shrewd leadership he proceeded to transform the summer into one of the most memorable in the history of the game. The Ashes appeared to be on their way back to Australia in the third Test at Headingley when Botham, who had already taken six wickets for 95 in Australia's first innings and scored 50 of England's first innings 174, came in at 105 for 5. England, who had followed on, were still 122 runs behind and soon they were 92 behind with only three wickets left. A furious assault by Botham on a difficult pitch against hitherto rampant fast bowlers now turned the match and the series upside down. A heroic, smiling figure, bare-headed and defiant on a grey Leeds afternoon, he took England to an eventual lead of 129 by driving of staggering power. His 149 not out included a six and 27 fours. England then bowled out Australia to win the game. The following Test at Edgbaston was finally decided by a spell of five wickets for one run in 28 balls by England's inspired all-rounder and in the fifth Test at Old Trafford he lifted the man-of-the-match award for the third successive Test by playing one of the great innings of history. This time on a very good wicket England's second innings lead of 205 was by no means certain to be enough when Botham came in to bat. He played himself in quietly for a time and then unleashed another volley of blistering strokes which owed nothing to luck and everything to rare strength and skill. Only Jessop could have equalled the power of his hitting as he moved from 28 to 100 in 37 minutes, reaching three figures off his 86th ball with his fifth six. Some huge hooks off Lillee and searing drives through the offside field, straight past or straight over the bowler, will live for ever in the memory of those who watched spellbound. His 118 included 13 fours and six sixes, the most in any Test innings. England won again and Botham, who also took many fine catches, was assured of immortality. Further successes against India away in 1981 (he hit 142 in the Kanpur Test) and at home the following summer maintained his reputation as the world's best all-rounder despite strong individual challenges by India's Kapil Dev, Pakistan's Imran Khan, and New Zealand's Richard Hadlee. He scored two more centuries against India, 128 at Old Trafford and 208 at The Oval. For Somerset against Warwickshire at Taunton in 1982 he hit a century in 52 minutes off 56 balls, the fastest in the county's history and a match-winning performance. After playing himself in, he scored 114 off his last 44 balls, including 30 off one over. Gradually his batting was becoming even more impressive than his bowling. He continued to perform well, if less consistently so, for England until 1984/5 when he voluntarily withdrew from England's winter tour to India and Sri Lanka in order to have a rest. His wickets had been gained increasingly expensively but he returned to form against Australia in 1985, taking 31 wickets in the Ashes' series to bring him close to the all-time record. Off the field a lifestyle, which had again landed him in serious trouble with the police, began to change. He prepared for the 1986 tour of West Indies by walking from John o' Groats to Land's End in aid of charity and then by travelling to America to launch a clothing business. Several more long-distance walks in aid of research into leukaemia raised thousands of pounds and sportsmen who joined him for short sections of these popular hikes marvelled at his amazing strength, both mental and physical. He had a record benefit of £90,000 with Somerset in 1984, but relinquished the captaincy after 1985. Somerset had fared poorly that season, but Botham himself had hit 80 sixes in first-class cricket—yet another record. Once more he failed to produce his best form in the West Indies, scoring 168 runs (16.80) and taking 11 wickets (48.63) in the 1986 Test series but he ended the tour with 354 Test wickets, just one behind Dennis Lillee's record total, before being suspended from first-class cricket for confessing in a newspaper article that he had occasionally smoked the illegal drug, marijuana. His punishment meant that he was obliged to make a swift impact on his return to county cricket at the end of the 1986 season if he was to regain his Test place. He immediately bludgeoned a century off 65 balls at Weston-super-Mare, hit another, even quicker one in a Sunday League game and, on being recalled to the England team for the last Test against New Zealand at The Oval, took a wicket—Edgar's—with his first ball before breaking the record when having Jeff Crowe lbw in his next over. For good measure, he hit a rapid 59 not out off 36 balls. After 1986 he left Somerset because of their decision to part with their West

Indian pair, Richards and Garner. Botham moved to Worcestershire and during a successful last tour for England in Australia in 1986/7 (he made a brilliant 138 at Brisbane) he decided also to play for Queensland. There he was not a success, by his normal high standards and his behaviour off the field was criticized. He took 29 wickets (27.75) and scored 646 runs (34), however, and Queensland came close to winning the Sheffield Shield for the first time. A serious back operation caused him to miss most of the 1988 season, but he returned to international cricket in 1989 and did not play his last Test until 1992. Especially effective in limited-overs cricket for Worcestershire, who won four trophies during his five years at the club, it was evident that the magic was fading before his move to Durham for their inaugural year of first-class cricket in 1992. He retired half-way through the 1993 season, a wealthy man now well known also as a television personality and occasional pantomime star. His elder son, Liam, made his first appearances for Hampshire 2nd XI as his father's almost uniquely high-profile career was ending.

First-class career (1974–93): 19,399 runs (33.97) including 38 centuries, 1,172 wickets (27.22), and 354 catches

Test matches (102): 5,200 runs (33.54) including 14 centuries, 383 wickets (28.40), and 120 catches

BOWDEN, Montague Parker

(b. 1865, Stockwell, Surrey; d. 1892, Umtali, Rhodesia) *Surrey, Transvaal, and England*

An Old Alleynian, Monty Bowden's right-handed batting and wicket-keeping for Surrey raised hopes which were never quite realized, although in his last home season, 1888, he hit 797 runs (31.22), making 189 not out in only $3\frac{1}{2}$ hours against Sussex at The Oval. He kept for Gentlemen v. Players at Lord's and at The Oval, and for Gentlemen v. Australians at Lord's. He toured South Africa with the first-ever team, led by Major Warton, 1888/9, and when he captained England in the second Test at Cape Town (in the absence of C. Aubrey Smith) he became, at 23 years and 144 days, England's youngest-ever Test captain. Remaining behind in South Africa, he formed a stock-broking firm with Aubrey Smith in Johannesburg, and they both played in the first Currie Cup Challenge match, for Transvaal v. Kimberley at Kimberley, when Monty scored 63 and 126 not out, his début in South African first-class cricket. Bitten by the pioneering 'bug', he went to Rho-

desia with the Pioneer Column of Cecil Rhodes. For three years he led a very adventurous life before falling heavily from his cart and dying at Umtali hospital, a primitive first-aid station little more than a mud hut. A man with a revolver had to stand guard over the body in case lions snatched it, and Monty Bowden was buried in a coffin knocked together out of whisky cases.

First-class career (1883–90): 2,316 runs (20.14) including 3 centuries, and 87 dismissals (73 c., 14 st.)

Test matches (2): 25 runs (12.50) and 1 catch

BOWES, William Eric

(b. 1908, Elland, Yorkshire; d. 1987, Otley, Yorkshire) *Yorkshire and England*

Bill Bowes, tall, raw-boned, and bespectacled, was a bowler of great ability with the new ball, having control of swing either way, although not quite as fast as some of his contemporaries. He could make the ball kick and would bowl a few bumpers to test out a batsman's nerve and technique. Sometimes (in the early 1930s) he bowled leg-theory to a packed leg-field and was involved in his share of controversy, but he spearheaded Yorkshire's attack during years of great Championship success. Touring Australia with MCC's 1932/3 side, he took only one wicket in the Tests, forcing Bradman to play on first ball at Melbourne in the second Test. But in England, against Australia in 1934 and 1938, South Africa in 1935, and West Indies in 1939, he was an integral part of the attack. Bill had an air of remoteness on the field, but underneath lay an educated, intelligent, and mathematical mind. His fielding was moderate and his batting such that he took more wickets than he scored runs. During the war, in which he reached commissioned rank, he was a POW and returned, not in full health, as a medium-paced bowler for two first-class seasons. He had a very good benefit and became a respected cricket journalist on Yorkshire newspapers. One of his books was his autobiography, *Express Deliveries*.

First-class career (1928–47): 1,528 runs (8.58) and 1,639 wickets (16.76)

Test matches (15): 28 runs (4.66), 68 wickets (22.33), and 2 catches

BOWLEY, Edward Henry

(b. 1890, Leatherhead, Surrey; d. 1974, Winchester, Hampshire) *Sussex, Auckland, and England*

One of the finest back-foot, right-handed batsmen of his time, Ted Bowley would raise his left elbow quite remarkably high, pushing the ball away with almost truculent force or leaning back to square-cut for four from right in front of his off-stump. Very quick on his feet, he could also drive powerfully off the front foot. He stiffened his county's batting and adapted himself as an opening batsman. A more than useful change-bowler, he was always liable to get wickets, tossing up deceptively flighted right-arm leg-spinners; and as a slip field he was superb. He reached 1,000 runs in a season 15 times and he shared in 15 partnerships exceeding 200, most notably 490 with John Langridge, opening for Sussex against Middlesex at Hove in 1933. Several great opening batsmen—from Hobbs and Sutcliffe down —stood in his way for representative honours, and he never played against Australia. But, as a veteran, he scored 2,360 runs (43.70) and appeared against South Africa in 1929, and that winter toured Australasia with MCC, appearing in three of the earliest Tests against New Zealand, and scoring 109 at Auckland. On retirement he became an outstanding coach at Winchester.

First-class career (1912–34): 28,378 runs (34.94) including 52 centuries, 741 wickets (25.99), and 373 catches

Test matches (5): 252 runs (36.00) including 1 century, 0–116, and 2 catches

BOYCOTT, Geoffrey

(b. 1940, Fitzwilliam, Yorkshire) *Yorkshire, Northern Transvaal, and England*

One of the greatest opening batsmen in cricket history, Geoffrey Boycott followed Herbert Sutcliffe and Len Hutton as the third Yorkshire opener to score 100 first-class centuries and, on an occasion which stirred deep emotions in every Yorkshire breast, he achieved this rare feat on his home ground at Headingley in a Test match against Australia. A model of the on-driven four which took him to his century was cast into bronze. A profoundly sensitive man for whom outstanding success and world-wide fame created intense personal problems, Boycott aroused extraordinary passions during a controversial career. His fan club had loyal members in many countries yet his single-minded and occasionally selfish approach to cricket sometimes caused animosity among fellow players. He was dropped by England after scoring 246 not out against India at Leeds in 1967 because the selectors felt that the innings was compiled too slowly for the good of the side. Eleven years later, after a bitter civil war in which Boycott enjoyed considerable support

among the Yorkshire CCC members, the committee held firm in their decision to dismiss him as club captain after eight years under his leadership, during which Yorkshire were, for many reasons, unable to win any major competitions. He and his supporters eventually overthrew the Yorkshire Committee and he himself became the most influential member of a completely new committee after 1983. At times Boycott seemed to see the middle of a cricket ground as the one place where he could escape from the intense publicity which hounded him. One part of his nature enjoyed the limelight; the other longed to run away and hide from it. Yet no one set his mind towards success with equal dedication and his decision to replace spectacles with contact lenses symbolized the development of a carefully cultivated public personality. Every run he scored in a long and prolific career was the result of a conscious act of will. A deep study of the game, a frugal life-style, and a fetish for daily practice in the nets were the hallmarks of his approach to cricket. (For many years until his mother's death he lived with her in Fitzwilliam in a simple terraced house although he was long since a man of substantial wealth.) Faults, such as an early fallibility around the off-stump, a tendency to run partners out too often, and moderate fielding performances, were all ruthlessly eradicated. Bowling in a cap, he was a useful medium-pace, in-swing bowler, though restricted by a recurrent back injury, but his main business was batting. Right-handed, 5 ft. 10 in., and with a strong, spare frame, he was especially good square on the off-side. His runs were churned out as from a highly reliable machine. All shots were at his command but only the safe ones used often. His first Test innings was 48 against Australia in 1964 two years after his début for Yorkshire. He became a more or less automatic selection as England's opening batsman until going into a self-imposed exile from Test cricket in 1974. He missed thirty Tests before returning against Australia in 1977, with scores of 107, 80, 191, 39, and 25. In the 1970/1 series against Australia he scored 657 runs, a major factor in England's success. He scored centuries against all the other six Test-playing countries of his era. In 1971 he scored 2,503 runs at first-class level, becoming the only English batsman to average better than 100 (100.12) in a season. He repeated this feat (102.53) in 1979. His highest score was 261 not out for MCC against the West Indian Board President's XI at Bridge-town in 1974, a great though pitch-monopolizing performance early in the tour. Though his performances for Yorkshire became slightly less prolific, and he became involved in yet another controversy at the end of the 1981 season when Ray Illingworth suspended him for publicly complaining about being left out of Yorkshire's Sunday side, he continued to hold his own at Test level, scoring a particularly fine 137 against Australia in the sixth Test of 1981. This was his seventh Test hundred against Australia. He travelled to India despite some political objections because of his South African connections (he had often coached and holidayed there) but he publicly avowed his opposition to apartheid. In India in 1981/2 he scored 105 in the third Test at Delhi to pass the record of Gary Sobers and to become for a time the highest scorer in Test history. Thereafter he seemed to lose interest in the tour and was sent home early, apparently ill. A few weeks later he appeared in shining health in South Africa as the early leader of a team of English 'mercenaries' who took on the South African team in a series disapproved of by the main governing bodies. The TCCB suspended Boycott, along with 14 other English players, for three years. Yet in 1982 this complex man and master batsman was once again the leading English batsman in the averages with 1,913 first-class runs (61.70). In 1985 he reached 100 hundreds for Yorkshire alone and in 1986 became only the fifth batsman to hit more than 150 hundreds. His long and often turbulent Yorkshire career finally ended quietly when his contract was not renewed at the end of the 1986 season. Consistent to the very end he had, at the age of 45, and despite a serious hand injury, scored 890 Championship runs at an average of 52, overtaking Herbert Sutcliffe's record of 149 centuries in fewer matches. In all he exceeded 1,000 runs in 23 English seasons and 2,000 three times. Seven of his 10 double-centuries were for Yorkshire. He captained England in four Tests in Pakistan and India in 1977/8 because of injury to Mike Brearley. In retirement he quickly established himself as a shrewd and trenchant television pundit and his expertise on the art of batting was willingly passed on to aspiring champions, including Graham Gooch and Michael Atherton, successive England captains of the 1990s. No one thought more about the technique of batting than Geoff Boycott. He was awarded an OBE for services to English cricket. His outstanding one-day innings was an audacious, brilliant, and uncharacteristic 146 against Surrey in the 1965 Gillette Cup final.

First-class career (1962–86): 48,426 runs (56.83) including 151 centuries, 45 wickets (32.42), and 264 catches
Test matches (108): 8,114 runs (47.72) including 22 centuries, 7 wickets (54.57), and 33 catches

BRADLEY, Walter Morris

(b. 1875, Sydenham, London; d. 1944, Wandsworth, London) *Kent and England*

After doing remarkable things for Lloyd's Register—such as taking six wickets with consecutive balls against Mitcham—'Bill' Bradley played for Kent as a protégé of Lord Harris. He had an aggressively long run with both arms flung above his thrown-back head prior to the right-arm delivery from the full reach of his 6 ft. height. Pitching at the stumps and seldom short, he personified the attack in cricket. In a short career he played in two Tests against Australia, 1899; he was emphatically the best amateur bowler of the year with 156 wickets (19.10).

First-class career (1895–1903): 956 runs (6.01) and 633 wickets (22.65)
Test matches (2): 23 runs (23.00) and 6 wickets (38.83)

BRAUND, Leonard Charles

(b. 1875, Clewer, Berkshire; d. 1955, Putney, London) *Surrey, Somerset, and England*

Of Len Braund, C. B. Fry said, 'He was one of the greatest all-rounders—*and to think that Surrey let him go!*' Playing on and off for Surrey from 1896 to 1898, he joined Somerset after a qualifying season spent playing for London County and fought many a noble battle for them. At Taunton in 1901 Somerset were 239 in arrears when Braund and L. C. H. Palairet added 222 in 2 hours 20 minutes. An aggressive right-handed batsman with powerful strokes on the leg, a bowler who became much more effective on switching from fast-medium to slow-medium leg-spin, and the finest slip field in an era of remarkable slip fielders, he was a first choice for England from 1901 until 1908. There were many highlights; on his first tour of Australia, 1901/2, he averaged 36 with the bat and took 21 wickets in the Tests. In 1903/4 he hit a classic 102 at Sydney and took 8 for 81 at Melbourne. Against the South African googly attack, at Lord's in 1907, he scored 104. And in the field, darting across from slip to the leg-side, he made a historic catch off George Hirst in the Edgbaston Test against Australia in 1902. Even in his last playing season he could pick slip catches off his toes, while discussing the Derby with the wicket-keeper. In retirement, a first-rate umpire for 16 years, he was an arbiter of complete integrity, full of pleasant humour which turned away wrath. During the Second World War both his legs were amputated in turn, but such was his strength of body and spirit that he survived and attended play at Lord's in his bath chair. In 1949 he became one of the 26 retired professionals who were given honorary membership of MCC.

First-class career (1896–1920): 17,801 runs (25.61) including 25 centuries, 1,114 wickets (27.27), 545 catches, and 1 stumping
Test matches (23): 987 runs (25.97) including 3 centuries, 47 wickets (38.51), and 39 catches

BREARLEY, John Michael

(b. 1942, Harrow, Middlesex) *Cambridge University, Cambridgeshire, Middlesex, and England*

A brain as sharp as barbed wire, allied to a sensitive and sympathetic nature and a passionate interest in the game, produced in Mike Brearley, OBE, almost the ideal captain. He was the first to acknowledge his good fortune in inheriting an improving England team at a time when some countries were weakened by the defection of leading players to Kerry Packer's World Series Cricket, and he led England to ten wins and five draws before first tasting defeat as captain against Australia at Melbourne in the New Year Test of 1979. He accepted defeat on that occasion with the same philosophical calm with which he had greeted the other of Kipling's 'two impostors' and by the time that he had led England to an unprecedented 5–1 win in the series and come home with the Ashes, which had been regained under his leadership in England in 1977, he was being recognized as one of the greatest, if also one of the luckiest, of all captains. Clear thinking, calmness under pressure, and decisiveness were his major qualities on the field, fair-mindedness and consideration for others the main ones off it. It was all the more remarkable that he retained the complete faith of his team-mates despite failing to justify a place as a top England batsman. As a solid right-handed (usually opening) batsman he had the ability to stroke the ball effortlessly in his more felicitous moods as well as to work assiduously for long periods with rigid determination and concentration; he was good enough to be chosen for England in the first place as an opener capable of standing up squarely to one of the most fearsome fast bowling attacks in

cricket history, the West Indies side of 1976, when Holding, Daniel, Roberts, and Holder formed a truly formidable quartet. He was vice-captain to Tony Greig in the following winter and took over as captain when the latter defected to Packer. After he took on the extra responsibility, his batting became rather careworn, and, with his exaggerated early backlift and his belief in wearing copious protective 'armour', he sometimes seemed wooden. But his several useful innings at important times included a crucial 53 in a stand of 111 with Derek Randall in the fourth Test at Sydney, 1978/9, which led to England's unexpected victory and the retention of the Ashes. A wicket-keeper in his younger days, Brearley developed into an outstanding catcher at first slip. In his four years as a Cambridge blue, 1961–4, he scored 4,348 runs, a record aggregate for a university career. He hit ten centuries and averaged 38.14. He captained Cambridge in 1963 and 1964. He won his Middlesex cap in 1964 and toured South Africa with scant success that winter. He captained MCC's under-25 team in Pakistan in 1966/7 and averaged 132.16, scoring 312 not out against North Zone at Peshawar. But he played no cricket in England in 1966 and 1967 when he was pursuing an academic career at British and American universities. (At Cambridge he gained a first in Classics and an upper second in Moral Sciences.) From 1968 to 1970 he played only half a season's cricket but in 1971 he returned to captain Middlesex and their fortunes soon improved because Brearley was able to steer a talented, but hitherto rudderless, ship in the right direction. Middlesex won the Championship in 1976 and 1977 and the Gillette Cup in 1977. They were losing finalists in the Gillette and Benson and Hedges Cups in 1975. As a senior county captain he played a leading role in formulating policies in the administration of county cricket and, characteristically, he was fair but firm in his attitude to the formation of World Series Cricket. He opposed the victimization of those players who signed at the start for Packer but led moves to ensure that the Packer players did not have everything their own way. Brearley himself rejected a vague offer in 1977 to join Packer and recruit other members of the England team. He said of it, 'Kerry Packer is not my style. I prefer the chugging British coaster with a cargo of pig-iron to a monstrous supertanker, hurriedly constructed.' Anyone who doubted his capacity as a captain, or as a worthy Test cricketer, had to change his mind during the amazing 1981 season when Brearley was recalled to take over as captain from the beleaguered Ian Botham. Largely by utilizing the latter's prodigious all-round powers, Brearley guided England from a 1–0 deficit after two Tests to an eventual 3–1 win and thus again secured the Ashes. Twice, at Headingley and Edgbaston, in desperately tight, tense finishes, he pressurized the Australian batsmen by artful field-placing and by making the maximum use of his bowlers, notably of his main 'striker', Willis. The Australian barrackers who had ruthlessly harried and taunted him when England made an extra tour under his captaincy after the treaty with Kerry Packer in 1979/80 (England lost a series for which they were poorly prepared 0–3, although Brearley performed well personally as a batsman) must have squirmed as the scholar captain (and his brilliant protégé Botham) stole two matches which Australia had every right to win. Brearley's career came to an appropriate end in 1982 when he led Middlesex to another Championship, the fourth in his 11 years as captain. He left the game to develop a career as a psychotherapist, freelance writer, and lecturer. Having finished top in the 1964 Civil Service examination, he could have chosen almost any career but, as Rodney Hogg remarked, Brearley got a 'degree in People' and he wanted to make use of it.

First-class career (1961–83): 25,185 runs (37.81) including 45 centuries, 3 wickets (64.00), 418 catches, and 12 stumpings

Test matches (39): 1,442 runs (22.88) and 52 catches

BREARLEY, Walter

(b. 1876, Bolton, Lancashire; d. 1937, Marylebone, London) *Lancashire, Cheshire, and England*

If ever a man bowled his heart, soul, and 15-stone weight, it was Walter Brearley, whose belligerency was his natural state. A right-arm fast bowler, he took a short run, with a rolling gait, and used his body to the full as he delivered. He believed that no batsman could bat—'They are probably a lot of ruddy teetotallers, any-way!'—and he loved to see the middle stump fly. As a number eleven batsman himself, he was an inveterate jumper of pavilion gates on the way to and from his short lease of the crease. It was said that, when he hurried to the wicket at Old Trafford, the horse walked between the shafts ready to drag the heavy roller for use at the end of the innings. In the first of his handful of Tests against Australia and South Africa, spread between 1905 and 1912, he took eight wickets at

Old Trafford; Australia lost by an innings and England clinched the Ashes. Leaving Lancashire after 1911 following a row with the committee, his last Test, in 1912, was played whilst he was representing Cheshire. His last first-class match was for an England XI against the 1921 Australians. He appeared for Gentlemen v. Players five times and became a notable coach.

First-class career (1902–21): 907 runs (5.88) and 844 wickets (19.31)

Test matches (4): 21 runs (7.00) and 17 wickets (21.11)

BRENNAN, Donald Vincent

(b. 1920, Eccleshill, Yorkshire; d. 1985, Ilkley, Yorkshire) *Yorkshire and England*

In a career sadly cut short by the claims of business, Don Brennan's brilliance in leg-side stumping rivalled that of Godfrey Evans and his talent behind the stumps was exceptional. An amateur, he toured India with MCC, 1951/2, but his only Tests were in England against South Africa, 1951. One of the characters of the game, he was subsequently a very active member on the committee of Yorkshire CCC. He only played regular county cricket between 1947 and 1953. Peering over the shoulder of a nervous undergraduate batsman he once advised Johnny Wardle in a loud voice 'Don't get him out for a moment, Johnny; he smells so bloody lovely.'

First-class career (1947–64): 1,937 runs (10.52) and 440 dismissals (318 c., 122 st.)

Test matches (2): 16 runs (8.00) and 1 stumping

BRIGGS, John

(b. 1862, Sutton-in-Ashfield, Nottinghamshire; d. 1902, Cheadle, Cheshire) *Lancashire and England*

Johnny Briggs was one of the best loved of Lancashire's characters, a little skip-jack of a man (only 5 ft. 6 in.) but a magnificent all-rounder. A cheerful, simple man, he thought life great fun and adored cricket. He was an aggressive right-handed batsman, with a penchant for a slashing drive into the vicinity of cover-point, a puzzling left-arm slow bowler with a beautifully easy action and much guile, and a swift-footed field at cover-point. He made his début at 16, and hit his highest score, 186, against Surrey at Aigburth, three days after his marriage in 1885. A first choice for England, he toured Australia six times and South Africa once with the first team there, 1888/9; in the second Test at Cape Town he was unplayable with 15 for 28, England winning by an innings. He had a hat-trick and a century for England against Australia. When he took 11 for 74 in the Lord's Test of 1886, England triumphed by an innings. Also, he played a considerable part in England's story-book win at Sydney, 1894/5; Australia required only 64 to win with eight wickets standing, but England scraped home by ten runs, thanks to the bowling of Johnny Briggs and Bobby Peel. His ending was sad. During the Test against Australia at Headingley, 1899, he suffered an epileptic seizure which is believed to have started with a blow over the heart from a drive of Tom Hayward's. He had to retire from the game and, though he returned to first-class cricket the following year, he had a further breakdown and died in an asylum. There, the story goes, he would imagine himself bowling up and down the ward and at the end of the day would proudly announce his bowling figures to the nurses.

First-class career (1879–1900): 14,092 runs (18.27) including 10 centuries, 2,221 wickets (15.95), and 258 catches

Test matches (33): 815 runs (18.11) including 1 century, 118 wickets (17.75), and 12 catches

BRITTIN, Jannette Ann

(b. 1959, Kingston, Surrey) *Surrey and England*

A natural cricketer par excellence, Jannette Brittin, neatly built and fair-haired, has scored centuries against Australia, New Zealand, and India, bowled her occasional right-arm off-spin to Test-winning effect, and is a superb fielder, A flamboyant, right-handed opening bat who particularly relishes the cut shot, Brittin made her England début at number seven against the West Indies in 1979. By the time the New Zealand tourists arrived in England in 1984, Brittin was promoted to opener and scored her maiden Test century (144 not out) in the first Test at Headingley. She finished the three-Test series with an average of 112.67. In the 1984/5 Golden Jubilee series in Australia, Brittin scored a century (112) in the first Test in Perth and secured two vital top-order wickets in the second Test in Adelaide, a match England won by five runs. Australia eventually won the five-Test series 2–1 but it was Brittin who was named player-of-the-series. Equally successful in limited-over matches, Brittin has England's highest score in World Cup matches (138 not out in 1982 in New Zealand) and, with 410 runs at an average of 51.25, was the best-performed bat when England won the World Cup in 1993. During that tournament Brittin became the first

person to pass 1,000 World Cup runs and became England's highest international run-gatherer. She has also played indoor hockey for England.

Test matches (19): 1,193 runs (45.88) including 3 centuries, and 9 wickets (46.11)

One-day internationals (45): 1,596 runs (43.13) including 4 centuries, and 8 wickets (14.25)

BROAD, Brian Christopher

(b. 1957, Bristol) *Gloucestershire, Nottinghamshire, Orange Free State, and England*

A 6 ft. 4 in. left-handed opening batsman and, before muscle-stiffness restricted him, an occasional right-arm medium-paced bowler, Chris Broad sandwiched two successful stints for Gloucestershire with nine profitable years at Nottingham from 1984 to 1992, but his Test career was surprisingly short-lived for so sound a player. Relatively slow in the field and too independent to be an ideal team-man, his batting was not the only consideration and he was disciplined twice on tours for petulance. Opposing new-ball bowlers had more respect for this determined and single-minded batsman than the England selectors. After several successful seasons at Gloucestershire following his début in 1979, he felt he needed a change of county to enhance his Test chances. Within half a season at Trent Bridge he was selected to make his Test début against the West Indies at Lord's in 1984. Very still at the crease and sticking to a small repertoire, Broad's most productive shot was the clip off his legs through mid-wicket, but, with a stately, upright style, he also drove hard and straight. He did a fine job against the West Indian fast bowlers, never flinching, and while others failed he made a hard-fought 55 on his début and finished with 195 runs (24.38) in four matches. He made 86 in the Test against Sri Lanka at Lord's at the end of the 1984 season and was unlucky to be left out of the tour of India. He enjoyed another consistent season for Nottinghamshire in 1985, scoring 1,786 runs (40.59) and captained Orange Free State in 1985/6. Steady batting throughout 1986 (his 1,500 runs included six hundreds) led to a well-deserved recall to England colours for the tour of Australia in 1986/7. In 1986 he also scored 1,000 runs in limited-overs cricket and he killed the theory of a weakness against spinners by scoring runs against all types of bowlers in all conditions. The following winter saw the high point of his career as he stroked successive Test hundreds at Perth (162), Adelaide and Melbourne, and shared fully in England's limited-overs triumphs on the same tour. In 1987/8 he added three more Test hundreds, at Faisalabad (Pakistan), Sydney (against Australia in the 'Bicentennial' Test), and Christchurch. Amazingly, after only two Tests in 1988 he had become an ex-Test player. Having cashed in on the grassless pitches of 1990 to the tune of 2,226 runs (54.29) he returned to his native Bristol in 1993, but an arthritic hip forced an unwilling retirement after two more seasons. He organised a benefit for himself a year later.

First-class career (1979–94): 21,892 runs (38.07) including 50 centuries, 16 wickets (64.81), and 189 catches

Test matches (25): 1,661 runs (39.54), 6 centuries, and 10 catches

BROCKWELL, William

(b. 1865, Kingston-upon-Thames, Surrey; d. 1935, Richmond, Surrey) *Surrey, Kimberley, and England*

An integral part of the Surrey Championship-winning side of the 1890s, Bill Brockwell was a stylish and often brilliant right-handed batsman, strong in back play, and a free-hitter in front of the wicket. He was also a useful medium-paced bowler, and very smart at second slip. Maturing slowly and first appearing for England against Australia in 1893, he headed the national batting averages in the wet summer of 1894—'Brockwell's year'—with 1,491 runs (38.23), and toured Australia that winter with A. E. Stoddart's team. He had one good Test, but generally disappointed. He continued as an excellent county player, in 1897 putting up 379 with Bobby Abel for the first wicket against Hampshire at The Oval, and in 1899 was again selected for England. An early coach overseas, he was employed both at Kimberley in South Africa and by the Maharajah of Patiala in India for some years. Though a man of parts—well groomed, a theatre-goer, photographer, writer, and conversationalist—he fell on hard times after retirement and at the time of death was destitute.

First-class career (1886–1903): 13,285 runs (27.00) including 21 centuries, 553 wickets (24.74), 250 catches, and 1 stumping

Test matches (7): 202 runs (16.83), 5 wickets (61.80), and 6 catches

BROMLEY-DAVENPORT, Hugh Richard

(b. 1870, Chelford, Cheshire; d. 1954, Kensington, London) *Cambridge University, Cheshire, Middlesex, and England*

At Eton Bromley-Davenport was described by *Wisden* as 'the best Public School bowler of 1887'.

Fast, left-arm, and bespectacled, he subsequently gained a blue at Cambridge, and played intermittently for Cheshire and Middlesex, as well as for Gentlemen v. Players. He toured the West Indies twice, Portugal once, and South Africa with Lord Hawke's teams, 1895/6 and 1898/9, where he had his Test experience. He could be a useful batsman.

First-class career (1892–9): 1,801 runs (18.37) and 187 wickets (17.92)

Test matches (4): 128 runs (21.33), 4 wickets (24.50), and 1 catch

BROOKE, Rupert

(b. 1887, Rugby, Warwickshire; d. 1915, Lemnos, Greece)

The poet, Rupert Brooke, whose evocative lines 'If I should die, think only this of me . . .' were central to the contribution to literature of the war-poets of 1914–18, had topped the bowling averages for Rugby in 1906.

BROOKES, Dennis

(b. 1915, Kippax, Leeds) *Northamptonshire and England*

A Yorkshireman, Dennis Brookes's beginnings with his lowly adopted county were unspectacular but, just after the Second World War, he developed into one of the finest batsmen ever to play for Northamptonshire. His stance was upright and his immaculate on-drive and elegant deflected strokes a joy to watch. He scored most of his runs in front of the wicket, largely with variations of the drive. He had 'the look of an England batsman' but he chipped a finger bone in the first Test of MCC's visit to the West Indies in 1947/8 at Barbados. This ended his participation in the tour, and he was never selected for England again. In the Test he had scored 10 and 7 and held 1 catch. He was the county's first official professional captain from 1954 until 1959, and, in his last season, captained Players against Gentlemen at Lord's. No one had made more runs for Northamptonshire alone—28,980 (36.13), which included at least one century off each of the first-class counties. He scored six double hundreds and six times made over 2,000 in a season. In early days a superb outfield, latterly he fielded close in. He was coach at Northampton from 1961 to 1973 and president of the county from 1982 to 1985.

First-class career (1934–59): 30,874 runs (36.10) including 71 centuries, 3 wickets (42.33), and 205 catches

BROWN, Alan

(b. 1935, Rainworth, Nottinghamshire) *Kent and England*

Alan Brown was a right-arm, fast-medium bowler with a pronounced 'drag', and an occasionally useful batsman. In his youth he was one of the fastest bowlers to have played for Kent for years, but he did not fully live up to early promise. He toured India and Pakistan with MCC, 1961/2, and appeared in two of the Tests. He took four wickets in five balls against Nottinghamshire at Folkestone in 1959, and it was at Folkestone that he made his best score, 81 against Glamorgan in 1968.

First-class career (1957–70): 2,189 runs (9.72) and 743 wickets (24.66)

Test matches (2): 3 runs (—), 3 wickets (50.00), and 1 catch

BROWN, David John

(b. 1942, Walsall, Staffordshire) *Warwickshire and England*

Six feet four inches tall, a great enthusiast with a never-say-die spirit, 'Big Dave' was a robust, hustling, right-arm, fast-medium bowler without a pretty action but with a suitably aggressive outlook and an ability to make the ball bounce. Red-faced and cheerful, he was popular with opponents as well as with his own team, and few bowlers tried harder. He was a safe fielder and played many stubborn tail-end innings. Many of his best performances were on five overseas tours, when hot weather and hard pitches brought out his best qualities of courage and determination. He was vice-captain of an MCC side in Pakistan in 1966/7 and captained Warwickshire from 1975 to 1977. In 1968 his 5 for 42 helped bowl out Australia for 78 at Lord's in the 200th Test between the two countries. In 1975 he took 8 for 60 for Warwickshire against Middlesex, also at Lord's, and he would have had more wickets had not most of his work been done on the benign pitch at Edgbaston. Off the field he became an enthusiastic horse-breeder and for some years acted as a wise and reasonable chairman of the Cricketers' Association. He became manager of Warwickshire from 1980 to 1987, and briefly returned to first-class cricket in 1982 when Warwickshire were short of bowling. He was approached as a possible England manager in 1986, before the appointment of M. J. Stewart.

First-class career (1961–82): 4,110 runs (12.26), 1,165 wickets (24.85), and 157 catches

Test matches (26): 342 runs (11.79), 79 wickets (28.31), and 7 catches

BROWN, Frederick Richard

(b. 1910, Lima, Peru; d. 1991, Ramsbury, Wiltshire) *Cambridge University, Surrey, Northamptonshire, and England*

Burly, red-faced, and jolly, Freddie Brown took on the appearance and mien of an archetypal country squire. A dynamic personality, he was once nicknamed 'Ginger' for pluck. He was a hard-hitting right-hand batsman, whose uninhibited straight-driving was worth a page from an Edwardian text-book. He was also a bowler who proved effective on all sorts of wickets. Starting as a leg-spin and googly bowler, his medium-pace 'cutters' were a revelation later in his career. He was, too, an energetic and skilful fielder who as captain insisted on fielding of consistent excellence. Such was his zest for the game that, either in batting, bowling, or fielding, he could transform a match. The revival of Northamptonshire cricket began after the Second World War under his captaincy. Previously, he had earned a high reputation as a Cambridge blue and Surrey amateur who had toured Australia with Douglas Jardine's side in 1932/3 and appeared in six pre-war Tests against New Zealand and India. He captained MCC to Australia in 1950/1 and, if luck had veered only once or twice in his direction, the margin in the rubber could have been 3–2 in England's favour rather than Australia's 4–1. There was a force and inspiration about his captaincy that was immortalized in the Sydney barrow-boy's cry: 'Fine lettuces, fine lettuces! Hearts like Freddie Brown's.' After his retirement from cricket he served as president of MCC, chairman of the Cricket Council, and president of the National Cricket Association. Father of four, he did much good work for club and school cricketers and was awarded first an MBE then a CBE. He was president of MCC in 1971/2 and chairman of the Cricket Council, 1974–9.

First-class career (1930–61): 13,325 runs (27.36) including 22 centuries, 1,221 wickets (26.21), and 212 catches

Test matches (22): 734 runs (25.31), 45 wickets (31.06), and 22 catches

BROWN, George

(b. 1887, Cowley, Oxford; d. 1964, Winchester, Hampshire) *Hampshire and England*

Broad, tall, and immensely strong, George Brown once deliberately 'chested' two successive balls from a fast bowler, while holding his bat aside and laughing. He was an all-rounder in the truest sense. Not only was he a top-class left-handed batsman with a long, free sweep of the bat, and a useful right-arm, medium-paced bowler, but he was a wicket-keeper good enough to be selected for England and a splendid, fearless fielder. He shared in a three-figure stand for every Hampshire wicket except the sixth and third of his partnerships still stand as county records, including his 344 with Phil Mead against Yorkshire in 1927. In all his Tests he kept wicket, and was brought in to strengthen England's weak batting against Australia for the last three matches of 1921, hitting 250 runs in five innings. He toured South Africa in 1922/3, and the West Indies and India before those countries were given Test status. By his wish his ashes were scattered over the county ground at Southampton. For many years Brown, Mead, Alec Kennedy, and Jack Newman had been the main substance of the Hampshire team.

First-class career (1908–33): 25,649 runs (26.71) including 37 centuries, 626 wickets (29.81), 568 catches, and 78 stumpings

Test matches (7): 299 runs (29.90) and 12 dismissals (9 c., 3 st.)

BROWN, John Thomas

(b. 1869, Great Driffield, Yorkshire; d. 1904, Pimlico, London) *Yorkshire and England*

Short but strongly built, Jack Brown could make runs under all conditions of weather and wicket. A neat, polished right-hander specializing in the late cut, he was a pleasure to watch and, as an opening batsman, was a mainstay of the Yorkshire Championship-winning side at the turn of the century. With 'Long John' Tunnicliffe, he shared in 19 opening partnerships exceeding a hundred, the highest being 554 against Derbyshire at Chesterfield, 1898, a record which stood for 34 years. Jack's score in this match was 300, but his highest was 311 against Sussex at Sheffield in 1897. His greatest day in Tests was in 1894/5 at Melbourne (on his only tour of Australia) when he and Albert Ward put on 210 together. England, after early disasters, won both this match and the rubber. A useful change-bowler, he

cultivated the fashionable leg-break. A quiet, pleasant man, he was a heavy smoker and drinker but became a teetotaller. None the less, he died tragically young of 'congestion of the brain'.

First-class career (1889–1904): 17,920 runs (30.52) including 29 centuries, 190 wickets (29.65), and 230 catches

Test matches (8): 470 runs (36.15) including 1 century, 0–22, and 7 catches

BUCKENHAM, Claude Percival

(b. 1876, Herne Hill, Surrey; d. 1937, Dundee, Scotland) *Essex and England*

Tall and slim with a fine nose and a little, dark toothbrush moustache, Claude Buckenham bowled very fast right-arm with a good high delivery and aimed straight for the stumps, but he suffered more than most from an Essex inability to hold catches. A hard-hitting batsman, he often played a useful innings when required. He went to South Africa in 1909/10, with H. D. G. Leveson Gower's MCC team, and enjoyed heartening success, but unfortunately he was considered a little too old for MCC's tour of Australia in 1911/12. He took 100 wickets in a season six times, including 135 at 24 runs each in 1906.

First-class career (1899–1914): 5,666 runs (14.98) including 2 centuries, and 1,152 wickets (25.31)

Test matches (4): 43 runs (6.14), 21 wickets (28.23), and 2 catches

BULLER, John Sydney

(b. 1909, Leeds; d. 1970, Birmingham) *Yorkshire and Worcestershire*

It was during a match between Worcestershire and Essex at Chelmsford in 1939 that Syd Buller was badly injured in the car crash which killed his county colleague, Charles Bull. Thirty one years later, at a match between Warwickshire and Nottinghamshire at Edgbaston, while umpiring, Buller himself died during an interval for rain. As a wicket-keeper, competing with Arthur Wood, there was no place for him in his native Yorkshire after one appearance in 1930. Qualifying for Worcestershire, he served the county efficiently and unobtrusively in a brief career interrupted both by his injuries and the Second World War. He was a first-class umpire of unimpeachable authority from 1951 to 1970, standing with Frank Lee in the second Test at Lord's between England and South Africa in 1960. Lee no-balled the South African fast bowler Geoffrey Griffin eleven times for throwing. In a subsequent exhibition game, because the Test finished early, Buller called Griffin in four balls out of five and his career as a bowler effectively ended from that over. Feelings were aroused because Buller had applied the law in a friendly encounter and the South Africans refused to have him umpiring again in the Tests. The authorities, however, paid his fee and the county captains showed their confidence later in the year by nominating him again for the Test panel in 1961. Administrators and players alike placed him firmly in the tradition of great umpiring set by Frank Chester. The first umpire to be made an MBE, he was awarded a Winston Churchill Scholarship to visit Australia and New Zealand but died before he could take up the offer.

First-class career (1930–46): 1,746 runs (13.74) and 249 dismissals (178 c., 71 st.)

BUTCHER, Alan Raymond

(b. 1954, Croydon, Surrey) *Surrey, Glamorgan, and England*

A stocky, fair-haired, left-handed opening batsman, Alan Butcher had a full range of attractive strokes, and was especially strong off the back foot. He was also a fine fielder and useful left-arm bowler at either medium or slow pace. He took time to establish himself in the Surrey side, having spent some of his youth in Australia where his keen cricketing parents had emigrated for a while with their three sons, all highly promising cricketers. His brothers, Ian and Martin, also played county cricket and so did his sons Mark and Gary. He was selected for a Test trial in 1976 and in 1978 he attracted wide notice with an accomplished 188 against Sussex at Hove. After scoring consistently in 1979 he was awarded his sole Test cap in the final Test against India at The Oval. He scored 14 and 20 but did not look at ease and was left out of the Australia tour the following winter. In 1980 he was comfortably Surrey's top scorer with 1,713 runs in the season, hitting 216 not out against Cambridge, his highest score in first-class cricket. He continued to bat consistently well, scoring 1,000 runs in 12 seasons and 2,116 (58.77) in 1990 for Glamorgan, whom he had joined in 1987. He captained the Welsh county from mid-way through the 1989 season to 1992, when injury forced his retirement. Making use of his intelligence and cricketing acuity, Essex then appointed him as coach, in succession to Keith Fletcher, in 1993.

First-class career (1972–92): 22,633 runs (36.38), 46 centuries, 141 wickets (38.53), and 185 catches

BUTCHER, Roland Orlando

(b. 1953, St Philip, Barbados, West Indies) *Middlesex, Suffolk, Barbados, Tasmania, and England*

Roland Butcher became, in 1981, the first black cricketer of West Indian extraction to play for England, thus giving hope to thousands more of Britain's post-war immigrants. He came to England at the age of 14 and was taken on from his school by Middlesex, who recognized a right-hand batsman of rare panache. He played with modest success for Barbados in the 1974/5 Shell Shield but was not capped for Middlesex until 1979. The following year he played two brilliant match-winning hundreds in the County Championship and also two spectacular innings in limited-overs games, for England in the Prudential Trophy and for Middlesex in the last Gillette Cup Final. The latter effort clinched a place on the England tour to the Caribbean early in 1981 and his first Test Cap was won in his native Barbados where he was warmly welcomed. But the fairy-tale ended there. In three Tests against fierce fast bowling he averaged only 14, with a top score of 32, and although not a complete failure (he also fielded brilliantly) it was clear that he needed to develop a sounder technique if he was to return to Test cricket. He played for Tasmania in 1982/3. He suffered a horrific facial injury in 1983 when missing a hook against the Leicestershire fast bowler, George Ferris, but his attractive if very inconsistent batting and superb outfielding continued to give pleasure to spectators. Retiring after a benefit in 1990, he played for Suffolk in 1991.

First-class career (1974–90): 12,021 runs (31.22), 4 wickets (45.50), 290 catches, and 1 stumping
Test matches (3): 71 runs (14.20) and 3 catches

BUTLER, Harold James

(b. 1913, Clifton, Nottinghamshire; d. 1991, Lenton, Nottinghamshire) *Nottinghamshire and England*

When Harold Larwood was partially disabled as a result of his exertions in Australia during the 'bodyline' tour, Harold Butler was promoted to the county side, and on Larwood's retirement he shared the new ball with Bill Voce. Right-handed and genuinely pacey, Butler lost his best years to the war and tended to break down, but he played for England against South Africa in 1947, and toured the West Indies in 1947/8. Carrying considerable weight, his run-up was sag-kneed and uninspiring; but he was a highly respected opponent and his delivery was difficult to fault. His best performance for Nottinghamshire was 8 for 15 against Surrey at Trent Bridge, 1937 (six clean-bowled). In his first Test at Leeds in 1947 his analysis read: 52–24–66–7. He twice took more than 100 wickets in a season.

First-class career (1933–54): 2,962 runs (10.54) and 952 wickets (24.44)

Test matches (2): 15 runs (15.00), 12 wickets (17.91), and 1 catch

BUTT, Henry Rigden

(b. 1865, Fulham, London; d. 1928, Hastings, Sussex) *Sussex and England*

An undervalued wicket-keeper, at a time of great 'keepers, Harry Butt let only six byes while 1,938 runs were being made at Hove in 1895. Year after year his hands were badly knocked about, but he quietly maintained his form, and possessed a great reputation for fairness. He toured South Africa with Lord Hawke's team, 1895/6. On retirement he became a highly valued umpire from 1913 to 1928, standing in six Tests.

First-class career (1890–1912): 7,391 runs (12.83) and 1,228 dismissals (953 c., 275 st.)

Test matches (3): 22 runs (7.33) and 2 dismissals (1 c., 1 st.)

BYRON, George Gordon, 6th Baron

(b. 1788, London; d. 1824, Missolonghi, Greece)

Despite a malformed foot, Byron, a major poet of the English Romantic movement and the author of *Childe Harold*, played for Harrow against Eton in 1805. 'We have played at Eton and were most confoundedly beat' he wrote. After the match both teams 'dined together and were extremely friendly. How I got home God knows.' He made 7 and 2 according to the score-sheet, although by his own version of events, years later, he scored 11 and 7.

CADDICK, Andrew Richard

(b. 1968, Christchurch, New Zealand) *Somerset and England*

Disillusioned with cricket in his native New Zealand, Andrew Caddick decided to make his career in England. After undergoing a four-year qualification period to be eligible for his adopted country, he made an immediate impact in county cricket, and although he struggled initially to make the jump to Test level, he was showing signs of adjusting when his progress was slowed by injury. A tall, dark, aggressive, and single-minded seam and swing bowler with an action modelled on Sir Richard Hadlee, and an obdurate late-order batsman, Caddick appeared for New Zealand in the Youth World Cup in Australia in 1987/8, and then toured England the following summer, when he decided to stay. He played league cricket in London in 1989 as well as some matches for Middlesex's second team before joining Somerset. Still classed as an overseas player, his path to a first-team place was blocked by Jimmy Cook, but after taking 24 wickets in six second-team matches in 1990, he claimed 96 wickets the following summer to win the Rapid Cricketline Player of the Year award, and made appearances against the West Indian and Sri Lankan touring sides. In his first year of Championship cricket in 1992 he took 71 wickets to earn himself a place on the A tour of Australia. The outstanding fast bowler on the trip, he then made a sensational start to the new season, taking 32 wickets in his first three Championship matches, including a career-best 9 for 32 out of a match haul of 12 for 120 as Lancashire, chasing 88, were bowled out for 72. Rewarded by three one-day international caps against Australia, he made his first Test appearance at Old Trafford, but he quickly found the pitches and the players to be less co-operative. Taking only five wickets in four Tests at the cost of almost 100 runs each, he did at least produce an impressive burst at Trent Bridge, where his 3 for 32 almost gave England victory, but more notable was his batting as he occupied the crease for over 8 hours. Chosen for the tour of the West Indies in 1993/4, he finished as England's top wicket-taker in the Tests with 18 victims in four matches, including 6 for 65 in Port of Spain, and 5 for 63 in the victory in Barbados. A shoulder problem which required surgery forced him to miss the first half of the 1994 summer, and although he took 51 wickets during the season, a recurrence of the shin soreness which had afflicted him in the West Indies obliged him to undergo another operation, ruling him out of the tour of Australia.

First-class career (1992–): 919 runs (15.06) and 220 wickets (26.92)

Test matches (8): 170 runs (14.16) and 23 wickets (44.91)

CAESAR, Julius

(b. 1830, Godalming, Surrey; d. 1878, Godalming) *Surrey and Lancashire*

Bearing the burden of a great name, a nervous personality, and a lack of inches, the right-handed

Julius Caesar—'Julie' to his contemporaries—was a 'fine, free hitter' and an early exponent of the pull shot. He was a valued member of a strong Surrey side for nearly 20 years despite his own prevailing pessimism about his batting. On the other hand, he was the chief advocate of his own fast round-arm bowling but highly rated as a cover-point or long-stop. At the same time he played for the All-England XI until he joined the newly founded United South of England XI in 1864. Among his best performances was a century for England against Kent in 1853. He was a founder-member of the Cricketers' Fund Friendly Society (1857) designed to give relief in old age, although ironically he spent his own last years in abject poverty. He had shot a gamekeeper in a shooting accident and never fully recovered from the trauma. Twice, Caesar toured abroad with Parr's team, to America in 1859 and to Australia in 1863/4, the second trip earning him a fee of £250.

First-class career (1849–67): 4,879 runs (15.78) including 3 centuries, 6 + 8 wickets (22.33), and 181 catches

CAFFYN, William

(b. 1828, Reigate, Surrey; d. 1919, Reigate) *Surrey, New South Wales, Lancashire, and Kent*

William Caffyn, the last significant survivor of the All England and United England XIs (he played for both), lived until after the First World War. He was Surrey's leading all-rounder (1849–63) and the only player to go on all of the first three overseas tours. He elected to stay in Australia after his 1863/4 visit, as a hairdresser and highly-regarded coach. When he returned to England in 1873 he made a few appearances for Surrey but as *Wisden* wrote, 'his day was done'. He was remembered by contemporaries as 'one of the most brilliant batsmen in England, who would certainly have been chosen in a Test match' had one existed in his time. His attractive right-handed batting, and especially his cutting, was rewarded on the few good wickets of his day though one of his best performances was to make 90 for the South against the North at Lord's in 1857, facing the speed of John Jackson on a rough track. In the same year he took 9 for 29 for a Surrey and Sussex XI against England at The Oval. When put on to bowl his 'joy was unmistakeable' and his right-arm round-arm medium pace was particularly effective against odds. He took 100 wickets a season on three occasions for one or other of the 'England' XIs. His reminis-cences *Seventy-one Not Out* are an important source of information on mid-nineteenth-century cricket.

First-class career (1849–73): 5,885 runs (17.99) including 2 centuries, 577 + 24 wickets (13.47), and 149 catches

CAHN, Sir Julien, Bt.

(b. 1882, Cardiff, Wales; d. 1944, Stanford Hall, Nottinghamshire)

Cricket and cricketers benefited from the philanthropy in the 1930s of Sir Julien Cahn, a Midlands business man. He took teams of first-class calibre on overseas tours and entertained the visiting tourists to England on his private ground at West Bridgford, not far from Trent Bridge. He built another one, equally well appointed, at Stanford Hall with a theatre in the pavilion for evening entertainment. He made a few appearances in those of his matches accorded first-class status, bowling what E. W. Swanton—who toured with him to the US and Canada in 1933—has called a right-arm 'parabolic' slow delivery. His generosity was boundless and there were occasionally those who took advantage of a kindly, if eccentric, well-meaning benefactor. He served both Nottinghamshire and Leicestershire as president and financed new stands and a covered winter shed at Trent Bridge. During the Second World War he sat on the Advisory County Cricket Committee but did not live to see the results of its deliberations.

First-class career (1928–35): 70 runs (10.00) and 2 wickets (74.50)

CALTHORPE, Hon. Frederick Somerset Gough

(b. 1892, Kensington, London; d. 1935, Worplesden, Surrey) *Cambridge University, Sussex, and Warwickshire*

Described in 1911 at Repton as 'the backbone of a strong side's batting', the Hon. Freddie Calthorpe obtained his blue at Cambridge and, from 1920 until 1929, captained Warwickshire. Always enthusiastic, he was an attractive right-handed batsman, who went out to the half volley or cut the short ball with the panache of a true amateur. As a medium-paced bowler he had a peculiar corkscrew run, and his swerve with the new ball often worried batsmen. In 1920 he achieved the double, and in 1922 he took 4 for 4 when Hampshire were dismissed for 15 (and yet ultimately won an extraordinary match!). Captain of MCC teams to the West Indies in 1925/6 and 1929/30, he led England during the second tour in the first four Tests ever played in the Caribbean. He hit 1,000 runs in a season five times and hit 209 against Hampshire in 1921. He founded the Cricketers' Golf Society and his family owned the land on which Edgbaston Golf Club is laid out.

First-class career (1911–35): 12,596 runs (24.04) including 13 centuries, 782 wickets (29.90), and 216 catches

Test matches (4): 129 runs (18.42), 1 wicket (91.00), and 3 catches

CAPEL, David John

(b. 1963, Northampton) *Northamptonshire, Eastern Province, and England*

Primarily a batsman, David Capel worked on his bowling to the extent that he was given the chance to prove himself as a Test all-rounder. Inconsistency and a succession of unlucky injuries prevented this spirited cricketer from establishing himself at Test level. Modest yet fiercely determined, the fair-haired Capel made his county début in 1981, but it was not until 1986 that he attracted significant attention, scoring 853 runs, taking 63 wickets, and being awarded his county cap. The reward was a place on England's post-Ashes tour of Sharjah, for which he warmed up with a career-best 134 for Eastern Province against Western Province in Port Elizabeth. The following summer he was picked for the third Test against Pakistan at Headingley, and he celebrated with another career-best, 7 for 46 against Yorkshire at Northampton. In the Test which followed he batted defiantly, making 53—after England had slipped to 31 for 5—and 28, but his bowling on a helpful pitch was disappointing, as it was the following weekend in the Benson and Hedges Cup Final at Lord's. Capel took 0 for 66 as Yorkshire won a tight match, but that came after he had scored a thrilling 97, full of powerful drives. Regaining his England place for the winter tours of Pakistan, Australia, and New Zealand which followed the World Cup, Capel showed his character in Karachi when he followed a run of 0, 0, 1, and 2 with a Test-best 98 which defied the wiles of Abdul Qadir. His opportunities to bowl in Pakistan were limited—he managed 13 overs in three Tests—but in seven Tests that winter he took only nine wickets and scored just one fifty. Capel played two Tests against the West Indies in 1988 with minimal success and was left out of the party to tour India, a trip later cancelled, but the following summer he was rewarded for a fine season in which he scored 1,311 runs and took 57

wickets with a recall for the sixth Test at The Oval. In the early months of 1990 he did a sound job as a fourth seamer in the Caribbean, playing in all four Tests and bowling much better in the team plan than his nine wickets suggested. His 81 runs included a battling 40 in dreadful light in Trinidad. Still in the selectors' thoughts, he toured Australia with the A side in 1992/3, but a broken arm the following summer, followed by a broken thumb and a knee injury in 1994, suggested his international days were over.

First-class career (1981–): 10,322 runs (29.49) and 457 wickets (32.69)

Test matches (15): 374 runs (15.58) and 21 wickets (50.66)

CARDUS, Sir Neville

(b. 1888, Manchester; d. 1975, London)

A whimsical conversationalist who lived in his later years at the National Liberal Club, Neville Cardus was the Herodotus of cricket writers. On what had been a descriptive and narrative enterprise, he imposed criticism. To the diet of sights and sounds of the game, he brought the wine of his own romantic temperament. In his use of imagery and literary allusion, he created a mythology. He had his imitators, parodists, and revisionists and no serious cricket writer remains unaffected by what and how he wrote. The young Cardus seized his opportunities. The Mancunian paper-boy read in the Free Library; the theatre chocolates-seller watched the performance; the untutored off-break bowler became assistant coach at Shrewsbury School; the convalescent music critic spent a summer reporting cricket for the *Manchester Guardian*. The essayist successfully submitted his work to a publisher. By 1922 the course of his life's work was charted. With the publication that year of *A Cricketer's Book*, Cardus established the pattern of his writing in the inter-war years. Travelling 'summer after summer up and down England' he reported Lancashire and England's cricket for his paper, confidently asserting the talents of the players; diffidently getting to know them as people; shrewdly interpreting the moods of their supporters. Of some two million words in twenty seasons *Days in the Sun, The Summer Game, Good Days,* and other books gave permanency to his prose. He spent much of the Second World War in Australia. After it, the non-conformist who had been given a free rein relished less the conformity and urgency which editors now demanded. The 'MG' lured him out of retirement to report the 'Ashes' series in 1953 but he preferred more leisured schedules. The weekly, monthly, and annual needs of the *Sunday Times, Playfair Cricket,* and *Wisden* were now his *métier, Wisden* claiming an article from him almost every year between 1951 and 1975. Much of what he wrote echoed the past but a later generation of players, if less rapturously, received their plaudits. There remain elements of mystery. *Autobiography* and *Second Innings* are challenged in the authenticity of facts and recollections by his biographer, Christopher Brookes. His famous 'scoop' at Eastbourne in 1921 does not stand microscopic examination. The reader pays a price for romanticism. Cardus's simultaneous contributions to cricket and music play counterpoint. The melody of his cricket writing was innovative; that of his music, at first, imitative. Gradually 'NC' of the 'MG' did for music what he had done for cricket. Those who could not hear the Hallé Orchestra would learn of the substance and sounds they had missed. As in cricket, the past made a special appeal. Elgar and Delius worked hard to win his approval but he was not ungenerous to the rising reputations of Mahler (whose biography he wrote) and Strauss. Intellectually, music was his first string, but cricket had been his passport to fulfilment. Cardus received the CBE in 1964, and was knighted three years later.

CARPENTER, Robert Pearson

(b. 1830, Cambridge; d. 1901, Cambridge) *Cambridgeshire*

Bob Carpenter, 'the old gardener', was—with Tom Hayward—one of the principal batting mainstays of the powerful Cambridgeshire side which, in the 1860s, was able to meet all challengers. He was an attacking and watchful right-handed batsman, with an admirable defence, equally at home driving or cutting. His right-arm under-arm bowling merited little attention except when playing against odds but as a fielder he was outstanding—at long-stop when long-stops mattered and at 'old fashioned' point when instant reflexes were vital. It was said he took 800 catches in all cricket. Of four centuries made in important matches, two were the first ever made for the Players against the United England XI in their regular matches against the All-England XI though it was for the latter—for whom he would play when available—that he made his highest score of 134 against Yorkshire at Sheffield in 1865. He went with Parr's side both to America (1859) and to Australia (1863/4), as much in demand for

his cricketing skill as for his singing and card-playing. By 1871 Cambridgeshire's great days were over and the United XI was no more. Carpenter's final spell was with the All-England XI, usually against odds, for the Players and for the North. He opened the batting with W. G. Grace in 1872 for England against a Nottinghamshire and Yorkshire XI and the 'champion' rated him as 'one of our finest batsmen'. With a final flourish he made 89 on ice in 1878 for Cambridge Town against the University. He umpired in first-class cricket (and in two Test matches) until a few years before his death at the dawn of the twentieth century.

First-class career (1861–76): 5,220 runs (24.39) including 4 centuries, 18 + 1 wickets (16.11), and 191 dismissals (190 c., and 1 st.)

CARR, Arthur William

(b. 1893, Mickleham, Surrey; d. 1963, West Witton, Yorkshire) *Nottinghamshire and England*

The prototype of Lovelace in Alec Waugh's *The Loom of Youth,* Arthur Carr was a fine right-handed attacking batsman, a splendid field and a strong and inspiring—if provocative—captain. He played in all five Tests of his only MCC tour, to South Africa in 1922/3. There have been few fiercer straight-drivers, especially off the quicker bowlers; and in 1929 he led Nottinghamshire as Champion county (for the first time for 22 years). His team was devoted to him. He had a great year in 1925, when he made 2,338 runs (51.95), and hit 45 sixes. Aggression was his essential characteristic and he was at the centre of several controversies. He lost the England captaincy to Percy Chapman against Australia in 1926, after four Tests, ostensibly because of tonsillitis; and, eight years later, his uncompromising and undiplomatic support of Harold Larwood and Bill Voce in the bodyline controversy brought his career as player and administrator to a premature close.

First-class career (1910–35): 21,051 runs (31.56) including 45 centuries, 31 wickets (37.10), 393 catches, and 1 stumping
Test matches (11): 237 runs (19.75) and 3 catches

CARR, Donald Bryce

(b. 1926, Wiesbaden, Germany) *Oxford University, Derbyshire, and England*

After leaving Repton, Donald Carr, son of an Army cricketer, played in one of the 'Victory Tests' of 1945, and, after National Service, successively captained Oxford, Derbyshire, and an MCC A team in Pakistan. He was a classy right-handed batsman, particularly strong to the on, and a very good hooker, often at his best against fast bowling. He was also a useful, if erratic, unorthodox slow, left-arm bowler, and he was brilliant at either slip or short leg. He toured India and Pakistan in 1951/2, where he played his Test cricket. From 1962, when he retired from county cricket, until 1986 he was successively assistant-secretary of MCC and secretary of the Cricket Council and Test and County Cricket Board. Thus, he was immersed in the increasingly complex administration of the official game. He was a patient, fastidious, and cautious administrator who cared deeply about the game and its players but was also blessed with a sense of humour. He managed three major MCC tours —to South Africa in 1964/5, to India and Pakistan in 1972/3, and to the West Indies in 1974. He was awarded the OBE in 1985. His son John is an outstanding batsman and useful bowler who has played with such success for Oxford University and Middlesex that in a different era he would certainly have played Test cricket.

First-class career (1945–68): 19,257 runs (28.61) including 24 centuries, 328 wickets (34.74), and 500 catches

Test matches (2): 135 runs (33.75) and 2 wickets (70.00)

CARR, Douglas Ward

(b. 1872, Cranbrook, Kent; d. 1950, Sidmouth, Devon) *Kent and England*

Douglas Carr was virtually unknown outside club cricket in Maidstone before he entered first-class cricket in 1909 at the age of 37. Having developed and practised the googly, then not widely used in county cricket, he created consternation among batsmen. So successful was he for Kent that, in his first season, he was chosen for Gentlemen against Players at Lord's and played in the final Test at The Oval against Australia, where he took 7 for 282 in 414 balls (and failed to score—he was no batsman). This was his sole Test appearance, although he fully maintained his bowling form until 1914.

First-class career (1909–14): 447 runs (8.94) and 334 wickets (16.72)

CARTWRIGHT, Thomas William

(b. 1935, Coventry, Warwickshire) *Warwickshire, Somerset, Glamorgan, and England*

Tom Cartwright was a player's player. Starting his career as an effective batsman, he was good enough to make seven first-class hundreds, including 210 for Warwickshire against Middlesex at Nuneaton in 1962. But he was respected by a whole generation of county cricketers as a medium-paced bowler who never made life easy for opponents and who, in the right conditions, could make it hellish. His action, with a high, rhythmic leap into the delivery stride, was smooth as velvet and his variety, like Cleopatra's, infinite. Generally speaking, medium-pace bowlers do not prosper in Test cricket where the broader canvas and better pitches tend to demand greater speed or subtle spin. Hence, in five Tests, against Australia in 1964, and against South Africa, home and away, in 1964/5, Cartwright could average only three wickets a match, six of these (for 94) in one innings against South Africa at Trent Bridge in 1965. But in county cricket he did a useful job day after day for three counties —primarily for Warwickshire where he first played in 1952, was capped in 1958 and remained until 1969, taking over 1,000 wickets in ten seasons despite seldom using, or wanting, a new ball. He did the double in 1962, when he took 8 for 39 in Somerset's first innings at Weston-super-Mare. He became coach at Millfield School, then played for Somerset before becoming coach (1974–6), having much to do with the early development of Ian Botham, especially as a bowler. From 1977 to 1983 he was Glamorgan's coach, then director of coaching to the Welsh Cricket Association, helping to produce many good young Welsh players. It was his withdrawal from England's touring party in 1968/9 because of injury which led to Basil D'Oliveira being chosen in his place, the subsequent cancellation of the tour by the South African government, and the isolation of South Africa from Test cricket for 22 years.

First-class career (1952–77): 13,710 runs (21.32) including 7 centuries, 1,536 wickets (19.11), and 332 catches

Test matches (5): 26 runs (5.20), 15 wickets (36.26), and 2 catches

CHAMBERLAIN, Joanna Michelle

(b. 1969, Leicester) *East Midlands and England*

Jo Chamberlain will be forever remembered for her player-of-the-match performance when England won the World Cup at Lord's in 1993. Memories of a below-par start to the tournament were wiped away as the left-handed clean-hitting Chamberlain carved out 38 runs from 33 deliveries and then ran out New Zealand's key batsman Debbie Hockley with a direct hit from extra cover. Her left-arm quick deliveries had also accounted for Kirsty Bond, brilliantly caught in the gully by Suzie Kitson, and a tremendous natural talent had finally delivered. Always exciting to watch, Chamberlain likes nothing better than to clear the boundary when batting and, in a quirk of fate shared with few, has a right arm capable of landing the ball in the wicket-keeper's gloves from the perimeter. In her Test début series as an 18-year-old, Chamberlain and Karen Smithies (née Hicken, and also 18 at the time) established an all-comers' seventh-wicket record of 110 against Australia at Hove, but it was not until the 1991/2 tour of New Zealand that Chamberlain really came of age at Test level. Her 14 wickets at 15.92 runs each with two five-wicket bags played a substantial part in England's 1–0 series win.

Test matches (6): 113 runs (16.14) and 20 wickets (22.90)

One-day internationals (34): 398 runs (23.41) and 42 wickets (15.83)

CHAPMAN, Arthur Percy Frank

(b. 1900, Reading, Berkshire; d. 1961, Alton, Hampshire) *Cambridge University, Berkshire, Kent, and England*

Percy Chapman is remembered particularly as a person who brought *joie de vivre* and the dashing stroke-play associated with the Edwardian amateur to the first-class scene after the holocaust of 1914–18. Over 6 ft. tall, with a mass of curly blond hair, his presence was towering, yet his features cherubic, and he radiated a debonair gaiety which captured the public's imagination. Dominating cricket at Uppingham and Cambridge before going to Kent, he was a polished left-handed batsman, excelling in exciting off-drives and leg-side strokes, almost invariably willing to attack the bowling, and often to loft the ball vast distances. He showed amazing speed and brilliance at silly point, cover, slip, and, above all, gully, where his huge hands would swallow

almost anything. In his first match as England captain, at The Oval in 1926, he led the team that won back the Ashes which had been lost in 1920/1, and in Australia in 1928/9 he retained the Ashes when England triumphed 4–1. He was dispossessed of the captaincy in the final match at The Oval against Australia in 1930, but took charge again in South Africa in 1930/1, after which his representative career ended, although he captained Kent from 1931 until 1936. He will remain the only player to have scored a century at Lord's in the University match, Gentlemen v. Players, and in a Test match against Australia. He married a sister of Tom Lowry, New Zealand's first Test captain. In later years, disastrously employed by a brewery, he became an alcoholic and a sad shadow of the Adonis who had once been a true national hero. People who had once flocked to be near, now avoided him.

First-class career (1920–39): 16,309 runs (31.97) including 27 centuries, 22 wickets (41.86), and 356 catches

Test matches (26): 925 runs (28.90) including 1 century, 0–20, and 32 catches

CHARLWOOD, Henry Rupert James

(b. 1846, Horsham, Sussex; d. 1888, Scarborough, Yorkshire) *Sussex and England*

One of four Charlwoods who played for Sussex between 1860 and 1914, although two did not play first-class cricket, Henry was the most useful, known as 'the hope of Sussex' and 'the most dashing batsman in the south'. For seven seasons he had the highest aggregate of runs for his weak county and he was an outstanding cover-point. He toured Australia with James Lillywhite's team in 1876/7, appearing in the first two Tests ever played.

First-class career (1865–82): 7,017 runs (21.19) including 5 centuries, and 4 wickets (22.25)

Test matches (2): 63 runs (15.75)

CHATTERTON, William

(b. 1861, Thornsett, Derbyshire; d. 1913, Hyde, Cheshire) *Derbyshire and England*

It was largely due to William Chatterton's essentially watchful and steady right-handed batting that Derbyshire were reinstated among the first-class counties in 1894. For W. W. Read's team in South Africa in 1891/2 he was the most prolific run-getter with 955 runs in 31 innings (eight times not out), and in his sole Test, at Cape Town, he opened the batting and scored 48. Such was the strength of English cricket, he never toured again nor played in a Test in this country. A direct man, he called a spade a spade, whatever the company. He captained Derbyshire jointly in 1887 and solely in the next two seasons and during the county's years of subordination (1888–93) he regularly appeared for MCC. He also played soccer for Derby County. He was a speedy fielder and useful slow bowler. William died of consumption and his brother Joseph, who had also played for Derbyshire, was claimed by typhoid when only 19.

First-class career (1882–1902): 10,914 runs (23.17) including 8 centuries, 208 wickets (21.48), 239 catches, and 4 stumpings

CHESTER, Frank

(b. 1895, Bushey, Hertfordshire; d. 1957, Bushey) *Worcestershire*

When Worcestershire and Warwickshire 2nd XI's played on August Bank Holiday 1910 their respective sides included the 15-year-old Frank Chester and Jack Parsons, who made a double-century. Both men later served in Salonika. Three years later, Chester, as the youngest professional in first-class cricket, made over 700 runs and took nearly 50 wickets. His achievements as a left-handed batsman playing very straight and as a slow left-arm bowler with plenty of spin won him an exceptionally long tribute in *Wisden* with the expectation that he would 'be an England player'. In August 1914 he took 3 for 22 and scored 178 against Essex at Worcester. Sadly, only ten more days of playing cricket remained to him. He went to war, survived the battle of Loos only to lose his right arm at Salonika. In 1922 he became a first-class umpire, making his début when Essex played Somerset at Leyton and fearlessly gave both captains out. From that game onwards he brought new standards to his profession. He had come to the job at a far younger age than was usual and in the next 30 years he acquired an experience of umpiring none could match. Bradman called his own dismissal at Trent Bridge in 1938 by Sinfield (whose only Test wicket it was) off a catch by Ames 'the cleverest decision ever made' against him. When Chester retired in 1955 he had umpired over 1,000 first-class matches and 48 Tests.

First-class career (1912–14): 1,773 runs (23.95) including 4 centuries, 81 wickets (31.61), and 25 catches

CHILDS, John Henry

(b. 1951, Plymouth, Devon) *Devon, Gloucestershire, Essex, and England*

John Childs's selection in 1988, when, at 36 years and 320 days, he became England's oldest débutant since Dick Howorth in 1948, capped a remarkable transformation in fortune for the sturdy, orthodox left-arm spinner who, four years earlier, had seemed to be drifting out of the game. A cheerful and popular player and an old-fashioned 'specialist' with a balanced, natural action but few pretentions to batting or fielding, 'Charlie' Childs came late into first-class cricket, having undertaken an apprenticeship in sign-writing. Spotted playing Minor Counties cricket for his native Devon, he was taken on by Gloucestershire, but after ten largely unproductive years, he was released at the end of the 1984 season. Childs wrote to fifteen counties—all except Yorkshire—in the hope of being taken on, but was resigned to his career being over when the Essex captain Keith Fletcher contacted him in December 1984. Taken on for the following summer, he managed only five first-class wickets at 105.60 each and expected to be released; instead, he was sent to Lord's to work on his action with the former England off-spinner Fred Titmus, a move which proved to be the catalyst for a dramatic upturn in form. In 1986, with a slightly longer, straighter, and quicker approach to the crease, Childs took 89 wickets at 15 runs apiece including more than fifty wickets in the last month of the season. It helped Essex to the County Championship, Childs was named as one of *Wisden*'s Five Cricketers of the Year, and but for the presence of Phil Edmonds, he would surely have toured Australia. His call-up came in 1988, the summer in which England named four captains and used twenty-seven players in six Tests. Managing a wicket with his fourteenth ball when he removed Carl Hooper, he took 1 for 91 as England were crushed by an innings. Left out for the next Test at Headingley, he returned at The Oval, where he helped England to their first lead on first innings over the West Indies for 13 Tests, but his figures of 2 for 92 could not prevent another defeat. He was chosen for the winter tour of India, but it was cancelled because the Indian Government objected to several players' links with South Africa and he was not picked again, despite making the 12 for the Headingley Test of 1992. That season he was named as Essex Player of the Year when his 64 wickets helped the county to their sixth Championship.

CHRISTIAN VICTOR

First-class career (1975–): 1,576 runs (9.43) and 941 wickets (29.86)
Test matches (2): 4 runs (not dismissed) and 3 wickets (61.00)

CHRISTIAN VICTOR, HRH Prince

(b. 1867, Windsor Castle, Berkshire; d. 1900, Pretoria, South Africa) *I Zingari*

Prince Christian Victor captained Wellington College as a right-handed batsman and wicket-keeper. He played for the I Zingari, in his only first-class appearance, against the Gentlemen of England at Scarborough in 1887, in the year in which the Golden Jubilee of his grandmother, Queen Victoria, was celebrated. As a serving officer he played a lot of cricket in India, scoring several centuries and one double-century. He died of fever during the Boer War.

First-class career (1887): 35 runs (17.50) and 1 catch

CHRISTOPHERSON, Stanley

(b. 1861, Blackheath, London; d. 1949, St John's Wood, London) *Kent and England*

One of the ten brothers who, with their father, used to form a family eleven and play matches, mostly in the Blackheath district, Stanley Christopherson was among the best fast bowlers of the 1880s. Right-handed he took a long run, made full use of his height and, with a natural swing, acquired much pace. In 1884, for the Gentlemen against the Australians, he took 8 wickets; for Kent, the only county to beat the tourists, he played a decisive part; and, for England in the Test at The Oval (his sole Test), he took 1 for 69 and scored 17. A man of great personal charm and an important figure in the City, he was president of MCC from 1939 until 1946, which, thanks to the war, was the longest period anyone has held the office. He also played hockey for England.

First-class career (1883–90): 923 runs (9.51) and 241 wickets (22.12)

CLARK, Edward Winchester

(b. 1902, Elton, Cambridgeshire; d. 1982, King's Lynn, Norfolk) *Northamptonshire, Cambridgeshire, and England*

Tall and fair, and a natural left-arm fast bowler, 'Nobby' Clark's action was literally a picture, for during the 1930s he was the anonymous subject of a Worthington beer advertisement, which showed him at the moment before delivery, right shoulder pointing at the batsman, left arm almost brushing the ear. Oddly, however, there were batsmen who considered his action to be suspect. His pace was tremendous, and he could produce the almost unplayable ball that came across the batsman like a fast leg-break. He was highly strung and temperamental, he would worry about his foothold, his feet blistered easily, and, when he was out of luck, the fire would leave his bowling. Should birds come flying overhead, chirping merrily, 'Nobby' would hurl oaths at them and ask what they had to sing about. He caused some controversy on tour in Ceylon in 1933/4 when, according to the opposition, he deliberately roughed up the pitch. He made his Test début against South Africa at The Oval in 1929, and did well, but, as he tended to alternate between his county and the more lucrative Lancashire League, he could not always be considered for England. In the early 1930s, however, he appeared against West Indies, India (while touring with MCC, 1933/4), and Australia. As late as 1946, he was considered for five overs as fast as any bowler. Both as batsman and fielder he was moderate.

First-class career (1922–47): 1,971 runs (6.25) and 1,208 wickets (21.49)
Test matches (8): 36 runs (9.00) and 32 wickets (28.09)

CLARKE, William

(b. 1798, Nottingham; d. 1856, Wandsworth, Surrey) *Nottinghamshire*

The first 20 years of William Clarke's career belong to Nottinghamshire cricket, as a player and as the founder (1838) of the Trent Bridge ground, in the meadow next to the inn of which his wife was the landlady. Not till 1846 did he appear for the Players against the Gentlemen at Lord's, sharing all 20 wickets with William Lillywhite in the following year. Meanwhile, he had founded (1846) the All-England XI which, for nearly 30 years, played over 20 matches a season all over the British Isles against local XX's and XXII's. By so doing, he transformed cricket from a regional game with separate local interests into a national institution. The historian R. S. Holmes called him 'a missionary for cricket' and Lord Harris attributed to him 'cricket's hold on the hearts of the people'. Clarke recruited the best players in the land, including Mynn, Pilch, and Parr, together with Nicholas Felix whose drawings and reports in *Bell's Life* have left a vivid picture of the impact on a local community of these travelling cricketers. Special trains would be run, spectators walked for miles, hotels did a roaring trade, and mayors ran gala evenings. As the team departed from Hereford with their coach piled up with 'trunks, portmanteaux and implements of war, "on towards Gloucester," the General cried'. The players themselves received about £5 a match while Clarke, with £65 a match, became cricket's first successful entrepreneur. The United England XI, begun in 1852, was not so much a break-away group as a rival one created by others who saw the benefits of what Clarke had achieved. Losing an eye playing Fives when young, his bowling mattered much more than his batting. Long after under-arm bowling was unfashionable his own right-arm under-arm bowling 'whose spin or rise would beat any batsman', as William Caffyn noted, was effective. In his last seven seasons, he took 340 wickets or so each year, admittedly against all odds, and a wicket with the last ball of his last match, a few weeks before he died. What he established, and others emulated, became the pattern for organized, professional county cricket and of national sides travelling abroad.

First-class career (1826–55): 2,133 runs (10.35), 409 + 386 wickets (10.13), and 55 catches

CLAY, John Charles

(b. 1898, Bonvilston, Glamorgan; d. 1973, St Hilary, Glamorgan) *Glamorgan and England*

John Clay was a right-arm, slow bowler of infinite cunning (after a spell as an enthusiastic fast-medium bowler) and a very useful late-order batsman. He acted towards his adopted county as a kind of Lord Palmerston; for many years he was either captain or captain-secretary, forming a most dedicated partnership with Maurice Turn-bull in the 1930s, and playing a vital part in Glamorgan's first Championship title in 1948. In 1937 he captured 176 wickets (17.34)—including 17 for 212 against Worcestershire at Swansea. He had played in his sole Test against South Africa at The Oval two years previously, taking 0 for 75, holding 1 catch, and not batting. After nearly 30 years as a player, he continued to give great service to the game both in Wales (especially as Glamorgan's president from 1961 until his death) and at Lord's (notably as an England selector). A Wykhamist, he was a shrewd, urbane and witty contributor to the *Glamorgan C.C.C. Year Book*.

First-class career (1921–49): 7,186 runs (15.45) including 2 centuries, and 1,317 wickets (19.76)

CLOSE, Dennis Brian

(b. 1931, Rawdon, Leeds) *Yorkshire, Somerset, and England*

A tough, stubborn, likeable character, Brian Close will be remembered as a great captain and as an all-round cricketer who did not achieve what he might have done. He was a gifted, left-hand bat, versatile right-arm, medium-pace or off-spin bowler and a quite fearless close fielder. Born at Rawdon near Leeds, he achieved fame overnight at the age of 18 when he did the double for Yorkshire in his first season and was picked for England against New Zealand. He was seldom off the back pages of the newspapers for long there-after and remains the youngest player to be capped by England. He toured Australia in 1950/1 while still on National Service, and made 108 not out in the opening first-class match but 0 and 1 in his only Test. Many disappoint-ments followed: prematurely bald, he often seemed to be plagued by ill-luck. He was affec-tionately known for the elaborate excuses he would make for every dismissal. He was always being put off by someone in the crowd or dazzled by the sun; or he would receive the only 'unplay-able' ball of the day. He dabbled with professional football for a while and missed one cricket season due to a football injury. His appearances for England were sporadic, including one notorious innings in 1961 when England seemed to be sailing to victory against Australia at Old Trafford but collapsed against Benaud. Close tried reck-lessly to hit England to success but perished to an ungainly leg-side heave which the selectors took a long time to forget. Yet against Hall, Griffith, Sobers, Gibbs, and the other members of the strong West Indies side of 1963 he established himself at last, playing a heroic innings of 70 at Lord's, during which he drove Wes Hall to distraction by moving down the pitch towards him as he ran up to bowl. At times Close's courage was almost blind—the type which won VCs in wartime. The unpredictable nature of his own play did not extend to his captaincy. He became Yorkshire captain in 1963 and at once proved strong, shrewd, and able to lead by his own determined example. In 1966 he was asked to captain England in the last Test against the West Indies at The Oval. He did an outstanding job, England won, and he continued successfully as captain the following summer against India and Pakistan. But he lost the position as a disciplinary measure after using delaying tactics in a Championship match against Warwickshire. He was involved in controversy again when he lost the Yorkshire captaincy after 1970, but in 1971 he began a successful twilight career with Somerset, whom he captained with the old skill, audacity, and occasional eccentricity from 1972 to 1977. In 1976 he played three more Tests for England, batting with his usual bravery against some ferocious fast bowling. He became a Test selector in 1979. Happily married, with two children, he was awarded the CBE for his services to cricket. He returned to his native county first as manager, then as cricket chairman from 1984 involving himself in yet more controversy. His invitational side's matches were a regular end-of-season event at the Scarborough Festival for several years and enabled him to play first-class cricket in his mid-fifties. His spare time activities were golf and backing race-horses, usually a triumph for hope over experience.

First-class career (1949–86): 34,994 runs (33.26) including 52 centuries, 1,171 wickets (26.42), and 814 dismissals (813 c., 1 st.)

Test matches (22): 887 runs (25.34), 18 wickets (29.55), and 24 catches

COBDEN, Frank Carroll

(b. 1849, Lambley, Nottinghamshire; d. 1932, Capel Curig, Caernarvonshire, Wales) *Cambridge University*

Towards half-past seven on a dull June evening at Lord's in 1870, Oxford needed four runs to beat Cambridge. They had three wickets in hand and a day to spare. Cobden, a quick right-arm bowler from Harrow, in his first year, came on for his 27th over. Off the first ball came a single; off the second a catch while the third clean bowled the batsman. The Oxford captain, it was learnt, had told his last man 'to put the bat straight in the block-hole and keep it there without moving it'. But the instinct to lift the bat was too strong and, with his fourth ball, Cobden dismissed 'Mr Stewart, the *spes ultima* of Oxford'. Cambridge had won against the odds, by two runs, through Cobden's hat-trick. Others had played a part too—William Yardley, who made the first century in the University series and The MacKinnon of MacKinnon who would play for England and live to be 98—but it was, for all time, 'Cobden's match'. In two more appearances against Oxford, he would only take one wicket although he would make Cambridge's top score in 1871. After leaving Cambridge, he played no more first-class

cricket, enjoying his game in the rural fastnesses of Shropshire and Herefordshire.

First-class career (1870–2): 471 runs (14.27), 65 wickets (17.20), and 9 catches

COLDHAM, James Desmond Bowen

(b. 1924, London; d. 1987, London)

Jim Coldham, a civil servant, was also a meticulous researcher and prolific writer in the tradition of F. S. Ashley-Cooper. His work included a history of Northamptonshire and a much-praised biography of Lord Harris. Many editors and authors were the beneficiaries of his statistical analyses, indexing, and obituary notes and he kept a large collection of cricket books at his family home in Woking. Some of his own scholarly articles appeared in the *Cricket Society Journal* which he edited for 14 years and which set standards in high-quality cricket writing. He had been amongst the Society's earliest and keenest members.

COLDWELL, Leonard John

(b. 1933, Newton Abbot, Devon) *Devon, Worcestershire, and England*

A medium-fast bowler in the Tate/Bedser mould, Len Coldwell was a strongly built, right-arm in-swing bowler with a whippy action, accurate length, and considerable stamina. Nearly bowling his county to her first-ever Championship in 1962—with 139 wickets from county matches alone—he was selected for MCC's tour of Australia in 1962/3. He achieved little on the tour, however, and, though he received further chances against Australia, it was only against Pakistan in 1962 that he had any real success at Test level. Later in the 1960s he and Jack Flavell formed Worcestershire's attacking spearhead in Championship wins in two successive seasons.

First-class career (1955–69): 1,474 runs (5.96) and 1,076 wickets (21.18)

Test matches (7): 9 runs (4.50), 22 wickets (27.72), and 1 catch

COLLINS, Arthur Edward Jeanne

(b. 1885, India; d. 1914, France)

By making 628 not out over five afternoons in a junior house match at Clifton College in 1899, Collins hit what is still the highest score in any class of cricket. Later he played for the school XI and, as a regular soldier, made a fifty at Lord's for the Royal Engineers against the Royal Artillery the year before he was killed in action.

COMPTON, Denis Charles Scott

(b. 1918, Hendon, Middlesex) *Middlesex and England*

One of the great artists and characters the game has known, Denis Compton was a warm-hearted, carefree, vague, charming, sometimes careless, genius. He was a dazzling right-handed batsman, a natural fielder with swift reactions, and occasionally a destructive bowler of left-arm unorthodox spin. He was a first choice for England, injuries permitting, from 1938 until 1956. His batting had a poetic quality mixed with the spirit of the eternal schoolboy. His most publicized stroke was the sweep, which he played perilously late, his most pleasing the cover-drive, placed exquisitely out of the reach of fielders; and, like all perfect timers of the ball, his leg-glance seemed not so much a stroke as a caress. He was a good hooker and cutter and was never tied to the crease; he loved to do battle, especially with the best wrist-spin bowlers. But for all his occasional unorthodoxy he had a sound basic technique, playing the ball watchfully and very late. The only uncertainty about his batting lay in his running between wickets and, while he was in, the air tended to be filled with call and counter-call. As Trevor Bailey said: 'A call from Denis was merely the basis for negotiation!' Punctuality for the start of play was never his strong suit, and he was once surprised to hear from another motorist on Vauxhall Bridge that the last day's play in a Test match at The Oval, starting half an hour earlier than usual, was already in progress. But his skill, good looks, charm and natural generosity brought him a fan club of unrivalled proportions. He became the original 'Brylcreem boy', feature of a thousand advertisements. The agent who organized him, Bagenal Harvey, founded a successful business around him, so much so that many subsequent sports 'stars' have called upon agents to look after their business affairs. Denis Compton first turned out for Middlesex against Sussex at Lord's in 1936, as a slow bowler batting at number eleven. Soon he was moving up the order and he made over 1,000 runs in his first season. He was to make at least 1,000 runs a season 17 times (three times overseas). On his Test début against New Zealand at The Oval in 1937 he hit 65 (run out); in his next Test, against Australia at Trent Bridge the following year, he hit his first century for England, 102. He could not tour South Africa in 1938/9 owing to his football contract with Arsenal. After the war and particularly in the halcyon summer of 1947

his cricket reached a breath-taking maturity. That year he scored 753 runs (94.12) against the South Africans in the five Tests; and in all first-class matches he made 3,816 runs (90.85), including 18 centuries, both of which constituted records for a first-class season. He also took 73 wickets (28.12)! Against Australia, the major power in those years, Compton was often England's mainstay, with 459 runs (51.00) in 1946/7 and 562 runs (62.44) in 1948. At Old Trafford he edged a ball from Ray Lindwall into his own face and had to retire before returning, still bleeding, to hit 145 not out (out of 363). About this time an old football injury to his knee flared up and the 'Compton knee' became a serious news topic. Some of his mobility was impaired, though not before he had slammed 300 in three hours for MCC against North-East Transvaal at Benoni in South Africa, 1948/9, the fastest triple-century known. But some of the old dash left his play, and he had a disastrous Test series in Australia in 1950/1, making 53 runs in eight innings. He fought back and, with Bill Edrich at The Oval in 1953, made the winning hit which enabled England to win back the Ashes after 20 years. In his last Test against Australia, at The Oval in 1956, after an operation to remove his right knee-cap, Compton top-scored with 94 (and hit 35 not out in the second innings). His highest score in a Test was 278 against Pakistan at Trent Bridge in 1954 and his best bowling 5 for 70 against South Africa in 1948/9. He captained Middlesex jointly in 1951 and 1952 with Edrich. His benefit realized £12,200 in 1949. He was awarded the CBE and became a PR consultant, occasional BBC commentator, and cricket correspondent of the *Sunday Express*. He played much charitable cricket for The Lord's Taverners. With Arsenal FC he won a League medal and Cup-winner's medal and earned 14 wartime England soccer caps. His elder brother, Leslie, also played cricket for Middlesex and soccer for Arsenal and England. He married three times and as a parent and husband was ever devoted and disorganized. No one could ever dislike Denis Compton, despite the often trenchant views he expressed as he grew older.

First-class career (1936–64): 38,942 runs (51.85) including 123 centuries, 622 wickets (32.27), and 416 catches

Test matches (78): 5,807 runs (50.06) including 17 centuries, 25 wickets (56.40), and 49 catches

CONAN DOYLE, Sir Arthur Ignatius

(b. 1859, Edinburgh; d. 1930, Crowborough, Sussex) *MCC*

Standing 6 ft. and weighing over 17 stone, Conan Doyle had the figure of a powerful sportsman rather than that of a distinguished man of letters. But the medical man who created Sherlock Holmes was both. He was a boxer, a footballer, and a cricketer who played a few first-class games for MCC. At Lord's, in minor matches, he made a century as an attacking right-handed batsman and on another occasion took 7 for 51 with his right-arm slow bowling. He and W. G. Grace —each of them possessing the Victorian quality of all-round talent in many things—clean bowled each other. It was Conan Doyle's only first-class wicket. He was dismissive of his own endeavours: 'I have never specialised and have therefore been a second-rater in all things.'

First-class career (1900–7): 231 runs (19.25), 1 wicket (50.00), and 1 catch

COOK, Cecil

(b. 1921, Tetbury, Gloucestershire) *Gloucestershire and England*

'Sam' Cook was a left-arm slow bowler, whose accuracy and flat trajectory meant that he was very difficult to attack successfully but, except when the wicket was extremely helpful, he was a dependable rather than a deadly bowler. Yet he took 9 for 42 against Yorkshire at Bristol in 1947 and in nine seasons claimed more than a hundred wickets. In his sole Test, against South Africa at Trent Bridge (of all places for his kind of bowling) in 1947, he scored 0 and 4 and took 0 for 127. He was a highly esteemed umpire from 1971 to 1986.

First-class career (1946–64): 1,965 runs (5.41), 1,782 wickets (20.52), and 153 catches

COOK, Geoffrey

(b. 1951, Middlesbrough) *Northamptonshire, Durham, Eastern Province, and England*

Geoff Cook escaped the Yorkshire recruiting system and made his way instead to Northamptonshire for whom he had five times scored 1,000 runs in a season when he was made captain in 1981. It turned out to be a momentous season for this cheerful individual, a neat, organized, right-hand opening batsman with a very solid technique, an occasional slow left-arm bowler, and brave short-leg fielder (twice in one season he was hit on the head and concussed when fielding short-leg). Cook first played for Northants in 1971 and was capped in 1975 when he established with Wayne Larkins one of the best and most attractive opening partnerships in county cricket. In 1978/9 he went to South Africa to captain Eastern Province in the Currie Cup and the following winter hit 172 against North Transvaal at Port Elizabeth. He was now showing confidence against all types of bowling and when the England selectors turned to him for the tour of India and Sri Lanka in 1981/2—impressed by his century in the 1981 NatWest Trophy Final —they saw him as a potential replacement for Geoff Boycott. Moreover, his captaincy of Northants had suggested that he had the qualities necessary for leading England and he reacted with good sense and maturity when for a time England's tour of India was threatened because of his connections with South Africa. Making his début against Sri Lanka at Colombo (Sri Lanka's first official Test) Cook scored 11 and 0, but against India in England in 1982 he scored 138 runs in five innings, making two fifties and sharing in two century opening stands. He toured Australia in 1982/3, played in three Tests, but enjoyed scant success. His Test career had been brief but he continued to be a capable opener for Northamptonshire and captain until 1988. His election as chairman of the Cricketers' Association underlined the respect of his fellow professionals. In 1991 he was appointed Director of Cricket at Durham as the county prepared for first-class status. Happy to be back in his native north-east, he played minor county cricket and in 1992, the county's first season on the major stage, appeared in some one-day games. The toughness of his new role was underlined, however, when Durham finished bottom of the Championship table in 1992 and 1993.

First-class career (1971–90): 23,277 runs (31.97) including 37 centuries, 15 wickets (53.73), 419 catches, and 3 stumpings
Test matches (7): 203 runs (15.61), 0–27, and 9 catches

COOK, Nicholas Grant Billson

(b. 1956, Leicester) *Leicestershire, Northamptonshire, and England*

Dark haired and of pink complexion, a dedicated cricketer, Nick Cook was an accurate, slow left-arm orthodox bowler and a correct lower-order right-hand batsman, who had a remarkable start to his Test career. He suffered along with many spinners from constant switches to one-day cricket with its requirement for negative bowling. Hurriedly called into the England side in 1983 after Phil Edmonds had strained his back getting out of his car, he took 5 for 35 and 3 for 90 on his début against New Zealand at Lord's. In his second Test at Trent Bridge he produced figures of 5 for 63 and 4 for 87, to take his tally to 17 in two matches. He collected four more wickets in the Wellington Test on the 1983/4 tour, and then in the first Test in Pakistan at Karachi he had an outstanding match. He took 6 for 65 in the first innings, and in the second almost brought England a sensational victory. With Pakistan needing only 65 to win, Cook captured 5 for 18 and they scraped home by three wickets. He had taken five or more wickets four times in his first four Tests and a total of 32 wickets. But he found Test cricket a lot harder against the West Indies in 1984 and lost his place to Edmonds. Returning to Pakistan in 1987/8 he bowled usefully in three more Tests, keeping up team spirit with his vibrant personality, but in later years leg injuries plagued him. He toured Sri Lanka with England's B team in 1985/6. Making his county début in 1978, he collected 75 wickets (24.74) in 1980, 90 (23.25) in 1982, and 73 (25.46) in 1983. But he did not keep a regular place in the Leicestershire side in 1985 when they preferred to rely on a seam attack, so he joined Northamptonshire for the 1986 season.

First-class career (1978–): 3,137 runs (11.66) and 879 wickets (29.02)

Test matches (15): 179 runs (8.52), 52 wickets (32.48), and 5 catches

COPE, Geoffrey Alan

(b. 1947, Leeds) *Yorkshire, Lincolnshire, and England*

An exceptionally accurate, bespectacled off-spin bowler, determined tail-end batsman, and sound fielder, Geoff Cope proved himself a cricketer of immense character. His career was twice interrupted by official judgements declaring his action illegal but he reacted with humour and courage. On the first occasion he remodelled his delivery successfully enough to earn a place on MCC tours to India and Australia in 1976/7—he took 23 wickets (19.52) in India—and to Pakistan and New Zealand in 1977/8, when he played his three Tests. Prevented from bowling in county cricket again in 1978, he returned to the Yorkshire side at the end of 1979 and earned a benefit with the county in 1980. But further criticisms of his

action forced his retirement from first-class cricket and he enjoyed four seasons with Lincolnshire instead.

First-class career (1966–80): 2,383 runs (14.01) and 686 wickets (24.70)

Test matches (3): 40 runs (13.33), 8 wickets (34.62), and 1 catch

COPSON, William Henry

(b. 1908, Stonebroom, Derbyshire; d. 1971, Clay Cross, Derbyshire) *Derbyshire and England*

Bill Copson was a link in his county's strong chain of fast or fast-medium bowlers; he bowled above medium-pace right-arm and, though his arm was not high, he could make the ball whip up or break back alarmingly. His fiery red hair matched his bowling, though he had a quiet and happy temperament. He left coal-mining during the General Strike of 1926, when he played cricket for the first time, and he worked up to the county eleven. He took a wicket with the first ball he bowled in first-class cricket, that of Andy Sandham at The Oval in 1932. From that point he improved steadily, developing his late swerve and pace off the pitch. His 160 wickets in 1936 contributed much towards Derbyshire's first Championship win, and in 1936/7 he toured Australia with MCC. Though he headed the averages for the tour, he did not make his Test début until 1939, when he was selected against the West Indies. In his first match at Lord's he captured 5 for 85 and 4 for 67, and England won handsomely. In 1937 he had some startling performances: 8 for 11 against Warwickshire at Derby, including four wickets in four balls, and hat-tricks in two other matches. He appeared for England again after the war, against South Africa and, on retirement, was an umpire from 1958 to 1967.

First-class career (1932–50): 1,711 runs (6.81) and 1,094 wickets (18.96)

Test matches (3): 6 runs (6.00), 15 wickets (19.80), and 1 catch

CORK, Dominic Gerald

(b. 1971, Newcastle under Lyme, Staffordshire) *Staffordshire, Derbyshire, and England*

Dominic Cork's all-round potential gained him a place in England's one-day side, but, hampered by injuries, he struggled to convince the selectors of his potential worth as a Test cricketer, despite his county captain Kim Barnett's assertion that 'of all the players I have seen in my career, he has the opportunity to go furthest'. Picked for a Test for the first time against the West Indies in 1995, Cork took 7 for 43 in the second innings at Lord's, a matchwinning spin, and at Old Trafford in his third game performed the hat-trick. A swing bowler operating from close to the stumps with a high, lissome action and a batsman with a keen eye and a savage pull shot, the combative Cork learnt the game in the North Staffordshire and South Cheshire League before making his début for Staffordshire in the Minor Counties Championship in 1989. Taking 23 wickets in four matches, he was hurriedly signed by Derbyshire before he toured Australia with Young England in the winter. On his first appearance for the county in 1990 he took a wicket in his first over against the New Zealanders, and later that summer he scored a century as nightwatchman for Young England against Pakistan at Taunton. It was in 1991, however, that Cork truly 'arrived' in county cricket with a career-best 8 for 53 before lunch against Essex on his twentieth birthday. Finishing the season with 57 wickets, he gained a place on the A tour of the Caribbean. The following summer he was named in the senior squad for the last three one-day internationals of the season against Pakistan, playing in the final match at Old Trafford and taking 1 for 37. Chosen for the A tour of Australia, he was handicapped by a knee injury, which recurred during the 1993 season, but it was still a notable summer for him. He played in two one-day internationals against Australia, and he demonstrated his continued improvement with the bat by making his maiden first-class century, 104 against Gloucestershire at Cheltenham, and producing a match-winning 92 not out, full of audacious leg-side shots, in the Benson and Hedges Cup Final against Lancashire to win the man-of-the-match award. Another A tour, this time to South Africa, followed, but a family bereavement cut short his trip before further knee trouble led to surgery which sidelined him for much of the first half of the summer. He returned in time to play in two one-day internationals against South Africa at the end of the summer, taking 3 for 49 at Old Trafford. He had to be content with an A tour to India in 1994/5 but it was the prelude to his dramatic breakthrough.

First-class career (1990–): 2,195 runs (23.35) and 209 wickets (27.97)

CORNFORD, Walter Latter

(b. 1900, Hurst Green, Sussex; d. 1964, Brighton, Sussex) *Sussex and England*

'Tich' Cornford was only just above 5 ft. high. A wicket-keeper, he incredibly stood right up to all bowling, even that of Arthur Gilligan and Maurice Tate at their best, and one of his happiest memories was at Hastings, when he stumped Jack Hobbs twice on the leg-side and also took five catches. At Worcester in 1928 he had eight victims. He was 'keeper in the inaugural Tests against New Zealand in 1929/30, but had the doubtful distinction of being behind the stumps at Auckland (the fourth Test) when extras numbered 57 (byes 31), for many years the largest ever in a Test innings. A useful later-order right-handed batsman, he hit 82 at Eastbourne in 1928, against Yorkshire. He retired from first-class cricket in 1939, but reappeared once in an emergency in 1947.

First-class career (1921–47): 6,554 runs (14.96) and 1,017 dismissals (675 c., 342 st.)
Test matches (4): 36 runs (9.00) and 8 dismissals (5 c., 3 st.)

COTTAM, Robert Michael Henry

(b. 1944, Cleethorpes, Lincolnshire) *Hampshire, Northamptonshire, and England*

A tall, right-arm, fast-medium bowler of fire, persistency and stamina, Bob Cottam took 9 for 25 for Hampshire against Lancashire at Old Trafford in 1965, the best bowling figures ever in an innings for Hampshire, and three times exceeded 100 wickets in a season, all for Hampshire. But he was not happy there and joined Northamptonshire in 1971. Reducing his pace and cutting the ball, he was part of a strong attack which made his new county Championship contenders for several years. He was also very effective in limited-overs cricket. He toured India once and Pakistan twice, playing his only Test cricket on those tours. He became the NCA's chief coach in the West Country, and coach respectively to Warwickshire (1988–90) and Somerset (1992–). His son Andrew, a promising left-arm spinner, moved from Somerset to Northamptonshire in 1994.

First-class career (1963–76): 1,278 runs (6.98), 1,010 wickets (20.91), and 153 catches
Test matches (4): 27 runs (6.75), 14 wickets (23.35), and 2 catches

COVENTRY, Hon. Charles John

(b. 1867, Marylebone, London; d. 1929, Earls Croome, Worcestershire) *Worcestershire and England*

After assisting Worcestershire, then a minor county, and MCC, Charles Coventry toured South Africa with Major Warton's team in 1888/9, playing in the first two Tests against

South Africa, batting at number ten and not bowling. In the first of these matches he made his début in first-class cricket, and was described as a 'fair bat with a free style who can hit hard'. Returning to South Africa in 1896, he took part in the Jameson Raid. He was reported dead—having been seen under a blanket 'kicking like a shot hare'—and arrangements were made at his home in Worcestershire for a funeral service; but news came through shortly before the service began —with all the mourners in attendance—that he was alive. The funeral became a celebration, and dancing on the village green, top hats, frock-coats and all, was hastily arranged.

Test matches (2): 13 runs (13.00)

COWANS, Norman George

(b. 1961, Jamaica) *Middlesex, Hampshire, and England*

Norman Cowans's performance in the fourth Test against Australia at Melbourne in 1982/3, when he took a match-winning 6 for 77, bowling with pace and hostility on a pitch keeping low, suggested that England had at last found a genuine fast bowler to rival the West Indians and eventually to replace Bob Willis as the spearhead of the English attack. If his pace was variable, he almost always swung the ball when conditions allowed. He came with his family to England when he was 7, and he was selected to tour Australia having taken only 43 first-class wickets. But he had shown great promise for Middlesex since his début at the age of 19 in 1980 as a raw but strong right-arm fast bowler. He took 5 for 28 and 5 for 34 in consecutive matches in 1982. He was an immediate success on the hard, bouncy Australian pitches and wickets against the state sides gained him a place in the Test team. Although only able to sustain his pace and accuracy for short spells, he showed his potential by constantly troubling a batsman of Greg Chappell's class. Then, with England desperate for victory at Melbourne, 2–0 down in the series, 21-year-old Cowans was their hero. Australia needed 292 to win in their second innings, but Cowans raced in and took 4 wickets for 19 runs in one devastating seven-over spell. He finished with figures of 6 for 77, as England eventually squeezed home by three runs. Despite this performance he was unable to develop as England's premier strike bowler, as he struggled to bowl quickly and consistently against Test opposition. He took 12 wickets (37.25) in the four Tests against New Zealand in 1983, and on the tour to

New Zealand and Pakistan the following winter he took 5 for 42 in the Lahore Test. But he played in only one Test against the West Indies in 1984, and after struggling manfully in India to capture 14 wickets (44.78) in the five Tests, he was dropped after only one match against Australia in 1985. Although he had the best striking rate of all bowlers in English first-class cricket in both the 1984 and 1985 seasons, he was selected for the England B tour to Sri Lanka in 1985/6 rather than for the main tour of the West Indies. In his benefit season of 1993 he took only a belated part in Middlesex's Championship triumph but his 16 first-class wickets (14.62) were enough to move him top of the national averages. He moved to Hampshire the following season, but with limited success. A useful squash and Real Tennis player, his first objective with the bat was usually to hit sixes and he sometimes did so, although he managed only one fifty.

First-class career (1980–): 1,605 runs (8.91), 662 wickets (24.86), and 63 catches
Test matches (19): 175 runs (7.95), 51 wickets (39.27), and 9 catches

COWDREY, Christopher Stuart

(b. 1957, Farnborough, Kent) *Kent, Glamorgan, and England*

Although lacking the prodigious run-scoring ability of his father, Chris Cowdrey was an attractive right-handed batsman, useful medium-pace bowler, and a fielder of breathtaking speed and brilliance, who followed his father both into the England side and to the Kent captaincy. Also educated at Tonbridge, he played for the Kent 2nd XI at the age of 15, captained a Young England side in the West Indies in 1976 and made his first-class début in 1977. In his first season, still only 19, he made 101 not out against Glamorgan at Swansea. Particularly impressive in one-day cricket, he produced several fine performances in the 1984 season, including a superb knock of 125 not out against Essex at Colchester in the Championship. So he was given the unenviable task of replacing Ian Botham on the 1984/5 tour of India. Playing in all five Tests, although his record was moderate, he was a valuable member of the series-winning side with bat, ball, and in the field. A character of charm and *joie de vivre*, he was appointed Kent captain in 1985 when his youngest brother, Graham, was just beginning to establish himself, leading the county until 1990, after which he played one season for Glamorgan. His experience as England captain in 1988 was disappointing, even bizarre. At Leeds on the day before his only match in charge, the gateman did not recognize him and would not let him enter the ground. England were overwhelmed by the West Indies. A subsequent bruised foot made him doubtful for the following fifth Test, but he had not declared himself unavailable when it was announced that he was 'unfit' and that the captaincy had passed to Graham Gooch.

First-class career (1977–): 12,252 runs (31.90) including 11 centuries, 124 wickets (39.33), and 205 catches

Test matches (6): 101 runs (14.42), 4 wickets (77.25), and 5 catches

COWDREY, Sir Michael Colin

(b. 1932, Ootacamund, India) *Oxford University, Kent, and England*

A great player, and a greatly loved one, before becoming an influential cricket administrator in the tradition of Lord Harris and Sir Pelham Warner, Colin Cowdrey's life has centred around cricket. The youngest player ever to appear in a Public Schools match at Lord's at 13, he dominated Tonbridge cricket for five years, scoring 2,894 runs and, with leg-breaks and googlies, taking 216 wickets. The initials, M.C.C., given to him by a cricketing father after his birth in Ootacamund, continued to fit him well. He was a prolific run-getter at Oxford, making a century in the Varsity match and serving as captain in his last year, and he was the youngest player capped by Kent. His emergence at Oxford followed soon after Peter May's at Cambridge and led directly to many prosperous years for England's cricket. He was the most felicitous and effortless of strokeplayers, yet few worked harder on their technique. Indeed there were times when he was too introspective, and, had he given fuller play to his natural genius, he could have been even greater. Plumply built, he was none the less a superlative first slip and in his early days a skilful, flighty legspinner. Perhaps only Jack Hobbs has been as popular in Australia, where he toured six times between 1954/5 and 1974/5—the latter visit when he was called for as emergency replacement in the battered and shell-shocked England side. Though only moderately successful, his patience, technique, and courage against Lillee and Thomson justified the choice. His first Test century was a saving 102 out of an innings of 191 at Melbourne, 1954/5, and he made three other centuries against Australia. For Kent at Canterbury against the Australians in 1961 he was at his best with a century in each innings, and his last century against the Australians, in 1975, also at Canterbury, was a match-winning innings. Among his twenty-two Test centuries one of the best remembered is his 154 at Edgbaston against the West Indies in 1957, when he and Peter May, by putting on 411 in 8 hours 20 minutes, laid the Ramadhin bogey and deprived their opponents of victory. Another magnificent exhibition of strokeplay against South Africa at The Oval in 1960, when he hit 155, saved his side. Cowdrey captained England in the West Indies, 1967/8, a happy and successful tour, and on other occasions, but, to his chagrin, he was never appointed captain on any of his tours of Australia. He lost the job for the final time in 1969 because of an injury, and never regained it. He captained Kent from 1957 until 1971, leading the county to the Championship in 1970. He was and is revered by the legions of Kent cricket supporters. Gentle, friendly, and polite, he has a way of charming young, old, rich, and poor, and his public speeches are models, laced with humour. Twenty-seven times he exceeded 1,000 runs in a season (six on tour). He went on eleven official MCC tours and numerous others. He has served on several Lord's committees, written a number of cricket books, been an active supporter of youth and charity cricket and was first awarded the CBE for his services to the game before being knighted in the 1992 New Years honours list. He was President of MCC in 1986/7 and from 1989 to 1993 was a dedicated, though unpaid, chairman of the International Cricket Council. To him goes the credit for easing control out of the experienced hands of England and Australia to make the organization a genuine world authority, with power to control the increasingly commercial professional game. Referees for Test matches and 'independent' umpires were introduced under his supervision, along with a code of conduct for players. Two of his sons, Christopher and Graham, followed him into the Kent side and he was such a proud father when Christopher took his first Test wicket in India in 1984/5 that, listening to the radio commentary, he accidentally drove the wrong way up a one-way street.

First-class career (1950–76): 42,719 runs (42.89) including 107 centuries, 65 wickets (51.21), and 638 catches

Test matches (114): 7,624 runs (44.06) including 22 centuries, 0–104, and 120 catches

COX, George

(b. 1911, Horsham, Sussex; d. 1985, Burgess Hill, Sussex) *Sussex*

'Not merely a chip off the old block but the old block itself,' Edmund Burke said of Pitt the Younger when he followed in his father's wake as a politician. So, too, was George Cox whose 25 years (1931–56) as a regular Sussex all-rounder followed almost immediately upon his father's retirement in 1928. His right-handed batting, and especially his off-drives, had the freedom of an old-style amateur while his refusal to surrender to an average—and possibly the loss of the war years as well—may have denied him an England cap. On 13 occasions he made 1,000 runs in a season and there were 4 double-centuries. One of his best came when Sussex were in trouble at 40 for 3 against Glamorgan at Hove in 1947: his undefeated 205 won the match. As a left-arm medium-pace bowler he was more in demand in the post-war period and his fielding at cover-point secured many a run-out. On retiring from Sussex —though he made a few appearances there-after—he was coach at Winchester College (1957–60) before returning to the county as their own coach. A brilliant after-dinner speaker and an engaging enthusiast for the game, especially when it involved the young, he had a total commitment to cricket and to his fellow-men.

First-class career (1931–61): 22,949 runs (32.92) including 50 centuries, 192 wickets (30.91), and 139 catches

COX, George Rubens

(b. 1873, Warnham, Sussex; d. 1949, Dorking, Surrey) *Sussex*

Two great achievements stand out in the long period (1895–1928) in which George Cox served Sussex. In 1906 against Hampshire at Chichester he scored 167 not out, sharing in a tenth wicket partnership of 116 with Harry Butt and playing, said *Wisden* 'the innings of his life'. Twenty years later, at the age of 52, he took 17 wickets for 106 against Warwickshire at Horsham, his home town, hitting the stumps on nine occasions and joining a select band of 19 first-class cricketers. 'What about giving me another turn?' he would say to his skipper Arthur Gilligan when Sussex were in difficulties. As a right-handed batsman he was stolid and dependable for twenty runs or so. As a left-arm bowler, gradually getting slower, he commanded flight and accuracy, forcing batsmen

to play him. Representative opportunities were fewer in his day but a whole generation took his regular appearances for Sussex as axiomatic. His loyalty was absolute and in later years, after a spell as county coach, he was made a life member. His portrait hung in the pavilion at Hove.

First-class career (1895–1928): 14,643 runs (18.77) including 2 centuries, 1,843 wickets (22.86), and 549 catches

COXON, Alexander

(b. 1916, Huddersfield, Yorkshire) *Yorkshire, Durham, and England*

Alec Coxon was a hostile, whole-hearted, tireless, right-arm, fast-medium bowler and a well-equipped late-order batsman. In his sole Test against Australia at Lord's in 1948, he scored 19 and 0 and took 3 for 172. After taking 131 wickets at 18.60 in 1950 he left county cricket to go into the leagues and played for Durham as a professional from 1951 to 1954.

First-class career (1945–50): 2,814 runs (18.15) and 473 wickets (20.91)

CRANMER, Peter

(b. 1914, Birmingham; d. 1994, Peacehaven, Sussex) *Warwickshire*

Peter Cranmer succeeded to the captaincy of Warwickshire in 1938 after the 'graceless dismissal' of Bob Wyatt. His playing record in first-class cricket up to that point was modest and his chief claim to leadership was his captaincy of England at rugby football. He had already won 16 caps as a strong, bustling centre three-quarter. Leadership proved the key: not only did his own game, as an aggressive right-hand batsman, improve but the players responded to his cheerful personality and adventurous style of captaincy in four seasons in command—two before the war and two after (1938–47). On three occasions he made 1,000 runs and after his first-class days were over he led the 2nd XI. He won a separate reputation as a commentator on cricket and rugby. After his glittering early career he was dogged by ill-fortune and ill-health but he bore even the amputation of both legs with humour and courage.

First-class career (1934–59): 5,855 runs (21.59) including 4 centuries, 29 wickets (41.65), and 126 catches

CRANSTON

CRANSTON, James

(b. 1859, Bordesley, Birmingham; d. 1904, Bristol)
Gloucestershire, Worcestershire, Warwickshire, and England

Late in his career (in 1889 and 1890), despite greatly increasing weight, James Cranston was regarded as one of the best left-handed batsmen in county cricket, but he was seized with a fit on the field of play in 1891 and much of his old brilliance thereafter left him. In his sole Test, against Australia at The Oval, 1890, he scored 16 and 15 and held 1 catch. His cricket for Worcestershire in 1885 and Warwickshire, 1886/7 was played before they became first-class.

First-class career (1876–99): 3,450 runs (19.71) including 5 centuries

CRANSTON, Kenneth

(b. 1917, Aigburth, Liverpool) *Lancashire and England*

Ken Cranston, amiable and rubicund, had appeared for the Navy, Combined Services, and Club Cricket Conference with distinction, but he was completely new to first-class county cricket when he accepted the captaincy of Lancashire in 1947. It was a great blow to the game when he had to resign at the end of the 1948 season owing to the claims of his dental practice, and subsequently his only appearances were in occasional Festival matches. He was a gifted all-rounder, a forcing right-handed batsman and a fast-medium opening bowler. In the two years he captained his county he played for England against South Africa in 1947 and against the West Indies in 1947/8, when he captained the side at Barbados in the first Test.

First-class career (1947–50): 3,099 runs (34.82) including 3 centuries, and 178 wickets (28.00)
Test matches (8): 209 runs (14.92), 18 wickets (25.61), and 3 catches

CRAPP, John Frederick

(b. 1912, St Colomb Major, Cornwall; d. 1981, Knowle, Somerset) *Gloucestershire*

A Cornishman, Jack Crapp was a countryman of unruffled calm. He was an extremely sound left-handed batsman and a brilliant first slip. He provided the middle-order 'graft' for his county for twenty years. Altogether he reached 1,000 runs in a season 14 times, and he captained the county in 1953 and 1954, the first professional to do so. He appeared in Test cricket between 1948

and 1949, against Australia at home and in South Africa on tour; he visited India with the Commonwealth side in 1953/4, but had to return home ill after two matches. On retirement he became a highly respected umpire (1957–80), standing in four Tests. Once asked for his name at a hotel, he replied 'Crapp' and was directed to the second door on the left.

First-class career (1936–56): 23,615 runs (35.03) including 38 centuries, and 385 catches
Test matches (7): 319 runs (29.00) and 7 catches

CRAWFORD, John Neville

(b. 1886, Cane Hill, Surrey; d. 1963, Epsom, Surrey) *Surrey, South Australia, Otago, Wellington, and England*

A prodigy at Repton where, in four seasons, he scored 2,098 runs and took 224 wickets, Jack Crawford first appeared for his county at 17. He was, perhaps, the greatest school cricketer in the history of the game, and, at 19, was the youngest player until Brian Close to achieve the double in first-class cricket (in 1906). He was a fine, orthodox, firm-footed, right-handed batsman with an upright stance, who delighted in straight-driving. He was also a medium-paced bowler who possessed nearly every gift: an easy delivery, accuracy, and ability to make the ball move considerably. He always played in spectacles. In his first season for his county in 1904 he bowled unchanged with H. C. McDonell in the match against Gloucestershire at Cheltenham, taking 10 for 78. Two years later he hit a ball on to the top balcony of the pavilion at Lord's. He toured South Africa in 1905/6—before he was 20—and Australia in 1907/8, when he headed the bowling in the Tests with 30 wickets (24.79) and was considered by many to have been the finest orthodox medium-paced bowler ever on Australian 'shirt-front' wickets. After a sharp dispute with Surrey over the composition of the county's XI which he was captaining against the Australians in 1909, he settled in Australia, playing Sheffield Shield cricket with distinction and touring New Zealand with an Australian side in 1914, when, against XV of Canterbury, he scored 354, 254 of which came from sixes and fours. He and Victor Trumper were recorded as adding 298 in 69 minutes. Returning to England when war broke out, he had three more seasons with Surrey, and at The Oval in 1919 he hit impressively against the Australian Imperial Forces, driving Jack Gregory back over his head into the pavilion and scoring 144. That season he came

208

third in the national batting averages with 61. His father, an uncle, and two brothers all played county cricket.

First-class career (1904–21): 9,488 runs (32.60) including 15 centuries, 815 wickets (20.66), and 162 catches

Test matches (12): 469 runs (22.33), 39 wickets (29.48), and 13 catches

CRAWLEY, Aidan Merivale

(b. 1908, Benenden, Kent; d. 1993, London) *Oxford University and Kent*

H. S. Altham called the Harrovian Aidan Crawley 'a beautiful player to watch with his correct footwork, long true swing and flashing acceleration from his wrists'. As a right-handed batsman at Oxford he won four blues, scored a double-century with ten sixes against Northamptonshire at Wellingborough in 1929, and achieved the second highest aggregate by an Oxford undergraduate. The tantalizing prospect of playing for England against the South Africans at Lord's in 1929 ended in disappointment when he was made 12th man. In strictly cricketing terms, these standards were not remotely matched in some 30 appearances in first-class cricket over the next 20 years. Instead, Crawley's diverse and brilliant career would be as a pilot who served in 601 Squadron, a politician (both Labour and Conservative) who became a parliamentary undersecretary, a cameraman who filmed the early period of Indian Independence, a journalist who became the first editor-in-chief of Independent Television News and Chairman of London Weekend, and a writer whose biography of de Gaulle has not been surpassed in the English language. Yet he was not lost to cricket as the first chairman of the National Cricket Association, a co-founder of the National Village Cricket Competition, and president of MCC. This was renaissance man writ new.

First-class career (1927–49): 5,061 runs (37.48) including 11 centuries, 15 wickets (37.66), and 44 catches

CRAWLEY, John Paul

(b. 1971, Malden, Essex) *Cambridge University, Lancashire, and England*

Not since David Gower's Test début in 1978 had so much been expected of an English-born batsman as it was when John Crawley made his senior international bow against South Africa at Lord's in 1994. In the event, his achievements in three matches were disappointing, but his selection for the winter tour to Australia still came as no surprise. Modest, tall, fair-haired, and strong through the leg-side, Crawley came from a cricketing family. His father was a well known league cricketer, his eldest brother Mark captained Oxford University and played for Lancashire and Nottinghamshire, and another brother, Peter, won a blue at Cambridge. John himself closely followed the footsteps of Michael Atherton, whom he succeeded as captain of Manchester Grammar School and Cambridge. At school, where he also kept wicket, Crawley scored over 1,800 runs in two years, including, in 1989, six centuries, five of them in consecutive innings. In the same season, he made his début for Young England against New Zealand, and in 1990, Majid Khan, managing a tour of Pakistan Young Cricketers to England, hailed him as the best young player in the country. Crawley captained the side in New Zealand that winter and during the following summer against Australia, making two centuries in the latter series, including 130 as England chased 401 to win, in the process becoming the first player to pass 1,000 runs in under-19 'Tests'. 1991 also saw the first of his three years at Cambridge in which he scored consistently but never made a first-class hundred at Fenner's. Having already represented Lancashire the previous year, he ended the 1991 summer with a maiden century for his county, 130 against Surrey. Assuming the Cambridge captaincy for 1992, Crawley produced an unbeaten 106 to win the Varsity match and then scored another century against Surrey, 172, as he passed 1,000 first-class runs for the first time. Another outstanding season in 1993 earned him an A tour to South Africa. For Cambridge he had scored 828 runs in nine matches, including an unbeaten 187 against Sussex at Hove, and for Lancashire a sparkling 109 secured one of only two victories over the touring Australians, after which Bobby Simpson, the Australian manager, immediately echoed Majid's verdict. Crawley enhanced his reputation in South Africa, batting for over 10 hours in Port Elizabeth to make 286 against Eastern Province, the highest score by an England player on tour in almost 30 years. Topping the tour averages with 779 runs, he returned home to score an unbeaten career-best 281 against Somerset at Southport, but Test recognition was delayed until July by which time he had lost form. Crawley's liking for the leg-side was exploited by South Africa and he made only 59 runs in five innings with a best of 38 at Headingley, but another major innings,

250 against Nottinghamshire, ensured his tour place.

First-class career (1990–): 5,950 runs (49.58) and 1 wicket (108.00)

Test matches (6): 230 runs (23.00), and 5 catches

CRAWLEY, Leonard George

(b. 1903, Nacton, Suffolk; d. 1981, Worlington, Suffolk) *Cambridge University, Worcestershire, and Essex*

Both at Harrow and Cambridge University, Leonard George, the brother of Aidan, displayed his all-round games ability and, in his second season with Worcestershire (1923) was averaging 86.20 when his qualification to play for them was challenged by Lord Harris. Subsequently Crawley went to Essex. He was a powerful and elegant right-handed batsman with a particular penchant for fast bowling, shown especially in his 228 for Essex against Glamorgan at Swansea in 1928. In 1932, though appearing infrequently because he was a schoolmaster, his average was over fifty and he was approached about his availability to go to Australia. As headmaster of his own preparatory school, he would have given himself leave of absence but in the event he was not selected. Instead, he wrote a strong letter to *The Times*, after the controversial Test at Adelaide in January 1933, declaring 'that our shock bowlers bowl deliberately at the body cannot honestly be denied'. He was among the first to appreciate the implication of events in Australia under Jardine's captaincy. Although he played first-class cricket until 1936, Crawley's fame rests on his golf. He won the English championship in 1931 and was the only British player to score a point (by his singles' victory) in the Walker Cup in 1932. Twice, in 1938 and 1947, he was a victor in the Walker Cup foursomes. He chose golf when in 1946 he was offered the choice of being cricket or golf correspondent for *The Daily Telegraph*.

First-class career (1922–36): 5,227 runs (31.11) including 8 centuries, and 42 catches

CURTIS, Timothy Stephen

(b. 1960, Chislehurst, Kent) *Worcestershire, Cambridge University, and England*

Tim Curtis could not have chosen a tougher baptism in Test cricket. A diligent, upright, right-handed opener with a sound temperament and a flowing off-drive, he was picked to face rampant, high-class West Indian and Australian sides in successive summers, and after modest returns in

five Tests, was dropped. Nevertheless, in county cricket he continued to be a model of consistency his batting a feature of a successful Worcester-shire side. After a sound cricketing education at the Royal Grammar School, Worcester, where he later returned as a teacher, he led Durham University to the UAU Championship in 1981 alongside future county cricketers Simon Hughes, Robin Dyer, and Gordon Lord—later his opening partner at Worcestershire. From there, Curtis moved to Cambridge University where he spent a year as a postgraduate, gaining a blue for cricket in 1983. Making his début for Worcester-shire in 1979 whilst still at Durham, he was awarded his cap in 1984, and by 1987 he had established a reputation as a possible future England opener. That season he made 1,601 first-class runs, and was also the leading run-scorer in the Sunday League, which Worcestershire won. His chance arrived the following summer, the season England used twenty-seven players and named four captains. Playing in the fourth and fifth Tests of the series against the West Indies, he scored 69 runs in four innings, sharing two half-century stands with Graham Gooch, but was then dropped for the Lord's Test with Sri Lanka and overlooked for the scheduled winter tour to India. He was recalled for the third Test against Australia in 1989 and produced a fighting Test-best 41 to help save a rain-affected match. Subsequently however, he, like many other of the England batsmen, had his technique ruthlessly exposed by Geoff Lawson and Terry Alderman, and after 30 runs in his next four innings, he was once more dropped. Settling to a consistent county career, he scored 1,731 runs the following summer, captained Worcestershire from 1992–5, and in 1993 a century against Durham meant he had completed hundreds against all the other seventeen counties. The following season he led Worcestershire to victory in the NatWest Trophy, and the respect in which he was held by fellow professionals was reflected in his election as chairman of the Cricketers Association.

First-class career (1979–): 17,910 runs (41.55) and 11 wickets (65.64)

Test matches (5): 140 runs (15.55)

CUTTELL, Willis Robert

(b. 1864, Sheffield, Yorkshire; d. 1929, Nelson, Lancashire) *Yorkshire, Lancashire, and England*

Robert Cuttell was a first-rate all-rounder, a right-handed batsman who could defend strongly and hit hard, a slow bowler of good length who could turn the ball either way, and an excellent field. In 1898 he became the first Lancashire player ever to achieve the double. He toured South Africa in 1898/9 with Lord Hawke's team, where he had his Test match experience. His father played for Yorkshire but after two matches for them in 1890, Robert crossed the Pennines.

First-class career (1896–1906): 5,938 runs (21.83) including 5 centuries, and 791 wickets (19.47)
Test matches (2): 65 runs (16.25), 6 wickets (12.16), and 2 catches

DAFT, Richard

(b. 1835, Nottingham; d. 1900, Radcliffe on Trent, Nottinghamshire) *Nottinghamshire*

Had there been no W. G. Grace, the fame of Richard Daft would have been greater. He was second to the 'champion' in the national averages on four occasions. Although he played first-class cricket as late as 1891, his best years were in the era before Test matches began. He took a team to North America in 1879 but never visited Australia. *Wisden* agonized in its obituary notice as to who was the greatest batsman of Tom Hayward, Bob Carpenter, or Daft. He played as an amateur at the beginning and at the end of his career with Nottinghamshire and as a professional from 1859 to 1880: thus, he appeared for both the Gentlemen and the Players. Daft was a stylish right-handed batsman, 'a model of grace and execution'; a wristy player exceptionally effective against fast bowling on fiery wickets. His 118 for the North v. the South on a poisonous pitch at Lord's in 1862 was the talk of the summer while his highest score was 161 for Nottinghamshire against Yorkshire at Trent Bridge in 1873. His book, *Kings of Cricket* (1893) has a great deal to say about his contemporaries and the transition in English cricket from the travelling 'England' XIs to the established county championship. In 1891 Daft made his final appearance in first-class cricket, in Nottinghamshire's August Bank Holiday match against Surrey at The Oval, 'the veteran batting with much of his old style'. He played in the match with his son, Harry, who was in the Notts County side which won the FA Cup in 1904 and who earned three international caps.

First-class career (1858–91): 9,788 runs (25.42) including 7 centuries, 51 wickets (20.98), and 155 catches

DAVIES, Jack Gale Wilmot

(b. 1911, Broadclyst, Devon; d. 1992, Cambridge) *Cambridge University and Kent*

After 4 years in the Tonbridge XI, Jack Davies's career at Cambridge—quite apart from a First in Classics—had several unusual features. His withdrawal through injury from the side to play Oxford in 1931 allowed A. Ratcliffe to come in and break the record for the match. 24 hours later the Nawab of Pataudi eclipsed it. In 1934 Davies ran out the unknown Hutton for nought on Hutton's first-class début and a week later bowled the famous Bradman for nought. He was a stylish right-handed batsman who straightaway played for Kent. His best season was 1946 when his post at the War Office as Chief Psychologist in the selection of Personnel did not preclude his making 1,246 runs as an opener. As a right-arm off-break bowler he continued to take wickets in the post-war years. His last first-class match was for MCC against his old university in 1961 of which he had become secretary to the Appointments Board and treasurer of the Cricket Club. Davies's personal modesty meant that many were unaware that he had variously worked at the United Nations and been an executive director of the Bank of England. Nor, indeed, that he had played Rugby for Blackheath and Kent. Cricket benefited from his experience and intellect when late in life he served on the TCCB and became treasurer and then president of MCC. But to several generations of undergraduates, he was an unassuming elder statesman of Cambridge cricket, quietly awaiting his cup of tea at Fenner's after the players had had theirs.

First-class career (1931–61): 5,982 runs (23.92) including 4 centuries, 258 wickets (30.41), and 87 catches

DAWSON, Edward William

(b. 1904, Paddington, London; d. 1979, Idmiston, Wiltshire) *Cambridge University, Leicestershire, and England*

While still at Eton, where he made centuries against Harrow and Winchester in the same year, Eddie Dawson appeared for his county and, later, captained Cambridge. A very sound right-handed batsman—a visiting Australian said that he had never seen such a broad bat when he played forward—he was equally valuable in the field. County captain for four years, he was claimed by business after 1933. He toured South Africa in 1927/8, and Australasia in 1929/30, playing in the earliest Tests against New Zealand. His twin nephews, keen club cricketers, run a famous Prep school at Sunningdale.

First-class career (1922–34): 12,598 runs (27.09) including 14 centuries
Test matches (5): 175 runs (19.44)

DEAN, Harry

(b. 1884, Burnley, Lancashire; d. 1957, Garstang, Lancashire) *Cheshire, Lancashire, and England*

Suiting his methods to the conditions of pitch and play, Harry Dean would bowl either his left-arm, fast-medium with its deceptive swerve, or slow spinners. Eight times he took more than a hundred wickets in a season, and was generally at his best in the 'Roses' match. Against Yorkshire at Aigburth in 1913—a special match arranged to coincide with the visit to Liverpool of King George V—he captured 17 for 91. His only Test appearances were in the Triangular Tournament of 1912 and at The Oval against Australia in the first 'timeless' Test in England, where he took 4 for 19 and the visitors were skittled out for 65. He was also a League cricketer of note and played for Cheshire for two years after retiring from Lancashire in 1921.

First-class career (1906–21): 2,559 runs (10.31) and 1,301 wickets (18.14)
Test matches (3): 10 runs (5.00), 11 wickets (13.90), and 2 catches

DEFREITAS, Phillip Anthony Jason

(b. 1966, Scotts Head, Dominica, West Indies) *Leicestershire, Lancashire, Boland, Derbyshire, and England*

Phillip DeFreitas's outstanding form in 1994, when he scored 207 runs and took 30 wickets in six Tests, suggested the promise he had shown when he first arrived on the international scene in 1986 was finally being fulfilled. A lithe swing and seam bowler with a whippy action capable of lively pace, a hard-hitting, largely orthodox lower-order batsman, and a brilliant fielder, 20-year-old 'Daffy' made his Test début in Brisbane and announced himself by taking 5 wickets and scoring 40, giving rise to the view that England had a new all-rounder in the making. Until his efforts against New Zealand and South Africa eight years later however, DeFreitas had done little else to justify those early predictions, aside from offering another frustrating glimpse of his potential when he took 30 Test wickets in the summer of 1991, leading him to be named as one

of Wisden's Five Cricketers of the Year. Success came relatively quickly to DeFreitas, and his inability to handle it may have been one of the reasons for his initial failure to live up to the expectations. Born in Dominica before emigrating to England with his parents in 1975, DeFreitas played club cricket in London before joining the MCC ground staff, and he played for Middlesex's second team before opting to join Leicestershire. Making his début for the county in 1985, he only became a regular the following season, but by the end of it, he had claimed 94 wickets, scored 645 runs, including a maiden first-class century, 106 against Kent, and was named Britannic Assurance Player of the Season. Selection for the Ashes tour followed, but after his promising beginning, DeFreitas managed only four more wickets in three Tests before he was dropped, although he remained a key figure in the one-day side as Mike Gatting's side retained the Ashes and won both limited-overs competitions. DeFreitas regained his Test place in 1987, but then lost it again after one rain-affected Test, the start of a frustrating three-year period as he was dropped and recalled at regular intervals, unable to convince the selectors he was worth an extended run in the side. DeFreitas's disappointment spilled over into county cricket and he was dropped by Leicestershire for disciplinary reasons. DeFreitas continued to enhance his reputation as a one-day bowler, helping England reach the World Cup Final in 1987 and named man-of-the-match against the West Indies at Lord's the following summer after bowling five successive maidens, but he was dropped from the Test side in both 1988 and 1989, and frustrated, he opted to join the unofficial tour of South Africa set for 1989/90 before opting out following threats against him. By now he had moved to Lancashire, arriving at Old Trafford at the start of the 1989 season, but although he bowled impressively to take 5 for 53 against New Zealand in the first Test of 1990, he then suffered with injury, and not even 5 for 26 in the NatWest Final at Lord's could convince the selectors to take him to Australia that winter; he eventually joined the tour as a replacement, but his efforts were modest. DeFreitas finally delivered at Test level in 1991, his 30 wickets in six matches that summer including match figures of 8 for 93 at Headingley as England beat the West Indies at home for the first time in 22 years, and a Test-best 7 for 70 against Sri Lanka at Lord's, as well as a first Test 50 at Trent Bridge. DeFreitas went to New Zealand and the World Cup as England's premier bowler, but early in the tour he picked up a persistent groin injury which was to hamper him for almost 18 months. Playing in only two Tests in 1992, he was still picked for the tour of India and Sri Lanka, but, again restricted by injury, he went through the whole trip without taking a first-class wicket, and after being called in as a late replacement for the first Test against Australia the following summer, he was dropped once more and missed the winter tour to the Caribbean. DeFreitas wintered in South Africa playing for Boland and changed counties again, this time moving to Derbyshire. After a chat with the new chairman of selectors Raymond Illingworth at the start of the season, he achieved the first hat-trick of his career, against Hampshire, and returned for the first Test against New Zealand at Trent Bridge. Swinging the ball away, he took 9 for 165, including his 100th Test wicket in his 34th match, and also scored a quickfire 51, only the second half-century of his Test career. A Test-best 69 followed at Old Trafford and after 21 wickets in three matches, New Zealand captain Ken Rutherford said he had been the difference between the two sides. Nine more wickets in three Tests against South Africa and an aggressive 37 in 31 balls at The Oval which helped tip the final match England's way made DeFreitas a certainty for the tour of Australia, and he ended the summer by claiming his 100th one-day international wicket.

First-class career (1985–): 5,826 runs (22.32) and 687 wickets (27.89)

Test matches (43): 910 runs (14.91), 138 wickets (32.33), and 14 catches

DEMPSEY, Sir Miles Christopher

(b. 1896, New Brighton, Cheshire; d. 1969, Yattendon, Berkshire) *Sussex*

General Dempsey commanded the Second Army in the Invasion of Normandy (1944) and the Fourteenth Army in the Far East (1945–6). He had captained the XI at Shrewsbury in 1914 as a right-handed batsman and slow left-arm bowler. After the First World War he made two appearances for Sussex and several for Berkshire and for the Staff College.

First-class career (1919): 5 runs (1.66) and 1 catch

DENISON, William

(b. 1801, London; d. 1856, Lee, Kent)

'Stickem-up' Denison was a good enough player to be chosen by William Clarke for his All-England XI and he appears in Felix's painting of the side in 1847, a diminutive figure next to Alfred Mynn. He was the first cricket reporter and the first to publish regular statistics. In 1827 he had opposed the prospect of round-arm bowling in *Sporting Magazine*, calling it 'throwing, pure and simple'. Its advocates called it the 'liberal' method or the 'intellect system'. His *Cricketer's Companion* covered the seasons 1843–6, with some matches not in Haygarth's *Scores and Biographies*. *Sketches of the Players (1846)* included pen-pictures of his contemporaries. Denison was also secretary of Surrey and something of an eccentric, wearing a wig long after such head-dress was no longer fashionable.

DENNESS, Michael Henry

(b. 1940, Bellshill, Lanarkshire) *Scotland, Kent, Essex, and England*

Mike Denness was unfortunate to become England captain in an age when the conduct of the man in the hot seat is open to almost as much scrutiny from press and public as that of the prime minister. An outwardly tough but inwardly sensitive Scotsman with no flair for handling the demands of the press and not a natural 'man manager', he nevertheless captained Kent with outstanding success, notably in one-day cricket, and was a generally sound, orthodox, and enthusiastic captain on the field who set a shining example with his athletic fielding in the covers. His batting limitations, like those of all his colleagues, were exposed by the exceptional pace and fury of Lillee and Thomson in Australia in 1974/5 but he was a player of high quality with a beautiful array of off-side strokes off front foot and back. A crowd-pleaser, his batting exuded confidence, style, and his own uninhibited delight in hitting a cricket ball hard to the boundary. He was an outstanding schoolboy player at Ayr Academy and made his début for Scotland in 1959, playing his first game for Kent in 1962 and winning his cap in his third season. For much of his career at Kent he formed a successful opening partnership with Brian Luckhurst, although he batted most often at number four in his twenty-eight Tests for England, in nineteen of which he was captain. He often played skilfully against the Indian spinners when vice-captain on his first tour of India, Pakistan, and Sri Lanka in 1972/3 but his form was mercurial in the two tours in which he captained England in the next two winters. He presided over some remarkable recoveries in the Caribbean which enabled England to draw a series against a much stronger

West Indies side, but dropped himself at Sydney in the fourth Test in which Australia regained the Ashes in 1975. Yet in the last match of the rubber he made a brilliant 188 at Melbourne and on the tour overall averaged 54. He made 1,000 runs in a season fourteen times in England and once abroad. Under his captaincy Kent won the John Player League three times, the Benson and Hedges Cup twice and the Gillette Cup once. He moved to Essex in 1977, and played a significant role in their winning of two competitions in 1979. He has worked in insurance, finance, public relations, and as a manager for World Series Cricket teams, and from 1981 to 1984 was coach of the Essex 2nd XI, becoming an honorary cricketing life member of MCC.

First-class career (1959–80): 25,886 runs (33.48) including 33 centuries, and 411 catches
Test matches (28): 1,667 runs (39.69) including 4 centuries, and 28 catches

DENTON, David

(b. 1874, Wakefield, Yorkshire; d. 1950, Wakefield) *Yorkshire and England*

'Lucky' Denton was so audacious in his right-handed batting that many people said that he was 'playing at Scarborough all the time' and taking too many risks, yet his aggregate of runs for Yorkshire alone (33,608) remained the highest until surpassed by Herbert Sutcliffe. Lightly built, of medium height, and possessing very flexible wrists, Denton was a stroke-maker of considerable power all round the wicket. On fast wickets he would cut brilliantly and, when the ground was slow, he employed the pull and the hook very effectively. In the field, especially in the deep and at third man, none of his contemporaries could chase the ball at greater speed, or return it more quickly and accurately. He played only once for England at home, against Australia at Headingley in 1905, J. T. Tyldesley generally being preferred to him. His other Test experience was with MCC in South Africa, 1905/6 and 1909/10, and on the latter occasion, at Johannesburg, he hit 104 in 100 minutes, his sole Test century. He exceeded 1,000 runs in a season 21 times and 2,000 five times. He was an occasional medium-fast bowler. On retirement he became a first-class umpire (1925–36).

First-class career (1894–1920): 36,440 runs (33.40) including 69 centuries, 34 wickets (27.58), 396 catches, and 1 stumping
Test matches (11): 424 runs (20.19) including 1 century, and 8 catches

DEWES, John Gordon

(b. 1926, North Latchford, Cheshire) *Cambridge University, Middlesex, and England*

A sound left-handed batsman and fine outfield, John Dewes scored 1,000 runs in May 1945, for Cambridge University (all in minor matches) and played for England in the Lord's 'Victory Test' that year. One of the powerful Cambridge side after the war, he shared an unbeaten second-wicket partnership of 429 with Hubert Doggart against Essex at Fenner's in 1949, at that time an English record, and the following year made his highest score, 212 against Sussex at Hove, adding 349 for the first wicket with David Sheppard. In 1950 he scored 2,432 runs (59.31), including nine centuries. Though he also scored quite heavily for Middlesex, he proved a class below Test cricket. On his début against Australia at The Oval in 1948, he opened with Len Hutton when England were routed for 52. He appeared against the West Indies in 1950 and toured Australia in 1950/1, but he was disappointing and his career faded. Also a hockey blue, he was an assistant master at Tonbridge before becoming a headmaster in Australia.

First-class career (1945–57): 8,564 runs (41.78) including 18 centuries
Test matches (5): 121 runs (12.10)

DEXTER, Edward Ralph

(b. 1935, Milan, Italy) *Cambridge University, Sussex, and England*

A T. E. Lawrence of the cricket field, Ted Dexter is an adventurer who will try anything once. The sixth Cambridge blue to captain Sussex after the Second World War, he was known as Lord Edward, as befits his naturally aristocratic air, but he was more shy than arrogant. A gifted all-round sportsman, born in Milan, he was one of the few 'box-office' draws in the 1960s, but retired while still in his prime to pursue an extraordinary variety of interests and careers, including flying private planes, riding motorbikes, playing brilliant amateur golf in high company, writing, broadcasting, modelling clothes, running a PR company, and owning first horses and then greyhounds. In 1989 he became the first chairman of the England Committee, a challenge taken on with enthusiasm and a quiverful of new ideas—'all my life has prepared me for this job'—only to leave it in disillusion and failure in 1993, let down, he felt, by a cynical press and a mercurial England team. In between heavy home defeats by Australia in his first and last year in the job, which involved strategic planning as well as team selection, there were also high points, notably the best record against the West Indies of any England teams since his own era as a player. England were unfortunate to lose 2–1 in the West Indies in 1989/90 and, still under the captaincy of Graham Gooch, held them to a 2–2 drawn series in England in 1991. A handsome figure, he was a right-handed batsman who often demonstrated that the best answer to great bowling is attack, although he seldom did so recklessly and his defence was firm and clean. In the right mood he could destroy any attack by orthodox assault, driving with immense power off front and back foot. He was always at his best when challenged by outstanding bowling or a race against time. As a medium-pace bowler, though handicapped by injury, he was an effective partnership-breaker. In his last stride he was reminiscent of Keith Miller, the ball unleashed in a final orgy of muscular activity after a brief, languid approach. Although apt to practise golf shots in the outfield he was a fine cover-point and an athletic fielder anywhere. His air of apparent disdain and aloofness and a tendency to over-theorize limited his success as a captain, but his players and his opponents always respected him. In a few short years he captained England against Australia, India, New Zealand, Pakistan, and the West Indies. In a Test career ranging from 1958 until 1968 it was sad that such a great attacking player should frequently have been forced to try to save matches rather than to win them. He came to the fore in the West Indies in 1959/60, heading the Test averages and making two centuries. His outstanding big innings were 180 at Edgbaston in 1961, and the even more remarkable 174 in 8 hours at Old Trafford in 1964, both of which saved England against Australia. More characteristic were his brilliant, indeed breathtaking, innings of 76 against Australia at Old Trafford in 1961, and his daring 70 against the West Indies at Lord's in 1963. Against Pakistan he shared in the record partnerships for the second and fourth wickets, the former being 248 with Colin Cowdrey at The Oval, 1962, and the latter 188 with Peter Parfitt at Karachi in 1961/2, when Dexter scored 205 which was to remain his highest in first-class cricket. Curiously, he first made his mark as a bowler in a representative match, for Gentlemen v. Players at Lord's in 1957, when he took 5 for 8 and 3 for 47. At Headingley, 1962, he secured 4 for 10 against Pakistan. Captain of Sussex from 1960 until 1965, he made 1,000 runs or more in a season ten times

(twice overseas). There were times when his heart was not in the game and he would give his wicket away. Although a brief sortie into politics turned out to be a failure—when he stood as a candidate in Cardiff against the future Prime Minister, James Callaghan—there are few things that he would not do better than most. He twice won the President's Putter at Rye. He lacked only the persistence to see every challenge through, but a gifted dilettante, was a hero too, and a misunderstood one, who in his role as England's cricket chairman was unfairly pilloried when light-hearted asides at press conferences were used to mock him.

First-class career (1956–70): 21,150 runs (40.75) including 51 centuries, 419 wickets (29.92), and 233 catches
Test matches (62): 4,502 runs (47.89) including 9 centuries, 66 wickets (34.93), and 29 catches

DICKENS, Charles

(b. 1812, Portsea, Hampshire; d. 1870, Gadshill, Kent)

The match between Dingley Dell and All-Muggleton, watched by Mr Pickwick, is the best-known example of the cricketing passages in Charles Dickens's novels. The game, he wrote, brought 'a thousand joys within the reach of those who would find existence a very humdrum and monotonous affair'. In an oil-painting of his home at Gadshill in Kent, he is shown bowling the first ball in a charity match and in another one, acting as scorer, which he did frequently. Curiously, the first English tour of Australia, in 1861/2, only came about because Dickens had refused an offer of a sponsored lecture tour from the sponsors, Spiers and Pond, so they turned to cricket instead.

DILLEY, Graham Roy

(b. 1959, Dartford, Kent) *Kent, Worcestershire, Natal, and England*

A 6 ft. 3 in., blond-haired, right-arm fast bowler from Dartford, Graham Dilley emerged in the late 1970s as the first in a new crop of English fast bowlers after a lean period. A very determined competitor, with a dangerous out-swinger, he could be very fast despite a rather rough action with a very long final stride and an open chest. A good fielder anywhere and an effective hard-hitting left-hand batsman, many English hopes for the 1980s rested on him. Making his first appearance for Kent in 1977, he was still uncapped by his county when picked to tour

Australia in 1979/80, when he became, at 20 years and 210 days, the youngest to play for England for 30 years. The tyro fast bowler took 11 wickets (16.63) against the mighty West Indies in three Tests in 1980, spearheading England's attack with encouraging hostility. The following winter he played in all four Tests in the Caribbean, taking only ten wickets (45.00), but again bowling some aggressive spells. He collected another 14 wickets in the first three matches against the 1981 Australians and he also batted belligerently. His 56 in the second innings at Headingley was the catalyst for Botham's series-turning 149 not out. After this match, Dilley lost fitness and form, and he performed only moderately on the tour to India and Sri Lanka in 1981/2. He spent two difficult seasons in county cricket, but seemed to have recovered his lost pace and rhythm, when he took five wickets on a featherbed wicket in the Faisalabad Test against Pakistan in 1983/4. But soon afterwards he was forced to return home with a serious injury requiring an operation in which bone was removed from his hip to his neck. He made his come-back in 1985, taking a hat-trick against Surrey at The Oval and after a successful season in South Africa, for Natal, he returned to the England team in 1986, taking 19 wickets in four Tests against India and New Zealand and establishing himself as England's main fast bowler. The following winter in Australia he played a major part in the retention of the Ashes with 16 wickets at 31. He played for Worcestershire from 1987 to 1992 after disagreeing with Kent's decision to dismiss his brother-in-law, Graham Johnson. He had another good home series against West Indies in 1988, taking 5 for 55 at Lord's when he swung the ball dangerously, but after two ineffective Tests against Australia in 1989, and worried by constant knee injuries, he went on the controversial tour to South Africa and was duly banned from Test cricket on his return. Unable to bowl for much of his later time at Worcester, he reappeared on the county scene in 1994 as coach to Surrey.

First-class career (1977–92): 2,339 runs (14.71), 648 wickets (26.84), and 75 catches

Test matches (41): 521 runs (13.35), 138 wickets (29.76), and 10 catches

DIPPER, Alfred Ernest

(b. 1885, Apperley, Gloucestershire; d. 1945, London) *Gloucestershire and England*

Alfred Dipper came into his county's XI by chance, as a last-minute substitute against Kent at Tonbridge in 1908. He was straight from village cricket but stemmed a disastrous collapse, and for 24 years remained a pillar, especially at number one, with his watchful right-handed batting. Of three double-centuries, his highest was 252 not out against Glamorgan at Cheltenham in 1923. Having to bolster a weak batting side, he tended to become rigidly defensive, until the advent of Walter Hammond encouraged him to deploy more strokes. Five times he exceeded 2,000 runs in a season and ten other times scored over 1,000 runs, but he was a poor fielder. 'There goes my whippet', would comment the laconic Charlie Parker as Alfred trotted after his ball at mid-on. He was a useful change-bowler. His sole Test was against Australia at Lord's in 1921, when he scored 11 and 40. On retirement he stood as an umpire for some years.

First-class career (1908–32): 28,075 runs (35.27) including 53 centuries, 161 wickets (30.45), and 210 catches

DOGGART, George Hubert Graham

(b. 1925, Earls Court, London) *Cambridge University, Sussex, and England*

A stylish and forcing right-handed batsman, useful right-arm off-break bowler, and a fine slip fielder, Hubert Doggart made a sensational début for Cambridge when he scored 215 not out against Lancashire in 1948. The following year his unbroken second-wicket stand of 429 with J. G. Dewes against Essex became an English record, and at the same time he made the highest score of his career, 219 not out. In all first-class matches that season he scored 2,063 runs at an average of 45.00, including a record 1,280 runs for Cambridge University. In 1950, while captain of Cambridge, he played in the first two Tests against the West Indies. He captained Sussex in 1954, but teaching at Winchester later curtailed his appearances. An erudite extrovert, he became headmaster of King's School, Bruton. Both his father, A. G., and his son, S. J. G., were Cambridge blues. Hubert himself also won a soccer blue as well as representing Cambridge at squash, rugby, fives, and rackets. A most generous giver of his private time to any cricketing cause, he served as both president (1981/2) and treasurer of MCC, and as president of the Cricket Society, the English Schools Cricket Association—a post he had held for 30 years by 1995—and the Friends of Arundel Cricket Club. He compiled a worthy book, *The Heart of Cricket*, in memory of his mentor, H. S. Altham. He was an indefatigable speaker at cricket dinners and meetings, always apposite, witty, and, with his commanding voice and slow delivery, audible to all.

First-class career (1948–61): 10,054 runs (31.51) including 20 centuries, 60 wickets (34.28), and 197 catches

Test matches (2): 76 runs (19.00) and 3 catches

D'OLIVEIRA, Basil Lewis

(b. 1931, Signal Hill, Cape Town, South Africa)
Worcestershire and England

An immensely talented and popular cricketer, Basil d'Oliveira moved from poverty in Cape Town to prosperity in Worcestershire with unwavering dignity. Few sportsmen in the public eye have given a better example of how to react to success, failure, and the problem of being a controversial figure. Debarred, despite his ability, from playing cricket against the best in South Africa because of being a 'Cape Coloured', he nevertheless performed with such dazzling success in minor cricket on very poor grounds and matting wickets that word reached England via John Arlott and Peter Walker and he was offered £450 in 1960 to play for the Central Lancashire League Club, Middleton. Two hundred pounds were needed for the air-fare and the sum was partially raised by raffles, fêtes, and matches held in the region of his tenement home, but for 'Dolly', as he affectionately became known, it was a wise investment. Already 25 years old, he had to leave his wife and first child behind in South Africa for his first season. It took him some time to adapt to English conditions but by the end of the season he was ahead of Garfield Sobers at the top of the league averages. He played with great success for Middleton for four years, made his first-class début in Rhodesia on a Commonwealth XI tour in 1961/2 and on a later Commonwealth tour Tom Graveney persuaded him that he could make the grade in county cricket. He spent 1964 qualifying for Worcestershire, making a century against the Australians, and in 1965, at the age of 33, he hit five Championship hundreds. He also took 35 wickets and some brilliant slip catches. In 1966 he played his first Test for England at Lord's, making an accomplished 27 before being unluckily run out.

With a beautifully relaxed, sideways-on stance and a very short backlift, his powerful forearms nevertheless gave him command of all the strokes and after a steady, watchful start to an innings he would accelerate to score freely and attractively. His bowling, again with a classic sideways-on action, was steady, medium pace with swing either way and disconcerting wobble. He was more or less a regular England all-rounder until 1972, making three major overseas tours, playing many crucial innings and always taking useful wickets. But in 1968 he was the innocent cause of an international incident when, picked to replace Tom Cartwright for the MCC tour of South Africa after he had been controversially omitted in the first place, he was refused entry and the tour was cancelled. Long after losing his place in the England team to Tony Greig he continued to display his class for Worcestershire, whose full-time coach he became when finally forced to stop regular county cricket because of age and injury at the end of 1979. Even in later years he was capable of anything when the mood was right, once almost winning a Benson and Hedges Cup Final at Lord's single-handed, despite a severe leg injury, and on another occasion keeping Yorkshire in the field for more than a day while compiling 227 (at Hull in 1974) purely because a Yorkshire bowler had annoyed him with a reference to his colour. He was awarded the OBE in 1969 for his services to cricket and his benefit in 1975 was worth £27,000. He was county coach from 1980 to 1991, a period of continued success for Worcestershire. He had the pleasure of seeing his son, Damian, establish himself in the side. On days of success, few people celebrated harder than 'Dolly'.

First-class career (1961–80): 18,919 runs (39.57) including 43 centuries, 548 wickets (27.41), and 211 catches

Test matches (44): 2,484 runs (40.06) including 5 centuries, 47 wickets (39.55), and 29 catches

DOLLERY, Horace Edgar

(b. 1914, Reading, Berkshire; d. 1987, Edgbaston, Birmingham) *Berkshire, Warwickshire, and England*

Known as 'the schoolboy wonder' at Reading School, 'Tom' Dollery was playing for Berkshire at 15 and Warwickshire at 20. For many years the best and most consistent right-handed batsman in the county with a wide range of strokes, he was forceful in approach and eminently dependable; at number five he was prepared equally to push home the advantage already gained or to retrieve the disaster of a sudden collapse, and he was a fine slip field and useful deputy wicket-keeper. Fifteen times he exceeded 1,000 runs in a season. Always greatly respected, he extracted the best that each man had to give when he became the first-ever professional captain of Warwickshire (a post he held from 1949 to 1955) and was an outstanding success. In 1951 he led the county to her first Championship title for 40 years. He was selected for England, however, in only a handful of Tests against South Africa, Australia and the West Indies between 1947 and 1950. On retirement he served as county coach.

First-class career (1933–55): 24,413 runs (37.50) including 50 centuries, 291 catches, and 13 stumpings

Test matches (4): 72 runs (10.28) and 1 catch

DOLPHIN, Arthur

(b. 1885, Wilsden, Yorkshire; d. 1942, Bradford, Yorkshire) *Yorkshire and England*

Contemporary with Herbert Strudwick, E. J. 'Tiger' Smith, and George Brown, Arthur Dolphin played only once for England, against Australia at Melbourne, 1920/1, when he scored 1 and 0 and held one catch, but he was an outstanding wicket-keeper in a great tradition of Yorkshire 'keepers, and a member of eight Championship-winning sides. His playing days over, he became an efficient and popular umpire who never wore a hat, even on the hottest days. Between 1933 and 1937 he stood in six Tests.

First-class career (1905–27): 3,402 runs (11.30) and 882 dismissals (609 c., 273 st.)

DOUGLAS, John William Henry Tyler

(b. 1882, Clapton, London; d. 1930 at sea, Denmark) *Essex and England*

Nearly 6 ft. tall, strongly built, with dark hair parted down the middle, piercing blue eyes, and a square jaw, Johnny Douglas was, mentally and physically, as tough as he looked. 'Johnny Won't Hit Today'—the initials were so converted in Australia—became an axiom. A born fighter, he became a dour right-handed batsman, blocking with obstinacy and only occasionally revealing his hitting powers; and the more he was barracked the more dour became his defence. With his rather cramped style and limited number of strokes, he was never an attractive player, though very effective. As a fastish bowler he worked untiringly, regularly rubbing the new ball vigorously against his left arm during the first overs

with it. He could bowl for hours without losing either speed or length and, with a new ball, he imparted an awkward swerve both ways. Always extremely fit, 'J.W.H.T.' was a rare fighter and had to be; England under his captaincy lost the first seven Tests off the reel against Australia after the First World War. Before 1914, however, he had led England in the regaining of the Ashes in Australia in 1911/12, standing in for P. F. Warner, who was ill, and he was also the victorious captain against South Africa in 1913/14. He captained Essex from 1911 to 1928, scoring 1,000 runs in a season ten times and 100 wickets in seven seasons (five doubles). A notable boxer, he won the Olympic Middleweight Championship in 1908, and also represented England in amateur Association Football. He was drowned at sea while trying to save his father, after their ship had collided with another in fog, seven miles south of the Laeso Trindel lightship.

First-class career (1901–30): 24,531 runs (27.90) including 26 centuries, 1,893 wickets (23.32), and 364 catches

Test matches (23): 962 runs (29.15) including 1 century, 45 wickets (33.02), and 9 catches

DOWNTON, Paul Rupert

(b. 1957, Farnborough, Kent) *Kent, Middlesex, and England*

The son of a noted club cricketer who played briefly for Kent, Paul Downton was an acrobatic wicket-keeper and a useful and determined right hand batsman whose career was ended prematurely after a bail had flown into his left eye in a match in 1990 and impaired his vision. Courteous and genuine by nature in an increasingly competitive cricket world, he was much missed. Educated at Sevenoaks School and Exeter University, he toured the West Indies with the England Young Cricketers in 1976 and played for Kent the following year, winning a cap in 1979. The return of Alan Knott, however, persuaded him to move to Middlesex. Already he had so impressed J. T. Murray, then an England selector, that he was chosen to tour Pakistan and New Zealand as deputy to Bob Taylor in 1977/8, and after playing a major role in his first season with Middlesex in 1980, he toured the West Indies the following winter, winning his first Test cap in Trinidad and playing two more games in the series. His 26 not out in the final Test in Jamaica helped England to save the game. In the first Test against Australia at Trent Bridge in 1981, however, he dropped a very easy catch which proved decisive in a low-scoring game. It cost him his place. But when Bob Taylor retired from Test cricket he was recalled to face the West Indies in 1984. In the first Test at Edgbaston, following Andy Lloyd's injury, he opened the batting in the second innings, and courageously responded with his first Test fifty. In fact, he resisted the West Indies pace attack for over 16 hours in the series. He had a good series in India with the bat, scoring 74 at Delhi, and kept tidily to the England spinners. He made his maiden first-class century for Middlesex in 1985 and it was his ability with the bat which made him England's first-choice wicket-keeper for 22 Tests in a row between 1984 and 1986. He took 19 catches and one stumping in the 1985 series against Australia. He had a difficult tour of the West Indies in 1986, scoring just 91 in the five Tests, and he contrived to mar capable wicket-keeping performances by missing the occasional vital chance. He nevertheless returned to the England team for the 1986/7 World Cup, helping his country into the final in Calcutta despite sustaining a black eye when he was struck by an errant ball during practice. He lost his Test place in 1988 but continued to give loyal and effective service to Middlesex until his accident in 1990 obliged him to retire half-way through the following season. He began a second career in the City, but retained links with cricket through broadcasting.

First-class career (1977–91): 8,270 runs (25.13) including 6 centuries, and 779 dismissals (690 c., 89 st.)

Test matches (30): 785 runs (19.62) and 75 dismissals (70 c., 5 st.)

DRUCE, Norman Frank

(b. 1875, London; d. 1954, Milford-on-Sea, Hampshire) *Cambridge University, Surrey, and England*

A right-handed batsman, Frank Druce captained Cambridge in 1897, averaging 66, an exceptional figure in those days. *Wisden* commented: 'He plays his own game without any rigid over-adherence to rule, scoring on the on-side from straight balls in a fashion only possible to a batsman with a genius for timing.' He toured Australia in 1897/8 with A. E. Stoddart's team and fared reasonably well in the Tests, but he retired from regular cricket after the tour, occasionally reappearing, with success, in such matches as the Free Foresters versus the Universities. He made 227 not out for Cambridge against C. I. Thornton's XI in 1897, and also

toured N. America in 1895. His elder brother, W. G., captained Cambridge two years before him, and also got a Rugger blue. Both were educated at Marlborough, as was their cousin, E. A. C., who won cricket and hockey blues.

First-class career (1894–1913): 3,416 runs (35.21) including 9 centuries

Test matches (5): 252 runs (28.00) and 5 catches

DUCAT, Andrew

(b. 1886, Brixton, London; d. 1942, St John's Wood, London) *Surrey and England*

With his glistening, dark hair firmly parted and seemingly never out of place, Andy Ducat was a dapper and attractive right-handed, fast-scoring batsman, who used his height (5 ft. 10 in.) well. An all-round stroke-maker, he was an occasional bowler and a fast-moving field. All his centuries were scored for Surrey, and when he received a telegram inviting him to play for England against Australia at Headingley in 1921, he thought it was a leg-pull and asked his Surrey colleagues which of them had done it. The invitation was genuine, but in this, his sole Test, he scored but 3 and 2, holding one catch. A double international, he appeared six times for England at football as a half-back, and he led Aston Villa to victory in the 1920 Cup Final. Cricket coach at Eton for several years, he died at Lord's while batting in a match between Home Guard units.

First-class career (1906–31): 23,373 runs (38.31) including 52 centuries, 21 wickets (43.00), and 206 catches

DUCKWORTH, George

(b. 1901, Warrington, Lancashire; d. 1966, Warrington) *Lancashire, Cheshire, and England*

It was said that there was only one greater appealer than George Duckworth and that was Dr Barnardo. Built like a miniature and very mobile tank, he was indeed a very demonstrative and vocal 'keeper, his right hand going affirmatively on high, but he was likened to the quieter Herbert Strudwick for swiftness of execution. At his best for his county between 1926 and 1930, when Lancashire won the Championship four times, he took some remarkable leg-side catches standing back to Ted McDonald. He toured Australia with MCC in 1928/9, 1932/3 and 1936/7—as second-string to Leslie Ames on the two latter tours—and South Africa in 1930/1. He was a very shrewd Lancastrian, always highly regarded for his cricket sense. He later became county scorer, a BBC commentator and a popular baggage-master for touring teams.

First-class career (1923–47): 4,945 runs (14.58) and 1,096 dismissals (753 c., 343 st.)

Test matches (24): 234 runs (14.62) and 60 dismissals (45 c., 15 st.)

DUGGAN, Mary Beatrice

(b. 1925, Worcester; d. 1973, Colwall, Worcestershire) *Yorkshire, Middlesex, and England*

Believed by many observers to be the best bowler England has produced, Mary Duggan started her career as a left-arm medium-fast opener. By the time she took over the England captaincy from Molly Hide in 1957/8, she was an orthodox spinner. Duggan took 77 wickets in an international career that lasted 11 years and remains the leading wicket-taker in Test cricket. She took five or more wickets in an innings on five occasions with best bowling figures of 7 for 6 from 14.5 overs in the second Test against Australia in Melbourne in February 1958. In a remarkable match at a damp St Kilda ground, Australia recorded their lowest total in an innings, 38, thanks to Duggan, and then England did likewise with 35, Betty Wilson taking 7 for 7 including a first Test hat-trick. The Oval was a particularly happy hunting ground for Duggan. In 1951 she made front page news in taking match figures of 9 for 104 as England beat Australia and in 1963 ended her international career in a blaze of glory by winning back the mythical Ashes with a challenging declaration after scoring a century in England's first innings herself. Described by Netta Rheinberg in *Fair Play* as: 'Big in build, big in heart, kind, generous and gentle,' Duggan developed into a very fine all-rounder. A positive right-handed middle-order bat, her first century, against New Zealand on her début tour as captain, came up in a rapid 135 minutes. In 1962, she and Ruth Prideaux (née Westbrook and coach of the 1993 World Cup-winning side) became the first women to be awarded the MCC Advanced Coaching certificate. She was much sought after as an outstanding teacher, lecturer, and coach. Duggan was president of the Women's Cricket Association when illness forced her to stand down just prior to the 1973 World Cup, which England won.

Test matches (17): 662 runs (24.51) including 2 centuries, and 77 wickets (13.49)

DULEEPSINHJI, Kumar Shri

(b. 1905, Sarodar, India; d. 1959, Bombay, India) *Cambridge University, Sussex, and England*

Born to the purple, Duleep was nephew of the great Ranji; cricket was in his blood, bones, and sinewy wrists. An elegant and artistic right-handed batsman, lithe and quick on his feet, with the ability to sight the ball a fraction earlier than most other players, he combined a basically sound defence with a fascinating variety of stroke-play, rivalling his uncle in many ways. An occasional leg-break bowler, he was panther-like at slip. He owed much to the prince of coaches G. A. Faulkner. Had his cricketing life not been harassed and cut short by ill-health, he might have risen to even greater heights. He captained Sussex in 1931/2. A Cambridge blue, he averaged some 2,000 runs a season for Sussex for several seasons, and was not afraid to go for the bowling. He hit 333 in a day at Hove, against Northamptonshire in 1930; but his greatest innings was at Lord's that year against Australia when he made 173 comfortably off the deadliest of Australia's bowlers. When caught off a big hit, Ranji gnawing his umbrella handle in the pavilion muttered: 'The boy was always careless!' Duleep captained Sussex for two seasons before his health failed, and he toured Australasia with MCC's team in 1929/30, playing in the earliest Tests against New Zealand. He had appeared against South Africa in the first Test of 1929, but this was one of his few failures at representative level. In 1950 Duleep was appointed High Commissioner for India in Australia and, three years later, returned to India to take high office in the State of Saurashtra. He also won a rackets blue.

First-class career (1924–32): 15,485 runs (49.95) including 50 centuries, 28 wickets (48.03), and 243 catches

Test matches (12): 995 runs (58.52) including 3 centuries, 0–7, and 10 catches

DURSTON, Frederick John

(b. 1893, Clophill, Bedfordshire; d. 1965, Norwood Green, Middlesex) *Middlesex and England*

A ground-staff boy at Lord's in 1914, Jack Durston blossomed slowly as a right-arm fast bowler when peace returned. Six foot five inches tall and powerfully built, he commanded greater control of length as his career progressed and, with speedy break-back, took many wickets on hard pitches at Lord's and elsewhere. He was a major influence in Middlesex's Championship victories of 1920 and 1921 and, in the latter year, having taken 11 wickets for the county against the Australians at Lord's, he played in the second Test there, scoring 6 not out and 2, and taking 5 for 136; this was his sole Test. Towards the end of his career, he put on a lot of weight, turning the scale at nearly 20 stone, and he changed from fast to off-break bowling. He took 100 wickets in a season six times and also kept goal for Brentford.

First-class career (1919–33): 3,918 runs (11.91), 1,329 wickets (22.03), and 257 catches

EAGAR, Patrick

(b. 1944, Cheltenham, Gloucestershire)

Patrick Eagar, whose father E. D. R. Eagar (1917–77) captained Hampshire (1946–57) and was a much-respected county secretary until his death, began his brilliant photographic career immediately after leaving Cambridge in 1965. He has photographed every day of every Test match in England since 1972 and has over a quarter of a million images. His ten books include *An Eye for Cricket* (1979) with John Arlott. He has twice won Sports Photographer of the Year awards for cricket portfolios. A disciple of John Arlott, he also has a renowned portfolio of photographs of vineyards, chateaux, and bottles.

ECKERSLEY, Peter Thorp

(b. 1904, Newton-le-Willows, Lancashire; d. 1940, Eastleigh, Hampshire) *Lancashire*

A century against Gloucestershire at Bristol in 1927, top scores in both innings against the 1930 Australians at Liverpool, a courageous 40 at Trent Bridge against Nottinghamshire in 1934 with Larwood and Voce bowling very fast, and an appearance for an England XI v. the 1938 Australians at Blackpool were personal landmarks in Peter Eckersley's career. A lively personality, he captained Lancashire from 1929 to 1935, winning the Championship in 1934—an amateur in a side of professionals, leading by personality and example in the field and making modest late-order contributions as a right-handed batsman. In his last full season he made cricket history by chartering a plane to fly Lancashire from Swansea to Southampton. He resigned the captaincy (1935) on being elected Member of Parliament for Manchester Exchange, a seat he retained until his death while serving with the Fleet Air Arm in the Second World War.

First-class career (1923–38): 5,629 runs (19.54) including 1 century, 7 wickets (49.71), and 141 catches

EDINBURGH, HRH The Duke of

(b. 1921, Corfu, Greece)

Prince Philip, Duke of Edinburgh, was captain of cricket at Gordonstoun as a right-handed batsman and right-arm off-spin bowler. He has retained a close association with the game so far as royal duties permit. As 'Twelfth Man' for the Lord's Taverners, he helped their fund-raising for the National Playing Fields Association by captaining, for some years, a side against one led by the Duke of Norfolk. He was twice (1949, 1974) president of MCC and served on the committee (1950–3).

EDMONDS, Philippe Henri

(b. 1951, Lusaka, Northern Rhodesia) *Cambridge University, Middlesex, Eastern Province, and England*

A tall, strongly built, gifted cricketer, Phil Edmonds was an orthodox slow left-arm spinner with a high, classical action, a hard-hitting, right handed batsman, and a brilliant all-round fielder. He was born of an English father and Belgian mother and brought up in Zambia (then Northern Rhodesia) before finishing his schooling at Cranbrook and proceeding to a Cambridge blue as a freshman. He captained Cambridge in 1973, and after success for Middlesex was picked for England against Australia at Headingley in 1975. In the match, which was ended when vandals poured oil on the pitch under cover of darkness on the fourth evening, Edmonds took 5 for 17 in his first 12 overs in Test cricket. He finished with 5 for 28 but took only one more Test wicket in three innings later in the series. It was not until Derek Underwood (who had bowled in harness with Edmonds in his first Test) decided to join World Series Cricket that Edmonds gained a regular place as England's left-arm spinner, but Underwood superseded him again for the tour of Australia in 1979/80. Against Pakistan and New Zealand, both away and at home in 1977/8, Edmonds had developed into an exceptionally accurate bowler who would turn the ball given the slightest help from any pitch. He took 7 for 66 against Pakistan at Karachi in the third Test, 1977/8. After the 1978 series against Pakistan and New Zealand, when he had again bowled superbly, he had an outstanding Test record, having taken 43 wickets at an average of 20.95 in 13 matches, and he looked set to become one of England's greatest slow left-arm bowlers. But his Test career suddenly ground to a halt. He surprisingly lost his place on the 1978/9 tour of Australia partly because of a personality clash with the then Middlesex and England captain, Mike Brearley, and before his selection for the 1984/5 tour of India he had played just five Tests since 1979, seemingly an awful waste of his enormous talent—he took over 70 first-class wickets every season after 1981. Perhaps it was the independent spirit and argumentative nature of this highly intelligent and articulate man, who was always ready to voice his opinions and to compete vociferously, that made the selectors wary of including him. Happily, he returned to favour, bowling beautifully and with great accuracy throughout the 1984/5 Test series in India, his most valuable performance coming at Delhi when he took 4 for 60 off 44 overs as England won their first Test in 13 matches. In the 1985 Ashes series, with his Middlesex colleague John Emburey restored to the side, Edmonds again played a significant part in England's triumph, taking 15 important wickets. On his first tour to the West Indies in 1986, he could take only three wickets in his three Test matches, but he never allowed the batsmen to dominate, bowling with great control, and he often batted bravely. Fifteen more Test wickets came his way against India and New Zealand in 1986, including 4 for 31 in the Indian second innings at Edgbaston, but his Test career ended in 1987 and Middlesex refused to give him the part-time career he sought thereafter as he developed a wide variety of business interests. He reappeared for the county once in 1992 in an emergency. His wife, Frances, also made a name for herself as a writer and broadcaster. They eventually had children but their family was delayed, she would claim, tongue-in-cheek, because Philippe insisted on listening all night to the BBC World Service news.

First-class career (1971–92): 7,347 runs (19.13) including 3 centuries, 1,185 wickets (25.24), and 332 catches

Test matches (41): 765 runs (17.79), 106 wickets (33.16), and 37 catches

EDRICH, John Hugh

(b. 1937, Blofield, Norfolk) *Norfolk, Surrey, and England*

Small, chunky and strong, John Edrich was like a left-handed version of his first cousin, Bill, but he became a more prolific batsman and was only the third left-hander, after Phil Mead and Frank Woolley, to score a hundred first-class centuries. He achieved this feat in 1977, the same year as Geoff Boycott, batting against Derbyshire at The Oval in a County Championship match. Much less of a song and dance was made about Edrich's milestone than about Boycott's and this was somehow typical, for Edrich was always a quiet, undemonstrative cricketer, his remarkably consistent success being based on a great natural ability, an iron self-discipline, courage, and unwavering concentration. Unlike most players he could shut everything from his mind except the advent of the next ball. Moving from his native Norfolk to London, John immediately made his mark for Surrey, scoring a century in each innings of only his second Championship match, against Nottinghamshire at Trent Bridge in 1959. At the age of only 22 he averaged 52 that season and had already made twenty-four centuries by the time he played the first of his 77 Tests, against the West Indies in 1963. The following summer, playing his first Test against Australia at Lord's, he demonstrated the ideal temperament which he possessed for cricket, scoring 120, the first of seven centuries against Australia, four of them on different grounds in Australia where he was a key member of three MCC touring teams in 1965/6, 1970/1, and 1974/5. On the last tour he captained England at Sydney after Mike Denness had dropped himself and, although England lost the match (the fourth Test of that rubber) and thereby relinquished the Ashes, he played an innings of immense courage on the final day of the match, making 33 not out in two and a half hours after suffering broken ribs from the first ball he had received from Lillee. Good-looking, with dark eyebrows above piercing light-blue eyes and flashing white teeth, he was seldom satisfied or fully convinced that the odds were in his favour. The strong points of his technique were very powerful forearms, watchfulness, and a rigid adherence to the principle of getting in line with the ball. His most productive strokes were placements off his toes either side of square-leg (and, as the innings progressed, through mid-wicket), a controlled cut behind the wicket on the off-side and a decisively punched cover-drive. In difficult batting conditions he would never lose patience, but in top form he could also be a devastating attacking player, most notably in 1965 when in the course of nine innings he made 1,311 runs including 310 not out at Leeds against New Zealand when his 5 sixes and 52 fours amounted to more runs in boundaries than any other player has scored in a Test innings. His lofted straight driving at this time was a revelation. A few weeks later he was hit on the head by a ball from Peter Pollock of South Africa at Lord's, but was soon scoring freely again. He scored more than 1,000 runs in a season 21 times (twice in Australia), and more than 2,000 six times. He scored centuries against all other countries and in all the overseas countries which he toured except New Zealand. He captained Surrey for five seasons between 1973 and 1977, a relatively lean period for the county although they won the Benson and Hedges Cup in 1974. Always safe and tidy in the field, he was an especially good gully. He retired after the 1978 season to concentrate on a number of business interests. He was awarded the MBE in 1977 and two separate testimonials by a grateful county club. He became an England selector in 1981 but resigned after one season to pursue his business activities. Successful though these were, his personal life was clouded by tragedy. His son, Justin, was killed in a road accident and his second wife, Judy, plagued by serious illness. In 1995 he returned to the circuit as England's batting coach.

First-class career (1959–78): 39,790 runs (45.47) including 103 centuries, and 311 catches
Test matches (77): 5,138 runs (43.54), 0–23, and 43 catches

EDRICH, William John

(b. 1916, Lingwood, Norfolk; d. 1986, Chesham, Buckinghamshire) *Norfolk, Middlesex, and England*

Bill Edrich, John's cousin, is remembered for his great courage and determination, especially on the international scene. Short, chunky, and alert, he was a right-handed batsman whose favourite shots were the pulled drive, the hook, and the late cut. Watchfulness and grit were the keynotes, and his skill, especially on bad wickets in Australia, endeared him to the crowds. With his Middlesex 'twin', Denis Compton, he was a great box-office draw immediately after the Second World War. His fast bowling was explosive and tearaway. Operating from a short run, he was capable of great speed in short bursts, almost hurling himself at the batsman as he delivered the ball. Later in his career he bowled slow off-breaks. He was also a slip field and, therefore, always in the game. He scored 1,886 runs in five seasons for Norfolk, including 111 against the South Africans in 1935. In his first full season for Middlesex in 1937 he made 2,154 runs in all

matches, and also exceeded 2,000 in the last two seasons before the Second World War. He made over 1,000 runs for Lord Tennyson's side in India in 1937/8, but his early Test performances were disastrous. Before the end of May 1938 he hit 1,010 runs, all at Lord's, but in the Tests that year he made only 67 in six innings, followed by consecutive scores of 4, 10, 0, 6, and 1, before he produced a magnificent 219 in the 'timeless' Test at Durban. In his earlier days he was frequently an opening batsman, but he settled down at first or second wicket down; and in Australia, 1946/7, he consolidated his place as a Test cricketer, especially at Sydney with 71 and 119, besides dismissing three of the first four batsmen. 1947 marked the zenith of his career as it did of his Middlesex 'twin', Denis Compton. The two of them seemed to be spending the whole summer at the crease, either for Middlesex, the county champions, or for England against South Africa. All bowling was put to the sword. Edrich scored 3,539 runs (80.43) with 12 centuries, took 67 wickets (22.58), and held 35 catches. In 1948 he battled against Australia, hitting 111 and 54 at Headingley (a match that England should have won). He did not tour Australia under Freddie Brown in 1950/1—a glaring omission—but he was at the other end when Denis Compton hit the winning run at The Oval in 1953 by which England regained the Ashes. In the first Test of the 1954/5 tour he scored a fighting 88 at Brisbane. Generally, however, he never quite recaptured his 1947 form again, although he captained Middlesex from 1953 until 1957. He returned to his native Norfolk, and for more than a decade enjoyed minor county cricket again (1959–71). During the war he served in the RAF and was awarded the DFC for daylight bombing over Germany as a Squadron Leader. Although not a footballer of Compton's class, he played for Tottenham Hotspur. A man of charm and intelligence, he lived life to the full and had four wives. Three of his brothers, Brian, Eric, and Geoff, also played first-class county cricket.

First-class career (1934–58): 36,965 runs (42.39) including 86 centuries, 479 wickets (33.31), 529 catches, and 1 stumping
Test matches (39): 2,440 runs (40.00) including 6 centuries, 41 wickets (41.29), and 39 catches

ELLIOTT, Harry

(b. 1891, Scarcliffe, Derbyshire; d. 1976, Derby) *Derbyshire and England*

Harry Elliott made his county place secure as wicket-keeper, although his early promise as a batsman was not realized, despite the fact that he often played well in a crisis. He appeared in 194 consecutive matches for his county up to 1928, when his selection for the Test against West Indies at Old Trafford broke the sequence. Subsequently he made 232 consecutive appearances until he was injured in 1937. In an emergency he reappeared for Derbyshire aged 55 after the war, while he was senior coach. In 1936, when the county won the Championship for the first time, he conceded only one bye in 25 completed innings. He toured South Africa with MCC (when the skipper himself was a 'keeper) in 1927/8, and India, 1933/4, when he kept in the first Test on Indian soil. His nephew, Charlie Elliott, played for Derbyshire and became well known as an umpire.

First-class career (1920–47): 7,580 runs (13.93) and 1,206 dismissals (904 c., 302 st.)

Test matches (4): 61 runs (15.25) and 11 dismissals (8 c., 3 st.)

ELLISON, Richard Mark

(b. 1959, Willesborough, Kent) *Kent, Tasmania, and England*

In the final analysis it was the performance of Kent's Richard Ellison in the Tests at Edgbaston and at The Oval in 1985 which enabled England to regain the Ashes. In the first four Tests the England attack, with the exception of Ian Botham, had lacked penetration; Ellison provided it in sensational style. In the Australian first innings at Edgbaston he took 6 for 77, exploiting a heavy cloud cover on the second morning in a lethal spell of 4 for 15, mesmerizing the Australian batsmen with his swing bowling. Then, after England had piled up 595 for 5 declared, he took four wickets for one run in the space of half an hour to reduce Australia to 36 for 5. He finished with match figures of 10 for 104 and seven more wickets at The Oval gave him a total of 17 wickets (10.88) in his two Tests, as decisive a contribution as any in recent years. But his period of ascendancy in Test cricket, in common with other swing bowlers, was brief, due in part to back injuries and a lack of any exceptional pace. Educated at Tonbridge and Exeter University, Ellison made his first-class début in 1981 and, with his height and athleticism, impressed as an authentic right-arm medium-fast swing bowler and a powerful left-handed middle-order batsman. He was capped by his county in 1983, and some consistent performances with the ball and his maiden first-class century in 1984 won him his

Test début in the fifth Test against the West Indies. He bowled impressively, taking 5 for 94 in the match. He was rather unlucky on the 1984/5 tour of India, bowling boomerang away-swingers with little success. But, following an early season injury in 1985, he concentrated on bowling faster to make the ball move later. As well as his devastating form in the Tests, he had career-best bowling figures of 7 for 87 against Northamptonshire and headed the 1985 first-class bowling averages with 65 wickets at an average of 17.20, the first Englishman to lead the averages for some time. In the West Indies in 1986 he took five wickets in the first innings at Sabina Park but was then rather disappointing, though his batting showed signs of developing. Losing form in 1986, he played in only one Test and one limited-overs international for England, and was left out of the team to tour Australia in 1986/7, spending the winter as a guest player for Tasmania. The magic swing never returned for long enough—partly because of frequent back strains—and he did not regain his Test place, but after missing all the 1987 season he took 71 wickets for Kent (average 21) a year later. His younger brother, C. C., was a Cambridge blue as a bowler of similar type and Richard followed him into the teaching profession in 1995.

First-class career (1981–93): 5,046 runs (23.80) including 1 century, 475 wickets (28.99), and 86 catches

Test matches (11): 202 runs (13.46), 35 wickets (29.94), and 2 catches

EMBUREY, John Ernest

(b. 1952, Peckham, London) *Middlesex, Western Province, and England*

Twenty years after becoming an established county cricketer, John Emburey's shrewd, determined, and dogged all-round cricket helped Middlesex to win the County Championship in 1993, the sixth title to which he had made a major contribution. At the age of 42 he had proved himself his country's most durable professional cricketer, fuelled by an intense interest in the game and its skills. The following winter he suffered a detached retina in his right eye whilst reading a book in Guyana, but although his batting suffered he took 52 wickets at 27 each for Middlesex in 1994 and was recalled for a final, 64th, Test in 1995. Although he had been a capped Middlesex player for less than two years when he was picked for England in 1978, he was already generally recognized as potentially one of the best slow bowlers in the world. A tall off-spinner with a classical high action causing awkward bounce, he turned the ball sharply enough whenever conditions permitted, could vary his speed and trajectory without losing control, and curved the ball disconcertingly away from the right-hander. Forced to play much of his cricket in limited-overs matches and thus to spend much of his time bowling to contain, he was a leading representative of the new school of tight, mean spinners that modern cricket demanded. But that he could also be a destructive attacking bowler he amply proved in Australia in 1978/9 when he forced his way into England's Test team against all expectations and in four matches took 16 wickets at 19 each. Surprisingly, he had to wait over a year for his next Test appearance, but, before he joined the rebel tour of South Africa in March 1982, he had established himself as England's leading off-spin bowler. In the Caribbean, he bowled with skill and stamina to take 5 for 124 at Port of Spain, and then played a valuable all-round part in England's triumphs in 1981. His best bowling in Test cricket, 6 for 33, came in the Sri Lankan Test on the 1981/2 tour, his last appearance before being banned from Test cricket for three years for taking part in an officially disapproved tour of South Africa. During his absence from the England side he continued to bowl tightly and effectively for Middlesex, taking 103 wickets in 1983, and his batting also improved considerably. He once hit six sixes in seven balls for Western Province against Eastern Province in the Currie Cup and almost saved England from defeat by New Zealand at Trent Bridge in 1986 by making an inventive 75. He was immediately welcomed back into the Test side in 1985. He took 7 for 105 in the first Test at Headingley and enjoyed a successful series against Australia, collecting 19 wickets (28.63). He was England's leading wicket-taker in the 1986 series in the West Indies, taking 14 wickets at an average of 32.00, in every Test tying down and frustrating all the home batsmen except Viv Richards. His best figures came in the second Test at Port of Spain, when he took 5 for 78. In a series in which England were thrashed, he was the one cricketer to come home with an enhanced reputation and he was rewarded with the England vice-captaincy for the 1986/7 tour of Australia. A shrewd and experienced cricketer, he was a sound choice and in 1988, during a one-sided series against the West Indies, he captained England at Lord's and Old Trafford, only to be displaced as England failed to press home a

dream start in the second Test, and lost even more heavily in the third. After the following season he undertook another disapproved tour of South Africa and was banned again, but he reappeared for England against Australia in 1993 and in India in 1993/4. Although by now his bowling was bland when pitted against skilled and confident Test batsmen, he regularly scored useful runs and did so again against the threatening leg-spin of Shane Warne of Australia.

First-class career (1973–): 11,395 runs (23.59) including 7 centuries, 1,503 wickets (25.91), and 434 catches
Test matches (63): 1,705 runs (22.73), 147 wickets (37.85), and 33 catches

EMMETT, George Malcolm

(b. 1912, Agra, India; d. 1976, Knowle, Somerset)
Devon, Gloucestershire, and England

A short, slightly built right-handed opener, George Emmett knew every shot in the book, and often, perhaps, tried to play too many of them. Extremely quick on his feet, he was never afraid to go down the wicket to slow bowlers. He was at a disadvantage against the really quick bowlers, but he was a fine hooker and cutter and he could hit the ball extremely hard. An occasional slow left-arm bowler, he was also a very safe field. After four seasons with Devon he joined Gloucestershire. He made his début for his adopted county in 1936, and fourteen times exceeded 1,000 runs in a season, mainly as opening batsman. He toured India twice with Commonwealth teams, but his selection as opening batsman against Australia at Old Trafford in 1948 caused a sensation because he replaced Len Hutton. In this, his sole Test, George scored 10 and 0. Captain of Gloucestershire from 1955 until 1958, he became coach on retirement in 1959.

First-class career (1936–59): 25,602 runs (31.41) including 37 centuries, 60 wickets (44.01), and 296 catches

EMMETT, Thomas

(b. 1841, Halifax, Yorkshire; d. 1904, Leicester)
Yorkshire and England

Tom Emmett was a vigorous left-arm fast bowler with a round-arm action, who could pitch on the leg-stump and hit the off. In a long career he remained effective even after he had lost his pace, by imparting greater spin to the ball. A cheery and humorous professional, his verbal exchanges with W.G. and others were as belligerent as those of his contemporaries, Gladstone and Disraeli. Tom called his ball that pitched on the leg-stump his 'sostenuter'—'What else would you call it?' he would ask. His motto was 'First a wide and then a wicket', and so it often proved. A useful, free-scoring batsman and good field, he captained Yorkshire from 1878 to 1882. In 1886 he took 124 wickets at 12.83, one of four seasons in which he exceeded 100 wickets. Tom did not appear for England against Australia at home, but toured Australia with three teams, and appeared in the first Test at Melbourne in 1876. Later, he coached Leicestershire CCC and at Rugby, where one of his pupils was P. F. Warner. His son, Arthur, played three matches for Leicestershire in 1902.

First-class career (1866–88): 9,053 runs (14.84) including 1 century, 1,571 wickets (13.56), and 276 catches

Test matches (7): 160 runs (13.33), 9 wickets (31.55), and 9 catches

EVANS, Alfred John

(b. 1889, Newtown, Hampshire; d. 1960, Marylebone, London) *Oxford University, Hampshire, Kent, and England*

An Oxford blue who captained the University in 1911, John Evans was a tall, lissom, right-handed, hard-driving batsman and a lively medium-paced bowler. In 1921, on the strength of an innings of 69 not out for MCC against the overwhelming Australians at Lord's, he played for England in the Test at Lord's, but was not a success, scoring 4 and 14, and was not selected again. He also won golf and rackets blues. He escaped from POW camps in the First World War, about which he wrote *The Escaping Club*, a classic of its genre. His father played for Oxford University, Hampshire, and Somerset and his brother and three cousins also played first-class cricket.

First-class career (1908–28): 3,499 runs (24.64) including 6 centuries, and 110 wickets (27.83)

EVANS, Thomas Godfrey

(b. 1920, Finchley, Middlesex) *Kent and England*

An irrepressible extrovert and the outstanding wicket-keeper of his day, Godfrey Evans made nonsense of the convention that wicket-keepers should be sound rather than showy, for he was, on most big occasions, both sound as a bell *and* spectacular as a Catherine wheel. Until Alan Knott surpassed him, he held the record for the most Test dismissals. Of stocky build and a quicksilver character, his darting movements

flowed from his natural exuberance, and he made acrobatic catches which few others, and certainly no other contemporary, could have reached. He always kept a game alive, and he stood up to anything less than a genuinely fast bowler, most notably to Alec Bedser. It is doubtful if there has ever been a more brilliant wicket-keeper, though he had the occasional bad day. He was a talented batsman, being very quick on his feet and having a wonderful eye. Two of his seven centuries were made in Tests, 104 against West Indies at Old Trafford in 1950 and 104 against India at Lord's in 1952, when he failed by only two runs to complete the hundred before lunch. Yet in a crisis at Adelaide in 1946/7 he stayed in for 95 minutes without scoring. He scored more than 1,000 runs in a season four times and claimed his 1,000th victim in 1959. Having first played for Kent in 1939, he was England's automatic choice as wicket-keeper between 1946 and 1958/9, making four tours of Australasia and two each to South Africa and the West Indies. Whether 'keeping or batting, his name was synonymous with entertainment and he was awarded the CBE. In retirement he lent his boundless energy to many a charity match and was for many years employed by Ladbrokes, the bookmaker, to fix the odds at big matches.

First-class career (1939–69): 14,882 runs (21.22) including 7 centuries, and 1,060 dismissals (816 c., 250 st.)

Test matches (91): 2,439 runs (20.49) including 2 centuries, and 219 dismissals (173 c., 46 st.)

FAGG, Arthur Edward

(b. 1915, Chartham, Kent; d. 1977, Tunbridge Wells, Kent) *Kent and England*

A very sound right-handed opening batsman, Arthur Fagg had strokes all round the wicket and, being a fine hooker, was particularly severe on fast bowlers. He was also a reliable slip field and occasionally kept wicket. After playing two Tests against India in 1936 he toured Australia with MCC in 1936/7, playing in two Tests, but had to be invalided home with rheumatic fever and missed the 1937 season. He recovered to perform the unique feat of scoring 244 and 202 not out for Kent against Essex at Colchester in 1938. He had to turn down the offer of a place in the side to South Africa that winter and played only one more Test, but he remained a first-rate county batsman, exceeding 1,000 runs thirteen times. For 18 years he was one of the best umpires, standing in many Tests, although latterly he was troubled by the lack of good behaviour on the field; he temporarily walked out of a Test at Edgbaston in 1973 when the West Indian players complained at one of his decisions.

First-class career (1932–57): 27,291 (36.05) including 58 centuries, 425 catches, and 7 stumpings
Test matches (5): 150 runs (18.75) and 5 catches

FAIRBROTHER, Neil Harvey

(b. 1963, Warrington, Lancashire) *Lancashire and England*

Neil Harvey Fairbrother—named after the Australian left-hander, his mother's favourite cricketer—found himself labelled a one-day specialist, a reputation borne of his ability to score quickly both through clever improvisation and, despite a slight though wiry frame, shots of withering power. A dashing left-hander, he is also an outstanding cover fielder, but 12 years after his Lancashire début in 1982 his was to some extent an unfulfilled promise. In 1985 he scored 1,400 first-class runs, the only Lancashire batsman to top a thousand in a miserable year for the county, and when he showed equal consistency the following summer he was selected for England's short tour of Sharjah. Test recognition followed, albeit briefly, that summer, when, on his home ground at Old Trafford he went out to bat with 25 minutes left on the first day. Overcome by nerves, he lasted four balls without touching any of them, fell lbw, and was promptly dropped. Returning for the tours of Pakistan and New Zealand which followed the World Cup that Autumn, he endured an equally lean time with scores of 3, 1, and 1 in his three Test innings. He reappeared in Test cricket in 1990, following a remarkable innings of 366 against Surrey at The Oval. He had revelled in perfect batting conditions to produce the then third-highest score in Championship cricket behind Archie MacLaren and Graeme Hick (since surpassed by Brian Lara's 501 not out), scoring a century in each session of the third day. Against New Zealand, however, the confidence of that innings deserted him and he was dropped after managing only 59 runs in five innings, although 1,740 runs that summer earned him a place as vice-captain on the A tour of Pakistan and Sri Lanka. The trip was a disappointment, and he was dropped for the 'Test' in Kandy. Another good start to the season in 1991 earned him a place in the one-day squad against the West Indies, and in the third match at Lord's he responded with a flowing 113

in a partnership of 213 with Hick, the highest third-wicket stand in limited-overs internationals in England. Overlooked for the Tests which followed, he was selected instead for the tour of New Zealand and the World Cup, and once the latter started he came into his own, making 285 runs at an average of 57, including a brilliant, match-winning 75 not out against South Africa and 62 in a losing cause in the final against Pakistan. The following summer, Fairbrother, now Lancashire captain, was restricted by a pulled hamstring but in India in the early months of 1992 he forced his way into the Test side, and produced a Test-best 83 on a turning pitch in a losing cause in Madras. It was an unhappy tour for England, however, and although he played in all three one-day games against Australia in 1993, he had a wretched season with the bat and resigned the Lancashire captaincy. He returned to England's one-day team against South Africa in 1994, and as a replacement for injured players in Australia the following winter. By 1994/5 he had played in 44 internationals, scoring 1,268 runs (38.42), with a century and 9 fifties.

First-class career (1982–): 14,317 runs (41.38) and 5 wickets (85.20)
Test matches (10): 219 runs (15.64)

FANE, Frederick Luther

(b. 1875, Curragh Camp, Co. Kildare, Ireland; d. 1960, Brentwood, Essex) *Oxford University, Essex, and England*

For two decades Frederick Fane's attractive right-handed, front-foot style was a familiar feature on Essex grounds. As an opening batsman he enjoyed success against googly bowlers on matting in South Africa in 1905/6, when he more than held his own and headed the Test averages with 342 runs (38.00). He visited South Africa again in 1909/10, but without the same success. He led MCC in Australia in 1907/8, when A. O. Jones fell ill and, though he did not relish having the captaincy thrust upon him, made 774 runs on the tour. He captained Essex from 1904 to 1906 and went to New Zealand and the West Indies on minor tours. He scored two double-centuries for Essex. Curiously, both his father and he read their own obituaries, owing to confusion over family initials.

First-class career (1895–1924): 18,548 runs (27.39) including 25 centuries, and 194 catches
Test matches (14): 682 runs (26.23) including 1 century, and 6 catches

FARNES, Kenneth

(b. 1911, Leytonstone, Essex; d. 1941, Chipping
Warden, Oxfordshire) *Cambridge University, Essex,
and England*

Ken Farnes was one of the most mourned of the
international cricketers lost in the Second World
War. Six feet five inches tall, but well proportioned, he took a run of 11 paces and, moving at a
great pace at the moment of delivery, could bowl
at a ferocious speed. His right-arm deliveries, with
the ball coming down from a height of above 8 ft.,
rose very sharply from a hard wicket, and, to add
extra nip, he flicked his wrist down at the last
moment. On his day he bowled as fast as any
man—Bill Edrich said that there was little to
choose between Farnes and Frank Tyson—but he
had to cope with unresponsive pitches and powerful batting. He played in three series against
Australia, one against the West Indies and one
against South Africa, the last being the 'timeless'
Test at Durban. After three years in the Cambridge side, he joined Essex and, by taking 11 for
131 at Southend against the all-powerful Yorkshire
side, he enabled his county in 1934 to beat the
Tykes for the first time for many years. Then
chosen for England against Australia at Trent
Bridge—his first Test—he captured five wickets in
each innings. In the 1936 Gentlemen v. Players
match at Lord's his bowling was reckoned the
fastest seen at Lord's since the time of C. J.
Kortright, and he took a sensational 8 for 43 in the
first innings. His best bowling in Tests was 6 for 96
in a total of 604 in the fifth match against Australia
at Melbourne in 1936/7, on a perfect wicket. He
was a safe field near the wicket but rarely of much
account as a batsman. Nevertheless he hit 97 not
out for Essex against Somerset at Taunton in 1936,
helping to add 149 for the last wicket, and laughed
at just missing his century. A master at Worksop
College after coming down from Cambridge, he
played as an amateur. Pilot Officer Farnes was
killed on active service while flying during the
Second World War.

First-class career (1930–9): 1,182 runs (8.32), 690
wickets (21.45), and 84 catches
Test matches (15): 58 runs (4.83), 60 wickets
(28.65), and 1 catch

FARRIMOND, William

(b. 1903, Daisy Hill, Lancashire; d. 1979,
Westhoughton, Bolton, Lancashire) *Lancashire and
England*

Second-string wicket-keeper at Lancashire to
George Duckworth, Bill Farrimond was still good
enough to represent England abroad against
South Africa, 1930/1, against the West Indies,
1934/5 and, at home, against South Africa in
1935. On Duckworth's retirement he stepped into
his shoes in 1938, but by the end of the war he
was too old for county cricket. He was a very
sound, quietly confident 'keeper, and a better
batsman than Duckworth. In the present era, no
doubt, he would simply have moved to another
county to ensure a regular place in the first
team.

First-class career (1924–45): 2,908 runs (23.64)
and 333 dismissals (256 c., 77 st.)
Test matches (4): 116 runs (16.57) and 7
dismissals (5 c., 2 st.)

FELIX, Nicholas

(b. 1840, Camberwell, Surrey; d. 1876, Wimborne
Minster, Dorset) *Kent and Surrey*

Felix, whose real name was Nicholas Wanostrocht, of Flemish origin, became headmaster of
the school his uncle had founded as a young man.
The 'facetious, jostling, merry, notch-making
Felix, lively and amusing' was a character far
removed from the notion of a nineteenth-century
headmaster, which explains the happy pseudonym with which he concealed his cricketing
activities from the parents of his pupils. His first
match at Lord's (1828), suitable enough for a
classical scholar, was marked by him, as a left-arm
under-arm slow bowler, and one Pontifex taking
13 wickets between them. From 1831 onwards he
played for the Gentlemen for over 20 years
besides being a member of the powerful Kent XI.
In 1846 a match was played in his honour at
Lord's between his XI and that of Fuller Pilch
visited by Prince Albert and 'some of the élite of
the land'. His left-handed batting was, thought
Pilch, 'a beautiful thing to see and if he did get
the ball, you heard her hit the palings on the off-
side almost as soon as she left the bat'. The grace
and fluency of Felix's batting was mirrored in his
skill as an artist. Of some 200 pictures in pastel or
watercolours, many show his cricket contemporaries while his group portraiture created a har-
monic unity letting each individual be a solo
performer in his own right. Thus, the All-England
XI of 1847 shows the elegance and authority of
Mynn and Pilch, as pillars on either side of the
picture, with the busy journalist Denison and
Felix himself modestly in the second row. He
commissioned the rising young artist, G. F. Watts
—who attended evening classes at Felix's
school—to produce a series of lithographs in

stone to illustrate batting technique. Felix himself was the model and, as a left-hander, knew that the printed image in reverse would be more useful. His own *Felix on the Bat* was a technical book including instruction on how to use the Catapulta, the bowling machine he invented. He illustrated it himself, some of his drawings exemplifying what not to do.

First-class career (1830–52): 4,556 runs (18.15) including 2 centuries, 0 + 9 wickets (no average), and 112 catches

FENDER, Percy George Herbert

(b. 1892, Balham, London; d. 1985, Exeter, Devon) *Sussex, Surrey, and England*

Percy Fender will be best remembered for his inspired captaincy. Tall, dark, with a long nose, moustache, glasses, and a long sweater, he was a gift to cartoonists and a calculating showman. In private life his habit and speech were of a conventional, even serious turn, but on the field he was adventurous, loved a gamble, and possessed one of the most acute brains ever applied to cricket. Most of his career was with Surrey, whom he helped to the Championship in 1914 and captained from 1921 until 1931. His expert handling of a rather thin Surrey attack on the perfect wickets at The Oval was a source of mystery; and when he sighted victory on the horizon, he would ride straight for it. In eight seasons he achieved the double six times. A right-handed batsman, he lived on risk and his wrists, and could hit with tremendous power; as a bowler he sometimes lost himself in search of variety, but was at his best as a slow leg-breaker; and he was superb in the slips. His century in 35 minutes at Northampton in 1920 remains the 'genuine' world record—he and H. A. Peach added 171 in 42 minutes—and at Lord's in 1927 he dismissed five Middlesex batsmen in seven balls. When he hit 185 against Hampshire at The Oval in 1922, the innings included three sixes, three fives and 25 fours. Surprisingly, he never captained England, although he appeared against Australia and South Africa. He bowled as successfully as any Englishman in Australia on the 1920/1 tour, taking 12 wickets in the Tests, and on matting in South Africa he took 4 for 29 at Cape Town, 1922/3. A writer with an analytical mind, he wrote several classic books about Test matches: *Defending the Ashes*, *The Turn of the Wheel*, *The Tests of 1930*, and *Kissing the Rod*, besides a text-book, *The ABC of Cricket*. Still quick-witted in very old age, he lived in Horsham with

his daughter where he retained an interest in his wine business. Although almost totally blind, he attended the 1977 Centenary Test in Melbourne as the oldest player able to travel. He was the oldest living Test player when he died in 1985 aged 92. His fastest century was equalled in artificial circumstances by Lancashire's Stephen O'Shaughnessy in 1983.

First-class career (1910–36): 19,034 runs (26.65) including 21 centuries, 1,894 wickets (25.05), and 600 catches
Test matches (13): 380 runs (19.00), 29 wickets (40.86), and 14 catches

FENNEX, William

(b. *c*.1764, Gerrards Cross, Buckinghamshire; d. *c*.1838, London) *Hambledon and Middlesex*

'A fine, free and elegant' right-handed batsman and a fast right-arm under-arm bowler whose action came very close to round-arm, Fennex appeared for Hambledon in 1786 and for Saffron Walden 40 years later. He achieved most success in single-wicket matches for England in the 1780s and 1790s while scoring 74 for England against Surrey at Lord's in 1797. As a coach he influenced Fuller Pilch and as a raconteur he recalled the great players of his day in conversation with John Mitford, which became source-material for James Pycroft's *The Cricket Field*.

First-class career (1801–16): 90 runs (6.00), 16 wickets (average not known), and 7 catches

FERRIS, John James

(1867–1900) *New South Wales, South Australia, Australia, Gloucestershire, and England*

See Australia section.

FIELDER, Arthur

(b. 1877, Plaxtol, Tonbridge, Kent; d. 1949, Lambeth, London) *Kent and England*

Arthur Fielder could bowl fast right-arm for hours without fatigue. He bowled off-cutters and out-swingers and he was fortunate in that Kent abounded with almost infallible slip fielders. He toured Australia twice and, in 1907/8, secured 25 wickets (25.08) in the Tests; all his Test cricket was confined to these tours. Taking 186 wickets (20.19) in 1906, he was prominent in Kent's winning of the Championship for the first time, and that year, uniquely for Players against Gentlemen at Lord's, he captured all ten wickets (for 90) in the first innings. He rarely achieved much as a batsman, but by scoring 112 not out he set up an English record for the last wicket by assisting Frank Woolley to add 235 runs against Worcestershire at Stourbridge in 1909.

First-class career (1900–14): 2,320 runs (11.31) including 1 century, and 1,277 wickets (21.02)
Test matches (6): 78 runs (11.14), 26 wickets (27.34), and 4 catches

FINDLAY, William

(b. 1880, Liverpool; d. 1953, Tenterden, Kent) *Oxford University and Lancashire*

After captaining Eton and Oxford, William Findlay had 5 years with Lancashire as a middle-order right-handed batsman and wicket-keeper before succeeding the redoubtable C. W. Alcock as secretary of Surrey (1907–19). There followed 7 years at Lord's as assistant to Sir Francis Lacey before Findlay himself became MCC secretary (1926–36). He was involved in the drafting of the club's replies to the Australian cables over the bodyline controversy (1932–3) and his diplomatic skills and tact had much to do with taking the heat out of a crisis which had assumed political and imperial proportions. After his retirement he chaired the important Findlay Commission (1937) on the financial problems of first-class cricket and at one time he served simultaneously on four different county committees. Sir Pelham Warner, whose own presidency of MCC (1950) had represented a departure from the tradition of noblemen and servicemen holding the office, persuaded a reluctant and modest Findlay to succeed him in 1951.

First-class career (1901–6): 1,984 runs (19.45) and 167 dismissals (140 c., 27 st.)

FISHLOCK, Laurence Barnard

(b. 1907, Battersea, London; d. 1986, Sutton, Surrey) *Surrey and England*

Laurie Fishlock was a left-handed stroke-maker with a style quite free from fuss. He bowled occasionally, slow left-arm. His emphasis was always on attack, whether batting or fielding—in his heyday he was a magnificent outfield—and he had a wonderfully consistent record for his county. Unfortunate with injuries in representative cricket, he perhaps did not quite have the patience for Test matches. As an opening batsman, he toured Australia with MCC in 1936/7, appearing in one Test, and again in 1946/7. His other Test cricket was at home against India. He

toured India with the Commonwealth team in 1950/1, and made over 1,000 runs; in England he exceeded 1,000 runs in a season twelve times. He also gained an England Amateur Football cap and played professionally for five clubs.

First-class career (1931–52): 25,376 runs (39.34) including 56 centuries, 11 wickets (45.81), and 216 catches
Test matches (4): 47 runs (11.75) and 1 catch

FITZGERALD, Robert Allan

(b. 1834, Purley, Berkshire; d. 1881, Chorley Wood, Hertfordshire) *Cambridge University and Middlesex*

Bob Fitzgerald became secretary of MCC (1863) at a time when the club's fortunes were at a low ebb, its membership small and there were calls for a 'Cricket Parliament' to replace it as the game's arbitrator. In 1869 Fitzgerald was influential in securing the membership of the young W. G. Grace, whose reputation was already established but who would have been unlikely —in the social context of the times—to have gravitated to Lord's. He took Grace with him to the United States and Canada on an unofficial MCC tour (1872) in which he was the 'champion batsman of cricketdom'. Fitzgerald's book on the tour, *Wickets in the West*, is a classic. As secretary, he pursued a practical, forward-looking policy. The pavilion was extended, the grandstand built, press accommodation provided, the freehold of the ground secured and membership increased threefold. Only an attempt to get Middlesex to play their home matches at Lord's failed. As an attacking right-handed batsman, Fitzgerald won his blue at Cambridge but work and ill-health limited his first-class appearances thereafter. It was illness which forced his resignation in 1876 when members recognized what he had achieved through his 'zeal, ability and popularity'. These qualities were matched by his wit, humour, and, when occasion demanded, brusqueness. He had become, in 1868, the first paid secretary of MCC.

First-class career (1854–74): 1,123 runs (15.59), 4 wickets (28.00), and 34 catches

FLAVELL, John Alfred

(b. 1929, Wall Heath, Staffordshire) *Worcestershire and England*

Jack Flavell, a strong, red-faced, red-headed man, was among the fastest right-arm bowlers in England in the 1950s. Starting as something of a tearaway, whose control was rather suspect, he later slowed down a little and became a steadier and more consistently successful performer. His 101 wickets in 18 matches in 1964 helped Worcestershire become county champions for the first time. However, 1961 had been his best year—171 wickets (17.79). In 1965, when the county won the Championship again, he took 132. Three times in his career he took nine wickets in an innings, all for his county. A left-handed batsman, he seldom detained his opponents for long. He appeared in Tests against Australia in 1961 and 1964, but seldom got helpful conditions and was a disappointment. He played soccer for Walsall and later became landlord of a pub.

First-class career (1949–67): 2,032 runs (6.51) and 1,529 wickets (21.48)

Test matches (4): 31 runs (7.75) and 7 wickets (52.42)

FLETCHER, Keith William Robert

(b. 1944, Worcester) *Essex and England*

A likeable Londoner, Keith Fletcher (nicknamed 'the gnome') had a Test record of which any batsman could be proud, but the impression remains that he could have been even more successful given a greater determination to take the initiative from the bowlers. Test match atmosphere often sent his shy character into its shell, and he was usually at his best in the second innings rather than the first. Three of his finest innings were 178 against New Zealand at Lord's in 1973, 129 not out against the West Indies at Bridgetown in 1974, and 58 not out against India at Bombay in 1977—defiant defensive innings which saved each match for his country. He also shone brightly in defeat at Lord's in 1973 against the West Indies, making 68 and 86 not out during the heaviest home defeat in England's history. From his youth this slightly built, fair-haired right-hander had a gift of perfect timing which aroused expectations of more match-winning innings than he eventually achieved. But he became an accomplished craftsman and an especially fine player of spin. He bowled some leg-spin himself, once taking 5 for 41. Born in Worcestershire of London parents whose home was bombed in the War, he was brought up in Cambridgeshire and played first for Royston, also Jack Hobbs's first club. He first played for Essex in 1962, was capped the following year and was an astute and successful county captain from 1974 to 1985, leading Essex to their first major triumphs in 1979. Always a valuable adviser to England captains, he himself led skilfully on the field and

kept his players happy off it with a philosophical approach to setbacks and a wry London humour. On eight overseas tours for MCC he was a key member of a frequently struggling batting side. In a stronger one he would have flourished more than he did. A fine all-round fielder for Essex, he caught some brilliant slip catches in Tests but also missed many important chances. He lost his appetite for Test cricket after the battering he received from Lillee and Thomson in 1974/5 but, though he was often a poking, prodding shadow of the batsman he could be, one prefers to remember the days when, with a complete repertoire of glorious strokes, he would look too good for any attack, glancing the ball off his toes forward of square, driving through extra-cover or wide of mid-on, and, above all, square-cutting with punishing power and a brilliance which glittered. He finished the 1974/5 tour in this form, with a century in Melbourne and a double in Auckland. He was recalled to the England side as captain for the tour of 1981/2 and, although England lost a grim, dilatory series against India 1–0, he led England to success in the first-ever Test played against Sri Lanka, in February 1982. He was then hastily and harshly discarded. As a batsman he held his own with several timely innings and he completed 3,000 Test runs. He hit 1,000 runs in a season 20 times (best 1,890 in 1968) and twice scored double-centuries, 228 not out against Sussex at Hastings in 1968 and 216 for England against New Zealand at Auckland in 1974/5. Under his shrewd captaincy Essex dominated English cricket in the early 1980s. He led them to the Championship again in 1983 and 1984, and their NatWest Trophy win in 1985 completed Fletcher's set of domestic trophies, but he stayed on as vice-captain in 1986, played an important part in bringing the County Championship pennant back to Chelmsford, and for a season in 1988 returned as captain to allow Graham Gooch to regain confidence. He became Essex's coach and guru until, in 1992, following the management of several England A and B tours, he became the England manager/coach in succession to Micky Stewart in 1992. His contract was prematurely terminated in 1995, after England's defeat in Australia and he returned, cheerful as ever, to Essex. He was awarded the OBE for his services to the game.

First-class career (1962–88): 34,665 runs (37.77) including 63 centuries, 51 wickets (45.01), and 644 catches

Test matches (59): 3,272 runs (39.90) including 7 centuries, 2 wickets (96.50), and 54 catches

FLOWERS, Wilfred

(b. 1856, Calverton, Nottinghamshire; d. 1926, Carlton, Nottingham) *Nottinghamshire and England*

Wilfred Flowers was the last survivor of the Nottinghamshire XI that in 1878 played the opening match with the first Australian touring team. He was a resolute right-handed batsman, a steady off-break bowler who was extremely difficult to play on a soft wicket, and a very safe field, either at third man or mid-wicket. In 1879 he demolished Middlesex at Lord's, taking 7 for 16 in 22 overs, 12 of which were maidens; and in 1883 he became the first professional ever to complete the double in a season (with 1,144 runs and 113 wickets). He played only once in a Test against Australia in England—in 1893—but he toured Australia twice. On retirement he became a first-class umpire. His nephew, Emmott Robinson, was a Yorkshire stalwart.

First-class career (1877–96): 12,891 runs (20.07) including 9 centuries, 1,188 wickets (15.89), and 222 catches

Test matches (8): 256 runs (18.14), 14 wickets (21.14), and 3 catches

FORD, Francis Gilbertstone Justice

(b. 1866, Paddington, London; d. 1940, Burwash, Sussex) *Cambridge University, Middlesex, and England*

Described as 'six feet two of don't care', Francis Ford, or 'Stork' as he was known, was the youngest of seven cricketing brothers (all Reptonians) and an elegant left-handed batsman, who used his height so effectively that, despite his very spare physique, he put exceptional force into his stroke-play. He turned many good-length balls into half-volleys. His most brilliant display was 191 for Cambridge against Sussex at Hove (out of 703 for 9) in 1890. A slow left-arm bowler, he caused trouble sometimes by dropping the ball on an accurate length from a great height, with plenty of spin and curl. He toured Australia with A. E. Stoddart's side in 1894/5, but did not enhance his reputation. He held strong views about 'leg before wicket', and his influence at Lord's was considerable in amending Law 39 (the lbw Law) in 1937. An outstanding goalkeeper, he also won a soccer blue.

First-class career (1886–1908): 7,359 runs (27.06) including 14 centuries, and 200 wickets (23.78)

Test matches (5): 168 runs (18.66), 1 wicket (129.00), and 5 catches

FOSTER, Frank Rowbotham

(b. 1889, Birmingham; d. 1958, Northampton) *Warwickshire and England*

In an age rich in genuine all-rounders, Frank Foster, no relation of the seven Foster brothers, was among the best. A natural hitter, he was a right-hand batsman who did not bother over-much about technique yet was good enough to hit 305 not out against Worcestershire at Dudley in 1914. He bowled left-arm, fast-medium, with a short run and beautifully easy action, his delivery seeming to hurry off the ground and rush batsmen into their strokes. He was also a fine slip. One of the pioneers of leg-theory bowling, he was consulted by Douglas Jardine before the 'bodyline' tour of Australia in 1932/3. As captain of Warwickshire from 1911 until 1914 he was an inspiration and led his county to their first Championship triumph in 1911. He made 1,383 runs and took 116 wickets for Warwickshire that season, topping both batting and bowling averages. In Australia in 1911/12 he and Sydney Barnes won the Ashes for England, Foster taking 32 wickets (21.62) in the series. Foster and Barnes formed one of the best bowling combinations England has ever had, and, incidentally, were a remarkable exception to the rule that all-out pace is the answer in Australian conditions. He did the double in 1911 and 1914. His career was finished by a crash on a motor-cycle early in the First World War.

First-class career (1908–14): 6,548 runs (26.61) including 7 centuries, 717 wickets (20.75), and 121 catches

Test matches (11): 330 runs (23.57), 45 wickets (20.57), and 11 catches

FOSTER, Neil Alan

(b. 1962, Colchester, Essex) *Essex and England*

Neil Foster was a sparky and spirited right-arm fast-medium bowler who overcame a serious spinal injury to become a leading member of the successful Essex side of the 1980s. Tall and slim, he had a classical bowling action, could bowl very accurately, and was able to move the ball both ways off the wicket, but although for at least five years he was the most consistently dangerous bowler of his type in England, suspect knees plagued him and eventually led to early retirement. He made his county début in 1980 at the age of 18. Problems with his back, requiring major surgery and the insertion of several metal plates, restricted his appearances in the next two years. But in 1983 he showed himself to be an outstanding young fast bowler, taking 51 wickets (22.37) in only 12 matches for Essex. He made his Test début at Lord's in the third Test against New Zealand, having played in only 19 first-class matches. He took a wicket in the second innings but a recurrence of his back injury ended his season. He went on the 1983/4 tour of New Zealand and Pakistan, producing his best bowling figures to date, 6 for 30 against Northern Districts, and in the third Test against Pakistan at Lahore he bowled magnificently to take 5 for 67. He played in only one Test against the West Indies in 1984, failing to take a wicket, but collected 87 wickets (24.11) in first-class cricket as Essex won the Championship. Then in India in 1984/5, in the fourth Test at Madras, he produced a match-winning performance: playing his first Test of the series, he took 6 for 104 and 5 for 59, running through the strong Indian batting side with an outstanding display of sustained hostility. But he did not establish himself in the Test side of 1985, bowling disappointingly in his only Test of the summer at Lord's where all three of his home Tests had been played, none with much luck. A chequered tour of the West Indies followed, some good early performances being spoiled by too little consistency of line and length. But in 1986 he consistently fulfilled his promise, taking over 100 first-class wickets—the only Englishman to do so—playing in two Tests and also making useful runs in the County Championship. He well deserved his place on England's tour to Australia in 1986/7, but even on that tour could gain a place in only one Test match. Against Pakistan in 1987 he topped the England bowling averages, taking 8 for 107 at Leeds, and he was in the England team which reached the World Cup Final in Calcutta the following winter. Anxiety about his frequently injured knees led to his accepting an unofficial tour of South Africa in 1989/90, and with it a three-year Test ban. After another operation, he had a brilliant season for Essex in 1991, taking 100 wickets and scoring a belligerent century against Sussex—on his day he could drive the ball with handsome style. But a last Test appearance at Lord's in 1993 finally finished his knees and his benefit season for the county he had whole-heartedly served proved to be his last.

First-class career (1980–93): 4,343 runs (20.68) including 2 centuries, 908 wickets (24.44), and 116 catches

Test matches (29): 446 runs (11.73), 88 wickets (32.85), and 7 catches

FOSTER, Reginald Erskine

(b. 1878, Malvern, Worcestershire; d. 1914, London) *Oxford University, Worcestershire, and England*

In the early years of the century Worcestershire were known as 'Fostershire' as the seven sons of a clergyman at Malvern all played for the county. It is said that when the family did the washing-up, the plates and cups were thrown from one to another to be dried and put away. R. E. Foster —'Tip'—the third in age, was undeniably the greatest of the septet. His right-handed batting was of the cultured, polished kind associated with Malvern; he has been described by a contemporary as a more flexible and sounder version of Ted Dexter, hard on the latter perhaps but an indication of Foster's class and style. He was also a useful fast bowler. At Oxford he won his blue as a freshman, played four times against Cambridge at Lord's and hit 171 in 1900, the record score in the match up to that date. A few days later, for Gentlemen against Players at Lord's, he scored 102 not out and 136. On his Test début, at Sydney in 1903/4, he held England's batting together in scoring 287, fours cascading from his bat. It was the highest score ever made by an Englishman in Australia. Although he captained England against South Africa in 1907, he had ceased to play regularly, business and illness successively curtailing his career. He died, sadly young, a victim of diabetes, three months before the First World War broke out. Also a brilliant footballer, he gained blues for soccer, golf, and rackets, as well as for cricket. He gained six full England soccer caps and is the only man to have captained England at both soccer and cricket. Three of his nephews, and his brother-in-law, also played county cricket.

First-class career (1897–1912): 9,076 runs (41.82) including 22 centuries, 25 wickets (46.12), and 179 catches

Test matches (8): 602 runs (46.30) including 1 century, and 13 catches

FOTHERGILL, Arnold James

(b. 1854, Newcastle upon Tyne; d. 1932, Newcastle) *Northumberland, Somerset, and England*

A medium-paced left-arm bowler and hard-hitting batsman, Arnold Fothergill was employed by Somerset when they were elevated to first-class rank. He toured South Africa with Major Warton's team in 1888/9 and played in the first two

Tests ever held against South Africa. He represented Players against Gentlemen at Lord's in 1882 and was on MCC's ground staff.

First-class career (1882–9): 843 runs (14.05) and 119 wickets (18.18)

Test matches (2): 33 runs (16.50) and 8 wickets (11.25)

FOWLER, Graeme

(b. 1957, Accrington, Lancashire) *Lancashire, Durham, and England*

A neat, jaunty left-handed opening batsman and a fine athlete, as befits his other profession as a teacher of PE, Graeme Fowler, a product of Accrington Grammar and Durham University, took advantage of TCCB bans on Graham Gooch, Geoff Boycott, Wayne Larkins and others by scoring consistently for Lancashire throughout the 1982 season and earning a place in the England team for the last Test of the summer, the decisive third match at Headingley against Pakistan. He was bowled for nine in the first innings but, showing confidence and good technique against Imran Khan, he made 86 in the second innings to inspire an England win and make sure of his place on the plane to Australia. A useful reserve wicket-keeper but also a fine all-round fielder, he first played for Lancashire's second eleven in 1973 at the age of 16 and made his opening appearance in a first-class match in 1979, but was not capped until 1981 when he hit 1,560 runs at an average of 40. Shrewdly advised by his friend David Lloyd, Fowler's three hundreds in his first full season were followed by five in 1982, including two in one match against Warwickshire at Southport when he batted with an injured leg and a runner in each innings. He hit the ball very hard, especially on the off-side. Although never appearing totally secure, he was England's regular opening batsman until 1985; he always performed grittily and often to great effect. He scored 207 runs (34.50) in his three Tests in Australia in 1982/3, including two fifties, and he made his maiden Test century against New Zealand at The Oval in 1983 when he shared an opening stand of 223 with Chris Tavaré. After touring New Zealand and Pakistan in the winter he batted staunchly in the 1984 series against the West Indies, making a defiant century at Lord's. He had a happy series in India in 1984/5, scoring 438 runs (54.75) in the five Tests, including 201 at Madras. But he lost form totally in 1985 due to a neck injury, losing his place for both England and, temporarily, Lancashire. He returned to form in 1986 with 1,163 runs (38.76) but was never again in serious contention for England. Leaving Lancashire in disillusionment at the end of 1992, he moved to Durham. A sharp dresser with an eye for the girls he was always one of English cricket's more unconventional characters.

First-class career (1979–   ): 16,663 runs (35.60) including 36 centuries, 10 wickets (36.60), 182 catches, and 5 stumpings

Test matches (21): 1,307 runs (35.52) including 3 centuries, 0–11, and 10 catches

FOWLER, Robert St Leger

(b. 1891, Enfield, Co. Meath, Ireland; d. 1925, Enfield) *The Army and Hampshire*

No schoolboy feat of fiction matched the performance of the Irish-born Eton captain, Bob Fowler, on a Saturday afternoon at Lord's against Harrow in 1910. His 64 runs in Eton's second innings—after following-on 165 runs behind—had ensured Harrow would have to bat again. Eton's last pair then put on 50 and 10,000 stayed to see Harrow knock off the 55 they now needed; but Fowler's off-breaks secured him 8 for 23 in 10 overs and his team won by nine runs. His next appearance at Lord's was anti-climactic, for on his first-class début three years later for MCC against Hampshire he scored 10 and did not bowl. As a career soldier his 24 matches for the Army and Hampshire were spread over 11 years culminating in an invitation to captain MCC in the West Indies in 1924/5. The tour was postponed for a year by which time Fowler was dead.

First-class career (1913–24): 957 runs (28.14), 59 wickets (24.77), and 21 catches

FRASER, Angus Robert Charles

(b. 1965, Billinge, Lancashire) *Middlesex and England*

Having established his credentials at the highest level by taking 47 wickets in his first ten Tests, Angus Fraser overcame a career-threatening hip injury to become once more a match-winner for England. When fully fit he was a fast-medium bowler of exemplary accuracy whose minatory bounce gave batsmen no respite. Essentially he aimed to hit the pitch hard, seam-down, on the right line and length, waiting for batsmen to make mistakes or the ball to move. A friendly, lumbering giant of a man, with a fierce will-to-win and a lugubrious air, Fraser and his younger brother Alastair, who played for Middlesex and Essex, both attended the Gayton High School in Harrow, as later did another future

Middlesex player Mark Ramprakash. The Frasers also learnt their cricket at Stanmore, with Angus progressing through the Middlesex Schools side to the county's Young Cricketers and eventually the staff at Lord's, making his début in 1984. Two years later came the setback of a back injury, but by 1988 'Gus' Fraser was being spoken of as a Test bowler, taking 80 wickets in the season, as well as 3 for 36 in Middlesex's NatWest Final victory over Worcestershire. He was 12th man for the second Test against Australia at Lord's, and in 1989 he made his début in the third match at Edgbaston, claiming the hitherto invincible Steve Waugh as his first wicket on the way to an impressive 4 for 63 in 33 overs. Five more wickets in two Tests followed before injury ruled him out of the final Test of the summer, but, chosen for the West Indies tour which followed, Fraser quickly showed he had become a key member of the attack. In Jamaica, his 5 for 29 set England on the way to their first Test win over the home side in 16 years, and he took five more wickets in the rain-ruined third Test in Trinidad before a rib-cartilage injury ruled him out for the rest of the tour; without Graham Gooch as well, England lost both remaining Tests and the series. When he returned for the series against India in 1990, Fraser took 16 wickets in three Tests including 5 for 104 and 3 for 39 as England won the Lord's match made famous by Gooch's 333. His selection for the winter tour of Australia was a formality, but with the hard grounds jarring his big frame, he broke down in December 1990 with the injury that was to cast doubt on his future. It happened during a marathon spell in the second Test in Melbourne which yielded him 6 for 82. Originally thought to be inflammation of the hip joint, Fraser struggled on to the end of the trip, missing two of the remaining three Tests, and then broke down again after only two matches in 1991. Surgery followed, and during his enforced lay-off, Fraser kept himself busy working for City Fund Managers Whittingdale. When he returned to action in 1992, his bowling was said to lack the 'nip' which had made him so dangerous at Test level, a suggestion supported by the figures as he took only 23 wickets that summer. It looked set to be a similar story in 1993, when suddenly, in August, Fraser took 16 wickets in two matches, including a then career-best 7 for 40 against Leicestershire. The selectors placed him on stand-by for the final Test of the summer against Australia at The Oval, and when Martin Bicknell pulled out through injury, Fraser played, responding with 8 for 131 to win the man-of-the-match

award as England beat Allan Border's side for the first time in 6½ years. The following winter in the Caribbean, Fraser again underlined his value, when, having missed the first Test of the series with a broken hand, he claimed 8 for 75 in the West Indies first innings in Barbados, the best-ever figures by an England bowler against the West Indies as the home side lost in Bridgetown for the first time in 59 years. By the end of 1994 however, after just 14 wickets in five Tests against New Zealand and South Africa, the selectors felt his bowling had lost its edge once more and left him out of the final Test of the summer against South Africa. Bitterly disappointed by his subsequent omission from the tour of Australia, he went to Sydney to play club cricket but was soon recalled as a replacement and in three Tests took 14 wickets, including 2 for 26 and 5 for 73 at Sydney.

First-class career (1984–): 1,502 runs (11.29) and 486 wickets (26.02)
Test matches (24): 233 runs (7.76), 99 wickets (27.86), and 6 catches

---

FREDERICK, Prince of Wales

(b. 1707, Hanover, Germany; d. 1751, London)

Forever satirized as 'Poor Fred', the Prince of Wales—in typical Hanoverian fashion—quarrelled with his father, George II, who called him 'the greatest ass in the world'. Frederick was banished from Court and had plenty of time to play cricket. He gave royal patronage to a game which was appealing to the aristocracy and led Surrey in various matches from 1735 onwards, wagering £1,000 on the results. A blow from a ball when playing cricket at Cliveden House in Buckinghamshire caused an abscess from which he died.

FREEMAN, Alfred Percy

(b. 1888, Lewisham, London; d. 1965, Bearsted, Kent) *Kent and England*

'Tich' Freeman must have bowled more balls that looked as if they could be hit for six than any bowler who ever lived, but his records in domestic cricket were simply fantastic. Regularly he took more than 200 wickets a season for Kent when the next most successful bowler managed about 60. In eight seasons between 1928 and 1935 he took 2,090 wickets. He bowled wonderfully well-controlled, right-arm leg-breaks, mixed with a skilfully disguised googly and top spinner. Against the best county batsmen he was a threat, against the worst a tyrant. Only 5 ft. 2 in. tall, he had small hands but very strong fingers which enabled him to turn the ball sharply. Ian Peebles described how after hitching up his trousers he would run up five paces and deliver the ball with a neat rotary action, 'like a spring snapping'. The quick feet could beat him, however, and the Australians were not afraid of him. He took 304 wickets (18.05) in 1928, a record in first-class cricket, but that winter, in Australia, he did not appear in a single Test. In his first tour of Australia, 1924/5, he had taken 8 wickets at 57.37 in two Tests. Such triumph set off by such failure is practically without parallel. He mesmerized the West Indies in their first Test series in 1928, heading the bowling with 22 wickets (13.72); and against South Africa, 1927/8 and 1929, he captured 14 and 22 wickets respectively. Only Wilfred Rhodes has taken more wickets in first-class cricket, and no one has taken more than his 3,151 in the County Championship.

First-class career (1914–36): 4,961 runs (9.50), 3,776 wickets (18.42), 238 catches, and 1 stumping
Test matches (12): 154 runs (14.00), 66 wickets (25.86), and 4 catches

FRENCH, Bruce Nicholas

(b. 1959, Warsop, Nottinghamshire)
Nottinghamshire and England

The youngest to play for Nottinghamshire when he made his first-class début at the age of 16 years 10 months in 1976, Bruce French was an experienced craftsman by the time that he finally won his spurs at Test level a decade later. Understudy to Paul Downton on two tours, to India in 1984/5 and West Indies in 1985/6, he won his first cap against India at home in 1986 and quickly proved himself to be more than just a polished and unfussy wicket-keeper. He held some brilliant catches and he was most unlucky to lose his place as the first-choice wicket-keeper in the team to tour Australia, the consequence of being no more than an occasionally useful right-handed tail-end batsman. Born to cricket—his father and four brothers played with him for Welbeck Colliery CC in his native Nottinghamshire before he joined the county staff—he was the country's leading wicket-taker in 1984, with 87 victims, 11 of them stumped. He took seven catches and three stumpings in a match, a Notts record. A family man, his hobbies are mountaineering and pipe-smoking. He showed his toughness when recovering quickly from mild concussion after being hit on the head by a ball from his Nottinghamshire colleague, Richard Hadlee, during the Lord's Test of 1986 against New Zealand. He was replaced for a time as wicket-keeper by Bob Taylor, who had retired but was allowed to play as substitute by permission of the New Zealand captain, Jeremy Coney. A finger injury, requiring surgery, obliged him to miss most of the 1988 season and, having given way to Jack Russell as England's wicket-keeper, he went instead to South Africa in 1989/90, thus earning a three-year ban. In 1995 he announced his retirement and his intention to begin a second career as a climbing instructor.

First-class career (1976–): 7,141 runs (18.94) including 2 centuries, 1 wicket (70.00), and 914 dismissals (814 c., 100 st.)
Test matches (16): 308 runs (18.11) and 39 dismissals (38 c., 1 st.)

FRINDALL, William Howard

(b. 1939, Epsom, Surrey)

Born on the first day of the 'Timeless Test' at Durban in 1939, Bill Frindall, styled 'the Bearded Wonder' by Brian Johnston, joined the BBC *Test Match Special* team as scorer in 1966 and became its longest serving member. His vast store of information has been profitably used by many. His *Wisden Book of Test Cricket*, listing all Test score-cards from 1877 to 1989, has assisted hundreds of researchers. His numerous works, all meticulously researched, include *The Wisden Book of Cricket Records*. He has edited the *Playfair Cricket Annual* since 1986 and the records section of Wisden since 1986. His Scoring Book, based on an idea of the Australian scorer Bill Ferguson in 1905, gives to each over a line across a series of vertical columns. The neatness and accuracy of his own scoring is legendary. A useful, very keen club cricketer, he was an aggressive right-handed batsman and medium-fast bowler whose own team, the Maltamaniacs, has toured abroad. Either as player or commentator, he spends much time supporting benefit and charity matches and he is president of British Blind Sport.

FRITH, David Edward John

(b. 1937, London)

A lifelong cricket addict and useful club cricketer, David Frith has been a prodigious and meticulous cricket writer. After editing *The Cricketer* (1972–8) he founded *Wisden Cricket Monthly* which he has edited since 1979. His *Pageant of Cricket* (1987), in the view of Sir Donald Bradman went 'closer to providing a complete picture of the past' than any other work and contains a majestic collection of pictures with shrewd, sometimes out-of-the-way, comment. His biographies of A. E. Stoddart (1970) and Archie Jackson (1974) reflected his talent as an indefatigible researcher and, in *The Fast Men* (1975), he offered the first thorough study of fast bowling from Lumpy Stevens to Thomson and Lillee.

FRY, Charles Burgess

(b. 1872, West Croydon, Surrey; d. 1956, Hampstead, London) *Oxford University, Surrey, Sussex, Hampshire, London County, Europeans, and England*

One of the legendary figures of cricket, C. B. Fry was a man of such majesty that he was actually offered the Kingdom of Albania. Unfortunately for that country Fry declined and King Zog ruled in his stead. His talent as a batsman blossomed gloriously during the early years of this century. He studied with a scholar's application the technique of batting and had the concentration and determination, as well as the physical strength and fitness, to master most bowlers in most conditions; science applied to genius was formidable indeed. Pre-eminently a back-foot player, he had a powerful straight drive but scored mainly on the leg-side and he had a cast-iron defence. A critic once said he had only one stroke. 'True,' replied Charles Fry, 'but I can send it in 22 places.' Ranji and C. B. Fry were the twin champions of Sussex: on what one likes to think of as a typical day at Hove, Fry would win the toss, open with Joe Vine and, as a matter of course, have an exhilarating stand later with Ranji. At close of play Sussex would be 500 for 2, with Fry some 200 not out. Six times between 1899 and 1905 he scored more than 2,000 in a season, in 1901 reaching 3,147 runs (78.67) which included thirteen centuries, six of them in succession. Although he could never spare the time for a tour of Australia, he played in Tests against 'the ancient enemy' in England in 1899, 1902, 1905, 1909, and 1912, in the latter year leading England to victory. He toured South Africa in 1895/6 and played against them at home in 1907 and 1912. He captained Sussex in 1904, 1905, 1907, and 1908. He made magnificent centuries against Australia and South Africa, 144 at The Oval in 1905, and 129 at The Oval in 1907, and as late as 1921, while playing for Hampshire, he was again

invited to play against Australia, but declined on grounds of age. A fine field, he had a chequered career as a bowler, being labelled a 'thrower' and, for a time, had his bowling arm in splints. Fry himself insisted that all his deliveries were fair. Although it was his cricket that captured the public imagination, Charles Fry was the complete all-round man. He was a dazzling and, if Neville Cardus is to be believed, domineering conversationalist, and a brilliant scholar (placed above a future Lord Chancellor, F. E. Smith, on the scholarship roll to Wadham College, Oxford). In 1893 at Oxford he equalled the long jump record of 23 ft. 6.5 in. He also played Association Football for England, and also earned a Cup Final medal (with Southampton). He would have added a rugby blue to those won for cricket, soccer, and athletics, but for an injury sustained just before the 'Varsity match. He edited *Fry's Magazine*, wrote several books of permanent cricket interest, an autobiography, and a novel (the latter with his wife), served on the League of Nations, stood as a Liberal candidate for Parliament and, the great purpose of his life, trained the young on TS *Mercury* on the Hamble. Only look at his photograph and you will see why H. S. Altham wrote of him, 'Fry could, alike in form and feature, have stepped out of the frieze of the Parthenon.'

First-class career (1892–1921): 30,886 runs (50.22) including 94 centuries, 166 wickets (29.34), and 240 catches

Test matches (26): 1,223 runs (32.18) including 2 centuries, 0–3, and 17 catches

GASTON, Alfred James

(b. 1854, Sussex; d. 1928, Brighton, Sussex)

'Leather Hunter', which was Gaston's pseudonym in the *Sussex Daily News* and Brighton *Evening Argus*, published the first printed *Bibliography of Cricket* (1895) in a limited edition of 25 copies. Besides writing benefit pamphlets for Sussex players, he wrote a history of Sussex county cricket and was an extensive collector and dealer. Arthur Gilligan called him 'one of the pillars of Sussex cricket off the field'. His lantern-lecture tours of the country on winter evenings anticipated the modern Cricket Society talks. Irving Rosewater called his monograph on him in 1975 'A study in enthusiasm'. It was a fit epithet for a man who combined painstaking research, collecting, authorship, journalism, lantern slide lectures, and bookselling, all in the name of cricket.

GATTING, Michael William

(b. 1957, Kingsbury, Middlesex) *Middlesex and England*

A very successful captain of Middlesex who led England to the Ashes, and all other prizes besides, in Australia in 1986/7, and in 23 Tests in all, Mike Gatting was a natural games player, one of a group of exceptionally talented batsmen who graduated from the England school sides of the early 1970s. A cheerful Londoner, short but very sturdily built, he was a tenacious, hard-hitting right-handed batsman, useful medium-pace bowler, and good all-round field. Playing his first match for Middlesex in 1975, he won his cap in 1977 when he scored more than 1,000 runs despite not scoring a century and gained the last place in the England touring team to Pakistan and New Zealand, playing in a Test in each country without success. As soon as he had scored his initial Championship hundred, 103 not out against Yorkshire in 1978, he added another immediately and developed into one of the few English batsmen who could be relied upon to trade blow for blow with the overseas stars in county cricket. In 1980 he made a determined 51 not out in the Centenary Test against Australia at Lord's and, although he failed against ferocious bowling in the West Indies in 1980/1, he played attractively and consistently for England throughout the 1981 Ashes series, scoring 370 runs in 12 innings at 30.83. In that season he started a remarkable sequence of heavy scoring in county cricket, finishing eighth in the first-class averages; he finished sixth in 1982, third in 1983 and he reached the peak of his form in 1984, scoring 2,257 runs with eight centuries, a top score of 258 against Somerset, heading the averages at 68.39. Capable of destroying any county bowling attack, he nevertheless struggled to establish himself in Test cricket, partly because he was never allowed to settle into a regular place and partly because of some careless shots. When he fell cheaply twice in the Lord's Test against the West Indies and was again dropped, he had scored 1,144 runs (23.83) in his 30 Tests with a top score of 81. But, at last, on the 1984/5 tour to India, Gatting made the breakthrough in Test cricket. In the first Test at Bombay, playing his 54th innings, he made his first Test century, a magnificent 136. He made 207 at Madras and scored 575 runs (95.83) in the series. He completed another two hundreds in England's powerful batting displays against Australia in 1985 out of a total of 527 runs (87.83). In eleven Tests he had scored 1,102 runs at 91.83.

But his tour to the West Indies in 1986 was dogged by misfortune, as first a broken nose which required surgery back in England and then a broken thumb kept him out of action until the final Test. His absence was a desperate blow to England's chances in the series. He made 15 and 1 in his only Test, although ironically he topped the tour batting averages and, when England lost the first Test to India in 1986, he succeeded David Gower as captain of his country. His first taste was bitter—defeat by India at Headingley, despite a defiant 31 not out as England were whipped out for 128 in their second innings. But at Edgbaston he showed his true mettle by scoring 183 not out in a total of 390 after England had been 61 for 3, and after that innings his appointment as captain of England in Australia in 1986/7 was certain. Although England lost the second series of 1986 to New Zealand, Gatting made 121 at The Oval, sharing a stand of 223 for the fourth wicket with David Gower to salvage some pride at the end of a dismal run of eleven Tests without a win in 1986. Under his command in Australia, England's fortunes changed. The Ashes were retained, and two one-day tournaments also won, but at home in 1987 England lost the five-match series by losing the only match which was not drawn, despite an innings of 124 by Gatting at Edgbaston. He followed this with 150 not out to save The Oval Test and for good measure scored a handsome century at Lord's in the MCC Bicentenary match. The ascendant star then plummeted with sad speed: in Pakistan the following winter he was goaded into a furious row with a provocative and mulish Test umpire named Shakoor Rana. Gatting's finger-wagging retort to an alleged insult from the official was officially exonerated although it led to the temporary suspension of the Test match, at Faisalabad. His career never quite recovered. He was sacked from the captaincy in England in 1988 for inviting a barmaid to his room during a Test match in Nottingham. The liaison had reached a Sunday tabloid newspaper, but the events of the winter's cricket undoubtedly played their part in Gatting's downfall. Disillusioned, he accepted an invitation to lead a team to South Africa in 1989/90, thus incurring a three-year ban from Test Cricket under an edict of the International Cricket Council. He resumed his Test career in India in 1992/3, and in Australia, 1994/5. but was out of luck until hitting 117 at Adelaide in a rare England win. For Middlesex he was as dominating as ever, leading them in 1993 to the third Championship under his command. Each of the one-day trophies also reached the Middlesex sideboard during the reign of this pugnacious, open-hearted, and likeable cricketer. His brother, Steve, played professional football for, amongst others, Arsenal.

First-class career (1975–): 31,785 runs (50.94) including 82 centuries, 156 wickets (29.43), and 423 catches

Test matches (74): 4,227 runs (36.75) including 9 centuries, 4 wickets (79.25), and 56 catches

GAY, Leslie Hewitt

(b. 1871, Brighton, Sussex; d. 1949, Sidmouth, Devon) *Cambridge University, Hampshire, Somerset, and England*

In a rather short, irregular career, Leslie Gay won a blue at Cambridge and kept wicket in one Test, for England in Australia, 1894/5, scoring 33 and 4, catching 3 and stumping one. A Corinthian, he kept goal for England at Association Football in three matches in 1893/4, and is thus a double international.

First-class career (1891–1900): 1,005 runs (15.46) and 89 dismissals (69 c., 20 st.)

GEARY, George

(b. 1893, Barwell, Leicestershire; d. 1981, Leicester) *Leicestershire and England*

One of a family of sixteen, George Geary thought of emigrating. But fortunately he remained and, with Ewart Astill, carried Leicestershire on his shoulders for many seasons, taking more than 100 wickets in 11 seasons. Big, strong, and cheerful, despite suffering some unpleasant injuries, he was a right-arm, fast-medium bowler with a high action and unwavering accuracy. He could also turn off-spinners if the conditions warranted. As a batsman he played many valiant innings with a good range of strokes; and he was a superb slip field, his long reach enabling him to hold some dazzling catches. Eleven times he took 100 wickets in a season. In his first Test against Australia, at Headingley in 1926, he shared in an invaluable ninth-wicket partnership of 108 with George Macaulay; and the same year, at The Oval, his two excellent catches in the last innings helped England to win the rubber. In Australia in 1928/9 he broke his nose but played on and, in the first innings of the final Test at Melbourne, took 5 for 105 in 81 overs, 36 of which were maidens, a remarkable feat of endurance. At Sydney in the second match he captured 5 for 35 and scored 66, and he headed the bowling aver-

ages for the series, with 19 wickets (25.10). On matting in South Africa, 1927/8, he was quite deadly, taking 12 for 130 in the first Test at Johannesburg, when the South Africans considered him the best in the world under those conditions. Later, elbow trouble incapacitated him. For his county he took all 10 for 18 against Glamorgan at Pontypridd, 1929, which was a world record until eclipsed by Hedley Verity (10 for 10) three years later. In retirement he was coach at Charterhouse, where he put Peter May on the road to success.

First-class career (1912–38): 13,504 runs (19.80) including 8 centuries, 2,063 wickets (20.04), and 451 catches

Test matches (14): 249 runs (15.56), 46 wickets (29.41), and 13 catches

GEORGE VI, King

(b. 1895, Sandringham, Norfolk; d. 1952, Sandringham)

The king performed a royal hat-trick at Windsor when he bowled Edward VII, the future George V, and the future Edward VIII in consecutive balls. He won the RAF tennis doubles with Louis Greig, in 1920.

GETTY, John Paul

(b. 1932, United States of America)

A philanthropist who was made an honorary KBE in 1986, J. Paul Getty has shown his vast enthusiasm for cricket in such ways as establishing his own ground and making immense donations to the game. He provided the largest private donation to the new Mound Stand at Lord's, where he has his own box—one frequently visited by a diverse collection of celebrities—and his beautiful ground at Wormsley on the Oxfordshire/Berkshire border is as perfectly conceived and laid out as any country-home ground has ever been. After a life full of difficulties and sadness, despite his enormous wealth, Paul Getty has found happiness in giving generously of its facilities on summer sundays since its inauguration in 1992. In the same year he acquired the ownership of Wisden Cricketers' Almanack.

GIBB, Paul Anthony

(b. 1913, Brandsby, Yorkshire; d. 1977, Guildford, Surrey) *Cambridge University, Yorkshire, Essex, and England*

Awarded his blue at Cambridge in 1935, Paul Gibb became, in the same year, the first Yorkshire amateur to make a century on his début for the county, scoring 157 against Nottinghamshire at Bramall Lane. In 1938/9 he further proved his appetite for the big occasion when he scored 93 and 106 in his first Test against South Africa at Johannesburg. He was a right-handed batsman who defended stoutly and drove admirably, and also a very competent wicket-keeper. He toured Australia in 1946/7, but retired from the game on his return home. He reappeared in 1951 as a professional for Essex and played with success until becoming an umpire in 1956. He travelled the country in a caravan. At the time of his death he was a bus driver, and had been so reserved that none of his workmates knew of his origins.

First-class career (1934–56): 12,520 runs (28.07) including 19 centuries, and 548 dismissals (425 c., 123 st.)

Test matches (8): 581 runs (44.69) including 2 centuries, and 4 dismissals (3 c., 1 st.)

GIFFORD, Norman

(b. 1940, Ulverston, Lancashire) *Worcestershire, Warwickshire, and England*

With his relatively flat trajectory and low delivery, often from wide of the crease, Norman Gifford was never a beautiful left-arm spinner to watch, but for 28 years he earned the respect of county batsmen for his unerring accuracy and his ability to bowl sides out whenever the wicket helped him. He was also a determined and resourceful left-handed tail-ender. A Lancastrian from the Furness district, his career began when he answered an advertisement in *The Cricketer* placed by Worcestershire, who quickly saw his ability. Lancashire also offered him terms but he never regretted his choice and in 1974 he captained Worcestershire to an exciting win in the County Championship. Ruddy-faced, and a pipe-smoker whose curly hair soon receded, he is a witty man with a cool temperament and astute cricket brain; his captaincy was outstanding although marked at one point by a dispute between players and committee over pay. In his first full season he took 133 wickets. In 1964 he played in two Tests against Australia, doing creditably but, with Derek Underwood barring the way for other left-arm spinners after 1966, he did not play again until 1971. However, he bowled particularly well in India, Pakistan, and Sri Lanka in 1972/3, and two England captains, Illingworth and Lewis, thought there was little to choose between Gifford and Underwood on good pitches. Worcestershire released him after the 1982 season when his

appearances had been restricted because of his elevation to the England selection committee. However, he was offered terms by Warwickshire for the 1983 season and so gave up his selector duties. In his first season with his new county he took over a hundred first-class wickets and he was captain of the club from 1985 to 1987. He was England's assistant manager on the tours to Australia (1982/3), New Zealand and Pakistan (1983/4), and India (1984/5), and he managed the A team to Australia in 1992/3. He was Sussex's manager-coach 1989–95. He was appointed Warwickshire captain following Bob Willis's retirement, and he captained an England side in two one-day internationals in Sharjah in 1984/5. He was awarded the MBE for his services to the game.

First-class career (1960–88): 7,048 runs (13.02), 2,068 wickets (23.58), and 319 catches

Test matches (15): 179 runs (16.27), 33 wickets (31.09), and 8 catches

GILLIGAN, Alfred Harold Herbert

(b. 1896, London; d. 1978, Shamley Green, Surrey) *Cambridge University, Sussex, and England*

A determined right-handed batsman, often opening the batting, a useful change-bowler, and a keen field, Harold Gilligan succeeded his brother Arthur as captain of Sussex in 1930 for one season. In 1929/30 he led England in the first-ever Tests against New Zealand, England winning the rubber. During the First World War, as a pilot in the Royal Navy Air Service, he piloted the first plane to fly over the German fleet at Kiel; engine trouble developed and he spent three days and nights in the North Sea before help came. One of his daughters, Virginia, married P. B. H. May.

First-class career (1919–31): 8,873 runs (17.96), 115 wickets (33.66), and 123 catches

Test matches (4): 71 runs (17.75)

GILLIGAN, Arthur Edward Robert

(b. 1894, London; d. 1976, Pulborough, Sussex) *Cambridge University, Surrey, Sussex, and England*

The most famous of three brothers who gained distinction at the game, Arthur Gilligan was a happy ambassador for cricket in England, Australia, South Africa, and India. A fighter but endlessly cheerful, he got the best out of Sussex, whom he captained from 1922 until 1929, by making the county one of the best fielding sides. He led England to success in the rubber against

South Africa in 1924 and also to her first win over Australia after the First World War, at Melbourne in 1924/5. While his health lasted, he was a lively right-arm fast bowler, accurate and always bowling at the stumps or for catches in the slips. He was a courageous batsman anywhere in the order—his initial hundred in first-class cricket was made at number eleven—and believed that all bowlers were made to be hit. Fielding at mid-off he ranked among the best. In 1924 at Edgbaston he took 6 for 7, with Maurice Tate dismissing South Africa for 30 (and in the second innings he claimed 5 for 83), but some weeks later he was hit badly over the heart while batting and his doctor advised him to stop bowling fast. As a bowler he was never the same force again. He later became immersed in the administration of the game and was successively president and patron of Sussex CCC and president of MCC (in 1967). He was popular as a radio commentator, especially in Australia, and, while teamed with Victor Richardson, 'What do you think, Arthur?' became a catch-phrase. He wrote a study of Sussex cricket and some well-received tour books, *Collins's Men*, *The Urn Returns*, and *Australian Challenge*. A keen golfer, he was president of West Sussex Golf Club where his photograph still hangs in the members' lounge.

First-class career (1919–32): 9,140 runs (20.08) including 12 centuries, and 868 wickets (23.20)
Test matches (11): 209 runs (16.07), 36 wickets (29.05), and 3 catches

GILLINGHAM, Canon Frank Hay

(b. 1875, Tokyo, Japan; d. 1953, Monaco) *Essex*

The only Anglican clergyman to make a double-century at Lord's—against Middlesex in 1904—Frank Gillingham, through a curacy at Leyton—qualified for Essex and in 25 years (1903–28), scarcely 'a season went by when he did not make a contribution'. He was a tall, powerfully built right-handed batsman, at his best against pace bowling. Like his clerical counterpart, Canon Jack Parsons, he was a fierce driver. His best season was 1908 when he hit four centuries, and during his career he made three appearances for the Gentlemen against the Players. In 1927 he gave the first BBC cricket commentary in a broadcast from Leyton during Essex's match against the New Zealanders. Canon Gillingham, much of whose work was in the east end of London, was appointed chaplain to King George VI in 1939. At the memorial service to him in 1953 a lady in the congregation

appreciated 'that lovely chapter out of the book of *Wisden*'.

First-class career (1903–28): 10,050 runs (30.64) including 19 centuries, and 112 dismissals (111 c., 1 st.)

GIMBLETT, Harold

(b. 1914, Bicknoller, Somerset; d. 1978, Verwood, Dorset) *Somerset and England*

When only a young farmer, Harold Gimblett hit 123 against Essex at Frome in 1935, his first county match, treating the bowling with unbecoming levity for 63 minutes. A right-hander, he cut, drove, pulled and hooked in a manner which gave him fame overnight. He soon opened the batting and continued his swashbuckling way, once hitting three sixes in an over during which his partner appealed against the light. Also a versatile fielder, he blazed a trail in 1936 which many thought would lead to regular international honours, and, indeed, on his Test début against India at Lord's he hit 67 not out on a frisky wicket. But he played in only two more Tests and never against Australia. His highest first-class score was 310 against Sussex at Eastbourne in 1948, and he exceeded 1,000 runs in twelve English seasons and once with a Commonwealth team in India. On retirement he held his county's record for runs and centuries in a career. Prone to melancholy, he killed himself.

First-class career (1935–54): 23,007 runs (36.17) including 50 centuries, 41 wickets (51.80), and 246 catches
Test matches (3): 129 runs (32.25) and 1 catch

GLADWIN, Clifford

(b. 1916, Doe Lea, Derbyshire; d. 1988, Chesterfield, Derbyshire) *Derbyshire and England*

Always remembered for his Derbyshire partnership with Les Jackson, Cliff Gladwin was a tall, rather gangling, lively right-arm in-dipping seam bowler, who achieved greater cunning and accuracy as the years went by, seriously begrudging the batsman every run. As a tail-end batsman, he was more light-hearted, his best efforts usually being saved for times of crisis. Generally a cheerful extrovert, he was given to impulsive gestures. He toured South Africa with MCC in 1948/9, and it was a leg-bye off his thigh that won the Durban Test off the last ball of the match. He took 100 wickets or more in a season 12 times.

GODDARD

First-class career (1939–58): 6,283 runs (17.36) including 1 century, and 1,653 wickets (18.30)
Test matches (8): 170 runs (28.33), 15 wickets (38.06), and 2 catches

GODDARD, Thomas William John

(b. 1900, Gloucester; d. 1966, Gloucester)
Gloucestershire and England

Originally Tom Goddard was an undistinguished right-arm fast bowler for his county. But at 27 he began bowling off-breaks and the effect was dramatic. In his first season he took 184 wickets (16.38) and never looked back. Six foot three inches tall with enormous hands, he could turn the ball sharply, coming fast off the pitch, and was a master of flight. His appeal, a rolling, burring 'How wer're it?' was West Country incarnate. Tom played once for England against Australia in 1930—his first Test—and occasionally against New Zealand, West Indies, and South Africa; he toured South Africa in 1930/1 and 1938/9, when he achieved the hat-trick in the first Test at Johannesburg. His impressive statistics might have been better had he not already been 36 when the new lbw Law from 1937 gave encouragement to off-spinners, and he was nearing 50 when off-spin began to replace leg-spin in Tests. Sixteen times he took over a hundred wickets in a season.

First-class career (1922–52): 5,234 runs (9.37) and 2,979 wickets (19.84)
Test matches (8): 13 runs (6.50), 22 wickets (26.72), and 3 catches

GOOCH, Graham Alan

(b. 1953, Leytonstone, Essex) *Essex, Western Province, and England*

A big, dark, fresh-faced man whose trade-marks became a droopy black moustache and a large, faded, cream-coloured sunhat, Graham Gooch needed only the bushy beard he sometimes wore to give him, from a distance, the appearance of a youthful W. G. Grace. After an uncertain start in Test cricket he developed as a magnificent right-handed opening batsman who loved to attack and hit the ball immensely hard, especially excelling in the drive and hook. Through dedication and skill he became England's highest Test scorer and most-capped player. The older he got, the harder he worked, becoming a less dominating player but one of formidable concentration and determination. He based his technique on the front foot, with a heavy bat which was already uplifted

as the bowler ran in. Personal fitness became almost a fetish. He insisted on equal commitment to practice and fitness from his players after becoming the England captain in 1989/90, a post he held with mixed success until resigning in 1993 after 34 Tests in charge. Although his captaincy was as inflexible as it was determined he had proved himself one of the most durable players of all time. When he scored his 100th hundred in 1993 there was no sign of any decline, nor any thought of retiring from his beloved Essex, although he chose not to tour the West Indies in 1994 after a disastrous trip to India in 1992/3 when illness and domestic strife added to his problems. Returning to the Test team at home against New Zealand in 1994, he scored 210 at Trent Bridge and kept his place through the summer to ensure a final tour of Australia. He was a useful medium-paced seam bowler and a fine fielder anywhere. After a distinguished schoolboy career in Essex and for the Young England side, with whom he toured the West Indies in 1972, he came to prominence with Essex. He played a commanding innings for MCC against the Australians in 1975, hitting both Jeff Thomson and Gary Gilmour for towering sixes into the grandstand, and was picked for England following his maiden Championship hundred against Kent. But he was out of his depth against Lillee and Thomson, scoring a pair on a spiteful rain-affected wicket in his first Test at Edgbaston. Dropped after one more match, he was retarded by this premature taste of life at the top but found form again as an opening batsman in 1978 and played consistently enough on his return to the England side to earn a place in Mike Brearley's successful touring team to Australia in 1978/9. There the extra bounce of Australian pitches, many of them unreliable, resulted in a succession of low scores but, dropping down the order to number four, he justified the selectors' faith with his fine 74 in the sixth Test which helped England to their historic 5–1 win in the series. He was desperately close to making his maiden Test century in Melbourne on the 1979/80 tour, when he was run out for 99, but the next summer he succeeded in triumphant style against the West Indies. He made 123 in the Lord's Test with a magnificent display of powerful driving against fierce fast bowling. He followed that with a fine series (460 runs, average 57.50) in the Caribbean, hitting 116 at Bridgetown and a scorching 153 at Kingston, and after struggling rather against Australia in 1981, he enjoyed a consistent series in India, making 487 runs (54.11) in the Tests on the

1981/2 tour. He was at his peak when he decided to join the disapproved tour to South Africa in March 1982, where he was elected captain and played a series of brilliant innings. During his three-year Test ban, while the England selectors struggled to find a replacement opener, he was in imperious form for Essex. He scored 2,559 first-class runs (67.34) in 1984, the highest aggregate in an English season since 1961, and consistently made big scores in the one-day competitions. Back in the England side in 1985 he returned to international cricket in style with two centuries in the one-day matches against Australia. Aware of the enormous expectation placed upon him by the English public, he was understandably nervous when he played Test cricket once more. But, in the final Test at The Oval he was at his glorious best, hitting 196 with 27 crushing boundaries, his highest Test score. Troubled by the controversy that arose over his part in the tour to South Africa, he had an unhappy visit to the Caribbean in early 1986, apart from a brilliant innings of 129 not out which brought England victory in a one-day international in Port of Spain. He fared better than most of the England batsmen, scoring 276 runs (27.60) in the five Test matches. At home in 1986 he scored hundreds in both the Lord's Tests—against India, 114 and New Zealand, 183—but made himself unavailable for the subsequent tour to Australia after his wife, Brenda, had given birth to twin girls. In his first year as captain of Essex, the county won the Championship for the third time in four years, all titles which owed much to Gooch's positive batting. Despite a century in the MCC bicentenary match, he resigned the captaincy after 1987 because he felt it was affecting his batting, but after returning to the post in 1989 he found himself in charge of England too by the end of the season. It was the start of a remarkable transformation of his form as a Test batsman. Playing with renewed purpose and authority he enjoyed four seasons and four winters of personal success not always shared by his team. In the West Indies in 1989/90 he led England to their first success there for 16 years in the first Test at Sabina Park, but a broken hand suffered when England seemed likely to go two up at Trinidad proved the turning point of the West Indian revival. Unabashed, Gooch scored 1,058 runs in six home Tests against New Zealand and India in 1990, including a monumental and virtually flawless innings of 333 against India in the Lord's Test, the highwater mark of his career. It was one of twelve hundreds he scored in that burning summer. In 1991 against the West Indies his superb 154 in difficult batting conditions at Leeds won England the match and hundreds against Australia followed at Adelaide (1990/1) and at Old Trafford and Lord's in 1993. There was, too, another match-winning hundred against Pakistan at Headingley in 1992. English cricket owed much to his intense devotion to the cause.

First-class career (1973–   ): 40,174 runs (49.23), 236 wickets (34.77), and 510 catches

Test matches (118): 8,900 runs (42.58) including 20 centuries, 23 wickets (46.47), and 103 catches

GOUGH, Darren

(b. 1970, Barnsley, Yorkshire) *Yorkshire and England*

Few England cricketers since the arrival of Ian Botham have made as much of an impact as Darren Gough when he burst onto the international scene in 1994. His dynamic fast bowling, cavalier batting, and obvious love of playing for his country gained him instant popularity with spectators and commentators alike. Short (5 ft. 11 in.) by the standards of contemporary fast bowlers, but strong and broad-shouldered, Gough's first senior outing, against New Zealand in a one-day international on a cold day at Edgbaston, saw him produce a hostile opening spell and he picked up the wicket of Martin Crowe with his sixth ball. Gough suffered a side strain through his exertions, delaying his entry into Test cricket, but after missing the first two Tests of the summer he appeared at Old Trafford, taking 4 for 47 and six wickets in the match. A barn-storming 65 in his first Test innings had helped turn the game in England's favour. Eleven more wickets followed in three Tests against South Africa, including eight in a defeat at Lord's, while his unbeaten 43 at The Oval as part of a thrilling counter-attack with Phillip DeFreitas was the catalyst for England's series-levelling win at the end of the summer. Gough's name was one of the first inked in for the winter tour to Australia. After collecting 39 wickets in the second half of the 1993 season, he had gained a place on the A tour of South Africa. Hard work made him second top wicket-taker on the tour with 23 victims, including 5 for 81 in the unofficial 'Test'. As a youngster, Gough's talents also included football, and he had trials with Rotherham United, but he embarked on a career in cricket when he joined Yorkshire on a Youth Training Scheme at the age of 17. In his first first-class match, at Lord's in 1989, he took 5 for 91 in the match, including the wicket of the Middlesex captain Mike Gatting. Young England recognition followed, including a tour to Australia, but his progress became less marked and by the end of 1992 Gough had still to win his county cap. Acting on advice from Yorkshire's overseas player, the West Indies captain Richie Richardson, he concentrated on bowling flat out, but also developed his lethal in-swinging yorker and a cunning slower ball.

First-class career (1989–): 1,228 runs (16.37) and 223 wickets (30.51)

Test matches (7): 244 runs (34.85) and 37 wickets (26.78), and 4 catches

GOULD, Ian James

(b. 1957, Taplow, Buckinghamshire) *Middlesex, Sussex, and Auckland*

An energetic and nimble wicket-keeper and batsman, with a quick wit, 'Gunner' Gould played a key role for England during the 1983 World Cup. In all he played in 18 one-day internationals scoring 155 runs (12.91), and claiming 18 dismissals (15 c., 3 st.). He also toured with England in Australia in 1982/3. Although he did not win a Test cap, he made significant Test appearances as a substitute fielder. Born and educated in Buckinghamshire, he joined the MCC ground staff from school, was taken on by Middlesex, and was capped in 1977. In 1981 he joined Sussex, whom he helped to second place in the Championship that year and to one-day trophies in 1982 and 1986, returning to Middlesex to captain the 2nd XI in 1991 after 10 years at Hove. His friendly disposition made him a popular figure throughout his career, and as a left-handed batsman he could hit the ball with style and vigour; but as a wicket-keeper he was just short of being in the top class. He captained Sussex in 1987 and played in New Zealand in 1979/80.

First-class career (1975–90): 8,756 runs (26.05) including 4 centuries, 536 catches, and 67 stumpings

GOVER, Alfred Richard

(b. 1908, Epsom, Surrey) *Surrey, Bedfordshire, and England*

In retirement Alf Gover became world famous for his London cricket school near Clapham Junction, where many of the world's great players practised in their time. Well into his seventies he got into cricket whites almost daily to coach in the nets. A right-arm fast bowler, he spent half his

career bowling on 'shirt-front' wickets at The Oval. He had pace, length, direction, and frequent 'devil'; what he lacked was co-operation in the Surrey slips. In his first Test, against India at Old Trafford in 1936, two catches were dropped off his bowling on the first morning. Running in like a man pursuing but not catching a bus, he would pound away with his arms working like pistons—his 'cocktail-mixing action'—culminating in some dangerous break-backs and late awayswingers. He took at least 100 wickets in eight seasons and in 1935 he took four wickets with successive deliveries at Worcester. The following year, by taking 200 wickets at 17.73, he was the first English fast bowler in 39 years to take as many wickets in a season. His batting caused vast amusement; the crowd hoped for beefy, agricultural blows and often saw them, but he rarely stayed for long. He toured India with Lord Tennyson's team in 1937/8. For many years he wrote a coaching column in *The Cricketer*, and in 1992 published a readable memoir of his playing days. He was president of Surrey in 1980.

First-class career (1928–48): 2,312 runs (9.36), 1,555 wickets (23.63), and 171 catches

Test matches (4): 2 runs (—), 8 wickets (44.87), and 1 catch

GORDON, Sir Home Seton Charles Montagu

(b. 1881, London; d. 1956 Rottingdean, Sussex)

Home Gordon's *Cricket Form at a Glance* was a prodigious piece of statistical research covering the careers of first-class cricketers from 1878 to 1937, the royalties from which he gave to charity. It was a pioneering work of its kind but many inaccuracies have been revealed by later statisticians. The diminutive, immaculate, and garrulous twelfth baronet devoted his life to watching and writing on the game. He knew everyone in it from W. G. Grace onwards and rode in a silver coach with Ranji to the Delhi Durbar in 1911. Though he was no player, Sussex, whose secretary he was, gave him his county 'cap' and made him president. He wrote a history of the club.

GOWER, David Ivon

(b. 1957, Tunbridge Wells, Kent) *Leicestershire, Hampshire, and England*

A casual, friendly man, David Gower was a left-handed batsman of rare brilliance and a superb fieldsman who left the game after 1993 when cricket supporters in England and outside were still begging the selectors to choose him for the Test side. For a brief period in the year before, he had enjoyed the distinction of being England's highest-ever Test scorer and when he was omitted from the tour to India in 1992/3 protesting members of MCC forced a special General Meeting to debate the issue. It uncovered wide feelings of public dissatisfaction with the organization and approach of the England team. Gower was the *cause célèbre*, but he was not picked for England again. He had not, perhaps, achieved all that his ability suggested he would when first he arrived in Test cricket, partly through lack of concentration, partly through lazy footwork; but he was, like Frank Woolley, as much an entertainer as a breaker of records. Indeed he was one of the few players whom spectators, young and old, looked forward to seeing every time he played. There was a touch and elegance about his batting which was uniquely his. Tall, with fair curly hair and the body of a natural athlete who could play any game well, his timing had the exquisite touch of a Menuhin. He stood straight and still at the crease, moved easily into the line of the ball and played it late with the relaxed air of a man always in control. The son of a District Officer in East Africa, he was educated at King's School, Canterbury, and with eight 'O' levels and three 'A' levels he began a Law course in London. He abandoned it after a year to take up a professional career with Leicestershire, who were quicker than Kent to offer him terms. Outstanding in the England Schools and Young England teams, notably on tours to South Africa and the West Indies (1974/5), he first played for Leicestershire in 1975 and for some time scored more runs for them in limited-overs cricket than he did in the Championship where he tended to get himself out to rash strokes outside the off-stump. He became England's outstanding player in his first home series against Pakistan and New Zealand in 1978 and also in Australia 1978/9. His first Test century at The Oval against New Zealand was followed by another in Perth and by 200 not out against India at Edgbaston in 1979. A lean period followed, especially in home Tests, and he was dropped during the 1980 series against the West Indies. But on the tour of the Caribbean early in 1981 he played with a new maturity, hitting 187 against Young West Indies in the first match of the tour and 154 not out in the fifth and final Test, at Sabina Park. He did not add to his four Test hundreds in India and Sri Lanka in 1981/2, or at home against India and Pakistan in 1982 but, though he still succumbed to the occasional

loose stroke, he was steadily becoming a more consistent batsman. He became vice-captain of England in 1982 and at the age of 25 led his country for the first time that season in the Lord's Test against Pakistan, when Bob Willis, the officially appointed captain for the series, was injured. On the 1982/3 tour of Australia, he finally cast off the tag of being a careless and inconsistent batsman. He was England's outstanding player, composing a series of magnificent innings, often as the rest of the batting was collapsing around him. He scored 441 runs (44.10) in the five Tests, with 114 at Adelaide and three fifties. Runs continued to flow off his bat against New Zealand in 1983 (404, average 57.71) including two more centuries. When Bob Willis was forced to return home from Pakistan, Gower once more took on the England captaincy. He had a difficult task—the side had just lost the series in New Zealand and the first Test against Pakistan, but the new captain responded heroically, scoring 152 at Faisalabad and 173 not out at Lahore, almost retrieving the series. Suitably impressed, the selectors appointed him captain for the 1984 series against the mighty West Indians, but he had a disappointing series with the bat and England were thrashed 5–0. His team recovered splendidly in India in 1984/5 and Gower made a timely return to form in the last Test with a defiant 78 to ensure England's series win. In 1985, both Gower's and his team's fortunes came magnificently right. Having hit a confidence-boosting century in the one-day international at Lord's, he made 732 glorious runs (81.33) in the Tests, a new record total for a home series against Australia and the highest aggregate ever scored by an England captain. His three Test centuries were highlights of the series—166 at Trent Bridge, 215 at Edgbaston, his highest Test score, and 157 at The Oval, as England regained the Ashes. His fortunes as captain turned dramatically for the worse in the Caribbean as he was at the helm for a second successive 5–0 mauling by the West Indies. He was the most accomplished of the English batsmen, scoring 370 attractive runs (37.00) with a top score of 90, but when England lost the first Test of the 1986 season against India at Lord's, Gower lost the captaincy after a brief, busy, bitter-sweet reign. He accepted the decision with characteristic good grace and finished the summer's Tests with a glorious innings of 131 against New Zealand at The Oval, but, jaded by too much cricket and worried by domestic matters, he resigned the Leicestershire captaincy and missed the last few weeks of the season—though he was named in the party to tour Australia, 1986/7. There he scored a hundred in Perth and shared fully in the all-round success of Mike Gatting's team, but he went two more summers (having opted out of the 1986/7 winter's cricket) without a Test hundred before being reappointed England captain by Ted Dexter in 1989. It transpired that he was second choice to Gatting, who had lost the job in controversial circumstances and when England were beaten nil-four, Gower, despite a courageous hundred at Lord's, was dropped and not chosen to tour the West Indies. Returning to the side against India in 1990, he scored a match-saving 157 not out at The Oval and in Australia in 1990/1 made high-class hundreds in successive Tests at Melbourne and Sydney. He had joined Hampshire in 1990 and played for them for four seasons, inconsistently but often brilliantly. He married and settled to a prosperous life in rural Hampshire, so the fact that Graham Gooch tired of his flippant attitude and refused to pick him for further terms after the Ashes were resoundingly won by Australia in 1990/1 was less of a blow to him. During his 73 at Old Trafford in 1992 against the incisive Pakistan attack he became, until Gooch overtook him, England's highest scorer. When he heard that, even with a change of captain, he had been overlooked for the 1993/4 tour to the West Indies, he announced his retirement and began a busy second career as a journalist and television commentator.

First-class career (1975–93): 26,339 runs (40.09) including 53 centuries, 4 wickets (56.75), and 281 dismissals (280 c., 1 st.)

Test matches (117): 8,231 runs (44.25) including 18 centuries, 1 wicket (20.00), and 74 catches

GRACE, Dr Edward Mills

(b. 1841 Downend, Bristol; d. 1911, Thornbury, Dorset) *Gloucestershire and England*

Barring his younger brother, W.G., it would be hard to name anyone who was—in his time—a more remarkable match-winner than Dr Edward Grace. 'The Coroner', as he was called, was primarily an attacking right-handed batsman, a lob-bowler who took thousands of wickets in club cricket, and an outstanding field at point (then a far more important position than it is today). Fame came early; in 1862 he was the most dangerous batsman in the country and a dominant all-rounder, and for MCC against Gentlemen of Kent he scored 192 not out and took all ten wickets in an innings. In 1863 he made over

3,000 runs in all matches and, that winter, toured with George Parr's team to Australia, the second such side, but failed to enhance his reputation, a bad hand and reckless hitting being the main causes. Later he was put in the shade by W.G., but he played for Gloucestershire from 1871 until 1896, serving also as secretary from 1871 (when the club was founded) until 1908. He and his brothers G.F. and W.G. represented England in the first-ever Test in England, against Australia at The Oval in 1880, and he made 36 (putting on 96 with W.G. for the first wicket) and 0.

First-class career (1862–96): 10,025 runs (18.67) including 5 centuries, 305 wickets (20.37), 369 catches, and 1 stumping

GRACE, George Frederick

(b. 1850, Downend, Bristol; d. 1880, Basingstoke, Hampshire) *Gloucestershire and England*

Frederick Grace was tall, handsome, and muscular and was the most charming of the Graces. His right-handed, free-hitting batting was more attractive to the eye than that of his elder brothers, though he did not have W.G.'s tremendous concentration and tempered-steel defence. The fifth and youngest of the brotherhood, he had a great career opening before him, but in 1880 a severe cold, caught while engaged in a club match, developed into congestion of the lungs, and he was dead within three days. A fortnight previously he had played with E.M. and W.G. in the first Test against Australia at The Oval and had failed to score in either innings, but his great catch off a soaring hit by George Bonnor is part of the legend of the game. The batsmen were on their third run when the steepler landed in Fred's hands, which his speed and judgement had brought precisely into the right position close on the boundary. He also held another catch in the match. He toured Australia with W.G.'s team in 1873. He was also successful for Gentlemen against Players, scoring 1,008 runs (31.50), including one century, in 24 matches, and appeared for his county from 1870 to 1880, scoring 3,216 runs (30.6).

First-class career (1866–80): 6,906 runs (25.02) including 8 centuries, 329 wickets (20.06), 170 catches, and 3 stumpings

GRACE, Dr William Gilbert

(b. 1848, Downend, Bristol; d. 1915, Mottingham, Kent) *Gloucestershire, London County, and England*

'W.G.' is still, a century after his prime, the most famous cricketer of all. His tall, broad, bearded figure is instantly recognized today wherever the game is played. No one else has ever dominated the field so long and indisputably by prowess and personality alike; he was for years, with W. E. Gladstone, the best known of all Englishmen and, in a sense, he epitomized the British passion for sport, the seeds of which were sown in every part of the Empire. He possessed colossal physical energy and an unappeasable appetite for every department of the game; and he put cricket 'on the map' as a public spectacle. He played lustily and within the law, but at times, with a twinkle in his eye, he stretched the rules. In the 1870s and 1880s particularly, he was head and shoulders above his fellows. The fourth of five brothers, who were all devoted to the game and whose father and mother coached and encouraged them, he burst into first-class cricket early and retained his power for 40 years. Tall and strong, he made his first century at 15—170 for South Wales against Gentlemen of Sussex at Hove —and, at 46, bearded and burly, he made his 100th in first-class cricket, 288 for Gloucestershire against Somerset at Bristol. In 1871 he became the first man ever to reach 2,000 runs in a season, 2,739 runs (78.25), which remained his own highest aggregate. In 1873 he was the first to achieve the double—2,139 runs and 106 wickets—a feat he achieved each year until 1878, and twice in the 1880s. In 1876 he made 2,622 runs (62.42), including 344 for MCC against Kent at Canterbury. This innings was followed in the next week by scores of 177 against Nottinghamshire and 318 not out against Yorkshire. In 1895, his 'Indian Summer', he was the first to achieve 1,000 runs in May (the month in which he also hit his 100th century), and so spontaneous was the public reaction that four testimonials were started. Many of these colossal performances were achieved on pitches which were dangerous and unpredictable. He captained Gloucestershire for 25 years and led them on the two occasions they have won the Championship. When he first played for Gentlemen in 1865, they had lost their last 19 matches. When he last played in 1906 they had lost only four more. He took a side to Australia in 1872/3 and captained Lord Sheffield's Test-playing side in 1891. He hit the first century in Tests in England, 152 at The Oval in 1880, in the first match; and in 1886, in the Oval Test, his 170 was the highest of three centuries he made against the touring team that year. He led England most times between 1880 and 1899, with success. He retired from the Tests in the latter year because 'the ground was getting too far

away'. A natural athlete in his younger days, he was a first-rate hurdler and runner. Grace's right-handed batting was based on a correct technique and an assertive attitude. At times he undoubtedly overawed his opponents as on the occasion when he was bowled early in a minor match but at once replaced the bails and batted on, pointing out that the crowd had come to watch him bat and not the unfortunate bowler! But his true genius is not in doubt; no one sighted the ball and assessed its length earlier, or timed it more truly than he did, and he was equally at home on the back or front foot—'the faster they bowl, the better I like them'. As a bowler with a round-arm action, he varied his flight skilfully, his pace usually very slow, turning the ball in from leg. He was a magnificent catcher off his own bowling. In first-class cricket he exceeded 1,000 runs 28 times and 100 wickets ten times. He kept up with club cricket to the last, played bowls for England, followed all sports, and ran with the beagles. Stories of 'The Champion' abound, of course. Most are true. In his last great season, 1898, he suddenly 'declared', for no apparent reason, when 93 not out and on his way to his fourth century of the season. Asked why, he said that he had just remembered that 93 was the one score between nought and a hundred he had never got. On the day that his wife produced their second child he was playing for the United South against 22 local players at Grimsby. He celebrated by making 400 out of his side's total of 681. Given out once at The Oval he remonstrated in his loud, squeaky voice: 'Shan't have it, can't have it, *won't* have it.' The riposte from Walter Read was: 'But you'll *have* to have it.' Once he had cooled down, W.G. would have seen the humour in this; he could always laugh at himself. He died of a heart attack after an air raid in 1915 and it was appropriate that this symbol of the British Empire should die during the war which marked the beginning of the end of Britain's dominant role in the world.

First-class career (1865–1908): 54,896 runs (39.55) including 126 centuries, 2,876 wickets (17.92), 875 catches, and 5 stumpings

Test matches (22): 1,098 runs (32.29) including 2 centuries, 9 wickets (26.22), and 39 catches

GRAVENEY, Thomas William

(b. 1927, Riding Mill, Northumberland)
Gloucestershire, Worcestershire, Queensland, and England

For many years the bearer of Gloucestershire's (and later Worcestershire's) post-war torch, Tom

Graveney was a tall, stylish right-handed batsman with a complete array of elegant strokes played mainly off the front foot. A cheerful character with the ruddy complexion of a countryman, he was also a good slip and occasionally useful leg-spin bowler. Whether making 0 or 90, he looked as if he enjoyed his cricket and such was his grace and touch that few batsmen have given more pleasure to spectators. Early in his Test career he would too often give his wicket away, and he did less well in Australia than elsewhere partly because the high bounce tended to undermine the effectiveness of his front-foot technique, yet he was the most prolific craftsman of his generation and the first of only nine to have scored 100 centuries since the Second World War. Twenty-one times he exceeded 1,000 runs in a season (twice on tours), and four times scored two centuries in the same match. Two of these were overseas—153 and 120 at Bombay in 1956/7 (for C. G. Howard's XI) and 164 and 107 not out at Lahore in 1963/4 (for a Commonwealth XI against Pakistan). Such performances in extreme heat proved his ability to concentrate. Against Australia he scored only one Test century—his superb 111 in about two hours in the fifth Test at Sydney, 1954, when the Ashes had already been decided. Against the West Indies, on the other hand, he was often outstanding when others struggled. His 258 against them at Trent Bridge in 1957 silenced those critics who had questioned his temperament. Three years earlier he had shared in a record partnership of 402 with Willie Watson against British Guiana and in 1966 he made a highly successful return to Tests with 459 runs in 7 innings at 76.50. He captained Gloucestershire in 1959 and 1960 and Worcestershire from 1968 to 1970; and he led England against Australia at Headingley in 1968 (in an emergency). He played for and coached Queensland where he lived for some time and, on returning to the UK, became landlord of a pub near Cheltenham. He was awarded the OBE for his services to cricket, and he became an articulate and justly popular commentator on the game for the BBC. His brother, Ken (J.K.) was a fast-medium bowler for Gloucestershire, captaining them in 1963/4 and his nephew (Ken's son) David also captained the county before becoming the first captain of Durham when they joined the Championship.

First-class career (1948–72): 47,793 runs (44.91) including 122 centuries, 80 wickets (37.96), 550 catches, and 1 stumping

Test matches (79): 4,882 runs (44.38) including 11 centuries, 1–167, and 80 catches

GREEN Stephen Edgar Alexander

(b. 1943, Ryde, Isle of Wight)

Educated at Oxford and Liverpool Universities, Stephen Green trained as an archivist and became curator and librarian of Marylebone Cricket Club in 1968. He established himself as a leading authority on cricket history, always willing to help fellow researchers, and the Museum at Lord's was thoughtfully modernized and adapted under his guidance.

GREENHOUGH, Thomas

(b. 1931, Rochdale, Lancashire) *Lancashire and England*

Tommy Greenhough (the second syllable pronounced 'hoff'), was one of the outstanding right-hand leg-break bowlers of the 1950s and early 1960s until he became handicapped by sundry injuries to fingers and feet. He was also unfortunate in that his was a dying art in England. He ran in a long way for a leg-spinner, with bouncing strides and the ball cradled in both hands until delivery, and spun the ball considerably. He played for England against India in 1959 and South Africa in 1960, taking 5 for 35 in the first innings against India at Lord's. He toured the West Indies with MCC in 1959/60 after taking 122 wickets in the 1959 season, but was not selected for the Tests.

First-class career (1951–66): 1,913 runs (8.39), 751 wickets (22.37), and 84 catches
Test matches (4): 4 runs (1.33), 16 wickets (22.31), and 1 catch

GREENWOOD, Andrew

(b. 1847, Huddersfield, Yorkshire; d. 1889, Huddersfield) *Yorkshire and England*

Andrew Greenwood had family associations with Lascelles Hall, a nursery of Yorkshire cricket. A small man, he was a plucky, sound batsman and a brilliant outfield. He toured Australia in 1873/4 and 1876/7, appearing in the first two Tests ever played. He was nephew of the more famous Luke Greenwood. For Yorkshire, from 1869 until 1880, he scored 2,780 runs (17.82).

First-class career (1869–80): 4,307 runs (18.32) including 1 century
Test matches (2): 77 runs (19.25) and 2 catches

GREIG, Anthony William

(b. 1946, Queenstown, South Africa) *Border, Eastern Province, Sussex, and England*

A 6 ft. 7 in., fair-haired all-rounder, Tony Greig was both one of the best and most influential cricketers of his generation. He was born in South Africa, the son of a Scottish father and South African mother, and lived there until 1966 when he moved to Sussex. From the start of his always controversial career he was a Jekyll-and-Hyde character, a dashing handsome man in a hurry to succeed, charming and multi-talented yet also ruthless and at times disingenuous. He was a brave, determined, and skilful all-round cricketer who seldom failed in Tests and many times seemed to be holding England's fortunes on his shoulders. He was never happier, indeed, than when he was doing so, for few other cricketers have so relished a fight against odds. Coming in at number six in the order he would immediately impose his personality on any match; with his giant figure almost always topped with a cap, he would march out swinging his bat round his shoulders as he prepared for battle. After the 1972/3 tour of India he adopted a policy of lifting the bat beyond stump height as the bowler approached and from the first ball he would be looking to drive. His batting was based on the front foot and his particular glories were the off-drive and the lofted straight drive, which he could produce at a moment of tension in a Test match (like the monstrous hit off Ashley Mallett into the outer at Melbourne in 1974/5) or in up-country matches, when he would delight crowds of all nationalities with his ability to hit the ball immense distances with no concern for the risks he was taking with his own average. His Test average was much better, in fact, than his career average—a testimony to his flair for the biggest challenge and the biggest occasion. He scored 226 for Sussex against Warwickshire at Hastings in 1975 and scored 1,000 runs in seven seasons. Many of his best innings were played on two tours of India and one each to the West Indies and Australia. In the five Tests in the West Indies in 1974 he made 430 runs, with two centuries, at an average of 47.77, took 24 wickets at 22.62 each—whereas England's next best bowler, Pocock, took nine wickets at 61—and held seven catches. Yet his copy-book was blotted by his notorious running out of Alvin Kallicharran after the final ball of the day had been bowled in the first Test in Port of Spain. Greig publicly apologized and Kallicharran was reinstated. He was normally a medium-fast bowler, unpredictable but able to swing the ball a great deal and to get steep bounce, but in the Caribbean tour he turned to quickish off-spinners, and with inspired bowling won the fifth Test, also at Port of Spain, for England by taking 13 wickets in the match. Later in 1974 he scored a buccaneering 110 at Brisbane against Lillee and Thomson in their primes. As a slip fielder he was superlative, the safest and also the most brilliant of his era. Unsuccessful as a captain of Sussex, he was an inspiring captain of England in 14 Tests, although in the field he was inclined to make wildly inappropriate moves on a sudden impetuous whim and tended either to attack or to defend with no policy in between. Nevertheless he led England brilliantly on and off the field in India in 1976/7 and had the world of cricket at his feet when he accepted Kerry Packer's secret offer to become the catalyst for the cricket revolution of 1977. While already earning upwards of £50,000 a year from various cricket contracts and allied business activities, and while a hundred per cent certain to be England's captain against Australia in 1977, he spent some of his time, between the Centenary Test in Melbourne, March 1977, and the new English season, in travelling the world on Mr Packer's behalf helping to sign up many of the world's best cricketers to play in a newly promoted cricket series known at first as Packer's Circus but later by its official name, World Series Cricket. Greig was well aware that, by doing this in secret and by actually signing up members of his own England team for series which he knew would be bitterly opposed by the organizers of established cricket, he was burning the boats of his career in England. He was dismissed as captain of England for what was regarded as his betrayal of trust, but continued to play for England (successfully) under Mike Brearley in 1977. Banned for a time from playing for Sussex in 1978 because of his outspoken remarks in a newspaper article in breach of his county contract—he could never resist saying what he thought in public—he played only a few more matches for Sussex that year before emigrating to Australia and starting a career as chairman of an insurance company and successful TV pundit. Although fiercely loyal to Kerry Packer himself, Greig eventually had the courage to question the wisdom of Australia's over-emphasis on one-day internationals.

First-class career (1965–78): 16,660 runs (31.19) including 26 centuries, 856 wickets (28.85), and 345 catches
Test matches (58): 3,599 runs (40.43) including 8 centuries, 141 wickets (32.20), and 87 catches

GREIG, Ian Alexander

(b. 1955, Queenstown, South Africa) *Cambridge University, Sussex, Surrey, Border, Griqualand West, and England*

Destined in cricket always to live in the shadow of his brother Tony, Ian Greig was a strong and capable right-handed all-round cricketer, without his brother's natural flair but an equally strong character. Personable, he was an outstanding captain at Cambridge in 1979 and led his team to an innings victory over Oxford at Lord's. He also won two blues at Rugby Union. He had to work hard for a regular place in the Sussex side. A medium-fast bowler with a good action, unexpected nip, and a good command of swing and cut, he was also a determined middle-order batsman. An outstanding all-round season for Sussex in 1981 forced his name into the notebooks of England's selectors. In 1982 he won his first cap for England at Edgbaston against Pakistan, taking 4 for 53 in the first innings, identical figures to those returned by Tony Greig in *his* first official Test (4 for 53 in second innings v. Australia, 1972). He was released by Sussex at the end of the 1985 season, and eventually settled, like his brother, in Australia, but not before he had enjoyed a successful run in county cricket for Surrey, whom he captained from 1987 to 1991. In 1990 he scored 291 against Lancashire at the Oval, and 1,259 runs in the season (54.73).
First-class career (1974–91): 8,301 runs (28.72) including 8 centuries, and 419 wickets (31.08)
Test matches (2): 26 runs (6.50) and 4 wickets (28.50)

GREIG, Canon John Glennie

(b. 1871, Mbow, India; d. 1958, Milford on Sea, Hampshire) *The Europeans and Hampshire*

One of several soldiers who combined active service with first-class cricket for Hampshire when duties permitted, 'Jungly' Greig made his county début in 1901 while on sick leave from India. From 1893 onwards he had already appeared for the Europeans in India, whose matches were counted as first-class. His first season for Hampshire proved his best. A slightly built, opening right-handed batsman, with strong wrists, Greig scored five centuries that summer

including 249 not out against Lancashire at Liverpool, in which his late cutting was 'a marvel of safety and brilliance'. From then until 1921, the Europeans and the county shared his talents. His was the wicket Indian sides needed to get in the Quadrangular Tournaments in which he scored 1,478 runs (41.05) besides taking 55 wickets with his slow right-arm bowling. His controversial stumping by a Hindu, given by a Hindu umpire, in 1916 led to the tournament committee appointing neutral umpires. On retiring from the Army and from cricket in 1921, Greig became Hampshire secretary until 1930. He encouraged his old friend General Poore to found Bournemouth CC in 1928. In 1930 Greig became a Roman Catholic priest, serving twice as Hampshire's president.
First-class career (1898–1922): 7,348 runs (36.37) including 15 centuries, 138 wickets (23.46), and 102 catches

GRIEVE, Basil Arthur Firebrace

(b. 1864 Kilburn, d. 1917 Eastbourne) *MCC*

A member of the Harrow XI of 1883 and of MCC for many years, and a wine merchant, Basil Grieve toured South Africa with Major Warton's team in 1888/9, and appeared in the two Tests, which were the first played on South African soil and also his earliest excursions in first-class cricket. He never represented a first-class county.
Test matches (2): 40 runs (40.00)

GRIFFITH, Stewart Cathie

(b. 1914, London; d. 1993, Felpham, Sussex) *Cambridge University, Surrey, Sussex, and England*

'Billy' Griffith was in the XI at Dulwich for four years, keeping wicket in the last two, and making 1,300 runs. A Cambridge blue, he toured Australasia with MCC's 'goodwill' team in 1935/6 and, after a handful of county games, served as a glider pilot in the Airborne Division, being awarded the DFC for his services at Arnhem. He kept wicket in the five 'Victory Tests' against Australia in 1945. Appointed captain and secretary of Sussex in 1946, he led the side for only one season but was secretary until 1950 and briefly a journalist until starting his long and dedicated secretarial career at Lord's. He toured the West Indies with MCC, 1947/8, as player and assistant-manager. Pressed into service as opening batsman in the second Test at Port of Spain, he hit his maiden century in first-class cricket, a resolute

140, which remained his career highest. In South Africa, 1948/9, he kept so well that he replaced Godfrey Evans in two Tests. Appointed assistant-secretary of MCC in 1952, he succeeded Ronald Aird as secretary in 1962, retiring in 1974. At a time of rapid change and many tensions (especially during the 'Stop the South African tour' campaign in 1970) it was fortunate that a man of his integrity, patience, and expertise should have been the pilot of English cricket. His son Mike became a Cambridge blue and later Sussex captain. He was president of Sussex in 1950 and of MCC in 1979/80.

First-class career (1934–54): 4,846 runs (16.42) including 3 centuries, and 408 dismissals (328 c., 80 st.)

Test matches (3): 157 runs (31.40) including 1 century, and 5 dismissals (5 c.)

GUISE, John Lindsay

(b. 1903, Calcutta, India; d. 1991, Eastbourne, Sussex) *Oxford University, Europeans, and Middlesex*

In scoring 278 for Winchester against Eton at Eton in 1921, John Guise made what is still the highest score in a 1st XI schools' match in England. Despite his effort, which contained 45 boundaries, Eton won by eight wickets. He was a very correct, opening right-handed batsman and, as a Freshman at Oxford, made 120 against the West Indians in 1923. His right-arm medium-paced 'floaters' got him a lot of schoolboy wickets and he took 4 for 19 in the University match at Lord's in 1924. After a short spell in India, he became a master at Winchester and made a few appearances for Middlesex.

First-class career (1923–34): 3,775 runs (26.21) including 4 centuries, 63 wickets (28.11), and 53 catches

GUNN, George

(b. 1879, Hucknall Torkard, Nottinghamshire; d. 1958, Tylers Green, Cuckfield, Sussex) *Nottinghamshire and England*

George Gunn was an original—a small, slim right-hander and for most of his long career an opening batsman. His style had sound classical foundations, but, as Sir Neville Cardus wrote, his mind and nature were whimsical, so that one day he would play an innings correct in every movement and principle, the next day produce something entirely unorthodox such as cutting a ball square from the leg-stump or walking out to the fastest bowling. Possessed of remarkable eyesight

and judgement, he made his début in Test cricket by chance. During the 1907/8 MCC tour he happened to be in Australia for health reasons; England's captain fell ill, and George was called in as reserve batsman. In the five Tests he included such scores as 119, 74, 65, and 122, heading the batting with an average of 51.33 and making the 119 and 74 in his first Test match. An official member of MCC's team to Australia in 1911/12, he averaged 42.33 in the Tests, but he only appeared once against Australia in England. His only other tour was to the West Indies in 1929/30, and the season before he had celebrated his fiftieth birthday with a century off Worcestershire. Twenty times he exceeded 1,000 runs in a season. For several seasons with Nottinghamshire he appeared with his son, George Vernon Gunn, who predeceased him. His uncle William and elder brother John were also Test cricketers.

First-class career (1902–32): 35,208 runs (35.96) including 62 centuries, 66 wickets (35.68), and 473 catches

Test matches (15): 1,120 runs (40.00) including 2 centuries, 0–8, and 15 catches

GUNN, John Richmond

(b. 1876, Hucknall Torkard, Nottinghamshire; d. 1963, Basford, Nottingham) *Nottinghamshire and England*

A hard-working all-rounder, John Gunn was a stubborn left-handed batsman with a variety of strokes, a slow-medium bowler with skilful variation of flight and spin, and an excellent field at cover-point. He remains the only Nottinghamshire player to have scored 20,000 runs and taken 1,000 wickets for the county. In 1903 he shared with William Gunn in a record third-wicket stand of 369 against Leicestershire at Trent Bridge, his own share being his first county century and career highest, 294. Two years later he added 361 for the fourth wicket with A. O. Jones against Essex at Leyton, still also a record. In the same week in 1903 he took 14 for 142 against Surrey at The Oval and 14 for 174 against Essex at Leyton. He achieved the double four times but, in an age of great all-rounders, his sole tour was to Australia in 1901/2 with A. C. Maclaren's team. Like his brother, George, he appeared only once in England, in 1905. Though he ceased playing for Nottinghamshire after 1925, he played further first-class cricket for Sir Julien Cahn's team.

First-class career (1896–1932): 24,557 runs (33.18) including 40 centuries, 1,242 wickets (24.52), and 248 catches

Test matches (6): 85 runs (10.62), 18 wickets (21.50), and 3 catches

GUNN, William

(b. 1858, St Anne's, Nottingham; d. 1921, Nottingham) *Nottinghamshire and England*

In organized county cricket Billy Gunn was perhaps the first of the great 'classic' batsmen, with a commanding height and reach, upright stance, and whip-cord wrists. A right-handed batsman, he set the pattern of beauty through technical perfection in English batting, and would exhibit a perfectly straight bat and finished style wherever he played. He was also a useful slow, round-arm bowler and a splendid, fast-moving field in the deep. He had no sudden jump to fame, but he was at his best in the 1890s, when no England side was complete without him; and he enjoyed many great partnerships with Arthur Shrewsbury. He played a commanding innings of 228 for Players against Australians at Lord's in 1890 and his 102 not out for England against Australia in 1893 was the first Test century at Old Trafford. As a veteran, he shared with John Gunn in a record third-wicket stand of 369 against Leicestershire at Trent Bridge in 1903. Owing to the claims of his growing bat-making business, Gunn and Moore, he could afford to visit Australia only once. In earlier years a mainstay of Notts County, he represented England twice at soccer—one of the rare double internationals. He also became a director of Notts County. Starting his career with nothing, when he died he was worth £60,000.

First-class career (1880–1904): 25,691 runs (33.02) including 48 centuries, 76 wickets (23.68), 333 catches, and 1 stumping
Test matches (11): 392 runs (21.77) including 1 century, and 5 catches

HAIG, Nigel Esmé

(b. 1887, London; d. 1966, Eastbourne, Sussex) *Middlesex and England*

Lean, wiry and enthusiastic, Nigel Haig would bowl tidy right-arm medium pace for long spells without showing any signs of fatigue. He was also a dangerous forcing batsman with strong wrists, whose upper-cut shocked the purists, and a fielder of feline prowess. He achieved the double three times, captained Middlesex with varying success from 1929 until 1934—he was a member of the Championship-winning sides of 1920 and 1921—toured the West Indies with MCC, 1929/30, appearing in the first Tests in the Caribbean, and represented England against Australia once in 1921. He was something of a

sporting all-rounder and was also extremely well-read. Not a brave batsman, he received congratulatory telegrams when once he was lbw to a fast bowler!

First-class career (1912–36): 15,220 runs (20.90) including 12 centuries, 1,117 wickets (27.48), and 221 catches
Test matches (5): 126 runs (14.00), 13 wickets (34.46), and 4 catches

HAIGH, Schofield

(b. 1871, Huddersfield, Yorkshire; d. 1921, Huddersfield) *Yorkshire and England*

Dubbed 'the sunshine of the Yorkshire eleven', Schofield Haigh was a thorough sportsman, who loved the game. A member of the powerful side that won the Championship regularly at the turn of the century, he was a right-arm, medium-fast bowler whose off-cutters on sticky wickets would make him practically unplayable. He believed in bowling at the stumps and his observation after inspecting a sticky pitch remains embedded in the folklore of cricket, 'Methinks they'll deviate somewhat.' He developed as a good utilitarian batsman, able to defend stubbornly or attack briskly as the occasion demanded, and he was a keen field. In his four Tests against Australia he was not the force he was for Yorkshire, but on two tours of South Africa he had considerable success in all matches. In 1898/9 he captured 107 wickets (8.18), including 6 for 11 in the second innings of the Test at Cape Town when he and Albert Trott, unchanged, dismissed South Africa for 35. He took at least 100 wickets in a season 11 times, and achieved the double once. After retiring from the county cricket he loved, he became a popular coach at Winchester.

First-class career (1895–1913): 11,713 runs (18.65) including 4 centuries, 2,012 wickets (15.94), and 299 catches
Test matches (11): 113 runs (7.53), 24 wickets (25.91), and 8 catches

HALLOWS, Charles

(b. 1895, Little Lever, Lancashire; d. 1972, Bolton, Lancashire) *Lancashire and England*

'Good-looking in a sporting sort of way', as Sir Neville Cardus put it, Charlie Hallows was tall and slim, a stylish left-handed batsman and a fast fielder. He was opening batsman when Lancashire won the Championship three years in succession, 1926, 1927, and 1928. In 1928 he hit 1,000 runs in May—a feat which, up till then, had only been performed by W.G. and Walter Hammond —and, with effortless ease, he once hit a Nottinghamshire fast bowler over mid-on for six at Old Trafford, the ball dropping on to the platform at Warwick Road Station. Unlike many batsmen, he made it clear how much he was enjoying himself at the wicket. Although he scored heavily and passed 1,000 runs in a season six times, he was chosen only twice for England, both matches played at home, against Australia in 1921, and the West Indies in 1928. He earned the unique distinction of holding professional posts in Leagues in England, Scotland, Ireland, and Wales. His uncle, James, also a left-handed all-rounder, had done the double for Lancashire in 1904.

First-class career (1914–32): 20,926 runs (40.24) including 55 centuries, 19 wickets (41.26), and 140 catches

Test matches (2): 42 runs (42.00)

HAMMOND, Walter Reginald

(b. 1903, Buckland, Dover, Kent; d. 1965, Durban, South Africa) *Gloucestershire and England*

Walter, or Wally, Hammond was simply one of the greatest cricketers ever. He was a product of Cirencester Grammar School and, although he had a chequered start to his career—appearing for Gloucestershire without birth or residential qualification and falling seriously ill in the Caribbean during his first tour with MCC—his immense natural talent was evident at once. Muscular and well proportioned, he was from the beginning a daring and brilliant right-handed batsman: in 1927 at Old Trafford he put to the sword Champion county Lancashire's attack including McDonald, hitting 187 in three hours. His style ripened, as Sir Neville Cardus said, 'to an almost statuesque nobility, easy and powerful of stroke-play but absolutely correct in its observance of first principles'. He reached 1,000 runs in the May of 1927—only W.G. had previously achieved this in 1895—and, on his first tour of Australia with MCC in 1928/9, he made 905 runs (113.12) in the series, which became a longstanding record. On his second tour in 1932/3 he hit 336 not out against New Zealand at Auckland, which remained for five years the highest in Tests. In addition, he hit six Test double-centuries. He made three highly successful tours of South Africa, the last in 1938/9 as captain. Although often disappointing in Tests in England, no one who saw it will forget his classical and dignified batting against Australia at Lord's in 1938 when he scored 240, destroying the bowling with regal

authority. Having turned amateur he captained England for the first time in this series. He also captained both Players and Gentlemen. During the Second World War he served in the RAF before playing with all his old freedom in the 'Victory Tests' against Australia in 1945. After a magnificent season in 1946, averaging 108 in the Championship, he led MCC in Australia that winter but, despite many successes outside the Tests, was very disappointing in the series itself and, on his return home, retired from regular first-class cricket. He had exceeded 1,000 runs in 22 seasons (five times overseas). Throughout, he was a nippy medium-fast bowler, especially effective with the new ball, and as a slip field he was swift and sure, one of the best ever. In 1928 he caught 10 batsmen in the match against Surrey, a record. In 1929 he held 78 catches and, for more than a decade, 'c. Hammond b. Parker' was a regular feature of Gloucestershire's score-book. He played soccer for Bristol Rovers. On retirement from English cricket he settled in South Africa, where he died, sadly rather a faded star and somewhat impoverished.

First-class career (1920–51): 50,551 runs (56.10) including 167 centuries, 732 wickets (30.58), 819 catches, and 3 stumpings

Test matches (85): 7,249 runs (58.45) including 22 centuries, 83 wickets (37.80), and 110 catches

HAMPSHIRE, John Harry

(b. 1941, Thurnscoe, Yorkshire) *Yorkshire, Derbyshire, Tasmania, and England*

John Hampshire (frequently called Jackie although he prefers his true name) is the only Englishman to have scored a century on his Test début at Lord's, but most of his life has been devoted to Yorkshire cricket. He was a fine fielder and a powerfully built right-hander who always made batting look relatively easy and hit the ball blisteringly hard, notably off the front foot. A failure to concentrate at times kept down the number of really big scores, but by the time he was made Yorkshire captain in 1979 he had scored 1,000 runs or more in 13 seasons, and all his runs had come at a healthy pace with the best interests of Yorkshire, rather than of himself, in mind. The one exception was his controversial 'go slow' at Northampton in 1978 when he blocked resolutely in order to draw public attention to what he considered to be selfish batting by his captain, Boycott. His début Test innings was a courageous one of 107 against the West Indies in 1969 which helped to rescue his side after a poor start. But his appearances for England were sporadic and, after his bright start, disappointing. He toured Australasia with Ray Illingworth's side of 1970/1, batting well without doing quite enough to win a regular Test place. He spent several winters in Tasmania, helping the island develop a team worthy of a place in the Sheffield Shield. Earlier in his career he was a useful leg-spin bowler. He was captain of Yorkshire for two seasons (1979–80), but could not hasten the county's longed-for new dawn and in 1982 he joined Derbyshire. He retired at the end of the 1984 season and became a first-class umpire.

First-class career (1961–84): 28,059 runs (34.55) including 43 centuries, 30 wickets (54.56), and 446 catches

Test matches (8): 403 runs (26.86) including 1 century, and 9 catches

HARDINGE, Harold Thomas William

(b. 1886, Greenwich, London; d. 1965, Cambridge) *Kent and England*

Wally Hardinge was a sound and reliable right-handed opening batsman at a time of plenty. He made his début at 16 and was at his best in late Edwardian days when Kent were often Champion county. He reached 1,000 runs in a season 18 times, but played only once for England, against Australia at Headingley in 1921, scoring 25 and 5. As a slow left-arm bowler he could break dangerous partnerships and he was a fleet-footed fieldsman, as befitted a soccer international, who played against Scotland as centre-forward in 1910. For many years he was on the staff of John Wisden & Co.

First-class career (1902–33): 33,519 runs (36.51) including 75 centuries, 371 wickets (26.48), and 297 catches

HARDSTAFF, Joseph, jun.

(b. 1911, Nuncargate, Nottinghamshire; d. 1990, Worksop, Nottinghamshire) *Nottinghamshire, Auckland, and England*

'Young Joe' Hardstaff was a polished right-hander in the highest company and, although invaluable years were lost to the Second World War, he showed some magnificent form afterwards, notably in the first Test in peacetime, when he hit 205 not out against India at Lord's in 1946. His partnership of 215 with Len Hutton against Australia at The Oval in 1938 had revealed both the upstanding right-handed attacking style and the defensive qualities which augured so well. Joe

toured Australia three times, 1935/6, 1936/7 and 1946/7, and the West Indies once, 1947/8. When he retired no one had made more runs for Nottinghamshire. He exceeded 1,000 runs 14 times (once overseas) and his own son, another Joseph, also appeared in first-class cricket for the Combined Services, before becoming secretary of Middlesex.

First-class career (1930–55): 31,847 runs (44.35) including 83 centuries, and 36 wickets (59.47)

Test matches (23): 1,636 runs (46.74) including 4 centuries, and 9 catches

HARDSTAFF, Joseph, senior

(b. 1882, Kirkby-in-Ashfield, Nottinghamshire; d. 1947, Nuncargate, Nottinghamshire) *Nottinghamshire and England*

Joseph Hardstaff earned the name 'Hotstuff' during MCC's Australian tour of 1907/8, when he was the most successful batsman, scoring 1,384 runs (51.25), including 311 in the Tests. A brilliant field in the deep, he was short but strongly built and a right-hander capable of scoring freely all round the wicket. Despite his successes in Australia and for his county, he never toured or played for England again, such was England's strength in the middle order. From 1927 until his death he stood as a first-class umpire, 17 times in Tests until prevented by the selection of his son, 'Young Joe', for England.

First-class career (1902–24): 17,146 runs (31.34) including 26 centuries, 58 wickets (38.69), 187 catches, and 2 stumpings

Test matches (5): 311 runs (31.10) and 1 catch

HARGREAVES, Reginald Gervis

(b. 1852, Accrington, Lancashire; d. 1926, Lyndhurst, Hampshire) *Hampshire*

While still at Oxford, Reginald Hargreaves made his début for Hampshire (1875). He was 'a good hitter' whose right-handed batting earned him a highest score of 94. He married Alice Liddell, Lewis Carroll's inspiration for *Alice in Wonderland*.

First-class career (1875–85): 544 runs (13.94), 15 wickets (28.40), and 17 catches

HARRIS, David

(b. 1755, Elvetham, Hampshire; d. 1803, Crookham, Hampshire) *Hambledon and Hampshire*

The 27 runs made for Hambledon against Kent at Sevenoaks in 1782 were the first recorded for

David Harris and probably remained his highest score. For his fame rests, not on his left-handed batting, but on his fast right-arm under-arm bowling, described in some detail by John Nyren. Bringing the ball 'from under his arm by a twist', he achieved length, lift, and leg-spin, forcing the batsman to play forward. 'Unless a batter were of the very first-class, he could do little or nothing with Harris.' Many were caught, for which, in those days, the bowler received no credit. In later years, troubled with gout, Harris would arrive on crutches, bowl his deliveries, and rest in an armchair. 1798 was his last season and in his final appearance at Lord's, for Hampshire against MCC, he took four wickets and two catches in the county's comprehensive victory. Nyren has left us a picture of a 'man of genius' who won 'the admiration of every cricketer in Hambledon'.

HARRIS, 4th Lord

(b. 1851, St Anne's, Trinidad, West Indies; d. 1932, Faversham, Kent) *Oxford University, Kent, and England*

George Robert Canning, 4th Lord Harris, was perhaps the greatest administrator and 'missionary' in the history of cricket, remaining in the game all his life. After a thoroughly sound grounding at Eton and Oxford, he revived Kent CCC; led a team to Canada and USA and the fifth team (1878/9) to Australia; collected and captained the team for the first Test in England; advanced the game in India while Governor of Bombay; befriended the professionals; opposed 'throwing' in bowling; upheld the Laws; contributed to the literature; served successively as president of Kent and of MCC and as a trustee and honorary treasurer of the Premier club; played from 1862 (his first net at Lord's) until 1930; appeared in four early Tests with success; and played for Gentlemen against Players and for Kent from 1870 to 1889 when he was frequently captain. He appeared intermittently from 1895 to 1906 and once in 1911, against the first All Indian team. Of genuinely high rank as a player, he was a forcing right-handed batsman, especially severe on fast bowlers, a brilliant field and a useful change-bowler. Autocratic and unable to suffer fools gladly, he none the less promoted the honour and skill of the game at all levels. He served as Under-Secretary of State for India and Under-Secretary of State for War in the Administrations of the Marquess of Salisbury. He was

also Governor of Bombay where he was a great patron of the game. He was GCSI and GCIE.

First-class career (1870–1911): 9,990 runs (26.85) including 11 centuries, and 75 wickets (25.11)
Test matches (4): 145 runs (29.00), 0–29, and 2 catches

HARTLEY, Col. John Caborn

(b. 1874, Lincoln; d. 1963, Woodhall Spa, Lincolnshire) *Oxford University, Sussex, Devon, and England*

A right-arm leg-break bowler, Col. John Hartley took a leading part in Oxford's win over Cambridge in 1896, with 11 wickets. During a career in which he could rarely play regularly, he played for Sussex from 1895 to 1898, toured America with Frank Mitchell's team in 1893, and South Africa with MCC in 1905/6, where he fared poorly in the Tests. He served during the Boer War and the First World War, being four times mentioned in despatches. He played a final first-class match for MCC in 1926, also represented Devon in 1909/10, and gained a Rugby blue.

First-class career (1894–1926): 1,380 runs (12.89) and 227 wickets (25.40)
Test matches (2): 15 runs (3.75), 1–115, and 2 catches

HAWKE, 7th Lord

(b. 1860, Gainsborough, Lincolnshire; d. 1938, Edinburgh) *Yorkshire and England*

A great friend and colleague of Lord Harris, Martin Bladen, 7th Lord Hawke, played for Eton and Cambridge University (as captain in 1885) and was associated with Yorkshire from 1881 until his death. He served as captain from 1883 to 1910, leading eight Championship sides, and as president from 1898 to 1938. He was successively president, trustee, and honorary treasurer of MCC, besides being an England selector and captaining teams to America, South Africa, India, the West Indies and Australia in 1887/8, when he had to return early owing to the death of his father. He was a very competent right-handed batsman, and represented England in some of the early Tests against South Africa. He was a far-sighted pioneer of winter payments and other benefits, helping to give cricketers the stability they would otherwise have lacked in their profession. He was born in Lincolnshire, one of the few exceptions to the Yorkshire rule that all their players must be born within the county.

HAYES

First-class career (1881–1911): 16,749 runs
(20.15) including 13 centuries
Test matches (5): 55 runs (7.85) and 3 catches

HAYES, Ernest George

(b. 1876, Peckham, London; d. 1953, London)
Surrey, Leicestershire, and England

One of the six aspirates that adorned the batting
line-up at The Oval in Edwardian days—Hayward, Hobbs, Hayes, Holland, Harrison, and
Hitch—Ernie Hayes was an attractive right-
handed batsman with a strong drive and fierce
pull, a useful leg-break bowler and a brilliant slip.
It was because he damaged his hands in the latter
position—he had to field to such as Tom Richardson, Bill Lockwood, and Bill Hitch—that he
retired from Surrey in 1919. Sixteen times he
exceeded 1,000 runs in a season, the best being
2,309 runs in 1906. His highest was 276 against
Hampshire at The Oval in 1909, when he added
371 with Jack Hobbs for the second wicket, the
year in which he made his only appearance in a
Test against Australia. He toured South Africa
1905/6, and Australia in 1907/8. He captained
Players against Gentlemen at The Oval in 1914.
Serving with the Sportsmen's Battalion in the
First World War, he was commissioned,
wounded, and awarded the MBE. In 1924 he
became coach to Leicestershire after a period at
Winchester and appeared as an amateur for his
new county a few times in 1926, unfortunately
being run out on 99 in his first innings. Later, he
returned and coached at The Oval.

First-class career (1896–1919): 27,318 runs
(32.21) including 48 centuries, 515 wickets
(26.70), 608 catches, and 2 stumpings
Test matches (5): 86 runs (10.75), 1–52, and 2
catches

HAYES, Frank Charles

(b. 1946, Preston, Lancashire) *Lancashire and
England*

Frank Hayes, despite a very successful career by
most standards, was one of the major disappointments of modern English cricket. Fair-haired, of
medium height, he was a right-handed batsman
with a natural balance and flair, and an athletic
cover fielder. He was for a while the 'great white
hope' of English batting, following innings of 94
and 99 in his first two Championship matches for
Lancashire in 1970. In 1973 he played a brilliant
innings in a Test trial at Hove, hitting the ball
impressively off the back foot. He was selected

for England for the first time against the West
Indies at The Oval that year and scored 106 not
out in the second innings although England were
soundly beaten. Hayes was destined to play all of
his Test cricket against strong West Indian sides
and for losing causes. The following winter in the
Caribbean he had little luck, found no consistent
form, was handicapped by nervousness to the
point of physical sickness before going in to bat,
and never commanded a regular Test place again.
Yet once or twice, as when he hit Malcolm Nash
of Glamorgan for 34 runs in one over (the four
came off the second ball), he suggested a rare
talent. An intelligent introvert with a science
degree from Sheffield University, he became captain of Lancashire in 1978 when he was given sole
power of first-team selection. But he was replaced
after three relatively unsuccessful years as captain
and the feeling that he was not a lucky cricketer
was underlined when, in 1982, he suffered a
complex fracture of an ankle when running
between the wickets in a match at Lord's. It was
a moment of great sadness when he announced
his retirement from first-class cricket, after injury
had restricted him to just one match in 1984. He
became a schoolmaster and master-in-charge of
cricket at Felsted.

First-class career (1970–84): 13,018 runs (35.86)
including 23 centuries, 0–15, and 176 catches
Test matches (9): 244 runs (15.25) including 1
century, and 7 catches

HAYGARTH, Arthur

(b. 1825, Hastings, Sussex; d. 1903, London) *MCC,
Middlesex, and Sussex*

Born a week after the fire at Lord's which
destroyed the existing records, Arthur Haygarth
seemed destined, if not from the cradle, at least
from his days at Harrow to devote his life to
salvaging the past and recording the present. The
first volume of his *Scores and Biographies* covered
the years 1746 to 1826 and the remaining fourteen, reflecting the great increase in the game,
took the story through the nineteenth century. At
first, Haygarth struggled to find a publisher until
Fred Lillywhite produced the first four volumes
before Haygarth transferred his allegiance to
MCC. The final volume, put together from
Haygarth's notes by F. S. Ashley-Cooper,
appeared appropriately in 1925, the centenary of
his birth. Their importance, as the title implies,
lies in the scores recorded and in Haygarth's
shrewd and pertinent biographies. On himself,
he wrote 'his patience and perseverance proved

trying to his adversaries' and many instances abound of his stone-walling tactics. For the Gentlemen in 1846—in one of his sixteen appearances for them—against the Players at Lord's he scored 26 in 4 hours. His defensive right-hand batting was dictated by his physique: he was fearless against fast bowlers on tricky pitches but unable to hit their bowling hard.

First-class career (1850–61): 3,042 runs (13.05), 19 wickets (7.63), and 65 catches

HAYMAN, Francis

(b. 1708, Exeter, Devon; d. 1776, London) *MCC, The Gentlemen*

Francis Hayman, a founder member of the Royal Academy, was prominent at a time when the first generation of major English artists were establishing their reputations. Hogarth was his friend and Gainsborough his pupil. Hayman's 'Cricket at Marylebone Fields' (c.1743) is important for its depiction of double-wicket play, its accuracy, its technical qualities, and its detail on dress. It was used frequently until early in the nineteenth century to illustrate editions of the Laws. The picture probably came into the possession of Thomas Lord, certainly of William Ward and appropriately hangs in the Long Room at Lord's. The artist's 'Cricket in the Artillery Ground' has been lost, only a copy from an engraving by Benoist surviving.

HAYWARD, Thomas

(b. 1835, Chatteris, Cambridgeshire; d. 1876, Cambridge) *Cambridgeshire*

The slight, frail figure of Tom Hayward opening the batting for Cambridgeshire with Robert Carpenter in the middle years of the nineteenth century belied the fact that he was one of the best batsmen in England. A 'fine, free and graceful' right-handed batsman who scored strongly in front of the wicket, he was of the second generation of cricketers in a family with strong Cambridgeshire links, and it was playing as a given man for the Gentlemen of that county against the University at Fenner's in 1859 that he scored 220. It was 'not against the best bowling of the day' commented *Scores and Biographies*, 'still the undergraduates were young and active, and by no means to be despised'. He made centuries in successive years (1862–3) for the Players against the Gentlemen at Lord's and in 1868 achieved the rare feat of 1,000 runs in a season. He also made

a century for All-England against Surrey at The Oval in 1862, on the first occasion a side totalled over 500. It was a match memorable for the Surrey bowler, Edgar Willsher, being no-balled for raising his arm above the level of his shoulder. The law was changed in 1864. As a right-arm off-break bowler, in the round-arm tradition, Hayward got many wickets for the All-England XI against odds. Never blessed with good health, he did not play after he was 37 and died at the age of 41. His nephew, Tom Hayward, followed him both in style and in reputation.

First-class career (1854–72): 4,789 runs (25.33) including 6 centuries, 249 + 18 wickets (15.80), and 62 catches

HAYWARD, Thomas Walter

(b. 1871, Cambridge; d. 1939, Cambridge) *Cambridgeshire, Surrey, and England*

Tom Hayward, a powerful influence on the young Jack Hobbs, was himself one of the most prolific right-handed batsmen in the history of the game. He came from a famous Cambridgeshire cricketing family, son of Daniel and nephew of Thomas, regarded in the 1860s as the finest professional of the time. He was tallish and well built, with a military moustache and bearing, and his off-drive and cut were handsome and correct. Patient and watchful, he reached his 1,000 runs for 20 successive seasons. Although he enjoyed several profitable years early in his career as a medium-pace off-break bowler, achieving the double in 1897 and the hat-trick twice in 1899, he felt he had to work too hard as both batsman and bowler and said so. In the field he was a reliable catcher. In 1906 he hit two separate centuries at Trent Bridge and Leicester in successive matches during Whitsun week, and altogether amassed 3,518 runs (66.37) in the season, which remained a record until Denis Compton and Bill Edrich beat it 41 years later. In 1913 he became the first professional to reach his 100th century in first-class matches. His opening partnerships with Hobbs were prolific; and he averaged 46 in 33 matches for Players against Gentlemen. A first choice for England from 1896 until 1909, he toured Australia three times and South Africa once, making three centuries in Tests. These included 122 against South Africa at Johannesburg in 1895/6—his second match for England—and 137 at The Oval against Australia in 1899 when he put on 185 with F. S. Jackson for the first wicket. In retirement he returned to

Cambridge but later became coach in the Parks at Oxford.

First-class career (1893–1914): 43,551 runs (41.79) including 104 centuries, 481 wickets (22.96), and 492 catches

Test matches (35): 1,999 runs (34.46) including 3 centuries, 14 wickets (36.71), and 19 catches

HEARNE, Alec

(b. 1863, Ealing, Middlesex; d. 1952, Beckenham, Kent) *Kent and England*

A younger brother of George and Frank, both of whom, like himself, appeared in early Tests between England and South Africa, Alec Hearne was a right-arm, medium-paced, leg-break bowler with an excellent command of length, flight, and spin. A neat batsman, he was strong in back play, a precise cutter, and, particularly on slow pitches, a quick and accurate hooker. Most of his best work was done for his county and he was prominent in Kent's victories over the Australians in 1884, 1886, 1890, and 1893. Yet he was never selected for a Test against Australia, despite the fact that his highest-ever score was 168 for W. G. Grace's side against the Australians at Crystal Palace in 1893. He toured South Africa with W. W. Read's team in 1891/2, and appeared in his sole Test at Cape Town in company with brother, George, and cousin, John Thomas, although his other brother Frank was representing South Africa; he scored 9, held one catch and did not bowl. In retirement Alec Hearne was coach at Kent's Nursery and later scorer to the club for many years.

First-class career (1884–1906): 16,346 runs (21.65) including 15 centuries, 1,160 wickets (19.93), and 404 catches

HEARNE, Frank

(b. 1858, Ealing, Middlesex; d. 1949, Cape Town, South Africa) *Kent, Western Province, England, and South Africa*

Brother of George and Alec Hearne, Frank had the rare experience of representing both England and South Africa in Tests. Only 5 ft. 5 in., he was a sound, defensive right-handed batsman, with many fine off-side strokes, and a useful, fast round-arm bowler who enjoyed ten good years (1879–89) with Kent before ill-health forced him to retire. He toured South Africa with Major Warton's team in 1888/9 and appeared in the first Tests between the two countries. Subsequently he settled in South Africa and represented his adopted country against England in 1891/2 and 1895/6. In 1894 he was a member of the first South African team to visit England, scoring 508 runs in 33 completed innings. His son, George Alfred Lawrence Hearne, was a member of the 1924 team to England.

First-class career (1879–1904): 4,760 runs (17.96) including 4 centuries, and 57 wickets (23.61)

Test matches (England—2): 47 runs (23.50) and 1 catch. (South Africa—4): 121 runs (15.12), 2 wickets (20,00), and 2 catches

HEARNE, George Gibbons

(b. 1856, Ealing, Middlesex; d. 1932, London) *Kent and England*

The eldest of three brothers—Frank and Alec being the others—George Hearne was primarily a left-arm medium-pace bowler with a round-arm action, who could bat correctly and whose batting improved as he got older. Throughout his career he was a very good field at point or mid-wicket. He was a participant in the Lord's match in May 1878 which established the reputation of Australian cricket, when a strong MCC eleven was defeated in a day. With W. W. Read's team in South Africa, 1891/2, he failed to score and did not bowl in his sole Test at Cape Town.

First-class career (1876–1903): 9,022 runs (17.51) including 5 centuries, and 686 wickets (16.76)

HEARNE, John Thomas

(b. 1867, Chalfont St Giles, Buckinghamshire; d. 1944, Chalfont St Giles) *Middlesex and England*

Brother of Herbert and Walter who played for Kent, J.T., Jack, or 'Old Jack' Hearne had 20 years as a loyal and successful servant of Middlesex. He bowled right-arm medium pace with considerable nip, and his action was perfect with left arm thrust out and left shoulder pointing towards the batsman. At times a useful batsman, he was also a reliable fielder. He captured 257 wickets (14.28) in 1896, including 56 wickets in all games against the Australians (15 in the three Tests): and on 14 other occasions he took 100 wickets in a season. In Australia, 1897/8, he headed the Test averages with 20 wickets (26.90). In 1899 he made history in the Test at Headingley with a hat-trick, accounting for Clem Hill, Syd Gregory, and Monty Noble. His life-aggregate of wickets is the fourth highest in the history of the game. Quiet, dignified, and controlled, he was considered by his old Middlesex captain, A. J. Webbe, to have 'a wonderfully kind nature'. On retirement 'Old

Jack' was elected to the county committee, in those days an almost unprecedented honour for a professional. He was a cousin of George, Frank, and Alec Hearne of Kent.

First-class career (1888–1923): 7,205 runs (11.99), 3,061 wickets (17.76), and 426 catches
Test matches (12): 126 runs (9.00), 49 wickets (22.08), and 4 catches

HEARNE, John William

(b. 1891, Hillingdon, Middlesex; d. 1965, West Drayton, Middlesex) *Middlesex and England*

A distant cousin (it is said) of J. T. Hearne, 'Young Jack' was slightly built, a serious and prolific all-rounder. As a right-hand batsman he was patient, business-like and undemonstrative. As a leg-break and googly bowler he was at his very best from 1911 to 1914 and, after the war, was one of the most erratic but also the most potent leg-break bowlers around. 'Joe' Murrell who kept to him for many years said, 'You can have 'em all, here and overseas. When he was pitching the leg-break "Nutty" Hearne was away on his own.' Before his twenty-third birthday Hearne had already played for England against either Australia or South Africa thirteen times. He toured Australia three times, and South Africa once, opening his Test career with 76 and 43 at Sydney and 114 at Melbourne in 1911/12 when he was twenty. Largely self-taught, he started his career as a ground-boy at Lord's and would have gone further had he not suffered from indifferent health. As it was, he reached 1,000 runs in a season 19 times, 100 wickets five times, and achieved the double on five occasions. After the war he relied increasingly on the off-spinner.

First-class career (1909–36): 37,252 runs (40.98) including 96 centuries, 1,839 wickets (24.42), and 348 catches
Test matches (24): 806 runs (26.00) including 1 century, 30 wickets (48.73), and 13 catches

HEMMINGS, Edward Ernest

(b. 1949, Leamington Spa, Warwickshire) *Warwickshire, Nottinghamshire, Sussex, and England*

Eddie Hemmings was 33 when he won his first Test cap after a career with many vicissitudes and he carried on year after year to become one of the most durable of all the players of his era. A smallish, slightly plump man with a lively sense of humour and liable to clown during the most serious match, he was the son of a good club cricketer from Leamington Spa. A useful right-hand batsman, he began as a medium-paced bowler but developed his main skill as an off-spinner and he had learnt all the tricks of his trade by the time that he began bowling for England in 1982. Running in mechanically, he bowled at subtly varied pace from close to the stumps with a good action and curved the ball away from the right-hander in the air as well as turning the off-spinner sharply enough when conditions allow. Yet when he left Warwickshire, for whom he had first appeared against Scotland at the age of 16 in 1966, he did so in some disillusionment after becoming the butt of the Edgbaston crowd on more than one occasion. He moved to Nottinghamshire in 1979 and there began to make the most of a tough apprenticeship on the bland Edgbaston pitches. In Nottinghamshire's Championship-winning year of 1981 he took 90 wickets at 20.63 each and he was by now an effective bowler in limited-overs matches, too. The first chances for England came in two one-day internationals against Pakistan in 1982. He did well and confirmed his growing confidence with a maiden hundred for Notts against Yorkshire: 127 not out at Worksop. Ironically, his first Test was at Edgbaston where he took three wickets against a strong Pakistan batting side. He went to Australia in 1982/3 as England's first-choice off-spinner, and he bowled steadily but with little luck. He had a fine all-round match at Sydney in the final Test of the rubber, taking three wickets in both innings and, going in as night-watchman in the second innings, making an accomplished and spirited 95. He lost his place but bowled expertly for Nottinghamshire to take 94 wickets in 1984. His return to Test cricket came in unhappy circumstances in 1987/8 after he had helped England to the World Cup Final in India and Pakistan. His first Test for five years was the bitter match in Faisalabad when tempers flared after Mike Gatting had moved an England fielder whilst Hemmings was running in to bowl. His chief rival, John Emburey, earned himself a ban from Test cricket after 1989, which enabled Hemmings to extend his career. In the West Indies in 1989/90 he only played in one-day internationals but in 1990 he took 6 for 58 in the first innings to set up victory at Edgbaston. Against India at Lord's he was struck for four successive sixes by Kapil Dev, but he played in all six Tests in 1990 and finished the Indian series by making an important 51 at The Oval when England were in trouble. He toured Australia again the following winter, playing only in the

HENDREN

Sydney Test (6 for 199). His professionalism was proved by his finishing top of the first-class averages for England's second tour in succession and even when Nottinghamshire released him in 1992 he was in demand. Sussex signed him in 1993 to improve their spin attack and he seldom let them down, taking 12 for 58 in the match against Leicestershire at Horsham. Playing for an International XI against a powerful West Indian XI at Kingston in 1982/3 he took all 10 wickets for 175.

First-class career (1966–   ): 9,463 runs (18.59) including 1 century, and 1,500 wickets (29.31)

Test matches (16): 383 runs (22.52), 43 wickets (42.44), and 5 catches

HENDREN, Elias Henry

(b. 1889, Turnham Green, Middlesex; d. 1962, Tooting Bec, London) *Middlesex and England*

A Cockney with Irish blood, 'Patsy' Hendren was a true immortal with 170 centuries, though a largely self-taught cricketer. His outstanding early talent was his speed and skill in the field. Only when cricket was resumed in 1919 did he really establish himself as a county batsman. He was a stocky scrum-half of a figure and Ian Peebles has recalled how he 'stood at the wicket with a slight crouch, a sharply protruding rump proclaiming his resolution'. He was a nervous starter but, as his innings lengthened, so his stance grew more upright and he seemed to achieve in his determined right-handed forward strokes a height and reach not in fact possessed. Very quick-footed, he was a skilled player of slow bowling and weaker against speed. With his short, strong forearms he made the hook his finest shot but all strokes were at his command, reinforced by a strong and orthodox defence. The crowd loved his short, square build, busy movements and low-slung run, and he enjoyed the occasional piece of slapstick for their amusement. He toured Australia in 1920/1, 1924/5, and 1928/9, South Africa once, and the West Indies twice. For Middlesex he reached 1,000 runs in a season 21 times, 15 times exceeding 2,000, and three times exceeding 3,000. His highest score was 301 not out for Middlesex against Worcestershire at Dudley in 1933. He was inconsistent for England until 1924 when he hit 132 and 142 at Headingley and The Oval respectively against South Africa, then a succession of fifties in Australia that winter and 127 not out against Australia at Lord's in 1926. From that point he was considered genuine England material and hit his highest score, 205 not out, against

the West Indies at Port of Spain in 1929/30. In 1934 against Australia he made 132 at Old Trafford, stabilizing the middle batting with a stand of 191 for the fifth wicket with Maurice Leyland, and, earlier at Trent Bridge, enabled England to save the follow-on by adding 101 for the seventh wicket with George Geary. In retirement he coached at Harrow and, later, at Lord's and at Hove (for Sussex). As a footballer, he was a wing-forward who played for Brentford, Manchester City and other clubs and was capped for England in a 'Victory' international in 1919. His brother Denis played cricket for Middlesex and Durham and became a first-class umpire.

First-class career (1907–37): 57,611 runs (50.80) including 170 centuries, 47 wickets (54.77), and 754 catches

Test matches (51): 3,525 runs (47.63) including 7 centuries, 1–31, and 33 catches

HENDRICK, Michael

(b. 1948, Darley Dale, Derbyshire) *Derbyshire, Nottinghamshire, and England*

With a truly model action, high and sideways-on, Mike Hendrick was one of the finest fast-medium bowlers of his generation yet in an era of very strong competition in his department he only made certain of his England place at the age of 30 during his fourth major overseas tour. Although 6 ft. 3 in. tall and strongly built, in his youth he was not physically fit enough to bowl at his best throughout the demanding county season. He first came to prominence with Derbyshire (that great breeding-ground of fast bowlers) in 1969 when Alan Ward looked more likely to become a regular England fast bowler. Hendrick, under the guidance of the England physiotherapist Bernard Thomas, had already decided that he must drive himself to go through a daily running and exercise routine when he experienced a humiliating moment in Australia in 1974/5. He had enjoyed a successful start to the tour and was running in to bowl his first over in the third Test at Melbourne when a hamstring snapped. The rest of the tour was a miserable anti-climax for him, but when, after some fine performances in England against Australia in 1977, his chance came again overseas, he took it with the eagerness of a man presented with a feast after a long and weary journey without food. Playing in five successive Tests against Australia in 1978/9 he was a key figure in England's success, driving the young Australian batsmen almost to despair with his remorseless accuracy. He took 19 wickets at 15.73 each in the series, but actually took credit for several more at the other end because the batsmen were forced to play rash shots against other bowlers in order to break the stranglehold imposed by 'Hendo'. Not only was he accurate, but he also got bounce and movement off the pitch. Thus, five years after his Test début against India in 1974 (when he took a wicket with his third ball at Old Trafford, and followed with figures of 4 for 28 at Edgbaston), he could mentally relax and consider himself established. Although a genuine tail-end batsman who thoroughly enjoyed a hearty long-handled swing, his value to any side as a bowler was enhanced by his exceptional brilliance in any close-fielding position, and also by his quick-witted repartee in the dressing-room. He left Derbyshire after his benefit season of 1981, having helped his native county to a thrilling victory in the first final of the NatWest Trophy. He went to South Africa with the English 'rebels' in March 1982, and on his return started a new career with Nottinghamshire. Injury, his constant bugbear, restricted his appearances for his new county, and he finally gave up his battle for fitness after playing only three matches in 1984. He became a first-class umpire, and for a time the manager-coach of Nottinghamshire, as well as commenting shrewdly on the game for BBC radio.

First-class career (1969–84): 1,601 runs (10.13), 770 wickets (20.50), and 176 catches

Test matches (30): 128 runs (6.40), 87 wickets (25.83), and 25 catches

HESELTINE, Lt-Col. Christopher

(b. 1869, London; d. 1944, Lymington, Hampshire) *Hampshire and England*

Neither in the XI at Eton nor winning a blue at Cambridge, Christopher Heseltine was 27 before making a name as a right-handed fast bowler. Fully utilizing his height, he brought the ball over at the extreme extent of his arm, sometimes with deadly effect, but he required careful nursing, being apt to tire. Three times he dismissed Bobby Abel (Surrey and England) for a duck. Touring India, South Africa, and the West Indies with teams captained by Lord Hawke, he appeared in two Tests against South Africa, 1895/6. 'The Colonel' was president of Hampshire from 1936 until his death. He was in the Boer War and the First World War, when he was mentioned in dispatches.

First-class career (1892–1914): 1,390 runs (12.30) and 170 wickets (24.54)

Test matches (2): 18 runs (9.00), 5 wickets (16.80), and 3 catches

HEYHOE FLINT, Rachael (née Heyhoe)

(b. 1939, Wolverhampton, Staffordshire) *East Midlands and England*

At The Oval in 1963, Rachael Heyhoe Flint scored the first six in women's Test match history, this single stroke amply illustrating a playing career that knew no bounds. Bold and adventurous, if not cavalier, Heyhoe Flint's strong, witty personality and media awareness brought the women's game into the public eye while carving out a career for herself in journalism and public relations. Accidentally brushed on a private part of her anatomy by a bat being held by the president of MCC at a public ceremony after a match at Edgbaston, she squealed over the public address system and brought the house down with her instant remark: 'Good thing it wasn't a long handle.' Taking over the England captaincy from the unfortunate Mary Duggan in 1966, Heyhoe Flint did not lose a Test in six series and was instrumental not only in winning the 1973 World Cup but founding the competition itself. It was Heyhoe Flint who made the first contact with a benefactor, Sir Jack Hayward, the tournament going from strength to strength if without the financial backing that had looked so promising at the outset. Renowned as an aggressive right-handed bat, Heyhoe Flint could also dig in when necessary, once spending 521 minutes over 179 to see England through to a series draw against Australia at The Oval in 1976. She was, by any standards, a most accomplished technical player. Some 15 years after her retirement, Heyhoe Flint still holds the women's Test record of 1,814 runs, included in which are 13 fifties. The public still perceive Heyhoe Flint and women's cricket as one and the same. In the late 1970s there were those within the game who took umbrage at this and others perceived impropriety, replacing her as England captain for the 1978 World Cup in India with Mary Pilling. She was recalled to play under Sue Goatman in the 1979 home series against the West Indies and the 1982 World Cup in New Zealand before having a spell as England manager and as an officer of the Women's Cricket Association. There was an apparently final parting of the ways after New Zealand toured in 1984, a sad situation for a sport that could ill afford to lose people who move in such influential circles. She also represented England at hockey, playing in goal. She was awarded the MBE in 1972.

HICK

Test matches (25): 1,814 runs (49.02) including 4 centuries
One-day internationals (23): 643 runs (58.45) including one century

HICK, Graeme Ashley

(b. 1966, Salisbury, Rhodesia) *Zimbabwe, Worcestershire, Northern Districts, Queensland, and England*

Billed as the batting saviour of English cricket thanks to his phenomenal performances during his seven-year qualification period, the entry of Graeme Hick into Test cricket could not have been more of an anticlimax. Having destroyed bowling attacks and changed record books following his arrival in the first-class game, his first three years on the international stage proved a severe test of his resolve. Technically, he was exposed as suspect against the short ball, and, by nature modest, quiet and not especially articulate, he struggled under the media spotlight. At times, Hick appeared to be retained as much for his underrated off-spin and near-flawless catching, especially at second slip, as for his batting, and it was only late in the summer of 1994 that he seemed truly to have established himself. Tall, powerful, and a magnificent driver both in the air and along the ground between mid-off and mid-on, Hick's performances prior to his Test début in 1991 were little short of phenomenal. He was the youngest player to top 2,000 runs in an English season in 1986; scorer of 1,000 runs before the end of May two years later, becoming only the sixth player to achieve the feat which included an unbeaten 405 against Somerset, the highest score in England for 93 years; the youngest player to reach fifty first-class centuries; and the quickest to 10,000 runs in county cricket, taking only 179 innings. In Rhodesia as a child, Hick had been highly rated at tennis and a schoolboy international at hockey, but cricket soon became his first love. Only 6 when he made his first century for Banket Junior School, he continued that progress at Prince Edward High School, averaging 185 with the bat in 1979. Whilst still a student, he became the youngest player to be selected for a World Cup squad when chosen by Zimbabwe in 1983, and the following year he arrived at Worcestershire on a scholarship. Eleven centuries in League and second-team matches led to a Championship début, and he made 82 not out against Surrey. In 1985 he made over 1,000 runs for Worcestershire and the touring Zimbabweans, including a maiden first-class century, 230

against Oxford University, but during the following winter, having grown frustrated at his country's failure to gain Test status, he decided to qualify for England. He celebrated that decision by topping 2,000 runs in 1987, was named as one of Wisden's Five Cricketers of the Year, and over the next four summers he never scored less than 1,800 runs. During the winters he played first in New Zealand—where he was offered and rejected a four-year qualification period—making 2,055 runs with ten centuries in two seasons, and then Australia, where after a slow start he scored 904 runs with three hundreds. When he became available for England in 1991 the early signs were good: in the third match at Lord's he made an unbeaten 86, and he and Neil Fairbrother added a record 213 for the third wicket. Test cricket, however, proved much tougher. A début at Headingley brought scores of 6 and 6, easily forgotten as England won their first Test at home against the West Indies in 22 years, but although his catching was excellent, and he took a wicket in his first over, he was first dropped down the order and then dropped altogether after making only 75 runs in seven innings, apparently demoralized by a regular bombardment from balls rising towards his upper body. The selectors persevered and so did he. In India and Sri Lanka in 1992/3 he scored 409 runs in four Tests, including his first Test century in his 22nd innings, a majestic 178 in Bombay after arriving with the score at 58 for 4. He topped the bowling averages as well, and when the new season began, scored 187 for Worcestershire against the Australians. It proved a false dawn as, struggling against the aggression of Merv Hughes and Shane Warne's leg-spin, he was dropped after two Tests, and although he returned for the final match at The Oval, given a vote of confidence by a new captain, Michael Atherton, and restored to his favoured number three position, his dismissal for 80 to a careless shot when a century looked certain gave his critics fresh ammunition. The 1993/4 tour of the Caribbean saw the graph continue upwards with 96 in Jamaica and 316 runs in the series, and in 1994 he finally made a Test hundred in England, 110 against South Africa at Headingley.

First-class career (1984–   ): 23,124 runs (57.23), 77 centuries, and 176 wickets (41.28)
Test matches (32): 1,933 runs (35.79) including 2 centuries, 19 wickets (51.21), and 50 catches

HIDE, Mary Edith

(b. 1913, Shanghai, China; d. 1995, Godalming, Surrey) *Surrey and England*

A positive, strong character, Molly Hide captained England at home and abroad between 1937 and 1954 and became a women's cricket legend in her own lifetime. Just how her tough, disciplined, but painstakingly fair handling of players would go down in today's world is debatable but Hide's peers admired her deep knowledge of the game and regarded her captaincy skills as inspired. Hide herself said her main objectives were to try to play bright, attractive cricket always, and to get a definite result. To this end she tried to instil into her teams how essential it was for whoever batted first to set an adequate rate of scoring. A classic right-handed bat and right-arm off-spin bowler, Hide was a talented all-rounder. But it was her batting that drew the crowds, full of crashing drives and flamboyant shots off the back foot. A second-wicket partnership with Betty Snowball of 235 in 142 minutes against New Zealand in Christchurch in 1934 remains an all-time Test best. On the 1948/9 tour of Australia, Hide performed with such distinction in the third Test at the Sydney Cricket Ground with innings of 63 and 124 not out, that her portrait was hung in the pavilion. Neville Cardus, who watched the game, offered a comparison with Denis Compton. This was some recompense for England losing the series when Hide suffered the most resounding defeat of her captaincy, by 186 runs in the first Test in Adelaide. She brought her long and successful career with England and Surrey to a close in 1954 but before that and for many years afterwards she worked tirelessly in an administrative capacity for the Women's Cricket Association. Hide, who attended Wycombe Abbey School, was the first woman to obtain a Diploma in Agriculture. This was achieved at Reading University and during the Second World War she ran the family 200-acre farm.

Test matches (15): 872 runs (36.33) including 2 centuries, and 36 wickets (15.25)

HIGGS, Kenneth

(b. 1937, Kidsgrove, Staffordshire) *Lancashire, Leicestershire, Staffordshire, and England*

An undemonstrative cricketer with firm views and a tough approach, Ken Higgs had two separate careers, each in its own way equally successful. He was a very sturdily built, right-arm, medium-fast bowler, and his short, well-grooved approach was the economical launching pad for a strong, thrusting body-action. The result was a jarring pace off the pitch. This, allied to formidable accuracy, made him one of the most respected and successful bowlers in county cricket for Lancashire between 1958 and 1969 and he won 15 England caps between 1965 and 1968, touring Australia and the West Indies. After two seasons of League cricket in his native Staffordshire Higgs was persuaded back into county cricket with Leicestershire where he became captain after Ray Illingworth in 1979. A fine slip fielder and stubborn tail-end left-hander, he showed what can be done with a straight bat and a front-foot technique by making 63 and sharing a last wicket stand of 128 with John Snow for England against the West Indies in 1966 (two short of England's record for the tenth-wicket partnership) and again by putting on a record 228 with Illingworth for Leicestershire's last wicket against Northants at Leicester in 1977 when he made 98. Remarkably he also has three first-class hat-tricks to his credit—two for Lancashire and one for Leicestershire—plus one in the 1974 Benson and Hedges Cup Final. He made another appearance in 1982, still bowling medium-fast seamers, and became Leicestershire's coach, returning for two matches in 1986 because of injuries to Leicestershire's other bowlers and taking 5 for 22 from 11 overs in the first innings against Yorkshire.

First-class career (1958–86): 3,648 runs (11.29), 1,536 wickets (23.61), and 311 catches
Test matches (15): 185 runs (11.56), 71 wickets (20.74), and 4 catches

HIGNELL, Alastair James

(b. 1955, Cambridge) *Cambridge University and Gloucestershire*

The son of a doctor who had made one appearance for the county, Alastair Hignell was the first man to captain Cambridge University at both cricket and rugby football. Subsequently he won 14 caps at full-back for England and played cricket for Gloucestershire as a rumbustious right-handed batsman who exceeded 1,000 runs on three occasions, making his first century against the West Indies at Bristol in 1976. He was a brilliant fielder.

First-class career (1974–83): 7,459 runs (29.48) including 11 centuries, 3 wickets (76.66), and 150 catches

HILL, Allen

(b. 1843, Kirkheaton, Yorkshire; d. 1910, Leyland, Lancashire) *Yorkshire and England*

The man who took the first-ever Test wicket, Allen Hill was one of the best right-arm 'seamers' of his day and, with a far shorter run-up than most bowlers of his type, he could deliver a sharp break-back from the off. For Yorkshire against Surrey at The Oval in 1871 he took 12 wickets, all bowled. For Players against Gentlemen at Lord's in 1874 he performed a memorable hat-trick, dismissing three of the best amateurs of the day with successive balls. He was a good slip but an erratic batsman, who captained his county occasionally. He toured Australia with James Lilly-white's side in 1876/7, and appeared in the two Tests, hitting 49 and taking 4 for 27 in the first innings of the second. For Yorkshire (1871–83) he took 537 wickets (12.96).

First-class career (1871–83): 2,478 runs (8.94) and 744 wickets (14.36)

Test matches (2): 101 runs (50.50), 7 wickets (18.57), and 1 catch

HILL, Arthur James Ledger

(b. 1871, Bassett, Hampshire; d. 1950, Sparsholt House, Hampshire) *Cambridge University, Wiltshire, Hampshire, and England*

A Cambridge cricket blue, Arthur Hill was a true sporting all-rounder, being also a fine player at rugby, hockey, boxing, rackets, and tennis, a good man to hounds and an expert fisherman. Tall and stylish, he was a splendid right-handed batsman with a free, natural approach to the game, a useful fast bowler before taking up lobs, and a reliable slip. He toured India, America, and South Africa with teams captained by Lord Hawke, and went with MCC to Argentina. He appeared in the Tests against South Africa in 1895/6, and in the last at Cape Town he hit 124 and took 4 for 8 in 40 balls in the second innings; remarkably the only occasion he ever bowled in a Test! In 1920 he and his son, A. E. L. Hill, turned out to play for Hampshire together and in 1929 he became president of Hampshire.

First-class career (1890–1921): 10,353 runs (27.98) including 19 centuries, and 305 wickets (27.99)

Test matches (3): 251 runs (62.75) including 1 century, 4 wickets (2.00), and 1 catch

HILTON, Malcolm Jameson

(b. 1928, Chadderton, Lancashire; d. 1990, Oldham, Lancashire) *Lancashire and England*

A devastating slow left-arm spinner on a turning wicket, Malcolm Hilton hit the headlines when he dismissed Don Bradman twice for Lancashire at Old Trafford in 1948. The great man was among the ten Test batsmen who constituted Hilton's first ten wickets in first-class cricket and he could never live this down, although he formed with Roy Tattersall one of the most effective spin-bowling partnerships in county cricket. He was disappointing on the tour of India under Nigel Howard in 1951/2, except at Kanpur where he and Tattersall bowled England to victory. At home he played against both the West Indies and South Africa. His best year was 1956, when he secured 158 wickets (13.96). For Lancashire 2nd XI in 1949 he took more than a hundred wickets, a very unusual feat in minor county cricket. One of the best close-in fields, and a fast runner and accurate thrower from the deep field, he was selected several times as 12th man for England because of these skills. He was also an aggressive right-handed, tail-end batsman with a slashing off-drive (he hit 100 not out against Northamptonshire at Northampton in 1955). His best bowling was 8 for 19 for his county against the New Zealanders at Old Trafford in 1958.

First-class career (1946–61): 3,416 runs (12.11) including 1 century, 1,006 wickets (19.41), and 202 catches

Test matches (4): 37 runs (7.40), 14 wickets (33.64), and 1 catch

HIRST, George Herbert

(b. 1871, Kirkheaton, Yorkshire; d. 1954, Lindley, Huddersfield, Yorkshire) *Yorkshire and England*

George Hirst was one of the legends of Yorkshire cricket, a fighter on the field and a friendly soul both on and off it. 'The happy warrior, this is he', read a caption on a contemporary photograph. The exploits of Hirst and Wilfred Rhodes, both from Kirkheaton, have a story-book quality about them. George combined toughness and loyalty with a sense of humour, kindness, and integrity and was a great influence for good over young people. He was a fastish, left-arm bowler with nip off the pitch and devastating late in-swing. As a right-handed batsman his remarkable quickness of eye and feet enabled him to hook and pull magnificently. He frequently gave of his best when the pitch helped bowlers. He was a dauntless field, notably at mid-off. In 19 seasons he made over 1,000 runs and in 15 took over a hundred wickets; he achieved the double 14 times, a feat surpassed only by Rhodes. In the years of Yorkshire's Championship 'hat-trick', 1900–2, he made 5,323 runs and took 328 wickets. No one has exceeded or will exceed his record of 2,385 runs (45.86) and 208 wickets (16.50) in 1906. His highest score, 341 against Leicestershire at Leicester including 54 boundaries, in 1905, remains unbeaten by any other Yorkshire batsman. In his first match after the First World War he made 180 not out against MCC at Lord's, aged 48. He toured Australia twice, 1897/8 and 1903/4, and, although his overall Test record was comparatively modest, two of his performances were outstanding. At Edgbaston in 1902 Rhodes and he bowled out Australia for 36 and, in the next match for Yorkshire against the tourists, he and F. S. Jackson dismissed them for 23, Hirst capturing 5 for 9. At The Oval in the same year his unbeaten 58 rescued England from a desperate position and with Rhodes he made the famous 15 runs for the last wicket to win the match; he always disclaimed the famous remark, 'We'll get 'em in singles', attributed to him on this occasion. On retirement he coached at Eton for 18 years. His benefit from Yorkshire in 1904 amounted to £3,703 and was the highest for 21 years.

First-class career (1891–1929): 36,356 runs (34.13) including 60 centuries, 2,742 wickets (18.72), and 604 catches

Test matches (24): 790 runs (22.57), 59 wickets (30.00), and 18 catches

HITCH, John William

(b. 1886, Radcliffe, Lancashire; d. 1965, Rumney, Cardiff, Wales) *Surrey and England*

John Hitch, called 'Bill' or 'Billitch', was a firm favourite at The Oval. Despite a hesitant run-up punctuated by two or three hops, he became one of the fastest right-arm bowlers in England. Always a spectacular hitter in the lower order, he more than once hit a ball out of The Oval. He was quite outstanding at short-leg, where he stood perilously close to the bat. He toured Australia twice, in 1911/12 and 1920/1, and also appeared in Tests against Australia and South Africa in England before and after the First World War. On leaving Surrey, he became a professional in the Lancashire League and later coach to Glamorgan.

First-class career (1907–25): 7,643 runs (17.81) including 3 centuries, 1,387 wickets (21.56), and 230 catches

Test matches (7): 103 runs (14.71), 7 wickets (46.42), and 4 catches

HOBBS, Sir John Berry

(b. 1882, Cambridge; d. 1963, Hove, Sussex) *Cambridgeshire, Surrey, and England*

A model cricketer in the widest sense, Jack Hobbs is remembered with affection not just as a master batsman but also as a man of natural dignity and charm, who through years of success remained unspoilt and unselfish. His father was a groundsman at Fenner's and his boyhood idol was a fellow Cambridge man, Tom Hayward, who led the youthful Hobbs to Surrey. Hayward was the first of his opening partners in first-class cricket and together they shared in four three-figure opening stands in one week in 1907. In his first two matches for Surrey in 1905, Hobbs hit 88 against Gentlemen of England (captained by W.G.) and 155 against Essex, both at The Oval, and was awarded his county cap. He never looked back. Hobbs saw the ball early and moved into each stroke calmly and comfortably. Before the First World War he was quick to attack, on springing feet, playing strokes all over the field. After the war, his batting lost any rough edges and he scored his centuries with serene poise. Ninety-eight of his 199 centuries were made after the age of 40. Though appearing to be a frail man, his strength, fitness, and powers of concentration were considerable. A magnificent field in the covers and a master of the art of luring batsmen into a run by his apparent lethargy, he ran out 15 batsmen on MCC's tour of Australia, 1911/12. He was only an occasional bowler, but with an easy and rhythmic action he could nevertheless make the ball swing away late and, in 1909/10 in South Africa, he opened both batting and bowling in three of the Tests. In 1920 he headed the national first-class bowling averages—with 17 wickets (11.82)! But it is his batting records which still make statistical minds boggle. No one has scored more runs in first-class cricket; his 316 not out for Surrey against Middlesex in 1926 remains the highest-ever at Lord's; his 266 not out at Scarborough in 1925 was the highest in the Gentlemen and Players match, and his aggregate of 4,052 runs is unbeaten in that fixture; no one has exceeded 12 centuries in Tests against Australia; and, until Denis Compton exceeded it, his 16 centuries in 1925 were a record for a season. He was the first man to score more centuries than W.G.—in a season when, aged 42, he made 3,024 runs. In 14 Test series between 1907 and 1930 he made 2,493 runs in Australia alone, including nine centuries. Andy Sandham succeeded Tom Hayward as his opening partner for Surrey, and they shared 63 opening three-figure stands, the highest being 428 against Oxford University at The Oval in 1926. In Tests Hobbs shared in 23 opening partnerships of over 100, eight with Wilfred Rhodes and 15 with Herbert Sutcliffe, the most memorable being his 323 with Rhodes at Melbourne in 1911/12, which remained the record for 37 years. His batting mastery was revealed in the challenge of a really difficult wicket, formidable bowling or a crisis, as at The Oval in 1926 or at Melbourne in 1929, when he and Sutcliffe led England from the prospect of inevitable defeat to victory on a treacherous pitch. With Sutcliffe he shared 26 opening stands of more than 100, including three in succession against Australia in 1924/5. Twenty-six times in a season (twice overseas) Hobbs himself exceeded 1,000 runs. Jack Mercer recalled how Glamorgan decided one day to try to run him out rather than bowl him out. A trap was laid on the off-side, with cover-point lurking closer than usual to cut off the off-side push with which Hobbs was wont to start an innings. Mercer bowled the first ball just outside the off-stump, but Hobbs moved across, pushed to mid-wicket and took an easy single! He received three benefits from Surrey which he used to finance a sports outfitters business which still flourishes. Honorary life member of Surrey and honorary member of MCC, he was knighted for his services to cricket in 1953.

First-class career (1905–34): 61,237 runs (50.65) including 193 centuries, 108 wickets (24.89), and 332 catches

Test matches (61): 5,410 runs (56.94) including 15 centuries, 1–165, and 17 catches

HOBBS, Robin Nicholas Stuart

(b. 1942, Chippenham, Wiltshire) *Essex, Glamorgan, Suffolk, and England*

Robin Hobbs would have been a typical county spinner if he had been born sixty years earlier. As it happened he was for much of his career unique: the only English leg-spinner good enough to command a regular place in a county side. Red-faced and jovial with large ears and sharp blue eyes, he was a popular character wherever he travelled. Not only was he a conviv-

ial companion on four overseas tours, but also a skilful and flighty leg-spinner with a useful, if not baffling, googly; as well as a superb, irrepressibly enthusiastic cover-fielder and a spirited hitter. He scored a century in 44 minutes against the Australians in 1975 at Chelmsford, then the fourth fastest ever. He left Essex at the end of 1975 but returned to first-class cricket in 1979 as Glamorgan's captain.

First-class career (1961–81): 4,940 runs (12.10) including 2 centuries, 1,099 wickets (27.09), and 295 catches

Test matches (7): 34 runs (6.80), 12 wickets (40.08), and 8 catches

HODGES, Carole Ann

(b. 1959, Blackpool, Lancashire) *Lancashire, Cheshire, and England*

Carole Hodges's finest hour came during England's successful 1993 World Cup campaign. Having lost to New Zealand and just squeezed past India the day before, pundits were predicting the end of the road for England as they prepared to take on the holders, Australia, who quickly claimed an early wicket. With her large and deliberate pace, Hodges strode to the crease to play what she later described as her best innings for her country, an unbeaten 105 from 141 deliveries. On the county ground at Guildford, she went from 50 to 100 in just 46 balls to complete her first century against the old enemy in seventeen Test innings, five one-day internationals, and three World Cups. Emotion bubbled constantly under the surface throughout her career but this time the Hodges tears were of joy and after England beat New Zealand in the World Cup final at Lord's on August 1, she announced her retirement from international cricket as her country's most capped player. A right-handed bat with strong shots all round the wicket, Hodges first represented England against New Zealand in 1984, scoring 158 in the third Test at Canterbury, the highest Test score against the Kiwis on home soil. A remarkably accurate off-spinner, Hodges took the first hat-trick in the World Cup in 1993. She also wheeled down 122 overs in the three Tests of England's 1991/2 tour to New Zealand, 83 of which were maidens. As a close-to-the-wicket fielder, Hodges was without parallel at point, setting a women's cricket record with 25 catches in Tests and 11 in one-day internationals. She was also particularly adept off her own bowling. There were some low points, the most pertinent being her removal from the

England captaincy after leading the side in the 1986 drawn home series against India and to a 1–0 defeat by Australia in 1987.

Test matches (18): 1,164 runs (40.13) including 2 centuries, and 23 wickets (29.47)

One-day internationals (47): 1,073 runs (32.51) and 58 wickets (15.08)

HOLLIES, William Eric

(b. 1912, Old Hill, Staffordshire; d. 1981, Chinley, Derbyshire) *Warwickshire, Staffordshire, and England*

A sturdy and exceptionally accurate right-arm, leg-break bowler, Eric Hollies was for many years the pivot of the Warwickshire attack. Although his googly was unexceptional, his top-spinner was devastating. He exceeded 100 wickets in a season 14 times. In his first county match he took 1 for 150, delivering a plethora of no-balls, and in his fourth match was often hit out of the Gloucester ground by Walter Hammond. Thereupon Hollies decided to accelerate his pace a little and so counteract the movements of quick-footed batsmen. This method made him one of the brisker slow bowlers of his time and he would no doubt have prospered equally well in one-day cricket. He toured the West Indies in 1934/5 and next played for England against South Africa in 1947, when he was preferred to Doug Wright. Hollies was the bowler when Don Bradman came out at The Oval to play his last Test innings against England. The first ball was a leg-break, which the Don played with a dead bat. The second, a googly of perfect length, bowled the great man and so deprived him of a glorious exit and reduced his Test career average to a mere 99! Though this was Eric Hollies's most famous moment, he preferred to talk about the rare occasions when he made runs. His best bowling was 10 for 49 in an innings against Nottinghamshire at Edgbaston in 1946, all without assistance from the field.

First-class career (1932–57): 1,673 runs (5.01), and 2,323 wickets (20.94)

Test matches (13): 37 runs (5.28), 44 wickets (30.27), and 2 catches

HOLMES, Errol Reginald Thorold

(b. 1905, Calcutta, India; d. 1960, London) *Oxford University, Surrey, and England*

A tall right-hander, Errol Holmes batted as one would have expected an Oxford Malvernian to bat: with style and panache—and in a Harlequin cap. His hallmark was the drive through the covers with the left leg well out and the bat following right through, but he could hit all round the wicket delightfully. Especially while at Oxford he had some triumphs with his medium-fast bowling; his was a tearaway action with a long run which did not produce quite as speedy a ball as promised. Succeeding Douglas Jardine as Surrey captain in 1934, he was a revitalizing influence. He believed that everyone should *enjoy* the game. He toured the West Indies as vice-captain, 1934/5, and led MCC's 'goodwill' tour of Australia, 1935/6. Retiring in 1938, he returned as Surrey captain for two seasons after the war. Some idea of his approach may be gained from his conversation with some Oxford cricketers long after he had retired. He was recalling the virtues of Harold Larwood: his searing pace, ferocious bounce, formidable accuracy, etc. 'How on earth did you play him, then?', asked a timid undergraduate. 'Drove him through the covers, me boy,' replied Holmes 'drove him through the covers.'

First-class career (1924–55): 13,598 runs (32.84) including 24 centuries, 283 wickets (33.67), and 192 catches

Test matches (5): 114 runs (16.28), 2 wickets (38.00), and 4 catches

HOLMES, Percy

(b. 1886, Oakes, Huddersfield, Yorkshire; d. 1971, Marsh, Huddersfield) *Yorkshire and England*

Chiefly remembered as Herbert Sutcliffe's opening partner, Percy Holmes seldom got the credit due to him. Technically, he was possibly Sutcliffe's equal, but he was an attacking right-hander without the monumental calm and concentration which made Sutcliffe so exceptional. Good footwork made Holmes a particularly successful hooker and cutter and he was a good fielder. A jaunty character, he was always on the look-out for runs. With Sutcliffe he set up the record first-wicket partnership of 555 against Essex at Leyton in 1932. In all they shared 18 partnerships exceeding 250, and 69 exceeding 100. His highest score was 315 not out for Yorkshire against Middlesex at Lord's in 1925, and he exceeded 1,000 runs in a season 15 times—once overseas when he made 1,200 runs (51.14) for MCC in South Africa, 1927/8, his sole Test-playing tour for MCC. In England he appeared once against Australia in 1921, and against India in 1932, but was not selected again.

HOME OF THE HIRSEL

First-class career (1913–35): 30,573 runs (42.11) including 67 centuries, and 342 catches
Test matches (7): 357 runs (27.46) and 3 catches

HOME OF THE HIRSEL, Alexander Frederick, Lord

(b. 1903, London; d. 1995, Hirsel, Scotland) *Oxford University and Middlesex*

A distinguished career in public life—he had accompanied Neville Chamberlain to Munich in 1938—brought Alec Douglas-Home to the British premiership (1963), relinquishing his hereditary peerage to return to the House of Commons. Subsequently, he sat again in the Lords as a life peer. In company with 'Gubby' Allen, Lord Dunglass (then heir to the Home earldom) enjoyed his cricket at Eton and in the nets at Plum Warner's garden nearby. Against Harrow at Lord's in 1922, his polished right-handed batting brought him 66 runs and his right-arm medium-paced away swingers 4 for 37. In modern parlance, he was 'man of the match'. At Oxford a blue 'seemed likely' (in his own words) but in the penultimate match before meeting Cambridge, Perrin of Essex hit him for three towering sixes and that was that. He had played occasionally for Middlesex and later toured South America with MCC under Warner's captaincy in 1926/7, being reprimanded by Warner for using a razor blade to clean a bat—'as bad as pouring water into port'. He continued to play at club level and for Lords and Commons until after the Second World War. In 1966 he became president of MCC, later remarking that there was as much paperwork to review as in his premiership. Two years later, as shadow foreign secretary, he visited South Africa and acted for MCC in meeting that country's prime minister and making an assessment on the likelihood of Basil d'Oliveira being allowed to enter with an MCC side. In speeches he liked to recall Canon Edward Lyttelton, 'who could never walk up the nave of his cathedral without speculating whether it would take spin'.

First-class career (1924–7) 147 runs (16.33), 12 wickets (30.25) and 9 catches

HONE, Leland

(b. 1853, Dublin, Ireland; d. 1896, Dublin) *Ireland and England*

An old Rugbeian and member of a famous Irish cricketing family, Leland Hone was the first player to represent England in Tests who never played for a first-class county. He was a wicket-keeper/batsman and, when Lord Harris found himself short of a 'keeper at the last moment to tour Australia in 1878/9, he invited Hone. He acquitted himself well as a 'keeper, but failed with the bat, in the sole Test at Melbourne scoring 7 and 6 and holding 2 catches. He played with success for Phoenix, Dublin and All Ireland.

First-class career (1878–80): 85 runs (7.08), 10 catches, and 2 stumpings

HOPWOOD, John Leonard

(b. 1903, Newton Hyde, Cheshire; d. 1985, Denton, Lancashire) *Lancashire and England*

Len Hopwood was a very competent right-handed batsman and a left-arm medium-pace bowler. Patient and determined, he took several years to establish himself in the strong Lancashire Championship-winning side, but in 1933 he made 1,972 runs (46.95), and in 1934 and 1935, his peak years, he achieved the double. Chosen for England against Australia in 1934, he played at Old Trafford and Leeds but was disappointing. Ill-health prevented his return to first-class cricket in 1946.

First-class career (1923–39): 15,548 runs (29.90) including 27 centuries, 673 wickets (22.45), and 198 catches
Test matches (2): 12 runs (6.00) and 0–155

HORNBY, Albert Neilson

(b. 1847, Blackburn, Lancashire; d. 1925, Nantwich, Cheshire) *Lancashire and England*

Small, truculent, bellicose, adventurous, rash, and a poor runner between wickets, 'Monkey' Hornby was a right-handed batsman with an attractive front-foot style and splendid punishing powers which he used freely. He was a magnificent field, but when he played for Harrow against Eton in 1864 he was of such slight physique that he weighed—'bat and all'—less than 6 stone. Captain of Lancashire from 1880 until 1891 and again in 1897 and 1898, he was firm, keen and genial, generally getting the best out of his men. He led the county to the Championship in 1881 and 1897, and to tied first place in 1882 and 1889. He opened the batting for many years with Dick Barlow—a partnership that has been immortalized in verse by Francis Thompson. Barlow said of him, 'First he runs you out of breath; then he runs you out; then he gives you a sovereign; then he runs out of sovereigns.' A double international, he appeared nine times for England at rugby football and three times at cricket against Australia. He was involved in a serious incident during a match between Lord Harris's team and New South Wales at Sydney, 1878/9, when Lord Harris was struck on the field of play by a 'larrikin' because of an umpire's decision on a run out; 'Monkey' was something of a pugilist, seized the offender and, despite being hit in the face and having his shirt nearly torn off his back, conveyed his prisoner to the pavilion. He captained England in the legendary 1882 Oval Test and in the Test at Old Trafford in 1884, and also captained England against Scotland in his last Rugby international.

First-class career (1867–99): 16,109 runs (24.07) including 16 centuries, 11 wickets (23.45), 313 catches, and 3 stumpings
Test matches (3): 21 runs (3.50) and 1–0

HORTON, Martin John

(b. 1934, Worcester) *Worcestershire, Northern Districts, and England*

Martin Horton was a strongly built and effective all-rounder. As a right-handed opening batsman he could hit powerfully on both sides of the wicket and his cutting was devastating despite a somewhat ungainly stance and short backlift. He was also a valuable off-break bowler and versatile field. He achieved the double twice, and, when making his highest score, 233 against Somerset at Worcester in 1962, he added 314 for the third wicket with Tom Graveney. His best bowling performance was 9 for 56 in an innings against the South Africans at Worcester in 1955. He appeared in two Tests against India in 1959 and, on leaving his county in 1966, became National Coach in New Zealand for nearly two decades, presiding over a great improvement in New Zealand cricket.

First-class career (1952–71): 19,945 runs (29.54) including 23 centuries, and 825 wickets (26.94)
Test matches (2): 60 runs (30.00), 2 wickets (29.50), and 2 catches

HOWARD, Nigel David

(b. 1925, Hyde, Cheshire; d. 1979, Douglas, Isle of Man) *Lancashire and England*

One of the two sons of Major Rupert Howard (sometime secretary of Lancashire and manager of MCC touring teams) who appeared for the county, Nigel Howard was a stylish and forcing right-handed batsman and a fine, zealous field. Soon after his début he was opening the batting with Cyril Washbrook and captained Lancashire unselfishly from 1949 until 1953. He captained MCC to India, Pakistan and Ceylon in 1951/2

when, although he struggled to justify his place in the side as a batsman, he did a good job on and off the field, relieving his players of most of the considerable diplomatic chores.

First-class career (1946–54): 6,152 runs (24.70) including 3 centuries, 1 wicket (52.00), and 153 catches
Test matches (4): 86 runs (17.20) and 4 catches

HOWELL, Henry

(b. 1890, Hockley, Birmingham; d. 1932, Birmingham) *Warwickshire and England*

Taking a fairly long run, 'Harry' Howell bowled distinctly fast right-arm with a nice easy action. At his best in the early 1920s, he enjoyed such hauls as 161 and 152 wickets in a season. In 1923 he took all 10 for 51 in Yorkshire's first innings at Edgbaston and, in 1922 on the same ground, captured 6 for 7, when Hampshire fell for 15, but eventually won the match. He visited Australia with MCC in 1920/1, when the slip fieldsmen often failed him, and in 1924/5.

First-class career (1913–28): 1,679 runs (7.81), 975 wickets (21.23), and 67 catches
Test matches (5): 15 runs (7.50) and 7 wickets (79.85)

HOWORTH, Richard

(b. 1909, Bacup, Lancashire; d. 1980, Worcester) *Worcestershire and England*

A versatile and canny all-rounder, Dick Howorth was a left-handed batsman of uncompromising style based on the straight bat in defence and solid front-foot strokes in attack. He drove powerfully and batted anywhere either as an opener or as low as number nine; he usually bowled slow left-arm, turning the ball from a steady length but could also bowl seamers if required; and he could field near the wicket or in the deep. There was an air of competence about everything he did. Off the field he was a notable raconteur. In 1947 he scored 1,510 runs, took 164 wickets, made his Test début against South Africa—securing a wicket with his first ball at The Oval—and toured the West Indies with MCC. He achieved the double three times and nine times took more than 100 wickets in a season. He opened a newsagents shop, which still bears his name, close to the Worcester ground by the River Severn.

First-class career (1933–51): 11,479 runs (20.68) including 4 centuries, 1,345 wickets (21.87), and 197 catches
Test matches (5): 145 runs (18.12), 19 wickets (33.42), and 2 catches

HUDSON, Robert Cecil

(b. London, 1920)

One of the stalwarts of BBC Radio outside Broadcasts, Robert Hudson devised *Test Match Special* (1957) as a continuous coverage of Test cricket. Having only just squeezed a hat-trick by Fred Trueman onto the air two years previously before being obliged to hand back to the studio, he realized that cricket's most exciting moments often come unpredictably. In 1958 he joined the radio team himself. His first TV commentary had been Bradman's last Test at The Oval in 1948. He was Head of BBC Radio Outside Broadcasts (1969–75) and for some 20 years a major commentator on royal and national occasions, including 66 rugby internationals. He conscientiously studied the commentator's art and his meticulous preparation for every broadcast was both exemplary and evident from his faultless performances at the microphone. In retirement he filled the void left by his wife's early death by speaking widely, giving all his fees to Cancer Research.

HUGHES, Thomas

(b. 1822, Uffington, Berkshire; d. 1896, Brighton, Sussex)

Thomas Hughes had played in the match between Rugby School and MCC (1841) which he immortalized sixteen years later in his *Tom Brown's School Days*. The book advocated the Victorian cult of muscular Christianity: the pursuit of Christian ideals through manly endeavour on the sports field. After leaving Rugby, Hughes won an Oxford blue in 1842 and stroked the University crew in the following year. In the 1870s, by now an established barrister, author, and politician, he set up a colony in Tennessee as an outpost of his ideas which he called Rugby. He created a cricket ground there and also visited the cricketers of Haverford College, Pennsylvania, a more enduring outpost of the game in the United States.

HUMPHRIES, Joseph

(b. 1876, Stonebroom, Derbyshire; d. 1946, Chesterfield, Derbyshire) *Derbyshire and England*

A feature of Joe Humphries's wicket-keeping was the way he stood up to fast bowlers like Arnold Warren and Bill Bestwick. At one time he seemed destined for the highest honours but, though he kept in three Tests in Australia, 1907/8, and at Melbourne added 34 for the ninth wicket with

Sydney Barnes to enable England to win, ultimately, by one wicket, he was not selected again. But at home he performed admirably for his county until 1914. He returned for a benefit match in 1920, but rain prevented a single ball from being bowled.

First-class career (1899–1914): 5,464 runs (14.19) and 674 dismissals (564 c., 110 st.)

Test matches (3): 44 runs (8.80) and 7 dismissals (7 c.)

HUNTER, Joseph

(b. 1855, Scarborough, Yorkshire; d. 1891, Rotherham, Yorkshire) *Yorkshire and England*

Though never taking the same rank as such contemporaries as Richard Pilling and Mordecai Sherwin, Joe Hunter was a good enough wicket-keeper for any county team. He toured Australia with Shaw and Shrewsbury's side, 1884/5, when he played for England. Ill-health caused his retirement and he was succeeded by his brother, David.

First-class career (1878–88): 1,330 runs (7.86) and 356 dismissals (232 c., 124 st.)

Test matches (5): 93 runs (18.60) and 11 dismissals (8 c., 3 st.)

HURST, Geoffrey Charles

(b. 1941, Ashton under Lyne, Lancashire) *Essex*

The score-book entry 'T. Greenhough c. Hurst b. Laker 5' in Lancashire's innings against Essex at Liverpool in 1962 has a unique quality. The catcher—in his sole appearance in first-class cricket—would perform a hat-trick of goals for England in the World Cup Final at Wembley in 1966 and the bowler had already taken 19 wickets for England against Australia at Old Trafford in 1956. Geoff Hurst played 49 times for England as a centre-forward in a career with West Ham United, West Bromwich Albion, and Stoke City.

First-class career (1962): 0 runs (0.00) and 1 catch

HUSSAIN, Nasser

(b. 1968, Madras, India) *Essex and England*

It took Nasser Hussain over three years to regain his England place after a traumatic first tour of the West Indies in 1990 and, when his second tour there four years later ended in failure, the international future of this gifted cricketer appeared bleakly empty. It would be a waste of a player of rare flair if he never established himself for England. A strong driver through the covers, fierce hitter backward of point, and brilliant fielder, the Anglo-Indian's first senior tour came about before he had played a full season of county cricket. Playing in three Tests in the series, two of them with a fractured wrist suffered in a freak tennis accident in Guyana, the combative Hussain impressed with his courage, but the injury kept him out for much of the next season, before, in 1992, disciplinary problems hindered his progress. One of three brothers—one of them, Mel, played once for Worcestershire and for the England Amateur side—Hussain's family moved from India to England when he was 5, and he quickly developed, first as a bowler. At the age of 15 he was considered the most promising leg-spinner in the country, but as he grew he lost his flight, and gradually batting took over. That benefited Young England in Sri Lanka in 1986/7, when Hussain made 170 in the second 'Test', and the following winter he was the team's leading run-scorer in the Youth World Cup as they reached the semi-finals. He made his début for Essex in 1987, after studying at Durham University. Keith Fletcher, the county captain, was sufficiently impressed with the youngster to drop himself, and in 1988 Hussain made an unbeaten 165 against Leicestershire. In 1989 Hussain rose to national prominence with 118 against Somerset as the Combined Universities narrowly failed to reach the semi-finals of the Benson and Hedges Cup, and he ended the summer on stand-by for the sixth Test against Australia at The Oval. With 990 runs in 15 matches, he was chosen for the Caribbean tour and after an early dispute, when he was reprimanded for refusing to walk when given out in an island game, he made his Test début in Jamaica, scoring 13 in England's first victory over the West Indies in 16 years. As the tour continued, however, his wristy technique, with the face of the bat not always straight, let him down, and his wrist injury proved a further hindrance. In the next two winters he toured with the A side, first to Pakistan and Sri Lanka, and then to the Caribbean. Seven centuries in 1993 led to a Test recall and he scored 71 and 47 not out against Australia at Trent Bridge. The West Indies tour which followed was a desperate disappointment. Hussain failed to pass 20 in any match leading up to the first Test, and although he scored a century in Guyana, he was unable to break into the side.

First-class career (1987–   ): 7,833 runs (43.04) and 2 wickets (153.50)

Test matches (7): 284 runs (25.81)

HUTCHINGS, Kenneth Lotherington

(b. 1882, Southborough, Kent; d. 1916, Ginchy, France) *Kent and England*

Although Kenneth Hutchings did not fulfil all the expectations for him after his brilliant years at Tonbridge, he was an outstanding right-handed batsman amid a galaxy of amateur talent the like of which has never been seen since. His driving was outstanding, and his fielding in the slips or the deep equally so. He was a regular choice for England for several years, touring Australia with MCC in 1907/8 and playing against Australia again in 1909. He hit 126 at Melbourne, when England eventually won by one wicket. He was killed in action in France at the height of the First World War.

First-class career (1902–12): 10,054 runs (33.62) including 22 centuries, 24 wickets (39.08), and 179 catches

Test matches (7): 341 runs (28.41) including 1 century, 1 wicket (81.00), and 9 catches

HUTTON, Sir Leonard

(b. 1916, Fulneck, Pudsey, Yorkshire; d. 1990, Norbiton, Kingston, Surrey) *Yorkshire and England*

A strong, dour, and painstaking character with a whimsical sense of humour, Len Hutton will perhaps be best remembered for two among many great achievements: as the maker of the record score in England and Australia Tests—364 at The Oval in 1938—and, as the first professional to be regularly appointed captain of England, the man who won back the Ashes in the Coronation year of 1953 and then successfully defended them in Australia in 1954/5. He was also the first professional to be elected to membership of MCC before his career had finished and the second (after Jack Hobbs) to be knighted for his services to cricket. A product of Pudsey St Lawrence and a protégé of Herbert Sutcliffe, Len Hutton (together with Denis Compton) towered above contemporary England batsmen. Tenacity, concentration, and perfect balance marked his play. The stylist always, with a wide repertoire of strokes, he did not venture anything unreasonably risky, but he could, according to the conditions, be either austerely defensive or a versatile handsome stroke-player. In the latter vein he played one of the most regal innings ever seen at Lord's, when he made 145 against Australia in 1953. Controversially, however, he was almost the first great player who habitually, after 1945, played slow bowling from the crease. He was a good close fielder and a useful leg-break bowler who often obtained valuable wickets. In his first Test, against New Zealand at Lord's in 1937, he made 0 and 1, but in the next match at Old Trafford he hit 100 and did not look back. In 1938 against Australia he averaged 118.25, and, in 1939, 96.00 against the West Indies. A wartime accident left his left arm permanently shorter and weaker than his right but, except for one occasion when he was controversially dropped from the England side against Australia in 1948, he was at the forefront of England's gradual revival after 1946. Head and shoulders above anyone else in Australia, 1950/1, he averaged 88.83 (the next best being 38.77); and he was captain in the 1953 and 1954/5 series, when the Ashes were won back and retained. In 1953 he averaged 55.37 (the next best being 39.00). Against Australia alone he made 2,428 runs (54.46). Altogether he captained England 23 times—more than any other player previously—and did not lose a rubber. He twice shared in three-figure stands with Cyril Washbrook in each innings of Tests against Australia, at Adelaide in 1946/7 and at Headingley in 1948. They made the then highest opening stand in Tests, when they scored 359 together at Johannesburg in 1948/9, Len's contribution being 158. Despite three successive ducks, he hit 1,294 runs in June 1949, the highest aggregate for a batsman in any one month. In retirement he became a successful businessman and was for a time an England selector.

First-class career (1934–60): 40,140 runs (55.51) including 129 centuries, 173 wickets (29.51), and 400 catches

Test matches (79): 6,971 runs (56.67) including 19 centuries, 3 wickets (77.33), and 57 catches

HUTTON, Richard Anthony

(b. 1942, Pudsey, Yorkshire) *Cambridge University, Yorkshire, Transvaal, and England*

Born, like his father, at Pudsey, Richard Hutton inevitably lived in his father's illustrious shadow. Yet he had the independence of character to forge his own career and he qualified as a chartered accountant and banker. An outstanding schoolboy all-rounder at Repton, he was a Cambridge blue from 1962 to 1964 and was for ten years a respected and aggressive Yorkshire all-rounder. Although a powerful driver, his batting had little of his father's exceptional balance, but he played an outstanding innings of 81 against India at The Oval in 1971 when he appeared in five of the six Tests of the summer. He played for the Rest of

the World team against Australia the following winter. Tall, strong, and belligerent (not incapable of some earthy language on the field) he was a steady fast-medium bowler in all conditions and a dangerous swinger and cutter of the ball in helpful ones. His opposition to the Yorkshire captain Geoff Boycott hastened his retirement. After working for many years for Barclays Bank, he became Editor of the game's oldest and best-known magazine, *The Cricketer*, in 1991.

First-class career (1962–76): 7,561 runs (21.48) including 5 centuries, 625 wickets (24.01), and 216 catches

Test matches (5): 219 runs (36.50), 9 wickets (28.55), and 9 catches

IDDON, John

(b. 1902, Mawdesley, Lancashire; d. 1946, Madeley, Staffordshire) *Lancashire and England*

Jack Iddon was a right-handed hard-driving batsman, a natural who reached 1,000 runs in twelve successive seasons up to 1939 (thirteen in all). Also a slow left-arm bowler, he was particularly effective on a wearing pitch at Bramall Lane in 1937, when he took 9 for 47 in Yorkshire's second innings. He toured the West Indies with MCC in 1934/5 and represented England against South Africa in 1935. He was killed in a car accident.

First-class career (1924–45): 22,681 runs (36.76) including 46 centuries, 551 wickets (26.90), and 217 catches

Test matches (5): 170 runs (28.33) and 0–27

IGGLESDEN, Alan Paul

(b. 1964, Farnborough, Kent) *Kent, Western Province, Boland, and England*

A succession of injuries prevented Alan Igglesden from staking a claim for a regular Test place. From the time he made his first team début for Kent in 1986 only to be ruled out by a side strain after only five matches, the personable Igglesden, a tall, lean swing- and seam-bowler with a vigorous approach to the crease and a high action, struggled to make it through the rigours of a county season without breaking down, a fact best illustrated in 1993 when he was consistently sidelined in sight of a second Test cap. He eventually won it in the West Indies the following winter. Starting as a genuinely fast bowler, he was gradually forced to adopt a more measured approach when he broke down again in 1987 and 1988. By the time he made his Test début he was fast-medium, but he compensated for that by learning to swing the ball during his winters in South Africa. Ironically, given Igglesden's fitness record, his selection for the sixth Test against Australia at The Oval in 1989 came thanks to three bowlers—Devon Malcolm, Angus Fraser, and Phillip DeFreitas—all pulling out injured. Drafted in on the eve of the match to become the 31st player and the 13th seam-bowler to be called up during the summer, he performed creditably on a flat pitch, taking 3 for 146, and was rewarded with an A tour to Zimbabwe after returning 56 wickets that summer. Further injuries meant he failed to pass fifty wickets in any of the next three seasons, but after topping the South African first-class averages whilst playing for Boland in 1992/3, taking 39 wickets at only 11 apiece, including a career-best 7 for 28 against Griqualand West in Kimberley, Igglesden began the 1993 season back in the Test reckoning. Chosen for the first Test against Australia that summer, he suffered a groin injury on the eve of the match. Picked again for the third Test, a side strain ruled him out, but he played in the first two Tests of the Caribbean tour. A stomach bug and a return of only three wickets cost him his place.

First-class career (1986–): 800 runs (8.51) and 462 wickets (26.37)

Test matches (3): 6 runs (3.00) and 6 wickets (54.83)

IKIN, John Thomas

(b. 1918, Bignall End, Staffordshire; d. 1984, Bignall End) *Staffordshire, Lancashire, and England*

A lantern-jawed left-hander, Jack Ikin was a player of lion-hearted courage, whose career was cut short by ill-health. He fought to uphold England's middle batting in the crucial years immediately after the Second World War, and was also a useful right-arm leg-break and googly bowler, and a brilliant and daring field in the short-leg area. He played for England against India in 1946, before receiving his county cap, and toured Australia with MCC in 1946/7. He also toured the West Indies, 1947/8, and India with the Commonwealth side, 1950/1. He exceeded 1,000 runs in a season 11 times—1952 was his best year with 1,912 runs (45.52)—and in 1946 he held 55 catches. He last appeared for England in 1955 against South Africa and later became a notable coach. His son, Michael, played with great success for Staffordshire.

First-class career (1938–64): 17,968 runs (36.81) including 27 centuries, 339 wickets (30.27), and 419 catches

Test matches (18): 606 runs (20.89), 3 wickets (118.00), and 31 catches

ILLINGWORTH, Raymond

(b. 1932, Pudsey, Yorkshire) *Yorkshire, Leicestershire, and England*

Never has an Indian summer burned so brightly or so long as in the case of Ray Illingworth. A shrewd and polished craftsman, he was a flawlessly accurate off-spinner, sound batsman and safe field, especially good in the gully. He might easily have ended his career merely as an outstanding county all-rounder with a moderate record as an England player. Yet he became captain of England and was one of the few players whose personal form has been enhanced by the responsibility of captaining a Test side. The opportunity came when he left Yorkshire (like Len Hutton he was Pudsey born) after 18 years to become captain of Leicestershire in 1969. For ten years under his leadership Leicestershire were always among the top counties, winning the Championship in 1975 and four other major trophies. In his momentous year of 1969 he took over the England captaincy from the injured Colin Cowdrey and, although he was envisaged originally as merely a caretaker, 'Illy' proved himself so tough a leader and so skilful a tactician that he was to lead England in 31 Tests, plus five games against the Rest of the World when the South African tour of 1970 was cancelled through political pressure. The pinnacle of his career was reached the following winter when England beat Australia by two Tests to nil to regain the Ashes which had been lost 12 years before. Popular alike with players and with press, Illingworth was every inch a professional both in his fastidious attention to his own and his players' legitimate interests and in his approach to the game itself. A formidable opponent, stubborn and fearless, he was also a loyal and considerate friend. His batting was solid, rugged, utilitarian, and determined, especially in a crisis. His bowling action started with a chassé, followed by a poised, relatively lengthy run and a classic delivery reminiscent of Laker. He varied his pace and mixed his stock off-break with the ball which floated away to slip. He took 100 wickets or more in a season ten times and scored more than 1,000 runs eight times. His highest Test score was 113 against the West Indies at Lord's in 1969 and his best bowling 6 for 29 against India in 1967, but it was for the useful, businesslike performance rather than the spectacular one that he was treasured—this and for his skill as a captain. He practically never lost his grip on any match and his competence improved the record of a moderate England side under his command. Awarded the CBE in 1973, he became Yorkshire manager in 1979. This was not the panacea all Yorkshiremen had sought, however, and in 1982, at the age of 50, he took over the Yorkshire captaincy, the oldest man to be officially appointed a county captain for any substantial period. But even under his leadership Yorkshire's decline could not be halted, and the county of the White Rose finished bottom of the Championship for the first time ever. Yet, the same year, one of the great cricket tacticians brought his county their first major success for 14 years as they won the John Player League, with two spinners, one of them the captain himself, to the fore. Still superbly fit, he continued to play in League cricket well into his fifties. He resigned as Yorkshire's manager after 1983 and became a shrewd observer of the game on radio and television. In 1986 he turned down an opportunity to become England's team manager, believing he would be allowed insufficient independence to do the job his way, and feeling also that the recompense offered was inadequate. In 1993, however, he took over as chairman of the England selection committee, immediately imposing his own stamp on what had become a somewhat thankless job. Characteristically, he was now a paid incumbent and he stuck by his young Lancashire captain, Mike Atherton, having first fined him for failing to give the match referee the full facts during an inquiry after England's Test against South Africa at Lord's (1993). He became manager as well as Chairman in 1995, relishing the challenge and stiffening the team's resolve.

First-class career (1951–83): 24,134 runs (28.06) including 22 centuries, 2,072 wickets (20.28), and 446 catches

Test matches (61): 1,836 runs (23.24) including 2 centuries, 122 wickets (31.20), and 45 catches

ILLINGWORTH, Richard Keith

(b. 1963, Bradford, Yorkshire) *Worcestershire, Natal B, and England*

Richard Illingworth's entry into international cricket was the stuff of Boy's Own fiction. On his début, in a one-day match against the West Indies at Edgbaston in 1991, he struck the winning runs; then, in his first Test appearance later that summer at Trent Bridge, he became only the eleventh man to take a wicket with his first ball

when he bowled Phil Simmons. A stocky and determined left-arm spinner, he struggled to maintain that sort of impact at the top level, but although he was dropped after only one further Test, he remained a member of England's one-day team and played a steady part in helping his side to the 1992 World Cup final. Illingworth attended Jim Laker's old school at Salts near Bradford, and, encouraged by his father Keith, made his Bradford League début at the age of 13, before going on to play for the Yorkshire under-15 side, which also included a future Worcestershire team-mate, Steven Rhodes. Spotted by the Worcestershire coach, Basil D'Oliveira, he was offered a contract by Worcestershire, believing that Phil Carrick would deny him a place for Yorkshire. Capped by Worcestershire in 1986, he took 11 for 108 on his début for Natal against Boland two years later. Two A tours for England preceded his promotion in 1991 when he played in all three one-day internationals against the West Indies, scoring an obdurate 9 not out at number eleven to win the first match, before returning figures of 3 for 115 in his first Test. Retained for Edgbaston, he found a pitch which offered little help; but the Test place he lost for four years to Philip Tufnell was regained in 1995.

First-class career (1982–): 4,941 runs (21.48) and 642 wickets (30.89)

Test matches (2): 31 runs (15.50) and 4 wickets (53.25)

ILOTT, Mark Christopher

(b. 1970, Watford, Hertfordshire) *Essex and England*

Lean, fit, keen, and amiable, Mark Ilott recovered from a stress fracture of the back to win Test recognition. A left-arm over-the-wicket fast bowler with a loose, whippy action he represented Hertfordshire Schools before Essex offered him a contract for 1988. He was the natural successor to his fellow left-armer John Lever, whose own career was coming to a close. In 1990 he broke into the Essex side in late season and ended with 25 wickets including a career-best 5 for 34 against Derbyshire before returning to Adelaide for a second winter in Australia, only to be called up for the A tour of Sri Lanka the following February when Steve Watkin was injured. He immediately impressed in humid conditions, taking 4 for 42 in the second innings after suffering from dehydration. For some time, however, he had suffered pain in his lower back, the result of a sideways-on action but a back foot which pointed down the pitch. A stress fracture was diagnosed and although Ilott tried to play on in one-day matches, he broke down completely in May. Surgery followed in August, and with a modified action he claimed 64 wickets in 1992. Ilott spent the winter touring Australia with the A side, before finally winning Test recognition in 1993. Twelfth man for the first two Tests of the summer against Australia, he was one of four new caps to appear in the third match at Trent Bridge, showing good stamina to take 4 for 152 in the match as England gained a morale-boosting draw following two defeats. In the next two matches, in company with the rest of the England bowlers, he laboured as the Ashes were lost. Ilott's response was to take 37 wickets at 15 apiece on the A tour of South Africa that winter, but after being named twelfth man for the first Test of 1994 against New Zealand, he was side-lined again by a persistent groin injury. Coming back strongly with 59 wickets in the season, he still had to be content with another A tour to India rather than the senior visit to Australia.

First-class career (1988–   ): 883 runs (13.80) and 274 wickets (29.36)

Test matches (3): 28 runs (7.00) and 8 wickets (51.50)

INSOLE, Douglas John

(b. 1926, Clapton, London) *Cambridge University, Essex, and England*

Doug Insole was a powerfully built, right-handed batsman with no frills but plenty of courage and resolution. He was one of the most prolific run-getters in the first two decades after the Second World War, a useful medium-pace change-bowler and a fine all-round field, especially at slip. He captained Cambridge University in 1949 and Essex from 1950 until 1960. A resourceful captain with up-to-date ideas, he had a first-class cricketing brain and his sense of humour and lack of pomposity kept the game in proper perspective. As Essex captain he pulled the county up from the bottom of the Championship to a regular position in the top half. His best season was 1955 with 2,427 runs (42.57), and he exceeded 1,000 runs in a season 13 times. At Clacton against Surrey in 1956 he scored eight runs off one ball from Tony Lock. He appeared in occasional Tests in the 1950s against Australia, South Africa, and the West Indies in England, and in South Africa, 1956/7, when he was MCC's vice-captain, scoring 110 not out at Durban. He was a Test selector for

many years from 1959, chairman of the TCCB when the controversy over Kerry Packer's World Series Cricket arose, and manager of the 1978/9 and 1982/3 teams to Australia, where he did a good job in awkward circumstances. A trustee of MCC, he remained a regular member of influential cricket committees and was chairman of Essex from 1976 to 1978 and 1984 to 1993. He was awarded a CBE for his services to the game, services always quietly rendered in his bluff, low-key style. When the TCCB lost their case in the High Court against Mr Packer he disarmed waiting news reporters expecting an angry reaction with the comment: 'We've had a good stuffing.' Also a football blue, he played in the 1955/6 FA Amateur Cup Final.

First-class career (1947–63): 25,241 runs (37.61) including 54 centuries, 138 wickets (33.95), 366 catches, and 6 stumpings

Test matches (9): 408 runs (27.20) including 1 century, and 8 catches

JACKMAN, Robin David

(b. 1945, Simla, India) *Surrey, Western Province, Rhodesia, and England*

Robin Jackman was born in Simla, the son of a British colonel in the Indian army. Never was there a more determined cricketer than this short, stocky, red-faced, fast-medium bowler with the strident appeal who loves the game with a rare devotion and achieved his great ambition when asked to play for England at last after seventeen seasons in the game. Educated at St Edmunds, Canterbury, Jackman deliberately became 'just one of the lads' in The Oval dressing room. His apprenticeship was long and hard as he worked to make the most of modest abilities. Accuracy, the ability to swing the ball away from the bat and delivery from close to the stumps helped him to pick up a healthy harvest of wickets every year after winning his cap in 1970, six seasons after his début. Also a capable fielder and useful tail-end batsman, he played for Western Province in 1971/2 and for Rhodesia between 1972/3 and 1979/80, taking 8 for 40 against Natal in 1972/3. These connections, and his marriage to a South African girl, created political problems in Guyana when Jackman was flown out to join England's team in the West Indies in 1980/1. But he achieved his ambition when chosen for the third Test in Barbados, getting a wicket with the fifth ball of his first over. He took three first-class hat-tricks, against Kent, Yorkshire and Natal, and in 1980 took 121 wickets at 15.40. He made sure of achieving another ambition, a tour to Australia, by taking three wickets for 74 in Pakistan's first innings in the Headingley Test of 1982. With characteristic doggedness Jackman bowled unchanged for 35 overs. However, he retired at the end of the 1982/3 tour of Australasia and emigrated to South Africa, becoming manager of Western Province and a successful television pundit.

First-class career (1964–82): 5,681 runs (17.69), 1,402 wickets (22.80), and 177 catches
Test matches (4): 42 runs (7.00) and 14 wickets (31.78)

JACKSON, Sir Francis Stanley

(b. 1870, Chapel Allerton, Leeds; d. 1947, London) *Cambridge University, Yorkshire, and England*

Tall and well built, Sir Stanley Jackson was a graceful right-handed batsman with superb timing, a medium-paced bowler with a model run-up and action who varied his pace subtly, and a keen field especially at cover. In many ways he personified the late Victorian and Edwardian approach to the game. From the time that 'Jacker' (fagmaster of Winston Churchill) enabled Harrow to overwhelm Eton at Lord's in 1888, he went from strength to strength. Son of Lord Allerton, a member of the Cabinet in Lord Salisbury's second Government, he led Cambridge to decisive victory in the 1893 University match. He also played for Yorkshire and England against Australia that year, making 91 and 103 in his first two Tests, at Lord's and The Oval respectively. He hit 118 at The Oval in the 1899 Test. After war service in South Africa he returned to cricket and in 1902 he was the best batsman in the series against Australia, redeeming the dreadful England start in the famous 'three run match' at Old Trafford. His career was crowned in 1905—'Jackson's Year'—when he led England to victory in the rubber, winning the toss in all five matches against Australia, and heading the batting averages with 70.28 and the bowling with 15.46. He appeared regularly for the Gentlemen, and for Yorkshire he was prolific. Subsequently, 'Jacker' was MP for a Yorkshire constituency, Lieutenant-Colonel of a West Yorkshire Regiment, Governor of Bengal (where he narrowly escaped an assassin's bullet), chairman of the Conservative Party, president of MCC and Yorkshire, and chairman of the England selectors (1934 and 1946).

First-class career (1890–1907): 15,901 runs (33.83) including 31 centuries, 774 wickets (20.37), and 195 catches
Test matches (20): 1,415 runs (48.79) including 5 centuries, 24 wickets (33.29), and 10 catches

JACKSON, Herbert Leslie

(b. 1921, Whitewell, Derbyshire) *Derbyshire and England*

After Cliff Gladwin's retirement in 1958 Les Jackson took over the extra responsibility and labour of 'stock' as well as 'shock' bowler, even though he was at an advanced age for a right-arm, fast-medium bowler. But his skill seemed to increase and, when he retired five years later, he held all the main records for a Derbyshire bowler. Strong, with a slingy action, he was accurate, hostile, and moved the ball wickedly off the seam; the game was never dull or negative when he was bowling on a 'green 'un' and he had a few in Derbyshire. For many years he was among the meanest and best seam bowlers in England. A miner who started in first-class cricket at the late age of 27, he exceeded 100 wickets in a season ten times, 20 times took ten or more wickets in a match, and 19 times seven or more wickets in an innings. He was not chosen for an overseas tour with MCC and appeared only twice for England at home—against New Zealand in 1949 and Australia in 1961. This was scant honour for so good a bowler.

First-class career (1947–63): 2,083 runs (6.19) and 1,733 wickets (17.36)
Test matches (2): 15 runs (15.00), 7 wickets (22.14), and 1 catch

JACKSON, John

(b. 1833, Bungay, Suffolk; d. 1901, Liverpool) *Nottinghamshire*

For a few years, until injury brought early retirement, John 'Foghorn' Jackson was the best fast bowler in England. His right-arm action was, by the law as it then stood, round-arm but his height allowed him to achieve elevation combined with pace and accuracy. While playing for Nottinghamshire (1855–66), he also travelled with the All-England XI playing against odds. His greatest haul was 17 for 63 against XVI of Oxford University in 1862. He toured with George Parr to America in 1859 and to Australia in 1863/4.

First-class career (1855–67): 1,993 runs (12.61) including 1 century, 650 + 5 wickets (11.52), and 106 catches

JAMES, Cyril Lionel Robert

(b. 1901, Tunapuna, Trinidad, West Indies; d. 1989, London)

C. L. R. James, winning an island scholarship to Queen's Royal College, became one of Trinidad's first black intellectuals, widely known in both England and the United States as a journalist and political commentator. In the 1960s he was closely associated with the nationalist movement within the West Indies. In his own words, he was 'at eighteen, a good cricketer' but it was journalism rather than cricket which took him abroad and to Nelson in Lancashire in 1932 to stay with the club's Trinidadian professional, Learie Constantine. There was some tension in the friendship, the young cricketer initially reluctant to be drawn into the politics of black nationalism by his lodger. Not till he was 62 and a respected contributor to the *Manchester Guardian* did James make a resounding mark as a cricket writer when his *Beyond A Boundary* was called by John Arlott 'the finest book' ever written on the game. It was praise akin to Lord David Cecil's evaluation of the novelist Barbara Pym. The book—Arlott apart—won acclaim for its classical style, the catholic nature of the author's interests, and his interpretation of West Indian cricket within the ethos of Caribbean society. In 1980 James's collected writings were published under the simple title, *Cricket*.

JAMESON, John Alexander

(b. 1941, Byculla, Bombay, India) *Warwickshire and England*

John Jameson was a modest man off the field but assertive and dominating on it. Barrel-chested and strong, he was a right-handed opening batsman with a brutal approach to the new ball. He got many a Warwickshire innings off to an exceptionally fast start, notably in 1974 when he dominated a world-record stand of 465 for the second wicket with Rohan Kanhai against Gloucestershire at Edgbaston, hitting 240 not out. His opening partnerships with Dennis Amiss were often prolific. On ten occasions he exceeded 1,000 runs in a season, but his tendency to inconsistency deterred the England selectors. He toured the West Indies in 1973/4, and his first ball in the Test at Kingston, a Boyce bouncer, he mishooked for six over fine third man. His best Test innings was 82 against India at The Oval in 1971, a characteristic effort including two straight-driven sixes off Bedi into the pavilion. He bowled occasional off-spinners. He became a first-class umpire from 1984 to 1987, coach of Sussex in 1988, and assistant secretary of MCC since 1989, with special responsibility for the Laws, the ground, and all the club's cricketing activities. Despite badly injured knees, he played with success for Warwickshire's over-fifties team in 1994.

First-class career (1960–76): 18,941 runs (33.34) including 33 centuries, 89 wickets (42.49), 255 catches, and 1 stumping
Test matches (4): 214 runs (26.75) and 1–17

JARDINE, Douglas Robert

(b. 1900, Bombay, India; d. 1958, Montreux, Switzerland) *Oxford University, Surrey, and England*

Douglas Jardine was an austere character of iron will with an inflexible self-discipline which extended to his captaincy. His name will forever be linked with bodyline. 'The Iron Duke' was a remarkably mature batsman and captain at Winchester before becoming—like his father—an Oxford blue. For Surrey he finished at the head of the national averages in 1927 and 1928 with 91 and 87 respectively; and he captained Surrey in 1932 and 1933. As England's captain he was a cold authoritarian figure, who yet inspired the loyalty of his team and the grudging admiration of most opponents—the 1932/3 Australians *not* included! As a right-handed batsman he was upright and correct, especially strong on the leg side, a solid defender and a particularly fine player of fast bowling—invariably wearing his Oxford Harlequin cap. He was a heavy scorer in Australia in 1928/9 and in 1932/3 (as captain), on the former tour hitting centuries in his first three innings. After talking with bowlers like Harold Larwood, he devised the bodyline method of attack—short fast bowling aimed at the body with a ring of short-leg fielders—both to counteract the menace of Don Bradman in Test cricket and as a concerted plan to bring back the Ashes in 1932/3. The campaign was successful but the tactics widely condemned. Despite much hostility, Jardine stuck to his convictions that such bowling was not unlawful, and in 1933 he scored 127 for England against the West Indies at Old Trafford facing and overcoming the fast leg-theory (or bodyline) of Learie Constantine and Manny Martindale. He captained MCC in the first Test-playing tour of India, 1933/4, but thereafter he appeared in very little first-class cricket.

JARVIS

First-class career (1920–48): 14,848 runs (46.83)
including 35 centuries, 48 wickets (31.10), and
188 catches
Test matches (22): 1,296 runs (48.00) including 1
century, 0–10, and 26 catches

JARVIS, Paul William

(b. 1965, Redcar, Yorkshire) *Yorkshire, Sussex, and
England*

A combination of injuries, harsh treatment by the
selectors, and the weight of expectations of a
Yorkshire public longing for a successor to Fred
Trueman combined to ensure that Paul Jarvis
failed to live up to the early promise which had
prompted his county to make him their youngest-ever player. Short and wiry, with a rapid
approach to the crease and a quick arm action,
Jarvis made his début at Scarborough at the end
of the 1981 season only 75 days past his sixteenth
birthday. The following summer, he became the
youngest Yorkshire bowler to achieve a hat-trick
in the Sunday League, and in 1985 he repeated
the feat in the county Championship. The strain
of leading the attack at such a young age did tell,
and in both 1984 and 1985 he was affected by
injuries, but in 1986 he took 11 for 92 against
Middlesex and was subsequently awarded his
county cap. The following season he took 81
wickets as well as turning in an eye-catching
performance in the Benson and Hedges Cup
Final when he took 4 for 43 in a narrow win over
Northamptonshire, and gained a place on the
winter tours of Pakistan, and New Zealand and
Australia which followed the World Cup. He
played just one first-class match in Pakistan, but
after missing out on a place in the Bicentennial
Test in Sydney, he appeared in the first two Tests
in New Zealand, bowling with genuine speed to
take six wickets, only to be surprisingly dropped
for the final match in Wellington. He returned to
play in the first two Tests of 1988 against the West
Indies, taking six more wickets, including a best
of 4 for 107 at Lord's, and making an unbeaten 29
in a losing cause in the same match. A serious
back strain ruled him out for the rest of the
summer. Recalled in 1989, he was dropped again
after taking only two wickets in two matches.
Frustrated, he signed up for the unofficial tour of
South Africa the following winter, thereby incurring a three-year ban from Test cricket. When the
ban on the 'rebels' was lifted in the autumn of
1992, Jarvis, having taken only 89 wickets in three
seasons, was surprisingly chosen to tour India
and Sri Lanka. Easily England's best seamer in the

first two Tests against India, taking four wickets,
he was then dropped for Phillip DeFreitas, who
failed to take a first-class wicket on the tour.
Jarvis regained his place for the Test in Sri Lanka,
and for the one-day series against Australia in
1993, only then to be dropped again, and after
further injury problems he was released by Yorkshire at the end of the season. Signing for Sussex,
he took 51 wickets in 1994.

First-class career (1981–   ): 2,474 runs (16.28)
and 546 wickets (28.17)
Test matches (9): 132 runs (10.15) and 21 wickets
(45.95)

JEEVES, Percy

(b. 1888, Earlsheaton, Yorkshire; d. 1916,
Montauban, France) *Warwickshire*

Discovered playing village cricket by Warwickshire's secretary, R. V. Ryder, Percy Jeeves was
hailed by *Wisden* as 'an absolute prize' and in three
seasons (1912–14) established himself as one of the
best right-arm fast-medium bowlers in England. In
1913 he topped the county averages with 106
wickets (20.88) and a year later he, and his young
county colleague Jack Parsons, both played in the
Gentlemen v. Players match at The Oval and were
seen as 'the great hopes of Warwickshire cricket'.
Jeeves attracted attention from the two 'Plums':
'Plum' Warner saw him as a future England
bowler and 'Plum' Wodehouse used his name for
the character of his famous gentleman's gentleman. In his last match, when the war which would
claim his life was already a month old, Jeeves clean-
bowled Tom Hayward (twice) and Jack Hobbs, to
help his county to victory against Surrey, the
county champions. As a right-handed batsman, he
often got quick runs when they were needed.

First-class career (1912–14): 1,204 runs (16.05),
199 wickets (20.03), and 49 dismissals

JENKINS, Roland Oliver

(b. 1918, Worcester; d. 1995, Worcester)
Worcestershire and England

A sound right-handed batsman but better known
as one of the last outstanding English leg-spinners, 'Roley' Jenkins was the local boy made good
par excellence. He had immense energy, every
ounce of which went into every ball he bowled,
and when he batted he did it with the same
cheerful determination. He approached the
stumps in a cap with a nautical roll, taking
childlike pleasure in each wicket. He achieved the
double twice, in 1949 and 1952, and per-

formed the hat-trick three times, two of them in the same match, and all against Surrey. He played at home for England against the West Indies and India, and toured South Africa with MCC, 1948/9, when he took 16 wickets in the Tests. 183 wickets followed in 1949.

First-class career (1938–58): 10,073 runs (22.23) including 1 century, 1,309 wickets (23.64), and 213 catches

Test matches (9): 198 runs (18.00), 32 wickets (34.31), and 4 catches

JESSOP, Gilbert Laird

(b. 1874, Cheltenham, Gloucestershire; d. 1955, Fordington, Dorset) *Cambridge University, Gloucestershire, and England*

The most famous hitter in cricket history, Gilbert Jessop, 'The Croucher', was a devastating match-winner and superb entertainer. Although he won one Test with his century at The Oval in 1902 his overall average was only 21. Yet for 20 years before the First World War he was the most exciting figure in the game. A right-handed batsman, he was short and compact with great strength about the shoulders, large, strong hands, and exceptionally long arms. He would sight the ball very early from his crouched stance, and by daring and speedy footwork completely invalidate the bowler's length and field-placings. Most of his shots were unorthodox, played with a straight bat, and he was consistent as well as pulverizing. Away from Tests he topped 1,000 runs in a season 14 times. In five innings of over 200—the highest being 286 against Sussex at Hove in 1903—he maintained a scoring-rate of only just under 100 runs an hour. Three of his other double-centuries were reached in under $2\frac{1}{2}$ hours. Each of his 53 centuries averaged an almost unbelievable 82.7 runs an hour. A fast but unremarkable bowler, he opened the bowling in his first Test against Australia at Lord's in 1899, when he was captain of Cambridge University. In 1897 and 1900 he achieved the double. His most famous performance came in the Oval Test of 1902. Seeking 273 to win, England were 48 for 5 when he went in on a none-too-easy pitch. In 75 minutes against bowling of the highest class he hit 104, making it possible for England to win amid almost unbearable tension with the last pair together. The previous winter in Australia he had met with only moderate success. He was one of the greatest fielders and throwers there has ever been, and few dared to take risks with 'Jessopus' at cover. He captained Gloucestershire from 1900

until 1912. His son, the Revd G. L. O. Jessop, played for Hampshire and Dorset.

First-class career (1894–1914): 26,698 runs (32.63) including 53 centuries, 873 wickets (22.79), and 463 catches

Test matches (18): 569 runs (21.88) including 1 century, 10 wickets (35.40), and 11 catches

JOHNSTON, Brian Alexander

(b. 1912, Hertfordshire; d. 1994, London)

Not till after the Second World War in which he won an MC as a Grenadier Guards officer, did 'Johnners' find his vocation as a broadcaster. For 24 years (1946–69) he commentated on Test matches, home and abroad, for BBC television, becoming the Corporation's first official commentator in 1963. At the same time, his versatility led to his broadcasting on a range of musical and light variety radio shows including the prestigious *In Town Tonight*. He shared in the commentaries on major royal occasions. At the age of 60, he began a new career as a freelance broadcaster, quickly becoming the cheerful and engaging guiding spirit of *Test Match Special* (1970–93), winning the Pye Sports Personality award in 1981 and hosting the immensely popular Outside Broadcast, *Down Your Way* (1972–87). Both programmes, threatened with closure because of internal changes of policy, were reprieved because of public pressure upon the BBC. A bubbly character of simple tastes with an irresistable charm and an irrepressible sense of gaiety, humour, and fun, he became an institution. Old Etonian though he was, narrowly missing the 1st XI as a wicket-keeper, he was classless in his approach to his fellow men and women. His humour matched that of professional comedians and like them he had his own stock-in-trade: cake. An England collapse, depressing his listeners, was redeemed by the mention of the cake, usually chocolate, he had received that morning. His laughter on the air reduced listeners—sometimes driving their cars—to helplessness. He had neither the moral thrust of an Arlott nor the compelling authority of a Swanton, but he was his own man, and the professional behind the microphone was never betrayed by his impish, even frivolous, approach. His first autobiography, *It's been a Lot of Fun*, one of scores of successful books, encapsulated his approach to life. When he died after a heart attack at a time when he was still leading a full life as a broadcaster, after-dinner speaker, and entertainer, the whole world of cricket mourned. Westminster Abbey was full to the gunwales for his memorial service and the Prime Minister, John Major, pronounced in his address that 'Summers would never be the same.'

JONES, Alan

(b. 1938, Velindre, Glamorgan, Wales) *Glamorgan*

Among those with claims to be the finest batsman in the British Isles not to play for England none can come technically closer than the left-handed opening batsman for Glamorgan (1957–83), the Welsh-speaking Alan Jones. He appeared for England against the Rest of the World at Lord's in 1970, and was awarded his cap and blazer. But the series—a replacement for that against South Africa—was retrospectively denied Test match status and Jones had been only a *de facto* England Test player. His 36,000 runs stand —and are likely to stand for ever—as the most scored in first-class cricket by a player without having been a Test batsman. On 23 successive occasions he scored 1,000 runs for Glamorgan, two achievements standing out—161 not out against the West Indies at Swansea in 1966 and 204 not out against Hampshire at Basingstoke in 1980. In a varied career he captained Glamorgan (1976–8), played for West Australia (1963–4), Northern Transvaal (1975–6), and Natal (1976–7), toured Ceylon with MCC (1969/70), and even appeared for an Australian Combined XI against South Africa at Perth (1963). In 1984 he was appointed county coach to Glamorgan.

First-class career (1957–83): 36,049 runs (32.89) including 56 centuries, 3 wickets (110.00), and 288 catches

JONES, Arthur Owen

(b. 1872, Shelton, Nottinghamshire; d. 1914, Dunstable, Bedfordshire) *Cambridge University, Nottinghamshire, and England*

Despite a rather cramped stance, Arthur Jones was a brilliant but sometimes impetuous opening batsman, especially strong on the off-side. He was also a very useful leg-break bowler and one of the finest all-round fieldsmen ever seen—said to be unequalled in the slips and to have invented the position of gully. A Cambridge blue, he led Nottinghamshire to the Championship in 1907, and that winter led MCC to Australia, where he had a serious illness. He had also toured Australia in 1901/2 with Archie MacLaren's team but his real *métier* was county cricket and, with James

Iremonger, shared in 24 opening stands of 100 or more for Nottinghamshire. He captained his county from 1900 until within a few months of his death from tuberculosis in 1914.

First-class career (1892–1914): 22,935 runs (31.54) including 34 centuries, 333 wickets (32.81), 577 catches, and 2 stumpings
Test matches (12): 291 runs (13.85), 3 wickets (44.33), and 15 catches

JONES, Ivor Jeffrey

(b. 1941, Dafen, Carmarthenshire, Wales) *Glamorgan and England*

A well-built, strapping Welshman, Jeff Jones was a fast and graceful left-arm bowler, who had immense fire, speed and sustained hostility. He matured into a first-choice England bowler between 1963 and 1967 and toured Australia and New Zealand in 1965/6, taking 15 wickets in four Tests against Australia, and also the West Indies, India, and Pakistan. His best bowling was 8 for 11 at Leicester in 1965, and in his last full season, 1967, he took 100 wickets (19.49). But in May 1968, he tore the ligaments in his elbow, and he never bowled effectively again.

First-class career (1960–8): 513 runs (3.97) 511 wickets (25.98), and 46 catches
Test matches (15): 38 runs (4.75), 44 wickets (40.20), and 4 catches

JUPP, Henry

(b. 1841, Dorking, Surrey; d. 1889, London) *Surrey and England*

Henry Jupp or 'Young Stonewall' of Dorking was once clean-bowled first ball in a local match. Instead of going out, he coolly turned, replaced the bails and prepared to receive the next ball. 'Ain't you going, Juppy?' asked the umpire. 'No,' replied Juppy, 'not at Dorking I ain't'—and he did not! Short, broad-shouldered, powerful, and a rough diamond, Harry Jupp was at his best defending, but he was a stylish and sound right-handed batsman, who could drive powerfully. He opened for Surrey for about 20 years. He was very good at cover-point or in the outfield. Touring Australia with James Lillywhite's team in 1876/7, he appeared in two Tests, top-scoring in the first at Melbourne with 63.

First-class career (1862–81): 15,319 runs (23.78) including 12 centuries, 228 catches, and 19 stumpings
Test matches (2): 68 runs (17.00) and 2 catches

JUPP, Vallance William Crisp

(b. 1891, Burgess Hill, Sussex; d. 1960, Spratton, Northamptonshire) *Sussex, Northamptonshire, and England*

A short, prematurely bald man, Vallance Jupp or 'Juppy' had broad shoulders, long arms, great strength, and a rough humour. He was an enterprising right-handed batsman of blazing energy, a penetrating slow-medium off-break bowler with a rolling gait, and a very agile field at cover. Starting as a professional with Sussex—his first century was against Northamptonshire—he turned amateur after the First World War and went to live in Northampton, where he had a business. He became secretary/captain of his new county and, during years of cricket depression at Northampton, was always ready to carry on the fight. He achieved the double ten times, more than any other amateur, and eight of them while with his new county, and, although he was unable to tour Australia with MCC in 1920/1 or 1924/5, he went to South Africa in 1922/3, taking 14 wickets in the four Tests. He appeared twice against Australia in 1921 and against the West Indies in 1928.

First-class career (1909–38): 23,296 runs (29.41) including 30 centuries, 1,658 wickets (23.01), and 222 catches

Test matches (8): 208 runs (17.33), 28 wickets (22.00), and 5 catches

KEETON, William Walter

(b. 1905, Shirebrook, Derbyshire; d. 1980, Forest Town, Nottinghamshire) *Nottinghamshire and England*

Walter Keeton was a quick-footed right-handed opening batsman, stylish, wristy, and consistent, who shared 45 century opening stands with Charlie Harris. His highest score was 312 not out at The Oval against Middlesex in 1939, the only triple hundred ever scored for Notts. He scored at least one century against each of the other first-class counties. With Reg Simpson he added 318 for the first wicket against Lancashire at Old Trafford in 1949 and besides his 312 he hit six other double-centuries. He played twice for England, against Australia in 1934 and against the West Indies five years later. He also played soccer for Sunderland and Nottingham Forest.

First-class career (1926–52): 24,276 runs (39.53) including 54 centuries, 2 wickets (51.50), and 76 catches

Test matches (2): 57 runs (14.25)

KENNEDY, Alexander Stuart

(b. 1891, Edinburgh, Scotland; d. 1959, Southampton) *Hampshire and England*

One of the most durable and consistent of all county all-rounders, Alex Kennedy was a dapper little man with sleek, dark hair, and an india-rubber physique, which nothing seemed to tire. He was a right-handed batsman, who could be either studious or violent and who appeared in every position from one to eleven. As a dedicated right-arm medium-fast bowler he varied his pace subtly and could swing the new ball very late either way. His accuracy, freshness, and intelligence were remarkable. He took a relatively long run-up, which included a sort of chassé in the middle. For years Newman and Kennedy *were* Hampshire's bowling and often, with Phil Mead, the batting too! Kennedy took 100 wickets in 15 seasons and did the double five times, in 1922 taking 205 wickets and scoring 1,129 runs. He took all 10 for 37 for Players against Gentlemen at The Oval in 1927; but represented England only in South Africa, 1922/3, when his bowling was very effective on the matting. (For Lord Tennyson's team in South Africa, 1924/5, he took 21 wickets in the unofficial Tests.)

First-class career (1907–36): 16,586 runs (18.53) including 10 centuries, 2,874 wickets (21.24), and 530 catches

Test matches (5): 93 runs (15.50), 31 wickets (19.32), and 5 catches

KENYON, Donald

(b. 1924, Wordsley, Staffordshire) *Worcestershire and England*

A right-handed, opening batsman, Don Kenyon was a craftsman with a shrewd cricket brain. He scored more runs and centuries than any other Worcestershire player, 19 times exceeding 1,000 runs in a season. His highest score was 259 against Yorkshire at Kidderminster in 1956; and three years previously, in the opening match of the tour, he hit 122 off the Australians. He toured India in 1951/2 and represented England against Australia and South Africa occasionally at home. He led Worcestershire for nine years, and was at the helm when the county won the Championship in 1964 and again in 1965. He served for several years as a Test selector and was president of his county from 1986 to 1989.

First-class career (1946–67): 37,002 runs (33.63) including 74 centuries, 1 wicket (187.00), and 327 catches

Test matches (8): 192 runs (12.80) and 5 catches

KEY, Sir Kingsmill James

(b. 1864, Streatham, Surrey; d. 1932, Wittersham, Kent) *Oxford University and Surrey*

Playing for Surrey while still a schoolboy at Clifton College, Key was four years in the Oxford XI. His 181 for the university against Middlesex at Chiswick Park in 1887 provided 'the most remarkable batting of the season' in a (then) record first-class partnership with H. Philipson of 340 for any wicket. He was a highly successful captain of Surrey (1894–9), but after disagreeing with the Committee, he resigned on a matter of principle. He believed amateurs were excluding deserving professionals from places in the side.

First-class career (1884–1909): 13,008 runs (26.22) including 13 centuries, 12 wickets (28.08), and 113 catches

KILBURN, James Maurice

(b. 1909, Sheffield, Yorkshire; d. 1993, Harrogate, Yorkshire)

Jim Kilburn, as cricket correspondent of the *Yorkshire Post*, accompanied the county team on its travels from 1934 onwards for over forty years. A reserved and, to those who did not know him, austere character, he knew Yorkshire cricket in all its moods, from the great days of Sutcliffe, Mitchell, Verity, Bowes, and the young Hutton to the less equable 1950s and 1960s. He was as early as any in predicting that Hutton would be 'a future Colossus regaining for England records which Bradman made his own'. He was in the tradition of 'Old Ebor', A. W. Pullin of an earlier era, whose history of the county he continued up till 1949. In it he summed up the changes he saw in players' attitudes. To the pre-war generation 'concerns were community concerns. Help in a period of struggle was freely given'. In the post-war world, 'the tradition [was] abandoned in the new cricketing world of easy satisfaction'. In a largely pre-television age, journalists of his calibre were vital in retaining the links between players and their county supporters. They told the tale, pertinent to the game itself without frills, sensation, or irrelevant asides. His own cricket had been played for Sheffield University and for Barnsley and Bradford in the Yorkshire Leagues principally as a right-arm off-break bowler. His *Thanks to Cricket* (1972) was at once autobiographical, historical, nostalgic, and critical.

KILLICK, Revd Edgar Thomas

(b. 1907, London; d. 1953, Northampton) *Cambridge University, Middlesex, and England*

A graceful, right-handed stroke-player, Tom Killick's first-class career was all too short. Few contemporaries executed the off-drive and square-cut with such ease and he was a swift mover in the outfield. A Cambridge blue, he enjoyed a short but distinguished career as opening batsman for Middlesex. In 1931, in his only game for the county that season, he shared in an opening stand of 277 with G. T. S. Stevens against Warwickshire at Lord's, his own score being 206. In 1929 he went in first with Herbert Sutcliffe in two Tests against South Africa, as successor to Jack Hobbs. He died while batting in a match between the diocesan clergy of St Albans and Coventry at Northampton.

First-class career (1926–46): 5,730 runs (40.35) including 15 centuries, 3 wickets (76.33), and 50 catches

Test matches (2): 81 runs (20.25) and 2 catches

KILNER, Roy

(b. 1890, Wombwell, Yorkshire; d. 1928, Barnsley, Yorkshire) *Yorkshire, Europeans, and England*

With his long chin, merry eyes, and cap askew, Roy Kilner said of a typical Roses match—which he relished—'What we want is no umpires and fair cheating all round!' He was a man of rare charm, humour, and generosity. A left-hander, he could not only drive powerfully on the off-side and pull very hard, but he could also play a dogged game and, as a slow bowler, his spin and accuracy made him at times unplayable. On true pitches he would plug away on a length for long spells with slight variations of flight and pace. A member of Yorkshire's Championship-winning sides of the early 1920s, he achieved the double three times, and his benefit in 1925 realized £4,014, a record for many years. He played for England against Australia and South Africa at home, and against Australia in Australia in 1924/5, when he was prominent in England's win at Melbourne in the fourth match, scoring 74 and taking 5 for 70. He died of enteric fever, contracted on his way home from India after a coaching engagement.

First-class career (1911–27): 14,707 runs (30.01) including 18 centuries, 1,003 wickets (18.46), and 266 catches

Test matches (9): 233 runs (33.28), 24 wickets (30.58), and 6 catches

KING, John Herbert

(b. 1871, Lutterworth, Leicestershire; d. 1946, Denbigh, Denbighshire, Wales) Leicestershire and England

John King had a long and honourable career as player and umpire. A grand left-handed batsman, strong on the leg side and gifted with a powerful square-cut, a left-arm slow bowler and reliable in the field, he was the pivot of his county's cricket for 30 years, scoring 205 against Hampshire at the age of 52. He exceeded 1,000 runs in a season 14 times and twice he took 100 wickets. For Gentlemen v. Players at Lord's in 1904, he hit 104 and 109 not out against some terrific fast bowling. In his sole Test, against Australia at Lord's in 1909, he scored 60 and 4. In the absence of a fast bowler, he also opened the bowling and took 1 for 99 (but Ransford and Trumper were both dropped off him in the same over).

First-class career (1895–1925): 25,122 runs (27.34) including 34 centuries, 1,204 wickets (25.16), and 340 catches

KINNEIR, Septimus

(b. 1871, Corsham, Wiltshire; d. 1928, Birmingham) Wiltshire, Warwickshire, and England

Coming into first-class cricket at 27, 'Paul' Kinneir was an orthodox left-handed batsman who rivalled Willie Quaife at the head of Warwickshire's batting averages for more than a decade. Touring Australia with MCC in 1911/12, he appeared in one Test at Sydney, scoring 22 and 30, but did not represent England again, partly because his fielding was considered poor.

First-class career (1898–1914): 15,641 runs (32.72) including 26 centuries, 48 wickets (31.08), and 181 catches

KNIGHT, Albert Ernest

(b. 1872, Leicester; d. 1946, Edmonton, Middlesex) Leicestershire and England

An outstanding character among the professionals of his day, Albert Knight was a very good hard-wicket player. A right-handed batsman, strong on the off-side with a favourite square-drive, he was also a good cover who threw in belligerently. He scored 1,000 runs in ten seasons, making his highest score, 229 not out, against Worcestershire at Worcester in 1903. He toured Australia in 1903/4, and played a heroic part in the fourth and critical match of the rubber at Sydney, making 70 not out after an early collapse. A Methodist lay preacher, he would pray before going in to bat and, sometimes, at the wicket—Walter Brearley threatened to report him to MCC for taking unfair advantage! He tended to forget the name of his batting partner to everyone's confusion. Once, a puzzled George Hirst, ball in hand, said to Knight's partner 'Won't you tell him your name, sir? Then we'll all be happy!' A widely read man, Knight became coach successively at Highgate School and Belvedere College, Dublin.

First-class career (1895–1912): 19,357 runs (29.24) including 34 centuries, 4 wickets (29.25), and 132 catches

Test matches (3): 81 runs (16.20) and 1 catch

KNIGHT, Barry Rolfe

(b. 1938, Chesterfield, Derbyshire) Essex, Leicestershire, and England

A vigorous all-rounder who enjoyed life off the field as well as on it, Barry Knight was an attractive forcing right-handed batsman, dangerous right-arm fast-medium bowler and an excellent field. Capable of hard work despite his slim, trim build, he achieved the double four times between 1962 and 1965. Leaving Essex after a dispute in 1966, he had three years with Leicestershire and then went to live in Sydney, where he established an indoor cricket school. He had toured Australia twice, India once, and Pakistan once. By scoring 125 against New Zealand at Auckland in 1962/3 he shared in the record sixth-wicket stand of 240 with Peter Parfitt, and he hit 127 against India at Kanpur in 1963/4.

First-class career (1955–69): 13,336 runs (25.70) including 12 centuries, 1,089 wickets (24.06), and 263 catches

Test matches (29): 812 runs (26.19) including 2 centuries, 70 wickets (31.75), and 14 catches

KNIGHT, Donald John

(b. 1894, Sutton, Surrey; d. 1960, London) Oxford University, Surrey, and England

Donald Knight was an amateur opening batsman of high distinction and his classic right-handed method, learned at Malvern, made him one of the outstanding players in immediate post-1918 cricket. After a bad blow to his head in 1920 when fielding at short-leg he was never quite the same although he played in the first two Tests of 1921 against Australia with some success before dropping out of the regular first-class game and becoming a highly respected cricket master at Westminster.

First-class career (1911–37): 6,231 runs (30.84) including 13 centuries, 3 wickets (8.33), and 74 catches

Test matches (2): 54 runs (13.50) and 1 catch

KNIGHT, Roger David Verdon

(b. 1946, Streatham, London) *Cambridge University, Surrey, Gloucestershire, and Sussex*

Signalling his arrival at Cambridge from Dulwich College with 86 (run out) on his début against Essex at Fenner's in 1967, Roger Knight, in his fourth year in the side, took 6 for 65 and then made 164 against the same opponents in 1970. No other Cambridge batsman topped 20. After struggling to hold a place with Surrey, this tall, stylish left-handed batsman took his services to Gloucestershire and then Sussex, one of a dying breed to combine schoolmastering with county cricket. His contribution to Gloucestershire, in five seasons, was to secure five man-of-the-match awards in one-day cricket and score 5,610 runs in the first-class game. On song, moving imposingly and invariably onto the front foot, he was a difficult man to bowl to and lesser batsmen played for England in his time. He returned to The Oval in 1978, taking over a weakened Surrey. In five seasons they went from bottom of the county Championship to four appearances in one-day finals at Lord's and to victory against Warwickshire in 1982. His captaincy did not flinch from unpopular decisions and was marked by calm resolve and steely determination. Knight's right-arm medium-pace bowling commanded a nagging accuracy and was valuable in one-day cricket where he achieved a total of 10 'man-of-the-match' or 'Gold' awards. He retired from county cricket after 1984 but played two seasons of minor county cricket for Bedfordshire in 1987–8. An assistant master at Eastbourne College and Cranleigh, where he ran a house and the cricket, he became headmaster of Worksop College in 1990, running a successful 1st XI himself and staging the 1992 European Cup at the College. In 1994 his considerable skills in leadership and administration were translated firmly from academia to cricket when he was appointed secretary of MCC.

First-class career (1967–89): 19,558 runs (32.00) including 31 centuries, 369 wickets (36.13), and 295 catches

KNOTT, Alan Philip Eric

(b. 1946, Belvedere, Kent) *Kent and England*

Alan Knott surpassed all previous records for an England wicket-keeper during the 11 hectic years between 1967 and 1977, when he played in 89 Tests. Soon after the Centenary Test at Melbourne he became one of the first recruits to Kerry Packer's World Series Cricket. Small, nimble, and dark-eyed, he was a serious family man off the field and an impish genius on it. He was preferred to all his wicket-keeping rivals, notably his immediate successor Bob Taylor, because of his exceptional batting ability. At his best in a crisis (and England faced many a crisis in his era) 'Knottie' applied hawk-eyed defence, an instinct for survival, and formidable powers of concentration, and with brilliant attacking flair was often able to turn the course of a game. His right-handed batting was shrewd, increasingly unorthodox (his top hand holding the bat with the palm facing the bowler) and often outrageous, as when he repulsed the dangerous swing bowling of Bob Massie by carting him to all parts of the leg-side field in 1972, or on two tours of India when he broke the stranglehold imposed by the Indian spinners by moving his feet to the pitch of the ball and hitting it over the top. He was an even better player of fast bowlers. Against Lillee and Thomson in 1974/5 he was England's second highest scorer. His wicket-keeping was as quick and dazzling as the flight of a hornet. He ignored the advice of wicket-keepers of other eras to stand up to the wicket to medium-paced bowlers, believing he got far more catching chances standing back. He frequently dived to pick up the half-chance, sometimes with positively demonic dexterity; up to the stumps he could be equally brilliant although he was undoubtedly more fallible. Much of his 'keeping for Kent and England was to the awkward bowling of Derek Underwood—the two were an almost inseparable partnership. Knott's fetish for fitness included sticking to a careful diet. He was prone to stiff muscles and therefore exercised constantly to keep his limbs supple. Off the field he was almost paranoiacally suspicious of breezes and draughts. He went on six major overseas tours, and scored more than 1,000 runs twice, hitting 127 not out and 118 not out in one Championship match against Surrey at Maidstone in 1972. Only Rodney Marsh has bettered his total of 269 Test victims which began with seven catches in his first Test against Pakistan at Trent Bridge in 1967. Yet he only began to dedicate himself to his 'keeping when he joined the Kent staff, having been a successful schoolboy off-spinner. Still regarded as the best wicket-keeper in the world, he announced his retirement from first-class cricket at the end of the 1985 season to concentrate on running his sports shop, and, appropriately, a keep-fit gym. He helped a succession of England wicket-keepers as a part-time coach and his son, James, began playing for Kent's 2nd XI in 1993.

First-class career (1964–85): 18,105 runs (29.63) including 17 centuries, 2 wickets (43.50), and 1,344 dismissals (1,211 c., 133 st.)

Test matches (95): 4,389 runs (32.75) including 5 centuries, and 269 dismissals (250 c., 19 st.)

KNOX, Neville Alexander

(b. 1884, London; d. 1935, Surbiton, Surrey) *Surrey and England*

From Dulwich College Neville Knox burst into Surrey cricket and had a big share in bringing the county out of a deep depression. Over 6 ft. tall and loose-limbed, he was probably the fastest bowler in England for several years. With a long and peculiar run, which started from near deep mid-off, he bowled at a great pace with a sharp break-back, and his good-length deliveries often reared up straight *à la* Jeff Thomson. He took twelve Players wickets for Gentlemen at Lord's in 1906—seven clean-bowled—and appeared the following year in two Tests against South Africa. His career ended rather abruptly: he had developed an acute form of shin soreness and was struggling against chronic lameness. Only sheer pluck enabled him latterly to keep going.

First-class career (1904–19): 905 runs (10.16), 411 wickets (21.55), and 32 catches

Test matches (2): 24 runs (8.00) and 3 wickets (35.00)

KORTRIGHT, Charles Jesse

(b. 1871, Ingatestone, Essex; d. 1952, Brentwood, Essex) *Essex*

Regarded by contemporaries as the fastest bowler of his time, Kortright was a right-armer who aimed at the off-stump, bowling very few short-pitched balls—advice he passed on to his Essex successor, Kenneth Farnes, in the 1930s. Among his best achievements, both at Leyton, were 13 for 64 against Surrey in 1893 and 8 for 57 against Yorkshire in 1900. In 1898 his bowling ruffled W.G. Grace but a few days later the pair batted together for the Gentlemen v. the Players at Lord's and shared in a tenth-wicket partnership of 78. The right-handed Kortright batted aggressively, taking 158 runs off Hampshire, then a second-class county, at Southampton in 1891 in 100 minutes. An amateur with sufficient private means, he was asked what he did when not bowling fast. He replied 'bowled leg-breaks and played golf'.

First-class career (1893–1907): 4,404 runs (17.61) including 2 centuries, 489 wickets (21.05), and 176 catches

LACEY, Sir Francis Eden

(b. 1859, Wareham, Dorset; d. 1946, Sutton Veny, Wiltshire) *Cambridge University and Hampshire*

To the secretaryship of MCC in 1898 Francis Lacey, a barrister, brought a formidable playing record. He had scored six centuries in a season at Sherborne, won a blue at Cambridge and made both a double-century and a triple-century for Hampshire. His 211 and 92 not out against Kent in 1884 at Southampton established his credentials in first-class cricket as a stylish front-foot right-handed batsman. On the same ground in 1887 his 323 not out against Norkolk still stands as the highest score in a county match not deemed first-class. His flighted slow bowling, in the round-arm style, brought him 11 for 181 for Hampshire against Sussex at Brighton in 1882 in a match in which he also made 207 for once out. During his time at Lord's (1898–1926) he established the Easter coaching classes and saw the Mound and Grand Stands completed. The structure of first-class cricket and the role of the Imperial Cricket Conference called for his decisive guidance. He was businesslike, austerely efficient, and painstaking and on his retirement became the only holder of the office to have been knighted.

First-class career (1882–97): 2,589 runs (32.77) including 4 centuries, 52 wickets (21.59), and 34 catches

LAKER, James Charles

(b. 1922, Bradford, Yorkshire; d. 1986, Putney, London) *Surrey, Essex, and England*

Jim Laker will forever be remembered for his amazing analysis of 19 for 90 against Australia in 1956. In his prime he was perhaps the best of all off-spinners, with a model high action, sharp spin, great accuracy, flight and the intelligence to think batsmen out. A Yorkshireman of few words, his approach to cricket and to life was independent, detached, cool. His figures did his talking for him. Eleven times he exceeded 100 wickets in a season. His best season was 1950, when he took 166 wickets (15.32), including 8 for 2 in the Test Trial at Bradford; and, from 1952 until 1958 when Surrey reigned as Champions, he shared the main attack with Alec Bedser, Peter Loader, and Tony Lock, personally taking 327 wickets (15.62). Partly because he had been punished heavily by the 1948 Australians, he could not find a regular place for England until 1956, but in this *annus mirabilis* his revenge was fearsome. In seven games against the Australians, many on rain-affected pitches, he took 63 wickets, including 46 at 9.60 in the Tests, the record against Australia. His performance at Old Trafford (9 for 37 and 10 for 53) is unique. He also took all ten against the hapless 1956 Australians for Surrey. Leaving Surrey in 1959, he reappeared after three years for Essex, finally retiring in 1964. He became a popular cricket commentator for BBC Television and wrote several books, one of which got him into trouble with Surrey and MCC, but his sins were soon forgiven. He was an active member of Surrey's Cricket Committee. Throughout his playing career, he was a useful, sturdy tail-end batsman and a reliable catcher.

First-class career (1946–65): 7,304 runs (16.60) including 2 centuries, 1,944 wickets (18.40), and 270 catches

Test matches (46): 676 runs (14.08), 193 wickets (21.24), and 12 catches

LAMB, Allan Joseph

(b. 1954, Langebaanweg, Cape Province, South Africa) *Western Province, Northamptonshire, and England*

Born of English parents in the Cape Province in South Africa, Allan Lamb had already attracted several plaudits for his batting for Western Province when he came to England in 1977 and qualified to play for Northamptonshire by special registration in 1978. Despite breaking an arm in his first season he immediately impressed as a compact, naturally gifted right-hand batsman with a simple method and a desire to take the initiative from bowlers whenever possible. Five feet eight, stocky, confident, and brave, he was a live-wire character in whose company there was never a dull moment. Debarred from playing Test cricket by the boycott of South Africa, he set his heart on playing for the land of his parents instead. He acquired a British passport, bought a cottage in Northamptonshire and in 1982 won a

place in the England side immediately he became available. Having averaged 66.55 in 1980 and 60.26 in 1981 in English first-class cricket, he had already proved himself a class above the run-of-the-mill county player. He confirmed his ability by scoring his first Test hundred against India at The Oval. He often impressed in Australia, playing on the fast wickets he was used to in South Africa, making 414 runs (41.40) in the Tests with four fifties. He had a fine series against New Zealand in 1983, topping the England batting averages, and hitting two centuries. After a disappointing tour of New Zealand and Pakistan he had a remarkable summer in 1984, displaying immense resolution and skill to score three gritty hundreds against the fierce and unrelenting West Indies fast attack. He made his fourth Test hundred of the summer against Sri Lanka. After making useful contributions in England's victories over India and Australia, he could not reproduce his heroics of 1984 on the tour to the West Indies in 1986, averaging only 22.40 in the Test series, and after 45 successive Tests for England he was dropped after failure in the first two matches against India the following summer. However, he reacted with a spate of brilliantly acquired runs for Northamptonshire and was recalled for the last Test of the summer against New Zealand and for the subsequent visit to Australia. If that tour was personally disappointing, he was far from finished, returning to add steel against the West Indies fast bowlers in 1988 and scoring 113 at Leeds. He made 125 against Australia on the same Headingley ground in the first Test of 1989—his ninth Test hundred, all scored in England—but pulled a muscle and missed the rest of the series. Vice-captain to Graham Gooch in 1989/90 in the West Indies he took over as captain for the last two Tests of the tour and scored superb hundreds at Sabina Park, in victory, and Bridgetown (in defeat) in his first Test as England captain. Only Colin Cowdrey has equalled Lamb's six Test hundreds against the West Indies. Throughout his career he was a superb limited-overs batsman, pacing his innings calmly and shrewdly and once stunning a Sydney crowd by hitting 18 off the final over from Bruce Reid, to win the match (1986/7). He played in the World Cup finals of 1983, 1987, and 1992. He became captain of Northamptonshire in 1989, leading them to victory at Lord's in the 1992 NatWest Trophy final. He accused Pakistan bowlers of tampering illegally with the ball in 1992 and successfully defended himself in court the following year.

First-class career (1972–): 31,131 runs (48.64) including 84 centuries, and 438 catches
Test matches (79): 4,656 runs (36.09) including 14 centuries, and 75 catches

LANG, Andrew

(b. 1844, Selkirk, Scotland; d. 1912, Banchory, Aberdeenshire, Scotland)

To the Badminton Library volume on *Cricket* (1888) Andrew Lang contributed the opening chapter on the history of the game. From a Scottish literary and academic background (his father was a friend of Sir Walter Scott) Lang came south in 1865. His enthusiasm for cricket was aroused while briefly at Oxford. Within a few years he was elected a member of MCC and settled upon a career as a writer in London. 'He would turn into the pavilion during the intervals of a match and write on the corner of a table.' Books and articles flowed from his pen and he had equal claims as a poet, essayist, historian, anthropologist, classical translator, and novelist. Cricket knew his prose and his verse in what he saw as 'the most catholic and diffused, the most innocent, kindly and manly of popular pastimes'.

LANGFORD, Arthur William Tanfield

(b. 1896, Ilford, Essex; d. 1976, Banstead, Surrey)

But for Arthur Langford 'there would be no *Cricketer*' wrote E. W. Swanton while its founder, Sir Pelham Warner, declared that the magazine owed everything to him. What has remained the game's longest standing monthly publication, *The Cricketer* was founded in 1921 by Warner. Two years later Langford began to write for it. In 1928 he became assistant editor to the founder. While Warner remained the 'front' man with a finger in many pies—journalist, selector, broadcaster—Langford did the backroom work. During the Second World War the paper was run as a cottage industry from his home in Surbiton, with devoted help from his wife, and even after his retirement in 1966 Langford wrote occasional pieces. He was a useful all-rounder in club cricket playing for MCC, Hampton Wick, and the Jesters, and southern club cricket was his special interest. He was immensely proud of his one appearance at Lord's.

LANGRIDGE, James

(b. 1906, Chailey, Sussex; d. 1966, Brighton, Sussex) *Sussex, Auckland, and England*

A genuine all-rounder, Jim Langridge was a fine fielder, a very sound, combative, but rather slow batsman, and a formidable left-arm bowler with flight, accuracy, and spin, despite an odd action which had the suggestion of a curtsy about it. The first of the modern professional Sussex captains, he led the county from 1950 until 1952, but Hedley Verity barred his way to regular Test cricket. Langridge played against the West Indies, South Africa, and India in England, and toured India in 1933/4, the first Test-playing tour to the Subcontinent, appearing in the three Tests. He also toured Australia, 1946/7, without playing a Test. He was called 'a fine, sturdy character, a real part of Sussex'. Twenty times he exceeded 1,000 runs in a season, and he did the double six times. He became county coach, his son Richard also played for Sussex and his brother John was another Sussex stalwart who was certainly amongst the best batsmen never to play for England, and who became a long-serving and highly regarded umpire.

First-class career (1924–53): 31,716 runs (35.20) including 42 centuries, 1,530 wickets (22.56), and 384 catches
Test matches (8): 242 runs (26.88), 19 wickets (21.73), and 6 catches

LANGRIDGE, John George

(b. 1910, Chailey, Sussex) *Sussex*

For nearly 30 years, under eleven different captains, John Langridge produced figures which cried aloud for England selection. He made 1,000 runs a season on seventeen occasions, 2,000 on eleven of them, and over 34,000 runs in his career. He would set himself a target of 500 runs a month; an orthodox, resolute, opening right-handed batsman with powers of great concentration, he usually succeeded. The nearest he got to being chosen for England was his selection for the MCC tour to India in 1939–40, cancelled because of the Second World War. In 1933 he shared with Ted Bowley in a Sussex first-wicket record stand of 490 against Middlesex at Hove, making 195 himself. Two weeks later on the same ground he made his highest score of 250 not out against Glamorgan. In 1949 he had a magnificent summer, scoring twelve centuries, four of them in succession. At last, he won some recognition at representative level, being selected that year for the Players against the Gentlemen at Lord's to open the batting with Len Hutton. He was, too, a most efficient slip catcher: 'c. Langridge (John), b. Langridge (James)' found its way into the score books on 133 occasions. After retiring, he became a first-class umpire, amiable, reliable and fit. In 1978 he completed 50 years in the first-class game.

First-class career (1928–55): 34,380 runs (37.45) including 76 centuries, 44 wickets (42.00), and 784 catches

LARKINS, Wayne

(b. 1953, Roxton, Bedfordshire) *Northamptonshire, Durham, Western Province, Eastern Province, and England*

A cheerful character from Bedfordshire, Wayne Larkins was a right-handed opening batsman of medium height and wiry build who possessed a rare gift of timing and loved to attack the new ball with bold, thrilling, but orthodox strokes. For more than 20 years he was one of the most attractive and destructive batsmen in county cricket, but consistency eluded him. Also a fine fielder and occasional medium-pace swing bowler, he undoubtedly had the ability to establish himself at Test level but a batting average of 16 after six Tests did not do him justice. He took a long time even to cement a regular place in the Northamptonshire side, making his first appearance in 1972 but not being capped until 1976. Once established, he became a consistently high scorer, forming an attractive opening partnership with Geoff Cook and putting on a county record of 322 for the second wicket with Richard Williams against Leicestershire in 1980. He toured Australia in 1979/80, played his first Test at Melbourne and his second against India in Bombay on the way home. He had three further opportunities against the West Indies in England in 1980, achieving a top score of only 33 but occasionally driving or playing the ball off his legs with crisp strokes which bore the hallmark of true class. He was recalled for the last Test of 1981 against Australia, scoring 34 and 24 at The Oval, and he was distinctly unlucky to be left out of the team for the subsequent tour of India. His disappointment no doubt persuaded him to take a hefty financial inducement to play on the officially disapproved-of South African tour of March 1982. This earned him a three-year ban from Test cricket, but he underlined what might have been by scoring five hundreds and 1,863 runs in first-class cricket in 1982. He made a

career-best 252 against Glamorgan at Cardiff in 1983 and in 1986 was called into England's side to play against India, only to be forced to withdraw before the match, having broken a thumb. He returned to Test cricket in the Caribbean in 1990 under Graham Gooch, touring Australia the following winter where he made 64 at Melbourne, one of three Test fifties. He joined Durham when they first entered the County Championship in 1992.

First-class career (1972–): 26,405 runs (34.51) including 57 centuries, 42 wickets (45.59), and 295 catches

Test matches (13): 493 runs (20.54) and 8 catches

LARTER, John David Frederick

(b. 1940, Inverness, Scotland) *Northamptonshire and England*

An extremely tall man (6 ft. 7$\frac{1}{2}$ in.), David Larter approached the crease with ten easy strides in a run of 20 yards, generally maintaining control over his length and mixing his pace. But his build was not ideal and he did not possess either the dynamism or speed of his predecessor, Frank Tyson. He took 121 wickets (16.76) in 1963 and in his first Test, against Pakistan at The Oval in 1962, he captured nine wickets. He toured Australia and New Zealand in 1962/3 and 1965/6 and India in 1963/4, but he broke down frequently through injuries, the last time during a Gillette Cup match in May 1967, and he retired from the game that year, briefly returning in 1969. His best bowling was 8 for 28 against Somerset at Northampton in 1965.

First-class career (1960–9): 639 runs (6.08), 666 wickets (19.53), and 56 catches

Test matches (10): 16 runs (3.20), 37 wickets (25.43), and 5 catches

LARWOOD, Harold

(b. 1904, Nuncargate, Nottinghamshire; d. 1995, Sydney, Australia) *Nottinghamshire and England*

A gentle, modest character, Harold Larwood is linked forever with one of the most violent episodes in cricket history. Of a little below medium height and wiry rather than powerful, he remains, perhaps, the most heroic England right-arm fast bowler. With a run-in of about 18 yards and with accelerating yet controlled rhythmical strides, his action built up like a long-jumper's to the explosive moment of delivery. He appeared to have abnormally long arms and in his prime his right hand would swing through from low on his right leg to a point so low after delivery that, according to D. R. Jardine and other contemporaries, his knuckles would actually touch the pitch on his follow-through. He was exceptionally fast—his contemporaries believe the fastest of all. Representing England against Australia in his first full season in 1926, he toured with Percy Chapman's team, 1928/9, and appeared again on the next Australian visit in 1930, but it was not until his second tour of Australia with Douglas Jardine, 1932/3, that he reached his best. He was at the centre of the bodyline controversy, the man who made the ruthless policy work. Bowling his short-pitched balls to a packed leg-side field with great pace and accuracy, he reduced Bradman to a mere mortal and in the five Tests he took 33 wickets at 19.51. He did not play for England again after this tour; this was partly political, but the constant pounding on the hard pitches, caused an injury to his left foot from which he never fully recovered. In 1936, however, he headed the national first-class averages with 119 wickets at 12.97 runs each. A useful but underrated hard-hitting batsman, he hit 98 at Sydney in his last Test. In eight full domestic seasons he exceeded 100 wickets each time. After the Second World War he took his wife and five daughters to Australia, and settled in Sydney. Belatedly, and through the influence of the cricket-mad Prime Minister, John Major, he was awarded an MBE in 1993.

First-class career (1924–38): 7,290 runs (19.91) including 3 centuries, 1,427 wickets (17.51), and 234 catches

Test matches (21): 485 runs (19.40), 78 wickets (28.35), and 15 catches

LATHWELL, Mark Nicholas

(b. 1971, Bletchley, Buckinghamshire) *Somerset and England*

Having enjoyed a rapid rise to prominence, Mark Lathwell, quiet and prone to introspection, struggled to come to terms with the prospect of international recognition, and after playing in two Tests against Australia in 1993, his form faded. A stocky little opener, particularly strong off the back foot and reliant on quick hands, excellent timing, and a superb eye rather than classical foot movement, Lathwell was schooled in Devon and spent a year on the MCC ground-staff before joining Somerset. The presence of the South African Jimmy Cook meant he played just twice in 1991 although compensation came in the form of Young England recognition, but the

following summer he made 1,176 runs, was awarded his cap and was selected to tour Australia with the England A team. Lathwell responded with two centuries, including a career-best 175 against Tasmania, and *Wisden* hailed him as a 'major discovery'. Beginning the 1993 season well, Lathwell was included in England's squad for three one-day internationals with Australia, but through insensitive leadership he did not play in any of the matches—despite the fact that Australia won all three—and loathed the experience of feeling unwanted. Returning to county cricket, he produced some spectacular displays, making 84 out of 105 runs scored while he was at the crease against Glamorgan and 132 out of an innings total of 197 against Essex. Lathwell was brought in to open the innings in the third Test against Australia at Trent Bridge, one of four debutants as the selectors responded to the call for new talent in the wake of two Test defeats, even though his inclusion meant breaking up the top-order pairing of Michael Atherton and Graham Gooch. Briefly the plan worked: Lathwell made 20 and 33, and Gooch, from number five, made a century as England drew the match. At Headingley, however, Lathwell could only manage a third ball duck and a diffident 25, and, with critics remarking on his lack of footwork, he was dropped. Included on the A tour to South Africa in 1993/4, he managed only 215 runs at an average of 17.91, but he looks too good not to rise again.

First-class career (1991–): 4,025 runs (35.00) and 9 wickets (57.22)

Test matches (2): 78 runs (19.50)

LAWRENCE, David Valentine

(b. 1964, Gloucester) *Gloucestershire and England*

David Lawrence's Test career ended abruptly in Wellington on 10 February 1992 when his left knee-cap split apart as he bowled during the Third Test against New Zealand. Even though the match was heading inexorably towards a draw, 'Syd', as he was universally known after the bandleader of the same name, was still charging in, typifying the spirit which made him one of the most popular cricketers of his time. He fell like a wounded elephant, a terrible moment for everyone on the ground and a personal disaster. For two years he worked to get back into cricket but failed when the kneecap broke again. Not only did it rob the game of an engaging, larger than life character, but England also lost a genuinely fast bowler. In an era of numerous medium-pacers, he had possessed real speed, the product of a lengthy run and the brute strength produced by an imposing frame of over 6 ft. and 16 stone. Born in Gloucester of Jamaican parents, David Lawrence made his début for Gloucestershire as a raw 17-year-old, but he first came to prominence in 1985 when he took 85 first-class wickets, forming a potent new-ball partnership with the West Indian fast bowler Courtney Walsh. It led to his being named by the Cricket Writers as their Young Player of the Year, and he gained a place on the England B tour of Sri Lanka that winter. A first Test cap followed against Sri Lanka at Lord's in 1988, and although he managed only three wickets, he impressed sufficiently to gain selection for the tour of India, only for the trip to be cancelled when the Indian Government objected to several players' links with South Africa. He had to wait until 1991 to reappear at Test level, playing twice against the West Indies and then once more against Sri Lanka. He justified his recall by taking 14 wickets, seven of them—including a Test-best 5 for 106—coming at The Oval when England levelled the series 2–2 with Viv Richards's side. Lawrence's selection for the winter was assured and he made an early impression by breaking opener Trevor Franklin's arm at Napier on the way to a five-wicket haul. Later in the same match, however, he strained his side and had to sit out the first two Tests of the tour as England clinched the series. Lawrence returned for the final Test, a week after his twenty-eighth birthday, determined to show what the side had been missing. It was to be his last first-class match, although he regained sufficient fitness to play club cricket after his enforced retirement.

First-class career (1981–92): 1,819 runs (10.70) and 507 wickets (31.87)

Test matches (5): 60 runs (10.00) and 18 wickets (37.55)

LEADBEATER, Edric

(b. 1927, Lockwood, Huddersfield, Yorkshire) *Yorkshire, Warwickshire, and England*

Eddie Leadbeater was that Yorkshire rarity, a right-arm leg-break bowler. Accurate, his 'wrong 'un' was usually a top-spinner instead of a googly. He was also a very useful batsman and a zealous fielder anywhere. He joined the MCC team in India in 1951/2 as replacement for the injured 'Dusty' Rhodes, playing in two Tests. He did not maintain his early success in county cricket, however, and had a short career for Warwickshire, without enhancing his figures.

First-class career (1949–58): 1,548 runs (15.18) including 1 century, 289 wickets (27.50), and 74 catches

Test matches (2): 40 runs (20.00), 2 wickets (109.00), and 3 catches

LEARY, Stuart Edward

(b. 1933, Cape Town, South Africa; d. 1988, Cape Town) *Kent*

At the age of 16, Stuart Leary left his native South Africa to join Charlton Athletic as a footballer. For them, and for Queen's Park Rangers, he would make 470 appearances in League matches. His success in cricket came more slowly—not till 1957 did he have an assured place in the Kent side for whom he scored 1,000 runs on nine occasions. He usually batted at number five, a right-hander who swept and steered. He was a leg-break bowler, whose best performance was against Glamorgan at Swansea in 1961 when he took 5 for 22. As a short-leg fielder he was nothing short of brilliant, his six catches in an innings against Cambridge University at Fenner's in 1958 equalling the Kent record. He returned home in 1972 where he directed coaching for the Western Province Cricket Union, doing much to encourage the game among children of all races besides managing a winning Currie Cup side. He was found dead on Table Mountain.

First-class career (1951–71): 16,517 runs (31.10) including 18 centuries, 146 wickets (33.80), and 362 catches

LEE, Frank Stanley

(b. 1905, London; d. 1982, London) *Middlesex and Somerset*

One of three brothers who played first-class cricket, Frank Lee, together with Jack, joined Somerset when Middlesex offered no prospects of permanent employment. He was an unhurried, solid, right-handed opening batsman, scoring 1,000 runs in a season on eight occasions. In 1931 he, Jack, and Harry (for Middlesex) all achieved this feat and in 1938 Frank became the first Somerset player to score 2,000 runs in a season and to make three consecutive centuries. After the Second World War—in which Jack had been killed in Normandy—Frank made his highest score of 169 against Nottinghamshire at Trent Bridge in 1946, receiving a record benefit a year later. He made few claims with his right-arm medium-paced bowling although securing five wickets on one occasion. From 1948 to 1963 he was an umpire, standing in 29 Tests. In 1960 he no-balled the South African fast bowler G. M. Griffin eleven times for throwing in the second Test match at Lord's. Griffin had already been no-balled seventeen times on the tour and earlier in his own country but Lee's decision effectively ended his career and led to an ICC statement on throwing. Lee was a man with a generous nature who had the moral courage to do something he disliked doing, even no-balling Griffin in an exhibition game after the Test match for not warning the batsman he was about to bowl under-arm.

First-class career (1925–47): 15,310 runs (27.93) including 23 centuries, 25 wickets (34.48), and 170 dismissals (158 c., 12 st.)

LEE, Henry William

(b. 1890, London; d. 1981, London) *Middlesex and England*

During the First World War, Harry Lee, who had been an ordinary right-handed batsman and off-spinner, was seriously wounded, reported killed, and taken prisoner by the Germans. On returning to England with a permanent limp, he became Middlesex's opening batsman and a member of two Championship-winning sides, hit two centuries against Surrey at The Oval in 1919, and for 15 years played third string to Patsy Hendren and 'Young Jack' Hearne. A very sound opener, he exceeded 1,000 runs in a season 13 times. His highest score was 243 not out against Nottinghamshire at Lord's in 1921. While coaching in South Africa, he was co-opted by MCC in 1930/1, after Andy Sandham had been injured in a car accident; and, playing in the fourth Test at Johannesburg, he scored 18 and 1. Often a useful change-bowler, he took 6 for 53 against the 1921 Australians. He was the elder brother of Frank and Jack (killed in action, 1944), both of whom played for Middlesex and Somerset.

First-class career (1911–34): 20,158 runs (29.95) including 38 centuries, 401 wickets (30.61), and 181 catches

LEES, Walter Scott

(b. 1875, Sowerby Bridge, Yorkshire; d. 1924, West Hartlepool, Co. Durham) *Surrey and England*

On the quick side of right-arm medium pace, Walter Lees had an easy, untiring action and plenty of 'devil' under all conditions, and he was also a dashing and fearless batsman, who won nearly all his fame playing for Surrey. He toured

South Africa with MCC in 1905/6, when the whole team was baffled by googly bowlers on matting, but he added to his laurels in the Tests, the only ones he played.

First-class career (1896–1911): 7,642 runs (17.13) including 2 centuries, 1,402 wickets (21.39), and 125 catches
Test matches (5): 66 runs (11.00), 26 wickets (17.96), and 2 catches

LEGGE, Geoffrey Bevington

(b. 1903, Bromley, Kent; d. 1940, Brampford Speke, Devon) *Oxford University, Kent, and England*

A former Oxford captain, Geoffrey Legge led Kent ably for three seasons from 1928 and, in a short career, off-drove and cut effectively as a right-handed batsman as well as catching almost anything within reach in the slips. He toured South Africa in 1927/8, and Australasia in 1929/30. He played in the earliest Tests against New Zealand, hitting 196 in the fourth match at Auckland. Unable to play much cricket after 1930, he was killed in action in 1940.

First-class career (1924–31): 4,955 runs (24.89) including 7 centuries, 8 wickets (22.62), and 122 catches
Test matches (5): 299 runs (49.83) including 1 century, 0–34, and 1 catch

LESLIE, Charles Frederick Henry

(b. 1861, London; d. 1921, London) *Oxford University, Middlesex, Shropshire, and England*

A capable all-rounder, Charles Leslie's career was all too short. He toured Australia in 1882/3 with Hon. Ivo Bligh's team, making 54 (run out) in the second Test at Melbourne and 144 against New South Wales.

First-class career (1881–8): 1,860 runs (22.96) including 4 centuries, 8 wickets (20.62), and 18 catches
Test matches (4): 106 runs (15.14), 4 wickets (11.00), and 1 catch

LEVER, John Kenneth

(b. 1949, London) *Essex, Natal, Cambridgeshire, and England*

After being for many years a respected county opening bowler, John Lever, known as 'J.K.', seized with both hands his chance to break through at the highest level. Steady bowling and stamina earned him selection in the first Test against India at Delhi in 1976/7 but no one was prepared for his match-winning performance. On his first active day in Test cricket he made 53 and took 4 for 16 in his opening spell, undermining India with late in-swing. He finished the match with 10 for 70, and the series with 26 wickets at 14.61. Tallish, fair-haired, and lithe, a fast-medium left-arm bowler, brilliant outfielder, and staunch right-hand tail-ender, he was not able to live up to that remarkable start but was unfortunate in having to fight for an England place against some outstanding rivals, notably Willis, Old, Botham, and Hendrick. His untarnished reputation survived a whipped-up 'scandal' at Madras in 1976/7 when, unwisely prescribed strips of vaselined gauze by the England physiotherapist—they were placed above his eyes to stop sweat pouring into them—he was accused of using the grease to help him swing the ball. He was officially exonerated. On five major tours between 1976 and 1982, indeed, Lever never let anyone down. He never seemed to be worried by minor injuries, could bowl long spells despite an excessively long run-up, was always accurate and could swing the ball both ways in helpful conditions. In both 1978 and 1979 he took 106 wickets and was the chief inspiration in Essex's first County Championship title in 1979. After being banned from Test cricket for going on the tour to South Africa in 1982, he continued in devastating form for Essex. Using his great experience to the full, he took 106 wickets in 1983 and 116 in 1984. He passed 1,500 first-class wickets in 1985, and a year later was dramatically recalled to the England side at the age of 37. He took six wickets in the match against India at Headingley, but England lost and Lever returned to faithful service for Essex as the county achieved another Championship title. At the end of the season, however, he was obliged to have a second operation to remove an abscess on his stomach. Nothing daunted, he continued for Essex until the end of the 1989 season, played two seasons of minor county cricket and became coach at an Essex school. Fit, loyal, and reliable, he had bowled only one no-ball in his first-class career and believed it to have been the umpire's mistake.

First-class career (1967–89): 3,678 runs (10.53), 1,722 wickets (24.25), and 187 catches

Test matches (21): 306 runs (11.76), 73 wickets (26.72), and 11 catches

LEVER, Peter

(b. 1940, Todmorden, Yorkshire) *Lancashire, Tasmania, and England*

A whole-hearted and aggressive right-arm fast bowler, 'Plank' Lever was an important member of the 1970/1 side in Australia which brought back the Ashes, and four years later his bowling in the sixth Test at Melbourne (6 for 38 in the first innings) restored some lost prestige for a battered team. Back trouble restricted him in his last few seasons and hastened his retirement, but he possessed a dangerous late out-swing and fierce pace. He was at his best when he pitched the ball up and used the seam, rather than trying to dig the ball in, and he restricted his use of the bouncer after very nearly killing the New Zealand tail-ender, Ewan Chatfield, with a short ball in 1975. After years as a respected county opener, notably in partnership with Ken Shuttleworth, he was picked for England against the Rest of the World in 1970 and took 7 for 83 in the World XI's first innings. He was 30 by the time he reached Australia for the first time but he proved the ideal support for John Snow. His batting successes in Tests included a merry innings of 88 not out against India at Old Trafford in 1971. He could be a determined and useful right-hand batsman. He became Lancashire's coach, but was dismissed in 1986 only to return to cricket in 1995 as England bowling coach.

First-class career (1960–76): 3,534 runs (14.25), 796 wickets (25.59), and 106 catches

Test matches (17): 350 runs (21.87), 41 wickets (36.80), and 11 catches

LEVESON GOWER, Sir Henry Dudley Gresham

(b. 1873, Titsey Place, Surrey; d. 1954, London) *Oxford University, Surrey, and England*

Known as 'Shrimp', Leveson Gower was for about 60 years a considerable personality in English cricket. Short and slight but effervescent, he was a right-handed batsman with a good eye and supple wrists, who revelled in the cut and, as a slow-medium bowler, he could make the ball drift. As both player and administrator, he was a naturally friendly and cheerful character. Successively captain of Winchester, Oxford, Surrey, and England in South Africa in 1909/10, he had a long playing career and afterwards served as president of Surrey for ten years and chairman of the England Selection Committee. He frequently toured with private teams, and for nearly 50 years ran the popular Scarborough Cricket Festival. In 1953 he was knighted for his services to the game.

First-class career (1893–1931): 7,638 runs (23.72) including 4 centuries, 46 wickets (29.96), and 103 catches

Test matches (3): 95 runs (23.75) and 1 catch

LEVETT, William Howard Vincent

(b. 1908, Gondhurst, Kent) *Kent and England*

One of the characters of the game, a tireless conversationalist behind the stumps or in the pavilion, 'Hopper' Levett brought a store of nervous energy to everything he undertook, and had days of brilliance when he was the best wicket-keeper in the land. He appeared four times for Gentlemen against Players, but the presence of Les Ames limited his opportunities for Kent. He toured India with MCC in 1933/4, and appeared in a sole Test at Calcutta, scoring 5 and 2 not out and holding 3 catches. After a 'heavy' night he is once said to have remained totally motionless whilst the first ball of the match whistled by him for four byes. The batsman tickled the next delivery down the leg-side, 'Hopper' dived, caught it and came up triumphantly with the ball in his hand saying, 'Not bad for the first ball of the morning, eh?'

First-class career (1930–47): 2,524 runs (12.25) and 478 dismissals (283 c., 195 st.)

LEWIS, Anthony Robert

(b. 1938, Swansea, Wales) *Cambridge University, Glamorgan, and England*

Dark, with a smile which would charm a statue, Tony Lewis is a man of many talents. An attacking right-hand batsman, he drove impeccably, cut well, and could work the ball anywhere on the leg-side with easy timing. An occasional leg-break bowler, he once had 3 for 18 against Somerset. Captain of Cambridge in 1962, he scored 2,190 runs (41.32) in 1966 and led Glamorgan to her second Championship title in 1969. He was captain from 1967 to 1972. His belated chance to play for England came when he took over as captain from Ray Illingworth, who was not available on the tough tour of India and Pakistan in 1972/3. He made 0 and 70 not out in his maiden Test at Delhi and 125 at Kanpur—and he included two half-centuries during the three drawn Tests with Pakistan. He failed in the first home Test against New Zealand in 1973 but it was because of injury that he did not represent England again. A gifted cricket writer and broad-caster, he also won a Rugby blue and was a violinist with the Welsh National Youth Orchestra. He became chairman of the Welsh Tourist Board and for many years the 'front-man' of BBC television's Test coverage.

First-class career (1955–74): 20,495 runs (32.42) including 30 centuries, 6 wickets (72.00), and 193 catches

Test matches (9): 457 runs (32.64) including 1 century

LEWIS, Clairmonte Christopher

(b. 1968, Georgetown, Guyana) *Leicestershire, Nottinghamshire, Surrey, and England*

Lithe and tall, Chris Lewis had all the attributes of a genuine right-handed all-rounder: an orthodox, clean striker of the ball, a genuinely fast bowler when the mood took him, and an outstanding fielder equally at home close-in or in the deep. Frequently, however, he failed to last a series either through injury or poor form, and his critics questioned his temperament because several of his best efforts came when the pressure was off. The son of a church minister, Lewis came to England aged 10 and was initially only a batsman. He went to Willesden High School in London, the same school as his future Leicestershire and England team-mate Phillip DeFreitas. Leicestershire offered him a contract in 1987, and although his progress was slowed by Raynaud's Phenomenon, a blood-circulation problem which required occasional hospital treatment, he still gained a place in the Young England side for the Youth World Cup the following winter, helping his side reach the semi-finals. After taking 45 wickets in just eleven matches in 1989, he was chosen for the A tour of Zimbabwe and Kenya before being switched to the senior tour of the Caribbean following an injury to Ricardo Ellcock. Lewis played in two one-day internationals, and retained his place for two more limited-overs matches against New Zealand at the start of the following summer. In the second game on a quick pitch at The Oval, he showed how menacing he could be by hitting Ken Rutherford on the head and then breaking one of Richard Hadlee's fingers, but he had to wait until the final match of the New Zealand series before he made his Test début, scoring 32 and 1 and taking four wickets in a comfortable win. Five more wickets followed in two Tests against India before he pulled out of the final Test of that series feeling unwell. Then, on the 1990/1 winter tour of Australia, he flew home with a stress fracture of the back after playing in only one Test. The following summer he again pulled out of a Test feeling unwell, this time the first match of the series with the West Indies, but after being recalled for the fourth Test at Edgbaston, he produced a superb all-round performance, taking 6 for 111 and following it up with a dashing 65 to lend respectability to a defeat. Lewis continued that good form into the winter in New Zealand, scoring a fluent 70 in an innings win in Christchurch, and taking ten wickets in two Tests, including a hostile 5 for 31 in Auckland, before missing the final match of the series to have treatment for Raynaud's Phenomenon. In the World Cup which followed, his bowling was hampered by a side strain but he still played a key role as England reached the final. In 1992 he joined Nottinghamshire, but although he had his moments in the summer's Tests against Pakistan—3 for 43 as England lost narrowly at Lord's and 55 to help save the follow-on at Old Trafford—his efforts were generally disappointing. On the winter tour to India and Sri Lanka he took only three wickets in three Tests in India but bowled better than those figures would suggest on a losing side, whilst in Madras he made a glorious 117 on his twenty-fifth birthday, his first Test century, reached with a straight six. England still lost by an innings. Five wickets followed in another Test defeat, this time in Sri Lanka and Lewis retained his place against Australia in 1993, only to be dropped after two listless performances including his first Test duck in England. A career-best 247 against Durham earned him a place on the winter tour of the West Indies, but, handicapped by a heel injury, he took only 14 wickets in five Tests and produced his best score of the series, 75 not out in Antigua, when the game was drifting to a draw. In 1994, although he played in one-day internationals against both New Zealand and South Africa and scored an unbeaten 220 against the county champions Warwickshire, he was overlooked for the winter until, playing club cricket in Australia, he was an eleventh hour replacement at Adelaide and took 11 wickets in the last two Tests.

First-class career (1987–): 5,343 runs (31.24) including 7 centuries, and 392 wickets (29.46)

Test matches (27): 1,009 runs (24.02) including 1 century, 77 wickets (37.27), and 23 catches

LEYLAND, Morris or Maurice

(b. 1900, Harrogate, Yorkshire; d. 1967, Harrogate)
Yorkshire and England

Few men have relished a fight more than Leyland, whose Christian name was registered as Morris but usually published as Maurice. A tough and cheerful Yorkshireman with one of the best records against Australia of any English batsman (1,705 runs at 56.83 in 20 matches), he was a left-hander with a wide stance and great strength, his strokes being weighty and decisive. He particularly liked hitting powerful skimming drives and, before the ball had thumped into the boundary fence, he would be standing still as a statue, his right arm at his side and his bat close to his body. He also bowled left-handed chinamen, which were a little less friendly than they looked—he once performed a hat-trick at Headingley. Apart from holding England together in many Tests—usually at number four—he was part of twelve Yorkshire Championship-winning sides. He exceeded 1,000 runs in 17 seasons with a highest score of 263 against Essex at Hull in 1936. After making 0 in his first Test innings against West Indies in 1928, he scored 137 and 53 not out in his second Test at Melbourne in 1928/9. He made two further tours of Australia, averaging 55.12 in the Tests of 1936/7. In his prime against Australia in 1934 he made 109 at Lord's and 110 at The Oval. He also toured South Africa and the West Indies. In his last Test—against Australia at The Oval in 1938—he contributed 187, his highest score for England, to England's record 903 for 7.

First-class career (1920–48): 33,660 runs (40.50) including 80 centuries, 466 wickets (29.31), and 246 catches

Test matches (41): 2,764 runs (46.06) including 9 centuries, 6 wickets (97.50), and 13 catches

LILLEY, Arthur Frederick Augustus

(b. 1866, Birmingham; d. 1929, Brislington, Bristol)
Warwickshire and England

From 1896 until 1909 'Dick' Lilley monopolized the position as England's wicket-keeper; and he toured Australia twice. He took the infinitely varied bowling of his period calmly, soundly and without fuss. For his county against MCC at Lord's in 1896, he took eight catches and, though he kept continuously for 23 years, he was such an artist that at the end of his career his hands and fingers showed scarcely a trace of the heavy strain to which they had been subjected. As a right-handed batsman, he was often invaluable and he continued to play for Warwickshire as a batsman when 'Tiger' Smith replaced him as 'keeper.

First-class career (1891–1911): 15,597 runs (26.30) including 16 centuries, 41 wickets (36.22), and 911 dismissals (716 c., 195 st.)
Test matches (35): 903 runs (20.52), 1–23, and 92 dismissals (70 c., 22 st.)

LILLYWHITE, Frederick William

(b. 1792, Westhampnett, Sussex; d. 1854, London) Sussex

Although nothing is known of his career till he was 30 and he did not play at Lord's till he was 34, William Lillywhite, the 'nonpareil' bowler, made up for lost time by still playing when he was 60. The diminutive 5 ft. 4 in. right-arm bowler was an early exponent of round-arm when, with James Broadbridge, he used it in three 'experimental' matches between Sussex and England in 1827. Although a lively debate in the press followed, the law approved the innovation eight years later. Lillywhite's skills lay in his 'accuracy of pitch' and the straightness of his round-the-wicket deliveries. On 154 occasions at least, he took 5 wickets in an innings and he secured 18 wickets when the Players defeated XVI Gentlemen at Lord's in 1837 by an innings. He could bat anywhere in the order and, as a right-handed opener for Sussex, carried his bat for 42 not out against MCC at Lord's in 1839. When reproached by his captain for failing to make a catch off his own bowling he allegedly replied, 'Look here, sir, when I've bowled the ball I've done with her, and I leave her to my field.' Starting life as a bricklayer on the Duke of Richmond's estate at Goodwood, he eventually became a ground bowler for MCC, combining this by being the first professional coach at Winchester College. His headstone in Highgate cemetery, erected by the noblemen and gentlemen of MCC, paid high tribute to his reputation, character, and 'teaching by precept and example'.
First-class career (1825–51): 2,352 runs (7.28), 215 + 1,355 wickets (10.89), and 140 catches

LILLYWHITE, Frederick

(b. 1829, Hove, Sussex; d. 1866, Brighton, Sussex)

Fred Lillywhite, the third son of Frederick William, the 'nonpareil' bowler, reported cricket for Bell's Life. He introduced the printing of scorecards with a portable press on the ground itself when MCC played Sussex at Lord's in 1848. Subsequently he took his equipment, including a tent, with him on George Parr's tour of North America (1859), on which he wrote a book. As a publisher, he produced (1862–3) the first four volumes of the Scores and Biographies which Arthur Haygarth was compiling but a dispute between the two men led to MCC publishing the remaining volumes. His Guide to Cricketers (1849–66) was incorporated, after his death, into the Cricketers' Companion (the 'Green' Lillywhite) —produced by his brother John. Fred was also in partnership with John Wisden (1855–8) who would later publish his Almanack (1864).

LILLYWHITE, James

(b. 1825, Hove, Sussex; d. 1882, Cheltenham, Gloucestershire) Sussex

James Lillywhite (senior), the eldest of Frederick William's three sons, played for Sussex for ten years (1850–60) as a right-handed batsman and round-arm bowler. Later he coached at Cheltenham College but his main contribution to cricket was as senior partner in the family publishing firm which produced the Annuals.
First-class career (1850–60): 169 runs (6.25), 21 + 10 wickets (15.42), and 11 catches

LILLYWHITE, James, jun.

(b. 1842, West Hampnett, Sussex; d. 1929, Westerton, Chichester, Sussex) Sussex and England

The last survivor of the team which he captained in the first two Tests ever against Australia, 1876/7, Jim Lillywhite came from a notable cricketing family. His uncle was William, the 'Nonpareil'. Five of the family played for Sussex and in one match three generations—father, son and grandson—took part. From 1862 until 1881 Jim appeared in every match played by the county. A left-arm slowish bowler with a high and exceptionally accurate delivery, he was also a vigorous left-handed batsman and a good field, either at slip or mid-on. Altogether, he visited Australia six times, the first being as a member of W. G. Grace's 1873/4 side, and four being in business partnership with Alfred Shaw and Arthur Shrewsbury, when he tended to have his fingers burned financially. He also toured America in 1868 and for some years was secretary of the United South of England XI. He became an efficient umpire.
First-class career (1862–83): 5,523 runs (14.30) including 2 centuries, 1,210 wickets (15.23), and 109 catches
Test matches (2): 16 runs (8.00), 8 wickets (15.75), and 1 catch

LILLYWHITE, John

(b. 1826, Hove, Sussex; d. 1874, London) *Sussex and Middlesex*

John was the most talented cricketer of Frederick William's three sons. He made exactly 100 appearances for Sussex (1850–69), a few for Middlesex and played for W. G. Grace's XI against Kent the year before he died. He was a right-handed batsman good enough to top the national averages in 1856 and a right-arm round-arm fast bowler who later turned to slow bowling. It was, however, as an umpire that he brought to a head the issue of bowlers who raised their arm above the shoulder. When England played Kent at the Oval in 1862, he called Edgar Willsher six times. All the professionals left the field and play was not resumed until the following day with another umpire. But Lillywhite had made his point, and the law was changed in 1864.

First-class career (1848–73): 5,127 runs (17.43), and 210 + 13 wickets (11.43) including 94 catches

LLOYD, David

(b. 1947, Accrington, Lancashire) *Lancashire, Cumberland, and England*

A chirpy, intelligent Accrington lad, affectionately known as 'Bumble' (he talks a lot and with an engaging Lancashire burr), David Lloyd had a high promise but this was blighted in mid-career by being a front-line batsman against Thomson and Lillee on the daunting 1974/5 tour of Australia, and by the responsibility of being county captain between 1973 and 1977, a job which on the whole he relished little. A neat, strong left-hander with all the shots and sometimes exceptional flair in attack, he was also an under-used, slow, left-arm orthodox spinner and a brilliant close fielder. For several seasons he was a specialist in the dangerous short-leg position. He made an immediate impact on Test cricket in 1974, scoring 214 not out in only his second Test against India at Edgbaston, an innings full of handsome driving, pulling and cutting, all based on quick, incisive footwork. But like all the England batsmen who had to face the ferocious pace of Thomson and Lillee the following winter, sometimes on difficult pitches, he seemed to be shell-shocked by the experience. Not that it affected his humour. Seeing Keith Fletcher signing an autograph the day after he had painfully 'headed' a bouncer far into the covers, Lloyd asked: 'What are you signing, Keith, Nat Lofthouse?' Under Lloyd's cheerful captaincy Lanca-

shire reached three successive Gillette Cup Finals, winning in 1975. He scored a century in his last first-class match in 1983, 123 against Northamptonshire. A witty and much-sought-after speaker at cricket dinners, he became an umpire in first-class cricket and continued to play for Cumberland before accepting a number of official cricket assignments. A live-wire coach with a gift for direct communication, he made a name for himself as a radio pundit and returned to Old Trafford as Lancashire's coach in 1994. By now his son Graham, a gifted right-handed batsman, was a capped Lancashire player and had played for England 'A'.

First-class career (1965–83): 19,269 runs (33.33) including 38 centuries, 237 wickets (30.26), and 334 catches

Test matches (9): 552 runs (42.46) including 1 century, 0–17, and 11 catches

LLOYD, Timothy Andrew

(b. 1956, Oswestry, Shropshire) *Warwickshire, Orange Free State, and England*

This left-handed, opening batsman made a most unlucky start to his Test career. Making his début in front of his home crowd at Edgbaston in 1984 he was hit on the side of the head by a ball from the West Indian Malcolm Marshall when he had reached 10, his sole Test innings to date. Suffering from blurred vision, he was forced to retire hurt, spent more than a week in hospital and was unable to play first-class cricket again that season, due to reduced sight in one eye. Since his first appearance for Warwickshire in 1977 Lloyd had been a solid and dependable player, and helped by two seasons for Orange Free State, 1978–80, he developed into a competent and compact opening batsman when Dennis Amiss moved down the order. A consistent season in 1983 won him a call-up into the England squad for the Lord's Test against New Zealand, but he was made 12th man. He scored 60 and 102 not out for the MCC against Essex at the beginning of the 1984 season, and he coped well with the West Indian fast bowlers in the one-day internationals to secure his place in the Test side. Following his accident, he resumed his first-class career in Zimbabwe and, playing his first match back at Edgbaston, scored 160 against Glamorgan in 1985. Red-haired and perky, and a keen follower of the sport of kings, he took his misfortune without complaint but the suspicion lingered that his brief hour of glory had come and gone, especially when two more, unconnected, injuries restricted his appearances for Warwickshire in 1986. He fought back again to become county captain from 1988 to 1992, shaping the team which two seasons later won three of the four major county competitions.

First-class career (1977–92): 17,211 runs (34.28) including 29 centuries, 23 wickets (73.13), and 147 catches

LOADER, Peter James

(b. 1929, Wallington, Surrey) *Surrey, Western Australia, and England*

A hostile, wiry, right-arm fast bowler with a long, high-stepping run, Peter Loader spearheaded Surrey's attack with Alec Bedser during the triumphant Championship years of 1952–8. When the swing went from the new ball he varied his pace cleverly. Against West Indies at Headingley, 1957, he achieved the first hat-trick in post-war Test cricket. He took 9 for 17 against Warwickshire at The Oval in 1958, and 9 for 28 against Kent at Blackheath, 1953—each in an innings—and seven times exceeded 100 wickets in a season. He toured Australia in 1954/5 and 1958/9, South Africa in 1956/7, and it was only because England had a cache of fast bowlers that he received so few chances in Test cricket. On leaving Surrey in 1963, he emigrated to Western Australia, where he is now a family man, businessman, and former cricket broadcaster.

First-class career (1951–63): 2,314 runs (8.51), 1,326 wickets (19.04), and 120 catches
Test matches (13): 76 runs (5.84), 39 wickets (22.51), and 2 catches

LOCK, Graham Anthony Richard

(b. 1929, Limpsfield, Surrey; d. 1995, Perth, Australia) *Surrey, Leicestershire, Western Australia, and England*

Tony Lock's remarkable career had as many dramatic turning-points as an epic family saga. Sturdily built, with reddish sandy hair which thinned early, he was an orthodox slow left-arm spinner possessed of an aggression seldom found in the fastest of bowlers. Fiery, rash, and quick-witted, he was quite phenomenal fielding at short-leg. At The Oval in 1957 he caught eight Warwickshire batsmen. Starting as a 16-year-old slow left-arm bowler with a good flight, Tony Lock, or 'Beau', first altered his technique to suit the slow turning wickets at The Oval, fizzing the ball at the batsman with sharp spin accompanied by shouts and gestures. He played a prominent

part when England recovered the Ashes against Australia at The Oval in 1953, taking 5 for 45 in the second innings, and the partnership of Lock and Laker kept the Ashes in England in 1956. His quicker ball, however, was suspected as a 'chuck' and—after seeing a film of his action during MCC's tour of Australia in 1958/9—he decided to end any controversy by returning to his slower style. He became notably more successful on hard overseas pitches by giving the ball more air. He had seven overseas tours, only one to Australia. Fourteen times he took more than 100 wickets in a season. He took four hat-tricks and reached his 1,000th wicket at the age of only 26—the fourth youngest ever. He was also the most prolific catcher among his contemporaries and always a useful, hard-hitting batsman. The final phase of his career began when he emigrated to Western Australia in 1963, although he returned to join Leicestershire in 1965, becoming captain the following year. His exuberant personality brought out the best in every member of the side both at Leicester and at Perth, where he captained Western Australia to success in the Sheffield Shield and broke their wicket-taking record.

First-class career (1946–71): 10,342 runs (15.88), 2,844 wickets (19.24), and 830 catches
Test matches (49): 742 runs (13.74), 174 wickets (25.58), and 59 catches

LOCKWOOD, William Henry

(b. 1868, Old Radford, Nottingham; d. 1932, Old Radford) *Nottinghamshire, Surrey, and England*

A 'rough diamond' with an impressive high action, Bill Lockwood was noted for a tremendous body-swing in delivery, followed by a sharp off-cutter or break-back, so that the ball often pitched outside the off-stump and caused the wicket-keeper to jump to take it on the leg-side. He had a chequered career. He was a great bowler for Surrey and England for three seasons, but on tour in Australia with A. E. Stoddart's team in 1894/5 he failed badly and the slide continued until 1897, when he lost his place in the county side. A narrow escape from being maimed by a shark and the tragic death of his wife and one of his children had led him to try to find too great a solace in alcohol. He made a courageous comeback, however, in 1898 when he took 134 wickets, scored nearly 1,000 runs and regained his place for England against Australia, not retiring until 1904. Against Australia at Old Trafford in 1902 he captured 11 for 76, one of the

LOHMANN

greatest feats in Anglo-Australian matches. Had
he not done so much bowling, he would have
been an impressive run-getter; he seven times
took more than 100 wickets in a season, and
twice achieved the double.

First-class career (1886–1904): 10,673 runs
(21.96) including 15 centuries, 1,376 wickets
(18.34), and 140 catches
Test matches (12): 231 runs (17.76), 43 wickets
(20.53), and 4 catches

LOHMANN, George Alfred

(b. 1865, Campden Hill, London; d. 1901,
Worcester, Cape Province, South Africa) *Surrey,
Western Province, and England*

Before he died of tuberculosis in South Africa,
where he had gone in search of health six years
before, George Lohmann had built a magnificent
reputation as a cricketer's cricketer who always
threw himself into a game. A fair, blue-eyed,
square-shouldered, and altogether handsome
man, he had jumped to the top early and remained
there. He was a right-handed, quick-footed,
match-winning batsman, a fielder who held slip
catches no one else would have thought possible
and, above all, a graceful medium-pace bowler
with an occasional fast ball, who used every
variety of deception. He was an integral part of
Surrey's Championship-winning side of the late
1880s and early 1890s. He toured Australia three
times between 1886 and 1892 and South Africa in
1895/6 when in the three Tests he was complete
master on the matting with 35 wickets (5.80),
taking 15 for 45 (7 for 38 and 8 for 7) at Port
Elizabeth. Against Australia at The Oval in 1886
he took 7 for 36 in the second innings, bowling
unchanged with Johnny Briggs to help England
win by an innings. At Sydney he took 8 for 25 in
1886/7 and 8 for 58 in 1891/2. Altogether he took
eight or more wickets in an innings 20 times (four
times in Tests) and 14 times 13 or more wickets in
a match. He managed the South African team to
England in 1901.

First-class career (1884–97): 7,247 runs (18.68)
including 3 centuries, 1,841 wickets (13.74), and
337 catches
Test matches (18): 213 runs (8.87), 112 wickets
(10.75), and 28 catches

LORD, Thomas

(b. 1755, Thirsk, Yorkshire; d. 1832, West Meon,
Hampshire)

Improbably, it was a Yorkshireman who gave his
name to Lord's cricket ground. William Lord, a

modest yeoman farmer, had raised 500 horsemen
to support the Jacobite Rising of 1745 and its
failure brought him to ruin and the sequestration
of his land. The family moved to Norfolk, whence
his son Thomas made his way to London where
he bowled to the members of the White Conduit
Club and sold wine. The aristocrats there, especially the Earl of Winchilsea and Charles Lennox,
later Duke of Richmond, harnessed his cricket
enthusiasm and business acumen by promising
him the backing to establish a private ground.
Lord took out a lease on land which became
Dorset Square and its new landlord played in the
first match in May 1787, opening the batting for
Middlesex against Essex and making 36 runs. By
the standards of those who would play for the
newly-formed MCC, which replaced the White
Conduit Club, he was not an outstanding performer and a half-century for Middlesex against
MCC in 1790 was probably his highest score. By
1810 London was growing fast and Thomas
Lord's lease had expired. Building development
led him to take his turf to a new Lord's at
Regent's Park. But the ground proved unpopular,
little cricket was played there and Parliament's
proposal to build a canal through it allowed
Lord's turf to find a third and final resting place in
1814, beside the newly consecrated St John's
Wood church. By 1825 Lord, a man of 70 and
a successful wine merchant, contemplated building houses around Lord's as a further business
venture. William Ward, banker, politician, and
cricketer himself, bought him out for £5,000. The
Yorkshireman who had given his name to
cricket's most famous ground ended his days
farming near Hambledon, whose eighteenth-
century players had only known underarm bowling. Lord let it be known he had no time for the
new-fangled round-arm which was being tried
out on 'his' ground in experimental matches in
1827.

First-class career (1801): 12 runs (12.00) and 1
wicket (average not known)

LOWSON, Frank Anderson

(b. 1925, Bradford, Yorkshire; d. 1984, Pool-
in-Wharfedale, Yorkshire) *Yorkshire and England*

Frank Lowson was a quiet, compact and stylish
right-handed opening batsman who produced
some superb innings for his county, notably his
highest score—259 against Worcestershire at
Worcester in 1953. At its best his batting was
marked by firm driving and attractive cutting, but
somehow lacked the spark which would have

turned him from an extremely competent performer into an outstanding one. He received several chances for England and toured India with MCC in 1951/2, reaching 1,000 runs on the tour. In England he exceeded 1,000 in a season eight times.

First-class career (1949–58): 15,321 runs (37.18) including 31 centuries, and 192 catches
Test matches (7): 245 runs (18.84) and 5 catches

LUCAS, Alfred Perry

(b. 1857, London; d. 1923, Great Waltham, Essex)
Cambridge University, Surrey, Middlesex, Essex, and England

A classic, though defensive, batsman who had a long career, 'Bunny' Lucas captained MCC against Australia at Lord's in 1902 having toured Australia with Lord Harris's team in 1878/9, and played in the first two Tests in England at The Oval in 1880 and 1882. Normally a change-bowler, he performed wonders for Lord Harris's team, having to do practically all the bowling with the two professionals, Tom Emmett and George Ulyett.

First-class career (1874–1907): 10,263 runs (26.38) including 8 centuries, 155 wickets (18.38), and 152 catches
Test matches (5): 157 runs (19.62), 0–54, and 1 catch

LUCAS, Edward Verrall

(b. 1868, Eltham, Kent; d. 1938, London)

Formative years as a young bookseller and journalist gave E. V. Lucas a love of literature and a way with words which bore fruit in some three-dozen collections of essays and anthologies including the classic *The Hambledon Men*. Among the travelogues, *belles-lettres*, critiques, and poetry may be found such cricketing nuggets as the essay 'Lord's and Ladies'—'there are three kinds of cricket-match girls!'—in *Willow and Leather* (1898). The essence of all his writing was optimism, nostalgia, and light-heartedness. That other devotee, the lawyer Norman Birkett, put him 'in the highest class' as a cricket writer. As a player, his boast was making 30 runs for the Passengers against the Officers on SS *Avelonia* in 1928.

LUCKHURST, Brian William

(b. 1939, Sittingbourne, Kent) *Kent and England*

Brian Luckhurst was a staunch, loyal, honest cricketer and a determined right-handed opening

batsman with a particularly fierce square-cut. He had been a solid performer for Kent for many years when he was selected for England against the Rest of the World in 1970 at the age of 31. In the second match of the series, at Trent Bridge, he made his reputation, his 113 not out steering England to victory against formidable opposition. Luckhurst's official Test career began in Australia the following winter when he was a stalwart of Illingworth's Ashes-winning side, making 455 runs at 56.87 in five Tests and hitting determined centuries at Perth and Melbourne. Four years later against much fiercer fast bowling he was a sad failure but the story of his career is one of consistent run-getting with an occasional purple patch. He scored 1,000 or more runs in a season 14 times and was a key member of the successful Kent side in limited-overs cricket, not least because of his excellent athletic fielding in any position. On his day he could also be a useful, slow, left-arm bowler; at Gravesend in 1962 he took 4 for 32 against Somerset. His highest score was 215 against Derbyshire at Derby in 1973. He became manager of Kent, and an injury crisis in 1985 led to his making an unexpected comeback, nine years after his retirement, against the Australians at Canterbury. He batted at number nine, making 1 and 9 not out. He remained on Kent's staff as a marketing manager after being replaced as coach.

First-class career (1958–85): 22,303 runs (38.12) including 48 centuries, 64 wickets (42.87), and 391 catches
Test matches (21): 1,298 runs (36.05) including 4 centuries, 1–32, and 14 catches

LYNCH, Monte Allan

(b. 1958, Georgetown, Guyana) *Surrey, Gloucestershire, Guyana, and England*

Born in Guyana but raised in Surrey, Monte Lynch was a surprise choice for England's one-day team against the West Indies in 1988. An attractive middle-order batsman with a distinctive, high back-lift, his call might have come sooner, but for the fact that he was banned from international cricket for three years after taking part in the unofficial tour of South Africa by a West Indian side led by Lawrence Rowe in 1983/4. Lynch's decision to join the trip may have come in part as a result of being overlooked by the England selectors after scoring 1,558 runs in 1983, but over the next two years he showed them what they were missing by scoring 3,218 runs, including 11 centuries. Lynch's brief chance in official international cricket in 1988 followed an explosive innings of 73 against the then England captain Mike Gatting. However, Gatting managed to run him out for nought on his début at Edgbaston, and, ill-at-ease in making 2 and 6 in the remaining matches, he was dropped. Breaking a leg playing football cost Lynch much of the 1989 season, although he returned with a career-best 172 not out against Kent. In his absence Graham Thorpe became established, and gradually Lynch found himself squeezed out. In 1994 he moved to Gloucestershire, but his popularity could be seen by his benefit, in 1991, which raised £107,000.

First-class career (1977–94): 16,281 runs (35.55) including 34 centuries, and 26 wickets (53.65)

LYON Beverley Hamilton

(b. 1902, Caterham, Surrey; d. 1970, Balcombe, Sussex) *Oxford University and Gloucestershire*

In the words of Walter Hammond, the ace in the county pack, Bev Lyon 'galvanised Gloucestershire cricket'. Taking over the captaincy in 1929, he brought the county within striking distance of the Championship title in three successive years, an honour which has eluded them ever since the days of Grace. He dared to lose in order to win and (Hammond again) took 'breathtaking risks'. Some of these won him some notoriety as when he persuaded the Yorkshire captain at Sheffield in 1931 to agree upon a 'freak first innings' declaration when each side had scored four off a boundary bye. This allowed the pursuit of maximum points in a rain-affected match. Lyon was not only an outstanding captain as a tactician but a right-handed batsman and close-in fielder who was totally worth his amateur place in the side. He could attack or defend, reached his 1,000 runs on four occasions and against Surrey at Cheltenham in 1934 made 189. He was a man ahead of his time, accompanying his men out from the professionals' gate at Lord's, advocating county cricket on Sundays and suggesting a knock-out competition long before either was introduced. Robertson-Glasgow declared that 'he made people talk about Gloucestershire. He clothed a routine in the finery of rollicking adventure.'

First-class career (1921–47): 10,694 runs (24.98) including 16 centuries, 52 wickets (45.02), and 263 catches

LYON, Malcolm Douglas

(b. 1898, Caterham, Surrey; d. 1964, St Leonards) *Cambridge University and Somerset*

Showing early promise at Rugby football and playing for the Lord's schools, Malcolm Lyon made his Somerset début before getting his blue at Cambridge. As an attacking right-handed batsman and wicket-keeper, he was one of the best amateurs in England in the 1920s. A century against the 1926 Australians and a double-century against Gloucestershire in 1930—both at Taunton—were among his best performances. In the Gloucestershire match his fierce driving brought him 210 runs at almost one a minute while his brother, Beverley, made a century for the visitors. In professional life, Lyon was a barrister and from 1932 onwards played little county cricket: he served as a magistrate in Gambia and Kenya and as a judge in the Seychelles and Uganda.

First-class career (1920–38): 7,294 runs (29.29) including 14 centuries, 8 wickets (71.75), and 192 dismissals (149 c., 43 st.)

LYTTELTON, Rt. Hon. Alfred

(b. 1857, London; d. 1913, London) *Cambridge University, Middlesex, and England*

A member of a strong cricketing family—his seven brothers also played either first-class or good class cricket—Alfred Lyttelton was in the Cambridge side that defeated the 1878 Australians, and was a right-handed, front-foot batsman in the classical mould. Moreover, he was the foremost amateur wicket-keeper of his day, standing up without a long stop, and he appeared in four of the first five Tests played against Australia in England. At The Oval in 1884, after the regular bowlers had been mastered by the Australian batsmen, he bowled in his pads and, with lobs, finished off the innings, taking 4 for 19 in 12 overs. Alfred Lyttelton was the best contemporary tennis player, excelled also at racquets and played for England at Association football. A lawyer, politician, and philanthropist, he held office as Colonial Secretary in A. J. Balfour's Conservative administration, 1903–5.

First-class career (1876–87): 4,429 runs (27.85) including 7 centuries, and 204 dismissals (134 c., 70 st.)

Test matches (4): 94 runs (15.66), 4 wickets (4.75), and 2 dismissals (2 c.)

LYTTELTON, Charles John, 10th Viscount of Cobham

(b. 1909, London; d. 1977, London) *Worcestershire*

Despite not being in the XI at Eton, Charles Lyttelton, by diligent application to first principles, treating bowlers on their merits rather than their reputations, and sheer enthusiasm became a reliable county player. To this he added an astute and popular captaincy (1936–9) at a time when Worcestershire's fortunes needed raising. His own adventurous right-handed batting helped the county, at Stourbridge in 1936, to their first win against Yorkshire in 27 years. As Governor-General of New Zealand (1957–62), he captained his own XI against MCC at Auckland in 1961, making 44 in 21 minutes in partnership with Ray Lindwall in what was his last first-class appearance. He had already been president of MCC (1954) and would be elected that of Worcestershire six days before he died. His idea of heaven, he said, was to bat against his own bowling.

First-class career (1932–61): 3,181 runs (20.26) including 1 century, 32 wickets (41.18), and 52 dismissals

LYTTELTON, Revd Hon. Edward

(b. 1855, London; d. 1942, Lincoln) *Cambridge University and Middlesex*

One of eight brothers, seven of whom played for Eton, Edward Lyttelton was a right-handed batsman who cut and drove with aristocratic grandeur. His best season was in 1878 when he captained Cambridge University to victory in all their matches, beating Oxford at Lord's by 238 runs and the Australians—at Lord's before 10,000 spectators—by an innings and 72 runs. He was also top scorer for the Gentlemen against the Players and completed his appearances at Lord's by scoring for Middlesex the only century made against the Australians. *Wisden* wrote: 'the glass stood at 105 in the sun. He made 31 runs in 14 minutes! (a fact). When he was out for 113, all present applauded him most lustily.' Lyttelton's last match, four years later, was also against the Australians, for Cambridge Past and Present at Portsmouth. He was outstanding at athletics and fives and had played football for England against Scotland in 1878, his 'annus mirabilis'. Later he became headmaster successively of Haileybury (1890–1905) and Eton (1905–16). His decision to leave Eton, though he was by then over 60, was influenced by public criticism of a sermon he had preached upon Germany at the height of the First

World War. For a further 15 years he was much in demand as a pastor and preacher.

First-class career (1875–82): 2,013 runs (22.36) including 1 century, 1 wicket (50.00), and 43 catches

MACAULAY, George Gibson

(b. 1897, Thirsk, Yorkshire; d. 1940, Sullom Voe, Shetland Islands) *Yorkshire and England*

Relentless and self-confident, George Macaulay was a versatile right-arm bowler. After a short, breezy run to the wicket, he could open the attack with lethal swing and then turn to off-spin, bowling round the wicket to utilize his vast break from the off. A tenacious batsman, he showed his fighting spirit in his only Test against Australia, at Leeds in 1926 when the two Georges, Macaulay and Geary, came together for the ninth wicket, added 108 and saved the game. Macaulay was also a daring close field. He was an integral part of Yorkshire for 15 years, eight years of which the county was Champion. In 1925 he took 211 wickets (15.48). His sole MCC tour was to South Africa in 1922/3—he took 16 wickets in four Tests—and he took a wicket with his first ball in Tests at Cape Town as well as making the stroke which brought victory by one wicket. He appeared in two Tests against the West Indies.

First-class career (1920–35): 6,056 runs (18.07) including 3 centuries, 1,837 wickets (17.65), and 373 catches
Test matches (8): 112 runs (18.66), 24 wickets (27.58), and 5 catches

MacBRYAN, John Crawford William

(b. 1892, Box, Wiltshire; d. 1983, Cambridge) *Cambridge University, Somerset, and England*

Taken prisoner in August 1914, Jack MacBryan played much cricket in Holland when interned there as a POW. A Cambridge blue, he became a mainstay of Somerset as a neat and polished right-handed batsman. His sole Test appearance at Old Trafford against South Africa in 1924 was ruined by rain, and he did not bat. He deserved many more opportunities.

First-class career (1911–36): 10,322 runs (29.49) including 18 centuries, and 128 catches

McCAGUE, Martin John

(b. 1969, Larne, Northern Ireland) *Western Australia, Kent, and England*

Born in Northern Ireland of British parents, but raised in Australia, Martin McCague attended the

Australian Cricket Academy and made his first-class début in the Sheffield Shield competition before turning his back on his adopted country to play Test cricket for England. As this strong, burly fast bowler prepared for his first Test, ironically against Australia, at Trent Bridge in 1993, one Sydney newspaper labelled him 'a rat joining a sinking ship'. After only two Tests, he suffered a stress fracture of the back, but impressive form the following season earned him a place on the Ashes tour. McCague's family had emigrated to Western Australia, whose coach, Darryl Foster, about to start a spell with Kent and aware of McCague's dual qualification, introduced him to county cricket in 1991. He took 16 wickets in six matches before returning to Australia for the winter. He played in eight of Western Australia's ten matches during the season, but after taking only 17 wickets was made 12th man for the Sheffield Shield final. He was still upset at the decision when he returned to England and in the 1992 season took 53 wickets, including 8 for 26 against Hampshire. By now he had found an English wife and he confirmed that he wanted to play for England. He got his chance in 1993 after impressive form, and although set back by his back injury and a shoulder injury the following season, his genuine speed, intelligent variations and 57 wickets, 15 of them in one match against Derbyshire including a career-best 9 for 86, earned him a return to Australia in 1993/4.

First-class career (1990–): 771 runs (13.53) and 204 wickets (26.48)
Test matches (3): 21 runs (4.20), 6 wickets (65.00), and 1 catch

McCONNON, James Edward

(b. 1922, Burnopfield, Co. Durham) *Glamorgan and England*

A tall right-arm off-spinner with an ideal action, Jim McConnon, or 'Mac', had long, strong fingers and impressive flight. Rather highly strung, he needed encouragement to produce his best. He was an excellent gully and a late-order batsman who once scored 95 against Middlesex at Cardiff in 1951. In the same season he took 136 wickets (16.07) and performed the hat-trick against the South Africans at Swansea. He toured Australia with MCC, 1954/5, and India with a Commonwealth team, but had to return home early with injury each time. His only Tests were against Pakistan in 1954.

First-class career (1950–61): 4,661 runs (14.38), 819 wickets (19.88), and 151 catches
Test matches (2): 18 runs (9.00), 4 wickets (18.50), and 4 catches

MACDONELL, Archibald Gordon

(b. 1895, Poona, India; d. 1941, Oxford)

In his satirical *England, Their England* (1933), Macdonell looked at the English social and sporting scene through the eyes of a Scotsman which he himself was. It was published at a time when romantic escapist literature was in vogue in reaction to the realities of the First World War. The characters in the classic description of a cricket match, which gave the book its wide fame, were thinly disguised members of Sir John Squire's cricket team, 'The Invalids', composed largely of literary men who had survived that war. When the book appeared, Macdonell was already an established dramatic critic and detective novelist. It was his only incursion into cricket-writing but it was instantly accepted as a classic. Later he wrote a scholarly work on *Napoleon and his Marshals*. In 1940, the year before he died, he broadcast thrice weekly for the BBC short-wave service to the United States and the British Empire. He made no claims to be a cricketer but was a first-rate golfer.

McGAHEY, Charles Percy

(b. 1871, Bethnal Green, London; d. 1935, Whipps Cross, Leytonstone, Essex) *Essex and England*

A cheerful, careless extrovert, Charlie McGahey was a tall, right-handed, hard-hitting, front-foot batsman, a useful, slow leg-break bowler, and a good field. The crowd loved him. His highest score was 277 against Derbyshire at Leyton in 1905, and he six times shared stands of over 200 for his county. He made more than 1,000 runs in a season ten times. Early in his career he suffered a threat of tuberculosis, and partly for medical reasons toured Australia with Archie MacLaren's team in 1901/2. There he appeared in his only Tests and came home cured. Over 6 ft. and weighing 14 stone, he played full-back for Arsenal and Millwall.

First-class career (1894–1921): 20,723 runs (30.20) including 31 centuries, 330 wickets (31.21), and 151 catches
Test matches (2): 38 runs (9.50) and 1 catch

MacGREGOR, Gregor

(b. 1869, Edinburgh, Scotland; d. 1919, London)
Cambridge University, Middlesex, and England

Gregor MacGregor or 'Mac' was famous before
the age of twenty. A wicket-keeper of extraordinary ability, he played for Cambridge for 4 years,
becoming captain in the fourth when Oxford
were defeated. He first played for England against
Australia in 1890, while still an undergraduate.
He would stand up close to the fastest deliveries
of such as Sammy Woods and Charles Kortright,
gathering the ball with an air of ease on either
side of the wicket. He led Middlesex from 1899
until 1907. Sometimes a very useful batsman, he
toured Australia with Lord Sheffield's team in
1891/2. He was also a Scottish Rugby international.

First-class career (1888–1907): 6,381 runs (18.02)
including 3 centuries, and 559 dismissals (411 c.,
148 st.)
Test matches (8): 96 runs (12.00) and 17
dismissals (14 c., 3 st.)

McINTYRE, Arthur John William

(b. 1918, Kennington, London) *Surrey and England*

Originally a leg-spinner, Arthur McIntyre first
kept wicket in an emergency. Stocky, his build
was right and his hands eminently safe. In 1947
he became Surrey's regular 'keeper and played a
principal part in Surrey's unrelenting triumphs of
the 1950s. He is specially remembered for some
brilliant stumpings off Alec Bedser's cutters,
though he was also a sound right-handed batsman. Only Godfrey Evans stood in the way of a
regular England place. He appeared in only three
Tests, once each against the West Indies, South
Africa, and Australia in 1950/1, when he was
played as a batsman. In 1947 he claimed 95
victims; and three times he exceeded 1,000 runs
in a season. For many years he was Surrey's
coach, a wise, sober presence in the dressing-
room at The Oval, a good judge of a cricketer but
sparing with his praise.

First-class career (1938–63): 11,145 runs (22.83)
including 7 centuries, and 795 dismissals (639 c.,
156 st.)
Test matches (3): 19 runs (3.16) and 8 dismissals
(8 c.)

MacKINNON, Francis Alexander (The 35th MacKinnon of MacKinnon)

(b. 1848, London; d. 1947, Morayshire, Scotland)
Cambridge University, Kent, and England

Francis MacKinnon played for Cambridge in the
historic 'Cobden's Match' of 1870 and was a
good, steady batsman who, from 1875 until 1885,
appeared for Kent in 78 matches, scoring 2,184
runs (16.42), including two centuries. He toured
Australia with Lord Harris's team in 1878/9 and,
in his sole Test at Melbourne, made 0 and 5. He
was president of Kent in 1889 and always kept in
close touch with the game.

First-class career (1875–85): 2,310 runs (15.71)
including 2 centuries, and 38 catches

MACLAGAN, Myrtle Ethel

(b. 1911, Ambala, India; d. 1993, Farnham, Surrey)
Surrey and England

Myrtle Maclagan was a tower of strength in the
game, her military background helping attain an
ideal temperament and unwavering concentration during 17 celebrated years as an England
player. A right-handed opening bat who saw her
first duty to be there when the first 50 of the
innings was posted, Maclagan scored the first
century in women's Test cricket in Australia in
1934 and some 29 years after this début series had
the strength and character to score 81 not out for
the Services against the 1963 Australian tourists.
Maclagan also recorded the first Test century in
England, at Blackpool in 1937, and with the ideal
foil in the nimble and aggressive Betty Snowball,
England's openers became known as the Hobbs
and Sutcliffe of the women's game. Maclagan
became the first English player to score 1,000 Test
runs. Batting was far from being the only string
to her powerful bow and her right-arm precisely
floated off-spin saw her become the first player to
post 1,000 Test runs and 50 Test wickets. In her
first Test on that momentous 1934/5 tour of
Australia, Maclagan took 7 for 10 to help skittle
the hosts for just 47. Captain of England for two
Tests due to injury to Molly Hide, Maclagan
represented the Army at hockey, lacrosse, badminton, and tennis while serving as an officer in
the WRAC. She was awarded an MBE. Her
obituary published in the *Daily Telegraph*
recorded that Maclagan's life was spartan and she
made no concession to age. On her eightieth
birthday so many people turned up to con-
gratulate her that she had to make a speech from

the top of a stepladder, which she announced with the blast of a whistle.

MacLAREN, Archibald Campbell

(b. 1871, Whalley Range, Manchester; d. 1944, Bracknell, Berkshire) *Lancashire and England*

Archie MacLaren was the true model of the classic batsman. A right-hander with a handsome face and figure, a high backlift, and an array of strokes all round the wicket (his particular glory being the off-drive and straight drive), he was in charge from the moment he got to the crease. He led Lancashire from 1894 until 1896, and again from 1899 until 1907. He succeeded W. G. Grace as England captain against Australia in 1899, took his own team to Australia in 1901/2—he had been there with A. E. Stoddart's teams, 1894/5 and 1897/8—and was captain in England in 1902 and 1909. He led Lancashire to Championship victory, but failed to win a rubber for England. He was a calculating attacker and sound tactician but his leadership was authoritarian. He reached 1,000 runs eight times in a season in England, and once in Australia. Throughout, he was an opening batsman. He made 108 on his début in first-class cricket, for Lancashire against Sussex at Hove in 1890; 228 on his début in Australia, for A. E. Stoddart's team against Victoria at Melbourne in 1894/5; 149 on his début in a first-class match in America; and 200 not out for MCC against a New Zealand Eleven at Wellington in 1922/3, his last first-class match. His 424 against Somerset at Taunton in 1895 remains the highest score in a first-class match in England. He hit five Test hundreds, four in Australia and one, his highest —140—at Trent Bridge in 1905. In 1921, at the age of 49, he raised and captained the famous amateur side which at Eastbourne defeated Warwick Armstrong's hitherto undefeated Australians. But away from cricket he found little pleasure or success in business.

First-class career (1890–1922): 22,236 runs (34.15) including 47 centuries, 1 wicket (267.00), and 453 catches

Test matches (35): 1,931 runs (33.87) including 5 centuries, and 29 catches

McMASTER, Joseph Emile Patrick

(b. 1861, Gilford, County Down, Ireland; d. 1929, London) *England*

An Irishman, McMaster toured South Africa with Major Warton's team of 1888/9 and appeared in the second Test at Cape Town. Going in at number nine he failed to score and did not bowl. This Test is believed to have been his only experience of first-class cricket!

MAJOR, The Rt. Hon. John

(b. 1944, Carshalton, Surrey)

After a career in banking, John Major entered British politics in 1979, becoming prime minister in 1990. As a schoolboy, he had won a London *Evening Standard* award at Rutlish Grammar School for taking 7 wickets for 9 in a match and his enthusiasm for the game never waned despite having to stop playing after receiving serious leg injuries in a car accident in Nigeria. He greatly values his membership of both MCC and Surrey, speaking regularly at fund-raising occasions for his home club, watching Test cricket whenever his busy life allows and contributing articles and forewords for a wide variety of cricket publications.

MAKEPEACE, Joseph William Henry

(b. 1881, Middlesbrough, Yorkshire; d. 1952, Spital, Cheshire) *Lancashire and England*

A thoughtful, right-handed opening batsman, 'Harry' Makepeace relied chiefly upon placing the ball and seldom put much power into his strokes. He was masterly against the turning ball on a difficult pitch. To him defence was the best method of attack. He was also an excellent cover-point. In 1926, when Lancashire won the Championship for the first time in 22 years, he made 2,340 runs (48.75) and in all he made more than 1,000 runs in 13 seasons. He toured Australia with MCC in 1920/1, hitting 117 in the fourth Test at Melbourne, but never appeared for England at home. In retirement he served as county coach. A double international, he played soccer for England four times, against Scotland and Wales, and with Everton won an FA Cup Winner's medal.

First-class career (1906–30): 25,799 runs (36.23) including 43 centuries, 42 wickets (46.92), and 194 catches

Test matches (4): 279 runs (34.87) including 1 century

MALCOLM, Devon Eugene

(b. 1963, Kingston, Jamaica, West Indies) *Derbyshire and England*

Few who witnessed Devon Malcolm's international début against the 1989 Australians at Trent

Bridge when he took 1 for 166 could have guessed that five years later he would be cheered off at The Oval after taking 9 for 57 against South Africa. Yet these two performances were typical of a career in which his very fast bowling has veered between the profligate and the precise. Off a long run and on a quick pitch, Malcolm produced a burst of sustained hostility against South Africa in 1994 to secure the sixth best Test figures of all time, underlining his ability as a match-winner. It confirmed not only his return to full effectiveness after suffering a knee injury in the Caribbean the previous winter, but also Derbyshire's wisdom in plucking him from League cricket in South Yorkshire. An amiable man of massive strength, Malcolm was born in Jamaica, but emigrated to England aged 16 to join his father in Sheffield, and soon began playing club cricket in the area. Even then, Malcolm was very fast yet also very erratic; after joining Sheffield United in the Yorkshire League, he gained a place in a representative side which beat Yorkshire, and bowled both Geoffrey Boycott and Martyn Moxon with yorkers. An approach from Derbyshire and their coach Phil Russell followed, and he first played for the county in 1984. Some members grew impatient at his lack of progress, but Russell and captain Kim Barnett maintained their faith in him, and in 1988, he took 56 wickets and helped the county to the Benson and Hedges Final. Capped the following summer Malcolm was called up for the fifth Test at Nottingham, but England still lost by an innings. At this stage of his career he bowled in glasses, later in contact lenses. His eyesight has made batting a lottery for him, but his fielding, once dreadful, has become almost a strength. In the West Indies in 1989/90 he took 19 wickets in four Tests, five of them—including Viv Richards twice—in a remarkable win in Jamaica, England's first against the West Indies in 16 years, followed by 10 for 137 and the man-of-the-match award in a rain-ruined third Test in Trinidad. He maintained that form against New Zealand the following summer, taking 15 wickets in three Tests. In the winter, he took a then career-best 7 for 74 against an Australian XI in Hobart and won the respect of Allan Border's men with 16 wickets in the Ashes series, bowling more overs than anyone else. Jaded after 18 months of non-stop international cricket, he was omitted after two Tests of 1991 and not recalled before the Oval Test against Pakistan in 1992. He responded with 5 for 94. Retained for the winter tour of India and Sri Lanka, Malcolm, along with the rest of the

bowlers, endured a wretched time as he took only three wickets in three Tests. Again, he had to wait until the Oval Test the following summer for a recall, but again he excelled, this time with 6 for 170 to help secure a consolation victory over Australia and confirm his tour place to the West Indies, only to be forced home for surgery to a knee injury sustained in the first Test in Jamaica. Back at his favourite Oval in August, 1994 he was fired up after being hit on the helmet by a bouncer whilst batting and reduced South Africa to 1 for 3 at one stage in their second innings, their captain Kepler Wessels later placing the performance alongside the best he had seen from the West Indians of the 1980s. It guaranteed him a second tour of Australia.

First-class career (1984–): 1,035 runs (7.78) and 528 wickets (31.46)

Test matches (28): 158 runs (5.85) and 98 wickets (35.08)

MALLENDER, Neil Alan

(b. 1961, Kirk Sandall, Doncaster, Yorkshire)
Northamptonshire, Somerset, Otago, and England

Neil Mallender's brief Test chance came against Pakistan in 1992 when he was selected on a 'horses for courses' basis to exploit a Headingley pitch expected to offer seam movement. A steady fast-medium bowler, he repaid the selectors' faith by engineering a victory, his 8 for 122 being the best figures by an England débutant for 9 years. Retained for the final Test at The Oval, he took two more wickets, but was then overlooked for the winter tour of India and Sri Lanka, and a combination of injury and advancing years counted against his recall. Nicknamed 'Ghost' for his pale complexion and fair hair, Mallender had learned the game at Beverley Grammar School and Hull Cricket Club. Yorkshire were slow to respond to his potential, despite his selection for a tour of the West Indies with England Young Cricketers. Instead, he joined Northamptonshire, playing in the NatWest Final against Derbyshire in 1981. After seven seasons at Wantage Road, during which he took 305 wickets for the county, Mallender moved to Somerset in 1987 and topped their bowling averages in his first two seasons at Taunton. For 10 years he spent his winters playing first-class cricket for Otago in New Zealand. He took over 250 wickets, including a career-best 7 for 27 against Auckland in 1984/5, captained the side for two seasons and, greatly liked and respected, earned himself a testimonial. In 1991/2, the best form of Mallender's career coincided with the

England tour of New Zealand. During the winter, he scored his maiden first-class hundred and took 49 wickets, easily topping the bowling averages. The touring side were struggling with injuries, but he did not play. It was the second time he had come close to helping England in New Zealand. On a previous tour he had almost played in England's calamitous defeat in Christchurch (1983/4). His eventual opportunity therefore came belatedly, at Leeds. With his 3 for 72 and 5 for 50 he played a major role in England's six-wicket victory. On a truer pitch at The Oval, he finished with 2 for 93.

First-class career (1980–): 4,557 runs (17.33) including 1 century, and 916 wickets (26.22)
Test matches (2): 8 runs (2.66) and 10 wickets (21.50)

MANN, Francis George

(b. 1917, Byfleet, Surrey) *Cambridge University, Middlesex, and England*

The elder son of F. T. Mann, George was a superb fielder and a very competent right-handed batsman who had established himself as one of the most popular and successful England captains when the demands of the family brewery forced him to leave the first-class game. More slightly built than his father, he was a balanced, attacking batsman, particularly strong on the leg. He captained Middlesex in 1948 and 1949 but his greatest triumph came in the fifth Test in South Africa at Port Elizabeth in 1948/9 when, as skipper, he saved England with 136 not out and turned a possible defeat into victory. This team remained unbeaten and was one of the finest fielding sides of modern times. His integrity and experience made him an invaluable chairman of the TCCB and president of MCC and he was awarded a CBE.

First-class career (1937–58): 6,350 runs (25.92) including 7 centuries, 3 wickets (129.66), and 72 catches
Test matches (7): 376 runs (37.60) including 1 century, and 3 catches

MANN, Francis Thomas

(b. 1888, Winchmore Hill, Middlesex; d. 1964, Milton-Lilbourne, Wiltshire) *Cambridge University, Middlesex, and England*

Remembered as a popular captain and massive hitter, Frank Mann, in fact, did not always score fast—his highest score, 194 against Warwickshire at Edgbaston in 1926, took five hours—but, when he did open out, the results were startling. A powerful right-hander, his most notable display of 'fireworks' was against Nottinghamshire at Lord's in 1921 when he hit 53 in 19 minutes. Burly and a delightful personality, he captained Middlesex from 1921 until 1928—leading them to the Championship title in 1921—and also MCC in South Africa, 1922/3, when the rubber was won. He was a Test selector and Middlesex president.

First-class career (1908–33): 13,235 runs (23.42) including 9 centuries, 3 wickets (83.00), and 174 catches
Test matches (5): 281 runs (35.12) and 4 catches

MANN, Sir Horatio

(b. 1744, Kent; d. 1814, Margate, Kent) *Kent*

> At last Sir Horace took the field,
> A batter of great might
> Moved like a lion, he a while
> Put Surrey in a fright.

These lines are the only evidence of Mann's batting abilities, written when he had opened the batting with the Duke of Dorset, for Kent against Surrey in 1773. The match was played at one of his country estates, Bishopsbourne Paddock, near Canterbury. The Duke made 25 and the Baronet 22, only three other Kent batsmen making double figures in the two-innings match. Mann's patronage of the game earned him the title 'the King of Cricket'. He employed players on his estates in Kent, cared for their families, wagered huge bets, participated in the revision of the laws in 1774 and was one of the founder members of MCC. Although he was an MP for 27 years, his life, said *The Gentleman's Magazine* in its obituary 'was rather dedicated to pleasure than business' and his gambling had made him a bankrupt.

MANNING, Henry Edward

(b. 1808, Totteridge, Hertfordshire; d. 1892, London)

A leading figure in the Oxford Movement, Manning became Cardinal-Archbishop of Westminster and was the most influential Roman Catholic in nineteenth-century Britain. He played in the first Harrow match against Winchester in 1825 at Lord's and immediately afterwards against Eton, getting a few runs and one wicket in a week in which the pavilion was burned down between the two matches. At Oxford, his friend Charles Wordsworth presented him with a bat to which Manning replied, in some well-known lines, 'And if there's anything on earth can mend my wretched play, it is that piece of wood'. He maintained his interest in the game all his life.

MARKS, Victor James

(b. 1955, Middle Chinnock, Somerset) *Oxford University, Somerset, Western Australia, and England*

The innate modesty of Vic Marks hid an intelligent and resolute all-round cricketer. At Blundell's, and at Oxford, where he was a popular and determined captain in 1976 and 1977, he was mainly a middle-order batsman, effective in a rugged and rough sort of way. But for Somerset he has become steadily more useful as an off-break bowler, giving the ball an almost old-fashioned amount of air and, despite this, proving highly effective in limited-overs cricket. He first represented England in a one-day international against the West Indies in 1980 and won his first Test cap against Pakistan in 1982. He has often been England's most dangerous bowler in one-day matches, luring the batsmen into a fatal mistake with his inviting flight. Having made 37 runs in seven Test innings, he took on the Pakistan spinners to such effect that he made three consecutive fifties on the 1983/4 tour. He was an accomplished county player, shining even in the company of Richards and Botham. He scored 1,262 runs at an average of over 50 and took 86 wickets in 1984, and captained Somerset frequently in 1985 in the absence of Ian Botham. He became captain in his own right in 1989 and played with great success for Western Australia in 1986/7. Leaving the game relatively early for family reasons, he became cricket correspondent of the *Observer* and a radio pundit characterized by an engaging giggle.

First-class career (1975–89): 12,419 runs (30.29) including 5 centuries, 859 wickets (33.28), and 144 catches

Test matches (6): 249 runs (27.66) and 11 wickets (44.00)

MARRIOTT, Charles Stowell

(b. 1895, Heaton Moor, Lancashire; d. 1966, Dollis Hill, Middlesex) *Cambridge University, Lancashire, Kent, and England*

Charles Marriott (known as 'Father') learned his cricket in Ireland and was a skilful right-arm, leg-break bowler with a rare googly. A schoolmaster, he played most of his cricket for Kent in the month of August. His style was odd: starting in the region of mid-off, he would prance up to the wicket with high, finnicky steps, but his length was immaculate, and his leg-break deadly on any responsive wicket. He played for England once, against the West Indies at The Oval in 1933,

when he made a duck, held 1 catch but took 11 for 96, England winning by an innings. He toured India with MCC, 1933/4, performing the hat-trick against Madras.

First-class career (1919–38): 574 runs (4.41), 711 wickets (20.11), and 47 catches

MARSHALL, Howard Percival

(b. 1900, Sutton, Surrey; d. 1973, Newbury, Berkshire)

After Oxford, where he had won a Rugby football blue and played in the first university match at Twickenham in 1921, Howard Marshall began a career in journalism and, later, broadcasting. In the 1930s, his deep, mellifluous, and measured voice was the one most associated with cricket by listeners to the BBC. He had, at first, no colleagues and for hour after hour, notably when Verity took 14 wickets in a day at Lord's against the 1934 Australians, he gave regular reports. 'The engineers were very helpful—always ready to fetch me a glass of beer or a cup of tea, or get the bowling figures from the scorers.' By 1938, when he had been joined by Arthur Wrigley as scorer, reports were becoming more like commentaries and he was able to interview Len Hutton after he had made his 364 at The Oval. When war broke out in 1939, Marshall became director of war reporting and in the post-war years was a journalist rather than a broadcaster, writing on rugby, boxing, and cricket. To the BBC he was a great loss: his spontaneity, in an age of scripted broadcasting, was a novelty and he not only set the pattern for future Test match commentaries but also proved to the many doubters that ruminative descriptions of a 'slow' game might actually be more pleasurable to listen to than those on more frenetic activities than cricket.

MARTIN, Frederick

(b. 1861, Dartford, Kent; d. 1921, Dartford) *Kent and England*

Frederick Martin (known as 'Nutty') had a long career as a left-arm, medium-pace bowler with a high, easy action that seemed part of himself. Most of his best work was done for Kent and MCC, on whose groundstaff he served for many years. He captured 436 wickets in three seasons from 1889 until 1891. In 1890 his haul was 190 wickets (13.05) and against Australia at The Oval he took 12 for 102, yet never represented England against Australia again. He toured South Africa with W. W. Read's team in 1891/2, bowling unchanged with J. J. Ferris in the second innings of the only Test at Cape Town.

First-class career (1885–1900): 4,545 runs (12.15), 1,317 wickets (17.38), and 120 catches
Test matches (2): 14 runs (7.00), 14 wickets (10.07), and 2 catches

MARTIN, John William

(b. 1917, Catford, London; d. 1987, Woolwich, London) *Kent and England*

A right-arm, fast-medium, in-swing bowler and a hard-hitting, tail-end batsman, Jack Martin was regarded as an England 'hope' at a time of dearth of fast bowlers. He appeared in the first Test at Trent Bridge against South Africa in 1947, taking 1 for 129 and scoring 0 and 26, but he was not selected again.

First-class career (1939–53): 623 runs (11.53), 162 wickets (24.00), and 32 catches

MARTINEAU, Gerard Durani

(b. 1896, Lahore, Pakistan; d. 1976, Lyme Regis, Dorset)

A schoolmaster by profession, Martineau was a regular contributor to cricket periodicals, and an essayist whose books included *Bat, Ball, Wickets and All* and *The Field is Full of Shades*.

MASON, John Richard

(b. 1874, Blackheath, Kent; d. 1958, Cooden Beach, Sussex) *Kent and England*

One of the best amateur all-rounders who never played in a Test in England, Jack Mason stood over 6 ft. and was essentially a right-handed, front-foot player, possessing a drive rarely surpassed for cleanness and power, and a most effective cut. A fast-medium bowler with a model action and high arm, he moved the ball away from the batsman; he was also a high-ranking slip fielder. He was a popular Kent captain from 1898 until 1902, and toured Australia with A. E. Stoddart's 1897/8 team.

First-class career (1893–1919): 17,337 runs (33.27) including 34 centuries, 848 wickets (22.39), and 390 catches
Test matches (5): 129 runs (12.90), 2 wickets (74.50), and 3 catches

MASTERMAN, Sir John Cecil

(b. 1891, Kingston Hill, Surrey; d. 1977, Oxford) *Leveson-Gower's XI, Harlequins, and Free Foresters*

As Provost of Worcester College, Oxford and the university vice-chancellor, as an adviser to governments, industry, and broadcasting and as a committee chairman of M.I.5, 'J.C.' was one of the most distinguished figures in mid-twentieth-century England. Academia and public service apart, he won an athletics blue at Oxford and represented England at lawn tennis and hockey. 'Cricket was my first and most enduring passion,' he wrote. As a left-handed batsman and a right-arm medium-pace bowler, he played for Harlequins and Free Foresters and toured with MCC to Canada in 1937. Cricket, both in fact and fiction, featured in some of his books.

First-class career (1926–30): 77 runs (19.25), 4 wickets (59.00), and 7 catches

MATTHEWS, Austin David George

(b. 1904, Penarth, Glamorgan, Wales; d. 1977, Penrhyn Bay, Caernarvonshire, Wales) *Northamptonshire, Glamorgan, and England*

Tall and with powerful shoulders, Austin Matthews was a right-arm fast-medium bowler who could make the ball do a little both ways, a hard-hitter, and a fine slip. After taking 14 for 132 on a batsman's wicket at Hastings for Glamorgan against Sussex, he played for England against New Zealand at The Oval in 1937 scoring 2 not out, taking 2 for 65 and holding 1 catch. This was his sole Test appearance.

First-class career (1927–47): 5,919 runs (15.70) including 2 centuries, 816 wickets (23.40), and 124 catches

MAY, Peter Barker Howard

(b. 1929, Reading, Berkshire; d. 1994, Liphook, Hampshire) *Cambridge University, Berkshire, Surrey, and England*

Perhaps the finest English batsman since the Second World War, Peter May was a prodigy at Charterhouse, where he was coached by George Geary, and was a prolific run-getter at Cambridge for three years (1950–2) amid a galaxy of talent never since equalled. During his National Service he played for the Royal Navy and Combined Services. He made his début for Surrey in 1950. Six foot tall, with broad and strong shoulders, he was exceptionally straight in defence, and a quite superb driver anywhere between cover and mid-wicket, but especially wide of mid-on and straight back past, or over, the bowler. He was an effortless timer of the ball and his approach to batting, as indeed to all his affairs, was disciplined and fastidious. Gentle, good-mannered, and self-effacing in character, he always had a hard, almost ruthless streak as a cricketer—very much an amateur with a professional approach. He captained Surrey from 1957 until 1962, and England against Australia and New Zealand, 1958/9, against the West Indies, 1959/60, and against South Africa, 1956/7. Altogether he led England 41 times in only six years. A regular England player during the 1950s, he toured Australasia and the West Indies twice each and South Africa once with MCC. On his Test début he made an impressive 138 against South Africa at Headingley in 1951, when England were chasing a large total. He overcame Ray Lindwall eventually in 1953, and was a key figure in England's victory at The Oval which regained the Ashes. Thereafter, he was the chief thorn in Australia's flesh, in 21 Tests against them making 1,566 runs (46.05) including three centuries, each scored when runs were badly needed. At Edgbaston against the West Indies in 1957, England were 288 behind on the first innings, when May and Cowdrey added 411 superbly for the fourth wicket, May's share being 285 not out, his highest score. In that series he averaged 97.80. Such was the responsibility that always seemed to rest on his shoulders that he seldom allowed himself to 'let loose', although for MCC against An Australian XI at Sydney in 1958/9 he made his second hundred of the match between lunch and tea on the third day, with batting which only a few players in history could have equalled. He exceeded 1,000 runs in a season fourteen times (three times overseas), five times exceeding 2,000. Illness forced him to withdraw from the tour of the West Indies in 1959/60 and this, together with the need to give more attention to his insurance business in the City, caused his premature retirement from the first-class game. He married Virginia, daughter of Harold Gilligan, and had four daughters, one of whom was European Three-Day-Event Junior Champion in 1979. He was chairman of both the TCCB's and the MCC's cricket committees, president of MCC in 1980/1 and became chairman of England's selectors from 1982 to 1988. They were difficult years for England, because many leading players had to be overlooked because of association with the politically unacceptable South Africa. As a sensitive man, Peter felt the stinging criticisms of his teams acutely. He had never much enjoyed any public role but he took them

on from duty. He was awarded a CBE for services to cricket.

First-class career (1948–63): 27,592 runs (51.00) including 85 centuries, and 282 catches
Test matches (66): 4,537 runs (46.77) including 13 centuries, and 42 catches

MAYNARD, Matthew Peter

(b. 1966, Oldham, Lancashire) *Glamorgan, Northern Districts, and England*

Full of *joie de vivre* and one of the most talented and accomplished batsmen in county cricket, Matthew Maynard scored a century in 98 balls against Yorkshire on his first-class début but struggled to carry his ability to destroy bowling attacks into the Test arena. Athletically built, a powerful driver of the ball off either foot, and a brilliant fielder close-in or in the deep, he was raised in North Wales, but spent two years with Kent before moving to Glamorgan. He scored 1,000 runs in his first full season in 1985, and two seasons later, in 1987, was capped as he totalled 1,626 runs. Voted Young Cricketer of the Year by the Cricket Writers Club in 1988, he was chosen for the fifth Test against the West Indies, making a nervous 3 and 10 as England were crushed. Instantly, and harshly, dropped he had a disappointing summer in 1989 when he barely topped 1,000 runs, and for pressing financial reasons joined the unofficial tour of South Africa that winter, thus incurring a lengthy ban from international cricket. For three years, he spent his winters playing and coaching in New Zealand while scoring heavily for Glamorgan during the summer. For much of 1992 he captained the county and a century before lunch against the touring Australians earned him a recall for the fifth Test. Struggling to concentrate after his daughter was born on the first morning of the match he made nought, then chipped a finger while fielding and made only 10 in the second innings. Retained for the final Test, he made 20 and 9, and was retained for the winter tour of the West Indies. A neck injury hampered his early tour form, but a rapid cameo of 22 not out in 15 balls in the first one-day international won him a place in the first Test in Jamaica, where he made an assured Test-best 35 and nought. Poor form in the four one-day internationals which followed cost him his place.

First-class career (1985–): 13,817 runs (41.49) and 6 wickets (114.33)
Test matches (4): 87 runs (10.87)

MEAD, Charles Philip

(b. 1887, London; d. 1958, Boscombe, Hampshire)
Hampshire, Suffolk, and England

Phil Mead was the imperturbable and unbowl-able backbone of Hampshire's batting for some 30 years. His 48,892 runs for Hampshire is a record number for any county. Left-handed, his defence was strong and his strokes firm and clean. A tall, heavily-built man, he would, wrote Ian Peebles, 'move deliberately into a wide range of strokes, sound, safe and unspectacular . . . Between each ball he would glance round the field, pluck his cap as if in salutation and shuffle his feet into a somewhat crouching stance.' Twenty-seven times he exceeded 1,000 runs in a season, eleven times 2,000, and twice 3,000. His best year was 1921 when he made 3,179 runs (69.10), including his highest score, 280 not out against Nottinghamshire at Southampton. In 1921, when English batsmen were generally fail-ing against Australia, he scored 182 not out at The Oval in the fifth Test. He toured Australia in 1911/12 and again in 1928/9. He visited South Africa twice also, averaging 54 in the Tests of 1913/14 and hitting 181 at Durban in 1922/3. He was hardly a sprightly wit, but one little quip gave him constant pleasure. The county offered £1 in talent money to every scorer of 50 runs and, as Phil reached his inevitable half-century, he would murmur: 'Well, that's another ton of coal for the winter!' Latterly, he became totally blind.

First-class career (1905–36): 55,061 runs (47.67) including 153 centuries, 277 wickets (34.70), and 671 catches
Test matches (17): 1,185 runs (49.37) including 4 centuries, and 4 catches

MEAD, Walter

(b. 1868, London; d. 1954, Shelley, Ongar, Essex)
Essex and England

'The Essex Treasure', Walter Mead was a short man with a drooping moustache who bowled right-arm, slow-medium with a deceptively easy action and a remarkable command of length; he could make the ball turn on the best of pitches, generally off-breaking but sometimes sending down a leg-break or a googly to good effect. He was excellent at cover and occasionally a useful tail-end batsman, who made 119 against Leices-tershire at Leyton in 1902. Twice he took 17 wickets in a match, against the Australians at Leyton in 1893 for 205 runs, and against Hamp-shire at Southampton in 1895 for 119 runs. His

sole Test was against Australia at Lord's in 1899, when he took 1 for 91 in 53 overs (24 of them maidens), scored 7 and 0 and held 1 catch. His son, Harold, who died of war wounds, played with him for Essex in 1913.

First-class career (1892–1913): 4,991 runs (10.61) including 1 century, 1,916 wickets (18.99), and 194 catches

MEYER, Rollo John Oliver

(b. 1905, Clophill, Bedfordshire; d. 1991, Bristol)
Cambridge University, Somerset, Western India, Bombay, and Europeans

There were three phases to Jack Meyer's cricket-ing career. In the 1920s he was a talented school-boy captain at Haileybury, in whom H. S. Altham detected 'a certain class', and for three years a Cambridge blue who with skilfully varied right-arm medium-paced bowling took six for 65 and two for 5 against the 1926 Australians. He also won a blue for rackets. Then came some years of cotton-broking and teaching in India with a little first-class cricket thrown in: he got 16 wickets for 188 for the Europeans against the Muslims at Bombay in 1927/8. The late 1930s with Somerset, included a double-century against Lancashire at Taunton in 1936 and 5 for 66 for the Gentlemen against the 1938 Australians. As at Fenner's in 1926 his victims included top men: Collins, Mac-artney, Ponsford, and Bradman. Meanwhile, he had founded Millfield School, a brave and success-ful experiment in independent education by a man of independent thinking. It became a nurs-ery for games-players, a pioneer in co-educational boarding, and an innovator in understanding dyslexia. Somerset appointed him captain in 1947 and he stood out as an imaginative and colourful cricketer in a county with more than its fair share of that genre. Two of the kind were Robertson-Glasgow, who rated him in the 1930s as 'the most experimental of modern cricketers' and Peter Roebuck, to whom tales of the 'unlucky adven-turer' still abounded in his own Somerset playing-days. Both Meyer's batting and bowling—like the man—defy conventional labels. A right-hander in all things, he could drive, hook, and plunder and he could find pace, swerve, and spin. Had he not gone to India, he might have played for England. But Millfield inexorably followed in the wake of India and there lay his life's real endeavour.

First-class career (1924–50): 4,621 runs (23.69) including 2 centuries, 408 wickets (25.39), and 85 catches

MIDWINTER, William Evans

(1851–90) *Victoria and Gloucestershire*

See Australia section.

MILBURN, Colin

(b. 1941, Burnopfield, Co. Durham; d. 1990, Aycliffe Village, Co. Durham) *Durham, Northamptonshire, Western Australia, and England*

A massively built Geordie, as jolly as he was large, Colin or 'Ollie' Milburn was both a right-handed, scientific hitter, and a character who, in his short career, became a 'box office' draw. Rotund as Billy Bunter he first attracted attention by making a century for Durham against the Indians in 1959, while still in his teens, and, on joining Northamptonshire, became a refreshing attacking opening batsman. Technically sound and straight, he was a fearless hooker, savage square-cutter and drove as immaculately as anyone through the cover region. He was also a useful medium-pace bowler and a reliable, forward short-leg, although his relative lack of mobility in the field certainly restricted his appearances for England. His best year was 1966: he scored 1,861 runs (48.97), including 203 against Essex at Clacton, hit a century before lunch on three occasions, and made his Test début, against the West Indies at Old Trafford, scoring 0 and 94. In the next Test, at Lord's, he scored 6 and 126 not out. He showed his mettle against India, Pakistan, and Australia—in his first Test against the latter, at Lord's in 1968, he hit a ferocious 83—but he was disappointing in the West Indies in 1967/8. The following winter he played with success for Western Australia, scoring 243 before tea—including a record 180 in the record two-hour session—against Queensland at Brisbane, an innings of rare brilliance, and joined MCC in Pakistan, hitting 139 at Karachi. He opened 1969 with 158 (including five sixes) for his county against Leicestershire at Northampton but, a few days later, he was involved in a car accident and lost his left eye. Reacting with incredible good humour to this shattering misfortune, he fought back and reappeared for Northamptonshire in 1973, but his batting was severely handicapped and his bowling not quite good enough to justify a regular place. He retired after the 1974 season and his benefit realized £20,000. He was greatly missed. In 1979 he became part-time coach to Oxford University and he was in great demand as an entertaining public speaker. His warmth of character and sociability were legendary but he was too thirsty for his health's sake and died of a heart attack.

> **First-class career** (1960–74): 13,262 runs (33.07) including 23 centuries, 99 wickets (32.03), and 224 catches
> **Test matches** (9): 654 runs (46.71) including 2 centuries, and 7 catches

MILLER, Audley Montague

(b. 1869, Brentry, Gloucestershire; d. 1959, Clifton, Bristol) *Wiltshire, MCC, and England*

An all-rounder, Audley Miller captained Wiltshire for 25 years and served also as honorary secretary. He played many times for MCC (mainly in minor matches) and toured South Africa in 1895/6 with Lord Hawke's team, in his sole Test at Port Elizabeth scoring 4 not out and 20 not out at number ten, and not bowling.

> **First-class career** (1896–1903): 105 runs (15.00) and 1 wicket (49.00)

MILLER, Geoffrey

(b. 1952, Chesterfield, Derbyshire) *Derbyshire, Essex, Cheshire, and England*

Geoff Miller, known as Dusty, had a long apprenticeship at Test level which he thoroughly justified by emerging as a key all-rounder during England's 5–1 win in Australia in 1978/9. Tallish, slim, and dark with a droopy moustache, he toured both India and the West Indies with the England Young Cricketers, first playing for Derbyshire in 1973. A tidy off-spinner, reliable fielder and a right-hand batsman with a natural gift of timing and a greater willingness than most English contemporaries to play strokes off the back foot, he made only a modest start in county cricket. But the arrival of the ebullient and dynamic Eddie Barlow as Derbyshire captain proved the catalyst he needed. He played promisingly in his first Test for England in 1976, but on two official tours in the next two winters he was often starved of opportunity as a bowler. On the 1977/8 tour to New Zealand and Pakistan he showed himself to be a very capable batsman, being left stranded on 98 not out in the Test at Lahore. He came into his own as a spin bowler in Australia in 1978/9. Bowling with great confidence and tight control, he used the Australian breezes skilfully to flight the ball and took more wickets than any other bowler on the tour, including 23 in the Test series. Relatively unsuccessful on tours to Australia in 1979/80, when he returned early through injury, and the West

Indies in 1980/1, he regained his England place in 1982 and scored 98 against India at Old Trafford, again just missing his maiden hundred. He went on his third tour to Australia in 1982/3 and performed usefully with 13 wickets and nearly 200 runs in the Test series. He made a brief reappearance in Test cricket against the West Indies in 1984, but he was never able to hold a regular place in the England side, perhaps not quite good enough either as a batsman or a bowler. In 1984, his long struggle to make his maiden first-class hundred was successful when in his 380th innings he scored 130 against Lancashire at Old Trafford. A thoughtful and witty character, he captained Derbyshire between 1979 and 1981 and was briefly England vice-captain on the tour of the West Indies. At the end of the 1986 season, seeking a renaissance of his career, he moved to Essex, but he was more useful than prolific in a strong team.

First-class career (1973–90): 12,027 runs (26.49) including 2 centuries, 888 wickets (27.98), and 309 catches

Test matches (34): 1,213 runs (25.80), 60 wickets (30.98), and 17 catches

MILLIGAN, Frank William

(b. 1870, Farnborough, Hampshire; d. 1900, Ramatlhabama, South Africa) *Yorkshire and England*

Frank Milligan was very much the ideal of the nineteenth-century amateur cricketer. He bowled fast, batted aggressively, if somewhat impatiently, and fielded superbly. But he was also a national symbol, for he was killed in action whilst serving as a lieutenant under Colonel Plumer in a bid to relieve Mafeking in the Boer War. He toured South Africa with Lord Hawke's team in 1898/9, playing in two Tests, and settled there.

First-class career (1894–8): 2,232 runs (17.85), 144 wickets (23.54), and 52 catches

Test matches (2): 58 runs (14.50), 0–29, and 1 catch

MILLMAN, Geoffrey

(b. 1934, Bedford) *Bedfordshire, Nottinghamshire, and England*

Joining Nottinghamshire after playing for Bedfordshire and Combined Services, Geoff Millman was a most accomplished wicket-keeper and a useful, stubborn batsman, who often opened. He captained Nottinghamshire from 1963 until 1965, when he left cricket to concentrate on his business career. He toured India and Pakistan in

1961/2 and also appeared in Tests, against Pakistan in England in 1962. However, John Murray and Jim Parks both had the edge on him.

First-class career (1956–65): 7,771 runs (18.86) including 3 centuries, and 656 dismissals (559 c., 97 st.)

Test matches (6): 60 runs (12.00) and 15 dismissals (13 c., 2 st.)

MILTON, Clement Arthur

(b. 1928, Bedminster, Somerset) *Gloucestershire and England*

Small and fair-haired, Arthur Milton was a neat and accomplished right-hand opening batsman, a steady and skilful accumulator of runs. Watching each ball with the greatest care, he always appeared to have plenty of time to play his strokes, preferring the back foot. An occasional medium-pace bowler, he was also a brilliant short-leg, extremely agile, with a very safe pair of hands. He exceeded 1,000 runs in a season sixteen times, and twice made two centuries in a match. In his first Test, against New Zealand at Headingley in 1958, he made 104 not out, a real scrambler's innings, full of luck but also of character. He toured Australia with MCC in 1958/9 but suffered a finger injury after playing in two Tests, although he reappeared against India the following year. Also a soccer international, he played with success for Arsenal. He captained Gloucestershire in 1968, but the extra responsibility did not suit him. He became coach to Oxford University, where he was greatly respected for his homespun wisdom; a postman; and a talent scout for the England selection committee. In 1993 they picked the young Somerset batsman Mark Lathwell despite Milton's advice that he was 'not quite ready'. Nor was he.

First-class career (1948–74): 32,150 runs (33.73) including 56 centuries, 79 wickets (45.94), and 758 catches

Test matches (6): 204 runs (25.50) including 1 century, 0–12, and 5 catches

MITCHELL, Arthur

(b. 1902, Basildon Green, Yorkshire; d. 1976, Bradford, Yorkshire) *Yorkshire and England*

Arthur or 'Ticker' Mitchell—so named because of his habit of 'ticking-on' (nattering) while play was in progress—often carried 'caution to excess' (as *Wisden* put it), although he could drive as well and as hard as anyone. His right-handed batting was generally grave and determined. In the slips he became a legend. On ten occasions he exceeded 1,000 runs in a season, including 1933, when he made 2,300 runs (58.97), 508 of them coming in a purple patch between 30 August and 7 September. He toured India with MCC in 1933/4 and appeared in the first Test series in that country without distinction, but as a late replacement in the Test against South Africa at Headingley in 1935—he was literally called from his garden to take part—he made 58 and 72. On retirement he became county coach, guarding the traditional values with an endearing severity.

First-class career (1922–47): 19,523 runs (37.47) including 44 centuries, 7 wickets (46.71), and 438 catches

Test matches (6): 298 runs (29.80), 0–4, and 9 catches

MITCHELL, Frank

(b. 1872, Market Weighton, Yorkshire; d. 1935, Blackheath, Kent) *Cambridge University, Yorkshire, Transvaal, and England*

A triple blue at Cambridge, Frank Mitchell played cricket for both England and South Africa and Rugby football for England. While captain of Cambridge in 1896 he helped to make history by instructing E. B. Shine to give away extras so that Oxford should not follow on. Despite the uproar it caused, his action helped the law to be changed so that the enforcement of the follow-on became voluntary. A heavy scorer in a strong Yorkshire side, Mitchell toured South Africa with Lord Hawke's team in 1898/9, served there in the army during the Boer War, returned to Yorkshire, then went back to South Africa, captaining the teams to England in 1904 and 1912. He also played for MCC, earned distinction in the First World War and was a prolific journalist on war, cricket and rugby.

First-class career (1894–1914): 9,176 runs (31.97) including 17 centuries, 36 wickets (23.17), 148 catches, and 2 stumpings

Test matches (England—2): 88 runs (22.00) and 2 catches. (South Africa—3): 28 runs (4.66)

MITCHELL, Thomas Bignell

(b. 1902, Creswell, Derbyshire) *Derbyshire and England*

A bespectacled former coal-miner, Tommy Mitchell was a resourceful right-arm leg-break and googly bowler who spun the ball as much as any bowler and could make it turn on any wicket.

He flighted the ball well and could bowl the off-spinner for variety. His quirks and quips could make a batsman lose his balance with laughter. He took more than 100 wickets in ten of his twelve seasons of first-class cricket, including 116 in Derbyshire's first Championship year, 1936. He toured Australia and New Zealand in 1932/3, playing against Australia and New Zealand once each; he also appeared against Australia and South Africa in England.

First-class career (1928–39): 2,431 runs (7.97), 1,483 wickets (20.59), and 132 catches

Test matches (5): 20 runs (5.00), 8 wickets (62.25), and 1 catch

MITCHELL-INNES, Norman Stewart

(b. 1914, Calcutta, India) *Oxford University, Somerset, Scotland, and England*

Norman Mitchell-Innes was a stylish and confident, right-handed batsman and a medium-pace change-bowler. His first-class cricket was limited by severe hay-fever and by his career in the Sudan Civil Service. He captained Oxford and Somerset occasionally. In his sole Test innings against South Africa at Trent Bridge in 1935 he scored 5, and he toured Australasia with the MCC 'goodwill' side of 1935/6.

First-class career (1931–49): 6,944 runs (31.42) including 13 centuries, 82 wickets (34.70), and 152 catches

MITFORD, Revd John

(b. 1781, Richmond, Surrey; d. 1859, Benhall, Suffolk)

John Mitford, 'no more fit to be a parson than I am the Angel Gabriel', as a friend observed, was the prototype of the cricket-playing parson: 'I lose industry and all other virtues so long as summer lasts.' He is an important source of our knowledge of late eighteenth-century and early nineteenth-century cricketers, and especially of William Fennex (whom he employed). Mitford passed his manuscript notes on to James Pycroft who incorporated them in his *The Cricket Field* (1851).

MOLD, Arthur Webb

(b. 1863, Middleton Cheney, Northamptonshire; d. 1921, Middleton Cheney) *Northamptonshire, Lancashire, and England*

A great humorist and betting man, Arthur Mold was one of the deadliest right-arm fast bowlers of his day, but, even while he was with his native

Northamptonshire, his action was suspect. Qualifying for Lancashire, he spearheaded the attack so well that he took 13 or more wickets in a match fourteen times, taking four wickets in four balls at Trent Bridge in 1895. He was selected for the three Tests against Australia in 1893. In 1900, however, when the county were playing Nottinghamshire at Trent Bridge, umpire Jim Phillips no-balled him for throwing, and he sent down only one over in the match. Later, the county captains condemned his delivery by 11 votes to 1, and his first-class career was over.

First-class career (1889–1901): 1,850 runs (7.14), 1,673 wickets (15.54), and 111 catches
Test matches (3): 0 runs (—), 7 wickets (33.42), and 1 catch

MONCKTON, Walter Turner, 1st Viscount of Brenchley

(b. 1891, Plaxtol, Kent; d. 1965, Folkington, Sussex)

Viscount Monckton's remarkable batting average in first-class cricket was achieved through his solitary appearance for Oxford and Cambridge and for the Navy and Army at Portsmouth in 1911. As a right-handed batsman, going in at number eleven, he made 29 not out and 43. He had kept wicket for Harrow in 'Fowler's match' in 1910 and won a Harlequin cap at Oxford. He was president of MCC (1956) and of Surrey (1950–2; 1959–65) and had come to the public notice as a personal legal adviser to the Prince of Wales who, as Edward VIII, abdicated in 1936. Subsequently, he held three cabinet posts and chaired the Commission on the future of the Rhodesias and Nyasaland (1959–60).

First-class career (1911): 72 runs (72.00) and 2 dismissals (1 c., 1 st.)

MONTGOMERY, Bernard Law, Field Marshal, Viscount Montgomery of Alamein

(b. 1887, London; d. 1976, Isington, Hampshire)

'Monty', the allied commander in North Africa and Europe in the Second World War who has been called 'the best British field commander since Wellington', was born at St Mark's Vicarage, Kennington Oval. His father, Bishop Henry Hutchinson Montgomery (1847–1932) wrote *Old Cricket and Cricketers* (1890), an account of the game's history and its virtues. The son was in the St Paul's School XI (1905–6) as an opening right-handed batsman, later playing hockey for the Army. His troops at El Alamein were instructed to 'hit Rommel's corps for six'. Surprisingly Montgomery, unlike several other wartime leaders, did not become president of MCC.

MOON, Leonard James

(b. 1878, London; d. 1916, Salonica, Greece)
Cambridge University, Middlesex, and England

One of the many amateurs of quality who flourished in Edwardian days, Leonard Moon was a vigorous right-handed batsman, whose speciality was the cut, and a useful wicket-keeper. A prolific run-getter at Westminster and Cambridge—where he hit 138 against the 1899 Australians—he was equally at home with Middlesex, sharing in two opening stands in excess of 200 with Sir Pelham Warner. He toured America in 1905 and South Africa in 1905/6; on the latter tour he made 826 runs and had his Test experience. He died of war wounds.

First-class career (1897–1913): 4,166 runs (26.87) including 7 centuries, 1 wicket (55.00), and 85 dismissals (72 c., 13 st.)
Test matches (4): 182 runs (22.75) and 4 catches

MORLEY, Frederick

(b. 1850, Sutton-in-Ashfield, Nottinghamshire; d. 1884, Sutton-in-Ashfield) *Nottinghamshire and England*

A left-arm fastish bowler, Fred Morley was the first Nottinghamshire player to take 100 wickets in a season, when in 1878 he captured 126 at 9.92. In America in 1879 he took 100 wickets for 354 runs! His success lay in his length and direction. 'If Morley bowled like a machine,' said his captain, Richard Daft, 'he certainly resembled a machine that was well oiled and in perfect working order.' He played in the first Test in England at The Oval in 1880, opening the attack and taking 8 for 146, the best analysis of the match. In 1882/3 he was a member of Hon. Ivo Bligh's team to Australia but he was knocked out and badly hurt in a collision at sea on the way out. A simple soul, he struggled on throughout the tour but it turned out that he had fractured a rib. On his return home his health deteriorated and he died of 'congestion and dropsy'.

First-class career (1872–83): 1,404 runs (5.40), 1,273 wickets (13.43), and 107 catches
Test matches (4): 6 runs (1.50), 16 wickets (18.50), and 4 catches

MORRIS, Hugh

(b. 1963, Cardiff, South Glamorgan, Wales)
Glamorgan and England

Hugh Morris gained Test recognition through sheer weight of runs. A chunky immensely likeable left-hander, who was also an outstanding schoolboy and club Rugby player, he achieved the highest aggregate ever by a Glamorgan batsman (2,276) including ten centuries in 1990 and when he maintained that consistency the following season, selection became almost inevitable. Given three Tests in 1991, he struggled to match his county performances, but a brave innings of 44 on a fiery pitch against the West Indies at The Oval helped England to win and he remained on the fringes of further recognition, making three A tours, two of them as captain. Educated at Blundell's, he played his first game for Glamorgan in 1981 whilst still at school and he captained the England Schools under-19 side before going on to play for Young England, leading them against Australia in 1983. In 1986 he topped 1,000 runs for the first time and became Glamorgan's youngest-ever captain at the age of 22. He relinquished the post from 1990 to 1992, but resumed as captain in 1993, when he led Glamorgan to a heady success in the Sunday League and to a prosperous season all round. Chosen to captain the A tour of Pakistan and Sri Lanka in 1990/1, he was called to join the senior party in Australia following a hand injury to Graham Gooch, but, played only two one-day games in almost a month. A knee injury, a legacy of a first-class rugby union career with Aberavon and the South Glamorgan Institute in the mid-1980s, hampered him during the 1993/4 A tour of South Africa and during a hectic 1994 season which included his Benefit.

First-class career (1981–   ): 15,192 runs (37.60) and 2 wickets (190.00)

Test matches (3): 115 runs (19.16)

Morris, John Edward

(b. 1964, Crewe, Cheshire) *Derbyshire, Durham, Griqualand West, and England*

It was John Morris's misfortune that despite being a talented and powerful middle-order batsman, he was more likely to be remembered for what became known as the 'Tiger Moth incident' than for his performances in three Tests against India in 1990 and on the subsequent tour of Australia. He had the talent to be a successful Test batsman, but not, perhaps, the persistence or the necessary luck. Confident, irrepressibly perky, stockily built, and a particularly strong puller and driver, he celebrated scoring a century against Queensland in Carrara in 1990/1 by joining David Gower as a passenger aboard two hired vintage aeroplanes, urging the pilots to fly low over the ground to acknowledge a hundred by Robin Smith. It was lighthearted, but both players were fined £1,000 for leaving the ground without permission. Gower, an established star, played only five more Tests for England—two of them coming later on the tour: Morris was still waiting for his fourth cap four years later. He had first played for Derbyshire in 1982, becoming the youngest player to score a Sunday League hundred. He was awarded his county cap in 1986, when he scored 1,739 runs. Over the next four summers Morris totalled more than 7,000 runs, but he continued to be overlooked, even for an A tour, despite the 'defection' of sixteen players to join the unofficial tour of South Africa in 1989/90. Recognition finally arrived the following summer, however, when he played in all three Tests of a record-breaking series against India. In his first, which included Graham Gooch's 333 at Lord's, he batted at number six and had time only to score four not out before England declared. At Old Trafford, after scoring 13 in the first innings, he was forced to retire hurt when 15 not out after being struck by a straight drive by Smith. At The Oval, he could manage only 7, and a Test-best 32 before being caught down the leg-side. In Australia he was inconsistent and neither as fit or as earnest as the tour managers would have wished. He played no more Tests, despite a hard-hitting unbeaten 63 on his one-day international début against New Zealand (in a triangular tournament). Although he made 1,398 runs the following summer, and 1,461 in 1993 including five centuries and a career-best 229 against Gloucestershire at Cheltenham, there was no recall. After wintering in South Africa, he joined Durham. Again he comfortably topped 1,000 runs, including a double-century against the county champions Warwickshire.

First-class career (1982–   ): 16,004 runs (39.71) and 7 wickets (128.85)

Test matches (3): 71 runs (23.66)

MORTIMORE, John Brian

(b. 1933, Bristol) *Gloucestershire and England*

A tall, slim all-rounder, John Mortimore was a right-arm off-break bowler, who spun the ball enough to be dangerous on helpful pitches and kept batsmen quiet at other times by dint of considerable accuracy and a good away-drifter. He was a contemporary of another Gloucestershire and England off-spinner, David Allen, with whom he made a formidable partnership. Mortimore was also a solid middle-order batsman, who loved to drive, and a very reliable field. His usefulness on hard wickets was proved in Australia in 1958/9, when he went as a reinforcement for a side hard pressed by injuries. Mortimore took four wickets in five balls against Lancashire at Cheltenham in 1962 and was always coming up with useful performances, achieving the double three times between 1959 and 1964. He led his county from 1965 to 1967, doing the job well in his studious, undemonstrative way.

First-class career (1950–75): 15,891 runs (18.32) including 4 centuries, 1,807 wickets (23.18), and 348 catches

Test matches (9): 243 runs (24.30), 13 wickets (56.38), and 3 catches

MOSS, Alan Edward

(b. 1930, Tottenham, Middlesex) *Middlesex and England*

Alan Moss, or 'Amos', was the spearhead of the Middlesex attack in the 1950s and early 1960s. Tall and strong, he was a very competent right-arm, fast bowler, who could always be relied on to do a steady job and was very quick indeed for a few overs, once hitting the sight screen first bounce with a bumper at Sabina Park. He was a great trier, working hard and learning how to move the ball about and increase his accuracy. He toured the West Indies twice and Pakistan once with MCC and, at home, played against Australia, South Africa and India.

First-class career (1950–68): 1,671 runs (6.99), 1,301 wickets (20.78), and 143 catches

Test matches (9): 61 runs (10.16), 21 wickets (29.80), and 1 catch

MOXON, Martyn Douglas

(b. 1960, Stairfoot, Barnsley, Yorkshire) *Yorkshire, Griqualand West, and England*

A tall, orthodox, and determined right-handed batsman, Martyn Moxon had to live with the highest expectations from the moment that he scored centuries in his first two Championship games in Yorkshire: 116 against Essex at Headingley (his début match) and 111 against Derbyshire at Sheffield, in 1981. His temperament was proved again when he made 153 in his first Roses

match in 1983 and when scoring an accomplished 74 in his first Test innings, at Lord's against New Zealand in 1986. He had been picked to play for England two years earlier, at Lord's against the West Indies, but had to withdraw from the team because of a broken finger. The following winter, in India and Australia, he batted consistently but his chances of making the Test team were retarded when he had to return home early in the tour because of the death of his father. A softly spoken and popular cricketer from Barnsley, he initially played in glasses but switched to contact lenses. He can also bowl right-arm medium pace usefully and is a fine all-round fielder. He was unlucky not to be selected for the 1986/7 tour of Australia, having been out four times out of four to Richard Hadlee in his two Tests against New Zealand. He spent two winters in South Africa between 1982 and 1984. His ill-fortune continued. Touring New Zealand in 1987/8 he actually 'reached' a Test hundred in Auckland but an umpire signalled leg-byes when a firm sweep went for three runs off his bat: he was later out for 99 and rain stopped play in the following Test at Wellington when he was 81 not out and in confident command. He played only one more Test, the fifth against Australia in 1989, but high-scoring seasons in 1990 and 1991 (1,669 runs) kept him in contention and in both 1991/2 and 1992/3 he was chosen to captain England 'A' sides. On the first tour he broke a thumb in Bermuda in a beer match en route to the West Indies and that was that. In Australia the following winter he at least played in three matches, averaging 48, still managed to break a finger. Accident-prone or not, he presided over a relatively harmonious period in Yorkshire's history as captain of the county from 1990 to 1995. His 1994 season started with yet another injury but ended with a career-best 274 not out against Worcestershire.

First-class career (1981–): 18,301 runs (41.97) including 38 centuries, 28 wickets (52.89), and 203 catches

Test matches (10): 455 runs (28.43) and 10 catches

MUNTON, Timothy Alan

(b. 1965, Melton Mowbray, Leicestershire) *Warwickshire and England*

Leicestershire's loss was Warwickshire's gain in the case of Tim Munton. A tall, fit, swing- and seam-bowler, he played 2nd XI cricket for his native county for three years, before his move to Warwickshire, which brought over 500 first-class wickets over the next ten years, two Test caps against Pakistan in 1992 and a triumphant peak in 1994. With his high action after a long run-up, he made steady progress and was awarded his cap in 1989 after passing 50 wickets in a season for the first time. The following summer, one dominated by batsmen, he took 78 wickets and was rewarded with selection for the A tour of Pakistan and Sri Lanka. He was joint-second highest wicket-taker with 10 victims, including 4 for 61 in the first 'Test' in Kandy. Despite another 73 wickets in 1991, Munton was initially overlooked for the winter tours, but gained a place on the A trip to the Caribbean when his county colleague Dermot Reeve was elevated to the senior squad. This time he managed only four wickets, but his Test chance came the following summer against Pakistan, in the third match at Old Trafford. Rain, which washed out the second day's play, moistened the atmosphere and helped Munton pick up his only wicket, Javed Miandad, caught at slip, before he produced a defiant unbeaten 25 to help ensure a draw. Retained for the next Test at Headingley, he took three wickets, including his Test-best two for 22 as England levelled the series with a six-wicket win, but he was left out for the final match. Warwickshire appointed him vice-captain the following summer and in 1994, with the captain, Reeve, frequently absent through injury, he led the side to many victories on the way to their first Championship title since 1972. Munton himself took 81 wickets, and could consider himself unlucky not to be chosen to tour Australia.

First-class career (1985–   ): 1,096 runs (9.87) and 502 wickets (26.72)

Test matches (2): 25 runs (25.00) and 4 wickets (50.00)

MURDOCH, William Lloyd

(1855–1911) *New South Wales and Sussex*

See Australia section.

MURRAY, John Thomas

(b. 1935, London) *Middlesex and England*

John Murray, or 'J.T.', was a stylist—indeed a perfectionist—both as a right-handed batsman and wicket-keeper. Immaculately turned-out always, he went through a careful ritual of touching his gloves together and describing a graceful curve with his hands before settling on to his haunches. His very passing of the ball to

the slips when he had taken it was an elegant and studied performance and he was a 'keeper of exceptional agility, bringing off some spectacular diving catches. He scored 1,025 runs and took 104 dismissals in 1957, only one other (Leslie Ames) having ever achieved this double in a season. Unfortunate injuries, both in India in 1961/2 and Australia in 1962/3, deprived him of a regular England place after he had done well against Australia in 1961, as virtual heir-apparent to Godfrey Evans. At his best he was a batsman of very high class, a lovely driver both to off and on, and a brave hooker. He made a timely and memorable hundred for England against the West Indies at The Oval in 1966. In 1975, his final season, he established the world record for the most dismissals in a career, broken by R. W. Taylor in 1982/3. He has served as a Test match selector and been awarded the MBE for services to the game.

First-class career (1952–75): 18,872 runs (23.59) including 16 centuries, and 1,527 dismissals (1,270 c., 257 st.)

Test matches (21): 506 runs (22.00) including 1 century, and 55 dismissals (52 c., 3 st.)

MYNN, Alfred

(b. 1807, Goudhurst, Kent; d. 1861, London) *Kent*

Powerful in size and personality, Alfred Mynn, 'the Lion of Kent', was, for a quarter of a century, the prelude to W. G. Grace. At Brighton, for MCC v. Sussex in 1836, he scored 45 and 92 and took nine wickets. Immediately afterwards, at Leicester, 'with his leg doctored up for the match', he scored 21 not out and 125 not out for the South v. the North. The subsequent journey to London laid out on top of a stage-coach brought the threat of amputation and a premature end to his career. But in two years he was back, a formidable right-handed batsman and a right-arm bowler who, off a short run in the era of round-arm, achieved great pace and late movement. The Gentlemen, for whom the hop farmer appeared on 20 occasions, had their diminishing fortunes revived by two successive wins against the Players in 1842 and 1843 through his all-round contributions. On his death *Bell's Life* printed W. J. Prowse's stanzas, 'In Memoriam', ending with the oft-quoted epitaph, 'Lightly lie the turf upon thee, kind and manly Alfred Mynn.'

First-class career (1832–59): 4,955 runs (13.42) including 1 century, 292 + 741 wickets (10.23), and 125 catches

NEWHAM

NEWHAM, William

(b. 1860, Shrewsbury, Shropshire; d. 1944,
Portslade, Brighton, Sussex) *Sussex and England*

Of medium height and well built, Billy Newham
drove hard on either side of the wicket, cut
brilliantly, and was specially adept, when playing
back, at forcing strokes past mid-on or turning
the ball to leg. At Leyton in 1902 he and Ranji
added 344 against Essex, which remains the
record seventh-wicket stand in England. As amateur player, captain, secretary or assistant-secretary, his connection with his county lasted 63
years. Touring Australia with Shaw's and Shrewsbury's team in 1887/8, he appeared in his sole
Test, at Sydney, scoring 9 and 17.

First-class career (1881–1905): 14,657 runs
(24.42) including 19 centuries, 10 wickets (61.50),
and 183 catches

NEWPORT, Philip John

(b. 1962, High Wycombe, Buckinghamshire)
*Buckinghamshire, Worcestershire, Boland, and
England*

One of the best swing bowlers of his generation,
as well as a handy lower-middle order batsman,
Phil Newport found himself unable to live up to
the promise of his Test début against Sri Lanka at
Lord's, when he took 7 for 164. Tall and phlegmatic, he made his county début in 1982 after
representing Buckinghamshire in the Minor
Counties Championship, honing his skills by
wintering abroad in South Africa, New Zealand,
and Australia. By adding a sharp pace to his
outswing, he became a highly effective performer, at his happiest coming on as first change,
once the initial gloss had gone from the ball. His
performance in his first Test, in 1988, together
with 93 first-class wickets that season, earned him
selection for the winter tour to India, but it's
subsequent cancellation, after the Indian Government had objected to the South African links of
several of the party, robbed him of the opportunity to establish himself. Nevertheless, he gained
selection for the first Test of the following summer, engineering an Australian defeat in two days
in the their opening first-class fixture by taking
eleven wickets, albeit on an unreliable surface.
Along with the rest of England's attack, however,
Newport performed poorly and was dropped,
and he had to wait almost two years for his next
chance. Injuries to Martin Bicknell and Angus
Fraser led to his being summoned from the A
team tour of Sri Lanka to play in the Perth Test

of 1991. Although he batted defiantly, making an
unbeaten 40 in a losing cause, he once again
struggled with the ball, failing to come to terms
with the local sea breeze, 'the Freemantle Doctor'. Newport's performance in bowling the 1992
Pakistanis to defeat at Worcester kept him in
contention for England, but despite taking 60
wickets at 24 in 1993 and scoring six Championship fifties to underline his batting ability, and
then taking 53 wickets the following summer, he
could not convince the selectors.

First-class career (1982–): 4,978 runs (25.72)
and 703 wickets (27.56)

Test matches (3): 110 runs (27.50) and 10 wickets
(41.70)

NICHOLS, Morris Stanley

(b. 1900, Stondon Massey, Essex; d. 1961, Newark,
Nottinghamshire) *Essex and England*

Morris Nichols was a fast right-arm bowler who
never knew when he was beaten. He kept the ball
up, either moving it away or bringing it back, and
sometimes pitched in a yorker. He was a left-
handed batsman, not elegant but businesslike and
a shrewd hitter. His walk back for his run-up had
something of the rollicking gait of a sailor. He
always looked relaxed and proved it was no
illusion by prospering in many a crisis. Eight
times, between 1929 and 1939, he achieved the
double. In 1935 at Huddersfield he took 11 for 54
and scored 146, the county champions, Yorkshire,
losing by a large innings margin. He toured New
Zealand, 1929/30, and India, 1933/4, playing in
the first Test series in those countries. He
appeared only once against Australia in 1930, and
twice against the West Indies. But he played four
times against South Africa in 1935 and at Trent
Bridge in the first Test, took six wickets for only
35 runs.

First-class career (1924–39): 17,827 runs (26.56)
including 20 centuries, 1,833 wickets (21.63), and
326 catches

Test matches (14): 355 runs (29.58), 41 wickets
(28.09), and 11 catches

NORFOLK, 16th Duke of

(b. 1908, Arundel, Sussex; d. 1975, Arundel)

The premier English duke and Earl Marshal
showed a devotion to cricket comparable to that
of the eighteenth-century aristocratic patrons.
Rank, inclination, and commitment inevitably
declared he would be president both of

MCC (1955) and of Sussex. Less likely was his role as manager of the MCC's tour of Australia in 1962/3. With Alec Bedser, as his assistant, he was responsible for the public relations of a team which included the mercurial Ted Dexter as captain and such divergent personalities as Fred Trueman and (Bishop) David Sheppard. The vice-captain, (Sir) Colin Cowdrey, thought him 'the kindest and most considerate of men' and *Wisden*, in objective and tempered prose, praised his 'dry wit and friendliness'. To cricketers as a whole, his private ground at Arundel was the symbol of his enthusiasm. His father, Duke Henry, had arranged for the ground's construction in 1895. Magnificent in its setting, it has often been the venue for the opening match of visiting touring teams, a castle in Sussex rather than a cathedral in Worcester, where the opening first-class match of a tour is usually played, becoming their gateway to the English scene. The Duke's widow, Lavinia, was determined to keep cricket going at Arundel Park and the scope in fact greatly increased after the Duke's death. 'The friends of Arundel' and other charities financed a new cricket school beside the ground and the field was also used from the early 1990s for some of Sussex's Championship fixtures. Since the creation of the Arundel Castle Cricket Foundation in 1985, over 70,000 different cricketers, mainly schoolboys, have enjoyed the facilities.

NYREN, John

(b. 1764, Hambledon, Hampshire; d. 1837, London)
Hambledon

John Nyren, son of Richard, was a left-handed batsman, who usually fielded at point or cover. He played a few times for Hambledon in its closing years and later for Homerton. He appeared at Lord's for England (1802–5) and for the Gentlemen in the first match against the Players in 1806. His highest score was 50. But it is as the author of *The Cricketers of My Time* (1833), an essay added to his instructional book *The Young Cricketer's Tutor* that his fame rests. In it are vivid and evocative character-sketches of the Hambledon cricketers whom he had known in his youth. 'Those annointed clod-stumpers the Walkers, Tom and Harry' and Lamborn, the shepherd, 'a plain spoked little bumpkin' whose off-breaks were too good for the Duke of Dorset, have become enshrined in a book which was a classic in its own time. Written when Nyren was almost 70, it owed something to the editorial hand of the Shakespearian scholar, Charles Cow-

den Clarke, and won immediate praise from John Mitford in his *The Gentleman's Magazine* and from the essayist Leigh Hunt in *The London Journal*. To John Arlott, over a century later, 'even at the twentieth reading, the epic quality, the nostalgia, the vitality' remained.

First-class career (1802–5): 159 runs (8.36) and 7 catches

NYREN, Richard

(b. *c*.1734, Slindon, Sussex; d. 1797, Leigh, Kent)
Hambledon and Hampshire

Learning his cricket from his uncle, Richard Newland, at Slindon, Nyren's move to Hambledon in 1772 came at a time when the club was not prospering. He became the 'chosen General of all the matches' and a left-handed all-rounder, good enough to score 70 in Hambledon's defeat of England in 1776 at Sevenoaks and to take three wickets. More important than his talent as a player was his 'knowledge of the game' and the role he played as intermediary between Hambledon's patrons and Hambledon's players. As his son, John Nyren, wrote in an objective character-study: 'He placed a full and just value upon the station he held in society, and he maintained it without insolence or assumption.' As captain, secretary, groundsman, and landlord successively of the 'Bat and Ball' and the 'George', he steered Hambledon through its greatest years. The detailed club accounts bear record to his stewardship, whether buying bottles of claret for the members, paying the players or providing dinner for the ladies. He was 'a thoroughbred old English yeoman' and a kinsman of the Jacobite fugitive from the 1745 Rebellion, Lord Nairne. In happier times the sixth Lord Nairne met Nyren's son John at Lord's in 1824 and their watch-chains both bore the same family crest.

OAKMAN, Alan Stanley Myles

(b. 1930, Hastings, Sussex) *Sussex and England*

Exceptionally tall and gangling, Alan Oakman was a right-handed batsman, at his best on hard wickets against medium and fast-medium bowling when, using his immense reach, he would unleash a stream of drives. His coolness in a crisis often served Sussex well. A useful off-break bowler, he took 99 wickets in 1954 (his best season) and, superb as a close field, held 57 catches in 1958. He appeared in two Tests against Australia in 1956, when his catching in Laker's leg-trap was outstanding, and he toured South Africa in 1956/7, where he was hampered by back trouble. He became a respected coach at Warwickshire.

First-class career (1947–68): 21,800 runs (26.17) including 22 centuries, 736 wickets (27.63), and 594 catches

Test matches (2): 14 runs (7.00), 0–21, and 7 catches

O'BRIEN, Sir Timothy Carew, Bt.

(b. 1861, Dublin; d. 1948, Ramsey, Isle of Man) *Oxford University, Middlesex, Ireland, and England*

A fiery Irishman, Tim O'Brien went up to Oxford only to obtain a blue for cricket but he was dismissed for a pair in his first University match. He was a dashing right-handed batsman, who loved the pull, at his best on 'sticky' wickets. His great resource and splendid physique made him at times a terror to the best of bowlers. Hitting 92 in Oxford's win against the Australians in 1884, he played in two Tests that year. Amid a galaxy of Middlesex amateur talent, his most notable performance was against Yorkshire at Lord's in 1889, when he hit 92 and 100 not out, his last 83 runs coming in 35 minutes, allowing Middlesex to win very unexpectedly. He toured Australia with G. F. Vernon's team in 1887/8 and South Africa with Lord Hawke's in 1895/6.

First-class career (1881–1914): 11,397 runs (27.01) including 15 centuries, 4 wickets (85.00), 173 catches, and 2 stumpings

Test matches (5): 59 runs (7.37) and 4 catches

O'CONNOR, Jack

(b. 1897, Cambridge; d. 1977, Buckhurst Hill, Essex) *Essex, Buckinghamshire, and England*

A small man from a notable cricketing family, Jack O'Connor was a right-handed batsman, quick on his feet, a good driver on both sides of the wicket and a fine hooker. He exceeded 1,000 runs in 16 seasons, reaching 2,000 runs four times between 1928 and 1934. He bowled a mixture of off- and leg-breaks which looked simpler than they were. A mainstay of Essex during the interwar years, he toured the West Indies in 1929/30 and, in England, appeared once against South Africa in 1929.

First-class career (1921–39): 28,764 runs (34.90) including 72 centuries, 557 wickets (32.89), 226 catches, and 1 stumping

Test matches (4): 153 runs (21.85), 1–72, and 2 catches

OLD, Christopher Middleton

(b. 1948, Middlesbrough, Yorkshire) *Yorkshire, Northern Transvaal, Warwickshire, Northumberland, and England*

Tall, strongly built, and the brother of an international Rugby Union player, Chris Old was immensely gifted in all three departments of cricket. But although in, or on the fringe of, the England side between 1972 and 1981, he achieved less than he might have done because of persistent injuries. He had operations on both knees in 1970 and 1971 and frequently suffered from strains in the shoulders or side. Often injuries came just before a Test match, suggesting that they might have been psychosomatic, yet once involved in an important match he often showed exceptional determination and seldom failed to justify his selection. A modest, charming, friendly, and amusing companion and prolific imbiber of ale, he talked eloquently about his own ills but never had a bad word to say about anyone else. A left-handed batsman, he was effective against all but top-class fast bowling and he drove gloriously: in 1977 he made the third fastest first-class century ever, in 37 minutes against an indifferent Warwickshire attack (his second 50 came in 9 minutes). He was also a brilliant fielder, athletic in the deep and superb in the slips, but his main value to Yorkshire and England was as a right-arm, fast-medium bowler. Approaching the wicket with heavy tread but lissom rhythm, he delivered with a classical sideways-on action, moving the out-swinger late and often bringing the ball back in wickedly off the pitch. Genuinely fast in his early years, he slowed his pace to fast-medium and was able to bowl long and accurate spells, as in 1978 against Pakistan at Edgbaston when his 7 for 50 included four wickets in five balls. If he lacked anything (apart from that elusive fitness) it was the mean or malicious streak which turns some fast bowlers into devils. In 1981 he became captain of Yorkshire in difficult circumstances and played a valuable all-round role in two exciting Test victories over Australia at Headingley and Edgbaston. But a year later his career went into a sudden decline. Having spent the 1981/2 winter playing for Northern Transvaal, he joined the so-called 'rebel' tour of South Africa and, along with the other English players concerned, was banned from Test cricket for three years. He did little for Yorkshire the following season, was deposed from the captaincy and replaced by Ray Illingworth and then harshly discarded by his county at the end of the season. He moved to Warwickshire and must have gained great satisfaction from taking ten wickets against Yorkshire at Headingley in 1984. Again troubled by injury he announced his retirement from first-class cricket after the 1985 season, though continuing to play league and Minor Counties cricket in Northumberland.

First-class career (1966–85): 7,756 runs (20.84) including 6 centuries, 1,070 wickets (23.48), and 214 catches

Test matches (46): 845 runs (14.82), 143 wickets (28.11), and 22 catches

OLDFIELD, Norman

(b. 1911, Dukinfield, Cheshire) *Lancashire, Northamptonshire, and England*

Had he not lost his best years to the Second World War, 'Buddy' Oldfield would no doubt have appeared in more Test cricket. In his sole Test, against the West Indies at The Oval in 1939, he scored 80 and 19, rippling the ground with lovely strokes. Short but stylish, a right-handed batsman rich in natural gifts, he was a versatile stroke-maker all round the wicket. Specially registered for Northamptonshire in 1948, he toured India with the Commonwealth team of 1949/50, making a century in three successive matches against India.

First-class career (1935–54): 17,811 runs (37.89) including 38 centuries, 2 wickets (60.50), and 96 catches

OLDROYD, Edgar

(b. 1888, Batley, Yorkshire; d. 1964, Truro, Cornwall) *Yorkshire*

Of 'Little Ark' Oldroyd, *Wisden* wrote in the middle years of his career 'he did not fall far below Sutcliffe in efficiency' but he was 'not half so good to look at'. Sutcliffe would reach great heights but Oldroyd remained a dependable middle-order Yorkshire right-handed batsman. He got his 1,000 runs a season on ten occasions and in 1922, his best year, he shared a record second-wicket partnership of 333 with Percy Holmes against Warwickshire at Edgbaston. When at 43 he left the county scene, he returned to his roots in the Bradford League. The mayor of Pudsey lured him back to open the batting for Pudsey St Lawrence with the 14-year-old Len Hutton. Under Oldroyd's tutorship, Hutton learnt the art of batting on difficult wickets. Occasionally Oldroyd took wickets in county cricket with his brisk right-arm off-breaks.

First-class career (1910–31): 15,925 runs (35.15) including 36 centuries, 42 wickets (39.47), and 203 dismissals

PADGETT, Douglas Ernest Vernon

(b. 1934, Dirk Hill, Bradford, Yorkshire) *Yorkshire and England*

A Yorkshire stalwart, Doug Padgett played for England twice against South Africa in 1960. At 16 the youngest man ever to play for Yorkshire, he became a very successful county batsman at a time of transition. He was a dapper, neat right-hander with an exemplary technique which he passed on to the next generation as the Yorkshire coach. He exceeded 1,000 runs in a season twelve times and toured New Zealand in 1960/1.

First-class career (1951–71): 21,124 runs (28.58) including 32 centuries, 6 wickets (36.00), and 261 catches

Test matches (2): 51 runs (12.75) and 0–8

PAINE, George Alfred Edward

(b. 1908, London; d. 1978, Solihull, Warwickshire) *Middlesex, Warwickshire, and England*

A slow left-arm bowler, George Paine thought much about his craft and, when he was practising, he would place white tape round the ball so that he could see how much he was spinning it. His Test match experience was for England in the West Indies in 1934/5 but, despite his success, he never represented his country at home.

First-class career (1926–47): 3,430 runs (11.95), 1,021 wickets (22.85), and 160 catches

Test matches (4): 97 runs (16.16), 17 wickets (27.47), and 5 catches

PALAIRET, Lionel Charles Hamilton

(b. 1870, Broughton East, Lancashire; d. 1933, Exmouth, Devon) *Oxford University, Somerset, and England*

A tall and graceful right-handed opening batsman, Lionel Palairet combined strong defence with elegant cutting and driving. After four years in the Oxford XI, two as captain, he joined Somerset as an undergraduate, and his drives into the river and churchyard at Taunton are still remembered. In 1892 he shared a then record opening partnership of 346 with H. T. Hewett against Yorkshire at Taunton. His highest score was 292 against Hampshire at Southampton in 1896 and seven times he exceeded 1,000 runs in a season, but his sole Test appearances were against

Australia at Old Trafford and The Oval in 1902, when England lost by three runs and won by one wicket respectively. A useful change-bowler and deputy wicket-keeper, 'Stork' captained Somerset in 1907.

First-class career (1890–1909): 15,777 runs (33.63) including 27 centuries, 143 wickets (33.90), and 263 dismissals (248 c., 15 st.)
Test matches (2): 49 runs (12.25) and 2 catches

PALAIRET, Richard Cameron North

(b. 1871, Grange-over-Sands, Lancashire; d. 1955, Budleigh Salterton, Devon) *Oxford University and Somerset*

Awarded his blue at Oxford by his brother, Lionel, Dick Palairet was a stylish right-handed opening batsman who played for Somerset for a dozen seasons (1891–1902). His highest score was 156 against Somerset at Taunton in 1896 in which he shared a second-wicket partnership of 249 with his brother Lionel. A football injury at Oxford was something of a handicap and he never quite fulfilled the promise he had shown as a schoolboy at Repton. For twelve years (1920–32) he was secretary of Surrey, 'a most able and tireless administrator'. He was appointed, together with 'Plum' Warner, as joint manager of the MCC tour to Australia in 1932/3. His responsibility was finance—Warner's weakness in this direction was recognized. Although very much the junior—and silent—partner in the controversy over 'bodyline' it was he, rather than Warner, whom the captain, D. R. Jardine, asked to write a foreword to his account of the tour and, indeed, to be a guest at his wedding.

First-class career (1891–1902): 4,000 runs (21.16) including 2 centuries, 3 wickets (55.66), and 108 catches

PALMER, Charles Henry

(b. 1919, Old Hill, Staffordshire) *Worcestershire, Leicestershire, and England*

Diminutive and bespectacled but a cricketer of character, Charles Palmer was an attractive right-handed batsman, his cutting and driving on the off-side being particularly effective. His size was deceptive, for he had very strong wrists and could hit very hard. As captain of Leicestershire from 1950 until 1957, he underrated himself as a bowler, delivering useful medium-pacers of immaculate length and—occasionally—'donkey drops'. Against Surrey, the Champion county, at The Oval in 1955 he wreaked havoc, taking 8 for

7. In making two centuries for Gentlemen against Players he joined a select band. He toured South Africa in 1948/9 and the West Indies in 1953/4 as player/manager. In his sole Test, against the West Indies at Barbados, he scored 22 and 0, and took 0 for 15. He has served both as secretary and chairman of Leicestershire and was president of MCC in 1978/9. Also chairman of the TCCB, he headed a committee which in 1986 proposed several changes in English cricket to improve the quality of the Test team. He was awarded a CBE for his services to cricket.

First-class career (1939–59): 17,458 runs (31.74) including 33 centuries, 365 wickets (25.15), and 147 catches

PALMER, Kenneth Ernest

(b. 1937, Winchester, Hampshire) *Somerset and England*

Ruddy faced and very much a 'Zomerset' man with a rich West Country burr, Ken 'Pedlar' Palmer was a hard-working, right-arm, fast-medium bowler and a useful batsman. He was coaching at Johannesburg when he was brought to Port Elizabeth and used as the new ball spearhead in the fifth Test against South Africa in 1964/5 after England's team had been weakened by injuries. He scored 10 and took 1 for 189. The previous winter he had toured Pakistan with a Commonwealth side. He achieved the double in 1961 with 1,036 runs and 114 wickets. Against Nottinghamshire at Trent Bridge in 1963 he took 9 for 57 in an innings. He became a first-class and Test umpire of high repute standing in a Test for the first-time in 1972 and despite more than one controversy involving Pakistan he was one of only four English umpires nominated for the first international Panel of umpires, from 1993. His brother, Roy, also a Test umpire, and son, Gary, both played for Somerset.

First-class career (1955–69): 7,771 runs (20.72) including 2 centuries, 866 wickets (21.34), and 158 catches

PARDON, Sydney Herbert

(b. 1855, London; d. 1925, London)

The editorship of the Pardon brothers, C. F. and S. H. rescued *Wisden*, if not from oblivion at least from mediocrity, establishing its publication as a corner-stone of the cricket year. Succeeding his brother after only four years in charge, Sydney's term of office (1891–1925) has outdistanced that of every other editor. His annual 'Notes' were authoritative and tackled squarely such issues of the day as the follow-on (1897), throwing (1901), overseas players (1921), and covered pitches (1925). Pardon was the quintessential late Victorian gentleman with a characteristic range of interests. His opera-glasses did duty at Lord's and Covent Garden while *The Times* published his articles on music, the theatre, and racing. Above all, he was a stylist—in deportment and manners, his command of the English language, and his appraisal of a cricketer.

PARFITT, Peter Howard

(b. 1936, Billingford, Fakenham, Norfolk) *Norfolk, Middlesex, and England*

Following the Edrich path from Norfolk to Middlesex, Peter Parfitt was a left-handed batsman of high class, a useful off-spinner and a superb close fielder. A chirpy character, he broke through with 2,007 runs in 1961, including eight centuries. In form like this he was a handsome and complete player with a very straight bat which seemed unusually broad. He represented England periodically between 1962 and 1972, visited Australia, New Zealand and India twice and South Africa and Pakistan once. He scored three centuries in successive innings against Pakistan in 1962, as part of a sequence of seven consecutive fifties. He scored two centuries in a match twice, including 122 and 144 against Pakistan at Lord's in 1962, and 15 times exceeded 1,000 runs in a season, including the tour of India and Pakistan in 1961/2. From 1968 until 1970 he captained Middlesex. For a time he ran a pub on the Yorkshire Moors and as an eager and amusing raconteur also organised corporate hospitality at Test matches where his hearty presence enlivened the dullest games.

First-class career (1956–74): 26,924 runs (36.33) including 58 centuries, 277 wickets (30.32), and 564 catches

Test matches (37): 1,882 runs (40.91) including 7 centuries, 12 wickets (47.83), and 42 catches

PARKER, Charles Warrington Leonard

(b. 1882, Prestbury, Gloucestershire; d. 1959, Cranleigh, Surrey) *Gloucestershire and England*

Charlie Parker, or 'Parlie Charker', became with A. E. Dipper one of the 'grand old men' of his county's cricket. He was a prolific left-arm slow-medium bowler with an immaculate length and enough spin to catch the edge of the bat, so that 'c. Hammond b. Parker' became a frequent entry in the score-book. He performed some extraordinary feats: 10 for 79 in an innings against Somerset at Bristol in 1921; 17 for 56 against Essex at Gloucester in 1925; nine wickets in an innings on eight occasions; five wickets in successive balls (one a no-ball) against Yorkshire at Bristol during his benefit match in 1922, and many more. There was always guile and accuracy in his bowling, and no one loved a sticky wicket more. He was underrated by England selectors, playing only one Test, against Australia at Old Trafford in 1921, when he made 3 not out and took 2 for 32 in 28 accurate overs. Having taken over 100 wickets for the sixteenth year in succession he became coach at Cranleigh School. Only two bowlers in history have taken more first-class wickets.

First-class career (1903–35): 7,951 runs (10.48), 3,278 wickets (19.47), and 247 catches

PARKER, Paul William Giles

(b. 1956, Bulawayo, S. Rhodesia) *Cambridge, Sussex, Durham, Natal, and England*

An outstandingly brilliant fieldsman and attractive right-handed middle-order batsman, Paul Parker comes from a large and talented family based near Horsham. His father was a journalist in Rhodesia when Paul was born in Bulawayo. His career had a spectacular start with two big innings as a freshman at Cambridge against Yorkshire, and Essex, whom he hit for 215 at Fenner's in 1976. He made his début for Sussex the same year and has been a regular member of the side since coming down from Cambridge for whom he also played Rugby, missing a blue only because of injury. Inconsistency and an apparent frailty against fast bowling early in an innings held him back, but overseas experience first in South Australia then in South Africa matured him enough to make him a candidate for England throughout 1981, when he scored 1,416 runs (45.67) and hit four championship hundreds. Eventually picked for the final Test of the summer against Australia, his only Test to date, he was out for 0 and 13 and was not selected for the subsequent tour of India. An intense, principled, intelligent man, he had two prolific seasons in 1984 and 1986 and his positive, attractive and orthodox batting, added to his electrifying, India-rubber fielding, helped Sussex to win the John Player League in 1982 and the NatWest Trophy in 1986. For some years he was a stockbroker in the winter months but never had a quicker return than in 1986 when one of his sixes hit a large artificial egg placed on the boundary at

Hove, for which the sponsors, an egg company, awarded him £2,000. Captain of Sussex from 1988 to 1991, he moved to Durham in 1992, playing for them in their first two seasons before retiring to a teaching post at Tonbridge School.

First-class career (1976–93): 19,419 runs (35.05) including 47 centuries, 11 wickets (69.90), and 257 catches

PARKHOUSE, William Gilbert Anthony

(b. 1925, Swansea, Glamorgan) *Glamorgan and England*

Gilbert Parkhouse was a sound right-handed opening batsman. He was also a brilliant slip field. For England he hit 69 against the West Indies at Trent Bridge in 1950 and—recalled to the Test arena after nine years—a memorable 78 against India at Headingley in 1959, putting on 146 with Geoff Pullar for the first wicket. But his failure in Australia in 1950/1 hung like a cloud over his career. For Glamorgan he shared many a long opening stand with Bernard Hedges. He exceeded 1,000 runs in a season fifteen times.

First-class career (1948–64): 23,508 runs (31.68) including 32 centuries, 2 wickets (62.50), and 324 catches
Test matches (7): 373 runs (28.69) and 3 catches

PARKIN, Cecil Harry

(b. 1886, Egglescliffe, Co. Durham; d. 1943, Cheetham Hill, Manchester) *Durham, Yorkshire, Lancashire, and England*

Although born in County Durham, 'Ciss' Parkin played once for Yorkshire before joining Lancashire, and also devoted much time to Staffordshire and other league cricket. Of medium height and rather slim, he was a splendid natural bowler. A clown and an eccentric, he relied mainly on the off-break, cleverly varying pace and spin. He toured Australia in 1920/1 with MCC and, although England were outplayed, Parkin took most wickets—16 (41.87)—in the series. He headed the bowling against the almost equally devastating Australians in 1921, with 16 wickets (26.25) from four Tests. But, after criticizing his captain, Arthur Gilligan, in the Test against South Africa at Edgbaston in 1924 (in a national newspaper), he was dropped from the England side and, two years later, returned full-time to league cricket. Cricket's chief comedian at that time, he could talk almost as well as he bowled, and was forever playing to the gallery, conjuring the ball out of his pocket or flicking it from his toe to his head. His son, Reginald, also played for Lancashire.

First-class career (1906–26): 2,425 runs (11.77), 1,048 wickets (17.58), and 126 catches
Test matches (10): 160 runs (12.30), 32 wickets (35.25), and 3 catches

PARKS, James Horace

(b. 1903, Haywards Heath, Sussex; d. 1980, Cuckfield, Sussex) *Sussex, Auckland, and England*

Short and stocky, James Parks was a solid and fearless right-handed opening batsman, a medium-pace in-swing bowler and a brilliant fielder. Although generally a workaday all-rounder, he made 3,003 runs (50.89) in 1937, including 11 centuries, and took 101 wickets (25.83), besides holding 21 catches—a performance which is unlikely to be repeated. His sole Test was against New Zealand at Lord's in 1937, when he scored 22 and 7 and took 3 for 36 (all lbw). He toured Australasia in 1935/6. In 1937 he added 297 for the fifth wicket with his brother, Harry, against Hampshire at Portsmouth, a long-standing Sussex record. His son, Jim, played for Sussex, Somerset, and England and his grandson, Bobby, for Hampshire.

First-class career (1924–52): 21,369 runs (30.74) including 41 centuries, 852 wickets (26.74), and 325 catches

PARKS, James Michael

(b. 1931, Haywards Heath, Sussex) *Sussex, Somerset, and England*

A sunny character, Jim Parks was a brilliant right-handed stroke-maker, especially quick on his feet to slow bowlers, who scored more than 2,300 runs in 1955 and 1959. He put the wicket-keeper's gloves on for the first time to help out when the regular Sussex 'keeper was injured and proved so safe and efficient standing back that he took over the post the following year, 1959. He played for England as batsman against Pakistan in 1954, and ten years later was picked as first-choice wicket-keeper. He dismissed 93 batsmen in both 1959 and 1961. A replacement for MCC in the West Indies, 1959/60, he came into the Test side at the eleventh hour and hit a match-saving 101 not out. When John Murray was injured in 1963, he established himself as England's 'keeper, taking some brilliant catches standing back, doing an adequate job to the spinners and making many useful runs. Between 1963 and 1967 he toured Australia, New Zealand, India, South Africa, and the West Indies. On twenty occasions he exceeded 1,000 runs in a season and he was a prolific scorer in limited-overs matches. In 1967 and 1968 he captained Sussex and later he played a few games for Somerset (1973–6). His father played for England, his uncle for Sussex and his son for Hampshire. He became commercial manager of Sussex.

First-class career (1949–76): 36,673 runs (34.76) including 51 centuries, 51 wickets (43.82), and 1,181 dismissals (1,088 c., 93 st.)

Test matches (46): 1,962 runs (32.16) including 2 centuries, and 114 dismissals (103 c., 11 st.)

PARR, George

(b. 1826, Radcliffe-on-Trent, Nottinghamshire; d. 1891, Radcliffe-on-Trent) *Nottinghamshire*

An effective rather than elegant right-handed batsman, George Parr—'the Lion of the North' —scored many of his runs by sweeping the ball to leg. This happened so frequently at Trent Bridge that a tree was named after him and a branch from it buried with him. He combined his cricket for Nottinghamshire with playing for the All-England XI. For the county, his best performance was 130 against Surrey at The Oval in 1859 while his right-arm under-arm slow bowling had earned him 23 wickets in a match for the All-England XI against odds at Boston two years earlier. He succeeded William Clarke as captain of the travelling side in 1856 and his own successor, Richard Daft, said of him 'a more honest and straight cricketer never took hold of a bat'. It is to Daft that we owe the story of Parr stranded on a Cornish moor and threatened at gun-point by a local. He also captained both Nottinghamshire and the Players (against the Gentlemen), and took the first and the third English teams overseas, to America in 1859 and to Australia in 1863/4. To lead men across moors, seas, and continents in the mid-nineteenth century called for particular qualities. Parr, as a player, was ranked by his contemporaries 'the best batsman in England' and regarded as 'shrewd, business-like and enterprising'. His colleagues in Australia were rewarded for their efforts with £250 apiece.

First-class career (1845–70): 6,626 runs (20.20) including 1 century, 29 wickets (15.34), and 126 catches

PATAUDI, NAWAB OF (Iftiqar Ali Khan)

(b. 1910, Pataudi, India; d. 1952, New Delhi) *Oxford University, Worcestershire, Southern Punjab, England, and India*

Coached by Frank Woolley when he came to England at the age of 16, Pataudi's fluent right-handed stroke-play was based on a patient and correct technique. Naturally gifted, he loved a challenge. He scored 238 not out for Oxford against Cambridge at Lord's in 1931, the record innings in the contests, a typical response to Alan Ratcliffe's double-century for Cambridge in the same game. In his first Test, against Australia at Sydney in 1932/3, he made 102. In a short career for Worcestershire he scored heavily, making 224 not out, 231 not out and 222 against Kent, Essex and Somerset respectively in 1933, and having an average of 91 in 1934. He represented England against Australia at Trent Bridge in 1934. Thereafter, he was handicapped by ill-health. Returning to India, he appeared in only one Ranji Trophy match, but captained the Indian team to England in 1946, when he reached 981 runs (46.71), including four centuries, on the tour, but achieved little in the Tests. He died of a heart attack while playing polo. His son also captained India.

First-class career (1928–46): 8,750 runs (48.61) including 29 centuries, 15 wickets (35.26), and 58 catches

Test matches (England—3): 144 runs (28.80) including 1 century. (India—3): 55 runs (11.00)

PAYNTER, Edward

(b. 1901, Oswaldtwistle, Lancashire; d. 1979, Keighley, Yorkshire) *Lancashire and England*

A perky left-handed batsman with an unquenchable Lancastrian spirit, Eddie Paynter had a perfect temperament. Amazingly enough, for a batsman with a Test average of 59, he only played his first game for his county at 24 and did not gain a regular place until he was 29. Small and wiry, he invested his strokes with remarkable power and drove, cut and pulled with delightful facility. Against Australia in seven Tests he averaged 84.42, his highest score being 216 not out at Trent Bridge in 1938, when he was a natural counter to the prevailing Australian leg-spin. In that series he averaged 101.75. In South Africa in 1938/9, he made 243 at Durban and 653 runs (81.62) in the series. Paynter's most legendary performance, however, was during his only tour of Australia in 1932/3, when he rose from a sick-bed at Brisbane, played a heroic first innings of

83, and in the second hit the winning six just before rain began falling heavily. Between 1932 and 1938 he exceeded 2,000 runs in a season four times; his career highest was 322 (in 5 hours) against Sussex at Hove in 1937. Although he had lost the tops of the first and second fingers of his right hand in an accident, he was a good cover-point and deep field.

First-class career (1926–50): 20,075 runs (42.26) including 45 centuries, 30 wickets (45.70), and 160 catches

Test matches (20): 1,540 runs (59.23) including 4 centuries, and 7 catches

PEARCE, Thomas Neill

(b. 1905, Stoke Newington; d. 1994, Worthing, Sussex) *Essex*

The need for a regular captain of Essex brought Tom Pearce to prominence in 1933 when he shared the office with Denys Wilcox. Pearce's employer in the wine trade, T. G. Grinter and a former Essex player himself, released him until Wilcox, a preparatory school headmaster was free in July. The arrangement worked well, not least because both men were thoroughly worth their place in the side, coming first and second in the averages in 1937. After the war Pearce took sole charge and full-time of an Essex side without the strong bowling attack the county had enjoyed in the 1930s. Three players had been killed (including Kenneth Farnes) and he rebuilt the side. Again, as a free-scoring right-handed bats-man he set the example, scoring 1,597 runs in 1948 and making his highest score of 211 not out against Leicestershire at Westcliffe. A few weeks earlier he had led Essex (and made 79 himself in the match) at Southend when the Australians made 721 but 'no other county in 1948 bowled them out in a day', he later remarked. Mean-while, he was grooming the young Douglas Insole and Trevor Bailey for future leadership and in 1949 he resigned the captaincy while embark-ing on a spell as an England selector. His other contributions included being chairman and presi-dent of the Club, selecting an annual side for the Scarborough Festival and managing the MCC tour of 1961/2 to India, Pakistan, and Ceylon (Sri Lanka). His genial, generous and imperturbable character was also displayed as a distinguished international rugby referee. He gained a TD and an OBE.

First-class career (1929–52): 12,061 runs (34.26) including 22 centuries, 15 wickets (61.80), and 153 dismissals

PEATE, Edmund

(b. 1855, Holbeck, Leeds; d. 1900, Horsforth, Leeds) *Yorkshire and England*

Although Ted Peate began with a troupe of Treloar's 'Clown Cricketers', he graduated in Yorkshire circles as the first of that county's line of famous left-arm slow bowlers. His bowling was extremely accurate and marked by just enough break to beat the bat. He toured Australia in 1881/2; and in the classic Oval Test of 1882 he opened the bowling and had a match record of 8 for 71. Until 1886 he was a first choice for Tests in England. Six times he took more than 100 wick-ets in a season. His career was brilliant but short. According to *Wisden*, 'he would have lasted longer if he had ordered his life more carefully.'

First-class career (1879–90): 2,384 runs (10.64), 1,076 wickets (13.48), and 132 catches

Test matches (9): 70 runs (11.66), 31 wickets (22.03), and 2 catches

PEEBLES, Ian Alexander Ross

(b. 1908, Aberdeen, Scotland; d. 1980, Speen, Bucks) *Oxford University, Middlesex, Scotland, and England*

Ian Peebles was a tall and talented leg-spinner from Scotland, who became one of the most brilliant and humorous of all cricket writers. He toured South Africa in 1927/8—and played in Tests—before appearing for Middlesex and Oxford. He learned his trade as secretary of the Aubrey Faulkner School of Cricket. There he developed a bowling action which was a model of its kind, flowing and easy. He was educated at Glasgow Academy and joined Middlesex in 1928, taking his first 100 wickets the following year. In the University match at Lord's in 1930 he cap-tured 13 Cambridge wickets. Always a severe test for batsmen with his deceptive googly and loop-ing flight, he dismissed Don Bradman for 14 at Old Trafford in 1930, after the great man had been floundering against him, and at The Oval took 6 for 204 in 71 overs. He revisited South Africa with MCC in 1930/1 and emerged with honour. Subsequently, he toured India, America, Ceylon, Malaya, and Egypt (usually with Sir Julien Cahn's team), enjoying a vast amount of cricket. He captained Middlesex successfully in 1939, but played less regularly after the War. Cricket correspondent of *The Sunday Times* for many years, his writing was always witty, shrewd, and polished whether it appeared in newspapers or in the many books he wrote.

First-class career (1927–48): 2,213 runs (9.66), 923 wickets (21.38), and 172 catches
Test matches (13): 98 runs (10.88), 45 wickets (30.91), and 5 catches

PEEL, Robert

(b. 1857, Churwell, Leeds; d. 1941, Leeds)
Yorkshire and England

Small and sturdy, Bobby Peel (no relation of the Prime Minister) was second in line to the great Yorkshire left-arm spin bowlers. To him length was the key; and he kept it no matter how severely he was attacked. Moreover, he was a punishing left-handed batsman, and an excellent cover-point. He visited Australia four times between 1884 and 1895 and never had a poor tour. In 1894/5 he took 27 wickets (26.70) in the five matches. In England he was equally successful. At Old Trafford in 1888 his 11 for 68 won the match, and at The Oval in 1896 Australia collapsed for 44 in the second innings, Peel taking 6 for 23. He achieved the double once, in 1896, when he hit his career highest, 210 not out against Warwickshire at Edgbaston, adding 292 for the eighth wicket with Lord Hawke. But one day in 1897 he came on the field under the influence of alcohol, and, it is reputed, urinated on the pitch in front of his lordship, who thereupon banished him from the Yorkshire XI. Years later, Lord Hawke said: 'He never bore me any malice.'

First-class career (1882–99): 12,191 runs (19.44) including 7 centuries, 1,775 wickets (16.20), and 214 catches
Test matches (20): 427 runs (14.72), 101 wickets (16.98), and 17 catches

PENN, Frank

(b. 1851, Lewisham, London; d. 1916, Patrixbourne, Kent) *Kent and England*

Although his career in first-class cricket was cut short by a heart disorder, Frank Penn achieved some very good performances for his county and the Gentlemen as a free, commanding batsman who hit to all parts of the field, a good cover-point or long-leg and a useful slow, round-arm bowler. He toured Australia with Lord Harris's team in 1878/9, but his only Test was the first Test in England at The Oval, 1880, when he bowled three overs for 2 runs and hit 23 and 27 not out, cutting for four the ball which gave England victory. The following year he retired from first-class cricket. In 1905 he was president of Kent; and his two brothers and son, Frank, also

played for the county. In 61 matches for Kent between 1875 and 1881, he scored 2,906 runs (29.35), including six centuries, and took eight wickets (38.87).

First-class career (1875–81): 4,291 runs (27.15) including 6 centuries, 10 wickets (37.10), and 49 catches

PERKS, Reginald Thomas David

(b. 1911, Hereford; d. 1977, Worcester)
Worcestershire, Herefordshire, Monmouthshire, and England

Tall and broad-shouldered, Reg Perks bowled right-arm fast-medium with very good control. Attacking the stumps, he had a long smooth run, a perfect high action with a sweeping follow-through and a sharp late in-swing. He took at least 100 wickets in a season sixteen times, taking more wickets for his county than anyone else. As a left-handed batsman, he was a bold and sometimes effective hitter. He toured South Africa with MCC in 1938/9 and played in the last Test against the West Indies in 1939 which was his best year with 159 wickets (19.22). Still a force after the War, he captured 14 for 96 (including 9 for 42) against Gloucestershire at Cheltenham in 1946.

First-class career (1930–55): 8,956 runs (12.20), 2,233 wickets (24.08), and 240 catches
Test matches (2): 3 runs (—), 11 wickets (32.27), and 1 catch

PHILIPSON, Hylton

(b. 1866, Tynemouth, Northumberland; d. 1935, London) *Oxford University, Middlesex, Northumberland, and England*

An Old Etonian, 'Punch' Philipson was a competent and versatile batsman and an excellent wicket-keeper who, standing up to most bowlers, took the ball with easy grace. Though only an irregular with Middlesex, he toured Australia with Lord Sheffield's and A. E. Stoddart's teams of 1891/2 and 1894/5. He also got blues for rackets, tennis, and soccer.

First-class career (1887–99): 1,951 runs (17.41) including 2 centuries, and 150 dismissals (103 c., 47 st.)
Test matches (5): 63 runs (9.00) and 11 dismissals (8 c., 3 st.)

PIGOTT, Antony Charles Shackleton

(b. 1958, London) *Sussex, Surrey, Wellington, and England*

A 'never-say-die' right-arm fast-medium bowler and a right-handed lower-order batsman, Tony

Pigott was in New Zealand playing for Wellington when an injury crisis led to his unexpected call-up into the England side for the Christchurch Test in 1983/4. He tried his hardest, taking 2 for 75 and scoring 4 and 8 not out, but England were humiliatingly beaten by New Zealand. This was so far, his only Test appearance. He postponed his marriage in order to make it. Educated at Harrow, Pigott enjoyed his best seasons in 1983, when he took 72 wickets (26.23), and 1988 (74 wickets at 28.08). He took a hat-trick against Surrey at Hove in 1978, not only in his first match, but with his first three balls of the 2nd innings. 1986 was another successful season: he made his maiden hundred and helped Sussex to victory in the NatWest Trophy Final at Lord's. A less happy bowling performance in the 1993 Final led to Sussex releasing him, but Surrey snapped up his services and he soon justified their confidence with some useful performances.

First-class career (1978–   ): 4,765 runs (19.77) including 1 century, and 650 wickets (31.02)

PILCH, Fuller

(b. 1804, Horningtoft, Norfolk; d. 1870, Canterbury, Kent) *Norfolk and Kent*

Arthur Haygarth's writing and G. F. Watts' engraving have left us a vivid image of Fuller Pilch, a tall slim and graceful right-handed batsman, 'very commanding, extremely forward'. Beginning his career with Norfolk by fielding to William Ward's 278 at Lord's in 1820, Pilch went north to Sheffield where the Hambledon veteran, William Fennex coached him. In 1834 he twice vanquished Thomas Marsden, hitherto the undisputed single-wicket champion of the country. In the following year round-arm bowling was legalized: Pilch learnt to play it and to bowl it himself. Coming south to Kent, he became a key figure in a side capable of beating the Rest of England and often doing so. W. J. Prowse's stanza said of Kent:

And with five such mighty cricketers, 'twas but
   natural to win,
As Felix, Wenman, Hillyer, Fuller Pilch and Alfred
   Mynn.

James Pycroft used him as the model of classic batting in his *The Cricket Field* while countless players tried to emulate him as he played against odds for William Clarke's All-England XI. He would travel with his own scythe to give an extra cut to the crude pitches on which he had to play. After he had retired, he umpired a match in which the young W. G. Grace played his first important game—against the All-England XI.

First-class career (1820–54): 7,147 runs (18.61) including 3 centuries, 9 + 133 wickets (20.44), and 121 catches

PILLING, Richard

(b. 1855, Old Warden, Bedfordshire; d. 1891, Manchester) *Lancashire and England*

Dick Pilling was, perhaps, the outstanding professional wicket-keeper of his day. He was known as 'The Prince of Wicket-Keepers' and his style was described as 'the perfection of neatness and rapidity'. He visited Australia with Shaw's and Shrewsbury's teams of 1881/2 and 1887/8 (besides appearing in three Tests in England) and, when his never robust health was seen to be failing, he went there on medical advice in 1890. His case, however, was hopeless and he returned home to die.

First-class career (1877–89): 2,572 runs (9.85) and 667 dismissals (459 c., 208 st.)

Test matches (8): 91 runs (7.58) and 14 dismissals (10 c., 4 st.)

PINTER, Harold

(b. 1930, London)

To write that 'cricket is the greatest thing that God ever created on earth' places the distinguished playwright, actor, and director Harold Pinter firmly in the front rank of the game's devotees. In plays such as *No Man's Land* (1975) ('In other words, did she google?') cricket is found in his lines. For his own club, the Gaieties, he was, paradoxically, an extremely serious cricketer, and sometime president. He was awarded a CBE for services to the theatre.

PLACE, Winston

(b. 1914, Rawtenstall, Lancashire) *Lancashire and England*

Winston Place was a discovery of 1946. Before the Second World War he was just an ordinary right-handed batsman, but when the game was resumed he became the perfect foil to Cyril Washbrook as Lancashire's opener. Dependable, self-effacing, conscientious, he could drive high over the bowler's head, indulge in a hefty pull and produce a classic cover-drive. Sure defence against the turning ball was another characteristic of his batting. In 1947/8 he toured the West Indies with MCC, scoring 107 in the fourth Test at Kingston (when the West Indies won the rubber) and in 1949/50 he visited India with the Commonwealth team. Place passed 1,000 runs in a season eight times, his best year being 1947 when he made 2,501 runs (62.52). He became a first-class umpire.

First-class career (1937–55): 15,609 runs (35.63) including 36 centuries, 1 wicket (42.00), and 190 catches
Test matches (3): 144 runs (28.80) including 1 century

POCOCK, Patrick Ian

(b. 1946, Bangor, Caernarvonshire, Wales) *Surrey, Northern Transvaal, and England*

Both as a gauche teenager on the Surrey staff and as a mature Test player, Pat, or 'Percy', Pocock remained the same cheerful, open, friendly, talkative character. It was obvious from an early age that he had outstanding ability as an off-spinner. Tall and strong, he was a sharp spinner of the ball despite persistent bother from blisters on his spinning finger, and possessed a perfect, high, sideways-on action, but he disappointingly failed to develop his full potential at the highest level. He bowled impressively on the demanding pitches of the Caribbean on his first tour of 1967/8, taking over from F. J. Titmus when the latter was injured, but was dropped despite taking 6 for 79 in the second innings of the first Test against Australia in 1968. (Lawry had punished him in the first innings.) In helpful conditions Pocock would bowl a side out quicker than most off-spinners in the world, but overseas he tended to experiment too much rather than just wheel away and let his action take wickets for him. Equally effective for Surrey in both three-day and one-day cricket, he took two hat-tricks, one during an amazing spell against Sussex in 1972 when he took four wickets in four balls, five in six, six in nine and seven in 11—the last two are records. Significantly this was at Eastbourne, not The Oval where wickets gave him little assistance. He was a capable fielder and a stylish, sometimes useful right-hand batsman. There was a well-deserved postscript to Pocock's Test career. The most consistent and long-serving of all England's off-spinners, he was rewarded with a place in the Test side in 1984 at the age of 37, eight times after his last appearance. He contained the West Indian batsmen expertly and played an important part in England's triumph in India in 1984/5. He bowled 237 accurate overs and took 13 wickets in the five Tests. He was appointed county captain in 1986, and his widespread popularity was recognized when he was

elected to an executive position on the Cricketers' Association. Having taken Surrey to third place in the Championship and into the semi-final of the NatWest Trophy, he retired after a quarter of a century as a professional cricketer.

First-class career (1964–86): 4,867 runs (11.34), 1,607 wickets (26.53), and 186 catches
Test matches (25): 206 runs (6.24), 67 wickets (44.41), and 15 catches

POLLARD, Richard

(b. 1912, Westhoughton, Lancashire; d. 1985, Westhoughton) *Lancashire and England*

Dick Pollard was a right-arm, fast-medium bowler with a long, padding, flat-foot run, who could move the ball either way and seemed to bowl faster as he warmed to his task; and his stamina was immense. But he lost his best years to the War. In his first Test, against India at Old Trafford in 1946, he took 5 for 24 (in 27 overs) in the first innings. He toured Australasia in 1946/7, appearing in one Test in New Zealand, and played twice against Australia in 1948. He dismissed Don Bradman twice for low scores.

First-class career (1933–50): 3,522 runs (13.29), 1,122 wickets (22.56), and 225 catches
Test matches (4): 13 runs (13.00), 15 wickets (25.20), and 3 catches

PONSONBY FANE, Sir Spencer Cecil Brabazon

(b. 1824, London; d. 1915, Yeovil, Somerset) *Surrey and Middlesex*

Making his début for MCC at the age of 15 in 1839 (the year before his election), Ponsonby Fane was a member for 75 years, and treasurer for 36 of them. He was responsible for building-up from scratch the valuable collection of pictures and prints at Lord's. As a right-handed batsman, he was 'a free and lively hitter, forward and leg' but with a reputation for running out both himself and his partners. His only century was for the Gentlemen of England against those of Kent and Sussex at Canterbury in 1856, a place where he figured more frequently on the stage, as a founder member of the Old Stagers who performed regularly at the Canterbury Week. He was also a founder member and player of both Surrey and the I Zingari and nearly 50 years later he became president of Somerset. Cricket apart, Ponsonby Fane had been private secretary to Lord Palmerston, the bearer of the Treaty of Paris to England after the Crimean War, British attaché at Washington, and comptroller of the Lord Chamberlain's Office.

First-class career (1841–64): 1,359 runs (11.92) including 1 century, 2 + 12 wickets (24.00), and 32 dismissals (30 c., 2 st.)

POOLE, Cyril John

(b. 1921, Mansfield, Nottinghamshire)
Nottinghamshire and England

At his peak in the 1950s, Cyril Poole was one of the best left-handed attacking stroke-makers in county cricket and, as befitted a professional footballer, he was brilliant in the deep. He toured India with MCC in 1951/2, making two fifties in three Tests, and made his highest score, 222 not out, for his county against the Indians at Trent Bridge in 1952, an uncharacteristically grim effort. In contrast he reached a century in sixty minutes (154 not out in 97 minutes) against Leicestershire at Trent Bridge in 1949.

First-class career (1948–62): 19,364 runs (32.54) including 24 centuries, 4 wickets (86.75), 224 catches, and 5 stumpings
Test matches (3): 161 runs (40.25), 0–9, and 1 catch

POPE, George Henry

(b. 1911, Tibshelf, Derbyshire; d. 1993, Chesterfield, Derbyshire) *Derbyshire and England*

Tall and spare, George Pope was one of three brothers who played for Derbyshire, Alfred and Harold being the others. He was a lively, right-arm, medium-pace bowler and, as a batsman, seemed a natural hitter who had schooled himself into a necessary restraint, without overdoing it. He possessed considerable speed in the field and when he 'bent' to pick up a ball from the ground, his back was completely straight. He achieved the double twice and in 1937 he hit three centuries in a month. In his sole Test, against South Africa at Lord's in 1947, he scored 8 not out and, as opening bowler, took 1 for 85. He also played in the three 'Victory Tests' against the Australian Services in 1945, and toured India with the Commonwealth team in 1949/50. In 1948 he did the double for the second time, scoring 207 not out at Portsmouth, but retired from full-time cricket because of his wife's ill-health. He became, however, something of a legend in northern League cricket, making skilful use of the leg-cutter which Alec Bedser had first learned from his brother Alfred.

First-class career (1933–48): 7,518 runs (28.05) including 8 centuries, 677 wickets (19.92), and 157 catches

POUGHER, Arthur Dick

(b. 1865, Leicester; d. 1926, Leicester)
Leicestershire and England

An all-rounder, Dick Pougher achieved much of his best work before his county became first-class in 1894. Bowling right-arm medium-pace with a high action, his stock ball was the off-break which came sharply off the pitch; he could also turn enough from leg to beat the bat. As a batsman, he used his height, reach and straightness of bat to play many useful innings. For MCC at Lord's in 1896 Pougher and Jack Hearne dismissed the Australians for 18; Pougher took 5 for 0 in 15 balls, coming on to bowl with the score at 18 for 3! Yet he never represented England against Australia. He toured Australia with Shrewsbury's team in 1887/8 and South Africa with W. W. Read's in 1891/2. At Cape Town in his sole Test he scored 17, took 3 for 26 and held 2 catches. He became owner of the pub which adjoined the county cricket ground at Leicester.

First-class career (1886–1902): 4,555 runs (18.59) including 5 centuries, 535 wickets (19.02), and 98 catches

PRICE, John Sidney Ernest

(b. 1937, Harrow, Middlesex) *Middlesex and England*

Strongly built, John Price was a determined, right-arm fast bowler with a long, crescent-shaped run-up who, unhappily, was never free from injury for long. He was a willing work-horse, however, distinctly sharp when firing on all cylinders and lacking only an especially steep bounce. He toured India and South Africa, but his appearances for England were spread over nine years and he never made his place secure. His best performance was at Calcutta in 1963/4 when he took 5 for 73 in India's first innings in his second Test. In the previous match he had taken 3 for 66 and 2 for 47 and, normally a left-hand batsman of no account, scored 32 going in at number eight for a team stricken by illness and injuries. In 1966 he took 94 wickets (18.74) including 8 for 48 against Derbyshire at Lord's.

First-class career (1961–75): 1,108 runs (8.39), 817 wickets (23.52), and 103 catches
Test matches (15): 66 runs (7.33), 40 wickets (35.02), and 7 catches

PRICE, Wilfred Frederick Frank

(b. 1902, London; d. 1969, Hendon, Middlesex)
Middlesex and England

A very safe wicket-keeper, Fred Price became a distinctly useful batsman—known as the 'Rock of Gibraltar' because of his defensive methods—and he often opened his county's batting. In 1937 he created a then world record by taking 7 catches in Yorkshire's first innings at Lord's. Afterwards a lady congratulated him. 'I was so thrilled with your performance, Mr Price, that I nearly fell over the balcony.' 'If you had, Madam,' replied Fred, 'I would have caught you as well!' He joined MCC as a replacement in the West Indies in 1929/30 and India in 1937/8, but his sole Test was against Australia at Headingley in 1938, when he scored 0 and 6 and held 2 catches.

First-class career (1926–47): 9,035 runs (18.33) including 3 centuries, and 987 dismissals (666 c., 321 st.)

PRIDEAUX, Roger Malcolm

(b. 1939, London) *Cambridge University, Kent, Northamptonshire, Sussex, Orange Free State, and England*

A gifted, natural, right-handed opening batsman, Roger Prideaux was outstanding both at Tonbridge and at Cambridge. He had an attractive upright style, was particularly strong off the front foot and played with an air of calm authority. Indeed it is surprising that he played in only three Tests. He scored two centuries in the match between Cambridge and Somerset at Taunton in 1960 and again for Northamptonshire against Nottinghamshire at Trent Bridge in 1966. His century in 52 minutes (118 in 60 minutes), for South against North at Blackpool in 1961, was the fastest in first-class cricket since 1937. His highest score was 202 not out for Northamptonshire against Oxford in the Parks in 1963. He played for Northamptonshire from 1961 until 1970, and as captain from 1967. In his first Test, against Australia at Headingley in 1968, he hit an outstanding 64, adding 123 for the first wicket with John Edrich. But he was unfit for the next match at The Oval, being replaced by Basil d'Oliveira and, because of the events which followed, Prideaux missed the chance to tour South Africa the following winter, when the tour was cancelled for political reasons. He did, however, tour Pakistan in 1968/9, and Canada and New Zealand with non-Test-playing MCC sides. Thirteen times he

exceeded 1,000 runs in a season. He settled in South Africa. His ex-wife, Ruth, was coach and manager of the England women's team.

First-class career (1958–75): 25,136 runs (34.29) including 41 centuries, 3 wickets (58.66), and 303 catches
Test matches (3): 102 runs (20.40) and 0–0

PRINGLE, Derek Raymond

(b. 1958, Nairobi, Kenya) *Cambridge University, Essex, and England*

An all-round cricketer of great strength and ability, Derek Pringle was a broadly built man of 6 ft. 5 in. who used his physical advantages to good effect. He was given sudden promotion to the England side in 1982 after captaining Cambridge with flair early in that season. He played for Cambridge for four years (1979–82) as a hard-striking right-hand batsman and a right-arm fast-medium bowler with an excellent action. He bowled impressively in his first series against India, taking four wickets on his début at Lord's, and he played several determined innings on the 1982/3 tour of Australia. Briefly recalled to the Test side in 1984, he had his finest match for England, scoring 46 not out and taking 5 for 108 against the West Indies at Edgbaston. But he was a much more mature cricketer when, in 1986, he resumed his Test career, with more success. His maiden Test fifty was scored against India at Lord's and in four Tests that season he scored 166 runs (20.75) and took 13 wickets (28.92). It was not enough to earn him a second tour to Australia. His father, Donald, played for East Africa in the 1975 World Cup. Derek himself probably enjoyed his finest hour in the World Cup in Australia and New Zealand, 16 years later, his second successive appearance in the final. Bowling superbly throughout with a white ball which he swung dangerously, he might have bowled his country to victory had not Javed Miandad been given not out when apparently plumb in front early in Pakistan's innings. Throughout his career he was consistently useful for Essex in the most successful period of their history but he could never hold down a regular England place, perhaps because his batting did not develop at the highest level. An intelligent, unconventional, amiable man and an insatiable reader and photographer, he became cricket correspondent of *The Sunday Independent* in 1994 and broadcasting opportunities followed.

PULLAR

First-class career (1978–93): 9,243 runs (28.26)
including 10 centuries, 761 wickets (26.58), and
153 catches
Test matches (30): 695 runs (15.10), 70 wickets
(35.97), and 10 catches

PULLAR, Geoffrey

(b. 1935, Swinton, Lancashire) *Lancashire,
Gloucestershire, and England*

A tall, strong left-handed batsman, Geoff Pullar
was known as 'Noddy' because of his ability to
fall asleep in almost any situation. But he was
awake enough at the crease, playing mainly off
the front foot and accumulating runs assiduously
on the leg-side. He started as a middle-order
batsman but his solid technique and phlegmatic
temperament persuaded the England selectors to
choose him as an opening batsman in 1959. He
responded with 75 against India at Headingley,
followed by 131 at Old Trafford, the latter being
the first Test century scored by a Lancastrian
batsman at Old Trafford. After withstanding the
West Indian fast bowlers calmly and successfully
in 1959/60, he made 175 against South Africa at
The Oval in 1960 (his career-highest), sharing in
an opening stand of 290 with Colin Cowdrey. He
toured India and Pakistan in 1961/2—reaching
1,000 runs—and Australia in 1962/3. But both in
the latter series and in the 1961 series in England
he failed against Australia, his highest score being
63 from nine matches. His 28 Tests were concentrated between 1959 and 1963. Giving up opening, he found form again. He played for
Gloucestershire in 1969 and 1970. Ten times he
exceeded 1,000 runs in a season.

First-class career (1954–70): 21,528 runs (35.34)
including 41 centuries, 10 wickets (38.70), and
125 catches
Test matches (28): 1,974 runs (43.86) including 4
centuries, 1–37, and 2 catches

PULLIN, Alfred

(b. 1860, Yorkshire; d. 1934, London)

Pigeons had to be strong to bear the weighty
reports 'Old Ebor' sent from the Yorkshire
county grounds in his early days to the offices of
the *Yorkshire Post* and *Evening Post*. The public
wanted their money's worth—at least two columns—and for 40 years Pullin travelled with the
Yorkshire team, giving them long and detailed
factual reports. His several books included a
History of Yorkshire County Cricket (1924). Two of
them, *Talks with Old Yorkshire Cricketers* (1898)
and *Talks with Old English Cricketers* (1900) high-

lighted the poverty which might face professionals in old age. He had found one of them
destitute and in rags. Both Lord Hawke and Sir
Leonard Hutton—spanning the generations
—paid him warm tributes in their memoirs. In
winter, he played an equal role as a Rugby
football reporter.

PYCROFT, Revd James

(b. 1813, Wiltshire; d. 1895, Brighton, Sussex)
Oxford University

While still an undergraduate at Oxford, James
Pycroft published in 1835 his *Principles of Scientific
Batting*. In the following year he organized (after
a gap of seven years) the match against Cambridge, opened the batting and probably captained Oxford. His 85 not out in the same year for
Non-Wykhamists against Wykhamists at Oxford
is his highest recorded score and in 1838 he again
played at Lord's for Left-Handed Batsmen against
MCC. Thereafter, he played club cricket, principally for Lansdown CC in Bath. In his last match
for them he was—in the modern phrase—being
subjected to 'sledging' by the opposition. He
replied, 'I'll tell you what gentlemen: I am here to
guard three stumps, so I claim to play accordingly.' *The Cricket Field*, published in 1851 and
running to nine editions, including an American
one in 1859, is his main claim to fame. Lord
Harris did not know of a theoretical treatise on
batting 'one whit better or more readable'. To
instruction, Pycroft adds history. He is one of the
major sources of our knowledge of the early days
by his recording the reminiscences of John Nyren,
the thoughts of John Mitford, the anecdotes of
William Beldham and the exploits of Fuller Pilch.
The game to Pycroft was 'a standing panegyric
on the English character . . . and of good
fellowship'. Like many a Victorian writer, his
interests were eclectic, including *The Advantages
and Temptations of a University Education*, *The
Public Health Act of 1863*, *Oxford Memories*, and the
novel *Elkerton Rectory*. Moving to Brighton, he
served for 30 years on the Sussex Committee.
E. V. Lucas remembered seeing 'a tall, erect
clerical figure, with a cape and a silk hat'.

QUAIFE, William

(b. 1872, Newhaven, Sussex; d. 1951, Birmingham)
*Sussex, Warwickshire, Griqualand West, and
England*

Adding the initial 'G' to differentiate between his
elder brother, Walter, and himself when they

were both with Sussex, Willie Quaife joined Warwickshire after one season and played for them for 35 years. In his first match for the Midland county he made 115 not out against Durham in 1893, and in his last, 115 against Derbyshire in 1928. A model right-handed batsman, a slow leg-break bowler and a fine coverpoint, he was, perhaps, the smallest man to play for England against Australia. Very sound in defence, he played with a very straight bat, demonstrating perfect balance, footwork and control. On 25 occasions he exceeded 1,000 runs in a season, his best year being 1905 with 2,060 runs (54.21) including his career-highest, 255 not out against Surrey at The Oval. However he was rarely successful in Tests, his best performances being 68 and 44 at Adelaide in 1901/2.

First-class career (1894–1928): 36,012 runs (35.37) including 72 centuries, 931 wickets (27.32), 354 catches, and 1 stumping
Test matches (7): 228 runs (19.00), 0–6, and 4 catches

RADFORD, Neal Victor

(b. 1957, Luanshya, Northern Rhodesia) *Lancashire, Worcestershire, Transvaal, and England*

Neal Radford was educated in Johannesburg but settled in Britain after playing league cricket in Lancashire and joining the county club in 1980. A wiry, swarthy, vigorous, hustling, accurate right-arm fast-medium bowler, good fielder, and useful right-handed batsman, he relied mainly on swing and clever changes of pace. He rightly prided himself on his fitness, and gave Worcestershire loyal and useful service in all types of cricket after five years with Lancashire during which he never fully established himself. For Transvaal, he took 32 wickets in 1984/5 prior to becoming the most successful bowler in county cricket in 1985 in his first year at Worcester. His 101 wickets in that season were followed by 42 more by the end of June the following summer when he played in the third Test against India at Edgbaston and the first against New Zealand at Lord's. He bowled with perseverance and stamina but lacked the devil his bowling usually possesses. His sole tour for England was to New Zealand in 1987/8, but the bland pitches there did not suit him, or any bowler.

First-class career (1978–): 3,407 runs (15.77) and 972 wickets (26.63)
Test matches (3): 21 runs (7.00) and 4 wickets (87.75)

RADLEY, Clive Thornton

(b. 1944, Hertford) *Norfolk, Middlesex, and England*

A small, chunkily built right-handed batsman from Norfolk, Clive Radley was always a consistent accumulator of runs. Effective rather than attractive, he watched the ball intently, cut well, and played skilfully within his limitations, often inventing his own strokes and running brilliantly between the wickets. Although a natural fighter, he proved suspect against the fast lifting ball in Australia. He was a fine close field. He scored 1,000 runs in a season 16 times and until 1994 he shared the sixth-wicket partnership record for the county, 227 with Fred Titmus, against the South Africans at Lord's in 1965. He toured Pakistan and New Zealand 1977/8 and Australia 1978/9 and in his second Test, against New Zealand at Auckland in 1977, he made a marathon score of 158. His second century was 106 against Pakistan at Edgbaston in 1978. As the elder statesman of the Middlesex side, he made his first double-century in 1985, exactly 200 against Northamptonshire at Uxbridge, and was rewarded with a new contract in 1986 when he often captained the county. Retiring a respected professional, he succeeded Don Wilson as head coach at Lord's.

First-class career (1964–87): 26,441 runs (35.44) including 46 centuries, 8 wickets (20,00), and 517 catches
Test matches (8): 481 runs (48.10) including 2 centuries, and 4 catches

RAIT KERR, Rowan Scrope

(b. 1891, County Wicklow, Ireland; d. 1961 Constantine, Cornwall) *The Army and Europeans*

'R.K.' was a right-handed batsman who carried his bat for Rugby School, with 54 not out, against Marlborough at Lord's in 1908 and returned there as MCC secretary in 1936. In between, his career as a 'sapper' had brought him a DSO and MC and plenty of runs in club cricket, especially while serving in India. After three years at Lord's, he returned to the army on the outbreak of war and became chairman of the War Office Selection Board for officers. In the post-war years he was mainly responsible for the Revised Code of Laws (1947) and later wrote a guide to them. Sir Pelham Warner, a fellow Rugbeian, who had held the fort at Lord's while Rait Kerr was away, called him 'the ablest secretary' MCC had had. His daughter, Diana (1918–), was the first curator at Lord's (1946–68), an authority on its collection of books, pictures, and cricketana and the joint-author (with Ian Peebles) of *Lord's, 1946–70*.

First-class career (1913–31): 89 runs (7.41) and 3 catches

RAMPRAKASH, Mark Ravindra

(b. 1969, Bushey, Hertfordshire) *Middlesex and England*

A prodigy at schoolboy level, and a prolific run-getter for his county, Mark Ramprakash struggled to convert his great talent into high scores in the Test arena. A compact right-hander, of intense temperament, he began promisingly by batting for over 17 hours in his first series against the West Indies in 1991, but three years later he had not established himself despite a burning will to do so. The good-looking son of a Guyanese father and English mother, he only took up the game aged 9, but was soon spotted by a Middlesex Colts coach, and in 1985, at the National Cricket Association Guernsey Festival Tournament, made an unbeaten 204. Chosen for the Young England tour of Sri Lanka in 1986/7, Ramprakash made 118 in $5\frac{1}{2}$ hours in the final 'Test' in Galle, and he made his début for Middlesex in 1987, scoring 63 not out against Yorkshire at Lord's. A-level studies limited his appearances both in that season and the next, although he still found time to play in the Youth World Cup in Australia, but it was in 1988 that he came to national prominence as he made 56 in the NatWest Final to win the man-of-the-match award on his début in the competition, helping Middlesex to victory after they had been 25 for 4 chasing 162. In 1989, he captained Young England against New Zealand, and after 1,541 runs the following summer, he was chosen for the A tour of Pakistan and Sri Lanka. Responding with 158 in a 'Test' in Kandy, he made his senior début in 1991, and played in all five Tests against the West Indies, scored 210 runs, despite never passing 30. His brace of 27s in his first match at Headingley were worth double as England beat the West Indies for the first time at home in 22 years. Ramprakash's brilliant fielding at cover was also a joy, with a diving catch and a run-out, also at Headingley, the highlights. There, however, his progress at Test level stopped. After a wretched tour of New Zealand, where he did not play a Test, he was omitted from the World Cup team and in 1992, three Tests against Pakistan brought just 31 runs. After losing his temper with a Cambridge off-spinner at Fenner's and a female spectator at Uxbridge, he was left out of both the next winter tours, despite having previously signed a winter

contract with the Test and County Cricket Board worth £15,000. In August 1993, his luck appeared to change when, set to play for Middlesex at Lord's, he was called up on the morning of The Oval Test against Australia when Graham Thorpe broke his thumb. Ramprakash made 64, his first Test fifty, England won, and he was chosen for the West Indies. Bafflingly omitted for the first Test despite a century in a warm-up match, he scored an unbeaten 154 in his father's country of origin to regain his place, but then scored only 73 runs in the rest of the series. Left out again throughout 1994, despite scoring 1,271 runs for Middlesex, he was vice-captain of the A tour to India, 1994/5, and made 72 and 42 as a replacement batsman against Australia in the last Test in Perth.

First-class career (1987–): 8,938 runs (40.63), 8 wickets (84.75), and 83 catches

Test matches (15): 498 runs (19.92) and 11 catches

RANDALL, Derek William

(b. 1951, Retford, Nottinghamshire) *Nottinghamshire, Suffolk, and England*

Of few cricketers can it be said with more truth that figures do not tell the full story. Derek Randall, first called 'Arkle' (after the great steeplechaser) when he lapped some of his Nottinghamshire colleagues on a training run, averaged only 26 after sixteen Tests for England before the tour of Australia in 1978/9, yet had already had an extraordinary effect on English cricket. In Australia, often faced with poor wickets, he made more runs (763 at 47.68) than anyone in the touring party and scored 385 Test runs at 38.50, returning home an established member of the side for the first time. Although he was a dedicated right-hand batsman with immense natural flair and a gift of timing, captains were always tempted to pick him for his fielding alone and he achieved many phenomenal run-outs. There was never a keener cover-point and it is difficult to think of any faster ones. Moreover his throwing became increasingly accurate. Covering some 15 yards towards the stumps as the bowler delivered Randall, was actually running as the batsman played his stroke and his acrobatics in the field inspired his colleagues in the MCC side on his first tour, to India and Australia in 1976/7. Although normally a somewhat diffident and self-conscious character, albeit irrepressibly talkative, he became a natural clown with an audience to play to, and, despite being a very nervous starter of an innings, he thrived on the big occasion. In March 1977 he played one of the great Test innings, cutting, driving, and hooking his way to a brilliant and audacious 174 in the second innings of the Centenary Test in Melbourne. Almost single-handed Randall took the fight to Dennis Lillee and turned potential anti-climax into a classic finish. A modest series against Australia at home in 1977, interrupted by an injury, was followed by failure on the winter tour of Pakistan and New Zealand but his second Test hundred, a staunch and patient 150 in the second innings of the fourth Test at Sydney in 1978/9, turned a series which was delicately balanced decisively England's way. Though he often got himself out with rash strokes, and would fidget about at the crease as the bowler delivered the ball, he was a character, an entertainer, and a batsman sometimes touched by genius, perhaps the spiritual son of another great but eccentric Nottinghamshire cricketer, George Gunn. He had a disastrous tour of Australia in 1979/80 and lost his place, but his Test career took on a new lease in 1982 when he hit entertaining and valuable hundreds for England against India at Lord's, going in at number six, and against Pakistan at Edgbaston when, against his will, he was tried as an opener. Making his fourth tour to Australia in 1982/3 he again enjoyed great success. Batting down the order once more he made 365 runs (45.62) in the series, including 115 at Perth, and headed the England Test averages. He played two important innings for England in the 1983 series against New Zealand, and in the winter scored two Test centuries against them. But, given the responsibility of going in at number three against the West Indies at Edgbaston in 1984, he made nought and one, and was immediately dropped. He always tried his heart out for England, but even 2,151 runs (53.77) in 1985 were not enough to win him a place on the tour of the West Indies and the rest of his days were cheerfully played out for Nottinghamshire. When the last over of the NatWest Final began in 1985, Nottinghamshire required 18 runs. Magically, Randall stroked 16 off the first five balls from the experienced England bowler Derek Pringle, but he was caught off the final ball and Essex won by one run.

First-class career (1972–93): 28,456 runs (38.14) including 52 centuries, 13 wickets (31.76), and 361 catches

Test matches (47): 2,470 runs (33.37) including 7 centuries, 0–3, and 31 catches

RANJITSINHJI, Kumar Shri (H. H. Jam Saheb of Nawanagar)

(b. 1872, Sarodar, India; d. 1933, Jamnagar)
Cambridge University, Cambridgeshire, Sussex, and England

The legendary Ranji came from ancient Rajput stock, and brought Eastern magic to the cricket fields of England, America, and Australia. Individual and distinctive in style, he possessed exceptionally keen eyesight besides flexibility and power of wrist, and he could glance the good length ball off the middle stump to leg in a way that no one else has equalled. His cutting and driving, too, were superb, models of feline grace. He was a useful change-bowler and a safe catcher in the slips. Throughout, he suffered from hay-fever. Awarded his blue at Cambridge by F. S. Jackson (and known in his university days as 'Smith') he soon announced his genius to the world. He made 77 and 150 on his début for Sussex against MCC at Lord's; and in his first Test against Australia at Old Trafford, 1896, he made 62 and 154 not out, rescuing England from two shaky starts. He was first in the national averages in 1896 with 2,780 runs (57.91), including ten centuries; in 1900 with 3,065 runs (87.57), including eleven centuries; and again in 1904 with 2,077 runs (74.17), including eight centuries. In 1899 he made 3,159 runs (63.18), including eight centuries. He passed 1,000 runs in all twelve seasons he was able to appear regularly, including his tour of Australia in 1897/8 with A. E. Stoddart's team, when he averaged 50.77 in the Tests. His highest score in Tests was 175 in the first match at Sydney in 1897, and his career-highest, 285 not out for Sussex against Somerset at Taunton in 1901. He captained Sussex for five seasons and somehow always seemed to be engaged in a stand at Hove with C. B. Fry, with whom he later served on the League of Nations. Ranji played his last match for Sussex in 1920 but by then he had lost an eye in a shooting accident, was overweight and no longer a force. K. S. Duleepsinhji was his nephew.

First-class career (1893–1920): 24,692 runs (56.37) including 72 centuries, 133 wickets (34.59), and 233 catches

Test matches (15): 989 runs (44.95) including 2 centuries, 1–39, and 13 catches

RATCLIFFE, Alan

(b. 1909, London; d. 1967, Toronto, Canada) *Wales, Cambridge University, and Surrey*

Coming into the 1931 Cambridge side against Oxford at Lord's at the last moment, through an injury to Jack Davies, Alan Ratcliffe, an opening right-handed batsman, made 201 to establish a new record in the University match. Twenty-four hours later, the Nawab of Pataudi, allegedly announcing his intentions in advance, eclipsed it with 238 not out, a record which still stands over 60 years later. In 1932, Ratcliffe again made a hundred against Oxford, perhaps entertaining hopes, before his dismissal for 124, of returning the compliment to Pataudi. He made occasional appearances for Wales and Surrey.

First-class career (1928–45): 1,969 runs (26.25) including 5 centuries, and 40 catches

READ, Holcombe Douglas

(b. 1910, Woodford Green, Essex) *Essex, Surrey, and England*

A Wykehamist, 'Hopper' Read took a long run with a somewhat tearaway right-arm action and his length was often erratic, but there was no doubt about his speed. A surprise choice for England against South Africa at The Oval in 1935—though earlier in the season he had been prominent in the débâcle of the champions, Yorkshire, at Huddersfield—he took 6 for 200 on a batsman's paradise and did not bat. He toured Australasia with MCC's 'goodwill' team of 1935/6, but he was unable to spare much time afterwards for first-class cricket. He had played two matches for Surrey in 1933 and 32 for Essex, 1933–5.

First-class career (1933–48): 158 runs (3.67), 219 wickets (22.93), and 21 catches

READ, John Maurice

(b. 1859, Thames Ditton, Surrey; d. 1929, Winchester, Hampshire) *Surrey and England*

Nephew of a prominent early player H. H. Stephenson, Maurice Read represented a new 'school' of professionals: well groomed, well mannered, articulate, sober, and thrifty. He was a free, hard-hitting, right-handed batsman with a sound defence, a useful fast-medium change-bowler, and a reliable outfield. For 15 years he was an integral part of the successful Surrey side and for more than a decade a regular choice for England against Australia and for Players against

Gentlemen. He had a large part in England's two-wicket victory at The Oval in 1890, on a sticky wicket making 35 of a total 95 for 8. He toured Australia four times between 1884 and 1892, and in all hit three centuries against the Australians, notably 186 for Surrey at The Oval in 1886, his career-highest, adding 241 with Bobby Abel for the fourth wicket. He toured South Africa with Major Warton's pioneer team of 1888/9, playing in the first Tests against that country.

First-class career (1880–95): 14,008 runs (24.66) including 11 centuries, 73 wickets (24.75), and 214 catches
Test matches (17): 461 runs (17.07) and 8 catches

READ, Walter William

(b. 1855, Reigate, Surrey; d. 1907, Croydon, Surrey) *Surrey and England*

A former schoolteacher, Walter Read or 'W.W.' was a bold and dashing character, no respecter of very important persons, and often in a high fury about something or other. He was a prime mover in the revival of Surrey cricket in the early 1880s, and for more than a decade one of the two best batsmen in the XI. He was a punishing front-foot player, with tremendous power in his right-handed off-drive. He was a safe field at point and purveyed lobs occasionally even in Tests. His career-highest score was 338 for Surrey against Oxford University at The Oval in 1888. In the previous season he had exceeded 200 in an innings twice. He toured Australia twice—captaining England in the sole Test of 1887/8 at Sydney, as the compromise leader agreed to by two rival touring teams. He also led his own team to South Africa in 1891/2. (Both Tests in which he was captain were won.) He represented England at home in each series from 1884 until 1893. In The Oval Test of 1884 he was furious at Lord Harris sending him in at number ten instead of three or four and 'took it out on' the Australian bowlers, slamming 117 in 2 hours.

First-class career (1873–97): 22,349 runs (32.06) including 38 centuries, 108 wickets (32.25), 381 catches, and 20 stumpings
Test matches (18): 720 runs (27.69) including 1 century, 0–63, and 16 catches

REEVE, Dermot Alexander

(b. 1963, Kowloon, Hong Kong) *Sussex, Warwickshire, and England*

Dermot Reeve tells the story against himself that the Pakistan captain Imran Khan, with whom he had played as a Sussex Junior, summoned him to his side after the World Cup final in 1992 and told him, 'You've done really well; for a player of such limited ability.' Originally a wicket-keeper-batsman, Reeve made the transformation first to a seam- and swing-bowler and then to a genuine all-rounder with dramatic results, winning three Test caps in New Zealand in 1992, before helping England to the final of the World Cup. Prior to 1995 he had played twenty-five one-day internationals for England. An optimistic, effervescent character and talented mimic, Reeve the batsman could drive a bowler to despair with his clever improvisation, while as a bowler he mixed his stock ball, the medium-paced outswinger, with clever changes of pace, making him difficult to hit, especially at the end of a one-day innings. He learned to bowl whilst on the MCC groundstaff at Lord's. After representing Hong Kong in the ICC Trophy in 1982, Reeve joined Sussex the following summer, taking 42 wickets in his first season. In 1986 he won the man-of-the-match award in the NatWest Final against Lancashire for a devastating spell of 4 for 20, including the potentially crucial wicket of Clive Lloyd, lbw for nought. Reeve moved to Warwickshire at the end of the 1987 season, and, after an injury-hit first summer, he again captured the NatWest headlines in 1989, once more winning the man-of-the-match award in the Final through tight bowling and an important innings of 42. Reeve topped 1,000 runs in a season in 1990, including a career-best 202 not out against Northamptonshire, and when he did it again the following summer as well as taking 45 wickets, he was named in the A team to the West Indies. Elevated to the tour of New Zealand following the failure of Angus Fraser to recover from injury, Reeve played in all three Tests, making 59 and taking a wicket with his eighth ball on his début, but it was in the World Cup which followed that he made his mark as one of England's host of all-rounders, bowling well and playing a crucial innings of 25 not out in 14 balls against South Africa which helped his side into the final. During the tournament, Reeve had fallen awkwardly whilst bowling, and the injury was later diagnosed as a stress fracture of the hip. It caused him to miss much of the following season, but with the winter tour of India and Sri Lanka including eight one-day internationals, he was chosen. The trip was unsuccessful for Reeve and for England, although his mother, Monica, who followed her son's career, took over as official scorer when the original choice became ill. He reappeared in one-

day internationals against Australia in the next summer and New Zealand in 1994, but it was as captain of Warwickshire after he was appointed in 1993 that he enjoyed further success. Reeve's bold, cool, unbeaten 81 led his side to a record victory target in that season's NatWest Final, before in 1994, despite struggling with injury, he and vice-captain Tim Munton helped the county to an unprecedented three titles: the County Championship, the Benson and Hedges Cup, and the Sunday League; they only missed out on the clean sweep when they were beaten by Worcestershire in the NatWest Final. Two more titles were won in 1995.

First-class career (1983–): 7,431 runs (33.93) and 409 wickets (27.76)

Test matches (3): 124 runs (24.80), 2 wickets (30.00), and 1 catch

RELF, Albert Edward

(b. 1874, Burwash, Sussex; d. 1937, Crowthorne, Berkshire) *Berkshire, Norfolk, Sussex, Auckland, and England*

Coming to Sussex from Norfolk at the age of 25, A. E. Relf was an immediate success and remained a mainstay of the team for 21 years, achieving the double eight times in ten seasons. Taking a short run with an easy, natural right-arm action, he bowled medium pace with perfect command of length and could keep an end going all day without becoming tired. He was also a prolific run-getter and brilliant in the slips. He toured Australia with the first MCC team of 1903/4, and his diary revealed his sore disappointment at receiving so few chances in the series. He appeared in two Tests, adding 115 for the ninth wicket with R. E. Foster in the first at Sydney. In his only Test against Australia in England, at The Oval in 1909, he took 5 for 85 in a total of 350. He toured South Africa in 1905/6 and 1913/14 with more satisfaction. For most of his life he was a happy, popular man but, while coach at Wellington College, he shot himself through the head in a mood of depression caused by the serious illness of his wife. He died a wealthy man and his wife recovered.

First-class career (1900–21): 22,238 runs (29.79) including 26 centuries, 1,897 wickets (20.94), and 537 catches

Test matches (13): 416 runs (23.11), 25 wickets (24.96), and 14 catches

RHODES, Harold James

(b. 1936, Hadfield, Glossop, Derbyshire) *Derbyshire, Nottinghamshire, and England*

Harold or 'Dusty' Rhodes first appeared for Derbyshire at 16 as a right-arm spin bowler, but subsequently altered his style, becoming a fast seam-bowler in the rich Derbyshire tradition. He represented England against India in two Tests in 1959, but his career was blighted. Doubts were expressed about his action, especially when he delivered his faster ball, and at Derby in 1960, while bowling against the South Africans, he was no-balled six times by umpire Paul Gibb. Both Gibb and Sid Buller called him in later matches; MCC investigated the matter and eventually decided that Rhodes had a 'hyper-extended arm'. He was officially cleared in 1968 but he did not play for England again. Three times he captured 100 wickets in a season, with 119 wickets (11.04) in 1965. After 1969 he went into league cricket and appeared for Nottinghamshire in several Gillette Cup and John Player League matches. He is the son of another Derbyshire cricketer, A. E. G. Rhodes, who became a Test umpire.

First-class career (1953–75): 2,427 runs (9.48), 1,073 wickets (19.70), and 86 catches

Test matches (2): 0 runs (—) and 9 wickets (27.11)

RHODES, Steven John

(b. 1964, Bradford, Yorkshire) *Yorkshire, Worcestershire, and England*

After being tipped to be a future England player from the time he became Yorkshire's youngest-ever wicket-keeper in 1981, Steve Rhodes had to endure a long wait before he finally won his first Test cap in 1994. He seized his chance with both hands. Having played for Young England in 1983, he found his way blocked at Yorkshire by David Bairstow and moved to Worcestershire in 1985. One B and four A tours with England followed, as well as selection for the cancelled 1988/9 tour of India and three one-day internationals against Australia in 1989, before the advent of Ray Illingworth as Chairman of England selectors. He wanted the 'tough little Yorkie' as he called him and was quickly proved right. Short, stocky, energetic and fiercely competitive, 'Bumpy' Rhodes inherited his love of wicket-keeping from his father Bill, who had kept for Nottinghamshire in the late 1950s and early 1960s. Rhodes junior learnt his cricket in the Bradford League with Farsley before joining the Yorkshire staff, but with

Bairstow still an England player in 1984, he left for Worcestershire with Yorkshire's blessing. He gave his new county loyal, determined, and consistent service as a wicket-keeper and the advent of four-day Championship cricket gave his dogged and orthodox batting more chance to flourish. Chosen as player of the A tour of South Africa in 1993/4, he began the 1994 season with a century against the New Zealanders at Worcester and was included in the one-day series which followed, keeping his place for the Tests. A début at Trent Bridge with 5 catches, plus 49 in an innings win was followed by a further 21 catches and 2 stumpings in the summer's five remaining Tests, as well as two fighting innings to help save the Lord's Test against New Zealand and a Test-best 65 not out on his 'home' ground at Headingley against South Africa. Sadly he completely lost form and confidence in Australia in 1994/5.

First-class career (1981–   ): 7,988 runs (33.42) and 711 dismissals (631 c., 80 st.)

Test matches (6): 222 runs (55.50) and 28 dismissals (26 c., 2 st.)

RHODES, Wilfred

(b. 1877, Kirkheaton, Yorkshire; d. 1973, Branksome Park, Dorset) *Yorkshire and England*

The exploits of Wilfred Rhodes and George Hirst are legendary in Yorkshire. As with Hirst, Rhodes's integrity was a prime quality but his character was even tougher and more complex. The third in his county's great tradition of slow left-arm bowlers, he was a natural psychologist. In his career of 32 years he learned and explored the weaknesses, rashnesses, and timidities of virtually every batsman in the Commonwealth. His action was balanced and economical with a natural flow. Formidably accurate, he would turn the ball on most surfaces but it was in the air that, by subtle variations of flight, he beat most of the 4,187 batsmen he dismissed. No man has equalled that gargantuan haul. Beginning with his county as a number eleven batsman, he rose to open for England against Australia and South Africa with Jack Hobbs. A tenacious right-hander, he was thorough in defence and calculated and certain in attack, notably so with a leaning off-drive which placed the ball accurately into the cover gaps. Apart from his bowling record only thirteen other batsmen have exceeded his total of runs; only six fieldsmen (excluding wicket-keepers) have held more catches. He passed 1,000 runs 21 times and took 100 wickets 23 times. His success was immediate, with 154 wickets in his first season, 1898, and 1,251 wickets in his first five seasons. He played in his first Test against Australia at Trent Bridge in 1899 (taking seven wickets) and his last at The Oval in 1926, when his 4 for 44 on the final day enabled England to regain the Ashes after 14 years. He toured Australia four times between 1903 and 1921; he visited South Africa twice; and his last tour was to the West Indies in 1929/30, when he appeared in the first Test series in the Caribbean. He captured 31 wickets (15.74) against Australia in 1903/4, when England won back the Ashes. Opening the batting for England for only the second time, in the first Test against South Africa at Johannesburg in 1909/10, he put on 159 with Jack Hobbs. In the fifth match at Cape Town these two added 221 and, in the fourth Test against Australia at Melbourne two years later, they created England's (then) first-wicket record of 323, Rhodes making 179. His most successful bowling returns were 8 for 68 at Melbourne in 1903/4 (15 for 124 in the match) and 7 for 17 at Edgbaston in 1902 when Australia were all out for 36. In later years he coached at Harrow before turning gradually blind. But he never repined and would attend matches regularly, 'reading' the game with remarkable accuracy by the familiar sounds around him. Of the many stories told about Rhodes one by Sir Neville Cardus stays in the mind. Rhodes and Emmott Robinson went out one day to inspect a rain-affected wicket. 'That'll be turning by four o'clock,' said Robinson sagely. 'Nay Emmott,' was the reply, 'half past four.'

First-class career (1898–1930): 39,802 runs (30.83) including 58 centuries, 4,187 wickets, (16.71), and 764 catches

Test matches (58): 2,325 runs (30.19) including 2 centuries, 127 wickets (26.96), and 60 catches

RICE, Sir Timothy Miles Bindon

(b. 1944, Amersham, Buckinghamshire)

Tim Rice wrote the lyrics for such outstanding stage musicals as *Jesus Christ, Superstar* (1970) and *Evita* (1978); and won an Oscar for the lyrics of the cartoon film *Aladdin*. His operetta *Cricket* (1986), written with Sir Andrew Lloyd Webber, was performed at Windsor Castle to celebrate the sixtieth birthday of Queen Elizabeth II. The contribution of this large man and genial character to cricket has been significant: as president of Lord's Taverners (1988–90); author of *Treasures of Lord's* (1989); MCC committee member (1991–4); and *Daily Telegraph* columnist. His cricket club, Heartaches CC, named after an Elvis Presley

song, was founded in the tradition of earlier clubs, with literary and artistic associations, such as J. M. Barrie's Allahakbarries and Sir John Squire's Invalids. A player of no pretensions his immense keenness ran to the production of an annual Heartaches handbook—à la *Wisden*—and he spread enjoyment on and off the field by his wit and bonhomie.

RICHARDS, Clifton James ('Jack')

(b. 1958, Penzance, Cornwall) *Surrey, Orange Free State, and England*

'Jack' Richards's first-class career ended abruptly in 1988 when he was released by Surrey after spending 13 years at The Oval. Talented and self-confident, his tendency to plain-speaking may well have counted against him, but his abilities as a punishing batsman and a wonderfully agile wicket-keeper with a distinctive upright style to the quicker bowlers could not be disputed, and he played a crucial part in England retaining the Ashes in Australia in 1986/7. Richards learnt the game at Penzance cricket club before being given a trial by Surrey, then coached by their former wicket-keeper Arthur McIntyre. Impressing, he joined the staff in 1976, and by 1978, he had taken over from Lonsdale Skinner as Surrey's first-choice behind the stumps. Initially, his performances with the bat were modest, but after scoring 668 runs in 1981, he was chosen to tour India and Sri Lanka as understudy to Bob Taylor. Richards played just six first-class matches on the whole tour but returned to score his maiden century, 117 not out against Nottinghamshire the following summer. In 1984, he made two centuries, but it was only in 1986, as he topped 1,000 runs for the first time with two more hundreds, that he gained international honours, playing in two one-day internationals against New Zealand. Selected for the tour of Australia which followed, Richards was chosen ahead of Bruce French for the first Test in Brisbane after England had struggled to score heavily in early matches. In the event, Richards made nought, bowled by a swinging full-toss, but England made 456, won the match, and with three catches and a stumping, he retained his place. In the next Test in Perth, he enjoyed his finest hour with an innings of 133, full of flowing strokes, adding 207 for the sixth wicket with David Gower. That Test was drawn, but in the fourth match in Melbourne, he took five catches in Australia's first innings, including a memorable effort sprinting back towards long-leg, as England won by an innings. Richards also helped Mike Gatting's side win the 'Perth Challenge', but his form dipped as the tour ended, and he lost his place to French for the World Series finals as the team completed the 'Grand Slam'. Richards kept in the one-day matches against Pakistan at the start of the 1987 season, but was then displaced by French for the Test series which followed, appearing in only the third match, which England lost, when his rival was struck down with chicken pox. Richards became Imran's 300th Test wicket. In 1988, after touring New Zealand as understudy to French, he returned for two Tests against the West Indies, but was unable to recapture the batting form which made him such an asset in Australia, making 13 runs in four innings. Failing to find a new county, he emigrated to Holland with his Dutch wife.

First-class career (1976–88): 8,012 runs (28.51) including 8 centuries, 5 wickets (44.80), and 676 dismissals (604 c., 72 st.)

Test matches (8) 285 runs (21.92) including 1 century, and 21 dismissals (20 c., 1 st.)

RICHARDSON, Derek Walter

(b. 1934, Hereford) *Worcestershire and England*

Fair-haired and with a countryman's complexion, 'Dick' Richardson was an attractive left-hand, middle-order batsman, who had a high backlift and a style quite unlike his brother Peter, his strokes tending to be more fluent. Possibly through rather careless stroke-play, he failed to fulfil his early great promise. He was a fine close fielder. He passed 1,000 runs in a season nine times and, in his sole Test against the West Indies at Trent Bridge in 1957, he scored 33 and held 1 catch.

First-class career (1952–67): 16,303 runs (27.40) including 16 centuries, 8 wickets (44.25), and 422 catches

RICHARDSON, Peter Edward

(b. 1931, Hereford) *Worcestershire, Kent, and England*

A patient and canny left-handed opening batsman, Peter Richardson was the eldest of three brothers to play county cricket. He established himself with 2,294 runs (39.55) in 1953, his second full season for Worcestershire. Three further times he exceeded 2,000 runs in a season, and twelve times altogether passed the 1,000 mark. Fair-haired and stocky with strong forearms, he pushed and deflected the ball with the minimum of backlift and loved to steal a quick

single. Captain of Worcestershire from 1956 until 1958, he also achieved much success in Tests. In his first match at Trent Bridge in 1956 he hit the Australian bowling for 81 and 73, putting on 151 for the first wicket with Colin Cowdrey in the second innings. At Old Trafford he made 104, again opening with Cowdrey, and adding 174 on the first day. England won by an innings. Richardson, however, was one of the disappointments of the 1958/9 tour of Australia. Moving afterwards from Worcestershire to Kent, he hit 111 and 115 for Kent against the Australians at Canterbury in 1964. He appeared in eight Tests during the 1961/2 tour to India and Pakistan and one more at home against the West Indies in 1963. A humorist, Peter had a penchant for sending deliberately faked cricket records to E. W. Swanton, for publication in the *Daily Telegraph*. On one occasion he also complained about excessive noise from Mr Swanton in the commentary box! He continued to attempt practical jokes on commentators.

First-class career (1949–65): 26,055 runs (34.60) including 44 centuries, 11 wickets (45.36), and 220 catches

Test matches (34): 2,061 runs (37.47) including 5 centuries, 3 wickets (16.00), and 6 catches

RICHARDSON, Thomas

(b. 1870, Byfleet, Surrey; d. 1912, Savoie, France) *Surrey, Somerset, and England*

One of the immortal fast bowlers, Tom Richardson was a black-haired, black-moustached gypsy of a fellow; lithe and supple, he pounded away with heart, hand, and magnificent muscle, not for a few overs with the new ball, but over after over all day. During his career Surrey were champions in four seasons. When asked if he approved of increasing the number of balls in an over from five to six, Tom said, 'Give me ten!' A glutton for work, he took 809 wickets in only three seasons from 1895 to 1897, in the former year taking 290 wickets (14.37), which is the largest number ever taken by a fast bowler and remained the highest by any bowler for 33 years. Seven times he passed 150 wickets in a season, ten times altogether 100 wickets. In his first Test against Australia, at Old Trafford in 1893, he took five wickets in each innings. On the first of his two tours in 1894/5 he headed the bowling with 32 wickets (26.53); in the second, also with A. E. Stoddart's team, he again took most wickets, capturing 22 (35.27). In the 1896 series he was again the most effective bowler, securing 24 wickets (18.29), and his great-hearted bowling at Old Trafford, when he took 13 for 244, one of the greatest sustained spells in the history of Test cricket, very nearly brought victory to England. At his peak, for some four or five years, he was certainly one of the greatest of fast bowlers. After a long run-up and high right-arm delivery, the combination of sheer pace with a pronounced off-break made him irresistible. Neville Cardus described his action memorably as being 'like a great wave of the sea about to break'. He died while on holiday walking in France; there was no question of the suicide that has sometimes been alleged.

First-class career (1892–1905): 3,424 runs (9.64), 2,104 wickets (18.43), and 126 catches

Test matches (14): 177 runs (11.06), 88 wickets (25.22), and 5 catches

RICHMOND, Duke of, Charles Lennox

(b. 1701, Goodwood, Sussex; d. 1750, Cobham, Surrey)

The second Duke of Richmond, grandson of Charles II, by issuing in 1725 a challenge to his Sussex neighbour, Sir William Gage, provided the first evidence of a nobleman playing cricket. Two years later, the 16 articles of covenant between him and Alan Broderick, the future Viscount Midleton, give the first historical record of how cricket should be played. In employing cricketers on his estate at Goodwood, Richmond set the fashion for the rest of the eighteenth century. The rise of Slindon, an obscure Sussex village, owed much to his patronage while one of its players, Richard Nyren learnt his cricket there before becoming the landlord of Hambledon's 'Bat and Ball' and the 'General' to its cricket. No record has survived of Richmond's own performances or abilities though a letter from Lord John Sackville suggested that if someone else had been 'stopping behind' a certain match might have been won. The Duke must have conceded rather too many byes!

RICHMOND, Thomas Leonard

(b. 1890, Radcliffe-on-Trent, Nottinghamshire; d. 1957, Saxondale, Nottinghamshire) *Nottinghamshire and England*

A right-arm, leg-break and googly bowler, who spun the ball considerably, Tom Richmond was under medium height and began to lose his skill when his increasing weight, combined with his lack of inches, made him very rotund indeed. Both as batsman and fielder he was a passenger.

From 1920 until 1926, however, he never took fewer than 113 wickets in a season. Eight times he had more than 12 wickets in a match. His sole Test was against Australia at Trent Bridge in 1921, when he scored 4 and 2 and took 2 for 86.

First-class career (1912–32): 1,644 runs (9.96), 1,176 wickets (21.22), and 39 catches

RIDGWAY, Frederick

(b. 1923, Stockport, Cheshire) *Kent and England*

A hard-working, right-handed, fast-medium bowler, Fred Ridgway was in his prime when many other fastish bowlers were available for England, and consequently his only tour for MCC was India in 1951/2 where his Test cricket was played. His short stature meant that some of his deliveries kept rather lower than the batsman expected. His best season was 1949 with 105 wickets (23.32) and he once took four wickets in four balls for Kent against Derbyshire at Folkestone in 1951. He was an excellent close field and could be a useful lower-order batsman.

First-class career (1946–61): 4,081 runs (11.00), 1,069 wickets (23.74), and 234 catches

Test matches (5): 49 runs (8.16), 7 wickets (54.14), and 3 catches

ROBERTSON, John David Benbow

(b. 1917, Chiswick, Middlesex) *Middlesex and England*

A man of modesty and natural dignity, Jack Robertson was a right-handed opening batsman of high class who would have played many more Tests had it not been his misfortune to be a contemporary of Len Hutton and Cyril Washbrook. He never failed England. He was a correct, consistent, and handsome batsman, and one of the best players of the new ball anywhere. Opening with Sid Brown for Middlesex during the 'Golden Summer' of 1947, he helped to wear down the bowling for Denis Compton and Bill Edrich to follow. When Brown and Robertson put on 310 against Nottinghamshire at Lord's that summer, it was a new record for the county and, although one thinks of 1947 as the year of the Middlesex twins, Robertson himself made 2,760 runs (52.47), including 12 centuries. His best season was 1951 when he scored 2,917 runs (56.09), including seven centuries. His highest score, 331 not out at Worcester in 1949, was made in the course of a day. Fifteen times (once overseas with MCC in India) he exceeded 1,000 runs in a season and nine times between 1947 and 1957 he passed 2,000 runs. Robertson's first Test

ROBERTSON-GLASGOW

was against South Africa in 1947. He headed the averages in the West Indies in 1947/8 with 390 runs (55.71), including 133 at Port of Spain. Against New Zealand at Lord's in 1949, when he replaced the injured Washbrook, he hit 121, putting on 143 for the first wicket with Hutton but was omitted for the rest of the series! His last Test series was against India in 1951/2, when he made over 300 runs. He was never selected against Australia. Also a useful off-break change-bowler and a fine field, he slid almost unnoticed from a game which his cultured and consistent play had graced for such a long time and became joint county coach with Jim Sims.

First-class career (1937–59): 31,914 runs (37.50) including 67 centuries, 73 wickets (34.74), and 350 catches

Test matches (11): 881 runs (46.36) including 2 centuries, 2 wickets (29.00), and 6 catches

ROBERTSON-GLASGOW, Raymond Charles

(b. 1901, Edinburgh; d. 1965, Buckhold, Berkshire) *Oxford University and Somerset*

Robertson-Glasgow and Douglas Jardine dismissed each other in the Charterhouse–Winchester match in 1919. Two more different figures in the English first-class scene between the wars could not be imagined: from Charterhouse, he won a Freshman blue at Oxford and his 5 for 29 against Somerset at Oxford in 1920 brought an immediate invitation to join that county—his cousin was MP for Bath, the best a Scotsman from Aberdeen could muster by way of a qualification. With a nickname secured because an Essex player had described himself as bowled by 'Robinson Crusoe', his gentle eccentricities blended with a formidable right-arm in-swinger which straightened out late at some pace. The chemistry of 'Crusoe' and Somerset worked. Middlesex were at the receiving end when he took 9 for 38 against them at Lord's in 1924 and he made five appearances for the Gentlemen against the Players. Long before his playing days were over he had become a journalist, working for the *Morning Post*, the *Daily Telegraph*, the *Observer*, and the *Sunday Times*. A. P. Singleton, Oxford captain in 1937, recalled a 'jovial figure in rough coat, grey flannels at half-mast and black dancing shoes (with) a small red memo book'. With his arrival at the Parks, 'cricket was fun'. 'Crusoe' found humour in small things, nostalgia made its appeal, a good story was worth telling and his own batting could be self-deprecated

though he shared in opening century partnerships in successive matches in 1928. While Neville Cardus drew his imagery from music, 'Crusoe' turned to the classics, especially Virgil. Simply because he had played the first-class game himself, the younger man had the edge in the dissection of technique. The journalist's language is, by definition, ephemeral but 'Crusoe' survives in his books, notably the autobiographical 46 Not Out. Behind the mask of laughter could lie black moods of depression and he took his own life one bleak winter's day in 1965.

First-class career (1920–37): 2,102 runs (13.22), 464 wickets (25.77), and 88 catches

ROBINS, Robert Walter Vivian

(b. 1906, Stafford; d. 1968, London) *Cambridge University, Middlesex, and England*

A forceful, dynamic, and influential cricketer, Walter Robins was an outstanding player at Highgate School, then a successful Cambridge blue, later a captain of both Middlesex and England, and finally an administrator as lively and enterprising as he had been player. Quick, short, with the walk and build of a cavalryman and a cheeky manner of batting, he used his feet freely and would go down the pitch to both fast and slow bowling. When he struck a length with his leg-breaks and googlies, he could go through any side. He was irrepressible, a believer in attack, whether batting, bowling, or fielding with energetic hostility in the cover. He led Middlesex from 1935 until 1938, in 1946 and 1947 and again in 1950, the county gaining the Championship in 1947. An old Middlesex player was once asked: 'What difference did Walter Robins make to a match?' He replied: 'The difference between the quick and the dead.' His first Test was against South Africa at Lord's in 1929. The following year he played against Australia twice, taking seven wickets in the match at Trent Bridge. Against the West Indies at Lord's in 1933, he took 6 for 32 in the first innings (West Indies falling for 97). He rescued England with 108 in just over 2 hours against South Africa at Old Trafford in 1935. He toured Australia in 1936/7, but was handicapped by injury. He led England victoriously against New Zealand in 1937. He achieved the double once, had a highest score of 140 against Cambridge at Fenners in 1930 and best bowling figures of 8 for 34 (13 for 115 in the match) against Lancashire at Lord's in 1929. He produced two hat-tricks at Lord's. He became honorary treasurer to Middlesex, a Test selector, manager of MCC in the West Indies, 1959/60 and served on the Cricket Inquiry Committee set up in 1960. A soccer blue at Cambridge, he played for Corinthians and Nottingham Forest. His son Charles also played for Middlesex.

First-class career (1925–58): 13,884 runs (26.40) including 11 centuries, 969 wickets (23.30), and 221 catches

Test matches (19): 612 runs (26.60) including 1 century, 64 wickets (27.46), and 12 catches

ROBINSON, Emmott

(b. 1883, Keighley, Yorkshire; d. 1969, Hinckley, Leicestershire) *Yorkshire*

Emmott Robinson was immortalized in Neville Cardus's famous phrase 'as the heap of Yorkshire clay' into whom the Lord breathed life in order to bowl at the pavilion end. At 35, he came to the first-class game late but, in a dozen seasons (1919–31), displayed a shrewdness, caution, and dedication which were part of the fabric of Yorkshire cricket in the 1920s. In a side full of stars, he was never top-billing but as a middle-order right-handed batsman and right-arm change-bowler his contribution was invaluable. His batting was firmly attuned to the immediate needs of the side and his bowling medium to fast, with inswingers forcing batsmen to play. His best performances came at the start of his career. He made 135 against Leicestershire at Leicester in 1921, while in the 'Roses' match at Bradford in 1920 he took 9 for 36 in Lancashire's second innings to give Yorkshire an unexpected victory by 22 runs before a huge Bank Holiday crowd. He was a first-class umpire (1937–51). Probably only a Yorkshire pre-war crowd could appreciate his worth—a cricketer with grit, but no glamour.

First-class career (1919–31): 9,744 runs (25.50) including 7 centuries, 902 wickets (22.05), and 321 catches

ROBINSON, Robert Timothy

(b. 1958, Skegby, Sutton-in-Ashfield, Nottinghamshire) *Nottinghamshire and England*

In the early stages of his first tour to India in 1984/5, Tim Robinson looked the ideal Test opening batsman. Right-handed, he played very straight and had a basically sound defensive technique, yet he could punish the bad ball very effectively with a wide range of attractive strokes and his first three Test hundreds—160, 175, and 148—were a glowing testimony to his powers of concentration. Dark-haired, wiry, quick in the field, and steady and reserved in character, he made his début for Nottinghamshire in 1978. After making modest progress during his days at Sheffield University, he won his county cap in 1983, aged 24, by making 1,545 runs (40.65) with 207 against Warwickshire. Splendid form in the next season, when he scored 2,032 runs (50.80) with five centuries, won him a place on the winter tour to India. Two hundreds in the games before the first Test gained him a place in the Test side. He did not allow himself to be unnerved by two low scores on his début, and in the next Test at Delhi made a magnificent 160, a superb display of concentration for almost 10 hours, playing England's young tormentor, Sivaramakrishnan, with great care and authority. This monumental innings by a batsman playing in only his second Test proved to be a match-winning contribution, and he made 444 runs (63.42) in the series. In his first Test in England, Robinson upstaged his new opening partner Graham Gooch, by taking the Australian pace attack apart at Headingley. With 27 marvellous boundaries, mostly through the off side, he made 175, forming the basis of a massive England total. He scored an undefeated 77 in the Trent Bridge Test and at Edgbaston made 148, putting on 331 with David Gower in an exhilarating display of strokeplay. With 490 runs (61.25) against Australia, he had scored 934 runs (62.27) in just 11 matches in his first year of Test cricket, but he came to earth with a solid bump in the West Indies in the early months of 1986. Bowled no fewer than nine times on the tour, he was upset by the extreme pace of the fast bowlers, scoring only 72 runs in his eight Test innings. His dedicated approach overcame the technical and mental flaws exposed by the world's most feared attack and he played another major Test innings —166—against Pakistan at Old Trafford in 1987. Two years later he settled for the large sum offered for an 'illegal' tour of South Africa and was banned from further Test cricket, but he took on the captaincy of Nottinghamshire in 1988 and maintained a consistently high quality of batsmanship in county cricket, sometimes opening, sometimes going in lower down.

First-class career (1978–): 22,637 runs (42.79) including 51 centuries, and 4 wickets (71.25)

Test matches (29): 1,601 runs (36.38) including 4 centuries, and 8 catches

ROEBUCK, Peter Michael

(b. 1956, Oxford) *Cambridge University, Somerset, and Devon*

Successfully catching an orange as he entered 'Boss' Meyer's study helped to secure Peter Roebuck a Free Scholarship at Millfield School from which he proceeded to Cambridge, making 158 against Oxford at Lord's in 1975 as a Freshman. Armed with three cricket blues (1975–7) and a first in law, this formidable intellectual chose to spend some summers making runs for Somerset and his winters teaching English in Australia. An adaptable and very determined right-handed batsman with abundant courage and a sound technique, he cannot have been far from the England selectors' thoughts, possibly as a captain in the Mike Brearley mould. He became captain of Somerset, having succeeded Ian Botham in 1986 and made a double-century against Nottinghamshire at Trent Bridge. In the subsequent furore which led to the departure of the county's three prima donnas—Botham, Viv Richards, and Joel Garner—Roebuck took his full share of the flak. After three seasons in command, during which the county had maintained 'an encouragingly high standard' he resigned believing he had done all he could. Meanwhile, with *Slices of Cricket* (1984), he had announced himself as an author whose 'sense of humour, clarity and irony' won warm praise from John Arlott. By 1991, when his first-class career ended, he had become the fourth highest scorer in Somerset's history and had taken many useful wickets with his off-spin, especially in limited-overs cricket. By 1994 he had acquired an established reputation as one of the shrewdest cricket journalists in both England and Australia besides writing the official history of the county, *From Sammy to Jimmy,* which he had adorned with his batting. He found time to captain Devon to a notable double in 1994, playing a leading all-round role.

First-class career (1974–91): 17,552 runs (37.26) including 33 centuries, 72 wickets (49.16), and 162 catches

ROOPE, Graham Richard James

(b. 1946, Fareham, Hampshire) *Berkshire, Surrey, Griqualand West, and England*

Tall, raw-boned, and curly haired, Graham Roope was a gifted all-round games player, probably just below the highest class as a right-hand, middle-order batsman, but he nevertheless did a useful job in 21 Tests for England between 1973 and 1978. He was also a noted goalkeeper in amateur football and it was his brilliant close fielding, especially at second slip, which often gave him the edge over others, when England teams were being picked. A genial if somewhat disorganized character off the field, he was a determined and tough competitor in any match and, although he did not make a century for England, seven fifties and thirty-five catches bear testimony to his usefulness. A right-hander, he was capable on his day of dominating an attack with glorious driving, but his batting for England was more often a question of a dogged struggle, as in 1975 when his solid 77 at The Oval helped to save England from defeat against Lillee, Thomson and the other Australians. A consistent county cricketer, Roope gave Surrey long and loyal service until 1982, often taking useful wickets with his medium-fast bowling. He returned to Minor County cricket for Berkshire.

First-class career (1964–82): 19,116 runs (36.90) including 26 centuries, 225 wickets (37.35), and 604 dismissals (602 c., 2 st.)
Test matches (21): 860 runs (30.71), 0–76, and 35 catches

ROOT, Charles Frederick

(b. 1890, Somercotes, Derbyshire; d. 1954, Wolverhampton, Staffordshire) *Derbyshire, Worcestershire, and England*

Fred Root was shot in the chest while serving as a dispatch-rider in the First World War, but he lived to become a leading exponent of right-arm, leg-theory bowling and a master of spin. Powerful and enduring in physique, he was contemptuous of adversity and pettiness, being himself a cheerful toiler. He delivered his in-swinger at a brisk medium pace, the ball dipping in at the toes unpleasantly late, and he had a complement of close leg-fielders. As a batsman, he loved to drive high and hard, and his defence was solid enough in a rough sort of way. He started first-class cricket with Derbyshire, where a familiar scoreboard line would be the suitably agricultural 'c. Beet b. Root', but he earned most of his fame with Worcestershire after the War. From 1923 until 1931 he took more than 100 wickets in every season, and in 1925 his haul was 219 wickets (17.21), a county record. Three times he took nine wickets in an innings, including 9 for 23 against Lancashire at Worcester in 1931. In 1928 he achieved the double. He toured the West Indies in 1925/6 and coached in South Africa, but his only Tests were against Australia in 1926. In retirement he played Lancashire League cricket for Todmorden. He became a journalist and his book, *A Cricket Pro's Lot*, expresses admirably the view of the professional then.

First-class career (1910–33): 7,911 runs (14.78) including 1 century, 1,512 wickets (21.11), and 244 catches

Test matches (3): Did not bat, 8 wickets (24.25), and 1 catch

ROSE, Brian Charles

(b. 1950, Dartford, Kent) *Somerset and England*

A tall, fair-haired, left-handed batsman, Brian Rose is likely to be remembered as the man who captained Somerset to their first wins in any major competitions: the Gillette Cup and John Player League in 1979. He first led the county in 1978 after playing his first Test cricket the previous winter on the England tour of Pakistan and New Zealand. Although he scored a century in both countries, he scored few runs in the five Tests in which he played. Lacking in neither courage nor application, he was at his best an attractive batsman with a pleasant, leaning, straight drive and a savage square-cut. A charming, rather dozy character, he was a captain who was popular both with opponents and with his own team, although he created a furore in 1979 by declaring the Somerset innings after one over to take advantage of a technicality in the rules of the Benson and Hedges Cup. Somerset were expelled from the competition but Rose was soon forgiven. His finest hour as a Test player came against the powerful West Indies attack of 1980 when, returning to England's team at Old Trafford, he hit a dashing 70 out of England's first-innings total of 150. He finished this series with 243 runs from six innings at an average of 48.60, but in the West Indies the following winter he could find no form, returning early with an eye defect. He later batted in glasses and, combining cricket with teaching, served under several captains.

First-class career (1969–87): 13,236 runs (33.25) including 25 centuries, 8 wickets (36.12), and 124 catches

Test matches (9): 358 runs (25.57) and 4 catches

ROSS, Alan

(b. 1922, Calcutta, India)

Haileybury 'were lucky to have such a good opening bowler' as Alan Ross who went up to Oxford before war-service in the Royal Navy. He was in the side got together at short notice to play a well-prepared Cambridge in a one-day game at Lord's in 1941. His career as cricket correspondent of the *Observer* took him on six MCC tours and enabled him to write three excellent tour books which combined felicitous writing on the matches with observant travelogue. He also wrote a penetrating biography of Ranjitsinhji (1983) which examined the dichotomy between the man as an English cricketer and an Indian prince. A poet of some distinction, and a publisher, he was for many years editor of *The London Magazine*, becoming also its managing director.

ROYLE, Revd Vernon Peter Fanshawe Archer

(b. 1854, Brooklands, Cheshire; d. 1929, Stanmore Park, Middlesex) *Oxford University, Lancashire, and England*

Brilliant fielding at cover-point brought Vernon Royle his fame; he was ambidextrous, very quick on his feet and to throw. 'Woa, mate, there's a policeman,' called out Tom Emmett to his batting partner in a 'Roses' match as Royle pounced on a shot in the covers. Just above average height, he was a right-handed batsman who got well over the ball, often hit powerfully and scored quickly. As a slow change-bowler, he helped Oxford to win the University match of 1875. He toured Australia with Lord Harris's team in 1878/9, and in his sole Test at Melbourne he scored 3 and 18, took 0 for 6 and held 2 catches.

First-class career (1873–91): 2,322 runs (15.48), 15 wickets (25.06), and 69 catches

RUMSEY, Frederick Edward

(b. 1935, London) *Worcestershire, Somerset, Derbyshire, and England*

Fred Rumsey was a large and enthusiastic left-arm fast bowler with a long run and a comfortable figure. He had two seasons with Worcestershire and, in his first full season for Somerset in 1963, took over 100 wickets and was prominent in what was then the county's most successful season. Against Nottinghamshire at Taunton he took 13 for 104. His best year, 1965, saw him take 119 wickets (16.18), but he left the county after 1968 to become Derbyshire's Public Relations Officer and for five years he appeared mainly in limited-overs matches. He played for England against Australia at Old Trafford in 1964 and in four more Tests against South Africa and New Zealand in 1965. An enthusiastic golfer, he ran a successful travel business in his retirement, frequently taking cricket teams to Barbados.

First-class career (1960–70): 1,015 runs (8.45), 580 wickets (20.29), and 91 catches

Test matches (5): 30 runs (15.00) and 17 wickets (27.11)

RUSSELL, Charles Albert George

(b. 1887, Leyton, Essex; d. 1961, Leytonstone, Essex) *Essex and England*

Born within a stone's throw of the Leyton ground, Charles Russell or 'Jack' was a master of on-side strokes. Although not specially attractive to watch, he became, soon after the First World War, one of the most dependable batsmen in the country. From 1919 until his retirement he never failed to reach 1,000 runs in a season, five times exceeding 2,000. His best year was 1922 when he was the most prolific batsman in England, scoring 2,575 runs (54.78), with nine centuries, including 273 against Northamptonshire at Leyton. On tour with MCC in Australia, 1920/1, he made 135 not out and 59 in the third Test at Adelaide (on the same ground he also made 156 and 201 against South Australia). In his first Tests in England, at Old Trafford and The Oval in 1921, he made 101 in the first and 13 and 102 not out in the second. On tour with MCC in South Africa, 1922/3, he made 9 and 96 in the fourth Test at Johannesburg and 140 and 111 in the fifth at Durban, the first time an English batsman had made two centuries in the same Test. A tree was planted to commemorate this feat. He was also one of the best slips of his time and a useful change-bowler.

First-class career (1908–30): 27,358 runs (41.57) including 71 centuries, 283 wickets (26.98), and 314 catches

Test matches (10): 910 runs (56.87) including 5 centuries, and 8 catches

RUSSELL, Robert Charles ('Jack')

(b. 1963, Stroud, Gloucestershire) *Gloucestershire and England*

Intensely patriotic, and also idiosyncratic like his mentor Alan Knott, Robert 'Jack' Russell frequently found himself left out of the England side despite being acknowledged from time to time as 'the best wicket-keeper in the world'. With a floppy white sun-hat and droopy moustache his appearance was often the opposite of his wicket-keeping, which was beautifully neat. Diminutive and agile behind the stumps, and with a crab-like,

fidgeting stance in front of them, Russell played in twenty consecutive Tests from his début against Sri Lanka at Lord's in 1988, claiming 58 victims, and also scored his maiden first-class century, 128 not out, against Australia at Old Trafford. He is a determined left-handed batsman who cuts and deflects effectively but for 4 years from January 1990, he missed fifteen Tests, because Alec Stewart, a superior batsman, was preferred behind the stumps. Eventually recognizing that Stewart's batting form was affected, the selectors recalled Russell for the tour of the West Indies in early 1994, but after a disappointing trip he lost his place again, this time to Steven Rhodes. First spotted by a Gloucestershire coach in 1972 playing for Stroud, Russell became the county's youngest-ever wicket-keeper at 17 years and 307 days when he played against the Sri Lankans in 1981, setting a record for most dismissals on a first-class début with seven catches and a stumping. Capped in 1985, he gained international recognition two years later when chosen as understudy to Bruce French for England's tour of Pakistan. He played just one match on the trip, but when French required surgery the following summer, first Paul Downton and then Jack Richards were preferred against the West Indies. Eventually picked to face Sri Lanka at Lord's, Russell kept tidily after a nervous start and made 94, then the highest score of his career, having come in as nightwatchman. Against Australia in 1989 he made a tentative start with the bat, but a fighting unbeaten 64 at Lord's was upstaged by his century at Old Trafford, spanning over 6 hours but ultimately in a lost cause. He finished the series with 21 victims and 314 runs, and was one of *Wisden*'s Five Cricketers of the Year. In the West Indies in 1989/90, there were 13 more catches, and a wonderfully spirited 5-hour innings of 55 in Barbados which so nearly saved the fourth Test, but after playing in all six Tests at home in 1990, he lost his place to Stewart during the tour of Australia which followed. Not, however, before he had taken six catches in an innings on a slow, low pitch in the second Test in Melbourne, and a remarkable stumping when standing up to the fast bowling of Gladstone Small. Russell missed only one of the next twelve Tests, making way for Stewart at The Oval in 1991 as England fielded a five-man attack against the West Indies, but he was left out of the World Cup which followed a winter series in New Zealand and then dropped from the Test team midway through the 1992 season and controversially and unwisely omitted from the tour to

India and Sri Lanka. His special skip up to the stumps on spinners' pitches, and his nimble batting against India's slow bowlers might have been invaluable. He was always a most conscientious and unselfish tourist, keeping strictly to pre-ordained diets (which mainly seemed to consist of cups of tea) and training routines. He was able to draw comfort from the success of his second career as an artist. What had started in 1987 as a way of passing the time during rain breaks became lucrative. From accurate pencil sketches he graduated to colourful and evocative oil paintings. In 1988 he held a three-week exhibition in Bristol, and the following year contributed the drawings to *Sketches of a Season*. Numerous commissions followed, including one from the Dean of Gloucester to draw the City's cathedral to raise funds for its 900th anniversary, and others from the Imperial War Museum to depict famous military actions.

First-class career (1981–): 9,469 runs (28.01), 1 wicket (53.00), and 795 dismissals (701 c., 94 st.)
Test matches (36): 1,255 runs (26.70) and 98 dismissals (90 c., 8 st.)

RUSSELL, William Eric

(b. 1936, Dumbarton, Scotland) *Middlesex, Berkshire, and England*

Eric Russell was the natural successor to Jack Robertson as Middlesex opener: a similarly modest man and often an equally handsome player. His right-handed, off-side hitting off either foot and his leg-glancing were, for a decade, among the delights of the game. In 13 seasons he exceeded 1,000 runs, with 2,342 runs (45.92) in 1964. With 'Pasty' Harris he put on 312 for the first wicket against the Pakistanis at Lord's in 1967, which was a county record. His major tours were to India and Pakistan in 1961/2, and Australia and New Zealand in 1965/6, when he played many fine innings, and at home he represented England against South Africa, West Indies and Pakistan. He later developed an old ground at Shenley in Hertfordshire into a magnificent cricket centre.

First-class career (1956–72): 25,525 runs (34.87) including 41 centuries, 22 wickets (45.14), and 304 catches
Test matches (10): 362 runs (21.29), 0–44, and 4 catches

SACKVILLE, John Frederick, 3rd Duke of Dorset

(b. 1745, Knole, Kent; d. 1799, Knole)

A patron of both cricket and the arts, Sackville was briefly an MP before inheriting the title from his uncle in 1769. Subsequently he became a privy councillor, lord-lieutenant of Kent, and in 1783, British ambassador to France. On his appointment, *Rambler's Magazine* satirized him as merely a cricketer. In 1789 he arranged for a team to visit Paris but on arriving at Dover they met the Duke retreating from the Revolution and the first overseas cricket tour was wisely abandoned. Although not a member of Hambledon, his aristocratic influence was evident. It was he who persuaded the club to switch from playing on Broadhalfpenny to Windmill Down. When Hambledon men were not required, he was able to recruit them for his own matches. He spent £1,000 a year in retaining on his Kent estate employees who were cricketers, including Minshull whom John Nyren called a capital bat but 'as conceited as a wagtail'. When the Duke's Kent XI played Hambledon in July 1774, he lost 500 guineas but more than recovered his money in the return match a month later, in which he made 77, his highest recorded score. He was an aggressive batsman and contemporary verse records that he could 'drive the ball beyond the booths' or send it 'across the Mead' and score 'six notches for the Deed'. Dorset was an advocate of ladies' cricket, declaring in 1797, 'What is human life but a game of cricket and, if so, why should not the ladies play it as well as we?' He was a founder member of both the White Conduit Club and Marylebone Cricket Club, playing himself certainly as late as 1787. On his death he left Sevenoaks Vine 'for the use of cricketers for ever'.

SALISBURY, Ian David Kenneth

(b. 1970, Northampton) *Sussex and England*

A determined late-order batsman and athletic fielder, Ian Salisbury was England's first specialist leg-spinner for 21 years. He started his Test career in heady fashion by taking five wickets at Lord's, almost helping his side to an improbable victory. Subsequently, a combination of injury and the ruthlessness of top-class batsmen in punishing anything other than perfect accuracy, limited his chances. He needed to play in a strong, winning side, because he lacked confidence. A zealous cricketer of great pluck, he only started playing regular club cricket when he was 14 and was at first a batsman who also bowled leg-spin. It was only after he joined the MCC groundstaff, following a spell with Northamptonshire 2nd XI, that he began to develop his bowling under the head coach, Don Wilson. Giving the ball a real snap from a good action, he bowls at a briskish pace, varies his leg-break with a well-disguised googly and can be a handful for the best players when pitching the ball right. He was selected for successive A tours before, in 1992, enjoying an outstanding season, capturing 87 wickets at 29 runs apiece. He earned his first Test cap and was named both Young Cricketer of the Year by the Cricket Writers and also one of Wisden's Five Cricketers of the Year. In his first match at Lord's he quickly had the great Javed Miandad caught at slip from a perfect leg-break, and took 3 for 49 in the second innings as Pakistan squeezed home by two wickets. Had his captain, Graham Gooch, had greater faith in him he would probably have been a match-winner. The following Test at Old Trafford brought him back to earth with a bump with 0 for 184, but he scored a spunky maiden Test 50 to save the follow-on. In India in 1992/3 he bowled very well at times, but not in the Tests, when his dogged batting was of greater use to a badly beaten side. Dogged by a shoulder injury during 1993, he was still selected for the winter tour to the West Indies. Although he claimed a Test-best 4 for 164 in Guyana and brilliantly caught Brian Lara in the Trinidad Test, he played in only two Tests on that tour, and then only once more, against South Africa at Lord's, in the summer of 1994.

First-class career (1989–): 1,801 runs (17.32) and 338 wickets (36.49)

Test matches (7): 205 runs (17.08) and 16 wickets (58.31)

SANDHAM, Andrew

(b. 1890, London; d. 1982, London) *Surrey and England*

Andy Sandham was the first batsman ever to make a triple-century in a Test, 325 for England against the West Indies at Kingston, 1929/30. He was a skilful opening batsman, small, neat, assured, a strong cutter and hooker, and deft deflector. Overshadowed by his county partner, Jack Hobbs, he was unlucky that Herbert Sutcliffe was also available to open for England. A self-effacing character who, paradoxically, drew attention to himself when batting, he shared in an opening stand of 428 with Jack Hobbs against Oxford University at The Oval in 1926, the

highest ever for Surrey's first wicket, and one of 66 century stands he shared with Hobbs. Twenty times (twice overseas) he exceeded 1,000 runs in a season, eight times exceeding 2,000 between 1921 and 1931. Besides his visit to the West Indies, he toured South Africa, 1922/3 and 1930/1, Australia, 1924/5, and India 1926/7 and represented England at home against Australia once in 1921, and South Africa twice in 1924. He was also a fine outfield. For many years he was Surrey's respected coach and later their scorer.

First-class career (1911–37): 41,284 runs (44.82) including 107 centuries, 18 wickets (31.11), and 158 catches

Test matches (14): 879 runs (38.21) including 2 centuries, and 4 catches

SCHULTZ (later STOREY), Sandford Spence

(b. 1857, Birkenhead, Cheshire; d. 1937, London) *Cambridge University and Lancashire*

A Cambridge blue who played occasionally for Lancashire, Schultz was more prominent in club cricket as a fast, round-arm bowler, good batsman and smart slip. A member of Lord Harris's team to Australia in 1878/9, he batted last, scoring 0 not out and 20, and taking 1 for 26 in his sole Test at Melbourne—but he helped to avert an innings defeat. As his German name 'Schultz' offended, he changed it to 'Storey'.

First-class career (1876–85): 1,046 runs (17.14), 28 wickets (40.82), and 29 catches

SCOTTON, William Henry

(b. 1856, Nottingham; d. 1893, London) *Nottinghamshire and England*

From 1884 until 1886 he was the best—or certainly the most successful—professional left-handed batsman in England, and he was an accomplished outfield. Few have ever played with so straight a bat or possessed such a strong defence but, as *Wisden* said, 'he carried caution to such extremes that it was often impossible to take any pleasure in seeing him play'. His finest hour—or rather $5\frac{3}{4}$ hours—was in The Oval Test in 1884. England's batsmen had faltered, confronted by a large Australian total, but Scotton, going in first, was ninth out for 90, a great chanceless defensive innings, adding 151 with the more dashing Walter Read for the ninth wicket, which made a respectable England total possible. Again, in the Oval Test of 1886, Scotton with W.G. put on 170 for the first wicket, taking about

4 hours over 34. The stand was immortalized in verse in *Punch*. Scotton visited Australia three times in the 1880s. He killed himself in a fit of depression due to domestic troubles and to losing his place in the Nottinghamshire XI.

First-class career (1875–91): 6,527 runs (18.97) including 4 centuries, 8 wickets (51.25), and 122 catches
Test matches (15): 510 runs (22.17), 0–20, and 4 catches

SELBY, John

(b. 1849, Nottingham; d. 1894, Nottingham)
Nottinghamshire and England

A first-rate right-handed batsman, especially on difficult wickets, Selby was at his best just before the Test era, although he appeared in the first two matches at Melbourne in 1876/7 with James Lillywhite's England XI, and top-scored with 38 in the second innings of the first Test. He revisited Australia in 1881/2, with Shaw's and Shrewsbury's side, but came home under a cloud, and never represented England again. There is some evidence that he misbehaved with his colleague's, W. H. Scotton's, wife. 'It is probable', said *Wisden*, 'that the stroke of paralysis which ended his life was partially due to a criminal charge . . . of which he was acquitted.'

First-class career (1870–87): 6,215 runs (18.83) including 4 centuries, 5 wickets (37.60), 128 catches, and 4 stumpings
Test matches (6): 256 runs (23.27) and 1 catch

SÉLINCOURT, Hugh de

(b. 1878; d. 1951, Pulborough, Sussex)

The Sussex village of Storrington, where Hugh de Sélincourt played his cricket, was immortalized as Tillingfold in his novels *The Cricket Match* (1924) and *The Game of the Season* (1931). They are marked by their characterization and presentation of a decent, orderly world. There is also an element of make-believe as when Tillingfold beat the 1921 Australians who 'created a very favourable impression' as they took their turn on the roller between innings. All this made an appeal to a generation in the 1920s and 1930s seeking escapism from the horrors of war and de Sélincourt's books have been accepted as classics in cricket fiction.

SELLERS, Arthur Brian

(b. 1907, Keighley; d. 1981, Bingley) *Yorkshire*

A tough, uncompromising Yorkshireman, Brian Sellers was an outstanding leader in the era of amateur county captains. He took over the acting leadership in 1932, without previous first-class experience, and promptly went 25 matches without defeat. While *Wisden's* prophecy that he would become 'one of the chief run-getters' in the side proved optimistic, he was worth his place for his captaincy and his brilliant close fielding. Yorkshire, in the 1930s, seldom had a batting crisis but Sellers, a right-hander, could rise to the occasion if needed, as when he made a century against the 1934 Australians or when he turned a possible defeat into victory against Kent in 1937 with a century and three fine catches. In the same year he made his only representative appearance, being undefeated in an eighth-wicket partnership of 63 with F. R. Brown for the Gentlemen v. the Players at Lord's. When his captaincy ended in 1947, he had led Yorkshire to six championships in nine seasons. His judgement made him an invaluable England selector over the period 1938 to 1955, while he served on the Yorkshire committee until 1972, as uncompromising as he had been on the field of play and closely involved in the turmoils which beset post-war Yorkshire cricket.

First-class career (1932–48): 9,270 runs (23.05) including 4 centuries, 9 wickets (75.11), and 273 catches

SELVEY, Michael Walter William

(b. 1948, Chiswick, Middlesex) *Cambridge University, Surrey, Middlesex, Glamorgan, Orange Free State, and England*

A dark, hirsute, hostile, and immensely strong, fast-medium bowler, Mike Selvey developed from modest beginnings with Cambridge and Surrey into one of the most consistent opening bowlers in England. Able to swing the ball both ways in the air, he often got a waspish pace and bounce off the pitch: a horrible man to face on a moist and cloudy morning at Lord's. He had a sensational start to his Test career: because of injuries to numerous other fast bowlers he was called up at the eleventh hour to play at Old Trafford against the immensely gifted West Indian team of 1976, and proceeded to dismiss Fredericks, Richards, and Kallicharran with his first 20 balls, finishing with 4 for 41. He toured India the following winter and bowled well without doing enough to earn more than one further Test cap. A safe, but by modern standards, ponderous fielder, he played with a straight bat and made some useful scores. He was captain of Glamorgan from 1983 to 1984. An intense and intelligent man, he became cricket correspondent of *The Guardian*, upholding a great tradition. He became a good, and immensely keen, golfer.

First-class career (1968–84): 2,405 runs (12.65), 772 wickets (26.66), and 79 catches

Test matches (3): 15 runs (7.50), 6 wickets (57.16), and 1 catch

SEWELL, Edward Humphrey Dalrymple

(b. 1872, India; d. 1947, London) *Essex, London County, and Buckinghamshire*

E. H. D. Sewell, as he was always known in his later career in journalism, played his early cricket—some of it under Ranjitsinhji's captaincy —while a civil servant in India. He became the first man there to make three consecutive centuries and twice made a double-century. Returning to England, he played as a professional (1900–4) for W. G. Grace's side, London County, and for Essex. For London County he made his highest score in first-class cricket, 188 against Surrey at The Oval in 1904 and in the same year participated in an extraordinary game for Essex at Chesterfield against Derbyshire. His own team, after scoring 597 in the first innings, lost the match by nine wickets, Sewell making top score in Essex's second innings. He was a powerful right-handed batsman with a devastating record for hard hitting in minor counties' cricket while playing for Buckinghamshire. He had played Rugby football for Blackheath and Harlequins and for many years reported on both sports for the daily press. He was also the author of over a dozen books. *Well Hit! Sir*, published in the year of his death, reflected on the personalities he had known. Of Lords Harris and Hawke, he wrote: 'The council chambers of cricket suffered their severest loss when the wickets of these two Englishmen fell.'

First-class career (1892–1922): 3,430 runs (24.50) including 5 centuries, 17 wickets (47.47), and 70 catches

SHACKLETON, Derek

(b. 1924, Todmorden, Yorkshire) *Hampshire, Dorset, and England*

A model professional, Derek Shackleton or 'Shack' was an apparently tireless right-arm stock bowler of uncanny accuracy who could both swing the ball in at medium pace and get it to leave the bat late. As a young player he was a batsman who could bowl erratic leg-spinners. But Hampshire were short of seam-bowlers and Shackleton became, for two decades, an awesome phenomenon of modern cricket, bowling 1,500 overs or so annually as though he were playing them on the pianola. Slim, trim, and immaculate, his action was light and easy. In his fortieth year (according to his captain, Desmond Eagar) he actually bowled a long-hop. In 1955, against Somerset at Weston-super-Mare, he took 14 for 29, including figures of 8 for 4 in the first innings. Twenty times consecutively he took more than 100 wickets in a season, a record, and no one has captured more wickets for Hampshire—2,669. Only Wilfred Rhodes has taken 100 wickets in more seasons. He took nine wickets in an innings on four occasions and ten or more in a match thirty-eight times. 'Shack' never represented England against Australia. However, he toured India in 1951/2, and appeared occasionally against South Africa and the West Indies at home. As a right-handed batsman, he added many runs when some of the acknowledged batsmen failed. His son, Julian, played for Gloucestershire. A modest, friendly man, he became coach at Canford School and from 1979 to 1981 a first-class umpire.

First-class career (1948–69): 9,574 runs (14.61), 2,857 wickets (18.65), and 221 catches

Test matches (7): 113 runs (18.83), 18 wickets (42.66), and 1 catch

SHARP, John

(b. 1878, Hereford; d. 1938, Wavertree, Liverpool) *Lancashire and England*

Short and thickset, Jack Sharp was a right-handed batsman who scored freely with hard, punching off-drives and powerful cuts and pulls. A good fast-medium bowler, he was also a brilliant field at cover-point. Ten times he exceeded 1,000 runs in a season and once—in 1901, a batsman's year—took more than 100 wickets. But against Australia at The Oval in 1909 he was chosen primarily as a fast bowler on a wicket hard and true. He took three good wickets and scored 105. He appeared in two other Tests that year. He also played soccer for Everton and England. Becoming an amateur cricketer, he captained Lancashire from 1923 until 1925, and was an England selector.

First-class career (1899–1925): 22,715 runs (31.11) including 38 centuries, 441 wickets (27.41), and 236 catches
Test matches (3): 188 runs (47.00) including 1 century, 3 wickets (37.00), and 1 catch

SHARPE, John William

(b. 1866, Ruddington, Nottinghamshire; d. 1936, Ruddington) *Nottinghamshire, Surrey, and England*

'One-eyed' Sharpe—he had lost an eye while a youth—came to Surrey as there was no room for him in his native Nottinghamshire XI. His right-arm, fast-medium bowling, with its remarkable break from the off and extra fast yorker, earned him two great seasons—1890 (139 wickets) and 1891 (108 wickets)—with the Champion county. After his tour of Australia, however, with Lord Sheffield's team, 1891/2, his talent evaporated as suddenly as it had developed. He returned to Nottinghamshire but, after a handful of matches, he was dropped. Of slight build, he had tried to bowl too fast, and had consequently worn himself out very quickly. He was an excellent field, with a good throw.

First-class career (1889–94): 657 runs (8.53), 338 wickets (16.06), and 48 catches
Test matches (3): 44 runs (22.00), 11 wickets (27.72), and 2 catches

SHARPE, Philip John

(b. 1936, Shipley, Yorkshire) *Yorkshire, Derbyshire, Norfolk, and England*

A cheerful, stocky, right-hand batsman renowned for his skill at hockey, cards, Gilbert and Sullivan performances, and witty repartee, Philip Sharpe was one of those players who was more impressive as a Test batsman than he was at county level. His outstanding claim to fame is as one of the greatest of all slip fielders, one amazing catch very close to the stumps off a full-blooded slash by Joey Carew of the West Indies at Old Trafford in 1969 living ineradicably in the memory. Sharpe's reactions were as his name and he so often got two sure hands to chances which others might have dived for in vain. His batting was full of enterprise: a good cover-driver, he was a particularly good hooker and cutter and many of his best innings for England were against the fast bowlers of the West Indies sides of 1963 and 1969. His defence was less impressive, hence perhaps his somewhat unpredictable form for Yorkshire. A brilliant boy cricketer at Worksop, he was capped by Yorkshire in 1960 and toured India

with MCC in 1963/4. He passed 1,000 runs in a season twelve times. He moved to Derbyshire for two seasons in 1975, hitting his highest score, 228, against Oxford University in his final season and also pleasing himself with a fine 126 against his old county colleagues. He then played Minor County cricket for Norfolk for two more seasons and served for many years as an England selector.

First-class career (1956–76): 22,530 runs (30.73) including 29 centuries, 3 wickets (65.66), and 617 catches
Test matches (12): 786 runs (46.23) including 1 century, and 17 catches

SHAW, Alfred

(b. 1842, Burton Joyce, Nottingham; d. 1907, Gedling, Nottinghamshire) *Nottinghamshire, Sussex, and England*

In old portraits Alfred Shaw looked the epitome of Victorian uncles: grave, portly, benign, a small cap perched on the top of rather a large head, and a short avuncular beard round his chin. He was *the* master of right-arm, slow-medium, good length bowling. He never delivered a wide in his life and in a long career bowled more overs than he had runs hit off them (25,699 overs and 5 balls, 24,873 runs). Nine times between 1870 and 1880 he took 100 wickets or more in a season; 1878 brought him 202 wickets (10.88) and his 186 wickets in 1880 cost only 8.54 runs each. He and Arthur Shrewsbury were the prime movers of a strike by the Nottinghamshire professionals against the county's committee; but in 1882 he was appointed county captain and, in the five years of his leadership, the county finished top of the Championship each time. He was shrewd, honest, obliging, and acquisitive. He toured Australia with James Lillywhite's team, 1876/7, captured 198 wickets (3.95) in all matches and appeared in the first Tests at Melbourne, taking 3 for 51 and 5 for 38 in 89.3 overs in the inaugural match. Later, he took three teams out to Australia as business ventures with either Lillywhite or Shrewsbury, though overall the ventures were financial failures. He appeared in the first Test in England at The Oval, 1880. He visited America with Edgar Willsher's side of 1868, and Richard Daft's of 1879. On the latter tour he was phenomenal, taking 178 wickets at the absurd average of 2.70. With his patron, Lord Sheffield, Shaw continued to tour the world, even playing cricket by the light of the midnight sun on the Ice Fiord at Spitzbergen. His professional connection with the game lasted more than 40 years, latterly as Sussex coach and a first-class umpire; at 53 he appeared for the weak Sussex side with some success.

First-class career (1864–97): 6,585 runs (12.44), 2,026 wickets (12.13), and 368 catches
Test matches (7): 111 runs (10.09), 12 wickets (23.75), and 4 catches

SHEFFIELD, 3rd Earl of

(b. 1831, London; d. 1909, Beaulieu, Hampshire)

Henry Holroyd, Earl of Sheffield, represented all that was best in nineteenth-century aristocratic paternalism. Anglo-Boer war orphans, the poor and hospitals benefited from his generosity as did Sussex cricket at both county and village level. When the county needed help in engaging professionals, the earl came to the rescue. In 1891–2 he financed a tour to Australia in order that the public there might see W. G. Grace. The venture left him £2,700 out of pocket—Grace's own expenses were £3,000—but he gave £150 which provided the Shield for which the Australian colonies (as they then were) competed. His own ground at Sheffield Park was the venue in which the Australians, on five occasions, and the South Africans, once, began their tours. He had, said the *Sydney Morning Herald* 'one of the most generous hearts that ever beat beneath a waistcoat'. Sheffield's idiosyncrasy was to shrink from photographers, but a surviving picture shows him with King Edward VII, the two men looking surprisingly alike.

SHEPHERD, David Robert

(b. 1940, Bideford, Devon) *Gloucestershire*

After five seasons with his home county of Devon, 'Shep' announced himself in first-class cricket with a century on début against Oxford University at the Parks in 1965. For fifteen seasons (1965–79), his rotund frame presented to bowlers a strong middle-order right-handed batsman who scored a thousand runs on two occasions. Some of his best performances were in one-day cricket. His humour, balanced temperament, and knowledge of the game made him just the right person to become a first-class umpire and, by 1985, he had joined the Test match panel. As character and umpire he is one of the best.

First-class career (1965–79): 10,672 runs (24.47) including 12 centuries, 2 wickets (53.00), and 95 catches

SHEPHERD, Donald John

(b. 1927, Port Eynon, Glamorgan, Wales)
Glamorgan

Leading Glamorgan in their victory against the 1968 Australians at Swansea and helping them to the Championship a year later, in the match in which he took his 2,000th wicket, were highlights in 'Shep's' twenty-three seasons (1950–72) in first-class cricket. When Worcestershire showed interest in the fast-medium seamer doing his national service locally, Glamorgan woke up to the fact that this was a bowler from the Gower peninsula they should employ. After five seasons, he switched to off-cutters, his spin surrendering little in pace and his high action retained. Wicket-keepers often stood back to him. A thousand overs a season was his regular diet and a hundred wickets an achievement on twelve occasions, including 177 in 1956—his first season as a spinner. Among many match-returns were 12 for 76 against Yorkshire at Cardiff in 1957. Other bowlers liked him because he caught batsmen out in the deep and wicket-keepers liked him because his throws came into their gloves. Everybody liked his quiet, friendly personality. He had his own unique brand of right-handed batsmanship. Two fifties, each with six sixes and each in a quarter of an hour, in 1961, against the Australians and Derbyshire, were samples of what he could do when he 'came off'. His representative cricket included matches for the Players (1952–7) against the Gentlemen and tours to East Africa, Pakistan, the Far East, and Zambia. No other bowler has taken so many wickets in first-class cricket without being picked for England. Like his fellow Welshman, the batsman Alan Jones, he stands on a lonely pinnacle.

First-class career (1950–72): 5,696 runs (9.67), 2,218 wickets (21.32), and 251 catches

SHEPPARD, Rt. Revd David Stuart

(b. 1929, Reigate, Surrey) *Cambridge University, Sussex, and England*

As a schoolboy at Sherborne, David Sheppard was a relatively modest batsman but mental tenacity drove him to the top. A tall, right-hand batsman he possessed many graceful off-side shots and limitless power of concentration, and became a leading figure in what one might term the 'Cambridge Movement' of the early 1950s. He shared opening partnerships with John Dewes of 343 against the West Indies at Fenners and 349 against Sussex at Hove in 1950, both records.

From 1951 to 1953 he scored 24 centuries, each season exceeding 2,000 runs. In 1952, as Cambridge captain, he hit 127 in the University match and topped the national first-class averages with 2,262 runs (64.62), including his career-highest, 239 not out for Cambridge at Worcester. Captain of Sussex in 1953, he was firm but kind and steered his team to second place in the Championship. He was selected for England in the final Test against the West Indies at The Oval in 1950, and toured Australia with MCC in 1950/1, but was disappointing. Against India at The Oval in 1952, he scored 119; and he led England in two Tests against Pakistan in 1954. In 1956, now ordained to the ministry of the Church of England, he was recalled for the fourth Test against Australia at Old Trafford and hit a memorable 113. He was the first ordained minister to play in Test cricket. Inevitably, his appearances in first-class cricket became fewer, but in 1962 he made 100 at Lord's in the last Gentlemen v. Players match, and that winter toured Australasia again, his 113 at Melbourne in the third Test contributing to England's only victory in the series. He made 1,074 runs (38.35) on the tour. One or two unfortunate dropped catches, however, led to Fred Trueman's affectionate jibe: 'It's a pity Reverend don't put his hands together more often in t'field.' David Sheppard was an inspiring organizer of the Mayflower Centre in London and was bishop of Woolwich before becoming bishop of Liverpool in 1975. In 1994, at a service marking his 25 years of ministry as a bishop of the Church of England, the service notes by the bishop of Warrington referred to his ecumenical work with Liverpool's Catholic archbishop, 'his deep concern for the underdog, his clear passion for the cause of the poor' and 'his willingness to challenge the very highest in the land'.

First-class career (1947–63): 15,838 runs (43.51) including 45 centuries, and 195 catches

Test matches (22): 1,172 runs (37.80) including 3 centuries, and 12 catches

SHERRIFF, Robert Cedric

(b. 1896, Hampton Wick, Surrey; d. 1975, Kingston-upon-Thames)

It is as the author of the anti-war play *Journey's End* (1928), that the reputation of Sherriff rests; a play which earned £75,000 for the £6-a-week insurance clerk. Two years later, *Badger's Green* appeared on the London West End stage while Bradman was making his mark against England in the 1930 Test series. The setting was village cricket, Badger's Green against Ragholt, and the play extolled the cardinal virtues of sportsmanship and loyalty. W. A. Darlington, the theatre critic—and a cricketer—called it 'brilliant' but on the day Bradman made his 334 at Leeds it was taken off. Sherriff would write many more plays, the scripts for several Hollywood films and some novels but he never again attained the fame which *Journey's End* had brought him. Like Alletson's 189 for Nottingham against Sussex in 1911, his fame rests on one performance.

SHERWIN, Mordecai

(b. 1851, Greasley, Nottinghamshire; d. 1910, Nottingham) *Nottinghamshire and England*

Less than 5 ft. 10 in. tall but weighing around 17 stone, Mordecai Sherwin was jocular, physically powerful and very hard-working. A surprisingly agile wicket-keeper, whose fleshy hands did not often suffer damage behind the stumps, he was quoted as saying: 'Oi'm not much with my pen myself, but Oi'd loike to bung my fist into the face of anyone wot says aught be wrong with my stumping.' He was the last of the old-time professionals of the county (1887 and 1888), and an ardent but unsuccessful Conservative candidate in Nottingham Municipal elections. For Players against Gentlemen at Lord's in 1888 he dismissed five batsmen in an innings; and represented England for the only time against Australia at home that year. In 1886/7 he toured 'down under' with Shaw's and Shrewsbury's team. He also kept goal for Notts County for many years.

First-class career (1876–96): 2,332 runs (7.59), 8 wickets (13.50), and 836 dismissals (611 c., 225 st.)

Test matches (3): 30 runs (15.00) and 7 dismissals (5 c., 2 st.)

SHREWSBURY, Arthur

(b. 1856, New Lenton, Nottinghamshire; d. 1903, Gedling, Nottinghamshire) *Nottinghamshire and England*

In the 1880s and 1890s Arthur Shrewsbury held a position of honour in the cricket world similar to that held by Jack Hobbs 30 to 40 years later. He stood head and shoulders above his fellow professionals in artistry and attainments on the field and second to none in the respect which his personal character had gained. He was one of the first right-handed batsmen to develop an impregnable quality in defence and combine it with powers of steady scoring. 'Bring me out a cup of tea at four o'clock,' he would say to the Trent Bridge pavilion attendant, in days before the interval was introduced, and he was generally still in when the time for his favourite beverage came round. When W.G. picked a Test team, Arthur was always his first choice—'Give me Arthur' has gone down in cricket lore. Sound rather than spectacular, he was a perfectionist, wanting every stroke to be played precisely right. Many of his finest innings were played on treacherous wickets, when he would go right forward, or right back to play the ball as late as possible. He was an excellent field either in the deep or, latterly, at point. A precise man, neat as a new pin, he was completely bald, but it was a joke among his colleagues that nobody had ever seen the top of his head. On the field he wore his cap, off it a neat bowler hat, and in bed a nightcap! Thirteen times he exceeded 1,000 runs in a season, his best year being 1887, when he made 1,653 runs (78.71), including eight centuries and headed the national averages. He hit no fewer than ten double-centuries, his highest being 267 for Nottinghamshire against Middlesex in 1887, and the same score against Sussex in 1890, both at Trent Bridge. He carried his bat through an innings nine times. Shrewsbury visited Australia with four teams in the 1880s, three times in partnership with Alfred Shaw, and also took a football team there. He played many fine Test innings. At Sydney in 1881/2 he top-scored each time with 82 and 47 in a losing contest. He made 164, a dominant innings, at Lord's in 1886 and in his last series in 1893 he made 106 and 81 at Lord's and 66 at The Oval. He shot himself through the mouth because he believed he was suffering from an incurable disease.

First-class career (1875–1902): 26,505 runs (36.65) including 59 centuries, and 377 catches
Test matches (23): 1,277 runs (35.47) including 3 centuries, 0–2, and 29 catches

SHUTER, John

(b. 1855, Thornton Heath, Surrey; d. 1920, Blackheath, London) *Kent, Surrey, and England*

A short man—5 ft. 6 in.—who did not care for averages or personal glory, John Shuter led Surrey from 1880 until 1893 and during the last seven seasons the county won the Championship five times and tied once. He was a popular leader and a singularly graceful right-handed batsman, with remarkable power on the off-side. He represented England once against Australia, at The Oval in 1888, scoring 28. On retiring from the Surrey

captaincy he received, as a testimonial, a grand piano and a brace of pistols. Shortly before his death he had been appointed secretary to Surrey.

First-class career (1874–1909): 10,206 runs (21.26) including 8 centuries, and 157 catches

SHUTTLEWORTH, Kenneth

(b. 1944, St Helens, Lancashire) *Lancashire, Leicestershire, and England*

A dark and well-built fast bowler with an action surely modelled on Fred Trueman's, Ken Shuttleworth was restricted by injuries throughout a career which never quite took off as it might have done. At the brief peak of his powers he was distinctly quick with a dangerous out-swing, flowing from a fine action with a long, final stride and sideways-on delivery. Also a capable batsman, he first played for Lancashire, a county with considerable fast bowling talent, in 1964, but did not establish himself until 1968. In 1970 he played an unofficial Test for England against the Rest of the World and was an important member of Illingworth's successful MCC side in Australia the following winter, taking 5 for 47 in the first Test at the Gabba ground in Brisbane. His best Championship performance was 7 for 41 for Lancashire against Essex in 1968. Lancashire grew tired of his persistent misfortune with injuries but he had his successes for Leicestershire after 1977.

First-class career (1964–80): 2,589 runs (16.59), 623 wickets (24.51), and 128 catches
Test matches (5): 46 runs (7.66), 12 wickets (35.58), and 1 catch

SIDEBOTTOM, Arnold

(b. 1954, Barnsley, Yorkshire) *Yorkshire, Orange Free State, and England*

Arnie Sidebottom made his only Test appearance against Australia at Trent Bridge in 1985 at the age of 31. He probably would have made his début much earlier if he had not concentrated so much on football—he played with success for Manchester United—and then joined the rebel tour to South Africa in March 1982, earning himself a three-year ban from Test cricket. Red-haired and raw-boned, he made his début for Yorkshire in 1973 and although not capped until 1980 he was a very effective right-arm seam-bowler of waspish pace and a more than useful lower-order batsman. Now committed to cricket, he played for Orange Free State in the winter seasons of 1981–4. He had not had a successful season in 1985 when he was called into the England side, but the selectors were mindful of his steady performances during his Test ban—he took 63 wickets (20.50) in 1984. Plagued with minor ailments throughout his career, he lasted only half an innings at Trent Bridge before a painful foot injury forced him to leave the field. He took 1 for 65 and scored two runs.

First-class career (1973–91): 4,508 runs (22.42) including 1 century, 596 wickets (24.42), and 63 catches

SILK, Dennis Raoul Whitehall

(b. 1931, Eureka, California, USA) *Cambridge University and Somerset*

After a distinguished school sporting career at Christ's Hospital in Horsham, an undefeated century by the right-handed Dennis Silk gave Cambridge University a last-minute victory at Lord's in 1953 against an Oxford team led by Alan Dowding, who would later serve as a housemaster under him at Radley College. Another century a year later, again in the University match, typified the batting of the future author of *Attacking Cricket* (1965). From 1956 to 1960 he was a welcome member of the Somerset side when schoolmastering duties at Marlborough permitted. There he was an inspiring teacher and avuncular housemaster. He captained MCC in Philadelphia (1959) and in New Zealand (1960/1). He also played rugby for Cambridge University and Sussex and as a Rugby Fives blue shared the National Open Doubles title with John Pretlove, the Kent batsman. After an outstanding wardenship of Radley (1968–91), Silk became the first president of MCC to serve a two-year term (1992–4) before being appointed chairman of the TCCB in 1994. A large frame and square-jaw might have made Dennis Silk a fierce figure; in fact he is a character of rare charm with a smile as bright as a rising sun.

First-class career (1952–61): 3,845 runs (29.80) including 7 centuries, 1 wicket (240.00), and 45 catches

SIMPSON, Reginald Thomas

(b. 1920, Nottingham) *Sind, Nottinghamshire, and England*

Making his début in first-class cricket in India, 1944/5, while serving with the RAF, Reg Simpson was already a well-equipped, right-handed batsman when he first played for Nottinghamshire in 1946. An opener, he was tall and slim with short, curly, dark hair. Possessing a neat, upright stance, he was a beautiful striker of the ball and a good player off the back foot, who had less trouble than most with the bouncer. He fielded superbly, usually at cover or in the deep. On fourteen occasions he exceeded 1,000 runs in a season (once overseas), and scored over 2,500 runs in both 1949 and 1950. At one period in 1949 Reg Simpson and Walter Keeton shared four successive century opening partnerships for Notts. From 1951 until 1960 he captained the county. He shared the record first-wicket partnerships for England against New Zealand with Len Hutton—147 at The Oval in 1949—and against the West Indies with Cyril Washbrook—212 at Trent Bridge in 1950. His most memorable innings, however, was 156 not out in the fifth Test at Melbourne in 1950/1, which was a major factor in England's first win over Australia for 13 years. He toured Australia twice, New Zealand and South Africa, and represented England against all the Test-playing countries at home but never fully established himself at the highest level. He became a director of Gunn and Moore Ltd and a shrewd observer of modern batting techniques.

First-class career (1944–63): 30,546 runs (38.32) including 64 centuries, 59 wickets (37.74), and 193 catches

Test matches (27): 1,401 runs (33.35) including 4 centuries, 2 wickets (11.00), and 5 catches

SIMPSON-HAYWARD, George Hayward Thomas

(b. 1875, Stoneleigh, Kenilworth, Warwickshire; d. 1936, Icomb Place, Gloucestershire) *Cambridge University, Worcestershire, and England*

George Simpson-Hayward was the last and one of the most successful lob-bowlers to represent England. He was very effective on the matting with H. D. G. Leveson-Gower's team in South Africa, 1909/10, which was his third, and only major, MCC tour. In 1909 he had taken 6 for 132 (in a total of 289) and top-scored when Worcestershire played the Australians; but he did not play for England at home.

First-class career (1899–1914): 5,556 runs (18.58) including 3 centuries, 503 wickets (21.39), and 133 catches

Test matches (5): 105 runs (15.00), 23 wickets (18.26), and 1 catch

SIMS, James Morton

(b. 1903, Leyton, Essex; d. 1973, Canterbury, Kent)
Middlesex and England

Jim Sims was lank, solemn, and lugubrious in the style of Alfred Lester, a master of understatement and a lively humorist, centre of many stories and a lovable character who spoke out of the side of his mouth. J. J. Warr once joined him as number eleven with Middlesex still requiring some 50 to win. Sims had had a good match and was playing well again. 'How do you want me to play it?' asked Warr. 'It doesn't really matter,' Jim replied, 'I'm already covered with bloody glory.' Starting in first-class cricket as a right-handed batsman, he developed more as an unusually consistent leg-break bowler with a tricky googly. He took all 10 for 90 in an innings for East against West at Kingston in 1948, and on eight occasions took more than 100 wickets in a season. As a lower-order batsman, he was sometimes invaluable. He toured Australia with MCC's 'goodwill' side of 1935/6 and the full side in 1936/7, and represented England at home against South Africa and India, his best performance being seven wickets in the match against India at The Oval in 1936. In retirement he became county scorer and died during a match at Canterbury.

First-class career (1929–53): 8,983 runs (17.30) including 4 centuries, 1,581 wickets (24.92), and 253 catches
Test matches (4): 16 runs (4.00), 11 wickets (43.63), and 6 catches

SINFIELD, Reginald Albert

(b. 1900, Benington, Stevenage, Hertfordshire; d. 1988, Ham Green, Bristol) *Hertfordshire, Gloucestershire, and England*

Year after year, Reg Sinfield served Gloucestershire with his mild-looking but persistent slow-medium, right-arm bowling and his obstinate and defensive batting, generally as an opener. Sometimes, however, he would attack to great effect. Ten times he exceeded 1,000 runs in a season and four times 100 wickets; twice he achieved the double. In 1938 in his sole Test, against Australia at Trent Bridge, he scored 6 and took 2 for 123. On retirement he became coach at Clifton and, later, at Coltston's School, also in Bristol, where he influenced the young Chris Broad.

First-class career (1921–39): 15,674 runs (25.69) including 16 centuries, 1,173 wickets (24.49), and 178 catches

SLACK, Wilfred Norris

(b. 1954, Troumaca, St Vincent, West Indies; d. 1989, Banjul, The Gambia) *Middlesex, Windward Islands, and England*

Wilf Slack embarked on his Test career in the most difficult of circumstances, flying out to the West Indies when his county captain, Mike Gatting, returned home for surgery on his broken nose, but this sound and determined left-handed opening batsman acquitted himself well in his two Tests. Born in St Vincent, he came to England as a boy in 1966, played for Buckinghamshire, and made his début for Middlesex in 1977, becoming a consistently heavy scorer in county cricket. He was unlucky to have missed selection in the original party for the tour of the West Indies, having scored 1,900 runs (54.28) in 1985, including a double-century against the Australian tourists. Instead, he went on the England B tour to Sri Lanka, and was the team's most successful batsman, scoring 382 runs (54.57) in four internationals, before his Caribbean call-up. Having played first-class cricket for the Windwards he hoped to adjust quickly to the barrage of fast bowling. He made a valuable 34 in England's victory in the Port of Spain one-day international, and made his Test début within a week of his arrival. He made only two in the first innings and was run out for nought in the second, but given a second chance in the last Test in Antigua, he made a valiant and patient 52, sharing in an opening stand of 127 with Graham Gooch. A dependable fielder, he bowled useful right-arm medium pace. Dropped after only one Test against India in 1986, his loss of form exacerbated by personal problems, this shy, likeable man finished the season well enough to earn a place on the tour of Australia in 1986/7. He had a tour on which little went right, but remained courteous and cheerful throughout. Two winters later, playing on a minor tour in The Gambia, he died suddenly of heart failure. He had more than once suffered black-outs during matches in previous years, but doctors had been unable to diagnose any illness.

First-class career (1977–88): 13,950 runs (38.96) including 25 centuries, 21 wickets (32.06), and 174 catches
Test matches (3): 81 runs (13.50) and 3 catches

SMAILES, Thomas Francis

(b. 1910, Ripley, Yorkshire; d. 1970, Starbeck, Harrogate, Yorkshire) *Yorkshire and England*

Frank Smailes was a right-arm, fast-medium bowler who could make the ball move either way. He was also capable of bowling useful off-breaks at slower speed and he was a hard-hitting, late-order, left-handed batsman. In the powerful Yorkshire side of the 1930s—seven times Champions—he took more than 100 wickets in a season four times and once reached 1,000 runs. In 1939 he captured all 10 for 47 in an innings against Derbyshire at Bramall Lane and he took 6 for 29 and 4 for 45 at Bramall Lane when his county nearly defeated the 1938 Australians; but his sole Test was against India at Lord's in 1946, when he scored 25 and took 3 for 62. He was picked in England's side of 13 for the 1938 Manchester Test, which never started because of rain.

First-class career (1932–48): 5,892 runs (19.25) including 3 centuries, 822 wickets (20.81), and 154 catches

SMALL, Gladstone Cleophas

(b. 1961, Barbados, West Indies) *Warwickshire, South Australia, and England*

Barbados-born but schooled in Birmingham, Gladstone Small has in no way been hampered by an apparent disability, the virtual lack of any neck between head and shoulders. A cheerful, willing, accurate, and determined right-arm bowler, he performed consistently well for Warwickshire at only a little below genuinely fast pace in the early 1980s, winning his county cap in 1982 when he was called into England's squad for the Edgbaston Test against Pakistan but did not play. He lost form through bowling far too many no-balls but when advised to shorten his run in 1985, he enjoyed a successful season with 69 wickets and followed this with 39 wickets in the Sheffield Shield as an overseas player for South Australia in 1985/6 including a career-best 7 for 42 against New South Wales at Adelaide. The following summer in England he was selected for the last two Tests of the season against New Zealand, taking four wickets for 98 on an unresponsive pitch at Trent Bridge and bowling tidily enough at The Oval to earn himself a place on the winter tour to Australia. Swinging the ball dangerously at times, he played in the last two Tests, taking 5 for 48 and 2 for 40 at Melbourne where England regained the Ashes when Small took a catch in the deep. He had another five-wicket analysis in

Sydney and although his appearances in Test cricket since have been sporadic, partly because of suspect hamstring muscles, he made two more overseas tours, to the West Indies in 1989/90, when he took 17 Test wickets (29.70) in four Tests, and Australia in 1990/1, when he again played in all but one Test. For Warwickshire his best season was 1988, when he took 80 first-class wickets but his most lucrative was 1994 when he helped his county to three titles: not always fit, he could still be relied upon to take wickets with the new ball, not least in limited-overs matches. A right-handed tail-end batsman, he has played some useful innings and he fields well with a strong throw.

First-class career (1980–): 4,269 runs (14.52) and 808 wickets (28.54)

Test matches (17): 263 runs (15.47), 55 wickets (34.01), and 9 catches

SMALL, John

(b. 1737, Empshott, Hampshire; d. 1826, Petersfield, Hampshire) *Hambledon and Hampshire*

John Nyren called John Small 'a star of the first magnitude'. Possibly his best years, as a right-handed batsman who pioneered the quick single, were the 1760s of which scant record exists. Not till he was 35 do any precise scores survive. In a five-a-side single wicket match between Hambledon and Kent on the Artillery ground in London in 1775 Lumpy Stevens 'bowled' him three times, the ball passing between the two stumps without disturbing the bails. Soon afterwards, the third stump was introduced while Small began both to use and to manufacture the more upright style of batting. Verses to his memory included the famous

John Small make bat and ball
Pitch a wicket, play at cricket
With any man in England.

Two of his best performances were in 1775 and 1776 in Hambledon's annual fixture with Surrey at Broad-Halfpenny Down when he made 136 not out and 85 respectively. At the age of 60 he made 23 for Hampshire against MCC at Lord's and probably played a few years longer. Cricket apart, he found time in a long life to be a gamekeeper, skater, draper, violinist, and, for 75 years, a chorister in Petersfield church. Once confronted by an aggressive bull on his return from a party he is said to have saved his life by playing his violin and calming the animal. (Arthur Haygarth, *Scores and Biographies*.) The Duke of Dorset and he exchanged gifts of a violin and a

357

pair of bats, that mutual respect in different walks of life which Nyren so much admired. His son, John, appeared in the first match between the Players and the Gentlemen at Lord's in 1806.

SMITH, Alan Christopher

(b. 1936, Hall Green, Birmingham) *Oxford University, Warwickshire, and England*

Three years in the Oxford University side and captain for two, Alan Smith or 'A.C.' was a 'complete cricketer'. He was a sound right-handed batsman always on the lookout for runs, a medium-pace bowler with an extraordinary knock-kneed run and a windmill action, and a top-class wicket-keeper. In 1962 he scored 1,201 runs (31.60) and had 82 dismissals (79 c., 3 st.) and in the following winter was first-choice 'keeper for England in Australia and New Zealand, as well as sharing in the second partnership of 163 unbroken for the ninth wicket with Colin Cowdrey against New Zealand at Wellington. He hit two centuries for Oxford against Hampshire at Bournemouth in 1959, held six catches in one innings against Derbyshire at Derby in 1970 and, on taking off his pads and going on to bowl against Essex at Clacton in 1965, he took a hat-trick. He was a keen, indeed hostile, captain who believed completely in himself and he led his county from 1968 until 1974, winning the Championship in 1972. He also had a flair for one-day cricket, and led Warwickshire to victory in the Gillette Cup in his first year as captain. He has been a director of Aston Villa FC, a Test selector, assistant manager of the MCC touring team to Australia in 1974/5, and manager of England sides in the West Indies in 1980/1 and in New Zealand and Pakistan in 1983/4, both unsuccessful tours for England, though he was praised for his management. Secretary of Warwickshire from 1976 to 1986, he was then appointed chief executive of the Test and County Cricket Board, a job to which he was devoted.

First-class career (1958–74): 11,027 runs (20.92) including 5 centuries, 131 wickets (23.46), and 776 dismissals (715 c., 61 st.)
Test matches (6): 118 runs (29.50) and 20 dismissals (20 c.)

SMITH, Cedric Ivan James

(b. 1906, Corsham, Wiltshire; d. 1979, Mellor, Lancashire) *Wiltshire, Middlesex, and England*

At 6 ft. 4 in. 'Big Jim' Smith was a burly man, who bowled fast and hit faster. A right-arm bowler he had stamina and a good action made his deliveries lift, swing and cut. In his first season for Middlesex in 1934 he took 172 wickets (18.88), and in six brief seasons for the county alone secured 676 wickets (17.75). His reputation as a smiter was richly deserved, and he was a great favourite at Lord's and elsewhere. He was as if 'hewn out of English oak', the personification of the village blacksmith. The violence of his favourite stroke between square-leg and mid-on was terrifying; at Lord's his hits would take the ball into the 'Q' stand, or over the Tavern into St John's Wood. Against Gloucestershire at Bristol in 1938 he hit 50 not out in 11 minutes (66 in 18 minutes), against Kent at Maidstone in 1935, 50 not out in 14 minutes; and his sole century, also against Kent at Canterbury, took 81 minutes. He appeared in one home Test against New Zealand in 1937, and toured the West Indies with MCC in 1934/5. At Bridgetown he took 5 for 15, enabling England to win her only match of the series.

First-class career (1930–9): 4,007 runs (14.68) including 1 century, 845 wickets (19.25), and 99 catches
Test matches (5): 102 runs (10.20), 15 wickets (26.20), and 1 catch

SMITH, Sir Charles Aubrey

(b. 1863, London; d. 1948, Beverley Hills, California, USA) *Cambridge University, Sussex, Transvaal, and England*

As well known in Hollywood as he was at Lord's Aubrey Smith was an old Carthusian and a Cambridge blue who appeared four times in the University match. Over 6 ft. tall, he was primarily a right-arm, fast-medium bowler whose sobriquet was 'Round the Corner', because he approached the wicket on a parabolic curve. He had a high action and persistent accuracy, cutting the ball in from the off. He was also a long-reaching batsman of both vigilance and power and excellent at slip. He played for Sussex for 13 years, as captain in 1887, 1888 and 1890. Against Cambridge at Fenner's in 1885 he took 5 for 8 and, five years later, 7 for 16 against MCC at Lord's. He toured Australia in 1887/8 and in 1888/9 he captained the first team (Major Warton's) to visit South Africa. In the first Test (his sole Test appearance) he scored 3 and took 5 for 19 and 2 for 42, thus playing a considerable part in England's victory. He remained in South Africa, stockbroking in Johannesburg for some years and played in the first Currie Cup tournament. Returning to London, he made his début on the London stage in

1896, and in the 1920s went to Hollywood, where in many films he typified the English gentleman —as he did in life. He became a one-man MCC in Hollywood, cricket in California revolving around him; he revitalized the game in the USA. His house at Beverly Hills was called 'The Round Corner'. He was knighted for his services to Anglo-American friendship and came to Lord's often. Once dropping a catch in America he called his butler for his glasses and, in missing another catch, expostulated 'the idiot brought my *reading* glasses!'

First-class career (1882–96): 2,986 runs (13.63), 346 wickets (22.34), and 97 catches

SMITH, Christopher Lyall

(b. 1958, Durban, South Africa) *Natal, Glamorgan, Hampshire, and England*

Born in Durban of British parents and learning his cricket in South Africa, Chris Smith set his heart on playing cricket in England. So successful was this fair-haired, stocky, and determined right-handed opening batsman that he forced his way into the Test side in 1983. He made his first-class début for Natal B in 1977/8 aged 18, and played regularly for Natal until 1982/3. Having made one appearance for Glamorgan in 1979, the following season he was engaged as Hampshire's overseas player in the absence of Greenidge and Marshall and he scored 1,048 runs (31.75) with three hundreds. He made only occasional appearances in the Hampshire first team in 1981 and 1982, but when he became qualified as an Englishman in 1983 he batted magnificently for his county. With almost 1,700 runs and six centuries by the beginning of August, he won a place in the third Test against New Zealand at Lord's. His Test career 'began' dramatically—he was out first ball, lbw to Richard Hadlee, but he recovered to make a composed 43 in the second innings. He batted resolutely on the 1983/4 tour to New Zealand and Pakistan, making 91 in the Auckland Test and scoring 280 runs (40.00) in his five Tests. He had a disappointing season in 1984 and lost his England place, but he scored exactly 2,000 runs (57.14) in 1985 and won a place on the England B tour to Sri Lanka, where he was one of the leading batsmen. He played a further Test in 1986, being called in as an eleventh hour replacement for the match against India at Headingley. He made 6 and 28, better than some in a dismal English batting performance—but this was not enough to save his place. Although not as naturally gifted as his younger brother Robin, who

had followed him to Hampshire, Chris worked exceptionally hard at his game and was a determined and technically watertight batsman as well as an occasional off-spin bowler. He retired shortly after guiding Hampshire to the NatWest Final at Lord's in order to take up a post as chief executive of the West Australian Cricket Association in Perth.

First-class career (1977–91): 18,028 runs (44.40) including 47 centuries, 50 wickets (53.70), and 176 catches

Test matches (8): 392 runs (30.15), 3 wickets (13.00), and 5 catches

SMITH, David Mark

(b. 1956, Balham, London) *Surrey, Worcestershire, Sussex, and England*

David Smith won a place on England's 1986 tour of the West Indies because of his ability to play fast bowling. He showed great courage in making 112 and 87 in 1985 for Worcestershire against Malcolm Marshall at his most hostile. A very tall and broad left-handed batsman with a high backlift, he made good use of his height and had a wide range of attractive shots. Brought up in Balham, and in his early days a useful medium-fast bowler off the wrong foot, he made his début for Surrey in 1973 when still only 17 and in his years at The Oval looked a most promising batsman, though prone to injury and sometimes temperamental. He moved to Worcestershire before the 1984 season and enjoyed two successful years for his new county. His fearless approach against fast bowling made him an ideal choice for the tour of the Caribbean, and he was thrust straight into Test cricket in the first Test at Kingston. Having played in only one first-class match on the tour, he could make only 1 and 0 on his début, but, brought back into the side for the fourth Test at Port of Spain, he responded with two fine innings of 47 and 32. A bad back prevented him from playing in the next Test. He returned to Surrey for two seasons in 1987, then took a final journey south to Hove where some fruitful innings culminated in one of 124, out of 321 for six, in the 1993 NatWest Final against Warwickshire. It should have been a match-winning performance, but did not prove so. After his first season at Hove, he was called out for a second tour to the West Indies as a replacement for Graham Gooch, only to break his thumb in his one and only innings. His highest score was 213 for Sussex against Essex in 1992.

SMITH

First-class career (1973–   ): 15,265 runs (36.17) including 28 centuries, and 30 wickets (52.47)
Test matches (2): 80 runs (20.00)

SMITH, David Robert

(b. 1934, Bristol) *Gloucestershire and England*

David Smith was a right-arm, medium-fast bowler with a very short run-up, whose pace was often considerably quicker than the batsman expected. Able to move the ball both ways, he was also able to maintain accuracy for long periods. He tended to be over-worked; in 1960, a rather wet season, he bowled not only 500 overs more than any of his colleagues, but more overs than any other Gloucestershire seam bowler since 1945. Moreover, he captured more wickets in a season, 143, than any other seam bowler since that time. He was a useful tail-end batsman and, as befitted a professional footballer with Bristol City and Millwall, a reliable field. He toured India with MCC in 1961/2 and did a useful job in the Tests on wickets totally unsuited to his style.

First-class career (1956–70): 4,970 runs (12.30), 1,250 wickets (23.72), and 292 catches
Test matches (5): 38 runs (9.50), 6 wickets (59.83), and 2 catches

SMITH, Denis

(b. 1907, Somercotes, Derbyshire; d. 1979, Derby) *Derbyshire and England*

A left-hander, Denis Smith became one of the most aggressive, stylish and successful batsmen in Derbyshire's history. At his best around the mid-thirties, he headed the batting averages with 42.42 when the county finished second in the Championship Table in 1935, and he was very prominent when they won the Championship for the first time in modern history the following year. His catching close to the wicket was invaluable throughout and he was a good deputy 'keeper. In 1935 he played two Tests against South Africa, in his first, at Headingley, putting on 128 for the first wicket with Arthur Mitchell. That winter he averaged 47.40 for MCC in the 'goodwill' tour of Australasia. He remained a county bulwark for many years, although no further Test honours came his way and on retirement he became county coach. He scored more than 1,000 runs in a season twelve times.

First-class career (1927–52): 21,843 runs (31.65) including 32 centuries, 20 wickets (36.70), 381 catches, and 5 stumpings
Test matches (2): 128 runs (32.00) and 1 catch

SMITH, Donald Victor

(b. 1923, Broadwater, Sussex) *Sussex and England*

Donald Smith spent several seasons when he was unable to consolidate himself in the Sussex side, but he suddenly found his form and runs flowed thereafter with great regularity. A left-handed opener, he struck 166 in less than 3 hours at Hove in 1957, an innings of electrifying brilliance, in which he hit nine sixes and 11 fours, winning the match unexpectedly against Gloucestershire. That season he scored 2,088 runs (42.61), playing in three Tests against the West Indies, although with scant success. He passed 1,000 runs in a season eight times with a highest score of 206 not out against Nottinghamshire at Trent Bridge in 1950. A useful left-arm medium-pace bowler, he took 7 for 40 for MCC against Oxford University at Lord's in 1956, including a hat-trick. Becoming a coach of some renown, he guided Sri Lanka's national side for some years.

First-class career (1946–62): 16,960 runs (30.34) including 19 centuries, 340 wickets (28.44), and 234 catches
Test matches (3): 25 runs (8.33) and 1–97

SMITH, Ernest James

(b. 1886, Birmingham; d. 1979, Birmingham) *Warwickshire and England*

For many years the oldest living Test cricketer, 'Tiger' Smith was the doyen of Edgbaston. He was wicket-keeper/batsman in 1911, when the county won the Championship for the first time, and he soon became England's 'keeper, standing up to the waspish bowling of Sydney Barnes and Frank Foster. In 1926 he dismissed seven batsmen in an innings (four caught and three stumped) against Derbyshire at Edgbaston and, over-all, his record is similar to that of his predecessor and mentor, Dick Lilley. A fine, confident, right-handed batsman, he opened the county's batting for many years, six times exceeding 1,000 runs in a season. He toured Australia in 1911/12 and South Africa in 1913/14, and represented England at home in 1912. He became a Test umpire and a much-respected Warwickshire coach. For many years after retirement he would sit in the Edgbaston pavilion, telling cricket stories or demonstrating batting techniques with a walking stick.

First-class career (1904–30): 16,997 runs (22.39) including 20 centuries, 2 wickets (51.00), and 878 dismissals (722 c., 156 st.)
Test matches (11): 113 runs (8.69) and 20 dismissals (17 c., 3 st.)

SMITH, Harry

(b. 1891, Bristol; d. 1937, Bristol) *Gloucestershire and England*

As a Bristol colt before the First World War, Harry Smith was asked to go behind the stumps in an emergency—and he blossomed as a consistently reliable 'keeper, besides being a sound batsman. His best work was in 1927 when in four consecutive innings he allowed only one bye while 1,374 runs were scored; and the following year he kept for England in the first match—his sole Test—against the West Indies at Lord's, scoring 7 and holding 1 catch.

First-class career (1912–35): 13,413 runs (22.35) including 10 centuries, and 722 dismissals (457 c., 265 st.)

SMITH, Michael John Knight

(b. 1933, Westcotes, Leicester) *Oxford University, Leicestershire, Warwickshire, and England*

Mike Smith was a modest but prolific and universally popular cricketer better known perhaps by his initials 'M.J.K.'. He always played in spectacles. He had three memorable years at Oxford —captain in his last year in 1956—hitting 201 not out, 104 and 117 against Cambridge in successive seasons at Lord's. His number of centuries and aggregate for these matches, 477, are records. A tall right-hander with great powers of improvisation and concentration he was always a prolific run-scorer, difficult to bowl to and especially punishing to the on-side where he unerringly found gaps. Once, batting for Warwickshire and going well, he expressed his concern to his partner, Ray Hitchcock, that the latter was getting bogged down. 'I don't seem to be able to find any gaps for the singles,' Ray complained. 'Well, chip them for threes instead,' Smith replied. To him this was no problem. He captained Warwickshire from 1957 until 1967, and in six consecutive seasons (1957–62) exceeded 2,000 runs each time, with 3,245 runs (57.94) in 1959. Twenty times he exceeded 1,000 runs in a season (once overseas). A brilliant short-leg field, he held 52 catches in 1961. He retired after 1967, but returned in 1970 to play regularly for another six seasons and was recalled for England against Australia in 1972. Taking longer to play himself in than most top-class players, he was particularly susceptible to the yorker early on in an innings. He toured Australia, South Africa, the West Indies, New Zealand, India, and Pakistan, captaining England in 25 Tests. Four times he was dismissed in the nineties but perhaps the best of his three Test centuries was 108 in the second Test against the West Indies at Port of Spain in 1959/60. A double blue and double international, he played Rugby once for England at fly-half against Wales. He was awarded an OBE for services to cricket. For many years he ran a Country Club but when he sold it he was able to devote time to cricket again, becoming chairman of Warwickshire and manager of England's tours to the West Indies (1993/4) and Australia (1994/5). He was in the right place to sign Brian Lara for Warwickshire in 1994, an adroit move with happy consequences for the county.

First-class career (1951–75): 39,832 runs (41.84) including 69 centuries, 5 wickets (61.00), and 593 catches

Test matches (50): 2,278 runs (31.63) including 3 centuries, 1–128, and 53 catches

SMITH, Robin Arnold

(b. 1963, Durban, South Africa) *Natal, Hampshire, and England*

A batsman of the highest class, Robin Smith was tormented by the Australian spinners Shane Warne and Tim May in 1993 to such an extent that his confidence suffered in the series against the West Indies and New Zealand which followed. His Test future stood in the balance when he was then omitted not only from three Tests against his native South Africa but also the tour to Australia in 1994/5. His first three years in Test cricket after his début in 1988 had been more or less a triumph, despite more self-doubt than most. Squarely-built, exceptionally strong and fearless, 'Judgie' Smith—so called because his hair had the appearance of a judge's wig—was born into a sporting family. Under the firm guidance of his father John, himself a first-class cricketer with Natal, young Robin soon developed into a superb athlete, breaking South African schools records at both the shot put and the 100 metres hurdles, and playing Rugby Union as an uncompromising full-back for Natal Schools. But it was as a cricketer that he showed exceptional gifts. With his elder brother Chris, who himself went on to play for Hampshire and England, he spent hours practising, and under the guidance of two Natal cricketing legends, Mike Proctor and Barry Richards, they flourished. Robin, indeed, scored 1,525 runs in a single schools season, eclipsing the record previously held by Richards. South Africa's sporting isolation persuaded him to follow his brother into county cricket with Hampshire, undergoing a four-year qualification period to become eligible for England. As an overseas player, and with Gordon Greenidge and Malcolm Marshall already established at the county, his appearances were initially restricted to the second team, but he soon made his mark with his trademark shot, a withering square cut, struck like the crack of doom. First appearing in Test cricket against the West Indies in 1988, he scored his first 50 on a pacey Oval pitch. In 1989 Smith truly established himself as an England regular, despite being left out of the original 12 for the first Test against Australia at Headingley. Called up following an injury to Mike Gatting, he scored a fifty. A gritty 96 at Lord's followed, and after missing the third Test through injury, he made his first Test century—143 out of a total of 260—at Old Trafford, adding another at Trent Bridge. England lost the series 4–0, but Smith's 553 runs (61.44) shone out. His importance to England now was well illustrated by the barrage of bouncers he received from the West Indies bowlers in Antigua towards the end of the 1989/90 series. He had only modest success in the Caribbean but against India in 1990 made two more centuries before failing for most of England's dismal tour of Australia in 1990/1. He returned to form in 1991 with 416 runs (83.20) against the West Indies, including a superb and probably match-saving 148 not out at Lord's, but the following summer he was uncertain against the leg-spin of Mushtaq Ahmed despite making a hundred at Edgbaston, and variations of flight and spin increasingly proved alien to a man brought up on a diet of pace and seam. Further struggles followed against India's Anil Kumble, and although Smith later made his first Test century abroad, 128 as an opener against Sri Lanka, his problems continued against Warne and May and he missed the sixth Test of 1993 after scoring 283 runs (28.30) in five matches. In the Caribbean, early in 1994, he made only 145 runs in four Tests before a face-saving 175 in Antigua, which came amid suggestions from the manager Keith Fletcher that he should concentrate more on making runs and less on making money. New Zealand were expected to provide easier opposition, but after 120 runs in three Tests, Smith made way for John Crawley. Although he scored 1,143 runs for Hampshire in 1994, he was left behind when England travelled to Australia. His absence showed and he returned with success in 1995.

First-class career (1980/1–): 17,813 runs (44.31), 45 centuries, and 12 wickets (57.75)

Test matches (53): 3,677 runs (44.30)

SMITH, Thomas Peter Bromley

(b. 1908, Ipswich, Suffolk; d. 1967, Hyères, France) *Essex and England*

Peter Smith was a right-arm, leg-break and googly bowler, who captured many wickets and seldom lost his length even when receiving heavy punishment. As a batsman, usually at number eight, he was a hitter who kept to rational laws. Four times he captured nine wickets in an innings, once against New South Wales for MCC in 1946/7. For Essex against Middlesex at Colchester in 1947—the season in which he achieved the double for the only time—he took 16 for 215, and against Derbyshire at Chesterfield, batting at number 11, he hit 163, his own top score and the highest-ever in that position, adding 218 with Frank Vigar for the last wicket, a record for Essex. In 1933 he arrived at The Oval prepared to play for England against the West Indies, only to learn that the invitation telegram was a hoax. He did not represent his country until 13 years later.

First-class career (1929–52): 10,142 runs (17.88) including 8 centuries, 1,697 wickets (26.55), and 346 catches

Test matches (4): 33 runs (6.60), 3 wickets (106.33), and 1 catch

SMITHIES, Karen (née Hicken)

(b. 1969, Ashby de la Zouch, Leicestershire) *East Midlands and England*

Karen Smithies became the second England captain to win the World Cup when she stepped forward to lift the trophy at Lord's on 1 August 1993. A forceful leader who has been highly successful at county level, Smithies took over the England captaincy from Helen Plimmer, who had led the side to a series win in New Zealand in 1991/2. In her words, leading her country was the realization of a dream but it was the opposing bats who became entranced by Smithies's right-arm medium pace deliveries during the World Cup. A shoulder injury had resulted in a slightly jerky delivery action and this, allied to a looping trajectory, produced 15 wickets whilst conceding just 1.55 runs per over. Not only was Smithies England's player of the series but her bowling performance was the best by an English player in World Cup history. Slight in stature, Smithies bats left-handed and it was in this department she was expected to make her international mark after teaming up with Jo Chamberlain to establish an all-comers' Test best seventh-wicket stand of 110 against Australia in 1987. Chamberlain and

Smithies were both 18 at the time and in their début series. She was awarded an OBE in recognition of England's success in 1993.

Test matches (5): 127 runs (25.40) and 5 wickets (45)

One-day internationals (31): 258 runs (16.13) and 30 wickets (15.00)

SMITHSON, Gerald Arthur

(b. 1926, Spofforth, Yorkshire; d. 1970, Abingdon, Berks) *Yorkshire, Leicestershire, Hertfordshire, and England*

While doing his National Service as a 'Bevin Boy', Gerald Smithson was selected for the MCC team to the West Indies in 1947/8, playing in two Tests. An attractive left-handed batsman, he had hit 169 for Yorkshire at Leicester. He injured his arm badly on the tour, however, missed the 1948 season, and could not consolidate his place with Yorkshire.

First-class career (1946–56): 6,940 runs (22.68) including 8 centuries, 1 wicket (117.00), and 131 catches

Test matches (2): 70 runs (23.33)

SNAITH, John Collis

(b. 1876, Nottingham; d. 1936, London) *Nottinghamshire*

Author of several novels, including *Willow the King*, Snaith, with his left-arm fast bowling, took 4 for 79 for Nottinghamshire against the 1900 West Indians in a three-day match ruled by MCC as not first-class. He appeared often for the county 2nd XI with a highest score, in club cricket, of 156 not out.

First-class career (1900): 21 runs (21.00) and 1 catch

SNOW, John Augustine

(b. 1941, Peopleton, Worcestershire) *Sussex, Warwickshire, and England*

Moody and intense, John Snow was the despair at times of even the most sympathetic captain, and quite unpredictable even to those who thought they knew him well. Yet he was unquestionably among the greatest of post-war English fast bowlers, on his day an irresistibly hostile match-winner. The son of a vicar, he was educated at Christ's Hospital, joining Sussex first as a right-

hand batsman. He continued even as a lower-order batsman to play many a useful innings both for his county and his country, and would sometimes open the batting for Sussex in limited-overs matches. He is of wiry build and his action, though far from classical, had a lovely rhythm. He approached the wicket with a relatively short run but with long, loping, relaxed strides and delivered the ball with a slightly open chest and a faint sway away from the stumps, all the force of a strong body going into the moment of propulsion. He varied his pace cleverly, bowling only a few really quick deliveries an over, but these few were genuinely fast. He could bowl the bouncer at will, but seldom overdid its use, even though he fell foul of umpires from time to time on the 1970/1 tour of Australia. He also moved the ball away from the bat and brought it back meanly from the off to right-handers or across the body and past the groping bat of left-handers. He seldom saw eye to eye with captains and had a habit of switching himself off and looking bored, though even in this mood he would swoop on the ball in deep field and throw it flat and hard to the top of the stumps or come on to bowl grudgingly and still produce a spell of devastating hostility. He played his first two Tests in England in 1965, but the first of many match-winning performances in Tests came at Sabina Park in 1967/8 when he took 7 for 49 in the second Test. He finished the series with 27 wickets in four Tests, quite outdoing his rival fast bowlers in the West Indies side. He was now England's first-choice fast bowler, reaching his peak under Illingworth in Australia in 1970/1 when his 31 wickets in six Tests did more than anything to regain the Ashes. The following summer he was dropped from the England side after knocking India's Gavaskar off his feet as the latter went for a quick run and he did not go on any more MCC tours, although he had made a successful home return against Australia in 1975. In his next season, 1976, he took 126 wickets at 19.09. He called the book he wrote at the end of his career *Cricket Rebel*, a role he rather relished. He was one of the first to join the Kerry Packer organization and he strongly criticized the status quo in the High Court case. Two volumes of his poetry have been published. He played in Warwickshire's John Player League winning side in 1980, before building up a successful business specializing in cricket travel.

First-class career (1961–77): 4,832 runs (14.17), 1,174 wickets (22.72), and 125 catches

Test matches (49): 772 runs (13.54), 202 wickets (26.66), and 16 catches

SNOWBALL, Elizabeth Alexandra

(b. 1906, Burnley, Lancashire; d. 1988, Colwall, Worcestershire) *Lancashire, Hampshire, and England*

Betty Snowball had no trouble combining opening the batting with wicket-keeping, performing the dual role with distinction for England in ten Tests either side of the Second World War. She became England's vice-captain. Her innings of 189 in 222 minutes with 22 boundaries, in 1935 in Christchurch, New Zealand, remains the highest individual score by an England Test player. This was the world-best mark until 1986 when Sandya Aggarwal scored 190 for India against England at Worcester. Fittingly, Snowball herself was there to see the opener's innings. Coaching from the magnificent West Indian, Learie Constantine, who was then with the Nelson club in Lancashire, is said to have turned Snowball from a cricket enthusiast into a maniac for the game. On the 1934/5 tour of Australia the home press likened her to the great Bert Oldfield and she was the only woman to be written about in C. D. Martineau's *The Valiant Stumper*. Small in stature and right-handed, the cut shot was one of her favourites while her wicket-keeping was neatness personified. Snowball was also immaculate in her attire, with gloves, bat and pads made to her own specifications. What transpired later in her career was a far cry from the duck she had made for the Rest of England against London and District at Beckenham in 1929, the first women's match played before a public audience. With Myrtle Maclagan and Molly Hide, the nimble and aggressive Snowball was to provide the backbone of English batting in the sport's formative years. On her death in 1988, Maclagan remarked that in 57 years of friendship she had never heard a cross word from the habitually cheerful Snowball, who also represented her native Scotland at lacrosse and squash.

Test matches (10): 613 runs (40.86) including 1 century, and 21 dismissals (13 c., 8 st.)

SOUTHERTON, James

(b. 1827, Petworth, Sussex; d. 1880, Mitcham, Surrey) *Surrey, Sussex, Hampshire, and England*

Short and sturdy, James Southerton was a student of cricket and a slow round-arm bowler, who spun his off-breaks considerably. He had an easy action and with the years, contrary to normal practice, his arm got higher and higher so that he developed from round-arm to over-arm. He was also a good middle-order batsman and a safe slip. He used to play for all his three counties in the same season before birth and residential qualifications became law. On ten occasions he took more than 100 wickets in a season. He toured Australia in 1876/7 with James Lillywhite's team and appeared in the first two Tests ever played, at 49 years 119 days the oldest ever to make a Test début.

First-class career (1854–79): 3,159 runs (9.03), 1,681 wickets (14.45), and 218 dismissals (215 c., 3 st.)

Test matches (2): 7 runs (3.50), 7 wickets (15.28), and 2 catches

SPOONER, Reginald Herbert

(b. 1880, Litherland, Lancashire; d. 1961, Lincoln) *Lancashire and England*

An outstanding schoolboy player at Marlborough, Reggie Spooner was one of the most handsome-looking right-handed batsmen of the Edwardian amateur heyday. Although he handled his bat 'as a lady would have handled her fan', there was a steely strength beneath his ease and rhythmic style. His superb off-drive had many a spectator purring with pleasure, many a fielder rubbing his hands. When he hit 224 against Surrey at The Oval in 1911, he drove Bill Hitch so straight and powerfully that Neville Cardus recalled Hitch having to 'leap into the air to save his shins time and again'. Rarely able to play a full season, Spooner exceeded 1,000 runs in a season six times, his highest score being 247 against Nottinghamshire at Trent Bridge in 1903. Unable because of injury or business to visit Australia, he appeared in seven Tests against them in England in 1905, 1909 and 1912. As one of the first batsmen to find the answer to the googly as perfected by the South Africans, he made 119 for England against South Africa at Lord's in 1912. A double international, he played Rugby for England against Wales in 1902/3.

First-class career (1899–1923): 13,681 runs (36.28) including 31 centuries, 6 wickets (97.00), and 142 catches

Test matches (10): 481 runs (32.06) including 1 century, and 4 catches

SPOONER, Richard Thompson

(b. 1919, Stockton-on-Tees, Co. Durham) *Durham, Warwickshire, and England*

As wicket-keeper and left-handed opening batsman, Dick Spooner was among the best since the

Second World War, but being of the same generation as Godfrey Evans he was at a disadvantage. First playing for Warwickshire at 29, he exceeded 1,000 runs in a season six times, 1,767 runs (43.09) in 1951 being the best. He toured India in 1951/2, and the West Indies in 1953/4, with MCC, and India with the Commonwealth side in 1950/1. He made 319 runs in the series against India in 1951/2, but represented England only once at home against South Africa in 1955, failing to score in both innings.

First-class career (1948–59): 13,851 runs (27.27) including 12 centuries, and 767 dismissals (589 c., 178 st.)

Test matches (7): 354 runs (27.23) and 12 dismissals (10 c., 2 st.)

SQUIRE, Sir John Collings

(b. 1884, Plymouth; d. 1958, Rushlake Green, Somerset)

John Squire was the inspiration behind A. G. Macdonell's *England, Their England* which was published in the year he was knighted. Squire had urged Macdonell to portray English life in its sporting context and the book was at once regarded as a classic. Squire, who was one of the earliest of the First World War poets, sought to recreate an England in which things of beauty, culture, and aesthetic appeal mattered. Cricket was an expression of this and the club he founded in 1920 called The Invalids attracted literary men, many of whom were survivors from the war. He is portrayed, though not unkindly, in Macdonell's book as the imperiously clumsy captain whose team comes down from London to play the villages: as, indeed, the Invalids still do. Neville Cardus once played for him near Taunton and recorded that the opposition were 'on the run', with five or six wickets down in an hour until someone discovered all had been in vain—no scorers had been appointed. Squire, a literary critic, dramatist and editor, was first and foremost a poet. His 'Rugger Match' was the first representation of that sport in verse while, in a different vein, he broadcast in the first running commentary on the Boat Race.

STANYFORTH, Lt-Col. Ronald Thomas

(b. 1892, London; d. 1964, Kirkhammerton Hall, Yorkshire) *Yorkshire and England*

An amateur wicket-keeper, Captain Stanyforth (as he was then) played much Army cricket and, although born in London, played for Yorkshire in three matches in 1928. He toured South America

with 'Plum' Warner's MCC team in 1926, and captained MCC in South Africa in 1927/8, when illness compelled the original selection, Captain G. R. Jackson, to withdraw. He also visited the West Indies with MCC in 1929/30 until injury forced him to return home early. His sole Tests were played in South Africa. A man of engaging enthusiasm, he wrote a text-book on the subject of wicket-keeping, and was a trustee of MCC.

First-class career (1914–33): 1,092 runs (17.33) and 93 dismissals (72 c., 21 st.)

Test matches (4): 13 runs (2.60) and 9 dismissals (7 c., 2 st.)

STAPLES, Samuel James

(b. 1892, Newstead Colliery, Nottinghamshire; d. 1950, Nottingham) *Nottinghamshire and England*

A right-arm, medium-pace bowler with a rather jumpy, shuffling run, Sam Staples bowled cutters on an excellent length for long spells, and was able to break the ball either way. A useful lower-order batsman, he was also a splendid field. At Canterbury in 1927 he took 9 for 141 in an innings against Kent. He toured South Africa with MCC in 1927/8, playing his only three Tests and visited Australia with MCC in 1928/9, only to return home before playing a single game, because of severe rheumatism. On retirement he was successively coach to Hampshire and a first-class umpire. His younger brother, Arthur, was also a Nottinghamshire stalwart.

First-class career (1920–34): 6,470 runs (17.03) including 1 century, 1,331 wickets (22.85), and 339 catches

Test matches (3): 65 runs (13.00) and 15 wickets (29.00)

STATHAM, John Brian

(b. 1930, Manchester) *Lancashire and England*

Honest, loyal, reliable, and the most undemonstrative of the great fast bowlers, Brian or 'George' Statham was a part of two outstanding partnerships within a decade. Both of them allowed England to recover constantly from the problems provided by a promising batting line-up which often disappointed in actual performance. First, with Frank Tyson, Statham tore through the Australians in the last four Tests of 1954/5, and he was later equally effective with Fred Trueman. Because of his remorseless accuracy, Statham was at least as much feared as his more ferocious partners. Known also as 'The Whippet', he was loose-limbed—indeed, double-jointed —and his action was beautifully fluid and smooth. He was content to bowl fast and straight, moving the ball both ways off the seam but working on the theory that if the batsman missed, *he* generally hit. He first burst into first-class cricket in 1950, and that winter flew to Australia as reinforcement for the MCC team, making his Test début against New Zealand. This was the first of four visits to Australia; and he also toured India, South Africa, and the West Indies. Only four England bowlers have taken more wickets than Statham in Tests. Thirteen times he took more than 100 wickets in a season. He had 15 for 89 against Warwickshire at Coventry in 1957 and 15 for 108 against Leicestershire at Leicester in 1964; and he performed the hat-trick three times. Very occasionally a useful tail-end, left-handed batsman, he was an outstanding fielder in the deep. He captained Lancashire from 1965 until 1967 and was awarded the CBE for his services to cricket. He shunned the limelight in his retirement, uneasy with the adulation which lesser cricketers craved.

First-class career (1950–68): 5,424 runs (10.80), 2,260 wickets (16.36), and 230 catches
Test matches (70): 675 runs (11.44), 252 wickets (24.82), and 28 catches

STEEL, Allan Gibson

(b. 1858, Liverpool; d. 1914, London) *Cambridge University, Lancashire, and England*

A member of the 'golden' Cambridge University XI that defeated the 1878 Australians, Allan Steel was reckoned in his day the greatest amateur all-rounder after W.G. Outstanding at Marlborough and a member of four good Cambridge sides, he was a first choice for Gentlemen against Players, and for England in the early home Tests from 1880 until 1888. Though never regularly captaining his county, he had a remarkable sequence as a winning skipper: Marlborough over Rugby, Cambridge over Oxford, Gentlemen over Players, Lancashire over Yorkshire, and England over Australia. In fact, he led England to victory in all three Tests of 1886. A remarkably accurate, right-arm, slow bowler, he spun the ball either way and kept a full length. He was also a quick-footed batsman and a superb driver on both sides of the wicket. He made 135 not out for England against Australia at Sydney in 1882/3, and 148 at Lord's in 1884—the former innings saved England and the latter helped to win the match.

First-class career (1877–95): 7,000 runs (29.41) including 8 centuries, 789 wickets (14.78), and 137 catches

Test matches (13): 600 runs (35.29) including 2 centuries, 29 wickets (20.86), and 5 catches

STEELE, David Stanley

(b. 1941, Bradeley, Staffordshire) *Staffordshire, Northamptonshire, Derbyshire, and England*

Grey-haired and bespectacled, David Steele was a right-hand batsman, fine close fielder, and slow left-arm bowler. Even if it had occurred in the pre-television age, his Test début in 1975 at Lord's at the age of 33 would have captured the national imagination. Only the regular followers of county cricket knew what a staunch and dependable player he was, until, coming in to bat against Australia in an all-too-familiar atmosphere of crisis (and after losing his way in the pavilion as he left the dressing room to bat), he made a heroic 50, putting on 96 with Tony Greig. That summer he topped England's averages with 365 runs from six innings at 60.83, playing Lillee and Thomson as if they were just another pair of county professionals. With a solid technique based on a firm forward defensive, plenty of shots once his eye was in, and limitless concentration and determination, he was one of the hardest of batsmen to dig out. Coming with further credit through a tough home series against the West Indies in 1976, making 106 at Nottingham, he was unlucky to be omitted thereafter as England rebuilt for the future; this was harsh but realistic and it meant that the unknown who became a household name overnight never played for England abroad. He moved to Derbyshire in 1979, starting as captain, soon resigning the post but doing well with bat and ball. After four seasons with Staffordshire from 1958 to 1962, he had played for Northamptonshire for 15 years, in nine of which he scored more than 1,000 runs, with 1,756 (48.7) in 1975 his highest aggregate. A cautious, moderate man, with printing as a secondary trade, Steele kept his feet firmly on the ground during his brief spell in the limelight. His 1975 benefit at Northants brought him £25,000 and a meat chop for every run he scored from a grateful local butcher. His brother, John Steele, and cousin, Brian Crump, have both played regular county cricket. He rejoined Northamptonshire in 1982 and, playing mainly as a slow left-arm bowler, took over 200 wickets in three seasons. He retired in 1984, returning to Minor Counties cricket and his other trade as a printer.

First-class career (1963–84): 22,346 runs (32.47) including 30 centuries, 623 wickets (24.89), and 546 catches
Test matches (8): 673 runs (42.06) including 1 century, 2 wickets (19.50), and 7 catches

STEPHENSON, Heathfield Harman

(b. 1833, Esher, Surrey; d. 1896, Uppingham, Rutland) *Surrey*

'H.H.' or 'Spurgeon' Stephenson (so-called because of his likeness to his contemporary, Charles, the Baptist evangelist), was an all-rounder in every sense. He was a technically sound right-handed batsman who used his height to drive well; a fast round-arm bowler who brought the ball back late; a wicket-keeper rated the second best in England and a fine fielder. Surrey used him as a conventional all-rounder because Tom Lockyer was their 'keeper but Stephenson got his chance when playing for the All-England XI (1854–64). His best year was 1864 when he made centuries at The Oval for both Surrey against Nottinghamshire and for the Players against the Gentlemen. He toured America in 1859 and captained the first English side in Australia in 1861/2. On the third occasion in 1858, in which he took three wickets in three balls for the All-England XI against odds, he was awarded a white hat: the origin of the 'hat-trick'. After his playing days were over, he became coach at Uppingham School (1872–96), acquiring an authority before which even masters quailed and producing, in 1877, five of the Cambridge XI.

First-class career (1853–71): 7,360 runs (17.90) including 3 centuries, 300 + 2 wickets (16.40), and 177 dismissals (152 c., 25 st.)

STEPHENSON, John Patrick

(b. 1965, Stebbing, Essex) *Boland, Essex, Hampshire, and England*

Brought into a dispirited England side as an opening batsman for the final Test of a disasterous summer in 1989, when the Australians swept almost all before them, John Stephenson did not disgrace himself, but neither did he do enough to win a place on the senior tour to the West Indies that winter. 'A' team recognition followed, but five years on, and despite becoming a capable medium-pacer, he found himself wondering whether he would ever add to his single Test cap. A determined and upright right-handed batsman with a preference for the front foot, Stephenson is also an athletic fielder, and succeeded Brian Hardie as Graham Gooch's opening partner at Essex after an education at Felsted and Durham University. Named as the county's outstanding young player in 1985, the year of his first team début, Stephenson went on to captain Durham to the UAU Championship in 1986, and the following year he led the Combined Universities in the Benson and Hedges Cup, the first time the side had been drawn from outside Oxford and Cambridge. After a winter's cricket in South Africa, he was capped by Essex in 1989 and fully deserved his Test call-up by making 1,354 runs, including four centuries. Innings of 25 and 11 (36 runs (18.00), no wickets or catches) helped England hold out for a draw, but led to no more than an A tour to Kenya and Zimbabwe where his batting disappointed. Like most good batsmen he prospered in the sun-soaked summer of 1990, scoring 1,887, and he went on a second A tour in early 1992 when he was drafted into the West Indies tour following Michael Atherton's withdrawl through injury. Having taken only 17 wickets with his whippy medium-pacers in 1991, he now swung the ball consistently to top the tour bowling averages with 20 wickets at only 13 runs each including returns of 4 for 57, 4 for 22, and 5 for 53 in the three 'Tests'. His batting suffered, however, and he averaged only 13.55. In 1993, he became the first Essex player to score 500 runs and take 20 wickets in a Sunday League season, thus reminding the selectors that he could prove a useful asset in any future one-day squad. He captained Essex several times as Graham Gooch's stand-in in 1994 but when he was passed-over as his successor he accepted an offer to join Hampshire from 1995.

First-class career (1985–   ): 10,230 runs (35.03) including 18 centuries, and 145 wickets (33.63)

STEVENS, Greville Thomas Scott

(b. 1901, London; d. 1970, London) *Oxford University, Middlesex, and England*

One of the greatest of all schoolboy prodigies, Greville Stevens was a right-handed batsman who, despite his short backlift, hit with surprising power. A leg-break and googly bowler, he foxed even the best batsmen when they failed to differentiate between his top-spinner and googly (let alone his well-disguised, fast, straight delivery) and he was also a safe field near the wicket. A member of the Middlesex Championship-winning sides of 1920 and 1921, he was the only schoolboy of modern times to play for Gentlemen against Players. His highlight as a batsman was 149 at number one for Middlesex against the Australians at Lord's in 1926 and, as a bowler, when he snatched victory by four runs over Yorkshire at Bradford in 1920. He was a member of the England team that regained the Ashes at The Oval in 1926, and he toured South Africa twice and the West Indies once.

First-class career (1919–33): 10,376 runs (29.56) including 12 centuries, 684 wickets (26.85), and 213 catches

Test matches (10): 263 runs (15.47), 20 wickets (32.40), and 9 catches

STEVENSON, Graham Barry

(b. 1955, Ackworth, Yorkshire) *Yorkshire, Northamptonshire, and England*

A right-handed all-rounder who bowled fast-medium, hit hard in an uncomplicated fashion and fielded athletically with a powerful throw, 'Stevo' was a down-to-earth character. Strongly built with a good, busy, orthodox action, he could be a match-winner on a helpful pitch and was a consistently useful performer in limited-overs cricket. First playing for Yorkshire in 1973, he was capped in 1978 and joined the England touring team to Australia as a replacement in 1979/80, playing his first Test against India in Bombay on the way home. The following winter he toured the West Indies but was selected for only one of the four Tests. In 1980 he took 8 for 57 in an innings against Northamptonshire and hit a rapid 111 against Derbyshire at Chesterfield. In 1982, going in at number 11, he hit 115 not out against Warwickshire and put on 149 with Geoff Boycott, a county record. He played a final season on the Northamptonshire staff in 1987, but only played one first-class game.

First-class career (1973–81): 3,965 runs (20.33) including 2 centuries, 488 wickets (28.84), and 73 catches

Test matches (2): 28 runs (28.00) and 5 wickets (36.60)

STEWART, Alec James

(b. 1963, Merton, Surrey) *Surrey and England*

Alec Stewart came relatively late to Test cricket, not making his début until he was almost 27, although that may have been due to 'reverse-nepotism': his father Micky, formerly of Surrey and England, being team manager. Once in the side, however, he was given every chance and

eventually justified that faith most handsomely. Not until his 26th innings did he score a Test century but, once established, despite some loss of form when he took over behind the stumps, he proved a high-class player with a steely determination. A superb timer of the ball, particularly strong through the covers and off the back foot, thanks to eight seasons playing grade cricket for the Midland Guildford Club in Western Australia and his upbringing at The Oval, he worked hard to cure an impetuous streak and a looseness outside the off-stump. Born into a sporting family —Micky also played a good standard of amateur football, and Alec's mother, Sheila, was an excellent netball and hockey player—he was educated at Tiffin School, joining Surrey as a batsman wicket-keeper in 1981. At the same time, he began wintering in Perth, playing alongside past and future Australian Test players including Bruce Yardley and Tom Moody, a spell which helped him to develop an overt competitiveness. At The Oval, with Jack Richards established behind the stumps, he was able to concentrate on his batting, topping 1,000 runs for the first time in 1985, and making 1,665 the following summer. His chance came early in 1990 in the West Indies, following the loss of several players to the tour of South Africa, and after a season in which he scored 1,637 runs, including a career-best 206 not out against Essex. He played with spirit in difficult circumstances, although his top Test score was no more than 45, as an opener in place of the injured Graham Gooch in Barbados. 1990 saw a maiden 50 against New Zealand at Lord's and, chosen again as deputy wicket-keeper to Australia and New Zealand in 1990/1, he made 91 in Sydney but failed to reach double figures in seven out of ten Test innings. He only returned for the fifth Test of the following summer, keeping wicket as England gambled on a five-man attack to level the series with the West Indies. He rose to the occasion with two crucial innings and four catches. Retained as a batsman for the final Test of the summer against Sri Lanka, he scored an unbeaten 113 at number three, his first Test century. Vice-captain on the tour of New Zealand, and promoted to bat alongside Graham Gooch in the absence of the injured Michael Atherton, he made 148, 4, 8, 107, and 63 in three Tests, leading the side in the final one-day international of the tour. Then, after a successful World Cup on either side of the stumps, and having taken over as Surrey's captain, he made a flawless 190, full of top-class driving and feathery strokes off his legs, in the first Test of the following summer against Pakistan. In the next match, at Lord's, he made 69 and 74 not out against Wasim Akram and Waqar Younis, becoming only the sixth Englishman to carry his bat in a Test, but his form dipped when he resumed wicket-keeping duties. At that stage he was Gooch's likely successor as England captain, but confusion over his role in the side during the following winter in India and Sri Lanka counted against him. Picked as number one wicket-keeper, he relinquished the gloves when Gooch fell ill and he led the side in the Second Test in Madras and the final Tests of a calamitous tour, in Sri Lanka. Fears over the depth of England's batting meant Stewart stayed behind the stumps against Australia in 1993, but after failing to score a century in the series, and with Gooch not touring, he played only as an opener in the West Indies. Four hundred and seventy seven runs in five Tests followed, including two epic innings of 118 and 143 in Bridgetown as the home side were beaten in Barbados for the first time in 59 years. Despite Gooch's return, Stewart, now a member of Surrey's executive board, kept the opener's berth for the first four Tests in 1994, making 119 against New Zealand at Lord's, and although he was dropped down the order for the last two Tests against South Africa, he still finished the summer averaging 52.75 in six matches.

First-class career (1981–): 15,524 runs (39.40), including 30 centuries, 3 wickets (125.00), and 355 dismissals (342 c., 13 st.)

Test matches (43): 2,982 runs (40.84), 53 catches, and 4 stumpings

STEWART, Michael James

(b. 1932, Herne Hill) *Surrey and England*

'Micky' Stewart became a regular member of the Championship-winning Surrey side in the late 1950s, as opening batsman and specialist short-leg fieldsman. A cheerful, plucky character, he was a neat and well-organized right-hander. His enthusiasm and agility in the field helped him to create a world record (since equalled) when he took seven catches in an innings at Northampton in 1957; that season he held 77 catches (one less than Walter Hammond's all-time record). His highest score was 227 not out against Middlesex at The Oval in 1964, and he passed 1,000 runs in a season fifteen times. He captained Surrey from 1963 until 1972 and visited India in 1963/4 as vice-captain of MCC but had to return early owing to illness. Between 1962 and 1964 he represented England against the West Indies,

India and Pakistan. As a footballer, he played for Charlton Athletic, Wimbledon, Hendon, and Corinthian Casuals, usually at inside-right. He returned to The Oval in 1979, as manager of Surrey, the county's fortunes instantly improving and his son Alec, a fine young batsman, has followed him into the Surrey side. In 1986 Micky Stewart was appointed to the post of assistant manager of the England side in Australia, with a brief to include planning, discipline, fitness and technical supervision and a promise that, if he did well, the job would be extended to cover home matches as well. In the event he remained England manager until 1992, a high-profile job which he carried out with typical dedication, but mixed success. He then became director of youth development with a brief to streamline the training of young cricketers throughout the country. He received an OBE for services to the game.

First-class career (1954–72): 26,492 runs (32.90) including 49 centuries, 1 wicket (99.00), and 634 catches

Test matches (8): 385 runs (35.00) and 6 catches

STODDART, Andrew Ernest

(b. 1863, South Shields, County Durham; d. 1915, London) *Middlesex and England*

England's captain at both cricket and Rugby football, Andrew Stoddart, or 'My dear victorious Stod' of the ballad, was a sporting Titan who led England to victory over Australia in 1894/5. He also scored 352 runs in the Tests, including 173 in the second Test at Melbourne, when he led a fight-back that resulted in a win, but was not so successful the next time in 1897/8. 'Stod' or 'Stoddie' was a dominating right-handed batsman with all the strokes, especially strong in driving and hitting to leg. He came into cricket seriously for the first time in 1885, when he made his début for Middlesex, and he hit 485 for Hampstead against Stoics the year after, then the highest score on record anywhere. He hardly knew a poor season and his last innings for Middlesex was a mammoth score of 221 against Somerset at Lord's in 1900; it was also his highest first-class score. He was a useful change-bowler and very reliable field. He toured Australia four times and the West Indies and America once each. His later years saw his hopes and health in decline, and he shot himself through the head in 1915.

First-class career (1885–1900): 16,738 runs (32.13) including 26 centuries, 278 wickets (23.63), and 257 catches

Test matches (16): 996 runs (35.57) including 2 centuries, 2 wickets (47.00), and 6 catches

STORER, William

(b. 1867, Butterley, Derbyshire; d. 1912, Derby) *Derbyshire and England*

One of the most polished wicket-keepers Bill, Storer was one of the first to stand up coolly to the fastest bowling, including that of Charles Kortright. Though he bent—without squatting—he appeared to be upright at the moment of receiving the ball. He would collect the ball off the edge of the bat as delicately as though picking a moth off a mink coat; and he had much experience facing fastish bowlers in Derbyshire's matches. He maintained a high reputation as a sound right-handed batsman always looking for runs. Twice he averaged over 50 in a season, scored 100 and 100 not out against Yorkshire at Derby in 1896, made his highest score, 216 not out against Leicestershire at Chesterfield in 1899, and seven times exceeded 1,000 runs in a season. He could take off his pads and become a useful change-bowler. Bill played in one Test against Australia in 1899 and toured there in 1897/8, but his career coincided with that of Dick Lilley, who was almost invariably given the preference as England's 'keeper. He spoke his mind and enjoyed his cricket, but his later years were dogged by ill-health.

First-class career (1887–1905): 12,966 runs (28.87) including 17 centuries, 232 wickets (33.89), and 431 dismissals (376 c., 55 st.)
Test matches (6): 215 runs (19.54), 2 wickets (54.00), and 11 dismissals (11 c.)

STREET, George Benjamin

(b. 1889, Charlwood, Surrey; d. 1924, Portslade, Sussex) *Sussex and England*

George Street joined MCC's team in South Africa in 1922/3 as a late replacement and played in his one and only Test at Durban, scoring 4 and 7 not out and making one stumping. He was then in his prime as a very competent county 'keeper—in 1923 having eight victims against Worcestershire at Hastings—and a useful tail-end batsman, but he was killed in a motorcycle accident just before the 1924 season started.

First-class career (1909–23): 3,984 runs (17.24) including 1 century, 3 wickets (22.00), and 429 dismissals (308 c., 121 st.)

STRUDWICK, Herbert

(b. 1880, Mitcham, Surrey; d. 1970, Shoreham, Sussex) *Surrey and England*

Bert Strudwick, or 'Struddie', held the world record, until beaten by John Murray in 1975, for the most dismissals in a career by a wicket-keeper. Neat, agile, dependable, and accomplished, he had 91 'scalps' in his first full season in 1903. Throughout his career Surrey had few spinners and he had to keep mainly to fastish bowlers, as most of his successors do today. As a right-handed batsman, he played some determined innings. He toured Australia with MCC four times between 1903 and 1924 and South Africa twice before the First World War. At Johannesburg in 1913/14 he dismissed seven in the match. His last Test was against Australia at The Oval in 1926, when England regained the Ashes after a long wait. He held a partnership in Alf Gover's Cricket School, and served Surrey for 60 years, latterly as scorer. During one of his Australian tours, a letter was addressed: 'Struddy, 'Stralia'—and it reached him safely without delay! There have been few more popular or respected cricketers.

First-class career (1902–27): 6,445 runs (10.89), 1 wicket (102.00), and 1,496 dismissals (1,242 c., 254 st.)
Test matches (28): 230 runs (7.93) and 72 dismissals (60 c., 12 st.)

STUDD, Charles Thomas

(b. 1860, Spratton, Northamptonshire; d. 1931, Ibambi, Belgian Congo) *Cambridge University, Middlesex, and England*

Charles Studd was the youngest and most famous of three brothers—the others were George and Kynaston—all of whom played for Eton, Cambridge (successively as captain) and Middlesex. Possessing a fine upright style, C.T. was a right-handed batsman, particularly strong on the off-side, and a medium-fast bowler who brought the ball over from a good height. While still at Cambridge, he played for England in the historic Oval Test of 1882—the year in which he became the second man ever (after W.G.) to achieve the double, with 1,249 runs and 128 wickets—and that winter he was a member of the Hon. Ivo Bligh's party to Australia which came home with the original Ashes. Studd achieved the double again in 1883, but a year later, greatly influenced by the evangelists, Moody and Sankey, he retired from regular first-class cricket to devote himself to overseas missionary work: he endured great hardship in China, Africa, and India.

First-class career (1879–1903): 4,391 runs (30.49) including 8 centuries, 441 wickets (17.36), and 73 catches

Test matches (5): 160 runs (20.00), 3 wickets (32.66), and 5 catches

STUDD, George Brown

(b. 1859, Netheravon, Wiltshire; d. 1945, Pasadena, California, USA) *Cambridge University, Middlesex, and England*

The eldest of the three brothers—George, Kynaston, and Charles—George Studd hit 120 against Oxford at Lord's, when he was captain in 1882. Essentially a front-foot player, he was a skilful and powerful driver, but in the field he was an uncertain catcher, though his picking-up was clean and quick. He toured Australia in 1882/3 with Hon. Ivo Bligh's team in search of the Ashes, but was very disappointing in the Tests. Called to the Bar, he did not practise but like his brother Charlie became a missionary; and from 1891 until his death he lived and worked in a notorious and squalid area of South Los Angeles in California.

First-class career (1879–86): 2,892 runs (21.91) including 3 centuries, 2 wickets (14.50), 74 catches, and 1 stumping

Test matches (4): 31 runs (4.42) and 8 catches

SUBBA ROW, Raman

(b. 1932, London) *Cambridge University, Surrey, Northamptonshire, and England*

Raman Subba Row was a key member of one of the last powerful Cambridge elevens. A tallish left-handed batsman, he was at first predominantly an on-side player but developed his off-side strokes and was particularly adept at placing the ball for singles. His high-flighted leg-breaks and googlies could break a stubborn stand—he took 5 for 21 against Oxford at Lord's in 1951—and, in the field, he alternated successfully between slips, gully, and the deep. On joining Northamptonshire—whom he captained from 1958 until 1961—he became a consistently heavy run-getter, with a strong defence. He made the highest-ever score for the county, 260 not out against Lancashire at Northampton in 1955, and in 1958 he broke his own record with 300 against Surrey at The Oval—adding 376 for the sixth wicket with Albert Lightfoot, the best for any wicket for the county. Six times he exceeded 1,000 runs in a season. After a rather disappointing start in Test cricket, he was pressed into service as an opening batsman against India at The Oval in 1959, scoring 94, and was an England regular until 1961, when he headed the batting against Australia with 468 runs (46.80), including his Test highest, 137 (in 7 hours 40 minutes) at The Oval. He resigned suddenly from county cricket for business reasons after the 1961 season, and has subsequently been a strong voice for reform within the establishment. A public relations executive, he was closely involved on various Lord's committees, chairman of Surrey and manager of England's tour of India in 1981/2. He was chairman of the TCCB, 1985–90, and was awarded a CBE.

First-class career (1951–61): 14,182 runs (41.46) including 30 centuries, 87 wickets (38.65), and 176 catches

Test matches (13): 984 runs (46.85) including 3 centuries, 0–2, and 5 catches

SUCH, Peter Mark

(b. 1964, Helensburgh, Dumbartonshire, Scotland) *Nottinghamshire, Leicestershire, Essex, and England*

Peter Such enjoyed a remarkable start to his Test career in 1993, taking 6 for 67 against Australia at Old Trafford, the best performance by an England débutant in ten years. A quietly-spoken steadfast character and an extremely accurate off-spinner with a long, straight approach to the wicket, Such's call-up was due reward for his perseverance after twice moving counties because of a lack of opportunity. Beginning his career with Nottinghamshire, where he had lived since the age of 5, he played for Young England in 1983 and a TCCB side against the 1986 New Zealanders, but found his way to the first team blocked by Eddie Hemmings, and left at the end of the 1986 season. For Leicestershire his chances were equally limited by the county's reliance on seam-bowling, his own poor batting and the presence of Peter Willey, and he played only 34 Championship matches in three seasons. The move to Essex in 1990 was not immediately productive but in 1992 he took 40 wickets and helped the county to the Championship alongside left-arm spinner John Childs, producing a career-best 6 for 17 against Nottinghamshire at Southend. Such and Childs were named jointly as Essex Players of the Year and Such was chosen for the A tour of Australia. The pick of the bowlers on the trip, he took 11 for 144, including 7 for 82 against the Australian Cricket Academy, although the game was declared not first-class. The following summer in the first Test he exploited a pitch which started damp to take 8 for 145 and produced two defiant innings, including a Test-best 14 not out as England battled vainly to save the match. He played in four of the five Tests that followed, and remained England's steadiest bowler, but took just eight more wickets, and despite finishing the season with 76 victims, Ian Salisbury and Philip Tufnell were picked ahead of him for the senior tour to the West Indies. Such went instead to South Africa with the A team, and after taking 19 wickets, he regained his Test place for the series with New Zealand in 1994. Again he was steady without being a sufficiently sharp spinner of the ball to dismiss top-class players on good pitches.

First-class career (1982–): 753 runs (6.55) and 459 wickets (30.14)

Test matches (8): 65 runs (9.28) and 22 wickets (36.59)

SUGG, Frank Howe

(b. 1862, Ilkeston, Derbyshire; d. 1933, Liverpool) *Yorkshire, Derbyshire, Lancashire, and England*

A fine all-round games player, Frank Sugg stood 6 ft. tall and was an enterprising right-handed batsman, hitting astoundingly hard off the back foot and never troubling himself about what the wicket was like, belonging to the hit-or-miss brigade. He was also a magnificent outfield. Five times he exceeded 1,000 runs in a season. His best work was for Lancashire, and he hit his highest score, 220, for Lancashire against Gloucestershire at Bristol. He appeared in only two Tests against Australia, both in 1888, making 31 at The Oval and 24 at Old Trafford, England winning by an innings each time.

First-class career (1883–99): 11,859 runs (24.45) including 16 centuries, 10 wickets (27.30), 167 catches, and 1 stumping

Test matches (2): 55 runs (27.50)

SURRIDGE, Walter Stuart

(b. 1917, London; d. 1992, Glossop, Derbyshire) *Surrey*

Stuart Surridge's alleged prophecy that Surrey would win the county championship five years running proved an understatement. For seven successive seasons (1952–8), often by a distance, they were undisputed champions, with Surridge himself in command for the first five. He inherited a side in 1952 not noticeably strong in batting and

he nailed his mast to the talents of the brilliant young star, Peter May, while inspiring confidence in lesser men and making his own useful contributions. The foundation of success lay in bowling and fielding. With Bedser, Loader, Laker, and Lock Surrey had an attack for all conditions, supported by Surridge's right-arm medium pace when needed—especially during Test match claims on any of his quartet. Surrey achieved such feats as the dismissal at The Oval of Warwickshire for 45 and 52 in 1953 and of Worcestershire for 25 and 40 a year later. A large, hearty man, Surridge set a prodigious example as a close-in fielder and in 1952 his 58 catches were a record for a season by a Surrey player not keeping wicket. An amateur captain in the tradition of great predecessors such as Fender and Jardine, he was worth his place for his fielding alone. Leadership was a bonus encompassing example, tactical skill, tremendous drive, and a sense of purpose which nearly always triumphed and—to opponents—occasionally jarred. He bore a famous name, for the family had begun to make bats in the 1870s and he and his son, 'Tiger', an excellent wicket-keeper, kept the business going.

First-class career (1947–60): 3,882 runs (12.94), 506 wickets (26.89), and 375 catches

SUTCLIFFE, Herbert

(b. 1894, Harrogate; d. 1978, Cross Hills, Yorkshire) *Yorkshire and England*

One of the game's immortals, Herbert Sutcliffe did not play for Yorkshire's first team until he was 24, due to the First World War. In his first season, 1919, he made 1,839 runs (44.85) and by 1924 he had eclipsed all rivals as opening partner for Jack Hobbs in Tests. Debonaire, well groomed, and unruffled, he was essentially a practical batsman, with a superb judgement of length, pace and direction. He lacked the polished elegance of Hobbs but certainly not his appetite for runs. He stood with the face of the bat very open, presenting its full width always, making few classical strokes, but hitting the ball firmly off the front foot especially to the off-side and cutting and hooking efficiently. A clever runner between wickets, he stole many a cheeky single with Jack Hobbs or Percy Holmes. Never flustered or intimidated, he had great courage, determination, and concentration, and was at his best on the big occasion. He shared in 145 first-wicket partnerships of 100 runs or more, 74 of them with Holmes and 26 with Hobbs. He first opened with Hobbs against South Africa in 1924, and they put on 136 together at Edgbaston and 268 at Lord's in his first two Tests. In the first Test in Australia, 1924/5, they put up 157 and 110 together at Sydney in the first match, followed by 283 in the second at Melbourne, when they batted all day facing a total of 600; at Melbourne Herbert made 176 and 127; and again at Melbourne, in the fourth Test, he scored 143 in another century opening partnership. He headed the Test averages with 734 runs (81.55). At The Oval in 1926, when England went in again, behind on the first innings, Hobbs and Sutcliffe put up 172, Sutcliffe going on to 161, thus laying the foundation for the victory that brought back the Ashes to England. In 1928/9 they remained reliable, Sutcliffe averaging 50.57 in the series. In 1930 he headed the England batting against Australia (who recovered the Ashes) with 436 runs (87.20); and against Australia, 1932/3 and 1934 (with a variety of opening partners), he still averaged over 50 per series, at Sydney, 1932/3, making his Test highest, 194. He hit centuries against New Zealand and South Africa, two in the match at The Oval in 1929; and his last Test of all was against South Africa in 1935. His stand of 555 with Holmes against Essex at Leyton in 1932 stood as the world record for 45 years, his score of 313 on this occasion remaining his highest, although it was only one of 17 scores above 200. He reached 1,000 runs in a season 24 times (including three times abroad). From 1922 until 1935 he scored over 2,000 runs each season, including 3,336 runs (74.13) and 14 centuries in the wet season of 1932. His average in Tests exceeds his overall average by nearly nine runs! Later a very successful businessman, he was also a Test selector and his son, christened William Herbert Hobbs, played for, and captained, Yorkshire. Herbert himself had been offered the Yorkshire captaincy; as a professional, he declined it. However, he became a major in the Second World War and later he deliberately took on the accents and manners of a 'gentleman'.

First-class career (1919–45): 50,138 runs (51.95) including 149 centuries, 10 wickets (52.70), and 473 catches

Test matches (54): 4,555 runs (60.73) including 16 centuries, and 23 catches

SUTTLE, Kenneth George

(b. 1928, London) *Sussex*

Ken Suttle had three things in common with his Sussex predecessor, John Langridge. Both scored over 1,000 runs in a season on seventeen occasions, both made over 30,000 runs for the county and both failed to win selection for England. Suttle was luckier in that his solitary MCC tour (to the West Indies in 1953/4) at least took place, unlike Langridge's which was cancelled because of World War One. An attractive, nuggetty little left-handed batsman who played very straight, Suttle made a record 423 consecutive appearances in the county championship (1954–69) with a highest score of 204 not out against Kent at Tunbridge Wells in 1962. His left-arm slow bowling was an asset, even more so his outstanding outfielding. He won three man-of-the-match awards in one-day cricket and his peremptory dismissal by the county in 1971—turning up at the ground to find he was not selected to play—did Sussex as little credit as their treatment of Maurice Tate a generation earlier.

First-class career (1949–71): 30,225 runs (31.09), 266 wickets (32.80), and 387 dismissals (38 c., 3 st.)

SWANTON, Ernest William

(b. 1907, London) *Middlesex*

Nearly 70 years as a cricket correspondent made 'Jim' Swanton the 'doyen' of them all. After leaving Cranleigh, he worked with the London *Evening Standard* (1927–39), representing his paper on the famous occasion when Holmes and Sutcliffe scored 555 for the first wicket for Yorkshire against Essex at Leyton in 1932. His paper was, in his own words, 'last in the queue' for the one public telephone box available and his copy missed the edition. For that omission, he lost the chance to report the controversial MCC 1932/3 tour of Australia. Had he gone instead of Bruce Harris, a tennis expert, the English public might have been given a quicker insight into the events of 'bodyline' bowling. This one failure was the exception which proved the rule, for Jim Swanton has ever been both immensely capable and exceptionally forthright. After the Second World War, in which he damaged a shoulder and was a prisoner in Japanese hands, although he managed to entertain stricken colleagues with reminiscences in his role as 'entertainments officer', he became the cricket correspondent of the *Daily Telegraph* (1946–75), reporting Rugby football as well, and remaining a contributor to the paper throughout his years of retirement. He became editorial director of *The Cricketer* in 1966 and the magazine, fuelled by Swanton's prodigious energy and broad cricket knowledge, soon embarked on its most prosperous era. He was an early pioneer of sports broadcasting in the late 1920s. He gave the first live commentary from a Test match in South Africa to England in 1938/9 and took part in the first ball-by-ball Test commentary in England (1939). In the post-war years his particular skill lay in summarizing a day's play on television or radio. Sheer professionalism was the hallmark of all his work and it declared his mastery of the game's technique. He was fair but penetrative in judgement and could be acerbic if necessary. His first book was the second volume of the *History of Cricket* (1938), the first volume of which had been written by Harry Altham in 1926. Later publications included his reports of tours in book-form; two meaty and wide-ranging volumes of autobiography, a biography of Sir George Allen and the co-editing of the magisterial *World of Cricket* (1966). A capable and regular club cricketer as an opening batsman and leg-spinner, he played first-class matches for Middlesex against the universities. He took teams of first-class calibre abroad and in 1935 founded the Arabs, a wandering club with an exclusive membership and unique flavour. Formidable, but generous, Swanton has been president of numerous distinguished cricket bodies and in frequent demand as a speaker. He was still on MCC's Arts and Library Committee at the age of 88. He remains cricket's *eminence grise*. His services to the game were recognized by the award of the OBE (1965) and the CBE (1994).

First-class career (1937–8): 67 runs (13.40) and 1 catch

SWETMAN, Roy

(b. 1933, London) *Surrey, Nottinghamshire, Gloucestershire, and England*

Slightly built, neat, and compact. Roy Swetman kept wicket confidently and creditably for three counties, and was also a useful batsman. He toured Australia and New Zealand with MCC in 1958/9, and the West Indies in 1959/60, but could not quite clinch the regular place as England's 'keeper.

First-class career (1953–74): 6,495 runs (19.21) including 2 centuries, 1 wicket (69.00), and 596 dismissals (530 c., 66 st.)

Test matches (11): 254 runs (16.93) and 26 dismissals (24 c., 2 st.)

TATE, Frederick William

(b. 1867, Brighton, Sussex; d. 1943, Burgess Hill, Sussex) *Sussex and England*

The 'tragedy' of Fred Tate's or 'Chub's' missed catch and mishandled innings in his sole Test, against Australia at Old Trafford in 1902, is well known to cricket students. He scored 5 not out and 4, took 2 for 51 and held one other catch in England's narrow defeat. 'I've a little lad at home who'll make up for that,' said the tearful Fred after the match—and so it proved 22 years later! Fred, however, was outstanding for Sussex. A slow to medium, right-arm, off-break bowler, with an easy action and good command of length, Chub remained the stock bowler for 17 years and, in the short programmes, exceeded 100 wickets in a season five times. His best (and most fateful year) was 1902, when he secured 180 wickets (15.71), his feats including 15 for 68 in a day against Middlesex at Lord's. On retirement he became coach to Derbyshire. Besides Maurice, one other son, C.F., played county cricket.

First-class career (1887–1905): 2,952 runs (9.58), 1,331 wickets (21.55), and 236 catches

TATE, Maurice William

(b. 1895, Brighton, Sussex; d. 1956, Wadhurst, Sussex) *Sussex and England*

Maurice Tate—who like his father was nicknamed 'Chub'—began as a right-handed batsman, but developed as one of England's greatest bowlers. At the outset he bowled right-arm, slow-medium, off-breaks like his father, interspersed by the occasional fast ball. But on being asked to concentrate on bowling fast-medium, he advanced overnight and in 1923 took 219 wickets (13.97). He was a big man with heavy shoulders and powerful thighs, whose feet delighted Tom Webster and other cartoonists but, when he turned to bowl, all was grace and co-ordination. His brisk run-up was a mere 8 yards, leading up to a high action as he leant back on his right leg with a fully extended left arm, his right arm catapulting over with a smooth elasticity, which gave an impression of immense momentum. He would swerve late from leg or bring the ball back from outside the off-stump; and it appeared that the ball gained pace off the pitch. From 1922 until 1925 inclusive he captured 848 wickets; and he exceeded 100 wickets in a season fourteen times. As a good, workmanlike, free-hitting batsman, who often opened for the county (besides being opening bowler) he exceeded 1,000 runs in a season twelve times; and he achieved the double eight times, seven seasons in succession in the 1920s. He toured Australia (three times), New Zealand, and South Africa. On his first tour in 1924/5 he took 38 wickets (23.18) in the five Tests, a record against Australia not broken until

1956. He took 13 wickets (18.92) in the first three Tests against the West Indies, and headed the bowling against South Africa in 1930/1 with 14 wickets (24.35). His best series at home was against South Africa in 1924, when he headed the bowling with 27 wickets (15.70) and in the first Test at Edgbaston he bowled unchanged with his England and county captain, Arthur Gilligan, to dismiss the visitors for 30 in 75 minutes. At The Oval in 1926 he was prominent in England's defeat of Australia when the Ashes were regained.

First-class career (1912–37): 21,717 runs (25.04) including 23 centuries, 2,784 wickets (18.16), and 284 catches

Test matches (39): 1,198 runs (25.48) including 1 century, 155 wickets (26.16), and 11 catches

TATTERSALL, Roy

(b. 1922, Bolton, Lancashire) *Lancashire and England*

Although he was never a vicious finger-spinner, Roy Tattersall's height combined with subtle variations of pace and great accuracy made him a first-rate, right-arm, off-break bowler. Emphatically the bowler of 1950—taking 193 wickets (13.59), which remained his career-best—he also headed the national averages. He was flown out as a replacement to Australia that winter. In the fifth Test at Melbourne his last-wicket stand of 74 with Reg Simpson, the left-handed Tattersall contributing 10, assured an English victory; and his 1 for 16 and 6 for 44 in the second Test against New Zealand at Wellington enabled England to win comfortably. Subsequently he toured India in 1951/2 and appeared in occasional Tests against South Africa, Australia, and Pakistan but Jim Laker was usually preferred. Against South Africa, on a rain-affected wicket at Lord's in 1951, he took 7 for 52 and 5 for 49, the outstanding performance of an underrated bowler. He exceeded 100 wickets in a season eight times and he performed the hat-trick while taking 9 for 40 in an innings against Nottinghamshire in 1953.

First-class career (1948–64): 2,040 runs (9.35), 1,369 wickets (18.04), and 146 catches

Test matches (16): 50 runs (5.00), 58 wickets (26.08), and 8 catches

TAVARÉ, Christopher James

(b. 1954, Orpington, Kent) *Oxford University, Kent, Somerset, and England*

A correct and determined right-handed batsman of phlegmatic temperament and a brilliant slip-fielder, Chris Tavaré seemed to be the answer to England's desperate need for a solid and reliable batsman. Educated at Sevenoaks School and Oxford, he was obviously destined for a cricket career and at Oxford quickly earned the respect of the professionals with his studious and disciplined approach to batting. An ability to get his head down and graft for runs, however, sometimes concealed the fact that he had a full array of attacking shots which were more often displayed in the one-day game. Tavaré scored a century for England Schools against All-India Schools at Birmingham in 1973 and won blues from 1975 to 1977, having made his first appearance for Kent in 1974. His first full season for Kent brought him 1,534 runs (45.11), and an innings of 150 not out in the Tunbridge Wells week against Essex, the 1979 county champions, underlined his ability to concentrate for long periods. His first chance at higher level came in a one-day international against the West Indies in 1980 when he played a fine innings of 82 not out at Headingley and won selection for the first two Test matches. A staunch innings of 42 in his second match at Lord's was considered too slow and strokeless, but England were thankful when he batted in much the same way against Australia in 1981, playing two dull but valuable innings of 69 and 78 on his recall at Old Trafford. He batted for nearly 12 hours in the match and his second 50 was the slowest in a Test in England, a 'record' he broke against Pakistan at Lord's in 1982 when, in a brave rearguard action, he took 350 minutes to reach 50. His 82 in 404 minutes very nearly saved England and underlined Tavaré's skill, courage and concentration. He toured India in 1981/2 and scored his first Test hundred, a patient and valuable 149, at Delhi, finishing the series with 349 runs (38.77), before scoring 85 in the second innings to steer England to success in the inaugural Test with Sri Lanka in Colombo. In England in 1982 the selectors asked him to open the innings and he did so with success, despite continuing at number three for Kent. He had an unsuccessful tour of Australia in 1982/3, although in his innings of 89 at Melbourne he revealed the whole range of his attacking repertoire. He was back at his determined best against New Zealand in 1983, and hit his second Test hundred. Then, recalled in the final Test against the West Indies in 1984, he showed all his courageous, defensive qualities in an innings of 49. But he was not chosen for the 1984/5 tour of India and was deposed as Kent's captain after only two seasons, despite having helped them to

TAYLOR

the NatWest Final. He moved to Somerset in 1989 and captained them for 4 years in his taciturn way before retiring and, having tested other possible careers, taking over the cricket at his old school. He was recalled as a last minute replacement for one Test at Edgbaston in 1989, a challenge for which he was not prepared.

First-class career (1974–93): 24,906 runs (38.79) including 48 centuries, 5 wickets (144.40), and 418 catches

Test matches (31): 1,755 runs (32.50) including 2 centuries, 0–11, and 20 catches

TAYLOR, Jonathan Paul

(b. 1964, Ashby-de-la Zouch, Leicestershire) *Derbyshire, Staffordshire, Northamptonshire, and England*

An inspired piece of talent-spotting by Northamptonshire rescued Paul Taylor from obscurity and allowed him to fulfill his ambition of playing for his country, albeit only briefly. A strong, quietly spoken left-arm fast-medium bowler, with the rare ability to swing the ball both ways, he began his county career at Derbyshire, but was released in 1987 after four relatively unproductive years, moving on to play for Staffordshire in the Minor Counties Championship. In 1990, coming up against eventual finalists Northamptonshire in the first round of the NatWest Trophy, he conceded 92 runs in his 12-over ration out of a total of 360 for two, but Allan Lamb and his colleagues were impressed enough for Taylor to be offered a contract the following season. 1991 was a summer of readjustment, but after wintering in Western Australia, briefly coming under the guidance of Dennis Lillee, he captured 68 first-class wickets in 1992, and gained a place on the winter tour of India and Sri Lanka. Winning his first cap in the first Test at Calcutta, he made more impression as an obdurate late-order batsman than as a bowler, on a pitch made for spin bowlers, finishing with figures of 1 for 74. Playing little cricket on the rest of the tour, Taylor seemed destined to join the realms of players with only one cap, but after taking 69 wickets in 1993, he was summoned to join the A tour of South Africa the following winter when Martin Bicknell broke down and, again as a late substitute, for the 1994 Lord's Test against New Zealand. Perhaps affected by nerves, he failed to do himself justice as a bowler despite producing a spectacular run-out. Again, however, his batting was staunch as England narrowly averted defeat.

First-class career (1984–): 455 runs (10.11) and 222 wickets (30.77)

Test matches (2): 34 runs (17.00) and 3 wickets (52.00)

TAYLOR, Kenneth

(b. 1935, Huddersfield, Yorkshire) *Yorkshire, Auckland, Norfolk, and England*

Ken Taylor served Yorkshire effectively either as an opening right-handed batsman or in the middle-order and, in his best innings, played with such fluency and authority that he looked to be of the highest quality. A bowler of 'little seamers' as he called his medium-pace swing bowling, he was also a cover fielder of uncommon mobility, as befitted a professional footballer. His highest score was 203 not out against Warwickshire at Edgbaston in 1961. He represented England against India in 1959 and against Australia in 1964. He taught at Gresham's School and later in South Africa. His son Nick played for Yorkshire, Surrey, and Somerset.

First-class career (1953–68): 13,053 runs (26.74) including 16 centuries, 131 wickets (28.72), and 150 catches

Test matches (3): 57 runs (11.40), 0–6, and 1 catch

TAYLOR, Leslie Brian

(b. 1953, Earl Shilton, Leicestershire) *Leicestershire, Natal, and England*

Les Taylor was possibly the last in a long line of England Test fast bowlers who had connections with the coal industry. A tall, strong, saturnine right-arm seam-bowler and tail-end batsman, he did not make his first-class début until the age of 23 in 1977, but he soon proved to be a fine county bowler. At a brisk medium pace, he bowled extremely accurately and could move the ball both ways off the pitch. He took 75 wickets (21.70) in the 1981 season, including a career-best performance of 7 for 28 against Derbyshire and was unlucky not to be selected for the tour of India and Sri Lanka the following winter. Instead, he joined the rebel tour of South Africa and showed how well he could bowl by being easily the English side's leading bowler with 11 wickets at an average of 18.72. He was banned from playing Test cricket for three years. After two very successful years in 1982 and 1983, he faced a desperate struggle for his fitness in 1984, when he could take only ten wickets in seven first-class matches. But, back near his best form for Leicestershire the following season, he was chosen for the Edgbaston and The Oval Tests against Australia. Not flattered by his figures (four wickets, average 44.50), Taylor took important wickets in both matches. Indeed, it was his wicket, when he caught and bowled Murray Bennett, which finally won the Ashes for England. Touring West Indies in the early months of 1986 he performed dependably, given scant opportunity, playing in only one limited-overs international. With 13 wickets at 19.92, he finished top of the first-class tour averages.

First-class career (1977–90): 1,061 runs (9.38), 581 wickets (25.21), and 53 catches

Test matches (2): 1 run, 4 wickets (44.50), and 1 catch

TAYLOR, Robert William

(b. 1941, Stoke-on-Trent, Staffordshire) *Derbyshire, Staffordshire, and England*

Of all the good and bad repercussions of the 'Packer Revolution', the happiest was that this perfect craftsman and ideal sportsman suddenly acquired a status which his exceptional ability warranted. Such a perfectionist as a wicket-keeper that he gave up the captaincy of his county the moment that he felt he was not keeping wicket as well as he could (though no one else had noticed any decline), Bob Taylor managed to be at once as keen as mustard and totally undemonstrative. A capable, orthodox batsman, lacking any great power of stroke, he was second choice to Alan Knott for almost a decade. He toured Australia with five England sides (and once with a Rest of the World side), the West Indies, Pakistan, India, and New Zealand. He three times dismissed eighty or more batsmen in a season (1962, 1963, and 1965). At Chesterfield in 1963 he dismissed ten Hampshire batsmen in the match and in 1966 at Derby caught seven Glamorgan batsmen in one innings. He had played just one Test in New Zealand in 1971 before his chance came to become England's regular 'keeper in Pakistan in 1977/8. He seized that opportunity unerringly and was a valuable member of the England team which defeated Australia 5–1 in 1978/9. At Adelaide England were in severe danger of losing the fifth Test when Taylor and his Derbyshire colleague, Geoff Miller, rescued England with a stand of 135, Taylor going on to make 97, equalling his highest score. In 1981, to his great delight, he scored a maiden first-class hundred in his 21st season, against Yorkshire at Abbeydale Park. He was

twice discarded by England after a relatively disappointing tour of Australia in 1979/80, amazingly enough after taking ten catches, seven in one innings, and scoring a priceless 43, in the Jubilee Test in Bombay. He re-established himself and in Australia in 1982/3 he broke J. T. Murray's all-time record of 1,527 first-class victims. He remained as England's wicket-keeper until the end of the 1983/4 tour, the senior member of the side and always ready to help the younger players; then announced his retirement from first-class cricket at the end of the 1984 season. Still fit and agile at the age of 43, it was typical of him that he wanted to give his long-serving deputies at Derbyshire their chance. He was awarded the MBE in 1981. In 1986 he made a welcome, but brief and unexpected reappearance in Test cricket when, attending the Lord's Test as a media relations officer for Cornhill Insurance, he took over the gloves in New Zealand's first innings as substitute for the injured Bruce French. He played a final first-class match at Scarborough in 1988.

First-class career (1960–88): 12,065 runs (16.92), including 1 century, 1–75, and 1,649 dismissals (1,473 c., 176 st.)

Test matches (57): 1,156 runs (16.28), 0–6, and 174 dismissals (167 c., 7 st.)

TAYLOR, Tom Launcelot

(b. 1878, Leeds; d. 1960, Leeds) *Cambridge University and Yorkshire*

The last distinguished pupil of the famous Uppingham coach, H. H. Stephenson, Taylor was the outstanding schoolboy cricketer of 1896. A right-handed batsman and an outstanding wicket-keeper, his century for Cambridge University against the 1899 Australians led to his playing for Yorkshire while still an undergraduate. His first-class career ended in 1906 but he was the county's tennis doubles champion 1922–4 and eventually became president of Yorkshire CCC.

First-class career (1897–1906): 5,968 runs (32.08) including 13 centuries, and 92 dismissals (86 c., 6 st.)

TENNYSON, Hon. Lionel Hallam (3rd Baron Tennyson)

(b. 1889, London; d. 1951, Bexhill, Sussex) *Hampshire and England*

Originally a fast right-arm bowler and heavy hitter in the lower rungs of the Eton batting order, Lionel Tennyson eventually made 19 centuries. He was a Regency figure and refused consistently to be trammelled by many of the considerations that bind most of humanity to a more prosaic existence. Captain of a depressed England for three Tests of 1921 and of Hampshire from 1919 until 1933 (the county's wicket-keeper, Walter Livsey, was his butler), he split a hand trying to stop an unstoppable shot from Charles Macartney in the Test at Leeds and batted one-handed against the thunderbolts of Gregory and MacDonald. He did not flinch in scoring 63 in just over an hour, while the other batsmen were hard pressed. He toured South Africa with MCC in 1913/14 and took his own team to the West Indies, India, and elsewhere. Seven times he reached 1,000 runs in a season. His two uninhibited and amusing volumes of autobiography are entitled *From Verse to Worse* and *Sticky Wickets*. R. C. Robertson-Glasgow said of him: 'his forward-stroke was, like the man, tough and determined'.

First-class career (1913–37): 16,828 runs (23.33) including 19 centuries, 55 wickets (54.10), and 172 catches
Test matches (9): 345 runs (31.36), 0–1, and 6 catches

TERRY, Vivian Paul

(b. 1959, Osnabrück, West Germany) *Hampshire and England*

A patient and correct right-hand batsman, Paul Terry established himself as Hampshire's opener only in 1984 when Gordon Greenidge was playing for the West Indies. He was so successful, scoring over 1,000 runs with five hundreds by the beginning of July, that the selectors gave him his chance in the Test side. Tall, fair-haired, and a quite brilliant fielder in any position, he had had a long apprenticeship after great success as a schoolboy at Millfield. With only limited first-class experience since his début in 1978, mostly down the order before 1984, he was not really ready for Test cricket. Batting at number three, his weakness outside the off stump was exposed by the West Indies. Two failures in his first Test at Headingley were followed by an even worse fate at Old Trafford—his left arm was broken by a short ball from Winston Davis. Bravely, he returned with his arm strapped up to allow Allan Lamb to complete his hundred and he even faced the bowling in a vain attempt to save the follow-on. He did not play again in the 1984 season, but toured Zimbabwe with an English Counties side in the winter. By 1986 he was vice-captain of Hampshire and over the next decade he was

perhaps their most consistent batsman, not to mention their most reliable catcher. He scored five centuries in 1994, his benefit season.

First-class career (1978–   ); 15,036 runs (37.13) including 36 centuries, and 290 catches
Test matches (2): 16 runs (5.33) and 2 catches

THOMAS, John Gregory

(b. 1960, Trebanos, Glamorgan, Wales) *Glamorgan, Northamptonshire, Border, and England*

A natural games-player, this strongly built, softly spoken fast bowler from Gorseinon was definitely the find of England's 1986 tour of the West Indies. Bowling with pace and hostility in his four Tests, he proved he was a genuine fast bowler, although a lack of control made him too expensive. As a right-handed all-rounder, Greg Thomas made his début for Glamorgan in 1979, and soon showed he could bowl quickly. He benefited from two winters playing in South Africa. He had rather a disappointing 1985 season, taking only 39 first-class wickets, but he had, on occasions, bowled with menacing speed. The selectors were impressed with his rhythmical approach and high action, so chose him for the West Indies tour as the spearhead of England's bowling attack. He took two wickets in each of the first two Tests, really troubling the West Indian batsmen. Then, at Bridgetown he took four wickets in five overs with the second new ball to finish with 4 for 70, as the West Indies collapsed from 361 for 3 to 418 all out. He made 31 not out in the second Test, playing the fast bowling with flair and composure. Sadly, he could find no consistent form in county cricket in 1986, no doubt held back by slow wickets in Wales, and played in only one Test, against New Zealand at Trent Bridge, before narrowly missing a place on the tour to Australia. He changed counties in 1989, playing three seasons for Northamptonshire, and went on the controversial unofficial tour to South Africa in 1989/90.

First-class career (1979–91): 3,419 runs (16.43) including 2 centuries, 525 wickets (31.05), and 74 catches
Test matches (5): 83 runs (13.83) and 10 wickets (50.40)

THOMPSON, George Joseph

(b. 1877, Cogenhoe, Northamptonshire; d. 1943, Bristol) *Northamptonshire and England*

A big, burly all-rounder with a drooping moustache, George Thompson or 'The Northampton

Nugget', bowled and batted Northamptonshire into first-class cricket. At Wellingborough School he bowled himself into the 1st XI at 13 and became one of the first public schoolboys to turn professional cricketer; he first played for the county at 17 as an amateur. Bowling right-arm medium to fast, rather at the pace of Tate or Bedser, his run was short but his delivery was high and whirling, like a windmill. His batting was solid and he was a great fighter in a tight corner. The first Minor Counties cricketer to take 100 wickets in a season, he performed this feat eight times in first-class cricket between 1905 and 1913. He achieved the double twice, in 1906 and 1910, and was prominent in the county's rise to second place in the Championship in 1912. He hit 125 for Players against Gentlemen at Scarborough in 1900; and, for an England XI against the Australians at Eastbourne in 1902, took 8 for 88 in one innings. But, such was the talent available, he represented England once only at home, against Australia at Edgbaston in 1909. His sole major tour was to South Africa in 1909/10 when, for a losing team, he came second to Jack Hobbs in the Test batting, averaging 33.37, and took 23 wickets (26.91). He toured Australasia with Lord Hawke's team in 1902/3 and the West Indies with Lord Brackley's in 1904/5, on the former tour routing the opposition with 177 wickets (6.50). He captained Northamptonshire occasionally in 1913 —the first professional to do so.

First-class career (1897–1922): 12,018 runs (22.01) including 9 centuries, 1,591 wickets (18.89), and 251 catches

Test matches (6): 273 runs (30.33), 23 wickets (27.73), and 5 catches

THOMSON, Arthur Alexander

(b. 1894, Harrogate, Yorkshire; d. 1968, London)

For a dozen years in the 1950s, the journalist and author A. A. Thomson had a considerable following as a cricket writer. His writing was romantic and heroic, with a lighter touch and more humour than Neville Cardus's, but within a narrower framework. The books he wrote on cricket were part of a literary output of nearly 60, which included plays, verse, novels, and travel-writing. Titles such as *Cricket my Pleasure* (1950), *Cricket my Happiness* (1954), *Pavilioned in Splendour* (1958), and *Cricket Bouquet* (1961) declare in graphic prose the enthusiasm and affection he conveyed.

THOMSON, Norman Ian

(b. 1929, Walsall, Staffordshire) *Sussex and England*

Ian Thomson was the best right-arm, medium-fast seam-bowler produced by Sussex since Maurice Tate, though not in Tate's exalted class. He took more than 100 wickets in a season 12 times. After a shuffling, unimpressive approach, his right arm came over high; his natural delivery was the in-dipper and, on a green top, he was able to make the ball dance off the seam bewilderingly, often bowling a good leg-cutter. He took all 10 for 49 in an innings (15 for 75 in the match) against Warwickshire at Worthing in 1964. A useful tail-end batsman, he hit 77 at Leicester in 1959. He was flown out to Pakistan, 1954/5, as a replacement, and in 1964/5 toured South Africa, where his only Tests were played. He won the 1964 Gillette Cup Final almost single-handed, taking 4 for 23 as he swung and seamed the ball almost unplayably.

First-class career (1952–72): 7,120 runs (14.74), 1,597 wickets (20.57), and 135 catches

Test matches (5): 69 runs (23.00), 9 wickets (63.11), and 3 catches

THORNTON, Charles Inglis

(b. 1850, Llanwarne, Herefordshire; d. 1929, London) *Cambridge University, Kent, and Middlesex*

Measurement and comparison across the generations present problems in cricket but there can be no doubt of the hitting powers of 'Buns' Thornton. As a right-handed batsman who drove strongly, he cleared the grounds at Lord's, The Oval, and Canterbury while landing a ball in Trafalgar Square, Scarborough, over the roofs of high Victorian houses. In practice at Hove in 1871, a hit of 168 yards was measured by the cricket antiquarian, James Pycroft. Three years in the Eton XI and four in the Cambridge side prefaced spasmodic appearances for Kent and Middlesex over 20 years. It was an innings of 107 out of 133 in 1866 for the Gentlemen of England against I Zingari at Scarborough which brought together the two things for which he is best remembered—hard hitting and the Scarborough Festival. He received presentations for his work in 1894 and in 1921, and the freedom of the borough. As a fast right-arm under-arm bowler he took over 600 wickets in all classes of cricket between 1866 and 1897.

First-class career (1867–97): 6,928 runs (19.35) including 5 centuries, 47 wickets (20.10), and 119 catches

THORPE, Graham Paul

(b. 1969, Farnham, Hampshire) *Surrey and England*

After four A tours, Graham Thorpe finally graduated to the senior side with flying colours in 1993 when he became only the fourteenth England player to make a hundred in his first Test. A dark, quietly spoken, compact left-hander, strong in the drive and adept at deflecting the ball on either side of the wicket, as well as being a sound slip-fielder and a tidy right-arm medium-pacer, Thorpe's promise was evident from an early age and by the time he was 11 he was involved in Surrey's youth programme. Also proficient at football, he played for England schoolboys, was offered trials by Brentford, but cricket won the day and he made his début for Surrey in 1988, scoring a century against Cambridge in his second match. In 1989, his first full season, he scored 1,132 runs to gain a place on the A tour of Kenya and Zimbabwe. Five fifties in ten innings, including 98 in the third unofficial 'Test' in Harare convinced the team manager, Keith Fletcher, of Thorpe's ability to progress, and that view was crucial in gaining him a place on the following winter's tour of Pakistan and Sri Lanka after he scored only 608 runs in a season dominated by batsmen. Thorpe justified his choice by topping the tour averages, but although he scored 1,203 runs the following summer, he had to be content with another A tour, this time to the Caribbean, where he, along with most of the rest of the side, struggled on uneven pitches. Thorpe's response in 1992 was to produce his best-ever aggregate, 1,895 runs including a career-best 216 against Somerset, but again he had to settle for an A tour rather than a winter with the senior squad. Topping the averages again, however, he returned on the brink of higher honours. They came in the three early-season one-day internationals against the Australians, and batting at number six, he made 31, 36, and 22. With Mike Gatting preferred in the first two Tests, Thorpe had to wait until the third match at Trent Bridge for his chance as one of four débutants and after a first innings failure he silenced the critics who felt his place belonged to David Gower with a battling, unbeaten 114, albeit against a below-strength attack. That helped England to a draw, but in his next match at Headingley, Thorpe came back to earth with a bump, making 0 and 13 as England lost the Test and the Ashes. Innings of 37 and 60 at Edgbaston cemented his place but he missed The Oval Test after breaking a thumb in the nets on the morning of the match. In the West Indies

early in 1994 a tendency to 'work' the ball across the line was ruthlessly exposed in the first two Tests. His response was 86 in the third Test in Trinidad, an innings of class and courage, and in the next Test in Barbados he revealed an aggressive streak, hitherto kept for one-day cricket as he hammered 84 in 129 balls with rare authority for an English batsman against West Indian fast bowling in an era and on a ground where the home side was used to ruling the roost. Remarkably, after a failure in the final Test in Antigua, Thorpe found himself dropped at the start of the new season despite scoring a century in his first match back for Surrey. Maintaining his form, he was recalled for the final two Tests of the summer against South Africa. Determined to prove his right to a regular Test place, he produced scores of 72, 73, 79, and 15 not out and in Australia, 1994/5, was England's outstanding batsman with 444 runs (49.33) including 123 at Perth.

First-class career (1988–): 8,414 runs (42.28) and 20 wickets (52.15)

Test matches (15): 1,152 runs (44.30) including 2 centuries, and 19 catches

TITMUS, Frederick John

(b. 1932, London) *Middlesex, Surrey, Orange Free State, and England*

Fred Titmus's long and distinguished career began with a first match for Middlesex at the age of 16 in 1949 and effectively ended with Middlesex winning the county championship for the first time since 1947 in his final full season, 1976. Small, dark, with twinkling brown eyes underneath prominent eyebrows, Fred was loved as a cheerful character with a quick if sometimes caustic wit, and revered as a master off-spinner and courageous batsman, with an effective method based upon a sound technique. He was good enough to open the batting for England in an emergency and, late in his career, his technique stood the searching test of the speed of Thomson and Lillee better than that of some more vaunted batsmen. Titmus first took 100 wickets in 1953, when he established himself in the Middlesex side on his return from National Service. He did the double of 100 wickets and 1,000 runs eight times, the last in 1967. He took 100 or more wickets in a season a further fifteen times, twenty-six times taking more than ten wickets in a match and 168 times five or more wickets in an innings. Keeping a perfect length, his special skill lay in his use of the air, making the ball float, drift and dip like a bird on the wing. But when a pitch was allowing the ball to turn he would bowl sides out as quickly as most—against New Zealand in 1965 at Headingley he took four wickets in six balls. First playing for England in 1955, he was on his sixth major MCC tour, as vice-captain, in 1967/8 when he lost four toes as his foot was caught in the propeller of a motor boat in the West Indies. If this accentuated his rather rolling gait, it hardly seemed to impair his skill and he was justifiably selected for a seventh tour (his third tour of Australia) in 1974/5, when he was more than 40. However he had less success with the ball than in 1962/3, when with 21 wickets he was England's leading wicket-taker in the Tests, and less success with the bat than in 1965/6, when he made 258 Test runs at an average of 64. That tour saw his highest score—137 not out against South Australia at Adelaide. In first-class cricket his best bowling returns were 9 for 52 against Cambridge in 1962, and 9 for 57 against Lancashire at Lord's in 1967. In Tests his best efforts were 7 for 79 at Sydney in 1962/3, and 84 not out against India at Bombay in 1963/4. He became Surrey's coach in 1977 but stayed in the job for only two seasons, feeling that he was not given enough independence. He retired to run a post office in Hertfordshire with his wife. All the time Fred was itching to play again and he did indeed play one game for Surrey in 1978, his thirtieth season in first-class cricket, and two for Middlesex in 1979. Still this was not the end, for he made further appearances in 1980 and 1982, in both of which years Middlesex won the Championship. He thus joined a small and select band of those who have played first-class cricket in five decades. He became a Test selector, and was awarded the MBE for his services to the game.

First-class career (1949–82): 21,588 runs (23.11) including 6 centuries, 2,830 wickets (22.37), and 473 catches

Test matches (53): 1,449 runs (22.29), 153 wickets (32.22), and 35 catches

TOLCHARD, Roger William

(b. 1946, Torquay, Devon) *Devon, Leicestershire, and England*

Roger Tolchard was a natural games player, although his wicket-keeping, judged by the highest standards, was good but not great. His batting form during MCC's tour of India and Pakistan in 1972/3 entitled him to a chance for England, but it did not come until four years later when he played a major role in England's first ever Test win in Calcutta. Normally a brilliant and often unorthodox stroke-maker with nimble footwork as his main asset, he was forced on this occasion to defend grittily, and did so for $5\frac{1}{2}$ hours to make 67 on a pitch which was rapidly deteriorating. He retained his place for the remainder of the series and shone, even in a brilliant fielding side, with his speedy work at short-leg or in the covers. In 1978/9 he toured Australia and again batted well in very different conditions. He was unlucky not to be chosen for more Tests before his tour was abruptly ended by a bouncer which caused a severely fractured cheek-bone. Coming from a Devonian family (his elder brother Jeff played for Leicestershire and younger brother Ray for Devon) he was an outstanding schoolboy player at Malvern and was capped by Leicestershire in his second season, 1966. He became captain of his county in 1981 and the following year led them to second place in the Championship. He was outstanding in limited-overs cricket. He retired in 1983, returned to Minor Counties cricket, and to his old school, Malvern, as cricket master. He captained the Old Malvernians to victory in the 1986 and 1990 *Cricketer Cup* finals.

First-class career (1965–83): 15,288 runs (31.13) including 12 centuries, 1–34, and 1,037 dismissals (912 c., 125 st.)

Test matches (4): 129 runs (25.80) and 5 catches

TOONE, Sir Frederick Charles

(b. 1868; d. 1930, Harrogate, Yorkshire)

Fred Toone set a standard for all secretaries of first-class counties and tour managers to emulate. He was appointed to the Yorkshire secretaryship (1903) after 6 years with Leicestershire, very much the personal choice of Lord Hawke from nearly 150 applicants. Under his influence, Yorkshire's administration, facilities, finances, and membership all benefited while his active concern for the professionals led to players such as George Hirst and Roy Kilner receiving unprecedented benefits. Yorkshire recognized all he had done for the county by awarding him a testimonial in 1926 of a similar value (£3,500). He and Hawke made a powerful duo. When war came in 1914, their energies were transferred to running the West Riding Volunteers from the club offices, with Hawke as colonel and Toone as adjutant. After the war Toone became manager of all three MCC tours to Australia in the 1920s. In an article in *Wisden* just before his death (1930), he wrote that 'sportsmanship was the keynote' of every tour and of his 'happy relations' with every MCC captain. Toone's wide-ranging abilities, his tact, objectivity, and experience were recognized by the Home Office in his appointment to the Committee to review crowd management after the Wembley Cup Final in 1923. For his promotion of good relations between England and Australia he was knighted in 1929. He would have been dismayed at the events on the 1932/3 MCC tour of Australia.

TOWNSEND, Charles Lucas

(b. 1876, Bristol; d. 1958, Stockton-on-Tees, Co. Durham) *Gloucestershire and England*

A lean and lanky schoolboy at Clifton, Charlie Townsend first played for his county at 16. A right-arm slow bowler and left-handed batsman, he was an immediate success in 1895. Such was his tidy length and exceptional degree of spin even the best batsmen were in serious trouble with his leg-breaks. He once did the hat-trick, all three victims being stumped. He frequently opened the bowling, and in the two matches against Nottinghamshire in 1895, he took 16 for 122 and 13 for 110. He achieved the double in 1898 when he took 101 wickets (29.06) and made 2,440 runs (51.91), including nine centuries, among which was his highest score of 224 not out against Essex at Clifton. He again did the double in 1899, when he made his only appearances in Tests against Australia. Although he was never able to appear regularly after 1900, as late as 1909 he hit 129 out of 169 in two hours for his county against the Australians at Cheltenham. His father was Frank Townsend, who played in the early years of the county club. His son, D.C.H., also represented England (see below) and his grandson, J.R.A., played for Oxford and Durham.

First-class career (1893–1922): 9,512 runs (30.29) including 21 centuries, 725 wickets (23.12), and 193 catches

Test matches (2): 51 runs (17.00) and 3 wickets (25.00)

TOWNSEND, David Charles Humphrey

(b. 1912, Norton-on-Tees, Co. Durham) *Oxford University, Durham, and England*

David Townsend is the last man to have represented England without ever having played for a first-class county. From Winchester he went to Oxford, and played against Cambridge in 1933 and 1934. Of fine physique, he was strong in defence and a powerful, right-handed stroke-player. He hit 193 against Cambridge at Lord's in 1934, and toured the West Indies in 1934/5, opening the batting in three Tests.

First-class career (1933–48): 1,801 runs (29.04) including 4 centuries, 6 wickets (83.50), and 16 catches

Test matches (3): 77 runs (12.83), 0–9, and 1 catch

TOWNSEND, Leslie Fletcher

(b. 1903, Long Eaton, Derbyshire; d. 1993, Nelson, New Zealand) *Derbyshire, Northumberland, Auckland, and England*

One of posse of all-rounders who were prominent in Derbyshire's first Championship win of 1936, Leslie Townsend was an attractive right-handed batsman, especially strong in front of the wicket and on the off-side. He was also a medium-pace, off-spin bowler and a very good field. Nine times he exceeded 1,000 runs in a season, four times took 100 wickets, and three times achieved the double, notably in 1933 when he made 2,268 runs (44.47) and took 100 wickets (18.71). He toured the West Indies with MCC in 1929/30 when he first represented England. He went to India with MCC in 1933/4, appearing in all three Tests on another inaugural tour, and altogether made 829 runs and took 65 wickets. He was never selected for a Test in England, however, and after the Second World War emigrated to New Zealand where he had played for Auckland and later coached in Nelson (South Island).

First-class career (1922–39): 19,555 runs (27.50) including 22 centuries, 1,088 wickets (21.12), and 237 catches

Test matches (4): 97 runs (16.16), 6 wickets (34.16), and 2 catches

TRAVERS, Benjamin

(b. 1886, Hendon, Middlesex; d. 1980 London)

With his play, *A Cuckoo in the Nest* (1925) Ben Travers began a series of highly successful and lucrative farces which ran at the Aldwych Theatre, London. His devotion to cricket started when he saw a Test match at The Oval in 1896 and continued throughout his life. He accompanied MCC teams abroad and was one of the few who could penetrate the reserve of Walter Hammond during the 1928/9 tour. In 1980 he talked about his cricket memories from the commentary box during a Test at Lord's and his reminiscences appeared, posthumously, as *94 Declared* (1981). John Arlott called them 'a collection of memories over a span of great cricket granted to few people and recalled with zest'. In particular, his description of Gilbert Jessop's epic hundred, against all odds at The Oval in 1902, was enthralling.

TREMLETT, Maurice Fletcher

(b. 1923, Stockport, Cheshire; d. 1984, Southampton) *Somerset, Central Districts, and England*

On his début for Somerset against Middlesex at Lord's in 1947, Maurice Tremlett impressed as a right-arm fast-medium bowler, taking 8 for 86 in the match. Well built and looking every inch a cricketer, he toured the West Indies that winter with MCC because of the great promise he had shown. Relatively inexperienced, however, he was always liable to be erratic and his bowling was severely mauled in the Caribbean. He again toured with MCC the following winter in 1948/9, and in South Africa, although he achieved little with the ball, his batting improved. Subsequently, while he lost his control as a bowler, he was worth playing for his batting alone. He passed 1,000 runs in a season ten times and his hard, straight driving, either lofted or along the ground, was most exhilarating. From 1956 until 1959 he served as the county's first professional captain. His son Tim played for Hampshire and England B before becoming Hampshire's coach.

First-class career (1947–60): 16,038 runs (25.37) including 16 centuries, 351 wickets (30.70), and 257 catches

Test matches (3): 20 runs (6.66) and 4 wickets (56.50)

TROTT, Albert Edwin

(1873–1914) *Victoria and Middlesex*

See Australia section.

TRUEMAN, Frederick Sewards

(b. 1931, Stainton, Yorkshire) *Yorkshire, Derbyshire, and England*

'I 'ear things about myself I'd never 'ave dreamt of in a million years, Sunshine, and I don't reckon to be short on imagination.' Thus did Fred Trueman, sitting back in a BBC commentary box, in affluent middle age, for once disclaim one of the numerous outrageous stories which have attached themselves to one of the game's greatest modern characters. If ever a man deserved his affluence it was F.S.T. He achieved international fame, first as one of the greatest fast bowlers of all time (only Kapil Dev, Richard Hadlee, Mal-

colm Marshall, Imran Khan, Ian Botham, Dennis Lillee, Bob Willis, and Lance Gibbs have taken more than Trueman's 307 Test wickets), secondly as a character who gave life and humour to every game he played, and thirdly as a naturally gifted radio commentator and raconteur, at his best when it was raining and he could delve into a rich memory; at his worst when trying in vain to be generous about most modern fast bowlers. He claimed both Jewish and Yorkshire blood and certainly kept a firm hold on his purse!. As his bowling developed from that of the wild young tearaway into the mature artist, so has his character developed from raw, reckless, boastful but fearless youth to international celebrity. For 'Fiery Fred', born at Stainton, cricket was the probable alternative to life down a coal-mine. His early days in the Yorkshire side—he was picked for nine matches in 1949 when just 18—showed him to be a hungry fighter. He always believed himself to be the best man for any job he wanted to do and after being left out of the Yorkshire side for the more experienced Bill Foord he was determined, as his colleague Bill Bowes recorded, to 'bloody well show 'em'. Much of the blustering talk, which accompanied his bowling and the over-use of bouncers in his early days, stemmed, Bowes believed, from a certain inferiority complex. At times this proved expensive, but hardly so during his dramatic entry on to the Test arena against India in 1952 when in three Tests he took 24 wickets, plainly terrifying some of his opponents. At Leeds four Indian wickets fell before a run was scored: they were bowled out in 1 hour 20 minutes for 58, Trueman taking 8 for 31. National Service interrupted his career; he fell foul of authority on Len Hutton's tour of the West Indies in 1953/4 and he was left out of the MCC sides which toured Australia in 1954/5 and South Africa in 1956/7. However, for ten consecutive seasons between 1957 and 1966 he took 100 wickets or more, including 175 in 1960 at 13.98, and became a more or less automatic selection for England. Neil Hawke, in 1964, was his 300th Test victim, pouched by Cowdrey at slip, the victim like countless others of a deadly, late outswing. Trueman is 5 ft. 10 in. tall and he had the ideal physique for fast bowling with immensely strong arms, legs, back, and shoulders. Added to this, he had mental aggression, sheer courage, and a beautiful, rhythmic action which built up from a rolling approach into an unforgettable long final stride with the body sideways-on. His fastest speed was genuinely quick, his length and line were good, and his swing formidable. In addition he was an effective right-hand batsman who hit the ball tremendously hard on the leg-side and scored three centuries. A brilliant natural fielder, he specialized at short-leg but also threw in hard and flat from the boundary with either hand. But it is as a bowler that he is immortal. He took four hat-tricks, ten or more wickets in a match 25 times and five wickets or more in an innings 126 times. After retiring from Yorkshire in 1968, he played successfully in a few limited-overs matches for Derbyshire. He was awarded an OBE.

First-class career (1949–69): 9,231 runs (15.56) including 3 centuries, 2,304 wickets (18.29), and 439 catches
Test matches (67): 981 runs (13.81), 307 wickets (21.57), and 64 catches

TUFNELL, Col. Neville Charsley

(b. 1887, Simla, India; d. 1951, London) *Cambridge University, Surrey, Norfolk, and England*

An Old Etonian and a talented wicket-keeper, Col. Neville Tufnell was a Cambridge blue who turned out occasionally for Surrey (when Bert Strudwick was not playing). While still at Eton, he toured New Zealand with Major E. G. Wynyard's team in 1906/7. He visited South Africa with MCC in 1909/10 and, deputizing for the injured Strudwick in the fifth Test at Cape Town—his sole Test—he made a stumping and scored 14.

First-class career (1907–24): 1,514 runs (14.28) including 1 century, 1 wicket (118.00), and 99 dismissals (59 c., 40 st.)

TUFNELL, Philip Clive Roderick

(b. 1966, Hadley Wood, Hertfordshire) *Middlesex and England*

Despite giving up cricket for three years in his mid-teens, and possessing an unstable temperament which led him into difficulties both on and off the field, Philip Tufnell proved himself a match-winner at Test level. A square-jawed but frail-looking orthodox left-arm spinner with a lengthy, slightly angled run starting with a skip, Tufnell's control of flight and a well-disguised, swinging arm-ball helped him become a worthy successor to Phil Edmonds for both Middlesex and England. He began as a fast bowler at Highgate public school, but lost interest in the game, gaining a qualification as a silversmith, until persuaded to try and bowl spin by the coaches at Finchley Indoor School. Showing

promise, he was taken on by MCC, named as their Young Cricketer of the Year in 1984, and made a Young England tour of the West Indies before making his début for Middlesex in 1986. In 1989 he took 51 wickets, although the pony-tail he sported that summer did not always meet with approval. The following year, in a season dominated by batsman, his 74 wickets earned him a place on the tour to Australia, but although he played in four of the five Tests, and came close to a hat-trick as he took 5 for 61 in his second Test in Sydney, he finished the tour with a question mark over his future. The Australian crowds loved to mock his inconsistent fielding and timorous batting and a lack of discipline off the field was criticized by the captain, Graham Gooch. He was dropped and told to smarten up but returned for the fifth Test against the West Indies at The Oval with England needing to win to level the series. Responding with a spell of 6 for 4 in 33 balls to help enforce the follow-on, Tufnell became an instant national hero as England won, and in the next Test at Lord's, he took 5 for 94 to bowl Sri Lanka out on the last day. Selected for the winter tour of New Zealand, Tufnell then won his third Test in a row in Christchurch with match figures of 11 for 147, including 7 for 47 in 46.1 second innings overs. The final wicket was that of Martin Crowe as Tufnell tossed the ball up to induce a miscued drive. He finished the series by bowling 71 overs in an innings in Wellington, a record in New Zealand first-class cricket, as England forced a draw, but he then lost his place during the World Cup which followed, often complaining of stomach cramps. The problem turned out to be a grumbling appendix which burst back in England to keep him out of the first half of 1992. Again he returned for the last Test of the summer against Pakistan and the winter tour of India and Sri Lanka which followed. The trip was a disaster for Tufnell, who disliked the subcontinent, was comprehensively out-bowled by his opposing spinners as he took only seven wickets in three Tests, and fined £500 after a show of petulance. Tufnell's mediocre Test form continued the following summer and he was dropped after two below-average performances against Australia, but his 64 wickets, including a career-best 8 for 29 against Glamorgan at Cardiff helped Middlesex to the County Championship and saw him return as 12th man for the final Test of the summer before being picked for the tour of the West Indies. Although his figures of four wickets in two Tests did not reflect the fact, he did a fine stock-bowling job in the

Caribbean, and enhanced his reputation, but in 1994 he returned home to face personal problems. A row with his former girlfriend led to a court appearance and a fine, and Middlesex gave him a two-month leave of absence to sort his life out. Remarkably, Tufnell managed to put those difficulties quickly behind him, taking 35 wickets in only eight matches for his county, and gaining a Test recall at the end of the summer. He remained his country's most dangerous spinner and nothing if not a character.

First-class career (1986–): 908 runs (10.09) and 594 wickets (31.56)

Test matches (18): 56 runs (5.09) and 58 wickets (38.43)

TUNNICLIFFE, John

(b. 1866, Pudsey, Yorkshire; d. 1948, Bristol) *Yorkshire*

'Long John of Pudsey' was the professional on whose advice and influence his Yorkshire captain, Lord Hawke, most relied. He was a man of strong character, a Methodist preacher, an opening right-handed batsman, and as infallible as a man could be at first slip. His strokes were 'few but mighty' and his height and reach brought him catches not many could have contemplated. Only ten cricketers in first-class cricket (other than wicket-keepers) have taken more. He reached 1,000 runs on twelve occasions and he shared in twenty-six century partnerships for the first wicket, most of them with J. T. Brown. In 1897 they put on 378 against Sussex at Sheffield and a year later achieved 554 against Derbyshire at Chesterfield—a world record for any wicket until beaten by Sutcliffe and Holmes in 1932. Tunnicliffe's 243 was the more remarkable in that he had not had a proper night's rest before going out to bat. He retired in 1907 to become coach at Clifton College. Later, he became one of the few professionals of his generation to serve on a county committee when elected to that of Gloucestershire—of which his son, W. G. became secretary (1921–35).

First-class career (1891–1907): 20,310 runs (26.95) including 23 centuries, 7 wickets (57.85), and 694 catches

TURNBULL, Maurice Joseph Lawson

(b. 1906, Cardiff; d. 1944, Montchamp, France) *Cambridge University, Glamorgan, and England*

To Maurice Turnbull batting was a gay adventure. He was a gifted right-hander who made runs when they were wanted and whose value could not always be assessed on figures. Initially an on-side player, he developed all the recognized strokes and added some of his own, and he was also a fine short-leg fielder. Always associated in the public mind with Glamorgan, he first appeared for them as a schoolboy in 1924. He captained Cambridge in 1929 and Glamorgan from 1930 until 1939. He passed 1,000 runs in a season ten times and three times hit double-centuries, the highest being 233 against Worcestershire at Swansea in 1937, a season in which Glamorgan finished higher than ever before thanks to his bold leadership and devoted example. For ten years he was an outstanding secretary to the Club. He toured Australia in 1929/30 and South Africa in 1930/1, and with Maurice Allom, wrote a lighthearted account of each tour. At home he represented England against the West Indies and India; and he was an England selector in 1938 and 1939. A Major in the Welsh Guards, he was killed in action in Normandy. A brilliant all-round sportsman, he also played for Wales at Rugby Union and hockey.

First-class career (1924–39): 17,544 runs (29.78) including 29 centuries, 4 wickets (88.75), and 280 catches

Test matches (9): 224 runs (20.36) and 1 catch

TWINING, Richard Haynes

(b. 1889, London; d. 1979, London) *Oxford University and Middlesex*

The first ball bowled in first-class cricket after the First World War was received by Dick Twining, so badly wounded in that conflict that his cricketing future had seemed uncertain. Captain of both Eton and Oxford University, he belonged to a generation who combined a business career with some county cricket and rather more country-house cricket. He was a right-handed opening batsman whose 'flawless' 135 in Middlesex's second innings ensured a victory against Surrey at Lord's in 1921. It was a match in which (for the second year running) the county championship went to whichever side won. Twining was a president of both Middlesex (1950–7) and MCC (1964).

First-class career (1910–28): 2,963 runs (22.96) including 3 centuries, and 50 dismissals (40 c., 10 st.)

TYLDESLEY, George Ernest

(b. 1889, Worsley, Lancashire; d. 1962, Rhos-on-Sea, Clwyd) *Lancashire and England*

The first Lancastrian to score 100 centuries, Ernest Tyldesley was the younger brother of J.T. He was an elegant right-handed stroke-player, fine hooker and engaging cutter whose chivalrous manner concealed a ruthless and belligerent approach. He reached 1,000 runs in a season nineteen times (once overseas), six times exceeding 2,000. His best years were 1928 with 3,024 runs (79.57), including ten centuries, and 1926 with 2,826 runs (64.22), again including ten centuries, four coming in successive innings. In July 1926 alone he scored 1,024 runs (128.00). His highest was 256 not out against Warwickshire at Old Trafford in 1930 (the season when Lancashire won the Championship for the fourth time in five years). In and out of the England team, he appeared in five Tests against Australia between 1921 and 1928/9, making 257 runs (42.83); and against South Africa in 1927/8, against vicious spin on matting, he achieved great things, making 520 runs (65.00) including 122 at Johannesburg, when he added 230 with Herbert Sutcliffe for the second wicket. He appeared against the West Indies in the first three Tests in England in 1928, scoring 122 in the first at Lord's. He should have played much more Test Cricket. Cardus called him an 'unobtrusive yet sterling character'.

First-class career (1909–36): 38,874 runs (45.46) including 102 centuries, 6 wickets (57.66), and 293 catches

Test matches (14): 990 runs (55.00) including 3 centuries, 0–2, and 2 catches

TYLDESLEY, John Thomas

(b. 1873, Worsley, Lancashire; d. 1930, Salford, Lancashire) *Lancashire and England*

J.T., or Johnny, Tyldesley brought to the battle the trained skill and aggressive spirit of a good professional soldier. Only 5 ft. 6 in. tall, not only was he a fine, attacking right-handed batsman on all wickets, particularly on the off-side, but he could also defend strongly. Moreover, he was a fine outfielder. He hit 152 in his second match for the county against Warwickshire at Edgbaston in 1895, and never looked back. Nineteen times he exceeded 1,000 runs in a season, five times the 2,000, 1901 bringing 3,041 runs (55.29), including nine centuries. He scored thirteen double-centuries, all for Lancashire, the highest being 295 not out against Kent at Old Trafford in 1906.

Three times he hit two centuries in a match. For several years, amid a rich profusion of amateur talent, he held the coveted post of number three in England's team. He toured Australia with A. C. MacLaren's team in 1901/2 and with the first MCC team in 1903/4 and South Africa with Lord Hawke's side of 1898/9. He was a regular against Australia in England between 1899 and 1909, and also appeared against South Africa in 1907.

First-class career (1895–1923): 37,897 runs (40.66) including 86 centuries, 3 wickets (70.33), and 355 catches

Test matches (31): 1,661 runs (30.75) including 4 centuries, and 16 catches

TYLDESLEY, Richard Knowles

(b. 1897, Westhaughton, Lancashire; d. 1943, Bolton, Lancashire) *Lancashire and England*

Dick Tyldesley's skill as a right-arm slow bowler increased like his bulk; he was a Falstaff from Westhaughton. Carrying his weight with remarkable ease, he toiled for long spells without tiring. Above medium height, he flighted the ball naturally and often got lbws with his top-spinner. His leg-break turned little under normal conditions but, on a responsive pitch, could be devastating. From 1922 until 1931 he took at least 100 wickets a season, his best being 1924, with 184 (13.98). At Derby in 1929 he dismissed two men with the last two balls of the first innings and two more with the first two balls he sent down in the second. He toured Australia in 1924/5, but played against Australia and South Africa at home with more success. He was one of four brothers—not related to G.E. or J.T.—who all played for Lancashire, the others being William, James, and Harry; all died young.

First-class career (1919–35): 6,419 runs (15.65) including 1 century, 1,509 wickets (17.21), and 337 catches

Test matches (7): 47 runs (7.83), 19 wickets (32.57), and 1 catch

TYLECOTE, Edmund Ferdinando Sutton

(b. 1849, Marston Moretaine, Bedfordshire; d. 1938, New Hunstanton, Norfolk) *Oxford University, Kent, Bedfordshire, and England*

While at Clifton, where he was in the XI for five years, finishing as captain, Edmund Tylecote made 404 not out in a house match. He led Oxford to victory in the University match. Besides his remarkably steady and free-hitting batting, he was a quiet and unobtrusive wicket-keeper who stood close-up unless the bowling was exceptionally fast, and he was one of the first to dispense with a long-stop. For Kent he hit a splendid 100 not out against the Australians at Canterbury in 1882; and that winter he toured Australia with Hon. Ivo Bligh's side in search of the Ashes, hitting 66 at Sydney in the match that decided the rubber. He hit a century at Lord's for Gentlemen against Players, and in the same fixture in 1876 he stumped two batsmen and caught five. He appeared twice for England against Australia in 1886, at Lord's and The Oval. In 22 matches for Kent from 1875 until 1883 he made 927 runs (24.39), including two centuries.

First-class career (1869–86): 3,065 runs (20.70) including 3 centuries, and 185 dismissals (127 c., 58 st.)

Test matches (6): 152 runs (19.00) and 10 dismissals (5 c., 5 st.)

TYLER, Edwin James

(b. 1864, Kidderminster, Worcestershire; d. 1917, Taunton, Somerset) *Worcestershire, Somerset, and England*

Playing a prominent part in Somerset's promotion to first-class rank in 1891, Edwin Tyler was a left-arm bowler of such slow pace that, had he not possessed a good head and great command of length, first-rate batsmen would have hit him all over the field. As it was, even the best batsmen respected him, and he achieved some outstanding performances. He captured all 10 for 49 in an innings against Surrey at Taunton in 1895, 9 for 33 against Nottinghamshire at Taunton in 1892 and 9 for 83 against Sussex at Hastings in 1907. Match figures included 15 for 95 against Sussex at Taunton in 1895 and 15 for 96 against Nottinghamshire at Taunton in 1892. There was some doubt about the legality of his action, but, as he was too slow to hurt anybody, it passed muster. For Lord Hawke's team in South Africa in 1895/6, he appeared in his sole Test at Cape Town, failing to score and taking 4 for 65.

First-class career (1891–1907): 2,952 runs (11.44), 895 wickets (22.09), and 118 catches

TYSON, Frank Holmes

(b. 1930, Farnworth, Lancashire) *Northamptonshire and England*

Frank Tyson was perhaps the only great fast bowler capable of quoting from Shakespeare or Wordsworth in between knocking stumps out of the ground. On his début for Northamptonshire at the county ground against the 1952 Indians, he swung his first ball so far that it went to first slip—and the slips moved back 5 yards! He was in the public eye thereafter as the fastest bowler in England. After trials for his native Lancashire, he had qualified for Northamptonshire and was soon to earn the designation 'Typhoon Tyson': his pace, originally after a run-up of more than 70 yards from the 'keeper, made spectators gasp and chatter, and batsmen turn to the wicket-keeper with a resigned smile after the first ball had whistled through. Although quite tall and immensely strong, Tyson tended to put excessive strain on his frame with his long final stride and a not quite fluent action and this, plus the need to bowl on too many featherbeds at Northampton, caused frequent injuries and a short career. But his partnership with Brian Statham, especially in Australia in 1954/5, has passed into the legend of the game. In the first Test at Brisbane he took 1 for 160 in 29 overs; the rest was a tale of unending success. There can have been few faster spells in cricket history than Tyson's in the second innings of the third Test at Melbourne. He skittled the opposition, taking 7 for 27 and, bowling down-wind off a shorter run, was literally as fast as a typhoon. He took most wickets in the series on either side: 28 (20.82). Against South Africa at Trent Bridge, in the first Test of 1955, he was almost equally devastating, taking 6 for 28 (off 21.3 overs) in the second innings. He toured Australia and New Zealand again, in 1958/9, with less success, and South Africa in 1956/7. Plagued by injuries, he played no more than a sprinkling of Tests in England between 1954 and 1956. A graduate of Durham University, he emigrated to Australia and has been assistant master and headmaster, as well as making an erudite author, journalist, and commentator. He gave up teaching for a time to become the chief cricket coach in Victoria.

First-class career (1952–60): 4,103 runs (17.09), 767 wickets (20.89), and 85 catches

Test matches (17): 230 runs (10.95), 76 wickets (18.56), and 4 catches

UDAL, Shaun David

(b. 1969, Farnborough, Hampshire) *Hampshire*

Raymond Illingworth's long-held admiration for Shaun Udal was well illustrated when the new chairman of selectors named the young off-spinner in his first squad, for the one-day international against New Zealand at the start of the 1994 season. Udal's response was to take two wickets, including that of the visiting captain Ken Rutherford for nought, and although he failed to break into the Test side during the summer, he later returned for the one-day series with South Africa before being named for the winter tour of Australia. Tall, fiercely determined, with a high action, a good fielder and rapidly improving batsman—his Hampshire colleague Robin Smith regarded him as the best timer of a ball he had ever seen—Udal's international recognition was reward for his consistency: 1994 was the third summer in a row in which he had taken over fifty first-class wickets. He had originally wanted to be a fast bowler like his grandfather, Geoffrey Udal, who played for Middlesex and Leicestershire, but soon switched to off-spin, although he retained a lethal quicker ball. First appearing in the championship début for Hampshire in 1990, a persistent groin injury restricted him to just one first-class match the following summer, although he quickly established a reputation as a miserly one-day bowler. In 1992, he began to make an impact in the Championship, taking a career-best 8 for 50 against Sussex at Southampton, and passing 100 wickets in all competitions. A year later he bowled 763.2 overs in first-class cricket alone —only three bowlers bowled more—taking 74 wickets. A continuation of that form in 1994, when he took 69 wickets, plus an improvement in his batting, with four fifties including a career-best 94 against Derbyshire, took him to the verge of Test cricket.

First-class career (1989–): 1,672 runs (22.29) and 225 wickets (31.79)

ULYETT, George

(b. 1851, Sheffield, Yorkshire; d. 1898, Sheffield) *Yorkshire and England*

George Ulyett, or 'Happy Jack', said of himself that Yorkshire played him for his whistling and good behaviour and that England played him to go in first with W. G. Grace, to give the doctor confidence. A tall, well-built man, he had the fun and zest of his generation of carefree professionals; and he was one of the foremost all-rounders of his day. His batting motto was high, wide, and handsome: at Edgbaston he off-drove a ball 130 yards and at Lord's straight-drove a ball over the old pavilion. His bowling was fast, the ball breaking sharply from the off and often rising uncomfortably, and he was a very reliable fielder, especially to his own bowling. Nine times he exceeded 1,000 runs in a season. His highest score was 199 not out against Derbyshire at Sheffield in

1887, when he carried his bat through the innings. A regular England player for a decade, he appeared in the first two Tests against Australia at Melbourne in 1876/7, taking 3 for 39 in the first Test and top-scoring with 52 and 63 in the second. Uniquely, he also played in the first Test against South Africa in 1888/9. At Lord's in 1884 he took 7 for 36 (in 39.1 overs) in the second innings, Australia being beaten by an innings. Altogether, he toured Australia five times, heading the batting averages as well as doing most of the bowling with 'Bunny' Lucas and Tom Emmett for Lord Harris's team in 1878/9, and hitting 149 and 64 at Melbourne in 1881/2. He also toured America with Richard Daft's team of 1879, when he frustrated a well-known baseball-pitcher by scoring 160 not out against him.

First-class career (1873–93): 20,823 runs (23.44) including 18 centuries, 653 wickets (20.14), and 368 catches

Test matches (25): 949 runs (24.33) including 1 century, 50 wickets (20.40), and 18 catches

UNDERWOOD, Derek Leslie

(b. 1945, Bromley, Kent) *Kent and England*

When Derek Underwood decided in 1977 to join World Series Cricket, he voluntarily interrupted one of the most remarkable of all Test careers. He left the Test arena after helping England to win the Jubilee series of 1977 against Australia and having taken 265 wickets in 74 Tests, but returned to play in 12 more Tests and to make two further tours—to Australia in 1979/80 and India in 1981/2—before joining an officially disapproved-of tour of South Africa in March 1982 which ended his Test career three wickets short of 300. A left-arm spin bowler, his pace was normally slow-medium but varied from brisk medium to slow according to conditions. His walk was rather flat-footed, the feet pointing towards mid-off and mid-on as he plodded thoughtfully back to bowl, and there was no beauty about the approach to the stumps—seven or eight paces—but the delivery was at once mechanical and fluid. What was exceptional was the totally unfailing length and carefully calculated direction, which drove thousands of batsmen to strokeless distraction and an often self-inflicted doom. Intensely dedicated, 'Deadly' first played for Kent in 1963 when not yet 18 and became the youngest player to take 100 wickets in his maiden season. By the age of 25 he had taken his 1,000th first-class wicket; only Wilfred Rhodes and George Lohmann had achieved this landmark at a younger age. He first played for England against the West Indies in 1966 and, as well as impressing as a bowler, he played the first of many determined and useful tail-end innings. He was a right-handed batsman with a strictly limited range of strokes, though cannily used. By sheer will-power, he also made himself into a reliable outfielder with safe hands and an accurate throw. Although it took him a long time to become as effective a bowler overseas as he was in England (he was for many years reluctant to give the ball the necessary extra air on good pitches) he travelled on eight overseas tours with official MCC teams. Among his many match-winning performances for Kent and England were his 7 for 50 against Australia in 1968 at The Oval (when he proved totally unplayable after a thunderstorm appeared to have deprived England of victory), 8 for 51 against Pakistan at Lord's in 1974 (again on a wet wicket), 9 for 28 against Sussex at Hastings in 1964, and 9 for 32 against Surrey at The Oval in 1978. Though his attack was based upon his miserly hatred of any batsman scoring any runs off him at any time, his bowling had endless subtle variations of pace, often of trajectory too, and his 'arm ball', which swung in to the right-hander, claimed many a victim. A dogged, steady character and an avid reader, he was a highly disciplined professional. Yet it was with the bat in 1984 that he achieved one of his greatest milestones. He made his maiden first-class hundred against Sussex at Hastings at the age of 39. He was awarded the MBE in 1981, and a second benefit in 1986, when, playing against Warwickshire at Folkestone, he returned a match analysis of 67.5 overs, 47 maidens, 9 wickets for 59.

First-class career (1963–87): 5,165 runs (10.12) including 1 century, 2,465 wickets (20.28), and 261 catches
Test matches (86): 937 runs (11.56), 297 wickets (25.83), and 44 catches

VALENTINE, Bryan Herbert

(b. 1908, Blackheath, Kent; d. 1983, Otford, Kent) *Cambridge University, Kent, and England*

Like his contemporary Percy Chapman, Bryan Valentine was a cheerful and sometimes great batsman. He often started hitting as soon as he went in, and averaged some fifty runs in an hour. Right-handed, he was essentially an in-front-of-the-wicket player with a penchant for the leg-side, and he could be a match-winner; he was also a brilliant fielder. He captained Kent from 1932 until 1934, jointly in 1937, and from 1946

until 1948. In 1946 he led a cavalry charge at Gillingham against Nottinghamshire, hitting 95 and 114, including nine sixes (seven in the century), allowing Kent to earn their first post-war points. He toured India and South Africa with MCC teams in 1933/4 and 1938/9 respectively, and made 136 on his Test début against India at Bombay, the first Test in that country. In his first two Tests against South Africa, he made 97 and 112. He did not represent England at home. He made 1,000 runs in a season nine times with a highest score of 242 against Leicestershire at Oakham in 1938. Also a brilliant lawn-tennis player, he won the Public Schools doubles with H. W. (Bunny) Austin. During the Second World War he was awarded the MC in North Africa.

First-class career (1927–50): 18,306 runs (30.15) including 35 centuries, 27 wickets (41.66), and 289 catches
Test matches (7): 454 runs (64.85) including 2 centuries, and 2 catches

VERITY, Hedley

(b. 1905, Headingley, Leeds; d. 1943, Caserta, Sicily) *Yorkshire and England*

Following in the great Yorkshire tradition of Peate, Peel, and Rhodes, Hedley Verity was one of the most skilful left-arm spin bowlers in history. His easy, springing run-up to the wicket suggested a cat preparing for the kill and his sheer accuracy of length and viciousness of spin reduced the best of batsmen to uncertainty and impotence. His average pace was slow-medium, on fast wickets about medium, and he could send down a virulent in-swinging yorker; on wet, crumbled or sticky wickets he reduced his pace and tossed the orthodox spinner higher. He was a great student of the game and, with Bill Bowes, the pivot of Yorkshire's attack in the great Championship-winning years of the 1930s. From 1935 to 1937 he exceeded 200 wickets each season. Twice he took all ten wickets in an innings, against Warwickshire at Headingley for 36 runs in 1931 and against Nottinghamshire on the same ground for ten runs in 1932—a world record. Against Essex at Leyton in 1933 his match haul was 17 for 91. In his last match of all he took 7 for 9 against Sussex at Hove on 1 September 1939. A regular for England for 7 years, he toured Australia twice and South Africa, India and New Zealand once each; and at home played in two series against Australia, the West Indies and New Zealand, and once each against South Africa and India. He was irresistible after rain at Lord's in

1934, when in one day he took 14 for 80 (15 for 104 in the match). Yet more than one witness has observed that he was almost happier bowling on a batsman's pitch than a bowler's: he loved a challenge. As a batsman, he was usually in the lower order. He had grit and technique and a casual observer could have mistaken him for Herbert Sutcliffe out of form. He was a sound all-round fielder, who could be brilliant to his own bowling or at backward point. During the 1936/7 Test series in Australia few regular opening batsmen could remain together for long. In the fourth match, at Adelaide, he was promoted to open with Charles Barnett, and they put up 53 and 45 together, the best first-wicket stands for England in the five Tests! A kindly, thoughtful, clean-living man, Captain Verity of the Green Howards died as a POW in Italy, having been wounded in an 8th Army attack in Sicily. There was no 'breaking-point' for him and his last reported words to his Company, 'keep going', were characteristic.

First-class career (1930–9): 5,605 runs (18.08) including 1 century, 1,956 wickets (14.90), and 269 catches
Test matches (40): 669 runs (20.90), 144 wickets (24.37), and 30 catches

VERNON, George Frederick

(b. 1856, London; d. 1902, Elmina, Gold Coast, Africa) *Middlesex and England*

George Vernon was a splendid, natural hitter, whose quickness of eye to some extent made up for his playing with a bat that was never quite straight. Clean, powerful driving was his forte. He toured Australia with the Hon. Ivo Bligh's team in 1882/3, and in his sole Test, the first at Melbourne, he batted number 11, scoring 11 not out and 3 and not bowling. He took his own side to Australia five years later, in conjunction with the Melbourne club, but Shaw and Shrewsbury took out another team at the same time, and the financial results were disastrous. He also took a team to India in 1889/90. He died young in West Africa. He also played Rugby for England.

First-class career (1876–98): 7,070 runs (19.11) including 4 centuries, 2 wickets (34.50), and 171 catches

VINE, Joseph

(b. 1875, Willingdon, Sussex; d. 1946, Aldrington, Sussex) *Sussex and England*

Originally a forcing right-handed batsman, the sturdy Joseph Vine curbed his natural instincts while partnering Charles Fry or Ranji and, in the early years of this century, was quite a stone-waller. Fry, his captain, told him that his job was to keep up one end and break the bowler's heart. Six times between 1901 and 1904, these two shaped double-century stands for the first Sussex wicket, each time the captain dominating the scoring. In a cartoon Joe was once likened to a snail. Late in his career, however, he emerged from his shell: in 1920 at Hastings against Northamptonshire he hit his highest score, 202, in 5 hours. Fourteen times he exceeded 1,000 runs in a season. He was also a useful slow leg-break bowler (he achieved the double in 1901) and an outfield of rare speed and certainty. He toured Australia in 1911/12 with MCC and appeared in two Tests. After retiring, he coached at Brighton College.

First-class career (1896–1922): 25,171 runs (29.92) including 34 centuries, 685 wickets (28.51), and 240 catches
Test matches (2): 46 runs (46.00)

VOCE, William

(b. 1909, Annesley Woodhouse, Nottinghamshire; d. 1984, Nottingham) *Nottinghamshire and England*

In a long career Bill Voce was three separate bowlers—slow left-arm, fast left-arm bowling over the wicket, and even faster bowling leg-theory round the wicket. At his peak he was the best fast left-arm bowler of his time: the famous foil to Harold Larwood, both for Nottinghamshire and, immortally, for England in Australia in 1932/3, the highly controversial 'bodyline' tour. Tall and strong, Voce had a beautiful action and his loose left arm made him also a glorious thrower from the deep. A more than useful batsman, he made several centuries for his county, and scored 1,020 runs in 1933. He took more than 100 wickets in a season six times, the first being 1929 when his county won the Championship. He toured the West Indies in 1929/30 and took most Test wickets—17. In South Africa, 1930/1, he was again chief bowler with 23 Test wickets. In the 'bodyline' series he took 15 wickets in four Tests; and four years later the first two Tests, at Brisbane and Sydney, both of which England won, brought him analyses of 6 for 41, 4 for 16, 4 for 10, and 3 for 66. In the five Tests he took more wickets than anyone on either side, 26 (21.53). In the second match he began by taking O'Brien, Bradman, and McCabe in four balls! After the Second World War England were short of bowlers and Bill Voce, hard-working as ever, but overweight, played against India and toured Australia in 1946/7. He finished his county career as he began it—as a slow bowler.

First-class career (1927–52): 7,590 runs (19.21) including 4 centuries, 1,558 wickets (23.08), and 286 catches

Test matches (27): 308 runs (13.39), 98 wickets (27.88), and 15 catches

WADDINGTON, Abraham

(b. 1893, Thornton, Yorkshire; d. 1959, Scarborough, Yorkshire) *Yorkshire and England*

Abe Waddington was a lively left-arm, fast-medium bowler, who gave no quarter and asked for none. His length was good, his action flowed, he made the ball swerve and rear awkwardly from the pitch, and he exceeded 100 wickets in six of his nine seasons with Yorkshire (the county winning the Championship four years in succession). A tail-end batsman, he hit his only century, 114 against Worcestershire at Headingley, in his last season. He was a very reliable close field. He toured Australia with MCC in 1920/1 where he played his only Test cricket.

First-class career (1919–27): 2,527 runs (12.89) including 1 century, 852 wickets (19.75), and 232 catches

Test matches (2): 16 runs (4.00), 1–119, and 1 catch

WAINWRIGHT, Edward

(b. 1865, Sheffield, Yorkshire; d. 1919, Sheffield) *Yorkshire and England*

Ted Wainwright belonged to Lord Hawke's great Yorkshire eleven. Tall, craggy, and blunt of tongue—but, to C. B. Fry, 'a charming character'—he was a fine right-handed batsman, a deadly off-break bowler on any wicket giving him assistance (although sometimes erratic) and an excellent field. In his first season, 1888, he took 105 off the Australians for his county at Bradford; and for more than a decade he was always scoring runs or taking wickets. He achieved the double in 1897. When he made his highest score, 228 against Surrey at The Oval in 1899, he added 340 for the fifth wicket with George Hirst in 3½ hours. He played once for England against Australia in 1893, and in the following season he took 166 wickets (12.73). He toured Australia with A. E. Stoddart's unsuccessful side in 1897/8.

First-class career (1888–1902): 12,513 runs (21.76) including 19 centuries, 1,071 wickets (18.24), and 353 catches

Test matches (5): 132 runs (14.66), 0–73, and 2 catches

WAKELAM, Henry Blythe Thornhill

(b. 1893, Hereford; d. 1963, Colchester, Essex)

'Teddy' Wakelam achieved a number of broadcasting 'firsts': a Rugby football commentary when England played Wales at Twickenham in 1927; one on Association football when Arsenal played Sheffield United at Highbury in the same year; and the first televised Test match between England and Australia at Lord's in 1938. He was lucky in having Walter Hammond's great innings of 240 on which to comment. From 1927 onwards the BBC also employed him annually to comment on the lawn-tennis championships at Wimbledon. He brought to the pioneer years of broadcasting the talents of a Harlequin Rugby football player and a useful all-round sportsman. He realized from the start that the secret of sound broadcasting was to conduct a personal conversation and the introduction of a blind man into the commentary box helped him to perfect this technique. In *Half-time* (1938) he described his experiences and adventures in broadcasting.

WALKER, Peter Michael

(b. 1936, Bristol) *Glamorgan, Transvaal, Western Province, and England*

Peter Walker was an all-rounder on and off the cricket field. He was a very tall (6 ft. 4 in.) left-arm, orthodox, slow bowler, a hard-driving right-hand batsman, and brilliant specialist short-leg fieldsman with octopus-like arms. Capped by Glamorgan in 1957, he won three caps for England against South Africa in 1960. In all he scored more than 1,000 runs in eleven seasons, doing the double in 1961 with 101 wickets, 1,347 runs, and 73 catches. His total in 1959 was 1,564 runs, 80 wickets, and 65 catches. He continued to be a key all-rounder in the Glamorgan side for a decade or more, taking more catches for the county than any other player, including eight in the match against Derbyshire at Swansea in 1970. A modest, personable man of wide interests, he lives in Cardiff, and became a successful broadcaster on cricket and current affairs, also forming his own film company.

First-class career (1956–72): 17,650 runs (26.03) including 13 centuries, 834 wickets (28.63), and 697 catches

Test matches (3): 128 runs (32.00), 0–34, and 5 catches

WALKER

WALKER, Vyell Edward

(b. 1837, Southgate, Middlesex; d. 1906, Arnos Grove, Middlesex) *Middlesex*

V. E. Walker was the most talented of seven cricketing brothers whose family ground at Southgate provided a focus for Middlesex cricketers and who played a major part in the formation of the county club. A strong, on-side right-handed batsman, V.E. was selected for the Gentlemen against the Players at Lord's when only 19, and had his greatest match for England versus Surrey in 1859, at the Oval. He made 20 not out and 108 and took 14 wickets, ten of them in the first innings for 74. He was to take all ten wickets twice in his career and was deprived of a third occasion only because, after a match was over, it was ruled that one batsman had been run out and not stumped. His right-arm slow under-arm bowling was described in *The Walkers of Southgate* as the finest since William Clarke of the All-England XI. After captaining Middlesex 'with skilful generalship' he became president both of the county and of MCC.

First-class career (1856–77): 3,384 runs (17.26) including 1 century, 304 + 30 wickets (15.77), and 188 catches

WALTERS, Cyril Frederick

(b. 1905, Bedlinog, Glamorgan, Wales; d. 1992, Neath, Glamorgan) *Glamorgan, Worcestershire, and England*

Joining Worcestershire as secretary after five seasons with Glamorgan, in which his overall batting average was 17, Cyril Walters blossomed as a flowing right-handed stroke-player. Slightly built, he played with wristy elegance and was admirably consistent, although he too often got out when he was well set. First playing for Worcestershire in 1928, he captained his new county from 1931 until 1935, scoring more than 2,000 runs in 1933 and 1934. His highest score was 226 against Kent at Gravesend in 1933. He made 51 in his first Test against the West Indies at Lord's in 1933. In India in 1933/4 he partnered Fred Bakewell and made 59 and 102 in the third Test at Madras. Against Australia in 1934 he captained England in the first Test at Trent Bridge because Bob Wyatt was injured and, partnering either Sutcliffe or Walter Keeton, was very successful throughout the series (401 runs at 50.12). Part way through the 1935 season, however, owing to ill-health and domestic commitments, he suddenly retired from first-class cricket.

First-class career (1923–35): 12,145 runs (30.74) including 21 centuries, 5 wickets (76.00), and 101 catches
Test matches (11): 784 runs (52.26) including 1 century, and 6 catches

WARD, Alan

(b. 1947, Dronfield, Derbyshire) *Derbyshire, Border, Leicestershire, and England*

Not many very tall fast bowlers have survived for long in top-class cricket, and Alan Ward is a case in point. On his day he could be very fast indeed, and one often felt that his spirit was willing but his flesh weak. His height, relatively slim build, and a right-arm action which somehow never looked natural—he almost seemed to over-balance as he delivered the ball—conspired to cause numerous injuries, especially in the legs. Derbyshire nursed him gently after a promising début in 1966. He was capped in 1969 and played for Derbyshire until 1976, when he moved to Leicestershire for two seasons without being able to command a regular place. His five Tests were spaced between 1969 and 1976, but injury plagued him when he had his big chance in Australia in 1970/1, and he had to return home early without sharing in the success of John Snow and England's other fast bowlers. His best bowling return in a Test was 4 for 61 against New Zealand at Trent Bridge in his second Test match. He took ten wickets in that short series at 21 each but the auspicious start was deceptive. For Derbyshire he took 7 for 42 against Glamorgan in 1974 and he also once took four wickets in four balls in a John Player League match. He was often useful as a tail-ender.

First-class career (1966–78): 928 runs (8.43), 460 wickets (22.81), and 51 catches
Test matches (5): 40 runs (8.00), 14 wickets (32.35), and 3 catches

WARD, Albert

(b. 1865, Leeds; d. 1939, Bolton, Lancashire) *Yorkshire, Lancashire, and England*

While an assistant schoolmaster, Albert Ward had some outings for Yorkshire, but was soon snatched for Lancashire by John Stanning, who was 'a naughty old boy', according to Lord Hawke, 'being an inveterate cricket poacher'. Thus Ward, a right-handed opening batsman, began a long, splendid, and honourable career for Lancashire. Six feet tall and of an ideal temperament—cool, patient, and persevering—he had a very sound defence and could drive powerfully and cut well. He seldom dropped a catch in the deep, and was a useful slow bowler. He carried his bat through an innings on five occasions (the best being 140 out of 281 against Gloucestershire at Bristol in 1893). His highest score was 219 for A. E. Stoddart's team against South Australia at Adelaide in 1894/5. He was prominent in England's success in Australia in 1894/5. In the first Test at Sydney he top-scored in both innings with 75 and 117—England winning by a mere ten runs. In the fifth match at Melbourne which decided the rubber, England, seeking 297 to win, lost two early wickets, but Ward, defending stoutly, scored 93, added 210 with J. T. Brown and victory was secured. He scored more runs than anyone else in the series, 419 (41.90) but never played for England again.

First-class career (1886–1904): 17,783 runs (30.08) including 29 centuries, 71 wickets (34.83), and 169 catches

Test matches (7): 487 runs (37.46) including 1 century, and 1 catch

WARD, Sir Leslie

(b. 1851, London; d. 1922, London)

Brought up in an artistic atmosphere, Ward exhibited at the Royal Academy while still at Eton. From 1878 onwards his cartoons appeared in *Vanity Fair* under the pseudonym of 'Spy' and included such famous cricketing names as Grace, Fry, Jessop, Warner, and Hobbs. His drawings were convincing portraits rather than mere lampoons and prints of them still hang on many walls.

WARD, William

(b. 1787, Islington, Middlesex; d. 1849, London)
Surrey and Hampshire

Born in the year in which Lord's and MCC began, William Ward made the first double-century (278) for MCC on their own ground against Norfolk in 1820: a score not surpassed there until Percy Holmes's 315 for Yorkshire v. Middlesex in 1925. He was a hard-hitting right-handed batsman who made nine centuries in all cricket, playing until shortly before his death. He adapted easily to facing round-arm bowling although he was one of those who opposed it in the 1827 trial matches and continuing as a slow right-arm bowler himself. When Thomas Lord in 1825 contemplated building development at Lord's, Ward, a director of the Bank of England and soon to be MP for the City of London, bought out his lease for £5,000. Exactly

20 years later, he was associated with the launching of Surrey CCC and its lease of The Oval while his son, Arthur, in the family tradition, negotiated the lease of Fenner's ground at Cambridge at a time when Caius College were contemplating building development on the site.

First-class career (1810–45): 4,022 runs (18.97) including 3 centuries, 49 wickets (average not known), and 53 dismissals (49 c., 4 st.)

WARDLE, John Henry

(b. 1923, Ardsley, Yorkshire; d. 1985, Doncaster, Yorkshire) *Yorkshire, Cambridgeshire, and England*

Johnny Wardle could bowl slow, left-arm orthodox *and* the chinaman and googly with equal facility. He was probably the best wrist spinner of his generation, and, excepting perhaps Tony Lock and Alf Valentine, the best orthodox left-arm spinner, too. He was a hard-hitting batsman and zealous close field, whose clowning would delight the crowd. He took his bowling seriously, however, and in 1954 he was very successful, taking 9 for 25 against Lancashire at Old Trafford, 9 for 48 against Sussex at Hove, and 16 for 112 against Sussex at Hull; and in ten seasons of his rather short career he captured at least 100 wickets, six times exceeding 150 wickets, 1955 bringing him 195 wickets (16.14). He had an outstanding tour for MCC in South Africa in 1956/7, taking 90 wickets (12.25), including 12 for 89 in the second Test at Cape Town. He toured Australia and New Zealand once and the West Indies twice; and occasionally represented England at home from 1950 until 1957. His career ended under a cloud: ill-advised articles in a national newspaper criticizing the Yorkshire captain and the other members of his team led to his being dropped by Yorkshire and the withdrawal by MCC of the invitation to tour Australia in 1958/9. Wardle retired to the Lancashire league, and later played for Cambridgeshire.

First-class career (1946–68): 7,333 runs (16.08), 1,846 wickets (18.97), and 256 catches

Test matches (28): 653 runs (19.78), 102 wickets (20.39), and 12 catches

WARNER, Sir Pelham Francis

(b. 1873, Port-of-Spain, Trinidad; d. 1963, West Lavington, Sussex) *Oxford University, Middlesex, and England*

'Plum' in his gracious old age was the very reverend dean of Cricket's Cathedral, but at the turn of the century he was young 'Plum' Warner, a polished batsman and the keenest of captains. 'Cricket's gentil knight', he became Sir Pelham for his services to the game world-wide in 1937. He was born in Trinidad where his father had been attorney-general, became captain of cricket at Rugby, earned a blue at Oxford, and played for Middlesex from 1894 until 1920, captaining the county between 1908 and 1920. He captained the first official MCC team to Australia in 1903/4, recovering the Ashes, and the first MCC team to South Africa in 1905/6. He was elected to the committee of MCC in 1904 and remained on it for most of the rest of his life. He founded and for many years edited *The Cricketer*, served as deputy-secretary of MCC from 1939 to 1945, and became president in 1950. In between, he travelled to many countries as an ambassador of the game. A neat, brave, balanced, and determined right-hand batsman of frail physique, 'Plum' first toured with Lord Hawke's team in the West Indies in 1896/7, and made his début in Tests for his Lordship's England side in South Africa in 1898/9. He was bitten by the travel bug and claimed to have made a duck in every British Dominion except India, as well as in Portugal. In successive Tests on the triumphant 1903/4 tour he made 68, 48, and 79. On his second tour of Australia in 1911/12, as captain, he was taken ill after scoring 151 against South Australia in the opening game and could play no more on the tour. He represented England against Australia at home in 1909 and 1912, and against South Africa in 1912; and was joint manager of MCC's team to Australia in 1932/3, the 'bodyline' tour, when he did not emerge from the controversy as a decisive figure. Well read and scholarly, he wrote or edited some twenty books on tours, history, and autobiography and was cricket correspondent of *The Morning Post* for nearly 20 years. His success as a batsman was as much due to concentration and will-power as to innate ability. He made 1,000 runs in a season fourteen times, his best season being 1911 with 2,123 runs (46.15), including his highest score of 244 for the Rest of England against Warwickshire at The Oval. On his Test début he carried his bat through the innings, making 132 (out of 237). He made three successive centuries at Lord's in 1910. In his last season as Middlesex captain, he led his county after a late burst to a sensational Championship win over Surrey at Lord's in his last match. It was said of Warner that he knew every blade of grass at Lord's: he certainly loved the game, and when he died his ashes were scattered at Lord's.

First-class career (1894–1929): 29,028 runs (36.28) including 60 centuries, 15 wickets (42.40), and 183 catches
Test matches (15): 622 runs (23.92) including 1 century, and 3 catches

WARR, John James

(b. 1927, Ealing, Middlesex) *Cambridge University, Middlesex, and England*

John Warr was discovered bowling in a humble match on Parker's Piece by a Cambridge captain desperate to find a fast bowler. He was something of a tearaway at University, captaining Cambridge in 1951, but developed into a much more controlled opening bowler, who could move the ball away from the bat from the extreme edge of the crease. As an undergraduate he was an unexpected choice for MCC's team to Australia, 1950/1, and failed in the Tests. Subsequently, he was a shrewd captain of Middlesex from 1958 until 1960; he took 116 wickets (18.17) in 1956, in which year he took 9 for 65 (14 for 92 in the match) against Kent at Lord's. A raconteur and wit, he has written entertainingly on the game in *The Sunday Telegraph* and other publications; he was also a very successful City businessman, a steward of the Jockey Club, and acted as Australia's representative on the ICC. He was President of MCC, 1987/8, and a trustee of the club.

First-class career (1949–60): 3,838 runs (11.46), 956 wickets (22.80), and 117 catches
Test matches (2): 4 runs (1.00) and 1–281

WARREN, Arnold

(b. 1875, Codnor Park, Derbyshire; d. 1951, Codnor Park) *Derbyshire and England*

Over 6 ft. and taking a long, bounding run, Arnold Warren was a fast right-arm bowler in the Derbyshire tradition. He was the first player ever to take 100 wickets in a season for the county—124 wickets (20.94) in 1904, including 15 for 112 against Nottinghamshire at Welbeck. In 1905 he represented England against Australia in the third Test at Headingley, scoring 7, taking 5 for 57 and 1 for 56—numbering Trumper (twice), Noble, Armstrong, and Darling among his victims—and holding 1 catch, but this was his sole appearance for England.

First-class career (1897–1920): 5,507 runs (13.73) including 1 century, 939 wickets (24.55), and 195 catches

WASHBROOK, Cyril

(b. 1914, Clitheroe, Lancashire) *Lancashire and England*

Shortish and strong around the chest and shoulders, Cyril Washbrook invariably wore his cap at a jaunty angle, and always put character as well as sound technique into his batting. He was neat and quick on his feet and a ruthless attacker of anything short, either with perfectly timed square-cuts or daring hooks. In the field he was a swift and accurate cover-point. In his second match for his county, against Surrey at Old Trafford in 1933, he hit 152. He made his Test début for England against New Zealand at The Oval in 1937. Despite losing invaluable years to the War, he enjoyed his best seasons straight after it, in 1946 and 1947 making 2,400 runs (68.57) including nine centuries, and 2,662 runs (68.25) including eleven centuries, one of which, 251 not out against Surrey at Old Trafford, remained his career-highest. He became Len Hutton's regular partner in Tests. They put on three successive century opening partnerships against Australia in 1946/7. Washbrook saved England in the third match at Melbourne with 62 and 112. Against Australia in England in 1948 he made 356 runs (50.85), including 143 and 65 in the fourth Test at Headingley, when he put on 168 and 129 with Hutton for the first wicket. In the second Test against South Africa, at Johannesburg in 1948/9, he made his highest Test score, 195, and with Hutton hit 359 for the first wicket, which became the new England record for the first wicket. In the five Tests he made 542 runs (60.22). He toured Australia in 1950/1 and, at home, appeared with success against India, New Zealand and the West Indies. Recalled to the England side in 1956 against Australia at Headingley, he came in when the score was 17 for 3, and shared in a stand of 187 with Peter May. When Washbrook was lbw to Benaud for 98 there were tears in many eyes. In all he made 996 runs in 17 Tests against Australia. He was the first professional Lancastrian captain, from 1954 to 1959. He had made 1,000 runs in a season 20 times (three times overseas) when he retired. He has served as a Test selector and as president of Lancashire and was awarded the CBE.

First-class career (1933–64): 34,101 runs (42.67) including 76 centuries, 7 wickets (44.14), and 212 catches

Test matches (37): 2,569 runs (42.81) including 6 centuries, 1–33, and 12 catches

WATKIN, Stephen Llywellyn

(b. 1964, Dyffryn Rhondda, Glamorgan, Wales) *Glamorgan and England*

Rarely injured and immensely popular with his colleagues, Steve Watkin forced his way into international contention through sheer weight of wickets, but despite playing a crucial role in securing wins in two of his first three Tests, he was unable to gain a permanent place in the England team. A tall, lean, seamer with a high action and a distinctive splay-footed run-up, Watkin first came to Glamorgan's attention at winter nets in Neath, and under Tom Cartwright's watchful eye he made his second team début in 1981. Keen to obtain qualifications, however, Watkin attended college and gained an honours degree in Human Movement Studies which delayed his entry into the county game, although he did tour the West Indies with a British Colleges side in 1987. A year earlier, he had made his first-team début for Glamorgan, with Graeme Hick as his first wicket, but it was not until 1988, after playing club cricket in South Africa during the winter, that he made a sizeable impact, taking 46 wickets including a career-best 8 for 59 against Warwickshire in the county's only victory of the season. The following year he finished as joint-highest wicket-taker in the country with 94 victims, including 6 for 42 as Northamptonshire were bowled out for 60 at Swansea. The effort gained him a place on the A tour of Kenya and Zimbabwe and the following summer, a further 60 wickets, albeit at almost 40 runs each in a batsman summer, earned him a spot on the A tour of Pakistan and Sri Lanka, although he flew home early injured. He won his first Test cap in 1991, taking 5 for 93 at Headingley as England recorded their first home win over the West Indies in 22 years. The second Test at Lord's was a more sobering experience and he was dropped having returned figures of 0 for 60. In 1993 he was the country's leading wicket-taker with 92 wickets and a key figure in Glamorgan's success in the Sunday League. Recalled for the sixth Test against Australia at The Oval, he took six wickets, including 4 for 65 in the second innings as England beat Allan Border's side for the first time since 1986. Watkin bowled 766.4 overs in the season—only two spinners bowled more—and his efforts gained further reward when he was voted Player of the Year by his fellow professionals. Selection for the West Indies tour was assured, but although he played in four of the five one-day internationals, he was unable to break into the Test side.

First-class career (1986–): 1,058 runs (9.04) and 526 wickets (29.61)

Test matches (3): 25 runs (5.00) and 11 wickets (27.72)

WATKINS, Albert John, known as Allan

(b. 1922, Usk, Monmouthshire, Wales) *Glamorgan and England*

A balding and genial 'Friar Tuck' of cricket, Allan Watkins was the first Glamorgan player to represent England against Australia (at The Oval in 1948, when England were dismissed on the first morning for 52, and eventually lost heavily by an innings). A genuine all-rounder, he was a sound and enterprising left-handed batsman, who often rallied his county, a penetrating, left-arm, medium-pace bowler and a dynamic fielder, brilliant at short-leg. He was an invaluable member of Glamorgan's first Championship-winning side in 1948. He achieved the double in both 1954 and 1955, and thirteen times exceeded 1,000 runs in a season. His highest score was 170 not out against Leicestershire at Swansea in 1954; and his best bowling feats were 7 for 28 against Derbyshire at Chesterfield and 7 for 29 against Gloucestershire at Gloucester, both in 1954. He toured South Africa, India and Pakistan. In South Africa, 1948/9, he made 111 in the fourth Test at Johannesburg; and he played especially well against India, 1951/2, when he was the foremost run-getter on either side, hitting 451 runs (64.42). Because of asthma, his doctor advised him to give up the game at first-class level, but he continued to play cricket for charity from time to time.

First-class career (1939–63): 20,361 runs (30.57) including 32 centuries, 833 wickets (24.48), and 462 catches

Test matches (15): 810 runs (40.50) including 2 centuries, 11 wickets (50.36), and 17 catches

WATSON, William

(b. 1920, Bolton-on-Dearne, Yorkshire) *Yorkshire, Leicestershire, and England*

A natural left-handed batsman, Willie Watson was both graceful and patient. Making batting look supremely easy, he was also a speedy runner between wickets. His bat met the ball with the measured straightness and certainty of a pendulum. He played for Yorkshire until 1956 and spent the rest of his career at Leicester as assistant-secretary and captain from 1958 until 1961. He represented England regularly from 1951 until 1958 against Australia, South Africa, the West Indies, New Zealand, and India. He toured Australasia in 1958/9 and the West Indies in 1953/4. In his first two Tests against South Africa in 1951, he hit 57 and 79, immediately strengthening the previously suspect English middle-batting. On his début against Australia, at Lord's in 1953, he made 109 and, with England facing defeat, he batted $5\frac{3}{4}$ hours, adding 163 with Trevor Bailey for the fifth wicket, one of the epic Test match stands. On his début against the West Indies, at Kingston in 1953/4, he made 116. He was vice-captain of the MCC non-Test-playing tour of New Zealand in 1960/1. When Yorkshire allowed him to join Leicestershire, he was an immediate success. He headed the averages of his new county each year, his best being 1959 with 2,212 runs (55.30). Altogether, he made 1,000 runs in a season 14 times with a highest score of 257 for MCC against British Guiana at Georgetown in 1953/4. Throughout, he was brilliant in the outfield, as befitted an international footballer. He played for Huddersfield Town and Sunderland, winning four caps for England, and he was a member of the World Cup side in 1950. He emigrated to South Africa in 1968, becoming coach at the Wanderers club in Johannesburg.

First-class career (1939–64): 25,670 runs (39.86) including 55 centuries, and 295 catches

Test matches (23): 879 runs (25.85) including 2 centuries, and 8 catches

WATTS, George Frederick

(b. 1817, London; d. 1904, London)

Watts's lithographs of two players (Alfred Mynn and Fuller Pilch) and of six strokes remain the finest examples of a form of cricketing art which immediately preceded photography. The batsman who posed for the strokes, with one exception, was Felix (Nicholas Wanostrocht), himself an artist and they were used in his instructional book, *Felix on the Bat* (1845). He was left-handed but Watts, drawing on stone, knew that printing would produce a reverse—and right-handed image—more useful in a coaching manual. Later Watts built up a reputation as an allegorical and portrait painter and sculptor, being elected to the Royal Academy (1967) and appointed, as one of the founder-members, to the Order of Merit (1902). Of his estimated 800 pictures, he himself presented 150 to the National Portrait Gallery.

WEBBE, Alexander Josiah

(b. 1855, London; d. 1941, Abinger Hammer, Surrey) *Oxford University, Middlesex, and England*

Perhaps the best batsman produced by Harrow, and captain of Oxford, Alexander Webbe or 'Webbie' crouched in ungainly fashion with legs wide apart at the wicket, but his defence was masterly and his cutting and driving outstanding. An opening right-handed batsman and useful change-bowler, he captained Middlesex from 1885 until 1898 and remained until his death the county's guide, philosopher and friend. His highest score was 243 not out against Yorkshire at Huddersfield in 1887 when he carried his bat through the innings. Altogether he carried his bat eight times, seven for his county. For Gentlemen against Players, at Lord's in 1875, he shared in an opening partnership of 203 with W. G. Grace, to whom on that occasion Webbe's defence and patience seemed perfect. He toured Australia with Lord Harris's team in 1878/9, and in his sole Test at Melbourne scored 4 and 0 and held 2 catches.

First-class career (1875–1900): 14,465 runs (24.81) including 14 centuries, 109 wickets (25.20), 228 catches, and 10 stumpings

WELLARD, Arthur William

(b. 1902, Southfleet, Kent; d. 1980, Eastbourne, Sussex) *Somerset and England*

Arthur Wellard was a valuable all-rounder, but is remembered largely as a hitter of 500 sixes. The record season was 1935 with 72 sixes and in both 1936 and 1938 he slammed 57; in 1933 he numbered 51; in 1935 he hit 5 off consecutive balls from T. R. Armstrong of Derbyshire and two years later he did the same to Frank Woolley. However, he was no rustic slogger, but a serious batsman with a respectable defence. Three times in 1933, 1935, and 1937, he achieved the double. A right-arm fast bowler with a fierce break-back, he varied his deliveries with medium-pace off-spinner. He was also a fine close field. Eight times he exceeded 100 wickets in a season, his best years being 1938 with 172 wickets (20.29) and 1937 with 156 wickets (23.55), and those years he represented England against Australia and New Zealand. He toured India in 1937/8 with Lord Tennyson's team. A native of Kent, Arthur as a young man asked the county club whether he could join the staff: he was told he would do better to go and be a policeman! He was still playing effective club cricket well into his sixties.

First-class career (1927–50): 12,485 runs (19.73) including 2 centuries, 1,614 wickets (24.35), and 376 catches
Test matches (2): 47 runs (11.75), 7 wickets (33.85), and 2 catches

WELLINGS, Evelyn Maitland

(b. 1909, Alexandria, Egypt; d. 1992, Basingstoke, Hampshire) *Oxford University and Surrey*

A good enough right-handed batsman to have made a first-class century and taken over 100 wickets as a right-arm bowler, Lyn Wellings was primarily a journalist. Fifteen years lay between his brief appearances for Surrey in 1931 and his final first-class match in 1946. He wrote for the London *Evening News* whose cricket coaching scheme he set up and which produced over a dozen professional cricketers. His criticism was rigorous and could be savage. For many years he wrote on public school cricket for *Wisden*. His prevailing theme was the lack of technique.

First-class career (1928–46): 836 runs (20.39) including 1 century, 108 wickets (30.14), and 10 catches

WHARTON, Alan

(b. 1923, Heywood, Lancashire; d. 1993, Colne, Lancashire) *Lancashire and Leicestershire*

A left-handed batsman who liked to attack, Alan Wharton had a full range of strokes and was also a more than useful, right-arm, medium-pace bowler. He made his reputation with Lancashire (1946–60) and then had a short—but prolific—stay with Leicestershire. Eleven times he exceeded 1,000 runs in a season, his best year being 1959 with 2,157 runs (40.69), including his highest score of 199 against Sussex at Hove. He made a century in each innings against Middlesex at Leicester in 1961. His best bowling was 7 for 33 in an innings against Sussex at Old Trafford in 1951. In his sole Test, against New Zealand at Headingley in 1949, he scored 7 and 13. He had to drop out of the Lord's Test through injury. A schoolteacher and JP, he was also a Rugby League footballer.

First-class career (1946–63): 21,796 runs (32.24) including 31 centuries, 237 wickets (31.59), and 288 catches

WHITAKER, John James

(b. 1962, Skipton, Yorkshire) *Leicestershire and England*

James Whitaker's misfortune was that his one senior tour coincided with England fielding a successful and settled side which completed a 'Grand Slam' of the Test series and two one-day competitions in Australia in 1986/7. An amiable man, he was unable to break into the team, his one chance coming when he replaced the injured Ian Botham in Adelaide. In excellent batting conditions, he made 11 in his only innings and never got another chance. His selection for the tour had been well earned, with 1,526 runs in 1986, despite missing five weeks of the season after fracturing both hands. His unbeaten 200 against Nottinghamshire remains his highest first-class score. He is a determined but limited player, powerful off both front and back foot and with strong forearms. Leicestershire were alerted to his talent by their former opening batsman Maurice Hallam, who was coaching at Uppingham school. Although he was born in Yorkshire, where the family's chocolate factory still flourishes, Whitaker was happy to go to Grace Road. At the end of the 1993 season, he was suggested as a candidate for the Somerset captaincy, but Leicestershire were reluctant to release him from his contract.

First-class career (1983–): 13,886 runs (37.42) and 2 wickets (134.00)

WHITE, Craig

(b. 1969, Morley, Yorkshire) *Victoria, Yorkshire, and England*

Yorkshire-born but raised in Australia, Craig White was hailed as the answer to England's lack of a genuine all-rounder by the new chairman of selectors Raymond Illingworth in 1994. Standing just over 6 ft. tall and with a powerful upper body, White played in the first four Tests of that summer bowling lively medium-pace and batting in the middle-order before missing the last two months of the season with a double stress-fracture of the left leg. Despite that injury, however, Illingworth and his colleagues were sufficiently impressed by what they had seen to bank on the player's fitness and pick him for the tour of Australia which followed. Selection for the Ashes tour as an England player represented the final step in a complete about-turn for White, who had spent most of his formative years hoping to play for Australia. Although born near Leeds, he emigrated to Australia with his parents at the age of 7 and quickly became assimilated, developing as a batsman, wicketkeeper, and occasional off-spinner, attending the Cricket Academy in Adelaide, representing his new country at youth level and latterly playing first-class cricket for Victoria. By 1990 Yorkshire, then still using only players born within the county, had got to hear about White and recruited him, ostensibly for a season at their Academy in Bradford. Quickly recognizing his talent, however, he was immediately given his first-class début before playing for the second team, an honour he shares with Fred Trueman. After modest beginnings, White's batting developed, whilst by 1992, helped by his disillusionment with cricket in Victoria and his marriage to a girl from Scarborough, he decided to stay in England. White's off-spin was sparingly used however, and this coupled with doubts about the legality of his action caused him to switch to medium pace for the 1993 season. Bowling only 120 overs, he still topped the Yorkshire averages that summer with 12 wickets, and after a winter spent weight-training he began the following season impressively with eight wickets and a fifty in an innings win over the touring New Zealanders, and six wickets in his next match against Essex. International recognition followed, and after taking time to find his feet, White compiled a mature half-century in a crisis against New Zealand at Lord's and followed it with a fiery three-wicket burst in the next Test at Old Trafford. His next Test, against South Africa, included a first-ball duck and the injury which kept him out for the rest of the season made his selection for Australia a gamble.

First-class career (1990–): 2,617 runs (33.99) and 63 wickets (28.11)

Test matches (4): 131 runs (21.83) and 8 wickets (32.25)

WHITE, David William

(b. 1935, Sutton Coldfield, Warwickshire) *Hampshire, Glamorgan, and England*

Unlucky to be a contemporary of Trueman, Statham and Tyson, 'Butch' White was powerfully built, and a genuinely fast right-arm bowler whose action was basically sound, although he was once no-balled for throwing, in 1960. A variable, inspirational performer, his career was sprinkled with fine achievements, including more than 100 wickets in a season four times, 9 for 44 in an innings against Leicestershire at Portsmouth in 1966, and 4 for 8 in a Gillette Cup contest. Although he toured India and Pakistan in 1961/2, playing in two Tests, he never represented his country at home. He joined Glamorgan in 1972, to play mainly in one-day matches. He was a cheerful and popular cricketer.

First-class career (1957–72): 3,080 runs (10.58), 1,143 wickets (23.54), and 106 catches
Test matches (2): 0 runs (0.0) and 4 wickets (29.75)

WHITE, John Cornish

(b. 1891, Holford, Somerset; d. 1961, Combe-Florey, Somerset) *Somerset and England*

A serene and cheerful character, looking, with his rosy cheeks and blue eyes, exactly like the yeoman farmer he was, Jack or 'Farmer' White was England's slow left-arm bowler between the reigns of Wilfred Rhodes and Hedley Verity. Remarkably, he spun the ball very little and succeeded instead by means of subtle variations of pace and trajectory. Nevertheless, he could make the ball 'do a little' each way on the truest pitch, and he often opened the attack for his county with the new ball. He developed into a competent batsman. He took 100 wickets in a season fourteen times, his best year being 1929 with 168 wickets (15.76). He captured all 10 for 76 against Worcestershire at Worcester in 1921, took nine wickets in an innings on four occasions and three times had fifteen or more wickets in a match. He twice did the double. He captained Somerset from 1927 until 1931, often coming from a morning's haymaking to play at Taunton. Playing fourteen of his fifteen Tests after the age of 37, he played for England against Australia in 1921 and 1930. He played against South Africa—as captain in 1929—and against the West Indies in 1928. He toured Australia in 1928/9 and exploded the theory that slow left-arm bowlers are of little use on Australian wickets; he was England's most successful bowler with 25 wickets (30.40) on the generally prevailing batsmen's pitches. In the blazing hot sun at Adelaide in the fourth Test his record was 124.5 overs, 37 maidens, 256 runs and 13 wickets, England winning by 12 runs. 'Farmer' White was an England selector in 1929/30, and became president of Somerset in 1960.

First-class career (1909–37): 12,202 runs (18.40) including 6 centuries, 2,356 wickets (18.57), and 426 catches
Test matches (15): 239 runs (18.38), 49 wickets (32.26), and 6 catches

WHYSALL, William Wilfrid

(b. 1887, Woodborough, Nottinghamshire; d. 1930, Nottingham) *Nottinghamshire and England*

After slow development as a right-handed batsman, 'Dodger' Whysall forged ahead after 1919 and he was at his peak by the time of his early death—he had fallen on a dance floor, injured his elbow, and died of septicaemia. Not a graceful batsman, he possessed unlimited patience, a strong defence and all the strokes. For 9 years he opened with George Gunn, and they shared in 40 three-figure stands together. He made 1,000 runs or more in ten seasons, reaching 2,000 between 1926 and 1930 inclusive. His best year, 1929, brought him 2,716 runs (51.24)—2,620 for Nottinghamshire alone, which remains a county record. His highest score was 248 against Northamptonshire at Trent Bridge in 1930, his last season. He played in one Test against Australia in 1930 having toured Australia with MCC in 1924/5 as batsman and emergency wicket-keeper. On his Test début, the third Test at Adelaide, he made 75 in the second innings, which nearly brought victory. In the next Test he made 76 at Melbourne.

First-class career (1910–30): 21,592 runs (38.76) including 51 centuries, 6 wickets (33.33), 316 catches, and 16 stumpings
Test matches (4): 209 runs (29.85), 0–9, and 7 catches

WILKINSON, Leonard Litton

(b. 1916, Northwich, Cheshire) *Lancashire and England*

A fair-haired, right-arm, leg-break bowler with a lively action, Len Wilkinson lost little time in making his presence felt in first-class cricket, taking 151 wickets (23.38) in 1938. He headed the bowling averages in all matches for MCC in South Africa, 1938/9, but he was very disappointing thereafter.

First-class career (1937–47): 321 runs (7.64), 282 wickets (25.25), and 53 catches
Test matches (3): 3 runs (3.00) and 7 wickets (38.71)

WILLEY, Peter

(b. 1949, Sedgefield, Co. Durham) *Northamptonshire, Leicestershire, Northumberland, Eastern Province, and England*

A cool, hard, self-possessed and philosophical north-easterner, Peter Willey was an exceptionally tough, right-hand, middle-order batsman who opted late in his career for a stance so open that he seemed to be looking at mid-wicket as the bowler approached. After beginning as a useful medium-pace bowler, severe knee injuries caused him to take up off-spin, which he developed with considerable success. Born in Durham, he first played for Northamptonshire in 1966 at the age of 16 years 5 months, making 78 against Cambridge in the second innings. A brilliant natural timer of the ball, his batting was at first inconsistent despite some electrifying innings in one-day cricket and several memorable first-class centuries, including his highest score of 227 against Somerset at Northampton in 1976, when he shared a record sixth-wicket stand for Northants of 370 with Roy Virgin. Making 1,115 runs (41.29) in this season, and playing a prominent part in Northamptonshire's victory in the Gillette Cup, Willey was selected for England against the immensely powerful West Indies side. He acquitted himself well in the circumstances, falling to a brilliant catch when well set on 45 in the second innings of his first Test at Headingley. After scoring 36, 45, 33, and 1 in matches which England lost, he was harshly treated when omitted from the MCC tour of India and Australia the following winter. But he earned a second chance against India at The Oval in 1979, played well and toured Australia in 1979/80. On a difficult tour he was a great success in the one-day internationals, hitting hard and handsomely and bowling usefully, but he failed in the Test matches. His wristy strength, determination, and glorious offside strokes were seen to better advantage against the West Indies fast bowlers, however. He scored 100 not out, his maiden Test century against them at The Oval in 1980 and saved England from possible defeat by adding 117 undefeated for the last wicket with Bob Willis. Eight months later he hit the same fierce West Indian attack for 102 not out, including a slashed square-cut six over third man. It was the first Test hundred ever scored in Antigua. He finished the four-Test series with an average of 47.87. He had lost his place in the Test team when he joined the lucrative tour to South Africa in March 1982. He joined Leicestershire in 1984, scoring six centuries in his first season for his new county and proving an able adviser and deputy for David Gower. After the end of his Test ban, he played in the first Test against Australia at Headingley and renewed his rivalry against the West Indies fast bowlers in the Caribbean in 1986. He showed all his fighting qualities in a magnificently brave knock of 71 on an untrustworthy pitch in the Kingston Test, but a knee injury forced his return to England. Despite a third operation, he was soon defying the odds with more successful performances for Leicestershire in 1986, taking over the captaincy from David Gower and returning to the England side for one Test—at Lord's—against New Zealand, preventing further England batting failures with scores of 44 and 42. He opted out of contention for the subsequent tour of Australia to give his knees a rest but gave Leicestershire staunch service before retiring to become a first-class umpire, one who quickly gained respect as a firm and fair official.

First-class career (1966–91): 24,361 runs (30.56) including 44 centuries, 756 wickets (30.95), and 235 catches

Test matches (26): 1,184 runs (26.90) including 2 centuries, 7 wickets (65.14), and 3 catches

WILLIAMS, Neil Fitzgerald

(b. 1962, Hope Well, St Vincent) *Middlesex, Essex, Tasmania, Windward Islands, and England*

Highly rated at county level, Neil Williams got his brief chance at Test level when he replaced an unfit Chris Lewis at The Oval in 1990. A loose-limbed seam-bowler, deceptively quick from a relatively short run-up and with an ability to swing the ball, Williams took two for 148 as India scored over 600, and was unable to break into the side again after being overlooked for the winter tours. Modest and friendly, Williams emigrated to Britain with his family at the age of 13. Taken on to the MCC staff after impressing the Middlesex coach Don Bennett whilst playing in the Middlesex County League, he joined the County in 1982 before returning to the Caribbean to play for the Windward Islands. In 1983, his first full season in county cricket, he helped Middlesex win the Benson and Hedges Cup and took 63 wickets to earn himself a place on stand-by for the England tour of New Zealand and Pakistan. To keep himself in shape in case of a call-up, he spent the winter playing for Tasmania in the Sheffield Shield competition. Although Williams took 54 Championship wickets in 1985, injuries then took their toll, but a return to full fitness in 1990 after a winter playing in the Caribbean and 49 wickets for Middlesex at 29 each earned him international recognition, and he took the wickets of Azharuddin and Tendulkar, also playing a spirited innings of 38 as a nightwatchman before the match ended in a draw.

First-class career (1982–   ): 3,907 runs (19.34) and 580 wickets (29.93)

WILLIS

WILLIS, Robert George Dylan

(b. 1949, Sunderland, Co. Durham) Surrey, Warwickshire, Northern Transvaal, and England

It is not easy to define what made Bob Willis, at his best, a great fast bowler. Will-power, intelligence, in recent years exceptional fitness, and a belief in bowling as fast and as straight as possible all played a part in his success. Unusually tall at 6 ft. 5 in., with his mop of brown, curly hair, he presented a hostile image to timid batsmen. He could bounce the ball awkwardly on most pitches and the unorthodox nature of his open-chested action made him that much more unpleasant for batsmen to face. He ran in a long way off a straight approach, moved the ball only a little but unpredictably—bowled a good yorker and an especially mean bouncer. On the field he locked himself into a cocoon of concentration, showing scant facial reaction in either triumph or dismay. Despite several shattering injuries, even at the end of his career he was still the spearhead of the England bowling attack, and he finished his career with 325 Test wickets. He made the first of his six tours to Australia as a slim youth of 21 in 1970/1 when he flew out late to replace Alan Ward and established himself as an important member of the Test side, bowling accurately and fielding brilliantly close to the wicket. Returning home he was dissatisfied with Surrey's unwillingness to give him his county cap and moved to Warwickshire in 1972. For several seasons he was handicapped by various injuries, notably to both knees, but he bowled with great consistency and courage on his second tour of Australia in 1974/5, taking 17 wickets (30.70). His next spell of success began with his recall to the England side in 1976, when he took 5 for 42 in the second innings, and eight wickets in the match, on a perfect Headingley pitch against the immensely powerful West Indies side. By now he was engaging in a daily routine of running and exercises and, during the Centenary Test in Australia in 1977, his rehabilitation was completed when a hypnotherapist taught him how to condition his mind for a major sporting occasion. In India, earlier in this tour, Willis had taken 20 Test wickets (16.75). At home against Australia in 1977 he took 27 wickets at 19.77 and in Australia in 1978/9 20 wickets (23.05), despite pain from blistered feet and a viral infection. His loyal support for Brearley and his own intelligent approach to the problems of touring had much to do with the team's well-being. Things did not go nearly so well in the hastily arranged tour of Australia the following winter when Willis could take only three Test wickets at 74 each when plagued by various ailments. But after returning home early for another knee operation, having taken little part in the 1980/1 tour of the West Indies, he bounced back into the limelight in 1981 to capitalize on Botham's famous innings at Headingley and, by taking 8 for 43 in Australia's second innings, he bowled England to a win which had seemed impossible. It was one of the great fast bowling spells of Test history. He ran down the slope from the Kirkstall End like a man possessed, achieving great pace and wicked lift. Australia, needing only 130 to win on a worn pitch, were 56 for 1 when Willis began bowling with the wind. They were bowled out for 111. Willis finished the series with 29 wickets to confirm the impression that his best efforts always tended to come against Australia. A loyal Test vice-captain, and captain of Warwickshire since 1980, he was appointed England captain in 1982. He had a fine summer, winning both series against India and Pakistan, and taking 25 wickets, and led his side to Australia in 1982/3. The Ashes were lost, but once again Willis was his side's most successful bowler. He was magnificent in 1983 against New Zealand, collecting 20 wickets (13.65) in four Tests, as he became the fourth bowler to take 300 Test wickets. He overtook Fred Trueman's total of 307 in the first Test of the 1983/4 tour to New Zealand and Pakistan, but later was forced home with a viral infection. He bravely returned to the side in 1984, before illness eventually forced his retirement. His performances for Warwickshire were rarely as outstanding as those in Test cricket and over thirteen seasons he took only 353 wickets for his adopted county. But his achievement for England, constantly recovering from serious injury, and still their fastest bowler at the age of 35, was enormous. His captaincy was criticized, but he always led by example, giving every ounce of his energy to his country's cause. Awarded the MBE in 1982, he was assistant manager on England's 1986 tour of the West Indies and became a very professional television commentator.

First-class career (1969–84): 2,690 runs (14.30), 899 wickets (24.99), and 134 catches

Test matches (90): 840 runs (11.50), 325 wickets (25.20), and 39 catches

WILSON, Revd Clement Eustace Macroe

(b. 1875, Bolsterstone, Yorkshire; d. 1944, Calverhall, Shropshire) *Cambridge University, Yorkshire, and England*

Outstanding at Uppingham, Clem Wilson soon gained his blue at Cambridge, and in his fourth University match in 1898 made 118. His brother Rockley also scored a century three years later, the only instance of brothers achieving this feat for Cambridge. Clem could bowl with either arm and, at The Oval against Surrey in 1895, ended a stand of 306 by holding a return catch when bowling left-arm. He played a little for Yorkshire, but the calls of the Ministry curtailed his appearances. He toured South Africa with Lord Hawke's team in 1898/9 when he played his Tests.

First-class career (1895–1900): 1,665 runs (23.78) including 1 century, 125 wickets (18.69), and 34 catches
Test matches (2): 42 runs (14.00)

WILSON, Donald

(b. 1937, Settle, Yorkshire) *Yorkshire and England*

A tall, slow, left-arm bowler, Don Wilson was in the Yorkshire tradition that stretches back to Edmund Peate, although he was not quite as dominant as his great predecessors. He took 100 wickets in a season five times. For Yorkshire against MCC at Scarborough in 1969, he took 7 for 19, and in the John Player League took 6 for 18 against Kent at Canterbury in 1969. He toured India 1963/4 and Australia and New Zealand in 1970/1, where he had his Test match experience. On a lesser tour, MCC to Sri Lanka in 1969/70, he took 8 for 36 (14 for 71 in the match) against the national side at Colombo. A left-handed, hard-hitting batsman, he hit his sole first-class century of 112 for MCC against South Zone at Hyderabad in 1963/4. For Yorkshire against MCC at Scarborough in 1966 he hit Robin Hobbs for 30 in one over. A highly regarded coach, who did notable work for non-white players in South Africa, he was chief coach at Lord's until 1991, when he moved to a job at Ampleforth College.

First-class career (1957–74): 6,230 runs (14.09) including 1 century, 1,189 wickets (21.00), and 250 catches
Test matches (6): 75 runs (12.50), 11 wickets (42.36), and 1 catch

WILSON, Evelyn Rockley

(b. 1879, Bolsterstone, Yorkshire; d. 1957, Winchester, Hampshire) *Cambridge University, Yorkshire, and England*

Rockley Wilson was a fine all-round cricketer and a unique character, whose conversation was full of anecdotes and wit. A remarkably accurate, slow-medium, right-arm bowler who could spin the ball a little either way, he was also a sound, determined batsman. At Cambridge he made 117 not out and 70 on his début in first-class cricket against A. J. Webbe's XI at Fenner's in 1899, and two years later scored 118 against Oxford at Lord's thus equalling the feat of his brother, Clem, in the University match three years before. For many years he ran the cricket at Winchester where he was a teacher, and played no first-class cricket from 1902 until 1913. He toured the Argentine with MCC and from 1913 until 1923 assisted Yorkshire regularly during August, when his bowling was very effective. He toured Australia in 1920/1 with MCC and in his sole Test, the fifth at Sydney, he scored 5 and 5 and took 3 for 36.

First-class career (1899–1923): 3,565 runs (22.00) including 4 centuries, 467 wickets (17.63), and 106 catches

WISDEN, John

(b. 1826, Brighton; d. 1884, London) *Sussex*

The obituary of John Wisden, 'the Little Wonder', in the *Almanack* which he founded called him 'a good bat and bowler unsurpassed, a fast friend and a generous employer'. As a right-arm medium-pace bowler in the days of round-arm delivery, his armoury included off-breaks and occasionally 'a very fast shooter'. For North v. South at Lord's in 1850 he clean-bowled all ten men in the second innings. Despite being only 5 ft. 4 in. he could hit hard, as he demonstrated in a century (four sixes) for Sussex against Kent at Tunbridge Wells in the same season. For much of his career he played for travelling sides against odds, with William Clarke's All-England XI and, after 1852, with the United England XI of which he was a founder. In a dozen seasons he took over 200 wickets a year for these sides including 455 in 1851. When he toured America with Parr's team in 1859 he did a double-hat-trick and took 29 for 60 against XXII of United States and Canada, at Rochester, New York. His *Almanack*, first published in 1864 from his cigar business in the Haymarket, and telling the reader on page 1 that the British Museum was closed on 1 January, was not seen by contemporaries as a serious rival to Lillywhite's *Cricketers Companion*. But soon after Wisden's death its association with the Pardon family ensured its future as the only long-term survivor of the nineteenth-century cricket periodicals.

First-class career (1845–63): 4,140 runs (14.12) including 2 centuries, 681 + 428 wickets (10.38), and 170 dismissals (169 c., 1 st.)

WOOD, Arthur

(b. 1898, Bradford, Yorkshire; d. 1973, Middleton, Yorkshire) *Yorkshire and England*

As a wicket-keeper, Arthur Wood was a master of the unexpected, full of uproarious humour, which, however, never interfered with his skill as a first-rate stumper or as a competent, right-handed batsman. His best season as a batsman was 1935, when he made 1,087 runs (36.23) for the champion county; and his best-known story concerns Yorkshire's game with the South Africans that year at Sheffield. Horace Cameron punished Hedley Verity for 30 runs in one over, at the end of which Arthur turned to Hedley and said: 'You've got him in two minds. He doesn't know whether to hit you for six or four!' As Leslie Ames was incapacitated, Arthur made his Test début against Australia at The Oval in 1938. Going in at 770 for 6 he hit 53 and stated afterwards: 'I'm always at my best in a crisis!' He kept in the three Tests against the West Indies in 1939, and at The Oval in the last match he took a most astounding catch; the ball soared up from the bat of Learie Constantine very high and Arthur sprinted, taking the catch at long-leg. 'By gow,' he panted, 'it's a good job I were standing back!'

First-class career (1927–48): 8,842 runs (21.20) including 1 century, and 888 dismissals (631 c., 257 st.)
Test matches (4): 80 runs (20.00) and 11 dismissals (10 c., 1 st.)

WOOD, Barry

(b. 1942, Ossett, Yorkshire) *Yorkshire, Lancashire, Derbyshire, Cheshire, Eastern Province, and England*

Very short, fair-haired, sturdy, and gutsy, Barry Wood lived for cricket. He was a correct and patient opening batsman, fine gully field, and useful slow-medium bowler who could swing the ball exceptionally in cloudy conditions. In all

three roles he was outstanding in limited-overs cricket, winning no fewer than six Gillette Cup man-of-the-match awards and eleven Benson and Hedges Gold awards for the outstanding individual performance in a match. Moreover he shared in all of Lancashire's Gillette Cup triumphs in the early 1970s after winning his cap in 1968, two years after crossing the border from Yorkshire, for whom he played in 1964. Wood's Test career began promisingly against Australia in 1972 when he made a good-looking 90, his highest Test score, against Dennis Lillee at his best at The Oval, driving immaculately through the covers. But a weakness against spin was cruelly exposed by the Indian spinners when he toured the East with MCC the following winter and his Test appearances afterwards were sporadic, although he was flown out very late in the winter of 1977/8 to reinforce the England team in New Zealand. After a successful benefit for Lancashire (£62,429) in 1979, he moved to Derbyshire and briefly captained the side. He was called into the England one-day side in 1982, but was not re-engaged by the county after the 1983 season, despite leading them to victory in the 1981 NatWest Trophy, and making 1,412 runs in the Championship that year. He played for Cheshire from 1986 to 1988. His son, Nathan, has played with success for England schools teams.

First-class career (1964–83): 17,453 runs (33.82) including 30 centuries, 298 wickets (30.73), and 283 catches
Test matches (12): 454 runs (21.61), 0–50, and 6 catches

WOOD, George Edward Charles

(b. 1893, Blackheath, Kent; d. 1971, Christchurch, Hampshire) *Cambridge University, Kent, and England*

Standing right up to the stumps for even the fastest bowlers, George Wood was a wicket-keeper who played for Cambridge both before and after the First World War, and a member of Archie MacLaren's amateur team which defeated the mighty Australians at Eastbourne in 1921. He had to decline a place in the MCC side to Australia in 1920/1 but was able to represent England in Tests against South Africa in 1924, and also played for Gentlemen against Players.

First-class career (1913–36): 2,773 runs (19.94) including one century, and 169 dismissals (116 c., 53 st.)
Test matches (3): 7 runs (3.50) and 6 dismissals (5 c., 1 st.)

WOOD, Henry

(b. 1853, Dartford, Kent; d. 1919, Waddon, Surrey)
Kent, Surrey, and England

Harry Wood was the third of four long-serving wicket-keepers who sustained Surrey for 70 years. He played during years when Surrey were either champion county or close to the leaders. He was painstaking to a degree and his hands often suffered horribly, but he never complained. He made the initial tour of South Africa in 1888/9, with Major Warton's team, appearing in the first Tests against that country and returned there in 1891/2. He was a useful batsman whose sole century in first-class cricket was 134 not out for England against South Africa at Cape Town on the second tour. His only appearance against Australia was at The Oval in 1888.

First-class career (1876–1900): 5,523 runs (16.94) including 1 century, and 674 dismissals (556 c., 118 st.)

Test matches (4): 204 runs (68.00) including 1 century, and 3 dismissals (2 c., 1 st.)

WOOD, Reginald

(b. 1860, Woodchurch, Cheshire; d. 1915, Sydney, Australia) *Lancashire, Victoria, and England*

When William Barnes was injured—he had aimed a blow at the Australian captain, Percy McDonnell, but connected with a wall instead —Reginald Wood, a native of Cheshire resident in Australia, was asked to play in the second Test at Sydney in 1886/7. Batting at number ten, he scored 6 and 0 and was not required again. Between 1880 and 1884 he had appeared with some success for Lancashire as a left-handed batsman and left-arm medium-pace bowler, scoring 166 runs (23.71) and taking four wickets (18.00) in six matches. Educated at Charterhouse, he played for Lancashire as an amateur but for Victoria as a professional.

First-class career (1880–7): 235 runs (15.66), 8 wickets (16.75), and 5 catches

WOODCOCK, John Charles

(b. 1926, Longparish, Hampshire)

An Oxford hockey blue as a goalkeeper, despite childhood illness which restricted his cricket ambitions, John Woodcock has written about cricket for *The Times* since 1954 (as cricket correspondent from 1954 to 1988) and he edited *Wisden Cricketers' Almanack*, 1981–6. He has reported well over 400 Test matches, covered forty overseas tours and was Sports Journalist of the Year, British Press Awards, in 1987. He is held in the highest regard by all who play and follow cricket. His technical judgement of players is outstanding and his day-to-day reporting has presented an acute appraisal in finely tuned prose. As editor of *Wisden* he tackled in his 'Notes' such subjects as dissent and undue appeals; over-rates; sponsorship; South Africa and the ICC; the decline in spin-bowling; four-day cricket; and overseas players. They represent a banner-roll of the issues of the 1980s and Woodcock pronounced on them in wise and sometimes sombre tones.

WOODS, Samuel Moses James

(1867–1931) *Cambridge University and Somerset*

See Australia section.

WOOLLER, Wilfred

(b. 1912, Rhos-on-Sea, Clwyd, Wales) *Glamorgan*

A Welsh Rugby international at 19, Wilfred Wooller returned from three years as a prisoner of war in Japanese hands to lead Glamorgan to their first county championship in 1948. As a right-handed batsman, in exactly 400 matches for the county, he adjusted his approach to the needs of the moment, scoring over 1,000 runs on five occasions. As a brisk right-arm medium-pace bowler, he took a stock of wickets annually, performing the 'double' in 1954. But it was Wooller the fielder, usually at forward short-leg, who secured over 400 catches: a massive figure threatening batsmen by his very presence and setting an example which led Glamorgan's fielding to be the pride of post-war county cricket. The courage, authority, and tactical skills which made him one of Wales' greatest three-quarters were translated to the cricket scene, both as a captain and as an England selector from 1955 to 1962. He retired from the county secretaryship in 1978 having steered Glamorgan through the triumphs of another championship success in 1969 and through some traumas in the 1970s.

First-class career (1935–62): 13,593 runs (22.57) including 5 centuries, 958 wickets (26.96), and 413 catches

WOOLLEY, Frank Edward

(b. 1887, Tonbridge, Kent; d. 1978, Halifax, Nova Scotia, Canada) *Kent and England*

Without question Frank Woolley rests among the half dozen or so great all-rounders of cricket history, although he did not dominate in Tests against Australia quite as much as he might have done. H. S. Altham has described how with his 'tall and graceful figure, his quiet air and unhurried movements, he brought to his left-handed batting an unmistakable air of majestic, almost casual, command. With his long reach and great gift for timing, he would with fascinating ease drive or force off the back foot what to other men was good-length bowling.' Neville Cardus managed at once to be romantic and succinct in his description: 'There was all summer in a stroke by Woolley.' His left-arm slow bowling was equally natural and elegant. His height enabled him to get bounce, his large hands considerable spin and he was accurate, too. In the field he became outstanding at slip—'c. Woolley b. Freeman' was a regular entry in the score-books, and no fielder has taken more catches. Only Sir Jack Hobbs has scored more runs. In four of the 13 seasons in which he made 2,000 runs, Woolley also took 100 wickets, a feat no one else has achieved more than twice. In all he scored 1,000 runs in 28 seasons and took 100 wickets in eight of them. His highest aggregate was 3,352 runs (60.94), including twelve centuries in 1928. His highest score, 305 not out for MCC against Tasmania at Hobart in 1911/12, remained for more than 50 years the highest by an Englishman in Australia. His last-wicket stand of 235 with Arthur Fielder, against Worcestershire at Stourbridge in 1909, remains the record for county cricket. Woolley toured Australia and South Africa three times each, and New Zealand once. He represented England from 1909 until 1934. His début was against Australia at The Oval in 1909, and his first Test century was 133 in the fifth Test at Sydney in 1911/12. In the first 'timeless' Test, against Australia at The Oval in 1912, he won the game with 62 and 10 for 49 in the match; and again in 1912, at The Oval against South Africa, he took 5 for 41 in the first innings. After the War he disappointed in Australia in 1920/1, but at Lord's the following season he held England together against Gregory and McDonald with the historic 95 (out of 187) and 93 (out of 283), two amazing performances against the irresistible Australian tide. One of only two English players to appear in all five Tests of 1921, he scored 343 runs (42.87). He hit hundreds against South Africa in 1924 and against Australia in 1924/5, his 123 at Sydney in the first Test coming in $2\frac{1}{2}$ hours. In the 1924/5 series he made 325 runs (36.11). He was, deservedly, a member of the England team at The Oval in 1926, which won back the Ashes after a long wait.

His highest score in Tests was 154 against South Africa at Old Trafford in 1929, a series when he made 378 runs (128.00). Woolley was a sober, cautious, introverted character, but a warmth and humour lay beneath the reserved exterior. He married a Canadian late in life.

First-class career (1906–38): 58,959 runs (40.77) including 145 centuries, 2,066 wickets (19.87), and 1,018 catches

Test matches (64): 3,283 runs (36.07) including 5 centuries, 83 wickets (33.91), and 64 catches

WOOLMER, Robert Andrew

(b. 1948, Kanpur, India) *Kent, Natal, Western Province, and England*

Bob Woolmer's Test career was blossoming handsomely when he took the decision to join Kerry Packer's World Series Cricket. A rosy-cheeked and genial man with great confidence in himself, Woolmer was a graceful right-handed batsman with a casual air and a delightful 'touch'—the comparison with Colin Cowdrey was often made —who drove fluently on the off-side and deflected with a delicate sense of timing. He was also a useful medium-fast bowler who swung the ball considerably in cloudy conditions, and a safe close fielder. His apprenticeship in the strong Kent side was a relatively long one and his breakthrough came when he began opening their batting after a long spell late in the order. Son of a British business executive who had captained Uttar Pradesh at cricket, Woolmer lived in India until he was 7, but was educated at Tunbridge Wells and first played for Kent in 1968. Capped in 1970, he began opening in 1976 when he made 1,749 runs (47.27). The previous year he had taken a hat-trick for MCC against the Australians at Lord's and also played his first Test as an all-rounder on the same ground. He was left out until the final match of the series when, going in at number five, he scored 149, reaching the slowest century for England against Australia in 6 hours 36 minutes. Two modest series followed, against the West Indies in 1976 and in India, 1976/7, but in 1977 he scored hundreds in successive Tests against Australia at Lord's and Old Trafford. Thus in only seven Tests against Australia (including the Centenary Test) he had already scored three centuries—as many as May, more than Washbrook, Woolley, Grace, Graveney. What he gained financially by joining World Series Cricket he lost in the momentum of his Test career. He played four more Tests for England at home, in 1980 and 1981, but could not establish himself again. Sadly, injury forced him to retire prematurely in 1984. He settled in South Africa and despite returning home to coach Kent in 1987 and Warwickshire between 1991 and 1994, he accepted a post as coach to the South African team towards the end of Warwickshire's triumphant 1994 season, in which they won three of the four county trophies. He was innovative and thorough as a coach, whether encouraging small boys at a multi-racial club in Cape Town (he did much good work at the Avondale club before apartheid barriers came down) or working on the technique of Test batsmen. Positive thinking was his forte, both as player and as coach.

First-class career (1968–84): 15,772 runs (33.55) including 34 centuries, 420 wickets (25.87), and 240 dismissals (239 c., 1 st.)

Test matches (19): 1,059 runs (33.09) including 3 centuries, 4 wickets (74.75), and 10 catches

WORDSWORTH, Charles

(b. 1806, London; d. 1892, St Andrews, Scotland) *Oxford University*

A contemporary described Charles Wordsworth as 'the best scholar, cricketer, oar, skater, racquet-player, dancer and pugilist of his day'. He captained Harrow in their first match against Winchester (1825) and was the main instigator of the first match between Oxford and Cambridge at Lord's two years later, his tutor having given him permission to go to London in term-time 'to consult a dentist'. His left underarm off-break secured him seven wickets though he made the first 'pair' in the series in the 1829 match, played at Oxford. Sixty years later he offered an explanation! 'I was suffering from the effects of my rowing which made it almost impossible for me to bat' and he recalled having a batting average at Oxford in 1828 of about 40. 'Batting (right-handed) was my forte.' He had rowed in the first Boat Race in 1828 and two years after these recollections were written (1888) he took up golf at the age of 84. Wordsworth, nephew of the poet, became warden of Glenalmond College (1847–54) and bishop of St Andrew's (1852–92). He may be seen as the prototype of the cult of muscular Christianity whose impact on nineteenth-century British and Imperial society was significant.

WORTHINGTON, Thomas Stanley

(b. 1905, Bolsover, Derbyshire; d. 1973, King's Lynn, Norfolk) *Derbyshire, Northumberland, and England*

Stan Worthington began as a right-arm, medium-fast bowler of accurate length and a late-order batsman, who indulged in the fast bowler's traditional 'dip'. He gradually learned to hit with more discrimination. When he made his first century, against Essex in 1928, he included four towering sixes. *Wisden* called him 'a serious-minded fellow'. Between 1928 and 1939 he reached 1,000 runs ten times, and in 1936 hit his highest score, 238 not out, against Sussex at Derby. Stan Worthington toured New Zealand in 1929/30 with MCC, playing in the earliest Tests against that country. In his next series, against India in 1936, he made 87 at Old Trafford, quickly adding 127 with Walter Hammond for the third wicket, and 128 at The Oval, this time adding a record 266 for the fourth wicket with Hammond in just over three hours. He toured Australia with MCC in 1936/7, playing and opening in three Tests, but was disappointing.

First-class career (1924–47): 19,221 runs (29.07) including 31 centuries, 682 wickets (29.22), and 340 catches

Test matches (9): 321 runs (29.18) including 1 century, 8 wickets (39.50), and 8 catches

WRIGHT, Charles William

(b. 1863, Harewood, Yorkshire; d. 1936, Melton Mowbray, Leicestershire) *Cambridge University, Nottinghamshire, and England*

'Chawles' Wright played four times for Cambridge against Oxford at Lord's, winning a medal for his faultless 102 in the 1883 match. After playing intermittently for Nottinghamshire for some 18 years, he lost the sight of an eye in an accident while shooting partridges. He was a very steady batsman who usually went in first, and his strong back-foot play on treacherous wickets often averted a collapse; he was also a good reserve wicket-keeper. He was one of the few county players given out 'handled ball', against Gloucestershire at Bristol in 1893, when the ball lodged in his pads and he picked it out, and, as captain of Notts (though never officially appointed) against Kent at Gravesend in 1890, he was the first ever to declare an innings closed. He toured with four teams led by Lord Hawke, two to America, and one each to India and South Africa in 1895/6 (his Tests).

First-class career (1882–1901): 6,989 runs (15.88) including 2 centuries, 195 catches, and 41 stumpings
Test matches (3): 125 runs (31.25)

WRIGHT, Douglas Vivian Parson

(b. 1914, Sidcup, Kent) *Kent and England*

Doug Wright was one of the enigmas of post-1945 cricket. At his destructive best, his impact on batsmen was devastating, as his record number of seven hat-tricks showed. His action was unusual, with skips and jumps in a long springy run, and he bowled much faster than the average leg-spinner, often turning and lifting the ball so sharply that it missed the stumps and even the wicket-keepers. It was this ability to beat even great batsmen when well set which kept him in Test cricket; his relatively modest figures do not reveal his ability to bowl the unplayable ball. Ten times he took more than 100 wickets in a season, the best being 177 wickets (21.12) in 1947, and twice he took nine wickets in an innings, his best match record being 16 for 80 against Somerset at Bath in 1939. He toured Australia and New Zealand twice and South Africa twice; from 1938 until 1951 he was an integral part of the England XI. In Australia, 1946/7, he took more wickets than anyone on either side, but at heavy cost—23 wickets at 43.04. Though he took his fair toll himself, Don Bradman had a tremendous regard for him. Again the most successful on both sides in 1947, he secured 19 wickets (25.47) from four Tests against South Africa, at Lord's taking 10 for 175 in the match. Time after time he bowled with skill and stubbornness, magnificent but—generally—ill rewarded. Also a useful tail-end batsman and a good field, he became a much-respected coach at Charterhouse, where Richard Gilliat and many other good players flourished in his care.

First-class career (1932–57): 5,903 runs (12.34), 2,056 wickets (23.98), and 182 catches
Test matches (34): 289 runs (11.11), 108 wickets (39.11), and 10 catches

WYATT, Robert Elliott Storey

(b. 1901, Milford, Surrey; d. 1995, Helston, Cornwall) *Warwickshire, Worcestershire, and England*

Cousin of the noted MP, Woodrow Wyatt, Bob Wyatt made runs, took wickets, and held catches in every quarter of the globe. Living to a great age in retirement in Cornwall, he held strong, independent, and shrewd views on the game. Though he often opened the batting, he is best remembered as a solid and dependable middle-order right-hander, who also bowled useful medium-pace swing. For sheer determination and concentration on all aspects of the game, he has had few equals; his study was scientific and intense. He captained Warwickshire, Worcestershire, and England. Instead of tossing the ball to a bowler and saying, 'All right, have a go,' he would at great length and with some eloquence outline the strategic masterplan. He toured India with MCC in 1926/7 and South Africa in 1927/8, making his first Test appearances. He hit 113 against South Africa at Old Trafford in 1929, toured the West Indies in 1929/30 with some success, and displaced Percy Chapman (against frantic newspaper disapproval) as England captain in the fifth Test against Australia at The Oval in 1930. He made 64, but England lost. He toured South Africa in 1930/1, as vice-captain to Chapman, and Australia the following year, as vice-captain to Douglas Jardine, making 51 and 61 not out in the fifth Test at Sydney. Captain against Australia in 1934, he was the less successful captain of two strong sides, and he lost series to the West Indies in 1934/5, and to South Africa in 1935. He hit 149, however, in the first Test at Trent Bridge. No longer captain, he appeared against India in 1936, and toured Australia with MCC in 1936/7. Bob Wyatt exceeded 1,000 runs in a season eighteen times (once overseas), five times reaching 2,000, his best being 2,630 runs (53.67) in 1929, including ten centuries. His highest score was 232 for Warwickshire against Derbyshire at Edgbaston in 1937. Among his writings is the widely acclaimed *The Ins and Outs of Cricket*. He served as a Test selector from 1949 to 1953 (chairman in 1950). He played for Warwickshire from 1923 to 1939, Worcestershire from 1946 to 1951, and made a final first-class appearance for Free Foresters in 1957.

First-class career (1923–57): 39,405 runs (40.04) including 85 centuries, 901 wickets (32.84), 415 catches, and 1 stumping
Test matches (40): 1,839 runs (31.70) including 2 centuries, 18 wickets (35.66), and 16 catches

WYNYARD, Major Edward George

(b. 1861, Saharanpur, India; d. 1936, Knotty Green, Beaconsfield, Buckinghamshire) *The Army, Hampshire, and England*

Over 6 ft. and finely built, Teddy Wynyard was a brilliant player of most games, excellent at cricket. A splendid right-handed forcing batsman using a wide variety of strokes, and an occasional lob-bowler, he stated that he had made 150 centuries in all kinds of cricket. For Hampshire against Somerset at Taunton in 1899, he made 225. He was a member of the winning England team, against Australia at The Oval in 1896, and he toured South Africa with MCC sides in 1905/6 and 1909/10, but his Test record was poor. A rather irascible man, he was not always popular and fell out with Ranji when the young Indian prince inadvertently ate some of his grapes! He played in the 1881 FA Cup Final for Old Carthusians as a forward and was also a skilful skater.

First-class career (1878–1912): 8,318 runs (33.00) including 13 centuries, 66 wickets (32.27), 163 catches, and 5 stumpings

Test matches (3): 72 runs (12.00) and 0–17

YARDLEY, Norman Walter Dransfield

(b. 1915, Barnsley, Yorkshire; d. 1989, Sheffield, Yorkshire) *Cambridge University, Yorkshire, and England*

A kindly, genial, unflappable character, Norman Yardley was a reliable cricketer who did valuable service during lean years for English cricket. A right-handed batsman, he was primarily an on-side player but had strokes all round the wicket. As a right-arm medium-pace bowler, he bowled at the wicket to a full length, and came through quicker than expected. After captaining Cambridge in his fourth year he toured South Africa with MCC in 1938/9 and, although he was wounded in the Western Desert in the Second World War, he returned to be vice-captain of MCC in Australia in 1946/7, and to captain England at home against South Africa in 1947, against Australia in 1948 and against the West Indies in 1950. He was Yorkshire skipper from 1948 until 1955, considered to be too nice a person at times and not severe enough on some of his senior professionals. In Australia against a very powerful side, he averaged 31.50 with the bat in the Tests and headed the bowling with ten wickets (37.20), dismissing Bradman three times running, twice before the great man had made a large score. He also came top of the bowling averages in 1948 with nine wickets (22.66), all accredited Australian batsmen. His highest Test score was 99 at Trent Bridge in 1947 against South Africa, after England had followed on and, with Denis Compton, he helped to save the day. For Yorkshire his highest was 183 not out against Hampshire at Headingley in 1951, and his best bowling was 6 for 29 for MCC against Cambridge

at Lord's in 1946. Eight times he exceeded 1,000 runs in a season. He was a good, versatile fielder. Chairman of the England Test selectors from 1951 to 1952 and again a selector from 1953 to 1954, he became a popular broadcaster on BBC radio. An all-round athlete, he was also North of England squash champion six times. He was president of Yorkshire CCC from 1981 to 1984.

First-class career (1935–55): 18,173 runs (31.17) including 27 centuries, 279 wickets (30.48), 328 catches, and 1 stumping

Test matches (20): 812 runs (25.37), 21 wickets (33.66), and 14 catches

YOUNG, Harding Isaac

(b. 1876, Leyton, Essex; d. 1964, Rochford, Essex) *Essex and England*

While serving in the Royal Navy, 'Sailor' Young bowled so well in minor matches and in the nets at Leyton that the Essex president, C. E. Green, bought him out of the Service to play for the county. A well-built man, he was a left-arm medium-pace bowler with 'a deceptive curl'. His best season was 1899, taking 139 wickets (21.79) and making 607 runs; against Warwickshire at Edgbaston he secured 15 for 154; and in his only two appearances in Tests, against Australia, he headed the England bowling averages, taking 4 for 30 in the first innings at Headingley. He also helped Essex beat the Australians at Leyton, taking 11 for 74. He toured the West Indies with MCC, 1910/11, and was on the ground staff at Lord's for many years, before becoming a first-class umpire from 1921 until 1931 and, latterly, a school coach. He umpired in three Test matches.

First-class career (1898–1912): 2,303 runs (11.99), 514 wickets (23.37), and 80 catches

Test matches (2): 43 runs (21.50), 12 wickets (21.83), and 1 catch

YOUNG, John Albert

(b. 1912, London; d. 1993, London) *Middlesex and England*

Small, dapper, and smiling in the style of a polished light comedian, Jack Young was a lively humorist and an orthodox, left-arm, spin bowler with a perky run-up and an excellent action. Like other slow spinners of his generation, his command of length and direction was complete. He could spin the ball considerably and if there was not quite enough guile in his flight to make him outstanding in Tests—although he bowled 11 consecutive maidens against Australia at Trent Bridge in 1948—he took many wickets for his county. Eight times he took more than 100 wickets in a season, four times between 1947 and 1952 exceeding 150 wickets, the best haul being 163 (19.88) in 1952. He toured South Africa in 1948/9, and played for England against Australia, South Africa and New Zealand at home. His best bowling in an innings was 9 for 55 for England against Commonwealth at Hastings in 1951.

First-class career (1933–56): 2,485 runs (8.93), 1,361 wickets (19.68), and 148 catches

Test matches (8): 28 runs (5.60), 17 wickets (44.52), and 5 catches

YOUNG, Richard Alfred

(b. 1885, Dharwar, India; d. 1968, Hastings, Sussex) *Cambridge University, Sussex, and England*

One of the few players to wear spectacles—the thickest conceivable—while representing England at both cricket and Association football, 'Dick' Young established a high reputation as a batsman/wicket-keeper at Repton and won his blue at Cambridge, playing four times against Oxford, and in his last year, 1908, as captain. In that season he scored 1,430 runs (35.07). First in and last out in 1906, he had hit 150. In the University match and for Sussex against Essex at Leyton in 1905 he scored 220. From 1905 until 1925 he assisted Sussex in the holidays. For 30 years he taught mathematics at Eton, where he was also cricket master. Though inclined to take risks, he got most of his runs in front of the wicket and in 1921 obtained one of the few centuries off the triumphant Australians, for Sussex at Eastbourne. He toured Australia with MCC in 1907/8, when he made his sole, disappointing, appearances in Tests. A fanatical theorist about cricket, he wrote a pamphlet, *Time for Experiment*, in which he suggested that captains should have the right to pour 100 gallons of water on any part of the pitch.

First-class career (1905–25): 6,653 runs (28.80) including 11 centuries, and 144 dismissals (115 c., 29 st.)

Test matches (2): 27 runs (6.75) and 6 dismissals (6 c.)

India

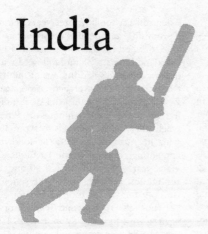

ABDUL HAFEEZ

(b. 1925) *Northern India, Oxford University, Warwickshire, India, and Pakistan*

See Kardar, A. H.

ABID ALI, Syed

(b. 1941, Hyderabad) *Hyderabad and India*

A stocky, barrel-chested all-rounder with a military moustache, Abid Ali was a careful stroke-maker who showed the full face of the bat to the ball and could drive well; he was also a medium-fast opening bowler who used the new ball particularly well in England but who in India merely fired a few preliminary shots before the army of spinners took over. Quick-moving and safe in the field, he also served as a deputy 'keeper. He toured England in 1971 and 1974, Australasia in 1967/8, and the West Indies in 1970/1, and at home he played against Australia in 1969/70, New Zealand in 1969/70, England in 1972/3, and West Indies in 1974/5. On his Test début in the first match at Adelaide he took 6 for 55 in the first innings total of 335. In England in 1971 he dismissed four of England's top batsmen for 15 runs on the first day of the Old Trafford Test. Less than three weeks later, in the final Test at The Oval, he cut the winning boundary when India defeated England for the first time on English soil. In the Ranji Trophy competition he scored more than 2,500 runs and took over 100 wickets. His career-highest was 173 not out for Hyderabad against Kerala in 1968/9 and his best bowling in an innings 6 for 23 against Surrey at The Oval in 1974.

First-class career (1959–79): 8,732 runs (29.30) including 13 centuries, 397 wickets (28.55), 190 catches, and 5 stumpings
Test matches (29): 1,018 runs (20.36), 47 wickets (42.12), and 33 catches

ACHREKAR, Ramakant

(b. Bombay)

Watching him conduct his nets in a small but very well-known corner of Shivaji Park, it is not easy to imagine that Ramakant Achrekar is the man who introduced names like Sachin Tendulkar, Vinod Kambli, Pravin Amre, and Chandrakant Pandit to Bombay cricket. Working in a bank by day and coaching boys every morning and evening, Achrekar extends this love for the game to meet the needs of some of his poorer wards. Hospitality in his house is always welcome and his pupils, many of them big stars now, never fail to see him before a major tour. Often, they return with little pieces of equipment which are immediately distributed among other cricketers. As coach of the Shardashram school near Shivaji Park he has nurtured Bombay cricket and, among young hopefuls, his name is spoken of in awe, almost as if entry to his 'net' would guarantee them a future. It often does, for he has continued to produce outstanding cricketers, most of whom tend to be bottom-handed, yet excellent players of spin. He has been the recipient of the Dronacharya Award, the highest state honour given to coaches. He believes in concentrating on a cricketer's natural strengths rather than in coaching heavily in a more English manner, and believes there is no substitute for match play.

ADHIKARI, Lt.-Col. Hemu Ramchandra

(b. 1919, Maharashtra) *Gujarat, Baroda, Services, and India*

Under average height, Hemu Adhikari was a neat, attractive right-handed batsman with a sound defence, especially good in a crisis; an occasional leg-break bowler and a brilliant cover or close field. He toured Australia in 1947/8 and England (as vice-captain) in 1952, and at home played against West Indies in 1948/9 and (once as captain) in 1958/9, against England in 1951/2, Pakistan in 1952/3, and Australia in 1956/7; but his duties as an officer in the Indian Army often prevented him appearing regularly. He achieved little in Tests on his two tours, but scored 114 not out against West Indies at New Delhi in his first Test in India, and against England in the fourth match at Kanpur in 1951/2, he helped to stave off an innings defeat with 60 in a total of 157. When Pakistan played India for the first time in official Tests in 1952/3, he hit 81 not out at number eight in the first Test, adding a record 109 in 80 minutes with Ghulam Ahmed for the last wicket. In his last Test against the West Indies at New Delhi in 1958/9, when he was skipper, he scored 63 and 40, sharing in a century partnership in each innings with Chandra Borde (besides taking 3 for 68), and steering India clear of defeat. His career highest was 230 not out for Services against Rajputana in 1951/2. Lt.-Col. Adhikari has been a popular and efficient manager of touring teams.

First-class career (1936–60): 8,683 runs (41.74) including 17 centuries, 49 wickets (37.93), and 97 catches

Test matches (21): 872 runs (31.14) including 1 century, 3 wickets (27.33), and 8 catches

AMARNATH, Mohinder Bharadwaj

(b. 1950, Patiala) *Punjab, Delhi, Durham, Wiltshire, and India*

Trim-figured, boyishly good-looking and of medium height, Mohinder Amarnath, Lala's younger son, was, like his father, a right-handed batsman and medium-paced bowler. With a short, relaxed run-up and good body action, he moved the ball through the air and off the pitch in helpful conditions, and he was an impressively solid orthodox batsman who drove handsomely and hooked bravely. One of the few players to have enjoyed success against the West Indies fast bowlers of the early 1980s, he made his first Test appearance in the fifth Test against Australia at Madras in 1969/70, having played for the Punjab

when still a schoolboy three years before. Despite a promising start he didn't reappear in Tests until 1975/6 when he quickly established himself. At Auckland he made 64 and followed with 4 for 63 in New Zealand's first innings of the next Test at Christchurch. He averaged 35.60 against New Zealand and 39.71 against the West Indies, including 85 in the second innings at Port of Spain when India defied the odds to score 406 for 4 to win. In Australia in 1977/8, following a disappointing series at home to England the previous year, Amarnath scored 90 and 100 in the second Test at Perth, and in the series made 445 runs (49.44). On the tour he was top scorer with 731 runs (48.73). A second Test century followed against West Indies at Kanpur in 1978/9, 101 not out, but he was desperately unlucky in England in 1979, missing the second and fourth Tests, at first because of an injured back and then more seriously because of a hairline fracture of the skull after being hit by a bouncer. This was a setback from which he took time to recover, but he continued to do well for Delhi and captained them to an incredible success in the final of the Ranji Trophy of 1981/2 when Delhi overhauled Karnataka's first innings score of 705 thanks primarily to Amarnath's heroic 185, the highest of six centuries in the first innings of either side! He returned to favour with India's selectors when picked to tour Pakistan in 1982/3 and began a triumphant season's cricket in which he hit 109 not out at Lahore, 61 and 64 in a heavy defeat at Hyderabad, 120 at Lahore in the fifth Test, and 103 at Karachi in the sixth. Then, against the fearsome West Indies fast bowlers he scored 58 and 117 at Port of Spain, 91 and 80 at Bridgetown, and 54 and 116 at St John's, Antigua. In all, he scored 2,355 runs in 1982/3, a record outside England. The West Indians got even with him when he failed dismally at home against them in 1983/4, but he held his place and hit his ninth Test hundred against Australia in 1985/6, 138 at Sydney. He played his full part in India's World Cup triumph in 1983, being man-of-the-match in the final at Lord's. He toured England again in 1986, scoring 69 in the first Test and 79 in the third. Helping Delhi to the final of the Ranji Trophy the following winter, he scored 85 in the final and in that same 1986/7 season played in series against Sri Lanka and Pakistan. At Nagpur his 131 helped India to their first Test victory over Sri Lanka, after five previous attempts. He completed 4,000 Test runs during this innings but he was left out of India's World Cup side in 1987/8 and after making only 56 in three Tests against

West Indies he faded from the scene he had graced both by his cricket and his manner.

First-class career (1966–88): 13,747 runs (43.22) including 30 centuries, 277 wickets (32.87), and 152 catches

Test matches (69): 4,378 runs (42.50) including 11 centuries, 32 wickets (55.68), and 47 catches

AMARNATH, Nanik, known as Lala

(b. 1911, Lahore) *Southern Punjab, Gujarat, Patiala, United Provinces, Railways, and India*

Described as a 'pure romantic, the Byron of Indian cricket', Lala Amarnath at his best was an all-rounder of international class and a bold and aggressive captain. A right-handed batsman whose driving and cutting were a rare delight, he would 'explode' with strokes all round the wicket. As a medium-pace bowler, he took an easy, alert run of four paces, gave a double hop as he delivered but maintained an almost impeccable length, moving his in-swingers greatly and mixing them with venomous leg-cutters. He was always desperately keen to get on with the game and could hardly wait for the ball to be returned to him before heading back for his next run-up. A reliable close fielder, he was also a useful deputy wicket-keeper. He toured England in 1936 and 1946 and Australia in 1947/8, and at home played against England in 1933/4 and 1951/2, West Indies in 1948/9, and Pakistan in 1952/3. For Southern Punjab against MCC in 1933/4 he scored 109 brilliantly, and in the first Test against England at Bombay he made 38 and 118 in $3\frac{1}{2}$ hours. He was the first Indian centurion in Tests, and his bowling talent was discovered at the nets before the start of this match. In England in 1936 the Indian team were rent by divisions and, although he had scored more runs (613) than anyone else and taken 32 wickets, he was sent home for disciplinary reasons before the first Test. After a special enquiry months later, he was exonerated, and he toured England again in 1946. In the first Test at Lord's he scored 50 and took 5 for 118 in the first innings, and in the second at Old Trafford he returned a match analysis of 8 for 167 in 81 overs. He captained India on the first visit to Australia in 1947/8, but although successive innings brought him 144, 94 not out, and 228 not out and subsequently he hit 172 not out, 171, and 135, he fared moderately with the bat in the Tests. At least he took most wickets in the series at lowest cost—13 wickets (28.15), twice taking four wickets in an innings, and at Melbourne in the third match 7 for 130. Against the first West

Indian side in 1948/9, he led India with flair, and scored 294 runs (36.75). No longer captain, he played once against England in 1951/2, but failed to score or to take a wicket. Restored to the captaincy, he led India successfully in the first series against Pakistan in 1952/3. A prolific all-rounder in India, he made 2,162 runs (39.50) and took 190 wickets (14.54) in the Ranji Trophy championship. The highest score of his career was 262 for India-in-England against Rest of India at Calcutta in 1946/7 and his best bowling figures in an innings, 7 for 30 for Patiala against Services in 1956/7. He served on the Indian Selection Committee from 1952 until 1960, for two years as chairman. He is the father of Surinder and Mohinder, both Test cricketers.

First-class career (1929–64): 10,426 runs (41.38) including 31 centuries, 463 wickets (22.98), 96 catches, and 2 stumpings

Test matches (24): 878 runs (24.38) including 1 century, 45 wickets (32.91), and 13 catches

AMARNATH, Surinder Bharadwaj

(b. 1948, Kanpur) *Punjab, Delhi, Baroda, and India*

The elder son of Lala Amarnath, Surinder was a skilful left-handed batsman and occasional right-arm medium-pace bowler. In 1963/4 he made his début for the Punjab while still a schoolboy. In 1972/3 he hit 202 not out for the Punjab against Delhi in the Ranji Trophy and in the same season made his unofficial Test début against Sri Lanka, scoring 118 at Ahmedabad. On his first appearance in an official Test he scored 124 against New Zealand at Auckland in 1975/6. That season he also toured the West Indies, playing in two of the Tests. A neat, wristy left-hander with aggressive instincts, he cover-drove and cut particularly well and it was surprising that he never maintained a regular place in India's Test team having stiffened up the batting against England in 1976/7. He was injured during the 1977/8 Australian tour and had to return home. His last Test cricket was played in Pakistan in 1978/9, but he was unlucky not to be picked for the next tour of Australia, in 1979/80, after scoring 235 not out against the Rest of India for Delhi in the Irani Trophy.

First-class career (1963–86): 8,175 runs (40.47) including 16 centuries, 4 wickets (65.00), and 47 catches

Test matches (10): 550 runs (30.55) including 1 century, 1–5, and 4 catches

AMAR SINGH

AMAR SINGH, Ladhabhai Nakum

(b. 1910, Rajkot; d. 1940, Jamnagar) *Nawanagar, Western India, and India*

Tall, of strapping build, and an entertaining, masterly all-rounder, Ladha Amar Singh could change the course of a game in a matter of minutes. Off a comparatively short, untidy run, climaxed with a sudden, almost frenzied action, he bowled right-arm fast-medium with an easy delivery, maintaining an immaculate length. Always bowling to his field, he could swing and cut the ball—especially in the heavier atmosphere of England—but it was his pace off the pitch which was most disconcerting to the batsman: 'He came off the pitch like the crack of doom,' said Wally Hammond. A right-handed hitter, he could score at a rapid pace off the best bowlers; and he was a very agile field in the close positions. He toured England in 1932, taking 111 wickets (20.78) and making 641 runs (22.89) in first-class matches. He took 12 for 211 against Gloucestershire at Bristol, and 11 wickets each against Cambridge and Worcestershire. He hit a rapacious 131 not out at number ten against Lancashire at Blackpool. At Lord's in India's first-ever Test, he took four wickets and, in an uphill fight, hit 51 at number ten in the second innings. Against England at Madras in 1933/4, he captured 7 for 86 (44.4 overs) in the first innings of 335 and hit 48 in the second innings. By now a popular and well-paid Lancashire League professional, he could be released only for a few games on the 1936 England tour, but made 143 runs and took ten wickets in the three Tests. In the first Test at Lord's, he took 6 for 35 in 25.1 overs in the first innings, and at Old Trafford in the second match saved India from suffering an innings defeat when he hit 48 not out. Against Lord Tennyson's team in 1937/8 he captured 36 wickets (16.66) in the five unofficial Tests. He died of pneumonia two years later.

First-class career (1930–40): 3,344 runs (24.23) including 5 centuries, 506 wickets (18.35), and 77 catches

Test matches (7): 292 runs (22.46), 28 wickets (30.64), and 3 catches

AMIR ELAHI

(b. 1908, Lahore; d. 1980, Multan, Pakistan) *Baroda, Northern India, Southern Punjab, India, and Pakistan*

Touring England with the 1936 team, Amir Elahi was not selected for the Tests, and on the 1947/8

Australia tour he played in one Test, as a bowler, yet was not called upon to bowl! He was in Pakistan's first team to visit India for an official series in 1952/3, but eight first-class matches brought him only 13 wickets. A right-arm medium-pace bowler who turned to leg-breaks and googlies, he was a prolific wicket-taker in the Ranji Trophy championship, taking 193 wickets (24.72). A lovable character, he was the first Pakistan Test player to die.

First-class career (1934–54): 2,562 runs (16.35), 513 wickets (25.77), and 67 catches

Test matches (India—1): 17 runs (8.50). (Pakistan—5): 65 runs (10.83) and 7 wickets (35.42)

AMRE, Pravin Kalyan

(b. 1968, Bombay) *Bombay, Railways, Rajasthan, and India*

A mild-mannered, soft-spoken style cloaks Pravin Amre's enormous determination to succeed. A wristy little right-hander, he first attracted attention as a schoolboy in Bombay, where he scored heavily for Shardashram Vidya Mandir and also had an excellent academic record. His début for Bombay in 1986/7 against Karnataka was inauspicious and he then accepted a job in the Railways in order to get more exposure to first-class cricket. It paid off as he made a brilliant 186 not out on a dirt track in his first match for them. He then played the Youth World Cup and returned to score heavily especially for Central Zone in the Duleep Trophy. He had three successive hundreds in the season of 1989/90 but was only picked for India two years later for the historic one-day series against South Africa at home in 1992. He hit a match-winning 55 on début. His first class average was 89.57 at that stage and it was enough to earn selection for the tour of Australia and the World Cup. He showed himself to be an excellent team-man, but had to wait another year for his Test début, which he celebrated with a typically gutsy century against South Africa at Durban. In the home season that followed he had scores of 76, 57, and 52 not out, making the most of the limited batting opportunities which middle-order Indian batsmen had in a highly successful period. But he had a disappointing tour of Sri Lanka after that and, with such competition for batting places, he rather surprisingly found himself forced out. He remains an outstanding player of spin bowling, often coming yards down the wicket to counter it.

First-class career (1986–): 3,862 runs (59.41) including 14 centuries, and 30 catches
Test matches (11): 425 runs (42.50) including 1 century, and 9 catches

ANKOLA, Salil Ashok

(b. 1968, Sholapur) *Maharashtra, Bombay, and India*

Tall, athletic, very good-looking but extremely soft-spoken, Salil Ankola made an immediate impact on his first-class début for Maharashtra against Gujarat in the Ranji Trophy season of 1988/9. He took a hat-trick and scored a career-best 43. He followed that up with figures of 6 for 51 against Baroda and was soon attracting national attention as a bowler of great pace and skill, taking 27 wickets in his first five Ranji Trophy matches. With just one season behind him he was picked in the Indian team to tour Pakistan, despite having been left out of the Rest of India team a week earlier. India's manager for that tour, Chandu Borde, also from Maharashtra, convinced the selectors that he would be responsible for the bowler's progress and when he took 6 for 77 in the opening match, it seemed he would be proved right. He played in the first Test, but faded out, mainly due to injury problems resulting from a very long run-up. He would remember that tour, however, for a six off Imran Khan from the first ball he faced in one-day internationals. He moved to Bombay in 1989/90 in quest of a better future and after a stint with Frank Tyson, he re-emerged with a shorter run-up, a more round-arm action, less pace but with greater control. He won back his place in the limited-overs games against England in early 1993 and came up with some consistent performances. He had a lovely throwing arm but his ground-fielding was not always of international class and he lost his place after tours to New Zealand and Sharjah in 1994, despite a career-best 6 for 47 against Gujarat in 1994/5.

First-class career (1988–): 381 runs (14.11), 138 wickets (24.83), and 17 catches
Test matches (1): 6 runs (6.00) and 2 wickets (64.00)

APTE, Arvind Laxmanrao

(b. 1934, Bombay) *Bombay and India*

A right-handed opening batsman with an array of brilliant strokes, Arvind Apte toured England in 1959, scoring 881 runs (27.53), including three centuries, but played in only one Test, at Headingley, when he scored 8 and 7.

First-class career (1955–71): 2,782 runs (33.51) including 6 centuries, 2 wickets (38.00), 14 catches, and 1 stumping

APTE, Madhav Laxmanrao

(b. 1932, Bombay) *Bombay and India*

A sound right-handed batsman who opened for Bombay with his brother Arvind, Madhav Apte played in two Tests against Pakistan in 1952/3 and toured the West Indies in 1952/3. Second to 'Polly' Umrigar in the West Indian Tests, making 460 runs (51.11), he reached 50 three times in the first two Tests and in the third, at Port of Spain, made 163 not out. After this tour he was discarded, although he continued for several years in Ranji Trophy championship matches, in all making 2,070 runs (39.80).

First-class career (1951–68): 3,336 runs (38.79) including 6 centuries
Test matches (7): 542 runs (49.27) including 1 century, 0–3, and 2 catches

ARSHAD AYUB, Mohammad

(b. 1958, Hyderabad) *Hyderabad and India*

Arshad Ayub was a slightly tubby off-spinner who tended to hit the deck rather than float the ball up to the batsman. He was an unusually determined cricketer whose greatest virtue was an awareness of his limitations, both as bowler and as batsman. He played to his strengths. Above all, he was an extremely effective bowler on turning pitches where his accuracy and control made him very difficult to play. But on flat batting surfaces he was far less penetrative due to his lack of variety, especially in the air. A prolific junior cricketer, he made an impressive first-class début for India Colts against Alvin Kallicharan's 1978 West Indies team to India, with 58 runs and 3 wickets. Shortly thereafter he played his first Ranji Trophy game for Hyderabad, and though he had an admirable first-class record, higher honours were blocked by his Hyderabad colleague Shivlal Yadav. He seemed to stagnate in first-class cricket until 1986/7 when he had an outstanding all-round season and took Hyderabad to victory in the Ranji Trophy, with 18 wickets and 621 runs (77.62) including consecutive scores in the semi-final and final of 206, 174, and 80. Performances of 8 for 65 in the Duleep Trophy and 6 for 105 in the Irani Trophy earned him a place in the first Test against the West Indies in 1987/8. He took 4 for 72 in the second innings but only managed one more in the remaining three Test matches. The following season was much better for him though. He took 5 for 21 against Pakistan at Dhaka, still the best figures by an Indian in limited-overs cricket against Pakistan, and in three Test matches against New Zealand on responsive pitches took 21 wickets. In an otherwise disastrous series against the West Indies he took 5 wickets in an innings at Georgetown and at Port of Spain and seemed set for better days. But a poor tour of Pakistan where he didn't get a wicket in two Tests led to his being dropped and though he figured in a few one-day internationals after that, he was never picked for the Test side again. He continued playing for Hyderabad and South Zone, picking up a hat-trick against Kerala in 1993/4, his last season in first-class cricket.

First-class career (1978–94): 3,014 runs (28.16) including 2 centuries, 361 wickets (28.51), and 44 catches

Test matches (13): 257 runs (17.13), 41 wickets (35.07), and 2 catches

ARUN, Bharati

(b. 1962, Vijayawada) *Tamil Nadu*

A heavily built, lumbering, new-ball bowler of medium pace and a useful lower-order batsman, Bharati Arun was considered extremely lucky to play two Test matches for India in the crowded domestic season of 1986/7. He only took 11 Ranji Trophy wickets in 1985/6 but began the next season with a hat-trick against lowly Goa. He was picked to play for India under-25 against Sri Lanka and bowled his out-swingers well in a high-scoring match to get 3 for 113. A hard-hitting century in the closing stages of the match ironically contributed more to his selection to the national team. He took 3 for 76 in the only innings of the Kanpur Test after an inauspicious beginning when he slipped heavily while running in to bowl his first ball in international cricket. He was dropped for the second Test but returned to play the third at Cuttack where he got his fourth Test wicket. He toured Sharjah with the Indian team in April 1987 playing in all three one-day internationals for a total of only eleven overs. Predictably, he didn't play for India again and retired in 1991/2 with only 110 wickets from 48 first-class matches.

First-class career (1982–92): 1,652 runs (30.59), 110 wickets (32.44), and 23 catches

Test matches (2): 4 runs (4.00), 4 wickets (29.00), and 2 catches

ARUN LAL, Jagdishlal

(b. 1955, Uttar Pradesh) *Delhi, Bengal, and India*

Arun Lal was fortunate to make his first Test appearance for India in his country's first-ever Test against Sri Lanka, on the excellent batting pitch at Madras in 1982/3. He made 63 in the first innings and subsequently played three Tests against Pakistan on India's tour of their neighbouring country, 1982/3, scoring 51 at Lahore as Gavaskar's partner. A right-handed opener and good close fielder, Arun was a consistent scorer in domestic cricket, hitting four Ranji Trophy hundreds in 1983/4 when he averaged 159 in the competition. Originally from Delhi, for whom he scored 102 in his opening first-class match against Services in 1975/6, he moved to Bengal in 1981, taking a job as a marketing executive with a firm in Calcutta. Arun also played at home against West Indies (1987/8) and New Zealand (1988/9), and four Tests in the West Indies in 1988/9, emerging with honour from a tough series, but not retaining his place thereafter.

First-class career (1974–94): 10,146 runs (47.41) including 29 centuries, 21 wickets (44.33), and 141 catches

Test matches (16): 729 runs (26.03) and 13 catches

AZAD, Kirtivardhan

(b. 1959, Purnea) *Delhi and India*

A nonconformist in life and in cricket, Kirti Azad, the son of an Indian Government minister, was an attacking right-hand batsman, quickish off-spinner, and fine outfielder. After an uneventful début against England for Combined Universities in 1976/7, he made his first Ranji Trophy appearance the following season and toured Australia and New Zealand in 1980/1. He played his first Test against New Zealand at Wellington, and back at home in 1981/2 he had an extended chance when playing in the first three Tests against England. Although he scored useful runs, and more elegantly than some of his colleagues, his bowling lacked guile or variety. After a successful time in India's World Cup-winning team in England in 1983 he played two Tests at home against West Indies the following season, with little reward, and one against Pakistan, but continued to be a force in Ranji Trophy cricket, scoring 186 against Tamil Nadu in 1982/3. His best bowling figures were 7 for 63 against an England XI, 1981/2.

First-class career (1976–91): 6,435 runs (40.98) including 20 centuries, 218 wickets (30.98), and 87 catches
Test matches (7): 135 runs (11.25), 3 wickets (124.33), and 3 catches

AZHARUDDIN, Mohammed

(b. 1963, Hyderabad) *Hyderabad, South Zone, Derbyshire, and India*

Seldom has any cricketer made quite so glittering a start to his Test career as the slim, humble, smiling genius who forced his way into the Indian team to play England at Calcutta in December 1984. He scored 110, followed this with 48 and 105 at Madras and completed his part in the series with scores of 122 and 54 not out at Kanpur. No one else has hit hundreds in each of his first three Tests. Nor was it a flash in the pan: boyish in look and demeanour, Azharuddin, a devout Muslim, matured into a great batsman and one of India's most successful captains. He first played for Hyderabad in 1981/2, delighting spectators from the first with the charm of his batting. He plays the ball very late and steers it into gaps on either side of the pitch with wondrous timing and a late turn of tensile wrists. Like most of the great players his first movement is back and across his stumps. Also a brilliant fielder, he held his place in a strong Indian batting side despite a relatively unsuccessful tour of Australia in 1985/6 and quickly established his class in England in 1986, making 83 not out in the first one-day international at The Oval. He toured England again as captain in 1990, playing an innings of 121 at Lord's which dazzled all who saw it with its brilliance, and at Old Trafford in the same three-match series he scored a commanding 179. England, indeed, has acted as his Codestone. In 1992/3 he returned home as captain of a defeated team in South Africa, under pressure from press and public after a loss of personal form. Yet in the final Test at Calcutta against Graham Gooch's England touring team 'Azhar', as they know him around the cricket world, responded with a brilliant century on the opening day of the series. He went on to score 179, an innings which dictated the terms of a triumphant series for India. Throughout his period in charge, India were a match for any opposition in Test cricket, especially when conditions favoured spin, and masters of most when it came to one-day internationals. By 1994 Azhar had played Tests and internationals at home against all the other Test countries and had toured, apart from England, Australia and South Africa, Sri Lanka in 1985 and 1993, West Indies in 1988, New Zealand in 1989 and 1993, and Zimbabwe in 1992. Only in his two Tests against Zimbabwe, and against West Indies —suggesting a fallibility against the very fiercest fast bowling—has he not scored a Test hundred. He was outstanding in his first stint for Derbyshire in 1991, scoring 2,016 runs (59.29) but in 1994, his second season for the county, despite a glittering 205 against Durham, he was subsequently disappointing. In one-day internationals he had scored 4,661 runs in 174 games by 1994, at an average of 35.85, with three hundreds. At home his highest score is 226 for South Zone v. East Zone in 1983/4.

First-class career (1981–): 11,617 runs (52.80) including 40 centuries, 7 wickets (84.71), and 156 catches
Test matches (65): 4,198 runs (46.64) including 14 centuries, and 268 catches

BAIG, Abbas Ali

(b. 1939, Hyderabad) *Hyderabad, Oxford University, Somerset, and India*

Of aristocratic Muslim lineage, Abbas Ali Baig was of small build yet could hit powerfully all round the wicket and his ability to hook fast bowling stamped him as a potentially great player. Equally sprightly in the field, his throwing was fast and accurate. As a teenager, he scored a century against Mysore in the Ranji Trophy competition, and in 1959 made 1,148 runs (45.92) as a freshman at Oxford. During the long vacation he replaced the injured Vijay Manjrekar in the rather weak Indian team touring England, making 102 in his first match against Middlesex at Lord's and 26 and 112 in his first Test, at Old Trafford, when he added 109 with Nari Contractor for the second wicket; at 20 years 131 days he became the youngest Indian to score a Test century. Subsequently, he played against Australia in 1959/60, Pakistan in 1960/1, and West Indies in 1966/7, but his 50 and 58 against Australia in the third match at Bombay were his only other significant performances for his country. He toured England again in 1971, but was left out of the Tests. In all first-class cricket he scored over 7,000 runs, with a career-highest of 224 not out for South Zone against North Zone in 1966/7. He managed a number of Indian teams after he had retired, and also wrote and commentated on the game.

BANERJEE

First-class career (1954–76): 12,367 runs (34.16) including 21 centuries, 9 wickets (48.00), and 154 catches
Test matches (10): 428 runs (23.77) including 1 century, 0–15, and 6 catches

BANERJEE, Sarobindu ('Shute') Nath

(b. 1913, Calcutta; d. 1980, Calcutta) *Bengal, Nawanagar, Bihar, and India*

The first Bengali to win a place in international cricket, Shute Banerjee was a right-arm fast bowler who thrived on hard work and was a generally useful tail-end batsman who defended with an honest straight bat and hit hard in front of the wicket. His sole Test was the fifth against West Indies at Bombay in 1948, when he scored 5 and 8 and took 5 for 127. He toured England in 1936 and 1946 when he shared in India's record tenth-wicket stand, against Surrey at The Oval. Coming in at number 11, with the score at 205 for 9, to join C. T. Sarwate, he hit 121, the two bowlers adding 249 in 3 hours 10 minutes in masterly fashion. His best bowling in an innings was 8 for 25 for Nawanagar against Maharashtra in 1941/2 and his career-highest, 138 for Bihar against Bengal out of 235 in 1952/3. He led Bihar from 1942 to 1958.

First-class career (1931–60): 3,671 runs (20.50) including 5 centuries, and 381 wickets (26.61)

BANERJEE, Subroto

(b. 1969, Patna) *Bihar and India*

Subroto Banerjee is a lively bowler with a lovely action who can swing the ball both ways and play some lusty shots late in the order. Playing for the relatively low-profile Bihar and East Zone teams in first-class cricket, he attracted very little attention in spite of the fact that he had been to Australia for the Youth World Cup and to New Zealand with an India under-19 team. But at the MRF Pace Academy under Dennis Lillee, he was highly rated. Though he took 29 wickets in the Ranji Trophy season of 1989/90 and had some consistent performances for East Zone, especially in one-day cricket his selection for the tour of Australia in 1991/2 as one of four new-ball bowlers came as a major surprise. So indeed was India's decision to go into the Sydney Test with four seamers and no spinner. It allowed Banerjee to make his Test début and he certainly made it memorable with the wickets of Mark Taylor, Geoff Marsh, and Mark Waugh on the first day. Oddly, he was not called to bowl again in the Test

even though India were switching bowlers around in the second innings in quest of victory. Since he did not play a Test after that, his figures of 3 for 47 give him an impressive average of 15.66. He scored 3 runs in the match (3.00). He had a good one-day début too, getting 3 for 30 against the West Indies at Perth, still the best figures by an Indian on début in one-day internationals. He played in the World Cup of 1992 and even toured South Africa in 1992/3 but only played occasionally in one-day internationals. His arrival coincided with that of Javagal Srinath and made him the fourth seamer for India; his bowling seemed to lose its sting completely thereafter, leading to one of the most modest domestic records for a player who has represented his country. Banerjee always seemed a little too laid-back to be competitive but he remained a very popular member of the side, though that had more to do with his singing skills!

First-class career (1987–): 844 runs (21.64), 87 wickets (29.52), and 19 catches

BANERJEE, Sudangsu Abinash

(b. 1919, Calcutta) *Bengal, Bihar, Maharashtra, and India*

A right-arm medium-pace bowler, 'Montu' Banerjee played in a sole Test against West Indies, at Calcutta in 1948/9, scoring 0, taking 5 for 181 and holding 3 catches.

First-class career (1941–54): 232 runs (7.03) and 92 wickets (23.28)

BAQA JILANI, Mohammed

(b. 1911, Jullundur; d. 1941, Jullundur) *Northern India and India*

In the course of taking 5 for 7 in 25 balls for Northern India against Southern Punjab (who totalled 22) in 1934/5, Baqa Jilani performed the first-recorded hat-trick in Ranji Trophy matches. A right-arm fast-medium bowler and useful lower-order batsman, he toured England in 1936, and in his sole Test, the last at The Oval, he scored 4 not out and 12 and took 0 for 55. He died before reaching the age of 30.

First-class career (1934–9): 928 runs (18.56) including 1 century, 83 wickets (19.93), and 12 catches

BEDADE, Atul Chandrakant

(b. 1966, Bombay) *Baroda*

A stocky man of medium height, Atul Bedade hit the ball harder than anyone else in contemporary

Indian cricket. A left-hander, his method was more blunt than elegant: even against the spinners, he relied more on power than footwork. Indeed, as he hit one huge six after another, it seemed he had no need to use his feet at all. He bulldozed his way into the Indian team in April 1994 after two highly productive years for Baroda, for whom he often batted as high as number four. In the 1993/4 season he hit three hundreds and two fifties in the Ranji Trophy, invariably at a rate faster than run-a-ball. He had more than thirty sixes that year and his progress was followed keenly by the national selectors who needed someone to bat like that for India at number six. They gambled on him for the Australasia Cup at Sharjah where, after a shaky start against fast bowling of the kind he had never faced, he almost got it right in the final against Pakistan, where he made 44 from 45 balls including four sixes. But in the easy batting conditions in India he discovered that there were few opportunities to bat at number six and invariably he was expected to hit a six every time he batted. Though he managed two good innings against the West Indies, including a top score of 51, he came under increasing pressure and towards the end of the season, and after a succession of poor scores, he vanished quite as dramatically as he had arrived. In 12 one-day internationals he scored 158 runs (22.57) and held 4 catches.

First-class career (1990–): 1,609 runs (43.48) including 7 centuries, and 10 catches

BEDI, Bishan Singh

(b. 1946, Amritsar) *Punjab, Delhi, Northamptonshire, and India*

One of the most popular cricketers of all time, Bishan Singh Bedi was for 12 years an almost indispensable bulwark of Indian cricket and also an aesthetic joy to watch. A very solidly built Sikh from Amritsar whose gaily coloured patkas adorned cricket grounds the world over and made him instantly recognizable, 'Bishy' was slim as a youth but filled out without losing an extraordinary looseness of limb and a balletic grace in movement. In the field he constantly flexed muscles and fingers to keep himself supple for the supreme moment when he delivered the ball. Easily the most subtle and artistic slow left-arm orthodox bowler of his generation, he ran in on the balls of his feet—they appeared indeed almost to be ball-bearings—and delivered from the highest possible point with a balance and poise which would catch the breath of the

connoisseur. Every nuance of the spinner's art was at Bedi's command at his peak: changes of pace; variations both of flight, and of degrees of spin; curve and loop through the air; the ball swinging in with the arm; the sudden faster one; and the orthodox leg-break to the right-hander, bouncing high because of the perfection of the action. He made his first-class début for Northern Punjab in the Ranji Trophy in 1961/2 at the age of 15 and subsequently transferred to Delhi. He played with success for Northamptonshire from 1972 to 1977 and captained India in twenty-two Tests from 1975/6, winning six. He created headlines more than once: objecting to the use of vaseline gauzes by two England bowlers in the Madras Test in 1976/7, and at Kingston, Jamaica in 1976 declaring India's first and second innings closed as a protest against the intimidatory tactics of the West Indian fast bowlers. Bedi was a consistent wicket-taker since playing his first Test in 1966/7. Against England at home in 1972/3 he took 25 wickets (25.28) including 5 for 63 in 40 overs in the second innings of the second Test at Calcutta. In the first innings of the fourth and fifth Tests of the series he delivered 68.5 and 69 overs respectively, having begun the series with figures of 86–43–109–5 in the match at Delhi. Against England in 1976/7 (when captain) he took 25 wickets again at 22.96, taking 6 for 71 in the second innings at Bangalore, where India won for the only time. Earlier the same season he had taken 22 wickets at 13.18 in three Tests against New Zealand. Thus in one Indian season he took 47 wickets in eight Tests. His most prolific series, again as captain, was in Australia in 1977/8 when he took 31 wickets (23.87) including 10 for 194 in the second Test at Perth. On his first encounter with Australia in 1969/70 he had headed the bowling averages with 21 wickets (20.57), following match figures of 9 for 108 at Delhi in the third Test with 7 for 98 in Australia's first innings in the fourth match, at Calcutta. He took more wickets for India than any other bowler, and, batting right-handed in spectacles, often contributed some hard-hitting innings at number ten in the order. He twice took 100 wickets in an English season with Northamptonshire and his best figures in first-class cricket were 7 for 5 (13 for 34 in the match) for Delhi against Jammu and Kashmir in 1974/5. He was pushed out of first-class cricket earlier than he would have wished, and was involved in disputes over the captaincy of Delhi before regaining a position of authority and not only continuing to play until 1981, but also fulfilling his wish to give something back to

Indian cricket by coaching young players. He was Manager/Coach to the national side in England in 1990.

First-class career (1961–81): 3,584 runs (11.37), 1,560 wickets (21.69), and 172 catches
Test matches (67): 656 runs (8.98), 266 wickets (28.71), and 26 catches

BHANDARI, Prakash

(b. 1935, Delhi) *Delhi, Bengal, and India*

An exciting, hard-hitting right-handed batsman and useful off-break bowler, Prakash Bhandari toured Pakistan in 1954/5, and at home played against New Zealand in 1955/6 and Australia in 1956/7, but did not establish himself in the Test team. He recorded the fastest century in Indian first-class cricket in 60 minutes for Bengal against Rajasthan at Udaipur in 1961/2; and his career-highest was 227 for Delhi against Patiala in 1957/8.

First-class career (1952–71): 2,453 runs (32.70) including 4 centuries, and 122 wickets (28.17)
Test matches (3): 77 runs (19.25), 0–39, and 1 catch

BHAT, Adwai Raghuram Bimba

(b. 1958, Mangalore) *Karnataka and India*

A slow left-arm spinner, Raghuram Bhat, despite his name, was very much a specialist bowler. Born at Mangalore, he made his first appearance in 1979/80 and figured prominently at once with 41 Ranji Trophy wickets in the season at 21.24. Two years later he bettered this by two and in 1983/4 was rewarded with a first Test cap, against Pakistan at Nagpur. In a drawn game, he took 2 for 65 from 39 overs. A few weeks later, in the first Test against West Indies at Kanpur, his worthy figures were 2 for 86 in 34 overs in a total of 454. He did not appear again, despite another good season in 1984/5 when he collected 47 first-class wickets at 20 each, including 11 for 141 in the match against Tamil Nadu. His six wickets in the Duleep Trophy final that year helped South Zone to defeat the North and confirmed his status as one of the best spinners in India. He turned the ball appreciably and used skilful variations.

First-class career (1979–93): 754 runs (13.00), 374 wickets (22.66), and 41 catches
Test matches (2): 6 runs (3.00), and 4 wickets (37.75)

BINNY, Roger Michael Humphrey

(b. 1955, Bangalore) *Karnataka and India*

The only Anglo-Indian to play for India, Roger Binny is an adaptable all-round cricketer. Quite tall, he bowled steadily, right-arm and medium-fast, fielded well, and batted capably in any position. As an opener for Delhi he scored 115, the first of six centuries in the two first innings of the historic 1981/2 Ranji Trophy final. Binny appeared first in first-class cricket in 1975/6, and a year later made a good impression for a Universities side against the MCC touring team at Nagpur. In the 1977/8 Ranji Trophy he proved his class as a batsman, scoring 563 runs (56.30) including an innings of 211 not out against Kerala when he shared an unbroken opening stand of 451 with S. Desai, a record in Indian cricket. He played in the full series of six Tests against the touring Pakistan team in 1979/80, scoring 143 runs (17.87) and taking 11 wickets at a cost of 36 each: he bowled the occasional good spell but on true pitches lacked the necessary control for a bowler of relatively mild pace. He opened the batting in the Golden Jubilee Test against England in Bombay (1979/80) and the following season toured Australia and New Zealand, playing a Test in each country without, however, making a really substantial contribution. It was his selection for India's Prudential World Cup team in England in 1983 which gave his career a new lease of life. With his accurate bowling, occasional contributions with the bat and strong arm from the deep, he proved a vital member of the XI which surprised the world not only by reaching the final at Lord's but actually winning it, against the 'unbeatable' West Indies. He was man-of-the-match in a crucial qualifying game against Australia, which India had to win to go through, and in the final removed the potential match-winner, Clive Lloyd, in addition to conceding only 23 runs in ten overs. He was equally effective when helping his country to win another rich prize in the World Championship in Australia in 1984/5 and shared also in various triumphs in the Middle East. Returning to Test cricket at home to Pakistan in 1983/4, he made 83 not out (top score) in the first innings in Bangalore, and 54 at Jullunder in his only other innings in the series. He kept his place throughout the home six-match series against West Indies in 1983/4, scoring 270 runs at an average of 24 and, although lightly bowled, taking seven wickets. His best bowling performance was 8 for 22 against Haryana in 1982/3. An inspiring captain of Karnataka, he sealed his place on the 1986 tour of England by scoring 115 for South Zone against West in the Duleep Trophy final, and at Headingley helped India to an unprecedented second successive Test victory by taking a career-best 5 for 40 in England's first innings of 102.

First-class career (1975–91): 6,579 runs (34.08) including 14 centuries, 205 wickets (36.02), and 91 catches

Test matches (27): 830 runs (23.05), 47 wickets (32.63), and 11 catches

BORDE, Chandrakant Gulabrao

(b. 1934, Maharashtra) *Maharashtra, Baroda, and India*

An attractive and unruffled right-handed batsman who showed no fear of fast bowling and drove and pulled to leg with assurance, a leg-break and googly bowler of excellent length, and a brilliant slip fielder, Chandra Borde made 55 and 61 not out for Maharashtra against Bombay in 1952/3 on his first-class début as a schoolboy, and from 1959 until 1967 played in 55 Tests. He toured England in 1959 and 1967, West Indies in 1961/2, and Australasia in 1967/8, and at home played against West Indies in 1958/9 and 1966/7, Australia in 1959/60, 1964/5, and 1969/70, Pakistan in 1960/1, England in 1961/2 and 1963/4, and New Zealand in 1964/5. In his first Test series, against West Indies in 1958/9, he made 109 and 96 in the fifth match at Delhi. In 1960/1 he headed the batting averages against Pakistan with 330 runs (82.50), including 177 not out in 9 hours (his Test-highest) in the fourth match at Madras. He tended to bowl less with time but his cultured (if sometimes slow) batting remained valuably consistent. Against England in 1961/2 he made 314 runs (44.85) and took 16 wickets (28.75); in the fourth match at Calcutta, when India defeated England for only the second time, he hit 68 and 61—top-scoring each time—and captured 4 for 65 in the first innings. In 1964/5 against New Zealand he made more runs than anyone, 371 (61.83), and in 1966/7 against the West Indies easily headed the batting averages with 346 runs (57.66). In his last tour, to Australasia in 1967/8, he was consistency personified, with 408 runs (31.38) in the Tests, although his highest score was a mere 69 in the first Test at Adelaide, when he captained India, unsuccessfully, for the only time. He was a prolific all-rounder in the Ranji Trophy competition, exceeding 4,500 runs (average 51) and 100 wickets. His career-highest was 202 for Maharashtra against Baroda in 1969/70

and his best bowling 7 for 44 for Baroda against Maharashtra in 1958/9.

First-class career (1952–74): 12,805 runs (40.91) including 30 centuries, 331 wickets (27.32), and 159 catches

Test matches (55): 3,061 runs (35.59) including 5 centuries, 52 wickets (46.48), and 37 catches

BOSE, Gopal

(b. 1947, Calcutta) *Bengal*

Gopal Bose was a steady and scholarly-looking opening batsman, a consistent scorer in Indian domestic cricket, who also bowled off-breaks. He played 10 years for Bengal, averaging 38.51 in the Ranji Trophy, but his best season was 1973/4 when he made 170 for the Rest of India in the Irani Trophy against Bombay and toured Sri Lanka with the Indian team. In the first unofficial Test he scored 104, suggesting that India had perhaps found a good partner for Sunil Gavaskar. But on the subsequent, and totally disastrous, tour of England he only managed 328 runs at 18.22. He did not play in the Tests but in the second one-day international at The Oval he scored 13 and bowled his off-breaks well to return figures of 1 for 39 from 11 overs. He played his last first-class match for East Zone in the Duleep Trophy in 1978/9, retiring from the game when he was still relatively young.

First-class career (1968–78): 3,741 runs (30.91) including 8 centuries, 71 wickets (26.83), and 39 catches

CHANDRASEKHAR, Bhagwat Subrahmanya

(b. 1945, Mysore) *Mysore and India*

Chandrasekhar, universally shortened to 'Chandra', was unique in style and, in his own era, in achievement too. No other leg-spinner, in an age when the art gradually became almost extinct, was so consistently a match-winner. This slim, handsome, bearded South Indian, undoubtedly one of the worst batsmen ever to play Test cricket (he alone 'achieved' four pairs of noughts), gave Indian cricket many of its finest hours, notably when he bowled his country to their first success both in England (he took 6 for 38 in England's second innings at The Oval in 1971, bowling them out for 101) and in Australia, when in the New Year Test of 1978 he took 12 for 104 in the match at Melbourne. Always likely to bowl an unplayable ball, Chandra's snake-like venom came partly from the extraordinary speed with which he turned his arm over. Right-handed, although he threw in with his left arm, his bowling arm was withered by polio at the age of 5 but he turned the handicap into an advantage. After a relatively lengthy run-up of some 10 yards, beginning with the ball held in front of his face in both hands as if he were taking aim at the stumps, the wasted limb twirled past his right ear in a vertical plane and the ball hummed out of the back of the hand, sending down googlies, fizzing top-spinners, and occasional leg-breaks at near medium pace. Full tosses and long-hops were not infrequent, yet such was his unorthodoxy and unpredictability that batsmen frequently missed the chance to put away his bad balls and indeed often hit them into the hands of a waiting fielder. Chandra first came to light for Mysore in the Ranji Trophy at the age of 17. Making his Test début against England at Bombay in 1963/4, he took 4 for 67 in 40 overs on a slow pitch. The following year against Australia he bowled India to victory on the same Bombay ground with 8 for 123 in the match. In 1966/7 he took 18 wickets (28.5) against the West Indies and in England in 1967 16 wickets (27.18) in the series and 57 wickets on the tour. In 1971 he took 50 wickets on the tour. His peak, however, was reached in India in 1972/3 when he took 35 wickets in five Tests against England, the most by an Indian in any series, at a cost of 18.91, beginning the series with 8 for 79 in England's first innings at Delhi. Having taken 17 wickets in three Tests against New Zealand in 1976/7, he lost form against England but it was significant that the moment that he recaptured his unique bite India did better. His 5 for 50 in the second innings at Madras came too late, but at Bangalore in the fourth match he took 6 for 76 and 3 for 75 as India won. Against Australia in 1977/8 he took 28 wickets (25.14) taking his 200th wicket in his 48th Test in the historic win at Melbourne. However, a recurring injury in his left heel restricted him the following season, and in England in 1979 he appeared to have lost his magic. He did not play Test cricket again and, after a little more domestic cricket, retired to the relative obscurity of work in a bank. A road accident later forced him to move about in a wheel-chair.

First-class career (1963–80): 600 runs (4.61), 1,063 wickets (24.04), and 107 catches

Test matches (58): 167 runs (4.07), 242 wickets (29.74), and 25 catches

CHANDRASEKHAR, Vakkadurai Bikshewaran

(b. 1961, Madras) *Tamil Nadu*

It is not difficult to see why V. B. Chandrasekhar was always referred to by his initials. His batting style, however, was less complicated than his name, and he was a much better batsman, at least, than his famous namesake, Bhagwat Chandrasekhar. Especially at the start of his career, he believed that every ball should, if possible, be hit to the boundary: in 1988/9 he scored a century off only 56 balls, playing for Tamil Nadu against the Rest of India in the Irani Trophy. It included eight sixes and eight fours and was part of an opening partnership of 154 in 22.4 overs that took the Tamil Nadu to victory. Not surprisingly, 'V.B.' and Srikkanth made a popular opening pair for Tamil Nadu. That century won him a place in the one-day games against New Zealand later in the year. But in four matches he only managed one fifty, scoring 73 runs in all at an average of 18.25. He was picked again, for the tour to New Zealand in early 1990 (where he also served as the reserve wicket-keeper), after centuries in the semi-final and final of the Duleep Trophy. He played in three of the four one-day internationals, making only 15 runs in all and even losing his opening spot. His opportunities dried up after that and having made such a late entry into first-class cricket (waiting till he completed a graduation course in engineering) he was not growing any younger.

First-class career (1986–): 3,690 runs (40.10) including 7 centuries, 43 catches, and 2 stumpings

CHAUHAN, Chetandra Pratap Singh

(b. 1947, Bareilly) *Maharashtra, Delhi, and India*

A small, solid, determined, and unflappable right-handed opening batsman, who cut vigorously and played in several successful opening stands with Sunil Gavaskar, Chetan Chauhan was also a fine fielder at short-leg, with very quick reflexes. After fleeting appearances against Australia and New Zealand in 1969/70 and England in 1972/3 he established himself on the 1977/8 tour of Australia, scoring 88 in the second Test at Perth, averaging 32.41 in the Tests and making 577 runs at 36.06 in all first-class games on the tour. Against Pakistan in 1978/9 he made 212 runs in three Tests, making 93 at Lahore and sharing with Gavaskar in an opening stand of 192. In six Tests against the West Indies in the same year he scored 331 runs, including 52 and 84 at Bombay, averaging 41.37 in the series. He batted steadily in England in 1979, his top score, in a series interrupted by rain, being 80 at The Oval when his partnership of 213 for the first wicket with Gavaskar passed the previous highest Indian opening stand in England and made possible India's remarkable attempt to score 438 in the fourth innings to win, although they eventually fell nine runs short. More valuable and consistent batting, not least in Australia in 1980/1 when Gavaskar was out of form, made him the only Test player to have scored more than 2,000 Test runs without scoring a century. When he was unaccountably dropped from the side before the series against England in 1981/2 (amid dark allegations of 'cricket politics') he had made sixteen Test fifties with a highest score of 97. In first-class cricket his highest score was 207 for Maharashtra v. Virarbha at Poona in 1972/3. He was an occasional off-spin bowler.

First-class career (1967–85): 11,143 runs (40.22) including 21 centuries, 51 wickets (34.13), and 190 catches

Test matches (40): 2,084 runs (31.57), 2 wickets (53.00), and 38 catches

CHAUHAN, Rajesh Kumar

(b. 1966, Ranchi) *Madhya Pradesh and India*

A big-hearted off-spinner with an unusual action, Rajesh Chauhan prefers to push the ball through rather than toss it up in the more traditional manner of Indian spinners. Strangely, he owes his emergence at international level to a sudden drought of off-spinners in India. After encouraging performances which included 6 for 62 against a powerful West Zone side in the Duleep Trophy in 1992 and five wickets in the Irani Trophy match, he found himself in the team for the first Test against England in early 1993. Playing the third spinner's role, he took nine wickets in the series but always kept the pressure up with some tight spells. He played thirteen consecutive Tests during a period in which India did not lose a single match, until he lost his place in the final Test against the West Indies in late 1994. India promptly lost. He often produces prodigious turn but lack of variation in flight tends to make him predictable. His style seems more suited to the one-day game where his fighting qualities add an extra dimension to his cricket. Chauhan made his first-class début at the age of 22 for Madhya Pradesh where, in partnership with Hirwani, he contributed to the emergence of a powerful regional team. He was a consistent wicket-taker,

though, ironically, he first attracted attention with a hard-hitting century, against Bombay, batting at number eight.

First-class career (1988–): 1,034 runs (20.68) including 1 century, 167 wickets (31.46), and 35 catches

Test matches (13): 64 runs (9.14), 33 wickets (34.87), and 8 catches

CHOWDHURY, Nirode Ranjan

(b. 1923, Jamshedpur; d. 1979, Durgapur, Pakistan) *Bengal and India*

A lively right-arm medium-pace bowler, Nirode Chowdhury toured England in 1952, taking 24 wickets (31.00) but not being selected for the Tests. At home he played one Test against West Indies in 1948/9 and one against England in 1951/2.

First-class career (1941–59): 419 runs (7.22), 200 wickets (25.15), and 22 catches

Test matches (2): 3 runs (3.00) and 1–205

COLAH, Sorabji Hormasji Munchersha

(b. 1902, Bombay; d. 1950, Ahmedabad) *Western India, Nawanagar, and India*

A fast-scoring right-handed batsman, medium-pace change-bowler, and brilliant fielder, Sorabji Colah toured England in 1932, playing in the Lord's Test. He also appeared in the first Test in India, against England at Bombay in 1933/4.

First-class career (1922–42): 3,578 runs (29.08) including 6 centuries, 6 wickets (46.50), and 51 catches

Test matches (2): 69 runs (17.25) and 2 catches

CONTRACTOR, Nariman Jehangirji

(b. 1934, Gujarat) *Gujarat, Railways, and India*

A watchful, left-handed opening batsman, Nari Contractor's timing and crisp stroke-play could be superb. He was an occasional right-arm medium-pace bowler and a very good close field. He captained India on 12 occasions with mixed success, until the match with Barbados at Bridgetown in 1961/2, when he was knocked senseless by a ball from Charlie Griffith into which he ducked: the back of his skull was fractured and for many hours he was gravely ill. Though he recovered, Contractor never played international cricket again; he had toured England in 1959, and at home played against New Zealand in 1955/6, Australia in 1956/7 and 1959/60, West Indies in 1958/9, Pakistan in 1960/1, and England in

1961/2. It was in 1959/60, in the home series against Australia, that he blossomed, scoring 438 runs (43.80), including 108 in the third match at Bombay. In 1960/1 against Pakistan he made 319 runs (53.16) in consistent vein. Although he made only 180 runs (22.50) in the 1961/2 series, he had the pleasure of leading India to their first win in a rubber against England. On his début in first-class cricket in 1952/3 he scored 152 and 102 not out for Gujarat against Baroda (equalling Arthur Morris's début record). His career-highest was 176 for Gujarat against Bombay in 1956/7, and the following season he made four hundreds in successive innings in the Ranji Trophy competition. In first-class cricket from 1952 until 1971—he captained Gujarat for some ten years—he made over 8,000 runs. His second name has wrongly appeared in earlier records as 'Jamshedji'. His son, H.W., played for Bombay.

First-class career (1952–71): 8,611 runs (39.86) including 22 centuries, 26 wickets (40.00), and 72 catches

Test matches (31): 1,611 runs (31.58) including 1 century, 1–80, and 18 catches

DALMIYA, Jagmohan

(b. 1940, Calcutta)

A shortish man with rimmed glasses and an unmistakable accent, Jagmohan Dalmiya brought to the Board of Control for Cricket in India a refreshingly contemporary air. Steeped in mistrust for many years, the relationship between the Board and the cricketers was immediately improved thanks in no small measure to an appreciation of the obvious, but hitherto unrecognized, need for financial stability. Dalmiya, who comes from a family of businessmen, achieved this by marketing cricket in India as it never had been before. Television rights were sold for the first time and sponsorship fees were hiked. But most important, through his persuasive powers, India started getting heard with more respect in world cricket. His detractors, of whom there are a few, complain that Indian cricket under him would sell itself to just about anything. But given the fact that it has been woefully undersold for decades, his aggressive approach was perhaps necessary. His bold organization of the Cricket Association of Bengal's Diamond Jubilee in 1993 and the conversion of the famous Eden Gardens to a floodlit cricket centre were memorable moments as was the 'acquisition' of the 1996 World Cup, in conjunction with Pakistan and Sri Lanka, by skilful financial inducements to the non-Test countries.

DANI, Hemchandra Tukaram

(b. 1933, Maharashtra) *Maharashtra, Services, and India*

A sound right-handed batsman and a fast-medium in-swing bowler who developed off-breaks and leg-breaks, 'Bal' Dani toured Pakistan in 1954/5 without being selected for the Tests. His sole Test appearance was the third against Pakistan at Bombay in 1952/3, when he did not bat, took 1 for 19 and held 1 catch. He has served on the Indian Board's Committee for Test Matches and Tours.

First-class career (1951–73): 6,459 runs (44.54) including 17 centuries, and 198 wickets (21.97)

DE MELLO, Anthony Stanislaus

(b. 1900, Karachi; d. 1961, Delhi) *Delhi*

Though he played first-class cricket for Delhi and led the Rest in the Bombay Pentangulars, Anthony de Mello played a far more crucial role in Indian cricket as an administrator with vision in the turbulent early decades of Indian cricket. He was one of the founders of the Board of Control for Cricket in India in 1928/9 and played a leading role in the setting up of the Ranji Trophy in 1934/5. He was the first secretary of the Indian Board, holding the job from 1928/9 to 1937/8, a period in which India toured England twice and hosted them once. But perhaps his most lasting contribution to Indian cricket was the construction of the Brabourne Stadium and the creation of the Cricket Club of India. It was he who persuaded Lord Brabourne to part with expensive land at virtually no cost for the setting up of a cricket stadium in return for which the stadium was named after the Governor of Bombay. It is a measure of his administrative skills that he was able to stay in control of Indian cricket in an era of the most fiendish manœuvring. He was president of the Board from 1946/7 to 1950/1 when he was finally toppled and left the Imperial Hotel in Delhi with a vow never to return to Indian cricket—a sad departure for a man who was in many ways a pillar of modern Indian cricket.

DEODHAR, Dinkar Balwant

(b. 1892, Pune; d. 1993, Pune) *Hindus and Maharashtra*

Till he died in August 1993 Professor D. B. Deodhar was the oldest surviving first-class cricketer, having made his first-class début as far back as 1911/12 for the Hindus in the Bombay Triangular tournament. In 1926/7 he became the first Indian to score a century (148) in an unofficial Test against Arthur Gilligan's MCC side. In fact Deodhar only appeared in two unofficial Tests, a record which does his great batting skills no justice. Sadly for him, by the time India played its first official Test he was 40 and, though he was one of the dominant personalities of Indian cricket, he was probably considered too old. Paradoxically, he led India against Ceylon in 1940/1 at the age of 48 and led Maharashtra to successive Ranji Trophy triumphs in 1939/40 and 1940/1 when armed with a young side, 'The Professor and his Boys' as they were called. He made 157 against Western India in 1939/40 and the following year, at the age of 48 years and 308 days, he flayed the Bombay attack to make 246. In the semi-final that year he scored 196. Indeed, age seemed to give birth to new pride and in 1944/5, at the age of 52 years and 233 days, he scored a century in each innings (105 and 141) against Nawanagar. When he retired in 1946/7, he had averaged 52.86 in the Ranji Trophy and both within his state of Maharashtra and indeed, all over India, he was greatly venerated. India's limited-overs zonal championship has been named after him since its inception in 1973/4. Apart from being a brilliant cricketer, the Professor, whose origins were humble, was a staunch nationalist, believing in the might of the Maratha movement.

First-class career (1911–47): 4,522 runs (39.32) including 9 centuries, 11 wickets (53.27), and 70 catches

DESAI, Ramakant Bhikaji

(b. 1939, Bombay) *Bombay and India*

In an outstanding first season in the Ranji Trophy in 1958/9 'Tiny' Desai took 50 wickets (11.10) and on his Test début in the final match at Delhi against West Indies took 4 for 169 in 49 overs in a total of 644 for 8. He was a slightly built but lissom right-arm fast-medium out-swing bowler who opened India's attack with endless liveliness, courage, and stamina. Though overworked on the 1959 England tour, he returned to India a much improved bowler. He also toured the West Indies in 1961/2 and Australasia in 1967/8; at home he played against Australia in 1959/60, Pakistan in 1960/1, England in 1961/2 and 1963/4, and New Zealand in 1964/5. Against Pakistan he took 21 wickets (29.80) including 8 for 190 in the match at Delhi. Against New

Zealand in 1964/5 he took 6 for 56 in the first innings at Bombay. A very popular man, he was often bowled into the ground, but usually came up smiling! Sometimes an equally spirited batsman, he made 85 at number ten against Pakistan in the first match in Pakistan in 1960/1. His best bowling figures were 7 for 46 (11 for 120 in the match) against Rajasthan in 1960/1.

First-class career (1958–72): 2,384 runs (18.19) including 1 century, 468 wickets (24.10), and 50 catches

Test matches (28): 418 runs (13.48), 74 wickets (37.31), and 9 catches

DILAWAR HUSSAIN, Dr

(b. 1907, Lahore; d. 1967, Lahore) *Central India, Muslims, Northern India, Uttar Pradesh, and India*

Of big physique, a wicket-keeper and right-handed defensive batsman, Dilawar Hussain had an ungainly crouching batting stance but possessed unwearying patience and admirable determination. A Cambridge undergraduate, he assisted India on the 1936 England tour, when the two other wicket-keepers were unfit; he made 620 runs (44.28) and, in his only Test at The Oval, scored 35 and 54. Yet he never represented the university in first-class cricket. On his Test début in India, against England in the second match at Calcutta, he opened the batting and made 59 and 57, the top score in each innings. Principal of MAO College, Lahore, Dr Hussain was a founder-member of the Board of Control of Cricket in Pakistan and a Test selector.

First-class career (1924–41): 2,394 runs (28.16) including 4 centuries, and 102 dismissals (70 c., 32 st.)

Test matches (3): 254 runs (42.33) and 7 dismissals (6 c., 1 st.)

DIVECHA, Ramesh Vithaldao

(b. 1927, Bombay) *Bombay, Northamptonshire, Oxford University, and India*

A well-built and versatile right-arm bowler, either fast-medium or off-break, and a useful batsman, 'Buck' Divecha played once for Northamptonshire against Australia in 1948. Touring England with the 1952 India team, he took 50 wickets (25.88), but achieved little in the Tests. At home he played against England in 1951/2 and Pakistan in 1952/3, also disappointingly.

First-class career (1948–63): 1,423 runs (20.32), 217 wickets (24.88), and 35 catches

Test matches (5): 60 runs (12.00), 11 wickets (32.81), and 5 catches

DOSHI, Dilip Razaklal

(b. 1947, Rajkot) *Bengal, Nottinghamshire, Warwickshire, Northumberland, Hertfordshire, and India*

A gentle, intelligent character, philosophical and humorous behind a studious front, Dilip Doshi's greatest virtue is patience. He needed it when waiting years after making his first-class début before getting his chance to succeed Bishan Bedi as India's first choice left-arm orthodox spinner, and he used it to great effect as a bowler. Playing cricket in glasses, and less liquid of movement than the great Bedi, Doshi nevertheless had an easy action, turning the ball sharply, and bowled with exceptional accuracy. Mixing flight and pace thoughtfully, he lured batsmen to destruction in a wide variety of cricket, not least in Test matches. He quickly made his mark at the highest level, reaching 100 wickets in his 28th Test, against Sri Lanka in 1982/3. His first series was against Australia in 1979/80 when he took 27 wickets (23.33) with eight wickets in both the first and last Tests of the series. A further 18 wickets at 28 each followed in another series against Pakistan the same season and at last Doshi, 11 years after his début, was on his way. He remained an automatic selection until 1982/3, doing well against England at home and away in 1981/2 when he took 35 wickets in nine Tests. He played four of the five Tests in Pakistan in 1982/3, before losing his place to the younger Maninder Singh, despite having taken six worthy wickets (including 5 for 90) in the drawn first Test in Lahore. Discarded after one Test against Pakistan in 1983/4, he continued to play for Bengal. His wide experience of cricket in England includes first-class cricket for Nottinghamshire and Warwickshire, 2nd XI appearances for two other counties and minor county cricket with Hertfordshire (in 1976, when he bowled them to a notable Gillette Cup triumph over Essex) and Northumberland. His best season was in 1980 when he took 101 wickets for Warwickshire at 26.73. Although apparently a rabbit with the bat, which he wields left-handed, he has been known to surprise opposing bowlers with stubborn defence or a few long-handled blows.

First-class career (1968–86): 1,442 runs (7.87), 898 wickets (26.58), and 62 catches

Test matches (33): 129 runs (4.60), 114 wickets (30.71), and 10 catches

DUNGARPUR, Raj Singh

(b. 1935, Dungarpur) *Rajasthan*

A man, or gentleman, of many parts in Indian cricket, Raj Singh would perhaps best like himself described as an obsessive cricket-lover. Hailing from the small princely state of Dungarpur in Rajasthan, he opened the bowling for his state side during their best years and thrice led them to the final of the Ranji Trophy. By his own admission, he was an average cricketer but his role in Indian cricket was to be crucial. He was a very popular manager of Indian touring teams, especially to England in 1982 and again in 1986 and to Pakistan in 1984/5. As a cricket commentator, his has been a mildly opinionated but always highly respected voice. But it was as a selector that he became genuinely controversial, especially as chairman of the committee in the late 1980s. His views were thought to be radical: he was influential in the dropping of Jimmy Amarnath in 1988 and in the appointment of Azharuddin as captain in 1990. But he could display a sense of caring, witnessed best in the manner in which Sachin Tendulkar was introduced to international cricket. As president of the Cricket Club of India he has been instrumental in giving the Brabourne Stadium a more contemporary yet dignified look and, indeed, for bringing the game back to what many believe is the real home of cricket in India.

First-class career (1956–71): 1,019 runs (17.27), 181 wickets (26.47), and 47 catches

DURANI, Salim Aziz

(b. 1934, Kabul, Afghanistan) *Saurashtra, Gujarat, Rajasthan, and India*

An erratically brilliant left-handed batsman who could hit courageously or defend dourly, Salim Durani was a slow left-arm bowler who, despite his rather lazy-looking action, could extract nip from the pitch and subtly vary changes of flight and line. Always aggressive, he often produced balls that beat batsmen at the top of their form. Tall and good-looking, he was offered the chance to become a film star. As a schoolboy, he made 108 and 41 on his first-class début for Saurashtra against Gujarat. He toured the West Indies in 1961/2 and 1970/1, and at home played against Australia in 1959/60 and 1964/5, England in 1961/2, 1963/4, and 1972/3, and New Zealand in 1964/5. His only visit to England was in 1960 to play for Stockport in the Lancashire League. Against England in 1961/2 he took 23 wickets

(27.04), besides making 199 runs (24.87). In the fourth match at Calcutta his match analysis was 8 for 113, and in the fifth at Madras 10 for 177. A few months later in the Caribbean he again took most wickets in the Tests, 17 (35.29) and finished third in the batting with 259 runs (28.77), which included his sole Test century, 104 in the fourth match at Port of Spain. In his second series against England he took only 11 wickets (42.81), but scored 230 runs (28.75). Losing his spinning place to Bishan Bedi, he came back in the early 1970s and in his final series, against England, made 243 runs (40.50).

First-class career (1953–78): 8,545 runs (33.37) including 14 centuries, and 484 wickets (26.09)

Test matches (29): 1,202 runs (25.04) including 1 century, 75 wickets (35.42), and 14 catches

ENGINEER, Farokh Maneksha

(b. 1938, Bombay) *Bombay, Lancashire, and India*

One of the best wicket-keepers India has produced, Farokh Engineer, known in England as 'Rooky', was a cricketer of immense character. Everything he did on a cricket field was alert and keen. He was an unorthodox right-handed batsman, who either opened or went in between six and nine, and his whole approach was brisk, confident, and aggressive. A good square-cutter and strong driver, his great strength was on the leg-side: he could 'work' practically any delivery to mid-wicket. As a wicket-keeper he was brash and brilliant, the enthusiastic pivot of all that went on in the field. He could reach the widest leg-glances with an acrobatic dive and have the bails off in an instant if the batsman's back foot was raised. He clearly revelled in taking and then disposing of the ball in the slickest and most stylish manner possible. He made his first-class début for Combined Universities against the West Indian touring team in 1958/9 and played for Lancashire from 1968 to 1976, later becoming a marketing executive with a textile firm. In his first Test series against England in 1961/2 he scored 65 batting at number nine in the Kanpur Test, and in the second Test against the West Indies later the same season he made 53 and 40 (top score against a rampant Wes Hall) at Kingston. However, he was not an automatic selection, facing strong rivalry from Budhi Kunderan and others. Not until 1965 did he finally play through a whole series, at home to New Zealand, making 90 in the first Test at Madras in only 115 minutes. Thereafter he began to move up the batting order and, opening for the first time at

Madras in the third Test against the West Indies in 1966/7, he hit 109, 94 coming before lunch, on the first day against an attack comprising Hall, Griffith, Sobers, and Gibbs. On the England tour of 1967 he opened with a different partner in each of the three Tests. On the 1971 tour of England he batted down the order, scoring 172 runs at 43.00 in three Tests. In 1974 he headed the averages with 195 runs in three Tests at 39.00, opening the batting at Lord's where he scored 86 in the first innings and shared an opening stand of 131 with Gavaskar. English opposition seemed to inspire his best form: opening the batting for the only time in the 1972/3 series, he scored 121 and 66 at Bombay. He headed the batting averages in the series with 415 runs (41.50) but he was discarded after a less successful series against West Indies in 1974/5. His highest score was 192 for the Rest of the World against a Combined XI at Hobart in 1971/2. He made his home in Lancashire and became a highly successful business executive.

First-class career (1958–76): 13,436 runs (29.52) including 13 centuries, and 824 dismissals (704 c., 120 st.)

Test matches (46): 2,611 runs (31.08) including 2 centuries, and 82 dismissals (66 c., 16 st.)

GADKARI, Chandrasekhar Vaman

(b. 1928, Poona) *Maharashtra, Services, and India*

An attacking right-handed batsman, medium-pace bowler and brilliant outfield, Gadkari toured the West Indies in 1952/3 and Pakistan in 1954/5, and made a defiant 50 not out in the fourth match at Georgetown against West Indies, rescuing his team from collapse. Most of his cricket from 1947 until 1960 was in the Ranji Trophy competition, in which he averaged 49.60 with the bat, but, as an officer in the Army, he could not appear regularly.

First-class career (1947–65): 3,024 runs (40.32) including 7 centuries, and 48 wickets (31.06)

Test matches (6): 129 runs (21.50), 0–45, and 6 catches

GAEKWAD, Anshuman Dattajirao

(b. 1952, Bombay) *Baroda and India*

The son of the former Indian captain, D. K. Gaekwad, Anshuman was a tall, bespectacled right-handed batsman with plenty of guts and determination, a fine fielder in the gully and an occasional off-break bowler, good enough to take 6 for 49 against Saurashtra in 1971/2. A charming, gentle character, he was full of strokes in his youth but the stern demands of Test cricket took much of the gaiety out of his batting and he became a steady but sometimes colourless player who, nevertheless, often produced a thoroughbred stroke through the covers off the back foot. He made his first-class début for Baroda in 1969/70 and became captain in 1975. An innings of 155 against Maharashtra in 1973/4 helped his selection for India against West Indies the following season when he made 80 at Madras in his second Test. He was disappointing on the tour of New Zealand and West Indies in 1975/6, yet played a most courageous innings on a dangerous pitch at Sabina Park, making 81 against Michael Holding at his most fearsome before retiring after being hit on the head. In 1976/7, after making 173 runs in three home Tests against New Zealand (43.25), he could not get going against the England fast bowlers, but in 1978/9, playing once as an opener and three other Tests lower in the order, he scored 293 runs (41.85) against the West Indies at home, including his first Test century, 102 at Kanpur. He could not maintain this form in England in 1979. A prolific 1982/3 season earned him a Test recall. He could make only two Test fifties on the tour of West Indies, but at Jullunder in 1983/4 he made 201 out of 374 in India's first innings, India's first double hundred against Pakistan. It took him 652 minutes and 426 balls, then the seventh-longest Test innings.

First-class career (1969–92): 12,136 runs (41.56) including 34 centuries, 143 wickets (32.07), and 160 catches

Test matches (40): 1,985 runs (30.07) including 2 centuries, 2 wickets (93.50), and 15 catches

GAEKWAD, Dattajirao Krishnarao

(b. 1928, Baroda) *Baroda and India*

Although under average height, Datta Gaekwad possessed a sure defence and delightfully crisp strokes, especially through the covers. He was a right-handed opening batsman of quiet efficiency. An occasional leg-break bowler, he was also an agile and fearless field. He toured England in 1952 and 1959 and the West Indies in 1952/3, and at home played against Pakistan in 1952/3 and 1960/1 and West Indies in 1958/9. When he was captain on his second England tour his side was heavily beaten, but he scored 1,174 runs (34.52) in all first-class matches. Modest and retiring, he did not have the verve and drive which are desirable in a captain and sometimes found the job a strain. His career-highest was 249 not out against

Maharashtra in 1959/60. In the Ranji Trophy competition, from 1947 until 1961, he made 3,139 runs (47.56), including 14 centuries. He is the father of A. D. Gaekwad.

First-class career (1943–64): 5,788 runs (36.40) including 17 centuries, 25 wickets (40.64), and 49 catches

Test matches (11): 350 runs (18.42), 0–12, and 5 catches

GAEKWAD, Fatehsinghrao Pratapsinghrao

(b. 1930, Baroda; d. 1988, Bombay) *Baroda*

A descendant of the royal family of Baroda (he was in fact often called 'Baroda'), Fatehsinghrao Gaekwad brought a genuine love for the game to his playing days, to his stints in commentary boxes, and, perhaps most valuably, to his role as the manager of the national team. A man of gentle manner with a characteristic chuckle, he played for Baroda schools and for a few years for Baroda in the Ranji Trophy, even leading them for four years. In 1959, only 29 years old, he was the manager of the Indian team to England but thereafter his political and corporate commitments seemed to overtake him. He was a member of parliament and a minister in the state of Gujarat and did pioneering work for the World Wildlife Fund in India. But perhaps his greatest contribution to Indian cricket was his role as manager on what could have been a very tricky tour of Pakistan in 1978. India and Pakistan were resuming cricket links after 17 years, during which two wars had taken place between them. India needed a mature manager with a feel for diplomacy and Fatehsinghrao, with his charming presence and great command over Urdu, did such a fantastic job that he was called upon again in 1982/3. He died in 1988, still young and widely admired.

First-class career (1946–58): 624 runs (22.28)

GAEKWAD, Hiralal Ghasulal

(b. 1923, Nagpur) *Central Provinces and Berar, Holkar, and India*

A cheerful personality known as 'C. K. Nayudu's devoted Gunga Din', Hiralal Gaekwad was India's short-term replacement for Vinoo Mankad; a left-arm medium or slow bowler of great stamina who could swing the new ball, he was also a hard-hitting batsman. He toured England in 1952 without appearing in Tests. His sole Test was the second at Lucknow in 1952/3 against Pakistan, when he scored 14 and 8 and took 0 for 47.

First-class career (1941–64): 2,487 runs (19.42), 375 wickets (23.62), and 43 catches

GANDOTRA, Ashok

(b. 1948, Rio de Janeiro, Brazil) *Delhi and India*

Born in Rio de Janeiro, Ashok Gandotra was a left-handed batsman and slow bowler who played in one Test each against Australia and New Zealand in 1969/70 and was then discarded.

First-class career (1965–75): 2,121 runs (28.66) including 2 centuries, and 21 wickets (26.71)

Test matches (2): 54 runs (13.50), 0–5, and 1 catch

GANGULY, Saurav Chandi

(b. 1973, Calcutta) *Bengal*

An extremely talented but flashy batsman, Saurav Ganguly often seems capable of scoring more runs than he actually does. He was successful at under-19 level, representing India in the Youth Asia Cup in 1989 and scoring a century of high quality. He made his Ranji Trophy début for Bengal immediately thereafter and though he scored only 22, it was immediately obvious that there was a bright future ahead. Later in the year he scored a century in the Duleep Trophy, where his selection was a gamble, and another in the final of the Deodhar Trophy. And then, in a stunning decision, he was picked for the tour to Australia in 1991/2. It turned out to be a traumatic tour for him: he seemed overcome by nerves in the only one-day international he played. Back home, a more mature player, he started scoring freely in domestic cricket, batting with confidence and style to go with his undoubted talent. His gentle medium pacers have begun to show their utility value in one-day cricket.

First-class career (1989–   ): 2,549 runs (47.20) including 6 centuries, 32 wickets (43.68), and 37 catches

GAVASKAR, Sunil Manohar

(b. 1949, Bombay) *Bombay, Somerset, and India*

A masterful little right-hand opening batsman of only 5 ft. 4¾ in., 'Sunny' Gavaskar was for most of his long career the best and most consistent opening batsman in the world. By the finish of the 1979 tour of England this softly spoken, courteous and gentle man had scored 20 centuries in 50 Tests: only Bradman had had a higher

ratio. When he returned to England in 1986 his collection of Test hundreds had reached 32, a world record, and in playing his 115th Test, at Edgbaston, he became the most-capped of all Test players. He became the first to pass 10,000 Test runs, in 1986/7, his final season as a Test cricketer, and his 34 hundreds remain the most ever. Thirteen of his hundreds were scored against West Indies, whose fast bowlers were for most of Gavaskar's career second to none. Despite his limited height he was a fine player of fast bowling, compact, balanced, patient, and a ruthless destroyer of the bad ball. With full use of the crease either forward or back he was also able to make what might be good-length balls to some players into short ones deserving of punishment. He seldom hooked, but cut, drove, pulled, and glanced with power and without flaw. Allied to his impeccable technique was an ability to set his eyes on distant targets and concentrate for long periods. He made a sensational start to his Test career after proving himself to be something exceptional in schools and representative cricket in Bombay. Thereafter he was the Indian batsman whom opposing bowlers most wanted to dismiss. Three times he amassed more than 1,000 Test runs in a calendar year: in eleven Tests in 1976 he scored 1,024 runs, in only nine Tests in 1978, 1,044 runs, and in eighteen Tests in 1983, 1,310 runs. Selected to tour the West Indies in 1970/1 he began with a mere 65 and 67 not out after missing the first Test but soon put such setbacks aside. His second Test brought 116 and 64 not out, his third, at Barbados, 1 and 117 not out and his fourth, at Port of Spain, Trinidad, 124 and 220 not out. His performance enabled India to win a rubber against West Indies for the first time and no Indian has scored more than the 774 runs he made in his first rubber. On the tour he scored five centuries, 1,169 runs and averaged 97.41. The tour to England in 1971 was an anticlimax, though he showed his ability with fifties at Lord's and Old Trafford, and he still made 1,141 runs, including two centuries. Even at home against England, in 1972/3, he was disappointing, but he made his first century against England at Old Trafford in 1974 in conditions ideal for seam-bowling. (In the match he scored 101 and 58 in totals of 246 and 182.) He broke a finger after the first Test against West Indies in 1974/5 and did not play again until the fifth. He was back to his prolific self in New Zealand in 1975 and in the West Indies the same season, scoring 921 runs (41.86) including Test centuries at Auckland, and two at Port of Spain, 156 in the second Test and

102 in the second innings of the third Test, helping India to a remarkable 404 for 4 which won them the match against the odds. Next in the Gavaskar saga came centuries at home against New Zealand and England in 1976/7, both at Bombay. On the tour of Australia in 1977/8 Gavaskar scored 113 in the first Test at Brisbane, 127 in the second at Perth, and 118 in the third at Melbourne. At home to the West Indies in 1978/9 he assumed the captaincy of India, after scoring 447 runs at 89.40 against Pakistan, and the new responsibility merely increased his prodigious appetite for runs. In the six Tests he scored 732 runs (91.50) including four more centuries, the highest being 205 at his beloved Bombay. Although India won the series 1–0, Gavaskar was replaced as captain for the 1979 tour of England, when he scored 542 runs (77.42) in four Tests. These included one of the greatest innings of modern times, a superlative 221 at The Oval, with twenty-one fours, when he batted without chance or error for 8 hours 10 minutes, bringing India close to a sensational victory. He regained the captaincy and fully established himself in the position, not just by virtue of his batting supremacy but also by tough and increasingly shrewd tactics. He slipped from grace in Australia in 1980/1 when, having finally contributed a substantial score after a run of failures, he was given out lbw in the Melbourne Test. Furious, Gavaskar ordered his opening partner, Chauhan, to leave the field as well, intending that India should withdraw from the Test, but saner counsels prevailed and India's captain apologized. Moreover, India went on to win the match, bowling Australia out for 83 in the second innings. At home against England in 1981/2 India won a turgid series 1–0, Gavaskar making 500 runs (62.50) including 172 in the Bangalore Test: here he batted for 708 minutes and was on the field for all but four minutes of the match. In the Ranji Trophy the same season he hit 340, sharing with Ghulam Parkar in an opening stand of 421, for Bombay against Bengal. In England in 1982 India contributed much on a short tour, though they lost the series 1–0, mainly because Gavaskar was less successful. In the third Test at The Oval he broke his leg when fielding close in on the off side, being hit by a ball struck with tremendous force by Ian Botham. He returned, however, to captain India in a Test against Sri Lanka at Madras, in which he scored his 25th Test hundred. Despite sharing the Test captaincy with Kapil Dev, he continued to play regular big innings, passing Geoff Boycott as the highest run

scorer in Tests; overtaking Sir Donald Bradman in 1983/4 with his 30th Test hundred, an innings of 236 not out against West Indies at Madras; and adding two more hundreds in Australia in 1985/6. He was by now the respected elder statesman of cricket, yet with an insatiable appetite for runs and an unfailing patience. He retired, with his many records, to a life as a media sage, having played his final major match at Lord's in the MCC Bicentenary match. He had never scored a hundred at Lord's but he did so now, to his and everyone's delight. He played for Somerset for one season in 1980, scoring 664 runs (33.20) in 14 matches and making many friends.

First-class career (1966–88): 25,834 runs (51.46) including 81 centuries, 22 wickets (56.36), and 293 catches

Test matches (125): 10,122 runs (51.12) including 34 centuries, 1 wicket (206.00), and 108 catches

GHAI, Rajinder Singh

(b. 1960, Amritsar) *Punjab*

Tall and bearded, Rajinder Singh Ghai was an energetic, medium-fast bowler who played most of his cricket in the north of India at a time when it was dominated by medium pacers. He made his début for Punjab at the age of 19 but only really made a mark at the national level in 1984/5 when he took 5 for 30 for North Zone against Central Zone. After a good match for India under-25 against David Gower's England team of 1984, he won a place in the Pune one-day international and three days later, playing for North Zone against England, he took 7 for 110. This helped him to get a place in the second one-day international but though he had a good year in 1985, touring with India to Sri Lanka, Sharjah, and Australia, he only played four other one-day internationals and by the age of 29 had given up playing first-class cricket.

First-class career (1979–89): 1,310 runs (27.29) including 1 century, 125 wickets (32.92), and 18 catches

GHAVRI, Karsan Devjibhai

(b. 1951, Rajkot) *Saurashtra, Bombay, and India*

Though he came from a relatively poor family, Karsan Ghavri soon made his mark in Indian cricket, touring Australia with the Indian Schools team in 1968/9. A chunky all-rounder, he bowled left-arm fast-medium, slanting the ball across the right-hander from over the wicket but also sometimes swinging the ball back in, and also batted capably left-handed. A very variable cricketer, he could sometimes look a real threat at Test level, at other times innocuous. There were allegations that his action was suspect when he bowled a bouncer, and also when he bowled slow left-arm (as at Bombay in 1976/7 when four of his wickets in his 5 for 33 against England were taken bowling slow) but he was never 'called'. First appearing for India in 1974/5 against the West Indies, he took 4 for 140 in a West Indies total of 604 for 6 at Bombay but was in and out of the side until taking 11 wickets in three Tests in Australia in 1977/8, including 7 for 138 in the fifth Test (in the match) at Adelaide after making 64 useful runs in India's only innings at Sydney. At home against the West Indies in 1978/9 he had by far his most successful series, with 27 wickets (23.48) in six Tests, including 5 for 51 in the second innings of the second Test at Bangalore and seven wickets in the match at Calcutta. In England in 1979 he was overshadowed by his opening partner Kapil Dev but often bowled well and the two formed as effective a seam attack as India had used for many years.

First-class career (1969–85): 4,500 runs (28.66) including 1 century, 452 wickets (29.01), and 60 catches

Test matches (39): 913 runs (21.23), 109 wickets (33.54), and 16 catches

GHORPADE, Jayasinghrao Mansinghrao

(b. 1930, Maharashtra; d. 1978, Baroda) *Baroda and India*

A bespectacled and attacking right-handed batsman, leg-break and googly bowler, and outstanding cover-point, Ghorpade toured the West Indies in 1951/2, joining the team as a replacement, and England in 1959, and at home played against New Zealand in 1955/6, Australia in 1956/7 and West Indies in 1958/9, without quite establishing himself. In England he made 833 runs (23.80), including 100 runs in six Test innings, which included his Test-highest, 41 in India's first innings of 168 in the second match at Lord's. His career-highest was 123 for Baroda against Rajasthan in 1957/8 and best bowling in an innings, 6 for 19 for Indian Universities against Pakistan in 1952/3. He was a national selector until his untimely death.

First-class career (1948–65): 2,631 runs (25.54) including 2 centuries, 114 wickets (30.83), and 33 catches

Test matches (8): 229 runs (15.26), 0–131, and 4 catches

GHULAM AHMED

(b. 1922, Hyderabad) *Hyderabad, Muslims, and India*

A tall, slim, handsome man, Ghulam Ahmed was a right-arm off-break bowler with an easy action and a mastery of subtle flight and variations of length and direction. One could almost feel him 'thinking' a batsman out but, except on certain types of matting pitches, he had to work extremely hard for his wickets in India: on the less helpful turf he was at least Jim Laker's equal. An aggressive tail-end batsman, he was also a fair field. He toured England in 1952 and Pakistan in 1954/5, and at home he played against West Indies in 1948/9 and 1958/9, England in 1951/2, Pakistan in 1952/3, New Zealand in 1955/6, and Australia in 1956/7. In England he was the best bowler, taking 80 wickets (21.92), including 15 (24.73) of the 39 wickets to fall to Indian bowlers in the Tests. In the first-ever official Test against Pakistan, at New Delhi in 1952/3, he made 50 at number eleven, adding 109 with H. R. Adhikari for the last wicket, and took 4 for 35 in the second innings. At Calcutta in the third match against Australia in 1956/7 he collected 10 for 130 (7 for 49 in the first innings). He captained India once against New Zealand in 1955/6 and twice against West Indies in 1958/9, his last series, when India were losing and he bowled listlessly. At one time he held the record number of balls bowled in an innings, 555, against Holkar in 1950/1. For many years he was secretary of the Indian Board of Cricket Control.

First-class career (1939–59): 1,379 runs (14.36), 407 wickets (22.57), and 57 catches

Test matches (22): 192 runs (8.72), 68 wickets (30.17), and 11 catches

GHULAM, Mohammad

(b. 1898, Lahore; d. 1966, Lahore) *Sind*

A lower-order right-hand batsman, Ghulam Mohammad was best known for his left-arm medium-pace bowling which was particularly effective on matting wickets in India. However, the decision to select him for India's first tour to England in 1932 backfired somewhat when he managed only three wickets on the tour. He played most of his cricket in Karachi and was the highest wicket-taker in the Karachi Quadrangulars which were, unfortunately for him, not accorded first-class status. He also played for the Muslims from 1924/5 to 1931/2.

GODAMBE

First-class career (1924–39): 677 runs (12.08), 99 wickets (25.73), and 18 catches

GODAMBE, Shankarrao Ramachandra

(b. 1899, Bombay; d. 1969, Bombay) *Bombay and Gujarat*

A right-arm fast-medium bowler and lower-order batsman, Godambe bowled manfully for Bombay and Gujarat, and for the Hindus in the Bombay Quadrangular. He first played for the Hindus at the age of 21 and continued playing for them till he was almost 43. He was picked for the Indian team on their first tour of England in 1932 but with only one Test match and rivalry from the outstanding Mohammad Nissar and Amar Singh, he did not play a Test match.

First-class career (1920–42): 848 runs (16.30), 103 wickets (22.80), and 49 catches

GOEL, Rajinder Singh

(b. 1942, Punjab) *Punjab and Haryana*

A small man who bowled his left-arm spinners with unbelievable control, Rajinder Singh Goel could bowl all day. He played in an era when spin was the motto of Indian cricket and when at least ten international-class spinners were available at any time. His peak coincided with that of Bishan Bedi and the closest he came to playing for India was in the first Test of 1974/5 against Clive Lloyd's West Indies side when Bedi was dropped for giving a live television interview in England a few months earlier. However India preferred to play two off-spinners in that match and Bedi returned for the second Test. But at first-class level he was rampant, dismissing sides with almost ridiculous ease. He came off a very short run-up and had an easy action which perhaps explains his great longevity. He took five wickets in an innings fifty-nine times and his tally of 640 wickets in the Ranji Trophy is still a national record and unlikely to be broken.

First-class career (1958–85): 1,043 runs (9.56), 750 wickets (18.54), and 66 catches

GOPALAN, Morappakam Joysam

(b. 1909, Maduranthakam) *Madras, Hindus, and India*

A right-arm fast-medium bowler of good length and stamina, Gopalan toured England in 1936 without much success, and his sole Test appearance was in the second match against England in 1933/4 at Calcutta, when he scored 11 not out and 7, took 1 for 39 and held 3 catches. He has served as a Test selector and he presented the 'Gopalan Trophy' which, since 1953/4, has been fought for by Madras and Sri Lanka.

First-class career (1926–52): 2,916 runs (24.92) including 1 century, 194 wickets (24.20), and 49 catches

GOPINATH, Coimbatarao Doraikannu

(b. 1930, Madras) *Madras and India*

A stylish right-handed batsman with a sound defence and strong off-side shots, an occasional medium-pace bowler, and fast outfield, 'Gopi' bagged 'a pair' on his first-class début for Madras in 1949/50, but he later captained his state and toured England in 1952 and Pakistan in 1954/5; at home he played against England in 1951/2, Pakistan in 1952/3, and Australia in 1959/60. In his first Test, the second against England at Bombay, he made 50 not out and 42, batting at number eight, but a few months later in England he was, perhaps, the biggest batting failure on the tour. One of the successes in Pakistan in 1954/5, however, he averaged 58.33 in all first-class matches. A heavy scorer in Ranji Trophy matches, he made 2,349 runs (51.06), including six centuries, his career-highest being 234 against Mysore in 1958/9. He has been chairman of the selectors and managed the 1979 tour to England.

First-class career (1949–63): 4,259 runs (42.16) including 9 centuries, 14 wickets (27.78), and 50 catches

Test matches (8): 242 runs (22.00), 1–11, and 2 catches

GOVINDRAJ, Devraj Devendraraj

(b. 1947, Hyderabad) *Hyderabad, Hyderabad Blues, and State Bank of India*

A fast-medium bowler with a beautiful bowling action, Govindraj, a nephew of the great C. K. Nayudu, did well to succeed in a zone that produced high-quality spinners as though from a production line. But like so many fast bowlers of this era he suffered from a general mistrust of anyone who did not bowl spin. He toured the West Indies in 1971 and retained his place on the victorious tour to England later that year where, in spite of the fact that India played in the first half of the season, his skills were not needed. He retired early, soon after completing 100 wickets in the Ranji Trophy.

First-class career (1964–75): 1,202 runs (13.50), 190 wickets (27.66), and 36 catches

GUARD, Ghulam Mustafa

(b. 1922, Surat; d. 1978, Ahmedabad) *Bombay, Gujarat, and India*

A large sub-inspector of Police, Ghulam Guard was a left-arm fast-medium bowler, very useful in Ranji Trophy matches, who appeared once each against West Indies in 1958/9 and Australia in 1959/60.

First-class career (1946–63): 238 runs (11.33) and 124 wickets (20.60)

Test matches (2): 11 runs (5.50), 3 wickets (60.66), and 2 catches

GUHA, Subroto

(b. 1946, Calcutta) *Bengal and India*

A tidy right-arm fast-medium swing-bowler, Subroto Guha toured England in 1967, taking 22 wickets in 13 matches but, owing to injuries, was available for only one Test. At home he played three times against Australia in 1969/70, but with moderate success.

First-class career (1965–77): 1,067 runs (12.70), 299 wickets (20.29), and 45 catches

Test matches (4): 17 runs (3.40), 3 wickets (103.66), and 2 catches

GUL MAHOMED

(b. 1921, Lahore; d. 1992, Lahore) *Baroda, Hyderabad, North India, Muslims, Lahore, India, and Pakistan*

A left-handed batsman with sparkling footwork and a spectacular cover-point and deep field, Gul Mahomed toured England in 1946 and Australia in 1947/8, and at home played against Pakistan in 1952/3, but his batting tended to be disappointing. In Ranji Trophy matches, however, he was a prolific run-getter. He made his career-highest, 319, for Baroda against Holkar in 1946/7 in the final of the Ranji Trophy, adding 577 with Vijay Hazare, which remains the world record for the fourth wicket. In Trophy matches he made 1,842 runs (37.38) until he took Pakistan citizenship in 1955. He played for Pakistan once, in the first match against Australia at Karachi in 1956/7, a low-scoring contest, in which he scored 12 and 27 not out, including the winning hit.

First-class career (1938–59): 5,614 runs (33.81) including 12 centuries, 107 wickets (27.20), and 60 catches

Test matches (India—8): 166 runs (11.06), 2 wickets (12.00), and 3 catches. (Pakistan—1): 39 runs (39.00)

GUPTE, Balkrishna Pandharinath

(b. 1934, Bombay) *Bombay, Bengal, Railways, and India*

Tall and sturdy, 'Baloo' Gupte was a right-arm leg-break and googly bowler of great stamina, whose flight and length were excellent. He once bowled more than 100 overs in an innings for Bombay against Delhi, in 1956/7, his match analysis being 15 for 302. Although in Ranji Trophy matches alone he took 257 wickets (23.47), he received few opportunities in Tests, playing once each against Pakistan in 1960/1, England in 1963/4, and New Zealand in 1964/5. He is the brother of S. P. Gupte.

First-class career (1953–70): 587 runs (9.17) and 414 wickets (24.95)

Test matches (3): 28 runs (28.00) and 3 wickets (116.33)

GUPTE, Subhash Pandharinath

(b. 1929, Bombay) *Bombay, Bengal, Trinidad, Rajasthan, and India*

The first of the world-class post-1946 Indian spin-bowlers, 'Fergie' Gupte was a slightly built right-arm leg-break bowler, supremely confident because of the control he developed; he flighted and spun the ball cleverly, his length remaining immaculate, though he was constantly experimenting in order to deceive. Despite an unpromising start against England in 1951/2, he toured the West Indies in 1952/3, Pakistan in 1954/5, and England in 1959, and at home also played against England in 1961/2, Pakistan in 1952/3 and 1960/1, New Zealand in 1955/6, Australia in 1956/7, and West Indies in 1958/9. He established himself in the West Indies, taking 50 wickets (23.64), including 27 wickets (29.22) in the Tests. In Pakistan he took 21 Test wickets (22.61) including 5 for 17 at Dacca in the second innings of the first Test, and in the third match at Lahore he sent down 110.2 overs (73.5 in the first innings) for 7 for 167. Shortly before the tour began, he took all ten wickets in an innings for Bombay against Pakistan Services and Bahawalpur CC. At his peak against New Zealand, he took 34 wickets (19.67) in the series (his colleagues took 34 wickets between them) including

7 for 128, in 76.4 overs in the first innings of the first Test at Hyderabad. Against West Indies he took 22 of the 53 wickets that fell in the Tests; and in England he captured 95 wickets (26.58) in all first-class matches. In 1981/2 a benefit match was held for him in Sharjah, United Arab Emirates.

First-class career (1947–64): 761 runs (8.18), 530 wickets (23.71), and 52 catches

Test matches (36): 183 runs (6.31), 149 wickets (29.55), and 14 catches

HADI, Syed Mohammad

(b. 1899, Hyderabad; d. 1971, Hyderabad)
Hyderabad and Madras

S. M. Hadi, like his younger brother, S. M. Hussain, was a right-hand middle-order batsman who, in 1934/5 became the first cricketer to score a century in the Ranji Trophy (132 not out against Madras). The fact that it was his début match makes the achievement more remarkable. He was the treasurer of the Indian team on its tour to England in 1936 and appeared in emergency in two matches. Though Hadi did not play cricket for Cambridge, he did win a blue for lawn tennis in the 1920s and played in the Davis Cup for India.

First-class career (1930–41): 1,043 runs (32.59) including 2 centuries, and 9 catches

HANUMANT SINGH (Maharajkumar of Banswara)

(b. 1939, Banswara) *Madhya Pradesh, Rajasthan, and India*

Hanumant Singh was a prince and bank executive to whom cricket was almost a religion. A charming man, he was a small, consistent right-handed batsman with a large repertoire of strokes, who was always ready to attack; he was also a useful leg-break bowler and a brilliant field in the deep. In the Ranji Trophy competition alone he scored over 5,000 runs for an average exceeding 50. He touched greatness in domestic cricket in 1966/7, scoring 869 runs (124.14) in Trophy matches, including his career-highest, 213 not out for Rajasthan against Bombay. In 1961/2, when Uttar Pradesh were outplaying Rajasthan, he stopped the rot with a flawless unbeaten 200. He toured England in 1967, and at home played in Tests against England in 1963/4, Australia in 1964/5, New Zealand in 1964/5 and 1969/70, and West Indies in 1966/7. As late as 1976 he captained Central Zone against the MCC touring team. On his Test début against England, in the fourth match at New Delhi in 1963/4, he made 105, never being afraid to play his strokes; he became the only Indian (until then) to make a century in his first Test innings. Against Australia he made 94 in a total of 193 in the first match at Madras and against New Zealand in 1964/5 he made 195 runs (48.75), including 75 not out at Bombay and 82 at Delhi.

First-class career (1956–79): 12,338 runs (43.90) including 29 centuries, 56 wickets (40.94), and 110 catches

Test matches (14): 686 runs (31.18) including 1 century, 0–51, and 11 catches

HARDIKAR, Manohar Shankar

(b. 1936, Baroda) *Bombay and India*

A right-handed batsman of sound technique and an occasional bowler of medium-pace or slowish off-breaks, Manohar Hardikar played in two Tests against West Indies in 1958/9 without distinction.

First-class career (1955–68): 3,602 runs (45.59) including 8 centuries, and 74 wickets (31.66)

Test matches (2): 56 runs (18.66), 1–55, and 3 catches

HAVEWALA, Dadabhoy Rustomji

(b. 1908, Nargol, Gujarat; d. 1982, Bombay)
Bombay

A hard-hitting left-handed middle-order batsman, Dady Havewala played for Bombay from 1934/5 to 1941/2 averaging 30.21. But it is really for one innings that his place in history is assured. In the Times of India Shield, Bombay's premier local tournament, in December 1933, playing for BB & CI Railway against St Xavier's College, he scored 515, still an Indian record for any class of cricket. He hit 32 sixes and 55 fours but sadly, he could not quite reproduce that kind of brilliance for Bombay, for whom he scored but one century (in 83 minutes!). He played two unofficial Tests against Lord Tennyson's team of 1937/8, with a highest score of 44.

First-class career (1934–42): 1,295 runs (26.42) including 2 centuries, 47 wickets (38.12), and 11 catches

HAZARE, Vijay Samuel

(b. 1915, Maharashtra) *Maharashtra, Baroda, Central India, and India*

A Roman Catholic and one of India's greatest batsmen, Vijay Hazare was small of stature but had all the strokes together with a very strong defence. Square-shouldered and with sinewy wrists and forearms, he would move his right foot back outside the leg-stump and hammer his square-cut through the covers. If the circumstances warranted it, he would forget his straight-bat orthodoxy but he rarely lofted the ball. His concentration was intense. He was also a very useful medium-pace bowler and a fine field. Retiring and gentlemanly, he was a conscientious captain of India for three years in the early 1950s; he led his country in fourteen Tests (nine against England and five against West Indies). He made his first big impact when scoring 316 not out for Maharashtra against Baroda in 1939/40 and an incredible 309 not out in a total of 387 for The Rest against Hindus in the same season. In 1946/7, when making 288 in $2\frac{1}{2}$ hours for Baroda against Holkar in the final of the Ranji Trophy competition, he added 577 with Gul Mahomed for the fourth wicket, a world record in first-class cricket—and he took 6 for 85 in the first innings. He toured England in 1946 and (as captain) in 1952, Australia in 1947/8 and the West Indies (as captain) in 1952/3, and at home played against West Indies in 1948/9, England in 1951/2, and Pakistan in 1952/3. On his first England tour he scored 344 runs (49.77), besides taking 56 wickets (24.75), but was disappointing in the Tests. In Australia he made most runs in the Tests, 429 runs (47.66), and in all first-class matches reached 1,056 runs (48.00). In the fourth Test at Adelaide he scored 116 and 145 (in a total of 277), the first time an Indian has made two centuries in a Test. Against West Indies in 1948/9 he headed the batting with 543 runs (67.87) in the Tests, his solid 134 not out in the second match at Bombay saving India from defeat after following on, and in the fifth match at Bombay his 122 nearly brought victory. At the top of the batting against England in 1951/2 with 347 runs (57.83), he hit dogged centuries in the first two Tests, 164 not out in 8 hours 35 minutes at Delhi, his Test-highest, and 155 at Bombay in 5 hours. As captain of a weak side in England, he was supreme in the Tests with 333 runs (55.50). In the first-ever Test against Pakistan, at Lucknow in 1953/4, he made 76, and in the third at Bombay, on turf that was far from easy, he contributed a steady 146 not out in $4\frac{1}{4}$ hours, adding 188 with 'Polly' Umrigar for the fourth wicket. After a not particularly successful tour of the West Indies, he was discarded both as captain and Test cricketer, but he had scored at least one Test century against each

country. His brother also played in Ranji Trophy cricket.

First-class career (1934–67): 18,740 runs (58.38) including 60 centuries, 595 wickets (24.61), and 165 catches
Test matches (30): 2,192 runs (47.65) including 7 centuries, 20 wickets (61.00), and 11 catches

HINDLEKAR, Dattaram Dharmaji

(b. 1909, Bombay; d. 1949, Bombay) *Bombay, Hindus, and India*

Never spectacular but always cheerful and sound, both behind the stumps and when batting, Dattaram Hindlekar toured England in 1936 and 1946. Despite suffering at different times from chipped fingers, blurred vision and many strains and bruises, he was India's first-string wicket-keeper. He was also a calm and courageous right-handed batsman who wore his cap at a bewildered angle, and stood with his left toe pointing up at an angle of 45 degrees. In 1936 he opened the batting in the Test at Lord's; ten years later at Old Trafford as number eleven he stood firm for 15 minutes with S. W. Sohoni to ward off defeat.

First-class career (1934–47): 2,439 runs (17.05) including 1 century, and 187 dismissals (128 c., 59 st.)
Test matches (4): 71 runs (14.20) and 3 catches

HIRWANI, Narendra Deepchand

(b. 1968, Gorakhpur) *Madhya Pradesh and India*

When Narendra Hirwani was picked for the fourth Test against the West Indies at Madras in January 1988, very few, even in India, had heard of him. Four days later he was a national hero and a statistician's delight having produced figures of 16 for 136, the best début figures in the history of Test cricket, and having bowled India to a comprehensive win against the West Indies. On an under-prepared wicket this small, stocky, bespectacled, owlish-looking leg-spinner bowled with great skill, getting the last eight wickets in the first innings for figures of 8 for 61. But the second effort was, if anything, more sensational. The West Indies were bowled out in 40.2 overs and Hirwani took 8 for 75 as the West Indians seemed to give up trying to read him. Before the year was out, he had taken 20 wickets in three Test matches against New Zealand for a staggering 36 wickets in four Tests. In spite of rather modest batting and fielding skills, he had made a presence in the Indian team in one-day cricket too. For an extremely shy young man who migrated from the small town of Gorakhpur to Indore, and who had worked very hard at his craft, this was a dream come true. Contrary to what those figures might suggest Hirwani was no genius, just a simple, small-town, hard-working boy who lived a hard life. With his bushy moustache and thick spectacles, he had quite a mysterious look about him, one that went rather well with the mystique associated with leg-spinners. He had made his first-class début at the age of 16 with 5 for 101 for Madhya Pradesh against Rajasthan. He was a consistent wicket-taker in the Central Zone but opportunities were limited because Madhya Pradesh rarely qualified for the knockout stage of the Ranji Trophy. He toured Australia with an India youth team in 1986/7 and was in New Zealand for the Youth World Cup in 1987/8. But it was a second-innings performance of 6 for 100 against the West Indies in a three-day game at the start of the tour that led the selectors to gamble with him in that last Test. Hirwani was not a big turner of the ball and it soon became apparent that on less responsive tracks he failed to come through off the wicket quickly enough. He had a disappointing tour of the West Indies in 1989 and though he played in all the Test matches in New Zealand and England in 1990, he never got five wickets in an innings again. He toured Australia in 1991/2 without playing a Test and thereafter the continued success of Anil Kumble meant there was no place for him.

First-class career (1984–   ): 684 runs (10.85), 384 wickets (27.99), and 28 catches
Test matches (14): 45 runs (5.62), 58 wickets (31.01), and 5 catches

HUSSAIN, Syed Mohammad

(b. 1909, Hyderabad; d. 1982, Hyderabad) *Madras and Hyderabad*

A right-hand middle-order batsman, S. M. Hussain made his first-class début for the Indians against the Europeans in the annual Madras Presidency match. He played a lot of cricket for Madras before moving to Hyderabad whom he lead with distinction to victory in the Ranji Trophy in 1937/8 and to the final in 1942/3. He also played for nine seasons for the Muslims in the Quadrangular and was selected for the 1936 Indian team to England where, unfortunately, he did not achieve much.

First-class career (1926–43): 1,724 runs (24.62), 3 wickets (38.33), and 24 catches

IBRAHIM, Khanmohammed Cassumbhoy

(b. 1919, Bombay) *Bombay and India*

A very sound right-handed opening batsman who scored prolifically in domestic cricket, Ibrahim played in four Tests against West Indies in 1948/9, scoring 85 and 44 in the first at Delhi. Soon afterwards, however, he dropped out of first-class cricket. In 14 years he had made 2,334 runs (66.69) in Ranji Trophy matches alone.

First-class career (1938–50): 4,716 runs (61.24) including 14 centuries
Test matches (4): 169 runs (21.12)

INDRAJITSINHJI, Kumar Shri

(b. 1937, Jamnagar) *Saurashtra, Madras, Delhi, and India*

A sound wicket-keeper and determined right-handed tail-end batsman who sometimes also opened, Prince Indrajitsinhji toured Australasia in 1967/8 without being selected for the Tests, but at home played against Australia in 1964/5 and New Zealand in 1969/70. For Delhi in the Ranji Trophy matches of 1960/1, while still a student, he gained 23 dismissals, then a record. He was unfortunate to have both Budhi Kunderan and Farokh Engineer as his rivals.

First-class career (1954–73): 3,694 runs (26.76) including 5 centuries, and 213 dismissals (133 c., 80 st.)
Test matches (4): 51 runs (8.50) and 9 dismissals (6 c., 3 st.)

IRANI, Jahangir Khan

(b. 1923, Karachi; d. 1982, Karachi) *Sind and India*

A very sound wicket-keeper, Irani won two caps on the first Indian tour of Australia in 1947/8, but did not represent his country again.

First-class career (1937–48): 399 runs (17.34) and 27 dismissals (21 c., 6 st.)
Test matches (2): 3 runs (3.00) and 3 dismissals (2 c., 1 st.)

JADEJA, Ajaysinghji Daulatsinghji

(b. 1971, Jamnagar) *Haryana and India*

A descendant of the families of Ranji and Duleep (he was even born in Jamnagar), Ajay Jadeja probably made cricket in his blood. He certainly made a very early start to his first-class career, playing for Haryana when he was 17. A successful period for the India under-19 team followed, but his first century in first-class cricket took three years to make. By then he had begun to show signs of being a very handy cricketer in the one-day game and toured Sharjah with the Indian team in 1990, though without getting a match. But his real break came in the World Cup of 1992 in which he played some tidy innings and fielded brilliantly; his catching of Allan Border at Brisbane was one of the fielding highlights of the tournament. Ajay was never really able to establish himself as a Test batsman in spite of three appearances in 1992 in the series against South Africa, where he averaged 24.75. In the build-up to that series he had scored 254 not out against a Combined Bowl XI, putting on a record 415 with Sanjay Manjrekar for the second wicket. Those three appearances remain his only Test matches, though he has since established a fair reputation in the one-day game, especially when accompanied by Sachin Tendulkar, as an enterprising opening batsman who can fill in some overs if needed, and as an outstanding fielder in an otherwise poor fielding side. However, in New Zealand in early 1994, when Prabhakar had to return with injury, he seized his opportunity with three fifties followed by an excellent innings of 87 against Australia at Sharjah. That meant the opener's slot was his again and in the home series against the West Indies and New Zealand, he produced a string of good starts including 104 against the West Indies at Cuttack. Having Tendulkar for company has often required him to play anchor, a role that suits his style of cricket quite well for he can move the strike around and is a very sharp runner between the wickets. In addition, his obvious enthusiasm for the game often perks up the side and while his chances in Test cricket may remain limited, he should play a valuable role in India's one-day sides in the years to come. Cricketing skills apart, his unusual upbringing has made him a good linguist too: he speaks Gujarati (at home), Hindi, Punjabi, Malayalam (his mother's language), and English —which makes 'sledging' in domestic cricket a bit difficult when he is around!

First-class career (1988–   ): 3,521 runs (53.34) including 7 centuries, 33 wickets (37.93), and 36 catches

Test matches (3): 99 runs (24.75)

JAHANGIR KHAN, Dr Mohammed

(b. 1910, Jullundur; d. 1988, Lahore) *Northern India, Cambridge University, Muslims, and India*

Prominent among the Muslim cricketers, Jahangir Khan was a hard-hitting right-handed bats-man, a tall, fast-medium bowler with a very effective 'flip' at the moment of delivery which made the ball kick off the pitch, and an alert field. He made 448 runs (19.47) and took 53 wickets (29.05) on his first tour of England in 1932 and in the first-ever Test at Lord's took 4 for 60 in the second innings. Going up to Cambridge, he won four blues between 1933 and 1936. He joined the 1936 Indians in England but was a failure in the Tests. His son is Majid Jahangir Khan of Pakistan.

First-class career (1928–46): 3,280 runs (22.31) including 4 centuries, 327 wickets (25.06), and 81 catches

Test matches (4): 39 runs (5.57), 4 wickets (63.75), and 4 catches

JAI, Laxmidas Purshottamdas

(b. 1902, Bombay; d. 1968, Bombay) *Bombay, Hindus, and India*

Jai was a graceful right-handed stroke-making batsman whose footwork was superb; his heyday coincided with that of the Bombay Quadrangular tournament. Selected for the 1932 tour of England, he refused on political grounds, most of the leaders of the National movement being in gaol. His sole Test was the first-ever in India, against England at Bombay in 1933/4, when he scored 19 and 0. He did tour England in 1936, but a broken finger impeded his progress. For some years he was a Test selector.

First-class career (1920–42): 3,231 runs (31.99) including 6 centuries, and 26 catches

JAISIMHA, Motganhalli Lakshminarsu

(b. 1939, Secunderabad) *Hyderabad and India*

A slim, stylish, wristy, and usually forceful right-handed batsman, a useful medium-pace bowler of out-swingers and off-breaks, and a brilliant field in any position, Jaisimha, or 'Jai', opened both batting and bowling for his state, which he captained for many years. An extrovert by nature, he was considered too 'flashy' sometimes to open in Tests and consequently often strengthened the middle batting instead, learning discretion with experience. On his first-class début at 15, against Andhra in 1954/5, he made 90 and took 3 for 56. He toured England in 1959, the West Indies in 1961/2 and 1970/1, and Australasia in 1967/8, and at home played against Australia in 1959/60 and 1964/5, Pakistan in 1960/1, England in 1961/2 and 1963/4, New Zealand in 1964/5 and 1969/70, and West Indies in 1966/7. In England he made only one unimpressive Test appearance, but in his next Test, the fifth against Australia, at Calcutta, in 1959/60, he hit 20 not out and 74. Two years later, in a battle of attrition with Pakistan in the second Test at Kanpur, he opened and was run out for 99, after 8 hours 20 minutes at the crease: he had made only five scoring strokes in the pre-lunch session on the third day. Against England in 1961/2 he impressed as an opening batsman with consecutive scores of 56, 51, 70, and 127, and made 399 runs (49.87) in the series. Against England in 1963/4 he was again very consistent, with 444 runs (44.40), including 129 in the third match at Calcutta. Flown out to join the team in Australia in 1967/8, he was pressed into service immediately for the third Test at Brisbane and kept the match alive at number six with dogged knocks of 74 and 101, India getting to within 39 runs of victory. But on his last tour, to the West Indies in 1970/1, he failed in the Tests. He has scored over 4,000 runs and taken over 200 wickets in Ranji Trophy matches.

First-class career (1954–77): 13,515 runs (37.54) including 33 centuries, 431 wickets (29.86), and 157 catches
Test matches (39): 2,056 runs (30.68) including 3 centuries, 9 wickets (92.11), and 17 catches

JAMSHEDJI, Rustomji Jamshedji Dorabji

(b. 1892, Bombay; d. 1976, Bombay) *Bombay and India*

A slow left-arm bowler, aged 41 years 27 days, Jamshedji played at Bombay in the first-ever Test in India against England. In this, his sole Test (he is still the oldest Indian to have made a Test début), he scored 4 not out and 1 not out, took 3 for 137 and held 2 catches.

First-class career (1922–39): 291 runs (11.19) and 134 wickets (22.11)

JAYANTILAL, Kenia

(b. 1948, Hyderabad) *Hyderabad and India*

Stockily built and slightly heavy on his feet, Jayantilal was a confident right-handed opening batsman partial to the off-side shots and the pull, and a fine field at slip. He made 153 against Andhra in 1967/8 on his début in the Ranji Trophy competition, and toured the West Indies in 1970/1 with the triumphant Indian team, coming fourth in the batting averages with 506 runs (56.22). However, he appeared in only one Test, the first at Kingston, scoring 5. In England

in 1971 he disappointed and was not selected for any of the Tests.

First-class career (1967–79): 4,687 runs (36.33) including 8 centuries, 6 wickets (51.83), and 66 catches

JEEJEEBHOY, Russi Ardeshir

(b. 1942, Calcutta) *Bengal*

A stylish wicket-keeper who played for Bengal, Russi Jeejeebhoy's selection for the tour to the West Indies in 1971 was one of the bigger surprises of Indian cricket, given that he had not played either in the Duleep Trophy for East Zone or in the Irani Trophy. Predictably, he had little to do on that tour and was not considered again. He resurfaced in Indian cricket many years later as a national selector.

First-class career (1965–73): 496 runs (10.33), 1 wicket (55.00), and 135 dismissals (105 c., 30 st.)

JOHNSTONE, Conrad Powell

(b. 1895, London; d. 1974, Kent, England) *Cambridge University, Kent, Europeans, and Madras*

C. P. Johnstone was a left-handed opening batsman and a right-handed medium-pace bowler who had an enormous influence on cricket, especially in Madras. He captained Madras in the first-ever Ranji Trophy match against Mysore in 1934/5. He also took them to the final of the Ranji Trophy in 1940/1 and was in fact awarded a CBE for his efforts on behalf of cricket in Madras. He played for the Europeans in India from 1926/7 to 1947/8. A noted golfer, he had captained Cambridge in 1920, won cricket blues in 1919 and 1920 and played 36 matches for Kent between 1919 and 1933. He was president of Kent in 1966.

First-class career (1919–45): 5,482 runs (30.62), 103 wickets (27.43), and 106 catches

JOSHI, Padmanabh Govind

(b. 1926, Baroda; d. 1987, Pune) *Maharashtra and India*

A stalwart who captained his state for several years, 'Nana' Joshi was a very sound wicket-keeper and useful right-handed batsman who opened the batting regularly during his early first-class years. He toured the West Indies in 1952/3 and England in 1959, and at home played against England in 1951/2, Pakistan in 1952/3 and 1960/1, West Indies in 1958/9, and Australia in 1959/60. On his Test début against England at

New Delhi, he had two catches and two stumpings in the first innings.

First-class career (1946–65): 1,724 runs (17.06) including 1 century, and 181 dismissals (120 c., 61 st.)

Test matches (12): 207 runs (10.89) and 27 dismissals (18 c., 9 st.)

KAMBLI, Vinod Ganpat

(b. 1972, Bombay) *Bombay and India*

An amazingly gifted left-hander, Vinod Kambli's career has run parallel to that of his great childhood friend, Sachin Tendulkar. Their friendship, established when Tendulkar was 13 and Kambli 14, might come straight from a soap opera. They played for the same school, Shardashram Vidyamandir, under the same coach, Ramakant Achrekar, and scored runs with the same appetite. The crowning glory, in every sense, of their partnership came on 24 February 1988 when, in the semi-finals of the Harris Shield, they added an unbroken 664 runs for the third wicket; a world record in any form of cricket and a partnership that was only broken on the orders of the coach who thought they had batted too long. Kambli was 349 not out and Tendulkar 326. But thereafter, they went different ways. Kambli made his Ranji Trophy début in 1989 and hit his first ball for six. He made 72 from 65 balls with four sixes and six fours. Later that year he played for the India under-19 team against Pakistan and was a notable failure, only scoring 12 from three innings. In the following year he scored 867 runs from eight matches in the Ranji Trophy, including a century in each innings in the semi-final, and finished the season with 1,087 runs from eleven matches with four centuries. He also hit twenty-six sixes that year, an amazing number for a small man but symbolic of the aggression he brought to the crease. He capped that performance with a place in the Indian team to tour Sharjah, where he did reasonably well before getting the shocking news that he was not in the team to tour Australia. He responded with 1,218 runs from seven first-class matches including a double-century and four centuries, and demanded a place in the team for the World Cup. Sadly, he struggled there, and in spite of an innings of 94 in a crucial Irani Trophy match was dropped for the tour to South Africa. Once again he produced a mountain of runs at home, including innings of 168 and 202. It won him a place in the first one-day international against England at Jaipur on his twenty-first birthday. He scored exactly 100, dedi-

cating the century to the already well-established Tendulkar, who egged him on in a partnership of 164. That was to be the beginning of an amazing run of scores in international cricket. He scored a bright 59 in the second Test at Madras and followed it up with 224 at Bombay and 227 against Zimbabwe at Delhi, both innings characterized by outstanding footwork and his trademark hunger for runs. He became only the third cricketer after Hammond and Bradman to score double-centuries in successive innings. In three innings in Sri Lanka, he scored 125, 4, and 120, achieving the feat of two double-centuries and two centuries in successive Test matches. He also acquired the highest aggregate by any international cricketer after five, six, seven, eight, nine, and ten Test innings and became the fastest Indian to 1,000 Test runs—getting there in his fourteenth innings. After that he faded somewhat, most notably against the West Indies at home where, even on the slow wickets, he was totally at sea against the bounce. He only managed 64 runs from six Test innings, placing a question mark against his ability to play bowlers who consistently bring the ball up. But on wickets in the subcontinent, he remains a rare talent and must definitely rank as one of the great players of spin bowling, in spite of being a predominantly bottom-handed batsman. His success is all the more remarkable, coming as he does from a very humble background. His father, a factory worker, was also a decent medium-pace bowler and in his simple lodgings, he planted the love for the game in a young boy. As a child, Kambli had to travel long distances in crowded trains for his practice sessions and that is perhaps where he built his great determination to succeed and acquire a better life. Yet he has always had an amazing zest for life. He often dresses outrageously and is quite proud of his nickname, 'Dessy', after his cricketing idol, Desmond Haynes.

First-class career (1989–): 4,898 runs (72.02) including 14 centuries, 4 wickets (50.75), and 30 catches

Test matches (14): 1,029 runs (57.16) including 4 centuries, and 6 catches

KANITKAR, Hemant Shamsunder

(b. 1942, Vidarbha) *Maharashtra and India*

Hemant Kanitkar learned cricket at college and was a stocky right-handed batsman of disciplined technique who played the late cut particularly well. He was also a competent deputy wicket-keeper but when not 'keeping was rather a liability in the field. In his first Test, against West Indies at Bangalore in 1974/5, he scored an adventurous 65 but he was discarded after the second match.

First-class career (1963–78): 5,007 runs (42.79) including 13 centuries, and 87 dismissals (68 c., 19 st.)

Test matches (2): 111 runs (27.75)

KANNAYIRAM, Natarajan

(b. Madras) *Madras*

Natarajan Kannayiram was a right-arm fast-medium bowler and a middle-order batsman who made his first-class début for the Indians versus the Europeans in 1947/8. However, it was his début in the Ranji Trophy for Madras that was more memorable, for he took 6 for 43 against Bombay in 1948/9. Those remained his best figures in a short first-class career, the highlight of which was selection for the Indian team that toured the West Indies in 1952/3. He was lucky to have made that tour since the original selection, G. V. Kasturirangan of Mysore, declined the invitation. On the other hand, Kannayiram had taken 14 wickets from two matches at 14.02 in the season of 1951/2.

First-class career (1947–57): 491 runs (18.18), 42 wickets (29.80), and 4 catches

KAPADIA, Bahadur Edulji

(b. 1900, Bombay; d. 1973, Bombay) *Bombay*

Bahadur Kapadia was a lower-order batsman, reliant on defensive skills, and a wicket-keeper who played for the Parsees in the Quadrangular Tournaments and for Bombay in the Ranji Trophy. Ironically, his wicket-keeping skills kept his elder brother Framji Kapadia out of the Parsees team. He was in the Indian team on the first tour to England in 1932 as reserve 'keeper to J. G. Navle, and since there was only one Test match he played no international cricket on that tour, nor indeed after that.

First-class career (1920–36): 522 runs (13.73) and 71 dismissals (47 c., 24 st.)

KAPIL DEV, Ramlal Nikhanj

(b. 1959, Chandigarh) *Haryana, Northamptonshire, Worcestershire, and India*

Kapil Dev was an all-round cricketer of charismatic brilliance, who became the greatest Test wicket-taker of all time. The best fast bowler produced by India, a gifted batsman, and a fine, athletic fielder, he was a strong six-footer who bowled fast-medium with an excellent action. A slow walk back to his mark was followed by a springy approach from some 20 yards culminating in a leap and a sideways-on delivery. His pace was lively, his length full, and the late out-swinger came naturally. Making his début for Haryana against Punjab in the Ranji Trophy in 1975/6, he took 6 for 39 in the first innings. In 1976/7 he took 7 for 20 against Bengal and in 1977/8 went one better with 8 for 38 against Services and 11 for 61 in the match. It was, therefore, no surprise when he made his Test début in Pakistan in 1978/9, although he soon learned to be philosophical about bowling on shirt-fronts against high-class batsmen. His seven wickets in three Tests against Pakistan cost 60.85 but his promise was clear and against the West Indies he took 17 wickets in six Tests at 33.00. Moreover, after making 59 in a run-feast at Karachi he revealed class and immense power with the bat against the West Indies, scoring 329 runs in the series at 65.80 including a magnificent 126 not out at Delhi, hard on the heels of some fine bowling on the fast pitch at Madras where he took 4 for 38 and 3 for 46. In England in 1979 he revelled in the bowling conditions, but failed to show the necessary restraint as a batsman against high-class English seamers, despite making a superb century in 74 minutes against Northamptonshire at Northampton. In each of the four Tests his bowling was both persistent and dangerous, even at Edgbaston where England scored 633 for 5 declared in their only innings, Kapil Dev taking all 5 for 146 in 48 overs. Back in India in 1979/80 he was again outstanding in two home series against Australia (28 wickets at 22) and Pakistan (32 wickets at 17 and 278 runs at 30). At 21 years and 27 days, in his 25th Test, he became the youngest man of any nationality to complete the Test double of 1,000 runs and 100 wickets. Against England at home in 1981/2 and away in 1982 he was India's key player—even ahead of Gavaskar—making 318 runs (53.00) in the home series and hitting 116 at Kanpur, taking 22 wickets in the series. In England his whole-hearted and clean-hitting batting was a joy: his Test innings were 41, 89, 65, and 97. At Lord's, he also took 8 of the 13 England wickets which fell. Lord's was also to be the scene of two of his greatest triumphs as captain of India. Returning there in 1983 he led the little-considered finalists to an amazing victory in the World Cup against West Indies, having already masterminded a defeat of West Indies in an earlier round. He had also produced an astounding innings of 175 not out after coming in against Zimbabwe at Tunbridge Wells when his side were 10 for 4 and seeing them decline further to 17 for 5 and 78 for 7. Three years after sending all cricket-lovers in India delirious, and having lost the captaincy for a while after several vengeful defeats at the hands of the West Indians, Kapil Dev returned to Lord's in 1986 and led his side to their first win against England there, following this with another success at Headingley to assure India of victory in the series of three games. Only ill-fortune with the weather had prevented his team from a similar success in Australia the previous winter when Kapil took 8 for 106 in Australia's first innings at Adelaide. He had gone one better when taking 9 for 83 against the West Indies at Ahmedabad in 1983/4. He took 29 wickets in the six Tests of this series at 18.51 and against the same invincible West Indies in 1982/3 took 4 for 45 and 4 for 73 at Kingston; furthermore, he scored 100 not out at Port of Spain and 98 in Antigua. Losing the captaincy, but keeping superbly fit, he chased Richard Hadlee's Test wicket record remorselessly, finally passing him against Sri Lanka at Ahmedabad in 1993/4. He is one of only three players to have taken 200 wickets and scored over 3,000 runs in Test cricket.

First-class career (1975–): 11,356 runs (32.91) including 18 centuries, 835 wickets (27.09), and 192 catches

Test matches (131): 5,248 runs (31.05) including 8 centuries, 434 wickets (29.64), and 64 catches

KAPOOR, Aashish Rakesh

(b. Madras, 1971) *Punjab, North Zone, and India*

A small right-handed all-rounder whose main strength is as an off-spinner although he can also bowl wrist-spin, Aashish Kapoor had done well in youth cricket before being called into the third and final Test at Chandigarh against the West Indies in December 1994. In this, his sole Test to date, he scored 15 and one and took one wicket for 122 in his 37 overs in the game, also taking a catch. In 1995, playing club cricket in the three counties league for Abergavenny on the Welsh border, he hit an amazing treble century in a single-innings afternoon match.

First-class career (1989–): 1,088 runs (32.00) including 1 century, 90 wickets (28.24), and 31 catches

KARDAR, Abdul Hafeez

(b. 1925, Lahore) *Northern India, Oxford University, Warwickshire, India, and Pakistan*

Abdul Hafeez Kardar is best remembered as the quiet, determined and orthodox captain of Pakistan in her first twenty-three Tests—quickly leading his country to a position of respect in the cricket world—and subsequently as an administrator of great, almost unimpeachable authority. He toured England with modest success for the 1946 Indian team as 'Abdul Hafeez', after hitting 173—his career-highest—for North Zone and 161 for Combined Universities against Australian Services in 1945/6. He was an attacking left-handed batsman, willing to back his eye against the bowler; tall, he had good wrists and a fine sense of timing. He bowled accurate left-arm slow or medium-slow and never relaxed in the field. At Partition in 1947 he became a citizen of Pakistan and, on the country's first tour of India in 1952/3, he made 416 runs (37.81), including 79 in the Madras Test, and took 13 wickets (23.53). The peak of his playing career was his successful leadership of Pakistan's first tour of England in 1954, when the rubber was tied. He knew English conditions extremely well, for besides his 1946 tour with India, he had won his blue at Oxford and played for Warwickshire from 1948 until 1950 with success. In the last Test at The Oval in 1954 he top-scored in the first innings with 36 in a total of 133—and led Pakistan to their first victory over England. In the indecisive 'war of attrition' with India on her first tour of Pakistan in 1954/5 he made 207 runs (25.87), including his highest score in Tests, 93 in the fifth match at Karachi. Again under his command Pakistan won the rubber against New Zealand in 1955/6, when he headed the bowling averages with ten wickets (15.00). In the sole match against Australia at Karachi in 1956, which Pakistan won, he top-scored with 69. In the West Indies in 1957/8 Pakistan lost a rubber for the first time under his captaincy, but he made 253 runs (31.62). He went into the third match at Kingston against doctor's orders with a broken finger, scoring 57 and bowling 37 overs. Subsequently, he was active for many years in cricket politics both in Pakistan and in the councils of ICC.

First-class career (1943–66): 6,832 runs (29.83) including 8 centuries, 344 wickets (24.55), and 110 catches

Test matches (India—3): 80 runs (16.00) and 1 catch. (Pakistan—23): 847 runs (24.91), 21 wickets (45.42), and 15 catches

441

KARIM, Syed Saba

(b. 1967, Patna) *Bihar and Bengal*

Karim was an early achiever, making his first-class début in the season of 1982/3, when only 15 years old. He led an India under-19 team two years later and has had a distinguished presence in domestic cricket since, keeping wicket with grace and batting solidly in the middle order as witnessed by his extremely impressive batting average. He scored two centuries in 1987/8 which earned him a place in the Indian team for the last one-day international against New Zealand at Jammu in early 1989, when the selectors were looking for an understudy to Kiran More. Unfortunately that match was washed out and though Karim was in the Indian team for the tour to the West Indies immediately afterwards, he played in none of the internationals and, as a result, never made it to the record books. He continued to score heavily, averaging 109.80, 79.83, and 75.50 in successive seasons. In 1994/5, he shifted from the relative obscurity of Bihar to the higher profile of the Bengal team in a come-back bid, but after 12 years in first-class cricket, it was perhaps too late.

First-class career (1982–   ): 4,538 runs (54.67) including 14 centuries, and 167 dismissals (137 c., 30 st.)

KENNY, Ramnath Bhaura

(b. 1930, Bombay; d. 1985, Bombay) *Bombay, Cumberland, and India*

A protégé of Duleepsinhji's, Ramnath Kenny was an elegant right-handed batsman, essentially a front-foot player with a sound defence, and an occasional off-break bowler. In 1956/7 he hit three successive centuries in Ranji Trophy matches, including 218 against Madras, his career-highest. He played in one Test against West Indies in 1958/9 and four against Australia in 1959/60, finishing third in the averages with 229 runs (32.71), his highest score being a well-fought 62 in the third Test at Calcutta. He hit three fifties against Australia, but did not represent India again. He became a highly respected coach and club professional at Penrith.

First-class career (1950–64): 3,079 runs (50.47) including 11 centuries, and 15 wickets (31.20)
Test matches (5): 245 runs (27.22) and 1 catch

KHANNA, Surinder Chamanlal

(b. 1956, Delhi) *Delhi*

A loyal player for Delhi for 12 years, Surinder Khanna kept wicket and scored heavily in domestic cricket, first in the middle order and then, more spectacularly, as an opener. He was rather surprisingly picked in the Indian team for the 1979 World Cup when Syed Kirmani was dropped for reasons still unknown. The high point in his career came when he made a come-back to the Indian team in 1984 for the first Asia Cup at Sharjah and was named 'man of the series' with scores of 51 not out and 56. But when the Australians toured later that year, he found the pace a little too hard to handle and finished his career with only ten one-day internationals. He continued to play for a further 3 years, ending his career as a pure batsman in 1987/8, a year in which he had scores of 143 and 220 not out.

First-class career (1976–88): 5,337 runs (43.39) including 17 centuries, and 233 dismissals (181 c., 52 st.)
One-day internationals (10): 176 runs (22.00) and 8 dismissals (4 c., 4 st.)

KIRMANI, Syed Mujtaba Hussain

(b. 1949, Madras) *Mysore (Karnataka), Railways, and India*

At his best a scintillating wicket-keeper and a sparkling and stylish right-handed batsman, Syed Kirmani spent many years as understudy to Farokh Engineer, touring England in 1971, 1974, and (for the World Cup) in 1975 without playing a Test. His first Test appearance for India was at Auckland in the first Test of 1975/6 and in the following game, the second Test at Christchurch, he equalled the Test record of six victims in an innings, five caught and one stumped. In the following Test he claimed four victims in New Zealand's only innings and also scored 49 in adding 116 for the seventh wicket with B. P. Patel. His first Test hundred was 101 not out against Australia in the sixth Test at Bombay, 1979/80. Against New Zealand in 1976/7, he headed the Indian averages with 196 runs (65.33), and in the five Tests against England which followed he kept wicket impressively, making six stumpings. In Australia in 1977/8 he made 411 runs (41.10) in first-class matches, batting with great consistency, his highest score being only 59 not out, 305 of his runs coming in Tests at 33.88. He lost form behind the stumps in the series against Pakistan and West Indies in 1978/9 and was omitted from the 1979 tour to England, but returned successfully at home to Australia in 1979/80. Outstanding against England both at home and away in 1981/2, he did not concede a bye for three successive Tests in the home series, while England scored 1,964 runs. In both series he made useful runs. He remained consistently useful to India in series against all the other Test opponents until finally giving way to younger rivals in the mid-1980s. By then he had added a second Test hundred—102 against England at Bombay in 1984/5 when he shared in a stand of 235 with Shastri, a record Indian seventh-wicket partnership against any opposition. He finished the series with 291 runs, an average of 58. In the previous season he and Gavaskar had added 143 without being parted for the ninth wicket against West Indies at Madras, a record for the series. A popular character, he shaved off all his hair for religious reasons.

First-class career (1967–): 9,620 runs (30.15) including 13 centuries, 1 wicket (126.00), and 479 dismissals (367 c., 112 st.)
Test matches (88): 2,759 runs (27.04) including 2 centuries, 1 wicket (13.00), and 198 dismissals (160 c., 38 st.)

KISCHENCHAND, Gogumal

(b. 1925, Karachi) *Delhi, Sind, Gujarat, Baroda, and India*

A diminutive right-hander with an ungainly crouching stance, Kischenchand's footwork was excellent and he could be a highly effective hooker and driver. He was a hard-working outfield and occasional leg-break bowler. He toured Australia in 1947/8, achieving little in the Tests, other than 44 on a difficult wicket at Sydney. At home he played in one Test against Pakistan in 1952/3; and for several seasons showed to good account in representative matches against Commonwealth sides, but his career faded. In Ranji Trophy matches he made 4,216 runs (54.05), including ten centuries; and for Hindus in three seasons of the Pentangular Tournament, early in his career, he amassed 611 runs (101.83).

First-class career (1940–70): 6,983 runs (46.86) including 14 centuries, and 37 wickets (31.16)
Test matches (5): 89 runs (8.90) and 1 catch

KULKARNI, Rajeev Ramesh

(b. 1962, Bombay) *Bombay and India*

'Raju' Kulkarni was not particularly well built for a fast bowler but he generated considerable pace

in his prime. A tearaway fast bowler at first, like so many of that tribe, he was too erratic, partly owing to a very unusual action, where after a rhythmic run-up he threw his head sideways just before delivery. But he settled down, as Indian new-ball bowlers must, to being a good swing bowler at just above medium pace with a stated preference for bowling with a ball that was a few overs old. He first attracted attention when, as a 20-year-old, he took 8 for 111 for Bombay against Delhi in what is traditionally a high-pressure game. It led to his one-day international début against West Indies in 1983 at Guwahati, where he took 0 for 17 from 7 overs. Kulkarni remained on the fringe of international cricket, being selected first for a very high quality Indian youth team to Zimbabwe in 1984 and then for the tour to Australia in 1985/6. Predictably his opportunities in Australia remained confined to the one-dayers and he only made his Test début in 1986 against Australia under unusual circumstances, receiving a telephone call on the morning of the match asking him to report immediately to the Wankhede Stadium. He bowled with spirit to get 3 for 85, a fair achievement considering India were playing with three spinners who bowled 116.4 overs between them. He wasn't picked for the series against Sri Lanka immediately afterwards but got two more Test caps against Pakistan. In a series dominated by spin, bowling opportunities were few and India could soon make do with a bowler who could bat better than Kulkarni. He seemed to fade after that, preferring to concentrate on a successful sports equipment business, but he gave it one last shot in 1990, after working hard on his control, and was picked for the Indian team for the shortened Asia Cup.

First-class career (1982–93): 1,396 runs (21.15), 232 wickets (32.99), and 25 catches
Test matches (3): 2 runs (1.00), 5 wickets (45.40), and 1 catch

KULKARNI, Umesh Narayan

(b. 1942, Maharashtra) *Bombay and India*

A left-arm fast-medium bowler, Kulkarni appeared suddenly but disappeared almost as quickly, like many others in India blunted by the prevailing slow wickets. He toured Australasia in 1967/8 but, despite the generally firm pitches, was innocuous. A left-handed batsman, he batted doggedly in the third Test at Brisbane for one not out in a last-wicket stand with M. L. Jaisimha which brought India within 39 runs of victory.

KUMAR

First-class career (1963–70): 158 runs (7.90) and 40 wickets (39.95)
Test matches (4): 13 runs (4.33) and 5 wickets (47.60)

KUMAR, Vaman Vishwanath

(b. 1935, Madras) *Madras (Tamil Nadu) and India*

A gifted right-arm leg-break bowler, Vaman Kumar played in only two Tests, in the first of which against Pakistan at New Delhi in 1960/1 he took 5 for 64 and 2 for 68, which brought India very close to victory. Believed by some critics to be the best leg-spinner in the country, his prime coincided with that of S. P. Gupte and the advent of B. S. Chandrasekhar. On his début in the Ranji Trophy competition in 1955/6 he took seven wickets against Andhra, and in each of five seasons exceeded 25 wickets. In 1974/5 he became the first to take 400 wickets in the competition.

First-class career (1955–77): 673 runs (7.64) and 599 wickets (19.98)
Test matches (2): 6 runs (3.00), 7 wickets (28.85), and 2 catches

KUMBLE, Anil

(b. 1970, Bangalore) *Karnataka, Northamptonshire, and India*

A tall, well-built man with a particularly studious look, especially when he wears his glasses, Anil Kumble is a fascinating and curious bowler. Unlike traditional leg-spinners, he is not a big turner of the ball, preferring to bowl a potent combination of googlies, top-spinners, and the occasional leg-break, at a brisk pace. He bowls off a very long delivery stride, a remnant of his fast-bowling days, and is almost unbelievably accurate—the secret of his impressive strike-rate in international cricket. He is always attacking the batsmen, giving them very little room to play shots. Kumble's entry into international cricket was rapid, even by Indian standards. He made his début for Karnataka against Hyderabad in November 1989, incidentally bagging a king pair, and took 24 wickets in five Ranji Trophy matches apart from scoring valuable runs in the late order. He played for India under-19 against Pakistan that year and was one of the successes with 245 runs (at 45.00), including a century, and also took 12 wickets. While playing for Wills XI in a domestic one-day tournament he attracted the attention of the chairman of the Selection Committee, Raj

Singh Dungarpur, who decided he was good enough to play for India in spite of somewhat unimpressive figures. It required getting a passport in record time, and in April 1990 Kumble was playing for India and playing well enough to make the tour to England later that year. He was man of the match in the first one-day international at Leeds and made his Test début in the second match at Lord's, taking 3 for 105 in the first innings. On his return from England, he met with little success and was disappointed that he had to miss the tour of Australia and the World Cup for he reckoned that on Australia's bouncy wickets he might have done well. He used the break to complete his engineering degree with a distinction and though he was dropped by South Zone in the season of 1992, he managed to find a place in the Rest of India team for the Irani Trophy. On a wearing pitch he ran through Delhi twice to produce figures of 7 for 64 and 6 for 74. This virtually guaranteed his selection for the tour to South Africa and this time he proved his worth. He produced a particularly good performance at the Wanderers in the second Test, taking 6 for 53 from 44 overs, and finished the tour with 18 Test wickets. In the four home Tests that followed, three against England and one against Zimbabwe, he took 29 wickets and emerged as the leader of an Indian attack that had rediscovered its roots in spin bowling. He has been remarkably consistent since then, needing only 10 Tests to reach 50 wickets. He has also been India's most consistent bowler in one-day internationals, often bowling before the field restrictions have ceased and returning in the 'slog' overs. His finest moment came before a 100,000 delirious spectators at the Eden Gardens in the final of the Hero Cup when he ran through the West Indies to produce sensational figures of 6 for 12, still the best by an Indian in one-day cricket. Despite the adulation top cricketers receive in India, stardom sits lightly on Anil Kumble. He remains mild-mannered and modest, far removed in character from the aggressive appealer on the field, and has already prepared for an alternative career. He works as an executive at one of India's leading watch companies and is at work every day he is not playing which, to be honest, is not often! He assumed the captaincy of Karnataka in 1994/5 and celebrated it with his best figures in first-class cricket, 16 for 99 (8 for 58 and 8 for 41) against Kerala, also the best match figures by an Indian in first-class cricket. He joined Northamptonshire in 1995 as the overseas successor to Curtly Ambrose, taking 105 wickets in 17 games.

First-class career (1989–): 1,643 runs (27.84) including 3 centuries, 266 wickets (23.85), and 30 catches
Test matches (20): 249 runs (14.64), 99 wickets (25.37), and 9 catches

KUNDERAN, Budhisagar Krishnappa

(b. 1939, Mangalore) *Railways, Mysore, and India*

A product of India's new mass-coaching scheme, 'Budhi' Kunderan was a sound and exciting right-handed batsman who could fit in anywhere in the order, a very capable wicket-keeper and occasional medium-pace bowler. He toured the West Indies in 1961/2 and England in 1967, and at home played against Australia in 1959/60, Pakistan in 1960/1, England in 1961/2 and 1963/4, New Zealand in 1964/5, and West Indies in 1966/7. As an opener, against Australia in the fourth Test at Madras, he hit a confident 71 in a total of 149 in a losing cause; and in the first match against England at Bombay in 1961/2, he caught three and stumped two in the first innings when only eight wickets fell—a record for an Indian 'keeper—yet was superseded by Farokh Engineer for the rest of the series. Opening against England in the first match at Madras in 1963/4 when Engineer was unfit, he was man of the match, making the then Indian highest score against England, a solid 192 in 6 hours 50 minutes, and of England's 15 wickets to fall, he caught three and stumped three. In this series he made more runs than anyone on either side, 525 runs (52.50) but claimed only eight dismissals. Later, when batting at number nine, with runs badly needed, he hit 79 in 92 minutes off the powerful West Indian attack in the first match at Bombay in 1966/7. In England in 1967 Engineer kept in the Tests, although Kunderan opened the batting with him in the third match at Edgbaston with some success. Stricken by injuries, India called on him to open the bowling on the first day of this Test; he had not bowled before on the tour and did not do so again. He thus became one of the few men who have opened both the batting and bowling in the same Test—even more surprising for a wicket-keeper who often batted low in the order! Prolific in the Ranji Trophy competition, he made 2,637 runs (48.83). He served as a professional in the North Lancashire League, before becoming a successful and popular professional at Drumpellier in the Western Union in Scotland.

First-class career (1958–76): 5,708 runs (28.97) including 12 centuries, and 261 dismissals (175 c., 86 st.)
Test matches (18): 981 runs (32.70) including 2 centuries, 0–13, and 30 dismissals (23 c., 7 st.)

KRIPAL SINGH, Amritsar Govindsingh

(b. 1933, Madras; d. 1987, Madras) *Madras (Tamil Nadu), Hyderabad, and India*

An orthodox, fluent, and aggressive right-handed batsman, a useful off-break bowler and a good field, Kripal Singh scored 636 runs (106.00) in the Ranji Trophy in 1953/4, including 208 against Travencore-Cochin, his career-highest. He toured England in 1959, and at home played against New Zealand in 1955/6, Australia in 1956/7 and 1964/5, West Indies in 1958/9, and England in 1961/2 and 1963/4. On his Test début—the first match between the two countries—he scored 100 not out against New Zealand at Hyderabad, and in the three Tests of his first series he averaged 99.50. But in England, although he made 879 runs (33.80), he appeared in only one Test, and was a disappointment, spending much time in the doctor's hands. Suffering from a sore spinning finger (he took ten wickets) he seldom looked happy in the field; this was his only overseas tour. Against West Indies in the fourth Test at Madras in 1958/9, facing a large total, he top-scored with 53, but the remainder of his Test career was anticlimax. He captained his state for several years, and in the Ranji Trophy competition made 2,581 runs (49.63) and took 115 wickets (21.77). His father was A. G. Ram Singh and his brother is A. G. Milkha Singh.

First-class career (1950–66): 4,939 runs (40.81) including 10 centuries, 177 wickets (28.41), and 57 catches
Test matches (14): 422 runs (28.13) including 1 century, 10 wickets (58.40), and 4 catches

KRISHNAMURTHY, Pallemoni

(b. 1947, Hyderabad) *Hyderabad, Services, and India*

A quietly efficient, lanky, quick-thinking wicket-keeper, who stood up to even the fastest bowlers, Krishnamurthy first appeared in the Ranji Trophy competition at seventeen and toured the West Indies in 1970/1 and England in 1971. In the Caribbean he played in all the Tests, but in England, although he had 24 dismissals in nine first-class matches, he was displaced in the Tests by Farokh Engineer.

LALL SINGH

First-class career (1966–79): 1,559 runs (14.84) and 218 dismissals (150 c., 68 st.)
Test matches (5): 33 runs (5.50) and 8 dismissals (7 c., 1 st.)

LALL SINGH

(b. 1909, Kuala Lumpur; d. 1985, Kuala Lumpur)
Southern Punjab, Hindus, and India

An enterprising and aggressive right-handed batsman of rather uncertain defence, born and bred in Malaya, Lall Singh was an extraordinarily quick mover in the field. It was said that he glided over the ground like a snake. He toured England in 1932, his sole Test being the first ever, at Lord's, when he scored 15 and 29 and held 1 catch. For many years he worked for the Cricket Club in Kuala Lumpur. He is the only Malaysian to have played Test cricket.

First-class career (1931–6): 1,123 runs (24.95) including 1 century, and 23 catches

LAMBA, Raman

(b. 1960, Meerut) *Delhi and India*

Raman Lamba could be adventurous, carefree, even reckless at times, often advancing down the wicket against the new ball. His success stemmed from a quickness of eye and a remarkable ability to hit through the line rather than on any great emphasis on technique. Indeed his footwork was most unconventional, for while he was willing to go down the wicket, he rarely moved across to be totally behind the line. This approach worked remarkably against any bowling that was short of the highest class. He was effective in one-day cricket but at Test level he was suspect against fast bowling. He made his first-class début at the age of 18 playing for an India under-22 side against Alvin Kallicharan's West Indies side of 1978. However he had to wait three more years before making his début for Delhi, a fifty against a strong Rest of India side, and only came into national reckoning after a successful domestic season in 1985/6 when, as part of Delhi's winning side, he scored 691 runs at 69.10. He toured Sharjah and England in 1986 but he had to wait till September that year to play his first international match in a one-day game against Australia at Jaipur. In a totally entertaining innings, he made 64 from just 53 balls and went on to win the man-of-the-series award after hitting 102 in the sixth one-dayer at Rajkot, making it the

shortest span for an Indian between début and a one-day century. It won him a Test place against Sri Lanka, where he made 101 from three Test innings without looking good enough to win a permanent place. Indeed, he managed only one more half century in the next fifteen one-day internationals before being dropped. He continued to plunder runs in domestic cricket, however, and in the 1987/8 season he made scores of 197, 114, and 320 in successive matches in the Duleep Trophy, the last of which is still a record for the tournament. He followed it up with 771 runs in the next domestic season at 64.25 and earned yet another recall to the Indian team. He seemed to have got it right this time when he scored three fifties in the limited-overs MRF World Series. He was picked for the Pakistan tour in 1989 but having been named in the XI in place of Azharuddin for the first Test at Karachi, he reported unfit on the morning. He never played for India again and in fact, earned a ten-month suspension from domestic cricket for his alleged provocation of the bowler Rashid Patel, who chased him to the boundary, brandishing a stump. Despite this, he was appointed captain of Delhi in 1994 and set up an Indian record partnership of 464 for the first wicket with R. Sahgal against a rather poor Himachal Pradesh side. Lamba himself made 312, his second triple-century, and ended the season with 744 runs at 74.40, but by then a successful new generation of Indian batsmen had arrived and Lamba was content to play out time for Delhi.

First-class career (1978–): 7,379 runs (55.48) including 27 centuries, 6 wickets (67.33), and 55 catches
Test matches (4): 102 runs (20.40) and 5 catches

LIMBDI, Kumar Shri Ghanshyamsinghji Daulatsinghji Jhalla of

(b. 1902, Limbdi; d. 1964, Bhavnagar) *Western India*

Vice-captain on the Indian tour to England in 1932, the Maharajkumar of Limbdi's cricketing credentials were a trifle better than those of his captain, the Maharaja of Porbandar, who was his brother-in-law. But like him, he showed good judgement in supporting the case for a proper cricket captain for the first Test. He was a right-hand middle-order batsman who played for Western India.

First-class career (1932–43): 505 runs (17.41) and 11 catches

MADAN LAL, Udhouram Sharma

(b. 1951, Amritsar) *Delhi, Punjab, and India*

A likeable and enthusiastic cricketer, Madan Lal bowled fast-medium with an excellent action, although lacking the physical strength to be a regular threat at Test level, and batted vigorously. He made his first Test appearance against England at Old Trafford in 1974, having taken 7 for 95 in an innings against Worcestershire, six of his victims being Test players. Though he had a good tour generally with 399 runs (33.25) and 31 wickets (40.74) he was a failure in the two Tests he played. On his return to the Indian side against West Indies at Calcutta in 1974/5 he took 4 for 22 in the first innings. The following year he took 5 for 134 in an innings of 403 in the second Test against New Zealand at Christchurch, and batted well on the tour of the West Indies, making 189 in the Tests at 47.25. He went on another tour to Australia in 1977/8, taking 9 wickets at 21.88 in the two Tests he played, including 5 for 72 in the second innings of the first Test at Brisbane, but failing against fast bowling. The arrival of the helmet as an acceptable form of cricket equipment, however, helped him greatly, and after consistent performances in Ranji and Duleep Trophy cricket he returned successfully to Test cricket against England in 1981/2, when his powers of swing were mainly responsible for the Indian victory in the only one of six Tests to reach a decision: he took 5 for 23 in England's second innings at Bombay. In England in 1982 he made 309 runs on tour (61.80), but as a bowler was accurate rather than dangerous. In 1983/4 his batting, improved by the wearing of the helmet, began to make a more regular mark. He scored 74 against Pakistan at Bangalore, establishing with Roger Binny a new seventh-wicket record for the series of 155, and later in the season scored a bold 63 not out against West Indies at Kanpur, easily India's top score. But his Test career seemed to be over when before the second Test at Headingley in 1986 he was called up at the eleventh hour to replace an injured player and, having had recent experience only of league cricket in Lancashire, proceeded to take 3 for 18 in England's first innings of 102, adding useful scores in both innings to help India to a sweeping victory. He was also valuable in India's 1983 World Cup triumph.

First-class career (1968–90): 10,204 runs, (42.87) including 22 centuries, 625 wickets (25.50), and 142 catches

Test matches (39): 1,042 runs (22.65), 71 wickets (40.08), and 15 catches

MAKA, Ebrahim Suleman

(b. 1922, Bombay) *Bombay and India*

A competent second-string wicket-keeper, Ebrahim Maka toured the West Indies in 1952/3 and at home played against Pakistan in 1952/3, without much distinction.

First-class career (1941–63): 607 runs (15.56) and 85 dismissals (59 c., 26 st.)

Test matches (2): 2 runs (—) and 3 dismissals (2 c., 1 st.)

MALHOTRA, Ashok Omprakash

(b. 1957, Amritsar) *Haryana, Bengal, and India*

A wristy, adventurous, and attractive little right-handed batsman cast in the mould of Viswanath, Ashok Malhotra twirls the bat like a spinning top before settling for each new ball. He announced his ability by scoring 724 Ranji Trophy runs (72.40) in 1979/80, including an innings of 224 not out against Jammu and Kashmir, and followed up with 515 runs (73.57) in 1980/1. He made his first Test appearance against England in the last two Tests of the 1981/2 series, but he was unluckily run out after making an impressive 31 at Madras and failed in his only innings at Kanpur. In England in 1982 he failed in the first Test at Lord's and lost his place. He toured the West Indies in 1982/3, not playing in a Test, but returned to score 32 and 72 not out in the fourth Test at Bombay against a powerful West Indies attack in 1983/4. He played in the remaining Tests, but in only one against England in 1984/5 as he struggled in vain to gain a regular place in what had become an outstanding Indian batting side.

First-class career (1973–   ): 9,613 runs (51.68) including 24 centuries, 1 wicket (340.00), and 75 catches

Test matches (7): 226 runs (25.11), 0–3, and 2 catches

MANINDER SINGH, Harbansingh Billa

(b. 1965, Poona) *Delhi and India*

After playing in a Test against Pakistan in Karachi in 1982/3 at the age of 17 years and 193 days, the second-youngest Indian to do so, this tall, athletic left-arm orthodox spinner who, like his mentor, Bishan Bedi, bowls in a patka, had developed by the mid-1980s into a high-class slow bowler and fine fielder. He is also a determined right-hand tail-end batsman. He toured the West Indies later in 1982/3 and did well against them at home in 1983/4, taking 10 wickets at 33, including 4 for 85 at Ahmedabad. Having taken 40 first-class wickets at 14.57 in 1981/2, including 8 for 48 (12 for 122 in the match) against Punjab, he matured noticeably during the 1984/5 and 1985/6 seasons, taking 46 and 39 wickets respectively, including 11 in the 1985/6 Ranji Trophy final for Delhi against Haryana. This earned him a recall to the Indian team for the 1986 tour of England where he topped the Test bowling averages with 12 wickets at 15. The following home season, 1986/7 Maninder played a prominent part in the second tied Test, against Australia, both with the ball and because he was lbw to the last ball of the match. In the same season he took 7 for 51, and 10 for 107 in the match against Sri Lanka at Nagpur. Superseded as India's regular left-arm spinner by V. Raju, Maninder nevertheless made further Test appearances against Pakistan, three matches in 1989/90, and Zimbabwe (1992/3).

First-class career (1980–   ): 1,387 runs (16.81) including one century, 606 wickets (23.85), and 59 catches
Test matches (35): 99 runs (3.80), 88 wickets (37.36), and 9 catches

MANJREKAR, Sanjay Vijay

(b. 1965, Mangalore) *Bombay and India*

A very highly accomplished batsman technically, Sanjay Manjrekar, a trim, dapper, neat right-hander, is always a delight to watch. An extremely intelligent cricketer who thinks deeply about the game, he can be something of an introvert on the field, in sharp contrast with his lighter approach off it where his singing skills have been widely praised. Always aware of his capabilities, Manjrekar sometimes did not hesitate to declare them, a trait that led many to believe that he was a little arrogant and closed to suggestion. He experienced a major dip in his career after raising hopes at one time of being India's next Gavaskar in terms of technical perfection and hunger for runs. His initiation into international cricket though was far more traumatic. In his first Test at Delhi against Viv Richards's West Indies side of 1987/8 he had to retire hurt in the second innings after a brave stay in the middle after his lip had been cut by a ball from Winston Benjamin. He did not play another

Test for 15 months when he was last to be picked for the tour to the West Indies in 1989. He returned as one of the few gains of the tour and drew wide praise for his approach to playing genuinely fast bowling. He scored an outstanding century at Bridgetown and produced two brave innings at Kingston in a series that was marked by some dismal Indian batting. It earned him the number three spot in the series against Pakistan which India drew 0–0 almost entirely because of his brilliant batting. He made 569 runs from seven innings, including a century in the first Test at Karachi and 218 in the third at Lahore. But his impact in that series went beyond those numbers for he was always battling a crisis and seemed to enjoy doing it. Sadly, he never recaptured those heights, scoring only one other Test century, against Zimbabwe in 1992. It took him 500 minutes, during which he was often unable to play a stroke, making it the slowest Indian century and the fourth slowest on record. He seemed to struggle on the bouncy wickets in Australia and South Africa and it came as no surprise when he was dropped on his return from South Africa. That coincided with Indian cricket's finest hour on slow and low home wickets. Consequently, it took him a year to regain his place and he seemed strangely ill at ease at number six, rarely looking like the batsman who had charmed connoisseurs of the game all over the world. He flowered for a while in one-day cricket where his technique did not permit the occasional need to be unorthodox. Still, he was man of the series at Sharjah in 1991 and played an uncharacteristically blistering innings against South Africa at Delhi where he made 105 from 82 balls. He continues to have an outstanding record in first-class cricket, having first appeared for Bombay in 1984/5 after a phenomenal run of scores in university cricket. Playing against Hyderabad in the semi-final of the Ranji Trophy in 1991, he scored 377, getting 227 out of those in boundaries, an Indian record. That is the highest score by a Bombay batsman and the second-highest in the history of the Ranji Trophy. Clearly, Manjrekar had cricket in his blood and, though he vehemently denies any influence from his father, old-timers believe the correctness in technique was a legacy of Vijay Manjrekar. Like his father he has kept wicket occasionally, doing the job a few times for India in emergencies and surprising many with his agility. Sadly, he did himself no credit when he was sent off in a Ranji Trophy match for using abusive language against an umpire when he was captain of Bombay.

First-class career (1984–): 8,353 runs (56.82) including 27 centuries, 3 wickets (79.33), and 68 dismissals (66 c., 2 st.)
Test matches (33): 1,855 runs (38.64) including 4 centuries, 21 catches, and 1 stumping

MANJREKAR, Vijay Laxman

(b. 1931, Bombay; d. 1983, Bombay) *Bombay, Bengal, Andhra, Uttar Pradesh, Rajasthan, Maharashtra, and India*

Vijay Manjrekar was one of the finest batsmen to represent India, a correct, fluent, right-handed stroke-player, with a sterling defence and a wide repertoire of strokes, who refused to be overawed by the big matches; he was also an occasional off-break bowler and, in his early days, a splendidly versatile field who could keep wicket when necessary. He toured England in 1952 and 1959, Pakistan in 1954/5, and the West Indies in 1952/3 and 1961/2, and at home he played against England in 1951/2, 1961/2, and 1963/4, Pakistan in 1952/3, and 1960/1, New Zealand in 1955/6 and 1964/5, West Indies in 1958/9, and Australia in 1956/7 and 1964/5. He first played in the Ranji Trophy competition at 18 and made 48 on his Test début against England in the third Test at Calcutta. As the youngest member on his first tour of England he hit 133 in the first Test, at Headingley (despite Fred Trueman), adding 222 with Vijay Hazare for the fourth wicket. In all first-class matches he made 1,059 runs (39.22). On his first West Indian tour he made 681 runs (56.75), including 118 at Kingston in the final Test when he added 237 for the second wicket with Pankaj Roy, an Indian record. In his first home series against Pakistan he made 270 runs (45.00) and in his first against New Zealand, 386 runs (77.20), including 118 in the first match at Hyderabad, adding 238 for the third wicket with 'Polly' Umrigar, an Indian record. In a low-scoring series at home against Australia he scored most runs—197 in six innings—and after a moderate series against Pakistan, he toured England for the second time. Although overweight and having to undergo an operation for the removal of a knee-cap after the second Test at Lord's, he was still the most attractive and prolific scorer for a weak side, scoring 755 runs (68.68) in nine matches. He again headed the batting averages in his second series at home against Pakistan, with 247 runs (49.40); and, when India defeated England for the first time in a series in 1961/2, he was the outstanding batsman on either side, with 586 runs (83.71), including a flawless 189 not out at

Delhi. He did not enhance his career on his second visit to the Caribbean and his only long innings against England in 1963/4 was an over-defensive 108 in the first match, at Madras; but against Australia in 1964/5 he made 59 and 39 in the second match, at Bombay, when at 122 for six wickets India looked beaten, but he and the Nawab of Pataudi turned the tide and India won by two wickets. In his final Test innings, against New Zealand in the first match at Madras in 1964/5, he hit a classic 102 not out. In the Ranji Trophy he made 3,686 runs (57.59), including 12 centuries.

First-class career (1949–73): 12,832 runs (49.92) including 38 centuries, 20 wickets (32.85), 72 catches, and 6 stumpings
Test matches (55): 3,208 runs (39.12) including 7 centuries, 1–43, 19 catches, and 2 stumpings

MANKAD, Ashok Mulvantri ('Vinoo')

(b. 1946, Bombay) *Bombay and India*

Flat-footed and cuddly-figured, Ashok Mankad, the eldest son of Vinoo Mankad, did not at first look as though seeds of greatness had created him. But though he never rose to the heights of his father, he became a very accomplished right-handed batsman with a good range of neat and well-timed strokes; always looking cheerful, he had a sound temperament and plenty of determination and concentration. Making his first Test appearance against New Zealand in 1969/70, he did not secure a place for India until scoring 74, 8, 64, 68, and 97 in successive innings in the first three Tests against Australia in 1969/70. In this, his first full series, he scored 357 runs as an opening batsman at 35.70, but the Test century he narrowly missed at Delhi never came so close again. In 1970/1 he was equally sound against the West Indies at home, making 180 runs in three Tests at 36.00, but though he scored 795 runs (41.84) in first-class matches on the 1971 tour of England, he failed in the Tests. His best Test score in England, 43 at Edgbaston in 1974, was most unluckily ended when his cap fell on the wicket as he tried to fend off a ball from Chris Old. In Australia in 1977/8 he headed the first-class averages with 508 runs (50.80) with a highest score of 92 but three Tests brought only 119 runs (23.80) and he was not picked for India again. However, having made his first-class début in 1963/4 he made over 6,000 Ranji Trophy runs, and nearly 13,000 in all first-class cricket, including 265 for Bombay against Delhi in 1980/1. Like his father, he played league cricket in England.

MANKAD

First-class career (1963–83): 12,980 runs (50.90) including 31 centuries, 72 wickets (45.50), and 126 catches
Test matches (22): 991 runs (25.41), 0–43, and 12 catches

MANKAD, Mulvantrai Himatial

(b. 1917, Jamnagar; d. 1978, Bombay) *Western India, Nawanagar, Maharashtra, Gujarat, Bengal, Bombay, Rajasthan, and India*

A team-man at all times and, perhaps, the greatest all-rounder produced by India, 'Vinoo' (his schoolboy nickname) was a right-handed batsman who varied from the stolid to the adventurous according to the state of the game: watchful in defence, the late-cut (or dab), leg-hit, and cover-drive earned him most of his runs. He was a high-quality, left-arm orthodox slow bowler with a slightly round-arm action who spun the ball unusually strongly and his flight and length were almost invariably perfect. His over would last little more than a minute; he never allowed a batsman to rest. He fielded beautifully. He captained India in six Tests (losing one and drawing five). Coached by A. F. Wensley (Sussex), he announced himself against Lord Tennyson's team in 1937/8 when he made 376 runs (62.66) and took 15 wickets (14.53) in the unofficial Tests. Touring England in 1946, he became the only Indian to achieve the double; as utility batsman, either at number one or anywhere else in the order, he made 1,120 runs (28.00) and he took 129 wickets (20.76) in 1,160.1 overs. In the Tests he captured 7 for 146 in the second match, at Old Trafford, and scored 63 in his first, at Lord's. He toured Australia in 1947/8, England in 1952 (Tests only), the West Indies in 1952/3, and Pakistan in 1954/5, and at home he played against West Indies in 1948/9 and 1958/9, England in 1951/2, Pakistan in 1952/3, New Zealand in 1955/6, and Australia in 1956/7. In Australia he was again the outstanding all-rounder, making 889 runs (38.65) and taking 61 wickets (26.14). In the Tests he made 116 in the third match at Melbourne to become the first centurion for India against Australia. Against England at home he took 34 Test wickets (at 16.97), collecting 8 for 55 (in 38.5 overs) and 4 for 53 (in 30.5 overs) at Madras where India won her first Test. On his second England tour his Lancashire League commitments allowed him to appear only in three Tests, including a historic performance at Lord's when he made 72 and 184 and bowled 97 overs for 231 runs and 5 wickets. In the first home series against Pakistan four Tests brought him 25 wickets (20.56) including a match-winning 13 for 131 in the first-ever match between the two countries at Delhi. Against New Zealand he scored 526 runs (105.20), and took 12 wickets (27.33); in the fifth Test at Madras he made 231 in $8\frac{3}{4}$ hours, putting on 413 for the first wicket with Pankaj Roy which remains a world record for all Tests. He also took 4 for 65 in 40 overs in the second innings. In the second match at Bombay he had made 223 in 8 hours in a total of 421 for 8 wickets declared, after an early batting collapse. Until Ian Botham of England did so in 21 Tests, no one had completed the Test double of 1,000 runs and 100 wickets in fewer games—he needed 23—and a few years later he joined two others with a tally of 2,000 runs and 100 wickets.

First-class career (1935–64): 11,591 runs (34.70) including 26 centuries, 782 wickets (24.53), and 190 catches
Test matches (44): 2,109 runs (31.47) including 5 centuries, 162 wickets (32.32), and 33 catches

MANSUR ALI KHAN

(b. 1941) *Oxford University, Sussex, Hyderabad, and India*

See Pataudi, Nawab of, jun.

MANTRI, Madhav Krishnaji

(b. 1921, Nasik) *Maharashtra, Bombay, and India*

The uncle of India's greatest modern batsman, Sunil Gavaskar, M. K. Mantri was himself a sound opening batsman and a neat wicket-keeper, who toured England in 1952 and at home played against England in 1951/2 and Pakistan in 1954/5, without quite establishing himself. In England he made 550 runs (22.91) and had 39 dismissals. In the Ranji Trophy competition he was consistently successful: he hit his highest score, 200, for Bombay against Maharashtra in 1948/9, the third of three centuries in successive matches; altogether in the competition he made 2,787 runs (50.67).

First-class career (1941–68): 4,403 runs (33.86) including 7 centuries, and 192 dismissals (136 c., 56 st.)
Test matches (4): 67 runs (9.57) and 9 dismissals (8 c., 1 st.)

MARSHALL, Nariman Dorabsha

(b. 1905, Bombay; d. 1979, Jaipur) *Western India and Nawanagar*

Nariman Marshall was a stylish middle-order batsman who occasionally bowled slow-medium off-cutters and kept wicket if necessary. He toured England with the 1932 Indian team, for whom he made 268 runs at 26.80.

First-class career (1928–38): 1,006 runs (22.58) including 2 centuries, 12 wickets (27.91), and 12 catches

MEHERHOMJI, Kharshed Rustom

(b. 1911, Bombay; d. 1982, Bombay) *Western India, Bombay, Parsees, and India*

As a competent deputy wicket-keeper, Meherhomji toured England in 1936, in his sole Test, the second, at Old Trafford, scoring 0 not out and holding 1 catch. He also played for the Parsees in the Bombay tournament. His uncle, Rustomji Meherhomji, was a batsman who toured England with All India in 1911.

First-class career (1933–46): 656 runs (15.61) and 71 dismissals (61 c., 10 st.)

MEHRA, Vijay Laxman

(b. 1938, Amritsar) *Eastern Punjab, Railways, and India*

A small but strong man, Vijay Mehra was a solid, crisp, right-handed opening batsman, who represented India for the first time in 1955/6 in the second Test against New Zealand at Bombay aged 17 years 265 days, the youngest ever to appear for the country. After two Tests against New Zealand he had to wait eight years before being selected again for his country—against England in the fourth match at Calcutta in 1961/2, when he made 62 and India defeated England for only the second time. He toured the West Indies in 1961/2, when his only real success was another 62 in the fourth Test at Port of Spain; and he played twice against England in 1963/4 with little success. His career faded, but in Ranji Trophy matches he amassed 3,222 runs (38.35), including ten centuries. He became a Test selector.

First-class career (1953–75): 5,636 runs (34.36) including 13 centuries, and 26 wickets (30.84)

Test matches (8): 329 runs (25.30), 0–6, and 1 catch

MERCHANT, Vijay Madhavji Thackersey

(b. 1911, Bombay; d. 1987, Bombay) *Bombay, Hindus, and India*

India's first outstanding Test batsman, Vijay Merchant's comparatively small physique did not handicap him, for what he lacked in reach he compensated for by perfect footwork and a quick eye. Right-handed, his cutting, both square and late, was brilliant, and he hooked, drove (especially the fast bowlers), and played the ball off his legs with masterly certainty. He was a careful builder of an innings and there was something softly feline about him at the wicket although, strangely enough, he appeared rather heavy-footed in the outfield. He appeared for Hindus in the Bombay Pentangular or Quadrangular tournaments (1929–46) and Bombay in the Ranji Trophy competition (1933–52); and he represented India in the first home Test series, against England in 1933/4, making 178 runs in three matches. In England in the wet summer of 1936, he was the outstanding batsman, with 1,745 runs (51.32), his 282 runs (47.00) in the Tests including a superb 114 at Old Trafford. In India he made his career-highest, 359 not out, against Maharashtra in 1943/4. Back in England in 1946 as vice-captain, another wet summer, he was superb with 2,385 runs (74.53), his seven centuries including two doubles—242 not out against Lancashire and 205 against Sussex. In the Tests he made 245 runs (49.00), with 128 in the rain-spoiled final Oval match as his highest. In his final Test, the first against England at Delhi in 1951/2, he scored 154, adding 211 for the third wicket with Vijay Hazare, a new Indian record for any wicket against England. It was felt, however, that the two were such rivals that they batted more for themselves than their team: England were able to save a match they seemed sure to lose. A recurrence of an old shoulder injury in this match, throwing himself full length while fielding, led to his retirement from active participation in the game, but he became a very prominent and outspoken administrator and writer. In Ranji Trophy matches he made 3,639 runs (98.75), including 16 centuries in only 47 innings. His first-class average is second only to Bradman.

First-class career (1929–52): 13,470 runs (71.64) including 45 centuries, 65 wickets (32.12), and 115 catches

Test matches (10): 859 runs (47.72) including 3 centuries, 0–40, and 7 catches

MILKHA SINGH, Amritsar Govindsingh

(b. 1941, Madras) *Madras (Tamil Nadu) and India*

A sound left-handed batsman and occasional right-arm medium-pace bowler in the sixties, Milkha Singh was the mainstay of the Madras (later Tamil Nadu) batting, together with his brother, A. G. Kripal Singh. He had a short Test career, playing at home against Australia in 1959/60, Pakistan 1960/1 and England 1961/2 without establishing himself. In the Ranji Trophy competition he made over 2,000 runs, averaging over 40 runs an innings.

First-class career (1958–69): 4,324 runs (35.44) including 8 centuries

Test matches (4): 92 runs (15.33), 0–2, and 2 catches

MISTRY, Kaikhushru Maneksha

(b. 1874, Bombay; d. 1959, Bombay) *Parsees*

One of India's earliest batting stars, Mistry was described as the Clem Hill of the Parsees and played for them with great success. He was employed by the Maharaja of Patiala, for whose team he once joined Ranji in making a double-century. Though he bowled left-arm medium pace well enough to have an excellent average, it is really as a left-handed batsman that he is remembered. As private secretary to the Maharaja, he toured England in 1911, but official engagements kept him away most of the time. He did, however, play the MCC match, making 78 out of 106 in 80 minutes with some bold stroke-play. It seemed India had a batting star but unfortunately for him the Maharaja fell sick and had to return home and Major Mistry played in only three games. He led India in their first unofficial Test match against MCC at Bombay in 1926–27. Now a colonel and aged 52, he scored 51.

First-class career (1893–1928): 1,600 runs (23.52), 104 wickets (13.17), and 34 catches

MODI, Rusi Sheriyar

(b. 1924, Bombay) *Bombay, Parsees, and India*

Tall and almost painfully thin, Rusi Modi was a careful, patient and wristy right-handed batsman with a sound defence, an elegant mover at the crease, who was beautifully light on his feet and quick to throw his whole body behind the ball and strike it to the boundary. He was an occasional bowler of medium-pace in-swingers. He toured England in 1946, and at home played against West Indies in 1948/9, England in 1951/2 and Pakistan in 1952/3. After scoring a record 215 for Parsees against Europeans in the Bombay Pentangular tournament in 1943/4, he made only one run on his début in the Ranji Trophy competition in 1944/5 but followed with a sequence of 168, 128, 160, 210, 245 not out (his career-highest, against Baroda), 31 not out, and 113. That season he had the record aggregate of 1,008 runs (201.60). In England in 1946, a wet summer, he scored 1,196 runs (37.37). Against West Indies he was the outstanding run-getter with 560 runs (56.00) in the Tests including his sole Test century, 112 in the second match at Bombay, when he added 156 for the third wicket and saved the match. His Test career came to an end, however, on a regrettable note of anticlimax. In Ranji Trophy matches he made 2,696 runs (81.69), including ten centuries.

First-class career (1941–62): 7,529 runs (53.02) including 20 centuries, 32 wickets (38.31), and 29 catches

Test matches (10): 736 runs (46.00) including 1 century, 0–14, and 3 catches

MOHOL, Sadanand Namdev

(b. 1938, Bassein) *Maharashtra*

Sadanand Mohol was a right-arm fast-medium bowler who played for Maharashtra in an era when spinners dominated Indian cricket completely. He took 112 wickets in the Ranji Trophy at 20.27, including a best of 8 for 42 against Saurashtra at Morvi in 1964/5. The following year, in a Defence Fund match at Poona, he became the first Indian bowler in first-class cricket to take four wickets in four balls. In the 1966/7 season he took 22 wickets and later that year toured England with the Indian team as one of just two opening bowlers. It was felt that his experience in the Lancashire League would be useful but he only appeared in seven matches on the tour, partly owing to a leg injury and partly due to a bias towards spinners. He retired in 1970/1 without having played any Test cricket.

First-class career (1959–71): 549 runs (12.76), 168 wickets (21.37), and 21 catches

MONGIA Nayan Ramlal

(b. 1969, Baroda) *Baroda and India*

A clean 'keeper who follows the Indian tradition of appealing loudly, and at every conceivable opportunity, Nayan Mongia is really two personalities meshed into one. On the field he can be aggressive and vociferous and has had ICC referees taking a close look at him more than once, but off it he is modest, polite, and eager to have a conversation on the game. Mongia's coach asked him while still a teenager to try his hand at wicket-keeping and pronounced him a natural. His progress thereafter was rapid, leading to a place in the Indian team for the Youth World Cup in 1987/8 and for a tour to Pakistan in 1988/9 with the India under-19 team, where he played the first two Tests as a pure opener and finished third in the batting list overall. He made his first-class début for Baroda the following year, due largely to the absence on national duty of Kiran More, and ended the season with a century against Delhi in the semi-final of the Ranji Trophy. Word of his ability had begun to spread but he was still a surprising selection for the tour to England in 1990, since both wicket-keepers came from the same Baroda team. Mongia missed the subsequent tours to Australia and South Africa, in spite of consistent performances in the Ranji Trophy and the Duleep Trophy in which he averaged 77.16 in 1990/1 and 80.80 in 1992/3. With More's decline becoming obvious, however, Mongia got his break during the Irani Trophy match of 1993/4. He not only scored an attractive century, but also picked up ten catches, still his best performance. In January 1994 he made his Test début against Sri Lanka, becoming India's 200th Test cricketer. He scored a quick 44 batting at number eight and 'kept well enough to suggest that India had discovered a long-term wicket-keeper. Two months later, he opened the batting in New Zealand, scoring 45 and 38. He quickly gets behind the line of the ball and though he tends to favour the on side, he has shots all round the wicket, as he showed again during a brave 80 against the West Indies at Bombay. His problems in international cricket have had less to do with the opposition and more with his occasional inexplicable ways. He was dropped from the Indian team for two matches in the winter of 1994 for apparently not trying to win a match in the closing overs which, in itself, was a departure from his normally aggressive style. Earlier that year he received a suspended one-match sentence during the Australasia Cup at Sharjah for showing dissent against an umpiring decision.

First-class career (1989–   ): 3,022 runs (47.96) including 7 centuries, and 132 dismissals (119 c., 13 st.)

Test matches (7): 342 runs (34.20), and 18 dismissals (16 c., 2 st.)

MORE, Kiran Shankar

(b. 1962, Baroda) *Baroda and India*

An accomplished wicket-keeper and right-handed batsman, Kiran More took to Test cricket like a duck to water. Having toured the West Indies as deputy to Syed Kirmani in 1982/3, he was unlucky to have to wait until the tour of England in 1986 to play his first Test cricket, having kept consistently, and batted well, during the tour of Australia the previous winter, when he played in nine one-day internationals. In England he was an immediate success, keeping wicket in the three Tests with neatness and sure-handed skill and batting with much confidence always in tune with the needs of his side. He made 156 runs at an average of 52 in his five Test innings, playing a vital role in the victories over England at Lord's and Headingley and in saving them from defeat with 31 not out on a difficult pitch at Edgbaston. His highest score is 181 not out against Uttar Pradesh in 1983/4 when he shared a last-wicket stand of 145 with V. Patel.

First-class career (1980–   ): 3,826 runs (28.76) including 4 centuries, and 318 dismissals (261 c., 57 st.)

Test matches (49): 1,285 runs (25.70) and 130 dismissals (110 c., 20 st.)

MUDDIAH, Venatappa Musandra

(b. 1929, Bangalore) *Services, Mysore, Hyderabad, and India*

A right-arm off-spin bowler, Venatappa Muddiah toured England in 1959 taking 30 wickets (29.46), but was not selected for the Tests. At home he played once each against Australia in 1959/60 and Pakistan in 1960/1 with little success. In Ranji Trophy matches he captured 101 wickets (23.49).

First-class career (1949–63): 805 runs (13.87), 175 wickets (23.76), and 62 catches

Test matches (2): 11 runs (5.50) and 3 wickets (44.66)

MUKHERJEE, Saradindu Purnendu

(b. 1964, Calcutta) *Bengal*

Saradindu Mukherjee was a tall off-spinner who bowled off a high action and with a distinctive jump in his delivery stride. He made a late but dramatic entry into first-class cricket. He was 25 when he first played for Bengal in the semi-final of the Ranji Trophy against Hyderabad but he finished that match with 5 for 132 including a hat-trick. With India looking for an off-spinner after Arshad Ayub, Mukherjee got his break in the Asia Cup in 1990 after only four first-class matches. He did reasonably well, only once going above four runs per over. But opportunities were limited since India played no more international cricket that year and the selectors did not consider him for the tour to Australia in 1991/2 where India had no off-spinner. He took 22 wickets in the Ranji Trophy that year but could not quite reproduce that form and was never really in contention thereafter.

First-class career (1989–): 527 runs (27.73), 66 wickets (36.69), and 13 catches

MUSHTAQ ALI, Syed

(b. 1914, Indore) *Holkar, Central India, Muslims, Maharashtra, Gujarat, Madhya Bharat, Uttar Pradesh, Madhya Pradesh, and India*

Despite sudden rushes of blood to the head—he had a tendency to jump out and hoist the ball straight to a fielder—Mushtaq Ali was a right-handed opening batsman of brilliance, flair, and a loose, easy grace. Very quick on his feet, he always introduced a spirit of adventure into his play. In his earlier days he was better known as a slow left-arm bowler, and he appeared as such in his first two Tests against England in 1933/4. In England in 1936 he made 1,078 runs (25.06), including four centuries, and formed a strong opening partnership with Vijay Merchant: in the second Test at Old Trafford, when India batted again 368 behind, they opened with a lively 203, Mushtaq hitting 112 in $2\frac{1}{4}$ hours. In the unofficial Test series against Lord Tennyson's team in 1937/8 he scored 101 and 55 at Calcutta. Back in England in 1946 he seemed too often to throw away his wicket attempting the impossible but he proved that he could bat with responsibility against the West Indies in 1948/9 when he came back as opener in the third Test at Calcutta, and scored 54 and 106, batting out of character for India to save the game. In a long career in the Ranji Trophy competition he made 5,013 runs (49.14), including seventeen centuries, his career-highest being 233 for Holkar against United Provinces in 1947/8.

First-class career (1930–64): 13,213 runs (35.90) including 30 centuries, 162 wickets (29.34), and 160 catches

Test matches (11): 612 runs (32.21) including 2 centuries, 3 wickets (67.33), and 7 catches

NADKARNI, Rameshchandra Gangaram

(b. 1932, Nasik) *Maharashtra, Bombay, and India*

A genuine all-rounder, 'Bapu' Nadkarni was a steady and determined left-handed batsman, a patient slow bowler of immaculate length and studious variations, and a courageous close field. He toured England in 1959, the West Indies in 1962/3, and Australasia in 1967/8, and at home played against New Zealand in 1955/6 and 1964/5, West Indies in 1958/9 and 1966/7, Australia in 1959/60 and 1964/5, Pakistan in 1960/1, and England in 1961/2 and 1963/4. A tall, neat cricketer who always bowled and batted with shirt-sleeves buttoned at the wrist, he was the most improved player on the otherwise ill-fated England tour of 1959 making 945 runs (23.62), taking 55 wickets (28.41), and holding 23 catches. In the last match at The Oval he fought for 4 hours for 76 in a vain attempt to avert defeat. In 1960/1 against Pakistan at Delhi he captured 5 for 67 in 84.4 overs (62 maidens). In the West Indies in 1961/2, when all five Tests were lost, he scored 286 runs (33.71) and also took nine wickets (35.11). Against England in 1963/4 he headed the batting with 294 runs (98.00—thanks to five not outs) and took nine wickets (30.88). In the fifth match at Kanpur he spent a total of 11 hours over 52 and 122, both times undefeated. In the first match at Madras his analysis read: 32–27–5–0, and he created a world Test record by bowling 131 balls (21.5 overs) without conceding a run. In 1964/5 against Australia he was the most successful bowler on either side with 17 wickets (13.70) in the three Tests: in the first at Madras he captured 5 for 31 and 6 for 91. Rather ineffective as a bowler against New Zealand in 1959/60, he hit 75 quickly in the first match at Madras but when he visited New Zealand he took 6 for 43 in the second innings of the third Test, at Wellington. In the Ranji Trophy competition he made 3,993 runs (62.39), his twelve centuries including 283 not out for Bombay against Delhi, 1960/1, and took 181 wickets (17.52). Captain of his two state teams, he later wrote about the allegedly shabby treatment meted out by the Board of Control to Indian Test players of his day.

First-class career (1951–72): 8,880 runs (40.36) including 14 centuries, 500 wickets (21.37), and 140 catches

Test matches (41): 1,414 runs (25.70) including 1 century, 88 wickets (29.07), and 22 catches

NAIK, Sudhir Sakharam

(b. 1945, Bombay) *Bombay and India*

A gritty right-handed batsman, whose main strength lay on the leg-side, Sudhir Naik toured England in 1974, making 730 runs (40.55) and, on his Test début at Edgbaston, scored 77. He also played against West Indies in 1974/5.

First-class career (1966–78): 4,376 runs (35.29) including 7 centuries, and 42 catches
Test matches (3): 141 runs (23.50)

NAOOMAL, Jeoomal Makhija

(b. 1904, Karachi; d. 1980, Bombay) *Sind, Northern India, Hindus, and India*

A diminutive and watchful right-handed batsman, who could defend doggedly and cut neatly, Naoomal was also a left-arm change slow bowler, and an outstanding fielder or deputy wicket-keeper. He toured England in 1932, making 1,297 runs (30.88), and 33 and 25 in the only Test, at Lord's. He played in two Tests against England in 1933/4. In 1938/9 he hit his career-highest, 203 not out, in $4\frac{1}{2}$ hours against Nawanagar in the Ranji Trophy.

First-class career (1926–45): 4,140 runs (32.44) including 7 centuries, 108 wickets (27.54), and 43 catches
Test matches (3): 108 runs (27.00) and 2 wickets (34.00)

NARASIMHA RAO, Modireddy Venkat

(b. 1954, Secunderabad) *Hyderabad, Ireland, and India*

A tall right-hander with a sound technique and a useful leg-spinner with a high action, Rao played in two Tests against West Indies in 1978/9, making only 11 runs in three innings, taking 1 for 107 and holding 5 catches. He has been a popular and successful professional in Ireland.

First-class career (1971–89): 4,845 runs (40.71) including 9 centuries, 245 wickets (28.05), and 111 catches

NAVLE, Janardhan Gnanoba

(b. 1902, Fulgaon; d. 1979, Poona) *Gwalior, Hindus, Rajputana, Central India, Holkar, and India*

A diminutive wicket-keeper, very quick, neat and safe in all that he did, and considered by Jack Hobbs to be in the same class as George Duckworth and Bert Oldfield, Navle was also a competent right-handed opening batsman. For many years he kept for Hindus in the Bombay Tournament and, touring England in 1932, he made 600 runs (15.78) and claimed 36 dismissals. He played for India in the first Test against England at Lord's in 1932 and at Bombay in 1933/4.

First-class career (1918–44): 1,976 runs (19.18) and 137 dismissals (101 c., 36 st.)
Test matches (2): 42 runs (10.50) and 1 catch

NAYAK, Suvendra Vithal

(b. 1954, Bombay) *Bombay and India*

With a smile never far away, 'Suru' Nayak conveyed his enjoyment of the game. He was a most capable all-round cricketer: a brilliant cover fielder with a strong throw; a stroke-playing right-hand batsman; and a bowler who specialized in medium-paced in-swing but could also bowl useful leg-breaks. Steady performances for Bombay and for West Zone earned him two appearances for India in one-day internationals against England at home in 1981/2. Touring England in 1982, he batted steadily in county matches and played in the second and third Tests with limited success.

First-class career (1976–89): 1,799 runs (28.10), including 2 centuries, 133 wickets (35.47), and 38 catches
Test matches (2): 19 runs (9.50), 1–132, and 1 catch

NAYUDU, Col. Cottari Kankaiya

(b. 1895, Nagrur; d. 1967, Indore) *Central Provinces and Berar, Holkar and United Provinces, Hindus, Rajputana, Hyderabad, Central India, Andhra, and India*

India's first captain in Test cricket and the best all-rounder at that time, 'C.K.' Nayudu was a tall and well-proportioned right-handed batsman, a front-foot player who hit the ball tremendously hard and was strong in driving on both sides of the wicket; he was also a more than useful slow-medium change-bowler, whose length was superb and spin well controlled. An all-round sportsman, retiring and modest but with a majestic gait, he proved an admirable leader in England in 1932, when he was the best batsman with 1,618 runs (40.45), including five centuries, besides taking 65 wickets (25.53). In the first home series against England in 1933/4 he made 160 runs (26.66) and, as captain, was exacting and thorough. In England in 1936, as vice-captain, he scored 1,102 runs (26.23) and took 51 wickets (31.78). In the third Test at The Oval, though hit

455

on the solar plexus by a ball from 'Gubby' Allen, he refused to retire and hit 81, his highest in Tests, in $2\frac{1}{2}$ hours. He was in his prime before the advent of Tests. From 1916 he played in the Bombay Quadrangular matches, making 155 for Hindus against Muslims in 1928/9. He hit 153 for Hindus against MCC in 1926/7, including eleven sixes and thirteen fours, in just over 100 minutes. In the Ranji Trophy he made his career-highest, 200, for Holkar against Baroda in 1945/6. His best bowling figures were 7 for 63 for Central India against Bengal in 1935/6. In his sixty-ninth year he returned to play in one first-class match. He became the elder statesman of Indian cricket, especially as Test selector and vice-president of the Indian Cricket Board of Control. His son, Prakash, played for Madhya Pradesh, his brother, C.S., for India, and his daughter became a cricket commentator. A huge monument to him stands at Indore, in the shape of a bat.

First-class career (1916–64): 11,825 runs (35.94) including 26 centuries, 411 wickets (29.28), 171 catches, and 1 stumping
Test matches (7): 350 runs (25.00), 9 wickets (42.88), and 4 catches

NAYUDU, Cottari Subbanna

(b. 1914, Nagpur) *Central India, Baroda, Holkar, Bengal, Andhra Pradesh, Uttar Pradesh, Madhya Pradesh, and India*

A bundle of energy, 'C.S.' Nayudu was a right-arm leg-break and googly bowler who was like a flail, spinning the ball fiercely. As a right-handed batsman, he was inelegant but waited for the right ball and then hit it hard; and in the deep he was brilliant. Between 1934 and 1961 he had an excellent record in the Ranji Trophy competition—2,575 runs (30.20) and 295 wickets (23.49), once taking 14 wickets in a match and twice exceeding 30 wickets in a season. But, despite his opportunities, he was very disappointing for India. He holds a record for bowling more balls in one match than anyone. For Holkar v. Bombay in 1944/5 he bowled 152.5 overs (917 balls).

First-class career (1931–61): 5,786 runs (23.90) including 4 centuries, 647 wickets (26.54), and 144 catches
Test matches (11): 147 runs (9.18), 2 wickets (179.50), and 3 catches

NAZIR ALI, Syed

(b. 1906, Jullundur; d. 1975, Lahore) *Southern Punjab, Sussex, Muslims, Patiala, and India*

An attacking right-handed batsman, who was a particularly fine driver, a fast-medium bowler who could move the ball both ways, and a splendid fielder, Nazir Ali attracted attention with good batting and even better bowling against MCC in India in 1926/7, and Arthur Gilligan suggested that he should qualify for Sussex. Some months later the secretary of Sussex was awakened at 1 a.m. by Nazir Ali asking for hospitality or to be sent where he could obtain it! Subsequently, he played once for the county and much cricket around London. He was a successful member of the Indian team in England in 1932—making 1,020 runs (31.87) and taking 23 wickets (21.78)—and played in the first-ever Test between the two countries, at Lord's. In 1933/4 he appeared in the final Test of the first series in India against England. In later years he was prominent in the administration of the game in Pakistan. He was younger brother of S. Wazir Ali.

First-class career (1923–54): 3,440 runs (30.17) including 7 centuries, 158 wickets (25.49), and 48 catches
Test matches (2): 30 runs (7.50) and 4 wickets (20.75)

NIMBALKAR, Bhausaheb Babasaheb

(b. 1919, Kolhapur) *Baroda, Holkar, Railways, and Maharashtra*

Bhausaheb Nimbalkar was a prolific scorer in domestic cricket where he enjoyed a long innings without really making a mark at the international level. He still holds the record for the highest individual score in Indian first-class cricket (443 not out for Maharashtra against Kathiawar) and indeed might have broken Bradman's prevailing record of 452 had it not been for the strange attitude of the rival captain. Kathiawar had made 238 in the first innings and by lunch on the fourth day, Maharashtra were 826 for 4, Nimbalkar 443 not out. The Kathiawar captain thought he had had enough and announced during the break that his side would concede the match if Maharashtra continued batting but would play on if they declared. Maharashtra declared, Bradman's record remained intact and Nimbalkar's score is still the fourth highest in first-class cricket after Lara, Hanif Mohammad, and Bradman. Apart from keeping wicket, he was also a right-arm medium-pace bowler. He played one unofficial Test against the first Commonwealth team in 1949–50, making 48 and taking one catch.

First-class career (1939–62): 4,577 runs (52.01) including 12 centuries, 52 wickets (34.23), and 86 dismissals (73 c., 13 st.)

NIMBALKAR, Raosaheb Babasaheb

(b. 1915, Kolhapur; d. 1965, Jalna) *Maharashtra and Baroda*

A right-handed middle-order batsman and wicket-keeper who also bowled leg-breaks occasionally, Raosaheb Nimbalkar was the elder brother of B. B. Nimbalkar who, unusually, was also a wicket-keeper. He was part of the Maharashtra team that won the Ranji Trophy in 1939/40 and 1940/1 and after moving to Baroda led them to two Ranji Trophy wins; in 1946/7 and 1949/50. He toured Ceylon in 1944/5 with the Indian team, playing in one unofficial Test and scoring 15 runs in two innings. He toured England with the 1946 Indian team but due to a fractured thumb, only played in seven matches and could not play in any of the Tests. The number of stumpings relative to the number of catches make his record quite remarkable.

First-class career (1934–53): 2,687 runs (30.19) including 4 centuries, 3 wickets (59.66), and 123 dismissals (82 c., 41 st.)

NISSAR, Mahomed

(b. 1910, Hoshiarpur; d. 1963, Lahore) *Southern Punjab, Muslims, Patiala, Uttar Pradesh, Railways, and India*

A tall, strapping man from the Punjabi hills, Mahomed Nissar was a right-arm fast bowler with a good, easy action who was able to make the ball swing and break back viciously. He came up a long way from park cricket, although hampered by the salwar he wore in his early days instead of a pair of flannels. In England in 1932 he and Amar Singh formed the attacking spearhead, Nissar heading the bowling with 71 wickets (18.09), and in the first-ever Test, at Lord's, he taking 5 for 93 in the first innings. In the first innings of the first-ever Test in India, against England at Bombay in 1933/4, he took 5 for 90. Back in England in 1936, he took 66 wickets (25.13) and headed the bowling in Tests with 12 wickets (28.58). For several years until 1940 he opened Muslims' attack in the Bombay Pentangular Tournament, and it was said that he could master all the batsmen except the Hindu, C. K.

Nayudu, who would walk down the wicket before the ball left his hand.

First-class career (1928–54): 1,120 runs (10.98) 396 wickets (17.70), and 65 catches
Test matches (6): 55 runs (6.87), 25 wickets (28.28), and 2 catches

NYALCHAND, Shah

(b. 1919, Dhangadhra) *Kathiawar and India*

A persistent, nagging left-arm medium-pace bowler, Nyalchand's sole Test was the second against Pakistan at Lucknow in 1952/3, when he scored 6 not out and 1 and took 3 for 97 in 64 overs (33 maidens) in the visitors' only innings.

First-class career (1939–64): 420 runs (7.63) and 235 wickets (22.57)

PAI, Ajit Manohar

(b. 1945, Bombay) *Bombay and India*

Tall, wiry, and fiery, a left-handed batsman and right-arm fast-medium bowler, Ajit Pai packed a terrific wallop in his shots off the back foot and could bowl at a stinging pace. He met with some success in both Ranji and Duleep Trophy competitions, but played in only a sole Test, the first against New Zealand at Bombay in 1969/70, scoring 1 and 9 and taking 2 for 31.

First-class career (1968–76): 872 runs (24.22) and 85 wickets (25.22)

PALIA, Phiroz Edulji

(b. 1910, Bombay; d. 1981, Bangalore) *United Provinces, Mysore, Parsees, Madras, Bombay, Bengal, and India*

An attractive left-handed batsman, useful slow bowler and quick fielder, Palia toured England in 1932 and 1936, playing in India's first-ever Test, at Lord's, and again at Lord's four years later. In 1932 he made 476 runs (21.63) and took 24 wickets (31.00). His highest score was also the best ever for United Provinces in the Ranji Trophy competition, 216 against Maharashtra in 1939/40. In this competition he made 1,501 runs (39.50). He was prominent for Parsees in the Bombay Quadrangular Tournament.

First-class career (1928–54): 4,536 runs (32.40) including 8 centuries, 208 wickets (24.06), and 40 catches
Test matches (2): 29 runs (9.66) and 0–13

PALWANKAR, Baloo

(b. 1876, Bombay; d. 1955, Bombay) *Hindus*

Probably the first of the great Indian spinners, Baloo Palwankar worked as a groundsman at a club in Bombay for a paltry salary. Unfortunately, social customs of that era meant that he was prevented from playing for the Hindus. Ironically, the Parsees allowed him to play and when the Hindus realized his ability, they called him back and in a delightful turn of fate, Baloo went on to lead the Hindus! He was on the first All-India tour of England in 1911 and his left-arm spin fetched him an amazing 114 wickets at a mere 18.86 each. He played first-class cricket till 1920/1 and his outstanding bowling average is an indicator of how good he must have been. He now has a road named after him in Bombay.

First-class career (1905–21): 753 runs (13.69), 179 wickets (15.21), and 12 catches

PANDIT, Chandrakant Sitaram

(b. 1961, Bombay) *Bombay and India*

Chandra Pandit, a smiling, neatly built cricketer, won his first Test cap at Headingley in 1986 as a batsman, although he is also a gifted wicket-keeper who in 1983/4 beat the then Ranji Trophy record with 31 dismissals. A right-hander, he made his début in 1979/80 but had to wait two more seasons before playing first-class cricket regularly. In 1983/4 he accounted for nine batsmen in the Board President's XI match against the West Indies and in the same season scored 398 runs at an average of 44. In 1984/5 he scored 610 runs and was again India's most successful wicket-keeper and it was clear that his chance had come at a higher level. Although not able to claim the wicket-keeping berth in the Tests in England, he 'kept with panache and tidiness in the two limited-overs internationals and, replacing the injured Mohinder Amarnath at Headingley, sparkled as a cover fielder and made 23 and 17 in difficult batting conditions, an important contribution to India's first Test victory at Leeds.

First-class career (1979–   ): 5,182 runs (49.35) including 14 centuries, 1 wicket (61.00), and 236 dismissals (206 c., 30 st.)
Test matches (5): 171 runs (24.42) and 16 dismissals (14 c., 2 st.)

PARKAR, Ghulam Ahmed Hasan Mohamed

(b. 1955, Kaluste) *Bombay and India*

A strict Muslim and a dedicated right-handed opening batsman, Parkar was one of the finest cover fieldsmen produced by India and appeared on the field as substitute several times against England at home in 1981/2 before making his first Test appearance officially in England in 1982. Unable, however, to deal with the awkward bounce of Bob Willis's best deliveries, he failed in the one-day internationals and in his only Test, at Lord's, where he scored 6 and 1 and held 1 catch. Opening partner with Sunil Gavaskar for Bombay, he shared in a first-wicket stand of 421 in the quarter-final of the 1981/2 Ranji Trophy against Bengal.

First-class career (1978–86): 4,167 runs (42.09) including 11 centuries, 2 wickets (65.50), and 47 dismissals (46 c., 1 st.)

PARKAR, Ramnath Dhondu

(b. 1946, Bombay) *Bombay and India*

Ramnath Parkar was a dapper and flowing stroke-making right-handed batsman, very light on his feet, who usually opened, and a fine cover-point. But his opportunities for India were limited to only two Tests against England, in 1972/3.

First-class career (1964–81): 4,455 runs (33.75) including 8 centuries, and 1 wicket (55.00)
Test matches (2): 80 runs (20.00)

PARSANA, Dhiraj Devshibhai

(b. 1947, Rajkot) *Saurashtra, Railways, Gujarat, Durham, and India*

An accurate left-arm seam-bowler capable of swinging the new ball considerably and a useful left-handed batsman, Dhiraj Parsana was discarded after two unsuccessful Tests against the West Indies in 1978/9.

First-class career (1965–83): 2,943 runs (26.51) including 2 centuries, and 320 wickets (22.26)
Test matches (2): 1 run (0.50) and 1 wicket (50.00)

PATANKAR, Chandrakant Trimbak

(b. 1930, Bombay) *Bombay and India*

A very competent wicket-keeper and useful right-handed batsman, Patankar's sole Test was the fourth at Calcutta against New Zealand in 1955/6. He dismissed four (three caught and one stumped), all in the first innings, and scored 13 and 1 not out.

First-class career (1945–68): 503 runs (15.71) including 1 century, and 58 dismissals (38 c., 20 st.)

PATAUDI, Nawab of, jun. (now Mansur Ali Khan)

(b. 1941, Bhopal) *Oxford University, Sussex, Hyderabad, Delhi, and India*

Recapturing for a time the aristocratic strain in Indian cricket, 'Tiger' Pataudi was a brave, vigorous, and adventurous right-handed batsman who attached greater importance to the productiveness of a stroke than its attractiveness. He was strong on the leg-side and not afraid to loft the ball, and he would have been much more prolific in Tests but for an accident before he had reached his prime. A freshman from Winchester in 1960, he hit 131 against Cambridge at Lord's and also made his début for Sussex, but the following year just before the Varsity match, when he was the first Indian to captain Oxford, he was involved in a car accident and lost the sight of his right eye. Having set his heart on playing for India, within a month he was back at the nets facing the bowling again, refocusing, adjusting his stance, experimenting with a contact lens, and practising very hard. He returned to Oxford's side in 1963, and went on to captain India in forty of his forty-six Tests. He also captained Sussex in 1966. He toured the West Indies in 1961/2, England in 1967, and Australasia in 1967/8, and at home played against England in 1961/2, 1963/4, and 1972/3, Australia in 1964/5 and 1969/70, New Zealand in 1964/5 and 1969/70, and West Indies in 1966/7 and 1974/5. In his third Test, against England at Madras in 1961/2, he hit 103 in only 2 hours 35 minutes. He succeeded to the Indian captaincy during the disappointing tour of the West Indies following Nari Contractor's serious injury, but made no large scores. He had a poor series against England in 1963/4 but a year later against Australia he was back in top form, scoring 270 runs (67.50), including a splendid 128 not out in a total of 276 in the first match at Madras and 86 and 53 at Bombay, when India beat Australia. A few weeks later he was equally effective against New Zealand with 317 runs (52.83), including 153 in the second match, at Calcutta, and 113 in the fourth, at Delhi. He led India to victory against New Zealand in two series. On his sole England tour, despite his shrewd captaincy and fine batting, his team suffered many misfortunes: he

made 777 runs (35.31), including 269 runs (44.83) in the Tests, when he stood out by himself, scoring 64 and 148 in a masterly fight-back in the first at Headingley. In Australia, batting under considerable personal and team difficulties, he headed the Test averages with 339 runs (56.50). Under his new name, Mansur Ali Khan, having been deprived by the Indian Government of his title, he returned to Tests against England in 1972/3 (but not as captain), making 147 runs (36.75) in three matches. Reappointed leader against West Indies in 1974/5, he was injured while fielding in the first Test and could not find his form. He was prolific in the Duleep Trophy competition, and he also made over 2,000 runs in the Ranji Trophy.

First-class career (1957–76): 15,425 runs (33.67) including 33 centuries, 10 wickets (77.60), and 208 catches

Test matches (46): 2,793 runs (34.91) including 6 centuries, 1–88, and 27 catches

PATAUDI, Nawab of, sen.

(b. 1910; d. 1952) *Oxford University, Worcestershire, Southern Punjab, and India*

See England section.

PATEL, Ashok Kurjibhai

(b. 1957, Bhavnagar) *Saurashtra*

Ashok Patel was a tall and thin man who bowled flat off-breaks with very good control. This made him an obvious choice for one-day internationals rather than for Test matches, in which his lack of penetration was likely to be more obvious. He played for Saurashtra and since only two teams qualified for the Ranji Trophy knockout, his chances on the national stage were few. But in 1983/4, he picked up 25 wickets and won a place in the West Zone team against the touring West Indians. Later that year, Australia toured India for a series of one-day matches and with his restrictive bowling, Patel did well against them, bowling the middle overs without giving away too many runs.

First-class career (1979–89): 1,506 runs (28.41), 109 wickets (34.57), and 24 catches

PATEL, Brijesh Parsuram

(b. 1952, Baroda) *Karnataka (Mysore) and India*

Capable on his day of touching the heights of batting, Brijesh Patel is a right-hander with a scintillating array of strokes played wristily and with a rare panache, but his best has been all too seldom displayed at the highest level. It took him a long time to establish a regular place in the Indian team following failures in the Tests in England in 1974. He made 73 not out in a losing cause against West Indies at Bombay in the fifth Test of 1974/5, 81 in similar circumstances against New Zealand at Wellington in 1975/6, and 115 not out against the West Indies at Port of Spain in the second Test of 1976. In four innings in this series he scored 207 runs, three times not out (average 207!). In 1975/6 he earned his place against New Zealand and England by scoring 601 runs in the Ranji Trophy (100.16) and, in the Tests, scoring 172 runs at 43.00 against New Zealand and 286 at 28.60 against England. These included a sparkling 83 in the fifth Test against England at Bombay. But he was disappointing both in Australia in 1977/8 and in England in 1979. He was a brilliant cover-point.

First-class career (1969–88): 11,911 runs (45.63) including 37 centuries, 7 wickets (30.71), and 86 catches

Test matches (21): 972 runs (29.45) including 1 century, and 17 catches

PATEL, Jasubhai Motibhai

(b. 1924, Ahmedabad; d. 1992) *Gujarat and India*

A right-arm off-break bowler who really spun the ball, Jasubhai Patel toured Pakistan in 1954/5 and headed the bowling averages with 35 wickets (10.68), but was selected for only one Test: indeed he had a chequered career in representative cricket. At home he played against New Zealand in 1955/6, and Australia in 1956/7 and 1959/60. A wrist injury sustained as a boy gave him a somewhat jerky action. His best series was against Australia in 1959/60, when he captured 19 wickets (17.21) in three matches; at Kanpur he came in at the last moment and, on newly laid turf, took 14 for 124 (9 for 69 and 5 for 55), the best-ever bowling performance for India, which made possible the first-ever win over Australia. In the Ranji Trophy competition he secured 140 wickets (21.46).

First-class career (1943–64): 787 runs (13.16) including 1 century, and 248 wickets (21.83)
Test matches (7): 25 runs (2.77), 29 wickets (21.96), and 2 catches

PATEL, Rashid Ghulam Mohammad

(b. 1964, Sabarkantha) *Baroda and India*

Rashid Patel was a left-arm fast-medium bowler who was rather surprisingly picked to play against New Zealand in the Bombay Test of 1988/9 two years after his début for Baroda. In 1987/8, he had taken 16 wickets from four matches but had done little else of note. His début, indeed his only Test, was disastrous. He only bowled 14 overs in the match, got no wickets and bagged a pair, falling to Hadlee both times, but took one catch. In the solitary one-day international that he played, he again failed to get any wickets and did not get his turn with the bat. At first-class level, Patel was an effective opening bowler but unfortunately for him, history will remember him more for his role in the infamous Raman Lamba–Rashid Patel affair when, armed with a stump, he chased Lamba all the way to third man. It was perhaps the ugliest moment in Indian cricket and earned him a one-year suspension. On his return to first-class cricket for Baroda, he was not the same bowler.

First-class career (1986–   ): 402 runs (10.05), 112 wickets (34.16), and 13 catches

PATIALA, Maharaja of, HH Sir Bhupendrasingh Rajindersingh

(b. 1891, Patiala; d. 1938, Patiala) *Hindus, Sikhs, Northern India, Patiala, and Southern Punjab*

A huge man with a weakness for the good things in life, the Maharaja was also a great lover and patron of cricket at a time when the game was just striking roots in India. It helped too that it was politically correct at that time to be involved in cricket! His largesse, probably inherited from his father, drew the finest cricketers to Patiala and the likes of Rhodes, Hirst, Leyland, Larwood, Tarrant, and Ranji played there. In 1911, he organized, and presumably paid for, the first Indian tour to England. In 1934, he donated a trophy for the national cricket championship of India, the Ranji Trophy, named after the great man who had died a year earlier. Poor health prevented his playing a lot more first-class cricket himself. At the time of his death, just 46 years old, he was president of the Cricket Club of India.

First-class career: (1915–38) 643 runs (17.37), 2 wickets (30.00), and 4 catches

PATIALA, Yuvraj of (Lt.-Gen. Yadavendra Singh)

(b. 1913, Patiala; d. 1974, The Hague, Holland) *Patiala, Southern Punjab, and India*

A great patron of the game, like his father, who donated the Ranji Trophy, the Yuvraj of Patiala was a tall, graceful right-handed batsman who played in a single Test, the third against England, at Madras, in 1933/4, scoring 24 and 60 and holding two catches. He was invited to tour England in 1932, but state business caused him to decline. He was India's Ambassador to Holland from 1971 until his death.

First-class career (1931–58): 1,602 runs (20.80) including 2 centuries, and 48 wickets (31.93)

PATIL, Sadashiv Raoji

(b. 1933, Kolhapur) *Maharashtra and India*

A right-arm fast-medium bowler, Sadashiv Patil played in a single Test, the second against New Zealand, at Bombay, in 1955/6, scoring 14 not out, taking 2 for 51 and holding 1 catch.

First-class career (1952–64): 859 runs (26.84) and 83 wickets (30.60)

PATIL, Sandeep Madhusudan

(b. 1956, Bombay) *Bombay, Madhya Pradesh, and India*

Tall and talented, a successful pop singer, film actor, and businessman as well as a brilliant attacking right-hand batsman, Sandeep Patil was a national idol whose first two Test centuries were absolute gems, the product of a player of very unusual flair. Having made his mark strongly for Bombay, and also in London club cricket, where his dominant batting led to Edmonton being voted out of the Middlesex League for playing 'guest artists', he toured Australia in 1980/1, and at Adelaide, despite being hit on the head by a ball from Len Pascoe in the previous Test, he hit a dazzling 174. On the tour he scored 802 runs (53.46). His powerful driving, cutting, and hooking were even more impressive against England at Old Trafford in 1982. After a run of failures, his Test future was at stake, but with no sign of nerves he hit India out of danger. His 129 not out included eighteen fours, six of them coming off one over from Willis which included a no-ball. This equalled the highest number of runs scored off one Test over of six legitimate balls. Two Tests later, against Sri Lanka at Madras, he hit another rapid century, 114 not out. His Ranji Trophy début was made in 1975/6, and four seasons later he hit his highest score, 210 against Saurashtra. Also a useful medium-paced bowler despite an awkward action, he swung the ball and even at Test level could be a worthwhile change bowler. Very much at home in England, he played for the Surrey second eleven in 1979 and was an important member of India's World Cup-winning team in 1983. He returned to England in 1986 but did not play a leading role.

First-class career (1975–92): 7,726 runs (43.40) including 20 centuries, 83 wickets (32.27), and 65 catches

Test matches (29): 1,588 runs (36.93) including 4 centuries, 9 wickets (26.66), and 12 catches

PHADKAR, Dattaray Gajaran

(b. 1925, Kolhapur; d. 1985, Madras) *Maharashtra, Bombay, Bengal, Railways, and India*

A genuine all-rounder of excellent temperament, Dattaray Phadkar was an attacking right-handed middle-order batsman, especially good against fast bowling, and a fast-medium bowler who could swing the ball either way, extract much life from the pitch and exploit a bad wicket with slower off-breaks. He toured Australia in 1947/8, England in 1952, the West Indies in 1952/3, and Pakistan in 1954/5, and at home played against West Indies in 1948/9 and 1958/9, England in 1951/2, Pakistan in 1952/3, New Zealand in 1955/6, and Australia in 1956/7. On the first tour of Australia he headed the batting in the Tests with 314 runs (52.33), in each of his four matches making at least one fifty, and took 8 wickets (31.75). On his Test début at Sydney in the second match he hit 51 and took 3 for 14, and in the fourth match at Adelaide he scored 123, adding 188 with Vijay Hazare for the sixth wicket after a batting collapse. Against West Indies in 1948/9 he made 240 runs (40.00) and took 14 wickets (29.35), in the fourth match, at Madras, collecting 7 for 159 in a total of 582. His only real success, however, against England in 1951/2 was in the third match, at Calcutta, when he scored 115 and took four wickets. In England the following season he did not do as well as expected, his only significant contribution to the Tests being a defiant 64 in the second innings of the first match at Headingley after Fred Trueman had broken through; joining Hazare at 26 for 5, these two added 105. Not helped by the lifeless matting pitches in the Caribbean in 1952/3, he yet headed the bowling in the Tests with 9 wickets (25.55). Making his début in the Ranji Trophy competition at 17, he later captained Bombay and, altogether, made 1,920 runs (46.82) and took 216 wickets (16.61), with a highest of 217 for Bombay against Maharashtra in 1950/1 and best bowling in an innings, 7 for 37 for Bengal against Bihar in 1956/7.

PORBANDAR

First-class career (1942–60): 5,377 runs (36.08) including 8 centuries, 466 wickets (22.04), and 92 catches
Test matches (31): 1,229 runs (32.34) including 2 centuries, 62 wickets (36.85), and 21 catches

PORBANDAR, Maharaja of, Rana saheb Shri Sir Natwarsinghji Bhavsinghji

(b. 1901, Porbandar; d. 1979, Porbandar)

The ruler of a little state in what is now Gujarat, the Maharaja of Porbandar's association with cricket is quite unique. Though classified as a right-hand middle-order batsman, he had no claims to cricketing greatness at all, being at best a club cricketer. But he was captain of the Indian team to England in 1932, pedigree rather than skill being the deciding factor, offering to take the job after the Maharaja of Patiala, who was the original choice, had to drop out. To his great credit he insisted that C. K. Nayudu should lead India in the first Test rather than himself.

First-class career (1931–3): 42 runs (6.00)

PRABHAKAR, Manoj

(b. 1963, Ghaziabad) *Delhi, Durham, and India*

One of the most consistent all-rounders in Indian domestic cricket since his first appearance in 1982/3 (taking 5 for 88 against Haryana) Manoj Prabhakar was only belatedly given an extended chance by the Indian selectors. A wiry medium-paced swing bowler and a right-handed batsman of sound technique who often opened for Delhi, he is one of very few cricketers to have opened both the bowling and the batting in Test cricket. Doing so with some success against England in 1992/3 (130 runs in four innings and 5 wickets in the three Tests) he was retained in his dual role in the following season. Chiefly a bowler, he shrewdly mixed inswingers and outswingers and possessed a skilful slower ball and a much quicker bouncer, a ball viewed with suspicion by his opponents, but never queried by umpires. He had made 122 in the Ranji Trophy final against Bombay in 1983/4 as well as taking the new ball and claiming a wicket in both innings. He played in two Tests at home against England in 1984/5, making 35 not out and, as an opener, 21, in the third Test at Calcutta but at this stage his bowling was not penetrative enough and he was considered only for limited-overs games for a time thereafter. He toured England in 1986 but was not chosen for the Tests. He finally established himself on tours of New Zealand and Pakistan in

1989/90. In 1991 in England his fighting 67 not out in the second innings at Old Trafford helped to save India from defeat. In 102 one-day internationals to 1993/4 he had scored 1,253 runs (21.98) including one century and taken 129 wickets (26.79). Against West Indies in 1994/5 he scored 120 in the first innings at Chandigarh, his maiden Test hundred but had to retire hurt in the second after being hit in the teeth by a bouncer. He joined Durham in 1995.

First-class career (1982–   ): 5,609 runs (43.82) including 15 centuries, 301 wickets (29.11), and 49 catches
Test matches (36): 1,490 runs (32.39) including 1 century, 94 wickets (37.58), and 19 catches

PRASANNA, Erapally Anantharao Srinivasa

(b. 1940, Bangalore) *Mysore (Karnataka) and India*

One of the famous quartet of Indian spin bowlers who graced their country's cricket in the 1960s and 1970s, Erapally Prasanna was a true artist, a subtle and flowing off-spin bowler with a neat, brisk, high action and marvellous control of line, length, and flight. Unlike his great rival, Venkataraghavan, he spun the ball in a classic high loop towards the batsman, increasing his chances of beating his adversary through the air. Moreover, through tossing the ball so high, Prasanna also made it bounce higher than expected. On the other hand the bold driver could attack him more easily than spinners with a flatter arc. His Test début was at Madras against England in 1961/2 in the fifth Test and as late as 1976/7 he was the leading Indian bowler in another series against England. His first overseas tour to the West Indies in 1961/2 proved a tough one and he did not play another Test for five years. He gained a regular place at last in England in 1967, where he took 7 for 111 in the Edgbaston Test and 45 wickets on the tour at 23.91. Against Australia and New Zealand away in 1967/8 he took 25 wickets (27.44) and 24 wickets (18.79) and was throughout the tour the leading Indian bowler. In successive Tests at Wellington and Auckland he took 8 for 88 and 8 for 76 (in the match). There followed 20 more Test wickets at home to New Zealand in 1969/70 and 26 at home to Australia also in 1969/70. A finger injury temporarily lost him his place in the West Indies in 1970/1 and thereafter he was never sure whether he or Venkat would earn the selectors' choice. His next full series were against the West Indies at home in 1974/5, when he took 15 wickets (40.06), including a match-winning 9 for 111 in the fourth game at Madras, and New Zealand away in 1975/6 when at Auckland he took 8 for 76 in the first innings and 11 for 140 in the match. Against England at home in 1976/7 he played in four of the five Tests and claimed 18 wickets at 21.61 including 4 for 93 in 57.4 overs at Calcutta but he gradually faded with youth and fitness no longer on his side. In domestic cricket he played first for Mysore (now Karnataka) in 1961/2, and captained them after 1969/70.

First-class career (1961–79): 2,476 runs (11.90), 957 wickets (23.45), and 127 catches
Test matches (49): 735 runs (11.48), 189 wickets (30.39), and 18 catches

PUNJABI, Pananmal Hotchand

(b. 1921, Karachi) *Gujarat and India*

A competent right-handed opening batsman who could keep wicket, Punjabi toured Pakistan in 1954/5, scoring 393 runs (23.11), but was disappointing in his sole Test series.

First-class career (1943–60): 1,953 runs (38.21) including 6 centuries
Test matches (5): 164 runs (16.40) and 5 catches

RAI SINGH, Kanwar

(b. 1922, Darkati) *Southern Punjab, India Services, and India*

A capable right-handed batsman, Rai Singh toured Australia in 1947/8 with little success, and in his sole Test, the third at Melbourne, scored 2 and 24.

First-class career (1940–61): 1,778 runs (30.13) including 4 centuries, and 21 wickets (33.33)

RAJINDERNATH, V.

(b. 1928, Amritsar; d. 1989, Madras) *Southern Punjab, Bihar, Northern India, and India*

A competent wicket-keeper and right-handed batsman, Rajindernath's sole Test was the third against Pakistan at Bombay in 1952/3, when he did not bat and made four stumpings (three off S. P. Gupte).

First-class career (1943–59): 844 runs (22.21) and 59 dismissals (36 c., 23 st.)

RAJINDER PAL

(b. 1937, Delhi) *Southern Punjab, Delhi, and India*

A right-arm fast-medium bowler who met with much success in the Ranji Trophy competition, Rajinder Pal's sole Test was the second against

England at Bombay in 1963/4, scoring 3 and 3 not out and taking 0 for 22.

First-class career (1954–74): 1,072 runs (11.28), and 339 wickets (21.88)

RAJPUT, Lalchand Sitaram

(b. 1961, Bombay) *Assam, East Zone, and India*

Making 94, 110, and 136 in successive Ranji Trophy matches, Lalchand Rajput, a steady but positive right-handed opening batsman, finished the 1984/5 season with 737 first-class runs at 40.94 and earned himself selection in the first two Tests of the three games played by India in Sri Lanka in September 1985. He began well with scores of 32 and 61 in his first Test but a duck and 12 in his second lost him his place in the strong Indian team. His high first-class average suggests that he would have played more Test cricket in eras when India was blessed with fewer high-class batsmen, although in four one-day internationals he managed only nine runs. He is an occasional bowler of medium pace who can also bowl slow off-breaks.

First-class career (1981–   ): 7,291 runs (49.26) including 18 centuries, 51 wickets (48.1), and 71 catches
Test matches (2): 105 runs (26.25) and 1 catch

RAJU, Sagilakshmi Venkatapathy

(b. 1969, Hyderabad) *Hyderabad and India*

An extremely slim little man with the ironic nickname 'Muscles', and a joyously carefree individual, Venkatapathy Raju is an outstanding match-winner on turning pitches. An orthodox slow left-arm spinner, he does not possess the gentle flight of a Bishan Bedi, but his great accuracy means he can be difficult to get away even on less responsive tracks. At first he suffered from not finding a regular place in the Indian team and from the moment that he became part of a spin-bowling trio in home conditions, his performances improved dramatically. He had 16 wickets in three Tests against England in 1993, an equal number against Sri Lanka in 1994, including 11 for 125 in the third Test, and topped that with 20 against the West Indies in 1994, when he looked India's best bowler. His finest moment was in his third Test in 1990 against Sri Lanka at Chandigarh where, on a vicious track, he took 6 for 12 in the first innings. His has been a steady rise in Indian cricket, having played with credit at under-15, under-17, and under-19 levels. He went to Australia with the India under-19 team in

1986/7 and played the Youth World Cup of 1987. He had made his début in the Ranji Trophy for Hyderabad in 1985/6 but it was in 1987 that he really began attracting attention. He took 20 and 24 wickets in successive seasons before outstanding performances on lifeless pitches in the Irani Trophy and the Duleep Trophy final saw him being picked for the tour to New Zealand in early 1990. He had 3 for 86 on début and as nightwatchman scored 31. In fact, his right-handed batting has often held up tottering innings for he can be a sticky and reasonably correct batsman. He invariably carries a smile out with him. He is a relaxed and extremely popular cricketer who has perhaps made more friends overseas than any other contemporary Indian player.

First-class career (1985–): 868 runs (14.00), 304 wickets (25.86), and 28 catches

Test matches (21): 228 runs (12.66), 81 wickets (28.03), and 5 catches

RAMAN, Woorkeri Venkat

(b. 1965, Madras) *Tamil Nadu, and India*

A tall, angular man with a most languid approach, Raman often gave the impression that he was disinterested. That façade hid a competitive streak and a delightful sense of humour. He was an attractive batsman who played the ball late and with silken timing, but, like so many left-handers, he was suspect against the moving ball outside off stump, especially given his tendency to hit on the rise. For years, Raman toured with Indian cricket teams, getting only stray opportunities and never acquiring a fixed place in the batting order. Indeed, his transition from a slow left-arm spinner who could bat to a specialist batsman was dramatic. From 1982/3, when he made his first class début (bowling left-arm spin with a bent arm alongside the leg-breaks of L. Sivaramakrishnan) to 1987/8, he batted in the lower middle order for Tamil Nadu and South Zone. On his one-day international début, against the West Indies at Calcutta, he batted at number eight but surprised everybody by walking out at number three just three days later. He had never batted that high before and made it a memorable occasion by scoring 95. A week later, he made his Test début at Madras with scores of 9 and 83 and almost immediately the bowler in Raman (who had taken 4 for 94 from 32 overs of left-arm spin against the West Indies a month before his début) vanished. Despite his promising start, he was only picked for one Test match each against New

Zealand in 1988/9 at home, and against the West Indies, where he flew as a replacement. In the same 1988/9 season he broke a 44-year-old record in the Ranji Trophy by scoring 1,018 runs in seven matches at 145.42 including innings of 313, 200 not out, and 238. In a desperate attempt to win back his place, Raman allowed himself to be converted into an opener during India's tour of New Zealand in 1990. He averaged 44 in that series including an innings of 96 at Christchurch but did not get another Test match for over two years. He was recalled to the side in 1992/3 for the tour of Zimbabwe and South Africa, where his bright moment came when he scored a typically classy century in the fourth one-day international at Pretoria. But when England toured India in early 1993, he was called out only to take some outstanding catches as a substitute at silly-point. He toured Sri Lanka in 1993 without playing a single match, yet continued to shine in domestic cricket, scoring three centuries in the Duleep Trophy in 1994/5. With a little faith from the selectors and a place in the middle order rather than at the top, where he was always a little too flashy and loose, there is little doubt that Woorkeri Raman would have scored many more runs for India.

First-class career (1982–): 6,510 runs (49.69) including 17 centuries, 80 wickets (36.51), and 69 catches

Test matches (8): 367 runs (30.58), 2 wickets (33.00), and 5 catches

RAMASWAMI, Cota

(b. 1896, Madras) *Madras, Indians, and India*

A sturdily built son of a pioneer of the game in Madras, Cota Ramaswami is the second-oldest Indian to make a Test début, at 40 years 37 days. In his prime, a free-scoring left-handed batsman and a fine driver on both sides of the wicket, he represented Hindus in the Bombay Tournament and toured England in 1936, though he claimed modestly that he had been chosen 'for other than cricket reasons' as he had become 'bulky and slow'. On the tour, however, he made 737 runs (30.70), and 40 and 60 on his Test début, at Old Trafford.

First-class career (1915–41): 2,400 runs (28.91) including 2 centuries, 30 wickets (33.06), and 33 catches

Test matches (2): 170 runs (56.66)

RAMCHAND, Gulabrai Sipahahimalani

(b. 1927, Karachi) *Sind, Bombay, and India*

Powerfully built, the whole-hearted 'Ram' Ramchand was a genuine all-rounder, a hard-hitting right-handed batsman, particularly forceful when playing off the back foot, and a medium-paced in-swinging bowler of very accurate length. He toured England in 1952, the West Indies in 1952/3, and Pakistan in 1954/5, and at home played against Pakistan in 1952/3, New Zealand in 1955/6, Australia in 1956/7 and 1959/60, and West Indies in 1958/9. He was captain in the five matches against Australia in 1959/60, his final series, winning one and losing two. A surprise choice for the England tour, he made 644 runs (24.76), took 64 wickets (25.85) and held 20 catches for a weak side, though he achieved little in the Tests, indeed being dismissed for a pair on his début at Headingley. In the Caribbean he made 249 runs (24.90) in the Tests, but his bowling was not penetrative. Against the Commonwealth team in 1953/4 he made 410 runs (58.57) in the unofficial Tests, and in Pakistan he headed the Test bowling averages with ten wickets (20.00), besides averaging 29.40 with the bat. At Bahawalpur in the second match, after India had lost seven wickets for 107 on the first day, he made 53 doggedly, and in the fifth match at Karachi he took 6 for 49 in 28 overs in the first innings, his best performance in Tests. His first century for India was a sparkling 106 not out against New Zealand in the third match at Calcutta in 1955/6. Against Australia in the second match, at Bombay, in 1956/7 he played a rescuing innings of 109. In his final series—as captain against Australia—he was disappointing with bat and ball but led his country to her first-ever win over Australia, in the second match at Kanpur. In the Ranji Trophy competition he made 2,599 runs (76.44), including ten centuries; he scored a century in each of the last four finals he played. He also took 73 wickets (22.27). His career-highest was 230 not out for Bombay against Maharashtra in 1950/1 and his best bowling in an innings, 8 for 12 against Saurashtra in 1959/60. On such occasions, he was inspired.

First-class career (1945–68): 6,026 runs (36.30) including 16 centuries, 255 wickets (29.48), and 105 catches

Test matches (33): 1,180 runs (24.58) including 2 centuries, 41 wickets (46.34), and 20 catches

RAMJI, Ladha

(b. 1900, Pidhar; d. 1948, Rajkot) *Western India and India*

A simple fellow with a massive physique and reckless love of the game, Ladha Ramji was a right-arm fast bowler who put everything into his opening overs and achieved considerable success for Hindus in the Bombay Quadrangular tournament. His sole Test was the first-ever in India against England at Bombay in 1933/4, when he scored 1 and 0, took 0 for 64 and held 1 catch. He was the brother of Amar Singh.

First-class career (1923–36): 316 runs (8.77) and 111 wickets (18.80)

RAMSINGH, Amritsar Govindsingh

(b. 1910, Madras) *Madras*

An outstanding left-arm spinner, A. G. Ramsingh was a central figure in Madras cricket. He played in two unofficial Tests in the 1930s, two of his sons (Kripal Singh and Milkha Singh) played Test cricket for India and a third (Satwendar Singh) was a very good Ranji Trophy cricketer for Tamil Nadu. Ramsingh reserved his best for the Indians v. Europeans matches in Madras. In 1936/7, he took 8 for 14 and two years later, scored a career-best 126. In 1934/5, in the first-ever Ranji Trophy match against Mysore he took 11 for 35 (6 for 19 and 5 for 16) and followed that up with 11 for 159 against Hyderabad. Two years later he took 10 for 141, also against Hyderabad. His ability to run through sides was reflected in at least three other ten-wicket hauls (10 for 80 against Mysore in 1939/40, 10 for 56 against Hyderabad in 1940/1, and 14 for 94 against Bengal in 1943/4). In all he took 164 wickets for Madras in the Ranji Trophy at an extremely low average and supplemented that with a very decent batting average.

First-class career (1934–47): 2,372 runs (34.88) including 6 centuries, and 235 wickets (15.91)

RANGACHARY, Commandur Rajagopalachari

(b. 1916, Madras; d. 1993, Madras) *Madras and India*

A strongly built police officer, Rangachary was a right-arm fast bowler with a round-arm flaying action and, always pacey, he had a useful out-swinger. No mean late-order batsman, he was an intrepid fielder at close quarters, swooping and tumbling near the bat. He toured Australia in 1947/8, but found that speed was not enough. At home against West Indies in 1948/9, he took 5 for

465

107 in a total of 631 in the first Test, at Delhi. In the next match, however, he conceded 148 runs without taking a wicket, and was not selected for India again. When he retired five years later, he had taken 104 wickets (20.79) in the Ranji Trophy competition.

First-class career (1938–54): 480 runs (7.74) and 200 wickets (25.98)

Test matches (4): 8 runs (2.66) and 9 wickets (54.77)

RANGNEKAR, Khanderao Moreshwar

(b. 1917, Maharashtra; d. 1984, Bombay)
Maharashtra, Bombay, Madhya Pradesh, Holkar, and India

An attacking left-handed batsman, occasional right-arm medium-pace bowler, and excellent field at cover, Rangnekar made 107 and 17 not out on his début in first-class cricket for Maharashtra against Western India in 1939/40. Touring Australia in 1947/8, he played in three Tests but could average only 10.81 for the tour and he was not selected for his country again. In a career of some 20 years he made 2,548 runs (49.96) in the Ranji Trophy competition.

First-class career (1939–64): 4,602 runs (41.45) including 15 centuries, and 21 wickets (40.95)

Test matches (3): 33 runs (5.50) and 1 catch

RANJANE, Vasant Baburao

(b. 1937, Poona) *Maharashtra, Railways, and India*

A very useful right-arm fast-medium bowler, able to swing both ways and cut the ball off the seam when the shine had gone, Ranjane made a sensational début in first-class cricket in 1956/7, taking 9 for 35 (including a hat-trick) and 4 for 36 for Maharashtra against Saurashtra in the Ranji Trophy competition. He toured the West Indies in 1961/2, and at home played against West Indies in 1958/9, England in 1961/2 and 1963/4 and Australia in 1964/5 without establishing himself. Altogether in the Ranji Trophy competition he took 116 wickets (22.11).

First-class career (1956–71): 698 runs (14.85) and 175 wickets (27.79)

Test matches (7): 40 runs (6.66), 19 wickets (34.15), and 1 catch

RANVIRSINGHJI, Maharaj Shri

(b. 1919, Nawanagar; d. 1962, Nawanagar)
Nawanagar and Services

A right-hand middle-order batsman, Ranvirsinghji was from the Nawanagar family and a cousin of Duleepsinghji. Not surprisingly he played in the Ranji Trophy for Nawanagar (once getting 6 for 84 against a strong Bombay batting line-up in 1946/7) for ten years before playing two more seasons for the Services. He played an unofficial Test against Lord Tennyson's team in 1937/8 scoring 10 runs in two innings but was lucky to tour Australia in 1947/8, being picked only because Merchant, Mushtaq Ali, and Modi declined to tour. It turned out to be a nightmare: he only scored 37 runs from three innings and was the only person on tour not to play in any of the Tests because, it is rumoured, the captain Lala Amarnath did not see eye to eye with cousin Duleep, who was covering that tour for the press!

First-class career (1936–47, 1950–2): 739 runs (18.02), 24 wickets (23.95), and 19 catches

RAO, Ramachandra Sudhakar

(b. 1952, Bangalore) *Karnataka*

A right-hand middle-order batsman, Sudhakar Rao modelled himself largely on his more illustrious team-mate, Gundappa Vishwanath. Like him, he too was very good square of the wicket and over the years became an extremely reliable batsman for Karnataka. Though he did not achieve as much as his hero, he did well enough to be picked by India for the tours to New Zealand and the West Indies in 1976. Playing as he did for a Karnataka side that also included Vishwanath and Brijesh Patel that was quite an achievement. Indeed the season of 1975/6 was undoubtedly his best for he made 449 (av. 149.09) runs in the Ranji Trophy from just four matches including 200 not out against Hyderabad. His national selection was helped by the fact that he could keep wicket if necessary, but on tour he missed the Tests and played only a one-day international in New Zealand, making just 4. He captained Karnataka for three years and when he retired in 1984/5, had made more than 3,000 runs in the Ranji Trophy.

First-class career (1972–85): 4,014 runs (39.74) including 7 centuries, 12 wickets (48.25), and 86 dismissals (85 c., 1 st.)

RAZDAN, Vivek Upendrakrishna

(b. 1969, Delhi) *Tamil Nadu, Delhi, and India*

Few people have reached international cricket as swiftly as Vivek Razdan. He was one of the trainees at the MRF Pace Academy when, on Dennis Lillee's recommendation, he was picked for the crucial Irani Trophy match for the Rest of India against Delhi on the eve of the tour to Pakistan in 1989. He was a well-built fast bowler who bowled a good out-swinger but had a most peculiar follow-through in which he seemed to stutter and end abruptly. He had not played a single first-class match till the Irani Trophy match. He took 3 for 113 and 2 for 75, enough, apparently, to convince the selectors that he was ready for Test cricket only 20 days after becoming a first-class cricketer. In the second Test at Faisalabad he had a forgettable match: out for a duck and no wicket in 13 overs. However, he was picked for the fourth Test and in Pakistan's only innings he bowled superbly to take 5 for 79. It seemed a promising career was ahead of him but strangely it proved to be his last Test. He played three one-day internationals on that tour of Pakistan and thereafter toured New Zealand in 1990 without getting into the side. After being dropped for the tour of England in 1990, he played one more one-day match against Sri Lanka at Nagpur. But by now his form in domestic cricket had waned. He made his Ranji Trophy début for Tamil Nadu almost a year after his international début and after one season moved to Delhi. His decline was as stunning as his ascent and he had figured in international cricket only because a selection committee was willing to gamble on raw talent.

First-class career (1989–): 700 runs (25.00) including 2 centuries, 67 wickets (33.79), and 8 catches
Test matches (2): 6 runs (6.00) and 5 wickets (28.20)

REDDY, Bharath

(b. 1954, Madras) *Tamil Nadu (Madras) and India*

A tall, slim wicket-keeper and competent right-handed batsman, who plays fast bowling calmly and with courage, Bharath Reddy spent much time in the shadow of Syed Kirmani but took over temporarily as India's first-choice wicket-keeper for the 1979 tour of England. An enthusiastic cricketer, his approach to keeping wicket was nevertheless calm and he did the job steadily and undemonstratively.

First-class career (1973–86): 1,743 runs (17.78) and 220 dismissals (171 c., 49 st.)
Test matches (4): 38 runs (9.50) and 11 dismissals (9 c., 2 st.)

REGE, Madhusudan Ramchandra

(b. 1924, Panvel) *Maharashtra and India*

A competent right-handed opening batsman, Madhusudan Rege made a sole appearance in Tests, against West Indies in the fourth match at Madras in 1948/9, when he scored 15 and 0 and held 1 catch.

First-class career (1944–55): 2,348 runs (37.26) including 6 centuries, and 33 wickets (42.96)

ROY, Ambar

(b. 1945, Calcutta) *Bengal and India*

A sound and consistent left-handed batsman who captained Bengal in the Ranji Trophy competition, Ambar Roy played in Tests against New Zealand and Australia in 1969/70. He made 3,811 runs (48.98) in the Ranji Trophy matches. Also a useful right-arm medium-pace bowler, he is a nephew of Pankaj Roy.

First-class career (1960–78): 7,163 runs (43.15) including 18 centuries, and 29 wickets (34.86)
Test matches (4): 91 runs (13.00)

ROY, Pankaj

(b. 1928, Calcutta) *Bengal and India*

A stocky, determined opening right-handed batsman and a forceful player off the back foot, Pankaj Roy never quite fulfilled his tremendous promise as a youth: he made 112 not out for Bengal against United Provinces on his début in the Ranji Trophy competition in 1946/7. He toured England in 1952 and 1959, the West Indies in 1952/3, and Pakistan in 1954/5, and at home he played against England in 1951/2, Pakistan in 1952/3 and 1960/1, New Zealand in 1955/6, Australia in 1956/7 and 1959/60, and West Indies in 1958/9. In his first series, against England, he batted excellently to score 387 runs (55.28), including 140 in his second match at Bombay and 111 in the fifth match at Madras, when India recorded her first-ever Test victory. The following English season, however, he suffered five 'ducks' in his seven Test innings, including 'spectacles' at Old Trafford. He rediscovered his touch against West Indies in 1952/3 when he made 383 runs (47.87), including 85 and 150 in the final run-feast at Kingston, adding 237 in 4 hours 15 minutes with Vijay Manjrekar, India's highest for the second wicket in Tests. In India's inaugural series in Pakistan, 1954/5, he made most runs, 272 (34.00) and again in a first series, against New Zealand in 1955/6, scored 301 runs (72.25), including 100 in the fourth match at Calcutta, followed by 173 at Madras, when he put on 413 in a day and a half for the first wicket with Vinoo Mankad, which remains a record for all Tests. Against West Indies in 1958/9 he made 334 runs (33.40), including 90 in 7 hours 25 minutes in the first match, at Bombay, as the mainstay of a negative policy; and in England the following season he scored 1,207 runs (28.73), though failing in all the Tests, bar the first at Trent Bridge, when he top-scored each time in an Indian débâcle with 54 and 49. In his last full series, against Australia, he made 263 runs (26.30). Much more consistent in the Ranji Trophy competition, he made 5,149 runs (65.18), including 21 centuries, his career-highest being 202 not out against Orissa in 1963/4.

First-class career (1946–68): 11,868 runs (42.38) including 33 centuries, 21 wickets (30.85), and 74 catches

Test matches (43): 2,442 runs (32.56) including 5 centuries, 1–66, and 16 catches

ROY, Pranab Pankaj

(b. 1957, Calcutta) Bengal and India

Son of Pankaj, Pranab was also a right-handed opening batsman from Bengal. A patient and technically correct player, he announced himself as a possible Test player by scoring 140 against a strong Commonwealth team in 1980/1 in a match to raise funds for flood relief. His chance for India came the following season against England at Madras, when he was out for six in a large Indian total of 481 for 4. He had, however, spent 82 minutes wearing down the new-ball fast bowlers, so if this was no success it was not a failure either. A confident 60 not out in the second innings confirmed that he could be at home in Test cricket; but in England in 1982 he could find no form at all, scoring only 174 runs from 12 first-class innings.

First-class career (1978–92): 4,056 runs (40.96) including 13 centuries, 1 wicket (134.00), and 42 catches

Test matches (2): 71 runs (35.50) and 1 catch

SANDHU, Balwindersingh Harbansingh

(b. 1956, Bombay) Bombay and India

A tall and strongly built Sikh, Balwindersingh Sandhu shared fully in the Indian triumph in the 1983 World Cup, taking two important wickets for 32 in the final at Lord's. A right-arm opening bowler, his temperament for the big occasion was apparent in his performances when first playing both for Bombay in 1980/1, when he took nine wickets in the match against Gujarat and scored 32, and in his first Test against Pakistan at Hyderabad, when he scored 71 and 12 and took two of the three wickets to fall. He toured the West Indies this same season (1982/3), taking some useful wickets with the new ball with his out-swingers bowled at a lively medium-fast but one home Test against West Indies the following season proved to be his last. As a right-handed tail-end batsman he believed in hitting the ball hard and played many spirited innings.

First-class career (1980–7): 1,003 runs (10.23), 168 wickets (27.91), and 19 catches

Test matches (8): 214 runs (30.57), 10 wickets (55.70), and 1 catch

SARDESAI, Dilip Narayan

(b. 1940, Margao) Bombay and India

A cool-headed right-handed batsman of sound technique, Dilip Sardesai was a wristy exponent of cover-drives and rippling glances, and a good gully or outfield. He was a very heavy scorer in the Ranji Trophy competition. On his début in first-class cricket in 1960/1 he scored 87 for Combined Universities against Pakistan. In 1961/2 he made the highest score of his career, 281 against Gujarat. He toured the West Indies in 1961/2 and 1970/1, England in 1967 and 1971, and Australia in 1967/8, and at home he played against England in 1961/2, 1963/4, and 1972/3, Australia in 1964/5 and 1969/70, New Zealand in 1964/5, and West Indies in 1966/7. His first success in Tests was not until his visit to the Caribbean in 1961/2 when, in the third match, at Bridgetown, he opened and scored 60 in a total of 187. Against England in 1963/4, he made 449 runs (44.90), five times exceeding 50. He accomplished little against Australia the following season, but he led the averages against New Zealand soon afterwards, with 359 runs (119.66); dismissed for 88—209 behind—in the third match, at Bombay, India were indebted to his 200 not out in the second innings, an effort which saved the match and almost made a victory possible. He had no luck in England in 1967, when after falling down the stairs at Lord's he had to miss the first Test, and he then broke a finger in the second which necessitated his return home. A poor tour of Australasia followed and he lost his regular place for India until he came back as his country's rescuer in every crisis during the series in the West Indies in 1970/1, his Test record being 642 runs (80.25); but for his partnerships with Eknath Solkar, India could well have lost the first, second, and fourth Tests. He made his Test-highest at Kingston, 212 in a total of 387, and also scored 112 at Port of Spain and 150 at Bridgetown. However, on his last tour, of England in 1971, he did not recapture this form, scoring 144 runs (29.40) in the Tests. After one match against England in 1972/3 he dropped out of Test cricket, but continued in the Ranji Trophy competition, reaching 3,599 runs (54.53).

First-class career (1960–73): 10,231 runs (41.75) including 25 centuries, 8 wickets (69.00), and 85 catches

Test matches (30): 2,001 runs (39.23) including 5 centuries, 0–45, and 4 catches

---

SARWATE, Chandrasekhar Trimbak

(b. 1920, Saugor) *Central Provinces and Berar, Maharashtra, Bombay, Holkar, Hindus, Madhya Bharat, Madhya Pradesh, Vidarbha, and India*

For one of his slight stature, Chandra Sarwate was a powerful right-handed batsman, often opening for his state, hitting hard between mid-on and mid-off and to square-leg. He was also a leg-break bowler with a generally low trajectory, able to turn the ball sharply. He toured England in 1946 and Australia in 1947/8, and at home he played against West Indies in 1948/9 and England in 1951/2. In England he took 37 wickets (25.37) and, usually batting at number ten, made 382 runs (23.87), appearing in one Test without distinction. His great match was against Surrey at The Oval when, with the score faltering at 205 for nine wickets, he and Shute Banerjee added 249 in 3 hours 10 minutes for the last wicket, which remains a record in England. Sarwate made 124 not out and took 5 for 54 in Surrey's second innings. In Australia he opened the batting regularly, in the third Test, at Melbourne, putting on 124 for the first wicket with Vinoo Mankad. At home, however, he achieved little in Tests. Making his début in the Ranji Trophy competition at 16, he took 5 for 33 for Central Provinces and Berar against Hyderabad, and subsequently became a prolific run-getter and wicket-taker, captaining Holkar (Madhya Pradesh) in due course. His career-highest was 246 for Holkar against Bengal in 1950/1. Against Mysore in 1945/6 he took 9 for 61 in an innings. In Ranji Trophy matches he made 4,923 runs (43.18), including twelve centuries, and took 281 wickets (27.42). He was a fingerprint expert.

First-class career (1936–69): 7,430 runs (32.73) including 14 centuries, 494 wickets (23.54), and 91 catches

Test matches (9): 208 runs (13.00) and 3 wickets (124.66)

SAXENA, Ramesh Chand

(b. 1944, Delhi) *Delhi, Bihar, and India*

A right-handed batsman of natural grace and skill, who made 113 aged 16 against Southern Punjab in 1960/1 on his début in the Ranji Trophy competition, Ram Saxena was also an occasional leg-break bowler and a good field at cover. He toured England in 1967, scoring 238 runs (23.80); in his sole Test, the first, at Headingley, he scored 9 and 16 and took 0 for 11.

First-class career (1960–82): 8,155 runs (40.37) including 17 centuries, and 33 wickets (28.27), and 65 catches

---

SCINDIA, Madhavrao

A descendant of the royal family of Gwalior, and effectively still the ruler in those parts of India, Madhavrao Scindia combines a great love for cricket with an active political career in which he has held several important portfolios in the Union cabinet. He has, however, always found time for a Sunday morning cricket match and was drawn towards Indian cricket administration. He was vice-president of the Board for 6 years before becoming president, a post he held for 3 years from 1990 to 1992. It was a period marked by India's proposal to readmit South Africa to the International Cricket Council, in itself an act unthinkable in years gone by, given India's strong and vocal opposition to apartheid. Being a powerful political figure, Scindia had access to the African National Congress and to Nelson Mandela, on whose approval, the decision was taken. Within two weeks South Africa were playing their first one-day international before delirious crowds in Calcutta, again a decision that only a political leader rather than a cricket administrator could have taken. It was also because of Scindia that Gwalior became a regular venue for international cricket. For all his commitments Scindia remained extremely accessible to the media and on completion of his tenure became chairman of the Organizing Committee of the 1996 World Cup.

SEKHAR

SEKHAR, Tirumalai Ananthan

(b. 1956, Madras) *Tamil Nadu and India*

Playing against Pakistan in 1982/3 after replacing the injured Madan Lal on the tour, Sekhar played in two Tests without scoring and without taking a wicket. A strong right-arm medium-pace swing bowler from Madras, he also played in three one-day internationals against England in 1984/5, taking 3 for 24 at Chandigarh.

First-class career (1976–90): 495 runs (14.14), 130 wickets (27.73), and 19 catches
Test matches (2): 0 runs (—) and 0–129

SEN, Probir Kumar

(b. 1926, Comilla; d. 1970, South Calcutta) *Bengal and India*

Rather stockily built, 'Khokhan' Sen's uncanny anticipation and nimble footwork as wicket-keeper led to catches and stumpings that altered the courses of many matches. A useful right-handed batsman, he was also an occasional bowler, and once, as captain of his state, performed a first-class hat-trick against Orissa in 1954/5 in the very last over, having given his gloves to a fielder. He toured Australia in 1947/8 and England in 1952, and at home played against West Indies in 1948/9, England in 1951/2, and Pakistan in 1952/3. In the fifth Test, at Melbourne, in 1947/8 he took 4 catches in Australia's sole innings of 575 for 8 declared—and let through only four byes. In the last Test at Madras against England in 1951/2, when India defeated England for the first time, he stumped five (four in the first innings), all off Mankad. Although he scored 1,796 runs (30.44) in the Ranji Trophy competition, he made no long scores in Tests. He died after a heart attack, following a day's cricket at Calcutta.

First-class career (1943–58): 2,580 runs (23.24) including 3 centuries, and 143 dismissals (107 c., 36 st.)
Test matches (14): 165 runs (11.78) and 31 dismissals (20 c., 11 st.)

SENGUPTA, A. K.

(b. 1939, Lucknow) *Services and India*

A very good all-rounder, right-handed opening batsman, leg-break and googly bowler, and slip field, Sengupta made his début in first-class cricket as a military cadet for Services against West Indies in 1958/9, scoring 35 and 100 not out, and in his first Ranji Trophy match—in the same season—he took 6 for 32 against Delhi. In his first season he played in the third Test, at Madras, against West Indies, scoring 1 and 8. After this bright start his career faded.

First-class career (1958–68): 1,695 runs (26.48) including 2 centuries, and 21 wickets (31.14)

SHARMA, Ajay Kumar

(b. 1964, Delhi) *Delhi and India*

Ajay Sharma is a short, stocky cricketer and a jack of all trades. He bats in the middle order for Delhi, often as high as number four, and scores runs as if from a well-run production line. Not very nimble on his feet, his main shots are played square of the wicket. In a higher category of cricket, such as his sole Test and the thirty-one one-day internationals he played in, he was better placed at number six. His limited skills were perhaps best reflected in the way he bowled. He came in off a rather mechanical short run and bowled flat left-arm spinners with the arm ball tending to dominate. But he was clearly a better batsman than bowler and seemed to continue bowling only to improve his chances of playing in the one-day game. The strategy seemed to work for he definitely played more international cricket than his talents suggested he would. His brightest moment came when he partnered Azharuddin in a partnership of 127 from just 13.5 overs against New Zealand at Baroda, where he scored a fifty in just 36 balls. He made his Ranji Trophy début in 1983/4 for Delhi and in the same season scored 131 against Bombay in the final of the Ranji Trophy. To find a regular place in a strong Delhi line-up through the mid-1980s was a credit and he topped that by winning a place in the Indian team for the third one-day international against West Indies at Calcutta in January 1988. He made his Test début in the same year, batting confidently in both innings and sharing a century partnership with Kapil Dev. It remained the only Test he played. In one-day internationals he managed only three fifties. He continues to be a dominant figure in domestic cricket and enjoyed an excellent season in 1994/5, making 1,288 runs at 92.00.

First-class career (1984–): 6,334 runs (67.38) including 24 centuries, 68 wickets (28.61), and 61 catches
Test matches (1): 53 runs (26.50) and 1 catch

470

SHARMA, Chetan

(b. 1966, Ludhiana) *Haryana and India*

A cricketer of tremendous spirit and a nephew of Yashpal Sharma, Chetan Sharma came from the stable which produced the great Kapil Dev. Coached by the same man, Dem Presh Azad, this wiry, 5 ft. 8 in., fast-medium bowler produces hostile pace from a brisk run-up and a slingy action which some opponents consider to be less than pure. A fine fielder and improving, aggressive right-handed batsman, he took a wicket with his fifth ball when making his first appearance in Test cricket against Pakistan in 1984/5, bowling Mohsin Khan, who was the first of many batsmen to be deceived by Sharma's surprising pace. He played against England later in the season with modest success, but against Sri Lanka in 1985/6 he took 17 wickets in three Tests. He then excelled himself in his first Test in England in 1986, taking 5 for 64 to help India to their first victory at Lord's, and by moving the ball both ways off the seam and maintaining his aggression, he took 16 wickets in his two Tests, becoming, at Edgbaston, the first Indian to take ten wickets in a Test in England. Subsequently he lost form, but time, talent and natural zest were all on his side and in 1987/8 he played seven Tests during home and away series against the West Indies. He played in sixty-two one-day internationals, playing a rampaging innings of 101 not out off 96 balls against England in the 1989/90 Nehru Cup at Kanpur, and taking 65 wickets (34.50).

First-class career (1982–): 3,047 runs (32.76), 405 wickets (25.47), and 59 catches
Test matches (23): 396 runs (22.00), 61 wickets (35.45), and 7 catches

SHARMA, Gopal

(b. 1960, Kanpur) *Uttar Pradesh and India*

A slightly built off-spin bowler with nice flight and good control, Gopal Sharma was named the best schoolboy cricketer in India in 1977/8, played for India's under-19 team two years later and showed himself to be a useful right-handed late-order batsman. Introduced to Test cricket at his birthplace, Kanpur, in the last Test against England in 1984/5, he bowled no fewer than sixty overs in the first innings, underlining his promise by taking the wickets of Gatting, C. S. Cowdrey, and Downton in the space of 29 balls, although, on a very slow pitch, these were his only victims. He played one more Test, against Sri Lanka,

before losing his place to the more experienced Shivlal Yadav, but he was recalled for two matches against Pakistan at home in 1986/7 and one more against Sri Lanka in 1990/1. In eleven one-day internationals he took 10 wickets.

First-class career (1978–): 2,309 runs (22.41) including 2 centuries, 353 wickets (30.01), and 48 catches
Test matches (5): 11 runs (3.66), 10 wickets (41.80), and 2 catches

SHARMA, Parthasarthy

(b. 1948, Alwar) *Rajasthan and India*

A solidly built and sound right-handed batsman, Sharma first played for India in one Test against the West Indies at Delhi in 1974/5 when he did well, scoring 54 and 49. In another Test in the West Indies in 1975/6 he was less successful, although on the tour he averaged 43.50. Against England's fast bowlers at home in 1976/7 he did as well as most after regaining his Test place with a century (111) at Ahmedabad against the touring team, but 62 runs in four innings were not enough and, after two Indian defeats, Sharma was one of the casualties. He was, however, a consistent batsman in domestic cricket, and a useful right-arm medium-paced bowler.

First-class career (1964–85): 8,614 runs (39.15) including 18 centuries, 191 wickets (24.49), and 146 dismissals (144 c., 2 st.)
Test matches (5): 187 runs (18.70), 0–8, and 1 catch

SHARMA, Sanjeev Kumar

(b. 1965, Delhi) *Delhi, Railways, and India*

Sanjeev Sharma was a hard-working right-arm medium pacer of average build. He bowled off a smooth run-up and moved the ball both ways but it was always apparent that he needed a lively pitch to be truly effective. He always bowled within his limitations, keeping the ball well up because he had neither the pace nor the temperament to bowl short. Indeed, his approach, after four steady rather than spectacular years for Delhi, was more suited to the one-day game. He made his début against West Indies at Calcutta in 1987/8 and took 5 for 26 against them at Sharjah a few months later, then the best figures for an Indian against them in limited-overs cricket. He made his Test début against New Zealand at Hyderabad in 1988 and in 1989 toured the West Indies where he had very little work to do. He lost his place immediately afterwards, only to regain it for the tour to England in 1990 after he had taken a career-best 8 for 76 for Delhi against Bihar. He played his second, and last, Test at Lord's, where, on a flat wicket, he seemed rather easy to get away. He could also be a valuable late-order batsman, scoring a first-class hundred after moving to Railways, but even he would look at his career average of 39.18 with a touch of surprise.

First-class career (1983–93): 1,685 runs (39.18) including 1 century, 149 wickets (35.91), and 22 catches

Test matches (2): 56 runs (28.00), 6 wickets (41.16), and 1 catch

SHASTRI, Ravishankar Jayadritha

(b. 1962, Bombay) *Bombay, Glamorgan, and India*

At the age of 19 Ravi Shastri made a sensational start to his Test career. Pulled out of a Ranji Trophy match to fly to New Zealand to take the place of two injured spinners, he arrived on the eve of the Wellington Test and took six wickets for 63 runs in the match, including a spell of three wickets in four balls. Nine more wickets followed in the next two Tests. A tall, erect figure, he bowled very accurate, rather flat, slow left-arm orthodox and batted right-handed with solid calm, sometimes opening the innings. He could be both a devastating hitter and a boring blocker, but he was for many years amongst the most respected all-rounders in International cricket. He had great charm and dignity, both on and off the field. He captained India's under-19 side in Sri Lanka in 1980/1 and is a future Test captain. At home against England in 1981/2 he played in all six Tests and was consistently useful with bat or ball. His 12 wickets, however, cost 38 runs each and he lacked the flight and subtlety of his spinning partner, Doshi. In the third Test in Delhi, batting at number eight, he made 93. In the final of the 1981/2 Duleep Trophy he confirmed his growing authority with the bat, scoring 134 for West Zone and he did well in England in 1982, making a valuable 66 in the Oval Test. His four Test wickets, however, were gained at 68 runs apiece. He was omitted from India's side in a Test against Sri Lanka in 1982/3, but subsequently toured both Pakistan and the West Indies. He hit 128 against Pakistan at Karachi and 102 against West Indies in Antigua, also taking ten wickets in the series, including 4 for 43 at Kingston. Renewing rivalry with Pakistan in 1983/4, he took 5 for 75 at Nagpur. He had a tremendous season in 1984/5, making 142

against England in the first Test at Bombay and averaging 54 in the series as well as hitting 200 not out off 123 balls, the fastest double-hundred in history, for Bombay against Baroda in the Ranji Trophy. His innings included thirteen sixes, six of them in one over from the left-arm spinner Tilak Raj, a feat achieved by only one other player, Gary Sobers. Later in the 1984/5 season he was 'player of the tournament' in the World Championship of Cricket in Australia, winning himself an expensive car. He was India's vice-captain in England in 1986, and in 1986/7, in the first of three home series, he averaged 231 in three innings against Australia. He hit a purple period around 1990–2, hitting 187 against England at The Oval (1990), 217 for the Rest of India against Bengal (1990/1, his highest score), 1,108 runs for Glamorgan in 1991, and 206 against Australia at Sydney (1991/2). He captained India once and played no fewer than 150 one-day internationals, scoring 3,108 runs (29.04), and taking 129 wickets (36.04).

First-class career (1979–94): 13,202 runs (44.00) including 34 centuries, 509 wickets (32.89), and 141 catches

Test matches (43): 3,830 runs (35.79) including 12 centuries, 151 wickets (40.96), and 36 catches

SHINDE, Sadashiv Garpatrao

(b. 1923, Bombay; d. 1955, Bombay) *Baroda, Bombay, Maharashtra, Hindus, and India*

Tall and rather frail in appearance, Sadu Shinde was a very thoughtful right-arm leg-break bowler whose googly—delivered in two different ways —was difficult to detect, but who tended to lose his length after punishment. He was also a useful tail-end batsman. He toured England in 1946 and 1952, playing in three Tests, and at home played against West Indies in 1948/9 and England in 1951/2 when, in the first Test, at Delhi, his flight and spin kept everyone struggling; he took 6 for 91 in 35.3 overs in the first innings. In the Ranji Trophy competition his most successful bowling was 8 for 162 for Bombay against Gujarat in 1950/1. He died suddenly of typhoid.

First-class career (1940–55): 871 runs (14.04), 230 wickets (32.59), and 16 catches

Test matches (7): 85 runs (14.16) and 12 wickets (59.75)

SHIVALKAR, Padmakar Kashinath

(b. 1940, Bombay) *Bombay*

Padmakar Shivalkar would have played for India had he been active in any other era. He was a wonderful spinner who was particularly unplayable on turning pitches and often bowled Bombay to victory from impossible situations, once claiming 8 for 16 against Tamil Nadu in the final of the Ranji Trophy in 1972/3. He toured Sri Lanka with an Indian team in 1974 and his best chance was perhaps when Bishan Bedi was dropped in 1979. But he was 39 then and the selectors picked the younger Dilip Doshi, who went on to take over 100 wickets for India. Shivalkar continued to be Bombay's best spinner after he had retired from first-class cricket in 1981. A full seven years later Bombay asked him to come out of retirement, at the age of 48, to play two crucial matches for them. He obliged and bowled with his usual accuracy. He took five wickets in an innings forty-two times and took a record 361 wickets for Bombay.

First-class career (1965–88): 515 runs (9.36), 589 wickets (19.69), and 63 catches

SHODHAN, Roshan Harshadial

(b. 1928, Ahmedabad) *Gujarat, Baroda, and India*

A competent left-handed batsman and medium-pace bowler, 'Deepak' Shodhan scored a spirited 110 in his first Test, the fifth against Pakistan, at Calcutta, in 1952/3, when runs were badly needed. He toured the West Indies a few months later but, although he hit 45 in the first Test at Port of Spain, he achieved little else and was not persevered with by the Indian selectors. In some 16 years in the Ranji Trophy competition he made 1,235 runs (33.37) and took 59 wickets (30.32).

First-class career (1946–62): 1,821 runs (31.94) including 4 centuries, and 73 wickets (34.05)
Test matches (3): 181 runs (60.33) including 1 century, 0–26, and 1 catch

SHUKLA, Rakesh

(b. 1948, Kanpur) *Delhi, Bihar, Bengal, and India*

A tidy and skilful right-arm leg-break and googly bowler, Rakesh Shukla was unlucky not to receive greater recognition for his useful all-round cricket over several years. His most heroic effort came in the 1981/2 Ranji Trophy final against Karnataka when, going in at number nine with the score at 548 for 7, he shared a ninth-wicket stand of 118 with Rajesh Peter to win the match on first innings. His sole Test was played against Sri Lanka at Madras in 1982/3. He did not bat but in a high-scoring draw took 0–70 and 2–82.

First-class career (1969–86): 3,798 runs (31.91) including 6 centuries, 295 wickets (24.53), and 71 catches

SIDHU, Navjot Singh

(b. 1963, Patiala) *Punjab and India*

An innings of 122 against the touring West Indians in 1983/4 earned Sidhu, sometimes known also as Navjot Singh, two Tests that season against the most powerful team in the world. A slim, bearded right-handed opening batsman who hits the ball very hard and frequently for six, he managed a top score of only 20 in four innings and was not persevered with, though he subsequently toured Zimbabwe with the Young Indian team. After vicissitudes which included surviving a trial for the alleged murder of a man after a car accident, he emerged as a highly successful Test opener following the eclipse of his rival, K. Srikkanth. He returned to the Indian team against West Indies in 1988/9, scoring 116 at Kingston and followed with 116 against New Zealand at Bangalore in 1988/9. By 1994 he had also scored Test hundreds against England (Madras, 1992/3) and Sri Lanka (104 at Colombo, 124 at Lucknow, both in 1993/4). His aggression and fierce driving were valuable also in limited-overs cricket and in seventy-two internationals to 1994 he had scored 2,743 runs, with four hundreds, averaging 42.40.

First-class career (1981–): 5,682 runs (41.77) including 15 centuries, and 35 catches
Test matches (34): 2,013 runs (40.26) including 6 centuries, and 8 catches

SIVARAMAKRISHNAN, Laxman

(b. 1965, Madras) *Tamil Nadu and India*

The first outstanding leg-spin bowler to emerge in world cricket in the 1980s, Laxman Sivaramakrishnan made his first Test appearance at the age of only 17 years 118 days, an Indian record, against West Indies in Antigua, 1982/3. A fine fielder and useful right-handed batsman, he scored 17 but his leg-breaks and googlies, delivered with a classical action, did not earn him any wickets on that occasion. It was different when he met England for the first time in 1984/5. His confident bowling at Bombay in the first Test earned him figures of 6 for 64 and 6 for 117. He finished the series as the top Indian bowler with 23 wickets at 31 and in a tournament in Australia later that season showed that he could be a force in limited-overs cricket too, playing a useful part in the Indian victory in the World Championship of Cricket. He was disappointing in league cricket in the north of England in 1985, finding the cold climate less than conducive to his brand of looping leg-spin, and in Australia in 1985/6 his three Test wickets in two games cost 70 each. He was not selected for the tour to England in 1986 and although the loss of control which had caused his eclipse was temporary, he gained a reputation for indiscipline off the field and played no more Test cricket. It was a deep disappointment not just to 'Siva' but to all who admired his style. He played in sixteen one-day internationals, taking 15 wickets.

First-class career (1981–   ): 1,785 runs (26.64) including 5 centuries, 147 wickets (37.51), and 57 catches

Test matches (9): 130 runs (16.25), 26 wickets (44.03), and 9 catches

SINGH, Bhupinder (Sen.)

(b. 1965, Hoshiarpur) *Punjab*

For a man from the tough Sikh community, and for someone who used the new ball, Bhupinder Singh (Sen.) was not a very big man. As a result he concentrated on bowling at a brisk medium pace with the ability to move the ball from just short of a length. Though he made his début in 1987/8, his breakthrough came in 1992/3 when his contribution of 36 wickets (at 19.97) helped Punjab win the Ranji Trophy. The following year, he took ten wickets in the Irani Trophy match and, although he was probably too old by Indian standards, the selectors thought that with his ability to bowl long spells under tough conditions he would be a good stand-in for Kapil Dev till someone younger and faster came along. But his initiation into international cricket, on the cruel surface of Sharjah, was a let-down. Though he took 3 for 34 against the UAE, he struggled against Pakistan. His unusual delivery stride, wherein he tended to fall away to his left, seemed to reduce his pace and he was not considered again.

First-class career (1987–   ): 1,256 runs (22.03), 186 wickets (23.59), and 27 catches

SINGH, Gursharan

(b. 1963, Amritsar) *Delhi, Punjab, and India*

Gursharan Singh was a small man, very light on his feet and capable of playing some exciting shots apart from being very good in the field. He showed a lot of promise as a youngster when he scored 101 not out against Keith Fletcher's 1981 England team. Later that year, in the final of the Ranji Trophy, he started off Delhi's pursuit of Karnataka's total of 705 with a brilliant 101 which laid the platform for Delhi's eventual victory with a score of 707 for 8! It saw him win a place in the Indian team to the West Indies in 1982/3 (a team in which Gundappa Vishwanath did not find a place) but he had a poor time there. He never really adjusted to the extra pace he was up against and scored only 123 runs in four matches, though he did manage a brave 89 against Barbados to prevent what would have been an embarassing defeat. His career had a bit of a revival after moving to Punjab in 1986/7 and in the 1988/9 season he scored 627 runs, including an innings of 298 not out against Bengal at Calcutta. It made him a somewhat surprise choice for the 1990 tour to New Zealand where he played in the third Test at Auckland and in a one-day international at Hamilton. He scored 18 (18.00) in his only Test and held 2 catches. In his only one-day innings he scored 4 and also held a catch. He was captain of the Punjab team that won the Ranji Trophy in 1992/3 and in fact holds the record for the number of catches held in a match while fielding as substitute (four against West Indies at Ahmedabad in 1983/4, including three in an innings).

First-class career (1981–   ): 5,719 runs (43.32) including 14 centuries, 4 wickets (30.00), and 105 catches

SINGH, Rabindra Ramnarayan 'Robin'

(b. 1963, Princes Town, Trinidad, West Indies) *South and Central Trinidad and Tamil Nadu*

Robin Singh brought to cricket in Madras, and to a lesser extent in India generally, the flavour of the West Indies. He actually made his first class début for South and Central Trinidad against North and East Trinidad in 1982/3 but moved thereafter to India where he enjoyed greater success. His attacking left-handed batting style and bustling right-arm medium pace immediately produced runs and he played a key role (555 runs at 69.37 with four centuries and 17 wickets at 18.17) in Tamil Nadu's Ranji Trophy win in 1987/8. He scored consistently thereafter and fielded brilliantly throughout and his infectious style was rewarded with a place in the Indian team to tour the West Indies in 1989. It was an emotional moment for him when he played the one-day international at Trinidad but he only played one other in his career, which surprised many considering his great utility value.

First-class career (1982–): 4,868 runs (53.49) including 19 centuries, 92 wickets (40.85), and 59 catches

SINGH, Randhir

(b. 1957, Delhi) *Orissa and Bihar*

Randhir Singh was a strong, medium-fast bowler who was very highly regarded in some cricketing circles in India in the early 1980s. He played for Orissa and Bihar, two low-profile teams, and did well to move into national reckoning within three years of his first-class début. He played in India's first home one-day international against England at Ahmedabad in 1981/2, making his début along with Ravi Shastri and Kris Srikkanth. Though he toured England in 1982, he only played for India again in 1983/4, against the West Indies at Guwahati where he took 1 for 30 (the wicket of Gordon Greenidge) from six overs. Thereafter, with Roger Binny, Madan Lal, and Chetan Sharma as rivals, he was ignored apart from a trip to Sharjah for the Champion's Trophy in 1986. He did not get a game and retired soon after.

First-class career (1978–89): 647 runs (12.94), 146 wickets (36.90), and 12 catches

SINGH, Rudra Pratap

(b. 1963, Lucknow) *Uttar Pradesh*

Rudra Pratap Singh (or R. P. Singh as he was better known) was a well-built medium pacer whose action reminded a few of Imran Khan's. Sadly, the resemblance did not go too much further for he only appeared in two one-day internationals for India against Australia in 1985/6. He got the wicket of Dean Jones in the last one-day international at Rajkot; a distinguished but solitary international wicket. He owed his rise in Indian cricket to a successful season in 1984/5 when he took 25 wickets in six matches including a career best 7 for 67 against Railways at Moradabad. He also had a hat-trick in the Ranji Trophy against Vidarbha at Nagpur in 1991/2 but by then he was no longer a contender for a national place, though he had also taken 6 for 21 against Bengal in a Wills Trophy one-day match in 1990/1, still the best figures in the tournament.

First-class career (1982–93): 1,406 runs (22.67) including 1 century, 149 wickets (32.24), and 22 catches

SOHONI, Sriranga Wasudeo

(b. 1918, Nimbosa) *Maharashtra, Baroda, Bombay, Hindus, and India*

Not tall, but exceptionally broad-shouldered and moving with a back straight as a guardsman's, 'Ranga' Sohoni was a right-arm fast-medium bowler with an effectively accelerating run and a good sideways action, who preferred bowling with the old ball. Confident and free-scoring, he usually opened the batting for his state, although in Tests he generally batted in the lower reaches. He was also an excellent outfield. He toured England in 1946 and Australia in 1947/8, and at home played against England in 1951/2. On the England tour he was rarely successful and also achieved little in Australia. Making his début in the Ranji Trophy competition at 17, he later captained Maharashtra and Bombay in turn, and altogether in the competition made 2,162 runs (34.87), including seven centuries, and took 139 wickets (24.11).

First-class career (1935–64): 4,307 runs (28.71) including 8 centuries, 232 wickets (32.96), and 69 catches
Test matches (4): 83 runs (16.60), 2 wickets (101.00), and 2 catches

SOLKAR, Eknath Dhondu

(b. 1948, Bombay) *Bombay, Sussex, and India*

Eknath Solkar was a solid, dogged, and courageous left-handed batsman, sound in technique, a left-arm medium-pace bowler and a brilliant, agile and fearless short-leg fieldsman. He rose from changing the score-boards at Bombay Hindu Gymkhana (where his father was an employee) to being coached at 12 by Vinoo Mankad, helping Bombay to win the Ranji Trophy for the tenth time in a row, and becoming first choice for India for six packed years. The figures he produced in runs and wickets were often less important than his fielding close to the leg-side to the Indian spinners. He toured the West Indies in 1970/1 and 1975/6 and England in 1971 and 1974, and at home played against Australia in 1969/70, New Zealand in 1969/70, England in 1972/3 and 1976/7, and West Indies in 1974/5. He first impressed as a batsman of Test calibre in the Caribbean on his first visit, with 224 runs from the five matches. With Dilip Sardesai he time and again rescued India from perilous positions. By now he was opening the bowling (with moderate results) with Abid Ali; and in England in 1971 these two gentle medium-pacers

475

saw the shine off the ball before the famous spin bowlers took over. In the Tests Solkar made 168 runs (42.00) and took 6 wickets (22.83); at Lord's he scored 67, sharing in a partnership of monumental patience with Gundappa Viswanath of 92 that saw India gain a first innings lead for only the second time in a Test in England, and at The Oval he bowled tightly in the first innings for 3 for 28 (his best for India) and hit 44, his country ultimately winning her first Test in England. Continuing to open the bowling with Abid Ali against England in 1972/3—although he failed to take a wicket in any of the five Tests—he hit 75 in the first, at Delhi. On his second England tour, although he was, perhaps, the best fielder on the side, he achieved little beyond taking the wicket of Geoffrey Boycott three times in successive innings. Against West Indies, in the fifth Test at Bombay in 1974/5, he made a dour 102—his sole Test century. The rest of his Test career was anticlimactic but he remained a force in the Ranji Trophy competition. Recommended to Sussex as a professional by the younger Nawab of Pataudi, he played for the 2nd XI for two seasons. With no vacancy for a further overseas player, his registration was then terminated.

First-class career (1965–81): 6,851 runs (29.27) including 8 centuries, 276 wickets (30.01), and 190 catches

Test matches (27): 1,068 runs (25.42) including 1 century, 18 wickets (59.44), and 53 catches

SOOD, Man Mohan

(b. 1939, Lahore) *Delhi and India*

A competent right-handed batsman, Sood's sole Test was the fourth against Australia, at Madras, in 1959/60, when he scored 0 and 3.

First-class career (1956–66): 1,214 runs (28.23) including 1 century

SRIKKANTH, Krishnamachari

(b. 1959, Madras) *Tamil Nadu and India*

A smiling cavalier of a batsman with a wide array of brilliant strokes, Srikkanth was a controversial choice to open India's innings against England in the first four Tests of 1981/2. He made a delightful 65 at Bangalore but his technique was more that of a gifted club cricketer than a hardened professional, and he temporarily lost his place. Srikkanth made his first-class début in 1978/9, and scored 90 and 37 against the Pakistan touring team a season later. In 1980/1 he scored more than 50 in five of his six Ranji Trophy innings,

including 172 against Karnataka. He missed selection for the Indian tour of England in 1982, but again showed his ability when hitting 57, 95, and 92 against Sri Lanka in three one-day internationals in 1982/3. He was selected for India's tour of Pakistan, but despite scoring 135, with five sixes and seventeen fours, against the Patron's XI in the second first-class match of the tour, he was not successful in the two Tests in which he played. He did well, however, in England in the 1983 Prudential World Cup, his aggressive and attractive 38 getting India away to a good start in the final against West Indies at Lord's. Against England at home in 1984/5, he played only two Tests but ended on a high note with rapid innings of 84 and 41 not out at Kanpur before going on to play a leading role in another World Championship of limited-overs cricket in Australia, which India again won. Touring Australia in 1985/6, he at last made a century in his fourteenth Test when he rattled up 116 off 117 balls, with nineteen fours and a six, in the third Test at Sydney. He averaged 72 in the three-match series but was never quite at his best in England in 1986. His other Test hundred was against Pakistan: 123 at Madras in 1986/7.

First-class career (1978–93): 7,349 runs (34.99) including 12 centuries, 29 wickets (49.72), and 93 catches

Test matches (43): 2,062 runs (29.88) including 2 centuries, 0–114, and 40 catches

SRINATH, Javagal

(b. 1969, Mysore) *Karnataka, Gloucestershire, and India*

The rise to prominence of Javagal Srinath in Indian and international cricket is a tribute to his ability to overcome conditions that are often designed to blunt fast bowlers. Unlike his contemporaries Kapil Dev and Manoj Prabhakar, who were basically swing bowlers, Srinath wanted to bowl fast and inevitably had to do so on pitches where bounce was often low. Unlike many other young Indian bowlers Srinath stuck to his task and soon word began going round about a tall, loose-limbed bowler from Karnataka who was making the wicket-keepers stand a couple of yards further back. He produced a hat-trick on his first-class début against Hyderabad and then took two wickets off successive balls in the second innings too. He finished the season of 1989/90 with 25 wickets from six matches and took 20 in the next year. In a bold move he was picked for the tour of Australia where he marked his Test début at Brisbane with 3 for 59. He finished that series with 10 wickets, a figure which does the quality of his bowling some injustice. He was particularly good bowling to left-handers, since his normal incoming ball goes away from them. With Kapil Dev and Prabhakar established, opportunities to take the new ball were few. When he did get the chance at Cape Town in the last Test on the tour to South Africa he produced a spell that may well be the quickest ever bowled by an Indian. He took 4 for 33 from 27 overs, making the opposing batsmen duck and fend. It was a rare moment in Indian cricket but it was to be followed by a dark one as Srinath found himself carrying the drinks for seven consecutive Test matches at home because turning pitches were the order of the day. He continued to play in the one-day internationals, producing an impressive strike rate of almost 1.5 wickets per match and becoming the quickest bowler in international cricket to a hundred wickets (3 years and 19 days). He only played his first Test match on Indian soil in late 1994 against West Indies, almost three years after making his Test début. The retirement of Kapil Dev and the subsequent assurance of a place in the side have brought out the best in him as he showed in the series against West Indies where he also batted boldly to score two half-centuries. In 1995 he joined Gloucestershire as the overseas replacement for Courtney Walsh.

First-class career (1989–   ): 796 runs (17.30), 144 wickets (30.36), and 23 catches

Test matches (15): 227 runs (22.70), 41 wickets (37.78), and 7 catches

SRINIVASAN, Thirumalai Echambadi

(b. 1950, Madras) *Tamil Nadu and India*

A sales executive with a Madras piston firm, Srinivasan was an unexpected choice as a utility batsman on the tour of Australia and New Zealand in 1980/1. A dashing right-hander, he gained his place with a century in the Irani Trophy. In his sole Test, against New Zealand at Auckland, he scored 29 and 19, but he distinguished himself in several appearances in one-day internationals on the tour, batting usefully and fielding brilliantly. Also an occasional leg-spinner, Srinivasan played league cricket for Woodhouse in the Yorkshire League, and has played Grade cricket in New South Wales.

First-class career (1970–83): 3,487 runs (34.18) including 5 centuries, and 3 wickets (48.66)

SUBRAMANYA, Venkatraman

(b. 1936, Bangalore) *Mysore (Karnataka) and India*

A tall, adventurous right-handed batsman with a good eye and powerful wrists, a medium-pace leg-break change-bowler and a reliable field, Subramanya toured England in 1967 and Australasia in 1967/8, and at home played against New Zealand in 1964/5 and West Indies in 1966/7. In the third match, at Madras, against West Indies he hit 61 courageously without inspiring much confidence. Generally disappointing overseas, his best effort in Tests was at Adelaide in the first Test of 1967/8 when he hit a gallant 75 in a losing cause. A prolific batsman in both Ranji and Duleep Trophy competitions, he made 213 not out against Madras in 1966/7. He made 2,261 runs (39.67) in the Ranji Trophy competition. His son, Pradeep, a fast-medium bowler, took 16 wickets for 154 in the 1985/6 Ranji Trophy match for Rajasthan against Vidharbha, the best match analysis ever recorded in India. He took 10 for 78 in the first innings.

First-class career (1959–70): 4,219 runs (31.48) including 8 centuries, 70 wickets (44.18), and 121 catches

Test matches (9): 263 runs (18.78), 3 wickets (67.00), and 9 catches

SUNDERAM, Gundibail Rama

(b. 1930, Mangalore) *Bombay and India*

A competent right-arm fast-medium bowler and useful tail-end batsman, Sunderam played in two Tests against New Zealand in 1955/6 with little success.

First-class career (1951–68): 558 runs (14.68) and 127 wickets (26.10)

Test matches (2): 3 runs (—) and 3 wickets (54.66)

SURENDRANATH, R.

(b. 1937, Meerut) *Services and India*

A happy cricketer, Surendranath was a slimly built right-arm fast-medium in-swinging bowler who had great stamina but tended to bowl too much down the leg-side, a tail-end batsman of good sense, and a very good close field. He toured England in 1959, and at home played against West Indies in 1958/9, Australia in 1959/60 and Pakistan in 1960/1. His best series was in England, when he headed the Test averages with 16 wickets (36.62). Swinging the ball in a sweltering atmosphere at Old Trafford in the fourth Test, he captured 5 for 115 in 47.1 overs (in a total of 490). Again in hot weather in the next match at The Oval, he took 5 for 75 in 51.3 overs (25 maidens) in a total of 361. In the Ranji Trophy he took 178 wickets (20.67).

First-class career (1955–69): 1,351 runs (15.70) including 1 century, 278 wickets (25.37), and 32 catches

Test matches (11): 136 runs (10.46), 26 wickets (40.50), and 4 catches

SURTI, Rusi Framroz

(b. 1936, Surat) *Gujarat, Rajasthan, Queensland, and India*

An exuberant character, Rusi Surti was a forceful left-handed batsman, especially at the expense of fast bowlers, a useful left-arm medium-pace or slow bowler who sometimes opened India's attack, and an excellent field at cover, often picking up the ball beautifully and hitting the wicket with an unerring throw. He toured the West Indies in 1961/2, England in 1967, and Australasia in 1967/8, and at home played against Pakistan in 1960/1, England in 1963/4, New Zealand in 1964/5 and 1969/70, Australia in 1964/5 and 1969/70, and West Indies in 1966/7. Outstanding for his ground fielding in the Caribbean, he made 246 runs (24.60) in the Tests. The climax of his career came in Australasia, when he scored more runs than anybody else, 967 (37.19), and took 42 wickets (29.73); in the Tests against Australia and New Zealand he was the most successful run-maker with 688 runs (45.50), besides taking 18 wickets (35.77). In the fourth Test at Auckland he was missed twice on 99 and was then caught still one short of his century (it remained his Test-highest). He was not considered for Tests after 1969 as he was, by then, living in Australia. His career-highest was 246 not out for Rajasthan against Uttar Pradesh in 1959/60. In all Ranji Trophy matches he scored 2,293 runs (32.75).

First-class career (1956–73): 8,066 runs (30.90) including 6 centuries, and 284 wickets (37.07)

Test matches (26): 1,263 runs (28.70), 42 wickets (46.71), and 26 catches

SWAMY, Venkatraman Narryan

(b. 1924, Calicut; d. 1983, Uttar Pradesh) *Services and India*

A competent right-handed batsman and fast-medium bowler, Swamy's sole Test was the first-ever against New Zealand at Hyderabad in 1955/6, when he did not bat and took 0 for 45.

First-class career (1951–9): 201 runs (14.35) and 68 wickets (22.16)

TALYARKHAN, Ardeshir Furdonji Sohrabji

(b. 1897; d. 1990, Bombay)

'A.F.S.T.', or 'Bobby' as he was affectionately called, was the first major media personality in Indian cricket and has perhaps been unrivalled since. He was doing live football and hockey commentaries in the 1930s but he was perhaps best known for his cricket broadcasts. Season after season, he would broadcast alone in his rich voice, his commentaries full of anecdotes. He captivated a whole generation. He created personalities out of cricketers and through the 1940s was almost single-handedly responsible for making cricket a mass-media sport. He stopped broadcasting in the 1950s because he refused to share the microphone with the All-India Radio panel. Specifically, he thought it insulting to have to share a microphone with 'Vizzy'—the Maharajah of Vizianagaram. However, he continued to have a long-running radio programme almost till his death and his voice retained its old magic. As a journalist, he was responsible for increasing the coverage of sports in newspapers, fighting for and getting a whole page, something unthinkable before. He wrote a daily column, first in the *Times of India* and then in *Mid-Day* of Bombay. It was perhaps symbolic of his commitment to his profession that the day his last column appeared was also the day that the papers carried the news of his death, at the age of 93.

TAMHANE, Narendra Shanker

(b. 1931, Bombay) *Bombay and India*

Originally a right-arm slow bowler, Tamhane became wicket-keeper in an emergency and developed as one of the best in India. His virtues were safe hands and neatness of execution. He was also a useful batsman. While still a Bombay student, he caught three and stumped four in the first unofficial Test against the Commonwealth at New Delhi in 1953/4, and he was a regular choice for official Tests from 1954 until 1960. He toured Pakistan in 1954/5 and England in 1959, and at home played against New Zealand in 1955/6, Australia in 1956/7 and 1959/60, West Indies in 1958/9 and Pakistan in 1960/1. Against Pakistan at Bahawalpur in the second Test he top-scored with 54 not out, his only substantial score in Tests. In the first match, at Dacca—his début—he had five victims; in the third at Lahore five; and in this (his first) series nineteen. In England he dismissed 49; in the two Tests he played he accounted for 6 of the 18 wickets to fall. On his début in the Ranji Trophy competition, against Baroda in 1953/4, he had seven victims (six caught, one stumped). He collected 253 dismissals in first-class cricket between 1951 and 1969; and his career-highest was 109 not out against Baroda in 1958/9.

First-class career (1951–69): 1,459 runs (18.35) including 1 century, 2 wickets (21.05), and 253 dismissals (175 c., 78 st.)
Test matches (21): 225 runs (10.22) and 51 dismissals (35 c., 16 st.)

TARAPORE, Keki Khursedji

(b. 1910, Bombay; d. 1986, Bombay) *Bombay and India*

A competent right-handed batsman and slow left-arm bowler, Tarapore's sole Test was the first against West Indies, at Delhi, in 1948/9, when he scored 2 and took 0 for 72. Active in cricket administration, he managed the Indian team to England (in 1967), the West Indies, and Australia and was secretary of the Indian Cricket Board. He took 8 for 91 against Nawanagar in 1939/40 and in his last Ranji Trophy match, the final against Baroda in 1948/9, he bowled 99 overs. He died in 1986 after being knocked down by a moped in Bombay.

First-class career (1937–49): 441 runs (11.30) and 148 wickets (28.77)

TENDULKAR, Sachin Ramesh

(b. 1973, Bombay) *Bombay, Yorkshire, and India*

If ever there was a prodigy in Indian cricket, it was Sachin Tendulkar. Perhaps only Don Bradman has matched his superiority over contemporaries. The saga started in 1985/6 when, aged 12, he scored a century for his school, Shardashram Vidyamandir, in the Harris Shield (under-17). The following year, he scored nine centuries including two double-centuries (and an innings of 276 in a day) for a total of 2,336 runs in a year. Already his was a familiar name in the newspapers and that was to continue dramatically through 1987/8 when he scored more than 3,000 runs, put on the world-record partnership of 664 with Vinod Kambli and scored a mind-boggling 1,028 runs in the Harris Shield in five innings (including scores of 207 not out, 329 not out, and 346 not out in the last three games!). It gave him the unimaginable

batting average of 1,028 and by now everyone, including Sunil Gavaskar, was convinced that this was a completely new cricketing phenomenon. Gavaskar said the boy would break all his own records and the Bombay selectors put him in the reserves for the state side before he was 15. His coach, Ramakant Achrekar, thought he was not yet ready for first-class cricket but not for the first time in his life, Tendulkar was to show his amazing mental strength. He made his first-class début for Bombay in the first match of the following season and, almost inevitably, made 100 not out. He finished the season with 583 runs from 11 innings at 64.77 and, not yet 16, said he was disappointed not to be picked for the tour to the West Indies in 1989. He did not have to wait long. He scored a brilliant century in the Irani Trophy match and later that evening became the youngest player to be picked for the Indian team. He played his first Test against Pakistan at Karachi (also Waqar Younis's début match) at the age of 16 years and 205 days and in the second Test became the youngest in cricket history to score a Test fifty. It was clear he had arrived when he scored a match-saving fifty in the last Test at Sialkot and later in the year narrowly missed becoming the youngest man to score a century in Test cricket. In the second Test at Napier he was out for 88 after being 80 not out overnight. He was just 16 years and 293 days old then but the world was already beginning to take notice of this stocky, boyish-looking batsman with a predominant bottom hand but an essentially orthodox technique. In the second Test against England at Old Trafford in 1990, India were set to score 408 to win on the last day and were struggling at 109 for 4 when he walked in. Soon they were 183 for 6 but Tendulkar stood firm, playing a most romantic innings even as the England bowlers attacked relentlessly. India saved the match and Tendulkar, with 119 not out, had played the first of many memorable Test innings. He was 17 years and 112 days old, still too young to have a driving licence, still unable by law to sign his tour contract, but old enough to save his country in a Test match. The following year, he toured Australia and moved to his favourite number four position, scoring centuries in the third Test at Sydney and the last at Perth. That was a particularly fascinating innings on an extremely lively wicket. With virtually every other Indian batsman struggling to cope with the bounce, Tendulkar seemed, mysteriously, to add inches to his small stature, rising up and playing some breathtaking shots to Perth's distant square boundaries.

He was ninth out for 114 and, not surprisingly, rates that as his best innings. By the time India returned from their pioneering tour to South Africa, Tendulkar was clearly India's number one batsman and the person around whom the fate of every Indian innings revolved. He was the only one to emerge with some credit and on a tour where every other Indian batsman struggled against the bounce. He scored 111 at Johannesburg and 73 at Port Elizabeth. Against England at home, he quickly showed that he was quite unaffected by the pressure as he batted with complete command. His innings of 165 at Madras was a classic for he was never in trouble at all. If that was the perfect Test innings, he cast another with 142 against Sri Lanka at Lucknow. It made him the only batsman in the history of the game to make seven Test centuries before he was 21. The only time that he has performed below expectations was when he joined Yorkshire as their first overseas cricketer in 1992. He made friends but did not score as many as Yorkshire hoped he would (1,070 at 46). Away from county cricket, caught up as he was in this almost frightening world of success, he remained strangely off-colour in the one-day game where he alternated between batting at numbers four and five. In a moment of inspiration, he asked to open the innings in New Zealand in 1994 and came up with an absolutely breathtaking innings of 82 from 49 balls. That was, in a way, the rebirth of Tendulkar in one-day cricket. In September he scored his first century, against Australia at Colombo in his 79th innings, but quickly followed that with three others, all scored in typically flamboyant style. Since moving to the top of the order, he has averaged more than fifty in one-day cricket at a strike rate of around 93 runs per hundred balls. However, when in flow, he seems to want to hit every ball and that has led to some rather undignified dismissals. Perhaps this is the penalty for having the ability to play more than one shot to every ball. Balls that are just short of a length may be driven on the rise one minute and pulled through mid-wicket the next. If, however, there is one shot which makes watching Tendulkar such a great joy, it is the drive in the arc from cover to mid-on, played with both grace and power, all along the ground. He loves bowling his little slow medium-pacers too, especially in the one-day game where in recent years he has often bailed out the Indian attack. In personal life, Tendulkar remains an extremely private man though that may derive in part from the fact that he is India's most public figure and can rarely venture outdoors without being mobbed. At such times his personal stereo seems to be his best friend and he has a very large collection of music to choose from. His frenetic lifestyle has left little time for the pursuit of education (his father is a professor of Marathi literature with little love for the game) but in the world of unbridled superstardom, that has as yet been no constraint.

First-class career (1988–   ): 7,707 runs (59.28) including 22 centuries, 22 wickets (68.86), and 64 catches

Test matches (35): 2,425 runs (52.71) including 8 centuries, 4 wickets (47.75), and 28 catches

UMRIGAR, Pahlan Ratanji

(b. 1926, Bombay) *Bombay, Gujarat, and India*

A tall, powerful right-handed batsman, 'Polly' Umrigar was especially strong in front of the wicket and could demoralize all but the fastest bowlers; he was also a medium-pace bowler of out-swing and off-cut who was dangerous on a helpful wicket, a brilliantly versatile field, and a sometimes very shrewd captain, especially when leading Bombay to five successive Ranji Trophy victories commencing in 1958/9. He scored 115 not out for Indian Universities against West Indies in 1948/9, and by the mid-1950s had become the sheet-anchor of India's batting. When he retired he had scored more runs for his country than any other batsman. He toured England in 1952 and 1959, the West Indies in 1952/3 and 1961/2, and Pakistan in 1954/5, and at home played against West Indies in 1948/9 and 1958/9, England in 1951/2 and 1961/2, Pakistan in 1952/3 and 1960/1, New Zealand in 1955/6, and Australia in 1956/7 and 1959/60. A heavy scorer against three Commonwealth sides, he first made his mark in official Tests, after several disappointing performances, in the fifth match against England, at Madras, in 1951/2 when he made 130 not out and India recorded their first-ever Test victory. On his first England tour he was easily the best batsman, in all first-class matches reaching, 1,688 runs (48.22), including five centuries, three exceeding 200, but he was a failure in the Tests. On his first visit to the Caribbean, he made 560 runs (62.22) in the Tests, including 130 and 69 in the first Test at Port of Spain. On the first visit to Pakistan he again headed the batting, in the Tests alone making 271 runs (54.20), including 108 in a total of 245 in the fourth match at Peshawar, besides taking 8 wickets (30.37), including 6 for 74 in 59 overs in the second match at Bahawalpur. In India's first Test against New Zealand at

Hyderabad he hit 223, his Test-highest, in about $8\frac{1}{2}$ hours, adding 238 for the third wicket with Vijay Manjrekar. In this series he scored 351 runs (70.20), and succeeded to the captaincy after the first match. Altogether, he led his country eight times against New Zealand, West Indies, and Australia, winning two games and losing two. On his second England tour he started in a blaze of glory, scoring over 800 runs, including two double-centuries, in May, but was overwhelmed by fast bowling more than once in the Tests and missed the last few matches through injury. Despite this, he was the heaviest run-getter with 1,826 runs (55.33), including three double-centuries and in four Tests he made 230 runs, including 118 in the fourth, at Old Trafford. A set-back against Australia was followed by 382 runs (63.66) against Pakistan including 115 at Kanpur, 117 at Madras and 112 at Delhi. In the second Test, at Kanpur, against England, he made 147 not out, his third century in successive Test innings; in this series he made 254 runs (50.80). On his second West Indies tour he headed the batting with 445 runs (49.44), besides taking nine wickets (27.66). In the fourth match, at Port of Spain, he scored 56 and 172 not out (the latter in about four hours) and captured 5 for 107 in 56 overs. A prolific all-rounder in the Ranji Trophy competition, he made 4,102 runs (70.72), including 14 centuries, the highest being 245 against Saurashtra in 1957/8, and took 138 wickets (19.72). He was a national selector and team manager.

First-class career (1944–68): 16,154 runs (52.27) including 49 centuries, 325 wickets (25.68), and 216 catches

Test matches (59): 3,631 runs (42.22) including 12 centuries, 35 wickets (42.08), and 33 catches

VALSON, Sunil

(b. 1958, Secunderabad) *Delhi, Tamil Nadu, and Railways*

Sunil Valson was a fast-medium bowler whose left-handedness, amidst a crop of right-handed medium pacers, perhaps ensured his selection to the Indian team for the 1983 World Cup. He did not play a single match but when India won the cup, he shared both in the glory and the spoils. Valson made his début for Delhi in 1977/8 and moved for a year to Tamil Nadu in 1981/2 when he took his career best 8 for 40 against Andhra. He returned to Delhi, playing for them for another four years before rounding off his career, prematurely in 1987/8 with a season for the Railways, for whom he took 19 wickets, including a performance of 7 for 59.

First-class career (1978–88): 376 runs (9.40), 212 wickets (25.35), and 34 catches

VENGSARKAR, Dilip Balwant

(b. 1956, Bombay) *Bombay, Staffordshire, and India*

A tall, slim, orthodox right-handed batsman, who early in his career often opened the batting but who developed into India's regular number three, Dilip Vengsarkar times the ball with the skill of a high-class player. He drives, glances and hooks gracefully and concentrates for long periods. He first toured New Zealand and the West Indies in 1975/6 as a very inexperienced batsman, with modest success. He showed his courage briefly against England in 1976/7, when his hand was broken by a ball from Bob Willis in the Madras Test, and established himself as a Test cricketer in Australia in 1977/8, making 589 runs (32.72) in first-class matches and 320 in the Tests at 35.55. At home against West Indies in 1978/9, he became a senior player after making 83 and 76 in the course of three Tests in Pakistan. In the six Tests against West Indies he made 417 runs (59.57), including two centuries, 157 not out at Calcutta and 109 in the fifth match, at Delhi. In England in 1979 he retained the number three position in the Indian order, hitting 103, including thirteen attractive fours, in the second innings of the Lord's Test and adding 210 for the third wicket with Viswanath to help save the match. In the series he scored 249 runs at 41.50 in four Tests. Further Test hundreds followed in 1979/80: 146 not out against Pakistan at Delhi, and 112 against Australia at Bangalore. He had a disappointing tour of Australia and New Zealand in 1980/1, but batted consistently well against England both at home and away in 1981/2, scoring 157 at Lord's. England remained his favourite opponents. He averaged 40 against them in the home series of 1984/5, including an innings of 137 at Kanpur, and then enjoyed a triumphant series against England in 1986, scoring yet another Lord's hundred—126 not out, his third in as many Tests there—a record; and following this up with another brilliant century at Headingley, 102 not out in difficult batting conditions. These performances were largely responsible for India's wins in both Tests and he finished the three Tests with an average of 90—and a Test batting average during three tours of England of over 50. In 1986/7 he scored 966 runs in home Tests at an average of 107.33. Not surprisingly he could not emulate these performances on his fourth tour of England in 1990, although he still averaged 57 in first-class games. His highest score was 284 for Bombay against Madhya Pradesh in 1991/2. He hit more than 1,000 runs in five Indian seasons, including 1,495 (57.50) in 1979/80. He captained India in ten Tests, and also played for Staffordshire in 1985.

First-class career (1975–92): 17,868 runs (52.86) including 55 centuries, 1 wicket (126.00), and 179 catches

Test matches (116): 6,868 runs (42.13) including 17 centuries, 0–36, and 78 catches

VENKATARAGHAVAN, Srinivasaraghavan

(b. 1945, Madras) *Tamil Nadu, Madras, Derbyshire, and India*

A charming, intelligent man with a natural dignity, 'Venkat' has been internationally popular except with commentators who do not like tongue-twisters. A slim, sinewy man with long fingers which he brushed through his long dark hair as he walked back before each delivery, Venkat was an orthodox and very accurate off-spinner; making a brief approach to the stumps before delivering with a high arm, he turned the ball more than most of his kind and was always liable to run through a side when conditions helped him. He took 530 wickets at 18.21 in the Ranji Trophy, the second-highest of all Ranji Trophy hauls, including five wickets in an innings 45 times. He captained India in England in 1979 and proved a calm, sensible, and shrewd leader, but was replaced as captain for the following series against Australia. Although beaten by an innings in the first Test at Edgbaston, India came close to what would have been the most glorious victory in all Test cricket when falling only nine runs short of the 438 they needed to win in the fourth innings at The Oval. Venkat had called for a 'positive attitude' from his batsmen and, partly as a result, a hitherto disappointing tour ended on a very high note. He made his first Test appearance against New Zealand in 1964/5 at Madras. In the following game at Calcutta he took 3 for 86 and 3 for 15 in 17 overs and in the fourth Test at Delhi he took 8 for 72 in the first innings and 12 for 152 in the match. Expensive against the West Indies at home in 1966/7, he toured England in 1967, playing in two Tests but taking only 20 wickets on the tour. A home series against New Zealand in 1969/70 again brought the best out of him, notably at Nagpur where he took 9 for 133. In the Hyderabad Test he top-scored with 25 in

India's total of 89. At home against Australia in the same season he was under-bowled but took 12 wickets at 26.66, and on the bland wickets of the Caribbean in 1970/1 he was outstanding, taking 22 Test wickets at 33.81. In the fifth Test at Port of Spain he not only took 6 for 111 but made 51 and 21. In 1971 in England he was preferred to Prasanna in all three Tests, taking 13 wickets at 26.92 and 63 in first-class matches. Against England at home in 1972/3 and 1976/7 and away in 1974 he was disappointing, and was overshadowed by Prasanna, yet against New Zealand in 1976/7 he took 11 wickets (28.00) in three Tests, and at Madras in the third made 64, his highest Test score. In 1978/9 he re-established himself as the first-choice off-spinner, taking 20 wickets in the six Tests at home to the West Indies. Apart from his sensible captaincy in England in 1979, he had once earlier captained India when they were defeated by an innings by the West Indies at Delhi in 1974/5. Such mercurial ups and downs were typical of his career. Away from Tests, Venkat also captained India in the 1975 Prudential World Cup and captained Tamil Nadu from 1970. He took five or more wickets in an innings 85 times in first-class cricket, his best figures being 9 for 93 against Hampshire at Bournemouth for the 1971 Indian team. In his three seasons in county cricket he took 189 wickets for Derbyshire. As a batsman, his best score was 137, made against Kerala in the 1970/1 season. Once he had retired there was little Venkat did not do in cricket: he coached and managed Indian teams; umpired and refereed in Test matches and occasionally commentated on them too. By the mid-1990s, however, his most important service to cricket was as the most respected of all Indian umpires.

First-class career (1963–85): 6,617 runs (17.73) including 1 century, 1,390 wickets (24.14), and 318 catches

Test matches (57): 748 runs (11.68), 156 wickets (36.11), and 44 catches

VENKATARAMANA, Margasaghayam

(b. 1966, Secunderabad) *Tamil Nadu and India*

A classical off-spin bowler with a relaxed run-up and a high action, Venkataramana had a dramatic rise in Indian cricket. He played for the first time for Tamil Nadu in the 1987/8 season when they won the Ranji Trophy. That meant greater exposure for the team and with 35 wickets from eight matches, including 7 for 94 in the final, Venkataramana was widely talked about. The following year, he made his début in a one-day international against New Zealand at Baroda taking 2 wickets (18.00) and two months later found himself in the West Indies making his Test début at Kingston, getting a solitary wicket when it was all over in the second innings (average 58.00) and remaining not out without scoring in both innings. He held a catch. He continued to bowl well on his return and though he missed out on the tour to Pakistan in 1989, he bowled well in the Duleep Trophy final that year to take 9 wickets in the match and displace Arshad Ayub from the team to New Zealand. He could not force a place in the internationals and faded dramatically on his return, bowling a very loose length. He continued to play first-class cricket for Tamil Nadu.

First-class career (1987–): 814 runs (14.53), 205 wickets (28.82) and 46 catches

VENKATESH PRASAD, Bapu Krishnarao

(b. 1969, Bangalore) *Karnataka*

A tall, extremely well-built fast-medium bowler, Venkatesh Prasad has the ability to get bounce out of even fairly dead wickets. In one-day internationals, the requirements of a defensive line have tended to cloak his attacking instincts. From the moment he made his first-class début for Karnataka in 1990/1, he was regarded highly in the south but it took him a while to convert that potential into wickets. With Javagal Srinath and Anil Kumble away most of the time, he got the opportunity to lead the Karnataka attack and in the season of 1993/4 he finally announced himself as a major new talent. He took 29 wickets in seven Ranji Trophy matches, including 7 for 37 against Kerala, and then had 7 for 38 against the North Zone at Valsad in the Duleep Trophy where he took 18 wickets from four matches, and 6 for 18 against them in the one day Deodhar Trophy at Surat. He was a stand-by for the Indian tour to New Zealand in 1993/4 and when Manoj Prabhakar returned with injury, he finally got his break. But his first few games suggested that he was not at home in limited-overs cricket and it was only in the home season against West Indies and in the Asia Cup at Sharjah in April 1995 that he finally convinced people that he was here to stay. Prasad is a man of very few words but very much a team man.

First-class career (1990–): 184 runs (10.22), 96 wickets (25.62), and 19 catches

VISWANATH, Gundappa Ranganath

(b. 1949, Bhadravati) *Mysore (Karnataka) and India*

Making 87 consecutive Test appearances between Georgetown, 1970/1 and Karachi, 1982/3, and the first Indian to score a century against all India's Test opponents, Gundappa Viswanath had a glittering Test career and seldom looked back for long from the day in Kanpur in November 1969 when, having made 0 in his first Test innings, he scored 137 in the second, becoming the sixth Indian to record a century in his first Test. A scintillating little player, 'Vishy', who married the sister of India's other little master, Sunil Gavaskar, was a right-handed number four batsman with wrists of steel who hit the ball with a wondrous touch and timing, especially through the covers off either foot. Like Gavaskar his judgement of length, his footwork and his balance were superb, but Vishy was the more likely to give the bowler a chance by flashing unwisely outside his off-stump. He stood only 5 ft. 4 in. high, a dark-eyed genius with a drooping black moustache. A leg-break bowler strictly in the nets only, he was a safe slip-fielder and a determined but philosophical competitor. After making 334 runs in his first Test series he toured the West Indies in 1970/1 and England in 1971 with relatively modest results. At home against England in 1972/3 he scored 365 runs (40.55) including 113 and 48 at Bombay, and after averaging 33 in the series in England in 1974 he hit 568 runs in ten Test innings in 1974/5 against West Indies, including 139 at Calcutta and 97 not out in a total of 190 at Madras. In the West Indies a year later he made 255 runs (42.50), including 112 at Port of Spain on the famous occasion when India scored 406 for 4 to win the match. In 1976/7 India played three Tests against New Zealand, in which Viswanath scored 324 runs at 64.80 with 103 not out at Kanpur, but in the five Tests against England which followed he suffered an inexplicable loss of form, his only substantial innings—79 at Bangalore—coinciding with India's only win in the series. Back to his best in Australia in 1977/8, he made 473 runs in six Tests at 52.55, with a highest score of only 89. However he scored 145 against Pakistan at Faisalabad in 1978/9 in the first Test between the two countries since 1961, and against West Indies at home the same season he made 124 out of 255 at Madras in the fourth Test and 179 at Kanpur in the sixth. In the series he scored 497 runs at 71.00 and he continued his good form in England in 1979 when he batted consistently throughout the series for 341 runs

(48.71), scoring 113 to save India from defeat at Lord's. He remained an automatic selection for India in the early 1980s, though there were clear signs that his concentration and speed of footwork were waning and his performances became increasingly inconsistent. Yet he enjoyed a successful home series against Australia in 1979/80, scoring 518 runs (74.00) in the six Tests, making 161 not out at Bangalore and 131 at Delhi. In Australia and New Zealand in 1980/1 he played only one major innings in six Tests, a brilliant 114 at Melbourne, but at home against England the following year he countered a threat to his place by hitting 107 when India were in trouble in Delhi and a dazzling 222 at Madras, his highest Test score, sharing a stand of 415 for the third wicket with Yashpal Sharma. He scored a century not only on his Test début but also in his first appearance in a first-class match, when, for Karnataka against Andhra in 1967/8, he made 230. He surpassed this exactly ten years later with 247 against Uttar Pradesh.

First-class career (1967–88): 17,970 runs (40.93) including 44 centuries, 15 wickets (48.50), and 226 catches

Test matches (91): 6,080 runs (41.93) including 14 centuries, 1 wicket (46.00), and 63 catches

VISWANATH, Sadinand

(b. 1962, Bangalore) *Karnataka and India*

No relation of his famous namesake, Sadinand Viswanath was a sparkling and competitive wicket-keeper and useful right-handed batsman who sometimes opened. After two tours for Young India, to Sri Lanka and Zimbabwe, he displaced Syed Kirmani in the one-day internationals against England in 1984/5 and subsequently toured Australia for the World Championship competition in which he kept well as India triumphed. He went on the tour to Sri Lanka in September 1985, playing in all three Tests, but could not hold his place.

First-class career (1980–90): 3,158 runs (30.66) including 1 century, and 179 dismissals (145 c., 34 st.)

Test matches (3): 31 runs (6.20) and 11 catches

VIZIANAGARAM, The Rajkumar of, Sir Gajapatiraj Vijaya Ananad

(b. 1905, Benares; d. 1965, Benares)

A lover of cricket capable of Machiavellian intrigue, 'Vizzy' was one of the more colourful characters of Indian cricket. In spite of a name that suggested some royal splendour, Vizzy was really a minor chieftain who had to leave his native land of Vizianagaram to settle down in Benares. But everything to him was larger than life and so, when political uncertainty caused the cancellation of the MCC tour to India in 1930/1, he organized a team of his own to tour India and Ceylon. That team had Hobbs and Sutcliffe in it apart from Nayudu, Deodhar, and Mushtaq Ali. Unfortunately, he also had ambitions as a cricketer despite the fact that his abilities on the field were notably less significant than his political skills off it. It was the latter that won him the captaincy of the Indian team for the tour to England in 1936 when he, unlike Porbandar and Limbdi, chose to play in the Tests. He scored a respectable 600 runs on the tour (16.21) but he is remembered more for his decision to send home the allegedly rebellious Lala Amarnath and for his shocking demand to Mushtaq Ali to run Vijay Merchant out in a Test match. Incidents such as these have clouded his reputation though he was also a generous contributor to the cause of Indian cricket. He continued to have a presence in the running of the game in India, being vice-president of the Board for many years and president from 1954 to 1956. In later years, he was also a commentator, heard rather than admired.

First-class career (1930–6): 1,228 runs (18.60) and 18 catches

Test matches (3): 33 runs (8.25) and 1 catch

WADEKAR, Ajit Laxman

(b. 1941, Bombay) *Bombay and India*

Standing a little over 6 ft. and strongly built, Ajit Wadekar, or 'Professor', was a cool, reserved character. A stylish left-handed batsman with a sound temperament, he was a hard-hitting stroke-player despite a short backlift, who treated each ball on its merits and seldom missed the chance to drive a half-volley. An occasional slow bowler, he was also an excellent close field and a calm and determined captain. He toured England in 1967, 1971 (captain), and 1974 (captain), Australasia in 1967/8 and the West Indies in 1970/1 (captain), and at home he played against West Indies in 1966/7, New Zealand in 1969/70, Australia in 1969/70 and England in 1972/3 (captain). Altogether he led India in 16 Tests. After a modest start to his Test career in 1966/7 he scored well in the Tests, making 242 runs (40.33) for the weaker side, his best effort being 91 in the second at Lord's after India had followed on. In

Australasia he scored freely but had only one notable Test innings—a brisk 99 in the second match, at Melbourne. In New Zealand, however, he made his maiden Test century, 143 in $6\frac{1}{4}$ hours, in the third match, at Wellington. He had dominated the bowlers in the first match at Dunedin with 80 and 71, India winning abroad for the first time. In a bowlers' series at home against New Zealand he was chief batsman with 167 runs (27.83); and again made most runs, 336 (37.33), when Australia toured soon afterwards. As skipper in the Caribbean, he made 625 runs (44.64) in all first-class matches, but was below his best in the Tests, though India won their first rubber against West Indies. In England in 1971 he scored 204 runs (34.00) in the Tests, more than anyone else, including 85 in the first match at Lord's, and 48 and 45 invaluably at The Oval when India won their first Test in England. At home a life-size statue was erected in his honour. In all first-class matches on the tour he made 1,057 runs (40.65) and held 23 catches. Against England in India—another victorious rubber—he made 312 runs (34.66) in the Tests. Captain for the last time against England in 1974, his team remained undefeated by any county, but lost all three Tests. At the end of this tour he retired from first-class cricket, having been deposed as captain of Bombay. He had won three series and lost one. Ajit Wadekar's highest score was 323 against Mysore in 1966/7 in a Ranji Trophy match, and in this competition he amassed more than 4,000 runs. He became India's cricket manager, resigning the post in 1994 after a most successful period. Cool as he appeared, Wadekar had suffered a slight heart attack shortly before this decision.

First-class career (1958–75): 15,380 runs (47.03) including 36 centuries, 21 wickets (43.23), and 271 catches
Test matches (37): 2,113 runs (31.07) including 1 century, 0–55, and 46 catches

WASSAN, Atul Satish

(b. 1968, Delhi) *Delhi*

A tall right-arm fast bowler who relied almost completely on his rhythm, Atul Wassan could be decidedly nippy at times. But he showed amazing fluctuations in form and when his rhythm deserted him, he could look ordinary at any level of the game. He made his first-class début at the age of 18 but from 1986 to 1989 he only played four times for Delhi, taking 11 wickets. Recovering form in 1989/90, he took 39 wickets in six matches and looked the most hostile bowler in

the country. It earned him a place in the Indian team to tour New Zealand, where he played in all three Test matches, but it was only in the third that he was able to make an impression. At one stage, he had figures of 4 for 32 but under an amazing onslaught from Ian Smith, he wilted and ended with 4 for 108, having conceded 24 in one over. He batted boldly at number ten to make the fastest fifty of the series, from 52 balls, but that was to be his brightest moment in international cricket. He toured England in 1990 and only picked up 8 wickets at great cost until he got it all right against Glamorgan, bowling a fiery spell to pick up 6 for 89 and earn a place in the team for the final Test. He bowled with hostility but on his return, after a couple of good performances in one-day internationals, seemed to have lost form completely. He was dropped by Delhi but staged a come-back in the 1994/5 season, being picked for India A against England A.

First-class career (1986–): 1,008 runs (21.00) including 2 centuries, 225 wickets (28.53), and 23 catches
Test matches (4): 94 runs (23.50), 10 wickets (50.40), and 1 catch

WAZIR ALI, Syed

(b. 1903, Jullundur; d. 1950, Karachi) *Southern Punjab, Patiala, Central India, Muslims, and India*

An attractive right-handed batsman with a keen eye and plenty of powerful strokes, including a splendid off-drive, a medium-pace change-bowler who maintained an excellent length and a good field, Wazir Ali toured England in 1932 and 1936, and at home played in the 1933/4 series against England. He led India against the unofficial Australians in 1935/6. He was the elder brother of S. Nazir Ali and the father of Khalid Wazir of Pakistan.

First-class career (1922–41): 7,193 runs (39.09) including 22 centuries, 34 wickets (30.67), and 59 catches
Test matches (7): 237 runs (16.92), 0–25, and 1 catch

WILLINGDON, Lord (Freeman-Thomas)

(b. 1866, Eastbourne; d. 1941, London) *Cambridge University and Sussex*

Of all the British rulers of India, Lord Willingdon had probably the longest involvement with Indian cricket. In those turbulent times, he looked upon cricket as a link between the English and the Indians and played an important role in the power struggle in the game, especially in the 1930s when he returned to India as the Viceroy (1931–6) and discovered that the princes could be manipulated using their cricketing links. Indeed, it has been claimed that some of the princes of that era took to cricket only to ingratiate themselves with the cricket-loving Viceroy. Apart from playing for Cambridge (1886–9) and Sussex (1886–90) as a steady right-handed batsman, he also played for an England XII in India in 1915/16 and for the Willingdon XI in 1918/19. It is said that he had a role to play in the sending back of Lala Amarnath in 1936 but, controversy apart, there is little doubt that Lord Willingdon did a pioneering job in spreading the awareness for cricket, and in acting as a patron for the game in an emerging India; a contrast to his harsh measures against the Indian freedom fighters. Christened Freeman Thomas, he changed his name to Freeman-Thomas in 1892 and was created the first Lord Willingdon in 1910. He was Liberal MP for Hastings, 1900–6 and for Bodmin, 1906–10, serving as a junior minister in the government from 1909 to 1912 until sent to India to be, successively, Governor of Bombay (1913–19) and Madras (1919–24). He was also Governor-General of Canada (1924–30). His father, F. F. Thomas, played for Sussex from 1860 to 1867.

First-class career (1886–1919): 1,587 runs (23.00) including 1 century, and 19 catches

YADAV, Nandlal Shivlal

(b. 1957, Hyderabad) *Hyderabad and India*

A steady off-spinner, Shivlal Yadav had a good action and was never afraid to give the ball air, but lacked any vicious spin and found taking wickets hard at top level—despite an auspicious first Test against Australia at Bangalore in 1979/80 when he took seven wickets for 81. He finished the series with 24 wickets at 24 runs each but was given little opportunity in Australia in 1980/1, playing in two Tests and breaking his toe while batting in the third and last game. He was disappointing against England, playing against them in the Golden Jubilee Test of 1979/80 and in one of the 1981/2 Tests without taking a wicket. In England in 1982 he took only 7 wickets at 86 each and was not chosen for the Tests. Recalled for the tour of Australia in 1985/6, he had an outstanding series, taking 15 wickets at 22.66 each, including 8 for 88 in the final Test at Sydney where his second innings figures were 33–12–19–3. He had excelled himself with the bat in the first Test at Adelaide, making 41 at number

eleven. After so successful a tour he was very disappointed to be given little opportunity on his second visit to England in 1986, when he did not play in a Test, but considerable further success came his way in home series against Sri Lanka and Pakistan in 1986/7. Against Sri Lanka he took 11 wickets at 13.63. In 1989/90 he crowned his career as a batsman by scoring 97 not out against Bengal in the semi-final of the Ranji Trophy.

First-class career (1977–90): 1,502 runs (18.31), 330 wickets (32.14), and 53 catches

Test matches (35): 403 runs (14.39), 102 wickets (35.09), and 10 catches

YADAV, Vijay

(b. 1967, Gonda) *Haryana and India*

Though he made his first-class début in 1987/8, Vijay Yadav was relatively unheard of until the 1990/1 season when Haryana won the Ranji Trophy for the first time. He had 30 dismissals that year and scored his first century. The next season was even more productive when he scored lots of runs to go with 25 dismissals. That was when his reputation as a wristy and aggressive batsman began to grow. For a man of such short stature Yadav can hit some massive blows and he once hit 191 from just 139 balls against Uttar Pradesh. He is particularly good at whipping balls through the on side and has always been an entertaining batsman to watch. In the 1991/2 season he hit 480 runs in the Ranji Trophy from seven matches, averaging 96.00 and topped that with 201 in the Duleep Trophy for North Zone against South Zone. He was picked for the Indian team that toured South Africa in 1992 and played his first international at East London after India had performed miserably until then. He had a hand in an unexpected victory, scoring an exciting 32 from 22 balls, playing some rousing shots against South African pace and adding an unbroken 74 for the sixth wicket with Pravin Amre. He won a Test place against Zimbabwe three months later, scoring 30 runs (30.00) and taking 2 catches and a stumping in his sole game. He toured Sri Lanka in 1993 and was the wicket-keeper in India's successful Hero Cup side but by then his impetuosity with the bat had become apparent. He lost his place to Nayan Mongia in early 1994 and only played two more one-day internationals when Mongia was banned for a while. In all he played 19 one-day internationals, scoring 118 runs (11.80) and claiming 19 dismissals (12 c., 7 st.).

First-class career (1987–): 2,559 runs (38.77) including 6 centuries, and 190 dismissals (163 c., 27 st.)

YAJURVINDRA SINGH, Jaswantsingh

(b. 1952, Rajkot) *Maharashtra, Saurashtra, and India*

A capable right-handed batsman, medium-pace change-bowler and brilliant close field, Yajurvindra Singh played twice against England in 1976/7, in his first Test at Bangalore taking 7 catches at short-leg, and equalling the innings and match catching records for non-wicket-keepers. Despite few opportunities on the 1979 tour of England, he took over from the injured Mohinder Amarnath at The Oval for the fourth and final Test and again showed his brilliance at short-leg, standing fearlessly still by the batsman's hip pocket.

First-class career (1971–82): 3,765 runs (42.30) including 9 centuries, 50 wickets (31.04), and 83 catches

Test matches (4): 109 runs (18.16), 0–50, and 11 catches

YASHPAL SHARMA

(b. 1954, Ludhiana) *Punjab, Haryana, Railways, and India*

Small but wiry, Yashpal Sharma was a neat and attractive right-handed batsman with good balance and timing, and a fine array of strokes, especially to the on-side. He was given little opportunity when he toured Pakistan at the end of 1978, but an innings of 135 not out for North Zone against the West Indies touring team at Jullundur early in 1979 helped him to earn a place in the touring team to England and he made rapid strides towards establishing himself as a regular Test batsman, making 884 runs at 58.93 on the tour and playing in the last three Tests of the series, scoring 102 runs at 25.50. He maintained consistent form against Pakistan at home in 1979/80, averaging 39 in the six Tests although a big score eluded him, and later in the same season scored his first Test century in his seventh Test, against Australia at Delhi. In Australia in 1980/1 he was a failure in the three Tests, despite scoring 201 not out against Victoria at Geelong, and at the end of the tour was dropped after one further failure against New Zealand. It was believed that he was particularly vulnerable to short-pitched fast bowling, but he seemed to lay that bogey against England at home in 1981/2, when he made a come-back to the Test team for the last two matches. In three innings he scored 220 runs, including a very determined 140 at Madras when he shared a record third-wicket stand of 415 with G. R. Viswanath. Less successful against England in 1982, he nevertheless held his place against Sri Lanka and on the 1982/3 tour of Pakistan.

First-class career (1973–93): 8,933 runs (44.88) including 21 centuries, 47 wickets (33.70), and 92 dismissals (90 c., 2 st.)

Test matches (37): 1,606 runs (33.45) including 2 centuries, 1 wicket (17.00), and 16 catches

YOGRAJ SINGH, Bhagsingh Bhundel

(b. 1958, Chandigarh) *Haryana, Punjab, and India*

A well-built right-arm fast-medium bowler and useful late-order batsman, Yograj was given an early chance at a representative level when playing for Combined Universities against MCC at Nagpur in 1976/7. For two years thereafter injury and poor form kept him out of first-class cricket but he re-emerged to win a place on the 1980/1 tour of Australia and New Zealand. He took 13 wickets in seven first-class matches on a disappointing tour for him. His sole Test, against New Zealand at Wellington, was relatively unsuccessful. He scored 6 and 4, and took 1 for 63. In 1979/80 he produced his best figures: 7 for 36 against Jammu and Kashmir.

First-class career (1976–85): 398 runs (15.30) and 67 wickets (26.22)

New Zealand

ALABASTER, John Chaloner

(b. 1930, Invercargill) *Otago and New Zealand*

A right-arm leg-break bowler, the best New Zealand have produced, and an occasionally useful batsman, John Alabaster toured India and Pakistan in 1955/6, England in 1958, South Africa in 1961/2, and West Indies in 1971/2. At home he played against the West Indies in 1955/6, England in 1962/3, and India in 1967/8. He reached his peak in South Africa, where, in all first-class matches, he took 86 wickets (25.80), more than anyone else, and scored 296 runs (16.44). In the five Tests he took 22 wickets (28.04), helping New Zealand to square a series for the first time.

First-class career (1955–72): 2,427 runs (13.33), 500 wickets (25.37), and 94 catches
Test matches (21): 272 runs (9.71), 49 wickets (38.02), and 7 catches

ALLCOTT, Cyril Francis Walter

(b. 1896, Lower Moutere; d. 1973, Auckland)
Hawke's Bay, Auckland, Otago, and New Zealand

A very good all-rounder, a left-handed batsman and left-arm orthodox slow bowler, Cyril Allcott visited England in 1927 and 1931 and at home played against England in 1929/30 and South Africa in 1931/2. In 1927 he hit his highest score, 131 against Warwickshire at Edgbaston, putting on 301 for the second wicket with C. S. Dempster, and one of his best pieces of bowling was also in 1927, at Weston-super-Mare, when Somerset, seeking 162 to win, collapsed for 67, Cyril Allcott taking 5 for 3 in five overs. He was very disappointing in Tests.

First-class career (1920–46): 2,514 runs (27.93) including 5 centuries, 220 wickets (26.78), and 61 catches
Test matches (6): 113 runs (22.60), 6 wickets (90.16), and 3 catches

Aldridge, Brian Leslie

(b. 1940, Christchurch)

New Zealand's senior Test umpire played cricket until he was 35, making his début as an umpire in 1975. Brian Aldridge is respected and popular with players and public, despite occasional, inevitable errors in major televised matches. He had stood in 22 Tests by 1994 and had the honour of standing in the final of the 1992 World Cup in Melbourne. He and Steve Dunne were the first members from New Zealand on the international umpires' panel.

ANDERSON, Robert Wickham

(b. 1948, Christchurch) *Canterbury, Northern Districts, Otago, Central Districts, and New Zealand*

At his best a handsome and hard-hitting player, a tall, strongly built, right-handed opening batsman, and athletic fielder, Robert Anderson is the son of W. M. Anderson who played in one Test for New Zealand. Anderson Junior played his early first-class cricket for Canterbury but later played for three other provinces in his determination to get to the top. Chosen to tour England in 1973, he did not make the Test side, but when he won his first cap at Lahore against Pakistan in

1976/7 he scored 92 in the second innings. He lost his place at the end of this three-Test series but returned to play with some success at home against England in 1978, making 28 and 26 in the low-scoring match at Wellington, when New Zealand defeated England for the first time, and 62, 15, 17, and 55 in his subsequent innings in the series. In England later that year he could make only 42 runs in six Test innings against top-class seam bowling and he was never thereafter able to win his place back.

First-class career (1967–82): 5,609 runs (30.65) including 8 centuries, 5 wickets (30.80), and 79 catches

Test matches (9): 423 runs (23.50) and 1 catch

ANDERSON, William McDougall

(b. 1919, Westport; d. 1979, Christchurch) *Canterbury*

A left-handed opening batsman and change-bowler, Bill Anderson's sole Test was against Australia at Wellington in 1945/6, when he scored 4 and 1 and held a catch. Lindwall dismissed him both times. His career-highest was 137 against Otago in 1945/6.

First-class career (1938–50): 1,973 runs (34.61) including 2 centuries, and 18 wickets (38.16)

ANDREWS, Bryan

(b. 1945, Christchurch) *Canterbury, Central Districts, Otago, and New Zealand*

For more than a decade a very useful right-arm medium-pace bowler, Bryan Andrews toured Australia in 1973/4, where he played in two Tests.

First-class career (1963–74): 474 runs (9.11) and 198 wickets (23.23)

Test matches (2): 22 runs (22.00), 2 wickets (77.00), and 1 catch

BADCOCK, Frederick Theodore

(b. 1897, Abbottabad, India; d. 1982, South Perth, Australia) *Wellington, Otago, and New Zealand*

Born in India, dying in Australia, and living for part of his childhood in England, Ted Badcock devoted many years to playing and coaching in New Zealand. There was a suggestion of Keith Miller in the dark lock flopping over his right eye, and in his dashing right-handed batting. As a bowler he had an easy, fluent action: his best ball was the medium-pace in-swinger which cut back slightly from leg and, although of a more leis-

urely pace, he was, at his best, as accurate as Alec Bedser. He played against England in the first-ever Test in New Zealand in 1929/30, again in 1932/3 and also against South Africa in 1931/2. Surprisingly he never toured England with New Zealand teams, although he was domiciled here during the Second World War, when he occasionally represented Northamptonshire with success. However, against South Africa at Christchurch and Wellington he made 64 and 53 respectively. For Wellington he enjoyed such performances as 5 for 54 and 7 for 59 against Otago in 1926/7, 7 for 50 against Canterbury in 1924/5 and 7 for 55 against Auckland in 1925/6.

First-class career (1924–45): 2,383 runs (25.62) including 4 centuries, 221 wickets (23.57), and 38 catches

Test matches (7): 137 runs (19.57), 16 wickets (38.12), and 1 catch

BARBER, Richard Trevor

(b. 1925, Otaki) *Wellington, Central Districts, and New Zealand*

A right-handed batsman, Trevor Barber played in only one Test, against the West Indies at Wellington in 1955/6, scoring 12 and 5 and catching the great Gary Sobers.

First-class career (1945–60): 1,966 runs (23.12) including 1 century

BARTLETT, Gary Alexander

(b. 1941, Blenheim) *Central Districts, Canterbury, and New Zealand*

A right-arm fast bowler whose pace off the pitch could be very disconcerting despite an open, dragger's action which did not satisfy purists, Gary Bartlett was a useful batsman and a safe field. He toured South Africa in 1961/2 and played against Pakistan at home in 1964/5, England in 1965/6 and India in 1967/8 with mixed success. In the five Tests against South Africa he scored 215 runs (23.88) but took only eight wickets (40.75). Against India, however, at Christchurch he took 6 for 38 in the second innings of 301, helping New Zealand to her fourth victory from 81 official Tests. At the age of 19 in an unofficial Test against Australia at Wellington in 1959/60, he put on an aggressive 71 in 45 minutes with John Reid and then took 5 for 51 in Australia's first innings. He performed the hat-trick against Northern Districts at Hamilton in 1959/60.

First-class career (1958–70): 1,504 runs (16.71) and 150 wickets (28.33)
Test matches (10): 263 runs (15.47), 24 wickets (33.00), and 8 catches

BARTON, Paul Thomas

(b. 1935, Wellington) *Wellington and New Zealand*

A composed, correct, and polished right-handed batsman, Paul Barton made a cultured 109 in the fifth Test against South Africa at Port Elizabeth in 1961/2, reaching his century with his 19th boundary despite a dislocated shoulder, and in all first-class matches on the tour made 675 runs (27.00). He achieved little in two Tests against England in 1962/3.

First-class career (1954–68): 2,824 runs (23.93) including 3 centuries
Test matches (7): 285 runs (20.35) including 1 century, and 4 catches

BEARD, Donald Derek

(b. 1920, Palmerston; d. 1982, Lancashire, England) *Central Districts, Northern Districts, Wellington, and New Zealand*

A run-saving, right-arm medium-pace bowler who rushed in to deliver the ball and who was by nature and physique a flamboyant hitter, Donald Beard played against the West Indies in New Zealand in 1951/2 and 1955/6. His persistent swing bowling in the fourth Test at Auckland in the latter season helped New Zealand to achieve her first-ever official Test victory. An All-Black Rugby trialist as a flank forward, he became principal at Te Aroha College.

First-class career (1945–65): 2,166 runs (22.10) and 278 wickets (21.58)
Test matches (4): 101 runs (20.20), 9 wickets (33.55), and 2 catches

BECK, John Edward Francis

(b. 1934, Wellington) *Wellington and New Zealand*

A hard-hitting left-handed batsman with rippling off and square drives but a reputedly flawed back-foot technique, John Beck toured South Africa in 1953/4 without having played in a first-class match. In his second Test at Cape Town he was run out for 99, having enjoyed four 'lives'. In the first Test against the West Indies at Dunedin in 1955/6 he scored an aggressive 66 to counter Ramadhin and Valentine.

First-class career (1953–62): 1,508 runs (23.93) including 2 centuries
Test matches (8): 394 runs (26.26)

BELL, William

(b. 1931, Dunedin) *Canterbury and New Zealand*

A right-arm leg-break bowler, William Bell toured South Africa in 1953/4 taking 12 wickets (52.66) but was ineffective in the two Tests he played.

First-class career (1949–59): 170 runs (10.00) and 44 wickets (40.52)
Test matches (2): 21 runs (—), 2 wickets (117.50), and 1 catch

BILBY, Grahame Paul

(b. 1941, Wellington) *Wellington and New Zealand*

A competent right-handed opening batsman who scored 161 against Otago in 1965/6, Grahame Bilby made an appearance in two Tests against England that season.

First-class career (1962–77): 2,936 runs (32.62) including 3 centuries
Test matches (2): 55 runs (13.75) and 3 catches

BLAIN, Tony Elston

(b. 1962, Nelson) *Central Districts, Canterbury, and New Zealand.*

Dedicating himself to a career in cricket, Tony Blain's first opportunity at international level came against Australia in the limited-overs games in 1985/6. He performed well enough, both behind the stumps and as an accomplished right-handed batsman, to earn the place as understudy to Ian Smith in England in 1986 and when Smith withdrew with a virus before the last Test of the tour at The Oval, Blain won his first cap, batting bravely for 37 in his sole innings and keeping tidily until he muffed a swirling skier off Ian Botham. He played two more Tests on tour of India in 1988/9, but Smith returned thereafter and Adam Parore emerged as a younger rival. His first appearance in first-class cricket was for Central Districts in 1982/3 but Smith barred his way to a regular place so he moved to Canterbury and helped them to win the Shell Trophy in 1983/4, averaging 61.00. Again unable to command a regular place, he moved back to Central Districts and in 1984/5 was leading run-scorer with 678, including centuries against Otago and Auckland. His Test career was given a second lease against Australia at home in 1992/3 and against Pakistan (home) and Australia (away) in the following season. He has also played in 38 one-day internationals, claiming 37 catches and a stumping and scoring 442 runs (16.37).

BLAIR

First-class career (1982–): 5,529 runs (35.21)
including 8 centuries, 2 wickets (59.50), and 232
dismissals (206 c., 26 st.)
Test matches (11): 456 runs (26.82) and 21
dismissals (19 c., 2 st.)

BLAIR, Bruce Robert

(b. 1957, Dunedin) *Otago*

This left-hand batsman and right-arm medium-pace bowler had a very successful 13-year stint for Otago. In 110 matches, he scored seven centuries and forty half-centuries. He was assertive in all he did and he won a place in fourteen one-day internationals. In these he had less success, scoring a modest 174 runs (12.50) and taking only one wicket. A stocky man, at times brutally aggressive, he was a very fine close-in fieldsman. He had several scores in the nineties before he scored a century in 1982/3, his best season (680 runs at 52.30). In 1986/7 he also exceeded 600 runs, a feat rare in a New Zealand season, scoring three centuries.

First-class career (1977–90): 5,995 runs (32.58)
and 55 wickets (31.81)

BLAIR, Robert William

(b. 1932, Wellington) *Wellington, Central Districts,
and New Zealand*

A hostile and accurate right-arm fast bowler and occasionally useful late-order batsman, Bob Blair toured South Africa in 1953/4 taking 30 wickets (25.40) and hitting 79 against Griqualand West at Kimberley, which remained his career-highest score. On the day that he heard his fiancée had been killed in a Christmas Eve train disaster back in New Zealand, he kept his end up bravely in the second Test at Johannesburg, adding 33 for the last wicket when everyone had to fight hard for runs. On the first day of his Test début, against South Africa at Wellington in 1952/3, he secured the wickets of Waite, Endean, and McLean on a batsman's wicket at a personal cost of eight runs. He toured England in 1958, taking 51 wickets (23.58), which included 6 for 19 when Cambridge were routed for 46 at Fenner's, but he achieved little in the Tests. Against South Africa at Auckland in the third Test of 1963/4 his match analysis was 7 for 141. He also played at home against England in 1954/5, 1958/9, and 1962/3 and the West Indies in 1955/6. His best bowling feats in an innings were 9 for 72 for Wellington against Auckland and 9 for 75 (14 for 136 in the match) against Canterbury in 1956/7, in which season he

captured 46 wickets (9.47), the greatest number taken in a Plunket Shield season. When injury eventually forced him out of the game, Bob Blair had taken more wickets in first-class cricket than any other New Zealand player. His batting put him amongst an élite company of players who have suffered the indignity of scoring three pairs of noughts in Test matches!

First-class career (1951–65): 1,672 runs (12.29),
537 wickets (18.54), and 46 catches
Test matches (19): 189 runs (6.75), 43 wickets
(35.23), and 5 catches

BLUNDELL, Sir Edward Denis

(b. 1907, Wellington; d. 1984, Townsville, Australia)
Cambridge University and Wellington

At 'windy Wellington', as it is known to those outside New Zealand's capital city, Denis Blundell always seemed to be bowling against the gale. Educated at Waitaki Boys School and Cambridge University, he became a successful lawyer and diplomat and he was knighted for his service to those professions. During the Second World War he rose to the rank of brigadier. He was at Cambridge when New Zealand made their first tour of England, in 1927 but the captain, Tom Lowry, included him in the New Zealand team for the game against the university. He was a Cambridge blue in 1928/9, taking 102 wickets in two seasons, including 6 for 25 against Leicestershire in 1928. He also won an athletics blue. He next played for New Zealand against E. R. T. Holmes's MCC team in 1935/6. He served as president of the New Zealand Cricket Council, 1959/62 and as New Zealand's High Commissioner in London, 1968–72, becoming Governor General of New Zealand, 1972–7.

First-class career (1927–38): 400 runs (8.69), 195
wickets (25.25), and 16 catches

BLUNT, Roger Charles

(b. 1900, Durham; d. 1966, Westminster, London)
Canterbury, Otago, and New Zealand

Dark and lithe, beginning his career in first-class cricket as a schoolboy, Roger Blunt was a very useful right-arm leg-break bowler who developed into a fine, stylish and adaptable batsman. He hit 42 from one eight-ball over for West Christchurch against Riccarton in 1923 (including seven sixes) and made three centuries in succession for Otago the following season. He toured England on the first-ever tour in 1927 and, as the most effective all-rounder, scored 1,540 runs (44.00) and took 78 wickets (24.97) in first-class matches. In 1929/30 he headed the bowling with nine wickets (19.00) in New Zealand's first Test series, against England. The first match at Christchurch brought him the top score of 45 not out in a total of 112 on the first day, besides a match record of 5 for 34. In England in 1931 he made 1,592 runs (43.02), and also took 34 wickets (34.76). In the first Test in England, at Lord's, a very watchful 96 helped to make an honourable draw. He played in the two Tests against South Africa in 1931/2 without distinguishing himself. In a dazzling display, however, in 1931/2 for Otago against Canterbury at Christchurch, he hit 338 not out at a run-a-minute, at that time the highest score by a New Zealander. Until Bert Sutcliffe surpassed him in 1953, he was the most prolific batsman in New Zealand cricket. He was awarded the MBE.

First-class career (1917–35): 7,953 runs (40.99) including 15 centuries, 214 wickets (31.01), and 88 catches
Test matches (9): 330 runs (27.50), 12 wickets (39.33), and 5 catches

BOLTON, Bruce Alfred

(b. 1935, Christchurch) *Canterbury, Wellington, and New Zealand*

A right-handed opening batsman with a sound defence and a useful leg-break bowler, Bruce Bolton played twice against England in 1958/9.

First-class career (1955–71): 2,092 runs (20.31) including 1 century, and 96 wickets (22.32)
Test matches (2): 59 runs (19.66) and 1 catch

BOOCK, Stephen Lewis

(b. 1951, Dunedin) *Otago, Canterbury, and New Zealand*

Tall and curly haired, Stephen Boock was a slow left-arm orthodox spin bowler with excellent control and considerable power of spin. Also an outstanding short-leg fieldsman, Boock (who pronounces his name to rhyme with 'Hock') became in 1977/8 only the third New Zealand bowler to take more than 50 wickets in a season and, by claiming 66 wickets at 16.48 in 13 matches, he surpassed the previous record of 57 wickets in a New Zealand season set by G. J. Thompson of Lord Hawke's 1902/3 touring team. After a début for Otago in 1973/4, he transferred to Canterbury in 1975/6, returning to Otago three seasons later, and taking 58 wickets at 21 each in 1978/9, another exceptional haul. He had the thrill of

winning a first Test cap at Wellington in February 1978 when New Zealand beat England for the first time. In the third Test in Auckland he took 5 for 67 in England's innings of 429 and in England a few months later took 39 wickets (22.17) in 13 matches on the tour. At Trent Bridge in an England innings of 429, he returned remarkable figures of 28–18–29–2. He toured Australia in 1980/1 and 1985/6. He had a prominent role in New Zealand's first win in a series against England, in 1983/4, taking 4 for 37 in the one-sided match at Christchurch. In March of the same season his 5 for 28 in the second innings at Kandy assured New Zealand of victory in their first Test match in Sri Lanka. In 1984/5 he played against Pakistan both away and at home, taking 7 for 87 from 37 overs in Pakistan's first innings at Hyderabad (17 wickets in the series) and six more in two Tests at home. He toured India again in 1988/9 but it was Boock's misfortune to coincide with an era favouring limited-overs cricket, a game which has not suited his rather old-fashioned virtues: indeed he left a tour of Australia early, seeing no prospect of playing. A genuine tail-ender, he nevertheless often batted grittily and at Sydney in 1985/6 he made 37 of a New Zealand record last-wicket stand of 124 against Australia.

First-class career (1973–90): 1,092 runs (8.53), 640 wickets (22.36), and 83 catches
Test matches (30): 207 runs (6.27), 74 wickets (34.64), and 14 catches

BRACEWELL, Brendon Paul

(b. 1959, Auckland) *Central Districts, Otago, Northern Districts, and New Zealand*

One of four brothers who played first-class cricket in New Zealand (B. P., J. G., D. W., and M. A.). Brendon Bracewell was a right-arm fast bowler who was chosen for the 1978 tour of England on the strength of his performances in only three matches. So well did he bowl that the selectors were handsomely rewarded for their gamble. In his first Test, aged only 18, he took the wicket of Graham Gooch with his third ball, and followed up by dismissing Mike Brearley to reduce England to 7 for 2. But he played too much too young and back injury restricted him thereafter. He played only three more Tests for New Zealand after his early tour. His brief peak had promised so much: 5 ft. 9 in. and of wiry build, every fibre of body and soul was thrown into his leaping delivery. His last Test was at home in 1984/5 but he made an unexpected tour of Australia in 1989/90, only to break down after one match.

First-class career (1977–90): 965 runs (11.76), 194 wickets (29.08), and 32 catches

Test matches (6): 24 runs (2.40), 14 wickets (41.78), and 1 catch

BRACEWELL, John Garry

(b. 1958, Auckland) *Otago, Auckland, and New Zealand*

The brother of Brendon Bracewell, John was a tall, resourceful, off-break bowler with a high action, and a useful, hard-hitting, right-handed batsman. Confidence was at the heart of his success. From 1980/1 he toured Australia four times and made three tours to England (1983, 1986, and 1990) in addition to visits to the West Indies, India, Pakistan, Sri Lanka, and Sharjah. His sharp spin and high bounce made him a match-winner on helpful wickets, as his 7 wickets for 9 runs for Otago against Canterbury in 1981/2 proved. Making his first-class début in 1978/9, he had twelve times taken more than five wickets in an innings and three times more than ten in a match by the end of the 1981/2 season. In three Test matches on his first tour of Australia he made little impact, but he took 4 for 61 and 5 for 75 against India at Auckland in 1980/1. Restored to favour for the tour of England in 1983, he took six, albeit rather expensive, wickets in the Trent Bridge Test. In Pakistan in 1984/5 he had little luck, taking only six wickets overall, but was Young New Zealand's leading bowler in Zimbabwe that same season, and when called out to reinforce the spin attack at Sydney in the second Test of 1985/6 he enjoyed a great personal triumph, driving powerfully for 83 not out and sharing a record (for New Zealand v. Australia) last-wicket stand of 124 with S. L. Boock. He took five wickets in the match and, promoted to number nine, made 28 not out to help New Zealand win the third Test and the series. In England in 1986, though he bowled well and played in all three Tests, it was his batting which most impressed: he followed a rumbustious century against Northamptonshire with an outstanding maiden Test century (110) at Trent Bridge. With 3 for 29 in the second England innings he played, with Hadlee, the leading role in New Zealand's first Test victory on the ground. His 6 for 59 at Bombay in 1988/9 levelled the series for New Zealand. An extrovert, he revelled in such triumphs.

First-class career (1978–91): 4,354 runs (25.91) including 4 centuries, 522 wickets (26.60), and 125 catches

Test matches (41): 1,001 runs (20.42) including 1 century, 102 wickets (35.81), and 32 catches

BRADBURN, Wynne Pennell

(b. 1939, Thames) *Northern Districts and New Zealand*

A sound right-handed opening batsman and slow-medium change in-swing bowler, Wynne Bradburn played in two Tests at home against South Africa in 1963/4.

First-class career (1957–69): 2,077 runs (20.36) including 1 century, and 19 wickets (42.31)

Test matches (2): 62 runs (15.50) and 2 catches

BROWN, Vaughan Raymond

(b. 1959, Christchurch) *Canterbury and New Zealand*

Vaughan Brown thoroughly earned his opportunity in Test cricket in 1985/6, when he toured Australia with the successful New Zealand side, playing in the first two Test matches. He began well, taking 1 for 17 from 12 overs in the first innings at Brisbane and making 36 not out in his inaugural Test innings. After this he was disappointing, especially on a pitch taking spin at Sydney, and lost his place to John Bracewell. A flighty, fair-haired off-spinner of shortish stature, Brown was a more than useful left-hand batsman.

First-class career (1978–90): 3,485 runs (29.28) including 6 centuries, 190 wickets (28.97), and 49 catches

Test matches (2): 51 runs (25.50), 1 wicket (176.00), and 3 catches

BURGESS, Mark Gordon

(b. 1944, Auckland) *Auckland and New Zealand*

Mark Burgess, a friendly, level-headed character and a fine cricketer, had been a Test player for more than a decade when he achieved the singular distinction of captaining New Zealand to their first victory over England at Wellington in 1978. In 1979 he led New Zealand into the semi-final of the Prudential World Cup when they lost only narrowly to England in their meeting at Old Trafford. Making his initial first-class appearance for the New Zealand under-23 side against his own province in 1963/4, Mark Burgess first played for Auckland three years later and in

1967/8 made his Test début against India, scoring 50 and 39 at Dunedin. A fair-haired right-hander with a sound technique and some handsome attacking strokes, especially adept at driving in the arc between cover and mid-wicket, he toured England in 1969, 1973, and 1978 (also appearing in the Prudential World Cup in 1979) as well as going to the West Indies, India, and Pakistan (twice). His first Test hundred was 119 not out against Pakistan at Dacca in 1969/70, and he hit a memorable 104 against England at Auckland in his next Test innings. Further centuries followed against the West Indies at Kingston in 1971/2 and Pakistan at Lahore in 1976/7, but his finest innings was a sparkling 105 against England on the Saturday of the Lord's Test in 1973. New Zealand ought subsequently to have won the game but let England off the hook. There was no such failure in 1978 when, amidst great excitement at the Basin Reserve, Burgess directed his fast bowlers Collinge and Richard Hadlee in a sensational demolition of England's second innings. Burgess's batting in Tests seemed to suffer from the extra responsibility of captaincy but he was popular with both his own team and his opponents. Essentially a dedicated amateur cricketer in a professional age, his attitude was that winning or losing was not life or death. Earlier in his career, as an occasional medium-paced bowler, he took 3 for 23 and 1 for 18 against India at Nagpur in 1969/70, during New Zealand's first Test win in India. He toured Australia under Geoff Howarth's captaincy in 1980/1, having some success.

First-class career (1963–81): 10,281 runs (35.82) including 20 centuries, 30 wickets (38.26), and 152 catches
Test matches (50): 2,684 runs (31.20) including 5 centuries, 6 wickets (35.33), and 34 catches

BURKE, Cecil

(b. 1914, Auckland) *Auckland and New Zealand*

A right-arm leg-break bowler consistent in length who delivered with plenty of 'air', Cec Burke or 'the Burglar' was also a useful batsman and a safe fielder in the gully or at third man. He toured England in 1949, securing 54 wickets (29.83)—including 6 for 23 in the first innings at Derby—but he was not selected for any of the Tests. His sole Test was the first after the Second World War, against Australia at Wellington in 1945/6, when he scored 1 and 3 and took 2 for 30. A rather fiery man, he was full of good fellowship and homespun philosophy.

First-class career (1937–54): 935 runs (17.43) and 200 wickets (25.99)

BURTT, Thomas Browning

(b. 1915, Christchurch; d. 1988, Christchurch) *Canterbury and New Zealand*

With his square, thickset figure, easy smile and general air of busy bustle, Tom Burtt was a favourite on many cricket grounds. A left-arm slow bowler of accurate length and flight with the ability to bowl to his field, he once said: 'I could bowl all day; I love it!' A useful and rugged batsman, he was prone to use his 'hockey-shot', a powerful cross-bat crack. He toured England in 1949, his only overseas tour, taking 128 wickets (22.88) in the dry summer, a record number for a New Zealander. Of his 1,245 overs, a third were maidens. In the Tests he took 17 wickets (33.41). At home he appeared against England in 1946/7 and 1950/1, against South Africa in 1952/3 and against the West Indies in 1951/2. He took 8 for 35 in an innings against Otago in 1953/4.

First-class career (1943–55): 1,644 runs (17.30), 408 wickets (22.19), and 53 catches
Test matches (10): 252 runs (21.00), 33 wickets (35.45), and 2 catches

BUTTERFIELD, Leonard Arthur

(b. 1913, Christchurch) *Canterbury and New Zealand*

A good all-rounder who was not able to play regular first-class cricket, Leonard Butterfield was a right-handed batsman and fast-medium bowler, whose sole Test was the first after the Second World War, against Australia at Wellington in 1945/6, when he made a pair and took 0 for 24.

First-class career (1934–46): 589 runs (22.65) and 38 wickets (19.65)

CAIRNS, Bernard Lance

(b. 1949, Marlborough) *Central Districts, Otago, Northern Districts, Durham, and New Zealand*

A massively built and enthusiastic all-rounder with enormous hands, Lance Cairns was primarily a right-arm medium-pace bowler. He swung the ball considerably in a heavy atmosphere, with a hopping, open-chested action reminiscent of a slow-motion Mike Procter. Though his swing was generally 'in' to the right-hander he could also bowl a Bedser-like leg-cutter. However, he could be equally valuable as a late-order batsman who hit the ball vast distances with a blacksmith's might and relish. In 1979/80 he hit a century in 52 minutes against Wellington for Otago—the fastest ever in New Zealand. He first played for Central Districts in 1972/3 and four years later moved to Otago. At Test level it was some time before he commanded a regular place because his bowling lacked penetration on good wickets, but between 1973 and 1984 he played in every other Test-playing country. He took 5 for 55 in 33.1 overs in India's first innings of 298 at Madras in 1976. He also took 6 for 85 against West Indies in 1979/80. He played for Durham in 1979 after proving an invaluable all-round member of the New Zealand side which reached the semi-final of the 1979 Prudential World Cup. He took 13 wickets in three Tests in Australia in 1980/1 and in the same season had 13 more victims (including 5 for 33 and 2 for 30 in the victory at Wellington) as New Zealand won a rubber against India for the first time in seven attempts. Against Australia at Auckland in 1981/2, he made 34 off 21 balls to settle the issue when New Zealand were faltering on the brink of their second win over Australia and a year later his 8 for 96 in the match helped to win New Zealand's first-ever Test against Sri Lanka. Then, in 1983 at Headingley, came his finest performance—7 for 74 in England's first innings, followed by 24 not out and 3 for 70 to inspire New Zealand's first victory in their 29th Test in England. Another seven-wicket haul, in the first Test against England at Wellington in 1983/4, included the first six wickets. He finished with 7 for 143 but England recovered and New Zealand were still in danger of defeat when Cairns joined Coney for the ninth wicket. Cairns made 64 of a partnership of 118, the game was saved and the rubber subsequently won.

First-class career (1971–86): 4,165 runs (20.72) including 1 century, 473 wickets (26.52), and 89 catches

Test matches (43): 928 runs (16.28), 130 wickets (32.91), and 30 catches

CAIRNS, Christopher Lance

(b. 1970, Picton) *Northern Districts, Canterbury, Nottinghamshire, and New Zealand*

A tall, right-handed all-round cricketer of high class, Chris Cairns's highly promising Test career was interrupted by a serious knee injury. Various physical handicaps have curtailed his progress since his first Test in Perth in 1989, but he followed Richard Hadlee not only as his country's leading all-rounder but also as Nottinghamshire's overseas player. Brilliant as a schoolboy and under-age representative player, he is, at his best, genuinely fast and a polished batsman, more so than his famous father, Lance, an in-swing bowler who could also hit the ball into the next parish. Making his first Test appearance in Australia in 1989/90 at the age of 19, Chris Cairns played home Tests against three other countries before injury struck. Against England at Christchurch in 1991/2 he scored 61 and added 117 with Dipak Patel for the seventh wicket, a record. For Nottinghamshire in 1993 he was consistently effective in all competitions, hitting 126 not out against Surrey in one Sunday League game and taking 6 for 52 against Kent in another. He topped the county's first-class bowling averages, with 53 wickets at 23.43, and with 962 runs at 43, including nine innings of 50 or more, he would have done the 'modern double' had he not had to return home after the sudden death of his sister.

First-class career (1988–   ): 3,415 runs (31.91) and 273 wickets (29.21)

Test matches (10): 349 runs (20.52) and 28 wickets (43.10)

CAMERON, Francis James

(b. 1932, Dunedin) *Otago and New Zealand*

A wily right-arm medium-fast bowler, able to swing the ball both ways, Frank Cameron toured South Africa in 1961/2, India and Pakistan in 1964/5, and England in 1965. In South Africa his tenacity as a stock bowler brought him 62 wickets (22.77) in first-class matches, including 20 wickets (24.65) in the Tests. His 5 for 48 in the first innings of the third Test at Cape Town materially assisted New Zealand's victory. In England, however, although he captured 47 wickets (24.42) he failed in the Tests. Usually a moderate number eleven batsman, he played twelve careful not-out innings out of 14 and finished at the top of the tour batting averages with 45! When Pakistan toured New Zealand in 1964/5, he headed the bowling in the three Tests with 13 wickets (15.61). At home he also played against England in 1962/3 and South Africa in 1963/4. On his way to South Africa in 1961/2, he took 7 for 27 in the first innings against Western Australia at Perth. He was later chairman of the New Zealand selectors and was awarded an MBE for services to the game.

First-class career (1952–67): 993 runs (11.82), 447 wickets (21.60), and 26 catches
Test matches (19): 116 runs (11.60), 62 wickets (29.82), and 2 catches

CAVE, Henry Butler

(b. 1922, Wellington; d. 1989, Wellington)
Wellington, Central Districts, and New Zealand

The best of a large family of cricketers—known as 'the Cavemen'—Harry Cave was an economical right-arm medium-pace bowler who was able to swing the new ball with a high, windmill-type action and was prepared to bowl until exhausted. He was a reliable and adaptable late-order batsman and a very good fielder. He toured England in 1949 and 1958 and India and Pakistan in 1955/6 and, at home, played against England in 1954/5 and the West Indies in 1955/6. He captained the team to India and Pakistan, and led New Zealand in one Test against the West Indies. In England in 1949 his four Test wickets cost 465 runs but he was much less expensive in 1958, taking 50 wickets (22.02) on the tour although he again lacked penetration in the Tests. In India and Pakistan he bowled with remarkable economy, taking 14 wickets in the Tests. Against India alone, 118 of his 255 overs were maidens. In his two Tests against England in 1954/5 at Dunedin and Auckland respectively, his figures were: 48–25–52–3. His most successful series was against the West Indies in 1955/6, when he took 12 wickets (15.50). In the fourth Test at Auckland he bowled New Zealand to their first-ever victory in Tests, by 190 runs, taking 4 for 22 (in 27.3 overs) and 4 for 21 (in 13.1 overs) with his hostile swing bowling. In three unofficial Tests against Australia in 1956/7, he captured 17 wickets (16.70). His highest score was 118 for Central Districts against Otago in 1952/3, and his most effective bowling 7 for 31 and 6 for 33 against Auckland—in a single day—during the same season.

First-class career (1945–59): 2,187 runs (16.08) including 2 centuries, 362 wickets (23.93), and 69 catches
Test matches (19): 229 runs (8.80), 34 wickets (43.14), and 8 catches

CHAPPLE, Murray Ernest

(b. 1930, Christchurch; d. 1985, Hamilton)
Canterbury, Central Districts, and New Zealand

A steady, stroke-making right-handed batsman, who frequently opened the batting, and a left-arm change slow bowler, Murray Chapple toured South Africa in 1953/4 and 1961/2 and, at home, played against South Africa in 1952/3 and 1963/4, England in 1954/5 and as captain in one match in 1965/6, and the West Indies in 1955/6. However, despite his experience, he had a disappointing Test record; his best effort was 76 at Cape Town in the third Test against South Africa in 1953/4, when he shared in an opening stand of 126 with G. O. Rabone. For Canterbury against the South Africans at Christchurch in 1952/3 he hit a fluent 165, his career-highest, and 88. He became involved in the national administration of the game and has managed New Zealand touring teams.

First-class career (1949–72): 5,344 runs (28.88) including 4 centuries, and 142 wickets (25.06)
Test matches (14): 497 runs (19.11), 1–84, and 10 catches

CLEVERLEY, Donald Charles

(b. 1909, Oamaru) *Auckland, Central Districts, and New Zealand*

A right-arm fast-medium bowler who could make the ball fly head-high, Donald Cleverley played in the first Test against South Africa at Christchurch in 1931/2 and also against Australia in the first Test after the Second World War at Wellington in 1945/6, but had little success. He was a national amateur boxing champion.

First-class career (1930–53): 157 runs (5.60) and 90 wickets (30.21)
Test matches (2): 19 runs (19.00) and 0–130

COLLINGE, Richard Owen

(b. 1946, Wellington) *Central Districts, Northern Districts, Wellington, and New Zealand*

When he retired, the most prolific wicket-taker in New Zealand Test cricket, Richard Collinge was at 6 ft. 5 in. a menacing prospect for any batsman. He approached the wicket off a notoriously lengthy, long-striding run, hands clawing the air, bowling left-arm fast-medium deliveries of consistent accuracy at a length full enough to make good use of any swing. He made his first-class début in 1963/4 and the following season at the age of 18 played in the three Tests against Pakistan, taking 15 wickets (24.33). A committed family man, later in his career he was sometimes a reluctant tourist and in 1971/2 had to return home early from the West Indies because of the illness of one of his children. However, he was almost always an automatic selection when he was available because his height and strength made him an opponent all batsmen respected though he was seldom genuinely fast, and sometimes looked rather ordinary on true batting pitches. Apart from the West Indies he toured Pakistan and India and England four times, in 1965, 1969, 1973, and as a replacement for the injured Dayle Hadlee in 1978. A determined and possibly underrated right-handed tail-end batsman, he had one great hour of glory against Pakistan in Auckland in 1972/3, when he made 68 not out, the highest score by a number eleven batsman in Test cricket, and shared a last wicket stand of 151 with Brian Hastings, still a record tenth-wicket stand in Tests. But Collinge's proudest moments must have been his participation in the first defeats ever inflicted by New Zealand on Australia and England. The victory by five wickets at Christchurch in March 1974 was New Zealand's first against Australia in 113 official Tests, and only the eighth in all Tests, Collinge taking 3 for 70 and 2 for 37. In the following match, which Australia won to level the series, he took 5 for 82 and 4 for 84. Three years and 11 months later, at Wellington, Collinge took 3 for 42 and 3 for 35 in the famous 72-run victory over England. The fast in-swinger with which he bowled Geoff Boycott for 1 in the second innings started the collapse of England to 64 all out amidst feverish excitement. It was entirely appropriate that this modest, calm stalwart of New Zealand cricket for 15 years should have had a strong hand in one of his country's finest cricketing hours.

First-class career (1963–78): 1,848 runs (14.43), 524 wickets (24.41), and 57 catches

Test matches (35): 533 runs (14.40), 116 wickets (29.25), and 10 catches

CHATFIELD, Ewen John

(b. 1950, Danniverke, Hawkes Bay) *Wellington and New Zealand*

A hard-working, tall, and reliably accurate fast-medium bowler who seemed to get better and better, Ewen Chatfield had a tragic experience on his Test début against England at Auckland in 1974/5. In a stubborn defensive innings at number eleven, he was struck on the temple by a ball from Peter Lever; his heart stopped and he swallowed his tongue. Following mouth to mouth resuscitation and heart massage by England's physiotherapist Bernard Thomas, he was taken to hospital and, happily, regained consciousness an hour later. Not selected for the

Prudential World Cup in England a few months later, he was fit enough to represent his country against Australia in 1976/7 and England in 1977/8, bowling steadily and industriously. He toured England with New Zealand's 1979 Prudential World Cup team. He took seven wickets in the match in New Zealand's win over Sri Lanka at Wellington (1982/3) and in England in 1983 bowled with great effect at Leeds (5 for 95 in the second innings) when New Zealand gained their first victory in England. His four wickets in the match for only 24 runs at Christchurch in 1983/4 helped in the humiliation of England and on tour in Sri Lanka later that season he was his usual reliable self, producing his best figures, 5 for 63, in the third test at Colombo. In the West Indies in 1984/5 he took 13 Test wickets at 33, including 4 for 51 and 6 for 73 in the first Test at Port of Spain, helping his team to draw, against the odds. Although always second fiddle to Richard Hadlee, few countries have had so effective an opening pair for so long. When Hadlee was injured in 1987/8 against England Chatfield took 13 wickets in three Tests at only 15 runs each. Unfailingly modest, he was awarded an MBE for his services to cricket.

First-class career (1973–90): 582 runs (9.09), 587 wickets (22.87), and 51 catches

Test matches (43): 180 runs (8.57), 123 wickets (32.17), and 7 catches

COLQUHOUN, Ian Alexander

(b. 1924, Wellington) *Central Districts and New Zealand*

A competent wicket-keeper and useful right-handed batsman, Ian Colquhoun appeared in two Tests against England in 1954/5.

First-class career (1953–64): 768 runs (14.76) and 136 dismissals (108 c., 28 st.)

Test matches (2): 1 run (0.50) and 4 dismissals (4 c.)

COMAN, Peter George

(b. 1943, Christchurch) *Canterbury*

A flamboyant opening batsman who usually scored at a furious rate, and an exuberantly enthusiastic fieldsman, Peter Coman had an array of hard-hit shots. He played in New Zealand's first-ever one-day international, against Pakistan in 1972/3 and started with a flourish. Sarfraz Nawaz opened the bowling and Coman took 16 off the over. A first-ball bouncer was hooked for six, and an amazing shot followed two balls later—a one-handed six. Coman scored two centuries and seventeen fifties for Canterbury and in his three internationals made 62 runs (20.66).

First-class career (1963–78): 2,635 runs (33.78) including 2 centuries

CONEY, Jeremy Vernon

(b. 1952, Wellington) *Wellington and New Zealand*

A very tall, fit, and enthusiastic all-rounder, Jeremy Coney was an organized and correct right-handed batsman, steady medium-paced bowler, and fine fielder who became an exceptionally astute captain. He had appeared in Tests against all the other countries before taking over as New Zealand captain from Geoff Howarth in Pakistan in 1984/5 and then leading the side to Australia in 1985/6 and to England in 1986. Very determined, he tended to produce his best when the chips were down. A good musician and qualified teacher, he became a regular selection after a successful home series against Pakistan in 1978/9 when he headed New Zealand's averages with 242 runs (48.40). Also outstanding as captain of Wellington in the Shell Series, Coney was named New Zealand's cricketer of the year that season and was an important member of the 1979 Prudential World Cup team which reached the semi-final and lost only narrowly to England. Against West Indies at home in 1979/80, he made 80 in a record seventh-wicket stand with Geoff Howarth at Christchurch and 49 not out at Auckland to help New Zealand to a most unexpected victory in the three-match series. He again batted consistently in Australia in 1980/1 and in England in 1983 he scored 238 runs in the four Tests (34) as well as taking wickets at important times and producing slip catches with his usual consistency. But it was not until the first Test against England at Wellington in 1983/4, with defeat facing his team, that he at last scored his initial Test century, a painstaking eight-hour marathon effort of 174 not out to save the game. He further enhanced his reputation by leading New Zealand to her first win in a series in England in 1986, endearing himself to spectators and opponents by his sunny disposition and also by allowing England to play two substitute wicketkeepers at Lord's when Bruce French was felled by a bouncer from Richard Hadlee. On tour he made 688 runs in 17 innings at an average of 57. He was awarded an MBE in 1986 and became a successful TV and radio sports commentator and presenter. Shrewd and witty he was streets ahead of most other players-turned-pundits. He wrote

an unusually good account of his playing career, *The Playing Mantis* (MOA, 1985).

First-class career (1970–87): 7,872 runs (35.14) including 8 centuries, 111 wickets (31.17), and 192 catches

Test matches (52): 2,668 runs (37.57) including 3 centuries, 27 wickets (35.77), and 64 catches

CONGDON, Bevan Ernest

(b. 1938, Nelson) *Central Districts, Wellington, Otago, Canterbury, and New Zealand*

One of the finest all-round cricketers produced by his country, Bev Congdon was a player of immense character and a fine ambassador for New Zealand. Thin, of medium height, and with a slightly stooping walk, he was a right-handed batsman who usually went in first wicket down. He had a sound technique, exceptional depths of concentration and determination, and delightful timing, notably when driving on the offside off either foot. A fine fielder anywhere, he was also a canny medium-paced bowler who swung the ball both ways and expected a wicket with every delivery. As a captain he was orthodox, tough, but never mean, and often shrewd. He led New Zealand in the first win against Australia and, had his fielders held their chances at Lord's in 1973, would also have inspired the first success against England. As it was, though no longer captain, he was a member of the team which eventually beat England for the first time in 1978. He scored more runs for his country than any other New Zealand cricketer. Of his seven Test centuries, three were scores of more than 150 and as captain of New Zealand in 17 Tests between 1971/2 and 1974/5 his batting actually seemed to grow in stature, rather than to suffer under the strain of captaincy. In 1973, in between scoring 176 and 175 in successive Tests, he cheerfully gave up his Sunday to play against a village side in Surrey. He made his début for Central Districts in 1960/1 and his first Test appearance in 1964/5. On the first of four official tours of England in 1965 he scored 1,040 runs as an opening batsman, and in the West Indies and Bermuda in 1971/2, he was a major success on a happy tour, scoring 992 runs at 82.66. In the second Test in Port of Spain, going in number three, he scored 166 not out and 82, and in the following Test at Bridgetown, taking over the captaincy from the injured Graham Dowling, he scored 126 not out. Scores of 61 not out, 11 and 58 followed, as New Zealand drew a series they had been expected to lose. It was really only in the 1970s that New Zealand went into Test matches without being considered the inevitable underdogs and Congdon's determined captaincy had much to do with this. In England in 1973 he scored a courageous 176, leading his side from the imminence of a crushing loss to one of the most honourable defeats in Test cricket. Facing a huge target and standing at 130 for four at one point on the fourth day, Congdon and Vic Pollard put on 177 for the fifth wicket. They amassed what was then the highest fourth innings score by a losing Test side (440) and New Zealand lost by only 38 runs. At Lord's ten days later New Zealand replied to England's 253 with 551, of which Congdon scored 175, but New Zealand's bowlers just failed to bowl England out a second time. The following winter (1973/4), after Congdon had scored 132 at Wellington in the first (drawn) Test against Australia, he led New Zealand to victory by five wickets at Christchurch. He accepted the ups and downs with the same good grace. He retired after a disappointing tour of England in 1978. He was awarded an OBE.

First-class career (1960–78): 13,101 runs (34.84) including 23 centuries, 204 wickets (30.02), and 201 catches

Test matches (61): 3,448 runs (32.22) including 7 centuries, 59 wickets (36.50), and 44 catches

COWIE, John

(b. 1912, Auckland; d. 1994, Lower Hutt, Wellington) *Auckland and New Zealand*

A well-built right-arm fast bowler, Jack Cowie, nicknamed 'The Bull', displayed invariable determination, stamina, accuracy, and outstanding skill. He could get the ball up from the most unresponsive turf, commanded the late outswinger and, from time to time, could made the ball snap back from the off viciously. For much of his career he was the one 'class' bowler in the New Zealand team. He toured England in 1937 and 1949 and, at home, played against Australia in 1945/6 and England in 1946/7. On his first England tour, he took 114 wickets (19.95) overall and in the Tests 19 wickets (20.78). Despite dropped catches, he took 10 for 140 in the second match at Old Trafford. At Wellington in 1945/6 he took 6 for 40 in Australia's sole innings (after New Zealand had been routed for 42); and in the sole England innings at Christchurch in 1946/7 he captured 6 for 83, besides hitting 45, by far his best score in Tests. His best analysis was 6 for 3 against Ireland at Dublin in 1937. He was also Auckland's goalkeeper and for 14 years served on New Zealand's FA council, seven of them as chairman. He was awarded an OBE in 1972.

First-class career (1932–50): 762 runs (10.16), 359 wickets (22.28), and 35 catches

Test matches (9): 90 runs (10.00), 45 wickets (21.53), and 3 catches

CRESSWELL, George Fenwick

(b. 1915, Wellington; d. 1966, Marlborough) *Wellington, Central Districts, and New Zealand*

Although he did not play in first-class cricket until he was 34, 'Fen' Cresswell toured England in 1949 after one trial match, taking 62 wickets (26.09). A right-arm medium-pace leg-theory bowler with an unusual chest-on delivery, he was invariably steady with his length and could swing or cut the ball either way. A rather poor left-handed batsman, he was nicknamed 'the ferret' because he went in after 'the rabbits' but also answered to 'Fritzy' because he stood to attention before bowling. In his sole Test on the 1949 tour, the last at The Oval, he took 6 for 168 in England's total of 482. He also played against England twice in 1950/1, taking 3 for 18 in 15 overs at Wellington. For a New Zealand XI against Australia at Dunedin in 1949/50 he took 8 for 100 in a total of 299. The soul of good fellowship in his cricketing days, he was found dead with a shotgun at his side.

First-class career (1949–55): 89 runs (5.23), 124 wickets (22.52), and 11 catches

Test matches (3): 14 runs (7.00) and 13 wickets (22.46)

CROMB, Ian Burns

(b. 1905, Christchurch; d. 1984, Christchurch) *Canterbury and New Zealand*

Well-built, loose-limbed, and high-spirited, Ian Cromb was a right-arm fast-medium bowler, whose action, though rather slingy, was likened to Maurice Tate's. He could swing the ball late, especially in England's heavy atmosphere and cut the ball a little, but his main asset was the ability to hurry the ball on to the bat. Unlike many New Zealand bowlers he could work up a 'hate' against the batsman. He was also a useful late-order batsman and good field. In England in 1931, he took 58 wickets (26.29) and scored 448 runs. At Wellington, in the second Test against South Africa in 1931/2, he hit a valuable 51 not out at number ten. He captained New Zealand in the unofficial Tests against MCC in 1935/6. His career-highest score was 171 for Canterbury against Wellington in 1939/40 and his most productive bowling 7 for 21 and 7 for 74 for South Island Army against North Island Army in 1942/3. He was a professional for several years in the East Lancashire League and in his fifties he played senior club championship cricket in Christchurch.

First-class career (1929–47): 3,950 runs (29.04) including 3 centuries, 222 wickets (27.71), and 103 catches
Test matches (5): 123 runs (20.50), 8 wickets (55.25), and 1 catch

CROWE, Jeffrey John

(b. 1958, Auckland) *Auckland, South Australia, and New Zealand*

Although the elder of the two Crowe brothers, Jeff first played Test cricket after his immensely gifted younger brother, though this was partly because he had launched his own career in South Australia, for whom he played with considerable success from 1977 to 1982, scoring 704 runs in 1981/2, including three centuries. He was certainly interesting the Australian selectors but decided to return to his own land to become a member of the first team to win a Test in England and also of the first to inflict a defeat on Australia on their own soil, both in a Test and in a series, in 1985/6. A tall and very solidly built, fair-haired, right-handed batsman, and most reliable fielder, who could also keep wicket, he looked so much like his younger brother that the pair delighted in swapping helmets in the field in order to confuse commentators when first appearing in Tests together, in 1983. Jeff scored his first Test hundred against England at Auckland in 1983/4, a determined innings of 128 which shut England out of the game. He was again very consistent on the short tour of Pakistan in 1984/5 (201 runs at 42.20). Given the daunting task of going in first wicket down against the West Indies fast bowlers in the Caribbean in 1985, he responded with some sound and courageous innings, notably in the fourth Test at Sabina Park when, with his side forced to follow-on, he hit 112, sharing a record stand of 220 for the second wicket with Geoff Howarth. He captained New Zealand in six Test matches, and although he last played Test cricket in 1989/90, he continued to be a dominating player at provincial level, scoring 1,063 runs (65.52) in 1991/2, a magnificent finale. His father, David, played first-class cricket for Wellington and Canterbury.

First-class career (1977–92): 10,233 runs (37.90) including 22 centuries, 1 wicket (55.00), and 199 catches
Test matches (39): 1,601 runs (26.24) including 3 centuries, 0–9, and 42 catches

CROWE, Martin David

(b. 1962, Auckland) *Auckland, Central Districts, Somerset, and New Zealand*

The son of a first-class cricketer, Dave, and Audrey, a gifted tennis player, Martin Crowe became the first of his family to play Test cricket for New Zealand when at the age of 19 he was selected at home against Australia at the end of the 1981/2 season. A right-handed batsman, he was also an athletic fielder; and, until back trouble forced him to stop, a brisk medium-fast bowler. Very soon he was being talked about as one of the best young batsmen in the world and he proved himself incomparably the classiest New Zealand batsman of his generation. In an age of almost constant international cricket he eventually broke most batting records, despite serious injuries which included a broken shin, back strain, frequent knee damage, and torn hamstrings. Tall, 14 stone, classically orthodox in method and with ample time to choose from a complete repertoire of strokes, he was masterful at the crease but modest and retiring off it. Consistent performances for Auckland after his first appearance for them in 1979/80 earned him a place in three Tests against Australia. He failed, but still looked a useful prospect. He quickly made himself indispensable for New Zealand both in Tests and limited-overs internationals. He broadened his experience in Yorkshire League cricket in 1982, hitting 102 at Scarborough on his first-class début in England that season and returning to score 819 runs (58.50) on the 1983 tour when he hit an accomplished 97 in defeat in the Prudential World Cup match against England. Against the same opponents at Wellington in 1983/4 he made his first Test hundred to help save a match which seemed lost and he batted steadily in a series at home and away against Pakistan in 1984/5 before hitting a brilliant 188 against West Indies in 1985 at Georgetown. He again scored 188 in the first Test at Brisbane in 1985/6, finishing the three-match series (New Zealand's first series win against Australia) with 309 runs (77.25). In the return series against Australia later in the same season, he scored 137 at Christchurch and he quickly hit impressive form in the 1986 series in England where he had already made a mark following a season on the MCC groundstaff. Deputizing for Viv Richards at Somerset in 1984 he had blossomed into rare brilliance after a poor start, hitting six hundreds, and 1,870 first-class runs (53.42) as well as many telling limited-overs contributions. He made a considerable impact at the club, starting a special weekly meeting for the younger uncapped players in order to encourage team spirit. He scored freely throughout the tour of England in 1986, making an elegant hundred in the Lord's Test and finishing the series with an average of 68. At the end of the tour he was offered, and accepted, a new contract with Somerset in 1987, a controversial decision since it meant the termination of the association between Somerset and the two great West Indians, Viv Richards and Joel Garner. These two had passed their peak; Crowe had yet to reach his, but there were frustrations as well as triumphs in the year ahead, especially when his attention to captaincy led to intrusions into his private life from a section of the press whom he despised. His highest score came against Sri Lanka at Wellington in 1990/1 when he made 299 and put on a record 467 for the third wicket with Andrew Jones. On the same Basin Reserve ground he scored 119 against the West Indies in 1986/7 (following this with 104 at Auckland) and in the next season 143 against England. Earlier that season his Test scores in a three-match series in Australia were 67, 23, 137, 8, 82, and 79. With Hadlee to bowl and Crowe to bat New Zealand were a match for any team throughout the 1980s, but even more depended on Crowe after Hadlee's retirement in 1990. Still, on a tour of Zimbabwe and Sri Lanka in 1992/3 he made a hundred in each country and against England in 1994, despite a constantly sore knee, he scored a beautifully constructed 142 at Lord's and, in tricky conditions against some hostile bowling, 70 and 115 at Old Trafford.

First-class career (1979–): 18,710 runs (55.85) including 67 centuries, 119 wickets (33.10), and 212 catches

Test matches (70): 5,230 runs (47.98) including 17 centuries, 14 wickets (48.42), and 63 catches

CUNIS, Robert Smith

(b. 1941, Auckland) *Auckland, Northern Districts, and New Zealand*

Although once described as 'neither one thing nor the other', Bob Cunis was a useful all-rounder. Broad-shouldered, he was a right-arm workaday fast-medium bowler apt to berate the batsman by word or look for some streaky shot,

and a determined, steady batsman. He toured England in 1969, India and Pakistan in 1969/70, and the West Indies in 1971/2 and, at home, played against South Africa in 1963/4, England in 1965/6 and 1970/1, and the West Indies in 1968/9. Despite the rain, riots, and rows which marred the third Test against India at Hyderabad in 1969/70 he returned a match analysis of 6 for 24. In the third match against Pakistan at Dacca he took 4 for 21, after adding 96 with Mark Burgess for the ninth wicket, saving New Zealand from defeat. On this 1969/70 tour he took 15 wickets (19.93) in the Tests. In the 1970/1 Test at Auckland against England he took 9 for 128, but he had to work hard for little reward in both Australia and the West Indies. He was also a Rugby centre-three-quarter of some reputation. He became coach of New Zealand's cricket team for a time, but arthritis of the hips and knees tempered his natural enthusiasm.

First-class career (1960–77): 1,849 runs (16.50) including 1 century, and 386 wickets (26.65)

Test matches (20): 295 runs (12.82), 51 wickets (37.00), and 1 catch

DACRE, Charles Christian Ralph

(b. Auckland 1899; d. Auckland, 1975) *Auckland, Gloucestershire, and New Zealand*

No one in New Zealand cricket has a better reputation as a hitter than Lance Cairns, but between the two World Wars, Charles Dacre was the big striker who delighted the crowds. He played his first representative game against Wellington in 1914, going to the ground by tram, wearing his short trousers, carrying his cricket gear, and playing in borrowed whites. He was only 15. A right-hand batsman, although he threw with his left hand, C. C. R. Dacre earned a name as a demolisher of bowlers and in 1925 he was the first New Zealander to score a century in each innings, 127 not out and 107 not out for Auckland against Victoria. He was an automatic choice for New Zealand's first tour of England in 1927. They opened the tour with a two-day game at Maidenhead and Dacre scored 101. During the second game, at Lord's, Dacre was asleep, with his pads on, when he was woken at the fall of the fourth wicket. The score was 107 and when he asked about the bowling, Dacre was warned 'Calthorpe (the Hon. F. S. G.) is swinging them.' 'I'll give him swing,' said Dacre and duly did, making 28 in 10 minutes. When joined by his captain, Tom Lowry, 115 runs were added in 59 minutes, Lowry making 106 and Dacre 107. In first-class matches on that tour he scored 1,070 runs at 31.5, including 90 against Leicestershire in 75 minutes, 64 against Gloucestershire in 25 minutes, and 176 against Derbyshire in 135 minutes, an innings containing twenty-one fours and eight sixes. Sadly, an injury to his right arm cut short his career with Gloucestershire in 1936. He was essentially cheerful in all that he did, even in retirement.

First-class career (1914–36): 12,230 runs (29.18) and 39 wickets (31.25)

D'ARCY, John William

(b. 1936, Christchurch) *Canterbury, Wellington, Otago, and New Zealand*

One of several young players 'blooded' on the 1958 England tour, John D'Arcy was a right-handed opening batsman of tremendous determination and concentration. Small and fair-haired, he often defended admirably, but an absence of forcing strokes, due partly to an unorthodox grip, reduced his effectiveness. His 522 runs in 22 matches included his career-highest score, 89 in about five hours against Glamorgan at Swansea.

First-class career (1955–62): 2,009 runs (23.09)
Test matches (5): 136 runs (13.60)

DAVIS, Heath Te-ihi-o-Te-Rangi

(b. 1971, Lower Hutt, Wellington) *Wellington and New Zealand*

The New Zealand selectors proclaimed their choice of Heath Davis for the tour to England in 1994 a calculated risk. He had played only twenty first-class games as a very strong and genuinely fast right-arm bowler. Tall and of Maori extraction, his potential was great but he had a reputation for wildness which was fully vindicated in England, despite earnest attempts to gain greater control. Playing for Bexhill against Chichester in the Sussex League two years before, he had sent down 42 no-balls and 8 wides in his 15 overs. His first ball in his only Test at Trent Bridge, a game he would not have played but for injuries to other bowlers, duly sailed down the leg side for four wides. He persevered but managed only one wicket for 93, and scores of nought not out in both innings. All tour he took only 9 first-class wickets at 79.85 each. His only other international experience was in a one-day tournament in Sharjah. Bowling a total of only 6 overs in games against Sri Lanka and Pakistan, his figures were 0 wickets for 51 runs.

First-class career (1991–): 141 runs (10.84) and 79 wickets (32.55)

DE GROEN, Richard Paul

(b. 1962, Otorohanga) *Auckland, Northern Districts, and New Zealand*

After seven years of sterling efforts, particularly for Northern Districts, Richard de Groen was rewarded with two New Zealand caps in Australia in 1993/4 and played against Pakistan at home in the same season. A right-arm fast-medium bowler and right-handed bat, he had many successes for Northern Districts. In 1992/3 he ended the Shell Trophy season with 46 wickets, a Northern Districts record, and in the match against Otago took 13 wickets, also a record for his team.

First-class career (1987–): 218 runs (7.51) and 154 wickets (26.10)
Test matches (4): 19 runs (4.75) and 8 wickets (53.12)

DEMPSTER, Charles Stewart

(b. 1903, Wellington; d. 1974, Wellington) *Wellington, Wanganui, Leicestershire, Scotland, Warwickshire, and New Zealand*

'Stewie' Dempster was generally an opening batsman and certainly one of the best players to have been produced by New Zealand. Indeed, at his best he was superb and amongst the finest batsmen in the world. Rather short and stocky, he was a right-hander who drove with tremendous power, rarely lifting the ball. He was always alert and reliable in the field. Never coached, he toured England with the first New Zealand team in 1927—when he said that he really learned cricket —heading the batting with 1,430 runs (44.68) in first-class matches and 2,165 runs (54.12) in all matches, including six centuries. During his 180 against Warwickshire at Edgbaston he hit W. G. Quaife for five fours in an over. In the first Test series in New Zealand, against England in 1929/30, when he headed the batting with 341 runs (85.25), he scored 136 at Wellington in the second match, putting on 276 for the first wicket with J. E. Mills, which remains his country's highest stand for any wicket against England. This was the first century in a Test for New Zealand and he followed it with 80 not out in the second innings. In England in 1931 he was brilliant, making 1,778 runs (59.26) in first-class matches, including seven centuries, his 212 against Essex at Leyton remaining his career-highest. In the first Test in England, at Lord's, he scored 53 and 120. Although not as dominant in the first series against South Africa in 1931/2, he hit 64 in the second match at Wellington; and in what was to be his last Test, at Auckland against England in 1932/3, coming in with two wickets down for 0, he hit 83 not out in a total of 156. After taking up a business appointment with Sir Julien Cahn, he played for his patron's team and qualified for Leicestershire, playing for the county from 1935 until 1939—as captain from 1936 to 1938—making 4,659 runs (49.04), including 18 centuries and heading the county's batting averages each year.

First-class career (1921–48): 12,145 runs (44.98) including 35 centuries, 8 wickets (37.5), 94 catches, and 2 stumpings

Test matches (10): 723 runs (65.72) including 2 centuries, 0–10, and 2 catches

DEMPSTER, Eric William

(b. 1925, Wellington) *Wellington and New Zealand*

A competent left-handed batsman and slow bowler, Eric Dempster toured South Africa in 1953/4, making 348 runs (21.75) and taking 22 wickets (32.00), and at home played against South Africa in 1952/3.

First-class career (1947–61): 1,592 runs (22.42) including 1 century, and 102 wickets (30.80)

Test matches (5): 106 runs (17.66), 2 wickets (109.50), and 1 catch

DICK, Arthur Edward

(b. 1936, Otago) *Otago, Wellington, and New Zealand*

An outstanding wicket-keeper and competent right-handed batsman, 'Art' Dick toured South Africa in 1961/2, England in 1965, and Pakistan in 1965/6 and, at home, played against England in 1962/3, South Africa in 1963/4, and Pakistan in 1964/5. In the series against South Africa in 1961/2 he equalled the then world-record number of dismissals in a rubber—23 (21 caught, 2 stumped). On his Test début, at Durban, his 7 dismissals (6 caught, 1 stumped) equalled the New Zealand record, In England in 1965, he had 27 dismissals from 13 first-class matches.

First-class career (1956–69): 2,315 runs (20.30) including 1 century, and 169 dismissals (148 c., 21 st.)

Test matches (17): 370 runs (14.23) and 51 dismissals (47 c., 4 st.)

DICKINSON, George Ritchie

(b. 1903, Dunedin; d. 1978, Lower Hutt, Wellington) *Otago and New Zealand*

This right-arm bowler and often useful batsman was, at his best, as fast a bowler as New Zealand has boasted, though when trying for top speed his arm would drop a little. He appeared in the first and second Tests in New Zealand against England in 1929/30, dismissing Frank Woolley twice, and once against South Africa in 1931/2. He took 11 for 89 against Canterbury in 1924/5.

First-class career (1921–44): 1,013 runs (18.75) including 1 century, and 150 wickets (26.96)

Test matches (3): 31 runs (6.20), 8 wickets (30.62), and 3 catches

DONNELLY, Martin Paterson

(b. 1917, Auckland) *Taranaki, Wellington, Canterbury, Oxford University, Middlesex, Warwickshire, and New Zealand*

Despite his lack of inches, Martin Donnelly was fit and strong and simply the best left-handed batsman in the world immediately after the Second World War. C. B. Fry volunteered that not one of the left-handers of his own day was superior. A complete batsman, he drove with punishing power and was merciless in pulling and cutting anything short. His footwork was superb. In the field he had speed, as befitted a rugby footballer, and a powerful, accurate throw: he was equally valuable at cover-point, gully, or in the leg-trap. First playing in the Plunket Shield at the age of 19, he was selected for the 1937 England tour, and was outstanding with 1,414 runs (37.21), though he started quietly in Test cricket with 121 runs from three matches. Whilst serving as a major, after war service in Egypt and Italy, he played a famous match-winning innings of 133 for the Dominions against England at Lord's. Already a graduate of University College, Canterbury, he went up to Oxford to read history in 1946 and won blues for cricket and rugby. Against Cambridge at Lord's that year, he hit a memorable 142 in a total of 261. He captained Oxford the following season and his feats in The Parks became legendary. In 1947 he scored a brilliant 162 not out in only 3 hours for Gentlemen against Players at Lord's. His career-highest, 208 not out for MCC against Yorkshire at Scarborough in 1948, took a mere 180 minutes. But he reached the zenith of a great career on New Zealand's England tour of 1949. He headed the batting with 2,287 runs (61.81), including five centuries. In the Tests, he made 462 runs (77.00), passing 50 in five out of six innings. In the second Test at his beloved Lord's, he scored 206, taking complete control of the attack. After coming down from Oxford he went into business and played only a little more first-class cricket— twenty games for Warwickshire and one for Middlesex. In 1946/7 he represented England against Ireland at rugby football in Dublin. His job in industry took him to Australia and he settled in Sydney. He was always equably tempered and treated cricket as a game, not a war.

First-class career (1936–61): 9,250 runs (47.44) including 23 centuries, 43 wickets (39.14), and 75 catches

Test matches (7): 582 runs (52.90) including 1 century, 0–20, and 7 catches

DOUGLAS, Mark William

(b. 1968, Nelson) *Central Districts, Wellington, and New Zealand*

The son of Graham Douglas, who played for Central Districts in the 1960s, Mark Douglas had often come close to national representation, before the absence of some key players in 1994 gave him the opportunity to win a one-day cap in Sharjah in the Australasia Cup. A left-handed batsman and a fast scorer by inclination, he scored 33 runs (11.00) in three internationals.

First-class career (1987–ʼ): 2,941 runs (31.92) and 4 wickets (30.00)

DOULL, Simon Blair

(b. 1969, Pukekohe) *Northern Districts and New Zealand*

A tall, right-arm fast-medium swing bowler, Simon Doull's career suffered through injury. He had to return home from Zimbabwe in 1992/3 after playing one Test, broke down in Australia in the following summer, and had to leave the tour to England in 1994 without playing a first-class match. Yet in 1993/4 he bowled with skill and stamina to take 5 for 66 and 2 for 48 in the first Test against Pakistan at Auckland. Further success followed against South Africa in 1994/5. A right-hand bat, he has scored one century.

First-class career (1989–ʼ): 654 runs (16.35) including 1 century, and 114 wickets (25.94)

Test matches (6): 115 runs (11.50), 16 wickets (35.81), and 5 catches

DOWLING, Graham Thorne

(b. 1937, Christchurch) *Canterbury, Prime Minister's XI (in India), and New Zealand*

Graham Dowling was a studious, methodical, and accomplished right-handed opening batsman, a brilliant field, usually at leg-slip, a proficient reserve wicket-keeper and a regular Test choice from 1961 until 1972. He became a thoughtful captain who led New Zealand in nineteen Tests, and was victor in four. He toured widely: to South Africa in 1961/2, India and Pakistan in 1964/5 and 1969/70, England in 1965 and 1969, and the West Indies in 1971/2. At home he played against England in 1962/3 and 1970/1, South Africa in 1963/4, Pakistan in 1964/5, India in 1967/8, and the West Indies in 1968/9. On both England tours—he was captain on the second—he made over 700 runs but, like his colleagues, struggled in the Tests. His three Test centuries were made against India: 129 in a total of 297 in the third match at Bombay in 1964/5; 143 in the first match at Dunedin and 239 in the second at Christchurch in 1967/8, when he led New Zealand to victory over India for the first time. His innings included five sixes and lasted 556 minutes. In this series against India he headed the batting with 471 runs (58.87), and in the season as a whole made 966 runs in ten first-class matches, a New Zealand record for a domestic season. During the tour of the West Indies in 1971/2 he was captain until back trouble forced his early return home and retirement from first-class cricket. A qualified Chartered Accountant, he became chief executive of the New Zealand Cricket Board, no sinecure in a country where Rugby Union was the major sport and professional cricket was not always a profitable business.

First-class career (1958–72): 9,399 runs (34.94) including 16 centuries, 9 wickets (42.00), and 111 catches

Test matches (39): 2,306 runs (31.16) including 3 centuries, 1–19, and 23 catches

DUNNING, John Angus

(b. 1903, Omaha; d. 1971, Adelaide, Australia) *Oxford University, Otago, and New Zealand*

A right-arm medium-fast bowler of off-cutters with an unlovely action but considerable heart, John Dunning toured England in 1937, taking 83 wickets (30.10) in 941.3 overs, the lion's share of the bowling. He captured 7 for 67 against Middlesex at Lord's, 9 for 64 against Cambridge at

EDGAR

Fenner's and 10 for 170 against Essex at Chelmsford; but in Tests against England between 1932/3 and 1937, his wickets were very costly. Though given a trial for Oxford in 1928, when he was a Rhodes scholar, he did not get a blue. He became a member of the Australian Cricket Board of Control.

First-class career (1923–38): 1,057 runs (13.04) and 228 wickets (27.58)

Test matches (4): 38 runs (7.60), 5 wickets (98.60), and 2 catches

EDGAR, Bruce Adrian

(b. 1956, Wellington) *Wellington and New Zealand*

On his first tour, to England in 1978, Bruce Edgar looked a player in the high tradition of New Zealand left-handers, worthy to follow in the footsteps of Donnelly and Sutcliffe. These were early days in his career, but this dark left-handed batsman played the rampant England fast bowlers with cool assurance, a very straight bat and the timing of a high-class player in the making. His selection for the tour followed a successful season in New Zealand domestic cricket in which he scored 612 runs (34.00), having made his first appearance for Wellington in 1975/6. In his first three Tests in England he scored 147 runs for a heavily defeated side at an average of 24.50 and did a capable job in the last Test as a stand-in wicket-keeper. On the tour he hit a maiden first-class hundred against Scotland and with 823 runs (37.40) in fifteen matches was his side's highest scorer. He scored his first Test century against Pakistan in 1978/9 with 129, and got his own back for a relatively disappointing tour of Australia in 1980/1 by making 161 against Australia at Auckland the following season, the basis for a New Zealand victory and the then highest score by a New Zealander against Australia. During the match he passed 1,000 Test runs in only his 17th match. In that 1981/2 season he scored 934 runs (51.88) in 19 innings. He enjoyed another consistently successful season in England in 1983, making a brave 84 in his country's first win in a Test in England, at Headingley—an innings interrupted by injury—and following this with scores of 70, 27, 62, and 76 in the next two Tests, when most of his fellow batsmen were failing. However, he could find no form on a tour of Pakistan in 1984/5 and lost his place in the Test team for the return series. Back in favour in Australia in 1985/6, he resumed his successful opening partnership with John Wright, scoring three fifties in three Tests. A chartered accountant, he announced his retirement from Test cricket after the 1986 tour of England, which he had started on a high note with a dogged 83 in the Lord's Test and a stand of 210 with Martin Crowe, the record for New Zealand's third wicket against England. He played on for Wellington, for whom his father, A. J., had also played.

First-class career (1975–90): 11,304 runs (40.22) including 24 centuries, and 2 wickets (46.00)

Test matches (39): 1,958 runs (30.59) including 3 centuries, 0–3, and 14 catches

EDWARDS, Graham Neil

(b. 1955, Nelson) *Central Districts and New Zealand)*

A short, heavily built wicket-keeper, very hard-hitting right-handed batsman and natural comic, 'Jock' Edwards first appeared for Central Districts in 1973/4 and was a useful member of the New Zealand side which participated in, and won, the 1974/5 Gillette Cup in Australia. He made his Test début against Australia in 1976/7 as a specialist batsman, but was selected for his wicket-keeping in 1977/8 and, on his return to the New Zealand side, celebrated with 55 and 54 in the drawn third match against England at Auckland. In England in 1978, however, he was rather disappointing, having an awkward match behind the stumps at Trent Bridge and losing his place for the third Test. On the tour he made 401 runs (22.27) and took 22 catches and a stumping. Somewhat harshly treated by some English critics, he enjoyed himself and kept the spirits of a beaten team high.

First-class career (1973–85): 4,589 runs (29.41) including 5 centuries, 0–32, and 142 dismissals (126 c., 16 st.)

Test matches (8): 377 runs (25.13) and 7 dismissals (7 c.)

EMERY, Raymond William George

(b. 1915, Auckland; d. 1982, Auckland) *Auckland, Canterbury, and New Zealand*

A competent right-handed opening batsman and occasional medium-pace bowler, Raymond Emery played in two Tests against the West Indies in 1951/2.

First-class career (1936–54): 1,177 runs (29.42) including 3 centuries, and 22 wickets (34.27)

Test matches (2): 46 runs (11.50) and 2 wickets (26.00)

FISHER, Frederick Eric

(b. 1924, Wellington) *Wellington, Central Districts, and New Zealand*

A useful all-rounder, a steady right-handed batsman and left-arm medium-pace bowler, Frederick Fisher played in a sole Test against South Africa at Wellington in 1952/3, scoring 9 and 14 and taking 1 for 78.

First-class career (1951–5): 485 runs (21.08) and 53 wickets (23.24)

FLEMING, Stephen Paul

(b. 1973, Christchurch) *Canterbury and New Zealand*

A left-hand bat, tall and stylish, born on 1 April but nobody's fool, Stephen Fleming matured rapidly as a batsman after dominating New Zealand's youth team. Like all accomplished batsmen he always seems to have ample time to make his strokes, his off-side shots are classic, and he is strong on the on-side. In 1990/1 he played in the Canterbury under-18 and under-20 teams with marked success. When Young England toured New Zealand that season Fleming scored 54 and 35 (run out) in the one-day matches and averaged over 40 in the three Youth Tests played. In his first Test, against India in 1993/4, he scored 92 in the second innings and in England a few months later he continued this promising start with 54 (top score) in New Zealand's first innings at Trent Bridge, 41 at Lord's, and 170 runs in the three-match series, at 28. He made 591 runs in his nine first-class matches on the tour, including 102 not out against Somerset and 118 not out against Middlesex in his first match at Lord's.

First-class career (1991–   ): 2,328 runs (37.55) and 40 catches

Test matches (4): 278 runs (34.75) and 3 catches

FOLEY, Henry

(b. 1906, Wellington; d. 1948, Brisbane, Australia) *Wellington and New Zealand*

A very sound left-handed opening batsman of limitless patience and a good slip fielder, Henry Foley played in a sole Test, the first-ever in New Zealand, against England at Christchurch in 1929/30 scoring 2 and 2. Ill-health curtailed his career.

First-class career (1927–33): 670 runs (33.50) including 1 century

FRANKLIN, Trevor John

(b. 1962, Auckland) *Auckland and New Zealand*

An exceptionally tall, lantern-jawed, right-handed opening batsman of sound technique, Trevor Franklin, a consistent player in provincial cricket and a popular one in league cricket in the north of England, scored 580 runs in only eight innings on a short tour of Australia with Young New Zealand in March 1983. These were three-day games and although the opposition in country districts was modest, his form earned him a place on the tour to England later that year. He fared well against the counties—539 runs at 35.93—but was out for 2 and 7 in his only Test, the fourth of the series at Trent Bridge. In 1984/5 he hit the highest score for Auckland for 37 years, 181 against Northern Districts, and after another good season the following year, he was selected for his second tour to England in 1986. He was most unlucky, breaking a thumb and then, as the team were about to leave for New Zealand from Gatwick Airport, being run over by a luggage trailer and breaking his leg. He fought his way back, although never able to run at full speed in the field again. Back in England in 1990, he scored 731 first-class runs (45.68) and 277 in the Tests (56.75) including a popular and painstaking 100 at Lord's, his only Test century. His bad luck returned when next he confronted England bowlers, at home in 1991/2: he had his left forearm broken by a ball from David Lawrence in the first over of an early tour match.

First-class career (1980–92): 7,484 runs (33.86) including 15 centuries, 1 wicket (51.00), and 75 catches

Test matches (21): 828 runs (23.00) including 1 century, and 8 catches

FREEMAN, Douglas Linford

(b. 1914, Sydney) *Nelson, Wellington, and New Zealand*

Australian by birth and a right-arm googly bowler, Doug Freeman appeared in only five first-class matches, two of which were Tests against England in 1932/3, at Christchurch and Auckland, when he had the misfortune to come up against Wally Hammond in supreme run-getting form. In his first Test, at 18 years 197 days, he became the youngest player to represent New Zealand, a record he still holds. On his first-class début in 1932/3, he took 9 for 187 in the match for Wellington against Auckland.

GALLICHAN

First-class career (1932–4): 28 runs (4.66) and 14 wickets (35.35)
Test matches (2): 2 runs (1.00) and 1–169

GALLICHAN, Norman

(b. 1906, Palmerston; d. 1969, Taupo) *Manawatu, Wellington, and New Zealand*

Over 6 ft. tall, Norman Gallichan was a hard-hitting, lower-order right-handed batsman and a steady, slow left-arm bowler who toured England in 1937, taking 59 wickets (23.92) and averaging 16.94 with the bat. In his sole Test, the second at Old Trafford, he scored 30 and 2 and took 3 for 113.
First-class career (1927–39): 636 runs (18.17) and 86 wickets (26.09)

GEDYE, Sydney Graham

(b. 1929, Auckland) *Auckland and New Zealand*

A competent right-handed opening batsman, Graham Gedye scored 52 on his Test début against South Africa at Wellington in 1963/4, and an equally fine 55 at Auckland in the same series. In that season he also scored 104 and 101 for Auckland against Central Districts. He played against Pakistan (once) in 1964/5.
First-class career (1956–65): 2,387 runs (30.21) including 3 centuries
Test matches (4): 193 runs (24.12)

GILLESPIE, Stuart Ross

(b. 1957, Wanganui) *Northern Districts, Northumberland, and New Zealand*

A tail-end right-handed batsman and accurate 6 ft. 1 in. right-arm medium-pace bowler, Stuart Gillespie made a somewhat belated appearance in international cricket, having demonstrated his keenness by playing for Northumberland in 1981. Going in fourth as a night-watchman against Australia in his sole Test to date he made a useful 28, but his bowling looked unlikely to disturb good Test players on good wickets. He took 1 for 79. Nevertheless his steadiness earned him four one-day internationals against Australia in the same season, although he narrowly missed selection on the 1986 tour to England.
First-class career (1979–90): 599 runs (14.97) and 99 wickets (27.16)

GRAY, Evan John

(b. 1954, Wellington) *Wellington and New Zealand*

A steady left-arm orthodox slow bowler and competent right-handed batsman, dark-haired and wiry, Evan Gray earned a place on the 1983 tour of England by dint of several good all-round performances in provincial cricket. At Lord's in his first Test he batted usefully and took 3 for 73 in England's second innings, enough to keep him in the side for the following Test. Although not chosen for the return home series against England he remained one of the best all-round players in New Zealand, taking 48 wickets at 21 in 1984/5, including 6 for 89 against Otago, 5 for 68 against the Pakistan touring team, and four other five-wicket hauls. He had an even better season in 1985/6, surpassing his previous highest score of 126 for Wellington against Central Districts in 1981/2 (when he shared a record sixth-wicket stand of 226 with R. W. Ormiston) with an innings of 128 not out against Otago. He also took 8 for 37 against Canterbury and his 545 runs (49.54) and 32 wickets at 22 each earned him a second tour to England in 1986. He played an important all-round role in New Zealand's first victory in a series in England, bowling steadily and batting stubbornly, a performance not fairly reflected in his figures.
First-class career (1975–92): 5,472 runs (28.80) including 6 centuries, 444 wickets (28.20), and 138 catches
Test matches (10): 248 runs (15.50), 17 wickets (52.11), and 6 catches

GREATBATCH, Mark John

(b. 1963, Auckland) *Auckland, Central Districts, and New Zealand*

A beefy, extrovert, fair-haired left-hander who hits the ball very hard and dedicated himself to an international career, Mark Greatbatch moved from Auckland to Central Districts and played league cricket in England to establish himself. He produced some heroic innings for his country before a chronic loss of confidence against short-pitched fast bowling temporarily lost him his Test place in 1994. With immense patience he ground out 107 not out in the second innings of his first Test against England in Auckland in 1988/9, playing the spinners with skill to save the match. Another marathon innings saved the day again in his first match against Australia, at Perth in 1989/90. Having hit 76 at number three in the first innings, he batted for 5 minutes short of 11 hours for a second innings of 146 not out. He was a regular member of the side for the next 4 years, until knee problems and loss of confidence coincided. A splendid 133 against a high-class Pakistan attack in 1992/3 confirmed his quality as had his several buccaneering innings as an opening batsman in the 1991/2 World Cup. His greatest one-day knock, however, was his 102 not out against England at Leeds in 1990 when, with booming drives, powerful hooks, and deft flicks off his legs he scored his runs off 104 balls. He followed this with 111 out of 224 in the second Texaco International on a rapid Oval pitch. A fine fielder anywhere, he has taken some spectacular catches in the slips. In 67 internationals to 1994 he had scored 1,748 runs (28.19).

First-class career (1982–): 8,069 runs (36.35) including 14 centuries, and 114 catches

Test matches (34): 1,858 runs (33.17) including 3 centuries, and 25 catches

GUILLEN, Simpson Clairmonte

(b. 1924) *Trinidad and Canterbury*

See West Indies section.

GUY, John Williams

(b. 1934, Nelson) *Central Districts, Wellington, Canterbury, Otago, Northern Districts, Northamptonshire, and New Zealand*

A fleet-footed left-handed batsman of very sound defence and concentration, John Guy hit the ball cleanly, relishing the lofted straight drive. At the age of nineteen he scored 57 and 115, which remained his career highest—hitting A. M. Moir for 36 in four overs—for Central Districts against Otago in 1953/4. He toured India and Pakistan in 1955/6, coping well with the dominant leg-spin and making 313 runs (34.77) in the Tests against India, including a stonewalling 102 in over 7 hours in the first match at Hyderabad on a perfect batting surface. His other tour was at South Africa in 1961/2, when he reached 533 runs (26.65) in all first-class matches, but failed in the Tests. At home he played against the West Indies in 1955/6 and England in 1958/9, scoring a bright 56 at Christchurch.

First-class career (1953–73): 3,923 runs (25.80) including 3 centuries, and 32 catches

Test matches (12): 440 runs (20.95) including 1 century, and 2 catches

HADLEE, Barry George

(b. 1941, Christchurch) *Canterbury*

The eldest son of Walter Hadlee, Barry was a particularly attractive right-hand batsman and had great success as an opener for Canterbury. A member of the New Zealand B team to Australia in 1971/2, he played in the 1975 World Cup in England. He had a magnificent season in 1978/9, when he scored 555 runs for his province. His top score was 163 not out against Otago in 1980/1. He held the Canterbury aggregate batting record for several seasons (4,429 runs at 31.6). He played twice for his country in one-day internationals. Ambidextrous, he once bowled right-arm spinners and left-arm in the same match. He scored six centuries.

First-class career (1961–81): 4,540 runs (30.54) and 3 wickets (56.67)

HADLEE, Dayle Robert

(b. 1948, Christchurch) *Canterbury and New Zealand*

One of five sons of Walter Hadlee, Dayle Hadlee was a right-arm fast-medium bowler in his youth. Forced by back trouble to reduce his pace, he became a fine swing bowler, but finally lost his battle against back pain and was able to play in only one match of his third tour of England in 1978. Keen and determined, like all the Hadlees, Dayle made his début for the under-23 XI against Central Districts in 1966/7, and in 1969 played in two Tests in England, followed by six in India and Pakistan. Performing with great consistency, his best Test was at Hyderabad where, in a match spoiled by poor weather, umpiring problems and some bad feeling, he took 4 for 30 and 3 for 31. India, bowled out for 89 and 76 for 7 in their second innings, escaped with a draw. In 1973 he played in all three Tests against England, taking ten wickets, showing characteristic accuracy and persistency and often swinging the ball a good deal. A safe fielder, he took a quite remarkable catch off his own bowling to dismiss Alan Knott at Lord's in 1969.

First-class career (1966–80): 2,113 runs (18.69) including 1 century, 351 wickets (25.22), and 40 catches

Test matches (26): 530 runs (14.32), 71 wickets (33.64), and 8 catches

HADLEE, Sir Richard John

(b. 1951, Christchurch) *Canterbury,
Nottinghamshire, Tasmania, and New Zealand*

A fast-bowling all-rounder famous for his superb control of pace, swing and cut, Richard Hadlee was one of the great bowlers of any era or nationality. Easily his country's highest wicket-taker, he gave New Zealand sides of the 1970s a chance to hold their own against the rest in an era increasingly dominated by fast bowlers and in the 1980s he inspired them to unprecedented success. He was also a capable fielder and a dynamic, hard-hitting left-handed batsman, though like most fast bowlers uncomfortable when tasting his own medicine. He played many a match-winning innings but his bowling was his special talent, one which by hard work, supreme dedication and rare intuition he polished and perfected. He would slice open the protective skin of an opposing batsman like an expert surgeon. Long-haired and untidy as a young cricketer, he developed from his experience in county cricket into an austere professional, setting himself stiff targets. With the South African, Clive Rice, he brought Nottinghamshire great success in the 1980s. Wiry rather than muscular in build, 6 ft. tall, and determined to the point of fierce hostility towards any batsman, his model right-arm side-on action engendered speed, lift, and late out-swing. One of five sons of Walter Hadlee, he first played for Canterbury in 1971/2, forming an effective opening partnership with his elder brother Dayle, whom he surpassed in speed, though at first not in accuracy. Touring in England in 1973 as the baby of the New Zealand party, Richard Hadlee's potential was clear, though he played in only one Test. The next time that he met England, in February 1978, he was the acknowledged spearhead of the New Zealand attack and it was his hostile bowling at the Basin Reserve which did most to bring New Zealand victory over England for the first time. Hadlee took 10 for 100 in the match, and with 6 for 26 bowled England out for 64 in the second innings. He had already been prominent, with 3 for 59 and 4 for 71, in New Zealand's first defeat of Australia, at Christchurch in 1974. In the series he took 15 wickets in three matches and in the three Tests in England later in the year was again easily England's biggest danger, taking 13 wickets at 20.76. His bowling was by now admirably consistent, in all conditions. He took 7 for 23 against India at Wellington in 1975/6, finishing the match with 11 for 58 and in India and Pakistan in

1976/7, he remained New Zealand's main weapon during an unsuccessful tour, although only at Madras where he took 3 for 37 and 2 for 52 did he have a pitch with much pace in it. He found a good deal more help from the conditions in England in 1978 when he joined Nottinghamshire, taking 36 wickets in six Championship matches at 14.47 (in the 1978 English season he took 78 wickets at 16.26). He also hit a sparkling 101 not out against Derbyshire and continued to be a highly effective county cricketer, taking 105 wickets (14.89) in 1981, and scoring 745 runs (32.39), including 142 not out against Yorkshire. He and Rice won the Championship for Notts after a 52-year wait. He surpassed this in 1984 with the first 1,000 run/100 wicket double in an English season since 1967. In 24 Championship matches he took 117 wickets (14.05) and made 1,179 runs, including 210 not out against Middlesex at Lord's, when he reached his hundred off 93 balls. His double was all the more remarkable for the fact that at the end of the previous season he had come close to a nervous breakdown. After a holiday, however, he returned to cricket in 1983/4 to take 12 wickets (19.33) to add to the 21 he had taken in four Tests in England the previous summer, when he also scored 301 runs (50.16). England were by no means his only victims. Against Pakistan in 1978/9 he took 18 wickets in only three Tests. Against West Indies in 1979/80 he took 19 wickets (19.00) and hit his maiden Test hundred at Christchurch, and in the Caribbean in 1984/5 he was, as usual, his country's leading wicket-taker—15 wickets at 27.26. He did it again in 1986/7, taking 17 wickets in three Tests (20.82). In Sri Lanka in the same season he took four wickets in the only Test and scored 151 not out, his highest Test score. But his most devastating performances of all were against Australia. In 1980/1 he took 19 wickets in three Tests in a losing series (away); in 1981/2, 14 more wickets at home in a drawn three-Test series; then, in 1985/6, came a quite phenomenal performance in Australia when, in another three-match rubber, he took 33 wickets at 12.15 each, including 9 for 52 and 6 for 71 (plus a brisk innings of 54) in the victory at Brisbane. Off a 12-pace run he bowled faster than anyone and moved the ball like a boy controlling a yo-yo. His good form continued with more incisive bowling in England in 1986. Like a woodpecker attacking the bark of a tree he jabbed away at the weak points of England's batsmen to take 19 wickets at a cost of only 20 each in the three Test matches. In New Zealand's decisive victory at Trent

Bridge, he made a typically hard-hitting 68 to lead a crucial batting revival by the team he had inspired for so long. In his last season for Nottinghamshire, 1987, he scored 1,111 runs and took 97 wickets. In eight seasons of county cricket he finished top of the national bowling averages five times and second twice. This final effort was followed by another successful visit to Australia in 1987/8—18 wickets in three Tests (19.61) and the following season, 1988/9, he achieved his ambition to become the (then) highest wicket-taker in Test history (12 November 1988, Bangalore; Arun Lal caught at third slip by Chris Kuggeleijn) with his 374th wicket. He took 18 wickets in the three Tests and against India in February 1990, at his home ground, Lancaster Park, he became the first bowler ever to take 400 Test wickets. That he did so in only 79 Tests emphasized his phenomenal striking rate. Awarded an MBE in 1980, he was made a KBE in 1990 during his final tour for New Zealand, in England. He retired to run a plant nursery in Christchurch with his wife, Karen.

First-class career (1971–90): 12,052 runs (31.71) including 14 centuries, 1,490 wickets (18.11), and 198 catches

Test matches (86): 3,124 runs (27.16) including 2 centuries, 431 wickets (22.29), and 39 catches

HADLEE, Walter Arnold

(b. 1915, Canterbury) Canterbury, Otago, and New Zealand

A tall and bespectacled right-handed batsman who frequently opened the batting, Walter or 'Wally' Hadlee could score rapidly with a variety of strokes or defend dourly. His most attractive shot was the off-drive, made either off his back foot or with the front foot planted firmly down the pitch and a graceful arc of the bat. In the field he was an inspiration, moving quickly and catching surely. He toured England in 1937 and returned as the enterprising and sporting captain of the 1949 side. He led New Zealand at home against Australia in 1945/6, and against England in 1946/7 and 1950/1. Pipe-smoking and kindly, he did all his work as leader without showmanship and fuss; he was fair-minded but could be ruthless with his team on the field, while driving himself hardest of all. In 1937 he made 1,225 runs (29.87) in first-class matches, and in the second Test at Old Trafford a dominating 93 in 2¼ hours until he had the misfortune to slip and tread on his wicket. In 1949 he made 1,439 runs (35.97), being at his best in difficult situations. Although

he made only one Test century he never failed to reach double figures. Against England at Christchurch he scored 116 in 2½ hours, opening with Bert Sutcliffe in a stand of 133. His highest-ever score was 198 in a total of 347 for Otago against the Australians at Dunedin in 1945/6. Very prominent in the administration of the game, Walter Hadlee has been an efficient chairman of the New Zealand Board of Control. He is the father of five cricketing sons, two of whom, Dayle and Richard, appeared in Tests, while Barry represented New Zealand in the Prudential World Cup. Spare of figure into his old age, he followed the phenomenal achievements of his son Richard closely, and with great pride. He was awarded a CBE.

First-class career (1933–52): 7,523 runs (40.44) including 18 centuries, and 67 catches

Test matches (11): 543 runs (30.16) including 1 century, and 6 catches

HARFORD, Noel Sherwin

(b. 1930, Otago; d. 1981, Auckland) Central Districts, Auckland, and New Zealand

A neat, well-balanced right-handed batsman who possessed a sparkling drive and pull but was rather unsound in defence, especially against spin bowlers, Noel Harford toured India and Pakistan in 1955/6 and England in 1958. On his Test début, against Pakistan at Lahore, he scored 93 and 64. Although he made 1,067 runs (26.02) in England he was very disappointing in the Tests. However, in making his maiden century, against Oxford University in The Parks, he added 204 brilliantly with John Reid in little more than two hours for the third wicket. He was a useful right-arm medium-pace swing bowler.

First-class career (1953–67): 3,149 runs (27.62) including 3 centuries, and 18 wickets (26.55)

Test matches (8): 229 runs (15.26)

HARFORD, Roy Ivan

(b. 1936, London) Auckland and New Zealand

A good wicket-keeper and moderate tail-end left-handed batsman, Roy Harford, born in London and no relation of Noel, played in Tests against India in 1967/8 in a short career. In his last Test, at Wellington, he dismissed seven, all through catches, of the 12 wickets to fall.

First-class career (1965–8): 143 runs (7.94) and 68 dismissals (60 c., 8 st.)

Test matches (3): 7 runs (2.33) and 11 dismissals (11 c.)

HARRIS, Chris Zinzan

(b. 1969, Christchurch) *Canterbury and New Zealand*

'Lugs' Harris comes from one of the most popular sporting families in New Zealand. His father P. G. Z. always seemed to be smiling. His elder brother, Ben, has represented Canterbury and Otago and shares his father's cheerful disposition with Chris, a left-hand bat with an aggressive outlook who bowls right-arm medium-paced in-swingers and is superb in the field. This has made him an effective one-day cricketer, but in Tests his bowling has been negligible. He headed the New Zealand bowling averages in the 1992 World Cup, with 16 wickets (21.37) including a particularly tidy 2 for 32 off 10 overs against the West Indies which virtually assured his team of a place in the semi-final. He came down to earth in that match, conceding 72 runs from his 10-over stint in Pakistan's late dash for victory, but by then both Harris and New Zealand had exceeded expectations. Three of his Tests were played in 1992/3, one each at home against Australia and Pakistan, and one on tour to Sri Lanka. He also played a match in Australia the following season. In 44 one-day internationals he has scored 687 runs (25.44) and taken 49 wickets (28.22).

First-class career (1989–): 1,867 runs (44.45) and 32 wickets (41.40)

Test matches (5): 116 runs (12.88), 0–103, and two catches

HARRIS, Parke Gerald Zinzan

(b. 1927, Christchurch) *Canterbury and New Zealand*

A right-handed batsman who could force the pace or defend stoutly, and a useful change-bowler, 'Zin' Harris toured India and Pakistan in 1955/6 without much success and South Africa in 1961/2, when he made 284 runs (31.55) in the Tests, including 74 in the first match at Durban and 101 in the third match at Cape Town. At home he played once against Pakistan in 1964/5. Immensely cheerful, he produced two cricketing sons who have represented Canterbury with distinction and, in the case of the younger boy, Chris, New Zealand too.

First-class career (1949–65): 3,122 runs (28.11) including 5 centuries, and 21 wickets (30.80)

Test matches (9): 378 runs (22.23) including 1 century, 0–14, and 6 catches

HARRIS, Roger Meredith

(b. 1933, Auckland) *Auckland and New Zealand*

A right-handed opening batsman and medium-pace change-bowler, Roger Harris played in two Tests against England in 1958/9, but was outclassed by the opposition's bowlers, such as Fred Trueman and Frank Tyson.

First-class career (1955–74): 3,863 runs (30.90) including 3 centuries, and 14 wickets (42.50)

Test matches (2): 31 runs (10.33)

HART, Matthew Norman

(b. 1972, Hamilton) *Northern Districts and New Zealand*

An accurate slow left-arm bowler with a model action, and a determined left-hand batsman, Matthew Hart lacked only the variety which deceives during a consistently useful first tour for New Zealand in England in 1994. In youth cricket he had bowled usefully but was often used as an opening batsman with considerable success. He was a member of the New Zealand under-19 squad on its tour of India, playing in both internationals. In three innings he scored 147 runs, and in India's four innings took 11 wickets. First picked against Pakistan and India in three home Tests in 1993/4, Hart took 4 for 84 in the match against Pakistan in Christchurch. In England he took 18 first-class wickets (47.22) and his influence on the Lord's Test, when he tied England's batsmen down for long periods, was greater than his match analysis of 85–44–105–2 suggests. This progress was checked in 1994/5 when, along with two other young members of the team, he was suspended for three games for allegedly smoking cannabis during a party in South Africa.

First-class career (1990–): 985 runs (18.58), 103 wickets (32.34), and 7 catches

Test matches (12): 317 runs (17.61), 27 wickets (49.85), and 7 catches

HART, Ronald Terence

(b. 1961, Lower Hutt, Wellington) *Central Districts and Wellington*

A neat, correct, right-handed batsman of unusual versatility, Ron Hart was also a wicket-keeper and an occasional off-spinner. He was selected for one tour, to the West Indies in 1985, but had to return home for family reasons after playing three games without success. Yet he had a consistent career, including a double-century for Central

Districts against Wellington in 1986, four other hundreds, and twelve fifties in 48 matches. He played in a single one-day international, scoring 3.

First-class career (1980–94): 2,686 runs (29.51) including 6 centuries, and 0–88

HARTLAND, Blair Robert

(b. 1966, Christchurch) *Canterbury and New Zealand*

A tallish, correct, right-hand opening batsman, Blair Hartland was unable in the early stages of his international career to fulfil all the promise he displayed as a youth, partly through illness and injury. He started with 22 and 45 on his first Test appearance against England in 1991/2, a match he played in the shadow of his cricketing father's terminal illness. He showed commendable courage when facing Wasim Akram and Waqar Younis in the following season. New Zealand hopes that the 1994 tour of England would finally establish him as a Test opener were not fulfilled. He played in the first Test at Trent Bridge after scoring 49 and 60 in the defeat against Yorkshire, but lost his place and managed only a modest 337 runs from sixteen first-class innings (21.05). His sole Test fifty was scored against Sri Lanka at Maratuwa in 1992/3. His 161 for Canterbury in 1993/4, however, was a record score for a provincial one-day match. He is a son of the late I. R. (Ian) Hartland, who also played for Canterbury and appeared for New Zealand Colts against Dennis Silk's MCC side in 1960/1. He has also played in 11 one-day internationals, scoring 212 runs (21.20).

First-class career (1988–   ): 3,019 runs (26.25) including 4 centuries
Test matches (9): 303 runs (16.83) and five catches

HASLAM, Mark James

(b. 1972, Bury, Lancashire) *Auckland and New Zealand*

Mark Haslam was chosen for New Zealand's tour of Zimbabwe and Sri Lanka in 1992/3 after having only a handful of first-class games. The young left-arm leg-spinner was also in the team for the Australian tour of 1993/4, but he was disappointing. In a single one-day international he scored 9 not out and took 1 for 28. His two Tests were played against Zimbabwe in 1992–3.

First-class career (1991–   ): 92 runs (7.66) and 29 wickets (48.10)
Test matches (2): 3 runs (3.00) and 1 wicket (153.00)

HASTINGS, Brian Frederick

(b. 1940, Wellington) *Wellington, Central Districts, Canterbury, and New Zealand*

A right-handed batsman, strongly built and prematurely bald, Brian Hastings was a delightful timer of the ball, quick to take any opportunity to cut or hook, or to clip medium-fast bowling off his legs. A superb gully, he was a regular choice at number four in the New Zealand order in the early 1970s, yet took a long time to convince the Test selectors of his ability, not being picked until 11 years after making his début for Wellington in 1957/8 at the age of 17. He played one season for Central Districts in 1960/1 and then transferred to Canterbury the following season. When he did win his Test cap against the West Indies in 1968/9, his scores were 21, 31, 8, 62 not out, 0, and 117 not out (at Christchurch). Equally consistent in the next few years, he toured England in 1969 and 1973, India in 1969/70, and the West Indies in 1971/2 where he scored an attractive 105 in the Bridgetown Test. He added further centuries against Pakistan at Auckland in 1972/3 (sharing in a record last wicket stand of 151 with Richard Collinge) and against England at Lord's in 1973. His highest first-class innings was 226 for Canterbury against New Zealand under-23 at Christchurch in 1964/5.

First-class career (1957–77): 7,686 runs (31.86) including 15 centuries, and 112 catches
Test matches (31): 1,510 runs (30.20) including 4 centuries, 0–9, and 23 catches

HAYES, John Arthur

(b. 1927, Auckland) *Auckland, Canterbury, and New Zealand*

A tall, right-arm genuinely fast bowler with a glorious action, much enthusiasm and a late outswing, Johnny Hayes or 'Haybag' toured England in 1949, but an injured groin muscle made him a passenger for half the tour. When he toured again in 1958, he headed the bowling with 62 wickets (20.20), although he captured only six in four Tests. Early in the tour he took 5 for 29 in the first innings against Essex at Ilford and 4 for 40 and 7 for 49 against MCC at Lord's. Later, at Cheltenham, he routed Gloucestershire, taking four wickets in five overs. He also toured India and

HENDERSON

Pakistan in 1955/6, and at home played against England in 1950/1 and 1954/5 and the West Indies in 1951/2. On the India and Pakistan tour he made good use of the new ball, taking 35 wickets (32.11) in the first-class matches, but his 13 Test wickets were very expensive. In New Zealand, his most memorable piece of bowling was in the first Test at Christchurch against the West Indies in 1951/2, when he disposed of Worrell, Walcott, and Gomez in eight balls. For Auckland against Wellington in 1957/8 he captured 14 for 65 (7 for 28 and 7 for 37).

First-class career (1946–61): 611 runs (9.54), 292 wickets (23.14), and 29 catches
Test matches (15): 73 runs (4.86), 30 wickets (40.56), and 3 catches

HENDERSON, Matthew

(b. 1895, Auckland; d. 1970, Lower Hutt, Wellington) *Wellington and New Zealand*

A left-arm fast bowler, often wayward but also unfortunate, Matthew Henderson toured England with the first New Zealand team in 1927, taking 33 wickets (24.21) in first-class matches. He played in the first-ever Test, against England at Christchurch in 1929/30, scoring 6 and 2 not out, taking 2 for 64 and 1 catch.

First-class career (1921–32): 495 runs (14.14) and 107 wickets (29.90)

HOCKLEY, Deborah Ann

(b. 1962, Christchurch) *Canterbury and New Zealand*

Debbie Hockley was the youngest woman Test captain ever appointed when she led the team to England in 1984, aged only 21. She has been outstandingly successful in New Zealand cricket. A right-hand bat, she showed very early promise and was selected for New Zealand at 15 whilst still at Avonside Girls' High School in Christchurch. She has fond memories of Ken Wadsworth whom she met only once but whose forthright approach she admired. Her own batting is stylish but vigorous. She went on to record the highest aggregate for New Zealand Tests and also had much success in one-day internationals. She studied for her physiotherapy examinations in Auckland for 5 years but most of her cricket has been played in Canterbury, who have dominated the national championship, winning it in 15 of the 16 years to 1994. She has won the Woman

Cricketer of the Year award three times, and shared it twice. She bowls usefully at slow-medium pace, and has also represented Canterbury at hockey.

Test matches (1979–94): 876 runs (46.11) and 5 wickets (26.40)

HORNE, Philip Andrew

(b. 1960, Upper Hutt, Wellington) *Auckland and New Zealand*

A left-hand opening bat, Philip Horne had a brief and disappointing Test career, but he travelled widely in pursuit of success. His first Test cap was earned in 1986/7 after he had made 81 for the Shell XI against the touring West Indies. He was chosen for the aborted Sri Lankan tour, for the Australian trip which followed, and for the tour of Zimbabwe by the New Zealand Young Internationals. After an absence of three years he was recalled for a tour of Pakistan in 1990/1. He made plenty of runs for Auckland, including the first double-century for his side in four decades, 209 against Northern Districts in 1988/9. He reached a century on four other occasions. Horne was an outstanding fieldsman, particularly in the covers. In four one-day internationals he scored 50 runs. He was also a New Zealand badminton player, taking part in the Commonwealth Games.

First-class career (1979–91): 2,879 runs (34.27) including 5 centuries, and 1 wicket (16.0)
Test matches (4): 71 runs (10.14)

HOUGH, Kenneth William

(b. 1928, Sydney) *Auckland, Northern Districts, and New Zealand*

A lively right-arm medium-pace bowler, Kenneth Hough's only Tests were against England in 1958/9, when he dismissed Cowdrey (twice), Watson, and Graveney, among others, for low scores. In his first Test at Christchurch he amused the crowd vastly by his impudent snatching of singles with E. C. Petrie when New Zealand were bordering on defeat by an innings. He took 12 for 146 against Central Districts in 1959/60, the same season in which he made his career-highest score of 91 against Otago.

First-class career (1956–60): 624 runs (16.42) and 119 wickets (20.87)
Test matches (2): 62 runs (62.00), 6 wickets (29.16), and 1 catch

HOWARTH, Geoffrey Philip

(b. 1951, Auckland) *Northern Districts, Auckland, Surrey, and New Zealand*

One of New Zealand's first fully professional cricketers, Geoff Howarth overcame many disappointments to become a successful Test batsman and an outstanding captain. A neat right-hander with some delightful offside strokes, and especially severe on the half volley which he would drive unerringly, he was also a fine fielder anywhere and a useful off-spin bowler. The younger brother of Hedley Howarth, he made his first-class début for New Zealand's under-23 XI in 1968/9 and, a few months after, came to England to join the Surrey ground staff. There he served a long and often frustrating apprenticeship. He eventually played for Surrey's 1st XI in 1971, was capped in 1974, in 1976 scored 1,554 runs in the dry summer at an average of 37.90 and in 1984 became Surrey captain. Not until 1972/3 did he represent a New Zealand provincial side, Auckland, and he subsequently transferred to Northern Districts in 1974/5 when he made his first Test appearances against England. After performing usefully in the 1975 Prudential World Cup, he was very disappointing on the 1976/7 tour of India and Pakistan but at last revealed his true ability when given possibly a final chance against England at Auckland in March 1978 (after playing only a minor role in the first New Zealand win against England at Wellington). He scored 122 and 102, saving New Zealand on a worsening pitch in the second innings and becoming only the second New Zealander after Glenn Turner to score two centuries in a Test. Confident, and sure of a place at last, he time and again kept New Zealand's boat afloat in a seething tide of English seamers in 1978, scoring a fine 123 at Lord's and 296 runs (74.00) in the three Tests, the most runs at the best average on either side. With a tour tally of 816 runs (45.33), this likeable and determined character finally justified his dedication to cricket. In the second of three Tests against Pakistan in 1979, he scored 114, his fourth century in six Test matches. He captained New Zealand against West Indies with outstanding success in 1980, scoring 239 runs (47.80) in the three-match series which New Zealand won 1–0, having led Northern Districts to the domestic double. Again captain in Australia in 1980/1, he led his side to the finals of the limited-overs competition but New Zealand were outplayed in the Test series. However, at Auckland in 1981/2 he led New Zealand to a rare Test win over

Australia and further triumphs followed against England: in 1983 the first Test win on English soil, at Headingley; and in 1983/4 the first win over England in a rubber. The win in England had taken 52 years and 29 matches to achieve, and Howarth's astute captaincy and personable nature had something considerable to do with it. Moreover, his side was unbeaten outside the Tests. By now wearing glasses, he made a brave 84 against West Indies at Kingston in May 1985 but his career ended in a sad anti-climax that year when, officially captain of Surrey, he was not chosen for any Championship matches. Nor was he reinstated as captain of his country. He was awarded the MBE in 1981, and the OBE in 1984 for his services to the game and became for a time in the early 1990s coach and manager of the national team.

First-class career (1968–86): 17,294 runs (31.90) including 32 centuries, 112 wickets (32.08), and 229 catches

Test matches (47): 2,531 runs (32.44) including 6 centuries, 3 wickets (90.33), and 29 catches

HOWARTH, Hedley John

(b. 1943, Auckland) *Auckland and New Zealand*

The elder brother of Geoff, Hedley Howarth was for many years New Zealand's leading slow bowler, and only Richard Hadlee has exceeded his 541 first-class wickets. He was an orthodox left-arm spinner who flighted the ball well, had good control and turned the ball enough to make the most of favourable conditions. He made his first appearance in first-class cricket in 1962/3 for New Zealand under-23 and the following season began a long career with Auckland. His first Test was at Lord's in 1969, the start of an unbroken sequence of 19 Tests in which he took 65 wickets by dint of steady reliability rather than any spectacular performances. He only twice took five wickets in a Test innings, both times during a successful tour of India and Pakistan in 1969/70 (on the way back from his first tour of England). His best performance came in the only Test ever played at Nagpur where Howarth, with 4 for 66 and 5 for 34, out-bowled the more highly rated Indian spinners and New Zealand gained their first success on Indian soil. Howarth was also in the team which beat Australia for the first time at Christchurch in 1974. In England, however, after taking 57 wickets on the 1969 tour, his return, as a senior member of the side, in 1973 was less successful. His best analysis was 7 for 43 against

Essex at Westcliff in 1969. A patient and philosophical temperament kept him smiling through many long and less fruitful bowling stints, notably a marathon one at Lord's in 1973 when, after taking 3 for 42 in the first England innings to set up a winning chance for his team, he battled away for 70 overs in England's second innings of 463 for 9, finishing with 4 for 144. As a batsman he would have a swing if asked to do so and often defended stubbornly, and in the field his hands were as safe as anyone's.

First-class career (1962–79): 1,668 runs (13.78), 541 wickets (25.27), and 138 catches

Test matches (30): 291 runs (12.12), 86 wickets (36.95), and 33 catches

JAMES, Kenneth Cecil

(b. 1904, Wellington; d. 1976, Palmerston) *Wellington, Northamptonshire, and New Zealand*

Coming to England in 1927 as a second-string wicket-keeper to captain Tom Lowry, Ken James made the post his own, claiming 85 dismissals (43 caught, 42 stumped), including eight victims at Derby. In a match at Colombo, on the way home, he had a hat-trick of catches off Bill Merritt's bowling. In all James caught or stumped 65 of Merritt's victims. Previously Ken had toured Australia with a New Zealand side in 1925/6 and, on his return, hit 107 not out, engaging in a record last-wicket stand of 138 with W. S. Brice for Wellington against Otago. He kept wicket for New Zealand in the first Tests in New Zealand, against England in 1929/30, and returning to England in 1931 had an immense amount of work to do but did the job with rare skill: his catching of Eddie Paynter in the third Test at Old Trafford being a classic. He kept against South Africa in 1931/2 and England in 1932/3 and then, coming to live in England, he qualified for Northamptonshire and played for the county from 1935 until 1939. In 1936 he had 65 dismissals and his batting improved considerably. In the four seasons he made 3,428 runs, besides collecting 173 catches and 45 stumpings. He was one of the first of the leading wicket-keepers habitually to stand back to medium-pace bowling. On the field he derived every possible scrap of enjoyment from every game he played. He later became a publican.

First-class career (1923–47): 6,413 runs (22.19) including 7 centuries, and 423 dismissals (311 c., 112 st.)

Test matches (11): 52 runs (4.72) and 16 dismissals (11 c., 5 st.)

JARVIS, Terrence Wayne

(b. 1944, Auckland) *Auckland, Canterbury, and New Zealand*

A ginger-headed, befreckled, right-handed opening batsman, Terry Jarvis was an elegant stroke-maker with a tendency to get stranded between back and front foot, and a fine fielder. He toured India and Pakistan in 1964/5, making 263 runs (32.87) in the Tests, but in England in 1965 was plagued by illness contracted in India. In the West Indies in 1971/2, with his captain Graham Dowling out of action through injury, he became Glenn Turner's opening partner and, in the fourth Test at Georgetown, hit his career-highest score of 182, putting on 387 for the first wicket with Turner, a New Zealand record. In this series Jarvis made 277 runs (46.16). He played against Pakistan at home in 1972/3, but unfortunately made a pair in the first match of the series, at Wellington.

First-class career (1964–77): 4,666 runs (29.34) including 6 centuries, and 102 catches

Test matches (13): 625 runs (29.76) including 1 century, 0–3, and 3 catches

JONES, Andrew Howard

(b. 1959, Wellington) *Central Districts, Otago, Wellington, and New Zealand*

An intense desire to succeed as a batsman runs strongly through 'Jed' Jones's veins, but it was not until he had played for three provinces and was on the eve of his twenty-eighth birthday that he was selected for New Zealand. He played in Sri Lanka in 1986, the tour which was abandoned after a bomb explosion in Colombo, killing more than 100 people. The following season he was in Australia and after scoring a laborious 45 in the second innings of the first Test, he did not receive rave notices from the more cynical of the Australian journalists. He had the right answer in Adelaide in the second Test: innings of 150 and 64. Thereafter he became, at number three, the mainstay of New Zealand's batting. A dark-haired right-hander of medium height, immensely hard to shift once set, he could not be called orthodox, with his 'jumping jack' style of defence—or attack—when the ball is pitched short. But his true quality has often been marked by this unorthodoxy; he is a master of his off-side strokes and also hooks powerfully and successfully. Brave and patient, he made his best Test score against Sri Lanka in 1990/1, when he put on 467 with Martin Crowe, a world Test record for any wicket: Crowe made 299, Jones 186. He followed this with a century in each innings at Hamilton and averaged 102 in the three Tests. Other notable innings included 143 against England at Wellington in 1991/2 and 170 not out against India at Auckland in 1989/90. In all these innings he revealed himself as a born fighter, with immense powers of concentration. He has supplemented his batting skills with occasional off-break bowling. He announced his retirement from Test cricket before the tour to England in 1994, but returned to the fray the following home season. By then he had played in 84 one-day internationals, scoring 2,739 runs (36.52) and taking 4 wickets (54.00).

First-class career (1979–): 8,723 runs (43.18) including 16 centuries, and 33 wickets (41.82)

Test matches (37): 2,898 runs (46.00) including 7 centuries, and 1 wicket (144.00)

KERR, John Lambert

(b. 1910, Hawkes Bay) Canterbury and New Zealand

A right-handed opening batsman of sound technique and stubborn defence, a good driver and strong on the leg-side, John Kerr was also a very good fielder. He toured England in 1931 and 1937. In the former year he made 804 runs (22.97) and played in the first Test in England, at Lord's. In the latter year he made 1,205 runs (31.71), almost 500 of them in his last seven matches, which included two of his three centuries. At home he played against South Africa in 1931/2 and England in 1932/3, when he made his highest Test score, 59 at Christchurch. More effective in the Plunket Shield competition, his career-highest was 192 against Wellington in 1932/3. He has been much involved in the administration of the game.

First-class career (1929–43): 4,289 runs (32.19) including 8 centuries, and 28 catches

Test matches (7): 212 runs (19.27) and 4 catches

KUGGELEIJN, Christopher Mary

(b. 1956, Auckland) Northern Districts and New Zealand

Stocky and fair-haired, Chris Kuggeleijn had a successful Shell Series career and captained Northern Districts, but he may be remembered best for the slip catch he took off Sir Richard Hadlee, giving the bowler the then world record for dismissals. A right-hand bat, he scored four centuries and was a useful off-spin bowler. His

finest innings was probably a dashing 102 off 89 balls in 70 minutes against Central Districts in 1989/90. He became a highly regarded coach for his district team. Of Dutch parentage, he also played for Holland in one-day matches. He played in 16 one-day internationals scoring 515 runs (15.77) and taking 12 wickets (54.00).

First-class career (1975–91): 3,747 runs (27.55) including 4 centuries, and 57 wickets (42.73)

Test matches (2): 7 runs (1.75) and 1 wicket

LARSEN, Gavin Rolf

(b. 1962, Wellington) Wellington and New Zealand

Known as 'Larceny' among his team-mates, Gavin Larsen's bowling is more like petty theft. Stocky, medium-paced and skilled at changing pace, he has dismissed many a good batsman without apparently being any great threat. A surprise choice as New Zealand vice-captain for the 1994 tour of England, he finally won a Test cap at Trent Bridge, and further Test chances came his way in 1994/5. He is also a determined batsman, a right-hander, whose top score was 161 against Central Districts in 1988. In this innings he shared with Ervin McSweeney in a New Zealand record of 341 for the fifth wicket. In 55 one-day internationals to 1994 he had scored 337 runs (19.82) and taken 40 wickets (45.25). He had conceded runs at an average of 3.67 an over in these games, better than most. This determined, cheerful cricketer, who enjoys life off the field without compromising his dedication to cricket, is deservedly popular.

First-class career (1984–): 2,895 runs (29.54), including 1 century, 111 wickets (31.07), and 55 catches

Test matches (1): 10 runs (5.00), 2 wickets (58.00), and 2 catches

LATHAM, Rodney Terry

(b. 1961, Christchurch) Canterbury and New Zealand

A nuggety, solidly built, and hard-hitting right-hand batsman, number four or five by preference for his province but an opening batsman in the one-day matches, 'Rottie' is immensely popular with Canterbury crowds for his forthright methods. When the 1994/5 season started he was less than 400 runs short of Canterbury's record aggregate of 5,940 set by Paul McEwan. He did well in his four Tests, making his first appearance against England in 1991/2 and scoring 119 and 48 against Zimbabwe at Bulawayo in 1992/3. He bowls steady right-arm slow-medium, generally when all seems lost for his side. He has also played in 33 one-day internationals, scoring 583 runs (20.10). As a sturdy centre three-quarter, he played Rugby for Canterbury.

First-class career (1980–): 5,931 runs (37.06) including 9 centuries, 34 wickets (43.26), and 94 catches
Test matches (4): 219 runs (31.28), 0–6, and 5 catches

LEES, Warren Kenneth

(b. 1952, Dunedin) *Otago and New Zealand*

Warren Lees had the difficult job of following Ken Wadsworth into the New Zealand side as wicket-keeper/batsman but immediately proved himself equal to the task, playing a resilient and determined role during his side's arduous and unsuccessful tour of Pakistan and India in 1976/7. In only his third Test, against Pakistan at Karachi, Lees came to the wicket when New Zealand were 104 for 5 in reply to a Pakistan total of 565. He responded by scoring 152, the highest individual score by a New Zealander against Pakistan, and sharing in a record seventh-wicket stand of 186 with Richard Hadlee. It was a heroic innings (his first century in first-class cricket), followed by 46 in the second innings which helped save the game. A bold hooker and driver, Lees was a right-hander whose record suggested that he might have been capable of earning a Test place as a batsman alone. Certainly he was extremely unfortunate to have been left out of the touring team to England in 1978, especially as his wicket-keeping was seldom less than proficient. He was, however, a vital member of the 1979 Prudential World Cup team which reached the semi-finals. He lost his regular place to I. D. S. Smith after the tour to Australia in 1980/1 but still played occasionally, notably a one-day series in Australia two years later, and the inaugural Tests against Sri Lanka in 1982/3, when he top-scored with a valuable 89 to rescue the New Zealand first innings at Christchurch. In the second Test at Wellington he held five catches in the second innings, and eight in the match, a record for New Zealand. His last two Tests were the first and last of the series in England in 1983. He was national coach for a time and also coached Otago. He was awarded an MBE.

First-class career (1970–88): 4,932 runs (24.66) including 5 centuries, 2 wickets (54.50), and 348 dismissals (304 c., 44 st.)
Test matches (21): 778 runs (23.57) including 1 century, 0–4, and 64 dismissals (57 c., 7 st.)

LEGGAT, Ian Bruce

(b. 1930, Invercargill) *Nelson, Central Districts, and New Zealand*

A useful right-handed batsman and medium-pace bowler, Ian Leggat toured South Africa in 1953/4. In eight first-class matches he scored 138 runs and took five wickets. In his sole Test, the third at Cape Town, he failed to score, took 0 for 6 and held 2 catches.

First-class career (1950–62): 1,319 runs (20.29) including 2 centuries, and 58 wickets (35.46)

LEGGAT, John Gordon

(b. 1926, Wellington; d. 1973, Christchurch) *Canterbury and New Zealand*

A burly, determined and sound right-handed opening batsman, Gordon Leggat toured India and Pakistan in 1955/6 and at home played against the West Indies in 1951/2 and 1955/6, South Africa in 1952/3 and England in 1954/5. Uniquely, he appeared against four different countries in his first four Tests. At his best on the India and Pakistan tour he made 652 runs (34.31), including 275 runs (27.88) in the Tests; his Test-highest was 61 at Madras in the fifth match. His career-highest was 166 against Central Districts in 1952/3. A highly successful manager in South Africa in 1961/2, he became chairman of the New Zealand Cricket Board of Control, but died suddenly.

First-class career (1944–56): 3,550 runs (36.97) including 7 centuries
Test matches (9): 351 runs (21.93)

LISSETTE, Alan Fisher

(b. 1919, Morrinsville; d. 1973, Hamilton) *Waikato, Auckland, Northern Districts, and New Zealand*

A competent left-arm slow bowler, Alan Lissette played in two Tests against the West Indies in 1955/6 with moderate results. His best performance was 7 for 45 (12 for 109 in the match) for Northern Districts against Otago in 1959/60. He was awarded the MBE for services to the Air Training Corps.

First-class career (1954–63): 476 runs (10.79) and 116 wickets (25.89)
Test matches (2): 2 runs (1.00), 3 wickets (41.33), and 1 catch

LOWRY, Thomas Coleman

(b. 1898, Napier; d. 1976, Hastings) *Wellington, Cambridge University, Somerset, Auckland, and New Zealand*

Born at Fernhill, Napier, Tom Lowry was a natural leader. Reserved but approachable, he was lion-hearted and a great sportsman. He captained New Zealand in her first two Tests against England—away in 1931 and at home in 1929/30. He always aimed at winning not drawing, abhorring any waste of time. A large, powerful man, he was a fine attacking right-handed batsman, who materially strengthened his defence over the years, always at his best in a crisis, ignoring frequent bruises to his hands. He could be either a very useful wicket-keeper or a good fielder close to the wicket; and he was a useful slow bowler, not afraid to give the ball plenty of 'air' if required. He promoted Ken James as first-string wicket-keeper on the 1927 tour in place of himself and, concentrating largely on captaincy and batting, made 1,277 runs (38.69), including four centuries. In the 1929/30 series he made a fighting 80 at Auckland in the fourth match in 210 minutes, and in 1931, when he made 1,290 runs (31.46) and took 15 wickets (18.26) on the tour, he contributed a gritty 62 in the second Test at The Oval. He came back in 1937 as player/manager and at Trent Bridge against Nottinghamshire hit 121 in 105 minutes. He did not appear, however, in the Tests. The highest score of his career was 181 for Wellington against Auckland in 1927/8. For several seasons he appeared with success for Somerset, and tradition has it that his sole qualification to play for the county was that he was 'born at Wellington'. Later he was president of the New Zealand Cricket Council.

First-class career (1917–38): 9,421 runs (31.19) including 18 centuries, 49 wickets (27.00), 188 catches, and 49 stumpings
Test matches (7): 223 runs (27.87), 0–5, and 8 catches

McEWAN, Paul Ernest

(b. 1953, Christchurch) *Canterbury and New Zealand*

A slim and very stylish right-handed batsman and good fielder, Paul McEwan made his first appearance for Canterbury in 1976/7. After a modest Test début against the West Indies in 1979/80, he went to Australia in 1980/1. Here he failed against fast bowling in both the Tests and the one-day internationals. Such a disappointment

might have set back one of less equable temperament, but he continued to bat usefully for Canterbury and, after scoring 713 runs (59.40) in the Shell Trophy in 1983/4, he represented his country on no fewer than three tours in the 1984/5 season. For Young New Zealand in Zimbabwe, he made 364 runs in only six first-class innings, including 153 in the three-day international at Harare. Joining the senior New Zealand side in Pakistan he played in only two games, scoring 33 not out and 44 against a Punjab XI, and 40 not out, his highest Test score, in the third Test in Karachi. This earned him another short tour to Australia for the World Championship based at Melbourne in 1985.

First-class career (1976–91): 6,677 runs (34.95) including 12 centuries, 29 wickets (38.79), and 82 catches
Test matches (4): 96 runs (16.00), 0–13, and 5 catches

MacGIBBON, Anthony Roy

(b. 1924, Christchurch) *Canterbury and New Zealand*

Tony MacGibbon spearheaded New Zealand's attack from 1950 until 1958, and proved himself a tremendous trier in a lean period in his country's cricket. A right-arm fast-medium bowler with a longish run, he could swing the ball either way and used his 6 ft. 5 in. to make it lift awkwardly. He was also a useful late-order batsman and a superb slip. He toured South Africa in 1953/4, India and Pakistan in 1955/6 and England in 1958, and, at home, played against England in 1950/1 and 1954/5, South Africa in 1952/3, and the West Indies in 1955/6. In South Africa in 1953/4 he was handicapped by enteritis, but still took 22 Test wickets (20.63). At Auckland in the fourth match against India in 1955/6, his 4 for 44 in the first innings and his knock of 35 in a low-scoring match contributed considerably to New Zealand's first-ever victory in an official Test (after 26 years and 45 matches). Playing at his best for the weak 1958 side in England, he took most wickets, 73 (21.35), on the tour and in the Tests, 20 (19.45). He made 670 runs (19.70), including a vigorous 66 at Old Trafford in the fourth Test, which was the highest score by a New Zealander in the series. On the first day of the first match at Edgbaston, he took 5 for 64 and England were all out for 221, only for New Zealand to collapse for 94. At the end of the tour, he remained in England to read Civil Engineering at Durham University. He briefly returned to New Zealand's

McGIRR

team. His best return in an innings remained 7 for 56 for Canterbury against Auckland in 1954/5.

First-class career (1947–62): 3,639 runs (19.56), 356 wickets (26.12), and 82 catches
Test matches (26): 814 runs (19.85), 70 wickets (30.85), and 13 catches

McGIRR, Herbert Mendelson

(b. 1891, Wellington; d. 1964, Nelson) *Wellington and New Zealand*

A dashing right-handed batsman and stock medium-pace bowler, Herb McGirr toured England with the first New Zealand team in 1927, making 737 runs (24.56) and taking 49 wickets (27.67). He played in two Tests against England in 1929/30, hitting 51 in his second at Auckland. His career-highest score was 141 for Wellington against Otago in 1930/1 and his best bowling figures in an innings were 7 for 45 against Canterbury in 1921/2. He continued playing club cricket until, after scoring 70 at the age of 67, he slipped when taking in the milk at home.

First-class career (1913–33): 3,992 runs (28.71) including 5 centuries, 239 wickets (27.49), and 54 catches
Test matches (2): 51 runs (51.00) and 1–115

McGREGOR, Spencer Noel

(b. 1931, Dunedin) *Otago and New Zealand*

A right-handed batsman, Noel McGregor had a wide range of strokes, including a handsome drive off the back foot, and he was a reliable deep fielder. He toured India and Pakistan in 1955/6 and South Africa in 1961/2. At home he played against England in 1954/5 and 1958/9, the West Indies in 1955/6, South Africa in 1963/4 and Pakistan in 1964/5. In India and Pakistan he established himself with 300 runs (25.00) in the Tests. In the second match against Pakistan at Lahore he made a painstaking 111 in 5 hours 40 minutes. He was disappointing against England, but when the 1963/4 South Africans toured he came second in the Test averages with 168 runs (28.00), including a fighting 62 at Auckland in the third match. On visiting South Africa in 1961/2 he made 709 runs (25.32) and contributed 242 runs (24.20) to the tied Test series. Often opening the batting he scored 68 at Cape Town in the third Test, a vital innings in his country's first-ever Test victory abroad. His career-highest was 114 not out against Wellington in 1959–60.

First-class career (1948–69): 6,487 runs (25.33) including 5 centuries
Test matches (25): 892 runs (19.82) including 1 century, and 9 catches

McINTYRE, John McLachlan

(b. 1944, Auckland) *Auckland, Canterbury*

An orthodox slow left-arm bowler, John McIntyre had a long and honourable career in domestic cricket, playing for Auckland at the beginning and end of his career and for Canterbury from 1965 to 1969. He made an impact in his first season for Auckland in 1961/2, taking 27 wickets. He was ineffective, however, on his one tour for New Zealand, to England in 1978, taking only 14 wickets in his nine matches. He was a determined and often effective lower-order left-handed batsman, scoring 87 not out against Otago in 1969/70. He captained Auckland in the last two matches of his final season.

First-class career (1961–83): 1,668 runs (17.93), 336 wickets (23.56), and 46 catches

McKECHNIE, Brian John

(b. 1953, Gore, Southland) *Otago*

A right-hand batsman and right-arm medium-pace bowler, Brian McKechnie played for Otago with success, although better known as an All Black full-back. Perhaps his most famous innings was one of nought not out at Melbourne in 1981. The teams were tied, one-all, in the international series, and New Zealand wanted six runs to win off the final ball when Greg Chappell instructed his brother Trevor to bowl underarm. McKechnie, or 'Colt' as he was known, was powerless but the Chappells were derided. He played in 14 one-day internationals in all, scoring 54 runs and taking 19 wickets at 26.05 each.

First-class career (1971–86): 1,169 runs (18.26) and 100 wickets (30.65)

McKELVEY, Patricia Frances

(b. 1942, Lower Hutt, Wellington) *Wellington and New Zealand*

Trish McKelvey captained New Zealand to their first Test victory over Australia at Melbourne in 1972. The team went on to South Africa, won their second Test and with the first and third matches drawn, took the series. McKelvey scored a century in the first Test. These were heady times for New Zealand who had lost, sometimes heavily, their first seventeen Tests. In 1969 at the

Basin Reserve in Wellington, McKelvey had recorded the first Test century by a New Zealand woman, 155 not out against England, and this remains her country's highest score. A phlegmatic right-handed bat, McKelvey was 24 and uncapped when she was named captain of New Zealand for the 1966 tour to England. She went on to lead her country in all her fifteen Test and fifteen one-day international appearances, including two World Cups, before retiring in 1982. McKelvey's involvement in cricket became even more intense during the 1980s and early 1990s, however, because she managed national teams and was a New Zealand selector. She also served on the New Zealand Women's Cricket Council and when the council merged with the men's body in 1992 was the only woman appointed a Board member. Also a radio and television commentator, McKelvey served national sporting organizations such as the Hilary Commission and the New Zealand Sports Foundation as well as becoming principal of Wellington High School.

Test matches (15): 681 runs (29.13) including 2 centuries
One-day internationals (15): 214 runs (21.40)

McLEOD, Edwin George

(b. 1900, Auckland; d. 1989, Auckland) *Auckland, Wellington, and New Zealand*

A competent left-handed batsman and occasional leg-break bowler, Edwin McLeod played in only one Test, the second at Wellington against England in 1929/30, when he scored 16 and 2 not out and took 0 for 5.

First-class career (1920–41): 1,407 runs (32.72) including 1 century, and 20 wickets (33.20)

McMAHON, Trevor George

(b. 1929, Wellington) *Wellington and New Zealand*

Played mainly for his wicket-keeping, Trevor McMahon toured India and Pakistan in 1955/6, keeping adequately but failing with the bat. His sole Test experience was during this tour.

First-class career (1953–65): 449 runs (9.97) and 98 dismissals (84 c., 14 st.)
Test matches (5): 7 runs (2.33) and 8 dismissals (7 c., 1 st.)

McRAE, Donald Alexander Noel

(b. 1912, Christchurch) *Canterbury and New Zealand*

A competent left-handed batsman and medium-pace bowler, Donald McRae played in one Test match, against Australia at Wellington in 1945/6—the first after the war—scoring 0 and 8 and returning figures of 0 for 44.

First-class career (1937–46): 354 runs (15.39) and 56 wickets (22.51)

McSWEENEY, Ervin Bruce

(b. 1957, Wellington) *Central Districts, Wellington, and New Zealand*

Wellington has a proud record of supplying New Zealand wicket-keepers, for example Ken James, Eric Tindull, Frank Mooney, and Trevor McMahon. Ervin McSweeney may never have played a Test, but he has been one of the most successful. His dismissals, 378 of them for Wellington, far exceed that of the other provincial record-holders. He is an assertive right-hand batsman with six centuries and twenty-three fifties to his credit. A tall, imposing figure, he has had a profound effect on many of the games he has played. He has had 41 dismissals in a season twice, easily a New Zealand provincial record. He was also one of the principals in the bizarre events during the Canterbury–Wellington Shell Trophy in 1989/90. This was the final fixture for each side, and Canterbury, with a first innings lead, faced a final task of scoring 291 in 59 overs. The score was 108 for 8 in 29 overs when Lee Germon, the wicket-keeper, and Roger Ford came together. They batted through until only two overs remained. Then McSweeney, the Wellington captain told Robert Vance, a very occasional bowler, to bowl deliberate no-balls; the over, laced with full tosses, consisted of 22 balls, from which Canterbury scored 77! The outcome was sad for Canterbury, frustrating for Wellington. The batsmen were undefeated, Germon hitting eight sixes and sixteen fours in a strange 160 not out, but the final scores were tied.

First-class career (1979–): 4,947 runs (33.65) including 6 centuries, and 385 dismissals (340 c., 45 st.)

MATHESON, Alexander Malcolm

(b. 1906) *Auckland and New Zealand*

A right-arm medium-pace bowler, always likely to whip in an unexpected quicker ball, and a useful tail-end batsman, Alexander Matheson played against England in the fourth Test at Auckland in 1929/30. He also toured England in 1931 when, despite being handicapped by a strained leg muscle, he took 44 wickets (23.81). In New Zealand, every Friday night, he motored 100

521

miles over rough country roads in order to play four hours' cricket in Auckland for his club.

First-class career (1926–47): 1,844 runs (23.64) including 1 century, and 194 wickets (28.53)
Test matches (2): 7 runs (7.00), 2 wickets (68.00), and 2 catches

MEALE, Trevor

(b. 1928, Auckland) *Wellington and New Zealand*

A tall left-handed opening batsman who concentrated grimly, Trevor Meale was a surprise choice for the 1958 England tour: he had appeared with success in London club cricket, but failed in his attempt to qualify for Kent. He made 502 runs (21.82) on the tour, playing in two Tests without luck.

First-class career (1951–8): 1,352 runs (27.59) including 2 centuries
Test matches (2): 21 runs (5.25)

MERRITT, William Edward

(b. 1908, Christchurch; d. 1977, Christchurch) *Canterbury, Northamptonshire, and New Zealand*

A cheerful and skilful right-arm leg-break and googly bowler of great stamina—perhaps the best of his kind produced by New Zealand—Bill Merritt had no great command of length but frequently had good batsmen in trouble. As a batsman he was rugged, unorthodox, but effective and he was a fine fielder. He represented Canterbury for the first time at 18, taking 8 for 68 in the match with Otago in 1926/7, and he toured England with the first New Zealand team in 1927 as its youngest and most successful bowler. He took 107 wickets (23.64), besides scoring 538 runs (26.90). In 1931 he again took most wickets in England, 99 (26.48), though he was less consistent, and scored 545 runs (18.79). In the two Tests he played, however, he failed. Likewise, in the first-ever series against England in 1929/30, he took only eight very expensive wickets and made few runs. He joined Rishton in the Lancashire League as a professional and later moved to Dudley. Recommended to Northamptonshire by his colleague, Ken James, he qualified for the county in 1939, but, because of the war, played for them only in 1939 and 1946. In 1939 he took 87 wickets (28.63) and made 926 runs (22.58). At his best he was a true match-winner. Figures of 13 for 181 for Canterbury against Otago in 1935/6; 12 for 161 for Northamptonshire against Cambridge University in 1939, when the county won a first-class match for the first

time since 1935; 12 for 130 for New Zealand against Essex; and 7 for 28 (second innings) at Lord's against MCC in 1931 illustrate his abilities. His highest score was a whirlwind 87 for Northants against Sussex in 57 minutes, including three sixes and ten fours, in 1939.

First-class career (1926–46): 3,147 runs (19.91), 536 wickets (25.50), and 58 catches
Test matches (6): 73 runs (10.42), 12 wickets (51.41), and 2 catches

MEULI, Edgar Milton

(b. 1926, Hawera) *Central Districts and New Zealand*

A competent right-handed opening batsman and occasional leg-break bowler, he played against South Africa in the first Test at Wellington in 1952/3, scoring 15 and 23, in his only Test appearance.

First-class career (1945–60): 1,914 runs (26.21) including 2 centuries, and 11 wickets (29.90)

MILBURN, Barry Douglas

(b. 1943, Dunedin) *Otago and New Zealand*

A neat, energetic and reliable wicket-keeper but moderate right-handed batsman, Barry Milburn toured England in 1969 and India and Pakistan in 1969/70, but Ken Wadsworth was preferred to him in the Tests. He represented New Zealand, however, at home in the series against the West Indies in 1968/9. He 'retired' in 1974 but came back for three more seasons in 1980.

First-class career (1963–83): 737 runs (11.51) including 1 century, and 195 dismissals (176 c., 19 st.)
Test matches (3): 8 runs (8.00) and 8 dismissals (6 c., 2 st.)

MILLER, Lawrence Somerville Martin

(b. 1923, Taranaki) *Central Districts, Wellington, and New Zealand*

A tall and likeable left-handed opening batsman, Lawrie Miller possessed a long reach and plenty of courage and, though seldom very impressive on a pitch with much life in it, he knew how to punish anything loose. Also a good field in the deep, he toured South Africa in 1953/4 and England in 1958 and, at home, played against South Africa in 1952/3 and the West Indies in 1953/4. Only coming into first-class cricket at 27, he was 35 when he toured England. He made 1,148 runs (30.21) with a highest of 76, but failed in the Tests there as he had in South Africa five years before. His best score in Tests, 47, was made in the fourth match against the West Indies at Auckland in 1955/6, when New Zealand won a Test for the first time. His career-highest, 144 against Auckland, was scored in the same season.

First-class career (1950–60): 4,777 runs (37.61), including 5 centuries, 3 wickets (25.00), and 33 catches

Test matches (13): 346 runs (13.84), 0–1, and 1 catch

MILLMOW, Jonathan Paul

(b. 1967, Wellington) *Wellington and New Zealand*

On his day, Jonathan Millmow could be a fast and hostile bowler. A member of the New Zealand team in England in 1990, he was stricken by injury and was seldom consistently fit thereafter. A tall man, he had a long, bucking run and an awkward, unorthodox action. In his comparatively brief career (37 matches) he took five wickets in an innings four times and ten in a match once, including 6 for 13 against Otago in 1989/90. He played in five one-day internationals, taking 4 wickets (58.00)

First-class career (1986/7–92): 129 runs (8.06) and 99 wickets (28.17)

MILLS, John Ernest

(b. 1905, Dunedin; d. 1972, Auckland) *Auckland and New Zealand*

An artist to his fingertips, John Mills was a left-handed opening batsman who played with a straight bat, drove beautifully and cut superbly, but tended to give the bowler a chance. He toured England with the first touring side in 1927, making 1,251 runs (37.90) and again in 1931, when he made 1,368 runs (31.81), being an effective opener with Stewie Dempster. On his Test début, the second match against England at Wellington in 1929/30, he scored 117 and with Dempster put on 276 for the first wicket, which remains the highest stand for any New Zealand wicket against England. His career-highest was 185 against Otago in 1929/30.

First-class career (1924–38): 5,025 runs (32.84) including 11 centuries, 4 wickets (30.75), and 30 catches

Test matches (7): 241 runs (26.77) including 1 century, and 1 catch

MOIR, Alexander McKenzie

(b. 1919, Dunedin North) *Otago and New Zealand*

A right-arm leg-break and googly bowler, Alex Moir delivered the ball, fingers snapping, with a studious air. As well as his slow bowling, often to a close-set attacking field, he doubled as a useful lower-order batsman. He toured India and Pakistan in 1955/6 and England in 1958. At home he played against England in 1950/1, 1954/5, and 1958/9, the West Indies in 1951/2 and 1955/6, and South Africa in 1952/3. In India and Pakistan his bowling failed against batsmen thoroughly comfortable in their home conditions; and in England, although he took 35 wickets (26.20), his increasingly unfashionable bowling proved ineffective in the Tests. His first Test was his best, against England at Christchurch in 1950/1, when he took 6 for 155 in 56.3 overs in a total of 550. Against Central Districts in 1953/4 he had a match record of 15 for 203 (7 for 84 and 8 for 119).

First-class career (1949–62): 2,102 runs (16.42), 368 wickets (24.56), and 44 catches

Test matches (17): 327 runs (14.86), 28 wickets (50.64), and 2 catches

MOLONEY, Denis Andrew Robert

(b. 1910, Dunedin; d. 1942, EL Alamein, North Africa) *Manawatu, Wellington, Otago, Canterbury, and New Zealand*

Denis Moloney was the leading all-rounder on the 1937 England tour. As well as being a bespectacled right-handed batsman, who often exercised a steadying influence, 'Sonny' was a useful medium-pace change-bowler and a fine field. He made 1,463 runs (34.83) and took 57 wickets (26.88). In the first Test at Lord's, his début, with his country 248 runs behind and seven wickets down, he hit a plucky 64. He was out immediately after the teams had been introduced to King George VI, to general dismay. His career-highest was 190 for Wellington against Auckland in 1936/7. He died of wounds while a prisoner of war at El Alamein in 1942. Walter Hadlee described him as a 'colourful personality who enjoyed the game for the game's sake'.

First-class career (1927–41): 3,219 runs (28.64) including 2 centuries, and 95 wickets (33.16)

Test matches (3): 156 runs (26.00), 0–9, and 3 catches

MOONEY, Francis Leonard Hugh

(b. 1921, Wellington) *Wellington and New Zealand*

A wicket-keeper without fuss or showmanship who was neat, clean, and efficient, sometimes stumping 'like a rattlesnake striking', Frank Mooney concentrated so hard, whether 'keeping or batting, that he rarely spoke or smiled. In the evenings, however, his energetic socializing and dancing helped to earn him the nickname 'Starlight'. A limited but extremely useful right-handed stroke-maker, he could drive hard straight back or through the covers. He toured England in 1949—his selection causing a strike among the Dunedin waterside workers who preferred one of their own number—and in the second first-class match at Worcester claimed seven dismissals (six in the second innings) and had a hand in a run out. He ended the tour with 66 victims (46 caught, 20 stumped), including ten from three Tests, and 774 runs (22.76). He toured South Africa in 1953/4, having nine victims in the five Tests, and at home played against England in 1950/1, the West Indies in 1951/2 and South Africa in 1952/3. His career-highest score was 180 against Auckland in 1943/4.

First-class career (1941–55): 3,143 runs (23.11) including 2 centuries, and 221 dismissals (168 c., 53 st.)

Test matches (14): 343 runs (17.15), 0–0, and 30 dismissals (22 c., 8 st.)

MORGAN, Ross Winston

(b. 1941, Auckland) *Auckland and New Zealand*

A sound right-hander whose favourite shot was a 'cuff' through mid-wicket, Ross Morgan was also an off-spin change-bowler with an exotic hop-skip run in and a reliable field. He toured India and Pakistan in 1964/5, England in 1965 and the West Indies in 1971/2. At home he played against Pakistan in 1964/5, England in 1965/6 and 1970/1, and the West Indies in 1968/9. His international career ended on a low note in the Caribbean, but at home in 1964/5 he headed the batting from two Tests with 187 runs (46.75). This included the top score, 66, in his first match at Auckland and an innings of 97 at Christchurch, when he was hitting hard in a vain attempt to force a win. His career-highest was 166 against Canterbury in 1968/9 and best bowling 6 for 40 against Central Districts in 1964/5.

First-class career (1957–77): 5,940 runs (27.50) including 8 centuries, 108 wickets (32.94), 85 catches, and 1 stumping

Test matches (20): 734 runs (22.24), 5 wickets (121.80), and 12 catches

MORRISON, Bruce Donald

(b. 1933, Lower Hutt, Wellington) *Wellington and New Zealand*

A combative right-arm medium-pace bowler and a left-handed batsman with an earnest (but, generally, unfulfilled) desire to hit boundaries, Bruce Morrison appeared in only one Test, at Wellington in the second match against England in 1962/3. Selected as replacement for the injured J. C. Alabaster, he scored 10 and 0, took 2 for 129, and held 1 catch.

First-class career (1953–65): 374 runs (9.35) and 167 wickets (24.03)

MORRISON, Daniel Kyle

(b. 1966, Auckland) *Auckland, Lancashire, and New Zealand*

Not tall for a right-hand fast bowler, but immensely big of heart, Danny Morrison studied under Sir Richard Hadlee and became New Zealand's main strike bowler after Hadlee had retired in 1990. Stocky and strong with a slingy action, he bowls at a very brisk pace and has command of a mean out-swinger. By 1994 he had taken five wickets in an innings 13 times, eight of them in Tests. Definitely a tail-end batsman, he lacks nothing in determination, scoring 42 against Pakistan in 1994. First appearing for New Zealand in Australia in 1987/8, he has since toured India, England, Pakistan, and Sri Lanka, always giving his side a cutting edge and never stinting himself. He played one season for Lancashire in 1992, bowling wholeheartedly as usual until he sustained a serious injury. His first really successful series, at home to India in 1989/90, brought him 16 wickets in three games, 13 more came against Sri Lanka in 1990/1, and the following season he bowled with outstanding fire and persistence at home to Australia. His 17 wickets in the series at 16.94 included a career-best 7 for 89 at Wellington. By 1994 Morrison's 67 one-day internationals had brought 85 wickets (29.01). Apart from learning a useful slow ball, he made few concessions to limited-overs tactics, bowling fast and straight to take wickets.

First-class career (1985–) 773 runs (9.78) and 337 wickets (31.50)

Test matches (41): 318 runs (7.95), 143 wickets (33.53). and 13 catches

MORRISON, John Francis Maclean

(b. 1947, Wellington) *Central Districts, Wellington, and New Zealand*

A very careful right-handed batsman, left-arm spin change-bowler and reliable field, John Morrison toured Australia twice, England (1979) and India and Pakistan (1976/7); and played at home against Australia in 1973/4 and 1981/2, England in 1974/5 and India in 1975/6. Over the years, his form was uneven, but on succeeding the injured Glenn Turner as opening batsman, he hit 117 in his second Test match, against Australia at Sydney, and headed the batting for the series with 249 runs (41.50). Two months later, in the first match at Wellington against Australia, he scored 66, sharing in a century stand for the second wicket with Turner. Against England in the first match at Auckland in 1974/5 he fought well in a losing cause, making 58 and 58 but in the next Test at Christchurch he was caught at third slip off the first ball of the match. His career-highest was 180 not out for Wellington against Northern Districts in 1972/3. In 1981/2 he was recalled: at Auckland his second innings figures of 35–16–52–2 helped his country to win.

First-class career (1965–84): 6,142 runs (30.71) including 7 centuries, 51 wickets (31.50), and 133 catches

Test matches (17): 656 runs (22.62) including 1 century, 2 wickets (35.50), and 9 catches

MOTZ, Richard Charles

(b. 1940, Christchurch) *Canterbury and New Zealand*

Although not of startling speed, Dick Motz was a big, tenacious right-arm fast bowler who combined lively pace with an out-swinger and movement off the pitch and was prepared to bowl until he dropped. He was also a late-order batsman who loved hitting sixes. Strongly built, he was a cricketer of great character. On his first-class début in the Plunket Shield competition in 1957/8 he took a wicket in his second over and two in his third. He toured South Africa in 1961/2, England in 1965 and 1969 and India and Pakistan in 1965/6. At home he played against England in 1962/3 and 1965/6, South Africa in 1963/4, Pakistan in 1964/5, India in 1967/8, and the West Indies in 1968/9. On his first tour, to South Africa, he headed the bowling with 81 wickets (17.77), including 19 wickets (26.57) in his country's most successful official Test series. In England in 1965 he was the attacking spearhead with 54 wickets

(22.98) from 14 matches, including 11 wickets from the three Tests. Against the 1967/8 Indians, he captured 15 wickets (28.86) in the four matches, and at Christchurch in the second match, he broke through to take 6 for 63 in the first innings and helped New Zealand to victory over India for the first time. In England in 1969, he had lost some of his edge but—in the last Test at The Oval—he became the first 'Kiwi' to take 100 wickets in official Tests. Near the end of the summer, it was discovered that he had been bowling for 18 months with a displaced vertebra, an injury which caused his retirement from first-class cricket on his return home. His best bowling in an innings was 8 for 61 against Wellington in 1966/7. His career-highest score was 103 not out against Otago in 1967/8 in 53 minutes, including seven sixes and eight fours, the fastest century ever recorded in New Zealand first-class cricket.

First-class career (1957–69): 3,494 runs (17.12) including 1 century, 518 wickets (22.72), and 41 catches

Test matches (32): 612 runs (11.54), 100 wickets (31.48), and 9 catches

MURRAY, Bruce Alexander Grenfell

(b. 1940, Wellington) *Wellington and New Zealand*

A tall, calm, and cautious right-handed opening batsman with a long reach, an occasional leg-break bowler and safe fielder, Bruce Murray toured England in 1969 and India and Pakistan in 1969/70. At home he played against India in 1967/8 and England in 1970/1. He scored 54 in his first Test against India at Dunedin and on his England tour made more runs than anyone else, 800 (40.00), although he had no substantial scores in the Tests. In India and Pakistan he was again prominent with 641 runs (37.70), including 329 runs (27.41) in the six Tests. At Lahore in the third Test against Pakistan he hit 90, his highest Test score, helping New Zealand to win for the first time against Pakistan. His career-highest was 213 against Otago in 1968/9.

First-class career (1958–73): 6,257 runs (35.55) including 6 centuries, 30 wickets (28.93), and 124 catches

Test matches (13): 598 runs (23.92), 1–0, and 21 catches

MURRAY, Darrin James

(b. 1987, Christchurch) *Canterbury and New Zealand*

A steady right-handed opening batsman, Darrin Murray broke into the Test team in South Africa in

1994/5 and played seven more Tests in a busy season, despite reaching 50 only once in 16 innings.

First-class career (1990–): 1,252 runs (43.17) including 2 centuries, and 11 catches

Test matches (8): 303 runs (20.20) and 6 catches

NASH, Dion Joseph

(b. 1971, Auckland) *Northern Districts, Otago, Middlesex, and New Zealand*

Dion Nash had a rapid rise to prominence after success with both bat and ball on an under-19 tour of India. He first appeared for Northern Districts in 1991/2 and in his third season was selected to tour Zimbabwe and Sri Lanka. A resolute right-hand batsman and a brisk right-arm away-swing bowler, he also appeared in the single Test against India in New Zealand in 1993/4 before going to England in 1994 and enjoying a marvellous match in the second Test at Lord's. Making 56 in New Zealand's first innings of 476, he took 11 wickets for 169 in several superb spells of bowling from the pavilion end. He was indubitably the man of a match which New Zealand were unlucky not to win and he finished the series with 17 wickets from three Tests at 25.23. Middlesex were sufficiently impressed to employ him as their overseas player in 1995, although the intervening winter had been difficult for Nash who, along with two other players, was dropped temporarily for experimenting with a soft drug during a party in South Africa.

First-class career (1991–): 676 runs (20.48) and 74 wickets (26.83)

Test matches (10): 176 runs (16.00), 32 wickets (31.68), and 7 catches

NEWMAN, Sir Jack

(b. 1902, Nelson) *Wellington, Canterbury, Nelson, and New Zealand*

A left-arm medium-pace bowler, Jack Newman played against South Africa in 1931/2, the first match between the two countries at Christchurch, and against England in 1932/3. Unfortunate to meet Wally Hammond in supreme form, he was hit for sixes off three successive deliveries in the second Test at Auckland. For Wellington against Otago in 1931/2 he took 10 for 96 in the match. He was president of the New Zealand Cricket Council from 1965 until 1967 and was knighted in 1978.

First-class career (1922–36): 206 runs (8.95) and 69 wickets (24.76)

Test matches (3): 33 runs (8.25) and 2 wickets (127.00)

O'SULLIVAN, David Robert

(b. 1944, Wellington) *Central Districts, Hampshire, Durham, and New Zealand*

An excellent slow left-arm bowler and often useful right-handed batsman, David O'Sullivan was a prolific wicket-taker in New Zealand domestic cricket. He also had one very successful season with Hampshire and, but for rivalry from two good, slow left-armers in Hedley Howarth and Stephen Boock and doubts about a slight kink in his action, he would have played more Tests. A sharp turner of the ball, he was particularly effective when conditions were wet or very dry. Born and educated in Palmerston North, he moved to England in 1969, and in 1971 made his first appearance as a specially registered overseas player with Hampshire. After taking 29 wickets in eleven Championship matches in 1972, his 47 wickets (20.59) in 1973 had much to do with Hampshire's success in the County Championship as he repeatedly bowled sides out late in the season. Ironically the county had to choose between O'Sullivan and Andy Roberts as their overseas bowler the following year and reluctantly dispensed with the services of the spinner. O'Sullivan's Test début was an unsuccessful one against Pakistan at Dunedin in February 1973 and it was not until his fourth Test, against Australia at Adelaide in 1973/4, that he took a wicket! His 5 for 148 in Australia's first innings in this match remained his best Test figures.

First-class career (1971–85): 2,174 runs (15.41), 523 wickets (25.91), and 46 catches

Test matches (11): 158 runs (9.29), 18 wickets (67.83), and 2 catches

OVERTON, Guy William Fitzroy

(b. 1919, Dunedin) *Southland, Otago, and New Zealand*

A right-arm bowler of considerable pace, able to swing the ball both ways, Guy Overton toured South Africa in 1953/4, taking 26 wickets (30.53). At Johannesburg in the fourth Test he had a spell of 3 wickets for 1 run in 13 balls. In all first-class matches he took more wickets than he scored runs.

First-class career (1945–56): 137 runs (4.15) and 169 wickets (25.14)

Test matches (3): 8 runs (1.60), 9 wickets (28.66), and 1 catch

OWENS, Michael Barry

(b. 1969, Christchurch) *Canterbury and New Zealand*

A strongly built and aggressive right-arm fast bowler with a long, direct approach to the stumps, 'Millie' Owens was not selected as a fast right-hand bowler for the tour of England in 1994 but eventually joined the team as a replacement and played in two of the three Tests, taking 4 for 99 at Old Trafford. After only a handful of matches he had been picked for New Zealand in 1992/3 when part of the New Zealand team returned home after a bomb blast in Colombo. As a replacement he did well in his first two Tests, taking 7 wickets on unhelpful pitches. In England in 1994 he took 17 first-class wickets at a cost of only 24 each.

First-class career (1991–   ): 45 runs (3.21) and 71 wickets (25.58)

Test matches (8): 16 runs (2.66), 17 wickets (34.41), and 3 catches

PAGE, Milford Laurenson

(b. 1902, Christchurch; d. 1987, Christchurch) *Canterbury and New Zealand*

A sound but painstaking right-handed batsman, strong on the leg-side, a useful slow change-bowler, and reliable slip field, 'Curly' Page toured England with the first touring team of 1927 and also went with the second of 1931 as chief lieutenant to Tom Lowry before captaining the 1937 side to England. At home he played in the first-ever Tests against England in 1929/30 and as captain in 1932/3; he was leader against South Africa in 1931/2 also. He succeeded Lowry as a sporting, popular, but firm skipper. He once said, 'People think more of a good sportsman who loses than a bad sportsman who wins.' A responsible middle-order batsman who restricted himself in the interests of the team, he made 1,154 runs (34.96) and took 23 wickets (21.65) in 1927; 990 runs (26.75) in 1931; and 666 runs (22.20) in 1937. At Lord's in 1931 he scored 104 in New Zealand's first official Test in England, helping New Zealand to an honourable draw by sharing in two century partnerships. His career-highest was 206 against Wellington in 1931/2. A double international, he was also an All Black Rugby half-back.

First-class career (1920–43): 5,857 runs (29.88) including 9 centuries, 73 wickets (32.39), and 117 catches

Test matches (14): 492 runs (24.60) including 1 century, 5 wickets (46.20), and 6 catches

PARKER, John Morton

(b. 1951, Dannevirke, Hawke's Bay) *Northern Districts, Worcestershire, and New Zealand*

The youngest of three brothers who have all played first-class cricket in New Zealand, John Parker made up his mind to follow the footsteps of Glenn Turner. A most determined, if limited, right-handed batsman with a short backlift and plenty of pluck, and a fine fielder, who could also keep wicket, he paid his way to England in 1971 and had a successful trial at Worcester, making 91 when he first appeared for them in that year against the Indian touring team. As a qualified player in 1972 he scored 869 runs (39.80) and remained a useful, if seldom a match-winning performer, for Worcestershire until 1975. In his first season in New Zealand in 1972/3 he batted outstandingly well to make 452 runs (45.20). He gained his first Test cap that season against Pakistan, but broke a bone in his hand while fielding, was unable to bat and took no further part in the series. Although on the 1973 tour of England he scored well in matches against the counties (648 runs on the tour at 29.45), he had a miserable three Tests against England's seam bowlers, failing to get into double figures in any one of his five innings. He redeemed himself by making 108 against Australia at Sydney a few months later and he was a member of the side which in the same season beat Australia for the first time, at Christchurch. However, he was inconsistent as an opener and did better when he dropped down the batting order. Touring Pakistan and India in 1976/7 as Glenn Turner's vice-captain, Parker led his country against Pakistan in the third Test at Karachi, which New Zealand did well to save, and in the following Test against India at Bombay he made 104 before being run out. His highest score for New Zealand was 121 against England at Auckland in 1974/5, but, although he again scored freely against the counties in the tour of England in 1978, his four Test innings brought him only 55 runs. He made fifties in the first and third Tests in Australia in 1980/1, and the following season he averaged over 100 in the Shell Shield and scored centuries in both innings against Central Districts. He continued to be effective in domestic cricket for several more seasons and became an amusing radio commentator on Tests.

First-class career (1971–84): 11,254 runs (34.84) including 21 centuries, 14 wickets (48.64), and 182 dismissals (177 c., 5 st.)

PARKER

Test matches (36): 1,498 runs (24.55) including 3 centuries, 1–24, and 30 catches

PARKER, Norman Murray

(b. 1948, Dannevirke, Hawke's Bay) *Otago, Canterbury, and New Zealand*

A right-handed batsman and good fielder, Murray Parker was chosen for the tough tour of Pakistan and India in 1976/7 and won his first Test cap in the third Test against Pakistan at Karachi when his younger brother John was captaining New Zealand for the first time. Opening the batting, he scored a steady 40 in the second innings which helped to save the game, but, although he played in New Zealand's next two Tests against India, he was not selected again.

First-class career (1967–79): 2,102 runs (25.02) including 1 century

Test matches (3): 89 runs (14.83) and 2 catches

PATEL, Dipak Narshibhai

(b. 1958, Nairobi, Kenya) *Worcestershire, Auckland, and New Zealand*

After a distinguished career for Worcestershire between 1976 and 1986—he was on stand-by for two England winter tours—the personable and stylish all-rounder Dipak Patel first played for Auckland on 6 January 1986 at Lancaster Park, Christchurch. He made 174, reaching his century from 130 balls. Those present have vivid memories of that innings: the polish, the assurance and the exquisite stroke-making. A right-hand batsman and tidy off-spinner, he took 8 wickets in the same match and Canterbury were heavily defeated. It was inevitable after this that he would play for New Zealand. His first Test was in February 1987, but he was only occasionally able to do himself justice. He had remarkable success in the 1990/1 World Cup, however, when New Zealand led on points after the qualifying rounds. He usually opened the bowling and the only time he was collared was in the semi-final against Pakistan. His bowling cost only 3.10 runs per over, the best of the tournament. He had played in 45 one-day internationals by 1994, scoring 346 runs (10.81) and taking 29 wickets (43.17). Patel first arrived in England as a schoolboy after his family had been forced to leave Kenya, along with many other Asians, by the policies of General Amin.

First-class career (1976–): 14,701 runs (30.50) including 26 centuries, and 603 wickets (33.47)

Test matches (25): 848 runs (20.68) and 45 wickets (45.11)

PETHERICK, Peter James

(b. 1942, Otago) *Otago, Wellington, and New Zealand*

An off-spinner who made his belated début for Otago in 1975/6, Peter Petherick assured himself of a permanent place in the record books by taking a hat-trick in his first Test match. He is one of only two people to have achieved this unlikely feat, M. J. C. Allom of England being the other. His victims were all distinguished Pakistani cricketers—Javed Miandad, Wasim Raja, and Intikhab Alam—in the first innings of the first Test at Lahore in October 1976. Petherick finished with 3 for 103 in the innings of 417. He was unfortunate not to be given more opportunity thereafter, missing the 1978 tour of England and playing only one home Test, against Australia at Auckland in 1976/7, when he bowled only four overs.

First-class career (1975–82): 200 runs (5.88) and 189 wickets (24.47)

Test matches (6): 34 runs (4.85), 16 wickets (42.93), and 4 catches

PETRIE, Eric Charlton

(b. 1927, Auckland) *Auckland, Northern Districts, Gentlemen, and New Zealand*

A neat, reliable wicket-keeper, Eric Petrie improved greatly during his tour of England in 1958, when he had 49 victims in 20 matches and played for Gentlemen against Players at Scarborough; he was one of the few real successes on the tour, and immensely popular. As a right-handed batsman good enough to hit two centuries, he was disappointing in representative cricket. In the Test at Christchurch during the 1965/6 tour, after an absence of five years from Test cricket, he hit 55—his top score in Tests.

First-class career (1950–67): 2,788 runs (17.98) including 2 centuries, and 234 dismissals (197 c., 37 st.)

Test matches (14): 258 runs (12.90) and 25 dismissals (25 c.)

PETRIE, Richard George

(b. 1967, Christchurch) *Canterbury and Wellington*

A tall, distinguished-looking cricketer, Richard Petrie looked a New Zealand Test prospect at the start of his career, but one-day internationals proved the limit of his achievements. A right-arm fast-medium bowler, and vigorous right-handed batsman, Petrie's progress was halted by an injury in the 1992/3 season. In Canterbury's match with Central Districts that same season he took 4 for 91 and made a century which included 18 fours. In 12 one-day internationals from 1990 he scored 65 runs (13.00) and took 12 wickets (37.41). He became a Wellington player in 1993/4.

First-class career (1988–): 329 runs (15.66), 70 wickets (31.61), and 7 catches

PLAYLE, William Rodger

(b. 1938, Wellington) *Auckland, Western Australia, and New Zealand*

A right-handed batsman with a wide range of strokes, and a good field, Bill Playle was a surprise choice for the 1958 England tour. In a less wet summer his stylish batting might have been more effective, but he failed in the Tests and 23 first-class matches brought him only 414 runs, despite 96 in the second match at Leicester. In his only other series, in 1962/3, against England at Wellington he made 65 in a losing cause, his best effort in Tests. Settling in Australia, his career-highest was 122 for Western Australia against Queensland at Perth in 1965/6.

First-class career (1956–68): 2,888 runs (21.87) including 4 centuries, 1 wicket (94.00), and 82 catches
Test matches (8): 151 runs (10.06) and 4 catches

PLUNKET, Lord

(b. 1864, Dublin, Ireland; d. 1920)

The fifth Baron Plunket was also Archbishop of Dublin and Primate of All Ireland before becoming Governor-General of New Zealand. While in office he awarded the Plunket Shield for major association cricket, having acquired an interest in the game during his university education. The first games were played in 1907/8 on a challenge basis. It was not until the 1921/2 season that all four teams—as it was then—were involved in a four-day competition. Lord Plunket also founded the Plunket Society, which is an important nation-wide organization caring for mothers in the pre-natal months and for children up to school age.

POLLARD, Victor

(b. 1945, Burnley, Lancashire, England) *Central Districts, Canterbury, and New Zealand*

Born in Lancashire, Vic Pollard grew up in New Zealand. Short and stocky with short-cut dark hair, he became a stubborn right-handed batsman

capable of nimble attacking stroke-play, square-cutting, off-driving and hooking with relish. He was, too, a very useful off-spin bowler and brilliant field, especially at cover. He toured India and Pakistan in 1964/5 and 1969/70, and England in 1965, 1969, and 1973, and at home he played against England in 1965/6 and 1970/1, India in 1967/8, and the West Indies in 1968/9. Making his first tour of England a year after leaving school, having been chosen primarily for his bowling, he was batting 'find' of the year, making 652 runs (31.31), including most runs in the Tests, 281 runs at 56.20. At Edgbaston, with New Zealand being out-played, he scored 81 not out, and at Lord's (twice) and Headingley he also passed 50. His bowling successes were negligible and for several years he did not fulfil his great promise. He made several fifties, and took 23 wickets (16.26) in matches against an Australian B team in 1966/7 but in England in 1969 as vice-captain he achieved very little in the Tests. On his third tour, however, in 1973, he performed nobly: he scored 629 runs (48.38) in all first-class matches and headed the Test averages with 302 runs (100.66) in the three matches. At Trent Bridge, when New Zealand, seeking 479 to win, lost four men cheaply, he scored 116 (including only nine fours), adding 177 with Bev Congdon for the fifth wicket. At Lord's in the next Test, when England came close to being beaten by the Kiwis for the first time, he contributed 105 not out, running out to hit Geoff Arnold and John Snow, and adding 117 for the sixth wicket with Mark Burgess, a New Zealand record. Finally at Headingley, with four wickets down for 78 on the first day, he added 106 for the fifth wicket with Burgess, this time making 62. He retired from international cricket after this tour. A teacher and Baptist lay-preacher, he was strongly opposed to the playing of first-class cricket on Sundays.

First-class career (1964–75): 5,314 runs (30.54) including 6 centuries, 224 wickets (30.94), and 81 catches
Test matches (32): 1,266 runs (24.34) including 2 centuries, 40 wickets (46.32), and 19 catches

POORE, Matt Beresford

(b. 1930, Christchurch) *Canterbury and New Zealand*

A competent right-handed batsman and useful off-spin change-bowler, Matt Poore toured South Africa in 1953/4 and India and Pakistan in 1955/6, and at home played against South Africa in 1952/3 and England in 1954/5. In South Africa

529

he made 550 runs (22.91) including 170 in the five Tests, but in India and Pakistan he was not quite so successful. Played mainly for his batting, he never reached a fifty in Tests. His career-highest was 142 against Central Districts in 1954/5.

First-class career (1950–62): 2,336 runs (23.12) including 2 centuries, and 68 wickets (26.67)
Test matches (14): 355 runs (15.43), 9 wickets (40.77), and 1 catch

PRIEST, Mark Wellings

(b. 1961, Greymouth) *Canterbury and New Zealand*

When he was selected to tour England in 1990, there were expectations that New Zealand would be well served by 'Popeye' Priest's slow left-arm bowling and his aggressive left-hand batting. Hard as he worked, he managed only 14 wickets on the tour, but in the seasons which followed he was generally the most successful spinner in New Zealand's inter-provincial cricket. In 1993/4 he averaged 55.80 and took 28 wickets from five matches at 16.35. His sole Test was the first against England at Trent Bridge in 1990. He made 26 at number six in his only innings and took one wicket for 26. He has also played in six one-day internationals, scoring 60 runs (10.00) and taking one wicket (210.00).

First-class career (1984–): 2,715 runs (32.32) including four centuries, and 202 wickets (33.15)

PRINGLE, Christopher

(b. 1968, Auckland) *Auckland and New Zealand*

Chris Pringle had barely begun his first-class career before he was selected for a touring team, as a replacement, in England in 1990. Several of the New Zealand players were injured when Pringle, who had been playing club cricket for Pudsey, wandered on to the Headingley ground during net practice and asked whether anyone had a ticket to spare. He was immediately mobilized and played in the two one-day internationals, but not the Tests. A burly swing bowler with a vigorous body action his brisk medium pace was insufficient for consistent success in Tests. Yet in Pakistan in 1990/1 he enjoyed a singular triumph when he took 7 for 52 in the Pakistan first innings at Faisalabad, and 11 for 152 in the match. Pringle later admitted to emulating the tactics of his opponents by tampering with the surface of the ball, action which had a dramatic effect on his ability to swing the old ball. He took 18 Test wickets at 23, success he was never to repeat, despite honest performances in

subsequent tours of Sri Lanka (1992/3) and England (1994). He has played with success, however, in 49 one-day internationals, taking 82 wickets (21.90).

First-class career (1989–): 600 runs (12.50) and 154 wickets (30.09)
Test matches (14): 175 runs (10.29), 30 wickets (46.30), and 3 catches

PRITCHARD, Thomas Leslie

(b. 1917, Kaupokonui) *Wellington, Warwickshire, and Kent*

Tom Pritchard was bitterly disappointed at not being chosen for the New Zealand tour of England in 1937. A genuinely fast right-hand bowler and big-hitting lower-order right-hand batsman, he played outside town, but he was devastating. He made his only New Zealand appearance against Sir Julien Cahn's team in 1938/9. After war service, with Tom Dollery as his mentor he joined Warwickshire and in his first appearance for the county against the 1946 Indian touring team he bowled Vijay Hazere, Vinoo Mankad, and Gul Mohammad. He enjoyed marked success in 170 matches for the county until 1955. When the New Zealand team went to England in 1949, Pritchard was in demand, but by now tied to his county. He did appear against the tourists, taking 6 for 96 in the first innings. His best bag was 8 for 20 against Worcestershire in 1950. He played four matches for Kent in 1956. He took 100 wickets in a season four times, including 172 in 1948 at 18.75 each.

First-class career (1937–56): 3,364 runs (13.34), 818 wickets (23.30), and 82 catches

PUNA, Narotam

(b. 1929, Surat, Gujarat, India) *Northern Districts and New Zealand*

Born at Surat near Bombay, Narotam Puna was a very good right-arm off-spin bowler, a brilliant field and a sometimes useful batsman. He played in the three Tests against England in 1965/6, in which season he captured no fewer than 34 wickets in the Plunket Shield competition. His best bowling in an innings was 6 for 43 against Auckland in 1959/60.

First-class career (1956–69): 1,305 runs (14.81) and 229 wickets (24.43)
Test matches (3): 31 runs (15.50), 4 wickets (60.00), and 1 catch

RABONE, Geoffrey Osbourne

(b. 1921, Otago) *Wellington, Auckland, and New Zealand*

Geoff Rabone was a forceful right-handed batsman, an off-spin bowler who could turn to leg-spinners or stock medium-pace as well, and a superb slip field who made extremely difficult catches look comparatively simple. Rabone, otherwise 'Bones' or 'Boney', toured England in 1949 and at home played against West Indies in 1951/2 and South Africa in 1952/3. He succeeded Mervyn Wallace to the regular captaincy, and was leader in South Africa in 1953/4 and at home against England in 1954/5. A sensitive, intelligent, genial, and courageous captain, he nevertheless lost four and drew one of the Tests during his captaincy. In England he was the best all-rounder, sometimes opening both batting and bowling, and collecting 1,021 runs (32.93), 50 wickets (35.70) and 24 catches; in the Tests his highest score was only 39 not out but he averaged 29.60. In the first three Tests in South Africa he was the most effective New Zealand batsman scoring 254 runs (50.80), including an exemplary innings of 107 lasting over 6 hours in the first match at Durban. He took 6 for 68 in 38.7 overs in a total of 326 in the third Test at Cape Town. When he broke a bone in his foot and had to return home, thirteen matches had brought him 547 runs and 28 wickets. His last Test as captain saw his country routed by England in the second match at Auckland in 1954/5, the second innings of 26 remaining the lowest total in Test cricket. His career-highest was 125 for Auckland against Central Districts in 1951/2 and best bowling in an innings 8 for 65 for Auckland against Australia B at Auckland in 1956/7.

First-class career (1940–61): 3,425 runs (28.30) including 3 centuries, 173 wickets (27.94), and 76 catches
Test matches (12): 562 runs (31.22) including 1 century, 16 wickets (39.68), and 5 catches

REDMOND, Rodney Ernest

(b. 1944, Auckland) *Wellington, Auckland, and New Zealand*

Rodney Redmond was a tall, left-handed, opening batsman who drove, cut and pulled off the front foot with tremendous confidence. Also a useful spin bowler and good field, he had a tremendous début against Pakistan in the third match at Auckland in 1972/3 when he made scintillating scores of 107 and 56—putting on opening stands

with Glenn Turner of 159 and 80. His century came in 2 hours 12 minutes. However, he never appeared again in a Test. No one has started better and fallen so quickly from form and favour. He toured England in 1973, but he had trouble with new contact lenses and his aggressive methods at the wicket were only rarely successful: in first-class matches he made 483 runs (28.41) and was not selected for the Tests. His career-highest was 141 not out for Auckland against Wellington in 1970/1 and best bowling in a match 10 for 110 for the New Zealand under-23 XI against Wellington in 1965/6. His troublesome eyesight caused early retirement.

First-class career (1963–76): 3,134 runs (33.69) including 5 centuries, 17 wickets (28.29), and 31 catches

REESE, Daniel

(b. 1879, Christchurch; d. 1953, Christchurch) *Canterbury, London County, Essex, New Zealand*

Dan Reese was one of New Zealand's greatest players and administrators. A gifted left-hand batsman and a slow-medium left-arm bowler with a distinctively smooth action, he was also an exceptionally fine fieldsman. He played first-class cricket for 26 years, yet appeared in only 72 matches. An engineer, he was often at sea. But he played, with his life-long friend Sir Arthur Sims for London County, for Essex, and in Melbourne for three years. He was first selected for Canterbury at the age of 16, and in his début match against Wellington had a match analysis of 6 for 65. In a trial match at Dunedin, for New Zealand against Otago, he took 9 for 14 off 93 balls in Otago's second innings. New Zealand had four matches in Australia in 1899, Reese taking 5 for 58 against South Tasmania and scoring 88 against Victoria in 110 minutes when the state side included Laver, Tarrant, and Armstrong. He had great success against Lord Hawke's team, captained by Warner in 1902/3, scoring one century for Canterbury and another for New Zealand. All four of his centuries were against overseas teams. After his marine excursions he went back to New Zealand in 1906 and was appointed captain of the national side, a position he held until the First World War. He was top of the batting and bowling figures for New Zealand's tour in 1913/14. He had spectacular success against South Australia, (96 and 130 not out) and Queensland (7 for 53 and 2 for 15). He played a leading role in administration as a member of the

Lancaster Park Board for many years, the Canterbury Cricket Association, and for nearly 30 years of the New Zealand Cricket Council. He was chairman for three years, president for four, a life member, and a national selector. He and his brother Tom, whose histories of New Zealand cricket proved invaluable—were successful business partners.

First-class career (1895–1921): 3,186 runs (25.28) and 196 wickets (19.86)

REID, John Fulton

(b. 1958, Auckland) *Auckland and New Zealand*

No relation of his prolific namesake, this calm and accomplished left-handed batsman played cricket like a professional but approached it in the spirit of an amateur. A geography master at Waitakere College, when turning down a chance to tour the West Indies in 1985 he gave his three priorities as: wife and children first, teaching second, cricket third. At that stage he had enjoyed a remarkable start to his Test career, scoring five centuries in thirteen Tests, three against Pakistan, and one each against India and Sri Lanka. If this suggests a relatively easy baptism, he also batted impressively in brief limited-overs encounters against the West Indian fast bowlers in Australia in 1984/5 and the following year shared fully in New Zealand's first series win in Australia, making 108, his sixth hundred in his 14th Test, in the innings victory at Brisbane. Tall and solidly built, Reid's method was orthodox and simple, based on quick and decisive movement of the feet into the correct position for every shot. After success in all grades of cricket, he made his first Test appearance against Pakistan at Auckland in 1978/9. He was dropped after this match but returned to make 123 not out against India in the second Test of 1980/1, his own third game, and at Colombo in the third Test against Sri Lanka (1983/4) he scored a match-winning 180. In 1984/5 he took heavy toll of Pakistan, scoring 106 and 97 in the Hyderabad and Karachi Tests, then 148 at Wellington and 158 not out at Auckland in the return series. In 1995 he took over, briefly, as New Zealand's national coach.

First-class career (1975–88): 5,650 runs (38.17) including 11 centuries, 6 wickets (36.83), and 125 dismissals (116 c., 9 st.)

Test matches (19): 1,296 runs (46.28) including 6 centuries, 0–7, and 9 catches

REID, John Richard

(b. 1928, Auckland) *Wellington, Otago, and New Zealand*

The best all-rounder produced by New Zealand before Richard Hadlee, John Reid, or 'Bogo', appeared in 58 consecutive official Tests, a world record. For 34 of these matches he was captain and he led New Zealand to her first three victories. He was a very strong, sturdily built, natural forcing right-handed batsman; a powerful driver and a sure hooker and cutter who never liked wasting time at the crease. Regularly having to face the job of redeeming lost causes, he often hit his side out of trouble. A medium-fast out-swing bowler, he turned sometimes to off-cutters, pitching an immaculate length. He was also a magnificent fielder, who sometimes served competently as a deputy wicket-keeper. At one time he held the New Zealand records simultaneously for making most runs, taking most wickets, holding most catches, scoring most centuries, and playing for and captaining the country most times, besides having made most runs in all first-class matches. He toured England in 1949, 1958, and 1965, South Africa in 1953/4 and 1961/2, and India and Pakistan in 1955/6 and 1965/6. At home he played against England in 1950/1, 1954/5, 1958/9, and 1962/3, West Indies in 1951/2 and 1955/6, South Africa in 1952/3 and 1963/4, and Pakistan in 1964/5. Altogether, he captained New Zealand in ten series between 1956 and 1965, several of unofficial standing. In England in 1949, his 1,488 runs (41.33) included four centuries, a fifty in his first Test, at Old Trafford, and an innings of 93 in his second, at The Oval. In the weak side of 1958, he stood head and shoulders above everyone else, amassing 1,429 runs (39.69), again including four centuries, besides taking 39 wickets (22.74). In South Africa in 1953/4 he became the first player to make 1,000 runs and take 50 wickets in a South African first-class season—1,012 runs (37.48) and 51 wickets (19.33). He also collected the first of his six Test centuries, 135 in the third match at Cape Town, when he added 176 with J. E. F. Beck for the fifth wicket in less than $2\frac{1}{2}$ hours. Against England in the first match at Dunedin in 1954/5, he took 4 for 36 in 27 overs. On the 1955/6 tour of India and Pakistan he headed the batting with 1,032 runs (54.31) and took 39 wickets (23.87), more wickets and runs than anyone else. Of this total, 493 runs (70.42) were made against India, including 119 not out in the third match, at Delhi, in which 222 was added in an unbroken stand for the third wicket with Bert Sutcliffe. When New Zealand won her first-ever official Test in the fourth match at Auckland against the West Indies in 1955/6, John Reid was top scorer with 84. In subsequent victories over South Africa in the third match at Cape Town and the fifth at Port Elizabeth in 1961/2, he again played a major part, making 92 at Cape Town and 69 at Port Elizabeth, besides taking eight wickets. In this series, he was by far the most successful all-rounder, making 546 runs (60.64) and taking 11 wickets (19.72), heading the bowling averages. On the whole first-class segment of the tour he eclipsed Denis Compton's record in South Africa, making 1,915 runs (68.39), including seven centuries, and taking 27 wickets (29.00). He continued to be the bane of South Africa, taking 6 for 60 in 35 overs against them in the second match at Dunedin in 1963/4. His career-highest was 296 for Wellington against Northern Districts in 1962/3—the second highest number of runs scored by one man in a day's play in New Zealand—and his best bowling in an innings 7 for 20 for Otago against Central Districts in 1956/7. Awarded an OBE, he settled in South Africa and became coach of Northern Transvaal, but he returned home to spend some of his retirement fishing in the South Island, and some of it as an ICC referee, quickly establishing a reputation for fairness and toughness.

First-class career (1947–65): 16,128 runs (41.35) including 39 centuries, 466 wickets (22.60), 240 catches, and 7 stumpings
Test matches (58): 3,428 runs (33.28) including 6 centuries, 85 wickets (33.35), 43 catches, and 1 stumping

REID, Richard Bruce

(b. 1958, Lower Hutt, Wellington) *Wellington, Auckland, and New Zealand*

The only son of the noted New Zealand captain, John Reid, this sturdily built batsman was distinctly his own man, no pale imitation of his famous father. Admittedly he was not as good, but he played some blistering innings for his provinces and in one-day internationals. Reid had a regrettably brief career—only 43 first-class games—but he was always entertaining, hitting one century and eleven fifties. In nine one-day internationals he scored 248 runs (27.55) and took a wicket (13.00).

First-class career (1979–92): 1,789 runs (24.84) and two wickets (7.00)

ROBERTS, Albert William

(b. 1909, Christchurch; d. 1978, Otago) *Canterbury, Otago, and New Zealand*

Albert Roberts was a right-arm medium-pace bowler who kept a good length, swung the ball and made it 'whip' off the pitch. As well as being a brilliant slip, he was also an effective batsman despite his peculiar technique—knees sagging, head apparently up—and represented New Zealand as a batsman in the first-ever Test at Christchurch. He was also selected for the first Test against South Africa in 1931/2 at Christchurch as a batsman when he scored 54. He toured England in 1937 primarily as a bowler, however, and, despite shoulder and finger injuries, captured 62 wickets (26.20), but also made 510 runs (25.50) and headed the Test averages with 142 runs (47.33). His career-highest was 181 for Canterbury against Wellington in 1931/2.

First-class career (1927–51): 3,645 runs (30.88) including 3 centuries, 167 wickets (28.51), and 78 catches
Test matches (5): 248 runs (27.55), 7 wickets (29.85), and 4 catches

ROBERTS, Andrew Duncan Glenn

(b. 1947, Te Aroha) *Northern Districts and New Zealand*

A right-handed all-rounder who batted in the middle order and bowled medium-pace, Andy Roberts made his Test début against India at Christchurch in 1976. His performances in this and the following Test were modest, but during the tour of Pakistan and India in 1976/7 he forced himself back into the side after missing the first Test against Pakistan. He played in the five remaining Tests of the tour, scoring 125 runs (31.25) against Pakistan and 112 (22.40) against India, which included his highest Test score, a determined 84 not out in the first innings of the second Test at Kanpur. In 1979 he hit 76 and 100 not out against the Pakistan touring team but was not selected for the Tests.

First-class career (1967–84): 5,865 runs (34.70) including 7 centuries, and 84 wickets (30.00)
Test matches (7): 254 runs (23.09), 4 wickets (45.50), and 4 catches

ROBERTS, Stuart James

(b. 1965, Christchurch) *Canterbury and New Zealand*

A right-hand batsman and, primarily, a right-arm fast bowler, Stuart Roberts has been a particularly popular player with the public and his contemporaries. Having represented New Zealand in one match at home in 1989/90 in a triangular one-day series against India and Australia, he briefly toured Pakistan in 1990, playing in one first-class match and a second one-day international. He also joined the 1994 tour of England as a replacement bowler. Roberts has given his province cheerful, loyal, and valuable service. In his two limited-overs games he scored one not out in his only innings but bowled only seven expensive overs (0 for 47).

First-class career (1985–   ): 367 runs (10.48), 166 wickets (28.90), and 13 catches

ROBERTSON, Gary Keith

(b. 1960, New Plymouth) *Central Districts and New Zealand*

Having played for New Zealand at under-23 level and on short tours to Australia for limited-overs games, Gary Robertson, a tall, right-arm fast-medium bowler and right-handed tail-ender, played two one-day internationals against England in 1983/4 and finally won a full Test cap against Australia in the third match at Auckland in 1985/6. In this, his sole Test, he scored 12 and took 1 for 91. An increasingly useful batsman, the highest of ten first-class fifties was 99 not out.

First-class career (1979–90): 1,875 runs (21.30), 252 wickets (29.63), and 22 catches

ROWE, Charles Gordon

(b. 1915, Glasgow) *Wellington, Central Districts, and New Zealand*

Born in Glasgow, Gordon Rowe was a right-handed batsman and medium-pace change-bowler whose sole Test appearance was in the first Test after the Second World War against Australia at Wellington in 1945/6, when he made a pair and held a catch. In a modest career he averaged 20.00 with the bat.

First-class career (1944–53): 380 runs (20.00)

RUTHERFORD, Kenneth Robert

(b. 1965, Dunedin) *Otago and New Zealand*

A slim, balanced and accomplished right-handed batsman, with dark, puckish features, who has sometimes opened, Ken Rutherford was also a fine fielder and occasional right-arm medium-paced swing bowler, had an unsuccessful tour of the West Indies in 1984 but in England in 1986 he

revealed his full potential with a dazzling innings of 317 against D. B. Close's XI at the Scarborough Festival, scoring his runs in only 4 hours. It was the highest-ever score at the Festival and the highest score by a New Zealander abroad. Already he had made a confident and attractive hundred against the England under-25 team (TCCB XI) at Edgbaston and, after making 63 in the second of the one-day internationals at Old Trafford, had played in the first Test at Lord's, making 0 and 24 not out. It was his only Test of that tour and he proved to be an inconsistent Test batsman despite the time he seemed to have to play the ball, a sure sign of class. The best of his three Test hundreds was 107 not out against England at Wellington in 1987/8. He also scored 102 against Australia and 105 against Sri Lanka, both in 1992/3. He captained New Zealand from 1992 to 1995, when he lost the job after a season of repeated setbacks for the national team. He had led them on his third tour to England with great good humour, nearly pulling off a memorable victory at Lord's.

First-class career (1982–   ): 10,433 runs (39.66) including 24 centuries, 22 wickets (45.45), and 124 catches
Test matches (56): 2,465 runs (27.08) including 3 centuries, 1 wicket (161.00), and 32 catches

SCOTT, Roy Hamilton

(b. 1917, Clyde) *Canterbury and New Zealand*

A competent right-handed batsman and medium-pace bowler, Roy Scott made his sole Test appearance against England at Christchurch in 1946/7, when he scored 18 and took 1 for 74.

First-class career (1940–55): 874 runs (24.97) and 94 wickets (25.47)

SCOTT, Verdun John

(b. 1916, Auckland; d. 1980, Auckland) *Auckland and New Zealand*

A tall, fidgety, right-handed opening batsman with the straight back of a guardsman, 'Scotty' or 'The Scotsman' had a short backlift but he was a fine on-side player, delivering most of his power from his huge wrists and forearms. This quiet, drily humorous man was also a good fielder, especially at first slip. He toured England in 1949, and at home played against Australia in 1945/6, England in 1946/7 and 1950/1, and the West Indies in 1951/2. On his England tour he made 1,572 runs (40.30), including four centuries, and contributed 178 runs (25.42) in the Tests.

Together with Bert Sutcliffe he gave New Zealand many good starts. His highest score in Tests was his last; a defiant 84 in over 4 hours in the second match at Auckland against the West Indies in 1951/2, which averted a rout. His career-highest was 204 against Otago in 1947/8. He also represented his country at Rugby League.

First-class career (1938–53): 5,620 runs (49.73) including 16 centuries, 10 wickets (27.10), and 42 catches

Test matches (10): 458 runs (28.62), 0–14, and 7 catches

SHRIMPTON, Michael John Froud

(b. 1940, Fielding) *Hawke's Bay, Central Districts, Northern Districts, and New Zealand*

A painstaking and confident right-handed batsman and occasional leg-break bowler, Michael Shrimpton toured Australia in 1973/4, and at home played against England in 1962/3, 1965/6, and 1970/1 and South Africa in 1963/4. In Australia he headed both batting and bowling averages with 426 runs (42.60) and seven wickets (24.28), but achieved little in the Tests. His highest Test score was 46 in the second match at Auckland against England in 1970/1, when he added 141 for the fifth wicket with Mark Burgess, a New Zealand record against England, but in his irregular Test career he failed to score on six occasions. His career-highest was 150 for Central Districts in 1962/3 and best bowling figures in an innings were 6 for 40 against Otago in 1969/70.

First-class career (1961–80): 5,812 runs (29.80) including 7 centuries, and 81 wickets (29.45)

Test matches (10): 265 runs (13.94), 5 wickets (31.60), and 2 catches

SIMS, Sir Arthur

(b. 1877, Spridlington, Lincolnshire, England; d. 1969, East Hoathly, Sussex) *Canterbury and London County*

A New Zealand captain before that country played Test cricket, a partner in the world-record eighth-wicket partnership, a multi-millionaire, a principal in the firm of Sims Cooper, and a philanthropist, Arthur Sims was, above all, a kindly man. He gave readily and generously to student scholarships, travelling professorships (for outstanding medical men from the Commonwealth), to cricket, and to a host of others. A right-hand batsman, he scored the first century for Christchurch Boys' High School, which subse-

quently produced sixteen Test players. His parents emigrated from Lincolnshire when he was 2. In 1894 he represented Canterbury and was New Zealand skipper in two matches against Australia in 1905. His career in industry took him all over the world, and he played for London County with W. G. Grace. In his last game with W.G. in 1912 Sims scored 127 not out. But he is best remembered as a more or less silent partner during Victor Trumper's ravishing 291 against Canterbury in 1914. Sims brought the Australia XI to New Zealand at his own expense. Canterbury made only 92, but the Australians lost their first 6 wickets for 118, the seventh at 209. Then Trumper scored his runs in 190 minutes (Sims 184 not out) and in that time 433 runs were scored. He played a full part in cricket's administration, being president of the New Zealand Cricket Council from 1936 to 1938 and the New Zealand representative on the Imperial Cricket Conference from 1926 to 1967. He played five matches for New Zealand, scoring 186 runs (23.25).

First-class career (1896–1914): 2,182 runs (26.28) and 19 wickets (21.52)

SINCLAIR, Barry Whitley

(b. 1936, Wellington) *Wellington and New Zealand*

Fair-haired and one of the smallest cricketers ever to appear in New Zealand, Barry Sinclair was a sound and often fluent right-handed batsman with an indomitable spirit, and an excellent field at cover. He was the immovable object of New Zealand's early middle batting for five concentrated seasons and captained the country against England and India. He toured India and Pakistan in 1964/5 and England in 1965, and at home played against England in 1962/3 and 1965/6 (captain), South Africa in 1963/4, Pakistan in 1964/5, and India in 1967/8 (captain). He established himself against South Africa in 1963/4, preventing a heavy defeat in the second match at Dunedin by scoring 52 out of 149. In the next Test, at Auckland, he made his Test highest, 138 (in a total of 263) in $5\frac{3}{4}$ hours. In India and Pakistan in 1964/5 he was rather disappointing with only 250 runs from six Tests, though he made 130 in the high-scoring second Test against Pakistan at Lahore. In England in 1965 he made 807 runs (36.68), but his only substantial Test innings was in the first match at Lord's, when runs were badly needed and he made 72 in less than $2\frac{1}{2}$ hours. In the third Test against England at Auckland in 1965/6 he scored 114 in 229 minutes when eight batsmen failed to reach 20, a characteristic piece of defiance, and headed the batting in the series with 218 runs (36.33).

First-class career (1955–71): 6,114 runs (32.87) including 6 centuries, 2 wickets (43.00), and 45 catches

Test matches (21): 1,148 runs (29.43) including 3 centuries, 2 wickets (16.00), and 8 catches

SMITH, Frank Brunton

(b. 1922, Rangiora) *Canterbury and New Zealand*

A stocky, cheerful, wristy right-handed batsman, Brun or 'Runty' Smith was a quick-eyed natural hitter, who tended to play with a cross-bat and his left foot insufficiently close to the ball; most of his runs came from cuts, hooks, and pulls. He was an excellent fielder, reliable in his catching and remorseless in pursuit of the hardest hit ball. He toured England in 1949, and at home played against England in 1946/7 and the West Indies in 1951/2. In England he made 1,008 runs (28.00) and at Headingley hit 96 in 2 hours and 54 not out in 50 minutes in the first Test.

First-class career (1943–53): 2,588 runs (33.17) including 4 centuries

Test matches (4): 237 runs (47.40) and 1 catch

SMITH, Horace Dennis

(b. 1913, Queensland; d. 1986, Christchurch) *Otago, Canterbury, and New Zealand*

A right-arm fast bowler from Queensland, Horace Smith played in only one Test, the first at Christchurch against England in 1932/3, scoring 4 and taking 1 for 113, something of an anticlimax after clean bowling Eddie Paynter with the first ball of his first over. His was a short first-class career.

First-class career (1931–4): 404 runs (22.44) and 17 wickets (33.52)

SMITH, Ian David Stockley

(b. 1957, Nelson) *Central Districts, Auckland, and New Zealand*

A neat, perky wicket-keeper and useful right-handed batsman, Ian Smith took over from Warren Lees as New Zealand's first-choice wicket-keeper on the tour of Australia in 1980/1. Some spirited innings in both the Tests and the one-day internationals justified his selection, as did his competent wicket-keeping, and not until he broke his finger during the Test in Christchurch against Australia in 1981/2 did his career

suffer a setback. He soon took over from Lees again and became one of the world's most reliable wicket-keeper/batsmen, excelling himself against England in 1983/4 with an innings of 113 not out in the third Test at Auckland, thus closing England out of a game they had to win to square the series. He toured England in 1983, 1986, and 1990; Australia in 1980, 1985, 1987, and 1989; plus the West Indies, India, Pakistan, and Sri Lanka. He maintained his spirit and fitness admirably. His greatest innings was played at Auckland against India in February 1990. Put in on a 'pitch like a lawn bowling green' New Zealand were 78 for 5 at lunch. Smith, with 38, then helped Richard Hadlee add 103 for the eighth wicket before producing a cascade of hooks, pulls, cuts, and drives to hit three sixes and twenty-three fours by the close of play, including 24 off one over from the fast bowler, Atul Wassan. His 173, off 136 balls, was the highest by a New Zealand wicket-keeper, and the highest by any Test number nine. The following season, 1990/1, he equalled a Test record by holding seven catches in an innings, against Sri Lanka at Hamilton. A tower of strength in one-day internationals too, he retired after New Zealand had reached the semi-final of the 1992 World Cup.

First-class career (1977–92): 5,570 runs (26.77) including 6 centuries, 0–38, and 452 dismissals (417 c., 35 st.)

Test matches (63): 1,815 runs (25.56) including 2 centuries, and 176 dismissals (168 c., 8 st.)

SMITH, Sydney Gordon

(b. 1881, San Fernando, Trinidad; d. 1963, Auckland) *Trinidad, West Indies, Northamptonshire, MCC, and Auckland*

New Zealand cricket owes much to the fact that his wife's asthma persuaded Sydney Smith to move to New Zealand in 1915. He was an assertive left-handed batsman, and a left-arm spin bowler. He had startling success for Trinidad and the West Indies against a team of English amateurs and against the MCC side in 1905. He headed the batting and bowling averages when he toured England in 1906. He settled in England in 1907 and, after qualifying, he became the first Northants batsman to reach 1,000 in a season and did the double in three seasons, also taking two hat-tricks. He captained Northants in 1913 and 1914 and in his last season, 1914, against Warwickshire, took wickets with four consecutive balls. He played for the Gentlemen four times, and once for the Rest of England. He added a new dimension to New Zealand cricket, taking plenty of wickets and making 256 in 330 minutes against Canterbury in a Plunket Shield match for Auckland. He played five matches for New Zealand in the pre-Test days and was New Zealand captain in his last appearance.

First-class career (1899–1926): 10,920 runs (31.28) including 14 centuries, 955 wickets (18.08), and 158 catches

SNEDDEN, Colin Alexander

(b. 1918, Auckland) *Auckland and New Zealand*

A medium-paced right-arm off-break bowler, and right-handed batsman, Colin Snedden, uncle of Martin and brother of Warwick (who also played for Auckland) played a Test against England at Christchurch in 1946/7, not batting and taking no wicket for 46. But for the war he would surely have played more.

First-class career (1938–49): 44 runs (8.80) and 31 wickets (25.41)

SNEDDEN, Martin Colin

(b. 1958, Mount Eden, Auckland) *Auckland and New Zealand*

Dark-haired and built for hard work, Martin Snedden bowled accurate, right-arm fast-medium and batted usefully left-handed, as his 70 runs at an average of 35 in two Tests at home against Australia in 1981/2 showed. In these two games his lively bowling also accounted for 11 Australian wickets. He toured Australia in successive seasons (1981/2 and 1982/3) to play in the one-day internationals. After playing against Sri Lanka at home in 1982/3, he toured England in 1983 but was unable to earn a regular Test place. An honest trier, he was more consistently effective as a one-day bowler, learning to change his pace and to bowl effective yorkers. On his second tour to England, in 1990, he played in all three Tests. His 23 first-class wickets on tour came at only 27 runs each. His father and grandfather played for Auckland and his uncle for New Zealand. Also a keen Rugby player, he is a qualified lawyer.

First-class career (1977–90): 1,792 runs (18.86), 387 wickets (25.62), and 55 catches

Test matches (25): 327 runs (14.86), 58 wickets (37.91), and 7 catches

SPARLING, John Trevor

(b. 1938, Auckland) *Auckland and New Zealand*

A short, fair-haired all-rounder, John Sparling was a gallant and dogged right-handed batsman, a useful off-spin bowler and very good field. He toured England in 1958 and South Africa in 1961/2, and at home played against England in 1958/9 and 1962/3, and South Africa in 1963/4. Showing promise on his England tour—making 513 runs, taking 38 wickets and holding 13 catches in 21 matches—he had his twentieth birthday on the first day of the fourth Test at Old Trafford, when he made a dour 50 in about 3 hours. Never again did he reach 50, or even achieve a bowling breakthrough in official Tests. His career-highest score was 105 against Canterbury in 1959/60, in which match he also took 7 for 98.

First-class career (1956–71): 4,606 runs (24.37) including 2 centuries, 318 wickets (22.71), and 86 catches

Test matches (11): 229 runs (12.72), 5 wickets (65.40), and 3 catches

STIRLING, Derek Alexander

(b. 1961, Wellington) *Central Districts, Wellington, and New Zealand*

Tall, dark, and strapping, Derek Stirling had already put in some impressive stints of fast-medium bowling in domestic cricket as well as having a successful season in Scotland in 1984, before getting his first taste of international cricket in Pakistan in 1984/5. He played in all three Tests, bowling with determination and stamina on unresponsive wickets, with a best performance of 4 for 88 in the third Test at Karachi. Later in 1984/5, Stirling also toured the West Indies and after an uncertain start, bowled well later in the tour, finishing with 13 first-class wickets at 23 and playing in the third Test. Although he was not chosen for New Zealand's next tour, to Australia, his 26 first-class wickets in the 1985/6 season earned him a place on the tour to England in 1986. Forcing his way into the Test team for the last two games, he had a notable success at Trent Bridge, taking 3 for 110 in the match, including vital wickets when England looked like saving the game, and scored 26, including two sixes, in a crucial New Zealand tail-end revival. On a quick wicket at The Oval, however, he bowled too short and was savaged for 24 off one over by Ian Botham.

STOTT

First-class career (1981–92): 1,651 runs (21.72), 206 wickets (33.72), and 27 catches
Test matches (6): 108 runs (15.42), 13 wickets (46.23), and 1 catch

STOTT, Leslie Warren

(b. 1946, Rochdale, England) *Auckland*

Warren Stott gave his adopted province signal service for 14 years and later served as a provincial selector and cricket broadcaster. He was an accurate medium-paced right-arm bowler, who took five wickets in an innings eight times in his 63 appearances, with a best of 6 for 68 and was sometimes very useful as a tail-end batsman. He took 3 wickets (16.00) in his only one-day international.

First-class career (1969–84): 591 runs (12.06) and 214 wickets (24.95)

SU'A, Murphy Logo

(b. 1966, Wanganui) *Northern Districts, Auckland, and New Zealand*

A strong and lively left-arm over-the-wicket bowler and aggressive left-hand tail-ender, Su'a started his first-class career in 1988/9 but after two years with very moderate success he moved to Auckland where, in his first season he had 28 wickets from his nine matches. His parents had moved to New Zealand from Western Samoa. He was picked for the first time against England at home in 1991/2, capturing eight wickets in his first two Tests. He subsequently toured Zimbabwe and Sri Lanka (1992/3) and took 5 for 85 in Zimbabwe's first innings at Harare, including a spell of 3 for 0 in seven balls. Such inspirational bursts have been a feature of Su'a's cricket. He took 5 for 73 against Pakistan at Hamilton in January 1993 including four of the top six wickets, swinging the ball dangerously both ways, but a drubbing by the Australian batsmen later that season set him back. He showed his versatility by bowling a few overs of left-arm spin against England at Wellington. He has also played in five one-day internationals scoring 17 runs (17.00) and taking 3 wickets (49.00).

First-class career (1988–): 678 runs (16.95), 120 wickets (31.62), and 9 catches
Test matches (13): 165 runs (12.69), 36 wickets (38.25), and 8 catches

SUTCLIFFE, Bert

(b. 1923, Auckland) *Auckland, Otago, Northern Districts, and New Zealand*

Craggy-jawed and fair-haired, Bert Sutcliffe was probably, with Neil Harvey, the best left-handed batsman of his generation in the world. His stroke-play was at once enterprising and cultured: his off- and cover-driving, hooking and pulling were models for a copy-book. This great opening batsman was genuinely modest yet also a character of sunny optimism. A left-arm slow bowler with a deceptive quicker ball, he was also rapid, clean and safe in the field. He became famous overnight by scoring 197 and 128 for Otago against MCC at Dunedin in 1946/7; and the following week, at Christchurch in his first Test, he made 58. During the next 20 years he proceeded to collect one New Zealand batting record after another. He toured England in 1949, 1958, and 1965, South Africa in 1953/4, and India and Pakistan in 1955/6 and 1965/6. At home he played against England in 1946/7, 1950/1, 1954/5, and 1958/9, the West Indies in 1951/2 and 1955/6, and South Africa in 1953/4. He was soon concerned in several records in New Zealand first-class cricket: for Auckland against Canterbury in 1948/9, he shared in opening stands of 220 and 286 with Don Taylor, a world record. Another record was an opening partnership of 373 with L. Watt, for Otago against Auckland in 1950/1. He made 355 for Otago against Auckland in 1949/50 only to exceed this score with 385 against Canterbury in 1952/3, which remains the highest-ever by a New Zealander. For more than a decade his 230 not out (in 9 hours) against India in the third Test at New Delhi in 1955/6, when he added 222 unbroken for the third wicket with John Reid, remained the highest score by a New Zealander in a Test. And in England in 1949 he amassed 2,627 runs (59.70), another New Zealand record on a tour, including seven centuries. When he hit 243 and 100 not out against Essex at Southend, it was the fourth time he had hit a century in each innings of a match. At Worcester in the opening match of the 1958 tour he hit 139, but a broken wrist—incurred while fielding against MCC at Lord's—impeded his progress. He emerged from retirement a few months before the 1965 tour, having made 151 not out brilliantly against India in the second Test at Calcutta. In the first Test at Edgbaston he was hit on the ear, while ducking into a ball from Fred Trueman and, although he returned after treatment to score 53, he had to miss most of the remainder of the tour. His only Test century at home against England was 116 in the first match at Christchurch in 1950/1. He captained New Zealand against the visiting West Indies in 1951/2 with little success. On touring South Africa in 1953/4, he took over the captaincy when Geoff Rabone became incapacitated. Specializing as a middle-order batsman at that time in order to counteract the weakness there, he made more runs than anyone else: in all first-class matches he scored 1,155 runs (46.20) including 305 (38.12) in the Tests. Opening the batting again in the five Tests in India in 1955 he amassed 611 runs (87.28). Successive Test innings brought him 137 not out, 73, 37, and 230 not out! In retirement Bert Sutcliffe proved himself a superb coach and was awarded an MBE.

First-class career (1941–66): 17,447 runs (47.41) including 44 centuries, 86 wickets (38.05), 160 catches, and 1 stumping

Test matches (42): 2,727 runs (40.10) including 5 centuries, 4 wickets (86.00), and 20 catches

TAYLOR, Bruce Richard

(b. 1943, Canterbury) *Canterbury, Wellington, and New Zealand*

A 6 ft. 3 in. all-rounder of outstanding quality, Bruce Taylor was an attractive, punishing left-handed batsman and an accurate right-arm fast-medium bowler with a command of swing both ways and a nasty bouncer. No matter what the state of the pitch or the ball, he would, with his high action, coax out at least a little movement. He was also an eager and determined field, and a character who enjoyed life to the full off the field. On his Test début against India at Calcutta in 1964/5 he created a sensation, hitting 105 freely in 158 minutes, adding 163 with Bert Sutcliffe for the seventh wicket, and then proceeding to take five for 86 in India's first innings. Not only was this his first century in first-class cricket, but he achieved the record of being the only player to score a hundred and take five wickets in an innings in his first Test. In the next match at Bombay he secured 5 for 26, India being routed for 88, and in his first Test against Pakistan at Rawalpindi he slammed 76 in 88 minutes in a total of 175. He visited England in 1965, 1969, and 1973, India and Pakistan again in 1969/70, and the West Indies in 1971/2. At home he played against England in 1965/6, India in 1967/8, West Indies in 1968/9, and Pakistan in 1972/3. He endured mixed fortune in his three England tours. Each time he exceeded 30 wickets in the short first-class programmes, but only in 1969 was his bowling a vital force in the Tests, especially in the last match at The Oval when, after injury had curtailed his appearances, he took 4 for 47 in the first innings. His best batting was at Lord's in 1965, his first Test in England, when he hit 51 after coming in with the score 62 for 6. When the West Indies visited New Zealand in 1968/9 he failed as a bowler, but headed the batting averages with 209 runs (69.66), including a swashbuckling 124 in the first Test at Auckland after six wickets had gone cheaply. His first 50 took 30 minutes and his century, reached with a six into the stand, 86 minutes. In the West Indies his bowling accounted for 27 wickets (17.70) in four Tests, including 7 for 74 in the first innings at Bridgetown. At home against Pakistan he took 13 wickets in three Tests, taking his tally past 100. He 'retired' in 1973, but returned successfully in 1978/9. His career-highest score was 173 for Wellington against Otago in 1972/3.

First-class career (1963–80): 4,579 runs (24.75) including 4 centuries, 422 wickets (25.13), and 66 catches

Test matches (30): 898 runs (20.40) including 2 centuries, 111 wickets (26.60), and 10 catches

TAYLOR, Donald Dougald

(b. 1923, Auckland; d. 1980, Auckland) *Auckland, Warwickshire, and New Zealand*

An attractive, enterprising right-handed batsman with strokes all round the wicket, occasional off-break bowler and good field, Don Taylor played against England in 1946/7 and the West Indies in 1955/6. Against the latter in the third match at Wellington, when he had been recalled to Tests after an interval of nine years, he scored 43 and 77 enterprisingly when runs were badly needed. For Auckland against Canterbury in 1948/9 he made 99 and 143, his career-highest, sharing in opening stands of 220 and 286 with Bert Sutcliffe, a world record. He appeared for Warwickshire as a professional from 1949 until 1953.

First-class career (1946–61): 3,772 runs (23.28) including 1 century, 32 wickets (33.21), and 62 catches

Test matches (3): 159 runs (31.80) and 2 catches

THOMSON, Graeme Bruce

(b. 1951, Invercargill) *Otago*

Graeme Thomson toured England in 1978, taking 15 wickets at 34 runs each with his left-arm medium pace after being injured early on the tour. He did not contend for an international place thereafter. He was a lower-order, left-handed batsman.

First-class career (1974–81): 340 runs (9.18), 110 wickets (28.90), and 23 catches

THOMSON, Keith

(b. 1941, Methven) *Canterbury and New Zealand*

A solid right-handed batsman, Keith Thomson played in two Tests against India in 1967/8, making 69 on his début at Christchurch. His career-highest was 136 not out against Northern Districts in 1968/9. He represented his country also at hockey.

First-class career (1959–74): 3,134 runs (28.23) including 5 centuries

Test matches (2): 94 runs (31.33) and 1–9

THOMSON, Shane Alexander

(b. 1969, Hamilton) *Northern Districts and New Zealand*

A squarely built, stylish right-handed all-rounder with very fair hair and a ready smile, Shane Thomson appeared first in a Test match when he had just celebrated his twenty-first birthday. All the mothers who watched the match on television were captivated by his looks! He has since belied his youthful appearance by mature batting, particularly in a crisis, and has bowled with success in two styles, first as a fast-medium bowler and then, after a back injury, as a slow off-spinner. He first appeared against India in 1989/90 and was an immediate success, subsequently touring England, although it was not until his second tour to England in 1994 that he played his first Test cricket overseas. He sealed his place with an attractive and brilliant maiden Test century, 120 not out, against Pakistan at Christchurch in February 1994, sharing a match-winning partnership with Bryan Young against long odds and hostile bowling from Wasim Akram and Waqar Younis. In England he had a useful tour, with 408 runs in ten first-class matches, including a belligerent and fluent 69 at Lord's, an innings ending in a run out. He made 38 not out in the second innings and bowled his off-breaks tidily, if without great venom, in both innings. This was an art, however, which he was still learning. In 24 one-day internationals he has scored 604 runs (30.10) and taken 19 wickets.

First-class career (1977–): 3,654 runs (41.05) including 6 centuries, 94 wickets (39.79), and 33 catches

Test matches (17): 856 runs (45.05) including 1 century, 19 wickets (45.05), and 7 catches

TINDILL, Eric William Thomas

(b. 1910, Nelson) *Wellington and New Zealand*

A lively left-handed batsman who often opened the innings, and a very competent wicket-keeper, Eric Tindill toured England in 1937, and at home played against Australia in 1945/6 and England in 1946/7. In first-class matches on his England tour, he averaged 18.34 with the bat and claimed 45 dismissals. The highest score of his career was 149 against Auckland in 1948/9. A versatile games player, he achieved his greatest renown as an All Black Rugby footballer.

First-class career (1933–50): 3,127 runs (30.35) including 6 centuries, and 128 dismissals (95 c., 33 st.)

Test matches (5): 73 runs (9.12) and 7 dismissals (6 c., 1 st.)

TROUP, Gary Bertram

(b. 1952, Auckland) *Auckland and New Zealand*

Tall and strong, a left-arm fast-medium bowler, Gary Troup toured India and Pakistan in 1976/7. In his sole Test on the tour, the second against India at Kanpur, he took 1 for 116, and was also unsuccessful at home against Pakistan in 1978, but his steady line and length proved useful to New Zealand in the 1979 Prudential World Cup and in the semi-final against England he was New Zealand's second most economical bowler. In 1979/80 he was outstanding against the West Indies, taking 18 wickets in three Tests. Injured after a good start to the 1980/1 tour of Australia, he returned there for the 1982/3 one-day internationals and, as one of New Zealand cricket's hardy perennials, returned to the Test team in the West Indies in 1984/5 and again in 1985/6 against Australia at home.

First-class career (1974–87): 925 runs (12.17), 272 wickets (27.72), and 39 catches

Test matches (15): 55 runs (4.58), 39 wickets (37.28), and 2 catches

TRUSCOTT, Peter Bennetts

(b. 1941, Pahiatua) *Wellington and New Zealand*

In a short first-class career as a right-handed opening batsman Peter Truscott made a single

Test appearance against Pakistan in the third match at Christchurch in 1964/5, scoring 3 and 26 and holding 1 catch. His career-highest was 165 for New Zealand under-23 against Auckland in 1963/4.

First-class career (1961–6): 870 runs (26.66) including 1 century

TURNER, Glenn Maitland

(b. 1947, Dunedin) *Otago, Worcestershire, Northern Districts, and New Zealand*

In two senses the most professional cricketer ever produced by New Zealand, Glenn Turner made himself a household name throughout the cricket world by dedicating himself to cricket from an early age and making best possible use of a considerable natural ability. Unswervingly single-minded in his pursuit of runs, unashamedly ambitious and often impatient of amateur administrators in New Zealand, his career with Worcestershire was the key to his success everywhere else. He deliberately enrolled in the hard school of county cricket, learned his lessons quickly and never forgot them. Almost frail-looking, pale-faced, and serious-minded, Turner was a right-handed opening batsman who played immaculately straight, defended with a solidity of technique which few contemporary players have matched, and, although a limited attacking batsman in his earlier days, eventually played every shot on demand and scored as fast as anyone when necessary. His most characteristic strokes were the off-drive and a beautifully timed drive to mid-wicket with the face of the bat turned on impact. He was also a high-class fielder either at slip or in the covers. Making his début for Otago in 1964/5 while still a schoolboy, he was recommended to Warwickshire by Billy Ibadulla, who coached in New Zealand, but was accepted by Worcestershire because their neighbours already had a full supply of overseas players. Worcestershire never had a more consistent performer than Glenn Turner, whose loyalty to his county was total. First appearing for them in 1967, he was qualified to play regularly in 1968, scored ten centuries in making 2,379 runs in 1970 (a county record), and hit centuries against the 16 other counties plus one for New Zealand against his own! In 1973 he scored 2,416 runs (67.11), including 1,018 runs (78.30) for the New Zealand touring team by the end of May, the first time this had been achieved in England since Bill Edrich did it in 1938. His Test career began against the West Indies in Auckland in February 1969 with a duck but he was soon scoring at the highest level as consistently as he did in all other forms of cricket. The broader canvas of the five-day match suited his tempo and his temperament, giving a painstaking and cultured craftsman the opportunity to build his innings steadily, soberly and coolly. He twice carried his bat through the completed innings of a Test match, and on a third occasion was last man out. He scored 43 not out in a total of 131 against England at Lord's in 1969, and 223 not out in a total of 386 against the West Indies at Kingston in 1971/2. On this tour of the Caribbean Turner hit four double centuries including two innings of 259 in successive matches at Georgetown, first against Guyana and then against the West Indies. Apart from this tour and his official visits to England in 1969, 1973, and for the Prudential World Cups of 1975 and 1979 (he missed the 1978 tour because he wanted to concentrate on his benefit with Worcestershire), he toured Australia twice (1973/4 and 1982/3) and India and Pakistan twice (1976/7 as captain). He captained New Zealand in ten Tests, relinquishing the job after a disagreement with cricket officials. He hit two centuries in the same match on four occasions: 122 and 128 against Warwickshire at Edgbaston in 1972; 101 and 110 not out for New Zealand against Australia at Christchurch in 1974 when Australia lost to New Zealand for the first time; 135 and 108 for Otago against Northern Districts in 1974/5 at Gisborne, and 105 and 186 not out for Otago against Central Districts at Dunedin in the same season. In 1975/6 he scored 1,244 runs (77.75), a record aggregate for a New Zealand season. Against Glamorgan at Swansea in 1977 he scored 141 not out in Worcestershire's total of 169, 83.4 per cent of the total, a first-class record. In 1982 he became only the nineteenth player, and only the second non-Englishman, to score 100 first-class hundreds. He did so in style, making 311 not out against Warwickshire at Worcester, where 33 of his 100 centuries had been scored. His goal achieved, he retired from county cricket, but made himself available again to New Zealand's selectors and toured Australia in 1982/3. He scored 1,000 runs in a season 18 times (15 in England). He has been New Zealand's most prolific player, yet if you passed this slight, pale figure in a crowd you might think him rather downtrodden. He managed New Zealand's teams in Australia (1985/6) and in England in 1986. His younger brother, Greg, became a successful professional golfer and Glenn returned to the front line of New Zealand cricket when reappointed as manager in 1995.

First-class career (1964–83): 34,346 runs (49.70) including 103 centuries, 5 wickets (37.80), and 410 catches

Test matches (41): 2,991 runs (44.64) including 7 centuries, 0–5, and 42 catches

UPHAM, Ernest Frederick

(b. 1873, Wellington; d. 1935, Paekakariki) *Wellington and New Zealand*

For almost 20 years Ernie Upham, a medium-fast right-arm bowler, picked up wickets like a Richard Hadlee. Unerring accuracy was the key to his great success. In only 49 games he averaged 5.4 wickets a match. In two games against the MCC touring team in 1906/7 he took 6 for 78 and 6 for 84, and against the same side, playing for Wellington, he had 7 for 78. He was invited at the turn of the century to go to England by an English umpire, Jim Phillips, who said 'he would be welcomed by any county side'. In 1901 Canterbury were left the simple task of scoring 92 to win against Wellington and reached 53 for no wicket. Then Upham set to work. Canterbury duly got home by three wickets but only after Upham had taken 7 for 24. In his final appearance, aged 36, he took 6 for 52 against Canterbury.

First-class career: (1892–1910): 716 runs (11.93) and 265 wickets (16.65)

VANCE, Robert Howard

(b. 1955, Wellington) *Wellington and New Zealand*

Like his father, Bob, Robert Vance gave Wellington cricket loyal and invaluable service, first as a wicket-keeper, then as an opening right-hand batsman and as a respected captain. His total of almost 7,000 runs is unusually large for a New Zealander. His top score was 254 not out, against Northern Districts in 1988/9. He made 119 appearances for his province. His Tests were played relatively late in his career, against England (1987/8) and Pakistan (1988/9) at home, and in Australia in 1989/90. He began with a sound and assured innings of 47 against England on his home ground, marked by positive running between the wickets, but, ironically, he was run out and did not establish a regular place, despite a calm and valuable innings of 68 against Pakistan at Auckland, made in the face of a Pakistan total of over 600. His father, R. A. Vance, gave many years of service to Wellington and New Zealand

cricket and was chairman of the Board of Control. The main stand at the Basin Reserve was named in his honour, rightly so for his vision and drive had transformed a once windy, cheerless ground into a delightful arena for cricket.

First-class career (1976–91): 6,995 runs (32.80) including 12 centuries, and 4 wickets (58.00)

Test matches (4): 207 runs (29.57)

VAUGHAN, Dr Justin Thomas Caldwell

(b. 1967, Hereford, England) *Auckland, Gloucestershire, and New Zealand*

A solid left-hand bat and a right-arm medium-pace bowler, Justin Vaughan was Auckland's captain during the 1993/4 season. His only Test was as one of the replacements for those who returned home in 1992/3 as a result of the bomb blast in Colombo. He scored 17 and 0 not out, batting at number seven, and had bowling figures of 0 for 56 from 14 overs. His British birth enabled him to play a season for Gloucestershire in 1992 and after recovering from a knee injury he proved a valuable member of the team, scoring 99 against Northamptonshire and 450 runs in his 16 innings. He would have been welcomed back had not his Test appearance turned him officially into an 'overseas' player. A qualified doctor, he gave up his job as a house surgeon at an Auckland hospital to concentrate for a time on his cricket. He first made his name by scoring 106 not out in his maiden first-class innings after coming in to bat against Wellington at 29 for five. He was out handled ball against England when playing for New Zealand's 'emerging players' in 1991/2. He has played in 3 one-day internationals scoring 51 runs (17.00) and taking no wickets at a cost of 53 runs.

First-class career (1989–): 2,020 runs (33.70), 60 wickets (30.53), and 50 catches

VIVIAN, Graham Ellery

(b. 1946, Auckland) *Auckland and New Zealand*

A left-handed stroke-playing batsman, superb deep fielder and a leg-spin bowler with a jerky action who delivered an exotic mixture of orthodox leg-breaks, sharp 'wrong 'uns' and the occasional double-bouncer, Graham Vivian toured England in 1965 at the age of 19. His selection followed a late search for a leg-spinner, but he found the pitches unsuitable and did not earn a Test place. He toured India and Pakistan in 1964/5 and in his first and only Test against India, in the second match at Calcutta, hit 43, adding 81 in 83 minutes with Vic Pollard for the eighth wicket. In the West Indies in 1971/2 he set a new high standard in fielding, but in nine matches made only 204 runs and took only four wickets, his Test record being particularly disappointing. Problems with his eyesight caused his retirement in 1979. His career-highest was 137 not out for New Zealand against Victoria in 1969/70 and best bowling in an innings 5 for 59 for Auckland against Central Districts in 1967/8. An excellent captain of Auckland, he came close to captaining New Zealand as well. He is the son of H. G. Vivian, also a Test player.

First-class career (1964–79): 3,259 runs (28.33) including 3 centuries, 58 wickets (38.00), and 41 catches

Test matches (5): 110 runs (18.33), 1–107, and 3 catches

VIVIAN, Henry Gifford

(b. 1912, Auckland; d. 1983, Auckland) *Auckland and New Zealand*

This attractive left-handed batsman had a sound defence and superb drive, and was particularly quick to punish the loose ball. A left-arm leg-spin bowler with an easy and rhythmical action and able to turn the ball sharply from a very good length, he was also a very alert field. Giff Vivian toured England in 1931 and made his Test début, the second match at The Oval, at the age of 18 years and 267 days. He took the wickets of Sutcliffe and Ames and top-scored with 51 in the second innings, when New Zealand were losing by an innings, hitting a six off Hedley Verity. On the tour he made 1,002 runs (30.36). This included 136 against Oxford and 101 (including four sixes) against the Champions, Yorkshire. He also took 64 wickets (23.75) on the tour. In his first and only Test against South Africa, in the second match at Wellington in 1931/2, he hit 100 and 73, the highest score in each innings. He also took 4 for 68 in a total of 410, but the South Africans won comfortably. Back in England in 1937 he made 1,118 runs (29.42) and took 49 wickets (36.91) and as an opener made 194 runs in the Tests (32.33), but his eight wickets (42.25) were expensive. His career-highest was 165 against Wellington in 1931/2 and best bowling 6 for 49 (10 for 108 in the match) against Wellington in 1938/9.

First-class career (1930–9): 4,443 runs (34.71) including 6 centuries, 223 wickets (27.62), and 71 catches

Test matches (7): 421 runs (42.10) including 1 century, 17 wickets (37.23), and 4 catches

WADSWORTH, Kenneth John

(b. 1946, Nelson; d. 1976, Nelson) *Central Districts, Canterbury and New Zealand*

A wicket-keeper who was made not born, but who was a safe athletic catcher standing back and who improved steadily, Ken Wadsworth was also a confident and aggressive right-handed batsman, who could, however, defend doggedly if necessary. Strongly built with a mass of fair hair, he was a pugnacious cricketer who hated losing. He was his country's regular 'keeper from 1969 until 1976, and when he died of cancer at the age of 29 he had not reached his peak. He toured England in 1969 and 1973, India and Pakistan in 1969/70, the West Indies in 1971/2, and Australia in 1973/4. At home he played against England in 1970/1 and 1974/5, Pakistan in 1973/4, Australia in 1973/4, and India in 1975/6. He was particularly successful behind the stumps on his two England tours, capturing 17 victims in the six Tests. His highest score in Tests was 80 in the first match at Melbourne against Australia in 1973/4. In the first match against the West Indies at Kingston in 1971/2, he made 78, with Glenn Turner adding 220 doggedly in about 5 hours, the country's record for the sixth wicket. His number of dismissals both in first-class and Test matches constituted records for New Zealand. He scored 103 for South Island against the West Indies at Dunedin in 1968/9 and 117 in the Shell Trophy final 1975/6. Ken Wadsworth was an inspiration to all those with whom he played, and his funeral at Nelson was attended by cricketers from the length and breadth of the country.

First-class career (1968–76): 3,664 runs (25.62) including 2 centuries, and 291 dismissals (265 c., 26 st.)

Test matches (33): 1,010 runs (21.48) and 96 dismissals (92 c., 4 st.)

WALLACE, Walter Mervyn

(b. 1916, Auckland) *Auckland and New Zealand*

Under average height and of hawklike visage, Mervyn Wallace, or 'Flip', was a right-handed attacking batsman with a wide range of attractive strokes, his cover-driving being immaculate, and his pulling and hooking exuberant, and an excellent field, particularly at cover-point. He toured England in 1937 and as vice-captain in 1949, and at home played against Australia in 1945/6, England in 1946/7 and 1950/1, and also captained the tour of South Africa in 1952/3. He headed the batting on the 1937 tour with 1,641 runs (41.02), and at Lord's on his Test début made 52 (including two pulls for six) and 56. On the 1949 tour he hit 910 runs before the end of May, but fell away so much that he did not reach his 1,000 runs until early July. Altogether on that tour he made 1,722 runs (49.20), including five centuries. In the last Test at The Oval his 55 and 58 were considerable factors in staving off defeat. His Test-highest was a solid 66 against England in the first match at Christchurch in 1950/1 in a high-scoring match. Despite his disappointments in Tests, he remained a cheerful enthusiast. His first-class career was more fruitful, with a career-highest of 211 against Canterbury in 1939/40.

First-class career (1933–61): 7,757 runs (44.32) including 17 centuries, and 68 catches

Test matches (13): 439 runs (20.90), 0–5, and 5 catches

WALMSLEY, Kerry Peter

(b. 1973, Dunedin) *Auckland and New Zealand*

A 6ft. 5in. blond-haired fast bowler, Kerry Walmsley came suddenly to prominence during a disastrous season for New Zealand cricket. Although his country were beaten at home by Sri Lanka, he bowled with fire and stamina in his first two Tests at Napier and Dunedin, with the experience of only three first-class matches behind him. He was, however, warned by the referee for bad language during his first Test.

First-class career (1994–   ): 36 runs (6.00) and 20 wickets (35.05)

Test matches (2): 8 runs (2.66) and 7 wickets (49.14)

WARD, John Thomas

(b. 1937, Timaru) *Canterbury and New Zealand*

A capable specialist wicket-keeper and, for his moderate capabilities, often an effective night-watchman, John Ward toured England in 1958 and 1965 as a reserve 'keeper playing in only one Test. He also went to India in 1964/5, when he played in four Tests before injury prevented him from continuing on the Pakistan leg of the tour. At home he appeared once each against South Africa in 1963/4, Pakistan in 1964/5 and India in 1967/8. He made his first tour, to South Africa, after only two first-class matches, including one for South Island in a trial match when he held five catches in the first innings.

First-class career (1957–71): 1,117 runs (12.41) and 257 dismissals (230 c., 27 st.)

Test matches (8): 75 runs (12.50) and 17 dismissals (16 c., 1 st.)

WATSON, William

(b. 1965, Auckland) *Auckland and New Zealand*

A tall, athletic, right-arm fast-medium bowler and tail-end right-handed batsman, Willie Watson was granted valuable experience by New Zealand's farsighted selectors when chosen for the tour of England in 1986 at the age of 20 and after very little first-class experience. A startling return of 7 for 23, including a hat-trick in the Shell Cup against Otago in 1984/5 had underlined his potential and in this, his first season, he took 24 first-class wickets. An injury to Ewan Chatfield gave him the chance of a first Test cap at Lord's and with his high action, lively pace and good control, he made a favourable impression, taking 2 for 70 in the first innings. Two more wickets for 51 followed in the next Test at Trent Bridge and it seemed that this keen young player was capable of becoming one of the successors to Richard Hadlee. He never quite lived up to that early promise but became a steady and reliably negative one-day bowler in 61 internationals in which he took 74 wickets (30.36). He suffered various injuries but always produced hard-working efforts in Tests. Apart from England he played abroad in Australia, India, Pakistan (three Tests in 1990), and Zimbabwe.

First-class career (1985–   ): 330 runs (7.17), 242 wickets (28.35), and 21 catches

Test matches (15): 60 runs (5.00), 40 wickets (34.67), and 4 catches

WATT, Leslie

(b. 1924, Otago) *Otago and New Zealand*

A right-handed batsman of monumental patience, Leslie Watt expected the same quality to be shown by spectators! He played in a sole Test, the first match against England at Dunedin in 1954/5, scoring 0 and 2. He achieved fame when he made his career-highest, 96 in 6 hours, against Auckland in 1950/1, establishing the record first-wicket stand of 373 with Bert Sutcliffe.

First-class career (1942–63): 1,972 runs (23.47)

WEBB, Murray George

(b. 1947, Invercargill) *Otago, Canterbury, and New Zealand*

Bounding in ferociously, tall and long-haired, Murray Webb was a hostile right-arm fast bowler who toured the West Indies in 1971/2, when the heat and heartless pitches took the sting out of his bowling. Off the field he devoted much of his time to a thesis for an MA degree. He played also at home against England in 1970/1 and Australia in 1973/4 but was superseded by the Hadlee brothers. His best bowling in an innings was 7 for 49 for Otago against Wellington in 1971/2.

First-class career (1969–74): 202 runs (10.10) and 133 wickets (23.39)

Test matches (3): 12 runs (6.00) and 4 wickets (117.75)

WEBB, Peter Neil

(b. 1957, Auckland) *Auckland and New Zealand*

Fair-haired and stocky, Peter Webb was a right-handed batsman, excellent fielder and occasional wicket-keeper who played his first two Tests against the West Indies in 1979/80, then returned to international cricket in 1982/3 when selected to tour Australia. He went to England in 1986 to learn the art of the groundsman, but remained captain of Auckland for another season.

First-class career (1976–87): 3,671 runs (33.07) including 5 centuries, 4 wickets (44.25), and 55 dismissals (53 c., 2 st.)

Test matches (2): 11 runs (3.66) and 2 catches

WEBB, Richard John

(b. 1952, Invercargill) *Otago*

A right-hand batsman and right-arm fast-medium bowler, Richard Webb's brother, Murray, played Test cricket, but he himself in just one one-day international—successfully so—for he took 4 wickets (26.25) and scored 6 not out. He appeared in 25 matches for Otago. His best performance was against Canterbury in 1984/5 when he took 6 for 20.

First-class career (1975–85): 79 runs (4.38) and 67 wickets (27.79)

WEIR, Gordon Lindsay

(b. 1908, Auckland) *Auckland and New Zealand*

Although thinning hair and a serious mien made him look older than his years, Lindsay, or 'Dad', Weir was an active as well as a sound right-handed batsman, and a medium-pace change-bowler who was unfailingly energetic in the field. He toured England in 1931 and 1937, and at home played against England in 1929/30 and 1932/3 and South Africa in 1931/2. On his first England tour he made 1,035 runs (25.87) and took 27 wickets (34.70), including knocks of 37 and 40 and 3 for 38 (as opening bowler with Ian Cromb at Lord's). In 1937, although he did not do

himself justice in making 893 runs (26.26) and taking 14 wickets (73.75), he hit 134 not out (including four sixes) at Worcester in $2\frac{3}{4}$ hours in a losing cause. At Auckland in the fourth match against England in 1929/30 he scored 63 in a run feast. In New Zealand's first Test against South Africa, at Christchurch in 1931/2, he hit 46 and, on a worn pitch, 74 not out in a total of 146. His career-highest was 191 against Otago in 1935/6 and his best bowling figures in an innings, 6 for 56 against Wellington in 1940/1.

First-class career (1927–47): 5,022 runs (32.19) including 10 centuries, and 107 wickets (37.35)

Test matches (11): 416 runs (29.71), 7 wickets (29.85), and 3 catches

WHITE, David John

(b. 1961, Gisborne) *Northern Districts and New Zealand*

A loyal and successful servant of Northern Districts cricket, David White was a solid right-hand batsman and an occasional right-arm off-break bowler, who scored four centuries and twenty-two fifties. He toured Pakistan with the New Zealand team in 1990 and had a brief recall—for an injured player—in Australia in 1993/4, but he was injured himself in his first game. Three one-day internationals brought him 37 runs (12.33).

First-class career (1979–94): 4,926 runs (28.97) and 33 wickets (41.48)

Test matches (2): 31 runs (7.75), 0–5, and five catches

WHITELAW, Paul Erskine

(b. 1910, Auckland; d. 1988, Auckland) *Auckland and New Zealand*

A sound and attractive right-handed opening batsman, Paul Whitelaw played in the two Tests against England in 1932/3 and, although he did not fail, was never tried again. In 1936/7, on a rain-damaged wicket, he made his career-highest, 195, in $5\frac{1}{2}$ hours, for Auckland against Otago. He added 445 for the third wicket with W. N. Carson in 268 minutes, which remained a world record for that wicket for 40 years.

First-class career (1928–47): 2,739 runs (37.52) including 5 centuries

Test matches (2): 64 runs (32.00)

WILSON, Jeffrey William

(b. 1973, Invercargill) *Otago and New Zealand*

Jeff Wilson became the golden boy of New Zealand sport; so much so that 'Goldie' was his nickname. Entering first-class cricket in 1991/2 as a personable, fair-haired youth abounding in talent and enthusiasm, he took five wickets in the second innings of his first match with his lively right-arm fast-medium bowling. He only played six games, but he took 26 wickets at 21.61 and his aggressive right-hand batting produced 188 runs at an average of 23. But he had an immediate conflict between cricket and rugby football, with indoor basketball making a second distraction. He is a talented athlete, one of the stars, as a right wing, of the All Blacks' tour of Scotland and England in 1993 and of their World Cup team in South Africa in 1995. In his second cricket season, he was chosen for the New Zealand one-day series with Australia, which finished two all. In the last match at Hamilton, Wilson scored 44 not out off 28 balls and helped his side to win with only two balls to spare. In four one-day internationals to 1994 he had scored 80 runs (26.66) and taken three wickets (45.00)

First-class career (1991–   ): 533 runs (16.65), 71 wickets (19.66), and 17 catches.

WRIGHT, John Geoffrey

(b. 1954, Christchurch) *Northern Districts, Derbyshire, Canterbury, Auckland, and New Zealand*

John Wright, an outstanding cricketer at Christ's College, Christchurch, and at Otago University, quickly came to the fore in New Zealand first-class cricket after representing Northern Districts for the first time in 1974/5 and became one of the world's most popular, respected and durable players. He was the first New Zealand batsman to score over 4,000 Test runs and led his country in fourteen Tests. The Editor of *Wisden*, Matthew Engel, wrote on his retirement that he had 'the most beautiful manners of his generation'. He was so successful on trial with Derbyshire and Kent in England in 1976 that the former county signed him as a specially registered overseas player in preference to two outstanding South African cricketers. Wright entirely justified the confidence shown in him by making 1,080 runs (32.70) for Derbyshire in his first season for them in 1977 and continued to bat with impressive consistency. A left-handed opening batsman of great determination with deep powers of concentration, and fine fielder, he had a sound defence and a full array of strokes, being notably strong, like many good left-handers, in punching the ball away to the on-side whenever a ball was pitched up near to his leg stump. Making his first appearances for his country against England, at

home and away, in 1978, he started with a solid 55 in the first Test at Wellington, the highest score for the New Zealand side in their first defeat of England. In England his best Test score was 62 in the first Test at The Oval, but against Pakistan in 1979 he batted consistently, scoring 88 in the second Test at Napier. He scored 110 against India at Auckland in 1980/1 and 141 against Australia at Christchurch in 1981/2. As New Zealand's regular opener in the 1980s, he maintained an admirable consistency, scoring 130 against England at Auckland in 1983/4, 107 against Pakistan at Karachi in 1984/5 and, in the West Indies later that season averaging 30 against the West Indies quick bowlers, by no means a disgrace. Vice-captain in England in 1986, he shared fully in New Zealand's first win in a series there, making an authoritative 58 in the victory at Trent Bridge and then helping to block England out of the third match at The Oval with a 7-hour century (119). He scored two further hundreds against England, at Auckland in 1987/8 and at Wellington in 1991/2, consolation for being stumped off Phil Tufnell for 99 at Christchurch, a mistake which triggered a fatal collapse. He toured every Test country (except South Africa and Zimbabwe) and by making 101 at Hamilton against Sri Lanka in 1990/1, completed a 'full set' of hundreds against all six of New Zealand's opponents. In county cricket he scored over 1,000 runs in six seasons, including 1,504 runs (48.51) in 1980 and 1,830 runs (55.45) with seven centuries in 1982. He also scored 1,019 runs (53.65) in New Zealand in 1986/7.

First-class career (1975–93): 25,073 runs (42.35) including 44 centuries, 2 wickets (169.50), and 192 catches

Test matches (82): 5,334 runs (37.82) including 12 centuries, 0–5, and 38 catches

YOUNG, Bryan Andrew

(b. 1964, Whangarei) *Northern Districts and New Zealand*

Bryan Young began his first-class career at the age of 19 as a useful lower-order right-handed batsman and a wicket-keeper. He gave up wicket-keeping in 1992/3 after a disappointing tour of Australia to concentrate on his batting and soon became recognized as one of the soundest opening batsmen in world cricket. He was the most successful wicket-keeper for Northern Districts, with 191 dismissals—71 clear of the second in the order. Included as an opener in the New Zealand team to Australia in 1993/4 he made 38 and 53 at

Brisbane in the only Test for which he was selected. But he played in all three Tests against Pakistan later in that season at home and finished the series with 120 in the second innings at Christchurch, winning the match for New Zealand in partnership with Shane Thomson. He followed this with 85 against India in a one-off Test at Hamilton, and a useful tour of England in 1994 during which he scored 122 against Essex and 94 in the second innings of the Lord's Test. He also fielded brilliantly at slip. To 1994 he had played in 26 one-day internationals, scoring 641 runs (27.86) and taking 13 catches.

First-class career (1983–): 4,725 runs (34.48) including 5 centuries, and 229 dismissals (218 c., 11 st.)

Test matches (16): 996 runs (32.12) and 25 catches

YUILE, Bryan William

(b. 1941, Wellington) *Central Districts and New Zealand*

Under average height, Bryan Yuile was a fair-haired left-arm slow bowler who relied much on flight and an immaculate length, a sturdy middle-order, right-handed batsman and a good field, especially at leg-slip. He toured South Africa in 1961/2, India and Pakistan in 1964/5 and 1969/70, and England in 1965 and 1969. At home he played against England in 1962/3, India in 1967/8, and the West Indies in 1968/9. He was rarely assured of a Test place. On his first England tour he headed the bowling averages with 24 wickets (22.91), and appeared in two Tests. On his second tour, however, although he headed the batting averages with 383 runs (63.83) and took 24 wickets (25.87), he was not selected for any of the Tests. On his second tour of India and Pakistan he captured 21 wickets (20.33), but played in only three Tests. He hit his Test-highest score of 64 in the first match against England at Auckland in 1962/3. He took 12 wickets (20.25) in the three Tests against Pakistan in 1964/5, including 6 for 112 in the third match at Christchurch. He also took nine wickets (27.11) in the three matches against the West Indies in 1968/9. In Tests he was rarely given the opportunity to dominate the scene, but, at least, was very good at the 'bits and pieces'. His career-highest was 146 for Central Districts against Canterbury in 1966/7 and his best bowling in an innings, 9 for 101 in a total of 311 against Canterbury in 1965/6.

First-class career (1959–72): 3,850 runs (24.67) including 1 century, 375 wickets (21.89), and 73 catches

Pakistan

AAMIR HANIF

(b. 1971, Karachi) *Karachi and Pakistan Automobile Corporation*

Aamir made his first-class début in 1989 for Karachi and by the end of the 1992/3 season had already made 3,196 runs in first-class matches for Karachi and PACO which included six centuries and nineteen fifties, not to mention his 44 wickets at 24.02 apiece. He was also averaging 50.22 in limited-overs matches. A very promising right-handed batsman in the middle order, he is a powerful driver of the ball and bowls right-arm medium-pace. In 1991 he bagged a hat-trick for Karachi Whites against Bahawalpur in the Quaid-e-Azam Trophy final. In the 1992/3 season he finished fourth in the national batting averages and was one of three men to pass 1,000 runs, totalling 1,042 runs (54.84) in 14 matches. For Karachi his 700 runs (70.00) effectively won the Quaid-e-Azam Trophy for the third season running. He toured Sharjah with Pakistan and made his one-day début in 1993/4 against Sri Lanka. He also toured with Pakistan B to Zimbabwe in 1990/1 but apart from an innings of 94 in the first 'Test' at Bulawayo, he could not come to terms with the conditions in that country.

First-class career (1989–): 3,719 runs (33.50), 63 wickets (23.04), and 50 catches

AAMER MALIK

(b. 1963, Mandi Bahauddin) *Lahore, Pakistan International Airline, and Pakistan*

Aamer Malik is three players rolled into one: a right-handed opening batsman who also bats in the middle order, a right-arm medium-pace bowler and, when required, a wicket-keeper. He has performed in all these roles not only at first-class level but also for Pakistan. He has immense powers of concentration and the stamina to play a long innings. An especially strong player on the off-side he is a team man and a good tourist. Making his first-class début in 1979/80 for Lahore he scored a century in each innings, emulating Arthur Morris of Australia and India's Nari Contractor. He went to Australia with the under-19 side in 1981/2, excelling as a batsman, and returned there twice to play grade cricket on a BCCP scholarship scheme. His breakthrough to international cricket followed his 938 runs (40.78) in 1985/6, when he hit four centuries. He earned his first Test cap against England in the Faisalabad Test, of 1987/8, the game which earned international notoriety because of the Gatting–Rana affair. Aamer took four close catches and in the next Test at Karachi batted for just short of 7 hours for an unbeaten 98 to earn Pakistan a draw. On the Caribbean tour of 1987/8 he kept wicket in the final Test at Bridgetown when Saleem Yousuf suffered an injury from a Marshall bouncer. He accounted for four dismissals. Earlier on the tour, against West Indies Cricket Board XI, he had six victims behind the stumps. He played in the first Test at Karachi against Australia in the 1988/9 season and toured Sharjah, Bangladesh, and Australia. He proved a match winner in Perth in a one-day international against Australia, making 90 and taking two wickets. At the Gabba he made 75 against West Indies to help Pakistan win. On the New Zealand tour following the Australian trip he played in two Tests without doing much but still finished with a first-class average of 72.20. In Pakistan he played in all four Tests against India in 1989, making centuries at Faisalabad and Lahore. In twenty-three one-day internationals to 1994/5 he had scored 536 runs (25.52), taken 3 wickets (28.66), and had 16 victims behind the stumps.

First-class career (1979–): 6,399 runs (42.94) including 20 centuries, 19 wickets (44.89), and 61 catches

Test matches (14): 565 runs (35.31) including 2 centuries, 1 wicket (89.00), 15 catches, and 1 stumping

AAMIR NAZIR

(b. 1971, Lahore) *Lahore, Allied Bank, and Pakistan*

Of medium build but with strong shoulders, Aamir Nazir emerged from Lahore's club cricket to play in the Patron's Trophy grade one matches in 1992/3 for the Income Tax department. As a right-arm medium-pace bowler who could bat right-handed in the lower middle order, he quickly made his mark. Swinging the ball away with surprising pace, he took 41 wickets in eight matches and was invited to join the Pakistan camp prior to the team's visit to the West Indies in 1992/3. Wasim Akram, the Pakistan captain, at once recommended him to the selectors. He made his one-day début at Port-of-Spain in the second match of the five-match one-day series, taking 3 for 43. Only a disputed umpiring decision deprived him of a hat-trick. On the same tour he made his Test début in the second Test at Bridgetown and took 2 for 79 in the first innings. In 1993/4 he was taken to New Zealand, where he took one wicket in the final Test at Christchurch, which Pakistan lost by five wickets. He has also toured Sharjah for one-day tournaments but with Waqar Younis, Wasim Akram, Aqib Javed, and Ata-ur-Rehman to the fore, he remained only a reserve.

First-class career (1992–): 7 runs (2.33) and 12 wickets (57.50)

Test matches (5): 15 runs (3.75) and 17 wickets (67.67)

AAMIR SOHAIL

(b. 1966, Lahore) *Lahore, Sargodha, Habib Bank, Allied Bank, and Pakistan*

Temperamental, tempestuous, and aggressive by nature Aamir could have played for Pakistan much earlier than he did. He made his one-day début at Sharjah in 1990/1 against Sri Lanka in the Wills Trophy. His progress to the top was hampered because of his instinctive aggression on and off the field. Infuriated at being dropped by the Lahore selectors, he was alleged to have vandalized the pitch by pouring oil on it and was temporarily banned. On a tour of Zimbabwe he was severely reprimanded for his loss of temper and on the 1994 tour of Sri Lanka he was reprimanded by referee Cammie Smith for showing dissent in the second Test after an appeal was rejected off his own bowling. A left-handed opening batsman and a slow left-arm bowler, he took time to establish himself at first-class level but once he did he was unstoppable. Possessing a wide array of strokes, he drove, cut, and hooked with tremendous relish to pulverize the bowlers on the domestic scene. In 1989/90 in thirteen first-class matches he mustered 680 runs (40.00) and in 1990/1 his contribution for his teams was 795 (41.84) in 12 matches. In 1991 he made a century for Pakistan A in Sri Lanka and played an attacking innings of 91 at Sharjah against India. He was ignored for the World Cup in 1991/2 but was rushed to reinforce an injury-stricken team. Against Zimbabwe he blasted a hurricane 114 in 136 balls and scores of over fifty in matches against India and Australia helped to establish him in the team. His 62 against India was in vain but his 76 against Australia at Perth brought a much needed win by 48 runs. Though his earlier form eluded him in the final stages, he still managed 326 runs (32.60) in ten matches, took 4 wickets, and fielded brilliantly to help Pakistan win the World Cup. In the final he bowled well without taking a wicket, conceding 49 runs in his 10 overs in one spell. A triumphant tour of England followed in 1992. He scored 1,110 runs in seventeen matches at an average of 42.69 and finished third in the Test averages. In the second Test at Lord's he made an attacking 73 with eleven fours and in the second innings, when Pakistan required 138 to win, he showed tremendous responsibility to make 39 before he played on to his wicket. In the Old Trafford Test he batted valiantly to make 205, his maiden century in only his fourth Test innings. He reached 100 off 127 balls, was 131 at tea, and hit thirty-two fours in his double-century. He did not have much of a series against Zimbabwe in the home series in 1993 but made two scores of over fifty in the series against New Zealand on Pakistan's 1993/4 tour and batted with his usual relish and aggression. In 49 one-day internationals to 1994/5 he had scored 1,573 runs (32.77) and taken 29 wickets.

First-class career (1983–   ): 7,136 runs (37.75) including 14 centuries, 100 wickets (34.83), and 93 catches

Test matches (23): 1,508 runs (35.90) including 2 centuries, 8 wickets (36.87), and 20 catches

AQIB JAVED

(b. 1972, Sheikhupura) *Lahore, Islamabad, Allied Bank, Pakistan Automobile Corporation, Hampshire, and Pakistan*

Incredibly, it is claimed that Aqib Javed made his first-class début for Lahore at the age of only 12 years, 76 days. Right-handed, he already bowled with reasonable pace and swung the ball away. In the under-19 competitions he was a star bowler. In 1987/8 he went to Australia to play in the Youth World Cup and in the next season he impressed Imran Khan, the Pakistan captain, while bowling in the nets and was taken to play in some charity matches in India with a team which Imran led. On his return, he was a surprise choice to tour Australia and New Zealand in 1988/9. He made his one-day début against West Indies at Adelaide in World Series Cricket and his Test début against New Zealand at Wellington at the age of 16 years and 189 days, to become the second-youngest Test player. With a long but easy run-up and high action he has fine control of line and length. In the Nehru Cup Final against West Indies in 1989/90 he gave away only 25 runs in ten overs in Pakistan's win by four wickets. He bowled with as much accuracy in the 1992 World Cup final against England, giving away fewer than three runs an over for the wickets of Alec Stewart and Neil Fairbrother. He was signed by Hampshire for the 1991 summer as a replacement for Malcolm Marshall, who was touring England with West Indies. He finished with 53 wickets at 31.24 and gained in experience which showed in domestic and one-day matches. He reserved his best, however, for the Wills Trophy in Sharjah in 1991/2 when in the final against India he took 7 for 37 in 10 overs in Pakistan's 72 run victory. It also included a hat-trick in his third over when he had Shastri, Azharuddin, and Tendulkar lbw from successive balls. He toured England in 1992 but took only nine wickets in five Tests, his best being 4 for 100 in the third Test at Old Trafford where he became the first player to be fined by an ICC referee, Conrad Hunte, for showing dissent after umpire Roy Palmer had warned him for intimidatory bowling at the tail-ender Devon Malcolm. He had 36 first-class wickets on tour at 26.83. On the 1992/3 tour of New Zealand he was once

again disciplined by a referee, this time by Peter Burge who suspended him for one match after the one-day international at Napier for using foul language to umpire Bryan Aldridge after an appeal was rejected. Thus he also became the first player to be suspended by a referee. Back injury prevented his participation in matches in the West Indies when Pakistan went there in 1992/3 and he had to withdraw from the team before the first Test. By 1994/5 he had already played in ninety-two one-day internationals, taking 99 wickets at 31.52.

First-class career (1984–   ): 157 runs (6.28), 134 wickets (33.62), and 5 catches

Test matches (18): 38 runs (2.37), 38 wickets (38.76), and 1 catch

ABDUL AZIZ DURRANI

(b. 1905, Rajasthan; d. 1979, Karachi)

Known as 'Master Aziz', he was both coach and father figure to most of the cricketers that Pakistan produced in its first 30 years. As a right-hand batsman and wicket-keeper, he played in the Ranji Trophy for Rajasthan and Maharashtra in pre-partition days, and played in an unofficial Test for India against the Australian Services XI, making 12 runs and taking two victims behind the wicket. An eye injury while keeping wicket prevented him from becoming a Test player. He moved to what became Pakistan in 1947 and became a cricket coach for the Sind Madaresah School, the school which produced the father of the nation, Mohammad Ali Jinnah. Here it was that Aziz met a little boy called Hanif Mohammad. He took him under his wing, and all his brothers, Wazir, Raees, Mushtaq, and Sadiq, and passed his knowledge and skill of the game to them. Most of the players who played in Tests for Pakistan from Karachi and also some from Lahore were his students. Devoted and dedicated, he was always available. His son, Salim Aziz Durrani, who prefered to stay in India, played with distinction in Tests for India as an all-rounder.

ABDUL KADIR

(b. 1944, Karachi) *Karachi and Pakistan*

A wicket-keeper and sound right-handed batsman, Abdul Kadir had a memorable Test début, against Australia at Karachi in 1964/5, when he was run out for 95, having put on 249 for the first wicket with Khalid Ibadulla on the first day. But in the first match ever between the two countries in Australia, at Melbourne six weeks later, he was dismissed for a duck. He also played against New Zealand in 1964/5, putting together a careful innings of 58 in the second match at Auckland.

First-class career (1961–72): 1,523 runs (28.73) including 1 century, and 59 dismissals (46 c., 13 st.)

Test matches (4): 272 runs (34.00) and 1 stumping

ABDUL QADIR KHAN

(b. 1955, Lahore) *Punjab, Lahore, Habib Bank, and Pakistan*

A stocky leg-spin and googly bowler of high class with a quirky, bounding action, an authentic looping flight and well-disguised 'wrong 'uns', Abdul Qadir was a true match-winner, as he first showed when taking 8 for 29 and 4 for 86 for Habib Bank against Universities at Lahore in 1977/8. In this same season he made his Test début against England at Lahore and in the second Test at Hyderabad took 6 for 44 to bowl England out for 191 in the first innings. In the series he took 12 wickets at 25.41 but, plagued by an injury early in the tour, he was a great disappointment in England in 1978, taking only six wickets on the tour at 66.00. He had been hampered by a shoulder injury which continued to worry him for some time; but it was a very different story when next he visited England four summers later. Then, he was the sensation of the tour, bamboozling county batsman quite unfamiliar with a good leg-break bowler, embarrassing England's best players too at times and always entertaining the crowd with his idiosyncratic approach to the stumps and boyish enthusiasm. With a flipper and two different top spinners to add to his basic repertoire of leg break and googly he was too much even for Australians brought up on a larger diet of this type of bowler. Following his 57 wickets in twelve matches in England, taken at 20.82 (his ten wickets in three Tests cost double this but had an effect of unsettling the batsmen which the figures do not reveal), he took 22 wickets in three home Tests against Australia in the same 1982/3 season in which he took 9 for 82 and 9 for 49 for Habib Bank against Karachi and Rawalpindi respectively in the space of three weeks to become the first Pakistan bowler to take 100 wickets in one season. His total of 18 wickets in three Tests, including 5 for 84 and 5 for 110 in the final match at Lahore, was largely responsible for bringing Pakistan their first win in a series against England, 1983/4. But he had a disappointing haul of 12 Test wickets at a cost of 61.5 each

on the Australian tour of 1983/4, when he seemed unable to come to terms with a predominantly left-handed batting line-up. A forthright nature sometimes brought him into conflict with the authorities—most notably in New Zealand in 1985 when he was sent home 'for disciplinary reasons' after the second Test. His volatile temperament also got him into trouble in the West Indies in 1987/8, when he became involved in a scuffle with a spectator during a tense Test in Barbados. He took 14 wickets in the three Tests of this series, an unofficial world championship, and deserved more. Earlier in that season he had become only the second Pakistan bowler to take 200 wickets, whilst returning an analysis of 9 for 56 against England at Lahore. He added 4 for 45 in the second innings and in three Tests took an amazing 30 wickets at 14.56, including 10 for 186 at Karachi. His Test appearances became less frequent owing to injuries and a dislike of touring but he made a return to domestic cricket in 1994/5. A useful right-handed batsman, he scored a century in his second first-class match and has two Test-match fifties to his credit.

First-class career (1975–91): 3,636 runs (18.74) including 2 centuries, and 897 wickets (23.43)

Test matches (38): 1029 runs (15.59), 236 wickets (32.80), and 11 catches

AFAQ HUSSAIN

(b. 1939, Lucknow) *Karachi Blues, Pakistan International Airline, and Pakistan*

A useful right-arm off-break bowler and batsman, Afaq Hussain played in the first official Test against England in Pakistan at Lahore in 1961/2, top-scoring with 35 not out in the second innings. He toured Australasia in 1964/5 with little success.

First-class career (1957–74): 1,448 runs (24.54) including 1 century, 214 wickets (19.42), and 52 catches

Test matches (2): 66 runs (—), 1–106, and 2 catches

AFTAB BALOCH

(b. 1953, Karachi) *National Bank of Pakistan, Pakistan International Airline, Karachi, Sind, and Pakistan*

A prolific batsman in domestic cricket, Aftab Baloch will no doubt be best remembered for his monumental innings of 428 for Sind against Baluchistan in 1973/4, the sixth-highest first-class score ever. A very sound right-handed batsman and occasional off-break bowler, he played in two Tests five years apart, against New Zealand at Dacca in 1969/70, when at 16 years 191 days, he became the second-youngest Test cricketer ever, and against West Indies in 1974/5, when he hit 60 not out. He was an outstanding captain of the National Bank side in the Qaid-e-Azam Trophy.

First-class career (1969–85): 9,166 runs (41.85) including 20 centuries, 223 wickets (31.46), and 137 dismissals (134 c., 3 st.)

Test matches (2): 97 runs (48.50) and 0–17

AFTAB GUL

(b. 1946, Gujar Khan, India) *Lahore, Punjab, Services, and Pakistan*

A stocky, right-handed opener, Aftab Gul, although over-impetuous on occasions, was often a reliable and effective batsman. He toured England in 1971, coming second in the batting with 1,154 runs (46.16), sharing in some splendid attacking opening partnerships with Sadiq Mohammad, but his highest score in the Tests was only 33. At home he played against England in 1968/9 and New Zealand in 1969/70 without much success. In 1968/9, while a Law student at Punjab University, he became the first player to appear in first-class cricket while on bail for alleged political activities. Such was his following, indeed, as a student leader that it was said that Pakistan officials did not dare to play the Lahore Test without him.

First-class career (1964–78): 6,129 runs (36.92) including 11 centuries, 14 wickets (33.21), and 46 catches

Test matches (6): 182 runs (22.75), 0–4, and 3 catches

AGHA SAADAT ALI

(b. 1929, Lahore) *Bahawalpur, Lahore, and Pakistan*

A sound right-handed batsman and reliable fielder, Agha Saadat Ali played in a single Test, the third against New Zealand at Dacca in 1955/6, scoring eight not out and holding 3 catches.

First-class career (1949–62): 325 runs (14.13)

AGHA ZAHID

(b. 1953, Lahore) *Lahore University, Habib Bank, and Pakistan*

A sound right-handed opening batsman and occasional medium-pace bowler, Agha Zahid played in a single Test, the first against West Indies, at Lahore, in 1974/5, scoring 14 and 1.

First-class career (1970–93): 13,475 runs (36.81) including 29 centuries, 108 wickets (32.18), and 130 catches

AHMED MUSTAFA

(b. 1944, Lucknow)

Mustafa Ahmed played against India for Pakistan Combined Schools XI in 1955/6 and for Karachi and Khairpur in the Quaid-e-Azam Trophy. As a right-handed batsman and wicket-keeper, he toured England with Pakistan Eaglets as vice-captain in the late fifties and scored over a thousand runs. Appointed as a selector and coach of the Karachi Cricket Association, he supervised BCCP coaching clinics and later in 1987 opened a coaching centre at Karachi for 12- to 16-year-olds.

AKRAM RAZA

(b. 1964, Lahore) *Lahore, Sargodha, Habib Bank, and Pakistan*

A wily and economical right-arm off-spin bowler and a useful late-middle-order right-handed batsman, Raza pushes the ball through at a low trajectory. He has a short, angled approach to the wicket. He made his first-class début in 1981/2 for Lahore, and in 1985/6 took 58 wickets at 20 runs apiece. In the 1988/9 season he bagged 64 wickets in thirteen first-class matches at 16.71 to finish fourth in the averages. He also made 358 runs (29.38) which included three fifties in the Quaid-e-Azam Trophy. He had 10 for 82 against Pakistan National Shipping Corporation to win the match for Habib Bank by 138 runs. He earned a place in the Pakistan B team against Sri Lanka in early 1988/9 and in the first match had 7 for 90 in Pakistan's impressive win. In 1989/90 he made his Test début against India at Lahore, without taking a wicket, and his one-day début at Bombay against Australia in the Nehru Cup. He played in two Tests against West Indies in the home series in 1990/1 and two seasons later took 71 wickets (24.28) and made 508 runs in seventeen matches. Joining the touring team to New Zealand in 1993/4 he played in the final Test at Christchurch, making two determined and correct inning of 29 and 26. He has played in twenty-six one-day internationals, scoring 92 runs (18.40) and taking 21 wickets (39.28). He had a successful tour of Sri Lanka in 1994.

First-class career (1981–): 4,070 runs (30.14) including 3 centuries, 428 wickets (26.47), and 107 catches

Test matches (9): 153 runs (15.30), 13 wickets (56.30), and 8 catches

ALIMUDDIN (or Alim-ud-Din)

(b. 1930, Ajmer, India) *Rajasthan, Gujarat, Karachi, Rajputana, Sind, Muslim, and Pakistan*

A stocky right-handed opening batsman, always ready to play his strokes, and a magnificent fielder, Alimuddin was amongst the earliest prominent Pakistani cricketers. He represented Rajasthan (Rajputana) in India's Ranji Trophy competition in 1942/3 aged 12! He hit 85 for Pakistan against Ceylon at Karachi in 1949/50 and toured England with the Pakistan Eaglets in 1953. In England, with the first Pakistan Test team in 1954, he started in tremendous form, scoring 142 at Worcester and 51 and 100 not out against Cambridge University at Fenner's in the opening matches and, although he failed in the Tests, he made 1,083 runs (30.94). Afterwards, he toured the West Indies in 1957/8, India in 1960/1 and England again in 1962, and at home played against India in 1954/5, New Zealand in 1955/6, Australia in 1956/7 and 1959/60, West Indies in 1958/9, and England in 1961/2. In the first official series in Pakistan, against India, he was the best batsman on either side, with 332 runs (41.50), including 103 not out in the fifth match at Karachi. In the West Indies he failed to find his best form but, after losing his place, he came back with 50, 109 and 53 in successive innings against England at Dacca and Karachi in 1961/2. On his second Test tour of England, his only notable achievement was in the third Test, at Headingley, when he scored 50 and 60 out of totals of 131 and 180 respectively. After captaining Karachi B, he became for a while National Cricket Coach. Taking up a career for Pakistan International Airline in London, he never missed a Test at Lord's.

First-class career (1942–68): 7,276 runs (32.77) including 14 centuries, 40 wickets (23.97), and 65 catches

Test matches (25): 1,091 runs (25.37) including 2 centuries, 1–75 and 8 catches

AMIR BI

(b. 1908, Surat)

The mother of the indomitable Mohammad brothers, Amir Bi, in her younger days was a badminton player of some distinction. When she moved to Pakistan with her family, the sudden death of her husband left her with the responsibility of raising her five sons, Wazir Mohammad, Raees Mohammad, Hanif Mohammad, Mushtaq Mohammad, and Sadiq Mohammad. With limited resources at her disposal she provided them with the facilities and the education which she could afford. Her passion for sport rubbed off on her children, four of whom played Test cricket. The fifth, Raees, was once 12th man in a Test. The brothers dominated the game at international level and both Hanif and Mushtaq led Pakistan. A proud mother, she followed their exploits at home and abroad and when one of her grandsons, Shoaib Mohammad, the son of Hanif, also played in a Test for Pakistan, she said, 'I can now die happily.'

AMIR ELAHI

(b. 1908; d. 1980) *Baroda, Northern India, and Southern Punjab*

See India section.

ANIL DALPAT SONAVARIA

(b. 1963, Karachi) *Karachi, Pakistan International Airline, and Pakistan*

The first of several wicket-keepers given their chance after the retirement of Wasim Bari, Anil Dalpat made his Test début against England at Karachi in 1984, becoming the first Hindu to represent Pakistan at cricket. A right-handed batsman and a neat and agile wicket-keeper, he graduated straight from the under-23 team into the Test side, where he coped well with the unfamiliar spin of Abdul Qadir, taking five catches and two stumpings in his first series. But he was replaced for the first two Tests of the 1984/5 season, against India, returning for the home and away series against New Zealand and recording his highest Test score of 52 in the third Test at Karachi. His total of 67 victims in the 1983/4 season was a Pakistan record. He emigrated to the United States.

First-class career (1976–): 2,550 runs (17.83) and 424 dismissals (301 c., 123 st.)

Test matches (9): 167 runs (15.18) and 25 dismissals (22 c., 3 st.)

ANWAR HUSSAIN

(b. 1920, Lahore) *Northern India, Bombay, Karachi, and Pakistan*

A sound right-handed batsman and fast-medium seam bowler, Anwar Hussain appeared in the Ranji Trophy before Partition—making his début for Northern India in 1940/1—and he played in Pakistan's first official home series, against India, in 1952/3, without much success.

First-class career (1940–55): 1,466 runs (27.14) and 34 wickets (36.32)
Test matches (4): 42 runs (7.00) and 1–29

ANWAR KHAN

(b. 1955, Karachi) *Sind, National Bank, Karachi, and Pakistan*

A tall, right-arm fast-medium bowler, Anwar Khan was a carefree lower-order batsman. Touring New Zealand and Australia in 1979, he played in one Test at Christchurch as substitute for the absent Imran Khan, Making 12 and 3 not out and bowling only four overs without taking a wicket.

First-class career (1972–85): 2,221 runs (21.35) including 1 century, and 209 wickets (29.01)

ARIF ALI KHAN ABBASI

(b. 1943, Ahmedabad, India)

Associated with the Board of Control for Cricket in Pakistan (BCCP) for more than 10 years in the capacity of secretary, treasurer, and chief executive, Arif was a useful right-handed middle-order batsman in Karachi club cricket. Educated at St Patrick's school and college in Karachi and at St Edmund Hall at Oxford between 1963 and 1967, he served as secretary of the BCCP from 1980 to 1984 and then from 1988 to 1991; and as treasurer from 1991 to 1994, when the chief justice Nasim Hassan Shah and the secretary of the BCCP, Shahid Rafi, were removed from office and the BCCP was dissolved. Arif instead became the member of the *ad hoc* committee to look after the affairs of the board. In both cricket and business he served his organizations with integrity.

ARIF BUTT

(b. 1944, Lahore) *Lahore, Railways, and Pakistan*

A persevering right-arm fast-medium bowler and useful tail-end batsman, Arif Butt was a member of the first-ever Pakistan team to visit Australasia, in 1964/5, when, despite an injury, he took 31 wickets (23.32) in nine matches, including 6 for 89 in the first innings of the first Test in Australia at Melbourne and 6 for 108 in the first against New Zealand, at Wellington.

First-class career (1960–78): 4,017 runs (29.10) including 4 centuries, 201 wickets (26.79), and 44 catches
Test matches (3): 59 runs (11.80) and 14 wickets (20.57)

ARSHAD KHAN

(b. 1971, Peshawar) *Peshawar, Islamabad, Railways, and Pakistan*

A right-arm off-spin bowler, Arshad made his first-class début in 1988 for Peshawar. In his first season he had 17 wickets at 27.35, with a best of 7 for 59, and he had further success in 1992/3, with 18 wickets at 17.77, and 1993/4 (28 wickets at 27.32). In the 1992/3 Sharjah Wills International Trophy he made his only one-day appearance, for Pakistan against Zimbabwe. He was out for a duck and conceded 43 runs in six overs without taking a wicket. Days later he was in South Africa with Pakistan's first-ever team there, ostensibly to take part in the Total Triangular series against South Africa and West Indies. In the event he did not play. His inclusion in the team was largely a political gesture to the people of the north, who had always protested that their part of the country was ignored by selectors.

First-class career (1988–): 271 runs (10.03), 76 wickets (26.39), and 15 catches

ASHFAQ AHMED

(b. 1973, Lahore) *Lahore, Pakistan International Airline, and Pakistan*

A tall, muscular, and energetic right-arm swing and seam bowler, Ashfaq has a long and fluent run-up and a side-on, high action. Guided by Wasim Akram while playing for his club Ludhiana Gymkhana in Lahore, he improved rapidly. In early 1993/4 he came into prominence for PIA in the Patron's Trophy when he had a haul of 27 wickets at 17.1. He made his Test début at Rawalpindi in the second Test against Zimbabwe, taking 2 for 31 in seventeen overs in the first innings. On the subsequent New Zealand tour he did well without playing a Test, partly through injury. He went to Sri Lanka with the Pakistan tourists of 1994/5, but did not add to his one Test appearance (2 wickets (26.50) and one run (1.00).

First-class career (1991–): 68 runs (7.55), 54 wickets (23.61), and 10 catches

ASHRAF ALI

(b. 1958, Lahore) *Lahore, Income Tax, Pakistan Universities, Railways, United Bank, and Pakistan*

Beefy of build, and unusually large for a wicket-keeper, Ashraf Ali came to national prominence in 1980/1 when, in addition to 37 dismissals, he scored 1,053 runs, topping the batting averages in the Qaid-e-Azam Trophy (49.19). A right-hander with considerable flair, his highest score in that season was 137 and he was chosen to tour Australia where, because of his superior batting, he was preferred to Wasim Bari as wicket-keeper in several one-day internationals. He made his first Test appearances in the last two games of Pakistan's inaugural (home) series against Sri Lanka, justifying his selection with scores of 58, 29 not out and 45 not out. But he had to wait nearly two years before he was recalled for the only two Tests of India's 1984 tour which was cut short by news of Mrs Gandhi's assassination. Again he did well with the bat, scoring 65 in the first Test, but his 'keeping was inconsistent and he lost his place again until returning for three home Tests against England in 1987/8. His fierce, bearded face is seen appealing to the umpire in many of the photographs of that bitter series.

First-class career (1974–94): 6,848 runs (38.68) including 5 centuries, 0–5, and 451 dismissals (371 c., 80 st.)

Test matches (8): 229 runs (45.80) and 22 dismissals (17 c., 5 st.)

ASIF IQBAL RAZVI

(b. 1943, Hyderabad) *Hyderabad, Karachi, Pakistan International Airline, National Bank, Kent, and Pakistan*

An exciting, stroke-playing, right-handed batsman, graceful, attacking, and very quick on his feet, Asif Iqbal was also a useful second-line seamer, brilliant all-purpose field, and shrewd captain who led Kent for more than one successful season and brought Pakistan close to the final of the 1979 Prudential World Cup. A smiling cavalier figure, there was charm in every action he made. Asif was at the forefront of the fight for better pay for Pakistan's professional cricketers, and a leading light in Kerry Packer's World Series Cricket, who came back to Test cricket after announcing his retirement. A nephew of Ghulam Ahmed, the Indian off-spinner, Asif was brought up in Hyderabad in Southern India and played for them in the Ranji Trophy from 1959 before emigrating to Pakistan in 1961. On his Test début for Pakistan against Australia at Karachi in 1964/5 he went in number ten, scoring 41 and 36, and formed a rather unlikely opening bowling partnership with Majid Khan: both became much better known for their batting. Asif, however, continued to be a serious bowler, taking 18 Test wickets in three matches in New Zealand in

1964/5, at Wellington taking 5 for 48 and 1 for 33. It was really in England in 1967 that he showed for the first time that he could be a batsman of world class, making 76 at number nine in the Lord's Test, sharing a stand of 130 with Hanif Mohammad (still a Pakistani record for the eighth wicket), and then at The Oval, when Pakistan were 65 for 8 in their second innings and still 159 behind England, sharing a dazzling stand of 190 in 175 minutes with Intikhab Alam for the ninth wicket and himself scoring 146, including two sixes and twenty-one fours. In the first innings of the same match, still taking the new ball, he had taken 3 for 66 in 42 overs. When he next met England at home in 1968/9 he batted at number four. But much of his best form over the years was shown in England, both for Kent and Pakistan. He joined Kent in 1968, playing a prominent role in many county successes, and scoring more than 1,000 runs in a season six times. His second Test century against England came at Edgbaston in 1971, 104 not out. He made two more Test centuries in the 1972/3 season, 175 against New Zealand at Dunedin and 102 against England at Lahore. But his best season was the busy one of 1976/7 when in three different series he hit four centuries. Touring Australia that season he made 313 runs in three Tests at 78.25, including 152 not out at Adelaide, and 120 in the third Test at Sydney when Pakistan defeated Australia away from home for the first time. The Pakistan team moved on to the Caribbean where Asif was less successful, yet still scored 135 in the fifth Test at Kingston. In 1978/9, returning to Test cricket after the Pakistan Packer players had been recalled, he made 104 at Napier to rescue his side against New Zealand and 134 not out in a total of 285 at Perth. Almost all Asif's greatest innings were played in perfect tune with the occasion and the position of the match. His stance at the crease became more open with the years and some of his strokes to the leg-side grew more rugged than graceful but the exceptional speed of eye and feet remained. He ran superbly between wickets. In retirement he has been heavily involved with the organization of international tournaments in Sharjah under the patronage of Abdul Rehman Bukhatir. He also represented Pakistan on the International Cricket Council. He lives in England, but travels widely.

First-class career (1959–82): 23,329 runs (37.26) including 45 centuries, 291 wickets (30.15), and 303 catches

Test matches (58): 3,575 runs (38.85) including 11 centuries, 53 wickets (28.33), and 36 catches

ASIF MASOOD

(b. 1946, Lahore) Lahore, Northumberland, Punjab University, Pakistan International Airline, and Pakistan

Tall, well-built, and with a flowing moustache and long black hair, Asif Masood was a right-arm fast-medium bowler, hostile with the new ball, who started his run with an eccentric double-chassis. His swing and movement off the pitch could have the best batsmen groping but he relied mainly on varying his angle of attack, using the full width of the crease. He toured England in 1971 and 1974 and Australia in 1972/3 and 1976/7, and at home he played against England in 1968/9 and 1972/3, New Zealand in 1969/70 and West Indies in 1974/5. His Test début was the first against England, at Lahore, in 1968/9 when, in a riotous atmosphere, he broke through the batting in the second innings, taking three good wickets. On his first England tour he took 13 Test wickets (26.46) but on his second England tour he was less effective. His Test career ended disappointingly on his second Australian tour. Among his best feats were 8 for 65 for Punjab University against Rawalpindi in 1970/1 and 5 for 65 for Pakistan against Rest of the World at Karachi the same season. Commentating during a Test in England, the BBC's Brian Johnston once mistakenly referred to him as 'Masif Asood'.

First-class career (1963–77): 635 runs (8.69), 305 wickets (29.02), and 38 catches

Test matches (16): 93 runs (10.33), 38 wickets (41.26), and 5 catches

ASIF MUJTABA MOHAMMAD

(b. 1967, Karachi) Karachi, Pakistan International Airline, and Pakistan

A diminutive left-hander Asif may be but he is big of heart. Primarily a batsman, with all the shots, he also bowls flattish slow left-arm. He made his mark in first-class cricket when an engineering student in 1984–5 and has since captained Karachi and PIA to domestic titles, and gone on tours to the West Indies and New Zealand as Pakistan's vice-captain. His first Tests and internationals were played at home in 1986/7 against the West Indies. His unbeaten 60 at Perth against Australia in an international tournament later that season brought victory for Pakistan. He toured England in 1987 with limited success and opportunity but at home against England the following winter he scored 157, hitting 27 fours, in a three-day match at Rawalpindi. He also played in a one-day match

and one Test against the tourists but failed, but did well on the domestic circuit by accumulating 840 runs during the season and finishing third in the batting averages. In the Quaid-e-Azam Trophy alone he averaged 51.00 and took 13 wickets at 24.07 but a tour of the West Indies in 1988 eluded him and he was in the shadows until chosen for the 1992 England tour. There he did very well, scoring 123 at Lord's against Middlesex and 59 in the second Test on the same ground in Pakistan's two-wicket win. In the Old Trafford Test his scores were 57 and 40 and he added another cool 50 in the final Test at The Oval in Pakistan's ten-wicket win. His 1,074 runs at 56.52 on the tour included two centuries. His last ball, a six off Steve Waugh at Hobart in the World Series Cup, enabled Pakistan to tie the match on their 1992/3 tour to Australia and New Zealand. On Pakistan's first tour to South Africa for a one-day series he made a belligerent 74, adding a record 165 for the fourth wicket, with Javed Miandad against South Africa at East London. On the 1992/3 West Indies tour he finished third in the batting averages, having played in all three Tests. He scored 102 against West Indies under-23 XI at Grenada. Against Zimbabwe at home in 1993/4 he topped the batting averages in a three-Test series. In the second Test at Rawalpindi he made fifty in each innings and in the final Test at Lahore in a drawn game he made an unbeaten 65. He was injured in the second Test against New Zealand at Wellington early in 1994 and on the tour of Sri Lanka did not do well. In fifty-one one-day internationals by 1994/5 he had scored 955 runs (30.80) and taken 7 wickets (90.14).

First-class career (1984–   ): 8,760 runs (48.13) including 23 centuries, 180 wickets (23.51), and 128 catches

Test matches (21): 762 runs (23.81), 2 wickets (76.00), and 17 catches

ATA-UR-REHMAN

(b. 1975, Lahore) Lahore, Allied Bank, and Pakistan

With a whipping, quick, arm action, as a right-arm fast-medium bowler, Ata generates considerable pace. Through under-19 competitions he developed into a very useful bowler. He toured Australia for the Youth World Cup in 1989 and also England, Zimbabwe, and Sri Lanka with second-string teams before being called as a replacement on the full tour of England in 1992. He made his début at Edgbaston in the first Test taking 3 for 69 in eighteen overs in the England total of 459, and took 18 wickets in nine first-class

ATHAR LAEEQ

matches. On the 1992/3 tour of the Caribbean, he played in all the three Tests, taking 6 wickets, including 3 for 28 in the first match at Port of Spain. He was retained in the side which toured New Zealand in 1993/4. In the first two Tests, both won by Pakistan, he bagged 6 wickets at 35.66 apiece before being injured. In the five one-day matches he took only 3 wickets. He was dropped for the 1994 Australasia Cup but was recalled when Waqar Younis had to withdraw because of an apendicitis operation. In four matches he took 7 wickets. With 3 for 32 against UAE he won the man-of-the-match award. In the final, his dismissal of Sachin Tendulkar paved the way for Pakistan's third successive win in the Australasia Cup. He made his one-day début in 1992/3.

First-class career (1990–   ): 114 runs (7.60), 66 wickets (36.37), and 9 catches
Test matches (9): 48 runs (8.00), 21 wickets (34.29), and 2 catches

ATHAR LAEEQ

(b. 1971, Karachi) *Karachi and National Bank*

A lively right-arm medium pace bowler and a right-handed batsman, Athar made his first-class début in 1989/90 against Sargodha for Karachi. He toured Bangladesh, India, and England with Pakistan under-19 sides and bowled with success. Against India he took 21 wickets in three under-19 Tests and against England, 17. He toured Zimbabwe and Kenya with the under-23 team and Sri Lanka with a Pakistan A team. He took 42 wickets in the 1991/2 season at 15.92 and finished third in the averages; he has been a consistent performer on the domestic circuit. He toured Sharjah with Pakistan in 1994 for the Australasia Cup but did not play in any match

First-class career (1989–   ): 538 runs (14.94), 175 wickets (22.74), and 14 catches

ATHAR VIQAR AZIM

(b. 1948, Karachi)

A club cricketer of some distinction, Athar became a dominant figure as a producer of sports and current affairs for Pakistan Television. Tall and good looking, a right-handed batsman with a variety of strokes, he has won five awards as the best TV producer, covering cricket, squash, and hockey. In the 1987 World Cup in Pakistan he was the chief producer, and he has also produced World Cup hockey and covered cricket at Sharjah for many years.

ATIF RAUF

(b. 1964, Lahore) *Lahore, Islamabad, Agricultural Development Bank, and Pakistan*

Atif Rauf made his first-class début in 1980/1 for Lahore but matured late as a right-handed middle-order batsman. Technically sound and very stylish, he is a front-foot player who loves to drive and can cut with immaculate precision. In ten matches in 1989/90 he averaged 43.08, in 1990/1 scored 699 runs in eleven games with two hundreds, and in 1992/3 his tally was 919 runs at an average of 41.77 in fifteen matches. But it was in 1993/4 that he really exploded, scoring 902 runs in ten matches at an average of 69.38. He took his team ADBP to the semi-final of the limited-overs Wills Cup with six unbeaten innings, including scores of 64 and 80. He finished the tournament with an average of 299.00. His 802 runs at an average of 66.83 in the Patron's Trophy won ADBP their first national title. In the final against Habib Bank in the first-class competition he made 118, and 85 in 97 balls, to demoralize the bankers. He was rewarded with a tour of New Zealand in early 1994. With Asif Mujtaba injured, he was given his first Test cap in the third and final match at Christchurch, scoring 16 and 9 in a match which Pakistan lost.

First-class career (1980–   ): 5,162 runs (40.32), 2 wickets (138.50), and 42 catches

AZEEM HAFEEZ

(b. 1963, Jhelum) *Karachi, Allied Bank, Pakistan International Airline, and Pakistan*

A tall and strong left-arm fast bowler with endless stamina, Azeem Hafeez was thrust into the considerable breach left by Imran's shin injury for the 1983/4 Test series against India, Australia, and England, despite his limited first-class experience. Born with two middle fingers missing on his right hand, he responded with the same courage and determination which had enabled him to overcome that disability. He made his début against India at Bangalore in 1983/4 and on the subsequent tour to Australia put in several marathon spells, heading the bowling averages with 19 Test wickets at 38.52, including 5 for 100 in the first Test at Perth. As the redoubtable Rod Marsh found out at the cost of a broken jaw at Adelaide, Azeem can get surprising pace and lift from a whippy action. His best Test figures of 6 for 46 against India at Lahore in 1984/5 secured his place for the two subsequent series against New Zealand when he took the respectable total of 22 wickets in six Tests. A fine ground fielder in the deep, he is also, despite his handicap, a safe catcher; and as a left-handed tail-ender, he has sometimes applied the long handle effectively.

First-class career (1982–90): 828 runs (11.66), 200 wickets (33.80), and 15 catches
Test matches (18): 134 runs (8.37), 63 wickets (34.98), and 1 catch

AZHAR KHAN

(b. 1955, Gujranwala) *Lahore, Punjab, Combined Universities, Pakistan International Airline, Habib Bank, and Pakistan*

A reliable and talented all-rounder, by the end of 1985/6 Azhar Khan had included a 209 not out among his 14 first-class hundreds. He has also on four occasions taken five or more wickets in an innings. A right-handed batsman and right-arm off-break bowler, he first played for Lahore in 1971/2. His sole Test was played against Australia at Lahore in 1979/80. In his only innings he scored 14 and, in his three overs in the game, took one wicket for two runs.

First-class career (1971–): 7,728 runs (37.69) including 16 centuries, 119 wickets (25.81), and 107 catches

AZMAT RANA

(b. 1951, Lahore) *Bahawalpur, Pakistan International Airline, Lahore, Muslim Commercial Bank, and Pakistan*

The younger brother of Shafqat Rana, Azmat was a neat and consistent left-hand batsman who played with steady success in Pakistan domestic cricket since his first appearance in 1969/70. His sixteen centuries included one of 206 not out, and also a century in each innings (100 and 100 not out) for Muslim Commercial Bank against Rawalpindi at 'Pindi in 1981/2. His only Test was played at Lahore against Australia in 1979/80. He scored 49 in his sole innings, did not bowl and took no catches

First-class career (1969–84): 5,984 runs (48.25) including 16 centuries, 0–85, and 74 catches

BASIT ALI

(b. 1970, Karachi) *Karachi, PACO, United Bank, and Pakistan*

Basit Ali's burgeoning Test career was in doubt in 1994/5 after he came home early from a controversial Pakistan tour of South Africa and Zimbabwe, amidst allegations of betting, bribery, and dressing-room rows. His action was a protest, but he decided against premature retirement when action was taken against the tour captain, Salim Malik. A dashing, dare-devil batsman who is never afraid to play his shots and improvise, Basit Ali modelled himself on his idol, Javed Miandad. Of similar build and height, his entry into international cricket was relatively late but very successful. A right-handed middle-order batsman and an occasional right-arm off-spin bowler, he showed early promise in club cricket in Karachi with massive scores in junior cricket. He was captain of the Pakistan Youth team for the World Cup in Australia in 1988 and toured Zimbabwe with the Pakistan B team in 1990, scoring a century in the last of the three matches. He announced his arrival on the domestic circuit with an unbeaten innings of 170 at the age of 15 for Pakistan Education Board in a grade two match in the Quaid-e-Azam Trophy and was selected to make his first-class début for Karachi in 1985/6. Against India in 1989 he was named captain of the under-19 team and at Gujranwala scored 189 against them in the mini-Test. In 1989/90 he made 1,479 first-class runs at 47.70 playing for Karachi and PACO but in 1990/1 he joined United Bank. His glut of runs at domestic level continued and in 1992/3 he made 860 runs (50.58) and was picked to tour the West Indies as a replacement for Salim Malik. He impressed everyone there with his attacking approach and maturity and topped the tour averages. In the opening four-day game against Jamaica, which Pakistan won by 144 runs, he scored 51 and 84. In the one-day internationals his contributions were consistently useful, with scores of 17, 34, 60, and 57. He started with a duck on his Test début at Port of Spain but in the second innings made 37 in a lost cause. In reply to West Indies 455 in the second Test at Bridgetown, Pakistan were tottering at 79 for 4 when he came in and batted valiantly to make an unbeaten 92 before he ran out of partners. He made 37 in the second innings but failed to save Pakistan from defeat. In the drawn final Test at Antigua he added another half-century and finished the tour making 222 in Tests at an average of 55.50. Against Zimbabwe, late in 1993 he was not much of a success but on the New Zealand tour in early 1994 he made 85 in Pakistan's win by an innings and 12 runs in the second Test at Wellington and later hit his maiden Test hundred (103) in the final Test at Christchurch and finished second in the batting averages (57.40), hitting a century and two fifties in the series. Later the same year he had further success with the bat on the Sri Lankan tour.

CHISHTY MUJAHID

First-class career (1985–): 5,928 runs (41.54) including 16 centuries, 6 wickets (65.00), and 51 catches
Test matches (14): 757 runs (34.40) including 1 century, and 4 catches

CHISHTY MUJAHID

(b. 1944, Delhi)

A gentle man but authoritative cricket commentator, Chishty Mujahid read law at Cambridge. His love for the game began when he played at club level as a right-hand batsman and right-arm leg-spin bowler. A frequent visitor to Tests in England during his student days in the late 1960s, he became a commentator renowned for being both articulate and knowledgeable. With Radio Pakistan he has toured Sri Lanka, India, Australia, South Africa, and England. He has worked in high-profile jobs in various national and international companies and became the director of corporate affairs and human resources in the UDL group of companies in Pakistan.

CORNELIUS, Alvin Roberts

(b. 1903, Allahabad, India; d. 1991, Lahore)

Justice Cornelius, 'Bobby' to his friends, was one of the founder members of the Board of Control for Cricket in Pakistan, instrumental in gaining the new nation's Test status in 1952. A Roman Catholic and an Anglo-Indian he had his education in the undivided India and at Cambridge in the 1920s. He was a judge at the time of Partition in the Lahore High Court. In the initial years of Pakistan cricket he served as the vice-president of the BCCP from 1948 to 1953. When the board was disbanded in the 1960s, he acted as the chairman of the *ad hoc* committee of the board and became its second president from 1961 to 1963. In his younger days, he played cricket at club level and loved the game. A father figure in Pakistan cricket, Justice Cornelius founded the Pakistan Eaglets Society and organized young Pakistan cricketers tours to England in the 1950s to gain experience. Pakistan's early cricket benefited a lot from his ability to find funds for the trips abroad by the cricketers. He was the country's Federal Law secretary and chief justice of the Supereme Court and had a brief stint as a law minister. Known in Lahore as the 'Judge Sahib' he had a sentimental attachment to the historic city, once the seat of the Moghul Emperors, and lived for 30 years in room number one of the Faletti's Hotel in Lahore.

D'SOUZA, Antao

(b. 1939, Goa) *Karachi, Pakistan International Airline, Peshawar, and Pakistan*

A very useful right-arm medium-fast bowler who sometimes bowled slower off-breaks, and a tail-end batsman difficult to dismiss, Antao d'Souza toured England in 1962, taking 58 wickets (34.79), though he was ineffective in the Tests. Undefeated in five of his six innings in the Tests, he headed the averages with 53. Against England at home in 1961/2 he took 9 wickets (22.88) from two Tests, in the third at Karachi capturing 5 for 112 in 57.5 overs in a total of 507, a truly heroic performance. He was always a tremendous trier. He played once against West Indies in 1958/9.

First-class career (1956–67): 815 runs (18.95), 190 wickets (26.03), and 20 catches
Test matches (6): 76 runs (38.00), 17 wickets (43.82), and 3 catches

EHTESHAM-UD-DIN

(b. 1950, Lahore) *Lahore, Punjab, Pakistan International Airline, National Bank, United Bank, Punjab University, and Pakistan*

A right-arm medium-paced bowler of portly build, but with a good action, Ehtesham belied his unathletic appearance with some steady performances for Pakistan until a tragi-comic appearance in the 1982 Leeds Test when, called from the Bolton Association as a late replacement but hopelessly overweight and unfit, he pulled a muscle in the field, after bowling tidily for figures of 1 for 46, and limped painfully out of the game. A record-breaker in the league, with 128 wickets in 1981 and 127 in 1982, he had been due to play in his own benefit match at Daisy Hill that same weekend, but instead of being a local hero he became something of a public laughing-stock. This was a shame for, in his previous Tests against Australia and India, he had performed a valuable stock bowling role, taking 14 wickets in three Tests at 19.28 against India in 1979/80. In domestic cricket in 1981/2 he took 77 wickets (18.18) in only thirteen matches.

First-class career (1969–86): 1,059 runs (11.38), 507 wickets (20.54), and 39 catches
Test matches (5): 2 runs (1.00), 16 wickets (23.43), and 2 catches

FAROOQ HAMID

(b. 1945, Lahore) *Lahore, Pakistan International Airline, and Pakistan*

A competent right-arm fast-medium bowler, Farooq Hamid toured Australasia in 1964/5, in all first-class matches collecting 11 wickets (33.09) and in his sole Test, against Australia at Melbourne, scoring 0 and 3 and taking 1 for 107.

First-class career (1961–70): 546 runs (13.00), 111 wickets (25.21), and 27 catches

FARRUKH ZAMAN

(b. 1956, Peshawar) *North West Frontier Province, Muslim Commercial Bank, and Pakistan*

A left-arm spinner, Farrukh Zaman took 3 for 80 and 4 for 37 for the NWFP Chief Minister's XI against New Zealand's touring team in 1976/7 and was impressive enough in winning the match to appear in the second Test at Hyderabad. However he was given very little chance, bowling only ten overs in the match, taking 0 for 15, not batting and not taking any catches. This was his sole Test.

First-class career (1971–92): 1,363 runs (10.90), 391 wickets (27.60), and 55 catches

FAZAL MAHMOOD

(b. 1927, Lahore) *Northern India, Punjab, Lahore, and Pakistan*

Solid in build and character, with striking green eyes, Fazal Mahmood became a senior police officer. He was known as 'the Alec Bedser of Pakistan' and was the most successful right-arm fast-medium bowler produced by his country before the 1970s. He was not so massive as Bedser in build, but his methods bore a distinct similarity. Both were masters of nagging, persistent length and concentrated on varied swing and a mixture of leg-cutters and break-backs. Fazal had no equal on matting and could be equally devastating on grass; determined, disciplined, and demanding, but always cheerful, he was also a hard-hitting lower-order batsman and very good field. Before Partition he represented Northern India in the Ranji Trophy competition. A certainty for the tour of Australia in 1947/8, he stood down owing to the announcement of Partition. In 1949/50 he was the leading bowler on Pakistan's visit to Ceylon, and, when Ceylon returned the visit in 1950, he took 20 wickets in two representative matches. In 1951/2 he captured 6 for 40 in 26 overs for Pakistan against MCC at Karachi, helping his country to victory. Once official Tests began, he toured India in 1952/3 and 1960/1, England in 1954 and 1962, and the West Indies in 1957/8, and at home played against India in 1954/5, New Zealand in 1955/6, Australia in 1956/7 and 1959/60, West Indies in 1958/9 and England in 1961/2. In the first official tour of India he was dominant with 20 wickets (25.51) in the Tests, besides making 173 runs (28.83). In the second match, at Lucknow, he had match-winning figures of 5 for 52 and 7 for 42. On the first tour of England he took 77 wickets (17.53) from sixteen first-class games, the four Tests bringing him 20 wickets (20.40), half of Pakistan's total of wickets. In the famous Pakistan victory at The Oval, Fazal took 12 for 99 (6 for 53 and 6 for 46). In the first official series at home against India, he captured 15 wickets (22.06) in four Tests. At Karachi against Australia in 1956/7 he was never mastered, taking 6 for 34 in 27 overs and 7 for 80 in 48 overs (13 for 114 in 75 overs), and Pakistan defeated Australia in their first-ever encounter. In a losing cause in the Caribbean he captured 20 wickets (38.20) in the Tests—in the third match at Kingston sending down 85.2 overs and taking 2 for 247—and hit a determined 60, his Test-highest, in the second match at Port of Spain. From 1958/9 until 1960/1 he led Pakistan in ten Tests against West Indies, Australia and India as A. H. Kardar's successor—winning two and losing two; he was dropped from the captaincy when all five Tests with India (in 1960/1) were drawn. Earlier he had led Pakistan to success against West Indies at home, taking 12 wickets (15.85) from his three Tests. In his final series as captain his bowling had lost penetration and he was severely criticized as leader. He played once against England in 1961/2; and, on the 1962 England tour, after two opening bowlers had broken down, he was flown over as replacement but, by this time, he was only a shadow of his former self and could not live up to expectations.

First-class career (1943–64): 2,602 runs (23.02) including 1 century, 460 wickets (19.11), and 38 catches

Test matches (34): 620 runs (14.09), 139 wickets (24.70), and 11 catches

GHAZALI, Mohammed Ebrahim Zainuddin

(b. 1924, Gujarat, India) *Services, Maharashtra, Muslims, and Pakistan*

A forcing right-handed batsman, useful off-break bowler and an excellent field, Mohammed Ghazali toured England in 1954, making 601 runs

GHULAM ABBAS

(28.61) and taking 17 wickets (39.64); he also played in two Tests, in his second at Old Trafford being dismissed for a pair and not taking a wicket

First-class career (1942–55): 1,569 runs (25.72) including 2 centuries, 61 wickets (33.65), and 17 catches

Test matches (2): 32 runs (8.00) and 0–18

GHULAM ABBAS

(b. 1947, Delhi, India) *Karachi, National Bank, Pakistan International Airline, and Pakistan*

A left-handed batsman, strong off the back foot and a splendid cover-driver, an occasional slow bowler and reliable field, Ghulam Abbas was a student when he toured Ceylon in 1964, Australasia in 1964/5 and England in 1967. In England he made 871 runs (34.84) and in his sole Test, the third at The Oval, scored 12 and 0.

First-class career (1962–85): 5,271 runs (35.61) including 9 centuries, 7 wickets (32.71), and 83 catches

GHULAM ALI

(b. 1966, Karachi) *Karachi and Pakistan Automobile Corporation*

A sound and compact right-handed opening batsman and a slow right-arm medium-pace bowler who is also used as a leg-spin bowler but only occasionally, Ghulam Ali possesses immense patience and concentration. Although he made his first-class début in 1983, his cricket flourished in 1990/1, with a flawless 101 against the New Zealand tourists for Karachi. In the 1991/2 season in twelve matches he piled up 988 runs (52.00), including three centuries, helping Karachi Blues to win the Quaid-e-Azam Trophy. In the following season in eleven matches he scored 595 runs (42.42) which also included two hundreds. Selected to tour Sharjah, he did not make the team. But in South Africa for the triangular one-day series in 1992/3 involving South Africa and West Indies, he made his only one-day appearance so far at Newlands against West Indies, scoring 2 in a total of 43, Pakistan's lowest score in one-day internationals.

First-class career (1989–): 3,332 runs (40.63) including 9 centuries, 6 wickets (35.50), and 31 catches

GHULAM MUSTAFA KHAN

(b. 1932, Lahore)

The longest serving official of the Board of Control for Cricket in Pakistan (BCCP), Mustafa joined the board in October 1957 and worked variously as assistant secretary, deputy secretary, and joint secretary. He was the first regular contributor to *Wisden Almanack* from Pakistan and compiled the *Pakistan Book of Cricket Records* in 1971, the first book of statistics on Pakistan cricket. He was assistant manager of the tour to Australia and New Zealand in 1979, and active in the administration of the 1987 World Cup.

GUL MAHOMED

(b. 1921) *Baroda, Hyderabad, and Punjab B*

See India section.

HAAFIZ, Shahid Yaqoob

(b. 1963, Lahore) *Lahore and Water and Power Development Authority*

His real name is Shahid Yaqoob but the title 'Haafiz' is added to his name because he learnt the Quran by heart at school. Against United Bank in 1984/5, his first season in first-class cricket, this right-arm fast bowler and right-handed batsman had an outstanding game with 11 wickets for 136 and an innings of 64. He toured Sri Lanka in the latter part of that year for an under-23 team and did well. In thirteen first-class matches in 1986/7 he scored 367 runs (19.31) and took 28 wickets (26.10). He was picked to tour the West Indies in 1987/8, making his one-day début at Antigua in the second one-day match of the five-match series. Fitness problems prevented his selection for the Tests.

First-class career (1984–90): 752 runs (25.06), 56 wickets (28.51), and 3 catches

HANIF MOHAMMAD

(b. 1934, Junagadh, India) *Bahawalpur, Pakistan International Airline, Karachi, and Pakistan*

Perhaps the best of four brilliantly gifted brothers who played cricket for Pakistan (Mushtaq, Sadiq, and Wazir were the others), Hanif Mohammad has been not just a national hero but a legend in Pakistan. Curly haired, with an open, boyish face, he was a small, compact, strong right-handed opening batsman with nearly all the shots in the use of which a rigid discipline was applied. He is one of only ten men to score a triple hundred in a Test match and has played both the longest and the highest innings in all first-class cricket. The latter was an innings of 499 for Karachi against Bahawalpur at Karachi in 1958/9. Always balanced and an unerring judge of the length of a ball, Hanif's bat often seemed impassable, certainly so even to the finest bowlers on the bland surfaces of his own land. But he proved his patience and skill all round the world. He scored 12 centuries in 55 Tests and 55 centuries in his career. He captained Pakistan in eleven Tests, winning two, losing two and drawing seven. He seldom took a risk, seldom gave an opponent a chance. Prolific even as a schoolboy, he first played for Pakistan at the age of 17 years 300 days against India at Delhi in 1952/3, scoring 287 runs (35.87) in the series and hitting four centuries on the tour, including 203 against the Bombay Cricket Association. He toured England for the first time in 1954, making 1,623 runs in first-class games but only 181 in the four Tests. He showed English spectators something of his monumental patience in making 59 in 314 minutes in the Lord's Test. Back at home he scored his first Test century, 142, against India at Bahawalpur in 1954/5 and the following season made 103 against New Zealand at Dacca. In the West Indies in 1957/8, in the same series in which Sobers scored his 365, he batted the record time of 16 hours 10 minutes to make 337 in a Pakistan total of 657 after they had followed on 473 runs behind. He shared in four century partnerships in that innings and his score is the third-highest in Test cricket. In the series Hanif made 628 runs at 69.77. When he injured his knee in the first Test against West Indies at Karachi in 1958/9, after scoring 103 in the first innings, he was forced to miss the rest of the rubber: he had to this point played in each of the 24 Tests played by Pakistan. The following season he scored 304 runs (60.80) at home against Australia (including 101 not out in a total of 194 for 8 declared in the third Test) and he was prolific in India in 1960/1, amassing 410 runs (51.25) in the series, including 160 in the first Test at Bombay. Against England in 1961/2 he drove bowlers to distraction, making 407 runs (67.83) including 111 and 104 in the second Test at Dacca when he batted in all for 14 hours and 53 minutes. English bowlers avenged themselves at home in 1962, when Hanif for once failed in the Tests. He captained Pakistan for the first time against Australia at Karachi in 1964/5 and later the same season at Melbourne he not only led the side but scored 104 and 93 and kept wicket

throughout in place of Abdul Kadir, who had injured himself batting, taking five catches, four in one innings! On the same tour he hit 100 not out at Christchurch to mark Pakistan's first visit to New Zealand, and when New Zealand paid a return visit in 1964/5 Hanif made 203 not out in a total of 385 for 7 at Lahore. He added 217 for the sixth wicket with Majid Khan. Captain in England in 1967 he made 187 not out at Lord's off 556 balls in 542 minutes, by now batting at number four. His last appearance in a Test, against New Zealand at Karachi in 1969/70, marked the first appearance of his youngest brother Sadiq, with whom he opened the batting. Mushtaq also played, only the third time that three brothers have played in the same Test. (The others were the Graces and the Hearnes.) There were some internal politics, according to some accounts, in his final departure. Later he became head of the national selectors. His son, Shoaib, is also a Test player.

First-class career (1951–76): 17,059 runs (52.32) including 55 centuries, 53 wickets (28.47), 178 catches, and 12 stumpings

Test matches (55): 3,915 runs (43.98) including 12 centuries, 1–95, and 40 catches

HAROON RASHID DAR

(b. 1953, Karachi) *Karachi, Sind, National Bank, Pakistan International Airline, United Bank, and Pakistan*

A tall, strapping man with heavy jowls and striking eyes, Haroon Rashid was a powerful right-handed batsman and a devastating destroyer on good wickets, but was a failure in England where the ball moves so much. A magnificent stroke-player, he first made his mark with an innings of 130 for National Bank against Bahawalpur at Bahawalpur in 1972/3. He toured Australia and the West Indies in 1976/7, scoring an impressive 57 in his first Test innings at Sydney where, in the third Test, Pakistan won a Test in Australia for the first time. He moved up the order to number three or four, playing in all five Tests against West Indies and making some useful scores. Against England at home the following season he became a senior batsman in the absence of players contracted to Kerry Packer, and Haroon responded with scores of 122, 45 not out (at Lahore), 108, 35 (at Hyderabad), and 27 in his only innings at Karachi. However, in England in 1978, Haroon's hitherto concealed technical deficiencies were exposed and he never mastered England's seam attack, making only 33 runs in five Test innings. Even then, however, he hooked one majestic six into the Lord's grandstand which will not be forgotten by those who saw it. He failed again in two home Tests against Australia in 1979/80; but a players' dispute over the national captaincy enabled him to rehabilitate himself in 1981/2 by scoring 153, a commanding innings, in the first Test against Sri Lanka at Karachi. He played only one Test in England in 1982 but had a useful middle-order role against Australia in 1982/3, scoring 148 runs in three innings at 49.33. An outstanding fielder, especially at short-leg, he was recalled for the fourth Test of the 1982/3 series against India but suffered the indignity of being bowled for 0 in a total of 581 for 3. Generally he suffered from inconsistent selection policies.

First-class career (1971–85): 7,500 runs (36.23) including 15 centuries, 8 wickets (31.87), and 126 catches

Test matches (23): 1,217 runs (34.77) including 3 centuries, 0–3, and 16 catches

HASEEB AHSAN

(b. 1939, Peshawar) *Peshawar, Karachi, Pakistan International Airline, and Pakistan*

A very capable, patient and accurate right-arm off-break bowler in university and trophy cricket, Haseeb Ahsan toured the West Indies in 1957/8, India in 1960/1 and England in 1962, and at home played against West Indies in 1958/9, Australia in 1959/60 and England in 1961/2. His best tour was that of India, when he took most wickets in the Tests, 15 (32.66). He never relaxed his grip when India made 404 in the second match at Kanpur, bowling 5 for 121 in 56 overs. In England he suffered a foot injury in the opening match at Worcester and soon had to return home without playing in a Test. A suspect action was an additional reason: there were suggestions that the umpires would 'no-ball' him if he bowled in Tests in England. He returned, however, as manager of the 1987 side, a role he carried out with much energy. Always smiling, he none the less preferred to fan the flames of the occasional controversy. For a time discredited in administrative circles at home, he returned as a member of the committee for the 1996 World Cup.

First-class career (1956–63): 242 runs (5.62), 142 wickets (27.70), and 9 catches

Test matches (12): 61 runs (6.77), 27 wickets (49.25), and 1 catch

IBADULLA KHALID

(b. 1935, Lahore) *Lahore, Warwickshire, Tasmania, Otago, Punjab, and Pakistan*

Although never possessing the rare talent which could take a match or an innings and shape it as he wished, 'Billy' Ibadulla proved himself a serviceable cricketer for many different teams. He played for Pakistan in New Zealand in 1964/5 and England in 1967, toured India in 1952/3 without playing in Tests, and at home played once against Australia in 1964/5. He represented Warwickshire for 16 years as a professional, and Tasmania and Otago as player/coach. A highly useful right-handed opening or middle-order batsman, medium-paced change-bowler and deputy wicket-keeper, he is a person of great natural dignity who has become an outstanding coach. He appeared in one match without success for Pakistan in India in 1952/3, but hit a splendid 166 on his official Test début against Australia at Karachi in 1964/5, having been specially called from England. His score equalled the Pakistan record against Australia, and his opening partnership of 249 with Abdul Kadir set a new record for his country and remains the first-class record for Pakistan. Essentially associated with Warwickshire (from 1956 until 1972), he exceeded 1,000 runs in a season six times, with 2,098 runs (33.83) in 1962 as his best; and shared in two record partnerships for the county: 377 unbroken for the first wicket with N. F. Horner against Surrey at The Oval in 1960, and 402 for the fourth wicket with Rohan Kanhai against Nottinghamshire at Trent Bridge in 1968. His best bowling figures were 7 for 22 against Derbyshire at Chesterfield in 1967. He settled as a coach in New Zealand, and in 1982 and 1983 stood on the English first-class umpires' panel. His son played first-class cricket for Gloucestershire and Otago.

First-class career (1952–72): 17,039 runs (27.31) including 22 centuries, 462 wickets (30.87), and 339 catches

Test matches (4): 253 runs (31.62) including 1 century, 1–99, and 3 catches

IJAZ AHMED

(b. 1968, Sialkot) *Gujranwala, Rawalpindi, Islamabad, Habib Bank, and Pakistan*

A gifted right-handed middle-order batsman and a left-arm medium-pacer, Ijaz Ahmed has drifted in and out of the Pakistan team. He is a hard-hitting batsman with a flourishing drive. After a quiet first-class début in 1983/4, he scored 983 runs in twelve matches in 1984/5 and toured Sri Lanka with the under-23 team. In the third limited-overs match he scored 79 with four sixes and seven fours. In the 1985/6 season he made a record 1,476 runs at an average of 46.12 in eighteen matches, with five centuries. In 1986/7 season he joined Habib Bank and effectively won the Wills Cup, with an unbeaten 123 in the semi-final and a fine all-round performance in the final. In the same season he made his one-day international début in his home town of Sialkot against West Indies. On the Indian tour in the 1986/7 season he made sizeable scores against the Zonal teams and finished with a tour average of 45.80, scoring a century against the Indian under-25 XI at Bombay. On his second début in the Madras Test he made only three but played well in the one-day matches, scoring 72 at Jamshedpur. On the England tour of 1987 he played in four Tests, making 150 runs, his highest being 69 at the Oval in the fifth and final match. On the West Indies tour in 1988 he played in the last two Tests and against Australia in 1988/9 made his first century (122) at Faisalabad. Another century against Australia at the MCG in 1989/90 confirmed his authority as a batsman but he could not maintain his form in later years at international level. Selection eluded him until he was recalled in 1994/5, when he toured South Africa and Zimbabwe with success. By the start of that season he had already played in 101 internationals scoring 1,750 runs (23.33) with two centuries, but taking only three expensive wickets (99.66)

First-class career (1983–): 6,753 runs (39.72), 33 wickets (29.60), and 85 catches

Test matches (24): 1,056 runs (31.05) including 2 centuries, 1 wicket (18.00), and 20 catches

IJAZ BUTT

(b. 1938, Sialkot) *Rawalpindi, Universities, Lahore, Multan, and Pakistan*

A sound and enterprising right-handed batsman and deputy wicket-keeper, Ijaz Butt opened the batting in his first Test, against West Indies at Karachi in 1958/9, and with 41 not out helped to hit off the runs needed for a ten-wicket victory. His Test-highest was 58 against Australia in the third match, at Karachi, in 1959/60. When he toured England in 1962, he made 21 dismissals and 1,016 runs (28.22), which included a century before lunch against Kent at Canterbury; he achieved little, however, in the Tests. He captained Rawalpindi for several years.

First-class career (1955–68): 3,842 runs (34.30) including 7 centuries, and 71 dismissals (51 c., 20 st.)

Test matches (8): 279 runs (19.92) and 5 catches

IJAZ FAQIH

(b. 1956, Karachi) *Karachi, Sind, Public Works Department, Muslim Commercial Bank, and Pakistan*

A skilful all-round cricketer, Ijaz was a forceful right-handed batsman and an off-break bowler with subtle variations on a steady theme. His promise was evident at home against West Indies in 1980/1 when he played his first Test at Karachi, though with little success. He toured with a Board of Control for Cricket in Pakistan XI in England in 1981 and played another Test in Australia in 1981/2, when he also bowled economically in the one-day internationals. In Pakistan he had a highest score of 183, in 1977/8, and in the following season he took 8 for 51 in an innings. In 1985/6 he collected 107 first-class wickets (16.06), as well as scoring 589 runs (34.64). He reappeared in international cricket in 1986/7, touring both India and the West Indies. In the Caribbean in 1987/8 he played in the first two Tests, taking 2 wickets in the first and making 10 not out in the second to keep out West Indies bowlers who were pressing for victory. His greatest triumph, however, had occurred at Ahmedabad in the fourth Test against India in March, 1987. Going in at number eight, he shared a seventh-wicket partnership of 153 with Imran Khan, going on to score 105, with four sixes.

First-class career (1973–92): 6,037 runs (32.80) including 18 centuries, 562 wickets (23.62), and 98 catches

Test matches (5): 183 runs (26.14) including 1 century, and 4 wickets (74.75)

IMRAN KHAN NIAZI

(b. 1952, Lahore) *Lahore, Pakistan International Airline, Dawood Club, Oxford University, Worcestershire, Sussex, New South Wales, and Pakistan*

The greatest of Pakistan's all-round cricketers, a captain who alone could unite the disparate factions of the game in his country, Imran Khan was not only the most influential cricketer Pakistan has produced, but also a household name throughout the world. A cousin of two other Pakistan captains, Majid Khan and Javed Burki, Imran was a proud, handsome, intelligent, and determined right-handed all-rounder. He bowled genuinely fast for long periods with a long run and leaping action, picked up and threw magnificently from the deep, and was a batsman of high class. He was educated at Aitchison College in Lahore and later at Worcester Royal Grammar School. At Oxford University he won blues from 1973 to 1975, captaining in 1974, and he was very much the outstanding Oxford cricketer of his generation, scoring 117 not out and 106 in the match against Nottinghamshire in the Parks in 1974, and on the same ground that season hitting 170 against Northamptonshire. He first played for Worcestershire in 1971, was capped in 1976, but in 1977 moved to Sussex whom he greatly helped to win the Gillette Cup in 1978 and the NatWest Cup in 1986. During a match for Sussex against Hampshire in 1981 he roughed-up one side of the ball with a bottle-top, a device to swing the old ball against the shine which was against the law. He admitted this in a newspaper article after his retirement in support of other Pakistan bowlers who had been accused of 'tampering' with the ball. Implicitly Imran suggested that such tactics were almost inevitable in conditions in Pakistan which generally favoured the batsmen—slow and grassless pitches—and he was equally outspoken in defence of fast bowlers who softened up batsmen with bouncers. Imran himself was one of the few fast bowlers who could take his own medicine. His fast bowling gradually assumed greater significance than his batting, although he often produced match-winning performances in both roles, as at Worcester in 1976 when he scored 111 not out and took 13 for 99 in the match against Lancashire. He played first for his country in England in 1971, toured the United Kingdom again in 1974, Australia and the West Indies in 1976/7, New Zealand and Australia in 1978/9, the first of several visits to all the Test-playing countries of his era. He was a prominent all-round figure in Kerry Packer's 'World XI' in 1977/8 and 1978/9. His first great triumph in Tests was at Sydney in 1976/7 when his superbly hostile efforts earned him 12 wickets for 165 in the third Test, enabling Pakistan to win on Australian soil for the first time. He consistently took wickets as Pakistan's main strike bowler, for many years forming an effective partnership with Sarfraz Nawaz, and would have scored still more prolifically in Tests if the batting strength above him had not been so great. He rescued Pakistan with his first Test century, 123 against West Indies at Lahore in 1979/80, and the early 1980s saw him fitter, stronger, and prouder than ever, reach-

ing new peaks. In Australia in 1981/2 he was heroic in a losing cause, taking 16 wickets in three Tests at 19.50 and comparing favourably with all the Australian fast bowlers. He also made a valuable 70 not out at Melbourne, where Pakistan won. Back home at the end of the same season he returned after a players' dispute to devastate Sri Lanka at Lahore, taking 14 wickets for 116 in the match, including 8 for 58, his best Test figures, in the first innings. Asked to captain Pakistan for the first time in England in 1982, he led from the front, learning from defeat in the one-day internationals and inspiring Pakistan to a memorable victory at Lord's. Pakistan were unlucky to lose the series 2–1, despite Imran's 21 wickets (18.57) including 7 for 52 at Edgbaston, and 212 runs (53.00). He went on to lead Pakistan in 48 Tests and in most of his 175 one-day internationals, in which he scored 3,709 runs (33.41) and took 182 wickets (26.62). At the height of his powers, he led his country to two crushing 3–0 wins in series against Australia and India in 1982/3 and in taking 40 wickets at 13.95 in the six Tests against the latter he became the first Pakistani to pass 200 Test wickets. In the third Test, his all-round performance of 117 and 11 wickets (for the second consecutive match) had been bettered only by Ian Botham. But the hard wickets and unrelenting schedule of cricket had taken their toll on even Imran's magnificent physique. An injury to his left leg, diagnosed as a stress fracture of the shin, refused to heal properly and he did not bowl a ball in Test cricket for nearly three years. Uncertainty about his fitness led to a series of internal wrangles over the selection of the team for the 1983/4 tour to Australia. The initial decision of the national selectors not to consider Imran and to make Zaheer captain having been summarily overturned by the president of the BCCP, and all the selectors sacked, Imran led a reselected team, but was unable to play until the fourth Test, and then only as a batsman. In hindsight, it would have been better if Imran had declared himself unfit and withdrawn, but that is not the nature of the man and it was a reminder of his ability, if any were needed, that in his first Test for almost a year, at Melbourne, he scored 83 and an unbeaten 72. In England the previous summer he had comfortably topped Sussex's batting averages, scoring 1,260 runs, despite playing only half a season, giving one remarkable display of competitive instinct in a very unremarkable late-season fixture at Edgbaston: only half-fit and bowling fourth change off a shortened run, he took 6 wickets for 6 runs in 23 balls including the hat-trick, and also top-scored in both Sussex innings with 94 and 64. He played for New South Wales in the 1984/5 season, helping them to win the Sheffield Shield. Almost restored to full fitness, but anxious to pace himself, he played in half Sussex's three-day and most one-day games in the 1985 season before returning to Pakistan colours for the Sri Lankan series, quickly re-establishing his positions as a bowler, with 17 wickets in three Tests, and as captain, after Javed Miandad's enforced resignation at the end of the series. In 1987 he captained Pakistan in England again and this time won the series, taking 21 wickets (21.66) in the five Tests, including 10 for 77 (7–40 in the second innings) in the decisive victory at Leeds. In the last Test at The Oval he hit an imperious 118. Away to the West Indies in 1987/8 he did even better, taking 23 wickets at 18, including 7 for 80 at Georgetown to set up a great victory in the first Test: he finished the job with 4 for 41 in the second innings but the West Indies, to Imran's chagrin, had a narrow win in the third Test to deny Pakistan their claim to be world champions. On the other hand, Imran bowled outstandingly to take Pakistan to the semi-final of the 1987 World Cup (17 wickets at 13) and then, in a final triumph, led his country to victory in the final of the 1992 quadrennial tournament when Pakistan defeated England in the final at Melbourne. By now Imran had embarked upon life after cricket. He had not played in domestic (only international) cricket in Pakistan since 1981 because he disapproved of their first-class structure and following the death from cancer of his mother, Shaukat Burki, in 1985, he began a massive campaign to raise money for the building of a cancer hospital in Lahore. The campaign had political overtones, in the opinion of many, and as Imran became a more serious adherent of the Muslim faith and spent less time in his London flat and more at home, the temptation to use his immense popularity as the basis of a political career became stronger. In 1995 he caused an international stir by marrying Jemima Goldsmith, the daughter of a wealthy Anglo-French financier.

First-class career (1969–92): 17,771 runs (36.79) including 30 centuries, 1,287 wickets (22.32), and 117 catches

Test matches (88): 3,807 runs (37.69) including 6 centuries, 362 wickets (22.81), and 28 catches

IMTIAZ AHMED

(b. 1928, Lahore) *Northern India, Services, Punjab, Pakistan Air Force, and Pakistan*

A shy man but one of the rocks on which Pakistan cricket was built, Imtiaz Ahmed missed only one of the first forty-two Tests played by his country. A right-handed batsman of great fighting qualities and a crowd-puller when in top form, he indulged in delightful sweeps and powerful hooks, especially against the best fast bowlers, but he was not always consistent. Safe and sound as a wicket-keeper, he played for Northern India at 16 in the Ranji Trophy competition. For Pakistan he toured India in 1952/3 and 1960/1, England in 1954 and 1962, and the West Indies in 1957/8, and at home played against India in 1954/5, New Zealand in 1955/6, Australia in 1956/7 and 1959/60, West Indies in 1958/9, and England in 1961/2. On the first tour of England, he had 86 victims (80 while keeping wicket), the record for a visiting team. In the final match at The Oval, when England were beaten for the first time, he caught 7 behind the stumps—all off Fazal Mahmood. At home against India he made 233 runs (25.88) and disposed of 12 victims—mostly off Fazal. Against New Zealand he headed the batting with 284 runs (71.00), including the highest-ever made by a wicket-keeper in a Test, 209 in the second match at Lahore in $6\frac{1}{2}$ hours. Facing a total of 348, Pakistan had been struggling at 111 for 6 when he and Waqar Hassan added 308 for the seventh wicket, which remains Pakistan's highest for that wicket. In the Caribbean he made 344 runs (38.22) in the Tests, including 122 as an opener in the third Test at Kingston. In India in 1960/1 he scored 375 runs (41.66) in the Tests. He was the rubber-losing captain against England in 1961/2, his only good score in the series being 86 in the third match at Karachi, but his 'keeping was as good as ever. In England the following season, though very disappointed at losing the captaincy, his Test record was 282 runs (35.25) and seven victims. He came out of retirement to lead Pakistan against the 1963 Commonwealth side and Ceylon in 1964. His career-highest was a forceful 300 not out for The Prime Minister's XI against Commonwealth at Bombay in 1950/1. He has been chairman of the Test selectors and has had a book of poems published.

First-class career (1944–74): 10,323 runs (37.26) including 22 centuries, and 393 dismissals (316 c., 77 st.)

Test matches (41): 2,079 runs (29.28) including 3 centuries, 0–0, and 93 dismissals (77 c., 16 st.)

INTIKHAB ALAM

INTIKHAB ALAM

(b. 1941, Hoshiarpur) *Karachi, Pakistan International Airline, Surrey, Sind, Punjab, and Pakistan*

A shy but engaging and universally popular character, Intikhab Alam, or 'Inti', was a high-class leg-spin and googly bowler and exceptionally hard-hitting right-hand batsman in the late middle order. With receding hair, just under medium height, and built, it seemed, of solid muscle, he was seldom injured. Intikhab first played in a first-class match for Karachi in 1957/8 aged 16 years 9 months, and apart from his wide experience with Surrey, where he was capped in his first year, 1969, he also played as a professional for West of Scotland. He captained Pakistan in seventeen Tests and with notable success in England in 1974 when the Pakistan team not only held their own in three drawn Tests but went through the seventeen matches of the tour without defeat, the only side to have achieved this since Sir Donald Bradman's of 1948. He had also been captain on the 1971 tour to England and he went on two earlier tours to England in 1962 and 1967. With other official Pakistan sides he toured Ceylon in 1964, Australia and New Zealand in 1964/5 and 1972/3, the second visit as captain, and Australia and the West Indies in 1976/7 where, after a split with other leading players who had demanded greater remuneration, he was a sad, isolated figure, given little opportunity. He had made a happier visit to Australia as vice-captain of the Rest of the World touring team in 1971/2. His long Test career began auspiciously when he bowled the redoubtable Colin McDonald of Australia with his first ball, but he was run out for 0 in his first innings. In his second Test, the third against India at Calcutta a year later, he hit 56 as well as taking 4 for 68 in the match, but it took a long time for him to establish a regular place in the Pakistan side, and not until he took 7 for 92 in the third Test against New Zealand, at Karachi, in 1964/5 can he be said to have been a match-winner as a leg-spinner. Test cricket was changing: the pitches in his native Pakistan were usually too slow to make him a real danger and in other countries often too green to allow the luxury of a flighty back-of-the-hand bowler. But his all-round efforts continued to be useful: 51 in a stand of 190 with Asif Iqbal at The Oval in 1967, the highest ninth-wicket stand in a Test; 4 for 117 in England's first innings at Lahore in 1968/9 and, as captain against New Zealand the following year, 10 for 182 (5 for 91 in each innings) in the

third Test at Dacca. He led Pakistan to their first win in a rubber overseas in New Zealand in 1972/3 when his own role was decisive. At Dunedin in the second Test he took 7 for 52 (his best Test figures) and 4 for 78, and at Auckland in the next match 6 for 127. In March 1973 he also made his highest Test score, 138, against England at Hyderabad, including four sixes, in a match in which he also took seven wickets. These early years of the 1970s saw him at his peak. He took 104 wickets (28.36) in England in 1971, 32 of them for Surrey in the County Championship, which they won after a long break. The following season he recorded career-best figures of 8 for 54 for Pakistan against Tasmania at Hobart. He retired from Surrey after the 1981 season and a year later became official manager of Pakistan. Simultaneously Imran Khan became captain and the partnership of the two at the helm of Pakistan cricket proved all-conquering. The role of 'Inti' in this success was often overlooked, but when Imran was not there to unite the various factions, there were many rows and controversies. They included the accusations of ball-tampering by Pakistani bowlers which reached their peak on the 1992 tour of England. Three years later Intikhab was dismissed after an unsuccessful and mercurial tour of South Africa and Zimbabwe during which the captain, Salim Malik (also dismissed) was accused of offering bribes to two Australian bowlers earlier in the 1994/5 season.

First-class career (1957–82): 14,331 runs (22.14) including 9 centuries, 1,571 wickets (27.67), and 227 catches

Test matches (47): 1,493 runs (22.28) including 1 century, 125 wickets (35.93), and 20 catches

INZAMAM-UL-HAQ

(b. 1970, Multan) *Multan, United Bank, and Pakistan*

An imposing figure, tall and broad-shouldered but baby-faced, Inzamam took the cricketing world by storm with his exploits in the semi-final and the final of the 1992 World Cup in New Zealand and Australia. Pakistan required 123 runs in 15 overs at 8.2 in the semi-final with little hope of winning the match but Inzamam's 60 in 37 balls, which included seven fours and one six, changed all that when he shared an 87-run fifth-wicket stand with Javed Miandad. Pakistan won the match by four wickets. Another brilliant innings of 42 in the final against England at the MCG helped Pakistan almost as much. A right-handed batsman and a left-arm slow bowler, he had been a dominating figure as a batsman of class in domestic cricket. His form in first-class cricket and in the one-day competitions at home earned him a Pakistan cap against West Indies in 1990/1, when he was included in the second one-day game at Lahore. He made 20 in the tied match but in the third game hit a blistering 60. Against the touring Sri Lankans in early 1992 he scored successive centuries in the fourth and fifth one-day matches in his home town Multan and at Rawalpindi. His 101 at Multan had come in 121 balls and 117 in the final match in 104 balls with thirteen fours. He could not carry his World Cup form into the tour of England a few months later (1992). He made his Test début at Edgbaston but in four Tests in the series could only score 66 runs and was dropped for the final Test at The Oval. He scored an unbeaten 200 at Fenner's against Combined Universities and 75 in the final Texaco Trophy game at The Oval. Touring Australia and Sri Lanka later in the year his 75 in the one-off Test at Hamilton helped Pakistan win the match by 33 runs. On the Caribbean tour of 1992/3 he made his maiden Test hundred in the final Test at Antigua. He came to the wicket with Pakistan reeling at 108 for 4 and in danger of a follow on. He averted that with 123, adding 96 for the ninth wicket with débutant Nadeem Khan. In the first two Tests he had made only 49 runs but had started the tour with a superb innings of 107 against Jamaica in the opening match of the tour. In the series against Zimbabwe at home late in 1993 his best effort was a modest 57 in the first Test but on the tour of New Zealand in early 1994 he made an unbeaten 135 in the second Test at Wellington, which Pakistan won by an innings. With an average of 74.33 he topped the batting for the tourists. Later the same year he made another century in a Test in Sri Lanka. In Pakistan's first-class cricket, his best season was 1989/90, when he finished sixth in the batting table with 1,645 runs at an average of 60.92. He hit six centuries and as many fifties in twenty-one matches. A man of gentle manners and cultured ways he soon established himself in the Pakistan batting line-up and in 1994/5, on a largely disastrous tour of Southern Africa, he played with a class and consistency which stamped him as one of the world's outstanding players. Prior to this season he had already played in sixty one-day internationals, scoring 2,020 runs (39.60).

First-class career (1985–): 6,084 runs (51.12) including 18 centuries, 37 wickets (33.51), and 77 catches

Test matches (23): 1,541 runs (48.15) including 4 centuries, and 22 catches

IQBAL QASIM, Mohammad

(b. 1953, Karachi) *Karachi, Sind, National Bank, and Pakistan*

Only 5 ft. 6 in. tall, Mohammad Iqbal Qasim was a very accurate left-arm spinner and a fine close fielder, who, despite some consistent performances, particularly on home ground, was seldom a regular member of the Test team. He toured Australia and the West Indies in 1976/7, taking 4 for 84 in his first Test at Adelaide and following up with 4 for 111 and 3 for 19 at Melbourne, which was also the venue for his best overseas performance, 7 for 148 in 1981/2. He toured England in 1978 and 1982, disappointing on both occasions, and New Zealand and Australia in 1979 without playing a Test, but he proved far more effective against Australia on his home wicket at Karachi, taking 7 for 49. He played two further series, against Sri Lanka in 1981/2 and Australia 1982/3, but then lost his place until the New Zealand series of 1984/5 when, unexpectedly recalled for the first Test at Lahore, he took 4 for 41 and 4 for 65 to win the match, ending the series with 18 wickets at 22.11. Inevitably, though, this performance was not repeated on the subsequent tour to New Zealand. Not noted as a batsman, he hit an unbeaten 45 in the third Test against New Zealand at Karachi. He toured England as assistant manager in 1987, playing in only one first-class match, but reappeared in three home Tests against Australia in 1988/9, taking 12 wickets at 14.83, including 5 for 35 and 4 for 49 in the first Test at Karachi, which Pakistan won by an innings. At 35 he was clearly as good a bowler as ever, but he was not called on again. He played one season for Cheshire, in 1981.

First-class career (1971–89): 2,403 runs (14.38), 998 wickets (20.38), and 166 catches

Test matches (50): 549 runs (13.07), 171 wickets (28.11), and 42 catches

IQBAL SIKANDER

(b. 1958, Karachi) *Karachi and Pakistan International Airline*

A useful right-arm leg-spinner and a right-handed middle-order batsman, he was a consistent wicket-taker at club level while playing for the Agha Khan Gymkhana. Always bowling with a tempting flight, he surprised many batsmen with his faster delivery which came into them. Soon he was playing first-class cricket for Karachi and then for the Pakistan Airline and with resounding success. His best season as a bowler was in 1986/7 when he bagged 78 wickets at 17.74 apiece. He chipped in with respectable scores as well, and in 1985/6 in twelve matches he scored 677 runs at 42.31 an innings. He toured India with the Pakistan team but did not play in a one-day or a Test match. In 1980/1 he appeared for the President's XI against the touring West Indians at Rawalpindi, taking 7 wickets in the match for 177. He also toured Sri Lanka with the Pakistan A team in 1991, but it was a surprise when he was selected in the Pakistan World Cup team to tour Australia and New Zealand in 1992. He played in four matches, and picked up a wicket each against Zimbabwe, South Africa, and New Zealand, the latter in the semi-final at Auckland. In his four internationals he scored one run and took three wickets (49.00).

First-class career (1976–   ): 4,011 runs (20.36) including 3 centuries, 638 wickets (23.14), and 122 catches

IRFAN BHATTI

(b. 1964, Faisalabad) *Rawalpindi*

A lively medium-fast swing bowler, Irfan Bhatti made his first-class début in 1990/1 for Rawalpindi. In 1993 he powered his lowly rated team into the final of the Wills Cup by taking 17 wickets at 14.11. His reward was a one-day international cap at Lahore against Zimbabwe. Bowling eight successive overs, he dismissed the openers Andy Flower and Mark Dekker, conceding 23 runs in the process.

First-class career (1987–   ): 82 runs (20.50), 2 wickets (138.00), and 3 catches

ISRAR ALI

(b. 1927, Jullundur) *Southern Punjab, Multan, Bahawalpur, and Pakistan*

A competent left-handed batsman, fast-medium bowler, and close field, Israr Ali made his début for South Punjab in the Ranji Trophy competition in 1946/7 before Partition. He toured India with the Pakistan side in 1952/3 but achieved little in two Tests. At home he appeared in two more Tests against Australia in 1959/60, taking five wickets inexpensively. Playing for Bahawalpur against Dacca University in 1957, he made 79 and took 6 for 1 in 11 overs, and took 9 for 58 against Punjab A team in the same season.

First-class career (1946–61): 1,132 runs (20.58) and 114 wickets (22.64)
Test matches (4): 33 runs (4.71), 6 wickets (27.50), and 1 catch

JALAL-UD-DIN

(b. 1959, Karachi) *Industrial Development Bank, Public Works Department, Karachi, Allied Bank, Railways, Customs, and Pakistan*

A right-arm fast-medium bowler who played in glasses, Jalal-ud-Din had an outstanding season in 1981/2. He was called into the 1982 Pakistan touring team to England as a replacement and was prevented only by injury from playing in the Headingley Test. He made his first Test appearance, however, against Australia at Lahore in 1982/3, taking 5 for 92 in the match. He played a further four Tests against India in the 1982/3 and 1983/4 series without much success and, despite some consistent domestic performances, including match figures of 11 for 129 against House Building Finance Corporation in the Quaide-Azam Trophy, he could not win back his place until the first Test against the Sri Lankans at Faisalabad in 1985/6. Both his father and brother played first-class cricket.

First-class career (1975–89): 696 runs (11.79), 268 wickets (23.86), and 12 catches
Test matches (6): 3 runs (3.00) and 11 wickets (48.81)

JAVED AKHTAR

(b. 1940, Delhi, India) *Rawalpindi, Services, and Pakistan*

A tall, well-built right-arm off-break bowler, Javed Akhtar flew to England on the eve of the third Test at Headingley in 1962 as replacement for the injured Haseeb Ahsan, but he met with little success and in his sole Test (at Headingley) scored 2 and 2 not out and took 0 for 52.

First-class career (1959–76): 835 runs (15.75), 187 wickets (18.21), and 38 catches

JAVED BURKI

(b. 1938, Meerut) *Oxford University, Karachi, Punjab, Lahore, Rawalpindi, North West Frontier Province, and Pakistan*

A solid and reliable right-handed middle-order batsman and an occasional medium-pace bowler, Javed Burki was an Oxford blue from 1958 to 1960. He toured India in 1960/1, England in 1962 and 1967, and Australasia in 1964/5, and at home he played against England in 1961/2, New Zealand in 1964/5 and 1969/70 and Australia in 1964/5. In his first series against India he made 325 runs (46.42) and in his second, against England in Pakistan, he was second to Hanif Mohammad with 340 runs (56.66), which included 138 in the first match at Lahore and 140 in the second at Dacca, both rather slow, painstaking knocks. Captain of the 1962 side in England, he played attractive cricket, making 1,257 runs (33.07), but his only success in the Tests was in the second match at Lord's when Pakistan, 270 behind on the first innings, lost four wickets cheaply and he made a defiant 101, adding 197 with Nasim-ul-Ghani. In Australasia he had a handsome tour aggregate of 843 runs (36.65), but failed in the Tests apart from a 'safety-first' 63 in the second match against New Zealand, at Auckland. On his second tour of England he had a lean time—582 runs from 29 innings. His career-highest was 227 for Karachi Whites against Khairpur in 1963/4. A coach of Imran Khan, he became chairman of an *ad hoc* committee set up to run Pakistan cricket after 1994. In this role he had to deal with the accusations of corruption against some of the players who toured southern Africa in 1994/5.

First-class career (1955–75): 9,421 runs (36.37) including 22 centuries, 35 wickets (44.37), and 101 catches

Test matches (25): 1,341 runs (30.47) including 3 centuries, 0–23, and 7 catches

JAVED MIANDAD KHAN

(b. 1957, Karachi) *Karachi, Sind, Habib Bank, Sussex, Glamorgan, and Pakistan*

A brilliant right-handed batsman with the full array of strokes and a buccaneering aggression, Javed Miandad had the time and the ability to become the highest scorer ever in Test cricket but in his later years his selection depended upon the quirks of selectors, his own uncertain fitness and wrangles over who should be captain. After Imran's retirement, first Wasim Akram then Salim Malik were appointed ahead of him, but by 1995 he had led Pakistan in 33 Tests, and was his country's most capped player. He had also played in the phenomenal member of 228 one-day internationals, scoring 7,327 runs (41.86) with eight centuries. Small but wiry, a fine athletic cover fielder and useful leg-spin bowler, he was a most glorious cover-driver and square-cutter, and so precocious was his talent that he had scored six Test centuries before his twenty-second birthday. He appeared for the first time in first-class cricket

for Karachi Whites in the Patron Trophy tournament at the age of $16\frac{1}{2}$. While qualifying for Sussex in 1975 he scored 227 against Hampshire at Hove for Sussex second XI, sending his opponents home gasping at his ability. Because of the glut of overseas players at Hove, however, his opportunities for Sussex were limited and in 1980 he moved to Glamorgan, captaining them for half the 1982 season and continuing to play for them until 1985. In his best season, 1981, he scored 2,083 runs (69.43) for the Welsh county, hitting a record eight centuries. A more than useful member of the 1975 Pakistan Prudential World Cup side, he was accurate enough to bowl twelve overs of leg-spin for 42 runs against the might of the West Indies batsmen, but since his first Test in 1976/7 it has been his batting which has made headlines. He scored 163 against New Zealand in his first Test, at Lahore, and then in his third match made 206 to become, at 19 years 4 months, the youngest ever to hit a double-century in a Test. Already, at the age of 17, he had scored 311 for Karachi Whites against National Bank. A relatively lean period followed his magnificent start in Test cricket, especially in England in 1978, but in 1978/9 he scored four more Test centuries: 154 not out against India at Faisalabad; 100 at Karachi in the third Test of the same series; 160 not out at Christchurch against New Zealand; and 129 not out against Australia at Perth. Prematurely made captain of his country, he was not helped by his volatile temperament during thirteen Tests as captain between 1979 and 1982, and he was deposed as a result of a players' revolt. He was involved in a flare-up with Dennis Lillee in Australia in 1981/2, when Pakistan lost the first two Tests, but won the last at Melbourne. Javed, with 205 runs in the Tests and 682 (75.77) in the first-class matches of a badly arranged tour, was the side's leading scorer. Not at his best in England, after being replaced as captain by Imran Khan in 1982, he returned to form with 138 against Australia at Lahore in 1982/3, although this was an uncharacteristically dogged innings. He contributed more than his share to a high-scoring series against India in 1981/2, following up his 126 in the third Test at Faisalabad with his highest Test score, an unbeaten 280 in the fourth Test at Hyderabad, and sharing in a record Test third-wicket stand of 451 with Mudassar Nazar. A fine innings of 131 in the third Test at Adelaide rescued an otherwise erratic series against Australia in 1983/4, though he topped the tour averages with 952 runs at 63.46. His formidable consistency returned for the home New Zealand

KABIR KHAN MOHAMMAD

series in 1984/5 when he scored two centuries in the same match at his favoured Hyderabad. Having regained the captaincy from Zaheer for the subsequent tour to New Zealand, which Pakistan lost 2–0, he had the unusual distinction of resigning it a second time after two successive wins against Sri Lanka in 1985/6. His stated reason that he wanted to concentrate on his batting did not entirely ring true as he had made an unbeaten 203 in the first Test and it was widely assumed that he had jumped before he was pushed by the selectors who wanted Imran back as captain. In 1987 he scored 260 against England in the fifth Test at The Oval, assuring Pakistan of a win in the series. Having played an important role in Pakistan's victory in the 1992 World Cup in Australia, Javed led the team to England later that year and again played with authority, despite occasional bursts of temper on the field. He made 364 runs in the series (60.66). One unusual career statistic is that Miandad's first adverse lbw decision in Pakistan came in his 35th home Test.

First-class career (1973–94): 28,647 runs (53.44) including 80 centuries, 191 wickets (33.48), 337 catches, and 3 stumpings
Test matches (124): 8,832 runs (52.57) including 23 centuries, 17 wickets (40.11), 93 catches, and 1 stumping

KABIR KHAN MOHAMMAD

(b. 1974, Peshawar) *Peshawar and House Building Finance Corporation*

A left-arm medium-pacer, Kabir Khan fashioned himself on Wasim Akram, although he bats right-handed. Of medium-height and strong build he made his first-class début in 1990 and once claimed 7 for 69 in the Quaid-e-Azam Trophy against Karachi. He played in the opening three-day match for Bank of Khyber XI against Zimbabwe at Peshawar, taking 2 for 48. He was selected to tour Sri Lanka with Pakistan in 1994 and made his Test and one-day début in Colombo. In neither match did he bat, but in the Test took 1 wicket (39.00) and in the international 1 wicket at 34.00.

First-class career (1990–): 238 runs (9.52), 54 wickets (29.51), and 3 catches
Test matches (4): 24 runs (8.00), 9 wickets (41.11), and 1 catch

KARDAR, Abdul Hafeez

(b. 1925) *Northern India, Oxford University, and Warwickshire*

See India section.

KHALID HASSAN

(b. 1937, Peshawar) *Punjab, Lahore, and Pakistan*

A promising right-arm leg-break and googly bowler and fine field, Khalid Hassan toured England with the first team in 1954, but never settled down, appearing to bowl a little too fast so that his length and direction suffered. In his sole Test, the second, at Trent Bridge, he scored 10 and 7 not out and took 2 for 116 (in 21 overs). At 16 years 352 days he remained for three years the youngest-ever to have played in a Test anywhere. He was not tried again for Pakistan.

First-class career (1953–4): 113 runs (11.30), 28 wickets (38.25), and 2 catches

KHALID WAZIR

(b. 1936, Jullundur, India) *Karachi and Pakistan*

A useful hard-hitting right-handed batsman, medium-pace change-bowler and good field, Khalid Wazir toured England with the first team in 1954 while a student, but achieved little; he played in two Tests but was not tried again for Pakistan. He is the son of S. Wazir Ali (India).

First-class career (1952–4): 271 runs (15.05), 14 wickets (53.28), and 12 catches
Test matches (2): 14 runs (7.00)

KHAN MOHAMMAD

(b. 1928, Lahore) *Bahawalpur, Somerset, Northern India, Punjab University, Karachi, Lahore, and Pakistan*

Helping to establish Pakistan cricket in company with his fast-medium bowling partner, Fazal Mahmood, Khan was also right-arm but, though steady and accurate and able to swing the ball considerably in a heavy atmosphere, was subject to strains, injuries and other cricket engagements. Soon after the commencement of the first tour of India in 1952/3, Pakistan lost him through injury and in the Caribbean in 1958/9 he could appear in only two Tests. On the first England tour in 1954 his Lancashire League engagement precluded him from playing in more than a handful of matches. However, in the first Test, at Lord's, bowling unchanged with Fazal, he took 5 for 61. In the first official series at home, against India in 1954/5, he was the most effective bowler on either side, securing 22 wickets (15.86) in four Tests. Specially penetrative in the first innings, he took 4 for 42 in 26.5 overs at Dacca, 5 for 74 at Bahawalpur, 4 for 79 at Peshawar, and 5 for 72 at Karachi. Against New Zealand in 1955/6 he captured 13 wickets (16.00). In the third match at Dacca with the ball swinging and keeping low on the soaked matting, he was unplayable with 6 for 21 in 16.2 overs and 2 for 20 in 30 overs (19 maidens). In his last home Test, the first against Australia, at Karachi in 1956/7, he bowled unchanged with Fazal in the first innings of 80, finished with a record 7 for 112, and Pakistan won comfortably. However, his last series, against West Indies in the Caribbean in 1957/8, he played in two Tests, at Kingston in the third sending down 54 overs and taking 0 for 259. He became a professional in the Lancashire League; captained Bahawalpur; and later became a professional in Canada.

First-class career (1946–61): 524 runs (11.39), 212 wickets (23.29), and 20 catches

Test matches (13): 100 runs (10.00), 54 wickets (23.92), and 4 catches

KHAWAJA ABDUR RAB

(b. 1915, Lahore)

A right-handed middle-order batsman and a right-arm slow bowler with the ability to bowl both off- and leg-spin, Abdur Rab played in the 1940s in the Ranji Trophy for Northern India Cricket Association and, after Partition, for the Punjab Cricket Association. It was as a coach that he gained greater distinction. He coached at the Lahore Club, Punjab University, Aitchison College and the Punjab Cricket Association, guiding such future stars as Khan Mohammad, Majid Khan, Imran Khan, Sarfraz Nawaz, Wasim Raja, and Ramiz Raja. An academic and a graduate of Punjab University, he also taught Mathematics, English, and Urdu at the Aitchison. From 1965 to 1980 he stood as an umpire in first-class matches in Punjab. Majid Khan described him as the best coach that he met during his formative years. Of medium height and strong physique, Abdur Rab always had a lot of time and patience.

KHIZAR HAYAT

(b. 1939, Amritsar) *Lahore, Punjab, and Railways*

A Test umpire, Khizar is a sports officer of Pakistan Railways. As a right-handed batsman he played first-class cricket for Punjab Cricket Association and Lahore City. He also captained Railways for three seasons and toured England with the Pakistan Eaglets in 1957. He made his début as a first-class umpire in 1974 and officiated his

first Test match in 1979. He stood in the 1987 and 1992 World Cups. In 1982 he was invited to England to umpire in eighteen county games. He learned much from the experience. A person of impeccable behaviour and character and sound judgement he was one of the first two men from Pakistan appointed to the panel of ICC international umpires. By 1994/5 he had stood in over 30 Tests and 53 one-day matches, the highest by any umpire from the subcontinent.

LIAQAT ALI KHAN

(b. 1955, Karachi) *Karachi, Habib Bank, Sind, Pakistan International Airline, and Pakistan*

A left-arm medium-paced seam bowler, Liaqat Ali made one appearance against West Indies at Karachi in 1974/5. But it was not until Imran Khan left Pakistan's side during Kerry Packer's two-year World Series Cricket experiment that he got his chance at Test level with any regularity. However, in four Tests against England in 1978/9, two at home and two away, he took only five wickets.

First-class career (1970–91): 737 runs (7.59), 485 wickets (25.63), and 63 catches

Test matches (5): 28 runs (7.00), 6 wickets (59.83), and 1 catch

MAHBOOB SHAH

(b. 1938, Delhi, India) *Karachi and Baluchistan*

As a right-handed middle-order batsman and right-arm medium-pace bowler, 'Shahji' made his first-class début in 1954/5. He played for Karachi University in the inter-varsity matches, besides Karachi and Baluchistan. He diverted his attention towards umpiring and first stood in a Test in 1975 at Karachi. In 1981 he officiated in county games in England. His crowning moment came when he was asked to umpire the 1987 World Cup final at the Eden Garden, Calcutta, in the match between England and Australia. Softly spoken and intelligent, he was one of the first two umpires from Pakistan to be appointed to the ICC panel of international umpires. In 1994 he stood in a Test between Australia and South Africa in South Africa. He holds courses for budding Pakistan umpires on a regular basis and works for Pakistan Steel as a General Manager. He has umpired 22 Tests and 26 one-day games.

MAHMOOD HUSSAIN

(b. 1932, Lahore; d. 1991, Harrow, England)
Karachi Whites, Universities, West Punjab, East Pakistan, and Pakistan

Faster than Fazal Mahmood, Mahmood Hussain was a tall, confident, fast-medium in-swinging bowler who could obtain lift from any type of wicket but tended to waste much energy with leg-theory and was subject to physical break-downs. He toured India in 1952/3 and 1960/1, England in 1954 and 1962, and the West Indies in 1957/8, and at home played against India in 1954/5, New Zealand in 1955/6, West Indies in 1958/9, and England in 1961/2. At his best in England in 1954 he took 72 wickets (21.30), including 4 for 58 in the first innings of the last Test at The Oval—sharing the ten wickets with Fazal—when Pakistan beat England for the first time. On his second England tour, however, he was overbowled and was not very successful in the Tests. In the first home series against India he took 14 wickets (26.57), including 6 for 67 in the first match at Dacca. In the Caribbean he was bowled into the ground, conceding at least 120 runs in each of the first three innings of the Tests, and then broke down after pulling a thigh muscle, having bowled only five balls in the next Test at Kingston. Against West Indies in the second Test at Dacca, his 4 for 48 in the second innings helped Pakistan to a narrow victory. Against India in the first Test, at Bombay, 1960/1, he sent down 51.4 overs and took 5 for 129 in the sole innings. His best bowling in an innings was 8 for 93 for Karachi Whites against Karachi Greens in 1956/7. He has been active in cricket adminis-tration and managed the ill-starred 1978 touring team to England.

First-class career (1949–69): 1,107 runs (10.74), 322 wickets (25.13), and 29 catches
Test matches (27): 336 runs (10.18), 68 wickets (38.64), and 5 catches

MAJID JAHANGIR KHAN

(b. 1946, Ludhiana) *Lahore, Pakistan International Airline, Punjab, Cambridge University, Glamorgan, Queensland, Rawalpindi, and Pakistan*

A dignified, intelligent, and amiably sleepy char-acter, Majid Khan was a richly gifted all-round cricketer with a composed, quietly confident approach. A brilliant attacking batsman, he was a powerful driver, cutter, and hooker, who in the later years of his career became an occasional opener. He was also a fine close fielder and a natural bowler who once opened for Pakistan but

later bowled flat, curling off-spinners which drifted awkwardly away from the right-handed batsman. At Cambridge he was the most success-ful captain for years and, until he lost his enthu-siasm and left the county in 1976 in an atmosphere of discord, he was also a good captain of Glamorgan, so it is surprising that he captained his country in only three Tests. The son of Dr Jahangir Khan, the former Indian Test cap and Cambridge blue, Majid was born in the year before Partition and at the age of 15 was making 111 not out and taking 6 for 67 on his first appearance for Lahore B. That he came from thoroughbred cricketing stock was underlined by the success of his cousin Imran Khan, his brother Asad, and another cousin Javed Burki, who also captained Pakistan. Batting for Punjab University against Karachi, Majid scored a double-century —undefeated—after his side had been 5 for 4! He was 18 years 26 days when he made his first Test appearance, against Australia at Karachi. He made 0 in his only innings but as an opening bowler took three wickets. However, it seems there was some suspicion about the bouncer which got him the wickets and Majid, who had so many strings to his bow, made his own decision to alter his bowling style. On his first visit to England with an official Pakistan side in 1967, he managed only 38 runs in Tests, but he showed his quality and power in scoring 973 runs (42.30) in other games including an amazing 147 not out in 89 minutes at Swansea, where he hit the off-spinner Roger Davis for 5 sixes in one six-ball over and in all hit 13 sixes. Glamorgan soon signed him and after making 1,258 runs in his first season, he scored 1,547 (39.66) in 1969. It was partly because he was already such a mature cricketer that his influence was so great when he arrived at Cambridge. Captaining the side in 1971 and 1972, he led them to the first victory against Oxford for 14 years. He captained by calm and confident example both in technique and spirit. In Australia, Queensland, eager for the same charisma to go to work, employed him for the 1973/4 Sheffield Shield season. He hit centuries in his first two matches but later lost form. The previous season Majid had scored a memorable 158 at Melbourne against Australia in his 20th Test innings, the highest score by a Pakistan player in Australia, and against New Zealand on the same visit his scores were 79, 79, 26, 110, and 33. Further Test centuries now began to flow: one against West Indies at Karachi in 1974/5; against New Zealand at Karachi and against West Indies at Georgetown, both in 1976/7, and against New Zealand at Napier and against Australia at Melbourne in 1978/9. He scored 89 and 110 not out in his only two Test innings at home against Australia in 1979/80. His brilliance shone more fitfully for Pakistan in the early 1980s, though he was at his best in making 74 in the third Test at Melbourne in 1981/2. He followed this with 63 against Sri Lanka at Lahore in the same season; but in England in 1982 he was a shadow of the magisterial player he had been for so many years and his career came to an unfittingly bleak end when he was recalled for the fifth Test against India in 1982/3 and failed to score in his only innings.

First-class career (1961–85): 27,444 runs (43.01) including 73 centuries, 224 wickets (32.12), and 410 catches

Test matches (63): 3,931 runs (38.92) including 8 centuries, 27 wickets (53.92), and 70 catches

MALIK NUR KHAN

(b. 1923, Tamman, nr. Rawalpindi)

Air Marshal Nur Khan, a professional soldier, has been a highly influential figure in Pakistan's sports and also in politics. A very efficient and articulate administrator, in his younger years he was an ace pilot in the Pakistan Air Force. He became chief of the Air Staff of his country from 1965, governor of West Pakistan, and chief executive of the Pakistan International Airline. His contribution to sports in his country is second to none. During his period as president of the Pakistan Hockey Federation (1966–9 and 1978–84) his teams won the hockey World Cup, Olympics, and Asia Cup. As an administrator of the airline he employed squash players and cricketers to promote the game and the company. He was the most respected and authoritative president of the Board of Control for Cricket in Pakistan (BCCP) from 1980 to 1984 and a very influential figure during the ICC meetings. He floated the idea of neutral umpires and neutral observers in international matches and introduced the Asia Cricket Cup. He appointed Javed Miandad, a young and junior player as captain of Pakistan against Greg Chappell's Australians in Pakistan in 1980 and on the tour of Australia in 1980/1. He stood firm in face of a rebellion by ten players against Javed Miandad's captaincy when he returned home to lead his country in the inaugural series against Sri Lanka. Without the majority of the rebels, which included Imran Khan and Majid Khan and all the stars of that era, Pakistan still won the series.

MANSOOR AKHTAR

(b. 1957, Karachi) *Karachi, United Bank, Sind, and Pakistan*

With Waheed Mirza, Mansoor holds the record for the highest-ever opening stand: 561 against Quetta for Karachi Whites in 1976/7. Mansoor's share was 224 not out. Slim, with a bushy moustache, he thus proved himself an exceptionally gifted right-handed batsman with a wide range of strokes, but he was not deemed to be quite ready for Test cricket when playing in Australia in 1980/1 after making his first two appearances at home against the West Indies. Still, in seven first-class innings in Australia he scored 345 runs (49.28) and he was even more successful in the tour of England in 1982, scoring 595 runs (39.66) in the first-class games and doing a useful job at number three in the Tests, topscoring with 58 in the first innings at Edgbaston and 57 in the first innings at Lord's. Having appeared to cement his Test place with a dashing 111 against the Australians at Faisalabad in 1982/3 and being selected for the 1983 Prudential World Cup, his career went into inexplicable decline, reaching its nadir when he played in only three matches, none of them Tests, on the tour of Australia in 1983/4. However, his performances in helping United Bank win the Quaid-e-Azam Trophy in 1984, which included a brilliant century in the semi-final, revived his career. He played in all five Tests against England in 1987, averaging 30, and was the only member of the team to score over 1,000 runs (1,156 at 55.04) on the tour. He also returned to Australia in 1989/90, but played in only one Test and in only two of the ten one-day internationals. In all he played forty-one internationals, scoring 593 runs (17.44).

First-class career (1974–   ): 12,462 runs (39.06) including 26 centuries, 30 wickets (37.60), and 146 dismissals (144 ct., 2 st.)

Test matches (19): 655 runs (25.19) including 1 century, and 9 catches

MANSOOR RANA

(b. 1962, Karachi) *Lahore, Bhawalpur, and Agricultural Development Bank*

The bearded Mansoor is a right-handed middle-order batsman and a useful right-arm medium-pace bowler. His father played first-class cricket before becoming a controversial umpire and his uncles Shafqat Rana and Azmat Rana played Tests for Pakistan. Azmat's twin, Sultan Rana,

MANZOOR ELAHI

also played first-class cricket. A compact little batsman with a wide range of strokes, he became a prolific scorer on the domestic circuit, reaching his peak in the 1985/6 season when he scored 1,124 runs at an average of 40.14. He toured Australia in 1981/2 with a Pakistan junior team. In 1988/9 he was the only batsman in the country to score over 1,000 runs, at an average of 67.31. His 809 runs (57.78) enabled the Agricultural Development Bank to win the Quaid-e-Azam Trophy. His performance earned him a spot in the Pakistan B team in the series against the visiting Sri Lankans the same year and he scored two centuries. He played two one-day internationals in Sharjah, scoring 15 runs (7.50).

First-class career (1978–): 8,396 runs (48.25) including 16 centuries, 19 wickets (32.52), and 61 catches

MANZOOR ELAHI

(b. 1963, Sahiwal) *Multan, Pakistan Railways, Allied Development Bank of Pakistan, and Pakistan*

A very strong and entertaining right-arm medium-pacer and right-hand batsman, Manzoor Elahi made his début against India at Faisalabad in the 1984/5 series, being run out for 26 and taking his first Test wicket. He subsequently played in the second Test against New Zealand at Hyderabad, where he batted at number eight and bowled only ten overs. A powerful hitter, who won the man-of-the-match award on his international début against India, he toured Sri Lanka with the under-23 side in 1983/4, India in 1986/7, England in 1987, and Zimbabwe and South Africa in 1994/5. He was also a regular visitor to Sharjah. In a charity match at West Bromwich in 1987 he hit six sixes in an over.

First-class career (1982–94): 6,260 runs (34.58) including 8 centuries, 241 wickets (30.69), and 112 catches

Test matches (6): 123 runs (15.37), 7 wickets (27.71), and 7 catches

MAQSOOD AHMED

(b. 1925, Amritsar) *Bahawalpur, Southern Punjab, Karachi, Rawalpindi, and Pakistan*

Maqsood was a stylish, attractive right-handed batsman, a natural hitter with a good eye, an occasional medium-pace bowler and a good field. He scored 137 for Pakistan against MCC at Lahore in 1951/2, came to England as a professional in the Staffordshire League, and toured India and England with the first Pakistan sides in

1952/3 and 1954 respectively. At home he played against India in 1954/5 and New Zealand in 1955/6. On the England tour he was second to Hanif Mohammad in the batting, making 1,314 runs (34.57) and often delighting the crowds, besides taking 20 wickets (43.95) and holding 14 catches; in the opening match at Worcester he hit a chanceless 111 in $2\frac{1}{4}$ hours. After his country had made a very shaky start against the visiting Indians at Lahore in the third Test, he added 136 with A. H. Kardar for the fourth wicket before he was stumped on 99.

First-class career (1944–64): 3,716 runs (32.03) including 6 centuries, 120 wickets (28.43), and 46 catches

Test matches (16): 507 runs (19.50), 3 wickets (63.66), and 13 catches

MAQSOOD RANA

(b. 1972, Lahore) *Lahore and Habib Bank*

Another of the cricketing Ranas, Maqsood is the son of the Test umpire Shakoor Rana and younger brother of Mansoor Rana. In his first match for Lahore in 1988/9 he captured 7 for 56 in the first innings against Faisalabad at Faisalabad. A right-arm medium-pace bowler and a right-handed tail-end batsman, he showed a lot of promise but never fulfilled it. To everyone's surprise he was named to tour Australia with the Pakistan team in 1989–90 and played his only one-day international match against Australia at the MCG without taking a wicket. He scored 5.

First-class career (1987–): 94 runs (7.23), 40 wickets (32.07), and 4 catches

MASOOD ANWAR

(b. 1967, Khanewal) *Multan, United Bank, Pakistan Automobile Corporation, and Pakistan*

A short and portly orthodox slow left-arm spinner and a left-handed lower-middle-order batsman Masood made his first-class début for his divisional team Multan in 1983/4 when aged only 16. A steady and accurate bowler, he soon became one of the frontline spinners on the domestic circuit. Born near Multan in a remote town of the Punjab province, he joined PACO to play three successive seasons for them before being employed by United Bank. With his spin and deceptive flight he mesmerized even the top batsmen of the country but always remained in the shadow of the left-arm spinner Iqbal Qasim until selected to play in the third and final Test of the 1990/1 series against West Indies, at Lahore. Pakistan and West Indies had won a Test each at Karachi and Faisalabad and in his one and only Test his gutsy and brave effort with the bat enabled Pakistan to save the match, and draw the series. In 193 minutes at the crease he made 37 off 127 balls against Bishop, Ambrose, Marshall, and Walsh at full throttle, until finally the spin of Carl Hooper accounted for him. In the first innings, batting at number nine, he made 2 in 54 minutes. His 3 wickets for 102 were those of Carl Hooper, Jeff Dujon, and Desmond Haynes. He remained an asset to his bank, taking 72 wickets at 23.22 apiece in 1991/2.

First-class career (1983–): 2,025 runs (18.24), 522 wickets (22.01), and 46 catches

MATHIAS, Wallis

(b. 1935, Karachi; d. 1994, Karachi) *Karachi, National Bank, Sind, and Pakistan*

An attractive and generally fast-scoring right-handed batsman, occasional medium-pace bowler and a particularly brilliant slip catcher, Wallis Mathias toured the West Indies in 1957/8, India in 1960/1, and England in 1962, and at home played against New Zealand in 1955/6, Australia in 1956/7 and 1959/60, West Indies in 1958/9, and England in 1961/2. In his first Test, against New Zealand at Dacca in 1955/6, he hit 41 not out in a rain-spoilt match, adding 96 in as many minutes with Hanif Mohammad for the sixth wicket. In the Caribbean he enjoyed his best series with 251 runs (27.88). When the West Indies toured Pakistan, he was at his best in the second Test at Dacca which Pakistan won narrowly; the first day he made 64 in a total of 145 and on the third day 45 in a total of 144. Afterwards, his career faded and, although he toured England, making 734 runs (30.58), he achieved little in his final series. He was, however, a popular and successful first captain of National Bank, whom he led from 1969 to 1976, later becoming coach, selector, and manager.

First-class career (1953–77): 7,520 runs (44.49) including 16 centuries, and 13 wickets (40.92)
Test matches (21): 783 runs (23.72), 0–20, and 22 catches

MIAN MOHAMMAD SAEED

(b. 1910, Patiala; d. 1979, Lahore) *Patiala, Northern India, Southern Punjab, India, and Pakistan (unofficial)*

Pakistan's first captain of the pre-Test era, Mian Saeed was a right-handed middle-order batsman and a right-arm medium-pace bowler. He played in the Ranji Trophy for Northern India, Patiala,

and Southern Punjab and for India in two unofficial Tests before becoming captain of Pakistan in unofficial Test matches against West Indies, Ceylon, and Commonwealth teams in the games played between 1948 and 1950. In 1948, when the West Indies team touring India under J. D. C. Goddard was invited on a detour of Pakistan, Mian Saeed led Pakistan's first-ever team against them in an unofficial Test at Lahore Lawrence Garden (now Baghe-Jinnah). In a drawn game he scored 101 in the second innings, sharing a second-wicket stand of 205 with Imtiaz Ahmed. He was captain of the Pakistan touring team to Ceylon in 1949, scoring 91 in a drawn game against a Ceylon XI at Colombo and 93 in the first 'Test'. Pakistan won by an innings and 192 runs. In 1950 when the Ceylon team made a return visit, he led Pakistan to an innings and 45 runs win at Lahore in the first 'Test' and by 10 wickets at Karachi. Mian Saeed's son, Yawar Saeed, played for Punjab and Somerset in the mid-1950s and his son-in-law, Fazal Mahmood, bamboozled many batsmen in official Tests while playing for Pakistan. Saeed later became chairman of selectors.

First-class career (1929–55): 2,338 runs (29.59), 5 wickets (53.60), and 31 catches

MIRAN BUX

(b. 1907, Rawalpindi; d. 1991, Rawalpindi) *Punjab, Rawalpindi, Services, and Pakistan*

A competent right-arm off-break bowler, Miran Bux played in two Tests against India in 1954/5—his final season of first-class cricket —and on his début in the third match at Lahore, he was, at 47 years and 275 days, the second-oldest Test débutant ever. A tall man, with large hands, he was for many years coach and groundsman at the Rawalpindi club. There, in his last season, he produced his best figures, 9 for 72 against Services. For, rather than against, services in 1956/7 Miran had taken 6 for 15 to help dismiss East Pakistan at Dacca.

First-class career (1949–54): 53 runs (3.31) and 48 wickets (19.45)
Test matches (2): 1 run (1.00) and 2 wickets (57.50)

MOHAMMAD ASLAM KHOKHAR

(b. 1920, Lahore) *Railways, Quetta, Northern India, Muslims, and Pakistan*

A very good right-handed, stroke-playing batsman, occasional leg-break and googly bowler and brilliant outfield, Mohammad Aslam Khokhar

MOHAMMAD FAROOQ

toured England with the first team in 1954, making 421 runs (28.06), and in his sole Test, the second, at Trent Bridge, scored 16 and 18.

First-class career (1938–64): 1,689 runs (29.39) including 1 century, 20 wickets (28.35), and 18 catches

MOHAMMAD FAROOQ

(b. 1938, Junagadh, India) *Karachi and Pakistan*

A hard-working right-arm fast-medium bowler who, in a short Test career, was one of the quickest of Pakistan's bowlers, and a hard-hitting tail-end batsman, Mohammad Farooq toured India in 1960/1 and England in 1962, and at home played against New Zealand in 1964/5. Although he took 33 wickets (26.42) from eight first-class matches in England, he broke down and could not complete the tour. When New Zealand were defeated in the first match at Rawalpindi by an innings, he flogged the bowling at number eleven, hitting 47 out of 65 for the last wicket with Pervez Sajjad in less than an hour, and in the match captured 5 for 82. He took 10 wickets (25.30) in the three Tests against New Zealand.

First-class career (1959–65): 173 runs (12.35), 123 wickets (26.98), and 7 catches

Test matches (7): 85 runs (17.00), 21 wickets (32.47), and 1 catch

MOHAMMAD ILYAS

(b. 1946, Lahore) *Pakistan International Airline, Punjab University, Lahore, and Pakistan*

An attacking right-handed opening batsman and useful leg-break and googly bowler, Mohammad Ilyas toured Australasia in 1964/5 and 1972/3, and England in 1967, and at home played against New Zealand in 1964/5 and England in 1968/9. On his first tour of Australasia he made 781 runs (31.24), including 154 against South Australia and 126 against Queensland, but his only notable Test performance was 88 in the third match against New Zealand on a tricky pitch. Against New Zealand in Pakistan he made 223 runs (44.60) in the three Tests. In the third match, at Karachi, as opening batsman, he raced to 126 in the second innings, having hit R. W. Morgan for four consecutive fours when his score was 97. In England, however, he shone only spasmodically until a foot injury laid him low. His Test career against England ended in 1968/9 on a low key against a background of rioting and chaos. Then, early in his second tour of Australia, a severe blow in the face by a bowler's delivery prevented him playing

for his country again, and he was accused of indiscipline. Instead of flying home, however, he applied for Australian citizenship and before the end of the season (1972/3) was playing first-grade cricket for Waverley in Sydney.

First-class career (1961–76): 4,607 runs (35.71) including 12 centuries, 53 wickets (31.00), and 48 catches

Test matches (10): 441 runs (23.21) including 1 century, 0–63, and 6 catches

MOHAMMAD MUNAF

(b. 1935, Bombay, India) *Karachi, Pakistan International Airline, and Pakistan*

A competent right-arm fast-medium bowler, a useful late-order batsman and a good close field, Mohammad Munaf toured the West Indies in 1957/8 and India in 1960/1 without appearing in any Tests, but at home he played against Australia in 1959/60 and England in 1961/2 with some success. At Lahore in the first Test against England he took four wickets for 42 in a total of 380.

First-class career (1953–71): 1,356 runs (17.61), 180 wickets (24.22), and 47 catches

Test matches (4): 63 runs (12.60) and 11 wickets (31.00)

MOHAMMAD NAZIR, jun.

(b. 1946, Rawalpindi) *Pakistan Railways, Punjab University, and Pakistan*

A right-arm off-spinner, with clever flight and fine control Mohammad Nazir proved the adage that spinners improve with age. Though his best Test figures remained the 7 for 99 he took on his début against New Zealand at Karachi (in the same match as Zaheer and Sadiq) in 1969/70, his consistent domestic performances, which included 86 wickets at 14.67 in 1981/2 and 70 wickets at 20.72 in 1982/3, earned him a Test recall against India at Bangalore in 1983/4 at the age of 37. In the third Test, he took 5 for 70 in the second innings and was selected for the tour to Australia where he only took one wicket in his three Tests. In the first phase of his career, he toured England in 1971, joining the team late, but played his only Test against England in Hyderabad in 1972/3. Recalled for the 1979/80 home series against the West Indies he had his most productive match at Faisalabad where he took eight wickets in the match. He had his best-ever season in 1985/6, aged 40, taking 88 wickets at 14.42, collecting ten wickets in a match no fewer than four times.

First-class career (1964–88): 4,211 runs (22.28) including 2 centuries, 829 wickets (19.26), and 84 catches
Test matches (14): 144 runs (18.00), 34 wickets (33.05), and 4 catches

MOHAMMAD TAHER MEMON

(b. 1939, India)

With advertising experience behind him and his knowledge of the game as a club cricketer in his student days, he successfully organized cricket sponsorship in the country on behalf of the Pakistan Tobacco Company, financing most of the domestic cricket competitions and international matches. He was deputy director of the 1987 World Cup and a member of the committee representing Pakistan in the 1996 World Cup.

MOHSIN HASAN KHAN

(b. 1955, Karachi) *Pakistan Railways, Karachi, Sind, Pakistan Universities, Habib Bank, and Pakistan*

Mohsin Khan was a relatively tall right-handed batsman with a wide range of graceful strokes, though early in his career he did not always play them at the right time. He earned a place in Pakistan's side against England in 1977/8 in the absence of several established batsmen who had signed to play for Kerry Packer in Australia. A determined, painstaking 97 for the Punjab XI against the England team earned him his first chance at Test level in the third Test, at Karachi, when he made an attractive 44 in Pakistan's only innings. In England in 1978 he played in all three Tests and batted consistently for a struggling, unsettled side, making 191 runs in five innings at 38.20, going in first wicket down and scoring more than 30 each time. Not selected against India on the return of the Packer players, Mohsin toured New Zealand and Australia in 1978/9 but played in only one Test in each country. His career suddenly blossomed anew in 1981/2 when he scored 1,160 runs (61.05) in the domestic season, flew to Australia as a replacement and reformed a highly successful Test opening partnership with Mudassar Nazar. Against Sri Lanka in the same season he scored 215 runs in three Test innings, including 129 at Lahore, his first Test hundred. In England in 1982 he played magnificently, scoring 1,248 runs in 20 innings on the tour at 73.41. He scored 203 not out against Leicestershire, and in the second Test at Lord's set up a famous win for Pakistan by hitting 200, with graceful driving and unerring strokes off his

legs. He hit a third Test century, 135, against Australia at Lahore in 1982/3 as well as scoring 104 in the first one-day international at Hyderabad. In the first innings of the Karachi Test he was given out 'handled the ball' after illicitly using his glove to prevent the ball hitting his stumps. In the first Test of the subsequent series against India he became the first Pakistani to reach 1,000 Test runs in a calendar year and in Australia showed his adaptability by scoring two of his side's four centuries in the series, 149 and 152 in the third and fourth Tests respectively. A man of moods and a perfectionist, he was so disillusioned by the end of the tour that he threatened to retire, but he put those thoughts behind him in the series against England, scoring his seventh Test century at Lahore and sharing in a record opening stand against England of 173. His partner on that occasion, Shoaib Mohammad, was selected ahead of him for the third Test against New Zealand in 1984/5, a reflection of a disappointing run which continued in New Zealand. Discarded again for the first Test against Sri Lanka in 1985/6, he renewed his opening partnership with Mudassar for the second Test. He was a prolific and popular professional with Walsden in the Central Lancashire League.

First-class career (1970–86): 11,254 runs (38.94) including 31 centuries, 14 wickets (39.00), and 135 catches
Test matches (48): 2,709 runs (37.10) including 7 centuries, 0–30, and 34 catches

MOHSIN KAMAL

(b. 1963, Lyallpur) *Allied Bank, Lahore, Pakistan National Shipping Corporation, and Pakistan*

Tall and strongly built, with a smooth run-up and fine action, Mohsin Kamal shot to prominence in taking 24 wickets in six matches in the Patron's Trophy in 1983/4. A graduate of the under-19 and under-23 sides, he became his country's 100th Test cap when he made his début against England in the third Test at Lahore in the 1983/4 series. It was a tough baptism for the 20-year-old because he was one of only three regular bowlers and his two wickets cost 125 runs in 32 overs. Not surprisingly, his confidence suffered and, though he toured New Zealand, he did not return to the Test side until the second Test in the home series against Sri Lanka in 1985/6 when, in a hostile spell, he tore through Sri Lanka's strong middle order to finish with 3 for 50, bowling straighter and quicker than on his début. In England in 1987 he took 36 first-class wickets (29.05) and played in

MOIN KHAN

four Tests. His enthusiasm in the field was contagious.

First-class career (1980–94): 1,144 runs (11.91), 270 wickets (32.07), and 27 catches
Test matches (9): 37 runs (9.25), 24 wickets (34.25), and 4 catches

MOIN KHAN

(b. 1971, Rawalpindi) *Karachi, Pakistan International Airline, Pakistan Automobile Corporation, and Pakistan*

A right-handed batsman and a reliable wicket-keeper, Moin made his first-class début for Karachi in 1986/7 when only 15 and within a short period established himself as a useful member of his team and later for his employers, the Pakistan Airline. Gutsy as a lower-middle-order batsman and equally good with the gloves, he served his apprenticeship and gained experience with Pakistan's under-19 and under-23 teams to Bangladesh, India, Zimbabwe, and England before being selected to make his international début against West Indies in 1990/1 in a home series. Leading the under-19 team to India in 1989/90, he scored a magnificent century (159) in 124 balls after half his side had been out for 129 in Bombay. That season he also helped Karachi Whites, his home team, clinch the Patron's Trophy from Karachi Blues by scoring his maiden first-class century (129). In the 1989/90 national under-19 championship, he scored 217 runs at an average of 72.33, which included an innings of 112 while batting at number eight. Leading the Pakistan B team to Zimbabwe, he took four catches in an innings victory in the final 'Test' at Harare. In the 1989/90 domestic season he scored 334 runs in six matches at an average of 33.40 but it was his 'keeping which impressed the selectors, with 23 victims behind the stumps. He was finally picked to play for Pakistan in the 1990/1 series against West Indies at home, when the regular wicket-keeper Saleem Yousuf sustained injuries. In his first match, the second Test at Faisalabad, he scored 24 and 32. Perhaps his noblest moments, however, came in the semi-final and final of the 1992 World Cup in New Zealand and Australia. In a pulsating match at Auckland Pakistan required 35 runs from the last five overs to beat New Zealand to the final. Moin hit twenty of them in eleven balls. In the final at the MCG he caught three England batsmen behind the stumps and finished the World Cup with 14 victims (three stumpings). Moin had an unsuccessful tour of England later in 1992 and it took him 3 years to regain his place.

First-class career (1986–): 2,176 runs (26.86) including 2 centuries, and 198 dismissals (182 c., 16 st.)
Test matches (13): 309 runs (19.13) including 1 century, and 36 dismissals (34 c., 2 st.)

MOIN-UL-ATIQ

(b. 1964, Karachi) *Karachi, United Bank, and Habib Bank*

A right-handed opening batsman of medium height and slim build, Moin started his cricket at club level for Nazimabad Colts. Possessing tremendous concentration he impressed the selectors and was picked to play in a two-day game at Sahiwal in the 1980/1 season against Laurie Potter's Australian Colts touring Pakistan. He top-scored with 34 but did not make his first-class début for Karachi until 1984/5, scoring 919 runs at an average of 41.77. No one before him had scored as many runs in his first domestic season. In 1985/6 he finished with 972 runs at an average of 81.00, hitting four centuries and finishing third in the batting averages, and in 1987/8, with 528 runs in only four matches, he topped the averages, scoring three hundreds and one fifty playing for various teams. In the 1986 Wills Cup one-day limited-overs final he blasted a hurricane 78 for United Bank against Habib Bank which prompted the selectors to include him in a hastily arranged limited-overs match in Quetta against the touring West Indies. He scored 67 scintillating runs and won the man-of-the-match award. In 1985 he toured Sri Lanka with Pakistan under-23 but was plagued by fitness problems and appeared in only three of the eight matches. He toured Sharjah as well but his big breaks came when he was selected to tour the West Indies in 1988 and New Zealand in 1988/9. Mudassar Nazar and Ramiz Raja were well established as the Test openers but he did manage to make his one-day début at Port of Spain in the fourth of the five-match series, making 46 in an opening stand of 109 with Ramiz Raja. In one-day internationals he scored 199 runs (39.80).

First-class career (1984–): 5,015 runs (32.99) including 10 centuries, 1 wicket (170.00), and 55 catches

MUDASSAR NAZAR

(b. 1956, Lahore) *Lahore, Punjab, Pakistan Universities, Habib Bank, Pakistan International Airline, United Bank, Cheshire, and Pakistan*

The son of another Test cricketer, Nazar Mohammad, Mudassar was a wiry, brave, and deter-

580

mined right-hand opening batsman with a savage square-cut, a useful bustling medium-pace bowler, and a good close-field. He carved a reputation as one of history's great stonewallers when in his third Test innings at Lahore in December 1977 he scored the slowest-ever Test hundred in nine hours 17 minutes. He proved later that he has plenty of strokes when in the remainder of the series against England he scored consistently, finishing with 309 runs from five innings. Like the other young players, bereft of experienced support because of the 'defections' to World Series Cricket, Mudassar struggled to find form in England in 1978. In the three Tests he scored only 86 runs (17.20), but on the tour made 677 runs from 21 innings and did enough to suggest a successful future. In 1979/80 he played further Tests against India, New Zealand, and Australia and he was a member of the Pakistan team in the 1979 Prudential World Cup. Against India at Bangalore in 1979/80 he scored 126, and in Australia in 1981/2 he showed how useful a bowler he could be when taking 12 wickets at a cost of only 13 each in one-day internationals against Australia and West Indies. Anyone doubting the worth of this performance had to keep quiet in England in 1982 when in the Lord's Test Mudassar, a man inspired, took 6 for 32 in England's second innings to win the match for Pakistan. He swung the old ball alarmingly. His ten wickets in the series cost only ten runs each and although he had only one substantial Test score with the bat he was unlucky. He formed an opening partnership of genuine Test quality with Mohsin Khan and on the tour averaged 82.50 with four hundreds, including 211 not out against Sussex at Hove. At home against Australia in 1982/3 he scored 198 runs in three Tests (66), the prelude to an orgy of self-indulgence on the docile home wickets against India when his aggregate of 761 runs in six Tests, which included a double-century and two hundreds in successive Tests, broke the Pakistan record for any rubber. During the course of his 231 in the fourth Test at Hyderabad, he equalled the world record for any wicket in Test cricket with a third-wicket stand of 451 with Javed Miandad. The imbalance of his performances at home and abroad was again illustrated on the 1983/4 tour of Australia when he struggled with bat and ball, scoring 261 runs in five Tests at 29.00 and taking three wickets at 96.00. But his Eddie Barlow-like ability to produce sudden wickets was again evident in the first Test against New Zealand in 1984/5 at Lahore. Opening the bowling on a benign wicket,

he took 3 for 8 off 11 overs. He had a mediocre series home and away with the bat, the highlight being a fine hundred in the second Test at Hyderabad, but he returned to form at home against Sri Lanka, averaging 84.33 for the three Tests. He did well in the three Tests in England in 1987, scoring 231 runs (57.75). These included a century at Edgbaston; and another followed at Lahore, against England once more, in 1987/8. A cheerful, irrepressible character, he played a good deal of league cricket in the north of England and was at the heart of Cheshire's revival in the Minor Counties competition. He married an English girl.

First-class career (1971–92): 14,078 runs (43.85) including 42 centuries, 152 wickets (34.34), and 141 catches

Test matches (76): 4,114 runs (38.09) including 10 centuries, 66 wickets (38.36), and 48 catches

MUFASIR-UL-HAQ

(b. 1944, Karnal; d. 1983, Karachi) *Karachi and Pakistan*

A steady left-arm fast-medium bowler, Mufasir-ul-Haq toured Australasia in 1964/5 but with moderate success, and in his sole Test, the third at Christchurch against New Zealand, he scored 8 not out, took 3 for 84 and held one catch.

First-class career (1960–76): 286 runs (7.15) and 105 wickets (26.78)

MUNIR MALIK

(b. 1934, Leih, India) *Rawalpindi, Punjab, Services, Karachi, and Pakistan*

A big-hearted right-arm fast-medium bowler, Munir Malik toured England in 1962, and at home played against Australia in 1959/60. In England he was overbowled, taking 43 wickets (39.93); in the third Test, at Headingley, he bowled without relief from 3 p.m. on the Thursday until 1.30 p.m. on the Friday, taking 5 for 128 in 49 overs in an innings of 428.

First-class career (1956–66): 675 runs (11.06), 197 wickets (21.75), and 23 catches

Test matches (3): 7 runs (2.33), 9 wickets (39.77), and 1 catch

MUSHTAQ AHMED

(b. 1970 Sahiwal) *Multan, United Bank, Somerset, and Pakistan*

A short, stocky, and skilful leg-spin and googly bowler, Mushtaq Ahmed had a hard act to follow

MUSHTAQ AHMED

in Abdul Qadir, but proved himself a world-class leg-spinner of rare accuracy and a cheery little cricketer too. He fields energetically and bats usefully, right-handed. Though he made his first-class début in 1986 for Multan, and played with success in domestic cricket for his provincial team and United Bank, he really came into the limelight in 1987 while playing for the Punjab Chief Minister's XI against England at Sahiwal, the town of his birth. The visitors had barely recovered from the demolition suffered at the hands of Abdul Qadir in the first Test at Lahore, where Qadir had taken 13 wickets, when a bowler with a similar bouncing action took 6 for 81. In the Youth World Cup in Australia in March 1988, Mushtaq confirmed this promise with 19 wickets. In the 1988/9 domestic season he bagged 29 wickets in five matches in the Patron's Trophy matches at an average of 20.00 apiece and finished the season with 52 wickets. The same year in the under-19 series against India he finished with 26 wickets at 19.76 and scored two fifties. He first appeared for Pakistan in a one-day game at Sharjah in March 1989 and toured Australia in 1989/90, making his first Test appearance at Adelaide. He was instrumental in Pakistan's success in the 1992 World Cup, taking 16 wickets at 19.43 and only months later played his part in Pakistan's 2–1 win in the five-match Test series against England in 1992 by bagging 15 wickets in the series at an average of 31.66. On the tour he took 66 wickets at 24.54. In his first season for Somerset in 1993 he finished with 85 wickets at 20.85, taking five wickets in an innings eight times and ten wickets in an innings on three occasions. Tipped as the trump card on Pakistan's tour of the West Indies in 1993, he started well by taking 5 for 86 and 3 for 43 in the 114-run win over Jamaica and 6 for 43 in the match against an under-23 XI at Grenada, but during this match he was arrested by police, along with Wasim Akram, Waqar Younis, and Aqib Javed on charges of 'constructive possession of a banned drug'. He was released when the charges were dropped but had to withdraw from the team after the first Test because of back injury. He had played in 77 one-day internationals by 1994/5, taking 89 wickets (31.98).

First-class career (1986–): 1,309 runs (13.49), 373 wickets (24.57), and 53 catches
Test matches (18): 163 runs (8.15), 44 wickets (36.47), and 5 catches

MUSHTAQ MOHAMMAD

(b. 1943, Junagadh, India) *Pakistan International Airline, Karachi, Northamptonshire, Staffordshire, and Pakistan*

The most versatile and, in all-round terms, the most prolific of the famous Mohammad brotherhood, five of whom played first-class cricket and four Test cricket for Pakistan, Mushtaq Mohammad disciplined his brilliant natural talent to become one of the most consistently successful Test cricketers of any nation in a long and very full career. He has scored over 30,000 runs and 70 centuries and was the first Pakistan player to have scored more than 25,000 first-class runs. A stocky right-handed batsman, he can play any stroke with superb timing, his wrists strong as steel yet flexible as a willow branch. Like his brother Hanif, his concentration and application are immense, but Mushtaq has often played fine attacking innings as well as dour defensive ones. As a leg-break bowler he has been one of the best in the world of a dying breed, taking his Test wickets much less expensively than most leg-spin contemporaries and, possessing a good googly, a genuine match-winner in the right conditions. The fourth of the brothers, Mushtaq showed unbelievable maturity at the age of 13 years 41 days by scoring 87 and taking 5 for 28 on his first-class début for Karachi Whites against Hyderabad, 1956/7. Two years later he became the youngest player ever to earn a Test cap, when in March 1959, at the age of 15 years 124 days, he played at Lahore in the third Test against the West Indies. Pakistan lost by an innings, Mushtaq made 14 and 4 and took no wickets but he was not in any way overawed and before the age of 19 he had scored 101 against India at Delhi and 100 not out against England at Trent Bridge in 1962. He played for Northamptonshire from 1966 to 1977, when after some criticism he resigned the captaincy which he had held for two years. Mushtaq had led Northamptonshire in 1976 to their first success in any major competition, the Gillette Cup, and also to second place in the Championship. In all matches for the county he had scored almost 16,000 runs (1,000 or more in a season 12 times) and taken 550 wickets. The Pakistan selectors restored him as captain for the tour to New Zealand and Australia in 1978/9 when those players who had signed contracts with World Series Cricket, Mushtaq amongst them, were recalled. Mushtaq, in fact, had travelled from Australia with Imran and Zaheer the previous season, apparently to play in the third

Test at Karachi but, after much politicking from both sides, the three 'stars' returned to Australia without playing. All missed the subsequent tour of England, where Mushtaq had played with official Pakistan sides in 1962, 1967, 1971, and 1974. His second tour as captain began on a high note with victory over New Zealand at Christchurch when Mushtaq's leg-breaks were the main instrument of victory: he took 4 for 60 and 5 for 59. He batted steadily in the two drawn games which completed the series, but as captain took responsibility for much of the acrimony in the two Tests in Australia, one won by each country, when, according to the spirit though not the letter of cricket, two Australian and one Pakistan players were 'cheated' out. He tried in vain to have one of the decisions reversed. But there can be no quibbling about Mushtaq's immense contributions to Pakistan cricket. Often more consistent than other more sparkling batsmen around him in the strong Pakistan batting sides of the 1970s, especially on green wickets in England, he scored 121 against Australia at Sydney in 1972/3, 201 against New Zealand at Dunedin on the same tour, and later the same season 157 against England at Hyderabad. In 1974/5 he made his first century against a West Indian attack, 123 at Lahore, followed by 121 at Port of Spain in 1976/7, when he also hit 101 and 107 in Tests at Hyderabad and Karachi against New Zealand. Apart from his skill on tricky pitches, it is hard to think of a more difficult batsman to dislodge than Mushtaq in the right mood on a good pitch. He continued to play a good deal including Minor County cricket, tours to the Middle East and North America, and club cricket in the Birmingham League. Fearless when facing a cricket ball arriving over a short pitch at 90 m.p.h., Mushtaq was afraid of dogs!

First-class career (1956–85): 31,091 runs (42.07) including 72 centuries, 936 wickets (24.34), and 349 catches

Test matches (57): 3,643 runs (39.17) including 10 centuries, 79 wickets (29.24), and 42 catches

NADEEM ABBASI

(b. 1964, Rawalpindi) *Rawalpindi and Pakistan*

An ebullient, bearded wicket-keeper and a reliable right-handed middle-order batsman, Abbasi made his mark through under-19 cricket. In his second season of first-class cricket in 1987/8 he finished seventh in the national averages, with 769 runs (54.92), helped by two centuries. He did not keep wicket much during the season although his additional talent of bowling with the new ball was used to the full. But it was as a wicket-keeper that he played against the Sri Lankan B team in 1988/9. He scored 113 at Lahore in the second 'Test'. The following season he played his three official Tests against India at home.

First-class career (1986–   ): 2,923 runs (31.09), including 4 centuries, 5 wickets (45.60), and 144 dismissals (119 c., 25 st.)

Test matches (3): 46 runs (23.00) and 6 dismissals (6 c.)

NADEEM GHAURI

(b. 1962, Lahore) *Lahore, Railways, Habib Bank, and Pakistan*

One of many left-arm spinners in Pakistan's domestic circuit, Nadeem had been on the scene for more than a decade when he toured Australia in 1989/90 and made his Test début at Sydney without scoring a run or taking a wicket. He played the first of his six one-day internationals (5 wickets at 46.00 in all) on the same tour. At the top level he was certainly disappointing for a man capable of taking 87 wickets for Railways in 1985/6 and 83 more for Habib Bank, at 18.86 apiece, the following year.

First-class career (1977–   ): 1,016 runs (12.39), 565 wickets (22.12), and 49 catches

NADEEM KHAN

(b. 1969, Rawalpindi) *Karachi, National Bank, and Pakistan*

The elder brother of the Test wicket-keeper Moin Khan, Nadeem is a left-arm spinner and right-handed late-middle-order batsman. Having made his first-class début for Karachi in the 1986 season he joined National Bank and was coached and guided by the experienced Iqbal Qasim. He was selected for a tour of the West Indies in 1993 along with his brother and played his sole Test in Antigua. He bowled 33 overs on the opening day and eventually finished with 2 for 147 in 38 overs in the first innings. In the match he scored 25 runs (25.00) and took 2 wickets (97.50). With Inzamam-ul-Haq he added a record 96 runs for the ninth wicket while making 25 at a time when Pakistan needed runs badly. He also played one limited-overs international, in Trinidad, but neither scored a run nor took a wicket.

First-class career (1986–   ): 1,120 runs (16.47), 240 wickets (28.87), and 45 catches

NASIM-UL-GHANI

(b. 1941, Delhi, India) *Karachi, Staffordshire, Universities, Dacca, National Bank, Public Works Department, and Pakistan*

A left-handed batsman, Nasim-ul-Ghani went for his strokes whenever possible in his younger, more cavalier days, but, on becoming a professional, tended to eschew risk; he was also a versatile, orthodox slow left-arm bowler, remarkably mature as a young player, of consistent length and much spin, and a good short-leg. He made his first-class début in 1956/7 at 15, bowling 79 overs in an innings (79–19–184–3) for Karachi Blues against Karachi Whites; and at 16 years 248 days, became the youngest Test player ever at that time on his début against West Indies in the first match at Barbados in 1957/8. He also toured India in 1960/1, England in 1962 and 1967 and Australasia in 1964/5 and 1972/3, and at home played against West Indies in 1958/9, Australia in 1959/60 and 1964/5, and England in 1961/2. In the Caribbean he headed the bowling in the Tests with 19 wickets (26.73), 6 for 67 in the second innings of the fifth match, at Port of Spain, which won the match with an innings to spare—Pakistan's first victory over West Indies. He did not then enhance his career until his first England tour, when he scored 247 runs (27.44) in the Tests, including a fine, stroke-making maiden century in the second match at Lord's. Pakistan were 77 for 4, 270 behind, when Nasim and his captain, Javed Burki, came together; in 3 hours they added 197 (Nasim 101), which remains the Pakistan record for the fifth wicket against England. On his second England tour he made spasmodic appearances without distinction, whenever his professional engagements allowed, and on his second tour of Australasia he made 200 runs (50.00) but rarely bowled on this unhappy visit. Among his best feats was 6 for 24 (12 for 54 in the match) for Karachi Whites against East Pakistan in 1961/2. For several years a professional in league cricket, he also played Minor County cricket for Staffordshire. In 1967 his 50 wickets for Longton cost only 12.32 each and included a hat-trick against Norton.

First-class career (1956–75): 4,490 runs (28.41) including 7 centuries, 343 wickets (25.16), and 104 catches

Test matches (29): 747 runs (16.60) including 1 century, 52 wickets (37.67), and 11 catches

NAUSHAD ALI RIZVI

(b. 1943, Gwalior, India) *Karachi, East Pakistan, Peshawar, Rawalpindi, Punjab, Services, and Pakistan*

A sound wicket-keeper and useful opening right-handed batsman, Naushad Ali toured England with Pakistan Eaglets in 1963 and Australasia in 1964/5, and at home played against New Zealand in 1964/5, his best score being 39.

First-class career (1960–79): 4,310 runs (36.83) including 9 centuries, and 170 dismissals (136 c., 34 st.)

Test matches (6): 156 runs (14.18) and 9 dismissals (9 c.)

NAVED ANJUM

(b. 1963, Lahore) *Lahore, Habib Bank, and Pakistan*

A penetrating right-arm medium-pace swing bowler and a right-handed batsman, Anjum has been a constant threat on the domestic scene, mainly as a bowler. Though he made his first-class début in 1979, he really came into his own in the 1983/4 season when he scored 828 runs and captured 55 wickets in first-class matches and was picked to make his one-day début for Pakistan against England at Karachi. His best outing was against National Bank in 1991/2 at Lahore where he took 9 for 45. Then, when his team were 69 for 5, he walked in to join Aamir Sohail and added 201 runs for the sixth wicket. He made 115 off only 125 balls taking his bank to the final against National Bank. He took 4 for 79 in the match and scored 43 and 33. He toured the West Indies in 1987/8 but without any success, but made his Test début against India in 1989/90 in the home series, taking 4 wickets in a drawn match for 149 runs. He toured England in 1992 but did not feature in the Tests. In thirteen one-day internationals he scored 113 runs (12.55) and took 8 wickets (43.00).

First-class career (1979–   ): 4,927 runs (27.67) including 6 centuries, 359 wickets (21.26), and 62 catches

Test matches (2): 44 runs (14.66) and 4 wickets (40.50)

NAZAR MOHAMMAD

(b. 1921, Lahore) *Northern India, Karachi, Sind, and Pakistan*

A generally attractive right-handed opening batsman and reliable close field, Nazar Mohammad played for Northern India in the Ranji Trophy competition from 1940/1 until Partition in 1947, and, when he toured India in 1952/3 on Pakistan's entry into official Test cricket, he was second to his opening partner Hanif Mohammad in the batting, making 687 runs (45.80), including three centuries. In his sole Test series, on this tour, he carried his bat through the innings of 331 for 124 not out in the second Test, at Lucknow, batting painstakingly for 8 hours 35 minutes. He retired from first-class cricket in 1953 after suffering a serious arm injury but became a National Cricket Coach, coaching his own son, Mudassar, who has also played for Pakistan.

First-class career (1940–53): 2,484 runs (40.06) including 7 centuries

Test matches (5): 277 runs (39.57) including 1 century, 0–4, and 7 catches

NIAZ AHMAD

(b. 1945, Benares, India) *East Pakistan, Dacca, Public Works Department, Railways, and Pakistan*

A competent right-arm fast-medium bowler and later-order batsman who could drive fearlessly and snick luckily, Niaz Ahmad toured England in 1967 and at home played against England in 1968/9. In England he took 25 wickets (34.52) and made 104 runs (20.80), but achieved nothing in his sole Test on the tour. He was the first indigenous East Pakistani to win a Test cap.

First-class career (1965–74): 466 runs (14.56) 62 wickets (38.45), and 31 catches

Test matches (2): 17 runs (—), 3 wickets (31.33), and 1 catch

NIAZ AHMED

(b. 1913, Azamgarh, India; d. 1964, Murree)

A member of the Indian Civil Service, Niaz Ahmed migrated to Pakistan after Partition in 1947 and worked in various high-profile jobs. At the time of his death in a car crash he was one of Pakistan's top civil officers in the capital Islamabad. Having played cricket at club level in his younger days, he maintained a keen interest in the game and was president of the Sind Cricket Association. His personal attention and his concern for the game helped cricket to grow in the Sind region. In his capacity as the administrator in that part of Pakistan he organized the building of the cricket stadium in Hyderabad which is named after him and became one of Pakistan's Test venues.

OMER KUREISHI

(b. 1927, Murree)

Having completed his education at Oxford and Harvard, Omer came back to Pakistan in the early 1950s and became his country's most liked and famous cricket commentator for nearly two decades. He toured Sri Lanka, England, Australia, and South Africa as a broadcaster and was manager of Pakistan's 1974 team to England. He worked as the editor of the *Karachi Times* and later as a director of public relations in the Pakistan International Airline. In the Lord's Test of 1974 when water leaked under the covers on to the pitch and Derek Underwood started to play havoc with the ball against the Pakistani batsmen, his strong protest as the manager of the team influenced the abandonment of the match. He also managed the 1979 team to New Zealand but came home early after criticism from his team.

PERVEZ SAJJAD HASSAN

(b. 1942, Lahore) *Pakistan International Airline, Lahore, Karachi, and Pakistan*

A graduate in psychology and a cunning slow left-arm leg-break bowler of accuracy and penetration even in unhelpful conditions, a rather moderate right-handed batsman but a good field, Pervez Sajjad toured Australasia in 1964/5 and 1972/3 and England in 1971, and at home played against Australia in 1964/5, New Zealand in 1964/5 and 1969/70, and England in 1968/9 and 1972/3. On his first visit to New Zealand he took 12 wickets (22.66) in the three Tests, including 5 for 42 in the second innings of the second match at Auckland, when he took four wickets in ten deliveries without cost. When Pakistan gained their first victory at home for six years, over New Zealand at Rawalpindi in 1964/5, he was prominent with 4 for 42 and 4 for 5 in 12 overs. In the three Tests against New Zealand five years later he was the outstanding bowler with 22 wickets (15.63); at Karachi he struck telling blows in the second innings with 5 for 33 in 24 overs, and at Lahore he took 7 for 74 in the first innings. In New Zealand, however, in 1972/3 his bowling was mastered. Including his visit with Pakistan Eaglets in 1963, he toured England three times —because of injury, joining the 1971 party later in the tour—and was not as effective as was hoped. His brother is Waqar Hassan.

QASIM ALI OMAR

First-class career (1961–74): 786 runs (10.48), 493 wickets (21.80), and 57 catches
Test matches (19): 123 runs (13.66), 59 wickets (23.89), and 9 catches

First-class career (1973–88): 6,704 runs (41.90) including 17 centuries, 6 wickets (38.16), and 70 catches
Test matches (26): 1,502 runs (36.63) including 3 centuries, 0–0, and 15 catches

QASIM ALI OMAR

(b. 1957, Nairobi, Kenya) *Karachi, Muslim Commercial Bank, and Pakistan*

A small, stocky and cheerful right-hander, with a crop of curly black hair advertising his East African origins, Qasim Omar (or Umar as he was sometimes known) in 1982/3 became the first player to score 1,000 runs in the Quaid-e-Azam Trophy in one season. His aggregate for nine matches was 1,078, including scores of 203 not out, 210 not out, 110, 174, and an unbeaten 110, and he was rewarded with a Test début against India the following season. But he did not get an extended run in the side until the tour to Australia. Batting at number three, and able to exploit his favourite hook and cut on the bouncier wickets, he recorded his maiden Test century at Adelaide, sharing in a record second-wicket partnership for Australia/Pakistan matches of 233 with Mohsin Khan, and showed such courage and enthusiasm in adversity that he quickly became a favourite with the home crowd, ending the series with 327 runs at 40.87 and a tour average of 42.61. Whilst having ice applied to various bruises on his body after his battle with Dennis Lillee in Adelaide, he said to the physiotherapist, 'Maybe you should just put me in the fridge!' He did not show the same qualities to his own crowd in the subsequent series against England, but proved against India in the aborted two-Test series of 1984, and against Sri Lanka at the beginning of the 1985/6 season that his ability to play big innings was not confined to domestic cricket when compiling 210 and 206 respectively, both at Faisalabad. In between, a poor home series against New Zealand was matched by a good tour to New Zealand where he topped the averages with 49.60, his fighting qualities being shown at their best in the third Test when innings of 96 and 89 were not enough to prevent his side's defeat. Quick and agile, he was a fine fielder. He was disappointing at home to the West Indies in 1986/7, scoring only 48 runs in six innings and after falling out of favour with Imran Khan and accusing team colleagues of discrimination and drug-trafficking, he never played for Pakistan again.

RAMIZ RAJA

(b. 1962, Lyallpur) *Lahore City Whites, Allied Bank, Service Industries, Punjab, and Pakistan*

A balanced and gifted right-handed batsman, the brother of all-rounder Wasim Raja, Ramiz Raja was one of three players to graduate from the under-23 side in Sri Lanka in 1983/4 to the Test team against England in the same season. His swift promotion was justified by weight of runs, 1,294 at 40.43 in the domestic season, including a magnificent 145 against the young Sri Lankans. A superb 60 in the semi-final of the one-day tournament in Australia against West Indies in 1984/5 proved his undoubted class, but he did not win back his Test place until the last Test of the 1985/6 home series against Sri Lanka when he made 52 in his only innings. Then, in the return series in Sri Lanka, he made his maiden Test hundred in the third Test in Colombo, 122 made in $6\frac{1}{2}$ hours, showing great adhesive qualities. Perhaps it was this innings which encouraged him to become an opening batsman. He took on the role in India in 1986/7 and made 114 at Jaipur on his way to 381 runs (42.33) in the series. In the one-day matches he frequently gave his side an enterprising start, with the wristy strokes all round the wicket which were to become familiar for the next few years. Although more Test hundreds proved elusive, he was outstanding in the limited-overs game, taking part in the 1987 and 1992 World Cup. He scored 349 runs at 49.85 in the first tournament and the same aggregate of 349, this time with an average of 58, in Australia and New Zealand in 1992. By 1994 he had played in 159 internationals, scoring 4,915 runs (33.43) with eight centuries. On Pakistan's 1992 tour of England he hit 1,036 first-class runs (43.16).

First-class career (1977–94): 8,424 runs (36.62) including 15 centuries, 5 wickets (55.80), and 79 catches
Test matches (48): 2,243 runs (30.72) including 2 centuries, and 27 catches

RASHID KHAN

(b. 1959, Karachi) *Public Works Department, Karachi, Pakistan International Airline, and Pakistan*

Making his first-class début in 1975/6, Rashid Khan was picked as a medium-fast right-arm bowler for two Tests against Sri Lanka in 1981/2, mainly because a players' revolt had deprived Pakistan of several top cricketers. Curiously, how-ever, it was as a tail-end batsman that he made most mark, scoring 59 and 43 not out when batting at number ten in his first two Test innings. He also bowled steadily and picked up three wickets in Pakistan's victory in the first Test, but just missed selection to England in 1982. He was a member of the 1983 Prudential Cup squad, opening the bowling in Imran's absence, and toured Australia in 1983/4, his one Test yielding a hard-earned 3 for 129 off 43 overs. He took 12 wickets on tour and was subsequently used mainly for one-day matches, though he was flown out as a replacement for Abdul Qadir on the tour of New Zealand in time to play in the final Test.

First-class career (1975–94): 2,153 runs (16.43), 426 wickets (25.74), and 82 catches
Test matches (4): 155 runs (51.66), 8 wickets (45.00), and 2 catches

RASHID LATIF

(b. 1968, Karachi) *Karachi and United Bank, and Pakistan*

One of many wicket-keeper/batsmen in Paki-stan's domestic cricket, Rashid Latif had a humble beginning and his early cricket was restricted to games for club, college, and Karachi University. In his inaugural first-class season in 1986/7 he played only three matches and bagged 12 victims while keeping wicket. In 1988/9 he played for the Combined Universities team against the touring Sri Lankan B team and his stylish, natural cricket attracted the attention of the United Bank, who at once employed him to play for them. In the Patron's Trophy grade one match against Paki-stan National Shipping Corporation (PNSC) he took seven catches in the Bank's ten-wicket win. In the semi-final he dismissed six batsmen and in the final a further nine. His all-round perform-ance enabled his Bank to win the Pentangular tournament at the end of the season. A total of 27 dismissals in eleven matches and 323 runs made 1990/1 a memorable season for him. Equally good against pace or spin, he was selected as Moin Khan's deputy for Sharjah matches and was taken to England on the 1992 tour where he played in eight matches. He made his one-day début in the third match at Nottingham, making 29 runs and in an auspicious Test début at The Oval scored an unbeaten 50 in 87 balls, which also included six fours. Before he went in to bat,

Geoff Boycott, a frequent visitor to the Pakistan dressing room, had asked him if he could bat. When he replied in the affirmative, Boycott promised him a five pound note if he made 35. Once he crossed that mark, Rashid waved his bat to Boycott in the commentary box and Boycott later handed him the promised prize money. On the 1992/3 tour to Australia and New Zealand he was as much a part of the team. In the one-off Test at Hamilton his contribution in Pakistan's sensational victory by 33 runs was 32 and 33. Plagued by back injury, he did not do much on the Caribbean tour later but averaged 56.33 in three Tests against Zimbabwe at home at the end of 1993, making an unbeaten 68 in the first Test at Karachi and 61 in the second Test at Raw-alpindi and had five dismissals in the final Test at Lahore in Zimbabwe's only innings. On the 1993/4 tour to New Zealand he dismissed 13 batsmen behind the wicket in three Tests and had a record haul of nine victims in the first Test at Auckland. Vice-captain to Salim Malik in South Africa and Zimbabwe in 1994/5, he twice had arguments with him about what to do after Pakistan had won the toss and, late in the tour, dramatically announced that he wished to retire from Test cricket. By 1994/5 he had already played in forty-five one-day internationals, scor-ing 339 runs (15.40) and claiming 60 victims, 11 of them stumped.

First-class career (1986–): 1,443 runs (26.72), 3 wickets (22.00), and 163 dismissals (139 c., 24 st.)
Test matches (16): 535 runs (26.75) and 49 dismissals (44 c., 5 st.)

REHMAN, Sheikh Fazalur

(b. 1935, Amritsar) *Lahore*

A sound right-handed batsman and leg-break bowler, Sheikh Rehman was flown out very late to the West Indies in 1957/8 as a reinforcement, Pakistan suffering at least three casualties, and in his sole Test, the fourth at Georgetown, scored 8 and 2, took 1 for 99 and held 1 catch.

First-class career (1954–62): 721 runs (19.51) and 91 wickets (21.65)

RIZWAN-UZ-ZAMAN

(b. 1962, Karachi) *Pakistan International Airline, Karachi, and Pakistan*

Quiet, soft-spoken and dedicated to cricket, an assiduous practiser, Rizwan was a small right-handed opening batsman with a good tempera-ment and excellent technique. He came to prominence after touring India in 1978/9 with Pakistan's under-19 side, topping the averages with 701 runs at 40.23. On his first senior tour, however, to Australia in 1981/2, he was less successful. Picked for the first Test in Perth he was lbw first ball to Alderman, the start of a collapse. He finished the tour with 431 first-class runs (43.10) and was not selected to tour England in 1982. He had two good first-class seasons in 1983/4 and 1984/5 when he averaged 57.60 and 78.64 respectively, but could not win back a Test place. However, following his most successful season, when he scored 1,198 runs (92.15), he toured Sri Lanka in 1985/6, and in 1986/7 played a home Test against West Indies and in five away to India. He made three fifties (197 runs at 24) but a double failure in the last Test cost him his place for good.

First-class career (1976–94): 12,050 runs (45.81) including 35 centuries, 81 wickets (22.60), and 105 catches

Test matches (11): 345 runs (19.16), 4 wickets (11.50), and 4 catches

SAADAT ALI

(b. 1955, Lahore) *Lahore, United Bank, Income Tax, and House Building Finance Corporation*

A right-handed batsman, Saadat was prolific in domestic cricket as an opening batsman. His brother, Ashraf Ali, played as wicket-keeper in Tests for Pakistan. In the 1977/8 season Saadat made a century in each innings of a first-class match while playing for Income Tax against Multan, 141 in the first innings and 222 in the second. In the 1983/4 season, which was his most successful, he made 1,649 runs (63.42), making four centuries, with 208 his highest score. The same year he made his one-day début against England at home making 44 and 78 in two one-day matches against them. He continued to bat with success in domestic first-class cricket but a Test cap eluded him.

First-class career (1973–88): 10,161 runs (38.87) including 21 centuries, 80 wickets (36.90), and 135 catches

SADIQ MOHAMMAD

(b. 1945, Junagadh, India) *Karachi, Pakistan International Airline, United Bank, Gloucestershire, Tasmania, Essex, Cornwall, and Pakistan*

The youngest of the famous Mohammad brothers, Sadiq was a left-handed opening batsman who hit the ball with a wristy brilliance and whose approach was generally more aggressive than that of his even more prolific brothers Hanif and Mushtaq. Good-looking, small, stocky, and a shy but personable character, Sadiq cut and glanced with crisp assurance, drove square of the wicket on the off-side and defended with determination when necessary, but he often fell to catches in the slips. With Zaheer Abbas he adorned Gloucestershire cricket after joining the county in 1972, the year after his first tour to England. He came with other official Pakistan sides in 1974 and 1978 and for the 1975 and 1979 World Cup tournaments. He also toured Australia and New Zealand in 1972/3 and Australia and the West Indies in 1976/7. More than most batsmen he was prone to peaks and troughs. Nevertheless, he consistently proved his quality in England, scoring more than 1,000 runs in seven seasons. Like his brothers he was playing first-class cricket as a schoolboy, making his début in 1959/60 at the age of 14 years 9 months. In addition to several sides in Pakistan he also played for Tasmania, where he was a player/coach. A useful leg-spinner, though seldom called upon in Test cricket, he took 5 for 29 for Karachi Blues against Lahore Greens in 1970/1 and 5 for 37 for Gloucestershire against Kent at Bristol in 1973. He scored four centuries in successive innings in 1976, including 163 not out and 150 in the match against Derbyshire at Bristol. In Test cricket he made his first appearance for Pakistan in 1969/70 against New Zealand, winning his first cap at Karachi in the same match as his future Gloucestershire colleague, Zaheer, also made his first Test appearance; Sadiq on this occasion did better with scores of 69 and 37 as opening partner for the only time with his elder brother Hanif. He scored the first of five Test centuries against Australia at Melbourne in 1972/3, following up later in the same tour with 166 against New Zealand at Wellington and then making 119 against England at Lahore when he got back home. In 1976/7 he hit 103 not out against New Zealand at Hyderabad and ten against Australia at Melbourne. He narrowly missed another Test hundred at Headingley in 1978 when, with 210 runs from five Test innings, his skill and experience saved an unsettled Pakistan side from even heavier defeat by England. It was, therefore, surprising, despite the return of the Packer players, that he should have lost his Test place after one appearance against India in 1978/9. He returned for three more Tests in India in 1979/80. He had a benefit with Gloucestershire in 1982, his last season. He had played one match for Essex in 1970 and had a season for Cornwall in 1984.

First-class career (1959–86): 24,160 runs (37.51) including 50 centuries, 235 wickets (31.85), and 326 catches
Test matches (41): 2,579 runs (35.81) including 5 centuries, 0–98, and 28 catches

SAEED AHMED

(b. 1937, Jullundur, India) *Lahore, Pakistan International Airline, Punjab, Railways, Universities, Karachi, Public Works Department, and Pakistan*

Though often in dispute with the Board of Control for Cricket in Pakistan, Saeed Ahmed was a resplendent stroke-making right-handed batsman of an upright stance with a particularly hard drive who thrived especially on firm pitches. He was also a useful slow to medium off-break bowler and a fine field at cover. Captain successively of Punjab University, Lahore and— briefly—of Pakistan, he toured the West Indies in 1957/8, India in 1960/1, England in 1962, 1967, and 1971, and Australasia in 1964/5 and 1972/3, and at home played against West Indies in 1958/9, Australia in 1959/60 and 1964/5, England in 1961/2 and 1968/9, and New Zealand in 1964/5. He enjoyed a highly successful first series, against West Indies in the Caribbean, making 508 runs (56.44) in the five Tests; on his début at Bridgetown he hit 65, and in other Tests he scored 64, 52, 44, 150 (at Georgetown in the fourth match), 12, and 97 in consecutive innings. When the West Indies toured Pakistan, he was the chief run-getter with 199 runs (39.80) from the three matches, including 78 in the first at Karachi, sharing in a then record second-wicket stand of 178 with Hanif; and he was also foremost in his first series against Australia, making 334 runs (55.66), which included a classic 166 in over 6 hours in the second match, at Lahore. In India he again scored most in a war of attrition, making 460 runs (51.11), including a painstaking 121 in the first match at Bombay, when he added 246 with Hanif in a then record second-wicket stand, and an attractive 103 in the fourth match at Madras. Although he faded rather against England at home, on his first England tour he was the second-best batsman, reaching 1,294 runs (34.97), including three centuries, making 302 runs (30.20) in the Tests. For Pakistan against the Commonwealth in 1963/4, he was head and shoulders above most of the other batsmen, but he was below his best on his first tour of Australasia. At home against New Zealand, however, in 1964/5 he made most runs, 286 (71.50),

including a glorious 172 out of 307 for eight wickets declared—his Test-highest—in the third match, at Karachi, when he battled for 5 hours 40 minutes, and saved his country from disaster, leading them, instead, to ultimate victory in both match and rubber. Generally competent in England on his second tour, he made 845 runs (33.80) altogether, and top-scored with two outstanding Test innings—44 out of 140 and 68 out of 114. Against a background of civil disorder he captained his country against England in 1968/9 in the three matches, the third being abandoned through rioting. He lost his place in the team against New Zealand and on his third England tour he did not find his form until late and played in the final Test only because Majid Khan was unable to appear. On the unhappy tour of Australia in 1972/3, he made 50 in the second Test at Melbourne, in which he had furious words with Dennis Lillee (who had Saeed uppermost in his thoughts for the series), claimed he was too unfit to appear in the third and final Test and was sent home for alleged indiscipline, ending his Test career. Younis Ahmed is his half-brother.

First-class career (1954–78): 12,847 runs (40.02) including 34 centuries, 332 wickets (24.74), and 122 catches
Test matches (41): 2,991 runs (40.42) including 5 centuries, 22 wickets (36.45), and 13 catches

SAEED ANWAR

(b. 1968, Karachi) *Lahore, United Bank, Agricultural Development Bank, and Pakistan*

A rumbustious left-handed batsman and a slow left-arm spin bowler, Saeed made his first-class début in 1986/7 and went through the grind of under-19 matches, later playing with great authority for Karachi, United Bank, and ADBP. Attacking and enterprising, he became one of the most entertaining and successful batsmen for Pakistan in one-day matches and later developed into a highly responsible opening batsman in Test cricket. A brilliant fielder near the wicket or in the outfield, he has the ability to destroy pace or spin with equal ease. He came into the limelight against the 1988 Australians by scoring 127 for NWFP Governor's XI at Peshawar in his first appearance against an international team. Taken to Australia for the World Series Cup, he made his one-day début against West Indies at Perth in 1988/9 where he did not make much impression. He was sent back home to play against Sri Lanka under-25 and scored heavily. The highlight of his

SAJID ALI

1989/90 season was his career-best 221 for Karachi Whites against Multan in the Patron's Trophy which was followed by 150 against India in a three-day match at Rawalpindi. His 42 in Pakistan's seven-run win at Gujranwala in the second one-day match against India earned him the man-of-the-match award. He toured Australia again in 1989/90 and batted magnificently in the World Series Cup. Against Sri Lanka he hammered a century in 99 balls at Adelaide, sharing a record 202 runs opening stand with Ramiz Raja. In his 126 he hit six sixes and eight fours. He finished the home season in 1989/90 making 1,082 runs (67.62) including five centuries and three fifties and later was a proud member of the Australasia Cup-winning team in Sharjah. He won his first Test cap against the West Indies in the second Test at Faisalabad, making a pair, and was ignored for the tour of England in 1992. He bounced back to regain his place for the 1993/4 tour of Australia and New Zealand and made his maiden Test century (169) in the second Test at Wellington, adding 197 for the third wicket with Basit Ali. An innings of 69 followed in the third Test at Christchurch. On the Sri Lankan tour in 1994 he made another Test century. In fifty-four one-day internationals he scored 1,811 runs (36.22).

First-class career (1986–): 4,360 runs (43.16) including 14 centuries, 9 wickets (42.11), and 36 catches
Test matches (12): 884 runs (40.18) including 2 centuries, and 4 catches

SAJID ALI

(b. 1963, Karachi) *Karachi and National Bank*

A right-handed opening batsman, Sajid emerged as the highest run-maker in the 1990/1 season with 1,460 runs at an average of 48.66, having notched up four centuries, including his first double-century in the Quaid-e-Azam Trophy against Multan. In only his second season, in 1983/4 he had aggregated 1,180 runs at an average of 49.16 and was in the reckoning for an opening spot for Pakistan. In 1984/5 he was in the Pakistan team to play against India at home in the second one-day international but the match and the rest of the tour was abandoned because of the assassination of the Indian Prime Minister Mrs Indira Gandhi and Sajid did not have the chance to bat. A few weeks later he played in the first one-day match against the New Zealand tourists and made 16 before being dismissed by Lance Cairns. He toured with Pakistan B to Zimbabwe in 1986/7 and batted well on the

tour. He also toured Sharjah in 1991. In 1992/3 he scored 1,232 (68.44) with five centuries to finish at the top of averages and in 1993/4 he hit three hundreds in his tally of 895 runs in twelve matches. Such form suggests that he should have had Test chances, but his ten one-day internationals by 1994/5 had produced only 83 runs (9.22).

First-class career (1982–): 10,435 runs (42.76) including 27 centuries, 7 wickets (43.57), and 137 catches

SAJJAD AKBAR

(b. 1961, Lahore) *Lahore, Sargodha, and Pakistan National Shipping Corporation*

One of many right-arm off-spin bowlers on the domestic scene, Sajjad remained in the shadow of Tauseef Ahmed and Ijaz Faqih but his success on Pakistan's slow wickets was finally rewarded when in 1989/90 he was selected to tour Sharjah for the Australasia Cup. His inclusion was well merited because he had taken 104 wickets in the 1989/90 season to become only the third man in his country's first-class history to take over 100 wickets in a season. He had also taken 96 wickets, at only 16.93, in sixteen matches in the 1985/6 season. In his two one-day internationals in Sharjah his 2 wickets cost only 22.50 runs each: he scored 5 runs. (5.00).

First-class career (1978–): 4,398 runs (28.93) including 4 centuries, 536 wickets (24.37), and 92 catches

SALAH-UD-DIN MULLA

(b. 1947, Aligarh, India) *Karachi, Pakistan International Airline, and Pakistan*

A stylish right-handed batsman with a specially fine on-drive, a useful slow off-break bowler, and good close field, Salah-ud-Din made his Test début at the age of 18 after only six first-class matches. Against New Zealand in the first match at Rawalpindi in 1964/5 he scored 34 not out and took 3 for 52 and 1 catch, but did not improve on this during the rest of his short Test career. He played against England in 1968/9 and New Zealand in 1969/70, and toured England in 1967 without appearing in a Test.

First-class career (1964–80): 5,729 runs (41.81) including 14 centuries, 155 wickets (28.45), and 63 catches
Test matches (5): 117 runs (19.50), 7 wickets (26.71), and 3 catches

SALEEM ALTAF BOKHARI

(b. 1944, Lahore) *Pakistan International Airline, Punjab University, Lahore, and Pakistan*

A very lively fast-medium right-arm bowler, using both in- and out-swingers, and an uninhibited batsman, generally at number eight, Saleem (or Salim) Altaf appeared in Test trials three times before being selected for his first Test against England in 1967. He toured England again in 1971, Australasia in 1972/3, Australia in 1976/7, and the West Indies in 1976/7, and at home played against New Zealand in 1969/70, England in 1972/3, and India in 1978/9. The fastest bowler of the 1967 side in England, he was handicapped by a torn muscle in the first Test, at Lord's. On his second England tour he was always dangerous with the new ball but suffered from illness. In the second innings of the third Test at Headingley he swept through the tail, taking 4 for 11 in 14.3 overs. In Australasia, swinging and seaming disconcertingly, he took 6 wickets (31.68) in the Tests, and in the third match at Sydney brought Australia close to defeat, taking 4 for 60 in the second innings. In the first Test against New Zealand at Wellington, he broke through in the second innings again, capturing 3 for 11 from his first 21 balls. In the final match at Auckland, he hit a steady 53 not out, his Test-highest, sharing in a last-wicket stand with Pervez Sajjad of 48. He played in one further Test against India at Lahore in 1978.

First-class career (1963–79): 3,067 runs (22.88) including 1 century, 334 wickets (28.29), and 61 catches

Test matches (21): 276 runs (14.52), 46 wickets (37.17), and 3 catches

SALEEM JAFFER

(b. 1962, Karachi) *Karachi, United Bank, and Pakistan*

A tall, slim, left-arm fast-medium bowler with a quick arm, 'Jeff' came to the top after having a series of match-winning performances in domestic cricket. An Ismaili Muslim (follower of the spiritual leader of the Ismaili sect, the Agha Khan), he soon made his mark after making his first-class début for Karachi Greens in 1983/4 against Lahore City in Lahore, where he took 5 for 11. In 1985/6 he had a tally of 80 wickets at 19 runs apiece in 18 matches for Karachi Whites and United Bank and played in one-day internationals for the first time against the West Indies. In the same series he made his Test début in the third

and final Test at Karachi, taking two wickets in a drawn game for 57 runs. He toured England in 1987 but had to go home injured before playing at home in the World Cup and suffering a mauling (57 runs from six overs) against Australia in the semi-final. He recovered to take five wickets against England in the Karachi Test of 1987/8 and toured the West Indies, playing in the final Test at Bridgetown. His best performance was 5 for 40 against New Zealand at Wellington in 1988/9. He played thirty-nine one-day internationals, taking 40 wickets at 34.55.

First-class career (1983–): 375 runs (8.15), 260 wickets (25.60), and 20 catches

Test matches (14): 42 runs (5.25), 36 wickets (31.63), and 2 catches

SALEEM MALIK

(b. 1963, Lahore) *Lahore, Habib Bank, Essex, Sargodha, and Pakistan*

A cricketer who bubbled over with keenness in his youth, Saleem (or Salim) Malik is a fine fielder and brilliant natural right-handed batsman with all the wristy strokes of the best Pakistan players and a silky timing. Appointed captain of Pakistan in 1993/4, in controversial circumstances, Saleem was eventually relieved of the job in 1994/5, after a disappointing tour of South Africa and Zimbabwe, during which he was accused of trying to bribe two Australians to bowl badly in the home series against Australia in October 1994. He denied the charge vehemently and it was his own superb batting which enabled Pakistan to win the series against the general run of play. He was chosen to tour Australia in 1981/2 at the age of 18 and scored 159 runs (39.75) in the only three first-class matches he played in. Later in the season he captained Pakistan's under-19 touring team in Australia and played his first Tests against Sri Lanka, making 100 not out in the second innings of his début Test at Karachi. He toured England in 1982 without making the Test team. A run of poor scores against India in the 1982/3 and 1983/4 series was relieved by a fine 107 in the third Test at Faisalabad, but it was not until the first of his five tours to Australia, when he joined the party late, that he began to establish himself in the middle order. In the final three Tests in Australia he had scores of 77, 35, 14, and 54 and against England looked easily the most impressive of the young Pakistani batsmen, scoring a patient and mature 116 in the second Test at Faisalabad and ending the series with 322 runs at 53.66. He scored his fourth Test century, an

SALEEM YOUSUF

unbeaten 102 against India in the second Test at his favoured Faisalabad, at the start of the 1984/5 season and averaged 68.00 in three home Tests against New Zealand, which included innings of 50 and 119 not out in the third Test at Karachi. Captain of the under-23 side to Sri Lanka in 1985, he made an unbeaten 140 in the first 'Test' at Kandy. In England in 1987 he was Pakistan's most consistent batsman, making a flawless 99 in tricky conditions at Headingley, an innings which paved the way for a famous victory. He scored 102 in the fifth Test at The Oval. In 1992 in England he did even better, scoring 488 runs (81.33) in five Tests and 1,184 (78.93) on the tour. For Essex in 1991 he had made 1,972 runs (73.03) including 215 against Leicestershire at Ilford. He also bowled his leg-breaks effectively at times. By the start of the 1994/5 season he had already played in 186 one-day internationals, scoring 4,532 runs (30.82) with five hundreds.

First-class career (1978–   ): 13,293 runs (47.47) including 35 centuries, 83 wickets (32.36), and 141 catches

Test matches (84): 4,804 runs (45.75) including 13 centuries, 5 wickets (49.20), and 54 catches

SALEEM YOUSUF

(b. 1959, Karachi) *Sind, Karachi, Industrial Development Bank of Pakistan, Allied Bank, and Pakistan*

An agile wicket-keeper and skilful hard-hitting right-hander, Saleem (or Salim) Yousuf played his Test cricket with the zest and naïvety of a schoolboy. He had to endure four years in the wilderness before regaining the Test place he had first won against Sri Lanka in 1981/2. He took five catches and two stumpings in that impressive début and showed that he had lost none of his ability by taking 12 more victims in his second and third Tests, also against Sri Lanka, in 1985/6 and he made enough runs in the lower order to suggest that Pakistan might have at last found a worthy successor to Wasim Bari. He toured England again in 1987, averaging 62 in the Test series, and also played in Australia, India, the West Indies, New Zealand, Bangladesh, and Sharjah. He was at his most valuable in the West Indies in 1987/8, scoring useful runs in every Test and a total of 196 (49.00) in his five innings. He blotted his copybook in England in 1987 when claiming a catch after the ball had bounced twice.

First-class career (1978–   ): 4,553 runs (28.63) including 6 centuries, 1 wicket (16.00), and 339 dismissals (298 c., 41 st.)

Test matches (32): 1,055 runs (27.05) and 104 dismissals (91 c., 13 st.)

SARFRAZ NAWAZ

(b. 1948, Lahore) *Lahore, Punjab, Public Works Department, United Bank, Northamptonshire, Railways, and Pakistan*

An amusing, unpredictable character, sometimes genial, sometimes liable to stormy tempers, Sarfraz Nawaz proved himself a fast-medium bowler of high class and was often extremely useful as a rugged, hard-driving, late-order batsman. By the time he finally retired (after a number of false starts) to take up a career in politics, he had become only the third Pakistani after Imran and Intikhab to take 100 Test wickets and score 1,000 Test runs. He was mentioned by Allan Lamb as being the man who taught others the effect of scratching one side of the surface of the ball in order to increase its propensity to swing. Sarfraz contested the allegation in the High Court in London, a suit he did not pursue to its conclusion. Very tall and strong, he allied with Imran Khan and Asif Masood in the 1970s to give Pakistan considerable seam-bowling strength. After a straight-backed wooden-legged run-up, he had a good high action and bowled at sharp pace, making the ball bounce and swing disconcertingly, and cutting it both ways off the seam. Not lacking courage (or was it foolhardiness?!) he once bowled a succession of bouncers for Northamptonshire against the Australian fast bowler Jeff Thomson. Although Thomson treated it as a joke and did not retaliate, Sarfraz found the massive West Indian Joel Garner less accommodating when he 'bounced' him in the 1979 Gillette Cup Final. Sarfraz's idiosyncrasies went further than this in 1977/8 when he flew from Pakistan to England in the middle of a Test series between the two countries (in Pakistan) as part of a one-man protest against the payment he was receiving, and the following winter he successfully appealed against Australian batsman Andrew Hilditch for handling the ball—Hilditch had picked up a gentle return from a fielder and thrown it back to Sarfraz, the bowler. Pakistan went on to lose the match and this incident marked a sad end to what had been for Sarfraz a highly successful tour, whose highlight had been a sensational spell at Melbourne on 15 March 1979 when he became the first visiting bowler to take nine wickets in a Test innings in Australia. His figures for the innings were 9 for 86 and, when Pakistan took the new ball at the start of the final day, Australia, with seven wickets left, needed only 99 to win. Cutting down his run and bowling seam up, Sarfraz took seven wickets for one run with the last 33 balls of his final spell. Pakistan won miraculously by 71 runs. Yet Sarfraz's career has also had its darker moments. He was not re-engaged by Northamptonshire in 1972, after first playing for them in 1969, but rejoined the county in 1974, was capped a year later and was a vital member of their team until 1982. First playing for Pakistan in 1968/9, he toured England in 1971, 1974, 1978, and 1982, Australia in 1972/3, 1976/7, 1978/9, 1981/2, and 1983/4, New Zealand in 1972/3 and 1978/9, and West Indies in 1976/7. Before his Melbourne performance his best figures in Test cricket were 6 for 89 against West Indies at Lahore in 1974/5. Troubled by injuries in England in 1982, he played only in the Lord's Test, taking 3 for 56 in the first innings. He was not re-engaged by Northants after 1982. Surprisingly left out of the touring side to India in 1983/4, he reacted predictably by launching a scathing attack on the selectors and was banned from Test cricket for six months, including the tour to Australia. But, equally predictably, after poor performances in the first two Tests in Australia, the ban was lifted in time for the third Test. It was not to be a fairy-tale return, however, and he took just eight wickets in the remaining Tests. Erratic to the last, 'Saf' topped the batting averages in his final series against England and his highest Test score, 90 in the third Test at Lahore, enabled him to complete the 1,000 run/100 wicket double. He became sports adviser to the government in the 1990s and promoted a campaign against alleged corruption in the Pakistan team.

First-class career (1967–85): 5,709 runs (19.35), 1,005 wickets (24.62), and 163 catches
Test matches (55): 1,045 runs (17.71), 177 wickets (32.75), and 26 catches

SHAFIQ AHMED

(b. 1949, Lahore) *Punjab University, National Bank, Lahore, Punjab, United Bank, and Pakistan*

An attractive right-handed opening or number three batsman and occasional medium-pace bowler, Shafiq Ahmed was a vigorous driver and cutter with a handsome, upright style, and a successful member of the strong National Bank team from 1974 to 1983. In all he scored more than 1,000 runs in nine domestic seasons. At Test level he was disappointing, though unfortunate to be competing with many brilliant players for a

batting place. After hitting 68 and a dominating 100 not out in the opening match of Pakistan's 1974 tour of England—against Leicestershire—he won his first cap at Leeds, making 7 and 18, but subsequently lost his place. In three Tests as a number three batsman at home against England in 1977/8 his highest score was 27 not out.

First-class career (1967–91): 19,555 runs (50.01) including 53 centuries, 98 wickets (33.36), and 211 catches
Test matches (6): 99 runs (11.00) and 0–1

SHAFQAT RANA

(b. 1943, Simla) *Pakistan International Airline, Lahore, and Pakistan*

A very good right-handed batsman adept at the cut and the drive, and an occasional off-break bowler, Shafqat Rana had a chequered Test career, playing five Tests over six years. He played at home against Australia in 1964/5, England in 1968/9, and New Zealand in 1969/70, and toured Australasia in 1964/5 and England in 1971 without appearing in a Test. His final series, against New Zealand, was his best: he made 167 runs (41.75) including his highest, 95, in the third match at Lahore, and 65 at Dacca in the next, his last, Test, on a pitch made of pounded mud. Minor rioting caused this match to be abandoned.

First-class career (1959–79): 4,947 runs (35.33) including 9 centuries, 16 wickets (35.00), and 83 catches
Test matches (5): 221 runs (31.57), 1–9, and 5 catches

SHAH MARDAN SHAH, 'Pir of Pagaro'

(b. 1928, Pir Jo Goth, Kairpur, Sind)

The spiritual leader of the 'Hurs', a warrior tribe in the province of Sind in Pakistan, the Pir of Pagaro (*Pir* means spiritual leader and *Pagaro* means turban or hat) was brought to England in the mid-1940s by the British after his father, the elder Pir, was arrested in 1943 and hanged in the Hyderabad central jail in Sind on 20 March 1943 for leading a rebellion against British rule. His children were brought to England and the present Pir was sent to school in Pinner where he took up cricket and played at club level. After India was divided and the British left, he returned to Pakistan and was initiated as the present Pir by his millions of supporters who live mainly in the Thar district of Sind Province. With his love of cricket he became a powerful figure in the formative years of Pakistan cricket. He was rich because of his lands and also because his followers showered money on him as a tribute. In his luxurious house in Karachi he installed cricket nets and became a patron of cricketers like the Mohammad brothers, Wallis Mathais, Khan Mohammad, and Mohammad Munaf, helping them with stipends to play cricket and bowl at him in the nets. Once, batting in the nets, he was hit by a Munaf delivery and his followers, some of the Hurs watching their Pir felled, advanced towards the bowler with sticks raised to avenge the insult. The Pir had to convince them that it was all in the game. In 1953, the initial year of Pakistan's first first-class tournament, the Quaid-e-Azam Trophy, he entered the Sind Cricket Association and played as captain against Bahawalpur scoring 15 and 1 in his only first-class match. When the three-day match against the visiting MCC A team, led by Donald Carr was abandoned against Sind because of rain at Hyderabad, he fielded his own team against them and played in it, presenting the England captain with an expensive watch as a gift.

SHAHID ISRAR

(b. 1950, Karachi) *Karachi and Pakistan*

A wicket-keeper, Shahid Israr scored 7 not out at number eleven and held 2 catches in his sole Test, the third against New Zealand at Karachi in 1976/7. Catches dropped by himself and others prevented Pakistan from translating their vast superiority into a victory in this match.

First-class career (1968–79): 847 runs (28.23) and 81 dismissals (61 c., 20 st.)

SHAHID MAHBOOB

(b. 1962, Karachi) *Karachi, Pakistan Automobile Corporation, Allied Bank, and Pakistan*

Bowling right-arm medium pace, Shahid could swing the ball viciously, with an especially good yorker. Also an attacking batsman, he was selected in the Pakistan World Cup team which played in England in 1983. He played against Sri Lanka, New Zealand, and West Indies, taking a wicket against each of them. In 1985/6 in sixteen matches he captured 72 wickets (29.00) and scored 518 runs (21.58). He took as many wickets the following season. In 1989/90 his 60 wickets at 31.00 enabled him to win a Test cap against India at home. He dismissed Mohammad Azharuddin and Ravi Shastri, finishing with match figures of 2

for 131 (65.5), but did not bat and was never picked again. He played league cricket in the north of England for a few seasons and in a total of ten one-day internationals, scoring 119 runs (23.80) and taking 7 wickets (54.57).

First-class career (1979–): 3,032 runs (16.93) including 3 centuries, 551 wickets (24.64), and 72 catches

SHAHID MAHMOOD

(b. 1939, Lucknow, India) *Karachi, Universities, Public Works Department, and Pakistan*

A competent left-handed opening batsman and medium-pace bowler, Shahid Mahmood toured England with the 1962 Pakistan team. Insufficient use, perhaps, was made of his talents; his confidence suffered and in his sole Test, the fourth, at Trent Bridge, he scored 16 and 9 and took 0 for 23. Playing for Karachi Whites against Khairpur at Karachi in 1969/70, he took all ten wickets for 58.

First-class career (1956–70): 3,117 runs (31.80) including 5 centuries, 89 wickets (21.65), and 25 catches

SHAHID SAEED

(b. 1966, Lahore) *Lahore, Railways, Pakistan Automobile Corporation, and Pakistan*

Of medium height and strong physique, an attractive right-handed opening batsman and right-arm medium-pace bowler, Shahid missed being part of the final Pakistan team which played in the 1992 World Cup. Having travelled to Australia as a member of a broader-based Pakistan squad which was to play a few warm-up matches before the Cup, he was axed in preference to Aamir Sohail. He had recaptured a Pakistan place for that trip after a very fruitful 1991/2 season at home when he scored 1,222 runs (58.19) in fourteen first-class matches for Lahore City and PACO. He made his first-class début in 1983 and in 1985/6 finished with 1,210 runs (48.40) for Railways. He played in Sharjah and in the Nehru Cup in India in 1989/90, and then won a Test cap against India at home in the same season, having made 730 first-class runs (48.66) and taken 27 wickets (29.70). In his only Test he scored 12 runs and bowled 15 overs, conceding 43 runs without taking a wicket. In ten one-day internationals he scored 141 runs (14.10) and took 3 wickets (53.00).

First-class career (1983–): 6,133 runs (39.56) including 12 centuries, 79 wickets (31.59), and 55 catches

SHAKEEL AHMED

(b. 1971, Daska, Sialkot) *Gujranwala, Bahawalpur, Islamabad, Habib Bank, and Pakistan*

While still a shy and unassuming youngster Shakeel shot into the limelight in the under-19 championship matches in 1989/90 as a right-handed opening batsman/wicket-keeper. On the 1990 under-19 tour to England he made 64 at Leeds in the second 'Test' and in the final 'Test' at Taunton hit a brilliant 190 in a total of 561 for 5 declared. In 1990/1 he toured Zimbabwe with Pakistan B and again impressed everyone with an unbeaten 50 against Zimbabwe B in the second match. The same year he played for Bahawalpur in the Quaid-e-Azam Trophy, scoring 422 runs (30.14). In the semi-final he contributed 73 and 92 as an opening batsman against Karachi Blues to help his team into the final. The following season in fifteen games for Bahawalpur and Habib Bank he mustered 788 runs (34.00) and bettered this in 1992/3 with 1,198 runs (54.45) as an opener, including five centuries. He thus earned a place in the Pakistan team for the Caribbean tour of 1992/3 and finished second in the averages in the first-class matches. He made 211 runs (70.33) which included 132 not out against West Indies under-23 XI at Grenada and an unbeaten 52 against the West Indies Board President's XI at Georgetown. In his Test début as an opener at Antigua, he was out for 0 in his only innings. He toured New Zealand in 1993/4 but played in only one first-class game, scoring 68 runs.

First-class career (1990–): 3,459 runs (43.78) including 8 centuries, and 59 dismissals (50 c., 9 st.)

Test matches (3): 74 runs (14.80) and 4 catches

SHAKEEL KHAN

(b. 1968, Lahore) *Lahore, Water and Power Development Authority, and Habib Bank*

Shakil's brother, Sohail Khan, was playing in Pakistan's top-grade cricket when this slim, shy youngster took up the game at the Model High School in Lahore which had produced cricketers like Mudaassar Nazar and Saleem Malik. A right-arm medium-pace bowler he played for WPDA at the age of 18 and was picked a season later for his only one-day international, taking 1 for 50 against England at Peshawar in 1986/7. He accompanied the Pakistan team to Australia in the Youth World Cup in early 1988 and bowled with steady success but he drifted rapidly into obscurity thereafter.

First-class career (1986–): 421 runs (11.07), 145 wickets (31.69), and 22 catches

SHAKOOR RANA

(b. 1936, Amritsar, India) *Punjab, Lahore, Khairpur, and Railways*

Suddenly world famous for the bitter and very public argument with the England captain Mike Gatting when umpiring at Faisalabad in 1987/8, Shakoor is a member of a well-known cricketing family. His brothers, Shafqat Rana and Azmat Rana, played Test cricket, another, Sultan Rana, played in first-class cricket as did Shakoor's own sons, Mansoor Rana and Maqsood Rana. He himself made his first-class début as a right-arm medium-pace bowler and a lower-middle-order right-handed batsman in 1957 for Punjab and later played for three other teams. Having made his début in a first-class match as an umpire in 1972/3 he first stood in a Test between Pakistan and West Indies at Lahore in 1975. Friendly, hospitable, fond of telling jokes but also temperamental, he had his differences with the authorities and also with players. Angered after he had disallowed an appeal for a catch at the wicket against Javed Miandad, the New Zealand captain Jeremy Coney walked his team off the playing area towards the pavilion in the third and final Test at Karachi in 1984/5. The game was held up for some time and it required a lot of persuasion by the cricket officials and some senior members of the team before Coney agreed that the Test should resume. The later clash with Gatting nearly resulted in the tour being called off. The incident happened on the second day of the Test, three balls from the end of play, with Pakistan struggling at 106 for 5. Gatting moved David Capel, behind the line of sight of the batsman, Saleem Malik, after Eddie Hemmings, the bowler, had started his run-up. Shakoor signalled from square leg to stop play, accusing the England captain, in terms alleged to be of crude abuse, of sharp practice. Gatting reacted furiously, play ceased and Shakoor refused to restart the Test on the third day unless the England captain apologized. The third day's play was lost by the time that, under protest, he did so. Shakoor was not given another Test until 1991.

First-class career 226 runs (12.58), 12 wickets (36.41), and 11 catches

SHARPE, Duncan

(b. 1937, Rawalpindi) *Quetta, Railways, Lahore, South Australia, and Pakistan*

An Anglo-Pakistani, Duncan Sharpe was an aggressive right-handed batsman and useful wicket-keeper, who top-scored in each innings of

SHOAIB MOHAMMAD

his first Test against Australia at Dacca in 1959/60, scoring 56 out of 200, and 35 out of 134—but after this series did not represent Pakistan again. He emigrated to Australia in 1960, and played for South Australia in the Sheffield Shield competition with success between 1961 and 1966.

First-class career (1955–66): 1,532 runs (27.35) including 2 centuries
Test matches (3): 134 runs (22.33) and 2 catches

SHOAIB MOHAMMAD

(b. 1962, Karachi) *Karachi, Pakistan International Airline, and Pakistan*

Son of Hanif, the 'little master', Shoaib Mohammad, a small and pugnacious right-hand opener, made his début against India in the second Test of the 1983/4 series at Jullundur. He scored just 21 runs in his first three Test innings, but soon showed that he had inherited all his father's legendary determination and concentration when putting on 173 for the first wicket with Mohsin Khan in the third Test against England, his own contribution being 80. A member of the under-23 side, he had a very consistent first-class season in 1983/4, scoring 1,118 runs at 48.60, but he played only one Test in each of the next three series, against New Zealand home and away and Sri Lanka, on each occasion replacing the popular Mohsin Khan and having to shoulder the additional burden of being the chairman of selectors' son. In the third Test against New Zealand on his home ground at Karachi, he had the unique distinction of opening the batting with Mudassar Nazar, the son of Nazar Mohammad, who with Hanif had formed Pakistan's first Test opening partnership. By far his greatest success in Test cricket has come against one country, New Zealand. In 1988/9 he scored 163 at Wellington and 112 at Auckland; in 1990/1, at home, he made 203 not out at Karachi, 105 at Lahore, and 142 at Faisalabad. Shoaib has also played in sixty-three one-day internationals, hitting 1,269 runs (24.49) with a highest score of 126 not out. At his best he looked a player from the top drawer, driving through the covers with glorious timing. An occasional off-spinner, he fields brilliantly.

First-class career (1976–): 10,161 runs (41.12) including 31 centuries, 19 wickets (47.21), and 72 catches
Test matches (42): 2,622 runs (46.82) including 7 centuries, 5 wickets (26.00), and 21 catches

SHUJA-UD-DIN BUTT, Lt.-Col.

(b. 1930, Lahore) *Northern India, Services, Punjab University, Bahawalpur, Rawalpindi, and Pakistan*

A very painstaking right-handed batsman and a useful slow left-arm bowler of great stamina who never hesitated to 'buy' his wickets, Shuja-ud-Din made his début at 16 for Northern India in the Ranji Trophy competition in 1946/7 before Partition. He toured England with the first Pakistan team in 1954 (and appeared in one match on the 1962 tour), and at home played against India in 1954/5, New Zealand in 1955/6, West Indies in 1958/9, Australia in 1959/60, and England in 1961/2. In the pioneering England tour, he accomplished little in the Tests, but in all first-class matches he was prominent with 67 wickets (28.85) and 366 runs (19.26), including his initial century, 135, against Somerset at Taunton. His highest in Tests was a determined 47 in the first match against New Zealand at Karachi, and in the second innings he captured 3 for 22 in 22 overs. With Pakistan heading for defeat at Lahore against Australia in the second Test in 1959/60, he made a grim 45 in 6 hours 18 minutes, adding 169 with Saeed Ahmed for the third wicket. Among his best scores was 147 for Services against MCC at Sargodha in 1955/6 and his best bowling was 8 for 53 (12 for 61 in the match) for Services against Lahore in 1961/2. He took 47 wickets in the 1961/2 Qaid-e-Azam matches, then a record. A Lieutenant-Colonel in the Pakistan Army, he was taken prisoner in the Indo-Pakistan War.

First-class career (1946–70): 3,342 runs (24.75) including 6 centuries, 298 wickets (22.53), and 69 catches
Test matches (19): 395 runs (15.19), 20 wickets (40.05), and 8 catches

SIKANDER BAKHT

(b. 1957, Karachi) *Public Works Department, Pakistan International Airline, Sind, Karachi, United Bank, and Pakistan*

A tall, pencil-thin, fast-medium bowler with tremendous enthusiasm and a good, high action after a long, zestful approach, Sikander Bakht could get lively pace from most pitches and outswing in most atmospheres. Though competing with sturdier fast bowlers like Imran, Sarfraz, Masood, and Saleem Altaf, Sikander played a prominent role in several Tests in the late 1970s and has tended to be underestimated. After a respectable début as third seamer against New Zealand at Karachi in 1976/7, he toured Australia and the West Indies, and took the new ball for the first time during the 'Packer Interregnum' in 1977/8 when he appeared in Tests at home and away against England. He hit the headlines by breaking the arm of the England captain Mike Brearley when one of his deliveries 'reared' during a one-day match at Karachi. His figures at home were disappointing, 3 for 136 in two Tests, but in England he took seven wickets in three Tests, and he missed only one of eight Tests played by Pakistan against India, New Zealand, and Australia in 1978/9. He performed manfully in India in 1979/80, taking 24 wickets in five Tests, including 11 in the second Test at Delhi where he had his best figures of 8 for 69 in the first innings. But on tours of Australia and England during 1981 and 1982 he was disappointing and he played only one more Test, against India at Faisalabad in the 1982/3 series.

First-class career (1974–90): 1,944 runs (14.18), 553 wickets (25.61), and 82 catches
Test matches (26): 146 runs (6.34), 67 wickets (35.98), and 7 catches

SOHAIL FAZAL

(b. 1967, Lahore) *Lahore and Habib Bank*

Tall and powerful looking, Sohail was selected as a hard-hitting right-handed batsman and an occasional right-arm medium-pace bowler. He was unsuccessful in first-class cricket but in the 1989 Wills Cup he hit a blistering unbeaten 89, out of 158 for 8, for Lahore against Habib Bank. Word got around and he was called to the Pakistan nets prior to a tournament in Sharjah. He made his one-day début there against West Indies, making 24. In Pakistan's win against India in the final he hit 32 in 24 balls but was not heard of after that.

First-class career (1985–   ): 495 runs (18.33), 19 wickets (37.00), and 17 catches

SYED FIDA HASSAN

(b. 1908, Lahore; d. 1977, Delhi, India)

A career diplomat and a high-ranking civil servant, Fida Hassan was a keen sportsman in his younger days and a useful cricketer at club level. He visited England as the manager of Pakistan's first cricket team to tour there in 1954 and was always proud of Pakistan achieving a draw in the series by winning the final Test at The Oval against the might of Hutton and Compton. One of the most revered cricket administrators, he became president of the Board of Control for Cricket in Pakistan (BCCP) and held the office from 1963 to 1969. He was keen to raise Pakistan's cricket standards through proper organization of his country's domestic cricket.

TAHIR NAQQASH

(b. 1959, Lahore) *Punjab, Lahore, Muslim Commercial Bank, Service Industries, and Pakistan*

A tall, wiry, right-handed all-rounder, Tahir would hit aggressively in the middle order; but his main strength was as a bowler, fast-medium and with a busy action, tending to fall away as he delivered, thus making the in-swinger his stock delivery. The son of a high-ranking journalist in Lahore, he began his career as an off-spinner but soon realized that he had natural ability as a quicker bowler. He made his first-class début in 1975/6, and in 1981/2 he toured Australia, making some appearances in the many one-day internationals on that tour. His first opportunity at Test level came when he returned home to play in all three Tests against Sri Lanka following a captaincy struggle in which several senior players refused to play under Javed Miandad. Tahir hit 57 in his first Test but took only 7 wickets in the series at 50 each. Against England at Edgbaston in 1982, however, he took 5 for 41 in the second innings, in one hostile spell removing five reputable batsmen in 43 balls at a cost of 20, including Ian Botham first ball. He became the first choice as Imran Khan's opening partner with the new ball, and again performed well against Australia in 1982/3. Hard-earned figures of 5 for 76 against India in Bangalore in 1983/4 secured him another visit to Australia where, despite topping the tour averages with 15 wickets, he played in only one Test. He toured New Zealand in 1984/5 and was a member of the Prudential World Cup squad in England in 1983. His best analysis was 9 for 45 for his Bank against Karachi in 1980/1.

First-class career (1975–89): 1,346 runs (18.43), 163 wickets (32.42), and 37 catches
Test matches (15): 300 runs (21.42), 34 wickets (41.11), and 3 catches

TALAT ALI

(b. 1950, Lahore) *Pakistan International Airline, Lahore, Punjab University, United Bank, and Pakistan*

A determined right-handed opening batsman and occasional medium-pace bowler, Talat Ali had a most unfortunate start to his Test career against

TANVIR MEHDI

Australia at Adelaide in 1972/3 when in his first innings his right thumb was fractured by a ball from Dennis Lillee. He retired hurt for 7 but in the second innings batted one-handed at number eleven to take the match into the last day. He played one further Test on the tour of Australasia, against New Zealand, again with little success, but in 1978/9 he returned and enjoyed his most successful match against New Zealand at Christchurch where he had scores of 40 and 61 in the first Test. He fell to Richard Hadlee in all his five innings in this series; on one occasion he claimed that he had been deceived by the latter's grunt as he delivered, thinking the grunt was a 'no ball' call by the umpire. He lost his place when the team moved to Australia. Having toured England in 1971 without playing a Test, he played a full series at home against England in 1972/3. He also appeared in two Tests in England in 1978. His highest score was 258 for PIA against Rawalpindi in 1975/6.

First-class career (1967–79): 7,296 runs (38.40) including 15 centuries, 2 wickets (123.50), and 42 catches

Test matches (10): 370 runs (23.12), 0–7, and 4 catches

TANVIR MEHDI

(b. 1972, Lahore) *Lahore and United Bank*

A thin and wiry right-arm fast-medium bowler and a right-handed lower-order batsman, Tanvir was spotted by United Bank's talent scout, Haroon Rashid, a former Test cricketer. He took him direct from club cricket into the bank team. In his initial first-class season in 1990/1 he finished with 36 wickets in eight matches in the Patron's Trophy grade-one matches, at 20.41 runs apiece. With a painfully long run-up he generated lively pace and impressed everyone with his ability to move the ball in both directions. He was picked to tour Sri Lanka with the Pakistan A team in August 1991 and there he appeared in three matches, taking 8 wickets for a mere 92 runs. He emerged as one of the leading wicket-takers in the 1991/2 first-class season by taking 45 wickets at 25.20 in 12 games while playing for United Bank and also Lahore. His best moment came against Bahawalpur, when he took 5 for 88 and 7 for 74 to enable Lahore to win by six wickets. Although he was not considered for the World Cup squad, he was selected to tour England in 1992. He made his only one-day international appearance at The Oval, scoring nought and taking one expensive wicket (72.00). After this he was sparingly used, but in Pakistan's five-wicket win against Somerset he took 5 for 64 in the match.

First-class career (1990–4): 458 runs (14.77), 135 wickets (25.79), and 15 catches

TASLIM ARIF

(b. 1954, Karachi) *Karachi, Sind, National Bank, and Pakistan*

In only his third Test match, against Australia at Faisalabad in 1979/80, Taslim Arif batted over 7 hours to hit an outstanding 210 not out, out of a Pakistan total of 382 for 2. He was on the field throughout the match. A wicket-keeper, opening batsman, and occasional right-arm medium-paced bowler, he made a youthful first appearance in first-class cricket in 1967/8 and played his first Test at Calcutta in the last match of the series against India in 1979/80. He started brilliantly, scoring 90 and 46, though he did not keep wicket in a Test until the following series against Australia. Playing two more home Tests against West Indies in 1980/1, he was less prolific.

First-class career (1967–90): 7,568 runs (33.63) including 13 centuries, 7 wickets (30.28), and 365 dismissals (309 c., 56 st.)

Test matches (6): 501 runs (62.62) including 1 century, 1–28, and 9 dismissals (6 c., 3 st.)

TAUSEEF AHMED

(b. 1960, Karachi) *Public Works Department, United Bank, and Karachi*

An off-spinner in the classical mould, Tauseef gives the ball a big tweak, and turns it sharply on helpful pitches. His promise was quickly recognized when he made his Test début as a teenager a season after his first appearances in first-class cricket. In three Tests against Australia at home in 1979/80 he took 12 wickets (29.66), including 7 for 126 in his first match at Karachi. He also played against Sri Lanka in 1981/2. Given the right conditions, he can be a devastating bowler as his match figures of 15 for 148 against Railways in the final of the 1984/5 Quaid-e-Azam Trophy proves, but he did not show the same form in his sporadic Test appearances during the same season, missed the tour to New Zealand and only returned for the third Test of the 1985/6 series against Sri Lanka when he took 5 for 54 in the second innings. Later that season he topped the Test bowling averages in Sri Lanka with nine wickets at 13.00, including 6 for 45 in Pakistan's victory at Kandy. In 1986/7 he was Pakistan's leading bowler in a full series in India and took 9 for 139 in the final Test which, by a mere 16 runs, gave Pakistan their first win in a series in India. At home against Australia in 1988/9 he took 11 wickets (24.27) in the three Tests and had match figures of 3 for 44 from 47.4 overs in the decisive opening match in Karachi; well over half his overs were maidens. In this match he also made his highest Test score, 35 not out.

First-class career (1978–94): 1,560 runs (15.75), 586 wickets (22.79), and 64 catches
Test matches (34): 318 runs (17.66), 93 wickets (31.72), and 9 catches

WAQAR HASSAN MIR

(b. 1932, Amritsar, India) *Services, Karachi, Punjab University, and Pakistan*

Appropriately, Waqar Hassan was an attractive stroke-making right-handed batsman, who was ideal in a crisis and a fine field either at cover or in the outfield. He made his début in first-class cricket at 17 and toured India in 1952/3, England in 1954 and West Indies in 1957/8. At home he played against India in 1954/5, New Zealand in 1955/6, Australia in 1956/7 and 1959/60, and West Indies in 1958/9. At Bombay in the third Test against India, when Pakistan were faltering at 60 for 6 on the first day, he made a stubborn 81, but even his 65 in the second innings failed to avert defeat. At Calcutta, however, in the fifth match his determined 97 in 5 hours saved Pakistan. In this first series he made most runs, 357 (44.62). On his England tour he scored 1,263 runs (32.38) in all first-class matches but, except for 53 in the first Test at Lord's, disappointed in the Tests. In the first official series in Pakistan, against India, he made 244 runs (30.50). Against New Zealand he finished second to Imtiaz Ahmed with 231 runs (57.75), including 189 in the second match at Lahore—his highest in Tests—when, after six wickets had fallen for 111, he and Imtiaz added a brilliant 308, which remains Pakistan's highest for that wicket in all Tests; New Zealand were beaten rather narrowly amid intense excitement. His highest score in the first-class game was 201 not out for A. V. M. Cannon's XI against Hasan Mahmood's XI at Karachi in 1953/4.

First-class career (1948–66): 4,620 runs (35.54) including 8 centuries, 2 wickets, and 45 catches
Test matches (21): 1,071 runs (31.50) including 1 century, 0–10, and 10 catches

WAQAR YOUNIS

(b. 1971, Burewallah) *Multan, United Bank, Surrey, and Pakistan*

That Waqar, one of the great fast bowlers of any nation or era, was plucked from obscurity is only a fairy-tale. When he hit the headlines he had already been playing first-class cricket for two seasons for Multan and United Bank. Just on 6 ft. tall and of wiry build, his accelerating run to the crease is long and uncompromising, culminating in a leap and a classical sideways-on action. A wicked in-swinging yorker with the old ball has been his trade mark but he has all the qualities: exceptional speed, stamina, insight into a batsman's weakness, and a wide variety of different balls at his command, each shrewdly used. Nor does he waste time with an excess of bouncers, generally bowling a full length and thereby claiming a large proportion of his wickets bowled or lbw. He comes from a remote cotton-growing and grain-trading town of Burewallah in the Vehari district of Multan which is known for its cottage industries and the tombs of Muslim saints. He had his schooling there at Sharjah where his father worked in a construction business. Having watched cricket at Sharjah, including his idol Imran Khan, he decided to bowl fast when he returned to Pakistan at the age of 12. With his approach and penetration, even as a youngster he frightened the life out of schoolboys. After his performance for Pakistan's under-19 side against India in 1987 the Pakistan captain invited him to join the Pakistan nets prior to the Champions Trophy in Sharjah and he made an immediate impact. He marked his Test début against India at home in 1989/90 at Karachi by taking 4 for 80. In 1990 he was offered to Sussex by Imran Khan, but they were already committed to another overseas player and Surrey at once signed him. In his first season in England he took over 90 wickets, 57 of them first-class, and in 1991 his 113 first-class wickets were bought at 14.65 apiece. His first fifty Test victims came from only ten Tests and he had already taken five wickets in an innings five times. A record 29 in a three-match Test series were claimed against New Zealand at home in 1990/1. He was past his 100th victim in the 20th Test and in his first series against England in England in 1992 he shattered them with a haul of 22 wickets, a record for a Pakistan bowler in England, to win the series for Pakistan. Allegations were made against him, Wasim Akram, and Aqib Javed of ball-tampering, after he had taken 3 for 36 and Akram 2 for 41, in

WASIM AKRAM

Pakistan's win at Lord's in the one-day match. In the one-off Test at Hamilton in January 1993, he demolished New Zealand with 9 for 81 in the match and on the West Indies tour of 1994 he was the highest wicket-taker with 19 in three Tests at 20.21 apiece. In the home series against Zimbabwe he led Pakistan in the first of the three Tests because of injury to Wasim Akram, and won the game with his 13 wickets. His 27 scalps in the series cost only 13.81 runs each. In another successful series against New Zealand months later he had a tally of 18 wickets at 22.50 in three Tests. In the first Test of that 1994 series, he reached 150 wickets in his 27th Test. In Pakistan's 2–0 win in the series against Sri Lanka in 1994 he took 11 wickets for 119 runs in the final Test. By 1994/5 he had taken 141 wickets (20.39) in 83 one-day internationals, hardly less remarkable than his Test performances. As umpires became more vigilant about illegal scratching of one side of the ball to make it swing against the shine, there was no convincing evidence of decline in Waqar's effectiveness. If his back can stand the strain his vigorous action imposes on it, he should continue to be successful even if his speed decreases. He and Wasim Akram, though they became rivals rather than friends, are amongst the immortal fast-bowling partnerships.

First-class career (1987–   ): 1,086 runs (12.77), 533 wickets (20.00), and 29 catches

Test matches (33): 312 runs (8.91), 190 wickets (19.16), and 4 catches

WASIM AKRAM

(b. 1966, Lahore) *Lahore, Pakistan Automobile Corporation, Lancashire, and Pakistan*

A cricketer of truly original talent, whose whippy ferocity with both ball and bat leaves an indelible impression on the spectator, Wasim Akram was the senior partner in one of the great fast bowling pairs in history. 'Wasim and Waqar' are to be mentioned in the same breath as Larwood and Voce, Gregory and McDonald, Lindwall and Miller, Trueman and Statham, Hall and Griffith, Heine and Adcock. With a brisk, eager run-up and whippy left-arm action, Wasim was the discovery of Pakistan's 1984/5 season, taking 7 for 50 in his first-class début at the age of 18 for the BCCP's Patron's XI against the touring New Zealanders. He had only just left the Cathedral school in Lahore. Though he did not play in the home series, this tall young fast bowler was a bold choice for the return tour to New Zealand, and more than justified the gamble by taking 12

wickets in his first two Tests, including 5 for 56 and 5 for 72 in the third Test at Dunedin. His fairy-tale first season continued in the one-day World Championships in Australia when he took the first 5 Australian wickets for 13 runs in the match at Melbourne. He had to work rather harder for his wickets in the first series of the 1985/6 season against Sri Lanka, taking eight in three Tests, but by now he was established as a key figure in any side chosen by Pakistan and, from 1988, by Lancashire, who signed him on a six-year contract during Pakistan's tour of England in 1987. He had already developed into a genuine all-rounder, capable of superb left-handed straight hitting, although his batting is more inconsistent. In England in 1987 he took 16 Test wickets at 29, forming a highly effective opening partnership with Imran Khan which was eventually to be superseded by his famous liason with Waqar Younis. The following season for Lancashire he scored a maiden first-class century in his second match and against Surrey at Southport scored a fifty in the first innings, 98 off 78 balls in the second, and took 5 for 15, including a hat-trick. At Adelaide in 1989/90, having taken 11 for 160 at Melbourne, he took 6 wickets in the second Test, also scoring 52 and, with Pakistan in big trouble, 123, his only Test century, an innings full of thrilling drives which earned him eighteen fours and a six. He shared a long stand with his mentor, Imran Khan, who promoted Wasim as captain of Pakistan after the 1992 World Cup, in which Wasim bowled with venom and accuracy for 18 wickets at 3.76 an over. In England in 1992, under Javed Miandad, he took 82 wickets on the tour at 16.21 and 21 in the four Tests for which he was fit. The Test captaincy duly came his way but he was reduced almost to mediocrity at times by the sheer volume of international cricket demanded of him and when Javed was left out of a tour in 1993/4, nine players rebelled against Wasim's 'domineering' captaincy, including Waqar. He was replaced as captain but played on under Saleem Malik, taking 11 wickets for 179 in the Wellington Test against New Zealand.

First-class career (1984–   ): 3,982 runs (21.75) including 4 centuries, 616 wickets (21.87), and 50 catches

Test matches (61): 1,398 runs (19.69) including 1 century, 261 wickets (23.21), and 21 catches

WASIM BARI

(b. 1948, Karachi) *Pakistan International Airline, Karachi, Sind, and Pakistan*

An outstanding natural wicket-keeper and most capable, late-middle-order, right-handed batsman, Wasim Bari was his country's automatic choice behind the stumps for almost a decade and a half after making his first Test appearance at Edgbaston in 1967. He proved marvellously reliable behind the stumps and, 12 years after that first match, he set a new world record when, in the first New Zealand innings at Auckland, he caught seven of the first eight batsmen. Strangely enough he did not claim another victim in the match, so, although breaking the record for an innings, he fell one short of his best match haul of eight (all caught) against England at Leeds in 1971. Five foot nine inches, Wasim was both balanced and agile, always ready to dive if necessary, but, unlike many, only if necessary. Few wicket-keepers had a safer pair of hands and he was better than most close to the stumps, having much more practice at keeping to spin bowlers in his native Pakistan than do the majority of contemporary Test wicket-keepers. He toured Australia five times, India and New Zealand twice, West Indies once, and England five times, including the 1978 tour when he captained an inexperienced side, unsettled by the ripples of the Packer affair, with commendable calm. As a batsman he was good enough to score 177 for PIA against Sind at Karachi in 1976/7 and in Tests has often played useful innings at around number eight in the Pakistan order, notably at Headingley in 1971 when, apart from his eight catches, he made 63, and at Adelaide in 1972/3 when his 72 was top score for Pakistan. Going in as nightwatchman at number three in Lahore against India in 1978/9, he made 85, his highest Test score. He continued to hold off challenges by younger wicket-keepers, although not immediately regaining his place after joining a players' revolt against the captaincy of Javed Miandad following the tour of Australia in 1981/2. Back in the side in England in 1982 he did not always keep wicket at his best, but he nevertheless remained first choice against Australia in the series won 3–0 early in the 1982/3 season. He played his last domestic cricket in Pakistan that season, but took part in two more tours, to Australia and the West Indies, in 1983/4.

First-class career (1964–84): 5,749 runs (21.69) including 2 centuries, 1 wicket (30.00), and 819 dismissals (674 c., 145 st.)

Test matches (81): 1,366 runs (15.88), 0–2, and 228 dismissals (201 c., 27 st.)

WASIM HAIDER

(b. 1967, Faisalabad) *Faisalabad, Railways, and Pakistan International Airline*

Wasim is a lanky right-arm fast-medium bowler and a right-handed middle-order batsman who scored 46 not out and took 5 for 116 against Sargodha in his first match for Faisalabad in 1983/4. Joining the airline team in 1987/8, his all-round performance in the final of the Qaid-e-Azam Trophy won them the title against United Bank. He made 38 and an unbeaten 45 and took 5 for 66 in the second innings. In 1989 he was named to tour Australia and New Zealand with Pakistan but on Imran Khan's insistence he was dropped from the team prior to the tour to accommodate Imran's choice, Aqib Javed. However, he featured prominently on the domestic circuit in the batting and bowling averages. By making 544 runs (34.00) and taking 55 wickets (21.12) in 1990/1 he earned a place in the World Cup squad for Australia and New Zealand the following season and made his one-day début at the MCG against the West Indies. He also played against England and India—full record 26 runs (13.00) and 1 wicket (79.00)—and although out of the side by the time that the final was played he received a plot of land from the Prime Minister, along with all the players, when he got home.

First-class career (1983–): 3,069 runs (30.38) including 3 centuries, 202 wickets (25.05), and 37 catches

WASIM HASAN RAJA

(b. 1952, Multan) *Lahore, Sargodha, Punjab University, Combined Universities, Pakistan International Airline, Punjab, National Bank, Durham, Northumberland, and Pakistan*

An explosive left-handed batsman, Wasim Raja was a dashing, popular, and attractive cricketer of superabundant talent, although sometimes lacking in application. He was also a gifted right-arm bowler of top-spinners and leg-breaks. Driving with a full follow-through of the bat or pulling ferocious, soaring shots whenever the bowler pitched short anywhere to the leg-side of middle, he played in such an uninhibited manner that he was always likely to be inconsistent. Yet in one series at least he disproved this, in the West Indies in 1976/7 when he scored 517 runs in five Tests at 54.44, as well as taking seven useful wickets at

WAZIR MOHAMMAD

18.71 each. He played in his usual free, indeed carefree way, though he often faced and overcame a crisis. Hitting no fewer than fourteen sixes in the series, he was consistency itself, top-scoring in five of Pakistan's ten innings in the series and hitting his highest, 117 not out, in the first Test at Bridgetown. Wasim first played for Pakistan in New Zealand, 1972/3, quickly establishing himself as a useful member of the side as a batsman at number six in the order, as a change-bowler, and as a brilliant fielder in the covers. His only other Test century was also against the West Indies, 107 not out at Karachi in 1974/5 when he put on a record 128 with Wasim Bari for the seventh wicket. But on his two tours of England in 1974 and, especially, in 1978 he was disappointing, although he was a key member of Pakistan's Prudential World Cup teams in England in 1975 and 1979. He again shone against India in 1979/80 (450 runs at 56.25) and against West Indies at home in 1980/1, scoring 246 runs in four Tests (61.50). He batted consistently in Australia in 1981/2; but both in this series and the subsequent one at home against Sri Lanka the big score eluded him and he lost his place after one Test in England in 1982. The flashes of brilliance, such as his 125 and 4 for 50 in the second Test against India at Jullundur in 1982/3 or his 112 against England in the second Test at Faisalabad in 1983/4, became rarer in his latter years and his decline was emphasized by an average of 9.66 on the tour to New Zealand in 1984/5. He married an English girl and took a post coaching cricket in the north-east.

First-class career (1967–86): 11,408 runs (35.20) including 17 centuries, 558 wickets (29.03), and 155 catches

Test matches (57); 2,821 runs (36.16) including 4 centuries, 51 wickets (35.80), and 20 catches

WAZIR MOHAMMAD

(b. 1929, Junagadh, India) *Bahawalpur, Karachi, and Pakistan*

The eldest of the Test-playing Mohammad brotherhood, Wazir was a determined, middle-order, right-handed batsman with a strong defence—invaluable in the early days of his country in international cricket—and an excellent outfield. He toured India in 1952/3, England in 1954, and the West Indies in 1957/8—the first three tours ever made by Pakistan—and at home he played against India in 1954/5, New Zealand in 1955/6, Australia in 1956/7 and 1959/60, and West Indies in 1958/9. In England he broke a finger in his

second innings, but recovered well to head the averages with 628 runs (39.25). A defiant 42 not out in $2\frac{3}{4}$ hours in the last Test at The Oval contributed to Pakistan's first and only win against England. In the first official series in Pakistan his only valuable contribution was 55 in the third match at Lahore. After several failures in representative matches, he played against Australia at Karachi in 1956/7 and hit 67, adding 104 for the sixth wicket with A. H. Kardar after five men had fallen for 70; Pakistan defeated Australia in the first match between the two countries. Back in good form in the West Indies, he headed the averages in all first-class matches with 70.83 from 850 runs, including 440 runs (55.00) in the Tests; he attempted gallantly to avert defeat in the third Test, at Kingston, scoring 106 in a total of 288; hit 97 not out in another losing cause at Georgetown; and in the final match at Port of Spain, which Pakistan won by an innings, he top-scored with 189—his career-highest—in $6\frac{3}{4}$ hours. The remainder of his Test career was an anti-climax.

First-class career (1949–64): 4,952 runs (40.26) including 11 centuries, and 35 catches
Test matches (20): 801 runs (27.62) including 2 centuries, 0–15, and 5 catches

YOUNIS AHMED, Mohammad

(b. 1947, Jullundur, India) *Pakistan International Airline, Surrey, Worcestershire, Glamorgan, South Australia, Karachi, Lahore, and Pakistan*

Thickset and strong, a dashing left-handed batsman with a large repertoire of strokes, including a magnificent off-drive, and an occasional bowler of either slow left-arm spin or medium-pace, Younis Ahmed played in two Tests against New Zealand in 1969/70, in the first of which at Karachi he made 62, and reappeared in Test cricket $17\frac{1}{2}$ years later, against India in 1986/7. One of the youngest players ever to appear in first-class cricket, he made his début in 1961/2 aged 14 years 4 months for Pakistan Inter-Board Schools against South Zone; but subsequently, despite his fleeting Test appearances, his cricket was for many years identified with Surrey for whom he played from 1965 until 1978. His quiet ambition was to qualify for England's Test team, but new qualification rules prevented this. He grew steadily less happy and less successful for Surrey but a move to Worcestershire in 1979 proved mutually beneficial, and he hit 1,539 runs at 69.95 in a triumphant season. He next moved to Glamorgan, leaving Worcester under a cloud after betting against his own team in an important match. He continued to bat with success in county cricket, however, after joining Glamorgan in 1984. By 1985 he had 13 times scored over 1,000 runs in a season, with a best of 1,760 runs in 1969 and a highest score of 221 not out for Worcestershire against Nottinghamshire in 1979. Always a controversial character, he was released by Glamorgan in 1986.

First-class career (1961–87): 26,073 runs (40.48) including 46 centuries, 49 wickets (42.87), and 244 catches

Test matches (4): 177 runs (29.50) and 0–6

ZAHEER ABBAS

(b. 1947, Sialkot) *Karachi, Public Works Department, Sind, Pakistan International Airline, Gloucestershire, Dawood Club, and Pakistan*

A cricket genius, Zaheer Abbas would have found a batting place in most people's imaginary 'World XI' for most of his career. Tall and lean, he batted for a long time in spectacles which he changed for contact lenses in the late 1970s. Both as batsman and a fine slip fielder he proved that a natural handicap to the sight need be no disadvantage. Only on bouncy wickets with a tinge of green in them, of a type which became more common in Australia in the 1970s, did he ever look unlikely to dominate the finest bowlers. But that he was a batsman of rare quality cannot be doubted, whether he is judged by figures or by style: calm, swift to judge line and length, very straight, moving easily either backwards or forwards, his strokes had a rippling, flowing grace all their own. So loose-wristed was he at the moment of impact that he seemed able to steer the ball at will through gaps in the covers or the leg-side, a high proportion of his runs tending to come in boundaries. Even on slow wickets he hit the ball very hard, especially off the back foot. Often in later years he wore a floppy white sun-hat on sunny days which increased the impression of cool, casual command. Zaheer, born at Sialkot, first played for Karachi Whites in 1965/6. His average in the Qaid-e-Azam Trophy in 1967 was 93.00, including an innings of 197 against East Pakistan, but he did not announce himself to a wider world until his second Test match, and his first in England, at Edgbaston in 1971 when he made a superlative 274; the mastery of his batting then was as remarkable as his unwavering concentration. He batted for 9 hours 10 minutes and hit 38 fours. It was strange that he had hitherto played only one Test, against New Zealand in

1969 at Karachi, but after his performance at Edgbaston Zaheer became an automatic selection at number three or four in the Pakistan order. He scored two more Test double-centuries, 240 against England at The Oval in 1974, when he never looked like getting out, and a majestic 235 not out against India at Lahore in October 1978. In the previous match Zaheer had scored 176 and 96 at Faisalabad in the first Test to have been played between Pakistan and India for 17 years. He scored Test centuries also in Australia—101 at Adelaide in 1976/7—and New Zealand—135 at Auckland in 1979. But nowhere is the name Zaheer more revered than in Gloucestershire where he was known by his team-mates simply as 'Z', a modest, gentle, affable destroyer of opposing bowlers. First playing for the county in 1972, he eleven times scored in excess of 1,000 runs, including 2,554 at an average of 75.11 in the dry summer of 1976. Eight times, a world record, he has scored hundreds in both innings of a match and four times, also a world record, he has scored a double-century and a century in the same match. He performed this unlikely feat twice in 1976, 216 not out and 156 not out against Surrey at The Oval and 230 not out and 104 not out against Kent at Canterbury, and did it again with 205 not out and 108 not out against Sussex at Cheltenham in 1977, and 215 not out and 150 not out against Somerset at Bath in 1981. He also scored four centuries in successive innings in 1970/1 and his aggregate of 1,597 runs (84.05) in 1973/4 is the record for a Pakistan season. In 1981 he scored 2,305 runs (88.69) in the English season. Early in the 1982/3 home season, he became only the 20th man to score more than 100 centuries, scoring an emphatic 215 against India, his fourth Test double-century, and, just for good measure, following up with two more hundreds in the next two Tests. He took over the captaincy when Imran was injured for the 1983/4 series against India and was initially selected as captain for the Australian tour, only to be replaced by Imran when the original selection panel was dismissed. 'Zed's' heart never seemed to be in that tour: he arrived late because of family commitments and returned home before the one-day international series. On the field, he seemed uncomfortable against the Australian fast bowlers and his highest score was 61, though his average was still 40.67. He captained the side for the first three Tests, but only as a stand-in for Imran as he had refused to take over as official captain in Australia when it had become clear that Imran would not be fully fit for most of the tour. Though he was often accused of lacking imagination as a captain, Zaheer led Pakistan to their first series win against England in 1983/4 and was captain again for home series against India in 1984/5, when he scored an unbeaten 168 at Lahore, and New Zealand. He did not tour New Zealand and announced after the second Test against Sri Lanka in 1985/6 that he would retire from Test cricket after the end of the three-Test series. However, on the eve of the third Test, he withdrew from the side, claiming that he had been forced to stand down 'by certain senior players'. His absence caused demonstrations among the crowd during the match. It was a sad and inelegant exit for a player who had, above all, been renowned for his grace

First-class career (1965–86): 34,843 runs (51.54) including 108 centuries, 30 wickets (38.20), and 278 catches

Test matches (78): 5,062 runs (44.79) including 12 centuries, 3 wickets (44.00), and 34 catches

ZAHID AHMED

(b. 1961, Karachi) *Pakistan International Airline, Karachi, Faisalabad and Lahore*

Gritty and aggressive, Zahid made his first-class début in 1978 for Karachi and played in two one-day internationals in 1986/7, scoring three runs and taking three wickets (23.33). A left-handed frontline batsman and a useful left-arm spinner, he toured Sri Lanka and India with under-19 teams and played against most of the visiting teams to Pakistan in the 1980s. In the 1986/7 season he scored 1,167 runs (43.22) and took 45 wickets at 23.57 to earn his one-day place against Mike Gatting's England team. He could not display the same form in 1987/8 but still managed to score 767 runs (54.78) in nine matches to help PIA win the Quaid-e-Azam Trophy and the Wills Cup.

First-class career (1978–): 6.413 runs (34.47) including 11 centuries, 299 wickets (25.90), and 85 catches

ZAHID FAZAL

(b. 1973, Sialkot) *Gujranwala, Lahore, Pakistan International Airline, and Pakistan*

A graceful, wristy, and attractive right-handed middle-order batsman and an occasional right-arm medium-pace bowler, Fazal has also opened the batting at first-class and international level. A fluent stroke-maker with a liking for cuts and cover-drives he was rated the most fluent driver and cutter of the ball since the legendry Zaheer

Abbas, but his inconsistency at higher levels made him only a stop-gap player. He was noticed in the grade two Patron's Trophy final of the 1988/9 season while scoring a superb 79 for Gujranwala, for whom he later made his first-class début in 1989/90. In that season he toured Bangladesh for the Asia Youth Cup and had a full under-19 tour of India, scoring over 400 runs in four Tests, including a superb innings of 152 at Bombay. In the Nagpur match he hit 109 in 65 balls and became an automatic choice for the under-19 tour to Engalnd in 1990. In the three main matches he made 212 runs at an average of 42.40. On his return he was sent to Zimbabwe with the Pakistan B team, making 115, 109, and 113 in the three first-class games. Before the tour was over he was called back home to play against New Zealand and made his one-day début against them at his home town in Sialkot. Later in 1990/1, he earned his first Test caps against the West Indies, but could manage only 75 runs in all, with a top score of 32. He scored 98 in the Wills Trophy international final in Sharjah in 1991 before retiring with cramp in the match against India, and later made a valuable 78 in the Faisalabad Test against Sri Lanka as an opening batsman. Apart from touring Sri lanka with Pakistan A in 1991/2, he also made the World Cup team where he played in the early matches against India and South Africa. In six matches on the 1992 England tour he contributed only 115 runs in the minor games, but more than 1,000 runs for Lahore and PIA in 1993/4, including 199 against Karachi Blues, which earned him another tour, to Sri Lanka. In seventeen one-day internationals to 1994/5 he had scored 333 runs (23.78).

First-class career (1989–): 2,918 runs (41.09) including 8 centuries, 1 wicket (168.00), and 39 catches

Test matches (8): 264 runs (18.85) and 5 catches

ZAKIR KHAN

(b. 1963, Bannu) *Agricultural Development Bank, Peshawar, and Pakistan*

A tall and well-built right-arm medium-pacer, Zakir Khan was a surprise choice for Pakistan's tour to Sri Lanka in 1985/6. But he justified his selection for his sole Test to date, in the third Test at Colombo, taking 3 for 80 in the first innings. He followed this with nought not out, and 0 for 70. He made his first-class début in 1982 and had his best season in 1984 when he took 16 wickets at 14.12. A right-hand batsman, he developed into a useful all-rounder, particularly in one-day cricket. He played in seventeen one-day internationals, scoring only 27 runs but being out only once, and taking 16 wickets (30.87).

First-class career (1982–93): 677 runs (11.67) including 1 century, 294 wickets (24.06), and 26 catches

Test matches (2): 9 runs (—), 5 wickets (51.80), and 1 catch

ZULFIQAR AHMED

(b. 1926, Lahore) *Bahawalpur, Pakistan International Airline, and Pakistan*

Primarily a right-arm, off-break bowler of great perseverance with a peculiarly deceptive action, Zulfiqar Ahmed would also try an occasional leg-break and there seemed such a slight change in his delivery that he could confuse even the best batsman; he was also a reliable late-order batsman. In a short but successful Test career he toured India in 1952/3 and England in 1954, and at home played against New Zealand in 1955/6 and Australia in 1956/7. In the first official tour of India he made 179 runs (59.66), including 108 runs in the Tests at an average of 108, thanks to several not out innings. His Test-highest was a hard-hitting 63 not out in the fourth match at Madras, when he shared in a last-wicket partnership of 104 in 85 minutes with Amir Elahi. The most successful spin bowler on the first England tour, he took 64 wickets (18.50), though his bowling was rarely used in the Tests. Second in the Test batting with 61 runs (20.33), however, he showed where the weakness of the team lay. His 34 was an essential ingredient to his country's first (and only) victory over England at The Oval,

by 24 runs. In the first series against New Zealand he was the best bowler, securing 19 wickets (15.10) in the three matches. In the first match at Karachi he was largely instrumental in the innings victory on a true matting pitch, capturing 5 for 37 in 37.2 overs and 6 for 42 in 46.3 overs, his best-ever performance.

First-class career (1946–65): 969 runs (19.00), 163 wickets (21.63), and 21 catches

Test matches (9): 200 runs (33.33), 20 wickets (18.30), and 5 catches

ZULQARNAIN

(b. 1962, Lahore) *Pakistan Railways, Lahore, and Pakistan*

Another in the long line of Pakistan wicket-keepers who were labelled as the next Wasim Bari, Zulqarnain leap-frogged over Saleem Yousuf, one of the other claimants to that title, on the 1985/6 tour to Sri Lanka, keeping in all three Tests and doing well enough with eight catches and two stumpings to hold his place for two subsequent one-day tournaments. Small, bearded, and perhaps closest in style to the illustrious Bari, Zulqarnain made his first-class début in 1980, graduating through the under-19 and under-23 national teams to the Test side after playing in two one-day internationals against West Indies. A right-hand batsman, he was not good enough to hold his place in the national side in an era when runs were expected from the wicket-keeper.

First-class career (1980–91): 922 runs (10.02) and 262 dismissals (207 c., 55 st.)

Test matches (3): 24 runs (6.00) and 10 dismissals (8 c., 2 st.)

South Africa

ACKERMAN, Hylton Michael

(b. 1947, Springs, Transvaal) *Border, Natal, Western Province, Northamptonshire, and Rest of World XI*

An attractive left-hand batsman, Hylton Ackerman had a prolific start to his first-class career which he did not quite manage to maintain. The youngest-ever South African Schools player at the age of 14 years and 8 months, he gained a record six Schools caps. He made his senior début for Border at the age of 16 and a year later made his maiden first-class century for the same province against the touring MCC team. He became only the second schoolboy to score a century against an international touring team, coincidentally both instances being provided by products of Dale College in King William's Town. He was selected for the cancelled tour of Australia in 1971/2 but took part in the replacement Rest of World Series, scoring 112 in the first representative match. Thereafter, he had to settle for the less appetizing fare of domestic cricket. One of the sharpest cricket brains in South African cricket during his era, he led Western Province to victory in the Currie Cup in the 1977/8 season, clinching the trophy in his 200th first-class match. A crucial part of this victory was his ability to take sharp catches off his champion fast bowler, Garth le Roux, and he participated in more than 150 dismissals in the field during his career. He played for Northamptonshire from 1967 to 1971, scoring over 1,000 runs in three of those seasons and making 208 against Leicestershire in 1970. His son, Hylton Deon, has played for Western Province.

First-class career (1963–82): 12,219 runs (32.49) including 20 centuries, 32 wickets (43.75), and 199 catches

ADCOCK, Neil Amwin Treharne

(b. 1931, Cape Town) *Transvaal, Natal, and South Africa*

Tall, wiry, and fit, Neil Adcock is one of very few South African fast bowlers to have exceeded 100 wickets in Test cricket. He had a smooth, rhythmic run, and a right-arm, upright delivery which involved little strain on the body. Fiery and hostile, he frequently bowled short and even off a length could make the ball lift to an awkward height. By comparison, his batting was boyishly lighthearted. He was an immediate success in Tests. In his first series against New Zealand in 1953/4 he took 24 wickets (20.21), being at his best in the second match at Ellis Park, Johannesburg, when he took 8 for 87 in the match, South Africa winning comfortably. Although he bowled fast but fairly, he hit Bert Sutcliffe and Laurie Miller before either had scored and they had to retire to hospital. He went on to tour England in 1955 and 1960, and to play at home against England in 1956/7, Australia in 1957/8, and New Zealand again in 1961/2. Handicapped by various injuries, he took special exercises to improve his performance, and on his second England tour in 1960 captured 26 wickets (22.57) in the Tests, equalling Hugh Tayfield's record, and 108 wickets (14.02) overall. He was a tower of strength when his colleague, Geoff Griffin, was no-balled out of the game for throwing. Four times during this season Adcock took two wickets with successive balls, yet he never performed the hat-trick. Earlier in his career, he and Peter Heine were a formidable opening pair. Against England in 1956/7, they took 39 wickets between them; in the final Test at Port Elizabeth they routed England's strong batting side in the first innings for 110, Adcock taking 4 for 20. He had mixed fortune against Australia in 1957/8 but in the third Test at Durban he broke the batting in the first innings with 6 for 43, his best single innings performance. In Currie Cup matches, his best feat was 13 for 65 for Transvaal against Orange Free State at Johannesburg in 1953/4. He became an incisive radio commentator on the game.

First-class career (1952–63): 451 runs (5.50), 405 wickets (17.25), and 23 catches
Test matches (26): 146 runs (5.40), 104 wickets (21.10), and 4 catches

ANDERSON, John Henry

(b. 1874, South Africa; d. 1926, Cape Province) *Western Province and South Africa*

A fast-scoring batsman, in his sole Test against Australia at Johannesburg in 1902/3, 'Biddy' Anderson scored 32 and 11 and held 1 catch.

First-class career (1894–1908): 511 runs (23.22) including 1 century

ASHLEY, William Hare

(b. 1862, Cape Colony; d. 1920, Southern Rhodesia) *Western Province and South Africa*

A left-arm slow-medium bowler, in his sole Test, the second-ever against England at Cape Town in 1888/9, 'Gobo' Ashley scored 1 and 0 and took 7 for 95, but South Africa lost by an innings and 202 runs.

First-class career (1888–91): 17 runs (4.25) and 20 wickets (14.10)

BACHER, Dr Aron (Ali)

(b. 1942, Johannesburg) *Transvaal and South Africa*

A man of Churchillian indomitability, Ali Bacher has been the most influential figure in international cricket since South Africa's return in 1992. For many years before this his single-minded determination, unstinting personal drive and commercial and political acumen had led the fight to keep South African cricket going during the period of isolation. At first his only objective was to provide the country's leading players—and spectators—with top-class cricket and Bacher

wheeled and dealed, using willing backers' money, to master-mind a number of unofficial Test series against overseas teams. Gradually he realized that by spreading the gospel of cricket to the Afrikaner Community on one hand and the 'black' townships on the other he could both achieve his objectives and perform a genuine social service to large numbers of young people. The programme of coaching courses introduced to the townships in the 1980s required foresight, drive, several political gambles, and the galvanizing of business supporters. Bacher won the trust of the more open-minded leaders of the disadvantaged black, coloured, and Asian communities, despite the enmity and suspicion of some, and was the first sporting leader to make contact with the African National Congress and thus to prepare the way for a smooth transition to 'normal' sport once the ANC became the country's dominant political force. Once South Africa's cricket was acceptable again there was no diminution of Bacher's enthusiasm or ambition. He had shrewdly assessed the best and worst aspects of commercial developments in cricket during the isolation period and applied the lessons as chief executive of the new United Cricket Board. As a player he had made his first-class début at the age of 18 and, in the following season, 1960/1, hit impressive centuries off Rhodesia and Natal. A small, stocky, and swarthy right-hander, he was mainly a back-foot player, very strong on the leg-side, partly as a result of his closed grip. He was a brilliant field and a competent second-string 'keeper. (Against a side of International Cavaliers, he held five catches and made one stumping in a single innings.) He toured England in 1965 and played in two series against Australia at home, captaining South Africa in the second of these in 1969/70, when Australia were routed. It was to be South Africa's final Test series, for political reasons. Bacher was selected to lead the attractive South African side to England in 1970, a tour that was cancelled at the eleventh hour after government intervention. In his second Test against England at Trent Bridge in 1965 his 67 helped materially in the victory; and in the third match against Australia at Durban in 1966/7, he was in at 'the kill' with 60 not out, having added 127 unbroken for the third wicket with Graeme Pollock. In South Africa's last Test innings of all, at Port Elizabeth in 1969/70, he hit 73 before giving 'Garth' McKenzie his sole wicket of the series. His highest score was 235 for Transvaal against the Australians at Johannesburg in 1966/7. A senior house-doctor in a Johannesburg multi-racial hospital, Bacher was aware of the need for political change long before most of his contemporaries. A heart by-pass operation in no way quenched his thirst for hard work.

First-class career (1959–74): 7,894 runs (39.07) including 18 centuries, 2 wickets (43.50), 110 catches, and 1 stumping

Test matches (12): 679 runs (32.33) and 10 catches

BALASKAS, Xenophon Constantine

(b. 1910, Kimberley; d. 1994, Johannesburg) *Griqualand West, Western Province, Border, Transvaal, North-Eastern Transvaal, and South Africa*

A thickset Greek, 'Bally', also known as 'Saxophone' took a short run-up and, for a right-arm slow leg-spin bowler, brought the ball off the ground unusually fast: he used a well-disguised googly sparingly. He was also a very useful lower-order batsman, good enough to score two double-centuries. His career was full of ups and downs. He first played for Griqualand West at 15, and in the 1929/30 Currie Cup matches took most wickets (39), and scored most runs (664). The following year he played in two Tests against England without success, and then toured Australia and New Zealand in 1931/2 without appearing in any Tests against Australia, but he hit 122 not out against New Zealand at Wellington. When he toured England in 1935, he could appear in only one Test because of injury, but his performance was memorable. He had exploited a worn spot at Bramall Lane to take 12 for 154 against Yorkshire and, just prior to coming to Lord's for the second Test, had collected 5 for 23 against Staffordshire. At Lord's in conditions favourable to bowlers, he took 5 for 49 and 4 for 54, and South Africa won her first-ever Test against England in England. It was his finest hour because he achieved little against Australia in 1935/6 or England in 1938/9. At home he made two double-centuries, 206 for Griqualand West against Rhodesia at Kimberley in 1929/30, and 200 not out for Rest of South Africa against Western Province at Cape Town in 1932/3. He took nine wickets against Australia in 1935/6 but at high cost and played in only one Test against England in 1938/9. A pharmacist by trade, he never lost his love for cricket and ran his own coaching school for 30 years.

First-class career (1926–47): 2,696 runs (28.68) including 6 centuries, 276 wickets (24.11), and 47 catches

Test matches (9): 174 runs (14.50) including 1 century, 22 wickets (36.63), and 5 catches

BARLOW, Edgar John

(b. 1940, Pretoria) *Transvaal, Eastern Province, Western Province, Boland, Derbyshire, and South Africa*

Known in his youth as 'Bunter' because of his spectacles and stout build, Eddie Barlow was supposed to be so short-sighted that he never saw further than the front wheel of his bicycle when he rode to school. But he developed into a magnificent all-round cricketer who positively revelled in every challenge the game set him. Burly and strong, he became a determined right-handed opening batsman with a solid defence, who was especially strong off the back foot, a right-hand medium-pace bowler who could make the ball swing prodigiously, and a brilliant slip fielder. Born in Pretoria, Barlow first played for the Transvaal in 1959/60. He later represented Eastern Province in the Currie Cup from 1964 to 1965, before moving back to Transvaal from 1966 to 1968, then on to Western Province, where he also ran a pig farm, and, finally, to Boland, a Province of only B class, where his influence brought swift improvements. In 1976 Derbyshire invited him to join them, paying what was then an unusually high salary of five figures, and he repaid them handsomely with inspiring all-round cricket during his three years at the county. Taking over the captaincy midway through his first year, during which he hit 217 against Surrey at Ilkeston, he drove the team to new standards of fitness. When he left he had taken them to a final at Lord's, three of their players were in the England side, and the club was imbued with the spirit of success. Barlow was a vital member of the strong South African side during the 1960s, scoring 1,900 runs at an average of 63.33 on the tour of New Zealand and Australia in 1963/4. He scored 201 against Australia at Adelaide. In England in 1965, on a short tour, he made 971 runs (38.84) in sixteen matches, but had a rather modest Test series. Back in England, however, playing for the Rest of the World in 1970 when the scheduled South African tour was cancelled, he was his usual dynamic self, doing the hat-trick and taking four wickets in five balls against England at Headingley. (His final figures were 7 for 64.) At Cape Town in 1966/7 he took 5 for 85 against Australia. On the field Barlow bubbled with self-belief and bristled with belligerence. Off it he is a modest and charming character who has been a great ambassador for the game and for his country. In 1984 he took up a post in London, promoting the cause of South African sport in the face of widespread political opposition. He stood unsuccessfully as an election candidate for the Progressive party. He coached Gloucestershire in 1990/1, returning home to concentrate on his vineyards in Cape Province. Reluctant to leave cricket, however, he applied, unsuccessfully, for the post of South African team manager in 1994.

First-class career (1959–82): 18,212 runs (39.16) including 43 centuries, 571 wickets (24.14), and 335 catches
Test matches (30): 2,516 runs (45.74) including 6 centuries, 40 wickets (34.05), and 35 catches

BAUMGARTNER, Harold Vane

(b. 1883, Henley-on-Thames, Oxfordshire, England; d. 1938, Accra, Gold Coast, Africa) *Bedfordshire, Orange Free State, Transvaal, and South Africa*

A tiny but tenacious left-arm slow bowler, Harold Baumgartner scored 16 and 3, took 2 for 99 (clean-bowling Jack Hobbs and J. W. H. T. Douglas) and caught 1 in his sole Test, the first against England at Durban in 1913/14.

First-class career (1903–14): 173 runs (7.86) and 70 wickets (18.51)

BEAUMONT, Rolland

(b. 1884, Natal; d. 1958, Durban) *Transvaal and South Africa*

When he played his natural game Rolland Beaumont would hit with positive brilliance but he tended to be over-cautious, especially in Tests, and failed to do himself justice. He came to England in 1912, playing against both England and Australia, and in the wet summer scored 510 runs (18.21) in all first-class matches. He also played against England in 1913/14.

First-class career (1908–14): 1,086 runs (25.25) including 1 century, and 11 catches
Test matches (5): 70 runs (7.77), 0–0, and 2 catches

BEGBIE, Denis Warburton

(b. 1914, Middleburg, Transvaal) *Transvaal and South Africa*

A quick-scoring but rather inconsistent batsman and change-bowler, Denis Begbie toured England in 1947, without reaching the Test side. On the tour he made 612 runs (30.60), including 132

against Essex at Southend. He played in Tests at home against England in 1948/9 and Australia in 1949/50, without quite fulfilling expectations.

First-class career (1933–50): 2,727 runs (35.88) including 6 centuries, 88 wickets (23.69), and 27 catches
Test matches (5): 138 runs (19.71), 1–130, and 2 catches

BELL, Alexander John

(b. 1906, East London; d. 1985, Cape Town) *Western Province, Rhodesia, and South Africa*

A right-arm fast-medium bowler of considerable grit—he once bowled on a hard wicket in a Test at Adelaide with a badly sprained foot—'Sandy' Bell toured England in 1929 and 1935 and Australasia in 1931/2. At home he played against England in 1930/1. Although not outstanding generally on his England tours his Test début was impressive. In his first innings at Lord's, maintaining an excellent length and making the ball swerve appreciably, he took 6 for 99. His best series, however, was against Australia in 1931/2 when he headed the bowling with 23 wickets (27.13). Four times he took four or more wickets in an innings but Australia won all five Tests, and 'Sandy' never dismissed Don Bradman! At Sydney, when he was hot and dripping with perspiration, and the scoreboard showed his figures to be no wickets for 96 runs, he said in trepidation to Herbie Taylor: 'What shall I do now, Herb?' The tongue-in-cheek reply was: 'Give him a fast one', and such was Bell's response that he finished his 46.5 eight-ball overs with 5 for 140. In Currie Cup cricket his best analysis was 8 for 34 in an innings for Western Province against Eastern Province at Cape Town in 1929/30. Twenty-six of his 69 Test runs were made in a record last-wicket stand of 103 with 'Tuppy' Owen-Smith at Leeds in 1929, enabling the latter to reach a hundred before lunch.

First-class career (1925–39): 311 runs (9.14), 228 wickets (23.29), and 27 catches
Test matches (16): 69 runs (6.27), 48 wickets (32.64), and 6 catches

BISSETT, George Finlay

(b. 1905, Griqualand West; d. 1965, Durban) *Griqualand West, Western Province, Transvaal, and South Africa*

Of wiry build and a right-arm fast bowler who could be devastating, George Bissett had a short career, but in his only Test series, against England in 1927/8, he did much to enable South Africa to draw the rubber after being two matches down. In the final match at Durban, he took a match-winning 7 for 29 in the second innings. He toured England in 1924 but a foot injury prevented him appearing in any of the Tests.

First-class career (1922–9): 294 runs (15.47), 67 wickets (27.10), and 8 catches

Test matches (4): 38 runs (19.00) and 25 wickets (18.76)

BISSET, Sir Murray

(b. 1876, Port Elizabeth; d. 1931, Salisbury, Rhodesia) *Western Province and South Africa*

Sir Murray Bisset, who captained Western Province with verve for several seasons, appeared in Tests against Lord Hawke's England side in 1898/9 and MCC in 1909/10. While the Boer War was still raging in 1901, he led a South African team to England. Controlling the side with skill and tact, he remained popular, despite some public criticism of the tour taking place at such a time, and reached 1,000 runs as a fine, forcing batsman. His highest score was 184 against Derbyshire at Derby. Also reserve wicket-keeper, he would stand right up to the fiery pace of the Boer fast bowler, J. J. Kotze, and execute stumpings at lightning speed. His final Test appearance was 11 years after his previous one. Sometime Chief Justice of Rhodesia, at the time of death he was Acting-Governor of that country.

First-class career (1894–1910): 1,436 runs (23.54) including 2 centuries, 5 wickets (24.40), and 64 dismissals (51 c., 13 st.)

Test matches (3): 103 runs (25.75) and 3 dismissals (2 c., 1 st.)

BLANCKENBERG, James Manuel

(b. 1892, Cape Town; d. c.1955, West Berlin, Germany) *Natal, Western Province, and England*

Jimmy Blanckenberg was a right-arm medium-paced bowler who could bowl for hours on end to a perfect length. A formidable proposition on matting, he was considered the best bowler in South Africa for several years. Against England in 1913/14 he was the most successful bowler with 19 wickets (22.52), as he was also in the three Tests against Australia in 1921/2 with 12 wickets, and again against England in 1922/3 with 25 wickets (24.52). At Johannesburg in 1922/3 his first innings analysis of 6 for 76 was his best in Tests and largely instrumental in South Africa's

victory. Failure in the Tests on the 1924 England tour, although he was dominant generally, taking 119 wickets (22.40), was followed by a felicitous spell playing in the Lancashire League.

First-class career (1912–24): 2,232 runs (22.32) including 1 century, 293 wickets (21.26), and 53 catches

Test matches (18): 455 runs (19.78), 60 wickets (30.28), and 9 catches

BLAND, Kenneth Colin

(b. 1938, Bulawayo, Rhodesia) *Rhodesia, Eastern Province, Orange Free State, and South Africa*

Colin Bland's fielding will never be forgotten by those who watched him. His speed at cover, perfect balance, and phenomenally accurate throwing caught the breath of spectators and often created panic amongst opposing batsmen. Six foot one and strong without being heavy, he was a crowd-puller, too, as a right-handed forcing batsman, though his penchant for lifting the ball, particularly in the arc between long-off and long-on, was often his downfall. Whatever he scored with the bat, his fielding was worth 50 runs to his side in any match. First playing in Tests against New Zealand at home in 1961/2, he toured Australasia in 1963/4 and England in 1965, besides appearing at home against England in 1964/5, and Australia in 1966/7. In his fourth Test against New Zealand at Johannesburg, the catch he held to dismiss John Reid, hurrying towards a century, was considered the finest seen in a representative match for many years. In Australia in 1963/4 he hit 126 in the final match at Sydney and made 367 runs (61.16) in the series. Against New Zealand he headed the batting with 207 runs (69.00) from the three matches. Against England in 1964/5 he was the dominant batsman, scoring 572 runs (71.50), including 144 not out in the second match at Johannesburg after South Africa had followed on 214 runs behind, which saved the match. In the short England tour of 1965, he made 906 runs (37.75) overall, hitting 286 runs (47.66) in the Tests, including 127 in the final Test at The Oval, which was to prove the last Test for 29 years between the two countries. It was his fielding, however, that captivated the public in England. At Lord's, England were 240 for 4 and heading for a match-winning lead, when Barrington, at 91, played perhaps the most fateful stroke in the series. He pushed the ball to leg and scampered down the pitch. Bland ran from mid-wicket towards mid-on and in one thrilling movement scooped up the ball, twisted and threw down the stumps at the bowler's end. He followed by running out Jim Parks, after which the match and the series changed course. England never again won a commanding position. Only Derek Randall, and for a time Clive Lloyd, have in recent times equalled the exploits of this lean, rangy, powerful Rhodesian who practised regularly by throwing at a single stump. In domestic cricket he excelled in 1964/5, when he created a new record of 1,048 runs from ten first-class matches. His highest score was 197 for Rhodesia against Border in 1967/8. Born at Bulawayo, though his grandparents were Scots, the man who had been a national hero in England in 1965 was a few years later refused entry to the United Kingdom.

First-class career (1956–74): 7,249 runs (37.95) including 13 centuries, 43 wickets (35.16), and 51 catches
Test matches (21): 1,669 runs (49.08) including 3 centuries, 2 wickets (62.50), and 10 catches

BOCK, Ernest George

(b. 1908, Kimberley; d. 1961, Transvaal) *Griqualand West, Transvaal, and South Africa*

A slow bowler, in his sole Test against Australia in the second match at Johannesburg in 1935/6, Ernest Bock scored 9 and 2, both times not out, and took 0 for 91.

First-class career (1928–39): 281 runs (14.05) and 32 wickets (27.78)

BOND, Gerald Edward

(b. 1909, Cape Town; d. 1965, Cape Town) *Western Province, Transvaal, North-Eastern Transvaal, and South Africa*

A fighting batsman, Gerald Bond scored 170 when Western Province faced Natal's record 664 for six wickets declared at Durban in 1936/7, 424 runs behind, but in his sole Test, against England in the first match at Johannesburg in 1938/9, he failed to score in his only innings and took 0 for 16.

First-class career (1929–39): 1,604 runs (41.12) including 1 century, and 20 wickets (35.35)

BOSCH, Tertius

(b. 1966, Vereeniging) *Northern Transvaal and South Africa*

Tertius Bosch was chosen as Allan Donald's understudy for the 1992 World Cup but only played in one match at Auckland where he suffered savagely at the hands of New Zealand's big-hitting Mark Greatbatch. A tall right-hander, he was a bowler of genuine pace who at times could be quicker than Donald. However, he never quite managed to solve the problem of his run-up which was short for a man who generated such pace and, apart from the Test match against West Indies which followed the World Cup, he has not seen further international action. In his sole Test he scored 5 runs, not out, and took 3 for 104 (34.66). He has played in two one-day internationals.

First-class career (1986–) 289 runs (8.50), 162 wickets (28.82), and 10 catches

BOTTEN, James Thomas

(b. 1938, Pretoria) *North-Eastern Transvaal and South Africa*

'Jackie' Botten was a right-arm medium-pace bowler, with subtle change of pace and the ability to make the ball run away to the slips. Also a useful batsman, he burst into Currie Cup cricket with 55 wickets in his first full season, 1958/9, a Cup record. He was also a star professional with Arcadia in the National Football League. He toured England in 1965, meeting with reasonable success, taking 33 wickets and scoring 227 runs in 12 matches.

First-class career (1957–72): 1,775 runs (15.84), 399 wickets (20.36), and 52 catches
Test matches (3): 65 runs (10.83), 8 wickets (42.12), and 1 catch

BRANN, William Henry

(b. 1899, Port Elizabeth; d. 1953, Port Elizabeth) *Eastern Province and South Africa*

A right-handed batsman, William Brann's sole Test experiences were against England in 1922. In his first match at Johannesburg, he scored 50 in the second innings, putting on 98 with Herbie Taylor in a fifth-wicket partnership, which did much towards winning the match. He represented his Province from 1920 until 1934 in the Currie Cup, doing nothing as memorable as hitting 97 and 83 not out against Western Province at Port Elizabeth in 1921/2.

First-class career (1920–34): 1,045 runs (22.23)
Test matches (3): 71 runs (14.20) and 2 catches

BRISCOE, Arthur Wellesley

(b. 1911, Johannesburg; d. 1941, Abyssinia) *Transvaal and South Africa*

A prolific scorer in Currie Cup matches, 'Dooley' Briscoe made such scores as 191 and 140 but could not reproduce such form in Tests, although for Transvaal he did hit 60 against the Australians in 1935/6 and 80 (for once out) against MCC in 1938/9. He was killed in action during the Abyssinian campaign.

First-class career (1931–40): 2,189 runs (45.60) including 6 centuries
Test matches (2): 33 runs (11.00) and 1 catch

BROMFIELD, Henry Dudley

(b. 1932, Cape Province) *Western Province and South Africa*

A competent right-arm off-spin bowler with a military appearance, and a fine close-in field, 'Brom' received many chances in Tests, appearing at home against New Zealand in 1961/2, and England in 1964/5. He also toured England in 1965. In the third Test at Cape Town in 1964/5, when England amassed 442, he took 5 for 88 in 57.2 overs, 26 of which were maidens. In England he enjoyed days of success outside the Tests, especially against Lancashire at Old Trafford, taking 8 for 69 in the match.

First-class career (1956–69): 374 runs (6.33), 205 wickets (25.63), and 68 catches
Test matches (9): 59 runs (11.80), 17 wickets (35.23), and 13 catches

BROWN, Lennox Sidney

(b. 1910, Transvaal; d. 1983, Durban) *North-Eastern Transvaal, Transvaal, Rhodesia, and South Africa*

A right-arm leg-spin bowler, who also bowled effectively at medium pace, Lennox Brown toured Australia and New Zealand in 1931/2, playing one Test in each country. He also played Lancashire League cricket and professional football for Huddersfield and Oldham.

First-class career (1930–48): 778 runs (16.91) and 147 wickets (24.77)
Test matches (2): 17 runs (5.66) and 3 wickets (63.00)

BURGER, Christopher George de Villiers

(b. 1935, Transvaal) *Natal and South Africa*

Chris Burger was a gifted stroke-player who toured England with the 1961 Fezelas (not first-class), but missed the official tour of 1965. Tall, strong, and possessed of a softly-spoken charm, his sole Tests were against the visiting 1957/8 Australians.

First-class career (1955–66): 2,073 runs (30.04) including 2 centuries, 1 wicket (17.00), and 47 catches
Test matches (2): 62 runs (20.66) and 1 catch

BURKE, Sydney Frank

(b. 1934, Pretoria) *North-Eastern Transvaal, Orange Free State, and South Africa*

A sporting, philosophical cricketer, Sydney Burke made his Test début in the third match against New Zealand at Cape Town in 1961/2, and, spearheading the bowling with his right-arm fast-medium deliveries, bowled 81 overs in taking 11 for 196. Despite this he was relegated to the position of purveyor of drinks and towels for the next Test and he had to wait until 1964/5 for his second and final Test appearance, against England. He managed the South African Universities team in England in 1967.

First-class career (1954–68): 2,334 runs (26.52) including 1 century, and 241 wickets (21.38)
Test matches (2): 42 runs (14.00) and 11 wickets (23.36)

BUYS, Izak Daniel

(b. 1895, Cape Colony; presumed dead) *Western Province and South Africa*

A slow to medium-paced bowler, Izak Buys's sole Test was the first against England at Johannesburg in 1922/3 when he scored 0 and 4 not out and took 0 for 52.

First-class career (1921–5): 37 runs (3.70) and 48 wickets (22.97)

CALLAGHAN, David John

(b. 1965, Queenstown) *Eastern Province*

David Callaghan, a right-hand all-rounder, can be compared with Australia's Simon O'Donnell in overcoming cancer to represent his country on the cricket fields of the world. The life-threatening illness caused him to miss most of the 1991/2 season and thus ruled him out of the 1992 World Cup. However, less than a year later he illustrated his determination by earning his place in the limited-overs squad against India, Pakistan, and West Indies. Of stocky build, he has been placed in the difficult position of being fifth- or sixth-choice batsman and bowler, which has made it difficult for him to consolidate his position. His ability in the outfield has helped to make him a natural for this type of cricket. He toured Australia in 1993/4 and in eighteen one-day internationals to 1994 had scored 217 runs (19.72) and taken 6 wickets (36.83).

First-class career (1983–): 3,564 runs (34.94), 43 wickets (36.51), and 65 catches

CAMERON, Horace Brakenridge

(b. 1905, Port Elizabeth; d. 1935, Johannesburg)
Transvaal, Western Province, Eastern Province, and South Africa

A high-ranking wicket-keeper/batsman, who learned his art on matting wickets, 'Jock' Cameron's stumping of a batsman was likened to the 'nonchalant gesture of a smoker flicking the ash from a cigarette'. Some of his stumping efforts dazzled the eye: he was neither flamboyant nor noisy and he took the ball cleanly. His style was described as 'the perfection of ease and rapidity without unnecessary show'. He was essentially a fast-scoring right-handed batsman, who could adapt his game and discipline his methods if necessary. Soon coming to the front in Currie Cup matches, he first represented South Africa against England in 1927/8: he toured England in 1929 and 1935; Australia and New Zealand in 1931/2; and played against England again at home in 1930/1. He began the 1929 tour with 102 at Worcester and, later, secured seven victims behind the stumps against Somerset at Taunton. In the second Test at Lord's, however, he was felled by a terrible blow on the head from a ball bowled by Harold Larwood. Although he missed the next Test, he appeared to make a full recovery, and in all matches reached 1,000 runs. Captaining his country once against England in 1930/1, he led the team to Australia in 1931/2 but found captaincy very burdensome. His wicket-keeping remained splendid and, on his second England tour, 1935, under Herbert Wade, he was at his peak. His powerful driving and pulling in the Test at Lord's, hitting 90 out of 126 in 105 minutes after four wickets had fallen cheaply, caught the public imagination: South Africa went on to win her first Test in England. He made headlines again when he hit Hedley Verity for 30 in an over at Sheffield in the game with Yorkshire. It was said that Verity had him in two minds—whether to hit him for four or six! A charming and strong personality, Jock Cameron died of enteric fever shortly after his return home from the tour in which he had scored 1,458 runs (41.65), including three centuries, and made 48 dismissals.

First-class career (1924–35): 5,396 runs (37.47) including 11 centuries, and 224 dismissals (155 c., 69 st.)

Test matches (26): 1,239 runs (30.21) and 51 dismissals (39 c., 12 st.)

CAMPBELL, Thomas

(b. 1882, Edinburgh, Scotland; d. 1924, Natal)
Transvaal and South Africa

A competent wicket-keeper though of small account as a batsman, Tom Campbell first appeared for his province at 24. He played against England in 1909/10 as the front-line 'keeper and also in 1912. While in England that year, however, rheumatism in the hands prevented him from showing his best form. He had toured Australia in 1910/11 without appearing in the Tests. He was killed in a Natal railway accident involving a mail train. This was uncanny for some years previously he had fallen out of a mail train.

First-class career (1906–12): 365 runs (12.16) and 52 dismissals (40 c., 12 st.)

Test matches (5): 90 runs (15.00) and 8 dismissals (7 c., 1 st.)

CARLSTEIN, Peter Rudolph

(b. 1938, Transvaal) *Orange Free State, Natal, Transvaal, Rhodesia, and South Africa*

Making his first-class début at 16 years 2 months and scoring 56 for Orange Free State against Natal at Bloemfontein in 1954/5, Peter Carlstein became the senior player in South African first-class cricket. A fine fielder and a slim, right-handed batsman, he could play some sparkling innings and seemed to have both the ability and the right temperament to succeed but consistency eluded him. He toured England in 1960, and Australia in 1963/4, and played once in a Test at home against Australia in 1957/8. He had a torrid time against the fast bowlers in Australia, and in England managed a Test average of only 13 despite scoring nearly 1,000 runs overall, including a magnificent 151 against Hampshire at Southampton. His best score in the Tests was 42. It cannot be said that he really 'came off' in Test cricket but he proved what he could do in the domestic first-class season of 1962/3 when he made 852 runs (71.00), including two double-centuries in three matches, the highest being 229 for Transvaal against the International Cavaliers at Johannesburg. He settled in Western Australia in his retirement.

First-class career (1954–80): 7,554 runs (31.60) including 9 centuries, 9 wickets (53.33), and 82 catches

Test matches (8): 190 runs (14.61) and 3 catches

CARTER, Claude Paget

(b. 1881, Durban; d. 1952, Durban) *Natal, Transvaal, Cornwall, and South Africa*

One of the most effective left-arm slow bowlers on matting, Claude Carter took 5 for 17 in 19 overs on making his début in first-class cricket at the age of 16 against Transvaal. Twenty-three years later he routed Border for 23, the lowest total recorded in Currie Cup matches: his analysis was 6 for 11. He toured England in 1912 and 1924—heading the bowling on his second visit with 65 wickets—and at home played against England in 1913/14 and Australia in 1921/2. When Australia amassed 450 at Johannesburg in 1921/2, he was at his best, taking 6 for 91. Also a hard-hitting batsman, he was professional to Cornwall for some years. For Natal he took 155 wickets.

First-class career (1897–1924): 1,333 runs (11.69), 366 wickets (18.56), and 64 catches
Test matches (10): 181 runs (18.10), 28 wickets (24.78), and 2 catches

CATTERALL, Robert Hector

(b. 1900, Port Elizabeth; d. 1961, Johannesburg) *Natal, Orange Free State, Transvaal, Rhodesia, and South Africa*

Though he was rarely a good starter, Bob Catterall's right-handed batting was delightfully free, marked by beautiful driving and strong hitting to leg, and he was also a fleet-footed and efficient deep field. Forthright and crinkly-haired, he was originally an opening batsman but later batted in the middle order, though he opened again throughout the 1929 series in England. All his Test cricket was against England between 1922 and 1931. He toured England in 1924 and 1929, and at home was an integral part of the 1922/3, 1927/8, and 1930/1 series. On his first tour, he was the only consistent batsman in the Tests, scoring 471 runs (67.28). In the first Test at Edgbaston, after South Africa had been routed for 30 and were following on 408 runs behind, he hit a handsome 120. At Lord's his second successive innings of 120 could not prevent another innings defeat. At The Oval he was again top scorer with 95: no other South African hit a century in this series. On his second tour, he again did well at Edgbaston, scoring 67 and 98 and sharing in first-wicket partnerships of 119 and 171 with Bruce Mitchell. His best Test innings in South Africa was a match-winning 119 in the fifth match at Durban in 1927/8. Not always in harmony with

officialdom, he not only captained Natal at cricket, but excelled also at soccer, hockey, tennis, golf, billiards, and baseball.

First-class career (1920–34): 5,849 runs (29.99) including 9 centuries, 53 wickets (30.73), and 52 catches
Test matches (24): 1,555 runs (37.92) including 3 centuries, 7 wickets (23.14), and 12 catches

CHAPMAN, Horace William

(b. 1890, Durban; d. 1941, Durban) *Natal and South Africa*

A useful right-handed batsman and googly bowler for Natal from 1911 until 1922, Horace Chapman played in two Tests, against England in 1913/14, and Australia in 1921/2, both at Durban.

First-class career (1910–22): 587 runs (20.96) and 30 wickets (25.23)
Test matches (2): 39 runs (13.00), 1–104, and 1 catch

CHEETHAM, John Erskine

(b. 1920, Cape Province; d. 1980, Johannesburg) *Western Province and South Africa*

A cheerful sportsman, respected captain, and very capable batsman whose straight drive was dominant, Jack Cheetham was also a superb versatile field. But it is as a captain who never allowed his men to lose faith in themselves that he is specially remembered. He toured England in 1951 and 1955, and Australasia in 1952/3; and at home played against England, Australia, and New Zealand between 1948 and 1953. He captained South Africa in England in 1955, when the touring team levelled the rubber after being two matches down. Never before had a South African team been so successful in England though, strangely, Cheetham was unfit to play in either victory. He led his country to a 4–0 victory over New Zealand in 1953/4. Against Australia in 1952/3, his team left home virtually written off as 'no hopers' but his firm, confident leadership, with its special emphasis on the value of first-rate fielding at all times, produced a side that very unexpectedly drew the series 2–2; and, as a bonus, New Zealand were defeated later in the tour. Although he hit 271 not out against Orange Free State at Bloemfontein in 1950/1, which remained a short-lived highest-ever in the Currie Cup competition—and averaged 83.14 that season—he was not prolific in Tests. He made five fifties, with a highest of 89 in the third Test

CHEVALIER

against New Zealand at Cape Town in 1953/4. On his first tour of England, 1951, he finished second in aggregate and average, 1,448 runs (38.10); and on his tour of Australasia he was second in the averages with 601 runs (40.06). President of the South African Cricket Association, 1969–72, he fought hard for the cause of South Africa in international cricket.

First-class career (1939–55): 5,697 runs (42.20) including 8 centuries, 8 wickets (47.00), and 67 catches
Test matches (24): 883 runs (23.86), 0–2, and 13 catches

CHEVALIER, Grahame Anton

(b. 1937, Cape Town) *Western Province and South Africa*

A left-arm slow bowler, Grahame Chevalier took the wicket of Paul Sheahan with the fifth ball he bowled in Test cricket, the first match at Cape Town against Australia in 1969/70. In this, his sole Test—the first that South Africa won at Newlands against Australia, the previous six having been lost—he scored 0 and 0 not out, took 5 for 100 and held 1 catch.

First-class career (1966–74): 84 runs (4.94) and 154 wickets (23.72)

CHRISTY, James Alexander Joseph

(b. 1904, Pretoria; d. 1971, Durban) *Transvaal, Queensland, and South Africa*

A tall, powerful, right-handed batsman and accomplished player of fast bowling, Jim Christy hit 68 and 107 not out in his first two matches for Transvaal in 1925/6. He toured England in 1929 and Australasia in 1931/2; and at home played against England in 1930/1. In the Lord's Test he impressed with 70 and 41 against Harold Larwood and Maurice Tate. After hitting 148 and 50 against Nottinghamshire at Trent Bridge, he suffered a finger injury which curtailed his appearances. His form was moderate in Australia, but he made 103 against New Zealand at Christchurch and 62 and 53 at Wellington, opening the batting each time, and in all first-class matches on the tour scored 1,178 runs (41.78).

First-class career (1925–36): 3,670 runs (37.07) including 11 centuries, 32 wickets (27.93), and 33 catches
Test matches (10): 618 runs (34.33) including 1 century, 2 wickets (46.00), and 3 catches

CHUBB, Geoffrey Walter Ashton

(b. 1911, East London; d. 1982, East London) *Border, Transvaal, and South Africa*

A fair-haired, bespectacled right-arm medium-pace bowler who moved the ball either way very late in flight or off the wicket, Geoff Chubb could bowl for long spells without losing accuracy. Originally an opening batsman, he turned to bowling after a rugby injury, and generally batted with the 'tail'. He toured England in 1951, taking 76 wickets (26.38), and, on making his Test appearance at Trent Bridge at the age of 40 years 56 days became the oldest South African on début. He had a very good series, taking 5 for 77 in the first innings at Lord's and 6 for 51 in the first innings at Old Trafford. After retirement at the end of the tour, he became involved in the management of the game. He served two terms as president of the South African Cricket Association.

First-class career (1931–51): 835 runs (18.15), 160 wickets (23.91), and 12 catches
Test matches (5): 63 runs (10.50) and 21 wickets (27.47)

COCHRAN, John Alexander Kennedy

(b. 1909, Johannesburg; d. 1987, Johannesburg) *Griqualand West, Transvaal, and South Africa*

A fast bowler, in his sole Test, the fifth against England at Durban in 1930/1, John Cochran scored 4 and took 0 for 47.

First-class career (1929–32): 25 runs (4.16) and 15 wickets (24.06)

COEN, Stanley Keppel

(b. 1902, Orange Free State; d. 1967, Durban) *Western Province, Orange Free State, Transvaal, Border, and South Africa*

For several years, 'Shunter' Coen was at the fringe of the Test XI. When Currie Cup matches were played on turf for the first time in 1926/7, he made 737 runs (73.70) for Orange Free State—a record for 20 years in the Cup—sharing in a stand of 305 for the second wicket with J. M. M. Commaille against Natal at Bloemfontein, a record for 40 years in South Africa. His sole Test appearances were against England in 1927/8. With a highest score of only 41 not out he averaged over 50!

First-class career (1921–39): 2,808 runs (32.65) including 6 centuries, and 22 wickets (49.40)
Test matches (2): 101 runs (50.50), 0–7, and 1 catch

COMMAILLE, John McIllwaine Moore

(b. 1883, Cape Town; d. 1956, Cape Town) *Western Province, Orange Free State, Griqualand West, and South Africa*

'Mick' Commaille represented South Africa at both cricket and Association football. Very popular throughout a long career, he was a consistently effective batsman, generally opening the innings, in Currie Cup cricket. After some 20 years with Western Province, he joined Orange Free State and shared in a stand of 305 for the second wicket with S. K. Coen against Natal at Bloemfontein in 1926/7, a record for 40 years. Though never very prominent in Tests, he played against England at home in 1909/10 and 1927/8, and in England in 1924 was vice-captain to Herbie Taylor. He toured Australia in 1910/11. On his England tour he made 1,202 runs (25.04).

First-class career (1905–30): 5,026 runs (32.21) including 9 centuries, 1 wicket (33.00), and 32 catches
Test matches (12): 355 runs (16.90) and 1 catch

COMMINS, John Brian

(b. 1965, East London) *Western Province B, Western Province, Boland, and South Africa*

Ten years after appearing in first-class cricket for the first time, John Commins made a surprising Test début against New Zealand at Durban in 1994/5. A stylish right-handed number three he did well in this and the following Test at Cape Town and would certainly have made the subsequent return tour of New Zealand had he not aggravated a groin injury in bizarre circumstances. Batting with a runner in his third Test against Pakistan, he struck his first ball for what he judged to be a two, forgetting that he had no need to run. His partner and runner were safe, but Commins dived in vain: run out nought, first ball. His father, Kevin, was formerly chief executive of Western province at Newlands.

First-class career (1964–): 2,571 runs (36.21) including 7 centuries, 4 wickets (42.50), and 18 catches
Test matches (3): 125 runs (25.00) and 2 catches

CONYNGHAM, Dalton Parry

(b. 1897, Durban; d. 1979, Durban) *Natal, Transvaal, Western Province, and South Africa*

Though handicapped by ill-health, 'Conky' Conyngham was one of Natal's best bowlers in the early 1920s. In his sole Test, the fifth against England at Durban in 1922/3, he scored 3 and 3 (both times undefeated), took 2 for 103 (in 61 overs) with his right-arm medium-pace bowling and held 1 catch.

First-class career (1921–31): 348 runs (15.13) and 86 wickets (20.67)

COOK, Frederick James

(b. 1870, Java; d. 1915, Gallipoli) *Eastern Province and South Africa*

A useful batsman, in his sole Test, the first against England at Port Elizabeth in 1895/6, Frederick Cook scored 7 and 0.

First-class career (1893–1905): 172 runs (17.20)

COOK, Stephen James

(b. 1953, Johannesburg) *Transvaal, Somerset, and South Africa*

Jimmy Cook, a right-hand batsman of rare quality and a dignified and disciplined character, succeeded Barry Richards and Eddie Barlow as South Africa's leading opening batsman. He had, in fact, started his career in the Transvaal middle-order but it was once that he switched to opening that his career really took off. He was a dominant player off the front foot, driving with perfect timing and placement, not that his game was restricted in any way. He smashed just about every Transvaal batting record that exists and his opening partnership with Henry Fotheringham could have been a great one for South Africa. He had to wait until 1989 to get his chance to play overseas and it was then that he really showed his worth on the perfect batting strips to be found in Somerset and elsewhere in England. In three seasons he scored more than 7,500 runs, improving his performance every year, and reached the century mark on no fewer than twenty-eight occasions. He was a first choice for South Africa in all the unofficial matches of isolation but had to undergo the disappointment of missing out on the 1992 World Cup after making South Africa's historic tour to India some four months previously. Nevertheless, he was recalled for his Test début against India at home in 1992/3 and also toured Sri Lanka in 1993. He was not able to maintain a permanent Test place although he remained for a time on the periphery of the national squad. In his youth he was a brilliant cover fieldsman, no doubt the result of his natural sporting talent as he also played professional soccer in South Africa with success. One of the hallmarks of his game was always his tremendous enthusiam and this showed no sign of diminishing during the last decade of a truly outstanding career. He succeeded Clive Rice as captain of Transvaal and took particular pleasure in trying to help the young hopefuls scale his own lofty heights. A genuine sportsman on and off the field, he was one of the key cricketers in maintaining high standards during isolation so that South Africa would be able to compete with the best with the dawning of the new era.

First-class career (1972–94): 20,676 runs (50.67) including 63 centuries, 3 wickets (35.66), and 151 catches

Test matches (3): 107 runs (17.83)

COOPER, Alfred Henry Cecil

(b. 1893, Johannesburg; d. 1963, Johannesburg) *Transvaal and South Africa*

A heavy scorer for Transvaal, hitting 171 not out against Western Province at Johannesburg in 1923/4, Alfred Cooper's sole Test appearance was against England at Durban in 1913/14, when he scored 6 and 0 and held 1 catch.

First-class career (1912–29): 1,788 runs (31.92) including 4 centuries, and 15 wickets (39.73)

COX, Joseph Lovell

(b. 1886, Pietermaritzburg; d. 1971, Bulawayo, Rhodesia) *Natal and South Africa*

Bowling a sharp right-arm fast-medium pace with a high action, Joe Cox achieved fame in the Currie Cup competition in 1910/11. Taking 8 for 20 (7 clean-bowled) against Transvaal in the second innings at Durban, he finished with 36 wickets from six matches, his province winning the trophy for the first time. He toured England in 1912 but was disappointing and his only Tests were played against England at home in 1913/14. He was an indifferent batsman and fielder.

First-class career (1910–22): 357 runs (8.30), 120 wickets (22.53), and 14 catches

Test matches (3): 17 runs (3.40), 4 wickets (61.25), and 1 catch

CRIPPS, Godfrey

(b. 1865, Mussoorie, India; d. 1943, Adelaide, Australia) *Western Province and South Africa*

An old Cheltenham boy and a dashing right-handed batsman, Godfrey Cripps hit 102 against Griqualand West at Kimberley in 1892/3 when his province carried off the Currie Cup at their first attempt. In a handful of Cup games he held

the then high average of 39.20. His sole Test was against W. W. Read's England side at Cape Town in 1891/2 when he scored 18 and 3 and took 0 for 23. He was vice-captain of the first South African team to England in 1894, making 394 runs (14.59).

First-class career (1891–4): 217 runs (31.00) including 1 century

CRISP, Robert James

(b. 1911, Calcutta, India; d. 1994, Colchester, England) *Rhodesia, Western Province, Worcestershire, and South Africa*

Debonair and good-looking, twice *Victor Ludorum* at St Edward's school in Salisbury, Rhodesia, Bob Crisp could swing the new ball either way and, bringing it down from a good height, make it lift awkwardly. In England in 1935 he took 107 wickets (19.58), including 13 in the five Tests. In the Currie Cup he twice took four wickets in four balls, respectively for Western Province against Griqualand West at Johannesburg in 1931/2, and against Natal at Durban in 1933/4, but after a season with Worcestershire in 1938, when he captured 42 wickets from eight matches, and a tour with Sir Julien Cahn, his activities were increasingly outside cricket. He climbed Kilimanjaro twice in a fortnight; became a reporter with the London *Daily Express*; founded the African magazine *Drum*; ran a mink farm; as a tank commander in the Western Desert was wounded five times and awarded the DSO and MC; published two books about his wartime experiences and another, *The Outlanders*, which traced the discovery of the Witwatersrand gold and the beginning of Johannesburg; and then, after living in England, 'opted out' and went to live in Greece. He ascribed his cure from cancer to 'plenty of red wine'. He mellowed after his restless life, which included a year walking round Crete, to become a pillar of the British Community at Stopa (Greece). He died in England at the house of a son, having just lost a £20 bet, with *The Sporting Life* on his knee. He had never lacked guts: in the 1935 Test at Trent Bridge, when Maurice Leyland and Bob Wyatt were in command at the crease in a record stand, Crisp limped off the field with a foot inflamed from a blood blister. The doctor warned him not to bowl again that day but he returned to take the wickets of both batsmen.

First-class career (1929–38): 888 runs (13.06), 276 wickets (19.88), and 27 catches

Test matches (9): 123 runs (10.25), 20 wickets (37.35), and 3 catches

CRONJE, Wessel Johannes

(b. 1969, Bloemfontein) *Orange Free State and Leicestershire*

A right-hand batsman and medium-pace bowler, son of another first-class cricketer and outstanding coach, 'Hansie' Cronje became the second-youngest South African captain of all time when he took over the leadership from an injured Kepler Wessels during the dramatic Sydney victory against Australia in January, 1994. Tall, dark, slim, and both very fit and intensely dedicated, Hansie has been a leader throughout his cricketing career and took over the reins of the Orange Free State with enormous success before he was 21 years old. Since then Free State has won the Currie Cup twice and most of the other domestic honours as well. As an international batsman he has established himself as one of South Africa's prolific scorers with centuries in each of his first full series against India, Sri Lanka, and Australia. He was the key to South Africa's drawn series against Australia when he took the fight to the leg-spinning ace, Shane Warne, with considerable success and his 122 at the Wanderers was a match-winning effort. He has not been quite as successful yet against the quicker men but such is his determination that it will be a major surprise if he does not work this out for himself in the seasons ahead, especially as his forcing strokes through the off-side off the back foot are an attractive feature of his batting. The desire to perfect his technique no doubt persuaded him to join Leicestershire as their overseas player in 1995.

First-class career (1987–): 4,689 runs (38.75) including 19 centuries, 30 wickets (37.23), and 50 catches

Test matches (21): 1,342 runs (39.47) including 5 centuries, 8 wickets (61.62), and 9 catches

CULLINAN, Daryll John

(b. 1967, Kimberley) *Border, Western Province, Transvaal, and South Africa*

Great expectations were probably heaped on Daryll Cullinan's shoulders at too young an age when he surpassed Graeme Pollock as South Africa's youngest first-class centurion at the age of 16 years 304 days. Much of his career has been frustratingly inconsistent for a player of such obvious talent. Occasionally the real talent blossoms such as when he made 337, a South African record, for Transvaal in a Castle Cup match at the Wanderers and then made 80 off the same

number of balls against West Indies in the Hero Cup in India. Both these achievements were in the 1993/4 season which suggests his game may finally be coming together consistently. A balanced right-hand batsman of medium height, he has wonderful gifts of timing and placement and both his 102 against Sri Lanka at Colombo in 1993/4 and his classy 94 at The Oval in 1994, when Devon Malcolm was too fast for most of his colleagues, revealed the true pedigree.

First-class career (1983–): 5,568 runs (38.93) including 11 centuries, 3 wickets (23.33), and 89 catches

Test matches (13): 777 runs (35.31) including 1 century, and 8 catches

CURNOW, Sydney Harry

(b. 1907, Transvaal; d. 1986, Perth, Western Australia) *Transvaal and South Africa*

Syd Curnow was an impressive batsman for several seasons in a strong Transvaal line-up. His career-highest score was 224 for North against South at Cape Town in 1932/3. He never toured England, but visited Australia in 1931/2, achieving little in the Tests. In three Tests at home against England in 1930/1, he had a highest score of 13. His cousin was a well-known statistician and record-keeper of South African cricket.

First-class career (1928–46): 3,409 runs (42.09) including 9 centuries

Test matches (7): 168 runs (12.00) and 5 catches

DALTON, Eric Londesbrough

(b. 1906, Durban; d. 1981, Durban) *Natal and South Africa*

More often than not a bad starter, at his best Eric Dalton was a determined and hard-hitting right-handed batsman and useful change-bowler. He toured England in 1929 and 1935, and Australasia in 1931/2. At home he played against England in 1930/1 and Australia in 1935/6. On his second England tour he made 1,446 runs (37.07) and in the final Test at The Oval played a magnificent innings of 117, adding a record 137 for the ninth wicket with 'Chud' Langton. Again against England, in the first Test at Johannesburg in 1938/9, he came to the rescue with 102 and in the tremendously high-scoring 'timeless Test' at Durban he took 4 for 59 in the first innings. On the Australian tour of 1931/2, playing against Tasmania at Hobart, he was hit first ball by a delivery from Laurie Nash which broke his jaw in two places and for more than a month his teeth were bound together with wire while he took liquid meals through a tube. A brilliant all-round sportsman, Dalton was South African amateur golf champion in 1950, and good at tennis and table tennis. He was also a musician with a fine baritone voice, and an accomplished pianist.

First-class career (1924–47): 5,333 runs (33.12) including 13 centuries, 139 wickets (25.81), and 72 catches

Test matches (15): 698 runs (31.72) including 2 centuries, 12 wickets (40.83), and 5 catches

DAVIES, Eric Quail

(b. 1909, Cape Colony; d. 1976, Cape Province) *Eastern Province, Transvaal, North-Eastern Transvaal, and South Africa*

A tall, athletic man—he was a hurdles champion —Eric Davies bowled right-arm fastish outswingers and, but for several dropped catches, might have achieved a sensational bowling analysis against Australia in his first Test at Johannesburg in 1935/6 when he spear-headed the attack and finished with 4 for 75 in a total of 439. For Transvaal against MCC in 1938/9, he took 6 for 82, but in the Tests that season achieved little.

First-class career (1929–46): 64 runs (3.55) and 47 wickets (27.70)

Test matches (5): 9 runs (1.80) and 7 wickets (68.71)

DAVISON, Brian Fettes

(b. 1946, Bulawayo, Rhodesia) *Rhodesia, Leicestershire, Gloucestershire, and Tasmania*

See Zimbabwe section.

DAWSON, Oswald Charles

(b. 1919, Durban) *Natal, Border, and South Africa*

Tall, broad-shouldered, fleet, and easy of movement, Ossie Dawson was a right-handed batsman of the classic upstanding school, a medium-pace bowler who could deliver the out-swinger from a smooth, long-striding run-up and a high delivery, and a fielder who would sprawl after catches and chase the ball to the last gasp. He toured England in 1947, opening the bowling in four of the Tests and hitting 55 in the final Test at The Oval, and at home played against England in 1948/9. His overall record on his England tour was 1,002 runs (32.32) including his career-highest score of 166 not out against South of England at Hastings, and 54 wickets (26.07), but ultimately, although a

power in Currie Cup matches, he disappointed in Tests.

First-class career (1938–62): 3,804 runs (34.58) including 6 centuries, 123 wickets (27.87), and 76 catches

Test matches (9): 293 runs (20.92), 10 wickets (57.80), and 10 catches

DEANE, Hubert Gouvaine

(b. 1895, Zululand; d. 1939, Johannesburg) *Natal, Transvaal, and South Africa*

A fine leader of South Africa against England in 1927/8, 1929, and 1930/1, 'Nummy' Deane—so called because of the loss of a finger-joint in boyhood, causing his hand to be numbed for some time—was an attractive, fast-scoring right-handed batsman and a brilliant field at cover. An experienced leader of Currie Cup-winning Transvaal sides, he won two Tests against England in 1927/8 largely through shrewd tactics and under his guidance the young 1929 side to England did much better than expected. In the fifth Test at The Oval he added 214 for the fourth wicket with Herbie Taylor, his share being 93. His first England tour, 1924, had been a moderate one for him. Prominent in the administration of the game, he was a member of the Selection board from 1929 until 1932.

First-class career (1919–31): 3,795 runs (30.11) including 6 centuries, 3 wickets (33.00), and 63 catches

Test matches (17): 628 runs (25.12) and 8 catches

DE VILLIERS, Petrus Stephanus

(b. 1964, Vereeniging) *Northern Transvaal, Kent, and South Africa*

'Fanie' de Villiers, a right-arm bowler of fast-medium pace with superb command of swing, is one of the great characters in the modern game. He always plays with a smile on his face, belying the gritty character underneath, and, as quicker bowlers go, has a better relationship with umpires than most. Set-backs have been a feature of his career, apart from the fact that he originally came from a totally non-cricketing background, being one of the many Afrikaans-speaking South Africans to blossom in this traditionally English game. Originally he was a bowler of genuine pace but a back injury cost him his sharper edge and then an unfortunate accident on military service that temporarily blinded him nearly put an end to his cricket career altogether. He resolved to make the most of every opportunity and to enjoy life to the full. On tour he goes out of his way to find out everything he can about every country he visits, to meet its people and to explore every corner. De Villiers started his international career as a limited-overs specialist, soon revealing an ability to concede fewer than four runs an over, even in the helter-skelter overs at the end of an innings. Injury to Brett Schultz gave him his Test match chance and he has never looked back. In only his second Test match he took 10 wickets at Sydney to bowl South Africa to an incredible, five-run victory over Australia. His secret is the amount of variety he brings to the crease, varying his angle of approach and using cut, swing, and seam, not to mention a change of pace to keep the batsman on his toes. To survive against de Villiers requires the most intense concentration upon every delivery. His batting is modest but again his fighting spirit shines through and, as a night-watchman, he once denied Australia for all of 3 hours with a broken finger. Sharp outfielding adds another dimension to his game and there is a direct comparison between the speed and accuracy of his throwing, often without any wind-up, and the fact that he was a champion javelin-thrower in his youth. It is indeed cricket's gain that he chose to concentrate on this summer sport rather than athletics. In 40 internationals to 1994 he had taken 44 wickets at 26.36, conceding runs at only 3.27 an over.

First-class career (1985–): 1,213 runs (15.75), 301 wickets (24.19), and 36 catches

Test matches (14): 230 runs (16.42), 70 wickets (24.75), and 8 catches

DIXON, Cecil Donovan

(b. 1891, Transvaal; d. 1969, Johannesburg) *Transvaal and South Africa*

A very good right-arm medium-paced off-spin bowler but a moderate batsman, in his sole Test, the third at Johannesburg against England in 1913/14, Cec Dixon failed to score in either innings, took 3 for 118 (including Jack Hobbs twice) and held 1 catch. Touring England in 1924, he took 37 wickets (25.97) but was disappointing. For the victorious Transvaal side, in 1923/4, however, he had 33 wickets (10.00).

First-class career (1912–25): 184 runs (5.93), 106 wickets (24.11), and 21 catches

DONALD, Allan Anthony

(b. 1966, Bloemfontein) *Orange Free State, Warwickshire, and South Africa*

Even before South Africa was readmitted to international cricket, Allan Donald was widely acknowledged to be a fast bowler of the highest class, carrying the unwanted title (for a South African) of the 'world's fastest white bowler'. His Test match record speaks for itself: he has outstripped all his South African colleagues in terms of strike rate and was only a matter of time before he joined Peter Pollock and Neil Adcock with more than 100 wickets to his name. Tall, blond, and wiry, he is a natural athlete on the cricket field and it is his perfect co-ordination, allied to his long arms, that enables him to bowl with both pace and accuracy. Donald bowls a fuller length than most international bowlers of his type but this does increase his chances of lbw decisions and it also enables him to swing the ball away from the bat. He seldom goes through a series without at least one match-winning performance and he carried South Africa to its first Test victory of the new era almost single-handed when he took 12 for 139, including 7 for 84 in the second innings, against India at Port Elizabeth in the 1992/3 season. His record for Warwickshire, once he claimed sole possession of the overseas spot, was even more remarkable, with 86 wickets at 16.25 in 1989 and 83 wickets at 19.68 in 1991. Having bowled with fire, and a willing capacity for hard work, he proved he was unlucky to lose his position as overseas player when his replacement Brian Lara (Donald was touring England for South Africa) produced such phenomenal form. Donald had married an English girl and settled in Birmingham and the club offered him a coaching position instead after a superb season for them in 1995. It was South Africa's misfortune that their return to international cricket did not come a bit earlier as they were likely to enjoy Donald for more than five years at his peak.

First-class career (1985–): 1,508 runs (11.42), 679 wickets (24.31), and 76 catches

Test matches (19): 132 runs (12.00), 84 wickets (26.50), and 5 catches

DOWER, Robert Reid

(b. 1876, Cape Colony; d. 1964, Cape Town) *Eastern Province and South Africa*

A fine batsman on matting and, at the time of death, the oldest surviving South African Test cricketer, Robert Dower's sole Test was the first against England at Johannesburg in 1898/9, when he scored 0 and 9 and held 2 catches.

First-class career (1896–1907): 82 runs (6.83).

DRAPER, Ronald George

(b. 1926, Cape Province) *Eastern Province, Griqualand West, and South Africa*

A wicket-keeper but primarily a fast-scoring right-handed opening batsman, Ronald Draper scored a century before lunch on four occasions: one for Eastern Province and three for Griqualand West in successive matches in 1951/2 and 1952/3. He had made 114 for Eastern Province against Orange Free State at Port Elizabeth in 1945/6 on his début in first-class cricket, and he became the first batsman to make two centuries in one Currie Cup match when he scored 129 and 177 for Griqualand West against Border at Kimberley in 1952/3. Despite this, his Tests were confined to two against Australia in 1949/50.

First-class career (1945–60): 3,290 runs (41.64) including 11 centuries, and 42 dismissals (32 c., 10 st.)

Test matches (2): 25 runs (8.33)

DUCKWORTH, Christopher Anthony Russell

(b. 1933, Que Que, Rhodesia) *Natal, Rhodesia, and South Africa*

For much of his career, Chris Duckworth was second-string wicket-keeper to John Waite, but he was also, like Waite, a capable batsman, having a sound defence and being a strong driver and puller. He toured England in 1955 and 1960 and, although not chosen for any of the Tests, played a magnificent 158 against Northamptonshire. His sole Tests were against England in 1956/7 when he was played for his batting.

First-class career (1952–62): 2,572 runs (22.96) including 3 centuries, and 104 dismissals (91 c., 13 st.)

Test matches (2): 28 runs (7.00) and 3 catches

DUMBRILL, Richard

(b. 1938, Wandsworth, London) *Natal, Transvaal, and South Africa*

A genuine all-rounder, Richard Dumbrill was born in London and was taken to South Africa at a very early age. His right-handed batting was naturally free, his medium-pace bowling steady and quicker than it appeared and his fielding good. He toured England with success in 1965,

on his Test début at Lord's—the 100th match between the two countries—taking 3 for 31 and 4 for 30. He played two more Tests against England and, at home, two against Australia in 1966/7, without repeating such a good performance.

First-class career (1960–8): 1,761 runs (23.48), 132 wickets (22.03), and 35 catches

Test matches (5): 153 runs (15.30), 9 wickets (37.33), and 3 catches

DUMINY, Jacobus Petrus

(b. 1897, Cape Province; d. 1980, Cape Town) *Transvaal, Western Province, Oxford University, and South Africa*

A good right-hand opening batsman, Duminy played for Oxford in 1921 and in two Tests against England in 1927/8 without distinguishing himself. While on a business trip to Europe in 1929, he was called on to play in the third Test at Headingley because the touring team was stricken with injury and illness: again he achieved little.

First-class career (1919–29): 557 runs (29.31) including 1 century, 12 wickets (30.66), and 11 catches

Test matches (3): 30 runs (5.00), 1–39, and 2 catches

DUNELL, Owen Robert

(b. 1856, Port Elizabeth; d. 1929, Lyon, France) *Eastern Province and South Africa*

Not in the XI at Eton or a cricket blue at Oxford, Owen Dunell became a useful batsman and good field. He appeared for South Africa in the first Tests against Major Warton's side in 1888/9, and was the country's first captain at Port Elizabeth. South African born, he died in France.

First-class career (1888–90): 79 runs (15.80)

Test matches (2): 42 runs (14.00) and 1 catch

Du PREEZ, John Harcourt

(b. 1942, Salisbury, Rhodesia) *Rhodesia and South Africa*

A fine all-rounder, being a very capable right-handed batsman and leg-break bowler, 'Jackie' Du Preez completed the Currie Cup 'double' of 2,000 runs and 100 wickets in 1973/4 (having made his début in 1961/2). Only eleven other players achieved this distinction. He made more than a hundred appearances for Rhodesia, scoring over 3,000 runs and taking over 200 wickets, which were all records for Rhodesia. His sole Test appearances were made against Australia in 1966/7.

First-class career (1961–80): 4,063 runs (23.76) including 1 century, and 296 wickets (31.07)
Test matches (2): 0 runs (0.00), 3 wickets (17.00), and 2 catches

Du TOIT, Jacobus François

(b. 1868, Orange Free State; d. 1909, Orange Free State) *Orange Free State and South Africa*

A natural leg-break bowler with a curly flight, 'Flooi' Du Toit appeared in a sole Test against England—and his only first-class match—at Cape Town in 1891/2, scoring 0 not out and 2 not out, taking 1 for 47 and holding 1 catch.

DYER, Dennis Victor

(b. 1914, Durban; d. 1990, Durban) *Natal and South Africa*

Powerfully built with a good eye, Dennis Dyer, an opening batsman, had immense patience and could hit quite majestically through the covers. He was a very serious and conscientious cricketer who suffered badly from the seven-year gap in top-class cricket caused by the Second World War. He hit 185 against Western Province at Durban in 1939/40 on his first-class début. He toured England in 1947 and in his first Test, the third at Old Trafford, defended doggedly for 3 hours for 62. Otherwise, his tour was disappointing; and at the end of the season, he underwent an operation for appendicitis.

First-class career (1939–49): 1,725 runs (37.50) including 3 centuries, and 20 catches
Test matches (3): 96 runs (16.00)

EKSTEEN, Clive Edward

(b. 1966, Johannesburg) *Transvaal and South Africa*

Clive Eksteen, a fair-haired, left-arm spinner who turns the ball sharply, albeit from a flat trajectory, seemed to be set for a major international career when South Africa rejoined the world fold in 1991. At the age of 24, he could have been said to have been born in the right place at the right time. He was selected for the initial tour of India but was only given two overs and was then discarded for the World Cup of 1992 on the strength of those twelve deliveries. Since then his chances have been few and far between and he has certainly not had the opportunity to establish himself. He toured Sri Lanka in 1993, making

only one Test appearance, and it was ironically as a right-hand tail-end batsman that he helped Jonty Rhodes save the day for South Africa in the first match at Moratuwa with a life-saving partnership. He was a slightly surprising omission for the 1994 tour of England but got further chances in 1994/5, helped by being second only to Rhodes among South Africa's best fieldsmen. He is the leader of a crop of younger spin bowlers, but on the short tour of New Zealand he took only one expensive wicket.

First-class career (1985–): 537 runs (10.74), 181 wickets (28.41), and 42 catches
Test matches (5): 72 runs (12.00) and 5 wickets (71.80), and 3 catches

ELGIE, Michael Kelsey

(b. 1933, Durban) *Natal and South Africa*

A very good right-handed batsman and useful slow left-arm change-bowler, 'Kim' Elgie played three Tests against New Zealand in 1961/2, hitting 56 in his second at Johannesburg. A prolific scorer in Currie Cup cricket, he was better known as a Rugby footballer. He studied at the universities of St Andrews and London and was capped for Scotland eight times.

First-class career (1957–62): 1,834 runs (36.68) including 3 centuries, 10 wickets (40.50), and 25 catches
Test matches (3): 75 runs (12.50), 0–46, and 4 catches

ENDEAN, William Russell

(b. 1924, Johannesburg) *Transvaal and South Africa*

A fine batsman and all-round fielder with very quick reflexes, Russell Endean toured England in 1951 and 1955 and Australasia in 1952/3. At home he played against New Zealand in 1953/4, England in 1956/7, and Australia in 1957/8. His 'keeping, although always very sound, never approached the brilliance shown by John Waite, but his batting developed so well that he became the sheet anchor of many a Springbok innings. Showing very good judgement against the new ball, his defence was sound and, although seldom a fluent stroke-maker, he dealt capably with the bad ball. During the 1952/3 Australian tour, he was the mainstay of South Africa's Test batting with 438 runs (48.66) including 162 not out in the second Test at Melbourne, and in all first-class matches he headed the batting with 1,496 runs (55.40) in Australia and New Zealand. He was also the best of an outstanding fielding side, holding 29 catches on the tour, some of them miraculous, in many different positions. He was known as 'Endless Endean'. Rather moderate in England in 1951, he was in excellent form in 1955, scoring 1,242 runs (34.50); at Headingley, his 41 at number eight and 116 not out at number six were important factors in South Africa's victory by 224 runs. His other Test century, 116, was off New Zealand at Auckland in 1952/3. He averaged 50.50 for Transvaal, his career-highest being 247 for his province against Eastern Province at Johannesburg in 1955/6. He was also a hockey international. Settling in England, he captained Malden Wanderers CC and this quietly-spoken man was very popular in a wide range of cricket. He is remembered also for two of Test cricket's oddities. In the second Test at Newlands in 1956/7 he was given out for 'handling the ball'. Having padded away a ball from Laker, the ball spun up towards the stumps and Endean used his hands to deflect it. He was also involved in the unique dismissal of Len Hutton in 1951 when Hutton was out 'obstructing the field' by deflecting a 'ballooned up' catch to Endean, the wicket-keeper.

First-class career (1945–64): 7,757 runs (37.83) including 15 centuries, 2 wickets (36.50), and 171 dismissals (158 c., 13 st.)

Test matches (28): 1,630 runs (33.95) including 3 centuries, and 41 catches

FARRER, William Stephen

(b. 1936, Cape Province) *Border and South Africa*

A hard-hitting right-handed batsman, 'Buster' Farrer made 77 on his début for Border against North-Eastern Transvaal in 1954/5, but was torn between cricket and tennis. Indeed, he dropped completely out of cricket between 1956 and 1960 during which time he reached number seven in South African tennis ranking and played at Wimbledon. But he returned to cricket, playing at home in three Tests against New Zealand in 1961/2, and touring Australasia in 1963/4. He captained his province on his return from tennis; made 888 runs (63.42) in nine matches in 1962/3; and hit his career-highest, 211, against Eastern Province at East London in his last first-class season, 1968/9.

First-class career (1954–69): 4,815 runs (43.37) including 12 centuries

Test matches (6): 221 runs (27.62) and 2 catches

FAULKNER, Major George Aubrey

(b. 1881, Port Elizabeth; d. 1930, Walham Green, London) *Transvaal and South Africa*

During the South African War, Aubrey Faulkner received professional coaching in Cape Town. During his career he was to become himself one of the great coaches and, as both player and coach, one of the dominating figures in South African cricket. One of the earliest exponents of the googly at slow-medium pace, he also used a well-concealed, and swift, yorker. At his best, with perfect length, spin in both directions and a puzzling variation of flight, he was master of some of the greatest batsmen. He bowled with a lively wheeling action. As a right-handed batsman he was solidity itself, and as a fielder versatile and reliable. He toured England in 1907 and 1912 and was called upon to strengthen the 1924 side in one Test. He toured Australia in 1910/11, and at home played against England in 1905/6 and 1909/10. On his Test début in the first match at Johannesburg in 1905/6, his 4 for 26 led to a victory by one wicket, South Africa's first Test win. With his googly-bowler companions, Vogler and Schwarz, he created something of a sensation in 1907. In the three Tests he took 12 wickets (18.16), besides averaging 23.40 with the bat in the low-scoring series. On the tour he took 64 wickets (15.82) and headed the batting with 1,163 runs (29.82). In the Headingley Test, he took 6 for 17 (England falling for 76) and 3 for 58. He was complete master against England in 1909/10, heading the batting with 545 runs (60.55) and sharing most of the bowling with Vogler, taking 29 wickets (21.89). In the first Test at Johannesburg—narrowly won by South Africa by 19 runs—he scored 78 and 123 and took 8 for 160 in the match. Now in his prime, he was an astounding success in Australia in 1910/11, taking 49 wickets (27.06) and amassing 1,651 runs (61.14), including four centuries. Head and shoulders above anyone else in the Tests, he made 732 runs (73.20), the record aggregate in a series at that time, which included 204 in the second Test at Melbourne and 115 in the third match at Adelaide, the first won by South Africa against Australia. He was not so successful against Sydney Barnes in the Triangular Tournament, though he made 122 not out against Australia at Old Trafford, and secured 17 wickets (26.70) in the six matches; in all first-class matches he achieved the double with 1,075 runs (23.88) and 163 wickets (15.42). Virtually his last bowl in Tests was at The Oval when he took 7 for 84 in England's first innings of 176. He did little when briefly recalled to the Test side in 1924. He had a distinguished record in the First World War, being awarded the DSO, and, after settling in England, opened his famous School of Cricket, later employing and bringing to the fore the young Ian Peebles. For Archie MacLaren's side at Eastbourne in 1921, he scored 153 and in the two innings took 6 for 63, helping to defeat the hitherto invincible Australians. He was subject to melancholia and died tragically by his own hand.

First-class career (1902–24): 6,366 runs (36.58) including 13 centuries, 449 wickets (17.42), and 94 catches

Test matches (25): 1,754 runs (40.79) including 4 centuries, 82 wickets (26.58), and 20 catches

FELLOWS-SMITH, Jonathan Payn

(b. 1932, Devon) *Oxford University, Northamptonshire, Transvaal, Hertfordshire, and South Africa*

Very strong and very competitive, 'Pom-Pom' Fellows-Smith toured England in 1960, playing in four Tests. One of the great modern hitters, he batted with immense gusto and freedom, specializing in stinging off-drives and rustic leg-swings. As a stock bowler, he could be waspish and he also bowled leg-spin. From Natal University he passed to Oxford, where he became a cricket and rugger blue. Making his championship début for Northamptonshire against Sussex at Hove in 1957, he rescued his adopted county by slamming 109 and 65 not out, innings which included six sixes and two sixes respectively. This century remained his career-highest. He disappointed in the Tests of 1960, but, on the tour, made 863 runs (31.96) besides taking 32 wickets. He settled in England.

First-class career (1953–64): 3,999 runs (29.40) including 5 centuries, 149 wickets (29.62), and 69 catches

Test matches (4): 166 runs (27.66), 0–61, and 2 catches

FICHARDT, Charles Gustav

(b. 1870, Bloemfontein; d. 1923, Bloemfontein) *Orange Free State and South Africa*

One of three cricketing brothers and educated at Bloemfontein, in Scotland and at Hamburg, Charles Fichardt was a vigorous batsman and useful lob-bowler. Once in a minor match at Bloemfontein he shared in a stand of 401 for the second wicket. He appeared in the third and fourth Tests played by his country, against England in 1891/2 and 1895/6.

First-class career (1891–1907): 87 runs (7.25)

Test matches (2): 15 runs (3.75) and 2 catches

FINLASON, Charles Edward

(b. 1860, London; d. 1917, Surbiton, Surrey) *Griqualand West, Transvaal, and South Africa*

Author, journalist, tennis champion, and a 'father' of Kimberley cricket, Charlie Finlason was a quick-scoring right-handed batsman and originally a fast bowler who later developed 'scientific break-bowling'. He played in the first-ever Test at Port Elizabeth in 1888/9, scoring 0 and 6 at number ten and taking 0 for 7. As a journalist when not on the field, he incurred the wrath of England's players with his acid comments. Undaunted, he became editor of the Johannesburg *Star*. He hit 154 not out for Kimberley against Transvaal in the second Currie Cup Tournament in 1890/1, his last innings in first-class cricket.

First-class career (1888–91): 213 runs (26.62) including 1 century, and 14 wickets (20.50)

FLOQUET, Claude Eugene

(b. 1884, Cape Colony; d. 1963, Port Elizabeth) *Transvaal and South Africa*

An opening right-handed batsman for his province, Floquet in his sole Test, the third match against England at Johannesburg in 1909/10, batted at number eight, scoring 1 and 11 not out and taking 0 for 24.

First-class career (1904–11): 104 runs (26.00)

FORTUNE, Charles

(b. 1905, Wiltshire; d. 1995, Johannesburg)

From 1951 until 1989 Charles Fortune's rich tones and flowery commentaries made him South Africa's voice of cricket. Originally a schoolmaster from England, he had a third career as a cricket administrator: from the age of 65 to 80 he was Secretary of the S.A. Cricket Association.

FOTHERINGHAM, Henry Richard

(b. 1953, Empangeni) *Natal and Transvaal*

Henry Fotheringham, instantly recognizable for his sturdy build, freckled complexion, and red hair, first made his mark for Natal as an attacking middle-order batsman. But it was when he switched to opening the batting for Transvaal with Jimmy Cook that his career really took off in the 1980s. As the lead-off men in a line-up of enviable strength which also included Alvin Kallicharran, Graeme Pollock, and Clive Rice, they regularly got the innings off to a cracking start, often averaging four to the over in both limited overs and first-class cricket. Just how well these two would have done together in international cricket is a matter of speculation. Fotheringham was one of the few top South African players of the isolation period not to try his hand on the England county circuit. With a correct technique, he hit the ball exceptionally hard, especially in the arc between mid-off and mid-on.

First-class career (1971–90): 8,814 runs (40.06), 7 wickets (70.00), and 135 catches

FRANCIS, Howard Henry

(b. 1868, Bristol, England; d. 1936, Cape Town)
Gloucestershire, Western Province, and South Africa

As a right-handed batsman, Howard Francis appeared generally with rather moderate success for Gloucestershire from 1890 until 1894, although he added 137 with Jack Board for the ninth wicket against Middlesex at Clifton in 1894, when he made 55. He emigrated to South Africa and from 1895 until 1902 often appeared in Currie Cup matches. He appeared in both Tests against England in 1898/9.

First-class career (1890–1902): 529 runs (12.90) and 14 dismissals (13 c., 1 st.)
Test matches (2): 39 runs (9.75) and 1 catch

FRANÇOIS, Cyril Matthew

(b. 1897, London; d. 1944, Pretoria) *Griqualand West and South Africa*

A hard-hitting right-handed batsman and fast-medium bowler, 'Froggy' François represented his province from 1920 until 1928. He gained prominence in 1922/3 when he took 7 for 114 for Griqualand West against MCC and he was selected for all five Tests that season. He had little return generally as a bowler, although he dismissed Frank Woolley, Arthur Carr, and Greville Stevens in the first innings of the first match at Johannesburg at a cost of 23 runs, but he enjoyed successive scores of 72, 41, 3 not out, and 43. In his last two appearances in first-class cricket in 1927/8, he hit 54 against MCC and 97 and 54 against Orange Free State. He was killed in a motor accident.

First-class career (1920–8): 1,232 runs (22.81) and 101 wickets (28.44)
Test matches (5): 252 runs (31.50), 6 wickets (37.50), and 5 catches

FRANK, Charles Newton

(b. 1891, Orange Free State; d. 1961, Johannesburg) *Transvaal and South Africa*

The diminutive Charlie Frank had been badly gassed during the First World War but fought his way back to fitness and, for several seasons, opened the batting for his province. He made 108 on his début in first-class cricket for Transvaal against Australia Imperial Forces at Johannesburg in 1919/20. He appeared in the three Tests against Australia in 1921/2—the tourists had been 'sweeping through South Africa like a raging veldt fire'—and in the second at Johannesburg he played an epic innings against Jack Gregory, Ted McDonald, and Arthur Mailey. His country had followed on 207 behind whereupon he batted for 8 hours 38 minutes to score 152, one of the slowest Test innings ever recorded, but Australia were thwarted.

First-class career (1919–26): 620 runs (28.18), including 2 centuries
Test matches (3): 236 runs (39.33) including 1 century

FRANK, William Hughes Bowker

(b. 1872, Cape Colony; d. 1945, Durban) *Transvaal*

An all-rounder, Billy Frank took part in only one first-class match: the second Test against England at Johannesburg in 1895/6 when he scored 5 and 2 and took 1 for 52.

FULLER, Edward Russell Henry

(b. 1931, Worcester, Cape Province) *Western Province and South Africa*

Fair-haired, well-built and determined, Eddie Fuller bowled an energetic right-arm fast-medium. He toured Australia in 1952/3 and England in 1955, and at home played against Australia in 1957/8. In the days before three seamers were automatically required in a Test team, he had to compete for a place with Neil Adcock and Peter Heine. Supported by superlative fielding in Australia, however, he headed the bowling averages both for the tour with 32 wickets (26.62) and for the Tests: appearing in two, he took 10 wickets (27.10). In the fifth Test at Melbourne, which South Africa won handsomely, he had a haul of 8 for 140. In England he had 49 wickets (19.51), including 6 in two Tests. He clinched a narrow victory over Transvaal at Johannesburg in 1955/6 by taking 11 for 70, Western Province winning the Currie Cup.

First-class career (1950–8): 1,062 runs (15.10), 190 wickets (26.45), and 29 catches
Test matches (7): 64 runs (8.00), 22 wickets (30.36), and 3 catches

FULLERTON, George Murray

(b. 1922, Johannesburg) *Transvaal and South Africa*

Short and almost delicate in build, George Fullerton was one of three wicket-keepers in the South African team to England in 1947, and the second in ranking. Neither spectacular nor stylish he, none the less, discharged this onerous task with credit. A right-handed batsman, his bat meticulously straight in defence, he was a handsome player on the off-side. He toured England again in 1951 and appeared at home against Australia in 1949/50. On his first England tour he made 698 runs (31.72) and had 24 dismissals; on his second tour he played as a batsman only, scoring 1,129 runs (31.36), including 167 against Essex at Ilford, his career-highest. He kept wicket during the last two Tests against Australia in 1949/50, hitting his highest Test score, 88, in the fourth match at Johannesburg. He hit two fifties against England in 1951.

First-class career (1942–51): 2,768 runs (31.10) including 3 centuries, 3 wickets (35.66), and 82 dismissals (64 c., 18 st.)
Test matches (7): 325 runs (25.00) and 12 dismissals (10 c., 2 st.)

FUNSTON, Kenneth James

(b. 1925, Pretoria) *North-Eastern Transvaal, Transvaal, Orange Free State, and South Africa*

A right-hander, Ken Funston always had the urge to hit but was not always at home against the rising ball and never quite realized his potential as a batsman. He was a magnificent outfield. He toured Australasia in 1952/3 and at home played against New Zealand in 1953/4, England in 1956/7, and Australia in 1957/8. In Australia he came third in the Test averages with 365 runs (36.50) and on the whole tour scored 673 runs (32.04), with a highest score of 92 in the fourth Test at Adelaide which remained his best in all Tests. On his début at Brisbane he hit 33 and 65 during a heatwave. He was a consistent scorer in Currie Cup matches.

First-class career (1946–61): 4,164 runs (30.39) including 5 centuries
Test matches (18): 824 runs (25.75) and 7 catches

GAMSY, Dennis

(b. 1940, Durban) *Natal and South Africa*

At an early age Dennis Gamsy showed himself to be an outstanding natural wicket-keeper. Bespectacled, he made his first-class début at 19. In his first Currie Cup match for Natal, against Transvaal at Johannesburg in 1959/60, he had nine victims—eight caught and one stumped. On two further occasions he collected nine 'scalps', and twice eight, in Currie Cup matches. Stockily built, he was always efficient. He toured England in 1965, having 25 victims in eleven matches, but Denis Lindsay, a better batsman, kept him out of the Tests. His only Tests were two against Australia in 1969/70, the last series played by South Africa before their isolation.

First-class career (1958–73): 3,106 runs (23.70) including 2 centuries, and 311 dismissals (278 c., 33 st.)
Test matches (2): 39 runs (19.50) and 5 catches

GLEESON, Robert Anthony

(b. 1873, Port Elizabeth; d. 1919, Port Elizabeth) *Eastern Province and South Africa*

A useful batsman, Robert Gleeson played against England in the first Test at Port Elizabeth in 1895/6, scoring 3 and 1 not out and holding 2 catches.

First-class career (1893–1905): 312 runs (18.35)

GLOVER, George Keyworth

(b. 1870, Wakefield, Yorkshire, England; d. 1938, Kimberley) *Griqualand West and South Africa*

Yorkshire-born, a slow right-arm bowler and steady batsman, George Glover was a member of the first South African team to tour England in 1894, scoring 337 runs (13.26) and taking 56 wickets (17.40) but the figures are not deemed to be first-class. He played in the third Test at Cape Town in 1895/6, scoring 18 not out and 3 and taking 1 for 28. In a Currie Cup match against Eastern Province at Cape Town in 1893/4, he took 15 for 68: he also made several fifties in the competition.

First-class career (1889–98): 621 runs (23.88) and 71 wickets (18.18)

GODDARD, Trevor Leslie

(b. 1931, Durban) *Natal, North-Eastern Transvaal, and South Africa*

A left-handed opener whether batting or bowling, and an excellent close-to-the-wicket fielder,

Trevor Goddard was the outstanding South African all-rounder of his period. Tall, with short hair, his batting was firmly based on the back foot and his medium-paced new ball or stock bowling was naggingly accurate. He toured England in 1955 and 1960, and Australasia in 1963/4; and at home between 1956 and 1969 played against England in two series and Australia in three. He captained South Africa in thirteen Tests, winning one and losing two. On his England tours, he made 1,163 runs (30.60) and took 60 wickets (21.85) in 1955 and 1,377 runs (37.21) and 73 wickets (19.71) in 1960. He also held 21 and 26 catches respectively. In each series Goddard scored more than 200 runs, often giving his country a sound start, and making 99 at The Oval in 1960. But his bowling was even more effective. He took 25 wickets (21.12) in 1955, taking 5 for 69 in 62 overs, 37 of which were maidens, in the second innings at Headingley, and 5 for 31 in the first innings at The Oval. His haul in 1960 was 17 wickets at 24.35. As captain in Australia in 1963/4, he scored 454 runs (64.86), with a top score of 93, and took 11 wickets (38.18) in the five Tests, South Africa drawing the series. In New Zealand he made 233 runs (46.60) and took 7 wickets (20.28). Well over half the overs he bowled in this series were maidens. His best bowling in Tests was 6 for 53 (in 32.5 overs) in the second innings of the first Test against Australia in 1966/7 at Johannesburg, winning the match for South Africa handsomely after they had been 126 behind on the first innings. In this series he collected 26 wickets (16.23), topping the averages, besides making 294 runs. In his last series as captain, against England in 1964/5, South Africa lost the first Test but, though they were at least as strong a side thereafter, at no time did he show himself prepared to take the slightest risk. For once his bowling failed, but he made 405 runs (40.50), including his sole Test century, 112, in his 62nd Test innings, in the fourth match at Johannesburg. In the same match he asked for an appeal against Mike Smith to be revoked after the England captain had been 'run out' when down the wicket 'gardening'. A heavy scorer and wicket-taker in the Currie Cup competition, Goddard's best season at home was 1966/7 with 830 runs and 45 wickets from ten matches. He was the first South African to have reached 10,000 runs and 500 wickets in first-class cricket and the only one to have reached 2,000 runs and 100 wickets in Tests. He became a Minister of the Church.

First-class career (1952–70): 11,279 runs (40.57) including 26 centuries, 534 wickets (21.65), and 175 catches
Test matches (41): 2,516 runs (34.46) including 1 century, 123 wickets (26.22), and 48 catches

GORDON, Norman

(b. 1911, Transvaal) *Transvaal and South Africa*

Towards the end of the 1930s, Norman Gordon made enough impression in the Currie Cup competition with his right-arm bowling to suggest that he would have done well in England had not the 1940 tour been aborted. His Test experience was limited to the five heavy-scoring matches against England in 1938/9 when he bowled tirelessly. In four innings he conceded at least 100 runs but he took more wickets (20) than anyone else on either side.

First-class career (1933–49): 109 runs (5.19) and 126 wickets (22.24)
Test matches (5): 8 runs (2.00), 20 wickets (40.35), and 1 catch

GRAHAM, Robert

(b. 1877, Grahamstown; d. 1946, Eastbourne, Sussex) *Western Province and South Africa*

An all-rounder, Robert Graham played in two Tests against England, at Johannesburg and Cape Town in 1898/9.

First-class career (1897–1901): 260 runs (10.83), 61 wickets (23.04), and 22 catches
Test matches (2): 6 runs (1.50), 3 wickets (42.33), and 2 catches

GRIEVESON, Ronald Eustace

(b. 1909, Johannesburg) *Transvaal and South Africa*

Ronnie Grieveson showed splendid form as wicket-keeper/batsman against England in the fourth and fifth Tests at Johannesburg and Durban respectively in 1938/9 but the Second World War robbed him of his best years. He scored 75 in the 'Timeless Test' at Durban.

First-class career (1929–40): 1,130 runs (33.23) including 1 century, and 36 dismissals (25 c., 11 st.)
Test matches (2): 114 runs (57.00) and 10 dismissals (7c., 3 st.)

GRIFFIN, Geoffrey Merton

(b. 1939, Natal) *Natal, Rhodesia, and South Africa*

An all-round athlete, the blond Geoff Griffin had an accident at school which left him with a distinct crook of the right elbow and he was totally unable to straighten the arm naturally. He persevered, however, as a fast bowler and in his second full season in the Currie Cup competition, 1959/60, headed the national averages with 35 wickets (12.23), despite some rumblings about his action. In England in 1960 he became the first touring player to be no-balled for throwing. This was at Lord's against MCC when he was called by Frank Lee and John Langridge. He was called again at Trent Bridge against Nottinghamshire, at Southampton against Hampshire and in the second Test at Lord's. At first, in this Test, he had done very well, achieving the first-ever hat-trick by a South African in a Test and, moreover, the first by anyone in a Test at cricket's headquarters. He was no-balled eleven times, by Frank Lee again, for throwing, and in an exhibition match played after the match, which finished early, he was persistently no-balled by Syd Buller and had to finish his last over underhand. This was the end of his career as a bowler in Test cricket: he completed the tour as batsman, making 353 runs in 22 innings, and as fielder.

First-class career (1957–63): 895 runs (17.90), 108 wickets (21.51), and 19 catches
Test matches (2): 25 runs (6.25) and 8 wickets (24.00)

HALL, Alfred Ewart

(b. 1896, Bolton, Lancashire, England; d. 1964, Johannesburg) *Transvaal, Lancashire, and South Africa*

A Lancastrian, Alf Hall was a left-arm fast-medium bowler who represented South Africa against England in the home series of 1922/3, 1927/8, and 1930/1. He also played for Lancashire in nine matches as a professional in 1923 and 1924 and for Transvaal for several seasons in the Currie Cup, capturing 52 wickets from six games in 1926/7 and 128 wickets (14.18) altogether in this competition. He loved matting, and on his Test début in the second match at Cape Town in 1922/3, was almost unplayable. When England were seeking 173 to win, he took 7 for 63 in the innings (11 for 112 in the match) and South Africa won by one wicket. Again, when South Africa won narrowly by four wickets in the fourth Test at Johannesburg in 1927/8, he took 9 for 167.

First-class career (1920–31): 134 runs (3.72), 234 wickets (19.23), and 13 catches
Test matches (7): 11 runs (1.83), 40 wickets (22.15), and 4 catches

HALL, Glen Gordon

(b. 1938, Pretoria; d. 1987, Natal) *North-Eastern Transvaal, Eastern Province, and South Africa*

A capable right-arm leg-break bowler and occasionally useful batsman, Glen Hall made a memorable first-class début in 1960/1, taking 9 for 122 in the first innings (13 for 146 in the match) for South African Universities against Western Province. His sole Test was in the third match at Cape Town against England in 1964/5 when he scored 0 and took 1 for 94.

First-class career (1960–8): 306 runs (7.84) and 110 wickets (29.66)

HALLIWELL, Ernest Austin

(b. 1864, Ealing, Middlesex, England; d. 1919, Johannesburg) *Transvaal, Middlesex, and South Africa*

'Barberton' Halliwell returned to England with the first South African team in 1894, the second in 1901 and the third in 1904, in the days before Tests were played in England between the two countries. At home he played for South Africa against England in 1891/2, 1895/6, and 1898/9, and against Australia in 1902/3. Captaining his adopted country in the first two Tests of 1895/6, he lost both. He ranked as one of the best wicket-keepers of the day, however, often standing up skilfully at the stumps to take the very fast bowler, J. J. Kotze. He considered that on South African matting it was better policy to stand up, whereas on English turf one could take more catches standing back. It was 'Barberton' who introduced the practice of having a piece of raw steak in the palm of the hand while keeping. A more than useful batsman, his highest score in Tests was 41 in the second match at Johannesburg in 1895/6. Having a birth qualification for Middlesex, for whom his father, R. Bissett Halliwell, had kept wicket in the early years, he appeared once for the county and also for Gentlemen against Players at Hastings in 1901.

First-class career (1891–1909): 1,702 runs (19.34), 3 wickets (58.33), and 112 dismissals (75 c., 37 st.)
Test matches (8): 188 runs (12.53) and 11 dismissals (9 c., 2 st.)

HALSE, Clive Gray

(b. 1935, Natal) *Natal and South Africa*

Born in Zululand and making his first-class début as a schoolboy, Clive Halse was a right-arm fast bowler who toured Australasia in 1963/4 in a team packed with fastish bowlers. He was expensive on the tour, but played in the last three Tests against Australia: at Adelaide when South Africa won by ten wickets, he took 3 for 50, including Bob Simpson and Norman O'Neill. His other sports were baseball and golf.

First-class career (1952–65): 321 runs (12.84) and 83 wickets (31.30)

Test matches (3): 30 runs (—), 6 wickets (43.33), and 1 catch

HANDS, Philip Albert Myburgh

(b. 1890, Cape Town; d. 1951, Orange Free State) *Western Province and South Africa*

As a right-handed batsman noted for his fearless hitting, Philip Hands toured England in 1924 but was disappointing, scoring only 436 runs in 26 innings. His best performance in a Test was a chanceless 83 against England in the fifth match at Port Elizabeth in 1913/14, made out of 98 in 105 minutes (but Syd Barnes was not playing!). In that series, he scored more runs, 281, than anyone other than Herbie Taylor. He represented his province in the Currie Cup competition from 1912 until 1927, hitting three centuries. Like his brothers, R. H. M.—with whom he appeared in the same Test—and K. C. M., he won a Rugby blue at Oxford. He was awarded the DSO and MC in the First World War.

First-class career (1906–27): 2,034 runs (25.11) including 3 centuries, 5 wickets (16.80), and 20 catches

Test matches (7): 300 runs (25.00), 0–18, and 3 catches

HANDS, Reginald Harry Myburgh

(b. 1888, Cape Town; d. 1918, France) *Western Province and South Africa*

A Rugby blue at Oxford and a good right-handed batsman, Reginald Hands made a sole Test appearance, against England in the fifth match at Port Elizabeth in 1913/14, scoring 0 and 7. His brother Philip also appeared in this match. He died of war wounds in France.

First-class career (1912–14): 289 runs (28.90)

HANLEY, Martin Andrew

(b. 1918, Cape Province) *Western Province, Border, and South Africa*

A right-arm off-break bowler who turned the ball at Newlands even more than Athol Rowan,

Martin Hanley took 128 wickets (18.86) in the Currie Cup competition alone. He wore the skin off his fingers in imparting his exceptional spin and, as he flighted the ball into a north-easter at Newlands, even the best batsman would grope like novices to cope with his 'bite' and flight. In his sole Test, against England in the third match at Cape Town (Newlands) in 1948/9, he achieved little, however, taking 1 for 88 and failing to score.

First-class career (1939–54): 308 runs (9.62) and 182 wickets (21.69)

HARRIS, Terence Anthony

(b. 1916, Kimberley; d. 1993, Plettenberg Bay) *Griqualand West, Transvaal, and South Africa*

A boy wonder without parallel in South Africa, Tony Harris rode a horse at 3, shot wonderfully well at 5, drove a lorry at 7, played tennis at 9, started Rugby at 12, won his province's junior tennis championship at the same age (for the first time out of five), represented his province at cricket at 16 (three times as a schoolboy) and went on to play soccer, squash, and golf, and to become one of only four men to have represented South Africa at both cricket and Rugby. Aged 17 years 4 months, he hit 114 not out in his first match in the Currie Cup for Griqualand West against Orange Free State at Kimberley in 1933/4. Only 5 ft. 6 in., he was an aggressive, right-handed fast-scoring batsman. On the tour of England in 1947, though he lacked consistency, he made 701 runs (36.89). His sole century, against Glamorgan at Swansea, was masterly, with conditions favouring the bowlers. On his Test début, at Trent Bridge, he hit 60 in a general run-feast. Very light on his feet, he was a splendid outfield and turned many a certain four into a quick single. During the Second World War he became a Spitfire pilot; his engine failed after action in the air and he bailed out to be taken POW.

First-class career (1933–48): 3,028 runs (41.47) including 6 centuries, and 52 catches

Test matches (3): 100 runs (25.00) and 1 catch

HARTIGAN, Gerald Patrick Desmond

(b. 1884, King Williamstown; d. 1955, Durban) *Border and South Africa*

A very competent right-handed batsman and fast-medium bowler, Gerald Hartigan shone like a beacon for the generally weak Border province side from 1903 until 1927, his highest score being

176 not out against Eastern Province in 1910/11. He toured England in 1912, playing in two of the Tests, but, in returning the ball from the deep, he fractured his arm and was out for the rest of the tour. He appeared in the first three Tests against England in 1913/14, top-scoring with 51 out of 160 in the second at Johannesburg (the match in which Syd Barnes took 17 wickets).

First-class career (1903–27): 1,544 runs (29.13) including 3 centuries, 92 wickets (21.08), and 19 catches

Test matches (5): 114 runs (11.40) and 1–141

HARVEY, Robert Lyon

(b. 1911, Orange Free State) *Natal and South Africa*

Sometime captain of his province, Robert Harvey was a very consistent right-handed batsman who, in a rather short career, made 740 runs (43.52) in the Currie Cup competition. He appeared in two Tests against Australia in 1935/6 without distinguishing himself, but for his province at Durban scored 104 in the first match and 138 in the second against the touring team.

First-class career (1933–40): 1,298 runs (38.17) including 2 centuries, and 37 wickets (26.10)

Test matches (2): 51 runs (12.75)

HATHORN, Christopher Maitland Howard

(b. 1878, Pietermaritzburg; d. 1920, Johannesburg) *Transvaal and South Africa*

A very sound right-handed batsman, usually at first or second wicket down, Maitland Hathorn toured England in 1901, 1904, and 1907 and Australia in 1910/11. At home he played against Australia in 1902/3 and England in 1905/6. He was very successful on his first two England tours (on neither of which Tests were played). He made 1,261 runs (35.02) in 1901 and 1,339 runs (37.19) in 1904. His sole Test century was 102 in the third match against England at Johannesburg in 1905/6. His health was never robust.

First-class career (1897–1911): 3,541 runs (26.62) including 9 centuries, 1 wicket (52.00), and 27 catches

Test matches (12): 325 runs (17.10) including 1 century, and 5 catches

HEARNE, Frank

(b. 1858; d. 1949) *Kent, Western Province, England, and South Africa*

See England section.

HEARNE, George Alfred Lawrence

(b. 1888, Catford, London, England; d. 1978, East Transvaal) *Western Province and South Africa*

A fast-scoring right-handed opening batsman, George Hearne made a promising start to his Test career against England at Johannesburg in 1922/3, making 28 and 27, but in the next Test he made 'a pair' and he was dropped for the rest of the series. He toured England in 1924 but his success was moderate and he appeared in only one Test. He was the son of Frank Hearne.

First-class career (1910–27): 1,981 runs (28.30) including 2 centuries, 14 wickets (28.64), 38 catches, and 2 stumpings

Test matches (3): 59 runs (11.80) and 3 catches

HEINE, Peter Samuel

(b. 1928, Natal) *Orange Free State, Transvaal, and South Africa*

Always associated with his new-ball partner Neil Adcock, Peter Heine was a well-built, 6 ft. 5 in., right-arm, genuinely fast bowler with a 'killer' streak. He first made news when he devastated the 1953/4 New Zealanders, taking 7 for 29 for Orange Free State. He toured England in 1955, securing 74 wickets (19.86), including 21 wickets (23.52) in four Tests. On his début, at Lord's, he took 5 for 60 on the first day, England collapsing for 133. In the next Test, at Old Trafford, Heine and Adcock collected 14 wickets between them, South Africa winning by three wickets. At home he played against England in 1956/7, Australia in 1957/8 and New Zealand in 1961/2. In the drawn rubber with England in 1956/7, the two fast bowlers took 39 wickets between them, Heine finishing with 18 (28.72). In the fifth match, at Port Elizabeth, they bowled out England for 110, Heine taking 4 for 22. Against Australia in 1957/8, he was more dominant than his partner, taking 17 wickets (18.88) and twice taking six wickets in an innings, certainly among his finest performances.

First-class career (1951–65): 1,255 runs (15.52), 277 wickets (21.38), and 34 catches

Test matches (14): 209 runs (9.95), 58 wickets (25.08), and 8 catches

HENRY, Omar

(b. 1952, Stellenbosch) *Western Province, Boland, Orange Free State, and South Africa*

It was inevitable that Omar Henry should gain as much attention for being the first player of colour to represent South Africa in the new dispensation as for his ability when he went to the World Cup in 1992. A wiry little left-arm spinner and determined left-hand batsman, he had, in fact, established himself previously at national level, making the South African side for unofficial international matches against the Australian XI in the late 1980s. He had, however, to wait until the age of 40 to play his first Test match against India and was selected for three of the four games during that summer, the exception being when South Africa opted for pure pace on the fast Wanderers track. A man of courage and dignity, he had to overcome both political and social obstacles to achieve the highest honours in cricket and that on its own was a considerable achievement. He played for Scotland for a while and thought of settling there before circumstances changed to enable him to lead a normal life in his own country. He was probably more effective in the limited-overs game than in the five-day version although he was given better opportunities in the latter.

First-class career (1977–94): 4,441 runs (28.65) including 5 centuries, 434 wickets (24.97), and 121 catches
Test matches (3): 53 runs (17.66), 3 wickets (63.00), and 2 catches

HIME, Charles Frederick William

(b. 1869, Bermuda; d. 1940, Pietermaritzburg) Natal and South Africa

Charles Hime was a reliable right-handed batsman and effective medium-paced bowler who, aged only 19, took 6 for 40 for a Pietermaritzburg XXII against the first England touring team in 1888/9. Amongst other good performances he also took 5 for 18 when captaining Natal against MCC in 1905/6 and added a very brisk 184 for the second wicket with Major R. M. Poore for Natal against Lord Hawke's England XI in 1895/6. His sole Test, however, was the first at Port Elizabeth in 1895/6 when he scored 0 and 8 and took 1 for 31.

First-class career (1889–1906): 358 runs (12.34) and 24 wickets (22.41)

HOBSON, Denys Laurence

(b. 1951, Port Elizabeth) Eastern Province and Western Province

Denys Hobson was South Africa's outstanding spin bowler through the late 1970s and early 1980s. A leg-spinner, who often operated at medium-pace, he made his home Newlands turf his happiest hunting ground. Here he took the bulk of his more than 200 first-class wickets. His ability to get the ball to bounce and to dip into the prevailing south-easterly wind were superb allies to his genuine turn. He once took 14 wickets in a single day's play (7 in each innings) for 113 runs against Natal, enabling Western Province to win outright after the loss of a virtual full day to rain. Three seasons later he took 9 for 64 in an innings against Eastern Province, his career-best return, and, in fact, dismissed all 11 Eastern Province batsmen during the course of the match. His international potential was recognized when he signed for World Series Cricket in 1977/8. However, like his countryman Graeme Pollock, he returned from Australia without playing a match. He had played some county 2nd XI cricket in an attempt to circumvent political considerations that eventually ruled him out.

First-class career (1970–85): 1,251 runs (13.30), 374 wickets (27.52), and 47 catches

HUDSON, Andrew Charles

(b. 1965, Eshowe, Zululand) Natal and South Africa

A right-hand opening batsman with a flowing range of attacking strokes, Andrew Hudson earned his place in South African cricket history when he became the first (and so far only) player to make a Test century on début. For good measure, he did so against West Indies on one of their favourite fast-bowling pastures at the Kensington Oval in Bridgetown in 1992. Hudson was a surprise selection, causing a shock in certain circles, when he was preferred to Jimmy Cook as Kepler Wessels's opening partner for the 1992 World Cup. However, he completely justified the faith of the wise men, becoming a first choice for South Africa until he unaccountably lost form on his first tour of England in 1994. He also became the first South African to score a century in a limited-overs international when he reached 108 against India at Bloemfontein's Springbok Park in the 1992/3 season. Hudson is a batsman who looks as though he may get himself into trouble as his first instinctive move is a half-pace forward and the positioning of his back foot would not satisfy the purist; but he has such gifts of stroke-play and timing that he has compiled an impressive Test career and a match seldom passes without his scoring at least a half-century. His ability to cut, pull, and hook gives him strong scoring strokes against the new ball and he always makes his runs attractively and at a cracking pace.

First-class career (1984–) 5,449 runs (34.70) including 10 centuries, and 84 catches
Test matches (19): 1,181 runs (34.73) including 2 centuries, and 15 catches

HUTCHINSON, Philip

(b. 1861, West Dean, Sussex, England; d. 1925, Durban) *Natal and South Africa*

One of the best right-handed batsmen in Natal and a useful bowler, Philip Hutchinson performed very well as an all-rounder in preliminary matches against the first England team and was one of the first two Natal men to receive international honours when he represented South Africa in the first two Tests at Port Elizabeth and Cape Town in 1888/9. These were his only first-class matches.

First-class career (2): 14 runs (3.50) and 3 catches

IRONSIDE, David Ernest James

(b. 1925, Mozambique) *Transvaal and South Africa*

David Ironside swung the ball at medium-pace and was able to bowl for long spells without losing accuracy. An effective seam bowler for his province in a short career, he made an impressive Test début in the second match at Johannesburg against New Zealand in 1953, proving irresistible in partnership with Neil Adcock, taking 5 for 51 and 3 for 37 in a winning cause. But after playing in two more matches in the series, he did not represent his country again.

First-class career (1947–56): 135 runs (6.42) and 130 wickets (21.13)
Test matches (3): 37 runs (18.50), 15 wickets (18.33), and 1 catch

IRVINE, Brian Lee

(b. 1944, Durban) *Natal, Transvaal, Essex, and England*

Son of a Natal baseballer, Lee Irvine was a marvellously free left-handed batsman with all the strokes and a versatile fielder who could keep wicket admirably. Trim and short-haired, he always cut a neat, dashing figure on the field. He burst suddenly into full flower in 1967/8 with 504 runs (56.00). He signed a three-year contract with Essex (although, in the event, he served only two years) and was a great success. He became known as a hitter of sixes, winning a competition in his

first English season, 1968, with 26. A 27-minute fifty brought him another prize. He made 1,439 runs (32.70) and 1,235 runs (37.42) in his two seasons with Essex and would assuredly have toured with South Africa had the 1970 visit gone ahead. Returning to his homeland, he continued to tear into bowling: he made 872 runs (54.50) in 1969/70, 882 runs (51.88) in 1972/3, and 890 runs (46.84) in 1974/5. He is one of the players who lost very severely when South Africa was banned from Test cricket. In his only series—the last played by his country—against Australia in 1969/70, he showed splendid form, hitting 79 and 73 in the third Test at Johannesburg and 102 in the fourth at Port Elizabeth. His career-highest was 193 for Transvaal against Eastern Province at Johannesburg in 1972/3.

First-class career (1962–77): 9,919 runs (40.48) including 21 centuries, 1 wicket (142.00), and 247 dismissals (240 c., 7 st.)
Test matches (4): 353 runs (50.42) including 1 century, and 2 catches

JACK, Steven Douglas

(b. 1970, Durban) *Transvaal and South Africa*

A strong, aggressive, red-headed right-arm fast bowler, Steven Jack might have played earlier for South Africa but for injuries. His first appearances at international level came in 1994/5 when his first Test matches at Durban and Cape Town against New Zealand were followed by limited-overs games in the Mandela Trophy, a triangular tournament with Sri Lanka and Pakistan. In his first Test series he bowled with fire, especially when taking 4 for 69 in the first innings of his second match at Newlands.

First-class career (1989–): 434 runs (16.07), 140 wickets (21.30), and 7 catches
Test matches (2): 7 runs (3.5), 8 wickets (24.5), and 1 catch

JEFFERIES, Stephen Thomas

(b. 1959, Cape Town) *Western Province, Boland, Lancashire, and Hampshire*

Stephen Jefferies teamed up with his great friend, Garth le Roux, to form the outstanding opening attack in South Africa for most of the 1980s. A dark-haired and broad-shouldered left-arm bowler of genuine pace, he possessed a lethal in-swinging yorker that earned him many critical breakthroughs. He is one of only two South Africans to take all 10 wickets in an innings (for 59 runs against Free State at Newlands in

1987/8). He had two spells of county cricket in England without achieving major success. A man of notable strength and stamina, he was able to bowl far longer spells than was the norm for a man of his pace. This may have accounted for a deterioration in his career once he reached the age of 30. His career came to a sad end in 1994 when he lost several fingers on his bowling hand in a domestic accident. He was an effective lower-order hitter as a left-hand batsman, coming into his own in this department as limited-overs cricket became more and more important in the modern game.

First-class career (1978–94): 3,807 runs (24.88), 478 wickets (27.62), and 54 catches

JENNINGS, Raymond Vernon

(b. 1954, Vanderbijlpark) *Transvaal and Northern Transvaal*

Unchallenged as South Africa's premier wicket-keeper for most of the isolation period, 'Jet' Jennings would surely have joined the ranks of the country's great stumpers had an international career been possible. A fierce competitor who put pressure on the opposing batsmen from behind the stumps, he was criticized in some quarters for standing too deep for his seamers. But it did enable him to cover an enormous arc on both sides of the stumps and he took acrobatic catches, seemingly covering 5 to 10 yards on both sides of the stumps, not to mention the miscued top edges that he pursued successfully 30 to 40 yards out. The iron ring he formed for Transvaal with first slip Alan Kourie and Graeme Pollock at second hardly missed anything of consequence over a 10-year period. He was a useful lower-order batsman although he was seldom needed in this role for his provincial side.

First-class career (1973–93): 4,160 runs (23.90) including 3 centuries, and 621 dismissals (567 c., 54 st.)

JOHNSON, Clement Lecky

(b. 1871, Co. Kildare, Ireland; d. 1908, Transvaal) *Transvaal and South Africa*

A well-known Irish cricketer—a good right-handed batsman and fast bowler—'Boy' Johnson was 5 years in the Dublin University XI and toured America with Gentlemen of Ireland. He settled in South Africa for health reasons but, within a year, was touring England with the first South African side of 1894 when he scored 508 runs and took 50 wickets: among his scores was

79 at the expense of Gentlemen of Ireland! His sole Test was the second at Johannesburg against England in 1895/6 when he made 3 and 7, took 0 for 57 and caught 1.

First-class career (1893–9): 117 runs (16.71)

KEITH, Headley James

(b. 1927, Dundee, South Africa) *Natal and South Africa*

A forceful left-handed batsman, strong in square-cutting and driving, and part of the powerful line-up of his province in the early 1950s, Headley Keith never quite made the grade in Tests. He toured Australasia in 1952/3 and England in 1955, and at home played against England in 1956/7. In the former tour he made 608 runs (33.77), including 111 and 113 not out against Victoria at Melbourne—the first South African to have achieved the feat in Australia—and in the latter tour he made 682 runs (24.35). On his Test début against England, at Lord's in 1955, he scored 57, and at Headingley 73, playing his part in a South African victory, but otherwise he was disappointing. His career-highest was 193 for Natal against Transvaal at Johannesburg in 1951/2. His left-arm bowling was rarely used in Tests but he was often a partnership breaker in Currie Cup matches. Before he made his first-class début he took 5 for 14 and 5 for 91 for Natal Country Districts against the visiting Australian team in 1949/50.

First-class career (1950–8): 3,203 runs (30.50) including 8 centuries, 79 wickets (27.51), and 61 catches

Test matches (8): 318 runs (21.20), 0–63, and 9 catches

KEMPIS, Gustav Adolph

(b. 1865, Port Elizabeth; d. 1890, Mozambique) *Natal and South Africa*

Many judges have affirmed that Gus Kempis was one of the best bowlers South Africa has ever produced: a left-arm medium-pacer who possessed great control over his length and turn, he could break either way with equal facility. His sole Test was the first between South Africa and England at Port Elizabeth in 1888/9 when he scored 0 and 0 not out and took 4 for 76. On tour with Natal through Cape Colony in 1889/90, he took 49 wickets (12.10), but he died some months later of fever at Chiloane on the East Coast. His brother, G. S., visited England with the first South African team in 1894.

First-class career (1888–90): 60 runs (6.00) and 46 wickets (12.71)

KIRSTEN, Gary

(b. 1967, Cape Town) *Western Province and South Africa*

A left-hand batsman who prefers the number three spot but has played all his cricket for South Africa as an opener, Gary Kirsten is a classic example of the cricketer who grabbed his opportunity with both hands when the opening occurred. He was surprisingly overlooked for South Africa's tour to India and Australia during the 1993/4 season but injury gave him the chance to make a late run as a replacement. Within three weeks of arriving in Australia he forced his way into the Test team and has been a first-choice ever since. His hunger for international cricket quickly became apparent as he filled the vacant spot as opening batsman, worked hard at becoming the specialist short-leg fielder with considerable success, and bowled vital overs of under-rated off-spin when South Africa opted for an all-pace attack, even on pitches that helped slow bowlers. No doubt he would have helped out behind the stumps had it been necessary! Initially during his Test career, he had trouble in covering his off-stump and was very vulnerable to catches in the slips, but he worked hard at his deficiencies and could be more than happy with his first season against Australia during which he made a memorable limited-overs century in the first leg of a triangular final against the host nation. His 201 not out against Durham helped make him the highest scorer on the tour of England in 1994, with 751 first-class runs (46.93). He and his half-brother, Peter, fulfilled a life ambition when they got the chance to open together for their country and he has always acknowledged that Peter is his favourite opening partner.

First-class career (1987–   ) 5,131 runs (43.85), 15 wickets (35.00), and 55 catches

Test matches (14): 948 runs (37.92), 2 wickets (66.50), and 15 catches

KIRSTEN, Peter Noel

(b. 1955, Pietermaritzburg) *Western Province, Sussex, Derbyshire, Border, and South Africa*

A right-hand batsman, occasional off-spin bowler, and one of South Africa's all-time fielding greats, Peter Kirsten was part of the golden era that never played international cricket and indeed he seriously considered emigrating to South Australia, in the late 1980s. When the chance finally came to play at the highest level in 1991, he was already 36 years old. Nevertheless he gave the

world a fleeting and tantalizing glimpse of what might have been during the 1992 World Cup in Australia and New Zealand. Playing in his favourite number three position, he was second only to Martin Crowe of New Zealand as the leading compiler of runs in the round robin section of the tournament. Although he was to play on-and-off for South Africa for several seasons thereafter, the world seldom saw this free-flowing batsman in full stride again. Short of stature, which helped to make his contests with fast bowlers all the more compelling, but a giant in terms of talent, he used powerful wrists to play every off-side stroke in the book and was capable of cutting any bowler to pieces regardless of the field settings. A successful schoolboy sprinter and stand-off half in Rugby, he also ran 'like greased lightning' between wickets and gave as much enjoyment to spectators with his athletic prowess as he did with his stroke-play. His lack of height proved a distinct advantage in the field where he was amazingly acrobatic and could drop quickly on the most blistering of cover drives. It was never worth chancing a single against his accurate, fast arm as he regularly threw down the stumps from any angle. He made his début for Western Province as an 18-year-old schoolboy at number five but quickly established himself at three, where he would have been a first choice for South Africa from 1976 onwards. The sign of great things to follow came in 1976/7 (his fourth first-class season) when he made five centuries in successive innings, six in seven, provided the first instance of scoring a century in both innings at Newlands, and joined Barry Richards and Graeme Pollock as the only South African batsmen to score 1,000 runs in a domestic first-class season. His prolific scoring continued when he signed for Derbyshire and made six double-centuries in the space of three seasons. He had a brief reign as South Africa's captain in rebel series against Sri Lanka and West Indies before being controversially dismissed, a move that played its part in his resigning the Western Province captaincy as well. By that time he had nevertheless become the first captain to do the double of Currie Cup and limited-overs success. His genius was not restricted to cricket as he could well have represented South Africa at Rugby. He had to wait almost until his fortieth birthday for the lifetime ambition of an international cricket tour of England and it was entirely fitting that he should score his maiden Test match century at Headingley in an innings that denied England their chance of enforcing the follow-on and thus of gaining victory. He was off the field for a while the next day with a headache! In 40 one-day internationals he scored 1,293 (38.02) with a century and 9 fifties.

First-class career (1973–): 20,920 runs (45.08) including 53 centuries, 117 wickets (39.73), and 181 catches

Test matches (12): 626 runs (31.30) including 1 century, 0–30, and 7 catches

KOTZE, Johannes Jacobus

(b. 1879, Cape Province; d. 1931, Cape Town) *Western Province, Transvaal, and South Africa*

A Boer farmer who preferred cricket to war, 'Kodgee' toured England with three South African teams in 1901 (while the Boer War was still raging), 1904, and 1907. Right-arm, and one of the fastest bowlers produced by South Africa, he could make the ball move even on the hardest pitches. Despite a vigorous body action and a very long run, he was able to keep going for long periods; he hated being punished by the batsman. 'Kodgee's best year was 1904 when he took 104 wickets (20.50)—he had taken 79 wickets in 1901—but it was not until 1907 that Tests were played in England and, as the googly bowlers were dominant that year, he appeared in only one Test. He had played twice against Australia, in 1902/3. A poor batsman, he was also a clumsy field. Remaining close to the game throughout his life, he was, perhaps, more responsible than anyone else for the introduction of turf wickets in South Africa, at Newlands in 1927/8. His most impressive bowling in an innings was for his province against Griqualand West at Port Elizabeth when he took 8 for 18 in 1902/3. His best home season was 1906/7—54 wickets (10.83) from six matches. He twice performed the hat-trick.

First-class career (1901–11): 688 runs (8.60), 348 wickets (17.86), and 31 catches

Test matches (3): 2 runs (0.40), 6 wickets (40.50), and 3 catches

KOURIE, Alan John

(b. 1951, Johannesburg) *Transvaal*

Something of a dour character who had his share of brushes with authority, Alan Kourie was a key member of the Transvaal side that carried all before it. A big man with huge hands, he was indispensable as a specialist first slip and left-arm spin bowler. As a right-hand batsman, he was at his best in crisis situations. He was not quite as successful in rebel series with the ball as many might have expected but this was probably caused by his sudden exposure to international batsmen who were not scared to use their feet. Had he had a proper international career from an early age, he would probably have adapted his game accordingly.

First-class career (1970–89): 4,470 runs (34.38) including 5 centuries, 421 wickets (23.44), and 148 catches

KUIPER, Adrian Paul

(b. 1959, Johannesburg) *Western Province, Derbyshire, and South Africa*

Often compared with England's Ian Botham as a champion hitter, Adrian Kuiper has not quite scaled the lofty heights he has often threatened. A powerfully built right-hand batsman, he launched himself in the major league with a remarkable all-round performance for South African Universities against Western Province in 1978/9. He first took 6 for 96 and then made his maiden first-class century (110 not out) to help his side to a South African record fourth innings winning total of 500 for 7, almost a world record. Regrettably that promise was never really fulfilled as he has made only seven first-class centuries although occasionally he explodes with a display of hitting that can devastate any side. This included a century off 49 balls at Bloemfontein's Springbok Park for South Africa against Mike Gatting's England XI in a limited-overs game. He subsequently disappointed at the 1992 World Cup when he was vice-captain and played his only Test against West Indies immediately thereafter. This was followed by a spell in the wilderness, caused in part by injury, but he returned for the limited-overs series against Australia at home in 1993/4, hitting 25 off the last five balls of the SA innings at Centurion Park, including sixes off the last three deliveries, and his future appearances were likely to be limited to this type of cricket. He bowls medium-pace away-swingers and possesses one of the better slower balls in South Africa, which makes him a useful back-up bowler. Unfulfilled though his talents may have been, he has still been one of the great entertainers of South African cricket. In 22 internationals he scored 414 runs (27.60).

First-class career (1977–): 6,613 runs (32.73) including 7 centuries, 183 wickets (28.73), and 95 catches

KUYS, Frederick

(b. 1870, Cape Colony; d. 1953, Cape Province) *Western Province and South Africa*

An all-rounder, Frederick Kuys played in one Test, the second against England at Cape Town in 1898/9, when he scored 26 and 0 and took 2 for 31.

First-class career (1896–9): 229 runs (16.35) and 11 wickets (18.72)

LANCE, Herbert Roy

(b. 1940, Pretoria) *North-Eastern Transvaal, Transvaal, and South Africa*

Tall, strongly built, determined and with the look of a GI with his crew-cut hairstyle, 'Tiger' Lance was a fine, upstanding, right-handed stroke-player and a useful change medium-fast bowler. He toured England in 1965 and at home played against New Zealand in 1961/2 and Australia in 1966/7 and 1969/70. In England he made 475 runs (26.38), running into form in the third Test at The Oval with 69 and 53, adding 96 with Colin Bland in the second innings for the fifth wicket in a very closely-fought contest. His best series, however, was his first against Australia when he made 261 runs (37.28) including 44 and 70 in the first match at Johannesburg, which South Africa won handsomely after being 126 behind on the first innings. A heavy scorer in domestic cricket —he made 729 runs (66.27) in seven matches in 1965/6—he scored 101 and 112 for Transvaal against Eastern Province at Johannesburg in 1966/7, becoming the third player to register two centuries in a Currie Cup match. His second knock included ten sixes and seven fours. He shared in the record tenth-wicket partnership in South Africa of 174 with D. Mackay-Coghill for Transvaal against Natal at Johannesburg in 1965/6.

First-class career (1958–71): 5,336 runs (34.87) including 11 centuries, 167 wickets (25.65), and 101 catches

Test matches (13): 591 runs (28.14), 12 wickets (39.91), and 7 catches

LANGTON, Arthur Beaumont Chudleigh

(b. 1912, Pietermaritzburg; d. 1942, Accra, Gold Coast) *Transvaal and South Africa*

The tallest—6 ft. 3 in.—and the youngest of the 1935 South African team to England, 'Chud' Langton took more wickets—115 (21.16)—than any of his colleagues and scored 537 runs. He

bowled accurate right-arm medium-pace and always needed careful watching for lift, break or change of speed. As a batsman, he could defend when necessary, but was at his best forcing the pace—pulling, driving and cutting. He was a fine field in any company. He played an important part in South Africa's first victory over England in England, at Lord's, when he took 6 for 89 and added 101 in two hours with Bruce Mitchell for the seventh wicket; and in the final Test at The Oval, he added 137 in seventy minutes with Eric Dalton, then a record, for the ninth wicket. In the 1935 series he took 15 wickets (41.53) and made 121 runs (30.25). He continued to put in useful all-round efforts against Australia in 1935/6 and England in 1938/9. He was killed in an air accident.

First-class career (1931–42): 1,218 runs (19.96), 193 wickets (25.74), and 41 catches

Test matches (15): 298 runs (15.68), 40 wickets (45.67), and 8 catches

LAWRENCE, Godfrey Bernard

(b. 1932, Salisbury, Rhodesia) *Natal, Rhodesia, and South Africa*

A 6 ft. 5 in. giant, the tallest player in South African cricket, 'Goofy' Lawrence was a right-arm opening fast bowler who, by dint of sheer hard graft, impressed successively the Mashonaland, Rhodesian, and Test match selectors. Also a useful batsman, it was unfortunate for him that his career should commence when Neil Adcock and Peter Heine were at peak form. He was sensational, however, in his sole Test series against New Zealand in 1961/2. He took 8 for 53 in the first innings of the second match at Johannesburg, and in the fourth Test, again at Johannesburg, his match analysis was 9 for 109. He only opened the bowling in one Test but in the fifth at Port Elizabeth he opened the batting in the first innings with Eddie Barlow, scoring 43. In ten first-class matches in 1961/2, he took 51 wickets (17.49). For more than a decade, he was Rhodesia's spearhead.

First-class career (1952–67): 1,079 runs (12.69) and 342 wickets (17.97)

Test matches (5): 141 runs (17.62), 28 wickets (18.28), and 2 catches

Le ROUX, Frederick Louis

(b. 1882, Durban; d. 1963, Durban) *Transvaal, Eastern Province, and South Africa*

An all-rounder and captain of Transvaal for several seasons, Fred Le Roux's sole Test was the fourth against England at Durban in 1913/14 when he scored 1 and 0 and (opening the attack) took 0 for 24. Before retiring officially, he captained a First League team in Durban at the age of fifty; and in 1950, acted as convener of the National Selection Committee.

First-class career (1908–29): 1,258 runs (28.59) including 2 centuries, and 93 wickets (19.75)

LE ROUX, Garth Stirling

(b. 1955, Cape Town) *Western Province and Sussex*

Garth le Roux burst on to the first-class scene with dramatic suddenness and for two seasons was as fast as any bowler in the world. A strapping, fair-haired, fast right-arm bowler, he gave an indication of what was to follow when he took 53 wickets for Western Province in only eight Currie Cup matches at an average of less than 15 and almost won the trophy single-handed. During that season he had his slip fielders standing a full pitch length behind the stumps, such was the pace he generated. Having qualified via the England county route, he was a natural for Kerry Packer's World Series Cricket (his powerful build and good-looking blond features made him perfect for the marketing men) and he did not disappoint, being voted man of the series ahead of countryman Clive Rice. A succession of serious injuries caused him to rely more on experience and an effective away-swinger during the second half of his career but, even operating at a lesser pace, he still gained enough bounce to be an extremely awkward customer to face. He took a hat-trick against the rebel Australians at the Wanderers in 1985/6. A savage hitter of the ball, he was a competent and reliable source of runs down the order at provincial level and came close to scoring a century on several occasions. He bowled with success for Sussex from 1978 to 1987, frequently forming a formidable opening partnership with Imran Khan. In 1981 he took 81 wickets (19.53).

First-class career (1975–89): 5,425 runs (25.71), 838 wickets (21.24), and 80 catches

LEWIS, Percy Tyson

(b. 1884, Cape Town; d. 1976, Durban) *Transvaal, Western Province, and South Africa*

At the time of his death the oldest surviving Springbok Test cricketer, 'Plum' Lewis was a right-handed batsman who could be brilliant at his best. He hit 151 for Western Province against

MCC in the opening match of the 1913/14 tour, and was selected for the first Test at Durban, but was 'c. Woolley b. Barnes' in each innings without scoring. This was his sole Test. He won the MC and bar as a Lieutenant-Colonel in France during the First World War and, being severely wounded in the leg, could play only club cricket on his return, using a runner.

First-class career (1907–14): 507 runs (26.68) including 1 century

LIEBENBERG, Gerhardus Frederick Johannes

(b. 1972, Upington) *Griqualand West and Orange Free State*

A stylish right-hand batsman who likes playing off the front foot, Gerhard Liebenberg had a dream first-class début for Griquas, scoring 84 and 108 in his first two matches. He gradually established himself as South Africa's best young batsman, playing in the A international against England at Port Elizabeth in 1993/4 and following that up with selection for the tour to England in the 1994 winter. He was, in fact, chosen as reserve wicket-keeper although he had seldom fulfilled these duties at higher than club level before his selection. It is as a batsman that South Africa will be hoping for him to achieve international recognition. He is a talented all-round sportsman who has also represented Griquas at tennis and athletics. On his tour of England in 1994, he scored 226 runs at 22.60.

First-class career (1989–   ): 2,117 runs (29.00), 1 wicket (10.00), 35 catches, and 3 stumpings

LINDSAY, Denis Thomson

(b. 1939, Transvaal) *North-Eastern Transvaal, Transvaal, and South Africa*

As wicket-keeper/batsman for the Fezelas in England in 1961, Denis Lindsay played the first ball from Bill Greensmith circumspectly back to the bowler in the opening match against Essex at Chelmsford. Then, opening his shoulders, he sent the last five deliveries soaring over the fence for six and, scoring 83 not out, won the match for his side. A year later he hit 48 and 84 for a Rhodesian Invitation XI against the Commonwealth tourists at Salisbury, the attack being of international calibre, and before long he was playing Test cricket. An upstanding right-handed attacking stroke-player, he was also a class wicket-keeper who had to wait for a Test place until John Waite retired, so for a time specialized as a batsman. He toured Australasia in 1963/4 and England in 1965, and at home played against England in 1964/5 and Australia in 1966/7 and 1969/70. In his first match on Australian soil, he hit a sparkling 104 (at number nine) against South Australia at Adelaide, but his sole notable Test innings was 65 in the fifth match at Sydney in a run-feast. On his England tour, when he was the first-string wicket-keeper, he made 779 runs (27.82) and had 24 dismissals, but he could not make runs in the Tests. He averaged only 22.80 against England in 1964/5, but in the home series against Australia in 1966/7 he blossomed as a well-organized as well as aggressive attacking force at the highest level. He hit 606 runs (86.57) in the series, more than anyone else on either side, the highest individual contribution by any wicket-keeper in a Test rubber. He also held 24 catches as South Africa beat Australia for the first time at home. Usually batting at number six, he hit 69 and 182 (including five sixes after the Springboks had been 126 behind) in the first match at Johannesburg; 81 in the second at Cape Town; 137 in the third at Durban; and 131 in the fourth at Johannesburg. His career-highest was 216 against Transvaal B at Johannesburg in 1966/7, his most prolific season, when he made 1,014 runs (72.42) in ten matches, including four centuries. The same season he had 46 dismissals (45 c., 1 st.), a South African record. He is son of J. D. Lindsay.

First-class career (1958–74): 7,074 runs (35.54) including 12 centuries, and 333 dismissals (292 c., 41 st.)
Test matches (19): 1,130 runs (37.66) including 3 centuries, and 59 dismissals (57 c., 2 st.)

LINDSAY, John Dixon

(b. 1908, Cape Province; d. 1990, Transvaal) *North-Eastern Transvaal, Transvaal, and South Africa*

A neat, businesslike wicket-keeper, Johnny Lindsay toured England in 1947 and although he began shakily on the early wet wickets he always gave the impression of much natural skill. On the tour he earned 27 dismissals and played in three of the Tests

First-class career (1933–49): 346 runs (11.16) and 55 dismissals (39 c., 16 st.)
Test matches (3): 21 runs (7.00) and 5 dismissals (4 c., 1 st.)

LINDSAY, Neville Vernon

(b. 1886, Orange Free State; d. 1976, Pietermaritzburg) *Orange Free State, Transvaal, and South Africa*

An all-round sportsman, outstanding at Rugby, hockey, golf, and bowls, Neville Lindsay was a sound right-handed batsman and brilliant cover field who represented either of his two provinces from 1906 until 1927, scoring 2,030 runs (33.00). He shared the South African ninth-wicket record partnership of 221 for Transvaal against Rhodesia at Bulawayo in 1922/3 with G. R. McCubbin. His sole Test was the second against Australia at Johannesburg in 1921/2 when he scored 6 and 29 and caught 'Horseshoe' Collins.

First-class career (1906–27): 2,030 runs (33.27) including 5 centuries, and 24 wickets (27.83)

LING, William Victor Stone

(b. 1891, Kimberley; d. 1960, Transvaal) *Griqualand West and South Africa*

Beginning as a promising right-arm googly bowler, William Ling developed into a very useful batsman in the Currie Cup competition, becoming the most effective batsman of his province for a decade. He appeared in the three Tests against Australia in 1921/2 and the first three against England in 1922/3, being marked 'absent' in the sole South African innings in the third match. He had been summoned home to Kimberley when his mother became seriously ill, and it proved to be his last Test.

First-class career (1910–30): 2,618 runs (31.76) including 3 centuries, and 72 wickets (31.52)
Test matches (6): 168 runs (16.80), 0–20, and 1 catch

LLEWELLYN, Charles Bennett

(b. 1876, Pietermaritzburg; d. 1964, Chertsey, Surrey) *Natal, Hampshire, and South Africa*

A notable all-rounder, being a left-handed forcing batsman, a left-arm slow to medium-paced bowler and a fine fielder, especially at mid-off, Charlie or 'Buck' Llewellyn first played for Natal at 18 and represented South Africa in five Tests against England and ten against Australia. His Test début was against England in the second match at Johannesburg in 1895/6; then from 1899 until 1910 he was a highly valued professional with Hampshire—ironically his career-highest was 216 for the county against the 1901 South

Africans at Southampton. For Hampshire he achieved the double in a season three times and twice registered two centuries in a match: he was among the 14 players chosen for the first Test for England against Australia in 1902 but was omitted in the final selection. Before qualifying for championship matches, he had created a sensation by taking 8 for 132 and then hitting 72 and 21 for Hampshire against the Australians at Southampton in 1899. He played for South Africa in the three Tests against Australia in 1902/3, taking 25 wickets (17.92), including 9 for 216 and scoring 90 in the first at Johannesburg, and 10 for 116 in the second, also at Johannesburg. After he had left Hampshire he toured Australia in 1910/11 and England in 1912. When South Africa defeated Australia for the first time, in the third match at Adelaide, he made 43 and 80, and clean-bowled Macartney, Ransford, and Trumper. In the Triangular Tournament, he hit fifties off England and Australia, but in his final Test, against England at The Oval, he was dismissed for 'a pair'. Subsequently, he played League cricket in England and died in Surrey where he had lived for many years. A story that 'Buck' was a coloured man ostracized by Jimmy Sinclair and other members of the South African team to Australia in 1910/11 was scotched by his daughter in *The Cricketer*. She confirmed that her father, though born at Pietermaritzburg, was of Welsh and English extraction and had no coloured blood. Moreover, he had been on good terms with all his cricket colleagues.

First-class career (1894–1912): 11,425 runs (26.75) including 18 centuries, 1,013 wickets (23.41), and 175 catches

Test matches (15): 544 runs (20.14), 48 wickets (29.60), and 7 catches

LUNDIE, Eric Balfour

(b. 1888, place unknown; d. 1917, France) *Western Province, Eastern Province, Transvaal, and South Africa*

A right-arm fast bowler, whose sole Test was against England in the fifth Test at Port Elizabeth in 1913/14, when he bowled 46 overs into the wind without being collared, 'Bill' Lundie took 4 for 107 and scored 0 not out and 1. He was killed in the First World War.

First-class career (1908–14): 126 runs (8.40) and 26 wickets (25.34)

MACAULAY, Michael John

(b. 1939, Durban) *Transvaal, Western Province, Orange Free State, North-Eastern Transvaal, Eastern Province, and South Africa*

A left-arm medium-paced seam bowler, Mike Macaulay appeared in one Test, the fifth against England at Port Elizabeth in 1964/5, scoring 21 and 12 and taking 2 for 73. He toured England in 1965, but took 25 wickets rather expensively and did not appear in any Tests, although he performed the hat-trick against Kent at Canterbury. He retired from first-class cricket with knee trouble after the 1968/9 season, but made a remarkable comeback in 1977/8, taking 42 wickets (23.14) for Eastern Province. He is the only player to have represented five provinces.

First-class career (1957–79): 888 runs (13.05) 234 wickets (22.89), and 45 catches

McCARTHY, Cuan Neil

(b. 1929, Pietermaritzburg) *Natal, Cambridge University, Dorset, and South Africa*

At 6 ft. 2 in., the tallest cricketer and fastest bowler of his time produced by South Africa, Cuan McCarthy tended to be very erratic in length, although he always maintained a good pace, and in his first Test series, against England, he took 21 wickets (26.71). In his first Test, at Durban, when England won by two wickets off the last ball, he had torn through most of the second innings batting, taking 6 for 43 out of 128 for 8. When Australia toured in 1949/50, however, this answer to Ray Lindwall had 11 catches dropped off his bowling in the Tests, and his figures failed to do him justice. In England in 1951 he was too erratic, and his persistence in bowling the bumper on a lively pitch probably cost his country the Test at Old Trafford. He collected only ten wickets (41.30) in the Tests and 59 wickets (23.96) in all first-class matches. Unfortunately, his fastest ball had in it some semblance of a throw and when he went up to Cambridge and played for the University as the attacking spearhead, rumblings grew about the legality of his action. Against Sussex his fiery bowling brought 8 for 36 including a hat-trick. He was no-balled only once, by Paddy Corrall, while bowling against Worcestershire at Worcester for Cambridge in 1952. He was also a boxing blue.

First-class career (1947–52): 141 runs (4.27), 176 wickets (25.85), and 23 catches

Test matches (15): 28 runs (3.11), 36 wickets (41.94), and 6 catches

McEWAN, Kenneth Scott

(b. 1952, Bedford, Eastern Province) Western Province, Eastern Province, Border, Essex, and Western Australia

One of the game's true gentlemen, Ken McEwan was a calm, cultured, and stylish right-hand batsman of the highest class who would surely have graced the world's greatest grounds at international level had circumstances permitted. Indeed, it was often suggested that he should take advantage of his Scottish heritage and follow the route taken by Allan Lamb, the Smith brothers, the Greig brothers and others into the England side. However, it was typical of the man's nature that he himself did not feel English enough to take such a step. Although he did well for a variety of South African provinces and scored a brilliant century against the rebel West Indians, his best performances were reserved for Essex in the county championship where he had a career of great distinction. He was equally successful and effective both in first-class and limited-overs cricket. His career reached a high point in England in 1976 when he scored six centuries including two before lunch on the first day and again the following season when he made eight centuries, four of which came in successive innings (there were, in fact, five in a row if one counted a non-first-class innings in the Sunday League). He ranks alongside Barry Richards as South Africa's most consistent and prolific scorer in county cricket. A personality of natural charm and dignity, he was liked and respected wherever he played, but never bitter that he played during the years of isolation. He retired to work on his father's cattle farm.

First-class career (1972–92): 26,628 runs (41.73) including 74 centuries, 4 wickets (77.25), 366 dismissals (359 c., 7 st.)

McGLEW, Derrick John

(b. 1929, Pietermaritzburg) Natal and South Africa

A dour and determined little opening batsman, 'Jackie' McGlew was appropriately named because there have been few tougher 'stickers' than he. He was also a brilliant fielder in the covers and an astute leader who captained his country in fourteen Tests, winning six of them and losing four. A right-hander, he had a good range of scoring strokes, but became noted instead for his concentration and powers of endurance. He toured England in 1951, 1955, and, as captain, in 1960; and Australasia in

1952/3. At home he played against New Zealand in 1953/4 and, as captain, in 1961/2; England in 1956/7; and Australia in 1957/8 (he captained South Africa against England and Australia in some earlier years when the regular leader was unable to play). He exceeded 1,000 runs in each of his England tours—1,002 runs (38.53) in 1951, 1,871 runs (58.46) including five centuries in 1955, and 1,327 runs (42.80) in 1960, heading the averages again. 1955 was by far his best Test series in England: he finished with 476 runs (52.88), including hundreds at Old Trafford and Headingley. In the third Test at Durban against Australia in 1957/8, two wickets had fallen very cheaply when McGlew 'stuck' there for 105 in 575 minutes: it was one of the slowest hundreds ever made, the first fifty taking 313 minutes, but his third-wicket partnership of 231 with John Waite was the highest to date for any South African wicket against Australia. He had made 108 in rather quicker time in the first match of the series at Johannesburg when he set up his country's first-wicket record stand of 176 against Australia with Trevor Goddard. His career-highest was 255 not out in the first Test against New Zealand at Wellington in 1952/3 when he carried his bat through an innings of 524 for 8 wickets declared, shared in the record seventh-wicket stand of 246 with A. R. A. Murray and was on the field throughout the match. Moreover, until it was exceeded by Graeme Pollock, this was the highest score for South Africa. On the 1952/3 tour, he made 1,138 runs (47.41). His best season at home was 1957/8 when he made 953 runs (50.15) including eight scores above fifty in 12 matches. He captained Natal for many years.

First-class career (1947–67): 12,170 runs (45.92) including 27 centuries, 35 wickets (26.62), and 103 catches

Test matches (34): 2,440 runs (42.06) including 7 centuries, 0–23, and 18 catches

MACKAY-COGHILL, Donald

(b. 1941, Kimberley) Transvaal

Don Mackay-Coghill would almost certainly have played for South Africa but for the extended career of Trevor Goddard. A tall left-arm bowler of fast-medium pace, he had impressive career figures, mixing his stock in-swinger with the delivery that went across the batsman. Under the inspiring captaincy of Ali Bacher, he was a feared spearhead of Transvaal, particularly at the Wanderers. He finished his career in a blaze of glory, taking 25 wickets in his last six matches. At one time he batted as high as number four for Transvaal (also left-hand) but generally preferred to be down the order and he set a Transvaal tenth-wicket record of 173 with 'Tiger' Lance. He completed the career double of 1,000 runs and 100 wickets.

First-class career (1962–74): 1,400 runs (17.72), 264 wickets (22.94), and 68 catches

McKENZIE, Kevin Alexander

(b. 1948, Pretoria) *Transvaal*

Isolation and the fact that he did not play first-class cricket outside South Africa meant that the name of Kevin McKenzie was hardly known in the greater cricketing world. Yet he developed into one of South Africa's outstanding right-hand batsmen of his time and had a rare (but always friendly) duel with Ken McEwan for the one middle-order vacancy in the rebel South African team (Peter Kirsten, Graeme Pollock, and Clive Rice were always certain selections). A fearless hooker, he was unique in modern South African cricket in that he was the only major South African batsman who declined to wear a protective helmet in an era of ever-increasing short-pitched fast bowling. The highlight of his career came at his home Wanderers ground in 1985/6 when he made 72 and 110 against the rebel Australians. This included a last-wicket stand of 31 with Graeme Pollock, who was batting one-handed after suffering a fracture, that is one of the legends of South African cricket. His son captained South Africa's under-19 team in England in 1995.

First-class career (1966–88): 6,756 runs (36.51) including 13 centuries, 1 wicket (133.00), and 141 catches

McKINNON, Atholl Henry

(b. 1932, Port Elizabeth; d. 1983, Durban) *Eastern Province, Transvaal, and South Africa*

A wily left-arm spin bowler and off-the-field humorist of burly build and rugged countenance, Atholl McKinnon took 278 wickets in Currie Cup matches alone. He toured England in 1960 and 1965; and at home played against New Zealand in 1961/2, England in 1964/5 and Australia in 1966/7. As successor to the late 'Tufty' Mann, he took 53 wickets (20.88) and 37 wickets (20.51) respectively on his England tours, while achieving very little in the Tests. In the high-scoring fourth Test against England at Johannesburg in 1964/5, he stuck manfully to his task, returning the following analysis: 86 overs—30 maidens—172 runs—7 wickets. In his early days, batting left-handed at net practice, he almost decapitated that famous old Springbok, Dave Nourse, at the next net. 'Son', growled the old man, 'turn round and bat the other way.' Atholl followed this instruction and, thus converted into a right-handed batsman of aggressive intent, he became a useful lower-order player! He became a popular coach before being struck down by a heart attack.

First-class career (1952–69): 1,687 runs (14.92), 470 wickets (21.14), and 32 catches

Test matches (8): 107 runs (17.83), 26 wickets (35.57), and 1 catch

McLEAN, Roy Alastair

(b. 1930, Pietermaritzburg) *Natal and South Africa*

Ebullient and a superb right-handed stroke-maker, Roy McLean was a beautifully balanced player and a cutter and hooker of immense power. A striking exception to the run of defensive-minded batsmen produced by South Africa from 1947 until 1960, he was, naturally, a great favourite with the crowds. Either on the boundary or close to the wicket, he was an outstanding fielder. He toured England in 1951, 1955, and 1960, and Australasia in 1952/3; and at home played against New Zealand in 1953/4 and 1961/2, England in 1956/7 and in two matches in 1964/5 and Australia in 1957/8. He was a potential match-winner whenever he played but he was also unreliable at times because of over impetuosity and in two series in South Africa was actually omitted from the side. He learned much of value from some ten century-partnerships he enjoyed for Natal with Dudley Nourse, under whose captaincy he first toured England in 1951, when in the fourth Test at Headingley, he repeatedly pierced the deep-set fields, hitting 67, 50 coming from sixes and fours. He finished second in the averages each time to Jackie McGlew in 1955 and 1960, finishing with 1,448 runs (38.10) and 1,516 runs (37.90) respectively, including eight centuries. Not prolific in the Tests, he managed to score 142 in the second Test at Lord's in 1955 when he took charge on a lively wicket in a dashing display, though he was missed several times; and in the third at Old Trafford, when South Africa sought 145 to win in two and a quarter hours, he hit 50 out of 72 with McGlew in 50 minutes, helping to ensure a narrow victory. In the 1960 Tests, he made 269 runs (33.62), more than anyone else. In a rain-restricted match at Old Trafford he hit 109 in a total of 229 in 2 hours

40 minutes. He hit the fastest century of that season, in 75 minutes against A. E. R. Gilligan's XI at Hastings after making only six in the first half-hour of his remarkable innings. He made his career-highest, 207, at 50 an hour, in the opening match at Worcester. On his tour of Australia in 1952/3, he had scored steadily before playing a decisive role in the six wicket win in the fifth Test at Melbourne, where he made 81 and 76 not out. His first Test century was against New Zealand at Durban in 1953/4—101 in 2 hours 25 minutes —South Africa going on to win by an innings. He also made 100 against England in the third match at Durban in 1956/7, and 113 in the third match at Cape Town against New Zealand in 1961/2. This was a superb almost solo fight against speed and spin, his century coming in less than 3 hours, but it could not prevent New Zealand winning her first-ever Test abroad. He scored 356 runs (39.55) in the series. In contrast to these occasional outstanding innings, McLean failed to score in eleven of his Test innings. Throughout his career, however, his fielding was superb. He represented Natal at Rugby football until 1953.

First-class career (1949–66): 10,969 runs (36.68) including 22 centuries, 2 wickets (61.00), and 132 catches
Test matches (40): 2,120 runs (30.28) including 5 centuries, 0–1, and 23 catches

McMILLAN, Brian Mervin

(b. 1963, Welkom) Transvaal, Warwickshire, Western Province, and South Africa

A gentle giant of a man but a tough competitor, who was in his element when he took the Australians on at their own 'sledging' game, Brian McMillan has proved himself to be an all-rounder of genuine Test calibre. He is a right-arm seamer of fast-medium pace who is capable of producing the occasional delivery that is genuinely quick, nor is he scared to use his physical attributes as an intimidating presence. As a right-hand batsman he has batted with success anywhere from number three to seven in first-class cricket. He played for Warwickshire in 1986, scoring 999 runs at 58.76, although his bowling was handicapped by a back injury. He had yet to score a Test century after three international seasons but had twice reached 90 and more often than not ran out of partners. His fighting 78 and 5 wickets in the match at Headingley in 1994 were typical of his all-round effectiveness. The elusive hundred came at last in January 1995 against Pakistan in Johannesburg, when his

match figures of 4 for 79 also helped towards a huge victory. He is never out of the game when on the field as his big hands have made him the safest slip fielder in the side, an important factor for a team that relies so heavily on pace.

First-class career (1984–): 4,743 runs (37.94), 230 wickets (27.12), and 94 catches
Test matches (17): 879 runs (36.62) including 1 century, 51 wickets (28.94), and 21 catches

McMILLAN, Quintin

(b. 1904, Transvaal; d. 1948, Transvaal) Transvaal and South Africa

A right-arm slow leg-spin and googly bowler and free-scoring batsman, Quintin McMillan packed a tremendous amount into his four years of first-class cricket. In his first two matches for his province, he scored 61 and took 9 wickets against Eastern Province and scored 185 against Orange Free State, both at Cape Town in 1928/9. He toured England in 1929, making 749 runs (26.75) and taking most wickets, 91 (25.45), including Hobbs, Carr, and Ames at low cost in the Oval Test. He played in all five Tests against England in 1930/1, top-scoring on the first day of the first match at Johannesburg with 45 not out in a total of 126: and he toured Australasia in 1931/2 taking 71 wickets in first-class matches, including 16 (20.18) in the two Tests against New Zealand. In the first Test played between the two countries, at Christchurch, he took 9 for 127 in the match, South Africa winning by an innings. Against South Australia at Adelaide, he took 9 for 53 in an innings. He retired for business reasons.

First-class career (1928–32): 1,607 runs (26.78) including 1 century, 189 wickets (26.63), and 30 catches
Test matches (13): 306 runs (18.00), 36 wickets (34.52), and 8 catches

MANN, Norman Bertram Fleetwood

(b. 1920, Transvaal; d. 1952, Johannesburg) Natal, Eastern Province, and South Africa

The bespectacled 'Tufty' Mann was a left-arm slow bowler who had no difficulty in pinning down English batsmen—his first spell of bowling in Tests, at Trent Bridge in 1947, consisted of eight successive maiden overs to Denis Compton and Bill Edrich in their peak year—but, as he admitted, he did not quite know where to bowl to Australians, although in the Tests against Australia in 1949/50, he headed the bowling averages with 17 wickets (25.29). He tended to seal up one end when conditions favoured batsmen and to extract full advantage when they offered him the slightest assistance. On the seven occasions when he bowled fifty or more overs in a Test, he only once gave away more than 100 runs. On both England tours, 1947 and 1951, well over a third of his overs were maidens: he took 74 wickets (25.25) on the former tour and, when his health was indifferent, 44 wickets (26.38) on the second. He headed the averages in both series of Tests—with 15 wickets (40.20) and 10 wickets (26.40) respectively from four matches. Against England at home in 1948/9 he again finished at the top with 17 wickets (25.29). His 4 for 24 in the second innings of the first Test at Trent Bridge in 1951 helped South Africa to her first victory for 16 years; and he also captured 6 for 59 in the first innings of the first match against England in 1948/9 at Durban—one of the most exciting of all Tests when England won by two wickets off the last ball. Despite indifferent eyesight, Mann could swing the bat to good purpose, hitting 97 in 55 minutes against Glamorgan at Cardiff in 1947. He made over 500 runs on the tour. In a short Currie Cup career, he took 75 wickets from 12 matches. During the Second World War, he was taken prisoner in Italy and escaped, being hidden by peasants. During the 1951 tour, he was taken ill and he died the following year after two operations. When hit for six by England's F. G. Mann, John Arlott described it as 'Mann's inhumanity to Mann'.

First-class career (1939–51): 1,446 runs (17.42), 251 wickets (23.71), and 25 wickets
Test matches (19): 400 runs (13.33), 58 wickets (33.10), and 3 catches

MANSELL, Percy Neville Frank

(b. 1920, St George's, Shropshire, England; d. 1995, Somerset West, Cape Province) *Rhodesia and South Africa*

Percy Mansell wore spectacles, looked vague and distracted and reminded people of a country vicar. Shropshire born, he was an all-rounder of high quality. He was a consistent right-handed batsman, being a fine driver, an inexpensive leg-break bowler and a most reliable slip field. He never represented his country at home, but toured England in 1951 and 1955 and Australasia in 1952/3. On his first England tour he held 21 catches and on his Test début, at Headingley, he hit 90 in 70 minutes. On his second tour, he was again the most reliable slip with 27 catches, but as a batsman did not approach his form in the

Currie Cup: over 25 years in this competition, from his début at 16, he made 2,245 runs (41.57) and took 160 wickets (19.83). He made 571 runs (43.92) and took 52 wickets (17.63) in 1951/2. With Hugh Tayfield in such prime form his opportunities, in Tests were blocked. He was prominent in the administration of the game and was awarded an MBE.

First-class career (1936–62): 4,598 runs (29.66) including 5 centuries, 299 wickets (26.08), and 156 catches
Test matches (13): 355 runs (17.75), 11 wickets (66.90), and 15 catches

MARKHAM, Lawrence Anderson

(b. 1924, Swaziland) *Natal and South Africa*

'Fish' Markham was an all-rounder who could bowl a prodigious leg-break and whose sole Test was against England in the fourth match at Johannesburg in 1948/9 when he scored 20 and took 1 for 72.

First-class career (1946–51): 268 runs (15.76) including 1 century, and 53 wickets (16.84)

MARTYN, Aubrey

(b. 1972, Pretoria) *Western Province*

A left-arm bowler of fast-medium pace and considerable promise, Aubrey Martyn started his international career the way any bowler dreads. Chosen for the 1994 tour of England, he broke down in the nets with a stress fracture without playing a single match.

First-class career (1992–   ): 72 runs (4.50), 54 wickets (26.51), and 7 catches

MARX, Waldemar Frederick Eric

(b. 1895, Johannesburg; d. 1974, Durban) *Transvaal and South Africa*

An old Malvernian, Eric Marx scored a brilliant 240 on his début for his province against Griqualand West at Johannesburg in 1920/1, including one six and thirty fours: it remains the highest first innings in first-class cricket anywhere. Although he made 119 against Orange Free State in the same season, his initial innings produced nearly half his total runs in an all too short first-class career. He was a useful right-arm medium-pace change-bowler. This meteor appeared in all the Tests against Australia in 1921/2.

First-class career (1920–2): 656 runs (41.00) including 2 centuries, and 13 wickets (30.84)
Test matches (3): 125 runs (20.83) and 4 wickets (36.00)

MATTHEWS, Craig Russell

(b. 1965, Cape Town) *Western Province and South Africa*

Craig Matthews is a tall and sturdy right-arm bowler of fast-medium pace. Once he gets into his rhythm he is difficult to score against with his accurate control of line and length from a high, over-the-top action. It is this which enables him to move the ball off the seam, causing problems for batsmen as, by his own admission, he is not always certain in his own mind which way the ball is going to track. He can be particularly effective on pitches with pace and bounce. After making the historic first tour to India in 1991, he was surprisingly omitted from the 1992 World Cup but bounced back against India the following season, playing in three out of four Tests. However, it was only in 1993/4 that he finally established himself as a Test regular, playing in five out of six matches against Australia and taking five wickets in an innings for the first time on his home Newlands pitch. He has made a first-class century and his batting is under-rated, something that became apparent in England in 1994 when he played several important Test innings. He has always impressed as a deep thinker about the game, emerging as one of Hansie Cronje's main advisers when the latter stood in for the injured Kepler Wessels as Test captain. He has led Western Province with distinction and it is a distinct possibility that he will get the chance to lead South Africa in the later stages of his career.

First-class career (1986–): 1,063 runs (20.05) including 1 century, 191 wickets (23.98), and 32 catches

Test matches (14): 318 runs (21.20), 46 wickets (27.28), and 1 catch

MEINTJES, Douglas James

(b. 1890, Pretoria; d. 1979, Johannesburg) *Transvaal and South Africa*

A very good all-rounder from a powerful province, Doug Meintjes played against England in two Tests in 1922/3. He was primarily a right-arm fast-medium bowler and in the second innings of his first Test at Johannesburg, he disposed of Arthur Carr, Philip Mead, and Percy Fender in quick succession and caught the next man, the captain, Frank Mann. He toured England in 1924.

First-class career (1910–26): 1,146 runs (16.14), 91 wickets (29.64), and 25 catches
Test matches (2): 43 runs (14.33), 6 wickets (19.16), and 3 catches

MELLE, Michael George

(b. 1930, Johannesburg) *Transvaal, Western Province, and South Africa*

Son of a former Western Province, Oxford University, Hampshire, and Transvaal cricketer who was one of the first exponents of leg-theory bowling, Michael Melle was a genuinely fast right-arm bowler in days when South Africa's attack could be as fast as any. He toured England in 1951 and Australasia in 1952/3 and at home played against Australia in 1949/50. On his Test début against Australia in the fourth match at Johannesburg in 1949/50, he captured 5 for 113 in the first innings of 465 for 8; but in England, where he was hampered by an operation, he was rather disappointing, although he headed the bowling averages with 50 wickets (20.28). In his only Test at The Oval he took 4 for 9 (three tailenders). In Australasia he tended to lack the extra life and fire required there but took 14 Test wickets (37.92). Against Tasmania at Launceston, he shone with 9 for 22 (12 for 56 in the match). His best effort was at Johannesburg in 1950/1: he took 8 for 8 for Transvaal against Griqualand West, who fell for 29.

First-class career (1948–54): 544 runs (11.33), 160 wickets (24.93), and 22 catches
Test matches (7): 68 runs (8.50), 26 wickets (32.73), and 4 catches

MELVILLE, Alan

(b. 1910, Cape Province; d. 1983, Transvaal) *Oxford University, Sussex, Natal, Transvaal, and South Africa*

A graceful right-handed batsman with a classical upright method, Alan Melville was a commanding player against fast bowling, his driving and hooking possessing a special grandeur. A cool and astute captain, he led South Africa in ten of his eleven Tests. After playing as a schoolboy for Natal, he went up to Oxford for whom he played in four University matches, captaining the 1931 and 1932 sides. He captained Sussex in 1934 and 1935. Immediately on his return home, he was appointed captain of South Africa for the series against England in 1938/9; and he was the very popular leader of the 1947 side to England. Brought up with cricket on the mat, and never having played on a turf wicket before, he nevertheless made an immediate impact in England with 132 not out in the Freshmen's match, 78 against Kent and 118 against Yorkshire in his first three innings in the Oxford Parks. He scored a memorable 114 for Sussex at Hove against the West Indian fast bowlers in $2\frac{1}{2}$ hours in 1933. Sussex were three times runners-up in the Championship in the five years he played for them. The highlights of his first Test series were innings of 78 and 103, in the 'Timeless Test' at Durban. In his next two Tests, in 1947, he made 189 (his career-highest) and 104 not out at Trent Bridge, and 117 at Lord's. Thus he achieved four centuries in successive Test innings. In the first innings at Trent Bridge he shared in the then-record partnership of 319 for the third wicket with Dudley Nourse. In this series he made 569 runs (63.22) and in all first-class matches on the tour 1,547 runs (40.71), including six centuries. His final Test appearance was against England in 1948/9. For many years he served as a Test selector

First-class career (1928–49): 10,598 runs (37.85) including 25 centuries, 132 wickets (29.99), and 156 catches
Test matches (11): 894 runs (52.58) including 4 centuries, and 8 catches

MIDDLETON, James

(b. 1865, Chester-le-Street, Co. Durham, England; d. 1913, Cape Town) *Western Province and South Africa*

'Bonnor' Middleton was the most prominent left-arm bowler in South Africa from 1894 until 1906, although he had a birth qualification for County Durham. Slow-medium in pace, he revelled in his nickname as his batting efforts resembled those of the famous Australian hitter, at least in style if not in effect and quantity. Bought out of the Army by Cape Town CC, his best feat was 12 for 100 for Western Province against Transvaal at Cape Town in 1897/8. He toured England with the 1894 and 1904 teams. In the former year, he took 83 wickets (15.79), including 12 for 83 against MCC and Ground at Lord's and 8 for 48 at Leicester. He played at home against England in 1895/6 and 1898/9, and Australia in 1902/3. On his Test début, the first match at Port Elizabeth in 1895/6, he took 5 for 64 and 4 for 66, England nevertheless winning handsomely. In the first Test at Johannesburg in 1898/9, he took 5 for 51 in the second innings and, in the next match at Cape Town, had 4 for 18, England falling for 92 but

again winning comfortably as South Africa's batting was even more ineffective. Eight years later he was completely overshadowed by the gaggle of googly bowlers and did not go on the first England Test tour.

First-class career (1890–1904): 176 runs (6.06), 140 wickets (18.02), and 14 catches
Test matches (6): 52 runs (7.42), 24 wickets (18.41), and 1 catch

MILLS, Charles Henry

(b. 1867, London, England; d. 1948, London) *Surrey and Western Province*

An all-rounder who appeared occasionally for Surrey in 1887 and 1888, Charles Mills emigrated to South Africa as professional to Kimberley CC. His sole Test was against England at Cape Town in 1891/2 when he scored 0 and 21, took 2 for 83 and held 2 catches. He toured England with the first-ever South African team in 1894, scoring 452 runs (14.18) and taking 28 wickets (23.20)

First-class career (1888–94): 160 runs (12.30), 29 wickets (15.55), and 11 catches

MILTON, Sir William Henry

(b. 1854, Little Marlow, Buckinghamshire, England; d. 1930, Cannes, France) *Western Province and South Africa*

An old Marlburian, William Milton was a hard-hitting right-handed batsman with a good defence—especially intolerant of loose bowling—and a fine fielder. He became a very prominent figure in the administration of the game in South Africa. He captained his province from 1885 until 1896 and was largely responsible for the first England team visiting the country in 1888/9. He appeared in the first three Tests—as captain in the second and third, both played at Cape Town in 1888/9 and 1891/2 respectively. He also represented England at Rugby against Scotland and Ireland. Sometime parliamentary secretary to Cecil Rhodes, he served as administrator of Southern Rhodesia for many years.

First-class career (1888–92): 152 runs (13.81)
Test matches (3): 68 runs (11.33), 2 wickets (24.00), and 1 catch

MITCHELL, Bruce

(b. 1909, Johannesburg; d. 1995, Johannesburg) *Transvaal and South Africa*

A neat, perfectly balanced right-handed opening batsman, Bruce Mitchell was a complete player who relished the Test match atmosphere. On his first tour of England in 1929, at the age of 20, he scored more runs in first-class matches—1,615 (32.95)—than any other member of the side. He toured England again in 1935 and 1947, and Australasia in 1931/2. At home he played against England in 1930/1, 1938/9, and 1948/9, and Australia in 1935/6. He played with a quiet, calm deliberation, making the most of his 5 ft. 10 in. to get well over the ball, and his footwork was superb. A useful experimental slow bowler, he was also a reliable close field. Originally he gained his place for his province for his leg-break bowling, taking 11 for 95 against Border at East London in 1925/6 at the age of 17, but he scarcely maintained this form in first-class matches. On his Test début at Edgbaston in 1929 he scored 88 and 61 not out, adding 119 and 171 respectively for the first wicket with Bob Catterall: he batted very slowly, however, and in later Tests went in first wicket down. He was reinstated as an opener against England in 1930/1, however, and he headed the batting averages with 455 runs (50.55) which included 123 in the second match at Cape Town when he put on 260 with I. J. Siedle for the first wicket. Although his overall record in Australia in 1931/2 was not outstanding, he headed the averages in the Tests, all five of which South Africa lost, with 322 runs (32.20). In the first Test played by South Africa against New Zealand, at Christchurch, he made 113, putting on 196 for the first wicket in 2 hours with J. A. J. Christy, his country winning by an innings. Mitchell's best match against Australia was the fourth at Adelaide, in which he made 75 and 95 in a losing cause. On his second England tour, in 1935, he scored 1,451 runs (45.34), including 195 (his career-highest) against Surrey at The Oval, when he put on 330 with Eric Rowan for the first wicket, a long-standing record, in 3 hours 40 minutes, and 488 runs (69.71) in the Tests, when he was far ahead of anyone else. He hit 128 in the final match at The Oval and at Lord's he had a major hand in South Africa's first victory in England, scoring a masterly 164 not out in the second innings out of a total of 278 for 7 declared. He could rarely get going against Australia in 1935/6 but headed the bowling averages with 10 wickets (33.00). In 1938/9 he again scored most runs in the series against England, 466 (58.25), including 109 in the third match at Durban and three other scores in excess of 50. Back in England in 1947, he was supreme, heading the tour averages with 2,014 runs (61.03), including eight centuries, the only time a South African has

topped 2,000 runs in England. In the Tests, opening the batting, he made 597 runs (66.33), including 120 and 189 not out in the final Test at The Oval, when he was on the field for practically the entire match. In his final series against England in 1948/9 he opened in only two matches, scoring 120 at Cape Town and 99 (caught behind) and 56 in his last Test at Port Elizabeth. In this series he made 475 runs (52.77). Bruce Mitchell was South Africa's most accomplished batsman of his time. Quiet and retiring though he was, neither the fiercest fast bowler nor the worst wet wicket ever dampened his determination.

First-class career (1925–50): 11,395 runs (45.39) including 30 centuries, 249 wickets (25.63), and 228 catches

Test matches (42): 3,471 runs (48.88) including 8 centuries, 27 wickets (51.11), and 56 catches

MITCHELL, Frank

(b. 1872; d. 1935) *Cambridge University, Yorkshire, and Transvaal*

See England section.

MORKEL, Denys Paul Beck

(b. 1906, Cape Town; d. 1980, Nottingham, England) *Western Province and South Africa*

Over 6 ft. tall, good-looking with broad shoulders and sleek black hair, Denys Morkel made excellent use of his reach and strength and, as a right-handed batsman, could defend soundly or hit very hard as the occasion demanded. Bowling fast-medium with a high delivery, he would make the ball nip off the pitch and always seemed likely to get two or three wickets cheaply at the start of an innings. He was also a very good versatile field. He toured England in 1929 and Australasia in 1931/2, and at home played against England in 1927/8. The best all-rounder on the England tour, he made 1,443 runs (34.35) and took 69 wickets (26.01), including 321 runs (45.85) and 14 wickets (32.71) in the Tests, more Test runs and wickets than anyone else. In the second Test at Lord's, he top-scored with 88 and took 7 for 156 in the match (all accredited batsmen) and in the final match at The Oval he hit 81. Soon after hitting 208 not out—not his career-highest, which was 251 for Cahn's XI—for his province against Natal at Cape Town in 1929/30, he settled in England—although he toured Australasia rather disappointingly a year later. Joining Sir Julien Cahn's team and doing extremely well in business under the aegis of Sir Julien, he was a considerable loss to South African cricket. He played for Gentlemen versus Players in 1931, 1932, and 1934. With S. S. L. Steyn he put on a record 222 for Western Province's eighth wicket against Border in 1929/30.

> **First-class career** (1924–38): 4,494 runs (34.30) including 8 centuries, 174 wickets (28.58), and 67 catches
> **Test matches** (16): 663 runs (24.55), 18 wickets (45.61), and 13 catches

MORRIS, Richard Edwin Tuffrey

> (b. 1947, Cape Town) *Western Province*

A dependable all-rounder, Richard Morris was South Africa's quality off-spin bowler of the 1970s along with Zimbabwean John Traicos. He was not a great spinner of the ball, relying on guile and flight to deceive his opponents. For variation he bowled a well-disguised in-swinger that gained him many leg-side stumpings. As a right-hand batsman he was at his best in a crisis and fought many successful rearguard actions for Western Province. He was one of many fine all-rounders to grace South African cricket during this period.

> **First-class career** (1967–79): 1,950 runs (25.32) including 2 centuries, 117 wickets (30.78), and 44 catches

MURRAY, Anton Ronald Andrew

> (b. 1922, Grahamstown; d. 1995, Cape Town) *Eastern Province and South Africa*

Although he was a nervous starter, Anton Murray used his 6 ft. 3 in. to good effect as a right-handed batsman and was also an impressive right-arm slow-medium bowler with shrewd variations. In the field he was astonishingly agile for such a big man, chasing the ball with knees high in the air like a wing three-quarter making for the line. He toured Australasia in 1952/3 and England in 1955, and at home played against New Zealand in 1953/4. He did not make the Test side in England but in Australasia made 592 runs (31.15) and took 39 wickets (30.97) in fourteen matches. In the second Test at Melbourne, when South Africa defeated Australia for the first time for 42 years, he top-scored in the first innings with 51, a solid rescue knock. Moreover, in the first Test against New Zealand at Wellington, when South Africa won even more comfortably, he hit 190, adding a record 246 for the seventh wicket with Jackie McGlew, and taking 5 for 49 in 51 overs in the match.

> **First-class career** (1947–56): 2,685 runs (29.83) including 4 centuries, 188 wickets (24.90), and 31 catches
> **Test matches** (10): 289 runs (22.23) including 1 century, 18 wickets (39.44), and 3 catches

MUZZELL, Robert Kendal

> (b. 1945, Stutterheim) *Western Province and Transvaal*

A right-hand batsman and under-used leg-spin bowler, Robbie Muzzell was considered unlucky not to tour England in 1965 or to play in the following series against Australia. Nevertheless he was still only 25 years old when South Africa disappeared from the international scene. Initially he played in the middle-order but he later distinguished himself for Transvaal as a fearless opening batsman and he was one of the few to handle Garth le Roux with confidence when the latter was bowling at his fastest. At the end of his first-class career he returned to his home province of Border and has distinguished himself in the administrative field. He was a popular manager of the South African team to Australia in 1993/4.

> **First-class career** (1964–78): 4,052 runs (34.93) including 7 centuries, 61 wickets (33.24), and 49 catches

NEL, John Desmond

> (b. 1928, Cape Town) *Western Province and South Africa*

A right-handed opening batsman, a fine player of fast bowling and a very reliable outfield, Jack Nel was chosen for all five Tests against Australia in 1949/50 to face Ray Lindwall and Keith Miller, but they were too good and his highest score was only 38. He made one further Test appearance, against Australia in 1957/8, and was then discarded, but he remained a true stalwart of Western Province whom he captained with much success for several years. He scored 217 not out against Eastern Province at Port Elizabeth in 1952/3.

> **First-class career** (1947–61): 1,839 runs (31.70) including 4 centuries
> **Test matches** (6): 150 runs (13.63) and 1 catch

NEWBERRY, Claude

> (b. 1889, Port Elizabeth; d. 1916, France) *Transvaal and South Africa*

Always a trier, with plenty of dash in the field, Claude Newberry erred in trying to bowl too fast and tended to throw his wicket away when batting in his short Test career against England in 1913/14. He was killed in the First World War.

First-class career (1910–14): 251 runs (11.95) and 49 wickets (24.75)

Test matches (4): 62 runs (7.75), 11 wickets (24.36), and 3 catches

NEWSON, Edward Serrurier

(b. 1910, Cape Town; d. 1988, Durban) *Transvaal, Rhodesia, and South Africa*

A hard-working right-arm fast-bowler, 'Bob' Newson appeared in Tests against England in 1930/1 and 1938/9 without taking many wickets, but in his first Test at Johannesburg, the first of the rubber, he added 45 invaluable runs for the last wicket with Quintin McMillan in the second innings, and South Africa won narrowly by 28 runs.

First-class career (1929–50): 553 runs (17.83) including 1 century, and 60 wickets (26.03)

Test matches (3): 30 runs (7.50), 4 wickets (66.25), and 3 catches

NICHOLSON, Frank

(b. 1909, Cumberland, England; d. 1982, Port Elizabeth) *Griqualand West and South Africa*

A competent opening batsman and wicket-keeper, 'Nipper' Nicholson played his sole Tests against Australia in 1935/6, when South Africa were looking for a successor to the recently deceased H. B. Cameron. He totalled 54 Currie Cup victims and hit four first-class hundreds including 185 against Orange Free State. He played for Griqualand West from 1927/8 to 1946/7, for several seasons as captain.

First-class career (1927–47): 2,353 runs (24.76) including 4 centuries, and 69 dismissals (32 c., 37 st.)

Test matches (4): 76 runs (10.85) and 3 dismissals (3 c.)

NICOLSON, John Fairless William

(b. 1899, Durban; d. 1935, Kilkeel, Co. Down, Northern Ireland) *Natal, Oxford University, and South Africa*

At Oxford, John Nicolson failed to win his blue, despite undoubted talent. A very competent left-handed batsman, strong on the leg-side and possessing an excellent defence, he became famous by putting up 424 for Natal's first wicket with I. J. Siedle against Orange Free State at

Bloemfontein in 1926/7, which remains a South African record for any wicket: his share was 252 not out. His Test experience was limited to three matches against England in 1927/8. On his début, the third match at Durban, he made 39 and (top-scoring) 78, sharing in several sizeable partnerships. A schoolmaster, he died young in Ireland.

First-class career (1923–30): 1,543 runs (37.63) including 3 centuries, 3 wickets (68.33), and 8 catches

Test matches (3): 179 runs (35.80) and 0–17

NORTON, Norman Ogilvie

(b. 1881, Grahamstown; d. 1968, East London) *Border, Western Province, and South Africa*

A capable all-rounder and captain of a weak province, Border, 'Pompey' Norton played in a sole Test, the fifth match against England at Durban in 1909/10, scoring 2 and 7 and taking 4 for 47. He got Jack Hobbs out when the batsman hit his wicket after making 187!

First-class career (1902–14): 347 runs (15.08) and 49 wickets (15.75)

NOURSE, Arthur Dudley

(b. 1910, Durban; d. 1981, Durban) *Natal and South Africa*

Dudley Nourse received no more coaching from his illustrious father, 'Old Dave', than a few words: 'I learned to play cricket with a paling off a fence. Now you go and do the same.' Dudley Nourse achieved even more than the old man. He was a talented right-handed batsman with all the strokes, built four-square with broad shoulders and blacksmith forearms. He seldom went right forward except when moving out to drive the slow bowlers, but off his back foot he hit exceedingly hard, whether hooking, forcing to the off or square-cutting. He was naturally bold and aggressive. He toured England in 1935, 1947, and 1951; and at home played against England in 1938/9 and 1948/9, and Australia in 1935/6 and 1949/50. Although he made 1,681 runs (41.00) including four centuries, on his first England tour, it was not until the powerful Australian side visited South Africa the following winter that he established himself in Tests. Australia won the series overwhelmingly but Dudley Nourse was the backbone of his country's batting, easily heading the averages with 518 runs (57.55) including 231 in the second Test in only 4 hours. He again headed the averages against England in 1938/9, scoring 422 runs (60.28) which included 120 in $4\frac{1}{2}$

hours in the second match at Cape Town, after England had topped 550. He hit an even more solid 103 in over 6 hours in the fifth, the 'Timeless Test' at Durban. A bout of pneumonia while serving in the Western Desert nearly cost him his life in the Second World War but he toured England as vice-captain in 1947 and made 1,453 runs (42.73), including four centuries, the highest being 205 not out against Warwickshire at Edgbaston. In the Tests he was supreme, with 621 runs (69.00), only Denis Compton scoring more runs in 'Compton's Year'. In the first Test at Trent Bridge, when he made 149, he added 319 for the third wicket with Alan Melville in just over 4 hours, a record that stood for 16 years. Succeeding Melville as captain, he led his country against England in 1948/9, scoring 536 runs (76.57), making 112 and 129 not out (in a total of 257 for nine wickets declared) in successive matches at Cape Town and Johannesburg. For the fifth successive time in a series he headed the averages against Australia in 1949/50 with 405 runs (45.00), in the second match at Cape Town making 65 and 114 for a beaten side. On his final England tour of 1951, again as captain, he had the misfortune to break a thumb early in the tour and was no longer the master. Yet in the first Test at Trent Bridge, the only one South Africa won and their first victory in 16 years, he made 208 in the first innings of 483 for 9 wickets declared, batting with a 'pinned' thumb. When the following year he retired, only his father and Herbie Taylor, both in longer careers, had scored more runs than Dudley Nourse. Altogether, he scored six double-centuries, the highest being 260 not out for Natal against Transvaal at Johannesburg in 1936/7. A born ball player, there were few better fieldsmen and safer catchers anywhere in the world.

First-class career (1931–53): 12,472 runs (51.53) including 41 centuries, and 135 catches

Test matches (34): 2,960 runs (53.81) including 9 centuries, 0–9, and 12 catches

NOURSE, Arthur William

(b. 1879, Thornton Heath, Surrey, England; d. 1948, Port Elizabeth) *Natal, Transvaal, Western Province, and South Africa*

The 'Grand Old Man' of South African cricket, 'Dave' Nourse was born at Croydon in Surrey and went to Africa as a 17-year-old trumpeter with the West Riding Regiment. From 1902 until 1924 he made 45 consecutive Test appearances. A left-handed batsman of rock-like stability and nerve, he could score all round the wicket. His swinging left-arm cutters were often useful—frequently he opened the bowling in Tests—and his enormous hands helped him to be a brilliant slip fielder. He toured England in 1907, 1912, and 1924, and Australia in 1910/11; and he appeared at home against England in 1905/6, 1909/10, 1913/14, and 1922/3 and Australia in 1902/3 and 1921/2. He scored 72 against Australia at Johannesburg in 1903/4 in his first Test and 18 not out and 93 not out in his first against England at Johannesburg in 1905/6, being in at the death when South Africa recorded their first Test victory by one wicket. A host in himself, Nourse contributed 62 out of a total of 140 in the first Test at Lord's in 1907; 92 out of 205 against Australia in the fourth match at Melbourne in 1910/11; 42 out of 93 in the third match at The Oval in 1912; and 64 and 111 (his only Test century) in the third match against Australia at Johannesburg in 1921/2, in the second innings adding 206 for the fourth wicket with C. N. Frank. In the 1905/6, 1907, 1910/11, 1921/2, and 1922/3 series he averaged 48.16, 31.75 (top), 38.00, 56.00 (top), and 33.77 respectively. Equally successful overseas, he made 1,762 runs (35.24) in England in 1912; and 1,928 runs (39.34) in England in 1924, one of the few successes. In Australia in 1910/11 he made 1,454 runs (60.58). On these three tours alone, he hit thirteen centuries and twenty half-centuries. In the Currie Cup competition, he made 3,482 runs (51.57), including twelve centuries, the highest being his career-best, 304 not out for Natal against Transvaal at Johannesburg in 1919/20. He scored more runs than anyone else in South African domestic cricket or for South African teams overseas.

First-class career (1896–1936): 14,216 runs (42.81) including 38 centuries, 305 wickets (23.36), and 171 catches

Test matches (45): 2,234 runs (29.78) including 1 century, 41 wickets (37.87), and 43 catches

NUPEN, Eiulf Peter

(b. 1902, Johannesburg; d. 1977, Durban) *Transvaal and South Africa*

Of Norwegian parentage and despite the loss of an eye—as a youngster, he was knocking two hammers together and a splinter flew off—'Buster' Nupen was regarded as one of the greatest bowlers on matting there has ever been. Tall and strongly built, he bowled right-arm fast medium round the wicket and, on the mat, his off-cutter would nip off quickly and lift sharply. His leg-cutter was more obvious, but also obtained many

wickets. He toured England in 1924, proving to
be very disappointing on turf and he played at
home against England in 1922/3, 1927/8, and
1930/1 (as captain in the first Test) and against
Australia in 1921/2 and 1935/6. In the three Tests
on matting in 1930/1 he captured 21 wickets
(19.66) but was omitted from the other two on
turf. In four 'unofficial Tests' against Hon. Lionel
Tennyson's team in 1924/5 he took 37 wickets
(11.45). In 27 Currie Cup matches, he took 184
wickets (12.75)—not all on matting—taking ten
or more wickets in a match nine times: he is one
of only two South Africans to have taken 16
wickets in a match (for 136 against Griqualand
West at Johannesburg in 1931/2). Rarely of much
account as a batsman, he managed to hit 51 and
69 in the third Test at Durban in 1927/8, sharing
in a new record stand with 'Nummy' Deane—95
for the eighth wicket and 123 for the seventh.

First-class career (1920–37): 1,635 runs (17.96),
334 wickets (18.19), and 34 catches

Test matches (17): 348 runs (14.50), 50 wickets
(35.76), and 9 catches

OCHSE, Arthur Edward

(b. 1870, Cape Colony; d. 1918, France) *Transvaal
and South Africa*

At 19 years and 1 day, the youngest-ever to
represent South Africa, Arthur Ochse played in
the first two Tests against Major Warton's England team in 1888/9. He was not closely related
to A. L. Ochse.

First-class career (1888–95): 231 runs (23.10)
Test matches (2): 16 runs (4.00)

OCHSE, Arthur Lennox

(b. 1899, Cape Province; d. 1949, Cape Province)
Eastern Province and South Africa

Muscle-bound and thickset, 'Oosh' Ochse was a
hostile right-arm fast bowler who headed the Test
averages in England in 1929 with ten wickets
(31.70) from two matches: he took 52 wickets
(35.36) on the tour. He made his Test début in
1927/8, the same season taking 5 for 31 for his
province against MCC when they collapsed for
49, only to win eventually by ten wickets! Coming from deep country, he was shocked by his
first sight of England, exclaiming outside Water-
loo Station: 'There are more people in this street
than in the whole of Graaff-Reinet!'

First-class career (1921–38): 564 runs (10.44),
140 wickets (28.33), and 20 catches
Test matches (3): 11 runs (3.66), 10 wickets
(36.20), and 1 catch

O'LINN, Sydney

(b. 1927, Cape Province) *Western Province,
Transvaal, Kent, and South Africa*

A left-handed batsman of strong defensive outlook and endless concentration, Sid O'Linn was
also a capable deputy wicket-keeper and fleet-
footed fielder in any position. After a season in
which he made 619 runs (68.78) for Transvaal, he
toured England in 1960, making 261 runs (32.62)
in the five Tests. He made 98 in just under 6
hours in the third Test at Trent Bridge, when
nearly everyone else was failing. He also played at
home against New Zealand in 1961/2. From 1951
to 1954, he was deputy to Godfrey Evans for
Kent, scoring 1,275 runs (31.09), catching 22 and
stumping 3. A good footballer, he played for
Charlton Athletic with distinction and represented the Springboks at soccer against Australia
in 1947.

First-class career (1945–66): 4,525 runs (35.62)
including 4 centuries, 2 wickets (59.50), and 103
dismissals (97 c., 6 st.)
Test matches (7): 297 runs (27.00) and 4 catches

OWEN-SMITH, Dr Harold Geoffrey Owen

(b. 1909, Cape Town; d. 1990, Cape Town) *Western
Province, Oxford University, Middlesex, and South
Africa*

Full of fun and adventure, 'Tuppy' Owen-Smith
who was later to qualify at St Mary's Hospital in
London as a doctor of medicine, did not remain
long in the Currie Cup competition. At 20, after
only five first-class matches, he became the most
exhilarating member of the South African team
to England in 1929 and, though on his return he
took 11 for 185 against a strong Natal side at
Newlands, he was soon back in England as a
Rhodes Scholar, going on to win three blues at
Oxford for cricket, Rugby, and boxing, captaining
England at Rugby and playing cricket for Middlesex. A dynamic personality, a daring and
plucky right-handed batsman who drove, cut, and
hit to leg brilliantly, he bowled slow leg-breaks
successfully and fielded with speed and accuracy
either at cover-point or in the deep. On the 1929
tour he made 1,168 runs (35.39) and took 30
wickets (25.80), in the third Test at Headingley
scoring a heroic 129 in the second innings in a
hopeless situation and putting on 103 in 63
minutes with the last man, 'Sandy' Bell, which
remains the country's record for the last wicket.
England nevertheless won by five wickets. His

651

son, Michael, became a well-known cricket journalist.

First-class career (1927–50): 4,059 runs (26.88) including 3 centuries, 319 wickets (23.23), and 93 catches

Test matches (5): 252 runs (42.00), 0–113, and 4 catches

PALFRAMAN, Steven John

(b. 1970, East London) *Eastern Province and Border*

Steve Palframan was the understudy wicket-keeper to David Richardson for South Africa on the 1993 tour to Sri Lanka where he had limited success from very limited opportunities. Since then, the selectors have opted for stand-by choices for their various tours, using batsmen who can keep wicket rather than the other way around. Nevertheless, he is a decade younger than virtually all the top stumpers in South Africa and will undoubtedly get his chance once the currently irreplaceable Richardson departs from the international scene. A right-hand batsman, he likes to play his shots and is particularly aggressive off the back foot.

First-class career (1990–   ): 803 runs (22.30) including one century, and 86 dismissals (78 c., 8 st.)

PALM, Archibald William

(b. 1901, Cape Town; d. 1966, Cape Province) *Western Province and South Africa*

A consistent batsman, who shared the unbroken sixth wicket Currie Cup record stand of 244 with J. M. M. Commaille starting at 27 for 5 against Griqualand West at Johannesburg in 1923/4, Palm appeared in one Test, the second against England at Cape Town in 1927/8, when he scored 2 and 13 and held 1 catch.

First-class career (1921–34): 1,958 runs (32.09) including 3 centuries

PARKER, George Macdonald

(b. 1899, Cape Town; d. 1969, New South Wales, Australia) *South Africa*

The bowling was not making much impact for the South Africans in England in 1924, so George Parker, who was born at Cape Town but a professional in the Bradford League, was asked to represent his country in the first Test at Edgbaston and the second at Lord's. He had played only one match previously in first-class cricket. In the first match he worked like a Trojan, taking 6 for

152 in England's only innings, becoming so exhausted that he had to leave the field before close of play on the first day. In the second match he took 2 for 121 (in 24 overs), being hit unmercifully by Jack Hobbs and Herbert Sutcliffe, though he obtained both their wickets in due course.

First-class career (1924): 3 runs (1.50) and 12 wickets (25.58)

Test matches (2): 3 runs (1.50) and 8 wickets (34.12)

PARKIN, Durant Clifford

(b. 1870, Port Elizabeth; d. 1936, Cape Province) *Eastern Province, Transvaal, Griqualand West, and South Africa*

A medium-paced bowler, 'Dante' Parkin played in a sole Test against England at Cape Town in 1891/2, scoring 6 and 0, taking 3 for 83 (in a total of 369) and holding 1 catch. He toured England with the first South African team in 1894 but failed on the turf wickets, taking only five wickets (50.00).

First-class career (1889–1903): 334 runs (15.18) and 48 wickets (20.29)

PARTRIDGE, Joseph Titus

(b. 1932, Bulawayo, Rhodesia; d. 1988, Zimbabwe) *Rhodesia and South Africa*

Sturdy, but bespectacled and looking like the bank official he was, Joe Partridge was a right-arm seam bowler of much honest endeavour who for more than a decade was a mainstay of Rhodesia's attack. After 12 years in first-class cricket, he made his belated Test début against Australia in 1963/4, on his only overseas tour, and he played at home against England in 1964/5. In 1962/3 he had set up a new record for the number of wickets taken in a South African season—64 wickets (16.68) from eleven matches. 1961/2 had brought him 53 wickets (13.98) from seven matches, including 14 for 101 against Natal at Salisbury. Against Border at Bulawayo in 1959/60 he had taken 7 for 9 in an innings. His was a long struggle for recognition at the highest level. In Australasia in 1963/4, however, he took more wickets than anyone else, 62 (25.91), relying on accuracy, stamina, and swing. In the five Tests against Australia he took 25 wickets (33.32), the same number as his opening partner, Peter Pollock, and against New Zealand he had 13 wickets (19.00) from three matches. In the third Test at Sydney, his match record was 9 for 211, and in the fifth at Sydney, swinging the ball in the heavy atmosphere, he took 7 for 91 in the first innings, his best Test performance. In the first innings of the third Test against New Zealand, he captured 6 for 86. His performances against England, however, were an anti-climax. He was unfortunate in that, while in his prime, he was overshadowed by such fast bowlers as Neil Adcock and Peter Heine.

First-class career (1951–67): 523 runs (9.17) and 376 wickets (20.77)

Test matches (11): 73 runs (10.42), 44 wickets (31.20), and 6 catches

PEARSE, Charles Ormerod Cato

(b. 1884, Pietermaritzburg; d. 1953, Durban) *Natal and South Africa*

A stylish batsman and useful change bowler, 'Ormy' Pearse toured Australia in 1910/11 but was not very successful, making 407 runs (20.35) and taking 10 wickets (26.80). He played in three of the Tests; and represented his province at intervals from 1905 until 1924.

First-class career (1905–24): 973 runs (23.73) and 11 wickets (31.18)

Test matches (3): 55 runs (9.16), 3 wickets (35.33), and 1 catch

PEGLER, Sidney James

(b. 1888, Durban; d. 1972, Cape Town) *Transvaal and South Africa*

A right-arm medium-pace leg-break bowler with a high delivery, well-varied pace, and quick break from leg, Sid Pegler was the last choice for the team to tour England in 1912 and was not an original selection to tour in 1924, but South Africa would have been in dire straits without him each time. On the former tour he sprang to the front rank taking 189 wickets (15.26)—the record for a South African on tour—and making 643 useful runs with his careful batting. In the latter tour he took 111 wickets (23.18). He headed the bowling in the 1912 Triangular Tournament Tests with 29 wickets (20.48), frequently opening the attack with his leg-breaks, and he took 9 wickets in the 1924 series, more than anyone else in another unduly rain-affected summer. Against England in the first Test at Lord's in 1912 he took 7 for 65 in the total of 337, only for South Africa to lose by an innings, and also at Lord's against MCC he captured four wickets in five balls, including the hat-trick, and finished with 11 for 119 in another losing cause. He

appeared against England at home in 1909/10 and toured Australia in 1910/11, but did not meet with the same degree of success. He was manager of South Africa's team to England in 1951.

First-class career (1908–30): 1,677 runs (12.70), 425 wickets (19.58), and 56 catches

Test matches (16): 356 runs (15.47), 47 wickets (33.44), and 5 catches

PIENAAR, Roy François

(b. 1961, Johannesburg) *Western Province, Northern Transvaal, Transvaal, and Kent*

A richly talented right-hand batsman, who was a very strong driver off the front foot, Roy Pienaar never did true justice to his ability although he played three successful seasons for Kent and represented South Africa in rebel series against the Australians and Mike Gatting's England XI. He was one of the few players of the isolation era who was still young enough to play for South Africa following the political settlement of the 1990s. Ironically, this opportunity coincided with a reversal of his own cricketing fortunes and he failed to make the grade.

First-class career (1977–): 9,538 runs (35.45), 153 wickets (33.19), and 71 catches

PITHEY, Anthony John

(b. 1933, Umtali, Rhodesia) *Western Province, Rhodesia, and South Africa*

A Rhodesian whose cricket was developed at Cape Town University, Tony Pithey was a tall right-handed batsman, either as an opener or later in the order. He had correct technique but scored slowly in Tests. On the other hand, he could withstand the most ferocious onslaught from fast bowlers. He toured England in 1965, and Australasia in 1963/4; and at home played against England in 1956/7 and 1964/5. Disappointing as an opener in England he batted lower in Australia, scoring 736 runs (33.45), including 170 (his career-highest) against Tasmania at Launceston. In the Tests, he made 208 runs (41.60), including a much-needed 76 in the second Test at Melbourne. His final Test series was his best, against England in 1964/5, when he made 462 runs (51.33). He tended to dawdle however, and took over 6 hours to score 154 in the third Test at Cape Town. In the next Test at Johannesburg, again in favourable conditions, he scored a sedate 95. In the Currie Cup competition he scored 2,786 runs (32.77), including five centuries, and captained Rhodesia for 7 years.

First-class career (1950–69): 7,073 runs (35.90)
including 13 centuries, and 59 catches
Test matches (17): 819 runs (31.50) including 1
century, 0–5, and 3 catches

PITHEY, David Bartlett

(b. 1936, Salisbury, Rhodesia) *Natal, Transvaal,
Rhodesia, Oxford University, Northamptonshire, and
South Africa*

Tony Pithey's younger brother David was a good
all-rounder, a right-handed forceful batsman and
off-break bowler who won a Rhodes Scholarship
to Oxford University in 1959 and was a cricket
blue in 1961 and 1962, hitting 67 against Cambridge at Lord's in the latter year. After making
fleeting appearances for Northamptonshire in
1962, he returned to Rhodesia, toured Australasia
with the South African side in 1963/4 and at
home played against Australia in 1966/7. He
made his first-class début in 1956/7 against Transvaal and in a career of some 10 years was
spasmodically brilliant. His career-highest score
was 166 in four hours against North-Eastern
Transvaal at Pretoria in 1962/3; and for Oxford
he hit 133 against Glamorgan in The Parks in
1961, the same year taking 7 for 47 against the
Australians. In three Tests against New Zealand
in 1963/4, he took 12 wickets (18.66) including 6
for 38 in the second innings of the second match
at Dunedin which was a major factor in South
Africa's win. In the second Test against Australia
at Cape Town in 1966/7 he made an invaluable
55 against periodic onslaughts from 'Garth'
McKenzie.

First-class career (1956–68): 3,420 runs (23.26)
including 3 centuries, 240 wickets (30.78), and 55
catches
Test matches (8): 138 runs (12.54) and 12 wickets
(48.08)

PLIMSOLL, John Bruce

(b. 1917, Cape Town) *Western Province and South
Africa*

Often looking like a Douglas Fairbanks pirate,
lean, sun-tanned, with a thin moustache and a
flicker of a grin, Jack Plimsoll was a left-arm fast-
medium bowler who toured England in 1947,
taking 68 wickets (23.32) and meeting with considerable success when the wicket gave him any
help. His sole Test appearance was at Old Trafford, the third match, when he scored 8 and 8 not

out and took 3 for 143. A successful manager of
the 1965 team to England, he would also have
managed the 1970 side if the tour had taken
place.

First-class career (1939–50): 386 runs (11.35),
155 wickets (23.10), and 9 catches

POLLOCK, Peter Maclean

(b. 1941, Pietermaritzburg) *Eastern Province and
South Africa*

A strapping, 6 ft. 2 in., fair-haired fast bowler,
good fielder and more than useful right-handed
tail-ender, Peter Pollock, elder brother of the even
more talented Graeme, played his initial first-class
match at the age of 17 and at the age of 20 took
3 for 61 and 6 for 38 in his first Test at Durban
against New Zealand. Genuinely fast with a good
high action after a long, straight approach, he had
mean bounce and a good away-swinger. He
continued to be successful throughout his Test
career, taking 40 wickets in eight Tests on one
tour of Australia and New Zealand in 1963/4. He
reached 100 wickets in only his 26th first-class
match, and in 1965 in England took 20 wickets in
three Tests and 50 in only twelve games on the
tour. He was relatively unsuccessful in two series
at home, taking 12 wickets in each, against
England in 1964 and Australia in 1966/7, but after
taking 44 wickets in ten domestic matches in
1968/9 (when the England tour was cancelled:
see Basil d'Oliveira), he and Mike Procter formed
a fearsome new-ball attack against Bill Lawry's
Australians in 1969/70. Pollock took 4 for 20 in
the first Test, 5 for 39 in the third and 15 in four
Tests as he and Procter took 41 of the 80
Australian wickets to fall in a 4–0 whitewash. By
the time that South Africa had been 'blackballed'
out of Test cricket, Peter Pollock had taken 116
wickets in 28 Tests, his country's third largest
haul. He showed his character when, in a losing
cause against Australia at Cape Town in 1966/7,
he scored 41 and 75 not out, going in at his
customary position of number ten. In the first
innings he shared a ninth-wicket stand against
Australia, putting on 85 with his brother, and his
second innings effort only just failed to save the
game. A committed Christian, he became chairman of South Africa's selectors when they
returned to Test cricket in 1992.

First-class career (1958–72): 3,028 runs (22.59),
485 wickets (21.89), and 54 catches
Test matches (28): 607 runs (21.67), 116 wickets
(24.18), and 9 catches

POLLOCK, Robert Graeme

(b. 1944, Durban) *Eastern Province, Transvaal, and South Africa*

Although he was tall, tough, and muscular, Graeme Pollock hit a cricket ball with the delicate touch and finesse of a surgeon. The sight of this fair-haired left-hander leaning effortlessly towards the path of the ball and sending it skimming through the covers or wide of mid-on with a relaxed swing through of a heavy bat was one of the most glorious sights of modern cricket but, after 1970, one sadly reserved for South African crowds only. Undoubtedly a genius, Pollock has been an exceptionally heavy scorer throughout his career. In a mere 23 Tests he scored seven centuries, two of which were double-hundreds and two more innings of more than 150. Like Gary Sobers, the only comparable post-war left-hander, Pollock did not need a half-volley or a long-hop to score fours: he would drive on the up, or cut, force, or pull anything even fractionally short of a good length. Said by his father, who kept wicket for Orange Free State, to have walked when he was 8 months, Graeme Pollock was in his school side at the age of 13 and at the age of 16 became the youngest player to score a hundred in the Currie Cup. By the time that he had arrived in Australia in 1963/4 he was broad shouldered and over 6 ft. tall and his inexperience meant little as he hit more than 1,000 runs on the tour at 53.27 and scored centuries in the Sydney and Adelaide Tests. He was not yet 20 and during his magnificent 175 at Adelaide he and Eddie Barlow added 341 for the third wicket in 4 hours 43 minutes, a record South African stand. His performances the following season in South Africa were relatively modest, yet although he often faced two top-class English off-spinners in Titmus and Allen on turning wickets, he made 137 and 77 not out in the final Test at his home ground in Port Elizabeth and reached 459 runs in the series. In England a few months later he scored 1,147 runs in 14 matches, including a breathtaking 125 in the Trent Bridge Test, scored in 2 hours 20 minutes out of 160 in cloudy, humid conditions when an acknowledged master of seam and swing, Tom Cartwright, had reduced the rest of South Africa's top batsmen to 43 for 4. Against Australia in 1966/7 he made 90 at exactly a run a minute in the first Test at Johannesburg, helping South Africa's talented side to gain the first home victory against Australia. A mere week later he was forced to bat with a runner because of a pulled thigh muscle and also to limit himself for much of his innings to strokes off the back foot. Coming in at his usual number four when South Africa, confronted by Graham McKenzie in top form, were 12 for 2, and soon after 85 for 5 in reply to Australia's 542, Pollock scored 100 off 139 balls and went on to score 209 out of 353 in 350 minutes, adding 85 with his brother for the ninth wicket. He later helped South Africa to win the rubber with 105 in the fifth Test at Port Elizabeth and when the countries next met in 1969/70 he savaged Lawry's bowlers to the tune of 517 runs in four Tests at 73.85. At Durban he scored 274, South Africa's highest individual Test score. After the isolation of his country from international sport, he continued to bat prolifically in South Africa, becoming the highest scorer in Currie Cup cricket, and once hitting a record 222 not out at Port Elizabeth in a 60-overs Gillette match. In 1974/5 he hit 1,097 runs (78.35) and he holds the record for a season's aggregate for both Eastern Province (984 runs in 1974/5) and Transvaal (961 runs at an average of 96.10 in 1978/9). He showed undiminished powers in high company with centuries in two of the unofficial Tests against the West Indian fast bowlers in 1983 and 1984 before finally announcing his retirement after a 1985/6 season in which he had also sounded some mellow echoes against the unofficial Australian touring team, including 59 off 44 balls in a one-day international at Johannesburg and 108—his 62nd 'first-class' century—in the four-day international at Durban. A naturally gifted fielder, he also bowled effective leg-spinners from time to time.

First-class career (1960–85): 20,940 runs (54.67) including 64 centuries, 43 wickets (47.95), and 248 catches

Test matches (23): 2,256 runs (60.97) including 7 centuries, 4 wickets (51.00), and 17 catches

POORE, Brigadier-General Robert Montagu

(b. 1866, Dublin, Ireland; d. 1938, Boscombe, Hampshire, England) *Hampshire, Wiltshire, Natal, and South Africa*

Before going to India as a young lieutenant, Robert Poore, an all-round sportsman and athlete, had not taken seriously to cricket. Thereupon, he studied textbooks avidly, practised strokes in front of his mirror and played in Army matches. Six feet four inches tall and with a large frame, his drive was one of the most powerful ever known. From 1892 until 1895, while ADC to Lord Harris, then Governor of Bombay, he averaged 80 for Government House. On going to

POTHECARY

South Africa, he hit centuries for Natal against Lord Hawke's eleven in 1895/6 and appeared for South Africa in the three Tests that season, but with little success. He might have appeared for either side, but the South Africans won a tug-of-war contest for his services. On returning to England in 1898, after scoring nine centuries in Natal, Major Poore, as he was always known, became the most successful batsman in the country in 1899. He hit 1,399 runs (116.58) for Hampshire, including seven centuries, and in all first-class matches scored 1,551 runs at 91.23, an average not exceeded in English cricket until 32 years later. With Captain Wynyard, he set up the English record for the sixth wicket—411 against Somerset at Taunton, the Major reaching 304, his career-highest. Military duties called him back to South Africa before the end of the season and, after occasional appearances, his career for Hampshire ceased in 1906. He had a distinguished record in the Boer War, kept fit and continued to play and coach cricket into old age. When asked the best method of playing bodyline bowling he replied: 'Charge the blighters!'

First-class career (1892–1914): 3,441 runs (38.66) including 11 centuries, 13 wickets (19.38), and 38 catches
Test matches (3): 76 runs (12.66), 1–4, and 3 catches

POTHECARY, James Edward

(b. 1933, Cape Town) *Western Province and South Africa*

A powerfully built right-arm fast-medium bowler, Jim Pothecary, who could swing a ball either way almost at will, shared the new ball with Neil Adcock for much of the England tour of 1960 but did not quite fulfil expectations, securing only 53 wickets (29.52). He played in three Tests on this tour, taking 4 for 58 in the first innings of the final Test at The Oval.

First-class career (1954–65): 1,039 runs (15.74), 143 wickets (28.34), and 42 catches
Test matches (3): 26 runs (6.50), 9 wickets (39.33), and 2 catches

POWELL, Albert William

(b. 1873, Kimberley; d. 1948, Cape Town) *Griqualand West and South Africa*

A good all-rounder, in his sole Test, the second at Cape Town against England in 1898/9, Albert Powell scored 5 and 11, took 1 for 10 and held 2 catches.

First-class career (1892–1905): 297 runs (9.90) and 12 wickets (34.33)

PRINCE, Charles Frederick Henry

(b. 1874, Orange Free State; d. 1949, Cape Town) *Western Province, Border, Eastern Province, London County, and South Africa*

A useful batsman and wicket-keeper, Charles Prince in his sole Test, the second at Cape Town against England in 1898/9, scored 5 and 1. He toured England in 1901, where he also played a match for London County.

First-class career (1894–1905): 730 runs (17.80) and 28 dismissals (14 c., 14 st.)

PRINGLE, Meyrick Wayne

(b. 1966, Adelaide, Eastern Cape) *Free State, Eastern Province, Western Province, Sussex, and South Africa*

Meyrick Pringle, a right-arm bowler of fast-medium pace, proved an instant success when he was selected as Allan Donald's new ball partner for the 1992 World Cup. He played in seven of the nine matches and it was his inspired spell of 4 for 11 at Christchurch that proved a match-winning effort against West Indies and a turning point in his country's fortunes after set-backs against New Zealand and Sri Lanka. He retained his place for three Test matches against West Indies and India but suffered concussion while batting at the Wanderers midway through the latter series and has struggled to reassert himself in a department in which South Africa has enormous depth. His stock delivery is an away-swinger that he bowls to a good line but he can also cut the ball back off the seam for variation and has seldom struggled to obtain bounce. He is a lively tail-end hitter. In fifteen one-day internationals to 1994 he had taken 21 wickets at 24.76.

First-class career (1985–): 1,119 runs (15.32), 221 wickets (24.25), and 17 catches
Test matches (3): 55 runs (18.33) and 3 wickets (57.00)

PROCTER, Michael John

(b. 1946, Durban) *Natal, Western Province, Rhodesia, Gloucestershire and South Africa*

One of the great all-rounders, an outstanding captain and a brave and admirable character, Mike Procter would have achieved colossal feats in Test cricket but the politics of his country and the rest of the cricket world's reaction to them deprived him of the opportunity to add to the 226 runs and 41 wickets he had gained in seven Tests against Australia in 1966/7 and 1969/70. In the latter four-match series he took 26 wickets at 13.57 and devastated the opposition with his furious pace. Nearly 6 ft. tall, but built like the trunk of an oak tree, Procter bowled straight and very fast, generally swinging the ball in to the right-hander after running in like a charging bull and delivering the ball, before his front foot landed, with a windmill twirl of his right arm, the chest facing the batsman but the arm coming past his right ear absolutely straight. On the quietest pitch he would suddenly produce an inspired spell of irresistible fast bowling. When the pitch took spin he could also be a match-winner, bowling orthodox off-spinners which turned sharply. As a batsman he was a glorious orthodox right-hander of the highest class, a commanding driver, and a superb striker off the back foot. Again, with rare dynamism, he could transform a match with a flurry of majestic strokes. As a 12-year-old at his prep. school in Natal, Procter scored five centuries, including 210 not out against a Transvaal under-13 side. Vice-captain of the South African Schools team to England in 1963, he returned in 1965 to qualify for Gloucestershire, top-scoring in his initial match for the 1st XI against the touring South Africans and from 1968 to 1981 was the pivot of the Gloucestershire side, their captain from 1977 to 1981. In the various county limited-overs competitions, he was frequently an irresistible match-winner and in the Championship, which Gloucestershire only narrowly missed winning under Procter's inspired leadership in both 1976 and 1977, he nine times passed 1,000 runs and twice took more than 100 wickets, despite recurring injuries to his knees. In South Africa, he scored six centuries in consecutive innings in 1970/1 to equal a world record, and, two seasons later, again playing for Rhodesia, scored two centuries in the match against the International Cavaliers. In 1972, 1977, and 1979 (twice in successive matches) he performed the hat-trick in Championship matches and in 1977 against Hampshire in the Benson and Hedges Cup, a competition which Gloucestershire went on to win. Against Worcestershire in 1977 he scored 108 and took 13 wickets in the match for 73. His highest score was 254 for Rhodesia against Western Province in 1970/1 and his best bowling figures, 9 for 71 also for Rhodesia, against Transvaal in 1972/3. He is the only player to have scored a century and performed the hat-trick on two occasions, for Gloucester-shire against Essex in 1972 and against Leicestershire in 1979. When South Africa emerged from the political and sporting wilderness, Procter, positive and popular, presided as Coach over a notably successful start in the World Cup in Australia in 1992 and remained in the job until 1994 when he was replaced after disagreements between himself and senior members of the team.

First-class career (1965–88): 21,936 runs (36.01) including 48 centuries, 1,417 wickets (19.53), and 325 catches
Test matches (7): 226 runs (25.11), 41 wickets (15.02), and 4 catches

PROMNITZ, Henry Louis Ernest

(b. 1904, Cape Colony; d. 1983, Cape Province) Border, Griqualand West, Orange Free State, and South Africa

A right-arm bowler of both off- and leg-spin, difficult to read, Henry Promnitz appeared twice for South Africa against England in 1927/8 and in the first innings of his first Test at Johannesburg, he took 5 for 58 in 37 overs. In his career, for a weak side, Border, in the Currie Cup competition, he took 125 wickets (22.80).

First-class career (1924–37): 592 runs (11.84) and 150 wickets (23.80)
Test matches (2): 14 runs (3.50), 8 wickets (20.12), and 2 catches

QUINN, Neville Anthony

(b. 1908, Orange Free State; d. 1934, Kimberley) Griqualand West, Transvaal, and South Africa

A left-arm medium-pace bowler who could make the ball swerve and spin but was happier on matting than on turf, Neville Quinn toured England in 1929, coming top of the bowling averages, though not taking most wickets, with 65 (23.89). In the first innings of the third Test at Headingley he took 6 for 19, including the first three batsmen. He played against England once at home in 1930/1, and in Australasia in 1931/2 he again headed the bowling averages with 42 wickets (23.90), including 13 in the Tests. Don Bradman held a high opinion of his capabilities, especially during the third Test at Melbourne when he took 4 for 42 in 31 overs in the first innings, including 'the Don' for 2. He died suddenly two years later.

First-class career (1927–34): 438 runs (9.12), 186 wickets (20.78), and 10 catches
Test matches (12): 90 runs (6.00), 35 wickets (32.71), and 1 catch

REID, Norman

(b. 1890, Cape Town; d. 1947, Cape Town) *Western Province and South Africa*

A zestful all-rounder in a first-class career lasting 4 years, Norman Reid played in a sole Test against Australia, the third match at Cape Town in 1921/2, mainly because of his brilliant fielding, usually at cover-point. He scored 11 and 6 and took 2 for 63. An Oxford rugby blue in 1912 and 1913, he was awarded the DSO and MC during the First World War, but died in tragic circumstances.

First-class career (1920–4): 395 runs (21.94) and 20 wickets (23.15)

RHODES, Jonathan Neil

(b. 1969, Pietermaritzburg) *Natal and South Africa*

When Jonty Rhodes arrived in Australia for the 1992 World Cup, South Africa's coach Mike Procter calmly announced to the international media that he was the best fielder in the world. At the time it was understandably received with a fair degree of scepticism but it did not take the young Natalian long to fulfil his coach's claim. He made the backward point position his own (short mid-wicket for the spinners), becoming a vital weapon in South Africa's limited-overs armoury and often being referred to as the sixth bowler, such was the number of runs that he saved. Unlike his great predecessor, Colin Bland, he is short and wiry, which was probably an asset in performing feats of great agility and athleticism. He is instantly recognizable in the field as he is constantly alive with motion, running on the spot, polishing the ball, retrieving the bowler's marker or delivering a cap to the umpire. And the impression is heightened when the ball is played within his range as he spends much time sprawled across the turf in the most unlikely of cricket positions, a probable reason why he does not hit the stumps as often as he would like, as he is nearly always off balance and often lying flat on his back when he makes his throw. His right-hand batting has often been criticized for lack of technique and he does play with a very strong bottom hand, no doubt the influence of his international-standard hockey ability. However, there is nothing much wrong with his batting average for South Africa. He has often been at his best in a crisis, notably when he scored a century against Sri Lanka (1993/4) to save a Test match and his major innings at Sydney and Johannesburg (1993/4) in Tests South Africa eventually won. His popularity is enormous wherever he has played cricket and he has attracted many admirers, simply because he has overcome epilepsy to achieve the highest honours in the game. In fifty-one one-day internationals to 1994 he had scored 1,201 runs (29.29).

First-class career (1988–): 3,544 runs (36.91) including 5 centuries, one wicket (49.00), and 42 catches

Test matches (16): 865 runs (39.30) including 1 century, 0–5, and 9 catches

RICE, Clive Edward Butler

(b. 1949, Johannesburg) *Transvaal, Natal, and Nottinghamshire*

A quick glance at the international record books would suggest that Clive Rice was an ordinary cricketer: three limited-overs internationals for 26 runs and 2 wickets. Nothing could have been further from the truth. It would be hard to choose between Rice and Mike Procter for South Africa's greatest all-rounder of the modern era. Procter was lucky to play seven Test matches before the isolation curtain came down. Rice was chosen for his first tour to Australia in 1971/2 shortly after his twenty-second birthday. Strangely enough, his choice was severely criticized as his first season of A section Currie Cup cricket had been relatively modest. Apparently, he owed selection partly to the fact that the wise men were worried about the age of their squad and wanted more youth in the field. Had the tour gone ahead, his selection would surely have turned out to be an inspired one. In a career that lasted for a quarter of a century he dominated the game wherever he played but particularly on Transvaal's home turf at the Wanderers Stadium and at Nottinghamshire's Trent Bridge ground where he formed a mighty foreign partnership with Sir Richard Hadlee of New Zealand. He would have been a top-order right-handed batsman in any international side while, in spite of his relatively short stature, he was able to generate plenty of pace and bounce as a fast-medium pace bowler. His greatest strength was that his temperament matched his talent in every way. He always played with controlled aggression and was a man of rare courage, never afraid to take on opponents or authority. He was involved in a Test legal case when he signed for Kerry Packer's World Series and this cost him the Nottinghamshire captaincy for a while and he was also involved in an acrimonious public exchange with former Springbok captain Peter van der Merwe, who was convener of the national selectors, when he was omitted from the team for the 1992 World Cup. He could never be kept down for any length of time and always bounced back as a renowned and respected cricketer. He twice won the all-rounder's challenge in Hong Kong and was also selected for the Bicentenary match between MCC and the Rest of the World in 1987 which was official acknowledgement of his contribution to the game. But he had to wait until that historic 10 November 1991 to represent South Africa in an official international match against India at Eden Gardens in Calcutta. At the age of 42, South Africa's international return had come almost too late for him and he was not to get another chance. Rice, however, was not a man to give up the game lightly and he continued to play, taking his career figures past 26,000 runs and 900 wickets. He has won every honour available to him, including successful captaincies of both Transvaal and Nottinghamshire. His highest score was 246 against Sussex at Hove and his best bowling return 7 for 62 against Western Province at the Wanderers. In that match he also played an innings of 90 and achieved the all-round feat of 100 runs and 10 wickets in the same match. He replaced Peter Kirsten as South Africa's captain in 1984 during the unofficial series against a West Indies XI and retained that position until 1991, apart from the Gatting XI series in 1990 when he lost his place in the Test side and Jimmy Cook took over. Aggressive on the field, he was almost shy away from it although he was a leading figure in marketing full-time professionalism in South Africa.

First-class career (1969–   ): 26,331 runs (40.95) including 48 centuries, 930 wickets (22.49), and 401 catches

RICHARDS, Alfred Renfrew

(b. 1868, Cape Colony; d. 1904, Salisbury, Rhodesia) *Western Province and South Africa*

A useful batsman, Alfred Richards appeared in a sole Test, the third at Cape Town against England in 1895/6, when he scored 6 and 0.

First-class career (1889–96): 346 runs (23.06) including 1 century, 13 catches, and 2 stumpings

RICHARDS, Barry Anderson

(b. 1945, Durban) *Natal, South Australia, Gloucestershire, Hampshire, and South Africa*

One of the most gifted batsmen in the history of cricket, Barry Richards found the difficult business of batting quite absurdly easy and all that prevented him from piling up records like a Bradman was his tendency to be bored if his supreme talent was not being fully tested by the mere mortals bowling at him. Forced by politics to play his cricket away from the Test arena during his prime, Richards became a wandering mercenary, playing only a little cricket in his native South Africa and instead revealing his magic in England and Australia. Born at Durban, the year before Mike Procter, Richards came to England as captain of the 1963 South African Schools side, played one month for Gloucestershire in 1965, and three years later, in his first full season for Hampshire, scored 2,395 runs (47.90). In his only Test series, in 1969/70, he dominated Bill Lawry's Australians, scoring his first Test hundred in his native Durban and reaching three figures in the first over after lunch. A tall, fair-haired, right-handed opening batsman with a casual and distracted air, Richards was separated from other batsmen by the almost unique amount of time he seemed to have to pick up the line and length of the ball. With a high backlift, full flow through of the blade, and quick movement of the feet either forward or back to get himself into the perfect position to play the ball, he was a technical paragon. He scored more than 1,000 runs in nine seasons in England and six in South Africa, twice scoring two hundreds in a match (against Northants in 1968 and Kent in 1976). Playing for South Australia in 1970/1 he was at his brilliant best, scoring 1,538 runs (109.86) and making 356 against Western Australia at Perth, including 325 in a single day. In 1977/8 and 1978/9 he returned to Australia to play with success in World Series Cricket and in 1978 abruptly left county cricket because he was bored with the workaday grind. From time to time, as at Bournemouth against the Rest of the World team in 1968, when he took 7 for 63, he proved devastating as an off-spin bowler, and he consistently picked up brilliant catches in the slips with minimum effort or fuss. Ironically, since the politics of their two countries prevented any form of dialogue, the West Indies cricket team owed a great debt to South Africa, for Richards had an immense influence on the batting of his Hampshire opening partner Gordon Greenidge, who developed into a magnificent batsman of world stature partly thanks to the example set by the graceful and regal presence at the other end. Hampshire crowds in the 1970s were privileged to see one of the most brilliant opening partnerships in cricket history. Richards scored a century before lunch nine times and made 1,000 runs in a season 15 times, on nine occasions in England; five in South Africa (including the record—1,285 at 80.31 in 1973/4); and once (in his only season) in Australia (see above). Generally smiling and charming, sometimes moody, even petulant, Barry Richards was determined to earn the money his talents merited. The genius is seldom a straightforward or an equable character, and never a dull one, but, on becoming coach to Natal, Richards admitted he had not previously appreciated the problems of cricket administration. Later he became director of cricket in Queensland, and a shrewd observer of the modern game, more receptive than most to new techniques and methods.

First-class career (1964–83): 28,358 runs (54.75) including 80 centuries, 77 wickets (37.48), and 367 catches

Test matches (4): 508 runs (72.57) including 2 centuries, 1–26, and 3 catches

RICHARDS, William Henry Matthews

(b. 1862, Cape Colony; d. 1903, Cape Town) *Western Province and South Africa*

A useful batsman, 'Dicky' Richards played in the second Test against Major Warton's England side at Cape Town in 1888/9, scoring 0 and 4. It was his only first-class match.

RICHARDSON, David John

(b. 1959, Johannesburg) *Eastern Province and South Africa*

Although Kepler Wessels and Allan Donald are generally regarded as the key men in South Africa's return to international cricket, the role filled by Dave Richardson was just as important. Not being a fast bowler or major batsman he did not achieve the same publicity as those who occupy the glamour positions, but as wicket-keeper and as a dependable right-hand batsman who can open in a crisis he has been vital to the team's success. This is borne out by the fact that he and Donald were the only two to have played in every Test contested by South Africa in the first four years of the new era. He was just as irreplaceable as the other two and has developed his wicket-keeping to the level where he does not have to yield to any of the world's leading stumpers. It may be argued that he has kept almost exclusively to pace but, in the modern game, even that requires a degree of acrobatics and athleticism that was not always necessary in

previous years. A wristy batsman, he likes to play an attacking game and it has normally paid off, particularly against New Zealand in 1994/5 when he scored 109 at Newlands and averaged 82 for his 4 innings. His quiet, almost reticent, nature belies a very tough competitor who has also shrewdly advised his captains.

First-class career (1977–): 5,340 runs (25.67) and 470 dismissals (438 c., 32 st.)

Test matches (22): 825 runs (26.61) including 1 century, and 92 dismissals (92 c.)

ROBERTSON, John Benjamin

(b. 1906, Cape Town; d. 1985, Cape Town) *Western Province and South Africa*

With his accurate and sustained spin bowling, Jack Robertson took 8 for 96 in the Australian innings of 318 for his province at Cape Town in 1935/6, thus earning Test selection for the first three matches.

First-class career (1931–7): 450 runs (18.00) and 65 wickets (24.20)

Test matches (3): 51 runs (10.20), 6 wickets (53.50), and 2 catches

ROUTLEDGE, Thomas William

(b. 1867, Liverpool, England; d. 1927, Stockton-on-Tees, Co. Durham, England) *Transvaal and South Africa*

A fine right-handed batsman with a very forceful approach and a useful change-bowler, Tommy Routledge played in Tests against England in 1891/2 and 1895/6 without living up to his reputation. On the day the meeting was held to select the first-ever South African side to visit England in 1894, he made a century and clinched his place.

First-class career (1889–97): 492 runs (21.39)

Test matches (4): 72 runs (9.00) and 2 catches

ROSE-INNES, Albert

(b. 1868; d. 1946) *Transvaal and South Africa*

A polished and reliable batsman and a slow left-arm bowler who 'terrorized most batsmen' (as a contemporary report put it), Bertie Innes made 55 and took 5 for 98 for Kimberley against Transvaal at Kimberley in the first Currie Cup Tournament of 1889/90. A year before he had appeared in the two Tests against England at Port Elizabeth and Cape Town and took 5 for 43 in the first innings of the first match. In a different era, he might have become a household name.

First-class career (1888–94): 70 runs (7.77) and 18 wickets (17.27)
Test matches (2): 14 runs (3.50), 5 wickets (17.80), and 2 catches

ROWAN, Athol Matthew Burchell

(b. 1921, Johannesburg) *Transvaal and South Africa*

With his shambling run—because of war wounds gained in the Western Desert he sometimes bowled with his leg in irons—Athol Rowan delivered right-arm slow-medium off-breaks from a good height. His grip was unusual in that he laid his index finger on, rather than across, the seam of the ball, which he delivered with a sharp and complete turn of the wrist; he imparted genuine spin and 'bite', varying these with a deceptive leg-cutter. He was also a very useful late-order batsman. For five post-war years he was a major factor in South Africa's attacking strategy. He toured England in 1947 and 1951 and played at home against England in 1948/9, not missing a Test. On his first tour he was the bowling mainstay, taking 102 wickets (24.97) in 1,075.4 overs. Although his twelve Test wickets were very expensive, most of his victims were the best batsmen. On the second tour his results were better in the Tests—18 wickets (34.44)—although he had a poor tour as a whole with 53 wickets (26.58). He made 432 runs (24.00) as some compensation. Often he was in pain with his leg and retired from first-class cricket at the end of the tour. In the in-between series at home he was the pivot of the attack with 24 wickets (33.08). His best performance was 9 for 19 (15 for 68) for Transvaal against the Australians at Johannesburg in 1949/50. The pitch took sharp spin and he baffled everyone in a match in which he also made 31 out of 125 and top-scored with 15 not out when Transvaal, seeking a mere 69 to win, lost by 15 runs. Through his exertions in this match he injured himself and could not play in any of the Tests in that series. He is Eric's younger brother.

First-class career (1939–51): 1,492 runs (24.06) including 1 century, 273 wickets (23.47), and 25 catches
Test matches (15): 290 runs (17.05), 54 wickets (38.59), and 7 catches

ROWAN, Eric Alfred Burchell

(b. 1909, Johannesburg; d. 1993, Johannesburg) *Transvaal and South Africa*

Superbly confident, a colourful, forthright character who was both a teetotaller and a non-smoker, Eric Rowan had an insatiable appetite for runs, which he collected with patience and an often dogged defence. His right-handed batting could be entertaining, however. He loved to carry on a running commentary as he was batting. His stance was easy and, very quick-footed, he could drive fearlessly and fluently against the fastest bowlers, chop or cut through the slips, and spoon strokes impudently from off-spinners safely over the heads of the leg-trap. Despite having broken his right arm when young, he was a first-rate field in any position. He toured England in 1935 and 1951, and in South Africa played against England in 1938/9 and 1948/9, and Australia in 1935/6 and in 1949/50. On his first England tour he amassed 1,948 runs (44.27) which included six centuries, more runs than anyone else, but he averaged only 27.33 in the Tests. Although he made 66 and 49 in the first Test against Australia at Durban in 1935/6, he was dropped after the third match and did not have an impressive series until 1938/9 when in four Tests he made 284 runs (47.33). In trouble with the authorities, he did not play another series against England till 1948/9. He opened the batting in the first two Tests but during the course of the second at Johannesburg the selectors announced that he had been dropped for the third match—only for Rowan to make an invaluable 156 not out on the last day in 6 hours, adding 162 unbroken with Dudley Nourse for the third wicket and saving South Africa after they had been 293 behind on the first innings. He was back for the fourth match at Johannesburg, scoring 86 not out, when things were again looking difficult for his country. Against Australia in 1949/50 he came second to Dudley Nourse with 404 runs (44.88), facing Ray Lindwall, Keith Miller, and Bill Johnston as the opening batsmen in all five Tests. Mainly on the losing side, he made 60 in a total of 137 in the first match at Johannesburg, and, in the third, 143 in a total of 311 at Durban. On his final England tour in 1951, he headed the batting with 1,852 runs (50.05) which included five centuries. In the Tests he scored 515 runs (57.22), including 236 and 60 not out at Headingley. In his first-class career he exceeded the double-hundred five times, his highest being 306 not out for Transvaal against Natal at Johannesburg in 1939/40 which remains the highest score by anyone in South Africa. Prolific in the Currie Cup competition, his best season was 1952/3 with 899 runs (74.91) from eight matches shortly before he retired. In hitting 176 against Rhodesia at Salisbury in 1950/1 he reached a century before lunch on the first day. He was the elder brother of Athol.

First-class career (1929–54): 11,710 runs (48.58) including 30 centuries, 4 wickets (42.00), and 83 catches
Test matches (26): 1,965 runs (43.66) including 3 centuries, 0–7, and 14 catches

ROWE, George Alexander

(b. 1874, Cape Colony; d. 1950, Cape Town) *Western Province and South Africa*

A left-arm slow bowler in early Currie Cup days, George Rowe was one of the first consistently successful bowlers in representative cricket. He played against England in 1895/6 and Australia in 1902/3. On his début in the second Test at Johannesburg he opened the bowling and took 5 for 115 in an innings of 482. Touring England in 1894 with the first South African side, he was the outstanding bowler in a wet summer, securing 136 wickets (12.87) in all matches and he was again the most successful on his second tour in 1901 in a warm, dry summer taking 136 wickets again (18.54). Bowling unchanged with George Lohmann for Western Province against Griqualand West at Johannesburg in 1896/7, he took 10 for 48—and in the next match, against Natal, 10 for 103, but perhaps his best feat was 13 for 155 against Cambridge University at Fenner's in 1901.

First-class career (1893–1907): 303 runs (7.04) and 170 wickets (21.12)
Test matches (5): 26 runs (4.33), 15 wickets (30.40), and 4 catches

RUNDLE, David Bryan

(b. 1965, Cape Town) *Western Province*

A right-arm off-spin bowler and useful lower-order hitter, Dave Rundle was South Africa's best slow bowler for all types of cricket in 1990 when Mike Gatting's rebel England XI toured and he was chosen for the five-day unofficial Test at the Wanderers, even though the pitch was unprepared and totally green. Ironically, South Africa's readmission to official Test cricket coincided with his own loss of form and he fell from favour apart from the tour to Australia in 1993/4 when he played in two limited-overs internationals, scoring 6 runs (3.00) and taking 5 wickets (19.00) but conceding almost six runs an over. He only became a bowler of any note in the second half of his career, having been chosen twice for SA Schools but exclusively as a middle-order batsman. Not a great turner of the ball, he has relied largely on flight for his success.

First-class career (1984–): 1,945 runs (23.15) including 1 century, 179 wickets (31.07), and 55 catches

RUSHMERE, Mark Weir

(b. 1965, Port Elizabeth) *Eastern Province, Transvaal, and South Africa*

Mark Rushmere, a tall right-hand batsman, is sufficiently versatile to open the innings or bat lower down. He was chosen as the cover batsman for the 1992 World Cup and was then rather harshly thrust into the most demanding of Test débuts against the new ball in the one-off Test against West Indies at Bridgetown, Barbados, later the same year. He scored six runs (3.00) and was not selected again. He is a solid rather than spectacular batsman but he has the application and concentration to play long innings once set. He has long been regarded as one of South Africa's best captains and his recent move to Transvaal will give him new opportunities in this regard. He made South African first-class history when he scored 150 not out in both innings for a South African Invitation XI against the Mike Gatting XI at Maritzburg in 1990. This is the only instance of this happening in this country although rebel statistics have since been annulled by the ICC. He comes from a distinguished cricketing family, his father, Colin having played for both Eastern Province and Western Province as well as being president of the former and serving on the national control board. Mark has played in four one-day internationals, scoring 78 runs (19.50)

First-class career (1983–): 5,770 runs (43.05), 2 wickets (20.50), and 52 catches

SAMUELSON, Sivert Vause

(b. 1883, Natal; d. 1958, Durban) *Natal and South Africa*

A slow bowler, Sivert Samuelson played in only one Test against England, the fifth at Cape Town in 1909/10, scoring 15 and 7, taking 0 for 64 and holding a catch. The following season he was devastating in the Currie Cup competition, taking 13 for 111 and 13 for 147 for Natal against Griqualand West and Orange Free State respectively at Durban, and finishing with 41 wickets (13.87).

First-class career (1908–23): 193 runs (12.06) and 57 wickets (21.05)

SCHULTZ, Brett Nolan

(b. 1970, East London) *Eastern Province and South Africa*

Brett Schultz is a powerfully built left-arm fast bowler who made a dramatic impact on South Africa's fortunes when he took 20 wickets in just three Tests on the normally unsympathetic pitches of Sri Lanka. Prior to that he had taken four wickets in two Tests against India which had not suggested he would become such an immediate success. He is a bowler who can match Allan Donald for pace but his biggest attribute is his ability to obtain bounce from the most placid of surfaces and to bowl a toe-breaking yorker. In many ways his bowling reminds one of a left-handed Mike Procter in that he is an enormously strong man with an unorthodox action and an ability to frighten batsmen. Possibly because of his catapult-like action, he has suffered more than his fair share of injuries and, following operations on both knees and an enforced absence from action for more than 12 months, there were doubts about his long-term future until early 1995 when he made a successful comeback against Zimbabwe in Harare.

First class career (1989–): 201 runs (10.05), 124 wickets (23.78), and 5 catches

Test matches (5): 6 runs (2.00) and 24 wickets (17.79)

SCHWARZ, Reginald Oscar

(b. 1875, London, England; d. 1918, Etaples, France) *Oxfordshire, Middlesex, Transvaal, and South Africa*

Few men did so much to establish the reputation of South African cricket as Reggie Schwarz. A quiet, retiring character, he learned the game in England at St Paul's School and played for Middlesex occasionally—averaging a mere 17.80 with the bat and taking 7 wickets in 14 matches for the county—before going to South Africa. He returned to England with the 1904 team and from that tour dates his fame. Studying the methods of B. J. T. Bosanquet, he learned most successfully the art of bowling off-breaks out of the back of the hand and then taught his fellow South Africans. He himself was unusual in that he bowled the googly only, without mixing in any leg-breaks. The ball moved slowly through the air, fast off the pitch, and often lifted awkwardly. Schwarz headed the averages in 1904 and in 1907, taking 65 wickets (18.26) and 137 wickets (11.79)

respectively, and with six men on the leg-side he was very difficult to play, although he was not so successful in 1912. At home he appeared against England in 1905/6 and 1909/10; and he toured Australia in 1910/11. In Australia he took 59 wickets (25.00), heading the bowling in the Tests with 25 wickets (26.04). In the first Test at Sydney, when South Africa were completely outplayed, he took 5 for 102 in a total of 528 and scored 61, coming in at 49 for 7 and adding 100 with Aubrey Faulkner. In the fifth match at Sydney, again in a losing situation, he secured 6 for 47 in a total of 364. Often opening the bowling, he took 18 wickets (17.22) in the 1905/6 series. He was often a useful batsman. He was also an England Rugby football international.

First-class career (1901–14): 3,798 runs (22.60) including 1 century, 398 wickets (17.58), and 108 catches

Test matches (20): 374 runs (13.85), 55 wickets (25.76), and 18 catches

SECCULL, Arthur William

(b. 1868, Cape Colony; d. 1945, Johannesburg) *Transvaal, Western Province, and South Africa*

A competent right-handed batsman and useful change-bowler, Arthur Seccull visited England with the first South African side in 1894, making 355 runs (15.10). His sole Test was the third against England in 1895/6 when he scored 6 and 17 not out, took 2 for 37 and held 1 catch.

First-class career (1889–97): 229 runs (22.90) and 15 wickets (16.86)

SEYMOUR, Dr Michael Arthur

(b. 1936, Cape Province) *Western Province and South Africa*

A right-arm off-break bowler who made his first-class début in 1960/1, 'Kelly' Seymour toured Australasia in 1963/4 and at home played against England in 1964/5 and Australia in 1969/70. On the tour he was expensive, taking 32 wickets (34.90), and none of his Test performances equalled the feat for South African Universities against New Zealand at Pretoria in 1961/2, when his accuracy helped him to figures of 7 for 80 in the first innings and 12 for 152 in the match.

First-class career (1960–70): 569 runs (14.22) and 111 wickets (29.52)

Test matches (7): 84 runs (12.00), 9 wickets (65.33), and 2 catches

SHALDERS, William Alfred

(b. 1880, Kimberley; d. 1917, Cape Province)
Griqualand West, Transvaal, Cape Colony, London County, and South Africa

A very impetuous right-handed opening batsman possessing strokes all round the wicket, William Shalders toured England with the 1901, 1904, and 1907 teams, often helping to give the side a good start before getting himself out in the 20s and 30s. On each tour he made over 700 runs in the first-class matches but he was disappointing in the first Test series in England in 1907. At home he played against England in 1898/9 and 1905/6, and against Australia in 1902/3. His highest score in Tests was 42 in the second match against Australia at Johannesburg in 1902/3, but his most invaluable knock was 38 in the first Test at Johannesburg in 1905/6 when South Africa beat England by one wicket. He was a useful change-bowler and very good fielder.

First-class career (1897–1909): 3,351 runs (23.27) including 2 centuries, 6 wickets (23.16), and 38 catches

Test matches (12): 355 runs (16.13), 1–6, and 3 catches

SHAW, Timothy Gower

(b. 1959, Empangeni) *Eastern Province*

A lanky left-arm spinner, Tim Shaw must wonder whether he will ever get beyond the role of a substitute in Test match cricket. He and Clive Eksteen appeared to have the inside lane for the Test side when both were chosen for the whistle-stop limited-overs tour to India in 1991. But Shaw was discarded for the World Cup the following year and, when he remained sidelined for successive series against India, Sri Lanka, and the first half against Australia, he seemed to have become a forgotten man. But perseverance has always been one of the features of his bowling and he was back in the squad for the home half of the series against Australia. Although he did not play in a Test match he bowled with impressive control and economy in limited-overs opportunities. He kept his squad place for the 1994 tour of England. Nagging accuracy and the ability to use his height to gain bounce have made him a difficult bowler to attack and his ability to push the ball through quickly makes him a difficult opponent on a turning wicket. By provincial standards he is no mean performer as a left-hand batsman and he is a genuine specialist fielder in the gulley position, having made many sharp stops and catches. He has taken a Test match catch as a substitute.

First-class career (1980–   ): 2,581 runs (22.05) including 1 century, 354 wickets (27.69), and 92 catches

SHEPSTONE, George Harold

(b. 1876, Pietermaritzburg; d. 1940, Transvaal)
Transvaal and South Africa

In the XI at Repton as a free hitter and fast bowler, George Shepstone returned to South Africa to play later in Tests against England in 1895/6 and 1898/9. He came back to England with the South African side in 1904 but illness curtailed his appearances. He represented his province with some distinction from 1898 until 1905, hitting 104 against Griqualand West at Cape Town in 1897/8 and taking 10 for 39 in the match against Border at Port Elizabeth in 1902/3.

First-class career (1895–1905): 693 runs (21.00) including 1 century, 42 wickets (16.23), and 11 catches

Test matches (2): 38 runs (9.50), 0–47, and 2 catches

SHERWELL, Percy William

(b. 1880, Natal; d. 1948, Bulawayo, Rhodesia)
Cornwall, Transvaal, and South Africa

Although born in Natal, Percy Sherwell came to England in childhood for his education and he played cricket for Cornwall before going to the Transvaal as a mining engineer. Slight, but well-built, with a clear-eyed face, Kitchener moustache and kindly expression, he was a wicket-keeper specially adept at taking googly bowling and a good batsman in a crisis. As South Africa's captain he managed his battery of googly bowlers admirably and batted heroically, leading South Africa to her first Test victory over England in 1905/6. In fact, he led South Africa in all the Tests he played—against England in 1905/6 and 1907, and in Australia in 1910/11. His first Test, at Johannesburg in 1905/6, was one of the legendary contests: South Africa, 95 behind on the first innings, needed 48 for victory when Sherwell came in as last man to join Dave Nourse. Amid great excitement the match was won by one wicket. Promoting himself to opening batsman at Lord's in 1907, the first Test in England, he made a sparkling 115 after South Africa had followed on 288 runs behind and saved the game. In Australia, while 1,479 runs were being made in two of the Tests, he allowed only four byes (all off one ball). In the 1907 Tests he made more runs than any of his colleagues—154 runs (30.80). He served on the Test Selection Committee from 1907 until 1924, was South Africa's Lawn Tennis singles champion in 1904, and represented his country against England at tennis in 1908/9. He was one of several brothers who made their mark at cricket, the best known being Noel, of Tonbridge, Cambridge University, and Middlesex, also a wicket-keeper.

First-class career (1902–13): 1,808 runs (24.10) including 3 centuries, and 120 dismissals (67 c., 53 st.)

Test matches (13): 427 runs (23.72) including 1 century, and 36 dismissals (20 c., 16 st.)

SHORT, Arthur Marun

(b. 1947, Graaff-Reinet) *Natal and Eastern Province*

A right-hand opening batsman, Arthur Short occupies a unique position in the history of South African cricket. He was the only uncapped player chosen for both the cancelled tours of England and Australia in 1970 and 1971/2 respectively. He also came agonizingly close to international recognition when he was made 12th man for the final Test against Australia in 1970. During that season he made 496 runs in just six matches. In the end his only overseas tour was with South African Universities to England in 1967. He retired prematurely because of his farming commitments.

First-class career (1969–75): 3,318 runs (27.88) including 2 centuries, 3 wickets (20.66), and 51 catches

SIEDLE, Ivan Julian

(b. 1903, Durban; d. 1982, Durban) *Natal and South Africa*

A solid right-handed opening batsman, 'Jack' Siedle never looked an easy man to get out. He watched the ball intently and had a good variety of strokes. He toured England in 1929 and 1935, each time being beset by illness and injuries to a knee, and at home played against England in 1927/8 and 1930/1, and Australia in 1935/6. On both England tours he was an admirable partner for Bruce Mitchell, scoring 1,579 runs (35.88) and 1,346 runs (39.58) respectively—including five centuries—though achieving little in the Tests. In South Africa, however, it was a different story: he made 384 runs (42.66) in the 1930/1 series, in the second Test at Cape Town putting on 260 with Mitchell for the first wicket, which remains the first-wicket record. Against Australia in 1935/6 he

was the only batsman besides Dudley Nourse to show any degree of consistency, making 332 runs (33.20) in the series, with a highest score of 59. A heavy scorer in domestic cricket, he hit three double centuries and shared in the record South African partnership of 424 with J. F. W. Nicolson for Natal against Orange Free State at Bloemfontein in 1926/7. His career-highest was 265 not out against Orange Free State at Durban in 1929/30. He made centuries in his last three innings in first-class cricket in 1936/7, including 207 against Western Province at Durban. A large and attractive clock on the ground at Kingsmead, Durban was erected in his memory. His son, John, made a century for Western Province against Eastern Province at Newlands on his first-class début in 1955/6.

First-class career (1922–37): 7,730 runs (40.05) including 17 centuries, 1 wicket (35.00), 57 catches, and 1 stumping

Test matches (18): 977 runs (28.73) including 1 century, 1–7, and 7 catches

SIMONS, Eric Owen

(b. 1962, Cape Town) *Western Province and Northern Transvaal*

Eric Simons, after persistently knocking on the door for a number of seasons, finally convinced the selectors of his ability when he was called up for the home limited-overs series against Australia in 1994 at the age of 32. A tall right-arm fast-medium pace bowler (at one time he was quick enough to take the new ball for Northern Transvaal while on national service and pick up 51 wickets in the season at an average of little more than 14), he has gradually developed his middle-order batting to the standard where he can be considered a genuine all-rounder. He has excelled in rescuing Western Province from top-order collapses, including a record ninth-wicket partnership of 157 against Northern Transvaal with Craig Matthews. He more than justified the selectors' faith in his first limited-overs series and his next ambition was to establish himself in the five-day side as well. He toured Pakistan in 1994.

First-class career (1982–): 2,944 runs (26.52), 258 wickets (25.65), and 56 catches

SINCLAIR, James Hugh

(b. 1876, Swellendam, Cape Province; d. 1913, Johannesburg) *Transvaal and South Africa*

Big and strapping, one of the first men to make South African cricket famous, Jimmy Sinclair was a prodigious right-handed hitter and an excellent fast bowler, combining a nice variety of pace with a high delivery. He first attracted attention against Lord Hawke's team in 1898/9 with scores of 86 (as an opening batsman) and 106 in a total of 177—the first Test century by a South African —in the Tests at Johannesburg and Cape Town respectively, together with 9 for 89 at Cape Town. Touring England in 1901, 1904, and 1907, he rather disappointed overall with the bat, though his great hitting remained a special feature—once he smote Wilfred Rhodes so hard out of the Harrogate ground that a cabby was knocked off his cab. But his bowling was very successful on the first two tours. He took 107 wickets (16.69) and 100 wickets (22.85) respectively in all matches. Twice in 1901, he took 13 wickets in a match and four times seven or more wickets in an innings. Taken prisoner by the Boers in the war, he escaped from the POW camp and reached the British lines thoroughly dishevelled but in time for the 1901 tour! Against the 1902/3 Australians he hit 101 in the second Test at Johannesburg and 104 (which included ten sixes and eight fours) in an innings of 225 in the third at Cape Town, heading the batting with an average of 47.66. In 1905/6 he took 21 wickets (19.90) against England. In England in 1907 his bowling was completely overshadowed by the quartet of googly bowlers but at times his hitting was as brilliant as ever. His Australian tour showed moderate results, but two years later he was dead. He also represented both South Africa and England at Rugby football and he was highly skilled at hockey and soccer.

First-class career (1892–1912): 4,483 runs (21.55) including 6 centuries, 491 wickets (21.43), and 65 catches

Test matches (25): 1,069 runs (23.23) including 3 centuries, 63 wickets (31.68), and 9 catches

SMITH, Anthony John Shaw

(b. 1951, Johannesburg) *Natal*

'Tich' Smith would have been the natural successor to Denis Lindsay as South Africa's premier wicket-keeper/batsman from the mid-1970s. His career reached a high point during the 1975/6 season when he played for the unofficial national XI against a powerful International Wanderers side made up of leading international cricketers. During that season he made 45 dismissals, only one short of the then South African record. But he impressed even more as a batsman, having the back-foot technique to handle bowlers of genuine

pace, and he could easily have held a place as a specialist batsman. It was his heroic defence against a fired-up Dennis Lillee that enabled the South African side to gain a draw at the Wanderers when the great Australian had swept the top order, including Richards, Barlow, and Pollock, aside. A talented all-round sportsman, Smith also represented Natal at Rugby.

First-class career (1971–84): 3,909 runs (27.33) including 2 centuries, 1 wicket (35.00), 320 dismissals (309 c., 11 st.)

SMITH, Charles James Edward

(b. 1872, Cape Colony; d. 1947, Johannesburg) *Transvaal and South Africa*

A useful middle-order right-handed batsman, Charlie Smith represented his province for 12 years. Against the Australians in 1902/3 he made 58 and 71 not out for a Transvaal XV and was selected for the three Tests against the touring team.

First-class career (1893–1905): 409 runs (24.05)

Test matches (3): 106 runs (21.20) and 2 catches

SMITH, Frederick W.

(No details available) *Kimberley, Transvaal, and South Africa*

Successively captain of Kimberley and Transvaal, Fred Smith collided with another player on the field in 1894 and broke his collar bone. A competent middle-order batsman, his first Test was also the first-ever played by South Africa, against Major Warton's England side in 1888/9. He appeared in the second Test and also in the second match at Johannesburg in 1895/6, by which time he was fully recovered.

First-class career (1888–96): 140 runs (15.55)

Test matches (3): 45 runs (9.00) and 2 catches

SMITH, Vivian Ian

(b. 1925, Durban) *Natal and South Africa*

A very steady right-arm leg-break bowler but without the googly, Ian Smith could be deadly on a helpful wicket. He toured England in 1947 and 1955 and at home played against Australia in 1949/50 and 1957/8. At Derby on his first England tour, he took 13 for 66, including a second innings analysis of 4.5–1–1–6 (including a hat-trick). He took 7 for 189 in 78.1 overs on his Test début at Trent Bridge (when England had to fight their way out of trouble) and on the tour headed the bowling averages with 58 wickets (23.17). When he visited England again he had fewer opportunities with Hugh Tayfield available. In the Currie Cup competition he took 190 wickets (19.53).

First-class career (1945–58): 547 runs (10.32), 365 wickets (22.55), and 37 catches

Test matches (9): 39 runs (3.90), 12 wickets (64.08), and 3 catches

SNELL, Richard Peter

(b. 1968, Durban) *Natal, Transvaal, Somerset, and South Africa*

A right-arm swing bowler of fast-medium pace, Richard Snell was more or less a regular member of the South African squad after the resumption of international cricket, without managing to establish a permanent place in the Test XI. He also had a disappointing season for Somerset in 1992, taking only 22 wickets in 16 championship games, although he proved a genial team man. His stock delivery is the in-swinger although he can also run the ball away to the slips and he can be deceptively quick off the pitch. His biggest bowling success came in limited-overs cricket when he took 5 wickets in a World Series final between South Africa and Australia at Melbourne. He probably played his best cricket to date on that Australian tour when he proved effective at bowling around the wicket at Australia's key left-handers. As a batsman he is normally good for quick runs at the end of a limited-overs innings although he underlined his natural talent by nearly scoring a century before lunch for South Africa against Glamorgan in 1994. Casual in appearance, with his shirt tails always hanging out and his dark hair permanently in his eyes, he is a good competitor. By 1994 he had played in thirty-six one-day internationals, taking 36 wickets (37.94).

First-class career (1987–): 1,104 runs (17.25), 191 wickets (28.01), and 16 catches

Test matches (5): 95 runs (13.57), 19 wickets (28.36), and 1 catch

SNOOKE, Sibley John

(b. 1881, Tembuland; d. 1966, Port Elizabeth) *Border, Western Province, Transvaal, and South Africa*

A stylish right-handed stroke-playing batsman, a useful fast-medium bowler and a reliable fielder, 'Tip' Snooke was a bulwark of his country for nearly 20 years. He made his first-class début in

the Currie Cup competition at 16, toured England in 1904, 1907, and 1912, and Australia in 1910/11. At home he played against England in 1905/6, 1909/10, and 1922/3. His first Test triumph was in the third match at Johannesburg in 1905/6 when he took 8 for 70 in the first innings (12 for 127 in the match), South Africa winning handsomely, and in the series he took most wickets, 24 (15.37). He helped his side avert defeat at The Oval in 1907 (when he appeared with his brother, Stanley), scoring 63 and 36. In the third Test at Adelaide in 1910/11, when South Africa beat Australia for the first time, he hit 103. In his last series, 1922/3, he opened South Africa's batting and bowling in three Tests, securing 3 for 17 and 2 for 41 in the fifth match at Durban, his final Test, and he headed the bowling averages.

First-class career (1897–1923): 4,821 runs (25.91) including 7 centuries, 120 wickets (25.14), and 82 catches

Test matches (26): 1,008 runs (22.40) including 1 century, 35 wickets (20.05), and 24 catches

SNOOKE, Stanley De La Courtte

(b. 1878, Tembuland; d. 1959, Cape Town) *Western Province, Transvaal, and South Africa*

A competent batsman, and captain of Western Province for some years, Stanley Snooke toured England in 1907, and in his sole Test at The Oval, batting at number eleven, failed to score in his single innings but held two catches. In the wet summer and on turf wickets, he was a great disappointment, averaging only 11.30 for the tour. He was elder brother of 'Tip'—S. J.—with whom he was often confused.

First-class career (1904–21): 798 runs (16.62), 19 wickets (11.78), and 31 catches

SOLOMON, William Rodger Thomson

(b. 1872, Cape Colony; d. 1964, Cape Province) *Transvaal, Eastern Province, and South Africa*

Largely because of two courageous innings, 64 for a Johannesburg XI and 52 for Transvaal against Lord Hawke's team in 1898/9, William Solomon played in the first Test at Johannesburg about a fortnight later, his sole Test appearance. He scored 2 and 2 and held 1 catch.

First-class career (1892–1906): 73 runs (9.12)

STEWART, Errol Leslie Rae

(b. 1969, Durban) *Natal*

Errol Stewart is an attacking right-hand batsman who became a wicket-keeper almost by mistake,

667

yet it is in this role that he has represented South Africa in five limited-overs internationals. As a schoolboy he achieved provincial and national honours strictly as a batsman and he only took over the gloves at senior level for Natal because there were no specialists of sufficient ability available. In a sense he is wasted behind the stumps as he is a brilliant outfielder, having the speed and safe hands of a man who has played both first-class cricket and Rugby (as a centre three-quarter). He toured Australia in 1993–4. He kept wicket in four of his five internationals, scoring 57 runs (14.25) and taking 3 catches.

First-class career (1988–   ): 1,430 runs (26.98) and 61 dismissals (59 c., 2 st.)

STEWART, Major Robert Bernard

(b. 1856, England; d. 1913, Cape Province) *Eastern Province and South Africa*

Captain of cricket at Wellington College, the Major was stationed in South Africa for many years and was a stylish batsman and brilliant cover-point. His only first-class match was a Test, the first-ever for South Africa against Major Warton's England team at Port Elizabeth in 1888/9, in which he scored 4 and 9 and held 2 catches.

STEYN, Philippus Jememia Ruddolf

(b. 1967, Kimberley) *Griqualand West, Orange Free State, and South Africa*

A late-developing right-handed opening batsman, Philippus Steyn played Nuffield Schools cricket from 1983 to 1987 and for South African Universities in 1989/90, but did not win a Test cap until the series against New Zealand in 1994/5. Taking over from Andrew Hudson, he scored 38 and 12 at Cape Town in the third Test, his only one to date. A brilliant fielder and good all-round sportsman, he also played tennis and Rugby at schoolboy provincial level. He bowls medium pace and has also kept wicket.

First-class career (1985–   ): 3,298 runs (27.03), 1 wicket (24.00), and 32 dismissals (31 c., 1 st.)

STRICKER, Louis Anthony

(b. 1884, Kimberley; d. 1960, Cape Town) *Transvaal and South Africa*

A forcing right-handed opening bat, Louis Stricker toured Australia in 1910/11 and England in 1912. At home he played against England in

1909/10. Despite his opportunities, he failed to reach a fifty in Tests, his highest score being 48 in the third match against Australia at Adelaide in 1910/11. However, he hit a fine 101 for Transvaal against MCC at Johannesburg in 1909/10, putting on 215 in 2 hours and 20 minutes with J. W. Zulch for the first wicket, which constituted a record at that time against a touring team.

First-class career (1906–12): 2,105 runs (22.88) including 2 centuries, 8 wickets (37.87), 29 catches, and 2 stumpings
Test matches (13): 342 runs (14.25), 1–105, and 3 catches

SUSSKIND, Manfred John

(b. 1891, Johannesburg; d. 1957, Johannesburg) *Middlesex, Cambridge University, Transvaal, and South Africa*

A tall right-handed batsman, often cramped in style, whose proneness to pad-playing caused much criticism, 'Fred' Susskind went to Cambridge, where he failed to win his blue, although, in his teens, he played in six matches for Middlesex (averaging 9.90). On returning home, he had a long and prolific career with Transvaal, making 2,595 runs (49.90) in the Currie Cup alone. He toured England in 1924 and although his method of batting did not arouse enthusiasm, he made 1,469 runs (32.64) in the wet summer, being one of the few successes. In this, his only Test series, he hit four scores between 51 and 65. He was a useful deputy wicket-keeper. As late as 1931/2 he made 769 runs (64.08) including four centuries for Transvaal.

First-class career (1909–37): 4,775 runs (34.60) including 11 centuries, 1 wicket (81.00), 85 catches, and 3 stumpings
Test matches (5): 268 runs (33.50) and 1 catch

SWART, Peter Douglas

(b. 1946, Bulawayo) *Rhodesia, Western Province, and Glamorgan*

One of the many ex-Zimbabweans to seek his cricketing fortune south of the border, Peter Swart was an all-rounder of genuine class although whether he would have broken into the Test side in the same era as Mike Procter and Clive Rice is a matter for speculation. However, he would have been a natural for any limited-overs squad. A feature of his cricket was his outfielding: very powerful wrists enabled him to throw the ball flat over the stumps with uncanny accuracy from the boundary's edge. He operated mainly as first-change and stock bowler for Western Province and his stamina enabled him to bowl long spells at fast-medium pace. A graceful driver of the ball, he is one of the few to have completed the Castle/Currie Cup double of 2,000 runs and 200 wickets.

First-class career (1965–85): 6,093 runs (25.60) including 6 centuries, 370 wickets (25.31), and 114 catches

SYMCOX, Patrick Leonard

(b. 1960, Kimberley) *Griqualand West, Northern Transvaal, Natal, and South Africa*

A tall right-arm off-spin bowler and useful lower-order hitter, Pat Symcox suddenly emerged as South Africa's leading spin bowler at the age of 33. Although he tends to dig the ball in, he has become an effective wicket-taker with his ability to turn the ball and gain natural bounce from his height. In successive away series against Sri Lanka and Australia, he did not play in a losing Test match and played a vital role in South Africa's dramatic five-run victory at Sydney in January, 1994. In a sense he is an old-fashioned cricketer who likes to enjoy himself both on and off the field but there is no doubting his commitment or character. He is not afraid to lead with his chin and a feature of his game is his appealing, which is both vociferous and convincing. He had to sacrifice his business career as a hospital administrator to achieve his dream of becoming an international cricketer. His father, Roger, was a first-class umpire in South African domestic cricket. In thirteen one-day internationals to 1994 he had taken only 11 wickets (32.18) but had conceded runs at under four an over, (3.89).

First-class career (1977–): 2,604 runs (25.03) including 1 century, 141 wickets (31.46), and 42 catches
Test matches (5): 160 runs (26.66) and 8 wickets (47.87)

TABERER, Henry Melville

(b. 1870, Cape Province; d. 1932, Cape Province) *Oxford University, Essex, Natal, Rhodesia, Transvaal, and South Africa*

Although he represented Oxford against Cambridge at athletics and Rugby football, 'Tabs' Taberer did not win his cricket blue and, after playing for Essex very usefully all-round (in their pre-first-class days) as a good batsman and fast bowler, he returned to South Africa. In his sole Test, the first against Australia at Johannesburg in

1902/3, he was appointed captain, scored 2 and took 1 for 48 (clean-bowling Victor Trumper). An exceedingly powerful man, he once, for a wager, threw a cricket ball 100 yards while standing in a tub.

First-class career (1891–1903): 222 runs (13.05), 22 wickets (20.27), and 5 catches

TANCRED, Augustus Bernard

(b. 1865, Port Elizabeth; d. 1911, Cape Town) *Kimberley, Griqualand West, Transvaal, and South Africa*

The eldest of the well-known brotherhood of five in the earlier annals of South African cricket, Bernard Tancred was regarded by some contemporaries as the first of the 'great' batsmen produced by his country. At least, in the first two Currie Cup Tournaments, 1889/90 and 1890/1, he averaged 74.75 with the bat in the generally rather low-scoring matches. An opening batsman, he had a sure defence and a splendid range of strokes. He was also an outstanding fielder at point. He played in the first-ever Tests against Major Warton's England side. He was unable to visit England in 1894 with the first touring team, owing to the claims of business.

First-class career (1888–98): 708 runs (35.40) including 1 century, 8 wickets (27.50), and 6 catches
Test matches (2): 87 runs (29.00) and 2 catches

TANCRED, Louis Joseph

(b. 1876, Port Elizabeth; d. 1934, Johannesburg) *Transvaal and South Africa*

The best-known of the brotherhood of five, Louis Tancred possessed abundant patience as an opening batsman and could wear down the bowling for others to punish. Although a pronounced crouch spoilt his style, he could hit powerfully, being especially good against fast bowling. He toured England in 1901, 1904, 1907, and 1912, the year of the Triangular Tournament, taking over the captaincy from Frank Mitchell in three of the six Tests on the last visit. At home he played against England in 1905/6 and 1913/14, and Australia in 1902/3. On his four tours he made 3,526 runs (25.18) in first-class matches, his best being in 1904 when he reached 1,217 runs (41.96). Not consistently successful in Tests—he was dismissed for a 'pair' in his first Test in England at Headingley in 1907—he did make 97 in the first innings of his first Test against Australia at Johannesburg in 1902/3, adding 173 for the second wicket with 'Buck' Llewellyn. In the third match against England at Johannesburg in 1905/6 he hit 73. In the Currie Cup he scored 1,231 runs (38.46), including four centuries, being the first man to reach 1,000 runs in the competition.

First-class career (1896–1920): 5,695 runs (27.51), including 11 centuries, 8 wickets (23.75), and 73 catches

Test matches (14): 530 runs (21.20) and 3 catches

TANCRED, Vincent Maximillian

(b. 1875, Port Elizabeth; d. 1904, Johannesburg) *Transvaal and South Africa*

A member of the well-known brotherhood, Vincent Tancred was a useful batsman, bowler, and wicket-keeper whose sole Test appearance—as an opening batsman like his other two brothers who represented their country—was in the first match against England at Johannesburg in 1898/9 when he scored 18 and 7. He took his own life in June 1904, while the South African team was in England.

First-class career (1897–9): 292 runs (24.33)

TAPSCOTT, George Lancelot

(b. 1889, Kimberley; d. 1940, Kimberley) *Griqualand West and South Africa*

A hard-hitting right-handed batsman who enjoyed his cricket, 'Dusty' Tapscott scored 106 quickly against Natal and 111 (in sixty-five minutes) and 60 for Rest of South Africa against Transvaal in 1911/12. But he was not selected for the 1912 England tour and his sole Test appearance was at Durban in the first match against England in 1913/14 when he made 4 and 1 and held 1 catch. He was the elder brother of 'Doodles'.

First-class career (1910–23): 934 runs (26.68) including 2 centuries, and 47 wickets (21.40)

TAPSCOTT, Lionel Eric

(b. 1894, Kimberley; d. 1934, Cape Town) *Griqualand West and South Africa*

A sparkling right-handed batsman and a fleet-footed fielder without a superior in South Africa, 'Doodles' Tapscott first played for his province in 1911/12 and was almost selected for the 1924 England tour. He played twice against England in 1922/3, hitting 50 not out on his début in the fourth match at Johannesburg. He represented South Africa also at lawn tennis.

First-class career (1910–29): 1,759 runs (26.25) including 2 centuries, and 34 wickets (23.91)

Test matches (2): 58 runs (29.00) and 0–2

TAYFIELD, Hugh Joseph

(b. 1929, Durban; d. 1994, Pietermaritzburg) *Natal, Rhodesia, Transvaal, and South Africa*

In the 1950s, Hugh or 'Toey' Tayfield—so-called because of his habit of stubbing his toe into the ground before bowling or receiving a ball—was in the top flight of right-arm off-spin bowlers and a major figure in the renaissance of South African cricket. Tall, trim, and with immaculate black hair, he would kiss his cap for luck before each over. His greatest assets were meticulous accuracy, mastery of subtle flight and pace variations, and the ability to bowl to his field. He hated being hit. He was a very useful lower-order batsman, especially in a crisis, and a brilliant field. A nephew of S. H. Martin (Natal, Rhodesia, and Worcestershire), he made his début at 17 in first-class cricket and was soon among the wickets. He toured England in 1951, 1955, and 1960, and Australasia in 1952/3; and at home played against Australia in 1949/50 and 1957/8, and New Zealand in 1953/4. Four times in the series against Australia in 1949/50 he conceded at least a hundred runs in an innings—in the five matches his 17 wickets were very expensive—but in the first innings of the third match at Durban, he routed the tourists for 75 on a 'sticky dog', capturing 7 for 23 in 8.4 overs. Australia won, however, Tayfield being 'pasted' in the second innings. He established himself in Australasia in 1952/3. Despite breaking a thumb (and falling in love) he took 30 wickets (28.10) in the Tests against Australia as the pivot of the attack, and 84 wickets (26.14) in all first-class matches: two Tests against New Zealand yielded ten wickets. He was the match-winner when South Africa won the second Test at Melbourne by 82 runs, taking 13 for 165. He took 26 wickets (21.84) in the Tests and 143 wickets (15.75) in all first-class matches in England in 1955. During this tour he collected his 100th wicket in only his 22nd Test. In the fourth Test at Headingley he bowled remarkably well on a batsman's wicket taking 9 for 164 in 78.1 overs in the match, South Africa earning an unexpected victory. He took 14 for 126 against Hampshire at Southampton and 13 for 98 against Surrey at The Oval. In the fifth Test on the same ground he hailed an unbroken spell of 53.4 overs, taking 5 for 60. Against England in 1956/7 he was even more dominant, taking 37 wickets (17.18) in the series—the most ever taken by a South African. His returns included 8 for 69 in the second innings at Durban and match figures of 13 for 192 at Johannesburg. When England wanted only 189 to win in the final match at Port Elizabeth, he took 6 for 78 and England lost decisively. On his last tour of England in 1960, however, he was almost innocuous in the Tests, although in all first-class matches he was as dangerous as ever with 123 wickets (21.65). More batsmen were using their feet to him but South African fielding around this period was brilliant. Three times he took 50 or more wickets in a home season, and he twice did the hat-trick. He has taken more wickets for South African teams, including Test teams, than anyone else.

First-class career (1945–63): 3,668 runs (17.30), 864 wickets (21.86), and 149 catches

Test matches (37): 862 runs (16.90), 170 wickets (25.91), and 26 catches

TAYLOR, Alistair Innes

(b. 1925, Johannesburg) *Transvaal and South Africa*

Sometime captain of his province and a sound opening batsman, 'Scotch' Taylor played in one Test against England, the first on the new Wanderers' ground at Johannesburg in 1956/7, scoring 12 and 6.

First-class career (1949–61): 2,717 runs (31.59) including 6 centuries, and 32 wickets (30.87)

TAYLOR, Daniel

(b. 1887, Durban; d. 1957, Durban) *Natal and South Africa*

A sound batsman, Dan Taylor played in the fourth and fifth Tests at Durban and Port Elizabeth respectively against England in 1913/14. In the first, he batted effectively for two scores of 36, when Sydney Barnes with 14 wickets was the menace. He also batted courageously for his province when MCC were beaten by four wickets. His father, Daniel, was a South African cricketing pioneer and his younger brother was the gifted Herbie.

First-class career (1907–20): 394 runs (21.88)
Test matches (2): 85 runs (21.25)

TAYLOR, Herbert Wilfred

(b. 1889, Durban; d. 1973, Cape Town) *Natal, Transvaal, Western Province, and South Africa*

Herbie Taylor was the undisputed master on matting wickets. Of average height, strong in defence and off the back foot, he blossomed as a free-scoring right-handed opening batsman with a perpendicular swing of the bat and all the orthodox scoring strokes: imperturbable, he was one of the most cultured batsmen of his time, his footwork so quick and sure that he was seldom forced into a hurried stroke. He displayed remarkable powers of concentration as a 21-year-old in making 173 for Natal against Griqualand West at Durban in 1910/11 and he hit 250 not out, his career-highest in 1912/13 against Transvaal at Johannesburg in 3 hours 45 minutes. He toured England in 1912, 1924 (captain), and 1929, and Australasia in 1931/2. At home he played against England in 1913/14 (captain), 1922/3 (captain), 1927/8, and 1930/31, and Australia 1921/2 (captain). In his three tours of England, he amassed 5,249 runs (34.30) including seven centuries: his aggregate in 1924 was 1,898 runs (42.17) and in 1929, 1,575 runs (38.41). From the day he hit a fighting 93 against Australia at Lord's in 1912 in nearly 3 hours, he never knew a poor series. Against England in 1922/3 and 1927/8 he made 582 runs (64.66) and 412 runs (41.20) respectively, by far the best batsman each time, in the former series scoring 176 in the first match at Johannesburg (helping in South Africa's then-highest against England), and 101 in the fourth and 102 in the fifth matches respectively: in the latter innings he batted solidly for 270 minutes but he received little support and his country lost the rubber. His 101 in the fourth match at Johannesburg in 1927/8, however, was a major factor in his country's victory. As late as 1929 he averaged 55.25 for the three Tests he played, making 121 at The Oval in the final Test, and adding 214 for the fourth wicket with 'Nummy' Deane after the scoreboard read 20 for 3 in face of a good total by England. In his last full series in Australia in 1931/2, he finished second to Bruce Mitchell in the Tests with 314 runs (31.40), in the fourth match at Adelaide making 78 and 84, only for South Africa to lose convincingly. His final Test was the first-ever by South Africa against New Zealand in 1931/2 at Christchurch. It was the 1913/14 series against England that established his fame. Captain for the first time at 24, he was the only batsman Sydney Barnes (49 wickets from four Tests) could not subdue, making 508 runs (50.80), including a chanceless 109 in the first Test at Durban. When Natal at Durban inflicted the only defeat on MCC (including Barnes), he was dominant with 91 out of 153 (the next highest score being 11), and 100 out of 216 for 6. In one match the mercurial Barnes dashed the ball to the ground: 'It's Taylor, Taylor, Taylor, all the time!' he exclaimed. The ideal model for all aspiring batsmen, in retirement he coached several generations of schoolboys. During the First World War he served in the Royal Field Artillery and the Royal Flying Corps, was commissioned and awarded the MC. His aggregate of runs in Test cricket has only been exceeded in South Africa by Bruce Mitchell and Dudley Nourse junior.

First-class career (1909–36): 13,105 runs (41.86) including 30 centuries, 22 wickets (25.45), and 75 catches
Test matches (42): 2,936 runs (40.77) including 7 centuries, 5 wickets (31.20), and 19 catches

THEUNISSEN, Nicolaas Hendrik Christaan, de Jong

(b. 1867, Cape Colony; d. 1929, Transvaal) *Western Province and South Africa*

A right-arm fastish bowler with a good length and disconcerting off-break and a hitter who often succeeded when others failed, Nicolaas Theunissen played in a sole Test, the second against Major Warton's England side at Cape Town in 1888/9, scoring 0 and 2 not out and taking 0 for 51. In all matches against the touring team that season, he took 34 wickets (10.73).

First-class career (1888–90): 66 runs (22.00) and 20 wickets (12.35)

THORNTON, Dr Patrick George

(b. 1867, Skipton, Yorkshire, England; d. 1939, London, England) *Yorkshire, Middlesex, Scotland, Transvaal, Ceylon, and South Africa*

A much-travelled general medical practitioner, George Thornton was a left-handed batsman and slow left-arm bowler of considerable skill. He played occasionally for Yorkshire and Middlesex, being at his best for the latter county in 1895 when he took 9 for 72 in the match against Gloucestershire (including W.G.). One of the first doctors to volunteer for service when the South African War broke out, he was made head of the Government Hospital at Pretoria and spent 9 years in South Africa, representing Transvaal at cricket. His sole Test appearance was in the first match against Australia at Johannesburg in 1902/3 when he scored 1 not out, took 1 for 20 and held 1 catch.

First-class career (1891–1903): 1,263 runs (22.55) including 1 century, and 32 wickets (31.47)

TOMLINSON, Denis Stanley

(b. 1910, Umtali, Rhodesia; d. 1993) *Rhodesia, Border, and South Africa*

A right-arm slow leg-break bowler and useful batsman, Denis Tomlinson toured England in 1935—the first from Rhodesia to do so—but did not receive many opportunities to shine, though he took 52 wickets (28.53). In his sole Test, the first at Trent Bridge, he scored 9 and took 0 for 38. In a long career, he was a very effective bowler for Rhodesia. On the way home he and Jock Cameron both contracted enteric fever. Cameron died; Tomlinson survived, but he had to miss the next season and was affected for years. His one century was scored as an opening batsman (not his regular position) for Rhodesia against Eastern Province in 1931/2.

First-class career (1927–48): 912 runs (16.88) including 1 century, 156 wickets (28.32), and 17 catches

TRAICOS, Athanaisios John

(b. 1947) *Rhodesia, Zimbabwe, and South Africa*

See Zimbabwe section

TRIMBORN, Patrick Henry Joseph

(b. 1940, Durban) *Natal and South Africa*

A lively right-arm fast-medium bowler and fine close catcher, Pat Trimborn was 26 years old when he made his Test début against Australia in the third match at Durban in 1966/7 to be one of his country's *six* seam bowlers. In the fifth Test at Port Elizabeth, he removed the 'bogeyman' Bob Cowper in the first innings and captured 3 for 12 in 10.1 overs of sustained effort in the second, South Africa winning the match and their first rubber against Australia. His last Test appearance was against Australia in 1969/70. His best season was 1966/7 when he took 36 wickets (18.94) in nine matches. Professional for East Lancashire in 1969, he took 91 wickets (7.89) and scored over 500 runs. He also played for the International Cavaliers.

First-class career (1961–76): 880 runs (11.89), 314 wickets (22.61), and 79 catches
Test matches (4): 13 runs (6.50), 11 wickets (23.36), and 7 catches

TUCKETT, Lindsay

(b. 1919, Durban) *Orange Free State and South Africa*

A right-arm fast-medium bowler with a run of 12 yards, covered with a loping, almost lolling, lazy stride and his eyes half-closed, Lindsay Tuckett had a high, smooth and easy action, and his main danger to the batsmen lay not in his swing but in his pace off the wicket and his tirelessness. He toured England in 1947, and at home played against England in 1948/9. The Second World War robbed him of precious years. In England, his lift, sustained hostility, and in-swingers troubled many batsmen on the prevailing good batting wickets, but a groin injury minimized his effectiveness later in the tour: he captured 69 wickets (25.78) including 15 at high cost in the Tests. He was ineffective in the series in South Africa; but in domestic cricket he took 13 wickets in a match twice—for 66 runs against Griqualand West at Kimberley in 1951/2 and for 105 runs against North-Eastern Transvaal at Bloemfontein in 1946/7. His father 'Len' also played for South Africa.

First-class career (1934–55): 1,496 runs (17.60) including 1 century, 225 wickets (23.07), and 38 catches

Test matches (9): 131 runs (11.90), 19 wickets (51.57), and 9 catches

TUCKETT, Lindsay Richard

(b. 1885, Durban; d. 1963, Bloemfontein) *Orange Free State, Natal, and South Africa*

A persevering right-arm stock bowler who from 1910/11 bowled tirelessly for his state, 'Len' Tuckett did not make his name until 1925/6, and then as a more than useful tail-end batsman: he shared in a century stand for the last wicket in each innings of a match, a unique performance. Playing for Orange Free State against Western Province at Bloemfontein, he added 115 with L. Fuller in the first and 129 with F. Caulfield in the second innings. In the same season he returned his best bowling feat, 13 for 136 against Griqualand West, also at Bloemfontein. In his sole Test, the third match against England at Johannesburg in 1913/14, he made 0 and 0 not out, took 0 for 69 and held 1 catch. In Currie Cup matches, he took 111 wickets (20.06).

First-class career (1909–30): 1,219 runs (18.19) and 167 wickets (30.07)

TWENTYMAN-JONES, Percy Sydney

(b. 1876, Cape Colony; d. 1954, Cape Town) *Western Province and South Africa*

A sound right-handed batsman, Percy Jones top-scored with 33 and 50 (in a total of 80!) for his province against the Australians in 1902/3 on a treacherous pitch, and he was selected for the third Test at Cape Town (his sole Test), when he was dismissed without scoring in either innings. It was enough, however, for he had joined the select band of Springboks who had represented their country at both cricket and Rugby football.

First-class career (1897–1906): 306 runs (18.00)

VAN DER BIJL, Pieter Gerhart Vintcent

(b. 1907, Cape Town; d. 1973, Cape Province) *Oxford University, Western Province, and South Africa*

A lanky 6 ft. 4 in., Pieter van der Bijl won a Rhodes Scholarship to Oxford and was awarded his cricket blue in 1932, making 540 runs (45.00) for the University. A very patient opening batsman, he returned home in time for the 1933/4 season. He scored 603 runs in the 1937/8 Currie Cup matches and the following season was opening batsman for the Test series against England. In the fifth 'Timeless Test' at Durban and despite bodily punishment from Ken Farnes, he made 125—at 17 runs an hour—and 97, sharing in opening stands of 131 with his captain, Alan Melville, and 191 with Bruce Mitchell who opened the second innings. During the Second World War he was badly wounded in Italy and was awarded the MC. His 6 ft. 7 in. son, Vintcent was South Africa's outstanding bowler in the wilderness years.

First-class career (1925–43): 2,692 runs (40.17) including 5 centuries, 5 wickets (31.60), 36 catches, and 2 stumpings

Test matches (5): 460 runs (51.11) including 1 century, and 1 catch

VAN DER BIJL, Vintcent Adriaan Pieter

(b. 1948, Cape Town) *Natal, Transvaal, and Middlesex*

One season for Middlesex in 1980, when he helped them win the Championship and headed the England first-class bowling averages with 85 wickets at 14.72, was sufficient to give the outside world a brief taste of what 'Big Vince' could have achieved during a full international career. At 6 ft.

7 in., built like an ox, he was a giant of a man, prematurely bald, who had been selected for the cancelled tour of Australia in 1971/2. He was brought up in a cricketing tradition second to none as both his father and grandfather played first-class cricket. Only four other families in South Africa have produced three generations of first-class cricketers. Later Vintcent was coached by Trevor Goddard at Natal University and helped further on the way to a great career. A right-arm bowler of fast-medium pace, he caused tremendous problems with his bounce allied to the swing and seam he was always able to impart. He was probably the best bowler of his type in the world at the peak of his career and a South African attack of Le Roux, Procter, Rice, and Van der Bijl would have been formidable indeed. His best first-class return was 14 for 111 but he also had figures of 13 for 53 and 11 for 33: economy was a feature of his bowling as much as his wicket-taking rate. He seldom conceded more than two to the over. He holds the South African record for a first-class season of 75 dismissals (11 more than anybody else) and his tally of 767 first-class wickets is exceeded only by those who had long careers in county cricket. His figures for South Africa alone are more than 100 better than anybody else. He was also a deep thinker on the game who enjoyed success as Natal's captain and later became a respected newspaper columnist.

First-class career (1968–83): 2,269 runs (16.20), 767 wickets (16.54), and 51 catches

---

VAN DER MERWE, Edward Alexander

(b. 1904, Transvaal; d. 1971, Johannesburg) *Transvaal and South Africa*

A versatile sportsman who represented Witwatersrand University at Rugby, soccer, cricket, and athletics and, later, Transvaal at Rugby, Edward van der Merwe was a very good wicket-keeper who toured England in 1929 and Australasia in 1931/2 as second-string to H. B. Cameron. He played in one Test in England and, on Cameron's death, one against Australia in 1935/6.

First-class career (1927–38): 287 runs (10.62) and 64 dismissals (35 c., 29 st.)
Test matches (2): 27 runs (9.00) and 3 catches

VAN DER MERWE, Peter Lawrence

(b. 1937, Cape Province) *Western Province, Eastern Province, and South Africa*

Well-built and bespectacled, Peter van der Merwe made his mark originally as a left-arm slow bowler and his solid, reliable right-handed batsmanship developed rather later: going in late in the middle order, he could defend or attack as the occasion demanded. His fielding was versatile and brilliant. He captained the University of Cape Town and Western Province and—quietly and without fireworks—led his country against England in 1965 and Australia in 1966/7, winning both rubbers, the second being the first-ever victory over Australia. A chartered accountant, he was a thoughtful and shrewd captain who inspired a zealous team-spirit, but unfailingly courteous and an excellent ambassador. He also toured Australasia in 1963/4 and at home played against England in 1964/5, learning much about leadership from Trevor Goddard. He first toured England in 1961 with the Fezelas when he earned the nickname 'Murphy' after the team's sponsor. On his Australian tour he made 506 runs (29.76), but accomplished little in the Tests. His best series as a batsman, by which time he had practically given up bowling, was in 1966/7 when he scored 225 runs (32.14) against Australia, including his Test highest, 76, which he made in the first match at Johannesburg. He became chairman of South Africa's selectors for some of the unofficial international matches against invited teams in the 1980s, remaining in the post for a time when the country returned to Test cricket.

First-class career (1956–68): 4,086 runs (29.18) including 4 centuries, 82 wickets (25.70), and 73 catches
Test matches (15): 533 runs (25.38), 1–22, and 11 catches

VAN RYNEVELD, Clive Berrange

(b. 1928, Cape Town) *Oxford University, Western Province, and South Africa*

An outstandingly versatile sportsman, Clive van Ryneveld was generally regarded as the greatest natural athlete produced by South Africa since 'Tuppy' Owen-Smith. By the time he was 23 he had won nine international caps—four as a Rugby footballer for England (as a brilliant three-quarter) and five as a cricketer for South Africa. Modelling his batting style on that of Herbie Taylor, he was an enterprising batsman with a long reach, and a particularly good player of slow bowling. His leg-breaks were sometimes erratic but often unplayable. He was an outstanding field anywhere because of his quick reflexes. He toured England in 1951 and at home played against New Zealand in 1953/4, England in

1956/7 (captain) and Australia in 1957/8 (captain for four Tests). Before touring England he had earned a double blue. For South Africa on his England tour, he made 983 runs (29.78), including a faultless 150 against Yorkshire at Bramall Lane, his career-highest. His best innings in the Tests was at Headingley when he hit 83, adding 198 for the second wicket with Eric Rowan. Against New Zealand in 1953/4 he was consistency personified, with a highest score of 68 not out, averaging 46.80 for 234 runs, besides taking 10 wickets (30.50). By this time, he was hard at work on his profession, in due course gaining admission as an advocate at the Cape Bar. He was able to lead his country, however, in four Tests of a shared series with England in 1956/7, his boyish enthusiasm permeating to his players. Trevor Bailey, indeed, recalled how, in the middle of his Test match he admonished one of his players with a schoolmasterly phrase, 'Pull your socks up, Tony Pithey.' In his final series, against Australia the following season, South Africa lost 3–0. He retired from first-class cricket and entered politics, being elected to the House of Assembly.

First-class career (1946–63): 4,803 runs (30.20) including 4 centuries, 206 wickets (30.24), and 71 catches

Test matches (19): 724 runs (26.81), 17 wickets (39.47), and 14 catches

VAN ZYL, Cornelius Johannes Petrus Gerhardus

(b. 1961, Bloemfontein) *Orange Free State and Glamorgan*

Corrie van Zyl, a tall right-arm seam bowler, was literally plucked off the beach where he was holidaying with his family to make his international début in 1992 as a replacement for the injured Brian McMillan. It was rather appropriate that the opponents should be the West Indies, many of whose stars learned their cricket on the beach front. In the circumstances too much should not have been expected of his two limited-overs appearances. Subsequently, persistent back trouble brought a premature end to his career. At his best in the mid-1980s, he bowled quickly enough to share the new ball with Garth le Roux in a rebel series against the Australian XI. As he lost pace, he relied more on swing and seam for his considerable success and the Free State attack of the late 1980s and early 1990s of Allan Donald, Franklyn Stephenson, and van Zyl was outstanding by any standards, leading to that province becoming South African champions for the

first time. For Glamorgan, however, he was a disappointment. He was in the party which visited Barbados in 1992 for a one-off Test match, but was not chosen for the match.

First-class career (1981–   ): 2,312 runs (18.06) including 1 century, 349 wickets (23.38), and 41 catches

VARNALS, George Derek

(b. 1935, Durban) *Natal, Eastern Province, Transvaal, and South Africa*

A mature right-handed batsman and fine close-in field, Derek Varnals scored 111 in $4\frac{1}{4}$ hours when several of his colleagues were in trouble for Natal against MCC at Durban in 1964/5, and subsequently appeared in the Test series without enhancing his career. His best seasons were 1957/8 when he made 519 runs (51.90) and 1964/5, 447 runs (40.63)

First-class career (1955–65): 2,628 runs (30.20) including 4 centuries

Test matches (3): 97 runs (16.16) and 0–2

VILJOEN, Kenneth George

(b. 1910, Griqualand West; d. 1974, Transvaal) *Griqualand West, Orange Free State, Transvaal, and South Africa*

A youthful prodigy who played his first game for Griqualand West at 16, Ken Viljoen became a confident and stylish right-handed batsman, possessing a remarkably sound defence, and very strong on his legs. He was also a brilliant outfield. He toured Australasia in 1931/2, England in 1935 and 1947, and at home played against England in 1930/1, 1938/9, and 1948/9, and Australasia in 1935/6. His first Test success was 111 in the third Test at Melbourne in 1931/2 when all his colleagues made double-figures but only he exceeded 47—in the next two Tests he made 0, 1, 1, and 0! On his first England tour in 1935 he ended the wettish season in a blaze of run-getting, heading the averages with 1,454 runs (46.90) which included five centuries; 280 runs came in four Tests, including 124 at Old Trafford when runs were badly needed. Twelve years later in England, he had a rather similar record—1,441 runs (49.68), including six centuries and 270 in five Tests, his best effort again being at Old Trafford when he made 93, with runs still badly needed. He was rather disappointing against the varied attacks of Australia in 1935/6 and England in 1938/9. He was consistently successful in the Currie Cup competition, making 2,658 runs

(59.07), his best domestic season being 1936/7 with 743 runs (92.87). The highest of his three double-centuries was 215 for Griqualand West against Western Province at Kimberley in 1929/30. Ken Viljoen was a very significant figure in the administration of the game.

First-class career (1926–49): 7,964 runs (43.28) including 23 centuries, 29 wickets (24.89), and 50 catches
Test matches (27): 1,365 runs (28.43) including 2 centuries, 0–23, and 5 catches

VINCENT, Cyril Leverton

(b. 1902, Johannesburg; d. 1968, Durban) *Transvaal and South Africa*

In the tradition of top-class left-arm spin bowlers, and a competent batsman, Cyril Vincent flourished in provincial competitions and in Tests both at home and abroad, but for 12 years he never appeared in a Currie Cup match because his employer refused to allow him the time to play. After two feats for Transvaal against MCC in 1927/8—18 wickets from two games and, subsequently, 23 wickets (22.47) and 134 runs (33.50) in the Tests—he took leave again to play in two trial games at Durban and was selected for the 1929 England tour, when he took 13 wickets from four Tests and made a belligerent 60 in the third Test at Headingley. He toured Australasia in 1931/2 and England again in 1935, and at home played against England in 1930/1. In the latter series, he took 18 wickets (20.77), which included 6 for 51 in the first innings of the fifth match at Durban. On his second visit to England, at 33 the veteran of the side he took 111 wickets (20.19) in all matches, including 18 (33.38) from four Tests. On this his last tour, he continued to be a model of accuracy, highly skilful in flighting and spinning the ball. In the third Test at Headingley, he took 8 for 149 in the match, all recognized batsmen. He was sometime chairman of the South African and Transvaal selection committees. He also once represented South Africa at baseball against Australia.

First-class career (1920–43): 1,582 runs (17.97), 293 wickets (23.91), and 68 catches
Test matches (25): 526 runs (20.23), 84 wickets (31.32), and 27 catches

VINTCENT, Charles Henry

(b. 1866, Cape Colony; d. 1943, Cape Province) *Griqualand West and Transvaal*

An Old Carthusian and left-handed both as batsman and bowler, Charles Vintcent played in the first three Tests for South Africa, against England in 1888/9 and 1891/2, without distinguishing himself.

First-class career (1888–1905): 119 runs (11.90) and 11 wickets (33.09)
Test matches (3): 27 runs (4.50), 4 wickets (48.25), and 1 catch

VOGLER, Albert Edward Ernest

(b. 1876, Cape Province; d. 1946, Pietermaritzburg) *Natal, Eastern Province, Transvaal, Middlesex, Aberdeenshire, and South Africa*

Bert Vogler was a high-class right-arm leg-break and googly bowler. After a jerky approach his delivery was very difficult to read and he could vary his stock-in-trade with a top-spinner and a deceptive slow yorker. A useful hard-hitting batsman, he was also a good fielder. On his first-class début at 27 for Natal against Transvaal at Johannesburg in 1903/4 in the Currie Cup competition, he took 5 for 86 (four of them top-class batsmen). He turned professional, came to England and joined the MCC ground staff, bowling several times in MCC matches with brilliant success. He intended qualifying for Middlesex but appeared only once for the county in 1906, scoring 87 and taking 5 for 91, as the county already had two colonial players. There was some friction and Sir Abe Bailey found a position for him in South Africa. He met with startling success in domestic cricket. He took all 10 for 26 in 12 overs (16 for 38 in the match) all in one day for Eastern Province against Griqualand West at Johannesburg in 1906/7. A regular member of South Africa's winning team against England in 1905/6, though he only took 9 wickets in the five Tests (but scored 137 runs at 34.25), he toured England in 1907 as one of the 'googly quartet' and was called by England's captain, R. E. Foster, 'the best bowler in the world'. Second to Reggie Schwarz in the averages, he took 119 wickets (15.62) and scored 723 runs (21.26): in the three Tests he was supreme with 15 wickets (19.66). In the first Test at Lord's, he captured 7 for 128 in the total of 428. Against England in 1909/10 he was at his peak with 36 wickets (21.75) in the five Tests, a record that stood until Hugh Tayfield broke it 47 years later. He took 12 for 181 in the first and 8 for 207 in the third matches, both at Johannesburg. But in Australia in 1910/11 he fell away considerably. Later he was associated with various Scottish, Irish, and English clubs and in 1912 even appeared against the South African tourists for an Irish club.

First-class career (1903–12): 2,375 runs (20.29)
including 1 century, 393 wickets (18.27), and 81
catches
Test matches (15): 340 runs (17.00), 64 wickets
(22.73), and 20 catches

WADE, Herbert Frederick

(b. 1905, Durban; d. 1980, Johannesburg) *Natal and
South Africa*

Herby Wade was a tower of strength to Natal
as a dashing right-handed batsman and captain.
In representative cricket it was his gift of leadership that was his greatest asset. Moreover, he
was a fearless close-in field. He played in ten
Tests, against England in 1935 and Australia in
1935/6, in each as captain. At Lord's in 1935
he led the eleven that registered the first-ever
victory in a Test in England. On this tour, he
made 1,042 runs (28.94) and showed an understanding knack of being able to 'read' the character of turf pitches. He inspired loyalty
amongst all his team. His experience against
Australia, however, was not quite so happy. For
some years he played cricket and Rugby football in Yorkshire. He was elder brother of
W. W. His highest score was 190 for Natal
against Eastern Province in 1936/7. In all he
scored 1,912 Currie Cup runs (44.46).
First-class career (1924–37): 3,858 runs (35.39)
including 9 centuries, and 50 catches
Test matches (10): 327 runs (20.43) and 4 catches

WADE, Walter Wareham

(b. 1914, Durban) *Natal and South Africa*

A very competent wicket-keeper/batsman, 'Billy'
Wade was unable to tour, but kept wicket at
home against England in 1938/9, and Australia in
1949/50. When England amassed 559 for 9 wickets declared in the second Test at Cape Town in
1938/9, he did not allow a single bye, an outstanding performance. In the 1948/9 series, he
made 407 runs (50.87), including 125 in the fifth
Test at Port Elizabeth. He had eight victims (one
caught, seven stumped) for Natal against Griqualand West at Durban in 1947/8. His highest score
was 208 against Eastern Province at Pietermaritzburg in 1939/40. He became an umpire and
'stood' in Test cricket.
First-class career (1935–50): 2,859 runs (48.45)
including 8 centuries
Test matches (11): 511 runs (28.38) including 1
century, and 17 dismissals (15 c., 2 st.)

WAITE, John Henry Bickford

(b. 1930, Johannesburg) *Eastern Province,
Transvaal, and South Africa*

Perhaps the best wicket-keeper/batsman to
have represented South Africa, John Waite was
a quiet, self-effacing perfectionist, neat though
relatively tall for his trade, taking the slow
bowlers unobtrusively and efficiently and capable of the spectacular diving catch standing
back. As a right-handed batsman he was very
sound defensively, had a complete range of
strokes despite a limited backlift, and was particularly strong off his legs. His powers of concentration were intense. He is the only player
to have appeared in 50 Tests for South Africa
and his representative career was spread
between 1951 and 1965. He toured England in
1951, 1955, and 1960, Australasia in 1952/3 and
1963/4, and at home played against New Zealand in 1953/4 and 1961/2, England in 1956/7
and 1964/5, and Australia in 1957/8. On his
first England tour he came as reserve 'keeper,
but was selected for the first Test at Trent
Bridge and never looked back, opening the batting on his début (later he strengthened the
middle order) and hitting 76. He scored 1,011
runs (33.70) on this tour and had 148 victims
(124 caught and 24 stumped). He had the
record 26 dismissals against New Zealand in
1961/2; 23 against New Zealand in 1953/4; and
16, 15, and 15 against England in 1956/7 and
1955 and against Australia in 1957/8 respectively. No other South African 'keeper has had
as many, either in Tests or first-class cricket
generally. In the fifth Test at Melbourne in
1952/3 he did not concede a bye in a total of
520. In two Tests against New Zealand, the
fifth at Port Elizabeth in 1953/4 and the third
Test at Cape Town in 1961/2, he had seven
dismissals. His first Test century was 113 in the
third Test at Old Trafford in 1955, a very
patient effort, after a middle-order collapse. He
headed the averages and scored most runs
against Australia in 1957/8 with 362 runs
(40.22), including 115 in the first match at
Johannesburg and 134 in the third match at
Durban when he added 231 for the third
wicket with Jackie McGlew. In England in 1960
he headed the Test averages with 38.14, though
his highest score was only 77. His fourth and
last Test century was 101 in the second match
against New Zealand at Johannesburg in
1961/2. Prolific in Australasia in 1963/4, he
scored 552 runs (42.46) in all first-class

matches; and his last dominant role as a batsman in Tests was in the fourth match against England at Johannesburg in 1964/5 when, in making 64, he added 157 for the fifth wicket with Tony Pithey in 3 hours 40 minutes, a South African record.

First-class career (1948–65): 9,812 runs (35.04) including 23 centuries, 511 dismissals (427 c., 84 st.)

Test matches (50): 2,405 runs (30.44) including 4 centuries, and 141 dismissals (124 c., 17 st.)

WALTER, Kenneth Alexander

(b. 1939, Johannesburg) *Transvaal and South Africa*

A right-arm fast-medium bowler who took 165 wickets (19.55) in the Currie Cup competition in 9 years, Ken Walter played in two Tests at home against New Zealand in 1961/2.

First-class career (1957–66): 594 runs (13.50) and 217 wickets (21.22)

Test matches (2): 11 runs (3.66), 6 wickets (32.83), and 3 catches

WARD, Thomas Alfred

(b. 1887, Rawalpindi, India; d. 1936, Transvaal) *Transvaal and South Africa*

A wicket-keeper who was at times badly knocked about, and a dogged batsman with a strong defence, Tommy Ward toured England in 1912 and 1924, and at home played against England in 1913/14 and 1922/3, and Australia in 1921/2. While opening the batting he made a rugged 64 in the fourth Test against England at Johannesburg in 1922/3 and 50 in the fourth Test at Old Trafford. He was electrocuted while working in a gold-mine.

First-class career (1909–27): 1,635 runs (15.42) and 175 dismissals (107 c., 68 st.)

Test matches (23): 459 runs (13.90) and 32 dismissals (19 c., 13 st.)

WATKINS, John Cecil

(b. 1923, Durban) *Natal and South Africa*

Of lean and hungry appearance, John Watkins was a right-handed batsman with a fine range of scoring strokes—his batting, like the man himself, was cavalier and joyous. He was a medium-paced swing bowler who could keep all but the most gifted batsmen quiet, and a fine slip fielder. He toured Australasia in 1952/3, and played at home against Australia in 1949/50, New Zealand in 1953/4 and England in 1956/7. The pinnacle of his career was the tour of Australasia with the team of 'no hopers' who performed so valiantly. He made 679 runs (28.29) and took 31 wickets (27.74) on the tour. Supported by tigerish fielding, he secured 4 for 41 in the first Test at Brisbane; hit 76 in the fourth at Adelaide; and in the fifth at Melbourne, despite the large Australian total of 520, he struck hard for 92 and 50, and was prominent in the victory by six wickets. In this series, he scored 408 runs (31.38) and took 16 wickets (29.06); and in the first Test against New Zealand at Wellington, which South Africa won by an innings, he captured 4 for 22 in 23.5 overs in the second innings. With Neil Adcock, he broke the back of New Zealand's first innings of the fifth Test in 1953/4 at Port Elizabeth, taking 4 for 34, and ensured victory by adding 107 in 75 minutes with Ken Funston.

First-class career (1946–58): 2,158 runs (24.80) including 2 centuries, and 96 wickets (28.52)

Test matches (15): 612 runs (23.53), 29 wickets (28.13), and 12 catches

WESLEY, Colin

(b. 1937, Durban) *Natal and South Africa*

A squat left-handed opening batsman and a brilliant field 'Tich' Wesley was chosen for the 1960 England tour for his aggression, but he proved uncertain against the best bowlers. Brian Statham dismissed him first ball in each innings of the third Test at Trent Bridge. His career-highest was 131 for Natal against New Zealand at Pietermaritzburg in 1961/2.

First-class career (1956–66): 1,892 runs (27.02) including 3 centuries, 15 wickets (23.60), and 20 catches

Test matches (3): 49 runs (9.80) and 1 catch

WESSELS, Kepler Christoffel

(b. 1957, Bloemfontein) *Orange Free State, Northern Transvaal, Western Province, Sussex, Queensland, Eastern Province, Australia, and South Africa*

A left-hand batsman of stoic and courageous qualities, Kepler Wessels was followed by controversy wherever his cricket career took him. However, by the time he had finished distinguished careers for both Australia and South Africa, he had earned the respect of even his harshest critics. A staunch Christian of the

Dutch Reformed Church, he was a member of a tightly-knit Afrikaner family, gifted also at tennis and boxing. Fair-haired, he had a pugilist's broken nose throughout his career and he would tell his teams in later years that what matters is not how often you fall, but how often you rise. It was evident that a cricketer of unusual character had arrived on the scene when he made his first-class début at age 16 for Orange Free State against Northern Transvaal whilst still at Grey College. He was flattened by the second ball he received but he got up, bloody but unbowed, refused to leave the field and completed a useful début. After a good season in 1976/7 under the tutelage of Eddie Barlow at Western Province, when he made 511 runs at an average of 36, he decided to look for an international future. He played for Sussex, 1976–80, scoring 1,800 runs (52.94) in 1979 and 1,562 runs (65.08) in 1980. In his first season in Australia, 1978/9, he played World Series Cricket and for the next season was an outstandingly successful opener for Queensland, scoring 1,094 runs (60.77) in 1981/2. He made his home in Brisbane and married his Australian wife, Sally. In a memorable Test début for Australia at Brisbane in 1982, he made 162 against England, falling only five short of the début record for an Ashes Test. Coincidentally, that series featured the Ashes début of another South African-born cricketer, Allan Lamb, who had been Wessels's colleague at Western Province in 1977. In all he was to play 24 Tests for Australia up to 1985, making centuries against four different countries. He had not always been regarded as truly Australian in some quarters and, when he also got accused of recruiting players for that country's rebel tour to South Africa, he decided he had had enough and returned home. He played for Australia in the second 'rebel' series of 1986/7 and built a new career for himself as captain and driving force behind the resurgence of Eastern Province, taking them to their first ever Currie Cup success in 1988/9 and to a clean sweep of all three South African domestic trophies the following season. Even in South Africa, controversy pursued him when he withdrew from the South African team against Mike Gatting's rebels in 1990, claiming he felt uncomfortable playing with team-mates who resented his presence. The SACU had cut his qualification period from four years to two and there was a strong feeling among South Africa's leading players of the time that he should not be let back into the national squad so quickly. His greatest hour for South Africa was still to come, however, when the selectors sacked previous captains Clive Rice and Jimmy Cook and gave him the honour of leading a unified South Africa to their first ever World Cup tournament in 1992. Apart from Peter Kirsten, he was given a team of youngsters and international greenhorns and this was where the toughness of Wessels was seen at its best. They stunned the world when they thrashed Australia by nine wickets in their opening round robin match at Sydney and went on to be unlucky losers of a controversial semi-final against England. This was followed by a one-off Test defeat against West Indies when South Africa came desperately close to becoming the first side to win at Bridgetown in 47 years. Wessels then led South Africa in unbeaten series against India, Sri Lanka, Australia (twice), and England although the last three ended in 1–1 draws. Throughout his career, Wessels displayed a single-purposed determination and fortitude to overcome whatever barriers were put in his path to reach the top in international cricket—and those barriers were huge, stretching from politics outside the game to the politics within. By the end of his career he was playing on courage alone, as his knees became irreparable after more than a dozen operations. The keynote of his game and his captaincy was discipline, with a total focus on cricket to the exclusion of everything else, but he found willing disciples among his team, who followed him unquestioningly. His discipline was best reflected in his own batting where he cut out any shot that represented a threat to his occupation of the crease. More than any other South African batsman of the united era, he made a scientific study of the art of batsmanship, presenting a resolute and uncompromising defence to the good deliveries but being quick to exploit any delivery that strayed off line or length. His favourite shots were the pull and the cut although he was also a very effective driver. Few would regard him as an attractive batsman but most would admire his effectiveness. It was typical of the man that he practised karate and boxing to improve his reaction skills in facing fast bowling and, towards the end of his career, he became a successful boxing promoter in his home town of Port Elizabeth. In 103 one-day internationals for his two countries he scored 3,224 runs (35.04).

First-class career (1973–94): 21,318 runs (49.80) including 55 centuries, 12 wickets (46.33), and 232 catches
Test matches (Australia, 24): 1,761 runs (42.95) including 4 centuries, 0–42, and 18 catches. (South Africa, 16): 1,027 runs (38.03) including 2 centuries, and 12 catches. (Overall: 40): 2,788 runs (41.00) including 6 centuries, and 30 catches

WESTCOTT, Richard John

(b. 1927, Lisbon, Portugal) *Western Province and South Africa*

Dick Westcott was a stylish and fluent right-handed opening batsman who played his best cricket at Newlands: he was also a useful medium-paced change-bowler. Early in his career he was seriously injured in a car accident, but despite considerable damage to his left arm, he fought his way back to health and international honours. He played in Tests at home against New Zealand in 1953/4 and Australia in 1957/8. In his initial Test, the third at Cape Town in 1953/4, he scored 62 after New Zealand had forced South Africa to follow on.

First-class career (1949–62): 3,225 runs (36.23) including 4 centuries, and 10 wickets (31.40)
Test matches (5): 166 runs (18.44) and 0–22

WHITE, Gordon Charles

(b. 1882, Cape Province; d. 1918, Gaza, Palestine) *Transvaal and South Africa*

Around 1910 Gordon White was considered to be South Africa's leading right-handed batsman. He had a sound defence and perfect timing, besides possessing a great variety of strokes, notably clean drives to both sides and crisp late cuts. He was also one of his country's battery of leg-break and googly bowlers. He never quite lived up to his reputation as a batsman on tour in England in 1904, 1907, and 1912. On his first visit to England, he scored 773 runs (29.73) in first-class matches and did the hat-trick against Kent at Canterbury, but three years later he found the prevailing soft wickets not to his liking. His experience was similar in 1912. He took 56 wickets (14.73) in 1907, as one of the googly quartet who carried most before them (except in the Tests). At home in 1905/6, however, when South Africa first won a Test rubber, he headed the batting with 437 runs (54.62), hitting 147 in 4 hours at Johannesburg in the third match when the rubber was decided; and he averaged 35.50 in the 1909/10 Tests, making 118 in the second match at Dur-

ban. In Currie Cup matches he averaged 38.10 with the bat and took 27 wickets. Gordon White died of war wounds a month before the Armistice.

First-class career (1902–12): 3,740 runs (27.70) including 4 centuries, 155 wickets (20.05), and 46 catches
Test matches (17): 872 runs (30.06) including 2 centuries, 9 wickets (33.44), and 10 catches

WILKINS, Christopher Peter

(b. 1944, King William's Town) *Border, Eastern Province, Natal, and Derbyshire*

A powerfully built right-hand all-rounder, Chris Wilkins would have been a must for any South African World Cup squad in the 1970s. And it would have needed the presence of Barlow and Richards to keep him out of Test line-up. An opening batsman, he always believed that attack was the best form of defence and it was a common sight to see him loft the new ball on the up to the long-on and long-off boundaries. He made the fastest century of the 1970 England season, scoring 120 in 73 minutes for the Rest of the World at Scarborough and he once enabled Eastern Province to score a batting bonus point (175 runs or more) on the first morning of a Currie Cup match. He bowled an effective out-swinger at above medium-pace and, to complete his repertoire as a useful cricketer, he seldom missed anything in the slips.

First-class career (1962–83): 10,966 runs (32.63) including 18 centuries, 142 wickets (35.30), and 217 dismissals (211 c., 6 st.)

WILLOUGHBY, Joseph Thomas

(b. 1874, Aldershot, Hampshire, England; d. c.1955) *Western Province and South Africa*

A useful bowler, Joseph Willoughby played for South Africa in two Tests against England in 1895/6, which were his only first-class matches. In his first match at Port Elizabeth he dismissed George Lohmann for 'a pair', and when he batted George did the same to him.

Test matches (2): 8 runs (2.00) and 6 wickets (26.50)

WIMBLE, Clarence Skelton

(b. 1864, Cape Colony; d. 1930, Johannesburg)
Transvaal and South Africa

Generally regarded as a consistent run-getter and superior field, Clarence Wimble's sole Test was against England at Cape Town in 1891/2 when he did not score in either innings or hold a catch.

First-class career (1890–2): 108 runs (27.00)

WINSLOW, Paul Lyndhurst

(b. 1929, Johannesburg) *Sussex, Transvaal, Rhodesia, and South Africa*

One of the most effective right-handed hitters seen in South African cricket, Paul Winslow once hit 'Toey' Tayfield for two consecutive sixes in a Currie Cup match and was caught by the same spectator each time. Six feet three inches and lean, this aggressive batsman played a few games for Sussex in 1949, having been coached by 'Patsy' Hendren, but was unable to qualify and, on returning to South Africa, was selected for two Tests against the 1949/50 Australians because of his bold methods and also his exceptionally versatile fielding. He was not a success, however. Touring England in 1955, though his overall figures were rather moderate—785 runs (23.68)—he hit magnificently in two matches at Old Trafford. Against Lancashire, he struck 40 off eight balls, including 30 off an over of Jack Ikin's, and in the third Test, coming in after a severe middle-order collapse, he scored 108 in 3 hours 10 minutes, reaching his century with a hit over the sightscreen, one of the biggest ever seen on the ground—before waving joyfully to his fellows in the pavilion. He added 171 with John Waite for the sixth wicket. During this tour, he hit no fewer than twenty-seven sixes. In his first match for Rhodesia, he hit 81 and 139 against Australia at Salisbury in 1957/8, showing greater discernment in his selection of balls to punish; but he did not represent his country again. He also excelled in golf, tennis, Rugby, and hockey.

First-class career (1949–62): 2,755 runs (23.34) including 2 centuries, 1 wicket (61.00), and 85 catches

Test matches (5): 186 runs (20.66) including 1 century, and 1 catch

WYNNE, Owen Edgar

(b. 1919, Johannesburg; d. 1975, Cape Province)
Transvaal, Western Province, and South Africa

A solid right-handed opening batsman, Owen Wynne was primarily an on-side player. He scored his career-highest of 200 not out for Transvaal against Border at Johannesburg in 1946/7. In the first match of MCC's tour in 1948/9, he made 108 for Western Province at Cape Town and, a few days later on the same ground, 105 for Cape Province against the tourists. Selected for the first three Tests, he accomplished nothing until the third at Cape Town when he scored 50 and 44—and was then dropped from the side! The following season he was the only man to face Ray Lindwall with confidence, while batting for a South African XI at Salisbury, and played in three Tests against Australia, but failed to distinguish himself. He was tragically lost at sea when yachting.

First-class career (1937–59): 2,268 runs (37.18) including 7 centuries

Test matches (6): 219 runs (18.25) and 3 catches

YACHAD, Mandy

(b. 1960, Johannesburg) *Transvaal and Northern Transvaal*

Mandy Yachad was a busy right-hand opening batsman, smallish, and quick on his feet, who excelled against fast bowling, largely because of his ability to pull and hook the quickest. This gained him an unofficial début for South Africa against the West Indian XI in 1984 when he made a brilliant century in a limited overs match on the pacey Wanderers strip. His best season did not come until 1990/1 when he made 994 runs at an average of 49.70. This proved to be the perfect run to gain selection for the historic India tour in November 1991. In spite of playing only one of the three limited-overs internationals, he was not summoned for international duty again. He also represented South Africa at hockey.

First-class career (1978–94): 6,365 runs (34.78) including 14 centuries, 1 wicket (26.00), and 76 catches

ZULCH, John William

(b. 1886, Transvaal; d. 1924, Natal) *Transvaal and South Africa*

An excellent right-handed opening batsman, with a wide range of strokes and sound defence, a very good field and useful change-bowler, 'Billy' Zulch, surprisingly, never came to England, his sole overseas tour being to Australia in 1910/11. At home he played against England in 1909/10 and 1913/14 and Australia in 1921/2. In Australia he scored 354 Test runs (39.33), including 105 in the third Test at Adelaide. In the fifth match at Sydney he made 150, which prevented a runaway Australian victory. Against England in 1913/14 he made 239 runs (39.83) in four Tests, sharing two century opening stands with Herbie Taylor. He scored an invaluable 80 in the first Test against Australia at Durban in 1921/2. In the next match, at Johannesburg, he was dismissed 'hit wicket' in an unusual manner—a splinter from his bat was sliced off by a ball from Ted McDonald and dislodged a bail. Consistently successful with Transvaal, in Currie Cup matches alone he averaged 59.33. He died young after a severe nervous breakdown.

First-class career (1908–24): 3,558 runs (41.85) including 9 centuries

Test matches (16): 985 runs (32.83) including 2 centuries, 0–28, and 4 catches

Sri Lanka

AHANGAMA, Franklyn Saliya

(b. 1959, Colombo) *Sinhalese and Sri Lanka*

A right-arm medium-paced bowler and left-hand tail-end batsman, Saliya Ahangama made a sensational début in Test cricket against India in the first Test of the 1985/6 series at Colombo, taking a wicket with his fourth ball. Remarkably, too, he had only made his first-class début for the Sri Lankan Colts, also against India, two weeks earlier. He had match figures of 5 for 109 in his first Test and at the end of that triumphant series topped the bowling averages with 18 wickets at 19.33, including 5 for 52 in the third Test at Kandy. He was selected for the subsequent tour of Pakistan but did not play a Test and injuries restricted his opportunities on tours of England in 1988 and 1991. He remained an effective bowler for Sinhalese Sports Club.

First-class career (1985–92): 211 runs (12.41), 115 wickets (19.15), and 10 catches
Test matches (3): 11 runs (5.50), 18 wickets (19.33), and 1 catch

AMALEAN, Kaushik Nagindas

(b. 1965, Colombo) *Colombo and Sri Lanka*

Bowling right-arm in-swing, and batting right-handed, Kaushik Amalean made a surprise Test début in the third match against Pakistan in Colombo in 1985/6, being called up as a late replacement. His figures of 3 for 59 suggested that he was not out of his depth at that level and his pace certainly impressed members of the England B team earlier in the season, one of whom likened him to a young Imran Khan; yet

his only other Test match was played in Perth two years later. Sri Lanka were beaten by an innings, but Amalean took a highly creditable 4 for 97. In seven one-day internationals he took 7 wickets (27.42) and scored 15 runs (7.50).

First-class career (1985–8): 13 runs (6.50), 13 wickets (27.84), and 2 catches
Test matches (2): 9 runs (9.00), 7 wickets (22.28), and 1 catch

AMERASINGHE, Mudalige Jayantha Gamini

(b. 1954, Colombo) *Nomads and Sri Lanka*

A phlegmatic, bearded, left-arm spinner who came into Test cricket at the age of 30, Amerasinghe made more of a mark with the bat than the ball on his Test début against New Zealand at Kandy in 1983/4 when, batting at number 11, he put on a Sri Lankan record tenth-wicket score of 60 with Vinodhan John in the first innings and top-scored with 34. On his first-class début in the same season, he returned match figures of 10 for 130 for the Sri Lankan Board's President's XI against Zimbabwe. In his second and last Test, he bowled tidily to take 2 for 73 against New Zealand at Colombo.

First-class career (1983–9): 104 runs (11.55) and 41 wickets (16.19)
Test matches (2): 54 runs (18.00), 3 wickets (50.00), and 3 catches

ANURASIRI, Sangarange Don

(b. 1966, Panadura) *Panadura and Sri Lanka*

An accurate left-arm spinner, who was not frightened to give the ball some air, and a right-hand tail-ender, Don Anurasiri served a hard apprenticeship as an 18-year-old on the slow wickets in England during the 1984 tour, his one wicket costing 336 runs, before he made his Test début two years later against Pakistan in the second Test in Colombo. In a match dominated by seam bowlers, he bowled only four overs, but in the third Test, though he did not take a wicket, his 15 overs cost just nine runs. Able and willing to give the ball a good tweak, he played in the first and last unofficial 'Tests' against the England B team in 1985/6, taking 2 for 207 in total. He returned to England in 1988 and 1991. A capable fielder with a strong arm, and a useful tail-end batsman, he performed reliably in all forms of cricket until losing an argument with the Sri Lankan Cricket Board over a controversial fitness test. In 45 one-day internationals to 1994 he had taken 32 wickets (45.75).

First-class career (1984–): 776 runs (11.24), 226 wickets (23.84), and 3 catches
Test matches (17): 88 runs (5.17), 37 wickets (38.97), and 3 catches

ATAPATTU, Marvan Samson

(b. 1970, Kalutara) *Sinhalese and Sri Lanka*

Probably the greatest disappointment in the short Test history of Sri Lanka, Marvan Atapattu is without doubt one of the most brilliant stroke-players in the country. Yet this talented right-hander, excellent fielder in the covers, and useful right-arm leg-spinner has been able to score only a single run in six Test innings. Rumour has it that even that single was a leg-bye—but for the umpire's charity. This amiable man scores heavily on the domestic circuit, however, and on the tour to England in 1990, he made three unbeaten half-centuries against counties, going in at number seven, and was second in the tour batting averages. The next year Sri Lanka toured England again for the customary single Test, but Atapattu had a poor trip, registering only a single fifty. Most observers feel that a suspect temperament has shackled him, but the enigmatic saga of a potential champion may not yet be over.

First-class career (1988–): 2,729 runs (44.73) including 7 centuries, 14 wickets (40.14), and 35 catches
Test matches (3): 1 run (0.16)

DASSANAYAKE, Pubudu Bhatiya

(b. 1970, Kandy) *Bloomfield and Sri Lanka*

After pussyfooting for almost a decade with the all-important post of wicket-keeper, the national selectors picked Dassanayake as a specialist with few pretensions as a batsman. Picked for the first time against the touring South Africans in 1993, he confirmed their faith in him. Stumping the last three South Africans consecutively to end the innings, he equalled the previous record-holder, Mahes Goonetilleke, whose career tally—in five Tests—was also three stumpings. Then, sent in at number three to counter the rampaging fast bowling pair, Donald and Schultz, Dassanayake batted doggedly. A quiet and efficient practitioner, who works very hard at his profession, he has not, however, managed a score higher than 36.

First-class career (1989–): 760 runs (19.48) and 42 dismissals (29 c., 13 st.)
Test matches (11): 196 runs (13.06) and 24 dismissals (19 c., 5 st.)

De ALWIS, Ronald Guy

(b. 1959, Colombo) *Sinhalese and Sri Lanka*

Bearded and tall for a wicket-keeper, Guy de Alwis made his début along with six other Sri Lankans, against New Zealand at Christchurch in 1982/3, taking 1 catch and scoring 0 and 3. He played in the inaugural Test against Australia at Kandy and then against the New Zealanders in 1983/4, taking nine dismissals in the three Tests. He was a useful lower- middle-order right-handed batsman, but lost his Test place, after being injured just before the Lord's Test on the 1984 tour, to Amal Silva, a more accomplished batsman but an inferior wicket-keeper. He was recalled, however, for the second Test of the 1985/6 series against Pakistan, taking four catches in the match and another four in the third Test, both at Colombo. He toured India in 1986/7 and Australia the following season.

First-class career (1982–90): 673 runs (15.29) and 74 dismissals (68 c., 6 st.)
Test matches (11): 152 runs (8.00) and 23 dismissals (21 c., 2 st.)

De MEL, Asantha Lakdasa Francis

(b. 1959, Colombo) *Sinhalese and Sri Lanka*

A product of Colombo's Royal College, and the best Sri Lankan fast bowler of his generation, Asantha de Mel was fortunate in reaching the top just as his country's long battle to attain Test status had been won. Fast-medium rather than genuinely quick, but with a free, high action and a good out-swinger, he toured England in 1981 with only modest success but quickly made his mark in Sri Lanka's first official Test, against England at Colombo in February 1982. He took 4 for 70 in England's first innings, including the first three batsmen. He then went to Pakistan and picked up more wickets than many more vaunted fast bowlers in that land of slow pitches, including 11 in the three Test matches. Injury kept him out of both the following Test series against New Zealand, though he took 2 for 113 in the inaugural Test against Australia at Kandy in 1982/3, and he returned to almost his best form in England in 1984, with 19 wickets on tour at 24.73, including a hard-earned 4 for 110 in the Lord's Test when not fully fit, and sealed his come-back with a career-best 5 for 64 against India at Colombo in 1985/6, ending the series with 12 wickets in three Tests at 36.50. Returning to Pakistan in 1985/6, he took the first six wickets for 109 in the first innings of the third Test at Karachi, his only wickets of the series, but presented rather more consistent problems to the same opposition on his own pitches a few months later, taking ten wickets at a cost of 25.80 in three Tests. An aggressive late-order right-handed batsman, he had a first-class century to his name and was a genuine all-rounder in anything other than the highest class.

First-class career (1980–8): 918 runs (19.12) including 1 century, 109 wickets (37.98), and 22 catches

Test matches (17): 326 runs (14.17), 59 wickets (36.94), and 9 catches

De SARAM, Douglas Lea

(b. 1882, Colombo; d. 1934, Colombo) *Sinhalese and Ceylon*

One of the most colourful personalities in Ceylon cricket during the early part of the century, Douglas de Saram was the captain of his school, St Thomas' College, and led the Combined Colleges XI in 1902. He played for and led the Sinhalese Sports Club from 1904 to 1908 and later captained the All-Ceylon team against MCC on their way to New Zealand in 1922, the first time a Ceylonese had skippered the national side. 'D.L.' was highly respected by all, and as the former Somerset all-rounder W. T. Greswell once commented: 'No better model cricketer and sportsman ever donned flannels in Ceylon.' He was a quiet but forthright character, and as a hard-hitting batsman a delight to watch. He was credited with throwing a cricket ball a distance of 118 yds 10 in. in 1913.

De SARAM, Frederick Cecil

(b. 1912, Colombo; d. 1983, Colombo) *Oxford University, Hertfordshire, Sinhalese, and Ceylon*

One of the best batsman ever to be produced on the island, 'Derrick' de Saram developed into one of the most talked about batsmen and captains in the game. A stylish, wristy right-hand batsman, he made his first-class début for Oxford University in 1934 (blue 1934 and 1935) having captained his school, Royal College. His first season in England was memorable: he aggregated 1,119 runs at an average of 50.86, with a highest score of 208 against Leveson-Gower's XI at Reigate. It was during the same season that de Saram gave a brilliant exhibition of batsmanship against the visiting Australians, scoring 128 in a total of 216—the next highest contribution being 16. The Australian attack, comprising Grimmett, Fleetwood-Smith, McCabe, and Ebeling, had bowled Oxford out for 70 in the first innings. *The Cricketer* wrote of De Saram: 'He made beautiful strokes all round the wicket and after reaching his hundred went for the bowling in an heroic manner so that when he was eventually caught he had hit four fine sixes and 18 fours in a superb piece of batting. It was indeed an innings which raised the drooping spirits of the Oxford supporters.' De Saram toured India with the Ceylon team in 1940/1, captained the Sinhalese Sports Club in 1949 and also led Ceylon. Very astute, he enjoyed pitting his wits against the opposition and a chat with Derrick after the game was over in the shade of the pavilion was invariably enlightening. He served as a selector after his retirement from the game and did yeoman service to his club as an administrator in their cricket affairs. In 1962 he was arrested and imprisoned for his alleged complicity in a plot to overthrow the government, but he was acquitted on appeal. A man with a sharp sense of humour, he was truly an officer (he was a colonel in the army) and a gentleman. His brother, F. J., and two uncles, D. L. and F. R., also played for Ceylon. He played matches for Hertfordshire between 1933 and 1936.

First-class career (1930–54): 2,789 runs (39.84) including 6 centuries, and 17 catches

De SILVA, Ashley Matthew

(b. 1963, Colombo) *Colombo and Sri Lanka*

A sturdy wicket-keeper and batsman, Ashley de Silva made his Test début in a single Test played at the SSC grounds when Sri Lanka registered her

De SILVA

first-ever win against England in 1992/3. A proficient wicket-keeper and a sound right-hand middle-order batsman, he did not impress at Test level sufficiently to be retained for long.

First-class career (1984–): 1,430 runs (26.00) and 74 dismissals (63 c., 11 st.)

Test matches (3): 10 runs (3.33) and 5 dismissals (4 c., 1 st.)

De SILVA, Dandeniyage Somachandra

(b. 1942, Galle) *Moratuwa, Lincolnshire, Shropshire, and Sri Lanka*

The younger brother of D. P. de Silva, who played for Ceylon, Somachandra, known familiarly as D.S. to distinguish him from his unrelated spinning partner Ajith, was born in Galle and was already a well-known and widely respected right-arm leg-break bowler when the era of Test cricket dawned for Sri Lanka. He had made his initial first-class appearance as early as 1966/7 for the Ceylon Board President's XI against the Hyderabad Blues of India and toured England in 1975, 1979, 1981, and 1984, when in the Lord's Test, despite an ankle injury, he bowled 45 overs for 85 runs, taking two wickets; as well as Pakistan in 1973/4 and 1981/2, India in 1975/6 and 1982/3, Australia and New Zealand in 1982/3, and Australia in 1984/5 for his final tour. Also a very useful right-handed late-middle-order batsman, he was an automatic choice for Sri Lanka's representative teams from the mid-1970s, his well-flighted leg-spinners and googlies commanding respect from even the finest batsmen. He became a popular figure and a respected Minor County bowler playing for Lincolnshire from 1975 to 1979, and for Shropshire from 1980. Playing for the Sri Lankan touring team against Oxford University at Guildford in 1979, he took 8 for 46 in an innings and 12 for 59 in the match. Though wickets came less easily to him in official Tests, he still picked up his share in 1981/2, including 3 for 54 in the first innings against England in the inaugural Test in Colombo and 17 wickets in three Tests against Pakistan. He captained Sri Lanka in Mendis's absence for two Tests in New Zealand on the 1982/3 tour, playing two of his best Test innings, 52 in the first Test at Christchurch and 61 in the second at Wellington.

First-class career (1966–84): 1,735 runs (21.96), 238 wickets (28.21), and 34 catches

Test matches (12): 406 runs (21.36), 37 wickets (36.40), and 5 catches

De SILVA, Ellewelakankanange Asoka Ranjit

(b. 1956, Kalutara) *Colombo and Sri Lanka*

A leg-spinner who bowled faster and flatter than many of his countrymen, and a left-hand batsman, Asoka de Silva finally emerged from the shadow of his namesake, D.S., to make his Test début in the first Test against India at Colombo in 1985/6 at the relatively ripe age of 29. Despite not taking a wicket, he bowled very tightly and was unlucky to be dropped for the second Test. He returned for the first Test of the next home series against Pakistan at Kandy, taking 1 for 37, but his appearances since have been sporadic, including two Tests in Australia in 1989/90 in which he batted at number four.

First-class career (1983–): 1,027 runs (17.11), 138 wickets (26.25), and 27 catches

Test matches (10): 185 runs (15.41), 8 wickets (129.00), and 4 catches

De SILVA, Ginigalgodange Ramba Ajith

(b. 1952, Ambalangoda) *Bloomfield and Sri Lanka*

Born and educated in Ambalangoda, Ajith de Silva was a very steady, orthodox, slow left-arm bowler and useful late-order left-handed batsman. He was already an experienced cricketer when picked for Sri Lanka's early Test matches in the 1980s. He toured Pakistan in 1973/4 and 1981/2, England in 1975 and 1979 (playing in the Prudential World Cup in those years), India in 1975/6, and Bangladesh in 1977/8. An effective bowler in one-day cricket because of his commendable accuracy, he disappointed his supporters in the inaugural Test in Colombo, being reluctant to take chances by flighting the ball on a pitch taking some spin. Nevertheless, he took four wickets; but in Pakistan he played in the first two Tests, taking only three wickets at 69 each. These were disappointing returns for so highly rated a bowler and one who in 1975/6 dismissed Viswanath of India in six successive innings, four times in Sri Lanka and twice in India. He joined the Sri Lankan tour of South Africa in 1982/3.

First-class career (1973–83): 317 runs (7.73), 161 wickets (27.44), and 21 catches

Test matches (4): 41 runs (8.20) and 7 wickets (55.00)

De SILVA, Pinnaduwage Aravinda

(b. 1965, Colombo) *Nondescripts, Kent, and Sri Lanka*

Two Test hundreds against Pakistan in the 1985/6 series and a century against the 1984/5

England touring team, all made before his twenty-first birthday, marked out Aravinda de Silva as the most precocious of the many talented young batsmen on whom Sri Lanka's Test future would be based. A wristy, flashy, quick-footed, brilliant but inconsistent little right-hander who loves to cut and hook, he made his Test début against England at Lord's in 1984 after scoring three consecutive fifties in the tour matches. He scored 16 and 3, making rather less impact than he did on the England touring team to India in 1984/5 when scoring 105, his maiden first-class century, despite being hit on the cheek second ball by Foster and being taken to hospital for examination. He had a steady series against India in 1985/6, averaging 33.6 for the three Tests, but really thrived on the docile Faisalabad pitch in the first Test of the subsequent series against Pakistan, hitting 122, his maiden Test century, and reaching his 100 with a typically belligerent hook for six off Imran. Promoted to number three for the final Test of that series at Karachi, he responded with a faultless 105 in the second innings against the pace of Imran and the guile of Abdul Qadir on a pitch which proved too difficult for the rest of his countrymen. He made a high reputation in Australia at Brisbane in 1989/90 with a brave and brilliant innings of 167 and it was also overseas that he played his largest Test innings, 267 against New Zealand at Wellington in 1990/1. He has captained Sri Lanka in four Tests and led the 1990 and 1991 tours to England, scoring 221 not out against Hampshire in the first year. He bowls briskish off-breaks, which have often been useful in the mass of one-day internationals in which Sri Lanka took part at an increasing rate in the 1990s. By February 1995 Aravinda had played 149 such matches, scoring 4,226 runs (32.25) with three hundreds and 31 fifties and taking 34 wickets (46.38). For Kent in 1995 he batted superbly for 1,781 runs (59.36), hitting 7 centuries. He also recorded a brilliant 112 in the Benson and Hedges Final at Lord's.

First-class career (1983–94): 7,466 runs (48.48) including 18 centuries, 50 wickets (27.98), and 70 catches

Test matches (48): 2,965 runs (37.53) including 17 centuries, 11 wickets (38.56), and 22 catches

DHARMASENA, Handunnettige Deepthi Priyantha Kumara

(b. 1971, Colombo) *Bloomfield and Sri Lanka*

A tall, right-hand bowler, and a middle-order batsman, Dharmasena purveys medium-pace off-

cutters with military precision. Making his début in the second Test against South Africa in 1993 at the SSC grounds, he had a fearful baptism when Sri Lanka were thrashed by an innings and 208 runs and he bowled a marathon spell of 45 overs without capturing a wicket, though he conceded only 91 runs. A player with a competitive spirit who gives very little away, he is prepared to fight to the bitter end. In eight one-day internationals to February 1995 he had taken eight wickets (31.87) with a best of 4 for 37.

First-class career (1988–): 561 runs (20.03), 67 wickets (22.05), and 16 catches

Test matches (6): 139 runs (13.90), 17 wickets (37.47), and 2 catches

DIAS, Roy Luke

(b. 1952, Colombo) *Colombo and Sri Lanka*

A slim, elegant and exceptionally gifted right-handed batsman with a marvellous sense of timing and a style a little reminiscent of Rohan Kanhai, Roy Dias was an automatic selection in Sri Lankan sides in the second half of the 1970s and in the team which played his country's first Test matches. Also a fine cover-point fielder and occasional right-arm medium-paced bowler, he toured India in 1975/6, Bangladesh in 1977/8, Pakistan in 1981/2, India in 1982/3, and England in 1979 and 1981 when he scored 608 runs (40.55). His experience was further widened by three seasons in England between 1977 and 1979 playing in league cricket. Against England in Sri Lanka's first-ever Test he scored a brilliant 77 in the second innings, and he went on to make 295 runs in three Tests against Pakistan, including 109 in the third Test at Lahore. He toured New Zealand and Australia in 1982/3 (but was injured), England in 1984 and Pakistan in 1985/6. At home, he made an uncharacteristically dogged 108 in the second Test against New Zealand at Colombo in 1983/4, helping to stem the run of three consecutive New Zealand victories, and 95 and an unbeaten 60 against India in Sri Lanka's first Test victory at Colombo in 1985/6. A fine 106, in a record fifth-wicket partnership of 216 with his captain Mendis, saved the third Test at Kandy, ensuring Sri Lanka's first series win.

First-class career (1974–92): 4,296 runs (32.05) including 5 centuries, 1 wicket (118.00), and 36 catches

Test matches (20): 1,285 runs (36.71) including 3 centuries, 0–17, and 6 catches

DISSANAYAKE, Lionel Gamini

(b. 1952, Kandy; d. 1994, Colombo)

A prominent member of parliament and cabinet minister, the Hon. Gamini Dissanayake was the president of the Board of Control for Cricket in Sri Lanka when the country was elected as a full member of the ICC in 1981. It was widely reported and accepted that his speech at that ICC meeting was well received. Educated at Trinity College, Kandy, he helped his alma mater by helping to convert the school grounds to an international stadium capable of staging Test matches. He also founded the Sri Lanka Cricket Foundation, and was its chairman until his untimely death. He was president of the Board of Control for a continuous spell of 8 years in the 1980s until his waning political career eased him out. His political star back in the ascendant, he was re-elected in 1994, only for a terrorist bomb cruelly to kill him, along with many others, at a political rally.

DUNUSINGHE, Chamara I.

(b. 1970) *Western Province North and Sri Lanka*

A neat, agile wicket-keeper and useful right-handed batsman, Chamara Dunusinghe rose nobly to the challenge of his first Test match, top scoring with 91 in the second Sri Lankan innings against New Zealand at Napier, and taking 7 catches in the match. He thus played an important part in Sri Lanka's victory and in what became their first win in an overseas series. He also played in the three one-day internationals on the tour and his form throughout suggested that Sri Lanka had found the answer to the long-standing problem of who should be their wicket-keeper.

First-class career (1990–): 712 runs (21.57) and 61 dismissals (52 c., 9 st.)
Test matches (2): 113 runs (28.25) and 8 dismissals (8 c.)

FERNANDO, Ellekutige Rufus Nemesion Susil

(b. 1955, Colombo) *Sri Lankan Air Force and Sri Lanka*

A right-handed batsman and a wicket-keeper, Susil Fernando was one of the 'second wave' of Sri Lankans who made their début on the New Zealand tour of 1982/3. An opener by trade, he batted at number three in his first Test at Christchurch, making 0 and 46, his highest Test score,

and did not keep wicket. He reverted to his natural position as opener against Australia and in the home series against New Zealand but without notable success, his names generally proving rather longer than his innings.

First-class career (1982–4): 312 runs (19.50)
Test matches (5): 112 runs (11.20)

FOENANDER, Samuel Peter

(b. 1882, Colombo; d. 1967, Colombo) *Colombo Colts*

Referred to as the 'Wisden of the East', Foenander was a journalist and veritable treasure trove of cricket statistics. Having captained Wesley College and been picked to represent Combined Colleges XI in 1902, he joined Colts CC where he became a vice-president after his playing days were over. His abiding interest was in cricket statistics and athletics. He was a founder member of the Ceylon Amateur Athletic Association and its first honorary secretary, in 1921. The next year he was elected honorary recorder of the Ceylon Cricket Association, a post he held until 1947. Foenander wrote several books on Ceylon's cricket history. After a stint as a schoolmaster at Royal College (1907 to 1927) he became the Sports editor of the *Ceylon Observer* for a period of 35 years, ending in 1963. In 1954 he was awarded an MBE and is believed to be the first Asian sportswriter to have been officially honoured. A versatile and reliable writer, he was known and respected for his integrity and assiduity.

GOONASEKERA, Yohan

(b. 1957, Colombo) *Nondescripts and Sri Lanka*

One of several batsmen tried out during the 'dark ages' of Sri Lankan Test cricket, Yohan Goonasekera played two Tests against New Zealand on the 1982/3 tour. He averaged 12 for the Tests and the tour, but was his side's outstanding fielder, taking a Sri Lankan record four catches in the gully in the first innings of the second Test at Wellington.

First-class career (1980–7): 445 runs (29.66), 3 wickets (32.66), and 12 catches
Test matches (2): 48 runs (12.00) and 6 catches

GOONATILLEKE, Hettiarachige Mahes

(b. 1952, Kegalla) *Kandy and Sri Lanka*

Born in Kandy and educated at St Anthony's College, Mahes Goonatilleke was an accomplished wicket-keeper, polished and swift, and a stolid right-handed batsman good enough to be given the responsibility of opening the innings in Test cricket. Picked to tour India in 1975/6, his first-class début was made on that tour. He toured Bangladesh two years later and England in 1981, by which time he had made himself first-choice wicket-keeper. Although not an automatic selection for one-day internationals, he played in five of Sri Lanka's early Tests before ending his Test career by going to South Africa.

First-class career (1975–83): 430 runs (13.43) and 54 dismissals (36 c., 18 st.)

Test matches (5): 177 runs (22.12) and 13 dismissals (10 c., 3 st.)

GUNASEKARA, Channa Hemasiri

(b. 1931, Colombo) *Sinhalese and Ceylon*

Son of Dr C. H. Gunasekara, Channa went through the same channels: Royal College, Sinhalese Sports Club and finally the Ceylon team. He opened the batting for Ceylon and first represented the country in 1951, playing against a succession of international teams from India, Australia, England, and the Commonwealth with fair success. A notable performance was an attractive 66 in 1953 against an Australian attack comprising Lindwall, Miller, Johnston, and Benaud. He was elected a member of MCC in 1961. A keen and a serious student of cricket, Gunasekara has served as a national selector (1983), writes part-time on the game, and has been both a radio and TV commentator.

GUNASEKARA, Dr Churchill Hector

(b. 1894, Colombo; d. 1969, Colombo) *Sinhalese, Middlesex, and Ceylon*

Patriarch of the most outstanding cricketing family in the island, C. H. Gunasekara graduated as a doctor of medicine in England just before the First World War. The young medical graduate was the first Ceylonese to represent an English county. The outbreak of war probably prevented him from being the first Ceylonese to win a cricket blue. However, while playing for the Indian Gymkhana, Sir Pelham Warner was duly impressed and he was picked as an amateur for Middlesex. Playing as a medium-paced right-arm bowler and lower-order right-hand batsman alongside stalwarts such as 'Patsy' Hendren, Jack Hearne, F. T. Mann, and G. T. S. Stevens, the mercurial Gunasekara excelled as a cover fielder. He played 39 games for the county between 1919

and 1922. He was instrumental in forming the Ceylon Cricket Association in the early 1920s and captained All-Ceylon in 1928 against Percy Chapman's English side. Earlier, in 1920, he became the first Ceylonese to become a member of MCC. In 1932/3 he captained the first Ceylonese team to tour India. He was also a keen tennis player and represented Ceylon against visiting teams in the 1930s. His son, Channa, also played for Ceylon as an outstanding opening batsman.

First-class career (1919–33): 957 runs (15.68), 90 wickets (31.94), and 32 catches

GUNASEKARA, Conroy Ivers

(b. 1920, Colombo) *Sinhalese and Ceylon*

Considered the best all-rounder produced by the country, the Revd David Sheppard commented in his autobiography that 'C.I.' could very easily have played for any country in Test cricket if he had been born in the right place. A hard-hitting right-hand middle-order batsman, versatile right-arm leg-spinner, and brilliant fielder anywhere, with hands like shovels, 'C.I.' was a captain's dream. Handsome, tall, and proportionately built, he was born for sports and also excelled at lawn tennis. His Jessop-like batting with his extra-heavy bat made life for fielders within a radius of 30 yards extremely hazardous. His two double-centuries against Madras in the Gopalan Trophy—including the highest score of the series of 212—bear testimony, not forgetting another blazing innings of 135 scored for a Commonwealth XI against MCC at the P. Saravanamuttu Stadium in 1952. Hitting one six and 20 boundaries, 'C.I.' put on 207 runs with another brilliant all-rounder, the Australian Keith Miller (106) in a mere 150 minutes. As Miller commented: 'I was particularly impressed by his temperament. He did not let the occasion overawe him and he played his strokes with power. I can say very few top-ranking cricketers put as much power behind their shots as Gunasekara does. His secret lies in the heavy bat he wields (I would not be able to use it) and his perfect timing. When he hit the ball, it travelled like a bullet.' Lindsay Kline, the Australian left-arm spinner, was another who felt the fury of Gunasekara. Richie Benaud's 1961 England-bound team stopped in Colombo for a one-day game and 'C.I.' plundered 24 runs—3 fours and 2 sixes—in an over from Kline in front of a delirious crowd. A dynamic all-rounder, he was not a slogger, but an entertainer who attracted crowds wherever he played. Equally important, he was a modest, self-effacing soul and a complete sportsman.

GUNERATNE, Roshan Punyajith Wijesinghe

(b. 1962, Colombo) *Nondescripts and Sri Lanka*

A leg-spinner and right-hand batsman, Roshan Guneratne made his only Test appearance against Australia at Kandy in 1982/3. On the receiving end of a large Australian total, he took 0 for 84 and was not out 0 in both Sri Lankan innings.

First-class career (1982–3): 9 runs (9.00) and 2 wickets (120.50)

GURUSINHA, Asanka Pradeep

(b. 1966, Colombo) *Sinhalese, Nondescripts, and Sri Lanka*

A tall but compact left-handed batsman, right-arm medium bowler and also, occasionally, a competent wicket-keeper, Asanka Gurusinha was one of the best of the crop of talented young batsmen who graduated from schoolboy to Test cricket during 1985. He announced his class with a fine 106 for the under-23 side against Pakistan under-23 in the second 'Test' at Colombo in 1984/5 and made his Test début at Karachi on the 1985/6 tour, acquitting himself capably with innings of 17 and 12 and taking two catches as wicket-keeper. After making 111 against the England B team in the first unofficial Test at Colombo, he was recalled as a batsman for the second Test of the home series against Pakistan and in the following Test at Colombo made an accomplished hundred, batting throughout the last day to save the match in an unbeaten fourth-wicket stand of 240 with Ranatunga, then the highest for any Sri Lankan wicket, of which his own share was 116. Thus establishing himself as more-or-less a fixture in both the Test and one-day games, Gurusinha scored further centuries against New Zealand and Australia. Against New Zealand at Hamilton in 1990/1 he enjoyed the rare distinction of scoring a hundred in each innings (119 and 102) and his 137 against Australia at the SSC grounds in Colombo two years later helped Sri Lanka to their highest Test score, 547 for 8 declared.

First-class career (1984– : 5,436 runs (43.14) including 15 centuries, 102 wickets (20.38), and 67 catches

Test matches (33): 1,952 runs (39.83) including 6 centuries, 18 wickets (33.50), and 26 catches

HATHURUSINGHE, Upul Chandika

(b. 1968, Colombo) *Tamil Union and Sri Lanka*

A stroke-playing right-hand opening batsman and right-arm slow-medium opening bowler who excels as a fielder both in the slips and in the covers, Chandika Hathurusinghe has the unique distinction of having represented the national under-19 team in England in 1988 even before he had played for the 1st XI of his school, Ananda College, Colombo. Joining the Sri Lankan squad as a replacement for the 1990/1 tour of New Zealand, Hathurusinghe began his career on an auspicious note, scoring 81 at Hamilton in the second Test and 74 in the final Test at Auckland. In his next Test, at Lord's, he played a lone hand of a top-score of 66. After a poor series against the touring South Africans 2 years later, however, he was sidelined, and, *inter alia*, a promising opening alliance with Roshan Mahanama was nipped in the bud. He returned to form in 1993/4, but in 10 more Test innings he managed only 157 runs.

First-class career (1988–): 4,206 runs (33.38) including 6 centuries, 138 wickets (23.46), and 48 catches

Test matches (18): 840 runs (28.96), 16 wickets (35.00), and 2 catches

INMAN, Clive Clay

(b. 1936, Colombo) *Nondescripts and Leicestershire*

A forceful left-hand batsman and a very occasional off-spinner who shot to prominence whilst at his school when he smashed a swashbuckling 204 runs in their annual match against St Joseph's in 1954. Having represented Ceylon in 1956 and toured India in 1957/8, he joined fellow-countryman Stanley Jayasinghe as a professional at Leicestershire in 1961. *Wisden* records: 'Leicestershire drew inspiration from the introduction to Championship cricket of Clive Inman, a talented left-hander from Ceylon. A model of consistency, Inman came third in the main averages with 1,708 runs at 42.7 per innings and he alone appeared in every match. Moreover, Inman, despite lack of support, always played attractively.' But his most productive season was in 1968 when he aggregated 1,735 runs (36.91). He hit 51 in 8 minutes in 1965 against Nottinghamshire, who gave away cheap runs in the hope of a declaration. Inman reached 1,000 runs in a season eight times and was the bulwark of a struggling county for many a year. He appeared briefly for Derbyshire in the John Player League in 1973 (not first-class). He settled in England. His father, H. C., also played for Ceylon.

First-class career (1956–71): 13,112 runs (34.50) including 21 centuries, 1 wicket (89.00), and 108 catches

JAYASEKERA, Rohan Stanley Amarasiriwardena

(b. 1957, Colombo) *Tamil Union and Sri Lanka*

An aggressive right-handed opening batsman and dependable wicket-keeper, Stanley Jayasekera, a product of Royal College, had a successful tour of England in the World Cup year of 1979, scoring 205 at an average of 51 in five innings. He narrowly missed selection for the first-ever Sri Lankan Test against England as a specialist batsman, but played in that role in the third Test against Pakistan at Lahore in March 1982. Going in at number three, he was bowled by Imran Khan for 0 and 2.

First-class career (1978–82): 356 runs (29.67) and 8 dismissals (6 c., 2 st.)

JAYASINGHE, Stanley

(b. 1931, Badulla) *Nondescripts and Leicestershire*

Stanley Jayasinghe played for Leicestershire between 1961 and 1965 as a forceful right-hand batsman and off-break bowler. He had represented Ceylon as an 18-year-old schoolboy from Nalanda College, when he toured Pakistan in 1949. After a stint in the leagues he signed for Leicestershire and represented them with distinction in 112 matches. Excelling on the back-foot, Jayasinghe was always on the offensive and was a delight to watch when in full flow. He hit 1,000 runs in each season he played except 1963 and 1964, when illness hampered him. Together with his compatriot Clive Inman he propped up the county's batting and in his final year, 1965, the two Ceylonese led the batting averages. Jayasinghe's best season was in 1962 when he scored 1,499 runs (29.9). In 1964, against Northamptonshire, he hit 106 out of 157 in 88 minutes, including sixteen fours and a six. During this innings he put on 100 with the opening batsman Brian Booth, whose contribution was nine runs. In retirement, though he served as manager of the Sri Lanka team to New Zealand in 1990/1, Jayasinghe has preferred a private life which includes his private coaching school and his farm in the south of Sri Lanka.

First-class career (1949–69): 6,811 runs (27.91) including 6 centuries, 34 wickets (35.20), and 109 catches

JAYASURIYA, Sanath Teran

(b. 1969, Matara) *Bloomfield and Sri Lanka*

A forceful, broad-shouldered, left-hand batsman and a part-time left-arm spinner, Sanath Jayasuriya has been in and out of the Test team since making his début in 1990/1 against New Zealand at Hamilton when he scored second-highest in the first innings with a face-saving 35 runs. A brilliant fielder with a strong arm, he has been shunted up and down the batting order, including a trial as an opener. A determined and dedicated performer, he has done his utmost to oblige the varying demands made on him though it has naturally affected his performances. A man who hit the first delivery he faced, from England's Phil Tufnell, for six to win the Test in 1992 at the SSC grounds, Jayasuriya can also put up the shutters when the occasion demands.

First-class career (1988–   ): 3,941 runs (39.41) including 8 centuries, 40 wickets (36.12), and 53 catches

Test matches (16): 611 runs (30.55), 4 wickets (86.25), and 17 catches

JAYAWICKREMA, Sagaradaththa Sudirukku

(b. 1911, Colombo; d. 1983, Colombo) *Sinhalese and Ceylon*

'Sargo', as he was universally known, and Derrick de Saram were contemporaries who emerged from Royal College, via the Sinhalese Sports Club to the national side where both ended up as captains. They were the May and Cowdrey of Ceylon. 'Sargo', unlike Derrick, was heavily built and dark; a shy personality whose right-hand batting and slow-medium bowling coupled with his magnificent fielding identified him more as an all-rounder. A quaint story demonstrates the respect Derrick had for 'Sargo'. During de Saram's first match for Oxford University, in 1934, he was massacring a Gloucestershire attack including three Test bowlers, Sinfield, Goddard, and Parker, on his way to a scintillating 176. While at the non-striker's end he was seen laughing silently to himself, prompting the umpire, J. H. King, to ask him what the matter was. De Saram replied: 'If I can make runs so easily against this lot, I was wondering what a buddy of mine back in Ceylon would do if he had a go.' That buddy was 'Sargo'. On the first official tour of India, in 1932/3, under the captaincy of Dr C. H. Gunasekara, Jayawickrema blasted a masterful 56 in 53 minutes and hammered the Indian Test fast bowler Mohammad Nissar for successive boundaries off the first three deliveries he faced. In the first unofficial Test match he scored a masterly 130, the first scored at Delhi's Ferosha Kotla ground, which enabled the Ceylon team to earn an honourable draw. On the next tour of India, which he led, in 1940/1, he scored a brilliant 138 at Eden Gardens and maintained his reputation. Unlike Derrick, 'Sargo's' cricket was essentially a home-grown product, cradled at Royal College and nurtured at the SSC. It was said that his 'bat was as broad as the plains of Tissamaharama and his cover drives as clean and sparkling as the waters of the Menik Ganga (river)'. There was a Hammond-like gait about him and once he hit the ball it normally stayed hit.

JEGANATHAN, Sridharan

(b. 1951, Colombo) *Nondescripts and Sri Lanka*

Selected for the New Zealand tour of 1982/3 at the age of 31, an enterprising 74, in a stand of 140 for the eighth wicket, against Tasmania on the first leg of the tour won him a Test début as an all-rounder at Christchurch. A forceful left-hander and a slow left-arm spinner, he was not given a chance to show either of his skills, batting at number nine and bowling only five overs, and he was dropped for the next home Test against Australia. He made his first-class début against Pakistan under-25 in 1973/4.

First-class career (1973–88): 437 runs (13.65), 49 wickets (31.61), and 14 catches

Test matches (2): 19 runs (4.75) and 0–12

JOHN, Vinothen Bede Jeyarajasingham (formerly J. V. B. Jeyarajasingham)

(b. 1960, Colombo) *Bloomfield and Sri Lanka*

A sturdy and accurate right-armed medium-pacer, Vinothen John, a Tamil, proved a useful opening partner for the more hostile de Mel on many occasions, most notably on the tour to England in 1984 when he topped the tour averages, with 26 wickets at 23.19. At Lord's, despite not being fully fit, he bowled with spirit to take four wickets, bringing his tally to a highly creditable 28 in six Tests since his début at Christchurch in 1982/3. In his second series against New Zealand in 1983/4, his total of 16 wickets in three Tests at a cost of 23.31, including match figures of 8 for 159 in the first Test at Kandy, was bettered only by Richard Hadlee. Not noted as a batsman, he shared in a Sri Lankan record last-wicket stand

of 60 in the same match at Kandy, ending up unbeaten on 27.

First-class career (1981–7): 127 runs (9.07), 74 wickets (25.33), and 4 catches

Test matches (6): 53 runs (10.60), 28 wickets (21.92), and 2 catches

JURANGPATHY, Baba Roshan

(b. 1967, Colombo) *Royal College and Sri Lanka*

A diminutive right-hand batsman and off-break bowler, Roshan Jurangpathy became the first member of the Malay community to play first-class cricket in Sri Lanka when he made his début for the under-23 side against Pakistan under-23 at Kandy in May 1985. By scoring 102, he also became, at 17 years and 342 days, the youngest Sri Lankan to score a first-class hundred and in the second 'Test' showed his all-round abilities by taking 8 for 103 in the match which Sri Lanka won by an innings. Just four months later, he completed the transition from Royal College schoolboy to Test player when selected for the third Test against India at Kandy. He had little chance to show his precocious talents, making 1 and 0 and not taking a wicket.

First-class career (1984–93): 1,483 runs (25.13) including 2 centuries, 104 wickets (20.62), and 27 catches

KALPAGE, Ruwan Senani

(b. 1970, Kandy) *Bloomfield and Sri Lanka*

A forceful left-handed batsman, thoughtful, and flighty off-spin bowler and brilliant fielder, Ruwan Kalpage played with great success for his school, St Anthony's College, Kandy, alongside two other potential Test cricketers, Muttiah Muralitharan and Piyal Wijetunge. A fearless hooker and a batsman who is always on the lookout for runs, Kalpage's shrewd off-breaks have been especially useful in the limited-overs game. For instance he skilfully deceived Mike Gatting in a day/night match in 1992/3, one of 38 victims in his 43 internationals to 1994. His first Tests were played against India at home in 1993/4. He also played at home against South Africa and Pakistan in that busy season, and toured India, scoring 63 and 18 at Bangalore when Sri Lanka were heavily defeated. A second Test fifty, 62 on his home ground at Kandy, followed, again a spirited effort in the face of some devastating fast bowling by Waqar Younis.

First-class career (1988–): 1,882 runs (27.27) including 3 centuries, 142 wickets (24.82), and 33 catches
Test matches (8): 265 runs (20.38), 6 wickets (67.50), and 6 catches

KALUPERUMA, Lalith Wasantha

(b. 1949, Colombo) *Bloomfield and Sri Lanka*

A skilful right-arm off-break bowler, gritty late-order right-handed batsman, and good close fielder, Lalith Kaluperuma dismissed the Indian captain Ajit Wadekar with the first ball he bowled in an unofficial 'Test', in 1975/6, and by the time that Sri Lanka's Test status was recognized he had firmly established himself as a steady off-spinner with good control of flight. However, he was disappointing when asked to dismiss good batsmen on good pitches, failing to take a wicket in his two Tests, against England (Colombo) and Pakistan (Faisalabad). He joined the Sri Lankan tour to South Africa in 1982/3.

First-class career (1970–83): 1,023 runs (17.33), 129 wickets (30.47), and 48 catches
Test matches (2): 12 runs (4.00), 0–93, and 2 catches

KALUPERUMA, Sanath Mohan Silva

(b. 1961, Colombo) *Bloomfield and Sri Lanka*

A right-handed middle-order batsman, Sanath Kaluperuma made his Test début against New Zealand in the home series of 1983/4 after scoring an unbeaten 132 in the third under-23 Test against Pakistan at Rawalpindi. He found difficulty in adapting to the higher level, however, scoring just 82 runs in the three Tests against New Zealand at 13.6, but taking 2 for 17 with his off-breaks in the first Test at Kandy. He made one appearance against the England B team in 1985/6, scoring 70 in the first innings of the second unofficial Test at Colombo.

First-class career (1983–9): 797 runs (31.88), 10 wickets (62.90), and 14 catches
Test matches (4): 88 runs (11.00), 2 wickets (62.00), and 6 catches

KALUWITHARANA, Romesh Shantha

(b. 1969, Colombo) *Galle and Sri Lanka*

Picked as a wicket-keeper against Allan Border's touring Australians in the 1992/3 season for the first Test at the SSC grounds, Kaluwitharana made a sensational début, not with the gloves but with the bat. Scoring a dazzling unbeaten 132,

including 26 fours, in 158 balls, he thumped Warne and McDermott with 'breathtaking arrogance'. Yet his ability behind the stumps was way below what he was capable of in front, and he was dropped from the side one Test later. His inability to cement his place in the side has been a source of great disappointment to most followers of the game.

First-class career (1988–): 1,609 runs (39.24) including 3 centuries, and 65 dismissals (59 c., 6 st.)
Test matches (3): 177 runs (59.00) including 1 century, and 6 catches

KARUNARATNE, Edwin Mendis

(b. 1881, Galle; d. 1977, Galle) *Galle*

The Grand Old Man of Galle cricket, Edwin Karunaratne 'carried' the game in Galle on his shoulders for nearly 50 years. After captaining his school, Richmond College, he captained Galle C.C. from 1922 to 1945 and became the first from outside Colombo to be elected president of the Ceylon Cricket Association, in 1933 and 1934. 'E.M.K.' as he was remembered, dedicated his life to the game and was the island's representative at the inaugural meeting of the Asian Cricket Council held in Calcutta in 1949.

KURUPPU, Don Sardha Brendon Priyantha

(b. 1962, Colombo) *Bloomfield and Sri Lanka*

This soft-spoken right-hand opening batsman-cum-wicket-keeper announced himself to the international cricket world when he scored an unbeaten 201 against a New Zealand attack comprising Hadlee, Chatfield, Snedden, and Bracewell on his Test début at the Colombo Cricket grounds in 1986/7. The series was eventually abandoned at the end of this Test due to a terrorist bomb blast which occurred in proximity to the hotel occupied by the tourists. Kuruppu's marathon innings lasted 776 minutes, the third-longest Test innings in the history of the game, behind Hanif Mohammad (970 minutes) and Leonard Hutton (797). There were more records: Kuruppu's double-century was the slowest in first-class and Test cricket and he became the first Sri Lankan to register a century on Test début. After Kuruppu's batting performance he did duty behind the stumps while New Zealand amassed 406 for 5, without conceding a single bye. This was the first occasion in a Test match when a player in pads was on the field for every minute of all five days. Despite this magnificent effort he played in only three further Tests, due mainly to the fact that Sri Lanka played so few Tests at that time.

First-class career (1984–92): 2,671 runs (37.09) including 5 centuries, and 57 dismissals (47 c., 10 st.)
Test matches (4): 320 runs (53.33) including 1 century and 1 catch

KURUPPUARACHCHI, Ajith Kosala

(b. 1964, Colombo) *Nondescripts and Sri Lanka*

One of several younger players blooded internationally against the England B team in 1985/6, the tall and curly-haired left-arm medium-pacer made a sensational start to his Test career when taking 5 for 44 in the first innings of the second Test to set up Sri Lanka's first win against Pakistan, at Colombo in 1985/6. He ended the match with figures of 7 for 85, and made nought not out, but was injured before the third Test and did not play.

First-class career (1985–94): 70 runs (5.83), 60 wickets (26.70), and 5 catches
Test matches (2): 0 runs and 8 wickets (18.62)

LABROOY, Graeme Fredrick

(b. 1964, Colombo) *Colombo and Sri Lanka*

A medium-fast right-arm opening bowler with a classical high-arm action and a useful lower-order batsman, Graeme Labrooy had the makings of a budding all-rounder. But, due to personal tragedy, his promising career was curtailed. On his only appearance against England, at Lord's in 1988, he helped Ravi Ratnayeke to add 64 for the last wicket which was a record for Sri Lanka against all countries. Labrooy's innings of 42, including six boundaries, was described by *Wisden* as one 'surprising perhaps even himself with the quality of stroke-play . . . and caused Gooch to make five bowling changes'. The high point in his career was during the New Zealand tour of 1990/1 at Auckland when he blasted an unbeaten 70 from 80 balls with two sixes and twelve fours, reaching his half-century in a record thirteen strokes. The staid *Wisden* commented: 'It was scary stuff for the fielders', reminiscent of Stan McCabe's incandescent innings of 189 at Johannesburg in the 1935/6 series when Springbok skipper Herbie Wade appealed against the light fearing physical danger to his fielders by the ferocity of the marauding Australian batsman.

First-class career (1986–): 924 runs (20.53), 124 wickets (33.56), and 17 catches
Test matches (9): 158 runs (14.36), 27 wickets (44.22), and 3 catches

LIYANAGE, Dulip Kapila

(b. 1972, Kalutara) *Colombo Colts and Sri Lanka*

A right-arm medium-fast bowler from the outstations, Dulip Liyanage made quite an impact at the beginning of his career with his aggressive brand of cricket, but due to injury has been sidelined. A useful batsman in the lower order who is capable of using the long handle, and an active fielder.

First-class career (1991–): 378 runs (15.12), 79 wickets (24.22), and 3 catches
Test matches (8): 66 runs (8.25) and 17 wickets (36.58)

MADUGALLE, Ranjan Senerath

(b. 1959, Kandy) *Nondescripts and Sri Lanka*

Born in Kandy but educated at Royal College in Colombo, Ranjan Madugalle was an effective off-spin bowler as a schoolboy. He developed into a specialist right-handed batsman of high quality and, having gained experience in the Saddleworth League in England and on the Sri Lankan tours to England of 1979 and 1981, he was ready to claim a batting place in the Test side with a delightful innings of 142 not out for the President's XI against Keith Fletcher's touring team at Kandy in 1981/2. In the inaugural Test his 65 helped to bail out Sri Lanka after a disastrous start to their Test 'career' and he went on to enjoy a successful tour of Pakistan, scoring 91 not out in the second Test at Faisalabad. He topped the Test and tour averages in New Zealand and Australia in 1982/3, making 79 in the second Test at Wellington, but had a less happy time in England in 1984 when, after starting promisingly, he was attacked by a drunken passer-by outside his hotel in Canterbury and suffered injuries to his face and his confidence, disappointing at Lord's. A fine century in the first Test against India at Colombo at the beginning of the 1985/6 season proved his well-being, but a subsequent run of low scores was broken only by a 65 in the second innings of the second Test against Pakistan at Sialkot on the 1985/6 tour and he did not play in the return series, thus ending his run as the only ever-present in the Sri Lankan side since their first Test in 1981.

First-class career (1979–89): 3,301 runs (32.04) including 2 centuries, 2 wickets (79.50), and 42 catches
Test matches (21): 1,029 runs (29.40) including 1 century, 0–38, and 9 catches

MADURASINGHE, Wijayasiri Ranjith

(b. 1961, Kurunegala) *Kurunegala Youth and Sri Lanka*

A tall right-arm off-spinner who hailed from the outstations, Madurasinghe possibly lacked the competitive edge required to stay at the top though he enjoyed tours to England in 1988, New Zealand and India in 1990/1, and a Sri Lanka B team tour of Zimbabwe in 1988. Sadly, after playing a mere three Tests he faded.

First-class career (1988–   ): 883 runs (16.35), 155 wickets (26.65), and 32 catches
Test matches (3): 24 runs (4.80) and 3 wickets (57.33)

MAHANAMA, Roshan Siriwardene

(b. 1966, Colombo) *Bloomfield and Sri Lanka*

A tiny right-handed opener, whose size belies his power, Roshan Mahanama had such an impressive series against England B in 1985/6, when he averaged 52.25 in three matches and scored a magnificent 111 out of 181 in the fourth one-day international, that the selectors had little hesitation in drafting him into the Test side for the second Test against Pakistan at Colombo. Opening the innings, he made 10 and 8, but improved on that in the third Test with a mature 41, employing his favourite cut stroke to good effect. He learned discretion without spoiling his attacking flair, reaching 153 and 109 in successive Tests against New Zealand at home in 1992/3, not to mention 204 runs for once out in three one-day internationals.

First-class career (1984–   ): 4,110 runs (34.25) including 5 centuries, and 76 catches
Test matches (32): 1,687 runs (31.83) including 3 centuries, and 19 catches

MENDIS, Louis Rohan Duleep

(b. 1952, Moratuwa) *Sinhalese and Sri Lanka*

A strong, stocky, wristy right-handed batsman of exceptional talent, Duleep Mendis was vice-captain of Sri Lanka in the country's early Tests and took over as captain for the second Test against Pakistan in Faisalabad in 1981/2 when Warnapura was injured. A fine fielder, he can also bowl

right-arm medium pace and keep wicket when required. Born in Moratuwa, he was a key member of Sri Lankan sides to England in 1975, 1979, and 1981, and also toured Pakistan and India in the 1970s, producing ample evidence of his quality both in first-class cricket and in one-day internationals. His start to his official Test career was disappointing until, in September 1982, he hit 105 runs in both innings in the first Test against India at Madras, thus becoming only the third batsman ever to score hundreds in both innings against India, after Bradman and Weekes. He nearly repeated the feat at Lord's in 1984 when in two memorable innings he made 111 and 94, his hundred taking only 112 deliveries and including three majestic hooked sixes off Ian Botham all played in light the umpires considered unfit! He led Sri Lanka by example to their first Test and series win over India in 1985/6, topping the averages with 310 runs at 62.00, including 124 in the third Test at Kandy, but then lapsed into a poor run of form in the subsequent two series against Pakistan. A highly experienced campaigner, he took over as official captain for the tour of New Zealand in 1982/3, but broke a finger in an early tour match and was unable to play in the two Tests.

First-class career (1972–91): 6,233 runs (35.82) including 12 centuries, 1 wicket (52.00), 49 catches, and 1 stumping
Test matches (24): 1,329 runs (31.64) including 4 centuries, and 9 catches

MURALITHARAN, Muttiah

(b. 1972, Kandy) *Tamil Union and Sri Lanka*

Muttiah Muralitharan is a prodigious spinner of the ball, a flighty off-spinner who could claim to be the best in the world in the early 1990s. Also a brilliant fielder, he has caused many a headache to leading batsmen with his sharp turn, though his action, with an extraordinary twist of a flexible right wrist, has raised eyebrows. If there is any help from a pitch he will practically turn the ball square and the degree of his spin also creates drift and dip in the air. Making his first appearance in first-class cricket for Central Province in 1989/90, he toured England in 1991 when still a teenager. His quality was evident despite modest returns and his performances in Test cricket have been consistently successful. Despite murmurs about his action—and public questioning of its legality by the New Zealand captain, Martin Crowe—he has not been no-balled by umpires. Against England at Colombo in 1992/3 he took five wickets in Sri Lanka's first win against the former mother country. Against South Africa in 1993/4 he took sixteen wickets in three Tests (22.25) also conceding under two runs an over in 54 overs in the second match at the SSC grounds in Colombo. Another successful season in 1994/5 put him amongst the best twenty bowlers in world cricket according to the 'official' computer ratings. In 18 Tests he had 4 five-wicket returns.

First-class career (1989–94): 330 runs (11.00), 147 wickets (23.98), and 25 catches

Test matches (18): 161 runs (16.10), 63 wickets (31.53), and 7 catches

OUTSCHOORN, Ladislaus

(b. 1918, Colombo; d. 1994, London, England) *Worcestershire*

A remarkable self-taught cricketer who made his début in competitive cricket in England at the age of 27 after being captured by the Japanese in Malaya, 'Laddie' Outschoorn became the first Ceylonese to play as a professional in the county circuit. After a brief stint in the leagues, he played for Worcestershire from 1946 to 1959, winning his cap in 1948. As an early-order right-hand batsman, a brilliant slip-fielder, and an occasional right-arm slow-medium bowler, he did yeoman service, scoring over 1,000 runs in nine seasons, with a career-best of 1,761 in 1951 (35.90). A man full of theories and ideas on the game, he was appointed national coach in 1966 when he returned to Ceylon. His quality was evident despite Worcestershire's innings defeat against the 1948 Australians. Outschoorn held the rampaging Australian attack—Lindwall, Miller, McCool, Toshack, and Johnson—with a top-score of 54. He hit two double-centuries, the higher being 215 not out against Northamptonshire at Worcester in 1949.

First-class career (1946–59): 15,496 runs (28.59) including 25 centuries, 33 wickets (61.51), and 278 catches

PIERIS, Percival Ian

(b. 1933, Colombo) *Sinhalese, Cambridge University, and Ceylon*

A right-arm medium-pace opening bowler who won his cricket blue at Cambridge in 1957 and 1958, Ian Pieris was a member of the team which beat Oxford in 1957 under the captaincy of his compatriot, Gamini Goonesena. Relying for his wickets on movement rather than pace, 'P.I.' was a lanky, bespectacled Old Thomian, who was also

a hard-hitting lower-order batsman. He represented Ceylon in the mid-1960s and toured both India and Pakistan in 1966/7. Later, he was elected president of the Board of Control for Cricket in Sri Lanka, in 1989/90 and 1990/1, but could not give of his best due to the hurly-burly of the country's cricket politics. Since then, as head of a large business enterprise, 'P.I.' has preferred to stay away from the spotlight of national cricket.

First-class career (1956–67): 917 runs (17.30), 101 wickets (34.95), and 14 catches

PUSHPAKUMARA, Kuruppuarachchige Ravindra

(b. 1975, Panadura) *Nondescripts and Sri Lanka*

A sturdy right-arm fast-medium opening bowler who has been trained at the famed MRF Pace Foundation in Madras, India, under the direction of Dennis Lillee, Pushpakumara appeared in one-day internationals in 1993/4 before winning his first Test caps the following season. Touring Zimbabwe in October 1994, he took eight wickets in two Tests, seven of them for 116 in the only innings of the third match at Harare, a performance which showed that he has heart and stamina as well as strength and speed.

First-class career (1992–): 22 runs (5.50) and 15 wickets (41.33)

Test matches (5): 39 runs (7.80) and 14 wickets (29.50)

RAMANAYAKE, Hewage Champaka Priyadarshi

(b. 1965, Colombo) *Tamil Union and Sri Lanka*

A well-built, right-arm medium-fast bowler capable of bowling long spells, Champaka Ramanayake carried the brunt of the Sri Lankan fast attack for quite a while. Bowling at a lively pace he was able to keep the batsmen in check but gave very little away—à la Statham. A good fielder in the deep with an accurate throw, he is a competitor who gives his all to the team although 18 Tests produced only one five-wicket analysis. He first appeared for Sri Lanka in 1987 after making his initial appearance in first-class cricket for Sri Lanka Colts in 1985/6. He toured England in 1988, 1990, and 1991, New Zealand 1990/1, Pakistan 1991/2, and also played non-first-class cricket overseas in Sharjah, Bangladesh and in the 1991/2 World Cup in Australia and New Zealand.

First-class career (1985–): 1,513 runs (19.90), 269 wickets (25.98), and 35 catches
Test matches (18): 143 runs (9.53), 44 wickets (42.72), and 6 catches

RANASINGHE, Anura Nandana

(b. 1956, Kalutara) *Bloomfield, Burgher, and Sri Lanka*

Twelfth man in Sri Lanka's first official Test, Anura Ranasinghe was a fighting all-round cricketer with considerable experience in the leagues of the north of England. He first played for Sri Lanka in 1974/5 when still a schoolboy, but did not fully live up to the high expectations held of his right-handed batting and medium-pace left-arm seamers. He toured England three times and India once before making the country's first official tour to Pakistan where he played in one Test, at Faisalabad, making 6 and 5 and taking one wicket in the match for 40 runs. He ended his international career by going to South Africa in 1982/3, thus incurring what was initially a 'life' ban.

First-class career (1974–90): 1,664 runs (23.77), 39 wickets (42.64), and 26 catches
Test matches (2): 88 runs (22.00) and 1 wicket (69.00)

RANATUNGA (or RANATUNGE), Arjuna

(b. 1963, Colombo) *Sinhalese, Western Province North, and Sri Lanka*

Having played in Sri Lanka's inaugural Test against England at the age of 18, Ranatunga missed only three of his country's first twenty-one Tests, and went on to become the captain who led the country to their first Test victory against England, at the SSC grounds in Colombo in 1992/3. An elegant left-hander of small, rather tubby build, he announced his precocious talent by scoring 54 in that first Test and, though subsequent efforts were less successful, the selectors' faith was rewarded when he hit 90 against Australia in 1982/3 and then 50, 84, and 111, his maiden century, in successive Tests against New Zealand, England, and India respectively in 1984 and 1985. Besides his hard-hit 84 at Lord's he had a successful tour of England in 1984, averaging 41.90 and picking up six wickets with his improving right-arm medium-pace. Seventy-nine at Faisalabad in the first Test and 77 in the second at Colombo were his best scores in the two series against Pakistan in 1985/6 until the final Test at Colombo when he rode his luck to record his second Test century, an unbeaten 135 in a record

fourth-wicket stand of 240 with Gurusinghe which saved the match. He captained Sri Lanka from 1989 (briefly relinquishing the post and becoming involved in a row with officials about the alleged unfitness of his players) and scored 127 at the SSC grounds in Colombo in 1992/3 when Sri Lanka made 547 for 8 declared but could not force the victory which they had threatened.

First-class career (1981–94): 6,087 runs (39.27) including 11 centuries, 83 wickets (32.90), and 63 catches
Test matches (56): 3,134 runs (35.21) including 4 centuries, 14 wickets (67.50), and 22 catches

RANATUNGA, Dhammika

(b. 1962, Colombo) *Sinhalese, Western Province North, and Sri Lanka*

A dour right-hand opening batsman and elder brother of Test captain Arjuna, Dhammika made his Test début against Australia during the 1989/90 tour. Though having scored a painstaking 40 in each of the two Tests he played, he was not picked thereafter for national duty, despite success at club levels.

First-class career (1984–94): 2,408 runs (30.10) including 2 centuries, 6 wickets (25.66), and 23 catches
Test matches (2): 87 runs (29.00)

RANATUNGA, Sanjeewa

(b. 1969, Colombo) *Nondescripts and Sri Lanka*

The third of the Ranatunga brothers to appear for Sri Lanka in Test cricket, Sanjeewa is a stubborn left-hand batsman. Though a free-scoring batsman before making his début at Test level, Sanjeewa has now been given the all-important number three position, and scored consecutive centuries against Zimbabwe, saving Sri Lanka the shame of losing the series with his dogged batsmanship. Having edged Asanka Gurusinha from the number three slot, the youngest Ranatunga is determined to cement his place, and the selectors have helped by switching Gurusinha to the opener's berth—a move not appreciated by most.

First-class career (1988–94): 1,926 runs (31.06), 30 wickets (20.23), and 21 catches
Test matches (6): 346 runs (34.60) and 2 catches

RATNAYAKE, Rumesh Joseph

(b. 1964, Colombo) *Nondescripts and Sri Lanka*

A right-arm fast bowler and right-hand bat, Rumesh Ratnayake proved one of Sri Lanka's most consistent performers in Test and one-day cricket after his début at the age of 19 against New Zealand on the 1982 tour. Wiry and aggressive, with a slingy action reminiscent of Jeff Thomson, he broke John Wright's nose with a bouncer, taking 4 for 81 in the second Test of that series at Wellington, but then betrayed his innocence by fainting at the sight of the blood! Dropped after the first Test against New Zealand in 1983/4, he performed well enough for the under-23 side against Pakistan to be recalled for the series against India, playing a major part in his country's first Test win with match figures of 9 for 125 in the second Test at Colombo. By the end of that triumphant series, in which he took twenty wickets at 22.95 including 6 for 85 in the first Test, he had become de Mel's established opening partner, a position he maintained in Pakistan on rather less responsive pitches. His six wickets at 45.83 were a tribute to his stamina and persistence and he showed hitherto hidden ability with the bat, making a stubborn 56 in the first Test at Faisalabad. He missed out on Sri Lanka's second triumph, against Pakistan at home in 1985/6, but he had the youth and potential to lead Sri Lanka's attack for some time. His pace would be vouched for by Larry Gomes of West Indies, some of whose teeth where removed by a Ratnayake bouncer during the 1984/5 World Championship in Australia.

First-class career (1982–92): 925 runs (16.81), 174 wickets (27.37), and 16 catches

Test matches (23): 433 runs (14.43), 73 wickets (35.10), and 9 catches

RATNAYEKE, Joseph Ravindran

(b. 1960, Colombo) *Nondescripts and Sri Lanka*

A tall right-arm fast-medium bowler and useful left-hand batsman, Ravi Ratnayeke graduated from the under-19 side, making his first two Test appearances in Pakistan in 1981/2. On unresponsive pitches he plugged away with determination to take 4 for 180 but met with rather more success when recalled for the second Test against New Zealand at Colombo, taking 5 for 42 in the first innings. On his second tour of Pakistan in 1985/6 he had the remarkable figures of 8 for 83 in the second Test at Sialkot (his near namesake R. J. Ratnayake took the other two wickets to add to the confusion for the statisticians) and in the return series his 5 for 37 broke the back of Pakistan's second innings at Colombo as Sri Lanka recorded their second Test win. He ended the three-Test series with 11 wickets at 18.90. He

spent several seasons as a professional in the north of England, and was highly rated by Sri Lanka's sometime coach, Sir Garfield Sobers.

First-class career (1980–90): 2,225 runs (28.52) including 1 century, 133 wickets (36.77), and 18 catches

Test matches (22): 807 runs (25.21), 56 wickets (35.21), and 1 catch

ROCKWOOD, Dr John

(b. 1882; d. 1935) *Tamil Union*

One of the greatest benefactors to cricket in Ceylon, Dr Rockwood was educated at Royal College and was one of the founder-members of the Tamil Union Cricket and Athletic Club in 1899. He captained the club from 1909 to 1912 and was the first honorary secretary. In 1922 he was elected the first president of the Ceylon Cricket Association, the forerunner to the present Board of Control for Cricket. Dr Rockwood organized many tours, footing the bill on most occasions. In addition, his own teams met most of the leading clubs in the country during the period after the First World War. He was also the president of the Ceylon Swimming Association in 1921 and the ADC to the Governor-General from 1927 to 1930. The Nondescripts Cricket Club was also a recipient of his munificence: he gave them money to develop the grounds and the pavilion. Contemporary newspaper reports supply plentiful evidence of his commitment to sport in general and cricket in particular.

RODRIGO, Mahesa

(b. 1928, Colombo) *Sinhalese and Ceylon*

A diminutive right-hand opening batsman and reserve wicket-keeper from Royal College, and nephew of the famous 'Sargo' Jayawickrema, 'Mahes' Rodrigo represented the country both at cricket and Rugby football (scrum-half)—captaining the Ceylon rugger side in 1952. He was a member of a powerful SSC side, which helped him to mature fast. In 1949 the 21-year-old opener bathed himself in glory by carrying his bat against the formidable West Indian touring team with a brilliant 135 and two months later made another century against the touring Pakistanis, led by Saeed Mohammad. Later, he helped his alma mater as coach of both the cricket and rugby teams, whilst looking after his lucrative restaurant business.

SAMARASEKERA, Matipage Athula Rohan

(b. 1961, Colombo) *Colombo and Sri Lanka*

Affectionately known as 'Big Sam', Samarasekera is a powerfully built, hard-hitting right-hand batsman who opens the batting when required and is a handy right-hand medium-slow bowler. Having played in the 1983 World Cup team that beat New Zealand, he made his Test début against England at Lord's in 1988, during which tour he scored a whirlwind 104 in 124 balls against Surrey at The Oval. Having failed to score in his first Test innings 'Big Sam' made amends in the second innings with a bright 57 which included a six and seven fours. However, an erratic Test match calendar coupled with frequent changes in the batting order, did not help his cause when he decided to play professional cricket in Bangladesh and thus ended what promised to be a great career at the international level.

First-class career (1982–): 2,466 runs (34.73) including 6 centuries, 36 wickets (38.27), and 29 catches

Test matches (4): 118 runs (16.85), 3 wickets (34.66), and 3 catches

SAMARAWEERA, Dulip Prasanna

(b. 1972, Colombo) *Colombo Colts and Sri Lanka*

A right-hand opening batsman and competent close-in fielder, Samaraweera was picked to replace the experienced Hathurusinghe, the latter having failed against the South Africans. Though failing against the West Indians on his Test début at Moratuwa, when his two innings earned him 21 runs (10.50) and he held a catch, his capacity for hard work and application promised better.

First-class career (1991–): 1,319 runs (32.97), 24 wickets (16.00), and 5 catches

Test matches (7): 211 runs (15.07)

SARAVANAMUTTU, Pakiasothy

(b. 1892; d. 1950) *Tamil Union*

Hailing from a distinguished family of cricketers, 'P. Sara' as he was universally known was a pioneer who helped the island's cricket in many ways. His greatest contribution was the building of the Colombo Oval, later to be named the P. Saravanamuttu Stadium. A product of St Thomas's College, he represented the Tamil Union and was the president of the Ceylon Cricket Association from 1937 until he was elected the first president of the Board of Control for Cricket in 1948. A man of vision, he built The Oval—as it

was then known—on marshy land and with it a scoreboard that is still regarded as one of the best anywhere in the world.

SATHASIVAM, Mahadeva

(b. 1916; d. 1977) *Tamil Union, Ceylon, and Malaysia*

The most flamboyant cricketer produced in the country, 'Satha' had the unique distinction of having captained two countries, namely Ceylon and Malaysia. Though his ability as a captain is debatable, his uncanny prowess with the bat has never been in question. Sir Frank Worrell once commented that if he was to pick a World XI, one of the first batsmen he would include would be Sathasivam. The Indian off-spinner, Ghulam Ahmed, who had bowled against the best batsmen in the world, rated 'Satha' as the best he had bowled against. In the late 1940s 'Satha' had scored a magnificent double-century against him at the Chepauk Stadium in Madras and beat the then highest score there, a record previously held by England's Joe Hardstaff. Though he had many dazzling innings in his glittering career, most experts rate as the best 'a faultless innings lasting nearly four hours' (*Wisden* 1951) against a Commonwealth XI attack of Freer, Worrell, Pope, and Tribe at the P. Saravanamuttu stadium in Colombo in 1950. Hitting eleven boundaries, he missed a well-deserved century by four runs: the next highest score was a mere 17 in a total of 153. His favourite stroke was the late-cut, which he played with panache. Later, he led the Malaysian national team during an extended stay in that country. He played for the sheer enjoyment of the game and thrilled spectators with his uncanny stroke-play and many are the stories of his derring-do. Soon his Bohemian life-style caught up with him when he was falsely implicated in the murder of his wife. Acquitted on all charges 'Satha' still used to haunt most grounds and hold court to adoring fans and friends until a heart attack at a seaside restaurant claimed one of the country's greatest batsmen.

SENANAYAKE, Charith Panduka

(b. 1962, Colombo) *Colombo and Sri Lanka*

Senanayake is a left-hand opening batsman with a penchant for driving the ball on both flanks, but due to a weak defence could not survive at the highest level and faded after one series in New Zealand in 1990/1. His best performance was at Hamilton when he scored his only half-century in

SENANAYAKE

Test cricket (64) and was associated in a 95-run opening partnership with Chandika Hathurusinghe (81) who was making his Test début.

First-class career (1982–): 747 runs (25.75) and 8 catches

Test matches (5): 97 (19.40) and 2 catches

SENANAYAKE, Robert Parakrama

(b. 1913, Colombo; d. 1986, Colombo) *Sinhalese and Ceylon*

An enthusiastic cricketer who represented St Thomas's College, Robert Senanayake later turned out for Sinhalese Sports Club as a reliable opening batsman. After captaining St Thomas's in 1932 he emigrated to England and played for the Cambridge University Crusaders in 1933 and 1934. He also represented Surrey Club and Ground. After his return, Robert devoted all his spare time and a lot of personal wealth to the cause of Ceylon cricket. He was president of the Ceylon Cricket Association from 1957 to 1966, when the Board of Control for Cricket in Sri Lanka was formed, and continued as president of the newly constituted Board until 1975. His charming disposition and his endearing character enabled him to overcome many obstacles, and he made use of his personal relations with his contemporaries at Cambridge. He made frequent trips on behalf of the Board of Control, at his own expense. MCC honoured him as a Life Member, a rare accolade for a Ceylonese. His father, Don Stephen, was the first Prime Minister of independent Ceylon.

SILVA, Sampathwaduge Amal Rohitha

(b. 1960, Moratuwa) *Nondescripts and Sri Lanka*

A wiry and hard-hitting left-hander and an agile wicket-keeper, Amal Silva joined an exclusive list of cricketers when he made his maiden first-class hundred against England at Lord's in 1984. Ironically, it was only an injury to first-choice wicket-keeper, Guy de Alwis, which gave him the chance to play at Lord's, but he proved that his unbeaten 102 in the second innings of the drawn Test was no fluke by making 161 not out and 70 off Warwickshire in the following match and topped the tour averages with 558 runs at 62.00. In the following three-Test series against India, he took a remarkable 22 dismissals (21 catches, one stumping), including nine victims in each of the first two Tests, a Test record, and his 111 in the second Test at Colombo played a large part in bringing Sri Lanka their first Test victory. In his

first five Tests (he made his début against New Zealand at Wellington in the second Test of the 1982/3 series) he took an average of 5.4 victims per match, making a better start than Marsh, Knott, or Bari. Perhaps inevitably, the responsibility of opening the batting and keeping wicket then proved too heavy and he was unable to live up to such heady beginnings. He toured Pakistan in 1985/6 and then was taken ill during the first Test of the return series, losing his place for the final two Tests to the original incumbent, de Alwis.

First-class career (1982–): 2,211 runs (29.87) including 5 centuries, and 111 dismissals (102 c., 9 st.)

Test matches (9): 353 runs (25.21) including 2 centuries, and 34 dismissals (33 c., 1 st.)

TENNEKOON, Anura Punchi Banda

(b. 1946, Anuradhapura) *Sinhalese and Ceylon*

At the age of 17, Anura Tennekoon was adjudged the most outstanding schoolboy cricketer of the year, a reputation which he amply justified in later years. In 1965, when 19, he was picked to represent Ceylon against MCC, led by Mike Smith, and four years later he batted for 5 hours against an England attack comprising John Snow, David Brown, Basil D'Oliviera, Derek Underwood, and Pat Pocock, at the P. Saravanamuttu stadium in Colombo, posting his first century against a foreign team. A balanced and accomplished right-handed batsman, Tennekoon also scored hundreds against India and West Indies. His 169 against Ajit Wadekar's Indians was a classic innings. In 1979, Sri Lanka won the inaugural ICC Trophy under Tennekoon's captaincy and qualified to participate in the World Cup, which greatly helped towards the granting of full-member status two years later. It was a great pity that Tennekoon retired from the game while there was much cricket left in him and Sri Lanka thereby lost an experienced and high-class batsman before taking their first steps in the Test arena. This softly-spoken, retiring man none the less served the cricket administration first as a selector and then as secretary to the Board of Control.

First-class career (1965–79): 3,481 runs (36.26) including 5 centuries, and 60 catches

TILLEKERATNE, Hashan Prashantha

(b. 1967, Colombo) *Nondescripts and Sri Lanka*

A versatile and talented cricketer who began his career as a brilliant close-in fielder and left-handed middle-order batsman, Hashan Tillekeratne was conscripted to keep wicket and did so willingly until he was dropped from the side. Not a regular 'keeper for his own club, he naturally found doing so for the Test team no easy task. Recalled to the side without wicket-keeping responsibilities in 1992/3, Tillekeratne excelled himself, scoring consistently well in the middle-order and fielding superbly at short-leg. Against England he made 66 not out in the first one-day international, and 93 not out and 36 not out in the subsequent Test victory at the SSC ground, dominating the attack with fierce square-cutting and quick movement of his feet. In the same 1992/3 season he had scored 82 in the only Test innings he played against Australia and 93 in the nine-wicket defeat of New Zealand at the SSC. In this match he equalled the record of 7 catches in a Test by a non-wicket-keeper, eagerly seizing chances at short-leg off the spin bowling of Warnaweera and Muralitharan. Tillekeratne himself also bowls useful left-arm spin. In 82 one-day internationals between 1986 and 1994 he had scored 1,522 runs (26.24).

First-class career (1984–94): 4,602 runs (44.67) including 12 centuries, 17 wickets (28.82), and 138 dismissals (133 c., 5 st.)
Test matches (30): 1,640 runs (39.04) including 2 centuries, and 66 catches

TISSERA, Michael Hugh

(b. 1939, Colombo) Nondescripts and Ceylon

An elegant right-hand batsman, useful right-arm leg-spinner, and charming man, Michael Tissera blossomed after a relatively modest career at St Thomas's College. Picked first time for the national side against Peter May's men in 1958, his début was also inauspicious, but his graceful batsmanship got him many runs on the domestic scene and an unbeaten century scored against a team of West Indian cricketers passing through Ceylon, including Wesley Hall and Gary Sobers, shot him to prominence. There was no looking back now. In 1964/5 he led Ceylon on a tour of India. After three defeats and one near defeat in five games, Ceylon were given little chance in the final 'Test' at Ahmedabad, but in a low-scoring game Tissera's declaration triggered a sensational win, as India collapsed for 66. In 1965 against Mike Smith's team, only rain prevented Ceylon from registering their first win against MCC. However, it was not long in coming: in 1969, under his leadership, Ceylon beat Colin Cowdrey's side in the first limited-overs encounter.

Four years later came another one-day win against Tony Lewis's men. Tissera later served as selector, manager, and vice-president of the Board of Control. A successful businessman in the tea trade, he still turns out in his flannels whenever the opportunity arises.

First-class career (1958–75): 1,394 runs (28.44), 27 wickets (31.70), and 15 catches

VAAS, Warnakulasooriya Patabadige Ushantha Joseph Chaminda

(b. 1974, Colombo) Colombo Colts and Sri Lanka

A diminutive, but nippy, medium-fast, left-arm over the wicket bowler, and a capable lower-order left-handed batsman, Chaminda Vaas had a very successful start to his Test career in 1994/5. Given seaming conditions he showed the ability to trouble the best batsmen with an in-swinger and a ball which leaves the right-hander sharply. He took 10 wickets at 23 runs each in three Tests in Zimbabwe in October 1994 and later did even better in New Zealand.

First-class career (1990–   ): 98 runs (19.60), 46 wickets (18.17), and 2 catches
Test matches (6): 160 runs (22.85), 26 wickets (18.92), and 1 catch

VANDERSPAR, George Augustus Hunter

(b. 1858; d. 1940, Bournemouth, England) Somerset and Ceylon

With Ashley Walker, George Vanderspar helped to organize Ceylon cricket around the turn of the century. A versatile sportsman, he excelled at Rugby and cricket and played for Somerset in 1880 (pre-first-class) and MCC. He not only captained the Colombo Cricket Club (1891) but also led the All-Ceylon team to Calcutta and twice to Madras (1885/6 and 1891/2). He was instrumental in persuading touring MCC and Australian teams to play in Colombo against All-Ceylon teams, two of which (1891 and 1894) he captained.

First-class career (1893): 7 runs (7.00)

WALKER, Ashley

(b. 1844, Bradford, Yorkshire; d. 1927, Harrold, Bedfordshire) Cambridge University, Staffordshire, Yorkshire, and Ceylon

A doughty Yorkshireman who also played minor county cricket for Staffordshire, Ashley Walker was one of the true founders of Ceylon cricket, and became assistant to the principal of Royal College. There he taught cricket, founded the school team and was instrumental in organizing the now famous Royal–Thomian cricket encounter, against St Thomas's College, in 1879. Today it is a three-day match and a national event, the second-longest uninterrupted cricket fixture in the world. He gathered together a joint team from the two schools to play a team of Europeans from the Colombo Cricket Club in 1881, one of many acts encouraging young cricketers and coaching budding youngsters. Walker continued to play in Ceylon, captaining a team of Ceylon-based Europeans to Madras in 1885 and to Bombay the next year. In 1884 he had captained the All-Ceylon team against the Australians. He was elected president of the Colombo Cricket Club in 1882, but his first love was Royal College.

First-class career (1863–70): 531 runs (15.61), 18 wickets (16.05), and 6 catches

WARNAPURA, Bandula

(b. 1953, Rambukkana) *Bloomfield and Sri Lanka*

A popular and respected cricketer, Bandula Warnapura succeeded the prolific Anura Tennekoon as captain of Sri Lanka after some consistent performances as an opening batsman in the years leading up to the achievement of Test status. He thus had the honour of leading his country in her first official Tests. Also a steady, right-arm, medium-paced bowler and good fielder, Warnapura, a balanced and correct right-hand batsman, was an automatic selection for most of Sri Lanka's representative teams through the 1970s, touring England in 1975, 1979, and 1981 (the latter tour as captain), India in 1975/6 and Pakistan in 1973/4 and 1981/2. In this last tour Sri Lanka were beaten but not disgraced in two matches though Warnapura, who missed the second Test through injury, did not show his best form. He made 106 in a one-day international against Australia in 1980. He fell from grace when choosing to tour South Africa in 1982/3, a decision which cost him and several colleagues a life ban from Sri Lankan cricket.

First-class career (1970–83): 2,280 runs (25.05) including 2 centuries, 13 wickets (48.30), and 23 catches
Test matches (4): 96 runs (12.00), 0–46, and 2 catches

WARNAWEERA, Kahakachi Patabendige Jayananda

(b. 1960, Matara) *Galle and Sri Lanka*

An off-spinner who bowls at a similar pace to Derek Underwood, though with a rather more jerky action, Warnaweera was the most successful of the Sri Lankan bowlers against the England B team in 1985/6. He topped the 'Test' averages with 14 wickets at 19.36, including match figures of 9 for 125 in the third match at Kandy which prompted the selectors to give him a Test début on the same ground against Pakistan just over two weeks later. At the SSC grounds in 1992/3 his match figures of 8 for 188 from 65 overs were chiefly responsible for Sri Lanka's first defeat of England.

First-class career (1985–   ): 230 runs (6.20), 264 wickets (19.64), and 10 catches
Test matches (10): 39 runs (4.33) and 32 wickets (31.90)

WEERAKODDY, Ajith Priyantha

(b. 1970, Colombo) *Nondescripts*

A right-arm fast-medium bowler, Ajith Weerakoddy was chosen to tour Sharjah in 1993/4 and played in one limited-overs international, taking no wicket for 41 in six overs. Despite useful first-class performances, he has not been selected since. A right-hand lower-order batsman, in his only international innings he scored two.

First-class career (1990–   ): 187 runs (8.13), 96 wickets (18.33), and 13 catches

WEERASINGHE, Colombage Don Udesh Sanjeewa

(b. 1968, Colombo) *Issipathana and Sri Lanka*

Sanjeewa Weerasinghe made his début against India at Colombo in 1985/6 as a 17-year-old schoolboy and seemed the likely successor to D. S. de Silva as Sri Lanka's leg-spinner, but his hopes were not fulfilled. Though Sri Lanka recorded a historic win he did not take a wicket, scored only 3, and was left out for the next Test. He was selected for the tour to Pakistan in the same season without playing a Test, but a fine performance in the third unofficial Test against England B on a helpful pitch at Kandy when he took 5 for 49 off 30.3 overs apparently put him back in contention. Sadly, he could not repeat this sort of success.

First-class career (1984–   ): 239 runs (12.57), 41 wickets (24.51), and 19 catches

WETTIMUNY, Mithra de Silva

(b. 1951, Colombo) *Sinhalese and Sri Lanka*

A diminutive right-hander, Mithra Wettimuny made his Test début against New Zealand in Christchurch on the 1982/3 tour, opening the innings with his younger brother Sidath, only the third fraternal opening partnership in the history of Test cricket (after E. M. and W. G. Grace and Hanif and Sadiq Mohammed). They put on 49 for the first wicket in the first Test, of which Mithra made 17, but subsequent innings of 5, 6, and 0 ensured that the partnership was short-lived.

First-class career (1982–3): 268 runs (17.86) and 0–25
Test matches (2): 28 runs (7.00) and 2 catches

WETTIMUNY, Sidath

(b. 1956, Colombo) *Sinhalese and Sri Lanka*

The younger brother of two other Sri Lankan openers, Sunil and Mithra, and a sound right-hand opener, Sidath Wettimuny won a place in the record books and in the hearts of English spectators at Lord's in 1984 when he made the highest score ever by any batsman on his first appearance in a Test in England. In all, he batted for 10 hours 42 minutes for his 190, displaying a wide range of strokes and a depth of concentration which belied his youthful features. He had, however, given notice of his ability to play long innings when making Sri Lanka's first Test century, 157 against Pakistan at Faisalabad in 1981/2. He toured England in 1981, New Zealand in 1982/3 and Pakistan again in 1985/6, but understandably found it hard to live up to expectations in the three series against Pakistan and India in 1985/6 and made only one score over 50 in sixteen Test innings in that period.

First-class career (1975–87): 2,859 runs (33.63) including 6 centuries, 2 wickets (37.50), and 21 catches
Test matches (23): 1,221 runs (29.07) including 2 centuries, 0–37, and 10 catches

WICKREMASINGHE, Anguppulige Gamini Dayantha

(b. 1965, Delduwa) *Nondescripts and Sri Lanka*

A wicket-keeper who should have played as a regular for many years, having made his Test début against Australia at Brisbane in the 1989/90 tour, Wickremasinghe was a victim of the national selectors who preferred playing batsmen

who can keep wicket rather than the other way around. Ironically, he kept wicket for his club where Tillekeratne used to field, but in Test matches the latter was, for a time, preferred. Even as a more than useful tail-ender who could have developed, Wickremasinghe was overlooked and Sri Lanka lost an efficient glove artist.

First-class career (1984–): 1,687 runs (21.35) including 1 century, 2 wickets (9.50), and 173 dismissals (150 c., 23 st.)
Test matches (3): 17 runs (8.50) and 10 dismissals (9 c., 1 st.)

WICKREMASINGHE, Gallage Pramodya

(b. 1971, Matara) *Burgher RC, Sinhalese, and Sri Lanka*

A fast-medium right-arm bowler with a long run and classical action, Gallage Wickremasinghe is also a useful fielder and a tail-end batsman who likes to use the long handle. After the exit of Rumesh Ratnayake, he has carried the brunt of Sri Lanka's fast bowling, his zest and enthusiasm tending sometimes to an excess of no-balls when straining for an extra yard of pace. First appearing in 1988/9 for Burgher RC, he was a regular tourist after his trip to England in 1990 and in 1991/2 took all 10 wickets for 41 for Sinhalese against Kalutara in Colombo. By 1994 he had played in 43 one-day internationals, taking 33 wickets (44.18).

First-class career (1988–94): 489 runs (12.86), 131 wickets (26.74), and 19 catches
Test matches (17): 199 runs (9.04), 32 wickets (50.06), and 7 catches

WIJEGUNAWARDENE, Kapila Indika Weerakkody

(b. 1964, Colombo) *Colombo and Sri Lanka*

A right-arm medium-paced opening bowler who was able to move the ball in the air and off the pitch, Wijegunawardene did not possess sufficient pace to pose danger to batsmen at Test level. Having made a tour of England in 1991, he played a further Test against Pakistan when he captured 7 for 98, but his career ended abruptly. A tail-end batsman with few pretensions, he was a tidy fielder.

First-class career (1987–92): 231 runs (9.24), 126 wickets (25.03), and 15 catches
Test matches (2): 14 runs (4.66) and 7 wickets (21.00)

WIJESURIYA, Roger Gerrard Christopher Ediriweera

(b. 1960, Moratuwa) *Sinhalese and Sri Lanka*

A slow left-arm bowler and right-handed tail-ender, Roger Wijesuriya played in all five games that the Sri Lankan under-19 side played against the Pakistan touring team of 1978/9, taking 25 wickets. But when he visited Pakistan with the senior Sri Lankan side three years later, he was less successful and was discarded by the selectors for Sri Lanka's next tour, of India. In Pakistan he played his only Test to date, taking no wickets for 105 at Lahore and making 0 and 3. He toured Pakistan in 1981/2, making his début in the third Test at Lahore, and New Zealand in 1982/3, but did not play another Test until 1985/6 when, again in Pakistan, he played in all three Tests, picking up just one wicket for 189.

First-class career (1978–   ): 486 runs (16.20), 107 wickets (25.77), and 27 catches

Test matches (4): 22 runs (4.40), 1 wicket (294.00), and 1 catch

WIJETUNGE, Piyal Kashyapa

(b. 1971, Mahiyangana) *Sinhalese and Sri Lanka*

A slow left-arm spinner who showed great promise as a schoolboy at St Anthony's College, Kandy bowled in tandem with off-spinner Muttiah Muralitharan and wreaked havoc in school cricket along with Ruwan Kalpage. A formidable trio at school levels, they played a single Test together, against South Africa at Moratuwa in 1993. Forced to change his bowling action, he lost form and was not picked again for national duty.

First-class career (1988–   ): 325 runs (9.55), 128 wickets (29.89), and 19 catches
Test matches (1): 10 runs (5.00) and 2 wickets (59.00)

West Indies

ACHONG, Ellis Edgar

(b. 1904, Port of Spain, Trinidad; d. 1986, Port of Spain) *Trinidad and West Indies*

Of Chinese extraction, 'Puss' Achong was a slow left-arm bowler of immaculate length. He toured England in 1933 and played at home against England in 1929/30 and 1934/5. Although working hard on the tour, he accomplished little in the Tests and was generally expensive, taking 71 wickets (36.14) in nearly 1,000 overs. He had a long experience of Lancashire League cricket in which he secured over 1,000 wickets. Possibly the expression 'Chinaman' for the left-arm bowler's 'wrong 'un' originated with 'Puss' in mind.

First-class career (1929–35): 503 runs (14.37), 110 wickets (30.23), and 20 catches

Test matches (6): 81 runs (8.10), 8 wickets (47.25), and 6 catches

ADAMS, James Clive

(b. 1968, Jamaica) *Jamaica, Nottinghamshire, and West Indies*

Affectionately known as 'Jimmy the Cricket' for his all-round ability as left-hand batsman, slow left-arm bowler, occasional wicket-keeper, and exceptional fielder, Adams himself prefers to concentrate on batsmanship. A product of Kingston High School, Jamaica College, and the Kingston Cricket Club, he was a gifted sportsman before graduating to the Jamaica team in 1985. Six seasons later he finally registered a maiden first-class century, the slowest ever in the Caribbean, but since then his range of shots has improved markedly. An energetic runner between wickets with a trade-mark slide and turn, the furrowed brow and bearded jaw set firm in the cleft of his shoulder enhance an image of solid application and determination in his middle-order batting. His Test début, alongside Kenny Benjamin and David Williams, in the historic South Africa match at Kensington Oval, Barbados, in 1992 set the tone for his advance at the top level. An undefeated 79 and 4 for 43 with orthodox, barely acknowledged, left-arm spin (including Hansie Cronje caught at slip off his fourth ball) ensured a trip to Australia that winter and a confirmed place in the home series against England in 1994. He made 95 not out in the first Test on his home ground, Sabina Park, held a record-equalling 6 catches, and followed up with a match-winning 52 not out in the one-day international, finally notching his first Test century at Bourda, Georgetown, a supreme 137 full of flowing off-drives spanning almost 7 hours of unflustered style and concentration. Adams finished with 374 runs at 62.33 in the series. He spent five seasons as professional at Eppleton in the Durham Senior League where he regularly topped the batting averages and earned a one-year contract at Nottinghamshire in 1994, surprisingly recording only one championship century, 121 against Sussex. A heavier-built clone of compatriot Jeffrey Dujon at a distance, his outlook is not dissimilar. Introspective, mannered, and courteous, he is a committed Christian, an avid reader of the Bible and seems set to form the counterpoint to the West Indian middle-order stroke-players for years to come. Later in 1994 he had a brilliant tour of India, scoring 615 first-class runs (153.75), 520 of them, including hundreds at

ALEXANDER

Nagpur and Chandigarh, in the Tests. He showed the character of a future captain.

First-class career (1985–): 5,076 runs (43.02) including 12 centuries, 43 wickets (38.25), and 94 catches

Test matches (18): 1,456 runs (72.80) including 4 centuries, 9 wickets (49.88), and 23 catches

ALEXANDER, Franz Copeland Murray

(b. 1928, Kingston, Jamaica) *Cambridge University, Jamaica, and West Indies*

An aggressive right-handed batsman and sound, sometimes brilliant, wicket-keeper, 'Gerry' Alexander was a Cambridge blue in 1952 and 1953. His initial first-class match in the West Indies was for Jamaica versus the Duke of Norfolk's XI in March 1957. He toured England in 1957, India and Pakistan in 1958/9 (captain), and Australia in 1960/1, and at home played against Pakistan in 1957/8 (captain) and England in 1959/60 (captain). The first-choice wicket-keeper for several years, he was a popular and astute leader, especially against England in 1959/60 when he secured 23 victims, thus equalling the world record, though he lost the rubber. In Australia in 1960/1 he did not once fail to register at least one 50 in the Tests, his best score being 108 in the third match at Sydney, and he headed the batting with 484 runs (60.50), besides dismissing 16 (including 6 in the fourth match at Adelaide). In all first-class matches on this tour he made 734 runs (52.42). He was also a blue at Association football and he won an England cap and an FA Amateur Cup Winner's medal.

First-class career (1952–61): 3,238 runs (29.17) including 1 century, and 256 dismissals (217 c., 39 st.)

Test matches (25): 961 runs (30.03) including 1 century, and 90 dismissals (85 c., 5 st.)

ALI, Imtiaz

(b. 1954, Trinidad) *Trinidad and West Indies*

A slim, right-arm leg-spin and googly bowler, with a fine action and a distinct loop in his flight, Imtiaz Ali looked an outstanding prospect in the Trinidad spin attack in the early 1970s but was tried in only one Test, the third against India at Port of Spain in 1975/6, when he scored 1 not out and took 2 for 89.

First-class career (1971–80): 558 runs (11.16) and 157 wickets (26.24)

ALI, Inshan

(b. 1949, Trinidad; d. 1995, Port of Spain, Trinidad) *Trinidad and West Indies*

A small, left-hand back-of-the-hand spinner, Inshan Ali never quite turned out to be the match-winner the West Indies selectors hoped he would be. He was a most unusual bowler, difficult to read, with a deceptive flight, but he lacked the control to trouble Test batsmen consistently. Cricket was never dull with Inshan for he seemed either to beat the bat or to be punished with a boundary for a full toss or long hop. Like all unorthodox spinners he seldom seemed to have much luck. He did, however, have one real Test triumph, figures of 5 for 59, against New Zealand in the first innings of the fifth Test at Port of Spain in 1971/2. He was certainly no failure on his two major tours, to England in 1973, when he took 38 wickets in eleven matches, and Australia in 1975/6, where he finished second in the tour averages with 22 wickets at 25.54. But on both tours he played only one Test.

First-class career (1965–80): 1,341 runs (13.82), 328 wickets (28.93), and 44 catches

Test matches (12): 172 runs (10.75), 34 wickets (47.67), and 7 catches

ALI, Sayed Mubarack

(b. (?); d. 1993, San Fernando, Trinidad) *Trinidad*

No bowler has been called for throwing more times in a first-class innings than Ali was by umpire Eddie Ward at Kensington Oval on 25 July 1942 in Trinidad's match against Barbados. An off-spinner who delivered with a bent arm, he was no-balled thirty times and eventually forced to bowl underarm. When his captain, Victor Stollmeyer, switched Ali to the opposite end, Ward's partner, the former Test player Herman Griffith, did not call him and he completed the innings, taking 3 for 99 from 25 overs. He had played four first-class matches by then, all in Port of Spain, but this was to be the end of his career as he was never chosen for Trinidad again.

First-class career (1941–2): 56 runs (9.33) and 16 wickets (32.25)

ALLAN, David Walter

(b. 1937, Christ Church, Barbados) *Barbados and West Indies*

Fair-haired and strong, David Allan came to England as a first-string wicket-keeper in 1963, but lost his place to Deryck Murray for all the Tests, despite a successful haul of 45 catches and eight stumpings. On his second visit in 1966 he shared duties with Jackie Hendriks, playing in two Tests. He played once against Australia in 1964/5 when Hendriks was out through injury. In his first two Tests, against India at Bridgetown and Kingston in 1961/2, he had ten victims and hit 40 not out in the first match. He could be a very useful batsman.

First-class career (1955–66): 764 runs (14.69) and 141 dismissals (117 c., 24 st.)

Test matches (5): 75 runs (12.50) and 18 dismissals (15 c., 3 st.)

ALLEN, Ian Basil Alston

(b. 1965, St Vincent) *Windward Islands and West Indies*

Ian Allen sprang to prominence early in 1991 when he took 4 for 51 for the West Indies Board XI against Australia in Barbados, but never fulfilled his promise as a genuinely quick right-arm opening bowler. He made his first-class début against the Leeward Islands in 1989, toured with West Indies B to Zimbabwe later that year and took 7 for 48 including a hat-trick against Trinidad and Tobago at Pointe à Pierre in 1991. This feat, and Ian Bishop's back injury, earned him a surprise selection on the summer tour to England where he made his Test début at Lord's, becoming only the fourth Vincentian after Alfie Roberts, wicket-keeper Michael Findlay, and Winston Davis to earn a Test cap. He operated as the second change-bowler and appeared again in the third Test at Trent Bridge, recording his best figures of 2 for 69 before being displaced by Patrick Patterson. In March 1992 he took 8 wickets, spearheading the Windward Islands attack in the opening first-class game of the England A tour in Grenada, once striking John Stephenson on the shoulder with a beamer apparently never acknowledged as accidental. As a right-handed batsman he was capable of useful lower-order runs, and rejoiced in the fact that he was never dismissed in his brief Test career.

First-class career (1989–   ): 394 runs (11.94) and 86 wickets (37.77)

Test matches (2): 5 runs and 5 wickets (36.00)

AMBROSE, Curtly Elconn Lynwall

(b. 1963, Swetes Village, Antigua) *Leeward Islands, Northamptonshire, and West Indies*

Curtly Ambrose is assured of a place in the pantheon of fast-bowling greats, an immortal already in the most demanding facet of the game. Aptly dubbed 'the tall destroyer', he stands an intimidating 6 ft. 7 in., delivering steepling bounce from a classic high right-arm action, and, as the eighth West Indian to claim 200 Test wickets, specializing in legendary feats in unlikely situations. A country boy, with a smile like a sliced melon, he comes from Swetes Village in the parched interior of Antigua. He came to cricket relatively late, having considered migration to the United States to pursue a career in basketball. His advance from inter-parish cricket and the family carpentry business at the age of 21, was rapid. He made an unremarkable début for the Leewards in 1986, played on an overseas scholarship for the Chester Club, Boughton Hall, in the Liverpool Competition that summer, and was signed as professional by Heywood in the Central Lancashire League the following year, a demanding role he never really enjoyed despite several startling performances. In early 1988 he was still virtually unknown but became almost an overnight sensation with 35 wickets at 15.51 in the domestic Red Stripe Cup tournament, a record for a regional season, after being called for throwing by the Test umpire Clyde Cumberbatch. A fortnight afterwards, he was thrust into the Test spotlight at Georgetown against Pakistan, later earning 22 wickets at 20.23 on his first England tour, and 26 at 21.46 in Australia. His output in home series against India and Pakistan was less prolific, a shortfall remedied in dramatic fashion on England's tour of the Caribbean in 1990 when Ambrose single-handedly took control in the final session of the fourth Test in Barbados. England had batted with dogged determination for a draw which would have ensured at least a share of the series but the Antiguan, armed with the new ball, cut down England with a coruscating, deadly accurate spell of 5 for 18 in 7.4 overs, including four lbws, which so undermined their spirit and morale that total capitulation and a 2–1 defeat ensued in Antigua. Ambrose's final figures of 8 for 45 were the fourth best by any West Indian in Tests. England were to become his favoured opposition, but he demolished South Africa with 6 for 34 in the inaugural Test in 1992, again at Kensington, and against Australia at Adelaide in 1993 he took 10 wickets, bowling to the point of exhaustion, before Courtney Walsh grabbed the final wicket to gain victory by one run, the narrowest winning margin in Test history. Subsequently, in the fifth Test at Perth, he shattered Australia with a burst of 7 for 1 in 32 balls, a devastating first-innings effort which assured the retention of the Frank Worrell Trophy. He capped these memorable exploits at Port of Spain in March 1994 when England were again swept away in a quite astonishing spell of 6 for 22 off 7.5 overs late on the fourth day of the third Test. England were chasing a victory target of 194 but retired hurt that evening at 40 for 8, after a riveting piece of cricket theatre, arguably the most exciting passage of play in modern times. Ambrose has the ability to wrest the psychological initiative, the shock factor a priceless asset encouraged by his mentor Andy Roberts, and when the force is with him he becomes a fearsome prospect. Fast and uncompromising off a loping approach, with a loose bowling arm and a characteristic wave of the hand towards the batsman just before delivery, he has a high angled yorker and nasty bouncer, and also bowls a skidding delivery at pace, responsible for a high proportion of bowled and lbw victims. He takes great pride in not conceding runs. The equally characteristic trouser tug, pulling vigorously at the waistband, is usually the hint of something dramatic, a signal that he's shifted into higher gear. He considers himself a rhythm bowler, but his frame, and particularly the stork-like legs, belie a tremendous resilience and fitness. In 49 Tests after his début, he missed just one, through haemorrhoids. His left-handed batting, producing a Test-best of 53, is spirited and full of self-belief. When Andy Caddick bowled him, heaving across the line, at the Queens Park Oval in that third Test in 1994, it stoked the fires of revenge and focused his mind on a triumph to come. This is the real legend of Ambrose—he produced awesome performances when it really mattered. He consigned himself to the English county cricket treadmill with Northamptonshire in 1989, 1990, 1993, and 1994, when his late arrival after the rigours of England's tour of the Caribbean caused dressing room friction and team instability. Shy, often lugubrious, an inveterate late arriver in his early career, seldom friendly to the press, he loves music, plays the guitar and takes readily to the microphone during parties.

First-class career (1986–): 2,301 runs (14.94), 651 wickets (20.39), and 51 catches
Test matches (48): 680 runs (11.92), 219 wickets (21.07), and 10 catches

ANDERSON, Cecil Alva

(b. 1910, Kingston, Jamaica; d. 1978, Kingston)

'Jack' Anderson's obvious knowledge and feel for the game earned his writing widespread readership and respect in the Caribbean and beyond. Like other cricket correspondents of his time, well before the introduction of local television coverage, Anderson covered matches in great detail. His views were sometimes controversial but never uninformed. He joined the Jamaica *Daily Gleaner* in 1933 and rose to become city editor of the *Gleaner*'s afternoon paper, *The Star*, at his retirement in 1976. He covered the West Indies' tours of England in 1957, 1963, 1966, and 1969 and, apart from the West Indian press, was West Indies' correspondent of *Wisden* for many years. He died when assailants broke into his home, the evening after he had watched a day's play in the fifth Test between Australia and the West Indies at Sabina Park, and shot him. One of his four sons, Alva, was a boxing blue at Cambridge and a national Jamaica hockey representative.

ARCHER, David Myrton

(b. 1931, St Michael, Barbados; d. 1992, Bridgetown, Barbados)

David Archer was one of the few West Indian umpires to have played first-class cricket. While resident in Grenada, he played in the annual Windward Islands tournament and his quickish leg-spin bowling earned him a place on the Windward Islands team for two matches in the 1967 Shell Shield. When he was no-balled for throwing against Trinidad and Tobago, he was not picked again. Returning to his native Barbados, he turned his attention to umpiring and stood in his first first-class match in the 1976 Shell Shield. He umpired the first of his 28 Tests in England's Bridgetown Test in 1981 and the last in 1992, South Africa's historic return to Test cricket, also at Kensington Oval, only 6 months before his death. Only the Jamaican, Douglas Sang Hue, of West Indian umpires, officiated in more Tests (31), but Archer also stood in 10 matches in the English county championship in 1982, the Australasian Cup in Sharjah in 1986, and the World Cup in India and Pakistan in 1987. A publican, Archer called his bar 'The Umpires' Inn'.

ARTHURTON, Keith Lloyd Thomas

(b. 1965, Charlestown, Nevis) *Leeward Islands and West Indies*

Keith Arthurton was only the third player, after Elquemedo Willett and Derick Parry, from the tiny island of Nevis (pop. 15,000) to graduate to Test status. His father in the village of Jessups actively discouraged his participation but his mother was a constant source of inspiration. A stylish left-handed bat with the chiselled, strong-shouldered physique of the natural athlete, his advance at the top level was marred by a $2\frac{1}{2}$-year hiatus before Sir Garfield Sobers advised a moderation in shot-making outside the off stump, and for a time he formed with Brian Lara and Jimmy Adams a triumvirate of middle-order left-handers. A first-class début on home ground at Grove Park in 1986 against Barbados preceded consistent run scoring over the next seven seasons, when he averaged 53.25 in regional domestic cricket. In 1988 he toured England as an unscheduled 17th player, justifying the selectors' faith with an overall average of just under 50 and making 27 in his Test début on a typical seamer's pitch at Headingley, when Gordon Greenidge was injured. He had little scope on the following tour of Australia, then suffered a poor home series against India in 1989. Towards the end of 1991, with Richards and Greenidge omitted from a plethora of one-day tournaments in Sharjah, Pakistan, and Australia, Arthurton earned a recall and enjoyed a relatively successful World Cup campaign. Supreme in the cover-drive and square-cut, he stroked ten offside boundaries in a top score of 59 in the first innings of the one-off Test against South Africa in early 1992, but was dropped once and caught twice at slip off no balls. His second tour of Australia was therefore a test of character and, heeding Sobers's words, he did not disappoint. He started well, with an undefeated century against Western Australia, but owed a great debt to vice-captain Gus Logie, who proposed his selection for the first Test ahead of himself. Arthurton duly delivered a maiden Test century, 157 not out in nearly $7\frac{1}{2}$ hours of intense concentration, the highest score by a West Indian in Tests at Brisbane. If this innings was a pivotal point in his career, his second century, an expansive 126 against England in the first Test at Sabina Park in February 1994, completed on his 29th birthday, seemed to mark his final coming-of-age as a Test batsman. A lightning quick mover in the field, with the graceful stride of a panther, he has a magnificent throwing arm and his slow-to-medium left-arm spinners had earned him 20 wickets (23.45) in 78 one-day internationals to 1994.

First-class career (1986–): 5,097 runs (44.71) including 15 centuries, 15 wickets (29.27), and 44 catches

Test matches (28): 1,210 runs (31.84) including 2 centuries, 1 wicket (107.00), and 16 catches

ASGARALI, Nyron Sultan

(b. 1920, Port of Spain, Trinidad) *Trinidad and West Indies*

A sound right-hand opening batsman though a late developer, Nyron Asgarali established himself by scoring 103, 128, and 83 in successive matches for Trinidad against British Guiana in 1951/2. Touring England in 1957, he disappointed in the Tests, but in all first-class matches made 1,011 runs (29.73). He became a professional in the Lancashire League.

First-class career (1940–62): 2,761 runs (32.86) including 7 centuries, 23 wickets (42.00), and 29 catches

Test matches (2): 62 runs (15.50)

ATKINSON, Denis St Eval

(b. 1926, Christ Church, Barbados) *Barbados, Trinidad, and West Indies*

A very sound right-handed batsman and medium-pace bowler of off-cutters and off-breaks, Denis Atkinson toured India in 1948/9, Australasia in 1951/2 and 1955/6, and England in 1957, and at home played against England in 1953, Australia in 1954/5, and Pakistan in 1957/8. He captained the West Indies in three Tests against Australia in 1954/5 in the absence of Jeff Stollmeyer through injury, losing two of them; and he led in the series against New Zealand in 1955/6, winning the rubber by three to one. His finest hour came in the fourth Test against Australia at Bridgetown in 1954/5. Facing a total of 668, West Indies collapsed and were 146 for 6 when Atkinson and C. Depeiaza came together and, in more than a day, added 348 for the seventh wicket, for 40 years a world record: Denis Atkinson contributed 219, his career-highest. He also took 7 for 164 in this match, which was drawn. In the series he headed the bowling with 13 wickets (35.30) and made 311 runs (44.42). In the fourth Test against New Zealand at Auckland in 1953/4 he took 7 for 53 (in 40 overs) in the second innings. On his sole tour of England in 1957 he began memorably taking 10 for 62 in the first match at Worcester with his off-cutters, but later he was overworked and a strained shoulder affected his performance. He achieved little in the Tests, but took 55 wickets (22.45) in all first-class matches and averaged 17.05 with the bat. Against England in the West Indies three years before, he had made 259 runs (43.16) in the Tests. He is the elder brother of Eric Atkinson.

ATKINSON

First-class career (1946–61): 2,812 runs (28.40) including 5 centuries, 200 wickets (26.45), and 39 catches

Test matches (22): 922 runs (31.79) including 1 century, 47 wickets (35.04), and 11 catches

ATKINSON, Eric St Eval

(b. 1927, Christ Church, Barbados) *Barbados and West Indies*

A right-handed batsman and fast-medium bowler, Eric Atkinson toured India and Pakistan in 1958/9, and at home played against Pakistan in 1957/8. In the third Test against Pakistan at Kingston (dominated by batsmen, including the innings of 365 not out by Gary Sobers) he took 8 for 78 in the match. In the two Tests in Pakistan he took nine wickets (13.22).

First-class career (1949–59): 696 runs (21.75) and 61 wickets (26.72)

Test matches (8): 126 runs (15.75), 25 wickets (23.56), and 2 catches

AUSTIN, Sir Harold Bruce Gardiner

(b. 1877, St Michael, Barbados; d. 1943, St Michael) *Barbados*

No individual has had more influence over West Indies cricket than Harold Austin during his prodigious lifetime. He was one of five brothers of an established Barbadian business family, all of whom played first-class cricket. He made a name for himself at Harrison College as a tall, correct right-hand batsman and right-arm medium-pace bowler and his début for Barbados was at the age of 17, against the first English team to visit the West Indies, led by R. Slade Lucas, in 1895. A commanding personality, a capacity to relate to people, and a wide knowledge of most subjects also stood him in good stead in politics and commerce and made him an obvious leader. In addition to being captain of Barbados and of the West Indies team on its tours to England in 1907 and 1923 and against MCC in the West Indies in 1926, he was member of the House of Assembly for the city of Bridgetown for 26 years, eventually serving as Speaker, and, as head of the family firm, president of the Chamber of Commerce. His knighthood, bestowed in 1933, was an anticipated honour. 'H.B.G.', as he was widely known, would certainly have been on the inaugural West Indies tour of England in 1900 as well had he not been fighting at the time in the Boer War for the British Army, in which he rose to the rank of Major. According to C. L. R. James, he was 'the natural captain of the West Indies for as long as he chose to play'. But he was more than that. He was also chief selector and benefactor, often helping to underwrite Barbados and West Indies cricket. If he was autocratic in some of his selections, he was a good judge of a cricketer and his insistence on the inclusion on the 1923 England tour of the 21-year-old Learie Constantine and George Francis, then known only as Austin's practice bowler in Barbados, proved particularly perceptive. The West Indies' improving performances against English teams, on tour and at home, prompted Austin and others to move towards the formation of a formal board of control to administer the game on a regional level, replacing the *ad hoc* committees that were previously charged with the job. At his instigation and under his chairmanship, a steering committee met in Bridgetown in January 1927 to discuss the matter, and the West Indies Cricket Board of Control was officially established in Port of Spain in June of that year with Austin as its first president. C. L. R. James's 1963 assessment of Austin as 'the man who has more than any other made West Indies cricket what it is' was appropriate praise. In his native Barbados, he served as vice-president of the Barbados Cricket Association from 1935 until his death and president of Wanderers Club from 1930.

First-class career (1895–1928): 2,643 runs (28.42) and 15 wickets (20.13)

AUSTIN, Richard Arkwright

(b. 1954, Jamaica) *Jamaica and West Indies*

A sound and stylish right-handed batsman and adaptable bowler who could turn from medium pace to off-spin, Richard Austin had just found a place in the West Indies side when he signed for Kerry Packer in controversial circumstances. He was then omitted from the West Indies Test side for the third Test against Australia at Georgetown in 1977/8, causing other Packer players to withdraw from the side on the eve of the match. He was the outstanding batsman in the Shell Shield that season, starting the season as Jamaica's opening batsman with scores of 74, 127, 88, and 56, and finishing with an average of 61.50. He also took 18 Shield wickets, including 4 for 45 and 8 for 71 against Trinidad. He toured South Africa with the first unofficial team in 1982/3.

First-class career (1974–83): 2,097 runs (33.82) including 4 centuries, and 73 wickets (31.21)

Test matches (2): 22 runs (11.00), 0–5, and 2 catches

BACCHUS, Sheik Faoud Ahumul

(b. 1954, Georgetown, British Guiana) Guyana, Border, Western Province, and West Indies

After showing exceptional promise from an early age in cricket in Guyana, Faoud Bacchus was capped against Australia in 1977/8 after the World Series cricketers had withdrawn. In the last two Tests of this series his achievements were modest but as a right-handed opening or middle-order batsman and superb cover fielder he was outstanding on the tour of India in 1978/9, finishing second in the Test averages with 472 runs (47.20). On a batsman's paradise at Kanpur he hit 250 in 512 minutes, the highest score ever made in a Test on this ground. Even then he contributed to his own downfall, slipping and hitting his stumps as he attempted a sweep. He toured England in 1979 with the victorious West Indies Prudential World Cup squad, and during 1981/2 toured England, Pakistan, and Australia without establishing a regular place in a powerful team. He captained the West Indies under-26 team to Zimbabwe in 1981 and was still on the fringe of the Test team when he decided to join the unofficial team in South Africa in 1983/4, when his batting was outstanding—664 runs from 12 matches.

First-class career (1971–86): 5,944 runs (35.17) including 8 centuries, 8 wickets (24.50), and 88 catches

Test matches (19): 782 runs (26.06) including 1 century, 0–3, and 17 catches

BAICHAN, Leonard

(b. 1946, Berbice, British Guiana) Guyana and West Indies

A cautious left-handed opening batsman possessing unwavering concentration, Len Baichan toured India and Pakistan in 1974/5 and Australia in 1975/6. On his first tour he made 711 runs (50.78), scoring two centuries in his first two innings in India, but, unfortunately, he was injured in a car accident and missed several matches, including the Tests. Back in time for the first Test against Pakistan at Lahore—his début in Test cricket—he made a very confident 105 not out. His tour of Australia was an anti-climax.

First-class career (1968–80): 4,449 runs (51.73) including 13 centuries

Test matches (3): 184 runs (46.00) including 1 century, and 2 catches

BAPTISTE, Eldine Ashworth Elderfield

(b. 1960, Liberta, Antigua) Leeward Islands, Kent, Northamptonshire, Eastern Province, and West Indies

A relatively slimly built right-handed all-rounder from Antigua, Eldine Baptiste made his initial first-class appearance for Kent in 1981 before playing for the Leeward Islands in 1982. A fast-medium bowler of unusual accuracy and stamina and a batsman who hit the ball with typical Caribbean relish and style, he was also a fine fielder who, on his first appearance in a Lord's Test, ran out England's Geoff Miller with a lethal throw from 80 yards. After a successful first full season for Kent in 1983, he toured India and Australia and made his first Test appearances. He made a slow start but in England in 1984 was an important 'utility' member of an all-conquering team, thrashing 87 not out in the first Test at Edgbaston and taking eight wickets in the series as the stock bowler. Injury prevented him from challenging for a place at home to England in 1985/6.

First-class career (1981–92): 6,180 runs (28.21) including 3 centuries, 522 wickets (25.41), and 88 catches

Test matches (10): 233 runs (23.30), 16 wickets (35.18), and 2 catches

BARRETT, Arthur George

(b. 1944, Kingston, Jamaica) Jamaica and West Indies

A good and accurate if relatively straightforward right-arm leg-break bowler, Arthur Barrett toured India and Pakistan in 1974/5 and at home played against India in 1970/1 and England in 1973/4, but, in an age of fast-bowling dominance, his leg-spinning talents were rarely reflected in his figures.

First-class career (1966–81): 1,086 runs (17.51) including 1 century, 169 wickets (31.21), and 54 catches

Test matches (6): 40 runs (6.66) and 13 wickets (46.38)

BARROW, Ivan

(b. 1911, Kingston, Jamaica; d. 1979, Kingston) Jamaica and West Indies

A neat, sound, and unobtrusive wicket-keeper and steady right-handed opening batsman, Ivan Barrow did not have a wealth of strokes but watched the ball closely and could drive powerfully when necessary. He toured Australia in

1930/1 and England in 1933 and 1939 and played at home against England in 1929/30 and 1934/5. He made 54 dismissals and scored 1,046 runs (23.77) on his first visit to England but on his second, after he had lived for several years in the United States, he averaged only 13.21. His third-wicket partnership of 248 for Jamaica with George Headley against Lord Tennyson's side in 1932 at Kingston remains a Jamaican first-class record. Barrow scored 169—his highest innings. In the second Test at Old Trafford in 1933 he scored 105, showing a greater range of stroke-play than usual, and putting on 200 for the second wicket with George Headley.

First-class career (1928–46): 2,551 runs (23.84) including 3 centuries, and 100 dismissals (73 c., 27 st.)

Test matches (11): 276 runs (16.23) including 1 century, and 22 dismissals (17 c., 5 st.)

BARTLETT, Edward Lawson

(b. 1906, St Michael, Barbados; d. 1976, St Michael) *Barbados and West Indies*

A slightly built, right-handed batsman, quick-footed, a hard-hitter in front of the wicket and a neat cutter, 'Barto' Bartlett toured England in 1928 and Australia in 1930/1. His best effort in Tests was 84 against Australia in the first match at Adelaide. He added 216 for the eighth wicket with C. R. Browne when Barbados registered 715 for 9 against British Guiana at Bridgetown in 1926/7.

First-class career (1923–39): 1,581 runs (23.25) including 1 century, and 8 catches
Test matches (5): 131 runs (18.71) and 2 catches

BAYLEY, Herbert Peter

(b. 1916, Georgetown, British Guiana) *British Guiana*

From a cricketing family in which his father, Benjamin Bayley, and uncle, Herbert Bayley, had been outstanding batsmen for British Guiana, Peter Bayley was a stylish right-hander who scored heavily while at St Stanislaus College in Georgetown. He made his first-class début for British Guiana in 1936, aged 19, and the following year amassed 268 against Barbados at his home ground, Bourda, an innings that remains the highest individual first-class score made for the country, either as British Guiana or Guyana. His fourth-wicket partnership of 381 with C. S. Persaud, who made 174, was the highest for any wicket in West Indies first-class cricket at the time

and has only been surpassed since for Guyana by the 390 added by Leslie Wight and Glendon Gibbs for the first wicket against Barbados at Bourda in 1951. Although he never came close to matching such scoring again, he was chosen for the West Indies tour of England in 1939. Affected by illness and a knee injury, he played only 15 innings from which he averaged a modest 20.46 and was not chosen for any of the three Tests. His one major score was 104 against Oxford University. Because of the Second World War, British Guiana did not resume inter-territorial cricket for four years and, when they did, Bayley was made captain, leading the team in two matches each against Trinidad and Barbados in 1944. His next, and last, appearance in first-class cricket was not until 1951. He later became a popular radio commentator on the game, both in Guyana and in Jamaica. An able manager with a personable manner and a keen sense of humour, Bayley headed the British Guiana Rice Board for many years and was mainly responsible for a significant increase in exports. Differences with the government led to his emigration to Jamaica where he became chief executive officer of the Matalon group of companies before retiring to New Jersey.

First-class career (1936–51): 1,577 runs (34.28) including 3 centuries

BECCA, Lascell Anthony

(b. 1940, Kingston, Jamaica)

As sports editor of the Jamaica *Daily News* throughout the 10 years of its existence between 1973 and 1983 and subsequently senior sports editor of the Jamaica *Gleaner*, Tony Becca has specialized in writing on cricket. He has earned respect for his straightforward style, his fair, forthright views, and his common sense approach to the controversies that so often afflict West Indies cricket. In addition to covering every home series for the past 21 years, he has toured Australia, England, and India and reported on the last three World Cups, marking his 100th Test during the 1994 England series in the Caribbean. His soft-spoken, unpretentious nature made him popular in press boxes wherever he went. Actively involved in sports administration, he became president of one of Jamaica's leading cricket clubs, Melbourne, having previously been secretary; he was also a member of the Table-Tennis Association council and sits on the National Sports Council. He was awarded a national honour in 1994, the Order of

Distinction, for his services to sport, especially cricket.

BENJAMIN, Kenneth Charlie Griffith

(b. 1967, Antigua) *Leeward Islands, Worcestershire, and West Indies*

Kenny Benjamin is one of a number of West Indians to gain international recognition after only limited exposure at first-class level. A right-arm fast bowler with a muscular frame and relatively short, rolling run-up, he played a handful of Red Stripe Cup matches before an encouraging series fronting the West Indies A attack against England in 1992 earned him a Test match début in the historic encounter with South Africa soon afterwards. The dramatic series in Australia later that year was a personal disappointment because a strained Achilles tendon and cartilage problem curtailed his involvement and necessitated an early return home after arthroscopic surgery. However, he was preferred to the troubled Patrick Patterson in the climactic fourth Test at Adelaide and performed with verve and aggression in a torrid match for the batsmen. Justin Langer, the young West Australian débutant, was struck several times about the head and body and likened one of his deliveries to 'being hit by a gun shot'. A fierce competitor and disciplined trainer, he bowls a fuller length than most West Indians of his genre, hits the pitch hard, and has the ability to skid the ball in and away. In only his third Test, in the opening match of the England series at Sabina Park, Kingston, in 1994, he claimed 6 for 66, incurring the wrath of umpire Steve Bucknor in the process for a brace of nasty bouncers at the tail-ender Alan Igglesden. His overall output, including match figures of 7 for 94 in the second Test at Bourda, was 22 wickets at 25.73. Benjamin played club cricket in England at Sheffield Collegiate in the Yorkshire League, then Netherfield in the Northern League before accepting a contract at Worcestershire in 1993, having endeared himself to the committee over a bottle of brandy. Later, he signed for Denton in the Lancashire County League and in 1994 performed the hat-trick for them three times. Yorkshire had shown interest but he was deemed to be 'not of international stature', a myopic viewpoint. His right-handed batting is not without substance: he topped the averages at Netherfield, after scoring 52 not out against Trinidad and Tobago in 1992, and made 96 in a 2nd XI match for Worcestershire. His background is not dissimilar from other fast-bowling Anti-guans like Ambrose, Baptiste, Merrick, and unrelated namesake, Winston Benjamin, the other eminent old boys from All Saints Secondary School. He was actually considered a better basketballer than the lofty Ambrose. He abhors even the mention of his middle names 'Charlie Griffith', a great fast bowler whom he considers passé.

First-class career (1989–): 592 runs (12.33), 188 wickets (25.32), and 10 catches
Test matches (16): 110 runs (6.87), 57 wickets (31.71), and 1 catch

BENJAMIN, Winston Keithroy Matthew

(b. 1964, St John's, Antigua) *Leeward Islands, Leicestershire, Hampshire, and West Indies*

Winston Benjamin, a direct, compact, fast right-arm bowler and dangerous right-hand lower-order batsman, spoiled a revived Test career when sent home from England in 1995 for reasons of unfitness and indiscipline. No relation of his teammate, Kenny, Winston Benjamin, like his countryman Ambrose, played for the Chester club, Boughton Hall, on an overseas scholarship instigated by Vivian Richards and a local travel company, and was drafted into a Rest of the World XI against D. B. Close's XI for his first-class début at Scarborough in 1985. He first represented the Leewards against Jamaica at Kingston early in 1986, and was engaged by Leicestershire for the subsequent five seasons though his undeniable all-round talents never quite flourished at Test level. His career did not run smoothly, in fact, and he was used largely as stock bowler and one-day specialist after his rapid rise to Test status at Delhi in 1987. A reputation for moodiness and temperamental problems did not help matters, and he took a year off from county obligations in 1991 with the express objective of regaining his Test place. In January, however, he was injured in a shooting incident at the Leewards' team hotel in Barbados. In 1992 he rejoined Leicestershire, recapturing his Test place after four seasons, against Pakistan. Then, in late July 1993, he was told he was being replaced the following year by Phil Simmons. Benjamin, already disaffected by the standard of Grace Road pitches, made public utterances about shabby treatment and lost motivation. He superseded Malcolm Marshall at Hampshire in 1994 after playing in all five Tests of the home series against England taking 12 wickets, making a typically belligerent Test career-best of 44 at Bourda in the second match and also scoring a potentially vital 35 at Port of Spain.

BEST

First-class career (1985–): 3,640 runs (22.19) including 1 century, 459 wickets (25.46), and 87 catches

Test matches (21): 470 runs (18.80), 61 wickets (27.01), and 12 catches

BEST, Carlisle Alonza

(b. 1959, St Michael, Barbados) *Barbados, Western Province, and West Indies*

Lantern-jawed and with a typically sunny Bajan smile, Carlisle Best worked his way into the powerful West Indies Test team in 1986 after two successful years in the Shell Shield. Captaining Barbados in 1984 and 1985, he was a great student of the game who like to commentate to himself as he batted. Best was a correct right-hander who sometimes opened, and a useful, if only occasional, off-spin bowler. On his first Test appearance at Sabina Park against England in 1985/6 he got off the mark in Test cricket with a hook for six, but he lost confidence after his promising start and lost his place after three games in which his slip fielding had been outstanding. He reappeared against England in 1989/90, this time making his mark with the bat with a memorable and classical century (164) on his home ground at Bridgetown. He broke a finger in this match, however, and played only two more Tests, in Pakistan in 1990/1. He played for Western Province in South Africa in 1993/4.

First-class career (1979–92): 5,439 runs (38.85) including 13 centuries, 24 wickets (32.16), and 107 catches

Test matches (8): 342 runs (28.50) including 1 century, and 8 catches

BETANCOURT, Nelson

(b. 1887, Trinidad; d. 1947, Trinidad) *Trinidad and West Indies*

A useful right-handed batsman and a bowler good enough to take the new ball against Barbados in 1922, Nelson Betancourt's sole Test was against England at Port of Spain in 1929/30. He batted soundly in a losing cause, scoring 39 and 13. He captained West Indies for this match because of a policy of having a different captain for each match in the series.

First-class career (1905–30): 444 runs (17.07)

BINNS, Alfred Phillip

(b. 1929, Kingston, Jamaica) *Jamaica and West Indies*

A competent right-handed batsman and wicket-keeper, Alfred Binns toured New Zealand in

1955/6, and played at home against India in 1952/3 and Australia in 1954/5, but rarely produced his best form in Tests.

First-class career (1949–57): 1,446 runs (37.07) including 4 centuries, and 65 dismissals (47 c., 18 st.)

Test matches (5): 64 runs (9.14) and 17 dismissals (14 c., 3 st.)

BIRKETT, Lionel Sydney

(b. 1904, Barbados) *Barbados, British Guiana, Trinidad, and West Indies*

An attractive right-handed batsman and a useful medium-pace change-bowler, Lionel Birkett first attracted wide attention by his splendid 253 for Trinidad against British Guiana at Georgetown in 1929/30. He was vice-captain of the first team to Australia in 1930/1 and on his début in the first Test at Adelaide scored 64, but did little in the others.

First-class career (1924–45): 1,295 runs (33.20) including 3 centuries

Test matches (4): 136 runs (17.00), 1–71, and 4 catches

BISHOP, Ian Raphael

(b. 1967, Port of Spain, Trinidad) *Trinidad and Tobago, Derbyshire, and West Indies*

Ian Bishop, a tall, strong right-arm pace bowler with a classical side-on action, was destined to become a fixture in the front line of the West Indian pace battery until a serious debilitating stress fracture of the lower back twice interrupted an already expansive career at the age of 26. A staunch Christian and intelligent man, he made his first-class début in 1987 against Guyana, and within two years his ability to swing the ball away late at pace earned Test recognition against India at Georgetown, and figures of 6 for 87 at Kensington in only his second Test. In January 1993 he bettered this with 6 for 40 at Perth in the fifth Test victory, generating extreme pace and movement from a modified action tending more to chest on, but broke down again during the second Test of the ensuing home series against Pakistan after match figures of 6 for 71 in Port of Spain. Another successful come-back followed in England in 1995. Already his Test career figures of 83 wickets at a mere 20.46 bore witness to an outstanding talent. He had withdrawn from the Australian leg of a winter tour in early 1991 with a cracked lower vertebra, an increasingly common injury amongst fast bowlers, and spent over a year on a rehabilitation programme which involved swimming and prayer. Derbyshire had released him from a 5-year contract in 1991 in the expectation that he would be in the West Indian touring party, but he returned in 1992 and took 64 wickets at 17.46. In fact, he bowled through a persistent Achilles tendon injury, but suffered no apparent reaction from the back problem and was fortunate that the rotational system operated by the Derbyshire seamers lessened the workload. Bishop even produced a devastating career best 7 for 34 against Hampshire at Portsmouth and 6 for 18 in an epic final match against Essex, the eventual champions. He returned to the Trinidad side in 1994/5, but his inevitable reinstatement as a West Indies player was delayed. As an orthodox, capable right-handed batsman he made a career-best undefeated 103 against Yorkshire at Scarborough in his second season for Derbyshire in 1990, a nice complement to finishing with the best strike rate in the country, 59 wickets at a rate of a wicket every 40 balls.

First-class career (1987–93): 1,452 runs (15.44) including 1 century, and 358 wickets (20.68)

Test matches (18): 231 runs (11.55), 83 wickets (20.46), and 3 catches

BLAIR, Philbert David

(b. 1943, Georgetown, British Guiana) *Demerara and Guyana*

Tall and with the muscular physique of a heavyweight boxer, Philbert Blair was one of the fastest bowlers produced by Guyana. He arrived as a virtual unknown at the Demerara Cricket Club but quickly made his mark. He was 24 when he first played for Guyana, against the touring MCC in 1968, and his only wicket was the number eleven Jeff Jones. His return of 23 wickets in four matches in the next year's Shell Shield coincided with the decline of Wes Hall and Charlie Griffith on the simultaneous tour of Australia and New Zealand and, when they were dropped for the 1969 tour of England, Blair was an obvious choice. His speed and hostility promised a bright future but his inexperience was a hindrance in England and he never overcame problems with his run-up. In nine matches, he took 14 wickets at 36.35 each, flattering to deceive after he clean-bowled openers Colin Milburn and Roger Prideaux for ducks in his first spell of the tour against D. H. Robins's XI at Eastbourne. He was not picked for any of the three Tests and, back home, never reproduced his 1969 Shield form again. He soon lost his position as spearhead of

the Guyana attack although, when recalled in 1973, showed what he was capable of once everything was right with match figures of 7 for 79 against the Combined Islands.

First-class career (1967–74): 142 runs (5.91) and 77 wickets (34.15)

BOYCE, Keith David

(b. 1943, St Peter, Barbados) *Barbados, Essex, and West Indies*

Truly a dynamic cricketer, right-handed as a batsman and bowler, Keith Boyce was an exciting all-rounder who played much of his best cricket for Essex but who also proved himself at Test level as a hostile fast bowler, volatile hitter of the ball and superb all-purpose field. Strongly built, with a lithe, athletic approach, he put everything into his fast bowling, and his muscular hitting from a high backlift was truly spectacular. He adored hitting sixes and was a master in limited-overs cricket, the first man in England to reach 1,000 runs and 100 wickets in this class of game. After playing with Trevor Bailey for the International Cavaliers, he joined Essex and from 1966 until 1977 was always a potential match-winner for them. His highest score was 147 not out against Hampshire at Ilford in 1969. He reached a century in 58 minutes and had a match double of 113 and 12 for 73 against Leicestershire at Chelmsford in 1975. His 8 for 26 against Lancashire at Old Trafford in 1971 was the record for the John Player League. He toured England with West Indian teams in 1973 and 1975, India and Pakistan in 1974/5, Australia in 1975/6, and at home played against India in 1970/1, Australia in 1972/3, and England in 1973/4. In the Prudential World Cup Final in 1975 he was a major factor in the West Indies' defeat of Australia at Lord's. He had shattered England in 1973, taking 19 wickets (15.47) in the three Tests. His highest Test score was 95 not out in the fifth match at Adelaide in 1975/6, a brilliant innings.

First-class career (1964–77): 8,800 runs (22.39) including 4 centuries, 852 wickets (25.02), and 215 catches

Test matches (21): 657 runs (24.33), 60 wickets (30.01), and 5 catches

BRANCKER, Rawle Cecil

(b. 1937, Bridgetown, Barbados) *Barbados*

A left-handed all-rounder good enough to be an important member of the powerful Barbados team of the 1960s (alongside Sobers, Hunte,

Nurse, Hall, Griffith), Rawle Brancker was a solid, unspectacular batsman and very slow bowler who depended on flight rather than spin for his wickets. He first came to notice at Combermere School, alma mater of Sir Frank Worrell, playing in a strong team from which Wes Hall and Peter Lashley also went on to play for Barbados and the West Indies. He made his first-class début, aged 18, for Barbados against E. W. Swanton's XI but only became assured of a regular place somewhat later on the basis of his consistent performances for the famous Empire club, whom he successfully captained for many seasons. Although he was a surprise choice as one of nine Barbadians in the West Indies team to England in 1966, his reliable batting, adaptability to any position in the order, from opening to number eight, and his effective, if innocuous-looking, bowling had made him one of the leading all-rounders in the region. His returns on the England tour were disappointing—329 runs at 18.27 and 33 wickets at 26.09—and he wasn't selected for a Test. Yet his 7 for 78 against Kent at Canterbury were his best figures in first-class cricket. He returned to England in 1969 as player-manager of the Barbados team and retired after the Shell Shield the following year. Brancker possessed an impish sense of humour and delighted in practical jokes. Always elegantly attired, he controls a successful import business in Bridgetown and has served as a senator in the Barbados parliament and as chairman of the Barbados Industrial Development Corporation.

First-class career (1955–70): 1,666 runs (27.31) including 5 centuries, 106 wickets (27.31), and 21 catches

BROWN, Errol Earl

(b. 1952, St Catherine, Jamaica) *Jamaica*

Like several others, Errol Brown, an off-spinner and right-hand batsman, owed his selection for the West Indies team to India and Sri Lanka in 1978/9 to the absence of the leading players who were contracted to Kerry Packer's World Series Cricket at the time. Even so, it came as a surprise since it was based on his performances in his début season when he returned 12 wickets at 35.16 for Jamaica in the Shell Shield and three for 74 in the match against the touring Australians. In eight first-class matches on tour, he managed only 8 wickets (57.25) and he lost his place in the Jamaica team after taking 5 at 60 runs each in the 1979 Shell Shield. Consistent returns in club cricket earned him a recall six years later but,

although he took 4 for 44 against Trinidad and Tobago in his first innings, he lasted only two matches.

First-class career (1977–85): 290 runs (17.05) and 34 wickets (41.23)

BROWNE, Courtney Oswald

(b. 1970, London) *Barbados and West Indies*

A slim, tallish, keen, and stylish wicket-keeper and right-handed batsman, Courtney Browne was made captain of Barbados before his 24th birthday and responded by taking the island from the bottom to the top of the Red Stripe Cup in 1994/5. Selection for his first major tour, to New Zealand, soon followed and he was called into the Test side against Australia at Kingston when Junior Murray fell ill on the eve of the fourth Test. Despite uncharacteristically missing a comfortable catch, with expensive results, he kept better than Murray in England in 1995 and replaced him for the fifth and sixth Tests. In his sole Test before that tour he scored 1 and 31 not out and held one catch.

First-class career (1990–): 726 runs (23.41) and 79 dismissals (74 c., 5 st.)

BROWNE, Cyril Rutherford

(b. 1890, Bridgetown, Barbados; d. 1964, Georgetown, British Guiana) *Barbados and British Guiana*

'Snuffy' Browne was a right-handed hard-hitting batsman and medium-pace leg-break bowler of quality. He toured England in 1923 and 1928 and played at home in the 1929/30 series, playing in the earliest West Indies Tests in both England and the Caribbean. He took 75 wickets (22.29) in 1923, and five years later, though past his best, took 8 for 81 at Derby, and against Kent at Canterbury had—literally—an hour of glory in which he hit a match-winning 103. Despite a severe blow on the head from a rising ball, he hit 102 not out for the West Indies against MCC at Georgetown in 1925/6, in pre-Test days. In 1937/8 he took 7 for 13, Barbados collapsing for 99. A magistrate, 'Snuffy' Browne was the first black West Indian to be elected to honorary life membership of MCC.

First-class career (1908–39): 2,077 runs (19.97) including 3 centuries, 278 wickets (22.40), and 59 catches

Test matches (4): 176 runs (25.14), 6 wickets (48.00), and 1 catch

BURNETT, Harold John Beverley

(b. 1915, Port of Spain, Trinidad; d. 1981, Port of Spain)

An outstanding schoolboy sportsman, Harold Burnett was captain of the Queen's Royal College teams that won both cricket and football island championships in 1933 and proceeded to represent Trinidad and Tobago in both sports. As a right-handed batsman and flighty off-spin bowler, he had only modest success and it was as an administrator that he was to make more of a name for himself. He was a member of the Queen's Park Cricket Club's management committee for many years and assistant manager of the successful West Indies team to England in 1963 under Frank Worrell's captaincy. When his old friend and team-mate, Jeffrey Stollmeyer, became president of the West Indies Cricket Board of Control in 1975 and the headquarters moved to Port of Spain, Burnett was appointed secretary. Known for his efficiency and attention to detail, Burnett's tenure coincided with some of the busiest and most turbulent times in West Indies cricket, involving the continuing controversy over South Africa and the trauma caused by the creation of Kerry Packer's World Series Cricket. Although his health had deteriorated, he remained WICBC secretary to his death.

BUTCHER, Basil Fitzherbert

(b. 1933, Berbice, British Guiana) *British Guiana and West Indies*

A supple, wristy, and resolute right-handed batsman and an occasional leg-break bowler, Basil Butcher became a consistently reliable performer at four or five in the West Indies order. In his first Test against India at Bombay in 1958/9, he made 28 and 64 not out and in the whole series he made 486 runs (69.42), including 103 in the third match at Calcutta and 142 in the fourth at Madras. Thereupon, he had a chequered career in representative cricket until the 1963 England tour when his 1,294 runs (44.62), including 383 in eight completed Test innings, one of which was 133 in a total of 229 in the memorable draw at Lord's, established him in the side. During an interval in the Lord's match he opened a letter which advised him that (against a background threat of civil war) his wife back home had had a miscarriage. Very upset, Butcher continued to play a solid and masterly innings which saved his side. Against Australia in 1964/5 he made 405 runs (40.50), including 117 at Port of Spain in the

second Test; Richie Benaud considered he was the most difficult of all the West Indians to get out. This was confirmed in Australia in 1968/9 with an identical Test record, 405 runs (40.50), including two centuries, and in all first-class matches he made 1,505 runs (51.89). He remained at his best on two further tours of England in 1966 and 1969. In the former year he scored 1,105 runs (48.04), including 420 (60.00) in the Tests; his 209 not out at Trent Bridge in the third match was a heroic innings in 7¾ hours, which won the match after West Indies had been 90 behind on the first innings. In the short tour in 1969 he headed the batting with 984 runs (61.50), including three centuries. The only Test wickets he took were 5 for 34 (four coming in three overs), when he finished off England's total for 414 at Port of Spain in 1967/8. He was a reliable outfielder with a remarkably powerful and accurate underarm throw. For many years he was a professional in the Lancashire League.

First-class career (1954–72): 11,628 runs (49.90) including 31 centuries, 40 wickets (30.42), and 67 catches

Test matches (44): 3,104 runs (43.11) including 7 centuries, 5 wickets (18.00), and 15 catches

BUTLER, Lennox Stephen

(b. 1929, Port of Spain, Trinidad) *Trinidad and West Indies*

A right-arm fast-medium bowler, 'Bunny' Butler took 5 for 93 for his island against Australia at Port of Spain in 1954/5, and his bowling was compared so favourably with that of Ray Lindwall that he played in the second Test on the same ground, when he took 2 for 151 in a run-feast, scored 16 and was not selected again.

First-class career (1948–56): 161 runs (14.63) and 29 wickets (33.34)

BUTTS, Clyde Godfrey

(b. 1957, Perseverance, British Guiana) *Guyana and West Indies*

The last of ten children from a village named Perseverance, some 30 miles east of Georgetown, Clyde Butts needed plenty of 'strength to persevere' when bowling in his first Test, against New Zealand on a typical batsman's paradise at Bourda in April 1985. A tall, slim off-spinner in the Lance Gibbs mould, he had won a place ahead of the younger Roger Harper, also from Guyana, on the strength of several skilful pieces of bowling in the Shell Shield. That season he took 45 wickets, more than anyone else, in first-class matches at 22 each but in the only New Zealand innings he toiled 47 overs for a return of 0 for 113. In his only innings, promoted to number three to give him a chance in a match heading inevitably for a draw, he scored 9. He was married on the rest day of the Test. He was chosen to tour Pakistan in 1986/7 where he proved himself to be the best off-spinner in the Caribbean, and when it came to a straight choice between himself and Harper soon after, Butts was preferred. He also toured New Zealand in 1986/7 and India in 1987/8 when he played in three Tests, but he never improved on his 4 for 73 at Karachi, and despite loyal and consistent service for Guyana until his retirement after the 1994 Red Stripe Cup, no more home Tests came his way in an era dominated by fast bowlers.

First-class career (1981–94): 1,431 runs (15.90), 348 wickets (24.20), and 42 catches

Test matches (7): 108 runs (15.42), 10 wickets (59.50), and 2 catches

BYNOE, Michael Robin

(b. 1941, Christ Church, Barbados) *Barbados and West Indies*

A stylish right-handed opening batsman and left-arm medium-pace change-bowler, Robin Bynoe toured India and Pakistan in 1958/9, scoring 515 runs (34.33) and made his Test début as an 18-year-old schoolboy against Pakistan. After being left in the background, he toured India again in 1966/7, but achieved little in the Tests and, because of a vulnerability against spin bowling, was not selected again.

First-class career (1957–72): 3,572 runs (41.05) including 6 centuries, 9 wickets (27.33), and 45 catches

Test matches (4): 111 runs (18.50), 1–5, and 4 catches

CAMACHO, George Stephen

(b. 1945, Georgetown, British Guiana) *Guyana and West Indies*

A very sound, bespectacled, right-handed opening batsman, normally rather sober, steady and slow in uncharacteristic West Indian vein, Steve Camacho's first innings in the Shell Shield Tournament in 1965/6 was 106 against Trinidad at Port of Spain. Two years later he made 328 runs (32.80) against England in his first Test series, including 87 in the fourth match at Port of Spain. He toured England in 1969 as the opening partner to Roy Fredericks, heading the batting in

the Tests with 187 runs (46.75). But in Australia in 1968/9 he did not quite come up to expectations. His last Tests were at home against India in 1970/1 when he made 68 runs in four innings. He became secretary of the West Indies Cricket Board but never let life become too serious.

First-class career (1964–79): 4,079 runs (34.86) including 7 centuries, 8 wickets (27.00), and 47 catches

Test matches (11): 640 runs (29.09), 0–12, and 4 catches

CAMERON, Francis James

(b. 1923, Kingston, Jamaica) *Jamaica, Canada, and West Indies*

A stocky right-handed batsman and off-break bowler, who played much club cricket in England, Jimmy Cameron toured India and Pakistan in 1948/9, scoring 330 runs (25.38) and taking 18 very expensive wickets. His best performance was a punishing 75 not out in the second Test against India at Bombay.

First-class career (1946–60): 551 runs (25.04), 29 wickets (48.65), and 9 catches

Test matches (5): 151 runs (25.16) and 3 wickets (92.66)

CAMERON, John Hensley

(b. 1914, Kingston, Jamaica) *Cambridge University, Jamaica, Somerset, and West Indies*

Something of a cricketing prodigy at Taunton School, John Cameron played in the University matches in 1935, 1936, and 1937 and put Cambridge on the road to victory in his first year with 7 for 73 in the first innings. He also appeared with success for Somerset. A punishing right-handed batsman and reliable field, he bowled off-breaks and, in his earlier years, back-of-the-hand spin as well. He was selected as vice-captain of the 1939 side to tour England.

First-class career (1932–47): 2,772 runs (18.23) including 4 centuries, 184 wickets (30.77), and 63 catches

Test matches (2): 6 runs (2.00) and 3 wickets (29.33)

CAMPBELL, Sherwin Legay

(b. 1970, Barbados)

A small, stylish, and wristy right-handed opening batsman of obvious quality, Sherwin Campbell began what promised to be a long Test career in New Zealand in 1994/5 with 51 in his first innings and 88 in his second.

First-class career (1990–): 855 runs (35.62) including 4 centuries, and 20 catches
Test matches (3): 145 runs (36.25) and 1 catch

CAREW, George McDonald

(b. 1910, Bridgetown, Barbados; d. 1974, Barbados) *Barbados and West Indies*

A sound right-handed batsman, George Carew came to the fore in 1934/5 with impressively consistent scores of 46, 43, and 68 against MCC. His Test appearances were scattered: against England in 1934/5 and 1947/8 at home, and against India on tour in 1948/9. In the second Test at Port of Spain in 1947/8 he played the innings of his life. Wearing his chocolate-coloured felt hat and chewing gum rhythmically, he smashed into England's attack with some high-class batsmanship and hit 107, sharing in an opening stand of 173 with Andy Ganteaume.

First-class career (1934–49): 2,131 runs (34.37) including 3 centuries, and 13 wickets (46.15)
Test matches (4): 170 runs (28.33) including 1 century, 0–2, and 1 catch

CAREW, Michael Conrad

(b. 1937, Port of Spain, Trinidad) *Trinidad and West Indies*

An attractive left-handed opening batsman, who struck the ball cleanly, notably through the covers off the back foot, 'Joey' Carew first impressed with 114 against Jamaica at Georgetown in 1958/9 and the following season hit 102 not out and 70 in two matches against MCC. He toured England in 1963, 1966, and 1969 and Australasia in 1968/9. At home he played against England in 1967/8 and India in 1970/1. He was not an overall success in English conditions, though in 1969 he made 677 runs in 12 matches, including three centuries, despite a damaged finger. By far his best season in representative cricket was 1968/9. In the fourth Test against Australia at Adelaide, he demonstrated to his colleagues the answer to John Gleeson's mysterious spin: hitting him straight, he made 90. In the fifth Test at Sydney he and Roy Fredericks put on 100 for the first wicket and at Auckland in the first Test against New Zealand he made a studious 109, adding 172 for the second wicket with Seymour Nurse. In the six Tests on the tour he made 643 runs (49.94) and in all first-class matches 1,222 runs (45.25). He was a useful right-arm leg-break bowler and later became a Test selector. Perhaps his greatest legacy to West Indies cricket, how-ever, lies in the advice and encouragement which he gave to a young left-hander from Santa Cruz, near his own home; Brian Lara rewarded Joey Carew richly for the interest he showed in him.

First-class career (1955–74): 7,810 runs (38.47) including 13 centuries, 108 wickets (29.76), and 83 catches
Test matches (19): 1,127 runs (34.15) including 1 century, 8 wickets (54.62), and 13 catches

CHALLENOR, George

(b. 1888, St Michael, Barbados; d. 1947, St Michael) *Barbados and West Indies*

George Challenor was the originator of the great tradition of West Indian batsmanship. An opening batsman of medium height and powerful build, he was essentially an off-side player of perfect timing and a punisher of any loose balls with pulls or on-drives; he had everything—style, hitting power, and strength of defence, all based on superb footwork. He toured England in 1906 (at 18), 1923, and 1928, the year Tests were first played between the two countries. On his second tour he made 1,556 runs (51.86), his six centuries including a match-winning 155 against Surrey at The Oval. He was specially elected to membership of MCC in 1923. Past his best in 1928, he made 1,074 runs (27.53). In his early days Barbados was already a home of brilliant batting. Against the strong 1912/13 MCC team he scored 118 and 109. Seven years later in two successive club finals he made 261, 204, and 133; and as late as 1926/7, after C. A. Wiles (a Barbadian batting for Trinidad) had hit the highest-ever in intercolonial cricket, Challenor responded with 220. A schoolteacher, he influenced the play of young Frank Worrell.

First-class career (1905–30): 5,822 runs (38.55) including 15 centuries, 54 wickets (23.87), and 25 catches
Test matches (3): 101 runs (16.83)

CHANDERPAUL, Shivnarine

(b. 1974, East Bank, Demerara, Guyana) *Guyana and West Indies*

Graduating to the Test arena as a teenager signifies a special talent and Shivnarine Chanderpaul, a frail left-hander from Unity-Lancaster near Georgetown on the east coast of the Demerara, displayed it in abundance with scores of 52, 50, and 77 in his first three appearances at the age of 19. A diminutive 5 ft. 5 in., and weighing only 120 lbs, his stature belied a maturity way beyond his tender years, a cultured technique under-pinned by supreme footwork, fine placement, and nerveless, wristy stroke-play. He has been seen as an Alvin Kallicharran reincarnate, not least because of his ancestry, and he became the first West Indian of East Indian descent to represent West Indies since Faoud Bacchus in Australia in 1981/2. As the first teenager to play for West Indies since Elquemedo Willett in 1972/3, and only the ninth in all (the sixth youngest), he displaced Phil Simmons in the second Test against England in 1994 on home soil at Bourda, Georgetown, a significant event for his country where a racist undercurrent still rails at the perceived 'Africanness' of the regional team. His undoubted ability as a right-arm leg-spinner, pushed through quickly with a flattish trajectory, was also a factor, but a penchant for big hundreds since his emergence at 17 supported his case admirably. He dominated the Northern Telecom Youth Championship in the Caribbean, opening his first-class career with a duck and 90 against the Leewards in 1992, then claimed four wickets and a maiden century (an undefeated 140) for the President's XI against Pakistan in 1993. On the West Indies Youth tour of England later that year he compiled 203 not out in the first 'Test' at Trent Bridge, and 153 against a Development of Excellence XI. In 1994 he was effectively the leading all-rounder in the regional Red Stripe Tournament with 389 runs at 55.57, plus a dozen wickets at 16.92. His meteoric rise was also a tribute to his utter dedication and commitment and, not least, to the selectors for appreciating precocious youth and allowing it to blossom.

First-class career (1992–): 1,310 runs (46.78) including 2 centuries, and 28 wickets (35.93)
Test matches (7): 433 runs (61.85), 2 wickets (141.00), and 4 catches

CHANG, Herbert Samuel

(b. 1952, Jamaica) *Jamaica and West Indies*

A diminutive left-hander with considerable powers of concentration and plenty of strokes, Herbert Chang was rewarded for several years of consistent batting in the Shell Shield with a tour to India in 1978/9 but was disappointing in his sole Test, the fourth at Madras, scoring 6 and 2. Despite his size, he was a brave player of fast bowling, and after nine years in first-class cricket he was still looking one of Jamaica's best batsmen, in the 1981/2 Shell Shield scoring 426 runs in ten innings (47.33). He joined the first team of West Indians to tour South Africa (1982/3).

First-class career (1972–83): 3,273 runs (35.19) including 5 centuries

CHRISTIANI, Cyril Marcel

(b. 1913, Georgetown, British Guiana; d. 1938, Georgetown) *British Guiana and West Indies*

Cyril Christiani toured England in 1933 as a very promising wicket-keeper/batsman. When MCC visited West Indies in 1934/5, he kept in all four Tests to a hostile and penetrating attack, and his seven dismissals helped to win the series. He and one of his brothers, E. S. Christiani, put on 196 for the first wicket for British Guiana against East India CC in 1936/7, a British Guiana record. Little more than a year later, he died of malaria. He was the elder brother of R. J. Christiani.

First-class career (1931–8): 658 runs (16.45) and 64 dismissals (44 c., 20 st.)
Test matches (4): 98 runs (19.60) and 7 dismissals (6 c., 1 st.)

CHRISTIANI, Robert Julian

(b. 1920, Georgetown, British Guiana) *British Guiana and West Indies*

A bespectacled and attractive stroke-playing right-handed batsman, quick-footed and specially strong in front of the wicket, an occasional off-break bowler, a brilliant close field, and a reserve wicket-keeper, Robert Christiani narrowly missed the 1939 England tour. On his Test début, the first match against England at Bridgetown in 1947/8, he made 1 and 99 and the following season, in India, scored 107 in the first Test at Delhi. On this tour he made 785 runs (41.31). On his sole visit to England in 1950 he batted usually at number seven and made 1,094 runs (45.58), with 30 catches, mostly as 'keeper, and three stumpings. He toured Australasia in 1951/2, making 261 runs in the five Tests against Australia and at home played against India in 1952/3 and England in 1953/4.

First-class career (1938–54): 5,103 runs (40.50) including 12 centuries, 18 wickets (60.44), and 108 dismissals (96 c., 12 st.)
Test matches (22): 896 runs (26.35) including 1 century, 3 wickets (36.00), and 21 dismissals (19 c., 2 st.)

CLARKE, Dr Carlos Bertram

(b. 1918, Bridgetown, Barbados; d. 1993, London) *Barbados, Northamptonshire, Essex, and West Indies*

Tall and lanky, 'Bertie' Clarke was a right-arm slow leg-break bowler with a high delivery and a pronounced 'loop' and a googly that nipped quickly off the pitch, a batsman who could hit very hard, and a brilliant and versatile field. He was a surprise selection for the 1939 England tour but he proved to be one of the few successes with 87 wickets (21.81). He played much wartime cricket in England, and appeared from 1946 until 1949 for Northamptonshire—taking 156 wickets —and for Essex in 1959 and 1960. A popular doctor, albeit in trouble for a while for carrying out merciful abortions, he continued playing club cricket in the south of England well into his sixties, mainly for the BBC.

First-class career (1937–61): 1,292 runs (12.30), 333 wickets (26.37), and 42 catches

Test matches (3): 3 runs (1.00) and 6 wickets (43.50)

CLARKE, Sylvester Theophilus

(b. 1954, Christ Church, Barbados) *Barbados, Surrey, Transvaal, Orange Free State, Northern Transvaal, and West Indies*

Tall and strapping, Sylvester Clarke was a right-arm fast bowler with a strange, in-swinger's action in which the arm came over rapidly and very high, despite the fact that the batsman saw the chest instead of the left shoulder in the delivery stride. Genial off the field 'Sylvers' was a man to have on *your* side. Very fast and hostile when fit and firing, he played a prominent part in Surrey's first success in a county competition for several years, in the Benson and Hedges Cup, 1982. He first played for Barbados in 1978 and against Trinidad that season his 6 for 39 in an innings included a hat-trick. In his first Test, against Australia in 1977/8, he took 3 for 58 and 3 for 83, and only injury (to which, despite his powerful physique, he was prone) prevented him from playing further games in the series. In India in 1978/9 he headed the Test bowling averages with 21 wickets (33.85) and he made further tours of Pakistan (1980/1) and Australia (1981/2). He did well in Pakistan, taking 14 wickets (17.28) in four Tests and hitting an important 35 not out in 30 balls with three consecutive sixes at Faisalabad. But he seriously blotted his copybook when, furious at being pelted by oranges and other missiles when fielding on the boundary during the last Test in Multan, he picked up a brick being used as a boundary marker and hurled it at a spectator, who happened to be a student leader, and who was taken to hospital, seriously injured. Fortunately for Clarke he recovered and the bowler, normally a genial man, escaped with a

short suspension by the West Indies Cricket Board. An unashamed hitter as a batsman, he made a rapid 100 not out for Surrey against Glamorgan in 1981. In the 1982 season he took 85 wickets (19.95) but the following winter he burnt the boats of his career for West Indies, signing to play for Transvaal and for the unofficial West Indian team in South Africa. He was an outstanding success, equalling a Currie Cup record with 58 wickets at 13.00 in 1984/5, but a serious back injury prevented his reappearance for Surrey in 1985. He recovered, and continued to bowl with great success for Surrey and Transvaal.

First-class career (1977–90): 3,269 runs (14.79) including 1 century, 942 wickets (19.52), and 146 catches

Test matches (11): 172 runs (15.63), 42 wickets (27.85), and 2 catches

COHEN, Rudolph Alexander

(b. 1942, Kingston, Jamaica) *Jamaica*

A tall, slim, right-arm bowler with a genuine turn of speed, Rudy Cohen was chosen for the West Indies tour of England in 1966. He was not in the original 16 but was summoned when his fellow Jamaican, Lester King, required an operation on his knee. At 23, he was the youngest member of the team and, with an exuberant personality and a store of stories, one of the liveliest. With Wes Hall and Charlie Griffith past their peak, Cohen was clearly to be seen as the one best equipped to spearhead the attack when the time came. Hall and Griffith, however, with support from captain Gary Sobers, ensured that Cohen was not required for Test duty, but he had a satisfactory tour, nevertheless, his 40 wickets in 18 matches taken at 24.22 each. His 6 for 71 against Sussex on a lively Hove pitch on that tour remained his best figures in the 30 first-class matches. He first played for Jamaica in 1964, not yet 21, and it was his pace and his potential, rather than his record, that recommended him to the West Indies selectors for he had not taken more than three wickets in an innings prior to the England tour. The standard of his batting is accurately reflected in his final first-class average. The effect of the experience gained in England was obvious in the 1967 Shell Shield, in which he took 15 wickets, but it was to be his last season. A career in law superseded his cricket and he qualified in the United States where he carries on a successful practice in Connecticut.

First-class career (1963–7): 160 runs (7.27) and 81 wickets (31.80)

COLLYMORE, Rickford Charles

(b. 1939, East Bank, Demerara, British Guiana)
Guyana

A tall, accurate left-hander, 'Rex' Collymore was a member of Guyana's exceptionally strong spin attack of the 1960s and 1970s that revolved around Lance Gibbs. He competed for a place mostly with another orthodox left-arm spinner, Edwin Mohammed, over whom he gained selection in the West Indies team to India in 1966/7. It was a welcome vote of confidence by the selectors as he had been no-balled five times for throwing in the match against Jamaica by umpire Douglas Sang Hue. It was a surprising censure since he possessed a high, seemingly pure action, the legality of which had never been questioned. In India, he was not chosen for any of the three Tests, in spite of an innings analysis of 37.4–4–88–4 against a strong West Zone team in his first match. Although he remained in the Guyana team until 1976, and was a useful left-handed, lower-order batsman, he was never picked again by the West Indies selectors. He was, for many years, a government cricket coach and also served as a Guyana selector before emigrating to England.

First-class career (1964–77): 688 runs (16.38) and 106 wickets (31.14).

CONSTANTINE, Sir Learie Nicholas (Lord, Baron of Maraval and Nelson)

(b. 1901, Diego Martin, Trinidad; d. 1971, London)
Trinidad, Barbados, and West Indies

A compelling, magnetic, and inspiring cricketer of extraordinary zest and dynamism, Learie or 'Connie' Constantine was the son of Lebrun Constantine, a plantation foreman and son of a slave, who had toured England with the first two West Indian teams of 1900 (when he scored the first century by a West Indian in England) and 1906. Learie himself played with his father for Trinidad in 1922 and some months later toured England with the third West Indian team, where he impressed with some amazingly good fielding at cover-point. Returning to England in 1928, he established himself as a great but volatile all-rounder. He always became the centre of attraction and could change the course of a match by startling brilliance but in Test cricket he was inconsistent. Muscular, lithe, stocky but long-armed, and with distinctly beady eyes, he was a brilliant, if unpredictable and unorthodox, right-handed hitter with powerful drives, pulls, and hits to leg. As a bowler he had a bounding run, a high smooth action, and, in his prime, considerable pace, sometimes bowling bodyline. Later he used every variation of medium pace, with an occasional fast ball. As a fielder, his contemporaries believe that he was the best of all time; by anticipation, feline reflex, and elastic movement, he brought off close catches no other fielders could have reached, and in the deep he picked up while going like a sprinter and threw with uncanny accuracy. He made 1,381 runs (34.52), took 107 wickets (22.95), and held 33 catches on the 1928 England tour. Only in the three Tests—89 runs in six innings and five expensive wickets—did he fail. His essential quality was seen at Lord's against Middlesex. The West Indians were 122 behind on the first innings, although Learie had slammed 86 in half an hour, going in at 79 for 5. In the Middlesex second innings he took 7 for 57, 39 balls bringing him 6 for 11. Set 259 to win, the touring team were 121 for five wickets when he hit 103 out of 133 in an hour, including 2 sixes and 12 fours, and the West Indians won by three wickets. In the first series in the West Indies in 1929/30 he took 18 wickets (27.61), including 9 for 122 at Georgetown when West Indies beat England for the first time. In the first tour of Australia in 1930/1 he made 708 runs (30.78), took 47 wickets (20.23) and fielded brilliantly, but he again failed in the Tests. By now a professional with Nelson in the Lancashire League, Learie was permitted to appear in a handful of matches on the 1933 tour; in his only Test, at Old Trafford, he hit a confident 64 in the second innings and prevented an England victory. His highest score in Tests was 90 in the second match against England at Port of Spain in 1934/5, and his 3 for 11 (in 14.5 overs) in the second innings put the West Indies on the road to handsome victory. In the fourth match at Kingston he captured 6 for 68 and in the series took 15 wickets (13.13). Appearing regularly on the 1939 tour, making 614 runs (21.17) and heading the bowling with 103 wickets (17.77), he was scintillating in his last Test of all at The Oval, hitting 79—the last 78 coming in 57 minutes—and taking 5 for 75 in England's first innings. Prominent in welfare work among coloured people in England during the Second World War, he captained the Dominions team that defeated England at Lord's in 1945; he wrote books and broadcast; he studied doggedly and was called to the Bar by the Middle Temple; he returned to Trinidad and became an MP and the Minister of Works in the Trinidadian Government. Later he came back to England as High Commissioner for Trinidad and Tobago; he was awarded the MBE, knighted, and created a

Life Peer. Posthumously, Trinidad awarded him the Trinity Cross, the country's highest honour.

First-class career (1922–45): 4,475 runs (24.05) including 5 centuries, 439 wickets (20.48), and 133 catches

Test matches (18): 635 runs (19.24), 58 wickets (30.10), and 28 catches

CONSTANTINE, Lebrun Samual

(b. 1874, Port of Spain, Trinidad; d. 1942, Port of Spain) *Trinidad*

Constantine's son, Learie, went on to greater fame but 'Old Cons' was, according to C. L. R. James, 'the most loved and most famous cricketer' in Trinidad in his time. A measure of the public's affection for him was evident in the story of how he got to England on the first West Indies tour in 1900. Although chosen, he remained behind as the boat was about to set sail. The team comprised either wealthy white men or black professionals whose way was paid for. Constantine, an overseer at an agricultural estate in Diego Martin, just outside Port of Spain, was neither wealthy nor professional and considered he could not afford the trip. Realizing the situation, those on the quayside to see the team off immediately raised a public subscription and a launch managed to get Constantine to the ship before it reached high seas. The inevitable fairy-tale ending was that 'Old Cons' hit 113 in the first match against Gentlemen of MCC, the first batsman to score a century for the West Indies in England, and at Lord's to boot. A batsman with a wide range of strokes, many of his own invention, he returned with the 1906 team, passing 1,000 runs in all matches at an average of just over 29. His influence on his sons—Elias, the youngest, also played for Trinidad—was obvious, especially in fielding in which he excelled when not keeping wicket. It was an especially proud moment for the family when Lebrun and Learie played together once for Trinidad against Barbados in Georgetown in 1922, father, aged 48, in his last first-class match, son, aged 20, in his third. Also in the team was Victor Pascall, brother-in-law and uncle respectively, a rare occurence.

First-class career (1893–1923): 2,433 runs (25.34) including 1 century, 46 wickets (13.73), and 113 dismissals (95 c., 18 st.)

COZIER, Winston Anthony Lloyd

(b. 1940, Bridgetown, Barbados)

For a generation the most able, articulate, and respected West Indian cricket journalist, Tony Cozier also gained a world-wide reputation as a commentator, both on radio and television. By any standards he is an accomplished professional: intelligent, fair, thorough, witty, and authoritative. A useful games-player himself, he kept goal in the Barbados hockey team and has been president of the island's Hockey Association (1971–9). He played first-division cricket in Barbados for Lodge School, Carlton, and Wanderers as a batsman with attacking inclinations. The son of a well-known journalist, Jimmy Cozier, Tony was managing and sports editor of the *Barbados Daily News* (1960–8), editor of the *Barbados Sunday Sun* (1981–4), founder and editor of the *West Indies Cricket Annual* (1971–91)—the first such publication worthy of Caribbean cricket—and from 1991 has edited, with the help of his son Craig, the *Red Stripe Caribbean Cricket Quarterly*. His opinions have often been deemed controversial in the West Indies, where parochial passions run deep, but he has been, rightly, quite the most influential commentator on cricketing affairs in the region. Overseas his radio commentaries, made with a still-youthful, lively voice have gained him wide popularity and the occasional rude letter. Being white-skinned but possessing a pure Bajan accent, nothing amused him more than the one calling him a 'black bastard'. He was awarded the Barbados national award, the Silver Crown of Merit, and the parties given by him and his wife Gillian at their beach-house on the rest days of Barbados Tests have become legendary.

CROFT, Colin Everton Hunte

(b. 1953, Demerara, British Guiana) *Guyana, Lancashire, and West Indies*

A tall, strong, hostile right-arm fast bowler with a chest-on action with a pronounced sway-away from the stumps in the delivery stride, though his apparent in-swingers often 'left' the right-handed batsmen, Colin Croft had a sensational start to his Test career, forming a devastating fast-bowling partnership with Joel Garner and Andy Roberts. Starting with 3 for 85 and 4 for 47 in his first Test against Pakistan at Bridgetown in 1976/7, he followed up with 8 for 29 in 18.5 overs in the first innings of the next Test at Port of Spain, the best analysis by a West Indian fast bowler in Test cricket. He took 33 wickets at 20.48 in the series, and began his second series the following season against Australia equally well until withdrawing with other players who had signed for Kerry Packer. In the first Test at

CUFFY

Port of Spain he dismissed 3 Australians in his first eight overs for 9 runs on the first morning of the match, and finished with 4 for 15, Australia collapsing for 90. Later on the same tour he drew a strong protest from the Australian manager after bowling an excess of bouncers when playing for Guyana against the touring team, hitting one batsman on the head and fracturing the jaw of another. In England in 1978 and 1979 he played for Lancashire, with a total of 56 wickets in first-class games in 1978 at 22.60. He returned to the county in 1982. He was steadily successful in two years of World Series Cricket. He toured Australia and New Zealand in 1979/80, England in 1980, Pakistan in 1980/1, and Australia again in 1981/2. In all these tours he was one of the most feared members of a powerful four-man West Indies fast attack, his three main partners being Roberts, Holding, and Garner. Against England at home in 1980/1 he was easily the most successful of the four, taking 24 wickets in four Tests (18.45). He disgraced himself, under provocation, in New Zealand in 1979/80, deliberately barging into an umpire as he ran in to bowl after a controversial decision had gone against him. He left Lancashire after 1982 with a back injury which threatened his career, a fact that may have made him accept a big pay-off for touring South Africa in 1982/3. He was the unwitting cause of a stir when thrown out of a 'whites only' carriage on a train. A qualified airline pilot, he settled in the United States. However, he returned to the Caribbean cricket scene in the 1990s as an occasional journalist and as a commentator on both radio and television.

First-class career (1971–84): 865 runs (10.55), 428 wickets (24.60), and 25 catches
Test matches (27): 158 runs (10.53), 125 wickets (23.30), and 8 catches

CUFFY, Cameron Eustace

(b. 1970, South Rivers, St Vincent) *Windward Islands, Surrey, and West Indies*

A 6 ft. 7 in. fast right-arm bowler, Cameron Cuffy bowled with spirit for Surrey in 1994 and made his Test début in India the following winter.

First-class career (1990–): 108 runs (4.69), 88 wickets (27.25), and 4 catches
Test matches (2): 1 run (0.50), 5 wickets (38.00), and 1 catch

CUMMINS, Anderson Cleophas

(b. 1966, Barbados) *Barbados, Durham, and West Indies*

A right-arm fast-medium bowler with a good-looking, fluent action, Andy Cummins seems perennially cast as a specialist one-day performer in deference to the emergence of Kenneth Benjamin as part of the four-man Test attack. He made a first-class début against Trinidad and Tobago in 1989, toured Sharjah in 1991, and made the first of several one-day international appearances against Pakistan in Karachi later in 1991. He took 12 World Cup wickets in Australia and New Zealand in 1992 in a generally disappointing West Indian performance then made his Test début in the series, clinching the fifth Test victory over Australia in February 1993. Cummins played in the first Test of the next home series against Pakistan, lost his place, and was then recalled for the third Test while Ian Bishop was indisposed through recurrent back trouble. Having taken 4 for 54 in Pakistan's only innings of a match ruined by rain at the Recreation Ground in Antigua, he was probably surprised not to be selected again. A year previously his omission from the historic South African match on home soil in Barbados had caused another eruption of ill-informed inter-island factionalism. Cummins had managed only five wickets in the three preceding one-day encounters and he found himself replaced, along with Winston Benjamin, by Courtney Walsh and Kenny Benjamin for the big occasion. The Bajan populace sadly boycotted a stirring match, but this was a mere catalyst in a long-running saga of discontent over the omission of Carlisle Best and Roland Holder, and the failure of Desmond Haynes to gain the captaincy. A placard reading 'No Cummins, No Goings' lightened the impact only slightly. Cummins served Durham industriously in 1993 and 1994, his well-ordered right-hand batting coming more to prominence.

First-class career (1989–): 1,470 runs (19.60), 180 wickets (30.55), and 14 catches
Test matches (5): 98 runs (19.60), 8 wickets (42.75), and 1 catch

DA COSTA, Oscar Constantine

(b. 1907, Kingston, Jamaica; d. 1936, Kingston) *Jamaica and West Indies*

A very talented all-rounder, being a reliable right-handed batsman, useful medium-pace bowler and versatile field, Oscar da Costa appeared in the fourth Test against England in 1929/30 with some success. On the 1933 England tour he made 1,046 runs (26.82), including his maiden century, 105 against Essex at Leyton, and took 31 wickets (34.03), but did little in the Tests. He was, however, the comedian of the party: he had a rubber stamp made so that no autograph-hunter should be disappointed. He appeared in one Test against England in 1934/5 and had the melancholy distinction of being the first West Indian Test cricketer to die.

First-class career (1928–35): 1,563 runs (29.49) including 1 century, 44 wickets (40.13), and 30 catches

Test matches (5): 153 runs (19.12), 3 wickets (58.33), and 5 catches

DANIEL, Wayne Wendell

(b. 1956, St Philip, Barbados) *Barbados, Middlesex, Western Australia, and West Indies*

The 'Black Diamond', as Wayne Daniel was known, came to England in 1976 as a raw young fast bowler and took 13 wickets in four Tests as part of a formidable quartet of fast bowlers who gave their opponents no respite. On this tour Wayne Daniel took 52 wickets (21.26) and Middlesex eagerly signed him on to their staff. A massively built, good-looking man, friendly off the field but hostile (though fair and sensible) on it, Daniel had a fine, muscular action after a long and heavy-footed approach. Relatively predictable, he was very fast indeed, generally bowling straight and keeping the ball well up to the bat but testing the courage and technique of the finest players. In 1977 he was a key figure in Middlesex's retaining a share of the County Championship title, taking 75 wickets at 16.44. A year later his figures were still better, 76 at 14.65, and he twice took seven cheap wickets in the Benson and Hedges Cup. In World Series Cricket in Australia, however, he was not consistently successful and, after a poor season in the Shell Shield in 1979, he was surprisingly omitted from the West Indies squad which won the Prudential World Cup in England in 1979. Against formidable competition, he did not regain his Test place until 1983/4 when he reappeared in three Tests in India and in two at home against Australia. At Ahmedabad in the third Test that year his 5 for 39 helped to win the match. He continued to bowl with whole-hearted endeavour for Middlesex.

First-class career (1975–88): 1,551 runs (11.48), 867 wickets (22.47), and 63 catches

Test matches (10): 46 runs (6.57), 36 wickets (25.27), and 4 catches

DAVIS, Bryan Alan

(b. 1940, Port of Spain, Trinidad) *Trinidad, Glamorgan, and West Indies*

A sound right-handed batsman, who often opened the batting, an occasional leg-break bowler, and excellent close-in field, Bryan Davis carried his bat through the innings when he scored 188 for North against South of Trinidad at Port of Spain in 1966/7. In this same season he toured India without playing in any of the Tests. When Australia toured in 1964/5, however, he appeared in four Tests, hitting 54 and 58 in the second Test at Port of Spain and on his début putting on 116 and 91 for the first wicket with Conrad Hunte. In two full seasons for Glamorgan in 1969 and 1970 he made well over 1,000 runs each time. He is the elder brother of Charlie Davis. He became a journalist and commentator.

First-class career (1959–71): 6,231 runs (34.81) including 5 centuries, 9 wickets (48.22), and 127 catches

Test matches (4): 245 runs (30.62) and 1 catch

DAVIS, Charles Alan

(b. 1944, Port of Spain, Trinidad) *Trinidad and West Indies*

A sound but slow right-handed batsman and useful medium-pace bowler, Charlie Davis was a schoolboy when he scored 115 in the Beaumont Cup match for North Trinidad in 1960/1. After prolific scoring for Trinidad against Guyana and the 1964/5 Australians, followed by a half-century for Trinidad and 158 not out for The President's XI against MCC in 1967/8, he was selected for the Test team at last to tour Australasia in 1968/9, only to fail with the bat. Although a change-bowler at home, he did nevertheless head the overall bowling averages with 24 wickets (32.58), including 7 for 106 against South Australia at Adelaide, his career-best. In England in 1969 he proved himself with the bat, making 103 in the second Test at Lord's in a stay of $6\frac{1}{4}$ hours, the only West Indian century of the series. Altogether, he made 848 runs (42.40). Although India won the rubber in the West Indies in 1970/1, Davis headed the batting with 529 runs (132.25) in four Tests, being almost unbowlable. He reached at least 50 in five innings out of seven, including 125 not out in the third match at Georgetown and 105 in the fifth at Port of Spain. When the New Zealanders toured in 1971/2, he made 466 runs (58.25) in the series, including 183 in the third match at Bridgetown, his career-highest, when he added 254 with

Gary Sobers for the sixth wicket. He played his last Test in 1972/3.

First-class career (1960–76): 5,538 runs (41.32) including 14 centuries, 63 wickets (39.36), and 44 catches

Test matches (15): 1,301 runs (54.20) including 4 centuries, 2 wickets (165.00), and 4 catches

DAVIS, Winston Walter

(b. 1958, Kingstown, St Vincent) *Windward Islands, Glamorgan, Tasmania, Northamptonshire, Wellington, and West Indies*

Lean, lithe, and, off a relatively short run with a quick arm action, liable to bowl the occasional ball of lethal whiplash speed, Winston Davis, a St Vincentian, would have been a regular Test bowler for most countries in most eras but his appearances in the early 1980s were limited by the extraordinary depth of fast-bowling talent in the Caribbean. After a first Test cap in Antigua in 1982/3, in which season he took a Shell Shield record of 33 wickets, he toured India the following year and took 14 wickets at a cost of 40 each in the Tests on unresponsive wickets. His hostility and speed had been shown in better light in the 1983 World Cup match at Headingley when he took 7 for 51 against Australia. Coming back into the Test side against England for the fourth match of the 1984 rubber he had a remarkable match, taking two useful wickets, breaking the arm of the England batsman, Paul Terry, with a sharply rising delivery, and, although a batsman of few pretensions, making 77 after going in as night-watchman. Davis had only joined the touring party from Glamorgan after injury to a rival fast bowler but his 14 first-class wickets at 14 each earned him a tour to Australia in 1984/5: here he was less successful, his 8 wickets costing 52 each, but in two Tests at home against New Zealand later that season he took ten wickets, including 4 for 19 in the first innings at Sabina Park. Glamorgan did not renew his contract in 1985 but the following winter he played for Tasmania, from 1987 to 1990 for Northamptonshire, and in 1990–1 for Wellington.

First-class career (1979–92): 2,346 runs (14.13), 608 wickets (28.48), and 57 catches

Test matches (15): 202 runs (15.53), 45 wickets (32.71), and 10 catches

DE CAIRES, Francis Ignatius

(b. 1909, British Guiana; d. 1959) *British Guiana and West Indies*

A sound right-handed batsman, Frank de Caires was masterly with 80 and 70 in the first-ever Test in the West Indies, against England at Georgetown in 1929/30. He toured Australia in 1930/1, but was not selected for the Tests.

First-class career (1928–39): 945 runs (28.63) including 1 century

Test matches (3): 232 runs (38.66), 0–9, and 1 catch

DEPEIAZA, Cyril Clairmonte

(b. 1927, St James, Barbados) *Barbados and West Indies*

Played mainly as a wicket-keeper in the West Indies, Clairmonte Depeiaza is remembered primarily for his historic seventh-wicket stand of 348 with his captain, Denis Atkinson, in the fourth Test against Australia at Bridgetown in 1954/5; it remained a world record until broken in a relatively obscure match in India in 1994/5 and was made when West Indies, in facing a total of 668, were 146 for 6 wickets. The two batsmen were defiant for more than a day, and Depeiaza's contribution was 122. He appeared in a handful of Tests against Australia and New Zealand in the mid-1950s.

First-class career (1951–7): 623 runs (32.78) including 1 century, and 40 dismissals (31 c., 9 st.)

Test matches (5): 187 runs (31.16) including 1 century, 0–15, and 11 dismissals (7 c., 4 st.)

DEWDNEY, David Thomas

(b. 1933, Kingston, Jamaica) *Jamaica and West Indies*

A tall, well-developed right-arm fast bowler, Tom Dewdney maintained a good control of length and possessed great stamina. His Test début against Australia in 1954/5 was only his third first-class match, and in a total of 668 he returned impressive figures of 33–7–125–4. He toured New Zealand in 1955/6 and, generally used sparingly, took 5 for 21 in the fourth Test at Auckland in 19.5 overs. He was disappointing on the 1957 England tour and when Pakistan visited the West Indies in 1958/9 he met with little success. He was injured in a car accident (also involving Gary Sobers) in England in September 1959, in which 'Collie' Smith was killed.

First-class career (1954–61): 171 runs (5.70), 92 wickets (30.73), and 6 catches

Test matches (9): 17 runs (2.42) and 21 wickets (38.42)

DHANRAJ, Rajindra

(b. 1969, Barrackpore, Trinidad) *Trinidad and West Indies*

The first specialist leg-spin bowler to play in a Test for the West Indies for 17 years, Rajindra Dhanraj was rewarded for consistent performances for Trinidad from the age of 18 by selection on the tour to India under Courtney Walsh in 1994/5. Slim, of medium height and Indian descent, he is dedicated to his difficult craft. Coming from a village near San Fernando in the south of Trinidad, he moved to Port of Spain to play cricket and to work in the accounts office of the Angostura Bitters company. Very accurate, he spins the ball vigorously, though lacking the well-disguised variations of the great wrist spinners. He had played with steady success for the West Indies Youth team and for West Indies A and B elevens when the selectors finally found the courage to abandon the successful policy of fielding four fast bowlers in all conditions when he played Tests in India, New Zealand, and England on successive tours in 1994/5. His success in the domestic season of 1994—30 wickets at 15.70, including 8 for 51 against Barbados—was repeated against the counties in England, and when Curtly Ambrose withdrew from the fifth Test with back pain he played his third Test at Trent Bridge. On a true pitch he was ineffective but ran out the England captain with a good piece of work at mid-on.

First-class career (1987–): 256 runs (8.25), 130 wickets (30.43), and 13 catches

Test matches (2): 5 runs (2.50) and 6 wickets (39.83)

DOS SANTOS, Sir Errol Lionel

(b. 1890, Port of Spain, Trinidad; d. 1992, Kew, England)

A Trinidadian of Portuguese descent, Errol dos Santos was a single-minded individual with obvious management skills. He was financial secretary, first locally born colonial secretary, commissioner of income tax, and acting governor in Trinidad's British colonial administration between 1941 and 1948, appointments indicative of the esteem in which he was held. As a member of the Queen's Park Cricket Club, then controlling body for the game in Trinidad, he was one of the prime movers behind the 'goodwill' series between Trinidad, Barbados, and British Guiana that kept first-class cricket going in the southern Caribbean during the Second World War. On retiring from the civil service, he became chairman of one of the country's largest companies but also concentrated his attention on the administration of the game at island and regional level. He was elected president of the West Indies Cricket Board of Control in 1954 and remained in the position for six years, making his mark mostly for his work in revising its financial structure. As president of Queen's Park, and once describing himself as 'a benevolent dictator', he set about improving facilities for members and expanding the Queen's Park Oval into one of the best-appointed cricket grounds in the world. Mainly through his initiative, new stands were erected, increasing the capacity to 25,000. One stand, on the western side of the Oval, was fittingly named in his honour. He was active as club president well into his eighties and, as such, was a key figure in the formation in 1956 of the Trinidad and Tobago Cricket Council, an umbrella body to administer domestic cricket, serving as its president for 19 years. However, he stoutly resisted later efforts to make the WICBC replace Queen's Park as its agent for organizing regional and Test matches with the democratically elected Trinidad and Tobago Cricket Board of Control, a successor to the Council. The change, however, was inevitable and it was formalized in May 1981, the year Sir Errol emigrated to England.

DOWE, Uton George

(b. 1949, St Mary) *Jamaica and West Indies*

A solidly built right-arm fast-medium bowler, with a fierce appearance and long run, Uton Dowe played at home against India in 1970/1, New Zealand in 1971/2, and Australia in 1972/3, without establishing himself in the Test team. So wild was he when bowling against Australia that the Jamaican crowd was driven to inventing an eleventh commandment: 'Dowe shalt not bowl'.

First-class career (1969–77): 128 runs (7.11) and 97 wickets (27.86)

Test matches (4): 8 runs (8.00), 12 wickets (44.50), and 3 catches

DUJON, Peter Jeffrey Leroy

(b. 1956, Kingston, Jamaica) *Jamaica and West Indies*

A natural cricketer, a graceful, orthodox right-handed batsman and acrobatic wicket-keeper, Jeffrey Dujon was a pivotal member of the great West Indies team of the 1980s. A product of

Wolmer's School in Kingston, he made an impressive start to his international career on tours to Zimbabwe and Australia in 1981/2. In Australia he scored 227 runs in three Tests (45.40), though his highest score was only 51. It was already clear that in this cool-headed cricketer West Indies had found the obvious successor to the long-serving Deryck Murray. Dujon's wicket-keeping steadily improved as he leapt about to make gymnastic catches off the fast bowlers, a key figure in the all-conquering West Indies team which won a record 11 Test matches in succession in 1984/5. The first of several felicitous Test hundreds came in his eighth Test, 110 against India in Antigua in 1982/3 and other memorable innings were his 101 against England at Old Trafford in 1984 and 139 against Australia at Perth in 1984/5 after being hit on the head by a bouncer before scoring: he retired with dizziness soon after but returned to play superbly. He made three full (Test-playing) tours of both England (1984, 1988, 1991) and Australia (1981/2, 1984/5, 1988/9) and also toured New Zealand, India, and Pakistan. He never played in a West Indian side which lost a Test series and there was controversy when he was finally omitted after an occasional uncharacteristic lapse in England in 1991. He was never fully tested as a wicket-keeper to spin bowling, because West Indian teams of his era won their matches through fierce fast bowling, but he could have been a Test player as a batsman alone and scored hundreds against all his Test opponents except New Zealand. In 169 one-day internationals he made 1,945 runs (23.15) with six fifties and a highest score of 82 not out, and claimed 204 dismissals (183 c., 21 st.).

First-class career (1974–92): 9,308 runs (38.14) including 19 centuries, 1 wicket (45.00), and 453 dismissals (434 c., 19 st.).

Test matches (81): 3,322 runs (31.94) including 5 centuries, and 272 dismissals (267 c., 5 st.).

EDUN, Wilfred Vincent

(b. 1930, Georgetown, British Guiana; d. 1990, Georgetown, Guyana) *British Guiana*

Tall (6 ft. 5 in.) and strongly built, 'Sonny' Edun was a mild, soft-spoken man whose appearances for British Guiana as useful batsman and steady, right-arm medium-pace bowler were limited by the dearth of organized first-class cricket in the West Indies prior to 1966. On the flimsy statistical recommendation of three first-class matches, in which he took three wickets and had a highest score of 36, he was one of the younger players chosen for the experimental West Indies team to

New Zealand in 1956. He played only two first-class matches and no Tests on tour, although his six wickets placed him at the head of the bowling averages. On his return home, he found the emergence of an exciting new generation of Guyanese batsmen—Rohan Kanhai, Basil Butcher, and Joel Solomon—kept him out and he played only one more first-class match. He later turned his attention to administration, was a member of the Guyana Cricket Board of Control, a national selector and manager of Guyana teams and West Indies teams for Tests in Georgetown. He was a consistent performer for and a life member of the Everest Club and it was there, while speaking at a cricket function, that he was stricken with the heart attack that claimed his life. He died in the arms of his son, Brian, a Guyana youth team player.

First-class career (1955–6): 119 runs (19.83) and 10 wickets (30.80)

EDWARDS, Richard Martin

(b. 1940, Christ Church, Barbados) *Barbados and West Indies*

A strong, barrel-chested, and lively right-arm fast-medium bowler, 'Prof' Edwards toured Australasia in 1968/9 but lacked penetration on the Australian leg of the tour, taking only 14 wickets (57.71). In New Zealand, however, he captured 6 for 129 in the first Test at Auckland and 7 for 126 in the second at Wellington, taking most wickets, 15 (23.48). Pale-skinned and prematurely bald, 'Prof' is a skilled carpenter and builder and has supervised the care of ground and pitches at the Kensington Oval.

First-class career (1961–70): 389 runs (11.78), 78 wickets (36.29), and 15 catches

Test matches (5): 65 runs (9.28) and 18 wickets (34.77)

FERGUSON, Wilfred

(b. 1917, Longdenville; d. 1961, Port of Spain, Trinidad) *Trinidad and West Indies*

A short, burly man who caused much merriment among spectators when, occasionally, he removed his cap and revealed a bald head, Wilf Ferguson was a purveyor of slow, right-arm well-pitched leg-breaks and a hard-hitting late-order batsman. The pivot of the attack against England in 1947/8, he took 23 wickets (24.65), in the second Test at Port of Spain securing 11 for 229 in 73.2 overs, when, on an easy-paced matting wicket, he tossed his deliveries skilfully into the wind. In the fourth match at Kingston he hit a spectacular 75 in $1\frac{3}{4}$

hours. He toured India in 1948/9 and played once against England at home in 1953/4 without distinction.

First-class career (1942–56): 1,225 runs (23.55) and 165 wickets (31.55)

Test matches (8): 200 runs (28.58), 34 wickets (34.26), and 11 catches

FERNANDES, Maurius Pachaco

(b. 1897, British Guiana; d. 1981, Georgetown, Guyana) *British Guiana and West Indies*

A right-handed batsman of class, with a strong defence and strokes all round the wicket, and a safe catcher, 'Maurice' Fernandes was a lynchpin of the 1923 side to England, despite an attack of malaria, scoring 523 runs (34.86). Back again in 1928, in a longer tour he made only 581 runs (18.15), but played in the first Test between the two countries, at Lord's. He led West Indies in the third Test against England at Georgetown in 1929/30, the first West Indian Test victory. For British Guiana he scored centuries against Barbados and Trinidad.

First-class career (1922–32): 2,087 runs (28.20) including 4 centuries, 5 wickets (36.60), and 30 catches

Test matches (2): 49 runs (12.25)

FINDLAY, Thaddeus Michael

(b. 1943, St Vincent) *Windward Islands and West Indies*

A genial and intelligent man from St Vincent, competent both as a wicket-keeper and right-handed batsman, Mike Findlay made his début in first-class cricket against Australia in 1964/5, and toured Australasia in 1968/9 as reserve wicket-keeper. He toured England in 1969, superseding Jackie Hendriks as first-string wicket-keeper during the series, but when India toured in 1970/1 he was replaced by Desmond Lewis. He returned for a full five-Test series at home to New Zealand in 1971/2 but was dropped again after one Test in Australia in 1972/3. He remained, however, 'Mr Cricket' in St Vincent and made a second tour of England as reserve 'keeper to Deryck Murray in 1976. Arnos Vale in Kingstown, where one-day internationals have been played, has a stand in his honour. He was awarded an MBE for his services to the game.

First-class career (1964–78): 2,927 runs (20.18) and 252 dismissals (209 c., 43 st.)

Test matches (10): 212 runs (16.30) and 21 dismissals (19 c., 2 st.)

FOSTER, Maurice Linton Churchill

(b. 1943, St Mary) *Jamaica and West Indies*

A cheerful character, Maurice Foster was a determined right-handed batsman, who often opened, and a flat but accurate off-break bowler. He captained Jamaica for several years. He made his début in three matches against International Cavaliers in 1963/4, scoring 136 not out in the second game. He toured England in 1969 and 1973 and at home played against India in 1970/1, New Zealand in 1971/2, Australia in 1972/3 and 1977/8, England in 1973/4, and Pakistan in 1976/7. Not so brilliant or flamboyant a player as many of his contemporary batsmen, Foster in Tests often provided the solid ballast in the middle order. Against Australia he scored 125 in the first Test at Kingston in 1972/3 when he made 210 for the fifth wicket in even time with Rohan Kanhai, and scored 262 runs (43.66) in the series. He became a popular cricket commentator.

First-class career (1963–78): 6,731 runs (45.17) including 17 centuries, 132 wickets (30.72), and 37 catches

Test matches (14): 580 runs (30.52) including 1 century, 9 wickets (66.66), and 3 catches

FRANCIS, George Nathaniel

(b. 1897, St James, Barbados; d. 1942, St Michael, Barbados) *Barbados and West Indies*

On the 1923 England tour George Francis established himself with George John as a first in the long line of outstanding fast-bowling partnerships from the West Indies. A professional cricketer, he was a right-hander who, avoiding any theory, unemotionally and undemonstratively bowled fast at the stumps. He fielded with characteristic West Indian zest. He was far and away the best bowler on the 1923 tour, collecting 96 wickets (15.32) and he put the touring team on the road to a brilliant victory against Surrey at The Oval, taking 10 for 76 in the match. When Test status was attained in 1928, he was a little past his best, taking 60 wickets (31.33), including only six in the Tests. Able to play only once in the first Caribbean Test series in 1929/30, he took 4 for 40 in 21 overs in England's first innings of 145 in the third match at Georgetown, which witnessed West Indies' first-ever victory. Touring Australia in 1930/1, he captured 11 wickets (31.81) in the first series there and, while engaged as a professional by Radcliffe in the Bolton League, he appeared in the first Test at Lord's in 1933 but was not a success. A truer reflection of his ability was his performance for

FREDERICK

Barbados against MCC in 1925/6 when he took 9 for 56 in an innings victory.

First-class career (1924–33): 874 runs (12.85), 223 wickets (23.11), and 42 catches
Test matches (10): 81 runs (5.78), 23 wickets (33.17), and 7 catches

FREDERICK, Michael Campbell

(b. 1927, St Peter, Barbados) *Barbados, Jamaica, Derbyshire, and West Indies*

A sound opening batsman, Michael Frederick made a sole Test appearance in the first Test against England at Kingston in 1953/4, scoring 0 and 30. He made two appearances as an amateur for Derbyshire in 1949.

First-class career (1944–54): 294 runs (29.40) and 3 catches

FREDERICKS, Roy Clifton

(b. 1942, Berbice, British Guiana) *Guyana and Glamorgan*

Roy Fredericks was a small but very tough left-handed opening batsman of high class who hit the ball exceptionally hard, an occasional slow left-arm bowler, and a brilliant close fielder, especially on the leg-side. Both dashing and dependable he hit 26 fifties and 8 centuries in his 59 Tests between 1968 and 1977. He played for Glamorgan between 1971 and 1973, scoring 1,377 runs (45.90) in his first season of county cricket and in his second sharing in a record opening stand of 330 with Alan Jones against Northants at Swansea when Fredericks scored 228 not out. He tended, indeed, to run into inspired bursts of form as when he hit two hundreds in a match against MCC for Guyana in 1973/4, a feat he had already achieved against Barbados in 1966/7. He toured Australasia in 1968/9 and 1975/6, England in 1969, 1973, 1975 (for the Prudential Cup), and 1976, and India, Pakistan, and Sri Lanka in 1974/5. From his first tour of Australia and New Zealand in 1968/9 when he made 1,131 runs, he never had a bad tour or an unsuccessful series, although he had to wait until February 1972 and the first Test at Kingston to record his maiden Test century, 163 against New Zealand. A score of 150 against England at Edgbaston in 1973 was followed by two hundreds against India, at Calcutta and Bombay, and then in 1975/6 came one of the great innings of Test history. On the fast pitch at Perth the West Indies, already a Test down in the series, batted second against the all-conquering combination of Lillee and Thomson supplemented by Walker, Gilmour, Mallett, and Ian Chappell. Fredericks reached his hundred in 4 minutes under 2 hours, off only 71 balls, with a six and 18 fours, and when he was out he had scored 169 out of 258. In such moods there was no stopping this pocket Hercules, who played every shot from the late cut to the leg-glance with immense gusto. He became Minister for Sport, temporarily reappearing for Guyana in 1982/3 and helping them to win the Shell Shield with scores of 103 and 217—at the age of 40. He also coached and managed Guyana sides and was a West Indies selector.

First-class career (1963–83): 16,384 runs (45.89) including 40 centuries, 75 wickets (37.94), and 177 catches
Test matches (59): 4,334 runs (42.49) including 8 centuries, 7 wickets (78.28), and 62 catches

FULLER, Richard Livingstone

(b. 1913, St Anne's Bay; d. 1987, Kingston, Jamaica) *Jamaica and West Indies*

A useful right-handed batsman and fast-medium bowler, Dickie Fuller's sole Test was the fourth match against England at Kingston in 1934/5 when he scored 1 and took 0 for 12. For Jamaica against MCC, also at Kingston, he had struck hard for 113 not out, hitting Jim Smith for four fours in succession.

First-class career (1934–47): 280 runs (28.00) including 1 century, and 12 wickets (43.66)

FURLONGE, Hammond Alan

(b. 1934, Apex Oilfields, Trinidad) *Trinidad and West Indies*

A right-handed opening batsman, given the forename 'Hammond' by keen cricket parents, Furlonge staved off defeat for Trinidad at the hands of Australia at Port of Spain in 1954/5 by scoring 57 and 150 not out, his maiden first-class century. He played Test cricket against Australia that season and the following, when he toured New Zealand with West Indies. He made a painstaking 64 (in a total of 145) in the fourth Test at Auckland, but won no more Test caps.

First-class career (1954–62): 808 runs (32.32) including 2 centuries
Test matches (3): 99 runs (19.80)

GANTEAUME, Andrew Gordon

(b. 1921, Port of Spain, Trinidad) *Trinidad and West Indies*

A diminutive, consistent right-handed opening batsman and deputy wicket-keeper, Andy Ganteaume marked his Test début against England at Port of Spain in the second match in 1947/8 with a dogged 112, his only Test innings. Not only was he discarded for the rest of the series, but he was never selected for another Test, such was the power of West Indian batting at the time. However, he toured England in 1957 without playing in a Test.

First-class career (1940–63): 2,785 runs (34.81) including 5 centuries, 0–51, and 37 dismissals (34 c., 3 st.)

GARNER, Joel

(b. 1952, Christ Church, Barbados) *Barbados, Somerset, South Australia, and West Indies*

At 6 ft. 8 in. one of the tallest Test cricketers of all time, Joel 'Big Bird' Garner was not just a *fast* bowler but a very accomplished one with a good action off a relatively short run and remarkable control for one whose stature might easily have made him ungainly. Strongly built as well as very tall, high bounce came naturally and he also swung and cut the ball to present batsmen with very exceptional problems. He first appeared for the West Indies at home against Pakistan in 1976/7, taking 25 wickets at 27.52, including 8 for 148 in the match in the third Test at Georgetown. In the first two Tests against Australia in 1977/8 he took 13 wickets, including 8 for 103 at Bridgetown, but missed the remainder of the series following the split which resulted from Packer players being unavailable for the official West Indies tour the following winter. In Australia Garner was consistently successful in World Series Cricket and in England in 1979 he ensured that West Indies retained the Prudential World Cup by taking 5 for 38 in the final at Lord's against England, four of them bowled. In England, after representing Somerset part-time in 1977 and 1978, he joined the county full-time in 1979. His devastating yorker ('the only consolation,' wrote Scyld Berry, 'of being bowled by Garner is that you haven't been hit on the boot') was frequently a match-winner for his county on the big occasion. After 1979 he was always one of the first men chosen in the West Indies team, bowling with success in Australia, New Zealand, England, and Pakistan. A shoulder injury handicapped him for a while but, after a rest, he returned to take 31 wickets (16.87) at home to Australia in 1983/4; 29 in five Tests in England in 1984 (at 18 each) and another 19 in five Tests in Australia in 1984/5. He played a leading role in the 11 consecutive Test victories by West Indies in

this period. A sunny character, popular wherever he played, he was also a big-hitting late-order batsman who scored 104 against Gloucestershire for the 1980 West Indies touring team and made an impressive 60 against Australia in the Brisbane Test of 1979/80. Amidst controversy, he was released by Somerset after the 1986 season, his benefit year. He was awarded an MBE in 1985 and although he did not play Test cricket after a final home series against England in 1986, he was still playing regularly in both Barbados and England in 1994, also making occasional appearances for 'old' West Indies.

First-class career (1975–88): 2,964 runs (16.74) including 1 century, 881 wickets (18.53), and 129 catches
Test matches (58): 672 runs (12.44), 259 wickets (20.97), and 42 catches

GASKIN, Berkeley Bertram McGarrell

(b. 1908, Georgetown, British Guiana; d. 1979, Georgetown, Guyana) *British Guiana and West Indies*

A steady right-arm medium-pace bowler, Berkeley Gaskin—in his fortieth year—played in two Tests against England in 1947/8, opening the attack. He was manager of the successful 1963 touring team to England.

First-class career (1928–54): 782 runs (14.21) and 138 wickets (31.89)
Test matches (2): 17 runs (5.66), 2 wickets (79.00), and 1 catch

GIBBS, Glendon Lionel

(b. 1925, Georgetown, British Guiana; d. 1979, Georgetown, Guyana) *British Guiana and West Indies*

A consistent left-handed opening batsman and occasional slow left-arm bowler, Glendon Gibbs made 216 for British Guiana against Barbados at Georgetown in 1951/2, putting on 390 with Leslie Wright for the first wicket, still an overall West Indian first-class record. He appeared in his sole Test, the first match at Kingston against Australia, in 1954/5, scoring 12 and 0, taking 0 for 7, and holding 1 catch.

First-class career (1949–63): 1,730 runs (38.91) including 5 centuries, and 23 wickets (53.47)

GIBBS, Lancelot Richard

(b. 1934, Georgetown, British Guiana) *Guyana, South Australia, Warwickshire, and West Indies*

For some years the highest wicket-taker in Test history, Lance Gibbs was a lithe, lean right-arm off-spinner with long fingers which gave him exceptional spin and bounce. With an unorthodox chest-on action and with the left arm down by his side as the right arm came over 'good and high', he exploited every conceivable change of pace, flight, and length and eventually developed the essentially English off-spinner's art of being able to bowl the ball which drifts away from the right-handed batsman. Only relatively late in his career did he relish bowling round the wicket on turning pitches. His stamina and courage were virtually unlimited, despite such handicaps as a painfully sore spinning finger and a nagging groin injury, and he was a very loyal team-man. He was a negligible batsman but a fine fielder in the gully. Only Gary Sobers, who caught many batsmen off his bowling 'round the corner' at short-leg, and Clive Lloyd had appeared in more Tests for the West Indies when Gibbs retired. Lance Gibbs toured India in 1958/9, 1966/7, and 1974/5, Australia in 1960/1, 1968/9, and 1975/6, Pakistan in 1958/9 and 1974/5, England in 1963, 1966, 1969, and 1973, and New Zealand in 1968/9; and at home he played against Pakistan in 1958/9, India in 1962/3 and 1970/1, Australia in 1965/6 and 1972/3, New Zealand in 1971/2, and England in 1967/8 and 1973/4. He played his cricket with a quiet, dignified air, only rarely showing much emotion. In his first Test series, against Pakistan in 1957/8, he headed the bowling averages with 17 wickets (23.05) from four Tests. He was top again in Australia in 1960/1 with 19 wickets (20.78) from three Tests, including three wickets in four balls in the second innings at Sydney. In the next Test at Adelaide he performed the hat-trick. In 1961/2 he captured 24 wickets against the visiting Indians, in the third Test at Barbados assuring his country of the rubber by taking 8 for 38 in the second innings; he took these eight wickets for six runs in a spell of only 15.3 overs, 14 of these being maidens. This was to remain his best Test performance. In England in 1963 he secured 26 wickets (21.30) in the Tests—78 wickets (20.05) in all first-class matches —and in 1966, 21 Test wickets (24.76). Despite the plethora of fast bowling, he more than held his own in later years, always liable to bowl a side out in the later stages of the match. In Tests he took five or more wickets in an innings on eighteen occasions and twice ten or more wickets in a match. Though generally of little account as a batsman, he and Gerry Alexander added 74 for the eighth wicket against Australia at Sydney in 1960/1, a West Indian record against Australia. In England, after experience in the Lancashire and Durham Leagues, he qualified for Warwickshire in 1968, remaining with the county until 1973, enjoying his best season in 1971, with 131 wickets (18.89). He was a popular club-man, his expertise at forecasting horse-racing results being almost on a par with his knowledge of cricket strategy. He is a cousin of Clive Lloyd and settled in the USA after he retired from cricket.

First-class career (1953–76): 1,729 runs (8.55), 1,024 wickets (27.22), and 203 catches

Test matches (79): 488 runs (6.97), 309 wickets (29.09), and 52 catches

GILCHRIST, Roy

(b. 1934, Seaforth, Jamaica) *Jamaica, Hyderabad, and West Indies*

Stockily built, 'Gilly' Gilchrist was a mean and hostile fast right-arm bowler with a smooth effortless action, considered to be the most able fast bowler since 'Manny' Martindale. He briefly formed a formidable partnership with Wes Hall. Gilchrist toured England in 1957 and India in 1958/9, and at home played against Pakistan in 1957/8. In England, despite his venomous bouncer, he was not particularly successful, but he unsettled Pakistan, taking 21 wickets (30.28) in the five Tests. In India he collected 71 wickets (13.57) from all first-class matches. In four Tests he took 26 wickets (16.11), including 9 for 73 in the third match at Calcutta. He was sent home in disgrace from this tour for bowling fast 'beamers' (full tosses around the batsman's head) and for other misdemeanours. He seemed to attract conflict and abuse, even in the Lancashire League, where he took hundreds of wickets and numerous hat-tricks. He played no more Test cricket after 1959.

First-class career (1956–63): 258 runs (7.81), 167 wickets (26.00), and 10 catches

Test matches (13): 60 runs (5.45), 57 wickets (26.68), and 4 catches

GLADSTONE, George

(b. 1901, Jamaica; d. 1978, Kingston, Jamaica) *Jamaica and West Indies*

A useful left-arm slow bowler and moderate batsman, Gladstone's 'bag' for Jamaica Colts XV against MCC at Kingston in 1929/30 was four good wickets. A few days later, for Jamaica, he took 9 for 252 in 75.3 overs, also against MCC. Thereupon, he made his sole Test appearance at Kingston (a 9-day affair), scoring 12 not out and taking 1 for 189. His birth certificate states his name as George Gladstone Morais.

First-class career (1929–30): 26 runs (—) and 10 wickets (44.10)

GODDARD, John Douglas Claude

(b. 1919, St Michael, Barbados; d. 1987, London) *Barbados and West Indies*

A considerable figure for many years in Barbados and West Indies cricket, John Goddard was a vigilant and determined left-handed batsman, usually batting at number eight in strong Test sides and a useful right-arm medium-pace in-swinging or off-break bowler. Also an excellent fielder, notably at silly mid-off, he was captain in 22 of his 27 Tests. A formidable but popular leader, he was capable of pressing home every advantage his men had gained, and he will be remembered particularly for his captaincy of the 1950 side to England when West Indian cricket 'came of age' and won a rubber in England for the first time. In India in 1948/9 he won all five tosses and the rubber. He also toured England in 1957, besides Australasia in 1951/2 and New Zealand alone as player-manager in 1955/6; and at home he played against England in 1947/8. He not only let his batsmen and bowlers have their head, but also repeatedly brought off the boldest and most difficult catches, made runs, and took wickets when needed. Making his début in first-class cricket at 16 in 1936/7, he shared in a large unbroken stand of 502 for the fourth wicket with Frank Worrell for Barbados against Trinidad at Bridgetown in 1943/4, his own score of 218 not out remaining his career-highest. In the third Test against England at Georgetown in 1947/8 he took 5 for 31 in the first innings, taking 11 wickets (26.09) in the series. Against India in 1948/9 with a highest score of only 44 he averaged 47.50 for the series; and against New Zealand in 1955/6 he headed the batting in the three Tests with 147.00, thanks to three not outs. He hit his highest Test score of 83 not out in the second match at Christchurch.

First-class career (1936–58): 3,769 runs (33.35) including 5 centuries, 146 wickets (26.33), and 94 catches

Test matches (27): 859 runs (30.67), 33 wickets (31.81), and 22 catches

GOMES, Hilary Angelo

(b. 1953, Arima, Trinidad) *Trinidad, Middlesex, and West Indies*

A slim, shy, artistic cricketer, 'Larry' Gomes was a left-handed batsman who timed the ball with natural ease, a good fielder and useful right-arm bowler who switched from medium pace to slow off-breaks. The brother of Sheldon Gomes, who has also played for Trinidad, Larry made his first appearance for the island in 1971/2. He was a member of one of the strongest touring teams, the formidable West Indies side to England in 1976. Although making 1,393 runs on the tour, including five centuries, of which the highest was 190 against Derbyshire, he was unable to gain a regular Test place, indeed failed in two Tests when the England bowlers (who had little success generally) exposed some technical frailties around Gomes's off-stump. Moreover, in three years on the Middlesex staff between 1973 and 1976 he did not score more than 93 not out and never entirely established himself in another very strong team. Yet in 1977/8 he emphasized his class, becoming a regular member of the Test team in the brief Packer interregnum, scoring 265 runs (44.16) against Australia in 1977/8 and 405 runs (40.50) in five Tests in India in 1978/9. Proper recognition came when he established a regular place in the full West Indies team at home against England in 1980/1, scoring 199 runs in four Test innings (49.75). Thus encouraged, he convinced everyone of his quality by scoring two Test hundreds in Australia in 1981/2, at Sydney and Adelaide. He finished top of both the tour and Test averages, scoring 200 not out against Queensland at Brisbane and in the Test scoring 393 runs (78.60) in six innings. More outstanding success followed in England in 1984 when, after hours of practice against a bowling machine to ensure that his bat was coming through straight, he began the series with scores of 143, 10, 92 not out, and 104 not out in the first three Tests. Back in Australia the following winter, he made a brave century on a bouncy pitch at Perth and another at Adelaide to lift his number of Test hundreds against Australia to six. His value as the quiet foil to the more spectacular West Indian stroke-players had never been better displayed. Against the modern trend, he seldom wore a helmet. He played in 83 one-day internationals, scoring 1,415 runs (28.87) with one century, and taking 18 wickets with a best performance of 5 for 46.

First-class career (1971–88): 12,982 runs (40.56) including 32 centuries, 107 wickets (39.32), and 77 catches

Test matches (60): 3,171 runs (39.63) including 9 centuries, 15 wickets (62.00), and 18 catches

GOMEZ, Gerald Ethridge

(b. 1919, Port of Spain, Trinidad) *Trinidad and West Indies*

A strong, craggy, middle-order right-handed batsman, an energetic fast-medium swing bowler who cantered in to bowl with his head nodding, and a superb close catcher, Gerry Gomez toured England in 1939 and 1950, India in 1948/9, and Australasia in 1951/2, and at home played against England in 1947/8 and 1953/4, and India in 1952/3. In his 1939 tour he did not bowl a ball but scored 719 runs (25.67) and, during and immediately after the Second World War, scored heavily at home. He shared in a partnership of 434 for the third wicket with Jeffrey Stollmeyer for Trinidad against British Guiana at Port of Spain in 1946/7, which remains the highest for that wicket in the Caribbean. Against England in 1947/8 he made 232 runs (46.40) and served as captain in the second match at Trinidad. In India in 1947/8 he began to come into his own as an all-rounder, scoring 256 runs (36.57), including 101 in the first Test at New Delhi—the first-ever Test between the two countries—and he sometimes shared the new ball, taking 16 wickets (28.58) in all first-class matches. In England in 1950 he made 1,116 runs (42.92) and took 55 wickets (25.58) in all first-class matches, including 207 runs in four Tests, and held 32 catches. At his best for a losing side in Australia in 1951/2, he headed the batting in the Tests with 324 runs (36.00), besides taking 18 wickets (14.22), which included 7 for 55 and 3 for 58 in the fifth match at Sydney, a magnificent performance in sweltering heat, when he bowled faster than usual and made the ball swing appreciably either way in the humid atmosphere. Gerry Gomez was a sage and active administrator on the West Indies Cricket Board of Control for many years, and an able radio commentator. He also stood as a Test umpire as an eleventh-hour replacement in 1964/5. He has done much work for umpires and other sporting associations.

First-class career (1937–57): 6,764 runs (43.63) including 14 centuries, 200 wickets (25.26), and 92 catches
Test matches (29): 1,243 runs (30.31) including 1 century, 58 wickets (27.41), and 18 catches

GOSEIN, Ralph Godfrey

(b. 1931, Port of Spain, Trinidad)

Ralph Gosein, a slimly-built civil servant from Trinidad, was the first West Indian of East Indian descent to umpire Test cricket and, throughout the 1970s, he and Douglas Sang Hue, the Chinese-Jamaican, formed a familiar and respected partnership for home series. Encouraged to take up umpiring by Eric Lee Kow, the Chinese-Trinidadian who was the leading umpire in the West Indies at the time, Gosein made his first first-class début as umpire in 1962 and stood in the first of his 25 Tests three years later, at Port of Spain in the Australian series. By the 1971 Indian tour, he had created such a reputation for himself that he was appointed to four of the five Tests and he officiated in 12 of the 14 Tests in the Caribbean between 1976 and 1978. A stickler for the laws, Gosein was backed by MCC when he overruled a decision by the West Indies Cricket Board of Control to make up lost play on an unscheduled sixth day when a crowd disturbance prematurely ended the fifth Test between Australia and the West Indies at Sabina Park. Another six overs and five balls remained when the crowd reacted violently to umpire Wesley Malcolm's caught behind decision against Vanburn Holder that left Australia one wicket away from victory and when bottles came flying onto the ground play was abandoned for the day. On the Australians' insistance, the West Indies Board agreed to conclude the match the next day but Gosein refused to comply, ruling that there was no such provision in the conditions of play. He and Sang Hue umpired all five so-called 'Super Tests' when Kerry Packer's World Series Cricket came to the West Indies in 1979 and it was widely felt that player pressure led to his retirement, aged 48, soon afterwards. He then concentrated on administration and remains the executive vice-president of the West Indies Cricket Umpires' Association.

GRANT, George Copeland

(b. 1907, Port of Spain, Trinidad; d. 1978, Cambridge) *Cambridge University, Trinidad, Rhodesia, and West Indies*

A Cambridge cricket and Association football blue, 'Jackie' Grant played against Oxford at Lord's in 1929 and 1930. He later captained the team in Australia in 1930/1 (the first visit to Australia), in England in 1933, and at home against England in 1934/5. A good and plucky right-handed batsman, whose spirits were never depressed, and a brilliant field in the gully where he brought off some amazing catches, he was an enthusiastic and astute captain. He played the game in the most sporting spirit and also insisted on those under him doing the same. In his first

Test, against Australia at Adelaide, he made 53 not out and 71 not out, and headed the averages in the series with 255 runs (42.50). In all first-class matches he made 738 runs (36.90) and was a sound leader. On his England tour he achieved little as a player in the Tests, but altogether scored 1,195 runs (30.64), including 115 against an England XI at Folkestone, when he added 226 with George Headley for the third wicket. He had the great pleasure of leading an underrated West Indian team to victory in the rubber against England in 1934/5. For many years he was engaged in missionary work in Africa.

First-class career (1928–35): 3,831 runs (32.19) including 4 centuries, 19 wickets (51.00), and 71 catches

Test matches (12): 413 runs (25.81), 0–18, and 10 catches

GRANT, Sir Kenneth Lindsay

(b. 1899, Port of Spain, Trinidad; d. 1989, Port of Spain)

Although Lindsay Grant did not reach the playing standard of his brothers, 'Jackie' and Rolph, both of whom captained the West Indies, and Fred, who led Trinidad, he made a sizeable contribution to the administration of West Indies cricket during a varied and active life. A member of a distinguished business family whose connection with West Indies cricket was perpetuated in the sponsorship of the limited-overs tournament for the Geddes Grant Shield, his cricket was no more than club standard. He devoted his energies to umpiring and administration. He officiated in several intercolonial tournaments in the 1930s and in the 1930 Port of Spain Test between England and the West Indies. Later, he was a foundation member of the Trinidad Umpires' Council, forerunner of the West Indies Cricket Umpires' Association. He was on the management committee of the Queen's Park Cricket Club for many years, was founder-member and president of the Trinidad Cricket Council, and Trinidad and Tobago's representative on the West Indies Cricket Board of Control from 1959 to 1970. A veteran of both world wars, in which he served in the Royal Air Force, he was awarded the OBE in 1956 and knighted in 1962 for his services to business, cricket, and social work. The former West Indies captain and WICBC president, Jeffrey Stollmeyer, described him as 'a gentleman of rare qualities and high principles'.

GRANT, Rolph Stewart

(b. 1909, Port of Spain, Trinidad; d. 1977, Ontario, Canada) *Cambridge University, Trinidad, and West Indies*

Tall and handsome, Rolph Grant was an all-round sportsman who won blues at Cambridge for cricket and Association football and a half-blue for boxing, later becoming goal-keeper for England amateurs and Trinidad's heavyweight boxing champion. On the cricket field he was a superb field, especially at short-leg, a very useful right-handed batsman generally in the lower-half of the order, and a slow off-spin change-bowler round the wicket. He toured England in 1939 as an admirable captain, and appeared at home against England in 1934/5. He hit his highest Test score of 77 in the fourth match at Kingston, adding 147 with George Headley for the seventh wicket. In England he solved the awkward problem of finding an opening partner for Jeffrey Stollmeyer by undertaking the task himself. His best effort was in the second Test at Old Trafford; after England declared at 164 for 7 wickets on a worsening wicket for the batsmen, he proceeded to hit 47 out of 56 in 38 minutes, including three sixes off Tom Goddard.

First-class career (1932–9): 1,883 runs (28.53) including 1 century, 79 wickets (25.17), and 66 catches

Test matches (7): 220 runs (22.00), 11 wickets (32.09), and 13 catches

GRAY, Anthony Hollis

(b. 1963, Trinidad) *Trinidad and Tobago, Surrey, and West Indies*

A tall, lanky right-arm bowler with an orthodox economical action, Tony Gray was one of a phalanx of West Indian quick-bowlers who strained for long-term recognition at the interface of two eras of great fast bowlers in the late 1980s. Hampered by persistent injury problems, his Test record of 22 wickets at 17.13 was impressive after three appearances in Pakistan in 1986 (including a Test-best 4 for 39 at Faisalabad on his début) and two in New Zealand in early 1987. Thereafter, he was overtaken in the pecking order by the rapid development of his compatriot Ian Bishop and although he formed part of the four-man A team fast attack in the home series against England in 1992, he never featured again in full Tests. At 6 ft. 6 in. and weighing 15 stone, 'Big Man' was capable of genuine speed and disconcerting bounce. He played for Surrey for four seasons from 1985, then again in 1990. He took a hat-trick in a devastating career-best 8 for 40 against Yorkshire at Sheffield in his first year, and prided himself on restrictive one-day spells. In 25 one-day internationals he took 44 wickets (18.97). An inordinately long reach assisted his right-handed batting but Gray reserved his best performances for Warner Park, Basseterre, in St Kitts where he scored 54 not out against the Leewards in 1986 and took 58 off the Australians for the West Indies Board President's XI in 1991. In the first 'unofficial' Test of the A series on an under-prepared pitch in Port of Spain, he struck an enterprising 50 which helped to secure the highest total in the match and West Indies' victory. He gave up a job as government youth coach in Trinidad for a post with the Development Programme of the United Cricket Board of South Africa in Western Transvaal during the winter of 1993/4.

First-class career (1984–): 1,571 runs (14.02), 434 wickets (22.66), and 57 catches

Test matches (5): 48 runs (8.00), 22 wickets (17.13), and 6 catches

GREENIDGE, Alvin Ethelbert

(b. 1956, Barbados) *Barbados and West Indies*

A right-handed batsman, like his namesakes Gordon and Geoffrey, but no relation to either, Alvin Greenidge, a tall man, had an impressive season for Barbados in 1977/8, scoring consistently in the Shell Shield and making a fine 96 for the island against the touring Australian team. When the Packer players left the West Indies team after two Tests of that series, Greenidge fitted well into the Test atmosphere despite his inexperience, scoring 56 in his first innings in the third Test and 69 in the second innings of the fourth, but in India the following year he was a disappointment, making only 80 runs in four Tests. A professional in Holland, he was top scorer for Barbados in the 1982 Shell Shield, scoring 172 against Jamaica.

First-class career (1974–84): 2,309 runs (30.51) including 4 centuries, and 5 wickets (29.40)

Test matches (6): 222 runs (22.20) and 5 catches

GREENIDGE, Cuthbert Gordon

(b. 1951, St Peter, Barbados) *Barbados, Hampshire, Scotland, and West Indies*

Gordon Greenidge moved with his parents to England at the age of 12, was brought up and educated in Reading, and was once approached on the initiative of Ray Illingworth to play for England. But he preferred to await his chance in his native West Indies (though, by his own admission, he never felt entirely at home there and often felt an outsider in the dressing-room) and developed into one of the finest of all players. With Desmond Haynes he formed one of the great opening pairs. They shared 16 century-partnerships in 89 Tests together, one every five and a half matches. No other pair matched them for durability, indeed they batted together in 53 more Tests than their nearest challengers. 298 against England in Antigua in 1990 was their best partnership. A compact, strong right-handed opening batsman with a marvellous temperament, Greenidge grafted on to his natural West Indian flair the fruits of a wide experience and became a magnificent and mature batsman with an immaculate technique who always sought to take immediate control at the start of an innings yet would seldom give his wicket away. His scorching square-cut, bold hooking, and driving in the arc between cover and mid-wicket are abiding memories, but he could make even a forward defensive stroke look beautiful. On two occasions he has hit thirteen sixes in a first-class innings. A loyal servant of Hampshire, the club which gave him his start in cricket, he also owed a debt to county cricket generally and in particular to his regular opening partner for Hampshire, the South African Barry Richards. Not so much a natural genius as Richards, Greenidge improved each year, and in the later years of his partnership with the South African he seldom suffered by comparison, performing many spectacular deeds, including 259 against Sussex in 1975; 136 and 120 (in 91 minutes) against Kent in 1978; 177 in a 60-over Gillette match against Glamorgan in 1975; a record 173, not out in 55 overs in the Benson and Hedges Cup against the Minor Counties South in 1973 and a record 163 not out in 40 overs in the John Player League in 1979, an innings which included ten sixes. Having played for Hampshire since 1970, he made a relatively late Test appearance but made 93 and 107 in his first match against India at Bangalore in 1974/5. In this series he scored 371 runs (41.22) and on the tour, 909 runs (45.45). In England in 1976 he made 1,952 runs in a season of brilliant batting, hitting nine centuries and averaging 55.77. In the Tests his 592 runs (65.77) were topped only by Viv Richards. On an awkward pitch at Old Trafford in the third Test he produced the most masterly performance of his career, making 134 and 101, his 134 coming out of a total of only 211. He followed this with a brilliant 115 in the fourth Test at Headingley. Against Pakistan in the West Indies in 1976/7 he was the supreme West Indian batsman with 536 runs (53.60), which included, strangely enough, only one century, 100 in the fifth Test at Kingston. When his Test career was interrupted by his signing for World Series Cricket he had shared in eight century opening partnerships. He continued to play with success for West Indies after the disbandment of WSC, despite an increasing proneness to injury. In Australia in 1979/80, however, it seemed that the more he limped with a knee strain, the harder he hit the ball. He made 80 and 98 not out against England in the finals of the one-day Triangular tournament. In New Zealand later in the tour he scored 274 runs in three Tests (45.66). In the fifth Test of the 1982/3 series against India in Antigua, he had to retire when 154 because his daughter, who subsequently died, was seriously ill. In England in 1984 he played brilliantly throughout the tour, hitting a wonderful 214 not out off 242 balls with 29 fours and two sixes to win the Lord's Test against the clock, and a painstaking 223 in almost 10 hours of faultless batting when West Indies were in trouble at Old Trafford. He was always at his best in English conditions and in 1986 enjoyed one of his finest seasons: he topped the national batting averages with 2,035 runs at 67.85, hitting four hundreds in successive innings. He scored 572 runs in the five Tests at 81.71 and on the tour scored 1,069 runs (82.33) from only 16 innings. The only country in which Greenidge did not score heavily was Australia but he finally put the record straight in 1988/9, with 104 at Adelaide. His last great Test innings was 226 against Australia at Bridgetown in 1990/1. He had a benefit with Hampshire in 1982. Throughout his career he was a dependable slip catcher. He was given an OBE in 1985.

First-class career (1970–91): 37,354 runs (45.88) including 92 centuries, 18 wickets (26.61), and 516 catches

Test matches (108): 7,558 runs (44.72) including 19 centuries, 0–4, and 96 catches

GREENIDGE, Geoffrey Alan

(b. 1948, Bridgetown, Barbados) *Barbados, Sussex, and West Indies*

A sound, right-handed opening batsman and occasional leg-break bowler, Geoff Greenidge had an amazing first-class début for Barbados in 1966/7, hitting 205 against Jamaica at Bridgetown and taking 7 for 124 in the first innings. In his first Test, against New Zealand at Georgetown in 1971/2 (a match of bottle-throwing incidents), he

scored a good-looking 50 and 35 not out but, although he received other opportunities, he did not make his Test place secure. From 1968 until 1975 he played for Sussex, usefully if unpredictably.

First-class career (1966–76): 9,112 runs (29.29) including 16 centuries, 13 wickets (72.92), and 95 catches

Test matches (5): 209 runs (29.85), 0–75, and 3 catches

GRELL, Mervyn George

(b. 1899, Trinidad; d. 1976, Cocorite) *Trinidad and West Indies*

A sound right-handed batsman and medium-pace bowler, Mervyn Grell's sole Test was the second against England at Port of Spain in 1929/30 when he scored 21 and 13, took 0 for 17 and held 1 catch.

First-class career (1929–38): 489 runs (28.76)

GRIFFITH, Charles Christopher

(b. 1938, St Lucy) *Barbados and West Indies*

One of the most feared fast bowlers of his time, Charlie Griffith began as a right-arm spinner. But he once filled a gap for his new club side as a fast bowler and, after taking seven wickets for one run with his new mode of attack, seldom looked back. The fast-bowling partnership of Griffith and Hall became one of the finest and fastest of all time in international cricket. Griffith was 6 ft. 2 in. tall, of massive build with powerful legs and shoulders, clean-living and very fit. He thundered along his 20-yard run to the wicket and delivered the ball with a chest-on action, which caused some controversy. His deadly ball was a fast yorker but it was his bouncer which caused greater consternation, especially after an incident in Barbados in 1961/2 when Nari Contractor, India's captain, was knocked senseless by one of his balls into which he had ducked: his skull was fractured and for many hours his life was in danger. Happily he recovered, but, in the same match, Griffith was no-balled for 'throwing'. Although some critics (especially the Australians) considered that he sometimes threw his faster ball, which batsmen found difficult to sight, he was only called in one other first-class match, by Arthur Fagg at Old Trafford, in the match with Lancashire in 1966. Volatile in his reactions to problems, Griffith gained a reputation as 'the big bad boy of cricket', and provided some good copy for the tabloids. He toured England in 1963 and 1966, India in 1966, and Australasia in 1968/9, and at home played against England in

1959/60 and 1967/8, and Australia in 1964/5. On his first-class début in 1959/60, for Barbados against MCC at Bridgetown, he dismissed Colin Cowdrey, Mike Smith, and Peter May in two overs, and soon added Ken Barrington to his 'bag'. In England in 1963 he was often unplayable, heading the bowling with 119 wickets (12.83), including 32 wickets (16.21) in the Tests. In the highly dramatic drawn second Test at Lord's he took eight wickets, and in the fourth at Headingley and fifth at The Oval nine wickets each time, including 6 for 36 in the first innings at Headingley. Against Gloucestershire at Bristol, he captured 13 for 58. Against Australia in 1964/5 he took 15 wickets (32.00). Very disconcerted by the continued rumblings over his action, he was not generally as effective on the 1966 England tour and in subsequent Test series.

First-class career (1959–69): 1,502 runs (17.26), 332 wickets (21.60), and 39 catches
Test matches (28): 530 runs (16.56), 94 wickets (28.54), and 16 catches

GRIFFITH, Herman Clarence

(b. 1893, Port of Spain, Trinidad; d. 1980, Bridgetown, Barbados) *Barbados and West Indies*

Short in build but also powerful and exuding a sturdy confidence, Herman Griffith was a fast bowler who also bowled brisk medium-fast out-swingers and off-breaks, cleverly changing pace and maintaining a good length. He once clean-bowled Herbert Sutcliffe with a ball which swung from middle-and-leg to the off stump. 'Griff' was the first consistently successful West Indian bowler in Test cricket. No man hated being hit more than he did and he had the reputation of being ready to call anybody anything which seemed to him to apply. Probably because of his temperament, or because he was rumoured to be a communist, Griff was omitted from the 1923 West Indian team to tour England despite causing a sensation with his 7 for 38 against Trinidad in 1921/2. Touring England in 1928, he took 76 wickets (27.89) in first-class matches (103 in all matches). In the third Test at The Oval he took 6 for 103 in England's total of 438. Against England in the first Test series in the Caribbean in 1929/30, he secured 16 wickets (31.75), including 8 for 162 at Port of Spain in the second match. On the first tour of Australia in 1930/1 he headed the Test bowling figures with 14 wickets (28.07), bowling Don Bradman for a duck in the fifth match at Sydney. (As he had dismissed the Don for 4 in an earlier Test, he was fond of referring to the great

man as his 'rabbit'.) In his fortieth year, in 1933, he toured England again. He had lost something of his pace and nip off the pitch, though his language remained as pungent as ever.

First-class career (1921–41): 1,204 runs (15.05), 258 wickets (28.27), and 36 catches
Test matches (13): 91 runs (5.05), 44 wickets (28.25), and 4 catches

GUILLEN, Simpson Clement

(b. 1924, Port of Spain, Trinidad) *Trinidad, Canterbury, West Indies, and New Zealand*

A very competent wicket-keeper and useful right-handed batsman, 'Sammy' Guillen toured Australasia in 1951/2, playing in five Tests with success. The tour brought him 34 dismissals (24 caught, 10 stumped) from 11 matches. He became a permanent resident of New Zealand, keeping wicket for Canterbury, and he appeared for New Zealand in three official Tests against West Indies in 1955/6 and three unofficial Tests against Australia in 1956/7. The West Indians raised no objections to Sammy playing for New Zealand, although he had not then lived for four years in his adopted country. The highest score of his career was 197 for Canterbury against Fiji in 1953/4.

First-class career (1947–61): 2,672 runs (26.97) including 3 centuries, and 134 dismissals (100 c., 34 st.)
Test matches (West Indies—5): 104 runs (26.00) and 11 dismissals (9 c., 2 st.). (New Zealand—3): 98 runs (16.33) and 5 dismissals (4 c., 1 st.)

HALL, Wesley Winfield

(b. 1937, St Michael, Barbados) *Barbados, Trinidad, Queensland, and West Indies*

The ideal of right-arm fast bowlers, a muscular 6 ft. 2 in. man with a classical action and good temper, Wes Hall was a fearsome prospect, especially in partnership with Charlie Griffith. Possessing a long, athletic approach, with eyes bulging, teeth glinting, and a crucifix swinging across his chest, Hall was an aesthetic joy to the spectator, but an intimidating sight to a waiting batsman. He bowled as though he meant to take a wicket with every delivery; his speed was measured as 91 m.p.h. and he was consistently fast and hostile. Curiously enough, he was in early days a batsman/wicket-keeper: indeed, when he first toured England in 1957, with moderate results, he had never taken a single wicket in first-class cricket. Success did not come quickly and it was only as a very late replacement that he toured India and Pakistan in 1958/9. Soon establishing his superiority, he took 46 wickets (17.76) from eight Tests and 87 wickets (15.08) on the whole tour, more wickets than anyone else. He captured 11 for 126 in the second Test at Kanpur against India and 8 for 77 in the second at Dacca against Pakistan. Against England in 1959/60 his haul was 22 wickets (30.86), including 7 for 69 in the first innings of the third match at Sabina Park. In the great tied match, the first Test at Brisbane in 1960/1, he took 9 for 203. With his shirt hanging out, he bowled the last over when six runs were needed for victory with three wickets left. He took one wicket and there were two run-outs. Earlier in the match he had hit 50 in 69 minutes. In this series Hall took 21 wickets (29.33), again more than any of his colleagues. He was again at the centre of the high drama at Lord's in 1963. He brought West Indies back into the game when, in England's second innings, he bowled unchanged throughout the 3 hours 20 minutes' play on the last day, taking 4 for 93. Unintentionally he had further hurt England's chances of winning when one of his deliveries broke Colin Cowdrey's forearm. With India as visitors in 1961/2 he was in his best form throughout, taking 27 wickets (15.74), including 5 for 20 in the first innings of the fourth match at Port of Spain. He was a first choice for his country for ten years, and until the later stages of his career he never had a poor series. Altogether, he toured England in 1957, 1963, and 1966, India and Pakistan in 1958/9, Australia in 1960/1 and 1968/9, and New Zealand in 1968/9. At home he played against England in 1959/60 and 1967/8, India in 1961/2, and Australia in 1964/5. He struck the ball hard and was sometimes a useful run-getter. A popular man wherever he played, he had several seasons for Queensland in the Sheffield Shield competition and several also in the Lancashire League. He later became a politician, was for many years a senator in the Barbados Parliament, and has frequently managed West Indies teams abroad with passion and wisdom.

First-class career (1955–71): 2,673 runs (15.10) including 1 century, 546 wickets (26.14), and 58 catches

Test matches (48): 818 runs (15.73), 192 wickets (26.38), and 11 catches

HARPER, Roger Andrew

(b. 1963, Georgetown, Guyana) *Guyana, Northamptonshire, and West Indies*

Roger Harper's approach to cricket was summed up when he faced the final ball of a crucial County Championship match in 1985. The last Northamptonshire pair were together and Northants still needed six to win. Harper pulled it far over long-on. The possibility of playing for a draw, despite the odds against his side, had not entered his head. An intelligent and very tall allrounder of strapping build, his aggressive batting is complemented by brilliantly athletic fielding in the deep or spectacularly good close catching; but his primary skill is as an off-spin bowler, the first since his fellow-Guyanan Lance Gibbs to claim a regular place on merit in a national team dominated by fast bowlers. He was expected to become Test captain, but his relatively innocuous bowling gradually became a luxury in so aggressive a team and he was dropped. He first played Shield cricket at the age of 17 and made his first Test appearance against India away in 1983, visiting Australia later in the same tour and then touring England in 1984, taking 6 for 57 in the England second innings at Old Trafford. In May 1986 he had barely stepped off the plane from the Caribbean when he hit 234 against Gloucestershire with 12 sixes. The following season, in the MCC Bicentenary match at Lord's, he brought off a typically virtuoso piece of fielding to run out Graham Gooch off his own bowling after Gooch had driven the ball hard back at him. Stopping the ball one-handed, Harper swivelled and threw directly at the stumps, with the startled batsman stranded. He made a surprise return to the West Indies team in 1993/4, touring Sharjah, Sri Lanka, and India. He played in a total of 81 oneday internationals, scoring 555 runs (15.00) and taking 72 wickets (35.90). His 4 for 40 against England in Port of Spain in 1994/5 was his only four-wicket analysis, but overall he conceded only 3.97 runs per over and it was as a one-day cricketer that Harper especially excelled. He has captained Guyana since 1986. His elder brother has also played Shield cricket for Guyana.

First-class career (1979–): 6,811 runs (33.55) including 8 centuries, 513 wickets (26.67), and 243 catches

Test matches (25): 535 runs (18.44), 46 wickets (28.06), and 36 catches

HAYNES, Desmond Leo

(b. 1956, St James, Barbados) *Barbados, Middlesex, Western Province, and West Indies*

A solidly muscled, right-handed opening batsman, Desmond Haynes played more Tests for the West Indies than all except Viv Richards; scored more runs in West Indies domestic cricket than anyone (3,961 runs at 50.78); and scored more runs in one-day internationals than any other player. A fine driver, he also hit hard off the back foot, cutting and hooking majestically. His long career began at the Carlton Club in Barbados. His début for the island was made in 1977 and a season later he made his first Test appearances against Australia, making 61, 66, and 55 in his first three innings. At Bridgetown he put on 131 with Gordon Greenidge for the first wicket in the second innings, the first of 16 century-partnerships they were to put together for the West Indies first wicket in 89 Tests together. Their average partnership was 47.32, fit to rank with some of the best of all time, and no pair has matched them for length of service. Greenidge and Haynes were as important a part of the West Indian domination of world cricket in the 1980s as the fast bowlers. Haynes, a vibrant character with a smile never far away, although also quick to anger and emotional, enjoyed the fruits of his and his team's success to the full, but kept himself fit and worked hard on his technique, spending many hours in the nets. He fitted comfortably into the shoes of Roy Fredericks as Greenidge's regular Test opening partner. Going on all the major West Indies tours after 1979, he also visited Zimbabwe in 1981, with the West Indies under-26 team, when he was vice-captain. At Lord's in 1980, he batted 490 minutes for 184, the solid foundation on which West Indies based a first-innings score of 518. Many of his finest hundreds have been scored in one-day internationals, especially against Australia (three in a row in 1983/4) and his most productive Test series was also at home against Australia in 1983/4 when he hit 468 runs (93.60), including 103 not out at Georgetown and 145 at Bridgetown. Against England at home in 1986, his 469 Test runs (78.16) included a sheet-anchor innings of 131 at Antigua in the fifth Test. Such is his love for cricket that as soon as the official West Indies tour of England had finished in 1984, Haynes led his own side, Carlton, in another tour of the country. Five of his Test hundreds were scored against England, the last a powerful 167 at St John's, Antigua, in 1989/90, when he and Greenidge added 298 together, their highest partnership. Another five centuries were scored against Australia, including two in 1988/9, at Perth and Sydney. Haynes had played in 239 one-day internationals, scoring a record 17 centuries, and in 116 Tests when in 1995 the West Indies Board banned him from playing at home against Australia because he had arrived back from South Africa, where he had

played for Western Province, too late to play in the first match of the Red Stripe Competition. He also played in World Series Cricket in 1978/9 and for Middlesex, with great success, from 1989 to 1990 and 1992 to 1994. He captained West Indies in one Test against England at Port of Spain in 1990, as stand-in for Viv Richards, and on the tour of Pakistan in 1990. He was awarded the Barbados Silver Crown of Merit in 1989.

First-class career (1976–): 24,219 runs (45.95) including 59 centuries, 8 wickets (33.50), and 184 dismissals (183 c., 1 st.)

Test matches (116): 7,487 runs (42.29) including 18 centuries, 1 wicket (8.00), and 65 catches

HAYNES, Robert Christopher

(b. 1964, Kingston, Jamaica) *Jamaica*

A tall, right-arm leg-spinner, aggressive left-hand batsman, and a catcher with fly-paper hands, Robert Haynes was one of Jamaica's youngest first-class cricketers when first selected, aged 17 and still at Kingston College, in the 1982 Shell Shield. It was to be a sensational début as he had figures of 11 for 206 against Guyana and nine for 140 against the Leeward Islands in his first two matches but his full all-round potential has never materialized. He toured England that summer with the West Indies youth team, under Roger Harper, but, while he was one of the outstanding players, he was suspended for the first two matches of the following season for indiscipline. It earned him an early reputation of being difficult to handle that he never shook off. He has remained a regular, and essential, member of the Jamaica team and has been clearly close to Test selection more than once, never more so than against England in the Caribbean in 1990. He hit his highest score, 98, against the touring team for Jamaica and took 8 for 147 in the match against them for the President's XI immediately preceeding the third Test at Port of Spain. The team was announced without him prior to the end of the match and Haynes's reaction was to smash 30 in 20 minutes with five fours as the President's XI slumped to defeat. He was picked for the West Indies tour of Pakistan later that year but his frustration was further heightened when he was ignored for the decisive final Test at Lahore, in spite of a pitch obviously prepared to assist spin. He was confined to one one-day international and the solitary first-class match and it seems his dream of playing Test cricket has passed. He has also played one-day internationals in Sharjah, India, and Australia; eight games in all with disappointing results: 26 runs (5.20) and 5 wickets (44.80). For several years, Haynes has been a popular and successful professional in the north of England, playing for clubs in the Lancashire, Central Lancashire, and Northern Leagues.

First-class career (1982–): 1,973 runs (21.44) and 197 wickets (29.32)

HEADLEY, George Alphonso

(b. 1909, Panama; d. 1983, Kingston, Jamaica)
Jamaica and West Indies

Born in Panama, George Headley was taken to his mother's island of Jamaica at the age of 10 and soon revealed a genius for cricket. Arguably still the greatest of all the West Indies' specialist batsmen, he was to become the dominant West Indian batsman from 1929 until 1948. A compact right-hander with every shot at his command, he never failed in a series of Tests. At the age of 18 he scored 71 and 211 in two matches for Jamaica against the Hon. Lionel Tennyson's side in 1927/8, and, rather than study dentistry in the USA, he played in the first-ever Test on West Indian soil against England at Bridgetown in 1929/30, making 21 and 176. In the third match at Georgetown he made 114 (adding 196 for the second wicket with Clifford Roach) and 112, West Indies winning a Test for the first time. In the next match at Kingston he amassed 223 in $6\frac{1}{2}$ hours, after the West Indies were set 836 runs to win. In this first home series he made 703 runs (87.87), only three men ever having reached a higher aggregate. He became known as 'Atlas' as the rest of his country's batting rested on him. Essentially a back-foot player, he almost always sought to attack the bowling, although he was also a sound defender. He was a fine cutter but his outstanding feature was his powerful and well-placed driving. He occasionally bowled enthusiastic and useful leg-breaks and fielded well anywhere; in his earlier days he would sometimes make a complete somersault in taking catches, Constantine-fashion. It was on the first tour of Australia in 1930/1 that, after mastering Clarrie Grimmett, he was given the sobriquet, 'The Black Bradman'. All first-class matches on this tour brought him 1,066 runs (44.41) including 102 not out (out of 193) in the second Test at Brisbane and 105 in the fifth at Sydney. At Kingston in 1931/2 he made his career-highest score of 344 not out for Jamaica against Lord Tennyson's side, adding a record unbroken 487 for the sixth wicket with C. C. Passailaigue. His other scores against these tourists were 84, 155 not out and 140. In

England in 1933 he made 2,320 runs (66.28), including seven centuries. In hitting 169 not out in the second Test at Old Trafford—the second century by a West Indian in a Test in England—he added 200 for the second wicket with Ivan Barrow who had preceded him to 100 by a few minutes. In the three Tests he made 277 runs (55.40). Once more the heart of the batting against England in 1934/5, he scored 485 runs (97.00), including his Test-highest score of 270 not out in the first Test at Kingston, an outstanding innings, which lasted nearly eight hours. A few days before he had hit 127 for Jamaica against the tourists. On the 1939 England tour he was still master, no one else approaching his total of 1,745 runs (72.70), including six centuries. To the Tests he contributed 334 runs (66.80), including 106 and 107 in the first match at Lord's; no West Indian had previously hit two centuries in the same Test. By the time the Second World War had come, George Headley had not missed a Test played by the West Indies for ten years and in the first post-war Test at Bridgetown against England he was appointed captain; the first black man ever to lead the side. Hampered, however, by a bad back, he missed the remaining Tests. In India in 1948/9 he appeared in the first Test at Delhi, but missed most of the tour through injury. His next and final Test was the first against England at Kingston in 1953/4 when, at 44 years and 236 days, he became the oldest-ever West Indian Test cricketer. He coached on behalf of the Government of Jamaica, and was the father of Ron Headley.

First-class career (1927–54): 9,921 runs (69.86) including 33 centuries, 51 wickets (36.11), and 76 catches
Test matches (22): 2,190 runs (60.83) including 10 centuries, 0–230, and 14 catches

HEADLEY, Ronald George Alphonso

(b. 1939, Kingston, Jamaica) *Jamaica, Worcestershire, Derbyshire, and West Indies*

Most of Ron Headley's cricket was played in England where in 1973 he joined a West Indian team, which had been depleted by injury, to appear in two Tests, but without luck. An attractive left-handed opening batsman, with a handsome cover-drive, full backlift and high follow-through, he moved on to his front foot as much as possible. He was a brilliant fielder anywhere and an occasional leg-break bowler. He was registered with Worcestershire from 1958 until 1974 and then briefly joined Derbyshire to play in the one-day games. He appeared for Jamaica in the Shell Shield in 1965/6 and 1973/4. His father George was an immortal cricketer and his son, Dean, has played with success for Middlesex and Kent.

First-class career (1958–74): 21,695 runs (31.12) including 32 centuries, 12 wickets (49.00), and 356 catches

Test matches (2): 62 runs (15.50) and 2 catches

HENDRIKS, John Leslie

(b. 1933, Kingston, Jamaica) *Jamaica and West Indies*

A tall, cheerful, extrovert wicket-keeper specially adept at taking slow bowling and a useful right-handed batsman, 'Jackie' Hendriks toured Pakistan in 1958/9 and Australia in 1960/1 as reserve 'keeper. When he finally made his Test début against India in 1961/2 in the first match at Port of Spain, he broke his finger, though he top-scored with 64. He did not regain his place until 1964/5 when, in the fourth Test at Bridgetown against Australia, he was struck by a ball from 'Garth' McKenzie and removed to hospital for brain surgery: his life was in the balance during this series. He recovered completely, touring England in 1966 and 1969, India in 1966/7 and Australasia in 1968/9, playing in 15 further Tests before Deryck Murray replaced him. He managed the record-breaking 1984 team to England, and several other successful teams, reacting with notable dignity to an unexpected defeat by Pakistan in 1986/7. He also chaired the West Indies selection committee for many seasons.

First-class career (1953–69): 1,568 runs (17.42) and 190 dismissals (140 c., 50 st.)

Test matches (20): 447 runs (18.62) and 47 dismissals (42 c., 5 st.)

HOAD, Edward Lisle Goldsworthy

(b. 1896, St Michael, Barbados; d. 1986, Bridgetown, Barbados) *Barbados and West Indies*

A sound, defensive right-handed batsman and leg-break change-bowler, Teddy Hoad was a prolific scorer in the West Indies. In the Intercolonial Tournament in 1926/7, for instance, he made 115 against British Guiana and 174 not out against Trinidad at Kensington. In England in 1928 he took a long time to find form, playing in only one Test, but finished at the head of the averages with 765 runs (36.42) including three centuries. He captained the West Indies in the first-ever Test in the Caribbean, against England at Bridgetown in

1929/30. He toured England again in 1933 as vice-captain, making 1,083 runs (27.76). He was, however, very disappointing in Test cricket.

First-class career (1921–38): 3,502 runs (38.48) including 8 centuries, 53 wickets (36.28), and 26 catches

Test matches (4): 98 runs (12.25) and 1 catch

HOLDER, Roland Irwin Christopher

(b. 1967, Trinidad) *Barbados*

A compact, well-organized middle-order right-hand batsman, Roland Holder had been touted as a player of genuine Test class for some years before forcing his way into the one-day international scene. A product of Combermere School in Barbados, an establishment of strong cricketing pedigree, Holder toured England and Australia with West Indies Young Cricketers, and has made runs consistently in regional domestic cricket since his début in 1989. An occasional right-arm medium pacer and a splendid fielder anywhere, he has acted as a substitute in Test matches on home ground at Kensington. Immaculately turned out with buttoned down sleeves, Holder always looked the part and he supplemented his best ever Red Stripe season, 376 runs averaging 41.77 in 1992, his first year captaining Barbados, with scores of 54, 77, and 40 in three 'unofficial' Tests against the England A tourists. He made his one-day international début in Sharjah in 1993, and played in the Hero Cup in India, scoring 50 against Zimbabwe at Hyderabad. Inexplicably, he suffered a downturn in form in 1994 until the final Red Stripe match when an unbeaten rearguard 116 against Trinidad and Tobago heralded a belated selection for the fifth one-day match against England at Queens Park. He had played 11 one-day internationals by 1994/5, scoring 187 runs (20.77), but he played in only one first-class match on the 1994 tour of India. He has captained Barbados since 1992.

First-class career (1986–): 2,708 runs (42.58) including 10 centuries, and 20 catches

HOLDER, Vanburn Alonza

(b. 1945, St Michael, Barbados) *Barbados, Worcestershire, Orange Free State, and West Indies*

A dignified and sporting cricketer, Vanburn Holder bowled with outstanding consistency during a long career. Tall and raw-boned, he bowled fast-medium with a good high action after a bandy-legged approach, moving his away-swinger dangerously late and seldom getting the luck he deserved. He fielded capably and batted right-handed in text-book manner, sometimes playing such good-looking strokes that it was surprising he did not get more runs, although he did score 122 against Trinidad at Bridgetown in a Shell Shield match in 1974. First playing for Worcestershire in 1968, he was capped in 1970 and was prominent in the county's win in the County Championship in 1974 when he recorded his best first-class bowling figures of 7 for 40 against Glamorgan at Cardiff. With the West Indies he toured England in 1969, 1973, and 1976. On his Test début at Headingley in 1969 he took 4 for 48 in England's first innings in 26 overs. In 1973 he took 4 for 56 in the first innings of the third Test at Lord's. In 1976 he took 15 wickets (24.46) in four Tests and shared with Holding, Roberts, and Daniel in a remorseless attack of fast or fast-medium bowling. On this tour he took 52 wickets in all first-class games at 19.30 each. Against New Zealand in 1971/2 he headed the Test bowling averages with 12 wickets (23.75) including 4 for 41 in 26 overs in the second innings of the fifth Test at Port of Spain where his 42 in the second West Indies innings was top score. In all first-class matches on the tour of India, Sri Lanka, and Pakistan in 1974/5 his accuracy and ability to move the ball off the seam on normally unresponsive wickets enabled him to take 40 wickets at 23.42. In four Tests against India he took 17 wickets (18.52), including 6 for 39 in the second innings of the deciding Test, the fifth at Bombay, paving the way for West Indian victory. The arrival of players like Garner and Croft pushed the reliable Holder out of the Test side for a time but when the Packer players left the fold he bounced back to take 6 for 28 in Australia's first innings of 290 in the fourth Test in 1977/8. In India the following winter, however, he was very expensive, age clearly starting to take its toll of a much-respected cricketer. He became a first-class umpire in England.

First-class career (1966–86): 3,593 runs (12.97) including 1 century, 950 wickets (24.52), and 99 catches

Test matches (40): 682 runs (14.21), 109 wickets (33.28), and 16 catches

HOLDING, Michael Anthony

(b. 1954, Kingston, Jamaica) *Jamaica, Lancashire, Derbyshire, Tasmania, Canterbury, and West Indies*

It is difficult to believe that anyone has made the strenuous business of bowling very fast seem as effortless as Michael Holding. Tall and slim, with his arms resting comfortably by his sides and his head nodding like a new-born baby's, he approached the stumps down a long, floating run which had the fragile grace of an antelope, then leapt high and bowled with fearsome speed and exceptionally high bounce. Few of the adjectives normally applied to fast bowlers apply, for Holding was not overtly ferocious and had none of the normal broad-shouldered, muscular power of most great exponents of his art. Since he is also a university graduate and was a 400-metre runner of potentially Olympic class, West Indian cricket was fortunate to hold his interest. He developed dramatically in England in 1976 after a tour to Australia in 1975/6 when his accuracy did not begin to match his youthful speed. At Brisbane in his first Test he took no wickets for 127 and his ten wickets in the series cost 61.40 each. Later the same season, however, he headed the Test averages against India on his home pitches, taking 19 wickets (19.89) which included 6 for 65 in the first innings of the third Test at Port of Spain. In England, in the hot summer of 1976, he was the most formidable of a fierce quartet of fast bowlers (Roberts, Daniel, and Holder being the others), taking 55 wickets on the tour at only 14.38 and 28 in the Tests at 12.71. Early in the season, playing against MCC at Lord's, he bowled with awesome pace, once splitting open the side of Dennis Amiss's head with a bouncer. His 5 for 17 in 14.5 overs in the Old Trafford Test on a treacherous pitch hustled out England for 71. In the final Test, in totally different conditions at The Oval on a slow and lifeless pitch, he produced one of the most remarkable fast bowling feats in modern times, taking 14 for 149 in the match by unforgettable bowling which was simply very fast and very straight. His 8 for 92 was the best analysis by a West Indian against England and his match figures the best by any West Indian in a Test. He bowled with further success against England on tour in 1980 (44 first-class wickets on the tour and 20 in the Tests), at home in 1981/2 (17 wickets in four Tests at 18.52), and in 1984 when in addition to 15 wickets, which included a vital spell of three wickets for five runs in 17 very fast balls at The Oval, he also scored 158 runs (31.60) with a highest score of 69 at Edgbaston when he hit four sixes. When required to do so, he hit with a straight bat and considerable flair. Despite his relatively slender build he also stood up well to tours of Australia (four times), New Zealand, India, and Pakistan between 1975 and 1985, although he fell from grace when expressing his displeasure with the

New Zealand umpires by kicking over the stumps (even this he did with elegance!). He split his time between county cricket and the Lancashire League in England, and in 1982/3 played with success for Tasmania. Faced with increasingly slow pitches and having relinquished the new ball for West Indies he generally bowled off a shorter run in the 1980s, relying on skilful swing and cut plus the occasional very fast ball, but when called on to take the new ball again in India in 1983/4 he responded characteristically by taking 30 wickets at 22.10. Vice-captain at home against England in 1986, he took 16 wickets at 24 and in Antigua smashed 73 with four sixes and six fours. Not the least remarkable fact about a very unusual bowler is that the umpires said that they could not hear him approaching behind them, so light-footed was the approach. Hence his sou-briquet, 'Whispering Death'. His charm and good looks enabled him to make a successful second career as a television and radio pundit and wherever he travelled he was never short of attractive female company. His other great hobby off the field was horse-racing.

First-class career (1972–89): 3,600 runs (15.00), 778 wicket (23.43), and 125 catches

Test matches (60): 910 runs (13.78), 249 wickets (23.68), and 22 catches

HOLFORD, David Anthony Jerome

(b. 1940, Bridgetown, Barbados) *Barbados, Trinidad, and West Indies*

A tall, slim right-arm leg-break bowler with a generally good command of length, David Holford developed more as a reliable right-handed batsman with a superb drive. Throughout, he was a fine close field and a cheerful and attractive cricketer. He toured England in 1966, India in 1966/7, and Australasia in 1968/9, and at home played against England in 1967/8, India in 1970/1 and 1975/6, New Zealand in 1971/2, and Pakistan in 1976/7. His finest hour came early, at Lord's in his second Test, in 1966; with the West Indies only nine runs ahead and five second-innings wickets gone, he joined his cousin Gary Sobers, and they added 274 in an unbroken partnership—a West Indian record against England—in 5 hours 20 minutes. Holford made a fighting 105 not out. On the tour he made 759 runs (37.95) and took 51 wickets (28.60). The series brought him 227 runs (37.83). Against India in the first Test at Bombay in 1966/7 he made a determined 80 and took five wickets, but soon afterwards an attack of pleurisy kept him out of

the rest of the tour. In the first Test against India at Bridgetown in 1975/6 he took 5 for 23. These successes tended to come spasmodically, and although consistently a respected and successful all-rounder for Barbados, whom he captained, he never fully established himself in Tests. However, he became chairman of the West Indies selectors and a manager of West Indies teams.

First-class career (1960–79): 3,821 runs (31.31) including 3 centuries, 253 wickets (32.00), and 83 catches

Test matches (24): 768 runs (22.58) including 1 century, 51 wickets (39.39), and 18 catches

HOLT, John Kenneth Constantine, jun.

(b. 1923, Jamaica) *Jamaica and West Indies*

Unlike his father, J.K. senior, who made the trip in 1923, John Holt did not visit England but he toured India and Pakistan in 1958/9, and at home played against England in 1953/4 and Australia in 1954/5. A right-handed batsman with strokes all round the wicket, he scored 94 in his first Test against England at Kingston in 1953/4 before being given out lbw to Statham by umpire P. Burke, whose wife and son were assaulted by spectators in reaction to the decision. In the next Test, at Bridgetown, he hit 166, adding 222 with Frank Worrell for the second wicket. In the series Holt made 432 runs (54.00). In India and Pakistan in 1958/9 he made 1,001 runs (43.52), including three centuries, one of which was 123 in the first Test against India at Delhi, when, in facing a total of 415, he and Conrad Hunte put on 159 for the first wicket.

First-class career (1946–62): 4,256 runs (41.32) including 9 centuries

Test matches (17): 1,066 runs (36.75) including 2 centuries, 1–20, and 8 catches

HOOPER, Carl Llewellyn

(b. 1966, Georgetown, Guyana) *Guyana, Kent, and West Indies*

Acknowledged as a graceful right-handed batsman of the classical mould from his early days at Georgetown Cricket Club, Carl Hooper's career expectations never quite reached their full flourish and there were only intermittent glimmers at Test level of an extraordinary talent until a successful period as Kent's overseas player from 1992 to 1994, and marriage to an English girl, enhanced his self-confidence and enabled his ability to mature. The 'enigmatic stylist' nourished the faith of the selectors through a long fallow period where he regularly appeared in full command before unexpectedly losing his wicket. His versatility as a genuine off-spin bowler with an easy, languid action undoubtedly supported his retention, especially in limited-overs cricket, and his consistency as a marvellously athletic slip fielder was always a major asset. Six feet tall and not bothering to wear a helmet, Hooper is assurance personified at the crease, with seemingly unlimited time for stroke-making which affords his batsmanship a veneer of rare nobility. He was arguably the best all-rounder to graduate from the regional youth tournament, the Northern Telecom Trophy, and in 1985 made a supreme maiden century, 126 run out, on his first-class début against Barbados. Effortless timing and placement mask an inherent power and the ability to improvise, and he was drafted into the World Cup squad in India and Pakistan in 1987, before making his Test début in Bombay shortly afterwards. In his second match at Calcutta a few days after his twenty-first birthday, he recorded a maiden century, an undefeated 100, and the cognoscenti sat back in anticipation of further artistic canvases. Yet the masterpiece failed to materialize, and another 37 innings were to pass before he reached the landmark again. Amid a welter of theory on technique and temperament Hooper himself, quiet and charmingly unassuming off the field, equated that relative lack of productivity to the burden of expectation and rising tide of hero worship at a tender age. He was also shuttled between number three and six in the order and injury played a part, too; he missed India's tour of the Caribbean in 1989, then later, England's entire series there in 1994, returning to England for treatment on a back problem while the West Indies Board were roundly condemned for a supposed lack of interest in players' welfare. On his first tour of England, in 1988, he struck a classy 84 at Trent Bridge but could muster only 82 in a further six innings. The selectors' judgement was rewarded in December 1990 at Lahore when Hooper scored 134 off 220 balls against Pakistan, an effort of huge significance as West Indies were on the verge of surrendering their first series for nearly a decade. The pitch was 'low and slow' but he batted, alongside the débutant Lara, with renewed confidence against the feared trio of Imran, Akram, and Younis. In the second innings of the previous Test, he had made 33 not out, the 'watershed' knock, wherein he had experienced an upliftment of spirit in consort with his captain, Richie Richardson. In England in 1991 he aver-

aged 85.46, the highest there by a West Indian, his output no doubt improved by experience as professional at Werneth in the Central Lancashire League where he broke Sir Frank Worrell's aggregate run record for a season. At Lord's in the second Test he made 111 after a nervous start, then produced a stupendous cameo on the fourth morning of the final Oval Test, striking three sixes, including a brace off Tufnell, in the first 20 minutes with West Indies following on. His off-spin bowling had gained greater credence in county matches and his variation developed further during the World Cup in Australia in 1992. In May 1993 in Antigua he duly delivered what many in the Caribbean had feared he never would: an innings of poetic majesty on home territory, 178 not out, after initial good fortune against Waqar Younis's in-swing. This highest Test score, off 247 balls over nearly 5 hours, contained every shot in the book (and some that were not when he needed to retain the strike). Hitting four sixes and nineteen fours, he also added 106 with Courtney Walsh for the last wicket, a West Indian record against all-comers. Under Walsh's captaincy in India at the end of 1994 he was the outstanding player in the one-day internationals and with 262 runs in three Tests did better than all but Jimmy Adams for a struggling side, also taking 9 wickets. His highest score was 236 not out for Kent against Glamorgan in 1993.

First-class career (1983–): 10,714 runs (45.02) including 25 centuries, 294 wickets (34.56), and 188 catches
Test matches (47): 2,238 runs (30.65) including 4 centuries, 48 wickets (52.56), and 53 catches

HOWARD, Anthony Bourne

(b. 1946, Barbados) *Barbados and West Indies*

Tony Howard was a right-arm off-break bowler who bowled well for his island against the New Zealand touring team in 1971/2. He played in one Test, the fourth against New Zealand at Georgetown, when he did not bat and took 2 for 140 in 62 overs in one innings.

First-class career (1965–75): 310 runs (10.00) and 85 wickets (27.30)

HUNTE, Conrad Cleophas

(b. 1932, Belleplaine, Barbados) *Barbados and West Indies*

By inclination an aggressive right-handed batsman who loved to let his natural talent flow,

Conrad Hunte realized, as an opener, that it was more important for West Indies to be given a sound, solid start, and he adapted his technique accordingly. He was very reliable, though he seldom had a completely satisfactory partner. His strength was primarily off his legs, either glancing fine or punching to mid-wicket, but he also hooked with power and timed his off-drive perfectly. He was a fine fielder, especially close to the bat, and occasionally bowled slow-medium cutters. He toured India and Pakistan in 1958/9, Australia in 1960/1, England in 1963 and 1966, and India in 1966/7. At home he played against Pakistan in 1957/8, England in 1959/60, India in 1962/3, and Australia in 1964/5. Although making his first-class début in 1950/1, he waited seven years before being selected for Tests and in his first series, against Pakistan in 1957/8, amassed 622 runs (77.75), including 142 in the first match at Bridgetown, 260 in the third at Kingston—his highest in Tests, when he added 446 for the second wicket with Gary Sobers (365 not out), a record stand for West Indies—and 114 in the fourth at Georgetown. In Australia in 1960/1 he hit 110 in a total of 233 in the second Test at Melbourne; and in England in 1963 he was at his peak, making more runs than anyone else, 1,367 runs (44.09), including 471 runs (58.87) in the Tests, when he headed the averages. He scored 182 in the first Test at Old Trafford and 108 not out in the fifth at The Oval. Against Australia in 1964/5 he was the outstanding batsman with 550 runs (61.11) and a highest score of 89: consistency personified. On his second tour of England in 1966, as vice-captain, he was not as dominant as before, but, again in the first Test at Old Trafford, he made a century—108. The highest of his three double-centuries was 263 for Barbados against Jamaica at Georgetown in 1961/2. He later worked for the Moral Rearmament movement, coached in South African townships, and has been an ICC match referee.

First-class career (1950–67): 8,916 runs (43.92) including 16 centuries, 17 wickets (37.88), and 69 dismissals (68 c., 1 st.)

Test matches (44): 3,245 runs (45.06) including 8 centuries, 2 wickets (55.00), and 16 catches

HUNTE, Errol Ashton Clairmore

(b. 1905, Port of Spain, Trinidad; d. 1967, Port of Spain) *Trinidad and West Indies*

A good opening batsman and useful wicket-keeper, Errol Hunte toured Australia in 1930/1 but all his Test cricket was played at home against England in 1929/30. In his second Test at Port of Spain he kept wicket and hit 58 and 30

First-class career (1928–34): 472 runs (20.52) and 36 dismissals (28 c., 8 st.)

Test matches (3): 166 runs (33.20) and 5 catches

HUNTE, Julian Robert

(b. 1940, Castries, St Lucia)

A self-made businessman and politician, Julian Hunte has vigorously represented the cause of the so-called 'small islands'—the Leewards and Windwards—on the West Indies Cricket Board of Control for the past 21 years, rising to the newly created post of vice-president in 1994. He joined the St Lucia Cricket Association at the age of 19, became president two years later, and president of the Windward Islands Association in 1970. His ambition led to the formation of his own company when he was 24 and his commitment to hard work has turned it into one of the largest in St Lucia with interests in shipping and insurance. He was Mayor of Castries from 1971 to 1972 as a member of the United Workers' Party which he later left to join the St Lucia Labour Party, becoming leader in 1984. He was elected to parliament in 1984, since when he has been leader of the opposition. Considered a candidate for the presidency of the WICBC when Sir Clyde Walcott resigned in 1993 to become chairman of the International Cricket Council, he withdrew his nomination, but he was widely regarded as a future president.

HYLTON, Leslie George

(b. 1905, Kingston, Jamaica; d. 1955, Kingston) *Jamaica and West Indies*

Heavy-set, Leslie Hylton delivered the ball at great pace. Learie Constantine, Manny Martindale, and he were ranked the most formidable right-arm fast-bowling trio in the world when MCC toured the Caribbean in 1934/5; the trio secured 47 wickets between them in the four Tests, of which Hylton's 'bag' was 13. Touring England in 1939, however, he could rarely find his form. He was executed for the murder of his wife.

First-class career (1926–39): 843 runs (18.73) and 120 wickets (25.62)

Test matches (6): 70 runs (11.66), 16 wickets (26.12), and 1 catch

JAMES, Cyril Lionel Robert

(b. 1901, Tunapuna, Trinidad; d. 1989, Brixton, London)

Known to acquaintances and the public simply as 'C.L.R.', and to close friends and colleagues as 'Nello', James was the author of *Beyond a Boundary*, published in 1963, which John Arlott described in his *Wisden* review of 1964 as 'the finest book written about the game of cricket'. It is that book, with its story of the relationship between the rise of West Indian cricket and the rise of West Indian political independence, that guaranteed James a place in cricket history. Yet he wrote on the game for many years for the *Manchester Guardian* after coming to England in 1932 and attracting the attention of Neville Cardus, and collaborated with his close friend, Learie (Lord) Constantine, on his books. As editor of *The Nation*, the organ of the ruling People's National Movement in Trinidad and Tobago, he mounted a strident and controversial campaign in 1959 to have Frank Worrell appointed West Indies captain over the fair-skinned Gerry Alexander, his motives being interpreted in some quarters as racial. James was vindicated by the huge success of the West Indies team when Worrell was appointed, with Alexander as his deputy, for the 1960–1 tour of Australia. James's interests and writing were not confined to cricket. Educated at Port of Spain's Queen's Royal College, where he was a useful all-rounder, he developed a zeal for left-wing politics in which he was actively involved in England and the United States, where he lived for 15 years. He wrote several political books and articles and was expelled from the USA in 1953 at the height of McCarthyism. He returned to his native Trinidad and Tobago in 1958 for the first time in 26 years to edit *The Nation* but soon fell out with the Prime Minister, Dr Eric Williams, whom he had taught as a student at Queen's Royal College, and returned to England in 1961. When he came back to Trinidad four years later to cover the Australian tour for the British press, he was put under house arrest. He departed for England within a few days and lived there until his death.

JOHN, George

(b. *c*.1883; d. 1944, Port of Spain, Trinidad)
Trinidad

Clifford Goodman, the massively built, free-living white Barbadian, and the black Trinidadian professionals, 'Float' Woods and C. P. Cumberbatch,

preceded him but justifiable claims can be laid for George John as the first of the great West Indian fast bowlers. C. L. R. James, in his classic *Beyond a Boundary*, described him as 'just the right height, about five ten, with a chest, shoulders and legs on him all power and proportion' and summed up the general impression of him in his heyday as 'one of the most formidable fast bowlers who ever handled a ball'. James rated him, at his peak, as fast as Frank Tyson but he had very little opportunity to demonstrate his worth outside Trinidad where he was head groundsman at the Queen's Park Oval. When he was chosen for the West Indies tour of England in 1923 he was somewhat past his best yet he took 55 first-class wickets at just under 19 each and 90 in all matches at 14.68. With George Francis and the young Learie Constantine, he formed a fast attack that Pelham Warner wrote he wished he could have for England's subsequent Ashes tour of Australia. In the final match of the 1923 tour, at Scarborough, the bowling of Francis and John that reduced a virtual England team, playing as H. D. G. Leveson-Gower's XI, to 19 for 6, requiring 28 for victory, soon became part of West Indian cricket folklore. He later played league cricket in England. One of his sons, Errol, is one of the West Indies' most distinguished playwrights; another, George, a leading journalist.

JOHNSON, Hophnie Hobah Hines

(b. 1910, Kingston, Jamaica; d. 1987, Miami)
Jamaica and West Indies

A 6 ft. 3 in. right-arm fast bowler, Hines Johnson toured England in 1950 with moderate success. His best performance in Tests was in his first match, against England at Kingston in 1947/8, when he took 5 for 41 and 5 for 55, maintaining a great pace and never attempting to intimidate by pitching short.

First-class career (1934–51): 316 runs (17.55), 68 wickets (23.36), and 13 catches

Test matches (3): 38 runs (9.50) and 13 wickets (18.30)

JOHNSON, Tyrell Fabian

(b. 1917, Tunapuna, Trinidad; d. 1985, Caura, Trinidad) *Trinidad and West Indies*

A very tall left-arm fast bowler, Johnson toured England in 1939 and looked better than a meagre reward proved him to be. In his sole Test, the third at The Oval, he scored 9 not out, took 3 for 129 and held 1 catch. He took a wicket with his first ball of the tour and also his first ball in a Test.

First-class career (1935–9): 90 runs (9.00), 50 wickets (21.50), and 8 catches

JONES, Brunell Rudolph Matthew

(b. 1914, Port of Spain, Trinidad; d. 1988, Arima, Trinidad)

Brunell Jones was one of the most prolific and widely read cricket writers in the West Indies for close to 40 years. Although he specialized in cricket, he covered all sports as well as the entertainment beat for Trinidad's leading papers, the Trinidad *Evening News* and the *Guardian*, on both of which he was sports editor. A tireless worker, he represented several overseas newspapers and the Associated Press as sports correspondent as well as editing and publishing annual magazines in the 1940s covering sport and entertainment. He wrote books on every home Test series between 1971 and 1977. He also arranged private tours of Bermuda and New York for his own Brunell Jones touring teams, comprising leading West Indian players, and was a member of the organizing committee for the Central American and Caribbean Games and the Commonwealth Games in Jamaica in the 1960s. He was awarded a national Trinidad and Tobago honour in 1974.

JONES, Charles Ernest Llewellyn

(b. 1902, British Guiana; d. 1959, British Guiana)
British Guiana and West Indies

A competent left-handed batsman and left-arm slow bowler, Charles Jones played against England in 1929/30 and 1934/5 without much success.

First-class career (1925–39): 917 runs (21.83) and 24 wickets (44.12)
Test matches (4): 63 runs (9.00), 0–11, and 3 catches

JONES, Prior Erskine Waverley

(b. 1917, Princes Town; d. 1991, Port of Spain, Trinidad) *Trinidad and West Indies*

Prior Jones was a strong, persevering right-arm fast bowler who moved the ball either way, both in the air and off the seam. He was a stubborn tail-end batsman and a fine slip field with a terrific throw and was expected to be a successful spearhead in England in 1950, but received few opportunities in 'Ramadhin and Valentine's year'. He played against England at home in 1947/8 and toured India in 1948/9, taking 51 wickets (18.54) on the slowish wickets, including 17 in the Tests.

In Australasia in 1951/2, however, as a veteran, he was virtually bowled into the ground.

First-class career (1940–52): 775 runs (14.09), 169 wickets (26.81), and 33 catches
Test matches (9): 47 runs (5.22), 25 wickets (30.04), and 4 catches

JORDAN, Hugh Beaumont deCourcey

(b. 1921, St Michael, Barbados; d. 1982, Bridgetown, Barbados)

Universally known as 'Cortez', because of the pencil-slim moustache he took to wearing in the fashion of Ricardo Cortez, the 1940s movie actor, Jordan was one of the leading West Indian umpires from 1950 to 1975. Invariably wearing a white panama hat and sunglasses, and always seemingly calm and efficient, Jordan stood in 22 Tests on every West Indian ground between 1953 and 1974. Neat and soft-spoken, he earned the players' confidence with his undemonstrative manner and was generally regarded as a 'batsman's umpire'. He was the first umpire in the West Indies appointed to a Test outside his home island, officiating the Port of Spain match in the 1955 Australian series. Ten years later, when he was appointed for the Georgetown Test between the West Indies and Australia, the local umpires' association protested at the appointment of an outsider by withdrawing the services of its members at the last moment. With no time to get an official umpire to Georgetown in time, the West Indies Board appointed Gerry Gomez, the former Test all-rounder, then a West Indies selector, to stand with Jordan. In 1968 Jordan officiated four of the five Tests between the West Indies and England, the first time a West Indian umpire had stood in so many in one series. His no-balling of Charlie Griffith for throwing a single ball in Barbados's match against India on the same day that a ball from Griffith caused a life-threatening head injury to the touring captain, Nari Contractor, caused great controversy. He had similarly censured the left-arm spinner, Tony Lock, on England's 1954 tour. As a slow-medium swing bowler, he was captain of the Harrison College second team as a schoolboy and arranged his own team comprising mainly Test and Barbados players for exhibition matches in the country districts.

JOSEPH, Harold

(b. 1956, Carapo, Trinidad) *Trinidad*

Although he did not play competitive cricket until he was 18, occupied instead with his interest in horse-racing at the Arima Race Club track near his home, Harold Joseph developed the bowling style similar to Sonny Ramadhin's by which he spun the ball both ways from the front of the hand with no perceptible change in action. He had been fascinated by an article he read on Ramadhin and, with practice, found he could emulate his style: to master it was more difficult, however, and it was not until 1981 that he finally convinced the selectors he was ready for first-class cricket in the Shell Shield. He swiftly made up for lost time, claiming 18 wickets in four Shield matches. More significantly, he bowled Geoff Boycott for 70 in a five-wicket haul in the match against the touring Englishmen and returned figures of 10–5–7–3 in the final of the limited-overs tournament against a Barbados team including Gordon Greenidge, Desmond Haynes, Thelston Payne, and David Murray. It was enough to earn him a place on the West Indies team to Australia in 1981/2 but, with an attack comprising Roberts, Holding, Garner, and Croft, there was never any realistic chance of his gaining a Test place. He played only two first-class matches, taking three for 45 in an innings against Tasmania and bamboozling batsmen in up-country matches. A jovial, uncomplicated character known to team-mates as 'Joe' or 'Harry Joe', he probably gained more satisfaction from the fact that he hit his first ball in a first-class match in Australia, against New South Wales, for six and from his winnings on the races around Australia. His interest in the game waned—he gave up even club cricket for a time—but he returned to confuse batsmen with the mystery of his each-way turn.

First-class career (1975–84): 263 runs (13.15) and 73 wickets (32.82)

JULIEN, Bernard Denis

(b. 1950, Carenage Village, Trinidad) *Trinidad, Kent, and West Indies*

A typical West Indian all-rounder, Bernard Julien was a quickish left-arm seam bowler of wiry build, who swung the ball both ways and could also bowl slow orthodox or unorthodox spin. He was an exhilarating and ebullient right-handed stroke-maker, lacking consistency, and an excellent fielder anywhere. A happy-go-lucky character, with an unerring eye for pretty girls, he did not quite fulfil early promise. His first-class début was for North Trinidad against South Trinidad in 1967/8. Playing for Kent between 1970 and 1977, he was always doing something useful, though

seldom sustaining his performances for long. He took 7 for 66 against Sussex at Hove in 1975 and 7 for 78 against the same opponents a year later when playing for the West Indian touring team. By now, however, his inconsistency had lost him his more-or-less regular place in the West Indies team. He played the first two Tests in England in 1976 but only once more represented the West Indies, against Pakistan at home later that year. He toured England twice in all, 1973 and 1976, went to India, Sri Lanka, and Pakistan in 1974/5 and Australia in 1975/6. His most brilliant performance in four Tests was a superb innings of 121 against England at Lord's in 1973 off only 127 balls. He added a second Test century against Pakistan at Karachi but he was more often successful in Test cricket as a dangerous swing bowler, especially with the new ball. His 16 wickets against England at home in the 1973/4 series included 5 for 57 at Bridgetown in an England total of 395. He returned to the Trinidad team in the 1981–2 season and bowled with success, taking 9 for 97 against Jamaica, his best figures. He was already fading as a cricketer when he toured South Africa (1982–4) though he was as popular as ever.

First-class career (1967–84): 5,792 runs (24.44) including 3 centuries, 483 wickets (28.72), and 126 catches

Test matches (24): 866 runs (30.92) including 2 centuries, 50 wickets (37.36), and 14 catches

JUMADEEN, Raphick Rasif

(b. 1948, Gasparillo) *Trinidad and West Indies*

An accurate slow left-arm orthodox bowler who turned the ball a good deal on helpful pitches, Raphick Jumadeen was a steady rather than a venomous bowler. He had little chance to shine in England in 1976 because the fast bowlers dominated a hot summer (when spin, in theory, should have proved fruitful). In all first-class matches on the tour he took 58 wickets (30.00). However, he took 11 wickets in two Tests against Australia in 1977/8, including 4 for 72 in a first innings of 343 at Kingston. At home against India in 1976 he took only nine wickets (31.00) in four Tests. In two more Tests against India in 1978/9, he took only three wickets but bowled long, economical spells.

First-class career (1967–81): 604 runs (8.50), 347 wickets (27.91), and 45 catches

Test matches (12): 84 runs (21.00), 29 wickets (39.34), and 4 catches

KALLICHARRAN, Alvin Isaac

(b. 1949, Paidama) *Guyana, Warwickshire, Queensland, Transvaal, Orange Free State, and West Indies*

One of the many great cricketers to prove that a lack of inches need be no disadvantage, Alvin Kallicharran comes from the same area as Rohan Kanhai, Berbice in Guyana. A brilliant, natural left-handed batsman, fine fielder with a deceptively strong throw from the deep, and an occasional slow right-arm off-break bowler, he developed a straight, text-book technique at an early age and this, plus his natural flair and an excellent temperament, enabled him to score attractive runs round the world. He was a determined competitor with a full armoury of strokes and immaculate timing whether driving, hooking, cutting, or glancing. Off the field he is a sunny, smiling character though he did not always see eye-to-eye with West Indian team-mates. His Test career began in Georgetown against New Zealand in 1971/2 when he hit 100 not out on a lifeless pitch, his last 41 coming in an hour after part of his innings had been interrupted by bottle-throwing. In the next Test, and his own second Test innings, he made 101 at Port of Spain. He played his first full Test series against Australia in the West Indies in 1972/3, scoring 294 runs in the series at 36.75. In England in 1973 he hit three hundreds against county sides and 889 runs (64.78) on the tour, although his highest score in the Test matches was 80. A shoulder injury restricted him on his second official tour of England in 1976, although he made a valuable 97 at Trent Bridge. Despite consistent batting for Warwickshire, for whom he scored 1,000 or more runs in five of his first seven seasons, his major successes have been on harder pitches away from England. In India, Sri Lanka and Pakistan in 1974/5 he made 1,249 runs (56.77) and 454 runs in the Tests at 56.75, including 124 in the first Test at Bangalore. In two Tests against Pakistan his scores were 94, 44, and 115. At home against England in 1973/4 he made 397 runs (56.71), never playing so well again after his brilliant hundred in the first Test at Port of Spain where, after Julien had played the last ball of the first day to Greig at short-leg, Kallicharran carried on walking towards the pavilion from the non-striker's end, never having grounded his bat. On Greig's unsporting throwing down of his wicket, he was given run out by umpire Douglas Sang Hue, although some of the fielders had turned towards the pavilion unaware of what had hap-

pened. After tempestuous scenes and in a heated atmosphere of crisis, Sang Hue diplomatically allowed his (technically correct) decision to be overruled. Not out 142 overnight, 'Kalli' was out for 158 the next day. He made 119 in the third Test at Bridgetown, adding 249 for the second wicket with Lawrence Rowe, a record for that wicket against England. In Australia in 1975/6 he scored 730 runs (36.50) and 421 in the Tests at 38.27. Later that season against India he scored 237 runs (47.40) with 103 not out at Port of Spain. Less successful against Pakistan at home in 1976/7, he signed without conviction for Kerry Packer's team, then later discovered that this contravened a contract which he had already signed with a radio station in Queensland. He escaped from his contract with Mr Packer's company, thus splitting with the main body of top West Indies players and assuming his country's captaincy in 1977/8 when Clive Lloyd resigned over the Packer issue on the eve of the third Test at Georgetown. 'Kalli' had already scored his customary hundred at Port of Spain in the first Test and he added 126 at Kingston in the fifth when a riot ended play early. On a happier tour of India in 1978/9 Kallicharran learned quickly the difficult art of captaincy and led by example with 538 runs (59.77), once again scoring a century in the first Test of a rubber, 187 at Bombay. Ignoring criticisms, he began playing, with great success, for Transvaal in 1981/2, and was a key member of two 'rebel' tours to South Africa. For Warwickshire in 1984 he scored 2,301 runs (52.29) including nine centuries, a Warwickshire record. He made Birmingham his family home and his son, Rohan, showed early promise but in 1986 Alvin failed to persuade the TCCB to allow him to play for Warwickshire as a qualified Englishman, a decision reversed in 1988.

First-class career (1966–90): 32,650 runs (43.64) including 87 centuries, 84 wickets (47.97), and 323 catches

Test matches (66): 4,399 runs (44.43) including 12 centuries, 4 wickets (39.50), and 51 catches

KANHAI, Rohan Bholalall

(b. 1935, Port Mourant) *British Guiana, Trinidad, Warwickshire, Western Australia, Tasmania, and West Indies*

Rohan Kanhai had a natural genius for batting. A small, neat right-hander with every cricket stroke and a few inventive ones of his own (notably a full-blooded sweep which swung him off his feet and the ball out of the ground), he possessed a wonderful gift of timing and scored runs consistently all over the world. A steely determination and huge appetite for runs made him one of the most consistent of batsmen to come from the Caribbean and he did much personally to dispel the general impression that West Indies batsmen would waste their natural brilliance from time to time and either throw their wickets away or fold up quickly in a crisis. Though he was not a particularly successful captain when that honour came his way, his occasionally stormy temperament being wrong for the job, Rohan Kanhai was in this sense highly significant in the development of West Indian cricket at international level. He made his first appearance for British Guiana in 1954/5, for Western Australia in 1961/2, for Warwickshire in 1968, for Tasmania in 1969/70, and for the West Indies in 1957. He played, indeed, in 61 of his 79 Tests without a break from his first series on the tour of England in 1957 when he was used as a makeshift wicket-keeper. Apart from his 15 Test centuries, he passed 50 on 28 other occasions, averaging 50 every third innings. On his second tour of England in 1963 he scored 1,149 runs (41.03) and 497 runs (55.22) in the Tests. In 1966 he scored a century at The Oval in the only Test of the series which the West Indies lost and in 1973, as captain, made 223 runs (44.60), including 157 in the third Test at Lord's. He had a prolific winter's cricket in 1958/9, scoring 538 runs (67.25) in five Tests in India, including his highest score of 256 at Calcutta. This was also his maiden Test century and the entire innings occupied only $6\frac{1}{2}$ hours. It included 42 fours and remains the highest score in a Test in India. Moving to Pakistan, Kanhai hit 217 in the third Test at Lahore, helping to inflict Pakistan's first home defeat. At home against England the following season he scored 110 out of 244 in the second innings of one of the bottle-throwing Tests, the second at Port of Spain, England winning an infamous contest. In Australia in 1960/1 he scored 117 and 115 at Adelaide to become the first West Indian to reach hundreds in both innings of a Test match. This series brought him 503 runs (50.30) and the tour 1,093 runs at 64.29 with four centuries. The following year, at home against India, he made two Test centuries and an aggregate of 495 runs (70.71), more than anyone else on either side. Against Australia at home in 1964/5 he made big scores in each of the last three Tests—89, 129, and 121, but he showed he was capable of a loss of form in India in 1966/7. He scored only 463 runs on the tour, although 227 of these came in the three

Tests at 56.75. He played in several English (and Scottish) leagues, and married a Lancashire girl. He became a more reliable player as his experience grew and his temperament became less volatile. In the West Indies in 1967/8 he scored 535 runs in the Tests against England at an average of 59.44, including 143 in the fourth Test at Port of Spain, and 150 in the last at Georgetown. As successor to Sobers as captain in Australia in 1972/3, he had successive Test scores of 84, 105, and 56, finishing with 433 runs (54.12), but Australia won the series. A successful series followed in the second half of the English summer of 1973, Kanhai's 653 runs helping his side to two Test wins out of three, but at home the following winter he personally had a poor series and his team failed to follow up several apparently winning situations against England who, having lost the first Test at Port of Spain, squared the rubber by winning the last on the same ground. His sequence of 61 Tests was broken only because he had to return to England for a cartilage operation. He was immensely valuable to Warwickshire for ten years, scoring 1,000 runs ten times, his best aggregate being 1,894 runs (57.39) in 1970, and in 1972 he scored eight centuries to equal the county record. In 1968 at Trent Bridge against Nottinghamshire, he added 402 with Billy Ibadulla, a record for Warwickshire's fourth wicket (Kanhai making 253), and in 1974 put on a world-record second-wicket stand of 465 with John Jameson against Gloucestershire at Edgbaston, his own contribution being 213 not out. He also played as a club professional in Melbourne, Australia. He coached and managed West Indies teams in the early 1990s.

First-class career (1954–82): 28,774 runs (49.01) including 83 centuries, 18 wickets (56.05), 319 catches, and 7 stumpings
Test matches (79): 6,227 runs (47.53) including 15 centuries, 0–85, and 50 catches

KENTISH, Esmond Seymour Maurice

(b. 1916, Westmoreland) *Jamaica and Oxford University*

A well-built right-arm fast bowler, Esmond Kentish played in two Tests against England, one in 1947/8 and the other in 1953/4. At Kingston in his second match he took 5 for 49 in 29 overs in the second innings, by bowling medium-fast at or outside the leg-stump to an on-side arc of seven men. He was a blue in 1956.

First-class career (1947–57): 109 runs (13.62), 78 wickets (26.71), and 6 catches
Test matches (2): 1 run (1.00), 8 wickets (22.25), and 1 catch

KING, Collis Llewellyn

(b. 1951, Christ Church, Barbados) *Barbados, Glamorgan, Worcestershire, Natal, and West Indies*

Though he played in four Test matches before the 1979 Prudential World Cup Final at Lord's, it was not until that occasion that many people outside Barbados appreciated quite what an explosive hitter of a cricket ball Collis King could be. Coming in when the West Indies were struggling at 99 for 4, he made a superb 86 in 66 balls, adding 139 with Viv Richards in 21 spectacular overs and quite outshining his partner, probably the finest contemporary batsman. A right-hander who, whatever the contest, wasted little time before launching a tallish, spare but muscular frame into all kinds of exotic drives, cuts, hooks, and pulls, King also bowled useful medium pace with a busy but far from classical action. He fielded well, with an infectious enthusiasm he brought to any match. He first appeared for Barbados in 1972/3, and played as a specially registered player for Glamorgan in 1977. On his first tour of England in 1976, King hit six centuries in his 1,320 runs (55.00), the highest being 163 at Northampton, and took 27 wickets (34.37). In three Tests he scored 167 runs (41.75), in the second Test at Headingley making a valuable 58 (50 off 39 balls) in the second innings out of 196. In 1979 he was banned from playing for Ponthlyddyn in the North Wales League because he was too good! (In one afternoon match in 1978 he had made 283.) He was banned from cricket in the West Indies for touring South Africa with the two 'rebel' teams (1982–4). On both tours he was the leading run-scorer in first-class matches, making 518 (51.80) in 1982/3 and 450 (40.90) the following year. He enjoyed life off the field, sometimes too much for the good of his cricket.

First-class career (1972–87): 6,770 runs (38.24) including 14 centuries, 128 wickets (34.21), and 98 catches
Test matches (9): 418 runs (32.15) including 1 century, 3 wickets (94.00), and 5 catches

KING, Frank McDonald

(b. 1926, Bridgetown; d. 1990, Walsall, England) *Barbados, Trinidad, and West Indies*

A right-arm fast bowler, Frank King received his opportunities but failed to establish himself. He toured India in 1952/3 and New Zealand in 1955/6, and at home played against England in 1953/4 and Australia in 1954/5. He possessed much stamina and bowled a considerable number of bumpers but only in his first series, against India in 1952/3, was he consistently effective, taking 17 wickets (28.23); at Port of Spain, in the third match, he took 5 for 74 in the first innings.

First-class career (1947–57): 237 runs (9.11) and 90 wickets (28.75)
Test matches (14): 116 runs (8.28), 29 wickets (39.96), and 5 catches

KING, Lester Anthony

(b. 1939, St Catherine Parish) *Jamaica, Bengal, and West Indies*

A bustling right-arm fast-medium bowler, Lester King had a short but productive Test career. He appeared twice against India in 1961/2 and once against England in 1967/8: in the former match, at Kingston, facing a total of 253, India lost five wickets for 26 runs in about an hour, all to King, who finished with 5 for 46. He toured England in 1963, taking 47 wickets (27.31) but, overshadowed by Charlie Griffith and Wes Hall, was not selected for any of the Tests. He also toured India in 1966/7 and Australia and New Zealand in 1968/9.

First-class career (1961–9): 1,404 runs (20.64), 142 wickets (31.42), and 38 catches
Test matches (2): 41 runs (10.25), 9 wickets (17.11), and 2 catches

LAMBERT, Clayton Benjamin

(b. 1962, Guyana) *Guyana, Northern Transvaal, and West Indies*

A chunky, well-muscled left-hander with an exciting array of strokes, Clayton Lambert was a prolific run-scorer in West Indian regional cricket for nigh on a decade without ever convincing the West Indian selectors he was the natural successor to Gordon Greenidge at the head of the order. A forthright, powerful driver and puller, he had made ten first class centuries before gaining belated international recognition on the West Indies B tour to Zimbabwe in 1989 where he made 219 in Harare. Midway through the West Indies tour of England in 1991, when Greenidge's knee could no longer take the strain, Lambert was plucked from the obscurity of Blackhall in the North Yorkshire and South Durham League, scoring 99 in his first match against Glamorgan then 116 against Essex which earned a middle-order slot in the first Test at the Oval. It was to be but a brief dalliance at the top level, in a Test when England squared the series, and Lambert was guilty of a horrendous slog off Phil Tufnell's first ball of the third day which heralded a collapse and follow-on. His sole Test resulted in a record of 53 runs (26.50), 1 wicket (4.00) (with his third ball just before lunch on day won), and 2 catches. He superseded Desmond Haynes in the Wills Trophy matches in Sharjah shortly afterwards, playing, in all, five one-day internationals for the West Indies (132 runs at 26.40) but lost his place and was relegated to the 'A' team for England's visit in early 1992, managing a top score of 83 in the three 'unofficial' Tests. His bulk lends itself naturally to a station at short leg, and in the second Test at Arnos Vale, St Vincent, he was responsible for a quite stunning dismissal, John Stephenson caught in the crook of his arm, unwittingly, from a full bloodied pull off Nehemiah Perry. Lambert continued to score heavily for Guyana in the Red Stripe tournament and having returned from grade cricket in New South Wales, opened his account in 1993 with an undefeated 263, including five sixes and sixteen fours, against the Windward Islands, surpassing the record of another Guyanese, Roy Fredericks. He finished with 441 runs at 73.50 but, at 31, he failed to make the Test squad for the Pakistan series, and, no doubt realizing his time was past, plumped for provincial cricket with Northern Transvaal in South Africa the following winter. His performances there included an innings of 214 against Transvaal.

First-class career (1982–): 5,488 runs (44.98) including 14 centuries, 4 wickets (26.00), and 108 catches

LARA, Brian Charles

(b. 1969, Santa Cruz, Trinidad) *Trinidad and Tobago, Warwickshire, and West Indies*

In the space of a few weeks in 1994 Brian Lara broke the two most romantic and significant of all batting records and thereby achieved a pre-eminence amongst his contemporaries equalled only by W. G. Grace and Sir Donald Bradman. A left-hander of innate genius, he was only 24 when he made the highest individual score in 117 years of Test cricket, 375 against England in the fifth Test in Antigua in 1994, surpassing Sir Gary Sobers's previous record of 365 not out. Exactly seven weeks later he recorded the biggest score ever in first-class cricket, an undefeated 501 for

Warwickshire against Durham at Edgbaston. This was run-feasting of gargantuan proportions, when seemingly unattainable landmarks in cricket history were bypassed, the unthinkable became almost commonplace, and memories of Bradman's appetite for long innings were rekindled. Like Bradman, Lara was hailed as a cricketing God, his batting invested with a style and panache that his contemporaries could never hope to match. Short in stature at 5 ft. 5 in., with a schoolboyish demeanour, Lara's sublime skills are underpinned by steely wrists and excellent footwork and have established him as an icon to all those who appreciate the aesthetics of batsmanship. A master of technique, his placement all around the wicket is unerring, his attacking shots are unfurled from a flamboyant high backlift, and his trademark whip stroke is played with ease and élan off the back or front foot. At the crease and off the field a handsome, shy smile adds greatly to the charm of a cricketer whose most serious threat after 1994 was likely to be too demanding an exploitation of his commercial potential. Born in the tiny village of Cantaro, in picturesque Santa Cruz, 4 miles east of Port of Spain, he grew up as one of eleven children and was taken to the Harvard club coaching clinics by an elder sister from the age of 7. He was effectively foster-fathered by Joey Carew, the former West Indies opener and selector, and displayed a bent for heavy run-scoring at the age of 14 when he made six centuries at Fatima College. In 1985 he toured India with a Trinidad schools team, later topped the batting averages in the West Indies Youth tournament in 1988, and led the full side to the inaugural Youth World Cup in Australia. His time was nigh. He made a first-class début the following year, soon taking 92 off the Barbados attack, Garner and Marshall included, and compiled a splendid 182 as captain, admittedly on a very flat pitch at Warner Park, St Kitts, for the West Indies under-23 XI against India in 1989. His leadership qualities had been recognized earlier when he took the West Indies B side to Zimbabwe and he was finally drafted into the full Test squad for the third Test on his home ground at Queens Park Oval against India in 1989. Sadly he was made twelfth man and simultaneously suffered the death of his father, Bunty. The Test selectors delayed his entrance for what seemed an interminable age to most Caribbean followers, but he eventually stepped out at Lahore in December 1990 where his 44 against Wasim Akram, Waqar

Younis, and Imran Khan 'made it feel like a century. If I could come through that, I could survive anything', he recalled. Initially, he was spared the so-called damaging effects of one-day cricket but he blossomed as an opener in the World Cup, and hundreds plundered off South Africa, Australia, and Pakistan in the shortened game are testimony to a flexible talent. Lara played 24 one-day internationals, in fact, before his next Test, the one-off match against South Africa in Barbados when he made 64 in the second innings. In 1992/3, in the third Test at Sydney, he duly delivered a maiden Test century in remarkable circumstances in only his fifth appearance. Australia were 1–0 ahead in the series, won the toss for the third time and amassed 503 before Lara transformed his hundred into a mammoth 277, a graceful monument to craft and concentration, a *tour de force* which was the fourth highest by any West Indian. Many considered it the best innings played in Australia in a decade or more whilst Rohan Kanhai, the team manager, classed it one of the greatest innings he had ever seen. 'Back foot, front foot, timing, placement, against spin and pace alike, he was simply magnificent.' He subsequently judged the innings worthier even than the 375 not out in Antigua. Before his next century, a withering 167 against England in the second Test at Bourda in 1994, Lara had made another which gained less widespread coverage. In the preceding domestic Red Stripe tournament, wherein he claimed the record aggregate runs for a season, 715, he notched three centuries, the first against Jamaica at Queens Park Oval when only a few hundred spectators enjoyed the privilege. After regaining the captaincy he had lost in 1991, he led from the front, never more so than on this occasion. Trinidad and Tobago were 103 for 6 replying to 206. Lara, 49 not out overnight, proceeded to score 180 of the 219 which gave them the lead, nearly 90 per cent of the runs from the bat. He faced 249 balls, making 131 on the second day while five other batsmen totalled a dozen. Controlling the strike to perfection with delicate chip shots for singles, Lara's effort was seen by David Holford, the chairman of selectors, as 'an incredible performance. He reduced the game to a farce. I've never seen anything like it.' The record-breaking innings on a lifeless pitch at the Recreation Ground in St John's was finally achieved from an imperious pull off Chris Lewis after equalling Sobers's 365 milestone with a nerveless extra-cover drive, a true moment of destiny. Caught behind, eventually, off a tired-looking drive, he struck 45 fours off 538 balls over $12\frac{3}{4}$ hours. Fittingly, Sir Gary was there to offer congratulation. To follow that with another, barely credible, run-gathering feat, erasing Hanif Mohammed's 499 set in 1959 in Karachi, was the stuff of dreams but for Lara, reality. Replacing the injured Indian all-rounder Manoj Prabhakar, he began his first county engagement at Warwickshire with a succession of hundreds, taking advantage of a match for which the captains had failed to contrive a finish. Durham, too, had a depleted attack on the final day and the wicket was bland, but nothing can detract from the enormity of his achievement. Anderson Cummins bowled him off a no ball when he was 10 then Chris Scott, the wicket-keeper, dropped a simple chance when he was 18 as Lara advanced to an overnight 111. The third day was washed out, but he moved easily to 150 on the resumption and, in a quite extraordinary passage, smote five sixes and fifteen fours in a savage 45 minutes which Phil Bainbridge, a seasoned campaigner and Durham captain, reckoned was simply the best batting he'd ever seen. He added 174 in the morning session, ate a light lunch of mashed potato and blackcurrant juice, and set his sights on the ultimate target. Michael Burns, a colleague and substitute fielder, almost caught him when his score was 413, but Lara went relentlessly on, surpassing the highest score in England, Archie Maclaren's 424, and Bradmans's 452. He had reached 497 by the last over of the day then inexplicably blocked the first three balls and was struck on the head by the fourth from John Morris, an occasional seamer. Peter Wight, one of the umpires, confirmed play was about to finish but later, it transpired, it could have been allowed to continue. Lara appreciates history and the next delivery was dispatched in classic style through cover. He batted for 7 hours 54 minutes, hitting 62 fours and 10 sixes off 427 balls, finishing the season with 2,066 first-class runs and 9 hundreds as part of his contribution to an unprecedented 'treble' by Warwickshire. Acclaimed and fêted from all quarters, 'The Prince' retained a singular unassuming exterior but, as a cult figure at the heart of 'Laramania', the tension sometimes shows. He was the youngest ever Trinidad captain in 1990 but lost the captaincy after an altercation with Gus Logie, and there were rumblings of discontent in the Warwickshire dressing room when mushrooming commercial interests lessened his appetite for fielding. He is, in fact, a very fine slip fielder but his leg-breaks and slow right-arm seamers are mainly a net option. Courteous and humble to the point of shyness in his early days, Lara is charmingly unaffected by his world-wide celebrity and, as names sometimes evoke the man, his does just that—ebony smooth with a dismissive brevity, words rolling off the tongue like runs off his bat. Already, with never a suggestion of arrogance, he has talked of reaching 400 in a Test Match.

First-class career (1987–): 7,320 runs (58.09) including 22 centuries, 1 wicket (215.00), and 102 catches

Test matches (25): 2,283 runs (55.68) including 4 centuries, and 53 catches

LASHLEY, Patrick Douglas

(b. 1937, Christ Church, Barbados) *Barbados and West Indies*

A determined left-handed batsman, patient and correct, an occasional medium-pace bowler and an excellent field, 'Peter' Lashley scored 200 for Barbados against Guyana at Bridgetown in 1959/60, thus earning a place to Australia in 1960/1, but he was only a modest success, averaging 19.40 despite a valuable 41 in the very exciting fifth Test at Melbourne. He toured England in 1966 and in the third Test at Trent Bridge took over three hours for 49. He became an executive with the Cable and Wireless company, which sponsored Test cricket in the West Indies, and was an expert player at Bridge and Dominoes.

First-class career (1957–75): 4,932 runs (41.44) including 8 centuries, 27 wickets (35.48), and 66 catches

Test matches (4): 159 runs (22.71), 1–1, and 4 catches

LAWRENCE, Roy

(b. Jamaica; d. 1994, Harrogate)

For 20 years, prior to his emigration in 1977 to England, Roy Lawrence was the voice of West Indies cricket. A tall, amiable man with a typically melodious Jamaican delivery, he was a general broadcaster. His work as cricket commentator made him hugely popular throughout the Caribbean, but particularly in Jamaica where he was an institution, his prestige enhanced by his hosting of a highly successful annual radio programme that raised money for the needy. He did his first commentary on Radio Jamaica on the 1948 England Test at Sabina Park. On the following England tour, in 1954, he became the first West Indian to join the Test broadcast outside his home island, going to Trinidad. He covered the West Indies' tour of England in 1957 for Radio Jamaica and was part of the Test Match Special team on the 1963 and 1966 tours. In Jamaica, his propensity for spoonerisms became part of local folklore. As the station joined him at the ground, his welcome was: 'It's another beautiful day here at Sabina Park, the sun is blowing and the breeze is shining all over the ground.' One, unauthenticated version has an excited Lawrence 'broadfighting this cast from the Stational Nadium' for one world title bout in Kingston. When Trevor Bailey reached 10 in 1954, he told listeners that 'nine of them are singles'. He was, in his heyday, one of Jamaica's better tennis players, a left-hander. Later resident in Harrogate, he was a member of Yorkshire and seldom missed a Leeds Test.

LEGALL, Ralph Archibald

(b. 1926, St Michael, Barbados) *Trinidad and West Indies*

A competent wicket-keeper and right-handed batsman, Legall's sole Test experience was against India in the Caribbean in 1952/3. Born in Barbados, he never played for the island.

First-class career (1946–58): 485 runs (22.04) and 42 dismissals (32 c., 10 st.)

Test matches (4): 50 runs (10.00) and 9 dismissals (8 c., 1 st.)

LEQUAY, Alloy Remigus

(b. 1924, Port of Spain, Trinidad)

Alloy Lequay was an elected representative of the Trinidad and Tobago parliament between 1966 and 1971, nominated Senator from 1976 to 1986, headed several charitible organizations, and, after a successful career in insurance, rose to the position of managing director of a large printing firm; but it was in sport that he was best known. He worked his way through the ranks to become president of both the Trinidad and Tobago and the Caribbean table-tennis associations, positions he resigned to become president of the Trinidad and Tobago Cricket Board of Control, which he has been since it succeeded the Trinidad Cricket Council as national controlling body in 1981. He remains the only serving member of the Council that was established in 1956. A small man of part Chinese descent, he has a reputation for hard work, organizational skill, and outspokenness. In 1992 he was made head of the cricket committee of the West Indies Cricket Board of Control, on which he has been Trinidad and Tobago's representative for more than a decade. He and his

Board have, more than once, voiced their dissatisfaction at perceived selection bias against Trinidad and Tobago players, Lequay countering criticism of his stand on one occasion with the assertion: 'The Trinidad and Tobago Cricket Board, born in an environment of injustice, had at times to be aggressive to achieve its objectives. This is why were are stable and respected today.' He was honoured with his country's second-highest award in 1988 for his public service.

LEWIS, Desmond Michael

(b. 1946, Kingston, Jamaica) *Jamaica and West Indies*

An accomplished right-handed batsman and wicket-keeper of high potential, Desmond Lewis had a meteoric Test career. His sole Test series was against India in the Caribbean in 1970/1 when his diligent batting was more than useful. In his first Test, at Georgetown, he made 81 not out; in his second, at Bridgetown, 88 as opening partner for Roy Fredericks; and in his third, at Port of Spain, 72, again as opening batsman. In the next series he was superseded by Deryck Murray.

First-class career (1970–6): 1,623 runs (31.82) and 78 dismissals (67 c., 11 st.)
Test matches (3): 259 runs (86.33) and 8 dismissals (8 c.)

LLOYD, Clive Hubert

(b. 1944, Georgetown, British Guiana) *Guyana, Lancashire, and West Indies*

Captain of West Indies in 74 Tests, more than any man of any nationality, Clive Lloyd led his side to a record number of successive victories, 11 in 1984, including a 5–0 clean sweep in England. These unique records owed much to both his fatherly leadership of a richly talented team and also to his own batting; fourteen of his Test hundreds were made as captain. A tall and commanding left-handed batsman and useful right-arm medium-paced bowler, Clive Lloyd revealed a quite phenomenal speed and reach in the covers in his early days and throughout a distinguished career thrilled spectators all over the world with his batting and, indeed, with his sheer presence. Instantly recognizable with his heavy spectacles, lean gangling figure, and loping walk with head bowed, he would explode into sudden exciting action—whether swooping to cut off an apparent four and throw down the wicket, diving to take a slip catch, or hitting the ball with murderous power, using a heavy bat to bludgeon fours and sixes with basically orthodox drives, hooks, and cuts. Despite persistent pain in his knees—which caused him to move from the covers to the slips in his later years—he remained a most successful batsman, especially on the big occasion, and he became a calm and able captain who usually got the most from a talented side and who twice led West Indies to success in the Prudential World Cup Final at Lord's. He was ruthless in his deployment of an attack usually comprised mainly or wholly of fast bowlers, sometimes allowing them to intimidate excessively with short-pitched bowling. A cousin of Lance Gibbs, 'Hubert' first appeared in first-class cricket for British Guiana in 1963/4 and first played for Lancashire in 1968. His first Test series was in India in 1966/7 and in his first game at Bombay he scored 82 and 78 not out. His second innings was a masterly performance by one so young—he added 102 with Gary Sobers to win the match on a turning wicket. In the three Tests he scored 227 runs (56.75). Lloyd has toured England in 1969, 1973 and as captain in 1976, 1980 and 1984. His 904 runs (56.50) in 1969 included 201 not out against Glamorgan at Swansea and, although he disappointed in the Test matches, his fielding was always worth scores of runs. In 1973 he made 318 runs (63.60) in the three Tests and hit 1,128 runs on the entire tour (59.36). His 132 in the first Test at The Oval helped to end a period of 20 Tests in which the West Indies had failed to win. During the World Cup Final at Lord's in 1975 Lloyd scored a superb match-winning century, and a year later made 1,363 first-class runs (61.95) on the tour but only 296 runs (32.88) in the Test series. For the second time he scored 201 not out against Glamorgan at Swansea, on this occasion in 120 minutes, equalling the record for the fastest double hundred in first-class cricket. He had first met England at home in 1967/8, making 369 runs (52.71), which included 118 in the first Test at Port of Spain and 113 not out at Bridgetown. He marked his first appearance against Australia in 1968/9 by scoring 129 at Brisbane and against Australia at home in 1972/3 he made 178 out of 366 at Georgetown. His most prolific series was his first as captain in India in 1974/5 when he scored 636 runs in the Tests (79.50) including 163 in the first match at Bangalore, reaching his century in only 85 balls, and a superb 242 not out in the fifth Test at Bombay. This was the true Clive Lloyd—an explosive match-winner, but never a consistent grinder out of records. Yet when he led West

Indies again in India, in 1983/4, he frequently baled his side out of trouble with long and responsible innings. West Indies won the series 3–0, with Lloyd scoring 496 runs at an average of 82, including 103 at Delhi and 161 not out at Calcutta, having come in at 41 for 4 (soon it was 63 for 6 but West Indies reached 377 and won by an innings). Captaincy had added responsibility to his batting and, although defeated heavily by Australia in 1975/6, Lloyd scored 469 runs (46.90) in the six Tests, including 149 at Perth and 102 at Melbourne. His tenth Test hundred came in his fiftieth Test, against India at Bridgetown in 1975/6, and the following year he made 151 on the same ground against Pakistan, hitting three sixes and 21 fours. He resigned as captain on the eve of the third Test at Georgetown against Australia in 1977/8 after disagreement with the selectors over the bitter Packer issue, but returned successfully in the World Cup in 1979 and led the West Indies again in Australia the following winter. A knee operation in Australia during the tour successfully dealt with a recurring problem, and for the next three years he played as well as he had ever done. He hit a beautiful hundred in Adelaide, and in England in 1980 also scored one in the Old Trafford Test, a performance which, as Lancashire was his second home, he was especially pleased with. In the 1980/1 season, following a successful tour of Pakistan, he played nine first-class innings in the West Indies and failed to reach 50 only once: when he was run out for 49! He averaged 76 in the Test series against England—hitting a marvellous hundred in the Barbados Test—and 172.50 in the Shell Shield. He held seven catches in the Tests, all in the slips, to show that his reactions were as quick and his hands as sure as ever. When the period of West Indian supremacy in world cricket, which had coincided with his captaincy, seemed in danger of being threatened during the final Test against Australia at Adelaide in 1981/2, Lloyd added a match-winning 77 not out to his first-innings 58 and was carried off the field on the shoulders of his fast bowlers, the main cause of the team's extraordinary run of success. The action, however, signified the importance of Lloyd's calm captaincy. Although he had a relatively simple task in the field, manipulating a succession of fit, hostile, and accurate fast bowlers, and pointing to the results when criticized for the tactical use of slow over-rates and frequent bouncers, his own batting was often a crucial element in the team's overall success. He scored 407 (67.83) against England in 1984 and 356

(50.85) in his final series in Australia in 1984/5. In England he was frequently a match-winner for Lancashire, notably in the Gillette Cup. He became captain of Lancashire in 1981 and continued to make the county his domestic base. He scored 1,000 runs in a season 14 times (ten in England). He was awarded an OBE and was appointed to several bodies promoting sport and social and community relations.

First-class career (1963–86): 31,232 runs (49.26) including 79 centuries, 114 wickets (36.00), and 377 catches

Test matches (110): 7,515 runs (46.67) including 19 centuries, 10 wickets (62.20), and 90 catches

LOGIE, Augustine Lawrence

(b. 1960, Sobo Village, Trinidad) *Trinidad and West Indies*

Only 5 ft. 4 in. tall and weighing 120 lbs, Gus Logie might have been taken for a jockey rather than a Test cricketer, but consistent scoring for Trinidad in the Shell Shield earned this little right-hander a full Test sequence at home against India in 1982/3 and he eventually established a regular place at number six in a powerful team, often at his best when more celebrated batsmen had failed. After a sequence of low scores in his first series, he survived the simplest imaginable slip catch off his glove in the fourth Test at Bridgetown when he had scored 7: he went on to make a sparkling 130. Logie toured India, Australia, and England in the next 18 months (making 585 runs in the first-class matches in England at an average of 73) and charmed crowds with his dashing stroke-play and dazzlingly quick outfielding. The last in a family of ten from the small village of Sobo in the far south of Trinidad, he had first confirmed his promise with an innings of 163 in St Lucia for Young West Indies against Young England in 1980 and it was against England that he was often at his most useful. At Lord's in 1988 he rescued the West Indies from a position of 54 for 5, making 81 out of 209 and in the second innings his 95 not out led to victory, the first of four in succession. With 364 runs at 72 in the series he was the most successful West Indian batsman. Again, in Trinidad in 1990, he saved his side from a disastrous start of 29 for 5 on a drying pitch, making a sparkling 98 after being dropped at the wicket early in his innings. His two Test hundreds were both scored against India: 130 at Bridgetown in 1982/3 and 101 at Calcutta in 1987/8. In the latter series, when India's leg-spinner Hirwani ran through the West Indies,

Logie, with 67 out of 160, alone offered significant resistance. In 158 one-day internationals he scored 2,809 runs, with one century, at an average of 28.95, also taking 61 catches.

First-class career (1977–92): 7,514 runs (35.11) including 13 centuries, 3 wickets (42.66), and 104 dismissals (103 c., 1 st.)

Test matches (52): 2,470 runs (35.79) including 2 centuries, 0–4, and 57 catches

LYON, John Randall

(b. 1952, Port of Spain, Trinidad) *Trinidad*

A small, neat wicket-keeper and low-order right-handed batsman, Randall Lyon's opportunities for Trinidad and Tobago depended on the availability of Deryck Murray. Murray's absence with the West Indies in Australia first opened a place for him in the 1976 Shell Shield and he began with two catches and three stumpings in his début match against Barbados. With Murray engaged in Kerry Packer's World Series Cricket, he was chosen as second-string wicket-keeper to David Murray for the 1978/9 West Indies tour of India and Sri Lanka, the last white cricketer to represent the West Indies. He played seven first-class matches on tour. He became Trinidad's 'keeper after Deryck Murray's retirement in 1981 but his job in insurance demanded more and more of his time and he was succeeded by David Williams in 1983. Throughout his time, Trinidad invariably fielded a strong spin attack (Raphick Jumadeen, Inshan and Imtiaz Ali, Ranjie Nanan, Harold Joseph) and his remarkably high percentage of stumpings was a reflection of his efficiency in this regard.

First-class career (1974–83): 614 runs (13.34) and 81 dismissals (55 c., 26 st.)

McMORRIS, Easton Dudley Ashton St John

(b. 1935, Kingston, Jamaica) *Jamaica and West Indies*

A right-handed opening batsman who could be difficult to dismiss when well set, Easton McMorris did not quite fulfil expectations for West Indies; he was inclined to weakness against high-class swing bowling. A year after his first-class début he scored 114 for Jamaica against the strong Duke of Norfolk's side at Kingston in 1956/7. He toured England in 1963 and 1966, and at home played against Pakistan in 1957/8, England in 1959/60 and India in 1961/2. In England he made 878 runs (36.58) in 1966, but each time

he fared poorly in the Tests. By far his best series was against India in 1961/2: he made 439 runs (58.16), including 125 at Kingston when he added 255 in a record second-wicket stand with Rohan Kanhai. Active in cricket administration in Kingston, he became a Test selector in 1995.

First-class career (1956–72): 5,906 runs (42.18) including 18 centuries, and 36 catches

Test matches (13): 564 runs (26.85) including 1 century, and 5 catches

McWATT, Clifford Aubrey

(b. 1922, British Guiana) *British Guiana and West Indies*

A competent wicket-keeper, Clifford McWatt was a left-handed batsman who could hit brilliantly, as when scoring 56 and 123 not out for British Guiana against Trinidad at Port of Spain in 1946/7. He appeared as first-string 'keeper against England in 1953/4 and Australia in 1954/5.

First-class career (1943–57): 1,673 runs (28.84) including 2 centuries, and 51 dismissals (45 c., 6 st.)

Test matches (6): 202 runs (28.85) and 10 dismissals (9 c., 1 st.)

MADRAY, Ivan Samuel

(b. 1934, Berbice, British Guiana) *British Guiana and West Indies*

A useful all-rounder, being a right-handed batsman and leg-break bowler, Madray's only Tests were against Pakistan in the Caribbean in 1957/8.

First-class career (1954–8): 73 runs (9.12) and 16 wickets (38.87)

Test matches (2): 3 runs (1.00), 0–108, and 2 catches

MANLEY, Michael Norman

(b. 1924, Kingston, Jamaica)

Son of the Jamaican Prime Minister and national hero, Norman Manley, Michael followed in his father's footsteps in politics and trade unionism and in his love of cricket. He could not master the game as a player, reaching no higher than Jamaica College's 2nd XI while at school, but he understood, and was fascinated by, its history, its importance to West Indian development, and its politics. Staunchly anti-apartheid, he was a pivotal figure during the years when the South African problem threatened to split international, and indeed West Indies, cricket. Clive Lloyd and

Michael Holding consulted him prior to accepting contracts with World Series Cricket because South Africans were also included and Manley brokered a deal with Kerry Packer by which only South Africans who played English county cricket would be engaged. His advice on the subject was often sought by the West Indies Board whose president, Allan Rae, was a close friend. On retiring from active politics in 1988, he wrote the voluminous *History of West Indies Cricket*. Only pressing government business kept him away from Sabina Park during big matches.

MARLEY, Robert Cecil

(b. 1909, Kingston, Jamaica) *Jamaica*

A tall, right-hand opening batsman who had played and captained Jamaica, Cecil Marley had been a member of the Jamaica Cricket Association for 25 years and president for five when he was elected president of the West Indies Cricket Board of Control in 1971 in succession to Noel Peirce. He had been Jamaica's representative on the WICBC since 1950 and was a West Indies selector in 1948. He was one of Jamaica's most successful lawyers and, according to his presidential successor, Jeffrey Stollmeyer, 'his trained legal mind enabled him to conduct meetings with admirable facility'. He remained only three years in the post before retiring for personal reasons, soon emigrating to Florida where he still resides. The first sign of the problems the WICBC would face over cricketing relations with South Africa surfaced during his term when Gary Sobers, at the time West Indies captain, visited Rhodesia under the illegal government of Ian Smith. The Guyana government under Forbes Burnham declared Sobers *persona non grata* until he apologized and it took all Marley's legal skills, with help from Prime Minister Eric Williams, to settle the matter to the satisfaction of all concerned.

MARSHALL, Malcolm Denzil

(b. 1958, Bridgetown, Barbados) *Barbados, Hampshire, Natal, and West Indies*

A lithe, whippy bowler of electric speed, natural athleticism, and rare determination, and a stylish and useful right-handed batsman, Malcolm Marshall became the most successful, and certainly amongst the very best, of all the great West Indian fast bowlers. He made his first appearance for Barbados in the final match of the 1977/8 Shell Shield competition and took 6 for 77 against

Jamaica at Bridgetown. His ability was such that he was taken to India in 1978/9 with only this one first-class match behind him and played in three Tests although the slow wickets drew all his youthful sting. However, his success for Barbados in the 1978/9 Shell Shield persuaded the West Indian selectors to prefer him to Wayne Daniel in their Prudential World Cup squad. Marshall was not selected for any of the matches but in his first season of county cricket he several times bowled with genuine pace and hostility to show that he would be a worthy successor to Andy Roberts as a match-winning opening bowler. His right-arm action, following a quick sprint to the stumps, lacked a classical final stretch and was not quite side-on enough to satisfy the purists but he had a very quick arm and natural rhythm which gave him extreme pace to hustle the batsman and he swung and cut the ball sharply. He would work like a surgeon on a batsman's weak points, remaining a master of his craft even when his pace began to drop. By the end of 1982 he had been on five major tours for the West Indies, plus one to Zimbabwe, but played in only 12 Tests, being considered only first reserve for the quartet of Roberts, Holding, Croft, and Garner. However, after his performance for Hampshire in 1982 he became a regular member of the West Indies side. He was easily the most successful bowler in county cricket that season with 134 wickets, the most ever taken by a county bowler in a 22-match Championship. His only full Test series before this had been a successful one on the slow wickets of Pakistan in 1980/1, when he took 25 wickets on the tour and 13 in the Tests at 24 each. A period of phenomenal success began at home against India in 1982/3. In this series his 21 wickets at 23.57 included 5 for 37 in the second Test in Trinidad. Against India (away) in 1983/4 his supremacy increased—33 wickets (18.81) including 6 for 37 at Calcutta. Returning home, tired but still full of zest, he took 21 wickets against Australia (22.85) and in England in 1984 he followed up with 24 wickets at 18.20 as West Indies brutally swept aside apparently feeble opponents. At Headingley he broke his left thumb fielding close to the wicket early in the match but not only did he return to bat one-handed, hitting a four and enabling Larry Gomes to reach a century at the other end, he also produced his finest Test figures of 7 for 53. Against Australia in 1984/5 he had 28 wickets (19.78) and was given a trophy as Man of the Series, having taken 10 for 107 in the Adelaide match. Back home against New Zealand in 1985, he took 7 for 80 on a fast pitch at Barbados and 27 wickets (18.16) in only four Tests. He was by now recognized as the most persistently dangerous fast bowler in the world and against England in 1986 he took 27 wickets at 17.85 as well as making 62 not out in the second Test and 76 in the fifth. Success continued almost unabated until he was left out following the 1991 tour of England, much to his dismay, with 400 Test wickets in his sights. He had taken 20 wickets in the series. He played on for Hampshire until 1992 and became captain of Natal in 1993/4, bowling with much of his old snap and scoring 420 runs at an average of 60, including a career-best of 120 not out against Western Province.

First-class career (1977–   ): 10,620 runs (24.64) including 7 centuries, 1,602 wickets (19.08), and 139 catches

Test matches (81): 1,810 runs (18.85), 376 wickets (20.94), and 25 catches

MARSHALL, Norman Edgar

(b. 1924, St Thomas) *Barbados, Trinidad, and West Indies*

A useful right-handed batsman and off-break bowler, Norman Marshall's sole Test was the third against Australia at Georgetown in 1954/5 when he scored 0 and 8 and took 2 for 62. In a short first-class career confined to the Caribbean, he made 1,110 runs (27.75) and took 78 wickets (33.51). He is elder brother of the better known Roy Marshall.

First-class career (1940–59): 1,337 runs (30.38) including 2 centuries, and 90 wickets (31.72)

MARSHALL, Roy Edwin

(b. 1930, St Thomas; d. 1992, Taunton, Somerset) *Barbados, Hampshire, and West Indies*

An attractive and forceful right-handed opening batsman with a variety of strokes, the tall and bespectacled Roy Marshall was also a useful change-bowler of off-breaks and a very good field. He made his début for Barbados at 15, and at 19 he scored 191 for Barbados against British Guiana at Bridgetown in 1949/50. He toured England in 1950 with much success, as the youngest member, making 1,117 runs (39.89), including 188 at Leicester but, owing to the great strength of the batting, was not selected for any of the Tests. In Australasia in 1951/2 his best score from Tests was 30, although he scored 114 against New South Wales at Sydney and 102 not

out against Otago at Dunedin. In 1951 he became professional to Lowerhouse in the Lancashire League, two years later began his qualification for Hampshire, and his international career was ended at 21 since at that time the West Indies did not call on players engaged in English first-class cricket. For nearly twenty years, as an essentially adventurous batsman, he was a 'box-office' draw for his adopted county and, on his day, the best bowlers in the world found it difficult to bowl to him; against anyone of less than high calibre, he was a complete destroyer. Hampshire's first Championship title, in 1961, owed much to his opening partnership with Jimmy Gray. Staying in England, he became chairman of Somerset's Cricket Committee.

First-class career (1945–72): 35,725 runs (35.94) including 68 centuries, 176 wickets (28.93), and 294 catches

Test matches (4): 143 runs (20.42), 0–15, and 1 catch

MARTIN, Frank Reginald

(b. 1893, Kingston, Jamaica; d. 1967, Kingston) *Jamaica and West Indies*

A left-handed opening batsman, 'Freddie' Martin watched the ball closely and hit hard off the back foot. Steady, calm, and sober, he was a difficult man to dislodge; and his slow bowling often kept down the runs. On his first-class début for Jamaica in 1925/6 he scored 195 against Barbados at Bridgetown and, the following year, made his career-highest, 204 not out, against the Hon. Lionel Tennyson's team at Kingston. He toured England in 1928 and 1933, and Australia in 1930/1, and played at home against England in 1929/30. In the former year he headed the batting in the first-ever Test series with 175 runs (29.16) and on the tour scored more runs than any of his colleagues, 1,481 (34.44), besides taking 22 wickets. In Australia he carried his bat for 123 in the fifth Test at Sydney, batting for about six hours, adding 152 with George Headley for the second wicket, and showing marked skill with the wicket becoming treacherous; Australia lost for the first time to West Indies. During his second visit to England, after scoring well and taking wickets in his first six matches, he wrenched an ankle and missed the Tests.

First-class career (1924–33): 3,589 runs (37.78) including 6 centuries, 74 wickets (42.55), and 19 catches

Test matches (9): 486 runs (28.58) including 1 century, 8 wickets (77.37), and 2 catches

MARTINDALE, Emmanuel Alfred

(b. 1909, St Lucy; d. 1972, St Peter, Barbados)
Barbados and West Indies

A small man for a fast bowler—5 ft. 8½ in.
—'Manny' Martindale was an impressive spearhead with an excellent right-arm action and a
dangerous in-swinger; his pace could be terrific.
He toured England in 1933 and 1939, and played
against England at home in 1934/5. In the second
Test at Old Trafford in 1933 he and Learie
Constantine caused a sensation by bowling a
form of bodyline—short-pitched bowling towards
the batsman's body with an accompanying arc of
leg-side fieldsmen—'Manny' taking 5 for 73 and
splitting Walter Hammond's chin in the process.
In this series he took 14 wickets (17.92) and on
the tour, 103 wickets (20.98), three times taking
eight wickets in an innings. He captured 19
wickets (12.57) against England in 1934/5. In the
first Test at Bridgetown his 'haul' was 3 for 39 and
5 for 22. In England in 1939 he fell away in pace
and accuracy and endured a poor season. By far
his best performance as a batsman was a well-
struck 134 against Trinidad at Bridgetown in
1935/6, when he added 255 with E. A. V. Williams for the eighth wicket which remains a West
Indian record. For some years he was a professional with Burnley in the Lancashire League,
and on his return to Barbados became a coach.

First-class career (1929–39): 972 runs (15.18)
including 1 century, 205 wickets (25.64), and 29
catches
Test matches (10): 58 runs (5.27), 37 wickets
(21.72), and 5 catches

MATTIS, Everton Hugh

(b. 1957, Kingston, Jamaica) *Jamaica and West
Indies*

Tall, a cultured right-hand batsman, particularly
strong off the back foot, and a useful off-break
bowler, Everton Mattis did not quite live up to his
distinguished West Indian Christian name, nor
the high hopes held of him, when selected to
replace Alvin Kallicharran in the West Indian
team against England in the home series of
1980/1. His best effort in the four-Test series was
a solid 71 at Antigua. He had served an apprenticeship in Shield cricket, scoring an impressive
132 against Guyana in 1980 and, although not
selected to tour Australia in 1981/2, he was
Jamaica's highest scorer in the Shell Shield in both
1980/1 and 1981/2. He threw away any further
chance of playing Test cricket by agreeing to tour

South Africa in 1982/3, pleading financial hardship as his reason for going.

First-class career (1977–84): 2,064 runs (33.29)
including 3 centuries, and 9 wickets (9.88)
Test matches (4): 145 runs (29.00), 0–14, and 3
catches

MENDONCA, Ivor Leon

(b. 1934, British Guiana) *British Guiana and West
Indies*

A capable wicket-keeper and right-handed batsman, Ivor Mendonca replaced the injured Jackie
Hendriks as 'keeper in two Tests against India in
1961/2 and, in his first Test at Kingston, hit 78,
adding 127 for the seventh wicket with Gary
Sobers. He also claimed five dismissals (four
caught and one stumped), but he never represented West Indies again, there being an abundance of wicket-keeping batsmen available.

First-class career (1958–62): 407 runs (31.30) and
30 dismissals (25 c., 5 st.)
Test matches (2): 81 runs (40.50) and 10
dismissals (8 c., 2 st.)

MERRY, Cyril Arthur

(b. 1911, Scarborough; d. 1964, Port of Spain,
Trinidad) *Trinidad and West Indies*

At his best a brilliant right-handed batsman, Cyril
Merry toured England in 1933, making 856 runs
(28.53) which included 146 against Warwickshire
at Edgbaston when, by exhilarating batting, he
and George Headley added 228 in 2 hours for the
fifth wicket. He met with little success, however,
in the Tests.

First-class career (1929–39): 1,547 runs (27.14)
including 1 century, 33 wickets (22.60), and 33
catches
Test matches (2): 34 runs (8.50) and 1 catch

MILLER, Roy

(b. 1924, Jamaica) *Jamaica and West Indies*

A competent all-rounder, a right-handed batsman
and fast-medium bowler, Roy Miller's sole Test
appearance was in the fourth match at Georgetown against India in 1952/3 when he scored 23
and took 0 for 28.

First-class career (1950–4): 231 runs (25.66) and
14 wickets (45.00)

MOODIE, George H.

(b. 1915, Jamaica) *Jamaica and West Indies*

A left-handed batsman and medium-paced or
slow spin bowler, George Moodie scored 94 and

60 not out respectively in Jamaica's two matches against MCC in 1934/5; and his sole Test was the fourth at Kingston on this tour, when he scored 5 and took 3 for 40.

First-class career (1931–52): 578 runs (22.23) and 42 wickets (35.45)

MOSELEY, Ezra Alphonza

(b. 1958, Barbados) *Barbados, Glamorgan, Eastern Province, North Transvaal, and West Indies*

A right-arm fast bowler with a wonderfully lissom, classical action, Ezra Moseley was recommended to Glamorgan after outstanding all-round performances in English festival cricket in Barbados. He made his début on an extremely cold morning at Swansea in 1980 and took 6 for 102 against Essex, finishing the season with 51 wickets at 26.27. He bettered these figures in 1981 when he totalled 52 at 18.11, including 6 for 23 against the Australians, before injury caused him to miss the last seven matches. Moseley generated real speed and late movement from a deceptively short approach, but the arched back in delivery stride caused untold stress and his career suffered accordingly. He was forced to withdraw when chosen for the West Indies under-25 XI to Zimbabwe in 1981, but recovered to join the front-line pace battery of Clarke, Garner, Daniel, and Stephenson for Barbados in 1982. Having opted for the first of two rebel West Indian tours to South Africa in 1983 he was ostracized by the West Indies Cricket Board for seven years. He filled the hiatus with professional engagements at Oldham, Littleborough, and Radcliffe, where he gained a reputation among Central Lancashire League followers for astonishing pyrotechnics as a powerful right-hand batsman, and destructive bowling on greentops. He played Currie Cup cricket for Eastern Province in 1984. In 1990 he was welcomed back into the fold and made a late Test début at Port of Spain in the third Test against England, an acrimonious encounter during which one ball from Moseley inadvertently altered the course of the match and the series. A freak downpour played a part too, in preventing an England victory, but Moseley's ball which reared off a length and broke Graham Gooch's hand ensured the England captain played no further part in the series. This delivery, a wicked, unplayable missile, even entered folklore in Australia, and an Ezra Moseley fan club was instituted in perverse celebration. He bowled well without luck in the fourth Test at Kensington before a hamstring pull kept him out of the final match and, though he played two one-day internationals and a three-day match on the following tour of Pakistan, it signalled the end of an all too brief Test career. After representing Northern Transvaal in 1991–2, and finishing second overall in the Castle Cup averages, with 36 wickets at 16.88, a recurrent back problem denied him further engagements.

First-class career (1980–92): 1,431 runs (17.45), 279 wickets (21.31), and 21 catches

Test matches (2): 35 runs (8.75), 6 wickets (43.50), and 1 catch

MURRAY, David Anthony

(b. 1950, Bridgetown, Barbados) *Barbados and West Indies*

A right-handed wicket-keeper/batsman with cricketing blood of high pedigree in his veins, David Murray was only prevented from playing a substantial number of Tests by the rivalry of his namesake Deryck. First choice for Barbados for many seasons, he toured England in 1973 and in the short tour scored 285 runs (35.62), including 107 not out against Kent at Canterbury. In 20 games on the tour he took 26 catches and made 5 stumpings. Belatedly given a chance in Test cricket in 1978 when Deryck Murray was dropped because of the row about the Packer players being unavailable to tour India, David caught six and stumped three in a capable display behind the stumps in the last three Tests against Australia, and again proved his ability in India in 1978/9 with 18 victims. In this series of six Tests he scored 261 runs (29.00), including 84 in the first Test at Bombay when he added 167 for the fifth wicket with Alvin Kalicharran after an early batting collapse. In India's only innings in the fifth Test at Delhi, he took five catches. Against Central Zone at Jamshedpur, he made his career-highest score: 206 not out. He finally took over from his namesake Deryck as senior West Indies wicket-keeper in 1980/1, playing a useful part in successes against Pakistan away, and England at home. Against Pakistan he scored 142 runs in six innings, despite a pair at Multan, having started with a valuable 50 in the first Test at Lahore. Married to an Australian, he was banned from cricket in the West Indies for playing in South Africa. Apparently addicted to drugs, his personal life went into a decline.

First-class career (1970–84): 4,503 runs (30.84) including 7 centuries, and 333 dismissals (292 c., 31 st.)

Test matches (19): 601 runs (21.46) and 62 dismissals (57 c., 5 st.)

MURRAY, Deryck Lance

(b. 1943, Port of Spain, Trinidad) *Trinidad, Cambridge University, Nottinghamshire, Warwickshire, and West Indies*

A cricketer of marvellous composure, Deryck Murray was a steady member of the West Indies team for upwards of 15 years and a strong influence on the game in the Caribbean as the leader of a movement to increase the earnings of leading West Indian players and to give them a greater say in cricketing affairs at home. Quiet, reserved, diminutive, and boyish, Murray looked barely out of his school clothes when Frank Worrell entrusted him with the duties of the main wicket-keeper/batsman role in England in 1963. He responded with a record 24 victims in the series (22 caught and 2 stumped) and afterwards proved a reliable wicket-keeper who seldom missed a chance, though without approaching the effervescent brilliance of many of the finest 'keepers. As a right-handed batsman he was a watchful, determined player, limited in the power if not the range of his strokes, but always liable to get runs when they were needed. He played for Cambridge University in his two years there in 1965 and 1966, proving more successful in the middle at Fenner's than he was in the examination room. However, he later got his degree at Nottingham University and played for the county from 1966 to 1969. He three times scored 1,000 runs in an English season, including 1,358 runs in 1966 when he made his highest score of 166 not out against Surrey at The Oval. He returned to play for Warwickshire from 1972 to 1975, playing an important role in the winning of the Championship in 1972. His highest score in a Test was 91 against India in the fifth Test at Bombay in 1974/5 when he added 250 with Clive Lloyd, the West Indian record for the sixth wicket against India. For a short while he opened the batting for West Indies but the experiment was not a success. Nevertheless Deryck Murray was an outstanding case of a cricketer making the most of his ability: behind the calm, gentle, and almost retiring exterior lay a calculating and determined character. He was the first secretary of the West Indian Cricketers Association and the first West Indian to have claimed over 100 Test victims behind the stumps. When he was left out of the side against England at Port of Spain in 1980/1, local spectators boycotted the match, and vandals damaged the pitch in protest. He retired at the end of the season and became one of Trinidad's representatives at the United Nations

before settling in England. Still very fit in his fifties, he played for various 'old West Indies' teams, carrying not an ounce of extra weight.

First-class career (1960–81): 13,291 runs (28.33) including 10 centuries, and 848 dismissals (740 c., 108 st.)

Test matches (62): 1,993 runs (22.90) and 189 dismissals (181 c., 8 st.)

MURRAY, Junior Randälph

(b. 1968, Grenada) *Windward Islands and West Indies*

Tall for a 'keeper, Junior Murray owed his accession to the Test team to his prowess as an orthodox, solid, right-handed batsman after David Williams failed to deliver middle-order runs in the wake of Jeffrey Dujon's abdication. Murray won his first cap in January 1993 in the third Test at Sydney, then scored an accomplished 49 not out in West Indies' unforgettable one-run victory at Adelaide. Waqar Younis put things back into perspective, trapping him for a pair, both lbw, in the first Test of the following Pakistan tour at Port of Spain, but Murray's development as a reliable, thoroughbred wicket-keeper with excellent foot movement continued apace during the home series against England, 1993/4. He made his first-class début against Barbados in 1987 and scored a maiden hundred against the Leeward Islands, Ambrose and Winston Benjamin included, at St John's in 1992, finishing with a season's average of 47.87 from 383 runs. He complemented this batting with consistent, high-class displays with the gloves during England's 'A' tour of the Caribbean. He was aware that the West Indian policy of four quick bowlers was only workable with a productive batsman at number seven, and he dedicated himself through a punishing fitness regime and practice to claim the spot. Fulfilment came with an even-time 101 not out against New Zealand in 1994/5, at Wellington, but he lost form and confidence in subsequent series at home to Australia and away in England (1995). Awarded the MBE for services to sport and dubbed a national hero with attendant commendations, 'Ninja' became the first Grenadian to gain Test status, a remarkable achievement when one considers that his impoverished homeland had not possessed a single net facility over the grooming period. Another, W. G. Mignon, went on the first tour to England in 1900.

MURRAY

First-class career (1987–   ): 2,015 runs (24.88) including one century, and 138 dismissals (130 c., 8 st.)
Test matches (20): 628 runs (28.54) including 1 century, and 74 dismissals (72 c., 2 st.)

MURRAY, Lance Hamilton

(b. 1921, Caroni, Trinidad) *Trinidad*

Lance Murray is Deryck Murray's father but this is by no means his only contribution to Trinidad and Tobago and West Indies cricket. A member of Queen's Park CC, of which his brother, 'Sonny', was secretary for many years, Murray was a right-hand batsman and wrist spinner good enough to have played regularly for North Trinidad in the annual Beaumont Cup match against South, as captain four times. He only represented Trinidad once, against Barbados, in 1956. He joined the administration of the Trinidad Cricket Council, later to become the Trinidad and Tobago Cricket Board of Control, in 1962 and served as a member of the management committee for more than 30 years. He was vice-president of the Board and has been one of Trinidad and Tobago's representatives on the West Indies Cricket Board of Control since 1968, occasionally representing the WICBC at the International Cricket Council. He was nominated as candidate for the WICBC presidency in 1993 but eventually withdrew so that the incumbent, Peter Short, could be elected unopposed. A land surveyor who spent his working life in the civil service, Murray is known for his forthright views and his hard-working nature.

NANAN, Ranjie

(b. 1953, Trinidad) *Trinidad and West Indies*

A right-arm off-break bowler and useful right-hand batsman, Ranjie Nanan is a policeman who would have been seen in more cricket for West Indies than his one Test in Faisalabad in 1980/1, had he not played in an era when the islands produced a phenomenal number of outstanding fast bowlers. In 1981/2 he had a record number of wickets in the Shell Shield, 32 from five matches, taking all his wickets away from the relaid pitch at the Queen's Park Oval, once a haven for the spinner. In his sole Test at Faisalabad, he scored 8 and 8, took 2 for 54 and 2 for 37, and held 2 catches, playing a valuable part in the West Indies' victory. He became captain of Trinidad in 1984 and in 1985 led them to their first win

in the Shell Shield since 1971. No man has taken more Shell wickets than Nanan for Trinidad.
First-class career (1973–91): 2,607 runs (20.85) including 1 century, 366 wickets (23.10), and 61 catches

NEBLETT, James Montague

(b. 1901, St Michael, Barbados; d. 1959, Mackenzie, British Guiana) *Barbados, British Guiana, and West Indies*

A competent all-rounder, batting right-handed, bowling leg-breaks and invariably keeping a good length, James Neblett toured England in 1928 but with little success, and his sole Test appearance was in the third match at Georgetown against England in 1934/5 when he scored 11 not out and 5 and took 1 for 75.
First-class career (1925–39): 526 runs (18.78), 29 wickets (41.55), and 16 catches

NETHERSOLE, Noel Newton

(b. 1904, Kingston, Jamaica; d. 1959, Jamaica) *Jamaica and Oxfordshire*

'Crab' Nethersole, a nickname acquired from his running style while an outstanding all-round sportsman at Jamaica College, managed successfully to combine an active political life with his cricket as player and administrator. He was a founder member of the People's National Party and, at the time of his early death, Minister of Finance under whom Jamaica's national income tripled. As a left-handed, bespectacled all-rounder, he bowled fast and batted with aggression and was a regular in the Jamaica team which he captained in the 1930s. As a Rhodes Scholar, he attended Oxford where he just failed to gain his blue but did play minor county cricket for Oxfordshire. He became a member of the Jamaica Cricket Board during his playing days and was Jamaica's representative on the West Indies Board for several years, serving as a West Indies selector from 1939 to 1955.

NORIEGA, Jack Mollison

(b. 1936, St Joseph, Trinidad) *Trinidad and West Indies*

As an ageing right-arm off-break bowler, Jack Noriega replaced Lance Gibbs—temporarily out of form—in the series against India in 1970/1 with dramatic success. In the second match at Port of Spain, which was dominated by spin bowlers, he captured 9 for 95 in 49.4 overs in the first innings of 352. In the second innings of the fifth match he took 5 for 129 in 53.4 overs on a turning wicket, most of the runs being scored by Sunil Gavaskar. He did not represent West Indies again.

First-class career (1961–75): 181 runs (9.05), and 68 wickets (29.67)
Test matches (4): 11 runs (3.66), 17 wickets (29.00), and 2 catches

NUNES, Robert Karl

(b. 1894, Kingston, Jamaica; d. 1958, London) *Jamaica and West Indies*

A fine left-handed opening batsman with a sound defence and plenty of stroke power, Karl Nunes was in the XI at Dulwich College. He toured England with the 1923 West Indian team as vice-captain and again in 1928 as captain and wicket-keeper, when West Indies were first accorded Test status, but scored only 87 in six Test innings. At home in 1926/7, he hit 200 not out and 108 in successive games for Jamaica against the Hon. Lionel Tennyson's team. His was a notable swan-song: in the fourth Test against England at Kingston in 1929/30, when he was again captain (each Test saw a different West Indian captain), he scored 66 and 92 as opener. When West Indies were set 836 runs to win, he added a gallant 228 with George Headley for the second wicket; then the clouds began banking over the Blue Mountains, the rains came and the match was saved. A member of the Jamaica Board of Control from its inception in 1926, and president of the West Indies Board of Control from 1945 until 1952, he received the CBE for public services.

First-class career (1920–32): 2,695 runs (31.34) including 6 centuries, 3 wickets (27.66), and 39 dismissals (31 c., 8 st.)
Test matches (4): 245 runs (30.62) and 2 catches

NURSE, Seymour McDonald

(b. 1933, St Michael, Barbados) *Barbados and West Indies*

A tall, powerfully built, right-handed stroke-playing batsman, a superb driver off the back foot, an occasional off-spin bowler, and a specialist close-to-the-wicket field, Seymour Nurse made a considerable impact on West Indian cricket early in his career, lost his place for a time, then re-emerged as a Test cricketer worthy to rank with the best of his generation. He made 128 not out in his second first-class match, against Jamaica at

Kingston in 1957/8; and 213 against MCC at Bridgetown in 1959/60, when in his first Test he hit 70 against England at Kingston. He toured Australia in 1960/1, England in 1963 and 1966, India in 1966/7 and Australasia in 1968/9, and at home played against England in 1967/8 besides 1959/60, India in 1961/2 and Australia in 1964/5. Injured and taking to crutches in Australia in 1960/1, he pulled a muscle early in the 1963 England tour and did not make the Test side. In the fourth Test against Australia at Bridgetown in 1964/5 he scored 201 and finally established himself in England in 1966 with 1,105 runs (44.20), including 501 runs (62.62) in the Tests; in the fourth match at Headingley he made 137. Against England at home in 1967/8 he made 434 runs (43.40) and, the next winter in Australia, he registered 348 runs (34.80) in the series, followed by complete dominance of New Zealand's attack: in the first match at Auckland he hit 95 and 168 (in 3 hours 35 minutes) and in the third at Christchurch, 258, his career-highest, a magnificent 8-hour innings in a total of 417. On this final tour he made 1,520 runs (52.41), including four centuries.

First-class career (1958–72): 9,489 runs (43.93) including 26 centuries, 12 wickets (32.41), and 116 catches
Test matches (29): 2,523 runs (47.60) including 6 centuries, 0–7, and 21 catches

OLIVIERRE, Charles Augustus

(b. 1876, Bequia Island; d. 1949, Pontefract, England) *St Vincent, West Indies, and Derbyshire*

Charles Olivierre, who came from a cricketing family in which his father and two brothers, Helon and Richard, also played first-class cricket, was the first West Indian 'import' in the English county championship. He remained after the first West Indies tour of England in 1900 to qualify by residence for Derbyshire, having impressed the county with his crisp, wristy stroke-play on a tour in which he headed the averages (853 runs at 32.7 including 159 against Leicestershire in an opening stand of 238 with the Trinidad-born P. F. Warner, who was making a solitary guest appearance). In six seasons for Derbyshire before eye problems forced a premature retirement, he scored consistently. His name will always be associated with one astonishing match against Essex at Chesterfield in 1904. Percy Perrin scored 343 not out as Essex amassed 597 and Olivierre responded with 229 out of Derbyshire's 548. Essex then collapsed to 97 all out and Olivierre led his county's nine-wicket victory with 92 out of the required 149. He never returned to the Caribbean, coaching in Holland every summer from 1924 to 1939.

First-class career (1894–1907): 4,830 runs (23.56) including 3 centuries, 29 wickets (22.89), and 109 catches

PADMORE, Albert Leroy

(b. 1946, St James, Barbados) *Barbados and West Indies*

A tall off-spinner with an action clearly reminiscent of, and modelled on, that of the great Lance Gibbs, Albert Padmore was unfortunate to become the best off-spinner in the Caribbean at a time when the islands were producing an unprecedented number of top-class fast bowlers. After making his Test début against India at home in 1975/6 he toured England as the main spinner in 1976 but, in a very dry summer when spinners were prospering, he played in only one Test and even then was granted only three overs! Padmore, however, took 59 wickets (23.40) on the tour and became contracted along with bigger names to World Series Cricket. He was banned from all West Indian cricket after 1983 for managing tours of South Africa.

First-class career (1972–84): 562 runs (13.06), 193 wickets (29.94), and 29 catches
Test matches (2): 8 runs (8.00) and 1–135

PAIRAUDEAU, Bruce Hamilton

(b. 1931, Georgetown, British Guiana) *British Guiana, Northern Districts, and West Indies*

A bespectacled and stylish right-handed opening batsman, Bruce Pairaudeau scored his maiden century, 130, against Jamaica in 1947/8 aged 16 years 5 months: his first-class début had been the previous season, a month before his sixteenth birthday. He hit three consecutive centuries in 1952/3, including 115 at Port of Spain against India on his Test début. Subsequently, although he remained quite a heavy scorer for British Guiana and toured New Zealand in 1955/6 and England in 1957, and at home played against England and India, he did not fulfil his early promise in Tests. He had several seasons as a professional in the Lancashire League, and from 1958 until 1967 he played for Northern Districts in New Zealand.

First-class career (1946–67): 4,930 runs (32.01) including 11 centuries, 0–82, and 64 catches
Test matches (13): 454 runs (21.61) including 1 century, 0–3, and 6 catches

PARRY, Derick Recaldo

(b. 1954, Charlestown, Nevis) *Leeward Islands, Cambridgeshire, and West Indies*

A right-arm off-spin bowler who turned the ball prodigiously and a determined right-handed batsman, Derick Parry came from the tiny island of Nevis, only 36 square miles in size, and was the second man from this Leeward island to represent the West Indies. First representing the Combined Leeward and Windward Islands in the Shell Shield in 1977, he had an outstanding season in 1978, taking nine wickets in the first Shield match against Barbados (7 for 100 in the first innings) and making 94 in the same match. He had a nightmarish start to his Test career, being out first ball in the first 1978 Test against Australia and bowling a wide first ball when called on to turn his arm. Returning to Port of Spain for the fourth Test, however, after the World Series players had left the team, Parry made sure that West Indies would win the series by making 65 in the second innings and then by taking 5 for 15 in 10.3 overs, helping to bowl out Australia for 94. All five wickets were taken in a single spell of 4.4 overs, 4 of them bowled. In India in 1978/9 he scored 193 runs in the six Tests but his nine wickets were very expensive. In further tours of England, Australia and Pakistan from 1979 to 1981, he suffered the frustration of never being seriously considered for the Test team because of the policy of playing four fast bowlers, and even his 40 wickets at a cost of only 20 each against the English counties in 1980 did not change things. He was, at least, well paid for his role as a reserve, but, seeing no international future for himself, he joined the two 'rebel' tours of South Africa in 1983 and 1984. He played Minor County Cricket from 1979–85.

First-class career (1975–84): 2,552 runs (26.86), 251 wickets (28.96), and 50 catches
Test matches (12): 381 runs (22.41), 23 wickets (40.69), and 4 catches

PASSAILAIGUE, Clarence Charles

(b. 1902, Jamaica; d. 1972, Montego Bay, Jamaica) *Jamaica and West Indies*

A very good right-handed forcing batsman, Clarence Passailaigue was unfortunate in missing selection for the first team to visit Australia in 1930/1 because in the previous home season he had hit 183 for Jamaica against MCC at Kingston and in his sole Test, the fourth match against England, also at Kingston, had made 44 and 2 not out, held 3 catches and taken 0 for 15. He is best remembered, however, for his outstanding performance of 261 not out for All Jamaica against the Hon. Lionel Tennyson's side again at Kingston in 1931/2. The Island amassed 702 for five wickets and with George Headley he added 487 in an unfinished sixth-wicket partnership, which remains the world record for that wicket.

First-class career (1929–39): 788 runs (56.53) including 2 centuries

PATTERSON, Balfour Patrick

(b. 1961, Portland, Jamaica) *Jamaica, Lancashire, Tasmania, and West Indies*

Six feet two, barrel-chested, and a magnificent athlete, Patrick Patterson forced his way into pole position amidst the formidable queue of West Indian fast bowlers in the early months of 1986 when, bowling with fearsome pace in the Shell Shield, he had the best batsmen of the other West Indian islands, Viv Richards included, dancing to his tune. Selected to play in the first one-day international against England at his home ground, Sabina Park, he took 2 for 17 in seven hostile overs and in his first Test a few days later had match figures of 7 for 73, sprinting to the wicket like a man possessed and hurling thunderbolts of crimson fire at the hapless English batsmen on a devil of a pitch. On his very first day in Test cricket he took 4 for 29, stimulated by a roaring crowd which included his parents, brothers, and sisters. Hailing from the coastal town of Portland, Patrick Patterson had not before this season established a regular place in the Jamaican side, despite making his first appearance in 1983. He had always wanted to bowl fast and few men can ever have put quite so much energy into every ball, the sprint being followed by a leap and a follow through which seemed to carry him almost to the batsman. He learned his cricket at his two schools—Happy Grove, followed by the famous Wolmers School in Kingston—as well as, in his own words, 'on street corners and the beach'. He joined Lancashire in 1985, sharing the duties of the overseas player with Clive Lloyd. But slow English wickets suited his out-and-out pace less well and he seldom produced spectacular returns, with no other genuinely quick bowlers to support him. Having taken 19 wickets at 22 each in his first Test series, he was chosen to tour Pakistan at the end of 1986 and subsequently played in England (1988), Australia (1988 and 1992) and India (1987). At home, he played against England a second time in

1989/90, but only for one Test, and also against Pakistan, South Africa, and Australia. He shared the new ball with Curtly Ambrose throughout the home series against Australia in early 1991, taking 5 for 83 at Sabina Park by means of a rapid demolition of the tail. In the series his 18 wickets at 22.77 represented his best effort since his first series but he drifted out of cricket after only one more season and a disappointing tour of Australia. He was not out in 58 of his 164 first-class innings. In 59 one-day internationals, he took 90 wickets (24.51).

First-class career (1982–93): 618 runs (5.83), 493 wickets (27.51), and 32 catches
Test matches (28): 145 runs (6.59), 93 wickets (30.91), and 5 catches

PAYNE, Thelston Rodney O'Neale

(b. 1957, Foul Bay, Barbados) *Barbados and West Indies*

A compact left-hander and capable wicket-keeper, Thelston Payne shot to prominence in 1983 when he became the first Barbadian to score three hundreds in one Shell Shield season. Ironically, though he made his first-class début in 1978, he only got his chance of a regular place in the first team when three players went to South Africa, but he took it firmly, scoring 517 runs at an average of 73.85. This consistency and the ability to keep wicket put him in line for the reserve 'keeper's spot on the 1984 England tour on which he did not get much opportunity to shine, playing seven games and averaging 38.2. But he was a cheerful tourist and starred on the team's record 'The West Indies are back in town' made to accompany the England tour. He also toured Australia and Pakistan as Jeff Dujon's reserve and his sole chance in Test cricket came at home against England in 1985/6 when he played in the second Test at Port of Spain after Dujon had broken a finger. He made five in his only innings and held five catches.

First-class career (1978–90): 3,391 runs (36.85) including 6 centuries, and 111 dismissals (103 c., 8 st.)

PEIRCE, Thomas Noel Malcolm

(b. 1916, Christ Church, Barbados; d. 1988, St Philip, Barbados) *Barbados*

As player and administrator, Noel Peirce, also known in some circles as 'Tom', was closely involved in West Indian cricket for most of his adult life. He was elected to the Barbados Cricket Association's board of management in 1939 at the age of 23 and served continuously for 25 years, the last six as president, before retiring in 1965 to undertake the presidency of the West Indies Cricket Board of Control. He was joint manager, along with Cecil De Caires, of the West Indies team to England in 1957. A useful, low-order batsman and leg-spinner who believed in giving the ball generous flight, he was also a specialist close fielder, but it was his captaincy that made him exceptional. He was made captain of the famous Wanderers Club at the age of 21 in 1938, a position he held until 1947. He took over the Barbados captaincy in 1942 and led the island team for four years before handing over to John Goddard although he was recalled for two matches in 1949 when Goddard was leading the West Indies in India. Peirce's time as captain coincided with some remarkable matches. He himself held five catches in the innings as Trinidad were routed for 16, the lowest first-class score in West Indies cricket, at Kensington Oval in 1942 and took seven in the match, still a West Indies record. Later, he watched his young batsmen compile two 500-plus fourth-wicket partnerships against Trinidad in the space of a year—502 unbroken between Frank Worrell and John Goddard and 574 unbroken between Worrell and Clyde Walcott. An insurance executive, he was a soft-spoken, mild-mannered man, respected for his sense of fair play. He was awarded the CBE in 1967 for his services to cricket and horse-racing: he was also a steward and, latterly, president of the Barbados Turf Club.

First-class career (1942–9): 261 runs (15.35) and 29 wickets (37.75)

PERREIRA, Joseph Anthony

(b. 1939, Georgetown, British Guiana)

'Reds' Perreira—a youthful nickname influenced by his hair colour—overcame a severe stammer to become one of the most familiar commentators on West Indian cricket. Years of practice virtually eliminated his speech impediment so that he broadcast his first first-class match, between British Guiana and Trinidad, in Berbice, in 1961. The first Test of the 1994 series between England and West Indies in Jamaica was the 100th he had described on radio, in every Test-playing country except South Africa and Zimbabwe. In addition to Caribbean Broadcasting Union stations he has been a guest commentator on the BBC, the Australian Broadcasting Corporation, Radio New Zealand, and All India Radio. Keen and knowledgeable on all sport, a unique charac-

teristic of his cricket commentaries is his regular updates on other regional and international sporting events. He was once Guyana's national soccer coach and chairman of the National Sports Council in Guyana. Since 1985 he has headed the sports desk at the Organization of Eastern Caribbean States, stationed in St Lucia, that envelops the Leeward and Windward Islands.

PHILLIP, Francis Mindoo

(b. 1929, Castries, St Lucia) *Windward Islands and West Indies*

Mindoo Phillip is unique as the only living cricketer to have a first-class ground named after him. Victoria Park, the main sporting centre in his native St Lucia, became the Mindoo Phillip Park in 1979 in recognition of a player once described as the island's Gary Sobers but who could be more accurately compared to his unrelated namesake, Norbert Phillip. A strong, athletic man from humble background, Phillip's reputation was founded mainly on his fierce hitting. A right-hander, he scored heavily for St Lucia in the annual Windward Islands' Cork Cup competition and was also a useful medium-pace bowler and brilliant fielder. At a time when the Windwards and Leewards had not yet been brought into the mainstream of West Indies cricket, he played only two first-class matches for the Windwards, against the touring Australians in 1955 and the Pakistanis in 1958. As a national representative in football, he filled every position, from goalkeeper to striker. On his retirement from the game in 1969, he was appointed government coach and head curator at Victoria Park. The renaming of the Park was timed to coincide with St Lucia's independence from Britain.

PHILLIP, Norbert

(b. 1948, Dominica) *Windward Islands, Essex, and England*

A tall, fit, and spirited all-rounder, Nobby Phillip was a lively fast-medium right-arm bowler and hard-hitting right-handed batsman. Spare-framed and seldom injured, he performed with great consistency for his native Dominica, the Windward Islands, the Combined Islands and for Essex, first appearing in first-class cricket in 1970. But his great advance really came in 1978: he averaged 76.66 in scoring 230 runs in the Shell Shield, took 21 wickets (17.71), including ten in the match against Guyana when he also scored 70 and 90 not out, won his Test cap against Australia, and had an excellent first season with Essex. To crown a hectic year he had a successful tour of India in 1978/9, taking 19 wickets in six Tests at 34.21, including 4 for 48 and 3 for 37 on the fast Madras wicket, besides making 177 runs (35.40). This followed a successful Test début against Australia at Georgetown where he took 6 for 140 in the match. For Essex Norbert Phillip fitted comfortably into the shoes left behind by his fellow West Indian Keith Boyce, taking 71 wickets (22.40) in 1978 and scoring 645 runs (26.87), including 134 against Gloucestershire, and in 1979 playing a prominent all-round role in Essex's double of Schweppes County Championship and Benson and Hedges Cup. He also played a prominent role in Essex's John Player League success in 1981, hitting violently to play the match-winning innings in the decisive last match at The Oval and, when the Windward Islands entered the Shell Shield under their own banner for the first time in 1982, he took 21 wickets at 16 and averaged 31 with the bat. He became captain of the Windwards in 1983.

First-class career (1969–85): 7,013 runs (23.61) including 1 century, 688 wickets (24.75), and 75 catches

Test matches (9): 297 runs (29.70), 28 wickets (37.18), and 5 catches

PIERRE, Lancelot Richard

(b. 1921, Port of Spain, Trinidad; d. 1989, Port of Spain) Trinidad and West Indies

A tall, well-built, right-arm seam bowler, Lance Pierre moved the ball either way, mostly outswinging. He toured England in 1950 but was not selected for any of the Tests. His sole Test was in the third match against England at Georgetown in 1947/8 when he did not bat and took 0 for 28.

First-class career (1940–50): 131 runs (6.23), 102 wickets (24.72), and 14 catches

PYDANNA, Milton Robert

(b. 1950, Berbice, British Guiana) Berbice and Guyana

Milton Pydanna first came on to the regional scene in the annual youth tournament under the surname Primo but, by the time he made his first-class début in 1971, he had taken the name by which he was known throughout his lengthy career as Guyana's wicket-keeper. His consistency is evident from his record of 58 matches in 18

seasons in the Shell Shield and Red Stripe Cup. A sound, unobtrusive 'keeper, he had to be adept standing up to the stumps, taking the succession of quality spinners Guyana possessed during his time, from Lance Gibbs through to Roger Harper and Clyde Butts. A conscientious cricketer, popular with his fellow players, he succeeded in improving his batting to the extent that he scored two first-class centuries. He was unlucky not to have been chosen for the tour of India in 1978/9 when the West Indies team was denuded by the loss of its main players to Kerry Packer's World Series cricket. Following Deryck Murray's retirement, he was number two to David Murray on the tour of Pakistan in 1980/1, playing two one-day internationals and actually topping the batting averages in his three first-class matches. But the selectors turned to Jeffrey Dujon on the strength of his batting to fill the spot in the Test team vacated when David Murray joined the 'rebel' tours to South Africa. He was Dujon's deputy in India in 1983 but he again had to content himself with the minor matches and a single one-day international at the end of the tour. A policeman when he first came into the Guyana team, Pydanna later transferred to the Guyana Defence Force and is currently a government coach.

First-class career (1971–88): 2,220 runs (19.82), and 183 dismissals (149 c., 34 st.)

RAE, Allan Fitzroy

(b. 1922, Kingston, Jamaica) Jamaica and West Indies

A modest, friendly, and generous-hearted man and a patient and wholly commendable left-handed opening batsman, very safe in defence and a strong driver, Allan Rae provided solidity at the start of West Indies' innings from 1948 until 1953, when the claims of his legal career caused his early retirement from the first-class game. Quite tall and broad-shouldered, he toured India in 1948/9, England in 1950 and Australasia in 1951/2, and at home played against India in 1952/3. Before touring England in 1950, he had batted in only three first-class innings in the Caribbean, and against Barbados in 1946/7 he had scored 111 and 128. His initial Test century, 104, was in the second Test against India at Bombay in 1948/9; in the fourth match at Madras he contributed 109, sharing in an opening partnership of 239 with Jeff Stollmeyer, which led to an innings victory. This was the first victory over India, and the opening stand was not bettered by

West Indies until 1984. In the series Rae made 374 runs (53.42). In the 1950 series against England —when West Indian cricket 'came of age'—he reached 377 runs (62.83) in the series, including 106 in the second match at Lord's, when the West Indies won their first Test in England, and 109 in the fourth match at The Oval, when he added 172 with Frank Worrell for the second wicket. In all first-class matches on this tour Rae made 1,330 runs (39.11), including four centuries, the highest of which was 179 against Sussex at Hove, which remained his career-highest. He had a rather disappointing series in Australia in 1951/2. In the second Test against New Zealand at Auckland, however, he hit 99, and his opening stand with Stollmeyer was worth 197 in less than $3\frac{1}{2}$ hours. His father, E. A. Rae, toured England in 1928, but was not selected for the Tests. A barrister, Allan was for many years a prominent figure in Jamaican and West Indies cricket administration. From 1981 to 1988, he was president of the West Indies Cricket Board. He remained cool and clear-headed during several cases of a political or financial nature.

First-class career (1946–60): 4,798 runs (39.65) including 17 centuries, 0–26, and 42 catches
Test matches (15): 1,016 runs (46.18) including 4 centuries, and 10 catches

RAE, Ernest Allan

(b. 1897, St Andrew, Jamaica; d. 1969, Kingston) *Jamaica*

A big man, over 6 ft. in height and 200 lbs in weight, Ernest Rae used his strength to full effect as a hard-hitting right-hand batsman. He developed such a reputation in Jamaica for six-hitting that fans called him 'Nash 6', a reference to the popular American car for which his family's garage was agent. He was also a deceptive bowler of slow off-breaks and a brilliant fielder, particularly in the slips. His all-round performances for Jamaica in three matches in Barbados in 1925 and against the touring MCC team in 1926 gained him selection on the West Indies team to England in 1928, the first tour on which they were granted Test status. Rae never came to terms with the slower pitches, achieving nothing with either bat or ball, and was not chosen for any of the three Tests. He continued playing for Jamaica until 1936 and for Kingston in the club competition until 1942, sharing several partnerships with his left-handed son, Allan, who proceeded to play 15 Tests for the West Indies between 1948 and 1953 as opening batsman and who followed his foot-

steps as president of Kingston CC and the Jamaica Cricket Association. Rae senior was also a Jamaica selector for many years.

First-class career (1924–36): 1,118 runs (30.21) including 1 century, 10 wickets (36.80), and 27 catches

RAMADHIN, Sonny

(b. 1929, Esperance Village, Trinidad) *Trinidad,. Lancashire, Lincolnshire, and West Indies*

With Alf Valentine, Sonny Ramadhin gripped the attention of the world of cricket on the 1950 England tour, when West Indies won her first-ever series there. A friendless orphan, he was helped as a budding cricketer and in other ways by a Barbadian intercolonial cricketer. The first East Indian to represent the West Indies, and only 5 ft. 4 in. tall, he was a right-arm off-break and leg-break bowler of impeccable length and line, excellent flight and subtle variations of pace, who could hide his intentions so well that wicket-keepers could rarely tell which way he would turn the ball; sometimes he would even succeed with the plain straight ball. Both his leg-break and the off-break, his more regular ball, were finger spun rather than wrist spun, yet appeared to come from the back of the hand. Two trial games before the 1950 England tour were his only experience of first-class cricket, yet he took 135 wickets (14.88), and in the Tests alone his 'haul' was 26 wickets (23.23) from the four matches. When West Indies won for the first time in England—at Lord's in the second match—Ramadhin took 11 for 152 in 115 overs, 50 of which were maidens. His bowling (and that of Valentine) was brilliant, and once the success had been gained on the final afternoon, there was impromptu calypso singing and dancing on the hallowed turf. 'Those two little pals of mine, Ramadhin and Valentine' became a widely sung calypso. Until 1961, when he was supplanted by Lance Gibbs, he was regular choice for his country. He toured Australasia in 1951/2, New Zealand in 1955/6, England again in 1957, India and Pakistan in 1958/9, and Australia in 1960/1, and at home he played against India in 1952/3, England in 1953/4 and 1959/60, and Australia in 1954/5. He tended to be more effective the first time that he came up against an opposing country, although Pakistan and New Zealand never mastered him. In New Zealand in 1955/6 he took more wickets in the Tests and all first-class games than anyone else—20 wickets (15.80) and 40 wickets (16.40) respectively. In the first innings of the first Test at Dunedin he took 6 for 23 in 21.2 overs. Against England in 1953/4 he was the most successful bowler on either side, in the five matches taking 23 wickets (24.30) in 304.3 overs, of which 133 were maidens. In England in 1957 he took 7 for 49 in 31 overs in the first innings of the first Test at Edgbaston, being as mesmeric as ever, but in the second innings he had a traumatic experience at the hands of Peter May and Colin Cowdrey who decided to play him as an off-spinner and added 411 in one of the most famous stands in Test history. Ramadhin bowled a record 98 overs and England almost won a match they had appeared certain to lose. Ramadhin was never so effective in Test cricket again, although he did take 17 wickets (28.88) against England in the 1959/60 series. He continued to master the lesser batsmen: indeed, in 1957, he headed the bowling in all first-class matches in England with 119 wickets (13.98). Altogether, in the first Test at Edgbaston, he sent down 774 balls (129 overs): no one has ever bowled more in a Test. After several years of Lancashire League cricket, he appeared for Lancashire with some success in 1964 and 1965 and later for Lincolnshire, and in 1979, his fiftieth year, was still operating in the Bolton Association. He first played in the Central Lancashire League in the early 1950s. Until his retirement he was the tenant landlord of a pub in Lancashire. A benefit for himself and Alf Valentine was organized in 1995.

First-class career (1949–65): 1,092 runs (8.66), 758 wickets (20.24), and 38 catches

Test matches (43): 361 runs (8.20), 158 wickets (28.98), and 9 catches

RICHARDS, Isaac Vivian Alexander

(b. 1952, St John's, Antigua) *Leeward Islands, Somerset, Queensland, Glamorgan, and West Indies*

The scorer of most runs in Test cricket for West Indies, their most capped player, and their captain from 1985 until 1991, Viv, or as Antiguans call him 'Vivi' Richards goes down in cricket history as one of the greatest of all time. Proud, fit and dignified, with a fine physique and an aquiline nose, he never wore a helmet, never shirked a challenge, and was always confident of his ability to come out on top of the best bowlers when conditions were equal. He could be emotional, even volatile, when his own, or West Indian supremacy was challenged, but he earned everyone's respect in a long, high-profile career. He played always not just for himself but for the prestige of his country and his people at a time when black sportsmen everywhere were asserting their prowess. At the time when he joined the other West Indian Test stars and signed for Kerry Packer's World Series Cricket, Richards was batting with a dominance which perhaps only Sir Donald Bradman had hitherto revealed. In eight months of 1976 he scored 1,710 runs (90.00) in Tests, a record for a calendar year. In the last three Tests of a losing series against an Australia spearheaded by Lillee and Thomson he scored 44, 2, 30, 101, 50, and 98; against India, when he got back home to the Caribbean, he scored 142, 130, 20 not out, 177, 23, and 64. Then against England in England and against an attack which at different times included Snow, Willis, Underwood, Pocock, Old, and Hendrick, he made a further 829 runs in seven innings: 232 and 63 at Trent Bridge; 4 and 135 at Old Trafford; 66 and 38 at Headingley; and 291 in 472 minutes off 386 balls at The Oval. He missed the Lord's Test through illness. His average in the series was 118.42. On the tour he hit four other centuries and totalled 1,724 runs (71.83). He was simply magnificent. Basically an orthodox right-handed batsman with perfect timing and immense power, he almost always looked to attack from the very first ball of his innings and possessed such an amazing range of strokes that he was practically never tied down. More often than not he got himself out but, frequently, miscued strokes which would have been fatal to others were struck by Richards with such force that they cleared the field. An imperious driver through extra cover, and a fearless and brilliant hooker, he would unfailingly hit any ball of fullish length which strayed to legward of his middle-stump for four runs between square-leg and mid-on, according to the positioning of the field, casually placing the full face of the bat through the intended line. He was the most likely match-winner in any contest, whoever he was representing. The son of Malcolm Richards, who was for many years Antigua's leading fast bowler, he had two brothers who also played for the island. Viv himself did so both at cricket and football while still at school and was so much the idol of the crowd that, when he was given out caught behind at the age of 17 in a Leeward Island tournament, they protested, stopped play and forced local officials to overrule the umpire's decision. He was subsequently given a two-year suspension—a harsh lesson that cricketers must keep their feelings to themselves—so it was not until 1972 that he made his first-class début, at once scoring freely. A new maturity came with his qualification for Somerset. In his first season for the county in 1974, under shrewd advice and roughly affectionate encouragement from Brian Close, Richards scored 1,223 runs and scored 1,000 runs or more in every subsequent English season until 1988 when, amidst much bitterness, Somerset released him. He scored 2,161 runs (65.48) in 1977. In 1979 Richards helped Somerset win their first major trophies in the Gillette Cup and the John Player League, which gave him as much pleasure as his match-winning hundred (138 not out) in the Prudential World Cup Final against England. His Test experience began in India, Sri Lanka and Pakistan in 1974/5. Picked largely to be blooded for the future, he in fact replaced the injured Lawrence Rowe, scoring 192 not out in his third Test innings at Delhi. In the 1980s, partly owing to an eye complaint, there were signs of at least a temporary bending beneath the heavy load he carried as the potential match-winner in each game he played. Yet he seldom failed to produce something memorable on the big occasion. In England in 1980 he was the leading batsman in both the Tests and first-class matches, hitting a superb 145 in the Lord's Test with a six and 25 fours. He hit 120 not out, out of 249, against Pakistan at Multan in 1980/1 and later in the same season, almost inevitably, marked the first-ever Test in his native Antigua with a century against England. In the previous Test he had scored 182 not out in Barbados. He was totally dominant in Australia in 1979/80, magnificent in both Tests and one-day internationals and scored 1,077 runs (71.09) in 15 matches on the tour. In the Tests his scores were 140, 96, 76, and 74—386 runs at an average of 91. But he was much less successful on a similar tour of Australia two years later. He was clearly in need of a rest and wisely took a long one after the end of his successful benefit season in England in 1982. Another loss of form, in Australia in 1984, was ended by a memorable innings of 208 in the fourth Test at Melbourne. Earlier that year, on an otherwise relatively moderate tour of England, he played his most breathtaking one-day innings, murdering a reputable England attack on a slow pitch at Old Trafford to score 189 chanceless runs off 170 balls out of a total of 272 for 9. The ninth wicket had fallen at 161. He hit 5 sixes and 21 fours. He became official captain of the West Indies in April 1985 against New Zealand and the following year emulated his predecessor Clive Lloyd by leading his country to a five out of five whitewash of England (at home). On his home ground in the final Test his eighth and last Test century against England was also the fastest and most spectacular, a piece of hitting at once

murderous and joyous. Reaching three figures off 56 balls, it was the fastest Test hundred (by this yardstick) ever. He also scored eight hundreds against India, and five against Australia. Under his captaincy, during which he deployed his fast-bowling strength ruthlessly, no series was ever lost under his command and when, occasionally, a Test defeat occurred he would smile and say, 'We have lost a battle but we will win the war.' Either close to the wicket or in the covers, he was a fielder of the highest class and also a capable slow-medium off-spinner who could bowl seam-up if necessary. He played for Glamorgan from 1990–3, and for Queensland in 1976/7. All this marvellous, bubbling talent was seldom boastfully used. At the crease he appeared relaxed to the point of insouciance; off the field a generally charming and justly popular figure, he enjoyed the fruits of his success in a relaxed fashion. When he married his childhood sweetheart at St John's in Antigua in 1980, the ceremony was given as much attention as a royal wedding. Richards was, indeed, the island's unofficial king.

First-class career (1971–93): 36,212 runs (49.33) including 114 centuries, 223 wickets (45.15), 464 catches, and 1 stumping

Test matches (121): 8,540 runs (50.23) including 24 centuries, 32 wickets (61.37), and 122 catches

RICHARDSON, Richard Benjamin

(b. 1962, Five Islands Village, Antigua) *Leeward Islands, Yorkshire, and West Indies*

Like the Australians who followed Bradman, Richie Richardson, a well-built and quick-footed right-handed batsman of abundant talent and aggressive style, inevitably found it hard to emerge from the shadow of his mentor, Vivian Richards, from whose island of Antigua he comes. But emerge he did, succeeding Richards as captain first of the Leewards and then in 1991/2, of the West Indies. He is a gentler, more sensitive soul than Richards; shy, modest, courteous and sportsmanlike and his batting lacks the steel of some of his contemporaries, although few of them can match him for glittering natural talent. His square-driving is explosive and irresistible. He toured India and Australia in 1983/4, making a duck in his first Test innings at Bombay, but after some brilliant batting in one-day internationals in Australia in the same season he played in the entire home series against Australia, scoring 327 runs in five innings at an average of 81.75. He hit his first Test century, an unbeaten

131, at Bridgetown and followed up with 154 in his native Antigua, matching the great Richards stroke for stroke as they put on 308 together. He failed to win a Test place on a relatively disappointing tour of England in 1984 but remained an important member of the West Indies 'squad', equally happy when opening the innings or going in first wicket down. After the retirement of Clive Lloyd he was the home team's leading batsman against New Zealand in 1985, making a determined 78 in difficult circumstances in the first Test at Port of Spain and then a brilliant 185 in the second Test at Bourda, square-cutting and off-driving with dazzling flair. Against England in 1986 he hit 387 runs (55.28) in the home series, including a superb 160 at Bridgetown, despite occasional difficulties against spin bowling. Only on his third tour of England, in 1991, did he do himself full justice, scoring 121 at The Oval in the defeat which was followed by the controversial dethronement of Viv Richards. Richardson led a reshaped West Indies side in the World Cup in 1991/2 and they took time to gel, almost losing a subsequent home Test against South Africa. However, in Australia in 1992/3 he established his position, winning the series 2–1 and scoring 109 at Sydney, his eighth Test 100 against Australia. None was better, however, than the devastating 182 at Georgetown in 1990/1, perhaps his greatest innings. By 1994 he had toured every Test country except Zimbabwe. Apart from 76 Tests he had played in 190 one-day internationals, scoring 5,430 runs (33.94) with five centuries. The non-stop pressures of international cricket began, however, to bear down on this guitar-playing, retiring character. Having led the West Indies to a 3–1 win in the home series against England in 1994, he joined Yorkshire as their second overseas player but could not summon the concentration to do his talent justice. Halfway through the season he was diagnosed as having 'acute fatigue syndrome' and told to have a complete six-months rest. He returned to duty as captain of the Leewards and West Indies in 1994/5.

First-class career (1981–): 12,280 runs (41.91) including 32 centuries, and 6 wickets (39.16)
Test matches (80): 5,674 runs (45.03) including 16 centuries, and 86 catches

RICKARDS, Kenneth Roy

(b. 1923, Kingston, Jamaica) *Jamaica, Essex, and West Indies*

A confident right-handed batsman, Kenneth Rickards scored 67 in his first Test at Kingston against England in 1947/8 and toured Australasia in 1951/2, but had little success. He played one game for Essex in 1953.

First-class career (1945–59): 2,065 runs (38.96) including 2 centuries, 1 wicket (128.00), and 10 catches
Test matches (2): 104 runs (34.66)

ROACH, Clifford Archibald

(b. 1904, Port of Spain, Trinidad; d. 1988, Port of Spain) *Trinidad and West Indies*

Possessing a reasonably strong defence and a variety of dazzling strokes, powerful drives, hooks, and crisp cuts, Clifford Roach was a right-handed opening batsman and a brilliant field, especially at cover-point. He stood as the second-best batsman to George Headley in the early Test series engaged in by West Indies. In the Tests he hit 50 in the second against England at Old Trafford in 1928; 122 and 77 in the first against England at Kensington Oval, Barbados, and 209, his career highest, which included 3 sixes and 22 fours in less than 5 hours, in the fourth match at Georgetown in 1929/30. In the first series against England in the Caribbean, he finished second to Headley, with 467 runs (58.37). Though inconsistent, he reached 1,000 runs in each of his 1928 and 1933 tours—1,222 runs (26.56) and 1,286 runs (25.72) respectively, including, in the latter year, a characteristically free 180 in 2 hours 50 minutes against Surrey at The Oval, when he reached his century before lunch on the first day. In Australia in 1930/1 he made 637 runs (24.50).

First-class career (1923–38): 4,851 runs (28.04) including 5 centuries, 5 wickets (105.20), and 43 catches
Test matches (16): 952 runs (30.70) including 2 centuries, 2 wickets (51.50), and 5 catches

ROBERTS, Alphonso Theodore

(b. 1937, Kingstown, St Vincent) *Windward Islands, Trinidad, and West Indies*

Slim and rather frail-looking, a steady right-handed batsman, Roberts toured New Zealand in 1955/6 and, in his sole Test, the fourth at Auckland, aged 18 years 173 days, he made 28 and 0. He was the first player from the 'small islands' to play in a Test. He made only 137 runs (19.55) on the tour and was not selected for West Indies again.

First-class career (1955–60): 153 runs (13.90)

ROBERTS, Anderson Montgomery Everton

(b. 1951, Urlings Village, Antigua) *Leeward Islands, Hampshire, New South Wales, Leicestershire, and West Indies*

Andy Roberts was the third West Indian to take 200 Test wickets. From 1974 to 1980, a period of intense activity throughout the cricket world, he was one of the most feared bowlers in the world, and between the English winter of 1974 and summer of 1976 he took 100 wickets in 19 Tests, the fastest in terms of time (two years, 142 days) until Ian Botham surpassed him. A tall, strong Antiguan with exceptionally broad shoulders, he had an action which was the perfect example of speed through economy: a quick sprint to the stumps, a spring into the air and a powerful thrust of the body, sending the ball very fast and very straight to its target. He used the bouncer frugally but intelligently. Behind a bland, expressionless, but chilling exterior lay a cool cricketing brain. A teetotaller, who favoured a special orange-flavoured soft drink from Antigua, he is as phlegmatic off the field as he was on, where a wicket merited only a quick, hastily dismissed smile, and a near miss no apparent frustration or excitement. At the age of 19 in January 1970, he made his first-class début for the Leeward Islands, taking 4 for 50 from 29 overs in the first innings. He played his first Test, against England, in Barbados early in 1974, taking 1 for 75 and 2 for 49 on a good batting wicket, and the fact that he was discarded for the rest of the series had much to do with England managing to draw a series in which they were much the weaker side. However, he was now on his way to the top, the first Antiguan to play for the West Indies. In England in 1974 Roberts took 119 wickets in 21 matches for Hampshire at an average of only 13.62, besides being a prolific wicket-taker in limited-overs matches. The following winter he was by far the most successful West Indian bowler in India, Sri Lanka, and Pakistan, with 32 wickets in five Tests against India and 12 more in two matches against Pakistan. At Madras he took 12 for 121 (7 for 64 and 5 for 57). In Australia in 1975/6 Roberts was again the best West Indies bowler, with 22 wickets (26.36). In England in 1976 he had better fast bowling support and took 28 Test wickets (19.17) in a triumphant tour for his team. Already, however, the strain of bowling fast for more than one team was beginning to dull the keen edge of his pace. At home against Pakistan in 1976/7 his 19 Test wickets were expensively gained (40.15). For Hampshire he remained a potential match-winner in each game that he played but, never one to convey great enjoyment, he often began to give an impression of a jaded and disillusioned man, and he left the county half-way through the 1978 season to concentrate on cricket for Kerry Packer. Bowling for West Indies in the Prudential World Cup in England in 1979 he looked like a fast bowler whose best days were already behind him. However, he learned to take wickets through movement, and thoughtful probing of a batsman's weakness, as well as through speed and bounce. He held his place as Holding's new-ball partner in Australia (1979/80 and 1980/1) and in England in 1980 but was dropped for the final home Test against England in 1980/1. He was also left out in the second of three Tests in Australia in 1981/2 but returned in the final match to take 4 for 43 in the first innings at Adelaide and set up a win for his side. Later in that season he took 24 wickets in only four matches for the Leeward Islands in the Shell Shield, including 6 for 54 against Jamaica, and he continued to prove that he was not yet to be written off as a spent force by bowling well for Leicestershire in 1982, his second year at the county on a part-time contract. Sure enough, he returned to Test cricket the following winter for the home series against India, leading the wicket-takers with 24 wickets at 22.70. In the Shell Shield he captained the Leewards in the absence of Viv Richards and led from the front, with 28 wickets at 18 each. He played in two further Tests, in India in 1983/4, at Calcutta passing 200 wickets in his 46th Test, celebrating with an innings of 68, his highest first-class score, sharing a record ninth-wicket stand of 161 with Clive Lloyd. No more than a capable fielder, he could indeed be a useful right-hand bat, as he showed also in the 1975 Prudential World Cup when he saved his side from elimination at the hands of Pakistan. Awarded a CBE for services to cricket, he became a fisherman, as well as cricketing sage, in Antigua but increasingly in the 1990s he drew closer again to the heart of West Indies cricket, becoming a regional selector, supervising the preparation of Test pitches at St John's and, in 1995, replacing Rohan Kanhai as coach to the West Indies team. He played, part-time, for Leicestershire from 1981–4 and for New South Wales in two matches in 1976/7.

First-class career (1969–84): 3,516 runs (15.69), 889 wickets (21.01), and 52 catches

Test matches (47): 762 runs (14.94), 202 wickets (25.61), and 9 catches

ROBERTS, Lawrence D.

(b. Kingston, Jamaica; d. 1993, Kingston)

As the sports editor and chief cricket writer of Jamaica's only daily newspaper of the time, the *Gleaner*, 'Strebor' Roberts exercised considerable influence on the game in Jamaica. He covered all series in the West Indies from 1948 to his retirement in 1969 as well as those in England in 1957 and 1963 and Australia in 1960/1. The Australian tour, featuring the tied Test, prompted him to write his only book, *Cricket's Brightest Summer*. Fiercely nationalistic, he was always alert to any perceived selectorial injustices against Jamaican players at West Indies level, occasionally putting forward the view that Jamaica apply on its own for Test status. He was also a specialist writer on horse-racing and boxing and, on his death, was described by Jamaica's Prime Minister Patrick Patterson as 'a legend in the field of sports'.

ROBERTS, Pascall Ronald

(b. 1937, Port of Spain, Trinidad) *Trinidad*

A tall, slim, left-arm bowler who used the new ball with fast-medium swing before changing to orthodox spin, Pascall Roberts was a regular, and vital, member of the Trinidad and Tobago team for nearly ten years after his first appearance in 1961. A tireless and uncomplaining campaigner, he never seemed happier than when wheeling away for 30 overs an innings, as he often did. He was also a useful right-hand batsman low in the order. He spent the summer of 1963 with Lowerhouse in the Lancashire League, replacing Basil Butcher, who was on tour of England with the West Indies, but otherwise remained at home where he was an outstanding performer in club cricket and the annual matches between South and North, which he captained. Douglas Sang Hue, the Jamaican Test umpire with a reputation for strictness in ruling on the legality of bowling actions, no-balled him for throwing three times in one over of his slower style in the match against Jamaica in 1967. It was an isolated incident and no other umpire found fault with his delivery. He was chosen for the West Indies team to England in 1969, aged 31, after a fruitful Shell Shield season and after a selection shake-up following a disastrous West Indies tour of Australia and New Zealand. Used principally as a spinner, he managed only 16 expensive wickets in 11 matches and did not play in a Test. He faded from the scene on the emergence of Bernard Julien, a left-arm bowler of identical versatility, and the left-arm spinner Inshan Ali, in the early 1970s.

First-class career (1961–79): 871 runs (13.82) and 211 wickets (25.05)

RODRIGUEZ, William Vincente

(b. 1934, Port of Spain, Trinidad) *Trinidad and West Indies*

A competent and steady right-handed batsman and useful leg-break bowler, Willie Rodriguez toured England in 1963 and went down with cartilage trouble before the first Test, but he was fit enough to appear in the fifth at The Oval when he helped to lay a solid foundation in an opening stand of 78 with Conrad Hunte. At home he played in occasional Tests against India in 1961/2, Australia in 1964/5 and England in 1967/8. He managed the West Indies side in Australia and New Zealand in 1979/80.

First-class career (1953–70): 2,061 runs (24.83) including 1 century, 119 wickets (28.08), and 36 catches

Test matches (5): 96 runs (13.71), 7 wickets (53.42), and 3 catches

ROWE, Lawrence George

(b. 1949, Kingston, Jamaica) *Jamaica, Derbyshire, and West Indies*

One of the enigmas of Test cricket, Lawrence Rowe had an extraordinary career, the zenith of which was an unforgettable triple-century against England in Barbados, one of only eleven scores of 300 or more in Tests. Soon after he spent several seasons in the wilderness due to trouble with his eyesight, injuries, and, most eccentric of cricketing complaints, an allergy to grass! Nurtured as a rare talent in his native Kingston, Rowe first played for Jamaica in 1968/9, toured England with the Jamaican side in 1970 and in 1971/2 broke through dramatically with four consecutive centuries, all at Kingston, including the unique achievement of a century and a double century on his Test début—214 and 100 not out against New Zealand. Probably a more nervous character than his cool, casual appearance at the crease would suggest—he infuriated opposing bowlers by humming or whistling a tune to aid his concentration—he was much less successful for a time outside his beloved Sabina Park. Against New Zealand he averaged 69.83, scoring 419 runs, but missed the later part of the 1972/3 series against Australia after scores of 76, 4, and 16, and a knee injury again caused him to miss the series against England in 1973. But it was England who learned the true quality of his batting the following winter in the Caribbean. A beautifully balanced right-handed batsman who either opened or went in at number three or four, he had a lazy-looking backswing of the bat, and drove with graceful certainty and impeccable timing through the covers or wide of mid-on, but the bulk of his runs came from strokes off the back foot. At his best, he was thrillingly quick to pick up the short ball and hook it to some distant part of the leg-side boundary. After making 120 in Kingston against England in the second Test of the 1974 series, he played an innings at Bridgetown which none who saw it can forget. His 302 out of 596 for 8 declared was his 11th first-class century but the first away from Sabina Park. Conditions were all in the batsman's favour and England subsequently drew the game, but Rowe batted for 612 minutes in an impeccable display of masterly batting, hitting a six and 36 fours in 302, made off 430 balls. In the fifth Test of the series, which the West Indies lost, he played the England spinners with cool skill, making 123 in the first innings (opening the innings, as he did throughout the series). His aggregate in the five Tests was 616 runs at 88.00. After a century in the Brisbane Test of 1975/6 he fell away, scoring only 270 runs in the series (24.54). His first season for Derbyshire in 1974 was quite successful, but in 1975 the problems with his eyesight began and, although he played in two Tests in 1976 in England, scoring a fifty in each, he never again seemed to be without some sort of ailment. However, after some success in World Series Cricket he toured Australia and did well in 1979/80, only to miss most of the tour to England in 1980 because of yet another injury. He became captain of Jamaica in 1981 but a year later he turned his back on official West Indies cricket and became a successful and diplomatic captain of the West Indies 'rebel' team in South Africa.

First-class career (1968–84): 8,755 runs (37.58) including 18 centuries, 2 wickets (112.00), and 118 catches

Test matches (30): 2,047 runs (43.55) including 7 centuries, 0–44, and 17 catches

ST HILL, Edwin Lloyd

(b. 1904, Port of Spain, Trinidad; d. 1957, Manchester, England) *Trinidad and West Indies*

A right-arm medium-paced bowler and useful batsman, Edwin St Hill played in two Tests against England in 1929/30 with moderate suc-cess. He toured Australia in 1930/1, but was not selected for any of the Tests: he took the field in four games, taking 16 wickets (29.81).

First-class career (1923–31): 274 runs (11.91) and 64 wickets (28.62)

Test matches (2): 18 runs (4.50) and 3 wickets (73.66)

ST HILL, Wilton H.

(b. 1893, Port of Spain, Trinidad, d. 1957) *Trinidad and West Indies*

About 6 ft. tall, slim and elegant, but with forearms like whipcord, Wilton St Hill was a strong back-foot player, a superb late-cutter and leg-glancer, and the possessor of some splendid off-side strokes. He scored 105 in $2\frac{1}{2}$ hours at Port of Spain for Trinidad against MCC in 1926/7, and Lord Harris considered that he was the best batsman in the West Indies. In 1929/30 he made a more cautious 102 on the same ground against MCC and in his only Test of the series, the second at Port of Spain, he opened with steady efforts of 33 and 30. On the 1928 England tour he had been selected for the first two Tests ever between the two countries, but he was a big disappointment, in first-class matches making only 262 runs (10.91). He vanished into obscurity.

First-class career (1911–30): 1,928 runs (27.15) including 5 centuries

Test matches (3): 117 runs (19.50), 0–9, and 1 catch

SANG HUE, Douglas

(b. Jamaica)

For nearly twenty years, Douglas Sang Hue, a diminutive, unassuming Chinese-Jamaican, was universally accepted as the best umpire in the West Indies and, arguably, the world. His unmistakeable stance, crouching low over the stumps with coat drawn up around the waist, was a familiar sight to West Indian crowds between 1961 and 1982 in which time he officiated in 31 Tests, a West Indian record. The Australian, Ian Chappell, not known for his generosity towards umpires, made a point of publicly praising his work after the 1973 series in which Sang Hue stood in all five Tests, the first time it had occurred in the West Indies. Perhaps because of his fearlessness, he also happened to be involved in a series of controversial incidents. His correct decision for a leg-side catch by the wicket-keeper that accounted for Basil Butcher against England in the 1968 Sabina Park Test touched off a crowd disturbance that prompted the riot police to resort to tear-gas. When Tony Greig threw down Alvin Kallicharran's wicket at the bowler's end off the last ball of the day in the 1974 Port of Spain Test, Sang Hue rightly ruled him run out and it needed hours of persuasion before he would accept England's withdrawal of the appeal, necessitated by the fear of crowd trouble. He called more bowlers for throwing than any West Indian umpire, among them the Australian off-spinner, Bruce Yardley, in 1978, an action that led to an Australian protest and the cancellation of his appointment for the subsequent Test. He was employed by Kerry Packer's World Series Cricket for two seasons in Australia and on its tour of the West Indies in 1979 and officiated in his last Test in the 1981 home series against England. By the following year, declining health obliged him to quit altogether.

SCARLETT, Reginald Osmond

(b. 1934, Kingston, Jamaica) *Jamaica and West Indies*

A mountainous figure of a man, Reg Scarlett was a useful right-handed batsman and off-break bowler, who hit two fifties and took three good wickets for Jamaica against MCC at Kingston in 1959/60, and appeared in three Tests that season against England. He settled in England and continued to play cricket into his fifties as well as being a prominent organizer of sporting activities for the Greater London Council. He was the inspiration of the 'Haringey Cricket College' which produced a number of county cricketers of West Indian origins in the 1980s.

First-class career (1951–60): 477 runs (23.85) and 48 wickets (34.12)
Test matches (3): 54 runs (18.00), 2 wickets (104.50), and 2 catches

SCOTT, Alfred Phillip Horner

(b. 1934, Jamaica) *Jamaica and West Indies*

A right-arm leg-break bowler who dismayed the Indian tourists by taking seven wickets for Jamaica against them at Kingston in 1952/3, Al Scott played in his sole Test against India at Kingston that season, scoring 5 and taking 0 for 140. His father was O. C. Scott

First-class career (1952–4): 38 runs (12.66) and 18 wickets (33.00)

SCOTT, Oscar Charles

(b. 1893, Kingston, Jamaica; d. 1961, Kingston) *Jamaica and West Indies*

A genuine all-rounder, being a very useful right-handed batsman and slow leg-break bowler, 'Tommy' Scott toured England in 1928 and Australia in 1930/1, and played at home against England in 1929/30. His performances were rather moderate in England—322 runs (20.12) and 25 wickets (36.24), although he finished second in the batting averages in the Tests with 74 runs (24.66)—but his leg-spin worked in Australia, where he took 40 wickets (33.22), including 11 wickets in the Tests. In the first Test at Adelaide he finished off the first innings by dismissing four batsmen in nine deliveries without cost. In the fourth Test against England at Kingston in 1929/30, he took 9 for 374, including figures of 80.2–13–266–5 in a total of 849 in the first innings.

First-class career (1910–35): 1,317 runs (24.38), 182 wickets (30.52), and 14 catches
Test matches (8): 171 runs (17.10) and 22 wickets (42.04)

SEALEY, Benjamin James

(b. 1899, St Joseph, Trinidad; d. 1963, Port of Spain, Trinidad) *Trinidad and West Indies*

A lively, hard-hitting right-handed batsman, medium-paced leg-break bowler and sound field anywhere—he was one of the fastest runners in Trinidad—Ben Sealey was in his late twenties before playing first-class cricket for the first time and soon became an all-round 'treasure of his island'. He toured England in 1933, scoring 1,072 runs (39.70), including three centuries, and taking 19 wickets (38.15). In his sole Test, the last at The Oval, he made 29, the highest score in a total of 100, and 12, and took 1 for 10.

First-class career (1923–41): 2,115 runs (29.37) including 4 centuries, 78 wickets (25.97), and 22 catches

SEALY, James Edward Derek

(b. 1912, St Michael, Barbados; d. 1982, Palo Seco, Trinidad) *Barbados, Trinidad, and West Indies*

A powerfully built and polished right-handed batsman, with a strong defence and forcing strokes all round the wicket, Derek Sealy was also a useful medium-paced bowler with unusual nip off the pitch, and a brilliant and versatile fielder who sometimes served as reserve wicket-keeper.

SHEPHERD

He became the (then) youngest Test player in history, when, at 17 years 122 days, he played in the first match at home against England at Bridgetown in 1929/30, scoring 58 and 15. He remains the youngest West Indian to have played in Tests. In Australia in 1930/1 he failed in the Tests, but he was at his best against England in 1934/5 when he made 92 in the second Test at Port of Spain, scoring 270 runs (45.00) in the series. Touring in England in 1939, he achieved little in the Tests, but in all first-class matches reached 948 runs (27.88), including a brilliant 181, his career-highest, in $3\frac{1}{2}$ hours against Middlesex at Lord's. For Barbados against Trinidad in 1942 he bowled brilliantly on a wet pitch to take 8 for 8, the best analysis in a first-class match in the West Indies. He moved to Trinidad after teaching games at his old school, Combermere, in Barbados, where one of his pupils was Frank Worrell.

First-class career (1928–49): 3,831 runs (30.40) including 8 centuries, 63 wickets (28.60), and 80 dismissals (67 c., 13 st.)

Test matches (11): 478 runs (28.11), 3 wickets (31.33), and 7 dismissals (6 c., 1 st.)

SHEPHERD, John Neil

(b. 1943, Belleplaine, Barbados) *Barbados, Rhodesia, Kent, Gloucestershire, and West Indies*

An irresistibly enthusiastic all-round cricketer, John Shepherd gave much of his best cricket to England after joining Kent in 1965. A vigorous right-arm medium-fast swing bowler and very hard-hitting right-hand batsman, his stocky, powerful frame was the key to his success. His first-class début for Barbados was in 1964/5, his début for Kent in 1966 and his first full season for them, 1967, when he won his county cap and Kent won the Gillette Cup. His Test career was all too brief: he played three games in England in 1969 when he bowled excellently with consistent hostility and movement through the air and off the seam, taking 12 wickets (22.16), including 5 for 104 in 58.5 overs in England's first innings of 413 at Lord's. At home the following winter he played in two Tests against India. He became the first black cricketer to tour South Africa, in 1973 with the Derrick Robins team, stirring up much opposition in the Caribbean, and played in the Currie Cup for Rhodesia (1975/6) as well as having two very successful seasons playing Grade Cricket for the Melbourne club, Footscray. Outstanding performances for Kent included 170 against Northamptonshire in 1968, at Folkestone, and 8 for 83 against Lancashire at Tunbridge Wells in 1977.

He moved to Gloucestershire in 1982 and made many valuable contributions, being capped in 1983. Thereafter he was employed mainly as a coach, most recently at Eastbourne College.

First-class career (1964–87): 13,359 runs (26.34) including 10 centuries, 1,157 wickets (27.71), and 292 catches

Test matches (5): 77 runs (9.62), 19 wickets (25.21), and 4 catches

SHILLINGFORD, Grayson Cleophas

(b. 1944, Dublanc) *Windward Islands and West Indies*

An enthusiastic right-arm fast-medium bowler who batted left, Grayson Shillingford toured England in 1969 and 1973. Despite a torn muscle, which kept him idle for a month during his first tour, he took 36 wickets (18.58) and bowled well in two Tests. At home he played against India in 1970/1 and New Zealand in 1971/2, but failed to establish himself.

First-class career (1967–79): 791 runs (10.14), 217 wickets (26.54), and 22 catches

Test matches (7): 57 runs (8.14), 15 wickets (35.80), and 2 catches

SHILLINGFORD, Irvine Theodore

(b. 1944, Dominica) *Windward Islands and West Indies*

The first cousin of Grayson Shillingford, with whom he played for many seasons for Dominica and the Windward Islands, Irvine Shillingford was a fine, orthodox right-handed batsman who was a consistently high scorer following his début against the Australians in 1965. He played three Tests against Pakistan in 1976/7, scoring 120 in his second Test at Georgetown. In 1978 he scored 238 against the Leeward Islands at Castries but was dropped after only one Test against Australia at Georgetown.

First-class career (1961–82): 5,449 runs (36.57) including 11 centuries, and 1 wicket (85.00)

Test matches (4): 218 runs (31.14) including 1 century, and 1 catch

SHIVNARINE, Sew

(b. 1952, British Guiana) *Guyana and West Indies*

A gifted little cricketer, Sew Shivnarine bowled slow left-arm orthodox, batted right-handed and made the transition to Test cricket without difficulty when suddenly elevated in 1978 after the withdrawal of the Packer players in the middle of the series against Australia. His scores in the series included 53 and 63 on his début at George-town and 53 at Kingston, but in India in 1978/9 he was disappointing, and his bowling proved to be not up to Test standards.

First-class career (1970–81): 2,182 runs (32.56) including 3 centuries, and 67 wickets (36.52)
Test matches (8): 379 runs (29.15), 1–167, and 6 catches

SHORT, Peter Desmond Bowen

(b. 1926, Port of Spain, Trinidad)

Peter Short was the longest serving president of the Barbados Cricket Association before resigning to take up the presidency of the West Indies Cricket Board of Control in 1993, a post for which he had been twice previously nominated. His election broke a sequence of former out-standing Test players—Jeffrey Stollmeyer, Alan Rae, and Clyde Walcott—serving as presidents. He himself was a right-hand opening batsman who played for Wanderers in Barbados club competition, for the British Army during his service between 1945 and 1957 when he was commissioned into the Royal Artillery, serving in Malaya and rising to the rank of captain, and for Northumberland in the minor counties championship. He was first elected to the board of management of the BCA in 1964 and became president in 1973, succeeding Eric Inniss who had died suddenly in office. The membership returned him at 21 consecutive annual general meetings at only two of which was there an opposing candidate. Between 1966 and 1971, he was WICBC secretary under the presidency of Noel Peirce, like himself and the first president, Sir Harold Austin, a Wanderers man. If his distinctive handle-bar moustache suggests a stern military approach to the way he conducts his affairs, it is misleading. He is very much a diplomat who attributed the success of the BCA under his leadership to teamwork in which each member pulled his weight. It was a philosophy in keeping with his parallel career in business management. If the reversion to a white West Indian as WICBC president caused some adverse comment, Short dismissed it as an irrelevant and minority opinion, asserting that racial issues are no longer prominent in West Indies cricket.

SIMMONS, Philip Verant

(b. 1963, Trinidad) *Trinidad, Leicestershire, and West Indies*

A tall, powerfully built, right-hand opening batsman, Phil Simmons never quite established him-self as the successor to Gordon Greenidge after suffering a horrific head injury at Bristol on the 1988 tour to England. His tendency to play across the line reduced his effectiveness at Test level but consistently heavy scoring in the Red Stripe tournament and the ability to bowl right-arm, nagging medium-pace out-swing assured him of a regular one-day international slot. A punishing stroke-player off either foot, who loves to drive in the air to long-off or long-on, he made his début in the World Cup at Lahore in 1987, making 50 off 51 balls against Pakistan, then 89 against Sri Lanka, and played in the first two Texaco limited-overs internationals on the summer tour to England before the fateful mishap against Gloucestershire. Simmons was batting without a helmet in poor light on the second day when he lost sight of a short ball from David Lawrence which fractured his skull. He was rushed imme-diately to Frenchay hospital, one of the leading neurosurgical units in Europe, where he under-went a life-saving operation to remove a blood clot on the brain. He missed the remainder of the tour. He made an unspectacular Test début at Madras in January 1988 in the fourth Test and failed to reach 50 in his next eight appearances. He was again selected for the 1991 tour of England as reward for his earlier courage and recuperation but, despite three centuries in county matches, he was troubled by away move-ment and spin alike in the Tests. In the short home series against South Africa, however, in 1992, he was twice 'man of the match' after thunderous centuries in one-day internationals in Kingston (where he struck five sixes in his favoured sector between long-on and deep-extra) and Port of Spain. Finally he scored a maiden Test century, in his twentieth innings, at Melbourne in late December 1992, prefaced by a bowling analysis that may never be bettered in one-day internationals, 4 for 3 off 10 overs, including 8 maidens, against Pakistan in a World Series day/night match at Sydney. In 93 one-day inter-nationals to the end of the 1994 tour of India he had scored 2,577 runs (30.32) with four centuries and had taken 40 wickets (34.72). A deceptively sharp fieldsman for his size, and a reliable per-former in the slip cordon, his all-round talents also drew admiration in three leagues in the North of England, latterly at Haslingden in the Lancashire League, and Leicestershire engaged him for the 1994 season where this amiable 'gentle giant' of a man quickly endeared himself to colleagues and supporters alike with an innings of 261 in his first Championship match against Northamptonshire at Grace Road.

First-class career (1983–   ): 7,219 runs (33.73) including 13 centuries, 78 wickets (34.87), and 128 catches

Test matches (22): 919 runs (23.56) including 1 century, 2 wickets (79.00), and 21 catches

SINGH, Charran Kamkaran

(b. 1935, San Juan) *Trinidad and West Indies*

A left-arm slow-bowler, Charran Singh had an unusual Test début against England as a 'local boy' on his home ground, Port of Spain, in the second Test of 1959/60. It was when he was given run out for 0 to make the West Indies total 98 for 8 against England's total of 382, that the crowd's shattered emotions got the better of them: bottles and missiles rained on to the field, spectators invaded the playing area and riot police had to quell the mob. A few weeks earlier Singh had taken 5 for 57 in 34 overs in the MCC first innings against Trinidad.

First-class career (1959–62): 102 runs (8.50) and 48 wickets (23.93)

Test matches (2): 11 runs (3.66), 5 wickets (33.20), and 2 catches

SMALL, Joseph A.

(b. 1892, Princes Town; d. 1958, Forest Reserve) *Trinidad and West Indies*

Joe Small was a tall, loose-limbed all-rounder, being a dashing right-handed batsman, who off-drove, cut, and glanced fluently, a medium-pace off-break bowler, and an agile slip fielder. He toured England in 1923 making 776 runs (31.04), including a classic 94 off Lancashire at Old Trafford, and taking 19 wickets (33.47). In the 1928 tour he totalled 595 runs (18.59) and was more successful as a bowler, taking 50 wickets (28.88). In the first Test between West Indies and England, at Lord's, he made a defiant 52 in a losing cause. He played his last Test, the second at Port of Spain against England, in 1929/30. He epitomized the spirit of West Indies cricket.

First-class career (1909–32): 3,063 runs (26.18) including 4 centuries, 165 wickets (27.81), and 72 catches

Test matches (3): 79 runs (13.16), 3 wickets (61.33), and 3 catches

SMALL, Milton Aster

(b. 1964, St Philip, Barbados) *Barbados and West Indies*

Another one off the production line of fast bowlers from Barbados, Milton Small took 8 for 110 in his first Shell Shield match in 1983/4. Tall, despite his name, he was a surprise choice in the West Indies team against Australia for the second Test of that season and, after a modest performance in this match (1 for 75), was an equally unexpected selection as one of six fast bowlers sent to England in 1984. An inswing bowler both accurate and hostile, though not especially fast, he replaced the injured Michael Holding for the second Test at Lord's and with 3 for 40 in the second innings made an important contribution to the victory. But a knee injury forced an early return home and he was able to play in only one Shell Shield match the following home season.

First-class career (1983–92): 51 runs (4.75) and 56 wickets (28.23)

Test matches (2): 3 runs (—) and 4 wickets (38.25)

SMITH, Cameron Wilberforce

(b. 1933, Christ Church, Barbados) *Barbados and West Indies*

An ever-smiling insurance salesman, 'Cammie' Smith was a tall and attractive right-handed opening batsman and wicket-keeper, who toured Australia in 1960/1 and scored 55 in the third Test at Sydney. He kept wicket in the first Test at Port of Spain against India in 1961/2 after Jackie Hendriks had broken a finger on the first day. He has managed various West Indian teams.

First-class career (1951–65): 2,277 runs (37.32) including 5 centuries, 3 wickets (32.33), and 35 dismissals (32 c., 3 st.)

Test matches (5): 222 runs (24.66) and 5 dismissals (4 c., 1 st.)

SMITH, O'Neil Gordon

(b. 1933, Kingston, Jamaica; d. 1959, Stoke-on-Trent, England) *Jamaica and West Indies*

Stocky and strong, 'Collie' Smith decided as a schoolboy to give up fast bowling and become an off-break bowler, like his hero, Jim Laker; so, for a time, he was called 'Jim'. He developed as a punishing right-handed batsman, a scintillating stroke-maker, and a brilliant versatile field. After only two games for Jamaica he hit 169 against the front-line Australian attack at Kingston in 1954/5, and a few days later, also at Kingston, he made 44 and 104 in his first Test against Australia. In his second match, however, he failed to score in either innings and, after being dropped for one match, returned with variable success for the remainder of his tragically curtailed career. A very cheerful and optimistic cricketer, he toured New Zealand in 1955/6, taking 13 wickets (18.53) in the four Tests, but achieving little with the bat. He consolidated his place in England in 1957, and scored more in the Tests than any of his colleagues, 396 runs (39.60), including 161 at Edgbaston in the first Test and 168 at Trent Bridge in the third. At home against Pakistan in 1957/8 he was the best all-rounder with 283 runs (47.16) and 13 wickets (38.00). Touring India and Pakistan in 1958/9, he scored 901 runs (34.65) and took 25 wickets (26.44) in all first-class matches. In the eight Tests he was second as an all-rounder to Gary Sobers, making 368 runs (28.30) and taking 12 wickets (27.25), although he was not particularly successful against Pakistan. In the first Test against India at Delhi he hit 100 in less than 3 hours and took 8 for 184. During 1958 and 1959 he was highly successful as professional to Burnley in the Lancashire League. His batting had now matured, his exciting stroke-play was used with greater discrimination and he had not yet reached his prime when in September 1959 he died of injuries received in a car accident involving also his great friend Gary Sobers. Smith's body was taken back to Jamaica, where 60,000 people attended the funeral.

First-class career (1954–9): 4,031 runs (40.31) including 10 centuries, 121 wickets (31.02), and 39 catches
Test matches (26): 1,331 runs (31.69) including 4 centuries, 48 wickets (33.85), and 9 catches

SMITH, Sydney Gordon

(b. 1881, Port of Spain, Trinidad; d. 1963, Auckland, New Zealand) Trinidad, Northamptonshire, MCC, Auckland, West Indies, and New Zealand

Only Garfield Sobers and, possibly, Learie Constantine, would rank above Sydney Smith as all-rounders produced by the West Indies. He was also unique among West Indians of the time in that he played for teams in three countries. A big man, left-handed in both skills, he was a strong back-foot batsman of aggressive intent and a bowler capable of medium-pace swing with the new ball or orthodox spin, the style in which he was most successful. His consistent form in the West Indies, including match figures of 16 for 85

for a Combined West Indies XI against R. A. Bennett's English touring team in Port of Spain in 1902, gained him his place on the West Indies tour of England in 1906. His 1,107 runs (33.54) and 116 wickets (19.31) were impressive figures but directly led to his loss to West Indies cricket. Smith remained in England after the tour to qualify by residence for Northamptonshire, against whom he had gained a 12-wicket match return. In his career for Northamptonshire between 1909 and 1914, he was among the leading all-rounders in county cricket, achieving the 'double' of over 1,000 runs and 100 wickets three times, the hat-trick twice, and was named one of Wisden's Five Cricketers of the Year in 1915. He returned to the Caribbean with A. F. Somerset's MCC team in 1910/11 and, after the First World War, emigrated to New Zealand where he also played with distinction for Auckland, representing New Zealand against the touring Australians in 1921, MCC in 1923, and New South Wales in 1924.

First-class career (1899–1926): 10,920 runs (31.28) including 14 centuries, 955 wickets (18.08), and 158 catches

SOBERS, Sir Garfield St Aubrun

(b. 1936, Bridgetown, Barbados) Barbados, South Australia, Nottinghamshire, and West Indies

Generally considered to be the greatest-ever all-round cricketer, the achievements of Gary, later Sir Garfield, Sobers stand alone. Blessed with every necessary attribute for greatness as a cricketer, he had rare natural genius, determination, stamina, and a remarkable capacity to continue to produce high-quality performances despite an exceptionally heavy workload, intense pressure from publicity, and the burden of always being the player whom the crowd most wanted to see and the opposition feared most. Tall, supple, athletic, and strong, with a buck-toothed smile never far away, he enjoyed his cricket and conveyed this to crowds, team-mates, and opponents, and though he played the game with a proper competitiveness and never lost his appetite for runs and wickets until late in his career, he made no enemies. His immortality rests on his all-round success, the style and panache with which he compiled the dazzling figures, and on his unique versatility. A left-hander, he was one of the greatest batsmen of all time and a marvellous new-ball fast-medium left-arm over-the-wicket bowler, who was equally good as a slow left-arm orthodox bowler (although he bowled much less in this style in later years), and also capable of bowling high-quality left-arm unorthodox (back of the hand) spin. As a fielder he was brilliant, with feline reflexes close to the wicket, especially on the leg-side. His very walk was internationally famous: a graceful, relaxed, long-striding walk, leaning forward, bent at the knees. He was born in Barbados with five fingers instead of four on each hand. The extra two were removed in boyhood. One of seven children of a merchant seaman, he was brought up by his mother after his father had died at sea in the War when Gary was only 5. Encouraged by a number of people who at once appreciated his genius, first shown in cricket matches played with other youngsters with a tennis ball, Sobers played golf, soccer, and basketball for Barbados and in 1953 first appeared for the island at cricket against the Indian touring team, aged 16. He made his first Test appearance at the age of 17 at the end of March 1954, in the fifth Test against England at Kingston, taking 4 for 75 in England's first innings of 414. Four years later, having steadily established himself, he made the final step from a highly promising player to a great one when he scored 365 not out at Kingston against Pakistan (1957/8). It was his first three-figure score in a Test, made at the age of 21, and it surpassed by one run Sir Leonard Hutton's record 364 which had stood since 1938. Gerry Alexander, the West Indies' captain, declared when the achievement was complete, at 790 for 3. Sobers batted for just over 10 hours, 3 hours less than Hutton, hit 38 fours and shared a stand of 446 for the second wicket with Conrad Hunte. In this series Sobers made 824 runs (137.33) and hit two other centuries. He scored more than 500 runs in five other series: against India in 1958/9 (557 at 92.83); England in 1959/60 (709 at 101.28); England in 1966 (722 at 103.14); England in 1967/8 (545 at 90.83); India in 1971 (597 at 74.62). In 13 of the 22 Test series in which he played for the West Indies he took ten or more wickets and in three series held more than ten catches. In England in 1966, as captain of the touring team, in addition to his 722 runs in five Tests at an average of 103, he took 20 wickets at 27.25, bowling 269.4 overs and often taking the new ball in an attack which also included Hall and Griffith, and he held ten catches. He made 161 in the first Test at Old Trafford, saved his side with 163 not out in the second at Lord's, and at Leeds, in the match which decided the rubber, hit 174 and took eight wickets for 80 in the match. Something of the man's intense competitiveness may be gleaned from his performance in the final match

of this series. He made 81 in the first innings, and, when he might have been expected to relax a little, with the series already won, he bowled no fewer than 54 overs, ten more than anyone else, in England's innings of 527. As a Test captain he was enterprising, once allowing England to win the decisive match of the series with a bold declaration at Port of Spain in 1967/8, but his attacking gestures often had happier results. He had one less successful tour as captain in Australia, although his loss of form and concentration was probably due to falling in love: he married a pretty Australian girl whom he had first met in England. But he is as much a legend in Australia as anywhere else: he is the only man to have achieved the double of 1,000 runs and 50 wickets in an Australian season, and he did it twice. He also played an innings of 254 for the Rest of the World against Australia at Melbourne in 1971/2, which was one of the most magnificent and masterly ever seen in a big match. In domestic cricket in England he was as inspirational for Nottinghamshire as he had been for South Australia. He captained the county from 1968 until 1974, although by the time of his retirement in the latter year, damaged knees and staleness had reduced his effectiveness. Against Glamorgan at Swansea in 1968 he hit Malcolm Nash, bowling slow left-arm, for six sixes in one six-ball over. It is unlikely that one man will again possess so wide a variety of cricketing skills as Sir Gary, who was knighted by the Queen in Barbados for his services to cricket in 1975. In retirement he had his ups and downs, including operations to his knees and his eyes, but he was never without a friend in the cricket world, and certainly not in his home island. Racing and golf were his chief recreations.

First-class career (1952–74): 28,315 runs (54.87) including 86 centuries, 1,043 wickets (27.74), and 407 catches

Test matches (93): 8,032 runs (57.78) including 26 centuries, 235 wickets (34.03), and 109 catches

SOLOMON, Joseph Stanislaus

(b. 1930, Berbice, British Guiana) *British Guiana and West Indies*

A steady right-handed batsman whose ability to shut up one end could stem a possible collapse, Joe Solomon was also a useful medium-pace leg-break change-bowler and excellent field. A slim East Indian, he batted around number six, though he twice opened for West Indies with Conrad Hunte, without success. He toured India and

Pakistan in 1958/9, Australia in 1960/1, and England in 1963; and at home played against England in 1959/60, India in 1961/2, and Australia in 1964/5. His one outstanding series was his first, against India in 1958/9 when in four Tests he headed the batting averages with 351 runs (117.00), including 100 not out in the fifth match at Delhi, which remained his sole Test century. On his Test début at Kanpur in the second match he had made 45 and 86. Thereafter he was always useful in the West Indies team, often when the need was greatest, for example in the dramatic Test at Lord's in 1963 when he hit a valuable 56 and in the famous tied Test at Brisbane when he ran out two Australian batsmen in the final crisis. His career-highest was 201 not out for Berbice against MCC at Blairmont in 1959/60.

First-class career (1956–69): 5,318 runs (41.54) including 12 centuries, 51 wickets (38.23), and 46 catches

Test matches (27): 1,326 runs (34.00) including 1 century, 4 wickets (67.00), and 13 catches

STAYERS, Sven Conrad

(b. 1937, British Guiana) *British Guiana and West Indies*

A tall all-rounder, a good right-handed batsman and fast-medium bowler of loose, somewhat gangling action, 'Charlie' Stayers played with moderate success in Tests against India in 1961/2.

First-class career (1957–63): 485 runs (28.52) including 1 century, and 68 wickets (26.10)

Test matches (4): 58 runs (19.33) and 9 wickets (40.44)

STOLLMEYER, Jeffrey Baxter

(b. 1921, Santa Cruz, Trinidad; d. 1989, Florida, USA) *Trinidad and West Indies*

Captain of West Indies in 13 Tests from 1951 until 1955 and the holder of the highest score in intercolonial matches, 324 against British Guiana in 1946/7 when he added a record 434 for the third wicket with Gerry Gomez, Jeffrey Stollmeyer was a tall, elegant, and stylish right-handed opening batsman, particularly strong on the on-side, a useful leg-break bowler, and a fine fielder. He first toured England at 18 in 1939, making 59 in his first Test innings. In 1946/7 he scored 324 for Trinidad against British Guiana at Port of Spain. In the first post-war Test against England at Bridgetown in 1947/8 he scored 78

and 31, but he missed half the series through injury. In India in 1948/9 he made 342 runs (68.40) in the Tests, including his maiden century, a faultless 160 at Madras in the fourth match, when he laid the foundations of victory by sharing in a then record first-wicket stand of 239 with Allan Rae. He hit 244 not out against South Zone at Madras, and in all reached 1,091 runs (64.17) for the tour. In England in 1950, again with Rae as his opening partner, he shared in first-wicket stands worth 52, 32, 37, 48, 77, 103 unbroken, and 72 in the four Tests, thus paving the way for 'the three Ws' in the year that West Indian cricket 'came of age'. In this series he scored 305 runs (50.83), including a highest score of 78 at Old Trafford on a poor pitch. In all first-class matches he made 1,334 runs (37.05) including 198 against Sussex at Hove, when he engaged in another record-breaking opening stand with Rae—355 in 4 hours and 40 minutes. As captain he batted well against Australia and New Zealand in 1951/2, against England in 1953/4 (a drawn series), and against Australia in 1954/5. In Australia in 1951/2 he hit a splendid 104 in the fifth Test at Sydney in a losing cause. He led West Indies to victory over India in 1952/3, scoring 354 runs (59.00) including 104 not out in the third match at Port of Spain. A senator in the Trinidad Legislature, he was for several years the widely respected president of the West Indies Cricket Board of Control and prominent in the councils of the ICC. He was shot in the head by armed robbers at his home in Trinidad and died in hospital in the USA without having recovered consciousness.

First-class career (1938–57): 7,942 runs (44.61) including 14 centuries, 55 wickets (45.13), and 93 catches

Test matches (32): 2,159 runs (42.33) including 4 centuries, 13 wickets (39.00), and 20 catches

STOLLMEYER, Victor Humphrey

(b. 1916, Santa Cruz, Trinidad) *Trinidad and West Indies*

A stylish, stroke-making, fast-scoring right-handed batsman, Vic Stollmeyer was troubled by illness on his sole England tour in 1939, but he made 542 runs (30.11). In his only Test, the third at The Oval, he hit his tour-highest, a brilliant 96 in $2\frac{1}{2}$ hours. It was his only innings at the highest level. He was a prolific scorer in intercolonial cricket and is the elder brother of Jeff Stollmeyer.

First-class career (1935–46): 2,096 runs (42.77) including 4 centuries, 15 wickets (40.80), and 16 catches

TARILTON, Percy Hamilton

(b. 1885, St John, Barbados; d. 1953, St Michael, Barbados) *Barbados and West Indies*

'Tim' Tarilton came to prominence as the first batsman to score a triple-century in first-class cricket in the West Indies, 304 not out against Trinidad at the Queen's Park Oval in 1920. He was one half of the most famous opening partnership in West Indies cricket before the Second World War. George Challenor was the other. Both right-handers, they perfectly complemented each other, Tarilton orthodox, patient, and defensive, Challenor dashing and aggressive. They first played together for Barbados in 1906 and were the regular opening pair for 21 years, until the legendary '700' series in Bridgetown in 1927 when Barbados amassed over 700 in successive matches against British Guiana and Trinidad. Scoring centuries each time, they added 183 in the first instance and 292 in the second, then a West Indies first wicket record. He was a disappointment on the West Indies tour of England in 1923, managing just 554 runs at 21.3 with an unbeaten 109 against Nottinghamshire his one major score but refound his form once back home. Although past 40, he hit 178 against MCC in their first representative match against West Indies on their 1926 tour, the highest score against the visitors, continued his heavy scoring the following year in the '700' series and ended his career with an innings of 105 against the touring MCC in 1930, aged 45, sharing an opening stand of 261 with E. L. G. Hoad. Tall and slim, Tarilton also occasionally kept wicket for Barbados.

First-class career (1905–30): 2,777 runs (38.56), 33 catches, and 5 stumpings

TAYLOR, Jaswick

(b. 1932, Trinidad) *Trinidad and West Indies*

A right-arm fast-medium bowler, Jaswick Taylor toured India and Pakistan in 1958/9 but, although he captured 35 wickets (18.31), he appeared in only two Tests. At home, in the previous season, he had made his Test début against Pakistan at Port of Spain in the fifth match when, by dint of pace and persistency, he took 5 for 109 in a total of 496.

First-class career (1953–60): 62 runs (5.63) and 50 wickets (26.22)
Test matches (3): 4 runs (2.00) and 10 wickets (27.30)

THOMAS, Frank Gilbert

(b. 1924, St Michael, Barbados) *Barbados and Windward Islands*

Although born and educated in Barbados, where he was a contemporary of Frank Worrell at Combermere School and for whom he played one match against Trinidad in 1945, Frankie Thomas's major contribution to West Indies cricket was for St Vincent and the Windward Islands as player and administrator. He left Barbados in 1947 to join the St Vincent civil service. A compact right-hand batsman and right-arm medium-pace bowler, he quickly made his mark in St Vincent club cricket and represented the island in the Cork Cup Windward Islands' tournament from 1948 to 1956, in that time also playing in the few first-class matches scheduled for the Windwards, in his last as captain. He served in various capacities on the St Vincent and Windward Islands associations and as a Windwards' delegate to the West Indies board. At West Indies level, he was selector for a time, assistant manager to England in 1976 and manager of the team against Pakistan in 1977. As cabinet secretary, he is credited with convincing the government to establish the playing field at Arnos Vale in 1972 that has become such a well-appointed ground and is now an established venue for one-day internationals. Awarded the OBE in 1980 for public service, Thomas's role in cricket was recognized in 1994 when a new stand at Arnos Vale was named in his honour.

TRESTRAIL, Kenneth Basil

(b. 1927, Port of Spain, Trinidad; d. 1992, Toronto, Canada) *Trinidad and Canada*

From a well-off business family, Kenny Trestrail was one of those gifted individuals capable of excelling at any ball game without much effort and yet failing to fulfil his potential for lack of endeavour. His talent was so obvious that he was chosen for Trinidad, aged 16, in 1944. By the time he was 20, he had already made four first-class centuries in the limited inter-territorial competition. His unbeaten 161 against Jamaica in Port of Spain during which he shared an unbroken second wicket stand of 295 with Jeffrey Stollmeyer was enough to earn him his place in the strong batting team to England in 1950. While eight other batsmen passed 1,000 runs on the tour, Trestrail could manage only 629 at 27.34 and failed to score a century. Within two years, he had emigrated to Canada, living the rest of his life in Toronto, much of it as a dedicated member of the Jehovah Witness church. He played club cricket in Toronto for some time and toured England with the Canadian team in 1954, enjoying a much happier time than with the West Indies four years earlier. He was also an outstanding tennis player who was Trinidad's champion in his teens. 'In Ken Trestrail, there were many, including myself, who felt we had another batsman in the class of the three Ws,' Jeffrey Stollmeyer wrote in his autobiography. A carefree attitude to the game, and life in general, in his youth spoilt his potential.

First-class career (1943–54): 2,183 runs (38.29) including 5 centuries

TRIM, John

(b. 1915, Berbice, British Guiana; d. 1960, Berbice) *British Guiana and West Indies*

A right-arm fast-medium bowler, John Trim toured India in 1948/9 and Australia in 1951/2, and at home played against England in 1947/8, after taking 4 for 68 and 5 for 36 for British Guiana against MCC. On his few Test appearances he was almost invariably inexpensive and penetrative. In the fourth Test at Melbourne in 1951/2 he broke through with the new ball, taking 5 for 34 in the first innings. On the Indian tour he took 37 wickets (22.10), including 7 for 76 in the fourth Test at Madras, bowling throughout with life and pace.

First-class career (1943–53): 386 runs (11.69) and 96 wickets (30.01)
Test matches (4): 21 runs (5.25), 18 wickets (16.16), and 2 catches

VALENTINE, Alfred Lewis

(b. 1930, Kingston, Jamaica) *Jamaica and West Indies*

Alf Valentine was coached in Jamaica by Jack Mercer of Glamorgan, Sussex and Northants, who taught him the value of spin, and he soon became one of the best left-arm slow bowlers since the Second World War. Fairly tall and slim, with sloping shoulders, and always bespectacled, he took a few steps and delivered easily, almost square to the batsman, keeping an immaculate length and giving the ball a sharp finger tweak,

treating his often very sore spinning finger regularly after play with surgical spirit. Prior to touring England in 1950 as the youngest member, he had taken only two wickets at 95 runs each in two first-class matches in the Caribbean, but in a historic partnership with Sonny Ramadhin he enjoyed a triumphant tour, securing 123 wickets (17.94), including 33 wickets (20.42) from 422.3 overs in the four Tests, three times dismissing Len Hutton when he was looking set for a long innings. Ramadhin and Valentine captured 59 wickets between them in the series. After a disappointing start Alf Valentine took 13 for 67 against Lancashire at Old Trafford, followed by 8 for 104 in the first innings of the first Test on that ground and he did not look back—he had seven wickets at Lord's and 10 for 160 (6 for 39 in the second innings) at The Oval. West Indian cricket 'came of age' in 1950 with its first win in England and the names 'Ramadhin and Valentine' were on everyone's lips. He toured England again in 1957 and 1963, Australasia in 1951/2, New Zealand in 1955/6, and Australia in 1960/1, and at home played against India in 1952/3 and 1961/2, England in 1953/4, Australia in 1954/5, and Pakistan in 1957/8. In Australia in 1951/2 he maintained his high skill, securing 24 wickets (28.79) in the Tests—more than anyone else on either side —and 61 wickets (23.83) in all first-class matches. In the third Test at Adelaide he took 6 for 102 in the second innings, West Indies enjoying a comfortable win. Then he had a relatively lean period though he took his 100th wicket in Tests in only 3 years 263 days. In England in 1957 he was plagued by ill health and injury. After three years out of favour he toured Australia in 1960/1 and his bowling was always valuable. On his last tour of England in 1963 Garfield Sobers kept him out of the Test team. He later settled in the USA.

First-class career (1949–65): 470 runs (5.00), 475 wickets (26.20), and 45 catches
Test matches (36): 141 runs (4.70), 139 wickets (30.32), and 13 catches

VALENTINE, Vincent Adolphus

(b. 1908, Buff Bay; d. 1972, Kingston, Jamaica) *Jamaica and West Indies*

A right-arm fast-medium bowler of a congenial disposition, Vincent Valentine made the batsman play every ball, keeping a perfect length, turning the ball both ways, and swinging it astutely. He was also a forcing lower-order batsman and a reliable field. He toured England in 1933 as a substitute for Learie Constantine (who had league commitments), taking 36 wickets (42.80) and making 391 runs (17.00): he played in two of the Tests without distinction.

First-class career (1931–9): 500 runs (17.85), 49 wickets (40.40), and 11 catches

Test matches (2): 35 runs (11.66) and 1–104

WALCOTT, Sir Clyde Leopold

(b. 1926, Bridgetown, Barbados) *Barbados, British Guiana, and West Indies*

With his schoolmate, Frank Worrell, Clyde Walcott added an unbroken 574 for the fourth wicket for Barbados against Trinidad at Port of Spain in 1945/6, which remains the record West Indian stand for any wicket; he was just 20 years of age and his score of 314 not out remained his career-highest. From 1947/8 for a decade, this brilliant and compellingly attractive cricketer was an integral part of the Test team, immortalized as one of 'the Three Ws'—Walcott, Weekes, and Worrell. Standing 6 ft. 2 in. and weighing about 15 stone, Clyde Walcott had a commanding presence, though a crouching stance, and his powerful physique enabled him to drive with tremendous force; right-handed, he had a strong defence, a peerless off-drive, and a dazzling square-cut. He was rarely lost for a stroke. Off either foot he bombarded fielders from mid-on to covers. He served reliably either as a wicket-keeper or first slip and he was a very useful fast-medium change-bowler. He toured India in 1948/9, England in 1950 and 1957, and Australia in 1951/2; and at home played against England in 1947/8, 1953/4 and 1959/60, India in 1952/3, Australia in 1954/5, and Pakistan in 1957/8. Originally, his wicket-keeping kept him in the Test side, but in India in 1948/9 he made 452 runs (64.57) in the Tests and 1,366 runs (75.88), including five centuries, in all first-class matches. On the 1950 England tour he made 1,674 runs (55.80), including seven centuries, the highest being 168 not out in the second Test at Lord's when he put on a record 211 for the sixth wicket with Gerry Gomez. After a lean period against the Australian shock attack of Lindwall and Miller in 1951/2, it was in the West Indies against England in 1953/4 and Australia in 1954/5 that he assumed an unrivalled supremacy. Against England he scored 698 runs (87.25), including three centuries, the highest, 220, being his own Test-highest, scored at Bridgetown in the second match. Against Australia he achieved the then-record West Indian aggregate of 827 runs (82.70), including no fewer than five centuries in three Tests, 126 and 110 in

the second match at Port of Spain and 155 and 110 in the fifth at Kingston; with Everton Weekes he added 242 for the third wicket at Port of Spain, which remains a record. He started the 1957 season in England in fine form, but injured himself in the first Test at Edgbaston when scoring 90, and, though he ended the tour with 1,414 runs (45.61), he seemed like a massive machine not quite functioning as it should. Back in the West Indies, against Pakistan in 1957/8, he returned to his best form, making 385 runs (96.25), including 145 in the fourth Test at Georgetown. At one time in his career he had hit 12 centuries in 12 consecutive Tests. He was a great favourite in the Lancashire League from 1951 until 1954, managed several West Indies touring teams in the 1970s, and was awarded the OBE for his services to cricket. He became a commentator and coach and served the Barbados and West Indies Cricket Board for many years, becoming president of the WICBC before, in 1993, he succeeded Sir Colin Cowdrey as chairman of the International Cricket Council. Clyde Walcott was himself knighted in 1994.

First-class career (1941–63): 11,820 runs (56.55) including 40 centuries, 35 wickets (36.25), and 208 dismissals (175 c., 33 st.)

Test matches (44): 3,798 runs (56.68) including 15 centuries, 11 wickets (37.09), and 64 dismissals (53 c., 11 st.)

WALCOTT, Leslie Arthur

(b. 1894, Barbados; d. 1984, Barbados) *Barbados and West Indies*

A competent all-rounder, right-handed batsman and quickish off-break bowler, Leslie Walcott's sole Test was the first ever played in the Caribbean, against England at Bridgetown in 1929/30, when he scored 24 and 16 not out and took 1 for 32.

First-class career (1925–36): 555 runs (30.83) and 16 wickets (29.50)

WALLACE, Philo Alphonzo

(b. 1970, Barbados) *Barbados*

Philo Wallace, a charismatic 6 ft. tall, right-handed opening batsman, enjoyed a meteoric rise to international status, graduating from club cricket with Spartan and the Hotel Association in Barbados to the senior team and appearances in one-day internationals in little over a year. Powerfully built, with an attacking outlook, he made 135 off 191 balls against the Leewards in 1991, a performance which hastened a trip to Pakistan, aged 21, for three limited-overs matches and a World Series Cup tournament in Australia where he struck 52 in a partnership of 128 in 24 overs with Desmond Haynes against India at Adelaide. His flamboyant style attracted severe criticism, however, highlighting a lack of judgement and shot selection, and his ambition was not helped by a substandard domestic season in 1992. Sir Garfield Sobers advised him during long hours in the nets and he did well in league cricket for Sunderland with over 1,000 runs in 1994, but he struggled to make disciplined big scores. In ten one-day internationals he has scored 214 runs (21.40).

First-class career (1990–): 1,439 runs (32.70) including 1 century, and 13 catches

WALSH, Courtney Andrew

(b. 1962, Kingston, Jamaica) *Jamaica, Gloucestershire, and West Indies*

A cool head and a high action enabled Courtney Walsh to mature early and rise quickly to a place amongst the élite of the finest squad of fast bowlers in world cricket. His remarkable consistency and durability were rewarded later in his career with the captaincy of Jamaica, Gloucestershire, and the West Indies, challenges to which he rose manfully and effectively. He captained West Indies in one match against England in 1993/4 and the following season on tours of India and New Zealand, although only as caretaker for Richie Richardson. Having made his mark on tours of England with the Young West Indies team in 1982 and on the B tour to Zimbabwe in 1983, he bowled well in England in 1984 and even better in Australia the following winter, earning his first Test caps. He took 13 wickets at 33 each in the five Tests and 37 on the tour, more than anyone else. Tall, slim, and with a detached, rather stately air and a ready smile, he also settled quickly in county cricket in England, helping Gloucestershire to climb 14 places in the Championship in his first full season, 1985, when he took 85 first-class wickets. Against England in 1985/6, his lethal bowling for Jamaica in an early match at Sabina Park helped to undermine confidence and in the second Test at Port of Spain, as deputy for Michael Holding, he bowled superbly on a good wicket in the second innings, taking 4 for 74. In England in 1986 he was the best bowler in the country, taking 118 Championship wickets at 18.17, including 9 for 72 against Somerset at

Cheltenham and five or more wickets in an innings on 11 other occasions. His year-long workload continued without interruption into the mid-1990s, by which time he had made four trips to England (1984, 1988, 1991, 1995), four to Australia (1984/5, 1986/7, 1988/9, 1992/3), three to Pakistan, two to New Zealand, one to Sri Lanka, and two to India, the second, in 1994 as captain. The depth of his character and physical stamina were never more evident than on the latter trip when he took 17 Test wickets at 21 in three matches and bowled more overs than anyone. On the eve of the third Test at Chandigarh, with the West Indies one-down after going 27 series without a defeat, he told his men that he had never played in a losing Test series and would 'rather lose 2–0 than go home 1–0 losers'. Walsh took five wickets in the match and West Indies won it by 243 runs. In the next two Tests in New Zealand, Walsh took 16 wickets, including 7 for 37 and 6 for 18 at Wellington where West Indies won by an innings and 322 runs. Although Walsh was much better known for his steadiness, the two and three wickets an innings which showed he had always played a part, he was frequently capable of inspired spells, like the 4 for 31 which pulled the chestnuts from the fire when West Indies seemed certain to lose to South Africa in their first-ever meeting, in Barbados in April 1992, or the devastating burst of hostility against Michael Atherton which turned the Sabina Park Test in 1993/4. His 36 wickets in 1992 are a record for the Shell Shield/ Red Stripe Cup.

First-class career (1982–): 3,682 runs (12.52), 1,230 wickets (22.37), and 77 catches
Test matches (74): 622 runs (8.88), 275 wickets (24.53), and 11 catches

WATSON, Chester Donald

(b. 1939, Jamaica) *Jamaica, Delhi, and West Indies*

A right-arm fast bowler, specially awkward because of his wristy action which made him faster than his run-up suggested, Chester Watson toured Australia in 1960/1 but with poor results. His only full series was against England at home in 1959/60 when he secured 16 wickets (37.06), including 4 for 62 in the second innings of the third match at Kingston.

First-class career (1958–64): 197 runs (7.57) and 85 wickets (32.07)
Test matches (7): 12 runs (2.40), 19 wickets (38.10), and 1 catch

WEEKES, Sir Everton De Courcey

(b. 1925, St Michael, Barbados) *Barbados and West Indies*

Short and thickset with an engaging charm, number two of 'the Three Ws'—Walcott, Weekes, and Worrell—Everton Weekes was immensely quick on his feet and possessed a whole armoury of attacking strokes on both sides of the wicket. For long periods he attacked all bowlers in the same relentless manner as Don Bradman; and he was a brilliant, versatile field. He toured India in 1948/9, England in 1950 and 1957, Australasia in 1951/2, and New Zealand in 1955/6; and at home he played against England in 1947/8 and 1953/4, India in 1952/3, Australia in 1954/5, and Pakistan in 1957/8. His 141 against England in the fourth Test at Kingston in 1947/8 earned him a place to India in 1948/9 where he hit the then-record West Indian aggregate in a series, 779 runs (111.28), including four centuries in succession—128 at New Delhi, 194 at Bombay and 162 and 101 both at Calcutta—and he only missed the fifth when he was run out for 90 at Madras. In England in 1950, when 'the Three Ws' were a tremendous draw, he again headed the batting, with 2,310 runs (79.65) and seven centuries, including 304 not out, his career-highest, against Cambridge at Fenner's, 279, 246 not out, 232 and 200 not out. In the Tests he registered 338 runs (56.33), including 129 at Trent Bridge in the third match. He fell below his own high standards in Australia in 1951/2 and in England in 1957, but otherwise he continued to score heavily. At home, against England in 1953/4, he made 487 runs (69.57), including 206 at Port of Spain in the fourth match when he and Worrell added 338 for the third wicket, a record for any wicket against England. Against India in 1952/3 he was far above anyone else, making 716 runs (102.28), including 207 at Port of Spain in the first match, 161 at Bridgetown in the third and 109 at Kingston in the fifth. Against Pakistan in 1957/8 he contributed 455 runs (65.00), including 197 at Bridgetown in the first match. In New Zealand in 1955/6 he was completely dominant, hitting 940 runs (104.44), including six centuries, in eight first-class matches. In the Tests alone he made 418 runs (83.60), which included 123 at Dunedin in the first match, 103 at Christchurch in the second and 156 at Wellington in the third. He also played in English League cricket, toured with various Commonwealth sides, coached in Barbados and was awarded the MBE and CBE. He made sage comments on the radio on all home

Tests in Barbados and also served as an ICC referee. He was knighted in 1995.

First-class career (1944–64): 12,010 runs (55.34) including 36 centuries, 17 wickets (43.00), 125 catches, and 1 stumping
Test matches (48): 4,455 runs (58.61) including 15 centuries, 1–77, and 49 catches

WEEKES, Kenneth Hunnell

(b. 1912, USA) *Jamaica and West Indies*

A barrel-chested, stylish and fast-scoring, though unorthodox, left-handed batsman, with a good variety of stroke-play all round the wicket, 'Bam Bam' Weekes was also a good reserve wicket-keeper. He toured England in 1939. He made 803 runs (29.74), which included 146 against Surrey, his career-highest, and a buccaneering 137 in $2\frac{1}{4}$ hours against England in the third Test, both at The Oval.

First-class career (1938–48): 1,731 runs (40.26) including 4 centuries, 12 wickets (38.66), and 22 dismissals (21 c., 1 st.)
Test matches (2): 173 runs (57.66) including 1 century

WHITE, Wilbur Anthony

(b. 1938, Brighton, Trinidad) *Barbados and West Indies*

A competent and tenacious all-rounder, Tony White was a robust right-handed hitter, a purveyor of stock medium-pace or off-break bowling and a good field. He joined the team in England in 1963 as a replacement for an injured player but, although he collected 228 runs and 28 wickets from nine matches, he did not appear in a Test on this tour. His sole appearances for West Indies were against Australia in 1964/5; he hit 57 not out in his first at Kingston.

First-class career (1958–66): 996 runs (25.53) and 95 wickets (28.05)
Test matches (2): 71 runs (23.66), 3 wickets (50.66), and 1 catch

WIGHT, Claude Vibart

(b. 1902, Georgetown, British Guiana; d. 1969, Georgetown, Guyana) *British Guiana and West Indies*

A good right-handed batsman, Vibart Wight was appointed vice-captain of the team to England in 1928 although he had never captained a first-class side. He made only 343 runs (20.17) but played in the third Test at The Oval, when he scored 35 in the match for once out. At home he appeared once against England in 1929/30, again reaching double figures in each innings. His overall average in first-class cricket was 30.94. He was the senior member of a well-known British Guiana cricketing family.

First-class career (1925–39): 1,547 runs (30.94) including 3 centuries, 3 wickets (69.66), and 20 catches

Test matches (2): 67 runs (22.33) and 0–6

WIGHT, George Leslie

(b. 1929, Georgetown, British Guiana) *British Guiana and West Indies*

Leslie Wight was a dour, defensive, right-handed batsman whose sole Test appearance was against India in the fourth Test at Georgetown in 1952/3 when he scored a very slow 21 in his only innings. Against Barbados at Georgetown in 1951/2 he amassed 262 not out, putting on 390 for the first wicket with G. Gibbs, which remains the record in the West Indies. He is brother of H. A., P. B., and Norman Wight, all of British Guiana. P. B. (Peter) became a well-known umpire. (After playing for Somerset from 1953 to 1965, he was on the first-class list from 1966 to 1995.)

First-class career (1949–53): 1,260 runs (66.31) including 4 centuries

WILES, Charles Archibald

(b. 1892, Bridgetown, Barbados; d. 1957, Diego Martin, Trinidad) *Barbados, Trinidad, and West Indies*

A sound, stylish, defensive right-handed batsman, Archie Wiles had some good performances against MCC in 1925/6 and helped Trinidad to win the Intercolonial Tournament in 1931/2. Touring England in 1933, however, he was disappointing. He was aged 40 years 346 days when, at Old Trafford in his sole Test appearance, he scored 0 and 2. His overall overage in first-class cricket was 27.16.

First-class career (1919–36): 1,766 runs (27.57) including 2 centuries

WILKIN, Calvin Lucien Addison

(b. 1924, Basseterre, St Kitts) *Leeward Islands and Leewards and Windwards Combined*

Calvin Wilkin, who captained St Kitts in the annual Leeward Islands' tournament for the Hesketh Bell Shield from 1963 to 1960 and who led the Leewards against the touring Pakistanis in 1958, was the first Leeward Islander on the West

Indies selection panel between 1979 and 1981. His leadership qualities were evident off the field as he was president of the St Kitts Cricket Association and the Leeward Islands Cricket Association between 1947 and 1978 and assistant manager of the West Indies team to England in 1988. His son Charles, a left-arm spinner, won a blue at Cambridge and took 16 wickets in the 1977 Leewards Islands tournament.

First-class career (1969–77): 302 runs (15.10), 30 wickets (48.00), and 4 catches

WILLETT, Elquemedo Tonito

(b. 1953, Charlestown, Nevis) *Leeward Islands and West Indies*

A steady, slow left-arm orthodox spin bowler, Willett toured England in 1973 and, although taking 30 wickets (23.13), did not make the Test XI. At home he appeared against Australia in 1972/3 at the age of only 19 and toured India and Pakistan in 1974/5 with some success. Coming from the tiny island of Nevis (36 square miles, population about 15,000), Willett was the first Leeward Islander to represent the West Indies, and his success was a much-needed inspiration to many others from the smaller West Indian Islands. His nephew, Stuart Williams, became the fourth player from Nevis to win a Test cap.

First-class career (1970–89): 1,100 runs (12.94), 286 wickets (28.43), and 66 catches

Test matches (5): 74 runs (14.80) and 11 wickets (43.81)

WILLIAMS, Alvadon Basil

(b. 1949, Kingston, Jamaica) *Jamaica and West Indies*

An attractive right-handed opening batsman with plenty of strokes, Basil Williams had an outstanding season in 1977/8, making 399 runs in the Shell Shield for Jamaica at an average of 79.80. He had his reward with a place in the Test side earlier than he might have hoped, when the World Series Cricket players were dropped before the third Test against Australia at Georgetown. He showed both his ability and his temperament by hitting a century in the second innings of his first Test and in three matches made 257 runs (42.83). In India in 1978/9 he scored 212 runs (35.33), including 111 in the third Test at Calcutta.

First-class career (1969–): 2,702 runs (36.00) including 4 centuries, and 19 catches

Test matches (7): 469 runs (39.08) including 2 centuries, and 5 catches

WILLIAMS, Cecil Beaumont

(b. 1926, St Michael, Barbados) *Barbados*

Known from his days at Harrison College as 'Boogles', Williams was a fine all-round sportsman who represented Barbados at both cricket and soccer. As a schoolboy, he was founder of the Carlton Club, of which he has been president since 1990, and has served on the Barbados Cricket Association board of management. An accredited diplomat, he was Barbados High Commissioner in London and Ottawa and Ambassador in Washington. A solid right-hand batsman especially strong off the back foot and a wrist spinner who specialized in googlies and top-spinners, Williams was a regular member of the Barbados team from 1947 to 1956, except for three years between 1950 and 1953 when he was studying at Durham University in England. His all-round performances in regional cricket merited his selection for the 1950 tour of England but the team's powerful batting and the presence of the spin pair, Sonny Ramadhin and Alf Valentine, limited his chances in both departments. His bowling in the MCC second innings at Lord's when he took 7 for 55 from 32.1 overs was the highlight of his trip and his best figures in first-class cricket but he could only score 152 runs in 18 first-class innings and was not called on in the Tests. Appointed Barbados captain for two matches against E. W. Swanton's team of English players in 1956, Williams hit his highest score, 133, against an attack spearheaded by Frank Tyson in what was his last year in first-class cricket. Among his six brothers, all of whom were also sportsmen, the eldest, Denys, is Chief Justice of Barbados. After retiring from the diplomatic service, 'Boogles' Williams joined one of Barbados' largest companies in an executive position.

First-class career (1947–57): 987 runs (29.02) including 2 centuries, and 75 wickets (29.10)

WILLIAMS, David

(b. 1963, Trinidad) *Trinidad and West Indies*

A diminutive wicket-keeper and right-hand batsman, David Williams waited in the wings for an inordinate length of time while Jeffrey Dujon held centre stage in the Test match arena and then, when his understudy role was apparently over, discovered that his batting was not of sufficient quality for a number seven and was superseded by Junior Murray. Nevertheless, he was probably the most accomplished all-round wicket-keeper in the Caribbean after his first-class début in 1983, standing up to an array of high-class Trinidadian spinners. A perennial tourist, Williams came to England with the West Indies Young Cricketers in 1982, went to Zimbabwe twice in 1986 and 1989 with the B team, and made senior trips to India (1987/8), England (1988 and 1991), Australia (1988/9 and 1992/3), Pakistan (1990), and Australia and New Zealand for the World Cup in 1992. Dapper and cheerful despite his relative lack of involvement, he eventually made his Test début, alongside Kenneth Benjamin and Jimmy Adams, in the historic South Africa match in Barbados in 1992, dropping a catch but snaring five other victims. He held 12 catches in the first Test of the tour to Australia in 1992/3, but then lost his place to Murray after a pair at Melbourne in the second Test. In 29 one-day internationals he scored 119 runs (10.82), held 33 catches, and made eight stumpings.

First-class career (1983–): 1,764 runs (16.18) and 212 dismissals (181 c., 31 st.)
Test matches (3): 21 runs (3.50) and 16 dismissals (15 c., 1 st.)

WILLIAMS, Ernest Albert Vivian

(b. 1914, Bridgetown, Barbados) *Barbados and West Indies*

'Foffie' Williams was a very sound, hard-hitting right-handed batsman with a specially powerful drive, a fast-medium bowler who attacked the stumps at all times and could bowl at speed for long periods, and a fine, athletic field. His career was seriously impeded by the Second World War. He hit 131 not out against Trinidad at Bridgetown in 1935/6, adding 255 for the eighth wicket with 'Manny' Martindale, which remains a West Indian record, and toured England in 1939, playing in one Test. In the first Test after the War, against England at Bridgetown in 1947/8, he scored 72—opening his scoring with 6, 6, 4 and 4 off the first four balls from Jim Laker and 4 and 4 off the next balls from Jack Ikin, a unique opening to an innings in Test cricket. When he bowled, his first spell was 11–8–3–1 and he finished with 3 for 51 off 33 overs. He had only joined the team for this match because Frank Worrell was down with food poisoning.

First-class career (1934–49): 1,479 runs (26.69) including 2 centuries, 116 wickets (29.20), and 19 catches
Test matches (4): 113 runs (18.83), 9 wickets (26.77), and 2 catches

WILLIAMS, Stuart Clayton

(b. 1968, Nevis) *Leeward Islands and West Indies*

A stylish right-handed opening batsman with a swaggering swivel-hipped hook shot, Stuart Williams is only the fourth Nevisian to play Test cricket after Elquemedo Willett (his uncle), Derick Parry, and Keith Arthurton. He owed his selection for the final Test against England in April 1994 at Antigua (Lara's record-breaking game) to a series of high-class performances after his first-class début in 1989 and injuries to Desmond Haynes and Richie Richardson. Williams made a maiden first-class century against the Windwards at St John's in 1990, but his development was hampered when Ottis Gibson shattered his left forearm at Kensington in 1992. In 1994, however, he was back to his authoritative best, making 157 and 60 against Barbados then taking another high-quality century off the Windwards, outstanding performances which prefaced his late appearance in the fifth Test at St Johns where his preference for the hook undermined him early in his only innings. Further opportunities came his way on tours of India, New Zealand, and England in 1994/5. In ten one-day internationals to the end of the 1994 tour of India he had scored 302 runs (30.20).

First-class career (1989–): 1,956 runs (33.72) including 4 centuries, and 21 catches
Test matches (10): 294 runs (19.60) and 9 catches

WISHART, Kenneth Leslie

(b. 1908, British Guiana; d. 1972, Georgetown, Guyana) *British Guiana and West Indies*

A careful left-handed opening batsman, Ken Wishart scored 88 and 77 in successive games for British Guiana against MCC at Georgetown in 1929/30 against heavy odds each time, but did not represent West Indies until the third Test at Georgetown against England in 1934/5 when he made a dogged 52 (followed by 0 in the second innings), and he was not tried again. He was British Guiana's (later Guyana's) representative on the West Indies Board of Control from 1949 to 1971.

First-class career (1928–47): 706 runs (23.53)

WORRELL, Sir Frank Mortimore Maglinne

(b. 1924, Bridgetown, Barbados; d. 1967, Kingston, Jamaica) *Barbados, Jamaica, and West Indies*

Three years before he died of leukaemia Frank Worrell was knighted for his services to cricket. He was a great cricketer, a great captain, an exemplary ambassador for West Indies cricket, and a man of strong convictions. Had he lived he would surely have become a statesman in world affairs. His captaining and his cricket always conveyed a monumental calm, even at the height of a crisis, and, as captain, he was involved in two of the most breathtaking finishes in Test history—at Brisbane in 1961 and Lord's in 1963. He first played for Barbados in 1941/2 at 18 as a slow left-arm bowler. The following season, as nightwatchman, he carried his bat for 64 and was soon opening the innings. In the same month he scored 188 (in five hours) and 68 against Trinidad at Port of Spain. At 19 in 1943/4, he amassed 308 not out, his career-highest, against Trinidad at Bridgetown, adding 502 for the fourth wicket with John Goddard in just under $6\frac{1}{2}$ hours without being separated. This world record for the fourth wicket was broken again by Worrell with 255 not out when he put on 574, again unbroken in less than 6 hours, this time with Clyde Walcott against Trinidad at Port of Spain in 1945/6; it remains the West Indian record for any wicket. Modestly, he dismissed both achievements: 'The conditions were loaded in our favour. I wasn't all that delighted about it.' Modelling himself on the youngest-ever West Indian Test cricketer, Derek Sealy, a master at his school, Frank Worrell was slim, lithely built, elegant, and stylish. A right-handed batsman, he commanded every orthodox stroke, was perfectly balanced, and possessed quick judgement and footwork. His timing was exquisite and he would sometimes embark upon an onslaught at once furious and yet graceful. As a left-arm bowler, he could be either a spinner or, more often, a fast-medium swing bowler with an easy, relaxed action. He was accomplished at cover or in the close catching positions. He toured England in 1950, 1957, and 1963. Australasia in 1951/2, and Australia in 1960/1; and at home he played against England in 1947/8, 1953/4, and 1959/60, India in 1952/3 and 1961/2, and Australia in 1954. He captained the West Indies in 15 Tests between 1960 and 1963, on his third tour of England and second of Australia and at home in his second series against India. Altogether nine of these matches were won. He was a quietly authoritative and yet dynamic leader who earned the respect of all with whom he played. In 1947/8 he scored 97 against England on his Test début at Port of Spain and in his next at Georgetown, 131 not out; thanks partly to notouts he averaged the record 147 in this series. In 1950 when 'the Three Ws' legend was born, he was above everyone else in the Tests, making 539 runs (89.93), including his scintillating Test-highest of 261 in 5 hours 35 minutes at Trent Bridge in the third match, sharing in seven records, including the partnership of 283 for the fourth wicket with Weekes. On the whole tour he took 39 wickets and made 1,775 runs (68.26) which included six centuries and a record stand of 350 for the third wicket with Weekes against Cambridge University at Fenner's. In the Tests against Australia in 1951/2 he was the heaviest scorer with 337 Test runs (33.70), including 108 in the fourth match at Melbourne, and in the two Tests against New Zealand, he made 71, 62 not out and 100 (at Auckland). He captured 19 wickets (21.57) in the Australian Tests, including 6 for 38 in the first innings of the third match at Adelaide, when he bowled throughout and Australia collapsed for 82. Against India in 1952/3 he had one great innings of 237 in the fifth match at Kingston, adding 197 and 213 respectively with Weekes and Walcott. After several years of inconsistency he returned to his best form in England in 1957, heading the batting in all first-class matches with 1,470 runs (58.80), including four centuries, and taking 39 wickets (24.33); in the Tests he registered 350 runs (38.88), including a masterly 191 not out in the third match at Trent Bridge, carrying his bat through the innings of 372. At Headingley in the fourth match he captured 7 for 70 in England's sole innings. At his best on an uncertain pitch at Lord's against Middlesex, he hit 66 not out in a total of 176 and 61 in a total of 143 for 8—besides taking 5 for 34 in the first innings. Against England at Bridgetown in the first Test of 1959/60 he scored 197 not out in 11 hours 29 minutes and, with Gary Sobers, added 399 for the fourth wicket. His immortal fame as a captain dates from the tour of Australia in 1960/1 when the popular West Indies side helped to revive flagging interest in the game in Australia. In the classic tie at Brisbane, the first Test, Worrell encouraged an attacking approach and himself made two hard-hit scores of 65 in the match. He led West Indies to a 5–0 victory over India in 1961/2 (only three times had this decisive margin been achieved in Test history) and headed the averages with 332 runs (88.00), making 98 not out in the fifth Test at Kingston, batting at number six which was now his usual position. In England in 1963, although he was seldom truly fit, he continued as a remarkably effective captain, West Indies winning the rubber 3–1. He retired from regular first-class cricket at the end of this tour, and was knighted the following year. Sir Frank Worrell had been a professional in the Lancashire League; studied sociology at Manchester University; been appointed Warden of the University College of the West Indies; and elected a senator in the Jamaican Parliament. When he died in 1967, a memorial service was held in Westminster Abbey. Twenty-seven years after his death a series of Frank Worrell Memorial Lectures were begun at the University of the West Indies 'to perpetuate his memory and influence'. The first two lectures were given by Michael Manley and Richie Benaud in 1994 and 1995.

First-class career (1941–64): 15,025 runs (54.24) including 39 centuries, 349 wickets (28.98), and 139 catches

Test matches (51): 3,860 runs (49.48) including 9 centuries, 69 wickets (38.73), and 43 catches

Zimbabwe

ARNOTT, Donald Brian

(b. 1936, Bulawayo) *Rhodesia*

Don Arnott has made an immense contribution to Rhodesia/Zimbabwe cricket both as player and administrator. He was first and foremost a wicket-keeper, who at his best was close to selection for South Africa. Indeed, he was summoned to Durban for the Test match against England in 1956/7 as cover for John Waite, who was a doubtful starter through injury. Had he not decided to retire to concentrate on farming, he would probably have followed Waite into the South African team. He also turned himself into a useful right-handed batsman. He learnt his cricket at Plumtree School, played for the South Africa Schools XI and first represented Rhodesia while still at school. Thereafter he played for Salisbury (Harare) Sports Club and for Mashonaland Country Districts. A tobacco farmer at Guruve until 1993, he was also a stalwart member of the Horseshoe club for whom he played winter cricket. He took up umpiring after his retirement from first-class cricket, and is thought by many to have been Rhodesia/Zimbabwe's finest, before he turned to administration in the early 1980s, managing Zimbabwe's successful ICC Trophy quest in 1986 and their World Cup party in 1987. After chairing the Zimbabwe Cricket Union Coaching Committee from 1987 to 1990, he was appointed the ZCU's first chief executive officer in 1994. His son, Kevin, played in Zimbabwe's first Test match.

ARNOTT, Kevin John

(b. 1961, Salisbury (Harare)) *Mashonaland Country Districts and Zimbabwe*

The second Zimbabwean to score a Test hundred, Kevin Arnott has a fine cricketing pedigree. His father, Don, was a wicket-keeper for Rhodesia in the 1950s and 1960s before turning to umpiring and subsequently becoming a leading administrator. Educated at Prince Edward School, where Graeme Hick was his fag in his last year, and Cape Town University, where he read Law, he played most of his senior cricket for Old Hararians. In recent years he has represented Mashonaland Country Districts. A technically correct right-hand batsman and brilliant fielder in the cover/mid-wicket region, Arnott made his first-class début in 1979/80. He played for Zimbabwe in the World Cups of 1987 and 1992 with a top score of 60 against India at Ahmedabad in 1987. Although capable of playing an attacking innings when well set, he is essentially an accumulator of runs with a style more suited to the three- or five-day match. Throughout his career he has been plagued with brittle fingers and many of his innings have been played in considerable pain. Arnott was selected for Zimbabwe's inaugural Test against India in 1992/3 with just one first-class hundred behind him (121 against Pakistan B in 1990) and was an immediate success. Scores of 40 and 32 at Harare were followed in the Bulawayo Test against New Zealand by 30 and then 101 not out to save the game. Business commitments (he is a lawyer) curtailed his future Test career, but Zimbabwe could ill afford to lose the adhesive qualities of this excellent team man.

First-class career (1979–): 1,592 runs (31.21) including 3 centuries, and 19 catches
Test matches (4): 302 runs (43.14) including 1 century, and 4 catches

BRAIN, David Hayden

(b. 1964, Salisbury (Harare)) *Mashonaland and Zimbabwe*

A tall, lanky, blond, left-arm medium-pace bowler and useful right-hand lower-order batsman, David Brain came late into Zimbabwe's national side. For some years he had played second fiddle to Malcolm Jarvis in the Harare Sports Club side. When Jarvis failed to make the most of his opportunities in Zimbabwe's first two Test matches, Brain was called up to replace him for the second Test against New Zealand at Harare in 1992/3. Four wickets in that Test were sufficient to book him trips for Zimbabwe's first overseas Test in India in 1992/3 and in 1993/4 to the Bengal Jubilee tournament and the Test tour of Pakistan. He returned figures of 4 for 41 in Pakistan's first innings of the second Test at Rawalpindi and then bettered that with 5 for 42 in Pakistan's first innings in the third Test at Lahore.

First-class career (1986–): 318 runs (17.66), 42 wickets (29.16), and 5 catches
Test matches (4): 74 runs (10.57) and 18 wickets (23.94)

BRANDES, Eddo Andre

(b. 1963, Port Shepstone, Natal, South Africa) *Zimbabwe*

A burly, barrel-chested, straight-backed, right-arm fast-medium bowler, on his day Eddo Brandes was capable of unsettling the very best batsmen. He learnt his cricket at Prince Edward School and subsequently Alexandra Sports Club, Harare, and made his first-class début against the visiting New South Wales side in 1985/6. A gifted all-round sportsman, who can hit a golf ball prodigious distances, he never quite realized his full potential as a cricketer. For some time a key member of the Zimbabwe side, being the spearhead of the attack as well as a hard-hitting right-hand lower-order batsman, he sometimes had difficulty living up to his advance billing. Brandes has suffered more than his fair share of injuries, some of which he

seemed to allow to get the better of him. But on a hard or helpful pitch, with the inspiration of an early wicket under his belt, he could be a real proposition, generating pace off a short run and disconcerting batsmen by getting lift from good length deliveries, as England discovered in the World Cup at Albury in 1992—his 4 for 21 in that game being largely responsible for Zimbabwe's victory. With 14 wickets Brandes was the fifth leading wicket-taker in the tournament. He broke down in Zimbabwe's inaugural Test match against India in 1992/3, bowling just two overs. However, although yet to encounter a wicket to suit him, he seemed to be coming to terms with Test cricket by the time of the three-Test series in Pakistan in 1993/4, for which he was appointed vice-captain to Andy Flower. His best Test figures to that date were 3 for 45 in Pakistan's first innings in the third Test in Lahore. In 23 one-day internationals to 1991 he had scored 177 runs (13.64) and taken 28 wickets (35.21)

First-class career (1985–): 540 runs (11.02), 104 wickets (34.25), and 21 catches
Test matches (6): 60 runs (6.66), 17 wickets (35.17), and 3 catches

BRIANT, Gavin

(b. 1969, Salisbury (Harare)) *Zimbabwe*

At his best a fine stroke-player and outstanding cover fielder, Gavin Briant's early internationals for Zimbabwe suggested that he might be just short of the requisite class to make the grade in Test cricket. A product of Eaglesvale High School, followed by Old Hararians, he later moved on to join the Flower brothers at Old Georgians. Briant first came to prominence when putting together an excellent 103 not out to secure a draw for Zimbabwe B against England A in the last match of the latter's 1989/90 tour. After helping Zimbabwe win the ICC Trophy in 1990 he lost form in 1990/1 but had a productive domestic season in 1991/2. However, he narrowly missed selection for the World Cup party in 1992 and had to wait until Zimbabwe's first overseas Test, against India in New Delhi in 1992/3, to win his only Test cap to date on his début in first-class cricket. Innings of 1 and 16 appeared to confirm a reputed frailty against spin. In five one-day internationals to 1994 he had scored 33 runs (11.00).

First-class career (1990–3): 262 runs (23.81) and 7 catches

BROWN, Robin David

(b. 1951, Gatooma (Kadoma)) Rhodesia/Zimbabwe

A classic right-handed batsman capable of cultured flowing shots, Robin Brown's first-class record did not do justice to his talents. Making his début in 1976, he scored four centuries for Rhodesia/Zimbabwe, the most notable perhaps being 102 against Young West Indies at Bulawayo in 1981/2, when he was the Zimbabwe captain. Educated at Umtali (Mutare) Boys High School, he played most of his cricket for Old Georgians and Mashonaland Country Districts as well as playing for his local side Karoi when his duties as a tobacco farmer permitted. He played seven matches for Zimbabwe in the World Cups of 1983 and 1987, with a highest score of 36 against Australia at Southampton in 1983. Brown at his most fluent played a finely crafted innings of 65 to help a Zimbabwe Country Districts XI defeat an England A side containing an all-Test player attack at Harare South in 1989/90. He was also a useful wicket-keeper.

First-class career (1976–90): 2,597 runs (23.60) including 4 centuries

BRUK-JACKSON, Glen Keith

(b. 1969, Salisbury (Harare)) Mashonaland Country Districts and Zimbabwe

A determined right-hand batsman, Glen Bruk-Jackson was a surprise choice for Zimbabwe's three-Test tour of Pakistan in 1993/4. A product of Falcon College, Bulawayo, he played his club cricket for Alexandra Sports Club before moving to Harare Sports Club in 1993/4. Appearances for Young Zimbabwe and Zimbabwe B against visiting sides in the early 1990s did not suggest that a Test career was around the corner. However, good form in the 1993/4 domestic season earned him selection to Pakistan. He played in the first two Test matches at Karachi and Rawalpindi with a top score of 31 and then in the third one-day international at Lahore.

First-class career (1987–): 593 runs (28.23) including 1 century, and 3 catches
Test matches (2): 39 runs (9.75)

BURMESTER, Mark Greville

(b. 1968, Durban, South Africa) Mashonaland and Zimbabwe

Mark Burmester learnt his cricket at Eaglesvale High School, Harare before joining the Old Georgians Club. Slimly built with fair hair, he is principally a right-arm medium-pace bowler, although at club level his right-hand batting is often put to use opening the innings. Although some way short of Test match class he is a wholesome and enthusiastic cricketer, who is useful anywhere in the field. These qualities earned him selection for the Zimbabwe World Cup party in 1992. He played in four matches with best figures of 3 for 36 against New Zealand at Hamilton. In 1992/3 he was selected for Zimbabwe's inaugural Test against India at Harare and became the first Zimbabwean bowler to take a wicket in Test cricket when he dismissed Ravi Shastri for 11. His 3 wickets for 78 in India's one innings represent his only successes in Test cricket to date. He played in the subsequent two Tests against New Zealand.

First-class career (1990–): 244 runs (22.18), 6 wickets (66.50), and 5 catches
Test matches (3): 54 runs (27.00), 3 wickets (75.66), and 1 catch

BUTCHART, Iain Peter

(b. 1960, Bulawayo) Zimbabwe

Iain Butchart was particularly deserving of a belated Test cap, because he had been at the heart of Zimbabwe's cricket in the years leading up to his country's elevation, playing 18 one-day internationals and a full part both in the World Cups of the 1980s and Zimbabwe's ICC Trophy successes. Tall and upright in bearing, he was principally a right-arm fast-medium bowler. However, he was no mean performer with the bat (right-handed), capable of playing quickly compiled attacking innings. Plumtree School led on to cricket for Matabeleland, followed by stints with Harare Sports Club and Mashonaland Country Districts. Butchart made his first-class début in 1980/1 and represented Zimbabwe in the World Cups of 1983, 1987, and 1992. Against India at Hyderabad in the 1987 World Cup, he and David Houghton put on 117 for the eighth wicket. His Test chance came 8 years later, against Pakistan in Harare. In his sole game to 1995, he scored 23 runs (11.50), took 0 for 11, and held a catch.

First-class career (1980–): 1,292 runs (20.18), 66 wickets (32.66), and 42 catches

CAMPBELL, Alistair Douglas Ross

(b. 1972, Salisbury (Harare)) Mashonaland Country Districts and Zimbabwe

Alistair Campbell's début for Zimbabwe in the 1990/1 season, when still a schoolboy, could not have been better timed. Not only was Zimbabwe's bid for Test status fast becoming a serious proposition, but also one or two of the senior established batsmen were approaching the end of their careers. Little more than a cursory glance at his batting would inform the educated onlooker that he was witnessing a class act. A left-hander in the mould of Gower and Pollock, with all the time in the world to play his shots, when in form he is nothing less than sheer delight to watch. As a purveyor of occasional right-arm off-breaks there are even pretensions, not yet realized, to all-rounder status. His father, Iain, at the time Headmaster of Lilfordia Prep School and an experienced coach to countless schoolboys, set him on his way. Eaglesvale High School helped to fine-tune the talent. His maiden first-class century came that first season at the early age of 18 against the visiting Glamorgan side in Bulawayo. For a time he flattered only to deceive: a few sweetly timed shots, before perishing to an unworthy waft, became something of a pattern. Some thought his temperament suspect. In a Zimbabwean side upholding a national reputation for superb fielding he looked sluggish and out of condition. Poor form against the visiting Australia B in 1991/2 seemed to bear out the critics. But hefty scores for his club, Old Hararians, just before the team was selected, earned him a trip to the 1992 World Cup. However, he made no impression in that tournament, batting largely down the order. Test cricket though might have been made for him. Leaner and fitter, he was restored to his preferred position at number three for Zimbabwe's inaugural Test match at Harare in 1992/3 and made an assured 45 in their first innings of 456. From this moment a greater maturity was to be observed in his approach to batting although, Gower-like, he still seemed able to keep the scoreboard ticking over at a faster rate than lesser players. By the end of Zimbabwe's three-Test tour of Pakistan in 1993/4 he had scored five fifties in seven Test matches, the best of them a scintillating 75 in the second innings at Rawalpindi, when he and Mark Dekker with their second century-partnership of the match threatened to carry Zimbabwe to victory until Waqar Younis and Wasim Akram had other ideas. He has played professional league cricket in England.

First-class career (1990–): 1,349 runs (36.45) including 2 centuries, 3 wickets (54.66), and 16 catches

Test matches (13): 732 runs (36.60) and 9 catches

CARLISLE, Stuart Vance

(b. 1972, Salisbury (Harare)) *Mashonaland Under-24 and Zimbabwe*

A specialist right-handed opener, Stuart Carlisle rather bizarrely did not bat when he made his first Test appearance against Pakistan in January 1995. Due to go in at number seven, he sat and watched for hours as the fifth wicket pair added 233 and Zimbabwe won by an innings, a match result later overshadowed by accusations that some Pakistan players had been bribed to lose. Carlisle made up for lost time by scoring 46 from 74 balls in his second match, again batting at number seven. This convinced the selectors to allow him to open in his third Test.

First-class career (1993–): 385 runs (38.50) including 1 century, and 6 catches

Test matches (3): 78 runs (26.00) and 5 catches

CHINGOKA, Peter Farai

(b. 1954, Salisbury (Harare))

It fell to Peter Chingoka to assume the mantle of President of the Zimbabwe Cricket Union in 1992 just as Zimbabwe had been granted Test match status. His was a popular and timely appointment. He was one of the very few black Zimbabweans with a background both as a competent player and as an administrator. He learnt his cricket at both Chishawasha Mission School and St George's College, following which he represented the Universals club. A right-arm medium-pace bowler and lower-order right-handed batsman, he captained the South African XI in 1974/5 against the visiting Derek Robins's XI and in provincial Gillette Cup matches. In more recent years he has been a regular member of the XX Club side in the Saturday League in Harare. Appointed to the ZCU Board in 1982, he became convenor of domestic cricket in 1989 and vice-president of the ZCU the following year.

CROCKER, Gary John

(b. 1962, Bulawayo) *Mashonaland Country Districts and Zimbabwe*

Gary Crocker was a last-minute surprise inclusion in Zimbabwe's XI for their first Test match, against India in Harare in 1992/3, when Ali Shah withdrew with a groin strain. He competed well with both bat and ball. A left-hander in both departments, he learnt his cricket at Hamilton High School and later with the Old Miltonians (Bulawayo) and Matabeleland before moving to

Alexandra Sports Club in 1993/4. Bowling is his stronger suit, although his medium pace seems likely to prove somewhat short of the requisite standard for Test cricket. After playing in Zimbabwe's first three Tests, he was omitted for the away Test in India in 1992/3 and the tour of Pakistan in 1993/4.

First-class career (1993–): 83 runs (27.66) and 8 wickets (20.12)
Test matches (3): 69 runs (23.00) and 3 wickets (72.33)

CURRAN, Kevin Malcolm

(b. 1959, Rusape) *Zimbabwe, Gloucestershire, Natal, and Northamptonshire*

A talented all-round cricketer, Kevin Curran is the son of K. P. Curran, who played for Rhodesia. The major part of his career has been played out in English County Cricket. Indeed, by 1994 he had become an England-qualified player. A right-handed middle-order batsman and wiry right-arm fast-medium bowler, he learnt his cricket at Marondellas (Marondera) Boys High School and subsequently played for Harare Sports Club. Curran first played for Zimbabwe in 1980 and represented them in the World Cups of 1983 and 1987, as well as on two tours to Sri Lanka and one to England in the early 1980s. His most successful World Cup appearance was against India at Tunbridge Wells in 1983 (the match in which Kapil Dev rescued India with 175) when he took 3 for 65, followed by an innings of 73 as Zimbabwe fell just short of India's total of 266. His relationship with both fellow players and administrators could be awkward. However, he was a highly effective performer for Gloucestershire from 1985 to 1990 and for Northants from 1991, regularly appearing high up in both the batting and bowling averages. He acquired an English qualification by 10 years of residence, but despite the precedent of Graeme Hick, the selectors were not tempted. He would, otherwise, have been an obvious choice for Zimbabwe's early Tests.

First-class career (1980–): 11,026 runs (36.03) including 19 centuries, 507 wickets (26.32), and 131 catches

DAVISON, Brian Fettes

(b. 1946, Bulawayo) *Rhodesia, Leicestershire, and Tasmania*

An aggressive, fast-scoring right-handed batsman, Brian Davison had successful careers in England,

Rhodesia, and Australia. After school at Gifford Technical High School, Bulawayo during which time he represented the Rhodesian Nuffield XI, he was selected for Rhodesia in 1967/8. He started in England with Northants but was spotted by Leicestershire whom he joined in 1969 and played for from 1970 to 1983. Only rarely did he reproduce the form for Rhodesia that he showed habitually in England where he averaged comfortably over 40 and scored 1,000 runs in a season 13 times. One occasion, and probably his finest hour, was in the final of the 1977/8 Datsun Shield against Eastern Province at Johannesburg when he guided Rhodesia to its first major South African trophy with a superb undefeated innings of 102. Scorer of 53 first-class centuries in his career, the most by a Rhodesian-born cricketer until Graeme Hick overtook him in 1990, he was also an occasional right-arm medium-pace bowler, an outstanding all-round fielder, and captained Rhodesia on 25 occasions between 1974 and 1977. In addition he represented Rhodesia at hockey. In his later years he accepted contracts to play for Tasmania, in which island he eventually settled and became an MP.

First-class career (1967–88): 27,453 runs (39.96) including 53 centuries, 82 wickets (32.78), and 338 catches

DEKKER, Mark Hamilton

(b. 1969, Gatooma (Kadoma)) *Matabeleland and Zimbabwe*

After a début for Zimbabwe in one-day internationals in 1992/3, Mark Dekker shot to prominence with two gritty performances in the second Test against Pakistan in Rawalpindi in 1993/4. He was involved in century partnerships in each innings with Alistair Campbell, in the second being left stranded on 68 not out when Zimbabwe, chasing 240 to win, crashed from 135 for 1 to 187 all out. He thus achieved the rare feat of carrying his bat through a complete Test innings in only his second Test match. A sound left-hand top-order batsman and occasional left-arm orthodox spinner, he opened the innings in his first three Test matches. Fast running between the wickets has always been a feature of his batting and he is a top-class cover fielder. He learnt his cricket at Christian Brothers College, Bulawayo, and now represents Matabeleland in Zimbabwe's Rothman's National League and Logan Cup. In 12 internationals to 1994 he had scored 250 runs (22.72) and taken 3 wickets at 22.

DUERS

First-class career (1990–): 349 runs (21.81), 6 wickets (66.83), and 12 catches
Test matches (8): 208 runs (20.80) and 10 catches

DUERS, Kevin Gary

(b. 1960, Lusaka, Zambia) *Mashonaland and Zimbabwe*

A product of Ellis Robins School, Kevin Duers, known to his colleagues as 'Swampy', played his domestic cricket initially for Matabeleland and subsequently for Alexandra Sports Club. He first made a name for himself during his début season in 1984/5, when he burst on to the Zimbabwe cricket scene with a stack of wickets against a strong Young New Zealand side, including 8 for 102 in the visitors' first innings of the fourth three-day match at Harare. A series of injuries subsequently hampered his further development and it was not until 1989/90 that he regained a regular place in the Zimbabwe side when the then captain, Peter Rawson, departed for Natal. A blond, athletically built, right-arm fast-medium bowler of rather more than 6 ft. he invariably bowled a good line. He was also capable of achieving regular movement away from the bat. A right-handed batsman, he did not, generally speaking, often trouble the scorers. After missing selection for the 1987 World Cup, Duers gained a late call-up for the 1992 event, to replace the injured Grant Flower. He played in six matches, taking three wickets, returning best figures against South Africa when he conceded only 19 runs from 8 overs.

First-class career (1984–): 116 runs (8.28), 77 wickets (32.36), and 10 catches

ELLMAN-BROWN, David Alan

(b. 1938, Bulawayo)

Without David Ellman-Brown's driving enthusiasm it is doubtful whether Zimbabwe's application for Test match status would have succeeded. When he was elevated from vice-president to president of the Zimbabwe Cricket Union in 1990, Zimbabwe's application was on the agenda of the ICC but was not reckoned by many judges to be likely to succeed. By dint of sheer hard work and persistent lobbying of the full-member countries he managed to turn the climate to Zimbabwe's advantage to such an extent that at the crucial ICC meeting in July 1992 the only country still opposed to Zimbabwe's application was England. An accountant by profession, his qualifications were well used, for he became Treasurer both of the ZCU and of the Mashonaland Cricket Association. He managed Zimbabwe sides on and off throughout the 1980s, including the World Cup party of 1983. His decision to stand down as President of the ZCU in 1992, shortly after Zimbabwe had secured Test match status, surprised many people. While domestic considerations played a part in this, the principle reason was that he had just been appointed senior partner of his firm, Coopers and Lybrand, a job which was not compatible with active cricket administration. He was appointed an honorary life member of MCC in 1993 and a 'life president' of the ZCU.

ESSOP-ADAM, Ebrahim Ali

(b. 1968, Salisbury (Harare))

A small, slightly built, right-handed batsman and quicksilver fielder, 'Eboo' Essop-Adam has thus far played one one-day international for Zimbabwe against New Zealand at Harare in 1992/3 scoring 14 not out and taking two catches. He plays his domestic cricket for the Universals Club for whom he is also a talented hockey player.

EVANS, Craig Neil

(b. 1969, Salisbury (Harare)) *Mashonaland Under-24 and Zimbabwe*

A talented all-round sportsman, Craig Evans has not, to date, made the most of his cricket abilities. A tall, strong, athletic figure, he was both a scratch golfer and a Rugby international for Zimbabwe (full-back) by the time he made his three brief appearances in one-day internationals against India and New Zealand at home in 1992/3. After school at Falcon College, he represented Old Georgians and Mashonaland in domestic cricket. He appeared to be equally talented with both bat and ball. A powerful right-handed batsman and right-arm medium-pace bowler, he seemed to lack the application and motivation to realise his potential—perhaps it all came too easily

First-class career (1990–): 212 runs (17.66), 4 wickets (27.00), and 6 catches

FLETCHER, Duncan Andrew Gwynne

(b. 1948, Salisbury (Harare)) *Rhodesia/Zimbabwe*

The pinnacle of Duncan Fletcher's career was as captain of Zimbabwe in the 1983 World Cup, when he led his country to victory in their very first one-day international, against Australia at Trent Bridge. He led by example too, scoring 69 not out when Zimbabwe batted and following it with figures of 6 for 42 as Zimbabwe won by 13 runs. A left-handed middle order batsman, right-arm fast-medium seam bowler and outstanding fielder in almost any position, his all-round figures in first-class cricket were surpassed for Rhodesia/Zimbabwe only by Mike Procter and Percy Mansell. A product of Prince Edward School, he played his domestic cricket for Old Hararians and for Mashonaland. As a batsman, he was a good driver of the ball but his chief quality was a tenacious fighting spirit, which stood him in good stead when elevated to the captaincy. This determination was never better displayed than in his second first-class match against Transvaal at the Police Ground in Salisbury in 1969/70 when he scored a match-saving fifty with a broken hand. The scorer of twenty first-class fifties, Fletcher never succeeded in converting one of them into a century—93 against Young New Zealand at Bulawayo in 1984/5 being his highest score. Many rated him his country's best ever fielder after Colin Bland. In particular he took many blinding catches off his own bowling. After retiring from Zimbabwe cricket he emigrated to South Africa where he continued to be involved in the game, latterly becoming director of cricket for Western Province.

First-class career (1969–85): 4,097 runs (23.68), 215 wickets (28.03), and 75 catches

FLOWER, Andrew

(b. 1968, Cape Town, South Africa) *Mashonaland and Zimbabwe*

To Andy Flower fell the honour of leading Zimbabwe to their first Test victory, against Pakistan on 3 February 1995. The captain scored 156 in his only innings, embellishing his younger brother's double-century. It was Zimbabwe's good fortune that Andy should have matured into a high-class wicket-keeper and batsman just when the country was admitted as a full member of the International Cricket Council in 1992. Fair-haired and slightly built, he followed Dave Houghton in becoming his country's second full-time cricket professional. A neat and compact left-handed batsman, who favours the back foot and is a prolific cutter and sweeper, he made his first-class début in 1986/7 against Young West Indies. He learnt his cricket at Vainona High School, Harare, and at the hands of his father, Bill, before joining Old Georgians, the club he now captains. A

regular member of the Zimbabwe side since the tour by Young West Indies in 1989/90, he took over wicket-keeping duties later that season from Dave Houghton, when the latter was appointed captain for the visit of England 'A'. At the same time he also dropped down the order from his favourite position opening the innings. He is an accomplished wicket-keeper of great agility, his light frame enabling him to take many astonishingly athletic catches. But it is as a batsman that Andy Flower has begun to fashion a career of genuine Test class. A half-century in his first innings in Test cricket against India at Harare in 1992/3 was swiftly followed by 81 in Zimbabwe's next Test against New Zealand at Bulawayo. A predictable first century duly followed, in Zimbabwe's first overseas Test against India in New Delhi the same season, when he made 115 and put on 192 for the fourth wicket with his younger brother, Grant. However, Flower's success, and Dave Houghton's relative decline as a batsman, prompted the selectors to give him the captaincy for the 1993 tour of England, and the Bengal Jubilee and Test tour of Pakistan in 1993/4. Whether he could sustain the triple burden of captain, leading batsman, and wicket-keeper remained to be seen—only two fifties in the three Tests in Pakistan being rather less than he would have hoped for. Nevertheless, an average of 55.44 after 7 Tests spoke for itself and presaged a bright future. He is also a more than useful one-day player, quite capable of playing attacking innings —his most accomplished to date being 115 not out against Sri Lanka at New Plymouth in the 1992 World Cup, when he carried his bat through Zimbabwe's innings. In 34 internationals to 1995 he had scored 1,028 runs (33.16).

First-class career (1986–): 1,817 runs (41.29) including 4 centuries, and 53 dismissals (47 c., 6 st.)
Test matches (13): 835 runs (49.11) including 2 centuries, and 31 dismissals (29 c., 2 st.)

FLOWER, Grant William

(b. 1970, Salisbury (Harare)) *Mashonaland Under-24 and Zimbabwe*

Grant Flower's 201 not out at Harare in the first Test against Pakistan in 1994/5 was the base on which his country's first victory was gained. Like his elder brother, Andrew, Grant is one of Zimbabwe's growing band of professional cricketers. His natural skills were in evidence from an early age and his advance through Zimbabwe's junior teams from St George's College, to the national side seemed preordained. A right-hand opening batsman, orthodox left-arm slow bowler, and outstanding fielder in virtually any position, he seemed likely to be a key member of the Zimbabwe side for many years to come. While not as fluent a stroke-maker as his brother, he possesses a sound orthodox technique and infinite powers of concentration. The latter have not always endeared him either to his opponents or to spectators but they have already stood his country in good stead. He made his first-class début against the visiting England A side in 1989/90, making his first half-century in the third unofficial 'Test' at Harare. Second to his brother as a run-scorer in Zimbabwe's third successive ICC Trophy win in Holland in 1990 he had by then, still short of his 20th birthday, cemented his place as his country's opening batsman. Good form against the strong Australia B side in 1991/2, when he made his highest first-class score to up to that point, 84 in Bulawayo, marked him as a certainty for the World Cup party in 1992. Unfortunately, a broken forearm sustained while playing as a replacement for a Zimbabwe under-23 side in Transvaal shortly before the World Cup denied him the trip. His most satisfying performance to date came in Zimbabwe's inaugural Test match against India at Harare in 1992/3 when, opening the innings with Kevin Arnott, they put on exactly 100—the first occasion when a country has recorded a three-figure opening partnership in its first Test match. He went on to make 82, having batted for all but 9 minutes of Zimbabwe's first day of Test cricket. Later that season, he came within a whisker of recording his maiden first-class century in a Test match, when making 96 in Zimbabwe's first innings against India in New Delhi. This was another impressive feat of concentration, during which he was involved in a stand of 192 with his brother and took Zimbabwe to within an ace of saving the follow-on in response to India's massive first innings of 536 for 7 declared. He was less successful during Zimbabwe's tour of Pakistan in 1993/4 and recorded a pair in the Rawalpindi Test, but his immediate future at Test level seemed assured. Fourteen internationals to 1994 had brought him 353 runs (29.41) with four fifties in 12 innings.

First-class career (1989–): 1,551 runs (33.00) including 1 century, 21 wickets (41.19), and 17 catches

Test matches (13): 627 runs (31.35) including 1 century, 2 wickets (86.50), and 6 catches

GRIPPER, Raymond Arthur

(b. 1938, Salisbury (Harare)) *Rhodesia*

An elegant right-handed opening batsman, Ray Gripper played for and captained Rhodesia between 1957 and 1971. While at St George's College, he represented the South Africa Schools XI. In domestic cricket he played for Old Georgians and Mashonaland. By far his most noteworthy performance was an innings of 279 not out for Rhodesia against Orange Free State at Bloemfontein in 1967/8, when he put on 268 for the first wicket with J. K. Clarke and an unbroken 281 for the second wicket with R. B. Ullyett, which remains the highest partnership for any wicket for Rhodesia/Zimbabwe. Gripper's innings was the highest score in Currie Cup cricket until Alan Lamb bettered it in 1987/8.

First-class career (1957–72): 4,353 runs (30.44) including 7 centuries, and 58 catches

HERON, John Gunner

(b. 1948, Salisbury (Harare)) *Rhodesia/Zimbabwe*

Jack Heron was an accomplished right-handed opening batsman, very strong on the front foot especially through the 'V'. He was also a superb out-fielder in an era of high-class Rhodesian fielding. He came to prominence as a schoolboy at Churchill School, during which time he captained South African Schools. In a career which lasted from 1967 to 1983 his figures do not do justice to a considerable talent. A stocky, stylish batsman, who often played with dash and daring, Heron's finest season was in 1975/6, when he passed Brian Davison's Currie Cup runs record and became the first Rhodesian to exceed 700 runs in a Currie Cup season. His innings of 153 against Eastern Province and 175 against Transvaal each displayed classic batsmanship of a high order. His swan-song was the 1983 World Cup when he played in all Zimbabwe's matches without ever making his mark. Shortly after retirement he emigrated to Perth in Australia.

First-class career (1967–83): 2,830 runs (26.20) including 5 centuries, and 39 catches

HOGG, Vincent Richard

(b. 1952, Salisbury (Harare)) *Rhodesia/Zimbabwe*

Vince Hogg has been a devoted servant of Zimbabwe cricket both as player and administrator since his first-class début in 1971. Educated at the Alan Wilson High School, Harare, he played most of his cricket for Alexandra Sports

Club and Mashonaland. He had more than respectable bowling figures, his right-arm fast-medium inswing bowling earning him 104 first-class wickets at 25.51. However, it was one event in a mostly undistinguished right-handed batting career for which posterity may chiefly remember him. Playing for Zimbabwe B against Natal B at Pietermaritzburg in 1979/80 he recorded the longest duck in first-class cricket, batting for 87 minutes without scoring. Indeed only one other batsman, Godfrey Evans, for England v. Australia at Adelaide in 1946/7, has batted longer for 0, taking 97 minutes to get off the mark. Hogg afterwards served the Zimbabwe Cricket Union with distinction, being a national selector and managing the Zimbabwe tour to England in 1993.

First-class career (1971–84): 181 runs (5.32), 123 wickets (26.29), and 12 catches

HOUGHTON, David Laud

(b. 1957, Bulawayo) *Mashonaland and Zimbabwe*

As the captain who took Zimbabwe into Test cricket, Dave Houghton will forever have a special place in the annals of his country's cricket history. Indeed his whole career has been one of breaking new ground. Zimbabwe's first local professional, he became its first full-time national coach in 1984. An unorthodox right-hand batsman of outstanding natural ability, Houghton would have almost certainly have had a full Test career had he been born in any other Test match country. As it was, the bulk of his best years were spent helping Zimbabwe demonstrate that its cricket was worthy of exposure at the top level. For the most part he was saddled with a double responsibility, since he was Zimbabwe's wicket-keeper in his early years, only giving up the gloves in 1989/90 when he succeeded Andy Waller as captain. For a batsman of his gifts his career has been surprisingly inconsistent, but on his day he could dominate with the best and loved nothing more than to demonstrate his repertoire of extravagant shots including the reverse sweep and the lofted drive over extra cover reminiscent of Viv Richards, making room for himself by stepping outside leg stump. Never was this better demonstrated than in his innings of 141 in 136 balls against New Zealand at Hyderabad in the 1987 World Cup, which took Zimbabwe to the brink of victory. He made his first-class début for Rhodesia against Transvaal in 1978/9 but had to wait until 1985 to register his maiden century, against Oxford University. By the

late 1980s Houghton was an accomplished batsman and usually performed well against visiting sides. His best season was 1989/90 when he began with a string of good scores against Young West Indies, including 165 in the first four-day match in Harare. Later in the season, England A felt the full force of his batting, when he followed 108 in the first five-day unofficial 'Test' in Harare with 202 at Bulawayo when Zimbabwe replied to England A's 529 for 9 declared. After a brief spell as Zimbabwe's captain between 1985 and 1987, his significant period in command was between 1989/90 and 1992/3. His strength was his technical awareness on the field but he was never an inspirational leader. Nevertheless, he fully deserved the honour of leading Zimbabwe in its first Test match against India at Harare in 1992/3 and, fittingly, he became his country's first century-maker, scoring 121 out of Zimbabwe's scarcely believeable 456 in their first innings of that match. Thereafter, he seemed to struggle somewhat with his batting and did not score another Test half-century until his seventh Test, against Pakistan in Lahore in 1993/4, by which time Andy Flower had replaced him as captain. In 1993/4 he announced his retirement from Test cricket but subsequently retracted this after resolving contractual differences with the Zimbabwe Cricket Union. He spent the 1994 English season with Worcestershire as senior coach and 2nd XI captain and in October 1994 scored 58, 266, and 142 in his three innings in the three home Tests against Sri Lanka, averaging 155 for the series. In 36 one-day internationals to 1994 he had scored over 1,000 runs.

First-class career (1978–): 5,181 runs (34.31) including 9 centuries, 148 catches, and 16 stumpings
Test matches (13): 912 runs (48.00) including 3 centuries, and 9 catches

JAMES, Wayne Robert

(b. 1965, Bulawayo) *Matabeleland and Zimbabwe*

Wayne James won his first Test cap against Pakistan at Lahore in 1993/4, keeping wicket and making 8 runs in his only innings. Slimly built with fair hair, he is a stylish right-hand bat and outstanding fielder. He learnt his cricket at Plumtree High School and with Old Miltonians in Bulawayo and now plays for Matabeleland. James made his first-class début in 1986/7, and has since remained on the fringe of the Zimbabwe side without establishing himself as a regular member. A brillant fielder anywhere, he also keeps wicket and could be a candidate to replace Andy Flower if the latter gives up the gloves to concentrate on his batting and captaincy. James was a member of Zimbabwe's World Cup party in 1992, playing in four matches with a highest score of 17. His highest score in first-class cricket is 215 in the Logan Cup for Matabeleland v. Mashonaland Country Districts during Zimbabwe's inaugural season of domestic first-class cricket in 1993/4. Although he initially disappointed at the highest level, he is a good player of fast bowling.

First-class career (1986–): 1,088 runs (37.51) and 30 catches

Test matches (4): 61 runs (15.25), 11 wickets (35.72), and 2 catches

JARVIS, Malcolm Peter

(b. 1955, Fort Victoria (Masvingo)) *Mashonaland and Zimbabwe*

Malcolm Jarvis was one of the stalwarts of Zimbabwe cricket who, with Traicos, held the bowling attack together in the late 1980s and early 1990s when the country was on the brink of Test cricket. His career was properly crowned with his selection for Zimbabwe's first Test match against India at Harare in 1992/3, aged 36. But after one more Test, against New Zealand, when he took 3 for 38 in New Zealand's second innings, he was omitted for Zimbabwe's next five Tests. A left-arm medium-pace swing bowler he was capable of achieving great movement and on his day could trouble the best. He batted right-handed in the lower order and had a strong arm in the outfield. His best first-class figures were 7 for 86 (12 for 160 in the match) for Zimbabwe against a strong Pakistan B side in 1990/1 at Bulawayo. After a relatively late first-class début in 1979/80, he progressed through the ranks of a strong Harare Sports Club side to earn selection for the World Cup in India and Pakistan in 1987, where he played in five out of six of Zimbabwe's games. He also played in five of Zimbabwe's eight games in the 1992 World Cup.

First-class career (1979–): 437 runs (10.92), 119 wickets (30.50), and 11 catches

Test matches (5): 2 runs (2.00), 11 wickets (35.72), and 2 catches

KASCHULA, Richard Herbert

(b. 1946, Gwelo (Gweru)) *Rhodesia/Zimbabwe*

A product of Chaplin School, Gwelo (Gweru), Richard Kaschula was one of the characters of Rhodesian cricket in the 1970s and early 1980s. A man of enormous bulk, he was a purveyor of tight and economical left-arm orthodox spin, which frequently saw him as the leading wicket-taker of the Rhodesia/Zimbabwe season. Thanks to a good 'arm ball' and natural ability to vary the trajectory, he was rarely collared in Currie Cup cricket in a period in which South African batsmanship was at its zenith. He played much of his domestic cricket for Hartley (Chegutu) and Midlands, where he farmed, but also represented Alexandra Sports Club and latterly, Old Georgians, in Harare. A right-handed batsman with genuine number eleven credentials, he could occasionally 'give it a whack'. With his relative immobility, his fielding was also in the same league.

First-class career (1970–82): 273 runs (7.18), 196 wickets (25.72), and 21 catches

LEWIS, David John

(b. 1927, Bulawayo) *Rhodesia and Oxford University*

David Lewis made an outstanding contribution to Rhodesia's cricket both on and off the field. After Plumtree School, he read law at Capetown University for whom he played both cricket and Rugby. He then went up to Oxford University for whom he played from 1949 to 1951, winning his blue in 1951. An effective and tenacious right-handed middle-order batsman he became, arguably, the best captain Rhodesia ever had—astute, popular and uncompromising. An all-round sportsman, he also gained a Rugby blue at Oxford and played fly-half for Rhodesia. Despite a busy career as a lawyer he maintained his involvement with cricket once his playing days were over, culminating in his being president of the Rhodesian Cricket Union, 1973–5. He was also an elected member of the board of the South African Cricket Union from 1976 to 1980

First-class career (1945–64): 3,662 runs (28.16), 8 centuries, and 39 catches

MEMON, Mohamed Ahmed

(b. 1952, Lundazi, Zambia) *Shropshire and Zimbabwe*

A right-arm off-spin bowler and right-handed lower-order batsman, 'Babu' Memon played just one one-day international for Zimbabwe, against India at Bombay in the 1987 World Cup. Educated at Morgan High School, Harare, he played his domestic cricket for the Universals club and for Mashonaland. His short first-class career lasted from 1985 to 1988, following which he became involved in cricket administration, including a spell as national selector. He managed the Zimbabwe side on their one Test tour to India in 1992/3. He played for Shropshire, 1978–80.

First-class career (1985–8): 68 runs (11.33), 4 wickets (48.75), and 3 catches

MORGANROOD, Leslie George

(b. 1903, Cape Town, South Africa)

Les Morganrood was for many years a leading administrator of Rhodesian cricket and devoted much of his life to cricket and cricketers. He was secretary of the Mashonaland Cricket Union. He was also secretary of the Cricket Society (Zimbabwe Branch). In his youth he represented Rhodesia at hockey, tennis, swimming, and water polo.

OLONGA, Henry Rhaaba

(b. 1976, Lusaka, Zambia) *Matabeleland and Zimbabwe*

The first black player to appear in Test cricket for Zimbabwe, Henry Olonga attracted widespread sympathy when he was called for throwing by the home umpire Ian Robinson in his only Test before 1994/5, which was against Pakistan in Harare. He did not bat and bowled only in the first innings, taking one for 27. A talented athlete and capable of bowling with sharp speed, he ran the 100 metres in 10.6 seconds at the age of 16.

First-class career (1993–): 1 run (1.00), 5 wickets (18.80), and 1 catch

OMARSHAH, Ali Hassimshah

(b. 1959, Salisbury (Harare)) *Mashonaland and Zimbabwe*

Ali Shah, as he is usually known, is a deceptively useful cricketer, many of whose better performances have occurred when his country has needed them most. A left-handed batsman with experience ranging from opener right the way down the order, he is also an equally accomplished right-arm medium-pace bowler. A member of Zimbabwe's first side to compete in the World Cup, against Australia in 1983, his career extended into the Test match era with appearances to date against New Zealand (home) and India (away) in 1992/3. A product of Morgan High School, Harare, Shah went on to become a key member of the Universals Club and to play for Mashonaland. He made his first-class début

for Zimbabwe against the Young Australians in 1982/3 and has a highest score of 185 against Gloucestershire at Bristol in 1990. His most significant bowling success to date was a return of 4 for 56 in the final of the ICC Trophy against Holland in The Hague in 1991. In good company, his best innings probably remains his 98 against a strong England A side at Harare in the First unofficial 'Test' in 1989/90. In 26 internationals he scored 390 runs (16.25) and took 18 wickets (44.10).

First-class career (1979–): 1,279 runs (23.25) including 2 centuries, 20 wickets (61.95), and 14 catches

Test matches (2): 59 runs (19.66) and 1 wicket (125.00)

PATERSON, Grant Andrew

(b. 1960, Salisbury (Harare)) *Mashonaland Country Districts and Zimbabwe*

Grant Paterson is a tall, elegant, hard hitting right-handed batsman, who was a regular member of the Zimbabwe side until just before the Test match era began. He could either open or bat in the middle order. After Prince Edward School, he played for both Harare Sports Club and Mashonaland Country Districts in domestic cricket, the latter courtesy of his occupation as a tobacco farmer. Although he played in all Zimbabwe's matches in both the 1983 and 1987 World Cups, Paterson was seldom at his best at the highest level, where his temperament seemed suspect. Perhaps his finest hour was in scoring 122 off 147 balls in a one-day match for Zimbabwe against West Indies B at Harare in 1986/7.

First-class career (1981–): 1,404 runs (21.93) and 11 catches

PEALL, Stephen Guy

(b. 1970, Salisbury (Harare)) *Mashonaland Country Districts and Zimbabwe*

Peall learnt his cricket at Falcon College, Bulawayo. A right-arm off-spin bowler and left-handed lower-order bat of occasionally violent disposition, he came to prominence in the shadow of John Traicos. Short and stocky, the antithesis of Traicos's wiry athleticism, he nevertheless acquired a similar ability to bowl a consistent line and length for long periods. Peall played his first one-day international against New Zealand in 1992/3. After missing the tour of India later the same season for disciplinary reasons, he won the first of four Test caps to date against

Pakistan in Karachi in 1993/4, when he had figures of 41–10–89–2 in Pakistan's first innings. In Zimbabwe's domestic cricket, after a spell with Mashonaland Country Districts, he joined Harare Sports Club where he formed an off-spin partnership with Traicos.

First-class career (1990–): 423 runs (20.14), 34 wickets (47.76), and 8 catches

Test matches (4): 60 runs (15.00), 4 wickets (75.75), and 1 catch

PECKOVER, Gerald Edward

(b. 1955, Salisbury (Harare)) *Rhodesia/Zimbabwe*

A fine all-round sportsman, Gerald Peckover represented his country at both cricket and hockey. After learning his cricket at Churchill School, he represented Standard Bank and Mashonaland. A wicket-keeper and batsman, his right-handed batting was noted for its stubborn grafting qualities. However, he compensated for this with outstanding running between the wickets. He played three matches for Zimbabwe in the 1983 World Cup without making much of a mark. Shortly after retiring from serious cricket, he emigrated to South Africa.

First-class career (1982–3): 478 runs (21.72) and 31 dismissals (27 c., 4 st.)

PICHANICK, Alwyn Leonard Arthur

(b. 1933, Salisbury (Harare))

During his long and distinguished spell as an administrator of Rhodesian and Zimbabwean cricket, Alwyn Pichanick was popularly known as 'Mr Cricket'. Although he handed over the reins as president of the Zimbabwe Cricket Union in 1990, a couple of years before Zimbabwe obtained Test status, his was probably the greatest single contribution, off the field, towards that goal. A quiet, self-effacing lawyer, he was brought up in a cricket environment, his father, Harry Pichanick, a former mayor of Salisbury, having preceded him as a leading cricket administrator. A more than useful right-handed opening batsman in club cricket, he played for Old Hararians, whom he captained, and Mashonaland. He was appointed a Rhodesian selector in 1962 and continued until 1975, when he became vice-president of the Cricket Union, moving upwards to be president the following year. He managed the Rhodesian side from 1966 until 1972/3 and occasionally thereafter. His decision to stand down from being president of the ZCU was precipitated by his appointment in 1990 as chairman of the Zimbabwe Sports and Recreation Commission. He was subsequently made a life president of the ZCU in addition to being appointed an honorary life member of MCC in 1993.

PYCROFT, Andrew John

(b. 1956, Salisbury (Harare)) *Western Province, Rhodesia, and Zimbabwe*

A right-handed batsman of high pedigree, Andy Pycroft's misfortune was that by the time of Zimbabwe's entry into Test cricket his best days were behind him and the demands of career and family were already limiting the time he could devote to the game. His Test career was therefore restricted to Zimbabwe's first three Test matches, which left him with a respectable batting average of 30.4 and a highest score of 60 in the first innings of the second Test against New Zealand at Harare in 1992/3. Pycroft first came to notice during schooldays at Diocesan College in Cape Town and subsequently at Cape Town University, where he developed into a prolific run scorer and represented Western Province as well as South African Universities. His national first-class career spanned three distinct phases of Zimbabwe's cricket, his début season being Rhodesia's last in the Currie Cup in 1979/80. For the most part he was confined to contests against touring sides to Zimbabwe and the occasional overseas trip. Nevertheless he managed a career total of 4,054 runs at 42.67. Pycroft's batting exuded class. Of medium height and solidly built, his strength was on the back foot and he particularly favoured the late cut, which he would play with delicacy and finesse. He could be something of a loner and was not afraid to speak his mind. For a while in the late 1980s he appeared to have retired permanently, but the tour by England A in 1989/90 enticed him back to the fold and by the time Australia B toured Zimbabwe in 1991/2 he was somewhere near his best. Although one-day cricket was never his forte, he can rarely have bettered his superb 104 in 109 balls against an Australia B attack including Shane Warne, Paul Reiffel, and Steve Waugh, which took Zimbabwe to the brink of winning the one-day series at Harare Sports Club in September 1991. He captained Zimbabwe in 1984/5 and again in England in 1985 but he never quite seemed comfortable in the job. After retiring from first-class cricket Pycroft quickly moved into administration, managing the Zimbabwe under-19 side on their 1993 tour of England and Denmark, and becoming a national selector in 1993/4.

First-class career (1975–93): 4,374 runs (38.03) including 5 centuries, 1 wicket (52.00), and 63 catches
Test matches (3): 152 runs (30.40) and 2 catches

RANCHOD, Ujesh

(b. 1969, Salisbury (Harare)) *Mashonaland and Zimbabwe*

A right-arm off-spin bowler and lower-order right-hand bat, Ranchod has been a stalwart of the Universals Club in Harare. Having the unusual distinction of making his first-class début in a Test match, he owes his one Test to date, against India at New Delhi in 1992/3, to the decision to drop Steven Peall from the touring party for disciplinary reasons. Although probably always well short of the requisite class, his bowling figures in that Test match of 12–0–45–1, including the wicket of Mohamed Azharuddin, in an Indian innings of 536 for 7 declared, were creditable. He scored 8 runs in his two innings (4.00). He has played three one-day internationals to date, against New Zealand in Harare, and Pakistan and Sri Lanka in Sharjah in 1992/3, and was a member of the Zimbabwe party for the tour of Pakistan in 1993/4.

First-class career (1992–): 223 runs (22.30), 10 wickets (54.60), and 2 catches

RAWSON, Peter Walter Edward

(b. 1957, Salisbury (Harare)) *Zimbabwe and Natal*

Peter Rawson was a fine competitive cricketer with a big heart, who captained Zimbabwe in the late 1980s. He also captained his country at hockey. Nicknamed 'Wrecker', he was an attacking right-arm medium-fast bowler, who seemed to have the knack of making things happen. His right-handed batting was not much to write home about early in his career but by dint of hard work and application he made himself into an effective grafter. After Churchill School, where he was a wicket-keeper and batsman, he played for Rhodes University in Eastern Province, South Africa, where he developed his bowling skills, and in club cricket for Alexandra Sports Club, Harare Sports Club, and Manicaland. He had an exceptional first-class bowling record for Zimbabwe between 1982 and 1989/90, taking 159 wickets at an average of 20.98. He played in both the 1983 and 1987 World Cups, with a best bowling performance of 3 for 47 against India at Tunbridge Wells in 1983 when he helped to reduce India to 17 for 5 before Kapil Dev rescued them

with an innings of 175. His sudden departure for South Africa to pursue a commercial career after captaining Zimbabwe against Young New Zealand and Lancashire in 1988/9 did not exactly enhance his reputation. However, he resumed his first-class career for Natal with considerable success, including a period as their captain.

First-class career (1982–): 1,976 runs (20.80), 257 wickets (23.90), and 40 catches

RENNIE, John Alexander

(b. 1970, Fort Victoria (Masvingo)) *Matabeleland and Zimbabwe*

John Rennie was a surprise selection for Zimbabwe's touring party for the Bengal Jubilee tournament in 1993/4 and the subsequent Test tour of Pakistan. In the event he justified the selectors' faith with competent performances on both legs of the itinerary and forced his way into the Test side. An accurate right-arm medium-pace seam bowler and lower-order right-handed bat, he is a product of St George's College, Harare, and the Old Georgians Club. By the 1993/4 season he had moved to Bulawayo and thus played for Matabeleland in Zimbabwe's inaugural season of domestic first-class cricket. He made his début in the first Test against Pakistan at Karachi and played again in the third Test at Lahore, where he returned his best figures to date, 2 for 22, in Pakistan's first innings.

First-class career (1993–): 309 runs (28.09), 5 wickets (48.00), and 3 catches
Test matches (3): 24 runs (8.00) and 3 wickets (85.33)

ROBERTSON, Stuart David

(b. 1947, Salisbury (Harare)) *Rhodesia*

Stuart Robertson was a stylish, left-handed middle-order batsman and outstanding slip-fielder, whose career ended prematurely in 1979 as a result of persistent back trouble. After Churchill School, he played most of his domestic cricket for Salisbury Sports Club and Mashonaland. Despite his early retirement, he ranks third in the list of run-scorers for Rhodesia/Zimbabwe, his 4,343 being bettered only by David Houghton and Brian Davison. He captained Rhodesia eleven times and also kept wicket for them when the occasion demanded. After retirement he had a spell as a national selector and was coach of the World Cup team in 1983, which managed a fine win against Australia.

First-class career (1968–80): 4,343 runs (33.15) and 111 catches

ROBINSON, Ian David

(b. 1947, Oxford, England)

Zimbabwe's leading umpire, Ian Robinson was appointed to the inaugural National Grid International Panel in January 1994 and stood in the first Test between West Indies and England at Kingston, Jamaica the following month. He had previously umpired in 6 matches of the 1992 World Cup in Australia and New Zealand and had made his début as a Test umpire in Zimbabwe's first Test match against India at Harare in 1992/3. He turned to umpiring after playing club cricket and stood in some of Rhodesia's last games in the Currie Cup prior to Zimbabwe's independence, having been appointed to the Rhodesian first-class panel in 1978.

STRANG, Bryan Colin

(b. 1972, Bulawayo) *Mashonaland Country Districts and Zimbabwe*

Bryan Strang had the fun of making his first Test appearance, against Pakistan at Bulawayo in 1994/5, in the same side as his brother, Paul. It was also his first first-class match but he returned the impressive match figures of 26.4–12–50–5. A left-arm seamer with good control but no great pace, he took four more wickets for 70 in his only other Test to date.

First-class and Test (2) career (1994–): 6 runs (2.00), 9 wickets (13.33), and 1 catch

STRANG, Paul Andrew

(b. 1970, Bulawayo) *Mashonaland Country Districts and Zimbabwe*

Paul Strang is a sturdy, skilful right-arm leg-spin bowler and a brilliant fielder. He was a member of the Zimbabwe touring party to Pakistan in 1993/4 but, bizarrely, was not given a single game on the tour. Things were different the following season when he played his first Test cricket, and had an outstanding tour of Australia in the one-day series. He learnt his cricket at Falcon College, Bulawayo, but now plays his domestic cricket for Mashonaland Country Districts. He bats right-handed in the lower-middle order. His brother, Bryan, a fast-medium left-arm bowler, also made his first Test appearances in 1994/5.

First-class career (1992–): 225 runs (17.30), 22 wickets (37.04), and 10 catches
Test matches (4): 74 runs (14.80), 9 wickets (13.33), and 3 catches

STREAK, Heath Hilton

(b. 1974, Bulawayo) *Matabeleland, Hampshire, and Zimbabwe*

A 'child of the African Bush' in his mother's words, Heath Streak keeps fit by playing soccer with the farm labourers with whom he grew up. The Africans call him 'Mgibise', Sindehele for 'warrior'. Only the fact that the exams clash with his cricket has prevented him from qualifying as a professional hunter on his father's cattle farm, an hour's drive from Bulawayo. The most exciting young cricketer to emerge since Zimbabwe's elevation to Test cricket, the aptly named Streak rapidly developed into a quality Test-match bowler, with pretentions to being an all-rounder. Having learnt his craft at Falcon College, Bulawayo, he now represents Matabeleland in Zimbabwe's domestic cricket. His father, Dennis, played for Rhodesia in the Currie Cup. A right-arm medium-fast bowler, he is ideally built for the purpose—standing just over 6 ft., broad-shouldered and immensely strong. He runs in uncompromisingly fast and the action is vigorous and classical. After representing Zimbabwe at school and junior level, he was selected for the senior tour of England in 1993 and then for the Bengal Jubilee and Pakistan tours of 1993/4. He played in all three Tests in Pakistan, achieving a best return of 5 for 56 in Pakistan's first innings of the second Test at Rawalpindi. A right-handed batsman, he never got going against Pakistan but he was to have an exceptional 1994/5 season, taking Test and international wickets in large numbers. By the time that he joined Hampshire for the 1995 season he had proved his quality by taking 22 wickets, 9 more than the next most successful bowler on either side in three Tests at home to Pakistan, each at a cost of only 13. His 9 for 105 in the first Test helped bring Zimbabwe's first Test victory.

First-class career (1992–): 204 runs (15.69), 20 wickets (38.25), and 4 catches
Test matches (9): 103 runs (10.30), 43 wickets (20.60), and 3 catches

TRAICOS, Anthanasios John

(b. 1947, Zagazig, Egypt) *Rhodesia, South Africa, Mashonaland, and Zimbabwe*

By any yardstick, John Traicos is the most accomplished bowler to have come out of Zimbabwe in the modern era. When he walked on to the field in Harare in October 1992 against India, 22 years and 222 days after playing the last of his three Test matches for South Africa, he was probably as fit as any member of the Zimbabwean side and still capable of astonishing reflex fielding in the gully. It seemed then to be commonplace to describe him as the best (right-arm) off-spin bowler in the world but, in an age where the spin bowler seemed to be a vanishing breed, that tag scarcely did him justice. Traicos has a model action. Off a maximum of four or five paces, he seems perfectly balanced and in control of line and length, even if, by the time of Zimbabwe's arrival in Test cricket, his normal line of attack had perhaps shifted too much towards leg stump for the purists—a reflection of the one-day tread-mill which had been his country's chief diet before elevation. A lean and hungry six-footer, he fielded like a panther to his own bowling and, while his right-handed batting was never more than modest, he brought to it the same dedica-tion and attention to detail that made him such an example to successive younger generations of Zimbabwe's cricketers. School at Thornhill in Gwelo (Gweru) was followed by Natal University, where he read Law and played for the South African Universities side which toured England in 1967. In his first-class début, against Cambridge University at Fenner's, he took 5 for 54 in 30.4 overs in the first innings. In 1968/9 for Rhodesia he twice took 8 wickets in an innings. The three South African caps came while he was at Natal during the victorious 1969/70 home series against Australia. Whereas some might have drifted into retirement, content to bask in the glory of that brief golden age when South Africa was at the pinnacle of world cricket, Traicos soldiered on, through Rhodesia's isolation, when the Currie Cup provided a lifeline for its cricket, and into Zimbabwe's independence and appear-ances in three World Cups. While Traicos himself often doubted whether Zimbabwe ever would, or even deserve to, be awarded Test status, its realization probably owed as much to himself as to any other player. It was fitting therefore that he should mark Zimbabwe's inaugural Test with figures of 5 for 86 in 50 immaculate overs in India's only innings. He played in Zimbabwe's first four Tests at the age of 45 but was not available for selection for the 1993/4 tour of Pakistan due to the demands of his new job as a company director. If retirement now beckons, cricket will be the poorer, for he has graced its fields with consummate skill, immaculate man-ners, and an iron determination. By 1994 he had played in 27 one-day internationals and although his 19 wickets were expensive (51.94) he con-ceded runs at only 3.88 an over.

First-class career (1967–): 1,190 runs (11.55), 289 wickets (34.19), and 109 catches
Test matches (7): 19 runs (3.16), 18 wickets (42.72), and 8 catches

WALLER, Andrew Christopher

(b. 1959, Salisbury (Harare)) *Mashonaland Country Districts*

Andy Waller, universally known as 'Bundu', was a happy and popular cricketer, whose career might have been more illustrious but for persistent back problems and the demands of his profession as a farmer in the Centenary district of northern Zimbabwe. A tall, good-looking, athletic figure he was a fine attacking right-handed batsman, occasional right-arm medium-pace bowler, and outstanding all-round fielder. School at Falcon College was followed by cricket for Harare Sports Club and Mashonaland Country Districts. He made his first-class début for Zimbabwe in 1984/5 and was appointed captain for the 1989/90 home series against Young West Indies. However, injury forced him to miss the England A series later that season and he never regained the captaincy. He played in all Zimbabwe's matches in the World Cups of 1987 and 1992, including an innings of 83 not out when putting on an unbroken 145 for the fifth wicket with Andy Flower against Sri Lanka at New Plymouth in 1992.

First-class career (1984–): 995 runs (24.87), 2 wickets (20.00), and 18 catches

WHITTAL, Guy James

(b. 1972, Chipinga (Chipinge)) *Matabeleland and Zimbabwe*

Guy Whittal scored 113 not out in Zimbabwe's first Test victory against Pakistan in 1995 and followed this with bowling figures of 2 for 49 and 3 for 58. A slight, right-handed batsman and right-arm medium-pace seam bowler, he was a product of Falcon College, Bulawayo. He made his first-class début for Zimbabwe in 1990/1 against Worcestershire shortly after leaving school, where he had established a reputation as a clean striker of the ball. He was selected for the Bengal Jubilee one-day series in India in 1993/4, playing in three of the matches, and the subsequent tour to Pakistan. He made his début in the first Test against Pakistan at Karachi and went on to play in all three Tests and the three one-day internationals. Also against Pakistan, at Harare in February 1995, his 113 not out contributed to Zimbabwe's first Test victory.

First-class career (1990–): 373 runs (17.76), 18 wickets (24.77), and 3 catches
Test matches (9): 304 runs (27.63) including 1 century, 18 wickets (32.66), and 5 catches

Rest of The World

ARGENTINA

AYLING, Cecil Douglas

(b. 1912, Buenos Aires, Argentina; d. 1990, Buenos Aires) *Argentina*

The omission of Cecil Ayling from the South American tour to England in 1932 was 'difficult to understand' even 40 years after the event. He was the most consistent batsman in Argentine domestic cricket between 1930 and 1963 and the only man to make over 2,500 runs (62.51) in the annual North v. South contests. His right-handed batting brought him 226 not out in a first-wicket partnership of 292 with his brother Cyril for the North at Belgrano in 1940. Three years earlier at Belgrano, in the same fixture, he had made hundreds in both innings. In 1954 he made centuries for Argentina in both matches against the visiting Brazilian side and repeated the performance two years later against a combined team from Brazil, Chile, and Peru. As a yardstick for comparison, he made 86 against the 1958 MCC tourists, all of whom were current first-class county cricketers.

First-class career (1937–8): 2,280 runs (38.00) including 3 centuries, 2 wickets (69.50), and 3 catches

AYLING, Cyril Edgar

(b. 1910, Buenos Aires, Argentina; d. 1993, Buenos Aires) *Argentina and South America*

One of five brothers who belonged to the second generation of Argentine cricketers, Cyril Ayling was an attacking right-handed batsman and a right-arm medium-pace bowler. Touring England with the South American side in 1932 he took 5 for 72 in MCC's first innings and scored 95 not out in a two-day (non-first-class) match at Lord's. He played for 30 years (1930–4) in the annual North v. South matches in Argentina, sharing in a record (for all wickets) partnership of 292 with his brother, Cecil, for the North at Belgrano in 1940 and making his only century (136) in major Argentine cricket.

First-class career (1932–8): 200 runs (15.38), 24 wickets (28.08), and 8 catches

AYLING, Dennet Ernest

(b. 1906, Buenos Aires, Argentina; d. 1987, Cordoba, Argentina) *Argentina and South America*

Dennet Ayling's right-arm off-spin bowling first came to prominence when his match analysis of 8 for 52 helped Argentina to defeat MCC at Palermo in 1926/7, his victims including three England captains of different eras (P. F. Warner, R. T. Stanyforth, and G. O. Allen). When South America toured England in 1932, he topped the bowling averages, taking 10 for 87 in a ten-wicket defeat of Oxford University at Oxford. His greatest performance in first-class cricket came when Argentina played Sir Theodore Brinckman's touring team in 1937/8. Ayling took 6 for 10 in the second innings to give Argentina victory by 222 runs. Twice in the match he added another England captain to his scalps—R. E. S. Wyatt. His 88 against the same opposition at Belgrano a week later staved off defeat. As a right-handed batsman he averaged over 50 in his annual appearances in the domestic matches between North and South (1926–47). His 256 not out for the North at Belgrano in 1939 remains the highest score by any player in the country and he made another double-century in 1929 on the same ground against Chile.

First-class career (1926–38): 653 runs (24.18), 79 wickets (16.41), and 6 catches

DORNING, Herbert

(b. 1875, Lancashire, England; d. 1955, Truro, England) *Argentina*

In a playing career in Argentina spanning over 40 years, Herbert Dorning appeared thirty-three times in the annual North v. South fixture (1894–1935), taking a record 210 wickets (13.45) and scoring almost 1,000 runs. His late-order left-handed batting brought him one century. As a left-arm medium-paced bowler—fast in his younger years—he took 6 for 65 in Argentina's defeat of MCC at Hurlingham in 1911/12. When the next MCC side visited the country in 1926/7, Dorning, though in his fifties, was again the most successful bowler in another victory for Argentina. His match analysis of 10 for 67 included the wickets of four former or current England players. He later became president of the Argentine Cricket Association. Of the many British expatriates who pursued business careers in the country, his contribution to cricket was among the greatest, one Buenos Aires obituary notice calling him the 'W.G.' of Argentine cricket.

First-class career (1911–30): 190 runs (14.61), 39 wickets (20.25), and 3 catches

GARNETT, Harold Gwyer

(b. 1879, Liverpool, England; d. 1917, Cambrai, France) *Lancashire, MCC, and Argentina*

Sydney Pardon, in *Wisden*, wrote that Harold Garnett seemed likely, in 1901, 'to become the best left-handed bat in England'. He had had an excellent season for Lancashire as an opening batsman though he achieved little with A. C. MacLaren's team in Australia (1901/2). For many years business took him to Argentina where he led them to a four-wicket defeat of Lord Hawke's MCC side at Buenos Aires in 1912. Back in England—and seldom any more a left-arm slow bowler—he played again for Lancashire and was selected to keep wicket for the Gentlemen against the Players at Lord's in 1914. His stumping of J. W. Hitch off F. R. Foster 'would have been wonderful even if done by Blackham at his

best'. He was killed in action in the First World War.

First-class career (1899–1914): 5,798 runs (26.00) including 5 centuries, 8 wickets (28.00), and 203 dismissals (185 c., 18 st.)

GIBSON, Clement Herbert

(b. 1900, Entre Rios, Argentina; d. 1976, Buenos Aires, Argentina) *Cambridge University, Argentina, South America, Sussex, and MCC*

Wisden in 1918, unable to nominate five cricketers of the year in wartime, chose five schoolboys of whom C. H. Gibson 'stood out by himself' as a fast bowler with all the classic virtues and the ability to swerve the ball very late. At Eton, he took 122 wickets in his four years in the XI including 9 for 30 against Harrow at Lord's in 1919 in the first post-war two-day match. While in the Cambridge side in 1921, he was picked to play by A. C. MacLaren for his England XI against the Australians at Eastbourne. This was the famous match in which the tourists were beaten by 28 runs against all expectations. Gibson took 6 for 64 in the Australian second innings. He toured Australia and New Zealand (1922/3) and made a few appearances for Sussex. Gibson's family and business interests lay in the Argentine. He made a dozen appearances up to 1940 in the annual North v. South matches, taking 6 for 16 for the South in 1922. He captained Argentina against the MCC in 1926/7 and the South American side in England in 1932, opening the bowling and making 99 against the Gentlemen of Surrey at the Oval. He was a late-order right-handed batsman capable of quick runs when needed.

First-class career (1920–39): 1,369 runs (15.04), 249 wickets (28.55), and 53 catches

BERMUDA

HAYWARD, Whitfield Frederick

(b. 1912, Pembroke, Bermuda)

After captaining the Bermudan Athletics Association at cricket before the Second World War, 'Chummy' Hayward played a major role as an administrator and benefactor and was awarded an OBE for these services. He served on the Bermuda Board of Control and organized both the first tour (1960) to England and five subsequent overseas tours in the 1960s and 1970s.

HAZEL, Nigel Le Roy

(b. 1921, Somerset, Bermuda)

After playing for Somerset in his native Bermuda, 'Chopper' Hazel became a professional in Scotland for Mannofield (1948–54) and Strathmore (1955–74). As an attacking right-handed batsman and right-arm fast-medium bowler he scored nearly 19,000 runs and took over 350 wickets for the second club. For Bermuda against MCC, in Bermuda in 1954, he secured the wicket of Len Hutton.

HORTON, Kenneth Howard Randolph

(b. 1945, Somerset, Bermuda)

Randy Horton, a left-handed middle-order batsman and an attacking right-arm medium-fast bowler, played for Bermuda between 1968 and 1979. As a centre-forward he represented his country (1967–75) at football and played professionally for the New York Cosmos (1970–5). After holding two headmasterships, he became assistant director of tourism in Bermuda.

HUNT, Alma Victor

(b. 1910, Somerset, Bermuda) *Scotland*

The greatest cricketer produced by Bermuda, 'Champ' Hunt played at Port of Spain in two trial matches in 1933 for the West Indies tour of England, as a left-handed batsman and right-arm fast-medium bowler. Despite making the highest aggregate in one match he was not selected. No official reason was given but it was suggested, on the one hand, that he had had insufficient experience and, on the other, that Bermuda did not 'qualify' as the West Indies. He became a professional with Aberdeenshire (1934–47) and appeared for Scotland in 1938 against the Australians and Yorkshire. He twice performed the 'double' in a Scottish season and had the unusual record of scoring the entire runs off the bat in Aberdeenshire's defeat of West Lothian by ten wickets in 1939. He served as secretary, and then president, of the Bermuda Board of Control (1966–83) and captained and managed Bermuda teams to England, the West Indies, the United States, Canada, Denmark, Holland, and Scotland. He represented Bermuda on the ICC (1967–82) and campaigned for many years, with eventual success, for the introduction of the associate members' tournament. His industry was recognized in the award of an OBE. He was twice (1979, 1989) on a delegation to South Africa to investigate the progress of integrated cricket. As a player, he had many of the qualities—especially in fielding—of Learie Constantine.

First-class career (1932–8): 65 runs (16.25), 2 wickets (35.50), and 3 catches

PARFITT, Clarence Leon

(b. 1943, St George's, Bermuda) *Bermuda*

After a domestic career for St George's which established him as Bermuda's most successful bowler, 'Tuppence' Parfitt became a professional in Scotland (1977–91) for Arbroath and Stenhousemuir. On his début at Lord's, in 1990, his left-arm swing bowling earned him a match analysis of 9 for 128 for Scotland against MCC. His left-handed batting usually brought up the tail. Bermuda's match against New Zealand at Hamilton in 1972 was accorded first-class status by the New Zealand Board, Parfitt taking 5 for 61.

First-class career (1971–2): 2 runs (not dismissed), 5 wickets (12.20), and 1 catch

CANADA

BELL, Llwelleyn Clarke

(b. 1910, Alliston, Ontario, Canada; d. 1942, Dieppe, France)

As a left-handed batsman, Clarke Bell made 109 not out for Ridley College (Past and Present) against the 1932 Australians at St Catherine's, Ontario, an innings singled out for special mention by Sir Donald Bradman. Four years later, he led the batting averages on the Canadian tour of England. Having scored more centuries than any other Canadian cricketer, he was killed at the battle of Dieppe.

KIRMANI, Farouk

(b. 1958, Karachi, Pakistan) *Karachi and Sind*

A right-handed batsman and right-arm off-spin bowler, Farouk Kirmani played for Canada (1982–93), leading the side on several occasions. He has scored centuries for Canada against East Africa, Bermuda, and the United States. In Pakistan he captained the under-19 side, with Javed

Miandad as his vice-captain, and appeared at first-class level (1971–5) for Karachi and Sind.

First-class career (1971–5): 729 runs (27.00), 1 wicket (32.00), and 9 catches

KYLE, John Henderson

(b. 1930, Vancouver, Canada)

A right-handed batsman and right-arm medium-paced bowler, Jack Kyle represented British Colombia on five occasions and appeared for Western Canada against Eastern Canada in 1958. As president of the Canadian Cricket Association (1978–93) he was responsible for organizing major overseas tours, a youth coaching programme, and raising Canadian cricket to a major position among associate members of ICC.

LAING, John Melville

(b. 1874, London, Ontario, Canada; d. 1947, Toronto, Canada)

Jack Laing was Canada's outstanding all-rounder at the turn of the century. He first appeared in representative cricket at the age of 17 and, as a middle-order left-handed batsman made 43 not out against the powerful Australian side at Toronto in 1893. Two years later his left-arm fast swerve bowling achieved the first international hat-trick for Canada against the United States at Toronto. In 1896 he set another record for the same fixture when he took 14 for 54 at Philadelphia. His highest score in domestic cricket was 249 for the Wanderers at Chicago against Douglas Park in 1903. His 77 wickets for Canada remains a record.

STEVENS, Richard John

(b. 1945, London, England)

A middle-order batsman and left-arm medium-fast bowler who swung the ball well, Rick Stevens captained Canada in their 1974 English tour and was a member of the Eastern Canadian side which beat the 1975 Australians by five wickets at Toronto on their way to England. For Canada against USA on the same ground in 1977 he took 7 for 29.

TERRY, Francis William

(b. 1860, Wells, Somerset, England; d. 1936, Mimico, Ontario, Canada) *Somerset*

After a few appearances for Somerset (1882–5), Francis Terry, a right-handed batsman and

wicket-keeper, emigrated to Canada. His 1,509 runs in 1892 was a Canadian record for 40 years and in 1893 he scored the first century for Canada against the United States. His only hundred in first-class cricket was for Somerset against Hampshire at Taunton in 1883.

First-class career (1882–5): 552 runs (32.47) including 1 century, and 15 dismissals (13 c., and 2 st.)

DENMARK

BUCHWALD, Charles

(b. 1880, Denmark; d. 1951, Denmark)

Charles Buchwald was Denmark's greatest batsman in the first quarter of the twentieth century. Making his début for Akademisk Boldklub (AB) at the age of 16, he scored the first century in Danish senior cricket four years later. In 1918 he scored the first double-century. As an opening right-handed batsman, he was a powerful driver and employed the 'draw' stroke long after it had gone out of fashion. He captained the Gentlemen of Denmark on the country's first tour of England in 1926. Although aged 46 and with no experience on grass wickets, he averaged over 50. In his career he made nearly 10,000 runs (49.79) and 28 centuries. He had some success as a right-arm bowler and played football for Denmark against England in the Final in the 1908 Olympic Games. As a civil servant, he reached the top of his profession and was a Knight of the Order of Danneborg.

HILARIUS-KALKAU, Harald

(b. 1852, Denmark; d. 1924, Denmark)

One of several Army officers playing Danish cricket in the mid-nineteenth century, Harald Hilarius-Kalkau was a leading figure in the Copenhagen Games Club. Wherever his military postings took him, the game would flourish and its growth in Jutland early in the twentieth century owed much to his coaching and influence.

HOSKIAER, Otto Valdemar

(b. 1829, Copenhagen, Denmark; d. 1895, Copenhagen)

Valdemar Hoskiaer, a young Danish engineering officer, was introduced to cricket by British engineers constructing the Danish Railways. He was an influential member of the Copenhagen Games Club and he wrote an article in 1866 arguing the 'beneficial physical exercise' of cricket. His ideas were taken up by the Ministry of Culture and welcomed by schools and colleges. In the same year, the Games Club published a manual of cricket—probably written by him—and in October he umpired the first match at Copenhagen, between the Games Club and the Soro Academy. Not surprisingly, he is known as 'the father of Danish cricket'.

MORTENSEN, Ole Henrik

(b. 1958, Vejle, Denmark) *Derbyshire and Denmark*

A lower-order right-handed batsman and a hostile and loquacious right-arm fast-medium bowler, 'Stan' Mortensen became the first Danish cricketer to play at first-class level. His country's membership of the European Community allowed Derbyshire to register him in 1983 while still retaining another 'overseas' player. An innings of 207 not out as a 15-year-old schoolboy and some outstanding bowling performances paved the way to selection for Svanhol, one of Denmark's premier clubs and for his country from 1975 onwards. In his first season, against Yorkshire at Sheffield—admittedly on a pitch reported for being sub-standard—he had a match analysis of 11 for 89, only G. Boycott resisting with 33 in the first innings and an undefeated century in the second. The match coincided with Wimbledon and led to a press caption which recorded Derbyshire's victory, as 'Dane, Set and Match'. He was a bowler of Test class.

First-class career (1983–94): 709 runs (8.86), 434 wickets (23.86), and 47 catches

NEILSEN, Kurt

(b. 1912, Denmark; d. 1992, Denmark)

In 1953, after two years of negotiation, Kurt Neilsen persuaded Danish cricketers to break away from the Copenhagen Games Club (of which he himself was chairman) and form their own association. Neilsen became the first chairman of the Danish Cricket Association (1953–67) and subsequently honorary president (1967–92). Under his influence, Denmark became an associate member of ICC, regular tours took place and clubs from all over the country participated in the two domestic divisions.

POCKENDAHL, Borge

(b. 1906, Copenhagen, Denmark; d. 1989, Copenhagen)

Borge Pockendahl was Denmark's finest batsman in the years spanning the Second World War. As a right-handed opening batsman, with a narrow but effective range of strokes, he scored 13,126 (38.83) runs, making 33 centuries including one double-century. In 1944—when cricket continued despite the German occupation—as a right-arm bowler, he took all ten wickets (for 12 runs) in a match.

STEPTOE, Douglas George

(b. 1923, Copenhagen, Denmark; d. 1994, Copenhagen)

Douglas Steptoe, a British citizen resident in Denmark, translated the laws of cricket into Danish and, just before his death, completed *The Story of Danish Cricket*. He had been secretary of the Danish Cricket Association, and represented Denmark on the ICC.

SYLOW, Ludwig

(b. 1861, Denmark; d. 1933, Denmark)

Ludwig Sylow, a right-handed batsman and right-arm bowler played his early cricket at Soro Academy, a school which had participated, in 1866, in Denmark's first cricket match in Copenhagen. His influence kept the game going in that city in the early 1880s at a critical time. He took part (1890) in Denmark's first tour abroad—to Germany—and his score of 92 in the following year remained the highest score in Danish cricket in the nineteenth century. In a career of 70 matches, he made 1,465 runs, took 307 wickets, and was the premier Danish all-rounder of his day. He contributed to the establishment of FIFA in the world of Association Football.

FIJI

BULA, Ilikena Lasarusa

(b. 1921, Fiji) *Fiji*

Credited with the longest surname in cricket (59 letters), the abbreviated version of Bula belongs to Fiji's finest batsman. His attacking right-handed batting was distinguished by a prolific number of sixes, largely through pulls. He made over 1,000 runs on Fiji's tour of New Zealand (1948) and his 88 against Wellington contributed to Fiji's second victory in first-class cricket (a status retrospectively accorded). His 253 in 1953 remains the highest score in Fijian domestic cricket.

First-class career (1948–54): 702 runs (41.29) including 2 centuries, and 7 catches

CAKOBAU, Ratu, Sir Edward Tugi Tuivanuavou

(b. 1908, Fiji; d. 1973, Fiji) *Auckland and Fiji*

Ratu ('Prince') Sir Edward Cakobau, a son of King George II of Tonga, made his début in first-class cricket for Auckland in 1931. After service in the Second World War he was an Oxford University Authentic and was filmed for a news-reel playing with 'Patsy' Hendren for Sir Pelham Warner's XI against London Public Schools in 1946. Returning home, he played as a middle-order right-handed batsman and right-arm medium-paced bowler on the 1948 Fiji tour of New Zealand. Five of the matches were retrospectively accorded first-class status so that 17 years separated his first and second appearances at this level. He later became Deputy Prime Minister of Fiji.

First-class career (1931–48): 89 runs (22.50), 11 wickets (18.63), and 2 catches

CAKOBAU, Ratu, Sir George Kadavulevu

(b. 1912, Fiji; d. 1989, Fiji) *Fiji*

Ratu, ('Prince') Sir George Cakobau, a paramount chief, had captained (1939) an undefeated Fiji Rugby Football tour of New Zealand and he returned there in 1948 as vice-captain of the representative cricket team led by P. A. Snow. A stylish right-handed batsman and right-arm swing bowler, he was the most successful all-rounder in a tour whose five matches against the provinces were retrospectively accorded first-class status. His 105 runs for once out, tight bowling, and a brilliant catch—when taking over as wicket-keeper—played a major part in Fiji's defeat of Wellington. He served as Governor-General of Fiji (1973–80).

First-class career (1948): 176 runs (25.14), 5 wickets (52.00), and 3 catches

MATAIKA, Viliame Savu

(b. 1906, Fiji; d. 1986, Fiji) *Fiji*

One of Fiji's finest medium-fast right-arm bowlers, Viliame Mataika had a match analysis of nine wickets for 109 for Fiji against Wellington during their 1948 tour of New Zealand. His right-handed batting, at number eleven, ensured Fiji's success by one wicket when 19 runs were required. The five major provincial matches were subsequently accorded first-class status.

First-class career (1948): 50 runs (16.66) and 11 wickets (19.27)

SNOW, Philip Albert

(b. 1915, Leicester, England) *Fiji*

A career in Fiji as a colonial administrator (1938–52) led to Philip Snow being a founder-member and secretary (1946–52) of the Fiji Cricket Association. He captained the Islands on their New Zealand tour (1948) in which five of the provincial matches were retrospectively accorded first-class status. As an orthodox right-handed batsman and a right-arm slow googly bowler, he led Fiji to victories against Wellington and Auckland. On his return to England he became Bursar of Rugby School (1952–76). He was Fiji's representative on the ICC (1965–74) a founder-member of the World Cup committee and eventually chairman and doyen of the ICC associate members. He had earlier (1934–8) captained Leicestershire's 2nd XI and his many books include *Cricket in the Fiji Islands* (1949).

First-class career (1948): 121 runs (17.28), 4 wickets (25.75), and 1 catch

SUKUNA, Ratu, Sir Josefa Lalabalavu Vanaaliali

(b. 1888, Fiji; d. 1958, at sea)

Ratu ('Prince') Sir Josefa Sukuna won the Médaille Militaire serving with the French Foreign Legion in the First World War. He became a Fijian District Commissioner, Secretary for Fijian Affairs, and Speaker of the Legislative Council. He lent his considerable influence towards the foundation of the Fiji Cricket Association in 1946. He became its first president and played a major role in securing the Fijian tour of New Zealand in 1948. The historian of Fiji cricket, P. A. Snow, has acknowledged his debt to Sir Joseph in recording the story of the game in the Islands in the first half of the twentieth century.

HOLLAND

de BEUS, Anthony Marius Justus

(b. 1899, Padang, Indonesia; d. 1971,
's Gravenhage, Netherlands)

De Beus made 25 appearances for Holland up to
1960 as a right-handed batsman, right-arm googly
bowler and, in his earlier years, as a wicket-
keeper. He scored over 1,000 runs and took about
500 runs in all Dutch cricket. He wrote (1928) a
coaching book for youth—*Jongens, Wat is
cricket?*

GLERUM, Herman Wilhelm

(b. 1911, Amsterdam, Holland) *Free Foresters*

Herman Glerum, a middle-order right-handed
batsman and a right-arm medium-pace bowler,
was the first of his countrymen to score over
1,200 runs in a season (1935). He made 10,895
runs in Dutch domestic cricket, 30 appearances
for Holland, and 20 centuries. In his one first-class
match, he took 3 for 32 for the Free Foresters
against Oxford University in 1957. This was the
last occasion R. E. S. Wyatt played first-class
cricket.

First-class career (1957): 1 run (0.50) and 3
wickets (10.66)

LEFEBVRE, Roland Philippe

(b. 1963, Rotterdam, Holland) *Somerset,
Glamorgan, Canterbury, and Holland*

A wiry, fair-haired, right-handed all-rounder, very
keen and fit, Roland Lefebvre played in the ICC
Trophy for Holland in both 1988 and 1989 and
with success both for Somerset (1990–2) and
Glamorgan (1993–). In the 1990/1 season he
took his talents to New Zealand and produced a
career-best bowling performance of 6 for 53 for
Canterbury against Auckland. A controlled seam
bowler of medium-fast pace off a relatively short
run-up, he took 7 for 15 in a NatWest match
against Devon in his first season at Taunton. He
was capped by the county in his second season
but moved to Glamorgan in 1993 to be more
certain of first-team cricket. A good outfielder
and aggressive batsman, he scored exactly 100
against Worcestershire at Weston-super-Mare in
1991.

First-class career (1990–): 1,439 runs (20.55)
including 1 century, 143 wickets (36.50), and 36
catches

LUBBERS, Steven Willem

(b. 1953, Emmastad, Curaçao)

Between 1968 and 1994 he made 154 appearances
for Holland, captaining his country to victories
against England B, West Indies, and South Africa.
As a middle-order right-handed batsman and a
right-arm off-spin bowler, he has scored over
14,000 runs and taken over 600 wickets in all
Dutch cricket.

MULIER, Willem Johan Herman

(b. 1865, Witmarsum, Netherlands; d. 1954,
Haarlem, Netherlands)

'Pim' Mulier was the major pioneer in establishing and promoting cricket and football in Holland. He founded clubs in both sports and wrote
(1897) a history of early Dutch cricket.

POSTHUMA, Carst Jan

(b. 1868, Haarlem, Netherlands; d. 1939,
Heemstede, Netherlands) *London County*

Nicknamed 'The Lion', Posthuma made 72
appearances for Holland up to 1928. As a left-
handed batsman, he made the first century in
Dutch domestic cricket (1894). He was the first
Dutchman to take 100 wickets in a season (1900)
and his left-arm fast bowling earned him a record
2,339 wickets (8.66). In 1903 he played for W. G.
Grace's London County side, taking 23 wickets
and coming second to G. W. Beldam in the
averages.

First-class career (1903): 45 runs (7.50), 23
wickets (15.04), and 1 catch

VAN MANEN, Hugo

(b. 1903, 's Gravenhage, Netherlands; d. 1983,
Wassenaar, Netherlands)

Van Manen made 36 appearances for Holland up
to 1958 as a right-handed batsman and right-arm
slow bowler. He captained his country, scored
over 13,000 runs (with 22 centuries) and took
over 300 wickets in all Dutch cricket.

VAN TROOST, Adrianus Pelrus

(b. 1972, Schiedam, Holland) *Somerset and Holland*

Had Adrianus Van Troost been born in a Rugby-
playing country he would surely have become a
second-row forward. Six foot seven inches and
powerfully built, this dark-haired giant instead

became one of the fastest right-arm bowlers ever seen in county cricket. Having played for Holland in the ICC Trophy in 1990, he announced his intention of qualifying for England, a process due to be completed by 1998. A lack of accuracy has hampered his bowling progress and his batting, with his body moving to leg against anyone even half as aggressive as himself, is of the hit and hope variety, but he is a potential match-winner on a pitch giving him any help.

First-class career (1991–): 258 runs (9.55), 93 wickets (36.54), and 9 catches

VAN WEELDE, Wally

(b. 1924, Amsterdam, Netherlands; d. 1992, Rotterdam, Netherlands)

Van Weelde, who made 32 appearances for Holland as a right-handed batsman and right-arm slow bowler, was in the national XI which defeated the Australians in 1964. He made nearly 14,000 runs (including 27 centuries) and took over 400 wickets in all Dutch cricket.

IRELAND

ANDERSON, Ivan John

(b. 1944, Armagh, Ireland) *Ireland*

An outstanding right-handed batsman and stroke-player and a right-arm off-break bowler, Ivan Anderson scored almost 4,000 runs for Ireland (1966–85). He shared, with A. J. O'Riordan, in a fourth-wicket partnership of 222 against Scotland at Glasgow in 1976 and his 198 not out against a Canadian XI at Toronto in 1973 is a record at Irish representative level. He made a 'magnificient century'—said *Wisden*—against Sri Lanka at Eglinton, in 1979.

First-class career (1966–82): 947 runs (37.88) including 3 centuries, 17 wickets (14.64), and 9 catches

BOUCHER, James Chrysostom

(b. 1910, Dublin, Ireland) *Ireland*

Capped for Ireland while still a schoolboy at Belvedere College, Dublin, Jimmy Boucher, together with E. Ingram, provided Ireland's greatest bowling combination for virtually a

quarter of a century. Between 1929 and 1954, for Ireland, his right-arm off-break bowling brought him 307 wickets at 15.25. His best performance in first-class cricket was at Dublin in 1937 against the New Zealanders. On a rain-affected wicket, the three-day match was concluded in one day, Boucher taking 7 for 13 in 12 overs. In the New Zealanders' 8-wicket victory, only 219 runs were scored in the entire match. He was a lower-order right-handed batsman but, as a bowler, he headed the English first-class bowling averages on two occasions (1937 and 1948). He was later secretary to the Irish Cricket Union (1954–73).

First-class career (1930–54): 625 runs (13.58), 168 wickets (14.04), and 23 catches

GWYNN, Lucius Henry

(b. 1873, Ramelton, Ireland; d. 1902, Davos, Switzerland) *Dublin University, Gentlemen, and Ireland*

In a brief career cut short by contracting tuberculosis at the age of 29, Lucius Gwynn sprang to fame in 1895 during Dublin University's tour of England. With successive centuries against Cambridge University and Leicestershire (and 346 runs in the two matches) he was invited to play for the Gentlemen against the Players at The Oval. He made 80, sharing in a fifth-wicket partnership of 133 with C. B. Fry. *Wisden* wrote of 'a wonderfully good innings' and, on his death 7 years later, declared 'he would have earned a high place among batsmen of his day'. He headed the national batting averages for 1895, with A. C. MacLaren, W. G. Grace (in his *annus mirabilis*), and K. S. Ranjitsinhji immediately below him. An academic post at Trinity College, Dublin limited his career and in his final match in England, 7 months before he died, he made an undefeated 81 for Ireland against London County at Crystal Palace. He represented Ireland as a Rugby three-quarter on seven occasions and an unsubstantiated report suggested he had declined an invitation to play cricket for England against Australia in 1896.

First-class career (1895–1902): 577 runs (44.38) including 2 centuries, 18 wickets (22.77), and 10 catches

INGRAM, Edward

(b. 1910, Dublin, Ireland; d. 1973, Basingstoke, England) *Ireland and Middlesex*

With Jimmy Boucher, his schoolboy contemporary from Belvedere College, Dublin, Eddie

Ingram shared Ireland's outstanding bowling combination for virtually a quarter of a century. In 48 matches for his country (1928–53) he scored over 1,000 runs and took over 150 wickets. His late-order right-handed batting was more effective at club level, both for Leinster and (after 1936) for Ealing, but his right-arm medium-pace leg-breaks and top-spin commanded respect at the highest standards. Against the Australians at Dublin in 1938 he took 7 for 83, including a spell of 5 for 29. During his years in England, he made a dozen appearances for Middlesex (1938–49).

First-class career (1928–53): 766 runs (15.01), 79 wickets (24.00), and 14 catches

LAMBERT, Robert James Hamilton

(b. 1874, Dublin, Ireland; d. 1956, Dublin) *Ireland and London County*

On his one appearance for W. G. Grace's London County, against Lancashire at Old Trafford in 1903, Robert Lambert, a right-handed batsman, made 84 for once out. A few years earlier he had scored over 2,000 runs and taken over 200 wickets in three successive seasons in Irish club cricket mainly for Leinster. His right-arm off-breaks earned him 179 wickets at 18.35 in his 52 appearances for Ireland (1893–1930), 13 of them as captain. In 1933, at the age of 59, he scored his hundredth century in all cricket. He had been Irish badminton champion (1911) and was later president of the Irish Cricket Union.

First-class career (1902–28): 1,121 runs (28.74) including 1 century, 70 wickets (24.08), and 19 catches

MONTEITH, James Dermott

(b. 1943, Lisburn, Ireland) *Ireland and Middlesex*

Between 1965 and 1984, Jimmy Monteith was an outstanding left-arm slow bowler in Irish representative cricket and a middle-order right-handed batsman. In 76 appearances he led his country 37 times. He also played on nine occasions for Middlesex (1981–2).

First-class career (1965–82): 530 runs (15.58), 94 wickets (20.64), and 23 catches

O'RIORDAN, Alec John

(b. 1940, Dublin, Ireland) *Ireland*

Alec O'Riordan, a right-handed batsman and left-arm medium-pace bowler, is the only player to have made over 2,000 runs and taken over 200

wickets in his 72 appearances (1959–77) in Irish representative cricket. In Ireland's match against the West Indians at Londonderry in 1969—which *Wisden* called the 'sensation of the season'—the visitors were dismissed on a damp and emerald green pitch for 25, by Douglas Goodwin and O'Riordan, whose figures were 4 for 18 in 13 overs. At one point, the West Indians were 12 for 9. In a drawn match between the two sides at Belfast he was the principal all-rounder.

First-class career (1958–77): 614 runs (15.74) including 1 century, 75 wickets (21.38), and 19 catches

SCOTLAND

AITCHISON, The Revd James

(b. 1920, Kilmarnock, Scotland; d. 1994, Glasgow, Scotland) *Scotland*

Like his earlier compatriot, John Kerr, James Aitchison, a minister in the church of Scotland and a graceful and technically strong opening right-handed batsman, would have had a distinguished career in first-class cricket had he not confined his playing career to Scotland. He was an automatic selection for his country (1946–63), scoring centuries against the South Africans (1947), the Australians (1956), Yorkshire, and Lancashire. In his 190 not out against Ireland at Dublin in 1959—still the highest score by a Scotland player in first-class cricket—he shared a partnership of 144 with the future England captain M. H. Denness, the first schoolboy to be capped for Scotland. Aitchison's club cricket was for Carlton, Grange, and Kilmarnock, for whom he compiled over 18,000 runs. His 3,669 runs for Scotland, and 56 centuries for his clubs, are both Scottish records.

First-class career (1946–63): 2,786 runs (32.77) including 5 centuries, and 22 catches

ALLAN, James Moffat

(b. 1932, Leeds, Yorkshire) *Kent and Scotland*

Jimmy Allen's right-handed batting could be found at number eleven (for Oxford University in 1953) and number one (for Kent in 1955). His left-arm slow bowling brought him a sensational start, spread over two matches for the University, against Yorkshire and the Australians at Oxford in

1953. He had taken the wickets of Vic Wilson (Yorkshire) and the Test cricketers Keith Miller and Ian Craig in ten overs before conceding a run. Subsequently he played four seasons for Kent (1954–7). In his nearly 20 years for Scotland he scored 1,494 runs, including 99 not out against the New Zealanders at Glasgow in 1965 when he ran out of partners.

First-class career (1953–72): 4,988 runs (22.36) including 5 centuries, 435 wickets (25.69), and 124 catches

BALFOUR-MELVILLE, Leslie Melville

(b. 1854, Edinburgh; d. 1937, North Berwick, Scotland) *MCC and Scotland*

One of the great sporting all-rounders of his time, 'L.M.' was an attacking right-handed batsman, who usually opened, and a wicket-keeper. He was in Scotland's national side for 40 years (1874–1914). As a schoolboy at Edinburgh Academy, he made top score for an Edinburgh XXII against George Parr's All-England XI and later, for the Gentlemen of Scotland, his 73 contributed to a defeat by 47 runs of the 1882 Australians at Edinburgh. He played mainly for Scotland's distinguished club, the Grange, and for I Zingari —both of whose averages *Wisden* often recorded. In his 60th year (1913), he made three centuries. For Scotland, he was also a Rugby international, a lawn-tennis champion, a long-jump title-holder, and the amateur golf champion in 1895 at St Andrew's. He was president of the Scottish Cricket and Rugby Unions.

First-class career (1888–1910): 121 runs (17.28) and 7 dismissals (6 c., 1 st.)

BROWN, James

(b. 1931, Perth, Scotland) *Scotland*

Jimmy Brown captained Scotland in 53 of his 85 appearances and is recognized as the best wicket-keeper the country has ever produced. As a right-handed middle-order batsman he made a free-scoring 90 against Yorkshire at Paisley in 1957 while not conceding a bye in the county's 374 runs. In club cricket for Perthshire he took 674 wickets (408 caught and 266 stumped). For his services to Scottish cricket he was appointed MBE.

First-class career (1953–73): 1,306 runs (19.49) and 106 dismissals (83 c., 23 st.)

KERR, John

(b. 1885, Greenock, Scotland; d. 1972, Greenock) *Scotland*

John Kerr, the 'Greenock Guv'nor'—in the view of (Sir) Jack Hobbs—was a right-handed opening batsman of near world-class in the 1920s. His opportunities for first-class cricket were limited to matches for Scotland and his highest score at that level was 178 not out against Ireland at Dublin in 1923. Against the formidable 1921 Australians he made 60 not out at Perth and 147 at Edinburgh, being one of only eight players that season to score a century against the attack of E. A. McDonald, J. M. Gregory, and A. A. Mailey. Three years later he made 80 not out against the South Africans. None of these matches was first-class. In Scottish club cricket, mainly for Greenock and for Carlton, he scored over 40,000 runs, while his right-arm slow bowling was often effective.

First-class career (1908–33): 1,975 runs (37.26) including 4 centuries, 7 wickets (36.00), and 31 catches

LAIDLAW, William Kennedy

(b. 1912, Edinburgh, Scotland; d. 1992, Edinburgh) *Scotland and Minor Counties*

An outstanding schoolboy cricketer at Melville College, William Laidlaw was the best right-arm slow leg-break bowler in Scotland, with great variety in his attack. He played for Scotland (1938–53) on thirty-two occasions, eleven of them as captain, and took 97 wickets. Against Yorkshire at Harrogate in 1938 his 7 for 70 confined the home team to a first innings lead of 17. After the Second World War he appeared for Durham (1948–52) and was in the Minor Counties representative side in 1950. His right-handed batting seldom disturbed the bowlers.

First-class career (1938–53): 132 runs (7.33), 42 wickets (29.16), and 8 catches

USA

BOHLEN, Francis Hermann

(b. 1868, Philadelphia, USA; d. 1942, Philadelphia) *MCC, London County, and Philadelphia*

A tall, classic right-handed batsman who drove 'with powerful ease' especially on hard, fast wickets, Francis Bohlen made 162 on his first-class début for Philadelphia against English Residents at Philadelphia in 1890. Three years later he made another century there in Philadelphia's historic defeat, by an innings, of the 1893 Australians. He made a few appearances in England for MCC (1894–1904) and shared in a brief partnership with W. G. Grace for London County against Cambridge University at Crystal Palace in 1904. But he was never as successful on English wickets and this was also demonstrated in his three tours to England with the Philadelphians (1897, 1903, 1908). He played on ten occasions for the USA v. Canada (1890–1907).

First-class career (1890–1908): 2,568 runs (23.34) including 3 centuries, and 20 catches

KING, John Barton

(b. 1873, Philadelphia, USA; d. 1965, Philadelphia) *Philadelphia*

Described by (Sir) Pelham Warner as 'one of the best fast bowlers' of all time, Barton King was unquestionably the greatest all-rounder in United States cricket. Tall, strong, and prematurely bald, his right-arm action made the ball swerve late from leg, a skill he developed from being a pitcher at baseball. His right-handed batting earned him two triple-centuries in American domestic cricket. In Philadelphia's historic defeat of the 1893 Australians by an innings and 69 runs, he took 7 for 168 and—batting at number eleven—made 36. He toured England on three occasions (1897, 1903, 1908) with distinct success. Against Sussex at Hove in 1897 he took 7 for 13 in 10 overs in the county's dismissal for 46, bowling W. L. Murdoch for 3 and 'Ranji' first ball. His fifty and match analysis of 13 for 115 played a major part in the Philadelphians' eight-wicket victory. Six years later, at The Oval, his 98 and 113 not out, together with match figures of 6 for 187, brought about Surrey's defeat by 110 runs. On his third tour he topped the national bowling averages and no bowler in first-class cricket has ever exceeded his career strike rate (wickets per balls) of 23.34. He made eleven appearances for USA v. Canada (1892–1912).

First-class career (1893–1912): 2,134 runs (20.51) including 4 centuries, 415 wickets (15.66), and 67 catches

LESTER, John Ashby

(b. 1871, Penrith, England; d. 1969, Philadelphia, USA) *Philadelphia*

During a visit to England in 1892 the president of Haverford College, Philadelphia, on seeing him bat, invited John Lester to become a student at his College. Cricket, although well-established there, was low in standard. Four years later Lester captained the College on their tour of England, averaging 84.64 himself, the next performer's average being nearly sixty runs behind. On his début at Lord's against MCC he made a century. Although he toured England again three times with the Philadelphians—on the last two occasions (1903, 1908) as captain—and topped the batting averages in both 1897 and 1903—he never quite fulfilled expectations. *Scores and Biographies* called him 'a watchful (right-handed) batsman who could hit'. As a right-arm slow bowler he came second in the tour averages in England on two of his visits. His *A Century of Philadelphian Cricket* (1952) is the definitive book on its subject. He retained a keen interest in cricket throughout a long life despite the fact that the game vastly declined in popularity and standard in Philadelphia from the 1920s onwards. It was his proposal which led to the establishment of the C. C. Morris Cricket Library at Haverford College in 1969.

First-class career (1896–1908): 2,552 runs (33.14) including 2 centuries, 57 wickets (22.72), and 15 catches

MARDER, John Israel

(b. 1909, Nottingham, England; d. 1976, London, England)

John Marder spent much of his life in the USA, becoming the first president of the USCA (later, the USACA). Two years later he was instrumental in reviving, after a lapse of 51 years, cricket's oldest international—the USA v. Canada—which had first been played in 1844. He published (1968) a history of the contest and had played a major role in getting the United States admitted as an associate member of the ICC in 1965. As an administrator, 'no one had done more for cricket in North America' wrote *Barclays World of Cricket*.

MORRIS, Charles Christopher

(b. 1882, Philadelphia, USA; d. Villanova, Pennsylvania, USA) *Philadelphia*

Christy Morris, the youngest of the leading players during Philadelphia's 'golden age' before the First World War, made 164 in the Philadelphians' substantial defeat of Nottinghamshire at Trent Bridge in 1903 while still a student at Haverford College. He was, said *Wisden*, 'a beautiful (right-handed) batsman' and—in his later years—a right-arm leg-break bowler who pioneered the googly in America. He led the Philadelphian Pilgrims' tour to England (1921)—by which time Philadelphian cricket no longer had first-class status—and made a century against the Incogniti. Despite the steady decline of cricket in most Philadelphian clubs, he retained his unflagging enthusiasm. Haverford College kept the flag flying and he turned out for their Alumni XI as late as his 70th year. In 1969, the Cricket Library at the College was opened and named after him. It holds his own extensive collection of cricket books.

First-class career (1901–8): 1,253 runs (20.54) including 1 century, and 22 catches

NEWHALL, Charles Allerton

(b. 1847, Philadelphia, USA; d. 1927, New York, USA) *Philadelphia*

Charles Newhall was the the last survivor of four cricketing brothers who played a major part in Philadelphian cricket in the years following the Civil War. Their contribution paved the way for the 'golden age' of the 1890s. Regarded as the best and fastest right-arm bowler America had produced, he toured England in 1884. His nephew, William, was the only one of the family to play first-class cricket in England (1908) and played in Germantown's defeat of the Australians in 1913, the last of Philadelphia's matches to be recognized as first-class.

First-class career (1878–86): 181 runs (9.05), 44 wickets (15.61), and 5 catches

PATTERSON, George Stuart

(b. 1868, Philadelphia, USA; d. 1943, Philadelphia) *Philadelphia*

George Patterson was regarded as one of America's finest all-round cricketers. He was a stylish right-handed batsman and a right-arm medium-pace bowler. At Haverford College in 1886 his batting average was 110.00. He toured England in 1889 with the Philadelphians and again in 1897 as captain. In between he made 271 in a first-class match for his own XI v. A. M. Wood's at Philadelphia in 1894. On his second tour of England both he and Wood made centuries against Nottinghamshire at Trent Bridge in a match drawn very much in the Philadelphians' favour.

First-class career (1885–97): 2,051 runs (40.21) including 5 centuries, 74 wickets (21.20), and 14 catches

WOOD, Arthur Machin

(b. 1861, Pye Bridge, Derbyshire; d. 1947, Philadelphia, USA) *Derbyshire and Philadelphia*

An 'effective rather than a graceful' opening right-handed batsman and a right-arm slow bowler, Arthur Wood appeared for Derbyshire before emigrating to the USA. He returned to England on three occasions with the Philadelphians (1897, 1903, 1908) scoring two centuries and topping the batting averages on his last visit. He made seven appearances (1893–1902) for USA v. Canada.

First-class career (1879–1909): 2,648 runs (22.44) including 3 centuries, 13 wickets (26.76), and 96 catches